Australia

Paul Smitz

Carolyn Bain, Sandra Bao, Susannah Farfor, Alan Murphy, Nina Rousseau,
Simon Sellars, Justine Vaisutis, Ryan Ver Berkmoes, Meg Worby

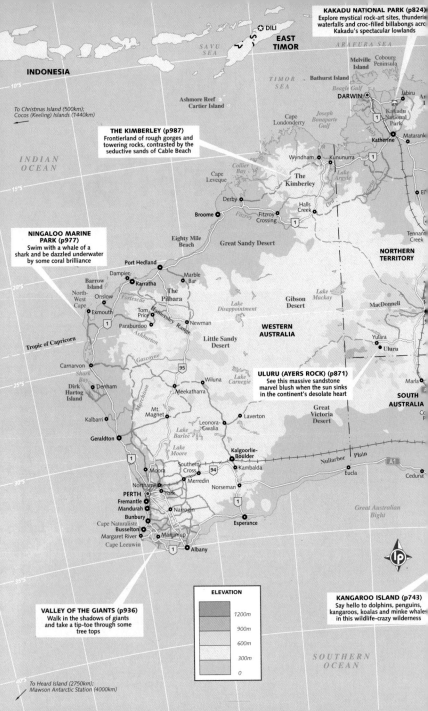

KAKADU NATIONAL PARK (p824)
Explore mystical rock-art sites, thunderin
waterfalls and croc-filled billabongs acro
Kakadu's spectacular lowlands

DILI

SAVU SEA

EAST TIMOR

ARAFURA SEA

INDONESIA

TIMOR SEA

Melville Island

Cobourg Peninsula

Bathurst Island

Beagle Gulf

DARWIN

Jabiru

Ar

Kakadu National Park

Mataran

To Christmas Island (500km);
Cocos (Keeling) Islands (1440km)

Ashmore Reef
Cartier Island

Cape
Londonderry

Joseph
Bonaparte
Gulf

Katherine

INDIAN OCEAN

THE KIMBERLEY (p987)
Frontierland of rough gorges and
towering rocks, contrasted by the
seductive sands of Cable Beach

Collier Bay

Cape Leveque

The Kimberley

Lake Argyle

El

Wyndham

Kununurra

Derby

Fitzroy Crossing

Halls Creek

Ord

Tennani Creek

Broome

Fitzroy

15°S

NINGALOO MARINE PARK (p977)
Swim with a whale of a
shark and be dazzled underwater
by some coral brilliance

Eighty Mile Beach

Great Sandy Desert

NORTHERN TERRITORY

Port Hedland

Marble Bar

Dampier

Barrow Island

Karratha

North-West Cape

Onslow

The Pilbara

Lake Disappointment

Gibson Desert

Lake Mackay

MacDonnell

Exmouth

Tom Price

Newman

Fortescue

Hamersley Range

Paraburdoo

Ashburton

Little Sandy Desert

WESTERN AUSTRALIA

Yulara

Uluru

20°S

Tropic of Capricorn

Gascoyne

Carnarvon

Shark Bay

Denham

Murchison

Lake Carnegie

ULURU (AYERS ROCK) (p871)
See this massive sandstone
marvel blush when the sun sinks
in the continent's desolate heart

Marla

SOUTH AUSTRALIA

Dirk Hartog Island

Wiluna

Kalbarri

Mt Magnet

Lake Barlee

Leonora-Gwalia

Laverton

Great Victoria Desert

Co

F

25°S

Geraldton

Meekatharra

Lake Moore

Kalgoorlie-Boulder

Nullarbor Plain

A1

Moora

Southern Cross

Kambalda

Eucla

Ceduna

Northam

Merredin

Norseman

Great Australian Bight

PERTH

Fremantle

Mandurah

York

Narrogin

Bunbury

Cape Naturaliste

Busselton

Margaret River

Manjimup

Cape Leeuwin

Albany

Esperance

30°S

35°S

VALLEY OF THE GIANTS (p936)
Walk in the shadows of giants
and take a tip-toe through some
tree tops

ELEVATION	
	1200m
	900m
	600m
	300m
	0

KANGAROO ISLAND (p743)
Say hello to dolphins, penguins,
kangaroos, koalas and minke whale
in this wildlife-crazy wilderness

SOUTHERN OCEAN

To Heard Island (2750km);
Mawson Antarctic Station (4000km)

105°E   110°E   115°E   120°E   125°E   130°E

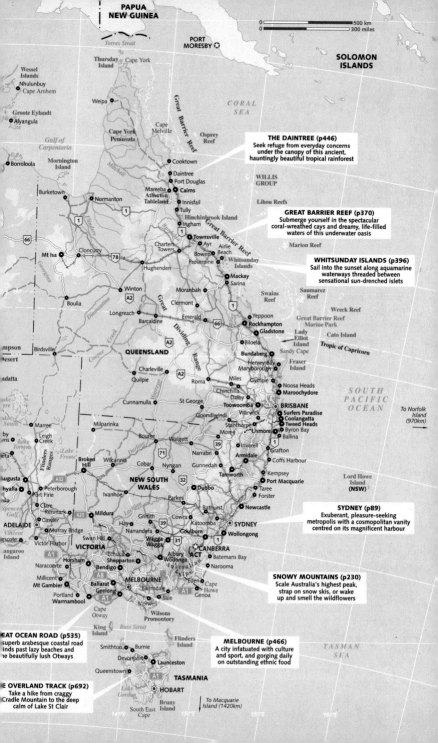

PAPUA NEW GUINEA

PORT MORESBY ○

SOLOMON ISLANDS

0 — 500 km
0 — 300 miles

THE DAINTREE (p446)
Seek refuge from everyday concerns under the canopy of this ancient, hauntingly beautiful tropical rainforest

GREAT BARRIER REEF (p370)
Submerge yourself in the spectacular coral-wreathed cays and dreamy, life-filled waters of this underwater oasis

WHITSUNDAY ISLANDS (p396)
Sail into the sunset along aquamarine waterways threaded between sensational sun-drenched islets

SYDNEY (p89)
Exuberant, pleasure-seeking metropolis with a cosmopolitan vanity centred on its magnificent harbour

SNOWY MOUNTAINS (p230)
Scale Australia's highest peak, strap on snow skis, or wake up and smell the wildflowers

GREAT OCEAN ROAD (p535)
A superb arabesque coastal road winds past lazy beaches and the beautifully lush Otways

THE OVERLAND TRACK (p692)
Take a hike from craggy Cradle Mountain to the deep calm of Lake St Clair

MELBOURNE (p466)
A city infatuated with culture and sport, and gorging daily on outstanding ethnic food

CORAL SEA

WILLIS GROUP

Lihou Reefs

Marion Reef

Swains Reef

Saumarez Reef

Wreck Reef

Great Barrier Reef Marine Park

Lady Elliot Island

Cato Island

Tropic of Capricorn

SOUTH PACIFIC OCEAN

To Norfolk Island (970km)

Lord Howe Island (NSW)

TASMAN SEA

To Macquarie Island (1420km)

Gulf of Carpentaria

Cape York Peninsula

QUEENSLAND

NEW SOUTH WALES

VICTORIA

ACT

TASMANIA

Wessel Islands
Nhulunbuy
Cape Arnhem
Groote Eylandt
Alyangula
Borroloola
Mornington Island
Burketown
Normanton
Weipa
Cape York
Thursday Island
Torres Strait
Cape Melville
Osprey Reef
Cooktown
Daintree
Port Douglas
Cairns
Mareeba
Atherton Tableland
Innisfail
Tully
Ingham
Hinchinbrook Island
Townsville
Charters Towers
Ayr
Bowen
Airlie Beach
Proserpine
Whitsunday Islands
Mackay
Sarina
Morahbah
Clermont
Emerald
Yeppoon
Rockhampton
Gladstone
Biloela
Bundaberg
Hervey Bay
Maryborough
Fraser Island
Sandy Cape
Gympie
Noosa Heads
Maroochydore
BRISBANE
Surfers Paradise
Coolangatta
Tweed Heads
Byron Bay
Ballina
Lismore
Grafton
Coffs Harbour
Kempsey
Port Macquarie
Taree
Forster
Newcastle
SYDNEY
Wollongong
Batemans Bay
Narooma
Eden
Cape Howe
Genoa
Mt Isa
Cloncurry
Hughenden
Winton
Boulia
Longreach
Barcaldine
Charleville
Quilpie
Cunnamulla
St George
Roma
Miles
Chinchilla
Dalby
Toowoomba
Warwick
Stanthorpe
Goondiwindi
Moree
Inverell
Armidale
Tamworth
Gunnedah
Narrabri
Walgett
Bourke
Nyngan
Cobar
Wilcannia
Broken Hill
Milparinka
Tibooburra
Birdsville
Marree
Leigh Creek
Peterborough
Port Pirie
Clare
Renmark
Mildura
Murray Bridge
ADELAIDE
Victor Harbor
Kangaroo Island
Naracoorte
Millicent
Mt Gambier
Portland
Warrnambool
Horsham
Bendigo
Ballarat
Geelong
MELBOURNE
Echuca
Shepparton
Wangaratta
Albury
Wodonga
Wagga Wagga
Narrandera
Griffith
Hay
Swan Hill
Dubbo
Parkes
Bathurst
Cowra
Katoomba
Goulburn
CANBERRA
Bairnsdale
Sale
Morwell
Wilsons Promontory
King Island
Bass Strait
Flinders Island
Smithton
Burnie
Devonport
Launceston
Queenstown
HOBART
Bruny Island
South East Cape
Quorn
Port Augusta
Whyalla
Spencer Gulf
Flinders Ranges
Cape Otway

145°E 150°E 155°E 160°E

Destination Australia

Australia is so big and so magnificently diverse that it could never merely be the sum of its icons. The stunning eggshell architecture of the Sydney Opera House, the surreal baked glow of Uluru (Ayers Rock) at dusk, the air-splitting pop of a crocodile snapping its jaws shut, a wave beautifully curled above a kaleidoscopic reef, suntanned bodies scattered like driftwood on a crisp white beach – these are only tiny parts of the whole experience that unfurls once your feet first crunch the soil of this awesome country-continent.

Many things about this faraway island are unforgettably different, even the things that sound familiar. You may have visited remote places before, but not the sublime isolation of the outback, with its dazzling salt pans, secretive reptiles, rough-cut canyons and sandstone towers. You've encountered wildlife before, but when was the last time you rode atop a camel among desert oaks, saw a rock wallaby hop up a cliff, floundered in the presence of a whale shark or had your camp site raided by a Tasmanian devil? Perhaps you've enjoyed seafood, but here you'll get your first taste of barramundi, crayfish and Moreton Bay bugs. And sip the local beer or wine (not the cheap plonk but the good stuff) and the flavours can leave your tongue lost for words. Even the humour is unpredictable: sneaky, subversive and loaded with double meanings.

One of the most intriguing things about Australia is that it's undiminished by its peculiarities. From its eerily tangled rainforest trails to its thought-provoking museums, vocal love of almost any sport and even its unbelievably annoying flies, the country is defiantly unique.

ROSS BARNETT

National Parks

OLIVER STREWE

Marvel at the distinctive striped rock towers at Purnululu (Bungle Bungle) National Park (p1002), Western Australia

JOHN BANAGAN

The unusual boab tree is common in the Kimberley (p987), Western Australia

OTHER HIGHLIGHTS

Overleaf: Art from the Warradjan Aboriginal Cultural Centre (p828), Kakadu National Park, Northern Territory

RICHARD I'ANSON

- Discover the extraordinary rock art and wildlife at Kakadu National Park (p824), Northern Territory
- Trek through the unique, majestic rock formations of the Flinders Ranges (p778), South Australia

Hike into the depths of Cradle Mountain-Lake St Clair National Park, Tasmania (p696)

RICHAR

ROB BLAKERS

Explore Kosciuszko National Park (p232), New South Wales' largest national park

Queensland's rugged Carnarvon National Park (p374) features sheer rock walls, deep pools, and Aboriginal rock art

CHRIS BELL

Be transfixed by colossal Uluru (Ayers Rock; p871), Northern Territory

ALAIN EVRARD

Islands & Beaches

Walk the wild, spectacular coast of Flinders Chase National Park (p749), South Australia

OTHER HIGHLIGHTS

- Enjoy endless walks along the endless beaches at Byron Bay (p189), New South Wales' northern utopia
- Stroll the sensational white-sand beaches at Wilsons Promontory (599), Victoria, the southernmost point of mainland Australia

Hovering over the Whitsunday Islands (p396), Queensland

Savour the endless pristine beaches of Freycinet National Park (p651), Tasmania

RICHARD I'ANSON

Stroll through the reflections of the Cathedrals in the Great Sandy National Park, Fraser Island (p354), Queensland

Take in the sinking sun on camel-back (p992) from Cable Beach, Broome, Western Australia

MICHAEL LAANELA

MICHAEL LAANELA

People-watching is the most popular activity at Bondi beach (p109), Sydney

Outdoor Activities

Carve it up along the New South Wales coast (p88)

DENNIS JONES

OTHER HIGHLIGHTS

- Tantalise your tastebuds and drink like a fish at the Margaret River wineries (p164), Western Australia

- Take an adventure tour through the limestone passages of South Australia's World Heritage–listed Narracoorte caves (p764)

- Scale the breathtaking heights of the iconic Sydney Harbour Bridge (p100)

Rock-climber ascends the Totem Pole on the Tasman Peninsula, (p615), Tasmania

GRANT DIXON

Bushwalking, climbing, wildlife: something for every outdoor enthusiast at the Grampians (p550), Victoria

JOHN BANAGAN

JOHN BANAGAN

Work on your snow tan on the slopes of
Thredbo (p235), New South Wales

RODNEY HYETT

Victoria's sinuous Great Ocean Road (p535) is a
spectacular road trip

Immerse yourself (literally) in the aqua waters of the Great Barrier Reef (p370), Queensland

NIGEL MARSH

City Life

Adelaide's Womadelaide festival (p723) showcases the musical talents of more than 400 international acts

OTHER HIGHLIGHTS

- Take a night stroll through hundreds of colourful food and craft stalls at Mindil Beach Sunset Market (p815), Brisbane
- Explore Canberra's National Gallery of Australia (p265) frame by frame

Celebrate horse racing and high fashion at Melbourne's annual Spring Racing Carnival (p500)

The Sydney Gay & Lesbian Mardi Gras (p136) attracts more than half a million spectactors to its annual colourful carnival

Contents

Northern Territory 794

Regional Map Contents

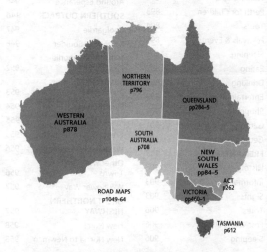

The Authors

PAUL SMITZ Coordinating Author, Australian Capital Territory & Northern Territory

Paul has stumbled, slipped and staggered all over Australia, leaving footprints of his soul in the unlikeliest places, but he knows there's still much of the country he has yet to even glimpse. His appreciative wanderings through Tasmanian forests, Canberra museums and Melbourne pubs, atop Bight-sized cliffs, across Queensland islands and along remote western beaches were mightily enhanced by his NT research, when he was able to visit isolated Aboriginal communities, get stalked by crocs, blink helplessly at the magnificence of flood plains and drive some sublimely empty Outback tracks.

My Favourite Trip

It's difficult to nominate a favourite trip in a country I find so rewarding to explore, but my first drive into central Australia would come close. I motored out of Adelaide with Juliana Hatfield blaring and headed north into the Outback, skirting blazing salt pans on my way to a night underground in Coober Pedy (p787). Further north I toasted the desert sky near the massive silhouette of Uluru (p871), trudged up the side of spectacular Kings Canyon (p867) and then trailed a dust storm as I rattled around the Mereenie Loop Rd (p866) and into the fascinating history of Hermannsburg (p865). I then introduced myself to enigmatic Alice (p845) before high-tailing it for the remote chasms of the West MacDonnell Ranges (p861).

CAROLYN BAIN Tasmania

Melbourne-born Carolyn has spent the last 16 years studying, travelling and, more recently, researching guidebooks in far-flung corners of the world, and on her first trip to Tasmania was thrilled to discover such a first-class destination so close to home. Later trips across stormy Bass Strait have given her the chance to yak with the friendly locals while exploring Tassie's scenic coastline, blissful national parks, sleepy historic villages, and – most importantly – excellent tearooms and wineries. She is currently based in Melbourne, getting her regular fix of Tasmanian heaven through King Island cheese and Boag's beer.

LONELY PLANET AUTHORS

Why is our travel information the best in the world? It's simple: our authors are independent, dedicated travellers. They don't research using just the Internet or phone, and they don't take freebies in exchange for positive coverage. They travel widely, to all the popular spots and off the beaten track. They personally visit thousands of hotels, restaurants, cafés, bars, galleries, palaces, museums and more – and they take pride in getting all the details right, and telling it how it is. For more, see the authors section on www.lonelyplanet.com.

SANDRA BAO   Sydney

Sandra has been an itinerant traveller since she was eight, when she first left her native Argentina to venture out into the world. After emigrating to the US she spent much of her life travelling in more than 50 countries and earned a psychology degree at the University of California Santa Cruz. Sydney reigns supreme among her favourite cities and Lonely Planet gigs, and during her research for this book Sandra has learned to appreciate echidnas, the Aussie accent and munching fish and chips at the beach.

SUSANNAH FARFOR   South Australia

Susannah is a Melbourne-based writer and editor whose work regularly appears in adventure-related travel and food publications. For this title she cruised, snorkelled and surfed the coasts; hiked the hills; explored caves; and put an oenology course to good use by quaffing wines along with SA's array of gourmet produce. Fascinated by the more remote regions of Australia, she has travelled in every state and also wrote Lonely Planet's *Northern Territory* and *Adelaide & South Australia* guidebooks.

ALAN MURPHY   Northern Western Australia

Alan is a born and bred West Australian who left Perth after hearing some vague notion about 'overseas' and 'the eastern states'. Although he now lives in Melbourne, he frequently visits WA and loves travelling around that vast and wondrous state. Lucky enough to have seen a bit of the world, Alan still finds the natural assets of northwest Australia, particularly Ningaloo, incomparable and at last understands the benefit of isolation. He was delighted to be given the opportunity of updating northern WA for this guide, and found writing about his home state a unique challenge.

NINA ROUSSEAU   Victoria

There's something truly satisfying about writing up your own backyard and Nina thoroughly enjoyed researching this chapter. Nina is a Melbourne-based writer who has also contributed to Lonely Planet's *Victoria*, *New Zealand* and *Australia & New Zealand on a shoestring* guidebooks. She is currently working as a Melbourne restaurant reviewer and freelance writer and editor.

SIMON SELLARS Coastal New South Wales

Simon has soft-focus memories of traversing the east coast as a callow lad, and was thrilled to be able to retrace his steps for this book. Simon wrote the NSW introductory text, North Coast and South Coast sections.

JUSTINE VAISUTIS Queensland

Justine first became a nomad when she lived in South Africa and South Korea as a little tacker; and in Canberra as a slightly bigger tacker, where she cultivated a craving for warm places. As a teenager she experienced her first Queensland winter and confused it with Utopia. This is her third jaunt to Queensland for Lonely Planet, having doused herself in the Queensland sun, dipped into its tepid beaches and ogled at the Great Barrier Reef for *Australia & New Zealand on a shoestring* and *Queensland & the Great Barrier Reef*. On her travels she accidentally left a snippet of her soul there so she's looking forward to heading back as soon as possible.

RYAN VER BERKMOES Inland New South Wales

Whether it is the sand of the shore or the red dust of the Outback, Ryan is always happy to have a bit of NSW caught in his shorts. A native of California, Ryan has covered a fair bit of the world during his long writing career. He was the coordinating author for Lonely Planet's *New South Wales* guide and was very happy to return to this amazing and diverse state for this guide.

MEG WORBY Perth & Southern Western Australia

One Australian trip took Meg from the Torres Strait Islands in the far north right down the east coast to Tasmania (two days and about 4000km), but this was her first trip to the wild west, the other smooth cheek of the end of the world, and she couldn't have dreamt up a better gig. When she's not on the road with the windows down, Meg lives in a state of bohemian bliss with Lonely Planet author Charles Rawlings-Way and works at Lonely Planet's Melbourne office as an editor.

CONTRIBUTING AUTHORS

Bob Brown wrote the boxed text 'Deforestation In Tasmania' (p697). Bob was elected to the Tasmanian parliament on the day after his release from Risdon Prison, during the Franklin Dam blockade in 1983. He was first elected to the Senate in 1996. His books include *Memo for a Saner World* and *The Valley of the Giants*.

Michael Cathcart wrote the History chapter (p38). Michael lectures in Australian history at the Australian Centre, University of Melbourne. His published work includes an acclaimed abridgement of Manning Clark's six-volume classic *A History of Australia*. Michael is well known as a former presenter on ABC Radio National and as the host of the ABC TV history series *Rewind*.

Simone Egger wrote the Culture chapter (p49). Simone freelances as a writer, editor and photographer in Melbourne. She's clocked up thousands of kilometres covering Australia for half a dozen Lonely Planet guidebooks. For this book she analysed thousands of words, notes, pictures, plays, manoeuvres and movements to uncover the essence of 'the Australians'.

Matthew Evans wrote the Food & Drink chapter (p73). Matthew was a chef before he crossed to the 'dark side' and became a food writer and restaurant critic. He is also the award-winning author of four food books, including Lonely Planet's *World Food Italy*, and there is little that he wouldn't eat (that isn't endangered), as long as he lives to tell the story.

Tim Flannery wrote the Environment chapter (p61). Tim's a naturalist, explorer and writer. He is the author of a number of award-winning books, including *Country* and *The Future Eaters*. Tim currently lives in Adelaide where he is director of the South Australian Museum (p717) and a professor at the University of Adelaide.

Dr David Millar wrote the Health chapter (p1071). Dr Millar is a travel medicine specialist, diving doctor and lecturer in wilderness medicine who graduated in Hobart, Tasmania. He has worked in all states of Australia (except the NT) and as an expedition doctor with the Maritime Museum of Western Australia. Dr Millar is currently a Medical Director with the Travel Doctor in Auckland.

Gary Presland wrote the boxed text 'Aboriginal Australians' (p40). After an early career at sea, Gary studied history and archaeology at university. He has written extensively on Aboriginal history and is the author of *Aboriginal Melbourne – The Lost Land of the Kulin People*.

Tony Wilson wrote the boxed text 'Sporting Australia' (p50). Tony is a freelance writer based in Melbourne and has worked in print, radio and TV, as well as playing in the Hawthorn Football Club (Aussie Rules) reserves. His published books include *Players* (a comic novel about Melbourne's fixation with Aussie Rules).

Thanks also to Steve Irwin (boxed text 'Crikey – Quarantine Matters!', p1017), Sally O'Brien (boxed text 'Chinese Whispers', p103), Andrew Tudor (boxed text 'Where to Surf in Australia', p1012), Virginia Jealous (boxed text 'Christmas Island', p923), Alan Fletcher (boxed text 'Just for Neighbours Fans', p511), George Dunford (boxed text 'Adnyamathanha Dreaming', p780) and Dave Burnett (boxed text 'Bush Doof', p525; also Lord Howe Island p215 and Norfolk Island p216).

Getting Started

Travel in Australia is not difficult thanks to a well-developed tourism industry that provides options for travellers on all budgets and to a certain entrepreneurial spirit that sees accommodation, cafés and other services sprouting up in the unlikeliest places – on the fringes of remote national parks, on outback cattle stations and across far-flung peninsulas and islands. Time is of the essence here, as travel times between points in remote areas or for cross-country trips can be as vast as the landscape. So think about what you want to see and how you're going to get there, and then make sure you don't underestimate how long you'll need for your visit.

WHEN TO GO

Truth be told, any time is a good time to be *somewhere* in Australia. Weather-wise, when it's cold down south, it's magnificent in the north and the Centre; when it's too hot and sweaty up north, the southern states are at their natural finest. There's also the numerous festivals and other public spectacles that are on show every month, from the summertime food-and-wine banquets and large-scale concerts that mark the start of the year, through mid-year arts celebrations and whimsical beer-can regattas to end-of-year footy finals, horse races and yachting contests.

See Climate Charts (p1014) for information.

The seasons in Australia are the antithesis of those in Europe and North America. It is summer from December to February, when the weather and longer daylight hours are tailor-made for swimming and other outdoor activities across much of the country; no prizes for guessing that this is Australia's tourism high season. The period from June to August is the winter season, with temperatures dropping the further south you travel – it's officially designated the tourism low season but it's also the time when travellers head north, where the humidity of the wet season has subsided and the temperature is highly agreeable (the Dry roughly lasts from April to September, and the Wet from October to March, with the heaviest rain falling from January onwards). Autumn (March to May) and spring (September to November) both enjoy a lack of climatic extremes.

DON'T LEAVE HOME WITHOUT...

- A willingness to call absolutely everyone 'mate', whether you know them, or even like them
- Double-checking the visa situation (p1031)
- Sunscreen, sunglasses and a hat to deflect fierce UV rays (p1076)
- Knowing what your embassy/consulate in Australia can and can't do to help you if you're in trouble (p1020)
- Taking yourself less seriously, for the inevitable times when locals 'take the piss'
- Sewing a pouch onto the front of your jeans, so that stray kangaroos have somewhere to rest when they hop into your hotel
- A travel insurance policy specifically covering you for any planned high-risk activities (p1024)
- A suitcase-sized wardrobe that anticipates the country's climatic variations (p1014)
- Extra-strength insect repellent to fend off merciless flies and mosquitoes (p1017)
- Memorising the meaning of the word 'irony'

Unless you want to be competing with hordes of grimly determined local holiday-makers in 'Are we there yet?' mode for road space, places on tours, seats on all forms of transport, hotel rooms, camp sites, restaurant tables and the best vantage points at major attractions, you should try to avoid Australia's prime destinations during school and public holidays. See Holidays (p1023) for more information. During these times, you're also likely to encounter spontaneous rises in the price of everything from accommodation to petrol.

COSTS & MONEY

In recent years the Australian dollar has been holding its own against major international currencies like the greenback and the euro, so the country is a less economical destination than it used to be in the days when the Aussie dollar was financially malnourished. That said, while manufactured goods tend to be relatively expensive, daily living costs such as food and accommodation are still fairly inexpensive. The biggest cost in any trip to Australia will be transport, simply because it's such an expansive country.

How much you should budget for depends on what kind of traveller you are and how you'll be occupying yourself. If you regard sightseeing and having a good time as integral parts of the travel experience, prefer to stay in at least midrange accommodation, and have a stomach for regular restaurant visits, then $90 to $110 per day (per person travelling as a couple) should do it. Travellers with a demanding brood in tow will find there are many ways to keep kids inexpensively satisfied, including beach and park visits, camping grounds and motels with pools and games rooms, kids' menus and youth/family concessions for attractions. For more information on travelling with children, see p1014.

At the low-cost end of travel, if you camp or stay in hostels, cook your own meals, restrain your urge for entertainment and touristy attractions, and move around by bus (or in your own vehicle), you could probably eke out an existence on $50 per day; for a budget that realistically enables you to have a good time, raise the stakes to $65 per day.

TRAVEL LITERATURE

Considering Australia's enormity and its social extremes – from city-scapes to isolation, yuppies to nomads – it's perhaps surprising that relatively little in the way of travel literature has appeared on this continental subject. That said, some inspiring, thought-provoking and just plain entertaining books have been written about this country.

Robyn Davidson's *Tracks* (1980) details her crazily self-indulgent but ultimately courageous trek across 2700km of the outback from Alice Springs to the West Australian coast, equipped with several wild camels and a burgeoning personal honesty.

Speaking of lunacy, read *Keep Australia On Your Left* (2000) by Eric Stiller for an enthralling though often overwritten account of an attempt by two men to circumnavigate Australia's daunting girth in a kayak.

Another raw experience is captured in *Songlines* (1998), by Bruce Chatwin, in which the solipsistic author writes engagingly about the nature of nomadic life and the memories and myths sung across the landscape of Aboriginal culture.

In Tasmania (2004) by Nicholas Shakespeare is a mixture of erudite history and the contemporary musings of the author, who moves to Tasmania's east coast and discovers a personal ancestry entwined with early explorations of the island.

TOP TENS

Must-See Movies

One of the best places to do your essential trip preparation (ie daydreaming) is in a comfy lounge with a bowl of popcorn in one hand, a remote control in the other and your eyeballs pleasurably glued to a small screen. Head down to your local video store to pick up these quintessential Australian flicks, which range from the intelligent and thrilling to the *über*-cheesy. See p54 for some reviews of these and other films.

- *Lantana* (2001)
  Director: Ray Lawrence

- *Japanese Story* (2003)
  Director: Sue Brooks

- *Picnic at Hanging Rock* (1975)
  Director: Peter Weir

- *Shine* (1996)
  Director: Scott Hicks

- *Mad Max II: The Road Warrior* (1981)
  Director: George Miller

- *Somersault* (2004)
  Director: Cate Shortland

- *Rabbit-Proof Fence* (2002)
  Director: Phillip Noyce

- *Muriel's Wedding* (1994)
  Director: PJ Hogan

- *Breaker Morant* (1980)
  Director: Bruce Beresford

- *The Castle* (1997)
  Director: Rob Sitch

Top Reads

When it comes to a good novel, even the most imaginative and unreal story will speak of truths that exist beyond the page. These page-turners have won critical acclaim in Australia and abroad, not least because they have something to reveal to the reader about contemporary Australian issues, culture and relationships. See p55 for reviews of some of these and other books by Australian authors.

- *True History of the Kelly Gang* (2000)
  Peter Carey

- *A Child's Book of True Crime* (2002)
  Chloe Hooper

- *Dirt Music* (2003)
  Tim Winton

- *Seven Types of Ambiguity* (2002)
  Elliot Perlman

- *The Hunter* (1999)
  Julia Leigh

- *Eucalyptus* (1999)
  Murray Bail

- *Journey to the Stone Country* (2002)
  Alex Miller

- *The Service of Clouds* (1997)
  Delia Falconer

- *Drylands* (1997)
  Thea Astley

- *Remembering Babylon* (1993)
  David Malouf

Top Sounds

Music has a knack for capturing (sometimes defining) the feel of an event or era. The following albums do this for many Australians, conjuring up the vibes of long breezy road trips in old cars, memorable backyard parties, summer afternoons spent face-down on a warm beach, endless nights in neon-lit clubs, and long arguments about politics in the wee small hours. See p57 for some reviews.

- *Swingshift* (1981) Cold Chisel

- *Back in Black* (1980) AC/DC

- *Little Birdy* (2003) Little Birdy

- *The Sound of White* (2004) Missy Higgins

- *Get Born* (2004) Jet

- *Cats & Dogs* (1981) Mental As Anything

- *Body Language* (2003) Kylie Minogue

- *Wayward Angel* (2004) Kasey Chambers

- *Tribal Voice* (1991) Yothu Yindi

- *Let's Wiggle* (1999) The Wiggles (just kidding…)

A different kind of journey is described in Tony Horwitz's entertaining *One for the Road* (1999), a high-speed account of life on and along the highway during a round-Oz hitchhiking trip.

In *Christmas Island, Indian Ocean* (2003), journalist Julietta Jameson relates how a mind's-eye fascination with this remote Australian territory during the Tampa refugee crisis evolved into a three-month exploration of the island's natural and multicultural history.

For comfortably predictable reading, pick up a copy of Bill Bryson's *Down Under* (2001), in which the mass-market humorist takes his usual well-rehearsed pot-shots at a large target.

Cold Beer and Crocodiles (2001) by Roff Smith is filled with empathetic sketches of the diverse Australian characters he meets during a nine-month cycling trip around the continent.

OK, Terry Pratchett's *The Last Continent* (2000) is actually a fantasy novel, but in a twisted kind of way it qualifies as a travel book with its imaginative, mischievous and often hilarious reinvention of Australia as a land called Fourex (a pun on XXXX beer).

INTERNET RESOURCES

Australian Government (www.gov.au) Gateway to all federal, state, territory and local government sites.

Australian Newspapers Online (www.nla.gov.au/npapers) National Library–maintained listing of Australian newspaper websites.

Australian Tourist Commission (www.australia.com) Official, federal government–run tourism site with nationwide info for visitors.

Department of the Environment & Heritage (www.deh.gov.au/parks/links/index.html) Links to info on Australia's national parks and reserves.

Guide to Australia (www.csu.edu.au/australia) Links to sundry domestic sites focusing on attractions, culture, the environment, transport etc.

Lonely Planet (www.lonelyplanet.com) Get started with summaries on Australia, links to Australia-related sites and travellers trading information on the Thorn Tree.

Itineraries

CLASSIC ROUTES

EAST COAST RUN
One Month / Sydney to Cairns

Hordes of travellers stay on the beaten track on Australia's sun-loving east coast, following a beach-sprinkled route from Sydney to Cairns.

Shed the big-city trappings of **Sydney** (p89) and meander along the Pacific Hwy through central and northern New South Wales (NSW) towns with idyllic beach locales. Soak up the serenity of **Port Stephens** (p169), the watersports-mad **Myall Lakes National Park** (p172) and the plateau-top rainforests of **Dorrigo National Park** (p205). Join the feral and famous in **Byron Bay** (p189), then head over the Queensland border into the brown-skinned state capital, **Brisbane** (p290), via the kitsch party town of **Surfers Paradise** (p325).

Bruce Hwy then wends along the coast into the far north. Nature lovers should visit the whale-watching haven of **Hervey Bay** (p350) and, further north, the blissful **Whitsunday Islands** (p396), the coral charms of the **Great Barrier Reef** (p370) and the scuba-diving nexus of **Cairns** (p420).

Most travellers fly into Sydney and head north, but there's no reason why you can't tackle the route from the other end and work your way down. See Sydney (p140), Brisbane (p315) and Cairns (p429) for information on transport to/from each city, or browse Getting Around (p1039).

The East Coast Run is jammed with holiday-making hurly-burly, all 2864 beachcombing, wave-riding, tree-hugging, late-rising kilometres of it. You could do the run in a matter of days, but why would you? Take a month or two and really chill out.

INTO THE OUTBACK

Two Months / Melbourne to Darwin

The Stuart Hwy is a must-do route for anyone longing for an outback experience. Locally understated as 'the Track', this hot, dusty piece of bitumen bisects the awesome central deserts as it stretches from the South Australian (SA) crossroads town of Port Augusta to the 'Top End' city of Darwin in the Northern Territory (NT).

Begin this Outback odyssey in **Melbourne** (p466), where you can stock up on superb food and be an inner-city barfly before riding the Princes Hwy west and diverting onto the magical contours of the **Great Ocean Road** (p535). Rejoin the highway and head across to **Adelaide** (p713), SA's mellow but artistically vibrant capital. The going gets sparser after you pass Port Augusta, with the empty terrain and soporific silence eventually broken by the opal-tinted dugout town of **Coober Pedy** (p787).

Once you've paid your respects to **Uluru (Ayers Rock)** (p871) and visited the spectacular, vertigo-inducing **Watarrka (Kings Canyon) National Park** (p867), make for the desert oasis of **Alice Springs** (p845) in the heart of the steep-sided **MacDonnell Ranges** (p859). Between 'the Alice' and the laid-back NT capital, **Darwin** (p800), you'll gawk at the bizarre **Devil's Marbles** (p845), down some beers at the **Daly Waters Pub** (p842) and marvel at the landscapes, wildlife and Aboriginal rock art of World Heritage–listed **Kakadu National Park** (p824).

You can do this route from top to bottom. See the individual Getting There & Away sections under Melbourne (p518), Adelaide (p731) and Darwin (p815) for information on transport to and from each city, or browse Getting Around (p1039) for general details, and Outback Travel (p1065) for specific tips on how to make this journey memorable but safe.

Don your sunnies, practise swatting flies and launch into this long, sweaty and utterly unique 5018km journey through the middle of the continent. Don't rush from coast to coast in a fortnight: give yourself two horizon-stretching months instead

THE GIANT LOOP
Six Months / Sydney to Sydney

After bidding *au revoir* to **Sydney** (p89) and following your suntanned nose up the east coast into Queensland (see p29), veer west from **Townsville** (p399) towards the tunnel-threaded Queensland mining town of **Mt Isa** (p376). Leave a vigorous trail of footprints (via **Tennant Creek**; p843) in the red centre, where you can inspect **Alice Springs** (p845) and the awesome splendour of **Uluru (Ayers Rock)** (p871) before doglegging it up to **Darwin** (p800). Cross into Western Australia (WA) for a pit stop at pretty **Kununurra** (p1003), then negotiate the Great Northern Hwy to the cosmopolitan beachside getaway of **Broome** (p989).

Take a peninsular sidetrack to the marine brilliance of **Ningaloo Reef** (p977) and snorkel-friendly **Cape Range National Park** (p981), followed by a date with a bottlenose dolphin at **Monkey Mia** (p972). Continue south to the 'life is a beach' city of **Perth** (p883) and the latte-flavoured enclave of **Fremantle** (p903), then wine away the hours at **Margaret River** (p929) until you're ready to tackle the flat immensity of the **Nullarbor Plain** (p954).

In SA bushwalkers can trudge towards the challenging **Flinders Ranges** (p778), while tipplers can refuel their palates in the **Barossa Valley** (p750). Beyond **Adelaide** (p713) it's a shortish trek into Victoria to check out surfboard-strewn **Torquay** (p535) and cultured **Melbourne** (p466), from where there's a ferry to the stunning island highlights of **Tasmania** (p611).

Further along the Victorian coast, enjoy the secluded wilderness of **Wilsons Promontory National Park** (p599) and spend a couple of days at **Ninety Mile Beach** (p603), then cruise around **Narooma** (p227) on the southern NSW coast, and bask in idyllic **Jervis Bay** (p225). After you've detoured to the national capital, **Canberra** (p263), return to the bright lights of Sydney.

Experiencing the farthest reaches of the land can mean tallying over 14,000km of highway, not counting side trips to beaches, forests, mountains, reefs, towns... Where you start and finish is up to your imagination, but allow for around six months of discovery.

ROADS LESS TRAVELLED

INLAND EAST COAST   One Month / Sydney to Cairns

This trip parallels the immensely popular east-coast route but avoids the almost perpetual traffic. It exposes you to introspective old settlements and some singular Australian back country.

If you're starting in **Sydney** (p89), breathe in the gorgeous indigenous scenery of the **Blue Mountains** (p149) and take a light-headed detour to the wineries of the **Lower Hunter Valley** (p164) before linking up with the New England Hwy to reach the nation's self-titled 'horse capital', **Scone** (p168).

A visit to the boot scootin', stretch-denim nexus of the country music scene, **Tamworth** (p201), is followed by stops in the cool, well-educated environs of **Armidale** (p203), and quaint **Tenterfield** (p207), the self-titled cradle of Australian Federation.

Over the Queensland border is the **Granite Belt** (p346), an elevated plateau of the Great Dividing Range that's renowned for its boutique wineries. Just up the road are the view-blessed historic buildings of **Toowoomba** (p347), while a trio of sunburnt roads (Burnett, Dawson and Gregory Hwys) takes you past the sandstone splendour of **Carnarvon Gorge** (p374). Then it's a long and dusty drive to the gold-rush town of **Charters Towers** (p409) and an equally long trek to the formidable lava tubes of **Undara Volcanic National Park** (p417) before you arch east to **Cairns** (p420).

See Getting There & Away for Sydney (p140) and Cairns (p429), or browse Getting Around (p1039) for transport details.

This route takes you away from the east-coast tourist clutter and through 2811km of variegated rural life, pioneering towns, vineyards and remote gorges. Suppress any need for speed and take a month to have a good, long look around.

ACROSS THE CONTINENT   One to Two Months / Cairns to Perth

Those who prefer solitude and travelling rough will love the Australian outback, which is crisscrossed with innumerable roads and tracks, some sealed and others little more than a pair of dirty ruts. There are many potential hazards in heading off the beaten track, so wherever you go, make sure you're well informed and fully prepared – see Outback Travel (p1065) for more information.

The following is a long, difficult route from the tropics to the Indian Ocean. Start in **Cairns** (p420), gateway to the arduous Peninsula Development Rd that (in case you're interested) snakes towards the tip of **Cape York** (p454). Head west to **Normanton** (p418), the biggest town in the Gulf of Carpentaria region, then south down the Matilda Hwy to the mining roughhouse of **Mt Isa** (p376).

To the southwest is the frontier outback town of Urandangi, after which you run into the **Plenty Hwy** (p1066), a monotonous – or to some, gloriously desolate – road with plenty of bone-jolting challenges (4WD recommended). Over 500km later you'll hit the Stuart Hwy and then the dead-centre city of **Alice Springs** (p845).

The Lasseter Hwy turn-off takes you to weighty **Uluru (Ayers Rock)** (p871) and the captivating **Kata Tjuta (the Olgas)** (p872) rock formations, beyond which is the beginning of the **Great Central Rd** (p1066). This lonely trail, suitable for well-prepared 2WDs and lined with saltbush, spinifex and desert oaks, stretches 750km to the tiny gold-mining town of **Laverton** (p952), from where it's another 400km to the gold-mining concern of **Kalgoorlie-Boulder** (p948). Finally, the ocean beckons from behind the beaches of Scarborough and Cottesloe in **Perth** (p883).

Few roads are less travelled than this monster 4560km trail from the tidal rivers of the Gulf Savannah to the pounding surf at the bottom of Western Australia, with undulating desertscapes in between. Conditions can be unpredictable, so plan on up to two months.

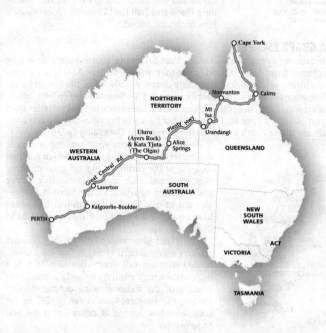

TAILORED TRIPS

WALK ON THE WILD SIDE

Appreciate Australia's stunning natural beauty from the inside with unhurried walks through its pristine national parks. Tasmania's wonderfully tangled interior is home to the famous 80.5km **Overland Track** (p697), a trail traversing the Cradle Mountain-Lake St Clair National Park and treating walkers to volcano-blasted peaks, crystal-clear tarns and wild moorlands. Tasmania is also the setting for the rugged **South Coast Track** (p701), which tiptoes around the edge of the sublime Southwest National Park. Jutting out from the Victorian coast is **Wilsons Promontory National Park** (p599), with over 130km of walking tracks and beautiful beaches, while the **Heysen Trail** (p709) runs for 1200km across SA from Cape Jervis on the tip of Fleurieu Peninsula to the rocky gorges and sawtooth ridges of the **Flinders Ranges National Park** (p778).

For another rough encounter, hit the 220km **Larapinta Trail** (p862) that follows the backbone of the West MacDonnell Ranges.

There's less strenuous walking on the rolling alpine plains of the Main Range in **Kosciuszko National Park** (p232), home to Australia's highest peaks. And for unadulterated beauty, don't miss being surrounded by granite mountains, tropical forests and thick mangroves on the 32km-long **Thorsborne Trail** (p412) across Queensland's Hinchinbrook Island.

A GRAPE ESCAPE

If nothing appeals to you more than following your bouquet-detecting schnozz from one vineyard to another, you'll find that Australia's grape-nurturing soil is soaked with tasty drops. A stalwart of the country's internationally praised viticulture scene is SA's **Barossa Valley** (p750), which is crowded with over 60 wineries and releases more bottled varieties than you can pop a cork at. The roll call of SA's worthy vine-covered bits continues to the north in the Riesling-proficient **Clare Valley** (p756).

Another prominent wine-making region is the **Hunter Valley** (p164) in NSW, which is home to some of the country's biggest glass-clinking concerns, and with some outstanding Shiraz and Semillon varieties. Victoria's rustic **Rutherglen district** (p565) specialises in fortified wines like muscat, Tokay and port that owe a debt to its hot climate.

The **Pipers River region** (p657) in Tasmania releases many superb vintages that are characterised by their full, fruity flavours. WA is a huge state which contributes only a small percentage of the national wine output. Nevertheless, the **Margaret River region** (p929) in the southwest has dozens of cellar doors for you to knock on.

CHILDISH DELIGHTS

There's a plethora of man-made and natural Australian sights and activities to capture the attention of the shrillest, most discerning child. For irresistible, top-of-the-Richter-scale distractions, head for Queensland's **Gold Coast** (p323) and the feisty rides of several big-budget theme parks. There's more stage-managed fun at period places like the pioneer settlement of **Swan Hill** (p561), with seats up for grabs on a paddle steamer, vintage cars and horse-drawn wagons. Kids enjoy the larger-than-life cheesiness of the country's 'big' things, like Nambour's **Big Pineapple** (p344), Ballina's **Big Prawn** (p188) and the **Big Rocking Horse** (p735) in the Adelaide Hills. Look in the index under 'big' for a listing of where to find other 'big' things in this book.

With its conspicuous natural assets, Australia is a great place to sit and watch wildlife go by, such as when southern right whales spout their way past King George Sound near **Albany** (p939) between July and October.

A refreshing ocean dip must be near the top of everyone's outdoor activities list, with beaches such as those at **Merimbula** (p228), in NSW, that are perfect for the occasion. And the **West Coast Wilderness Railway** (p692) is an unforgettable ride across some of west-coast Tasmania's most exhilarating terrain, between Queenstown and Strahan.

GET FESTIVE

Australians will seize on just about any excuse for a celebration, and while you're visiting this country it only makes sense to follow the light-hearted, self-indulgent lead of its inhabitants. The year gets off to a champagne-swilling start when fireworks explode high above Sydney Harbour on **New Year's Eve** (p115). The new year is also vigorously celebrated further south during the **Hobart Summer Festival** (p628), when Taswegians stuff themselves with food, wine and song.

In late January the streets of Tamworth in NSW are littered with broken guitar strings and broken hearts during its famous **Country Music Festival** (p201), while Sydney vamps itself up in February when the **Gay & Lesbian Mardi Gras** (p114) overwhelms Oxford St with rowdy, colourful glam.

The exuberant **Adelaide Festival of Arts** (p723) and its eccentric sibling, **Adelaide Fringe** (p723), fill the SA capital with culture and idiosyncratic performances in March every two years. And in April in Victoria, Melbourne repeatedly smacks its own funny bone with the outstanding **International Comedy Festival** (p499).

The outback Queensland town of Longreach droves itself crazy with dust-raising thrills during the three-day **Outback Muster** (p381) in May.

Meanwhile, for sheer quirkiness and dedication to silliness, the NT's long-running **Beer Can Regatta** (p809) in Darwin in July is an absolute must-see. Indigenous music is the highlight of **Stompen Ground** (p992), held September/October in the WA town of Broome.

Snapshot

Australians are becoming increasingly focused on personal finances and the nebulous concept of traditional values, if the results of the October 2004 federal election are anything to go by. The conservative Coalition (Liberal and National parties) was voted in for the fourth successive time by a comfortable margin, and John Winston Howard became the country's second-longest-serving prime minister, after Australia's mid-20th-century prime minister Robert Menzies. International issues such as Australia's involvement in the ongoing Iraq conflict had far less resonance with most voters than did the proceeds of the Coalition's firm-handed economic management. Conservative Christian voters also began to influence the outcome in many marginal seats, while the new Family First Party garnered strong, widespread support.

The no-contest result of the federal election had significant fallout for Australia's opposition parties. The largest of these, the Australian Labor Party (ALP), dealt with its failures by reverting to the tried-and-true tactic of howling for the blood of its own leader. To no-one's surprise, Mark Latham resigned from the ALP leadership in January 2005, citing ill health and a desire to rediscover family life. He was promptly replaced by Kim Beazley, the Lazarus of Australian politics, who led his party to resounding election defeats in 1998 and 2001 but somehow convinced himself and his peers that it simply wasn't his fault. Another casualty of the election was Pauline Hanson, former leader of the anti-immigration One Nation Party, who failed in her bid to become an independent senator. One Nation also lost its sole senator in the election.

The Australian economy is in good health, with the Coalition's aggressive pro-business policies encouraging steady economic growth, a relatively high-value Australian dollar, increased trade with China and some record-breaking profits for local businesses, including the posting by BHP Billiton in February 2005 of a stupefying *half-year* profit of $3.6 billion. This has been accompanied by low inflation and unemployment figures. On the downside, though, the country's trade deficit has ballooned to $20 billion, average household debt is soaring and, driven relentlessly by capitalist concerns, the price of real estate in many urban centres is bordering on the ludicrous.

Most Australians don't appear to be too bothered by the absence of any weapons of mass destruction in Iraq, even though this squarely contradicts the reasons initially given for Australia's military involvement there. But early in 2005 there were heated debates over the role of Australians in the 'forced interrogation' (as opposed to 'voluntary interviews') of Iraqi prisoners, a charge denied by Defence Minister Robert Hill but confirmed by a senior intelligence officer who claimed first-hand experience. In February 2005 Prime Minister Howard also announced the commitment of a further 450 troops to Iraq, going against the popular expectation that the Australian military contingent would be scaled back.

Environmental issues were expected to play a key role in the election's outcome, and they did – but not in the way many expected. In Tasmania, the often vitriolic disagreement between environmentalists and logging companies over the future of the state's old-growth forests, such as in the Styx Valley, resulted in the ALP being hauled over the proverbial coals for its proposal to protect most of these wilderness areas.

FAST FACTS

Population: 20,265,000

GDP growth: 3%

Inflation: 2.8%

Unemployment: 6%

Average gross weekly income (full-time work): $960

Tourism generates over $32 billion annually (4.2% of Australia's GDP)

Australia's coastline is 25,800km long and is dusted with over 7000 beaches

The perentie monitor lizard (*Varanus giganteus*) grows up to 2.5m in length and has been known to catch and eat small kangaroos

Tasmania is one of the world's biggest suppliers of opium – for legal purposes, primarily the production of medicines

Jobs and the welfare of families ('family' being a buzz word in contemporary Australian politics) were deemed the priorities by the electorate. To add insult to injury, a group of 20 environmental organisations and activists were sued in December 2004 for over $6 million by woodchipping giant Gunns Limited, which claimed corporate depression because of vigorous anti-logging campaigns. See p697 for further information about logging in Tasmania.

The earthquake-triggered tsunamis that struck Asia on 26 December 2004 and caused the deaths of an estimated 300,000 people (including 25 Australians) prompted an incredible local response, with individual donations to charities totalling over $140 million within a month of the disaster. Several large-scale events were organised to raise money for victims of the tsunamis, including the massive WaveAid concert at the Sydney Cricket Ground and a sell-out, all-star international cricket match played at the Melbourne Cricket Ground. Innumerable small-scale community events were also arranged around the country, with many set up as ongoing fundraisers.

South Australia bore the brunt of the country's deadliest bushfires in 22 years when flames raced across the Eyre Peninsula in January 2005, killing nine people, burning out 83,000 hectares of land and causing $50 million worth of property damage. It's thought that upwards of 30,000 sheep and cattle were also killed in the fires, which were fuelled by fiery temperatures and bone-dry scrub.

In mid-2004 the government signalled its intention to abolish the Aboriginal and Torres Strait Islander Commission (ATSIC), Australia's main indigenous body. The move will see the disbanding of Aboriginal-elected regional councils and their collective replacement with a government-appointed advisory board. Draft legislation to accomplish this has been introduced into parliament, although the exact date of ATSIC's demise and details of who will take over its responsibilities are yet to be finalised. ATSIC responded to the proposal defiantly early in 2005 by handing ownership of its multimillion-dollar art collection to a group of other Aboriginal organisations, prompting the government to pre-emptively seize the artworks from ATSIC offices. Indigenous frustration was also evident in November 2004 when the courthouse and police station of the large Aboriginal community of Palm Island, off the north Queensland coast, were burnt down after an Aboriginal man died from injuries allegedly sustained in police custody. Sparsely reported, however, are the entrenched poverty and housing shortages that afflict Aboriginal communities across the country, particularly in Northern Territory, Queensland and Western Australia.

The Australian infatuation with sport continues unabated. Headlines were created by the decision to expand the Super 12 international rugby union competition to a Super 14 event in 2006, with Perth chosen as the fourth local team to be included. Meanwhile, Melbourne was preparing for the XVIII Commonwealth Games in March 2006, an event involving around 4500 athletes from 71 countries and an estimated one million spectators.

History Michael Cathcart

Michael Cathcart presented the ABC TV history series *Rewind*. He is a lecturer in history at the Australian Centre, University of Melbourne.

INTRUDERS ARRIVE

By sunrise the storm had passed. Zachary Hicks was keeping sleepy watch on the British ship *Endeavour* when suddenly he was wide awake. He summoned his captain, James Cook, who climbed into the brisk morning air to a miraculous sight. Ahead of them lay an uncharted country of wooded hills and gentle valleys. It was 19 April 1770. In the coming days Cook began to draw the first European map of Australia's eastern coast. He was mapping the end of Aboriginal supremacy.

Two weeks later Cook led a party of men onto a narrow beach. As they waded ashore, two Aboriginal men stepped onto the sand, and challenged the intruders with spears. Cook drove the men off with musket fire. For the rest of that week, the Aborigines and the intruders watched each other warily.

Cook's ship *Endeavour* was a floating annexe of London's leading scientific organisation, the Royal Society. The ship's gentlemen passengers included technical artists, scientists, an astronomer and a wealthy botanist named Joseph Banks. As Banks and his colleagues strode about the Aborigines' territory, they were delighted by the mass of new plants they collected. (The showy banksia flowers, which look like red, white or golden bottlebrushes, are named after Banks.)

The local Aborigines called the place Kurnell, but Cook gave it a foreign name: he called it 'Botany Bay'. The fertile eastern coastline of Australia is now festooned with Cook's place names – including Point Hicks, Hervey Bay (after an English admiral), Endeavour River and Point Solander (after one of the *Endeavour*'s scientists).

When the *Endeavour* reached the northern tip of Cape York, blue ocean opened up to the west. Cook and his men could see the sea-route home. And on a small, hilly island ('Possession Island'), Cook raised the Union Jack. Amid volleys of gunfire, he claimed the eastern half of the continent for King George III.

Cook's intention was not to steal land from the Aborigines. In fact he rather idealised them: 'They are far more happier than we Europeans', he wrote. 'They think themselves provided with all the necessaries of Life and that they have no superfluities.' At most, his patriotic ceremony was intended to contain the territorial ambitions of the French, and of the Dutch, who had visited and mapped much of the western and southern coast over the previous two centuries. Indeed, Cook knew the western half of Australia as 'New Holland'.

In remote parts of Australia, many older Aborigines still speak their traditional languages rather than English.

The brilliant classic biography of Cook is JC Beaglehole's *The Life of Captain James Cook* (1974). Beaglehole also edited Cook's journals. There are several biographies online.

CONVICT BEGINNINGS

Eighteen years after Cook's arrival, in 1788, the English were back to stay with a fleet of 11 ships, packed with supplies including weapons, tools, building materials and livestock. The ships also contained 751 ragtag convicts, and around 250 soldiers, officials and their wives. This motley 'First Fleet' was under the command of a humane and diligent naval captain, Arthur Phillip. As his orders dictated, Phillip dropped anchor

TIMELINE	44,000 BC	8000 BC
	According to the most recent estimate, Aborigines settled in Australia	Tasmania's Aborigines are separated from the mainland when sea levels rise after the last Ice Age

at Botany Bay. But the paradise that had so delighted Joseph Banks filled Phillip with dismay. The country was marshy, there was little healthy water, and the anchorage was exposed to wind and storm. So Phillip left his floating prison and embarked in a small boat to search for a better location. Just a short way up the coast his heart leapt as he sailed into the finest harbour in the world. There, in a small cove, in the idyllic lands of the Eora people, he established a British penal settlement. He renamed the place after the British Home Secretary, Lord Sydney.

The intruders set about clearing the trees and building shelters and were soon trying to grow crops. Phillip's official instructions urged him to colonise the land without doing violence to the local inhabitants. Among the Aborigines he used as intermediaries was an Eora man named Bennelong, who adopted many of the white man's customs and manners. For many years Bennelong lived in a hut on the finger of land now known as Bennelong Point, the site of the Sydney Opera House. But his people were shattered by the loss of their lands. Hundreds died of smallpox, and many of the survivors, including Bennelong himself, succumbed to alcoholism and despair.

So what kind of society were the British trying to create? Robert Hughes' bestseller, *The Fatal Shore* (1987), depicts convict Australia as a terrifying 'gulag' where the British authorities tormented rebels, vagrants and criminals. But other historians point out that powerful men in London saw transportation as a scheme for giving prisoners a new and useful life. Indeed, under Governor Phillip's authority, many convicts soon earned their 'ticket of leave', a kind of parole which allowed them to live where they wished and to seek work on their own behalf.

But the convict system could also be savage. Women (who were out-numbered five to one) lived under constant threat of sexual exploitation. Female convicts who offended their gaolers languished in the depressing 'female factories'. Male re-offenders were cruelly flogged and could even be hanged for such crimes as stealing.

In 1803 English officers established a second convict settlement in Van Diemen's Land (later called Tasmania). Soon, reoffenders filled the grim prison at Port Arthur (p645) on the beautiful and wild coast near Hobart. Others endured the senseless agonies of Norfolk Island prison (p216) in the remote Pacific.

So miserable were these convict beginnings, that Australians long regarded them as a period of shame. But things have changed: today most white Australians are inclined to brag a little if they find a convict in their family tree. Indeed, Australians annually celebrate the arrival of the First Fleet at Sydney Cove on 26 January 1788, as 'Australia Day'.

FROM SHACKLES TO FREEDOM

At first, Sydney and the smaller colonies depended on supplies brought in by ship. Anxious to develop productive farms, the government granted land to soldiers, officers and emancipated convicts. After 30 years of trial and error, the farms began to flourish. The most irascible and ruthless of these new land-holders was John Macarthur. Along with his spirited wife Elizabeth, Macarthur pioneered the breeding of merino sheep on his verdant property near Sydney.

A likable observer of the settlement was Watkin Tench. His vivid journal is available as *Watkin Tench 1788* (edited by Tim Flannery).

The Fatal Shore (1987) is an exhilarating international bestseller, well worth the read. For the counterargument see Alan Atkinson's *The Europeans in Australia: Volume One* (1998).

The website www.port arthur.org.au is a vital guide for the visitor to this powerful historical site.

Early 1600s	1770
Dutch sailors reach Western Australia and Cape York, but are unimpressed with the harsh terrain	English captain James Cook maps Australia's east coast in the *Endeavour*

ABORIGINAL AUSTRALIANS Gary Presland

Recent estimates of Australia's Aboriginal population at the time of European invasion suggest that there were perhaps one million people across the continent.

The precise time of arrival in Australia of ancestral Aborigines will likely never be known. What is currently conjectured is that the initial landfall occurred perhaps about 46,000 years ago, at a time of lower sea levels, during the Ice Age. These people came via the region of Southeast Asia, and in order to reach continental Australia had to cross water passages at least 70km wide. From the point of arrival (now long since inundated by rising sea level) people spread through all of Australia's environmental zones within a comparatively short period. Archaeological sites close to Melbourne in the southeast and on the Swan River near Perth in the southwest have been dated to about 40,000 years ago. Two human burials at Lake Mungo (p260) in western New South Wales (NSW) have recently been re-dated to a similar figure.

Australia was a continent of hunters and gatherers. With regional variations in the country's diverse ecological zones, people made their living by focusing on the available natural resources. But this was not a purely passive exercise. There are many instances of Aborigines acting to maximise the returns of their hunting and foraging strategies. In western Victoria elaborate systems were devised for trapping eels; in the northern wetland environments it was common practice to replant tubers to promote future growth. And in every part of the continent fire was used as a tool in the clearing of vegetation, to aid movement and to promote new growth. In many regions this 'fire-stick farming' maintained a grassland environment.

Across the continent cultural elements were maintained and transmitted in oral forms. Of particular importance was the use of songs to convey stories of the creative activities of ancestor figures during the 'Dreaming'. Short songs containing powerful information might relate to specific localities or, when a series is strung together, a dreaming track. In this latter case, such series are sometimes called songlines and can refer to tracks extending over considerable distances. A detailed knowledge of such songs was held to be a sign of great power in an individual. See the boxed text, p53, for more information about traditional Aboriginal religion.

There were about 250 languages spoken in Aboriginal Australia, divided into approximately 700 dialects. The most important social group was the clan, as the group that identified with specific tracts of land. Because of their close identification with land and their day-to-day hunting and foraging strategies, clans were essentially localised in their operations. There was regular movement but Aborigines were not nomadic; rather, they moved within their estates according to a range of determinants, including seasonal variation and the need to be at specific places for ritual and totemic purposes. In many parts of the country early observers commented on the permanent 'villages' of local people.

Many clans were linked as part of exchange networks that saw the movement of objects and ideas over long distances. In this way pearl objects and baler shells from the Gulf of Carpentaria in the north found their way to Spencer Gulf, 3000km to the south.

Permanent European settlement in Australia began in Sydney in January 1788, but Aboriginal people had had occasional contact with other people for hundreds of years prior to this. From the 15th century onwards European ships periodically sighted Australian shores, and Dutch and English ships touched briefly on Australia's northwest coast in the 17th century. From the mid-18th century Southeast Asian fishermen regularly fished in coastal waters for *trepang* (sea cucumber). They also traded with local Aborigines and took a number of men back to Indonesia.

1788	1854
The First Fleet settles at Sydney Harbour with its cargo of convicts	Gold miners' rebellion brutally put down at the Eureka Stockade; most colonies are granted self-government soon after

Following the settlement of Sydney, the occupation of Aboriginal land occurred progressively across Australia. This invasion took place from a number of directions and was resisted by local Aboriginal groups. Frontier violence was not uncommon but there were also many instances of cooperation for mutual benefit.

In the more populated eastern colonies the impacts on the indigenous populations were dramatic and sudden, including death through introduced diseases and a dramatic decline in birth rate. The dispossession of land was a major factor in the rapid demise of most elements of traditional Aboriginal culture.

Through more than 40,000 years Aboriginal Australians had successfully adapted their way of life to many challenges. The European invasion brought rapid and massive changes but Aboriginal culture survived and continues in a wide variety of contemporary forms.

Since the late 1960s, use of the term 'Koori' (or Koorie) to refer to Aborigines has become widespread. The word means 'people' in a number of languages from southeastern Australia and is one of a number of such terms used to distinguish the indigenous people of specific regions. A Koori is an indigenous person from NSW or Victoria, just as a Murri is from Queensland, a Nunga is from South Australia (SA) and a Noongar from Western Australia (WA).

At the time of first occupation of Aboriginal land, beginning in 1788, the Australian continent had been regarded as *terra nullius* – land that was owned by nobody.

This fiction went largely unchallenged until the mid- to late 20th century. In 1968 a group of Gurundji stockmen on Wave Hill cattle station in the Northern Territory (NT) instigated the first Aboriginal land claim. Although this claim failed, it set in motion a still-continuing movement by Aboriginal people to reclaim their land.

In 1982 a small group of Torres Strait Islanders from Mer (Murray Island), headed by Koiki (Eddie) Mabo began legal proceedings in the Queensland Supreme Court to establish their traditional ownership of their land. The case eventually progressed to the High Court of Australia which, in 1992, upheld their claim. This landmark judgement refuted the legal fiction of *terra nullius* and established that Aborigines had the right to claim title to their traditional lands.

In the following years the federal Labor government enacted legislation to make the Mabo decision law. However, the legislation excluded pastoral leases, which led to confusion within the pastoral industry and a lack of confidence within the mining and resource industries. There was also widespread scaremongering regarding the rights of Aboriginal people to make claims on land, fuelled particularly by prominent individuals such as the controversial right-wing One Nation leader Pauline Hanson.

A conservative federal government led by John Howard was elected in 1996. Soon after, in another watershed case brought by the Wik people of northern Queensland, the High Court ruled that pastoral leases and native title could coexist.

Fearful of a deluge of Aboriginal land-rights claims, the Howard government moved quickly to diminish the rights of Aborigines in this respect. A 10-point plan was devised, which effectively eliminated many of the reforms of the previous Labor government and reduced the range of allowable claims. Under the plan, Aborigines have access to pastoral land for the purposes of visiting sacred sites and holding ceremonies, and to gather resources such as food and water. Native title was abolished on pastoral leases when it would interfere with the rights of the pastoralist.

Gary Presland has written extensively on Aboriginal history and is the author of Aboriginal Melbourne: The Lost Land of the Kulin People

1861	1901
Explorers Burke and Wills die in an ostentatious attempt to cross the continent – they become heroes	The Australian colonies federate; the federal parliament meets for the first time in Melbourne

Macarthur was also a leading member of the Rum Corps, a clique of powerful officers who bullied successive governors (including William Bligh of *Bounty* fame), and grew rich by controlling much of Sydney's trade, notably rum. But its racketeering was ended in 1810 by a tough new governor named Lachlan Macquarie. Macquarie also laid out the major roads of modern-day Sydney, built some fine public buildings (many of which were designed by talented convict-architect Francis Greenway) and helped to lay the foundations for a more civil society.

Macquarie also championed the rights of freed convicts, granting them land and appointing several to public office. But Macquarie's tolerance was not shared by the 'exclusives'. These land-holders, middle-class snobs and senior British officials observed a rigid expatriate class system. They shunned ex-prisoners, and scoffed at the distinctive accent and the easy-going manners of these new Australians.

By now, word was reaching England that Australia offered cheap land and plenty of work, and adventurous migrants took to the oceans in search of their fortunes. At the same time the British government continued to transport prisoners.

In 1825 a party of soldiers and convicts established a penal settlement in the territory of the Yuggera people, close to modern-day Brisbane. Before long this warm, fertile region was attracting free settlers, who were soon busy farming, grazing, logging and mining.

Tom Petrie's classic Reminiscences of Early Queensland (1904) is the vivid life story of a colonial bushman who grew up with Aborigines.

TWO NEW SETTLEMENTS: MELBOURNE & ADELAIDE

In the cooler grasslands of Tasmania, the sheep farmers were also thriving, and they too were hungry for more land. In 1835 an ambitious young squatter named John Batman sailed to Port Phillip Bay on the mainland. On the banks of the Yarra River, he chose the location for Melbourne, famously announcing 'This is the place for a village.' Batman then worked a staggering swindle: he persuaded local Aborigines to 'sell' him their traditional lands (a whopping 250,000 hectares) for a crate of blankets, knives and knick-knacks. Back in Sydney, Governor Burke declared the contract void, not because it was unfair, but because the land officially belonged to the British Crown. Burke proved his point by granting Batman some prime acreage near Geelong.

At the same time, a private British company settled Adelaide in South Australia (SA). Proud to have no links with convicts, these God-fearing folks instituted a scheme under which their company sold land to well-heeled settlers, and used the revenue to assist poor British labourers to emigrate. When these worthies earned enough to buy land from the company, that revenue would in turn pay the fare of another shipload of labourers. This charming theory collapsed in a welter of land speculation and bankruptcy, and in 1842 the South Australian company yielded to government administration. By then miners had found rich deposits of silver, lead and copper at Burra, Kapunda and the Mount Lofty Ranges, and the settlement began to pay its way.

The level of frontier violence is disputed in the acrimonious and highly political 'history wars', as detailed in Stuart Macintyre's The History Wars (2003).

THE SEARCH FOR LAND CONTINUES

Each year, settlers pushed deeper into Aboriginal territories in search of pasture and water for their stock. These men became known as squatters (because they 'squatted' on Aboriginal lands) and many held this territory with a gun. To bring order and regulation to the frontier, from the 1830s, the governments permitted the squatters to stay on these 'Crown lands' for payment of a nominal rent. Aboriginal stories tell of white men poisoning traditional water holes during this time, or slaughtering groups of Aborigines in reprisal for the killing of sheep or settlers. Across the country, people also tell stories of black resistance leaders, including Yagan of Swan River, Pemulwy of Sydney and Jandamarra, the outlaw-hero of the Kimberley.

In time, many of the squatters reached a compromise with local tribes. Aborigines took low-paid jobs on sheep and cattle stations as drovers and domestics. In return they remained on their traditional lands, adapting their cultures to their changing circumstances. This arrangement continued in outback pastoral regions until after WWII.

The newcomers had fantasised about the wonders waiting to be discovered from the moment they arrived. Before explorers crossed the Blue Mountains west of Sydney in 1813, some credulous souls imagined that China lay on the other side! Then explorers, surveyors and scientists began trading theories about inland Australia. Some spoke of an Australian Mississippi. Others predicted desert. An obsessive explorer named Charles Sturt (there's a fine statue of him looking lost in Adelaide's Victoria Sq; p713) believed in an almost mystical inland sea.

The explorers' journeys inland were mostly journeys into disappointment. But Australians made heroes of 'failed' explorers who died in the wilderness (Leichhardt, and the duo of Burke and Wills are the most striking examples), just as they did those who returned with news of fresh pastures. It was as though the Victorian era believed that a nation could not be born until its men had shed their blood in battle – even if that battle was with the land itself.

GOLD & REBELLION

Transportation of convicts to eastern Australia ceased in the 1840s. This was just as well: in 1851 prospectors discovered gold in New South Wales (NSW) and central Victoria. The news hit the colonies with the force of a cyclone. Young men and some adventurous women from every social class headed for the diggings. Soon they were caught up in a great rush of prospectors, entertainers, publicans, sly-groggers (illicit liquor-sellers), prostitutes and quacks from overseas. In Victoria, the British governor was alarmed – both by the way the Victorian class system had been thrown into disarray, and by the need to finance law and order on the goldfields. His solution was to compel all miners to buy an expensive monthly licence, in the hope that the lower orders would return to their duties in town.

But the lure of gold was too great. In the reckless excitement of the goldfields, the miners initially endured the thuggish troopers who enforced the government licence. After three years, however, the easy gold at Ballarat was gone, and miners were toiling in deep, water-sodden shafts. They were now infuriated by a corrupt and brutal system of law which held them in contempt. Under the leadership of a charismatic Irishman named Peter Lalor, they raised their own flag, the Southern

Acclimatisation societies of the 19th century tried to replace the 'inferior' Australian plants and animals with superior European ones. Such cute 'blessings' as rabbits and foxes date from this time.

The mystical and mad dimensions of exploration inspired Patrick White's *Voss* (1957), revered by some as the great Australian novel.

The Goldfields of Victoria website, www.goldfields .org.au, is a fabulous tourist guide. The key attraction is Sovereign Hill at Ballarat.

1948	1949
Ambitious programme of postwar reconstruction under way; the first Holden car leaves the factory	Robert Menzies' new Liberal Party begins an era of government lasting until 1972

Cross, and swore to defend their rights and liberties. They armed themselves and gathered inside a rough stockade at Eureka, where they waited for the government to make its move.

In the predawn of Sunday 3 December 1854, a force of troopers attacked the stockade. In 15 terrifying minutes, they slaughtered 30 miners and lost five soldiers. But democracy was in the air and public opinion sided with the miners. When 13 of the rebels were tried for their lives, Melbourne juries set them free. Many Australians have found a kind of splendour in these events: the story of the Eureka Stockade is often told as a battle for nationhood and democracy – again illustrating the notion that any 'true' nation must be born out of blood. But these killings were tragically unnecessary. The eastern colonies were already in the process of establishing democratic parliaments, with the full support of the British authorities. In the 1880s Peter Lalor himself became Speaker of the Victorian parliament.

The gold rush had also attracted boatloads of prospectors from China. These Asians endured serious hostility from whites, and were the victims of ugly race riots on the goldfields at Lambing Flat (now called Young) in NSW in 1860–61. Chinese precincts soon developed in the backstreets of Sydney and Melbourne, and popular literature indulged in tales of Chinese opium dens, dingy gambling parlours and oriental brothels. But many Chinese went on to establish themselves in business and, particularly, in market gardening. Today the busy Chinatowns of the capital cities (p77) and the presence of Chinese restaurants in towns across the country are reminders of the vigorous role of the Chinese since that time.

Gold and wool brought immense investment and gusto to Melbourne and Sydney. By the 1880s they were stylish modern cities, with gaslights in the streets, railways, electricity and that great new invention, the telegraph. In fact, the southern capital became known as 'Marvellous Melbourne', so opulent were its theatres, hotels, galleries and fashions. But the economy was overheating. Many politicians and speculators were engaged in corrupt land deals, while investors poured money into wild and fanciful ventures. It could not last.

MEANWHILE, IN THE WEST...

Western Australia (WA) lagged behind the eastern colonies by about 50 years. Though Perth was settled by genteel colonists back in 1829, their material progress was handicapped by isolation, Aboriginal resistance and the arid climate. It was not until the 1880s that the discovery of remote goldfields promised to gild the fortunes of the isolated colony. At the time, the west was just entering its own period of self-government, and its first premier was a forceful, weather-beaten explorer named John Forrest. He saw that the mining industry would die if the government did not provide a first-class harbour, efficient railways and reliable water supplies. Ignoring the threats of private contractors, he appointed the brilliant CY O'Connor as his chief engineer to design and build each of these as government projects. O'Connor's final scheme was a 560km pipeline and a series of mighty pumping stations that would drive water uphill from the coast to the dry goldfields round Kalgoorlie (p955). As the

There's a good Chinese Museum in Melbourne; see home.vicnet.net.au /~mcah/welcome.htm

O'Connor's pipeline is presented as a tourist experience at www .goldenpipeline.com.au

1950s	1956
Massive immigration programme from Europe transforms Australian cities; economic boom	Olympic Games held in Melbourne; TV arrives in Australia

work neared completion, O'Connor was subjected to merciless slander in the capitalist press. In 1902 the tormented man rode into the surf at South Fremantle and shot himself. A lonely statue in the waves marks the spot. His great pipeline continues to pump water into the thirsty gold cities of central WA.

GROWING NATIONALISM

By the end of the 19th century, Australian nationalists tended to idealise 'the bush' and its people. The great forum for this 'bush nationalism' was the massively popular *Bulletin* magazine. Its politics were egalitarian, democratic and republican, and its pages were filled with humour and sentiment about daily life, written by a swag of writers, most notably Henry Lawson and 'Banjo' Paterson.

Central to the *Bulletin*'s ethos was the idea of 'mateship'. At its most attractive, mateship was a sense of brotherhood reinforced by a profound egalitarianism. But there was also a deeply chauvinistic side to mateship. This was represented in the pages of the *Bulletin,* where cartoons and stories often portrayed women as sexy maidens or nagging wives. It parodied Aborigines as amiable simpletons and it represented the Chinese as goofballs or schemers. A more bruised and knowing account of women and the bush appeared in the short stories of Barbara Baynton.

The 1890s were also a time of great trauma. As the speculative boom came crashing down, unemployment and hunger dealt cruelly to working-class families in the eastern states. However, Australian workers had developed a fierce sense that they were entitled to share in the country's prosperity. As the depression deepened, trade unions became more militant in their defence of workers' rights. At the same time, activists intent on winning legal reform established the Australian Labor Party.

Some people feared that the nation was about to descend into revolution. But there was a broad liberal consensus in Australia that took democracy and fairness for granted. So the new century was ushered in, not with bombs, but with fireworks.

NATIONHOOD

On 1 January 1901 Australia became a federation. When the bewhiskered members of the new national parliament met in Melbourne, their first aim was to protect the identity and values of a European Australian from an influx of Asians and Pacific Islanders. Their solution was what became known as the White Australia policy. It became a racial tenet of faith in Australia for the next 70 years.

For those who were welcome to live here (ie whites), this was to be a model society, nestled in the skirts of the British Empire. Just one year later, white women won the right to vote in federal elections. In a series of radical innovations, the government introduced a broad social welfare scheme and it protected Australian wage levels with import tariffs. Its mixture of capitalist dynamism and socialist compassion became known as the 'Australian settlement'.

Meanwhile, most Australians lived on the coastal 'edge' of the continent. So forbidding was the arid inland, that they called the great dry Lake Eyre 'the Dead Heart' of the country. It was a grim image – as if the heart

For more on the painters and writers of the colonial bush legend, see www.cultureandrecreation .gov.au/articles/bush

The most vivid celebration of the contemporary bush legend is the Stockman's Hall of Fame at Longreach in central Queensland; see www .outbackheritage.com.au

Two very different, intelligent introductions to Australian history are Stuart Macintyre's *A Concise History of Australia* and Geoffrey Blainey's *A Shorter History of Australia.*

1966	1967
Australian troops sent to fight alongside US troops in Vietnam War; protest movement born	Popular referendum overwhelmingly gives Aborigines the status of full citizens

muscle, which should pump the water of life through inland Australia, were dead. No wonder that the green and pleasant fields of England still seemed like 'home' to so many. But one prime minister in particular, the dapper Alfred Deakin (1903–10), and many other 'boosters' were determined to overcome the tyranny of the climate. Even prior to Federation, in the 1880s, Deakin championed a scheme to develop irrigated farming on the Murray River at Mildura, and it was successful: the region developed a prosperous grape and dried-fruit industry. (Today, this massively productive region is facing an ecological crisis as the Murray struggles to meet the great demands made upon it.)

ENTERING THE WORLD STAGE

Living on the edge of a dry and forbidding land, and isolated from the rest of the world, most Australians took comfort in the idea that they were still a part of the British Empire. When war broke out in Europe in 1914, thousands of Australian men rallied to the Empire's call. They had their first taste of death on 25 April 1915, when the Australian and New Zealand Army Corps (Anzacs) joined other British and French troops in an assault on the Gallipoli Peninsula in Turkey. It was eight months before the British commanders acknowledged that the tactic had failed. By then 8141 young Australians were dead. Soon the Australian Imperial Force was fighting in the killing fields of Europe. By the time the war ended, 60,000 Australian men had been slaughtered. Ever since, on 25 April, Australians have gathered at war memorials around the country for the sad and solemn services of Anzac Day.

In the 1920s Australia embarked on a decade of chaotic change. Cars began to rival horses on the highway. In the new cinemas, young Australians enjoyed American movies. In an atmosphere of sexual freedom not equalled until the 1960s, young people partied and danced to American jazz. At the same time, popular enthusiasm for the British Empire grew more intense – as if Imperial fervour were an antidote to grief. As radicals and reactionaries clashed, Australia careered wildly through the 1920s until it collapsed into the abyss of the Great Depression in 1929. World prices for wheat and wool plunged. Unemployment brought its shame and misery to one in three houses. Once again working people experienced the cruelty of a system which treated them as expendable. For those who were wealthy – or who had jobs – the Depression was hardly noticed. In fact, the extreme deflation of the economy actually meant that the purchasing power of their wages was enhanced.

In the midst of the hardship, sport brought escape to a nation in love with games and gambling. A powerful chestnut horse called Phar Lap won race after race, culminating in an effortless and graceful victory in the 1930 Melbourne Cup (which is still known as 'the race that stops a nation'). In 1932 the great horse travelled to the racetracks of America, where he mysteriously died. In Australia, the gossips insisted that the horse had been poisoned by envious Americans. And the legend grew of a sporting hero cut down in his prime. Phar Lap was stuffed and is a revered exhibit at the Melbourne Museum.

The year 1932 saw accusations of treachery on the cricket field. The English team, under their captain Douglas Jardine, employed a violent

The most accessible version of the Anzac legend is Peter Weir's Australian epic film *Gallipoli* (1981), with a cast that includes a young Mel Gibson.

A favourite depression novel is George Johnson's *My Brother Jack* (1964).

Don't miss Phar Lap himself. This stuffed horse is a seriously odd spectacle. The legend is explored at www.museum.vic.gov.au /pharlap

new bowling tactic known as 'body-line'. His aim was to unnerve Australia's star batsman, the devastatingly efficient Donald Bradman. The bitterness of the tour provoked a diplomatic crisis with Britain, and became part of Australian legend. And Bradman batted on – achieving the unsurpassed career average of 99.94 runs.

WAR WITH JAPAN

After 1933 the economy began to recover. The whirl of daily life was hardly dampened when Hitler hurled Europe into a new war in 1939. Though Australians had long feared Japan, they took it for granted that the British navy would keep them safe. In December 1941, Japan bombed the US Fleet at Pearl Harbor. Weeks later the 'impregnable' British naval base in Singapore crumbled, and before long thousands of Australians and other Allied troops were enduring the savagery of Japan's prisoner of war camps.

As the Japanese swept through Southeast Asia and into Papua New Guinea, the British announced that they could not spare any resources to defend Australia. But the legendary US commander General Douglas MacArthur saw that Australia was the perfect base for American operations in the Pacific. In a series of savage battles on sea and land, Allied forces gradually turned back the Japanese advance. Importantly, it was the USA, not the British Empire, who saved Australia. The days of the British alliance were numbered.

VISIONARY PEACE

When WWII ended, a new slogan rang through the land: 'Populate or Perish!' The Australian government embarked on an ambitious scheme to attract thousands of immigrants. With government assistance, people flocked from Britain and from non-English speaking countries. They included Greeks, Italians, Slavs, Serbs, Croatians, Dutch and Poles, followed by Turks, Lebanese and many others. These 'new Australians' were expected to assimilate into a suburban stereotype known as the Australian way of life'.

This was the great era of the 'nuclear family', in which Australians basked in the prosperity of a 'Long Boom'. Many migrants found jobs in the growing manufacturing sector, under which companies like General Motors and Ford operated with generous tariff support. In addition, the government embarked on audacious public works schemes, notably the mighty Snowy Mountains Hydroelectric Scheme in the mountains near Canberra. Today, environmentalists point out the devastation caused by this huge network of tunnels, dams and power stations. But the Snowy scheme was a great expression of optimism and testifies to the cooperation among the men of many nations who laboured on the project. At the same time, there was growing world demand for Australia's primary products: metals, wool, meat and wheat. In time Australia would even become a major exporter of rice to Japan.

This era of growth and prosperity was dominated by Robert Menzies, the founder of the modern Liberal Party and Australia's longest-serving prime minister. Menzies was steeped in British history and tradition, and liked to play the part of a sentimental monarchist. He was also a vigilant

The official guardian of war history is the Australian War Memorial in Canberra – go to www.awm.gov.au

A wonderful novel set in wartime Brisbane is *Johnno* (1975) by David Malouf, one of Australia's best writers.

High Court rejects *terra nullius* and rules that some Aborigines have legal title to their traditional lands (Mabo case)

The Sydney Olympic Games

A popular and scathing commentary on Australia in the 1960s was Donald Horne's *The Lucky Country* (1964).

opponent of communism. The chill of the Cold War was extending across Asia, and Australia and New Zealand entered a formal military alliance with the USA – the 1951 Anzus security pact. When the USA hurled its righteous fury into a civil war in Vietnam, Menzies committed Australian forces to the battle, introducing conscription for military service overseas. The following year Menzies retired, leaving his successors a bitter legacy. The antiwar movement split Australia.

There was a feeling too among artists, intellectuals and the young that Menzies' Australia had become a rather dull, complacent country, more in love with American and British culture than with its own talents and stories. In an atmosphere of youthful rebellion and new-found nationalism, the Labor Party was elected to power in 1972 under the leadership of a brilliant, idealistic lawyer named Gough Whitlam. In just four short years his government transformed the country. He ended conscription and abolished all university fees. He introduced a free universal health scheme, no-fault divorce and equal pay for women. The White Australia policy had been gradually falling into disuse; under Whitlam it was finally abandoned altogether. By now, around one million migrants had arrived from non-English speaking countries, and they had filled Australia with new languages, cultures, foods and ideas. Under Whitlam this achievement was embraced as 'multiculturalism'.

Read more about the prime ministers, including Menzies, at www.primeministers .naa.gov.au

By 1975, the Whitlam government was enveloped in a tempest of inflation and scandal. At the end 1975 his government was controversially dismissed from office by the governor general. But the general thrust of Whitlam's social reforms was continued by his successors. From the 1970s, Asian immigration increased. Vietnamese communities became prominent, particularly in Sydney and Melbourne. China and Japan far outstripped Europe as major trading partners – Australia's economic future lay in Asia.

MATERIALISM

Today Australia faces new challenges. Since the 1970s the country has been dismantling its protectionist scaffolding. New efficiency has brought new prosperity. At the same time wages and working conditions, which used to be fixed by an independent authority, are much more uncertain. Egalitarianism is giving way to competition. And two centuries of development has placed great strains on the environment – on water supplies, forests, soils, air quality and the oceans (see p72). The country is closer than ever to the USA, as it demonstrated by its commitment to the war in Iraq (2003–). Some say that this alliance protects Australia's independence; others insist that it reduces Australia to a fawning 'client state'.

Though many Australians pride themselves on their tolerance, no-one talks as much of 'multiculturalism' any more. Under popular conservative prime minister John Howard, the majority of Australians have hardened their hearts to asylum seekers. At the same time, Howard's stance on Aboriginal issues has been marked more by confrontation than by sympathy. But since his first election in 1996, he has presided over secure economic growth, encouraging an atmosphere in which material self-advancement and self-reliance are the primary measure of what is right.

2001	**2002**
Norwegian ship *Tampa* rescues 460 asylum seekers from their sinking boat; Australian government prevents them landing on Australian soil	Death of 89 Australians when a Bali nightclub (in Indonesia) is bombed by Islamic militants

The Culture

THE NATIONAL PSYCHE
Colonisation & Myth Making

Convicts and colonists arriving in Australia must have felt as though they'd dropped over the edge of the world. A gruelling four-month odyssey had transported them away from familiarity, family and friends to a vast place of infernal heat, hemmed by seas and governed by a fledgling system with serious teething problems. To cope with this struggle against nature and tyranny, these new Australians forged a culture based on the principles of a 'fair go', with back-slaps for challenges to authority and eager ears for the legend of the Aussie 'battler'.

The Eureka Stockade (1854), one of Australia's first anti-authoritarian struggles, saw miners rebel against what they saw as unjust gold-mining licences. Ultimately the miners won out and the principles of democracy emerged, but not without a fight (p43). Some saw this battle as part of the age-old clash between the poor Irish Catholics and the ruling English Protestants, played out on foreign soil where the Irish had come to start afresh with no intention of returning to the status quo of old Britain.

The next major challenge to the Brits came with Gallipoli, fought on Turkish soil during WWI. The Australian and New Zealand contingent, the Anzacs, lost this bloody conflict, and accused the Brits of sending them to the slaughter in an unwinnable fight. The Anzacs are revered as heroic battlers, and remembered as those who showed the British and Europeans that Australians weren't just parochial colonials, but tough Aussies, fighting with courage, honour and tenacity.

Another of Australia's beloved historical heroes is Ned Kelly. The feisty bushranger has been the subject for much artistic exploration of Australian identity, depicted in literature, cinema and painting. Was Ned a murdering thief or a poor Irish hero, railing against a society diseased with injustice and poverty? Most Australians prefer to believe the latter account, of Ned as a true-blue Aussie battler, striving for equality and justice – and handsome to boot. See the boxed text p596 for the story.

The colonial battle with the parched land has been relived through tales of valour and misfortune. Burke and Wills' infamous, failed crossing of the continent is one much-told story. Its ironic twist was an illuminating illustration of the colonialists' disassociation with the Australian landscape: they died of starvation surrounded by 'bush' food.

> 'Australians forged a culture based on the legend of the Aussie battler'

Reality Check

In the last half-century the less-acknowledged layers of Australian culture and history have begun to achieve wider recognition, in particular

---

BEWARE THE BUNYIP

Please report any sightings of shaggy, one-eyed monsters you may see lurking in Australia's rivers and lakes. Although the last recorded sighting of the legendary bunyip was around 1850, white settlers had been spotting the menacing creatures since they heard about them from indigenous locals. In Aboriginal Dreaming (p53) the bunyip is a feared water spirit who had a hand in many creation stories. White settlers embraced the legend and the bunyip became a metaphorical expression of the collective fear of the strange land, its inhabitants, and their futures. Today the bunyip features in children's literature, and has been known to eat children who stray from their beds...

SPORTING AUSTRALIA *Tony Wilson*

Australians like sport just slightly less than we like winning, which is why we love the Commonwealth Games so much. If you are reading this just prior to the 2006 Melbourne Commonwealth Games, Australians will soon embark upon a gold glut that will leave visitors wondering if they've just visited the otter enclosure at feeding time. And if you're reading this after the Games, then we've already gorged ourselves, had a magnificent time, and are now sunning ourselves on a rock, grateful that every four years we get to show little fish like Botswana, Kiribati and Tuvalu who's boss. See www.melbourne2006.com.au for event and ticket details.

Of course some visitors might point out that Australians are feasting in the small Commonwealth pond. That each Olympiad, the big cats like the USA, Russia and China show the Aussies up on the medal table. And to these people we quote per capita statistics, explaining that at the Athens Olympics we finished with 17 gold and 49 medals in total, coming in at 2.4635 medals per million people, with only the Bahamas going better with two medals at 6.309 medals per million. To people from the Bahamas, quite hypocritically, we quote the medal table. Australians, you see, like a consistent, fair debate slightly less than we like winning.

Strangely, for all this national pride, the number-one watched sport in Australia is a local one: **Australian Rules Football** is akin to tribal warfare. Around Melbourne you can pass through Carlton, Collingwood, Hawthorn, North Melbourne, Footscray, Essendon, Richmond and St Kilda – all of which have a team in the elite **Australian Football League** (AFL; www.afl.com.au). Once this league was exclusively Victorian, but since 1982 it has expanded nationally. At first the nascent Sydney Swans produced a full forward in microscopic shorts and an owner who flew pink helicopters, and interstate footy all seemed a bit of a joke. But then teams from Western Australia and South Australia joined the competition, Brisbane received some assistance, and between 1992 and 2004, no less than eight premiership cups jetted interstate. The most spectacular aspects of the game are the long kicking, the high marking, and the brutal collisions (shirtfronts) that nobody wants to see ('blah, blah, blah, safety of the players') but that nevertheless get replayed 10 times on the evening news. Fans of panto will enjoy the crowd participation factor in the 'Baaaaaaaaaal-lll….yeees!' cry, offered lustily by the crowd at the slightest breath of opportunity.

If you think there are too many men with necks in AFL, think seriously about watching a game of **rugby league**. The **National Rugby League** (NRL; www.nrl.com.au) is the most popular sporting competition north of the Murray River. Indeed some people will argue that it is the national football code. The best way to deal with these types is to quietly tell them that they're wrong. Sometimes they'll be stocky types with forearms like Christmas hams, in which event I'd ask that you not cite me as your source. Undoubtedly the highlight of the season is the annual State of Origin series. To see one of these games is to acquire a grim appreciation of Newton's laws of motion: a force travelling in one direction can only be stopped with the application of an equal and opposite force. It's terrifying stuff. If Newton had been hit by a Queensland second rower, rather than an apple, science would have been very much the poorer.

Australians who can play **rugby union** dream of playing for our national team, the Wallabies. For a period, the Wallabies were so dominant that the whole nation was on first-name terms with the William Webb Ellis trophy – we just called it 'Bill'. But then Jonny Wilkinson hit the world scene, snatched the World Cup for England, and now nobody talks about Bill. He's like the fallen uncle who's run off with another woman, and no longer gets invited to Christmas dinner. While we wait for a reconciliation with Bill, **Bledisloe Cup** (www.rugby.com.au) games against New Zealand are the most anticipated fixtures and form part of a Tri Nations tournament that also includes South Africa. The same countries also share a club competition, the ever-popular Super 14, which comprises four Australian teams: the Waratahs (Sydney), the Reds (Brisbane), the Brumbies (Australian Capital Territory) and Western Force (a Perth franchise).

Australia is a nation of **swimmers** (www.swimming.org.au). Whereas any of you could be taken by a shark at any moment, we parry them away with skill and finesse. Okay, that might be a bit of a stretch, but girt by sea and public pools, Australians can swim. Our current golden girl is Jodie Henry. Our greatest ever swimmer is Dawn Fraser, who is known nationally simply as 'Our Dawn'. Jodie Henry actually swims Our Dawn's event, the 100m freestyle, and if she wins gold at two more Olympics, will quickly become Our Jodie. Australia's greatest male swimmer is Our Ian. If anyone says anything mean about Ian Thorpe (Thorpie), even if it's in relation to the quality of his acting in his guest-starring performance on *Friends*, the nation goes berserk.

The English (or possibly the French) invented **cricket**, and it's beautiful *(c'est magnifique)*. For a newcomer to the sport, perhaps the best advice is not to expect too much action. Like baseball, cricket is about accumulation. It can build to soaring crescendos, but sometimes it doesn't – so bring a good book. Until the 1930s, test matches could last up to nine days with no result, but through the Geneva Convention, they were cut back to a maximum of five. Today, one-day cricket (which is sometimes called 'the pyjama game') is popular, and 20-20 cricket, which is shorter still, is just bursting on the scene. The Australian team has dominated both test and one-day cricket, holding the number-one world ranking for the best part of a decade. The stars have been Shane Warne (who survived a sex scandal), Ricky Ponting (who survived a pub brawl), Glenn McGrath (who released a tasty hickory sauce) and Adam Gilchrist (who has ears like a kid from a 1930s comic strip).

Come January, somebody usually fries an egg on the **tennis** courts at Melbourne Park just to show you can. The **Australian Open** (www.ausopen.com.au) is one of tennis' four Grand Slams, and it attracts more people to Australia than any other sporting event (even more than the annual Easter goat race at Lightning Ridge). Lleyton Hewitt is the great Aussie star, even if he does have his critics for screaming 'C'mon' with the scattergun intensity of a kid with Tourette's. Still, with his love of *Rocky* movies (particularly *Rocky IV*), and his Wimbledon and US Open titles, it's hard to stay mad at Lleyton. In the women's game, Alicia Molik has been a huge improver, cracking the Top 10 for the first time in 2005.

The Socceroos have had a history of falling at the last hurdle in their bids to qualify for the World Cup. The problem for the Aussies has been that many of the early hurdles involved 16–0 thrashings of countries like American Samoa, so players weren't hardened to the cyclone that was an away tie in South America. Still, soccer fans pray and hope that Germany 2006 will be the dawning of a new era. From a participation viewpoint, **soccer** is one of the growth sports in Australia, and much hope is pinned on the new **A-League** (www.a-league.com.au). For years local soccer has suffered as young players choose the better competition, contracts and mineral water on offer in Europe. The A-League, however, may have the dollars and profile to reverse the trend.

On the first Tuesday in November, the nation stops for a horse race, the **Melbourne Cup** (www.racingvictoria.net.au). In Melbourne, Cup Day is a public holiday, albeit a holiday when too many people wear boardshorts with comedy tuxedo tops. Australia's most famous Cup winner was Phar Lap, who won in 1930 before dying of a mystery illness in America. Phar Lap is now stuffed – even more so than he was after carrying 10 stone (63.5kg) over 2 miles (3.2km) – and is a prize exhibit in the Melbourne Museum (p492).

Australian **netball's** (www.netball.com.au) biggest rivalry is with New Zealand's Silver Ferns. There are 1.2 million netballers in the country, which makes netball Australia's most popular participation sport.

Women's basketball (www.wnbl.com.au) is also popular, with most Australians believing that our own Lauren Jackson is the best player in the world. In the **men's basketball** (www.nbl.com.au), McKinnon and Bogut are big names and bigger men. Although recently retired, Andrew Gaze, the man who made the expression 'I'll have a good hard crack at it' his own, will be sorely missed.

The list of sports could go on. Our men's **hockey team** (www.hockey.org.au) finally won gold at the Athens Olympics. The **Bells Beach Surf Classic** (www.surfingaustralia.com) features the 'real' Bells Beach, as opposed to the pretend one in the movie *Point Break*. There's the **Sydney to Hobart Yacht Race** (www.rolexsydneyhobart.com) each Boxing Day and the **Formula One Grand Prix** in Melbourne each March. There's even **wife carrying**, although our wife carriers do not yet have the strength or racing smarts of the wife-carrying specialists over in Estonia and Finland…

But that will come. We'll get there eventually. And if we don't, we'll move on and crow about something else. In fact it'll be a big test for Australian wife carrying to see if it gets mentioned in the next edition.

Tony Wilson is the author of the novel Players, *a black comedy about football and the sports media.*

through art, literature and cinema; as a result, the iconic 'battler' has become less relevant. Migrants have brought their own stories, cultures and myths to meld with those of the colonial Australians. There's also a long-overdue acknowledgment that the original inhabitants of this country are fundamental to a true definition of Australian culture today.

For more information on mandatory detention of asylum seekers, see www.spareroomsfor refugees.com.

The immense prosperity the landscape has given has forged the title 'Lucky Country', the land of opportunity, and for most Australians this rings true. Australians enjoy a sophisticated, modern society with immense variety, a global focus, if not a regional one, and a sense of optimism, if tempered by world events.

The precept of a 'fair go' has more recently been challenged by Australia's policy to mandatorily imprison asylum seekers, including children. Processing applications can take time, sometimes years; this has led to humanitarian concerns for displaced individuals in Australia who are living without rights to health or employment for extended periods.

LIFESTYLE

Australians have been sold to the world as outdoorsy, sporty, big-drinking, thigh-slapping country folk, but despite the stereotypes, most Australians live in cities, watch a lot more sport than they play and wouldn't be seen dead in an Akubra hat. Peek into the Australian lounge room and you may be surprised by what you find.

The Great Australian Dream of owning an oversized house and carport on a quarter-acre block has meant that sprawling suburbia is endemic in Australian towns and cities. Inside the average middle-class suburban home, you'll probably find a married heterosexual couple, though it is becoming increasingly likely they will be de facto, or in their second marriage. Australian law doesn't recognise gay marriages, but most Australians are open-minded about homosexuality.

Our 'Mum and Dad' will have an average of two children (probably called Lachlan and Emily – Australia's names of the moment), although the number of childless couples rose by 30% in the last decade. The average full-time worker increasingly spends more time at work: averaging 41½ hours and earning $960 gross per week.

Our typical family owns two TV sets and a computer. They'll have a BBQ in the backyard and a pet Labrador. What rubbish the dog doesn't eat is recycled: 99% of Australians recycle their rubbish. Like most Australians our family probably loves the sun. Australians have the highest rate of skin cancer in the world, with one in two people affected. Our family drags a caravan off to the beach every holiday, and on weekends they probably watch sport, go to the movies or head to the shops. However, don't get the idea that they're particularly active: recent studies show up to 60% of Australians are obese or overweight (figures just behind the USA – world leaders in failing the pinch test). For more detail on Australians and their obsession with watching sports, see the boxed text, p50.

Our family not only travels domestically, they also love to travel overseas. In 2004 Australians made about 4.4 million overseas trips – up by 30% from the previous year. It's also probably fair to say that Australia has produced some of the most successful travel businesses in the world: Flight Centre, Intrepid and Lonely Planet, to name a few.

Our middle-Australia couple like a few quiet ones up the pub, though despite the long-held reputation that Australians are boozers, recent figures show they are relatively abstemious, drinking less than 30 litres a year per person (compared with the Czech Republicans, who have the highest alcohol consumption rate – an awe-inspiring 187 litres per person).

POPULATION

According to the Australian Bureau of Statistics, the population mid-2005 was around 20,265,000 – increasing by one person every two minutes and nine seconds. Population density is among the lowest in the world, with an average of 2.5 people per square kilometre – no-one's within cooee (shouting distance) in the outback. Most people live along the eastern seaboard, between Melbourne and Brisbane, with a smaller concentration on the coastal region in and around Perth. Despite the extraordinarily low population density, population policy is fiercely debated in Australia. Opponents of increased immigration argue the dry Australian landscape can't sustain more people (just one of their arguments); others say population growth is an economic imperative, particularly considering Australia's declining birth rates.

MULTICULTURALISM

Australia continues to reap the rewards of its multicultural make-up – one of the most diverse in the world – enjoying a wealth of ideas, cuisines and lifestyle opportunities. The last census reported that 23% of the population is foreign-born, and over 40% of Australians are of mixed cultural origins. Every four minutes and eight seconds Australia gains another international migrant. Many foreign-born Australians came from Italy and Greece after WWII, but recent immigrants have mostly come from New Zealand and the UK, as well as China, Vietnam, Africa and India, among many other places. Some 2.2% of the population identifies itself as of Aboriginal origin, and most live in the Northern Territory. Australia's other indigenous people, Torres Strait Islanders, are primarily a

ABORIGINAL DREAMING

Traditional Aboriginal religious beliefs centre on the continuing existence of spirit beings that lived on earth during creation time (or Dreamtime), which occurred before the arrival of humans. These beings created all the features of the natural world and were the ancestors of all living things. They took different forms but behaved as people do, and as they travelled about they left signs to show where they had passed.

Despite being supernatural, the ancestors were subject to ageing and eventually returned to the sleep from which they'd awoken at the dawn of time. Here their spirits remain as eternal forces that breathe life into the newborn and influence natural events. Each ancestor's spiritual energy flows along the path it travelled during the Dreamtime and is strongest at the points where it left physical evidence of its activities, such as a tree, hill or claypan. These features are called 'sacred sites'. These days the importance of sacred sites is more widely recognised among the non-Aboriginal community, and most state governments have legislated to give these sites a measure of protection.

Every person, animal and plant is believed to have two souls – one mortal and one immortal. The latter is part of a particular ancestral spirit and returns to the sacred sites of that ancestor after death, while the mortal soul simply fades into oblivion. Each person is spiritually bound to the sacred sites that mark the land associated with his or her spirit ancestor. It is the individual's obligation to help care for these sites by performing the necessary rituals and singing the songs that tell of the ancestor's deeds. By doing this, the order created by that ancestor is maintained.

Each person has their own totem, or Dreaming. These totems are the links between the people and their spirit ancestors, and take many forms, such as trees, snakes, fish and birds. Songs explain how the landscape contains these powerful creator ancestors, who can exert either a benign or a malevolent influence. They also have a practical meaning: telling of the best places and the best times to hunt, and where to find water in drought years. They can also specify kinship relations and identify correct marriage partners.

Melanesian people, living in north Queensland and on the islands of the Torres Strait between Cape York and Papua New Guinea.

RELIGION

Some 16% of Australians described themselves as having no religion in the most recent census. The largest religious affiliations in the country were Catholic (27%), Anglican (21%) and other Christian denominations (21%), with non-Christian religions including Buddhism (2%) and Islam (1.5%) making up another 5% of Australians. Proponents of New Age spirituality pervade many religious classifications, so you might meet a vegetarian Catholic who meditates, with more than a few self-help titles on the bookshelf. See the boxed text, p53 for information on traditional Aboriginal spiritual beliefs.

ARTS

Australians are conspicuous in their support for sport (it's hard to ignore a green-and-gold mob yelling 'oi oi oi'), but statistics also reveal them to have a quiet love affair with the arts. Australia Council figures show attendance figures for galleries or performing arts that are almost double those for all codes of football (though of course seasonal factors and TV coverage of sport has an effect on attendance). Cinema is the top pursuit, with 70% of the population lining up for flicks and popcorn annually. Bookworms all over Australia fork out about $1 billion on books each year, around 25% of Australians attend a music concert annually, and about 20% of Australians gallery-hop.

Cinema

Australia has a healthy art-house film industry, with the occasional croc-wrestling blockbuster bringing a smidge of khaki to Hollywood's red carpet.

One of the first established in the world, the industry really kicked off when social upheaval and cultural re-examination in the '60s and '70s led to the establishment of the Australian Film Commission, a cinematic forum for Australians to thrash out issues of identity. *Walkabout,* in the early '70s, was one of the first films to explore indigenous Australia. Other films focused on revisiting colonisation, war and the country's relationship to England, such as *Gallipoli* and *Breaker Morant,* which mythologised the gung-ho Aussie male as pawn to the British Empire. *Mad Max* and *Mad Max II* were genre-busters that referenced Australia's car culture, and were box-office hits that did well overseas – to everyone's surprise.

Government tax incentives in the early '80s introduced investor clout, spurring a handful of hopefuls desperate to secure the international success of the *Mad Max* movies. Examples include the appalling *Mad Max III,* and *Crocodile Dundee* – movies that did nothing to hose down stereotypes of stubbled Aussie blokes.

In the late '80s and '90s the spotlight was turned home to the suburban quarter-acre block, where the larrikin Aussie battler fought for a 'fair go' in side-splitting satirical celebrations of Australian myths and stereotypes. The best of these were *Muriel's Wedding* and *The Castle.* At the same time powerful films, such as *Ghosts of the Civil Dead* (co-written by Nick Cave and John Hillcoat) and Jane Campion's *Sweetie,* showed Australians could do more than take the piss out of themselves.

The presence of Fox Studios Australia (Sydney), Warner Roadshow Studios on the Gold Coast (Queensland) and Central City Studios (Melbourne)

'films such as... Jane Campion's *Sweetie* showed Australians could do more than take the piss out of themselves'

MUST-SEE AUSTRALIAN MOVIES

Lantana (2001, director Ray Lawrence) The stand-out film of recent years: a warts-and-all analysis of love, trust and betrayal in relationships.

Rabbit-Proof Fence (2002, director Phillip Noyce) A true story tracing three sisters' journey home along a 2400km stretch of the rabbit-proof fence; an important lesson in Australian history.

The Boys (1998, director Rowan Woods) One to make you squirm: this powerful film portrays a dysfunctional family and the circumstances that may have surrounded a real-life murder.

Muriel's Wedding (1994, director PJ Hogan) From bouquet bitch-fight to phony marriage, the bumpy ride towards self-discovery for ABBA-devotee Muriel is utterly hilarious one minute and despairingly bleak the next.

Proof (1991, director Jocelyn Moorhouse) A blind photographer, his obsessive carer and a doe-eyed gardener learn about trust in a torturous love triangle.

Gallipoli (1982, director Peter Weir) The definitive Aussie mateship movie, *Gallipoli* explores naivety, social pressure to enlist and ultimately the utter futility and human waste of this campaign.

Breaker Morant (1980, director Bruce Beresford) War crimes and justice are examined in this masterpiece, set during the late stages of the Boer War. It's based on the story of Lieutenant Harry Morant: hero or scapegoat of the British Empire, depending on your take.

Mad Max (1979, director George Miller) Don't miss this awesome thriller of the cult-classic *Mad Max* trilogy. *Mad Max II* (1981) is equally good: one of the best action movies ever produced. *Mad Max III* is – ahem – well anyway; stay tuned for *Mad Max IV*.

The Chant of Jimmie Blacksmith (1978, director Fred Schepisi) The screen adaptation of Thomas Keneally's novel represents the displacement experienced by an indigenous boy trying to fit into white society.

Picnic at Hanging Rock (1975, director Peter Weir) A ponderous period film that was one of the first to explore the influence of the Australian landscape; eerie, other-dimensional references.

---

has attracted big-budget US productions such as *Star Wars Episode II* and *III* and *Moulin Rouge* to the country. While the economic benefits are many, the local industry can only dream of the 80% box-office share that US releases claim in Australia. Government quotas regulate the amount of Australian material that's screened locally – without such quotas Australian audiences would see even less home-grown material.

In the last couple of years, most films made for an Australian audience have abandoned the worn-out ocker stereotypes and started to explore the country's diversity. Indigenous stories have found a mainstream voice on the big screen, with films such as *The Tracker*, *Beneath Clouds* and *Rabbit-Proof Fence* illustrating a nation starting to come to terms with its racist past and present. Cultural and gender stereotypes continue to erode in a genre of intimate dramas exploring the human condition, such as *Lantana* and *Head On*, the latter featuring a gay Greek-Australian as the lead character. By staying relevant to contemporary Australians, the industry continues to survive and thrive.

Literature

Stories and ballads in early postcolonial literature mythologised the hardships of pioneers and unjust governments. Nationalism was a driving force, especially in the late 1800s with the celebration of the country's centenary (1888) and Federation (1901). AB 'Banjo' Paterson was the bush poet of the time, famous for his poems *The Man from Snowy River*, *Clancy of the Overflow* and *Waltzing Matilda*. Henry Lawson, a contemporary of Paterson, wrote short stories evoking the era; one of his best, *The Drover's Wife*, is a moving tale of the woman's lot in the settling life. Barbara Baynton wrote first-hand of a woman's perpetual struggle against Australian conditions, which are also collected in a book of short stories. All these stories helped establish the motifs of traditional

Australian literature: the desert as 'heart' of a nation, the hardworking Aussie 'battler' as soldier against adversity.

By the 1940s a modernist movement known as the Angry Penguins charged onto the scene, headed by Max Harris and his magazine, *Angry Penguins*. It set out to deflower the conservative European-style expression that dominated Australian art and literature, determining a 'mythic sense of geographical and cultural identity'. The inevitable backlash took shape in the famous Ern Malley affair. Two traditionalist poets gleaned lines from disparate sources and submitted them as poems purporting to be the works of a recently deceased poet by the name of Ern Malley. The poems were published in *Angry Penguins* in 1944, and enthusiastically received. The pranksters believed their hoax discredited the modernist movement; however, the publishers stayed firm in their belief the poems had literary merit. Analysis of 'the Hoax' continues today; most recently in Peter Carey's novel *My Life as a Fake* (2005), which beautifully frames the relationship between art and artist, truth and fiction.

In the postwar era, Australian writers began to re-evaluate their colonial past. Patrick White, the country's only Nobel Prize winner for Literature, helped turn the tables on earlier writers' romanticism with *Voss* (1957) and his deeply despair-inducing *The Tree of Man* (1955). Later novelists, such as the Booker Prize winner Thomas Keneally, keenly felt the devastation and angst of indigenous Australians, as depicted in his excellent novel *The Chant of Jimmie Blacksmith* (1972); it was also made into an important film.

Australia's literary scene, long dominated by writers of British and Irish descent, has evolved to reflect the country's multicultural make-up. Many indigenous writers focus on coming to terms with identity in often intensely personal autobiographies. Sally Morgan's *My Place* (1988) is one of the most popular books ever written by an indigenous Australian, along with Ruby Langford's *Don't Take Your Love to Town* (1988), a moving autobiography of courage against adversity. Kim Scott's excellent *Benang* (2000) is a challenging but rewarding read. Malaysian-born Australian Hsu-Ming Teo's *Love and Vertigo* took out the *Australian/* Vogel literary award in 1999, while Hong Kong–born Brian Castro shared the award in 1982. Castro's novels, including *Shanghai Dancing* (2003), often explore issues of diversity and identity.

> 'Australia's literary scene, long dominated by writers of British and Irish descent, has evolved to reflect the country's multicultural make-up'

Other contemporary authors, such as Peter Carey and David Malouf, often focus on fictitious reinterpretations of Australian history to examine perceptions of the individual and society. Carey, Australia's best-known novelist and twice winner of the prestigious Booker Prize, writes knockout books; among his finest are *Oscar & Lucinda* and *True History of the Kelly Gang*. Thea Astley and Tim Winton (see p939), winners of Australia's most prestigious literary award, the Miles Franklin, usually focus on human relations, but with a strong sense of place in the Australian landscape.

Australian children's literature is popular worldwide. Classics such as Norman Lindsay's *The Magic Pudding* (1918) and May Gibbs' *Complete Adventures of Snugglepot and Cuddlepie* (1946) captivated imaginations by bringing the Australian bush to life; Gibbs' *Adventures of Bib & Bub* pits gumnut babies Snugglepot and Cuddlepie against the Australian bogeyman – the bunyip (p49). *Possum Magic* (1983) by Mem Fox reignited an interest in Australian bush creatures after a long hiatus; her picture book *Hattie & the Fox* has also become a modern classic. Jeannie Baker's sublime picture books convey environmental messages through collages; look for *Hidden Forest* (2000) and *Belonging* (2004).

ALL-TIME AUSTRALIAN LITERARY WONDERS

Elizabeth Costello (JM Coetzee, 2004) This cerebral novel, the first written by South African–born Coetzee since his immigration to Australia in 2002, traverses critical writings from the author's earlier writings, which makes for a fascinating read.

Gould's Book of Fish (Richard Flanagan, 2001) A gorgeously rendered tale that revisits Australia's convict days, early interactions with indigenous Australians and the country's corrupted history.

True History of the Kelly Gang (Peter Carey, 2000) This Booker Prize–winning interpretation of Ned Kelly's trials brings him to life in language and spirit, with Carey's take depicting him as ultimate victim of an unjust system. Beautifully told and paced – you won't be able to put it down.

Benang (Kim Scott, 2000) Through anecdote and documentation, the racist treatment of the narrator and Aboriginal people in general is explored in this complex, moving, but sometimes frustrating work.

Drylands (Thea Astley, 1999) Explores the self-destruction of a rural community through Astley's unadorned writing style, with her typical critique of contemporary society through the characters often forgotten.

Cloudstreet (Tim Winton, 1998) Winton's books are much loved by Australians. His gift is his ability to write earthy text superbly evoking a sense of place. In *Cloudstreet* – arguably his best – you're led through the poetic lives of two rural families living in the big smoke.

Remembering Babylon (David Malouf, 1993) A white man lives for 16 years with Aborigines, and when reunited with early colonial Australia begins a search for identity in a society filled with fear. Compelling insight into the social dynamics of the time.

Voss (Patrick White, 1957) By no means a light read, this richly metaphoric, superbly written novel explores the megalomania-fuelled era of exploration, which is contrasted with the starchy English-styled urban life. This honest insight into the colonial exploration era is a masterpiece, and a must for literature devotees.

Pamela Allen's books are frequently shortlisted for Children's Book of the Year awards for early readers. Libby Gleeson writes delightful picture books, as well as stories for older readers. For young adults, John Marsden's sci-fi *Tomorrow* series has gained a loyal following. Morris Gleitzman is deservedly popular: *Worm Story* is his 22nd bluntly humorous book. Paul Jennings is an award-winning author for kids whose gross-out books are worthy of your bookshelf.

Great for long flights, Australia's bestselling author, Bryce Courtenay, pumps out brick-sized blockbusters, such as *Matthew Flinders' Cat* and *The Potato Factory*.

Music

Australian rock was born on the sticky carpet of Australia's pubs, in the conservative climate of the flare-wearing seventies. This thriving live-music scene was thrashed out in local pubs, and popularised by the hugely successful *Countdown* – a music TV show that exposed local bands. Eff-off rock legends AC/DC started out in the early '70s; their 1980 album *Back in Black* blitzed, some 10 million sales in the US alone. Cold Chisel also started out around that time, and their gravelly Aussie blokedom and earnest rock was an instant success; *Cold Chisel* and *East* are their best albums. Paul Kelly's first forays into the music scene were in the '70s, too, though his solo album *Post* (1985) put his passionate folk-ballad blend on the map. Midnight Oil's politico-pop peaked at the time of *Diesel and Dust* (1987), while the Go Betweens – one of Australia's most artistically successful bands – endured the whole decade before splitting in 1989. Nick Cave & the Bad Seeds are among a number of indie performers who came to prominence in the late '70s and left for overseas in a diaspora of Aussie talent in the '80s.

By the late '80s, notably around the time that *Countdown* wound down (1987), Australian popular music began to be dominated by the lucrative

---

RECENT-RELEASE AUSTRALIAN ALBUMS

Lyre of Orpheus/Abattoir Blues (Nick Cave & the Bad Seeds) This double CD is gothic, gospel poetry that's agonisingly beautiful. Who cares if the band hasn't lived here in a while…

Ways & Means (Paul Kelly) The latest from one of Australia's finest songwriters, this double-CD set is a bumper introduction to Kelly's bluesy-ballad repertoire.

Get Born (Jet) Rollicking good old-school rock that belts out hits such as 'Are You Gonna Be My Girl'.

Vulture Street (Powderfinger) Apparently a more populist shift in this alternative-rock band's discography.

Sunrise Over Sea (John Butler Trio) This band has broad appeal, with songs that move from reggae to round the campfire.

---

ditty-pop market. Enter Kylie Minogue; one-time fluffy-haired nymphet from *Neighbours* (p511), she first hit the music stage with *Locomotion* in 1987, and, as they say, the rest is history. John Farnham released *Whispering Jack* in 1986 and it became the biggest-selling album in Australian history (there's no accounting for taste).

Throughout the '90s it seemed everybody had a box of vinyl and moonlighted as a DJ. This scene was dominated by loungey remixes and electronic beats that followed and reinterpreted overseas trends. The beginning of the millennium saw a backlash of sorts, with a rock revival. Melbourne band Jet is at the forefront of the genre, with other bands like Powderfinger, Something for Kate, Regurgitator, Gerling and Spiderbait also working hard on the local scene.

Contemporary indigenous music is thriving, and the annual 'Deadlys' awards are a good place to find out who's setting the pace (www.vibe .com.au). Jimmy Little, the country-folk stalwart, began his career in the '50s, taking out the Lifetime Achievement award in 2004. Indigenous music finally hit mainstream in the '90s thanks largely to the immense popularity of Yothu Yindi and the single 'Treaty', lifted from their excellent album, *Tribal Voice* (1991). Archie Roach is best known for albums such as *Sensual Being*, his latest, and *Charcoal Lane* (1991), arguably his best. With fellow singer-songwriter and partner Ruby Hunter, Archie has toured globally and collaborated on various performance projects. Compelling singer-storyteller Kev Carmody and the multitalented Christine Anu are also both worth looking out for. The winner of the popular *Australian Idol* TV talent show in 2004 was Casey Donovan – daughter of the lead guitarist in the indigenous band the Donovans.

Local radio stations have a content quota to play at least 15% Australian music, but for a 100% dose, tune into the national youth radio station **Triple J** (www.triplej.net.au/homeandhosed) for 'Home and Hosed', 9pm to 11pm Monday to Friday. Also check out **Message Stick** (www.abc.net.au/message) for 100% indigenous arts and music information. See Festivals & Events in individual state and territory chapters for information about Australia's many fabulous live-music festivals.

Theatre & Dance

Like most art forms in Australia, the country's performing arts were built on European traditions. Over time, both theatre and dance have developed into unique practices that have defined themselves through talented local playwrights, actors, designers, dancers, composers, choreographers and musicians. Australia has a broad range of companies – both fully funded and independent – and an abundance of venues to play out any drama.

Australian theatre has a long association with vaudeville that flourished in the late 19th century. The bawdy combination of comic skits and music entertained the influx of miners who'd arrived during the gold rush. The theatre scene turned the corner in 1967 when Betty Burstall founded La Mama theatre (p515), which spawned the Australian Performers Group – later known as the Pram Factory. The Pram Factory was dedicated to producing Australian works, written by Australians such as David Williamson and Stephen Sewell, set in Australia and using the Australian vernacular. Around the same time Sydney established the Belvoir Street Theatre Company (p134), which also continues to perform outstanding Australian works. And just when you thought things were getting too serious, Barry Humphries (aka Dame Edna) stormed Australian stages with his (her) inimitable satire of the Australian housewife, among other characters.

The 1990s hosted a revival in musical theatre, with wildly successful productions such as *Bran Nue Day* (about Australian Aboriginality) and the Peter Allen story *Boy from Oz,* which recently hit Broadway. The respected Bell Shakespeare Company also formed in the '90s, and continues to perform Shakespearean and other classically themed works.

Australia's exuberant dance scene is well versed in both classical and contemporary styles: check out **Australia Dancing** (www.australiadancing.org) for up-to-date information on companies and performances. Classically, the **Australian Ballet** (www.australianballet.com.au), established in 1964, is considered among the world's finest companies. Dance has long been influenced by Aboriginal traditions too; this is most accessible through the stellar Sydney-based **Bangarra Dance Company** (www.bangarra.com.au), which performs stories and characters of the Dreaming. Melbourne's contemporary company **Chunky Move** (www.chunkymove.com) is enjoying great success. It's been pushing the boundaries since 1998, redefining contemporary dance and popularising the medium with vital choreography, clever concepts firmly anchored in popular culture and extraordinary dancers.

The Australia Council funds a number of major state theatre and dance companies. If you add to that the huge number of independent companies and venues that produce works which, collectively, fill the gaps left by the mainstream, you have the vibrant, multilayered landscape of Australia's performing arts.

Visual Arts

Paintings in the early days of colonial Australia depicted the landscape through European eyes. It wasn't until the 1880s, in tune with the growing nationalist movement, that Australian-born artists began to capture the unique qualities of the Australian light and landscape. Known as the Heidelberg School, artists such as Tom Roberts and Arthur Streeton created a heroic national iconography from the shearing of sheep and visions of a wide brown land that offered opportunity to all. By the 1940s a cultural re-evaluation had taken place, with the modernist movement known as the Angry Penguins at the helm, which threw romantic Impressionist convention out and introduced a period of modernism: Arthur Boyd, Sir Sidney Nolan (who painted the well-known *Ned Kelly* series), Albert Tucker and Joy Hester were the main players.

Contemporary Australian artists are strongly concerned with an Australian sense of place, as well as being actively engaged in the more universal concerns of our contemporary, globalised world. Artists such as Jeffrey Smart and photographer Bill Henson are well known for their explorations of the urban environment. Other artists comment on the practice of making art, and the reflective nature between the real and the represented. The impact of technology is a common theme of such artists

'Barry Humphries (aka Dame Edna) stormed Australian stages with his (her) inimitable satire of the Australian housewife'

as Patricia Piccinini and Stephen Hunt, who are empowered by the digital world as well as being thoughtfully engaged with the ethical dilemmas it generates. And cross-cultural investigations are regularly represented, with artists drawing upon a range of personal cultural perspectives to find their own expressive language.

Indigenous culture has brought huge benefits to Australia's art. Visual imagery is a fundamental part of indigenous life, a connection between past and present, the supernatural and the earthly, and the people and the land. The early forms of indigenous artistic expression were rock carvings (petroglyphs), body painting and ground designs.

Arnhem Land, in Australia's tropical Top End, is an area of rich artistic heritage. Some of the rock-art galleries in the huge sandstone Arnhem Land plateau are at least 18,000 years old, and range from hand prints to paintings of animals, people, mythological beings and European ships. Two of the finest sites are accessible to visitors, the Ubirr and Nourlangie in Kakadu National Park. The art of the Kimberley is perhaps best known for its images of the Wandjina, a group of ancestral beings who came from the sky and sea and were associated with fertility. The superb Quinkan galleries at Laura on the Cape York Peninsula, in north Queensland, are also among the finest in the country. Among the many creatures depicted on the walls are the Quinkan spirits.

Painting in central Australia has flourished to such a degree that it is now an important source of income for indigenous communities. It has also been an important educational tool for children, through which they can learn different aspects of religious and ceremonial knowledge. Western Desert painting, also known as 'dot' painting, has partly evolved from 'ground paintings', which formed the centrepiece of dances and songs. These 'paintings' were made from pulped plant material and the designs were made on the ground using dots of this mush. Dot paintings depict Dreaming stories (see p53). Bark painting is an integral part of the cultural heritage of Arnhem Land indigenous people, and one of their main features is the use of *rarrk* designs (cross-hatching). These designs identify the particular clans, and are based on body paintings handed down through generations.

Environment Tim Flannery

Australia's plants and animals are just about the closest things to alien life you are likely to encounter on Earth. That's because Australia has been isolated from the other continents for a very long time – at least 45 million years. The other habitable continents have been able to exchange various species at different times because they've been linked by land bridges. Just 15,000 years ago it was possible to walk from the southern tip of Africa right through Asia and the Americas to Tierra del Fuego. Not Australia, however. Its birds, mammals, reptiles and plants have taken their own separate and very different evolutionary journey, and the result today is the world's most distinct – and one of its most diverse – natural realms.

The first naturalists to investigate Australia were astonished by what they found. Here the swans were black – to Europeans this was a metaphor for the impossible – while mammals such as the platypus and echidna were discovered to lay eggs. It really was an upside-down world, where many of the larger animals hopped, where each year the trees shed their bark rather than their leaves, and where the 'pears' were made of wood.

If you are visiting Australia for a short time, you might need to go out of your way to experience some of the richness of the environment. That's because Australia is a subtle place, and some of the natural environment – especially around the cities – has been damaged or replaced by trees and creatures from Europe. Places like Sydney, however, have preserved extraordinary fragments of their original environment that are relatively easy to access. Before you enjoy them though, it's worthwhile understanding the basics about how nature operates in Australia. This is important because there's nowhere like Australia, and once you have an insight into its origins and natural rhythms, you will appreciate the place so much more.

Tim Flannery is a naturalist, explorer and writer. He lives in Adelaide where he is director of the South Australian Museum and a professor at the University of Adelaide.

Pizzey and Knight's *Field Guide to Birds of Australia* is an indispensable guide for bird watchers and anyone else even peripherally interested in Australia's feathered tribes. Knight's illustrations are both beautiful and helpful in identification.

Tim Flannery's *The Future Eaters* is a 'big picture' overview of evolution in Australasia, covering the last 120 million years of history, with thoughts on how the environment has shaped Australasia's human cultures.

Australia's beautiful and unusual black swan
JOHN BANAGAN

A UNIQUE ENVIRONMENT

There are two really big factors that go a long way towards explaining nature in Australia: its soils and its climate. Both are unique. Australian soils are the more subtle and difficult to notice of the two, but they have been fundamental in shaping life here. On the other continents, in recent geological times processes such as volcanism, mountain building and glacial activity have been busy creating new soil. Just think of the glacier-derived soils of North America, north Asia and Europe. They feed the world today, and were made by glaciers grinding up rock of differing chemical composition over the last two million years. The rich soils of India and parts of South America were made by rivers eroding mountains, while Java in Indonesia owes its extraordinary richness to volcanoes.

All of these soil-forming processes have been almost absent from Australia in more recent times. Only volcanoes have made a contribution, and they cover less than 2% of the continent's land area. In fact, for the last 90 million years, beginning deep in the age of dinosaurs, Australia has been geologically comatose. It was too flat, warm and dry to attract glaciers, its crust too ancient and thick to be punctured by volcanoes or folded into mountains. Look at Uluru (p871) and Kata Tjuta (the Olgas p872). They are the stumps of mountains that 350 million years ago were the height of the Andes. Yet for hundreds of millions of years they've been nothing but nubs.

Under such conditions no new soil is created and the old soil is leached of all its goodness by the rain, and is blown and washed away. Even if just 30cm of rain falls each year, that adds up to a column of water 30 million km high passing through the soil over 100 million years, and that can do a great deal of leaching! Almost all of Australia's mountain ranges are more than 90 million years old, so you will see a lot of sand here and a lot of country where the rocky 'bones' of the land are sticking up through the soil. It is an old, infertile landscape, and life in Australia has been adapting to these conditions for aeons.

Australia's misfortune in respect to soils is echoed in its climate. In most parts of the world outside the wet tropics, life responds to the rhythm of the seasons – summer to winter, or wet to dry. Most of Australia experiences seasons – sometimes very severe ones – yet life does not respond solely to them. This can clearly be seen by the fact that although there's plenty of snow and cold country in Australia, there are almost no trees that shed their leaves in winter, nor do any Australian animals hibernate. Instead there is a far more potent climatic force that Australian life must obey: El Niño.

The cycle of flood and drought that El Niño brings to Australia is profound. Our rivers – even the mighty Murray River, the nation's largest river, which runs through the southeast – can be miles wide one year, yet you can literally step over its flow the next. This is the power of El Niño and its effect, when combined with Australia's poor soils, manifests itself compellingly. As you might expect from this, relatively few of Australia's birds are seasonal breeders, and few migrate. Instead, they breed when the rain comes, and a large percentage are nomads, following the rain across the breadth of the continent.

So challenging are conditions in Australia that its birds have developed some extraordinary habits. The kookaburras, magpies and blue wrens you are likely to see – to name just a few – have developed a breeding system called 'helpers at the nest'. The helpers are the young adult birds of previous breedings, which stay with their parents to help bring up the new chicks. Just why they should do this was a mystery, until it was

B Beale and P Fray's *The Vanishing Continent* gives an excellent overview of soil erosion across Australia. Fine colour photographs make the issue more graphic.

Uluru (Ayers Rock) is often thought to be the world's largest monolith. In fact, it only wins second place. The biggest is Mt Augustus (Burringurrah) in Western Australia, which is 2½ times the size.

The Devil's Marbles, enormous granite boulders seemingly tossed to the ground south of Tennant Creek in the Northern Territory, are believed by the local Warumungu Aboriginal people to be the eggs of the Rainbow Serpent.

Right-facing page:

Chambers Pillar, Northern Territory (p866)

PAUL SINCLAIR

A koala and her baby
MARK NEWMAN

R Strahan's *The Mammals of Australia* is a complete survey of Australia's somewhat cryptic mammals. Every species is illustrated, and almost everything known about them is covered in the individual species accounts, which have been written by the nation's experts.

What led to the extinction of the Tasmanian tiger? In *The Last Tasmanian Tiger: The History and Extinction of the Thylacine,* Robert Paddle investigates the role of rural politics in the animal's demise.

The saltwater crocodile is the world's largest living reptile – males can reach a staggering 6m long.

realised that conditions in Australia can be so harsh that more than two adult birds are needed to feed the nestlings. This pattern of breeding is very rare in places like Asia, Europe and North America, but it is common in many Australian birds.

Australia is, of course, famous as the home of the kangaroo (roo) and other marsupials. Unless you visit a wildlife park, such creatures are not easy to see as most are nocturnal. Their lifestyles, however, are exquisitely attuned to Australia's harsh conditions. Have you ever wondered why kangaroos, alone among the world's larger mammals, hop? It turns out that hopping is the most efficient way of getting about at medium speeds. This is because the energy of the bounce is stored in the tendons of the legs – much like in a pogo stick – while the intestines bounce up and down like a piston, emptying and filling the lungs without needing to activate the chest muscles. When you travel long distances to find meagre feed, such efficiency is a must.

Marsupials are so energy-efficient that they need to eat one-fifth less food than equivalent-sized placental mammals (everything from bats to rats, whales and ourselves). But some marsupials have taken energy efficiency much further. If you visit a wildlife park or zoo you might notice that faraway look in a koala's eyes. It seems as if nobody is home – and this in fact is near the truth. Several years ago biologists announced that koalas are the only living creatures that have brains that don't fit their skulls. Instead they have a shrivelled walnut of a brain that rattles around in a fluid-filled cranium. Other researchers have contested this finding, however, pointing out that the brains of the koalas examined for the study may have shrunk because these organs are so soft. Whether soft-brained or empty-headed, there is no doubt that the koala is not the Einstein of the animal world, and we now believe that it has sacrificed its brain to energy efficiency. Brains cost a lot to run – our brains typically weigh 2% of our body weight, but use 20% of the energy we consume. Koalas eat gum leaves, which are so toxic that koalas use 20% of their energy just detoxifying this food. This leaves little energy for the brain, and living in the tree tops where there are so few predators means that they can get by with few wits at all.

The peculiar constraints of the Australian environment have not made everything dumb. The koala's nearest relative, the wombat (of which there are three species), has a large brain for a marsupial. These creatures live in complex burrows and can weigh up to 35kg, making them the largest herbivorous burrowers on Earth. Because their burrows are effectively air-conditioned, they have the neat trick of turning down their metabolic activity when they are in residence. One physiologist, who studied their thyroid hormones, found that biological activity ceased to such an extent in sleeping wombats that, from a hormonal point of view, they appeared to be dead! Wombats can remain underground for a week at a time, and can get by on just a third of the food needed by a sheep of equivalent size. One day, perhaps, efficiency-minded farmers will keep wombats instead of sheep. At the moment, however, that isn't possible; the largest of the wombat species, the northern hairy-nose, is one of the world's rarest creatures, with only around 100 surviving in a remote nature reserve in central Queensland.

Among the more common marsupials you might catch a glimpse of in the national parks around Australia's major cities are the species of antechinus. These nocturnal, rat-sized creatures lead an extraordinary life. The males live for just 11 months, the first 10 of which consist of a concentrated burst of eating and growing. Like teenage males, the day comes when their minds turn to sex, and in the antechinus this becomes an obsession. As they embark on their quest for females they forget to eat and sleep. Instead they gather in logs and woo passing females by serenading them with squeaks. By the end of August – just two weeks after they reach 'puberty' – every male is dead, exhausted by sex and by carrying around

The largest roo that ever existed was the giant short-faced kangaroo, which lived during the Pleistocene era. It grew to heights of up to 3m!

Kangaroos sunbathing at Pebbly Beach near Jervis Bay (p226)
MITCH REARDON

A carpet of desert wild flowers in Western Australia (p957)

MITCH REARDON

Of Australia's 155 species of land snakes, 93 are venomous. Australia is home to 10 of the world's 15 most venomous snakes.

H Cogger's *Reptiles and Amphibians of Australia* is a bible to those interested in Australia's reptiles, and useful protection for those who are definitely not. This large volume will allow you to identify the species, and you can wield it as a defensive weapon if necessary.

swollen testes. This extraordinary life history may also have evolved in response to Australia's trying environmental conditions. It seems likely that if the males survived mating, they would compete with the females as they tried to find enough food to feed their growing young. Basically, antechinus dads are disposable. They do better for antechinus posterity if they go down in a testosterone-fuelled blaze of glory.

One thing you will see lots of in Australia are reptiles. Snakes are abundant, and they include some of the most venomous species known. Where the opportunities to feed are few and far between, it's best not to give your prey a second chance, hence the potent venom. Around Sydney and other parts of Australia, however, you are far more likely to encounter a harmless python than a dangerously venomous species. Snakes will usually leave you alone if you don't fool with them. Observe, back quietly away and don't panic, and most of the time you'll be OK.

Some visitors mistake lizards for snakes, and indeed some Australian lizards look bizarre. One of the more abundant, it's the sleepy lizard. These creatures, which are found throughout the southern arid region, look like animated pine cones. They are the Australian equivalent of tortoises, and are harmless. Other lizards are much larger. Unless you visit the Indonesian island of Komodo you will not see a larger lizard than the desert-dwelling perentie. These beautiful creatures, with their leopard-like blotches, can grow to more than 2m long, and are efficient predators of introduced rabbits, feral cats and the like.

Australia's plants can be irresistibly fascinating. If you happen to be in the Perth area in spring it's well worth taking a wildflower tour. The best flowers grow on the arid and monotonous sand plains, and the blaze of colour produced by the kangaroo paws, banksias and similar native plants can be dizzying. The sheer variety of flowers is amazing, with 4000 species crowded into the southwestern corner of the continent. This diversity of prolific flowering plants has long puzzled botanists. Again, Australia's poor soils seem to be the cause. The sand plain is about the poorest soil in Australia – it's almost pure quartz. This prevents any one fast-growing species from dominating. Instead, thousands of specialist plant species have learned to find a narrow niche, and so coexist. Some live at the foot of the metre-high sand dunes, some on top, some on an east-facing slope, some on the west and so on. Their flowers need to be striking in order to attract pollinators, for nutrients are so lacking in this sandy world that even insects like bees are rare.

If you do get to walk the wildflower regions of the southwest, keep your eyes open for the sundews. Australia is the centre of diversity for these beautiful, carnivorous plants. They've given up on the soil supplying their nutritional needs and have turned instead to trapping insects with the sweet globs of moisture on their leaves, and digesting them to obtain nitrogen and phosphorus.

If you are very lucky, you might see a honey possum. This tiny marsupial is an enigma. Somehow it gets all of its dietary requirements from nectar and pollen, and in the southwest there are always enough flowers around for it to survive. No one, though, knows why the males need sperm larger even than those of the blue whale, or why their testes are so massive. Were humans as well endowed, men would be walking around with the equivalent of a 4kg bag of potatoes between their legs!

> The whole eastern half of the Northern Territory is designated as the Arnhem Land Aboriginal Reserve. Apart from a few areas, it's not open to independent travellers.

NATIONAL & STATE PARKS

Australia has more than 500 national parks – nonurban protected wilderness areas of environmental or natural importance. Each state defines and runs its own national parks, but the principle is the same throughout Australia. National parks include rainforests, vast tracts of empty outback, strips of coastal dune land and rugged mountain ranges.

Public access is encouraged as long as safety and conservation regulations are observed. In all parks you're asked to do nothing to damage or alter the natural environment. Camping grounds (often with toilets and showers), walking tracks and information centres are often provided for visitors. In most national parks there are restrictions on bringing in pets.

Some national parks are so isolated, rugged or uninviting that you wouldn't want to go there unless you were an experienced bushwalker

> An eco-tourist's dream: Lord Howe Island (p215)
> CHRISTOPHER GROENHOUT

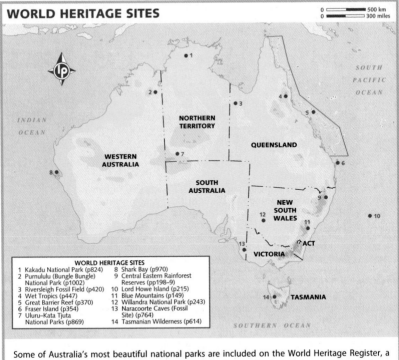

WORLD HERITAGE SITES

0 ——— 500 km
0 ——— 300 miles

SOUTH
PACIFIC
OCEAN

INDIAN
OCEAN

NORTHERN
TERRITORY

QUEENSLAND

WESTERN
AUSTRALIA

SOUTH
AUSTRALIA

NEW
SOUTH
WALES

ACT

VICTORIA

TASMANIA

SOUTHERN OCEAN

WORLD HERITAGE SITES

1 Kakadu National Park (p824)
2 Purnululu (Bungle Bungle) National Park (p1002)
3 Riversleigh Fossil Field (p420)
4 Wet Tropics (p447)
5 Great Barrier Reef (p370)
6 Fraser Island (p354)
7 Uluru–Kata Tjuta National Parks (p869)
8 Shark Bay (p970)
9 Central Eastern Rainforest Reserves (pp198–9)
10 Lord Howe Island (p215)
11 Blue Mountains (p149)
12 Willandra National Park (p243)
13 Naracoorte Caves (Fossil Site) (p764)
14 Tasmanian Wilderness (p614)

Some of Australia's most beautiful national parks are included on the World Heritage Register, a UN register of natural and cultural places of world significance. See http://whc.unesco.org/heritage .htm for more information about these sites.

or 4WD traveller. Other parks, however, are among Australia's major attractions.

State parks and state forests are other forms of nature reserves; owned by state governments they have fewer regulations than national parks. Although state forests can be logged, they are often recreational areas with camping grounds, walking trails and signposted forest drives. Some permit horses and dogs.

For the addresses of national and state park authorities, see the National Parks section in each destination chapter.

> Devil Facial Tumour Disease (DFTD), a facial cancer contracted by the Tasmanian devil through its aggressive eating habits, is thought to have been responsible for wiping out half the devil population in the past decade.

WATCHING WILDLIFE

Some regions of Australia offer unique opportunities to see wildlife. One of the most fruitful places is Tasmania. The island is jam-packed with wallabies, wombats and possums, principally because foxes, which have decimated marsupial populations on the mainland, were slow to reach the island state (the first fox was found in Tasmania only as recently as 2001!). It is also home to the Tasmanian devil – the Australian hyena, but less than one-third the size of its African ecological counterpart. They're common on the island. In some national parks you can watch them tear apart road-killed wombats. Their squabbling is fearsome, the shrieks ear splitting. It's the nearest thing Australia can offer to experiencing a lion kill on the Masai Mara.

For those intrigued by the diversity of tropical rainforests, Queensland's World Heritage sites are well worth visiting. Birds of paradise, cassowaries and a variety of other birds can be seen by day, while at night you can search for tree-kangaroos (yes, some kinds of kangaroo do live in the tree tops). In your nocturnal wanderings you are highly likely to see curious possums, some of which look like skunks, and other marsupials that today are restricted to a small area of northeast Queensland. Fossils from as far afield as western Queensland and southern Victoria indicate that such creatures were once widespread.

Australia's deserts are a real hit-and-miss affair as far as wildlife is concerned. If visiting in a drought year, all you might see are dusty plains, the odd mob of kangaroos and emus, and a few struggling trees. Return after big rains, however, and you'll encounter something close to a Garden of Eden. Fields of white and gold daisies stretch endlessly into the distance, perfuming the air. The salt lakes fill with fresh water, and millions of water birds – pelicans, stilts, shags and gulls – can be seen feeding on the superabundant fish and insect life of the waters. It all seems like a mirage, and like a mirage it will vanish as the land dries out, only to spring to life again in a few years or a decade's time. For a more reliable bird-watching spectacular, Kakadu (p824) is well worth a look, especially towards the end of the dry season around November.

The largest creatures found in the Australian region are marine mammals such as whales and seals, and there is no better place to see them than South Australia. In springtime southern right whales crowd into the head of the Great Australian Bight. You can observe them near the remote Aboriginal community of Yatala as they mate, frolic and suckle their young. Kangaroo Island (p743), south of Adelaide, is a fantastic place to see seals

The website of the Parks & Wildlife Commission of the Northern Territory (www.nt.gov.au/ipe /pwcnt) provides an abundance of info on the territory and its gems.

The dingo, which has never inhabited Tasmania, is thought to have been the world's first domesticated dog and the ancestor of all domestic dog breeds.

The educational website of the Australian Museum (www.lostkingdoms.com) holds a wealth of info on Australia's animal life from the Cretaceous period till now. Kids will love the online games, fact files and movies.

The unique (and cute?) Tasmanian devil
JOHN BANAGAN

The barramundi can reach lengths of over 1m and changes sex from male to female once it turns five or six years old.

and sea lions. There are well-developed visitor centres to facilitate the viewing of wildlife, and nightly penguin parades occur at some places where the adult blue penguins make their nest burrows. Kangaroo Island's beaches are magic places, where you're able to stroll among fabulous shells, whale bones and even jewel-like leafy sea dragons amid the sea wrack.

The fantastic diversity of Queensland's Great Barrier Reef is legendary, and a boat trip out to the reef from Cairns or Port Douglas is unforgettable. Just as extraordinary but less well known is the diversity of Australia's southern waters; the Great Australian Bight is home to more kinds of marine creatures than anywhere else on earth. A stroll along any beach, from Cape Leeuwin at the tip of Western Australia to Tasmania, is likely to reveal glimpses of that diversity in the shape of creatures washed up from the depths. The exquisite shells of the paper nautilus are occasionally found on the more remote beaches, where you can walk the white sand for kilometres without seeing another person.

Right-facing page:

The mystical waters of the Great Barrier Reef, Queensland (p370)

MICHAEL AW

A magnificent humpback whale breaching (p1011)

BOB CHARLTON

If your visit extends only as far as Sydney, however, don't give up on seeing Australian nature. The Sydney sandstone – which extends approximately 150km around the city – is one of the most diverse and spectacular regions in Australia. In springtime, spectacular red waratahs abound in the region's parks, while the woody pear (a relative of the waratah) that so confounded the early colonists can also be seen, alongside more than 1500 other species of flowering plants. Even in a Sydney backyard you're likely to see more reptile species (mostly skinks) than can be found in all of Great Britain – so keep an eye out!

ENVIRONMENTAL CHALLENGES

The European colonisation of Australia, commencing in 1788, heralded a period of catastrophic environmental upheaval, with the result that Australians today are struggling with some of the most severe environmental problems to be found anywhere. It may seem strange that a population of just 20 million, living in a continent the size of the USA minus Alaska, could inflict such damage on its environment, but Australia's long isolation, its fragile soils and difficult climate have made it particularly vulnerable to human-induced change.

Damage to Australia's environment has been inflicted in several ways, the most important being the introduction of pest species, destruction of forests, overstocking rangelands, inappropriate agriculture and interference with water flows.

Beginning with the escape of domestic cats into the Australian bush shortly after 1788, a plethora of vermin – from foxes to wild camels and cane toads – have run wild in Australia, causing extinctions in the native fauna. One out of every 10 native mammals living in Australia prior to European colonisation is now extinct, and many more are highly endangered. Extinctions have also affected native plants, birds and amphibians.

The destruction of forests has also had a profound effect on the environment. Most of Australia's rainforests have suffered clearing, while conservationists fight with loggers over the fate of the last unprotected stands of 'old growth'.

Many Australian rangelands have been chronically overstocked for more than a century, the result being the extreme vulnerability of both soils and rural economies to Australia's drought and flood cycle, as well as the extinction of many native species. The development of agriculture has involved land clearance and the provision of irrigation, and here again the effect has been profound.

Clearing of the diverse and spectacular plant communities of the Western Australian wheatbelt began just a century ago, yet today up to one-third of that country is degraded by salination of the soils. Between 70kg and 120kg of salt lies below every square metre of the region, and clearing of native vegetation has allowed water to penetrate deep into the soil, dissolving the salt crystals and carrying brine towards the surface.

In terms of financial value, just 1.5% of Australia's land surface provides over 95% of its agricultural yield, and much of this land lies in the irrigated regions of the Murray-Darling Basin. This is Australia's agricultural heartland, yet it too is under severe threat from salting of soils and rivers. Irrigation water penetrates into the sediments laid down in an ancient sea, carrying salt into the catchments and fields. If nothing is done, the lower Murray River will become too salty to drink in a decade or two, threatening the water supply of Adelaide, a city of over a million people.

Despite the enormity of the biological crisis engulfing Australia, governments and the community have been slow to respond. It was in the 1980s that coordinated action began to take place, but not until the '90s that major steps were taken.

The establishment of **Landcare** (www.landcareaustralia.com.au), an organisation enabling people to effectively address local environmental issues, and the expenditure of $2.5 billion through the National Heritage Trust Fund have been important national initiatives. Yet so difficult are some of the issues the nation faces that, as yet, little has been achieved in terms of halting the destructive processes.

Individuals are also banding together to help. Groups like the **Australian Bush Heritage Fund** (www.bushheritage.asn.au) and the **Australian Wildlife Conservancy** (AWC; www.australianwildlife.org) allow people to donate funds and time to the conservation of native species. Some such groups have been spectacularly successful; the AWC, for example, already manages many endangered species over its 5260-sq-km holdings.

So severe are Australia's problems that it will take a revolution before they can be overcome, for sustainable practices need to be implemented in every arena of life – from farms to suburbs and city centres. Renewable energy, sustainable agriculture and water use lie at the heart of these changes, and Australians are only now developing the road map to sustainability that they so desperately need if they are to have a long-term future on the continent.

Food & Drink Matthew Evans

Born during the poverty of the convict era and reared under a strong British influence, Australian cuisine has come a long way. Australia is now one of the most dynamic places in the world to have a feed, thanks to immigration and a dining public willing to give anything new, and better, a go. Sydney and Melbourne can rightfully claim to be destinations worthy of touring gourmands from New York to Paris, but travellers will feel the effects of a blossoming food culture right across the country.

However, this development has been a recent one. Despite its world-class dining opportunities, Australia doesn't live to eat. As a nation we're new to the world of good food, to being mesmerised by the latest TV chef, devouring cookbooks and subscribing to foodie magazines in the hundreds of thousands. The eating in Australia has never been better, and it's improving by the day.

Despite our new-found fascination with fine dining, at heart we're still mostly a nation of simple eaters, and the majority of Australians are still novices in anything beyond meat and three veg. This is changing, though, as the influx of immigrants (and their cuisine) has found locals trying (and liking) everything from lassi to laksa. This passionate minority has brought about a rise in dining standards, better availability of produce and a frenetic buzz about food in general. It's no wonder Australian chefs, cookbooks and food writers are so sought after overseas.

We've coined our own phrase, Modern Australian (Mod Oz), to describe our cuisine. If it's a melange of East and West, it's Mod Oz. If it's not authentically French or Italian, it's Mod Oz – the term is our attempt to classify the unclassifiable. The cuisine doesn't really alter from one region to another, but some influences are obvious, such as the Italian migration to Melbourne and the Southeast Asian migration to Darwin.

You'll find that dishes aren't usually too fussy, and flavours are often bold and interesting. Spicing ranges from gentle to extreme, coffee is great (though it still reaches its greatest heights in the cities), and meats are tender, full flavoured and usually bargain priced.

The truth may be that most Australians would rather a nice dip in the sea, followed by a bowl of potato wedges with sour cream, than the world-class fine dining that our cities boast, but at least now, for residents and travellers alike, there's the option of great dining if we want it.

> Matthew Evans was a chef, before becoming a food writer and restaurant critic. He is currently chief restaurant reviewer for the *Sydney Morning Herald* and co-editor of the *Sydney Morning Herald Good Food Guide*, and is the author of four food books, including Lonely Planet's *World Food Italy*.

> The first colonists from Europe nearly starved to death waiting for shipped-in supplies rather than finding out what the indigenous population was eating.

STAPLES & SPECIALITIES

Without a doubt, Australia's best food comes from the sea. Nothing compares to this continent's seafood, hauled from some of the purest waters you'll find anywhere, and usually cooked with care.

TALKING STRINE

The opening dish in a three-course meal is called the entrée, the second course (the North American entrée) is called the main course and the sweet bit at the end is called dessert, sweets, afters or pud. In lesser restaurants, of course, it's called desert.

When an Australian invites you over for a baked dinner it might mean a roast lunch. Use the time as a guide – dinner is normally served after 6pm. By 'tea' they could be talking dinner or they could be talking tea. A coffee definitely means coffee, unless it's after a hot date when you're invited up to a prospect's flat.

TRAVEL YOUR TASTEBUDS

Much of Australia's most interesting (if not always most delicious) produce is wild. Some unusual foods you may spy on your travels include wild mushrooms, such as bright-orange pine mushrooms and slippery jacks, so called because they can get quite slimy after rain. There's kangaroo, a deep purpley-red meat, which is deliciously sweet. Fillets are so tender and lean they have to be served rare. The tail is often braised in the same way oxtail is cooked. In the north, you may encounter crocodile, a white meat not dissimilar to fish with a texture closer to chicken. In the outback you may be encouraged to try witchetty grubs, which look like giant maggots and taste nutty, but with a squishy texture. In the tropics you may find green ants. The way to eat them is to pick them up and bite off their lightly acidic bottoms. Sugar ant abdomens are full of sweet sap, so again just bite off the tail end.

Much of the native flora has evolved to contain unpalatable chemicals. Despite this, you may enjoy fiery bush pepper, sweetly aromatic lemon myrtle, aniseed myrtle, coffeelike flecks of wattle seed, vibrant purple rosella flowers, supersour Davidson plums, lightly acidic bush tomato (akudjura) and, of course, the macadamia nut.

The wildest food of all is Vegemite, a frighteningly salty yeast-extract spread with iconic status. Most commonly used on toast, it's also not bad on cheese sandwiches. It's often carried overseas for homesick expats, or licked from fingers by freckle-faced youngsters. Outsiders tend to find the flavour coarse, vulgar and completely overwhelming. But what would they know?

Connoisseurs prize Sydney rock oysters, a species that actually lives right along the New South Wales (NSW) coast and even in Western Australia (WA). There are sea scallops from Queensland, and estuary scallops from Tasmania and South Australia (SA). Rock lobsters are fantastic and fantastically expensive, and mud crabs, despite the name, are a sweet delicacy. Another odd-sounding delicacy is 'bugs' – like shovel-nosed lobsters without a lobster's price tag; try the Balmain and Moreton Bay varieties. Marron are prehistoric-looking freshwater crayfish from WA, while their smaller cousins, yabbies, can be found throughout the southeast. Prawns are incredible, particularly sweet school prawns or the eastern king (Yamba) prawns found along the northern NSW coast. Add to that countless wild fish species and we've got one of the greatest bounties on earth.

Almost everything we eat from the land was introduced. Even superexpensive black truffles are now being harvested in Tasmania and WA, and there's a white-truffle harvest on at least one hazelnut farm in Tasmania. Australia is huge (similar in size to continental USA) and it varies so much in climate, from the tropical north to the temperate south, that at any time of the year there's an enormous variety of produce on offer. In summer, mangoes are so plentiful that Queenslanders actually get sick of them. Tasmania's cold climate means its strawberries and stonefruit are sublime. Lamb from Victoria's lush Gippsland is highly prized, the veal of White Rocks in WA is legendary, and the tomatoes of SA are the nation's best.

The Sydney Fish Market (p107) trades in several hundred species of seafood every day, second only to Tokyo in variety.

There's a small but brilliant farmhouse cheese movement, hampered by the fact that regulations ensure most milk must be pasteurised (unlike in Italy and France, the homes of the world's best cheeses). Despite that, the results can be great. Keep an eye out for goat's cheese from Gympie, Kytren and Kervella, cheddar from Pyengana (p656), sheep's milk cheese from Highland Farm, Milawa's washed rind, and anything from Woodside Cheesewrights or Bruny Island, among others.

Not many actual dishes can lay claim to being uniquely Australian. Even the humble 'pav' (pavlova), the meringue dessert with cream and passionfruit, may be from New Zealand. Ditto for lamingtons, large cubes of cake dipped in chocolate and rolled in desiccated coconut.

Yet anything another country does, Australia does, too. Vietnamese, Indian, Fijian, Italian – no matter where it's from, there's an expat community and interested locals desperate to cook and eat it. Dig deep enough, and you'll find Jamaicans using scotch bonnet peppers and Tunisians making tagine. And you'll usually find their houses are the favourite haunts of their locally raised friends.

Despite this, Australians' taste for the unusual usually kicks in at dinner only. Most people still eat cereal for breakfast, or perhaps eggs and bacon on weekends. They devour sandwiches for lunch with nearly the same verve as the British, and then eat anything and everything in the evening. Yum cha (the classic southern Chinese dumpling feast), however, has found huge popularity as a lunch option with urban locals in recent years, particularly on weekends. Some non-Chinese even have it with the traditional Chinese, first thing in the morning.

DRINKS

No matter what your poison, you're in the right country if you're after a drink. Once a nation of tea and beer swillers, Australia is now turning its attention to coffee and wine. In fact, if you're in the country's southern climes, you're probably not far from a wine region right now.

Australian beer, for years, was of the bland, chilled-so-you-can-barely-taste-it variety. Now microbrewers and boutique breweries are popping up as fast as hops after rain. Keep an eye out for WA's Little Creatures (a fragrant drop sometimes called the Sauvignon Blanc of beer; p907), James Squire amber ale from Sydney, Hazards from Hobart and Mountain Goat from Melbourne. More widespread is the robust, full-figured Cooper's from Adelaide. Most beers have an alcohol content between 3.5% and 5%. That's less than many European beers but stronger than most in North America. Light beers contain under 3% alcohol and are finding favour with people observing the stringent drink-driving laws.

The terms for ordering beer varies with the state. In NSW you ask for a 'schooner' (425mL) if you're thirsty and a 'middy' (285mL) if you're not quite so dry. In Victoria and Tasmania it's a 'pot' (285mL), and in most of the country you can just ask for a glass of beer and wait to see what turns up. Pints (425mL or 568mL, depending on where you are)

Australian Gourmet Pages (www.australiangourmetpages.com.au) is a website devoted to wine, food, restaurants and more in Australia run by a *Vogue Entertaining + Travel* contributor. Subscribe (for free) and you'll receive several weekly updates on subjects as diverse as food labelling, food stores and stories found overseas.

WINE REGIONS

Purists will rave about Cabernet Sauvignon from Coonawarra (SA; p763), Riesling from the Clare Valley (SA; p756), Chardonnay from Margaret River (WA; p929) and Shiraz from the Barossa Valley (SA; p750). SA is Australia's vinous heartland (visit the National Wine Centre in Adelaide, p720), but there are many more regions that produce fine wine.

The closest region to Sydney, the Hunter Valley (NSW; p164 and p168) first had vines in the 1830s, and does a lively unwooded Semillon that is best aged. Further inland, there's Cowra, Orange and Mudgee. Just out of Melbourne are the Mornington (p530) and Bellarine (p524) Peninsulas, Mount Macedon (p527) and the Yarra Valley (p528). WA is blessed with incredible wines around Denmark and Frankland in the Great Southern region. There's even a wine region in Queensland (p346), though not all of it is good.

Most wineries have small cellar doors where you can taste for free or a minimal fee. If you like the wine, you're generally expected to buy.

Although plenty of good wine comes from big producers with economies of scale on their side, the most interesting wines are usually made by small vignerons, where you pay a premium; the gamble means the payoff in terms of flavour is often greater. Much of the cost of wine (nearly 42%) is due to a high taxing programme courtesy of the Australian government.

TOP TEN FOOD FESTIVALS

Australia has a multitude of festivals to keep gastronomes gambolling year-round.

- Barossa Vintage Festival (SA; p752)
- Clare Valley Gourmet Weekend (SA; p756)
- Festivale (Tasmania; p660)
- Melbourne Food & Wine Festival (Victoria; p499)
- National Festival of Beers (Queensland; p306)
- Sardine Festival (WA; p906)
- Taste of Byron (NSW; p192)
- Tastes of Rutherglen (Victoria; p565)
- Taste of Tasmania (Tasmania; p628)
- Valley Fiesta (Queensland; p306)

---

aren't as common, though Irish pubs and European-style ale houses tend to offer pints for homesick Poms.

In terms of coffee, Australia is leaping ahead, with Italian-style espresso machines in virtually every café, boutique roasters all the rage and, in urban areas, the qualified *barista* (coffee maker) virtually the norm. Expect the best coffee in Melbourne, decent stuff in most other cities, and a 20% chance of good coffee in many rural areas. Melbourne's café scene rivals the most vibrant in the world – the best way to immerse yourself is by wandering the city centre's café-lined lanes.

CELEBRATIONS

Food and celebration in Australia are strongly linked, with celebrations often including equal amounts of food and alcohol. A birthday could be a barbecue (barbie, BBQ) of steak (or prawns), washed down with a beverage or two. Weddings are usually followed by a big slap-up dinner, though the food is often far from memorable. Christenings are more sober, usually offering home-baked biscuits and a cup of tea.

Food tourism and food festivals are blossoming. Melbourne, for instance, has its own month-long food-and-wine festival in March (p499). There are harvest festivals in wine regions, and various communities, such as Clare Valley (p756), hold annual events. See the boxed text, above.

For many an event, especially in the warmer months, Australians fill the car with an Esky (an ice chest, to keep everything cool), tables, chairs and a cricket set or footy, and head off for a barbie by the lake/river/beach. If there's a total fire ban (which occurs increasingly each summer), the food is precooked and the barbie becomes more of a picnic, but the essence remains the same.

Christmas in Australia, in midsummer, is less likely to involve a traditional European baked dinner, and more likely to be replaced by a barbecue, full of seafood and quality steak. It's a response to the warm weather. Prawn prices skyrocket, chicken may be eaten with champagne at breakfast, and the main meal is usually in the afternoon, after a swim and before a really good, long siesta.

Various ethnic minorities have their own celebrations. The Indian community brings out all the colour of the old country and the stickiest of sweets during Diwali; Greeks will embrace any chance to hold a spit barbecue; and the Chinese go off during their annual Spring Festival (Chinese New Year) every January or February (it changes with the lunar calendar).

WHERE TO EAT & DRINK

Typically, a restaurant meal in Australia is a relaxed affair. It may take 15 minutes to order, another 15 before the first course arrives, and maybe half an hour between entrées and mains. The upside of this is that any table you've booked in a restaurant is yours for the night, unless you're told otherwise. So sit, linger and live life in the slow lane.

A competitively priced place to eat is a club or pub that offers a counter meal. This is where you order at the kitchen, usually a staple such as a fisherman's basket, steak, mixed grill, chicken parmigiana or Wiener schnitzel, take a number and wait until it's called out over the counter or intercom. You pick up the meal yourself, saving the restaurant money on staff and you on your total bill.

Solo diners will find that cafés and noodle bars are welcoming and good fine-dining restaurants often treat you like a star but, sadly, some midrange places may still make you feel a little ill at ease.

One of the most interesting features of the dining scene is 'Bring Your Own' (BYO). If a restaurant says it's BYO, you're allowed to bring your own alcohol. If the place also sells alcohol, the BYO bit is usually limited to bottled wine only (no beer, no casks) and a corkage charge is added to your bill. The cost is either per person or per bottle, and ranges from nothing to $15 per bottle in fancy places. Be warned, however, that BYO is a declining custom, and many if not most licensed restaurants don't like you bringing your own wine, so always ask when you book.

Most restaurants open around noon for lunch and from 6pm or 7pm for dinner. Australians usually eat lunch shortly after noon, and dinner bookings are usually made for 7.30pm or 8pm, though in major cities some restaurants stay open past 10pm. Regularly updated, independent reviews can be found in local restaurant guides, or online at www.australian gourmetpages.com.au or through www.citysearch.com.au.

Quick Eats

There's not a huge culture of street vending in Australia, though you may find a pie or coffee cart in some places. Most quick eats traditionally come from a milk bar, which serves old-fashioned hamburgers (with bacon, egg, pineapple and beetroot if you want) and other takeaway foods. Fish and chips is still hugely popular, most often a form of shark (often called flake; don't worry, it can be delicious) either grilled or dipped in heavy batter and fried, and ideal for eating at the beach on a Friday night.

American-style fast food has taken over in recent times, though many Aussies still love a meat pie, often from a milk bar, but also from bakeries, kiosks and some cafés. If you're at a rugby league or Aussie Rules

---

CHINATOWNS

The best-value food in most cities is lurking in Chinatown. Arrange to be there for Chinese New Year (celebrated with copious fireworks in late January or early February) and you won't regret it!

- Melbourne's Little Bourke St (p479) is a squashy, bustling strip – like a bonsai Hong Kong. Beware of the Millennium Dragon who guards the Museum of Chinese Australian History.

- Restaurants in Adelaide's compact Chinatown (p726) are found near Gouger Market and patronised enthusiastically by faithful clientele.

- Guarded by an impressive archway, Brisbane's colourful Duncan St Chinatown (p300) is small but diverse, and the place to head for alternative medicines, authentic eateries and intriguing ingredients for your own kitchen.

- Sydney's Chinatown (p125) crowns the lot, both in size and offerings: you'll find many blocks' worth of everything from roast-duck takeaway and quick and tasty yum cha to fine seafood restaurants complete with live critters in aquariums.

AUSTRALIA'S TOP FIVE

Berardo's on the Beach (Queensland; p342) Great beach, great food, great dreaming you never have to go home again. Chef Bruno Loubet is doing everything from tomato *tarte tatin* to beef cheeks and sensational reef fish with his French flourish.

Circa, the Prince (Victoria; p509) Some of the best Modern Australian food in a lush designer setting. Gentle spicing, savoury jellies and the best game and sashimi-grade seafood.

Fins (NSW; p194) The freshest seafood, boldly spiced, in an iconic hotel.

Little Creatures (WA; p907) Watch the yachts bob at the marina as you sample flavoursome fare in a designer brewery's converted warehouse space. Think pizza, pasta and other drinking food.

Petaluma's Bridgewater Mill Winery & Restaurant (SA; p733) Impossibly deft, classy fare from the chef's Vietnamese background and love of Australian produce is served in a benchmark winery just out of Adelaide.

---

football match, a beer, a meat pie and a bag of hot chips are as compulsory as wearing your team's colours to the game.

Pizza has become one of the most popular fast foods; most pizzas that are home-delivered are of the American style (thick and with lots of toppings) rather than Italian style. That said, more and more wood-fired, thin, Neapolitan-style pizza can be found, even in country towns. In the city, Roman-style pizza (bought by the slice) is becoming more popular, but you can't usually buy the other pizza in anything but whole rounds.

There are some really dodgy mass-produced takeaway foods, bought mostly by famished teenage boys, including the dim sim (a bastardisation of the dim sum dumplings from China) and the Chiko Roll (a large, spring roll–like pastry).

> Most of Australia's finest chefs are qualified – as electricians, librarians, teachers and more.

VEGETARIANS & VEGANS

You're in luck: most cities have substantial numbers of local vegetarians, which means you're well-catered for. Cafés seem to always have vegetarian options, and even our best restaurants may have complete veggie menus. Take care with risotto and soups, though, as meat stock is often used.

Vegans will find the going much tougher, but local Hare Krishna restaurants or Buddhist temples often provide relief, and there are usually dishes that are vegan-adaptable at restaurants.

The **Australian Vegetarian Society** (www.veg-soc.org) has a useful website that lists a number of vegetarian and vegetarian-friendly places to eat.

Following are some of our recommended veggie hot spots:

Barking Cow (WA; p933) Mad vego options three hours from Perth in bluesy Bridgetown, in the southern forests region.

Bernadette's Café & Restaurant (Australian Capital Territory; p277) The simple aesthetic belies the effort that goes into making superhealthy meals here.

Bluegrass (Northern Territory; p856) Exceptional flavours, creative ingredients and warm surroundings for all vegetarians to relish.

Govinda's (NSW; p137) Healthy, all-you-can-eat Indian buffet, with movie option!

Shakahari (Victoria; p507) A pioneer in vegetarian eating, still going strong after 20 years. Try the tempura avocado rolls.

Sirens (Tasmania; p631) Deliciously creative food, plus feel-good extras (eg tips donated to charity).

Sprouts (SA; p727) Vegetarian (and vegan) is treated as a cuisine rather than a lifestyle choice at this small, stylish dining room serving dishes such as Cajun-spiced tofu and mushroom crepe wraps.

Veg Out (Queensland; p311) This little nook serves superb Middle Eastern and Asian veggie fare

EATING WITH KIDS

Dining with children in Australia is relatively easy. At all but the flashiest places children are generally welcomed, particularly at Chinese, Greek or

Italian restaurants. Kids are usually more than welcome at cafés, while bistros and clubs often see families dining early. Many fine-dining restaurants don't welcome small children (assuming they're all ill-behaved).

Most places that do welcome children don't have separate kids' menus, and those that do usually offer everything straight from the deep fryer – crumbed chicken and chips, etc. You might be best finding something on the normal menu (say a pasta or salad) and ask the kitchen to adapt it to your child's needs.

The best news for travelling families, weather permitting, is that there are plenty of free or coin-operated barbecues in parks. Beware of weekends and public holidays, when fierce battles can erupt over who is next in line for the barbecue.

> Run by two food writers who trained as chefs, www.campionandcurtis.com has information on cooking schools, restaurants and cookbooks plus plenty of their own Modern Australian recipes. They write a monthly newsletter, too.

HABITS & CUSTOMS

As a nation, Australians aren't really a fussy lot. And that extends to the way we approach dining, usually a casual affair and even at the finest of diners a jacket is virtually never required (but certainly isn't frowned upon). At the table, however, it's good manners to use British knife-and-fork skills, keeping the fork in the left hand, tines down, and the knife in the right, though Americans may be forgiven for using their fork like a shovel. Talking with your mouth full is considered uncouth, and fingers should be used only for food that can't be tackled another way.

If you are lucky enough to be invited over for dinner at someone's house, always take a gift. You may offer to bring something for the meal, but even if the host downright refuses – insisting you just bring your scintillating conversation – still take a bottle of wine. Flowers or a box of chocolates are also acceptable.

DOS & DON'TS

- Do shout drinks to a group on arrival at the pub.
- Do tip (up to 15%) for good service, when in a big group, or if your kids have gone crazy and trashed the dining room.
- Do show up for restaurant dinner reservations on time. Not only may your table be given to someone else, staggered bookings are designed to make the experience more seamless.
- Do take a small gift and/or a bottle of wine to dinner parties.
- Do offer to wash up or help clear the table after a meal at a friend's house.
- Do ring or send a note (even an email) the day or so after a dinner party, unless the friends are so close you feel it unnecessary. Even then, thank them the very next time you speak.
- Do offer to take meat and/or a salad to a barbecue. At the traditional Aussie barbie for a big group, each family is expected to bring part or all of their own tucker.
- Don't ever accept a shout unless you intend to make your shout soon after.
- Don't freak out when the waiter in a restaurant attempts to 'lap' your serviette (napkin) by laying it over your crotch. It's considered to be the height of service. If you don't want them doing this, place your serviette on your lap before they get a chance.
- Don't expect a date to pay for you. It's quite common among younger people for a woman to pay her own way.
- Don't expect servile or obsequious service. Professional waiters are intelligent, caring equals whose disdain can perfectly match any diner's attempt at contempt.
- Don't ever tip bad service.

BILLS & TIPPING

The total at the bottom of a restaurant bill is all you really need to pay. It should include GST (as should menu prices) and there is no 'optional' service charge added. Waiters are paid a reasonable salary, so they don't rely on tips to survive. Often, though, especially in urban Australia, people tip a few coins in a café, while the tip for excellent service can go as high as 15% in whiz-bang establishments. The incidence of add-ons (bread, water, surcharges on weekends etc) is rising.

'Shouting' is a revered custom where people rotate paying for a round of drinks. Just don't leave before it's your turn to buy! At a toast, everyone should touch glasses. You're supposed to look the person you clink with in the eye, too – failure to do so is reported to end in seven years' bad sex.

Australians like to linger a bit over coffee. They like to linger a really long time while drinking beer. And they tend to take quite a bit of time if they're out to dinner (as opposed to having takeaway).

Smoking is banned in most eateries in the nation, so sit outside if you love to puff. And most states and territories are bringing in nonsmoking sections in bars and clubs, too, so it's getting quite unlikely you'll be able to smoke inside – best to never plan on it. And never smoke in someone's house unless you ask first. Even then it's usual to smoke outside. See the boxed text, p79 for other tips on general food-and-drink etiquette.

COOKING COURSES

Many good cooking classes are run by food stores such as **Simon Johnson** (☎ 02-9319 6122) in Sydney, the **Essential Ingredient** (☎ 03-9827 9047) in Melbourne and **Black Pearl Epicure** (☎ 07-3257 2144) in Brisbane. Others are run by markets, such as the **Sydney Seafood School** (☎ 02-9004 1140) at the Sydney Fish Markets or the **Queen Victoria Market Cooking School** (☎ 03-9320 5835) at the Queen Victoria Market in Melbourne.

The following run longer courses for the inspired:

Elise Pascoe Cooking School (☎ 02-4236 1666; www.cookingschool.com.au; Jamberoo Valley, NSW) Food writer and remarkable cook Elise Pascoe runs mostly weekend cooking classes in a stunning setting just south of Sydney, near Kiama.

Howqua Dale Gourmet Retreat (☎ 03-5777 3503; Mansfield, Victoria) Highly regarded weekend cooking schools and tours are run by amazing chef Marieke Brugman.

Le Cordon Bleu (☎ 1800 064 802; Sydney, NSW) The original must-do French course is available thanks to a joint venture down under. Courses from 10 weeks to five years (part-time).

EAT YOUR WORDS

For a bit more insight into Australian cuisine, stick your nose into one or more of these books.

Australian Regional Food Guide (Sally and Gordon Hammond) – A great guide to where to buy good food at the source as you travel around.

Good Food Guide The *Age* and the *Sydney Morning Herald* newspapers both put out annual restaurant guides that rate over 400 restaurants in Victoria and NSW respectively.

Secret Men's BBQ Business (Alan Campion) – An insight into the way men and barbies come together in modern society.

Australian Fare (Stephen Downes) – Subtitled 'How Australian Cooking Became the World's Best', this is one man's one-eyed view, with interesting historical context going back to Melbourne's 1956 Olympics.

Australian Seafood Handbook (ed GK Yearsley, PR Last and RD Ward) – Don't know what fish that is? This tells you the real name, the local name and plenty more besides.

Penguin's Good Australian Wine Guide (Huon Hooke and Ralph Kyte-Powell) – Annual publication with lots of useful information on many readily available wines.

Wine Atlas of Australia and New Zealand (James Halliday) – Complete with CD-ROM, all about the antipodean wine regions and what to expect when you get there.
The Cook's Companion (Stephanie Alexander) – Australia's single-volume answer to Delia Smith. If it's in here, most Australians have probably seen it or eaten it.
Chalk and Cheese (Will Studd) – Everything you ever wanted to know about boutique cheese and cheesemakers in Australia's blossoming industry.

Food Glossary

Australians love to shorten everything, including peoples' names, so expect many other words to be abbreviated. Some words you might hear:
barbie – a barbecue (BBQ), where (traditionally) smoke and overcooked meat are matched with lashings of coleslaw, potato salad and beer
Chiko roll – a fascinating large, spring roll–like pastry for sale in takeaway shops; best used as an item of self-defence rather than eaten
Esky – an insulated ice chest to hold your *tinnies*, before you hold them in your *tinny holder*; may be carried onto your tinny, too
middy – a medium glass of beer (NSW)
pav – pavlova, the meringue dessert topped with cream, passionfruit and kiwifruit or other fresh fruit
pie floater – a meat pie served floating in thick pea soup (SA)
pot – a medium glass of beer (Victoria, Tasmania)
rat coffin – a meat pie, traditionally made with minced beef; compulsory eating (with White Crow tomato sauce) at footy matches
sanger/sando – a sandwich
schooner – a big glass of beer (NSW), but not as big as a pint
snag – (aka surprise bag) sausages
snot block – a vanilla slice
Tim Tam – a commercially produced chocolate biscuit that lies close to the heart of most Australians; best consumed as a Tim Tam Shooter, where the two diagonally opposite corners of the rectangular biscuit are nibbled off, and a hot drink (tea is the true aficionado's favourite) is sucked through the fast-melting biscuit like a straw – ugly but good
tinny – usually refers to a can of beer, but could also be the small boat you go fishing for mud crabs in (and you'd take a few tinnies in your tinny, in that case)
tinny holder – insulating material that you use to keep the *tinny* ice cold, and nothing to do with a boat

New South Wales

New South Wales (NSW) is Australia's most populous state and home to Sydney, with its attention-grabbing bridge and opera house and a cockiness that bites you on the bum. These are images that visitors conjure up, but the state is more than just a backdrop to Sin City. It was the site of Australia's first permanent European settlement, and as such, the New South Welsh often believe the rest of the country should come to them. That pose has spread from the swish capital to cities like Newcastle and Wollongong, once branded industrial backwaters, now reinventing themselves with tourism-fuelled gusto.

In between the urban sprawls, NSW is Australia's most diverse state, filled with outback vistas, alpine territory, verdant rainforests and golden surf. Pack your tent and hiking boots and lose yourself in the Blue Mountains or any number of rugged national parks. Or get a 'Brazilian', pack your wax and board and hotfoot it to the loose-as-a-goose coast. One of the state's most popular trails, the south coast is filled with dainty historical hamlets and fishing villages, while the north is home to unbroken beaches and resort towns. The hinterlands of the far north are filled with a heady mix of lush rainforest and alternative lifestyles.

Naturally, with such a geographical playground to explore, NSW is ideal for mainlining adrenaline – take your pick from canyoning, skiing, surfing, whale watching and even goanna pulling (not what it seems). This remarkable spread of attractions ensures that NSW is the gateway for most visitors to Australia, and with excellent road, rail and air networks, you can rest easy knowing you'll be able to whisk from place to place with consummate ease.

HIGHLIGHTS

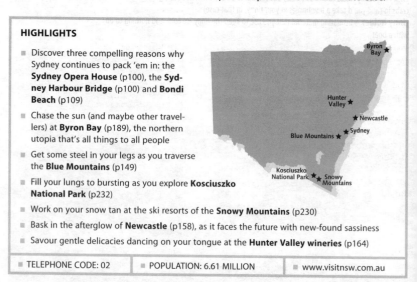

- Discover three compelling reasons why Sydney continues to pack 'em in: the **Sydney Opera House** (p100), the **Sydney Harbour Bridge** (p100) and **Bondi Beach** (p109)

- Chase the sun (and maybe other travellers) at **Byron Bay** (p189), the northern utopia that's all things to all people

- Get some steel in your legs as you traverse the **Blue Mountains** (p149)

- Fill your lungs to bursting as you explore **Kosciuszko National Park** (p232)

- Work on your snow tan at the ski resorts of the **Snowy Mountains** (p230)

- Bask in the afterglow of **Newcastle** (p158), as it faces the future with new-found sassiness

- Savour gentle delicacies dancing on your tongue at the **Hunter Valley wineries** (p164)

| ■ TELEPHONE CODE: 02 | ■ POPULATION: 6.61 MILLION | ■ www.visitnsw.com.au |

NEW SOUTH WALES FACTS

Eat: All manner of seafood, from Sydney rock oysters to the incredible eastern king (Yamba) prawns found along NSW's northern coast

Drink: James Squire beer, particularly the amber ale, and a lively unwooded Semillon from Hunter Valley

Read: *Cooking with Sky Prawns*, by Edward Joshua and Chris Carr, a cookbook that aims to ease NSW's locust plague via consumption (it claims the insects are more nutritious than beef)

Listen to: *Rose Tattoo* (1978) by Rose Tattoo, *10, 9, 8, 7, 6, 5, 4, 3, 2, 1* (1982) by Midnight Oil, *The Boys* (1998) by The Necks and *Highly Evolved* (2002) by The Vines

Watch: *Bliss* (1985), *Puberty Blues* (1981), *The Boys* (1998), *Lantana* (2001)

Avoid: Funnel-web spiders

Locals' nickname: Sin City (Sydney; p89)

Swim at: Bondi Beach (p109) for the glamour, Byron Bay (p189) for the views

Strangest festival: The Australian Goanna Pulling Championships (p186)

Tackiest tourist attractions: The Rock Roadhouse (p170) and the Big Prawn (p188)

HISTORY

The north and west coasts of Australia were charted in the 1640s by Abel Tasman, who named the continent New Holland. In 1770 Captain James Cook sailed up the east coast, landing at Botany Bay and naming the area New South Wales (it's actually a mystery as to why Cook chose this appellation, although the general assumption is that the area must have reminded him of Wales, despite the lack of leeks and male-voice choirs).

After the American Revolution, Britain was no longer able to transport convicts to North America. In 1786 Joseph Banks (the botanist on Cook's 1770 expedition) put forth the idea that NSW would be suitable as a repository for thieves, as it was considered 'uninhabited'. In January 1788 the First Fleet sailed into Botany Bay under Captain Arthur Phillip, who didn't appreciate what he found. Thus, the fleet – with its 750 male and female convicts, 400 sailors, four marine companies and enough supplies for two years – headed north and found 'the finest harbour in the world': Sydney Cove.

The early settlement suffered – soils were poor, souls were lost and no relief came from England for 2½ years. Then a farm was established at Parramatta, where the soil was more fertile, and gradually the situation improved. As crops began to yield, NSW became less dependent on Britain for food.

By the 1830s the general layout of NSW was understood, and the Blue Mountains had been penetrated. In addition the Lachlan, Macquarie, Murrumbidgee and Darling Rivers had been explored.

NSW eventually shrank. In the early 1800s it comprised about half the continent, before the mainland colonies were progressively carved from it (South Australia, Victoria, Queensland) and it became one among several.

The state ceased to be a dumping ground for convicts in 1848.

The large quantities of gold found at Ophir in 1851 caused a rush of hopeful miners from Sydney, and for the rest of the century there were rushes throughout much of Australia. Certainly, without gold, it's hard to imagine how places like Broken Hill would have reached the size they did.

By the turn of the 20th century, Sydney was a vigorous city of almost 500,000 people.

The last few years have seen Sydney boom beyond all expectations, helped immeasurably by the success of the 2000 Olympics.

Aboriginal People

When Captain Cook sailed into Botany Bay, so the story goes, he passed four Aboriginal men spearing fish from a canoe who took no notice of the alien ship. Cook, his head filled with notions of 'noble savages', was respectful towards the indigenous population and later reported back on their peaceable nature.

However, when Captain Phillip's penal settlement came to town, kidnappings and punishment became the norm, with the explicit aim of terrifying Aborigines into submission. Smallpox, introduced by the invaders, also decimated the local population, who had no resistance to such a disease. But there was resistance in other forms: Aboriginal freedom-fighting groups began to spring up, led by storied indigenous figures including Bennelong, Pemulwuy and Mosquito, a warrior

NEW SOUTH WALES

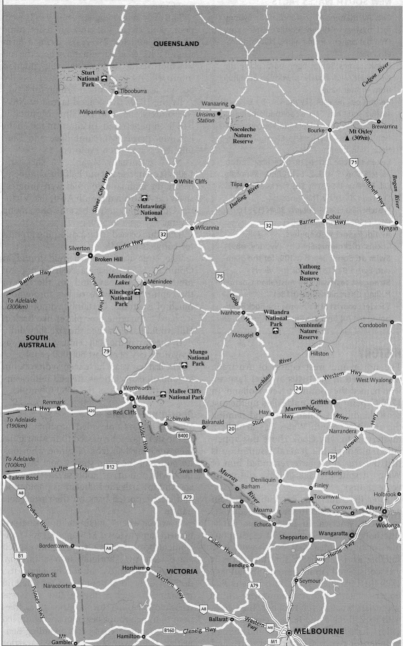

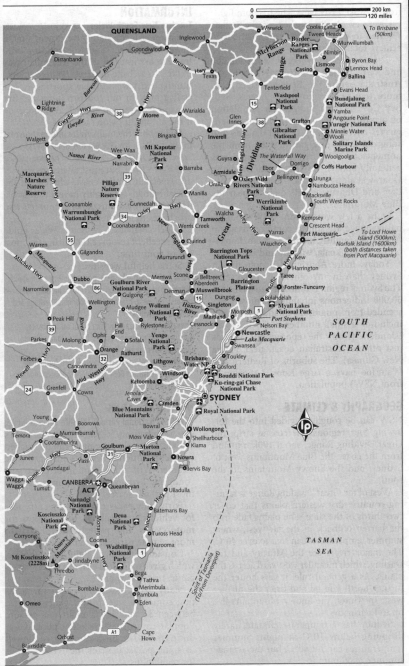

NEW SOUTH WALES

from a Broken Bay tribe. The freedom fighters were eventually crushed, as the settlers resorted to ever more barbaric methods to achieve total domination.

There were somewhere between 500,000 and one million Aboriginal peoples in Australia before the British arrived, and more than 250 regional languages. Sydney Cove had an indigenous population of around 3000, using three main languages encompassing several dialects and subgroups. Ku-ring-gai (derived from the nomenclature 'Koori'; see following) was generally spoken on the northern shore; Dharawal along the coast south of Botany Bay; and Dharug and its dialects near the Blue Mountains.

Quite a few words from NSW Aboriginal language are still in common usage in Australian English, including galah, kookaburra, dingo, koala, wallaby and billabong.

Today, more Aboriginal people live in Sydney than in any other Australian city. The Sydney region is estimated to have over 30,000 indigenous inhabitants, mostly descended from migratory inland tribes, and including a small number of Torres Strait Islanders (from the eponymous islands just off the Australian coast, near Papua New Guinea). The suburbs of Redfern and Waterloo have a large Koori (Aborigines from NSW) population.

GEOGRAPHY & CLIMATE

NSW can be roughly divided into the following four regions: the coastal strip; the Great Dividing Range, about 100km inland from the coast; the Blue Mountains west of Sydney; and the Snowy Mountains in the south.

West of the Great Dividing Range is farming country: dry western plains that cover two-thirds of the state. The plains fade into the barren outback in the far west, where summer temperatures can soar to over 40°C. The major rivers are the Murray and the Darling, which meander westward across the plains. As a general rule, it gets hotter the further north you go and drier the further west. In winter, the Snowy Mountains live up to their name.

Sydney has a temperate climate, rarely dropping below 10°C at night. Summer temperatures can hit 40°C, but the average summer maximum is 25°C.

INFORMATION

Tourism New South Wales (☎ 13 20 77; www.tourism.nsw.gov.au) is the state government's main marketing wing. 'Sport, recreation and tourism are integral to the Australian way of life', its website declares. 'Where opportunities exist we will use sporting events as flagships for our tourism industry.' But nonsporty types can enjoy NSW, too, even if the authorities won't admit it.

Sydney has the main **visitor information centre** (Map pp94–5; ☎ 1800 067 676, 02-9240 8788; www.sydneyvisitorcentre.com; 106 George St, The Rocks, Sydney; ⏱ 9.30am-5.30pm), but most towns are well set up, especially on the coast, where even the tiniest hamlets invariably have a tourist office and a Mt Kosciuszko of pamphlets and brochures to leaf through.

Lonely Planet's *New South Wales* guide is an excellent resource for getting the most out of your time.

Some helpful websites:

www.nationalparks.nsw.gov.au Information about national park access (including access for mobility-impaired visitors), camping, conservation, Aboriginal heritage and children's activities.

www.nrma.com.au Find out about car insurance; purchase road maps and guides; book accommodation, tours and event tickets online.

www.visitnsw.com.au General NSW information.

www.yha.com.au Book YHA-affiliated accommodation through this website.

NATIONAL PARKS

The **NSW National Parks & Wildlife Service** (NPWS; www.nationalparks.nsw.gov.au) controls the state's 70-odd national parks; most can be reached with conventional vehicles in reasonable weather. With the exception of those surrounding Sydney, public transport into most parks is scarce.

Forty-four parks charge daily entry fees for vehicles, generally $7 per car (less for motorcycles and pedestrians). Entry to more remote parks is often free.

Consider purchasing the annual pass, which gives unlimited entry to all the state's parks; prices start at $22.

Many parks have campsites with facilities; some are free, others generally cost between $5 and $10 a night per person. Popular camp sites are often booked out during holidays. Bush camping is allowed in some parks; contact the NPWS office for regulations.

ACTIVITIES

Bushwalking

NSW offers many standards, lengths and terrains for walking, and almost every national park has marked trails or wilderness walking.

In Sydney, you can try the beautiful Bondi to Coogee walk (p112) or the wonderful 9km-long Manly Scenic Walkway (p110). The wilderness areas of Wollemi National Park are near Sydney, as are the dramatic cliff-top walks in the Royal National Park (p145) and bushwalks around the inlets of Broken Bay in Ku-ring-gai Chase National Park (p147).

West of Sydney, the sandstone bluffs, eucalyptus forests and wildflowers of the Blue Mountains make for a thrilling experience, as does Barrington Tops National Park (p172) to the north. Kosciuszko National Park (p232), in the Snowy Mountains, has excellent alpine walks in summer, and you can walk to the summit of Australia's highest peak, Mt Kosciuszko (2228m).

In the state's northwest, the Warrumbungle National Park (p214), with its volcanic peaks, has over 30km of trails to keep you hale and strong.

Far west in the outback, the land's traditional owners will take you on a guided bushwalk in Mutawintji National Park (p247). Longer routes include the three-day Six Foot Track (p157) to the Jenolan Caves. The Great North Walk (p158) from Sydney to Newcastle can be walked in sections, or covered in a two-week trek.

Outdoor stockists are good sources of bushwalking information. Also try the **NPWS** (www.nationalparks.nsw.gov.au) and the **Confederation of Bushwalking Clubs NSW** (www.bushwalking.org.au/code.html).

Lonely Planet's *Walking in Australia* has further information.

Canyoning

This sport has been described as a mixture of rock climbing, abseiling, swimming and bushwalking. If negotiating narrow clefts filled with water is your bag, then consider the Blue Mountains (p152), with crevices around 90m deep but only a few metres wide. With designations like Cut-Throat Canyon, Crikey Canyon and Heart Attack Canyon, this terrain is probably not for the faint hearted. Try http://members.ozemail.com.au/~dnoble/canyoning.html for the complete rundown.

Cycling

Sydney has a recreational bike-path system and an abundance of hire outlets. Longer-distance rides abound – the coast is an obvious choice with its surfeit of parks, beaches and little towns. The Hunter Valley and Blue Mountains provide a challenge. In the more moderate months, you can enjoy long-distance rural rides on relatively untravelled roads.

Bicycle NSW (Map pp94-5; ☎ 02-9281 4099; www.bicyclensw.org.au; Level 5, 822 George St, Sydney) provides information on cycling routes throughout the state. It publishes the *Cycling Around Sydney* guide, as well booklets on cycle paths around the state.

The **Bicycles Network Australia** (www.bicycles.net.au) website is also worth a look, as is Lonely Planet's *Cycling Australia*.

Diving & Snorkelling

For shore diving in Sydney, there's the Gordons Bay Underwater Nature Trail, north of Coogee; Shark Point, Clovelly, and Ship Rock, Cronulla (p111). Good boat diving can be had at Wedding Cake Island, off Coogee, Sydney Heads and Royal National Park.

Elsewhere, try Terrigal, Port Stephens (p170), Seal Rocks in Myall Lakes National Park (p172), Coffs Harbour (p183), Byron Bay (p192), Jervis Bay (p225), Ulladulla, Narooma and Merimbula (p228).

Diving outfits typically offer four-day **PADI courses** (Professional Association of Diving Instructors; www.padi.com).

Goanna Pulling

The town of Wooli (p186) has revived this traditional sport. Watch grown men wearing leather harnesses try to pull each other's heads off, with nary a goanna in sight.

Sailing

Sydney has a plethora of sailing schools. Pittwater (p111) also offers exceptional sailing, as does Lake Macquarie, south of Newcastle, and Myall Lakes to the north.

The **Yachting Association of New South Wales** (☎ 02-9660 1266; www.nsw.yachting.org.au; 3rd fl, Grandstand, Wentworth Park, Wattle St, Glebe) in Sydney can help you find sailing clubs and courses.

Skiing

Snowfields straddle the NSW–Victoria border. The season is relatively short, mid-June to early September, and snowfalls can be unpredictable. Cross-country skiing is popular and most resorts offer lessons and equipment.

The Snowy Mountains (p234) feature hugely popular resorts including Charlotte Pass, Perisher Blue, Selwyn and Thredbo.

Skiing Australia (www.skiingaustralia.org.au) details the major resorts and race clubs.

Surfing & Swimming

Swells at Manly, Dee Why, Narrabeen and Avalon, and the areas around Bondi and Cronulla, are ideal for surfing (p112).

Practically any NSW coastal town can sate the needs of swimmers and surfers. Get wet at Byron Bay (p192), Lennox Head (p189), Angourie Point (p187), Nambucca Heads (p180), Coffs Harbour (p183), Wollongong (p220), Jervis Bay (p225), Ulladulla (p226), Merimbula and Pambula.

There are also multitudes of lakes and rivers where you can cool off. Most towns have an Olympic-sized pool.

Combining a holiday with learning to surf is becoming popular. Surf shops offering lessons can be found in most popular surfing spots around the state.

Surf carnivals start in December and run till April. Contact **Surf Life Saving New South Wales** (☎ 02-9984 7188; www.surflifesaving.com.au /surfnsw.html; PO Box 430, Narrabeen 2101) for details.

Useful websites include www.realsurf.com and www.coastalwatch.com.

Whale & Dolphin Watching

Migrating southern right and humpback whales pass near Australia's southern coast between the Antarctic and warmer waters, and whale-watching cruises allow you to get close to these magnificent creatures. Good spots are Eden (p229) in southern NSW and along the mid-north coast of NSW at Coffs Harbour (p183) and Port Stephens (p170).

Dolphins can be seen year-round at many places along the coast, such as Jervis Bay (p225), Port Stephens (p170) and Byron Bay (p190).

White-Water Rafting & Canoeing

For rafting, try the upper Murray and Snowy Rivers and the Shoalhaven River, south of Sydney; the Nymboida and Gwydir Rivers; Albury, Jindabyne and Nowra; Coffs Harbour (p183) and Nambucca Heads (p181) to the north.

For canoeing, Port Macquarie (p176), Barrington Tops (for white-water canoeing; p172), Myall Lakes and Jervis Bay are worthwhile. Contact the **New South Wales Canoeing Association** (☎ 02-9660 4597; www.nswcanoe.org.au; Rm 210, Sports House, Wentworth Park, Wattle St, Ultimo) in Sydney for info on courses and hire, or to buy *The Canoeing Guide to NSW*.

TOURS

NSW offers a bewildering variety of tours to suit all tastes: wineries, outback, whale watching, skiing, bushwalking, Aboriginal heritage and surfing. Various companies operate tours to popular destinations such as the Blue Mountains (p152) and the Lower Hunter Valley (p166); at the latter, you can choose from riding around wineries in a horse carriage or three-wheeled trike, ballooning over them or even skydiving into their midst. Sydney Harbour (p114) is another obvious choice. Less obvious packages allow you to make like Paul Hogan and climb the Harbour Bridge (p100).

Try Stockton Bight (p170), the 35km area of sand dunes around Anna Bay, for something extraordinary; a host of companies offer everything from sand boarding and quad biking to trekking in a 4WD around the dunes (with eco-sensitivity, naturally).

See www.visitnsw.com.au for a comprehensive list of touring options, and the regional sections in this chapter.

GETTING THERE & AROUND

Sydney's **Kingsford Smith Airport** (code SYD; ☎ 02-9667 9111; www.sydneyairport.com.au) is the obvious point of arrival for most international visitors to Australia. By car and motorcycle, you'll probably reach NSW via the Hume Hwy if you're coming from the south, or via the Pacific Hwy if you're coming from the north. The Princes Hwy heads south from the capital along the state's southern coast.

Air

Virgin Blue (☎ 13 67 89; www.virginblue.com.au), **Jetstar** (☎ 13 15 38; www.jetstar.com.au) and **Qantas** (☎ 13 13 13; www.qantas.com.au) fly all over Australia; fares are cheaper if booked online.

Regional Express (Rex; ☎ 13 17 13; www.regionalex press.com.au) flies to Sydney, Melbourne, Adelaide, Canberra and Devonport, as well as 12 other destinations in NSW, Victoria, SA and Tasmania.

Bus

Buses are often quicker and cheaper than trains, but not always. If you want to make stops on the way to your ultimate destination, look for cheap stopover deals rather than buying separate tickets. In remote areas, school buses may be the only option. The drivers will usually pick you up, but they're not obliged to.

Greyhound Australia (☎ 13 14 99; www.greyhound .com.au) operates regular services throughout Australia. It has a variety of discount passes available (p1042); consider purchasing the Central Coaster Pass, which covers the east coast north of Sydney to Brisbane and costs $167 for 90-days' usage.

Smaller regional operators:

Fearnes Coaches (☎ 02-6921 2316; www.fearnes.com .au) Runs between Sydney, Canberra and Wagga Wagga.

Firefly Express (☎ 1300 730 740; www.fireflyexpress .com.au) Runs between Sydney, Melbourne and Adelaide.

Murrays Coaches (☎ 13 22 51; www.murrays.com.au) Runs between Sydney and Canberra.

Port Stephens Coaches (☎ 02-4982 2940; www.ps coaches.com.au) Runs between Sydney and Port Stephens and Newcastle.

Premier Motor Service (☎ 13 34 10) Runs between Sydney and Melbourne along the east coast.

Train

CountryLink (☎ 13 22 32; www.countrylink.nsw.gov.au), the state rail service, will take you to most sizable towns in NSW, in conjunction with connecting buses. You need to book in advance, either by phone, online or in person at Sydney's Central Station (Map pp94–5) or one of the CountryLink Travel Centres at Circular Quay (Wharf 6; Map pp94–5), Wynyard Station (Map pp94–5) or Town Hall Station (Map pp94–5). CountryLink offers 1st- and economy-class tickets, as well as a quota of discount tickets; return fares are double the single fare. Australian students travel for half the economy fare.

The Backpacker Discovery Pass offers unlimited travel on the train and coach network in NSW for international travellers with a foreign passport. It costs from $217 (14 days) to $383 (six months). There's also the East Coast Discovery Pass (from $93.50), which can cover you from Melbourne to Cairns.

CityRail (p143; ☎ 13 15 00; www.cityrail.info), the Sydney metropolitan service, runs frequent commuter-style trains south through Wollongong to Bomaderry; west through the Blue Mountains to Katoomba and Lithgow; north to Newcastle; and southwest through the Southern Highlands to Goulburn.

SYDNEY

☎ 02 / pop 4 million

Vibrant and spectacular, brash and even boastful, Sydney throws off style like a catwalk supermodel on steroids. This amazing city absolutely buzzes with multicultural energy and offers practically everything anyone could ask for in a travel destination: a spectacular harbour spanned by an equally striking bridge, the famous Opera House, heavenly beaches and surf, plenty of great restaurants, hip bars and nightlife, and distinctly flavoured neighbourhoods. And while other capital cities such as Melbourne and Brisbane lay claim to being uniquely Australian cities, Sydney is Australia's international darling; many travellers who come for a week end up staying a year. Sydney is the place to combine relaxed hedonism, decadent industriousness and look-at-me antics.

HISTORY

It was at Sydney Cove, where the ferries run from Circular Quay today, that Sydney's first European settlement was established in 1788, so it's not surprising that Sydney has a strong sense of history. But that doesn't stop the city from being far brasher and livelier than many of its younger Australian counterparts.

The city is built on land once occupied by the Eora tribe, whose presence lingers in the place names of some suburbs and whose artistic legacy can be seen at many Aboriginal engraving sites around the city. Many ascribe Sydney's raffish spirit to the fact that the military were essentially in charge of things in the late 18th century and early 19th century. Paying for labour and local products in rum (hence their name, the Rum Corps), the soldiers upset, defied and outmanoeuvred three of the colony's early governors, including one William Bligh of *Bounty* mutiny fame.

NEW SOUTH WALES

SYDNEY'S TOP 11

- Walk around, photograph and tour the **Opera House** (p100) – like you wouldn't!
- Stroll across the **Harbour Bridge** (p100) and into the North Shore.
- Check out the **Rocks** (p101) – Australia's birthplace and tourist hot spot.
- Relax and picnic in the **Royal Botanic Gardens** (p105).
- Hang out, swim and eat fish and chips at **Bondi** (p109) or **Coogee** (p109).
- Take the ferry to Manly – and do the **Manly Scenic Walkway** (p110).
- Eat cheaply but well in **Chinatown** (p120) and **Surry Hills** (p120).
- Drink, party and stay up late in **Kings Cross** (p131).
- Take the train to Katoomba and the **Blue Mountains** (p149).
- Shop for souvenirs at **Paddy's Markets** (p139) in Chinatown.
- Strut up and down Paddington's fashionable **Oxford St** (p138).

ORIENTATION

The harbour divides Sydney into north and south, with the Sydney Harbour Bridge and the Harbour Tunnel joining the two shores. The city centre is roughly from Circular Quay to Central Station. To the west is Darling Harbour, while to the east lie Darlinghurst, Kings Cross and Paddington.

Three kilometres further southeast, along the coast, are the ocean-beach suburbs of Bondi and Coogee. Sydney's Kingsford Smith Airport is 10km south of the city centre. West of the centre are the gentrified suburbs of Pyrmont, Glebe and Balmain. The inner west includes Newtown and Leichhardt. Suburbs stretch 20km north and south of the centre, their extent limited by national parks. The suburbs north of the bridge are known collectively as the North Shore. The western suburbs sprawl for 50km to reach the foothills of the Blue Mountains.

For information on getting into the centre from Sydney's airport, see p141.

Maps

Just about every brochure you pick up includes a map of the city centre, but Lonely Planet's *Sydney City Map* is an exceptional choice. The *Sydney UBD Street Directory* ($40) is invaluable for drivers.

For a great selection of travel maps (and Lonely Planet guidebooks) check out **Map World** (Map pp94-5; ☎ 9261 3601; www.mapworld .net.au; 280 Pitt St; ✆ 8.30am-5.30pm Mon-Wed & Fri, to 6.30pm Thu, 10am-4.30pm Sat, 10am-3pm Sun). For aerial, topographic and many other maps,

visit the **Department of Land & Water Conservation** (DLWC; Map pp94-5; ☎ 9228 6360; 23-33 Bridge St; ✆ 8.30am-5pm Mon-Fri).

INFORMATION
Bookshops

Ariel (Map pp94-5; ☎ 9332 4581; 42 Oxford St, Paddington; ✆ 9am-midnight) Good for well-chosen art and design titles.

Desire Books (Map p98; ☎ 9977 0888; 3/3 Whistler St, Manly; ✆ 10am-6pm Mon-Wed, to 10pm Thu, to 6pm Fri & Sat, 11am-5pm Sun) Chess on Thursday nights, sofas in back and a small collection of new and used books (will take trade-ins).

Dymocks Books (Map pp94-5; ☎ 9235 0155; 424-428 George St; ✆ 9am-6.30pm Mon-Wed, Fri & Sat, to 9pm Thu, 10am-5.30pm Sun) In excess of 250,000 titles spread over three floors, including a Lonely Planet aisle! Several branches in town.

Gleebooks (Map p99; ☎ 9660 2333; 49 Glebe Point Rd, Glebe; ✆ 9am-9pm) Frequent winner of 'bookshop of the year' awards. Also has children's books and used books at its annexe at 191 Glebe Point Rd.

Travel Bookshop (Map pp94-5; ☎ 9261 8200; Shop 3, 175 Liverpool St; ✆ 9am-6pm Mon-Fri, 10am-5pm Sat, closed Sun) Crammed with, you guessed it, travel books. Also has used books (trade 'em in).

Emergency

Lifeline (☎ 13 11 14) Offers 24-hour phone-counselling services, including suicide prevention.

National Roads & Motorists' Association (NRMA; Map pp94-5; ☎ 13 21 32; www.nrma.com.au; 388 George St) For auto insurance and roadside service.

Police Station (Map pp94-5; ☎ 000) The Rocks (132 George St); Central Sydney (570 George St)

Rape Crisis Centre (☎ 1800 424 017, 9819 6565)
Wayside Chapel (Map p97; ☎ 9358 6577; 29 Hughes St, Potts Point; ☼ 7am-10pm) This crisis centre is in the heart of Kings Cross.

Internet Access

Internet cafés are common in Sydney, especially in Kings Cross, Chinatown and Bondi. Rates are around $3 an hour. Plenty of hostels and hotels offer Internet access to their guests.

Global Gossip (Map p97; ☎ 9326 9777; 61 Darlinghurst Rd, Kings Cross; ☼ 9am-1am) Also in Bondi, near Central Station and in the city centre.
Travellers Contact Point (Map pp94-5; ☎ 9221 8744; www.travellers.com.au; Level 7, 428 George St; ☼ 9am-6pm Mon-Fri, 10am-4pm Sat) Free email for the first 30 minutes.

Internet Resources

For more information on Sydney, check out the following websites:

www.cityofsydney.nsw.gov.au City news and politics.
www.sydney.citysearch.com.au What's happening in Sydney.
www.viewsydney.com.au Live images from around the city.
www.visitnsw.com.au Info on Sydney and NSW, including events.
www.whitepages.com.au Find a business or service anywhere in Australia.

Media

The 'Metro' lift-out in Friday's *Sydney Morning Herald* provides a comprehensive listing of what's on in the city over the coming week. The Wednesday 'SLM' inset in the *Daily Telegraph* does the same. Free music and entertainment papers include *Drum Media*, *Revolver*, *3D World* and *Sydney Star Observer* (the last is a gay publication).

There are plenty of guidebooks that cover Sydney. Lonely Planet's *Australia*, *Australia & New Zealand on a Shoestring* and *New South Wales* are general guides, but if you want more details check out *Sydney* and the handy-sized *Best of Sydney*.

Medical Services

Kings Cross Travellers Clinic (Map p97; ☎ 9358 3066; 13 Springfield Ave, Kings Cross; ☼ 9am-1pm & 2-6pm Mon-Fri, 10am-noon Sat) Bookings advised for morning-after pill scripts and dive medicals.
Sydney Hospital (Map pp94-5; ☎ 9382 7009; 8 Macquarie St) Has a 24-hour emergency ward.

Travellers Medical & Vaccination Centre (Map pp94-5; ☎ 9221 7133; www.traveldoctor.com.au; Level 7, 428 George St; ☼ 9am-5.30pm Mon, Wed & Fri, 8am-5.30pm Tue, 9am-7.30pm Thu, 9am-1pm Sat) The best place to get any travel-related shots and medical advice.

Money

There are plenty of banks and ATMs in Sydney. Change bureaus include the two found at **Central Station** (☼ 8am-5pm Mon-Fri, 9am-6pm Sat & Sun) and one opposite Wharf 6 at **Circular Quay** (☼ 8am-8.30pm). There are also several in the city centre, Kings Cross and at the airport (open until the last flight comes in; however, rates aren't as good as in the city).
American Express (Map pp94-5; ☎ 1300 139 060; 105 Pitt St; ☼ 9am-5pm Mon-Fri, 10am-1pm Sat) Helps with travel arrangements; has other branches throughout town, including an exchange booth inside the Travel Bookshop.

Post

There are plenty of post office branches throughout the city. Main offices:

General Post Office (GPO; Map pp94-5; 1 Martin Pl; ☼ 8.15am-5.30pm Mon-Fri, 10am-2pm Sat) Beautifully colonnaded Victorian.
Poste Restante Service (Map pp94-5; Level 2, Hunter Connection Bldg, 310 George St; ☼ 8.15am-5.30pm Mon-Fri) You will need identification to retrieve any post.

Tourist Information

All hours vary with the seasons. Longer summer hours are listed here.

City Host Information Kiosks (Map pp94-5) Circular Quay (cnr Pitt & Alfred Sts; ☼ 9am-5pm); Martin Pl (btwn Elizabeth & Castlereagh Sts; ☼ variable hours); Town Hall (George St; ☼ variable hours)
Darling Harbour Visitors Centre (Map pp94-5; ☎ 9240-8788; Darling Harbour; ☼ 10am-6pm) Behind the Imax theatre.
NSW Visitors Centre (Map p144; ☎ 9667 6053; www .visitnsw.com.au; Kingsford Smith International Airport; ☼ 6am-11pm) Book discounted hotel rooms and onward travel here.
Sydney Visitors Centre (Map pp94-5; ☎ 9240 8788; www.sydneyvisitorcentre.com; 106 George St, The Rocks; ☼ 9.30am-5.30pm) Very helpful and stuffed full of brochures.
Travellers Aid Society (Map pp94-5; ☎ 9211 2469; Platform 1, Central Station; ☼ 8am-2.30pm Mon-Sat) Provides general information, travel assistance, phone recharge and hot showers.

(Continued on page 100)

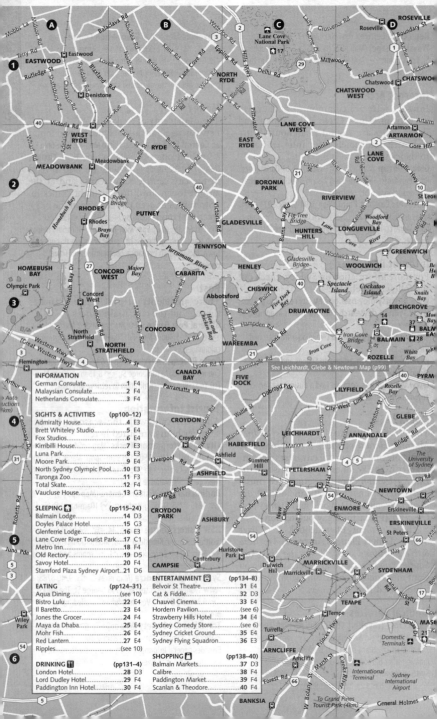

INFORMATION
German Consulate	1 F4
Malaysian Consulate	2 F4
Netherlands Consulate	3 F4

SIGHTS & ACTIVITIES (pp100–12)
Admiralty House	4 E3
Brett Whiteley Studio	5 E4
Fox Studios	6 E4
Kirribilli House	7 E3
Luna Park	8 E3
Moore Park	9 E4
North Sydney Olympic Pool	10 E3
Taronga Zoo	11 F3
Total Skate	12 F4
Vaucluse House	13 G3

SLEEPING (pp115–24)
Balmain Lodge	14 D3
Doyles Palace Hotel	15 E3
Glenferrie Lodge	16 E3
Lane Cover River Tourist Park	17 C1
Metro Inn	18 D5
Old Rectory	19 E3
Savoy Hotel	20 F4
Stamford Plaza Sydney Airport	21 D6

EATING (pp124–31)
Aqua Dining	(see 10)
Bistro Lulu	22 E4
Il Baretto	23 E4
Jones the Grocer	24 F4
Maya da Dhaba	25 E4
Mohr Fish	26 E4
Red Lantern	27 E4
Ripples	(see 10)

DRINKING (pp131–4)
London Hotel	28 D3
Lord Dudley Hotel	29 F4
Paddington Inn Hotel	30 F4

ENTERTAINMENT (pp134–8)
Belvoir St Theatre	31 E4
Cat & Fiddle	32 D3
Chauvel Cinema	33 E4
Hordern Pavilion	(see 6)
Strawberry Hills Hotel	34 E4
Sydney Comedy Store	(see 6)
Sydney Cricket Ground	35 E4
Sydney Flying Squadron	36 E3

SHOPPING (pp138–40)
Balmain Markets	37 D3
Calibre	38 F4
Paddington Market	39 F4
Scanlan & Theodore	40 F4

See Leichhardt, Glebe & Newtown Map (p99)

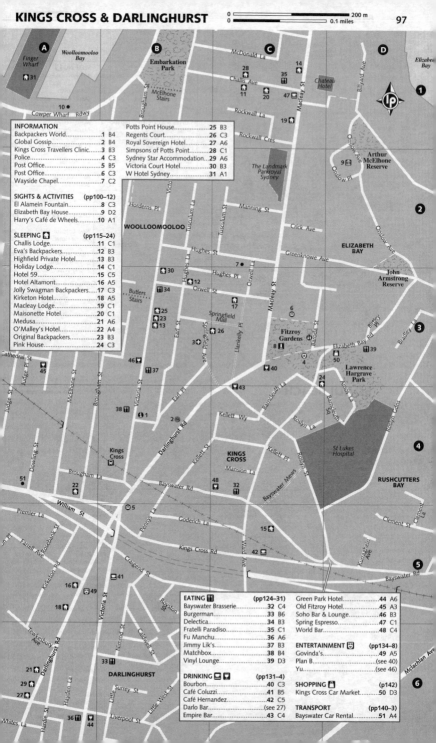

0	200 m	
0	0.1 miles	

INFORMATION
Backpackers World	1 B4
Global Gossip	2 B4
Kings Cross Travellers Clinic	3 B3
Police	4 C3
Post Office	5 B5
Post Office	6 C3
Wayside Chapel	7 C2

SIGHTS & ACTIVITIES (pp100–12)
El Alamein Fountain	8 C3
Elizabeth Bay House	9 D2
Harry's Café de Wheels	10 A1

SLEEPING (pp115–24)
Challis Lodge	11 C1
Eva's Backpackers	12 B3
Highfield Private Hotel	13 B3
Holiday Lodge	14 C1
Hotel 59	15 C5
Hotel Altamont	16 A5
Jolly Swagman Backpackers	17 C3
Kirketon Hotel	18 A5
Macleay Lodge	19 C1
Maisonette Hotel	20 C1
Medusa	21 A6
O'Malley's Hotel	22 A4
Original Backpackers	23 B3
Pink House	24 C3
Potts Point House	25 B3
Regents Court	26 C3
Royal Sovereign Hotel	27 A6
Simpsons of Potts Point	28 C1
Sydney Star Accommodation	29 A6
Victoria Court Hotel	30 B3
W Hotel Sydney	31 A1

EATING (pp124–31)
Bayswater Brasserie	32 C4
Burgerman	33 B6
Delectica	34 B3
Fratelli Paradiso	35 C1
Fu Manchu	36 A6
Jimmy Lik's	37 B3
Matchbox	38 B4
Vinyl Lounge	39 D3

DRINKING (pp131–4)
Bourbon	40 C3
Café Coluzzi	41 B5
Café Hernandez	42 C5
Darlo Bar	(see 27)
Empire Bar	43 C4
Green Park Hotel	44 A6
Old Fitzroy Hotel	45 A3
Soho Bar & Lounge	46 B3
Spring Espresso	47 C1
World Bar	48 C4

ENTERTAINMENT (pp134–8)
Govinda's	49 A5
Plan B	(see 40)
Yu	(see 46)

SHOPPING (p142)
Kings Cross Car Market	50 D3

TRANSPORT (pp140–3)
Bayswater Car Rental	51 A4

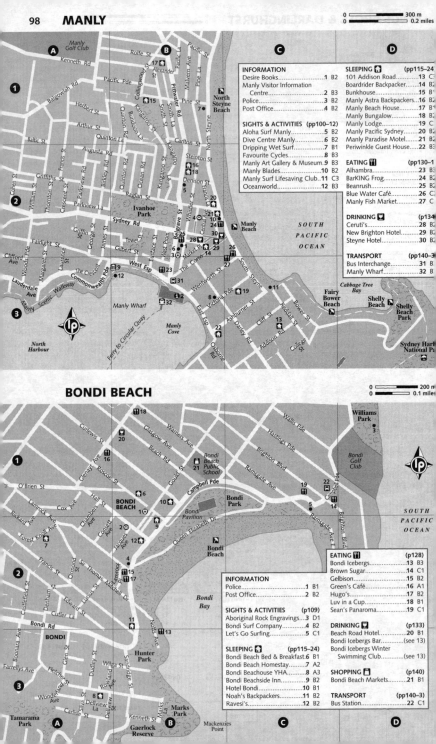

MANLY

0 — 300 m
0 — 0.2 miles

INFORMATION
Desire Books.....................1 B2
Manly Visitor Information
   Centre.........................2 B3
Police.............................3 B2
Post Office.......................4 B2

SIGHTS & ACTIVITIES (pp100–12)
Aloha Surf Manly................5 B2
Dive Centre Manly...............6 B2
Dripping Wet Surf...............7 B1
Favourite Cycles.................8 B3
Manly Art Gallery & Museum.9 B3
Manly Blades....................10 B2
Manly Surf Lifesaving Club...11 C3
Oceanworld.....................12 B3

SLEEPING (pp115–24)
101 Addison Road.............13 C
Boardrider Backpacker........14 B
Bunkhouse.....................15 B
Manly Astra Backpackers....16 B2
Manly Beach House............17 B
Manly Bungalow...............18 B
Manly Lodge....................19 C
Manly Pacific Sydney..........20 B
Manly Paradise Motel.........21 B
Periwinkle Guest House.......22 B3

EATING (pp130–1)
Alhambra........................23 B
BarKING Frog...................24 B2
Beanrush........................25 B2
Blue Water Café................26 C
Manly Fish Market.............27 C

DRINKING (p134)
Ceruti's..........................28 B
New Brighton Hotel...........29 B
Steyne Hotel....................30 B

TRANSPORT (pp140–3)
Bus Interchange................31 B
Manly Wharf....................32 B

BONDI BEACH

0 — 200 m
0 — 0.1 miles

INFORMATION
Police.............................1 B1
Post Office.......................2 B2

SIGHTS & ACTIVITIES (p109)
Aboriginal Rock Engravings...3 D1
Bondi Surf Company............4 B2
Let's Go Surfing..................5 C1

SLEEPING (pp115–24)
Bondi Beach Bed & Breakfast.6 B1
Bondi Beach Homestay........7 A2
Bondi Beachouse YHA..........8 A3
Bondi Beachside Inn.............9 B2
Hotel Bondi.....................10 B1
Noah's Backpackers...........11 B2
Ravesi's..........................12 B2

EATING (p128)
Bondi Icebergs..................13 B3
Brown Sugar....................14 C1
Gelbison.........................15 B2
Green's Café....................16 A1
Hugo's...........................17 B2
Luv in a Cup....................18 B1
Sean's Panorama..............19 C1

DRINKING (p133)
Beach Road Hotel.............20 B1
Bondi Icebergs Bar............(see 13)
Bondi Icebergs Winter
   Swimming Club.............(see 13)

SHOPPING (p140)
Bondi Beach Markets.........21 B1

TRANSPORT (pp140–3)
Bus Station......................22 C1

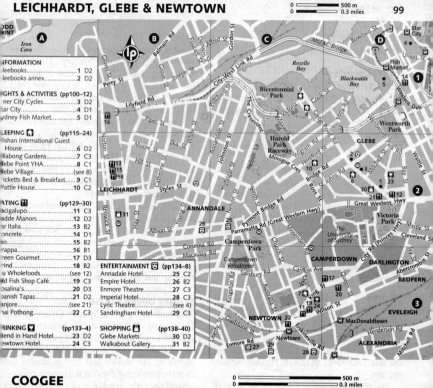

INFORMATION
Gleebooks......................1 D2
Gleebooks annex.............2 D2

SIGHTS & ACTIVITIES (pp100–12)
Inner City Cycles..............3 D2
Star City.......................4 D1
Sydney Fish Market..........5 D1

SLEEPING (pp115–24)
Alishan International Guest
  House.......................6 D2
Billabong Gardens...........7 C3
Glebe Point YHA.............8 C1
Glebe Village...............(see 8)
Tricketts Bed & Breakfast...9 C1
Wattle House................10 C2

EATING (pp129–30)
Acicalupo....................11 C3
Badde Manors...............12 D2
Bar Italia.....................13 B2
Concrete......................14 D1
Iku............................15 B2
Grappa.......................16 B1
Green Gourmet...............17 D3
Grind.........................18 B2
Iku Wholefoods............(see 12)
Old Fish Shop Café..........19 C3
Rosalina's....................20 D3
Spanish Tapas...............21 C3
Sanjore.....................(see 21)
Thai Pothong................22 C3

DRINKING (pp133–4)
Friend in Hand Hotel........23 D2
Newtown Hotel..............24 C3

ENTERTAINMENT (pp134–8)
Annandale Hotel.............25 C2
Empire Hotel.................26 B2
Enmore Theatre.............27 C3
Imperial Hotel...............28 C3
Lyric Theatre..............(see 4)
Sandringham Hotel..........29 C3

SHOPPING (pp138–40)
Glebe Markets...............30 D2
Walkabout Gallery..........31 B2

COOGEE

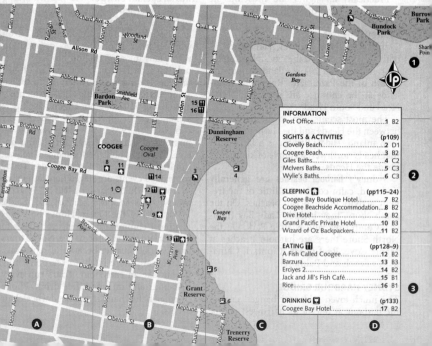

INFORMATION
Post Office....................1 B2

SIGHTS & ACTIVITIES (p109)
Clovelly Beach................2 D1
Coogee Beach................3 B2
Giles Baths...................4 C2
McIvers Baths................5 C3
Wylie's Baths.................6 C3

SLEEPING (pp115–24)
Coogee Bay Boutique Hotel.....7 B2
Coogee Beachside Accommodation..8 B2
Dive Hotel....................9 B2
Grand Pacific Private Hotel....10 B3
Wizard of Oz Backpackers.....11 B2

EATING (pp128–9)
A Fish Called Coogee.........12 B2
Barzura.......................13 B3
Erciyes 2.....................14 B2
Jack and Jill's Fish Café......15 B1
Rice..........................16 B1

DRINKING (p133)
Coogee Bay Hotel.............17 B2

(Continued from page 91)

Travel Agencies

Backpackers World (Map p97; ☎ 9380 2700, 1800 676 763; www.backpackersworld.com.au; 212 Victoria St, Kings Cross; ☺ 9am-7pm Mon-Fri, 10am-6pm Sat, 11am-5pm Sun) Five Sydney locations.

STA Travel (Map pp94-5; ☎ 9252 8022; www.statravel .com.au; Shop 1, 2 Bridge St; ☺ 9.30-5.30pm Mon-Sat) There are 20 Sydney branches.

Travellers Contact Point (Map pp94-5; ☎ 9221 8744; www.travellers.com.au; Level 7, 428 George St; ☺ 9am-6pm Mon-Fri, 10am-4pm Sat) Backpacker agency which holds mail and has a good bulletin board.

YHA Membership & Travel Centre (Map pp94-5; ☎ 9261 1111; www.yha.com.au/yhainfo/membership _travel.cfm; 422 Kent St; ☺ 9am-5pm Mon-Wed & Fri, 9am-6pm Thu, 9am-2pm Sat) Offers travel packages and YHA bookings worldwide; also try the travel agent in the Sydney Central YHA (see p116).

SIGHTS

Sydney's chock-full of things to see and do. Much of it doesn't cost a cent, but if you plan on seeing an exceptional number of museums, attractions and tours, check out the **Smartvisit card** (☎ 1300 661 711; www.seesydney card.com).

Practically all sights and museums in Sydney have good disabled access.

Sydney Harbour

Sydney's stunning harbour, **Port Jackson**, is both a major port and the city's playground. It stretches some 20km inland to join the mouth of the Parramatta River. The headlands at the entrance are known as North Head and South Head.

The most scenic part of the harbour is between the Heads and the Harbour Bridge, 8km inland. **Middle Harbour** is a large inlet that heads northwest a couple of kilometres inside the Heads.

Sydney's **harbour beaches** are generally sheltered, calm coves with little of the frenetic activity of the ocean beaches. On the south shore, they include Lady Bay (nudist), Camp Cove and Nielsen Park. On the North Shore there are harbour beaches at Manly Cove, Reef Beach, Clontarf, Chinaman's Beach and Balmoral.

SYDNEY HARBOUR BRIDGE

The much-loved 'old coat hanger' crosses the harbour at one of its narrowest points, joining central Sydney with the satellite business district in North Sydney. The bridge was completed in 1932 at a cost of $20 million and has been a favourite icon ever since, partly because of its sheer size, partly because of its function in uniting the city.

You can climb up almost 200 stairs inside the southeastern stone pylon, which houses a small (free) museum and the **Pylon Lookout** (Map pp94-5; ☎ 9240 1100; www.pylonlookout.com .au; admission $8.50; ☺ 10am-5pm), or you can join a climbing group and scale the bridge itself in a BridgeClimb (p114).

Cars, trains, cyclists, joggers and pedestrians use the bridge. The cycleway is on the western side and the pedestrian walkway is on the eastern; access is from the Argyle St stairs near Cumberland St, in the Rocks. The best way to experience the bridge is on foot, so put on your walking shoes.

SYDNEY OPERA HOUSE

The postcard-perfect Sydney Opera House (Map pp94–5) is dramatically situated on the eastern headland of Circular Quay. Its soaring shell-like exterior is one of *the* must-see sights in the world, and brings tingles the first time you clap eyes on it. Its construction was an operatic blend of personal vision, long delays, bitter feuding, budget blowouts and righteous politicking. Construction began in 1959 after Danish architect Jørn Utzon won an international design competition with plans for a $7 million building. After political interference, Utzon quit in disgust in 1966, leaving a consortium of Australian architects to design a compromised interior – at a cost of $102 million. Utzon hasn't personally seen the Opera House since. Finally completed in 1973, it was lumbered with an impractical internal design for staging operas. The first public performance here was, ironically, Prokofiev's *War and Peace*. Today some 3000 events are staged here annually.

A worthwhile hour-long **tour** (☎ 9250 7250; www.sydneyoperahouse.com; adult/concession $23/16; ☺ 9am-5pm) of the Opera House buildings is almost compulsory during your visit to Sydney and is very informative. Not all tours can visit all theatres because of rehearsals, but you are more likely to see everything if you take an early tour. Tours run every half-hour and include a free drink. Phone or email beforehand if you need wheelchair access.

SYDNEY HARBOUR NATIONAL PARK
This park protects the scattered pockets of bushland around the harbour and includes several small islands. It offers some great walking tracks, scenic lookouts, Aboriginal carvings and historic sites. On the south shore it incorporates South Head and Nielsen Park; on the North Shore it includes North Head, Dobroyd Head, Middle Head and Ashton Park. Fort Denison, Goat, Clarke, Rodd and Shark Islands are also part of the park. Pick up info at the **Sydney Harbour National Park Information Centre** (Map pp94–5; ☎ 9247 5033; 110 George St, The Rocks; ⏱ 9.30am-4.30pm Mon-Fri, 10am-4.30pm Sat & Sun), which is housed inside historic Cadman's Cottage.

Fort Denison (Map pp94–5) is a small, fortified island off Mrs Macquaries Point, originally used to isolate troublesome convicts. The fort was built during the Crimean War amid fears of a Russian invasion (seriously!). Two tours are available: the heritage tour (adult/child/family $22/18/72) or the brunch tour (adult/child $47/43).

There are also tours of **Goat Island** (Map pp94–5), just west of the Harbour Bridge, which has been a shipyard, quarantine station and gunpowder depot. Pick the heritage tour (adult/child/family $20/16/62) or a Gruesome Tales tour ($25).

All tours can be booked through the information centre.

The Rocks & Circular Quay

Sydney's first European settlement was established on the rocky spur of land on the western side of Sydney Cove, from which the Harbour Bridge now crosses to the North Shore. It was a squalid, raucous and notoriously dangerous place full of convicts, whalers, prostitutes and street gangs, though in the 1820s the nouveaux riches built three-storey houses on the ridges overlooking the slums, starting the city's obsession with prime real estate (which continues today).

The Rocks later became an area of warehouses and maritime commerce and then slumped into decline as modern shipping and storage facilities moved away from Circular Quay. An outbreak of bubonic plague in the early 20th century led to whole streets being razed, and the construction of the Harbour Bridge resulted in further demolition.

Since the 1970s redevelopment has turned much of the Rocks into a sanitised, historical tourist precinct, full of narrow cobbled lanes, fine colonial buildings, old pubs, fancy restaurants and Australiana shops. Despite the kitsch it's delightful to spend an afternoon strolling the poky backstreets and soaking up the atmosphere, especially on weekends when the **Rocks Market** (George St) is in full swing – see p139.

SYDNEY IN...

Two Days
Walk around the **Rocks** (above) historic area and nearby **Circular Quay** (above), stopping to snap photos of the iconic **Sydney Opera House** (opposite) and to revel in the atmosphere of the kitsch **Rocks Market** (p139). Head around to the lush **Royal Botanic Gardens** (p105) before scooting off to Australia's most famous beach, **Bondi** (p109) – remember to bring your swimsuit! If you have time, take the gorgeous, two-hour stroll from Bondi to **Coogee** (p112).

The next day, hop on a ferry to **Manly** (p110) and, if you like walks, do the 9km **Manly Scenic Walkway** (p110). For dinner and drinks there's either **Darlinghurst** (p126) or **Surry Hills** (p127). Then party the night away in brash **Kings Cross** (p138).

Four Days
On your third day, walk around the bustling **city centre** (p103) and scenic **Darling Harbour** (p106). For breathtaking views, climb the **Sydney Harbour Bridge** (opposite) on a BridgeClimb tour. Take a scenic ferry ride to Watsons Bay and sit down for lunch at the famous **Doyles Palace Hotel** (p133). Finish the day with a cheap, tasty dinner in **Chinatown** (p125).

Your fourth day should see you on a train to **Katoomba** (p152), in the majestic **Blue Mountains** (p149). Spend the day exploring caves and hiking among the gumtree forests before returning to Sydney.

A TALE OF TWO CITIES

Athens and Sparta, Paris and Milan, Springfield and Shelbyville – their struggles pale beside the epic 150-year rivalry between Sydney and Melbourne. Australia's biggest city, Sydney is also its oldest, having begun in 1788 as a convict colony. Melbourne, currently in the number-two slot, was founded in 1835. Sixteen years later prospectors struck gold in Victoria, and the ensuing rush rocketed Melbourne ahead of Sydney in both wealth and population. The SMR (Sydney-Melbourne Rivalry) had begun.

Competition flared when Melbourne became Australia's temporary capital following nationhood in 1901. Purpose-built Canberra didn't replace Melbourne until 1927, by which time a driven Sydney had begun catching up financially, having already re-taken the lead in population figures.

These days, the SMR plays out for the most part as friendly chaffing, though discussions can get heated. Melburnians will point to Sydney's convict origins, its high housing prices and what they see as a lack of culture, while talking up their own city's multi-ethnicity, great restaurants and lively arts scene. Sydneysiders will often either feign ignorance of any rivalry, or maintain that it's one-sided, an invention of envious Melburnians deluded enough to compare their boring burgh with the obviously superior Sydney. And each side accuses the other of being unfriendly and snobbish.

A few unhappy souls seem dead earnest in their enmity toward the opposing city, convinced that no friendship or even meaningful dialogue can take place between the two groups.

If you should get caught in the middle between such types, don't try to pour oil on the waters by saying the two cities are nearing parity in their ethnic diversity and culinary sophistication, or by claiming that Sydney's scenery is balanced by the fact that Melbourne is the birthplace of footy.

No, just put on your most innocent face and ask, 'Hey, does Canberra really suck as much as they say?'

The oldest house in Sydney (1816) is **Cadman's Cottage** (Map pp94-5; ☎ 9247 5033; 110 George St, The Rocks; ☽ 9.30am-4.30pm Mon-Fri, 10am-4.30pm Sat & Sun). It's also the former home of the last government coxswain, John Cadman; it now houses the Sydney Harbour National Park Information Centre.

Nearby, the **Museum of Contemporary Art** (MCA; ☎ 9250 8467; www.mca.com.au; 140 George St; admission free; ☽ 10am-5pm) is set in a stately Art Deco building. It has a fine collection of modern art from Australia and around the world (sculpture, painting, installations and the moving image) and temporary exhibitions on a variety of themes. The classy MCA Café is worth a stop (see p124).

A short walk west along Argyle Street, through the awe-inspiring **Argyle Cut** (excavated by convicts), takes you to the other side of the peninsula and **Millers Point**, a delightful district of early colonial homes with an English-village feel. Nearby lies the 1848 **Garrison Church** and the more secular delights of the Lord Nelson Brewery Hotel (see p131) and the Hero of Waterloo (see p131), which tussle over the title of Sydney's oldest pub.

Sydney Observatory (☎ 9217 0485; Watson Rd, Observatory Hill; admission free, daily tours $6; ☽ 10am-5pm), off Argyle St, has a commanding position atop Observatory Park overlooking Millers Point and the harbour. There's a pleasant garden and an excellent free astronomy museum. Nightly sky-watching visits (adult/child/family $15/12/40) must be paid in advance; there's also a 3-D theatre with daily shows (adult/child/family $6/4/16).

Close by, in the National Trust Centre, is the **SH Ervin Gallery** (☎ 9258 0173; www.nsw.national trust.org.au; Watson Rd, Observatory Hill; adult/concession $6/4; ☽ 11am-5pm Tue-Fri, noon-5pm Sat & Sun). It shows temporary exhibitions on Australian art and is also the home of the annual Salon des Refusés show, for rejected Archibald Prize contenders. The café here serves good food.

At Dawes Point, on Walsh Bay, just west of the Harbour Bridge, are several renovated wharves. **Pier One** now houses a luxury hotel; **Pier Four** is beautifully utilised as the home of the prestigious Wharf Theatre, Bangarra Dance Theatre, Sydney Dance Company and Australian Theatre for Young People (ATYP). Other wharves now appear to be getting the 'luxury waterfront apartments' treatment.

Circular Quay, built around Sydney Cove, is one of the city's major focal points. The first European settlement grew around the Tank Stream, which now runs underground into the harbour near Wharf Six. For many years this was the shipping centre of Sydney, but it's now both a commuting hub and a recreational space. It combines ferry quays, a train station and the Overseas Passenger Terminal (read: huge cruise ships) with harbour walkways, parks, restaurants, buskers and lots of tourists.

Central Sydney

Central Sydney (Map pp94–5) stretches from Circular Quay in the north to Central Station in the south. The business hub is towards the northern end, but most redevelopment is occurring at the southern end and this is slowly shifting the city focus.

Sydney lacks a true civic centre, but **Martin Pl** (Map pp94–5) lays claim to the honour by default. This grand, revamped pedestrian mall extends from Macquarie St to George St and is impressive with monumental financial institutions and the colonnaded Victorian GPO at No 1. There's plenty of public seating, a cenotaph commemorating Australia's war dead and an amphitheatre where lunchtime entertainment is sometimes staged.

The **Sydney Town Hall** (Map pp94-5; cnr George & Druitt Sts), about three blocks south of Martin

Pl, was built in 1874. The elaborate chamber room and concert hall inside matches its outrageously ornate exterior. Next door, the Anglican **St Andrew's Cathedral**, built around the same time, is the oldest cathedral in Australia.

The city's most sumptuous shopping complex, the Byzantine-style **Queen Victoria Building** (QVB; Map pp94-5; George St), is next to the town hall and takes up an entire city block. Another lovingly restored shopping centre is the much smaller **Strand Arcade** (Map pp94-5; cnr Pitt St Mall & George St). See p140 for information about these shopping icons.

For jaw-dropping views of Sydney and environs, whoosh to the top of **Sydney Tower** (AMP Tower; Map pp94-5; ☎ 8251 7800; www.sydney skytour.com.au; cnr Market & Castlereagh Sts; adult/concession $22/15.85; ☒ 9am-10.30pm, to 11.30pm Sat), the landmark needle visible from multiple spots in town (see the boxed text, p105).

The splendidly over-the-top **State Theatre** (Map pp94-5; ☎ 9376 6861; 49 Market St; tours $15) was built in 1929; tours are for groups of 10 or more, by appointment only. To the southwest is the tiny **Spanish Quarter** and larger **Chinatown** (Map pp94–5), dynamic areas breathing life into the city's southeastern zone, which includes the busy hub of Central Station.

On the eastern edge of the city centre is the formal **Hyde Park** (Map pp94–5), once the colony's first racetrack and cricket pitch. It has a grand avenue of trees, delightful fountains, and a giant public chessboard. It contains the dignified **Anzac Memorial** (☒ 9am-4.30pm), which has a free exhibition

---

CHINESE WHISPERS Sally O'Brien

The first Chinese came to Australia around 1840, when convict shipments stopped and labouring jobs were freely available. Initially the Chinese immigrants were considered a solution to the labour shortages; however, racial intolerance grew as the numbers of gold-seekers increased during the Gold Rush. State entry restrictions were enforced from the early 19th century and continued into much of the 20th century. In 1861 the NSW Government enacted the 'White Australia policy'. The framework of this policy, aimed at reducing the influx of Chinese immigrants, continued until the late 20th century and included Acts such as the 1861 *Chinese Immigration Regulation and Restriction Act*, which included a poll tax on Chinese immigrants, refusal of naturalisation and restricted work permits. As a result of this policy, the Chinese population remained low.

Sydney's Chinese community gravitated to Dixon St around 1870, and it quickly became a bustling commercial centre known for its opium dens and gambling. While the opium dens are long gone, you'll still find plenty of action in the area, and plenty of Australians of Chinese descent.

on the ground floor covering the 10 overseas conflicts in which Australians have fought. **St Mary's Cathedral**, with its new copper spires, overlooks the park from the east, while the 1878 **Great Synagogue** (☎ 9267 2477; www.great synagogue.org.au; 187a Elizabeth St; ☺ tours adult/child $5/3) stands on the west. Tours of the synagogue take place at noon Tuesday and Thursday (entry at 166 Castlereagh St).

MACQUARIE PLACE & SURROUNDS

Narrow lanes lead south from Circular Quay towards the city centre. At the corner of Loftus and Bridge Sts, under the shady Moreton Bay figs in Macquarie Place Park are a cannon and anchor from the First Fleet flagship, HMS *Sirius*. Here also is the **Macquarie Place Obelisk** (Map pp94–5), erected in 1818, indicating road distances to various points in the nascent colony. Nearby is the rear façade of the imposing 19th-century **Department of Land & Water Conservation** (DLWC; Bridge St), which has maps of the city (see p90).

Sydney buffs will enjoy the excellent **Museum of Sydney** (Map pp94–5; ☎ 9251 5988; www.hht.net.au; 37 Phillip St; adult/concession $7/3; ☺ 9.30am-5pm), two blocks east and on the site of the first government house, built by Arthur Phillip in 1788. Sydney's early history (including pre-1788) comes to life here in whisper, argument, gossip and artefacts. There's also a worthy café on the premises and a fine gift shop.

The 1856 **Justice & Police Museum** (Map pp94–5; ☎ 9252 1144; www.hht.net.au; 8 Phillip St; adult/concession $7/3; ☺ 10am-5pm Sat & Sun, daily in Jan), in the old water-police court and station, has fascinating exhibits on crime and policing, with a Sydney focus. The drug and addiction exhibition (with its creative bongs) is especially interesting. Wheelchair access is to the ground floor only, but Braille and audio guides are available.

MACQUARIE STREET

Sydney's greatest concentration of early public buildings grace Macquarie St, which runs along the eastern edge of the city from Hyde Park to the Opera House. Many of the buildings were commissioned by Lachlan Macquarie, the first governor to have a vision of the city beyond being a convict colony. He enlisted convicted forger Francis Greenway as an architect to realise his plans.

Two Greenway gems on Queens Sq, at the northern end of Hyde Park, are **St James Church** (1819–24; Map pp94–5) and the 1819 Georgian-style **Hyde Park Barracks Museum** (Map pp94-5; ☎ 8239 2311; www.hht.net.au; Macquarie St; adult/concession $7/3; ☺ 9.30am-5pm). The barracks were built originally as convict quarters, then became an immigration depot, and later a court. The museum details the history of the building and provides an interesting perspective on Sydney's social history, with the best use of rats you'll ever see in a display.

Next door is the lovely **Mint Building** (Map pp94-5; ☎ 8239 2288; 10 Macquarie St; ☺ 9am-5pm), which was originally the southern wing of the infamous Rum Hospital built by two Sydney merchants in 1816 in return for a monopoly on the rum trade. It became a branch of the Royal Mint in 1854. There's a fancy **café** (☺ breakfast & lunch) on the premises and a small historical collection.

The Mint's twin is **Parliament House** (Map pp94-5; ☎ 9230 2047; Macquarie St; admission free; ☺ 9am-4pm Mon-Fri), which was originally the northern wing of the Rum Hospital. This simple, proud building has been home to the NSW Parliament since 1829. The public gallery is open on days when parliament is sitting.

Next to Parliament House is the **State Library of NSW** (Map pp94-5; ☎ 9273 1414; www.sl .nsw.gov.au; Macquarie St; ☺ 9am-9pm Mon-Fri, 11am-5pm Sat & Sun), which is more of a cultural centre than a traditional library. It holds over five million tomes, and hosts innovative temporary exhibitions in its galleries. The library's modern wing also has a great bookshop filled with Australian titles. Free one-hour tours are available.

The **Sydney Conservatorium of Music** (Map pp94-5; ☎ 9351 1222; www.usyd.edu.au/su/conmusic; Macquarie St) was built by Greenway as the stables and servants' quarters of Macquarie's planned government house. Macquarie was replaced as governor before the house could be finished, partly because of the project's extravagance. See p134 for more information about the music recitals held here.

Built between 1837 and 1845, **Government House** (Map pp94-5; ☎ 9931 5222; www.hht .net.au; Macquarie St; admission free; ☺ grounds 10am-4pm daily, house 10am-3pm Fri-Sun) dominates the western headland of Farm Cove and, until early 1996, was the official residence of the

---

BEST VIEWS IN TOWN...

Sydney is an ostentatious city that offers visitors a dramatic spectacle. You can see the complete panorama by whooshing to the top of **Sydney Tower** (see p103), a needle-like column with an observation deck and revolving restaurants set 250m above the ground. The expansive views extend west to the Blue Mountains and east to the ocean, as well as to the streets of inner Sydney below. Skytour is a half-hour virtual-reality ride through Australia's history and landscape, and is included in the admission price. To get to the tower, enter the Centrepoint shopping mall from Market St and take the lift to the podium level where you buy your ticket.

The Harbour Bridge is another obvious vantage point. If you're pinching pennies, check out the spectacular view from the **Pylon Lookout** (p100). If you've got the bucks, however, you *must* do the once-in-a-lifetime **BridgeClimb tour** (p114). For those afraid of heights, there are impressive panoramas of the city and harbour from **Mrs Macquarie's Chair** (below) and from **Observatory Hill** (p102) in Millers Point. **Blues Point Reserve** and **Bradleys Head** are the best vantage points on the North Shore.

The most enjoyable, atmospheric and even romantic way to view Sydney is by boat. If you can't persuade someone to take you sailing (or don't want to pay for a cruise), jump aboard a ferry at Circular Quay. The Manly ferry offers the obligatory cruise down the length of the harbour, east of the bridge, for a mere $5.80.

If you're in the vicinity of Kings Cross, the northern end of Victoria St in Potts Point is an excellent vantage point to take in the cityscape and its best-known icons, especially at night.

---

governor of NSW. It's a marvellous example of the Gothic Revival style. Tours of the house depart every half-hour from 10.30am (unless there's a special event being held).

The **Domain** (Map pp94–5) is a pleasant grassy area east of Macquarie St that was set aside by Governor Phillip for public recreation. Today it's used by city workers as a place to escape the city hubbub, and on Sunday afternoon it's the gathering place for soapbox speakers who do their best to engage or enrage their listeners.

ART GALLERY OF NSW
The **art gallery** (AGNSW; Map pp94–5; ☎ 9225 1744; www.artgallery.nsw.gov.au; Art Gallery Rd; admission free; ۞ 10am-5pm, to 9pm Wed) has an excellent permanent display of 19th- and 20th-century Australian art, Aboriginal and Torres Strait Islander art, 15th- to 19th-century European and Asian art, and some inspired temporary exhibits. The frequently controversial Archibald Prize exhibition is held here annually, with portraits of the famous and not-so-famous bringing out the art critic in every Sydneysider. There's usually a charge for some temporary exhibitions; free tours are available (call for times).

AUSTRALIAN MUSEUM
This natural history **museum** (Map pp94–5; ☎ 9320 6000; www.amonline.net.au; 6 College St; adult/ concession $10/5; ۞ 9.30am-5pm) has an excellent Australian wildlife collection (including skeletons) and a gallery tracing Aboriginal history and the Dreamtime. It's on the eastern flank of Hyde Park, on the corner of College and William Sts. There's an indigenous performance at noon and 2pm every Sunday, and a range of kids' exhibits.

ROYAL BOTANIC GARDENS
The city's favourite picnic spot, jogging route and place to stroll is the enchanting **Royal Botanic Gardens** (Map pp94–5; ☎ 9231 8125; www.rbgsyd.nsw.gov.au; Mrs Macquaries Rd; admission free; ۞ 7am-sunset, gardens shop 10am-4pm), which borders Farm Cove, east of the Opera House. The gardens were established in 1816 and feature plant life from the South Pacific. They include the site of the colony's first paltry vegetable patch, which has been preserved as a First Farm exhibit.

Also here is one of Sydney's best harbour vantage points, the rocky ledge called **Mrs Macquarie's Chair**. It's near the tip of Mrs Macquarie's Point and offers fabulous views across the harbour.

There's a fabulous, leech-free **Sydney Tropical Centre** (Map pp94–5; adult/child $2.20/1.10; ۞ 10am-4pm) housed in the interconnecting Arc and Pyramid glasshouses. The multistorey Arc has a collection of rampant climbers and trailers from the world's rainforests, while the Pyramid houses the Australian collection, including monsoonal, woodland and tropical rainforest plants.

Free **tours** depart at 10.30am daily (or at 1pm Monday to Friday) from the information booth at the Gardens Shop. As far as wildlife goes, you can't fail to notice the gardens' resident colony of grey-headed **flying foxes** (*Pteropus poliocephalus;* also known as fruit bats), who spend their days chittering loudly and hanging around upside down until it's time to commute south across the city at dusk. Cockatoos, small reptiles and large orb spiders can also be seen. The park's paths are for the most part wheelchair accessible, although there are some flights of stairs scattered about.

Darling Harbour

This huge waterfront leisure park on the city centre's western edge, once a thriving dockland area, was reinvigorated in the 1980s by a combination of vision, politicking and big money. The supposed centrepiece is the **Harbourside Shopping Centre** (Map pp94–5), which houses shops and restaurants. More-interesting attractions are the aquarium, excellent museums and Chinese Garden.

The snazzy wining and dining precincts of **Cockle Bay Wharf** (Map pp94–5), built opposite Harbourside, and **King St Wharf** (Map pp94–5) have lent the area a bit more kudos with Sydneysiders and visitors alike. Stretching across the water is the unmissable **Pyrmont Bridge** (Map pp94–5), a pedestrian-and-monorail-only route once famous as the world's first electrically operated swingspan bridge.

The monorail and MLR (Metro Light Rail) link Darling Harbour to the city centre. Ferries from Circular Quay's Wharf 5 stop at Darling Harbour's Aquarium and Pyrmont Bay wharves ($4.80). If you're confused there's a **visitors centre** (Map pp94–5; ☎ 9240 8788; ⏲ 10am-6pm) under the highway and behind the Imax theatre.

SYDNEY AQUARIUM

Near the eastern end of Pyrmont Bridge, this good **aquarium** (Map pp94–5; ☎ 8251 7800; www.sydneyaquarium.com.au; Aquarium Pier, Darling Harbour; adult/concession $25/16; ⏲ 9am-10pm) displays the richness of Australian marine life. Three 'oceanariums' are moored in the harbour with sharks, rays and big fish in one, and Sydney Harbour marine life and seals in the others. There are also informative and well-presented exhibits of freshwater fish and coral gardens. The transparent underwater tunnels are mesmerizing.

AUSTRALIAN NATIONAL MARITIME MUSEUM

This wonderful thematic **museum** (Map pp94–5; ☎ 9298 3777; www.anmm.gov.au; 2 Murray St, Pyrmont; admission free; ⏲ 9.30am-5pm) tells the story of Australia's relationship with the sea, from Aboriginal canoes and whaling history to the First Fleet and surf culture. Keep an eye out for the beer-can boat. There is an admission fee to the nearby ships and submarine (adult/concession $20/10).

POWERHOUSE MUSEUM

Sydney's hippest **museum** (Map pp94–5; ☎ 9217 0100; www.powerhousemuseum.com; 500 Harris St, Ultimo; adult/concession $10/6; ⏲ 10am-5pm) covers the decorative arts, social history, and science and technology, with eclectic exhibitions ranging from costume jewellery and musical instruments to steam locomotives and space capsules. The collections are well displayed and the emphasis is on hands-on interaction. Find it behind the Sydney Exhibition Centre – it's in a former power station for Sydney's now-defunct trams.

CHINESE GARDEN OF FRIENDSHIP

The tranquil **Chinese Garden** (Map pp94–5; ☎ 9281 6863; www.chinesegarden.com.au; adult/child/family $6/3/15; ⏲ 9.30am-5.30pm), in the southeastern corner of Darling Harbour, was designed by landscape architects from Guangdong, and is an oasis of lush serenity. Enter through the Courtyard of Welcoming Fragrance, circle the Lake of Brightness and finish with tea and cake in the **Chinese teahouse** (⏲ 10am-4.30pm), or by having your photo taken in a Chinese opera costume ($10).

STAR CITY

Looking for subdued good taste and muted colour schemes? Dream on, at the mammoth temple of mammon that is **Star City** (Map p99; ☎ 9777 9000; www.starcity.com.au; 80 Pyrmont St, Pyrmont; ⏲ 24hr), which is on the northwestern headland of Darling Harbour. Star City includes a casino, two theatres and a lurid volcano, as well as the inevitable try-hard

nightclub, flash hotel and retail outlets (if
you have any money left over). There's a
MLR and monorail stop here, and bus No
888 also sweeps through.

SYDNEY FISH MARKET
Selling more than 15 million kilograms of
seafood annually, this large **fish market** (Map
p99; ☎ 9552 2180; www.sydneyfishmarket.com.au; cnr
Pyrmont Bridge Rd & Bank St, Pyrmont; ☷ 7am-4pm) is
the place to get on first-name terms with a
bewildering array of scaly critters. You can
see fish auctions (early mornings), eat sushi
or fish and chips, buy super-fresh seafood
and attend seafood cooking classes (call for
details). It's west of Darling Harbour, on
Blackwattle Bay. The MLR (stop: Fish Market) is the best way to get here.

Kings Cross
The Cross is a lovably raffish, fairly tame
cocktail of restaurants, cafés, backpacker
hostels, traveller services and pubs, though
at night you can add the elements of strip
joints, prostitution and drugs. It attracts
an odd mix of highlife, lowlife, tourists and
suburbanites looking for cheap services
and an adrenaline-charged party scene. On
Sunday a few stalls set up around **El Alamein
Fountain** (Map p97), in Fitzroy Gardens, for
a small flea market.

The Cross was the centre of Bohemian-
ism during the Vietnam War era, when it
became the vice centre of Australia. It still
appeals to the free-wheelin' spirit and to
those with devil-may-care attitudes seeking
24-hour drinking. Many budget travellers
begin and end their Australian adventures
in the Cross – many of Sydney's hostels are
here – and it's a good place to swap information, meet up with friends, find work,
browse notice boards and buy or sell a car.

In the dip between the Cross and the
city is **Woolloomooloo** (Map p97), one of Sydney's oldest areas and an interesting place
to stroll around. The **Finger Wharf** houses
apartments, restaurants and the ultra-fancy
W Hotel Sydney (p123). **Harry's Café de Wheels**,
next to the wharf, must be one of the few
pie carts in the world to be a tourist attraction. It opened in 1945, stays open 18 hours
a day (till way after midnight on weekends)
and offers the cheapest meals with water
views in town (you'll be sitting on a concrete bench with the seagulls though).

The easiest way to get to the Cross from
the city is by train. It's the first stop outside
the city loop on the line to Bondi Junction. Bus Nos 324, 325 and 327 from Circular Quay pass through the Cross. You
can stroll from Hyde Park along William
St in 15 minutes. A longer, more interesting route involves crossing the Domain,
traversing the pedestrian bridge behind the
Art Gallery of NSW, walking past Woolloomooloo's wharf and climbing McElhone
Stairs from Cowper Wharf Rd, ending up at
the northern end of Victoria St.

Inner East
The backbone of Darlinghurst, Surry Hills
and Paddington, **Oxford St** (Map pp94–5) is
one of the more happening places for late-
night action. It's a strip of shops, cafés, bars
and nightclubs whose flamboyance and
spirit can be largely attributed to the vibrant
and vocal gay community. The route of the
Sydney Gay & Lesbian Mardi Gras parade
(see the boxed text, p136) passes this way.

The main drag of Oxford St runs from
the southeastern corner of Hyde Park to the
northwestern corner of Centennial Park,
though it continues in name to Bondi Junction. Taylor Sq is the main hub. (An orientation warning: Oxford St's street numbers
restart on the Darlinghurst–Paddington border, west of the junction with South Dowling
and Victoria Sts.) Bus Nos 380 and 382 from
Circular Quay, and No 378 from Railway Sq,
run the length of the street.

Darlinghurst is a vital area of urban cool
full of bright young things. There's no better way to soak up its studied ambience
than to loiter in a few outdoor cafés and do
as the others do. Darlinghurst is wedged between Oxford and William Sts, and encompasses the vibrant 'Little Italy' of Stanley St
in East Sydney. The **Sydney Jewish Museum**
(Map pp94-5; ☎ 9360 7999; www.sydneyjewishmuseum
.com.au; 148 Darlinghurst Rd; adult/child/family $10/6/22;
☷ 10am-4pm Sun-Thu, to 2pm Fri, closed Sat & Jewish
holidays) employs multilingual guides who
are Holocaust survivors. Excellent, evocative displays run through Australian Jewish
history and the Holocaust.

South of Darlinghurst is **Surry Hills**, home
to a mishmash of inner-city residents, heaps
of cheap and tasty ethnic eateries (especially
on Crown St) and a swag of good pubs. Once
the undisputed centre of Sydney's rag trade

and print media, many of its warehouses have been converted into flash apartments. A small but atmospheric **market** (Map pp94-5; cnr Crown & Foveaux Sts; ⊙ first Sat of the month) is held in Shannon Reserve. The **Brett Whiteley Studio** (Map p144; ☎ 9225 1740; www.brettwhiteley .com; 2 Raper St; adult/concession $7/5; ⊙ 10am-4pm Sat & Sun) is in the late artist's old studio. You'll be able to identify it by the two large matches (one burnt, one intact) at the door. Surry Hills is a short (uphill) walk east of Central Station or south from Oxford St. Catch bus No 301, 302 or 303 from Circular Quay.

Next door to Surry Hills, **Paddington** is an attractive residential area of leafy streets, tightly packed Victorian terrace houses and numerous small art galleries. It was built for aspiring artisans, but during the lemming-like rush to the outer suburbs after WWII the area became a slum. A renewed interest in Victorian architecture and the pleasures of inner-city life led to its restoration during the 1960s and today many terraces swap hands for a million dollars.

Most facilities, shops, cafés and bars are on Oxford St but Paddington doesn't really have a geographic centre. Most of its streets cascade northwards down the hill towards Edgecliff and Double Bay. It's always a lovely place to wander around, but the best time to visit is on Saturday when the **Paddington Market** (see p139) is in full swing.

Just southeast of Paddington is Sydney's biggest park, 220-hectare **Centennial Park** (Map p144), which has running, cycling, skating and horse-riding tracks, duck ponds, BBQ sites and sports pitches.

Moore Park (Map p144) abuts the western flank of Centennial Park and contains sports pitches, a golf course, an equestrian centre, the **Fox Studios** (Map p144; ☎ 9383 4333; www.fox studios.com.au; Lang Rd; ⊙ 10am-midnight) film and entertainment complex, which includes cinemas, a bowling alley and a shopping/dining precinct, and the Aussie Stadium and Sydney Cricket Ground (SCG). **Sportspace Tours** (☎ 9380 0383; adult/child/family $23.50/15.50/62.50; ⊙ 10am & 1pm Mon-Fri) offers behind-the-scenes guided tours (1½ hours) of the SCG and Aussie Stadium.

Eastern Suburbs

A short walk northeast of the Cross is the harbourside suburb of **Elizabeth Bay**. **Elizabeth Bay House** (Map p97; ☎ 9356 3022; www.hht.net .au; 7 Onslow Ave; adult/concession $7/3; ⊙ 10am-4.30pm Tue-Sun) by architect John Verge, is one of Sydney's finest colonial homes and dates from 1839. It's open on Mondays if it's a public holiday.

Beautiful **Rushcutters Bay** (Map p144) is the next bay east. Its handsome harbourside park is just a five-minute walk from the Cross and a great spot for cooped-up travellers to stretch their legs.

Further east is the ritzy suburb of **Double Bay** (Map p144), which is well-endowed with old-fashioned cafés and exclusive stores. The

---

NORTHERN BEACHES LOWDOWN

Avalon Beach (Map p144; bus L88, L90) A big beach with good surf and orange-coloured sand. Back in the late 1990s, local residents told the producers of *Baywatch* (who wanted to film here) to shove it. Ten points. The suburb of Avalon is also a good spot to grab a coffee and check out cute local shops.

Bilgola (Map p144; bus L88, L90) This beach seems like a bit of a secret for everyone except locals. Lovely.

Collaroy (Map p144; bus L88, L90) A good spot to unwind, with a relaxed atmosphere. The beach stretches for two suburbs, meaning there's room for everyone.

Curl Curl (Map p144; ferry Manly, then bus 136 or 139) A well-balanced mix of family groups and surfers make this a quintessential Aussie beach.

Dee Why (Map p144; bus 176) Big and popular with local families, and with a good reputation for surfing breaks.

Freshwater (Map p144; ferry Manly, then bus 139) This is a nice beach, not too rough, and popular with local teenagers.

Narrabeen (Map p144; bus L88, L90) This is surfing turf, so if you want to learn, it might be best to wait before trying the breaks here.

Palm Beach (Map p144; bus L90) The tip of Sydney and supremely blissful. The fact that many scenes for the cheesy TV series *Home and Away* are filmed here doesn't detract from its astounding beauty.

Whale Beach (Map p144; bus L88 to Avalon, then bus 193) Heavenly and remote, this gorgeous beach is smack bang in the middle of paradise.

views from the harbour-hugging New South Head Rd as it leaves Double Bay, passes **Rose Bay** and then climbs east towards wealthy **Vaucluse** are stupendous. **Vaucluse House** (Map p144; ☎ 9388 7922; www.hht.net.au; Wentworth Rd, Vaucluse; adult/concession $7/3; ☷ 10am-4.30pm Tue-Sun), situated in Vaucluse Park, is a beautifully preserved colonial mansion dating from 1827.

At the entrance to the harbour is **Watsons Bay** (Map p144), a snug community with restored fisherman's cottages, a palm-lined park and a couple of nautical churches. If you want to forget you're in the middle of a large city, have a beer at the famous **Doyles Palace Hotel** (see p133). Nearby **Camp Cove** (Map p144) is one of Sydney's best harbour beaches, and there's a nude beach (mostly male) near South Head at **Lady Bay**. **South Head** (Map p144) has great views across the harbour entrance to North Head and Middle Head. **The Gap** (Map p144) is a dramatic cliff-top lookout on the ocean side, which has a reputation for suicides.

Bus Nos 324 and 325 from Circular Quay service the eastern suburbs via Kings Cross. Sit on the left side heading east to make the most of the views.

Southern Beaches

Bondi (Map p98) lords it over every other beach in the city, despite not being the best one for a swim, surf or, damn it, a place to park. Still, the crashing waves, flashy cafés, rocky scenic points, grassy picnic lawns and strutting boardwalks aren't shabby at all. The suburb itself has a unique atmosphere due to its mix of old Jewish and other European communities, dyed-in-the-wool Aussies, New Zealanders who never went home, working travellers and the good-looking beach bums.

The ocean road is Campbell Pde, home to most of the commerce. There are **Aboriginal rock engravings** on the golf course in North Bondi. Catch bus No 380, 382, L82 or 389 from the city to get to the beach or, if you're in a hurry, catch a train to Bondi Junction and pick up one of these buses as they pass through the Bondi Junction bus station.

Situated just south of Bondi is **Tamarama** (Map pp92–3), a lovely cove with strong rips. It is a stunning 15-minute walk from Bondi. Another 10 minutes further south is

Bronte (Map pp92–3), a nice beach hemmed in by a bowl-shaped park and sandstone headlands. The cafés with outdoor tables on the edge of the park make it a great chill-out destination. Further south again is **Clovelly Bay** (Map pp92–3), a narrow scooped-out beach with little surf and good swimming (especially for children). As well as the saltwater baths here, there's a wheelchair-access boardwalk so the chairbound can take a sea dip.

Something of a poor cousin to Bondi, **Coogee** (Map p99) has a relaxed air, a good sweep of sand and plenty of places to stay and eat. You might want to take a dip in the historic seabaths Wylie's Baths to cool down. You can reach Coogee by catching bus No 372 from Railway Sq or No 373 from Circular Quay. Alternatively, take a train to Bondi Junction and pick up bus No 314 or 315 from there. From Bondi, it's a beautiful two-hour walk.

Inner West

West of the centre is the higgledy-piggledy peninsula suburb of **Balmain** (Map pp92–3). It was once a notoriously rough neighbourhood of dockyard workers but has been transformed into an artsy, middle-class area of restored Victoriana flush with pubs, cafés and trendy shops. It's a great place for a stroll, and cars will actually stop when you cross the street. Catch a ferry from Circular Quay or bus No 442 from the QVB.

Cosy, Bohemian **Glebe** (Map p99) lies just southwest of the centre, boasting a large student population, a café-lined main street, a tranquil Buddhist temple, yuppies galore, and several decent places to stay. A market (see p139) is held at Glebe Public School, on Glebe Point Rd, every Saturday. Bus Nos 431 to 434 from Millers Point run via George St along Glebe Point Rd. The MLR also travels through Glebe.

Bordering the southern flank of the university is **Newtown** (Map p99), a melting pot of social and sexual subcultures, students and home renovators. King St, its relentlessly urban main drag, is full of recycled-funky clothes stores, bookshops, cheap cafés, pubs and Thai eateries. While it's definitely moving upmarket, Newtown comes with a healthy dose of youthful grunge, and harbours a decent live-music scene. The best way to get there is by train,

NEW SOUTH WALES

but bus Nos 422, 423, 426 and 428 from the city all run along King St.

Predominantly Italian **Leichhardt** (Map p99), southwest of Glebe, is becoming increasingly popular with students, lesbians and young professionals. Its Italian eateries have a citywide reputation, but the main drag, Norton St, also offers cafés, bookstores and boutiques without an elitist sneer. Bus Nos 436 to 438 run from Railway Sq to Leichhardt.

North Shore

On the northern side of the Harbour Bridge is **North Sydney** (Map pp92–3), a high-rise office centre with very little to tempt the traveller. **McMahons Point** is a lovely, forgotten suburb wedged between the two business districts, on the western side of the bridge. There's a line of pleasant alfresco cafés on Blues Point Rd, which runs down to Blues Point Reserve on the western headland of Lavender Bay. The reserve has fine city views.

Luna Park (Map pp92–3; ☎ 9922 6644; www.lunapark sydney.com; Milsons Point; admission free, rides extra; variable hours), on the eastern shore of Lavender Bay, is an amusement park and a highly visible landmark. At the end of Kirribilli Point, just east of the bridge, stand **Admiralty House** and **Kirribilli House**, the Sydney residences of the governor general and the prime minister respectively (Admiralty House is the one nearer the bridge; both are closed to the public). Northeast of here are the upmarket suburbs of **Neutral Bay**, **Cremorne** and **Mosman**, all with pleasant coves and harbourside parks perfect for picnics. Ferries go to all these suburbs from Circular Quay.

On the northern side of Mosman is the pretty beach suburb of **Balmoral**, which faces Manly across Middle Harbour. Here there are picnic areas, a promenade and three beaches.

In a superb harbourside setting, **Taronga Zoo** (Map pp92–3; ☎ 9969 2777; www.zoo.nsw.gov.au; Bradleys Head Rd, Mosman; adult/child/family $27/14/70; ☀ 9am-5pm) has some 3000 critters (from seals to tigers, koalas to giraffes, echidnas to platypuses) all in decent habitats and well cared for. Ferries to the zoo depart from Circular Quay's Wharf 2 every 30 minutes from 7.15am on weekdays, and 8.45am on Saturday and Sunday. Bus No 247 gets you there from the QVB building ($3.50). A

ZooPass ($33.50), sold at Circular Quay and elsewhere, includes return ferry rides and zoo admission. Bring a picnic if you want to avoid expensive zoo food.

Manly

The jewel of the North Shore, Manly is on a narrow peninsula that ends at the dramatic cliffs of North Head. It boasts harbour and ocean beaches, a ferry wharf, all the trappings of a touristy beach destination and a great sense of community. It's a sun-soaked place not afraid to show a bit of tack and brashness to attract visitors, and it makes a refreshing change from the prim upper-middle-class harbour enclaves nearby.

The **Manly Visitors Information Centre** (☎ 9977 1088; Manly Wharf; ☀ 9am-5pm Mon-Fri, 10am-4pm Sat & Sun), just outside the ferry wharf, has free pamphlets along with information on the 9km Manly Scenic Walkway. From Circular Quay, JetCats traverse the harbour in a mere 15 minutes, while the ferries do the trip in a relaxing 30 minutes – and offer great views.

Oceanworld (☎ 9949 2644; West Esplanade; adult/child/family $17.50/9/30; ☀ 10am-5.30pm), near Manly wharf, is a tacky aquarium whose big draw is divers feeding sharks and stingrays. After 3.30pm the admission price drops 15%. Nearby is the small **Manly Art Gallery & Museum** (☎ 9949 1776; West Esplanade Reserve; adult/concession $3.60/1.20, free Wed; ☀ 10am-5pm Tue-Sun), which focuses on the suburb's special relationship with the beach. Behind the gallery is the wonderful 9km-long **Manly Scenic Walkway**, which has a 2km-long wheelchair-accessible path. Bring water and snacks as there are no shops along the way.

A short walk from the Manly wharf brings you to the Corso, Manly's lively pedestrian mall, and trendy Manly Beach. A footpath follows the shoreline from South Steyne around the small headland to tiny **Fairy Bower Beach** and the picturesque cove of **Shelly Beach**.

North Head, at the entrance to Sydney Harbour, is about 3km south of Manly. Most of the dramatic headland is in Sydney Harbour National Park. The **Quarantine Station** represents an interesting slice of Sydney's social history; it housed suspected disease carriers from 1832 right up until 1984 and many people died here. To visit the station, book a **guided tour** (☎ 9247 5033; adult/child $11/7.70; ☀ 1.15pm Tue-Thu, 1.15pm & 3.30pm Sat &

Sun). The station is reputedly haunted and there are spooky three-hour night **ghost tours** (Wed $22, Fri-Sun $28) – over 12 years of age only. Kids' ghost tours (aged six to 12 years) are also available; call for details.

Northern Beaches
A string of ocean-front suburbs sweeps 30km north along the coast from Manly, ending at beautiful, well-heeled **Palm Beach** (Map p144) and the spectacular Barrenjoey Heads at the entrance to Broken Bay. Beaches along the way include **Freshwater**, **Curl Curl**, **Dee Why**, **Collaroy** and **Narrabeen**. The most spectacular are **Whale Beach** and **Bilgola** (near Palm Beach), both with dramatic, steep headlands. Several of the northernmost beach suburbs also back onto **Pittwater**, a lovely inlet off Broken Bay and a favoured sailing spot.

Bus Nos 136 and 139 run from Manly (near the wharf) to Curl Curl and Freshwater respectively. Bus No L90 from the Wynyard Park bus interchange in the city runs to Newport and then north to Palm Beach.

ACTIVITIES
Canoeing & Kayaking
Contact the **New South Wales Canoeing Association** (9660 4597; www.nswcanoe.org.au) for information on canoeing.

Alternatively, **Natural Wanders** (9899 1001; www.kayaksydney.com) has exhilarating half-day bridge and island paddling tours for $90.

Sydney Harbour Kayaks (9960 4389; www.sydneyharbourkayaks.com.au) offers lessons, sales and rentals, along with half-day eco-tours for $99 per person.

Cycling
Sydney is a big city and thus full of bike-unfriendly traffic; the best spot to get some spoke action is Centennial Park. Many cycle-hire shops require a hefty deposit on a credit card.

Cheeky Monkey (Map pp94-5; 9212 4460; 456 Pitt St; per day/week from $25/100; 8.45am-5.30pm Mon-Fri, 10am-4pm Sat)

Favorite Cycles (Map p98; 9977 4590; 22 Darley Rd, Manly; per hr/day $9/22; 9am-6pm Mon-Wed & Fri, to 7pm Thu, to 5pm Sat, 10am-4pm Sun)

Inner City Cycles (Map p99; 9660 6605; 151 Glebe Point Rd, Glebe; per day/week $33/90; 9.30am-6pm Mon-Wed & Fri, to 8pm Thu, to 4pm Sat, 11am-3pm Sun)

Wooly's Wheels (Map pp94-5; 9331 2671; 82 Oxford St, Paddington; per day/week $39/265; 9am-6pm Mon-Wed & Fri, to 8pm Thu, to 4pm Sat, 11am-4pm Sun) Across from Victoria Barracks and very handy to Centennial Park.

Diving
The best shore dives in Sydney are Gordons Bay Underwater Nature Trail, north of Coogee; Shark Point, Clovelly; and Ship Rock, Cronulla. Popular boat dives are Wedding Cake Island, off Coogee; around Sydney Heads; and off the Royal National Park.

Dive Centre Bondi (Map p98; 9369 3855; www.divesydney.com; 192 Bondi Rd, Bondi) Shore dives with gear start at $100; boat dives at $130. An open-water PADI course costs $345.

Dive Centre Manly (Map p98; 9977 4355; www.divesydney.com; 10 Belgrave St, Manly) Similar rates and offerings as its sister office in Bondi.

Pro Dive (Map pp94-5; 9264 6177; www.prodive.com.au; 478 George St) Offers shore dives with gear for $85, boat dives with/without gear $169/109 and diving courses from $295 to $495. Has several outlets in and around Sydney.

In-line Skating
The beach promenades at Bondi and Manly and the paths of Centennial Park are the most favoured spots for skating.

Manly Blades (Map p98; 9976 3833; 49 North Steyne, Manly; 9am-6pm) Rents blades (from $15), scooters (from $7) and skateboards (from $10).

Total Skate (Map p144; 9380 6356; 36 Oxford St, Woollahra; first hr $10, per hr thereafter $5) Near Centennial Park; fee includes safety equipment.

Sailing
There are plenty of sailing schools in Sydney and, even if you are not serious about learning the ropes, an introductory lesson can be a fun way of getting out on the harbour.

EastSail Sailing School (9327 1166; www.eastsail.com.au) Courses, charters, cruises, corporate events and overnight packages. Plenty of boats, but you'll need big bucks.

Sydney By Sail (9280 1110; www.sydneybysail.com) Offers plenty of courses, including a weekend introductory sail course for $425.

Scenic Flights
Viewing the harbour from the heavens is a memorable experience (especially on a sunny

day). It ain't cheap, but it is spectacular. **Sydney by Seaplane** (☎ 9974 1455, 1300 656 787; www .sydneybyseaplane.com) offers glorious tours of Sydney's harbour, the northern beaches and the coastline, plus areas further afield, like the Hawkesbury River and Ku-ring-gai Chase National Park. Flights start from adult/child $145/70 for 15 minutes; dinner packages are also available.

Surfing

South of the Heads, the best spots are Bondi, Tamarama, Bronte and Maroubra. Cronulla, south of Botany Bay, is also good. On the North Shore the best beaches are Manly, Curl Curl, Dee Why, North Narrabeen, Mona Vale, Newport Reef, North Avalon and Palm Beach itself. For current wave activity check www .wavecam.com.au.

Aloha Surf (Map p98; ☎ 9977 3777; www.aloha .com.au; 44 Pittwater Rd, Manly) Half/full day board hire $20/40; also sells and trades equipment.

Bondi Surf Company (Map p98; ☎ 9365 0870; 72-76 Campbell Pde, Bondi) Rents board and wetsuit for $15 per hour, bodyboards and flippers for $10 per hour.

Dripping Wet Surf (Map p98; ☎ 9977 3549; www .drippingwetsurf.com; Shop 2/93 North Steyne, Manly) Board rentals for $13/45 per hour/day, wetsuits for $5/20 per hour/day.

Let's Go Surfing (Map p98; ☎ 9365 1800; www .letsgosurfing.com.au; 128 Ramsgate Ave, Bondi) Private lessons from $95; also rents boards and wetsuits for $20 per hour.

Swimming

Sydney's harbour beaches offer sheltered swimming spots. Just remember that after heavy rains excess water gets washed into the harbour from city streets.

If you want to frolic in real ocean waves, stay within the flagged areas patrolled by lifeguards. There are some notorious but clearly signposted rips, even at Sydney's most popular beaches, so don't underestimate the surf just because it looks safe.

Andrew 'Boy' Charlton Pool (Map pp94-5; ☎ 9358 6686; Mrs Macquaries Rd, The Domain; adult/child $5/3.50; ☼ 6am-8pm Oct-Apr) Saltwater, smack bang on the harbour and popular with the gay crowd; Sydney's best pool and for serious swimmers only.

North Sydney Olympic Pool (Map pp92-3; ☎ 9955 2309; Alfred St South, Milsons Point; adult/child $4.70/ 2.30; ☼ 5.30am-9pm Mon-Fri, 7am-7pm Sat & Sun) Just near the entrance to Luna Park is this great pool complex with harbour views. There are indoor and outdoor pools plus sauna and gym services.

Wylie's Baths (Map p99; ☎ 9665 2838; Neptune St, Coogee; admission $3; ☼ 7am-6pm) The waves wash in, but the sharks don't. It's like swimming in the ocean, but you're in a saltwater pool.

WALKING TOUR

WALK FACTS
Distance: 5km
Duration: two hours

This beautiful coastal walk leads south from North Bondi, along Bondi Beach to the beaches of Clovelly and Coogee, via Tamarama and Bronte. It combines panoramic views, swimming opportunities and loads of chances for a cup of coffee or a freshly squeezed juice at a beachside café.

Begin at the Bondi Golf Course to see the **Aboriginal rock engravings (1)**. Follow Military Rd south and turn left into Ramsgate Ave to get to the **lookout (2)** and mind-blowing views of Bondi Beach. Follow the beach path along the boardwalk, dipping your toes in the water and checking out surfers. Soon you'll be going uphill past **Bondi Icebergs (3**; p128), which houses a lavish restaurant and two bars with sweeping views over the sea pool and along Bondi Beach. Keep following the path as its winds along the coast around dramatic cliffs; you'll eventually pass pretty **Tamarama Beach (4**; p109) and come to **Bronte Beach (5**; p109), which has a host of wonderful cafés to sustain you.

Continue south past the atmospheric sun-bleached **Waverley Cemetery (6)** and you'll soon reach **Clovelly Bay (7**; p109), where you can grab another coffee if you're lagging. Follow the footpath up through the car park, then head along Cliffbrook Pde to Gordons Bay. A few more minutes' walk south brings you to glorious **Coogee Beach (8**; p109). At the southern end of the beach are the historic seabaths, **Wylie's Baths (9)**, perfect for a refreshing dip.

SYDNEY FOR CHILDREN

Parents will find more than enough to keep the little ones busy, happy and worn out by day's end – just be sure they're smeared with sunscreen, especially at the beaches!

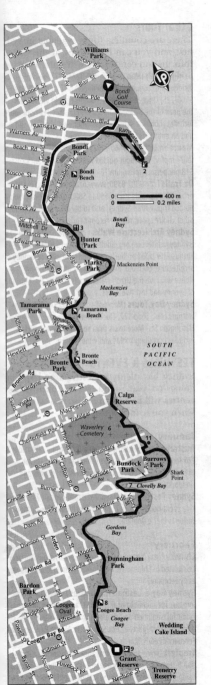

Helpful child publications include the excellent and free *Sydney's Child* magazine (www.sydneyschild.com.au), found at tot-oriented businesses, libraries and schools. Likewise, there's the *kidfriendly* mini-mag (www.kidfriendly.com.au), available at tourist offices; it's mostly full of ads, but has some useful coupons and a list of seasonal child-friendly events.

Many of Sydney's attractions have good children's exhibits. If you're up for museums, check out the **Powerhouse Museum** (p106) and the **Australian Museum** (p105). The **Art Gallery of NSW** (p105) has special kids' tours and workshops, while **Sydney Opera House** (p100) often puts on events for children. Star gazers will appreciate the **Sydney Observatory** (p102) and its educational events; thrill-seekers will love **Luna Park** (p494) and its roller-coaster rides. Finally, no child should leave the city without a visit to **Taronga Zoo** (p110) and its plethora of well-tended animals.

Darling Harbour (p106) is a wonderful destination for families. There are kids rides, playgrounds and activities, along with plenty of fast-food outlets. Big draws include the **Sydney Aquarium** (p106), an **Imax theatre** (p137), the **Chinese Garden of Friendship** (p106) and the **Australian National Maritime Museum** (p106). A trackless train called the **People Mover** (adult/child $3.50/2.50) snakes around Darling Harbour's attractions every 20 minutes or so, relieving tired little legs.

Further outside the city are some other good youngster attractions. Manly has the **Quarantine Station** (p110), which offers kids' ghost tours, and its own dinky aquarium, **Oceanworld** (p110).

If time allows, visit the **Sydney Children's Museum** (Map p144; ☎ 9897 1414; www.sydneykids.org; cnr Pitt & Walpole Sts, Merrylands; adult/child/family $5.50/5.50/20; ☎ 10am-4pm), located west of Sydney. Children can partake in interactive science exhibits, a large playground and craft workshops. Check the website for instructions on how to get there.

Another interesting destination, located an hour's drive north of Sydney, is the **Australian Reptile Park** (Map p144; ☎ 4340 1022; www.reptilepark.com.au; Pacific Hwy, Somersby; adult/child 4-15/family $20/10/52; ☎ 9am-5pm). Attractions include giant crocs, snakes and tortoises (along with more cuddly Aussie critters) and regular shows highlight spiders and koalas. Again, check the website for complete instructions on how to arrive.

Some of Sydney's best children's fun is free, however. There are always the popular beaches of **Bondi** (p109) or **Manly** (p110) – just keep an eye on warning flags, and don't let your children wander too far into the water by themselves. Glorious parks include the **Royal Botanical Gardens** (p105), with its riveting flying fox population; **Centennial Park** (p108), which offers activities along with picnic areas; and **Moore Park** (p108), which includes the Fox Studios complex.

With such a smorgasbord of kids' delights on offer, the only thing you're going to have to worry about is whether you've got the energy to keep up.

TOURS
City Bus Tours

The best bus tours are operated by the State Transit Authority (STA).

Bondi Explorer (☎ 13 15 00; www.sydneypass.info; adult/child/family $36/18/90; ☺ 8.45am-4.15pm) Runs a large circuit from Circular Quay to Kings Cross, Double Bay, Rose Bay, Vaucluse, Watsons Bay, the Gap, Bondi Beach and Coogee, returning to the city along Oxford St. Buses depart every 30 minutes; buy your ticket on board or at STA offices.

Sydney Explorer (☎ 13 15 00; www.sydneypass.info; adult/child/family $36/18/90; ☺ 8.40am-5.20pm) Red STA tourist buses navigate the inner city on a route designed to pass most central attractions. A bus departs from Circular Quay every 20 minutes but you can board at any of the 26 bus stops on the route. Tickets are sold on board and at STA offices, and you hop on and off the bus as often as you like. A running commentary helps you digest what you're seeing.

Harbour Cruises

There's an endless range of cruises on the harbour, from paddle-steamers to sailing yachts. Smart penny-pinchers just take the $5.80 ferry to Manly and call it a night.

Captain Cook Cruises (Map pp94-5; ☎ 9206 1111; www.captaincook.com.au; Aquarium Wharf, Darling Harbour or Wharf 6, Circular Quay; adult/child/family $25/12/55)

Harboursights Cruises (☎ 13 15 00; adult/child/family from $18/9/45) Run by the STA, these excellent short cruises let you take in the sights, sounds and smells of the harbour. Choose from the morning (one hour), afternoon (2½ hours) or evening (1½ hours) cruises. Tickets can be bought at ferry ticket offices in Circular Quay.

Magistic Cruises (Map pp94-5; ☎ 8296 7222; www.magisticcruises.com.au; King St Wharf 5, Darling Harbour or Wharf 6, Circular Quay; adult/child/family $22/16.50/60)

Matilda Rocket Express (Map pp94-5; ☎ 9264 7377; www.matilda.com.au; Aquarium Wharf, Darling Harbour; adult/child/family $22/14/50)

Other Tours

There are countless tours available in Sydney, and you can book some at the visitor information centres. Here are just a few:

BridgeClimb (Map pp94-5; ☎ 8274 7777; www.bridgeclimb.com.au; 5 Cumberland St, The Rocks; tours $160-225) Once-in-a-lifetime, unforgettable views from the peak of the Sydney Harbour Bridge. This 3½-hour tour includes thorough safety checks, your own climbing suit and an enthusiastic guide.

Maureen Fry (☎ 9660 7157; www.ozemail.com.au/~mpfry) Two-hour guided walks around Sydney cost $18 per person (minimum 10 people, or $180 per tour).

Oz Trails (☎ 9387 8390; www.oztrails.com.au; charter groups 1-10 people from $660 to $880) Tour operator with guided trips within Sydney, and to the Blue Mountains and other choice spots; reader-recommended .

Sydney Architecture Walks (☎ 9518 6866; www.sydneyarchitecture.org; adult/concession $20/15) These enthusiastic building buffs will open your eyes to Sydney's architecture, both old and new. Those into the Opera House will love the Utzon walk. Strolls start at the Museum of Sydney and last two hours.

Sydney Day Tours (Map pp94-5; ☎ 9251 6101; www.sdtours.com; Shop 122, Clocktower Center, cnr Argyle & Harrington Sts) More tours than you can shake a stick at, including cuddling koalas and wine tasting.

FESTIVALS & EVENTS

Sydney has plenty of festivals and special goings-on year-round. Visitor information centres will be able to advise you what's on when you're in town.

January

Australia Day (www.nadc.com.au) Australia's 'birthday' (26 January; the anniversary of the First Fleet's arrival in Sydney in 1788) is celebrated with BBQs, picnics and fireworks on the harbour.

Sydney Festival (www.sydneyfestival.org.au) This massive event floods the city with art, including free outdoor concerts in the Domain.

February

Chinese New Year (www.cityofsydney.nsw.gov.au/cny) Celebrated in Chinatown with fireworks in late January or early February.

Sydney Gay & Lesbian Mardi Gras (www.mardigras.org.au) The highlight of this world-famous festival is the colourful, sequined parade along Oxford St, culminating in a bacchanalian party at Fox Studios, in Moore Park, in late February or early March.

Tropfest (www.tropfest.com) This home-grown short-film festival ensures its flicks are fresh with the inclusion of compulsory props (announced just before the competition).

Big-name stars like Keanu Reeves, Nicole Kidman and Russell Crowe are often the judges.

March/April
Royal Easter Show (www.eastershow.com.au) This 12-day event is an agricultural show and funfair held at Homebush Bay. Bring the kids and pet the baby animals.

May
Sydney Writers' Festival (www.swf.org.au) Celebrates the literary in Sydney, with guest authors, talks and forums.

June
Sydney Biennale (www.biennaleofsydney.com.au) An international art festival held in even-numbered years at the Art Gallery of NSW, the Powerhouse Museum and other venues.
Sydney Film Festival (www.sydneyfilmfestival.org) A 14-day orgy of cinema held at the State Theatre and other cinemas.

July
Yulefest Christmas comes early, and is as close to white as Australia gets in this popular Blue Mountains celebration.

August
City to Surf Run (www.city2surf.sunherald.com.au) This 14km-long fun run takes place on the second Sunday in August and attracts a mighty 40,000 entrants who run from Hyde Park to Bondi Beach.

September
Carnivale There's plenty of colour at this multicultural arts festival held in early spring.
Royal Botanic Gardens Spring Festival (www.rbgsyd .gov.au) Spring into spring, with concerts, colourful flower displays and plenty of pollen.

October
Kings Cross Carnival Taking place in late October or early November, this central-city street fair includes a bed race.
Manly Jazz Festival Held over the Labour Day long weekend in early October and featuring lots of jazz performances, mostly free.
Rugby League Grand Final (www.nrl.com) The two best teams left standing in the National Rugby League (NRL) meet to decide who's best.

November
Sculpture by the Sea (www.sculpturebythesea.com) Held in mid-November, the Bondi-to-Bronte walk is transformed into an outdoor sculpture gallery.

December
Boxing Day On 26 December, Sydney Harbour is a sight to behold as hundreds of boats crowd its waters to farewell the yachts competing in the gruelling Sydney to Hobart Yacht Race (www.rolexsydneyhobart.com).
Christmas Day Thousands of backpackers descend on Bondi Beach on Christmas Day (25 December), much to the consternation of the civil authorities and the overworked lifesavers.
New Year's Eve The Rocks, Kings Cross and Bondi Beach are traditional gathering places for alcohol-sodden celebrations on New Year's Eve, although alcohol-free zones and a massive police presence are aimed to quell the rowdier elements.

SLEEPING
Sydney has a huge variety of accommodation. You can grab some shut-eye at a cheap hostel, cosy B&B, seedy motel, authentic Aussie pub or five-star luxury behemoth with breathtaking harbour views.

Exactly where you stay in Sydney will depend on your budget and holiday needs. For example, those travellers seeking hostels and party atmosphere should think about heading to Kings Cross or the beach destinations of Bondi or Manly, while those willing to spend more and wanting to be closer to tourist sights might wish to stay in the Rocks or the city centre. Areas such as Chinatown and Surry Hills are still close to the centre while offering distinctive atmosphere and more culinary and transport options. Decide what you want and read up a little on Sydney's many neighbourhoods before deciding where to settle in.

Prices are highest during the summer (December to January) and often drop during the slow winter months. Rates in this Sleeping section reflect mostly high-season – but not peak-season (say, Christmas) – tariffs. Some hotels have many rates that vary during the year and even change with demand, so it's a good idea to call ahead and get a quote – and a reservation. After all, Sydney is a top tourist destination and you'll do well to book in advance. This is especially crucial during Christmas and New Year's.

For long-stay accommodation, peruse the 'flats to let' and 'share accommodation' ads appearing in the *Sydney Morning Herald* on both Wednesday and Saturday. Hostel notice boards are also good sources of information. Alternatively, you can try www .gumtree.com.au, www.domain.com.au,

NEW SOUTH WALES

STAYING NEAR THE AIRPORT

Stamford Plaza Sydney Airport (Map pp92-3; ☎ 9317 2200; www.stamford.com.au; cnr O'Riordan & Robey Sts, Mascot; d from $145; ❄ ⬛ ⬛) This comfortable and modern high-rise hotel is a 10-minute walk from the airport's domestic terminals or a quick, free shuttle ride from all the terminals. Service is excellent, and there's broadband access in many rooms. Check the website for specials.

---

www.sleepingwiththeenemy.com or www .flatmates.com.au. Keep in mind that some long-term lodgings require deposits (or bonds) and don't come furnished.

Sydney will present a parking challenge. Many hotels offer a place for your car, but some charge dearly ($15 to $20 per day) for it. When you make your hotel reservation, ask if they offer parking, how much it costs and if you need to reserve a spot.

Budget

CITY CENTRE

Sydney Central YHA (Map pp94-5; ☎ 9281 9111; www.yha.com.au; 11 Rawson Pl; dm $28-33, d $82-94; ❄ ⬛ ❄ ⬛) The Cadillac of Sydney hostels, this huge heritage-listed building offers 500-plus beds, swank artsy spaces, a game room, nightly movies, all the services you'd expect (including a full-on travel agency) and even an ATM in the lobby. And don't forget the rooftop swimming pool! It's within spitting distance of Central Station and very popular, so be sure to reserve (especially for private rooms). The place is wheelchair accessible.

Railway Square YHA (Map pp94-5; ☎ 9281 9666; www.yha.com.au; 8-10 Lee St; dm 27-33, d $78-88; ❄ ⬛) Housed in a former parcels shed is this tastefully renovated, railroad-themed hostel. Original cargo doors, exposed ceilings, and dorms in reproduction train cars add flavour, while the spa, bathroom floor warmers, comfortable rooms and trendy common areas make your budget stay almost luxurious. It's right next to Central Station (look for it behind the Medina building) and much more intimate than its sister YHA just down the street.

Wake Up! (Map pp94-5; ☎ 9288 7888, 1800 800 945; www.wakeup.com.au; 509 Pitt St; dm 24-33, d $88-

98; ❄ ⬛) Trendy backpackers flock to this large, modern and artsy hostel right near Central Station. Spiffy spaces await them (the seven floors each have a theme and colour), as do all the services they could ask for. There's a sunny café on the main floor and a gloomy restaurant/bar downstairs; access to a small kitchen is also included.

Big Hostel (Map pp94-5; ☎ 9281 6030, 1800 212 244; www.bighostel.com; 212 Elizabeth St; dm $25-34, d $72-93; ❄) This 'boutique' hostel is a new concept in accommodation. It works, though, so you can expect good dorms with lockers, a very hip TV lounge/kitchen area and a great rooftop patio. A light breakfast is included. Most doubles come with bathroom, and all rooms have TV and air-con. It's *not* a party hostel.

Base Backpackers (Map pp94-5; ☎ 9267 7718, 1800 242 273; www.basebackpackers.com; 477 Kent St; dm $26-34, d $89; ❄ ⬛) Also known as Wanderers on Kent, this well-located hostel has good wheelchair-accessible rooms and great access to central Sydney. Dorms can get huge (the cheapest are 10 beds) and the girls-only dorm is called the Sanctuary. The common rooms are decent, and there's a solarium.

George Street Private Hotel (Map pp94-5; ☎ 9211 1800; www.thegeorge.com.au; 700a George St; dm $22-28, d $60-69, ste $80-90) This is a decent inner-city budget choice. A maze-like, no-frills place, George Street has clean dorms (no lockers) and OK doubles – all rooms share bathrooms. There's a cosy kitchen and dining area, and the place is popular with young travellers.

KINGS CROSS

Original Backpackers (Map p97; ☎ 9356 3232, 1800 807 130; www.originalbackpackers.com.au; 160-162 Victoria St; dm $25-28, d without bathroom $70; ⬛) Smack dab in the centre of Kings Cross and set in a wonderful historic mansion, this long-running hostel offers 176 beds, friendly staff, two small kitchens and great outdoor spaces. It's a maze-like place where rooms have high ceilings and fridges. Free pick-up from the airport is on offer.

Eva's Backpackers (Map p97; ☎ 9358 2185, 1800 802 517; www.evasbackpackers.com.au; 6-8 Orwell St; dm $24, d & tw $60; ❄ ⬛) This well-managed hostel has colourful halls, good small dorms and a communal kitchen/dining area. The TV lounge room is practically nonexistent, but the rooftop barbecue area with excellent city views makes up for it. It's often full, so book ahead. Doubles share bathrooms; breakfast is included.

Macleay Lodge (Map p97; ☎ 9368 0660; www.bud gethotelssydney.com; 71 Macleay St; s $50, d $60-70) This plain spot offers good-sized, good-value rooms with TVs, fridges and coffee-making amenities. Most rooms share bathrooms; some come with balcony. Overall you're looking at a quiet, clean and mostly unmemorable stay.

Jolly Swagman Backpackers (Map p97; ☎ 9358 6400, 1800 805 870; www.jollyswagman.com.au; 27 Orwell St; dm $24, d without bathroom $64; 🖳) Those looking for party atmosphere can find it at this slightly grungy hostel with more than 130 beds. All rooms come with fridge and lockers. If you're looking for work there's a system of sorts that will help. Flash a VIP card for $1 or so off rates.

Potts Point House (Map p97; ☎ 9368 0733; 154 Victoria St; dm from $15, d from $40) Budget, barebones and bleak, but basically bearable without breaking the bank.

O'Malley's Hotel (Map p97; ☎ 9357 2211; www .omalleyshotel.com.au; 228 William St; d $66-99; 🐾) This friendly Irish pub comes attached to 15 traditionally decorated, well-furnished rooms with fridge and TV; two have good harbour views. It's a great deal (breakfast is included) and surprisingly quiet given its location. One room with kitchenette is available.

Pink House (Map p97; ☎ 9358 1689, 1800 806 385; www.pinkhouse.com.au; 6-8 Barncleuth Sq; dm $23-25, d without bathroom $65; 🖳) Yes, it's pink, but it's also a beautiful historical mansion with charming personality and relaxing leafy patios. There's good atmosphere, a communal kitchen and light breakfast (with Vegemite!) included.

Royal Sovereign Hotel (Map p97; ☎ 9331 3672; www.darlobar.com; cnr Liverpool St & Darlinghurst Rd; d without bathroom $77-88; 🐾) Perched above one of Sydney's favourite drinking dens, these 19 small but sharply decorated rooms all come with TV. Upper rooms are quieter but more expensive, and come with fridge and coffeepot. Even the halls are nice.

Highfield Private Hotel (Map p97; ☎ 9326 9539; www.highfieldhotel.com; 166 Victoria St; s without bathroom $50-65, d without bathroom $65-80) A clean and welcoming hotel owned by a Swedish family (and therefore a Swedish magnet), this

well-run place offers good security, simple bright rooms, 24-hour access and a spot-on location. A common lounge sports fridge and microwave.

BONDI

Bondi Beachouse YHA (Map p98; ☎ 9365 2088; www .yha.com.au; 63 Fletcher St; dm $27, s/d from $60/70; 🖳) Bondi's best hostel, offering clean rooms (some boasting water views), two TV lounges and an unsurpassable rooftop terrace with spa. Cheap meals, free sporting-equipment rentals and nightly activities are also on tap. Catch bus No 380 from the city or Bondi Junction and alight at the Fletcher St stop.

Noah's Backpackers (Map p98; ☎ 9365 7100, 1800 226 662; 2 Campbell Pde; www.noahsbondibeach .com; dm $22-25, d without bathroom $55-65, tw $80; 🖳) Noah's is large, basic and somewhat impersonal, and the kitchen's well used and so not always spotless. The huge rooftop terrace, however, has great beach views, and there's a decent TV lounge. Doubles sport fridges and TVs; try to score one facing the ocean.

COOGEE

Coogee Beachside Accommodation (Map p99; ☎ 9315 8511, 1800 013 460; www.sydneybeachside.com .au; 178 Coogee Bay Rd; d without bathroom $75) Here's a good option for those seeking simple but clean rooms with fridge and TV. There's a small kitchen with counter seating, and a garden patio below. Family rooms are available ($95); check the website for current rates.

Wizard of Oz Backpackers (Map p99; ☎ 9315 7876, 1800 013 460; www.wizardofoz.com.au; 172 Coogee Bay Rd; dm $27) Just a few blocks from the hot beach sands, this laid-back hostel has OK dorms and a casual TV lounge. The sunny back patio is nice, but it's a quiet zone because of neighbours. Cheap airport pick-up is available; office hours are limited.

Grand Pacific Private Hotel (Map p99; ☎ 9665 6301; 136a Beach St; s/d without bathroom $35/45) Curt management rules at this very un-grand, gritty and down-and-out smelly joint. Yet that scruffy charm and those dirt-cheap prices keep the hordes coming, so reserve ahead and try to get a balcony (usually snagged by the regulars). All rooms come with TV and fridge; use of the kitchen is available.

NEW SOUTH WALES

GLEBE & NEWTOWN

Glebe Point YHA (Map p99; ☎ 9692 8418; www
.yha.com.au; 262-264 Glebe Point Rd, Glebe; dm $24-28, d
$68; 💻) Well run and pleasant, this large,
friendly hostel offers good facilities, lots of
activities and simple but clean rooms with
sinks. There's a covered rooftop area with
picnic tables and a BBQ, which feels airier
than the basement common rooms.

Glebe Village (Map p99; ☎ 1800 801 983; www
.glebevillage.com; 256 Glebe Point Rd, Glebe; dm $26-28,
d $75; 💻) Looking for a party hostel? This
is probably the place to come. Hang out
in the leafy front patio with good music
playing, and try not to stress the laid-back
staff. Rooms are quirky, breakfast is free
and occasional BBQ nights make folks even
merrier.

Wattle House (Map p99; ☎ 9552 4997; www.wat
tlehouse.com.au; 44 Hereford St, Glebe; dm $27, d $85; ☒)
Here's the homiest, most intimate hostel
you could hope for – all wrapped up in
a lovely Victorian house accommodating
just 26 people. It's also tidy, friendly and
efficient, and it comes with a kitchen and
a sweet little garden. It's not a party place,
so expect some quiet – and be sure to call
ahead (couples, reserve room No 4).

Billabong Gardens (Map p99; ☎ 9550 3236,
1800 806 419; www.billabonggardens.com.au; 5-11 Egan
St, Newtown; dm $23-25, s $49, d $66-85; 💻) This
brick-and-tile motel/hostel in Newtown
has some pleasant common spaces along
with a kitchen, a cosy TV room and a tiny
murky pool. Most importantly, however,
it's located close to hoppin' King St. From
Railway Sq catch bus No 422, 423, 426 or
428 up King St and get off at Missenden Rd.
By train, go to Newtown Station and turn
right; Egan St is four blocks up on the left.

MANLY

Boardrider Backpacker (Map p98; ☎ 9977 6077; www
boardrider.com.au; Rear 63, The Corso; dm $28, d $75-85;
💻) Smack-bang in the middle of the Corso,
Manly's happenin' pedestrian mall, is this
backpacker's, catering to the young and surfing. It has a large TV room and hires out
water-sports equipment. The rooftop patio
is pretty cool, and there's a balcony to check
on the waves.

Manly Bungalow (Map p98; ☎ 9977 5494; www
.manlybungalow.com; 64 Pittwater Rd; d/tw without bathroom $75/90) Just a handful of rooms are avail-
able for those who seek quiet, secure and

pleasant rooms with a small, serene garden
nearby. All come with kitchenette and TV,
and there's one family room for $100. Book
ahead; office hours are limited.

Manly Astra Backpackers (Map p98; ☎ 9977 2092;
www.manlyastra.com; 68 Pittwater Rd; d without bathroom
$65) On offer here are 12 decent, no-nonsense
rooms, a small living room and an even
smaller kitchen. It's a place for quiet couples
(as opposed to party animals). There's free
use of bodyboards. Call ahead, as reception
has limited hours.

Bunkhouse (Map p98; ☎ 9976 0472, 1800 657 122;
www.bunkhouse.com.au; 35 Pine St; dm $25, d $65; 💻)
Each dorm room here comes with its own
TV, kitchenette and bathroom, making
this place instantly unique. There's also a
common kitchen, a dining area and a TV
lounge. The Bunkhouse is about 200m from
the beach.

Manly Beach House (Map p98; ☎ 9977 7050; www
.manlybeachhouse.com; 179 Pittwater Rd; s/d/tr without
bathroom $50/70/80; 🅿 💻) Nine private rooms
welcome couples and families looking for
a more intimate and quiet Manly stay.
There's a homy front living room, a small
kitchen and a sunny patio. Rooms are basic
but good sized.

TEMPE

Old Rectory (Map pp92-3; ☎ 9559 7841, 8504 2615;
oldrectory.idx.com.au; 2 Samuel St; s $50-70, d $70-80;
☒ 💻) This place is great if you need to be
within a 10-minute drive of the airport. A
helpful couple manages nine basic, comfortable rooms (most with shared bathrooms)
in this modest yet historic Tempe house.
There's a communal kitchen and a grassy
lawn. It's on a very busy street, so traffic
(both ground vehicles and aeroplanes) is
noisy at times. Breakfast is free, but airport
pick-up is $10.

CAMPING & CARAVANNING

Sydney's caravan parks, most of which also
have sites for tents, are a fair way out of
town. The following are up to 26km from
the city centre. Note that peak seasons
(such as Christmas) see rate hikes.

Lane Cove River Tourist Park (Map pp92-3;
☎ 9888 9133; www.lanecoverivertouristpark.com.au;
Plassey Rd, North Ryde; powered sites $32-36, unpowered
sites $28-30; 💻) This cheery place lies 14km
north of the city and has good facilities (including over 150 caravan sites, plus cabins).

You can chill out in the pool when temperatures swelter.

Sydney Lakeside Caravan Park (off Map pp92-3; ☎ 9913 7845; www.sydneylakeside.com.au; Lake Park Rd, Narrabeen; powered sites $33-40, unpowered sites $28-33) Located 26km north of Sydney, this nifty place occupies prime real estate around the northern beaches. If roughing it doesn't appeal, there are good cabins and lakeside 'villas' ($150 to $240).

Grand Pines Tourist Park (off Map pp92-3; ☎ 9529 7329; www.thegrandpines.com.au; 289 The Grand Pde, Sans Souci; powered sites $35-45; 💻) This friendly, good-quality caravan park is 17km south of Sydney on beautiful Botany Bay. Take your pick from sites, vans and cabins ($66 to $154); high standards are maintained.

Midrange
THE ROCKS & CIRCULAR QUAY

Bed & Breakfast Sydney Harbour (Map pp94-5; ☎ 9247 1130; www.bedandbreakfastsydney.com; 142 Cumberland St; s $140-220, d $155-250; ⊠) Each of the nine rooms in these twin heritage buildings are charmingly unique, and all come with soft sheets, a full hot breakfast and relaxing moments in the leafy courtyard. The location is great, and there's a pleasant kitchen. Some rooms share bathrooms.

Russell (Map pp94-5; ☎ 9241 3543; www.therussell.com.au; 143a George St; d from $140-280; ⊠) Located smack in the middle of the Rocks' main tourist drag, this charming 29-room hotel offers creaky floors, modest flowery rooms, pleasant lounge areas and a sunny roof garden. There's an intimate feel and a narrow staircase (there's no elevator); the cheapest rooms share bathrooms.

Lord Nelson Brewery Hotel (Map pp94-5; ☎ 9251 4044; www.lordnelson.com.au; 19 Kent St; d $180; ⊠) This popular swanky pub, in a historic sandstone building, has its own brewery; there is also a restaurant on the 1st floor. The nine rooms are beautiful, and one small single with shared bathroom goes for $120. Breakfast is included.

Australian Hotel (Map pp94-5; ☎ 9247 2229; www.australianheritagehotel.com; 100 Cumberland St; d $125) Ten sweet rooms are on offer here, some with shared bathrooms. There's a rooftop terrace (great views) and a cosy communal lounge with tea- and coffee-making facilities, and breakfast is included. The highlight might just be the cool pub downstairs, however.

Mercantile Hotel (Map pp94-5; ☎ 9247 3570; www.mercantilehotel.com; 25 George St; s without bathroom $80-110, d without bathroom $110-140; ⊠) This green-tiled hotel is a restored pub with a strong Irish connection. It's right near the bridge and offers comfortable rooms; some have fridge and jets in the bathtub. There's also a sunny terrace; breakfast is included.

Palisade Hotel (Map pp94-5; ☎ 9247 2272; www.palisadehotel.com; 35 Bettington St; d/tw without bathroom $118/128) Standing sentinel-like at Millers Point, the Palisade Hotel has nine solidly furnished rooms, some with balcony and breathtaking views of the Harbour Bridge. It's a lovely heritage building (although the carpet shows its age) in a more isolated part of the Rocks. A decent pub is downstairs.

CITY CENTRE

Vibe Hotel (Map pp94-5; ☎ 9282 0987; www.vibehotels.com.au; 111 Goulburn St; d from $185; 🅿 ⊠ 💻) Rooms here are being remodelled into snazzy hip designs with three-colour design schemes, good use of mirrors and striped comforters on the beds; hopefully the dust will have settled by the time you arrive. Important: investigate the 'vibe-out room' and nifty rooftop pool.

Y on the Park (Map pp94-5; ☎ 9264 2451, 1800 994 994; www.ywcansw.com.au; 5-11 Wentworth Ave; dm $33, s $74-118, d $88-130; 🅿 ⊠ 💻) A family-friendly YWCA hotel (men are welcome), ideally located right near Hyde Park. Rooms are clean and modern, with deluxe versions sporting safes. Four-bed dorms (no bunks!) cost $33 per person. Breakfast is included; be sure to reserve parking.

Stellar Suites (Map pp94-5; ☎ 9264 9754, 1800 025 575; www.stellarsuites.com.au; 4 Wentworth Ave; rooms $135-360; 🅿 ⊠ 💻) Gorgeous, luxurious rooms in dark, rich colours heal well-travelled bones at this hip boutique hotel in a prime location right near Hyde Park. All 38 modern rooms have kitchenette, telephone, safe and Internet connection, and a three-bedroom apartment is available (along with free movies for all).

Wynyard Hotel (Map pp94-5; ☎ 9299 1330; www.wynyardhotel.com.au; 107 Clarence St; s/d without bathroom $77/88) Here's another pub offering 12 decent, no-frills rooms with TV, fridge, and tea- and coffee-making facilities. There's kitchen access and a basic roof terrace, and family rooms are available for $120. A light breakfast is included, and laundry is free.

Grand Hotel (Map pp94-5; ☎ 9232 3755; 30 Hunter St; s & d without bathroom $77-88) This well-located, heritage-listed hotel offers 19 cosy, flowery rooms above its decent pub. All are simple but comfortable and come with their own sink, fridge, tea- and coffee-making facilities, and TV; some have a balcony. One family room is available for $120.

CHINATOWN & DARLING HARBOUR AREA

Aarons Hotel (Map pp94-5; ☎ 9281 5555, 1800 101 100; www.aaronshotelsandresorts.com.au; 37 Ultimo Rd; d from $100; ⬛) In the heart of Chinatown (think good, cheap food) is this 94-room heritage-building hotel. The plain rooms vary in size but are clean and roomy; some have courtyard views. Aarons' is popular with group bookings, and rates go up by $10 on Friday and Saturday nights. Two disabled rooms are available.

Metro Hotel (Map pp94-5; ☎ 9283 8088, 1800 004 321; www.metrohospitalitygroup.com; 300 Pitt St; d from $150; ⬛ ⬛ ⬛) The location near Central Station and Chinatown is spot on, and rooms are nice, small, well lit and neatly decorated. There's a restaurant on the premises, but nearby parking costs an extra $21 per 24 hours. Check the website for specials.

Capitol Square Hotel (Map pp94-5; ☎ 9211 8633; www.rydges.com/capitolsquare; cnr George & Campbell Sts; d from $105; ⬛ ⬛ ⬛) Here's a very convenient place to stay near Chinatown and Darling Harbour, especially given the good deals that are sometimes available. Small rooms are average and hardly plush, but some do come with balcony. Rates skyrocket on weekends (to $150) and tend to change with demand, so call ahead.

Pensione Hotel (Map pp94-5; ☎ 9265 8888, 1800 885 886; www.pensione.com.au; 631 George St; d $125; ⬛) This hip new boutique hotel is a great contemporary choice in Chinatown, offering stylish and tasteful rooms with minimalist décor and basic services such as fridge and cable TV. Friday and Saturday nights see rate hikes to $140, however.

Glasgow Arms Hotel (Map pp94-5; ☎ 9211 2354; admin@glasgowarmshotel.com.au; 527 Harris St; s/d $120/135; ⬛) Just across the road from the excellent Powerhouse Museum, this pub hotel has 10 comfortable, good-sized and flowery rooms, some with small balcony and one with kitchenette. Tea and coffee are served all day, and breakfast is included.

Vulcan Hotel (Map pp94-5; ☎ 9211 3283; www.vulcanhotel.com.au; 500 Wattle St; d $99-150; ⬛ ⬛ ⬛) The location of this budget boutique hotel is a bit off-centre, but rooms are stunning in their simple design and décor. There's charm in this heritage-listed building, and a courtyard garden is in the works.

KINGS CROSS

Victoria Court Hotel (Map p97; ☎ 9357 3200; www.victoriacourt.com.au; 122 Victoria St; d $135-165; ⬛ ⬛) Looking for a quiet and comfortable room with a lovely Victorian air? Try this quaint boutique hotel, where at night plush floral-sheeted beds comfort you and in the morning a breakfast buffet is served in the indoor glass-covered patio. Budgeteers should ask for the one room with unattached but private bathroom ($85).

Hotel 59 (Map p97; ☎ 9360 5900; www.hotel59.com.au; 59 Bayswater Rd; d $88-165) This small, friendly hotel in the quiet stretch of Bayswater Rd has just nine pleasant rooms, all varying in size. The small café downstairs whips up great cooked breakfasts (included in room price). Family rooms – some with kitchenette – are available, but call ahead.

Maisonette Hotel (Map p97; ☎ 9357 3878; maisonettehotel@bigpond.com; 31 Challis Ave; s/d $60/95) Not a bad deal for this clean, friendly hotel, and the price gets better if you stay longer than one night. The small, bright doubles come with bathroom, kitchenette and TV, but singles share bathrooms.

Challis Lodge (Map p97; ☎ 9358 5422; www.budgethotelssydney.com; 21-23 Challis Ave; s/d $75/85, without bathroom $55/65) Subdued management greets you (keep ringing the bell) at this labyrinthine place with all manner of rooms – some are small and gloomy, while others are brighter and have amenities such as microwave or sink. Balcony rooms go for $110 to $120.

Holiday Lodge (Map p97; ☎ 9356 3955; www.holidaylodgehotel.com; 55 Macleay St; s $65-95, d $75-110; ⬛) Front rooms here have small balconies overlooking the street (though this means more noise). The cheapest rooms – the smaller ones out the back – are still decent value, though. All come with TV, fridge and bathroom, and family rooms are available. Parking costs $17 per night.

DARLINGHURST & SURRY HILLS

Kirketon Hotel (Map p97; ☎ 9332 2011; www.kirketon.com.au; 207 Darlinghurst Rd, Darlinghurst; d $140-190;

P ☒) Yet another boutique offering in Darlinghurst, this one has contemporary design, fluffy pillows, an elegant muted colour scheme and mirrored hallways. Renowned restaurant Salt is next door, and there are two bars on the premises.

Sullivans Hotel (Map pp94-5; ☎ 9361 0211; www .sullivans.com.au; 21 Oxford St, Paddington; d $135-150; P ☒ ☒) Situated in an area often referred to as 'Paddinghurst', this well-managed 64-room motel has simple, good rooms and a charming pool courtyard. The pricier rooms face inside, and those at the front have a balcony. Bookings are essential during Mardi Gras (late February to early March).

City Crown Motel (Map pp94-5; ☎ 9331 2433; www .citycrownmotel.com.au; 289 Crown St, Surry Hills; d $95-115; ☒) This basic motel offers clean, simple rooms – some with balcony or patio – that are acceptable enough, though unmemorable. Still, you're a stone's throw from Oxford St and the city centre. Reserve well ahead during Mardi Gras, when prices skyrocket.

Hotel Altamont (Map p97; ☎ 9360 6000; www .altamont.com.au; 207 Darlinghurst Rd, Darlinghurst; dm $20, d $89-130; ☒) Flashy in that rustic sort of way, this modern boutique hotel offers lovely rooms – some with patio – and a smart, intimate lobby strewn with leather chairs. There's a great terrace, and even cheap dorm rooms are available! Continental breakfast is included (dorms pay $2). A great deal considering the surroundings, services and location. Reception is open from 8am to 8pm.

Sydney Star Accommodation (Map p97; ☎ 1800 134 455; stay@sydneystar.com.au; 275 Darlinghurst Rd, Darlinghurst; dm $20, s $60-85, d $80-100) This well-located budget place is especially great for long-term guests seeking quiet, good-value and appealing rooms with TV, fridge and microwave (some have sinks). There's a small kitchen and a courtyard for socializing.

WATSONS BAY

Doyles Palace Hotel (Map pp92-3; ☎ 9337 5444; www .doyles.com.au; 1 Military Rd; d $145-420; P ☒) Located on some of Sydney's best real estate, this renovated, top-drawer hotel offers either park or water views – guess which costs more? The best thing about this place has to be the drinking and dining empire below, which attracts hordes of both tourists and locals – especially on sunny weekends. Breakfast is included; reserve ahead.

BONDI

Ravesi's (Map p98; ☎ 9365 4422; www.ravesis.com .au; cnr Campbell Pde & Hall St; d $125-275, ste $275-450; ☒) Gorgeous and sleek describes the 16 contemporary rooms and two-level suites at this posh place. Luxurious balconies offer five-star peeps at the ocean, and the modern bathrooms are spotless. It's a fabulous stay, and the trendy bar downstairs attracts beautiful crowds.

Bondi Beachside Inn (Map p98; ☎ 9130 5311; www.bondiinn.com.au; 152 Campbell Pde; d from $120; P ☒) The apartment-style rooms at this high-rise monstrosity are a bit worn and sterile, but most have good kitchenettes and plenty of space. Water views will cost you, however.

Bondi Beach Homestay (Map p98; ☎ 9300 0800; 10 Forest Knoll Ave; www.bondibeachhomestay.com.au; s without bathroom $80, d without bathroom $125-135; P ▭) In a charmingly decorated home with friendly owners, this is one of Bondi's hidden gems. Rooms are homy, bathrooms are immaculate, and the comfortable common areas include a lounge and a sunny deck. Breakfast is included, and there's kitchen access.

Hotel Bondi (Map p98; ☎ 9130 3271; www.hotel bondi.com.au; 178 Campbell Pde; s $75, d $110-120, ste $160-220; ☒) The beachfront, peach-coloured Hotel Bondi resembles a tasty layered cake and offers small, tidy rooms a cut above the usual pub standard. Choice front rooms have views, but note that the hotel is also home to three bars and a nightclub. Prices drop between April and September.

Bondi Beach Bed & Breakfast (Map p98; ☎ 9365 6522; www.bondibeach-bnb.com.au; 110 Roscoe St; s from $100, d from $129; P) Just five immaculate (and nonsmoking) rooms, all with TV, fridge, toaster and coffee maker, are offered by your in-house hosts Nadia and Michael. Two rooms share a bathroom, and one has a balcony. Light breakfast is included; be sure to reserve.

COOGEE

Dive Hotel (Map p99; ☎ 9665 5538; www.divehotel .com.au; 234 Arden St; d from $150; P ▭ ▭) The 14 rooms at this delightful boutique hotel are wonderfully luxurious, and come with kitchenette, small groovy bathroom, and breakfast; those at the front sport ocean views. There's an elegant kitchen for all, and a relaxing, Asian-flavoured back patio.

BALMAIN

Balmain Lodge (Map pp92-3; ☎ 9810 3700; www
.balmainlodge.com.au; 415 Darling St; s/d without bathroom
$65/80; **P**) Located on Balmain's backbone,
Darling St, this place offers capable management and clean, no-frills rooms with
kitchenettes and patios. It's popular with
long-term tenants, so call ahead (reception
is 'supposedly' open Monday to Friday from
8am to 6pm). There's wheelchair access.

GLEBE

Alishan International Guest House (Map p99;
☎ 9566 4048; www.alishan.com.au; 100 Glebe Point
Rd; dm $22-33, s $88-99, d $99-115; **꠸**) This well-
run gem, housed in an old building, offers
clean rooms with character and a communal kitchen. There's also a beautiful airy
balcony and a nice garden in which to hang
out, along with a bright dining area.

MANLY & NORTH SHORE

Manly Lodge (Map p98; ☎ 9977 8655; www.manly
lodge.com.au; 22 Victoria Pde, Manly; s & d $135-200;
꠸) Vaguely Spanish in appearance, Manly
Lodge is a labyrinthine guesthouse with 28
rooms and suites, all with kitchenette and
some with private patio. It's a comfortable
though not luxurious set-up, and sports a
spa, a sauna and a small, leafy patio. Family
rooms are available (from $150).

101 Addison Road (Map p98; ☎ 9977 6216; www
.bb-manly.com; 101 Addison Rd, Manly; s/d without bathroom $110/150) Only two rooms are available,
but if you snag one you'll have a peaceful,
cosy stay. There's a large living room with
piano, and your host, Jill, knows the area
inside and out. Breakfast is included, and
tea and coffee are served all day.

Manly Paradise Motel (Map p98; ☎ 9977 5799;
www.manlyparadise.com.au; 54 North Steyne, Manly; d
$110-160; **P ꠸ ꠸**) Just looking for a com-
fortable, bouncy bed right across from the
beach? This might be the place for you.
Rooms come with wicker furniture and are
narrow but spacious; bathrooms are downright tiny. Some have partial sea views.

Periwinkle Guest House (Map p98; ☎ 9977 4668;
www.periwinkle.citysearch.com.au; 18-19 East Esplanade,
Manly; s from $110, d from $135; **P**) This beautifully
restored Victorian house offers 18 pleasant
and well-appointed rooms, all with fridge
and TV (and some with stunning water
views). There's a family atmosphere and
a relaxing shady courtyard. Cook dinner

in the nifty kitchen, but remember that a
light breakfast is on the house.

Glenferrie Lodge (Map pp92-3; ☎ 9955 1685; www
.glenferrielodge.com; 12a Carabella St, Kirribilli; s/d without
bathroom from $60/105; **꠸**) This large, beautiful
old house lies on a quiet residential street
and has a wonderfully grassy back garden.
Rooms come with fridge, and bathrooms
are clean; dorm beds are available. Breakfast
is included, and cheap dinners are available,
but there's no kitchen access. Arrive via the
Milsons Point train station or by ferry from
Kirribilli wharf.

Sydney Beachouse YHA (off Map pp92-3; ☎ 9981
1177; www.yha.com.au; 4 Collaroy St, Collaroy; dm $26, d $64,
f $104; **P ꠸ ꠸ ꠸**) This clean hostel comes
with great outdoor spaces, including a solar-
heated pool! It's also wheelchair and child
friendly and lies close to some of Sydney's
best beaches (there's free surfboard hire).
To get here, catch bus No L90 or L88 from
Railway Sq, Town Hall or Wynyard train stations. From Manly, take bus No 155 or 156.

Top End

THE ROCKS & CIRCULAR QUAY

Four Seasons (Map pp94-5; ☎ 9238 0000; www
.fourseasons.com; 199 George St; d from $440; **P ꠸ ꠸**)
Easily one of the main contenders for the
title of 'best hotel in Sydney', the Four Seasons features an unbeatable location, luxurious rooms, professional staff and knockout
views (city, Opera House or harbour – take
your pick) from over half its rooms. Those
seeking spa services will find them here.

Park Hyatt (Map pp94-5; ☎ 9241 1234; www
.sydney.park.hyatt.com; 7 Hickson Rd; d from $585; **P ꠸**
꠸ ꠸) Contemporary designs. Futuristic
leather furniture. Flat-screen TVs. Deca-

dent views of the harbour. Around-the-clock butler service. Great location. The $6500 Government suite. Super-luxurious. What more is there to say?

CITY CENTRE

Establishment Hotel (Map pp94-5; ☎ 9240 3100; www.establishmenthotel.com; 5 Bridge Lane; d from $340; 🛇 💻) You'd never imagine these ultra-slick digs would be hidden behind an inconspicuous entrance off a dark, unwelcoming alley. You could imagine, however, secretive stars and low-key moguls slinking within the 33 silky rooms tricked out in simple modern lines and two-colour design schemes. Beds are lined with fine cotton linen, baths are encircled in marble or limestone, and two equally extravagant bars – right on the premises – provide a place to perch and quench your stylish thirst. If you're a celebrity, go for the deluxe split-level penthouse ($1100).

CHINATOWN & DARLING HARBOUR AREA

Hyde Park Inn (Map pp94-5; ☎ 9264 6001; www.hydeparkinn.com.au; 271 Elizabeth St; s/d from $155/170; 🅿 🛇 💻) Nicely located across from Hyde Park – the higher floors have awesome leafy views – this pleasant hotel offers good, spacious rooms with kitchenettes. Deluxe rooms come with balcony and offer the best views (and cost more). Two-bedroom apartments are available.

KINGS CROSS AREA & WOOLLOOMOOLOO

Regents Court (Map p97; ☎ 9358 1533; www.regentscourt.com.au; 18 Springfield Ave, Potts Point; d $187-255; 🅿 🛇) A loyal following keeps coming back to the spacious, luxurious rooms at this family-owned place. All are bright, and boast fully stocked kitchens and pleasant dining areas. The highlight, however, has to be the lush and lovely rooftop garden – it's a wonderfully relaxing spot in Kings Cross.

Simpsons of Potts Point (Map p97; ☎ 9356 2199; www.simpsonspottspoint.com.au; 8 Challis Ave, Potts Point; d $215-255, ste $355; 🅿 💻 🛇) A charming B&B despite the sniffy management, the plush communal areas and luxurious rooms here deliver comfort to those wishing to be spoilt. Some rooms have a balcony, and the breakfast room is glass-topped.

W Hotel Sydney (Map p97; ☎ 9331 9000; www.whotels.com; 6 Cowper Wharf Rdwy, Woolloomooloo; d from $335; 🅿 🛇 💻 🖳) With what must be the most impressive lobby in Sydney, this lavishly contemporary boutique hotel – housed in an old wool-processing warehouse – offers ultra-chic loft suites with stunning water views. Even standard rooms sport slick minimalist design, and surround an open central space fitted with airy bar and café. The elegant underground pool is a plus.

DARLINGHURST & SURRY HILLS

Medusa (Map p97; ☎ 9331 1000; www.medusa.com.au; 267 Darlinghurst Rd, Darlinghurst; d $270-385; 🛇 💻) This sultry 18-room boutique hotel is pure Sydney – glamorous, flashy, sexy and decadent. Lose yourself in the colourful, curvaceous furniture, and enjoy the chocolates on your pillow, soft linens on your bed and Aveda toiletries in your bathroom. A lovely, sunny fountain courtyard offers dreamy lounging; design buffs will be in heaven.

Medina on Crown (Map pp94-5; ☎ 9360 6666, 1300 300 232; www.medinaapartments.com.au; 359 Crown St, Surry Hills; apt from $218; 🅿 🛇 💻 🖳) The comfortable one- and two-bedroom apartments on offer here are all spacious and come with well-stocked kitchens, so they're great for families. Plenty of services and a peaceful courtyard pool area might turn Crown St into a holiday spot for you, especially if you consider the rooftop grass tennis court.

EDGECLIFF

Savoy Hotel (Map pp92-3; ☎ 9326 1411; www.savoyhotel.com.au; 41 Knox St; d $190-260; 🅿 🛇) This three-star hotel lies smack bang in Double Bay's coffee-lounge belt, which is just off busy New South Head Rd, and has nicely decorated rooms with balconies. There's a lovely atrium in the common lounge, and the feel is friendly and relaxed.

Metro Inn (Map pp92-3; ☎ 9328 7977; www.metrohospitalitygroup.com; 230 New South Head Rd; d $180; 🛇) Like many creatures of a certain age in this neighbourhood, the three-star Metro Inn has been getting some work done over the years. Some rooms (all neat and tidy) have great views of the harbour, and the Metro is close to Edgecliff train station. Prices are highly variable during the year, so check the website.

COOGEE

Coogee Bay Boutique Hotel (Map p99; ☎ 9665 0000; www.coogeebayhotel.com.au; 9 Vicar St; d from $220; 🅿 🛇) Those seeking swank on the beach need look no further than these trendy and contemporary digs. Most rooms come with balcony, while some sport jets in the tub – and the extra $10 for an ocean view is definitely worth it. In case the price is too high, call for specials, or check out the more down-to-earth (and noisier) wing at the Coogee Bay Hotel (p133; rooms cost from $130).

GLEBE

Tricketts Bed & Breakfast (Map p99; ☎ 9552 1141; www.tricketts.com.au; 270 Glebe Point Rd; s $176-190, d $198-220; ▢) Seven lovely rooms and the spacious, antique-filled common areas will make you feel right at home – if your home is a gorgeous 19th-century mansion. There's a great deck at the back, plenty of reading materials, and your gracious host, Liz. Be sure to reserve.

MANLY

Manly Pacific Sydney (Map p98; ☎ 9977 7666; www .accorhotels.com.au; 55 North Steyne; d from $250; Ⓟ ✖ ▢ ☎) This big hotel is across the beach and lays claim to Manly's fanciest digs. There's a gym, a business centre, a spa, a sauna and a real sense of seaside swank. The most expensive rooms come with balcony and ocean views; check the website for specials.

EATING

With great local produce, innovative chefs and BYO licensing laws, it's no surprise that eating out is one of the great delights of a visit to Sydney. The 'Spanish Quarter' consists of a cluster of seven or eight Spanish restaurants and bars on Liverpool St between George and Sussex Sts, and is a great spot to nibble on tapas and imbibe sangria.

The Rocks & Circular Quay

Many restaurants and cafés in the Rocks have tourists in their sights, but there are also plenty of options for diners seeking something different or even upscale.

Rockpool (Map pp94-5; ☎ 9252 1888; 107 George St; mains $54-60; ✆ dinner Tue-Sat) This is one of the best eateries in Sydney. Chef Neil Perry churns out beautiful (in all senses) dishes, and the seafood especially shines. Go for the southern rock lobster *tajine* with roast apricots and couscous for two while enjoying the cool, slick and modern atmosphere – you'll thank us later.

Sailor's Thai Canteen (Map pp94-5; ☎ 9251 2466; 106 George St; mains $25-36; ✆ lunch Mon-Fri, dinner Mon-Sat) Sit at the long, communal stainless-steel table and feast on some of the best Thai food this side of Bangkok. Consultant chef David Thompson whips up complex dishes fit for royalty, and you'll be sampling it with arts bureaucrats, politicians and fellow tourists. Upstairs is casual, while downstairs means white tablecloths.

MCA Café (Map pp94-5; ☎ 9241 4253; 140 George St; mains $16-27; ✆ 10am-4pm) Nicely located at the slick Museum of Contemporary Art, this hip and very popular café sports outside tables with views of the Opera House. Order eggs Benedict, muesli or fruit salad for breakfast, while lunch could be seared scallops, linguini with prawns or beer-battered fish and chips.

Sydney Cove Oyster Bar (Map pp94-5; ☎ 9247 2937; Circular Quay East; mains $17-40; ✆ breakfast, lunch & dinner) In a sunny spot close to the Opera House, this outdoor café specialises in oyster dishes (try the shots, $5.50) and other seafood temptations. It's all outdoor seating, so beware of cloudy days. If the menu's too expensive, consider the Portobello Café next door.

City Centre

There's no shortage of places for a snack or quick meal in the city, especially on weekdays, when most restaurants cater to the business crowds. Lots of cheap grub is hidden away in building food courts, however, so snoop around.

Wagamama (Map pp94-5; ☎ 9252 9593; cnr Bridge & Loftus Sts; mains $11-18.50; ✆ lunch & dinner) Long, no-nonsense picnic tables and minimalist décor help you concentrate on slurping those delicious chilli beef ramen noodles and *yakisoba*. There are also curry, rice and salad dishes. It's Japanese fast food, Sydney style.

Bodhi (Map pp94-5; ☎ 9360 2523; Cook & Phillip Park; yum cha $5-8, mains $6-8; ✆ lunch & dinner Tue-Sun, lunch Mon) Vegans need look no further than this flashy spot, located underneath the plaza in front of the cathedral. Lunch means tasty yum cha, though the outdoor seating can be windy. There's another (much smaller) branch at Central Station (there's no yum cha, but try the veggie laksa soup, $7.50).

Casa Asturiana (Map pp94-5; ☎ 9264 1010; 77 Liverpool St; tapas $8-14, mains from $22; ✆ lunch & dinner) Located in Sydney's tiny 'Spanish Quarter', this tapas joint reputedly serves the best tapas in town. Try small platefuls of seafood, meat and vegetarian titbits, and order a fine Spanish white (or red) to help wash it all down. If you're in the mood for a *cazuela*, paella or weekend flamenco you're also in luck.

Apartment (Map pp94-5; ☎ 9241 1488; 155 Macquarie St; mains $8-15) Nestled below some of Sydney's fanciest apartments (the building was designed by Renzo Piano) this airy café feeds local politicians, power businessmen and trendy fashionistas things like cajun chicken and salade niçoise. The coffee is good, and sidewalk tables make for breezy dining.

Chinatown

Much of Sydney's cheapest (and tastiest) food can be found in bustling Chinatown, though you could also spend a small fortune. Food courts, found at most large shopping centres, offer the best bargains.

Sea Bay Restaurant (Map pp94-5; ☎ 9267 4855; 382 Pitt St; mains $8-12; ⊗ lunch & dinner) The tacky décor isn't much to write home about, but the deliciously chewy homemade noodles are. One steaming, slurpy bowlful will fill you for less than $10, and there are steamed dumplings and wok-fried dishes too. Ask for the picture menu.

Marigold Citymark (Map pp94-5; ☎ 9281 3388; Levels 4 & 5, 683 George St; mains $14-46; ⊗ lunch & dinner) This posh 800-seat palace serves lunchtime yum cha daily and has an extensive menu of other dishes. Join the hordes – it's especially boisterous and interesting if you catch sight of a mammoth wedding banquet in full force.

Emperor's Garden BBQ & Noodles (Map pp94-5; ☎ 9281 9899; 213-215 Thomas St; mains $9-16; ⊗ lunch & dinner) Here's a busy eatery specialising in meat and poultry dishes. The little takeaway section out front has many goodies, including some crimson-hued offerings hanging in the window; give the duck and rice (takeout $9) a try – it's simply decadent.

Pho Pasteur (Map pp94-5; ☎ 9212 5622; 709 George St; mains $8-10; ⊗ lunch & dinner) Super spartan, super quick and super crowded at lunchtime, Pho Pasteur serves some of the best Vietnamese *pho* (noodle soup) around, though service *will* be gruff.

Xic Lo (Map pp94-5; ☎ 9280 1678; 215a Thomas St; mains $9-12; ⊗ lunch & dinner) Sleek lines, stainless-steel counters and muted colours translate into hip Vietnamese food, and the crowds drop in en masse during lunchtime. The crispy chicken with rice ($9) is a winner, but the *pho* and rice rolls are also popular.

BBQ King (Map pp94-5; ☎ 9267 2586; 18-20 Goulburn St; mains $12-24; ⊗ lunch & dinner) Vegetarians should give this place a wide berth, 'cause the roast duck and barbecued pork are the main attractions. It's an old-school Chinese eatery, with bustling service, generous pots of tea and a lack of fancy décor. It's open till 2am.

Golden Century Seafood Restaurant (Map pp94-5; ☎ 9212 3901; 393-399 Sussex St; mains $12-22; ⊗ noon-4am) This is the place for an upscale Chinese dinner, especially if you like your seafood fresh – it's sitting in nearby tanks (check out the abalone and giant crabs!). This is a favourite late-night eating spot for many of Sydney's chefs and hotel workers.

Darling Harbour & Pyrmont

The Harbourside Shopping Centre, Cockle Bay and King St Wharf have dining options as far as the eye can see – some hit, many miss. At least most have nice views, though they don't usually come cheap.

Blackbird Café (Map pp94-5; ☎ 9283 7385; Level 2, Cockle Bay Wharf, Darling Harbour; mains $8-19; ⊗ breakfast, lunch & dinner) Here's a good budget option with something for everyone – hot-stone pizzas, plenty of salads, wok stir-fries, a vegetarian list, and staples such as pasta and meat selections. The shady outdoor balcony is pleasant, as are the harbour views. It's open late.

Chinta Ria...Temple of Love (Map pp94-5; ☎ 9264 3211; Level 2, Cockle Bay Wharf, Darling Harbour; mains $10-26; ⊗ lunch & dinner) This ain't really cheap Malaysian food, but the atmosphere here sure is fun. An enormous Buddha greets you at the door, while the spicy chicken laksa ($16) is worth getting excited about. Jazzy music, colourful décor, clanging dishes and efficient service abound.

Zaaffran (Map pp94-5; ☎ 9211 8900; Level 2, 345 Harbourside, Darling Harbour; mains $17-26; ⊗ lunch & dinner) Indian food doesn't come fancier than at this air-con joint with its glassy views. Chef Vikrant Kapoor (of Singapore's Raffles fame) whips up both traditional and exotic selections. Try the tiger prawns with coconut and tamarind, or chicken biryani

NEW SOUTH WALES

with mint. The menu offers good descriptions and includes vegetarian choices.

Concrete (Map p99; ☎ 9518 9523; 224 Harris St, Pyrmont; breakfast $6-14, mains $14-17; ☿ breakfast & lunch) This slick, minimalist joint boasts tasty offerings such as buttermilk pancakes with grilled pineapple for breakfast; lunch means eggplant and roasted almond ravioli or Mediterranean lamb skewers. Enjoy it all at a shady outdoor table. The location is a bit off the tourist path, just a few blocks from Darling Harbour.

Kings Cross & Around

The Cross has a good mixture of tiny cafés, swanky eateries and fast-food joints serving greasy fare designed mainly to soak up beer.

Jimmy Lik's (Map p97; ☎ 8354 1400; 188 Victoria St; mains $26-29; ☿ dinner) A mirror image of its swanky bar next door, this upscale eatery offers exotic Asian-inspired tapas such as smoked eel in betel leaf ($3.50), while main dishes include crispy pork hock, Vietnamese braised *wagyu* beef and salmon salad.

Fratelli Paradiso (Map p97; ☎ 9357 1744; 12 Challis Ave; mains $11-20; ☿ breakfast, lunch & dinner) You can have lunch here, and it's great, but what keeps us getting out of bed in the morning is the idea of breakfast here. The eggs are magnificent, the rice pudding superb, the coffee from God. Just keep in mind that it closes at 6pm on weekends.

Delectica (Map p97; ☎ 9368 1390; 130 Victoria St; mains $7-14; ☿ breakfast & lunch daily, dinner occasionally) Breakfast is served all day, so get your blueberry pancakes with yogurt and honey for dinner if you like – or try the burger with beetroot or the pumpkin salad with hummus dressing. There's plenty of other less fancy stuff, such as omelettes, sandwiches and pasta.

Matchbox (Map p97; ☎ 9326 9860; 197 Victoria St; mains $10-12; ☿ breakfast & lunch) Tiny as a matchbox indeed – there are just four small sidewalk tables and a wraparound counter. And this trendy breakfast (served all day) place gets packed on weekends, so come early.

Bayswater Brasserie (Map p97; ☎ 9357 2177; 32 Bayswater Rd; mains $22-31; ☿ lunch Tue-Fri, dinner Mon-Sat) This classy restaurant has good service and a relaxing back-room bar for aperitifs. The menu is short and simple, and offers delicious things such as roast lamb rump, prosciutto-wrapped chicken, and barramundi with anchovy butter.

Vinyl Lounge (Map p97; ☎ 9326 9224; 17 Elizabeth Bay Rd; mains $8-13; ☿ breakfast & lunch) More a locals' café than a restaurant, this hip, white hole-in-the-wall place has shots of coffee guaranteed to kick. Enjoy your semolina with apples, currants and yogurt ($7.50) on the classic '60s yellow-plastic tables.

Darlinghurst & East Sydney

Victoria St sports the most eateries in Darlinghurst. There's a second cluster of (mostly Italian) restaurants on Stanley St, just south of William St between Crown and Riley Sts.

Bills (Map pp94-5; ☎ 9360 9631; 433 Liverpool St, Darlinghurst; mains $18-23; ☿ breakfast & lunch daily, dinner Mon-Sat) Beautifully presented gourmet food. Gleaming open kitchen. Fresh flowers and fashion 'zines. Large communal table for conversations about your sweet-corn frittata with bacon ($18.50) and his grilled Hiramasa kingfish with chickpea salad ($22.50). Unbearable weekend brunch crowds. No sign outside. Bill Granger.

Lure (Map pp94-5; ☎ 9361 3366; 381 Bourke St, Darlinghurst; mains $10-14; ☿ dinner Mon-Thu, lunch daily) This small fish shop will make you look good eating fish and chips and sipping organic coffee right near Taylor Sq. Its gleaming sidewalk tables are airy and attractive, while a fancier back area offers privacy for the celebrity in you. Order the salmon teriyaki salad and you'll feel even more special.

Fu Manchu (Map p97; ☎ 9360 9424; 249 Victoria St, Darlinghurst; mains $9-20; ☿ lunch Mon-Fri, dinner daily) This is the original Fu, with some of the best Asian eating in Darlinghurst. The vibe is 21st-century Hong Kong slick chic, with chopsticks and elbows getting a thorough workout (it's a narrow space). Grab some steamed barbecue pork or ginger buns ($7.50).

Bill & Toni's (Map pp94-5; ☎ 9360 4702; 74 Stanley St, East Sydney; mains $13-15; ☿ lunch & dinner) Folks come here because it's a tradition for basic Italian cuisine, a stalwart of the cheap and cheerful, and in our opinion a national treasure. The service is lightning-fast, you get your orange cordial for free, and everyone leaves with a smile. The café downstairs has good coffee.

Balkan (Map pp94-5; ☎ 9360 4970; 209 Oxford St, Darlinghurst; mains $21-39; ☿ lunch & dinner Wed-Mon) When you're craving fried calamari, grilled octopus or just a rib-eye steak, grab your padded wallet and head to Oxford

St. Meals at this longstanding place won't come cheap, but they'll satisfy your carnivore cravings.

Burgerman (Map p97; ☎ 9361 0268; 116 Surrey St, Darlinghurst; mains $9-12; ☻ lunch & dinner) Does a lamb fillet with eggplant, garlic and basil mayo sound good? How about a beetroot and horseradish mayo burger? This and other tasty treats are cooked up in a small, open space with simple yet smart décor. Grab a sidewalk table and enjoy.

Surry Hills

Crown St is the main thoroughfare through Surry Hills, but it's a long street, and the restaurants occur in fits and starts. It's definitely worth a wander, and if you're looking for cheap exotic grub there are half a dozen nondescript but good-value Lebanese eateries around the corner of Cleveland and Elizabeth Sts. Additionally, many cheap Indian and Turkish places spice up Cleveland St between Crown and Bourke Sts.

Longrain (Map pp94-5; ☎ 9280 2888; 85 Commonwealth St; mains $23-38; ☻ lunch Mon-Fri, dinner Mon-Sat) It seems that all of Sydney's beautiful set are keen to graze on the superb Thai-inspired offerings here. They'll sit at the communal tables or long counter, so don't expect much privacy; try the caramelized pork hock with chilli vinegar, however, and you'll be needing to gush to nearby ears. An excellent bar is icing on the cake.

Billy Kwong (Map pp94-5; ☎ 9332 3300; 355 Crown St; mains $16-39; ☻ dinner) One of Sydney's hardest restaurants at which to snag a table. It's small and chatty and sports hip staff – no reservations are taken except for one large table (choose between 6pm and 8pm sittings). The menu changes seasonally but usually includes treats such as silken tofu with mushrooms and ginger, crispy-skin chicken with shallots, and spicy octopus salad with baby herbs. The weekend surcharge is $2.20 per person.

Foodgame (Map pp94-5; ☎ 9380 8585; 185 Campbell St, Surry Hills; mains $7-15; ☻ lunch & dinner) The steel deli counters work well with the plush lounge area, communal table and sidewalk seating. Wherever you sit, you'll enjoy the salads (Thai to Caesar), burgers (satay to steak) and pasta (ravioli to fettuccini). And don't even think about leaving without dessert (lemon tart, sticky-date pudding, lime-infused coconut *panna cotta*…).

Bills 2 (Map pp94-5; ☎ 9360 4762; 359 Crown St; mains $19-28; ☻ breakfast, lunch & dinner) The loyal and eclectic crowd has followed Bill Granger's success from his Darlinghurst eatery to this shiny new upstart. This is an equally chic place with sidewalk seating and tea from 4pm to 6pm. Tasty selections might be the roasted lamb rump with baked eggplant or black mussels with *romesco* sauce. Enjoy!

Uchi Lounge (Map pp94-5; ☎ 9261 3524; 15 Brisbane St; mains $14-17; ☻ dinner Tue-Sat) Dress up creatively – your server certainly will, and so will the décor around you. Blissful Japanese food takes centre stage, however; start with chilled *udon* with lime *ponzu* and follow with kingfish sashimi, seared tuna or tempura oysters. The raspberry litchi or ginger sake goes down smoothly.

Red Lantern (Map pp92-3; ☎ 9698 4355; 545 Crown St; mains $12-20; ☻ lunch Tue-Fri, dinner Tue-Sun) Before anything else, call to make a reservation – and ask for a front patio table. This hot new Vietnamese joint serves up some great shrimp rolls in rice paper ($9) and an exotic *muc rang muoi* (chili salted squid, $14), all the while softly glowing in atmospheric lighting.

Mohr Fish (Map pp92-3; ☎ 9318 1326; 202 Devonshire St; mains $7-18; ☻ lunch & dinner) Don't expect a fancy eatery – this place takes up a space the size of your living room. It's very casual and has only a short, simple menu of fried seafood – can you say fish and chips ($7.50)? Expect the locals to join you at the crowded counter.

Il Baretto (Map pp92-3; ☎ 9361 6163; 496 Bourke St; mains $10-18; ☻ breakfast, lunch & dinner Tue-Sat, breakfast & lunch Sun) This place, packed to the rafters, dishes up some of the most heavenly pasta and gourmet sandwiches in Sydney. It's tiny and chaotic, but wait patiently at the pub across the road – they'll come and get you. Try the *spaghetti alle vongole* or homemade gnocchi – yum.

Maya Da Dhaba (Map pp92-3; ☎ 8399 3785; 431 Cleveland St; mains $8-15; ☻ dinner) Better-than-average Indian fare is served amongst natty surroundings covered in wall hangings at this popular restaurant. The Andrakhi lamb chops ($14.50) arrive sizzling and juicy, while the chicken Makhani ($13) is also quite tasty, but there are plenty of vegetarian choices as well.

Maltese Café (Map pp94-5; ☎ 9361 6942; 310 Crown St, Surry Hills; mains $6-7) For pasta on the cheap,

NEW SOUTH WALES

visit this casual and cheerful café near the intersection of Crown and Oxford Sts. The menu is simple, offering things such as ravioli and teriyaki, but don't leave without trying the *pastizzi* (80c) – delicious meat-filled pies that make great snacks.

Paddington & Woollahra

Bistro Lulu (Map pp92-3; ☎ 9380 6888; 257 Oxford St, Paddington; mains $26-30; ☯ lunch Thu-Sat, dinner daily) How does blue-eye cod wrapped in prosciutto sound? Or perhaps caramelized-fig tart, blue-cheese polenta or grilled sirloin sound better? And let's not forget the pan-fried gnocchi with cauliflower *polonaise* and truffle vinaigrette. Add some subdued lighting and you may think you're in a Paris bistro.

And the Dish Ran Away with the Spoon (off Map pp94-5; ☎ 9361 6131; 226 Glenmore Rd, Paddington; mains $5-10; ☯ breakfast, lunch & dinner) Local yuppies cram this charming little Paddington deli to lunch on great pasta, organic chicken and tofu burgers. It's a primo spot to pick up picnic fixings or takeaway lunches and dinners, and breakfast is served all day. Try the low-fat 'skinny burger' ($8) – it tastes too good to be true.

Jones the Grocer (Map pp92-3; ☎ 9362 1222; 68 Moncur St, Woollahra; mains $8-16; ☯ 8am-6pm Mon-Fri, 9am-5.30pm Sat, 9am-5pm Sun) With the lovely food on display it's easy to see why this is one of Sydney's favourite places to stock up on fancy deli goods, such as Asian groceries, chutneys, cheese, olives and exotic coffees. But it's also nice for the old coffee-and-cake break.

Bondi

The touristy eateries stretch along the Campbell Pde promenade, while fancy bistros can be found on side streets. You'll generally have to forgo a table with sea view if you're seriously pinching pennies, but a bag of take-away and patch of sand works just as easily.

Brown Sugar (Map p98; ☎ 9365 6262; 100 Brighton Blvd; mains $8-14; ☯ breakfast & lunch) This cramped space really churns out brekky to the smooth set on weekends – and one bite of their blackstone eggs ($13) will tell you why. Weekdays are much less frantic, but the linguine with asparagus and rocket tastes just as good.

Sean's Panaroma (Map p98; ☎ 9365 4924; 270 Campbell Pde; mains $25-39; ☯ dinner Wed-Sat, lunch Sat & Sun) Sean and his team have never let

us down when we're looking for complex dishes such as preserved duck with potato cake, cabbage and pickled cherries ($35) or just a simple *pici* (Tuscan pasta, $21). Sidewalk tables with views of the beach add a romantic element.

Hugo's (Map p98; ☎ 9300 0900; 70 Campbell Pde; mains $35-38; ☯ dinner daily, breakfast & lunch Sat & Sun) Everything is attractive here, from the views to the food to the crowd to the staff. The airy sidewalk seating is gold and a great place to enjoy your seared scallops, duck omelette and sour-cherry soufflé.

Luv in a Cup (Map p98; 106 Glenayr Ave; mains $8-13; ☯ breakfast & lunch) As cute and cramped as a bug's ear, this mostly breakfast joint cooks up some fantastic 'love eggs' ($12) and 'love waffles' ($7.50). Energetic drinks include Turkish or iced coffees and creamy milkshakes. The lunch menu is limited, but breakfast is served until 4pm.

Green's Café (Map p98; ☎ 9130 6181; 140 Glenayr Ave; mains $8-14; ☯ breakfast & lunch Wed-Mon) A green-hued, laid-back and homy experience awaits those seeking tasty and healthy salads, sandwiches and scrambles. The teas and peach lassis are special too. (It's not vegetarian only, despite the name.)

Gelbison (Map p98; ☎ 9130 4042; 10 Lamrock Ave; mains $11-16; ☯ dinner) This is an old favourite with many beach bums, celebrities and assorted gluttons looking for great Italian. There are pizzas galore (27 kinds), even more pastas, and a few veal and risotto dishes.

Coogee

There are a number of cheap takeaways on Coogee Bay Rd, but you're better off hitting the cafés in the streets running off it, which have healthier food, sunnier interiors and outdoor tables.

Barzura (Map p99; ☎ 9665 5546; 62 Carr St; mains $17-24; ✷ breakfast, lunch & dinner) Airy and modern, this popular café offers pleasant meals at any time of the day. Breakfast means corn fritters with bacon, tomato and avocado; lunch could be an open salmon sandwich with capers; and dinner temptations include grilled lamb liver with pancetta and chorizo-and-saffron risotto. The specials board has other interesting options.

A Fish Called Coogee (Map p99; ☎ 9664 7700; 229 Coogee Bay Rd; mains $4.50-8; ✷ lunch & dinner) This busy little fishmonger sells fresh seafood cooked many different ways. Grab some great takeaway fish and chips ($8), crumbed calamari ($6) or battered prawns ($4) and sit on the beach, 'cause you may not snag one of those gleaming sidewalk tables.

Erciyes 2 (Map p99; ☎ 9664 1913; 240 Coogee Bay Rd; mains $8-13; ✷ café lunch & dinner daily, restaurant dinner daily) The café up the front serves quick meat pies and kebabs, along with some excellent dips – try the *jajik* (cucumber, yogurt and garlic). At night, the restaurant out the back does similar fare but with belly dancing as well (Friday and Saturday only).

Rice (Map p99; ☎ 9664 6655; 100 Beach St; mains $11-17; ✷ lunch & dinner) Stunning in its dark colour scheme, this fancy noodle joint serves up the Asian goods to your specifications. Curries, salads, stir-fries and meat dishes are also available. It's up the hill from the beach, which puts it nicely away from the beach crowds.

Jack & Jill's Fish Café (Map p99; ☎ 9665 8429; 98 Beach St; mains $14-20; ✷ dinner daily, lunch Sun) Next door to Rice, this simple, homy place offers good seafood dishes at reasonable prices. We recommend the Cajun-spiced barramundi with rice ($19), but the tandoori perch ($20) is also a temptation.

Glebe

Glebe Point Rd was Sydney's original 'eat street', but what it now lacks in cutting-edge dining experiences it retains in laid-back, unpretentious atmosphere and good-value food.

Spanish Tapas (Map p99; ☎ 9571 9005; 28 Glebe Point Rd; tapas $8-14; ✷ dinner) Those in search of tapas need look no further, as this fancier joint offers those little Spanish dishes

that range from good to great. Sample the mussels in tomato, tuna croquettes, garlic mushrooms or spinach-and-onion omelettes. The low lights, music and convivial diners add to the festive atmosphere.

Tanjore (Map p99; ☎ 9660 6332; 34 Glebe Point Rd; mains $8-16; ✷ dinner Sat-Wed) A pioneer of South Indian food in Australia, Tanjore attracts a range of locals, Indian-food lovers and celebrities to its cosy, dark dining room. Worthy dishes include the tandoori prawns, mango chicken and lamb *saag* (with spinach). And don't forget the garlic naan and a mango lassi to wash it all down with.

Iku Wholefoods (Map p99; ☎ 9692 8720; 25A Glebe Point Rd; mains $3-9; ✷ lunch & dinner) Here's one of the best vegan places in town, offering cheap and healthy takeaway treats (mostly organic). Order the miso soup, tofu fritters and Japanese rolls, and have a picnic at nearby Victoria Park. Iku closes relatively early (between 7.30 and 8pm) at weekends.

Badde Manors (Map p99; ☎ 9660 3797; 37 Glebe Point Rd; mains $8-13; ✷ breakfast, lunch & dinner) This long-established corner haunt is especially hectic on market day, when sidewalk tables are the holy grail. There are plenty of choices to make; lentil or tofu burgers, focaccia, bagels, frappés, smoothies, cakes, gelato, sticky-date, fig and ginger pudding…

Newtown

A swag of funky cafés and restaurants lining King St offer an interesting introduction to the suburb's community life. Many cater to university students.

Thai Pothong (Map p99; ☎ 9550 6277; 294 King St; mains $8-26; ✷ lunch Tue-Sun, dinner daily) Still flush from its '2002 Best Thai restaurant in Sydney' trophy, this popular restaurant serves up an interesting and affordable range of veggie dishes, seafood, curries and salads. Check out the green mango barramundi salad ($26) or the pumpkin curry ($17).

Bacigalupo (Map p99; ☎ 9565 5238; 284 King St; mains $11-16; ✷ breakfast, lunch & dinner) This airy and casual place will satisfy your rumbling tummy with more choices than you can shake a breadstick at. Hearty breakfast selections tempt with three-egg omelettes, muesli, and corn bread with braised tomato. Light meals include risotto with eggplant and grilled octopus salad – wash it all down with a mocha or a flat white.

NEW SOUTH WALES

Old Fish Shop Café (Map p99; ☎ 9519 4295; 239a King St; mains $9-10; ☺ breakfast, lunch & dinner) Yep, it used to be a fish shop. Now it's a tiny corner café with tasty sandwiches and pizzas, garlic hanging from above, paint peeling off the walls and open windows to catch King St's fumes. The place opens early for simple breakfasts but closes at 7pm.

Green Gourmet (Map p99; ☎ 9519 5330; 115 King St; mains $11-15; ☺ lunch & dinner) A peaceful Zen-like atmosphere greets you at the door and, along with the soothing music and the simple aesthetics, makes the tofu dishes and soups go down easily. Great Chinese-Malaysian vegetarian food is the speciality here, with yum cha livening up weekend lunch. Come and enjoy; your chakra spirit will thank you.

Rosalina's (Map p99; ☎ 9516 1429; 30 King St; mains $14-16; ☺ dinner Tue-Sun) On King Street's less lively section lies the hardly chic Rosalina's, offering tasty traditional dishes such as chicken cacciatore and a tasy veal parmigiana and scallopine, plus of course heaps of spaghetti varieties. Service is charming and the wine's not bad, making it a popular stop on weekends.

Leichhardt

You can still get a cheap spaghetti on Norton St, but the classic bistros are now rubbing shoulders with upscale restaurants, plus a few Greek, Chinese and Thai interlopers.

Grappa (Map p99; ☎ 9560 6090; Shop 1, 267-277 Norton St; mains $23-38; ☺ lunch Tue-Fri & Sun, dinner Mon-Sat) Oddly located above a parking garage, this spacious eatery looks better on the inside – its open kitchen, snazzy bar and elegant décor will impress your date. Tasty mains include snapper in rock salt, buffalo *bocconcini* and tuna *carpaccio*; go for the excessive with the half roast duck or 450g T-bone steak. An award-winning wine list only adds to the appeal.

Elio (Map p99; ☎ 9560 9129; 159 Norton St; mains $22-30; ☺ dinner) Personal attention and informed service are a hallmark at this no-nonsense Italian institution, and the food's not bad either. Try the homemade gnocchi with creamed pumpkin ($22), the portobello-mushroom risotto ($25) or the Spring Bay black mussels with dill ($27). In winter the rabbit-and-olive pie with roast parsnips and green peas ($26) will warm you right up.

Bar Italia (Map p99; ☎ 9560 9981; 169-171 Norton St; mains $10-17; ☺ breakfast, lunch & dinner) This popular family-style restaurant, café and gelateria offers all the pastas and sauces, along with salads, focaccia and plenty of veal. During the day sidewalk tables fill with appreciative diners, while at night seafood such as garlic prawns and fish and chips is a big draw. The famous gelato is a must-have accessory for any Norton St stroll.

Grind (Map p99; ☎ 9568 5535; 151 Norton St; mains $9-15; ☺ breakfast & lunch) Try the delicious pasta dishes or go for the focaccia sandwiches (how does roast beef, aïoli, *arugula* and tomato chutney sound? Or perhaps the lamb skewers with Greek salad rings truer?) Either way you'll be golden, and if you're on the balcony above you can even smoke afterwards. An espresso bar ices the cake.

North Shore

Aqua Dining (Map pp92-3; ☎ 9964 9998; cnr Paul & Northcliff Sts, Milsons Point; lunch mains $31-39, dinner mains $41-42; ☺ lunch Sun-Fri, dinner daily) Soma design accomplished the fit-out here, with its muted mushroom tones and clean lines. It never really competes with the view of the Opera House and Harbour Bridge, however, let alone the Olympic swimming pool with bathers underneath. Expect sterling service and supreme food (the hickory-smoked Yamba prawns are especially good) – all worth the hike out to the North Shore. Reservations are a good idea.

Ripples (Map pp92-3; ☎ 9929 7722; Olympic Dr, Milsons Point; mains $20-28; ☺ breakfast, lunch & dinner) Primely located with killer views of the Harbour Bridge and Opera House, this mostly outdoor eatery offers Mod Oz cuisine with European and Asian influences. The chef-recommended prawn noodle salad and tempura garfish (both $26) promise to be great choices. Look for it under the North Sydney Olympic Pool.

Manly

The ocean end of the Corso (Manly's pedestrian mall) is jam-packed with takeaway places and outside tables. Manly Wharf and South Steyne have plenty of airy eateries that catch the sea breeze and bustle on sunny days. Note that weekends see restaurant surcharges of 10%.

BarKING Frog (Map p98; ☎ 9977 6307; 48 North Steyne; lunch mains $12-16, dinner mains $19-29; ☺ breakfast & lunch daily, dinner Wed-Mon) Right off the beach, this attractive place does good lunchtime fare (think pasta and burgers), while the evenings are more Mod Oz – things like sumach-crusted lamb on fig couscous ($28) and grilled wild barramundi with braised leek and fennel ($29).

Alhambra (Map p98; ☎ 9976 2975; 54a West Esplanade; mains $19-25; ◷ lunch & dinner) We love coming to Manly because it means we can make sure Alhambra has maintained its high standards. The Spanish- and Moroccan-inspired dishes (including tapas) are excellent – try the grilled octopus, the lamb salad with couscous or the potato aïoli. Choose the covered sidewalk tables, or admire the Moorish décor inside.

Manly Fish Market (Map p98; ☎ 9976 3777; Shop 1, Wentworth St; mains $9-13; ◷ breakfast, lunch & dinner) Near Ocean Beach is this tiny fish shop with just two tables, though with the beach so near most folks grab the delicious (and generous) fish and chips bag and head to the water. If you want to be fancy, however, there are the prawn cutlets or mixed seafood boxes, or just swing next door to the upscale restaurant.

Blue Water Café (Map p98; ☎ 9976 2051; 28 South Steyne; mains $16-27; ◷ breakfast, lunch & dinner) The huge portions are a major draw at this bustling, popular beach café. The whopping lemon chicken burger ($14) or the crispy-skinned ocean trout with cherry tomatoes ($24) will really satisfy a post-surf hunger, although the boards on the wall will remind you to get back into the foam.

Beanrush (Map p98; ☎ 9977 2236; 7 Whistler St; coffees $2.50-4, mains $7-10; ◷ breakfast & lunch Mon-Sat) This small hole-in-the-wall café has great coffee made from wonderfully exotic organic beans (think Sumatran or Nicaraguan); the snacks are mighty fine, too. It's worth a visit if your engine needs revving, but keep in mind that it closes at 5.30pm.

DRINKING

There's no shortage of watering holes in Sydney. The Rocks and Kings Cross are popular magnets, but attractive, low-key places can be found in inner-city suburbs such as Surry Hills and Darlinghurst. The beaches have their share, obviously, and ocean breezes to boot.

City Centre & The Rocks

Establishment Bar (Map pp94-5; ☎ 9240 3000; 252 George St) Flashier than greased lightning is this upscale yuppie bar that brings white columns, marble bars, leather sofas and dressed-up crowds together. The patio garden out the back is a fine place to enjoy the Aussie and Thai tapas, and the music is downright slick.

Tank Stream Bar (Map pp94-5; ☎ 9240 3109; 1 Tank Stream Way) Tucked away behind the swanky Establishment and down a dark alley is this upscale and nicely lit bar. It's a great place to unwind after the hard working day. Flashes of steel and high stools add elegance – an interesting blend of original features and new flourishes, with plenty of ventilation.

Australian Hotel (Map pp94-5; ☎ 9247 2229; 100 Cumberland St, The Rocks) Grab a pleasant sidewalk table at this classic pub (also a hotel, see p119) and order a Scharer's lager on draught – it's got a cult following here in Sydney. Exotic gourmet pizzas (try the crocodile, emu and roo toppings) help fill the time between drinks.

Lord Nelson Brewery Hotel (Map pp94-5; ☎ 9251 4044; 19 Kent St, The Rocks) The Lord Nelson is an atmospheric old pub (also a hotel, see p119) that claims to be the 'oldest pub' in town (although others do, too!) and brews its own beers (Quayle Ale, Trafalgar Pale Ale, Victory Bitter, Three Sheets, Old Admiral and Nelsons Blood). Go ahead and try them all.

Hero of Waterloo (Map pp94-5; ☎ 9252 4553; 81 Lower Fort St, Millers Point) Enter into the wonderful stone interior, meet the boisterous locals and enjoy the nightly music (piano, folk, jazz or Irish tunes). Downstairs is an original dungeon, where drinkers would sleep off a heavy night before being shanghaied to the high seas.

Kings Cross Area & Woolloomooloo

Jimmy Lik's (Map p97; ☎ 8354 1400; 188 Victoria St, Kings Cross) Long benches and a long cocktail list (try the Japanese pear with lemon juice, sake and vodka) fit well into the highfalutin atmosphere. It's a great place to wait for a table at Jimmy Lik's next door (see p126).

Bourbon (Map p97; ☎ 9358 1144; 24 Darlinghurst Rd, Kings Cross; ◷ to 6am) This place is flash to the max, attracting young, hip and uppercrust crowds that come to lounge in booths, sit back on sofas or overlook the park and bustling sidewalk. Hip music, mod lighting and swanky service are included.

NEW SOUTH WALES

Empire Bar (Map p97; ☎ 9360 7531; cnr Darlinghurst Rd & Roslyn St, Kings Cross) This place is hard to miss, with airy open windows offering great views of one of the Cross's busiest intersections. Inside, marble details and a cosy, classy feel welcome you, as do the daily drink specials. Ry Cooder might serenade you from the speakers, but if you need more action there's pool upstairs.

World Bar (Map p97; ☎ 9357 7700; 24 Bayswater Rd, Kings Cross) Three floors of cool spaces attract the backpacking crowd (especially on Tuesday), and happy hour's $2.50 schooners keep them rockin'. There's an airy tropical terrace out the front, free pool until 6pm, and DJs nightly. On weekends a live Latin band performs.

Soho Bar & Lounge (Map p97; ☎ 9326 0333; 171 Victoria St, Kings Cross) In an old Art Deco pub, the revamped ground-floor bar has played host to numerous Sydneysiders' social lives. It's a dark, relaxed drinking lounge with smooth leather chairs and sofas, so you'll want to wear your sleekest. Happy hour sees two-for-one cocktails.

Old Fitzroy Hotel (Map p97; ☎ 9356 3848; 129 Dowling St, Woolloomooloo) Is it a pub? A theatre? A bistro? Actually it's all three. Grab a bowl of laksa, see the acting stars of tomorrow and wash it all down with a beer, for about $30. The little balcony is unbeatable on a hot, steamy night, though there are also airy sidewalk tables.

Spring Espresso (Map p97; ☎ 9331 0190; Macleay St & Challis Ave, Potts Point; mains $8-12; ⌚ 6.30am-6.30pm) For good coffee and good snacks try this small and bustling café. Sidewalk tables are hot spots during the morning rush, but the wait is worth it.

Café Hernandez (Map p97; ☎ 9331 2343; 60 Kings Cross Rd, Kings Cross; snacks $5-9; ⌚ 24hr) This tiny place has classic atmosphere and grinds exotic Kenyan, Honduran and Colombian beans into great coffee. Everyone from taxi drivers to arty students comes to sip, and at 3am you'll think you're in Valencia.

Darlinghurst

Darlo Bar (Map p97; ☎ 9331 3672; 306 Liverpool St, Darlinghurst) Darlo's great vibe attracts a boisterous crowd on weekends. Service is friendly, the furniture is retro mix and match, and creative lighting makes things bright and cosy. Add an interesting neighbourhood and you've got a winner.

Kinselas (Map pp94-5; ☎ 9331 3100; 383 Bourke St, Darlinghurst) Set in what used to be a funeral parlour, this darkish place has come back from the dead more times than we can recall. The downstairs part is poker machines and bad carpet, but the bar upstairs is stylish, modern and incredibly popular with the bright young things. The cocktails are very good too. On hot summer nights, hanging on the minuscule balcony is *de rigueur*.

Green Park Hotel (Map p97; ☎ 9380 5311; 360 Victoria St, Darlinghurst) Mostly locals come to the good old Green Park, with its tiled walls and bar; it's also a popular hang-out for pool shooters (Wednesday night means comps). Loungey seating, hip-hop music, good draught beer and sidewalk tables are cool too.

Café Coluzzi (Map p97; ☎ 9380 5420; 322 Victoria St, Darlinghurst; snacks $5-7.50; ⌚ 5am-7pm) The traditional Italian coffee attracts the city's java-addicted; early on weekend mornings cyclists pedal in for their fix. Coluzzi has achieved legendary status by making coffee for over 50 years, and it claims to be the heart and soul of Sydney's coffee world.

Surry Hills & Paddington

Cricketers Arms (Map pp94-5; ☎ 9331 3301; 106 Fitzroy St) A cosy vibe fills this friendly pub with friendly locals (many gathered at the wraparound bar) and those appreciative of good DJ skills (displayed from Thursday to Sunday). There's also tapas, a small beer garden patio with wooden benches, and a nice upstairs area.

Hollywood Hotel (Map pp94-5; ☎ 9281 2765; 2 Foster St) This Art Deco pub looks nondescript from the outside, but its dark intimate inside reveals a somewhat Bohemian crowd happy to start the weekend with gusto. Eclectic live music is played at night from Monday to Wednesday.

Palace Hotel (Map pp94-5; ☎ 9361 3611; 122 Flinders St) On the junction with South Dowling St, this is a handy, low-key pub good for socialising with a mixed crowd. There is a nice Art Deco ambience, good beer (jugs go for $8) and cheap munchies. Upstairs are the cocktail lounge and pool tables.

Lord Dudley Hotel (Map pp92-3; ☎ 9327 5399; 236 Jersey Rd, Woollahra) The Lord Dudley is as close as Sydney gets to an English pub atmosphere, with dark wood details and good

AUTHOR'S CHOICE

Paddington Inn Hotel (Map pp92-3; ☎ 9380 5913; 338 Oxford St) Large, popular and pretty, this pub doesn't look like much from the outside – but it's surprisingly swanky on the inside. The airy window seats are gold, especially on weekend afternoons when the nearby Paddington market is in full swing. The food is fancy and the cocktails elaborate, while funky music helps it all go down easily. And if you need a change of pace, Oxford St's more rowdy (read: gay) bars are a stone's throw west.

beer in pint glasses. It gets packed with a noisy crowd, including Rugby Union fans (there's plenty of sport on the TV screens), and there's good food served downstairs. Needless to say, it draws a good share of Sydney's English expats.

Mars Lounge (Map pp94-5; ☎ 9267 6440; 16 Wentworth Ave) This futuristic-looking drinking hole doesn't quite fit its location, but if you feel like sitting at a modern booth with red-tinged atmosphere and sometimes deafening music, here you are.

Flinders Hotel (Map pp94-5; ☎ 9356 3622; 63-65 Flinders St) Risen from its ex-gay-enclave ashes, this remodelled drinking hole has prettified itself into a swanky new joint that welcomes a mixed crowd. Sophisticated furniture, two plasma TVs and weekend DJs comfort and entertain, and there's also plenty of fancy cocktails and Thai food. Happy hour runs from 3pm to 7pm on weekdays and offers $3 draught beers.

Watsons Bay

Doyles Palace Hotel (Map pp92-3; ☎ 9337 5444; 10 Mar-ine Pde) Surrounded by pricey seafood restaurants and home to a lovely boutique hotel (see p121), you'll be pleased to know that you can have the Doyles experience simply by buying a jug of beer, sitting down in the beer garden and enjoying the superlative view of Sydney Harbour. This is a time-honoured tradition, but avoid weekends, when the place is packed to the gills.

Bondi & Coogee

Beach Road Hotel (Map pp98; ☎ 9130 7247; 71 Beach Rd, Bondi) Reputedly *the* pub in Bondi, though it's well inland. Still, this huge but beautiful place

offers snazzy atmosphere, a large and pleasant beer garden, and a swanky cocktail bar upstairs with live music. Wednesday nights are especially popular with backpackers.

Bondi Icebergs Bar (Map pp98; ☎ 9365 9000; 1 Notts Ave, Bondi) You can't get more modern and trendy than this classy spot. The hanging chairs, colourful sofas and elegant cocktails are just fine, but the view's the killer. Make sure your bank account's up to snuff. And if you really want to lash out, check out the much-raved about Bondi Icebergs restaurant (see p128).

Bondi Icebergs Winter Swimming Club (Map pp98; ☎ 9130 3120; 1 Notts Ave, Bondi) Located just below the Bondi Icebergs Bar, this is a more affordable and laid-back place with practically the same views. Order café food (pizzas and burgers) and $3.50 beers. Bring ID, since if you're not a member you need to prove you live at least 5km away.

Ravesi's (Map pp98; ☎ 9365 4422; cnr Campbell Pde & Hall St, Bondi) Most likely Bondi's fanciest drinking spot, with glass walls that take in ocean views and the street crowd. Low black leather sofas and high chrome stools mean cocktails won't come cheap, but they guarantee a hip, good-looking crowd. The complex also includes a hotel (see p121).

Coogee Bay Hotel (Map pp99; ☎ 9665 0000; cnr Arden St & Coogee Bay Rd, Coogee) Four bars live on the premises here, so think about whether you want breezy (water view), casual (beer patio), classy (balcony) or sporty (TV screens). Whichever you choose, you'll be drinking with the popular crowd in the heart of Coogee.

Balmain & Glebe

London Hotel (Map pp92-3; ☎ 9555 1377; 234 Darling St, Balmain) Snag an outside counter stool overlooking the street at this gorgeous pub, located in a beautifully restored historical building. It's a good place for a cleansing ale (12 beers are on tap, including Cooper's, Stella and Redback), especially after a trawl through the nearby Saturday market. Sundays are good locals days, when live music plays.

Friend in Hand Hotel (Map pp99; ☎ 9660 2326; 58 Cowper St, Glebe) It's hardly yuppie and not very relaxing (what with all that betting going on), but you can enjoy the poetry slams on Tuesday, hermit-crab races on Wednesday or comedy gigs on Thursday. Or just grab

NEW SOUTH WALES

an eyeful of the bric-a-brac around you, and say hi to the cockatoo.

Manly

Ceruti's (Map p98; ☎ 9977 7600; 15 Sydney Rd) Weekends rock here, when the restaurant becomes part of the bar party and DJs fire up the youthful crowd with spinning house beats. Weekdays offer happy hour from 4pm to 7pm – a good time to try the speciality cocktail, called 42 below, which is made with New Zealand vodka.

New Brighton Hotel (Map p98; ☎ 9977 3305; 71 The Corso) This bar/nightclub's best feature is probably the upstairs wraparound balcony, offering primo views of the Corso and, in the distance, the rolling sea. Head inside and spin to DJs Captain Kirk and White Brothers, or play on the purple-felted pool tables. For quieter conversation stick to the crimson-hued bar downstairs; the elegant leather sofas are nice, and there's live music on Friday.

Steyne Hotel (Map p98; ☎ 9977 4977; The Corso) Nine bars on two levels – this place has a spot for everyone. Sport fanatics can glue themselves to the big-screen TVs in Harry's sports bar, while outdoor enthusiasts can check out the beer garden. Smoke-free Kelly's bar overlooks the beach, while Redheads bar offers cigar aficionados a place to light up. There's more, but you get the picture.

ENTERTAINMENT

The *Sydney Morning Herald* 'Metro' liftout (published on Friday) and the *Daily Telegraph* 'SLM' liftout (published on Wednesday) list events in town for the coming week. Free newspapers such as *Drum Media*, *Revolver* and *3D World* also have useful listings and are available from bookshops, bars, cafés and record stores.

Ticketek (Map pp94-5; ☎ 9266 4800; www.ticketek .com.au; 195 Elizabeth St; ⊙ 9am-7pm Mon-Fri, 9am-4pm Sat) The city's main booking agency for theatre, concerts, sport and other events. Book by phone, over the Internet or through agencies around town.

Halftix (Map pp94-5; ☎ 1300 668 413; 91 York St; ⊙ 9.30am-5.30pm Tue-Fri, 10am-3.30pm Sat) Sells discount tickets, though choices are limited. Phone and Internet bookings are available.

Classical Music & Theatre

Sydney Opera House (Map pp94-5; ☎ 9250 7777; www.sydneyoperahouse.com; Bennelong Point, East Circu-

lar Quay) The heart of performance in Australia, with the Concert Hall and Opera Hall holding about 2600 and 1500 people respectively. Witness theatre, comedy, music, dance and ballet, but it's opera that really shines. Box-office hours are from 9am to 8.30pm Monday to Saturday and two hours before a Sunday performance. And don't be late for your performance or you'll be shut out until intermission!

City Recital Hall (Map pp94-5; ☎ 8256 2222; www .cityrecitalhall.com; 2 Angel Pl) This is a purpose-built 1200-seat venue with wonderful acoustics that hosts live music performances. Its architecture is based on the 19th-century European blueprint, and it's an excellent place to hear the Australian Brandenburg Orchestra, among others.

Eugene Goossens Hall (Map pp94-5; ☎ 8333 1500; 700 Harris St, Ultimo) The ABC's intimate Eugene Goossens Hall often has good classical recitals that are broadcast live. It seats up to 500 on a good day, and is not the place to come with a cough. It's located in the ABC Ultimo Centre.

Sydney Conservatorium of Music (Map pp94-5; ☎ 9351 1222; www.usyd.edu.au/su/conmusic; Macquarie St) This historic music venue showcases the talents of its students and their teachers. Choral, jazz, operatic and chamber concerts are held here from March to September, along with a range of free lunch-time recitals Wednesdays at 1pm (March to November).

Sydney Theatre (Map pp94-5; ☎ 9250 1999; www .sydneytheatre.org.au; 22 Hickson Rd, Walsh Bay) This stylish venue, opened January 2004, seats 850 and is managed by Australia's largest theatre company, the Sydney Theatre Company. It works with both national and international companies to bring theatregoers the best in ambitious and artistic drama and dance.

Wharf Theatre (Map pp94-5; ☎ 9250 1700; www .sydneytheatre.com.au; Pier 4, Hickson Rd, Walsh Bay) Part of the Sydney Theatre; also home to the **Australian Theatre for Young People** (ATYP; ☎ 9251 3900), **Bangarra Dance Theatre** (☎ 9251 5333), the **Sydney Philharmonia Choirs** (☎ 9251 2024) and the **Sydney Dance Company** (☎ 9221 4811).

Belvoir Street Theatre (Map pp92-3; ☎ 9699 3444; www.belvoir.com.au; 25 Belvoir St, Surry Hills; tickets adult $27-45, concession $21-30) Located in a residential neighbourhood and sporting a cute café, this intimate venue hosts experimental Australian theatre and twists on original productions with big names such as Geoffrey Rush and Cate Blanchett.

Capitol Theatre (Map pp94-5; ☎ 9320 5000; www
.capitoltheatre.com.au; 13 Campbell St, Haymarket) This
large theatre – originally a marketplace –
has been lavishly restored after being saved
from demolition and is now is home to big-
name concerts (Sting, Natalie Merchant)
and long-running musicals (Chicago, the
Musical; The Lion King).

Lyric Theatre (Map p99; ☎ 9657 9657; Star City,
Darling Harbour) The large Lyric Theatre stages
flashy musical extravaganzas and has good
acoustics. It's located in the Star City Casino complex, so if you get bored with the
musical you could walk out and gamble
your money away nearby.

Sydney Comedy Store (Map pp92-3; ☎ 9357 1419;
www.comedystore.com.au; Fox Studios, Driver Ave, Moore
Park; tickets $15-30) In its purpose-built home
in the Fox Studios, this comedy venue has
stand-up and open-mike nights; international comedians have included Arge
Barker, Doug Stanhope and Jimeoin.

Live Music

Sydney doesn't have as dynamic a music
scene as Melbourne, but you can still find
live music most nights of the week. For detailed listings of venues and acts, see the
listings in the papers mentioned in the Entertainment introduction.

JAZZ & BLUES

Sydney has a healthy and innovative jazz
and blues circuit, with quite a few venues
worth a swing.

Wine Banq (Map pp94-5; ☎ 9222 1919; 53 Martin Pl)
Hands down, this is the sexiest place to hear
live jazz in Sydney. The whole place looks
like it was carved out of an architect's bunker dreams, and a brilliant wine list only
adds to the appeal. Past performers here
include Wynton Marsalis, Barbara Morrison and Harry Connick Jr.

Basement (Map pp94-5; ☎ 9251 2797; www.global
network.com.au; 29 Reiby Pl, Circular Quay; cover charge
$12-50) This subterranean place has decent
food, good music (plus the odd spoken-word
and comedy gig) and some big international
names occasionally dropping by – making
cover charges skyrocket. Exotic notes come
with the monthly Indian and African gigs.

Strawberry Hills Hotel (Map pp92-3; ☎ 9698 2997;
453 Elizabeth St, Surry Hills) This refurbished pub

features live jazz in the forms of the Eclipse
Alley Five from 4pm to 7pm on Saturday, and
Bill Dudley & the New Orleanians from 5pm
to 8pm on Sunday. Plus there's happy hour
from 2pm to 6pm, so throw down some $3
schooners before the show.

Empire Hotel (Map p99; ☎ 9557 1701; www.empire
live.com.au; 103a Parramatta Rd, Annandale; cover charge
Fri & Sat $5-15) Blues (along with ska, pop and
rockabilly) buffs should investigate the Empire for live acts – the venue is aided by
a very good sound system. It's trying to
diversify, with Tuesday nights seeing free
swing-dance lessons.

ROCK & POP

There's sometimes no charge to see young
local bands, while between $5 and $20 is
charged for well-known local acts, and at
least $60 for international performers.

Enmore Theatre (Map p99; ☎ 9550 3666; www
.enmoretheatre.com.au; 130 Enmore Rd, Newtown; tickets
$15-120) The Enmore hosts major Australian
and overseas acts such as Kiss, Oasis, Alicia
Keys and David Byrne, plus comedy and
jazz. The Rolling Stones played a brilliant
'intimate' concert here in early 2003.

Metro Theatre (Map pp94-5; ☎ 9287 2000; www
.metrotheatre.com.au; 624 George St; tickets $10-75) This
is easily the best place to see well-chosen
local and alternative international acts (plus
the odd DJ) in well-ventilated comfort.
Other offerings include comedy, cabaret,
music and theatre.

Hopetoun Hotel (Map pp94-5; ☎ 9361 5257; 416
Bourke St, Surry Hills; cover charge $6-12) This great
little venue offers flexibility for artists and
patrons alike, and features an array of modern musical styles from folk to rap to DJs.
Both local bands and the occasional international group plays; think Spiderbait, Tex
Perkins and You Am I.

Sandringham Hotel (Map p99; ☎ 9557 1254; 387
King St, Newtown) You can still pay a minimal
amount of money ($5 to $10) at this intimate, 150-seater venue to get your earwax
blasted out while you're munching on
tapas. Acts play mostly on weekends (along
with pool competitions), and you can expect local rock and pop bands; occasional
names such as Diesel and Jon Stevens will
show up, however.

Annandale Hotel (Map p99; ☎ 9550 1078; www
.annandalehotel.com; 17 Parramatta Rd, Annandale) This
venue plays host to a sometimes eclectic

GAY & LESBIAN SYDNEY

In Sydney one could be forgiven for thinking that gay is the new straight. Gay and lesbian culture forms a vocal, vital, well-organised and colourful part of Sydney's social fabric. In 2002 Sydney played host to the best-dressed Olympics ever – the Gay Games.

The colourful Sydney Gay & Lesbian Mardi Gras is Australia's biggest annual tourist event, and the joyful-hedonism-meets-political-protest Oxford St parade is watched by over half a million people. The Sleaze Ball (a Mardi Gras fundraiser) takes place in October, with leather taking the place of Lycra. The parties for both events are held in Moore Park, and tickets are restricted to Mardi Gras members. Gay and lesbian international visitors wishing to attend the parties should contact the **Mardi Gras office** (☎ 02-9568 8600; www.mardigras.org.au) well in advance – tickets sell fast.

The Taylor Sq region of Oxford St is the hub of gay life in Sydney, although there are pockets in suburbs such as Paddington, Newtown, Alexandria and Leichhardt. Gay beach life is focused on Lady Bay (nude) and Tamarama (also known as Glamarama). You may also want to check out Red Leaf Pool on New South Head Rd, just past Double Bay, or Andrew 'Boy' Charlton pool (p112). For men, tans and heavy pecs are a 'classic' look. The scene for women is a bit more inclusive.

However, there's still a homophobic side to some 'true blue' Aussies, and violence against homosexuals isn't unheard of, particularly during school holidays. For the record, in NSW the age of consent for homosexual sex is 16 for both men and women.

The free gay press includes the paper *Sydney Star Observer* and the website **Lesbians on the Loose** (www.lotl.com). These can be found in shops and cafés in the inner east and west. They all have excellent listings of gay and lesbian organisations, services and events. **Gay & Lesbian Tourism Australia** (GALTA; www.galta.com.au) can provide a wealth of information about gay and lesbian travel in Oz.

If you're keen to take part in Sydney's gay-nightlife scene you can find plenty of listings in the local gay press. The following represent a mix of old favourites and newer club nights that cover both low-key and out-there bases.

ARQ (Map pp94–5; ☎ 02-9380 8700; 16 Flinders St, Darlinghurst) Downstairs is cool and loungey, with amoeba-shaped sofas and pool tables. Upstairs you'll find the state-of-the-art light-and-sound system, along with drag shows and good DJs. This large club has it all, and is a popular place to recover on Sunday. It's open Thursday to Sunday.

assortment of local and international alternative music acts. Loud rock, heavy metal, dance and acoustic gigs jam nightly from Tuesday to Sunday (tickets $8 to $30), while cult movies (!) play Monday nights.

Hordern Pavilion (Map pp92–3; ☎ 9383 4063; www.playbillvenues.com; Fox Studios, Driver Ave, Moore Park) Its heyday is over, but the 80-year-old Hordern (which seats just over 4200 people) still hosts hot international acts such as Santana and the Chemical Brothers.

Cat & Fiddle (Map pp92–3; ☎ 9810 7931; 456 Darling St, Balmain) Nightly live music runs from 8pm, with local folk and acoustic bands providing the energy at this smoky venue. Tall stools and tables seat the crowd, happy hour runs from 4pm to 6pm on weekdays (from 10am to 4pm on Saturdays), and there's even a small theatre on the premises (about 35 seats).

Sydney Entertainment Centre (Map pp94–5; ☎ 13 61 00; Harbour St, Haymarket) This big concrete box has hosted superstars like Mark Knopfler, Bryan Adams, REM, Elton John and Cher. It seats just over 12,000 and, despite being purpose-built for these bigger gigs, the sound quality is only adequate at best. Sporting events play here too.

Cinemas

Generally, cinema tickets cost between $12 and $15 for adults (less for concession). Tuesday is often discount day, with tickets going for about $11. Chains such as Hoyts, Village and Greater Union also have numerous suburban theatres. Movie listings can be found in Sydney's daily newspapers.

Chauvel Cinema (Map pp92–3; ☎ 9361 5398; www .chauvelcinema.com.au; cnr Oxford St & Oatley Rd, Paddington) This cinema, with its association with the

Colombian (Map pp94–5; ☎ 02-9360 2151; cnr Oxford & Crown Sts, Darlinghurst) Insanely popular, this swanky drinking spot offers up an intoxicating mix of cute guys, thumping music and heady drinks. The décor is to die for, and the street-facing counter makes it oh-so-easy to check out the boisterous street scene. Women and handlebar moustaches welcome.

Exchange Hotel (Map pp94–5; ☎ 02-9331 1936; 34 Oxford St, Darlinghurst) You get four in one at this long-running temple. Choose from the Palace Lounge, a small and hip bar; Spectrum, a nightclub with DJs and live bands; and Q Bar and Phoenix, both gay magnets.

Imperial Hotel (Map p99; ☎ 02-9519 9899; 35 Erskineville Rd, Erskineville) The film *Priscilla – Queen of the Desert* was inspired by the world-class drag shows that run Thursday to Saturday here. There's also bingo on Tuesday and free pool Monday and Sunday, so it's got most of the week covered.

Midnight Shift (Map pp94–5; ☎ 02-9360 4319; 85 Oxford St, Darlinghurst) The ground floor is quite pubby despite the disco balls, but upstairs it's a licence to booze and cruise with less conversation. We like the fact that you can find a range of men here – it's especially popular with Asians and older gay dolls, and 'retro' nights add interest.

Newtown Hotel (Map p99; ☎ 02-9517 1728; 174 King St, Newtown) In Sydney's other gay enclave, the Newtown does a roaring trade with gay folk looking for Tuesday pool competitions, Wednesday-night trivia and DJs on Thursday. Good drag acts liven up the mostly gay crowd on weekends.

Oxford Hotel (Map pp94–5; ☎ 02-9331 3871; 134 Oxford St, Darlinghurst) This bustling corner locale can't be beat, especially if you land a patio table. Downstairs it's a hardcore gay crowd, while on the 2nd floor Gilligan's cocktail bar attracts a fancy mixed bunch. The top floor is open weekends only, and definitely worth a stop.

Stonewall (Map pp94–5; ☎ 02-9360 1963; 175 Oxford St, Darlinghurst) The nightly shows and good vibe make this friendly spot a popular one, and the nice airy location also helps. In recent times the ceiling has collapsed here, causing one DJ to proclaim 'I finally brought the house down!'

Taxi Club (Map pp94–5; ☎ 02-9331 4256; 40-42 Flinders St, Darlinghurst) Bring ID to present to door 'reception' – this is a club of sorts, but all are welcome. Upstairs are small but comfy areas, with too many pokies for our taste. Happy hour sees $2 draught beers and $3.50 spirits, and there's bingo on Monday nights. Taxi Club is popular with cross-dressers and gets boisterous after midnight.

Australian Film Institute (AFI), runs quality releases new and old (with a liberal dose of quirky and out-there), and has themed festivals (German, Israeli etc). Bargain days are Monday and Tuesday (tickets $9.50).

Verona Cinema (Map pp94–5; ☎ 9360 6296; www.palace.net.au; Level 1, 17 Oxford St, Paddington) This cinema also has a café and bar, so you can discuss the good (invariably nonmainstream) flick you've just seen. Mondays are bargain days, with $9.50 tickets.

Academy Twin Cinema (Map pp94–5; ☎ 9331 3457; 3a Oxford St, Paddington) This smaller cinema was fitted out in the 1970s; it has art-house and independent offerings. Mondays are bargain days, with $9.50 tickets.

Imax (Map pp94–5; ☎ 9281 3300; Southern Promenade, Cockle Bay; adult/child $17/12) This is the world's biggest movie screen. If you're into being wowed by massive images, some in 3-D, then Imax is for you. Movies shown tend to be either thrill-fests or nature docos.

Dendy (Map pp94–5; ☎ 9247 3800; www.dendy.com.au; Shop 9, 2 Circular Quay East; general/concession $14/10.50) This lavish cinema is within spitting distance of the Opera House. There's a great bar for ticket holders only. On Monday movies cost $9 for everyone.

Greater Union Hoyts Cinemas (Map pp94–5; ☎ 9273 7431; 505 George St) This monster-sized movie palace with 17 screens and plenty of eateries provides an orgy of popcorn-fuelled mainstream entertainment.

Govinda's (Map p97; ☎ 9380 5155; www.govindas.com.au; 112 Darlinghurst Rd, Darlinghurst; dinner & movie $20, movie only $11; ⏱ 6-10.30pm) Govinda's is a Hare Krishna–run, all-you-can-gobble vegetarian smorgasbord; the cinema here is floor cushions with incense and yoga in the atmosphere.

Nightclubs

Sydney's dance club scene is alive and kicking, with local and international DJs making thousands of people swing and grind their hips every weekend. Some places have strict door policies and a lot of attitude, while others are more casual and are great places to catch up with friends – or meet new ones.

Slip Inn (Map pp94-5; ☎ 8295 9999; 111 Sussex St; cover charge $15-18) Warrenlike and sporting three different lounges (and themes), this place struggles with a multiple-personality disorder – but that doesn't stop the cool kids from enjoying the funky house and hip-hop breaks on the turntable. The actual nightclub is called Chinese Laundry; there are several bars with separate names also.

Q Bar (Map pp94-5; ☎ 9360 1375; Level 3, 44 Oxford St, Darlinghurst; Fri & Sat cover charge $15-20) With more reincarnations than Cleopatra over the years, this funky and eclectic joint (located in the Exchange Hotel; see the boxed text, p136) has DJs playing nightly. Weekends mean house and dance music, but if you're not into that there's always the pool table and cocktail bar.

Home (Map pp94-5; ☎ 9266 0600; Cockle Bay Wharf, 101 Wheat Rd, Darling Harbour; cover charge $20-25) With gorgeous views of Darling Harbour, this huge club offers stupendous sound systems and special nights like Together on Saturday (funky house music) or Queer Nation on the Sunday of three-day weekends. Also check out the Mobo Bar, in a separate section.

Yu (Map p97; ☎ 9326 0333; 171 Victoria St, Potts Point; cover charge $10-20) Yu wants you to get down to the best of house and funk, played by some of Sydney's most venerable DJs. We love After Ours, which solves the dilemma of what to do on a Sunday night. The club itself is slick-looking and attached to a fancy Soho bar.

GoodBar (Map pp94-5; ☎ 9360 6759; 11a Oxford St, Paddington; cover charge $10) Two-level and trendy, this popular, hanky-sized club is still attracting crowds of pretty people. It boasts R&B, hip-hop and celebrity spotting. The best nights are Wednesday and Saturday.

Plan B (Map p97; ☎ 9358 1144; 24 Darlinghurst Rd, Kings Cross; cover charge $5-20) So hot and new the bouncers are working overtime, this classy disco sports a glowing pink bar, a lounge area for wallflowers and of course a hoppin' dance floor. Wear your best, and get ready for slammin' house and funk music.

Sport

Spend a day or two in Sydney and you'll notice a little something about its inhabitants. They're shiny, they're hard, they're psyched – and they get (and stay) this way through exercise. Sydney's sunshine, parks, beaches and love of showing off all conspire to make this a delightful city for staying fit or watching sport. If you like to watch, have a credit card handy and book tickets to a variety of sporting events, big and small. If you're the one being sporty, it can be as simple as putting your feet in some jogging shoes or doing some laps at a beachside pool, or as tricky as getting a golf game on a sunny weekend.

The Sydney Cricket Ground (SCG; Map pp92–3), Moore Park, is the venue for sparsely attended state cricket matches, well-attended five-day Test matches and sell-out one-day World Series cricket matches. Moore Park also has a golf course.

Sydney is one of rugby league's world capitals. **National Rugby League** (NRL; www.nrl.com.au) games are played from March to October at a variety of venues, including Aussie Stadium in Moore Park and Telstra Stadium in Homebush Bay.

The (sometimes) high-flying Sydney Swans, NSW's contribution to the **Australian Football League** (AFL; www.afl.com.au) play matches between March and September. Their home ground is the SCG.

The city's oldest and largest 18-footer yacht club is the **Sydney Flying Squadron** (Map pp92-3; ☎ 9955 8350; 76 McDougall St, Milsons Point). You can catch a ferry from there to watch skiff racing from 2pm to 4pm on Saturday between September and April (adult/child $15/5.50). Ferries are also provided for occasional special shows.

SHOPPING

The hub of city shopping is Pitt St Mall, with department stores, shopping centres and shops all within easy reach. It's much more relaxing to shop for fashion on popular inner-city strips such as Oxford St, Paddington; for furnishings and antiques on Queen St, Woollahra; for CDs around Crown St, Surry Hills; for outdoor gear near the corner of Kent and Bathurst Sts in town; or at Sydney's markets. The Rocks is where you'll generally find what's known as 'Australiana' (ie souvenirs), though it won't be cheap. Try Paddy's Markets in Chinatown instead.

Late-night shopping is on Thursday night, when many stores stay open until 9pm.

Aboriginal Art

Aboriginal & Tribal Art Centre (Map pp94-5; ☎ 9247 9625; 117 George St, The Rocks) Opposite the MCA, this gallery has a small but good-quality range of crafts for sale; look for bark paintings, didgeridoos, boomerangs and weavings. Free exhibitions are often on display in the open space. Overseas packing and shipping are available.

Gavala Aboriginal Art (Map pp94-5; ☎ 9212 7232; Ground Level, Harbourside Shopping Centre, Darling Harbour) Proudly proclaiming itself Sydney's only Aboriginal-owned retail centre and gallery, this is a great place to source everything from a T-shirt to a bark painting, a boomerang to an Aboriginal flag.

Walkabout Gallery (Map p99; ☎ 9550 9964; www.walkaboutart.com; 70 Norton St, Leichhardt) This friendly gallery is part of the World Vision Indigenous Programs, which means you can be sure that Aboriginal artists are getting properly paid. It offers mostly wall art, along with some jewellery, ceramics and small wood statues.

Australiana

RM Williams (Map pp94-5; ☎ 9262 2228; 389 George St) This is a long-established manufacturer and distributor of Aussie outdoor gear, such as drought-breakers (oilskin riding coats) and moleskin trousers. And of course it offers the classic elastic-sided riding boot beloved by almost every Australian.

Australian Wine Centre (Map pp94-5; ☎ 9247 2755; Goldfields House, 1 Alfred St, Circular Quay) Downstairs in this building, behind Circular Quay, the centre has wines from every Australian wine-growing region. It will package and send wine overseas, and of course you're welcome to sample a few drops.

Strand Hatters (Map pp94-5; ☎ 9231 6884; Shop 8, Strand Arcade, Pitt St Mall) Wearing a hat to protect oneself from the sun is a good idea in this country – wearing an authentic rabbit-felt Akubra from this shop will ensure that you'll look like you came straight from the outback. Plenty of other high-quality selections are ready to top your head.

Gowings (Map pp94-5; ☎ 9264 6321; cnr George & Market Sts) One of the most eccentric department stores you'll ever set foot in, offering five floors of dress shirts, outdoor gear, gag

gifts (vibrating soap anyone?), Speedos, rubber chickens, luggage, jester hats and flip-flops. You're bound to find something you like, if you've got the time.

Flame Opals (Map pp94-5; ☎ 9247 3446; 119 George St, The Rocks) If you've been seduced by the colourful opal, this is a good place to pick one up; it's been family-operated for over 30 years. Prices range from about $20 to 'if you have to ask, you can't afford it', and the staff are more than happy to help with any questions.

Clothing

Scanlan & Theodore (Map pp92-3; ☎ 9361 6722; 433 Oxford St, Paddington) Regularly topping the lists of favourite designers, Scanlan & Theodore excel in beautiful pieces for the evening or the office. Plenty of feminine patterns and colours such as pinks and reds complement fabrics you just can't help but fondle.

Calibre (Map pp92-3; ☎ 9380 5993; 416 Oxford St, Paddington) Smart suiting and hip weekend-wardrobe supplies for men are the specialty here. Even if you're a complete fashion misfit, the staff – complete with slicked-back hair – and full-length mirrors will make you look good. There are other locations as well.

Country Road (Map pp94-5; ☎ 9394 1818; 142 Pitt St) Now armed with hip designer Sophie Holt, Country Road's new designs sport a welcome youthful element alongside those old traditional lines. All ages and both sexes are catered to; plenty of CR branches dot the city.

Markets

Paddington Market (Map pp92-3; ☎ 9331 2923; www .paddingtonmarket.com.au; St John's Church, 395 Oxford St, Paddington; ☽ Sat) Very popular, upscale and pricey, with vintage clothing, creative crafts, beautiful jewellery, tasty food and holistic treatments. Don't even think about finding a place to park – this is one for public transport.

Paddy's Markets (Map pp94-5; ☎ 1300 361 589; www.paddysmarkets.com.au; cnr Hay & Thomas Sts, Haymarket; ☽ 9am-5pm Thu-Sun) Smack in the heart of Chinatown, this Sydney institution is a great place to find cheap souvenirs, clothing, cheap electronics, sheepskin rugs and plenty of knick-knacks. There's also a good selection of fresh fruit, vegetables and seafood available.

Rocks Market (Map pp94–5; ☎ 9240 8717; www
.therocksmarket.com; George St, The Rocks; ☯ Sat & Sun)
Held at the top end of George St, this touristy
market offers wonderful crafts made of metal,
ceramic, stone, leather and glass. Souvenirs
(including roo balls) are also available.

Balmain Markets (Map pp92–3; ☎ 0418 765 736; St
Andrew's Church, 223 Darling St, Balmain; ☯ Sat) This
small but good local market offers crafty
stuff like handmade candles and soaps,
jewellery, exotic textiles, artwork and used
clothing and books.

Glebe Markets (Map p99; Glebe Public School, cnr
Glebe Point Rd & Derby Pl; ☯ Sat) A large, popular
and slightly grungy market selling the usual
books, vintage clothing, leather goods,
hippy crafts and curios.

Bondi Beach Markets (Map p98; ☎ 9315 8988;
Bondi Beach Public School, cnr Campbell Pde & Warners Ave,
Bondi; ☯ Sun) At the northern end of Camp-
bell Pde, this small market is good for hip
clothing, exotic imports, jewellery, furniture, knick-knacks and people watching.

Shopping Centres & Department Stores
Queen Victoria Building (QVB; Map pp94–5; ☎ 9265
6864; 455 George St) The magnificent QVB takes
up a whole block with its late-19th-century
Romanesque grandeur, and boasts nearly
200 shops on five levels. It's the city's most
beautiful shopping centre, and you'll find
plenty of fashion outlets, along with stores
selling Australian knick-knacks. The lower
level, which connects to Town Hall Station,
has food bars, shoe-repair shops, newsagents
and dry-cleaners. Tours are available.

Skygarden Arcade (Map pp94–5; ☎ 9231 1811; 77
Castlereagh St) This large, modern complex has
a range of fashion shops and some food
outlets, plus a monster-sized branch of Borders for books and music.

Strand Arcade (Map pp94–5; ☎ 9232 4199; Pitt
St Mall) Several leading Australian fashion
designers and craftspeople have shops at
the narrow, thoughtfully restored Strand
Arcade. Designer boutiques nestle amid
old-fashioned cafés, shoe-repair shops and
hairdressing salons.

Market City (Map pp94–5; ☎ 9212 1388; Quay St,
Haymarket) This mammoth shopping centre
houses Paddy's Markets, a slew of restaurants, cinemas and heaps of retail outlets
(mostly the end-of-season variety).

Centrepoint (Map pp94–5; ☎ 9231 9300; cnr Pitt &
Market Sts) This shopping centre, situated beside the Imperial Arcade and beneath Sydney Tower, has four storeys of fashion and
jewellery shops. There are connecting above-
ground walkways to David Jones and Myer.

David Jones (Map pp94–5; ☎ 9266 5544; cnr Elizabeth
& Market Sts) Bright and sparkling, this is considered the city's premier department store.
It's a good place to look for top-quality goods;
there are two locations on Market St.

Myer (Map pp94–5; ☎ 9238 9000; 436 George St) At
seven storeys, Myer (formerly Grace Bros)
is one of Sydney's largest stores and a prime
venue for after-Christmas sales. You'll find
everything from cafés to cosmetics and
whatever's in between.

GETTING THERE & AWAY
Air
Sydney's Kingsford Smith Airport is Australia's busiest and has flights from all over
the country and the world. **Qantas** (☎ 13 13
13; www.qantas.com.au), **Jetstar** (☎ 13 15 38; www
.jetstar.com.au) and **Virgin** (☎ 13 67 89; www.virgin
blue.com.au) offer frequent flights to and
from other Australian cities. At the time of
writing, low-end, one-way fares started at:
Melbourne ($70), Brisbane ($80), Canberra
($95), Adelaide ($120), Perth ($220), Ho-
bart ($100), Alice Springs ($190), Darwin
($220) and Cairns ($160). (One-off specials
can be cheaper than the prices given here.)

For further details on air travel within
Australia, see p88. For air travel to/from
Australia, see p1035.

Boat
Heading to Tasmania? Check out the huge
freighter **TT Lines** (☎ 1800 634 906; www.spiritof
tasmania.com.au); fares vary depending on season but run about $180 to $320 one way;
check the website for more.

Bus & Train
All long-distance train and bus services operate from **Central Station** (Map pp94–5; ☎ 9379
1777); book tickets in advance. The **Sydney
Coach Terminal** (☎ 9281 9366) is also here.

CountryLink (Map pp94–5; ☎ 9379 9606, after hr
☎ 13 22 32; www.countrylink.info; Platform 1, Central Station; ☯ 6.15am-8.45pm), the government's network of trains and buses, offers discounts
of up to 50% with two weeks' notice. It
also has an office at **Circular Quay** (Map pp94–5;
☎ 9224 3400; ☯ 9.45am-5.30pm Mon-Fri). Sample
train fares (without discount) include Bris-

bane ($115, 14 hours), Byron Bay ($102, 13 hours), Canberra ($50, 4½ hours) and Melbourne ($115, 11 hours).

Major bus operators include **Greyhound Australia** (☎ 13 20 30; www.greyhound.com.au), **Premier** (☎ 13 34 10; www.premierms.com.au) and **Murrays** (☎ 13 22 51; www.murrays.com.au). Sample destinations include Brisbane ($90, 16 hours), Byron Bay ($85, 13 hours), Canberra ($35, 3½ hours) and Melbourne ($60, 13 hours).

GETTING AROUND

For information on buses, ferries and trains call **Transport Infoline** (☎ 13 15 00; www.131500 .com.au; ⏰ 6am-10pm). The operators can tell you exactly how to get from one point to another.

To/From the Airport

Sydney's **Kingsford Smith Airport** (☎ 9667 9111; www.sydneyairport.com.au) is 10km south of the city centre. The international and domestic terminals are a 4km bus trip apart on either side of the runway.

One of the easiest ways to get from the airport into the centre is with a shuttle company. These take you straight to your hostel/ hotel and cost $9 to $12. All go into the city centre; some reach surrounding sub-

urbs and beach destinations. Companies include **Kingsford Smith Transport** (KST; ☎ 9666 9988; www.kst.com.au), **Super Shuttle** (☎ 0500 513 789, 9311 3789; www.supershuttle.com.au) and **Shuttle Bus Services** (SBS; ☎ 0500 503 220; www.shuttle busservices.com).

If you're going to Bondi via the cheapest route, take bus No 400 or 400 express (both $4.30) to Bondi Junction, then the L82, 380, 381 or 382 to Bondi.

Airport Link (☎ 8337 8417; www.airportlink.com .au) is a train line that runs to and from city train stations to the domestic ($11) and international ($11.80) airport terminals every 10 to 15 minutes. Trains run from approximately 5am to midnight daily.

Taxi fares from the airport are approximately $25 to Circular Quay, $35 to North Sydney and Bondi, and $50 to Manly.

Bus

Sydney's bus network extends to most suburbs. Fares depend upon the number of 'sections' you pass through. As a rough guide, short jaunts cost $1.60 and most other fares in the inner suburbs are $2.70. If you plan on taking many buses it's cheaper to buy passes (see the boxed text, below). Regular buses run between 5am and midnight.

FARE DEALS

There's a confusing number of transport deal passes to be had in Sydney. Decide your preferences and do some research to save money.

The **SydneyPass** (adult/child/family 3 days $100/50/250, 5 days $130/65/325, 7 days $150/75/375) is oriented to tourists and offers three, five or seven days' unlimited travel over a seven-day period on all buses, trains (within the city centre and surrounding suburbs) and ferries as well as Airport Link, the Explorer hop-on/hop-off buses, the JetCats, RiverCats and three STA-operated harbour cruises.

TravelPasses (most tourist destinations $32, plus Manly ferry $40) are more commuter-oriented (but great for tourists who don't need frills) and offer cheaper weekly travel on the regular buses, trains and ferries. There are several colour-coded grades.

The **Daytripper** (adult/child $15/7.50) is good for one day only, and covers all buses, ferries and trains you're likely to need for sightseeing in central Sydney. It also offers discounts to some popular tourist destinations, like the zoo and aquarium.

If you're just catching buses get a **TravelTen** (5 sections $19.70), which gives a big discount on 10 bus trips and should get you to most tourist destinations. There are various colour codes for distances so check at a Transit Shop which is the most appropriate for you.

All the passes above are sold at train stations, bus Transit Shops and major newsagents.

Ferry Ten (10 inner-harbour ferry trips $30.30, plus Manly ferry $45.10) tickets are similar. They can be purchased at Circular Quay.

Several transport-plus-entry tickets are available, which work out cheaper than catching a ferry and paying entry separately. They include the **ZooPass** (adult/child $33.50/16.50) and the **AquariumPass** (adult/child $29.10/14.50). Buy them at Circular Quay.

The major starting points for bus routes are Circular Quay, Argyle St in Millers Point, Wynyard Park, Queen Victoria Building on York St and Railway Sq. Most buses head out of the city on George or Castlereagh Sts and return on George or Elizabeth Sts. Pay the driver as you enter, or use your prepaid ticket.

At Circular Quay there's a **Transit Shop** (Map pp94-5; Alfred & Loftus Sts, Circular Quay; 7am-7pm Mon-Fri, 8.30am-5.30pm Sat & Sun) that sells bus passes and dispenses bus route information. Look for this kiosk right in front of the McDonald's. Other bus Transit Shops around the city also sell passes. For more bus information you can call ☎ 9244 1991 or ☎ 13 15 00 or check www.sydneybuses.info.

Car

Cars are good for day trips out of town, but driving one in the city is like an anchor around your neck. Heavy traffic, elusive parking (even at hotels) and the extra costs just aren't worth the stress.

BUYING/SELLING A CAR

Sydney is the capital of car sales for most travellers. The **Kings Cross Car Market** (Map p97; ☎ 9358 5000, 1800 808 188; www.carmarket.com.au; cnr Ward Ave & Elizabeth Bay Rd, Kings Cross; 9am-5pm) gets mixed reports, but it seems popular with travellers. Always read the fine print on anything you sign with regards to buying or selling a car. Several dealers will sell you a car with an undertaking to buy it back at an agreed price – do not accept any verbal guarantees; get it in writing.

The *Trading Post,* a weekly rag available from all newsagents, is also a good place to look for second-hand vehicles. You can also check in the 'Classified' section of the *Sydney Morning Herald* (www.smh.com.au). Car prices will probably be a bit cheaper if you buy from a private party.

Yet another option is going to a car auction. One place is **Auto Auctions** (☎ 9724 9111; www.auto-auctions.com.au; 682 Woodville Rd, Guildford).

Before you buy any vehicle, regardless of the seller, we strongly recommend that you have it thoroughly checked by a competent mechanic. The **NRMA** (Map pp94-5; ☎ 13 21 32; www.nrma.com.au; 388 George St) charges $240 for nonmembers ($200 for members). We've heard some real horror stories from readers who've failed to get their vehicles checked.

The **Register of Encumbered Vehicles** (REVS; ☎ 9633 6333; www.revs.nsw.gov.au) is a government organisation that checks the car you're buying is fully paid-up and owned by the seller. Other helpful websites, especially if you have problems with your vehicle, are www.fairtrading.nsw.gov.au and www.accc.gov.au.

HIRE

Car-rental rates sometimes include insurance and unlimited kilometres, and some require you to be over 25 years old. Rates depend on time of year, so call ahead.

Avis (☎ 13 63 33; www.avis.com.au), **Budget** (☎ 13 27 27; www.budget.com.au), **Europcar** (☎ 1300 131 390; www.europcar.com.au), **Hertz** (☎ 13 30 39; www.hertz.com) and **Thrifty** (☎ 1300 367 227; www.thrifty.com.au) all have desks at the airport, and some have offices in the centre (most on William St). A good place to try is **Bayswater Car Rental** (Map p97; ☎ 9360 3622; www.bayswatercarrental.com.au; 180 William St, Kings Cross).

TOLL ROADS

The Harbour Tunnel and Harbour Bridge both impose a southbound toll of $3; if you're heading from the North Shore to the eastern suburbs, it's much easier to use the tunnel. The Eastern Distributor imposes a northbound toll of $4.

The new Cross City tunnel should soon be finished, with the hope that it will ease traffic congestion and slash travel times across the city. Tolls will be $1.10 or $2.50, depending on distance travelled.

Ferry

Sydney's **ferries** (☎ 9207 3166; www.sydneyferries.info) provide the most enjoyable way to get around the harbour. Many people use ferries to commute so there are frequent connecting bus services. Some ferries operate between 6am and midnight, although ferries servicing tourist attractions operate much shorter hours.

There are three kinds of ferry: regular STA ferries, fast JetCats that go to Manly ($7.90) and RiverCats that traverse the Parramatta River to Parramatta ($7.40). All ferries depart from Circular Quay. The **ferry information office** (Map pp94-5; ☎ 9207 3170; 7am-5.45pm Mon-Sat, 8am-5.45pm Sun) is at Wharf 4. Most regular harbour ferries cost $4.80, although the longer trip to Manly costs $6. There are some fare deals; see the boxed text, p141.

Metro Light Rail & Monorail

The **Monorail** (☎ 9285 5600; www.metromonorail .com.au) and **Metro Light Rail** (MLR; ☎ 9285 5600; www.metrolightrail.com.au) are other good means of transport within the centre.

The Monorail circles Darling Harbour and links it to the city centre. There's a monorail every three to five minutes, and the full loop takes about 14 minutes. A single trip costs $4.20, but for $8 you can have unlimited rides for the day. The monorail operates from 7am to 10pm Monday to Thursday, to midnight on Friday and Saturday and from 8am to 10pm Sunday.

The MLR operates 24 hours a day between Central Station and Pyrmont via Darling Harbour and Chinatown. The service runs to Lilyfield via the Fish Market, Wentworth Park, Glebe, Jubilee Park and Rozelle Bay from 6am to 11pm Sunday to Thursday (to midnight Friday and Saturday). Tickets cost $2.80 to $5.20, but for $8.40 you can have unlimited rides for the day.

Taxi

There are heaps of metered taxis in Sydney. Flag fall is $2.75, and the metered fair is $1.56 per kilometre. There is a 20% surcharge between 10pm and 6am and for heavy luggage, Harbour Bridge and Tunnel tolls. The radio booking fee is $1.15. The four big taxi companies offer a reliable service:

Legion (☎ 13 14 51)
Premier Cabs (☎ 13 10 17)
RSL Cabs (☎ 13 22 11)
Taxis Combined (☎ 8332 8888)

Train

Sydney has a vast suburban rail network and frequent services, making trains much quicker than buses. The underground City Circle comprises seven city-centre stations. Lines radiate from the City Circle, but do not extend to the northern and southern beaches, Balmain or Glebe. All city-bound suburban trains stop at Central Station, and usually one or more of the other City Circle stations as well (a ticket to the city will take you to any station on the City Circle). Trains run from around 5am to midnight.

After 9am on weekdays and at any time on weekends, you can buy an off-peak return ticket for not much more than a standard one-way fare. Staffed ticket booths are supplemented by automatic ticket machines

at stations. If you have to change trains, it's cheaper to buy a ticket to your ultimate destination – but don't depart from an intermediary station en route to your destination or your ticket will be invalid.

Any station has train information. Central Station has a good **information kiosk** (◷ 6am-10pm) near platforms 4 and 5. The **transport information booth** (☎ 9224 2649; ◷ 9am-5pm) at Circular Quay also hands out advice; it's right next to CountryLink. You can also check www.cityrail.info.

AROUND SYDNEY

There are superb national parks situated to the north and south of Sydney, and historic small towns to the west, which were established in the early days of European settlement. There is also the Hunter Valley, and many organisations run day trips from Sydney. It's easier to visit the Hunter from Newcastle, however.

BOTANY BAY

It's a common misconception that Sydney is built around Botany Bay. Sydney Harbour is actually Port Jackson, and Botany Bay is 10km to 15km south on the city's fringe. This area is a major industrial centre so don't expect too many unspoilt vistas. Despite this, the bay has pretty stretches and holds a special place in Australian history. This was Captain Cook's first landing point in Australia, and it was named by Joseph Banks, the expedition's naturalist, for the many botanical specimens he found here.

The **Botany Bay National Park** (www.national parks.nsw.gov.au) encompasses both headlands of the bay. At Kurnell, on the southern headland, monuments mark Cook's landing place. The 436-hectare park has bushland and coastal walking tracks, picnic areas and an 8km cycle track. The park's **Discovery Centre** (☎ 02-9668 9111; ◷ 11am-3pm Mon-Fri, 10am-4.30pm Sat & Sun) describes the impact of European arrival, and has information on the surrounding wetlands. During the winter months, you can watch whales migrating from the observation platform at Cape Solander, about 2km from the Discovery Centre.

The park is open from 7am to 7.30pm daily. Entry costs $7 per car but pedestrians

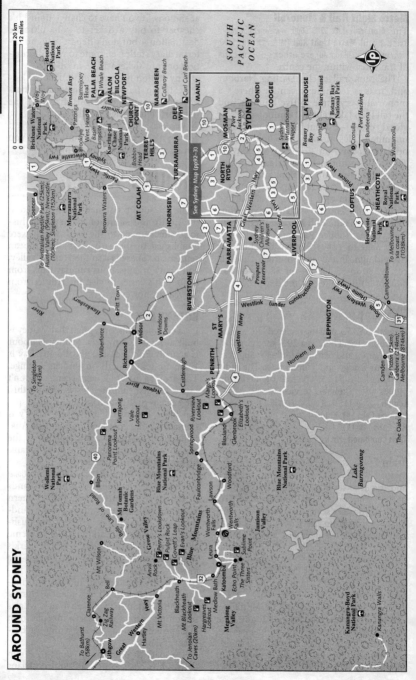

AROUND SYDNEY

are not charged and, since the monuments and most walking tracks are close to the entrance, you may as well park outside. From Cronulla train station (10km away), catch **Bus Link's** (☎ 02-9523 4047) No 987 bus.

La Perouse, on the northern headland, is named after the French explorer who arrived in 1788, just six days after the arrival of the First Fleet. Although the First Fleet soon sailed to Sydney Harbour, La Perouse camped at Botany Bay for six weeks before sailing off into the Pacific and disappearing. The fabulous **Laperouse Museum & Visitors Centre** (☎ 02-9311 3379; adult/child/family $5.50/3.50/13.20; ☻ 10am-4pm Wed-Sun), in the old (1882) cable station, charts the history of La Perouse's fateful expedition; there's also an excellent Aboriginal gallery with exhibits on local indigenous history.

Just offshore is **Bare Island** (☎ 02-9247 5033; adult/concession/family $7.70/5.50/22), a decaying concrete fort built in 1885 to discourage a feared Russian invasion. Entry is by guided tour only at 1.30pm and 2.30pm on Saturday and Sunday.

There's no entry fee to this northern segment of the national park. Catch bus No 394 from Circular Quay or No 391 from Eddy Av at Central Station.

ROYAL NATIONAL PARK

This coastal park of dramatic cliffs, secluded beaches, scrub and lush rainforest is the oldest gazetted national park in the world. It begins at Port Hacking, just 30km south of Sydney, and stretches 30km further south. A road runs through the park with detours to the small township of Bundeena on Port Hacking, to the beautiful beach at Wattamolla, and to windswept Garie Beach. The spectacular two-day, 26km coastal walking trail running the length of the park is highly recommended. Garie, Era and Burning Palms are popular surfing spots; swimming can be delightful at Wattamolla. A walking and cycling trail follows the Hacking River south from Audley, and other walking tracks pass tranquil freshwater swimming holes.

There's a friendly **visitors centre** (☎ 02-95 42 0666; www.nationalparks.nsw.gov.au; ☻ 9.30am-4.30pm) at the top of the hill at the park's main entrance, off the Princes Hwy near Audley. Staff can help you with camping permits, maps and bushwalking details.

You can hire exercise accoutrements at the **Audley Boat Shed** (☎ 02-9545 4967; Farnell Rd), where rowboats, canoes and kayaks cost $16/30 per hour/day, aqua bikes $12 per 30 minutes, and bicycles $14/30 per hour/day.

Entry to the park costs $11 per car, but is free for pedestrians and cyclists. The road through the park and the offshoot to Bundeena are always open, but the detours to the beaches are closed at sunset.

The **Bundeena–Maianbar Heritage Walk** is still awaiting completion; it promises good coastal views and some Aboriginal sites of interest.

Sleeping

Cronulla Beachouse YHA (☎ 02-9527 7772; www .cronullabeachyha.com; Level 1, 40 Kingsway, Cronulla; dm $25, d & tw $70; ℗ ☐) This friendly and intimate hostel offers 48 beds and a personal feel. Facilities are comfy and well maintained, with a cheery vibe from staff and travellers alike. You can also get the key for the Garie Beach YHA (see following), and it's a great place to join others doing the 26km coastal walk or get your surfing skills up. Catch the train to Cronulla Station, and keep walking left until you reach Kingsway. Wheelchair accessible.

Garie Beach YHA (☎ 02-9261 1111; www.yha.com .au; Garie Beach, Royal National Park; dm $13) This 12-bed, basic (no electricity, phone or shower; bring food) and secluded bush hut–like hostel is close to one of the best surf beaches in NSW. You need to book, collect a key and get detailed directions from the **YHA Membership & Travel Centre** (Map pp94-5; ☎ 02-9261 1111; www.yha.com.au/yhainfo/membership_travel.cfm; 422 Kent St; ☻ 9am-5pm Mon-Wed & Fri, to 6pm Thu, to 2pm Sat) in the city centre, or from Cronulla's YHA. The nearest food store is 10km away.

Beachhaven Bed & Breakfast (☎ 02-9544 1333; www.beachhavenbnb.com.au; 13 Bundeena Dr, Bundeena; d $200-250) Offering a choice of 'Tudor Suite' or 'Beachhouse', this quirky, kinda lavish place receives positive feedback and is right on heavenly Horderns Beach. Breakfast is included in room price.

The only **camp site** (adult/child $8/4) accessible by car is at Bonnie Vale, near Bundeena. **Bush camping** (adult/child $3/2) is allowed in several areas – one of the best places is Providential Head, at the end of the coastal walk – but you must obtain a permit from the visitors centre.

Getting There & Away

You can reach the park from Sydney by taking the Princes Hwy and turning off south of Loftus. From Wollongong, the coast road north is a spectacular drive, and there are fantastic views of the Illawarra Escarpment and the coast from Bald Hill Lookout, just north of Stanwell Park, on the southern boundary of the Royal National Park.

The Sydney–Wollongong railway forms the western boundary of the park. The closest station is at Loftus, 4km from the park entrance and another 2km from the visitors centre. Bringing a bike on the train is a good idea. Engadine, Heathcote, Waterfall and Otford are on the park boundary and have walking trails leading into the park.

A scenic route is to take a train from Sydney to the suburb of Cronulla (changing at Sutherland on the way), then a **Cronulla National Park Ferries** (☎ 02-9523 2990) boat to Bundeena in the northeastern corner of the park (adult/child $4.50/2.25). Ferries depart from Cronulla Wharf, just below the train station. Cronulla National Park Ferries also offers daily Hacking River cruises in summer (a reduced timetable in winter) for $17.50/12.50/50 per adult/child/family.

PARRAMATTA
☎ 02

Parramatta (an Aboriginal word meaning 'where the eels lie down'), 24km west of Sydney, was the second European settlement in Australia and contains a number of historic buildings dating from early colonial days. When Sydney proved to be a poor area for farming, Parramatta was selected in 1788 for the first farm. Now consumed by Sydney's westward sprawl, Parramatta is a thriving commercial centre, with some architectural gems (from eras past) nestled amongst the modern developments, which are, for the most part, forgettable.

The incredibly helpful and knowledgeable **Parramatta visitors centre** (☎ 9630 3703; 346A Church St; ☉ 9am-5pm) is the best place to get acquainted with the area. It has lots of brochures and leaflets, plenty of info on access for visitors with impaired mobility, and it's close to public transport.

On the western edge of the city, **Parramatta Park** was the site of the area's first farm and contains a number of relics. The elegant **Old Government House** (☎ 9635 8149; www.friends ofogh.com; adult/concession/family $8/5/18; ☉ 10am-4pm Mon-Fri, 10.30am-4pm Sat & Sun) sits atop a rise overlooking the Parramatta River. Built from 1799 as a country retreat for the early governors of NSW, it's the oldest remaining public building in Australia and now houses a museum with early colonial furniture and other fine objects.

St John's Cathedral (O'Connell St) and the **Parramatta Town Hall** (Church St Mall) form a pleasant civic centre near the junction of Church and Macquarie Sts. **St John's Cemetery** (O'Connell St), between the cathedral and the park, contains the graves of many of the first settlers.

There are more historic buildings east of the city centre. **Elizabeth Farm** (☎ 9635 9488; 70 Alice St, Rosehill; adult/child/family $7/3/17; ☉ 10am-5pm) is the oldest surviving home in the country. The founders of Australia's wool industry, John and Elizabeth Macarthur, built it in 1793 and its deep veranda and simple lines became the prototype for early Australian homesteads. There's wheelchair access to every part of the house except the kitchen.

The exquisite **Experiment Farm Cottage** (☎ 9635 5655; 9 Ruse St, Harris Park; adult/concession/ family $5.50/4/14; ☉ 10.30am-3.30pm Tue-Thu, 11am-3.30pm Sat & Sun) is a beautiful colonial bungalow built on the site of the first land grant issued in Australia.

Getting There & Around

The most scenic way to reach Parramatta is by RiverCat from Circular Quay ($7, 50 minutes) – otherwise catch a train from Central Station ($4.40). By car, exit the city via Parramatta Rd and detour onto the Western Motorway tollway ($2.20) at Strathfield.

PENRITH
☎ 02

Penrith, on the calm Nepean River, is at the base of the forested foothills of the Blue Mountains. Despite being 50km west of the city centre, it's virtually an outer suburb of Sydney. The **Penrith visitors centre** (☎ 4732 7671; ☉ 9am-4.30pm) is in the car park of the huge Panthers World of Entertainment complex on Mulgoa Rd.

The **Museum of Fire** (☎ 4731 3000; Castlereagh Rd; adult/child/family $6/4/15; ☉ 10am-3pm) is the best thing to see in the area, with equipment and memorabilia related to fire and fire fighting, which is all too relevant to the area.

You can reach Penrith by train from Central Station ($6.60) or by driving west along Parramatta Rd and then taking the Western Motorway tollway at Strathfield ($2.20).

CAMDEN AREA

Camden is promoted as the 'birthplace of the nation's wealth' because it was here that John and Elizabeth Macarthur conducted the sheep-breeding experiments that laid the foundation for Australia's wool industry. Camden is on the urban fringe, 50km southwest of the city centre, off the Hume Hwy. There's a **visitors centre** (☎ 02-4677 3962; www.stonequarry.com.au; cnr Argyle & Menangle Sts; ☼ 9am-3pm) that can give you a hand. **John Oxley Cottage** (☎ 02-4658 1370; Camden Valley Way, Elderslie; ☼ 9.30am-4pm) is an historic house on the town's northern outskirts.

The 400-hectare **Mount Annan Botanic Garden** (☎ 02-4648 2477; Mt Annan Dr, Mt Annan; adult/child/family $4.40/2.20/8.80; ☼ 10am-6pm Oct-Mar, 10am-4pm Apr-Sep) is the native plant garden of Sydney's Royal Botanic Gardens, and is midway between Camden and Campbelltown, to the east. Take a train to Campbelltown Station and Busways bus No 895 or 896 from there. By car, take tourist drive 18, off the F5 Fwy.

South of Camden is the small town of **Picton**. A number of historic buildings still stand, including the train station and the 1839 **George IV Inn** (☎ 02-4677 1415; 180 Old Hume Hwy/Argyle St; s/d $33/50), which brews great Bavarian-style beer in its own brewery and provides eight modest rooms. Menangle St West is listed by the National Trust and worth a wander.

KU-RING-GAI CHASE NATIONAL PARK

This 15,000-hectare national park, 24km north of the city centre, borders the southern edge of Broken Bay and the western shore of Pittwater. It has that classic Sydney mixture of sandstone, bushland and water vistas, plus walking tracks, horse-riding trails, picnic areas, Aboriginal rock engravings and spectacular views of Broken Bay, particularly from West Head at the park's northeastern tip. There are several roads through the park and four entrances. Entry is $11 per car.

The **Kalkari visitors centre** (☎ 02-9457 9853; Ku-ring-gai Chase Rd; ☼ 9am-5pm) is about 2.5km into the park from the Mt Colah entrance on Ku-ring-gai Chase Rd; it's staffed by friendly volunteers. The road descends from the visitors centre to the picnic area at **Bobbin Head** on Cowan Creek. **Halvorsen** (☎ 02-9457 9011; Bobbin Head) rents rowboats for $25/60 per hour/day and eight-seater motorboats for $50 for half a day.

Recommended walks include the America Bay Trail and the Gibberagong and Sphinx tracks. The best places to see **Aboriginal engravings** are on the Basin Trail and the Garigal Aboriginal Heritage Walk at West Head. There's a mangrove boardwalk at Bobbin Head. It's unwise to swim in Broken Bay because of sharks, but there are netted swimming areas at Illawong Bay and the Basin.

Sleeping

Pittwater YHA (☎ 02-9999 5748; www.yha.com.au; Ku-ring-gai National Park; dm $23, d & tw $60) This idyllic, beautifully situated hostel, a couple of kilometres south of the Basin, is noted for its friendly wildlife and considerate management. You should book ahead and bring food; reception's open 8am to 11am and 5pm to 8pm. To get here, take bus No 156 from Manly Wharf to Church Point, then the ferry from Church Point to Halls Wharf – after all that, you're in for a 10-minute uphill walk, but it's definitely worth the effort.

Basin campsites (☎ 02-9974 1011; adult/child Sep-April $9/4.50, May-Aug $7.50/4) Camping is permitted at the Basin (bookings essential) on the western side of Pittwater. Getting there takes a walk of about 2.5km from West Head Rd, or a ferry or water-taxi ride from Palm Beach.

Getting There & Away

There are four road entrances to the park: Mt Colah, on the Pacific Hwy; Turramurra, in the southwest; and Terrey Hills and Church Point, in the southeast. **Shorelink Buses** (☎ 02-9457 8888; www.shorelink.com.au) runs bus No 577 every hour from Turramurra Station to the park entrance ($2.70) on weekdays; one bus enters the park as far as Bobbin Head. The schedule changes on weekends with fewer buses going to the entrance but more to Bobbin Head.

The **Palm Beach Ferry Service** (☎ 02-9918 2747; adult/concession $10/5) runs to the Basin hourly from 9am to 5pm Monday to Thursday, 9am to 8pm Friday and 9am to 6pm Saturday, Sunday and public holidays. You can also

NEW SOUTH WALES

use 24-hour **Church Point Water Taxis** (☎ 0428 238 190; up to 6 people $42) for the trip between Church Point and Palm Beach. There is a $6 surcharge from midnight to 6am.

From the city centre, bus No E86 is a direct peak-hour service to Church Point, or catch bus No L88, L90 or 190 from Wynyard Park as far as Warringah Mall and transfer to No 156 from there.

HAWKESBURY RIVER

The mighty Hawkesbury River enters the sea 30km north of Sydney at Broken Bay. It's dotted with coves, beaches and picnic spots, making it one of Australia's most attractive rivers. Before reaching the ocean, the river expands into bays and inlets including Berowra Creek, Cowan Creek and Pittwater on the southern side, and Brisbane Water on the northern. The river flows between a succession of national parks – Marramarra and Ku-ring-gai Chase to the south, and Dharug, Brisbane Water and Bouddi to the north. Windsor is about 120km upstream.

A great way to get a feel for the river is to catch the **Riverboat Postman** (☎ 02-9985 7566; Brooklyn Wharf, Brooklyn; adult/child/family $38/20/85). This mail boat does a 40km round trip Monday to Friday, running upstream as far as Marlow, near Spencer. It leaves Brooklyn at 9.30am and returns at 1.15pm. There are also coffee cruises and all-day cruises (booking recommended). The 8.16am train from Sydney's Central Station gets you to Brooklyn's Hawkesbury River Station in time to meet the morning Riverboat Postman.

You can hire houseboats in Brooklyn, Berowra Waters and Bobbin Head. These aren't cheap, but renting midweek during the low season is affordable for a group. **Ripples** (☎ 02-9985 5555; www.ripples.com.au; 87 Brooklyn Rd, Brooklyn) has a good fleet of comfortable houseboats, with admirable reductions during quiet times and midweek. The cost for four people for a weekend is around $900.

The settlements along the river have their own distinct character. Life in **Brooklyn** revolves totally around boats and the river. The town is on the Sydney–Newcastle railway line, just east of the Pacific Hwy. **Berowra Waters** is a quaint community further upstream, clustered around a free 24-hour winch ferry that crosses Berowra Creek. There are a couple of cafés overlooking the water, and a marina where you can hire an outboard boat for around $60 for half a day. Berowra Waters is 5km west of the Pacific Hwy; there's a train station at Berowra, but it's a 6km hike down to the ferry.

Wisemans Ferry is a tranquil settlement overlooking the Hawkesbury River, roughly halfway between Windsor and the mouth of the river. Free 24-hour winch ferries are the only means of crossing the river here. **Wisemans Ferry Inn** (☎ 02-4566 4301; Old Northern Rd, Wisemans Ferry; d $72-88, without bathroom $60-72) is an historic inn with decent (if a little cramped) rooms. There's often a lot going on in the pub, from singers to live music to lingerie waitresses (this last one on Thursdays), if that's your thing.

Standards are high at the **Del Rio Riverside Resort** (☎ 02-4566 4330; www.delrioresort.com.au; Chaseling Rd, Webbs Creek, Wisemans Ferry; powered/unpowered sites $21/19, cabins $83-140), just 3km southwest of the village centre. The attractive cabins have tranquil water views. Take the Webbs Creek winch ferry and then follow the signs.

Yengo National Park, a rugged sandstone area covering the foothills of the Blue Mountains, stretches from Wisemans Ferry to the Hunter Valley. It's a wilderness area with no facilities and limited road access. North of the river, a scenic road leads east from Wisemans Ferry to the Central Coast, following the river before veering north through bushland and orange groves.

An early convict-built road leads north from Wisemans Ferry to tiny, delightful **St Albans**. **Settlers Arms Inn** (☎ 02-4568 2111; www.settlersarms.com.au; 1 Wharf St, St Albans; d $130-150) is a charming Georgian sandstone inn that dates from 1836. It has four pleasant rooms and there's a public bar that's worth visiting for a beer or a meal.

WINDSOR & RICHMOND
☎ 02

Windsor, Richmond, Wilberforce, Castlereagh and Pitt Town are the five 'Macquarie Towns' established on rich agricultural land on the upper Hawkesbury River in the early 19th century by Governor Lachlan Macquarie. You can visit them on the way to or from the Blue Mountains if you cross the range on the Bells Line of Road – an interesting alternative to the Great Western Hwy.

The **Hawkesbury visitors centre** (☎ 4588 5895; Bicentennial Park, Ham Common, Windsor Rd, Clarendon; ☽ 9am-5pm Mon-Fri, 10am-3pm Sat, 10am-2pm Sun) is across from the Richmond Royal Australian Air Force (RAAF) base. It's the main information centre for the upper Hawkesbury area and is immensely helpful.

Windsor has some fine old buildings, notably those around the picturesque Thompson Sq on the banks of the Hawkesbury River. The **Hawkesbury Museum & Tourist Centre** (☎ 4577 2310; 7 Thompson Sq, Windsor; adult/ child $2.50/50c; ☽ 10am-4pm) is in a building that dates from the 1820s, and was used as the Daniel O'Connell Inn during the 1840s. There are a variety of displays in the museum.

The 1815 **Macquarie Arms Hotel** has a nice veranda fronting the square and is reckoned to be the oldest pub in Australia, but there are quite a few 'oldest pubs' in NSW. Other old buildings include the convict-built **St Matthew's Church of England**, completed in 1822 and designed, like the **courthouse**, by the convict architect Francis Greenway.

You can reach Windsor by train from Sydney's Central Station, but public transport to other Macquarie Towns (apart from Richmond) is scarce. By car, exit the city on Parramatta Rd and head northwest on the Windsor Rd from Parramatta.

The next largest of the Macquarie Towns is **Richmond**, which has its share of colonial buildings and a pleasant village green–like park. It's 6km west of Windsor, at the end of the metropolitan railway line and the start of the Bells Line of Road across the Blue Mountains.

The office of the **National Parks & Wildlife Service** (NPWS; ☎ 4588 5247; Bowmans Cottage, 370 George St, Richmond; ☽ 9am-12.30pm & 1.30-5pm Mon-Fri) can give you information about national park facilities in the region.

The pretty **Ebenezer Church**, 5km north of Wilberforce, was built in 1809 and is the oldest church in Australia still used as a place of worship.

Wilberforce is the starting point for the Putty Rd, a 160km isolated back road that runs north to Singleton in the Hunter Valley. The **Colo River**, 15km north along this road, is a picturesque spot popular for swimming, canoeing and picnicking.

BLUE MOUNTAINS

The excellent natural habitat of the Blue Mountains has been Sydney's wilderness getaway for the past century. It's especially popular in summer, when Sydneysiders come to escape the heat. The area boasts magnificent scenery, excellent bushwalks, gum trees, gorges, outdoor activities, great eating and enough tourism infrastructure to keep you very comfortable, though much of the area is so precipitous that it's still only open to bushwalkers.

The Blue Mountains, part of the Great Dividing Range, were initially an impenetrable barrier to white expansion from Sydney. Despite many attempts to find a route through the mountains – and a bizarre belief among many convicts that China, and freedom, was just on the other side – it took 25 years before a successful crossing was made by Europeans. A road was built soon afterwards that opened the western plains to settlement.

The foothills begin 65km inland from Sydney and the mountains rise up to 1100m. Be prepared for the climatic difference between the Blue Mountains and the coast – you can swelter in Sydney but shiver in Katoomba. It usually snows sometime between June and August, when the region has a Yuletide Festival complete with Christmas decorations and dinners.

There are several national parks in the area. The Blue Mountains National Park has some truly fantastic scenery, excellent bushwalks, Aboriginal engravings and all the canyons and cliffs you could ask for. It's a favourite with adrenaline junkies, and is the most popular and accessible of the three national parks in the area. Great lookouts include Evan's Lookout and Govett's Leap Lookout near Blackheath – both are more spectacular than the Echo Point Lookout in Katoomba.

Wollemi National Park, north of the Bells Line of Road, is NSW's largest forested wilderness area and stretches all the way to Denman in the Hunter Valley. It has limited access and the park's centre is so isolated that a species of tree, the Wollemi Pine, was only discovered here in 1994.

Kanangra-Boyd National Park is southwest of the southern section of the Blue

NEW SOUTH WALES

WHAT'S IN A NAME?

The blue haze, which gave the mountains their name, is a result of the ultra-fine oily mist given off by eucalyptus trees. This haze, seen from a distance, makes the ranges look serenely blue.

Mountains National Park. It has bushwalking opportunities, limestone caves, including the famous Jenolan Caves, and grand scenery. It includes the spectacular Kanangra Walls Plateau, which is surrounded by sheer cliffs and can be reached by unsealed road from Oberon or from the Jenolan Caves.

For more information on these parks (including camping) contact the **National Parks & Wildlife Service Visitor Centre** (NPWS; ☎ 02-4787 8877; www.nationalparks.nsw.gov.au; Govetts Leap Rd, Blackheath; ☺ 9am-4.30pm), about 2.5km off the Great Western Hwy and 10km north of Katoomba.

Orientation

The Great Western Hwy from Sydney follows a ridge running east–west through the Blue Mountains. Along this less-than-beautiful road, the Blue Mountains towns merge into each other – Glenbrook, Springwood, Woodford, Lawson, Wentworth Falls, Leura, Katoomba, Medlow Bath, Blackheath, Mt Victoria and Hartley. On the western fringe of the mountains is Lithgow.

To the south and north of the highway's ridge, the country drops away into precipitous valleys, including the Grose Valley to the north, and the Jamison Valley south of Katoomba.

The Bells Line of Road is a much more scenic and less congested alternative to the Great Western Hwy. It's the more northerly of the two crossings, beginning in Richmond and running north of the Grose Valley to emerge in Lithgow, although you can cut across from Bell to join the Great Western Hwy at Mt Victoria.

Bushwalking

The roads across the mountains offer tantalising glimpses of the majesty of the area, but the only way to really experience the Blue Mountains is on foot. There are walks lasting from a few minutes to several days.

The two most popular areas are Jamison Valley, south of Katoomba, and Grose Valley, east of Blackheath. The area south of Glenbrook is also good.

The NPWS centre can help you pick a hike; for shorter walks, ask at the Katoomba visitors centre. It's rugged country, and walkers sometimes get lost, so it's highly advisable to get reliable information, not to go alone, and to tell someone where you're going. Many Blue Mountains watercourses are polluted, so you must sterilise water or take your own. Be prepared for rapid weather changes.

Good walking books on the area include *Exploring the Blue Mountains* (Key Guide, $30) and *Walks in the Blue Mountains* (Neil Paton, $11).

Sleeping

Accommodation ranges from camping grounds and hostels to guesthouses and luxury hotels. Katoomba is the main centre. Prices are fairly stable throughout the year, but most places charge more on weekends, public holidays and during Yulefest (July). Prices listed in the following sections are high-season rates. If you intend to camp in the national parks, check with the NPWS first.

Getting There & Away

Katoomba is 109km from Sydney's city centre, but it's still almost a satellite suburb. Trains run approximately hourly from Central Station. The trip takes two hours ($11.40) and there are stops at plenty of Blue Mountains townships on the way.

By car, leave the city via Parramatta Rd and detour onto the Western Motorway tollway (M4; $2.20) at Strathfield. The motorway becomes the Great Western Hwy west of Penrith.

To reach the Bells Line of Road, head out on Parramatta Rd, and from Parramatta drive northwest on the Windsor Rd to Windsor. The Richmond Rd from Windsor becomes the Bells Line of Road west of Richmond.

Getting Around

The **Blue Mountains Bus Company** (☎ 02-4751 1077; www.mountainlink.com.au) runs several buses to Katoomba, Leura, Blackheath, Mt Victoria, Faulconbridge and Penrith, among other Blue Mountains destinations. Check the website for details and schedules.

There are train stations in Blue Mountains towns along the Great Western Hwy. Trains run roughly every hour between stations east of Katoomba, and roughly every two hours between stations to the west.

For (tour) buses that cover the Katoomba/Leura area only, and for a package that includes a train ride from Sydney plus bus transport around these same areas, see p155.

Redicar (☎ 02-4784 3443; 80 Megalong St, Leura) is a budget option for those looking to hire a car, van or 4WD.

GLENBROOK TO LEURA
Information
To find books and guides on walking in the area, try **Megalong Books** (☎ 02-4784 1302; 183 The Mall, Leura; ☺ 9am-6pm Mon-Sat, 10am-6pm Sun). There are plenty of books on the Blue Mountains; *Exploring the Blue Mountains* and *Walks in the Blue Mountains* are both available at this bookshop.

Sights & Activities
From Marge's and Elizabeth's Lookouts, just north of Glenbrook, there are good views east to Sydney. The section of the Blue Mountains National Park south of Glenbrook contains **Red Hand Cave**, an old Aboriginal shelter with hand stencils on the walls. It's an easy 7km-return walk, southwest of the NPWS building.

The famous artist and author Norman Lindsay (1879–1969) lived in Springwood from 1912 until his death. His home is now the **Norman Lindsay Gallery & Museum** (☎ 02-4751 1067; www.hermes.net.au/nlg; 14 Norman Lindsay Cres, Faulconbridge; adult/child $9/4; ☺ 10am-4pm). It houses many of his risqué paintings, cartoons, illustrations and sculptures. The large grounds are well worth a wander, and include statues and fountains.

Just south of the town of Wentworth Falls there are great views of the Jamison Valley. You can see the spectacular 300m **Wentworth Falls** from Falls Reserve, which is the starting point for a network of walking tracks.

Leura is a quaint, tree-lined town full of country stores and cafés. The **Leuralla Gardens Toy and Railway Museum** (☎ 02-4784 1169; 36 Olympian Pde; museum & garden adult/child $10/5, garden only $6/3; ☺ 10am-5pm) is an Art Deco mansion that houses a fine collection of 19th-century Australian art, as well as a toy and model-railway museum. The historic house, set in 5 hectares of lovely gardens, is a memorial to HV 'Doc' Evatt, a former Labor Party leader and first president of the UN. There's also a nice lookout across the road, with two statues and an amphitheatre.

Sublime Point, south of Leura, is a great cliff-top lookout. Nearby, **Gordon Falls Reserve** is a popular picnic spot, and from here you can take the cliff-top path or Cliff Drive 4km west past Leura Cascades to Katoomba's Echo Point.

Sleeping & Eating
Hawkesbury Heights YHA (☎ /fax 02-4754 5621; www.yha.com.au; 836 Hawkesbury Rd, Hawkesbury Heights; d $40) This 12-bed, purpose-built hostel is surrounded by bush. It's an ecofriendly property with solar power, a 'green' toilet and a wood stove. Reservations are essential, but worth it; call between 7am and 8am or 5pm and 10pm only.

There are NPWS **camping areas** accessible by road at Euroka Clearing near Glenbrook, Murphys Glen near Woodford, Ingar near Wentworth Falls and at Perry's Lookdown near Blackheath. To camp at Euroka Clearing, you need a permit (adult/child $5/3 per day) from the **Richmond NPWS** (office ☎ 02-4588 5247, toll booth ☎ 02-4739 2950; Bowmans Cottage, 370 George St, Richmond; ☺ office 9am-4.30pm Mon-Fri, toll booth 9.30am-4.30pm Sat & Sun) and your own drinking water. The tracks to Ingar, Euroka and Murphys Glen may be closed after heavy rain.

Leura Gourmet (☎ 02-4784 1438; 159 The Mall, Leura; mains $3.50-15.50; ☺ 8am-5pm) A deli and a café, the Leura Gourmet has lovely views towards Katoomba and is a nice place to unwind with coffee while you ogle a selection of foodstuffs for an upscale picnic lunch. The fabulous breakfasts (which are served until 11am) include omelettes and vegetarian offerings.

Stock Market Café (☎ 02-4784 3121; 179 The Mall, Leura; ☺ 8am-4.30pm Mon-Fri, 8am-4pm Sat & Sun) This tiny eatery serves the best coffee in town, and has a great range of tasty and affordable snacks, salads, sandwiches and gourmet pies. Come in for breakfast and stock up on caffeine and carbs before you head out on a hike.

NEW SOUTH WALES

KATOOMBA

☎ 02 / pop 17,900

Katoomba and adjacent Wentworth Falls and Leura form the tourist heart of the Blue Mountains. Despite the number of visitors and its proximity to Sydney, Katoomba retains a friendly and otherworldly ambience that is accentuated by its Art Deco and Art Nouveau guesthouses and cafés, its thick mists and occasional snowfalls. **Yulefest** is celebrated in winter throughout the Blue Mountains, with Winter Magic (a street parade with market stalls etc) taking place on the Saturday nearest to June's Winter Solstice. Book your hotel room way in advance during this time.

The major scenic attraction is **Echo Point**, which is about 2km down Katoomba St from the train station. From here are some of the best views of the Jamison Valley and the magnificent **Three Sisters** rock formation – a photo session here is obligatory.

To the west of Echo Point is **Scenic World** (☎ 4782 2699; www.scenicworld.com.au; ☺ 9am-5pm), which includes a railway (steep inclinator), skyway and flyway (both cable cars). All offer breathtaking views from breathtaking heights; each costs $14/7/35 roundtrip per adult/child/family. Nearby eateries offer excellent views.

For information on local walks head to the **visitors centre** (☎ 1300 653 408; Echo Point; ☺ 9am-5pm), right near Echo Point. Katoomba has several ATMs and a post office, so you're not terribly out of touch with reality.

Information

There are Blue Mountains information centres open daily on the highway at **Glenbrook** (☎ 1300 653 408; Great Western Hwy; ☺ 9am-5pm Mon-Fri, 8.30am-4.30pm Sat & Sun) and at the spruced-up **Echo Point** (☎ 1300 653 408; ☺ 9am-5pm) in Katoomba, which has wheelchair access. The **Blue Mountains Heritage Centre** (☎ 4787 8877; Govetts Leap Rd, Blackheath; ☺ 9am-4.30pm) is about 3km off the Great Western Hwy. The website you'll want is www.bluemountains tourism.org.au.

Adventure Activities & Tours

Most Blue Mountain operators have offices in Katoomba – competition is steep, so shop around for the best deal. If you have a YHA card ask if you're eligible for a discount. For bus tours see p155.

Australian School of Mountaineering (ASM; ☎ 4782 2014; www.asmguides.com; 166 Katoomba St) Rock climbing from $165, abseiling from $125 and canyoning from $135.

Blue Mountains Adventure Company (☎ 4782 1271; www.bmac.com.au; 84a Bathurst Rd) A bit more expensive than ASM; also has bushwalking (from $135) and mountain biking (from $125).

Blue Mountains Walkabout (☎ 0408 443 822; www .bluemountainswalkabout.com; cash only $95) Eight-hour bushwalks with Aboriginal themes and spirituality. It can be strenuous at times. Twenty-five per cent of the price is donated to Aboriginal causes.

Katoomba Adventure Centre (☎ 1800 824 009; www.kacadventures.com.au; 1 Katoomba St) Canyoning and waterfall abseiling, among other things.

Tread Lightly Eco Tours (☎ 4788 1229; www.tread lightly.com.au; 100 Great Western Hwy, Medlow Bath) Eco-bushwalks and 4WD tours from two to eight hours ($30 to $165). Most tours operate from Katoomba and Blackheath.

Sleeping

There are heaps of places to stay in Katoomba; unless noted, all but budget offerings include breakfast. For more options ring the visitors centre or check www.blue mts.com.au.

BUDGET

Flying Fox (☎ 4782 4226, 1800 624 226; www.theflying fox.com.au; 190 Bathurst St; dm $21, d $58; P ⏛) This small, homy hostel is a few blocks from the centre and offers colourful spaces, laid-back atmosphere and a small deck out back. Spacious dorms and three private rooms share bathrooms, and grassy camping sites are available for $12 per person.

Blue Mountains YHA (☎ 4782 1416; www.yha.com .au; 207 Katoomba St; dm $26-32, d $72-80; P ⏛) An excellent hostel in a heritage-listed building, and comes complete with hip lounge areas in an old dance hall. The sunny terrace with fountain is a major plus. Plenty of services on offer, including area tours and activities; YHA cards earn $3.50 discount.

Hostel 14 (☎ 4782 7104; 14 Lovel St; www.bluemts .com.au/no14; dm $22, s/d $49/59) A charming, cosy old house with intimate common areas and comfy rooms (the cutest doubles are upstairs). The wooden deck on the side is a lovely place to hang out and read. It's about a 10-minute walk from the train station.

Katoomba Falls Caravan Park (☎ 4782 1835; www.bmcc.nsw.gov.au; Katoomba Falls Rd; powered/un-

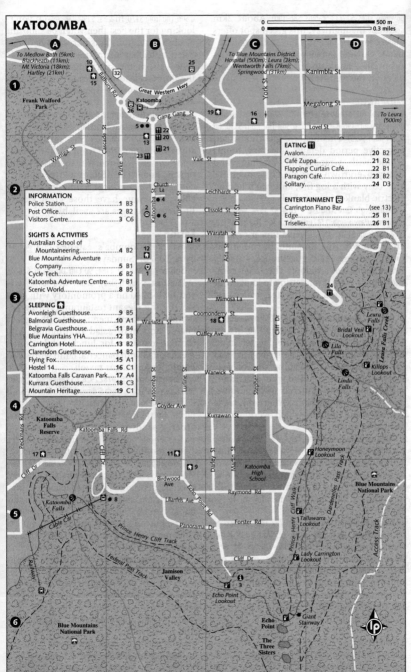

KATOOMBA

0 ——————— 500 m
0 ——————— 0.3 miles

To Medlow Bath (5km);
Blackheath (11km);
Mt Victoria (18km);
Hartley (21km)

To Blue Mountains District
Hospital (500m); Leura (2km);
Wentworth Falls (7km);
Springwood (31km)

Great Western Hwy

Gang Gang St

To Leura
(500m)

Frank Walford
Park

Kanimbla St

Megalong St

Lovel St

EATING 🍴
Avalon............................**20** B2
Café Zuppa.....................**21** B2
Flapping Curtain Café......**22** B1
Paragon Café..................**23** B2
Solitary..........................**24** D3

ENTERTAINMENT 🎭
Carrington Piano Bar........(see **13**)
Edge..............................**25** B1
Triselies.........................**26** B1

INFORMATION
Police Station..................**1** B3
Post Office......................**2** B2
Visitors Centre.................**3** C6

SIGHTS & ACTIVITIES
Australian School of
  Mountaineering...............**4** B2
Blue Mountains Adventure
  Company.........................**5** B1
Cycle Tech.......................**6** B2
Katoomba Adventure Centre...**7** B1
Scenic World.....................**8** B5

SLEEPING 🛏
Avonleigh Guesthouse..........**9** B5
Balmoral Guesthouse...........**10** A1
Belgravia Guesthouse..........**11** B4
Blue Mountains YHA............**12** B3
Carrington Hotel................**13** B2
Clarendon Guesthouse.........**14** B2
Flying Fox.......................**15** A1
Hostel 14........................**16** C1
Katoomba Falls Caravan Park...**17** A4
Kurrara Guesthouse............**18** C3
Mountain Heritage.............**19** C1

Church
La

Leichhardt St

Clissold St

Vale St

Waratah St

Ada St

Merriwa St

Mimosa La

Coomonderry St

Wanialda St

Oatley Ave

Warwick St

Leura
Falls

Bridal Veil
Lookout

Lila
Falls

Killops
Lookout

Linda
Falls

Katoomba
Falls
Reserve

Katoomba Falls Rd

Goyder Ave

Kurrawan St

Birdwood
Ave

Lilianfels Ave

Panorama Dr

Katoomba
High
School

Raymond Rd

Forster Rd

Honeymoon
Lookout

Blue Mountains
National Park

Tallawarra
Lookout

Lady Carrington
Lookout

Katoomba
Falls

Cable Car

Prince Henry Cliff Track

Federal Pass Track

Cliff Dr

Jamison
Valley

Echo Point
Lookout

Echo
Point

Giant
Stairway

Blue Mountains
National Park

The
Three
Sisters

NEW SOUTH WALES

powered sites $17/13, cabins $86-100) About 2km south of the highway, this green spot offers good camping facilities but sniffy management. Outside January and February rates drop 20%. Look under Recreational Services on the website.

MIDRANGE

Balmoral Guesthouse (☎ 4782 2264; www.balmoral house.com.au; 196 Bathurst Rd; d Sun-Thu from $110, Fri & Sat from $125) This historic guesthouse has attractive period details, charming rooms (some with wraparound veranda) and lushly overgrown gardens. In winter it's kept cosy with a log fire, and you'll find an electric blanket in your bed.

Avonleigh Guesthouse (☎ 4782 1534; www.blue mts.com.au/avonleigh; 174 Lurline St; d Sun-Thu from $120, Fri & Sat from $130; P) Twelve flowery rooms are waiting for the romantic in you at this quaint cottage-style guesthouse – teddy bears adorn your pillow. The large common room is great for getting to know your fellow guests, and the free tea, coffee and port helps.

Kurrara Guesthouse (☎ 4782 6058; www.kurrara .com; 17 Coomonderry St; d Sun-Thu $100-140, Fri & Sat $130-170; P) This guesthouse, located in an historic building, is a little shabby around the edges but in a charming sort of way. Rooms that may remind you of Grandma's house come cluttered with antiques, and some sport spa baths. Afternoon tea is served on the veranda, which overlooks the rampant garden.

Belgravia Guesthouse (☎ 4782 2998; www.blue mts.com.au/belgravia; 179 Lurline St; d $86-96; P) Just seven decent but no-nonsense rooms are available at this simple guesthouse, along with a small living-room area. It's no-frills and cheap, and not too far from Echo Point.

Clarendon Guesthouse (☎ 4782 1322; www.clare ndonguesthouse.com.au; 68 Lurline St; s/d $29/55, d incl breakfast Sun-Thu $70-130, Fri & Sat $130-176; P) Three very different types of rooms are offered at this odd hotel, from basic budget to modern motel-style to old-fashioned digs. Common facilities include fireplace with log fires, cocktail bar, swimming pool and even a cabaret theatre.

TOP END

Carrington Hotel (☎ 4782 1111; www.thecarrington .com.au; 15-47 Katoomba St; r without bathroom $119-139,

d Sun-Thu from $170, Fri & Sat $190; P) If you're looking for the best then you'll be snoozing at the Carrington. This gorgeous heritage-listed hotel has maintained its lavish old style – from the sparkling chandeliers to the stunning lead-light dome in the cocktail bar – yet luxurious spa services are also available.

Mountain Heritage (☎ 4782 2155; www.mountain heritage.com.au; cnr Apex & Lovel Sts; d Sun-Thu from $180, Fri & Sat from $238; P) Soft music, over-stuffed sofas and great front deck with awesome views welcome you to this friendly upscale hotel. The décor is a lovely country cottage, while the large rooms are comfortable (and some have those great views). Breakfast packages are available.

Eating

Most of Katoomba's eateries charge an extra 10% on Sundays.

Solitary (☎ 4782 1164; 90 Cliff Dr; mains $26-32; breakfast & lunch daily, dinner Wed-Sun) Awesomely located on a promontory with great views is this elegant restaurant offering Katoomba's fanciest menu. Order the goat's cheese and herb salad or linguine with roasted tomatoes for lunch, while dinner means quail with pancetta, lamb with sweet potato, or asparagus ravioli.

Paragon Café (☎ 4782 2928; 65 Katoomba St; mains $15-22; breakfast, lunch & dinner) The Paragon is Katoomba's undisputed Art Deco masterpiece. Settle in at a dark wood booth and order a sandwich, frittata, salad or meat pie – or just pop in for coffee and dessert. Check out the cocktail bar out the back.

Café Zuppa (☎ 4782 9247; 36 Katoomba St; mains $12-20; breakfast, lunch & dinner) Chalkboard specials proclaim house specialities: burgers, pizza, pasta and sandwiches. This casual and quirky spot boasts creaky wooden floors, bustling service and lots of families enjoying the good food and coffee (breakfasts are delicious).

Avalon Restaurant (☎ 4782 5532; 18 Katoomba St; mains $14-27; lunch Wed-Sun, dinner daily) Set upstairs in the old Savoy cinema is this Art Deco extravaganza, with a must-see cocktail bar in front. Too few lucky tables have views over the valley, but everyone can enjoy the funky art, creative lighting, rowdy weekend atmosphere and reasonable menu.

Flapping Curtain Café (☎ 4782 1622; 10 Katoomba St; mains $7-11; breakfast & lunch) If breakfast oddities like porridge, mushroom on toast, Welsh rabbit and fruit loaf appeal, this is your kinda joint. It's a casual place with friendly hippy service and colourful art, and there are also two sidewalk tables. Thick shakes will slow your walk to Echo Point.

Entertainment

Carrington Piano Bar (☎ 4782 1111; www.thecarring ton.com.au; 15 Katoomba St) Claim a seat on the great sunny patio in front of the fancy hotel and you'll be sitting pretty on the main street in Katoomba. There's also live music from Wednesday to Saturday. The Carrington empire also has another bar around the corner on Bathurst Rd, called the Main Bar.

Triselies (☎ 4782 4026; 287 Bathurst Rd) Right near the train station, this venue offers good live acts, predominantly funk and rock, on weekends. Thursdays see open mike, however, so jump up there and have some fun.

Clarendon Guesthouse (☎ 4782 1322; www.claren donguesthouse.com.au; 68 Lurline St) This guesthouse has an odd configuration of rooms, but is also known for its good cabaret acts.

Edge (☎ 4782 8900; www.edgecinema.com.au; 225 Great Western Hwy; adult/child $14.50/9.50) To experience peak thrills from the safety of a cushioned seat, come to the Edge. This giant-screen cinema shows a stunning 40-minute Blue Mountains documentary at 10.20am, 11.05am, 12.10pm, 1.30pm, 2.15pm and 5.30pm. Times may vary during holidays. There's also a regular screen that offers mainstream movies and costs less ($12.50/8.50).

Getting There & Around

Katoomba is 110km from Sydney's centre. Trains run approximately hourly from Central Station ($11.40 one way, $22.80 round trip). By car, leave the city via Parramatta Rd. At Strathfield detour onto the Western Motorway tollway (M4; $2.30), which becomes the Great Western Hwy west of Penrith.

If you like walking you can easily get around Katoomba on foot, and even walk to the quaint nearby town of Leura (2km away). If you only have a day or would rather ride, try the hop-on, hop-off **Trolley Tours** (☎ 1800 801 577; www.trolleytours.com.au; per day $12; ⌚ 9.15am-4.50pm). It's located next to the train station and stops at the major

sites in the area. The **Blue Mountains Explorer Bus** (☎ 4782 4807; www.explorerbus.com.au; adult/child/family $25/12.50/63; ⌚ 9.30am-5.30pm) does a similar circuit and costs much more, but boasts fun double-decker buses. They also have a one-time-around fare of $11.

For a complete transport package consider the Blue Mountains ExplorerLink ticket, which includes a round-trip train ticket from Sydney plus a Blue Mountains Explorer Bus pass. It costs $36/14.50 per adult/child, saving you a few bucks. Buy it at Central Station.

You can hire bicycles from **Cycle Tech** (☎ 4782 2800; 182 Katoomba St, Katoomba; half/full day $30/50), where prices include a spare kit and helmet.

Car hire is available from the nearby town of Leura. **Redicar** (☎ 4784 3443; 80 Megalong St, Leura) is a budget option for those looking to hire a car, van or 4WD.

BLACKHEATH AREA

The little town of Blackheath is a good base for visiting the Grose and Megalong Valleys. There are superb lookouts a few kilometres east of the town, such as **Govett's Leap** and **Evan's Lookout**. To the northeast, via Hat Hill Rd, are **Pulpit Rock**, **Perry's Lookdown** and **Anvil Rock**.

A cliff-top track leads from Govett's Leap to Pulpit Rock, and there are several walks from Govett's Leap down into the Grose Valley. Get details on the walks from the **NPWS visitors centre** (☎ 02-4787 8877; www.nation alparks.nsw.gov.au; Govetts Leap Rd, Blackheath; ⌚ 9am-4.30pm). Perry's Lookdown is the beginning of the shortest route (four hours return) to the beautiful **Blue Gum Forest** in the base of the valley.

The **Megalong Valley**, south of Blackheath, is largely cleared farmland, but it's still a beautiful place, with awesome sandstone escarpments. The road down from Blackheath passes through pockets of rainforest and you can walk the beautiful 600m **Coachwood Glen Nature Trail**. A couple of kilometres further on is the small valley settlement of Werribee, where there are several horse-riding outfits. **Werriberri Trail Rides** (☎ 02-4787 9171; horse@lisp.com.au; Megalong Rd, Megalong Valley; guided rides per hr/day $40/180) can show you the area on horseback and best of all, the horses are well looked after. They cater to all levels.

Blackheath is a short drive along the Great Western Hwy from Katoomba. It's also on the railway line from Sydney – two stops past Katoomba. From Blackheath, it's a 15-minute winding drive into the Megalong Valley via Shipley and Megalong Rds.

Sleeping

Gardners Inn (☎ 02-4787 8347; www.gardnersinn.com .au; 255 Great Western Hwy; s/d Sun-Thu $33/59, Fri & Sat $45/80) This cosy and friendly inn, opposite the train station, is the oldest hotel (1832) in the Blue Mountains. Rooms are reasonable (bathrooms are shared) and continental breakfast is included.

Blackheath Caravan Park (☎ 02-4787 8101; blkheath@tpg.com.au; Prince Edward St; powered sites per person $13-16, unpowered sites per person $10-12) This friendly caravan park is off Govetts Leap Rd, about 600m from the highway. It also has caravans ($60 to $70) available.

There's rudimentary backpack camping (no fired allowed) at Acacia Flat, in the Grose Valley near the Blue Gum Forest. It's a steep walk down from Govett's Leap or Perry's Lookdown. You can also camp at Perry's Lookdown, which has a car park and is a convenient base for walks into the Grose Valley, although you'll need to bring your own water. Bear in mind that you can only stay for one night.

MT VICTORIA & HARTLEY
☎ 02

Mt Victoria, the highest point in the mountains, is a small historical village with a semirural atmosphere 16km northwest of Katoomba on the Great Western Hwy.

Everything is an easy walk from the train station, where there's the **Mt Victoria Museum** (☎ 4787 1210; Mt Victoria Railway Station; 2-5pm Sat & Sun, plus holidays), which has an interesting collection of Australiana. Interesting buildings include the **Toll Bar Cottage** (1849) and the **church** built in the 1870s. The charming **Mt Vic Flicks** (☎ 4787 1577; Harley Ave; admission $10) is a cinema of the old school, with a small candy bar, real cups of tea and the occasional piano player.

About 11km past Mt Victoria, on the western slopes of the range, is the tiny, sandstone 'ghost' town of **Hartley**, which flourished from the 1830s but declined when bypassed by the railway in 1887. There are several historic buildings, including the 1837 courthouse.

The **NPWS visitors centre** (☎ 6355 2117; 10am-1pm & 2-4.30pm) is in the Farmer's Inn (1845). You can wander around the village for free, but to enter the **courthouse** you must book a tour – call the visitors centre for information.

Sleeping & Eating

Hotel Imperial (☎ 4787 1878; www.bluemts.com.au /hotelimperial; 1 Station St, Mt Victoria; dm $25, d $139-200, d without bathroom $109-139) This fine old hotel has arguably the best backpackers' rooms in the region, although there are only four beds in the dorm. The hotel faces the highway and quieter Station St, and the public bar is pretty good for a beer.

Victoria & Albert Guesthouse (☎ 4787 1241; www .ourguest.com.au; 19 Station St, Mt Victoria; d with/without bathroom $140/110;) This lovely and comfortable guesthouse (1914) is in the grand old style, but modern enough to offer a spa and sauna. Log fires warm up chilly nights, and there's a good restaurant on the premises. Breakfast is included.

JENOLAN CAVES

Southwest of Katoomba on the western fringe of Kanangra-Boyd National Park, the **Jenolan Caves** (☎ 02-6359 3311; www.jenolancaves .org.au; tours adult/child/family from $15/10/39) are the best-known limestone caves in Australia. One cave has been open to the public since 1867, although parts of the system are still unexplored. There are nine caves you can visit by guided tour. There are about a dozen tours between 9.45am and 5pm weekdays, between 9.30am and 5.30pm weekends, and a 'ghost tour' at 8pm Saturday; most tours last one to two hours. It's advisable to arrive early during holiday periods, as the best caves can be 'sold out' by 10am.

Sleeping

Jenolan Caves Resort (☎ 02-6359 3322; www.jenolan caves.com; Gatehouse $90-120, Mountain Lodge units $145-235, Caves House $125-280;) There's fully 10 kinds of rooms here – from the cheaper Gatehouse (sleeping up to six), to the lavish, old-fashioned Caves House. 'Low season' here means weeknights, two-night weekends and three-night long weekends; 'high season' means Saturday night only and bookings for two nights on public-holiday weekends. It's an atmospheric place to bed down no matter what choice you make.

Getting There & Away

The caves are on plenty of tour itineraries from Sydney and Katoomba. By car, turn off the Great Western Hwy at Hartley and the caves are a 45-minute drive along Jenolan Caves Rd. The Six Foot Track from Katoomba to Jenolan Caves is a fairly easy three-day walk, but make sure you get information from an NPWS visitors centre.

BELLS LINE OF ROAD

This back road between Richmond and Lithgow is the most scenic route across the Blue Mountains. It's highly recommended if you have your own transport. There are fine views towards the coast from Kurrajong Heights on the eastern slopes of the range, there are orchards around Bilpin, and there's sandstone cliff and bush scenery all the way to Lithgow.

Midway between Bilpin and Bell, the delightful **Mt Tomah Botanic Gardens** (☎ 02-4567 2154; adult/child/family $4.40/2.20/8.80; ☒ 10am-4pm May-Sep, 10am-5pm Oct-Apr) is a cool-climate annexe of Sydney's Royal Botanic Gardens. As well as native plants there are displays of exotic cold-climate species, including some magnificent rhododendrons. Parts of the park are wheelchair accessible.

North of the Bells Line of Road, and a 10-minute drive north of Mt Tomah, at the little town of **Mt Wilson** are formal gardens and a nearby remnant of rainforest known as the **Cathedral of Ferns**.

LITHGOW

☎ 02 / pop 20,000

Nestled in the western foothills of the Blue Mountains, Lithgow is an industrial town that straddles the border with NSW's Central West. It didn't really get going until the 1870s, when the Zig Zag Railway brought supply trains across the mountains, after which it promptly became a coal-mining centre. The highest scenic lookout in the Blue Mountains is at **Hassan Walls**, 4km south of town.

The **Lithgow visitors centre** (☎ 6353 1859; www .tourism.lithgow.com; Great Western Hwy; ☒ 9am-5pm Mon-Fri, 10am-4pm Sat, 11am-3pm Sun) is well stocked with brochures covering the entire region. Super-helpful staff advise on walking and driving routes and can point you towards the local attractions and a range of activities.

The **Zig Zag Railway** (☎ 6353 1795; Chifley Rd; adult/child/family return $20/10/50) is at **Clarence**, about 11km east of Lithgow. It was built in 1869 and was quite an engineering wonder in its day. Trains descended from the Blue Mountains by this route until 1910. A section has been restored, and steam trains run the 12km trip daily. One-way tickets are available for hikers wishing to walk the Zig Zag Walking Track. Trains depart Clarence station at 11am, 1pm and 3pm daily. Special steam trains operate only on Wednesday, Saturday, Sunday and holidays, and diesel trains on Monday, Tuesday, Thursday and Friday.

Down a side road behind the tourist office, there's **Lithgow Tourist & Van Park** (☎ 6351 4350; www.lithgowcaravanpark.com.au; Cooerwull Rd; powered/unpowered sites $21/16, cabins $59-88). It's well managed, with common TV room and on-site kiosk. If you don't feel like roughing it, try the decent one- and two-bedroom cabins.

Several pubs also have accommodation, including **Grand Central** (☎ 6351 3050; cnr Main & Eskbank Sts; per person incl breakfast $25). Standard rooms with shared bathrooms are available, all with breakfast.

Lithgow Valley Motel (☎ 6351 2334; www.lithgow valleymotel.com.au; 45 Cooerwull Rd; s $65, d & tw $72) is off the highway and has good rooms that are clean and serviceable, with a Japanese restaurant on the premises.

There are frequent CityRail trains between Lithgow and Sydney ($17). Regular trains between Lithgow and Katoomba cost $6.

NORTH COAST

The north coast is a utopian blend of sea and sand, shimmering lakes, sumptuous national parks, dolphins and whales, outdoor activities and alternative lifestyles. It's the 'acceptable face' of Australian tourism, attracting freedom-seeking internationals and jaded Aussies alike and, as such, parts of it have become overdeveloped. That is because its delights are worth returning to – over and over – and the region is very accessible; even the smallest towns are brimming with brochures and pamphlets for tourists.

The Pacific Hwy is the region's spine, a blacktop cable plugging you straight into the most electric destinations: Newcastle, Port

Macquarie, Byron Bay and the sultry climes of the tropical far north. Some of the best attractions are off the highway, though – the north coast is stuffed to its gilded tip with secluded inlets, dainty historical towns and a bit of fun-loving kitsch here and there. Maybe just fold the map away every now and then, take a few random right-hand turns and stop and smell the wax flowers.

SYDNEY TO NEWCASTLE

The central coast, between Broken Bay and Newcastle, combines splendid lakes, surf beaches, alluring national parks and the expected swathes of housing.

Gosford & Around

Leave the Sydney–Newcastle Fwy at **Brooklyn** to take a cruise on the **Riverboat Postman** (☎ 02-9985 7566; adult/child $33/16.50; ☖ departs 9.30am), Australia's last postal ferry, or visit historic **Dangar Island**, with bird-watching and bushwalks. **CityRail** (☎ 13 15 00; www.cityrail.nsw .gov.au) runs trains from Sydney ($6, one hour) and Newcastle ($12, one hour 40 minutes) to Brooklyn's Hawkesbury River station.

The largest town in the area is hilly **Gosford** (population 55,000), from where there are frequent CityRail trains to Sydney ($8) and Newcastle ($9.80). **Busways** (☎ 02-4368 2277; www.busways.com.au) services radiate frequently to nearby towns and the coast. The **Gosford visitor information centre** (☎ 02-4385 4074; www.cctourism.com.au; 200 Mann St, Gosford; ☖ 9.30am-4pm Mon-Fri, 10am-2pm Sat) covers all of the central coast.

Southwest of Gosford, there are trails rambling through rugged sandstone and between wildflowers at **Brisbane Water National Park**. **Bulgandry Aboriginal Engraving Site** is 6km along Woy Woy Rd from Kariong. CityRail trains stop at Wondabyne train station inside the park upon request. Southeast of Gosford, **Bouddi National Park** extends north along the coast from the mouth of Brisbane Water and has excellent coastal bushwalking and camping.

Both parks are managed by the **Gosford NPWS office** (☎ 02-4320 4200; central.coast@npws.nsw .gov.au; Suite 36-38, 207 Albany St N, Gosford; ☖ 8.30am-4.30pm Mon-Fri).

The National Trust–classified township of **Pearl Beach**, on the eastern edge of Brisbane Water National Park, is a quiet enclave with a sweet beach set in bushland. For holiday rentals, try www.pearlbeachreal estate.com.au.

Terrigal

☎ 02 / pop 5000

This beachside hamlet colonises your subconscious with its ocean beat – there's not much to do except surf and sunbake on the beautiful wide beach, or walk along the town's windswept headlands to **Skillion Lookout**.

Near the beach, **Terrigal Beach Lodge YHA** (☎ 4385 3330; yha@terrigalbeachlodge.com.au; 12 Campbell Cres; dm/d $25/60; ☐ Ⓟ) has peace-and-love exhortations plastered on the common-room walls, while **Tiarri Guest Rooms** (☎ 4385 9564; 16 Tiarri Cres; d from $89) has seven roomy doubles (all with courtyards) and a hilltop location near the beach.

Patcinos (☎ 4385 1960; cnr Church St & Campbell Cres; mains $7-12) is a modest little café with tasty vegetarian and deli-style meals, but **Onda** (☎ 4384 5554; www.onda.com.au; 150 Terrigal Dr; mains $22-34) is quality Italian, with alfresco dining in a courtyard perched above the beach.

From Gosford, **Busways** (☎ 4368 2277; www .busways.com.au) services run to Terrigal ($4) at least hourly.

NEWCASTLE

☎ 02 / pop 137,000

Newcastle has had some unflattering press over the years, due to its status as a former steel town. But the place has changed: it's now concentrating on promoting other assets, like its quality beaches, its harbour and its de facto status as capital of the Central Coast. It's really quite an appealing place, with outstanding heritage architecture in the CBD, a beautiful foreshore and some classy inner-city suburbs.

Like other industrial towns worldwide, Newcastle has spawned an innovative, often confrontational arts scene that has, all at the same time, reacted against and been inspired by the sights and sounds of heavy industry. It's also got a good reputation for live music; it was the stomping ground of silverchair, super-successful Nirvana clones, and there are loads of local bands hoping to surf similar sound waves today.

Finally, Newcastle is ideal for exploring the sumptuous Hunter Valley (p164).

NEWCASTLE

INFORMATION
Angus & Robertson.................1	E2
Battle Ground..........................2	E2
Cook's Hill Books & Records....3	D3
Newcastle Region Library..........4	D3
Newcastle Visitor Information	
Centre.................................5	D3
Post Office..............................6	F2
Royal Newcastle Hospital.........7	F2

SIGHTS & ACTIVITIES
Avago Sports...........................8	F2
Blue Water Sea Kayaking..........9	B2
Bogey Hole............................10	F3
Convict Lumber Yard..............11	F1
Fort Scratchley......................12	F1
Newcastle Region Art Gallery...13	D3
Newcastle Region Museum......14	B3
Newcastle's Famous Tram.......15	F2
Obelisk.................................16	E3
Ocean Baths.........................17	F2
Queens Wharf Tower.........(see 26)	

SLEEPING
Buchanan B&B......................18	F2
Clarendon Hotel...................19	D2
Newcastle Backpackers..........20	B3
Newcastle Beach YHA...........21	F2
Nomads Backpackers by the Beach..22	F2
Novocastrian.........................23	F1

EATING
Bi-Lo Supermarket.................24	C3
Bogie Hole Café....................25	F2
Brewery................................26	E2
Customs House Hotel.............27	F1
Goldbergs Coffee House........28	D3
Last Drop.............................29	F2
Mangrove Jacks....................30	B2
Niyon..................................31	A3
Paymaster's Café...................32	F1
Rendez-vu............................33	D3
Scratchleys...........................34	E2

DRINKING
MJ Finnegan's.......................35	D2

ENTERTAINMENT
Cambridge Hotel...................36	B3
Civic Theatre........................37	D3
Salarium Space.....................38	B3
Showcase City Cinemas..........39	E2
Wickham Park Hotel..............40	A3

TRANSPORT
Bus Station...........................41	F1
Stockton Ferry......................42	E2

STOCKTON

Griffith Park

Port
Hunter

Hunter River

Newcastle
Harbour

Wharf Rd

SOUTH
PACIFIC
OCEAN

Nobbys
Beach

Nobbys Rd

Newcastle Beach

Shortland Esp

Bathers
Way

King Edward
Park

EAST END

NEWCASTLE

Watt St

Scott St

Bond St

Stevenson Pl

Hunter St Mall

Newcomen St

Church St

Hunter St

Wolfe St

Perkins St

Brown St

Tyrrell St

Darby St

Civic

COOK'S
HILL

National
Park

Newcastle
Sports
Centre

HAMILTON

NEWCASTLE
WEST

WICKHAM

Wickham
Park

Pacific Hwy (Stewart Ave)

Pacific Hwy
(Hunter St)

Memorial Dr

To Wetlands Centre (15km);
Maitland (30km);
Williamtown (40km);
Williamtown Airport (40km);
Hunter Valley (50km)

To Belmont (40km);
Belmont Airport (40km);
Gosford (75km);
Sydney (150km)

To RAAF Base (4km);
John Hunter
Hospital (4km)

To Blackbutt
Reserve (5km)

To Bar Beach (1km);
Merewether Beach (2km)

To Nobbys
Head (1km)

500 m
0.3 miles

Orientation

The city centre is bordered by the Hunter River and the sea.

The train station, post office and banks stand at the CBD's northeastern edge. The shopping centre is Hunter St, a pedestrian mall between Newcomen and Perkins Sts. The lively suburb of Hamilton is adjacent to Newcastle West.

Information

BOOKSHOPS

Angus & Robertson (☎ 4929 4601; Shop 2, 147 Hunter St Mall)

Cook's Hill Books & Records (☎ 4929 5079; 72 Darby St) Mostly second-hand books and records.

INTERNET ACCESS

You can also try the hostels.

Battle Ground (☎ 4926 3898; Shop 2, 169-173 King St; per hr $6)

Newcastle Region Library (☎ 4974 5300; Laman St; per hr $5.50)

MEDICAL SERVICES

John Hunter Hospital (☎ 4921 3000; Lookout Rd, New Lambton) Emergency care.

Royal Newcastle Hospital (☎ 4923 6000; Pacific St) No emergency department.

MONEY

Banks are in Hunter St Mall; most have foreign exchange.

TOURIST INFORMATION

Newcastle visitor information centre (☎ 4974 2999; www.newcastletourism.com; 361 Hunter St; ⏱ 9am-5pm Mon-Fri, 10am-3.30pm Sat & Sun) Accommodation and extensive Hunter Valley information.

Sights

Queens Wharf Tower on the waterfront and the obelisk above King Edward Park afford commanding views of the city and the water. Across the river (five minutes by ferry) is Stockton, a modest settlement with striking views back to Newcastle and exposed shipwrecks lurking in its waters.

NOBBY'S HEAD

Nobby's was an island until it was joined to the mainland in 1846 to create a singularly pretty (and long) sand spit; it was twice its current height before being reduced to 28m above sea level in 1855. The walk along the spit towards the lighthouse and meteorological station is exhilarating, as waves crash about your ears and joggers jostle your elbows.

FORT SCRATCHLEY

This was one of Australia's few gun installations to fire a gun in anger during WWII. On 8 June 1942 a large Japanese submarine surfaced, raining shells on the city. Fort Scratchley returned fire, negating the threat after just four rounds. The complex houses the Military Museum, the Maritime Museum and underground defensive tunnels, but it's closed to the public for renovations until late 2005/early 2006. Visit the grounds, though, for a glimpse of the big guns and I-can-see-for-miles views of the city and coastline.

MUSEUMS

The **Newcastle Region Museum** (☎ 4974 1400; www.nrmuseum.com.au; cnr Wood & Hunter Sts; admission free; ⏱ 10am-5pm Tue-Sun, 10am-5pm Mon during school holidays; ▣), in a restored brewery, has a variety of exhibits including interactive science gadgets, an indigenous section and a shrine to local sports legends.

The excellent **Newcastle Region Art Gallery** (☎ 4974 5100; www.ncc.nsw.gov.au/services/culture/artgallery/index.cfm; 1 Laman St; admission free; ⏱ 10am-5pm Tue-Sun) collects works by revered Australian artists (Drysdale, Nolan, Whiteley) and hosts hip exhibitions by international stars and young local artists – recent showings included hyperreal photographs of Australian celebrities and a treatise on automobile fetishism.

WILDLIFE

Walking trails meander through grey gums and native wildlife enclosures at **Blackbutt Reserve** (☎ 4952 1449; www.ncc.nsw.gov.au; Carnley Ave, New Lambton Heights; admission free; ⏱ 9am-5pm); get up close and personal with koalas, wombats, emus, kangaroos, wallabies and quolls (legendary cat-shaped marsupials from Tasmania). The fastest bus from the CBD is No 363, but it stops at the Lookout Rd entrance, which is quite a hike from the creatures.

The **Wetlands Centre** (☎ 4951 6466; www.wetlands.org.au; Sandgate Rd, Shortland; adult/concession $5/3; ⏱ 9am-3pm Mon-Fri, 9am-5pm Sat & Sun) is a swampy wonderland, home to 200 bird and animal species; hire a canoe ($7.50 for two hours). Take the Pacific Hwy towards Maitland and turn left at the cemetery, or catch bus No 106 from the train station.

Activities

SWIMMING & SURFING

Right by the East End, **Newcastle Beach** sates the needs of surfers and swimmers, but if you're paranoid about sharks, the **ocean baths** are a mellow alternative, encased in wonderful, multicoloured 1922 architecture – there's a shallow pool for toddlers and a compelling backdrop of heaving ocean and chugging cargo ships. Surfers should goofy-foot it to **Nobby's Beach**, just north of the baths – the fast left-hander known as the **Wedge** is at its north end.

South of Newcastle Beach, below King Edward Park, is Australia's oldest ocean bath, the convict-carved **Bogey Hole**. If your swimsuit is chafing you, scramble around the rocks and under the headland to the (unofficial) nude beach, **Susan Gilmour Beach**.

The most popular surfing break is at **Bar Beach**, 1km south. At nearby **Merewether Beach**, home of famous grommet Mark Richards, the opening of the winter swimming season is heralded at its **ocean baths**, where blocks of ice are dumped into the water so that the cold-blooded freaks from the Merewether Mackerels Winter Swimming Club can strut their stuff. Frequent local buses from the CBD run as far south as Bar Beach, but only No 207 continues to Merewether.

Avago Sports (☎ 0404 278 072; www.avago.com .au; Newcastle Beach; 3hr/day/week $30/40/95; ☼ 7am-7pm) will deliver surfboards, bodyboards, sandboards and mountain bikes, including maps and local tips, to your Newcastle accommodation. Sailboards and windsurfers are also available for hire.

WALKING

The **Bathers Way** self-guided walk takes you from Nobby's Beach to Merewether Beach; signposts teach you about indigenous, convict and natural history in between swims. The **Newcastle East Heritage Walk** wanders around the East End for 3km, between the city's architectural treasures. Brochures for both walks are available at the visitor information centre, or just follow the signs.

SEA KAYAKING

Blue Water Sea Kayaking (☎ 4961 1233; www.sea kayaking.com.au; Shop 4, Newcastle Cruising Yacht Club Commercial Centre, Hannell St, Wickham) rents kayaks (from $20) and leads tours.

HANG GLIDING

Air Sports (☎ 0412 607 815; www.air-sports.com.au) offers tandem hang-gliding flights (from $165).

Tours

Newcastle's Famous Tram (☎ 4963 7954; tram@idl .net.au; adult/child $10/6) trundles around the East End for 45 minutes, taking in major historical sites. It leaves the train station on the hour between 10am and 2pm (last tram at 1.45pm Monday to Friday).

Festivals & Events

Electrofringe (www.electrofringe.org) Explores bleeding-edge electronic and digital realms: sound, video, online etc; late September.

Mattara Festival (www.mattarafestival.org.au) Celebrate Newcastle in early October.

National Young Writers' Festival (www.youngwriters festival.org) Cracking mix of established and emerging writers giving talks, workshops, panels; late September.

Newcastle Jazz Festival (www.newcastlejazz.com.au) Jam your horn in late August.

Newcastle Regional Show (☎ 4961 2085) 'Country fair'-type show; git on down early March.

Surfest (www.surfest.com) Hang ten in late March.

Sleeping

BUDGET

Newcastle Beach YHA (☎ 4925 3544; mail@newcastleyha .com.au; 30 Pacific St; dm/s/d from $24/42/60; ☐) This heritage-listed building is a bikini strap away from Newcastle Beach. Inside, it's a bit like an English public school (without the humiliating hazing rituals): grand and ostentatious, high ceilings, huge dorms and a plush-leather common room. There's also free surfboard hire, pub meals, quizzes, pizza nights etc, and a palm-tree courtyard with a BBQ.

Newcastle Backpackers (☎ 1800 333 436, 4969 34 36; www.newcastlebackpackers.com; 42 & 44 Denison St, Hamilton; dm/d from $18/55; ☐) Sprawling over three properties, this hostel has pleasant gardens, a pool, table tennis and the stuffed-to-the-gills feel of a thriving community. The managers are zealous surfers and will drive you to the beach, lend you a surfboard and give you a free lesson. They'll also pick you up and drop you off at any Newcastle train station. It's close to the Beaumont St restaurant district.

Nomads Backpackers by the Beach (☎ 1800 008 972, 4926 3472; www.backpackersbythebeach.com .au; 34 Hunter St; dm/d $25/55; 🖳) This one's also in a terrific location, right near the beach and some excellent Hunter St eateries. It's bright, clean, modern and relaxed and the staff hold court on Newcastle nightlife and surfing.

MIDRANGE

Clarendon Hotel (☎ 4927 0966; www.clarendonhotel .com.au; 347 Hunter St; s/d/ste $121/132/143; 🖳 🖳) In an old Art Deco building, the Clarendon is thickly atmospheric with mod furniture and lighting, and lavishly painted walls and stylish furniture; David Lynch (or James Ellroy) might feel at home here. There's a bar, a brasserie and lashings of conviviality downstairs.

Buchanan B&B (☎ 4926 5828; www.buchanan-bb .com.au; 20 Church St; s/d from $75/120; 🖳) This restored heritage house offers beautiful, high French beds and a tasty homemade breakfast. The outside is done up in those delightful pastel hues that characterise Australian coastal architecture, and the interior is 19th-century glam.

Novocastrian (☎ 1800 005 944, 4926 3688; 21 Parnell Pl; d $110-185, f $165; 🌣) It's part of the world's largest hotel chain, but at least its location is individual: right above Nobby's Beach.

Eating

Darby and Beaumont are the main eat streets, rammed to the gills with culinary establishments of all persuasions.

RESTAURANTS

Customs House Hotel (☎ 4925 2585; www.customs house.net.au; 1 Bond St; mains $12-27; 🕑 lunch & dinner) Once HQ for confiscating contraband, this lovely old building, with scenic alfresco patio, is now part pub, part classy bistro. The fusion menu might include Atlantic salmon (a Newcastle culinary staple) or roast supreme of duck.

Brewery (☎ 4929 6333; www.qwb.com.au; Queens Wharf; 150 Wharf Rd; mains $24-26; 🕑 lunch & dinner) Perched on Queens Wharf, the views and outdoor tables are naturally sought after. The food is good, hearty marine-type fare:

chargrilled rumps, fisherman's baskets, grilled fish. Features a good, NSW-centric wine list too. Wear your boat shoes for best results.

Niyon (☎ 4961 0825; 49 Beaumont St; mains $12-18; 🕑 dinner) This upstairs Thai restaurant has a prime balcony overlooking epicurean Beaumont. Great green curries (some without coconut milk, in a surprising non-traditional gambit) and laconic, likeable service.

Rendez-vu (☎ 4929 2244; 115 Darby St; mains $10-25; 🕑 lunch & dinner) Although good sandwiches and a wide-ranging cocktail list draw crowds to the sidewalk tables, the staff's rude phone manner may mean others never make it. Take your chances.

Scratchleys (☎ 4929 1111; www.scratchleys.com.au; 200 Wharf Rd; mains $13-28; 🕑 lunch & dinner) Claims to be Australia's most 'environmentally friendly restaurant', but can the seafood here cut it? Latest foodies awards say 'yes'.

Mangrove Jacks (☎ 4969 8181; www.mangrove-jacks.com.au; 97 Hannell Street, Wickham; mains $25-34; 🕑 lunch & dinner) The view here is undeniably breathtaking, overlooking the Honeysuckle Marina precinct; the food (Mod Oz seafood) less so, though still edible by all means. There's a takeaway service.

CAFÉS

Last Drop (☎ 4926 3470; 37 Hunter St; dishes $7-10) A gem of a café, packing on the charm with terrific smoothies and gourmet wraps, radiant staff and the comfy couch in back.

Paymaster's Café (☎ 4925 2600; 18 Bond St; mains $20-28; 🕑 lunch & dinner) Wicker chairs, sea breezes, heritage surrounds and an Asian-influenced menu. If they have it, promise you'll try the *char sui* pork, with bok choy and *udon* noodles.

Bogie Hole Café (☎ 4926 1790; cnr Hunter & Pacific Sts; mains $11-21; 🕑 breakfast, lunch & dinner) This place is always packed. It's metres from the beach, has masses of sidewalk tables and serves huge helpings of nicely prepared standards: pastas, salads, burgers, steaks, lamb and chicken.

Goldbergs Coffee House (☎ 4929 3122; 137 Darby St; meals $7-18; 🕑 breakfast & dinner) A smooth café, European style with open frontage, but featuring a typically earthy Novocastrian twist: a wrought-iron chandelier looming like an oversized arachnid. Attracts chatty crowds of all persuasions.

SELF-CATERING

Bi-Lo Supermarket (☎ 4926 4494; cnr King & National Park Sts)

Drinking

Brewery (☎ 4929 6333; 150 Wharf Rd) Right on the harbour, share the jetty with Novocastrian office workers and uni students; just as well there's that jetty and that view, as the upstairs bar is poorly designed, with pillars in the way of the bands on the stage.

MJ Finnegan's (☎ 4926 4777; www.irishpub.com.au; 21-23 Darby St) A comfy establishment, with Irish stylings that aren't as contrived as the typical Celtic chains.

Also recommended:

Clarendon (☎ 4927 0966; www.clarendonhotel.com.au; 347 Hunter St) Art Deco décor, in the Clarendon Hotel (see opposite).

Customs House Hotel (☎ 4925 2585; 1 Bond St) Foreshore atmosphere.

Entertainment

LIVE MUSIC

Hostel staff, music-store employees and Thursday's paper are your best bets for inside goss. Most pubs feature bands Wednesday to Sunday.

Salarium Space (☎ 4961 5191; www.angelfire.com /oz/salariumspace; Morrow Park Bowling Club, Station St, Wickham) Dripping with good vibes, Salarium is hosted in an old, converted bowling club. Dig it: cushions, candles, fairy lights…it's certainly a change from Newie beer pits. Diverse acts play here: jazz, world music, funk, noise. It's open when they 'feel like it'.

Live Sites (www.livesites.org.au; ☼ Jan-Apr) This council-led initiative has proved popular. In malls, squares and public spaces around town, expect a varied line-up of acts: Latin jazz, professional street performers, Indian raga music.

Cambridge Hotel (☎ 4962 2459; www.yourcam bridge.com; 789 Hunter St) The Cambridge launched silverchair and the tourist brochures won't let them forget it – but Newie's House of Rock has moved on, showcasing touring national bands and local acts.

Wickham Park Hotel (☎ 4962 3501; www.wph .com.au; 61 Maitland Rd) Features a welcoming, neighbourhood-pub feel, with acoustic shows in the beer garden and suchlike. There's a wacky website in bright colours which should give you an indication of the business.

CINEMAS

Showcase City Cinemas (☎ 4929 5019; 31 Wolfe St; tickets $9-10.50) Specialises in foreign and independent flicks.

Greater Union (☎ 4926 2233; 183-185 King St) Mainstream releases.

THEATRE

Civic Theatre (☎ 4926 1289; www.civictheatrenewcastle .com.au; 375 Hunter St) The Civic hosts theatre, musicals, concerts and dance in a typically evocative Newcastle heritage building. It was designed by specialist 'picture palace' architect Henry White, a man responsible for around 180 theatres in Australia, North America and New Zealand.

OTHER

Octapod (www.octapod.org) This is the mob behind the Newcastle Young Writers' Festival and Electrofringe. Creative and committed, they put on loads of events around town, including workshops, screenings and gigs.

Getting There & Away

AIR

Newcastle's main **airport** (☎ 4928 9800; www .newcastleairport.com.au) is at Williamtown, about 15km north of the city. **Virgin Blue** (☎ 13 67 89; www.virginblue.com.au) and **Jetstar** (☎ 13 15 38; www.jetstar.com.au) fly to Brisbane (from $70) and Melbourne (from $65), while **Qantas** (☎ 13 13 13; www.qantas.com.au) goes one better by flying to Sydney (from $95), as well.

BUS

Nearly all long-distance buses stop behind Newcastle train station.

Port Stephens Coaches (☎ 4982 2940; www.ps coaches.com.au) Nelson Bay to Newcastle ($10.40, 1¼ hours); Newcastle to Sydney ($24, two hours 10 minutes, once daily).

Rover Coaches (☎ 4990 1699; www.rovercoaches.com .au) To Cessnock ($12, 1¼ hours, four daily).

CAR

ARA (☎ 1800 243 122, 4962 2488; www.ararental.com .au; 86 Belford St, Broadmeadow) offers rentals from $29 a day; alternatively, Tudor St in Hamilton has the big rental agencies.

TRAIN

CityRail (☎ 13 15 00; www.cityrail.nsw.gov.au) operates frequent trains into Sydney ($17, three hours).

Getting Around

TO/FROM THE AIRPORT

Port Stephens Coaches (☎ 4982 2940; www.pscoaches .com.au) goes to and from Williamtown airport frequently ($5.90, 35 minutes) en route to Nelson Bay. Local bus Nos 310, 311, 322 and 363 go to Belmont airport from Newcastle train station ($2.50, 1½ hours).

Taxis (☎ 4979 3000) cost around $45 to Williamtown or Belmont airport.

BUS

Most **local buses** (☎ 13 15 00; www.newcastlebuses .info) operate every half-hour on weekdays, less frequently on weekends. Fares are time-based, with one-hour ($2.70), four-hour ($5.30) and all-day ($8.10) passes available. The main depot is near the train station.

FERRY

From Queens Wharf, the Stockton ferry ($2) runs every half-hour from 5.15am until midnight on Friday and Saturday, stopping at 11pm Monday to Thursday and 10pm on Sunday.

LOWER HUNTER VALLEY

The Hunter Valley is the oldest wine region in Australia, best known for its Semillon and Shiraz varieties, but sometimes it just can't get respect. Those loyal to SA's Barossa and Victoria's Yarra Valleys tend to look down their noses at the Hunter, and a recent newspaper article quoted a Melbourne restaurateur as saying the valley was only good for 'growing bananas'. That's their misfortune, because there are some top-class establishments here. All up, there are over 90 wineries in the Lower Hunter and around half a dozen in the Upper Hunter (p168).

Vines were first planted here in the 1820s; by the 1860s there were 20 sq km under cultivation. A Hunter sparkling wine made its way to Paris in 1855 and was favourably compared to the French product. However, most Hunter wineries gradually declined, and it wasn't until the 1960s that wine making again became an important industry; perhaps that's the root of all this tribal loyalty. Old perceptions die hard in Australia.

The Hunter has an important ace up its sleeve: these wineries are refreshingly attitude free and welcoming of viticulturists and novices alike.

Newcastle's hostels and the Hunter Valley visitor information centre can help you out with tours; make sure you take a copy of the latter's comprehensive *Hunter Valley Wine Country Visitors Guide*, featuring summaries of all the vineyards and an excellent map.

Orientation & Information

Most of the Lower Hunter's attractions lie in an area bordered to the north by the New England Hwy and to the south by the Wollombi/Maitland Rd. The area's main town is Cessnock, close to the southern edge of the vineyards. Most of the action happens along Broke Rd; the town of Pokolbin is at the intersection of Broke and McDonalds Rds.

The former coal-mining centre of Maitland is the northern gateway into the Hunter.

The **Hunter Valley visitor information centre** (☎ 02-4990 4477; www.winecountry.com.au; 455 Wine Country Dr, Pokolbin; ☉ 9am-5pm Mon-Sat, 9am-4pm Sun) is in a large complex with a café, and is very well organised. Information is posted outside for out-of-hours visitors.

Sights

WINERIES

Visit the following by all means, but remember: all of the Hunter's wineries are welcoming and worthwhile. Staff will rarely give you the evil eye if you leadenly twirl your glass once too often, or don't take the proper time

---

KNOCK IT BACK...HAVE ANOTHER ONE?

Before embarking on your voyage of the senses, keep in mind that drink-driving regulations are heavily enforced in New South Wales. If you are driving, know that to stay under the blood-alcohol limit of 0.05, the average man can have two standard drinks in the first hour and one every hour after. Most women can have one standard drink per hour. Wineries offer 20ml tastes of wine – five of these equals one standard drink. Other ways to minimise the damage: choose a designated driver, buy a bottle to take with you, use the spittoons provided, take a tour if you can, or give up the demon drink.

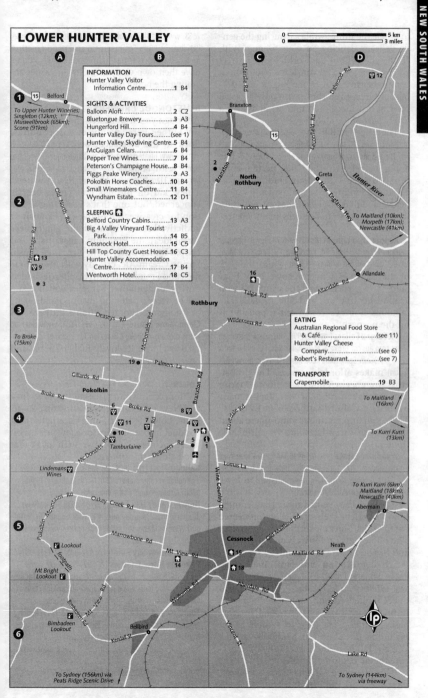

LOWER HUNTER VALLEY

0 — 5 km
0 — 3 miles

INFORMATION
Hunter Valley Visitor
Information Centre................1 B4

SIGHTS & ACTIVITIES
Balloon Aloft..........................2 C2
Bluetongue Brewery.................3 A3
Hungerford Hill.......................4 B4
Hunter Valley Day Tours.........(see 1) B4
Hunter Valley Skydiving Centre.5 B4
McGuigan Cellars....................6 B4
Pepper Tree Wines...................7 B4
Peterson's Champagne House...8 B4
Piggs Peake Winery..................9 A3
Pokolbin Horse Coaches.........10 B4
Small Winemakers Centre........11 B4
Wyndham Estate.....................12 D1

SLEEPING
Belford Country Cabins...........13 A3
Big 4 Valley Vineyard Tourist
Park.....................................14 B5
Cessnock Hotel........................15 C5
Hill Top Country Guest House..16 C3
Hunter Valley Accommodation
Centre..................................17 B4
Wentworth Hotel....................18 C5

EATING
Australian Regional Food Store
& Café................................(see 11)
Hunter Valley Cheese
Company.............................(see 6)
Robert's Restaurant...............(see 7)

TRANSPORT
Grapemobile.........................19 B3

To Upper Hunter Wineries;
Singleton (12km);
Muswellbrook (65km);
Scone (91km)

Belford

Branxton

North
Rothbury

Greta

Hunter River

To Maitland (10km);
Morpeth (17km);
Newcastle (41km)

Tuckers La

Allandale

Rothbury

Wilderness Rd

To Broke
(15km)

Deaseys Rd

Palmers La

Gillards Rd

Pokolbin

Broke Rd

To Maitland
(16km)

To Kurri Kurri
(13km)

Tamburlaine

Lindemans
Wines

To Kurri Kurri (6km);
Maitland (18km);
Newcastle (40km)

Abermain

Oakey Creek Rd

Marrowbone Rd

Cessnock

Neath

Maitland Rd

Lookout

Mt Bright
Lookout

Bimbadeen
Lookout

Bellbird

Kendall St

Aberdare Rd

Lake Rd

To Sydney (156km) via
Peats Ridge Scenic Drive

To Sydney (144km)
via freeway

to inhale the fumes while savouring the gentle delicacy dancing on your tongue. With all the goodwill in the world, they'll correct your technique. You can learn a lot from a comprehensive tour of the region and tastings are free. Even those with only a casual interest in wine should tour around – it's a lovely part of the state.

The **Hungerford Hill** (☎ 02-4998 7666; www.hungerfordhill.com.au; 1 Broke Rd, Pokolbin; 🕙 9am-5pm Mon-Fri, 10am-5pm Sat & Sun) winery is shaped like a big barrel, with its 'lid' permanently propped open – this commanding spectacle stands sentinel over the lakes and valleys below, and makes an excellent introduction to your winery tour. Features an on-site restaurant.

Pepper Tree Wines (☎ 02-4998 7539; www.peppertreewines.com.au; Halls Rd, Pokolbin; 🕙 9am-5pm Mon-Fri, 9.30am-5pm Sat & Sun) is just about the pick of the bunch, set in gorgeous, New England–style gardens. And the wine? It's won around 60 trophies and 500 medals. The fabulous Robert's restaurant (opposite) is on the property.

McGuigan Cellars (☎ 02-4998 7402; www.mcguiganwines.com.au; cnr Broke & McDonalds Rds, Pokolbin; tours $2; 🕙 9.30am-5pm, tours noon Mon-Fri, 11am & noon Sat & Sun) makes affordable wines. The proprietors are cheeky enough to quote Martin Luther for their *raison d'être*: 'Beer is made by men,' exclaimed Luther, 'wine by Gods!' There's an unpretentious atmosphere about the place that translates into very drinkable tipples.

Wyndham Estate (☎ 02-4938 3444; www.wyndhamestate.com.au; 700 Dalwood Rd, Dalwood; tours free; 🕙 10am-4.30pm, tours 11am), established in 1828, is Australia's oldest extant winery – you'd best believe they've had more than enough time to perfect their craft (they pioneered commercial Shiraz planting in Australia). The estate puts on festivals and jazz events and has an on-site restaurant.

Self-deprecating and informal, **Piggs Peake Winery** (☎ 02-6574 7000; www.piggspeake.com; 697 Hermitage Rd, Pokolbin; 🕙 10am-5pm) produces limited-edition, unwooded wines to impress your mates back home. In 2004 lucky swines were able to sample wines including the Sows Ear Semillon and the Wiggly Tail Marsanne. Post-2004, the porcine theme continues apace.

If the preceding wineries are 'major labels', then the **Small Winemakers Centre** (☎ 02-4998

7668; www.smallwinemakerscentre.com.au; McDonalds Rd, Pokolbin; 🕙 10am-5pm) is indie and proud, acting as a cellar door for 10 wine makers who don't have their own vineyards. Organic wines are among the booty on offer.

BLUETONGUE BREWERY
Although you won't catch the likes of Martin Luther here, plenty of mere mortals flock to the **Bluetongue Brewery** (☎ 02-4998 7945; www.hunterresort.com.au/bluetongue/index.htm; Hunter Resort, Hermitage Rd; 🕙 breakfast, lunch & dinner, tours 11am & 2pm) at Hunter Resort winery, a new kid on the block as far as beer is concerned, but one that's attracting attention for creative, refreshing and exquisitely addictive brews. Try alcoholic ginger beer (great idea); the Premium Lager, malty and crisp; Hunter Bitter, with a caramel finish; Spring Cream Ale, creamy with more caramel; and Framboise, with raspberries added during fermentation. Sample them all using the brewery's patented Tasting Paddle.

Another recommendation is the **Peterson's Champagne House** (☎ 02-4998 7881; www.petersonhouse.com.au; cnr Broke & Branxton Rds, Pokolbin; 🕙 breakfast & lunch) with its lovely-jubbly bubbly and on-site restaurant.

Tours
Visitors centres and places to stay in Sydney and Newcastle can help you organise a tour of the Lower Hunter. Some pubs in the area conduct informal tours for a low price, a bit like the classic 'pub crawl' with all of that good-time atmosphere.

Balloon Aloft (☎ 1800 028 568, 02-4938 1955; www.balloonaloft.com; Branxton Rd, North Rothbury; flights $280) Airborne tours of the vineyards.

Hunter Valley Day Tours (☎ 02-4938 5031; www.huntertourism.com/daytours; 455 Wine Country Dr, Pokolbin) Wine- and cheese-tasting tours; prices vary according to the size of your group.

Hunter Valley Skydiving Centre (☎ 02-4322 9884)

Pokolbin Horse Coaches (☎ 02-4998 7305; www.hunterweb.com.au/pokolbinhorsecoaches; McDonalds Rd, Pokolbin) Day tours in a quaint, open-air carriage (from $45), including pick-up, picnic lunch and tastings.

Tumbleweed Trike Tours (☎ 02-4938 1245) Motor around on extravagant, customised trikes – one seat in front, two in back. Rates start at $100 per couple for the first hour, decreasing in $50 increments each subsequent hour.

Vineyard Shuttle Service (☎ 02-4998 7779; www.vineyardshuttle.com.au) Bus tours from $33 per person.

Festivals & Events

Budfest September; held in Cessnock.
Harvest Festival February to May.
Jazz in the Vines (www.jazzinthevines.com.au) October.
Lovedale Long Lunch In May, seven wineries and chefs produce gut-bursting lunches, served with music and art.
Opera in the Vineyards (www.4-d.com.au) October.

Sleeping

As always, ask staff at the visitor information centre to match accommodation to your budget and standards. Prices at motels adjust to whatever the market will bear, and are higher on weekends; there's usually a minimum two-night stay. Maitland and Singleton are good alternatives to basing yourself in the vineyards or in Cessnock; they're further away, but cheaper.

VINEYARDS

Belford Country Cabins (☎ 02-6574 7100; www.belford cabins.com.au; 659 Hermitage Rd, Pokolbin; d from $100; P ✕) Choice accommodation in bushland, among kangaroos, possums and ironbark trees. The sense of space and the great outdoors on your doorstep is almost worth the price alone; added to that are the roomy and cosy cabins. Children are welcome (cots, high chairs and so forth are available) and there's a pool, BBQs and a games room.

Hill Top Country Guest House (☎ 02-4930 7111; www.hilltopguesthouse.com.au; 81 Talga Rd, Rothbury; d from $88; ✕ P ✑) Hill Top offers great views, horse riding, in-house massage, canoeing, a pool, self-drive buggies, wildlife safaris, double spas, a grand piano, cattle mustering and a billiard room. And you thought you were here for the wine.

Hunter Valley Accommodation Centre (☎ 02-4991 4222; www.huntervalleyaccommodation.com; 453 Wine Country Dr, Pokolbin; s/d from $60/80; P ✕ ✑) Well located, right by the visitor information centre. There's a pool and tennis courts.

CESSNOCK

Cessnock Hotel (☎ 02-4990 1002; 234 Wollombi Rd; s/d from $35/60) This classic restored pub has cottage-type rooms – a bit more cosy than your standard pub accommodation. Downstairs is a lively bar, with a bistro and expansive courtyard.

Wentworth Hotel (☎ 02-4990 1364; murphys@ wentworthhotelcessnock.com.au; 32 Vincent St; s/d from $50/70) The Wenty, dating from the 1920s,

is another pub that's tarted up its décor. Breakfast is included, there's a restaurant and live music some nights.

Big 4 Valley Vineyard Tourist Park (☎ 02-4990 2573; Mt View Rd; powered sites $24, deluxe cabins $60; ✕ ✑) A spacious, orderly park with a pool and on-site Thai restaurant. It's ideally placed for the wineries.

Eating
VINEYARDS

Many wineries have picnic tables and barbecues and a goodly proportion have onsite restaurants.

Robert's Restaurant (☎ 02-4998 7330; www.roberts restaurant.com; Halls Rd, Pokolbin; mains $36-40) Book ahead, as Robert's has quite the reputation – it's extraordinarily atmospheric, located in a settler's cottage in the Pepper Tree grounds (opposite). Its gourmet menu induces rapture, combining the best of French and Italian traditions with Aussie country produce.

Australian Regional Food Store & Café (☎ 02-4998 6800; www.australianregionalfoods.com.au; Small Winemakers Centre, McDonalds Rd, Pokolbin; mains $17-19; ✚ breakfast, lunch & dinner) Like the centre in which it's located, this food store champions 'indie', often organic, produce ('lean and green', they say). Stock up – you won't get the likes of the extraordinarily tangy dill-and-lemon mustard, salmon sauce or chilli olive oil in your standard supermarkets. Free tastings are available and the café makes good use of the store's products.

Hunter Valley Cheese Company (☎ 02-4998 7744; www.huntervalleycheese.com.au; McGuigans Complex, McDonalds Rd, Pokolbin; ✚ 9am-5.30pm) Enough of Martin Luther, already; this place anoints Monty Python as its patron saint: 'Blessed are the cheesemakers', quote the staff T-shirts, and the staff themselves will chew your ear about cheesy comestibles all day long. Using vegetarian rennet and no preservatives, there's a bewildering, sinful variety of styles on offer, including 'washed rinds to remember'. There are free tastings and more structured ones for $6. Watch your girth.

Getting There & Around

There's no public transport around the vineyards. Hire a car in Sydney or Newcastle, or join a tour.

Grapemobile (☎ 0500 804 039; www.grapemobile .com.au; cnr McDonalds Rd & Palmers Lane, Pokolbin) hires bikes ($5/30 per hour/day), while the

Vineyard Shuttle Service (☎ 02-4998 7779; www.vine yardshuttle.com.au) takes you from your accommodation to anywhere in the valley and back ($10).

BUS

Kean's (☎ 02-6543 1322) goes to Cessnock ($30, two hours 20 minutes, once daily), Muswellbrook ($39, 3½ hours) and Scone ($47, three hours, 50 minutes) from Sydney, and from Port Macquarie to Scone ($84, 11 hours).

Rover Coaches (☎ 02-4990 1699; www.rovercoaches.com.au) goes to Cessnock from Newcastle ($10.60, 1¼ hours).

Sid Fogg's (☎ 02-4928 1088; www.sidfoggs.com.au) runs services up the valley to Dubbo via Maitland ($59, six hours).

TRAIN

CityRail (☎ 13 15 00; www.cityrail.nsw.gov.au) runs trains from Newcastle to Maitland ($4.40, 30 minutes), and Sydney to Maitland via Newcastle ($21, 3½ hours).

UPPER HUNTER VALLEY

Rugged granite outcrops loom over the Upper Hunter's classic vineyard landscapes. Allow time to explore – the area is far more spread out than the lower valley.

The nearest town is Denman, 25km southwest of Muswellbrook. A great route into the Upper Hunter from Sydney follows the very winding Putty Rd from Windsor to Singleton, passing through some of the most breathtakingly scenic parts of Wollemi and Yengo National Parks.

Information

The **Muswellbrook visitor information centre** (☎ 02-6541 4050; www.muswellbrook.org.au; 87 Hill St; ☽ 9am-5pm) is at the north end of town.

Sights

WINERIES

Rosemount Estate (☎ 02-6549 6450; www.rosemount estates.com.au; Rosemount Rd, Denman; ☽ 10am-4pm), around 8km from Denman, is one of Australia's biggest exporters; it owns seven vineyards around Australia, so the depth and range of the wines is superlative.

Situated in a beautiful valley 18km west of Denman, **James Estate** (☎ 02-6547 5168; www .jamesestatewines.com.au; 951 Rylstone Rd, Sandy Hollow; ☽ 10am-4.30pm) is the quintessential independent wine maker. Try the White Syl-

vaner, an aromatic European drop unique to the Hunter Valley.

Arrowfield Estate (☎ 02-6576 4041; www.arrow fieldwines.com.au; Golden Hwy, Jerry's Plain; ☽ 10am-5pm) enjoys a loyal clientele, not only for its stellar wines but also for its super location: it's the only winery in the Hunter Valley actually located on the Hunter River.

GOULBURN RIVER NATIONAL PARK

At the southwestern edge of the Hunter Valley, this national park follows the Goulburn River as it cuts through sandstone gorges. The route was used by Aboriginal people travelling from the western plains to the sea – the area is rich in cave art. Emus may steal your sandwiches and if you're around early in the morning or late in the afternoon, you might spot a platypus or a cute red-necked wallaby (watch out for them on the roads). Look really hard and you might come face to face with a white-throated nightjar or perhaps a variegated fairy-wren.

There are short bushwalks to various lookouts, and basic **camp sites** (☎ 02-6372 7199; admission free) with no facilities or drinking water. The **Mudgee NPWS office** (☎ 02-6372 7199; Shop 1, 160 Church St, Mudgee) and **Mudgee visitor information centre** (☎ 1800 816 304, 02-6372 1020; www.mudgee-gulgong.org; 84 Market St, Mudgee; ☽ 9am-5pm Mon-Fri, 9am-3.30pm Sat, 9.30am-2pm Sun) have more information. The only partly sealed approach road is from Merriwa, 35km west of Sandy Hollow on the Denman road, but the unsealed portions are pretty decent.

BURNING MOUNTAIN

Off the New England Hwy, 20km north of Scone, is an underground coal seam that's been smoking for over 5000 years. A steep 3.5km-return walking track leads up through the nature reserve to puffing vents. The unusual nature of this area seems to uphold all kinds of biblical prophecies for deeply religious folk; it's undeniably mysterious.

Festivals & Events

The **Horse Festival** (☎ 02-6545 3688) is a 12-day event in May with racing carnivals, open studs, stock-horse shows and working events.

Sleeping

There are a few motels around the Muswellbrook visitor information centre.

Segenhoe B&B (☎ 02-6543 7382; www.segenhoe inn.com; 56 Main Rd, Aberdeen; d $190-220; ✖) In the hamlet of Aberdeen, near Scone, this big, sandstone house (from 1834) sits in a pretty Italianate garden. The sumptuous colonial rooms are all-frills, and there's a restaurant, a gift gallery and a 'coffee shop' to keep you otherwise occupied. This is really quite a lovely spot.

Morna May Cottage (☎ 02-6547 2088; www.morn amay.com.au; 310 Rosemount Rd, Denman; s/d from $80/110; P ✖) Both of these light, bright bungalow-style cottages have their own kitchen; one has two bedrooms. They're the last word in classy vineyard accommodation – interiors are plush, and you have the opportunity to relax in a claw-footed bathtub, looking out over remote wineries through huge windows.

Royal Hotel (☎ 02-6547 2226; www.upper-hunter .com/Denman/Royal; Ogilvie St, Denman; s/d $25/35) In the devastating fires of 1928, it's a fact that the Royal was unscathed while the rest of Denman burned; in 1955, when floods ravaged the town, blokes stood knee-high in water at the bar and continued nursing their beer, supremely confident the place would survive – which it did. Accommodation is simple but decent, and the restaurant does surf 'n' turf type meals.

Belmore Hotel (☎ 02-6545 2078; belmorehotel@ pubboy.com.au; 98 Kelly St, Scone) The rooms here are undergoing renovation, and should be available by late 2005. The pub has two bars (one with open fireplace), a restaurant, live bands and DJs, and the all-important meat raffle on Friday nights.

Getting There & Around

Kean's (☎ 02-6543 1322) runs buses from Sydney to Muswellbrook ($39, 3½ hours) and Scone ($47, three hours 50 minutes), and from Port Macquarie to Scone ($84, 11 hours). **CountryLink** (☎ 13 22 32; www.country link.nsw.gov.au) trains travel from Sydney to Scone ($49.50, two hours 10 minutes) and to Muswellbrook ($44, three hours 47 minutes).

NEWCASTLE TO PORT MACQUARIE
Port Stephens
☎ 02 / pop 55,000
This stunning sheltered bay is about an hour's drive north of Newcastle, occupying a submerged valley that stretches more than

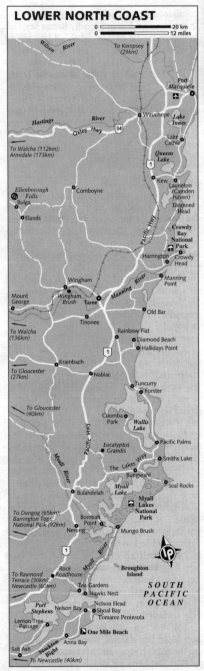

LOWER NORTH COAST

20km inland. It's a popular boating and fishing spot and takes in friendly **Nelson Bay**, the 'dolphin capital of Australia', and all kinds of adventure activities and several near-deserted beaches fringed by bungalows.

The **Port Stephens visitor information centre** (☎ 4980 6900; www.portstephens.org.au; Victoria Pde, Nelson Bay; ⏰ 9am-5pm) is near d'Albora Marina.

There's Internet access at **Abandon All Computer Frustrations** (☎ 4984 3057; Shop 2, 106 Magnus St, Nelson Bay; per hr $6) and the **CTC Centre** (☎ 4997 0749; Shop 4, Myall Plaza, Tea Gardens Masonic Centre, Tea Gardens; per hr $6; ⏰ 9am-4pm).

SIGHTS & ACTIVITIES

At the mouth of the Myall River, opposite Nelson Bay, are the small, pretty towns of **Tea Gardens**, on the river, and **Hawks Nest**, on the beach. **Jimmy's Beach** at Hawks Nest fronts a glasslike stretch of water, while **Bennett's Beach** has great views of Broughton Island.

On the southern side of the Tomaree Peninsula, **One Mile Beach** is a gorgeous semicircle of softest sand and bluest water, favoured by those in the know: surfers, beachcombers, idle romantics. Nearby **Samurai Beach** is popular with folks from the local nudist resort and has great surf.

Further south you can hang loose at the surfside village of **Anna Bay** – it's backed by the incredible **Stockton Bight**, the longest moving sand dunes in the southern hemisphere, stretching 35km to Newcastle. The tourist board refers to the dunes as '*Mad Max*'-style, but if you want to talk films, think *Lawrence of Arabia* – more Sahara than outback. In the heart of it, it's possible to get so surrounded by shimmering sand, you'll lose sight of the ocean and the townships. Other cultural reference points to help you paint a visual picture: an early Tintin book; a well-known Salvador Dali painting; one Pink Floyd album in particular – it's incredibly evocative, in short. At the far west end of the beach, the wreck of the *Sygna* founders in the water.

About half an hour by boat from Nelson Bay, **Broughton Island** is uninhabited except for muttonbirds, little penguins and an enormous diversity of fish species. The diving is great and the beaches are incredibly secluded.

The restored 1872 **Inner Lighthouse** at Nelson Head has a small **museum** with displays on the area's history and a **tea room**. The views of Port Stephens are suitably inspiring.

Back on the highway, a few kilometres before the turn-off to Tea Gardens and Hawks Nest, is the **Rock Roadhouse** – a replica of Uluru (Ayers Rock). This place is a marvel of…something. Inside, there are shops, a café and a Big Foot (although no-one seems to know what it does). It's Australiana at its finest and is highly recommended, even if your tank is full and your cynicism is in the red.

Activities available through the visitor information centre include fishing, helicopter rides and tours of Barrington Tops National Park, Hunter Valley wineries and Maitland architecture.

Try the following:

Blue Water Sea Kayaking (☎ 4981 5177; www .seakayaking.com.au; sunset/kayak tours from $30) Three-hour kayaking tours in Port Stephens and on the Myall River.

Hawks Nest Dive Centre (☎ 4997 0442; www.hawks nestdive.com.au; 87A Marine Dr, Tea Gardens) Hires gear, offers trips and provides many kinds of dive courses.

Horse Paradise (☎ 4965 1877; http://users.bigpond .com/horseparadise; Nelson Bay Rd, Williamtown; dune rides from $40) Ride through the dunes or Port Stephens bushland.

TOURS

Imagine (☎ 4984 9000; www.imaginecruises.com.au; 123 Stockton St, Nelson Bay; cruises from $20) Using sailboats, a 99% dolphin-watching success rate is claimed; also snorkelling tours. Eco-accredited.

Moonshadow (☎ 4984 9388; www.moonshadow.com .au; Shop 3, 35 Stockton St, Nelson Bay; cruises from $19) Dolphin watching, whale watching, dinner cruises, seven-hour trips to Broughton Island. Big catamarans with a bar. Eco-accredited.

Port Stephens 4WD Eco-Tours (☎ 4982 7277; tours from $18) Drive around Stockton sand dunes, visit the *Sygna* and go sand boarding.

Sand Safaris (☎ 4965 0215; www.sandsafaris.com .au; 173 Nelson Bay Rd, Williamtown; tours from $110) Eco-sensitive quad-bike forays out on the dunes.

SLEEPING

In Nelson Bay, Government St – between Stockton and Church Sts – is lined with motels and hotels, as is Ocean Beach in Hawks Nest. Shoal Bay, virtually a suburb of Nelson Bay, mixes accommodation with stores and restaurants. Anna Bay is the closest hamlet to One Mile Beach.

Nelson Bay B&B (☎ 4984 3655; www.nelsonbay bandb.nelsonbay.com; 81 Stockton St, Nelson Bay; d from $90) A cute little joint, more like a tiny boutique

THE GREAT PIE WARS: BEST PIES ON THE COAST

The Australian fetish for meat pies is legendary: Australians eat 260 million of them a year, around 13 per citizen. In the '70s, a song from a well-known TV commercial featured a continuous refrain: 'Football, meat pies, kangaroos and Holden cars' – everything that defined Australia at the time. Actually, it wasn't so long ago, before the current era of ultra-professionalism, that elite Australian sportsmen would turn up to training smoking a ciggy, drinking a beer and eating a pie (trailing their pet roo by a leash, no doubt). To sum up, pie crust in your moustache was a badge of pride – even if you were female.

Along the north coast, you're more likely to find kangaroo *in* your pie – this is Pie Country, make no mistake, and there's a lot of showmanship around that tries to convince us of that. During research for this book, it seemed that every one-horse town we visited claimed to make 'Australia's Best Pies', but often they were just the same old deal: insubstantial crust, watery filling, mystery meat.

If you're salivating already, make sure you visit the following three pie emporiums; all have won medals in the prestigious Great Aussie Pie Competition (www.greataussiepiecomp.homestead.com /Page1.html). Every pie they churn out is, truly, an enigma wrapped in a mystery wrapped in a crust: wondrous to behold and indisputably unquantifiable. It's not all about the flashy fillings, though: those creamy, flaky crusts are similarly breathtaking.

Red Ned's Pies (☎ 02-4984 1355; www.redneds.com.au; Shop 3, 17-19 Stockton St, Nelson Bay; pies $4-5; ✆ 6am-5pm) Fifty different kinds, baked fresh daily, everything from your standard savoury mince to the lobster, prawn and barramundi pie (with coconut-cream sauce, leeks and celery, and topped with caviar, no less). Don't forget the Indian butter-chicken pies, either, or the kangaroo teriyaki, the Thai satay vegetarian…Kingpin Pie King Barry Kelly learnt his trade in top-shelf international hotels and his philosophy is simple: he gets a kick out of watching people stare at his specials board, goggle-eyed (anyone for BBQ-bourbon-and-beef pie?).

Pie Man (Tea Gardens ☎ 02-4997 1733; Shop 3, 17-19 Stockton St; ✆ 24hr); Raymond Terrace (☎ 02-4987 1912; 26 Sturgeon St; ✆ 24hr) Motto: 'I only have pies for you'. The variety isn't as bewildering as Red Ned's, but the quality is right up there. The Pie Man sticks to favourites including prime beef, beef Burgundy and Thai chicken pies, peppered with a few innovative variations like the incredible oyster Kilpatrick. The Pie Man himself, Randall Smith, grew up in Adelaide, home of the notorious pie floater – a meat pie floating in pea soup. Anyone who has tasted one of these horror shows will know why he's now obsessive about creating the perfect pie.

Fredo Pies (☎ 02-6566 8226; www.fredopies.com.au; 75 Macleay St, Frederickton; pies $4-5; ✆ 7am-7pm) The Marilyn Monroe statues out the front will grab your attention, but the amazing pies will keep you here for evermore. 'Mrs Pie', Nola Turnbull, claims to have 160 recipes in her possession, with a rotating 50 made fresh daily. The emphasis is country-style, as witnessed by the superlative, never-to-be-matched lamb, mint and honey pie; and the rabbit mulligatawny; the emu; the ostrich… For vegos, the farmhouse potage is on a par, as is the asparagus, cheese and pasta pie and the vegetable mornay.

hotel, secluded among tall trees off a semiprivate drive. One room has its own spa bath.

Shoal Bay Holiday Park (☎ 1800 600 200, 4981 1427; www.beachsideholidays.com.au; Shoal Bay Rd, Shoal Bay; powered sites/d from $30/85; P ⊠ ⊡) Right on the bay, with top-notch cabins such as the Outrigger Villa: two bedrooms, bathroom, kitchen, TV, VCR, cable and air-con. There are daily activities for kids.

Melaleuca Surfside Backpackers (☎ 4981 9422; www.melaleucabackpackers.com.au; 33 Eucalyptus Dr, One Mile Beach; unpowered sites/dm/d $14/25/70) A gorgeous site. The wooden cabins, custom-built from red cedar, are set amid peaceful scrub right across from the beach. There's a huge, comfortable communal lounge area and

kitchen; and the camp sites are 'free range'– you pick your own and cars are not allowed near tents, which equates to purest bliss. The grounds are also inhabited by koalas, land mullets, sugar gliders and possums.

Samurai Beach Resort (☎ 1800 822 200, 4916 3400; www.samuraibeachresort.com.au; 288 Gan Gan Rd, Anna Bay; d from $99; P ⊡ ⊠) This new resort features luxury units, self-contained villas and studios. The décor is nothing to shout about, but again the woodland surroundings are a treat and the beach is close to hand.

O'Carrollyn's (☎ 4982 2801; www.ocarrollyns.com .au; 36 Eucalyptus Dr, One Mile Beach; d from $119) Self-contained villas, all wheelchair-accessible, with custom-built bathrooms, as well as TV and VCR, and wheelchair access to a beautiful, near-deserted beach. This is spruce, feel-good accommodation, surrounded by landscaped gardens teeming with koalas.

Shoal Bay Resort & Spa (☎ 1800 181 810, 4981 1555; www.shoalbayresort.com; Beachfront Rd, Shoal Bay; d from $160; P ✿) Offers a range of accommodation from comfy suites to luxury villas. There's also the gobsmacking Aqua Spa complex, which includes a 25m pool, health club, three spas (sea, mineral and fresh water), gym, racquet-ball court, and a hairdressing and beauty salon.

Tea Gardens Hotel Motel (☎ 4997 0203; cnr Marine Dr & Maxwell St, Tea Gardens; s/d $55/70) This place on the riverfront has cute pink-and-blue rooms set around a leafy garden out back. The hotel is a popular watering hole.

Tea Gardens Waterfront B&B (☎ 4997 1688; 117 Marine Dr, Tea Gardens; d incl breakfast from $100) With lovely Myall River views, this B&B has two large, spotless studio-rooms and is set in a leafy courtyard.

EATING

Sinclair's (☎ 4984 4444; d'Albora Marina, Nelson Bay; mains $12-27; ☽ lunch & dinner) The standout from several waterfront restaurants in Nelson Bay, Sinclair's is mainly seafood (including a raunchy selection of Port Stephens oysters), but there are Turkish and Mediterranean infusions, too, as well as a big, relaxed outdoor eating area.

Nicole's (☎ 4997 2922; 81 Marine Dr, Tea Gardens) In a 100-year-old cottage, this is a seriously sweet café that doubles as an art gallery, showcasing mainly beachy and aquatic art with a local flavour. Right on the banks of the Myall, the garden here is seductive, soundtracked by trickling water features, and is easy on the eye with birdbaths, much greenery and Roman statues. Good cakes, too.

Incredible Edibles (☎ 4981 4511; cnr Donald & Stockton Sts, Nelson Bay; sandwiches from $5) is a good deli with good sandwiches, while Red Ned's Gourmet Pie Bar and the Pie Man are (almost) unrivalled for pies along the east coast (see the boxed text, p171).

GETTING THERE & AROUND

To drive from Nelson Bay to Tea Gardens, you have to backtrack to Raymond Terrace.

Port Stephens Coaches (☎ 4982 2940; www.ps coaches.com.au) goes from Nelson Bay via Anna Bay to Newcastle ($10.40, 1¼ hours,

13 daily). The 9am bus from Nelson Bay continues to Sydney ($35, 3½ hours).

Port Stephens Ferry Service (☎ 4984 1262; cruisein@nelsonbay.com) chugs from Nelson Bay to Tea Gardens and back three times a day ($18 return, one hour).

Barrington Tops National Park

This World Heritage wilderness lies on the rugged Barrington Plateau, which rises to almost 1600m. Northern rainforest butts into southern sclerophyll here, creating one of Australia's most diverse ecosystems, with giant strangler figs, mossy Antarctic beech forests, limpid rainforest swimming holes and pocket-sized pademelons (note: it is illegal to put pademelons in your pocket).

There are walking trails and lookouts near Gloucester Tops, Careys Peak, Williams River (wheelchair accessible) and Jerusalem Creek. Be prepared for cold snaps, and even snow, at any time. All drinking water must be boiled.

Day tours to Barrington Tops can be organised through the **Port Stephens visitor information centre** (☎ 02-4980 6900; www.portstephens.org .au; Victoria Pde, Nelson Bay; ☽ 9am-5pm), while **Canoe Barrington** (☎ 02-6558 4316; www.canoebarrington.com .au; 774 Barrington East Rd) runs white-water trips out of its riverside lodge, 14km from Gloucester. Weekend packages including accommodation and guide cost $319, and kayaks can be rented from $50 daily. Accommodation-only deals start at $21 per person.

From Newcastle, the road through Morpeth and Paterson to Dungog is dreamy, passing by rolling green fields, historic towns, frolicking horses and stands of silver birch and ghost gums.

There's camping at various places, including **Devil's Hole** (free), **Junction Pools** (per person $3) and **Gloucester River** (per person $5). Contact **Gloucester NPWS office** (☎ 02-6538 5300; 59 Church St, Gloucester) for more information.

CountryLink (☎ 13 22 32; www.countrylink.nsw.gov .au) train/coach combos run from Newcastle to Dungog ($13, 1½ hours).

Myall Lakes National Park

Boaters, fishers, sailboarders and canoeists all love Myall, a patchwork of coastal lakes, islands, forest and beaches. There are bushwalks through coastal rainforest and past beach dunes at **Mungo Brush** in the south, perfect for spotting wildflowers and dingoes. The best beaches and surf are in the north around beautiful, secluded **Seal Rocks**, with emerald-green rockpools, epic ocean views and svelte, golden sand.

Take the short walk to the **Sugar Loaf Point Lighthouse** where you can enjoy the views to Seal Rocks; there's a water-choked gorge along the way and a detour to **Little Lighthouse Beach**. The path around the lighthouse leads to a lookout over the actual Seal Rocks – islets that provide sanctuary for Australia's northernmost colony of Australian fur seals. During summer breeding, the seals are out in abundance and you'll do well to bring binoculars. **Humpback whales** swim past Seal Rocks and can sometimes be seen from the shore.

Bulahdelah visitor information centre (☎ 1800 802 692, 02-4997 4981; tourbglc@nobbys.net.au; cnr Crawford St & Pacific Hwy; ☺ 9am-5pm) has guides for hikers and information about camp sites and houseboat, canoe, sailboard and runabout hire.

Well-outfitted **Myall Shores EcoPoint Resort** (☎ 1300 769 566, 02-4997 4495; www.myallshores .com.au; Lake Rd, Bombah Point; powered sites/d from $20/70), right on the water and in dense bushland, has ecofriendly cabins, a restaurant and bar, petrol, gas and basic groceries. The road from Bulahdelah is unsealed and lined with salmon gums and dairy farms.

Seal Rocks Camping Reserve (☎ 1800 112 234, 02-4977 6164; Kinka Rd, Seal Rocks; powered/unpowered sites $22/18, d from $50) is right on the wondrous Number One beach with on-site vans and comfy cabins; call ahead if you want one. The road from Bungwahl is largely unsealed.

Bulahdelah has several motels. You can drive from Tea Gardens to Bulahdelah via the **Bombah Point ferry** (per car/pedestrian $6/2.50), which crosses on the half-hour, 8am to 6pm. It only take five minutes, though – fancy a swim?

Lakes Way is a beautiful twisting road between Bulahdelah and Forster-Tuncurry with inspiring views of lakes and forest. The turn-off to Forster-Tuncurry leaves the Pacific Hwy 4km north of Bulahdelah. About 7km along this winding road, you'll see a turn-off to the 400-year-old **Eucalyptus grandis** along Stoney Creek Rd. It's a bumpy 5km drive to the massive flooded gum, one of NSW's tallest trees, but it's worth every bruise for the 25-minute, palm-treed rainforest walk.

Busways (☎ 02-4983 1560; www.busways.com.au) has services from Sydney and Tea Gardens

($49) or Newcastle and Tea Gardens ($31), dropping off at Hawks Nest ($19).

Forster-Tuncurry
☎ 02 / pop 17,996

These twin towns face off on either side of the sea entrance to Wallis Lake. Forster (pronounced Foster), the more popular of the two, is like a mini–Gold Coast – high rises everywhere, more development planned – but its beaches are pretty, there's an ocean bath, excellent fishing and an abundance of water sports.

The **Forster visitor information centre** (☎ 6554 8799; www.greatlakes.org.au; Little St, Forster; ☺ 9am-5pm) is on Forster's lake side. There's Internet access at **Leading Edge Computers** (☎ 6555 2064; Shop 3, cnr Head & Beach Sts, Forster; per hr $5) and the **library** (☎ 6591 7256; Breese Pde, Forster; ☺ Tue-Sun), near the Forster Shopping Village.

The **lake** is tops for paddling. **Nine Mile Beach** at Tuncurry is consistently the best for surf, but **Forster Beach** and **Pebbly Beach** can also be good. There are large **swimming pools** at Forster Beach and near the harbour entrance in Tuncurry.

Forster Dolphin Lodge YHA (☎ 6555 8155; dolphin_lodge@hotmail.com; 43 Head St, Forster; dm/s/d $23/38/54; ▣) has small common areas and very helpful staff. All rooms have bathrooms and the beach is right out the back; bike hire ($8) is available.

Forster Beach Caravan Park and Marina (☎ 1800 240 632, 6554 6269; www.escapenorth.com.au/forstercaravanpark; Reserve Rd, Forster; powered sites/d from $19/51) is a sprawling space, backed by the mighty breakwall; villas and cabins are available.

Forster is Motel City. Try the **Forster Palms Motel** (☎ 6555 6255; palmsmotel@pnc.com.au; 60 Macintosh St, Forster; d/ste from $60/65; P ▨ ▣), with its faux-tropical ambience, standard rooms and saltwater pool with BBQ, or the **Great Lakes Motor Inn** (☎ 6554 6955; glmotorinn@tsn.cc; 24 Head St, Forster; P ▨ ▣), handy for the beaches, with comfortable rooms and DVD facilities.

Escape motel madness at the lavish **Tokelau Guest House** (☎ 6557 6400; www.tokelau.com.au; 2 Manning St, Tuncurry; ste from $141), opposite Wallis Lake. It's furnished with Federation-period furniture and rooms open out onto lovely gardens.

On the lake front, **Poet's Corner** (☎ 6557 5577; 48 Wharf St, Forster; mains $26-32) offers substantial Mod Oz, while **Casa del Mundo** (☎ 6554 5906; 12 Wharf St, Forster; mains $14-29) does tapas and

NEW SOUTH WALES

Mexican dishes. Upstairs, **Casuarina** (☎ 6555 6522; 1st fl, 8 Little St, Forster; mains $13-16; ☒ lunch & dinner), with top lake views, churns out good Thai, Chinese and Malaysian food and hosts occasional blues performances.

CountryLink (☎ 13 22 32; www.countrylink.nsw.gov .au) operates a bus-train combination to Sydney ($50, six hours). **Busways** (☎ 4983 1560; www .busways.com.au) coaches stop in Forster between Sydney and Brisbane, as does **Greyhound Australia** (☎ 13 14 99; www.greyhound.com.au).

Manning Valley

From Forster-Tuncurry, the Pacific Hwy swings inland to riverside **Taree**, a large town serving the farms of the fertile Manning Valley. The **Taree visitor information centre** (21 Manning River Dr; ☒ 9am-5pm) is down the road from the **Big Oyster**, the weirdest car yard you'll ever see.

Further west up the valley, **Wingham Brush**, a patch of idyllic rainforest near the timber town of Wingham, is home to giant, otherworldly Moreton Bay figs and flocks of flying foxes. Its boardwalks are a thoroughfare from the town to the **Manning River**.

Near Wingham, **Tinonee** (population 670) is a tiny heritage town. It features a really unusual, multicoloured fish-shaped letterbox on its outskirts, 'prime horse poo' (according to roadside signs) and the 22-seat Terrace Cinema (see boxed text, above). On the coast near Taree, the cute resort town of **Old Bar** has long, quiet beaches.

PORT MACQUARIE
☎ 02 / pop 41,000

The tourist board will tell you that 'God lives here', conveniently forgetting that Port Macquarie was founded in 1821 as a penal colony for slack convicts who found life in

Sydney Cove too easy. This heavy-duty past is still visible in the frontier architecture (Port was the third town to be established on the Australian mainland), but these days, idle Aussies choose to serve time here; Port's the gateway to the subtropical coast, and its palm trees, rolling parklands, beach coves, swank restaurants and accommodation options attract scores of holiday-makers from around the country.

Port Macquarie is surrounded by koala habitat – parks, greenlands and so on – and the whole region is ideal for adventure activities.

Information
NPWS office (☎ 6584 2203; 152 Horton St; ☒ 9am-4.30pm Mon-Fri)
Port Macquarie visitor information centre (☎ 6581 8000, 1800 303 155; www.portmacquarieinfo .com.au; Clarence St; ☒ 8.30am-5pm Mon-Fri, 9am-4pm Sat & Sun)
Port Surf Hub (☎ 6584 4744; 57 Clarence St; per hr $6; ☒ 9am-7pm) Internet access.
Post office (Palm Court, cnr Short & William Sts)

Sights
MUSEUMS & HISTORIC BUILDINGS
Port's colonial past is apparent in the town centre, where you'll find the 1835 **garrison** (cnr Clarence & Hay Sts), now renovated with shops and cafés, and the 1869 **courthouse** (☎ 6584 1818; Clarence St; adult/child $2/50c; ☒ 10am-4pm Mon-Sat).

The 1836 **Port Macquarie Historical Society Museum** (☎ 6583 1108; 22 Clarence St; adult/child $5/2; ☒ 9.30am-4.30pm Mon-Sat) has some terrifying baby dolls, some commemorative china and an award-winning collection of Victorian frocks.

The 1824, convict-built **St Thomas' Anglican Church** (☎ 6584 1033; William St; adult/child $2/1;

PORT MACQUARIE

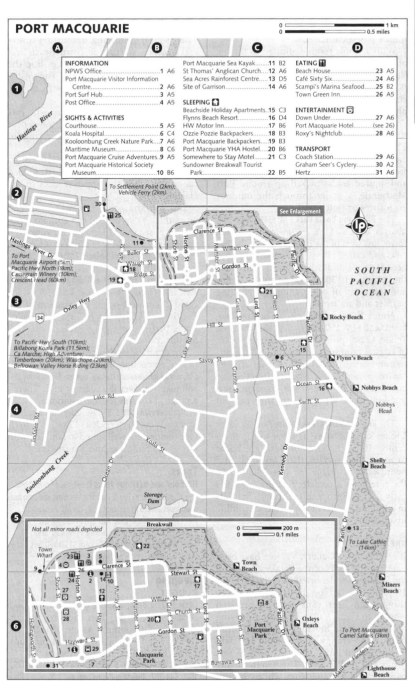

INFORMATION	
NPWS Office	1 A6
Port Macquarie Visitor Information	
Centre	2 A6
Port Surf Hub	3 A5
Post Office	4 A5

SIGHTS & ACTIVITIES	
Courthouse	5 A5
Koala Hospital	6 C4
Kooloonbung Creek Nature Park	7 A6
Maritime Museum	8 C6
Port Macquarie Cruise Adventures	9 A5
Port Macquarie Historical Society	
Museum	10 B6

Port Macquarie Sea Kayak	11 B2
St Thomas' Anglican Church	12 A6
Sea Acres Rainforest Centre	13 D5
Site of Garrison	14 A6

SLEEPING	
Beachside Holiday Apartments	15 C3
Flynns Beach Resort	16 D4
HW Motor Inn	17 B6
Ozzie Pozzie Backpackers	18 B3
Port Macquarie Backpackers	19 B3
Port Macquarie YHA Hostel	20 B6
Somewhere to Stay Motel	21 C3
Sundowner Breakwall Tourist	
Park	22 B5

EATING	
Beach House	23 A5
Café Sixty Six	24 A6
Scampi's Marina Seafood	25 B2
Town Green Inn	26 A5

ENTERTAINMENT	
Down Under	27 A6
Port Macquarie Hotel	(see 26)
Roxy's Nightclub	28 A6

TRANSPORT	
Coach Station	29 A6
Graham Seer's Cyclery	30 A2
Hertz	31 A6

9.30am-noon & 2-4pm Mon-Fri) is one of Australia's oldest churches.

With a whole room dedicated to the life of Matthew Flinders' cat Trim, the **Maritime Museum** (☎ 6583 1866; 6 William St; tour adult/child $6/4; 11am-3pm Mon-Sat) has its fair share of charm. Exhibits include wreck relics and photographs of early navigators.

NATURE RESERVES & PARKS

The **Koala Hospital** (☎ 6584 1522; www.koalahospital .org.au; Macquarie Nature Reserve, Lord St; admission by donation; feeding time 8am & 3pm) cares for sick and injured koalas picked up around Port Macquarie. Wander through the outdoor enclosures or watch feedings.

The **Billabong Koala Park** (☎ 6585 1060; 61 Billabong Dr; adult/child $10/6; 9am-5pm) is outside town, just west of the intersection of the Pacific and Oxley Hwys. Marsupials are bred here for zoos and private parks. Come for the pattings (10.30am, 1.30pm and 3.30pm) and the array of other animals, including parrots and wallabies.

About 3km south of town, **Sea Acres Rainforest Centre** (☎ 6582 3355; Pacific Dr; adult/child $10/6; 9am-4.30pm) protects a 72-hectare pocket of coastal rainforest alive with birds, goannas and brush turkeys. There's an ecology centre, a café and a wheelchair-accessible boardwalk. Take one of the excellent, free, one-hour guided tours to get the most out of your visit.

The **Kooloonbung Creek Nature Park** (cnr Gordon & Horton Sts; admission free) is close to the town centre. Its 50 hectares of bush are home to many bird species; there are trails and boardwalks (suitable for wheelchairs). In the reserve is a cemetery dating from the early days of European settlement. Exhibits in a hut nearby detail the variety of wildlife living here.

BREAKWALL

It's the People's Gallery. Visitors have been painting the rocks of the breakwall, behind the Sundowner Breakwall Tourist Park, for 10 years. The 'art' on display covers everything from beer cans and big-breasted women to Darth Vader. The accompanying texts range from touching eulogies to dead friends and crappy poems about the pain of unrequited love to bad-ass odes to sex, drugs and rock 'n' roll. There aren't many bare rocks left; brand yours while you can.

Activities

There's great swimming and surfing at several beaches, starting at Town Beach and running south. Cruise operators line the waterfront near Town Wharf. The visitor information centre can help with houseboat hire.

Hit the waves and learn to surf with **Port Macquarie Surf School** (☎ 6585 5453; www.portmac quariesurfschool.com.au), offering a wide range of lessons and prices.

Port Macquarie Sea Kayak (☎ 6584 1039; Sea Rescue Shed, Buller St; 2hr trips $30) conducts guided canoe trips into the upper reaches of the Hastings River.

Did you know that a camel's urine can be as thick as syrup and can contain twice the salt of sea water? Find out for yourself – camel rides are available south of town with **Port Macquarie Camel Safaris** (☎ 6583 7650; Matthew Flinders Dr; rides per 20min $20).

Bellrowan Valley Horse Riding (☎ 6587 5227; www.bellrowanvalley.com.au; rides from $50) is located 23km west of the intersection of the Pacific and Oxley Hwys, in a lush valley that's perfect for equine exploration. Call for directions.

For dramatic landscapes and a good injection of adrenaline, **High Adventure** (☎ 1800 063 648; www.highadventure.com.au; tandem flights from $99) will take you over the coast or hills. There's a range of courses for solo aspirants.

Timbertown (☎ 6585 1940; Oxley Hwy, Wauchope; admission by donation; 9.30am-3.30pm) is a heritage theme park well suited to families, with lots of old buildings and a steam train.

Tours

Harbour and heritage tours (adult/child from $12/6; 10.30am & 1pm Tue & Thu) The Maritime Museum runs good tours aboard its restored boat, the MV Wentworth.
Port Macquarie Cruise Adventures (☎ 6583 8483, 1300 555 890; www.cruiseadventures.com.au; Short St, Town Wharf; cruises adult/child from $15/10) Offers many tours, including nature and oyster variants.

Sleeping
BUDGET
Ozzie Pozzie Backpackers (☎ 6583 8133; 36 Waugh St; dm/d $20/48; P) This friendly joint has clean, bright rooms, a range of activities, free bike and bodyboard hire, free pick-ups, wheelchair ramps and BBQ nights.

Port Macquarie Backpackers (☎ 6583 1792, 1800 688 882; lindel@midcoast.com.au; 2 Hastings River

Dr; dm/d $21/48; (P) (Q) (Z)) Easily identified by the globe out the front, this heritage-listed house has pressed-tin walls, comfy bunks and a friendly atmosphere. The pool is surrounded by palms and you can rent bikes and fishing gear.

Port Macquarie YHA Hostel (☎ 6583 5512; www .yha.com.au; 40 Church St; dm/d from $22/55; (P) (Q)) A neat and compact hostel close to Town Beach. There's a shuttle bus to help you get around.

Somewhere to Stay Motel (☎ 6583 5850; wizbang ent@hotmail.com.au; cnr Lord & Burrawan Sts; s/d from $60/70; (P) (X) (Z)) The irreverent cheer here extends right down to the promotional materials showing a dolphin and koala sharing a bed. The rooms are comfortable and have balconies.

Sundowner Breakwall Tourist Park (☎ 6583 2755; 1 Munster St; sites/cabins from $26/60; (Q) (Z)) Extensive facilities, a roomy feel, and right by the river mouth. Get a load of that breakwall (opposite).

MIDRANGE

This is motel country and you get all makes and models, the cheapest furthest from the beaches along Hastings River Dr and the pricier lining the strip of sand.

Beachside Holiday Apartments (☎ 6583 9544; www.beachsideholidays.com; 48 Pacific Dr; 1-/2-room units $100/145; (P) (X) (Z)) A fun place right across the road from Flynn's Beach. The units are large, with balconies, and face either the ocean or the pool. The rooftop BBQ spot is a treat.

HW Motor Inn (☎ 6583 1200; www.hwport.com.au; 1 Stewart St; r from $105; (P) (X) (Q) (Z)) An older, lavishly renovated boutique motel with large rooms and numerous amenities. Many feature balconies with views right onto Town Beach. Rooms have wi-fi and broadband and the décor is chic.

Flynns Beach Resort (☎ 6583 3338; www.flynns beachresort.com.au; cnr Pacific Dr & Ocean St; units from $155; (P) (X) (Z)) This large complex has extensive gardens and a nice pool area. Units have spacious balconies and pleasant living spaces with full kitchens.

Eating

Beach House (☎ 6584 5692; Horton St; mains $10-18; (Y) breakfast, lunch & dinner) A great spot for a beer and a burger, or oysters and a glass of Chardonnay – take in the waterfront view from one of the huge number of tables outside.

Ca Marche (☎ 6582 8320; Cassegrain Winery, 764 Fernbank Creek Rd at Pacific Hwy; mains $26-32; (Y) lunch daily, dinner Fri) A justifiably popular place, Ca Marche has an inventive menu that brings international flavours to the region's bounty. Tables outside await balmy weather.

Scampi's Marina Seafood (☎ 6583 7200; Port Marina, Park St; mains from $20; (Y) lunch Fri-Sun, dinner daily; (X)) Packs 'em in on two levels inside and at pretty tables outside. The huge specials list always reflects what's fresh, and the **takeaway window** (meals $5-30; (Y) 5-10pm) sells everything from fresh oysters to lobster mornay and chips.

Town Green Inn (☎ 6583 1011; cnr Clarence & Horton Sts; mains $12-25; (Y) lunch & dinner; (X)) The bistro in the Port Macquarie Hotel has been given the 'stylish and bright' treatment. The long menu includes steaks you grill yourself and wood-fired pizzas.

Café Sixty Six (☎ 6583 2484; 66 Clarence St; meals $6-15; (Y) breakfast, lunch & dinner) This very agreeable Italian café has good coffee all day as well as a daily list of specials. The patio provides a good refuge from the pavement mobs and the staff are just plain cheery.

Entertainment

Things can get rowdy on weekends, so the council has imposed a 2.30am lock-out policy on bars and clubs.

Port Macquarie Hotel (☎ 6583 1011; cnr Horton & Clarence Sts) Has live bands on weekends and a trivia night on Sunday.

Down Under (☎ 6583 4018; cnr William & Short Sts; (Y) 6pm-4am) This veteran club is one big subterranean bar. There's karaoke many nights.

Roxy's Nightclub (☎ 6583 5466; Galleria Bldg, William St; after 10pm admission $5; (Y) 6pm-late) At this, the closest thing to a true club in Port, you might find yourself rubbing (massive) shoulders with Sydney rugby players.

Getting There & Away

QantasLink (☎ 13 13 13; www.qantas.com.au) flies to Sydney (from $115) several times a day from Port Macquarie Airport.

Greyhound Australia (☎ 13 20 30; www.greyhound .com.au) runs south to Sydney ($58, seven hours) and north to Byron Bay ($62, six hours). **Premier Motor Service** (☎ 13 34 10) has a similar service. **Kean's** (☎ 1800 625 587) has sporadic services from the coach station west to Tamworth and north to Kempsey,

Nambucca Heads and Coffs Harbour three times a week.

CountryLink (☎ 13 22 32; www.countrylink.nsw .gov.au) has a train service to Wauchope from Sydney, where you connect to a bus for the short ride to Port ($75, seven hours).

Getting Around

The **Settlement Point ferry** ($3 per car, passengers free, 10 minutes, operates 24 hours) operates on a flat punt, giving you access to the north beach and Pilots Beach. Four-wheel drives can drive to Point Plomer and on over unsealed roads to Crescent Head to the north.

Hertz (☎ 6583 6599; 102 Gordon St; per day $50-100) is one of several rental-car agents in town.

Prefer to cycle? Head to **Graham Seer's Cyclery** (☎ 6583 2333; Port Marina; per day $24).

PORT MACQUARIE TO COFFS HARBOUR
Kempsey

☎ 02 / pop 8460

About 45km north of Port Macquarie, Kempsey is the home of the fabled **Akubra hat** (www .akubra.com.au), the headwear of choice for a swag of Aussie icons – everyone from Paul 'Crocodile Dundee' Hogan and singer John 'Whispering Jack' Farnham to John 'Prime Minister' Howard (when he wants to bond with country folk). Unfortunately, the factory is not open to the public. However, if you're curious as to why the Akubra was birthed here, remember that farmers like hats – and that Kempsey is a large rural town serving the farms of the Macleay Valley.

Country-music legend, the late Slim Dusty (who also favoured an Akubra), was also born here. Thanks to John Howard's patronage (he must have been in a bonding mood), the wheels are in motion for the opening of a **Slim Dusty Heritage Centre** (☎ 6562 6533; www .slimdustycentre.com.au; Old Kempsey Showgrounds), due in late 2005. For more on Slim, see p180.

The **Kempsey visitor information centre** (☎ 65 63 1555, 1800 642 480; Pacific Hwy; ⏰ 9am-5pm Mon-Fri, 10am-4pm Sat & Sun) is at a rest stop on the south side of town, sharing space with a **sheepshearers museum** (adult/child $3.30/1.60).

Just 6km north is **Fredo Pies** (☎ 6566 8226; www.fredopies.com.au; 75 Macleay St, Frederickton; pies $4-5; ⏰ 7am-7pm). Few cars manage to get past this place, and sometimes it's not because of the outstanding pies (see the boxed text,

MID-NORTH COAST

p171) – standing guard outside are two life-sized statues of Marilyn Monroe, one squatting uncomfortably on a pole.

Crescent Head
☎ 02 / pop 1190

An intimate town on the coast 18km southeast of Kempsey, Crescent Head is the surf longboarding capital of Australia. This is where the Malibu surfboard gained prominence in Australia during the '60s, and today many come just to watch the longboard riders surf the epic waves of **Little Nobby's Junction** (there's also good shortboard riding off Plummer Rd).

The road to Crescent Head is near the Kempsey visitor centre. Alternatively, from the north take the very scenic Belmore Rd which leaves the Pacific Hwy at Seven Oaks and follows the Belmore River.

Crescent Head Accommodation Bureau (☎ 1800 352 272; www.pointbreakrealty.com.au) has vacation rentals.

Crescent Head Holiday Park (☎ 6566 0261; Pacific St; sites/cabins from $19/65) is right at the mouth of the river, but **Mediterranean Motel** (☎ 6566 0303; 35 Pacific St; r $80-120; P ✗ ⚊) is the best motel in town, with comfortable rooms. Groups up to eight may enjoy the 'surf shacks' out back ($90 to $200). The Mediterranean-influenced food served in the **restaurant** (meals $10-25; ☻ breakfast, lunch & dinner) is a cut above.

Busways (☎ 1300 555 611; www.busways.com.au) operates services two to three times daily Monday to Saturday to and from Kempsey (Belgrave St).

Hat Head National Park

The 6500-hectare Hat Head National Park runs from just north of Crescent Head to just south of South West Rocks. It protects scrubland, swamps and some excellent beaches backed by one of NSW's largest sand dunes. Bird life is prolific on the wetlands. Rising up from the generally flat landscape is Hungry Hill, near Hat Head, and sloping Hat Head itself, where there's a walking track. The park is accessible from the hamlet of Kinchela, on the road between Kempsey and South West Rocks.

You can pitch a tent in the **Hungry Hill camping area** (per person $3), 5km south of Hat Head. There are pit toilets and no showers, and you'll need to take your own water.

Surrounded by the national park, the quiet town of **Hat Head** with its paperbark-lined main street, has a gorgeous beach and great fishing. **Hat Head Holiday Park** (☎ 02-6567 7501; sites/cabins from $16/60) is large and close to the beautiful sheltered bay.

South West Rocks & Around
☎ 02 / pop 3500

Uncrowded beaches, native forests, cave diving and a relaxed atmosphere make South West Rocks a great place to hunker down for a few days; the entire town is pretty quiet, largely thanks to its location well off the Pacific Hwy. The spectacular beach here is one of the few places on the east coast where you can watch the sunset over the water, and Front Beach in the centre is a sandy crescent backed by a conservation area.

Just getting here may be more than half the fun. The area west of the Pacific Hwy is a rich river flatland lined with dense vegetation, appealing old farmhouses and vintage shacks built on stilts. It's a great drive and to fully appreciate it, leave the Pacific Hwy at Seven Oaks and take the 22km sinuous road along the Macleay River, which passes through a few quaint fishing villages.

SIGHTS & ACTIVITIES

Boatman's Cottage (☎ 6566 7099; cnr Ocean Ave & Livingstone St; ☻ 10am-4pm) dates from 1902 and has tourist information and a small maritime museum.

The waters off South West Rocks are great for divers, especially **Fish Rock Cave**, south of Smoky Cape. **South West Rocks Dive Centre** (☎ 6566 6474; 5/98 Gregory St; 1 dive $90) offers dive lessons and trips.

The 19th-century **Trial Bay Gaol** (☎ 6566 6168; Quarry Rd, Arakoon; admission $4.50; ☻ 9am-4.30pm, last entry 4.15pm), a kind of Dickensian version of Alcatraz, has an imposing past. In 1816 Sydney convicts stole a brig, the *Trial,* only for their bid for freedom to be dashed when a storm sank the vessel.

Later, the gaol was built to house 'well-behaved' convicts whose main task was to construct a breakwater around the bay. However, plans fizzled and except for a brief interlude in WWI when it housed Germans, it's been unoccupied for more than 100 years. It's now a museum and the ruins of the great, grey walls and still-intact cells loom over the choppy seas below.

NEW SOUTH WALES

The **Arakoon State Conservation Area** is behind the gaol and has primitive but picturesque camp sites.

Nine kilometres southeast of South West Rocks, the **Smoky Cape Lighthouse** is a landmark that shouldn't be missed, perched high above the ocean on a bracingly breezy cape.

SLEEPING & EATING

Seabreeze Hotel (☎ 6566 6909; www.macleaycbd.com .au/seabreeze.html; Livingstone St; r from $80; ☒) In a great spot at the front of town, the Seabreeze has 28 basic rooms, a large bar and a **bistro** (meals $8-18; ☺ lunch & dinner) with tables inside and out.

Rock Pool Motor Inn (☎ 1800 180 133; www.rock poolmotorinn.com.au; 45 Mcintyre St; r $82-160; ℗ ☒ ☒) Also boasting 28 rooms, the Rockpool features plenty of amenities as well as a good restaurant.

Smoky Cape Lighthouse Cottages (☎ 6566 6301; www.smokycapelighthouse.com; rates variable) Two beautifully restored cottages that were once used by the keepers.

Trial Bay Tourist Park (☎ 6566 6142; www.trial bay.com.au; 161-171 Phillip Dr; sites/cabins from $19/80; ☒) A great family feel and kiddie-oriented activities. Not so wholesome is its on-site takeaway, which features 'dirty burgers' (with chips and gravy in the bun) and deep-fried Mars Bars.

Horseshoe Bay Beach Park (☎ 6566 6370; Livingstone St; sites/cabins from $18/55) Right in town, on the sheltered Town Beach, with 82 sites and 12 cabins.

Geppy's (☎ 6566 6196; cnr Livingstone & Memorial Sts; mains $14-29; ☺ dinner) An award-winning restaurant that specialises in local seafood and game. There's live jazz on Wednesdays.

GETTING THERE & AWAY

Cavanaghs (☎ 6562 7800) has two bus runs daily to and from Kempsey.

Nambucca Heads & Around

☎ 02 / pop 6000

Nambucca Heads is a low-key place featuring stunning vistas, untrammelled coastline and perfect beaches surrounded by azure waters.

The Nambucca (meaning 'many bends') Valley was occupied solely by the Gumbainggir people until European timber cutters arrived in the 1840s. There are still strong Aboriginal communities situated in Nambucca Heads and to the west of the valley in Bowraville.

The very helpful **Nambucca Heads visitor information centre** (☎ 6568 6954; cnr Riverside Dr & Pacif Hwy; ☺ 9am-5pm) doubles as the main bus terminal and has a nice spot on the estuary.

The **Bookshop café** (☎ 6568 5855; cnr Ridge & Bowra Sts; meals $6-10; ☺ 8am-5pm; ☐) has used books, terrific fruit smoothies and Internet access.

SIGHTS & ACTIVITIES

The only patrolled beach in town is **Main Beach**. **Beilby's** and **Shelly Beaches** are just to the south, closer to the river mouth, where the best surf is; they can be reached by going past the **Captain Cook Lookout**, with its stunning views.

Off Bowra St, Wellington Dr leads down hill to the waterfront and the locally famous **V-Wall breakwall** with gentle graffiti by locals and travellers: the messages are like those in pub toilets, but in prettier colours.

The **Mosaic Wall** in the town centre was created by a local artist using material such as tiles and broken crockery. Look for Elvis.

Visit the **Headland Historical Museum** (☎ 6568 6380; Main Beach; adult/child $2/50c; ☺ Wed, Sat & Sun 2-4pm) for local-history exhibits, including a collection of over 1000 photos and displays of maritime equipment.

DETOUR: THE PUB WITH NO BEER

In 1957 Slim Dusty recorded a song that was a big hit in Australia and England, 'The Pub with No Beer'. This jaunty ditty concerns the Cosmopolitan – a pub in Taylors Arm, 25km west of Macksville – that's somehow missed out on its quota of beer. The lyric relates how this 'dry spell' causes big men to cry, wild animals to howl and women to look on in bemusement.

Now officially known as the **Pub With No Beer** (☎ 02-6564 2100; Taylors Arm Rd; ☺ noon-late), the Cosmopolitan has since done everything possible to propagate its fame, with scores of billboards and countless brochures along the coast trumpeting this unlikely attraction. The pub does have beer, of course, as well as meals and Dusty souvenirs.

Beachcomber Marine (☎ 6568 6432; Riverside Dr) has various boats available for rent by the hour or day.

Valley of the Mist (☎ 6568 3268; Macksville; tours $8-50) is a traditional farm set west of the village of Macksville and 10km south of Nambucca Heads. A variety of tours are offered, from learning the bush tucker possibilities of living off the land to exploring the rich wetlands by canoe. Call for times and directions.

SLEEPING

Beilby's Beach House (☎ 6568 6466; www.beilbys.com .au; 1 Ocean St; s/d from $45/60; 🏊 💻 🛁) The owners are tri-lingual (English, French and German), the rooms are very comfortable, the location is right near the beach, the brekky is all-you-can-eat and ankle-biters are welcome.

Marcel Towers (☎ 6568 7041; 12 Wellington Dr; r $70-130; 🅿) Bland architecture but dreamy location: overlooking the Inner Harbour, with the foreshore walk right across the street.

Miramar Motel (☎ 6568 7899; 1 Nelson St; s/d from $72/77; 🅿 🛁) The views are worth the premium – it's right on the headland. Rooms have useful amenities like fridges.

White Albatross Holiday Resort (☎ 6568 6468; www.white-albatross.com.au; Wellington Dr; sites/cabins from $22/55) This award winner is near the river mouth with an adjacent lagoon to swim in. A deluxe waterfront villa is $135.

EATING

Matilda's Restaurant (☎ 6568 6024; Wellington Dr; mains $15-25; 🕑 lunch & dinner Mon-Sat) Steaks and freshly caught seafood in a wooden building creaking with character.

Bluewater Brasserie (☎ 6568 6394; V-Wall Tavern, Wellington Dr; mains $18; 🕑 lunch & dinner) Located in a rough-and-tumble pub, this brasserie is slightly fancier and has Mod Oz aspirations.

Starfish Café (☎ 6569 4422; 5 Main St; mains $14-28; 🕑 breakfast, lunch & dinner) There's a great view from the back veranda, and a modern menu with local seafood, steaks and various fusion specials. Live music some nights.

Boatshed Seafood Brasserie (☎ 6568 9292; 1 Wellington Dr; 3-course set menu $30; 🕑 lunch & dinner Wed-Sun) On the waterfront, serving fried calamari and chips for takeaway or sumptuous barramundi fillets.

GETTING THERE & AWAY

Harvey World Travel (☎ 6568 6455; 16 Bowra St) handles bookings.

Nearly all southbound buses stop outside the visitor centre, northbound at the shopping centre nearby. **Kean's** (☎ 1800 625 587) runs three times a week to Tamworth, and **Premier Motor Service** (☎ 13 34 10) motors to either Sydney or Brisbane ($59, both eight to nine hours). **Greyhound Australia** (☎ 13 20 30; www.greyhound.com.au) is a bit pricier.

The train station is about 3km out of town: follow Bowra St then Mann St. **Countrylink** (☎ 13 22 23; www.countrylink.nsw.gov.au) goes north to Coffs Harbour ($5.50, 40 minutes) and beyond, and south to Sydney ($84, eight hours).

COFFS HARBOUR

☎ 02 / pop 60,000

Coffs Harbour is the biggest town between Newcastle and the Gold Coast and therefore an important regional centre. It's been working hard to tart up its image and is generally a clean, family-friendly place.

Bananas were first grown in the area in the 1880s, but no one made much money from them until the railway came to town in 1918. Banana growing is still big business – you'll see trees everywhere – but these days tourism is the mainstay of the local economy. Inevitably, bananas and tourism combine in the iconic Big Banana complex (p182).

The nearby Nymboida River has some of the wildest white-water rafting in Australia, while south of Coffs is Sawtell, a sprawl of housing developments fronting some fabulous surf beaches.

Orientation & Information

The Pacific Hwy turns into Grafton St and then Woolgoolga Rd on its run north through town. The city centre is around the Grafton St and Harbour Dr junction. Note that High St and Harbour Dr are one and the same, with both names used interchangeably by adjoining businesses. The Pacific Hwy is the best way to access the beaches and resorts to the north.

The **Coffs Harbour visitor information centre** (☎ 6652 1522; www.coffscoast.com.au; cnr Grafton & McLean Sts; 🕑 8am-5pm) has a complete rundown on accommodation, activities and tours.

There's Internet access at **Planet Games** (☎ 6652 5188; 7/20 Gordon St; per 20min $2; 🕑 10am-7pm)

NEW SOUTH WALES

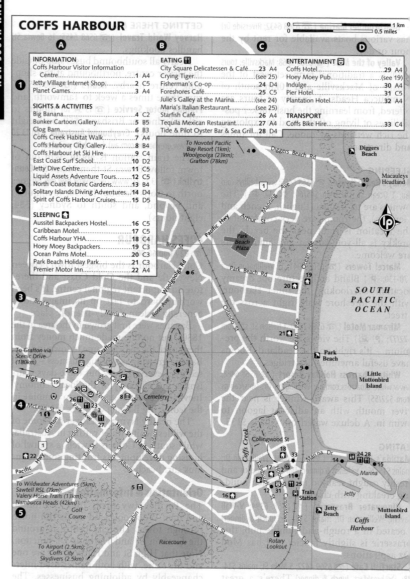

COFFS HARBOUR

INFORMATION
Coffs Harbour Visitor Information
  Centre..1 A4
Jetty Village Internet Shop...................2 C5
Planet Games.....................................3 A4

SIGHTS & ACTIVITIES
Big Banana...4 C2
Bunker Cartoon Gallery......................5 B5
Clog Barn...6 B3
Coffs Creek Habitat Walk...................7 A4
Coffs Harbour City Gallery.................8 B4
Coffs Harbour Jet Hire.......................9 C4
East Coast Surf School......................10 D2
Jetty Dive Centre..............................11 C5
Liquid Assets Adventure Tours..........12 C5
North Coast Botanic Gardens............13 B4
Solitary Islands Diving Adventures....14 D4
Spirit of Coffs Harbour Cruises..........15 D5

SLEEPING
Aussitel Backpackers Hostel..............16 C5
Caribbean Motel................................17 C5
Coffs Harbour YHA............................18 C4
Hoey Moey Backpackers.....................19 C3
Ocean Palms Motel............................20 C3
Park Beach Holiday Park....................21 C3
Premier Motor Inn.............................22 A4

EATING
City Square Delicatessen & Café.......23 A4
Crying Tiger...................................(see 25)
Fisherman's Co-op.............................24 D4
Foreshores Café.................................25 C5
Julie's Galley at the Marina............(see 24)
Maria's Italian Restaurant...............(see 25)
Starfish Café.....................................26 A4
Tequila Mexican Restaurant..............27 A4
Tide & Pilot Oyster Bar & Sea Grill...28 D4

ENTERTAINMENT
Coffs Hotel.......................................29 A4
Hoey Moey Pub.............................(see 19)
Indulge...30 A4
Pier Hotel...31 C5
Plantation Hotel...............................32 A4

TRANSPORT
Coffs Bike Hire.................................33 C4

---

and **Jetty Village Internet Shop** (☎ 6651 9155; Jetty Village, Harbour Dr; per 15min $2; ☯ 10am-8pm Mon-Sat, 10am-4pm Sun).

Sights
Welcome to 'Bananas 101'. Lesson 1: as Monty Python was the first to discover, the Earth is banana-shaped. Lesson 2: banana

oil is actually made from petroleum. Lesson 3: bananas are, in fact, herbs. Lesson 4: former prime minister Paul Keating envisaged Australia as a 'banana republic'. Lesson 5: Coffs Harbour boasts a ferrous-concrete **Big Banana** (☎ 6652 4355; www.bigbanana.com; Pacific Hwy; ☯ 9am-4.30pm) that's hailed by many a a national icon. The adjoining park offers ice skating ($12), a snow slope (adult/child $15/10) and many other attractions. Kids will love it, banana freaks will make a beeline for the over-stuffed gift store, while cynics and the easily bored will make like a banana and split. This joint, built in 1964, actually started the craze for 'Big Things' in Australia. Just so you know who to blame or praise, as you like…

The **North Coast Botanic Gardens** (☎ 6648 4188; Hardacre St; admission by donation; ☺ 9am-5pm) harbours many endangered species and examples of the region's rainforest types, as well as sections devoted to faraway places like Africa, China…and Queensland. It's a great spot to lie on the grass, surrounded by towering eucalypts full of kookaburras. The 6km **Coffs Creek Habitat Walk** passes by, starting from opposite the council chambers on Coff St and finishing near the sea.

The harbour's northern breakwall runs out onto **Muttonbird Island**, named for the more than 12,000 pairs of birds who migrate here from late August to early April, with cute offspring visible in December and January. It marks the southern boundary of the **Solitary Islands Marine Park**, where warm tropical currents meet temperate southern currents, attracting unusual varieties of fish and divers (look out for extremely rough conditions).

At the **Legends Surf Museum** (☎ 6653 6536; Pacific Hwy; adult/child $5/2; ☺ 10am-4pm), over 160 boards are on display as well as hundreds of surfing photos. It's 100m off the Pacific Hwy 10km north of Coffs; look for signs.

Clog Barn (☎ 6652 4633; www.clogbiz.com; 215 Woolgoolga Rd; adult/child $4.50/3.50; ☺ 7.30am-5pm) is a miniature Dutch village with windmills, a clog barn with a ridiculously large range of collectable spoons, and plenty of clogs. There's also a bunch of non-Dutch lizards and incessant polka music piped through the PA for your enjoyment. It has to be asked: why?

BEACHES
Park Beach has a picnic ground and is patrolled at weekends and during school holidays; be careful of rips. **Jetty Beach** is south and more sheltered. **Diggers Beach**, reached by turning east off the highway near the Big Banana, has a nude section. Surfers like Diggers and **Macauleys Headland**.

GALLERIES
The **Coffs Harbour City Gallery** (☎ 6648 4861; Rigby House, cnr Coff & Duke Sts; ☺ 10am-4pm Wed-Sat) has changing exhibits of regional art and travelling shows, while the **Bunker Cartoon Gallery** (☎ 6651 7343; City Hall Dr; admission $2; ☺ 10am-4pm), off Albany St, displays original cartoons in an old WWII bunker.

Activities
Coffs City Skydivers (☎ 6651 1167; www.coffscentral .dnet.tv/CoffsCitySkyDivers; Coffs Harbour airport; tandem jumps $320) Tandem skydiving and first-jump courses.

Coffs Harbour Jet Ski Hire (☎ 0418 665 656; Park Beach; per 15min $78) rents jet skis.

East Coast Surf School (☎ 6651 5515; Diggers Beach; lessons from $50) is run by noted east coast surfer Helene Enevoldson.

Jetty Dive Centre (☎ 6651 1611; www.jettydive .com.au; 398 Harbour Dr; open-water courses from $200) offers great-value PADI certification, exploring Solitary Islands Marine Park.

Liquid Assets Adventure Tours (☎ 6658 0850; www.surfrafting.com; 328 Harbour Dr; half-day surf rafting $40) offers national marine park kayaking.

Valery Horse Trails (☎ 6653 4301; Gleniffer Rd; 2hr rides from $40) has 60 horses and plenty of acreage in the hills behind town.

Festivals & Events
Catch the **Coffs Harbour International Buskers' Festival** (www.coffsharbourbuskers.com) in late September.

Watch tattooed men balance precariously on a unicycle, while juggling bearded ladies and chainsaws with one hand and nonchalantly eating an apple and directing traffic with the other hand.

Tours
Mountain Trails (☎ 6658 3333; tours from $60) Award-winning ecofriendly 4WD rainforest, waterfall and bush tucker tours.

Solitary Islands Diving Adventures (☎ 6651 2401; Marina Dr; 4 boat dives $129) Runs diving and snorkelling trips to the amazing marine park.

Spirit of Coffs Harbour Cruises (☎ 6651 4612; International Marina; whale-watching cruises $35; ☺ Jun-Nov) Watch for price wars among operators.

Wildwater Adventures (☎ 6653 3500; www.wild wateradventures.com.au; 754 Pacific Hwy; 1-day trips $153) Traverse the thrilling rapids of the Nymboida River in one- or multiday trips.

Sleeping

BUDGET

Coffs Harbour YHA (☎ 6652 6462; coffsharbour@yhansw
.org.au; 51 Collingwood St; dm/d from $25/70; ☐ ☒)
Clean, sparkling rooms and bike and surfboard hire.

Aussitel Backpackers Hostel (☎ 6651 1871; www
.aussitel.com; 312 Harbour Dr; dm/d $22/55; ☐ ☒)
Next to the jetty – take the canoes for a
paddle on the river or jump off the jetty as
you wish. The Internet café offers a range
of services.

Hoey-Moey Backpackers (☎ 6651 7966; Ocean
Pde; dm/d $22/50; ☐) Right on the beach, this
mob gives you a beer on arrival, but if that
doesn't suffice, there's also a pub (opposite)
and bottle shop. Oh, the place has clean,
four-bed dorm rooms, too.

Ocean Palms Motel (☎ 6651 5594; www.oceanpalms
motel.com.au; cnr Park Beach Rd & Ocean Pde; s/d from
$69/79; P ☒) The mature palms at this ma-
tured motel give it a South Seas feel. There's
a nice pool surrounded by lush gardens
and the rooms have been kept updated. A
charming choice among the many motels
near the beach.

Premier Motor Inn (☎ 6652 2044; www.premier
motorinn.com; Pacific Hwy; s/d from $70/78; P ☒ ☒)
One of the better choices among the thicket
of motels lining the Pacific Hwy, the Premier is back from the road in spacious
grounds that help to muffle the burble of
truck exhausts. Rooms are large and well
appointed, some with kitchenettes.

Park Beach Holiday Park (☎ 6648 4888; Ocean Pde;
sites/cabins from $21/52; ☐) Comprises 445 sites,
52 cabins and a first-class location.

MIDRANGE

Caribbean Motel (☎ 6652 1500; www.stayincoffs
.com.au; 353 Harbour Dr; r $75-115; P ☒ ☒) Close
to Coffs Creek, this clean, bright and cute
motel has a bit of style as shown by the
water-shooting statuary along the pool. It
also has a little restaurant. Some rooms
have balconies with ocean views, others
have spas.

TOP END

Novotel Pacific Bay Resort (☎ 6659 7000; www.pac
ificbayresort.com.au; cnr Pacific Hwy & Bay Dr; r $162-236;
P ☒ ☒) The large grounds feature tennis
and volleyball courts, cocktail bars, walking
trails and a fitness centre. The 180 rooms
have balconies, many with kitchens.

Eating

JETTY

The Jetty on Harbour Dr is the main restaurant strip and there's really no point
eating elsewhere; most of the CBD closes
down around 6pm. Kitchens start closing
around 8.30pm, so come early and make
a reservation if you have your heart set on
a particular place. Most places have pavement tables.

Foreshores Café (☎ 6652 3127; 394 Harbour
Dr; mains $6-20; ☺ breakfast & lunch) Quick and
friendly service, huge breakfasts (including
snazzy French toast) and ocean breezes on
the terrace make this a great spot to start
the day.

Crying Tiger (☎ 6650 0195; 386 Harbour Dr; mains
$8-16; ☺ dinner; ☒) Thai food is served in this
stylish restaurant, including more unusual
Thai items such as *choo choo talay* (red-
curry seafood).

Maria's Italian Restaurant (☎ 6651 3000; 366
Harbour Dr; mains $9-15; ☺ dinner) This is the
kind of old-fashioned Italian place that
never goes out of style. Families love it for
the long, satisfying and cheap menu (pizza
and spag bol).

MARINA

Second to the Jetty in popularity, with good
seafood.

Fisherman's Co-op (☎ 6652 2811; 69 Marina Dr;
meals $7 ☺ 9am-6pm winter, 9am-8pm summer) Fresh
fish right off the boats. Homemade gelato
and a nice picnic area add to the rapture.

Tide & Pilot Oyster Bar & Sea Grill (☎ 6651 6888;
Marina Dr; mains $20-30; ☺ breakfast, lunch & dinner)
Right on the ocean (if you're lucky, you
might spot a whale), this elegant seafood
restaurant has truly great food. The downstairs **café** (mains $6-12; ☺ breakfast, lunch & dinner)
has tables in and out and serves everything
from classic eggs and bacon to fresh fish.

Julie's Galley at the Marina (☎ 6650 0188; Marina
Dr; meals $4-7; ☺ 8am-6.30pm) Have your break-
fast egg-and-bacon roll with the blokes off
the boats. All kinds of burgers (several veggie options) are served by the cheery chef.

CITY CENTRE

The city centre is good for lunch, or for
coffee all day, but most places are closed in
the evening. The pedestrian area opposite
Palm Mall (part of High St pedestrian mall)
has lots of cafés.

Starfish Café (☎ 6651 5005; City Sq; mains $5-12; ☺ breakfast Mon-Sat, lunch Mon-Fri) The most up-scale of the cafés on the pedestrian zone off High St. Good coffee and meals presented with artistic touches. Superb eggs Benedict, sandwiches and salads.

City Square Delicatessen & Café (☎ 6652 5855; City Sq; sandwiches $6-8; ☺ breakfast Mon-Sat, lunch Mon-Fri) Create your own sandwich from the array of delicacies in the counter display cases or sip a tasty coffee while you decide which prepared foods and cheeses you want to take home to your holiday gaff.

Tequila Mexican Restaurant (☎ 6652 1279; 224B High St; mains $14-20; ☺ dinner Mon-Sat) This ser-viceable joint is one of the few places in the CBD that's open for dinner. They have all the standards: burritos, fajitas, and a fistful of margaritas. There's live, easy-listening music on Saturday nights.

Entertainment

See Thursday's edition of the *Coffs Harbour Advocate* for listings.

NIGHTCLUBS

Indulge (☎ 6658 6426; 15 City Blvd Mall; admission var-ies) Upstairs in an older part of the mall, you'll find foam parties, travelling acts and general mayhem until very late.

LIVE MUSIC

Hoey Moey Pub (☎ 6852 3833; Ocean Pde) This party pub satisfies the demanding, gagging-for-it backpacker crowd with local acts and cover bands, pool comps and trivia nights.

Coffs Hotel (☎ 6652 3817; cnr Pacific Hwy & West High St) This pub complex has bands, several bars, DJs and god-awful karaoke. It fully rocks on Friday nights.

Pier Hotel (☎ 6652 2110; cnr Hood & High Sts) The cover bands that aren't at Hoey Moey can often be found at this classic 1930s pub.

Plantation Hotel (☎ 6652 3855; www.plantation hotel.com.au; 88 Grafton St) This huge, gleaming joint gets sweaty most nights with loads of bands, booze and bad boys and girls. There's also a restaurant and backpacker accommodation on site.

Getting There & Away

AIR

Coffs Harbour Airport is just south of town. **Virgin Blue** (☎ 13 67 89; www.virginblue.com.au) has flights to Sydney (from $90) and Melbourne

(from $150). **QantasLink** (☎ 13 13 13; www.qantas .com.au) flies to Sydney (from $90), Mel-bourne (from $210), Adelaide (from $250) and Perth (from $375). **Sunshine Express** (☎ 13 13 13; www.sunshineexpress.com.au) goes to Brisbane (from $175).

BUS

Buses leave from a shelter adjacent to the information centre.

Greyhound Australia (☎ 13 20 30; www.greyhound .com.au) has several services a day running north, including Byron Bay ($43, four hours), and south to Sydney ($62, nine hours). **Premier Motor Service** (☎ 13 34 10) has similar runs.

Busways (☎ 6652 2744) has local school runs to Bellingen ($7, one hour, three daily Monday to Friday), while **Kean's** (☎ 1800 625 587) has services including Tamworth ($59), Armidale ($32) and Bellingen ($15) three times weekly.

TRAIN

Countrylink (☎ 13 22 32; www.countrylink.nsw.gov.au) goes north to Casino (where the train used to branch off to Byron Bay) and Brisbane ($75, 5½ hours), and south to Sydney ($84, nine hours).

Getting Around

Hostel shuttles meet all long-distance buses and trains.

There's pedal power at **Coffs Bike Hire** (☎ 6652 5102; cnr Orlando & Collingwood Sts; per day from $25; ☺ 8.30am-5.30pm Mon-Fri, 9am-2pm Sat & Sun).

Ryan's Buses (☎ 6652 3201) runs to Grafton ($19) twice a day and to the beaches ($8 to $9) north of Coffs several times daily.

Major car-rental companies are at the airport, or try the 24-hour **Coffs District Taxi Network** (☎ 13 10 08, 6658 5922).

COFFS HARBOUR TO BYRON BAY

With a nice beach in a deep cove, **Wool-goolga** (also known as Woopi; population 3800) is a less-developed coastal town just north of Coffs, known for its surf-and-Sikh community.

As you drive by on the highway you'll no-tice the impressive **Guru Nanak Temple**, a Sikh *gurdwara* (place of worship). Don't confuse it with the **Raj Mahal**, a decrepit, Indian-influenced concrete extravagance that has two giant elephant statues out the front; it's

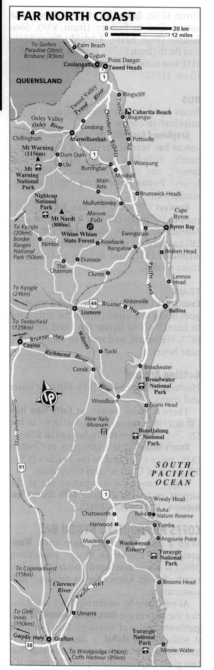

FAR NORTH COAST

actually an emporium of sorts, with arts and crafts, clothes and a restaurant.

If you drive straight through town up to the point, you'll get a magnificent view of the **Solitary Marine Reserve**.

Stay at the **Woolgoolga Beach Caravan Park** (☎ 02-6654 1373; Beach St; sites/cabins per 2 people $20/50) or the **Beach Motel** (☎ 02-6654 1333; 78 Beach St; r $85-175; P ⊠ ⊠) with its 10 comfortable rooms.

Get into the spirit of things at the **Maharaja Tandoori Indian Restaurant** (☎ 02-6654 1122; 10-12 River St; mains $26) opposite the temple – they do a suitably authentic curry. On the beachfront, **Bluebottles Brasserie** (☎ 02-6654 1962; cnr Wharf & Beach Sts; mains $10-30; ⊠ breakfast & lunch daily, dinner Thu-Sat) has live jazz and a changing and creative menu served throughout the day.

Red Rock (population 290), a sleepy village with a beautiful inlet and gorgeous surrounds, is a site sacred to the Gunawarri tribe. Soak up the sun or catch a fish while camping at **Red Rock Caravan Park** (☎ 02-6649 2730; 1 Lawson St, Red Rock; sites/cabins from $12/65).

The 20,000-hectare **Yuraygir National Park** covers the 60km stretch of coast north from Red Rock. The beaches are outstanding and there are some bushwalking paths where you can view endangered coastal emus. Walkers can bush camp and there are **basic camping areas** (per person $5) at Station Creek in the southern section; at the Boorkoom and Illaroo rest areas in the central section; on the north bank of the Sandon River; and at Red Cliff at the Brooms Head end of the northern section (these are accessible by car). There are also walk-in camp sites in the northern section: Plumbago Headland, Shelly Head and Shelly Beach. Self-service kiosks collect the park's $7 day-use fee.

Nearby **Wooli** (population 560) hosts the **Australian Goanna Pulling Championships** (☎ 02-6649 7575) over Easter. Rather than ripping the eponymous animal to shreds, participants, squatting on all fours, attach leather harnesses to their heads and engage in cranial tug-of-war. This sport was all the rage in the 19th century, until it was replaced in popularity by sheep worrying and dunny dodging.

Grafton (population 17,300), with its wide streets, big verandas and spectacular jacarandas, feels like the border post for the subtropics. The town is a graceful old beast nestled on the banks of the wide, imposing Clarence River, with parks and streets awash with an amazing variety of trees. The town's mainstay is in its agricultural roots: beef cattle inland and sugar cane in the Clarence River delta.

The **Clarence River visitor information centre** (☎ 02-6642 4677; www.clarencetourism.com; cnr Spring & Charles Sts; 9am-5pm) is on the Pacific Hwy south of town, near the turn-off to the bridge and sharing a parking lot with a McDonald's. There's a **NPWS office** (☎ 02-6641 1500; 49 Victoria St; 8.30am-5pm).

There's an interesting arts scene, which manifests in the **Grafton Artsfest** (www.artsfest grafton.com), held twice yearly with workshops and exhibitions.

Victoria St is the town's historical focal point, providing fascinating glimpses of 19th-century architecture.

The **Grafton Regional Gallery** (☎ 02-6642 6996; 158 Fitzroy St; admission free; 10am-4pm Tue-Sun) is a small regional art gallery in an 1880 house. The **Clarence River Historical Society** (190 Fitzroy St; adult/child $3/1; 1-4pm Tue-Thu & Sun) has displays of old housewares. The **Pelican Playhouse**, South Grafton, puts on amateur dramatics written by local playwrights.

Susan Island, in the middle of the river, is home to the largest fruit-bat colony in the southern hemisphere. Their evening departure is a spectacular summer sight. Hire a tinny from **Seelands Boat Hire** (☎ 02-6644 9381; Old Punt Rd; per day $60).

Busways (☎ 02-6642 2954) runs to Yamba ($10, 1¼ hours, six daily); **Ryan's Buses** (☎ 02-6652 3201) to Coffs Harbour ($18). **Greyhound Australia** (☎ 13 20 30; www.greyhound.com.au) and **Premier Motor Service** (☎ 13 34 10) stop at the train station.

Countrylink (☎ 13 22 32; www.countrylink.nsw.gov .au) stops here; Sydney is served three times daily ($90, 10 hours).

Angourie Point is one of the coast's top spots for experienced surfers and has a spring-water quarry pool; good views beckon over the rocky shore from the small cliffs at the end of the road. Further north at the river mouth, east of the highway through cane fields and sprawling channels, the fishing town of **Yamba** (population 4000) has beaches on three fronts, a relaxed pace and a burgeoning café culture.

Pacific Hotel (☎ 02-6646 2466; www.pacifichotel yamba.com.au; 1 Pilot St, Yamba; dm $18-20, d $50-130;

) is gorgeously situated on a hill overlooking Yamba Beach. There's a plethora of varying rooms and a superb bistro.

From Yamba, a passenger-only **ferry** (☎ 02-6646 6423; adult/child $5/2.50) runs four times a day to Iluka, on the north bank of the Clarence River.

Busways (☎ 02-6642 2954; tickets $10) and **Countrylink** (☎ 13 22 32; www.countrylink.nsw.gov.au; tickets $12) buses both service Grafton (1¼ hour, six daily).

Maclean (population 2463), between the Yuraygir and Bundjalung national parks, is worth a look. It's a picturesque little town, situated at the junction of the Clarence River's main and southern arms, where the river begins its lazy sprawl over the delta. The **Lower Clarence visitor information centre** (☎ 02-6645 4121; Ferry Park, Pacific Hwy, Maclean), at the edge of town, can help with accommodation.

Maclean is extremely proud of its Scottish background, going so far as to call itself the 'Scottish Town in Australia' (there must be another one). There's a Scots information and souvenir shop; haggis is available; street signs are bilingual (Gaelic and English); and there's a **Highland Gathering** every Easter, a **Scots Debutante Ball** every September and an **International Tartan Day** every July. Down the main street, there's also around 200 power poles painted with the tartans of various clans, and all of this ensures a steady stream of visitors anxious to reconnect with their Celtic roots.

The locals are particularly friendly and love to tell the story of why the main street has a big curve in it (they reckon one of the first settlers, a stubborn Scot, refused to get out of the way of development, forcing the roadworks to go around him). They also love to tell the story of the cows that got drunk from drinking the water next to a leaking brewery.

World Heritage–listed **Iluka Nature Reserve** is a short detour off the highway; it's the southern end of **Bundjalung National Park** (day-use fee per vehicle $7). Created in 1980, the park is almost 4000 hectares of coastal land, with 30km of unspoilt beaches for surfing and swimming.

Stay at the Woody Head **picnic and camping area** (☎ 02-6646 6134; per person $8), which has rock pools and is 6km north of Iluka.

No, it's not a mirage – the **New Italy Museum** (☎ 02-6682 2622; Pacific Hwy) actually exists. It's

19km north of the turn for Iluka and smack bang in the heart of Australiana. Here, you'll find a folk museum devoted to Italy and a copy of Michelangelo's *David* that has suffered from serious fondling.

There's also an unusual exhibition that sheds light on this oasis, tracking the Marquis de Ray's ambitious plan to colonise the New Guinea island of New Ireland. Although the Marquis managed to exploit over 300 Italian sailors in the process, his plan was foiled when he was sent to a lunatic asylum. Many of the sailors who survived settled around this area, and this compelling history was made into an opera, *The Mercenary*, in 2002, with music by Paul Grabowsky and a libretto by Janis Balodis.

There's also a **café** (9am-5pm) and an Aboriginal arts-and-crafts shop.

Ballina

☎ 02 / pop 16,500

Ballina is a sign of the times. Basing its appeal around family holidays and nature activities, it likes to tout itself as a quiet alternative to Byron, and is booming along the riverfront.

The **Ballina visitor information centre** (☎ 66 86 3484; www.discoverballina.com; cnr Lasbalsas Plaza & River St; 9am-5pm) is at the eastern end of town. Sip a smoothie and surf the net at the **Ice Creamery Internet Café** (☎ 6686 5783; 178 River St; meals $6-8; 8.30am-9pm;).

SIGHTS & ACTIVITIES

Behind the information centre, the **Naval & Maritime Museum** (☎ 6681 1002; Regatta Ave; admission by donation; 9am-4pm) has the remains of a balsawood raft that drifted across the Pacific from Ecuador as part of the Las Balsas expedition in 1973.

Shelley Beach is white, sandy and patrolled. **Shaws Bay Lagoon** is popular with families.

Ballina is also home to the awesome **Big Prawn** (☎ 6686 0086; Pacific Hwy; 24hr), which has it all over the Big Banana (p182), the Big Oyster (p174) and the Big Avocado (p200) in terms of scale and aesthetics (but not the 'little' Rock, p170). Check the Prawn when it's all floodlit at night, terrifying unsuspecting animals, scaring small children and putting the fear of God into local drunks; there's a 24-hour restaurant and plenty of prawn-related knick-knacks. It's bloody bizarre.

Richmond River Cruises (☎ 6687 5688; Regatta Ave; 2hr tours adult/child $20/10) is the most established cruise service.

SLEEPING & EATING

Ballina Manor (☎ 6681 5888; www.ballinamanor.com.au; 25 Norton St; r $150-210;) This beautiful hotel began in the 1920s as an Edwardian-style girls' school. It's been lovingly restored and the rooms boast many antiques. The creative restaurant serves fresh seafood.

Brundah (☎ 6686 8166; 37 Norton St; s/d $130/165;) This magnificent Federation-era homestead has impeccable rooms overlooking lush gardens and a huge acacia.

Ballina Heritage Inn (☎ 6686 0505; 229 River St; s/d from $80/90;) A modern place, right in the centre with 26 very comfortable units.

Ballina Travellers Lodge YHA (☎ 6686 6737; 36-38 Tamar St; dm/s/d $25/64/74;) Central and peaceful, with friendly owners, modern dorms, and bike and bodyboard hire.

Ballina Lakeside Holiday Resort (☎ 6686 8755; Fenwick Dr; sites/cabins $25/45;) Close to Shelley Beach, with access to fresh and saltwater swimming holes, and many amenities – spas, mini-golf course, gym, that kind of thing.

Shaws Bay Caravan Park (☎ 6681 1413; 1 Brighton St; sites/cabins from $22/50) Low-key, right on the lagoon.

Out of the Blue (☎ 6686 6602; 3 Compton Dr; mains $15-25; lunch Sun, dinner Wed-Sat) The good views of Shaws Bay complement the huge variety of fresh seafood.

Pelican 181 (☎ 6686 9181; 12-24 Fawcett St; meals $6-20; breakfast, lunch & dinner) A breezy, quality seafood restaurant and takeaway right on the river.

GETTING THERE & AWAY

Regional Express (☎ 13 17 13; www.regionalexpress .com.au) and **QantasLink** (☎ 13 13 13; www.qantas .com.au) fly to Sydney (from $100) from the airport near town. This is also the closest service to Byron Bay.

Greyhound Australia (☎ 13 20 30; www.greyhound .com.au) stops at the Big Prawn. **Premier Motor Service** (☎ 13 34 10) stops at the Ampol station (corner of Kerr St and Pacific Hwy).

Blanch's Bus Service (☎ 6686 2144; http://tropical nsw.com.au/blanchs) operates several daily services to Lennox Head, Byron Bay, Bangalow and Mullumbimby from the Tamar St bus stop.

Countrylink (☎ 13 22 32; www.countrylink.nsw.gov .au) has buses connecting to trains at the Casino train station.

If you're heading to Byron Bay, take the coast road through Lennox Head. It's much shorter and prettier than the highway.

Lennox Head
☎ 02 / pop 4500

Just a few kilometres south of Byron Bay, Lennox Head is light years away in terms of crowds, even though it has great beaches. It's a relaxing alternative. It also has some of the best surf on the coast, including long righthander breaks, especially in winter. **Lake Ainsworth**, a lagoon just back from the beach, has water that's softened – and made icky brown – by tannins from the tea trees along its banks (it makes your skin feel great). It's also popular for sailing and sailboarding, and has a sandy, shady little beach.

The **Lennox Head visitor information centre** (☎ 6687 5728; 90 Ballina St; ☼ 8am-5.30pm Mon-Fri, 8am-3.30pm Sat & Sun; ▣) has Internet access (with wi-fi).

The YHA-affiliated **Lennox Head Beach House** (☎ 6687 7636; www.yha.com.au; 3 Ross St; dm/d $24/60; ▣) has immaculate rooms and a great vibe; for $5 you can use the boards, sailboards and bikes. **Lake Ainsworth Caravan Park** (☎ 6687 7249; Pacific Pde; per 2 people sites/cabins $20/50) has a nice sea breeze flowing through it.

Ruby's by the Sea (☎ 6687 5769; 17-19 Pacific Pde; pub meal $9-16, bistro meal $12-24; ☼ lunch & dinner), part of the Lennox Point Hotel, has sandwiches and burgers in the pub downstairs and Mod Oz in the scenic bistro upstairs.

Café de Mer (☎ 6687 7132; Ballina St; mains $7-14; ☼ breakfast, lunch & dinner) is funky, while **Red Rock Café** (☎ 6687 4744; 3/60 Ballina St; mains $10; ☼ breakfast, lunch & dinner) is hip Mod Oz.

7 Mile Café (☎ 6687 6210; 41 Pacific Pde; mains $12-24; ☼ lunch & dinner) offers airy and shady seating.

Premier Motor Service (☎ 13 34 10) stops three times a day on request heading north and south; pick up is from the Countrylink Coach Stop. **Blanch's Bus Service** (☎ 6686 2144; http://tropicalnsw.com.au/blanchs) runs to Ballina, Byron Bay and Mullumbimby.

BYRON BAY
☎ 02 / pop 7030

OK, you've made it to the promised land. God's own Earth. Land of a thousand myths.

For many, Byron is a hedonistic pleasure park, a place to indulge one's wildest instincts. For others, it's hippy heaven, a utopian community blessed with a beautiful natural environment, healthful activities and pursuits, and socially conscious locals (McDonald's can't trade here, for example, due to local pressure groups). The truth is somewhere in-between.

When Byron Bay is good, it's unsurpassed: long days, balmy weather, endless beaches, delightful accommodation, delectable food, delirious nightlife. But when it's bad, let's just say it's very crowded. Even then, you can still take the opportunity for endless walks on the endless shore, or hightail it to the delightful little towns nearby that make the whole region greater than its parts.

It's worth remembering, though, that people actually live here year-round. For them, mass tourism is a necessary evil at best; at worst it's robbing their town of its innate charm. Property prices have soared, long-time residents are being priced out and developers are looking to the high-rise horrors of the Gold Coast to satisfy demand (residents have responded by electing Australia's first Green Party council).

Despite it all, the charisma and hospitality of the local community really makes Byron what it is – an asset worth bottling in its own right.

Information
Accommodation booking office (☎ 6680 8666; www.byronbayaccom.net; Suite 6, 75 Jonson St) A great service for booking in advance.

Backpackers World (☎ 6685 8858; www.backpackers world.com.au; Shop 6, Byron St; ☼ 9am-7pm Mon-Sat, 11am-5pm Sun; ▣) Has the Net, but is primarily a travel agent.

Byron Bay visitor information centre (☎ 6680 8558; www.visitbyronbay.com; Stationmaster's Cottage, 80 Jonson St; ☼ 9am-5pm) Ground zero for tourist information.

Byron Bus & Backpacker Centre (☎ 6685 5517; 84 Jonson St; ☼ 7.30am-7pm; ▣) Handles bus, train, accommodation and activity bookings and has currency exchange, left-luggage lockers ($5), car rental and Internet access.

Byron Environment Centre (Octagonal hut, Railway Park, Jonson St) Sporadic hours, passionate staff.

Internet Outpost (☎ 6685 6762; 58 Jonson St; per 10min $1; ☼ 9am-8pm Mon-Fri, 9am-6pm Sat & Sun; ▣)

NEW SOUTH WALES

Sights

CAPE BYRON

The grandfather of the 'mad, bad and dangerous to know' poet Lord Byron was a renowned navigator in the 1760s, and Captain Cook named this spot, Australia's most easterly, after him. (A star-struck clerk in Sydney thought the grandson was the one being honoured, and named the streets – and the town – after poets: Keats, Jonson, Shelley.)

Here, the views are far beyond perfection on all sides and the ocean is alive with schools of dolphins. Humpback whales pass nearby during their northern (June to July) and southern (September to November) migrations. Keep your peepers especially peeled: there's a whale they call Migaloo

that's been known to be fond of Byron waters. He's the only known all-white humpback whale in the world.

Drive right up to the picturesque 1901 **lighthouse** (☎ 6685 6585; Lighthouse Rd; ☽ 8am-sunset). It's $5 to park at the top, but free 300m below. Alternatively, walk to the summit (it's good exercise) but be wary of hoofing it back to town after dark, especially if alone: the terrain is isolated and you'll be dodging unseen cars on the narrow roads. There are good displays and you can stay overnight (p193).

The 4km circular walking track round the cape from the **Captain Cook Lookout** on Lighthouse Rd provides a good chance of seeing wallabies, bush turkeys and feral goats in the final rainforest stretch.

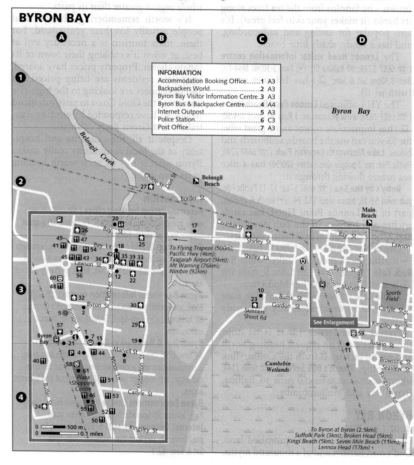

BYRON BAY

INFORMATION

Accommodation Booking Office........**1** A3
Backpackers World.................................**2** A3
Byron Bay Visitor Information Centre.**3** A3
Byron Bus & Backpacker Centre.........**4** A4
Internet Outpost.....................................**5** A3
Police Station...**6** C3
Post Office..**7** A3

To Flying Trapeze (500m);
Pacific Hwy (4km);
Tyagarah Airport (9km);
Mt Warning (76km);
Nimbin (92km)

To Byron at Byron (2.5km);
Suffolk Park (3km); Broken Head (5km);
Kings Beach (5km); Seven Mile Beach (11km);
Lennox Head (17km)

0   100 m
0   0.1 miles

BEACHES

Main Beach, immediately in front of town, is terrific for people watching and swimming. At the western edge of town, **Belongil Beach** is clothing-optional. **Clarkes Beach**, at the eastern end of Main Beach, is good for surfing but the best surf is at the next few beaches: the **Pass**, **Watego's** and **Little Watego's**.

Tallow Beach is an amazing stretch of beach that extends 7km south of Cape Byron to a rockier stretch around **Broken Head**, where a succession of small beaches dot the coast before opening onto **Seven Mile Beach**, which goes all the way to Lennox Head.

The suburb of **Suffolk Park** (with more good surf, particularly in winter) starts 3km south of town.

Kings Beach, a popular gay beach, is just off Seven Mile Beach Rd near the Broken Head Holiday Park.

Activities

Adventure sports abound and most operators offer free pick-up from local accommodation. It's cheapest to book through hostels.

Kidz Klub (☎ 6680 8585; 67 Shirley St) keeps kids thoroughly entertained with a 'no parents' rule strictly enforced. You can book your child (ages five to 12) by the hour ($10) or get rid of them for the entire day ($90). Activities include sandcastle making and bushwalking.

Take circus lessons at **Flying Trapeze** (☎ 0417 073 668; www.flyingtrapeze.com.au; Byron Bay Beach Club, Bayshore Dr; from $40).

0 ————————— 1 km
0 ————————— 0.5 miles

SIGHTS & ACTIVITIES		
Ambaji	8	B4
Blackdog Surfing	9	A4
Buddha Gardens	10	C3
Byron Bay Surf School	11	D3
Byron Surf Shop	12	B3
Cape Byron Lighthouse	13	F2
Captain Cook Lookout	14	E2
Dive Byron Bay	15	A3
Dolphin Kayaking	16	E3
Kidz Klub	17	B2
Pure	(see 45)	
Quintessence	18	B3
Sundive	19	B3
Surf Life Saving Club	20	B2
Surfing Byron Bay	21	A3

SLEEPING		
Aquarius Backpacker Resort	22	B3
Arts Factory Lodge	23	C3
Bamboo Cottage	24	A4
Bayview Lodge	25	B3
Beach Hotel	26	A2
Belongil Beachouse	27	B2
BreakFree Eco Beach Resort	28	C2
Byron Bayside Motel	29	B3
Cape Byron YHA	30	B3
Clarkes Beach Caravan Park	31	E2
Great Northern Hotel	32	A3
Hibiscus Motel	33	B3
Lighthouse Keeper Cottages	34	F1
LJ Hooker	35	B3
Main Beach Backpackers	36	A3
Professionals	37	B3
Rae's on Watego's	38	F2

EATING		
Blue Olive	39	B3
Byron Farmers' Market	40	A4
Byronian	41	A3
Café Wunderbar	42	B3
Cardamom Pod	43	A3
Dish	44	A4
Fins	(see 26)	
Fresh	45	A3
Ka-toush	46	A4
Mongers	47	A3
Olivo	48	A3
Orgasmic	49	A3
Orion	50	A4
Oz Bakehouse	51	A4
Red Ginger	52	A4
Santos	53	A4
Snap	54	A3
The Balcony	(see 45)	
Woolworths	55	A4

DRINKING		
Dish Raw Bar	(see 44)	
La La Land	56	A3
Railway Friendly Bar	57	A3

ENTERTAINMENT		
c-moog	58	A4
Cheeky Monkeys	59	D3
Cocomangas	60	A3
cuba lounge	(see 58)	
Pighouse Flicks	(see 23)	

TRANSPORT		
Byron Bay Bicycles	61	A4
Jetset Travel	(see 4)	

NEW SOUTH WALES

ALTERNATIVE THERAPIES

The *Body & Soul* guide, available from the visitors centre, is a handy guide to the many alternative therapies Byron has to offer.

Ambaji (☎ 6685 6620; www.ambaji.com.au; 6 Marvell St; massages from $60; ⌚ 9am-5pm Mon-Sat, 11am-3pm Sun) Blueprint healing, craniosacral balancing, crystal singing bowls and life coaching.

Buddha Gardens (☎ 6680 7844; www.buddhagardens .com; 21 Gordon St; ⌚ 10am-6pm) Balinese-style day spa in a secluded spot, with a long list of therapies.

Pure (☎ 6685 5988; cnr Lawson & Jonson Sts; massages from $40; ⌚ 9am-7pm) Swedish massage, reiki, facials and a vibrating sauna ($30).

Quintessence (☎ 6685 5533; 8/11 Fletcher St; massages from $45; ⌚ 10am-5pm) 'Please enter our tranquillity zone', they say.

Surf Life Saving Club (Main Beach; massages from $55; ⌚ 8am-6pm Mon-Sat) Therapeutic treats and yoga classes ($12).

DIVING

About 3km offshore, Julian Rocks Marine Reserve blends cold southerly and warm northerly currents, attracting a profusion of marine species and divers alike.

Dive Byron Bay (☎ 1800 243 483, 6685 8333; www .byronbaydivecentre.com.au; 9 Marvell St) Large selection of rental equipment.

Sundive (☎ 6685 7755; www.sundive.com.au; 8 Middleton St) Long-standing and respected dive school.

FLYING

Byron Airwaves (☎ 6629 0354, 0427 615 950; www .byronair.cjb.net) Tandem hang gliding ($145) and courses (from $1500).

Byron Bay Skydivers (☎ 6684 1323; www.skydive byronbay.com; Tyagarah Airport) Tandem dives from $239.

Byron Gliding Club (☎ 6684 7627; www.byrongliding .com; Tyagarah Airport) Joyrides in gliders from $80; lessons also offered.

KAYAKING

Paddle within 30m of dolphins with **Dolphin Kayaking** (☎ 6685 8044; www.dolphinkayaking.com .au; half-day tours $60; ⌚ 9am-2pm), located on the beach across from 56 Lawson St.

SURFING

Byron Bay waves are often quite mellow. Most hostels provide free boards to guests.

Blackdog Surfing (☎ 6680 9828; Shop 8, The Plaza, 85 Jonson St) Intimate group lessons; special courses for women.

Byron Bay Surf School (☎ 1800 707 274; www.byron baysurfschool.com; 127 Jonson St; classes from $60) Vast curriculum.

Byron Surf Shop (☎ 6685 7536; cnr Lawson & Fletcher Sts) They sell and rent boards (from $20).

Surfing Byron Bay (☎ 6685 7099; off 84 Jonson St)

Tours

Most tour companies will pick you up from where you're staying.

Byron Bay Eco Tours (☎ 6685 4030; www.byronbay ecotours.com; tours $85) Small tours to the World Heritage national parks.

Mountain Bike Tours (☎ 0429 122 504; www .mountainbiketours.com.au; tours from $90) Ride through the rainforest, lunch included.

Festivals & Events

Byron Bay Writers Festival (www.byronbaywriters festival.com.au) In late July/early August, this gathers together top-shelf writers and literary followers from across Australia.

East Coast International Blues & Roots Music Festival (www.bluesfest.com.au) At Easter, this is a major event, with renowned international stars and the cream of Aussie talent; book early.

Splendour in the Grass (www.splendourinthegrass .com) This high-dose mash-up of indie rock, electronica, hip-hop and other strains of sonic revolution takes place in July.

Taste of Byron (www.tasteofbyron.com) Along Byron's beachfront eateries, this celebration of produce from the Northern Rivers region rumbles the tummy in October.

Sleeping

The old mantra applies in Byron more than anywhere: always book ahead, especially in summer. Motels are clustered in town and south along Bangalow Rd, and there are scores of B&Bs and apartments along Belongil Beach.

Holiday houses during low/peak season cost from $400/600 per week and go much, much higher. Rental agents include the following:

Professionals (☎ 6685 6552; www.byronbaypro.com .au; cnr Lawson & Fletcher Sts)

LJ Hooker (☎ 6685 7300; www.ljhooker.com; Shop 1, Byron Arcade, 13 Lawson St)

BUDGET

Main Beach Backpackers (☎ 6685 8695; www.main beachbackpackers.com; cnr Lawson & Fletcher Sts; dm/d from $18/50; P 🅿 🖳 🎿) A modern, excellent place near the beach.

Arts Factory Lodge (☎ 6685 7709; www.artsfactory
.com.au; Skinners Shoot Rd; sites/dm/d per person from
$15/24/60; ☒) If you dig the alternative life-
style, this huge place is for you. Accommodation ranges from tepees to funky tents,
and amusements include permaculture gardens, didgeridoo lessons, DJs, yoga classes,
the atmospheric Piggery Café and Pighouse
Flicks (p195). There are free minibuses
around town.

Cape Byron YHA (☎ 1800 652 627, 6685 8788; www
.yha.com.au; cnr Middleton & Byron Sts; dm/d from $24/80;
☒ ☒ ☒) This excellent complex is situ-
ated close to the town centre and has its
own shops. Clean and orderly.

Belongil Beachouse (☎ 6685 7868; www.belongil
beachouse.com; Childe St; dm/d from $26/65, self-contained
cottages from $150; ☒) Across from Belongil
Beach, this is a fantastic place to stay, and
great value for money. Polished floorboards, stained glass in the dorm doors and
mosaics add to the atmosphere, all aimed at
a slightly more mature crowd.

Aquarius Backpacker Resort (☎ 1800 028 909,
6685 7663; 16 Lawson St; dm $18-35, d $55-200; ☒ ☒)
Close to Main Beach, with a bar, café, pool
and garden. Rooms have bathroom, TV
and fridge.

Great Northern Hotel (☎ 6685 6454; Jonson St;
s/d $45/55) Basic pub rooms and the perfect
place to crash after you have been listening to the great tunes and bands playing
downstairs.

Clarkes Beach Caravan Park (☎ 6685 6496; off
Lighthouse Rd; sites/cabins from $22/85) The 109 small
sites can be jammed here but it's quiet and
you are right on the beach.

MIDRANGE

Byron Bayside Motel (☎ 6685 6004; www.byronbay
sidemotel.com.au; 14 Middleton St; r from $75; ☒ ☒)
Right across from lush forest and close to
the beach, this new 20-unit motel has large
rooms with good balconies.

BreakFree Eco Beach Resort (☎ 6639 5700; www
.breakfree.com.au; 35 Shirley St; ste from $125;
☒ ☒ ☒ ☒) This 30-unit resort blends in
with the surroundings. Rooms are a bit chic;
it's a good place for couples.

Bamboo Cottage (☎ 6685 5509; www.byron-bay
.com/bamboocottage; 76 Butler St; r $75-200; ☒)
Bedrooms in this pretty 1930s house are
sumptuous and brightly coloured. French,
English, sign language and some Japanese
spoken.

Bayview Lodge (☎ 6685 7073; www.byron-bay
.com/bayview; 22 Bay St; 1-/2-bedroom units from $155/200;
☒) It's beachside, and some units have excellent views from their balconies. Units are
large and have full kitchens, some decorated
with clown art.

Hibiscus Motel (☎ 6685 6195; www.byronbayresorts
.com/hibiscus; 33 Lawson St; d $135-295; ☒) Excellent
location, right in town and right near Main
Beach. The seven clean rooms at this cheery
place have cable TV.

Lighthouse Keeper Cottages (The Professionals
☎ 6685 6552; www.byronbaypro.com.au; Cape Byron; 3-
day rentals from $550) These two historic 1901
cottages at the Byron Bay Lighthouse
have fabulous views. You've got the entire
grounds to yourself after dusk.

TOP END

Beach Hotel (☎ 6685 6402; www.beachhotel.com.au;
cnr Jonson & Bay Sts; r $220-700; ☒ ☒ ☒) Cen-
tral, beachfront hotel. Ground-floor rooms
open onto lush gardens and a heated pool,
upper-storey rooms have ocean views.

Rae's on Watego's (☎ 6685 5366; www.raes.com
.au; 8 Marine Pde; d $370-1150; ☒ ☒ ☒ ☒) This
dazzlingly white Mediterranean villa was
rated by *CondeNast Traveller* as one of the
world's top 25 hotels. The rooms here are
seriously gorgeous and breathtakingly luxurious. The restaurant (see p194) is worth
the trip alone.

Byron at Byron (☎ 1300 554 362; www.thebyron
atbyron.com.au; 77-97 Broken Head Rd; ste from $270;
☒ ☒ ☒ ☒) This swanky resort is a vi-
sion in white. South of Byron proper, the 60
suites are set among the rainforest and are a
15-minute walk from the beach. Rooms have
DVD players and many more luxuries.

Eating
CAFÉS
Café Wunderbar (6685 5909; 2 Fletcher St; treats $4;
☒ 7.30am-5pm) 'Byron's German café' offers
beguiling baked goods, beautiful Danish
pastries and Continental cakes, and Byron's
best coffee. Locals dig it and so will you.

Fresh (☎ 6685 7810; 7 Jonson St; meals $7-22;
☒ breakfast, lunch & dinner) They're pretty hip –
they reckon they serve 'designer fruit', for
example. Excellent pancakes and zesty salads, and the Mod Oz menu is sublime when
taken at the open-air tables at night.

Orgasmic (☎ 6680 7778; 11 Bay Lane; mains $6-
9; ☒ lunch & dinner) A simple Middle Eastern

place off the alley, perfect for escaping the hordes. Advocates swear this place makes the region's best falafels – 'orgasmic', in a word.

Orion (☎ 6685 6828; 5/2 Jonson St; mains $16-25; ☽ breakfast, lunch & dinner) A lovely little place, right across from the Beach Hotel, serving classic Indian for dinner: tandoori, curries, vindaloo. Does a hearty breakfast, too: Turkish toast, sausage, eggs.

Byronian (☎ 6685 6754; 58A Jonson St; mains $7-14; ☽ breakfast & lunch) A relaxing café with a gallery and great outdoor tables renowned for people watching on busy Jonson.

Snap (☎ 6680 9300; 13 Bay Lane; meals $6-16; ☽ breakfast & lunch) Settle into the amazing wicker chairs and you may never want to get up. Fusion specials make this a prime retreat to catch up on the newspaper or gossip.

RESTAURANTS

Fins (☎ 6685 5029; The Beach Hotel, cnr Jonson & Bay Sts; mains $25-35; ☽ dinner) Let the sounds of the sea and the buzz of the bar next door float over your table to create the perfect holiday indulgence. The fresh seafood here is rightfully considered the best on the coast.

Red Ginger (☎ 6680 9779; 109 Jonson St; mains $12-20; ☽ breakfast, lunch & dinner) Fragrant flowers greet you as you enter this open-air place, setting the mood for creative food, like organic bagels at breakfast, *soba* noodle salad at lunch or prawn linguine at dinner.

Rae's on Watego's (☎ 6685 5366; 8 Marine Pde; mains $36-46; ☽ lunch & dinner) Exquisite Mod Oz cuisine on a terrace overlooking the ocean. With the sound of surf providing ambience, sample the Moreton Bay bugs or baby snapper for a meal beyond compare.

Balcony (☎ 6680 9666; cnr Lawson & Jonson Sts; dinner $18-28; ☽ breakfast, lunch & dinner) With a commanding location overlooking Byron's pumping heart, the balcony (as in the architectural feature) affords voyeuristic views of the bustling thoroughfares. The terrific tucker is Mediterranean fusion, with global infusions.

Olivo (☎ 6685 7950; 34 Jonson St; mains $22-28; ☽ dinner) It's long and narrow, brick-walled and mirrored, with beige leather seating; it's chic, that's what it is. On arrival you're served garlic- and thyme-olives, setting the mood for a Mod Oz menu that runs rampant from Europe to Asia. It may be fancy, but they do kids well (grilled with

a Béarnaise sauce…just kidding; children are welcome).

Dish (☎ 6685 7320; cnr Jonson & Marvell Sts; mains $27-35; ☽ dinner) This opulent place has a Mod Oz menu and impressive wine list. Look for substantial seafood specials, or stake out the adjoining Dish Raw Bar (opposite).

Ka-toush (☎ 6680 7718; The Plaza, 85 Jonson St; mains $8-15; ☽ dinner) Pull up a pillow at the traditional low tables outside. The Middle Eastern food is excellent – try the mixed entrée plate.

QUICK EATS

Mongers (☎ 6680 8080; 1 Bay Lane; meals $9-15; ☽ lunch & dinner) Tucked behind the Beach Hotel, enjoy some of the best fish or calamari you'll ever have at the open-air tables.

Oz Bakehouse (☎ 6685 7717; 20 Jonson St; mains $8-12; ☽ 24hr; ▯) Ideal for those who get the munchies at all times, this bakery never closes. The pies and sandwiches are pretty good and you may even meet a new friend at 2am.

Cardamom Pod (Shop 8, Pier Arcade, 7 Lawson St; meals $10-15; ☽ lunch & dinner) Unassuming, with just a few tables, but a fistful of fantastic vegetarian and vegan Indian fare.

SELF-CATERING

Byron Farmers' Market (☎ 6685 9792; Butler St; ☽ 8-11am Thu) A great place to sample some of the amazing food produced in the region.

Other good sources of food to fill your holiday kitchen or picnic basket:

Red Ginger (☎ 6680 9779; 109 Jonson St; ☽ breakfast, lunch & dinner) A fine array of prepared Asian foods and ingredients.

Santos (☎ 6685 7071; 105 Jonson St; ☽ 8.30am-6pm Mon-Fri, 9.30am-5pm Sat, 10am-4pm Sun) Bright organic foods' grocery.

Blue Olive (☎ 6680 8700; 27 Lawson St; ☽ 9am-5.30pm Mon-Fri, 9.30am-4.30pm Sat, 9.30am-3.30pm Sun) Fine cheeses and deli items, prepared foods, fantastic pesto.

Woolworths supermarket (☎ 6685 7202; The Plaza, 85 Jonson St; ☽ 8am-9pm Mon-Fri, 8am-8pm Sat & Sun)

Drinking

Beach Hotel (☎ 6685 6402; www.beachhotel.com.au cnr Jonson & Bay Sts; ☽ 11am-late) This enormous beer garden draws everyone from grey pensioners and lobster-red British tourists to acid-soaked hippies and high-on-life earth mothers, beach bums and businessmen to

Champagne Charlies and Hooray Henrys. It's so close to the main beach you'll get sand up your clacker, and it's shot through with a fabulously infectious atmosphere that makes everyone your best mate. There's live music and DJs some nights.

Railway Friendly Bar (☎ 6685 7662; Jonson St; ✆ 11am-late) This is the other contender for Byron's finest drinking den. A ridiculously likeable indoor/outdoor pub with fine food, like smoked trout and linguine, live music (folk and rock) many nights, and a kooky trivia quiz on Sunday arvo.

La La Land (☎ 6680 7070; lalaland@bigpond.net.au; 6 Lawson St) Slinky soft couches, jaw-achingly cool tunes, orange-and-brown décor, sinfully low lighting…unpretentious attitudes. It's simply unreal.

Balcony (☎ 6680 9666; cnr Lawson & Jonson Sts; ✆ to late) A great restaurant and a fine bar. Drink in the view from stools, chairs or sofas while working through the long wine list.

Great Northern Hotel (☎ 6685 6454; Jonson St) This enormous, boisterous pub has live music many nights.

Dish Raw Bar (☎ 6685 7320; cnr Jonson & Marvell Sts) Take your cocktails with sushi or oysters and a large dollop of hip: the stylish black-and-white leather furnishings have red accents.

Entertainment

Byron Bay's nightlife rivals that of some Australian capital cities; along the coast it's unimpeachable. There's a gig guide in Thursday's *Byron Shire News* and Bay 99.9 FM details various events.

CINEMAS

Pighouse Flicks (☎ 6685 5828; Skinners Shoot Rd; admission $10) The cinema at the Arts Factory Lodge (see Sleeping, p193) shows second-run and arthouse flicks nightly.

NIGHTCLUBS

Cheeky Monkeys (☎ 6685 5886; www.cheekymonkeys .com.au; 115 Johnson St; ✆ 6pm-late) Cheap food, cheap meals, cheap drinks and table-top dancing mayhem, all of it aimed squarely between the eyes of backpackers.

Cocomangas (☎ 6685 8493; 32 Jonson St; ✆ 9pm-very late Tue-Sat) Dance the night away at this sweaty nightclub, with fusion, funk and techno nights.

c-moog (☎ 6680 7022; www.c-moog.com.au; 9-10 The Plaza, 85 Jonson St; ✆ 8pm-3am Tue-Sat) Spins funk and beats and has occasional gay-themed nights. Interestingly, they have a no-smoking policy on the dance floor.

cuba lounge (✆ 8pm-3am Thu-Sat) Next door, this is c-moog's new chill-out space devoted to 'sexy tunes' spun by 'mixologists'. They reckon you won't get in with shorts and a T-shirt.

Getting There & Away

AIR

The closest airport is at Ballina (p188) but most people use the larger Coolangatta airport on the Gold Coast (p324).

BUS

Greyhound Australia (☎ 13 14 19; www.greyhound .com.au) and **Premier Motor Service** (☎ 13 34 10) stop on Jonson St. Approximate times and fares for both: Brisbane ($30, three hours), Coffs Harbour ($43, four hours) and Sydney ($86, 12 to 14 hours).

Kirklands (☎ 6622 1499; www.kirklands.com.au) goes to Lismore ($13.20, 70 minutes), Murwillumbah (two hours) and Coolangatta Airport (two hours).

Blanch's (☎ 6686 2144; http://tropicalnsw.com.au /blanchs) goes to Ballina, Lennox Head, Bangalow and Mullumbimby.

Byron Bay Airbus (☎ 6684 3232; www.airlinkair bus.com) operates to/from Coolangatta (from $35, 50 minutes) and Ballina (from $30, 30 minutes) airports to Byron. Call to arrange pick-up.

Getting Around

Byron Bay Bicycles (☎ 6685 6067; The Plaza, 85 Jonson St) Hires mountain bikes for $25 per day.

Jetset Travel (☎ 6685 6554; Byron Bus & Backpacker Centre, 84 Jonson St) Rents new, small cars from $49.

Taxi (☎ 6685 5008; www.byronbaytaxis.com)

BYRON BAY TO TWEED HEADS

The Pacific Hwy continues north to the Queensland border at Tweed Heads. The pretty Coolamon Scenic Dr leaves the highway just south of Brunswick Heads, passing through **Mullumbimby** (population 2700). The hip and happening spill over from Byron into this town, with trendy cafés and bistros, and pricey organic treats. It's worth a look.

Stay at lushly shaded **Mullumbimby Motel** (☎ 02-6684 2387; 121 Dalley St; r $52-100; P ✆) or the good-value **Commercial Hotel** (☎ 02-6684 3229; cnr Burringbar & Stuart Sts; s/d $30/45). There's also the basic **Maca's Camping Ground** (☎ 02-6684 5211; Main Arm Rd, Main Arm; sites $18), 12km north of town in **Main Arm** (head out of town on Burringbar St, then follow Main Arm Rd and the blue 'camping' signs).

Try **Milk & Honey** (☎ 02-6684 1422; 59A Station St; mains $15-20; ☺ dinner Mon-Sat) for sublime wood-fired pizza.

Lulu's Café (☎ 02-6684 2415; Dalley St Plaza; mains $8; ☺ breakfast & lunch Mon-Sat) is a great vegetarian place and **Poinciana** (☎ 02-6684 4036; 55 Station St; meals $6-20; ☺ breakfast, lunch & dinner), shaded by two ancient poinciana trees, offers buckwheat crepes for brekky and savoury Mediterranean for dinner.

Blanch's Bus Service (☎ 02-6686 2144; http://tropicalnsw.com.au/blanchs) runs several times daily to Byron Bay, Lennox Head and Ballina.

Countrylink (☎ 13 22 32; www.countrylink.nsw.gov.au) provides train services.

Take the Chinderah Bypass to the legendary **Moo Moo Café** (☎ 02-6677 1230; Tweed Valley Way, Mooball; mains $8; ☺ breakfast & lunch), halfway between Brunswick Heads and Murwillumbah in the town of Mooball. This famous café has a bovine obsession, with cow and farm memorabilia aplenty.

Tweed Heads (population 73,800) marks the southern end of the Gold Coast strip. At Point Danger (named by Captain Cook to warn of the treacherous rocks and shoals) the towering **Captain Cook Memorial** straddles the state border. Tweed Heads accommodation options spill over into Coolangatta and up the Gold Coast, where there's more choice.

FAR NORTH COAST HINTERLAND

Byron Bay is not the only jewel in this part of the world. Shimmering in their own right the non-beach hinterlands lay claim to stunning, lush scenery (the area's three national parks – Border Ranges, Mt Warning and Nightcap – are all World Heritage–listed rainforest), organic markets, wilderness B&Bs and alternative lifestyles. This is far and away one of Australia's most desirable locales.

BANGALOW
☎ 02 / pop 900

Just 14km out of Byron Bay, Bangalow's appeal lies in the character of its main street Byron St, where a collection of old buildings is occupied by galleries, delis and yoga practitioners.

THE GLOWING CROSS OF LISMORE

In 1978 Lismore attracted global attention when a headstone in the local cemetery was discovered to be glowing luminescent, 24 hours a day. Word spread and soon the site was attracting hundreds of visitors a night, from far and wide, all looking for enlightenment (and not all of them high on the local weed). Some talked to the cross and even rubbed it for luck; others just sat and contemplated. The local papers devoted many column inches to the phenomenon, citing all manner of explanations, including the supernatural. Finally, the burning issue of Lismore being overrun by hippies and freaks had been pushed off the front pages by something even weirder.

The headstone belonged to the grave of William Steenson, who died in Mullumbimby in 1907 when he tried to stop an out-of-control train carriage. It turned out that the Steenson family had known about the spectral quality of William's cross, and had colluded for 60 years with locals to keep the mystery a secret for fear of vandalism, until an out-of-towner happened upon it.

The light was known locally as the 'ghost on the hill', but what really made it shimmer? Some say the granite must have had some kind of phosphorescent quality; tests were undertaken, with all manner of methods to control the angle of light on the grave, but nothing could be determined for sure. Sensationalism obfuscated serious investigation into the matter and it remained an oddity, deepening in 1986 when the cross suddenly vanished. It has never been recovered.

Two years later a replica was constructed from the same material, but inevitably there has never even been the hint of a glimmer from it.

There's a good weekly **farmers' market** (Byron St; ☼ 8-11am Sat) with top local organic produce on hand.

Riverview B&B (☎ 6687 1317; 99 Byron St; r $75-195) has lavish gardens, bubbling waters and a bright and cheery, yet traditional, interior.

Urban Café (☎ 6687 2678; 33 Byron St; meals $12-16; ☼ breakfast & lunch daily, dinner Thu-Sat) has the classic café menu (rocket salad, burger, bruschetta), a vast terrace, and live jazz, blues or country on weekends.

Fresca (☎ 6687 1711; Bangalow Hotel, 1 Byron St; mains $16-25; ☼ lunch & dinner) has already won raves for its changing daily menu of fresh seafood and Mod Oz cuisine.

Blanch's Bus Company (☎ 6686 2144; http://tropicalnsw.com.au/blanchs) runs to Byron Bay, Ballina and Mullumbimby.

LISMORE

☎ 02 / pop 27,360

Great for visiting the hinterland and Byron, Lismore is close to rainforest, beaches and the Wilson River. There's a thriving arts scene, and the Southern Cross University campus gives the town a youthful outlook, while numerous hip cafés serve the locally grown coffee.

The **Lismore visitors centre** (☎ 6622 0122; Ballina St; Internet access per 20min $3; ☼ 9am-5pm Mon-Fri, 10am-4pm Sat & Sun; ☐) has a rainforest display ($1), while kids groove on the **Heritage Park** playground, next to the centre, with its skate park and **train rides** (rides $1.80; ☼ 10am-2pm Thu, 10am-4pm Sat).

The **Lismore Regional Art Gallery** (☎ 6622 2209; www.lismore.nsw.gov.au/gallery; 131 Molesworth St; admission by donation; ☼ 10am-4pm Tue-Fri, 10.30am-2.30pm Sat & Sun) displays many local works.

The **Koala Care & Research Centre** (☎ 6622 1233; Rifle Range Rd; admission free; ☼ 9-10.30am Sat) is home to recovering koalas and well worth a visit. To get a glimpse of platypuses, head up the northern end of Kadina St and walk up to **Tucki Tucki Creek** at dawn or sunset.

Tucki Tucki Nature Reserve (☎ 6628 1177; Wyrallah Rd), 16km south of town, protects koala habitat. Initiation ceremonies were once held at the Aboriginal **bora ring** nearby.

Sleeping

Karinga Motel (☎ 6621 2787; 258 Molesworth St; r $62-100; ☒) Clean, affordable and central, with 31 comfortable rooms.

Tulloona House (☎ 6624 2897; 106 Ballina Rd, Goonellabah; s/d incl breakfast $80/100) This National Trust–classified Victorian mansion is packed to bursting with antique bric-a-brac. Outside are clutter-free gardens. It's 5km towards Ballina; pick-ups can be arranged.

Lismore Palms Caravan Park (☎ 6621 7067; 42-48 Brunswick St; sites/cabins from $15/50; ☒) This one has pleasant staff and atmosphere. It's right on the river, with 13 self-contained cabins.

Eating

Lismore stages its farmers market every Saturday at the Showground, which is off the Nimbin Rd.

Paupiettes (☎ 6621 6135; 56 Ballina St; mains $10-17; ☼ dinner Tue-Sat; ☒) This small bistro has been providing locals with superb Mod Oz cuisine that showcases local produce.

Left Bank Café (☎ 6622 2338; 133 Molesworth St; mains $8-16; ☼ breakfast & lunch Mon-Sat; ☐) The Left Bank (actually on the left bank by the art gallery and transit centre) is delightfully pretentious and makes a very good cup of coffee. It's wi-fi enabled.

Mega Pizza (☎ 6622 2900; 120 Ballina St; meals $8-12; ☼ dinner) This tiny takeaway joint cooks up some of the most tasty and innovative pizzas on the north coast, like the amazing meatball version.

20,000 Cows Café (☎ 6622 2517; 58 Bridge St; mains $6-10; ☼ dinner Wed-Sun) The décor is as eclectic as the menu of Indian and Middle Eastern delights.

Blue Tongue (☎ 6622 0750; 43 Bridge St; meals $8-20; ☼ breakfast & lunch daily, dinner Fri) A groovy little place with '50s kitsch and a big 'back-to-nature' garden out back. Tasty sandwiches, baked goods and live jazz Friday nights.

Drinking

Mecca Café (☎ 6621 3901; 80 Magellan St) On Friday and Saturday nights they close the kitchen at this splendid café and open the bar. Cosy booths make it even more special.

Northern Rivers Hotel (☎ 6621 5797; Bridge St) While you're nursing a beer, the in-house crèche (Thursday to Saturday nights) nurses your kids.

Entertainment

Tropical Fruits (www.tropicalfruits.org.au) A lesbian and gay group that stages parties through the year, climaxing in big-time New Year's revelry.

NORPA (Northern Rivers Performing Arts; ☎ 6622 0300; www.norpa.org.au; Lismore City Hall) Stages all manner of performing arts – musicals, classical concerts, theatre, comedy, more – at the Star Court Theatre and Lismore City Hall.

Winsome Hotel (☎ 6621 2283; 11 Bridge St) Enjoy live bands, DJs, pool competitions and all kinds of other entertainment under the benevolent eye of the Big Regina – a huge portrait of HM Queen Elizabeth II.

Getting There & Away

Rex (☎ 13 17 13; www.regionalexpress.com.au) has flights to Sydney (from \$100).

Greyhound Australia (☎ 13 14 99; www.greyhound .com.au) buses travel to Byron Bay (\$36, two hours); **Kirklands** (☎ 6622 1499; www.kirklands.com .au) to Ballina (\$11, 50 minutes) and Byron Bay (\$14, one hour 10 minutes); and **Waller's** (☎ 6687 8550) to Nimbin (\$9, 45 minutes).

CountryLink (☎ 13 22 32; www.countrylink.nsw.gov .au) runs buses from the disused train station to Casino.

AROUND LISMORE

The Channon is an intimate village between Nimbin and Lismore. Time your visit for the second Sunday of each month for the 'mother of all markets' (say the locals). **Havan's** (☎ 02-6688 6108; www.rainbowregion.com/havan; Lot 1, Lawler Rd; s/d \$75/115) is an eco-tourist retreat set in the heart of a rainforest. There are numerous walks near the property, where you can see platypuses and other exotic creatures.

NIGHTCAP NATIONAL PARK

This 8080-hectare park, south of Murwillumbah and north of Lismore, borders Nimbin and The Channon. It was World Heritage–listed in 1989 and is home to diverse subtropical rainforests and many species of wildlife, notably the wompoo fruit-dove and the red-legged pademelon. With NSW's highest annual rainfall, the park has spectacular waterfalls, gorgeous green gullies and sheer cliffs. The exposed rock pinnacles of the **Sphinx** can be seen from Lismore.

Mt Nardi (800m) offers a challenging climb, and the NPWS office in the visitor information centre in Murwillumbah (p200) has information on walks and picnics.

The **Whian Whian State Forest** (☎ 02-6627 0200) adjoins the southeast side of the park

and is home to the Albert's lyrebird and the **Minyon Falls**, which plunge 100m into a rainforest gorge surrounded by a flora reserve with several walking tracks.

The historic **Nightcap Track** (16km long) passes through both the state forest and Nightcap National Park and was originally used by postal workers in the late 19th and early 20th century. **Rummery Park** is not far off the road down from the falls and is a well-provided picnic spot with BBQs and cold showers. **Peate's Mountain Lookout**, just on from Rummery Park, gives you a great panoramic view from Jerusalem Mountain in the north, to Byron Bay in the east.

Southeast of the forest, **Mud Manor Forest Retreat** (☎ 02-6688 2205; www.mudmanor.com; Fox Rd, Rosebank; r from \$120; 🖳 🖳) has handcrafted luxuries, large decks, spa bathrooms and lush gardens.

NIMBIN

☎ 02 / pop 1300

Nimbin, the phenomenon, started in 1973, when the Australian Union of Students staged an experimental 'Aquarius Festival' in the Nimbin Valley – 'a total, cultural experience through the lifestyle of participation'. The event was a great success, attracting scores of jaded, disillusioned students and dropouts from all over the land; when it was all over, some couldn't bear to give up the dream and stayed on, determined to turn the sleepy town into a permanent haven for like-minded souls.

These days, young and old 'hippies' (or whatever they're called now) prowl the streets and there are numerous businesses and community centres attesting to the unique local culture. At noon, though, when Byron day-trippers are being hectored by pot-dealers, it can seem like a surreal theme park. But at other, quieter times, the 'real' Nimbin comes into its own, where anyone searching for their own piece of Utopia can find it.

Its reputation may be big, but Nimbin itself is tiny. The **Nimbin Connexion** (☎ 6689 1764; www .nimbinconnexion.com; 80 Cullen St; ⏰ 10am-6pm; 🖳) is at the northern end of town, with accommodation and tour information, bus tickets, bike hire and Internet (including wi-fi).

Nimbin Museum (☎ 6689 1123; 62 Cullen St; admission \$2; ⏰ 'Nimbin time, man'), ostensibly about the region's post-Aquarian era, is interpretive and expressionistic, more a work of art than of history. Across the street, the **Hemp Embassy** (☎ 6689 1842; www.hempembassy.net; 51 Cullen St; ☼ 'whenever') raises consciousness about marijuana legalisation, as well as providing tools and fashion items for getting high. The embassy leads the **Mardi Grass** festival each May, and smokers are welcome at the coffee shop next door.

Nearby is the **Nimbin Artists Gallery** (☎ 6689 1444; 47 Cullen St; ☼ 10am-4pm).

The **Nimbin market** is on every third and fifth Sunday, a spectacular affair of produce and art where locals revel in their culture. There's live music.

Djanbung Gardens (☎ 6689 1755; www.earthwise .org.au; 74 Cecil St; admission free; ☼ 10am-4pm Tue-Sat) is a permaculture education centre, café and bookshop.

There are nearly 100 local farms that host volunteers willing to yank weeds and perform other chores. Try **Willing Workers on Organic Farms** (www.wwoof.org).

Sleeping

Nimbin Rox Hostel (☎ 6689 0022; www.nimbinrox .com; 74 Thorburn St; sites/dm/d $10/24/60; P ☼) Everything is clean and the atmosphere is relaxed and friendly, with hammocks, permaculture gardens, craft workshops, live bands, Thai massage and a pool.

Rainbow Retreat Backpackers (☎ 6689 1262; 75 Thorburn St; sites/dm/d $8/15/40) Enter a time warp at Rainbow Retreat as you relax, chill out, play the didgeridoo or camp out in the gypsy vans. There's a free courtesy bus from Byron Bay.

Nimbin Backpackers at Granny's Farm (☎ 6689 1333; 110 Cullen St; sites/dm/d $10/20/48; P ☼) Granny's has two pools, cabins and train-carriage accommodation.

Nimbin Hotel (☎ 6689 1246; Cullen St; dm $25) Tidy two- and four-bed rooms and a great veranda.

Grey Gum Lodge (☎ 6689 1713; www.nimbinaust ralia.com/greygumlodge; 2 High St; r $40-60; ☼) All rooms in this 1927 weatherboard house have bathroom, TV and fridge.

Nimbin Caravan & Tourist Park (☎ 6689 1402; 29 Sibley St; sites from $19) A simple place next to the local swimming pool.

Eating & Drinking

Rainbow Café (☎ 6689 1997; 64A Cullen St; mains $4-8; ☼ breakfast & lunch) The original Nimbin

institution makes delicious cakes, breakfast, burgers and vegetarian fare and has a big backyard.

Aquarius Bakery/Café (☎ 6689 1566; 45 Cullen St; meals $4-8; ☼ 6am-5pm) Tuck into a tasty sandwich on fresh bread with delicious coffee out on the patio.

Nimbin Trattoria & Pizzeria (☎ 6689 1427; 70 Cullen St; mains $7-16, pizzas $4-23; ☼ lunch Thu-Sun, dinner daily) Tasty pizza, pasta and salads and groovy desserts.

Nimbin Hotel (☎ 6689 1246; Cullen St) This classic local boozer has a vast, new back porch overlooking the verdant valley below. Artistic photos of regulars grace the insides.

Getting There & Away

Nimbin Shuttle (☎ 6680 9189) operates to and from Byron Bay ($12 one way, Monday to Saturday). **Jim's Alternative Tours** (☎ 6685 7720; www.byron-bay.com/jimstours) is a long-running Byron outfit with a party bent, and **Grass Hoppers** (☎ 0500 881 881; www.grasshoppers.com.au) offers tours daily. **Waller's** (☎ 6687 8550) buses run to Lismore ($9, 45 minutes).

BORDER RANGES NATIONAL PARK

This 31,729-hectare World Heritage area covers the NSW side of the McPherson Range, with the park's wetter areas protecting large tracts of superb rainforest. It's estimated that a quarter of all Australian bird species can be found here.

The eastern section is the most accessible, via the gravel **Tweed Range Scenic Drive**, which begins at Barkers Vale, 40km southwest of Murwillumbah. The drive loops through the park from Lillian Rock to Wiangaree, through mountain forest most of the way, with steep hills and breathtaking lookouts over the Tweed Valley to Mt Warning and the coast.

There are basic **NPWS camp sites** (per person $3) on the Scenic Drive: Sheepstation Creek, 15km north of the turn-off at Wiangaree, and Forest Tops, 6km further on. There's free camping at Byrill Creek, on the eastern side of Mebbin State Forest.

MT WARNING NATIONAL PARK

Although only 2380 hectares, this is the most dramatic feature of the hinterland, with Mt Warning (1156m) towering over the valley. The peak is the first part of mainland Australia to be touched by sunlight each day.

Over 60,000 people a year make the 4.4km, five-hour round-trip trek to the top from Breakfast Creek. If you'd like a guide and a chance to learn much more about the local ecology, try **Mt Warning Eco Tours** (☎ 1800 097 587; www.myaussieadventures.com; tours from $60).

Captain Cook named this mountain in 1770 to warn seamen of the offshore reefs. The Aboriginal people called it Wollumbin, meaning, all at once, 'cloud catcher', 'fighting chief of the mountain' and 'weather maker'.

The **Mt Warning Caravan Park & Tourist Retreat** (☎ 02-6679 5120; Mt Warning Rd; sites/cabins from $18/50), on the Mt Warning approach road, has good kitchen facilities and a well-stocked kiosk.

Wallers (☎ 02-6687 8550) buses run from Lismore ($20) to Dum Dum, the tiny town at the turn-off for Mt Warning.

Uki (*uke*-eye) is a cute town in the shadow of Mt Warning's dominating peak. It's got an alternative feel typical of the region, as well as the **Uki visitor information centre** (☎ 02-6679 5399; Buttery Bldg, Main St; ☻ 10am-4pm; ▣).

MURWILLUMBAH

☎ 02 / pop 9000

This relaxed town may well take its cues from the Tweed River, which it straddles; the waters flow wide and slow here and views of the river are simply soothing. It is an agricultural focal point for the region, and has stunning views of Mt Warning.

Information

The **Murwillumbah visitor information centre** (☎ 6672 1340; www.tweed-coolangatta.com; 13 Commercial Way, off Old Pacific Hwy; ☻ 9am-4.30pm) has national park passes and a great rainforest display.

Sights

The **Tweed River Art Gallery** (☎ 6670 2790; www.tweed.nsw.gov.au/artgallery; cnr Mistral Rd & Tweed Valley Way; admission free) administers Australia's richest prize for traditional art, the $100,000 Doug Moran Prize. Works of past winners are on display. Check out the always-popular and enigmatic portrait of Jonathan Aatty by Hui Hai Xie.

The **Murwillumbah Museum** (☎ 6672 1865; 2 Queensland Rd; adult/child $2/1; ☻ Wed & Fri 11am-4pm) has a solid account of local history and an interesting radio room.

Tropical Fruit World (☎ 6677 7222; www.tropicalfruitworld.com.au; Duranbah Rd; adult/child $30/15; ☻ 10am-4.30pm) is a much-hyped family attraction 12km northeast of Murwillumbah; it's home to the **Big Avocado** but it's really a lemon. There are rides and various fruit displays but it never quite justifies the price of admission.

Northern Breeze (☎ 07-5524 2264; northernbreeze@omcs.com.au; per person $20-45) runs tours that pick you up at your door and take you through the local national parks, Nimbin and Tweed Valley attractions.

Sleeping

Murwillumbah YHA (☎ 6672 3763; 1 Tumbulgum Rd; dm/d $25/54) Beautifully located on the edge of the Tweed River, this friendly hostel cements its reputation by dishing out free ice cream every night. Canoe and bike hire is available, and there's free transport to the base of the Mt Warning climb if you stay more than two nights.

Town Palms Motel (☎ 6672 8600; 3 Wharf St; r $55-60; ☒) The pick of the motels, with position, facilities and 10 rooms.

Imperial Hotel (☎ 6672 2777; 115 Main St; s/d $25/40) Big and pink, it has standard (pink) rooms. However renovations are planned for 2005 so confirm prices – and room colours.

Eating

Austral Café (☎ 6672 2624; 88 Main St; mains $6; ☻ breakfast & lunch Mon-Sat; ☒) The motto at this 1950s icon is 'a great place to meet and eat'. That says it all.

Fish Bowl (☎ 6672 2667; 3 Wharf St; meals $5-10; ☻ 9am-7.30pm Mon-Sat, 9am-5pm Sun) This café and takeaway does fresh fish in many forms. The dory fillets are justifiably popular.

New Leaf (☎ 6672 4073; Shop 10, Murwillumbah Plaza; meals $5-10; ☻ breakfast & lunch Mon-Fri; ☒) The food here is creative and vegetarian, with many Middle Eastern dishes and a long list of salads. Enjoy inside, out on the courtyard or takeaway.

Getting There & Away

Greyhound Australia (☎ 13 20 30; www.greyhound.com.au) stops here on the Pacific Hwy run north to Brisbane ($24, three hours) and south to Sydney ($100, 13 hours). **Premier Motor Service** (☎ 13 34 10) runs a similar service.

Waller's (☎ 6687 8550) has school-day buses to Nimbin and Lismore.

NEW ENGLAND

Atop the Great Dividing Range, vast table-lands of sheep and cattle-grazing country dotted with rainforest tumble over the eastern escarpment onto coastal plains below. If you enjoy the seasons, this is the best spot in Australia as New England has all four. If you're travelling along the eastern seaboard, it's well worth diverting inland to visit some of the area's little towns and get a glimpse of the Australian lifestyle away from the coast. If nothing else you can enjoy the cheery chatter of cherubic-cheeked country folk.

The New England Hwy, which runs from Hexham (northwest of Newcastle) to Brisbane, has far less traffic than the coastal roads and is an inland alternative to the Pacific Hwy.

TAMWORTH

☎ 02 / pop 35,330

Tamworth's claim to fame is its massive Country Music Festival and that is the key to whether you'll like this town or not. If you're into country music, you'll be in heaven; if not, keep driving.

The **visitors centre** (☎ 6755 4300; www.visittamworth.com.au; cnr Peel & Murray Sts; ☯ 9am-5pm) is shaped like a guitar and has a diverting exhibit 'Walk a Country Mile' (adult/child $6/2).

Sights

If you really do love country music, visit the excellent **Australian Country Music Foundation Museum** (☎ 6766 9696; 93 Brisbane St; adult/child $5.50/3.30; ☯ 10am-2pm Mon-Sat), not far from the train station. Its Golden Guitar display has photos and lists of winners from every awards ceremony; the Hall of Fame features Slim Dusty, Tex Morton and Buddy Williams among others.

Off the New England Hwy in South Tamworth, the **Big Golden Guitar** stands in front of the **Gallery of Stars** (☎ 6765 2688; The Ringers; adult/child $8/4; ☯ 9am-5pm). Like Tamworth, if you like country music (or classic kitsch) you might enjoy the wax versions of various stars here. Some of the most loyal listeners are remembered at the **Truck Drivers' Memorial**, about 100m south.

There are recording studios, such as **Nashgrill** (☎ 6762 1652; nashgrill@bigpond.com.au; 75 Denison St), **Big Wheel Recording** (☎ 6765 5677; 24 Wilburtree St) and the new **Lindsay Butler Studio** (☎ 6762 1104; 336 Goonoo Goonoo Rd) that are open to the public by arrangement; one day's notice is usually enough.

Festivals & Events

Tamworth's population doubles during the **Country Music Festival** (www.tamworth.nsw.gov.au) held over a week in late January. Over 800 acts perform at more than 2000 events (most of them free), all culminating with the Australian country music awards, the Golden Guitars.

Sleeping

Unless you book years in advance, you'll be lucky to find a bed or camp site anywhere during the festival, when prices skyrocket. However the council makes large areas of river land available to campers, where it's rough and rowdy but fun. Most of the pubs in town have accommodation, and there are tons of motels on the highways out of town. The visitors centre can help with bookings.

Quality Hotel Powerhouse (☎ 6766 7748; www.qualityhotelpowerhouse.com.au; New England Hwy; r $130-165; ☒ ☐ ☒) A large and comfortable hotel with wi-fi, and not far from the visitors centre. A new wing has some very posh apartments that are good for long stays.

Ashby House Motor Inn & Restaurant (☎ 1800 027 947, 6762 0033; www.ashbyhousemotorinn.com.au; 83-85 Ebsworth St; s/d from $90/100; ☒ ☐ ☒) This boutique motor inn has lovely wide verandas and well-equipped rooms.

Motel 359 (☎ 6762 4100; 359 Goonoo Goonoo Rd; r from $45; ☒ ☐) This basic place has the right name if you can never remember your house number (but good luck with that street name). Rooms are basic and clean. There's public Internet access.

Tamworth YHA (☎ 6761 2600; www.yha.com.au; 169 Marius St; dm/d from $22/46; ☐) Opposite the train station, this place is clean and friendly. The managers have information on seasonal work.

Eating

Tamworth Hotel (☎ 6766 2923; 147 Marius St; mains $13-20; ☯ lunch daily, dinner Thu-Sat) The Art Deco front bar is gorgeous and the food at Ushers Brasserie is quite good, posh even. And this is one place where you want to slip out of the country music vibe as they want you to slip into something nice to wear.

Marigold Cafe (☎ 6765 8300; 146 Bridge St; mains $11-20; ◷ lunch & dinner) The typically long menu at this very popular Chinese restaurant has many items not always found, such as Singapore chicken. The dining room is simple; there's a big takeout business.

Stetson's Steakhouse & Saloon BBQ (☎ 6762 2238; Craigends Lane; mains $15-25; ◷ breakfast, lunch & dinner) Near the Golden Guitar, this busy cowboy-themed restaurant has massive steak dinners served in a suitable rustic atmosphere.

Ashby House (☎ 6762 0033; 83-85 Ebsworth St; mains $18-27; ◷ dinner) The lovely restaurant at Ashby House creates inventive dishes with local produce, game and meat. As a twist, you can order up a BBQ kit and cook up your own steaks out by the pool.

Entertainment

As you'd suspect, Tamworth always has live country music in its pubs: check Thursday's *Northern Daily Leader* (the visitors centre keeps a copy all week). Dress codes are stricter in Tamworth than elsewhere in the region – after all cowboys never go out smelling like cow poop.

Venues rotate, but good bets are the **City Tavern** (☎ 6766 2442; 211 Peel St), **Imperial Hotel** (☎ 6766 2613; cnr Brisbane & Marius Sts) and **Good Companions** (☎ 6766 2850; 9 Brisbane St). West of downtown, the **Pub** (☎ 6765 5655; 99 Gunnedah Rd) combines country charm with country music.

Getting There & Away

QantasLink (☎ 13 13 13; www.qantas.com.au) has flights to Sydney (starting from $95) from Tamworth.

Most long-distance buses stop beside the visitors centre; typically Sydney is $50 (eight hours). **Keans** (☎ 1800 043 339, 6543 1322) buses go north to Scone ($21, two hours), Armidale ($26, three hours) and Coffs Harbour ($59, 6½ hours). Buses also go south to the Upper Hunter Valley. **Greyhound Australia** (☎ 13 14 19; www.greyhound.com.au) goes to Sydney ($80, 7½ hours) and Brisbane ($85, nine hours).

CountryLink (☎ 13 22 32; www.countrylink.nsw.gov .au) trains coming from Sydney ($75, six hours) continue north to Armidale ($18, two hours).

AROUND TAMWORTH

If you like the Tamworth area, and figu you'll need a job if you move there, conside a jackeroo or jillaroo course. **Leconfield st.** **tion** (☎ 02-6769 4328; www.leconfield.com; Bimbod Kootingal) has programmes that cost $490 fe five days and include sheep shearing, lasso ing, milking and swimming the horses.

The **Dag Inn** (☎ 02-6769 3234; www.thedag.co .au; Crawney Rd), a 8093-hectare sheep and catt station, has three-day courses (from $40t that include the Dag Sheep and Roustabou experiences. The Dag also has a multitud of farm-stay and other options.

Australia's **national paragliding championship** are held in February and March at **Manill** 44km north of Tamworth along the Ne England Hwy. Godfrey Wenness, recoro holder for the world's longest paraglidin flight (335km), found that inland therma here make for excellent, long cloud-hoppin flights. **Sky Manilla** (☎ 02-6785 6545; www.flymani .com) offers tandem flights from $130.

More down to earth, the **Manilla Heritag Museum** (☎ 6785 1207; 197 Manilla St; adult/child $4/ ◷ 9am-noon Sat & Sun) has interesting display on local history.

About 45km to the southeast of Tam worth, **Nundle** is a charming town just o the Fossikers Way. There are a couple o decent museums and some cute little shop And town has scores and scores of other coun try towns, it has a **Hanging Rock** you ca climb for great views. The **Nundle Countr Cafe** (☎ 02-6769 3158; Jenkins St; meals $5-10; ◷ 7am 6pm Sun-Thu, 7am-7pm Fri & Sat) serves as the loc visitors centre and can direct you to accom modation. It also serves up some fine an filling country fare.

URALLA

☎ 02 / pop 2310

It seems like there's a surprise around ever corner in Uralla. And if you like used an vintage books, you'll really be in luck i this enticing little town. Bushranger Cap tain Thunderbolt, whose six-year caree included several episodes of holding u Uralla publicans then spending the pro ceeds on beer, was killed here in 1870. Th **visitors centre** (◷ 6778 4496; http://visituralla.co .au; New England Hwy; ☎ 9.30am-4.30pm) is next t the **Thunderbolt statue**. It hires out pans fo gold-panning in the rocky local stream and rivers ($10).

Sights

McCrossin's Mill Museum (☎ 6778 3022; Salisbury St; admission by donation; ☺ noon-5pm) has panache and humour to burn. There are full details on the late Captain Thunderbolt and other intriguing displays, such as the 'history of the cricket bat' and the story of one Uralla boy's experience of WWI. The **Brass & Iron Lace Foundry** (☎ 6778 5065; 6 East St; adult/child $4/2; ☺ 9am-5pm) has been churning out metal things since 1872. The owner gives very entertaining tours. South along the highway to Tamworth, **Thunderbolt's Rock** is where the captain used to wait for likely victims.

Uralla has three of Australia's best antiquarian bookstores. The anchor is **Burnet's Books** (☎ 6778 4682; 46 Bridge St; ☺ 9am-6pm), which offers superb customer service. The store organises the town's **annual book festival** in September.

An interesting loop goes southeast from Uralla to **Gostwyck**, an Australian sheep station that looks like an English country squire's hamlet, complete with photogenic vine-covered chapel. From there, go via **Dangar Falls** up to Armidale.

Sleeping & Eating

Chesterfields B&B (☎ 6778 3113; chesterfields1@ bigpond.com; Bridge St; s/d from $55/65) The five rooms at this gay-friendly place are adorable and there's a trampoline in the flower-filled back yard. It also has a delicious café that's open for breakfast and lunch.

Coachwood & Cedar (☎ 6778 4110; Bridge St; s/d from $35/60) Also known as the Top Pub, this place has nice motel-style rooms, with a shearing-shed motif in the bathrooms. Pub meals are served and the pub has regular bands.

Getting There & Away

Keans (☎ 1800 043 339) goes from Uralla to Coffs Harbour three times a week. **Edward's** (☎ 6772 3116) makes the Armidale run ($3, 25 minutes) on weekdays only.

ARMIDALE

☎ 02 / pop 22,300

The New England regional centre of Armidale is famous for its spectacular autumn foliage and heritage buildings. It has a split personality: beefy cattle heritage and twee Cotswolds aspirations. The 1000m altitude means it's pleasantly cool in summer and

frosty (but often sunny) in winter. Several parks and the Dumaresq River contribute to the pleasant charm.

The **visitors centre** (☎ 1800 627 736, 6772 4655; www.armidaletourism.com.au; 82 Marsh St; ☺ 9am-5pm) at the bus station runs free two-hour heritage tours of the city; buses depart at 10am.

Fast Track Computers (☎ 6771 1287; 209 Beardy St; per hr $5; ☺ 9.30am-5.30pm Mon-Fri, 9.30am-1.30pm Sat) has Internet access.

Sights

There are some elegant old buildings around the town centre. Pick up the heritage walking-tour pamphlet from the visitors centre. On the corner of Faulkner and Rusden Sts is the interesting **Armidale Folk Museum** (☎ 6770 3536; admission by donation; ☺ 1-4pm). Parts of Beardy St in the centre have been pedestrianised and make for good strolling, shopping and snacking.

At the southern edge of town, the **New England Regional Art Museum** (☎ 6772 5255; Kentucky St; admission free; ☺ 10am-5pm Tue-Sun), has a sizable permanent collection and good contemporary exhibitions. Downstairs, the **Museum of Printing** (☎ 6771 5965; admission $3.50; ☺ 11am-4pm Thu-Sun) has printing machines from all eras, historic prints and kitsch 20th-century labels from local products. Next door, the **Aboriginal Cultural Centre & Keeping Place** (☎ 6771 1249; Kentucky St; admission $3; ☺ 9.30am-4pm Mon-Fri) hosts changing exhibitions.

Sleeping

There are motels around the visitors centre and on Barney St. Head out of town on the Glen Innes Rd to find doubles under $60.

Sandstock Motor Inn (☎ 6772 9988; sandstock@ bigpond.com; 101 Dumaresq St; r $78-98; ⚡) The faux-heritage look is attractive and this 12-unit motel is close to the parks and centre. Some units have vintage pictures on the wall.

Smith House (☎ 6772 0652; www.smithhouse.com.au; 100 Barney St; s/d $35/50) Partly student accommodation, this is one of the best places to stay in Armidale. Large, comfortable motel-style rooms share bathrooms; one sprawling room sleeps six and has its own bathroom.

Creekside Cottages (☎ 6772 2018; 5 Canambe St; s/d from $80/95) Self-contained cottages with log fires, and you can get eggs and veggies from the organic garden. Kids are welcome, and there's a cubby house, tennis court and trampoline.

Pembroke Tourist & Leisure Park (☎ 6772 6470; www.pembroke.com.au; 39 Waterfall Way; sites/dm/cabins per 2 people $15/20/50; 🖳 🐾) East of town (2km) on Waterfall Way (Grafton Rd), it's YHA-affiliated, and has a clean kitchen, and masseur.

Eating

Restaurant Q (☎ 6771 1038; Girraween Shopping Centre; mains $20-30; 🕑 lunch & dinner Tue-Sat) The nicest place in town manages to make you forget it's in a shopping mall from the minute you walk into the classically simple surrounds. Dishes are Mod Oz with a French twist and mains are meaty – just like the tastes of the locals.

Armidale's pedestrian mall is a good place for a casual lunch.

Café Midalé (☎ 6772 8166; 173 Beardy St; mains $6-10; 🕑 breakfast & lunch) Midalé has a huge range of sandwiches, bagels and croissants and an equally extravagant coffee list.

Filling Groovy (☎ 6772 3343; 171 Beardy St; sandwiches $4-8) This stylish little place specialises in sandwiches and smoothies. Picnic tables outside are good places to enjoy the fare.

Courthouse Cafe (☎ 6772 0099; 162 Beardy St; mains $6-12; 🕑 breakfast & lunch Mon-Sat) In the shadow of the 1859 Courthouse, this open-air café has a changing Mod Oz menu. It's perfect for a little cultured lunch.

Drinking

Wicklow (☎ 6772 2421; 85-87 Marsh St) This complex of indoor and outdoor bars is very trendy and packed with university students.

New England Hotel (☎ 6772 7622; Beardy St Mall) At the other end of the scale, the Newie is your classic country pub, and in this case, one that dates to 1857.

Getting There & Away

QantasLink (☎ 13 13 13; www.qantas.com.au) flies to Sydney (from $100) from Armidale.

Harvey World Travel (☎ 6772 1177; East Mall Shopping Centre, 90-96 March St) books bus tickets.

Greyhound Australia (☎ 13 14 19; www.greyhound.com.au) goes to Sydney ($88, 10 hours) via Tamworth and the Hunter Valley. **Keans** (☎ 1800 625 587) runs east along the Waterfall Way via Bellingen to Coffs Harbour three times weekly.

CountryLink (☎ 13 22 32; www.countrylink.nsw.gov.au) buses run to Glen Innes ($14, 1¼ hours)

and Tenterfield ($32, 2½ hours). Trains g to Tamworth ($18, two hours) and Sydne ($84, eight hours).

Getting Around

Armidale Bicycle Centre (☎ 6772 3718; 244 Beardy S per day from $22) rents bikes and will deliver t wherever you're staying.

THE WATERFALL WAY

A spectacular set of World Heritage–liste national parks lines the Waterfall Way fron Armidale to Dorrigo and Bellingen, nea Coffs Harbour. The entire area is full o magnificent gorges and waterfalls; in sun mer the road is lined with yellow paper da sies. You can easily drive the 168km to th coast in a day, but as this is one of the lovel est parts of NSW, why not take a few?

From Armidale, the road heads ea 40km to **Wollomombi Falls**, one of Australia highest. Tame paths lead to nearby lookou and more-strenuous multiday tracks hea down into the wilderness gorges of **Oxle Wild Rivers National Park**. At the southern edg of the park is **Apsley Falls**.

New England National Park, 11km off th Waterfall Way and on a good gravel roac is home to platypuses, glider possums an grey kangaroos. Over 20km of bushwalk ing trails mostly begin from wheelchai accessible **Point Lookout**, where there ar views that surpass its mundane name b an order of magnitude. There are nearb **cabins** ($45-80), and sites at **Thungutti Campin Area** (adult/child $3/2). Bookings are handled b the Dorrigo **NPWS office** (☎ 02-6657 2309).

Cathedral Rock National Park has bou ders the size of…large churches; wetlan swamps here are perfect for bird-watchin **Camping** (adult/child $3/2) is also available. Ne Ebor township, **Ebor Falls** is a spectacula part of **Guy Fawkes River National Park**, deep i gorge country that's popular for canoein and bushwalking. Access is from Hernan 15km northeast of Ebor, then it's anothe 30km to Chaelundi Rest Area for campin and trailheads. There are great views fron Ebor Falls rest area, or stop to have a loo at the little old **graveyard** nearby.

Dorrigo

☎ 02 / pop 1190

Beautiful wide streets, lush green fores and a sleepy feel – that's Dorrigo in a nu shell. This is densely forested mountain country, bordering the eastern escarpment of the Great Dividing Range, and, not surprisingly, one of the last places to be settled by Europeans in the eastwards push across the New England tableland.

The **visitor information centre** (☎ 6657 2486; 36 Hickory St; ⊙ 10am-4pm) is run by volunteers who share a passion for the area. For queries about the World Heritage–listed national parks, there's a very useful **NPWS office** (☎ 6657 2309; Dome Rd; ⊙ 9am-4.30pm).

The town's main attraction is **Dangar Falls**, which pounds down into a swimming hole – think of it as aquatic massage.

SLEEPING & EATING

Dorrigo Hotel/Motel (☎ 6657 2017; www.hotelmotel dorrigo.com.au; cnr Cudgery & Hickory Sts; r $46-85) This classic country pub is a stately example of 1920s architecture. The hotel rooms have been restored to their original charm (and the bathrooms are still shared). The pub serves good food.

Dorrigo Mountain Resort (☎ 6657 2564; www .dorrigomountainresort.com.au; Waterfall Way; sites/ cabins from $18/48) Just north of the Dome road turn-off, this resort has basic, self-contained wooden cabins, camp sites, and sweeping views.

The Art Place (☎ 6657 2622; 18-20 Cudgery St; meals $7-14; ⊙ lunch) Right in the centre, this café has a gallery where you can ponder local works while you sip your excellent coffee.

Misty's (☎ 6657 2855; 33 Hickory St; mains $14-20; ⊙ lunch Sun, dinner Wed-Sat) This charming little restaurant has a changing regional menu and is in a renovated weatherboard house.

GETTING THERE & AWAY

Three times a week **Keans** (☎ 1800 625 587) heads east to Port Macquarie and west to Tamworth via Armidale.

Dorrigo National Park

This 11,732-hectare park is home to a huge diversity of vegetation because of its rich soil and subtropical conditions. All those trees mean there are plenty of places for birds to perch and at last count there were over 120 species present.

The turn-off to the park is just south of Dorrigo. The **Rainforest Centre** (☎ 02-6657 2309; Dome Rd; ⊙ 9am-5pm), at the park entrance, has

information about the park's many walks as well as a café. There's also an **elevated walkway**, the Skywalk, over the rainforest canopy. It's well worth making the drive down to the **Never Never rest area**, in the middle of the national park, from where you can walk to waterfalls or begin longer walks.

Bellingen

☎ 02 / pop 2731

Bellingen is a charming hill town that succeeds by not trying too hard. It's definitely worth the 12km drive off the Pacific Hwy to sample the laid-back vibe, spiced with a dose of art and alternative lifestyles. Spend a couple of hours wandering the streets and lazing by the Bellingen River. Movie fans may have read about Bellingen as a potential location for the filming of *Eucalyptus*, starring Russell Crowe and Nicole Kidman.

There is no visitor information centre in town, so stop at the centres in Dorrigo (opposite) and Uralla (p202).

Bellingen Book Nook (☎ 6655 9372; 25 Hyde St; ⊙ 10am-4pm Mon-Fri, market Sat 9am-3pm) is in a real nook. An amazing number of books are crammed into this small space. There are always a few itinerant readers lounging around while others gossip.

Between Bytes (☎ 6655 9821; Shop 7D, Church St; per hr $6; ⊙ 9am-4.30pm Mon-Fri) has Internet access.

SIGHTS & ACTIVITIES

To get a feel for the place, head to the magnificent **Hammond & Wheatley Emporium** (Hyde St), which looks like a musty old department store until you see the range of stylish goods for sale in the restored surrounds. It also has an art gallery and a café.

The historic **Old Butter Factory** (☎ 6655 2150; 1 Doepel Lane; ⊙ 9.30am-5pm) houses craft shops, a local art gallery, opal dealers, a masseur and a good **café**.

Bellingen Museum (☎ 6655 0289; adult/child $2/ free; ⊙ 10am-3pm Tue, 10am-noon Wed & Fri) is one of those places run by enthusiastic volunteers, who you suspect hang out there even when it's closed. For a nature fix, there's a huge colony of flying foxes on **Bellingen Island** from December to March.

On the third Saturday of the month the community **market** takes to the streets and is quite an event, with over 250 stalls. On the second and fourth Saturday of the month there's an **organic market**. Both markets are good reasons for a trip.

FESTIVALS & EVENTS

In January, Bellingen becomes a **Stamping Ground** (☎ 6655 2472; www.stampingground.com.au), a festival of international dance performances. The **Bellingen Jazz & Blues Festival** (www.bellingenjazzfestival.com.au) features a strong line-up of jazz names in late August. You'll find a multicultural mix of music and performances at **Global Carnival** (www.globalcarnival.com) held annually in early October.

SLEEPING

Koompartoo Retreat (☎ 6655 2326; www.midcoast.com.au/~koompart; cnr Lawon & Dudley Sts; chalet $135; 🐾) A delightful experience: four stylish, cosy timber chalets with private balconies. The champagne glasses in each room are suggestive in the extreme.

Rivendell Guest House (☎ 6655 0060; www.rivendellguesthouse.com.au; 12 Hyde St; r $85-135; 🐾) Right in town, you can escape civilisation on the flower-bedecked veranda and in the lush gardens. Everything is comfortable without being fussy.

Bellingen YHA (☎ 6655 1116; www.yha.com.au; 2 Short St; dm/d from $23/56; 🅿 💻) Backpackers flock here in droves and it's not hard to figure out why. A tranquil, engaging atmosphere pervades this renovated weatherboard house. There's a free shuttle to the bus stop and train station in Urunga.

Federal Hotel (☎ 6655 1003; Hyde St; s/d $25/40) There's a high degree of character at this place in the heart of town.

Bellingen Caravan Park (☎ 6655 1338; www.bellingen.com/caravanpark; Dowle St; sites $20) Perched next to Bellingen Island and the flying foxes, the sites here have a tranquil and green setting.

EATING & DRINKING

There are plenty of excellent options to choose from in this hedonistic town.

No 2 Oak St (☎ 6655 9000; 2 Oak St; mains $28) No 2 is renowned in the region for Modern Australian cuisine with a continental accent. Host Toni Urquart keeps the wine list as intriguing as the changing menu. As a bonus, it's housed in a 1910 heritage cottage with a verdant veranda.

Lodge 241 (☎ 6655 2470; 117-121 Hyde St; mains $16; 🕓 breakfast & lunch) Cool jazz plays inside

and there are valley views outside at this upmarket café set in an old masonic lodge. Much of the food is organic and there are extra touches, such as wood-fired sourdough bread.

Cool Creek Cafe (☎ 6655 1886; www.coolcreekcafe.com.au; 5 Church St; mains $16-20; 🕓 dinner Thu-Mon) A first and only in Bellingen! A place where you can expect to see a Joni Mitchell cover band. This upscale hippy joint is BYO and has live music (blues, folk, Mitchell) many nights. The food is organic and there is a kids menu.

Federal Hotel (☎ 6655 1003; 77 Hyde St; meals $8-15; 🕓 11am-late) A classic, filled with character *and* characters.

GETTING THERE & AWAY

Keans (☎ 1800 625 587) has buses east to Coffs Harbour ($15), and west to Dorrigo and Tamworth a measly three times a week.

Around Bellingen

There are some beautiful spots waiting to be discovered in Bellingen's surrounding valleys. The most accessible is the tiny hamlet of **Gleniffer**, 10km to the north and clearly signposted from North Bellingen. There's a good swimming hole in the **Never Never River** behind the small Gleniffer School of Arts at the crossroads. Then you can drive around Loop Rd, which takes you to the foot of the New England tableland – a great drive that words don't do justice to.

If you want to sweat, tackle the **Syndicate Ridge Walking Trail**, a strenuous 15km walk from Gleniffer to the Dorrigo Plateau, following the route of a tramline once used by timber-cutters. There's a very steep 1km climb on the way up. To get to the start, take the Gordonville Rd, turning into Adams Lane soon after crossing the Never Never River. The walking track commences at the first gate.

The remaining 14km drive from Bellingen to the Pacific Hwy and the coast runs through a pretty valley. Scattered through here are little shops that are worth a look.

NORTH OF ARMIDALE

Glen Innes (population 6250), is obsessed with Scotland and businesses with names like Glen This and Wee That are thick as whiskey after the haggis has fallen into the barrel. The **visitors centre** (☎ 02-6732 2397; www

.gleninnestourism.com; Church St; 9am-5pm Mon-Fri, 9am-3pm Sat & Sun), near Meade St, is with the bus stop. Overlooking the town and off the eastern end of the Gwydir Hwy, the **Standing Stones**, erected in 1990 to commemorate the town's Celtic roots, look strangely powerful among the gum trees.

The town centre is full of **heritage buildings**. The **Land of the Beardies History House** (02-6732 1035; cnr West Ave & Ferguson St; admission $5/1; 10am-noon & 1-4pm Mon-Fri, 1-4pm Sat & Sun) fills an old hospital to bursting with eclectic artefacts of old Glen Innes. If you're around on a weekend, take a **pub crawl on horseback** (02-6732 1599; www.pubcrawlsonhorseback.com.au; Bullock Mountain Homestead; tours from $265), a two-day tour that includes accommodation.

The **Australian Celtic Festival**, which features oodles of pipe bands, is held over the first weekend in May. The **Land of the Beardies Bush Festival** is celebrated in November with music, dancing and a long-beard competition.

There are several **motels** along the highway. For a brush with fame, have a pause at the **Tartan Tea Rooms** (02-6732 2047; 141 Church St; meals $10; 9.30am-dark), where your hosts are the cheery Leyland family, the same folks who wandered Australia for their TV travelogue.

Dramatic, forested and wild, **Gibraltar Range & Washpool National Parks** lie south and north of the Gwydir Hwy, about 80km east of Glen Innes on the road to Grafton. Walking tracks lead to camping areas (per person $5). Washpool has some beautiful swimming holes amid the cool, quiet World Heritage–listed rainforest.

TENTERFIELD

02 / pop 3191

At the junction of the New England and Bruxner Hwys, Tenterfield is the birthplace of both Federation (thanks to a speech given in town by 19th-century NSW premier, Henry Parkes) and of the flamboyant 'boy from Oz', Peter Allen. The **visitors centre** (6736 1082; cnr Rouse & Miles Sts; 9.30am-5pm Mon-Fri, 9.30am-4pm Sat & Sun) has bushwalking guides and can book tours to nearby national parks.

The **Tenterfield Saddler** (6736 1478; High St; 10am-4pm) celebrated by Peter Allen in his eponymous song is still open for business. About 12km outside town on the road north to Liston lies **Thunderbolt's Hideout**, where bushranger Captain Thunderbolt did just that. On your way there check out the **Tenterfield Weather Rock** near the baths.

Bald Rock National Park (per person $7) is 29km northeast of Tenterfield. You can hike to the top of Australia's largest granite monolith (which looks like a stripey little Uluru) and **camp** (per person $5) near the base.

Motels line Rouse St leading south out of town. **Peter Allen Motor Inn** (6736 2499; 177 Rouse St; s/d from $70/80;) has spotless, comfortable rooms and is close to the centre. For plenty of choice in accommodation, **Tenterfield Lodge** (6736 1477; 2 Manners St; sites/cabins per 2 people from $13/50, s/d $25/45) is a friendly place in a ramshackle 1870s farmhouse.

Long-distance buses that travel between Sydney and Brisbane along the New England Hwy stop in Tenterfield. **Kirklands** (6622 1499; www.kirklands.com.au) runs to Casino and Lismore (two hours 50 minutes, Monday to Friday). **CountryLink** (13 22 32; www.countrylink.nsw.gov.au) buses run to Glen Innes ($14, 1¼ hours) and Armidale ($32, 2½ hours).

TENTERFIELD TO CASINO

The exceedingly twisted road to Casino leads through the quietly beautiful Upper Clarence cattle country. The rolling hills are easy on the eyes, even if dinner time isn't easy on the grazing inhabitants.

Clarence River Wilderness Lodge (02-6665 1337; www.clarenceriver.com; Paddy's Flat Rd; sites $4-8, cabins from $50) is a long way from anywhere up a rough but scenic road (30km from Tabulam). This rustic lodge is in a beautiful river gorge with great swimming. There's also bushwalking, platypus-spotting, canoe and kayak expeditions and gold fossicking. Lights are solar-powered, hot water is heated with a wood fire, and guests need to bring bedding, food and drinks.

Richmond Range National Park contains some of the best-preserved old-growth rainforest in NSW. The 15,712-hectare park is part of a World Heritage–listed preserve and offers an array of chances to see what this part of Australia looked like before settlement. There is a good two-hour circular walk through the foliage from the Cambridge Plateau picnic area (some sections are steep). There are basic camp sites at **Peacock Creek** (per person $3). The park is 45km west of Casino via the Bruxner Hwy (which goes to Tenterfield); turn north onto Cambridge Plateau Dr.

'Australia's Beef Capital', **Casino** (population 11,900), celebrates its **beef festival** in late May and early June. The big beef locally is that this is now where the CountryLink train that once served Lismore and Byron Bay comes to an abrupt halt. Passengers transfer to buses for their onward journeys.

CENTRAL WEST

Stretching 400km inland from the Blue Mountains, NSW's central west gradually shifts from rolling agricultural heartland into vast plains, and finally the harsher outback soil of the far west. The vast region is steeped in bushranger and gold-rush history.

The Newell Hwy, the most direct route between Melbourne and Brisbane, passes through the central west. Dubbo is the main transit hub for the region. An alternative Sydney–Melbourne route, the Olympic Way, runs from Albury, on the Murray River, through Wagga Wagga to Cowra.

The central west may at first seem mundane, but as the heartland for a lot of high-value food production it has developed into something of a foodie centre. You can find interesting places to sample the fruits of the region in Mudgee, Orange and the historic town of Bathurst.

BATHURST

☎ 02 / pop 27,036

Laid out on a grand scale, Bathurst is Australia's oldest inland settlement. It's one of the more atmospheric of NSW inland towns. The broad streets, gas lamps, formidable Victorian buildings and leafy, manicured parks all reek of days gone by. Activities include bushwalking and searching for gold.

The **visitors centre** (☎ 6332 1444; www.bathurst .nsw.gov.au; 28 William St; ☯ 9am-5pm) has an exemplary range of local information.

Sights

The **Regional Art Gallery** (☎ 6331 6066; 70-78 Keppel St; admission free; ☯ 10am-5pm Tue-Sat, 11am-2pm Sun) focuses on artists from the area, with a particular interest in Hill End. The excellent **library** (☎ 6332 2130; ☯ 10am-6pm Mon-Fri, 10am-5pm Sat, 11am-2pm Sun) shares the building and has free Internet access.

Get off on the rocks at the **Australian Fossil and Mineral Museum** (☎ 6331 5511; 224 Howick St; adult/child $8/4; ☯ 10am-4pm Mon-Sat, 10am-2pm Sun) which has a real big draw: Australia's only tyrannosaurus rex skeleton.

The **Chifley Home** (☎ 6332 1444; 10 Busby St; admission $4; ☯ 11am-3pm Sat-Mon) is the sweet, simple suburban home Ben Chifley lived in while he was prime minister (1946–49) – Bathurst is no Kirribilli. The **historical museum** (☎ 6332 4755; Russell St; adult/child $2/1; ☯ 10am-4pm Tue, Wed, Sat & Sun) lives in the majestic courthouse building.

Gear-heads will be in heaven at the **National Motor Racing Museum** (☎ 6332 1872; Pit Straight; adult/child $7/3; ☯ 9am-4.30pm) – Bathurst's **Mt Panorama** has been Australia's street-car racing centre since 1917 and many of the winners are on display. The graffiti in the ladies' is well worth a look. You can drive the curvy 6.2km circuit yourself, though there's a sedentary 60km/h speed limit.

Sleeping

Sundowner Bathurst (☎ 6331 2211; www.sundowner motorinns.com.au; 19 Charlotte St; r $79-143; ☒ ☒) This classic motel rises above the norm with good service and large, well-appointed rooms. Close to the centre and shopping.

Commercial Hotel (☎ 6331 2712; 135 George St; www.geocities.com/commercialhotelbathurst; s/d $29/49) This family-run hotel has a cosy bar downstairs and small but inviting rooms upstairs.

A Winter-Rose Cottage (☎ 6332 2661; www.winter -rose.com.au; 79 Morrissett St; r from $90) A snug B&B with a well-loved garden. If you're staying a while, opt for the self-contained cottage out the back.

East's Bathurst Holiday Park (☎ 6331 8286; Great Western Hwy; sites/cabins per 2 people $19/68; ☒) This is the main caravan park, but at race periods other camping areas are open.

Eating

There's an upmarket café culture downtown as well as several good restaurants.

Good Catch Café (☎ 6331 1333; 85 George St; mains $8-16; ☯ 11am-9pm Tue-Sat) This cheerful café sells excellent fish and chips, salads and more.

Bernard's Bakery (☎ 6331 2042; 81 George St; snacks $4-6; ☯ breakfast & lunch) Bernard's packs the local workers in with crusty rolls and first-rate pies.

Restaurant Legall (☎ 6331 5800; 56 Keppel St; mains $25-28; ☯ lunch Thu & Fri, dinner Tue-Sat) Good French-provincial fare is created from the very best local ingredients and it's all served in a cute old house.

Crowded House Café (☎ 6334 2300; 1 Ribbon Gang Lane; mains $14.50-27; ☯ lunch Mon-Sat, dinner Tue-Sat) Tables in this restored 1850 church spill out into a secluded, shady courtyard. Food ranges from the adventurous Mod Oz inside to comfy café fare outside.

Getting There & Away

Selwood's (☎ 6362 7963; www.selwoods.com.au) has frequent links to Orange ($10, 45 minutes).

CountryLink (☎ 13 22 32; www.countrylink.nsw .gov.au) has one train a day to Sydney ($9, 3½ hours). Otherwise there are bus connections to the CityRail service at Lithgow.

AROUND BATHURST

About 70km south of Bathurst, along awesomely windy roads, are the famous **Abercrombie Caves** (☎ 02-6368 8603; www.jenolancaves .org.au; ☯ 10am-4pm). The complex has one of the world's largest natural tunnels, the Grand Arch. Admission is by a complex set of tickets that begin at $12. There's **camping** (per person $8) near the cave.

Australia's oldest surviving gold town, **Sofala** is a good-looking little place with some unusually well-preserved timber buildings. Peter Weir shot his 1974 film *The Cars That Ate Paris* here. Grab an Evans Shire tea while you're in town.

Some 35km down an unsealed road, the ghost town of **Hill End** was the scene of an 1870s gold rush. The **NPWS visitors centre** (☎ 02-6337 8206; Hospital Lane; ☯ 9.30am-12.30pm & 1.30-4.30pm), inside the old hospital, includes a fascinating **museum** (admission $2.50). Book here for the three **NPWS camping grounds** (powered sites per adult/child $7.50/4, unpowered sites $5/3). There are a few residents hanging on, and many of them can be found at the dusty **Royal Hotel** (☎ 02-6337 8261; Beyers Ave; r $35-90), the only pub that remains of the original 28.

ORANGE

☎ 02 / pop 31,970
Although pears, apples and stone fruits are grown here in profusion, you will find nary an orange. The town is actually named after Prince William of Orange. Banjo Paterson was born here, and his legacy is recalled by

a most-unusual talking monument next to the visitors centre that endlessly repeats his lyrics to *Waltzing Matilda*.

The **visitors centre** (☎ 1800 069 466, 6393 8226; www.orange.nsw.gov.au; Civic Sq, Byng St; ☯ 9am-5pm) is beside **Orange Regional Gallery** (☎ 6393 8136; admission free; ☯ 10am-5pm Tue-Sat, 1-4pm Sun), which collects Brett Whiteley paintings and sculptural ceramics. There's Internet access at **Orange City Library** (☎ 6393 8132; ☯ 10am-7pm Mon-Fri, 9.30am-4pm Sat, 1-5pm Sun) behind the centre.

Cook Park (Clinton & Summer Sts) is very manicured and a great place to see the autumn colours. **Orange Botanic Gardens** (☎ 6393 8680; Kearneys Dr; admission free; ☯ 7.30am-dusk) is on Clover Hill, 2km north of the city centre. The woodlands, which thrive in the mild weather, are preserved.

Many award-winning vineyards lie southwest of town towards **Mt Canabolas** (1395m), an extinct volcano. You can drive to the top or there are a couple of steep walking tracks. The visitors centre has information on the myriad of wineries and pick-your-own fruit orchards (but no oranges!) in the area. The local **taxi company** (☎ 6362 1333) will take you on a tour.

Australia's first real gold rush took place at **Ophir**, 27km north of Orange along mostly unsealed roads. The area is now a nature reserve of sorts, and it's still popular with fossickers.

Sleeping & Eating

Town Square (☎ 6369 1444; tsm@netwit.net.au; 246 Anson St; s/d $95/110; ⚟) In a convenient central location, the Town Square is one of the newer motels.

Parkview Hotel (☎ 6361 7014; 281 Summer St; r from $75; ⚟) Comfortable rooms in a beautiful restored hotel.

Metropolitan Hotel (☎ 6362 1353; 107 Byng St; mains $8-15; ☯ lunch & dinner) Affiliated with Town Square, the cheery Metropolitan has a good bistro on the veranda.

Lolli Redini (☎ 6361 7748; 48 Sale St; mains $15-30; ☯ lunch Fri & Sat, dinner Tue-Sat) The Italian-accented food here wins raves for its quality and presentation. One of the best restaurants in the region, be sure to book, especially for a table outside in summer.

Smoothie Break (☎ 6360 4860; 142 Summer St; dishes $3-8; ☯ 8am-8.30pm) Delicious sorbets are served up here, as well as fresh juices, salads and sandwiches.

Getting There & Away

Regional Express (☎ 13 17 13; www.regionalexpress .com.au) flies to Sydney (from $145) from Orange's airport, 13km southeast of the city.

Selwood's (☎ 6362 7963; www.selwoods.com.au) has services to Bathurst ($10, 45 minutes) leaving from the railway station.

CountryLink (☎ 13 22 32; www.countrylink.nsw .gov.au) trains go to Sydney ($47, five hours) and Dubbo ($23, 1¾ hours).

COWRA

☎ 02 / pop 8722

Ever since August 1944, when 1000 Japanese prisoners broke out of a POW camp here (231 of them died, along with four Australians in the ensuing melee), Cowra has aligned itself with Japan and the cause of world peace.

The **visitors centre** (☎ 6342 4333; www.cowra tourism.com.au; Olympic Park, Mid Western Hwy; ⏰ 9am-5pm) shows an unusual holographic film about the break-out. The tiny 3-D host is oddly chirpy – it's really quite a spectacle. Outside there's an aromatic rose garden.

Sights

The Australian and Japanese **war cemeteries** are 5km south of town; many of those who died were very young. A nearby **memorial** marks the site of the break-out, and you can still see the camp foundations. The superb **Japanese Garden** (☎ 6341 2233; Binni Creek Rd; admission $8.50; ⏰ 8.30am-5pm) on Bellevue Hill has beautifully maintained, traditional gardens, which smoothly incorporate local gum trees. There's a **sakura** (cherry-blossom festival) around the second weekend in October.

One of the darkest places for stargazing in all of Australia is **Darby Falls Observatory** (☎ 6345 1900; Mt McDonald Rd; adult/child $10/7; ⏰ 7-10pm, during daylight savings 8.30-11pm). From town, follow Wyangala Dam Rd for 22km and turn onto Mt McDonald Rd, then follow the signs.

The Mill (☎ 6341 4141; 6 Vaux St; ⏰ 10am-6pm) is Cowra's oldest building, and a winery to boot. Taste some of the region's famous Chardonnay as a reward for taking the interesting two-hour tour.

The small town of **Canowindra** lies 32km north of Cowra. The whole of its dogleg main street, Gaskill St, is heritage-listed. The **Age of Fishes Museum** (☎ 02-6344 1008; cnr Gaskill & Ferguson Sts; adult/child $7.70/3.50; ⏰ 10am-4pm) is very proud of its display of unique fossil fishes that have been found nearby.

Tours

Ideal Tours (☎ 6341 3350; www.australianacorner.com; 1 Kendal St) runs tours of wineries and other local attractions.

Sleeping & Eating

Country Gardens (☎ 6341 1100; 75 Grenfell Rd; s/d from $85/95; ⏰ 🖥 🐕) The most upmarket motor inn in town, with bright, comfortable rooms and helpful staff.

Imperial Hotel (☎ 6341 2588; 16 Kendal St; s/d incl breakfast from $30/50) This is the best of Cowra's pubs. Rooms are comfortable, modern and motel-like, and some have bathrooms.

Neila (☎ 6341 2188; 5 Kendal St; mains $28; ⏰ dinner Thu-Sat) A brief but innovative Mediterranean menu, fused with bold Asian flavours, is supported by proudly local produce at this small gem on Cowra's main drag. The owners grow much of the produce on their farm and the flavours are often simply amazing.

The Naked Lady (☎ 6341 1455; 14 Railway Lane; meals $7-10; ⏰ 9am-5pm daily, dinner Sat) Enjoy unique baked goods, creative sandwiches and daily specials inside or outside on the fountain-serenaded patio.

Getting There & Away

CountryLink (☎ 13 22 32; www.countrylink.nsw.gov.au) runs buses to Bathurst ($18, two hours).

FORBES

☎ 02 / pop 7102

Forbes is really a pretty place. It's perched on the banks of the Lachlan River and the wide streets are lined with grand 19th-century gold rush–funded buildings. The **visitors centre** (☎ 6852 4155; cnr Newell Hwy & Union St; ⏰ 9am-5pm) is inside the old train station and has local art exhibits.

Ben Hall, a landowner who became Australia's first official bushranger, was betrayed and shot near Forbes. He's buried in the town's cemetery; people still miss him, if the notes on his grave are anything to go by. The **historical museum** (☎ 6852 3856; 9 Cross St; adult/child $3/1; ⏰ 2-4pm Jun-Sep, 3-5pm Oct-May) houses Ben Hall relics and other memorabilia.

The **Bushrangers Hall of Fame** (☎ 6851 1881; 135 Lachlan St; adult/child $5/3; 10am-6pm), in the Albion Hotel, has guided tours of old underground tunnels that were used to transfer gold from banks into waiting coaches.

The **Albion Hotel** (☎ 6851 1881; 135 Lachlan St; s/d $35/60) has decent but basic rooms and a most enjoyable pub.

You may recognise Forbes from the popular Australian film *The Dish*, where much of the filming took place. To see the dish itself, head 60km north to **Parkes Radio Telescope** (☎ 6861 1777; www.outreach.atnf.csiro.au /visiting/parkes; Newell Hwy; admission free; ☼ 8.30am-4.15pm). Get mysteries about the film solved and find out more about Parkes' role in broadcasting the first moon landing from here.

DUBBO

☎ 02 / pop 31,000

Surrounded by sheep and cattle country, this large agricultural town stands at the regional crossroads of the Mitchell and Newell Hwys. Besides being a popular spot to bed down, it offers diversions such as its noted zoo.

The **visitor information centre** (☎ 1800 674 443, 6884 1422; www.dubbotourism.com.au; Macquarie St; ☼ 9am-5pm) is in a nice park.

Sights

Dubbo's star attraction is the **Western Plains Zoo** (☎ 6882 5888; www.zootopia.com.au; Obley Rd; adult/child $27/14; ☼ 9am-5pm, last entry 4pm), 5km southwest of town. It's the largest open-range zoo in Australia and has over a thousand animals, including its stars, the Bengal tigers. You can walk the 6km circuit or join the crawling line of cars, but to avoid the heatstroke of the first or the tedium of the latter, hire a bike ($14). Guided morning zoo walks start at 6.45am ($3 plus admission).

The animatronic characters at the **Old Dubbo Gaol** (☎ 6882 8122; adult/child $8/4; ☼ 9am-4.30pm), off Macquarie St, are just irritating enough for you to wish they would suffer the fate that once befell prisoners in this well-preserved 1871 gaol. The **Dubbo Regional Gallery** (☎ 6881 4342; cnr Talbragar & Macquarie Sts; admission by donation; ☼ 10am-6pm Mon-Fri, 10am-3pm Sat, noon-4pm Sun) has well-curated displays of thought-provoking local artists' works as well as Aboriginal art.

Dundullimal (☎ 6884 9984; Obley Rd; adult/child $6/3; ☼ 10am-5pm), about 2km beyond the

Western Plains Zoo, is a timber slab homestead built in the 1840s. Audio tours and exhibits bring alive what life was like back then (not fun but better than the gaol).

And to confirm that some things still smell the same, visit the **Livestock Saleyards** (☎ 6882 2155; Newell Hwy; ☼ sheep sales noon Mon, cattle 8.30am Thu), 5km north of town.

Sleeping

Dubbo Backpackers YHA (☎ 6882 0922; www.yha.com .au; 87 Brisbane St; dm/d $22/44; ☐) The cosy and homy rooms fill up quickly with transient backpackers. The friendly owner will sell discount zoo tickets, rent bikes and more.

Shearing Shed Motor Inn (☎ 6884 2977; 31 Cobra St; s/d from $66/75; ☒ ☒) You won't get fleeced at this motel that's typical of the family-run places along Cobra St and the Newell Hwy. Rooms are large and comfortable.

Westbury (☎ 6884 9445; westburyguesthouse.com .au; cnr Brisbane & Wingewarra Sts; r from $85-140; ☒) More a boutique hotel than a B&B, the Westbury is in a restored 1910 heritage building. The common rooms are uncommonly gracious.

Dubbo City Caravan Park (☎ 6882 4820; Whylandra St; sites/cabins per 2 people from $15/43; ☒ ☒) This pleasant caravan park on the riverbank is a 20-minute walk from town.

Eating

Grape Vine Café (☎ 6884 7354; 144 Brisbane St; mains $5-10; ☼ breakfast & lunch, dinner Fri & Sat; ☐) Enjoy snacks, wonderful meals and wi-fi inside in the vintage café area or out back in the lovely courtyard.

Three Snails (☎ 6884 9994; 7/36 Darling St; mains $15-25; ☼ lunch Wed-Sun, dinner Tue-Sat) Dubbo's best restaurant draws its inspiration globally for its careful and inventive Mod Oz menu. When it's balmy, book a veranda table.

Darbar (☎ 6884 4338; 215 Macquarie St; mains $7-17.50; ☼ dinner) The peals of joy aren't from the vibrator shop next door but from loud regulars lapping up tasty Indian fare at this long-time favourite.

Village Bakery Café (☎ 6884 5454; 113 Darling St; pies $4; ☼ breakfast & lunch) Excellent pies in too many flavours to choose from.

Getting There & Away

Dubbo has flights to/from Sydney from $110 with **QantasLink** (☎ 13 13 13; www.qantas

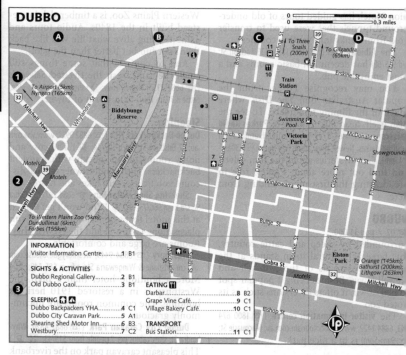

DUBBO

0   500 m
0   0.3 miles

To Three
Snails (200m)

To Gilgandra
(65km)

Train Station

Swimming
Pool

Victoria Park

Showgrounds

To Airport (5km);
Nyngan (165km)

Biddybunge
Reserve

Motels

Motels

To Western Plains Zoo (5km);
Dundullimal (6km);
Forbes (155km)

Elston
Park

To Orange (145km);
Bathurst (200km);
Lithgow (263km)

Motels

INFORMATION
Visitor Information Centre............**1** B1

SIGHTS & ACTIVITIES
Dubbo Regional Gallery.............**2** B1
Old Dubbo Gaol.....................**3** B1

SLEEPING
Dubbo Backpackers YHA............**4** C1
Dubbo City Caravan Park...........**5** A1
Shearing Shed Motor Inn...........**6** B3
Westbury...........................**7** C2

EATING
Darbar.............................**8** B2
Grape Vine Café....................**9** C1
Village Bakery Café................**10** C1

TRANSPORT
Bus Station........................**11** C1

.com.au) and **Regional Express** (REX; ☎ 13 17 13; www.regionalexpress.com.au). The latter also does a daily round-trip to Broken Hill (from $180).

Dubbo is located at the junction of the Newell (Melbourne–Brisbane) and Mitchell (Sydney–Adelaide) Hwys. Major coach companies all pass through Dubbo; expect to pay from $80 to $110 for tickets to Sydney (12 hours), Melbourne (11 hours), Adelaide (11 hours) and Brisbane (12 hours).

CountryLink (☎ 13 22 32; www.countrylink.nsw .gov.au) has daily trains to/from Sydney ($70, 6½ hours) via Orange ($23, 1¾ hours).

MUDGEE
☎ 02 / pop 8619

A really good-quality old country town, Mudgee lies amidst rolling hills on the scenic Castlereagh Hwy, which heads northwest from Lithgow. It's rapidly becoming a weekend destination for Sydney folks drawn by the pleasures of clean country living and still-low property prices. *Mudgee* is an Aboriginal word meaning 'nest in the hills'.

The **visitors centre** (☎ 1800 816 304, 6372 102 www.mudgee-gulgong.org; 84 Market St; ⏰ 9am-5pm Mon Fri, 9am-3.30pm Sat, 9.30am-2pm Sun) is near the pos office. It can help plan wine-tasting jaunts There's also a useful **NPWS office** (☎ 6372 719 160 Church St; ⏰ 9am-4pm Mon-Thu).

Sights
WINERIES

Most of the 20 or so wineries here are lo cally owned ventures and the vineyards are clustered together, making the region idea for cycling. There's a **wine festival** every Sep tember.

Host of the immensely popular **Chambe Music Festival** in December, **Huntington Estat** (☎ 6373 3825; www.huntingtonestate.com.au; Cassilis Rc ⏰ 9am-5pm Mon-Fri, 10am-5pm Sat, 10am-3pm Sun makes a fine Shiraz.

Poet's Corner (☎ 6372 2208; www.poetscorne wines.com; Craigmoor Rd; ⏰ 10am-4.30pm Mon-Sat, t 4pm Sun), 2.5km off Henry Lawson Rd, ha produced a vintage annually since 1858 making it one of Australia's oldest. (Thes days it's owned by the Pernod company. Try the Henry Lawson Shiraz.

Mudgee Growers (☎ 6372 2855; www.mudgee growers.com.au; cnr Henry Lawson Dr & Cassilis Rd; ⏰ 10am-5pm) is a new venture that utilises the grapes from many growers in the region. Sample the growing line of reds and whites in a rustic tasting room that's part of a historic winery.

Sleeping & Eating

Mudgee has lots of places to stay, from cute B&Bs to heritage hotels.

Lawson Park Hotel (☎ 6372 2183; cnr Church & Short Sts; s/d without bathroom from $50/65) This beautiful, historic hotel has comfortable rooms, most with direct access to the veranda.

Cobb & Co Court (☎ 6372 7245; www.cobbandco court.com.au; 97 Market St; r $110-240;) These former stables have been completely shovelled out and reborn as a vintage boutique hotel. Rooms are well-appointed in a gentleman-farmer kind of way (with spas, fridges etc).

Mudgee Riverside Caravan & Tourist Park (☎ 6372 2531; 22 Short St; sites/cabins per 2 people from $14/56;) In a leafy setting, this is a relaxed caravan park with a camp kitchen, and offers multiple-night discounts and bicycle hire.

Lawson Park Grill (☎ 6372 2183; Lawson Park Hotel; mains $12-18; ⏰ dinner) Sells steaks you can grill yourself. The pub has weekend live music.

Wineglass (☎ 6372 7245; Cobb & Co Ct; mains $25-30; ⏰ lunch & dinner) Serves refined regional cuisine on a changing menu.

Eltons (☎ 6372 0772; 81 Market St; mains $8-20; ⏰ breakfast, lunch & dinner) From the pavement tables you can partake of Mudgee's burgeoning café society; inside or out in the courtyard you can enjoy excellent pasta and wood-fired pizzas.

Getting There & Away

CountryLink (☎ 13 22 32; www.countrylink.nsw.gov.au) buses to/from Lithgow are timed to connect with Sydney trains ($48, 5½ hours).

GULGONG
☎ 02 / pop 2018
There was a time during the gold rush when Gulgong was so packed, dogs in the main street had to wave their tails up and down rather than side to side (or so they say). Things are much quieter these days (though the town does seem trapped in time), but staff at the **visitors centre** (☎ 6374 1202; 109 Herbert St; ⏰ 8am-4.30pm Mon-Fri, 9am-3pm

Sat, 9.30am-2pm Sun) can tell you all about the good old days, when Anthony Trollope, Elizabeth Jessie Hickman (Australia's only lady bushranger) and Cranky Sam Poo (an irritable Chinese bushranger) hung around these parts. Walk up the hill behind the centre to see where gold was discovered.

The huge **Gulgong Pioneer Museum** (☎ 6374 1513; 73 Herbert St; admission $5; ⏰ 9am-5pm) has more stuff in it than any other country-town museum in the state. Originally built from bark, the **opera house** (☎ 6374 1162; 99-101 Mayne St) has been running longer than any other in Australia. Poet Henry Lawson lived in Gulgong as a kid – find out about him at the **Henry Lawson Centre** (☎ 6374 2049; 147 Mayne St; admission $4; ⏰ 10am-3.30pm Wed-Sat, 10am-1pm Sun-Tue).

Rooms at the **Centennial Hotel** (☎ 6374 1241; 141-143 Mayne St; s/d $45/55) are comfortable enough, and you get a bathroom and breakfast for your tariff. Touristy but cute, the **Saint & Sinner** (☎ 6374 1343; 111 Mayne St; mains $4-12) makes a great egg sandwich (and even serves it on a green and yellow plate) and also serves pizzas. There are interesting 'Aussie Icon' paintings on the wall.

CountryLink (☎ 13 22 32; www.countrylink.nsw .gov.au) runs two buses to Mudgee ($5.50, 30 minutes).

NORTHWEST

Most people pass through this wedge of NSW on the Newell Hwy, barely pausing on their way to/from Queensland. The country is flat and dry but largely fertile, especially in the broad valley of the Namoi River. Cattle and cotton are the main industries.

The Northwest doesn't see many tourists, excepting those visiting Warrumbungle National Park and Lightning Ridge. The latter is getting an increasing stream of visitors who are drawn to its opal-mining culture, and is possibly the best reason to venture deep into the region. Otherwise you can drive for quite a way without seeing another car, on roads that follow incongruously sinuous routes across the flat landscape.

NEWELL HIGHWAY
The Newell Hwy is the quickest route between Melbourne and Brisbane, briefly

joining the Oxley Hwy from Tamworth at **Coonabarabran** (population 3000), the gateway to the Warrumbungles. It's at the junction of the Oxley and Newell Hwys. The **visitors centre** (☎ 02-6842 1441; www.coonabarabran.com; Newell Hwy; 9am-5pm), south of the clock tower, has the skeleton of a Diprotodon (a seriously giant prehistoric wombat) on display.

Coachman's Rest Motor Lodge (☎ 02-6842 2111; Newell Hwy; r $90-115;) is small and quiet, and has a good pool area as well as a restaurant. **Woop Woop Café** (☎ 02-6842 4755; 38A John St; mains $6-12; breakfast & lunch Tue-Sun, dinner Fri & Sat) serves organic salads, sandwiches and boasts good coffee and an art gallery. **Jolly Cauli Coffee Shop** (☎ 02-6842 2021; 30 John St; mains $4-8; breakfast Mon-Sat, lunch Mon-Fri;) This bustling place has tables inside, out on the footpath and on an adjoining patio.

One of the largest optical telescopes in the world is at **Siding Spring** (☎ 02-6842 6211; www.sidingspringexploratory.com.au; National Park Rd; 9.30am-4pm). Its visitors centre has some good educational displays and there are occasional tours ($11) of the site.

The **Skywatch Observatory** (☎ 02-6842 3303; Timor Rd; adult/child $14/9; exhibits 2-5pm), 2km west of Coona, has night-time telescope viewing. Viewing times vary by the season. Nongalactic-minded day visitors can try the mini golf.

Almost everyone is awed by the spectacular granite domes and spires of **Warrumbungle National Park**, 33km west of Coonabarabran. The 23,198-hectare park has over 30km of bushwalking trails (including some good short walks) and explosive wildflower displays during spring, as well as challenging rock-climbing routes (permit required). Park entrance fees ($7 per car) are payable at the **NPWS visitors centre** (☎ 02-6825 4364; 9am-4pm) in the park, which also handles camping registration ($5 to $8). It can get cold here, even on summer nights.

Tibuc Cabins (☎ 02-6842 1740; www.coonabarabran.com/tibuc; National Park Rd; cabins from $90) is a rustic place on an organic farm at the edge of the national park. Swim in a spring-fed pool, or cook yourself a BBQ. Beautiful **Gumin-Gumin** (☎ 02-6825 4368; gumin@tpg.com.au; r from $80), an 1870s homestead, rambles across a lovely setting 9km from the west entrance to the park.

Narrabri (population 7300), the cotton-growing centre, is home to the **Australian**

Cotton Centre (☎ 02-6792 6443; Newell Hwy; adult/child $7/5.50; 9am-5pm). This large exhibition is dedicated to the region's big cash crop. Among the compelling facts: one standard 225kg bale of cotton can be made into 3085 nappies. Some 20km west, the **Australia Telescope** comprises an array of radio telescopes used to map the universe far beyond the capabilities of optical telescopes. The **visitors centre** (☎ 02-6790 4070; admission free; 8am-4pm) has displays and a shop.

Sawn Rocks, a pipe-organ formation about 40km northeast of Narrabri (20km unsealed), is the most accessible and popular part of **Mt Kaputar National Park**. The southern part of the park has dramatic lookouts, climbing, bushwalking and camping.

Moree (population 20,000), a large town on the Gwydir River, has therapeutic **artesian spa baths** (☎ 02-6752 7480; cnr Anne & Gosport Sts; adult/child $5/3; 7am-8.30pm Mon-Fri, 7am-7pm Sat & Sun). In one of the town's attractive historic buildings, **Moree Plains Gallery** (☎ 02-6757 3320; admission by donation; 10am-5pm Tue-Fri, 10am-2pm Sat) specialises in Aboriginal art.

CASTLEREAGH HIGHWAY

The Castlereagh Hwy forks off the Newell at the pretty town of **Gilgandra**, and runs north into rugged opal country towards the Queensland border (its surfaced section ends soon after Lightning Ridge). Just north of Gilgandra, pull off the highway at the spot where, in 1818, John Oxley spat the dummy, when, expecting to find a giant inland sea, he instead discovered that the Macquarie River petered out into a boggy marsh. West of here, the prolific bird life of 200,000-hectare **Macquarie Marshes** is best seen during breeding season (usually spring, but it varies with water levels). Drive along the unsealed Gibson Way between Carinda and Coonamble, passing by Quambone. From there sealed roads go south to Warren.

Lightning Ridge

Near the Queensland border, this fiercely independent and strikingly imaginative mining community (one of the world's few sources of black opals) has real frontier spirit. It remains a place where hundreds of battlers dream of striking it rich underground, and now and again some of them even do. Certainly somebody is profiting from the estimated $35 million in opals that are removed each year. And indeed it is this kind of money that has local miners lobbying for more of the surrounding land to be opened up to mining – land that also contains scores of environmentally sensitive areas and sacred Aboriginal sites. The debate continues.

The fossicking season kicks off over the Easter long weekend, and is celebrated with horse and goat races. Several **underground mines** and **opal showrooms** are open to the public and there's a **gem festival** every July. In an example of the community's spirit, locals have mapped out four touring routes around town, using car doors as markers. Get details from the **Lightning Ridge visitors centre** (☎ 02-6829 1670; Morilla St; 9am-5pm).

Head 2km out of town along Pandora St to the boiling **artesian bore baths** (admission free; 24hr).

Black Opal Tours (☎ 02-6829 0368; half-day tours from $35; 9.30am) are a good way to see the fields, do a bit of fossicking, hear mining stories and visit oddities such as the **ironstone castle**.

There are a few motels and caravan parks in town. **Lightning Ridge Hotel Motel** (☎ 02-6829 0304; ridgehotel@hotmail.com; Onyx St; s/d $67/87;) is set on nicely landscaped grounds. There are **camp sites** (from $11), a popular pub and the **Ridge Rock Café** (mains $8-16; breakfast, lunch & dinner), which has the best food in town.

Bluey Motel (☎ 02-6829 0380; 32 Morilla St; r $40-55;) is a simple place, and one of several right in the centre of town. Rooms feature TVs and private bathrooms, and the motel has a BBQ area. The owner also operates a small bookstore on site, which has a good selection of books on opals and the folks who mine them. Drink with the eccentric locals at the **Diggers Rest Hotel** (☎ 02-6829 0404; Opal St).

CountryLink (☎ 13 22 32; www.countrylink.nsw .gov.au) buses go to/from Dubbo ($60, 4½ hours).

LORD HOWE ISLAND

☎ 02 / pop 350

Beautiful Lord Howe is a tiny subtropical island 550km east of Port Macquarie and 770km northeast of Sydney. Listed on the World Heritage Register for its rare bird and plant life, Lord Howe is an ecotourist's dream. It's also the kind of place that some visitors fall in love with, returning year after year for its first-name, bare-feet hospitality, perfect beaches and tropical-paradise ambience.

Lord Howe is not a budget destination, although prices fall considerably in winter. Unless you have a boat you'll have to fly here, and both food and accommodation are relatively limited and expensive. It's popular with older travellers and honeymooners, but there's plenty here for the active family.

Orientation & Information

Boomerang-shaped Lord Howe is dominated by three peaks: **Mt Lidgbird** (777m) and **Mt Gower** (875m) brood at its southern tip, and the spectacular spire of **Ball's Pyramid** (548m) juts from the sea 23km to the southeast.

The island is about 11km long by 3km wide, with most accommodation and services located in the flat area north of the airport. Island time is GMT plus 10½ hours, 30 minutes ahead of Sydney (except in summer).

The **visitor information centre** (☎ 1800 240 937, 6563 2114; www.lordhoweisland.info; cnr Lagoon & Middle Beach Rds; 9.30am-3pm) screens a worthwhile 20-minute audiovisual presentation. There's **Internet** (9am-4pm Sun-Fri) at the museum.

Nearby on Ned's Beach Rd you'll find the post office, Thompson's general store and Westpac Bank (no ATM).

Sights & Activities

Visit between September and April and you'll be amazed by the huge number of seabirds nesting in this tiny oasis. (Shout loudly enough at a Providence petrel and it will tumble out of the sky and crash at your feet, just to see what all the fuss is about.)

One of the pleasures of Lord Howe is **bushwalking** in the low hills and rainforests. The climb to the summit of Mt Gower is a candidate for Australia's finest one-day **walk** (licensed guide required; from $25) and takes eight to 10 hours return.

The daily **fish-feeding** frenzy takes place in late afternoon at Ned's Beach, where **sea kayaking** is popular. There's good **surf** at Blinky Beach, and off the island's western shore lies the world's southernmost **coral reef**, sheltered by a wide lagoon. You can inspect the brilliantly coloured sea life from **glass-bottom boats** (per adult/child $22.00/13.50) or rent snorkelling and diving equipment from outfitters at Lagoon Beach.

The **museum** (9am-4pm Mon-Fri, to 12.30pm Sat) has Internet facilities and a gift shop.

Tours

Thompson's store, near the visitor information centre, takes bookings for a range of tours and activities, from fishing charters to historical and nature walks.

Sleeping & Eating

Camping is prohibited and all accommodation must be booked in advance. There are plenty of lodges and self-contained apartments, some of which drop rates or close in winter. Eating out is expensive and bookings are essential.

The restaurants at Arajilla Retreat and Capella Lodge serve excellent modern Australian cuisine.

Ocean View Apartments (6563 2041; Lagoon Rd; d from $86, f apt from $135) In truth, these self-contained apartments don't have ocean views, but they do have tennis courts and a swimming pool.

Broken Banyan (6563 2024; Anderson Rd; d from $97) This is a reasonable kid-free budget option, with six self-contained units in three pairs set among lawns and pleasant gardens. A little way 'up the hill', but still no more than 10 minutes' walk from town, there are restaurants nearby.

Arajilla Retreat (1800 063 928, 6563 2002; www.lordhowe.com.au; Lagoon Rd; d $578-726) The plush apartments at this appealing, upmarket resort-style place have modern facilities. Beautifully situated, each suite has its own deck overlooking kentia palm forest.

Capella Lodge (9918 435; www.lordhoweisland.info/stay/capella.html; d from $427) Big money has been splashed around to make this luxury resort a haven for the cash-rich and time-poor. As well as offering spectacular views, it has a range of premium suites, and packages with all the extras from spa treatments to complimentary canapés and cocktails each evening.

Pinetrees (6563 2177) Serves up a three-course set meal ($40) and has a fish fry ($25) on Monday evening.

Blue Peters (Lagoon Beach; closed in winter) Serves simple tucker.

Coral Café (breakfast & lunch Sun-Fri, dinner Sun & Mon) This café at the museum is open late for pizza on Sunday and Monday.

Getting There & Away

Flight and accommodation packages are usually the only way to get a decent deal. Winter prices start from around $1069 for five nights.

Try **Fastbook Pacific Holidays** (1300 361 153; www.fastbook.com.au) in Sydney or **Oxley Travel** (1800 671 546; www.oxleytravel.com.au) in Port Macquarie.

QantasLink (13 13 13) has daily flights from Sydney (from $690 return via Internet advance purchase), and one or two direct flights a week from Brisbane (generally on Saturday and/or Sunday) for a similar fare. There's also a weekly flight from Coffs Harbour during the high season.

Getting Around

You can hire bicycles (per day $8) and cars (per day $50) on the island, but a bicycle is all you really need and most accommodation places will happily drive you somewhere. There is a 25km/h speed limit throughout the island. As there are few streetlights, the walk back to your digs after dark can be a challenge – bring a torch.

NORFOLK ISLAND

6723 / pop 1800

Norfolk Island is a green speck in the vast South Pacific Ocean, 1600km northeast of Sydney and 1000km northwest of Auckland. It's the largest of a cluster of three islands emerging from the Norfolk Ridge, which stretches from New Zealand to New Caledonia, the closest landfall, almost 700km north.

Norfolk Island is particularly popular with older Australians and New Zealanders on package holidays. Tourism accounts for more than 90% of the local economy but it is not a cheap destination. Airfares are expensive and there is no budget accommodation available.

Norfolk Island is not subject to Australian tax laws, which has led on the one hand to the strip of duty-free outlets in Burnt

Pine and on the other to the sprinkling of millionaires who live on the island.

History

Norfolk Island, which appears never to have been settled by Polynesians, was first sighted by James Cook on 10 October 1774. Fifteen convicts were among the first settlers who arrived on 6 March 1788, only weeks after the First Fleet reached Port Jackson to found Sydney. As a result of food shortages, shipwrecks and native timber that proved too brittle for building, many gave up and moved to New Norfolk, Van Diemen's Land (Tasmania).

Norfolk Island was abandoned for 11 years before colonial authorities decided to try again in 1825. Governor Darling planned this second penal settlement as 'a place of the extremest punishment short of death'. Under such notorious sadists as commandant John Giles Price, Norfolk became known as 'hell in the Pacific'.

The second penal colony lasted until 1855, when the prisoners were shipped off to Van Diemen's Land and the island was handed over by Queen Victoria to the descendants of the mutineers from the HMS *Bounty,* who had outgrown their adopted Pitcairn Island. About a third of the present population is descended from the 194 Pitcairners who arrived on 8 June 1856.

The island's musty tranquillity was disturbed in early 2002 when a young Australian was brutally killed there, the first murder recorded since convict days. At the time of writing no culprit had been found, a cause of much whispering and disquiet in the tiny community. The island's ghosts were also disturbed in 2004 when a Pitcairn descendant shot dead his father, a local MP.

Orientation & Information

The island measures only 8km by 5km, with vertical cliffs surrounding much of the coastline. Kingston, the principal settlement in convict days and now largely an open-air museum, is on the small coastal plain (once a swamp) on Slaughter Bay on the island's southern coast. The service town of Burnt Pine is at the centre of the island, near the airport, while Norfolk Island National Park encompasses the hillier northern part of the island.

The **visitor information centre** (☎ 22 147; www .norfolkisland.com.au; Taylors Rd; ☽ 8.30am-5pm Mon-Fri, to 3pm Sat & Sun) is next to the post office in Burnt Pine.

Westpac Bank (☎ 22 120) and the **Commonwealth Bank** (☎ 22 144) have branches nearby, the latter with an ATM. Most shops have Eftpos.

The **Communications Centre** (Norfolk Telecom; ☎ 22 244; ☐) on New Cascade Rd has telephone, fax and Internet facilities, and you can also access the Internet at **Norfolk Island Data Services** (☎ 22 427; Village Pl; per hr $3.50).

VISAS

The island is a self-governing external territory of Australia. Travelling to Norfolk Island from Australia (or New Zealand) means you will get an exit stamp in your passport and board an international flight. Upon arrival on Norfolk you automatically get a 30-day entry visa. You will need a re-entry visa or valid national passport upon return.

Sights & Activities

Kingston, built by convicts of the second penal colony, is Norfolk's star attraction. Many historic buildings have been restored and the finest of these along Quality Row still house the island's administrators, as well as four small but interesting **museums** (☎ 23 088; www.museums.gov.nf; single/combined tickets $6/18; ☽ 11am-3pm).

By the shore sits the ruins of an early pentagonal prison, a lime pit into which convict murder victims were sometimes thrown, and the picturesque **convict cemetery** with some poignant epitaphs, including that of 105-year-old Thomas Wright, a convict who at 101 had been sentenced to 14 years!

You could easily spend an hour poking around the **Bounty Folk Museum** (☎ 22 592; Middlegate Rd; admission $7.50; ☽ 10am-4pm), crammed with motley souvenirs from the convict era and *Bounty* mutineers.

A recent addition is **Fletcher's Mutiny Cyclorama** (☎ 23 871; Queen Elizabeth Ave; ☽ 9am-5pm Mon-Sat, 10am-3pm Sun), a 360-degree panoramic painting depicting the *Bounty* Mutiny and the Norfolk Islanders' unique history.

West of Burnt Pine, magnificent **St Barnabas Chapel** (Douglas Dr; tours adult/child $12/6) was built by the (Anglican) Melanesian Mission, which was based on the island from 1866 to 1920. It's never really closed; visitors are asked to close the door behind them.

Nature lovers will enjoy the island's lush vegetation and rugged coastline. The enriched volcanic soil and mild, subtropical climate provide perfect growing conditions for the 40-odd plant species unique to the island, including the ubiquitous Norfolk Island pine.

Covering the northern part of the island, **Norfolk Island National Park** offers various bushwalking tracks, with excellent views afforded from Mt Pitt (316m) and Mt Bates (318m).There's a sheltered beach with pristine waters at **Emily Bay** in the south, from where glass-bottom boats depart to view the coral reef.

The snorkelling in front of the Kingston breakwater is worthwhile; you can hire some gear in Burnt Pine, or several companies arrange snorkelling, diving and fishing trips.

Bounty Divers (☎ 22 751; www.bountydivers.nf) takes people out to the wreck of the HMS *Sirius*.

Sleeping

Accommodation is expensive and must be booked in advance. Most visitors come on package deals, starting from around $990 for seven nights in winter and around $1450 in summer, sometimes including car hire and breakfast.

Polynesian Motel (☎ 22 309; fax 23 040; New Cascade Rd; d from $88) This is one of a few cheaper, 1970s' motel-style resorts.

Auntie Em's (☎ 22 373; fax 22 827; Taylors Rd; d from $115) This family-run guesthouse, centrally located in Burnt Pine, has plenty of old-style charm.

Islander Lodge (☎ 22 114; fax 23 014; Middlegate Rd; d from $175) Perched on a hillside, these self-contained apartments enjoy fantastic views of Kingston and various bays.

Whispering Pines (☎ 22 114; fax 23 014; Mt Pitt Rd; d from $215) Several modern, self-contained cottages sit on a secluded ridge adjacent to the national park, a short drive from Burnt Pine.

Highlands Lodge (☎ 22 741; fax 22 045; Selwyn Pine Rd; d $173-270) This comfortable guesthouse, nestled on the hillside below the national park, has bright, airy rooms with pleasing bush views.

Eating

Interesting 'progressive' dinners ($40) at local residents' homes and the island fish fry ($25) – a sunset fish dinner held at Puppy's Point – can be booked through tour operators.

Brewery Bar & Bistro (☎ 23 515; Douglas Dr; meals from $8) Opposite the airport, this brewery serves cheap counter meals and brews its own beer. There are tours ($10) of the brewery every Thursday.

Cafe Pacifica (☎ 23 210; Cutters Corn Rd) Set inside a plant nursery near the Bounty Folk Museum, this upscale café serves delightful lunches, brunch and teas.

Hilli Lounge & Wine Bar (☎ 24 270; Queen Elizabeth Ave; mains $25) Good food served in cosy surroundings.

Homestead Restaurant (☎ 22 068; Hundred Acres; mains from $24) Out of town near the gates to the Rocky Point Reserve, the Homestead serves an excellent lunch.

Aquillo's (☎ 22 459; New Cascade Rd; mains from $17) This restaurant remains a popular choice.

There are cheap meals at various pubs and clubs, including the **Norfolk Island Leagues Club** (☎ 22 440; Ferny Lane; mains from $8).

Getting There & Away

Most flights are booked as part of a package deal. There's a departure tax of $30, payable at the airport or in advance at the visitor information centre.

Flight schedules to Norfolk Island were thrown into confusion with the collapse in June 2005 of Norfolk Jet Express, which used to fly to the island from Melbourne (via Sydney) and from Brisbane.

The slack was taken up by **Alliance** (☎ 1300 130 092), which has flights to and from both Brisbane (from $750) and Sydney (from $650) on Wednesday and Saturday. **Air New Zealand** (☎ 22 195, in New Zealand ☎ 0800 737 000) flies to and from Auckland on Wednesday and Sunday.There are no flights between Lord Howe and Norfolk Islands.

Getting Around

Car hire can be organised at the airport for as little as $30 a day. The speed limit around most of the island is 50km/h. Cows have right of way on the island's roads, and there's a $300 fine for hitting one.

Bicycle hire can be arranged through the visitor information centre.

SOUTH COAST

The nonchalant south coast, between Sydney and the Victorian border, is in a parallel universe to its rowdy northern counterpart. This is a far less hectic part of the world, with subtle attractions that are nonetheless shot through with a goodly dollop of charm.

There are popular beaches – such as Wollongong, Kiama, Ulladulla – but there's also the quiet, easy allure of fishing towns like Eden and Batemans Bay and the sharp tang of history wafting from settlements like Berry.

All this plus oodles of untrammelled nature: fabulous forests, nifty national parks and suchlike. How's the serenity?

If you are into the active life, then the benefits of the south coast region are clear and ever-present: take your pick from scuba diving, hang gliding, skydiving, horse riding, fishing, caving, bushwalking, scenic flights, island visits and whale and dolphin watching.

WOLLONGONG

☎ 02 / pop 228,800

Wollongong, NSW's third-largest city, is 80km south of Sydney. It's a sprawling industrial centre with Australia's biggest steelworks, but it also has fine surf beaches and striking hinterland; the Illawarra Escarpment – the hills behind the city – provides a super backdrop and coastal views.

The 'Gong is pleasantly low-rise and low-key; like Newcastle, it's shedding the skin of its industrial past and refocusing on the future of tourism, using its natural assets as bait. Like Melbourne, it's learnt the art of self-promotion: the tourist board touts Wollongong as 'Australia's most liveable regional city'.

Orientation & Information

Crown St is the main commercial street, and a large two-block pedestrian mall lies between Keira (part of the Princes Hwy) and Kembla Sts. There's a post office and ATMs on Crown St Mall.

The **Wollongong visitor information centre** (☎ 4227 5545, 1800 240 737; www.tourismwollongong .com; 93 Crown St; ⏰ 9am-5pm Mon-Fri, 10am-4pm Sat & Sun) can book accommodation.

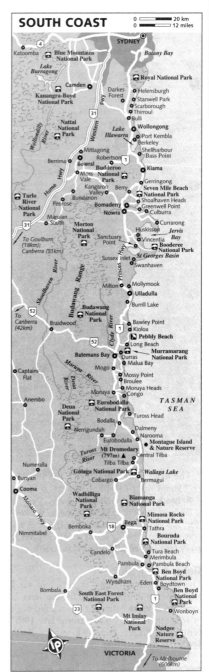

SOUTH COAST
0 ——— 20 km
0 ——— 12 miles

NEW SOUTH WALES

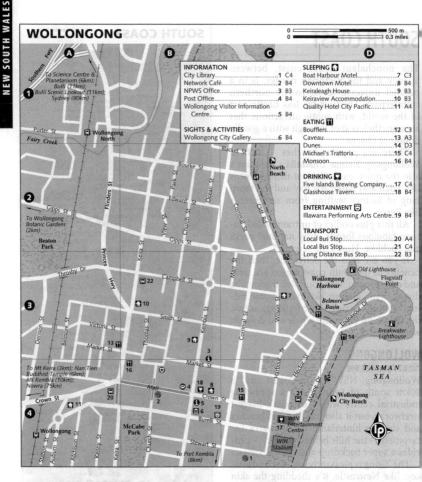

WOLLONGONG

0 — 500 m
0 — 0.3 miles

INFORMATION
City Library.................................1 C4
Network Café.............................2 B4
NPWS Office..............................3 B3
Post Office.................................4 B4
Wollongong Visitor Information
  Centre....................................5 B4

SIGHTS & ACTIVITIES
Wollongong City Gallery..............6 B4

SLEEPING
Boat Harbour Motel....................7 C3
Downtown Motel.......................8 B4
Keiraleagh House........................9 B3
Keiraview Accommodation.........10 B3
Quality Hotel City Pacific...........11 A4

EATING
Boufflers..................................12 C3
Caveau....................................13 A3
Dunes.....................................14 D3
Michael's Trattoria....................15 C4
Monsoon.................................16 B4

DRINKING
Five Islands Brewing Company.....17 C4
Glasshouse Tavern.....................18 B4

ENTERTAINMENT
Illawarra Performing Arts Centre..19 B4

TRANSPORT
Local Bus Stop..........................20 A4
Local Bus Stop..........................21 C4
Long Distance Bus Stop..............22 B3

The **NPWS office** (☎ 4225 1455; 4/55 Kembla St; ⊙ 8.30am-4.30pm Mon-Fri) has regional maps.

Network Café (☎ 4228 8686; Upstairs, Shop 4 & 5, 157 Crown St; per hr $3.50; ⊙ 10am-6pm Mon-Wed, 10am-9pm Thu-Sat, 10am-5pm Sun) has Internet access, but only the **city library** (Stewart St) gives it away free (no email support, though).

Sights & Activities

The shore offers empty expanses of sand and a pretty harbour. The fishing fleet is based in **Belmore Basin**, cut from solid rock in 1868; there are two handsome late-19th-century lighthouses on the foreshore. **North Beach** has the best surf.

The **Wollongong City Gallery** (☎ 4228 7500; www.wollongongcitygallery.com; cnr Kembla & Burelli Sts;

admission free; ⊙ 10am-5pm Tue-Fri, 12-4pm Sat & Sun) displays a permanent collection of Illawarra colonial, indigenous and Asian art, and diverse temporary exhibits.

The lavish **Nan Tien Buddhist Temple** (☎ 4272 0600; www.nantien.org.au; Berkeley Rd, Berkeley; admission free; ⊙ 9am-5pm Tue-Sun) is the southern hemisphere's largest (the name means 'Paradise of the South'; it's located here due to favourable feng shui between the escarpment and the ocean). It's an arresting sight as it overlooks Mt Keira and Mt Kembla, and features Japanese gardens, a pagoda, a vegetarian restaurant, 10,000 Buddhas and meditation and cultural activities.

The **Science Centre & Planetarium** (☎ 4283 6665; www.uow.edu.au/science_centre; Squires Way

Fairy Meadow; adult/child $10/6; ☺ 10am-4pm) covers everything from the dinosaur to the electrical age, with the motto 'Hands On' (that's 'interactive' to you, chief).

Enjoy the tranquil **Wollongong Botanic Gardens** (☎ 4225 2636; 61 Northfields Ave, Keiraville; admission free; ☺ 7am-4.45pm Mon-Fri, 10am-4pm Sat & Sun Apr-Sep, 10am-6.45pm Oct-Mar) among teeming bird life and a range of habitats.

Sleeping

Quality Hotel City Pacific (☎ 4229 7444; www.city pacifichotel.com.au; 112 Burelli St; d $175-200, f $200; ▣ ✕ ▤ ⬛) In an older, well-kept building, with bright, modern rooms, some with city and water views. There's a small saltwater pool.

Downtown Motel (☎ 4229 8344; info@downtown motel.net; 76 Crown St; s/d from $100/110; ▣ ▤) Straight out of the 1960s, this friendly option has clean, functional rooms in a very convenient spot.

Keiraleagh House (☎ 4228 6765; backpack@primus .com.au; 60 Kembla St; dm/s/tw $18/30/50) A ramshackle heritage house stuffed with ambience. Rooms are slightly faded, but comfortable, and there's a large kitchen, a sizable patio, bench seating and a BBQ.

Keiraview Accommodation (☎ 4229 1132; bookings@keiraviewacco.com.au; 75-79 Keira St; dm/d/f $24/72/77; ▣ ▤) Clean and modern, this complex contains the YHA hostel, with neat four-bed dorms. Doubles and family rooms have verandas and kitchenettes.

Boat Harbour Motel (☎ 4228 9166; www.boat harbour-motel.com.au; cnr Campbell & Wilson Sts; s/d $120/140; ▣ ✕) Get a load of the views at this comfortable motel. The rooms facing the water have nice balconies.

Eating

Keira St has the greatest concentration of restaurants, especially north of the mall.

Caveau (☎ 4226 4855; 122-124 Keira St; 3 courses $55; ☺ dinner Tue-Sat; ✕) Caveau has the essential ingredients for success: double storefront in a vintage building, smooth service and an ever-changing Modern Australian menu that makes use of the produce from nearby specialty farms.

Michael's Trattoria (☎ 4225 9542; 50 Crown St; mains $30; ☺ lunch Tue-Fri, dinner Tue-Sat; ✕) Atmospherically speaking, it's a slice of old Italy near the beach, but from a culinary point of view it's insanely popular with locals for meat dishes such as steak with rosemary.

Dunes (☎ 4228 7111; 1 Marine Dr; dinners from $35; ☺ breakfast Sat & Sun, lunch & dinner daily; ✕) This flash joint soars above City Beach with tremendous views, especially from the outside tables. Meat and fish dishes are prepared simply in an open kitchen.

Monsoon (☎ 4229 4588; 193 Kiera St; mains $12-20; ☺ lunch Tue-Sat, dinner Tue-Sun; ✕) The old wooden floors in this storefront have weathered to a golden brown, while the Vietnamese cuisine is seasoned with Mod Oz reality.

Boufflers (☎ 4227 2989; cnr Harbour St & Cliff Rd; mains $5-15; ☺ lunch & dinner) This place offers takeaway seafood at its best, but it isn't open late.

Drinking

Five Islands Brewing Company (☎ 4220 2854; www.fiveislandsbrewery.com; WIN Entertainment Centre, cnr Crown & Harbour Sts; ✕) Spacious and sleek, with tall plate-glass windows, a patio overlooking the sea and nine excellent draughts brewed on the premises…it's popular.

Glasshouse Tavern (☎ 4226 4305; 90 Crown St; ☺ 10am-late Mon-Sat) Smart café by day, febrile drinking, dancing and pick-up joint by night – particularly Saturday, when it heaves until 5am.

Entertainment

Illawarra Performing Arts Centre (IPAC; ☎ 4226 3366; www.ipac.org.au; 32 Burelli St) Excellent theatre, dance and music, including topical productions – a recent show addressed the plight of Australia's 'illegal' immigrants.

Getting There & Away

BUS

All long-distance buses leave from the **bus station** (☎ 4226 1022; cnr Keira & Campbell Sts). **Premier Motor Service** (☎ 13 34 10; www.premierms .com.au) operates to Sydney ($14, two hours, three daily weekdays, two daily weekends) and Eden (adult/child $60/38, 7½ hours, two daily). **Murrays** (☎ 13 22 51) travels to Canberra (adult/child $31/19, three hours, one daily).

TRAIN

CityRail (☎ 13 15 00; www.cityrail.nsw.gov.au) runs from Sydney to Wollongong (adult/child $9.80/4.90, 1¾ hours, frequent), continuing

SOUTH COAST: TOP FIVE CULTS OF PERSONALITY

The south coast's quiet charm has always attracted its fair share of unique individuals. Following are some of the most interesting historical figures to have graced the region since Charles Jackson (opposite) stretched a line across the Kiama blowhole, took a deep breath and hoped for the best…

■ **Ben Boyd** – Charismatic Boyd, a former London stockbroker, liked to gamble with other people's money. He sunk a small fortune into two whaling settlements at Twofold Bay – Boydtown and East Boyd – only for his British backers to get cold feet and vote him out of the syndicate. Boyd left Sydney in disgrace and was last seen in the Solomon Islands in 1851, after going ashore to hunt duck; his deserted rowboat was later found next to a gun and a multitude of footprints. They say Boyd was killed by headhunters, a salutary lesson that the spectacular, failed Aussie entrepreneurs of the 1980s singularly neglected to heed.

■ **Old Tom, the Killer Whale** – In the 1920s in Twofold Bay, Old Tom led a pod of killer whales (including Stranger, Hooky and Humpy) that was known as the 'Killers of Eden'. This mob was hell-bent on genocide. Finding stray baleen whales, they'd shepherd them into the bay, alerting whalers by thrashing the water with their tails. Once the baleen was harpooned, Tom would roll over its blowhole so it couldn't breathe; Stranger, Hooky and Humpy would swim below to prevent the victim from diving deeper. The pod's reward was the tongue and lips, leaving the carcass for the whalers.

■ **DH Lawrence** – In 1922 the famous English novelist took a break from scandalising the Poms to spend the winter in Thirroul. With wife Frieda, Lawrence lived in a house named Wyewurk, where he wrote almost all of his famous novel *Kangaroo*. Wyewurk still stands, looking much as Lawrence described it in the book: 'A real lovely brick house, with a roof of bright red tiles.' *Kangaroo* has become an unofficial guide to Thirroul, even though the town bears little resemblance to Lawrence's world. Rampant development, as always, threatens to turn it into an identikit suburb of Wollongong.

■ **Zane Grey** – This prolific American writer was the first to use the Western as a serious literary genre, but to Aussies he'll always be known for *An American Angler in Australia*, the book that put Bermagui on the global stage. In 1936, Grey, an obsessive fisherman, heard about the angling in Bermagui and decided to try his luck. The outsider was met with bemusement, but the locals changed their tune when he snagged a 460kg tiger shark, then the largest fish ever caught with rod and reel. Later, Grey caught the south coast's first-ever yellowfin tuna.

■ **Arthur Boyd** – This much-loved Australian artist was known for paintings that were deeply mired in personal experience: love, anger, religious attitudes. Later, he became immersed in the Australian landscape, buying the beautiful property Bundanon (p225) on the Shoalhaven River, before donating it for use as a gallery and artists' retreat. Boyd said that 'you can't own a landscape' and his decision to release Bundanon was borne from his desire for the public to be inspired by the place, rather than having it benefit only a chosen few.

south to Kiama, Gerringong and Bomaderry (Nowra).

The **Cockatoo Run** (☎ 1300 653 801; www.3801limited.com.au; adult/child/family $40/35/100; ⏰ Wed & Sun) heritage tourist train travels across the southern highlands, traversing the escarpment and dense rainforest.

Getting Around

The main local bus stops are on Marine Dr and the corner of Crown and Keira Sts.

You can reach most beaches by rail, and a cycle path runs from the city centre north to Bulli and south to Port Kembla. Alternatively, call a taxi (☎ 4229 9311).

AROUND WOLLONGONG

The **Illawarra Escarpment** comprises a number of separate sections from Bulli Pass (pronounced bull-eye) to Bong Bong; it isn't very large but the country is spectacular. There are **walking tracks** on Mt Kembla and Mt Keira, but you'll need your own transport to get there. Enjoy spectacular views over the town and coast from the **Bulli Scenic Lookout**, north off the Princes Hwy.

Get in touch with the **Wollongong visitor information centre** (☎ 02-4227 5545, 1800 240 737; www.tourismwollongong.com; 93 Crown St, Wollongong; 9am-5pm Mon-Fri, 10am-4pm Sat & Sun) or Wollongong's **NPWS office** (☎ 02-4225 1455; 4/55 Kembla St, Wollongong; 8.30am-4.30pm Mon-Fri) for information about the park and bush camping.

Wollongong's beachside suburbs are inviting: **Bulli** and **Thirroul** (where DH Lawrence once lived; see opposite) are especially popular.

At **Coalcliff**, the road heads up the escarpment; a short way along, near **Stanwell Park**, it enters thick forest and you drive through the Royal National Park.

Several excellent surf beaches lie north of Wollongong, including **Sandon Point**, **Austinmer**, **Headlands** (only for experienced surfers) and **Sharkies**.

On the road to Otford and Royal National Park, the views from **Lawrence Hargrave Lookout**, at Bald Hill above Stanwell Park, are superb. Hargrave, who was a pioneer aviator, made his first flying attempts in the area in the early 20th century; today **Stanwell Park** is used as a base for hang gliding.

HangglideOz (☎ 0417 939 200; www.hangglideoz .com.au) and **Sydney Hang Gliding Centre** (☎ 02-4294 4294; www.hanggliding.com.au) offer tandem flights from $180.

Symbio Wildlife Gardens (☎ 02-4294 1244; www .symbiowildlife.com; 7-11 Lawrence Hargrave Dr, Stanwell Tops; adult/child $17/9; 9.30am-5pm) has over 1000 critters. You are encouraged to touch, feed and pet the little bundles of joy.

Hit the trails with **Darkes Forest Riding Ranch** (☎ 02-4294 3441; www.horseriding.au.com; 84 Darkes Forest Rd, Darkes Forest; per hr from $35).

WOLLONGONG TO NOWRA

This region has some great beaches, state forests and, in the ranges to the west, the big **Morton National Park**.

Lake Illawarra is popular for water sports. Further south is **Shellharbour**, a popular holiday resort, and one of the oldest towns along the coast (its name comes from the number of shell middens, remnants of Aboriginal feasts, that the early Europeans found here).

There are beaches on the Windang Peninsula north of the town and scuba diving off **Bass Point** to the south.

Kiama

☎ 02 / pop 12,300

Kiama is a pretty seaside town boasting handsome old buildings, good beaches and an atmospheric ocean setting.

The **Kiama visitor information centre** (☎ 4232 3322; www.kiama.com.au; 9am-5pm) is on Blowhole Point.

Nearby is Kiama's **blowhole**, which can spout up to 60m and is floodlit until 1am. This attraction has drawn visitors for ages; in 1889 local freak, Charles Jackson, drew huge crowds for his shtick of traversing the mouth of the blowhole on a tightrope.

There's a good **lookout** from the top of Saddleback Mountain, and a small enclosed **surf beach** right in town. The broad **Werri Beach** is 10km south in Gerringong, while **Bombo Beach** is 3km north of the centre.

Minnamurra Rainforest Centre (☎ 4236 0469; car $10; 10am-5pm) is in **Budderoo National Park**, on the eastern edge, about 14km inland from Kiama. There's a **NPWS visitor centre**, from where you can take a 1.6km-loop walk on a boardwalk through the rainforest past several small waterfalls. There's a secondary 2.6km walk on a paved track to the Minnamurra Falls.

Kiama Terrace Motor Lodge (☎ 4233 1100; www .kiama.com.au/kiamaterrace; 45-51 Collins St; r from $125; P ⚫ ⚫) is a classic motel with comfortable units. It's in the heart of town, near the beach, shops and pubs.

Bellevue Accommodation (☎ 4232 4000; www .bellevueaccommodation.com.au; 21 Minnamurra St; r $140-250; P ⚫) has six large units in a traditional building with wide porches and good views. The rooms are plush with DVD and kitchen facilities.

Kiama Backpackers (☎ 4233 1881; tomtom@1earth .net; 31 Bong Bong St; dm/d $21/50; ⚫) has a street address that some hostels would murder for. In addition, it's only 25m from the station and a couple of minutes from the beach. There's accommodation for the disabled.

Terralong St and nearby Collins St have the largest concentration of eateries. Every fourth Saturday, the **Kiama Produce Market** (☎ 0409 377 132; Black Beach) offers an array of local organic produce, unusual baked goods and prepared foods.

Long-distance buses stop 3km north of Kiama at the Bombo Beach train station.

Frequent **CityRail** (☎ 13 15 00; www.citvrail.nsw .gov.au) trains run north to Wollongong and

Sydney ($13) and south to Gerringong and Bomaderry/Nowra ($4.40, 2½ hours).

Berry
☎ 02 / pop 1600

The small, pretty town of Berry is inland, about 20km north of Nowra. Founded in the 1820s, it remained a private town on the Coolangatta Estate (p331) until 1912. Try **Pottering Around** (☎ 4464 2177; Berry Stores complex, 99 Queen St; ☒ 10am-5pm) for tourist information. **Queen St** has some National Trust–classified buildings and the **museum** (135 Queen St; admission free; ☒ 11am-2pm Sat, 11am-3pm Sun), in an interesting 1884 bank building.

Mild to Wild (☎ 4464 2211; www.m2w.com.au; 84 Queen St) organises adventure trips: canoeing, canyoning, mountain biking, rock climbing, kayaking and abseiling.

The popular **Berry Country Fair** is held on the first Sunday of the month at the showgrounds. There are several **wineries** in the area and the **Hotel Berry** (☎ 4464 1011; berrypub@shoal.net.au; 120 Queen St; tours $15; ☒ 10.30am Sat) runs a short but exceptional wine tour.

Accommodation prices rise on weekends, so book ahead.

Bunyip Inn Guesthouse (☎ 4464 2064; 122 Queen St; s/d incl breakfast $60/120; ☒) is in an impressive old bank building, with distinctive, spacious rooms.

The **Hotel Berry** (☎ 4464 1011; berrypub@shoal.net.au; 120 Queen St; s/d from $30/40) has large, well-kept bedrooms, a pretty courtyard dining area and above-average meals.

Drinkers at the **Great Southern Hotel** (☎ 4464 1009; 95 Queen St; r $44) sit on saddle seats surrounded by hub caps, a torpedo hanging from the ceiling and a motorcycle on the bar. The wiggy ambience sets the tone for themed rooms.

Premier Motor Service (☎ 13 34 10; www.premierms.com.au) runs buses (between Kiama and Nowra) that stop at Berry on request.

Around Berry

There are scenic roads from Berry to pretty **Kangaroo Valley**. Canoe and swim on the Shoalhaven and Kangaroo Rivers; try **Mild to Wild** (☎ 02-4464 2211; www.m2w.com.au; 84 Queen St) for outdoor activities.

Near Berry lies **Seven Mile Beach**, a glorious stretch of sand backed by attractive forest. Just north is the **Seven Mile Beach National Park** stretching up to Gerroa.

The Shoalhaven River meanders through dairy country, reaching the sea at Crookhaven Heads. On the estuary's north side is **Shoalhaven Heads**, where the river once reached the sea but is now blocked by sandbars.

Just before Shoalhaven Heads is **Coolangatta**, the site of the south coast's earliest European settlement (and therefore founded before its more famous Queensland namesake).

Coolangatta Estate (☎ 02-4448 7131; www.coolangattaestate.com.au; 1335 Bolong Rd, Shoalhaven Heads; per person $45-160) is a slick **winery** (☒ 10am-5pm) with a golf course, a good restaurant and accommodation in convict-built buildings.

NOWRA
☎ 02 / pop 24,800

Nowra is a centre for dairy farms. It's workmanlike, but handy for excursions to beaches and villages around Jervis Bay, north to Berry and inland to Kangaroo Valley and Morton National Park.

There's a **Nowra visitor information centre** (☎ 4421 0778; www.shoalhaven.nsw.gov.au; cnr Princes Hwy & Pleasant Way; ☒ 9am-4.30pm), an office of the **NPWS** (☎ 4423 2170; 55 Graham St; ☒ 9am-4.30pm Mon-Fri), a **post office** (☎ 4429 4142; cnr Junction & Berry Sts) and the **Shoalnet Internet Café** (☎ 4422 5014; 46 Berry St; per hr $5; ☒ 9am-4.30pm Mon-Fri, 9-11am Sat).

Get cheek-by-jowl with native animals at **Nowra Wildlife Park** (☎ 4421 3949; 23 Rockhill Rd; adult/child $10/5; ☒ 9am-5pm). Heading north from Nowra, cross the bridge and immediately turn left, then branch left onto McMahons Rd at the roundabout; turn left again at Rockhill Rd.

Nowra Museum (☎ 4421 2021; cnr Kinghorne & Plunkett Sts; admission $1; ☒ 1-4pm Sat & Sun) features local history exhibits, while **Meroogal** (☎ 4421 8150; cnr West & Worrigee Sts; adult/child $7/3; ☒ 1-5pm Sat, 10am-5pm Sun Feb-Dec, 10am-5pm Thu Sun Jan), in an historic 1885 house, has artefacts from its four generations of female occupants.

The relaxing **Ben's Walk** starts at the bridge near Scenic Dr and follows the south bank of the Shoalhaven River (6km return). North of the river, the circular 5.5km **Bomaderry Creek Walking Track** runs through sandstone gorges from a trailhead at the end of Narang Rd.

Shoalhaven River Cruises (☎ 4447 1978; tour $23; ☒ 10.30am & 1.30pm Wed & Sun) has two tour up the beautiful river.

Amiable and old fashioned, the **White House Heritage Guest House** (☎ 4421 2084; www.

.whitehouseguesthouse.com; 30 Junction St; s/d from $55/77; (P) (巡)) is beautifully restored, while the **George Bass Motor Inn** (☎ 4421 6388; www .georgebass.com.au; 65 Bridge Rd; s/d $93/99; (P) (巡) (🖳)) is unpretentious and well appointed.

Grant's Seafood Café (☎ 4421 2742; 9 Egans Ln; mains $10-15; ☽ lunch daily, dinner Thu-Sat; (巡)) is a casual indoor/outdoor eatery serving superb fish and chips, pasta, salads and ribs.

Premier Motor Service (☎ 13 34 10; www.prem-ierms.com.au; Stewart Pl) runs to Sydney ($21, three hours) and Melbourne.

The **train station** (☎ 4421 2022) is 3km north at Bomaderry. Frequent **CityRail** (☎ 13 15 00; www.cityrail.nsw.gov.au) trains go to Sydney ($15, 2¾ hours). **North Nowra Bus Lines** (☎ 4423 5244; www.nowracoaches.com.au) links Nowra to the Bomaderry train station every one to two hours weekdays and only three times on Saturday. For a taxi, call ☎ 4421 0333.

AROUND NOWRA

West of Nowra is **Bundanon** (☎ 02-4423 0433; www.bundanon.com.au; 533 Bundanon Rd, West Cambewarra; ☽ 10.30am-4pm Sun), an art gallery and artists' retreat that was once the home of Australian painter, Arthur Boyd (see the boxed text, p222). Bundanon displays works by Boyd and his family as well as prominent Australian artists. Note: you may only arrive between 10.30am and 1.30pm. Weekday tours are available on request for a minimum of 15 people.

Just before Nowra, as you travel south through Bomaderry, turn right into Illaroo Rd at the set of lights before the Shoalhaven River bridge. Follow Illaroo Rd through the roundabout west of Nowra for 13km, then turn left off Illaroo onto Bundanon Rd.

Australia's Museum of Flight (☎ 02-4421 1920; www.museum-of-flight.org.au; 489A Albatross Rd; adult/ child $10/5; ☽ 10am-4pm) is 10km south of Nowra at an operational airfield. Its excellent displays include a Sopwith Camel WWI biplane (Snoopy's favourite).

JERVIS BAY

South of Nowra, Jervis Bay is a pleasing stretch of coastline with white sandy beaches, bush and forest. **Huskisson** (population 3300), one of the oldest towns on the bay, is attractive and handy for water sports and whale and dolphin watching. It retains old-world charm, despite extensive housing developments.

There's a boardwalk and museum near the **Lady Denman Heritage Complex** (☎ 02-4441 5675; www.ladydenman.asn.au; 1 Dent St, Huskisson; adult/ child $8/4; ☽ 10am-4pm), on the Nowra side of Huskisson. The complex boasts historic buildings, artefacts, Aboriginal crafts and boats including the *Lady Denman*, a ferry dating from 1912.

In 1995 the Wreck Bay Aboriginal community won a land claim and now jointly administers the vast **Booderee National Park** (Booderee is an Aboriginal word meaning 'plenty of fish').

On the bay's southeastern spit of land, it's quite lovely, with good swimming, surfing and diving on bay and ocean beaches. Much of the area is heathland, with small pockets of rainforest.

There's a **Booderee National Park visitor information centre** (☎ 02-4443 0977; www.deh.gov.au /parks/booderee; ☽ 9am-4pm) at the park entrance where walking trail and camping information is available.

Also located in the park, **Booderee Botanic Gardens** (☎ 02-4442 1122; ☽ 8.30am-4pm) offers picturesque, gentle walks around different habitats.

South of Huskisson, **Hyams Beach** is spectacularly white and secluded.

Dolphin Watch Cruises (☎ 1800 246 010; www .dolphinwatch.com.au; Owen St, Huskisson; adult/child $20/10) offers several dolphin and whale-watching trips, while **Deep 6 Diving** (☎ 02-4441 5255; deep6divingjervisbay.com.au; 64 Owen St, Huskisson) charges $90 for two boat dives plus equipment hire.

There's substantial accommodation in Huskisson and Vincentia; book ahead for weekends. Prices soar on weekends and holidays.

At **Jervis Bay Guesthouse** (☎ 02-4441 7658; www .jervisbayguesthouse.com.au; 1 Beach St, Huskisson; r incl breakfast $115-235; (巡)) most of the gorgeous, light and airy rooms have beach views and broad verandas overlooking the bay. Children under 12 are discouraged.

Husky Pub (☎ 02-4441 5001; www.thehuskypub .com.au; Owen St, Huskisson; s/d $40/60) is a good-time joint with good rooms, live music, outdoor picnic tables and tip-top bay views.

Huskisson Beach Tourist Resort (☎ 02-4441 5142; Beach St, Huskisson; powered/unpowered sites from $26/24, cabins from $68; (🐾)) has an awesome beach location, a little way out of Huskisson on the road to Vincentia.

AROUND JERVIS BAY

Ulladulla is an area of beautiful lakes, lagoons and beaches. There's swimming and surfing – try **Mollymook** beach, just north of town.

Accommodation includes **South Coast Backpackers** (☎ 02-4454 0500; 63 Princes Hwy, Ulladulla; dm/d $22/45) and **Ulladulla Guest House** (☎ 02-4455 1796; www.guesthouse.com.au; 39 Burrill St, Ulladulla; r from $180; **P** ✕ ☕), a luxury guesthouse set in beautiful gardens, with an on-site art gallery and a restaurant serving local grub with French stylings.

Premier Motor Service (☎ 13 34 10; www.premierms.com.au) runs from Ulladulla to Sydney ($28), Nowra ($15), Batemans Bay ($12) and Eden ($8).

Ulladulla Bus Lines (☎ 02-4455 1674) services the local area, mainly between Milton, Mollymook, Ulladulla and Burrill Lake.

Pebbly Beach, popular with surfers, is about 10km off the highway, in Murramarang National Park. Its charms include wild kangaroos and lorikeets that will eat from your hand (careful – the little buggers can get nippy).

Pebbly Beach camping ground (☎ 02-4478 6006; sites per person per night $5), in a lovely spot, is run by the NPWS, as is the **Depot Beach camping area** (☎ 02-4478 6582; sites per person per night $5), a beachside site with basic amenities. Turn off the highway onto North Durras Rd south of East Lynne; avoid rough Pebbly Beach Rd. Caravans can't be taken on the last section of the road to Pebbly Beach.

BATEMANS BAY

☎ 02 / pop 10,200

Batemans Bay is a fishing port that has become one of the south coast's largest holiday centres, with good beaches and a luscious estuary.

The **Batemans Bay visitor information centre** (☎ 4472 6900, 1800 802 528; cnr Beach Rd & Princes Hwy; ✆ 9am-5pm) is opposite Maccas, near the town centre, and features a gallery with local works.

DragNet (☎ 4472 7009; Shop B3, Stocklands Mall, Perry St; per hr $6) has the Internet (and wi-fi).

The **Old Courthouse Museum** (☎ 4472 8993; Museum Pl; adult/child $5/1; ✆ 1-4pm Tue-Thu) displays local history exhibits.

Just behind it is the **Water Garden Town Park** and a **boardwalk** through wetlands. The Mara Mia is a nice waterside walkway.

On the north side of the Clyde River estuary, just across the bridge, **Oyster Shed Boat Hire** (☎ 4472 6771; Last Shed, Wray St) hires out runabouts from $50.

Several boats offer **cruises** up the estuary from the ferry wharf just east of the bridge as well as sea cruises (and you might see penguins at the Tollgate Islands Nature Reserve).

Birdland Animal Park (☎ 4472 5364; 55 Beach Rd, near Batehaven; adult/child $14/7; ✆ 9.30am-4pm) has adorable wombat displays and koala feeding.

Corrigans Beach is the closest beach to the town centre. South of Corrigans, a series of small beaches dot the rocky shore, with longer beaches along the coast north of the bridge, leading into Murramarang National Park.

Surfers flock to **Surf Beach**, **Malua Bay**, the small **McKenzies Beach** and **Broulee**. The best surfing in the area is at **Pink Rocks** (near Broulee).

You can't beat the views from comfortable, friendly **Zorba Motel** (☎ 4472 4804; Orient St; s/d $75/85; **P** ✕), while amenities at the **Bay Waters Inn** (☎ 4472 6344; cnr Princes & Kings Hwys; from $90; **P** ✕ ☕) make up for its north-of-the-river location: mini golf, a playground, a spa, tennis courts and more.

Well-equipped **Shady Willows Caravan Park** (☎ 4472 4972; www.shadywillows.com.au; cnr Old Princes Hwy & South St; sites $18-30, cabins from $46; ☕) shares the site with the **Batemans Bay YHA** (☎ 4472 4972; www.yha.com.au; cnr Old Princes Hwy & South St; dm $22-28, d $48-56; ☕).

Bay River Houseboats (☎ 4471 2253; www.bayriverhouseboats.com.au; Wray St) offers eight- and 10-berth boats.

Sam's (☎ 4472 6687; Orient St; mains $10-12; ✆ lunch Wed-Fri, dinner Wed-Mon; ✕) is a classic Italian joint with fresh seafood, unpretentious pasta and excellent pizza.

Starfish Deli (☎ 4472 4880; Promenade Plaza, Clyde St; mains $13-26; ✆ breakfast, lunch & dinner; ✕) buzzes with its waterfront dining area serving Tuscan steak and gourmet wood-fired pizzas and pasta.

Premier Motor Service (☎ 13 34 10; www.premierms.com.au) runs south to Eden ($30, 3½ hours) and north to Sydney ($35, 5½ hours), twice daily.

Murrays (☎ 13 22 51) runs bus services to Narooma ($19, two hours) and Canberra ($24, 2½ hours) at least daily.

AROUND BATEMANS BAY

About 60km inland from Batemans Bay, on the scenic road to Canberra, is **Braidwood**, home to many old buildings and a thriving arts-and-crafts community. There's unspoilt coast down the side roads south of **Moruya**, including **Eurobodalla National Park**, an area of many lakes, bays and inlets backed by spotted-gum forests. Eurobodalla is an Aboriginal word meaning 'place of many waters' and there are Aboriginal middens here, as well as native wildlife including potoroos, hooded plovers and white-footed dunnarts. Don't miss the incredible rock formations at **Bingie Bingie Point**. Contact the Narooma NPWS (following) for more information.

NAROOMA

☎ 02 / pop 3400

Narooma is a seaside holiday town, especially popular for serious sport fishing. The natural beauty of the waterfront (forest-edged inlets and lakes, emerald-green waters and rugged coastline) fades as you head up to the commercial centre on the hill.

The **Narooma visitor information centre** (☎ 4476 2881; Princes Hwy; ☑ 9am-5pm) is just south of the bridge, and there's an **NPWS information office** (☎ 4476 2888; cnr Princes Hwy & Field St; ☑ 8.30am-4.30pm Mon-Fri).

The **library** (☎ 4476 1164; Field St; ☑ 10am-5pm Mon-Fri, 9.30am-2pm Sat) has free Internet.

Cruise up the Wagonga River on the **Wagonga Princess** (☎ 4476 2665; Riverside Dr; adult/child $20/14). Call for a schedule of the three-hour cruises, which include a stop for a walk through the bush and some billy tea.

There are several **boat-hire** places along Riverside Dr and a nice **walk** along the inlet and around to the ocean, with safe **swimming** just inside the heads.

For **surfing**, Mystery Bay (between Cape Dromedary and Corunna Point) is rocky but good, as is Handkerchief Beach, especially at the north end. Narooma's Bar Beach is best when a southeasterly blows. Potato Point is popular.

The small **Lighthouse Museum**, in the visitor information centre, features an old Fresnel light.

Near pretty Wagonga Inlet, **Forsters Bay Lodge** (☎ 4476 2319; 55 Forsters Bay Rd; d $68-85) has six simple but comfortable rooms. The **Bay St B&B** (☎ 4476 3336; 5 Bay St; d $140-190) is central, with modern rooms and wide sunny verandas.

Whale Motor Inn (☎ 4476 2411; www.whalemotorinn.com; 104 Wagonga St; s/d from $100/115; P ⊠ ⊠) may well have large, clean rooms and a restaurant offering room service, but **Lynch's Hotel** (☎ 4476 2001; 135 Wagonga St; s/d $40/60) has been serving the bushed and parched for over 100 years. It offers basic pub accommodation and cheap beers late at night.

East's Narooma Shores Holiday Park (☎ 4476 2046; www.easts.com.au; Princes Hwy; sites from $19, d cabins from $50) has over 260 camp sites and 43 cabins.

Casey's Café (☎ 4476 1241; 120 Wagonga St; meals $6-12; ☑ breakfast & lunch) does the best coffee in town alongside fantastic smoothies, burgers, salads and sandwiches.

The elegant interior at **Pelicans at the Marina** (☎ 4476 2403; 31 Riverside Dr; meals $10-17; ☑ breakfast & lunch Tue-Sun) yields enticing views of the harbour. The menu features oysters five ways and specials such as prawns in cumquat glaze.

Premier Motor Service (☎ 13 34 10; www.premierms.com.au) stops in Narooma on the run between Sydney and Melbourne. **Murrays** (☎ 13 22 51) stops on its daily run between Narooma and Canberra via Batemans Bay.

AROUND NAROOMA

About 10km offshore from Narooma, **Montague Island** was once an important source of food for local Aborigines (who called it Barunguba) and is now a nature reserve. **Fairy penguins** nest here and although you'll see some year-round, there are over 10,000 in late winter and spring. Many other seabirds and hundreds of sea lions make their homes on the island. There's also a historic **lighthouse**.

The only way to see the island is via a 30-minute **boat trip** (☎ 02-4476 2881; adult/child $89/69) and three-hour tours are conducted by a NPWS guide. Book ahead through the visitor information centre and take the afternoon trip if you want to see the fairy penguins.

The clear waters around the island are good for diving. **Island Charters Narooma** (☎ 02-4476 1047; www.islandchartersnarooma.com; 16 Old Princes Hwy) offers diving, snorkelling, whale watching and other tours starting from $65 per person. Attractions in the area include grey nurse sharks, sea lions and the wreck of the SS *Lady Darling*.

Off the highway, 15km south of Narooma, **Central Tilba** is perched on the side of **Mt Dromedary** (797m). It's a delightful 19th-century gold-mining boomtown.

There's information at the **Bates Emporium** (☎ 02-4473 7290; ☺ 8am-5pm), which is at the start of the main street. It also serves as a community centre and post office.

Visit the **ABC Cheese Factory** (☎ 02-4473 7387; Bate St, Central Tilba; ☺ 9am-5pm), producer of fine cheesy comestibles, like the smoked and honey varieties.

From the nearby town of **Tilba Tilba** you can hotfoot it to the top of Mt Dromedary (also called Gulaga). The return walk (11km) takes about five hours.

South of the beautiful bird-filled **Wallaga Lake** and off the Princes Hwy, **Bermagui** (population 2000) is a pretty fishing port, made famous when writer Zane Grey included it in his fishy tome, *An American Angler in Australia* (see the boxed text, p222).

The **Bermagui visitor information centre** (☎ 02-6493 3054; info@bigfoot.com.au; 18 Lamont St, Bermagui; ☺ 10am-4pm) is just beyond the marina.

Stay at **Horseshoe Bay Hotel/Motel** (☎ 02-6493 4206; 10 Lamont St, Bermagui; dm $10-20, motel r $49, pub r $60-135; P 🞶), with basic motel rooms, dorms and recently renovated pub rooms, some with balconies and spas overlooking the bay.

Eat at **Saltwater** (☎ 02-6493 4328; 59 Lamont St, Bermagui; mains $15-25; ☺ lunch Wed-Sun, dinner Thu-Sat, takeaway noon-8pm Tue-Sun), reason enough to come to town with the freshest seafood on the coast.

Bermagui is a handy base for visits to **Gulaga/Wallaga Lake** and Mimosa Rocks National Park (below).

On the Princes Hwy is **Cobargo**, another unspoilt old town. Near here is the main 2WD access to rugged **Wadbilliga National Park**, a sub-alpine wilderness area of 77,000 hectares.

SOUTH TO THE VICTORIAN BORDER

Just north of Tathra, the beautiful, thickly wooded **Mimosa Rocks National Park** hugs 17km of coastline ranging from dramatic weather-pounded volcanic rock to lagoons and beaches. There are several camping grounds here.

South of Tathra, the 2590-hectare **Bournda National Park** (admission per car $6) has got the flamin' lot: good beaches, walking trails, tea-tree forests, heaths, freshwater lagoons saltwater lakes, various headlands with good views, and interesting bird life including little terns and the intriguing pied oystercatcher.

Camping (per person $8) is permitted at Hobart Beach, on the southern shore of the big **Wallagoot Lagoon**. Contact the **Merimbula NPWS office** (☎ 02-6495 5000; cnr Merimbula & Sapphire Coast Drs; ☺ 8.30am-4.30pm Mon-Fri) for more information.

Merimbula
☎ 02 / pop 4900

Merimbula is a big and bustling holiday resort and retirement town, where locals love to big-up the impressive 'lake' (even though it's actually a large inlet) and the beaches speak for themselves. Despite mushrooming motel and apartment development, the setting remains appealing.

INFORMATION
The **Merimbula tourist information centre** (☎ 6497 4900; www.sapphirecoast.com.au; Beach St; ☺ 9am-5pm Mon-Sat, 9am-4pm Sun) is on the waterfront and has a **booking office** (☎ 1800 150 457 6497 4901) for accommodation, tours and activities.

Book park tours, walks and camp sites at the **NPWS Discovery Centre** (☎ 6495 5000; cnr Merimbula & Sapphire Coast Drs; ☺ 8.30am-4.30pm Mon-Fri).

DragNet (☎ 1300 662 344; Shop 3/11 Merimbula Dr; per hr $8; ☺ 9am-5pm Mon-Sat) has Internet access (with wi-fi).

SIGHTS & ACTIVITIES
At the wharf's eastern point is the small **Wharf Aquarium** (☎ 6495 4446; Lake St; adult/child $9/5; ☺ 10am-5pm), which holds shoals of tropical fish and sharks in large tanks.

A **nature boardwalk** follows the estuary southwest of the causeway and **diving** is popular, with plenty of fish and several wrecks including the large *Empire Gladstone*, which sunk in 1950. There are good views across the lake from near here and the jetty is a popular fishing spot.

The **Old School Museum** (☎ 6495 2114; Main St; adult/child $2/free; ☺ 2-4pm Tue, Thu & Sun) is a delightful volunteer-run museum featuring knick-knackery from over the years and local-history displays.

Nearby **Pambula Beach** is quiet, in a suburban kind of way.

SLEEPING & EATING

Town Centre Motor Inn (☎ 6495 1163; 8-10 Princes Hwy; s/d $60/70; **P** 🏊 🖥) Has 20 large rooms, with good views, over three levels.

Seachange B&B (☎ 6495 3133; www.sapphire coast.com.au/seachange; 49 Imlay St; s/d from $100/125; **P**) Comfortable, modern and 2km out of town, with fantastic water views and well-appointed rooms.

Wandarrah YHA Lodge (☎ 6495 3503; www.yha .com.au; 8 Marine Pde; dm $22-27, d $48-58; **P** 🖥) This spacious lodge near the surf beach, is good and clean and offers tours to Eden and nearby national parks.

Crown Apartments (☎ 6495 2400; www.crowna partments.com.au; 23 Beach St; d $125-225; **P** 🏊 🖥) Has a zingy design. One- and two-bedroom units come with full kitchens, balconies and great views.

Zanzibar Café (☎ 6495 4038; cnr Main & Market Sts; mains $22-30; 🕙 dinner Tue-Sat) Features a varied Mod Oz menu, huge plate-glass windows and a patio.

Donna's Cantina (☎ 6495 1085; 56 Market St; tapas $11, mains $22; 🕙 lunch & dinner) Features imaginative seafood and Spanish and Mediterranean dishes. Take your tapas outside and toast the throngs with a glass of vino.

GETTING THERE & AWAY

Regional Express Airlines (Rex; ☎ 13 17 13; www .regionalexpress.com.au) has several daily flights to Melbourne (from $120) and Sydney (from $150).

Greyhound Australia (☎ 13 20 30; www.greyhound .com.au) and **Premier Motor Service** (☎ 13 34 10; www.premierms.com.au) buses stop in Merimbula.

Countrylink (☎ 13 22 32; www.countrylink.nsw .gov.au) stops here on the four-times-weekly Eden to Canberra run.

Eden

☎ 02 / pop 3200

Eden, on Twofold Bay, is much less touristy than towns further up the coast; this old whaling port is a place of much charm.

The welcoming **Eden visitor information centre** (☎ 6496 1953; cnr Princes Hwy & Mitchell St; 🕙 9am-5pm) is in the same building as the **library** (☎ 6496 1687; per hr $6; 🕙 9am-5pm Mon-Fri, 9am-noon Sat), which has Internet access.

At the wonderful **Killer Whale Museum** (☎ 6496 2094; 94 Imlay St; adult/child $6/2; 🕙 9.15am-3.45pm Mon-Sat, 11.15am-3.45pm Sun), read about a modern-day Jonah, a heroic porpoise and,

perhaps most extraordinarily, treacherous Old Tom (see the boxed text, p222).

Cat Balou Cruises (☎ 6496 2027; 11 Cocora St) has whale-spotting cruises (adult/child $60/55) in October and November. At other times of the year, dolphins, sea lions and sea birds can usually be seen during the shorter bay cruise ($28/17).

There's a good whale **lookout** at the base of Bass St.

South of Eden, the road turns away from the coast and runs through beautiful forests. Inland is the gorgeous **South East Forest National Park**.

In October Eden comes alive for the **Whale Festival**, with a carnival, street parade and stalls, and oddball local events like the Slimy Mackerel Throw.

Twofold Bay Motor Inn (☎ 6496 3111; 164-166 Imlay St; r $77-165; **P** 🏊 🖥) is centrally located, with 24 units and a tiny indoor pool. Rooms are well equipped and some have nice views down to the water.

Dating from 1845, the **Crown & Anchor Inn** (☎ 6496 1017; www.crownandanchoreden.com.au; 239 Imlay St; s/d from $110/130; **P**) has been beautifully restored. It has a lovely Twofold Bay view from the back patio and five rooms with stylish period furniture.

Eden Tourist Park (☎ 6496 1139; Aslings Beach Rd; powered/unpowered sites $20/17, cabins from $55) has 160 sites and is situated on a spit separating Aslings Beach from Lake Curalo.

Eden is known for its oysters. Slurp the food of love down at **Oyster Bar** (☎ 6496 1304; 253 Imlay St; mains $15; 🕙 breakfast & lunch daily, dinner Thu-Sat), an atmospheric, tiny seafood café serving fresh and often garlicky treats.

Wheelhouse (☎ 6496 3392; 253 Imlay St; mains $25-30; 🕙 lunch & dinner) dishes up local seafood, served simply and done every which way. Oysters and mussels are specialities and there are good views of the harbour's tugs and fishing boats, too.

Greyhound Australia (☎ 13 20 30; www.greyhound .com.au) and **Premier Motor Service** (☎ 13 34 10; www.premierms.com.au) buses stop in Eden. **Countrylink** (☎ 13 22 32; www.countrylink.nsw.gov.au) runs four trains weekly to Canberra.

Ben Boyd National Park & Around

Protecting some of failed entrepreneur Ben Boyd's relics (see the boxed text, p222), this 10,407-hectare national park has dramatic coastline and isolated beaches. The main access road to the park is the sealed Edrom Rd, which leaves the Princes Hwy about 25km south of Eden.

Wonboyn Rd is 4km south of Edrom Rd, and gives access to **Nadgee Nature Reserve** and to **Wonboyn**, a small settlement on Wonboyn Lake at the northern end of the reserve. Many roads in the parks have unsealed sections that can be slippery after rain.

Wonboyn Cabins & Caravan Park (☎ 02-6496 9131; d sites $18-30, cabins $50-115; ☒) is spacious and has some friendly rainbow lorikeets.

Green Cape Rd is closer to the highway, off Edrom Rd; it runs right down to Green Cape, from where there are some good views and a **lighthouse**, of which you can take **tours** (☺ 1pm & 3pm). You can also spend the night here: two **cottages** (☎ 02-6495 5000; www.nationalparks.nsw.gov.au; cottages $165-250) that belonged to the lighthouse keepers have been lavishly restored, each sleeping six.

Nadgee Nature Reserve continues down the coast from Ben Boyd National Park. Much of it is official Wilderness Area, but vehicle access is allowed as far as the ranger station near the Merrica River, 7km from Newton's Beach.

SNOWY MOUNTAINS

The Snowy Mountains – the Snowies – form part of the Great Dividing Range where it straddles the NSW–Victorian border. After the flatlands of western NSW, the winding roads, steep canyons and jagged peaks are a welcome and dramatic change.

Mt Kosciuszko (pronounced 'kozzee-osko' and named after a Polish hero of the American War of Independence), in NSW, is Australia's highest mainland summit (2228m).

Much of the Snowies are contained within Kosciuszko National Park, an area of year-round interest, with skiing (p234) in winter, and a myriad of activities including bushwalking in summer.

The upper waters of the Murray River form both the state and national-park boundaries in the southwest. The Snowy River, made famous by Banjo Paterson's poem *The Man from Snowy River* and the film based on it, rises just below the summit of Mt Kosciuszko. The Murrumbidgee River also rises in the national park.

You can take white-water rafting trips on the Murray River in summer, when the water is high enough, and fishing and horse riding are quite popular. This is the start of serious snow country and it can truly become a winter wonderland.

Getting There & Away

Cooma is the eastern gateway to the Snowy Mountains. The most spectacular mountain views can be enjoyed from the Kosciuszko Alpine Way (sometimes closed in winter), running between Khancoban, on the western side of the national park, and Jindabyne. You'll need a car to use this road. There are restrictions on car use in the national park during the ski season; check with the NPWS or visitors centres at Cooma or Jindabyne before entering.

If you are just going to one place to ski, then public transport is an option. Otherwise you'll need a car, which does let you fully appreciate the region.

Canberra is the closest airport with decent service to the Snowies.

COOMA

☎ 02 / pop 6900

Cooma is part country town, part mountain town. As such it's a charming combination of both with good places to hang out, an attractive centre and a laid-back vibe. The drive on the Monaro Hwy from the south traverses rolling hills, whose beauty is the converse of their simplicity.

Cooma has a **visitors centre** (☎ 1800 636 525, 6450 1742; www.visitcooma.com.au; 119 Sharp St; ☺ 9am-5pm Sep-May, 7am-5pm Jun-Aug; ☐) and there are numerous ski shops that rent gear and offer an avalanche of advice.

SIGHTS & ACTIVITIES

The **Snowy Mountains hydro-electric scheme information centre** (☎ 1800 623 776, 6453 2004; www .snowyhydro.com.au; ☺ 8am-5pm Mon-Fri, 8am-2pm Sat & Sun), on the Princes Hwy 2km north of town, has hi-tech interactive exhibits and videos of this amazing project, which took 25 years and more than 100,000 people to build.

It's also a good place to find out about visits to the three power stations in the area. Portions of the project are now under renovation and you can learn about details of this complex process.

In town, the **Avenue of Flags**, in Centennial Park, flies the flags of the 28 nationalities involved in the construction.

The heritage walk around town is a good way to take in the sights and historical buildings, and to get a flavour for Cooma's late-19th-century history. Maps are available from the visitors centre, where you can also arrange to tour **Cooma Gaol** (although it sometimes is pressed back into use).

The **Cooma Monaro Railway** (☎ 1800 636 525; adult/child $12/5) is a surviving relic of the line that once went as far as Sydney (and it still should!). On most weekends volunteers fire up a train and take passengers north to Bunyan and Chakola (20km). Call for schedules.

Sleeping & Eating

Cooma has some excellent restaurants and one very good hotel in particular. Most pubs also have pretty good food.

Royal Hotel (☎ 6452 2132; cnr Sharp & Lambie Sts; r from $30) On a beautiful tree-lined street, the Royal is one of the few places in town where elaborate verandas survive (ask for a room with access). This grand 1858 pub has a delightful local character and there are lots of tables inside and out.

White Manor (☎ 6456 1152; www.whitemanor.com; 252 Sharp St; s/d from $65/70; ⚡) This is a very comfortable and central motel. The 12 units take in flower-scented breezes from the owners' container garden and have nice features such as satellite TV.

Bunkhouse Motel (☎ 6452 2983; www.bunkhouse motel.com.au; 30 Soho St; dm/d from $30/55) Each dorm in this friendly place has its own kitchen and bathroom, the doubles are comfortable and there's a quiet, vine-covered courtyard.

Sketches (☎ 6452 1477; Royal Hotel, cnr Sharp & Lambie Sts; meals $22-25; ⚡ lunch & dinner Tue-Sat) This bistro has Mediterranean-influenced steaks and pasta.

Elevation (☎ 6452 1466; 170 Sharp St; meals $12-24; ⚡ dinner Tue-Sat) The Art Deco interior fits right in with the artfully presented Mod Oz cuisine. Steaks come with a variety of sauces; pasta in variations that include creative numbers, such as 'Funghi' (mushrooms, garlic and shallots).

The Lott (☎ 6452 1414; 178-180 Sharp St; meals $6-12; ⚡ breakfast, lunch & dinner) This is the place for a cosy atmosphere, hearty meals and good coffee.

Getting There & Away

Transborder Express buses stop near Centennial Park, all others stop at Snowstop Village on Sharp St, a few blocks east of the visitor information centre.

Snowliner Travel (☎ 6452 1584; Sharp St), situated opposite the visitors centre, handles bus bookings. **Transborder Express** (☎ 6241 0033; www.transborderexpress.com.au) runs services for CountryLink and has services to/from Canberra and Canberra airport ($37, 90 minutes). Some runs continue into the hills via Jindabyne to Thredbo ('Alpinexpress' $31, 70 minutes) while others go south to Eden ($30, three hours) and the coast.

Victoria's **V/Line** (☎ 13 61 96; www.vline.com.au) has a twice-weekly run between Melbourne and Canberra via Cooma. The nine-hour trip from Melbourne goes by train to Sale, then on to Canberra by bus.

JINDABYNE

☎ 02 / pop 4400

Occupying a somewhat artificial location on an artificial lake, Jindabyne is the closest major town to the ski resorts. At peak times the population can quintuple. The rest of the year (temperatures permitting) you can take your pick from white-water rafting, horse riding, mountain biking, swimming, sailing and wakeboarding.

INFORMATION

The large NPWS-operated **Snowy Region visitors centre** (☎ 6450 5600; ⚡ 8.30am-5pm) is in the centre of town on Kosciuszko Rd and has good displays. The regional website (www.snowymountains.com.au) is also helpful.

Snowprint Bookshop (☎ 6457 1115; 141 Snowy Ave) manages to pack a café and a good selection of regional titles into its compact space.

ACTIVITIES

Dozens of local adventure companies offer a huge range of activities.

Snowy River Horseback Adventure (☎ 6457 8385; www.snowyriverhorsebackadventure.com.au), on the Barry Way about 30km southwest of Jindabyne, suits more experienced riders and has half-day rides ($95) plus much longer ones.

Upper Murray Rafting (☎ 1800 677 179; www.kos.com.au/rafting) operates white-water rafting trips out of Jindabyne with half-day trips starting at $65; longer trips are possible.

Paddy Pallin (☎ 6456 2922; www.paddypallin.com
.au; cnr Kosciuszko & Thredbo Rds) rents out tents
and other walking equipment, and offers
an impressive range of summer activities,
including guided alpine hikes (from $298)
through the mountains.

Kosciuszko Alpine Guided Walks (☎ 1800 020
524; Novotel Lake Crackenback Resort, Kosciuszko Alpine
Way) offers a tremendous range of guided
walks from $25.

Sleeping

Winter (high season) sees a huge influx
of visitors; prices soar, many places are
booked out months ahead and overnight
accommodation all but disappears. Prices
also rise on Friday and Saturday nights
throughout the year.

Banjo Paterson Inn (☎ 6456 046 275, 6456 2372;
www.banjopatersoninn.com.au; 1 Kosciuszko Rd; r $70-250)
Rooms at this snazzy lakefront place have
balconies and good facilities, and there's
a decent bar and onsite restaurant called
Clancy's.

Snowy Mountains Backpackers (☎ 1800 333 468,
6456 1500; www.snowybackpackers.com.au; 7 Gippsland
St; dm/d low season $20/50, high season $35/80; ☐) In
the heart of town, and with newish, clean,
bright rooms. Cafe Susu is a find (right).

Snowline Caravan Park (☎ 1800 248 148, 6456
2099; www.snowline.com.au; sites/cabins from $21/45;
☒) A very nice lakeside place with a huge
number of camping sites and cabins.

There are numerous places full of character scattered about the hills here. Some
recommendations:

Bimblegumbie (☎ 6456 2185; www.bimblegumbie
.com.au; Kosciuszko Alpine Way; d/cabins from $120/220)
Friendly place with comfortable cabins and B&B rooms.
Magical gardens.

Crackenback Farm (☎ 6456 2198; www.crackenback
.com; Kosciuszko Alpine Way; r from $150; ☒) Day spa,
great restaurant (book for lunch and dinner) historic cottage rooms, friendly farm animals and a maze.

USEFUL INFORMATION

The following telephone numbers provide
useful information about the park:

Weather (☎ 02-6450 5550)
Road conditions (☎ 02-6450 5551)
Park Snow Report (winter) (☎ 02-6450
5553)
Resort conditions (www.ski.com.au)

Eating

Il Lago (☎ 6456 1171; 19 Nugget's Crossing; mains $22-27;
☽ lunch winter, dinner Wed-Mon) A complex pasta
menu and pizza with many local fans.

Sundance Bakery & Café (Nugget's Crossing; snacks
$2-5; ☽ breakfast & lunch) A sweet-smelling
bakery with top breakfasts and good sandwiches and salads.

Cafe Susu (☎ 6456 1503; Gippsland St; meals $8-15;
☽ breakfast, lunch & dinner) Gorgeous breakfasts
set the daily pace for fine things later in the
day (burgers etc). There's live jazz some
nights.

KOSCIUSZKO NATIONAL PARK

The closest you'll get to Switzerland (but
without the attitude, just the altitude) is this
jewel in the national-park crown. NSW's
largest national park (6900 sq km) includes
caves, lakes, forest, ski resorts and the country's highest mountain at 2228m, Mt Kosciuszko. The busiest time is winter, but
it's also popular in summer when there are
excellent bushwalks and marvellous alpine
wildflowers (in January). Recently, people
have been drawn to see the park's regeneration after the horrible fires of 2002–03 (see
the boxed text, p234).

The major draw is Mt Kosciuszko and
the main ski resorts in the south of the
park. Charlotte Pass is the highest resort
village in Australia. It's less than 8km from
the top of Mt Kosciuszko, and there's an
18km round-trip walking track to the
summit. There are several other walking
tracks from Charlotte Pass, including a
20km walk, which includes Blue, Albina
and Club Lakes.

From Jindabyne, Kosciuszko Rd leads
through Sawpit Creek (15km) to Perisher
Valley (33km) and on to Charlotte Pass
(40km). The spectacular Kosciuszko Alpine Way runs from Jindabyne to Thredbo
(33km) and around to Khancoban (116km)
on the southwestern side of the mountains.
Accessibility on all roads is subject to snow
conditions.

Entry to the national park, including the
ski resorts, costs $16 per car, per day. There
are NPWS offices in Khancoban (p236) and
Tumut (p236) and the main visitors centre
is in Jindabyne (p231).

Take adequate clothing and be prepared
for all conditions; even in summer there is
sometimes snow on the ground.

Sleeping

In summer most of the resorts close, but good deals can be found at Thredbo (p235), and guesthouses and retreats elsewhere in the park. For the ski season, book as early as possible. Costs vary enormously: for example a two-bedroom apartment in Thredbo could cost about $3000 per week during the peak ski season (roughly mid-July to early September) and a double room in a lodge around $1000. It's unlikely that you'll find overnight accommodation on the mountain in peak season. There's a good chance that you'll pay considerably less than this if you shop around. Many agents book accommodation and packages on the ski fields.

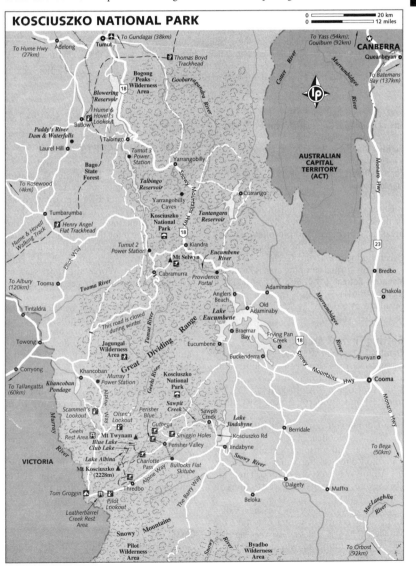

KOSCIUSZKO NATIONAL PARK

KOSCIUSZKO & FIRE

Six forest fires started in Kosciuszko National Park on 17 December 2002. Crews were easily containing these typical summer blazes, when on 8 January 2003, an electrical storm started 160 more in the park and surrounding region. Soon these fires combined and caused devastation over a vast area. By the time crews got control in March, over 321,000 hectares of the park's 690,000 hectares was damaged; 90% of the southern part of the park had burned.

As you drive the Kosciuszko Alpine Way you will see kilometre after kilometre of scorched land. However even under this scorched earth there are signs of life. The eucalyptus trees are actually designed with fires in mind. The heat triggers dormant buds under the tough bark, which sprout and make the scarred trunks look as though they are covered with odd vines. The fate of the other major tree in this region, the Alpine Ash, is more in doubt. A fire in 1984 wiped out much of the Alpine Ash population, which triggered seeds in the ground to sprout. However, the new trees normally don't drop their own replacement seeds for 20 years, so the fires of 2002–03 may have wiped out the ash before it could reseed itself.

Recommended specialists:

Snowy Mountains Reservation Centre (☎ 1800 020 622; www.snowholidays.com.au)

Perisher Blue Snow Holidays (☎ 1300 655 811; www.perisherblue.com.au)

Thredbo Resort Centre (☎ 1800 020 589; www .thredbo.com.au)

Bush camping is permitted in many areas of the national park. Some riverside picnic areas have fireplaces and pit toilets. There's a string of five along the Alpine Way between Bullocks Flat and Geehi.

The only formal camping area is **Kosciuszko Mountain Retreat** (☎ 02-6456 2224; www.kositreat .com.au; sites/cabins $16/$66), a tranquil place in bushland at Sawpit Creek, along the road to Perisher Valley.

Getting There & Around

Transborder Express (☎ 6241 0033; www.transborder express.com.au) runs services for CountryLink and has service to/from Thredbo via Jindabyne to Cooma ('Alpinexpress' $31, 70 minutes) and Canberra airport ($64, three hours).

In Cooma you can connect with V/Line (p231) for Melbourne.

In winter you must carry chains on Kosciuszko Rd to Perisher Valley as well as on the Alpine Way west of Thredbo. There are also severe winter parking restrictions in Perisher Valley.

The best way to get to Perisher Valley and nearby resorts in winter is to take the **Skitube** (☎ 02-6456 2010; same-day return trip adult/ child $32/$18), a tunnel railway up to Perisher Valley and Mt Blue Cow from below the

snow line at Bullocks Flat, 14km east of Thredbo on the Alpine Way.

SKIING & SKI RESORTS

Skiing or snowboarding are marginal activities in Australia. The winter ski season is short (July, August and early September and good snow isn't always guaranteed, although the increased use of snow-making machines is making it more so. Nor are the mountains ideal for downhill skiing – their gently rounded shapes mean that most long runs are relatively easy and the harder runs short and sharp. Worse, the short season mean operators have to get their return quickly, so costs are high.

The good news is that when the snow is there and the sun is shining, the skiing can be superb and the resorts are great fun. You'll find lively nightlife, decent restaurants, fine scenery and enough frightening slopes to keep you interested.

The resorts tend to be especially crowded on weekends because they're so convenient to reach, particularly when coming from Canberra.

The open slopes are a ski-tourer's paradise: Nordic (also known as cross-country or langlauf) skiing is popular and most resorts offer lessons and hire out equipment. The national park includes some of the country's best trails, and often old cattle herders' huts are the only form of accommodation apart from your tent.

Costs

Group lessons, including a lift ticket, cost about $110/60 a day per adult/child. Ski equipment such as boots, skis and stocks can be hired for around $40 a day. It will cost less for longer periods, and if you hire them away from the mountain (although if you have a problem with the fit, you may be stuck).

There are hire places in towns close to the resorts and many garages hire out ski equipment and chains.

Thredbo

☎ 02 / pop 2900

Thredbo has the longest run (3km through 670m of vertical drop) in the country and some of Australia's best skiing. As well as the long runs, the absence of T-bar lifts makes Thredbo popular with snowboarders. Turbo-charged snow-making machines have improved the ride.

The cost for lift tickets is adult/child $87/47 per day, or $374/215 per five-day pass. There is a plethora of packages, including lessons and access to special beginners' and children's areas.

The chairlift to the top of Mt Crackenback runs right through the summer (return adult/child $24/12). From the top of the chairlift it is about a 2km walk to a lookout point with good views of Mt Kosciuszko, or it's 7km to the top of the mountain itself.

Unlike other resorts, Thredbo is a good place to visit in summer, with many scenic bushwalking tracks and plenty of activities, including mountain biking, bobsledding, fly-fishing, platypus-spotting and golf. **Thredbo Resort Centre** (☎ 1800 020 589, 6459 4294; www.thredbo.com.au; Friday Dr) is well-stocked with visitor information. Services are in the compact centre, but the hills are lined with apartments and lodges.

SLEEPING & EATING

Trying to ferret out a winter place to stay may require a bit of digging through the booking websites. There are lots of dining choices in the centre.

Kasee's (☎ 6457 6370; www.kasees.com.au; r summer from $100, ski season from $160) A very cosy place. Rooms have kitchens and balconies, and guests can use the Finnish sauna or mellow out around the open fire.

Thredbo YHA Lodge (☎ 6457 6376; www.yha .com.au; 8 Jack Adams Pathway; dm/d summer $23/54, rates higher in ski season) Comfortable with a lively balcony. A ballot is held in April for high-season spaces; check the website for details.

Sante (☎ 6457 6083; Squatters Run, Mowamba Mall; mains $30; ✓ dinner Tue-Sat) The best place to eat soothes the spirits with a rustic and dark interior. To help recover from the day's exertions, the inventive menu is meaty – half the people order one of the superb steaks. Some even squeeze in one of the famous chocolate desserts.

Perisher Blue

☎ 02 / elevation 1720m

Perisher Blue (☎ 6459 4495, 1300 655 811; www .perisherblue.com.au), which includes Perisher Valley, Smiggin Holes, Mt Blue Cow and Guthega, has 53 lifts accessible with one ticket. There's alpine and cross-country runs, valley and bowl skiing, snowboarding areas (Dude!) and more.

Perisher Valley (1720m) has a good selection of intermediate runs. Guthega (1640m) is mainly a day resort best suited to intermediate and beginner skiers, as it's smaller and less crowded. Mt Blue Cow (1640m), between Perisher Valley and Guthega, has beginner to intermediate skiing.

Lift tickets cost $87/48 per adult/child for a day, and $376/219 for a five-day pass. Many types of packages are available. In winter you can only park in the resort if you have accommodation that provides it and you must carry chains – that's why daytrippers take the Skitube (opposite). This may change, however, as there are proposals to greatly expand the resort and plow the road through the winter. Locals and environmentalists contend that plowing will fill the pristine areas with cars and cause other damage.

Most accommodation is in Perisher Valley and Smiggin Holes.

Chalet Sonnenhof (☎ 6457 5256; www.sonnenhof .com.au; d summer $240) is one of the few Perisher lodges open in summer. Rates include breakfast and dinner.

Charlotte Pass

☎ 02 / elevation 1780m

At the base of Mt Kosciuszko, **Charlotte Pass** (☎ 6457 5458; www.charlottepass.com.au) is the highest, and one of the oldest and most isolated resorts in Australia. In winter you have to snowcat the last 8km from Perisher Valley (one way adult/child $35/25; you must book). Five lifts serve rather short but uncrowded runs and this is good ski-touring country. Daily lift passes cost $85/65 per adult/child.

Mt Selwyn

☎ 02 / elevation 1492m

Halfway between Tumut and Cooma, **Mt Selwyn** (☎ 1800 641 064; www.selwynsnow.com.au), in the north of the park, is a day resort only. There is no access during the summer. It has 12 lifts, is ideal for beginners and families, and is also the cheapest resort (adult/child lift tickets cost $65/32.50).

There are motels and cabins 45km east in Adaminaby.

For something completely different, try the **Historic Currango Homestead** (☎ 02-6947 7025; www.currango.asn.au; beds from $30), an historic 1895 homestead managed by the NPWS. Beds are in twin rooms and there are also cabins. The surrounds are about as natural as you'd expect for the park and staying here is a chance to fully commune with nature.

The Kosciuszko Alpine Way

From **Khancoban** on the western side of the ranges, this spectacular and twisting route runs through dense forest around the southern end of Kosciuszko National Park to Thredbo and Jindabyne.

Two of the best mountain views are from **Olsen's Lookout**, 10km off the Alpine Way on the Geehi Dam dirt road, and **Scammell's Lookout**, just off the Alpine Way at a good picnic spot.

Note that chains are required in winter for the portion of the Alpine Way west of Thredbo.

In Khancoban you won't have to wait to smell the roses as the scent from the many gardens permeates the air. The **NPWS office** (☎ 02-6076 9373; Scott St; ⏰ 8.30am-noon & 1-4pm) is very useful. Pick up the *Alpine Way Guide* and buy park-use tickets, books and maps. There are good displays on the 2002–03 fires.

There are several accommodation options at Khancoban.

The **Khancoban Alpine Inn** (☎ 02-6076 9471; www.alpineinn.com.au; Alpine Way; dm $20, s/d $55/65; ⏰) has a pleasant garden, a good **bistro** (mains $8-10) and a fun pub.

Tumut Area

☎ 02 / pop 6243

Tumut, a pretty town on the Snowy Mountains Hwy outside the northwestern side o the park, has a good regional **visitors centre** (☎ 6947 7025; www.tumut.nsw.gov.au; cnr Gocup & Ade long Rds; ⏰ 9am-5pm).

Yarrangobilly Caves (☎ 6454 9597; car entry $3 tours $11-14; ⏰ 9am-4pm), 77km south of Tumut are a complex of caverns in 440-million-year-old limestone. Three caves are oper and the sights are spectacular. Outside ir the open air, take one of the short walk and then enjoy the 27°C thermal pool beside the river.

The **NPWS office** (☎ 6454 9579; ⏰ 9am-5pm provides information for the northern par of the park, much of which wasn't affecter by the 2002–03 fires.

Near the fruit-growing town of Batlow south of Tumut, is **Hume & Hovell's Lookout** where the two explorers did just that ir 1824.

Paddy's River Dam, about 12km southeast off the road to Tumbarumba, was buil by Chinese gold-miners in the 1850s, anc there's a trail to the nearby **waterfalls**.

SOUTHWEST & THE MURRAY

This wide, endlessly rolling country ha some of the state's best farming areas anc its most interesting history. The Murray River forms the boundary between NSW and Victoria, with most of the larger town on the Victorian side. Part of this area i known as the Riverina because of the Mur ray and Murrumbidgee Rivers and thei tributaries.

Getting There & Around

Several roads run through the southwest the Hume Hwy being the major one. Ther are quieter routes such as Olympic Way which runs through Cowra, Wagga Wagg and Albury. Routes to Adelaide include th Sturt Hwy through Hay and Wentworth You'll also pass through the southwest i travelling between Brisbane and Melbourn on the Newell Hwy.

Major bus routes cross the region, run ning from Sydney and Brisbane to botl

Melbourne and Adelaide. Melbourne to Sydney bus services run on the Hume Hwy and trains run close to it.

THE HUME HIGHWAY

The Hume is the main road between Melbourne and Sydney, Australia's two largest cities. It's the fastest and shortest route, and although it's definitely not the most interesting, there are some worthwhile diversions along the way.

One of the simplest diversions is at the Sydney end: take the coastal Princes Hwy past Royal National Park to Wollongong. Just after Wollongong take the Illawarra Hwy up the picturesque Macquarie Pass to meet the Hume near Moss Vale.

Further south you can leave the Hume to visit Canberra or continue beyond Canberra through the Snowy Mountains on the Alpine Way, rejoining the Hume near Albury.

The Hume is a divided freeway most of the way from Sydney to the Victorian border, with a few stretches of narrow, two-lane road carrying a lot of traffic.

SYDNEY TO GOULBURN

The large towns of **Mittagong** and **Bowral** adjoin each other along the Hume Hwy. The Southern Highlands **visitors centre** (☎ 02-4871 2888; http://southern-highlands.com.au; 62-70 Main St, Mittagong; ◷ 9am-5pm Mon-Fri, 8.30am-4.30pm Sat & Sun) has comprehensive information.

The **Tulip Time Festival**, held in the area from the end of September to early October, is a brilliant show of spring colour.

Four kilometres south of town, a winding 65km road leads west to the **Wombeyan Caves** (☎ 02-4843 5976; www.jenolancaves.org.au; adult/child from $15/10; ◷ self-guided tour 8.30am-5pm), with their spectacular limestone formations. The drive up is through superb mountain scenery and there are pretty camp sites and cabins at the caves.

Bowral is where the late great cricketer Sir Donald Bradman, undoubtedly Australia's greatest sporting hero and the game's supreme batsman, spent his boyhood. There's a cricket ground here and the **Bradman Museum** (☎ 02-4862 1247; www.bradman.com.au; St Jude St; adult/child $8.50/4; ◷ 10am-5pm), which explores the history of the game downstairs while upstairs is dedicated to the life of 'the Don' himself.

Bowral has become quite popular with Sydney swells, and it has quite a renowned café and restaurant scene. Typical is the **Grand Bar & Brasserie** (☎ 02-4861 4783; Grand Arcade, 295 Bong Bong St; meals $9-27; ◷ breakfast Sat & Sun, lunch & dinner daily), an arcade café that has tables in and out, and serves up creative food throughout the day. There are lots of Mod Oz specials and the quality reflects the refined tastes of the locals.

A little further south along the Hume is tiny **Berrima**, founded in 1829 and remarkably little changed since then. It is full of art galleries, and interesting antique and used-book shops. The region boasts many wineries. The atmospheric **Surveyor General Inn** (☎ 02-4877 1226; Old Hume Hwy; r from $65) has comfy rooms with shared bathrooms and a fine bistro. The old sandstone **White Horse Inn** (☎ 02-4877 1204; www.whitehorseinn.com.au; Market Pl; r from $70) has tasteful rooms in white and yet another fine bistro.

South of Berrima is the small, appealing town of **Bundanoon**, one of the gateways to **Morton National Park**, which has the deep gorges and high sandstone plateaus of the **Budawang Range**. The park visitor centre is at **Fitzroy Falls** (☎ 02-4887 7270; Nowra Rd; vehicle entrance $3; ◷ 9am-5.30pm).

The **Bundanoon YHA Hostel** (☎ 02-4883 6010; www.yha.com.au; Railway Ave; sites per person $10, dm/d $22/52) occupies an old Edwardian guesthouse set in shady gardens.

CityRail has services from Bundanoon to Sydney ($15, 2½ hours); **CountryLink** (☎ 02-6041 9555, 13 22 32; www.countrylink.com.au) goes to Canberra ($27; two hours) via Goulburn. CountryLink buses run to Wollongong ($13, two hours).

GOULBURN

☎ 02 / pop 20,900

Founded in 1833, Goulburn is at the heart of a prosperous sheep-grazing district that's famous for its fine merino wool, hence the rather stern-looking three-storey **Big Merino** towering over the Old Hume Hwy in town. The shop attached will cater for all your sheep-based souvenir needs and you can even buy petrol. Venture up into the sheep's innards, which are packed with information about the wool trade. At the top you can gaze through his eyes at, appropriately enough, the giant woolsheds on the horizon.

Ask at the **visitors centre** (☎ 1800 353 646, 4823 4492; www.igoulburn.com; 201 Sloane St; ◷ 9am-5pm) for details on their much-loved organs. It also has a good self-guided walking-tour brochure taking in some of the town's handsome historic buildings, including the imposing 1887 **courthouse**. The **Old Goulburn Brewery** (☎ 4821 6071; 23 Bungonia Rd; adult $8; ◷ tours at 11am & 3pm), was designed in 1836 by convict and architect Francis Greenway, who also designed the Hyde Park Barracks in Sydney. After a tour, try the traditional ale in the fine pub.

YASS

☎ 02 / pop 4900

Another wool town, Yass is closely connected with the 1820s explorer Hamilton Hume, after whom the highway is named. The **visitors centre** (☎ 6226 2557; http://yass.nsw .gov.au; Comur St; ◷ 9am-4.30pm Mon-Fri, 9am-4pm Sat & Sun), on Coronation Park, has a historic town-walk map.

Next door is the **Yass & District Museum** (☎ 6226 2557; Comur St; admission $2), which has exhibits relating to Hume. The museum is run by volunteers, so check opening times at the visitors centre.

The **Hume and Hovell Walking Track**, which follows the route chosen by Hume and his sometime partner in exploration William Hovell, has some half-day and longer walks that begin here.

The National Trust–listed **Cooma Cottage** (☎ 6226 1470; adult/child $4.40/2.20; ◷ 10am-4pm Thu-Mon) was Hume's home from 1839 to 1873; the cottage is 4km out of town on the Yass Valley Way.

About 57km southeast of Yass, along some partially dirt roads, the limestone **Carey's Caves** (☎ 6227 9622; adult/child $11/7; ◷ tours noon & 1.30pm Fri-Mon) are at **Wee Jasper**. You can also join the Hume and Hovell Walking Track here.

GUNDAGAI

☎ 02 / pop 2000

Gundagai, 386km from Sydney, is a gem of a surviving 1860s town. The **visitors centre** (☎ 6944 0250; www.gundagaishire.nsw.gov.au; 249 Sheridan St; ◷ 8am-5pm Mon-Fri, 9am-noon & 1-5pm Sat & Sun) houses **Rusconi's Marble Masterpiece**, a 21,000-piece cathedral model. For the entry fee (adult/child $3/1.50) you get to hear a snatch of the tune 'Along the Road

to Gundagai', which you will then prob ably hum mindlessly for the next few day Rusconi also made the **Dog on the Tuckerbo** memorial, which you can see at the servic station situated 8km south of town on th Hume Hwy.

The impressive 1896 **Prince Alfred Bridg** (closed) and the adjacent 1903 Railwa Bridge span the flood plain of the Mu rumbidgee River. A series of floods cu minated in 1852 when Gundagai suffere Australia's worst flood disaster and 7 deaths were recorded. Only then were loca convinced to move the town to its curren spot on higher ground.

Gold rushes and bushrangers were pa of the town's colourful early history. Th notorious bushranger Captain Moonligh was tried in Gundagai's 1859 **courthouse** an is now buried in the town.

Other places of interest include **Gundag Historical Museum** (☎ 6944 1995; Homer St; admissi $3; ◷ 9am-3pm) and the **Gabriel Gallery** (☎ 69 1722; Sheridan St; admission free; ◷ 9am-5pm Mon-F 9am-noon Sat), which has a great display of hi toric photos. The latter is above the Mit 10 hardware shop.

Touches such as slate bathrooms an comfy furniture make **Poet's Recall** (☎ 69 1777; poets.recall@bigpond.com; cnr West & Punch Sts $65-100; ◷ ◷) the best motel in town.

Blue Heeler Guesthouse (☎ 6944 2286; bluehee ozemail.com.au; 145 Sheridan St; dm $20, d incl breakfa $40; ◷) is a refurbished backpackers lodg in what used to be the Hotel Gresham. has good kitchen and lounge areas, a ba cony overlooking the street, Internet acce and free bikes. The owners can help fin seasonal work in the surrounding orchar and farms.

Relive the 1930s at the **Niagara Cafe** (☎ 69 1109; 142 Sheridan St; mains $8-12; ◷ breakfast, lun & dinner), where the décor, and the men are frozen in time. Next door is a beautif fruit-and-veg shop.

HOLBROOK

☎ 02 / pop 1300

The halfway point between Sydney an Melbourne, Holbrook was known as Ge manton until WWI, during which it was r named after a British war hero; in Holbroo Park there's a replica of the submarine i which the brave deeds that earned him th Victoria Cross took place.

The **Woolpack Inn Museum** (☎ 6036 2131; 83 Albury St; adult/child $4/1; ☺ 9.30am-4.30pm) has tourist information and piles of donated old treasures'. Out back is an old schoolhouse: check out the artefact from a failed effort by kids long ago to realise every student's dream.

ALBURY WODONGA
☎ 02 / pop 69,880

Divided by the Murray River just below the Hume Weir, the towns of Albury (in NSW) and Wodonga (in Victoria) have merged. With many good restaurants, some lively bars (there are lots of university students) and a few places of interest, Albury is the more interesting bit of the conurbation. It's a good base for trips to the snowfields and high country of both Victoria and NSW, the vineyards around Rutherglen (Victoria), and the tempestuous upper Murray River (the river becomes languid below Albury). It's also a good spot to break the journey between Sydney and Melbourne.

Information
The large Albury Wodonga **visitors centre** (☎ 1300 796 222; www.destinationalburywodonga.com au; Hume Hwy; ☺ 9am-5pm), offering information on both NSW and Victoria, is over the bridge on the Wodonga side. It's in an interesting old butter factory called Gateway Village, which also has shops and cafés.

Sights & Activities
Albury Regional Museum (☎ 6021 4550; Wodonga Pl; admission free; ☺ 10.30am-4.30pm), in Noreuil Park, covers Aboriginal culture, the local ecosystem and 20th-century migration into the area. See the tree marked by explorer William Hovell on his 1824 expedition with Hume from Sydney to Port Phillip.

In town, the **Albury Regional Art Gallery** (☎ 6051 3480; 546 Dean St; admission free; ☺ 10.30am-5pm Mon-Fri, 10.30am-4pm Sat & Sun) has a small, permanent collection featuring Russell Drysdale and Fred Williams and contemporary Australian photography.

In summer you can swim in the Murray River in **Noreuil Park**. From September to April (water levels permitting) you can take a **river cruise** (☎ 6021 1113) on the replica paddle-steamer *Cumberoona*. Cruises start at $16 and schedules change, so ring ahead to check.

The gracious old **botanic gardens** (☎ 6023 8769) are at the north end of Wodonga Pl and have a worthwhile Rainforest Walk. Stroll up a small hill from the gardens to the small war memorial to enjoy good views of the fertile plain.

In November the annual **Ngangirra Festival**, which features Aboriginal art, music, dance and language, is held at Mungabareena Reserve.

Albury Backpackers (☎ 6041 1822; thecanoeguy@ hotmail.com) runs half-day to seven-day canoeing trips on the Murray and you don't have to stay at the hostel to join one. It's worth asking about bike hire as well; there are good cycling tracks around town and the visitors centre has a bike-track map.

See over 120 bird species in their native habitat at the **Wonga Wetlands** (☎ 6051 3800; Riverina Hwy, Splitters Creek), an innovative project to restore local wetlands using treated waste water. Call for tour information.

Oz E Wildlife (☎ 6040 3677; Ettamogah; adult/child $10/5; ☺ 9am-5pm), 11km north on the Hume Hwy, is a sanctuary for sick and injured local wildlife. The roos will enjoy your company.

A few kilometres north again, the cartoonesque **Ettamogah Pub** (☎ 6026 2366; Burma Rd; ☺ 10am-late) is just that: a real life version of the pub in Ken Maynard's old comic.

Jindera Pioneer Museum (☎ 6026 3622; Urana St; adult/child $5/1; ☺ 10am-3pm Tue-Sun) has lots of donated old stuff, in a somewhat better than usual setting; walk, don't run, to the 'poison cart'. It's 16km northwest of Albury, in Jindera.

Sleeping
Some motels are on busy streets such as Hume and Young and suffer from noise, especially from flatulent trucks.

Gundowring B&B (☎ 6041 4437; thudson@albury .net.au; 621 Stanley St; r $110-150) A great three-room B&B near the centre, and in a gorgeous Federation house a short walk from the botanic gardens.

Seaton Arms Motor Inn (☎ 6021 5999; cnr Olive & Wilson Sts; s/d from $90/100; ☒) Simple, unassuming and comfortable, this motel is in a good quiet spot in the centre.

Albury Backpackers (☎ 6041 1822; thecanoe guy@hotmail.com; 452 David St; dm/d $20/42; ☐) A well-run, central hostel with a good lounge area, a well-equipped kitchen and free bikes. The management organises adventure activities and can help you find farm work in the area.

Albury Motor Village (☎ 6040 2999; www.motor village.com.au/albury.htm; 372 Wagga Rd; sites/cabins per 2 people $21/65; 🔀 🐾) About 4.5km north of the centre, this is a tidy park with a range of cabins, caravans and backpacker beds in clean dorms.

Eating

Dean St has several fun blocks with good eateries and nightspots, especially around the junction with David St where quite a café culture has sprung up.

The Lounge (☎ 6021 5880; 453 Dean St; meals $14-24; 🕑 lunch Sat & Sun, dinner Tue-Sun) Open to midnight most nights, the Lounge is one of those new fusion places that combines comfy sofas, piles of glossy magazines, a bar and tables inside and out. The menu is as eclectic as the concept: sandwiches, pasta and Mediterranean-style snacks.

Thai Puka (☎ 6021 2504; 652 Dean St; mains from $13; 🕑 lunch & dinner) This upmarket Thai restaurant has an innovative menu, stylish surrounds and attracts a fun-filled young crowd.

Expresso Cafe (☎ 6041 4880; 449C Dean St; meals $5-10; 🕑 9am-9pm Mon-Sat, 9am-5pm Sun; 🖳) Burgers, Greek treats and excellent coffee. Survey the street scene from tables outside or surf the Internet inside.

Zen X (☎ 6023 6455; 467 Dean St; meals $7-15; 🕑 lunch Mon-Sat, dinner daily) A cute Japanese restaurant with quite good sushi and *teppanyaki*.

Sweet Chestnuts (☎ 6021 2977; Gateway Village; meals $9-20; 🕑 breakfast & lunch daily, dinner Thu-Sat) In a sparely furnished 150-year-old house near the visitors centre, this café-cum-restaurant has a great menu of regional food made with organic ingredients sourced locally.

Entertainment

Dean St has several good bars and pubs. The **New Albury Hotel** (☎ 6021 3599; 491 Kiewa St) has an Irish theme and live jazz on Sunday.

Getting There & Away

QantasLink (☎ 13 13 13; www.qantas.com.au) flies between Albury airport (code ABX) and Sydney (from $125). **Regional Express** (Rex; ☎ 13 17 13; www.regionalexpress.com.au) has ser-

vices to Sydney (from $120) and Melbourn (from $85).

CountryLink (☎ 6041 9555, 13 22 32; www.count link.com.au), at the grand Victorian train sta tion, books bus and train tickets. Buses sto here.

Greyhound Australia (☎ 13 14 99; www.greyhoun .com.au) runs between Sydney ($57, eigl hours) and Melbourne ($37, four hours).

V/Line (☎ 13 61 96; www.vline.com.au) has buse to Mildura (12 hours) along the Murra and trains to Melbourne (from $67, fou hours).

The nightly **XPT train service** (☎ 6041 955 between Sydney ($90, 7½ hours) and Me bourne ($60, 3½ hours) stops in Albur Most things are within walking distanc but you can call at taxi on ☎ 13 10 08.

WAGGA WAGGA

☎ 02 / pop 44,451

Wagga Wagga, on the Murrumbidge River, is the state's largest inland cit Despite its size, this very tidy city retai a relaxed country-town feel. The nam means 'place of many crows' in the loc Wiradjuri people's language and is us ally abbreviated to one word, pronounce 'wogga'. This is a good place to break you journey; forget your road cares at the man pubs in the centre.

Orientation & Information

The long main street, Baylis St, which run north from the train station, becomes Fitz maurice St at its northern end. The **visito centre** (☎ 6926 9621; www.tourismwaggawagga.cc .au; Tarcutta St; 🕑 9am-5pm) is close to the rive There's good Internet access at **Civic Vide** (☎ 6921 8866; 21 Forsyth St; 🕑 10am-10pm).

Sights & Activities

The excellent **botanic gardens** (☎ 6925 293 Baden Powell Dr; 🕑 dawn-dusk) are about 1.5k south of the train station. The interpretiv centre is open 11am to 3pm Thursday • Sunday; there's a small zoo and peacock roam free; and a kid-sized model railwa operates twice monthly.

The Civic Centre houses the **Wagga Wag** **Art Gallery** (☎ 6926 9660; admission free; 🕑 10ar 5pm Tue-Sat, noon-4pm Sun), home to the wonde ful National Art Glass Collection, whic provides an overview of the history an development of the studio glass moveme in Australia from the 1970s. Not only is the actual gallery space a superb configuration of water, light and glass, but the permanent exhibition is one of diverse colour and beauty.

The **Wiradjuri Walking Track**, which includes some lookouts, begins at the visitors centre (pick up a map here) and eventually returns here after a 30km tour of the area. There's a shorter 10km loop past Wollundry Lagoon.

From the **beach** near the Wagga Wagga Caravan Park you can go swimming and fishing. Wagga's flat, wide spaces make it suitable for cycling; pick up the bike-track brochure.

Military buffs will be interested in Wagga's long association with the armed forces; there's a self-guided drive brochure of **military sites** and **museums**.

Nearby wineries include **Wagga Wagga Winery** (☎ 6922 1221; Oura Rd; ☼ 11am-late), which has good wines and a great BBQ.

Sleeping

There are many motels to choose from. There are several along Tarcutta St, which fronts the Murrumbidgee River and is close to the centre of town.

Townhouse International (☎ 6921 4337; www .townhouseinternational.com.au; cnr Morgan & Fitzharding Sts; r $110-250; ☒ ☒) Right in the centre, this sleek place has modern and comfortable rooms. The pool is inside a health club. There's also a great restaurant, Three Chefs (right), here.

Centralpoint (☎ 6921 7272; 164-166 Tarcutta St; s/d from $87/108; ☒) There's nothing to sneeze at at this motel, which describes itself as 'allergy-conscious'. It's a solid choice and is across from the visitors centre.

Wagga Wagga Guesthouse (☎ 6931 8712; 149 Gurwood St; dm/d from $25/45; ☐) The only backpackers in town offers cheap weekly rates, if you have seasonal work in the area. Housed in a renovated weatherboard cottage, it has a friendly atmosphere and clean communal areas. The guesthouse also has bikes for hire.

Wagga Wagga Beach Caravan Park (☎ 6931 0603; 2 Johnston St; sites/cabins $15/55; ☒) Of the several caravan parks in the area, this one has the best location. It's on the river next to a swimming beach and is only a couple of blocks from the town centre.

EATING

Baylis/Fitzmaurice St has a diverse range of places to eat, including good coffee shops and bakeries.

Three Chefs (☎ 6921 5897; Townhouse International, 70 Morgan St; mains $14-22; ☼ breakfast & lunch Mon-Fri, dinner Mon-Sat) Two sisters and their husband are the namesakes of this excellent Mod Oz restaurant. The interior is slightly bland, which means there is no competition for the fine dishes using regional ingredients.

Magpies Nest Restaurant (☎ 6933 1523; cnr Old Narrandera & Pine Gully Rds; mains $20-27; ☼ lunch Wed-Sun, dinner Wed-Sat) Housed in restored stone stables, this place has outside seating that offers sweeping views of the town. The focus is on local produce: vegetables come straight from the garden and olive oil is crushed in-house.

Indian Tavern Tandoori (☎ 6921 3121; 176 Baylis St; dishes $8-17; ☼ dinner) Locals who love a tasty vindaloo support this popular eatery, perhaps the best regional Indian restaurant in NSW, in D'Hudson Arcade.

Getting There & Away

From Wagga Wagga (code WGA) **QantasLink** (☎ 13 13 13; www.qantas.com.au) flies daily to Sydney (from $105) and **Regional Express** (☎ 13 17 13; www.regionalexpress.com.au) flies to Sydney (from $100) and Melbourne (from $110).

Buses leave from the **train station** (☎ 13 22 32, 6939 5488; ☼ bookings 8.30am-5pm Mon-Fri). **Greyhound Australia** (☎ 13 14 99; www.greyhound.com.au) buses go to Sydney ($53, eight hours) and Adelaide ($110, 16 hours).

Wagga is on the railway line between Sydney ($78, six hours) and Melbourne ($78, 4½ hours) and there are two services daily with CountryLink and V/Line.

NARRANDERA

Near the junction of the Newell and Sturt Hwys, Narrandera is in the Murrumbidgee Irrigation Area (MIA). The **visitors centre** (☎ 1800 672 392, 02-6959 1766; www.narrandera.nsw .gov.au; Cadell St, Narrandera Park; ☼ 9am-5pm) hands out a walking-tour map of the town and **Lake Talbot**, which is partly a long, artificial lake, partly a big swimming complex. Bush (including a koala-regeneration area) surrounds the lake and a series of walking trails make up the **Bundidgerry Walking Track**. East St is good for cafés and motels.

GRIFFITH

☎ 02 / pop 16,005

Griffith was planned by Walter Burley Griffin, the American architect who designed Canberra, and it's the main town of the MIA.

Information

You'll find Griffith's helpful **visitors centre** (☎ 6962 4145; www.griffith.nsw.gov.au; cnr Banna & Jondaryan Sts; ☉ 9am-5pm) underneath a mounted WWII fighter plane. There's detailed information about local wine trails here.

The **NPWS office** (☎ 6966 8100; 200 Yambil St; ☉ 8.30am-4.30pm Mon-Fri) gives information about Cocoparra, Willandra and Oolambeyan National Parks.

Fast Internet access is available at the impressive and air-conditioned **library** (☎ 6962 2515; 233-237 Banna Ave; ☉ 9am-5.30pm Mon-Wed & Fri, 9am-7pm Thu, 9am-4pm Sat).

Sights & Activities

Descendants of the Italian farmers who helped to develop this area make up a large percentage of the population. You can visit eight local **wineries**; the visitors centre has opening times and a map.

On a hill northeast of the town centre, **Pioneer Park Museum** (☎ 6962 4196; Remembrance Dr; admission $7; ☉ 9am-4.30pm) is a re-creation of an early Riverina village. There's also a section on the contributions of Italians to the town (more than just cafés and wine!).

Cocoparra National Park, just east of Griffith, isn't large, but its forested hills and dry gullies provide some contrasts, and there's a fair presence of wildlife including turquoise parrots. There is a free camping ground on Woolshed Flat in the north.

Sample some of the lush local produce at **Catania Fruit Salad Farm** (☎ 6963 0219; Hanwood Cox Rd; adult/child $7.50/free; ☉ tours 1.30pm), 8km southeast of the centre.

Sleeping

Comfort In Gemini (☎ 6962 3833; www.choicehotels .com.au; 201 Banna Ave; r $80-130; ☒) This modern hotel is right in the centre of town and popular with business travellers.

Yambil Inn Motel (☎ 6964 1233; fax 6964 1355; 155-157 Yambil St; s/d $84/89; ☒ ☒) A pleasant motel in a quiet street near the main shops and restaurants.

Summit International Hostel (☎ 6964 4236; www .griffithinternational.com.au; 112 Binya St; dm from $19; ☐)

Across the road from the Anglican cathedral, this hostel is pretty rough around the edges and could use some maintenance.

Griffith Tourist Caravan Park (☎ 6964 2144; 91 Willandra Ave; sites/cabins $19/55; ☒ ☒) You can easily walk to the centre from this nicely laid-out park.

Eating

Italian is the region's dominant cuisine but there are alternatives.

Michelin (☎ 6964 9006; 72 Banna Ave; mains $20; ☉ brunch Sun, lunch & dinner Mon-Sat) All plate glass and minimal modernity, this stylish and modern French bistro works magic with local ingredients. The specials are always intriguing.

L'Oasis (☎ 6964 5588; 150 Yambil St; mains $15-20; ☉ lunch & dinner Tue-Sat) Diverse flavours (many from Asia), fresh produce and a wide selection of local wines make this place a local favourite. It's also open-air on balmy nights.

Vita's (☎ 6962 7999; 252-254 Banna Ave; meals $8-20; ☉ lunch & dinner) This elegant café and restaurant has a bit of glam about it. The wine list features many local favourites.

Il Corso (☎ 6964 4500; 232 Banna Ave; mains $15; ☉ breakfast, lunch & dinner) Eat inside or out at this traditional Italian café, which is known for its wood-fired pizza.

Getting There & Away

Regional Express (☎ 13 17 13; www.regionalexpress .com.au) flies between Griffith (code GFF) and Sydney (from $100).

All buses, except CountryLink (which stops at the train station), stop at the **Griffith Travel & Transit Centre** (☎ 6962 7199; 121 Banna Ave; ☉ 9am-5pm Mon-Fri, 9am-noon Sat, 9.30am-2.30pm Sun) at the service station opposite the visitors centre. Services include **Greyhound Australia** (☎ 13 14 99; www.greyhound.com.au) to Canberra ($54, seven hours) and Sydney ($77, 10 hours) via Dubbo and **V/Line** (☎ 13 61 96; www .vline.com.au) to Melbourne ($59, six hours). For a taxi, call ☎ 6964 1444.

LEETON

☎ 02 / pop 6927

Leeton is the MIA's oldest town (1913) and like Griffith, was designed by Walter Burley Griffin. It remains close to the architect's original vision and is developing into a thriving commercial centre.

The Leeton **visitors centre** (☎ 6953 6481; www.leetontourism.com.au; 10 Yanco Ave; ⌚ 9am-5pm Mon-Fri, 9.30am-12.30pm Sat & Sun) is on the main road into town from Narrandera. Ask here about presentations at the **SunRice Centre**, which may, among other things, tell you how to keep the stuff from sticking.

Lillypilly Estate (☎ 6953 4069; ⌚ 10am-5pm Mon-Sat) and **Toorak Wines** (☎ 6953 2333; ⌚ 10am-4pm Mon-Sat) are two good wineries on either side of Leeton.

WILLANDRA NATIONAL PARK

This World Heritage–listed national park, on the plains 160km northwest of Griffith as the crow flies, has been carved from a huge sheep station on a system of lakes that are usually dry. Its 19,400 hectares represent less than 10% of the area covered by Big Willandra station in its 1870s heyday. There are several short walking tracks in the park and the Merton Motor Trail loops around the eastern half. The NPWS in Griffith (opposite) has complete information, including road conditions and accommodation details.

Park entry costs $7 per car. There's a camping ground near the homestead, and with permission you can bush camp. There is also shared self-catering accommodation (bring supplies as there's no shop) in the former 'men's quarters', for four people in bunk rooms ($25). A cottage sleeping eight costs $40 for four people, plus $10 for each additional person.

If you want to enjoy this wilderness in style and comfort, try the lovingly restored and classic U-shaped historic **Willandra Homestead** (r $60). The main access is situated off the Hillston–Mossgiel road, around 64km northwest of Hillston. It takes very little rain to close roads here and winter rain, between June and August, often does.

The **Oolambeyan National Park** is a new national park being developed at another former station in the area to protect the Plains Wanderer, an endangered native bird.

HAY

☎ 02 / pop 2703

Hay stands out, and not just because it is surrounded by flat treeless ground at the junction of the Sturt and Cobb Hwys. It's an interesting and friendly place.

Information

News Agent (☎ 6993 1081; 142 Lachlan St) Has an Internet kiosk.

Visitor information centre (☎ 6993 4045; www.visithay.com.au; 407 Moppett St; ⌚ 9am-5pm Mon-Fri, 9am-2pm Sat, 9am-noon Sun) Off Lachlan St.

Sights & Activities

Shear Outback – The Australian Shearer's Hall of Fame (☎ 6993 4000; www.shearoutback.com.au; Sturt Hwy; adult/child $15/10; ⌚ 9am-5pm, shearing demonstrations 10.30am, 1pm & 3.30pm) is easily the most surprising sight you'll find in this part of NSW. It captures the sights, feel and even smells of a sheep-shearing shed and does a great job of evoking the tough lives of shearers who endure this physically punishing trade. The live shearing demonstrations by Billy, a local champ, are worth timing your visit for.

There are some fine swimming spots along the Murrumbidgee River, and interesting old buildings like the **Old Hay Gaol** (Church St; adult/child $2/1; ⌚ 9am-5pm) and **Bishops Lodge** (☎ 6993 1727; Roset St; admission $5; ⌚ 2-4.30pm Mon-Sat), an 1889 corrugated-iron mansion.

Hay was the location of three internment camps during WWII, and the **Hay Internment & POW Camps Interpretive Centre** (☎ 6993 2112; admission $2; ⌚ 9am-5pm Mon-Fri, 10am-4pm Sat & Sun), inside railway carriages at the **old railway station**, gives an insight into that period when 4000 Italian and Japanese POWs and internees were housed locally.

Sleeping & Eating

The **Nicholas Royal Motel** (☎ 6993 1603; 152 Lachlan St; s/d $75/83; ❄ 🏊) is right in the centre of town and has comfortable rooms set in gardens.

Cobb Inlander Motel (☎ 6993 1901; 83 Lachlan St; s/d from $60/68; ❄) has comfortable rooms and is also close to Hay's delightful centre.

The **Jolly Jumbuck** (☎ 6993 4718; 184 Lachlan St; meals $8-15; ⌚ lunch & dinner), in the friendly Riverina Hotel, has a long menu and good steaks.

Getting There & Away

Greyhound Australia (☎ 13 14 99; www.greyhound.com.au) buses on the Sydney to Adelaide route stop at the Caltex service station just near Shear Outback – The Australian Shearer's Hall of Fame.

DENILIQUIN

☎ 03 / pop 7786

Deniliquin is an attractive, bustling country town on a wide bend of the Edward River. It's also a place of pilgrimage for ute fetishists.

Sights & Activities

The Deniliquin **visitors centre** (☎ 1800 650 712, 5898 3120; deniliquin.visitnsw.com.au; cnr Napier & George Sts; ☻ 9am-4pm) is inside the **Peppin Heritage Centre**, which has the same opening times. The heritage centre has displays on irrigation, and the history of wool-growing in the area. There's Internet access at **Purtills Caltex** (☎ 5881 9000; 162 Hardinge St; ☻ 7am-9pm).

Island Sanctuary, on the riverbank in town, has pleasant walks among the river red gums and lots of animals, including flocks of boisterous white cockatoos.

Rural Australia has a love affair with the ubiquitous ute, a pick-up truck that has car-like qualities and which is the basis for infinite modifications big and small. They are as much a part of country life as worries about drought and dead kangaroos by the side of the road. Agricultural Deniliquin fancies itself the centre of ute culture and has gone so far as to mount one on a pole by the visitors centre. **Ute Muster** (☎ 5881 3388; www .utemuster.info), the climax of ute culture, occurs every October Labour Day long weekend when some 4000 utes and 20,000 ute fanciers show up from across the country. There are parades, contests and various cultural activities that are part of the concurrent **Play on the Plains Festival**, where you can't wrestle a ute but you can wrestle a bull.

Sleeping & Eating

There are several caravan parks and plenty of motels, but as trucks roll through town all night, choose one off the highway.

Riverview Motel (☎ 5881 2311; 1 Butler St; s/d from $58/68; ☒ ☒) This is a pretty, quiet spot with big verandas overlooking the river.

McLean Beach Caravan Park (☎ 5881 2448; Butler St; sites/cabins $16/55; ☒) At the northwestern end of Butler St, by a nice river beach and set in pleasant woodlands.

Crossing (☎ 5881 7827; Heritage Centre; mains $8-15; ☻ breakfast & lunch daily, dinner Fri & Sat) The best place to eat locally has tables inside and out, and a great menu of sandwiches, salads and more-complex items such as wood-fired pizzas and fresh fish. Or you can jus enjoy the river view over a coffee or drop of local wine.

Getting There & Away

Greyhound Australia (☎ 13 14 99; www.greyhoun .com.au) buses stop on Whitelock St near Napier St. **CountryLink** (☎ 13 22 32; www.countrylin .com.au) buses run to Wagga ($48, 3½ hours and Albury ($26, 3½ hours) several day each week. **V/Line** (☎ 13 61 96; www.vline.com.au runs daily buses to Melbourne ($34, fou hours). **TravelScene** (☎ 5881 7744; 358 Cressy St sells tickets.

JERILDERIE

Some 92km east of Deniliquin and on the Newell Hwy, Jerilderie is immortalised b the bushranger Ned Kelly, who held th whole town for three days in 1879. Kell relics can be seen in the **Jerilderie Museum** (☎ 03-5886 1511; Powell St; admission by donatior ☻ 9.30am-4pm). The town is 109km south o Narrandera (p241).

ALONG THE MURRAY

Most of the major river towns are on the Victorian side (see p557), but it's easy to hop back and forth across the river. You can cross the border at the twin towns o Moama (NSW) and Echuca (Victoria).

The **visitors centre** (☎ 1800 804 446, 03-548 7555; www.echucamoama.com; 2 Heygarth St; ☻ 9am 5pm) serves both towns and is located ir Echuca beside the bridge that crosses into NSW. Ask about trips on the paddle steam ers that ply these waters, and are reminder of when the Murray and Darling River were the main highways of communicatior and trade.

The largest NSW town on the river i Albury (p239). Downstream from here i **Corowa**, a wine-producing centre, whose Lindemans winery dates from 1860. To **cumwal**, on the Newell Hwy, is a quiet river side town with sandy beaches and a bi fibreglass Murray Cod in the town square The cod-stuffed Murray River has som good beaches.

WENTWORTH

☎ 03 / pop 1400

The old river port of Wentworth lies at th impressive confluence of the Murray an Darling Rivers, 30km northwest of Mildura

Enormous river red gums shade the banks, and there are numerous lookouts and walking tracks.

The **visitors centre** (☎ 5027 3624; www.wentworth .nsw.gov.au; 28 Darling St; ☒ 9.30am-4pm Mon-Fri, 10am-2pm Sat & Sun) is on the main road.

You can see some local history in the **Old Wentworth Gaol** (☎ 5027 3327; Beverley St; adult/ child $6/free; ☒ 10am-5pm) and across the road in the interesting **Rotary Museum** (☎ 5027 3337; adult/child $7/2; ☒ 10.30am-5pm Mon-Sat). The latter has a large collection of photos of the paddle steamers that once made this a major port.

The **Perry Dunes** are impressive orange sand dunes 6km north of town, off the road to Broken Hill.

Harry Nanya Tours (☎ 1800 630 864; www.harry nanyatours.com.au; Shop 11, Sandwych St) is based in town and runs full- and half-day tours (adult/child from $50/30) with Aboriginal guides to Mungo National Park (p260).

Red Gum Lagoon (☎ 5027 2063; 210 Adams St; d $110; ☒) has several peaceful and luxurious self-contained cottages on the waterfront.

OUTBACK

Should you get a chance to fly above this vast, flat land of sunburnt shades of red, orange and brown, it will suddenly hit you: you're looking at Aboriginal art. The swirls, dots and patterns of Aboriginal art all reflect the land itself, right down to the splotches of white where there was once water. Under these scorched features lies much wealth, and the fascinating town of Broken Hill has produced much of the state's wealth.

In the far west you'll find fascinating national parks that bring together amazing natural environments and significant Aboriginal heritage. This is a place where the road truly seems to stretch on forever. Seek local advice before travelling on secondary roads west of the Mitchell Hwy. Carry plenty of water, and if you break down stay with your vehicle. Many dirt roads are OK for 2WDs, but they can be very corrugated, and sandy or dusty in patches. Much of the country is flat and featureless as far as the eye can see, but there are plenty of birds, mobs of emus, and kangaroos along the roadside to watch – and to watch out – for.

BOURKE
☎ 02 / pop 2600

The relaxed town of Bourke, about 800km northwest of Sydney, is on the edge of the Outback; the Australian expression 'back of Bourke' describes anywhere that's remote. The land beyond is indeed flat and featureless, but it is also beautiful in a stark way: such nothingness can be exhilarating and it attracts more and more visitors every year.

The **visitors centre** (☎ 6872 1222; Anson St; ☒ 9am-5pm Easter-Oct, Mon-Fri Nov-Easter) is a mine of information. The local website (www .backobourke.com.au) is also useful. Half-day tours run from here, depending on numbers of people, or pick up the useful *Mud Map Tours* brochure.

The historical and agricultural **Mateship Country Tour** (adult/child $22/11) lasts 3½ hours. You can book paddle-steamer tours (unless the river's in flood or drought). Visit the **NPWS office** (☎ 6872 2744; 51 Oxley St; ☒ 8.30am-4.30pm Mon-Fri), if you plan to go to the Aboriginal art sites at **Mt Gunderbooka**.

Check out the progress of the **Back O'Bourke Exhibition Centre** (☎ 6872 1321; Kidman Way; www.backobourke.com.au), which has been under development for a couple of years. The centre follows the legends of the back country from both indigenous and settler perspectives by using oral histories and innovative displays.

Brewarrina (Bree) is 95km east of Bourke. Here you can see **The Fisheries**, which are stone fish traps in the Darling River that the Ngemba people used. Brewarrina means 'good fishing'.

Sleeping & Eating

Bourke Riverside Motel (☎ 6872 2539; www.bourke riversidemotel.com; 3 Mitchell St; r from $65; ☒ ☐ ☒) Occupying the historic Telegraph Hotel, this is a friendly place in an enchanting riverside garden setting.

Gidgee Guesthouse YHA (☎ 6870 1017; www.yha .com.au; 17 Oxley St; dm/d from $22/52; ☐) Located in the old London Bank building, Gidgee (also known simply as Bourke YHA) has a distinct arts focus with changing exhibitions, music gear for use and a peaceful sculpture garden.

Port O'Bourke Hotel (☎ 6872 2544; 32 Mitchell St; s $38, d with/without bathroom $85/59, mains $12-18; ☒ lunch & dinner Mon-Sat; ☒) Recently renovated pub accommodation in the best of Bourke's hotels. The bistro is the best in town.

Kidman's Camp Tourist Park (☎ 6872 1612; Kidman Way; sites/cabins from $18/69; 🔀) This quiet camping ground, situated 8km north of town, runs down towards the river; it has rustic cabins.

Getting There & Away

Air Link (☎ 13 17 13) has five flights a week from Dubbo to Bourke (code BRK). **Country-Link** (☎ 13 22 32) buses run four times a week to Dubbo ($56), where you can make onward connections. **Bourke Courier Service** (☎ 6872 2092; cnr Oxley & Richard Sts) sells bus and plane tickets.

BACK O' BOURKE – CORNER COUNTRY

There is no sealed road west of Bourke in NSW. The 713km from Bourke to Broken Hill, via Wanaaring and Tibooburra, are lonely, unsealed roads. The far western corner of the state is a semidesert of red plains, heat, dust and flies, and running along the border with Queensland is the Dog Fence, which is patrolled every day by boundary riders who each look after a 40km section.

Tiny **Tibooburra**, the hottest place in the state (average high temperature in January is 36°C), is in the northwestern corner and has a number of 19th-century stone buildings.

The **NPWS office** (☎ 08-8091 3308; Briscoe St; 🕑 8.30am-4.30pm Mon-Fri) is a good source for information on many things local, and has self-guided tours through the rolling redsand dunes. It also has info on **Sturt National Park**, on the northern edge of town.

There are a few accommodation options, including the sunny (!) **Granites Motel** (☎ 08-8091 3305; sites/cabins from $12/50, d $65).

Pubs here have rooms, including the 1880s **Family Hotel** (☎ 08-8091 3314; Briscoe St; r $30-70; 🔀) which has many facilities.

Dead Horse Gully (sites $5) is a basic NPWS camping ground 2km north of town; you'll need to bring drinking water (as you should everywhere).

You can normally reach Tibooburra (driving slowly and carefully) from Bourke or Broken Hill in a conventional vehicle, except after rain (which is pretty rare). The road from Broken Hill is partly sealed.

South of Tibooburra, **Milparinka**, once a gold town, now consists of little more than

a solitary hotel and some old sandston buildings.

Sturt National Park

Taking in vast stony plains, the tower ing red sand hills of the great Strzeleck Desert and the unusual flat-topped mesa around the Olive Downs, this far-north western park covers 340,000 hectares o classic outback terrain. Thanks to the pro tection of the dingo-proof fence, there ar large populations of western grey and re kangaroos.

It has 300km of driveable tracks, camp ing areas and walks around the **Jump Up Loo Rd** and **Gorge Loop Rd**. The NPWS at Tiboo burra has brochures for as well as inf on accommodation in old sheep shearers quarters. Park use and camping fees are $ and $3 per day respectively.

At **Cameron Corner**, 140km northwest o Tibooburra, there's a post to mark th place where all three states – Queensland SA and NSW – meet. It's a favourite goa for visitors and a 4WD is not always nec essary to get there.

Staff at **Cameron Corner Store** (☎ 08-809 3872) can advise on road conditions, an there's fuel and basic **accommodation** (r fro $45) here.

BARRIER HIGHWAY

The Barrier Hwy is the main sealed rout in the state's west, heading from Nynga 594km throught to Broken Hill. It's an al ternative route to Adelaide and the mos direct route between Sydney and Wester Australia.

Cobar still has a productive copper min and earlier mining history is revealed i old buildings like the Great Western Hote with its stretch of iron lacework ornament ing the veranda.

The **Great Cobar Heritage Centre** (☎ 02-683 2448; Barrier Hwy; exhibits $5.50/3.50; 🕑 8.30am-5p Mon-Fri, 9am-5pm Sat & Sun) does a good job o covering every aspect of local life.

Accommodation options include **Cros Roads Motel** (☎ 02-6836 2711; cnr Bourke & Louth Rd r $65-75; 🔀 🖵), a quiet option to the bigge motels along the main highway, and th **Great Western Hotel** (☎ 02-6836 2053; Marshall St; from $50; 🔀), a popular hotel that has bas motel-style units. Rooms include a break fast of chops and eggs.

Wilcannia, on the Darling River, was a busy, prosperous port in the days of paddle steamers. When river transport diminished, its wealth dried up and the town fell into decline. Today its historic buildings are in rough shape.

About 91km northwest of Wilcannia is **White Cliffs**, an opal-mining settlement, where many cool-seeking residents have moved underground. You can fossick for opals around the old diggings (watch out for unfenced shafts) and there are the underground homes and motels – 'dug-outs' – to look at. The general store has a mud map of the area.

Emus often graze by the hi-tech dishes of the **White Cliffs Experimental Solar Power Station** (☎ 08-8091 6633; admission by donation; ☺ tours 2pm), which provides the town's power.

For true local character, head out to Turkey Hill and **Jock's Place** (☎ 08-8091 6753; ☺ 9am-5pm). Jock is a local character who'll give you an entertaining tour of a dug-out home and mine.

Accommodation around here includes **PJ's Underground** (☎ 08-8091 6626; www.babs.com .au/pj; Turley's Hill; r $100-130), an old opal mine that's been converted into a surprisingly bright and cosy guesthouse. This place has bags of character, can provide meals for guests and has an interesting section of the old mine that has been left untouched.

Mutawintji National Park

This beautiful 69,000-hectare park in the sandstone Bynguano Range, 131km north of Broken Hill, has fairly reliable river red gum–shaded water holes and is therefore a focus for wildlife. It is well worth the two-hour drive from Broken Hill or White Cliffs on an isolated dirt road – but not after rain.

The Mutawintji National Park is Aboriginal land and contains ancient rock engravings and cave paintings, some at least 8000 years old. The major art site is off-limits to visitors, except when taking a guided tour (☺ tours 11am Wed & Sat Apr-Oct) run by the Mutawintji Aboriginal community. Check details with the **NPWS office** (☎ 08-8080 3200) in Broken Hill. Self-guided walking trails are provided, and rock paintings can be seen in some areas. The **Homestead Creek** (sites per adult/ child $5/3) camping ground has bore water and vehicle entry to the park is free.

BROKEN HILL
☎ 08 / pop 19,800

Out in the far west, Broken Hill, or the Silver City as it is known, is an oasis in the desert. Long a mining town, it's fascinating not only for its comfortable existence in a rugged environment, but also for its mining trade-union history.

Broken Hill has also become a major centre for Australian art and artists, who are drawn to the area's austere beauty, the intensity and reliability of the light and the cheap property prices. A visit here should be a priority. See the local art, learn the mining legacies and then just hit the highway in any direction to get a feel for this empty yet beautiful land.

History

The Broken Hill Proprietary Company Ltd (BHP) was formed in 1885 after Charles Rasp, a boundary rider, discovered a silver lode. Early conditions in the mine were appalling. Hundreds of miners died, and many more suffered from lead poisoning and lung disease. This gave rise to the other great force in Broken Hill: the unions. Many miners were immigrants, but all were united in their efforts to improve conditions.

The Big Strike of 1919 and 1920 lasted for over 18 months. The miners won a 35-hour week and the end of dry drilling, which was responsible for the dust that afflicted so many of them. The concept of 'one big union', which had helped to win the strike, was finally formalised in 1923 with the formation of the Barrier Industrial Council.

Today the world's richest deposits of silver, lead and zinc are still being worked here, though zinc is of greatest importance. However all of the mining operations are slowly being wound down and the gold of tourism is replacing the silver of the ground.

Orientation & Information

In many ways Broken Hill is more a part of SA than NSW. It's 1170km from Sydney but only 509km from Adelaide; its clocks are set on Adelaide (central) time, half an hour behind Sydney (eastern) time; and the telephone area code (☎ 08) is the same as that of SA.

NEW SOUTH WALES

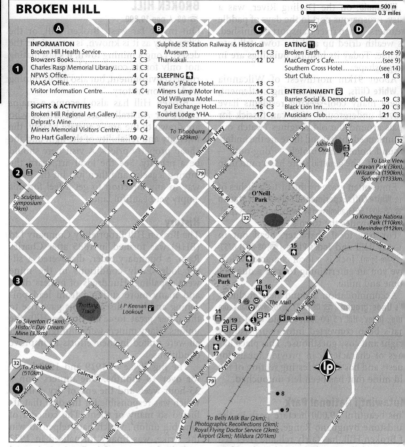

BROKEN HILL

0 — 500 m
0 — 0.3 miles

INFORMATION
Broken Hill Health Service	1 B2
Browzers Books	2 C3
Charles Rasp Memorial Library	3 C3
NPWS Office	4 C4
RAASA Office	5 C3
Visitor Information Centre	6 C4

SIGHTS & ACTIVITIES
Broken Hill Regional Art Gallery	7 C3
Delprat's Mine	8 C4
Miners Memorial Visitors Centre	9 C4
Pro Hart Gallery	10 A2

Sulphide St Station Railway & Historical Museum	11 C3
Thankakali	12 D2

SLEEPING
Mario's Palace Hotel	13 C3
Miners Lamp Motor Inn	14 C3
Old Willyama Motel	15 C3
Royal Exchange Hotel	16 C3
Tourist Lodge YHA	17 C4

EATING
Broken Earth	(see 9)
MacGregor's Cafe	(see 9)
Southern Cross Hotel	(see 14)
Sturt Club	18 C3

ENTERTAINMENT
Barrier Social & Democratic Club	19 C3
Black Lion Inn	20 C3
Musicians Club	21 C3

The city is laid out in a grid and the central area is easy to get around on foot. Argent St is the main street.

The **visitor information centre** (☎ 8088 9700; www.visitbrokenhill.com.au; cnr Blende & Bromide Sts; ⏱ 8.30am-5pm) is an area specialist. Pick up the excellent free booklet *Broken Hill's Accessible Outback* for a mass of helpful regional information. *Broken Hill Heritage Trails* tells the sometimes surprising stories of the town's buildings, with tours by car and on foot.

Broken Hill Health Service (☎ 8080 1333; cnr Thomas & Chloride Sts; ⏱ 24hr)

Browzer's Books (☎ 8088 7221; 345 Argent St; ⏱ 9am-5.30pm Mon-Fri, 9am-2pm Sat, 11am-1pm Sun) Huge selection of new and used books and maps.

Charles Rasp Memorial Library (Blended St; ⏱ 10am-8pm Mon-Wed, 10am-6pm Thu & Fri, 10am-1pm Sat, 1-5pm Sun) Charming staff, free Internet.

NPWS office (☎ 8080 3200; 183 Argent St; ⏱ 8.30am-4.30pm Mon-Fri) National park inquiries and bookings.

Royal Automobile Association of South Australia (RAASA; ☎ 8088 4999, ☎ road service 8087 2643; 261 Argent St; ⏱ 8.30am-5pm Mon-Fri & 8.30-11.30am Sat) Provides reciprocal service to other auto club members.

Sights
MINING

There's an excellent two-hour undergroun tour at the original BHP hole, **Delprat's Min** (☎ 8088 1604; adult/child $40/30; ⏱ tours 10.30a

(Continued on page 25)

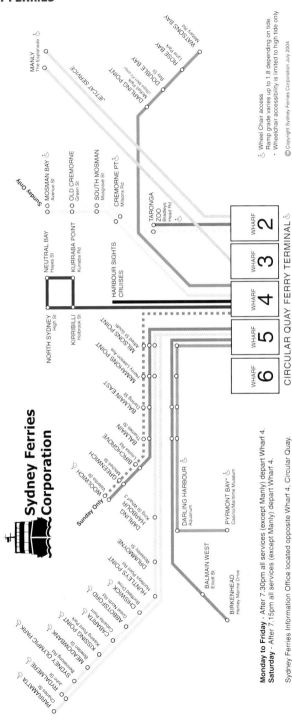

Sydney Ferries Corporation

Monday to Friday - After 7.30pm all services (except Manly) depart Wharf 4.
Saturday - After 7.15pm all services (except Manly) depart Wharf 4.

Sydney Ferries Information Office located opposite Wharf 4, Circular Quay.

CIRCULAR QUAY FERRY TERMINAL

WHARF 2
WHARF 3
WHARF 4
WHARF 5
WHARF 6

MANLY
The Esplanade

"JETCAT SERVICE"

WATSONS BAY
Militari Rd

ROSE BAY
Lyne Park

DARLING POINT
Mackell Park (rowy)

DOUBLE BAY
Bay St (Sooner Marr Rd)

MOSMAN BAY
Avenue St

OLD CREMORNE
Green St

SOUTH MOSMAN
Musgrave St

CREMORNE PT
Milsons Rd

Sunday Only

TARONGA ZOO
Bradleys Head Rd

NEUTRAL BAY
Hayes St

KURRABA POINT
Kurraba Rd

HARBOUR SIGHTS CRUISES

NORTH SYDNEY
High St

KIRRIBILLI
Holbrook St

MILSONS POINT
Alfred St South

McMAHONS POINT
Henry Lawson Ave

BALMAIN EAST
Darling St

BALMAIN
Thames St

BIRCHGROVE
Louisa Rd

GREENWICH
Mitchell St

WOOLWICH
Valentia St

DARLING HARBOUR
Aquarium

PYRMONT BAY
Casino/Maritime Museum

Sunday Only

DARLING HARBOUR
King St Wharf 3

BALMAIN WEST
Elliott St

DRUMMOYNE
Wolseley St

HUNTLEYS POINT
Huntleys Point Rd

CHISWICK
Great North Rd

ABBOTSFORD
Great North Rd

CABARITA
Cabarita Point Park

KISSING POINT
Kissing Point Park

MEADOWBANK
Bowden Rd

SYDNEY OLYMPIC PARK
Jonn St

RYDALMERE
Jonn St

PARRAMATTA
Charles St

BIRKENHEAD
Henley Marine Drive

- Wheel Chair access
- Ramp grade varies up to 1.8 depending on tide.
- Wheelchair accessibility is limited to high tide only

© Copyright Sydney Ferries Corporation July 2004

CITYRAIL'S SYDNEY SUBURBAN NETWORK

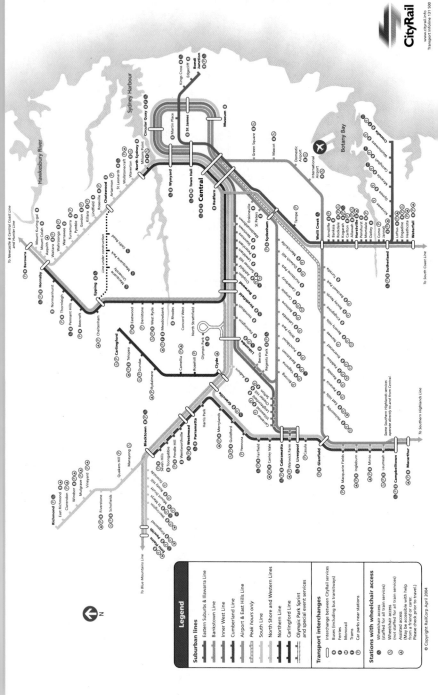

© Copyright RailCorp April 2004

White-petalled lotus, Royal Botanic
Gardens (p105), Sydney

Warehouses along the historic Rocks precinct
(p101), Sydney

Sydney Harbour Bridge (p100) and the city skyline from Milsons Point, Sydney

Sydney Harbour ferry (p142)

GREG ELMS

Byron Bay (p189), New South Wales

Minyon Falls, Nightcap National Park
(p198), New South Wales

Walls of China, Mungo National Park (p260), New
South Wales

Chardonnay grapes, Hunter Valley (p164), New South Wales

OLIVER STREWE

Stockton Bight sand dunes (p170), New South Wales

DALLAS STRIBLEY

Main street of Gulgong (p213), New South Wales

CLAVE

CHRISTOPHER GROENHOUT

Canberra Space Centre (p282), Australian Capital Territory

OLIVER STREWE

Australian War Memorial (p269), Canberra

Lake Burley Griffin (p267), Canberra

DENNIS JONES

National Museum of Australia (p265), Canberra

Parliament House (p268), Canberra

Floriade (p273), the spring garden festival in Commonwealth Park, Canberra

(Continued from page 248)

Mon-Fri, 2pm Sat), where you don miners' gear and descend 130m. Children under six years are not allowed. Delprat's is a short drive from the centre, on the road to the Miners Memorial.

The **Historic Day Dream Mine** (☎ 8088 5682; 1hr tour adult/child $15/8; ☺ 10am-3.30pm), begun in 1881, is 20km from Broken Hill along the Silverton Rd, and then another 13km north off Silverton Rd. All ages are allowed, and sturdy footwear is essential. Tours leave regularly.

Crowning the huge hill of mine rubble (or mullock as it's known locally) that looms over the centre is the **Miners Memorial Visitors Centre** (☎ 8088 6000; Federation Hill; memorial admission adult/child $2.50/2; ☺ 8.30am-10pm). It houses the impressively stark, Cor-Ten steel memorial to all the miners who have died since Broken Hill first became a mining town. Inside the monument, a sobering series of plaques for each year itemise an appalling litany of gruesome deaths.

The visitor information centre makes an excellent vantage point over Broken Hill and is a great spot to enjoy sunrise or sunset. There's a good café-restaurant, Broken Earth (p258), here.

GALLERIES

In late 2004, the must-see highlight, **Broken Hill Regional Art Gallery** (☎ 8088 6897; 404-408 Argent St; admission $3; ☺ 10am-5pm), moved to grand new quarters: an 1885 restored hardware store. And this isn't some musty old space either, but a two-level showplace with soaring vaulted ceilings. Some of the best works in the collection, like everybody's favourite *The Sack of Morocco*, by Arthur Hacker, now have the space to be fully appreciated. There are regular special exhibitions, and the Aboriginal art is superb.

There are more than a dozen private galleries, including the **Pro Hart Gallery** (☎ 8087 2441; 108 Wyman St; adult/child $2/1; ☺ 9am-5pm Mon-Sat, 1.30-5pm Sun). Pro Hart, a former miner, is Broken Hill's best-known artist. The gallery has an extensive collection of Australian art, and some minor works by major artists such as Picasso and Dali.

Thankakali (☎ 8087 6111; cnr Beryl & Buck Sts; ☺ 9am-4pm Mon-Fri, 10am-3pm Sat & Sun) is an extensive gallery in an old brewery, and features work by local Aboriginal artists.

The **Sculpture Symposium** was an international project by 12 sculptors who carved sandstone blocks on a hill top 9km from town. There are wide views over the plains from here, and it is a great place to watch one of Broken Hill's famous sunsets. The visitor information centre has gate keys and directions to drive to the top (per car $6), or follow the road signs and take a free steepish 15-minute walk.

ROYAL FLYING DOCTOR SERVICE BASE

You can visit the **Royal Flying Doctor Service Base** (RFDS; ☎ 8080 1777; tours adult/child $5.50/2.20; ☺ 9am-5pm Mon-Fri, 11am-4pm Sat & Sun) at the airport. The tour includes a film, and you can inspect the headquarters, aircraft and the radio room that handles calls from remote towns and stations.

OTHER SIGHTS

Over 650 vintage photos of Broken Hill have been displayed thematically at **Photographic Recollections** (☎ 8087 9322; Eyre St; adult/child $4.50/2; ☺ 10am-4.30pm Mon-Fri, 1-4.30pm Sat), in the old Central Power Station. It's an impressive show: check out the shots of mock graves dug by striking workers for scabs (derogatory term for strikebreakers).

A trainspotter's dream, the **Sulphide St Station Railway & Historical Museum** (☎ 8088 4660; cnr Bromide & Blende Sts; adult/child $2.50/2; ☺ 10am-3pm) is in the Silverton Tramway Company's old station. The tramway ran between Cockburn (SA) and Broken Hill (via Silverton) until 1970. There's an impressive array of locomotives and rolling stock and lots of good displays about life in the city.

Tours

There are free volunteer-led two-hour guided **walks** (☺ 10am Mon, Wed & Fri Mar-Oct) of Broken Hill; these leave from the visitor information centre.

The Broken Hill Council has opened a Cultural Walk Trail 9km from town. The 2km track goes through a protected area rich in plants and animals, and Aboriginal culture. Pick up the self-guiding map and directions at the visitor information centre.

Plenty of companies offer tours of the town and nearby attractions, some going further out to White Cliffs and Mutawintji National Park, and offering tours of several days' length to other outback destinations, such as Tibooburra.

Bush Mail Run (☎ 8087 2164; adults $77) Outback mail delivery service that operates every Wednesday and Saturday. The day starts at 7am and you cover over 500km, stopping at isolated homesteads for the occasional cuppa.

Tri State Safaris (☎ 8088 2389; www.tristate.com.au) Runs some good tours (for up to 20 days) into the surrounding outback, including day trips into White Cliffs ($159) and Mutawintji National Park ($147).

Sleeping

Pretty much every taste and budget is easily covered off at bedtime in Broken Hill. **Broken Hill Historic Cottages** (☎ 8087 9966; from $95; ☒) is a booking service for a range of homes available for holiday rentals, all fully equipped and sleeping up to six people.

BUDGET

Tourist Lodge YHA (☎ 8088 2086; www.yha.com.au; 100 Argent St; dm/d $22/50; ☒ ☲ ☒) This popular and central YHA has a laid-back atmosphere. The small pool may be empty (depending on the weather). There's bike rental.

Mario's Palace Hotel (☎ 8088 1699; www.marios palace.com.au; cnr Argent & Sulphide Sts; r $35-70; ☒) Star of the hit Australian movie *The Adventures of Priscilla, Queen of the Desert*, Mario's is an impressive old pub (1888) with amazing murals by the late owner Mario Celetto. Rooms are a bit ragged but that's part of the charm. Refurbishments are planned for 2005.

Lake View Caravan Park (☎ 8088 2250; 1 Mann St; sites/cabins $16/40; ☒) Three kilometres northeast of town, this park enjoys a quiet, prime location on the edge of the bush.

MIDRANGE

Miners Lamp Motor Inn (☎ 8088 4122; miners lamp@ozzienet.net; 357 Cobalt St; s/d $70/78; ☒ ☲) The motel units behind the historic Southern Cross Hotel (right) are comfortable and modern, and the pub serves excellent food.

Old Willyama Motor Inn (☎ 8088 3355; oldwilly@ pcpro.net.au; 30 Iodide St; s/d from $88/94; ☒ ☲ ☒) This central motel has wi-fi in each of its large and comfortable rooms and a good beer garden at the pub in front.

TOP END

Royal Exchange Hotel (☎ 8088 2308; www.royalex changehotel.com; 320 Argent St; r from $150; ☒ ☲) This elegant hotel has memorable Art Deco styling. There is also an impressive lounge bar that's quite popular.

Eating & Drinking

Broken Hill has several good food options that surpass most visitor's modest expectations.

Broken Earth (☎ 8087 1318; Miners Memorial Visitors Centre; meals $12-30; ☒ lunch & dinner) With its stunning views over Broken Hill, airy modern design and something-for-everyone menu of Mod Oz dishes, Broken Earth rises as high as its location.

Southern Cross Hotel (☎ 8088 4122; 357 Cobalt St; meals $7-17; ☒ dinner) Has a good pub restaurant menu, the standouts being the fresh fish. The rooms are open with classic design and there is a long cocktail list. This is a good mellow place to have a few drinks with friends.

Sturt Club (☎ 8087 4541; 321 Blende St; meals $16-25; ☒ lunch & dinner) This low-key club has an enormous 'club cut' steak that keeps locals coming back week after week. Frequent specials are good and often adventurous.

Bells Milk Bar (☎ 8087 5380; 160 Patton St; treats $2-6; ☒ 10.30am-10pm Tue-Thu, 10am-11pm Fri-Sun) A charming 1950s throwback on a street of charming throwbacks, Bells is a neighbourhood institution. Over a dozen flavours of ice cream are made here, and you can get classic milkshakes, sundaes, spiders and much more. About 2km from town, it's a real treasure. To get there, follow the main road, Silver City Hwy, to the airport for 2km from the centre and turn left at the junction with Patton St.

Royal Exchange Hotel (☎ 8087 2308; 320 Argent St) The bar here is as elegant as the hotel, and not what you'd expect in a mining town, but then again that's probably a famous artist over in the corner cutting a deal with an agent.

Entertainment

Many nightspots are open until 4am on weekends.

Barrier Social & Democratic Club (The Demo; ☎ 8088 4477; 218 Argent St) The Demo has live country music Friday, and on Saturday it's rock.

Musicians Club (☎ 8088 1777; 276 Crystal St) A slick social club caters to musicians of the cover type. You can add to the various games of chance by starting your own pool as to when 'Proud Mary' will be played. Gets crowded and fun.

Getting There & Away
AIR
Regional Express (☎ 13 17 13; www.regionalexpress .com.au) has flights to Broken Hill (code BHQ) from Sydney (from $335) via Dubbo and Adelaide.

BUS
The dog decamped so other services are filling in for Greyhound Australia, which stopped serving Broken Hill. **Buses R Us** (☎ 8262 6900) runs trips to/from Adelaide ($69, seven hours) and they depart from the visitor information centre.

TRAIN
Broken Hill is on the Sydney to Perth railway line, and the *Indian Pacific* passes through on Tuesday and Friday (departing 6.30pm central standard time) bound for Sydney ($163 to $450), and on Thursday and Sunday (departing 8.20am) heading for Perth via Adelaide. For timetables and fares, contact the **Great Southern Railway** (☎ 13 21 47; www.trainways.com.au).

There's a direct **CountryLink** (☎ 8087 1400, 13 22 32; www.countrylink.com.au; booking office 8am-5pm Mon-Fri) train service on Monday ($122, 13 hours) from Sydney which returns on Tuesday. The train station exterior is enlivened with dramatic murals by local artist Geoff DeMain.

AROUND BROKEN HILL
Silverton
☎ 08
Silverton, 25km northwest of Broken Hill, is a not-to-be-missed old silver-mining town that reached its peak in 1885, when it had a population of 3000 and public buildings designed to last for centuries. In 1889 the mines closed and the population (and many of the houses) moved to Broken Hill. Today it's an interesting little ghost town, and used as a setting in the movies *Mad Max II, A Town Like Alice* and 2002's *Dirty Deeds.*

In between wild donkeys wandering the streets, a number of buildings still stand, including the **old gaol** (adult/student $2.50/1.50; 9.30am-4.30pm), which is now the museum, and several **art galleries**. The friendly **Silverton Hotel** (☎ 8088 5313; 9am-9pm) has a display of photographs taken on the film sets and you mustn't leave without taking the infamous 'Silverton test' – or better yet getting someone else to take it while you watch. The hotel offers some bare-bones **accommodation** (s/d $33/44) overlooking the graveyard. **Penrose Park** (☎ 8088 5307; sites $15, 8-bed bunkhouse with/without kitchen $40/65) is a shady option 1km out of town.

The amiable Bill Cannard runs a variety of **camel tours** (☎ 8088 5316; www.silvertoncamels .com; Silverton Rd; 30min/1hr tours $15/25, 2hr sunset ride $50) from Silverton. Longer trips are available and he'll often pick you up in Broken Hill.

The road beyond Silverton becomes bleak and lonely almost immediately. The **Mundi Mundi Plains** lookout, 5km north of town, gives an idea of just how desolate it gets, and Mad Max fans will feel a pang of nostalgia. Further along, **Umberumberka Reservoir**, 13km north of Silverton, is a popular picnic spot.

Menindee Lakes
The nine lakes are part of a water-storage development on the Darling River, 112km southeast of Broken Hill. **Menindee** is the closest town to the area. Burke and Wills stayed at **Maidens Hotel** (☎ 08-8091 4208; Yartla St; s/d $30/45) on their ill-fated expedition north in 1860. The hotel has been renovated (the Burke and Willis bit burned down in 1999) but the front section is classic early 20th century.

Menindee Lakes Caravan Park (☎ 08-8091 4315; sites from $13) is a low-key camping ground on the edge of the water, where you can swim and fish. It's out of town on the Broken Hill road.

Kinchega National Park is close to town, and the lakes are a haven for bird life. The visitors centre is at the site of the old Kinchega woolshed, about 16km from the park entrance. There are three well-marked driving trails through the park, and accommodation at the shearers' quarters (book at the Broken Hill NPWS office; see p247) and plenty of good camp sites along the river. There's a daily-use fee of $7 per vehicle.

NEW SOUTH WALES

MUNGO NATIONAL PARK

Located southeast of Menindee and northeast of Mildura is **Lake Mungo**, part of the World Heritage–listed Willandra Lakes Region. Mungo is a dry lake that is the site of the oldest archaeological finds in Australia: human skeletons and artefacts date back 46,000 years or possibly more. A 25km semicircle ('lunette') of huge sand dunes has been created by the unceasing westerly wind, which continually exposes fabulously ancient remains. These shimmering white dunes are known as the **Walls of China** and their story traces that of humans in Australia.

Mungo is 110km from Mildura and 150km from Balranald on good, unsealed roads that become instantly impassable after rain. These towns are the closest places selling fuel.

Harry Nanya Tours (☎ 1800 630 864, 03-5027 2076; www.harrynanyatours.com.au; tours from adult/child $85/45) is well known, runs daily tours to Lake Mungo National Park from Mildura and Wentworth, and employs Aboriginal guides who give cultural information. Check ahead as tours may not run without sufficient numbers.

Several Mildura-based companies also offer tours; check at the Mildura visitors centre (see p558).

The **NPWS office** (☎ 03-5021 8900; ⏰ 8.30am-4.30pm Mon-Fri), on the corner of the Sturt Hwy at Buronga, near Mildura, has park information. There's a visitors centre (not always staffed) in the park, by the old Mungo woolshed. Pay your day-use fee of $7 per vehicle here.

From here a road leads across the dry lake bed to the Walls of China, and you can drive a complete 70km loop of the dunes when it's dry. There's a self-guided drive brochure at the visitors centre.

Accommodation fills up during school holidays; book camp sites through the NPWS office in Buronga.

Mungo Lodge (☎ 03-5029 7297; www.mungolodge .com.au; s/d from $108/118) On the Mildura road, about 4km from the visitors centre, this is a comfortable quiet spot with a restaurant (book ahead).

In the park, **Main Camp** (sites per person $3) is 2km from the visitors centre, and **Belah Camp** (sites per person $3) is on the eastern side of the dunes.

Australian Capital Territory

The Australian Capital Territory (ACT) is an intriguing and rewarding destination, a geo-political creation that's not yet 100 years old but has accumulated many lifetimes worth of memorable political events, social events and misadventures. It was originally established to confine a new national capital, Canberra – it's a spacious, orderly and well-scrubbed metropolis with a matter-of-fact personality contrasted by a deeply ingrained appreciation of cultural life. Needless to say, the territory has long since developed its own nature-loving sense of place, and many of its inhabitants – from government bureaucrats and opinion-ated artists to a lively population of university students – now regard it less a place they may have been 'forced', by circumstance, to inhabit and more an energising habitat they willingly enjoy. The territory and its active, entertaining small city (many say big town) have accomplished all this without embracing the parochialism of Sydney or Melbourne.

The ACT has made its home in a bushy inland plot in the southeast of New South Wales (NSW). It covers 2366 sq km and features rugged blue-grey ranges in the south and west, with Canberra wedged up in the northeast corner. Only a few gear shifts from the city are historic homesteads, hi-tech installations, wild physical activities and an abundance of camera-friendly natural sights. The splendid ridges, forests and pristine rivers and water-holes of Namadgi National Park cover 40% of the territory – bushwalkers, bird-watchers, cyclists, picnickers and others seeking a combination of isolation and endemic beauty will all find plenty to occupy them here.

AUSTRALIAN CAPITAL TERRITORY

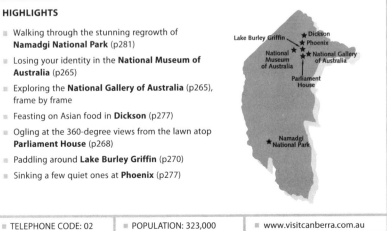

HIGHLIGHTS

- Walking through the stunning regrowth of **Namadgi National Park** (p281)
- Losing your identity in the **National Museum of Australia** (p265)
- Exploring the **National Gallery of Australia** (p265), frame by frame
- Feasting on Asian food in **Dickson** (p277)
- Ogling at the 360-degree views from the lawn atop **Parliament House** (p268)
- Paddling around **Lake Burley Griffin** (p270)
- Sinking a few quiet ones at **Phoenix** (p277)

Lake Burley Griffin ★ Dickson
★ Phoenix
National ★ ★
Museum ★★ National Gallery
of Australia   of Australia
Parliament
House

★ Namadgi
National Park

| ▪ TELEPHONE CODE: 02 | ▪ POPULATION: 323,000 | ▪ www.visitcanberra.com.au |

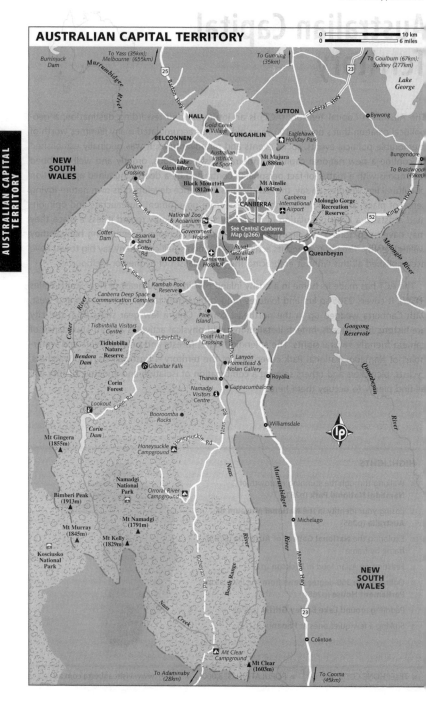

AUSTRALIAN CAPITAL TERRITORY

0   10 km
0   6 miles

Burrinjuck Dam

Murrumbidgee River

To Yass (35km); Melbourne (655km)

To Gunning (35km)

To Goulburn (67km); Sydney (277km)

Lake George

Bywong

HALL

Gold Creek Village

BELCONNEN   GUNGAHLIN

SUTTON

Eaglehawk Holiday Park

Federal Hwy

Bungendore

To Braidwood (49km)

Kings Hwy

NEW SOUTH WALES

Unarra Crossing

Lake Ginninderra

Australian Institute of Sport

Mt Majura ▲(888m)

Mt Ainslie ▲(843m)

Black Mountain (812m) ▲

CANBERRA

Canberra International Airport

Molonglo Gorge Recreation Reserve

Molonglo River

National Zoo & Aquarium

Government House

See Central Canberra Map (p266)

Royal Australian Mint

Queanbeyan

52

Cotter Dam

Casuarina Sands

Cotter Rd

WODEN

Canberra Hospital

Paddy's River Rd

Kambah Pool Reserve

Canberra Deep Space Communication Complex

Pine Island

Googong Reservoir

Tidbinbilla Visitors Centre

Tidbinbilla Rd

Point Hut Crossing

Tidbinbilla Nature Reserve

Bendora Dam

Gibraltar Falls

Lanyon Homestead & Nolan Gallery

Tharwa   Royalla

Corin Forest

Namadgi Visitors Centre

Cuppacumbalong

Lookout

Corin Rd

Booroomba Rocks

Williamsdale

Mt Gingera (1855m) ▲

Corin Dam

Honeysuckle Campground

Honeysuckle Rd

Murrumbidgee River

Queanbeyan River

Bimberi Peak (1913m) ▲

Namadgi National Park

Orroral River Campground

Naas Rd

Mt Murray (1845m) ▲

Mt Namadgi ▲(1791m)

Michelago

Monaro Hwy

Mt Kelly ▲(1829m)

Kosciusko National Park

Booth Range

Echbon Rd

Naas River

NEW SOUTH WALES

Naas Creek

Colinton

Mt Clear Campground ▲ Mt Clear (1603m) ▲

To Adaminaby (28km)

To Cooma (45km)

AUSTRALIAN CAPITAL TERRITORY

AUSTRALIAN CAPITAL TERRITORY FACTS

Eat: Italian, Malaysian, Turkish, Chinese, vegetarian, seafood…

Drink: 'Middy' (285mL) or 'schooner' (425mL) of any chilly beer

Read: How to be a Megalomaniac by Mungo MacCallum, The Point by Marion Halligan

Listen to: Koolism (hip-hop), The Gadflys (pop, rock, punk)

Watch: Somersault

Avoid: Swimming in algal blooms

Locals' nickname: Pubes (public servants)

Swim at: Cotter River (p281), which is overflowing with cool clean water and lined by serene picnic spots

Strangest festival: National Gospel Happening (November), which in 2004 featured an Elvis impersonator

Tackiest tourist attraction: Gold Creek Village (p282) souvenir shops

CANBERRA

☎ 02 / pop 320,000

Canberra is a city that thrives outdoors, amid lakeside parks, green hills and patches of naturally ragged bushland that lie in and around the suburbs. When the inhabitants aren't admiring the autumnal dressage of the millions of trees, the crisp and often clear-skied days of winter, the blooming colours of spring or the depths of a waterhole on a hot summer's day, they can take a cultural dip in Canberra's bewildering array of museums or satisfy their appetites and vices in one of the many healthily competitive restaurants, cafés and bars found here.

The relative serenity and orderliness of the Australian capital is not to everybody's taste, especially the unapologetically homogenous suburbia you'll find here. However, the days when Canberra was mostly an incubator for a uniform public service are long gone, with more than half of the the workforce here now employed in the private sector. And the thriving arts scene means that theatres and galleries are full of thoughtful, provocative and nicely designed fare.

HISTORY

When Australia's separate colonies were federated in 1901 and became states, the decision to build a national capital was written into the constitution. In 1908 the site was selected – diplomatically situated between the arch-rivals Sydney and Melbourne – and in 1911 the Commonwealth government created the Federal Capital Territory. American architect Walter Burley Griffin then beat 136 other entries to win an international competition to design the city. When the foundation stones of the new capital were being laid on 12 March 1913 the city was officially baptised 'Canberra', a name derived from 'Kamberra', believed to be an Aboriginal term for 'meeting place'.

Canberra took over from Melbourne as the seat of national government in 1927 and its land holdings were renamed the Australian Capital Territory in 1938. The city's expansion really got under way after WWII – in the next decade the population trebled to 39,000. The western and southern outskirts of the city were struck by devastating bushfires in January 2003, which were fuelled by the bushland that is a feature of Canberra's landscape. The fires claimed four lives, 530 homes, 30 farms and the historic Mt Stromlo Observatory, and decimated large swaths of Namadgi National Park. Almost all of the 5500 hectares of Tidbinbilla Nature Reserve, including most wildlife, was destroyed. The regeneration of the fire-scorched landscape, however, began quickly and the area is well worth exploring.

CLIMATE

Summer days across the ACT range from comfortably warm to uncomfortably hot, though the temperature doesn't often top 40°C. Winter days here are invariably cool and sometimes gloriously sunny, with little wind, and often kick off with early morning frost and fog – winter nights hover around 0°C during July. Canberra gets a lot of sunshine and receives an annual average rainfall of 630mm, most of it falling in the west of the territory. Snow in the city is rare, making fleeting appearances twice a year at most, but more common in the ranges of nearby Namadgi National Park.

ORIENTATION

The city of Canberra is arranged around Lake Burley Griffin. From the north side the main arterial road, Northbourne Ave, intersects compact Canberra City (also known as Civic). The pedestrian malls situated to the east comprise Canberra's main shopping areas.

South of the city, Northbourne Ave becomes Commonwealth Ave and crosses Lake Burley Griffin to Capital Circle. This road encircles Parliament House on Capital Hill, the apex of architect Walter Burley Griffin's parliamentary triangle. Located within and near the triangle are several of the country's important buildings, including Old Parliament House, the High Court of Australia and the National Gallery of Australia.

The rest of the city is made up of suburban clusters, each with their own 'town centres'. These comprise Gungahlin and Belconnen to the north of Civic, and Weston Creek, Woden Valley and Tuggeranong to the south.

Canberra International Airport is 7km southeast of the city; see Getting Around (p281) for transport information.

Maps

The **NRMA** (☎ 13 21 32; 92 Northbourne Ave, Braddon; ◷ 9am-5pm Mon-Fri) has a *Canberra & Southeast New South Wales* map ($7; free if you belong to an affiliated motoring organisation), good for tours of the countryside. The Canberra visitor information centre (opposite) stocks city maps and cartography for bushwalks. The Namadgi visitor information centre (p281) stocks regional topographic maps.

INFORMATION
Bookshops

Electric Shadows Bookshop (☎ 6248 8352; City Walk, Civic) Off Akuna St, this bookshop specialises in books on theatre and film, plus art-house videos.
Gilbert's (☎ 6247 2032; 102 Alinga St, Civic) Eclectic range of second-hand books.
Map World (☎ 6230 4097; Jolimont Centre, 65 Northbourne Ave, Civic) Stocks numerous maps and travel guides.
National Library Bookshop (☎ 6262 1424; Parkes Pl, Parkes) Superb selection of Australian fiction.
Paperchain Bookstore (☎ 6295 6723; 34 Franklin St, Manuka) All-purpose book list.

Smiths Alternative Bookshop (☎ 6247 4459; 76 Aling St, Civic) From New Age 'science' to gay and lesbian literature

Emergency

Ambulance (☎ 000, TTY Text Telephone 106)
Canberra Rape Crisis Centre (☎ 6247 2525, TTY 6247 1657) Help 24 hours.
Fire (☎ 000, TTY 106)
Lifeline (☎ 13 11 14) Crisis counselling available 24 hours
Police (☎ 000, TTY 106)

Internet Access

Hostels and the Jolimont Centre newsagency also provide Internet access.
Cafe Cactus (☎ 6248 0449; 1/7 Mort St, Civic; per min 20c, per hr $10; ◷ 7.30am-4pm Mon-Fri) You can get light meals here but the Internet access is pricey.
Cafe Jet (☎ 6257 3999; 7 Akuna St; per hr $7; ◷ 24hr Located inside Canberra City Accommodation (p274).
CivicPort Internet Cafe (☎ 6247 2366; Level 1, 16 Garema Pl, Civic; per 5min 30c; ◷ 10am-9pm Mon-Fri, noon-8pm Sat & Sun) There's a 15-minute minimum charge here.

Internet Resources

Canberra Arts Marketing (www.canberraarts.com.au) Comprehensive events listings.
Canberra Bed & Breakfast Network (www.canberra bandb.com) B&B options in and around Canberra.
National Capital Authority (www.nationalcapital.gov .au) Good for capital history and facts.

Media

The city's main broadsheet is the *Canberra Times*. If you prefer dance music to classic hits, listen to Raw FM (87.6).

Medical Services

Canberra Hospital (Map p262; ☎ 6244 2222, emergency dept ☎ 6244 2611; Yamba Dr, Garran)
Capital Chemist (☎ 6248 7050; Sargood St, O'Connor; ◷ 8.30am-11pm Mon-Fri, 9am-11pm Sat & Sun)
Travellers' Medical & Vaccination Centre (☎ 6257 7156; 5th fl, 8-10 Hobart Pl, Civic; ◷ 9am-4.30pm Mon-Fri, 9am-7pm Thu) Appointments essential.

Money

The following agencies and all banks exchange cash and travellers cheques:
American Express (Amex; ☎ 1300 139 060; Petrie Plaza, Civic; ◷ 9.30am-4pm Mon-Thu, 9.30am-5pm Fri) Located inside a branch of the Westpac bank.
Travelex (☎ 1800 637 642; Canberra Centre, Bunda St, Civic; ◷ 9am-5pm Mon-Fri, 9.30am-12.30pm Sat) Found inside the Harvey World Travel office.

Post

Main post office (☎ 13 13 18; 53-73 Alinga St, Civic)
Pick up your poste restante here. Mail can be addressed:
poste restante Canberra GPO, Canberra, ACT 2601.

Tourist Information

Canberra visitor information centre (☎ 1300 554
114, 6205 0044; www.visitcanberra.com.au; 330 Northbourne Ave, Dickson; ☺ 9am-5.30pm Mon-Fri, to 4pm Sat
& Sun) The city's official tourist centre. Ask visitor centre
staff and check the website for information on disabled
access in the ACT.

Citizens Advice Bureau ACT (☎ 6248 7988; www
.citizensadvice.org.au; Griffin Centre, 19 Bunda St, Civic;
☺ 10am-4pm Mon-Tue & Thu-Fri, to 1pm Wed) Happily
provides info on community services and facilities; plans to
shift to new premises next door early in 2006.

SIGHTS

Canberra's many significant buildings, museums and galleries are splayed out either
side of Lake Burley Griffin, while most natural features lie in the territory's west. Many
attractions can provide strollers and wheelchairs, and nearly all close Christmas day.

Those keen on visiting Questacon (p269),
the Australian Institute of Sport (AIS; p270)
and Cockington Green (p282) should pick
up a three-in-one ticket (adult/child/family
$36/20/105), which gives access to all three
attractions; buy it at any of the sites or the
visitor information centre.

Bus No 34 is handy for many of the following sights.

National Museum of Australia

This wonderfully engaging **museum** (☎ 6208
5000; www.nma.gov.au; Lawson Cres, Acton Peninsula,
Acton; admission free; ☺ 9am-5pm) is one big abstract Australian storybook. The museum
uses creativity, controversy, humour and
fearless self-contradiction to dismantle national identity and provoke visitors to come
up with ideas of their own. From the skewed
angles of the architecture to the use of interactive technology, it's an inspiring collision
of aesthetics. There are lots of attendants
on hand to help you navigate exhibitions
on environmental change, indigenous culture, national icons and more, and you can
take one-hour **guided tours** (adult/child/family
$7.50/5/20).

Bus No 34 runs here. There's a free bus on
school holiday weekends and public holidays,
departing regularly from 10.30am from platform seven in the Civic Bus Interchange.

National Gallery of Australia

The stunning **National Gallery** (☎ 6240 6502;
www.nga.gov.au; Parkes Pl, Parkes; permanent collection
free, various fees for visiting exhibitions; ☺ 10am-5pm)
has an Australian collection ranging from
traditional indigenous art (including burial
poles from the Tiwi Islands) to significant

AUSTRALIAN CAPITAL TERRITORY

CULTURE AT WAR

The National Museum of Australia began presenting its provocative social history in March 2001.
Within a year, over a million people had wandered over the fittingly uneven terrain of the Garden of Australian Dreams, pondered the consequences of 'first contact' between Aborigines and
Europeans, and looked behind simple icons such as the Hills Hoist and the quarter-acre block
to the complex circumstances that gave them meaning. But despite emphatic, ongoing public
interest, the museum's founding director, Dawn Casey, was effectively dismissed in December
2003, a casualty of a broader upheaval called the 'culture wars'.

Casey's contract was terminated by the museum board, which, despite the museum's success, had become the museum's biggest critic, claiming it promoted a 'black armband' history
and failed to appropriately applaud the achievements of European settlers and their offspring.
There were suggestions that Casey, an Aboriginal woman, was a victim of sexism and racism.
But another, more widely held, theory is that political pressure was exerted by the federal government via a board stacked with like-minded conservatives. This is thought to be symbolic of
a deepening schism in Australian society between those strongly aligned with the political left,
and those aligned with the right – a division that nurtures conflicting notions of social identity,
and growing political interference in public institutions.

In the face of all this, the museum continues to assert on its website that it intends 'providing
a dynamic forum for discussion and reflection'. Time will tell if the museum and its new director,
Craddock Morton, uphold this ideal.

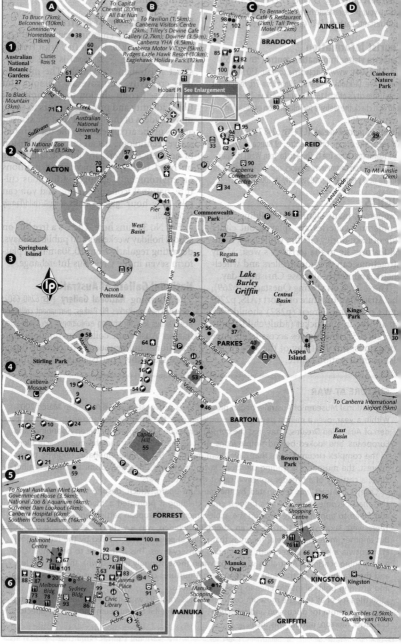

CENTRAL CANBERRA

20th-century works by the likes of Arthur Boyd and Albert Tucker, and impressive 21st-century creations from Marie Hagerty, Fiona Hall and Savanhdary Vongpoothorn. Contrasting with these are early nationalistic statements by Charles Conder and Tom Roberts, visiting exhibitions (with admission fees charged), and examples of fine glasswork (most notably by the influential Stephen Proctor), photography, fashion and furniture, plus a striking Sculpture Garden.

There are all-inclusive **guided tours** (☼ 11am & 2pm), plus a **tour** (☼ 11am Thu & Sun) focusing on indigenous Australian art. Visually impaired visitors should ask about the *Braille Guide*.

Lookouts

Black Mountain (812m), northwest of the city, is topped by the 195m-high **Telstra Tower** (☎ 1800 806 718; Black Mountain Dr; adult/child $3.30/1.10; ☼ 9am-10pm), which has a great windblown vista from 66m up its shaft. It also has a revolving restaurant, considered overpriced by many locals. In the northeast, **Mt Ainslie** (843m) has fine views day and night; walking tracks to the mountain start behind the War Memorial and end at **Mt Majura** (888m).

Lake Burley Griffin

Named after Canberra's architect, **Lake Burley Griffin** was filled by damming the Molonglo River in 1963. Around its 35km shore are many places of interest.

Built in 1970 to mark the bicentenary of Cook's landfall, the **Captain Cook Memorial Water Jet** (☼ 10am-noon & 2-4pm, also 7-9pm daylight-saving months) flings a 6-tonne column of water up to 147m into the air. At nearby **Regatta Point** is a skeleton globe on which Cook's three great voyages are traced; also close is the **National Capital Exhibition** (☎ 6257 1068;

www.nationalcapital.gov.au/experience/attractions/NCE/index.htm; admission free; ☯ 9am-5pm), displaying the city's history. Further east is the stone-and-slab **Blundells' Cottage** (☎ 6257 1068; Wendouree Dr; adult/concession $8/4; ☯ 11am-4pm), built in 1860 to house workers on the surrounding estate and now a reminder of the area's early farming history.

On Aspen Island is the 50m-high **National Carillon** (☎ 6257 1068; ☯ recitals 12.45-1.35pm Wed winter, 2.45-3.35pm Thu summer, 2.45-3.35pm Sat & Sun year-round), gifted from Britain on Canberra's 50th anniversary in 1963. The tower has 55 bronze bells, weighing from 7kg to 6 tonnes. Bookings are required for Carillon **tours** (adult/child/family $8/4/20; ☯ 12.30pm Tue & Thu, 11.30am Sat).

Australian National Botanic Gardens

Spread over 90 hectares on Black Mountain's lower slopes are these beautiful **gardens** (☎ 6250 9540; www.anbg.gov.au/anbg; Clunies Ross St, Acton; admission free; ☯ 9am-5pm Mar-Dec, 9am-8pm Jan & Feb). The **Aboriginal Plant Use Walk** (about 45 minutes, 1km) passes through the cool **Rainforest Gully** and has signs explaining how Aborigines relate to indigenous plants, while the **Eucalypt Lawn** is peppered with 600 species of this ubiquitous tree. Stretch your legs on the moderately steep **Black Mountain Summit Walk** (approximately 1¾ hours return, 5.5km).

The **visitor information centre** (☯ 9.30am-4.30pm) is the departure point for free **guided walks** (☯ 11am & 2pm year-round & 10am summer). Nearby is **Hudsons at the Gardens** (☎ 6248 9680; mains $7-14; ☯ 8.30am-6pm Jan, 8.30am-5pm Feb-Dec), a pleasant café popular with stroller-pushing parents.

National Zoo & Aquarium

This engaging **zoo and aquarium** (Map p262; ☎ 6287 8400; www.zooquarium.com.au; Lady Denman Dr, Yarralumla; adult/child/concession/family $21.50/11.50/17.50/62.50; ☯ 9am-5pm), which is nestled behind Scrivener Dam, is definitely worth devoting several hours to. Rambling outdoor enclosures contain attention-getting animals such as the diminutive sun (Malay) bear, a recently arrived giraffe and two tigons (the result of breeding tiger-lion crosses in captivity), while the aquarium provides sharks and access to a snow-leopard lair. You can have a brief encounter with a cheetah for a whopping $150, or take a 90-minute 'Animal Action' **tour** (adult/child from $40/30).

Parliament House

The symbolical and extravagant **Parliament House** (☎ 6277 5399; www.aph.gov.au; admission free; ☯ 9am-5pm) opened in 1988 after a $1.1 billion construction project. The building is dug into Capital Hill, its roof covered in grass and topped by a 81m-high flagpole with a flag the size of a double-decker bus. The rooftop lawn is easily accessible and provides superb 360-degree views of the city. You enter across a 90,000-piece fore court **mosaic** by Michael Nelson Tjakamarra, the theme of which is 'a meeting place'. The foyer's grey-green marble columns represent a forest, and the marquetry wall panels are inlaid with designs of Australian flora. The Great Hall is embellished with a 20m-long **tapestry**, inspired by the original Arthur Boyd painting of eucalypt forest hanging nearby. Also here is one of only four known 1297 copies of the **Magna Carta**.

Free 45-minute **guided tours** (☯ every 30min 9am-4pm) are available on nonsitting days and 20-minute tours on sitting days, but you're welcome to self-navigate and watch parliamentary proceedings from the public galleries. Tickets for question time (2pm on sitting days) in the **House of Representatives** are free but must be booked through the Sergeant at Arms (☎ 6277 4889); tickets aren't required for the **Senate Chamber**.

Old Parliament House

Engage with bygone political eras in the **Old Parliament House** (☎ 6270 8222; www.oph.gov.au; King George Tce, Parkes; adult/concession/family $2/1/5; ☯ 9am-5pm), Australia's seat of government from 1927 to 1988. Make yourself comfortable in the prime minister's suite; address the House of Representatives; or attend one of the *über*-pretentious yuppie cabarets sometimes held here. There's a free 40-minute **guided tour** (☯ 9.30am, 10.15am, 11am, 11.45am, 12.45pm, 1.30pm, 2.30pm & 3.15pm), or guide yourself via a free leaflet.

Inside you will find the **National Portrait Gallery** (☎ 6270 8236; www.portrait.gov.au), which exhibits painting, photography and new-media portraiture. There are 15-minute free **tours** (☯ 11.30am & 3pm). The gallery also has an intriguing annexe embedded in the hillside at **Commonwealth Place** (admission free; ☯ 10am-6pm Wed-Sun), where more of its valuable collection is displayed, in particular contemporary photography.

Opposite the main entrance to Old Parliament House is the sprawling **Aboriginal Tent Embassy**, established in 1972 in response to governmental refusal to recognise land rights. It's where the Aboriginal flag gained prominence.

Australian War Memorial

The hulking **war memorial** (☎ 6243 4211; www .awm.gov.au; Treloar Cres, Campbell; admission free; ☺ 10am-5pm) looks down Anzac Pde to Old Parliament House across the lake. Its immensity preserves the history and human toll of wartime. **Anzac Hall** confronts you with heavy machinery, including a Japanese midget submarine and a fortune-favoured Lancaster bomber called *George*. Entombed among the Hall of Memory's sombre mosaics and stained glass is the **Unknown Australian Soldier**, whose remains were returned from a WWI battlefield in 1993 and who symbolises all Australian war casualties.

Held throughout each day are free 90-minute **guided tours**; alternatively, purchase the *Self-guided Tour* leaflet ($3).

Along Anzac Pde, Canberra's broad commemorative way, are **11 memorials** to various campaigns.

Questacon – National Science & Technology Centre

This educational science **centre** (☎ 1800 020 603; www.questacon.edu.au; adult/child/concession/family $14/8/9.50/42; ☺ 9am-5pm) is a child magnet, with entertaining and interactive science and technology exhibits. Kids can learn bushcraft from the Burarra people of Arnhem Land, pretend to be scared by animatronic predators, explore the physics of fun parks and take shelter from earthquakes. There are also science shows, and puppet shows for the littlies.

Canberra Museum & Gallery

The stylish display space of the **museum and gallery** (☎ 6207 3968; www.museumsandgalleries.act .gov.au/museum/index.asp; Civic Sq, London Circuit, Civic; admission free; ☺ 10am-5pm Tue-Fri, noon-5pm Sat & Sun) is devoted to Canberra's social history and visual arts. The interesting permanent exhibition, 'Reflecting Canberra', includes the engine of a fire-brigade pumper truck melted in the 2003 bushfires. The museum also stages various talks and craft-oriented workshops.

Screensound Australia – National Screen & Sound Archive

If you are into celluloid, head here. This **archive** (☎ 6248 2000; www.screensound.gov.au; McCoy Circuit, Acton; admission free; ☺ 9am-5pm Mon-Fri, 10am-5pm Sat & Sun) preserves Australian moving picture and sound recordings for posterity. The permanent exhibition highlights include the 1942 Oscar awarded to high-voltage propaganda flick *Kokoda Front Line*; the old celluloid and glass slides comprising the Salvation Army's 1900 production *Soldiers of the Cross*; and the costumes worn by pugnacious TV icon Aunty Jack. There are also temporary exhibitions, talks and film screenings.

High Court of Australia

The grandiose **High Court** (☎ 6270 6811; www.h court.gov.au; Parkes Pl, Parkes; admission free; ☺ 9.45am-4.30pm Mon-Fri) was dubbed 'Gar's Mahal' when it opened in 1980, a reference to Sir Garfield Barwick, chief justice during the construction of the building. The rarefied heights of the main courtroom and foyer are in keeping with the building's name, though its authority is somewhat undermined by the photo gallery of chief justices attempting to look dignified while wearing sheepskin rugs on their heads. Sittings usually occur for two weeks each month (except January and July) and are open to the public; call for times.

National Library of Australia

This enormous **library** (☎ 6262 1111; www.nla .gov.au; Parkes Pl, Parkes; admission free; ☺ main reading room 9am-9pm Mon-Thu, 9am-5pm Fri & Sat, 1.30-5pm Sun) opened in 1901 and has accumulated more than six million items, most of which can be accessed in one of the eight reading rooms. Bookings are required for the free, 45-minute **behind-the-scenes tour** (☎ 6262 1271; ☺ 12.30pm Thu). The **Exhibition Gallery** (admission free; ☺ 9am-5pm) presents thematic displays collated mainly from the library's diverse collections.

National Archives of Australia

Canberra's original post office now houses the **National Archives** (☎ 6212 3600; www.naa.gov .au; Queen Victoria Tce, Parkes; admission free; ☺ 9am-5pm), a repository for Commonwealth government records in the form of personal papers, photographs, films, maps and paintings. The centrepiece **Federation Gallery** holds original

AUSTRALIAN CAPITAL TERRITORY

charters, including Australia's 1900 Constitution Act and the 1967 amendment that ended constitutional discrimination against indigenous Australians. Public research facilities include a **reading room**. High-profile raconteurs regale audiences here once or twice a month during **Speaker's Corner** (☎ 6212 3624); bookings are essential.

Royal Australian Mint

To check out the country's biggest money-making operation, visit the **mint** (Map p262; ☎ 6202 6891; www.ramint.gov.au; Denison St, Deakin; admission free; 9am-4pm Mon-Fri, 10am-4pm Sat & Sun). A gallery showcases the history of Australian coinage, including the 'holey dollar' and the 'dump', both minted in 1813. Also on show are mint-produced official insignia and Sydney Olympics medals, and you can view the production of proof (collector's) coins and circulating coins; production ceases on the weekend. As a souvenir, mint your own $1 coin (in the true spirit of capitalism, it'll cost you $2.50), or purchase one of the strange 'coinwatches' from the gift shop.

Australian National University

The attractive grounds of the **ANU** (☎ 6125 5111; Acton; www.anu.edu.au), founded in 1946, lie between Civic and Black Mountain and make for a pleasant wander. Drop into the **Drill Hall Gallery** (☎ 6125 5832; Kingsley St; admission free; noon-5pm Wed-Sun) to see special exhibitions and paintings from the university's art collection; a permanent fixture is the near-phosphorescent hue of Sidney Nolan's *Riverbend*. Collect the ANU *Sculpture Walk* brochure for a fine-arts appreciation of the university grounds.

Australian Institute of Sport

The country's elite and aspiring-elite athletes hone their sporting prowess at the **AIS** (Map p262; ☎ 6214 1444; www.ausport.gov.au/tours; Leverrier Cres, Bruce). **Tours** (adult/child/concession/family $13/7/10/36; 10am, 11.30am, 1pm & 2.30pm) are led by resident athletes. You'll absorb information on training routines, see displays on Australian champions and the 2000 Sydney Olympics, and encounter interactive exhibits where you can humble yourself at basketball, rowing and skiing. Check out the enormous steel sculpture called *The Basketballer* out the front.

Other Attractions

Peek through the gates of the prime minister's official residence, the **Lodge** (Adelaide Av, Deakin), and the governor-general's official residence, **Government House** (Map p262; Dunross Dr, Yarralumla). **Scrivener Dam lookout** (Map p262) gives a good view of both.

Canberra has 80-odd diplomatic missions, mostly in nondescript suburban houses in Yarralumla, but some are architecturally worthwhile and periodically open to the public. The **Thai embassy** (Empire Circuit, Yarralumla), with its pointy orange-tiled roof, is reminiscent of Bangkok temples. The **Papua New Guinea high commission** (☎ 6273 3322; Forster Cres, Yarralumla) resembles a *haus tamberan* (spirit house) from the Sepik region and has a **cultural display** (10am-12.30pm & 2.30-4.30pm Mon-Fri).

The 79m-tall **Australian-American Memorial** (Kings Ave, Russell), a pillar topped by an eagle, recognises US support for Australia during WWII.

The **Church of St John the Baptist** (Constitution Ave, Reid) was finished in 1845, its stained glass windows donated by pioneer families. The adjoining **St John's Schoolhouse Museum** (☎ 6249 6839; Constitution Ave, Reid; admission by donation; 10am-noon Wed, 2-4pm Sat & Sun) houses memorabilia from Canberra's first school.

The **Canberra Tradesmen's Union Club** (Tradies; ☎ 6162 5656; 2 Badham St, Dickson; 8am-5am) has rows of poker machines with a **Bicycle Museum** (admission free; 8am-5am), which includes the aptly named Boneshaker Tricycle. The Tradies also operates the Downer Club, where you can make planetary observations at **Canberra Space Dome & Observatory** (☎ 6241 5333; www.ctuc.asn.au/planetarium; 72 Hawdon Pl, Dickson; per venue adult/child/concession/family $10/6/8/28; observatory 7.30pm, 8.30pm & 9.30pm Tue-Fri, 8.30pm & 9.30pm Sat, planetarium 7.30pm & 8.30pm Tue-Thu, 7.30pm Fri & Sat); bookings are essential.

ACTIVITIES

Canberra partakes in plenty of vitalising activities. Bushwalking is plentiful, swimming in river-fed waterholes is a must, and you can hire bikes and skates to roam the city.

Boating

Lake Burley Griffin Boat Hire (☎ 6249 6861; Acton Jetty, Civic; 9am-5pm Mon-Fri, 8am-dusk Sat & Sun, closed May-Aug) has canoe, kayak and paddle boat hire (from $12 per hour); however swimming in the lake isn't recommended.

Bushwalking

Tidbinbilla Nature Reserve (p281), 45km south-west of the city, has marked walking tracks. Another great area for bushwalking is **Namadgi National Park** (p281), which is one end of the challenging 655km-long Australian Alps Walking Track.

Local bushwalking maps are available at **Mountain Designs** (☎ 6247 7488; 6 Lonsdale St, Braddon). The *Namadgi National Park* map ($4.40), available from the Canberra and Namadgi visitor information centres, details 23 walks.

Cycling

Canberra has an extensive cycle path network. One popular track circles the lake, while there are other tracks shadowing the Murrumbidgee River. The city's visitor information centre sells the *Canberra Cycleways* map ($6.50) and *Cycle Canberra* ($15), the latter published by **Pedal Power ACT** (www.pedalpower.org.au).

Mr Spokes Bike Hire (☎ 6257 1188; Barrine Dr, Civic; ⏰ 9am-5pm Wed-Sun, daily during school holidays) is near the Acton Park ferry terminal; bike hire per hour/half-day/full day costs $12/30/40. **Canberra YHA** (p274), **Canberra City Accommodation** (p274) and **Victor Lodge** (p274) also rent out bikes. **Row'n'Ride** (☎ 6228 1264) will deliver bicycles (hire per day/week $45/95) to your door.

In-line Skating

Mr Spokes Bike Hire (☎ 6257 1188; Barrine Dr, Civic; ⏰ 9am-5pm Wed-Sun, daily during school holidays) hires out skates for $11 for the first hour, then $5.50 for each subsequent hour. So does **Adrenalin Plus** (☎ 6257 7233; Shop 7, 38 Allara St, Civic; ⏰ 10am-5.30pm Mon-Thu, to 7pm Fri, to 5pm Sat, to 4pm Sun), which charges $17 for two hours' hire.

Swimming

There are 50m and 25m heated indoor swimming pools at the **Canberra International Sports & Aquatics Centre** (☎ 6251 7888; www .clubgroup.com.au/home; 100 Eastern Valley Way, Bruce; adult/child $4.80/3.50; ⏰ 6am-9pm Mon-Fri, 7am-7pm Sat & Sun).

You can also have a splash at the **Canberra Olympic Pool** (☎ 6248 6799; Allara St, Civic; adult/child $4.70/3; ⏰ 6am-8.30pm Mon-Thu, to 7.50pm Fri, 7am-6pm Sat, 8am-6pm Sun) and the National Trust–listed 75-year-old **Manuka Swimming Pool** (☎ 6295 1349; Manuka Circle, Manuka; adult/child

$4/3; ⏰ 6.30am-7pm Mon-Fri, 8am-7pm Sat & Sun Nov-Mar, usually closed Apr-Oct).

See Picnicking, Swimming & Walking Areas (p281) for information on some inviting waterholes around the city.

WALKING TOUR

Much of Canberra's architectural and political accomplishments are framed by the parliamentary triangle, the slice of the city defined by Kings Ave, Lake Burley Griffin and Commonwealth Ave, and overlooked by Capital Hill. Crowning the hill is the enormous bulk of **Parliament House** (**1**; p268). Head north along Commonwealth Ave towards the lake, passing the Canadian, New Zealand and UK high commissions on your left. Turn right (east) at Coronation Dr to King George Tce and **Old Parliament House** (**2**; p268); opposite the main entrance you'll see the **Aboriginal Tent Embassy** (**3**; p269), which was established more than 30 years ago.

Crossing diagonally (northwest) across the Old Parliament House lawn to King Edward Tce, you will arrive at the **National Library of Australia** (**4**; p269). Located beside it is **Questacon** (**5**; p269), Canberra's interactive science museum. Towards Kings Ave along King Edward Tce is the **High Court of Australia** (**6**; p269), while across Parkes Pl you'll find the wonderful **National Gallery of Australia** (**7**; p265).

Follow King Edward Tce to Kings Ave, then turn left (northeast) and keep following the avenue across the lake. You'll see the **National Carillon** (**8**; p268), on Aspen Island to your left. Before reaching the **Australian-American Memorial** (**9**; opposite), located at the end of Kings Ave, turn left (northwest) at the roundabout onto Parkes Way, which follows the northern shore of the lake. After 1km turn left (south) off Parkes Way to the historic 19th-century **Blundells' Cottage** (**10**; p268).

Continue your walk along Parkes Way to the next roundabout. **Anzac Parade** (**11**; p269), leading northeast from here, is lined with memorials and ends at the largest, the **Australian War Memorial** (**12**; p269). Return to Parkes Way and follow it to Commonwealth Ave. Turn left (south) and, after 500m, turn left (east) again onto Albert St and follow the path to the **National Capital Exhibition** (**13**; p267) at Regatta Point. Gaze at the

AUSTRALIAN CAPITAL TERRITORY

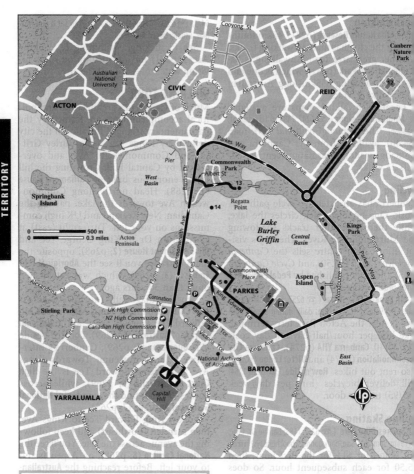

WALK FACTS

Distance: 12km

Duration: three hours

Captain Cook Memorial Water Jet (**14**; p267) on the lake. Continue southward along Commonwealth Ave to eventually return to Parliament House.

CANBERRA FOR CHILDREN

The hyperactive demands of children are easily met in Canberra, where there are enough reasonably priced activities to satisfy the highest energy levels without savaging your account balance. The visitor informa-

tion centre has factsheets (*Children's Activities* and *Parks & Playgrounds*).

For fresh air and exercise, stroll throug the lovely **Australian National Botanic Garden** (p268) or the wild, wonderful **National Zoo Aquarium** (p268). Energy levels can also be ac commodated by swimming at a **pool** (p271) o **waterhole** (p281), or by hiring **bikes** (p271).

For hands-on scientific fun, visit **Questaco** (p269). Another place with a child-friendl scientific bent is **CSIRO Discovery** (☎ 6246 464 www.discovery.csiro.au; Clunies Ross St, Acton; adult/chil family $6/3/15; ◷ 9am-5pm Mon-Fri), where you ca come to grips with virtual reality, gene tech nology and other cutting edge concepts.

Miniature steam-train rides can be take at **Gold Creek Village** (p282). And there is plethora of museums custom-built for active imaginations, including the **National Dinosaur Museum** (p282) and the brilliant **National Museum of Australia** (p265). The littlest littlies will appreciate a spin on Civic's landmark 1914 **merry-go-round** (☎ 6247 4527; City Walk; 1/3/10 tickets $2.50/6/17; ☺ 10am-4pm Tue-Thu, 10am-7pm Fri, 9.30am-4pm Sat, 11am-3pm Sun, hours reduced in winter).

For professional short-term childcare, look up 'Baby Sitters' and 'Child Care Centres' in the *Yellow Pages* directory.

TOURS

Aquila Helicopters (☎ 0412 066 766; Canberra International Airport; flights from $55) For aerial views.

Balloon Aloft (☎ 6285 1540; www.balloon.canberra .net.au; rides from $210) For quieter aerial views.

Canberra Day Tours (☎ 6298 3344; www.canberraday tours.com.au) This company shuttles you around select city sites for $45/70 per half-/full day, including entry fees. It also runs a daily hop-on, hop-off bus (☎ 0418 455 099) that loops around major attractions. Tickets (adult/child $35/25) are valid for 24 hours. After 12.30pm you can buy an afternoon ticket ($25/20), but you have limited time to make it really worthwhile. First departure is at 9.30am from the Melbourne Building, a block south of the Jolimont Centre; services run roughly every 1¼ hours, up to and including 3pm.

Destiny Tours (☎ 0414 232 244; www.destinytours.com .au; tours $50) On the last Friday and Saturday of each month (except for December), this outfit takes 90-minute circuits of Canberra's little-known crime and ghost sites in a Cadillac hearse.

Go Bush Tours (☎ 6231 3023; www.gobushtours.com .au) This reputable company takes tailored excursions around Canberra, including a day-long exploration of Namadgi National Park (adult/concession $120/80). It has a wheelchair-accessible vehicle.

Southern Cross Yacht Club (☎ 6273 1784; www.cscc .com.au; 1 Mariner Pl, Yarralumla), Provides a sightseeing lake tour aboard the MV *Southern Cross*, with cruises (adult/ child $15/9) departing 3pm from Wednesday to Sunday.

SS Maid Marion (☎ 0418 828 357) One-hour cruises (adult/child $12/5) that pick-up/drop-off at lakeside locales such as the National Museum of Australia and the National Library; there are usually around three cruises daily.

FESTIVALS & EVENTS

January
Summernats Car Festival (www.summernats.com.au) Revs up over three days in January at Exhibition Park.

February
Metal for the Brain (www.metalforthebrain.com) Australia's biggest all-ages heavy-metal festival, in early Feb.

National Multicultural Festival (www.multicultural festival.com.au) Celebrated over 10 days in February.
Royal Canberra Show (www.rncas.org.au/showwebsite /main.html) The country meets the city at the end of February.

March–April
Celebrate Canberra (www.celebratecanberra.com) The city's extended birthday party in mid-March.
National Folk Festival (www.folkfestival.asn.au) One of the country's largest folk festivals, held every March/April.

September–November
Canberra International Film Festival (www.canberra filmfestival.com.au) A 10-day international film festival held October/November at Electric Shadows cinema (p279).
Floriade (www.floriadeaustralia.com) Held in September/ October and dedicated to Canberra's spectacular spring flowers.
Stonefest (www.stonefest.au) Big-time two-day music festival staged at the end of October at the University of Canberra.

SLEEPING

There is only a handful of accommodation choices in the centre of Canberra. Most of the hotels and motels are either strung out along Northbourne Ave or ensconced in northern suburbs such as Ainslie, O'Connor and Downer. The other main accommodation areas lie around Capital Hill, particularly in Kingston and Barton.

Most places can supply cots and a room or two suitable for a family-sized stay. Travellers with limited mobility will find that few places outside top-end accommodation have true barrier-free rooms.

Local hotels and motels will often match each other's standby rates outside of public and school holidays (and when conferences aren't being held), normally offering $20 to $25 less than advertised rack rates.

Budget
HALLS OF RESIDENCE
Some of the ANU's halls of residence rent out rooms during the end-of-year university holidays. Ring ahead to check, because sometimes the halls are booked during conferences. Most offer similar facilities, with room prices starting from around $50 (up to $15 more for B&B).

Bruce Hall (☎ 6125 6000) and **Burton & Garran Hall** (☎ 6267 4333) are at the northern end of Daley Rd. **Ursula Hall** (☎ 6125 6200; Dickson Rd) and the affiliated **John XXIII College** (☎ 6279 4905; Dickson Rd) lie to the south, opposite Sullivans Creek. Civic is a brisk 15- to 20-minute walk (1.5km) across campus.

HOSTELS

Canberra City Accommodation (☎ 1800 300 488, 6257 3999; www.canberracityaccommodation.com.au; 7 Akuna St, Civic; dm/s/d from $24/55/70; 🤖 💻 🖳) This bright and well-managed complex includes Canberra Backpackers. And judging by its impressive roll call of services, it's mighty eager to please. Facilities include an indoor pool, gym, 24-hour reception, bar, Internet café (see Internet Access, p264), pay TV, continental breakfasts ($4.50) and bike hire ($16 per day).

Victor Lodge (☎ 6295 7777; www.victorlodge.com.au; 29 Dawes St, Kingston; dm/s/d $25/55/70; P 💻) This high-standard budget B&B is excellent value, offering lodgers an all-you-can-eat breakfast, spotless rooms (with linen) and reliable facilities. Guests can hire bikes ($15 per day) or simply stroll to the nearby Kingston cafés and shops. There's a pick-up/drop-off service, or catch bus No 38, 39 or 80.

Canberra YHA (☎ 6248 9155; canberra@yhansw.org.au; 191 Dryandra St, O'Connor; dm/d/f from $20/55/85; P 💻) This appealing purpose-built hostel is set in bushland beneath O'Connor Ridge, 6km northwest of Civic, and incorporates the 1960s Wattle Lodge – the newer grey-brick extensions are eerily reminiscent of an old Canberra public school. It's a peaceful place with an open-plan kitchen-lounge and pleasant outside decks. Take bus No 35; once there, you can hire bicycles ($15 per day).

HOTELS

City Walk Hotel (☎ 1800 600 124, 6257 0124; www.citywalkhotel.com.au; 2 Mort St, Civic; dm $22-24, s $45-75, d $60-85, f from $105) For an inner-city budget hotel, City Walk is in surprisingly good shape. The plain rooms have firm beds, and a recent lick of paint has improved the ambience. The interior climate is also enhanced by the fact that you can't light a cigarette or drink alcohol inside.

Kingston Hotel (☎ 6295 6844; 73 Canberra Ave, Griffith; dm $20; P) This is a basic southside pub option, with a bistro serving cheap roasts. You'll see blue-collar regulars whose utes (utility vehicles) bear stickers saying things like 'Lost wife and dog. Reward for dog'. Linen costs $5.50 extra.

CAMPING & CARAVANNING

Eaglehawk Holiday Park (Map p262; ☎ 6241 641 www.eaglehawk.contact.com.au; Federal Hwy, Sutto powered/unpowered sites per 2 people $22/17, s & $70-125, f $90-145; P 🤖 🖳) A friendly high wayside complex 12km north of town, ju over the NSW border. The camp sites a an afterthought, positioned on the edge of field. The villas are winners in the facilitie stakes, with full cooking amenities and ai con; cabins get only a microwave. A neigh bouring pub provides meals ($8 to $13).

Canberra Motor Village (☎ 6247 5466; canmot village@ozemail.com.au; Kunzea St, O'Connor; powered sit per 2 people $21-28, unpowered sites per 2 people $15, $60-125; P) Dozing in a peaceful bush se ting located 6km northwest of the centr this place has good amenities and an o derly arrangement of motel rooms and sel contained cabins.

Midrange

University House (☎ 6125 5211; www.anu.edu.au/u house; 1 Balmain Cres, Acton; s $80-130, d $115-18 P) This 1950s building, with furniture t match, is soothingly positioned in the mid of the rambling university grounds. Man of the spacious rooms have small balconie and there's a good selection of wine in th cellar bottle shop.

Olims Hotel Canberra (☎ 1800 020 016, 6248 551 www.olimshotel.com; cnr Ainslie & Limestone Aves, Braddo r $100-155; P 🤖) This 1927 National Trust listed building and its later refurbishmen surround a lovely terraced courtyard. Th ground-floor 'superior' rooms are quit comfortable here, but the 1st-floor, sel contained 'loft' rooms are more spaciou and have balconies looking over the inne garden.

Rydges Eagle Hawk Resort (☎ 6241 6033; ww .rydges.com/eaglehawk; Federal Hwy, Sutton; r from $10 P 🤖 🖳) This facility-laden resort is stowe away on a 52-hectare block of land 10kr northeast of Civic. We've been quoted excel lent walk-in rates here, but remember tha because it's a conference venue, rooms ca often be booked out midweek.

Tall Trees Motel (☎ 13 17 79, 6247 9200; ww .bestwestern.com.au/talltrees; 21 Stephen St, Ainslie; s/ from $100/120; P 🤖) The green grounds c this accommodating motel and its locatio in leafy Ainslie lend it a relaxed air. It's good place to base yourself if you want t be near but not in the centre.

AUSTRALIAN CAPITAL TERRITORY

AUTHOR'S CHOICE

Ginninderry Homestead (☎ 6254 6464; www
.ginninderry.com.au; 468 Parkwood Rd, Macgregor; r
$130-165; P ⊗) Four antique-filled rooms
are up for grabs at this thoroughly hospitable B&B, located 20km west of town on
a bucolic, 28-hectare spread. Three-course
dinners ($50) can be arranged on Friday
and Saturday, and picnic provisions can be
supplied. No need to hide the kids in your
suitcase, either – children are welcome.

Motel Monaro (☎ 6295 2111; www.bestwestern
.com.au/motelmonaro; 27 Dawes St, Kingston; r $125;
 P ⊗ ☐) Offers compact, well-maintained
rooms on a quiet street near the Kingston
shops. It has several large, multibed rooms
that are ideal for groups, and has good
walk-in rates when business is slow.

Miranda Lodge (☎ 6249 8038; book@parkview
canberra.com.au; 534 Northbourne Ave, Downer; s/d incl full
breakfast $100/120; P ⊗) Miranda has motel-
style rooms in decent condition (if a bit worn).
Rooms around the back are shielded from
Northbourne Ave noise. The owners also
run the nearby, equally priced **Parkview Lodge**
(526 Northbourne Ave, Downer; P ⊗); the 'view' is
mostly of the netball centre across the road.
Direct inquiries to Miranda Lodge.

Blue & White Lodge (☎ 6248 0498; blueandwhite
lodge@bigpond.com; 524 Northbourne Ave, Downer; s/d incl
breakfast $90/100; P ⊗) This lodge's pillared
façade does a good impression of a Masonic
temple. The rooms are prim and comfortable, and the owners also manage the similarly styled **Canberran Lodge** (528 Northbourne Ave,
Downer; s/d incl breakfast from $90/100; P ⊗).

Pavilion (☎ 1800 828 000, 6247 6888; www.pavilion
canberra.com; 242 Northbourne Ave, Dickson; r from
$115; P ⊗ ☒) The atrium garden of this
centrally located, midrange hotel is a nice
touch – the radioactive-green carpet running around its edge isn't. The Pavilion has
several wheelchair-accessible rooms, though
none are fully barrier-free.

Top End

Novotel (☎ 6245 5000; www.novotel.com.au; 65 Northbourne Ave, Civic; r from $180; P ⊗ ☐ ☒) The
Novotel is adjacent to the Jolimont Centre,
just a few minutes' stroll from Civic's restaurants and shops. Four-star conveniences
include in-room data points, a business cen-

tre, a pool and daily weather reports posted
in the elevators.

Hyatt Hotel Canberra (☎ 6270 1234; www.canberra
.park.hyatt.com; Commonwealth Ave, Yarralumla; r from
$250; P ⊗ ☒) A luxurious Art-Deco hotel.
Lavish facilities such as an impressive gym
and pool, a cigar bar and round-the-clock
room service, coupled with sycophantic
service, make it Canberra's only five-star
accommodation. Try for a room with a
view of the lake, and ask about the various
B&B packages.

Pacific International Apartments – Capital Tower
(☎ 1800 676 241, 6276 3444; www.pacificinthotels.com;
2 Marcus Clarke St, Civic; apt from $185; P ⊗ ☒)
Rooms on the southern side of this apartment complex's curving façade face Lake
Burley Griffin's wind-rippled waters. The
surrounding parkland makes a good place
to collect (or scatter) your thoughts. The facilities are excellent and apartments have up
to three bedrooms.

EATING

Canberrans fork in food and fork out cash
in several hundred diverse eateries. Most
restaurants are in Civic, which has raised its
menu standards to compete with upmarket
selections in Kingston, Manuka and Griffith. There's also a fantastic Asian strip in
Dickson and many other possibilities scattered throughout the suburbs.

On Monday and Sunday nights tumble-
weeds roll through town and it can be hard
to find a restaurant that's open.

Civic & Acton

Canberra's city-centre eateries have their
general location in common, but diverge
significantly when it comes to the type of
food they offer and how they offer it. Within
and around Civic you'll find everything
from food courts to no-fuss Italian restaurants and trendy chef-owned enterprises.
Garema Pl is not one of the world's greatest
outdoor plazas, but it's ringed by enough
restaurants and outdoor seating to appease
Canberrans. West Row restaurants are lively
at lunchtime and in the evening.

Caffe della Piazza (☎ 6248 9711; 19 Garema Pl,
Civic; mains $12-24; ⊗ lunch & dinner) The outdoor
tables at this well-established local favourite are usually crammed at lunchtime, and
often at dinnertime, too. Its tasty trademark
pastas come in big portions and there's a

heady wine list, so don't book yourself in for a ballroom dancing lesson afterwards.

Lemon Grass (☎ 6247 2779; 65 London Circuit, Civic; mains $9-17; ⏱ lunch & dinner Mon-Fri, dinner Sat) This is a small, informal Thai restaurant that's garnered culinary awards for its dependable cuisine. The spicy scents of stir-fries and curries pull you in by the nostrils from the front door. There's a sizable list of vegetarian mains.

Courgette (☎ 6247 4042; 54 Marcus Clarke St, Civic; lunch mains $18, dinner mains $30; ⏱ lunch & dinner Mon-Fri, dinner Sat) This fine-dining establishment may be named after a vegetable (the humble zucchini), but meat gets top billing here, from pan-seared calf liver to wonderful prawn ravioli. Frequented by an older clientele, this restaurant is earnest but low-key, and offers a splendid assortment of mature wines by the glass or bottle.

Gods Café & Bar (☎ 6248 5538; ground fl, ANU Arts Centre, Union Court, University Ave, Acton; mains $9-19; ⏱ breakfast & lunch Mon-Fri mid-Jan–mid-Dec) The menu changes every few months at this easy-going café, where academics, students and blow-ins eat well-prepared mains brimming with regional produce, and scan long lists of tea and wine. Eat in the main low-lit den or the light-filled side hall.

Asian Café (☎ 6262 6233; 32 West Row, Civic; mains $10-20; ⏱ lunch & dinner) The main room of this busy Chinese and Malaysian restaurant is cheerfully daubed with streaks of green and orange, while a smaller back room is brightened further by a skylight. It doles out accomplished laksa and soups, along with Western variations such as King Island steak and stuffed eggplant.

Little Saigon (☎ 6230 5003; cnr Alinga St & Northbourne Ave, Civic; mains $9-15; ⏱ lunch & dinner) A wide variety of Vietnamese cookery gets downed in this restaurant's big interior, and at reasonable prices. The popular 'lunch box' menu offers takeaway chicken, beef, pork or vegetarian ($5) accompanied by rice or noodles; to substitute squid or prawns costs a little extra ($7.50).

Fast food is trayed up at the **Canberra Centre Food Court** (Bunda St, Civic; meals $5-12; ⏱ lunch), including sushi, kebabs, burgers, gourmet rolls and smoothies.

Manuka

Southeast of Capital Hill is the well-groomed Manuka shopping centre, which pitches it-self as an upmarket hub for businesspeopl and professional socialites.

Alanya (☎ 6295 9678; 1st fl, Style Arcade, Frankl St; mains $18-26; ⏱ lunch & dinner Mon-Fri, dinner Sa The recipient of several industry accolade during its 20 years in the business, Alany is an excellent Turkish eatery with a vaguel formal air and some curious ceiling decora tions. Sample the *köfte* (meatballs) or som skewered chicken or lamb.

Atlantic (☎ 6232 7888; 20 Palmerston Lane; mai $28-31; ⏱ lunch & dinner Mon-Fri, dinner Sat) A se of white tablecloths is adrift in Atlantic quiet, intimate interior and up on the breez rooftop terrace. Dine on Atlantic salmo lobster and other fresh, expertly prepare catches, or keep your taste buds on dry lan with slow-braised Wagyu beef.

Abell's Kopi Tiam (☎ 6239 4199; 7 Furneaux § mains $14-20; ⏱ lunch & dinner Tue-Sun) This wel regarded Malay-Chinese partnership has colourful interior, pavement tables for a fresco grazing, a good selection of vegeta ian curries and intriguing daily specials tha have included stuffed baby cuttlefish.

My Café (☎ 6295 6632; Franklin St; mains $8-1 ⏱ breakfast, lunch & dinner) Rich daytime indu gences such as eggs Benedict and gourme focaccias make way at night for pastas an cooked meats. The food is reasonably price and there's usually a crowd packed unde the pavement marquee.

Legends (☎ 6295 3966; Franklin St; mains $16-2 ⏱ lunch & dinner Mon-Fri, dinner Sat) An upstair Spanish restaurant suffused with a jovial at mosphere and the strains of a flamenco gu tarist most nights. Nibble your way through the tapas menu ($7.50 to $9.50) or hoe int specialities such as *bacalao* (salted cod), Va encia paella or duck with fig sauce.

Kingston

Kingston has enough gleaming cafés an outdoor seating to give Manuka a run fo its latte.

Silo (☎ 6260 6060; 36 Giles St; meals $7-17; ⏱ brea fast & lunch Tue-Sat) This accomplished baker sells an outstanding range of breads an tartlets, and is a dab hand at coffee makin and egg-laden brunches. The only dowr side to eating here is the scarcity of empt chairs. Curd freaks drool at the window c the cheese room.

Santa Lucia (☎ 6295 1813; 21 Kennedy St; mains $1 22; ⏱ lunch & dinner Mon-Fri, dinner Sat) Establishe

25 years ago and still run by the same family, Santa Lucia and its red-and-white-checked tablecloths are an institution among local pasta lovers. It serves all the Italian staples, plus kids' meals and 'express lunches' for office dwellers.

First Floor (☎ 6260 6311; Green Sq, Jardine St; mains $18-22; ☺ lunch Tue-Fri, dinner Mon-Sat) This restaurant has an odd look, with its combination of weathered wooden tables, a steel bar, exposed brickwork and a bottle-glass back wall. But the effect is kind of disarming, and the wine list and meat-heavy mains are very good. Get a table looking out over Green Sq.

Dickson

Dickson's consumer precinct is a smorgasbord of Asian cuisine, where stomachs are filled with Chinese, Thai, Laotian, Vietnamese, Korean, Japanese, Turkish and Malaysian food.

Dickson Asian Noodle House (☎ 6247 6380; 29 Woolley St; mains $10-15; ☺ lunch & dinner) A perennially popular Laotian and Thai café, overflowing with customers and empty noodle bowls all week. Recent renovations have modernised the décor, but there are still no credit-card facilities and there's a $30 minimum charge or Eftpos.

Tak Kee Roast Inn (☎ 6257 4939; 10 Woolley St; mains $10-13; ☺ lunch & dinner) This one-room traditional Chinese affair, locally lauded for its skill in cooking meats, is recognisable by the skewered flesh hanging in the front window – this has the same effect on committed vegetarians that garlic has on vampires. Its won tons are superb, as is its barbecued beef brisket.

Other recommendations:

Au Lac (☎ 6262 8922; 39 Woolley St; mains $9-11; ☺ lunch & dinner Tue-Sun, dinner Mon) A simple Vietnamese vegetarian restaurant specialising in soya bean concoctions.

Kingsland Vegetarian Restaurant (☎ 6262 9350; Shop 5, Dickson Plaza, Dickson; mains $7.50-13; ☺ lunch & dinner Wed-Mon, dinner Sat) Located off Woolley St, this place serves Chinese vegetarian banquets.

Other Areas

Bernadette's Café & Restaurant (☎ 6248 5018; Wakefield Gardens, Ainslie; mains $9-17; ☺ lunch & dinner Tue-Sat, lunch Sun) This is a soothingly simple, uncluttered eatery preparing healthy vegetarian burgers, focaccias and soups, plus sal-

ads embellished with quail eggs and roast yam. Desserts are locked safely away from prying fingers in a glass-fronted strong box.

Green Herring Restaurant (☎ 6230 2657; Ginninderra Village, O'Hanlon Pl, Nicholls; mains $25-28; ☺ lunch Fri-Sun, dinner Tue-Sat) This place offers rustic cosiness in a large cottage with a memorable tumble-down look. Don't be put off by the name – it serves modern dishes with creative flourishes and exceptional desserts, and has a separate vegetarian menu.

DRINKING

Canberra's liberal licensing laws have nourished a vigorous drinking scene, with pubs and bars concentrated in Civic but some good establishments also setting themselves up in suburbs such as Dickson, O'Connor and Kingston.

Phoenix (☎ 6247 1606; 21 East Row, Civic) Regulars don't think twice about coming back to this pub after rising from the ashes of the night before, and we love it too. The mellow atmosphere, rustic decorations and armchairs incline you towards a good long sit, though it could cut back on the incense a little.

Hippo (☎ 6257 9090; www.hippobar.com.au; 17 Garema Pl, Civic) Appropriately located above Happy's restaurant, this small lounge-bar stirs up good feelings in its mixed-age crowd by mixing drinks with panache. After a few cocktails, it's harder to sit straight on the poufs and easier to be mesmerised by the ceiling fans. Wednesday night is greeted with live jazz ($10 admission).

Wig & Pen (☎ 6248 0171; cnr Alinga St & West Row, Civic) This convivial two-room brewery pub is packed with thirsty office workers on Friday night; at other times you'll come across a youthful, down-to-earth crowd. It produces several different styles of beer a year, including real English ale. Popular brews include an awarded pale ale, Bulldog Best Bitter and the 100% organic Mr Natural.

All Bar Nun (☎ 6257 9191; MacPherson St, O'Connor) A popular suburban tavern with big windows to illuminate its throng of drinkers, a covered back courtyard to retreat to, and pavement tables to snag passers-by. Despite its name, it would undoubtedly serve a nun if one ventured in.

Civic Pub (☎ 6248 6488; 8 Lonsdale St, Braddon) Some people think this place is rough as guts, while others think it's down to earth. Make up your own mind while you check out the 20-table pool room with a jukebox that's a rock'n'roll gold mine.

Durham Castle Arms (☎ 6295 1769; Green Sq, Jardine St, Kingston) At first the florals on the wall benches clash painfully with the floral carpet in 'the Durham', but after a few pints they complement each other beautifully. It stays open until at least 2am, which is good news for those stumbling around late at night looking for a pub with character rather than an image-conscious bar.

Trinity Bar (☎ 6262 5010; 28 Challis St, Dickson) A sleek bar with an intoxicating line-up of vodkas, martinis and cocktails, plus beer pulled from ceiling-hanging taps. Patrons deep in conversation or mutual infatuation array themselves along the polished bartop or slouch on comfy couches.

Knightsbridge Penthouse (☎ 6262 6221; 34 Mort St, Braddon) This bar is fun to visit because of the way it completely overdoes its quirky chic – no two couches are the same, optic fibres light up the windows, the cocktail list is bound in old *Encyclopedia Britannica* covers, and *Clockwork Orange*–style sculptures rest against the walls. It's New Orleans Gothic meets Bret Easton Ellis.

Other watering holes:

King O'Malley's (☎ 6257 0111; 131 City Walk, Civic) A labyrinthine Irish pub, with its name taking the piss out of the teetotalling bureaucrat who kept Canberra 'dry' until 1928.

PJ O'Reilly's (☎ 6230 4752; cnr Alinga St & West Row, Civic) Another place where pints of Irish beer get sloshed around; sometimes called 'Plastic McPaddy's'.

ENTERTAINMENT

Canberra's Friday night wind-down and Saturday night hangover sequel are the week's biggest social events. Mainstream music is as big here as anywhere else, but

the city is curiously good at nurturing m sical malcontents, and they pop up reg larly at various venues and festivals. F entertainment listings, see the 'Fly' sectic of Thursday's *Canberra Times* and the fr monthly street mag *bma*.

Ticketek (☎ 6219 6666; www.ticketek.com.au; Aku St, Civic) sells tickets to major events, inclu ing big-name gigs at the Royal Theatre the Canberra Convention Centre.

Live Music

Many pubs have free live music.

Toast (☎ 6230 0003; City Walk, Civic; admission 10) Diversity reigns supreme in this lai back little venue, where fans of industri goth, salsa, retro, cabaret and folk ming at the bar. The vibe is one of acceptanc all prejudices must be left to brood at t door. It's located upstairs behind Electr Shadows cinema (opposite).

ANU Union Bar (☎ 6125 2446; www.anuunion.c .au; Union Court, Acton; admission $5-20; ☺ gigs fr 8pm) Has energetic live music bouncing c its walls and into the ears of sozzled studen up to three times a week during semeste Significant student discounts usually app to gigs. It's also a good place for a game pool and a drink.

Tilley's Devine Cafe Gallery (☎ 6247 7753; ww .tilleys.com.au; cnr Wattle & Brigalow Sts, Lyneham; adm sion $20-40; ☺ shows from 9pm) You can eat this iconic, relaxed Canberra venue – th meals are sizable but fairly plain. Howeve the real reason to come here is to slide in one of the dark booths and choose fro an eclectic menu of singers, musicians ar comedians.

Nightclubs

Academy (☎ 6257 3355; www.academyclub.com.a Bunda St, Civic; admission $5-15; ☺ 10pm-late Thu-Su The old Center Cinema has been converte into this striking nightclub – the origin movie screen dominates the crowded ma dance space with frenetic, larger-than-li visuals. Upstairs is Candy Bar, a stylish coc tail dispenser with an extended 'happy hou (5pm to 7pm Wednesday to Friday). Yo can also chill out in Pod, which has a bar ar leather lounges to sink into.

icbm & Insomnia (☎ 6248 0102; 50 Northbour Ave, Civic; icbm admission free, Insomnia $5; ☺ icb 7pm-late Wed-Sat, Insomnia 9pm-late Wed-Sat) Th popular dual-club complex is on premis

nce inhabited by a legendary meat market called the Private Bin. Situated down-
tairs is icbm, where clubbers bounce to
ardrum-bursting disco and pop. Upstairs
s Insomnia, the nightclub proper where
DJs keep young groovers on their toes, and
tand-up comedians harangue the audience
n Wednesday nights.

Club Mombasa (☎ 0421 477 740; www.clubmom
asa.com.au; 1st fl, 128 Bunda St, Civic; events $5-10;
☺ 8pm-late Wed-Sat) A small, sociable club
with a dance floor and couches that haven't
changed since the height of disco fever, and
a commitment to all-night reggae, funk, R
& B, African and Latin rhythms.

Performing Arts

Canberra Theatre Centre (☎ box office 1800 802 025,
275 2700; www.canberratheatre.org.au; Civic Sq, London
Circuit, Civic; ☺ box office 9am-5.30pm Mon-Sat) There
are many dramatic goings-on within this
performing arts venue. Information and
tickets are supplied by Canberra Ticketing
in the adjacent North Building (Eftpos is
not available).

Gorman House Arts Centre (☎ 6249 7377; www
gormanhouse.com.au; Ainslie Ave, Braddon) This arts
centre hosts various theatre and dance
companies that regularly stage their own
self-hatched productions, including the innovative moves of the **Australian Choreographic
Centre** (☎ 6247 3103).

Cinemas

Electric Shadows (☎ 6247 5060; www.electricshadows
.com.au; Akuna St, Civic; adult/child/concession $14/8/9) A
venerable art-house cinema, long serving as
a foil to the multiplex mentality. Weekday
matinees (pre-5pm, excluding Wednesday)
cost adults only $9 and all Wednesday ses-
sions are $8.

Greater Union (☎ 6247 5522; www.greaterunion
.com.au; 6 Mort St, Civic; adult/child/concession $15/10/11)
This cinema venue is obsessed with main-
stream releases, but don't expect any big-
budget vitality in the aged premises. You'll
find other multiplex cinemas in suburban
shopping malls.

Sport

The Canberra Raiders are the home-town
rugby league side and during the league season (from March to September) they play
regularly at **Canberra Stadium** (☎ 6256 6700;
www.canberrastadium.com; Battye St, Bruce; P). Also

laying tackles at Canberra Stadium are the
ACT Brumbies rugby union team, who play
in the international Super 12 competition
(February to May). From October to February, catch the super-successful women's
basketball team, the Canberra Capitals, at
Southern Cross Stadium (☎ tickets 6253 3066; cnr
Cowlishaw St & Athllon Dr, Greenway; P); their com-
patriots, the AIS, play at the **AIS Training Hall**
(☎ 6214 1201; Leverrier Cres, Bruce; P).

Casino

Casino Canberra (☎ 6257 7074; www.casinocanberra
.com.au; 21 Binara St, Civic; ☺ noon-6am; P) You
can 'play to win' here, although there's no
money-back guarantee if you lose. The only
dress requirement is that you look 'neat and
tidy'.

SHOPPING

Canberra is a crafty city and a good place
for picking up creative gifts and souvenirs
from galleries, museum shops and markets.
At the time of research, a big new shopping
complex was slated for construction across
Bunda St from Garema Pl.

Canberra Centre (☎ 6247 5611; Bunda St, Civic)
Civic's main shopping centre contains dozens of speciality stores, including fashion
boutiques, department stores, jewellery
shops and an impressively stocked tea shop.
The ground-floor information desk can help
with wheelchairs and stroller hire.

Craft ACT (☎ 6262 9993; www.craftact.org.au; 1st fl,
North Bldg, Civic Sq, Civic) Presents cutting-edge
designs in the shape of bags, bowls, pen-
dants and prints. It's worth visiting just to
see the latest imaginative efforts of local
and interstate artists.

Old Bus Depot Markets (☎ 6292 8391; cnr The
Causeway & Cunningham St, Kingston; ☺ 10am-4pm
Sun) This popular, decade-old indoor mar-
ket specialises in hand-crafted goods and
regional edibles, including the output of the
Canberra district's 20-plus wineries.

Gorman House Markets (☎ 6247 3202; Gorman
House Arts Centre, Ainslie Ave, Braddon; ☺ 10am-4pm Sat)
Get a massage and your tarot read, then sift
through organic produce, vintage clothing,
books, crafts and assorted bric-a-brac.

Gold Creek Village (see p282) has many
cheesy souvenir shops, though a couple sell
good-quality crafts. Here you'll find **Aboriginal Dreamings Gallery** (☎ 6230 2922; 19 O'Hanlon
Pl, Nicholls), with an excellent selection of

Aboriginal works such as 'bush dolls' cobbled together from twigs, and eucalypt didgeridoos naturally hollowed out by termites; certificates of authenticity are provided where possible.

GETTING THERE & AWAY

Air

Canberra International Airport (☎ 6275 2236) is serviced by **Qantas** (☎ 13 13 13; www.qantas.com .au; Jolimont Centre, Northbourne Ave, Civic) and **Virgin Blue** (☎ 13 67 89; www.virginblue.com.au), with direct flights to Adelaide (from $170), Brisbane (from $120), Melbourne (from $80) and Sydney (from $95).

Brindabella Airlines (☎ 6248 8711; www.brinda bella-airlines.com.au) flies between Canberra, Albury Wodonga (from $90) and Newcastle (from $290).

Bus

The **interstate bus terminal** (Northbourne Ave, Civic) is at the Jolimont Centre, and has showers, left-luggage lockers, public Internet access and free phone lines to the visitor information centre and some budget accommodations. Inside is the **CountryLink travel centre** (☎ 13 22 32, 6257 1576; ☺ 9am-5pm Mon-Fri), which books seats on most services. Travellers headed to the south coast can board a CountryLink coach that travels via Cooma to Eden (adult/concession $45/25, 4¼ hours). **Travelscene** (☎ 1300 733 323, 6249 6006; 65 Northbourne Ave; ☺ 8am-6pm Mon-Fri, 9am-5pm Sat & Sun) takes bookings for Transborder, Sid Fogg's Coachlines and Rixon.

Greyhound Australia (☎ 13 14 99; www.greyhound .com.au; Jolimont Centre office ☺ 6am-9.30pm) has frequent services to Sydney (adult/concession $35/32, four to five hours) and also runs to/from Adelaide ($140/130, 20 hours) and Melbourne ($70/65, nine hours). At the time of writing it was unclear if its winter services to Cooma and Thredbo would continue.

Murrays (☎ 13 22 51; www.murrays.com.au; ☺ Jolimont Centre counter 7am-7pm) has daily express services running to Sydney (adult/concession $35/24, 3¼ hours) and also runs to Batemans Bay ($24/22, 2½ hours), Narooma ($36/32, 4½ hours) and Wollongong ($31/24, 3½ hours).

Transborder (☎ 6241 0033; www.transborderexpress .com.au) runs daily to Yass (adult/concession $13/9, 50 minutes). Its 'Alpinexpress' service runs to Thredbo ($65/55, three hours) via

Jindabyne ($45/35, 2½ hours) daily exce Tuesday and Thursday.

Sid Fogg's Coachlines (☎ 1800 045 952; www. foggs.com.au) runs between Canberra and New castle (adult/concession $55/50, 4½ hours **Rixon** (☎ 13 34 10) heads from Canberra Batemans Bay (adult/concession $30/27, 2 hours) and Moruya ($32/29, 3¼ hours).

Car & Motorcycle

The Hume Hwy connects Sydney and Me bourne, passing 50km north of Canberr The Federal Hwy runs north to connect wi the Hume near Goulburn and the Barto Hwy meets the Hume near Yass. To th south, the Monaro Hwy connects Canber with Cooma.

Rental car prices start at around $50 day. Major companies with city-centre o fices and desks at the airport include th following:

Avis (☎ 13 63 33, 6249 6088; 17 Lonsdale St, Braddon)
Budget (☎ 1300 362 848, 6257 2200; cnr Mort & Girrahween Sts, Braddon)
Hertz (☎ 13 30 39, 6257 4877; 32 Mort St, Braddon)
Thrifty (☎ 1300 367 227, 6247 7422; 29 Lonsdale St, Braddon)

Another option is locally-owned **Rumb** (☎ 6280 7444; 11 Paragon Mall, Gladstone St, Fyshwic Its office is usually open only on weekda (weekends by appointment).

Train

Kingston train station (☎ 6295 1198; Burke Cre located off Wentworth Ave, is the city's r terminus. Bus Nos 39 and 80 run betwee here and Civic. You can book trains an connecting buses inside the station at th **CountryLink travel centre** (☎ 13 22 32, 6239 70! ☺ 6.15am-5.30pm Mon-Sat, 10.30am-5.30pm Sun).

CountryLink trains run to/from Sydn (adult/child $50/25, 4¼ hours, two dail There's no direct train to Melbourne, but CountryLink coach to Cootamundra lin with the XPT train to Melbourne ($95/5 nine hours, one daily); the service leaves Jol mont at 10am. You can also travel via bus Yass Junction, then jump on an XPT train Melbourne ($105/55, nine hours, one dail A longer but more scenic bus/train servi to Melbourne is the V-Line Capital Lir ($60/38, 10½ hours) running every Tuesd and Friday via Cooma and the East Gipp land forests to Sale, where you board th

Melbourne-bound train. A similarly priced Canberra–Melbourne option that runs daily is the V-Line service that buses you to Albury, from where you catch a train heading southward (adult/concession $60/38, eight hours).

GETTING AROUND
To/From the Airport
Canberra International Airport is in Pialligo, 7km southeast of the city. Taxi fares to the city average $20.

Deane's Buslines (☎ 6299 3722) operates the AirLiner bus ($5, 20 minutes, 11 times daily Monday to Friday), which runs between the airport and the city interchange (bay 6).

Car & Motorcycle
Canberra has an annoyingly circuitous road system, but there are no one-way inner-city streets to further tax your sense of direction, and the wide, relatively uncluttered main roads make driving easy (even at the so-called 'peak hour' times).

There's plenty of well-signposted parking available in Civic. The visitor information centre has a *Motorbike Parking in Canberra* pamphlet.

Public Transport
BUS
Canberra's public transport provider is the **ACT Internal Omnibus Network** (Action; ☎ 13 17 10; www.action.act.gov.au) – the bus network of this organisation is often criticised by local users for its poor dependability. The main Civic Bus Interchange is along Alinga St, East Row and Mort St in Civic. Visit the **information kiosk** (East Row, Civic; ☿ 7.15am-5pm) for free route maps and timetables, or buy the all-routes *Canberra Bus Map* ($2.20) from newsagents.

You can buy single-trip tickets (adult/concession $2.40/1.30), but a better bet for most visitors is to buy a daily ticket (adult/concession $6/3). Pre-purchase tickets from Action agents (including the visitor information centre and some newsagents) or buy them from the driver.

Canberra Day Tours operates a hop-on, hop-off bus service; for details see p273.

Taxi
Canberra Cabs (☎ 13 22 27) has vehicles with access for wheelchairs. There's a convenient taxi rank on Bunda St, outside the Greater Union cinema. A typical taxi fare from Civic to Dickson should cost around $5 to $6.

AROUND CANBERRA

For information and maps on attractions around Canberra, ransack the visitor information centre.

PICNICKING, SWIMMING & WALKING AREAS
Spots for picnics and barbecues are scattered throughout the ACT, though they're rarely accessible by public transport. **Black Mountain** is handy for picnics, and swimming spots lie along both the **Murrumbidgee** and **Cotter Rivers**. Other popular riverside areas include **Uriarra Crossing**, **Casuarina Sands**, **Kambah Pool Reserve**, **Cotter Dam** and **Pine Island**.

Tidbinbilla Nature Reserve (☎ 02-6205 1233; ☿ reserve 9am-6pm, visitor information centre 9am-4.30pm Mon-Fri, 9am-5.30pm Sat & Sun), off Paddy's River Rd, 45km southwest of the city, is threaded with bushwalking tracks. However, recovery from the devastating January 2003 bushfires will take a long time. You can visit the only survivor from the reserve's koala enclosure, who was christened Lucky.

The facilities at **Corin Forest** (☎ 02-6235 7333; www.corin.com.au; Corin Rd; ☿ 10am-5pm Sat, Sun & public holidays, 10am-4pm Mon-Fri during school holidays) include picnicking areas and a café, but the main attractions are the various rides. There's a 1.2km bobsled track and a flying fox, both open year-round; a waterslide, open from December to Easter; and a 'snowplay' area cushioned by natural drifts and snow-making equipment, open June to September. See the website for prices and special packages.

Namadgi National Park includes eight peaks higher than 1700m and offers excellent opportunities for bushwalking and mountain biking. For more information, visit the **Namadgi visitor information centre** (☎ 02-6207 2900; Naas Rd; ☿ 9am-4pm Mon-Fri, 9am-4.30pm Sat & Sun), 2km south of Tharwa. There is **camping** (unpowered sites per person $3) available at Honeysuckle Creek, Mt Clear and Orroral River; bookings must be made in advance through the visitor information centre.

CANBERRA SPACE CENTRE

The Canberra Deep Space Communication Complex, 40km southwest of the city, is one of the three earth-bound facilities that comprise the National Aeronautics and Space Administration's (NASA's) Deep Space Network. Within the complex is the **Canberra Space Centre** (☎ 02-6201 7800; www.cdscc .nasa.gov; admission free; ◷ 9am-5pm), located off Paddy's River Rd, where there are interesting displays of spacecraft and deep-space tracking technology, plus a piece of lunar basalt scooped up by Apollo XI in 1969. A theatrette continuously screens short films on space exploration.

GOLD CREEK VILLAGE

There are several attractions at **Gold Creek Village** (Map p262; ☎ 02-6253 9780; Gold Creek Rd, Barton Hwy, Nicholls; admission free; ◷ 10am-5pm), a combination of colonial kitsch, interesting exhibits and knick-knack shops that gets overrun by families and tour groups.

Kids can get in touch with their prehistoric selves at the attention-getting **National Dinosaur Museum** (☎ 02-6230 2655; www.national dinosaurmuseum.com.au; adult/child/concession/family $9.50/6.50/7.50/30; ◷ 10am-5pm, last entry 4.30pm), where fossil workshops and some giant, chronologically arranged bones await discovery. The **Australian Reptile Centre** (☎ 02-6253 8533; adult/child/concession/family $8/5.50/6.50/28; ◷ 10am-5pm) is a fascinating showcase of reptilian life. Behind glass are tree skinks and scrub pythons, plus the world's three deadliest (yet surprisingly nonaggressive)

land snakes. The prehistory gallery bring you up to speed on trilobites and has th impressive skeleton of a 70 million-year-ol carnivorous fish, the *Xiphactinus*.

Ginninderra Village (admission free; ◷ 10am-5pr sported a few 'for lease' signs when we vi ited, but still had some worthwhile galleries, second-hand book shop and an 1883 schoo house. Nearby is **Cockington Green** (☎ 02-62 2273; www.cockington-green.com.au; adult/child/fam $14/7/37; ◷ 9.30am-5pm, last entry 4.15pm), an im maculately manicured miniature English vi lage saturated with quaintness.

LANYON HOMESTEAD & NOLAN GALLERY

Beside the Murrumbidgee, 20km south (Canberra, is the beautiful National Tru: property **Lanyon Homestead** (☎ 02-6235 567 Tharwa Dr; adult/concession/family $7/4/15; ◷ 10ar 4pm Tue-Sun), explorable via a guided tour. O site, but in a separate building, is the **Nola Gallery** (☎ 02-6237 5192; adult/concession/fami $3/2/6; ◷ 10am-4pm Tue-Sun), containing pain ings by celebrated Australian artist Sidne Nolan, including famous Ned Kelly art an spray-canned caricatures. You can buy combined ticket to both the homestead an gallery (adult/concession/family $8/5/19).

CUPPACUMBALONG

This 1922 **homestead** (☎ 02-6237 5116; Na Rd; ◷ 11am-5pm Wed-Sun & public holidays), nea Tharwa, has a National Trust–listed garde and a quality Australian craftware studi and gallery.

Queensland

Time and place tick into a languid dimension when you cross the Queensland border. Occupying Australia's northeast corner, this immense state dazzles visitors with a diversity of landscapes and colours, from the postcard beaches of the Sunshine Coast, to the rich greens of the Daintree and other rainforests, and the azure blues of the Great Barrier Reef. Beyond striking mountain ranges, the interior stretches into the sunburnt Outback, where the big empty reveals an ocean of pristine terra firma and humbling horizons.

Touted as Australia's 'Sunshine State', Queensland is allegedly blessed with 300 days of sunshine, and outside the deluge of the wet season, the sky seems unceasingly awash with an amber glow. With a touch of help from the unhurried Queensland psyche, it weaves a little magic to melt urban decay and winter chills. It's not all about rest and relaxation though. Flick off the beach towel and put your muscles and mettle to the test with a bout of white-water rafting, scuba diving, snorkelling, bushwalking, horse riding, surfing, bungee jumping, skydiving, abseiling…or whatever else your imagination can conjure.

Once you've exploited the landscape and the innumerable ways to enjoy it, indulge in Queensland's ever-changing culture. Brisbane, the brown-skinned capital, is lively and cosmopolitan. In the north, Cairns is a travellers' mecca, humming with the feel of a global village. Between the two are strings of towns and islands where you can indulge in fine dining, drinking and living. The one constant throughout? Queensland's affable and hospitable population.

HIGHLIGHTS

- Diving, snorkelling and meeting the aquatic locals in the **Great Barrier Reef** (p370)
- Frolicking in freshwater lakes and on the beach highway of **Fraser Island** (p354)
- Immersing yourself in **Cape Tribulation** (p449) and the ancient **Daintree rainforest** (p447)
- Navigating the azure **Whitsunday Islands** (p385)
- Sassy dining on the **Sunshine Coast** (p334) and heavy partying on the **Gold Coast** (p323)
- Exploring the bronzed Outback and finding a new mate in **Mt Isa** (p376)
- Navigating Queensland's national parks: platypus-spotting in **Eungella** (p391), ogling **Carnarvon Gorge** (p374) and bushwalking on **Hinchinbrook Island** (p412)

- Cape Tribulation & Daintree Rainforest
- ★ Great Barrier Reef
- ★ Hinchinbrook Island
- ★ Mt Isa
- ★ Whitsunday Islands
- Eungella ★
- Carnarvon Gorge ★
- ★ Fraser Island
- Sunshine Coast ★
- ★ Gold Coast

- TELEPHONE CODE: 07 ■ POPULATION: 3,860,100 ■ www.queenslandholidays.com.au

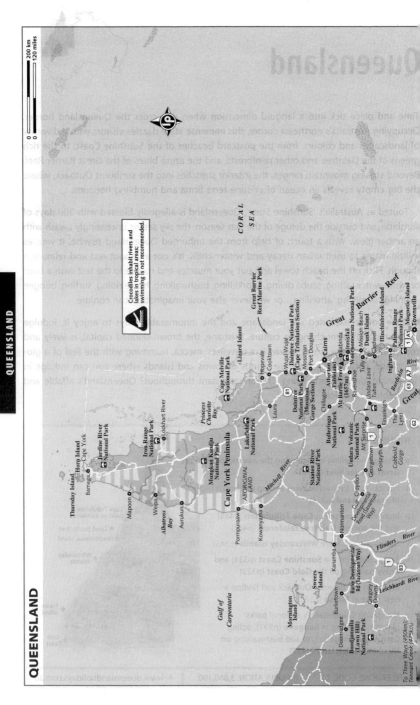

QUEENSLAND

Crocodiles inhabit rivers and lakes in tropical areas; swimming is not recommended.

QUEENSLAND

200 km
120 miles

CORAL SEA

Great Barrier Reef Marine Park

Great Barrier Reef

Lizard Island

Cape Melville National Park

Princess Charlotte Bay

Hopevale
Cooktown
Wujal Wujal
Daintree National Park
Cape Tribulation Section
Mossman
Cape Tribulation
Port Douglas

Laura
Daintree National Park (Mossman Gorge Section)
Atherton Tableland
Chillagoe
Mt Bartle Frere (1657m)
Babinda
Innisffail
Wooroonooran National Park
Mission Beach
Dunk Island
Tully
Cardwell
Hinchinbrook Island
Ingham
Paluma Range National Park
Magnetic Island
Townsville

Lakefield National Park

Mungkan Kandju National Park

Iron Range National Park

Lockhart River

Jardine River National Park

Horn Island
Thursday Island
Cape York
Bamaga

Cape York Peninsula

ABORIGINAL LAND

Staaten River National Park

Bullerringa National Park

Undara Volcanic National Park
Mt Surprise
Undara Lava Tubes
Georgetown
Forsayth
Cobbold Gorge

Ravenshoe

Mitchell River

Staaten River

Mapoon
Weipa
Aurukun
Albatross Bay

Pormpuraaw
Kowanyama

Normanton
Croydon
Cut

Gulf Burke Developmental Rd (Savanah Way)

Karumba

Sweers Island

Mornington Island

Gulf of Carpentaria

Burketown
Doomadgee

Boodjamulla (Lawn Hill) National Park

Gregory Downs

Flinders River

Georgetown
Gulf Developmental Road (Savanah Way)

Leichhardt River

To Three Ways (450km); Tennant Creek (475km)

Burdekin River
Burdekin
A1
A7
Great
The Lynd
62

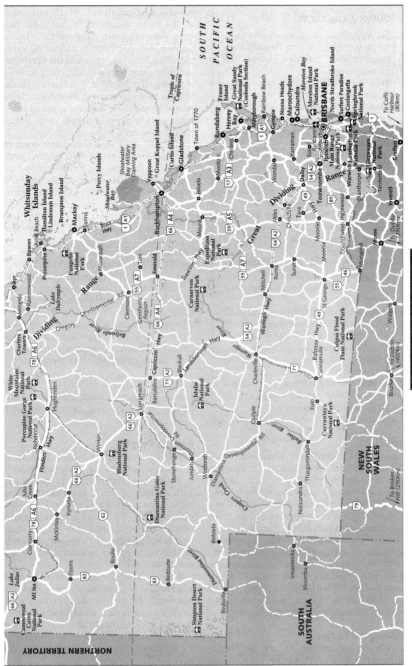

QUEENSLAND

QUEENSLAND FACTS

Eat: Moreton Bay Bugs, prawns and barramundi (especially at Lake Tinaroo), Rockhampton steak, mangoes, bananas and macadamia nuts

Drink: Pot of Four X, Bundaberg Rum, Granite Belt wines

Read: David Malouf's *Fly Away Peter*, Thea Astley's *It's Raining in Mango*, Andrew McGahan's *Praise*, John Birmingham's *He Died with a Felafel in His Hand*

Listen to: Powderfinger's *Vulture Street*, George's *Polyserena*, Pete Murray's *Feeler*, Christine Anu's *Stylin' Up*

Watch: *Crocodile Dundee, Gettin' Square, The Thin Red Line, Scooby Doo, Dead Calm*

Avoid: Surfers Paradise during Schoolies Week, cane toads, sunburn, stingers

Locals' nickname: Cane Toads, Banana Benders

Swim at: Fraser Island's Lakes McKenzie and Wabby, Sunshine Coast's Peregian and Noosa Beaches, Great Keppel Island, Great Barrier Reef

Strangest festival: Kynuna's (in outback Queensland) surf life-saving carnival every April, Brisbane's Story Bridge Hotel's Australia Day (January 26) Cockroach Races, Brisbane's National Festival of Beers in mid-September

Tackiest tourist attraction: Big Pineapple (p344), although the Big Mango and Big Gumboot come a close second

---

HISTORY

Queensland started as a penal colony in 1824, but by 1859 it had become a separate colony independent of New South Wales (NSW). Wholesale land acquisition by settlers (Queensland's early white settlers indulged in one of the greatest land grabs of all time) met with fierce, but ultimately futile, Aboriginal resistance. With the discovery of gold and other minerals in the '60s and '70s, and a highly successful experimentation with sugar-cane production, Queensland's economy and population began to explode – it has never looked back. Today, mining and agriculture still form the economy's backbone.

Aboriginal People

By the turn of the 19th century, the Aborigines who had survived the bloody settlement of Queensland, which saw some of the worst massacres in Australia, had been comprehensively run off their lands and the white authorities had set up evershrinking reserves to contain the survivors. A few of these were run according to well-meaning, if misguided, missionary ideals but the majority were strife-ridden places where people from different areas and cultures were thrown unhappily together as virtual prisoners.

It wasn't until the 1980s that control of the reserves was transferred to their residents and the reserves became known as 'communities'. However, these freehold grants, known as Deeds of Grant in Trust, are subject to a right of access for prospecting, exploration or mining.

Increasing visitor interest in indigenous culture has created opportunities for some contact with Aboriginals. In addition to the fantastic rock-art sites at various locations, you can encounter living Aboriginal culture at the Yarrabah community south of Cairns and the Hopevale community north of Cooktown, and take tours led by Aboriginal guides at Mossman Gorge and Malanda Falls. At the Tjapukai Cultural Park (p424) in Cairns, an award-winning Aboriginal dance group performs most days for tourists.

Perhaps the most exciting event is the Laura Aboriginal Dance Festival (p456), held every second year in June on Cape York Peninsula.

Kanaka People

Another people on the fringes of Queensland society are the Kanakas, descendants of Pacific islanders brought in during the 19th century to work, predominantly on sugar plantations, under virtual slave conditions. The first Kanakas were brought over in the 1860s, and soon a brisk business in kidnapping and transporting South Sea islanders (known as 'blackbirding') had sprung up.

About 60,000 Kanakas were kidnapped and brought to Queensland before the trade was finally banned by the 1901 Pacific Islands Labourers Act. Most were promptly shipped back to the South Pacific, but the descendants of the 1600 or so who stayed are concentrated in the coastal area to the north of Rockhampton.

GEOGRAPHY & CLIMATE

Queensland is dominated by the coast, and it's no surprise that most of the settlements and tourist attractions are concentrated in the narrow coastal strip. This strip has some amazing natural features such as the Great Barrier Reef, lush rainforests, endless fields of sugar cane and stunning national parks.

Inland is the Great Dividing Range, which comes close to the coast of Queensland before slicing its way down into NSW and Victoria, and the tablelands – fertile areas of flat agricultural land that run to the west. Finally, there's the barren Outback, which fades into the Northern Territory (NT).

In the far northern Gulf Country and Cape York Peninsula there are huge empty regions cut by countless dry riverbeds, which can become swollen torrents in the wet season. During this time, the network of waterways sometimes brings road transport to a complete halt.

Queensland seasons are more a case of hot and wet or cool and dry than of summer and winter. November/December to April/May is the wetter, hotter half of the year, while the real Wet, particularly affecting northern coastal areas, is January to March. This is also the season for cyclones and, if one hits, the Bruce Hwy can be blocked by the ensuing floods.

In the south, Brisbane and Rockhampton get about 450mm of rain from January to March, and temperatures in Brisbane rarely drop below 20°C. Queensland doesn't really experience 'cold weather', except inland or upland at night from about May to September. Inland, of course, there's also a lot less rain than near the coast.

INFORMATION

There are official tourist offices in just about every city and town in Queensland, staffed, largely, by friendly and knowledgeable volunteers. **Tourism Queensland** (Map pp296-7; ☎ 13 88 33, 3535 3535; www.tq.com.au, www.queenslandtravel .com; 30 Makerston St, Brisbane; ⏰ 8.30am-5pm Mon-Fri, 9am-1pm Sat) is the government-run body responsible for promoting Queensland interstate and overseas. Its Queensland Travel offices, which are located in state capitals, act primarily as promotional and booking offices. The Tourism Queensland website (www.accessiblequeensland.com) is also a good source of information for disabled visitors to the state. Another excellent online resource is www.queenslandholidays.com .au, which is devoid of any industry content and aimed squarely at tourists.

Adults travelling with children can check out the **Bub Hub** (www.qld.bubhub.com.au) website, which lists everything from clinic contacts and locations to prenatal care and activities for newborns to toddlers, or call the **Child Care Information Service** (☎ 1800 637 711, 3224 4225).

For safety tips on travelling in Queensland, check out the website www.police .qld.gov.au/toursafe

For comprehensive information about the state, it's worth picking up a copy of Lonely Planet's *Queensland & Great Barrier Reef* guidebook.

Some other useful contacts are the **Queensland Parks & Wildlife Service** (QPWS; ☎ 13 13 04; www.epa.qld.gov.au) and **Royal Automobile Club of Queensland** (RACQ; ☎ 13 19 05; www.racq.com .au). Also check out www.wotif.com.au for discounted accommodation and also www .quickbeds.com.au for last-minute accommodation.

NATIONAL PARKS

Queensland has some 220 national parks and state forests, and while some comprise only a single hill or lake, others are major wilderness areas. Many islands and stretches of coast are national parks.

Three of the most spectacular national parks inland are Lamington (p333), on the forested rim of an ancient volcano on the NSW border; Carnarvon (p374), with its 30km gorge southwest of Rockhampton; and, near Mackay, rainforested Eungella (p391), swarming with wildlife. The coast also boasts some spectacular nature haunts, including the Great Sandy National Park (p343), a dense tangle of mangroves, rivers and forest; and, of course, the jewel in the crown – the Great Barrier Reef Marine Park (see the boxed text, p370).

Big parks usually have a network of walking tracks. You can get information directly from park rangers, or from the **Queensland Parks & Wildlife Service** (QPWS; ☎ 13 13 04; www .epa.qld.gov.au) agencies in most major towns.

Many parks have camping grounds with toilets and showers, and there are often privately run camping grounds, motels and lodges on the park fringes. To camp anywhere in a national park you need a permit, available in advance either by calling QPWS or booking online. Camping in national parks and state forests costs $4/16 per person/family per night. Popular parks fill up at holiday times, so booking well ahead is advisable.

ACTIVITIES
Adrenaline-Charged Activities
Queensland has its fair share of activities to satisfy adrenaline junkies. Bungee jumping and similar thrill rides can be found at major tourist stops, such as Surfers Paradise, Airlie Beach and Cairns. If you need something a tad more heart-stopping, parachuting and tandem skydiving opportunities are also prolific; two of the best spots to jump out of a plane are Caloundra (p335) and Mission Beach (p414).

Bushwalking
There are excellent bushwalking possibilities in many parts of the state and national parks and state forests often have marked walking trails. Among the favourites are: Lamington (p333), Girraween (p346), Carnarvon (p374), Hinchinbrook Island (p412), home to the spectacular Thorsborne Trail, and Wooroonooran (p416), which contains Queensland's highest peak, Mt Bartle Frere (1657m).

The Queensland government has also developed the Great Walks of Queensland, six tracks designed to allow walkers to experience rainforests and bushlands without disturbing the ecosystem. They include the Whitsundays, Sunshine Coast Hinterland, Mackay Highlands, Fraser Island, Gold Coast Hinterland and the Wet Tropics (tropical North Queensland). The Whitsunday Great Walk and Fraser Island Great Walk are already completed and the rest should be up and running by mid-2006. Contact **QPWS** (☎ 13 13 04; www.epa.qld.gov.au) for more information.

There are bushwalking clubs around the state and several useful guidebooks, including *National Park Bushwalks of the Great South East* ($24.95), a QPWS publication with graded walks between Fraser Island and the NSW border. Lonely Planet's *Walking in Australia* includes three walks in Queensland, which range from two to five days in length.

Diving & Snorkelling
The Queensland coast is littered with enough spectacular dive sites to make you giddy and there are dozens of operators vying to teach you or provide you with the ultimate dive safari. Learning here is fairly inexpensive – a four- or five-day PADI (Professional Association of Diving Instructors) course costs anything from $170 to $500 – and you can usually choose to do a good part of your learning in the warm waters of the Barrier Reef itself.

Every major town along the coast has one or more diving schools – the three most popular places are Airlie Beach, Cairns and Townsville – but standards vary from place to place and course to course. Good instructors move around from company to company, so ask around to see which company is currently well regarded.

When choosing a course, look at how much of your open-water experience will be out on the reef. Many budget courses only offer shore dives, which are frequently less interesting. Normally you have to show you can tread water for 10 minutes and swim 200m before you can start a course. Most schools require a medical, which usually costs extra (around $50).

While school standards are generally high, each year a number of newly certified divers are stricken with 'the bends' and end up in the decompression chamber in Townsville. This potentially fatal condition is caused by bubbles of nitrogen that form in the blood when divers ascend too quickly to the surface – always ascend slowly and on dives over 9m in depth, take a rest stop en route to the surface.

For divers, trips and equipment hire are available just about everywhere. You'll need evidence of your qualifications, and some places may also ask to see your diving log book. You can snorkel just about everywhere, too. There are coral reefs off some mainland beaches and around several of the islands, and many day trips out to the Great Barrier Reef provide snorkelling gear free.

During the Wet (usually January to March) floods can wash a lot of mud out into the ocean, and visibility for divers and snorkellers is sometimes affected.

Lonely Planet's *Diving & Snorkelling Australia's Great Barrier Reef* is an excellent guide to all the dives available on the reef.

Sailing & Fishing

Sailing enthusiasts will find many places with boats and/or sailboards for hire, both along the coast and inland. Manly (near Brisbane), Airlie Beach and the Whitsunday Islands are possibly the biggest centres and you can indulge in almost any type of boating or sailing. The Great Barrier Reef has traditionally been a popular fishing ground, but a recent overhaul of the zoning laws has tightened the area that can be fished. For comprehensive information on where and when you can fish, contact the **Great Barrier Reef Marine Park Authority** (☎ 4750 0700; www.gbrmpa.gov.au), based at Reef HQ in Townsville (p401). The Whitsundays, with their plentiful bays and relatively calm waters, are particularly popular for sailing; day trips start at $80 and multiple-day trips from $350. Bareboat charters (sailing yourself) are also possible – see the boxed text, p397.

Fishing is one of Queensland's most popular sports and you can hire fishing gear and/or boats in many places. Karumba, Cooktown and North Stradbroke Island are some of the more frequented spots.

Surfing

The southeastern coast of Queensland has some magnificent breaks, most notably at Coolangatta, Burleigh Heads, Surfers Paradise, Noosa and Town of 1770. Various surf shops offer board hire, or you can buy cheap second-hands. Surfing lessons are a good idea before you hit the big surf; Surfers and Noosa are good places to learn. See the boxed text, p1012 for information on Queensland's best breaks.

Swimming

North of Fraser Island the beaches are sheltered by the Great Barrier Reef, so they're great for swimming but not good for surfing. The clear, sheltered waters of the reef hardly need to be mentioned. There are also innumerable good freshwater swimming spots around the state. Box jellyfish are a serious problem from Rockhampton north between October and April; see the boxed text (p366) for more information.

White-Water Rafting & Canoeing

The Tully and North Johnstone Rivers between Townsville and Cairns are the big ones for white-water rafting. You can do day trips for around $150.

Sea-kayaking is also a popular activity, with various trips running from Cairns, Mission Beach, Cape Tribulation, Noosa and Maroochydore.

Coastal Queensland is full of waterways and lakes, so there's no shortage of canoeing territory. You can rent canoes or join canoe tours in several places – among them Noosa, North Stradbroke Island, Townsville and Cairns.

TOURS

There are all sorts of tours offered around Queensland, although most of them concentrate on a small area. Many are connected with a particular activity (eg bushwalking or horse riding) or area (eg 4WD tours to Cape York), plus anything ranging from a 1½-hour trip around Surfers Paradise or a boat on wheels to a week-long outback adventure. There are also thousands of brochures in hostels, hotels and tourist information offices. Although choosing one can often be a hit-and-miss affair, you'll find some of the best the state has to offer mentioned throughout the chapter.

Good online resources for tours include www.queenslandholidays.com.au and www.queenslandtravel.com.

GETTING THERE & AROUND

Most travellers will arrive in Queensland from NSW, and while your car or bus can legally be inspected crossing the border, it hardly ever happens. You probably won't even notice that you've passed from one state to the other. Brisbane (p315) is the main port of call for inbound flights into Queensland and is the main international airport for the state, but Cairns and the Gold Coast airports also receive international flights. For more information, see the Transport chapter (p1035).

Air

The three national carriers, **Qantas Airways** (☎ 13 13 13; www.qantas.com.au), **Jetstar** (☎ 13 15 38; www.jetstar.com.au) and **Virgin Blue** (☎ 13 67 89; www.virginblue.com.au), fly to Queensland's major cities. There is also a multitude of smaller airlines operating up and down the coast, across the Cape York Peninsula and into the Outback.

QUEENSLAND

Alliance Airlines (☎ 3212 1212; www.allianceairlines
.com.au) Flies between Brisbane, Mt Isa and Townsville.
Australian Airlines (☎ 13 13 13; www.australian
airlines.com.au) Flies between Cairns and the Gold Coast.
Macair (☎ 13 13 13; www.macair.com.au) The major
outback carrier.
Sunshine Express (☎ 13 13 13; www.sunshineexpress
.com.au) Flies from Brisbane to the Sunshine Coast,
Maryborough and Hervey Bay.

Boat

It's possible, with difficulty, to make your
way along the coast or even over to Papua
New Guinea or Darwin by crewing on the
numerous yachts and cruisers that sail
Queensland waters. Ask at harbours, marinas or sailing clubs. Manly (near Brisbane),
Airlie Beach, Townsville and Cairns are
good places to try. You'll normally have to
contribute some money for your passage.
For information regarding crewing, see the
boxed text, p397.

Bus

Greyhound Australia (☎ 13 14 99; www.greyhound
.com.au), the largest bus company in Australia,
offers comprehensive coverage of Queensland and all the major tourist destinations, as
well as excellent interstate connections.

The busiest route is up the coast on the
Bruce Hwy from Brisbane to Cairns – there
are various passes that cover this route, allowing multiple stops along all or part of the
coast. Most passes involve interstate travel
and attract a 10% discount for members of
YHA, VIP, Nomads and other approved organisations, as well as card-carrying seniors/
pensioners. Useful passes for Queensland include the 'Mini Travellers Pass', which gives
you 30 days to travel from Sydney to Cairns
for $205. The 'Sunseeker Ex Sydney' enables
you to do the same thing in 183 days for
$385, and the 'Sunseeker Ex Brisbane' allows
you to travel between Brisbane and Cairns
within 183 days for $325. There are also
several passes that include outback destinations en route to the NT. Check the Greyhound Australia website for more details.
See Transport (p1044) for more information
on interstate bus passes.

Premier Motor Service (☎ 13 34 10; www.premier
ms.com.au) also covers the route between
Sydney, Brisbane and Cairns, with fewer
services than Greyhound, but often slightly
cheaper fares.

Car

Most locals enjoy the luxury of getting around
Queensland by car; therefore, roads are
generally in good condition, in particular
along the coast and main thoroughfares in
the hinterland and outback. However, they
can often turn into badly maintained sealed
roads or dirt tracks in the more remote
areas of the state. And it seems quite a few
drivers aren't much into speeding – in fact,
things are slow paced and they sometimes
don't make the speed limit.

For car hire information see individual
destinations.

Train

Queensland Rail (☎ 13 22 32, 1300 131 722; www.travel
train.com.au) operates seven services in total
throughout Queensland. The main railway
line is the Brisbane to Cairns run, which is
serviced by the *Tilt Train*, a high-speed connection that operates three times weekly,
and the *Sunlander*, a more leisurely option
with four services weekly. There are also inland services from Brisbane to Charleville,
Brisbane to Longreach, and from Townsville
to Mt Isa, plus a *Tilt Train* service between
Brisbane and Rockhampton. More detail is
listed under the relevant destinations.

BRISBANE

☎ 07 / pop 1.5 million

It's Australia's third-largest city, but while
other capitals compete vociferously in their
endeavour to reach top billing in the status
stakes, Brisbane quietly executes its evolution in true, casual Queensland style. There's
no need to advertise the virtues – locals already know it's one of the most desirable
places in Oz to live. For visitors, the city is an
outstanding précis of Australia; the big-city
package exists here but the pretensions and
speed are refreshingly absent.

Start with a metropolis that reclines
languidly over a tropical landscape. Dis-
sect it with the undulating Brisbane River
and mix in a climate that lures southerners by the chilly townload every winter.
Weave throughout a smorgasbord of cultural flavours, simmering in cafés, theatres,
art-house cinemas, concert halls, galleries,
museums and live music venues. Pepper the
vista with subtropical gardens and pano-

BRISBANE IN...

Two Days

Acquaint yourself with Brisbane's pace by milling about **Queen St Mall** (p303). Head into **Brisbane City Hall** (p295) to learn about the city's history and to get a bird's-eye view from the tower at the **Museum of Brisbane** (p295). Gape at the beautiful former **Treasury Building** (p295) and then fuel up at funky **Jorge** (p309) or fine **E'cco** (p309). After lunch head down to marvel at **Parliament House** (p295), ogle contemporary art at the **QUT Art Museum** (p295) and take an afternoon nap in the **City Botanic Gardens** (p298). Finish the day with a brew at the **Belgian Beer Cafe** (p312).

Start day two with an indulgent breakfast in **Fortitude Valley's** (p310) Brunswick St Mall and then do some window (or actual) shopping in the nearby boutiques. Make your way to the **South Bank Parklands** (p299) and delve into the **Queensland Cultural Centre** (p299). If it's the weekend, potter about the **South Bank Markets** (p315) before cooling off at **Streets Beach** (p299). Once you've soaked up the sun, head over to the West End and dine on native fare at **Cumquats** (p311), or experience organic bliss at **Mondo Organics** (p311).

Four Days

Day three, give the feet a rest and take a cruise up the Brisbane River to **Lone Pine Koala Sanctuary** (p301). Watch the city unfold around you and take a closer look at Brisbane's leafy sprawl.

On day four make your way to the top of **Mt Coot-tha** (p299) for far-reaching views. Take in a short bushwalk through the reserve and visit the beautiful **Brisbane Botanic Gardens** (p300). Dazzle your senses at the **Sir Thomas Brisbane Planetarium** (p300). Cap the day off with a banquet in Fortitude Valley's **Chinatown** (p310), or a chic dinner at **Anise** (p310) or **Sunbar Restaurant and Lounge** (p310). Work it all off at one of the Valley's clubs or catch a live gig at **Zoo** (p314).

ramic views from lookouts or river vessels. Add to this a calendar stocked with festivals and an anthology of eateries and you'll realise what all the low-key fuss is about.

HISTORY

The first settlement here was established at Redcliffe on Moreton Bay in 1824 – a penal colony for difficult convicts from the Botany Bay colony in NSW. After struggling with inadequate water supplies and hostile Aborigines, the colony was relocated to safer territory on the banks of the Brisbane River, before the whole colony idea was abandoned in 1839.

Moreton Bay was thrown open to free settlers in 1842, an action which marked the beginning of Brisbane's rise to prominence and the beginning of the end for the region's Aborigines.

ORIENTATION

Brisbane's city centre or CBD is bound by a U-shaped loop of the Brisbane River. The action is centred on pedestrianised Queen St Mall, which runs down to the former Treasury Building (now a casino) and Victoria Bridge to South Bank.

Across Victoria Bridge is South Brisbane and the South Bank Parklands; further south is the hip West End. Ann St runs northeast of the CBD into trendy Fortitude Valley. The Story Bridge (Brisbane's answer to the Sydney Harbour Bridge) connects Fortitude Valley with Kangaroo Point.

The Roma St Transit Centre, where you'll arrive if you're coming by bus, train or airport shuttle, is on Roma St, about 500m west of the CBD.

Brisbane airport is about 15km northeast of the city. There are shuttles to and from the city (see p317).

Maps

Visitors centres hand out free maps, with detail of the CBD but not much else. For more comprehensive detail pick up a copy of Lonely Planet's *Brisbane & Gold Coast City Map* ($6). Alternatively, *Brisbane Suburban Map* by UBD ($7.25), *Brisbane & Region* by Hema Maps ($5.95), or Gregory's *Brisbane Street Directory* ($24.50) are all good.

The definitive guide to Brisbane's streets is UBD's *Brisbane Street Directory* (known locally as 'Refidex', $39), which includes maps of the Gold and Sunshine Coasts.

QUEENSLAND

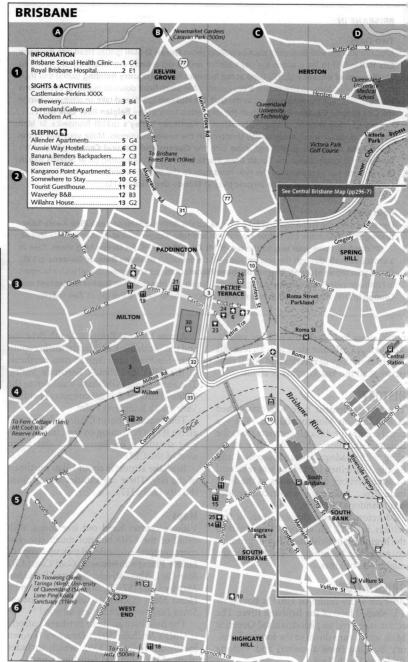

BRISBANE

INFORMATION
Brisbane Sexual Health Clinic.....**1** C4
Royal Brisbane Hospital.............**2** E1

SIGHTS & ACTIVITIES
Castlemaine-Perkins XXXX
 Brewery...............................**3** B4
Queensland Gallery of
 Modern Art..........................**4** C4

SLEEPING
Allender Apartments..................**5** G4
Aussie Way Hostel.....................**6** C3
Banana Benders Backpackers.....**7** C3
Bowen Terrace........................**8** F4
Kangaroo Point Apartments.....**9** F6
Somewhere to Stay..................**10** C6
Tourist Guesthouse..................**11** E2
Waverley B&B.........................**12** B3
Willahra House........................**13** G2

See Central Brisbane Map (pp296-7)

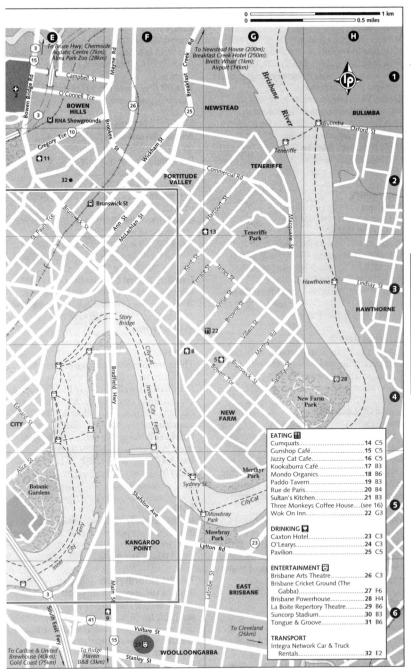

EATING 🍴
Cumquats.................................**14** C5
Gunshop Café..........................**15** C5
Jazzy Cat Cafe.........................**16** C5
Kookaburra Café......................**17** B3
Mondo Organics.......................**18** B6
Paddo Tavern..........................**19** B3
Rue de Paris............................**20** B4
Sultan's Kitchen.......................**21** B3
Three Monkeys Coffee House....(see 16)
Wok On Inn............................**22** G3

DRINKING 🍷
Caxton Hotel...........................**23** C3
O'Learys................................**24** C3
Pavilion..................................**25** C5

ENTERTAINMENT 🎭
Brisbane Arts Theatre................**26** C3
Brisbane Cricket Ground (The
  Gabba)..............................**27** F6
Brisbane Powerhouse.................**28** H4
La Boite Repertory Theatre..........**29** B6
Suncorp Stadium......................**30** B3
Tongue & Groove.....................**31** B6

TRANSPORT
Integra Network Car & Truck
  Rentals...............................**32** E2

QUEENSLAND

INFORMATION

Bookshops

Archives Fine Books (Map pp296-7; ☎ 3221 0491; 40 Charlotte St) A fantastic range of second-hand titles.

Book Nook (Map pp296-7; ☎ 3221 3707, 3221 6055; Lower Ground fl, 51 Edward St) Primarily selling top-quality performing arts and poetry books.

Borders Bookstore (Map pp296-7; ☎ 3210 1220; 162 Albert St) Sizable branch of this reliable chain.

Folio Books (Map pp296-7; ☎ 3221 1368; 80 Albert St) Small bookshop with eclectic offerings.

World Wide Maps & Guides (Map pp296-7; ☎ 3221 4330; Shop 30, Anzac Sq Arcade, 267 Edwards St) Comprehensive range of travel guides and maps.

Emergency

Ambulance (☎ 000, 1300 369 003)

Fire (☎ 000, 3247 5539)

Lifeline (☎ 13 11 14)

Police (☎ 000) City centre (Map pp296-7; ☎ 3224 4444; 67 Adelaide St); Headquarters (Map pp296-7; ☎ 3364 6464; 100 Roma St); Fortitude Valley (Map pp296-7; ☎ 3131 1200; Brunswick St Mall)

RACQ City centre (Map pp296-7; ☎ 13 19 05; GPO Bldg, 261 Queen St); Fortitude Valley (Map pp296-7; ☎ 13 19 05; 300 St Pauls Tce) Roadside service.

Internet Access

Internet cafés are fairly prolific in Brisbane, particularly in and around the city centre. Rates generally range from $4 to $6 per hour. Most backpacker hostels offer Internet access.

Central City Library (Map pp296-7; ☎ 3403 8888; Lower Ground fl, City Plaza Complex, 69 Ann St; ☺ 9am-6pm Mon-Fri, 10am-3pm Sat & Sun) Free but there's a two-hour limit and bookings are essential.

Global Gossip City centre (Map pp296-7; ☎ 3229 4033; 290 Edward St; ☺ 8am-midnight); Fortitude Valley (Map pp296-7; ☎ 3666 0900; 312 Brunswick St; ☺ 8am-midnight) Plenty of terminals and cheap-call phone booths.

Internet City (Map pp296-7; ☎ 3003 1221; Level 4, 132 Albert St; ☺ 24hr) Cheap broadband access.

State Library of Queensland (Map pp296-7; ☎ 3840 7666; Stanley St, South Bank; ☺ 10am-8pm Mon-Thu, to 5pm Fri-Sun) Free Internet access, but advanced booking is essential.

Internet Resources

www.brisbane-australia.com

www.brisbane.citysearch.com.au Good for up-to-the-minute information about entertainment, restaurants and drinking holes.

www.ourbrisbane.com Extensive online city guide.

Media

Rave (www.ravemag.com.au) Gig guide and entertainment section of Brisbane's *Courier Mail* newspaper.

This Week in Brisbane & South-East Queensland Available from the visitor information centre; good for cultural events.

Time Off (www.timeoff.com.au) Free weekly mag listing Brisbane's gigs and events.

Medical Services

Brisbane Sexual Health Clinic (Map pp292-3; ☎ 3227 8666; 270 Roma St)

Day & Night Pharmacy (Map pp296-7; ☎ 3221 4585; 141 Queen St; ☺ 7am-9pm Mon-Thu, to 9.30pm Fri, 8am-9pm Sat, 8.30am-5.30pm Sun)

Queensland Statewide Sexual Assault Helpline (☎ 1800 010 120)

Royal Brisbane Hospital (Map pp292-3; ☎ 3253 8111; Herston Rd, Herston; ☺ 24hr casualty ward)

Travel Clinic (Map pp296-7; ☎ 1300 369 359, 3211 3611; 1st fl, 245 Albert St; ☺ 7.30am-7pm Mon-Thu, to 6pm Fri, 8.30am-5pm Sat, 9.30am-5pm Sun)

Travellers' Medical & Vaccination Centre (TMVC; Map pp296-7; ☎ 3221 9066; 5th fl, 247 Adelaide St; ☺ 8am-5pm Mon & Fri, 10am-7pm Tue, 8am-9pm Wed, 8am-2pm Thu, 8.30am-2pm Sat) Vaccinations and medical advice for travellers.

Money

There are foreign-exchange bureaus at Brisbane airport's domestic and international terminals, as well as ATMs that takes most international credit cards. Most banks have exchange bureaus as well as ATMs.

Amex (Map pp296-7; ☎ 1300 139 060; 131 Elizabeth St)

Interforex Brisbane (Map pp296-7; ☎ 3221 3562; Shop Q 255, Wintergarden, 171-209 Queen St)

Travelex City centre (Map pp296-7; ☎ 3221 9422; 276 Edward St); City centre (Map pp296-7; ☎ 3210 6325; Shop 149F, Queen St Mall)

Post

Australia Post (☎ 13 13 18) GPO (Map pp296-7; 261 Queen St); Wintergarden Centre (Map pp296-7; Post Shop, 2nd fl, Wintergarden Centre, Queen St Mall; ☺ 8.30am-5.30pm Mon-Fri, 9am-4pm Sat)

Tourist Information

Brisbane Visitor Information Centre (Map pp296-7; ☎ 3006 6290; cnr Albert & Queen Sts; ☺ 9am-5.30pm Mon-Thu, to 7pm Fri, to 5pm Sat, 9.30am-4.30pm Sun) Great one-stop information counter for all things Brisbane.

Brisbane Visitors Accommodation Service (Map pp296-7; ☎ 3236 2020; 3rd fl, Roma St Transit Centre, Roma St; ☺ 7am-6pm Mon-Fri, 8am-5pm Sat & Sun)

QUEENSLAND

Privately run outfit specialising in backpacker travel, tours and accommodation in much of Queensland.

Naturally Queensland (Map pp296-7; ☎ 3227 7111; 160 Ann St; ☉ 8.30am-5pm Mon-Fri) The Environment Protection Agency's (EPA) information centre provides maps, brochures, books and permits for Queensland's national parks and state forests.

South Bank visitor information centre (Map pp296-7; ☎ 3867 2051; Stanley Street Plaza, South Bank Parklands; ☉ 9am-6pm, to 9pm Fri; ☐)

Travel Agencies

STA Travel (Map pp296-7; ☎ 3221 3722; www.sta travel.com; Brisbane Arcade, 111 Adelaide St)

Trailfinders (Map pp296-7; ☎ 1300 780 212, 3229 0887; 91 Elizabeth St)

YHA Membership & Travel office (Map pp296-7; ☎ 3236 1680; 450 George St) Tours, YHA membership and YHA hostel bookings.

SIGHTS

Most of Brisbane's major sights can be found in the **city centre** (also called the CBD) or within easy walking distance of it. Sandstone architecture revealing Brisbane's colonial history is scattered throughout the city and **South Bank** sits a short ferry ride across the river. **Fortitude Valley** with its cafés, culture, food and shopping is a popular stomping ground for locals and visitors, as is the **West End**. The freebie brochure *Brisbane's Living Heritage* (www.brisbaneliving heritage.com), available from the visitor information centres, highlights many of the sights Brisbane has to offer.

Brisbane City Hall & Museum of Brisbane

The **City Hall** (Map pp296-7; ☎ 3403 6586; btwn Ann & Adelaide Sts; admission free; lift & viewing tower ☉ 10am-3pm Mon-Fri, 10am-2.30pm Sat) is an historic sandstone edifice overlooking the sculptures and fountains of King George Sq. Built in 1930, its splendour is not only skin-deep; when you enter be sure to draw your eyes from the marble staircase upwards to the kaleidoscope roof and gothic Art Deco light fittings. There's an observation platform up in the bell tower which affords brilliant views across the city.

On the ground floor, the **Museum of Brisbane** (admission free; ☉ 10am-5pm) is split into two sections. One wing showcases the city's past, present and future through static and interactive displays. The Memory Theatre here features a film of various Brisbanites extolling personal accounts of their city. The second wing is a gallery, exhibiting art, crafts and photography by local and international artists. There are free guided tours of the museum on Tuesdays, Thursdays and Saturdays at 11am.

Former Treasury Building

There are many attractive historical buildings dotted around the city centre. The most grand of these is the **former Treasury Building** (Map pp296–7), near Victoria Bridge. Its Italian Renaissance–style façade and commanding balconies now enclose a different money maker: Conrad's 24-hour casino. In the block southeast of the casino, Conrad also occupies the equally gorgeous former **Land Administration Building** (Map pp296–7). Here, however, it's been converted into the Conrad Treasury, a five-star hotel (see the boxed text, p309).

Commissariat Stores Building

Just to the south of Treasury Building is another building of note, the **Commissariat Stores Building** (Map pp296-7; ☎ 3221 4198; 115 William St; adult/child $4/2; ☉ 10am-4pm Tue-Fri & Sun), built in 1829 and recently reopened as a convict and colonial museum.

Parliament House

Further south of the Commissariat Stores on George St is **Parliament House** (Map pp296-7; ☎ 3406 7562; cnr Alice & George Sts; admission free; ☉ 9am-5pm Mon-Fri), dating from 1868 with a roof clad in Mt Isa copper. You can watch the politicians in action (or inaction) from the public balcony on sitting days. Free tours leave on demand between 9am and 4pm Monday to Friday and 10am to 2pm weekends, unless parliament is sitting.

QUT Art Museum

Almost next door to Parliament House is the small but excellent **QUT Art Museum** (Map pp296-7; ☎ 3864 2797; 2 George St; admission free; ☉ 10am-4pm Tue-Fri, noon-4pm Sat & Sun), within the Queensland University of Technology (QUT) campus. The focus of the constantly changing exhibits is on contemporary and mostly Australian works, but exhibits by international artists are also displayed. Best of all are the displays of work by QUT students.

QUEENSLAND

CENTRAL BRISBANE

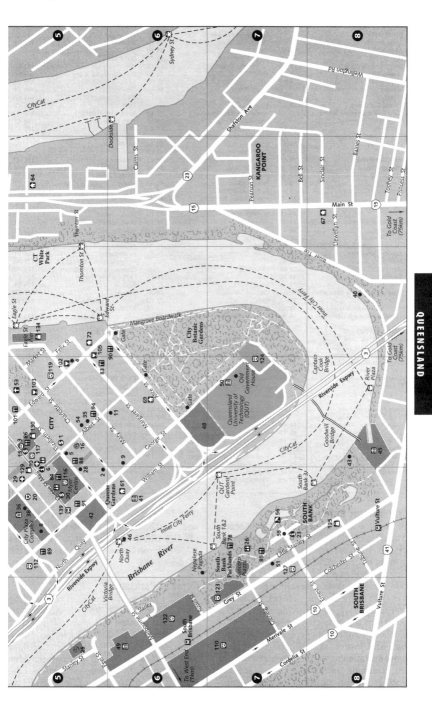

City Botanic Gardens

Brisbane's expansive **City Botanic Gardens** (Map pp296-7; ☎ 3403 0666; Albert St; admission free; ☼ 24hr, free guided tours 11am & 1pm Mon-Sat) are a mass of green lawns, towering Moreton Bay figs, bunya pines, macadamia trees and other tropical flora, descending gently from the QUT campus. The network of walking trails and shady sites provide plenty of respite from the busy city for lunching office workers, strollers, joggers, picnickers, cyclists and in-line skaters. The pretty **Mangrove Boardwalk**, a wooden walkway skirting the riverbank on the eastern rim, is lit up until midnight, affording good opportun-

ities to spot possums. Between October and March, the alfresco **Moonlight Cinemas** (☎ 1300 551 908; www.moonlight.com.au; adult/child $12.50/8; ☼ 6pm Tue-Sun) screens movies in the gardens.

Roma St Parkland

Another garden offering quiet respite is the **Roma St Parkland** (☎ 3006 4545; www.romastreet parkland.com; 1 Parkland Blvd; admission free; ☼ 24hr, free guided tours 10am & 2pm Thu-Sun Sep-May, 11am & 2pm Thu-Sun Jun-Aug), a veritable feast of flora inhabiting 16 hectares at the northern edge of the city, with subtropical gardens (the world's largest in a city centre), kid's play-

QUEENSLAND

grounds, plenty of public BBQs and a small outdoor theatre. Scattered throughout the park are works by local artists.

Old Windmill & Observatory

Just near the Roma St Parkland and north-east of the Roma St Transit Centre, the **Old Windmill & Observatory** (Map pp296-7; Wickham Tce), which is closed to the public, was built in 1828 and pips the Commissariat Stores at the post as Brisbane's oldest surviving building.

Queensland Cultural Centre

In South Bank the extensive Queensland Cultural Centre (Map pp296–7) encompasses several buildings and offers visitors a cultural smorgasbord.

At the back of the complex, the **Queensland Museum** (☎ 3840 7555; www.qmuseum.qld.gov.au; Grey St, South Brisbane; admission free; ☯ 9am-5pm) has an eclectic collection of exhibits, ranging from dinosaur skeletons to more recent relics of Queensland's history. Upstairs there's an enlightening if not distressing display on Queensland's endangered species, as well as a reconstruction of the host of mammoth marsupials that roamed these shores over 100,000 years ago. There are also good temporary exhibits on the likes of bug, beetle and butterfly parades from around the globe.

Within the museum is the excellent **Science-centre** (www.sciencentre.qld.gov.au; adult/child/family $9/7/28), a hands-on science exhibit with interactive displays, optical illusions, a perception tunnel and regular film shows.

Inside a concrete monolith, the **Queensland Art Gallery** (☎ 3840 7303; www.qag.qld.gov.au; Melbourne St, South Brisbane; admission free; ☯ 10am-5pm Mon-Fri, 9am-5pm Sat & Sun, free guided tours 11am, 1pm & 2pm Mon-Fri, 11.30am, 1pm & 2.30pm Sat & Sun) houses a fine permanent collection of mostly domestic and European artists. There are plenty of Australian masterpieces here, including works by Brett Whiteley, Sidney Nolan and Arthur Boyd. A constant parade of visiting exhibitions mixes the mediums and genres up.

At the time of writing the Queensland Art Gallery was constructing the new **Queensland Gallery of Modern Art** (Kurilpa Point), 200m north of the existing gallery. It's due to open in 2006 and will be the second-biggest public art museum in Australia. Its focus will be contemporary Australian, indigenous Australian, Asian, Pacific and international art. It also promises multimedia works and programmes for art enthusiasts of all ages.

South Bank Parklands

These impressive **parklands** (Map pp296-7; admission free; ☯ dawn-dusk) sit on the banks of the Brisbane River and consist of large smears of green, peppered with eateries, small rainforests, vivid foliage, BBQs, and climbing gyms where youngsters swarm like bees to honey.

The most distinctive feature here is **Streets Beach**, an artificial swimming hole that curls its way through the park before opening up into a lagoon. Behind the beach is **Stanley St Plaza**, a renovated section of historic Stanley St, with shops, cafés and a visitors centre.

The **Suncorp Piazza** is an open, outdoor theatre which screens free international sporting events regularly and free movies during school holidays. It also acts as a venue for concerts and performances.

The parklands are within easy walking distance of the city centre, but you can also get here by CityCat or Inner City Ferry (there are three jetties along the riverbank), or by bus or train from Roma St or Central stations.

Maritime Museum

At the western end of the South Bank promenade, this **museum** (Map pp296-7; ☎ 3844 5361; Sidon St, South Brisbane; adult/child $6/3; ☯ 9.30am-4.30pm) has a wide range of displays, including artefacts recovered from wrecks along the Queensland coast, ship models and the HMAS *Diamantina*, a restored 1945 naval frigate that you can clamber around to indulge your naval-battle fantasies. A daunting highlight is the sizable map showing the location of over 1500 shipwrecks in Queensland's waters since 1791, mostly victims of the reef.

Mt Coot-tha Reserve

About 7km southwest of the city centre out Milton Rd, **Mt Coot-tha Reserve** (off Map pp292–3) is a huge bush and parkland with oodles of picnic spots and a lookout with spectacular views; on a clear day you can see all the way to Moreton Bay and the bay islands. The lookout is accessed via Sir Samuel Griffith Dr and has wheelchair access.

QUEENSLAND

Just north of the road to the lookout, on Sir Samuel Griffith Dr, is the turn-off to **JC Slaughter Falls** (3.4km) reached by a short walking track. Also here is a 1.8km **Aboriginal Art Trail**, which takes you past eight art sites with works by local Aboriginal artists.

The very beautiful **Brisbane Botanic Gardens** (☎ 3403 8888; admission free; ☼ 8.30am-5.30pm Sep-Mar, 8am-5pm Apr-Aug, free guided walks 11am & 1pm Mon-Sat), at the foot of the mountain and the reserve, covers 52 hectares and includes over 20,000 species of plants. Highlights include cactus, Japanese and herb gardens, rainforests, an arid zone and an enclosed tropical dome.

Within the gardens is the **Sir Thomas Brisbane Planetarium** (☎ 3403 2578; adult/child/family $2/1/5; ☼ 2.30-4.30pm Tue-Fri, 10am-4.30pm Tue-Fri during school holidays, 11am-8.30pm Sat, to 4.30pm Sun), the largest planetarium in Australia. There's a great observatory here and the shows inside the **Cosmic Skydome** (adult/child/family $11.50/6.80/31) are a must for sci-fi nuts.

To get here via public transport take bus No 471 from Adelaide St, opposite King George Sq ($2.60, 30 minutes, hourly Monday to Friday, six Saturday and Sunday). The bus drops you off in the lookout car park and stops outside the Brisbane Botanic Gardens en route. The last trip to the city leaves at around 4pm on weekdays and 5pm at weekends.

Brisbane Forest Park

This 28,500-hectare natural bushland reserve (Map p319) in the D'Aguilar Range is a hugely popular recreation area for city dwellers, and starts around 10km from the city centre. The bird life is a big lure here and it's a beautiful spot for a BBQ. There are also walking trails ranging from a few hundred metres to 8km, including the 6km Morelia Track at the Manorina Bush Camp and the 5km Greene's Falls Track at Maiala National Park.

At the park entrance the **Brisbane Forest Park visitors centre** (☎ 3300 4855; www.brisbane forestpark.qld.gov.au; 60 Mt Nebo Rd; ☼ 8.30am-4.30pm Mon-Fri, from 9am Sat & Sun) has information about bush **camping** (per person/family $4/16) in the park and maps of walking trails.

Beside the visitors centre is **Walk-About Creek** (adult/child/family $5/2.50/12.50; ☼ 9am-4.30pm), a freshwater study centre where you can see a resident platypus up close, as well as turtles, green tree frogs, lizards, pythons and canoodling gliders.

To get here catch bus No 385 ($3.40, 30 minutes) from the corner of Albert and Adelaide Sts. The bus stops outside the visitors centre and the last departure back to the city is at 4.55pm. The actual park walks are a fair distance from the centre, so if you're planning on attacking them it's best to have your own transport.

Inner North

For over a decade the alternative neighbourhoods of Fortitude Valley and nearby New Farm have been the hub of all things contemporary and cool. During the day the action is concentrated on **Brunswick St Mall** (Map pp296–7), a pedestrianised arcade full of pavement cafés, bars and shops. This strip buzzes on Friday and Saturday nights, when it becomes the nerve centre for Brisbane's nightlife. On Saturday mornings the scent of cigarettes and beer is replaced by lattes and incense as weekend brunchers join the bustle of the **Brunswick St Markets** (Map pp296–7).

McWhirter's Markets (Map pp296–7) at the Wickham St end of Brunswick St Mall is a Brisbane landmark with an impressive Art Deco corner façade.

Alongside the funky restaurants and bars, Brisbane's very own **Chinatown** occupies only one street (Duncan St; Map pp296–7) but exhibits the same flamboyance and flavour of its counterparts in Sydney and Melbourne. The Ann St end is guarded by an exquisite Tang dynasty archway and oriental lions. The mall itself is populated by Chinese restaurants, herbalists, massage therapists and acupuncture businesses.

Southwest of the Valley, **St John's Cathedral** (Map pp296-7; ☎ 3835 2248; 373 Ann St; admission free; ☼ 9.30am-4.30pm Mon-Sat, 11am-4.30pm Sun, tours 10am & 2pm Mon-Sat, 2pm Sun) is a beautiful piece of 19th-century Gothic Revival architecture. Inside the church is a magnificent fusion of carved timber and stained glass.

New Farm (Map pp296–7), just east of the Valley along Brunswick St, became 'desirable' among young professionals a few years ago and is now chock-a-block with wine bars and restaurants.

At the eastern end of Brunswick St, **New Farm Park** (Map pp292–3) is a large, open parkland with playgrounds, picnic areas with gas barbecues, jacaranda trees and beautiful rose gardens.

The inner north is renowned for its profusion of private galleries and exhibition spaces. The best and biggest of these is the **Institute of Modern Art** (☎ 3252 5750; www.ima .org.au; ⏲ 11am-5pm Tue-Fri, to 4pm Sat), a non-commercial gallery with an industrial exhibition space and regular showings by local names. The gallery is housed inside the **Judith Wright Centre for Contemporary Arts** (Map pp296-7; ☎ 3872 9000; www.judithwrightcentre.com; 420 Brunswick St, Fortitude Valley), another excellent venue for live performance of all genres.

Newstead House

North of the centre, on the Brisbane River, is Brisbane's best-known heritage site, the lovely old **Newstead House** (off Map pp292-3; ☎ 3216 1846; Breakfast Creek Rd, Newstead; adult/child/ family $4.40/2.20/11; ⏲ 10am-4pm Mon-Fri, 2-4pm Sun). Set in attractive forested grounds, its historic homestead dates from 1846 and is beautifully fitted out with Victorian furnishings and antiques, clothing and period displays.

Wildlife Sanctuaries

LONE PINE KOALA SANCTUARY

About 11km southwest of Brisbane, this **wildlife sanctuary** (off Map p319; ☎ 3378 1366; Jesmond Rd, Fig Tree Pocket; adult/child/family $16/11/39; ⏲ 8.30am-5pm) is the largest koala sanctuary in the world. Set in attractive parklands beside the river, over 130 of the fuzzy bears live here, alongside kangaroos, dingoes and wombats. The koalas are undeniably cute and most visitors readily cough up the $15 to cuddle one and capture it on film, but you can also hand feed the tame kangaroos for around $1 for a bag of pellets. Talks are given on the animals at set times throughout the day.

To get here catch the No 430 express bus ($3.40, 35 minutes), which leaves hourly from the Queen St Mall bus station (under the Myer Centre) from around 8.30am to 3.45pm daily.

Alternatively, **Mirimar Cruises** (☎ 1300 729 742; incl park entry per adult/child/family $44/25/120) cruises to the sanctuary along the Brisbane River from North Quay, next to Victoria Bridge. It departs daily at 10am, returning from Lone Pine at 1.30pm.

BRIGHTENING UP THE CITY

What do you do with a dull grey box that sticks out like a sore thumb? Why, turn it into a piece of art of course. Tired of unimaginative traffic signal boxes (TSBs) scattered across the city, the city council formed a project to recruit volunteer artists to paint the TSBs. The idea was to create a street-side art gallery to charm the senses, and it has worked – most, if not all, of the 700 or so TSBs have been lovingly, colourfully and artfully painted. Some blend in well with their surroundings, while others stick out like sore thumbs (but well-dressed sore thumbs).

ALMA PARK ZOO

Twenty-eight kilometres north of the city centre off the Bruce Hwy (exit Boundary Rd), this **zoo** (Map p319; ☎ 3204 6566; Alma Rd, Dakabin; adult/child/family $23/15/55; ⏲ 9am-5pm, last entry 4pm) has a large collection of Australian native birds and mammals, including koalas, kangaroos, emus and dingoes, as well as exotic species such as Malaysian sun bears, leopards and monkeys. You can touch and feed many of the animals – feeding times are between 11am and 2.30pm.

To get here via public transport catch the Zoo Train (on the Caboolture line), which leaves from Roma St Transit Centre daily at 9am ($4, 45 minutes) and connects with the free zoo bus at Dakabin station. The bus departs the zoo at 1.30pm daily to connect with the 1.47pm service from Dakabin back to the city.

DAISY HILL KOALA CENTRE

About 25km southwest of the city, this **centre** (Map p319; ☎ 3299 1032; Daisy Hill Rd, Daisy Hill Forest Reserve; admission free; ⏲ 10am-4pm) has informative displays and a number of fat and happy-looking koalas, but it's no zoo. The surrounding area is an important koala habitat and an established conservation area. The idea here is to learn more about koalas rather than just settle for a cuddle and photo. You can spot them in the wild and there are lovely picnic and bushwalking spots, plus plenty of opportunities to see bird life and other furry natives.

To get here via public transport, catch Logan City Bus Services Route No 70 from the corner of Mary and Edwards Streets to the corner of Lyndale Rd and Davina Streets in Daisy Hill ($4, 45 minutes, five daily), from where it's about a 1km walk. You can also visit the centre with Araucaria Ecotours (p305).

ACTIVITIES

Brisbane has the perfect climate for outdoor activities, and these are as much a lure as the city's sights. Being a relatively flat city and blessed with numerous parks and gardens, cycling, in-line skating and walking are among the most popular free-time activities for locals and visitors.

Cycling

Brisbane has around 500km of bike tracks, many along the scenic Brisbane River. Pick up a copy of the city council's *Brisbane Bicycle Experience Guide* booklet from visitor information centres.

Bicycles are allowed on Citytrains, except on weekdays during peak hours. You can also take bikes on CityCats and ferries for free, but cycling in malls is a no go.

Brisbane bike rentals:

Brisbane Bicycle Sales (Map pp296-7; ☎ 3229 2433; www.brizbike.com; 87 Albert St; per hr/day $12/20; ☒ 8.30am-5.30pm Mon-Fri, to 4pm Sat, 10am-4pm Sun)

Riders (Map pp296-7; ☎ 3846 6200; Shop 9, Little Stanley St, South Bank; per hr/day $12/30; ☒ 8am-5pm Mon-Sat, 10am-4pm Sun)

Valet Cycle Hire (☎ 0408 003 198; www.valetcyclehire .com; per half/full day $30/40) Bikes delivered to your door. Also a daily afternoon guided tour ($38) offered for small numbers.

BRISBANE'S TOP FIVE PICNIC SPOTS

- **Mt Coot-tha Reserve** (p299) Pick and choose from a host of pretty picnic spots.

- **City Botanic Gardens** (p298) Munch on lunch beneath fig and macadamia trees.

- **Brisbane Forest Park** (p300) Take your BBQ out bush.

- **Roma St Parkland** (p298) Explore these global gardens then pull up a patch of grass for lunch.

- **South Bank Parklands** (p299) Sizzle some snags in between swims and soaking up the sun.

In-line Skating

For something a little different, take an in-line skate tour of Brisbane with **Sk8tours** (www.sk8tours.com; ☒ tours 7.30pm) or **Planet Inline** (☎ 3255 0033; www.planetinline.com). Both organise Wednesday night tours starting from the top of the Goodwill Bridge for $10, and Planet Inline also runs a Saturday morning breakfast club tour ($15), and Sunday afternoon tours which differ each week and last about three hours ($15).

You can hire skates and equipment from **Skatebiz** (Map pp296-7; ☎ 3220 0157; 101 Albert St; per 2/24hr $13/20; ☒ 9am-5.30pm Mon-Thu, 9am-4pm Sat, 10am-4pm Sun).

Rock Climbing

The **Cliffs rock-climbing area** (Map pp296–7) situated on the southern banks of the Brisbane River at Kangaroo Point, is an excellent climbing venue and extremely popular with avid scramblers. The pink volcanic cliffs are allegedly 200 million years old and quite spectacular in the evening when they're floodlit.

Several operators offer climbing and abseiling instruction in this area. **Torre Outdoor Adventures** (☎ 3870 3223; climbing $15), which runs a rock-climbing club, meets here every Wednesday night at 5.45pm; just make your way to the base of the cliffs.

Other operators:

K2 Extreme (☎ 3257 3310; k2extreme@k2basecamp .com.au; per person $30) Saturday morning sessions including safety procedures and a climb.

Worth Wild Rock Climbing (☎ 3395 6450; www .worthwild.com.au; group instruction per person $75)

Swimming

Streets Beach (p299) is the most scenic spot in Brisbane to cool off, but there are plenty of conventional swimming centres in the city to choose from.

Other recommendations:

Centenary Aquatic Centre (Map pp296-7; ☎ 3831 7665; 400 Gregory Tce, Spring Hill; adult/child $4.30/3.30; ☒ 5.30am-7.30pm Mon-Fri, 6am-6pm Sat & Sun) Large complex encompassing an Olympic-sized lap pool, a kids' pool and a diving pool with a high tower.

Chermside Aquatic Centre (off Map pp292-3; ☎ 3359 6134; 375 Hamilton Rd, Chermside; adult/child/ family $7.70/7/23; ☒ 10am-3pm Sat & Sun, 10am-5pm daily during school holidays) Waterpark with slides and tube rides. Great for families. Indoor swimming pool also open daily.

Other Activities

Brisbane's Chinatown offers travel-weary bones, muscles and minds some blissful respite in the form of free **tai chi** classes every Sunday morning at 11am in the Chinatown Mall (Duncan St; Map pp296–7).

There are free **aerobics** and **yoga** classes on the lawns at the South Bank Parklands (Map pp296–7) every Tuesday and Sunday morning between April and August. For more information, check www.south-bank .net.au.

You can take to the skies over Brisbane from $250 with any of the following places:

Brisbane Skydiving Centre (☎ 5464 6111; www .brisbaneskydiving.com.au) Tandem and solo skydiving.

Fly Me to the Moon (☎ 3423 0400; www.flymetothe moon.com.au) Balloon flights over Brisbane.

Ripcord Skydivers (☎ 3399 3552; www.ripcord-sky divers.com.au) Tandem and solo skydiving.

WALKING TOUR

Brisbane's relatively flat landscape makes it extremely walker-friendly, and navigating the historic buildings, mighty Brisbane River and laid-back CBD on foot is the best way to immerse yourself in the city. The city council produces the free *Experience Guide,* which suggests good itineraries. The following walk (Map p304) covers 5km to 6km and takes anything from a couple of hours to a full day. For more information on the individual sights, see p295.

Start your walking expedition at the imposing classical-style **Brisbane City Hall** (**1**; p295), where you can buff up on the city's history and take the lift up to the top of the bell tower to soak up the spectacular views over the CBD. Walk through the statues and lawns of **King George Sq (2)**, and cross Edward St into **Anzac Sq (3)**, where locals, city workers and ibises mill about the grassy patches and shady trees. Scattered throughout the square are touch-and-tell interactive displays where you can learn about the significance of the park. At the northwestern end of the park the **Shrine of Remembrance (4)** is a Greek Revivalist cenotaph where an eternal flame burns in remembrance of Australian soldiers who died in WWI.

Head over the pedestrian bridge at the eastern corner of the square, which connects Anzac Sq to **Post Office Sq (5)**. Continue heading southeast, across Queen St, to Brisbane's magnificent, historic **GPO (6)**, still in use. Walk down the small alley that skirts the eastern side of the post office through to Elizabeth St. Cross the road and explore the beautiful **St Stephen's Cathedral (7)** and the adjoining **St Stephen's Chapel**. Built in 1850, the chapel is Brisbane's oldest church and was designed by English architect Augustus Pugin, who designed London's Houses of Parliament. The cathedral was built in 1874.

From the cathedral, head southwest down Elizabeth St, then turn right onto Edward St and left into the **Queen St Mall (8)**. This busy pedestrian mall is the commercial centre of Brisbane, and is lined with fine façades dating back to Australia's federation, including the glorious frontage of the old **Hoyts Regent Theatre (9**; p313).

Continue exploring the length of Queen St Mall until you reach George St. Diagonally opposite you'll see the unmistakable Italian-Renaissance **former Treasury Building (10**; p295), now housing the casino. Turn left onto George St and you'll pass another spectacular Italian-Renaissance building, the **Land Administration Building (11)**, now the Conrad Treasury hotel (see the boxed text, p309). Take the small alley just south of the hotel (Stephens Lane) onto William St and head right, passing the historic **Commissariat Stores Building (12**; p295).

Continue down William St and cross Alice St to take in the splendour of Queensland's regal copper-topped **Parliament House (13**; p295). Further south is the excellent **QUT Art Museum (14**; p295) and the gracious **Old Government House (15)**, built in 1860. From here you can meander through the **City Botanic Gardens (16**; p298) and take the weight off your feet for a while under a magnificent Moreton Bay fig.

Once you've had enough respite, head back through the QUT campus toward the river and catch a ferry from QUT Gardens Point ferry stop to South Bank 3. This will land you at the southern end of the **South Bank Parklands (17**; p299). Meander north along the modernist walkway, past **Streets Beach (18**; p299) and **Stanley St Plaza (19**; p299). Just beyond here, tucked away among the trees, is an ornate wooden **Nepalese Pagoda (20)**, built during Brisbane 1988 Expo. Past the Queensland Cultural Centre, be sure to pop into the **Queensland Museum (21**; p299) and the **Queensland Art Gallery (22**; p299).

QUEENSLAND

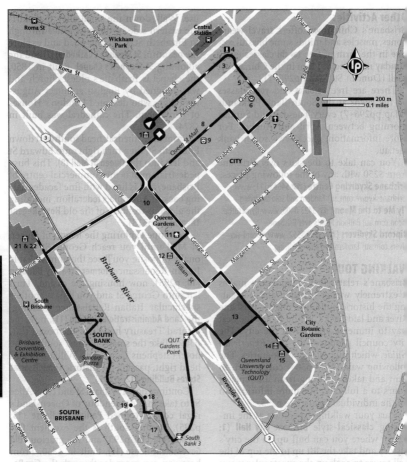

WALK FACTS

Distance: 5km to 6km

Duration: two to five hours

Once you've exhausted these, cross the Victoria Bridge back into the CBD, back past the former Treasury Building, turning left onto George St. Turn right onto Adelaide St and one block will land you back at your starting point at the Brisbane City Hall.

BRISBANE FOR CHILDREN

Brisbane is a family-friendly city, with plenty of options to keep kids happy and occupied. At the **Queensland Cultural Centre** (p299) you'll find fantastic, interactive programmes run by the Queensland Museum during school holidays. The incorporated Sciencecentre will keep inquisitive young minds inventing, creating and discovering.

Take budding Warholes to the **Queensland Art Gallery** (p299), where the Children's Art Centre runs regular programmes throughout the year as well as a bunch of excellent programmes during holidays. Alternatively, **Hands On Art** (☎ 3844 4589; www.handsonart.org.au; South Bank; per child $6; ☺ 10am-5pm Wed-Fri, 10am-5pm Mon-Fri during school holidays) is designed for kids to get creative with clay moulding, printing, painting, dancing, puppet-making and more in a workshop environment. Bookings are essential.

The river is a big plus; many children will enjoy a river cruise, especially if it's to the **Lone Pine Koala Sanctuary** (p301), where they can cuddle one of these lovable creatures. Imaginative playgrounds in the city centre include **Roma St Parkland** (p298) and the **South Bank Parklands** (p299), which has the safe and child-friendly Streets Beach and a scattering of jungle-gym playgrounds with rubber surfaces.

The **Sir Thomas Brisbane Planetarium** (p300) has exhibits and shows on stars, planets and other inter-galactic goo which will boggle young minds.

The **Brisbane City Council** (www.brisbane.qld.gov .au) runs Chill Out, a programme of activities for 10 to 17 year olds during the school holidays, and Visible Ink, an ongoing programme, with activities and events designed for 12 to 16 year olds.

The free monthly booklet *Brisbane's Child* (www.brisbaneschild.com.au) has information about Brisbane for parents.

Click onto Bub Hub (www.qld.bubhub .com.au) for comprehensive information for new parents, including everything from clinic contacts and locations, prenatal care and activities for newborns to toddlers.

For childcare listings see http://directory .ourbrisbane.com/directory/categories/63 .html or contact the **Child Care Information Service** (☎ 1800 637 711, 3224 4225; Level 4, 111 George Street).

TOURS
Brewery Tours
There are hugely popular guided brewery tours in and around Brisbane, and, yes, free samples are included, but we all know the real lure is to experience something as Australian as a kangaroo – beer.

Carlton & United Brewhouse (off Map pp292-3; ☎ 3826 5858; cnr Mulles Rd & Pacific Hwy, Yatala; entry without/with transfer bus $15/30; ☺ tours 10am, noon & 2pm Mon-Fri) This complex, 40km south of the city centre, pumps out about three million bottles of the good stuff a day – mmmmm all that culture!

Castlemaine-Perkins XXXX Brewery (Map pp292-3; ☎ 3361 7597; www.xxxx.com.au; cnr Black & Paton Sts, Milton; adult/child $18/10; ☺ tours hourly 10am-4pm Mon-Fri, also 6pm Wed) Tours at this brewery include four ales to quench your thirst (as long as you're over 18) so leave the car at home. The brewery is a 20-minute walk west from the Roma St transit centre or you can take the Citytrain to Milton station. Wear closed shoes.

City Tours
Artours (☎ 3899 3686; www.artours.coaus.com; adult/child $45/15; ☺ 9.15am & 1.15pm Tue-Sat) Focuses on Brisbane's art scene. Typical half-day tours take in five to six galleries and last 3½ hours.

Brisbane Walking Tours (☎ 0410 425 762; adult/ child $16/10) Two-hour, small-group walking tours around Brisbane.

City Nights tour (Map pp296-7; adult/child $20/15; ☺ 6pm Mar-Oct & 6.30pm Nov-Feb) Departs from the City Hall, goes a little further afield and includes Mt Coottha Lookout and a cruise on a CityCat. Tickets for both can be bought on the bus or at the tourism information kiosk in the Queen St Mall.

City Sights bus tour (Map pp296-7; day tickets adult/ child $20/15; ☺ 9am-3.45pm, every 45min) Hop-on, hop-off bus departs from the GPO and shuttles around 19 of the city's major landmarks. Day tickets can be bought on the bus and allow you to get off and on whenever and wherever you want. The same ticket covers you for unlimited use of conventional city bus and ferry services.

Ghost Tours (☎ 3844 6606; www.ghost-tours.com.au; adult/child from $30/15.50) Guided tours of Brisbane's haunted heritage.

Tours and Detours (☎ 1300 300 242, 3847 3666; www.toursanddetours.com.au; adult/child $50/30; ☺ 9am) Runs a Brisbane highlights tour which takes in many of the city's historical buildings, sights and gardens, as well as a river cruise. The tour lasts four hours and includes hotel pickup.

River Cruises
The Brisbane River provides a great medium to see the city's peaks and troughs.

Kookaburra River Queens (☎ 3221 1300; www.kook aburrariverqueens.com; 2hr lunch/2½hr dinner cruise per person $45/60) Restored wooden paddle steamers chug pleasantly up and down the river. A buffet meal or seafood platter is included. Lunch cruises depart from Eagle St Pier at noon daily. Dinner cruises depart from Eagle St Pier at 7pm, Monday to Saturday and 6.30pm Sunday and public holidays.

Mirimar Cruises (Map pp296-7; ☎ 1300 729 742; Queens Wharf Rd, North Quay; 1½hr cruise per adult/pensioner/child $18/16/10, day tour adult/pensioner/child $88/85/49). A popular option. This company also operates cruises to Lone Pine Koala Sanctuary (see p301).

River City Cruises (Map pp296-7; ☎ 0428 278 473; www.rivercitycruises.com; South Bank Pier 1 & 2; adult/ child/family $20/15/55; ☺ departs 10.30am & 12.30pm Mar-Nov, also 2.30pm Dec-Feb) For the sights without the fancy fuss, these are 1½-hour cruises with commentary.

Hinterland Tours
Araucaria Ecotours (☎ 5544 1283; www.learnabout wildlife.com; per person from $275; ☺ every Wed) Based

in the Gold Coast hinterland. Offers three-day naturalist-led wilderness tours in the Mt Barney National Park area, with stops at the Daisy Hill Koala Centre and the Karawatha Wetlands. Also operates day tours including 'Bushwalking in Brisbane' ($55) and 'Coochiemudlo Island' ($80). Both include lunch.

Rob's Rainforest Tours (☎ 3357 7061, 0409 496 607; http://homepage.powerup.com.au/~rogfbus7/index.html; per person $65) Hugely popular assortment of day trips operated by a former backpacking globetrotter. Tours take in the Gold and Sunshine Coast Hinterlands, including Kondalilla National Park waterfalls and the Glass House Mountains, Lamington National Park and Springbrook National Park.

FESTIVALS & EVENTS

Information on festivals and events in Brisbane can be found at the visitor information centres or check out www.ourbrisbane.com/whatson. The city's major events are listed here.

January
Cockroach Races This bizarre ritual takes place at the Story Bridge Hotel (see p313) on Australia Day, 26 January.

February
Chinese New Year Always a popular event in Fortitude Valley in February.
Tropfest (www.tropfest.com) Nationwide short film festival telecast live at South Bank in late February.

April
Queensland Winter Racing Carnival (www.queenslandracing.com.au) From late April to late July there are major horse-race meetings each weekend at both Doomben and Eagle Farm Racecourses, including the Brisbane Cup in mid-May.

June
Brisbane Pride Festival (www.pridebrisbane.org.au) Brisbane's fabulously flamboyant annual gay and lesbian celebration.

July
Brisbane International Film Festival (www.biff.com.au) Ten days of quality films in July.
Queensland Music Festival Huge celebration of world of music, held over 15 days in July on odd-numbered years.
Valley Fiesta Food and music festival held in Chinatown and Brunswick St Mall in mid-July.

August
'Ekka' Royal National Agricultural Show (www.ekka.com.au) The country comes to town in early August.

September
Brisbane Riverfestival (www.riverfestival.com.au) Brisbane's major festival of the arts, with buskers, performances, music and concerts.
National Festival of Beers (www.nfb.com.au) Held at the RNA Showgrounds over three days in mid-September.

October
Livid (www.livid.com.au) Annual one-day alternative rock festival.

December
Christmas Festival (www.south-bank.net.au) Massive Chrissy celebrations held during the week before Christmas at South Bank.

SLEEPING

Brisbane has an excellent selection of accommodation to suit any budget. Although the city centre offers mainly expensive options, there is a broad variety within walking distance or with good public-transport connections.

The inner suburbs have their own distinct flavour. Spring Hill, just north of the city centre, is quiet and close to the city centre and Fortitude Valley. Petrie Terrace and Paddington, just west of the city centre, combine trendy restaurants and lively bars. Fortitude Valley ('the Valley') is an alternative neighbourhood with Brisbane's best nightlife. New Farm, southeast beyond the Valley, is a mix of quiet suburbia and the upwardly mobile. West End, south of the river, has a decidedly chilled-out atmosphere and some great cafés and restaurants.

The main motel drags are Wickham St (Fortitude Valley) and Gregory Tce (Spring Hills), on the northern edge of the city, and Main St (Kangaroo Point), which is also the link road to the southern Gold Coast Hwy.

The Brisbane Visitors Accommodation Service (p294) has a free booking service, and brochures and information on hostels and other budget options in Brisbane and up and down the coast.

Budget
GUESTHOUSES
Tourist Guesthouse (Map pp296-7; ☎ 1800 800 589, 3252 4171; www.touristguesthouse.com.au; 555 Gregory Tce, Spring Hill; dm $20, s/d/tr $60/75/85; ⓟ ⌘ ⌑) A short walk from Brunswick St, this beautifully restored Queenslander is scrubbed-up rustic. More of a hotel-cum-hostel, it's

laden with faded pine but mod cons too. All rooms have TVs and fridges and the doubles are excellent value.

HOSTELS

Bunk Backpackers (Map pp296-7; ☎ 1800 682 865; www.bunkbrisbane.com.au; cnr Ann & Gipps St, Fortitude Valley; dm $23-26, s $40, d & tw $70; P ⊠ ⌨ ⌘) Brisbane's snazziest hostel has generous dorms with bathrooms, luscious mattresses, gleaming kitchens and funky décor. It's extremely secure and well organised and the faaaaabulous bar and swimming pool attract trendy locals. The hostel's also wheelchair friendly.

Palace Backpackers (Map pp296-7; ☎ 1800 676 340, 3211 2433; www.palacebackpackers.com.au; cnr Ann & Edward Sts; dm/s/d $22/$36/60; ⊠ ⌨) This huge institution caters to loners, party-goers and everyone in-between in an ageing, multi-storey labyrinth. You can't miss the theatresque façade and although the rooms are a little cramped, there are comfy TV rooms, a huge kitchen, a tour information desk, job centre and rooftop sundeck.

Tinbilly (Map pp296-7; ☎ 1800 446 646, 3238 5888; www.tinbilly.com; 462 George St; dm $22-27, tw & d $85; ⊠ ⌨) This funky, central hostel flaunts a modern, colourful interior, excellent facilities and clinical cleanliness. Each room has air-con, a bathroom and individual lockers, and are wheelchair-accessible. Downstairs, a happy, helpful buzz swims around the job centre, travel agency and popular bar.

Aussie Way Hostel (Map pp292-3; ☎ /fax 3367 0083; 34 Cricket St, Petrie Terrace; dm/s/d $22/36/50; ⊠) This small and homely hostel is housed in a picturesque, two-storey timber Queenslander and feels more like a guesthouse than a backpackers. Dorms are a tad more spacious than most and come with fridges and televisions. The friendly hosts are knowledgeable and can organise just about anything for you.

Banana Benders Backpackers (Map pp292-3; ☎ 1800 241 157, 3367 1157; www.bananabenders.com; 118 Petrie Tce, Petrie Terrace; dm $21-23, tw & d $50, 1-bed apt from $240; ⌨) Sporting one of Queensland's fruity mascots, this yellow-and-blue number is small, relaxed and personal. Rooms are spacious and functional; there's also an outdoor patio and BBQ area and the friendly owners can help you find work. It's a good spot to hang your hat for a while and the apartments are lovely.

Somewhere to Stay (Map pp292-3; ☎ 1800 812 398, 3846 2858; www.somewheretostay.com.au; 45 Brighton Rd, West End; dm $17-25, s from $32, d $45-65; P ⌨ ⌘) Set inside a mammoth Queenslander, this rambling hostel houses a good variety of rooms, from simple, six-bed dorms to indulgent doubles with TVs, bathrooms and fridges. The relaxed atmosphere is fashioned by breezy balconies and spectacular city views.

More budget options:

Bowen Terrace (Map pp292-3; ☎ 3254 0458; www .bowentceaccommodation.com; 365 Bowen Tce, New Farm; s $40, d $50-60) Quiet, family-run accommodation.

Prince Consort Backpackers (Map pp296-7; ☎ 1800 225 005, 3257 2252; www.nomadsworld.com; 230 Wickham St, Fortitude Valley; dm $21-24, d $48-52, tr $69; ⊠ ⌨) Character-laden hostel above a pub, with appealing dorms and good facilities.

CAMPING & CARAVANNING

Newmarket Gardens Caravan Park (off Map pp292-3; ☎ 3356 1458; www.newmarketgardens.com.au; 199 Ashgrove Ave, Ashgrove; powered sites per 2 people $21-23, unpowered sites per 2 people $20-21, d caravans $38, d cabins $70-90; P ⊠ ⌨) Sitting just 4km north of the city centre, this park lacks good tree coverage, but facilities include spotless bathrooms and BBQs. There is also a good range of cabins and some are wheelchair friendly. Buses to the city centre stop right outside.

Midrange

APARTMENTS

Dahrl Court Apartments (Map pp296-7; ☎ 3830 3400; www.dahrlcourt.com.au; 45 Phillips St, Spring Hill; s & d/f apt $100/110, 1-/2-bed townhouse $130/140; P ⊠) Tucked into a quiet and leafy pocket of Spring Hill, this boutique complex offers outstanding value. The self-contained apartments have stylish bathrooms, heritage aesthetics, air-con and cable TV. The commodious townhouses come with a courtyard or balcony. Ask about weekly rates.

Kangaroo Point Apartments (Map pp296-7; ☎ 1800 676 855, 3391 6855; www.kangaroopoint.com; 819 Main St, Kangaroo Point; apt per night/week from $80/390; P ⊠ ⌘) These contemporary, serviced and self-contained apartments are excellent if you're staying a week or more. Rates start with stylish 3½-star units and step up in style to sleek, spacious and indulgent 4½-star units (from $145), which come with balconies. Good disabled access.

Dorchester Self-Contained Units (Map pp296-7; ☎ 3831 2967; www.dorchesterinn.com.au; 484 Upper Edward St, Spring Hill; s/d/tr units $70/80/90; P ⊗) The units in this renovated, two-storey block are a tad dated in the décor department, but they're spotless, and for room, amenities and service this place is virtually unbeatable. There are also laundry facilities – and if the hosts were any friendlier you'd take them home.

Allender Apartments (Map pp292-3; ☎ 3358 5832; www.allenderapartments; 3 Moreton St, New Farm; r $100-135; ⊗) Behind a homely, yellow-brick façade, Allender offers tasteful and immaculate studios and one-bedroom apartments. The cool and shaded interiors are a fusion of funky décor and homely amenities and there's plenty of room to spread out.

Central Brunswick Apartments (Map pp296-7; ☎ 3852 1411; www.centralbrunswickhotel.com.au; 455 Brunswick St, Fortitude Valley; r $120-140; P ⊗) The studios and apartments in this modern complex have a fairly generic, business-traveller manner about them but are still very comfortable. Some have balconies and spas and week-long stays attract excellent discounts. The facilities include a sauna and gym and babysitting can be arranged.

B&BS

Thornbury House B&B (Map pp296-7; ☎ 3839 5334; thorn-b@bigpond.net.au; 1 Thornbury St, Spring Hill; d incl breakfast $90-100) Behind a trellised frontage lies this beautifully maintained two-storey Queenslander built in 1886, with polished timber throughout, clean rooms, and warm hosts. Little extras like televisions and bathrobes come free of charge and breakfast is served in a lovely courtyard.

Waverley B&B (Map pp292-3; ☎ 3369 8973; http:// babs.com.au/waverley; 5 Latrobe Tce, Paddington; s/d incl breakfast $90/110; P ⊗) This stylish B&B has cool rooms decorated in period furniture with gorgeous, plump beds. Each room also has a small sitting area and little trimmings such as pamper products in the exquisite bathrooms. There's also a great self-contained unit ($440 per week).

Fern Cottage (off Map pp292-3; ☎ 3541 6685; 89 Fernberg Rd, Paddington; s/d $90/120; ⊗) Inside an exquisitely renovated Queenslander, just west of the city centre, Fern Cottage has cushy and ornate rooms and an interior splashed with Mediterranean ambience. There's a lush garden retreat out the back with a

shady balcony. The friendly hosts here go to great lengths to make sure your stay is happy.

Also recommended:

Willahra House (Map pp292-3; ☎ 3254 3485; willahrahouse@mhpm.com.au; 268 Harcourt St, New Farm; s $75-100, d $95-125; P ⊗) Beautiful homestead-style house with plush rooms.

Ridge Haven B&B (off Map pp292-3; ☎ 3391 7702; http://uqconnect.net/ridgehaven; 374 Annerley Rd, Annerley; s $110-125, d $120-135; P ⊗) Historic Victorian home, south of the city, with atmospheric rooms.

HOTELS & MOTELS

Il Mondo (Map pp296-7; ☎ 3392 0111; www.ilmondo .com.au; 25 Rotherham St, Kangaroo Point; r $100-165; P ⊗ ⊛) This postmodern boutique hotel has contemporary rooms that are reminiscent of an Ikea showroom. There's plenty of block colours, minimalist design and space, and the bathrooms are quite blissful. Starting rates are for standard hotel rooms and increase to self-contained apartments.

Inchcolm Hotel (Map pp296-7; ☎ 3226 8888; www.inchcolmhotel.com.au; 73 Wickham Tce; s & d from $140; P ⊗ ⊛) This personable hotel is a converted block of medical offices. Much of the heritage structure and charm (and just a whiff of medicinal products) of its former ego remains, but the comfortable rooms have been renovated extensively. All come with kitchenettes and cable TV. Good standby deals.

Best Western Gregory Terrace (Map pp296-7; ☎ 3832 1769; ggtmotel@bigpond.net.au; 397 Gregory Tce, Spring Hill; r $98-130, f $110-145; P ⊗ ⊛) Out on Spring Hill's northern edge, this four-star establishment overlooks Victoria Park and has respectable and well-maintained rooms. The décor is fairly plain but some rooms have balconies and the family rooms are extremely accommodating. Prices increase with the views.

Acacia Inner-City Inn (Map pp296-7; ☎ 3832 1663; fax 3832 2591; 413 Upper Edward St; s/d incl breakfast $55/75; P) This reasonable B&B has small motel-style rooms in a functional environment. The singles are snug, but the doubles are roomier and there's not a speck of dirt to be found. All rooms come with TV and bar fridge.

Two good motel options on offer are the small and smart **Soho Motel** (Map pp296-7; ☎ 3831 7722; www.sohomotel.com.au; 333 Wickham Tce, Spring Hill; s/d $70/85; P ⊗ ⊡) which has compact but comfy rooms, and the cheerful

AUTHOR'S CHOICE

Conrad Treasury (Map pp296-7; ☎ 1800 506
889, 3306 8888; www.conradtreasury.com.au; 130
William St; r from $320; P 🏊) Brisbane's most
opulent hotel is housed in the beautifully
restored former Land Administration Building. This is the place to come if you're trying
to impress. Every room is unique, but each
is dressed in polished wood, marble, elegant furnishings and heritage atmosphere.
All rooms come with either a city or park
view. Rates start with standard rooms but a
step up takes you to the voluminous Parlour
Rooms; those on the 4th floor have balcony
access. The suites will make you giddy. The
hotel prides itself on being able to cater personally to couples, families, solo travellers,
business travellers and any and every other
breed of traveller.

Paramount Motel (Map pp296-7; ☎ 1800 636 772,
3393 1444; www.paramountmotel.com.au; 649 Main St,
Kangaroo Point; s/d/f $70/75/105; P 🏊 🍴).

Top End

Stamford Plaza Brisbane (Map pp296-7; ☎ 3221
1999; sales@spb.stamford.com.au; cnr Edward & Margaret
Sts; r from $280; P 🏊 🍴) The Stamford has a
gorgeous historic façade in front of a modern tower. Inside, indulgent rooms have
antique touches, large beds and plenty of
atmosphere. On site is a gym, sauna, spa and
several restaurants. There are often good
package deals up for grabs.

Quay West Suites Brisbane (Map pp296-7; ☎ 18
00 672 726, 3853 6000; reservations@qwsb.mirvac.com
.au; 132 Alice St; 1-/2-bedroom ste $250-320; P 🏊 🍴)
This sophisticated complex has very stylish
self-contained units with modern kitchens, fully equipped laundries, TVs, stereos,
modem ports and spectacular views. Recently refurbished, the refined interiors are
worth the price tag and the staff are utterly
gracious.

Also recommended:

Sheraton Brisbane (Map pp296-7; ☎ 3835 3535;
www.sheraton.com/brisbane; 249 Turbot St; r from $250;
P 🏊) One of the luxury chain, with restaurants, bars,
several rooms for the disabled and frequent specials.

Chifley on George (Map pp296-7; ☎ 3221 6044;
reservations.george@chifleyhotels.com; 103 George St;
r from $150; P 🏊 🍴) Pleasant and straightforward
hotel rooms, with a spa and a restaurant on site.

EATING

Brisbane's CBD has a number of fine and
pricey eating options but, like Brisbane's
accommodation options, many of the city's
best restaurants and cafés are in the neighbourhoods of Fortitude Valley, New Farm,
West End, Petrie Terrace and Paddington.
Most of the cafés in the CBD are closed at
the weekend.

City Centre

C (Map pp296-7; ☎ 3832 4722; 483 Adelaide St; mains
around $35; 🕐 lunch Mon-Fri, dinner Mon-Sat; 🍴) C
perfects the art of elegant eating, with a sun-
drenched interior of block white and polished wood. The menu is graced with delicate
infusions such as roasted barramundi fillet
with celeriac, capsicum and red wine jus, or
honey-glazed duck breast with peppercorn
sauce. The service is friendly and flawless.

F.I.X. (Map pp296-7; ☎ 3210 6016; cnr Edward & Margaret Sts; mains $15-25; 🕐 lunch Mon-Fri, dinner Mon-Sat)
This bustling brasserie delights office workers and social diners with its varied menu.
Try the prawn, *wakami* (Asian seaweed)
and ginger wontons or sticky duck shanks.
Veggie options are limited to pastas and
salads, but they're all good. The attached
bar doles out spiffy cocktails.

Grosvenor on George (Map pp296-7; ☎ 3236 2288;
320 George St; mains $17-25; 🕐 lunch & dinner) Sassy
suits love this classy bar during the week,
when they tumble in for creative fusions
like *hoi sin* duck pizza. The menu is in a
constant state of flux and the walls carry
work by local artists. Friday nights are rel-
egated to drinkers.

E'cco (Map pp296-7; ☎ 3831 8344; 100 Boundary St;
mains from $30; 🕐 lunch Tue-Fri, dinner Tue-Sat) One
of the finest restaurants in the state, E'cco is
a must book for any culinary aficionado. Expect
masterpieces like Flinders Island lamb, tomato and goat's cheese couscous and apple
tzatziki and olive jus. The interior is suitably swish and you'll need to book well in
advance.

Jorge (Map pp296-7; ☎ 3012 9121; 183 George St;
mains $15-25; 🕐 11am-late Mon-Fri, 3pm-late Sat & Sun)
Cast amid a sea of retail outlets, Jorge's
catchphrase is 'Groove, Lounge, Dine' and
this spunky restaurant-cum-bar fulfils all
three. The open kitchen sizzles up ingenious
creations like smoked kangaroo salads and
grilled prawn burgers. See p313 for Jorge's
after-dark activities.

QUEENSLAND

Verve Cafe & Bar (Map pp296-7; ☎ 3221 5691; 109 Edward St; mains $10-20; ☺ lunch Mon-Fri, dinner Mon-Sat) This funky subterranean venue is a bar/café/restaurant fusion with muted tunes and tones and excellent service. Stylish café fare is served in generous portions and the crowd is arty and relaxed.

Rush Lounge (Map pp296-7; ☎ 3211 9511; Post Office Sq; mains $10-20; ☺ breakfast, lunch & dinner Mon-Fri) A luscious injection of suede, oriental style and cut velvet makes this one of the most ambient spots in the city. Deli-standard quiches and sambos are served in sanguine surrounds and the humble steak sanga is turned into a work of art.

Customs House Brasserie (Map pp296-7; ☎ 3365 8921; 399 Queen St; mains $20-27; ☺ lunch daily, dinner Tue-Sat) Wedged at the base of Customs House and shielded from the city's high-rises, the menu at this brasserie is as impressive as the location. Prawn-and-green-papaya salad, or beef mignons wrapped in pancetta taste oh so much better with the uninterrupted views of the river.

Metro Cafe (Map pp296-7; ☎ 3221 3181; cnr Albert & Mary Sts; dishes $4-8; ☺ breakfast & lunch Mon-Fri) Deservedly popular with the office brigade, this petite diner dishes up mountainous breakfasts, sizzling burgers and kebabs and dozens of fresh and tasty sandwiches. You can munch slowly at the great window seating and watch the world go by.

You'll find **food courts** (Map pp296-7; dishes $5-8; ☺ 9am-5pm) on the ground floor of the Wintergarden Centre and also on Level E (ground floor) of the Myer Centre. Both places offer takeaway fare from around the globe, including sushi, curries, stir-fries and gourmet sandwiches.

More city eating:

Il (Map pp296-7; ☎ 3210 0600; Cnr Edward & Alice Sts; mains $33-40; ☺ lunch Mon-Fri, dinner Mon-Sat) Sunny, classy restaurant with a sophisticated menu.

Govinda's (Map pp296-7; ☎ 3210 0255; 1st fl, 99 Elizabeth St; Sun feast $6.50, all you can eat $8.50; ☺ lunch Mon-Sat, dinner Fri, Sun feast from 5pm) Hare Krishna eatery serving vegetarian curries, snacks, salads and stews.

Fortitude Valley & New Farm

Sunbar Restaurant and Lounge (Map pp296-7; ☎ 3257 4999; 367 Brunswick St; mains $28; ☺ lunch Tue-Fri, dinner Tue-Sat) Super slick and chic, Sunbar is an injection of style into the Valley's funky strip. Pack a fancy appetite for dishes such

as lobster and scallop ravioli with grilled scampi, parma ham and a truffle bisque sauce. See p312 for lounge activities.

Vietnamese Restaurant (Map pp296-7; ☎ 3252 4112; 194 Wickham St; mains $10-13; ☺ lunch & dinner) This popular restaurant serves spectacular authentic Vietnamese food in no-nonsense surrounds. Dishes come in every carnivorous, seafood and vegetarian version imaginable but the real delights are to be found on the 'Authentic Menu'. The shredded beef in spinach rolls are divine.

Spoon Deli & Café (Map pp296-7; ☎ 3257 1750; 22 James St; dishes $8-18; ☺ 11am-3pm Mon-Fri, 11.20am-4pm Sat & Sun) This upmarket, sun-drenched deli serves rich and lavish pastas, salads, soups, paninis and focaccias. The fresh juices are liquid meals. Diners munch their goodies at oversized square tables or low benches skirting the windows.

Anise (Map pp296-7; ☎ 3358 1558; 697 Brunswick St; tapas $10, mains $20-30; ☺ breakfast Sat & Sun, lunch Wed-Sun, dinner daily) Beginning the day as a stylish coffee haunt, Anise converts itself into a fashionable wine bar (see p312) for lunch and dinner. The menu is a work of French art, with dishes like smoked duck on Paris mash, and gorgonzola and mascarpone soufflé tart.

Main Squeeze (Map pp296-7; ☎ 3257 4429; 350 Brunswick St; mains $12-18; ☺ breakfast & lunch Mon-Sat) Young fashionistas head to this groovy and unpretentious café/bar to fill up on chickpea burgers, char-grilled, grain-fed sirloin and Asian dishes. Some just come for the drinks and coffee. The atmosphere is neo-meets warehouse.

BurgerUrge (Map pp296-7; ☎ 3254 1655; 542 Brunswick St; dishes $8-11; ☺ lunch Fri-Sun, dinner Tue-Sun) This is undeniably Brisbane's best burger joint. Although the menu is one dimensional, the varieties include Portabella mushroom, marinated free-range chicken or lamb and mint chutney burgers – plus the standard beef sort.

Garuva Hidden Tranquillity Restaurant & Bar (Map pp296-7; ☎ 3216 0124; 324 Wickham St; mains around $20; ☺ dinner) It's not just the food that attracts diners to this unique restaurant. A rainforested foyer leads to tables with cushioned floor seating, concealed by walls of fluttering white silk. Choices like Turkish shark and Chinese roast beef are consumed accompanied by dim lighting and smooth soundtracks. Debaucherous!

Wok On Inn (Map pp292-3; ☎ 3254 2546; 728 Brunswick St, New Farm; dishes around $8; ☺ lunch & dinner) This industrious noodle bar cooks up hot and tasty mains and soups, with a regular $6.50 lunch special.

Chinatown is sprinkled with tiny eateries serving Thai, Chinese and Korean dishes for around $10; recommended is **Thai Wi-Rat** (Map pp296-7; ☎ 3257 0884; Beirne Bldg, Chinatown Mall, Fortitude Valley; dishes $7-10; ☺ 10am-9pm).

For fresh fruit and vegies there's a great produce market inside **McWhirters Marketplace** (Map pp296-7; cnr Brunswick & Wickham Sts) in the Valley.

Also recommended:

Monsoon (Map pp296-7; ☎ 3852 6988; 455 Brunswick St, New Farm; mains $20-30; ☺ lunch & dinner Tue-Sat) Modern Asian and Australian in open-air surrounds.

Veg Out (Map pp296-7; ☎ 3852 2668; cnr Brunswick & Wickham Sts, McWhirters Marketplace; dishes $7-14; ☺ 7.30am-9pm Mon-Thu, to 10pm Fri & Sat, 10am-8pm Sun) Canteen-style café serving organic and vegetarian nosh.

South Bank

Cafe San Marco (Map pp296-7; ☎ 3846 4334; South Bank Parklands; mains $16-25; ☺ breakfast, lunch & dinner) With its picture-perfect position, this waterfront bistro is a great spot for a relaxed feed. The crowd-pleasing menu offers char-grilled steaks, Asian curries, salads and good seafood dishes; just the ticket for picky palates and the patter of little feet. Good for families.

There's a small outdoor **food court** (Map pp296-7; South Bank Parklands), where it's particularly pleasant to indulge in a cheapie lunch ($8 and under) in the sun.

West End

Cumquats (Map pp296-7; ☎ 3846 6333; 145 Boundary St; dishes $15-25; ☺ lunch & dinner Tue-Sat) This multi-award-winning restaurant cooks up a who's who of Australian game: seared wallaby, braised Tasmanian possum and emu fillets, to name a few. The talented chef fuses flavours and ingredients perfectly and there are also veggie dishes for the timid.

Gunshop Café (Map pp292-3; ☎ 3844 2241; 53 Mollison St; mains $15-20; ☺ breakfast, lunch & dinner Tue-Sat, breakfast & lunch Sun) Lovers of slothful breakfasts and brunches unite for group comas at this popular institution. Organic eggs and breads start the day, making way for mains like beef spare ribs with sticky plum sauce and potato mash. Wash it all down

with great coffee, microbrewery beers and good wines.

Jazzy Cat Cafe (Map pp292-3; ☎ 3864 2544; 56 Mollison St; mains $15-20; ☺ breakfast, lunch & dinner) Set in a beautifully restored Queenslander, this restaurant-cum-café oozes bohemian vibes, from the friendly staff to the scrummy food. The menu is multicultural and inventive, with a good balance of veggie and carnivorous risottos, Asian salads and pastas.

Three Monkeys Coffee House (Map pp292-3; ☎ 3844 6045; 58 Mollison St; dishes $8-18; ☺ breakfast, lunch & dinner) A far departure from the profusion of minimalist cafés, this laid-back alternative is a spacious warren of indoor and outdoor dining nooks. The décor is pseudo-Moroccan, but you'll munch on focaccias, paninis, pizzas, salads, nachos and more. Save room for the wicked cakes and good coffee.

Petrie Terrace, Paddington & Milton

Kookaburra Café (Map pp292-3; ☎ 3369 2400; 280 Given Tce; meals $10-25; ☺ lunch & dinner) There's a rustic edge to the classy timber-and-tin décor that compliments the distinctly Aussie menu of this great little eatery. Tourists and locals vacuum the perfect steaks, fancy fish and chips and lamb shanks. The pizzas have won awards, so bring your appetite.

Sultan's Kitchen (Map pp292-3; ☎ 3368 2194; 163 Given Tce; dishes $15-20; ☺ dinner) Serving up fragrant and authentic flavours from all corners of the subcontinent, this outstanding Indian restaurant offers more than the

Tikka, Tandoori and Madras norm. The atmosphere is intimate and simple and the service impeccable. Grab your vino from Paddo's bottleshop down the road.

Rue de Paris (Map pp292-3; ☎ 3368 2600; Shop 16, 30 Park Rd; mains $15-25; ☺ breakfast, lunch & dinner) Amidst Milton's flashy alfresco strip, this ambient spot has the wicker chairs and marble of a Parisienne café but the menu is an extensive list of Mediterranean, Middle Eastern, Mod Oz and Asian flavours. There's a wealth of breezy outdoor seating and the service is snappy.

The bistros at the **Caxton Hotel** (Map pp292-3; ☎ 3369 5544; 38 Caxton St; mains $10-25; ☺ lunch & dinner) and the **Paddo Tavern** (Map pp292-3; 3369 0044; ☎ 186 Given Tce; mains $8-15; ☺ lunch & dinner) serve good pub grub.

Breakfast Creek

Breakfast Creek Hotel (off Map pp292-3; ☎ 3262 5988; 2 Kingsford Smith Dr; dishes $13-17, steaks $20-25) This famous, sprawling hotel, on a photogenic bend of the Brisbane River just northeast of Fortitude Valley, dates from 1889 and is a Brisbane institution. The pub's open-air Spanish Garden Steak House serves incredible steaks, including the behemoth 450g rump.

Self-Catering

There's a **Coles Express** (Map pp296-7; Queen St), just west of the mall, and a **Woolworths** (Map pp296-7; Edward St) in the city centre. In Fortitude Valley, there's a great produce market inside **McWhirters Marketplace** (Map pp296-7; cnr Brunswick & Wickham Sts).

DRINKING

The Valley is Brisbane's undisputed nightlife centre, with ample drinking holes and music venues. There are also drinking spots clustered around the city centre, Petrie Terrace and the West End, although on weekends the centre is empty. Wine and style bars are making incursions into Brisbane's pub culture, but as an addition rather than replacement.

Belgian Beer Cafe (Map pp296-7; ☎ 3221 0199; cnr Edward & Mary Sts) Fussy connoisseurs of the liquid gold will be tickled tiddly at this swanky city bar. With 26 Belgian nectars available and a bevy of domestic beers and wines, the atmosphere is decidedly convivial. Plant yourself in the sunny courtyard, or lounge back in the capacious, brassy bar.

Anise (Map pp296-7; ☎ 3358 1558; 697 Brunswick St) You'll need to bring your fancy threads and palates to this trendy wine bar in the heart of New Farm. Patrons plant themselves a high-backed chairs along the long narrow bar and nibble on tapas (see p310) while plunging into the exhausting and excellent range of wines.

Sunbar Restaurant and Lounge (Map pp296-7; ☎ 3257 4999; 367 Brunswick St) Think chillout sessions and classy cool; muted, soft vinyl adorns Sunbar's luminescent orange bar around which you can perch your designer clad tush. If your tush is generically clad you're just as welcome but the emphasis is still on sophisticated fun. See also p310 for Sunbar's delectable dining.

Port Office Hotel (Map pp296-7; ☎ 3221 0072; 4 Edward St) The industrial edge at this renovated city pub is softened by swathes of dark wood and jungle print. Find a stool or bench early and settle in for the evening. When things get hectic (Thursday to Saturday night) the crowd fills the upstairs balcony and seating.

Press Club (Map pp296-7; ☎ 3852 4000; 339 Brunswick St, Fortitude Valley) This underworld setting is a mixture of minimal lighting, stylish Goth décor, comfy couches and plenty of dark corners. Heavenly beats throb, courtesy of live DJs, from Wednesday to Sundays and the atmosphere is more chilled-out drinking rather than beer vacuuming.

O'Learys (Map pp292-3; ☎ 3368 1933; 25 Caxton St, Petrie Terrace) Any hint of pretensions are left at the door of this atmospheric pub. Loud conversations take place inside the big brassy bar, with kegs for tables and lots of polished timber beneath a cavernous roof. There's also a great beer garden and live music throughout the week.

GPO (Map pp296-7; ☎ 3252 1322; 740 Ann St, Fortitude Valley) The dressed-up old post office in the Valley is the location of this fashionable gay-friendly bar. Downstairs you'll find strappy heels and trendy haircuts, while upstairs offers chilled tunes and the occasional live band.

Caxton Hotel (Map pp292-3; ☎ 3369 5544; 38 Caxton St, Petrie Terrace) This popular pub is a crowd pleaser with locals, and heaves on Friday and Saturday night, when the happy buzz wafts out the wide-open bay windows. Expect mainstream music in the background and sports on the TV.

Jorge (Map pp296-7; ☎ 3012 9121; 183 George St) After sunset from Wednesday to Sunday, the permanent decks at this venue get a good workout when DJs spin background funk into the wee hours. Suave punters sip boutique beers and cocktails in between buzzy conversations. See p309 for Jorge's snappy dining offerings.

Other good watering holes:

Pavilion (Map pp296-7; ☎ 3844 6172; cnr Boundary & Wilson Sts, West End) A jack of all drinking trades, with a bar, café and bistro. Popular with the 20- to 30-somethings.

Story Bridge Hotel (Map pp292-3; ☎ 3391 2266; 196 Main St, Kangaroo Point) Beautiful old pub with a fashionable back bar and a casual beer garden. Also the location for the annual Australia Day (26 January) cockroach race.

Exchange Hotel (Map pp292-3; ☎ 3229 3522; 131 Edward St) Spacious city pub that lures a good cross-section of drinkers and socialisers.

Down Under Bar & Grill (Map pp292-3; ☎ 3211 9277; cnr Ann & Edward Sts) Backpackers' haunt, which heaves on a nightly basis.

ENTERTAINMENT

Brisbane pulls all the international bands heading to Oz and the city's clubs have become nationally renowned. There's also plenty of theatre. Pick up the free entertainment papers *Time Off* (www.timeoff .com.au), *Rave* (www.ravemag.com.au) and *Scene* (www.sceneonline.com.au). Another good source of information is the website www.brisbane247.com.

The *Courier-Mail* also has daily arts and entertainment listings and a comprehensive 'What's On In Town' section in each Thursday's newspaper.

Ticketek (☎ 13 19 31; http://premier.ticketek.com .au) is a centralised phone-booking agency that handles bookings for many of the major events, sports and performances. You can pick up tickets from the **Ticketek booth** (Map pp296-7; Elizabeth St), at the back of the Myer Centre.

Nightclubs

Brisbane's club scene is well and truly concentrated in the Valley. Generally clubs are open Thursday to Sunday night, are adamant about photo ID and charge $5 to $15 entry.

Family (Map pp296-7; ☎ 3852 5000; 8 McLachlan St, Fortitude Valley) Family exhilarates dance junkies every weekend on four levels with two dance floors, four bars, four funky themed booths and a top-notch sound system. This club has been voted Australia's best club twice, and top DJs from home and away grace the hallowed decks here.

Fringe Bar (Map pp296-7; ☎ 3252 9833; cnr Ann & Constance Sts, Fortitude Valley) Too cool for skool, this is the kind of bar where the next afro will be invented. Retro décor swims with style and swaying punters and live DJs get their groove on from Wednesday to Sunday night. Long lines are standard at the weekend.

Empire (Map pp296-7; ☎ 3852 1216; 339 Brunswick St, Fortitude Valley) Within the confines of this long-standing club you'll find DJs working the decks and a dancing crowd in the Moon Bar upstairs, and trendy, lithe things mingling in the sceney Corner Bar downstairs. Things get going after 9pm at the weekend.

Monastery (Map pp296-7; ☎ 3257 7081; 621 Ann St, Fortitude Valley) From the outside this club resembles a generic office block, but there's nothing suit-and-tie about the dim interior with its soft suede couches and lucid soundscapes. Big domestic acts such as Endorphin intermittently play live, but it's the resident DJs that keep the fans coming back.

Source (Map pp296-7; 697 Ann St, Fortitude Valley) Less hardcore and more generic, this joint keeps clubbers of all ages and genres happy with live DJs from Thursday to Saturday night playing R&B, hip-hop and drum 'n' bass. There is an open-mic session on Sunday.

Cinemas

Both the **Dendy Cinema** (Map pp296-7; ☎ 3211 3244; 346 George St) and **Palace Centro** (Map pp296-7; ☎ 3852 4488; 39 James St, Fortitude Valley) play good arthouse films. The cheapest cinema for mainstream flicks is **South Bank Cinema** (Map pp296-7; ☎ 3846 5188; cnr Grey St & Ernest Sts, South Bank).

There are also open-air movies screened over summer in the South Bank Parklands (see p299) and the City Botanic Gardens (see p298).

Mainstream cinemas on Queen St Mall:

Greater Union (Map pp296-7; ☎ 3027 9999; Level A, Myer Centre, Queen St Mall) Mainstream blockbusters.

Hoyts Regent Theatre (Map pp296-7; ☎ 3027 9999; 107 Queen St Mall) A lovely old cinema worth visiting for the building alone.

Theatre

Many of Brisbane's theatre venues are located in or near South Bank. The Queensland Cultural Centre has a dedicated **phone line** (☎ 13 62 46) that handles bookings for all the South Bank theatres. Also keep an eye out for *Centre Stage*, the events diary for the complex, available from tourist offices.

Performing Arts Centre (Map pp296-7; ☎ 3840 7444; www.qpat.com.au; Queensland Cultural Centre, Stanley St, South Bank; P) This centre consists of three venues and features concerts, plays, dance and performances of all genres. Catch anything from international comedy acts to *Alice in Wonderland*.

Queensland Conservatorium (Map pp296-7; ☎ 3875 6375; 16 Russell St, South Bank) South of the Performing Arts Centre, this conservatorium showcases the talent of attending students.

Brisbane Powerhouse (Map pp292-3; ☎ 3358 8622, box office ☎ 3358 8600; 119 Lamington St, New Farm; P 🏃) A one-stop venue for contemporary arts and performance in the inner north. The Powerhouse presents an evolving schedule of theatre, dance, music and workshops.

Metro Arts Centre (Map pp296-7; ☎ 3221 1527; 109 Edward St; 🏃) This progressive venue hosts community theatre, local dramatic pieces, dance and art shows. It's a good spot to head for a taste of Brisbane's creative performance talent.

Also recommended:

QUT Gardens Theatre (Map pp296-7; ☎ 3864 4213; Queensland University of Technology, George St; P) Touring productions plus shows from the university's performing companies.

Brisbane Arts Theatre (Map pp292-3; ☎ 3369 2344; 210 Petrie Tce, Petrie Terrace) Amateur theatre performances along the lines of Shakespeare and Dickens.

La Boite Repertory Theatre (Map pp292-3; ☎ 3010 2611; 424 Montague Rd, West End) Intimate theatre presenting a range of art-house theatre.

Gay & Lesbian Venues

Brisbane has a small gay and lesbian scene, centred mostly around the Valley. Events are covered in the fortnightly *Q News* (www.qnews.com.au). *Queensland Pride*, another gay publication, takes in the whole of the state. *Dykes on Mykes* (www.queerradio.org), a radio show on Wednesday from 9pm to 11pm on FM102.1, is another source of information on the city.

Wickham Hotel (Map pp296-7; ☎ 3852 1301; 308 Wickham St, Fortitude Valley) This classic old Victorian pub is Brisbane's most popular gay and lesbian venue, with nightly events including drag shows, dancers and DJs. The Wickham celebrates the Sydney Mardi Gras and the Pride Festival in style and grandeur.

Sportsman's Hotel (Map pp296-7; ☎ 3831 2892; 130 Leichhardt St) Another popular gay venue, Sportsman's Hotel has shows, pool tables and a relaxed atmosphere.

Other good options include GPO (p312) and Family (p313).

Live Music

Brisbane is a good place to catch some live music, and rightly so considering its history. Groups such as the influential '70s punk band *The Saints*, and more recently *Powderfinger* and *Regurgitator*, all hail from here. The *Bee Gees* even spent some of their formative years here. Cover charges start at about $6 for local acts and go up from there.

Brisbane Convention and Exhibition Centre (Map pp296-7; ☎ 3308 3000; Glenelg St, South Bank; P) This is Brisbane's largest multi-functional entertainment complex. When the big guns are in town they strut their stuff here to swarming crowds, and you're likely to catch anyone from PJ Harvey to the Wiggles!

Zoo (Map pp296-7; ☎ 3854 1381; 711 Ann St, Fortitude Valley) This grungy institution is a favourite with musos of all calibre, and offers excellent opportunities to see some raw talent. The eclectic performances draw long crowds every weekend, and whether you're into hard metal or electronic soundscapes, Zoo has a gig for you.

Tongue & Groove (Map pp292-3; ☎ 3846 0334; 63 Hardgrave Rd, West End) This funky little venue in the West End hosts everything from reggae and blues to dance beats from Tuesday to Sunday. Jazz is another common theme and all nightlife takes place in the dimly lit subterranean bar.

Indie Temple (Map pp296-7; ☎ 3852 2851; 210 Wickham St, Fortitude Valley) The emphasis is on alternative music and rock at this raw student stomping ground. Metal nights and live music alternate with theme nights. It's also becoming the fashionable small venue for big international acts so keep an eye out.

More music venues:

Rev (Map pp296-7; ☎ 3852 3373; 25 Warner St, Fortitude Valley) Smallish venue hosting home-grown talent.

QUEENSLAND

Brisbane Jazz Club (Map pp296-7; ☎ 3391 2006; 1 Annie St, Kangaroo Point; cover $8-12) A must for jazz purists on Saturday and Sunday nights.

Sport

You can see interstate cricket matches and international test cricket at the **Brisbane Cricket Ground** (Gabba; Map pp292-3; ☎ 3008 6166; www.thegabba.org.au; Vulture St, Woolloongabba). The cricket season runs from October through to March.

During the other half of the year, rugby league is the big spectator sport. The Brisbane Broncos plays home games at **Suncorp Stadium** (Map pp292-3; ☎ 3331 5000; Castlemaine St, Milton).

Once dominated by Victorian teams, the Australian Football League (AFL) has been mastered by the Brisbane Lions; they won the flag in 2001, 2002 and 2003. You can watch them kick the ball and some southern butt at a home game at the Gabba between March and September.

SHOPPING

Brisbane boasts plenty of chain and independent outlets of all merchandise to keep the cash flowing. In the CBD, the confluence is on Queen St Mall. In the Valley, dozens of trendy fashion boutiques converge around the Ann and Brunswick Sts intersection.

Queensland Aboriginal Creations (Map pp296-7; ☎ 3224 5730; Little Stanley St, South Bank) This is probably Brisbane's best indigenous arts store, stocking a good range of authentic Aboriginal art, crafts and souvenirs, including paintings and prints, didgeridoos, boomerangs, jewellery, clap-sticks, bullroarers, woomeras and clothing.

Australian Geographic (Wintergarden Centre Map pp296-7; ☎ 3003 0355; Queen St Mall; Myer Centre Map pp296-7; ☎ 3220 0341; Queen St Mall) These stores stock everything from books and calendars on Australian flora and fauna to glow-in-the-dark dinosaurs.

Australia the Gift (Map pp296-7; ☎ 3210 6198; 150 Queen St Mall) This is the biggest vendor of Australiana in the city and carries extensive stock.

Dogstar (Map pp296-7; ☎ 3852 2555; 713 Ann St, Fortitude Valley) The Japanese-born designer of the beautiful pieces in this shop has infused more than a touch of her land of birth into the designs. Beautiful fabrics are used to make up pants, skirts and ensembles that will be envied anywhere.

Blonde Venus (Map pp296-7; ☎ 3216 1735; 707 Ann St, Fortitude Valley) Head here to pick up a piece of Zimmerman, Akira or Morrissey. Blonde also sells cutting-edge designers on the verge of being discovered.

Markets

Brunswick St Markets (Map pp296-7; Brunswick St Mall, Fortitude Valley; ☽ 8am-4pm Sat & Sun) At the weekend these funky markets fill the mall with a diverse collection of crafts, clothes and budding designer-ware…and the inevitable junk.

Crafts Village Market (Map pp296-7; Stanley St Plaza, South Bank; ☽ 5pm-10.30pm Fri, 10am-6pm Sat, 9am-5pm Sun) This market has a great range of clothing, arts and handmade crafts from Friday to Sunday.

The carnival-style **Riverside Centre Market** (Map pp296-7; Riverside Centre; ☽ 8am-4pm Sun) and **Eagle St Pier Market** (Map pp296-7; Eagle St Pier; ☽ 8am-4pm Sun) host over 150 craft stalls, including glassware, weaving and leatherwork. There are also children's activities.

GETTING THERE & AWAY

Air

Brisbane's main airport is about 16km northeast of the city centre at Eagle Farm and has separate international and domestic terminals about 2km apart, linked by the **Airtrain** (☎ 3215 5000; www.airtrain.com.au; ☽ 5.30am-7.30pm Mon-Fri, 5.30am-7pm Sat & Sun, every 15 min; per person $3). It's a busy international arrival and departure point with frequent flights to Asia, Europe, Pacific Islands, North America, New Zealand and Papua New Guinea. See p1035 for details of international airlines that service Brisbane.

Domestic airlines servicing Brisbane include **Qantas** (Map pp296-7; ☎ 13 13 13; www.qantas.com.au; 247 Adelaide St; ☽ 8.30am-5pm Mon-Fri, 9am-1pm Sat), **Virgin Blue** (☎ 13 67 89; www.virginblue.com.au), **Jetstar** (☎ 13 15 38; www.jetstar.com.au), **Macair** (☎ 13 13 13; www.macair.com.au) and **Sunshine Express** (☎ 13 13 13; www.sunshineexpress.com.au).

General one-way fares offered by Virgin Blue and Qantas between Brisbane and the other state capitals start from Sydney ($100), Melbourne ($130), Canberra ($120), Adelaide ($180), Perth ($270) and Darwin ($190). Within Queensland, there are flights available between Brisbane and Cairns,

($130), Rockhampton ($90), Townsville ($130) and Mt Isa ($230).

Jetstar has cheaper flights between Brisbane and Melbourne, Cairns and Rockhampton.

Bus

Brisbane's **Roma St Transit Centre** (Map pp296-7; Roma St), about 500m west of the city centre, is the main terminus and booking office for all long-distance buses and trains. The centre has shops, food outlets, ATMs, an accommodation booking service and a backpackers' employment service.

The bus companies have booking desks on the third level of the centre. **Greyhound Australia** (☎ 13 14 99; www.greyhound.com.au) is the main company on the Sydney–Brisbane run ($100, 16 hours). **Premier Motor Service** (☎ 13 34 10; www.premierms.com.au) often has cheaper deals on this route. You can also travel between Brisbane and Melbourne ($164, 24 to 28 hours) or Adelaide ($290, 40 hours), although competitive airfares may enable you to fly for the same price or less.

Within Queensland, buses head to Mt Isa ($155, 26 hours), Cairns ($200, 29 hours), stopping at Noosa Heads ($24, 2½ hours), Hervey Bay ($50, 5½ hours), Rockhampton ($70, 11½ hours), Mackay ($140, 16 hours) and Townsville ($180, 23 hours).

Car & Motorcycle

There are five major routes into and out of the Brisbane metropolitan area, numbered from M1 to M5. The major north–south route, the M1, connects the Pacific Hwy to the south with the Bruce Hwy to the north, but things get a bit confusing as you enter the city.

Coming from the Gold Coast, the Pacific Hwy splits into two at Eight Mile Plains. From here, the South East Freeway (M3) runs right into the centre, skirting along the riverfront on the western side of the CBD, before emerging on the far side as the Gympie Arterial Rd.

If you're just passing through, take the Gateway Motorway (M1) at Eight Mile Plains, which bypasses the city centre to the east and crosses the Brisbane River at the Gateway Bridge ($3 toll). From either direction, the Eagle Farm exit on the northern side of the bridge provides a quick route to Fortitude Valley and the city centre. Just north is the turn-off to Brisbane airport. The Gateway Motorway and Gympie Arterial Rd meet in Bald Hills, just south of the Pine River, and merge to form the Bruce Hwy.

Heading inland, the Ipswich Motorway (M2) branches off the M1 south of the centre, and crosses the M3 before snaking off southwest to Ipswich and the Darling Downs. For a quick route from the city, pick up Milton Rd at the northwestern tip of the CBD and follow it out to the M5, which runs south to meet the Ipswich Motorway at Wacol (this is also the way to Mt Coot-tha Reserve).

HIRE

All of the major companies – **Hertz** (☎ 13 30 39), **Avis** (☎ 13 63 33), **Budget** (☎ 13 27 27), **Europcar** (☎ 13 13 90) and **Thrifty** (☎ 1300 367 227) – have offices at the Brisbane airport terminals and throughout the city.

There are also several smaller companies in Brisbane, which advertise slightly cheaper deals:

Abel Rent A Car (Map pp296-7; ☎ 1800 131 429, 3236 1225; www.abel.com.au; Ground fl, Roma St Transit Centre)

Can Do Car Rentals (Map pp296-7; ☎ 3832 3666; www.candorentals.com.au; cnr Wickham & Warren Sts, Fortitude Valley)

Integra Network Car & Truck Rentals (Map pp292-3; ☎ 1800 067 414, 3620 3200; www.abcintegra.com.au; 398 St Pauls Tce, Fortitude Valley)

Train

Brisbane's main station for long-distance trains is the Roma St Transit Centre. For train reservations and information call into the **Queensland Rail Travel Centre** (☎ 13 22 32; www.qr.com.au; Central Station Map pp296-7; ☎ 3235 1323; Ground fl, Central Station, 305 Edward St; ☺ 7am-5pm Mon-Fri; Roma Transit Centre Map pp296-7; ☎ 3235 1331; Roma St; ☺ 7am-5pm Mon-Fri). You can also make reservations online or over the phone.

New South Wales' **CountryLink** (☎ 13 22 32; www.countrylink.nsw.gov.au) has a daily XPT (express passenger train) service between Brisbane and Sydney. The northbound service runs overnight, and the southbound service runs during the day (economy/1st class/sleeper $115/165/245, 15 hours).

Services within Queensland:

Spirit of the Outback (economy seat/economy sleeper/1st-class sleeper $165/230/350, 24 hours) Brisbane to Longreach via Rockhampton twice weekly.

Sunlander (economy seat/economy sleeper/1st-class sleeper/Queenslander class $190/240/380/690, 30 hours) Brisbane to Cairns via Townsville. The exclusive Queenslander class includes restaurant meals and historical commentary.

Tilt Train Brisbane to Cairns (business seat only $280, 25 hours) and Brisbane to Rockhampton (economy seat/business seat $95/140, seven hours).

Westlander (economy seat/economy sleeper/1st-class sleeper $90/145/225, 16 hours) Brisbane to Charleville via Roma.

Concessions are available to children under 16 years, students with a valid ISIC card, and senior citizens.

GETTING AROUND

Brisbane boasts a world-class public transport network, and information on bus, train and ferry routes and connections can be obtained from the **Trans-Info Service** (☎ 13 12 30; www.transinfo.qld.gov.au; ☺ 6am-10pm).

Bus and ferry information is available at the Brisbane Visitor Information Centre (p294), the **bus station information centre** (Map pp296-7; Queen St Mall bus station; ☺ 8.30am-5.30pm Mon-Thu, 8.30am-8pm Fri, 9am-4pm Sat, 10am-4pm Sun), and the Queensland Rail Travel Centre (opposite).

Fares on buses, trains and ferries operate on a zone system. There are 23 zones in total but the city centre and most of the inner-city suburbs fall within Zone 1, which translates into a single fare of $2/1 per adult/child.

If you're going to be using public transport more than once on any single day, it's worth getting a **daily ticket** (per adult/child zone 1 $4/2, zone 2 $4.80/2.40, zone 3 $5.60/2.80). These allow you unlimited transport on all buses, trains and ferries and are priced according to the number of zones you'll be travelling in.

You can also purchase **off-peak daily tickets** (per adult/child zone 1 $3/1.50, zone 2 $3.60/1.80, zone 3 $4.20/2.10), which allow you to do the same thing between 9am and 3.30pm and after 7pm from Monday to Friday, and all weekend.

A **Ten Trip Saver** (per adult/child zone 1 $16/8, zone 2 $20/9.60, zone 3 $23/11.20) gives you 10 trips for the price of eight.

To/From the Airport

The easiest way to get to and from the airport is the **Airtrain** (☎ 3215 5000; www.airtrain .com.au; per adult/child $10/5; ☺ 5am-8pm, every 15mins),

which runs between the airport and the Roma St Transit Centre and Central Station. There are also half-hourly services to the airport from Gold Coast Citytrain stops. **Coachtrans** (☎ 3238 4700; www.coachtrans.com.au) runs the half-hourly **Skytrans** (to city per adult/child $9/6, to city accommodation $11/7; ☺ 5.45am-10pm) shuttle bus between the Roma St Transit Centre and the airport. A taxi into the centre from the airport will cost around $30.

Boat

Brisbane's nippy blue CityCat catamarans run every 20 to 30 minutes, between 5.50am and 10.30pm, from the University of Queensland in the southwest to Bretts Wharf in the northeast, and back. Stops along the way include North Quay (for the Queen St Mall), South Bank, Riverside (for the CBD) and New Farm Park. The City Cats are wheelchair accessible at the University of Queensland, Guyatt Park, North Quay, South Bank 1 & 2 and Hawthorne.

Also useful are the Inner City Ferries, which zigzag back and forth across the river between North Quay, near the Victoria Bridge, and Mowbray Park. Services start at 6am from Monday to Saturday and from 7am on Sunday, and run till about 9pm from Sunday to Thursday and until about 11pm on Friday and Saturday. There are also several cross-river ferries; most useful is the Eagle St Pier to Thornton St (Kangaroo Point) service.

Like all public transport, fares are based on zones. Most stops you'll need will be city-based and will therefore cost $2/1 per adult/child for one trip.

Bus

The Loop, a free bus service that circles the city area, stopping at QUT, Queen St Mall, City Hall, Central Station and Riverside, runs every 10 minutes on weekdays between 7am and 6pm.

The main stop for local buses is in the underground Queen St Mall bus station (Map pp296–7) in the Myer Centre, where there's an information centre. You can also pick up many buses from the colour-coded stops along Adelaide St, between George and Edward Sts.

Buses run every 10 to 20 minutes Monday to Friday, from 5am till about 6pm, and with the same frequency on Saturday morning (starting at 6am). Services are less frequent at other times, and cease at 7pm Sunday and midnight on other days.

Car & Motorcycle

There is free two-hour parking on many streets in the CBD and in the inner suburbs, but the major thoroughfares become clearways (ie parking is prohibited) during the morning and afternoon rush hours. If you do park in the street, pay close attention to the times on the parking signs, as Brisbane's parking inspectors take no prisoners. Parking is free in the CBD during the evening.

Taxi

There are usually plenty of taxis around the city centre, and there are taxi ranks at the transit centre and at the top end of Edward St, by the junction with Adelaide St.

You can book a taxi by phone. The major taxi company here is **Black & White** (☎ 13 10 08). Rivals include **Yellow Cab Co** (☎ 13 19 24) and **Brisbane Cabs** (☎ 13 22 11). Most cabs have Eftpos facilities.

Train

The fast Citytrain network has seven lines, which run as far as Gympie North in the north (for the Sunshine Coast) and Nerang and Robina in the south (for the Gold Coast). All trains go through Roma St, Central and Brunswick St stations.

MORETON BAY

The Brisbane River ambles east from the city and enters into Moreton Bay, an area reckoned to have some 365 islands – one for each day of the year. It's a popular region for weekending Brisbanites and home to some of Queensland's highlights. Most people head for North Stradbroke, to exploit the photogenic beaches and surfing, and Moreton Island, to participate in the dolphin feeding at Tangalooma and dive some spectacular wrecks. The coastal suburb of Redcliffe is laced with history and blessed by a gorgeous esplanade, making it another popular haunt.

Tours

Humpbacks are a regular sight in the bay between June and November.

Manly Eco Cruises (☎ 07-3396 9400; www.manlyeco cruises.com; per adult/child $90/40) Takes folk out on the MV *Getaway* with boom nets, for full-day cruises. There's also a very popular Sunday BBQ breakfast tour (adult/child $30/15) which lasts two hours.

Moreton Bay Escapes (☎ 1300 559 355; www.more tonbayescapes.com.au; per adult/child/family incl lunch $110/90/335) Operates day tours in the racing yacht *Solo*, which include three hours sailing and three hours snorkelling, swimming or just being lazy on Moreton Island.

REDCLIFFE

☎ 07

Redcliffe is a pretty coastal town on a jutting peninsula, sitting 35km north of Brisbane. It was the first white settlement in Queensland, but today it's a popular haunt for day trippers. Doused in a relaxed ambience, it's also blessed with spectacular views of the bay and a string of pretty beaches.

The main **Redcliffe Visitor Information** (☎ 1 00 659 500; Pelican Park, Hornibrook Esplanade, Clontarf; ⊗ 7am-4pm) office is located at the base of the peninsula. There's also a smaller, central version in **Redcliffe** (cnr Redcliffe Pde & Irene St; ⊗ 9am-4pm).

The main drawcard in Redcliffe is the esplanade that skirts the shoreline. Along it you will discover the sizable **Redcliffe Jetty**, which has had several makeovers since its beginnings in 1885. A few hundred metres south of the jetty sits **Settlement Cove Lagoon**, a small man-made lagoon littered with barbecues as well as colourful climbing boats and castles for little tackers to climb all over.

Vehicle ferries to Bulwer on Moreton Island leave from **Scarborough**, at the northern tip of the headland.

NORTH STRADBROKE ISLAND

☎ 07 / pop 3500

Best known as 'Straddie', this tranquil sand island is peppered with residential settlements. By far it's the most popular of Moreton Bay's destinations and it's just a convenient 30-minute ferry ride from Cleveland, which lies 30km southeast of Brisbane.

Folk come to snorkel, surf and swim in the excellent surf beaches and the island offers a good range of places to stay and eat for longer visits. It can get pretty busy over Christmas and Easter though, when families converge for their annual holidays.

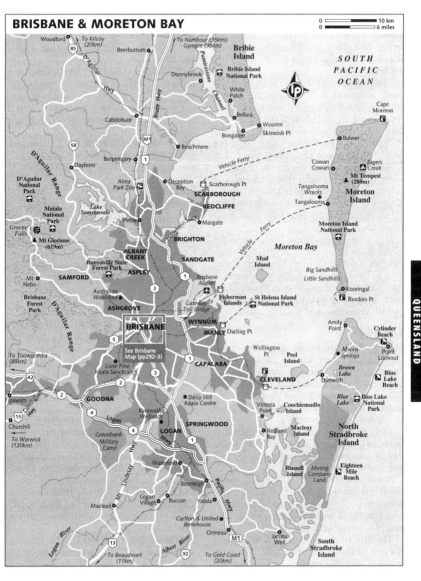

BRISBANE & MORETON BAY

The island's wild southeastern coast is a playground for 4WD drivers.

There are three small settlements on the island: Dunwich, Amity Point and Point Lookout. These are all grouped around the northern end. **Point Lookout**, on the main surf beach, is the nicest place to stay. The middle of the island boasts stunning vege-tation and is a divine spot for bushwalkers. Apart from the beach, the southern part of the island is closed to visitors because of sand mining.

The informative **Stradbroke Island Visitor Information Centre** (☎ 3409 9555; www.stradbroke tourism.com; ✆ 8.30am-5pm) is 200m from the ferry terminal in Dunwich.

Sights

Dunwich, on the western coast, is where the ferries dock. Here you'll find the tiny **North Stradbroke Historical Museum** (☎ 3409 9699; 17 Welsby St).

The eastern beach, known as **Eighteen Mile Beach**, is open to 4WD vehicles and campers, with lots of walking tracks and old 4WD roads in the northern half of the island. **Blue Lake** is reached by a sandy 4WD track – it's just off the road from Dunwich to the beach. Much more pleasant is the 2.7km walking trail through the forest. The freshwater lake is a beautiful spot for a swim, if you don't mind the spooky unseen depths. There's also good swimming at **Brown Lake**, about 3km along the Blue Lake road from Dunwich.

If you want to walk the 20km across the island from Dunwich to Point Lookout, a number of dirt-track loops break the monotony of bitumen roads. A pleasant diversion near the coast, about 4km north of Dunwich, is **Myora Springs**, which is surrounded by lush vegetation and walking tracks.

Activities

Endless stretches of white sand account for Straddie's best **beaches** around Point Lookout, where there's a series of points and bays along the headland. Cylinder and Amity Point generally provide calm swimming, while Main Beach churns some good swells and breaks for **surfing**.

You can hire surfboards and bodyboards from various places; kayak hire per hour/day is around $20/50, surfboards $15/40 and bodyboards $10/30.

Straddie Adventures (☎ 3409 8414; Point Lookout) offers sea-kayaking trips (including snorkelling stops $35) around Straddie, and sandboarding ($25), which is like snowboarding, except it's done on sand.

The island is also famous for its **fishing**, and the annual Straddie Classic, held in August, is one of Australia's richest and best-known fishing competitions. **Dunwich Sports & Hobbies** (☎ 3409 9252; Bingle Rd; ⌚ 7.30am-5pm Mon-Fri, to 4pm Sat & 3pm Sun) hires out fishing gear.

Stradbroke Island Scuba Centre (☎ 3409 8888; www.stradbrokeislandscuba.com.au; 1 East Coast Rd), based at Stradbroke Island Backpackers (right), offers snorkelling for $60 inclusive of a two-hour boat trip and all the gear. Open-water courses cost $350.

Tours

Awesome Wicked Wild (☎ 3409 8045; half/full day $35/50) Offers tours of Amity Point and the lakes in 20ft glass-bottom canoes.

North Stradbroke Island 4WD Tours & Camping Holidays (☎ 3409 8051; straddie@ecn.net.au) Operates tours by negotiation, based on numbers and the time of year. Generally the cost of half-day tours are $30/15 per adult/child. This outfit also operates half-day fishing tours for the same price.

Straddie Kingfisher Tours (☎ 3409 9502; www.straddiekingfishertours.com.au; adult/child $70/40) Operates eco-tourism based tours around the island lasting six hours.

Sleeping

Straddie Views B&B (☎ 3409 8875; www.northstradbrokeisland.com/straddiebb; 26 Cumming Pde; r per week night/weekend $100/120) Purpose-built rooms at this friendly B&B are spacious and classy. Creature comforts include bar fridges, tea and coffee facilities and a spot of port. Breakfast is served with views on the upstairs deck.

Whale Watch Resort (☎ 1800 450 004, 3409 8555; www.whalewatchresort.com.au; Samarinda Dr; r per 2/5 nights from $326/720; 🔲 🖳 🐾) Sublime and secluded apartments which will make you feel like a million bucks. Cavernous interiors contain three rooms, two bathrooms, large lounges and superb views of the ocean. The private decks have classy timber furniture so you can dine and admire your own views.

Stradbroke Island YHA (☎ 3409 8888; www.stradbrokeislandscuba.com.au; 1 East Coast Rd; dm $22, tw & d $50) This large beachside hostel is clean, well kept and has excellent facilities, including a dive school right on the doorstep. Guests can make use of surf- and boogie boards and rent bikes for $10/15 per half/full day. The hostel runs a pick-up bus from opposite the transit centre in Brisbane but you need to book.

Headland Chalet (☎ 3409 8252; 213 Midjimberry Rd, Point Lookout; d & tw cabins per person Sun-Thu $25, Fri & Sat $30; 🐾) An excellent cheap option is this cluster of simple cabins on the hillside overlooking Main Beach, near the roundabout. Cabins are attractive inside and have good views and there's also a pool, TV room and small kitchen.

If you're thinking of staying a while, a holiday flat or house can be good value, especially outside the holiday seasons. There are numerous real estate agents who manage the rentals, which vary from $170 to $500 per night, dropping significantly for multi-day stays:

Dolphin Holiday Accommodation (☎ 3409 8455; 1 Endeavour St)
Raine & Horne (☎ 3409 8213; 4 Kennedy Dr)
Ray White (☎ 3409 8255; Mintee St)

There are six camping grounds on the island operated by **Stradbroke Camping** (☎ 1300 551 253; powered sites per adult/child $12/5.30, unpowered sites $9/4.20, foreshore camping $5.30/3.20) on the island, but the most attractive are the places grouped around Point Lookout. The Adder Rock Camping Area and Thankful Rest Camping Area both overlook lovely Home Beach, while the Cylinder Beach Camping Area is right on Cylinder Beach and one of the most popular beaches on the island. Sites should be booked well in advance.

Eating

There are a couple of general stores selling groceries in Point Lookout, but it's worth bringing basic supplies. Note that few places to eat are open later than 8pm.

Whale's Way (☎ 3409 8106; mains $20-30; ☒ dinner Tue-Sat) Excellent restaurant which sets the benchmark on Straddie, serving delicate concoctions like Moreton Bay bugs and ocean king prawns layered between filo pastry with a light curry sauce. The elevated views are just as special.

Stonefish Cafe Bar & Restaurant (☎ 3409 8549; cnr Mooloomba Rd & Mintee St; ☒ breakfast & lunch) No boring bacon and eggs to be had at this funky spot, you'll be filling up on vanilla-bean French toast or an Israeli breakfast with coriander toast instead. The eclectic menu represents Middle Eastern, Thai and Aussie flavours and most of the seating is outdoor, which catches the sea breeze.

Point Lookout Pizza (☎ 3409 8179; Kennedy Dr; pizzas $12-22; ☒ dinner) Don't be fooled by the takeaway façade, the ladies here cook up a mean pizza and they don't hold back on the toppings. The usual suspects are up for grabs or you can delve into a garlic prawn, spicy chicken or smoked salmon pizza.

Getting There & Away

The gateway to North Stradbroke Island is the seaside town of Cleveland. Regular City-train services run from Central or Roma St Stations in Brisbane to Cleveland station ($4,

one hour), from where you can get a bus ($1) to the ferry terminal.

Stradbroke Ferries (☎ 3286 2666) runs a water taxi to Dunwich almost every hour from about 6am to 6pm ($13 return, 30 minutes). It also has a slightly less frequent vehicle ferry (per vehicle including passengers return $95, 45 minutes) from 5.30am to 6.30pm (later at weekends).

The **Stradbroke Flyer** (☎ 3821 3821; www.flyer.com.au) also runs an almost-hourly catamaran service from Cleveland to One Mile Jetty ($13 return, 45 minutes), 1.5km north of central Dunwich.

Getting Around

Local **buses** (☎ 3409 7151) meet the ferries at Dunwich and One Mile Jetty and run across to Point Lookout ($10.50 return). The last bus to Dunwich leaves Point Lookout around 6pm. There's also the **Stradbroke Cab Service** (☎ 0408 193 685), which charges $30 from Dunwich to Point Lookout.

MORETON ISLAND
☎ 07

North of Stradbroke, Moreton Island comes a close second to Fraser Island for excellent sand-driving and wilderness, and sees far fewer visitors. Apart from a few rocky headlands, it's all sand, with **Mt Tempest** towering to 280m, the highest coastal sand hill in the world. The island's bird life is prolific, and at its northern tip is a **lighthouse**, built in 1857. Ninety per cent of the island is national park. Off the western coast are the **Tangalooma Wrecks**, which provide good snorkelling and diving.

Moreton Island has no paved roads, but 4WD vehicles can travel along beaches and a few cross-island tracks – seek local advice about tides and creek crossings. You can get QPWS maps from the vehicle ferry offices or the **rangers** (☎ 3408 2710) at Tangalooma. Vehicle permits for the island cost $31 and are available through the ferry operators or from the Naturally Queensland office in Brisbane (p294). Note that ferry bookings are *mandatory* if you want to take a vehicle across; see p322 for operators.

Tangalooma, halfway down the western side of the island, is a popular tourist resort situated at an old whaling station. The main attraction is the **wild-dolphin feeding**, which takes place each evening at around sunset.

Usually about eight or nine dolphins swim in from the ocean and take fish from the hands of volunteer feeders, but you need to be a guest of the resort to be involved.

The only other settlements, all on the west coast, are **Bulwer** near the northwestern tip, **Cowan Cowan** between Bulwer and Tangalooma, and **Kooringal** near the southern tip. The shops at Kooringal and Bulwer are expensive, so bring what you can from the mainland.

Without your own vehicle, walking is the only way to get around the island, and you'll need several days to explore it. Fortunately, there are loads of good walking trails and decommissioned 4WD roads. It's worth making the strenuous trek to the summit of Mt Tempest, about 3km inland from Eagers Creek.

An area of bare sand known as the **Desert** is about 3km south and inland from Tangalooma, while the **Big Sandhills** and the **Little Sandhills** are towards the narrow southern end of the island. The biggest lakes and some swamps are in the northeast.

Tours

There are a couple of good outfits.

Gibren Expeditions (☎ 1300 559 355; 2-/3-day tours per person from $210/320) Activity-based tours by local guides.

Sunrover Expeditions (☎ 1800 353 717, 3880 0719; www.sunrover.com.au; adult/child incl lunch $120/90; ☺ Fri, Sun & Mon) 4WD tours departing from Roma St Transit Centre.

Sleeping

Bulwer Cabins (☎ 3203 6399; www.moreton-island.com; cabins from $90) These accommodating self-contained units, 200m from the beach at Bulwer, sleep up to six.

Tangalooma Wild Dolphin Resort (☎ 1300 652 250, 3410 6000; www.tangalooma.com; packages $230-330; ☒ ☒) If price is no obstacle, this resort has plush rooms, nice beaches and tame dolphins. Rates include transfers and dolphin feeding.

There are nine (including four on the beach) **QPWS camping grounds** (per person/family $4/16), all with water, toilets and cold showers. For information and camping permits, contact the Naturally Queensland office in Brisbane (p294) or the **ranger** (☎ 3408 2710). Camping permits are also available from the ferry operators (see right).

Getting There & Around

The **Tangalooma Flyer** (☎ 3268 6333; www.tangalooma.com/tangalooma/transport; return adult/child $60/30; ☺ 6am, 10am & 5pm Mon, 8am, 10am & 5pm Tue-Fri, 8am, 10am, noon & 5pm Sat & Sun) is the resort's fast catamaran. It departs from Holt St, off Kingsford Smith Dr (in Eagle Farm). A bus ($5) departs Brisbane's Roma St Transit Centre at 9am. Bookings are essential.

The **Moreton Venture** (☎ 3895 1000; www.moretonventure.com.au; return adult/child/vehicle plus 2 passengers $20/30/135; ☺ departs 8.30am daily, plus 6.30pm Fri & 2.30pm Sun) ferry leaves from Howard-Smith Dr, Lyton, at the Port of Brisbane.

The **Combie Trader** (☎ 3203 6399; www.moreton-island.com/how.html; return adult/child/vehicle plus 4 passengers $35/20/150; ☺ departs 8am & 1pm Mon, 8am Wed & Thu, 8am, 1pm & 7pm Fri, 6am & 11am Sat, 8am, 1pm & 5.30pm Sun) Sails between Scarborough and Bulwer and takes about 2½ hours to make the crossing. Saturday morning crossings are slightly cheaper for pedestrians.

You can hire 4WDs to explore the island from **Moreton Island 4WD hire** (☎ 3410 1338; www.moretonisland.com.au/4wd_page.htm; Bulwer; per day from $145).

BRIBIE ISLAND
☎ 07

This slender sand island at the northern end of Moreton Bay is joined to the mainland by a bridge at its southern end, where you'll find the small settlements of Woorim, Bellara and Bongaree. The northwestern coast of the island is protected as **Bribie Island National Park**, and has some beautifully remote **QPWS camping areas** (4WD access only, per person/family $4/16). There's a **ranger station** (☎ 3408 8451) at White Patch on the southeastern fringes of the park. You can pick up information at the **Bribie Island information centre** (☎ 3408 9026; www.bribie.com.au; Benabrow Ave, Woorim; ☺ 9am-4pm Mon-Fri, 9am-3pm Sat & 9.30am-1pm Sun).

You can stay overnight at **Sylvan Beach Resort** (☎ 3408 8300; www.sylvanbeachresort.com.au; 19-23 Sylvan Beach Esplanade; d $90-150; ☒ ☒), a good midrange resort with comfortable two- and three-bedroom, self-contained units and on-site BBQs.

Bribie Island SLSC (☎ 3408 4420; Rickman Pde; mains $8-15), at the southern end of the beach, overlooks the ocean and serves up Aussie tucker.

There are frequent Citytrain services between Brisbane and Caboolture. A Trainlink bus runs between the station and Bribie Island.

GOLD COAST

☎ 07 / pop 376,500

Heady, wild and pure fun, the Gold Coast is Australia's very own whiff of Las Vegas. Stretching 35km north from Coolangatta at the state's southern border, to Southport, the coast is skirted by the most aggressively developed patch of Australia, and the landscape is a sea of high-rise condominium clusters, theme parks, airport-sized shopping malls, and restaurants. It's all designed to provide constant commercial stimulus; a feat achieved with unapologetic aplomb so it's best to leave any delusions about discovering Australian culture behind.

This commercial overload doesn't appeal to everyone, but the Gold Coast receives more than two million visitors every year. Most are drawn by the surf, sun and fun, but there is also a spectacular hinterland less than 30km from the beach. Although little-visited, this densely forested region contains two of Queensland's best national parks; Lamington and Springbrook. The Gold Coast also has some excellent surfing breaks, particularly at Burleigh Heads, Kirra and Duranbah.

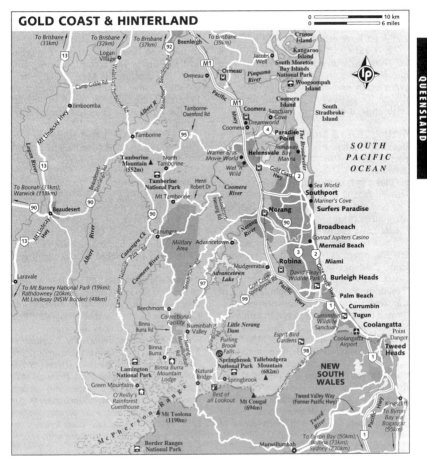

GOLD COAST & HINTERLAND

SEASONAL HIGHS FOR THE HIGH RISE

Most accommodation on the Gold Coast is reasonable throughout the year, but properties increase their tariffs by 20 to 50% during school holidays. The most expensive time of year is during Indy (late October) and Christmas Eve to late January, when a three-night minimum is the norm. These increases are adhered to most in Surfers Paradise and you may encounter more flexibility elsewhere. All prices in this section are based on 'normal' season (or any time other than the above).

Dangers & Annoyances

Car theft is a major problem all the way along the Gold Coast – park in well-lit areas and don't leave valuables in your vehicle.

The Gold Coast turns into party central for thousands of school leavers between mid-November and mid-December for an event locally known as Schoolies Week. Although it's generally a lot of fun for those celebrating, it can be hell for everyone else.

Getting There & Around

Based at Coolangatta, the Gold Coast airport is serviced by **Qantas** (☎ 13 13 13; www.qantas.com; 3047 Gold Coast Hwy, Surfers Paradise), **Virgin Blue** (☎ 13 67 89; www.virginblue.com.au) and **Jetstar** (☎ 13 15 38; www.jetstar.com.au). General one-way airfares start at Sydney ($100) and Melbourne ($130).

Gold Coast Tourist Shuttle (☎ 1300 655 655, 5574 5111; www.gcshuttle.com.au; per adult/child/family $15/8/38) operates door-to-door transfers from Coolangatta airport to most Gold Coast accommodation. It also offers a 'Freedom Pass' which includes return transfers to your accommodation plus unlimited theme park transfers and unlimited Surfside Buslines travel for three days per adult/child/family from $50/23/115.

Citytrain services link Brisbane to Helensvale station ($7.60, one hour), Nerang station ($8.40, one hour 10 minutes) and Robina station ($10, 1¼ hours) roughly every half hour. **Surfside Buslines** (☎ 13 12 30, 5571 6555; www.transinfo.qld.gov.au) runs regular shuttles from the train stations down to Surfers ($3 to $4) and beyond, and to the theme parks.

Coachtrans (☎ 13 12 30, 3238 4700; www.coachtrans.com.au) operates a shuttle between Coolangatta and Brisbane, with 18 stops along the way, including Wet 'n' Wild, Movie World and Dreamworld. It also operates the Airporter service from Brisbane airport to Surfers Paradise ($23, 1½ hours) or direct to your Gold Coast accommodation ($35).

Surfside Buslines (☎ 13 12 30, 5571 6555; www.transinfo.qld.gov.au) runs a frequent service up and down the Gold Coast Hwy from Coolangatta. You can buy individual fares or get an Ezy Pass ($10) for a day's unlimited travel, or a weekly pass ($43).

SOUTHPORT & MAIN BEACH

☎ 07 / pop 24,830

Sheltered from the ocean by a long sand bar known as the Spit, and from the commercialism further south by dense residential blocks, Southport is the northern gateway to the Gold Coast. It's a quieter alternative to Surfers for accommodation. Immediately southeast is Main Beach, where the tourist developments begin in earnest. From here, the Spit runs 3km north, dividing the Broadwater from the South Pacific Ocean.

There are ATMs dotted along Scarborough St and the **Gold Coast Hospital** (☎ 5571 8211; 108 Nerang St, Southport) is here.

Sights & Activities

On the spit jutting north from Main Beach is **Sea World** (see the boxed text, p327) and the **Marina Mirage**, an upmarket shopping and dining complex. On the ocean side of the spit, the beaches and surf are excellent, under-used and backed by a peaceful area of parkland.

Sea World Helicopters (☎ 5588 2224; Sea World; per adult/child from $50/40) offers chopper flights over the spit, plus longer turns over the Gold Coast area. Just up the road, **Dreamworld Helicopters** (☎ 5588 1111) does the same.

Various cruises depart the marinas at Main Beach and explore the surrounding canals. **Island Queen Showboat Cruises** (☎ 5557 8800; www.islandqueen.com.au; Marina Mirage; per adult/child from $55/35) offers a dinner and cabaret cruise, among others. **Wyndham Cruises** (☎ 5539 9299; www.wyndhamcruises.com.au; per adult/child/family $40/20/95) operates two-hour cruises up to and around the Broadwater with morning or afternoon tea included.

At **Mariner's Cove Booking Office** (☎ 5591 8883), near the Marina Mirage, you can book and organise just about any water activity:
Godfathers of the Ocean (☎ 5593 5661; www.god fathersoftheocean.com; Southport Surf Life Saving Club) Respected surf school.
Gold Coast Kayaking (☎ 0419 733 202; 2-3 hr kayak tours per person/family $35/95) Guided tours including breakfast or afternoon tea and snorkelling. Good for families.
Shane's Watersports World (☎ 5591 5225; shaneswatersports@retnet.net.au) Jet ski hire from $75 per half-hour. Jet ski and parasailing packages from $100.
Snorkelling Adventures (☎ 0405 427 174; snorkelling adventures@bigpond.com; 2-3 hrs per person $35) Snorkelling and fish feeding.

Sleeping & Eating

Palazzo Versace (☎ 1800 098 000, 5509 8000, www .palazzoversace.com; Sea World Dr, Main Beach; d $380-725, condominiums from $1200; P ✗ ⚐) The Palazzo is quite simply extravagance defined. Everything from the pool furniture to the buttons on the staff uniforms has Donatella Versace's glamorous mark on it. Rooms are sumptuous and equally spectacular are the restaurants and bars.

Sungold's Harbour Side Resort (☎ 5591 6666; www.harboursideresort.com.au; 132 Marine Pde; d per weeknight/weekend from $80/120; P ✗ ⚐) Within this sprawling brick property are bright, pastel-hued studios and apartments with oodles of room and charm. The kitchens are equipped with microwaves and dishwashers and the complex has good facilities.

Saks (☎ 5591 2755; Marina Mirage, 74 Seaworld Dr, Main Beach; mains $15-25; ☺ lunch daily, dinner Wed-Sun; P ✗) This smart bar/restaurant treats cultured palates to a brief but sophisticated menu boasting dishes such as roast duck and macadamia nut salad and spectacular gourmet wood-fired pizzas. Tall glass windows offer uninterrupted views of the marina.

Also recommended:
Trekkers (☎ 1800 100 004, 5591 5616; www.trekkers backpackers.com.au; 22 White St, Southport; dm $23, d & tw $60; 🖳 ⚐) Super friendly and relaxed hostel in a charming old Queenslander.
Peter's Fish Market (☎ 5591 7747; Sea World Dr, Main Beach; meals $10; ☺ lunch & dinner) Outstanding cooked and fresh fish.

SURFERS PARADISE & BROADBEACH

☎ 07

It may once have been a surfer's paradise, but this resort town is now the undisputed core of the Gold Coast's revelry. Here the bonanza of eateries, drinking holes and artificial attractions peak, and the dizzying fun sucks you into a relentless spin before spitting you back out exhausted.

For backpackers, Surfers is the headiest destination in Queensland and hostel staff do their best to ensure the place goes off every night of the week. A few kilometres down the road the lazy surf culture again predominates in relaxed and refined Broadbeach, which offers more space and some excellent eateries.

Orientation & Information

Cavill Ave, with a pedestrian mall at its beach end, is Surfers' main thoroughfare, while Orchid Ave, one block in from the Esplanade, is the nightclub and bar strip. The following are all based in Surfers Paradise.
Backpacker Tour Desk (☎ 1800 359 830, 5592 2911; Transit Centre, Surfers Paradise) Helpful accommodation booking service for backpackers.
Email Centre (☎ 5538 7500; Orchid Ave, Surfers Paradise; per hr $4; ☺ 9am-11pm) Internet access.
Gold Coast Accommodation Service (☎ 5592 0067; www.goldcoastaccommodationservice.com; Shop 1, 1 Beach Rd, Surfers Paradise) Accommodation booking service.
Gold Coast Tourism Bureau (☎ 5538 4419; www.gold coasttourism.com.au; Cavill Ave Mall, Surfers Paradise; ☺ 8.30am-5.30pm Mon-Fri, 8.30am-5pm Sat, 9am-4pm Sun) Helpful information booth.
Mercari Imaging (3189 Gold Coast Hwy, Surfers Paradise; per hr $4; ☺ 9am-7.30pm) Internet access.
Surfers Paradise Day & Night Surgery (☎ 5592 2299; 3221 Gold Coast Hwy, Surfers Paradise; ☺ 7am-10pm) Medical centre and pharmacy.
Travelex (☎ 5531 7917; Cavill Ave Mall, Surfers Paradise; ☺ 8.30am-9pm Mon-Fri, 9am-9pm Sat & Sun) Foreign currency exchange.

Sights

For the most part, the emphasis in Surfers is on entertainment and parting you from your cash. This said, the excellent **Gold Coast Art Gallery** (☎ 5581 6567; 135 Bundall Rd, Surfers Paradise; ☺ 10am-5pm Mon-Fri, 11am-5pm Sat & Sun), located beside the Nerang River, features two main galleries displaying excellent temporary exhibitions. The curatorship is insightful and inventive, with domestic and international works getting good coverage.

Space junkies can indulge their intergalactic fantasies at **Infinity** (☎ 5538 2988; www .infinity.com.au; Chevron Renaissance, cnr Surfers Paradise

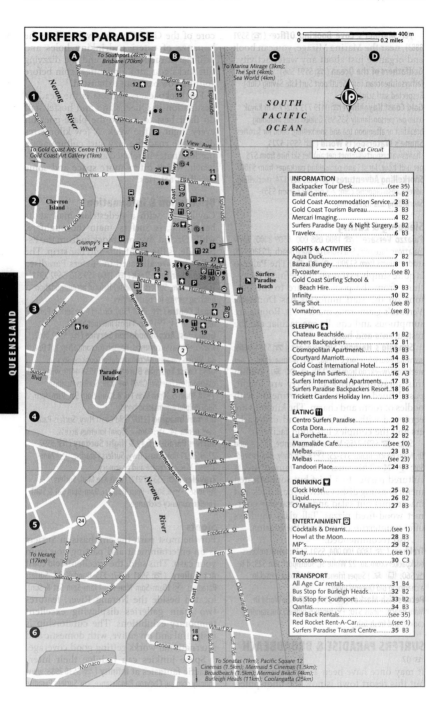

SURFERS PARADISE

INFORMATION

Backpacker Tour Desk	(see 35)	
Email Centre	1	B2
Gold Coast Accommodation Service	2	B3
Gold Coast Tourism Bureau	3	B3
Mercari Imaging	4	B2
Surfers Paradise Day & Night Surgery	5	B2
Travelex	6	B3

SIGHTS & ACTIVITIES

Aqua Duck	7	B2
Banzai Bungey	8	B1
Flycoaster	(see 8)	
Gold Coast Surfing School & Beach Hire	9	B3
Infinity	10	B2
Sling Shot	(see 8)	
Vomatron	(see 8)	

SLEEPING

Chateau Beachside	11	B2
Cheers Backpackers	12	B1
Cosmopolitan Apartments	13	B2
Courtyard Marriott	14	B2
Gold Coast International Hotel	15	B1
Sleeping Inn Surfers	16	A3
Surfers International Apartments	17	B3
Surfers Paradise Backpackers Resort	18	B6
Trickett Gardens Holiday Inn	19	B3

EATING

Centro Surfers Paradise	20	B3
Costa Dora	21	B2
La Porchetta	22	B2
Marmalade Cafe	(see 10)	
Melbas	23	B3
Melbas	(see 23)	
Tandoori Place	24	B3

DRINKING

Clock Hotel	25	B2
Liquid	26	B2
O'Malleys	27	B3

ENTERTAINMENT

Cocktails & Dreams	(see 1)	
Howl at the Moon	28	B3
MP's	29	B2
Party	(see 1)	
Troccadero	30	C3

TRANSPORT

All Age Car rentals	31	B4
Bus Stop for Burleigh Heads	32	B2
Bus Stop for Southport	33	B2
Qantas	34	B3
Red Back Rentals	(see 35)	
Red Rocket Rent-A-Car	(see 1)	
Surfers Paradise Transit Centre	35	B3

GOLD COAST THEME PARKS

Immediately northwest of Surfers Paradise is a string of big, American-style theme parks, all competing for the most thrilling ride or the most entertaining show. Discount tickets are sold in most of the tourist offices on the Gold Coast; the 3 Park Super Pass (adult/child $160/100), available at Sea World, Movie World and Wet 'n' Wild, covers entry to all three parks.

Dreamworld (☎ 07-5588 1111; www.dreamworld.com.au; Pacific Hwy, Coomera; adult/child $60/38; ⏱ 10am-5pm) On the Pacific Hwy 17km north of Surfers, this is thrill central. Screams of delight are derived from formidable rides such as the Tower of Terror, which takes just seven seconds to accelerate you to a speed of 161km/h. Children are kept entertained by the Nickelodeon Park and wildlife shows, including an eye-popping tiger show.

Sea World (☎ 07-5588 2222, show times ☎ 07-5588 2205; www.seaworld.com.au; Sea World Dr, Main Beach; adult/child $60/38; ⏱ 10am-5.30pm) A huge aquatic theme park, Sea World has loads of animal performances, including twice-daily dolphin shows, sea-lion shows, shark-feeding, and the real crowd-pleasers – two celebrity resident polar bears, Hudson and Nelson. You'll have to set a schedule though – the waterslides and rollercoasters are agonizingly addictive.

Warner Bros Movie World (☎ 07-5573 8485; www.movieworld.com.au; Pacific Hwy, Oxenford; adult/child $60/38; ⏱ 10am-5.30pm) Otherwise known as 'Hollywood on the Gold Coast', Movie World is a must for mainstream-movie junkies. You can mingle with your favourite Looney Tunes and movie characters here, all of whom leap at photo opportunities. There's a constantly changing 'ride of the moment' as well as stunt shows and movie-themed whizzing rides.

Wet 'n' Wild (☎ 07-5573 2255; www.wetnwild.com.au; Pacific Hwy, Oxenford; adult/child $38/24; ⏱ 10am-5pm Feb-Apr & Sep-Dec, 10am-4pm May-Aug, 10am-9pm 27 Dec–26 Jan) The best fun you can have getting wet. A colossal water-sports park, it offers loads of slippery rides, mammoth swimming pools and white-water rapids, which you can whizz down on a rubber ring. It all makes a trip to the beach comparable to sitting in the bathtub, but you can just soak up the sun too if you want.

Blvd & Elkhorn Ave, Surfers Paradise; adult/child/family $20/12/53; ⏱ 10am-10pm), a walk-through maze cleverly disguised as 'the future' by an elaborate sound and light show. It's great for families and regularly procures squeals of wonder from the kids.

Activities

BALLOONING & SKYDIVING
You can get high on life with **Tandem Skydive** (☎ 5599 1920) or **Skydive Queensland** (☎ 5544 6323; www.skydiveqld.com.au), both of which offer tandem jumps from 10,000ft to 14,000ft from around $250. More timid adventurers can opt for hot-air ballooning with **Balloon Down Under** (☎ 5593 8400; www.balloondownunder .com; 1hr flights per adult/child $255/210) or **Balloon Aloft** (☎ 5578 2244; www.balloonaloft.net; 1hr flights per adult/child $255/185). Both offer early morning flights over the Gold Coast Hinterland, ending with a hot breakfast.

BUNGEE JUMPING
Bungee jumping is almost a rite of passage in Surfers and you can initiate yourself at **Banzai Bungey** (☎ 5526 7611; cnr Cypress Ave & Ferny Aves; jumps from $100). But wait! On the same

block there are new and inventive ways to revisit your breakfast. **Flycoaster** (☎ 5539 0474; www.flycoaster.com; rides $39) swings you like a pendulum after you've been released from a hoist 20m up. **Sling Shot** (☎ 5570 2700; rides $30) catapults you into the air at around 160km and **Vomatron** (☎ 5570 2700; rides $30) warns you from the outset before it whisks you around in a giant arc at about 120km an hour. The continuous stream of delighted whoops serve as hearty recommendations.

HORSE RIDING
There are a couple of outfits that operate horse-riding treks in the Gold Coast Hinterland: **Numinbah Valley Adventure Trails** (☎ 5533 4137; www.numinbahtrails.com; 3hr treks adult/child from $60/50) and **Gumnuts Horseriding** (☎ 5543 0191; 2hr rides adult/child from $55/33).

SURFING
Behind the seemingly impenetrable wall of high rises, Surfers Paradise Beach has enough swell to give beginners a feel for the craft of surfing. Surf schools are abundant and charge between $40 and $50 for a two-hour lesson.

INDYCAR

Since 1991 Surfers Paradise has been host to what has been dubbed Queensland's biggest party – the Australian leg of the IndyCar series (the US equivalent of Formula One motor racing). Each October, the main streets of central Surfers are transformed into a temporary race circuit, around which hurtle some of the world's fastest cars – their drivers push them up to speeds of more than 300km/h.

On a good year around a quarter of a million spectators descend on Surfers for the race and the three-day carnival that precedes it. Surfers is fairly over the top at the best of times, but IndyCar gives the town a chance to *really* let its hair down. It's a great time to be there, or a great time to be anywhere else, depending on how you feel about the place.

General admission charges to the races range from $30 to $75 per day at the gate, cheaper if you book. Four-day grandstand seating is between $210 and $530. For more information call ☎ 1800 300 055 or check www.indy.com.au.

Cheyne Horan School of Surf (☎ 1800 227 873, 0403 080 484; www.cheynehoran.com.au) offers excellent tuition by a World Champion surfer.

Brad Holmes Surf Coaching (☎ 5539 4068, 0418 757 539; www.bradholmessurfcoaching.com) caters to travellers with disabilities also.

Gold Coast Surfing School & Beach Hire (☎ 1800 787 337, 5526 7077; www.goldcoastsurfing.com; Cavill Ave Mall, Surfers Paradise; ⏱ 9am-5pm) also rents out short boards and Malibu boards per hour/three hours/day for $15/25/40.

Tours

Several operators offer the curious experience of exploring Surfers by road and river in a boat on wheels. All charge around $35/26/90 per adult/child/family.

Aqua Duck (☎ 5538 3825; Orchid Ave)
Aquabus (☎ 5539 0222)
Eco Duck (☎ 5532 2444)

Festivals & Events

IndyCar Surfers Paradise's biggest motor-racing party (see above).

Quicksilver Pro-Surfing Competition Mid-March sees some of the world's best surfers out on the waves.

Schoolies Week Month-long party by school-leavers from mid-November to mid-December. Generally involves lots of alcohol and a few organised events in the first week.

Surf Life-Saving Championships Also in mid-March.

Sleeping

BUDGET

Sleeping Inn Surfers (☎ 1800 817 832, 5592 4455; www.sleepinginn.com.au; 26 Peninsular Dr, Surfers Paradise; dm $21, d with/without bathroom $65/55; 🖵) A wide choice of rooms is offered at this modern hostel, from basic dorms to classier doubles with TVs; in a converted motel. Its

size caters to party punters as well as those in dire need of a quiet sleep.

Cheers Backpackers (☎ 1800 636 539, 5531 6539; 8 Pine Ave, Surfers Paradise; dm/d $23/60; P 🖵 🏊) Amid the friendly blur of theme nights, karaoke, pool comps, pub crawls, happy hours and BBQs here, you're bound to find your bed. Rooms are reasonable, but the emphasis is on partying and it's dangerously close to Surfers' nightlife.

Surfers Paradise Backpackers Resort (☎ 1800 282 800, 5592 4677; www.surfersparadisebackpackers.com.au; Gold Coast Hwy, Surfers Paradise; dm/d/tr $22/55/80; P 🖵 🏊) Another converted motel, this place gets the thumbs-up for being a little distance from the mayhem and its great facilities, including a small gym and sauna, pool room and bar, tennis court and bright, spacious rooms (triples have a kitchen). The dorms are six-bed maximum.

MIDRANGE

Surfers International Apartments (☎ 1800 891 299; 5579 1299; www.surfers-international.com.au; 7-9 Trickett St, Surfers Paradise; r per 3-night stay $420-510; P ❌ 🏊) Balconies with spectacular beach views are standard at this high-rise, just off the beach. It has plush apartments bathed in classy blue hues. The interiors are modern and sizable and come with cable TV and modem ports. The complex has a small gym and poolside BBQ.

Cosmopolitan Apartments (☎ 5570 2311; cnr Gold Coast Hwy & Beach Rd, Surfers Paradise; r from $85; ❌ 🏊) This central complex contains privately owned, self-contained apartments. Each is uniquely decorated with personal touches, providing a refreshing departure from the generic mould. Standards include dishwashers, balconies, laundries and phones. Most also have cable TV. There's also a BBQ area, spa and sauna.

Trickett Gardens Holiday Inn (☎ 5539 0988; www .trickettgardens.com.au; 24-30 Trickett St, Surfers Paradise; d/f $85/150; P ⊠ ⊠) Friendly low-rise block which is great for families, with a central location and well-equipped self-contained units. The rooms are generic but roomy and comfortable. It's often full so bookings are advised.

Other recommendations:

Gold Coast International Hotel (☎ 1800 074 020, 5584 1200; www.gci.com.au; cnr Staghorn Ave & Gold Coast Hwy, Surfers Paradise; d $135-235; P ⊠ ⊠) Polished rooms with hinterland or ocean views.

Chateau Beachside (☎ 5538 1022; www.strand.com; cnr Elkhorn Ave & the Esplanade, Surfers Paradise; d $110-140, ste $120-150; P ⊠ ⊠) Seaside complex in the heart of Surfers with spacious units, good views and a cheap restaurant.

TOP END

Courtyard Marriott (☎ 1800 074 317, 5579 3499; www.marriott.com; cnr Gold Coast Hwy & Hanlan St, Surfers Paradise; d/ste from $155/165; ⊠) Right in the centre of Surfers, this plush top-end hotel is attached to the Paradise Centre Mall and offers all the luxury you would expect in this price range, including sea views, and spa baths in the dearer suites.

Eating

Surfers' many eateries generally offer quantity over quality, but there are a few gems.

Sonatas (☎ 5526 9904; cnr Surf Pde & Queensland Ave, Broadbeach; mains $15-25; ⊠ breakfast, lunch & dinner) This sunny café is a popular haunt for the locals, owing to a crisp, Mod Oz menu. Highlights include wok-tossed prawns and Moreton bay bugs, Cajun barramundi or brie and almond salad. Vegetarians get their slice of the pie too.

Marmalade Cafe (☎ 5504 7353; Shop 36, Chevron Renaissance, Surfers Paradise; mains $10-15; ⊠ lunch & dinner) A downright funky menu, with lunches such as Moroccan spiced lamb salad and breakfasts of homemade hot-cakes with cardamom and spiced bananas. This café has a pocket of sheltered outdoor seating and long cushioned benches inside.

Melbas (☎ 5592 6922; 46 Cavill Ave, Surfers Paradise; mains $25-35; ⊠ lunch & dinner; ⊠) Flashy Melbas' menu is pure spunk; forget focaccias, here you delve into Thai-baked lamb

rack with Tom Yum broth, or oven-baked, butter-curried snapper with cashews. The lunch menu (mains $12) is cheaper. It's also a popular drinking hole, see p330.

Costa Dora (☎ 5538 5203; 27 Orchid Ave, Surfers Paradise; dishes $12-22; ⊠ lunch & dinner; ⊠) This Italian eatery has earned a good reputation for its appetising pastas and pizzas. A splash of shellfish graces the menu as does a kids' selection and the $10 pasta-and-cappuccino lunch deal is a bargain. The Italian village frescos add kitschy ambience.

Tandoori Place (☎ 5592 1004; cnr Gold Coast Hwy & Trickett St, Surfers Paradise; mains $15-20; ⊠ lunch & dinner; ⊠) Popular Indian cuisine is embellished with a splash of Mod Oz here; ingredients such as kangaroo are infused into traditional *tandoors* (clay ovens) as well as offering other subcontinent fare. Vegetarians are also spoiled for choice and this place has deservedly won awards. The service is friendly and efficient.

Two kid pleasers serving cheap pizzas and pasta are **La Porchetta** (Orchid Ave ☎ 5527 5273; 3 Orchid Ave; Elkhorn Ave ☎ 5504 5236; Elkhorn Ave; meals $10-15; ⊠ breakfast, lunch & dinner; ⊠) and **Chateau Beachside** (☎ 5526 9994; cnr Elkhorn Ave & The Esplanade, Surfers Paradise; meals $6-10; ⊠ breakfast, lunch & dinner; ⊠), which also dishes up good burgers and an all-you-can-gobble $10 break-fast (see also left). There's a super-market in **Centro Surfers Paradise** (Cavill Mall, Surfers Paradise).

Drinking

O'Malleys (☎ 5570 4075; Level 1, 1 Cavill Ave, Surfers Paradise; ⊠) During the day this elevated theme pub offers blissful respite from the hectic heat of Cavill Ave with its medicinal $8 jugs. The network of booths and stools overlooking the ocean fill up at night when the atmosphere is happy and rowdy.

Liquid (☎ 5538 0111; Shop 1, 18 Orchid Ave, Surfers Paradise) Liquid's wide-open entrance parades a glossy bar highlighted by electric blue neon. Water cascades down the back walls and the trendy patrons sip cocktails before succumbing to the hip-luring soundtrack. Eventually it all ends up naughty and noisy.

Clock Hotel (☎ 5539 0344; 3282 Gold Coast Hwy, Surfers Paradise) At this institution an older crowd lingers over beer at the bar like an episode from *Cheers* by daylight, but the 20- and 30-somethings who dig the 'Latin Fire'

QUEENSLAND

Tuesday, 'Champers' Thursday, karaoke Sunday and consistent big-screen sports fill the joint at night.

Melbas (☎ 5592 6922; 46 Cavill Ave, Surfers Paradise; mains $25-35; ☺ lunch & dinner; ☒) After dinner this place gets glam in a *Miami Vice* kinda way, and pumps out neon-coloured cocktails and crowd-pleasing tunes.

Entertainment

Orchid Ave is Surfers' main bar and nightclub strip but venues change hands, names and orientation regularly. Many offer vouchers for backpackers and Wednesday to Saturday are generally the big party nights. Cover charges hover between $5 and $10.

Howl at the Moon (☎ 5527 5522; Shop 7, Upper Level, Centro Surfers Paradise) Surfers' 'it' bar of the moment, Howl at the Moon keeps the punters happy and the queues long with a talented line of musos belting out everything from rap to blues on the pianos. Unrequited howl-alongs are encouraged.

Cocktails & Dreams (☎ 5592 1955; Level 1, The Mark, Orchid Ave, Surfers Paradise) Others come and go but this club has been the stomping ground for young party goers for aeons. Drink deals, dancing and general debauchery pulls the crowds in and spits them out again in the wee hours after an exhausting good time. Linked by a stairway, the **Party** (☎ 5538 2848) offers more of the same with $2 drink deals from Thursday to Sunday nights, theme nights and bubbly prizes.

Troccadero (☎ 5536 4200; 9 Trickett St, Surfers Paradise) When the big guns are in town they strut their stuff at Troccadero. If it's not high profile Aussie and international acts playing, you'll catch live rock in all its genres.

Gold Coast Arts Centre (☎ 5588 4000) This is attached to the Gold Coast Art Gallery (p325) and regularly hosts impressive theatrical productions.

Conrad Jupiters Casino (☎ 5592 8100; www.conrad.com.au; Gold Coast Hwy, Broadbeach; admission free; ☺ 24hr) At this mammoth casino, countless optimistic gamblers try their luck and invariably leave with lighter pockets and a briefly satiated fix. Also here is **Jupiters Theatre** (☎ 1800 074 144), with live music and glamorous dinner shows.

More entertainment:

MP's (☎ 5526 2337; Forum Arcade, 26 Orchid Ave, Surfers Paradise) Popular gay club with cheap drinks and drag shows during the week.

Mermaid 5 Cinemas (☎ 5575 3355; 2514 Gold Coast Hwy, Broadbeach)

Pacific Square 12 Cinemas (☎ 5572 2666; Pacific Fair Shopping Centre, cnr Hooker Blvd & Gold Coast Hwy, Broadbeach)

Getting There & Around

Long-distance buses stop at the **Surfers Paradise Transit Centre** (cnr Beach & Cambridge Rds). **Greyhound Australia** (☎ 13 14 99; www.greyhound.com.au), **Premier Motor Service** (☎ 13 34 10; www.premierms.com.au) and **Kirklands** (☎ 1300 367 077) have frequent services to/from Brisbane ($15, 1½ hours).

Local car-rental outfits that consistently offer good deals include **All Age Car Rentals** (☎ 1800 671 361; 3024 Gold Coast Hwy, Surfers Paradise; used cars per day from $19), **Red Back Rentals** (☎ 5592 1655; Surfers Paradise Transit Centre; per day from $25) and **Red Rocket Rent-A-Car** (☎ 1800 673 682, 5538 9074; Shop 9, The Mark, Orchid Ave, Surfers Paradise; per day from $15), which also rents scooters and bicycles. Insurance costs extra.

See Getting There & Around (p324) for more transport information.

BURLEIGH HEADS

☎ 07 / pop 8430

Burleigh Heads is legendary for surfers. In the right weather conditions, the headland here produces a spectacular right-hand point break, famous for its fast and deep barrel rides, but it definitely isn't for beginners. The shore is lined with vicious black rocks and the rip is ferocious.

The town itself is a tranquil, surfie departure from the business of Surfers. You can get national park information from the **QPWS Information Centre** (☎ 5535 3032; 3032 Gold Coast Hwy; ☺ 9am-4pm) at the northern end of Tallebudgera Creek.

Sights & Activities

The **Burleigh Heads National Park** is a small but diverse forest reserve with walking trails around the rocky headland.

There are three wildlife sanctuaries in the vicinity. **Currumbin Wildlife Sanctuary** (☎ 5534 1266; www.currumbin-sanctuary.org.au; Gold Coast Hwy, Currumbin; adult/child $22/15; ☺ 8am-5pm) is an excellent spot to frolic with Australian native animals, including tree kangaroos, koalas, emus, wombats and other cute and fuzzies. They're joined daily by flocks of brilliantly coloured rainbow lorikeets, which take great delight in eating out of your hand. To get here catch Surfside Bus 1 or 1A in either direction.

Nestled into a dense enclave of bush, **David Fleay Wildlife Park** (☎ 5576 2411; West Burleigh Rd; adult/child/senior/family $13/6.50/8.50/33; ☼ 9am-5pm) is rich with the help of the QPWS. Four kilometres of walking tracks enable you to meander amid native wildlife and the park is an important breeding centre for platypuses.

Esprit Bird Gardens (☎ 5533 0208; 746 Currumbin Creek Rd; adult/child $2.50/free; ☼ 9.30am-5pm Fri-Sun, daily during school holidays) is an attractive sub-tropical garden with several aviaries housing exotic and native birds.

The right-hand point break at Burleigh Heads is the best wave here but it's usually crowded with pro surfers. There are plenty of other waves to practise on along the beach. The **Hot Stuff Surf Shop** (☎ 5535 6899; 1706 Gold Coast Hwy) rents out surfboards per half/full day for $20/30.

Sleeping & Eating
Hillhaven Holiday Apartments (☎ 5535 1055; www .hillhaven.com.au; 2 Goodwin Tce; r per week from $605; P ☒ ☐ ☒) These opulent apartments, perched high on the headland overlooking Burleigh Heads, are what holiday indulgence dreams are made of. Classic interiors with neutral tones are set off by the best views in town. Call for shorter stays.

Burleigh Gardens Holiday Apartments (☎ 5576 3955; www.burleighgardens.com; 1849 Gold Coast Hwy; 1-bedroom apt per night/week from $90/460, 2-bedroom apt from $100/550; P ☒) Comfortable, self-contained one- and two-bedroom units are solid value and their balcony views and proximity to the beach make them popular. Interiors vary but they all have plenty of room.

Oskars (☎ 5576 3722; 43 Goodwin Tce; dishes $19-30; ☼ lunch & dinner) Oskar's elegant restaurant is one of the Gold Coast's finest. Sweeping views of the coastline are complimented by a changing selection of seafood, depending on the day's catch, but expect something along the lines of snapper tempura with starfruit, coriander and red chilli salsa.

Burleigh Beach Club (☎ 5520 2972; cnr Goodwin Tce & Gold Coast Hwy; dishes $10-18; ☼ lunch Mon-Sat, dinner Sun-Thu) For pure beach bistro nosh and family-friendly surrounds, this club is hard to beat. The ubiquitous burgers, steak, fish and chicken dishes are on offer but it's all tasty and the portions are huge.

Also recommended:
Burleigh Beach Tourist Park (☎ 5581 7755; www .gctp.com.au/burly; Goodwin Tce; powered/unpowered sites per 2 people from $23/21, cabins $115; ☒) Snug council-run park with a smattering of shady sites.
Pantry (☎ 5576 2818; 15 Connor St; dishes $7-15; ☼ 6am-5pm) Cheery café good for families.

COOLANGATTA
☎ 07 / pop 6820
This friendly little surf resort is probably the most laid-back spot on the Gold Coast and it's a great place to kick back and catch a few waves. There are good views down the coast from **Point Danger**, the headland at the end of the state line.

The helpful **Coolangatta Visitors Centre** (☎ 5536 7765; infocoolangatta@gctb.com.au; cnr Griffith & Warner Sts; ☼ 8am-5pm Mon-Fri, 8am-4pm Sat, 9am-1pm Sun) can set you out with local info. You can get online at **PB's OZ Internet Cafe** (☎ 5599 4536; 152 Griffith St; per 30min $4; ☼ 9am-6pm).

Aside from Point Danger, the surf at Kirra Point often goes off and there are gentler breaks at Greenmount Beach and Rainbow Bay. You can rent boards for around $30 per day from **Retro Groove** (☎ 5599 3952; 3 McLean St) or **BKD** (backdoorsurfwear@yahoo.com; Boundary St).

Sleeping & Eating
Bella Mare (☎ 5599 2755; www.bellamare.com.au; 5 Hill St; r per 2-nights/week from $240/600, villas per 2-nights/week from $340/700; P ☒ ☒) A fancy apartment block with cool and crisp apartments and indulgent villas. Interiors contain a hint of the Med and plenty of mod cons, including cable TV. There's a two-night minimum stay and the weekly rates are very reasonable.

Aries Holiday Apartments (☎ 5536 2711; 82 Marine Pde; ste per night/week from $130/590; P ☒) Close to the beach, these sunny, self-contained units have two bedrooms and two bathrooms plus all the facilities you'd need for a long-term stay. The balconies catch the ocean breeze and vista, and they can accommodate a small army.

Jellies (☎ 5536 1741; 91 Griffith St; mains $20-30; ☼ breakfast, lunch & dinner) This sun-flooded restaurant has the most inventive menu in town; the fish of the day is topped with a chilli mango, macadamia and coriander salsa. Pizzas, snacks and kids' meals are also served.

Beaches Grill & Coffee Bar (☎ 5536 9311; Coolangatta Hotel, cnr Marine Pde & Warner St; mains $12-18; ☽ breakfast, lunch & dinner) The best spot in town for hungry, midrange wallets. The menu is snappy pub bistro, with dishes such as salt-and-pepper seared and curried chicken, or New York sirloin dusted with pepper and rosemary. Then, of course, there's the fish. It's very kid-friendly.

Also recommended:

Coolangatta YHA (☎ 5536 7644; booking@ coolangattayha.com; 230 Coolangatta Rd, Bilinga; dm $22-24, s/d $35/50; P 🖥 🖳) Well-equipped and functional hostel. Breakfast and courtesy transfers from Coolangatta and Surfers are included.

Coolangatta Beach Surf Life Saving Club (☎ 5536 4648; Marine Pde; mains $8-20; ☽ lunch & dinner) Club meals at club prices.

Kirra Beach Tourist Park (☎ 5581 7744; www.gctp .com.au/kirra; Charlotte St, Kirra; powered sites per 2 people $25-30, unpowered sites per 2 people $23-26, cabins from $70; 🐾 🖳) Spacious park with grassy sites and wheelchair access. Varying prices for cabins and lodgings.

GOLD COAST HINTERLAND

Only a short drive inland from Coolangatta, the Gold Coast takes a dramatic aesthetic and ambient turn in its spectacular hinterland. Riding the McPherson Range, which stretches back 60km to the NSW border, the wooded settlements that speckle this area are influenced by the mountain air and dense forests. Bohemian vibes flourish, the commercialism of the coast is microscopic and the national parks are a paradise for walkers. This unspoilt environment is easily accessible by car – a perfect antidote to the noise and clamour of the coast. Expect a lot of rain in the mountains from December to March, and in winter the nights can be cold.

Getting Around

The only way to access the Gold Coast Hinterland without your own wheels is on a tour. **Bushwacker Ecotours** (☎ 07-5520 7238; www .bushwacker-ecotours.com.au; tours adult/child from $90/50) has quite an extensive array of eco-tours, starting with day-long bushwalks and topping out at four-night excursions.

4X4 Hinterland Tours (☎ 1800 604 425, 0429 604 425; sales@hinterlandtours.com.au; day tours adult/child $130/80) specialises in small group 4WD eco-tours to either Springbrook or Lamington National Park and Mt Tamborine. **Australian Day Tours** (☎ 1300 363 436; www.daytours .com.au; day tours adult/child $70/40, 2-day tours $340/140) travels via Mt Tamborine and Canungra to O'Reilly's Guesthouse (opposite).

O'Reilly's (☎ 07-5524 4249; adult/child/family $45/25/120) operates day tours to O'Reilly's Guesthouse in Lamington National Park, via Mt Tamborine, with jump-out stops along the way.

See p305 for hinterland tours departing from Brisbane.

TAMBORINE MOUNTAIN

Just 45km northwest of the Gold Coast, this 552m-high plateau is on a northern spur of the McPherson Range. Patches of the area's original forests remain in nine small national parks. There are gorges, spectacular cascades including **Witches Falls**, **Cameron Falls** and **Cedar Creek Falls** near North Tamborine, and walking tracks to various lookouts with great views over the coast. Most settlements in the area are cutesy heritage communities set up for the benefit of tour groups.

The **visitor information centre** (☎ 07-5545 3200; Doughty Park; ☽ 10.30am-3.30pm Sun-Fri, 9.30am-3.30pm Sat) at North Tamborine has plenty of brochures and information on wineries in the area.

The fabulous **Tamborine Mountain Distillery** (☎ 07-5545 3452; 87-91 Beacon Rd, North Tamborine; ☽ 10am-3pm Wed-Sun) is a boutique distiller that manufactures its own schnapps, liqueurs and other spirits from organically grown fruits.

SPRINGBROOK NATIONAL PARK

This national park is perched atop a 900m-high plateau, which, like the rest of the McPherson Range, is a remnant of the huge volcano that once centred on Mt Warning in NSW.

The national park is in three sections: **Springbrook**, **Mt Cougal** and **Natural Bridge**. The vegetation is cool-temperate rainforest and eucalypt forest, with gorges, cliffs, forests, waterfalls, an extensive network of walking tracks and several picnic areas.

The village of Springbrook is balanced right on the edge of the plateau, with numerous waterfalls (when there's enough rain) that tumble more than 100m to the coastal plain below. There are several places where you can get the giddy thrill of leaning right out over the edge, including Purling Brook Falls, at the Gwongorella Picnic Area, just off Springbrook Rd, Canyon Lookout and Best of All Lookout, which is reached via Lyrebird Ridge Rd.

The **ranger's office and information centre** (☎ 07-5533 5147; 2873 Springbrook Rd; ☽ variable hours) at Springbrook provides copies of the National Parks walking tracks leaflet for all three sections. You can pitch a tent at the **Purling Brook Falls campground** (per person $4), near Gwongorella Picnic Area. It has no showers or bins. You need to book in advance through **QPWS** (☎ 13 13 04; www.smartservice.qld.gov.au/as).

The **Natural Bridge section**, off the Nerang–Murwillumbah road, has a 1km walking circuit leading to a rock arch spanning a water-formed cave, which is home to a huge colony of glow-worms.

Springbrook Mountain Lodge (☎ /fax 07-5533 5366; 317 Repeater Station Rd; s/d Mon-Thu $44/70, weekends $65/90, per extra person $22, d cabins $135) is 3km off the Springbrook Rd, and the highest place on the plateau (960m). The millionaire views from the chalet-style lodge are simply breathtaking. The comfortable split-level rooms have bathrooms and there are self-contained cabins.

English Gardens (☎ 07-5533 5244; 2832 Springbrook Rd; r $120-$140) has two quaint cottages set amid a sprawling English-cum-Australian garden. There's also a small **café** (mains $4-11; ☽ breakfast & lunch).

LAMINGTON NATIONAL PARK

West of Springbrook, this 200-sq-km park covers much of the McPherson Range and adjoins the Border Ranges National Park in NSW. The park includes most of the spectacular Lamington Plateau, which reaches 1100m in places, as well as densely forested valleys below.

Much of the vegetation is subtropical rainforest. There are beautiful gorges, caves, waterfalls and lots of wildlife. Commonly spotted animals include satin and regent bowerbirds, and pademelons (a type of small wallaby) in the late afternoon.

The two most popular and accessible sections of the park are **Binna Burra** and **Green Mountains**, both reached via paved roads from Canungra. Binna Burra can also be reached from Nerang. The park has 160km of walking tracks, ranging from an excellent tree-top canopy walk along a series of rope-and-plank suspension bridges at Green Mountains, to the 24km Border Trail that links the two sections of the park.

Walking trail guides are available from the **ranger stations** (Binna Burra ☎ 07-5533 3584; ☽ 1.30-3.30pm Mon-Fri, from 9am Sat & Sun; Green Mountains ☎ 07-5544 0634; ☽ 9-11am & 1-3.30pm Mon-Fri).

Sleeping & Eating

Binna Burra Mountain Lodge (☎ 1800 074 260, 07-5533 3622; www.binnaburralodge.com.au; Binna Burra Rd, Beechmont; d with/without bathroom incl breakfast $300/240) This excellent mountain retreat has rustic cabins clustered around a central **restaurant** (mains $13-18; ☽ lunch & dinner), all with good views over the national park. The tariff includes all meals, walking and climbing gear, and activities. There is also a **camp site** (powered/unpowered sites $27/20, on-site safari tents $40) that was closed at the time of writing, but should be operational by the time you read this.

O'Reilly's Rainforest Guesthouse (☎ 1800 688 722, 07-5544 0644; www.oreillys.com.au; Lamington National Park Rd; guesthouse s/d from $80/140, units from s/d $200/250) This famous guesthouse at Green Mountains is still run by the O'Reilly family and has been very stylishly redeveloped over the years. Tariffs include activities and 4WD bus trips. There's also a plush **restaurant** (mains $25-40), and the cheaper **Gran O'Reilly's Bistro** (snacks $5-15; ☽ breakfast & lunch).

There is a **QPWS camping ground** (per person/family $4/16) close to O'Reilly's. Limited numbers of camping permits must be obtained in advance from the ranger at Green Mountains or by booking online.

Getting There & Away

The **Binna Burra bus service** (☎ 07-5533 3622; one way adult/child $22/11) operates a daily bus for guests, picking up from Coolangatta airport (1.30pm) and Nerang trains station (2pm) daily.

Allstate Scenic Tours (☎ 07-3285 1777; return adult/child day trip only $55/35, overnight $44/33) runs a bus service between Brisbane and O'Reilly's from Sunday to Friday, leaving Brisbane's Roma St Transit Centre at 9.30am and arriving back at the transit centre at around 5.45pm.

Mountain Coach Company (☎ 07-5524 4249; return day trip adult/child/family $45/24/117) has a daily service from the Gold Coast to O'Reilly's via Tamborine Mountain (one hour). If you want to use this service to stay overnight at O'Reilly's the cost is $30 each way.

SUNSHINE COAST

Another weekend getaway from the Queensland capital, the coast north of Brisbane lives up to the tourist brochure images of euphoric families frolicking in the sand, couples engaged in romantic scenarios and singles wallowing in sun-kissed bliss. The area is less developed than the Gold Coast and consists of a string of low-rise resorts perpetuating a slow, coastal pace. The exception is the stretch from the concentrated area of Mooloolaba, an hour and a half from Brisbane, to Alexandra Headland and Maroochydore.

North of Maroochydore, there's a patch of still unspoilt coastline at Coolum and Peregian Beach. After this you arrive in Noosa, an exclusive, staunchly low-rise and leafy resort that resembles an antipodean answer to France's Nice.

Filling the space between the beach and the vast empty of Queensland's interior is the Sunshine Coast's undulating hinterland, where charming villages linger on the outskirts of national parks.

Getting There & Around

AIR

Sunshine Express (☎ 13 13 13; www.sunshineexpress .com.au) flies to the Sunshine Coast's Maroochydore airport from Brisbane ($95). **Jetstar** (☎ 13 15 38; www.jetstar.com.au) and **Virgin Blue** (☎ 13 67 89; www.virginblue.com.au) also have daily connections to Sydney ($90).

BUS

Greyhound Australia (☎ 13 14 99; www.greyhound .com.au) and **Premier Motor Service** (☎ 13 34 10; www.premierms.com.au) have daily services from Brisbane to Maroochydore ($19, 1½ hours), which then continue on to Noosa ($24, 2½ hours).

The **Suncoast Pacific** (www.suncoastpacific.com.au; Brisbane; ☎ 07-3236 1901; Caloundra ☎ 07-5491 2555; Maroochydore ☎ 07-5443 1011) runs between Brisbane's Roma St Transit Centre and airport to points along the Sunshine Coast. One-way trips from Brisbane include Caloundra

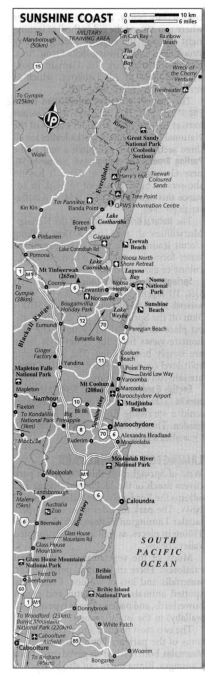

($25, two hours), Maroochydore ($25, two hours) and Noosa ($25, three hours). It also offers standby fares to the above from Brisbane airport but seats and fares are subject to availability.

The blue minibuses run by **Sunbus** (☎ 07-5492 8700) buzz frequently between Caloundra and Noosa ($5.20, 1½ hours), stopping along the way. Sunbus also has regular buses across from Noosa to the train station at Nambour on the Bruce Hwy ($4.40, one hour), via Eumundi and Yandina.

Henry's (☎ 07-5474 0199), **Noosa Transfers & Charters** (☎ 07-5449 9782; noosatransfers@powerup .com.au) and **Col's Airport Shuttle** (☎ 07-5473 9966; www.airshuttle.com.au) offer transfers from Maroochydore airport and Brisbane to Sunshine Coast locations. The cost per adult/child is around $40/25.

TRAIN

Citytrain has services from Nambour from Brisbane ($11.60, two hours). Trains also go to Beerwah ($7.60, 1½ hours), near Australia Zoo.

GLASS HOUSE MOUNTAINS
☎ 07 / pop 660

About 20km north of the small dairy township of Caboolture, the Glass House Mountains are 16 ethereally shaped volcanic crags which emerge from the humid green surrounds in sporadic and *Jurassic Park* style. Towering to over 500m, with sheer rocky sides, these peaks were believed by Aborigines to be a family of mountain spirits, the most distinctive of which is the father Tibrogargan. The fragmented Glass House Mountains National Park surrounds Mts Tibrogargan, Cooee, Beerwah, Coonowrin, Ngungun, Miketeebumulgrai and Elimbah, with picnic grounds, walking trails and lookouts. The peaks are reached by a series of sealed and unsealed roads known as Forest Dr, which heads inland from Glass House Mountains Rd.

There are walking trails (really low-grade mountain climbs) on Tibrogargan, Beerwah and Ngungun. The **QPWS Office** (☎ 5494 0150; Bells Creek Rd, Beerwah; ☽ 7am-3.30pm) in Beerwah has information on the area.

Nearby is one of the state's biggest tourist pullers – **Australia Zoo** (☎ 5494 1134; www .crocodilehunter.com; Glasshouse Mountains Rd, Beerwah; adult/child/family $29/19/90; ☽ 9am-4.30pm). Visitors

flock to this park in droves, as much to see Steve 'Crocodile Hunter' Irwin as the huge array of animals. It's unlikely you'll catch Mr Crikey here, but the park is impressive in its own right, with a menagerie including tigers, tortoises, macaws, crocs (of course) and many more critters from home and abroad. Phone about free transfers from Beerwah train station.

CALOUNDRA
☎ 07 / pop 75,000

At the southern end of the Sunshine Coast, Caloundra is a quiet little family resort with a curvaceous shoreline, offering good fishing and pleasant surf beaches. There are seven lovely beaches; **Bulcock Beach**, good for windsurfing, is near the main street.

Caloundra is a very popular spot for skydiving and **Sunshine Coast Skydivers** (☎ 5437 0211; Caloundra Aerodrome; per person from $180) will facilitate any urges to jump out of a plane (tandem) and whoop for joy. It's almost as much fun watching from the ground.

The **Caloundra Visitor Information Centre** (☎ 5491 9233; 7 Caloundra Rd; ☽ 9am-5.30pm) is located out on the roundabout at the entrance to town.

Sleeping

Belaire Place (☎ 5491 8688; www.belaireplace.com; 34 Minchinton St; r from $105-175; **P** ☒ ☒) Overlooking Bulcock Beach, these spacious and sunny apartments are great value. Rates increase as the views do but the bright and modern interiors all contain sparkling kitchens, cable TV and balconies big enough to park a truck on.

La Promenade (☎ 5499 7133; www.lapromenade .com.au; 4 Tay Ave; d/f from $140/170; ☒ ☒) These upmarket waterfront units near Bulcock Beach have terracotta-tiled floors, stylish furniture and spa baths. There's a trendy café and a communal rooftop area. Rates are lower for longer stays.

Tourist Accommodation (☎ 5499 7655; fax 5499 7644; 84 Omrah Rd; dm/tw/d $17/40/50) This hostel-cum-hotel gets rave reviews from readers and for good reason. Within the spotless and functional complex are comfortable dorms and snug doubles, some of which contain TVs. The facilities are excellent and there's a great BBQ area out the back.

Dicky Beach Family Holiday Park (☎ /fax 5491 3342; 4 Beerburrum St; powered/unpowered sites per 2 people from $24/20, cabins from $60; 🏊 🐕) Absolutely everything is in its place – this well-ordered park right on the beachfront could win a tidy suburbs competition. Aside from the immaculate cabins, there is plenty of green grass and tree cover for comfortable tent-pitching.

Other recommendations:

Anchorage Motor Inn (☎ 5491 1499; fax 5491 7279; 18 Bowman Rd; s/d $80/85; 🏊 🐕 🅿) Decent motel with simple, clean rooms.

Hibiscus Holiday Park (☎ 1800 550 138, 5491 1564; fax 5492 6938; cnr Bowman Rd & Landsborough Park Rd; powered/unpowered sites per 2 people from $23/18.50, caravans/cabins $55/60, units $75-85; 🏊) Reasonable sites, good facilities and lovely villas on the water.

Eating

Above Board (☎ 5491 6388; Shop 8, The Esplanade; mains $10-24; ☺ breakfast, lunch & dinner) A trendy eatery with a relaxed atmosphere and a sophisticated menu. You can rock up in jeans and dine on mahi mahi fillets with macadamia pesto dressing, or pistachio-stuffed pork fillets sitting on a wine-glazed mash. Brekky and lunch are simpler.

For inexpensive club food you can head to the gaudy **Caloundra RSL** (☎ 5491 1544; 19 West Tce; dishes $10-25; ☺ breakfast, lunch & dinner), which packs enough flamboyance to outdo Liberace, but has two excellent restaurants and a café. Alternatively, the **Caloundra Surf Club** (☎ 5491 8418; fax 5492 5730; Ormonde Tce; mains $12; ☺ lunch & dinner) and **Dicky Beach Surf Club** (☎ 5491 6078; Coochin St; mains $12; ☺ lunch & dinner) both dish up big portions on the cheap.

MAROOCHY

☎ 07 / pop 30,212

The most developed patch of the Sunshine Coast boasts sporadic bouts of apartment blocks and a growing suburban spread, which is happily inhabited by many a Sunshine Coaster. It's actually a conglomeration of suburbs, encompassing Maroochydore, Cotton Tree, Alexandra Headland and Mooloolaba. Although the surf culture here has been adulterated somewhat by shopping plazas and a commercial esplanade, the impact is relatively harmless. In summer Maroochy bursts with holidaying families.

Information

Maroochy Tourism Information Booths Mooloolaba (☎ 5478 2233; cnr Brisbane Rd & First Ave, Mooloolaba; ☺ 9am-5pm); Maroochydore airport (☎ 5448 9088; Friendship Dr, Marcoola; ☺ 9.30am-3pm)

Maroochy Visitors Centre (☎ 1800 882 032, 5479 1566; www.maroochytourism.com; cnr Sixth Ave & Melrose St, Maroochydore; ☺ 9am-5pm Mon-Fri, to 4pm Sat & Sun) Super helpful. Free accommodation booking service.

Sights & Activities

Underwater World (☎ 5444 8488; The Wharf, Mooloolaba; adult/child/family $23/13/60; ☺ 9am-6pm) is the southern hemisphere's largest oceanarium, and home to teeming schools of fish, grey nurse sharks and stingrays, plus touch pools and seal shows.

Scuba World (☎ 5444 8595; www.scubaworld.com.au; The Wharf, Mooloolaba) arranges shark dives at Underwater World (certified/uncertified divers $95/145) and takes certified divers on coral dives off the coast (from $55).

There are good surf breaks along the strip – probably the best is Pin Cushion near the mouth of the Maroochy River. **Robbie Sherwell's XL Surfing Academy** (☎ 5478 1337; 63 Oloway Cres, Alexandra Heads; per person $20; ☺ 9.30am Mon-Fri, 7.30am Sat) offers good, one-hour lessons.

The already-learned can rent boards from **Beach Beat** (☎ 5443 2777; 164 Alexandra Pde, Alexandra Headland; surfboards/bodyboards per day $35/25; ☺ 9am-5pm).

Sleeping

Coral Sea Apartments (☎ 5479 2999; www.coralsea-apartments.com; 35-37 Sixth Ave, Maroochydore; apt 2 nights from $290; 🏊 🐕) These yawning two- and three-bedroom apartments, with large balconies, occupy a lovely spot close to Maroochy Surf Club and the beach. Inside you'll find tasteful décor and extra goodies such as dishwashers, wide-screen TVs and videos.

Heritage Motor Inn (☎ 5443 7355; heritagemotorinn@hotmail.com; 69 Sixth Ave, Mooloolaba; r $85-95, 🏊 🐕) Push past the kitsch exterior – as motels go this one's a winner. The spacious rooms are cool, bright and spotless. The hosts are super friendly and if a spot of rain dampens your beach plans there are free in-house movies. Wheelchair friendly.

Argyle on the Park (☎ 5443 3022; www.argyleonthepark.com.au; 31 Cotton Tree Pde, Cotton Tree; r $140-160; 🏊 🐕) This bulbous condo complex contains classy units swimming in wicker furnishings, pale hues and sunlight. Some of the views on the upper levels are fantastic and several units have two balconies to exploit the scenery.

Cotton Tree Caravan Park (☎ 1800 461 253, 5443 1253; www.maroochypark.qld.gov.au; Cotton Tree Pde, Cotton Tree; powered/unpowered sites per 2 people from $22/19; villas minimum 2-night from $210; ☒) This mega-park, right on the beach, is actually a merger of two caravan parks. In summer it resembles a teeming suburb but it's a grassy spot with great facilities and it caters well to travellers with disabilities.

Other recommendations:

Cotton Tree Beachouse Backpackers (☎ 5443 1755; www.cottontreebackpackers.com; 15 The Esplanade, Cotton Tree; YHA members dm/d $19/42, nonmembers $21/46; ▣) Charming timber hostel with good facilities. Close to the beach.

Mooloola Motel (☎ 5444 2988; moolmool@bigpond .com; 45-56 Brisbane Rd, Mooloolaba; s $95-105, d$100-110; ▤) Decent and comfy motel.

Eating

Earth (☎ 5477 7100; Level 1, Mooloolaba International, cnr Venning St & The Esplanade, Mooloolaba; mains $26-30; ☺ lunch & dinner) More like heaven – this chic restaurant with its 90-degree ocean views, flawless service and sublime cuisine is immaculate ingestion. Expect creations like blue-swimmer crab risotto or twice-cooked pork curry with Thai basil and chilli. The wine list is suitably divine.

Hot Pipis (☎ 5444 4441; Shop 3/11 The Esplanade, Mooloolaba; dishes $15-24; ☺ breakfast, lunch & dinner) This is a breezy pavement eatery that exudes effortless style. The atmosphere is cool but the seafood-dominated menu positively sizzles with items such as red curry of Moreton Bay bugs, blacklip mussels, tiger prawns and barramundi. You better leave room for dessert.

Raw Energy (☎ 5446 1444; Shop 3, Mooloolaba Esplanade, Mooloolaba; dishes $6-13; ☺ breakfast & lunch) Just because it's good for you doesn't mean it's all alfalfa wraps and mung beans. Marinated tofu or macadamia and lentil burgers, savoury tartlets and toppling vegetable stacks are the order of the day, plus a smorgasbord of fresh juices and smoothies.

Sunshine Plaza (Horton Pde, Maroochydore; meals $5-8) has a whole host of quick-eat options in its large food court as well as supermarkets for self-caterers.

Also recommended:

Cracked Pepper (☎ 5452 6700; Shop 1, Mooloolaba International, cnr Venning St & The Esplanade, Mooloolaba; mains $10-20; ☺ breakfast, lunch & dinner) Sophisticated café fare and copious outdoor seating.

Maroochy Surf Club (☎ 5443 1298; 34-36 Alexandra Pde, Maroochydore; mains $10-18; ☺ lunch & dinner) Impressive club menu and spectacular views.

Getting There & Away

Long-distance buses stop at the **Suncoast Pacific bus terminal** (☎ 5443 1011; First Ave, Maroochydore), just off Aerodrome Rd.

AROUND MAROOCHY

With your own transport, you can easily base yourself in the less crowded, up-and-coming **Coolum** and **Peregian Beaches**. The area is good for surfing, but also offers wonderful coastal views from **Point Perry** or the chance to climb **Mt Coolum**. There's a **visitor information office** (David Low Way; ☺ 9am-1pm Mon-Sat) opposite the main drag.

In the heart of Coolum, **Coolum Beach Resort** (☎ 07-5471 7744; www.coolumbeachresort.com; 7-13 Beach Rd, Coolum Beach; r $175-235; ☒ ▤) has sunny, self-contained units with balconies and cable TV. Alternatively, **Villa Coolum** (☎ 07-5446 1286; www.villacoolum.com; 102 Coolum Tce, Coolum Beach; r $80; ▤) offers modest bungalows kitted out with simple gear.

Castro's Bar & Restaurant (☎ 07-5471 7555; cnr Frank St & Beach Rd, Coolum; mains $15-25; ☺ dinner) serves delicious woodfired pizzas alongside creative salads, risottos, pastas and mains. Radicals of all ages are welcome.

NOOSA

☎ 07 / pop 47,500

Steeped in a stunning landscape of tropical vegetation, interrupted by the ambling, crystalline waters of Noosa Sound, Noosa is one of Queensland's most scenic and sceney resorts. It has an exclusive vogue quality to it, and wealthy style cats have spent several decades making it their stomping ground. Thankfully, the locals have defended the area from high-rise development and it remains accessible to everyone, so the well-heeled simply share the beach with thongs and bronzed bikini bodies baring their bits.

The area north of Noosa River is preserved as the Cooloola Section of Great Sandy National Park, a haven for 4WD driving, hiking and kayaking.

Orientation

'Noosa' covers a group of communities around the mouth of the Noosa River. Most action focuses on Noosa Heads, but there are

QUEENSLAND

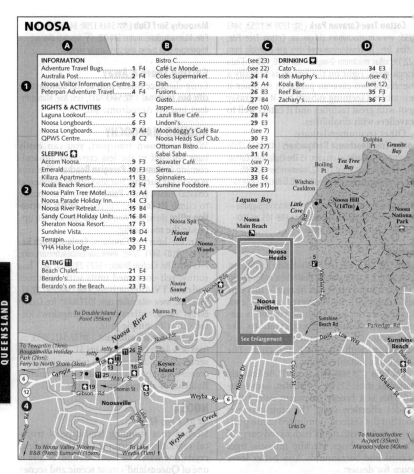

NOOSA

INFORMATION
Adventure Travel Bugs....................1 F4
Australia Post.................................2 F4
Noosa Visitor Information Centre..3 F3
Peterpan Adventure Travel.............4 F4

SIGHTS & ACTIVITIES
Laguna Lookout.............................5 C3
Noosa Longboards..........................6 F3
Noosa Longboards..........................7 A4
QPWS Centre..................................8 C2

SLEEPING
Accom Noosa..................................9 F3
Emerald..10 F3
Killara Apartments........................11 E3
Koala Beach Resort.......................12 F4
Noosa Palm Tree Motel.................13 A4
Noosa Parade Holiday Inn.............14 C3
Noosa River Retreat......................15 B4
Sandy Court Holiday Units............16 B4
Sheraton Noosa Resort..................17 F3
Sunshine Vista..............................18 D4
Terrapin.......................................19 A4
YHA Halse Lodge..........................20 F3

EATING
Beach Chalet.................................21 E4
Berardo's......................................22 F3
Berardo's on the Beach.................23 F3

Bistro C....................................(see 23)
Café Le Monde.........................(see 22)
Coles Supermarket......................24 F4
Dish...25 A4
Fusions..26 B3
Gusto...27 B4
Jasper......................................(see 10)
Lazuli Blue Café...........................28 F4
Lindoni's......................................29 E3
Moondoggy's Café Bar..............(see 7)
Noosa Heads Surf Club................30 F3
Ottoman Bistro.......................(see 27)
Sabai Sabai..................................31 E4
Seawater Café...........................(see 7)
Sierra...32 E3
Spinnakers...................................33 E4
Sunshine Foodstore..................(see 31)

DRINKING
Cato's..34 E3
Irish Murphy's...........................(see 4)
Koala Bar.................................(see 12)
Reef Bar......................................35 F3
Zachary's.....................................36 F3

---

places to stay and eat west along the Noosa River in Noosaville and Tewantin. Uphill from Noosa Heads is Noosa Junction. Over on the east coast of the Noosa headland is the peaceful resort of Sunshine Beach, with one of the best surf breaks in the area.

Information
You will find ATMs and banks in Noosa Junction.
Adventure Travel Bugs (☎ 1800 666 720, 5474 8530; 9 Sunshine Beach Rd, Noosa Junction; per hr $1; ☒ 8am-8pm Mon-Fri, 9am-7pm Sat & Sun) Internet access.
Australia Post (☎ 5473 8591; 91 Noosa Dr)
Noosa Visitor Information Centre (☎ 1800 448 833, 5447 4988; www.tourismnoosa.com.au; Hastings St; ☒ 9am-5pm) Extremely helpful and professional setup.

Peterpan Adventure Travel (☎ 1800 777 115; www.peterpans.com; Shop 3, 75 Noosa Dr, Noosa Junction; per hr $1; ☒ 9am-6.30pm Mon-Sat, 10am-6.30pm Sun) Internet access. Also offers tours (see opposite).

Sights
The small but beautiful **Noosa National Par** extends for about 2km southwest from th headland that marks the end of the Sun shine Coast. It has fine walks, great coasta scenery and a string of popular bays fo surfing on the northern side. **Alexandria Ba** on the eastern side has the best sands an is also an informal nudist beach.

The main entrance at the end of Park R (the eastern continuation of Hastings St has a car park, picnic areas and the **QPW**

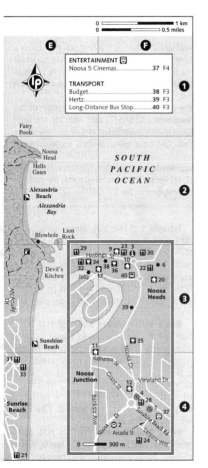

rental per hr/day $30/100). Conditions at the river mouth and Lake Weyba are best between October and January, but on windy days the choppy Noosa River is a playground for the serious daredevils.

The Noosa River is excellent for canoeing; it's possible to follow it up through Lakes Cooroibah and Cootharaba, and through the Cooloola Section of Great Sandy National Park to just south of Rainbow Beach Rd. **Noosa Ocean Kayak Tours** (☎ 0418 787 577) offers two-hour kayaking tours, either around Noosa National Park, or along Noosa River for $50. You can also hire kayaks from $40 per day.

Tours

Several companies run boats from the Noosa Harbour at Tewantin up the Noosa River into the 'Everglades' area; essentially the passage of the Noosa River that cuts into the Great Sandy National Park.

Companies include the following:

Beyond Noosa (☎ 1800 657 666, 5449 9177; www .beyondnoosa.com.au; day tours incl lunch adult/child $70/30)

Everglades Water Bus Co. (☎ 1800 688 045, 5447 1838; 4hr tours adult/child/family $55/40/180)

MV Noosa Queen (☎ 5455 6661; adult/child incl lunch $38/19)

For the more adventurous, **Peterpan Adventure Travel** (☎ 1800 777 115; www.peterpans.com; Shop 3, 75 Noosa Dr, Noosa Junction; per person $130) offers three-day canoe tours into the park including tents and equipment.

See the boxed text, p356, for information on trips to Fraser Island.

Sleeping

The vast majority of accommodation is in the form of self-contained units, although there are also several backpacker hostels and caravan parks. With the exception of these last two, accommodation prices can rise by 50% during school holidays and 100% in the December to January peak season.

BUDGET

YHA Halse Lodge (☎ 1800 242 567, 5447 3377; backpackers@halselodge.com.au; 2 Halse Lane, Noosa Heads; dm/d $27/70; 🖵) Elevated from Hastings St by a steeeep driveway, this 100-year-old Queenslander is legendary on the backpacker route for its colonial good looks. The dorms and kitchen are a tad cramped,

centre (☎ 5447 3243; 🕙 9am-3pm), where you can obtain a walking track map.

For a panoramic view, you can walk or drive up to the **Laguna Lookout** from Viewland Dr in Noosa Junction. From Sunshine Beach, access to the park is via McAnally Dr or Parkedge Rd.

Activities

Surfing lessons are big business in Noosa; see the boxed text, p340 for details. Masters of this art can also move onwards and upwards to kite-surfing. For lessons, call **Kitesurf Australia** (☎ 5455 6677; www.kite-surf.com .au; 2hr/4hr lessons per person $140/260) or **Noosa Adventures & Kite-Surfing** (☎ 0438 788 573; www.noosa kitesurfing.com.au; 2hr/8hr lessons per person $120/$380,

QUEENSLAND

SURFING NOOSA

With a string of fine breaks in an unspoilt national park, Noosa is a fine place to catch a wave. The best year-round break is probably Sunshine Corner, at the northern end of Sunshine Beach, though it has a brutal beach dump. The point breaks around the headland only perform during the summer, but when they do, expect wild conditions and good walls at Boiling Point and Tea Tree, on the northern coast of the headland.

There are also gentler breaks on Noosa Spit at the far end of Hastings St, where most of the surf schools do their training. Options include **Wavesense** (☎ 07-5474 9076, 1800 249 076; www .wavesense.com.au), **Noosing Surf Lessons** (☎ 0412 330 850; www.noosasurflessons.com.au) and **Merrick's Learn to Surf** (☎ 0418 787 577; www.learntosurf.com.au). Two-hour group lessons on longboards cost around $45.

If you just want to rent equipment, **Noosa Longboards** (www.noosalongboards.com; Noosa Heads (☎ 07-5447 2828; 64 Hastings St; Noosaville ☎ 07-5474 2722; 187 Gympie Tce) rents longboards per half/full day for $30/45 as well as surfboards for $20/30 and bodyboards for $15/20.

---

but the bar is a hive of social activity. The hostel offers a discount to YHA members.

Sandy Court Holiday Units (☎ 5449 7225; fax 54 73 0397; 30 James St, Noosaville; d $55-70; 🖳) Down a quiet residential street, these self-contained units offer unbeatable value. The décor is a wee bit weary and the furnishings and crockery are mix and match, but the units are clean, comfortable and well-managed. Longer stays attract bargain rates.

Also recommended:

Koala Beach Resort (☎ 1800 357 457, 5447 3355; www.koala-backpackers.com; 44 Noosa Dr, Noosa Junction; dm $22, tw & d $55; 🖳 🖳) Huge dorms, good facilities and plenty of party action.

Bougainvillia Holiday Park (☎ 1800 041 444, 5447 1712; jsjs@optusnet.com.au; 141 Coooroy-Noosa Rd, Tewantin; powered/unpowered sites per 2 people from $26/24, cabins $55-95; 🖳 🖳) Neat as a pin and meticulously landscaped.

MIDRANGE

Accommodation on Hastings St can be ridiculously expensive, but the tariffs drop markedly along Gympie Tce, the riverside main road through Noosaville. For private units to rent, call **Accom Noosa** (☎ 1800 072 078; www .accomnoosa.com.au; Shop 5, Fairshore Apartments, Hastings St, Noosa Heads). There's often a three-night minimum stay for these.

Noosa Parade Holiday Inn (☎ 5447 4177; www .noosaparadeholidayinn.com; 51 Noosa Pde, Noosa Heads; r $120; 🖳 🖳) No it's not part of the chain, but this small apartment complex certainly maintains similar standards. Tiled and spotless units are reminiscent of an Ikea showroom, with cool interiors and bold colours. Longer stays attract good discounts.

Terrapin (☎ 5449 8770; www.terrapin.com.au; The Cockleshell, Noosaville; r per night $160-200, per week $620-1200; 🖳) If you're hanging about for a week or so, these two-storey townhouses are a good option. The earthy interiors are lifted by bold furnishings and balconies or gardens. All contain mod cons plus either a video unit or DVD.

Noosa Valley Winery B&B (☎ 5449 1675; fax 5449 1679; 855 Noosa Eumundi Rd, Doonan; r $120; 🖳) This pretty B&B is away from the bustle of downtown Noosa, and is incorporated with a boutique winery. Thin pockets of bush surround the elegant rooms, which swim in sunlight. Each room has a private alcove where breakfast is served. The B&B is wheelchair friendly.

Noosa River Retreat (☎ 5474 2811; pauline@ escapesresorts.com.au; cnr Weyba Rd & Reef St, Noosaville; r $75-85; 🖳 🖳) An orderly complex housing spick, span and spacious one- and two-bedroom units, some of which are shielded by gardens. Those on the upper floor feature spa baths and there's a central BBQ. Bookings are advised.

Other recommendations:

Noosa Palm Tree Motel (☎ 5449 7311; fax 5474 3246; 233 Gympie Tce, Noosaville; r $80-95; 🖳 🖳) Sound motel rooms with kitchenettes or larger, fully-equipped units.

Killara Apartments (☎ 5447 2800; www.killaranoosa .com; 42 Grant St, Noosa Junction; r per 3-nights/week from $280/630; 🖳 🖳) Functional and modern units with plenty of space and colour.

Sunshine Vista (☎ 1300 551 999, 5447 2487; www.sun shinevista.com.au; 45 Duke St, Sunshine Beach; r per week $730-$1610; 🖳 🖳) Comfortable units in an excellent location. Generally weekly bookings only.

TOP END

Sheraton Noosa Resort (☎ 5449 4888; www.starwood
hotels.com/sheraton; 14-16 Hastings St, Noosa Heads; r from
$280-400; ❄️ 🔁) Elegance personified. This
five-star hotel's tastefully coordinated rooms
contain sueded fabrics, fabulous beds, balconies, kitchenettes and spas. The Sheraton also
has four bars, three restaurants, and a gym,
sauna and spa. There are some great deals if
you book online. Wheelchair friendly.

Emerald (☎ 1800 803 899, 5449 6100; www.emerald
noosa.com.au; 42 Hastings St, Noosa Heads; r $230-450;
❄️ 🔁) The stylish Emerald has indulgent
rooms bathed in ethereal white and sunlight. Expect clean and crisp edges and exquisite furnishings. All of the rooms are
self-contained and the mod cons are so lovely
you'll miss them when you leave.

Eating

RESTAURANTS

Ottoman Bistro (☎ 5447 1818; 249 Gympie Tce, Noosaville;
mains $18-27; 🕐 lunch & dinner) Fantastic Turkish-
bazaar-meets-Noosaville and gets a big
thumbs-up for Middle Eastern cred such as
Harissa spatchcock, traditional *labne* (yoghurt spread) or seafood *tagine* (stew). You
can recline on the wall couches, sit beneath
shady sailcloths or play a round of backgam-
mon while you dine.

Jasper (☎ 5474 9600; 42 Hastings St; mains $16-26;
🕐 breakfast, lunch & dinner) Dining under Jasper's
shady canopy, set behind a thin perimeter
of palms and water features, is definitively
tranquil. The menu carries blue-swimmer
crab cakes, sand-crab lasagne and excellent
laksas. The staff and prices are relaxed.

Lindoni's (☎ 5447 5111; Hastings St, Noosa Heads;
mains $20-30; 🕐 dinner) Wrought iron and over-
sized statues grace Lindoni's patio, adding
to the Italian theme. The classy menu mixes
authentic ingredients with Australian style;
pasta with Moreton Bay Bug meat and a
mild cream curry, or bocconcini-and-
prosciutto-stuffed veal with red wine jus.

Café Le Monde (☎ 5449 2366; Hastings St; mains $17-
28; 🕐 breakfast, lunch & dinner) There's not a fussy
palate or dietary need that isn't catered for
on Café Le Monde's enormous menu. The
large, open-air patio buzzes with diners digging into burgers, seared tuna steaks, curries, pastas, salads and plenty more. Great
for families and groups.

Fusions (☎ 5474 1699; 271 Gympie Tce; mains $15-20;
🕐 breakfast, lunch & dinner) Catching plenty of

beach breeze through the wide open doorways, families, couples, locals and tourists
sit at Fusions' high-backed Balinese chairs
inside or the oversized tables outside.
Gourmet sandwiches, woodfired pizzas and
spruced-up café fare graces the menu. Ideal
breakfast spot.

Dish (☎ 5449 0094; Shop 2, 14 Thomas St, Noosaville;
mains $16-25; 🕐 dinner Mon-Sat) Tucked into a quiet
corner, this diminutive restaurant serves
fabulous food on a wee wooden deck. The
menu is a work of art – think seared cara-
way and roasted coffee oil marinated kangaroo with roasted mash. There's also a kids
menu and plenty of veggie options.

Laid-back dining and Asian-infused
dishes are to be had at **Sabai Sabai** (☎ 5473
5177; 46 Duke St; mains $22-28; 🕐 lunch & dinner) or
Berardo's on the Beach (☎ 5448 0888; 49 Hastings
St, Noosa Heads; dishes $10-26; 🕐 lunch & dinner; ❄️),
which also boasts Italian and Middle Eastern flavours with beachside views.

Also recommended:

Bistro C (☎ 5447 2855; On the Beach Arcade, Hastings
St; mains $18-26; 🕐 breakfast, lunch & dinner) Boister-
ous bistro overlooking the beach.

Spinnakers (☎ 5474 5177; The Esplanade, Sunshine
Beach SLSC, Sunshine Beach; mains $15-25; 🕐 lunch &
dinner) Excellent club bistro.

Noosa Heads Surf Club (☎ 5474 5688; Hastings St;
mains $10-20; 🕐 breakfast Sat & Sun, lunch & dinner
daily) Popular surf club serving good club grub.

CAFÉS

Seawater Café (☎ 5449 7215; 197 Gympie Tce, Noosaville; meals $8-20; 🕐 breakfast, lunch & dinner) Noosa's
exclusive air hits planet earth at this kitsch
and colourful restaurant, which dishes out
excellent seafood in simple surroundings.
Amid a painted sea of mermaids and other
sea paraphernalia you can also dig into meal-
sized sandwiches or the bargain nightly
roast.

Lazuli Blue Café (☎ 5448 0055; 9 Sunshine Beach Rd,
Noosa Junction; meals $7-12; 🕐 breakfast & lunch) Slow
and lazy eating is mandatory at this relaxed
café, where colossal fresh juices and smoothies are the speciality. The breakfasts, Turkish
toasties, salads and meatier dishes including
Cajun chicken are pretty special too.

Sunshine Foodstore (☎ 5474 5611; 46 Duke St, Sunshine Beach; dishes $6-14; 🕐 breakfast & lunch) Local
sun-and-coffee addicts tackle newspapers
daily at the outdoor wooden benches of
this ambient café. It's not just the fix and

QUEENSLAND

NOT-TO-BE-MISSED NOOSA NOSH

Noosa's culinary constitution is legendary but you don't need to spend your holiday savings to enjoy it. The following are top picks, spanning all budgets and dress code.

Gusto (☎ 07-5449 7144; 257 Gympie Tce, Noosaville; mains $17-30; ✆ lunch & dinner) Gusto trumps Noosa's classy competition with effortless style, superior service and breezy water-views. The Mod Oz menu offers Hervey Bay scallops, opulent bangers and mash, Mooloolaba prawns or melt-in-your mouth cuttlefish, all marinated, cooked and served with passion.

Berardo's (☎ 07-5447 5666; Hastings St, Noosa Heads; mains $26-33; ✆ dinner) Beautiful Berardo's is culinary utopia, from the sun-dappled setting swimming in elegance to the heavenly food. Delicate dishes such as spiced local seafood hotpot with saffron and tomato or grilled eye fillet steak, with horseradish and thyme gallette and balsamic jus will lull you into a divine coma. Fingers dancing across the keys of a grand piano in the centre of the restaurant will keep you awake though.

Sierra (☎ 07-5447 4800; 10 Hastings St, Noosa Heads; mains $15-25; ✆ breakfast, lunch & dinner) This hot little café could have been plucked from any hip inner-city suburb with its funky vibes and food. Swimming in delicious smells, diners vacuum items from the eclectic menu, which boasts wok-tossed, char-grilled and marinated fare. All the seating is alfresco and it's incredibly popular.

Beach Chalet (☎ 07-5447 3944; 3 Tingira Cres, Sunrise Beach; dishes $5-8; ✆ breakfast & lunch) A sneeze south of Sunshine Beach at Sunrise Beach, this tiny café is just a small extension of a general store. The brekkies, burgers and sandwiches border on legendary though, as do the views of the breakers.

---

sunshine they come for though; brekkies here consist of eggs any way with fresh pesto and vegies, while for lunch you can savour gargantuan ciabattas.

Moondoggy's Café Bar (☎ 5449 9659; 187 Gympie Tce, Noosaville; meals $5-12; ✆ breakfast & lunch) This cute café serves tasty wraps, focaccias and other lunch fare with a gourmet twist.

SELF-CATERING
Self-caterers can head to **Coles Supermarket** (Noosa Fair Shopping Centre, Lanyana Way, Noosa Junction).

Drinking
Zachary's (☎ 5447 3211; 30 Hastings St, Noosa Heads) Slinky bar imbues a splash of urban cool into Noosa's coastal milieu. Dark colours, dim lighting and ambient beats swirl about trendy young things. Bar snacks are served, but who cares?

Koala Bar (☎ 5447 3355; 44 Noosa Dr, Noosa Junction) Noosa's backpackers and other free spirits start their nightly revelry at this popular hostel bar. Live rock fills every crevice several nights a week and when it doesn't the place hums to the harmony of beer jugs and beery banter.

Reef Bar (☎ 5447 4477; 9 Noosa Dr, Noosaville) A little bit country, a little bit coast, the Reef Bar is a cruisy watering hole with a strong local feel. You've every chance of grasping

the secrets of Aussie Rules football, while listening to Australian rock or dancing to doof doof.

Also recommended:

Irish Murphy's (☎ 5455 3344; cnr Sunshine Beach Rd & Noosa Dr, Noosa Junction) Irish theme pub with good ales.

Cato's (☎ 5449 4888; 12-14 Hastings St; Noosa Heads) Voluptuous bar serving thirsty style cats.

Entertainment
Noosa 5 Cinemas (☎ 1300 366 339; 29 Sunshine Beach Rd, Noosa Junction) Plush, comfortable cinema screens the latest blockbusters.

Getting There & Around
Long-distance buses stop at the bus stop near the corner of Noosa Dr and Noosa Pde; see p334 for fares. All hostels have courtesy pick-ups, except Halse Lodge, which is only 100m away.

Sunbus (p335) has frequent services between Maroochydore and Noosa ($4.40, one hour), and links Noosa Heads, Noosaville, Noosa Junction etc. Between 26 December and 10 January, and over Easter, there are free shuttle buses every 10 to 15 minutes stopping frequently between Noosa Junction and Tewantin.

Riverlight Ferry (☎ 5449 8442) operates ferries between Noosa Heads and Tewantin (one way per adult/child/family $9.50/4/25, all day pass $13.50/5/35, six to 10 crossings daily).

Noosa Bike Hire and Tours (☎ 5474 3322; www .noosabikehire.com) rents bicycles from several locations in Noosa including YHA Halse Lodge (p339). Alternatively, it will deliver and collect the bikes to/from your door for free.

The **Other Car Rental Company** (☎ 5447 2831; www.noosacarrental.com; per day from $45) delivers cars and 4WDs to your door.

Other rental agencies:

Budget (☎ 5474 2820; Bay Village Mall, Noosa Heads)

Hertz (☎ 5447 2253; Noosa Blue Resort, 16 Noosa Drive, Noosa Heads)

COOLOOLA COAST

Stretching north from Noosa to Rainbow Beach, the Cooloola Coast is a 50km strip of long sandy beaches, backed by the Cooloola section of the Great Sandy National Park. Remote, undeveloped and a good place for spotting kangaroos, it nevertheless attracts crowds at peak times.

With a 4WD you can drive up the beach at low tide to Rainbow Beach, passing the Teewah Coloured Sands and the wreck of the *Cherry Venture*, swept ashore in 1973.

Lake Cooroibah

About 2km north of Tewantin, the Noosa River widens out into Lake Cooroibah. From the end of Moorindil St in Tewantin, you can take the **Noosa North Shore Ferry** (☎ 07-5447 1321; pedestrian/car one way $1/5; ⏰ 5am-12.30pm Fri & Sat, 6am-10.30pm Sun-Thu) up to the lake in a conventional vehicle and camp along sections of the beach.

Camel Safaris (☎ 07-5442 4402; www.camelcompany .com.au; Beach Rd, Noosa North Shore; 1hr ride per adult/child $40/30, 2hr ride $55/45) operates glorious camel treks up the beach.

Set over a sprawling park with camping, cabins, motel rooms and more is **Noosa North Shore Retreat** (☎ 07-5447 1706; www.noosa northshore.com.au; Beach Rd; powered/unpowered sites per 2 people from $19.50/14, r from $70, cabins from $90; ☒ ☒). Backed by bush, it's a great spot for wildlife spotting, canoeing, bushwalking… or relaxing. There's also a **pub** (mains $8-15; ⏰ lunch & dinner) and small shop.

If really want to go bush, **Gagaju** (☎ 1300 302 271, 07-5474 3522; www.travoholic.com/gagaju; 118 Johns Dr, Tewantin; unpowered sites per 2 people $12, dm $18) is a riverside eco-wilderness camp with basic dorms constructed entirely out of re-cycled timber. Activities include canoeing, mountain biking and bushwalking. A courtesy shuttle runs to and from Noosa about three times a day.

Lake Cootharaba

North of Lake Cooroibah is the gorgeous Lake Cootharaba, which measures about 5km across and 10km in length. It's reached by driving northwest of Tewantin. **Boreen Point** is a relaxed little community with several places to stay and eat. The lake is the gateway to the Noosa Everglades.

From Boreen Point, an unsealed road leads another 5km up to **Elanda Point**, where there's a **ranger's station** (☎ 07-5485 3245; Elanda; ⏰ 7am-4pm), and the headquarters of the **Elanda Point Canoe Company** (☎ 1800 226 637, 07-5485 3165; www .elanda.com.au/noosa; Elanda Point; per day for 1 or 2 people $25), which rents canoes and kayaks. If it's just the transport you're after, they'll shuttle you up to Kinaba or Figtree (one way $25) and Harry's Hut (one way $45) camping grounds in the park.

Lake Cootharaba Gallery Units (☎ 07-5485 31 53; 64 Laguna St, Boreen Point; r per night/week from $80/400) are two self-contained units, which are homey and practical. The gallery the units are attached to is a tad on the eccentric side but the hosts are lovely.

The much-loved **Apollonian Hotel** (☎ 07-5485 3100; fax 07-5485 3499; Laguna St, Boreen Point; dm/d without bathroom $25/45, mains $12; ⏰ lunch & dinner) is a gorgeous old pub with sturdy timber walls, shady verandas and a beautifully preserved interior. Rooms are in the Queenslander out the back and the pub grub is tasty.

Great Sandy National Park (Cooloola)

East and north of the lakes is the Great Sandy National Park. This 54,000-hectare varied wilderness of mangroves, forest and heathland is traversed by the Noosa River. With a 4WD (available in Noosa), you can drive through the park all the way to Rainbow Beach, but kayaking from Boreen Point is a more relaxing way to sightsee. You can also take an organised tour – see p339. There are some fantastic walking trails starting from Elanda Point on the shore of Lake Cootharaba, including the 46km Cooloola Wilderness Trail to Rainbow Beach and a 7km trail to the **QPWS**

QUEENSLAND

information centre (☎ 07-5449 7364; ⏱ 7am-4pm) at Kinaba Island.

The park contains about 15 **QPWS camping grounds** (per person/family $4/16), including Fig Tree Point, at Lake Cootharaba's northern edge, Harry's Hut, 4km further up the river, and Freshwater, about 6km south of Double Island Point on the beach. You must purchase permits for all camping grounds along the river at Elanda **ranger's station** (☎ 07-5485 3245; Elanda; ⏱ 7am-4pm). You can purchase permits for Harry's Hut, Fig Tree Point, Freshwater and all beach camping at the **QPWS Great Sandy Information Centre** (☎ 07-5449 7792; 240 Moorindil St, Tewantin; ⏱ 7am-4pm), which can also provide information on park access, tide times and fire bans within the park. Apart from Harry's Hut and Freshwater, all sites are accessible by hiking or river only.

SUNSHINE COAST HINTERLAND

There are organised tours of this region, but with your own transport you can better explore the appealing landscape between towns and villages.

About 6km south of the commercial town of **Nambour** is the **Big Pineapple** (☎ 07-5442 1333; Nambour Connection Rd, Nambour; ⏱ 9am-5pm), one of Queensland's kitschy 'big things'. You can walk through the 15m-high fibreglass fruit for free, or take a plantation train tour (adult/child $11.50/9.50), which includes commentary on everything you wanted to know about growing a lot of pineapples. About 8km north of the Big Pineapple on the Bruce Hwy, you'll arrive at **Yandina**, where it's worth having a meal at the renowned Asian restaurant, **Spirit House Restaurant** (☎ 07-5446 8994; 4 Ninderry Rd, Yandina; mains $23-33; ⏱ lunch daily, dinner Wed-Sat). If travelling with children, also stop at the **Ginger Factory** (☎ 07-5446 7096; 50 Pioneer Rd, Yandina; admission free; ⏱ 9am-5pm).

Further north, both locals and visitors flock to the **Eumundi markets** (⏱ 8am-2pm Wed, 6am-2pm Sat), where you'll find everything from homemade cheese graters to aromatic sneeze abators, plus clothing, food and music in the 200-plus stalls. Sunbus 631 and 630 ($4, one hour, roughly hourly) head here from Noosa Heads. Both **Storeyline Tours** (☎ 07-5474 1500; www.sunshinecoastdaytours .com.au) and **Henry's** (☎ 07-5474 0199) arrange day tours from Noosa accommodation (adult/child $15/10).

Inland from Nambour, the Blackall Range creates a scenic hinterland with appealing national parks and rather chintzy rustic villages. The scenic Mapleton to Maleny road runs along the ridge of the range, past rainforests at **Mapleton Falls National Park**, 4km northwest of Mapleton, and **Kondalilla National Park**, 3km northwest of Montville. Both Mapleton and Kondalilla waterfalls plunge more than 80m, and their lookouts offer wonderful forest views.

In Maleny you'll discover the **Mary Cairncross Scenic Reserve** (☎ 07-5499 9907; Mountain View Rd; admission free; ⏱ 8am-6pm), a pristine rainforest shelter spread over 53 hectacres southeast of town, with a healthy population of bird life and unbearably cute pademelons.

Midway between Mapleton and Maleny is **Montville**, with potteries, dinky craft shops and restaurants. Ask the **information centre** (☎ 07-5478 5544; 168 Main St; ⏱ 10am-4pm) about nearby B&Bs.

The **Woodford Folk Festival**, held annually during the five days leading up to New Year's Eve, is the closest Australia has to Woodstock. Woodford is situated southwest of Maleny.

SOUTH BURNETT REGION

Further inland again, the South Burnett region includes Australia's leading peanut-growing area. The main attraction is the **Bunya Mountains National Park**, more than 1000m above sea level and accessible by sealed road from Dalby or Kingaroy. There are several **camping grounds** (per person/family $4/16), including at the lovely, green site adjacent to the station. There are also walking tracks to waterfalls and lookouts. The **ranger** (☎ 07-4668 3127; www.epa.qld.gov.au; Bunya Ave) is at Dandabah, by the park entrance.

DARLING DOWNS

West of the Great Dividing Range in southern Queensland stretch the rolling plains of the Darling Downs. The tranquil rural setting and vast horizons of rich pastoral land are an attraction in themselves, but this region of southeast Queensland is also awash with hidden gems. The dramatic landscapes of Girraween and Sundown National Parks provide spectacular bushwalking opportunities; the perfect precursor to spending a day with glass in hand at the scenic Granite Belt vineyards, Queensland's most promising wine-growing district. Warwick, Roma and Goondiwindi are typical country towns, but leafy Toowoomba and Stanthorpe have a more 'New England' feel.

Getting There & Away
AIR
Qantas (☎ 13 13 13; www.qantas.com.au) flies from Brisbane to Roma ($120).

BUS
Greyhound Australia (☎ 13 14 99; www.greyhound.com.au) has connections from Brisbane to Toowoomba ($25, two hours), Miles ($41, 5½ hours), Roma ($56, eight hours), Warwick ($40, four hours) Stanthorpe ($50, 4½ hours) and Goondiwindi ($55, five hours).

Crisps' Coaches (☎ 07-4661 8333; www.crisps.com.au) is the biggest local operator, offering services from Brisbane to Warwick ($33, 2¼ hours), Goondiwindi ($50, 5¼ hours) and Stanthorpe ($45, 3½ hours).

Brisbane Bus Lines has daily services from Brisbane into the South Burnett region.

TRAIN
The **Queensland Rail** (☎ 1300 131 722; www.traveltrain.com.au) *Westlander* runs twice weekly from Brisbane to Charleville (economy seat/sleeper $95/145, 16 hours) on Tuesday and Thursday, returning on Wednesday and Friday, stopping in Toowoomba (economy seat/sleeper $28/85, four hours) and Roma (economy seat/sleeper $65/120, 11 hours). There are connecting bus services from Charleville to Cunnamulla and Quilpie.

IPSWICH TO WARWICK
Almost an outer suburb of Brisbane, Ipswich was a convict settlement as early as 1827 and has some fine old houses and public buildings, described in the excellent *Ipswich Heritage Trails* leaflets available from the **Ipswich tourist information centre** (☎ 07-3281 0555; cnr Brisbane St & D'Arcy Doyle Pl; ☼ 9am-4pm Mon-Fri, 10am-3pm Sat & Sun), in the Post Office Building.

Southwest of Ipswich the Cunningham Hwy to Warwick crosses the Great Dividing Range at **Cunningham's Gap**. Here the road winds rather treacherously through the 1100m-high mountains of **Main Range National Park**, which has dense rainforest and numerous walking trails and lookouts. The

---

> ### THE FASTEST SHEARS IN THE WEST
> On the corner of the Cunningham Hwy and Glengallan Rd in Warwick is a giant pair of blade shears atop a block of stone. This monument commemorates Jackie Howe, born on Canning Downs Station near Warwick, and acclaimed as the greatest 'gun' (the best in the shed) shearer the country has ever seen. He holds the amazing record of having shorn 321 sheep with a set of hand shears in less than eight hours. Established in 1892, the record still stands today – it wasn't even beaten by shearers using machine-powered shears until 1950.
>
> Jackie had a habit of ripping the sleeves off his shirts when he was working and to this day the sleeveless blue singlets worn by many Australian workers are known as 'Jackie Howes'.

---

ranger station (☎ 07-4666 1133) is west of Cunningham's Gap on the southern side of the highway, and there's a small camping ground opposite.

WARWICK
☎ 07 / pop 12,000

Warwick, 162km southwest of Brisbane, is Queensland's second-oldest town and a good place to heed the adage about stopping to smell the roses. Its Leslie Park and Jubilee Rose Gardens are perfumed with many varieties, including the red City of Warwick (*Arofuto*) genus. The town is also known for its rodeos, as well as numerous historic buildings.

The **tourist information centre** (☎ 4661 3122; 49 Albion St; ☼ 9am-5pm Mon-Sat, 10am-3pm Sun) has plenty of material on the neighbouring South Downs historic towns and buildings.

Two B&Bs offering comfortable digs are the atmospheric **Abbey of the Roses** (☎ 4661 9777; www.abbeyoftheroses.com; cnr Locke & Dragon Sts; d midweek/weekend $90/110), which is National Trust–listed and filled with period furnishings, or the far simpler **Grafton Rose B&B** (☎ 4667 0151; 134 Grafton St; d $120).

Monopolising the main street is the insanely popular **Mussels** (☎ 4661 1525; Palmerin St; mains $13-22; ☼ breakfast, lunch & dinner), where locals dig into hefty gourmet burgers, steaks and seafood dishes. If you're after something a tad healthier, the charming, domed

Bramble Patch Cafe (☎ 4661 9022; 8 Albion St; snacks $10; ☷ breakfast & lunch) serves great sandwiches and homemade preserves.

STANTHORPE & THE GRANITE BELT

South of Warwick is the Granite Belt, an elevated plateau of the Great Dividing Range. This 'high country' is renowned for its fruit, vegetables and 40-plus boutique wineries.

The attractive highland town of Stanthorpe is most famous for being cold – it sits at an altitude of 915m and is one of the few places in the state that gets snow – and even celebrates its chilly climate with an annual **Brass Monkey Festival** every July. From October to mid-June (provided there's been plenty of rainfall in the year) Stanthorpe's fruit-picking opportunities lure plenty of backpackers.

Information

Oz Jobs (☎ 07-4681 3746; cnr Railway & Rogers Sts) Job placements on farms and vineyards.
Stanthorpe Visitor Information Office (☎ 07-4681 2057; Leslie St; ☷ 9am-3pm Mon, 8.30am-5pm Tue-Sat, 9am-4pm Sun) South of the river.

Sights & Activities

About 26km south of Stanthorpe, a sealed road turns off the highway, leading 9km east to the **Girraween National Park**, which fea-

tures towering granite boulders surrounded by pristine forests. Wildlife abounds, and the park adjoins Bald Rock National Park in NSW. **Grape Escape** (☎ 1300 36 1150; www .grapeescape.com.au; $60 per person) operates tours to five wineries, including lunch.

Sleeping

Escape on Tully (☎ 07-4683 7000; www.escapeontully .com; 934 Mt Tully Rd; d midweek/weekend $90/140) Take the name literally – this B&B is a great weekend retreat for couples or groups. Everyone will enjoy the sunny north-facing deck (complete with bathtub!) and gorgeous views. Despite absolute privacy, it's only 10 minutes into town and to the nearby wineries.

Happy Valley (☎ 07-4681 3250; www.happyvalleyre treat.com; Glenlyon Drive; d midweek/weekend $120/150) Set amid dense bush with granite outcrops, this fine resort offers modern homestead units or more secluded timber cabins, all with their own bathrooms and wood fires. There's also a tennis court and restaurant on site.

Camping options:
Top of the Town Caravan Village (☎ 07-4681 4888; fax 07-4681 4222; 10 High St; powered sites $18, dm $20, cabins from $72; ☐ ☒) Popular with seasonal workers.
Blue Topaz Caravan Park (☎ 07-4683 5279; New England Hwy, Severnlea; powered sites $15, cabins $50) Good for families; pets welcome.

GRANITE BELT WINERIES

The burgeoning cluster of vineyards scattered around the elevated plateau of the Great Dividing Range constitutes Queensland's best-known wine district. Moseying from one winery to the next amid some spectacular scenery is a must for visitors to the area.

Grapes were first grown in the district in the 19th century, but the wine industry really took off during WWII when Italian immigrants were brought into the countryside to work on farms (at the time, Australia was at war with Italy). These forced emigrees flourished, and there are now some 40 wineries dotted around the New England Hwy between Cottonvale and Wallangarra.

The area doesn't have a particular speciality, but Shiraz and Cabernet Sauvignon are becoming popular regional styles for red varieties, and Semillon, Verdehlo and Chardonnay the best white varieties.

Heading south from Stanthorpe, the following list includes just a few of the more highly regarded vineyards in the area.
Lucas Estate (☎ 07-4683 6365; Donges Rd, Severnlea; ☷ 10am-5pm)
Mountview (☎ 07-4683 4316; Mt Stirling Rd, Glen Aplin; ☷ 9.30am-4.30pm Fri-Sun)
Ballandean Estate (☎ 07-4684 1226; Sundown Rd, Ballandean; ☷ 9am-5pm)
Symphony Hill Wines (☎ 07-4684 1388; 2017 Eukey Rd, Ballandean; ☷ 10am-5pm)
Pyramids Road Wines (☎ 07-4684 5151; Pyramids Rd, Wyberba; ☷ 10am-4.30pm Sat & Sun)
Bald Mountain Winery (☎ 07-4684 3186; Hickling Lane, Wallangarra; ☷ 10am-5pm)
Robert Channon Wines (☎ 07-4683 3109; Bradley Lane, Stanthorpe; ☷ 10am-5pm, closed Jan) North of Stanthorpe.

There are two good **camping grounds** (per person/family $4/16) in Girraween National Park, plus numerous walking trails. The **visitors centre** (☎ 07-4684 5157; 1-3.30pm Mon-Fri, 9-5pm Sat & Sun) accepts camp site bookings.

Eating

Cooks, Gluttons & Gourmets (☎ 07-4681 2377; 137a High St; mains $12-24; dinner) An understated Mod Oz eatery with a creative menu and a warm, casual vibe. The food, however, is fine dining; a towering plate of Atlantic salmon and prawns comes served on handmade pappardelle, and the tea-smoked kangaroo fillet is tender and delicious.

Anna's Restaurant (☎ 07-4681 1265; cnr Wallangarra Rd & O'Mara Tce; dishes $9-17; dinner Mon-Sat) This family-run, Italian BYO restaurant is set in a cosy Queenslander. It is famous locally for the weekend buffets (adult/child $28/14) where you can gorge yourself on antipasto platters, hearty pasta and a vast array of veal, poultry and seafood dishes.

You can dig into good pub grub at **O'Mara's Hotel** (☎ 07-4681 1044; 45 Maryland St; dishes $7.50-16; lunch & dinner).

GOONDIWINDI
☎ 07 / pop 5500

Situated west of Warwick on the NSW border, Goondiwindi (*gun*-doo-windy) is something of a one-horse town, the horse in question being Gunsynd, a remarkably successful racehorse. There's a statue of the 'Goondiwindi Grey' in MacIntyre St.

The helpful **municipal tourist office** (☎ 4671 2653; Goondiwindi-Waggamba Library, 4 McLean St; 9am-5pm;) provides useful information and has Internet access (per hour $5).

While you're in town, pop into the **Customs House Museum** (☎ 4671 3041; 1 MacIntyre St; 10am-4pm Wed-Mon), which has a gorgeous flower-filled garden and a collection put together by the local historical society.

For reasonably priced accommodation, try **Country Comfort** (☎ 4671 1855; 110 Marshall St; s/d $85/89;), a modern motel just east of the junction with McLean St.

TOOWOOMBA
☎ 07 / pop 89,400

Perched on the edge of the Great Dividing Range, with breathtaking views of the Lockyer Valley 700m below, Toowoomba is a renowned garden city with a temperate climate. It's the largest town in the area and the birthplace of that archetypal Aussie cake, the lamington. The centre is graced with some stately buildings.

Information

Coffee On Line (☎ 4639 4686; 12 Russell St; per 30 min $6.60; 8.30am-8pm Mon-Fri, 8.30am-7pm Sat, 10am-7pm Sun) Internet access.

QPWS (☎ 4639 4599; 158 Hume St; 8.30am-5pm Mon-Fri)

Toowoomba Visitor Information Centre (☎ 4639 3797; www.toowoomba.qld.gov.au; 86 James St; 9am-5pm)

Sights & Activities

The inspiring and ever-expanding **Cobb & Co Museum** (☎ 4639 1971; 27 Lindsay St; adult/child $8/4; 10am-4pm) is more than a collection of carriages and traps from the horse-drawn age; it's also a showcase for Toowoomba's indigenous Australian and multicultural communities, and includes a children's play area.

Queen's Park (cnr Lindsay & Campbell Sts) houses the botanic gardens, although some might prefer the beautiful **Ju Raku En Japanese Garden** (☎ 4631 2627; West St; 7am-dusk), with its 3km of walking trails, waterfalls and streams.

Picnic Point, on the eastern edge of town just south of the Warrego Hwy, is the most accessible of the town's several 'escarpment parks', which all enjoy wonderful views. The annual **Carnival of Flowers** (☎ 4638 7143) is held in September.

Sleeping & Eating

Toowoomba's accommodation can fill surprisingly fast and it's best to book ahead, especially during festivals.

Vacy Hall (☎ 4639 2055; www.vacyhall.com.au; 135 Russell St; d $100-190) Just uphill from the town centre, this magnificent 1880s mansion offers heritage-style accommodation of the highest standard. The pricier rooms have bathrooms and verandas, and the extensive grounds are well worth a stroll.

Ambassador Motor Inn (☎ 4637 6800; 200 Ruthven St; s/d $100/110) Up a notch from the run-of-the-mill motel, this bustling four-star option has transformed its comfortable rooms into well-appointed suites which attract travellers and business people alike.

Settlers Inn (☎ 4632 3634; cnr James & Ruthven Sts; s/d/tr $30/40/45) At the time of writing, this busy motel was beginning to style itself as a backpackers place. The accommodation is plain and the service a touch abrupt, but it's a cheap, clean option.

GPO Café & Bar (☎ 4659 9240; 1/140 Margaret St; mains $12-25; ☒ breakfast & lunch daily, dinner Tue-Sat) Slick and modern GPO has an airy dining room and inner-city style. The food here is big on flavour. Corn, crab and chilli chowder comes with a polenta muffin, or try a gourmet burger.

Bon Amici (☎ 4632 4533; 191 Margaret St; light meals $4-10; ☒ 8am-late) Join Toowoomba's culture vultures at this sophisticated, red-walled café for delectable cakes, a stiff drink or a good coffee. Live music, poetry and jazz fill the afternoon and evening schedule.

Bindi Spot (☎ 4638 0044; 164 Margaret St; mains $12.50-18; ☒ lunch & dinner) This popular Indian joint dishes up colourful curries, an array of dependably good dishes, and some tasty standouts such as salmon steak served with pomegranate chutney and mango salsa.

TOOWOOMBA TO ROMA

About 45km west of Toowoomba, is the historic **Jondaryan Woolshed Complex** (☎ 07-4692 2229; www.jondaryanwoolshed.com; Evanslea Rd; adult/ child self-guided $9/5, guided $13/8; ☒ 9am-4pm, tours 1pm Wed-Fri, 10.30am & 1pm Sat, Sun & school holidays). A large complex with rustic old buildings, antique farm and industrial machinery, period displays, and daily blacksmithing and shearing demonstrations. You can stay in the basic **shearers quarters** (adult/child $12/6) or **camp** (up to 4 people $10).

A further 167km west in Miles is **Dogwood Crossing** (☎ 07-4627 2455; ☒ 8.30am-5pm Mon-Fri, 9am-4pm Sat & Sun), a $1.6 million dollar community project which combines visual arts, social history and literature into a museum, gallery, library and multimedia resource centre. Nearby, the excellent **Miles Historical Village** (☎ 07-4627 1492; Murilla St; adult/child/family $10/2/20; ☒ 8am-5pm) is well worth a visit.

You can bed down in a refurbished, underground bunker at **Possum Park** (☎ 07-4627 1651; Leichardt Hwy; s/d $55/60), where munitions were stored during WWII as part of Australia's prepared last line of defence against the advancing Japanese.

ROMA

☎ 07 / pop 5900

An early Queensland settlement, and now the centre of a sheep and cattle-raising district, Roma also has some curious small industries. There's enough oil in the area to support a small refinery, but the gas deposits are larger and Roma contributes to Brisbane's supply through a 450km pipeline.

The major landmark is the **Big Rig Complex** (☎ 4622 4355; www.thebigrig.com.au; Warrego Hwy; adult/ child $14/9, combined entry & night show $25/15; ☒ 9am-5pm, night show at 7pm), a museum of oil and gas exploration centred on the old, steam-operated oil rig at the eastern edge of town. There's also a nightly sound and light show. Inside the complex, the **visitor information centre** (☎ 1800 222 399; Warrego Hwy; ☒ 9am-5pm) can help with accommodation if you're stopping en route to the Carnarvon Gorge (p374).

FRASER COAST

In stark contrast to the heady 'coasts' further south, Queensland's Fraser Coast opens up to reveal a sparsely populated shoreline, backed by rural flavours and oceans of green space. The interior is peppered with towns steeped in history and the coast is thick with national parks.

The undeniable lure in this region is enigmatic Fraser Island; if you have even the slightest taste for bushwalking, 4WD driving and scenery ranging from dense rainforests to vast beaches, this destination is a must. Mellow Hervey Bay is the major access point for the island, but you can also get there from the tiny and picturesque fishing resort of Rainbow Beach. From July to October whales inundate the area to chill out before continuing their trek south to Antarctica.

By the time you reach Bundaberg further north, you've entered a region of sugar cane, rum and coral. Fruit-picking jobs also bring working travellers to this town.

GYMPIE

☎ 07 / pop 10,600

Gympie is a peaceful little town which played an important role in Queensland's history, thanks to its once-rich gold deposits. Most mining stopped in the 1920s, but the town is a lovely place to stretch the legs and encounter a whiff of rural Queensland.

It's worth dropping into the **Cooloola Shire Public Gallery** (☎ 5482 0733; 39 Nash St; admission free; ☒ 10am-4pm Wed-Fri, 11am-4pm Sat & Sun). Set in a big two-storey Queenslander, it displays temporary exhibits of Australian art, with a third of the gallery devoted to local works.

The principal reminder of Gympie's illustrious past is the **Gympie Gold Mining & Historical Museum** (☎ 5482 3995; 215 Brisbane Rd; adult/child/family $8.80/4.40/24; ⏱ 9am-4.30pm), which holds a diverse collection of mining equipment and steam engines. There's also a week-long **Gold Rush Festival** every October.

Just north of Gympie lies the well-curated **Woodworks Forestry & Timber Museum** (☎ 5483 7691; cnr Fraser Rd & Bruce Hwy; adult/student $4/2; ⏱ 9am-4pm Mon-Fri, 1-4pm Sun). One highlight is the cross-section of a huge bunya pine that lived through the Middle Ages, Columbus' discovery of America and the industrial revolution, only to be felled in the early 20th century.

There are three offices of the helpful **Cooloola Regional Development Bureau** (www.cooloola.org.au; Matilda ☎ 5483 5554; Matilda Service Centre, Bruce Hwy; ⏱ 9am-5pm; Lake Alford ☎ 5483 6411; Bruce Hwy, Gympie; ⏱ 8.30am-4pm; Gympie ☎ 5483 6656; 224 Mary St, Gympie; ⏱ 9am-5pm). Gympie has several motels and caravan parks, and it's on the main bus and train routes north from Brisbane.

RAINBOW BEACH
☎ 07 / pop 1050

Unspoilt and exceedingly laid-back, Rainbow Beach is named after a spectacular set of multicoloured cliffs. It's a smidgeon of a town and greets weary travellers like the pot of gold at the end of a rainbow. The pandanus tree–lined beaches and red-hued cliffs arc round Wide Bay, offering a sweeping panorama from the lighthouse at Double Island Point in the south to Fraser Island in the north.

The view from the Carlo Sandblow, a 120m-high dune on the hill overlooking this tiny town, has been known to make the most cynical sightseer gasp.

Information

QPWS Office (☎ 5486 3160; Rainbow Beach Rd; ⏱ 7am-4pm) Permits for Fraser Island.

Rainbow Beach visitors centre (☎ 5486 3227; 8 Rainbow Beach Rd; ⏱ 7am-6pm) Privately run and moderately helpful.

Rainbow Photographics (☎ 5486 8777; 12 Rainbow Beach Rd; per hr $4; ⏱ 9am-5pm Mon-Fri, 9am-3pm Sat, 9am-noon Sun) Internet access.

Activities

For those not wishing to hire a 4WD (p350), **Surf & Sand Safaris** (☎ 5486 3131; www.surfandsand safaris.com.au; per adult/child $55/28) runs half-day 4WD tours south down the beach, taking in the lighthouse at Double Island Point and the *Cherry Venture*, a freighter that ran aground here in 1973.

Paragliding above the Carlo Sandblow, where the national championships are held every January, is an unforgettable experience. **Rainbow Paragliding** (☎ 5486 3048, 0418 754 157; per person $130) offers tandem glides for those with the gumption.

Surfing is popular, as is scuba diving at Wolf Rock off Double Island Point, where you'll find gropers, turtles, manta rays and harmless grey nurse sharks. The **Wolf Rock Dive Centre** (☎ 5486 8004; wolfrockdive@bigpond.com) offers four-day PADI courses ($360) here.

Tours

Backpackers can arrange a self-drive tour to Fraser Island (see p356) from Rainbow Beach at **Dingo's Backpacker's Resort** (☎ 1800 111 126, 5486 8200; www.dingosatrainbow.com).

Sleeping & Eating

Rainbow Sands Holiday Units (☎ 5486 3400; fax 5486 3492; 42-46 Rainbow Beach Rd; d $80-100; ❄ ⚓) This low-rise, palm-fronted complex has neat and appealing motel rooms with poolside glass doors and bar fridges, or self-contained units with full laundries for comfortable longer stays. The owners are utterly genuine and helpful.

Rainbow Shores Resort (☎ 5486 3999; www.rainbowshores.com.au; 12 Rainbow Shores Dr; r from $115; ❄ ⚓) If you like a little luxury with your beach you've hit the jackpot with this sprawling resort. Accommodation options include standard holiday units, funky three-bedroom beach houses and polished split-level villas. On site is a nine-hole golf course, BBQs, children's playground, restaurant and plenty of bush.

Frasers on Rainbow YHA (☎ 1800 100 170, 5486 8885; bookings@frasersonrainbow.com; 18 Spectrum St; dm/d from $20/55; ❄ 🖳) In a nicely converted motel, this hostel has roomy dorms with fabulously comfy beds. Locals join travellers at the sprawling outdoor bar at night, but it won't stop you from getting a good night's sleep.

Rainbow Beach Hotel (☎ 5486 3125; 1 Rainbow Beach Rd; mains $15-25; ⏱ breakfast Sat & Sun, lunch &

dinner daily) The smoky public bar at this pub is a great spot to mingle with the locals, while the front beer garden and bistro are quiet and classy. A typical pub menu offers fresh fish alongside juicy steaks, calamari and chicken dishes.

Also recommended:

Rainbow Beach Holiday Village (☎ 1300 366 596, 5486 3222; www.beach-village.com; powered/unpowered sites per 2 people from $22/20, cabins from $90; 🈺 🖳) Excellent caravan park set in a small jungle.

Dingo's Backpacker's Resort (☎ 1800 111 126, 5486 8200; www.dingosatrainbow.com; 3 Spectrum Ave; dm/d $20/50; 🈺 🖳 🖳) Backpackers' menagerie with reasonable dorms and a festive bar.

Archie's (☎ 5486 3277; 12 Rainbow Beach Rd; mains $5.50-15; ☺ breakfast, lunch & dinner) Great takeaway.

To play castaway, get a permit from the QPWS (p349) and set up camp in one of the paradisiacal grounds along Inskip Point – Sarawak, Beagle, Natone or Dorrigo.

Getting There & Around

Greyhound Australia (☎ 13 14 99; www.greyhound .com.au) and **Premier Motor Service** (☎ 13 34 10; www.premierms.com.au) have daily services from Brisbane ($35, 5½ hours).

With a 4WD it's possible to drive south along the beach through the Cooloola section of the Great Sandy National Park (p343) to Noosa, or head for Fraser Island.

Aussie Adventure 4WD Hire (☎ 5486 3599; 4/54 Rainbow Beach Rd) and **Safari 4wd** (☎ 1800 689 819, 5486 8188; 3 Karoonda Ct) offer 4WD vehicle hire from $120 to $175 per day. For ferry details, see p358.

MARYBOROUGH
☎ 07 / pop 21,200

Known as 'the heritage town', Maryborough's streets brim with exquisitely maintained timber Queenslanders, which are an attraction unto themselves. Junk browsers will love the National Trust–classified **Brennan & Geraghty's Store** (☎ 4121 2250; 64 Lennox St; adult/child/family $5/3.5/12; ☺ 10am-3pm), which traded for 100 years before becoming a museum. It's filled with tins, bottles and packets, including early Vegemite jars and curry powder from the 1890s, all crammed onto the ceiling-high shelves.

The excellent **Maryborough visitor information centre** (☎ 4121 4111; City Hall, Kent St; ☺ 9am-5pm Mon-Fri) is staffed by knowledgeable locals.

There are several motels and caravan parks in the town, plus budget accommodation in some of the old hotels.

HERVEY BAY
☎ 07 / pop 36,100

You need to see the 10km stretch of idyllic beach for yourself to appreciate why Hervey Bay is such a popular holiday destination. The outskirts of the town are stymied by an industrial jungle, but this concrete sea dissolves quickly into a subdued suburban spread, which rubs shoulders with a flawless shoreline. Hervey Bay's infrastructure makes it the most popular launching pad to Fraser Island, but the town is populated by affable locals and it is a pleasant spot to hang out for a few days. Every year this notion is exemplified by the magnificent humpback whales, which churn in and tune out in the bay's tranquil waters. This spectacular sight complimented by sublime swimming, fishing and other water-related activities, lures Queensland families by the campervanload. It seems many have been coming for so long they've not bothered to leave and the town has a healthy percentage of retirees among its permanent population.

Information

There is only one official tourist office, but numerous booking agents in town also give out tourist information.

Adventure Travel Centre (☎ 1800 554 400, 4125 9288; 410 The Esplanade, Torquay; per hr $4; ☺ 7am-10pm) Internet access and booking agent.

Hervey Bay Tourism & Development Bureau (☎ 1800 811 728; www.herveybaytourism.com.au; cnr Urraween & Maryborough Rds; ☺ 8.30am-5pm Mon-Fri, 10am-4pm Sat & Sun) Helpful and professional tourist office on the outskirts of town.

Post Office (☎ 4125 1101; 414 The Esplanade, Torquay)

Whale Watch Tourist Centre (☎ 1800 358 595; Urangan Marina, Urangan; ☺ 9am-5pm) Privately run.

Sights

Hervey Bay is mostly about activities, but there are also a handful of attractions.

Reef World (☎ 4128 9828; Pulgul St, Urangan; adult/child $14/8, shark dives $50; ☺ 9.30am-5pm) is a small aquarium featuring some of the Great Barrier Reef's most colourful characters. You can get nose to nose with the fish and coral through glass, but the resident turtles reputedly love a good pat on the back. You

---

A WHALE OF A TIME

Viewed in the flesh, humpback whales certainly surpass anything watched in a nature documentary. Up to 15m in length and 40 tonnes in weight, they're majestic and awe-inspiring – and seen regularly around the waters of Hervey Bay.

Up to 3000 humpbacks (*Megaptera novaeangliae*) enter the bay between the last week of July and the end of October. They come to hang out in the sheltered waters to escape predators and rest before continuing their arduous migration south to Antarctica. Having mated and given birth in the north, they arrive in Hervey Bay in groups of about a dozen (known as pulses), before splitting into smaller groups of two or three (pods).

Their annual trek has endowed the whales with a surprising tolerance for spectators in the bay and it appears many indulge in extended bouts of showmanship to exact astounded ooohs and ahhs from above the water. You may see the same whale cruise around a boat for several hours before it breaks into a spontaneous bout of jumping and tail flipping. Young whales often mimic their mothers' antics, producing adorable half-jumps and almost-flips. Whales are also curious creatures and some even roll up beside the numerous whale-watching boats with one eye clear of the water, making those on board wonder who's actually watching whom.

---

can also take a dip with lemon, whaler and other nonpredatory sharks.

Run by the Korrawinga Aboriginal Community, the **Scrub Hill Community Farm** (☎ 4124 6908; Scrub Hill Rd; tours per adult/child/family $16.50/5.50/33; ☺ by appointment) produces organic vegetables, tea tree oil and excellent artworks, including didgeridoos. The guided tours offered (call ahead to arrange) detail how the farm operates.

For a dose of the region's history, potter through the cluttered but interesting **Hervey Bay Historical Museum** (☎ 4128 1064; 13 Zephyr St, Scarness; adult/child $2.50/50c; ☺ 1-5pm Fri-Sun), which encompasses several buildings and includes thousands of items.

Another worthwhile amble is through Hervey Bay's pretty **Botanic Gardens** (Elizabeth St, Urangan), which are a lush mix of small lagoons, dense foliage and walking tracks.

Activities

WHALE- & DOLPHIN-WATCHING

Between mid-July and late October, whale-watching tours operate out of Hervey Bay daily – weather permitting. Sightings are guaranteed from 1 August to 1 November, when you get a free subsequent trip if the whales don't show.

The boats cruise from the Urangan Harbour out to Platypus Bay and then zip around from pod to pod to find the most active whales. Most vessels offer half-day (four-hour) tours including lunch, that cost from $80 to $95 for adults and $45 to $65 for children. The larger boats run ¾-day trips

and the amenities are better, but they take around two hours to reach Platypus Bay.

Among the many available tours:

MV Tasman Venture (☎ 1800 620 322; www.tasman venture.com.au; ☺ tours 8.30am & 1.30pm) Maximum of 80 passengers, underwater microphones and viewing windows.

Spirit of Hervey Bay (☎ 1800 642 544, 4125 5131; www.spiritofherveybay.com; ☺ tours 8.30am & 1.30pm) Large vessel with underwater viewing rooms. Maximum 150 passengers.

Quick Cat II (☎ 1800 671 977, 4128 9611; www.hervey baywhalewatch.com.au; ☺ tours 8am & 1pm) Underwater cameras, maximum of 80 passengers and wheelchair accessible.

Whalesong (☎ 1800 689 610, 4125 6222; whalesong@ bigpond.com; ☺ tours 7.30am & 1pm) Maximum of 70 passengers. Caters to traveller with disabilities.

FISHING

The fishing in and around Hervey Bay is excellent and numerous vessels operate fishing safaris. **SilverStar Fishing Charters** (☎ 4128 9778; silverstar_fishing@bigpond.com; full day person $150) and **MV Fighting Whiting** (☎ 4124 6599; adult/child/family incl lunch $55/30/150) offer calm-water fishing trips that run for around eight hours. These also leave from Urangan Harbour.

Tours

Hervey Bay offers plenty of self-drive back-packer tours to Fraser Island. For more information see the boxed text, p356.

Hostels offering tours:

A1 Fraser Roving (☎ 1800 989 811, 4125 6386; www .fraserroving.com.au)

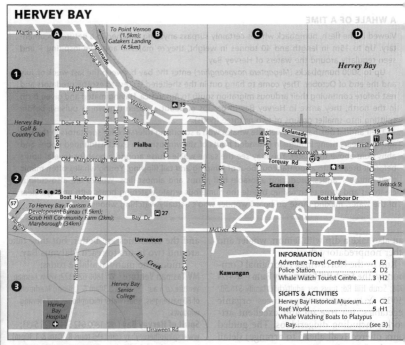

HERVEY BAY

INFORMATION	
Adventure Travel Centre	1 E2
Police Station	2 D2
Whale Watch Tourist Centre	3 H2

SIGHTS & ACTIVITIES	
Hervey Bay Historical Museum	4 C2
Reef World	5 H1
Whale Watching Boats to Platypus Bay	(see 3)

Colonial Log Cabins (☎ 1800 818 280, 4125 1844; www.coloniallogcabins.com)

Koala Beach Resort (☎ 1800 354 535, 4125 3601; www.koala-backpackers.com)

Sleeping
BUDGET
Most of the vast number of Hervey Bay hostels do pick-ups from the main bus stop, and organise trips to Fraser Island and other activities.

A1 Fraser Roving (☎ 1800 989 811, 4125 6386; www.fraserroving.com.au; 412 The Esplanade, Torquay; dm $20-25, d with/without bathroom $55/50; ☐ ☒) Friendly hostel has earned its place on the backpacker grapevine with utterly genuine owners, spartan but spotless dorms and an atmospheric bar. If you're after a quiet night there's plenty of space to buffer the noise. Good wheelchair facilities.

Colonial Log Cabins (☎ 1800 818 280, 4125 1844; www.coloniallogcabins.com; 820 Boat Harbour Dr, Urangan; dm $22, d & tw from $55, cabins from $80; ☒ ☐) Dorms, cabins and villas at this excellent YHA place are scattered throughout a tranquil pocket of bush in the 'burbs. Possums

and parrots entertain regularly and the con vivial bar and pool area give it a welcom ing vibe.

Other recommendations:

Happy Wanderer Village (☎ 1800 444 040, 4128 9048; hwanderer@hervey.com.au; 105 Truro St, Torquay; powered/unpowered sites per 2 people from $25/21, cabins from $50, villas from $85 ☒ ☒) Great range of accommodation. Wheelchair accessible.

Woolshed Backpackers (☎ 4124 0677; 181 Torquay Rd, Scarness; dm $17, d & tw $44) Small, private timber cottages.

Camping
Two appealing council-run caravan park along the Esplanade are **Pialba Beachfron Tourist Park** (☎ 4128 1399; www.beachfronttouris parks.com.au/parks/pialba.php; powered/unpowered site per 2 people from $22/17) and **Torquay Beachfron Tourist Park** (☎ 4125 1578; www.beachfronttouris parks.com.au/parks/torquay.php; powered/unpowered site per 2 people from $22/17).

MIDRANGE
Bay Bed & Breakfast (☎ 4125 6919; baybedandbrea fast@bigpond.com; 180 Cypress St, Urangan; s $65, d $95

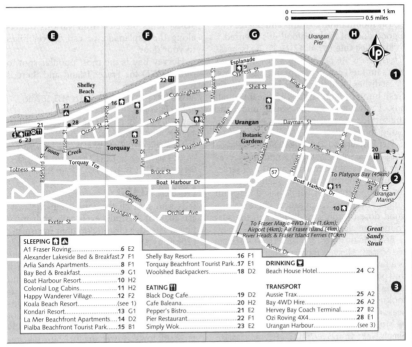

110;) Guests at this modern and comfortable B&B occupy cool rooms in a secluded annexe out the back. There's also a stylish share lounge, couches to sink into, guests' fridge, tea and coffee facilities and a lagoon-style saltwater pool outside.

La Mer Beachfront Apartments (1800 100 181, 4128 3494; www.lamer.com.au; 396 The Esplanade, Torquay; r per night/week $120/600;) Plenty of holiday units use the word luxury with creative licence, but La Mer comes up with the goods. Behind the generic façade are fresh and modern apartments with open plans and spanky new mod cons including full laundries, DVDs, cable TV and even coffee plungers!

Arlia Sands Apartments (4125 3778; www.arlia sands.com.au; 13 Ann St, Torquay; r $125;) This refurbished series of units contains plush furniture, wide-screen TVs, stereos and beautiful kitchens. They're the self-contained unit for the style cat and each has an ample balcony as well as a personal clothesline.

Boat Harbour Resort (4125 5079; www.boat harbourresort.com; 650 The Esplanade, Urangan; r $80-95;) This series of timber studios and two-bedroom villas all have mountain-flavoured exteriors, but they're bright and summery inside. The studios have sizable decks out the front and the roomy villas are great for families.

Kondari Resort (1800 072 131, 4128 9702; www .kondari.com.au; 49-63 Elizabeth St, Urangan; r $60-135;) Within this sprawling, low-rise resort are two pools, tennis courts, BBQs and a profusion of native bush. Rates start with simple and neat motel rooms, climb to bright studios, and peak at one-bedroom family villas. The style factor of each abode also increases with the tariff.

Also recommended:

Shelly Bay Resort (4125 4533; www.shellybayresort .com.au; 466 The Esplanade, Torquay; r $95-130;) Bold and cheerful units with sunkissed balconies.

Alexander Lakeside Bed & Breakfast (4128 9448; www.herveybaybedandbreakfast.com; 29 Lido Pde, Urangan; d/tr/f $105/120/140;) Quiet and friendly B&B.

Eating & Drinking

Cafe Baleana (4125 4799; Shop 7, Terminal Bldg, Buccaneer Ave, Urangan; mains $10-25; breakfast, lunch & dinner) Laid-back waterfront café that provides expensive views and atmosphere at wallet-friendly prices. The trendy menu boasts mountainous paninis and salads, with a good dose of fresh seafood. It's licensed.

Black Dog Cafe (☎ 4124 3177; 381 The Esplanade, Torquay; mains $10-20; ☽ lunch & dinner) Hervey Bay's funkiest eatery pumps out East-meets-West dishes including sushi, Japanese soups, fresh burgers, club sambos and seafood salads. There's a menu for 'young pups' and the service is so friendly you'll want to tip. Good for families.

Pier Restaurant (☎ 4128 9695; 573 The Esplanade, Urangan; mains $20-40; ☽ dinner) Arguably Hervey Bay's finest seafood restaurant, the Pier serves exquisite 'marine cuisine' such as mignon scallop kebabs, or whole baked fish with ginger and peppercorn sauce. There's also a good dose of nonfishy dishies and the surrounds are classy.

Beach House Hotel (☎ 4128 1233; 344 The Esplanade, Scarness) Hervey Bay's most relaxed pub is a favourite with loyal locals. Cable sports and pool tables entertain the stimulus-needy while ample tables accommodate those just looking for a quiet drink. The whole lot is seasoned nicely with sea breezes.

More eating options:

Simply Wok (☎ 4125 2077; 417 The Esplanade, Torquay; mains $7-15; ☽ breakfast, lunch & dinner; ⊠) Inventive sandwiches, salads, seafood and Asian cuisine.

Pepper's Bistro (☎ 4125 2266; 421 The Esplanade, Torquay; mains $10-20; ☽ lunch & dinner) Popular pub bistro.

Getting There & Away

Sunshine Express (☎ 13 13 13; www.sunshineexpress .com.au) has daily flights between Brisbane and Hervey Bay ($140). Hervey Bay airport is off Booral Rd, Urangan.

The **Queensland Rail** (☎ 1300 131 722; www.travel train.com.au) *Sunlander* ($55, five hours) and *Tilt Train* ($55, 3½ hours) connect Brisbane with Maryborough West, where a Trainlink bus ($5.90) transfers to Hervey Bay.

Hervey Bay is on a main bus route between Brisbane ($50, 5½ hours) and Rockhampton ($55, 5½ hours). **Wide Bay Transit** (☎ 4121 3719) has hourly services every weekday, with five on Saturday and three on Sunday, running between Maryborough and Hervey Bay marina ($5.90, 1½ hours).

Getting Around

Most places to stay will pick you up from the bus station if you call ahead.

Bay Bicycle Hire (☎ 0417 644 814; per half/full day $15/20) rents bicycles from various outlets along the Esplanade, or can deliver bikes to your door.

Hervey Bay is the most popular spot to hire a 4WD for Fraser Island and there is plenty of choice:

Aussie Trax (☎ 1800 062 275, 4124 4433; 56 Boat Harbour Dr, Pialba)

Bay 4WD Hire (☎ 1800 687 178, 4128 2981; www.bay 4wd.com.au; 52-54 Boat Harbour Dr, Pialba)

Fraser Magic 4WD Hire (☎ 4125 6612; www.fraser -magic-4wdhire.com.au; Lot 11, Kruger Court, Urangan)

Ozi Roving 4X4 (☎ 4125 6355; 10 Fraser St, Torquay)

FRASER ISLAND

It is said that all the sand from the eastern coast of Australia eventually ends up at Fraser Island, a gigantic sandbar measuring 120km by 15km and created by thousands of years of longshore drift. Seen from the coast this beautiful enigma appears too lush and green to be the world's biggest sand island, but the island's diverse ecology is one of the many wonders of the place. Rainforests and some 200 freshwater lakes dot the landscape, and dunes, known locally as 'sandblows', tower up to 224m tall, reminding you that the island contains more sand than the Sahara desert (allegedly). Offshore, whales, dolphins, sharks and turtles can often be seen from high points.

Coming here, there are certain essentials to know: 4WDs are necessary (see the boxed text, p356). The lakes are lovely to swim in, but the sea's lethal: undertows and man-eating sharks make it a definite no-go. And feeding the island's dingoes has made them increasingly aggressive in recent years (see the boxed text, p358).

Yet none of this detracts from the enjoyment of a location unlike any other on earth. If the dunes, the forests, the lakes, the birds and mammals aren't enough, gaze up at the night sky. With little light behind you, the Milky Way blazes bright.

History

Known to local Butchulla indigenous Australians as K'gari (Paradise), the island takes its European name from James and Eliza Fraser. The captain of the *Stirling Castle* and his wife were shipwrecked on the northwest coast in 1836. He died here, and she survived with help from the Aborigines.

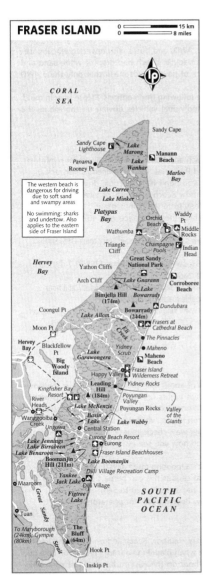

FRASER ISLAND

In the late 20th century the focus shifted from exploitation to protection. Sand mining ceased in 1975 and logging stopped in 1991, after the island was brought under the auspices of the QPWS, as part of the Great Sandy National Park. In 1993 native title was recognised and the island listed as a World Heritage area.

Information
General supplies and expensive fuel are available from stores at Cathedral Beach, Eurong, Kingfisher Bay, Happy Valley and Orchid Beach.

There are several ranger stations on the island:

Central Station (☎ 07-4127 9191; ☻ 10am-noon)
Dundubara (☎ 07-4127 9138; ☻ 8-9am)
Eurong (☎ 07-4127 9128; ☻ 10.30am-3.30pm Mon, 8am-3.30pm Tue-Thu, 8am-1pm Fri)
Waddy Point (☎ 07-4127 9190; ☻ 7am-8am & 4-4.30pm)

There are tow truck services at **Eurong** (☎ 07-4127 9188) and **Yidney Rocks** (☎ 07-4127 9167).

PERMITS
You'll need a permit for vehicles ($33) and camping (per person/family $4/16) and these must be purchased before you arrive; contact **QPWS** (☎ 13 13 04; www.epa.qld.gov.au) or purchase them from the following:
Bundaberg QPWS Office (☎ 07-4131 1600; 46 Quay St)
Naturally Queensland (Map pp296-7; ☎ 07-3227 7111; 160 Ann St, Brisbane; ☻ 8.30am-5pm Mon-Fri)
QPWS Great Sandy Information Centre (☎ 07-5449 7792; 240 Moorindil St, Tewantin; ☻ 7am-4pm)
Rainbow Beach QPWS Office (☎ 07-5486 3160; Rainbow Beach Rd; ☻ 7am-4pm) Permits for Fraser Island.
River Heads QPWS kiosk (☎ 4125 8485; ☻ 6.15-11.15am & 2-3.30pm)

Permits aren't required for the private camping grounds or resorts.

Sights & Activities
From the island's southern tip vehicles should use the high-tide access track between Hook Point and **Dilli Village**, rather than the beach. From here on, the eastern beach is the main thoroughfare. A short drive north of Dilli will take you to the resort at **Eurong**, the start of the inland track across to Central Station and Wanggoolba Creek (for the ferry to River Heads).

As European settlers awoke to the value of Fraser's timber, that same tribe of Aborigines was unfortunately displaced (although not without a fight) and tracts of rainforest were cleared in the search for turpentine (satinay), a waterproof wood prized by shipbuilders. The island was also mined for its mineral sand for many years.

QUEENSLAND

QUEENSLAND

NOTES FROM A SMALL ISLAND: EXPLORING FRASER

There's a sci-fi other-worldliness to Fraser Island, as 4WDs and buses with towering wheel bases and fat, chunky tyres all pull in to refuel against an idyllic beach backdrop of white sand and waving palm trees. The surfeit of sand and the lack of paved roads mean that only these 4WD vehicles can negotiate the island.

For most travellers transport comes down to the following three options. Please bear in mind, when choosing, that the greater the number of individual vehicles driving on the island, the greater the environmental damage.

Tours

Package tours leave from Hervey Bay, Rainbow Beach and Noosa and typically cover rainforests, Eli Creek, Lakes McKenzie and Wabby, the coloured Pinnacles and the *Maheno* shipwreck.

Advantages: Tours can be booked last-minute, you don't have to cook, drive…or think and you can jump on at Hervey Bay and return to Rainbow Beach or Noosa, or vice versa. You gain a much greater understanding of the island's ecology from the commentary.

Disadvantages: During peak season you could share the experience with 40 others.

Among the many:

Fraser Experience (☎ 1800 689 819, 07-4124 4244; www.safari4wdhire.com.au; 2-day tours $195) Small groups and more freedom regarding the itinerary.

Fraser Island Company (☎ 1800 063 933, 07-4125 3933; day tours adult/child from $105/60, 2-day tours from $195/140) Range of tours available, from small groups to coaches.

Fraser Venture (☎ 1800 249 122, 07-4125 4444, www.safari4wdhire.com.au; day tours adult/child from $105/55, 2-/3-day tours from $215/$305) Lively drivers and sizable coaches on strict schedules.

Kingfisher Bay Tours (☎ 1800 072 555, 07-4120 3353; www.kingfisherbay.com; Fraser Island; day tours per adult/child $125/65, 2-/3-day adventure tours per person from $230/305) Ranger-guided day tours in 4WDs. Multi-day tours targeted at 18 to 35 year olds.

Sand Island Safaris (☎ 1800 246 911; 3-day tours from $315) Well-regarded small group tours.

Self-drive Backpacker Tours

Hostels in Hervey Bay organise guests into groups of about nine per vehicle to drive their own convoy to the island and camp out, usually for two nights and three days. Some instruction about driving 4WD vehicles is given and drivers are nominated. Unfortunately, there have been complaints about dodgy vehicle-damage claims upon return, which can be quite costly. Booking through a local hostel reduces the risk of this. Either way, check your vehicle beforehand.

Advantages: Cheap! You get to choose when and how you see everything and if your group is good, even getting rained on is fun.

Disadvantages: If your group doesn't get along it's a looooong three days. Inexperienced drivers get bogged in sand all the time, although if it's not serious this can be part of the fun.

Rates hover around $140 and exclude food and fuel (usually $30 to $40).

See Tours under Hervey Bay (p351) and Rainbow Beach (p349) for operators.

4WD Vehicle Hire

Hire companies lease out 4WD vehicles in Hervey Bay, Rainbow Beach and on the island itself. A driving instruction video will usually be shown, but when planning your trip, reckon on covering 20km an hour on the inland tracks and 50km an hour on the eastern beach. Most companies will help arrange ferries and permits and hire camping gear.

Advantages: Complete freedom to roam the island, and escape the crowds.

Disadvantages: Having to drive in conditions where even experienced drivers often have difficulties, and being responsible for any vehicle damage.

Rates for multiple-day rentals start at around $120 per day for a Suzuki Sierra to $180 for a Landcruiser. If you want to hire while on the island, **Kingfisher Bay 4WD Hire** (☎ 07-4120 3366; Fraser Island) has a medium-sized fleet, from Suzuki Sierras to Landcruisers; all $195 per day. Also see Getting Around under Hervey Bay (p354) and Rainbow Beach (p349) for rental companies.

In the middle of the island is **Central Station**, the starting point for numerous walking trails. From signposted tracks head to the beautiful **Lakes McKenzie**, **Jennings**, **Birrabeen** and **Boomanjin**. Like many of Fraser's lakes, these are 'perched', formed by water accumulating on top of a thin impermeable layer of decaying twigs and leaves. They also join Iceland's famous Blue Lagoon as open-air beauty salons, where you can exfoliate your skin with the mineral sand and soften your hair in the clear water. Lake McKenzie is possibly the most spectacular, but Lake Birrabeen is also amazing, and usually less crowded.

About 4km north of Eurong along the beach is a signposted walking trail to **Lake Wabby**. An easier route is from the lookout on the inland track. Wabby is surrounded on three sides by eucalypt forest, while the fourth side is a massive sandblow, which is encroaching on the lake at a rate of about 3m a year. The lake is deceptively shallow and diving is dangerous – in recent years, several people have been paralysed by doing so. You can often find turtles and huge catfish in the eastern corner of the lake under the trees.

Driving north along the beach you'll pass **Happy Valley**, with many places to stay, and **Eli Creek**. After rainfall this becomes a fast-moving, crystal-clear waterway that will carry you effortlessly downstream. About 2km from Eli Creek is the wreck of the *Maheno*, a passenger liner that was blown ashore by a cyclone in 1935 while being towed to a Japanese scrap yard.

Roughly 5km north of the *Maheno* you'll find the **Pinnacles** – a section of coloured sand cliffs – and about 10km beyond, **Dundubara**. Then there's a 20km stretch of beach before you come to the rock outcrop of **Indian Head**, the best vantage point on the island. Sharks, manta rays, dolphins and (during the migration season) whales can often be spotted from the top of the headland.

From Indian Head the trail branches inland, passing the **Champagne Pools**, the only safe spot on the island for saltwater swimming. This inland road leads back to **Waddy Point** and **Orchid Beach**, the last settlement on the island. Many tracks north of this are closed for environmental protection. The 30km of beach up to **Sandy Cape**, the

northern tip, with its lighthouse, is off-limits to hire vehicles. The beach from Sandy Cape to Rooney Point is closed to all vehicles, as is the road from Orchid Beach to Platypus Bay.

Sleeping & Eating

Fraser Island Wilderness Retreat (☎ 07-4127 9144; www.fraserislandco.com.au; Happy Valley; d & tr $125-160, f $160-200, mains $10-20; ☻ breakfast, lunch & dinner; ☒) Small resort comprises a series of self-contained, timber lodges pocketed in tropical foliage. There's a rustic edge to them but they're a good, comfortable, midrange option. On site is a restaurant and shop.

Fraser Island Beachhouses (☎ 1800 626 230, 07-4127 9205; www.fraserislandbeachhouses.com.au; Eurong Second Valley; d per 2 nights $250-350, f per 2 nights from $400; ☒) This complex contains sunny, self-contained units kitted out with polished wood, cable TVs and ocean views. Rates start with studios and climb to $600 (per two nights) for six-bed beachfront houses. Low season attracts a two-night minimum stay and high season five nights.

Eurong Beach Resort (☎ 07-4127 9122; www.fraser-is.com; Eurong; r $100-170, mains $15-30; ☻ breakfast, lunch & dinner; ☒ ☒) Cheerful Eurong is the main resort on the east coast. The cheapest digs are in simple motel rooms and units, climbing in price to comfortable apartments and A-frame chalets. There's also a restaurant, lagoon-style pool and the popular Beach Bar.

Self-caterers should come well equipped, as supplies on the island are limited and pricey.

Other top-end options:

Sailfish on Fraser (☎ 07-4127 9494; www.sailfishonfraser.com.au; Happy Valley; d/f from $200/220; ☒) Sailfish is a plush and indulgent, 4½-star retreat.

Kingfisher Bay Resort (☎ 1800 072 555, 07-4120 3333; www.kingfisherbay.com; Kingfisher Bay; r from $270; ☒ ☒) This elegant eco-resort has smart hotel rooms, sophisticated 2- and 3-bedroom timber villas (three-night minimum from $820), restaurants, bars and shops.

CAMPING

The most developed **QPWS camp grounds** (per person/family $4/16), with coin-operated hot showers, toilets and barbecues are at Waddy Point, Dundubara and Central Station. Campers with vehicles can also use the more basic grounds at Lake Boomanjin, Lake Allom, and Ungowa and Wathumba on the

QUEENSLAND

DEADLY DINGOES

It's hard not to feel sorry for Lindy Chamberlain. If Australia had known in 1980 what it does now, perhaps her cry that 'A dingo's got my baby' would have been taken seriously and the Mt Isa mother might not have been convicted in Darwin for murder. Tragically, it took another death, of a nine-year-old Brisbane boy on Fraser Island in 2001, before the debate over whether Australia's native dogs are dangerous to humans was settled conclusively.

That fatal mauling at Waddy Point was the worst in an increasing number of attacks on Fraser in the preceding years. In response, around 30 of Fraser Island's estimated 160 dingoes were culled on the orders of the Queensland government, drawing condemnation from indigenous Australians and environmental groups. The saddest fact is that this event and the growing aggressiveness of the animals was surely brought about by tourists hand feeding or harassing the dingoes over the years.

There is now a minimum fine of $225 (and a maximum one of $3000!) for feeding dingoes or leaving food where it may attract them to camping grounds. The QPWS provides a leaflet on being 'Dingo Smart' in its Fraser Island information pack.

western coast. There is also a hikers-only camp ground at Lake McKenzie. Camping is permitted on designated stretches of the eastern beach (you also need a permit for these). Fires are prohibited except in communal fire rings at Waddy Point and Dundabara; you need to bring your own untreated, milled timber.

Two private camping grounds on the island are **Frasers at Cathedral Beach** (☎ 07-4127 9177; www.fraserislandco.com.au; Cathedral Beach; powered/unpowered sites per 2 people $28/18, cabins from $110), a spacious park with abundant grassy sites and excellent facilities; and **Dilli Village Recreation Camp** (☎ 07-4127 9130; Dilli Village; unpowered sites per 2 people $20, dm $20, cabins $100), which offers good camp sites and neat facilities.

Getting There & Away

Vehicle ferries connect Fraser Island to River Heads, about 10km south of Hervey Bay, or Inskip Point, near Rainbow Beach.

Fraser Venture (☎ 07-4125 4444; pedestrian/vehicle & 4 passengers return $18/115, additional passengers $6) makes the 30-minute crossing from River Heads to Wanggoolba Creek on the western coast of Fraser Island. It departs daily from River Heads at 9am, 10.15am and 3.30pm, returning at 9.30am, 2.30pm and 4pm. On Saturday there's an additional 7am service, which returns at 7.30am. This company also operates the **Fraser Dawn Vehicular Ferry** (pedestrian/vehicle & 4 passengers return $18/115, additional passengers $6) from the Urangan marina to Moon Point on Fraser Island.

Kingfisher Vehicular Ferry (☎ 1800 072 555, 07-4120 3333; pedestrian/vehicle & 4 passengers return $18/115) does the 45-minute crossing from River Heads to Kingfisher Bay, departing at 7.15am, 11am and 2.30pm, and returning at 8.30am, 1.30pm and 4pm. The **Kingfisher Fast Cat Passenger Ferry** (adult/child return $45/22) crosses between Urangan marina and Kingfisher Bay at 8.45am, noon and 4pm daily, returning at 7.40am, 10.30am, 2pm, 5pm and 8pm. There are additional services from Thursday to Sunday.

Coming from Rainbow Beach, **Rainbow Venture** (☎ 07-5486 3227; pedestrian/vehicle & 4 passengers return $10/60) and **Manta Ray** (☎ 0418 872 599; pedestrian/vehicle & 4 passengers return $10/60) both make the 15-minute crossing from Inskip Point to Hook Point on Fraser Island continuously from about 7am to 5.30pm.

Air Fraser Island (☎ 07-4125 3600) flies out of Hervey Bay airport and lands on the island's eastern beach.

CHILDERS

☎ 07 / pop 1500

Childers is an attractive strip of a town littered with heritage buildings that still thrive off the surrounding orchards. It is best known as a sure bet to earn some cash through fruit-picking work, but the town was marked indelibly by a devastating fire at the Palace Backpackers Hostel in June 2000, in which 15 backpackers died. There is now a beautiful memorial with extremely moving dedications to those who perished at the **Childers Palace Memorial Art Gallery and Information Centre** (☎ 4126 3886; ⏱ 9am-5pm

Mon-Fri, 9am-noon Sat & Sun), where you'll also find a good gallery.

Even if you're merely passing through, it's worth stopping at **Mammino** (☎ 4126 2880; 115 Lucketts Rd; ☿ 9am-6pm), whose macadamia-nut and other confectionery will leave you muttering a Homer Simpsonesque 'Mmmm, ice cream'. The company is just outside Childers; as you head along the Bruce Hwy to Bundaberg, turn left towards Woodgate.

If you are staying the night make a beeline for the **Three Big Fig Trees B&B** (☎ 4126 1838; www.the3bigfigtrees.com.au; 87 Hawes Rd; s/d $70/90), which sits atop a hill, commanding 360-degree views of the surrounding valleys. There's a range of purpose-built rooms, all in keeping with the house's heritage structure, and breakfast is a cracker!

Also recommended are **Avocado Motor Inn** (☎ 4126 1608; avocadomotorinn@bigpond.com; Bruce Hwy; r $56-65; ✖ ▓), which has comfortable and gleaming rooms, and **Palace Backpackers** (☎ 4126 2244; www.childersbackpackers.com; Churchill St; dm/d $25/60, per week $150/170; ✖), a new, modern hostel behind the site of the original.

BUNDABERG
☎ 07 / pop 44,550

Aside from the odd aesthetic alteration, this country town has remained relatively unaltered for the majority of its lifespan. The main strip, embellished with wide streets and swaying palms, is positively gracious and the suburban gridlock which extends outwards is still dominated by stoic old Queenslanders (that's the houses). From 'the hummock', the only hill in this flat landscape, the eye sees fields of waving sugar cane from Bundaberg to the coral-fringed coast.

'Bundy', as it's popularly known, attracts working backpackers with abundant work on the surrounding farms and orchards. But the town offers distractions for travellers of all ilk in the way of museums, spectacular gardens, scuba diving and the chance to see unbearably sweet turtles make their first stumble down the beach at nearby Mon Repos.

Information

Bundaberg visitors centre (☎ 1800 308 888; www .bundabergregion.info) 271 Bourbong St (☎ 1800 308 888, 4153 8888; ☿ 9am-5pm); 186 Bourbong St (☎ 4153 9289; ☿ 9am-5pm Mon-Fri, 9am-noon Sat & Sun)

Cosy Corner Internet Cafe (☎ 4153 5999; Barolin St; per hr $4; ☿ 8am-7pm Mon-Fri, 9am-5pm Sat, 11am-5pm Sun) Internet access.

QPWS Office (☎ 4131 1600; 46 Quay St) Permits for Fraser Island.

Sights

The **Botanic Gardens** (Mt Perry Rd; ☿ 5.30am-6.45pm Sep-Apr, 6am-6.30pm May-Aug), 2km north of the centre, are splendid. Their vast grounds are a network of lakes and small islands populated by colonies of ibises and geese. Within the reserve are three museums.

The **Hinkler House Museum** (☎ 4152 0222; adult/child $5/2.50; ☿ 10am-4pm) is devoted to Bundaberg's most famous son, the aviator Bert Hinkler; in 1928 he made the first solo flight between England and Australia.

Nearby, the interesting **Bundaberg & District Historical Museum** (☎ 4152 0101; adult/child $4/2; ☿ 10am-4pm) has plenty of antiques in a colonial-era setup.

At the park's southern end, the **Fairymead House Sugar Museum** (☎ 4153 6786; adult/child $4/2; ☿ 10am-4pm) has good displays about the sugar industry, including some frank displays on hardships endured by Kanaka workers.

The **Bundaberg Arts Centre** (☎ 4152 3700; www .bundaberg.qld.gov.au/arts; cnr Barolin & Quay Sts; admission free; ☿ 10am-5pm Tue-Fri, 11am-3pm Sat & Sun) displays temporary exhibits of Australian art. The works are eclectic, often using mixed media, and demonstrate considerable talent.

Bundaberg's biggest claim to fame in Australia is the iconic Bundaberg rum. You can see the vats where the sugary gold is made at the **Bundaberg Rum Distillery** (☎ 4131 2999; www .bundabergrum.com.au; Avenue St; adult/child $9.90/4.40; ☿ 1hr tours 10am-3pm Mon-Fri, 10am-2pm Sat & Sun). Tours follow the rum's production from start to finish and, if you're old enough (18), you get to sample the final product.

Activities

About 16km east of Bundaberg the small beach hamlet of Bargara entices divers and snorkellers with a dazzling bank of coral near the Barolin Rocks and in the Woongarra Marine Park. **Salty's** (☎ 1800 625 476, 4151 6422; www.saltys.net; 208 Bourbong St) and **Bundaberg Aqua Scuba** (☎ 4153 5761; www.aquascuba.com; Shop 1, 66 Targo St) both offer four-day, PADI open-water diving courses, which cost $170/245 for shore/open-water dives.

QUEENSLAND

QUEENSLAND

TALKING TURTLE

You almost expect to hear the hushed commentary of wildlife programme–maker David Attenborough during the egg-laying and hatching at Mon Repos, Australia's most accessible turtle rookery. But on this beach, 15km northeast of Bundaberg, it's no disappointment to be accompanied instead by the knowledgeable staff from the **EPA visitors centre** (☎ 07-4159 1652; ⏱ 7.30am-4pm Mon-Fri). From November to late March, when loggerhead and other marine turtles drag themselves up the beach to lay their eggs, and young then emerge, the office organises ranger-guided **tours** (adult/child/family $5.50/3/13; ⏱ 7pm-midnight). Bookings are mandatory through the Bundaberg visitors centre (p359). Alternatively, go with the highly recommended **Footprints Adventures** (☎ 07-4152 3659; www.footprints adventures.com.au; adult/child incl transfers $50/25).Either way, take warm clothing, rain protection and insect repellent.

Tours

Bundaberg Ferry Company (☎ 4152 9188; Quay St; adult/child/family $20/13/60; ⏱ 9.30am & 1.30pm) Operates pleasant 2½-hr river cruises aboard the *Bundy Belle*, an old-fashioned ferry.

Lady Musgrave Barrier Reef Cruises (☎ 1800 072 110, 4159 4519; www.lmcruises.com.au; Shop 1, Bundaberg Port Marina, Port Bundaberg; adult/child incl lunch $140/75) If you wish to snorkel among coral off one of the magnificent Southern Reef Islands (opposite), this company has day trips to Lady Musgrave Island. Cruises leave on Monday, Tuesday, Thursday, Saturday and Sunday at 7.45am, returning to the Marina at 6pm. Transfers to camp on the island cost $280/150 per adult/child.

Sleeping

Robbie's Place (☎ 4152 7511; www.babs.com.au/robbies place; 109 Woongarra St; d incl breakfast $100, f $120; 🏊 🖵) Guests at this lovely B&B occupy a stylish timber extension, which contains mock-period bedrooms, a new kitchen, lounge room with stereo and cable TV, and a large balcony with private BBQ. Families and groups can rent the whole lot out on a room-only basis.

Country Comfort Bundaberg (☎ 4151 2365; www .countrycomforthotels.com; 73 Takalvan St; d $95; 🏊 🖵) Bundaberg's most comfortable motel has enough space to make you feel like the only

sardine in the tin. The décor is a little dated but the rooms see plenty of sunlight and the bathrooms positively glisten.

Oscar Motel (☎ 4152 3666; oscarmotel@hotmail .com; 252 Bourbong St; d $71-85; 🏊 🖵) This reliable motel has a good range of rooms, from small and functional to utterly cavernous. All have cable TV and the proud and professional owners keep the whole place spotless.

Bundaberg Backpackers & Travellers Lodge (☎ 4152 2080; fax 4151 3355; cnr Targo & Crofton Sts; dm per night/week $20/110; 🏊 🖵) Cloaked within a bland brick exterior, this hostel perpetuates a warm, cheerful buzz with helpful owners and a constant stream of working travellers. Little extras like dressers in the dorms and oodles of couches create a homely environment.

Also recommended:

Lyelta Lodge & Motel (☎ 4151 3344; 8 Maryborough St; s/d $50/55, without bathroom $35/47) Clean and practical motel-cum-hostel.

Alexandra Park Motor Inn (☎ 1800 803 419, 4152 7255; alex.parkmotorinn@bigpond.com; 66 Quay St; d $85-95; 🏊 🖵) Quiet motel with standard and self-contained rooms.

Eating

Les Chefs (☎ 4153 1770; 238 Bourbong St; mains $20; ⏱ lunch Mon-Fri, dinner daily) One for the carnivores, this upscale and intimate restaurant goes global, treating diners to duck, veal, seafood, chicken and beef dishes á la Nepal, Mexico, France, India and more. It comes highly recommended by locals so dinner bookings are recommended.

Indulge (☎ 4154 2344; 80 Bourbong St; dishes $8-14; ⏱ breakfast & lunch) With a sophisticated ambience and intoxicating pastries, this narrow café adds a sliver of Europe to Bundaberg's main drag. Fancy brekkies and lunches are also on the menu and it all goes down well with a fresh coffee.

Talking Point Cafe (☎ 4152 1811; 79 Bourbong St; dishes $5-10; ⏱ breakfast & lunch) This inviting café keeps things uncomplicated, serving up great-value paninis, focaccias, soups and coffee. The couches by the front window can be difficult to climb out of, so you'll just have to stay for cake.

Good pub grub at good prices is up for grabs at the bistros at the **Grand Central Hotel** (☎ 4151 2441; 81 Bourbong St; mains $9-19) and the **Club Hotel** (☎ 4151 3262; cnr Tantitha & Bourbong Sts; mains $8-12; ⏱ lunch & dinner).

Other options:

IGA Supermarket (Woongarra St) For self-caterers.

Spices Plus (☎ 4154 3320; 1 Targo St; dishes $8-14; ☽ dinner) Authentic Indian food served inside the beautiful old Union Bank building.

Entertainment

Moncrieff Theatre (☎ 4153 1985; 177 Bourbong St) This big, old, one-screen cinema shows several films daily.

Getting There & Away

QantasLink (☎ 13 13 13; www.qantas.com.au) flies to Bundaberg several times a day from Brisbane ($135).

The main bus stop in Bundaberg is **Stewart's Coach Terminal** (☎ 4153 2646; 66 Targo St). **Greyhound Australia** (☎ 13 14 99; www.greyhound. com.au) and **Premier Motor Service** (☎ 13 34 10; www.premierms.com.au) have daily services between Bundaberg and Brisbane ($65, seven hours), Hervey Bay ($25, 1½ hours), Rockhampton ($55, four hours) and Gladstone ($45, 2½ hours).

The **Queensland Rail** (☎ 1300 131 722; www.traveltrain.com.au) *Sunlander* ($60, seven hours) and *Tilt Train* ($60, five hours) both make the journey from Brisbane to Bundaberg on their respective routes to Cairns and Rockhampton.

**DIVING IN QUEENSLAND –
FIVE OF THE BEST**

Green Island (p431) The entirety of Green Island is national park, made up of dense rainforest. The fringing reefs surrounding it are considered to be among the most beautiful off any island and the diving and snorkelling are quite spectacular.

Heron Island (p363) This exclusive and tranquil coral cay sits amid a huge spread of reef. You can step straight off the beach and join a crowd of colourful fish here.

Lady Elliot Island (p362) The most southerly of the Great Barrier Reef islands, and also a coral cay. It's home to 19 highly-regarded dive sites, so it's hard to know where to begin.

Lizard Island (p453) Remote and rugged, Lizard Island boasts what are arguably Australia's best-known dive sites – Cod Hole, famous for its resident giant and docile potato cod, and Pixie Bommie.

SS Yongala (p402) This eerie shipwreck has resided on the ocean shore since 1911, and now teems with marine life.

AROUND BUNDABERG

In many people's eyes, the beach hamlets around Bundaberg are more attractive than the town itself. Some 25km north is **Moore Park**, with wide, flat beaches. Some 16km east lies **Bargara**, a picturesque spot drawing increasing numbers of tourists who come for the seaside golf. Families find Bargara attractive for both the turtle-shaped playground on its main foreshore and for the sheltered swimming areas for kids at Kellys Beach.

Bargara Beach Dive (☎ 07-4159 2663; www.bargaradive.com; Shop 4, 16 See St) operates open-water dive courses with small classes for $300.

Bargara Shoreline Apartments (☎ 07-4159 1180; www.shorelineapartments.com.au; 104 Miller St, Bargara; d $75-90, 1-/2-bedroom apt $100/140; ⚄ ⚄) has clean and simple motel rooms as well as bright and breezy one and two-bedroom apartments.

The fabulous **Kacy's Restaurant and Bar** (☎ 07-4130 1100; cnr See & Bauer Sts; mains $10-25; ☽ lunch & dinner) at the Bargara Beach Hotel, is like a South Pacific oasis. Sitting on the capacious deck you can choose from New Orleans gumbo, Thai curry prawns and bugs done any way you please from the huge menu.

CAPRICORN COAST

It's called that because this coastal stretch of Queensland straddles the tropic of Capricorn. Latitude 23.5 South passes through Rockhampton, the area's major hub and Australia's brash beef-farming capital, where oversized bulls greet the visitor and raging bulls are ridden by locals. The region has a surprisingly diverse collection of environments; tropical isles such as Heron and Lady Elliot, which offer some of the best diving and snorkelling on the entire Great Barrier Reef, a fertile hinterland supporting grazing and cropping, rugged national parks and Queensland's best fossicking sites for gemstones, particularly sapphires.

SOUTHERN REEF ISLANDS

The southernmost 'Capricornia' section of the Great Barrier Reef begins 80km northeast of Bundaberg around Lady Elliot Island and continues 140km northwards to Tryon Island, east of Rockhampton. The cays here are fairly expensive to reach, but you'll be

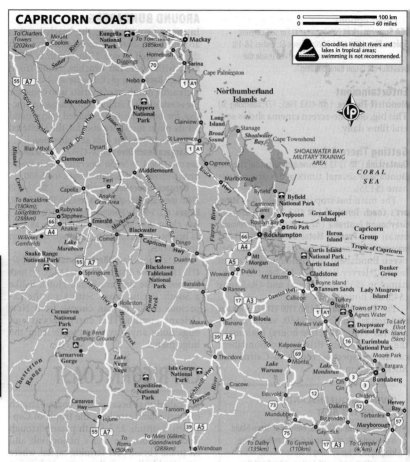

CAPRICORN COAST

Crocodiles inhabit rivers and lakes in tropical areas; swimming is not recommended.

rewarded with a Robinson Crusoe–style quiet, plus excellent snorkelling and diving among relatively untouched coral. Access is mainly from Bundaberg, Gladstone, Hervey Bay or the Town of 1770.

Lady Elliot Island

This 40-hectare vegetated coral island is possibly the region's most beautiful, with superb diving straight off the beach, as well as numerous shipwrecks, coral gardens, bommies (submerged rock) and blowholes. It's perfect for those who suffer seasickness (but not for nervous fliers) as it's reached by light plane.

Lady Elliot Island Resort (☎ 1800 072 200; www .ladyelliot.com.au; s/d tents $220/290, s/d incl breakfast &

dinner from $250/390) is a no-frills resort, which justifies its rates with vivid underwater scenery. There are basic tent cabins, simple motel-style units and self-contained suites with two bedrooms.

Scenic Air (book through the resort) flies guests to the resort from Bundaberg and Hervey Bay for $175/90 return per adult/child.

Lady Musgrave Island

This 15-hectare cay is an uninhabited national park about 100km north of Bundaberg. Surrounded by an aqua-blue lagoon, it's a popular destination for coral-spotting day trippers, and a desert-island camp for those on diving and snorkelling retreats.

The island also has a dense canopy of piso-nia forest, which brims with terns, shear-waters and white-capped noddies during nesting. The birds nest from October to April, and green turtles nest from Novem-ber to February.

A **QPWS camping ground** (per person/family $4/16) lies on the island's west side, with bush toi-lets and little else. Campers need a permit and to be totally self-sufficient, even bring-ing their own water. Numbers are limited to 40 at any one time, so apply well ahead for a permit at the Gladstone **QPWS office** (☎ 07-4971 6500; www.epa.qld.gov.au; 136 Goondoon St).

Lady Musgrave Barrier Reef Cruises op-erates day trips from Bundaberg; see p360 for more information.

Heron & Wilson Islands

Heron Island is a true coral cay, densely vegetated with pisonia trees and surrounded by 24 sq km of reef. There's a resort and research station on the northeastern third of the island – the remainder is national park. It is famed for superb scuba diving and snorkelling.

Heron Island Resort (☎ 07-4972 9055, 1800 737 678; www.heronisland.com; s/d from $350/480) covers the northeastern third of the island. Its com-fortable accommodation is suited to families and couples – the Point Suites have the best views. Prices include all meals, but guests will pay $180/90 per adult/child for launch transfer, or $495/248 for helicopter transfer. Both are from Gladstone.

Wilson Island (www.wilsonisland.com; 5 nights s/d from $2600/4000), also a national park, has been reinvented as an expensive wilderness re-treat with permanent tents. There are excel-lent beaches and superb snorkelling and all guests buy combined Wilson/Heron pack-ages of two nights on Heron and three on Wilson, with all meals included.

AGNES WATER & TOWN OF 1770

The twin coastal towns of Agnes Water and Town of 1770 are among Queensland's most appealing seaside destinations and rank among Australia's most talked-up, and bought-up, real estate. The popularity boom is kept in check by surrounding national parks, beaches and ocean, plus the location is a healthy distance from the beaten track.

The Town of 1770, 5km south of Agnes Water, is a little more laid-back than its sibling. The abundant shoreline and spec-tacular lookouts throughout the area lend themselves to stunning sunsets, which simply invite relaxation. Most people come here to do just that, along with a bout of fishing, boating or visiting the neighbour-ing national parks and southern cays of the Great Barrier Reef.

Information

Agnes Water Library (☎ 07-4902 1501; Rural Trans-action Centre, Round Hill Rd; $2.60 per 30mins; ☺ 9am-noon, 1-4pm) Internet access.

Agnes Water Visitor Information Centre (☎ 07-49 74 7002; Rural Transaction Centre, Round Hill Rd)

Discovery Centre (☎ 07-4974 7002; Shop 12, Endeav-our Plaza, cnr Round Hill Rd & Captain Cook Dr, Agnes Water) Privately run information service.

QPWS office (☎ 07-4974 9350; www.epa.qld.gov.au; Captain Cook Dr, Town of 1770)

Activities

Agnes Water is Queensland's northernmost **surf beach**. A surf life-saving club patrols the main beach and there are often good breaks along the coast. You can learn to surf with **Reef 2 Beach Surf School** (☎ 07-4974 9072; 1/10 Round Hill Rd, Agnes Water).

Round Hill Creek at the Town of 1770 provides a calm anchorage for **boats** and also offers good **fishing** and **mudcrabbing** up-stream. **1770 Marine Services** (☎ 07-4974 9227; per day/half-day $80/50) hires out aluminium dinghies. **Jetski 1770** (☎ 07-4974 7765) con-ducts jet-ski tours starting at $60 per half hour.

Tours

If you really need to get away from it all, try the unspoilt Fitzroy Reef Lagoon, a stunning coral outcrop on the Great Barrier Reef.

Recommended tour operators:

1770 Great Barrier Reef Cruises (☎ 07-4974 9077; Captain Cook Dr; adult/child incl lunch $130/65 plus $5 per person environment tax) Has excellent day trips to Lady Musgrave Island including snorkelling and fishing gear. Cruises depart the Town of 1770 marina. Island camping transfers are also available for $225 per person ($245 in school holidays).

1770 Holidays (☎ 07-4974 9422, 1800 177 011; www .1770holidays.com; 535 Captain Cook Dr; adult/child incl lunch $125/65 plus $5 per person environment tax; ☺ departs 8am) Operates day tours to Fitzroy Reef Lagoon including snorkelling (diving is a $65 optional extra). 1770 Holidays also runs enjoyable full-day tours in

QUEENSLAND

its *LARCs* (amphibious vehicles), taking in Middle Island, Bustard Head and Eurimbula National Park, costing $95/65 per adult/child including lunch, there are also daily one-hour sunset cruises ($22/12).

Sleeping & Eating

Beach Shacks (☎ /fax 07-4974 9463; beachshack@1770 .net; 578 Captain Cook Dr, Town of 1770; d from $150) Quite delightful self-contained 'shacks' are decorated in timber, cane and bamboo. They offer grand views and magnificent, private accommodation just a minute's walk from the water.

Hideaway (☎ /fax 07-4974 9144; thehideawaybb@ bigpond.com; 2510 Round Hill Rd; d incl breakfast $130; ☒) Immersed in an idyllic bush setting, just 4km west of Agnes Water, this colonial-style homestead has three luxurious double bedrooms with bathrooms, a lounge room, outdoor dining area and barbecue area.

Mango Tree Motel (☎ /fax 07-4974 9132; 7 Agnes St; s/d from $80/90; ☒) Only 100m from the beach, this motel offers large self-contained rooms (sleeping up to six per room) with the option of continental breakfasts. There's also a licensed restaurant.

Saltwater Café 1770 (☎ 07-4974 9599; Captain Cook Dr, Town of 1770; mains $10-26; ☺ lunch & dinner) This little salt-encrusted waterfront diner has plenty of charm and a bar. Choose between fish and chips or a delicious mud crab. Tuesday is pizza night and on Wednesday it's curry.

More accommodation:

Captain Cook Holiday Village (☎ 07-4974 9219; www.holidayvillage@bigpond.com; 385 Captain Cook Dr, Town of 1770; powered/unpowered sites per 2 people $19/16, dm bungalows $50, cabins from $75) Large, well-equipped park with a good restaurant.

Cool Bananas (☎ 1800 227 660; www.coolbananas.biz .com; 2 Springs Rd, Agnes Water; dm $22; ☐) Roomy dorms, and tropical gardens. Pick-ups from Bundaberg.

Getting There & Away

Greyhound Australia (☎ 13 14 99; www.greyhound .com.au) has one daily bus from Bundaberg ($24, 1½ hours). Other buses are met at Fingerboard Rd by a local **shuttle service** ('Macca' ☎ 07-4974 7540; $17).

GLADSTONE

☎ 07 / pop 27,660

Gladstone is one of the busiest ports in Australia, handling agricultural, mineral and coal exports from central Queensland. That it's an industrial town first and foremost can't be missed. The huge port with coal-and bauxite-loading terminals, oil tanks, the world's largest alumina refinery and a power station to represent a few of the town's big industries. But when the working clothes come off, Gladstone is well placed for exploring some beautiful coral cays and lagoons on the southern Great Barrier Reef.

The **Gladstone Visitor Information Centre** (☎ 4972 9000; Bryan Jordan Dr; ☺ 8.30am-5pm Mon-Fri, 9am-5pm Sat & Sun), located at the marina, is the departure point for boats to Heron Island. The **QPWS office** (☎ 4971 6500; 3rd fl, 136 Goondoon St; ☺ 8.30am-5pm Mon-Fri) has information on the southern Great Barrier Reef Islands. The **Gladstone City Library** (☎ 4976 6400; 39 Goondoon St; ☺ 9.30am-5.45pm Mon-Fri, 9am-4.30pm Sat) has free Internet access but you must book in advance.

The beautiful **Tondoon Botanic Gardens** (☎ 4979 3326; Glenlyon Rd; admission free; ☺ 9am-6pm Oct-Mar, 8.30am-5.30pm Apr-Sep), about 6km south of the town centre, comprises 83 hectares of rainforest and Australian native plants with walking trails and lakes. The **Auckland Hill Lookout** has good views over the Gladstone harbour, port facilities and shipping terminals. A brass tablet on the lookout maps the harbour and its many islands.

Auckland Hill B&B (☎ 4972 4907; www.ahbb.com .au; 15 Yarroon St; s/d incl breakfast $100/125; ☒ ☒) is a magnificent, sprawling Queenslander with six spacious rooms containing king-sized beds; one room is wheelchair accessible.

Gladstone Backpackers (☎ 4972 5744; 12 Rollo St; dm/d $22/48) is friendly, if a little scruffy, with a good kitchen and bathrooms. There's free use of bicycles and pick-ups from the marina, bus and train.

Buses connect Gladstone with Brisbane ($85, 10½ hours), and Rockhampton ($30, 1½ hours).

Alternatively, **QantasLink** (☎ 13 13 13; www.qantas .com.au) flies here from Brisbane ($125).

ROCKHAMPTON

☎ 07 / pop 59,500

The administrative and commercial hub of central Queensland, 'Rocky' is a little bit city and a whole lotta country. Proclaiming to be the beef capital of Australia, larger-than-life figurines of cattle greet the visitor at nearly every turn. There are more than

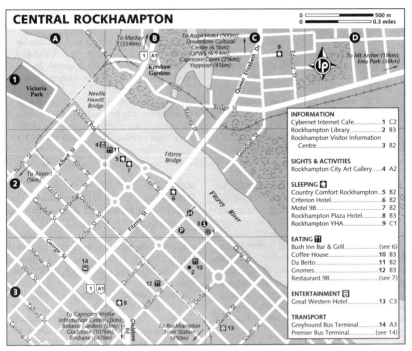

CENTRAL ROCKHAMPTON

INFORMATION	
Cybernet Internet Cafe	.............1 C2
Rockhampton Library	..............2 B3
Rockhampton Visitor Information	
Centre	....................3 B2

SIGHTS & ACTIVITIES	
Rockhampton City Art Gallery	.....4 A2

SLEEPING	
Country Comfort Rockhampton	..5 B2
Criterion Hotel	....................6 B2
Motel 98	...........................7 B2
Rockhampton Plaza Hotel	..........8 B3
Rockhampton YHA	..................9 C1

EATING	
Bush Inn Bar & Grill	.................(see 6)
Coffee House	......................10 B3
Da Berto	...........................11 B2
Gnomes	............................12 B3
Restaurant 98	.......................(see 7)

ENTERTAINMENT	
Great Western Hotel	................13 C3

TRANSPORT	
Greyhound Bus Terminal	...........14 A3
Premier Bus Terminal	..............(see 14)

two million cattle within a 250km radius of the city, and unsurprisingly, this is a great place to tuck into a steak.

Although Rocky styles itself as quintessentially Australian, there's an undeniable amalgam of US-influenced country and western music, Australian V8 utes, pig dogs and Bundaberg Rum. Nevertheless, the inhabitants are as true blue as you'll find anywhere in Australia.

Queensland's largest river, the mighty Fitzroy, flows through the heart of the city, giving it a lush ambience. There are several attractions worth taking in here and Rocky is also the gateway to Yeppoon and Great Keppel Island, but lingering a while will introduce you to the real, unburnished Australia.

Information

Capricorn Visitor Information Centre (☎ 4927 2055; Gladstone Rd; ☺ 8am-5pm) Helpful centre 3km south of the town.

Cybernet Internet Cafe (☎ 4927 3633; 12 William St; per hr $5; ☺ 10am-5.30pm)

QPWS (☎ 4936 0511; 61 Yeppoon Rd, North Rockhampton) About 7km northwest of central Rockhampton.

Rockhampton library (☎ 4936 8265; 69 William St; ☺ 9.15am-5.30pm Mon, Tue & Fri, to 8pm Thu, to 4.30pm Sat, 1-8pm Wed) Free Internet access, but you'll need to book.

Rockhampton Visitor Information Centre (☎ /fax 4922 5339; 208 Quay St; ☺ 8.30am-4.30pm Mon-Fri, 9am-4pm Sat & Sun) Helpful office in the beautiful former Customs House.

Sights

There are some fine old buildings, particularly on Quay St. Leaflets from the visitors centres map out walking trails.

The excellent **Rockhampton City Art Gallery** (☎ 4936 8248; 62 Victoria Pde; admission free; ☺ 10am-4pm Tue-Fri, 11am-4pm Sat & Sun) boasts an impressive collection of Australian paintings, including works by Sir Russell Drysdale, Sir Sidney Nolan and Albert Namatjira. The permanent collection is supplemented by innovative temporary exhibitions, for which there are varying admission charges.

About 6.5km north of the centre is the **Dreamtime Cultural Centre** (☎ 4936 1655; Bruce Hwy; adult/child $13/6; ☺ 10am-3.30pm Mon-Fri, tours 10.30am & 1pm), a rewarding indigenous Australian

STINGERS

It mightn't look or feel pretty, but unless you stay out of the water a 'stinger suit' is your only protection against Queensland's lethal jellyfish. There are two to be aware of; the rare and tiny (1cm to 2cm across) irukandji and the box jellyfish, also known as the sea wasp or stinger. They're found in coastal waters north of Rockhampton (occasionally further south) from around October to April, although the danger period can vary.

If someone has been stung, douse the stings with vinegar (available on many beaches or from nearby houses) and call an ambulance (artificial respiration may be required). Some coastal resorts erect stinger nets that provide small areas for safe swimming; otherwise stay out of the sea when the sea wasps are around. Or, if you simply must snorkel, visit a sports store for a clingy, Lycra all-body stinger suit.

and Torres Strait Islander heritage display centre, providing a fascinating insight into the region's indigenous history. The recommended 90-minute tours include boomerang throwing.

Rockhampton's wonderful **Botanic Gardens** (☎ 4922 1654; Spencer St; admission free; ☒ 6am-6pm, zoo feeding 2.30-3.30pm) are a beautifully landscaped oasis of Japanese gardens, lagoons and immaculate lawns. There is good access for those with disabilities, a kiosk, an attractive picnic area and a small **zoo** with koalas and a walk-through aviary.

Tours

Beef n Reef Adventures (☎ 1800 753 786; www.beefnreef.com; tours $85) operates highly recommended small-group day tours that deliver a taste of authentic Orstraalia. Capricorn Dave takes punters on a whirlwind tour around Rockhampton's hidden bush gems, including the Koorana Croc farm or Capricorn Caves. Overnight trips can also be arranged.

Sleeping

BUDGET

Rockhampton YHA (☎ 4927 5288; peter.karen@yhaqld .org; 60 MacFarlane St; dm members/nonmembers $19/23, d $50-59) This well-maintained hostel has spotless six- and nine-bed dorms and amenities. The kitchen is cavernous and there's a spacious lounge and dining area. It also has doubles and does courtesy pick-ups.

Also recommended:

Criterion Hotel (☎ 4922 1225; fax 4922 1226; 150 Quay St; s $40-45, d $60; ☒) Grand old pub with period rooms. Corner suites overlook the river.

Ascot Hotel (☎ 4922 4719; 117 Musgrave St; dm/d $18/36; ☒ ☐) Clean, friendly and comfortable backpackers accommodation with a good pub downstairs.

MIDRANGE

Coffee House (☎ 4927 5722; www.coffeehouse.com .au; 51 William St; d from $99; ☒ ☒) Popular with the business traveller, the Coffee House offers beautifully appointed motel rooms, self-contained apartments and spa suites in central Rocky. It has a restaurant (below) and wine bar and a café with Rocky's best coffee and cakes.

Country Comfort Rockhampton (☎ 4927 9933; fax 4927 1615; 86 Victoria Pde; d $105-180; ☒ ☐ ☒) Country Comfort boasts big rooms with views and excellent service. There are luxurious penthouses and family rooms available and downstairs you'll find a stylish restaurant and bar.

Motel 98 (☎ 4927 5322; www.motel98.com.au; 98 Victoria Pde; d $109; ☒ ☐ ☒) This smart motel has well-appointed, spacious rooms around the inviting pool. The elegant dining room (opposite) has a terrace overlooking the river.

Rockhampton Plaza Hotel (☎ 1800 001 800; 4927 5855; 161-7 George St; d $99-109; ☒ ☐ ☒) Overlooking a park, the Plaza has well-appointed, pretty typical four-star hotel rooms. There's a bar and restaurant and it's located a short stroll southwest of the centre and close to the railway station.

Eating

Coffee House (☎ 4927 5722; www.coffeehouse.com.au; 51 William St; mains $20-30; ☒ breakfast, lunch & dinner) Despite a perennial buzz from its ever-occupied tables, this popular and stylish café-cum-restaurant-cum-wine bar is extremely relaxed. Folk come for the big breakfasts and excellent coffee in the morning, and local seafood and beef mains plus an extensive wine menu for lunch and dinner.

Bush Inn Bar & Grill (Criterion Hotel; ☎ 4922 1225; 150 Quay St; dishes $10-20; ☒ lunch & dinner) The

Bush Inn serves some of the best pub food in town and is very popular with locals. There are huge steaks, slabs of barramundi, chicken dishes and pizzas on the menu.

Restaurant 98 (☎ 4927 5322; www.motel98.com.au; 98 Victoria Pde; mains $22-34 ☺ lunch & dinner) An elegant restaurant with a contemporary menu which is outstanding. Dishes here include chicken breast with a walnut and cashew crust, served with baby greens and a wasabi-scented sauce, inventive kangaroo, steak, lamb and seafood options. Sit inside or out on the terrace overlooking the Fitzroy River.

Also recommended:

Da Berto (☎ 4922 3060; Pilbeam Theatre, Victoria Pde; mains $19-29; ☺ lunch Tue-Fri, dinner Tue-Sun) Cosy Italian restaurant.

Gnomes (☎ 4927 4713; 106 William St; mains $13-19; ☺ lunch & dinner Tue-Sat) Casual BYO venue serving excellent seafood and vegetarian dishes.

Entertainment

Great Western Hotel (☎ 4922 1862; 39 Stanley St; admission $7.70) Looking like a spaghetti western film set, Lee Kernaghan's pub is a haven for cowboys and gals. DJs and occasional live acts feature on Friday nights,but the prime entertainment is watching poor brave fools try to ride bucking bulls and broncos in the bullring every Wednesday.

Criterion Hotel (☎ 4922 1225; 150 Quay St) Easily Rockhampton's favourite pub, the Criterion resonates with a good-time feel in its front bar and in the Bush Inn Bar & Grill. There's live music Wednesday to Saturday nights.

Getting There & Away

AIR

Rockhampton is serviced by **Jetstar** (☎ 13 15 38; www.jetstar.com.au), **Virgin Blue** (☎ 13 67 89; www.virginblue.com.au) and **Qantas** (☎ 13 13 13; www.qantas.com.au). General one-way fares include Brisbane ($89), Mackay ($80) and Sydney ($120).

BUS

Greyhound Australia (☎ 13 14 99; www.greyhound.com.au) and **Premier Motor Service** (☎ 13 34 10; www.premierms.com.au) have regular coach services along the Bruce Hwy, and the Rocky terminus for both carriers is at the **Mobil roadhouse** (91 George St). There are regular services to and from Mackay ($50, four hours), Bris-

bane ($85, 11 hours) and Cairns ($130, 16 hours).

Young's Bus Service (☎ 4922 3813) operates several services to Yeppoon including a loop that includes Rosslyn Bay. Young's also has buses to Mt Morgan, Monday to Friday. Buses depart from the Kern Arcade in Bolsover St.

TRAIN

The **Queensland Rail** (☎ 1300 131 722, 4932 0453; www.traveltrain.com.au) *Tilt Train* and *Sunlander* connect Rockhampton with Brisbane (from $95) and Cairns ($220). The journey takes seven to eleven hours, depending on which service you take.

The *Spirit of the Outback* also connects Rockhampton with Brisbane (economy seat/sleeper $150/95, 10 hours), Emerald (economy seat/sleeper $55/105) and Longreach (economy seat/sleeper $105/155) twice weekly.

AROUND ROCKHAMPTON

In the Berserker Range, which is 23km north of Rockhampton, are the **Capricorn Caves** (☎ 07-4934 2883; www.capricorncaves.com.au; Caves Rd; adult/child $16/8; ☺ 9am-4pm). This series of limestone caves and passages is spectacular year-round, but particularly during the summer solstice (1 December to 14 January), when the sun beams vertical light through the roof of the Belfry Cave. The informative one-hour Cathedral Tour is an easy guided walk leaving on the hour. For the more daring, the three-hour adventure tour ($60) takes you through tight spots with names like 'Fat Man's Misery'. You must book in advance and be at least 16 for this tour.

The complex also has barbecue areas, a pool and kiosk, and camping ground.

About 120km southwest of Rockhampton and 22km east of Baralaba, **Myella Farm Stay** (☎ 07-4998 1290; www.myella.com; Baralaba Rd; per person incl meals 1-/2-days $65/170) is a 1040-hectare beef property 120km southwest of Rockhampton that's popular among travellers looking to experience life on a working station. Accommodation is in a renovated homestead with polished timber floors and a wide veranda. Daily chores are an optional activity and rates include a large, home-cooked meal around the campfire. Ring for directions, or to arrange a pick-up.

Mt Morgan

☎ 07 / pop 2400

The historic gold- and copper-mining town of Mt Morgan is located 38km southwest of Rockhampton on the Burnett Hwy. Gold was found here in 1880 and the town experienced an ensuing boom. The open-cut gold and copper mine has lain fallow since 1981, but Mt Morgan still has a well-preserved collection of late-19th-century buildings, and is registered as a heritage town.

The **Mt Morgan Historical Museum** (☎ 4938 2122; 87 Morgan St; adult/child $5/1; ☽ 10am-4pm) has an extensive collection of artefacts, including a 1921 black Buick hearse, photographs tracing the mine's history and even an old fire engine.

There is an excellent half-hour **historic steam train ride** (adult/child/family $15/12/42) to Cattle Creek and back from the attractive old Mt Morgan train station. Pop into the helpful **visitor information centre** (☎ 4938 2312; Railway Pde; ☽ 8am-4pm) for more information.

Mt Morgan Tours (☎ 4938 2312; mine tours adult/child/family $25/20/70, mine & town tours $35/30/200; ☽ tours 2.30pm), based in the old railway station, runs around several value-packed day tours around the town.

Ferns' Miners Rest (☎ 4938 2350; 44 Coronation Dr; r $50; ☒) has small but comfortable self-contained units which sleep up to four.

Young's Bus Service (☎ 4922 3813; one way $7.50) operates a regular bus from Rockhampton to Mt Morgan and back Monday to Saturday.

Greyhound Australia (☎ 13 20 30; www.greyhound .com.au) connects Mt Morgan with Rockhampton ($11, 45 minutes) and Brisbane ($80, 12 hours) four times weekly.

YEPPOON

☎ 07 / pop 10,780

The gateway to Great Keppel Island, Yeppoon is an attractive seaside village in its own right. Its pleasant beaches give way in the north to rainforest around Byfield. Travelling south, you pass Rosslyn Bay, the departure point for Great Keppel, before wending your way along scenic coastline.

Information

Capricorn Coast Information Centre (☎ 1800 675 785, 4939 4888; www.capricorncoast.com.au; Scenic Hwy; ☽ 9am-5pm)

Click On Central (☎ 4939 5300; cnr Mary & James Sts) Internet access.

Sleeping

While Away B&B (☎ 4939 5719; www.whileaway bandb.com.au; 44 Todd Ave; d from $105; ☒) With four good-sized rooms and an immaculately clean house with wheelchair access, this B&B is a perfect quiet getaway – note that there are no facilities for kids. There are complimentary nibbles, tea, coffee, port and sherry as well as generous breakfasts.

Rydges Capricorn Resort (☎ 1800 075 902, 4925 2525; www.capricornresort.com; Farnborough Rd; d $250-320; ☒ ☒) This large and lavish golf resort about 8km north of Yeppoon has rooms ranging from standard hotel rooms to plush self-contained apartments. There's also a gym, several bars and restaurants and immaculate golf courses.

Driftwood Motel & Holiday Units (☎ 4939 2446; fax 4939 1231; 7 Todd Ave; s/d $75/85; ☒ ☒) Huge self-contained units at motel prices with absolute beach frontage make Driftwood a great bargain. There are good family units with separate bedrooms and there's a children's playground.

Budget options:

Yeppoon Backpackers (☎ 4939 4702, 1800 636 828; 30 Queen St; dm/d $20/42; ☒) Friendly hostel in a rambling old Queenslander. Free pick-ups from Rockhampton.

Beachside Caravan Park (☎ 4939 3738; Farnborough Rd; powered/unpowered sites per 2 people $18/15) Basic and neat park north of the town centre.

Getting There & Away

Young's Bus Service (☎ 4922 3813) operates a loop service from Rockhampton to Yeppoon, Rosslyn Bay, Emu Park and back ($7.70 one way, daily). **Rothery's Coaches** (☎ 4922 4320) does three runs per day from Rockhampton airport ($15/30 one way/return), or Rockhampton accommodation ($8.25/16.50) by arrangement to Rosslyn Bay.

AROUND YEPPOON

About 7km south of Yeppoon, **Rosslyn Bay Boat Harbour** is the departure point for ferries to Great Keppel Island. A great place to stay here is the **Rosslyn Bay Inn** (☎ 07-4933 6333; www.rosslynbayinn.com.au; Vin E Jones Dr; s/d from $79/99; ☒ ☒), offering comfortable studio rooms and one- and two-bedroom units, as well as a bar and restaurant.

Continuing southwards for 13km, you pass three headlands with fine views – **Bluff Point**, **Double Head** and **Pinnacle Point** – before arriving in **Emu Park**. This is the home to the

'Singing Ship' memorial to Captain Cook, a sculpture with drilled tubes and pipes that whistle or moan dolefully in the wind. Some 15km south of Emu Park is the turn-off to the **Koorana Crocodile Farm** (☎ 07-4934 4749; Coowonga Rd; adult/child $15/7; ☼ 10am-3pm, tours 10.30am & 1pm), a simple farm with lots of crocs destined to become fashion accessories or the odd restaurant meal.

Alternatively, drive 40km north from Yeppoon to the state forests of **Byfield**, where you can camp at **Waterpark Creek Camping Ground** (☎ 13 13 04; sites per family/adult $16/4) which must be pre-booked. It's 2km east from the main road to the creek crossing, beyond which is an attractive picnic area, with toilets, tables and gas barbecues.

GREAT KEPPEL ISLAND

Great Keppel's 18km of fine, white beaches rival any of Queensland's beautiful isles and it sits just 13km from the mainland. Around 90% of its 14 sq km is natural bushland. There's a wide range of activities and entertainment to keep you busy, but you can also find patches of overwhelming quiet. The fact that it's only semi-developed, gorgeous and cheap also makes this a flawless destination for many travellers.

Sights & Activities

The tips of air-tubes bobbing above the surrounding waters are testament to the popularity of **snorkelling**. Visitors usually start out investigating **Shelving Beach**, becoming

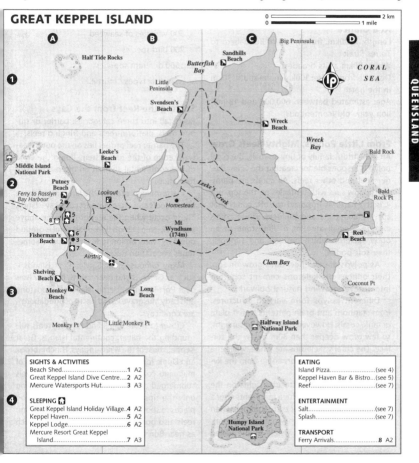

GREAT KEPPEL ISLAND

SIGHTS & ACTIVITIES	
Beach Shed....................................1	A2
Great Keppel Island Dive Centre...2	A2
Mercure Watersports Hut.............3	A3

SLEEPING	
Great Keppel Island Holiday Village..4	A2
Keppel Haven..............................5	A2
Keppel Lodge..............................6	A2
Mercure Resort Great Keppel	
Island......................................7	A3

EATING	
Island Pizza...........................(see 4)	
Keppel Haven Bar & Bistro...(see 5)	
Reef....................................(see 7)	

ENTERTAINMENT	
Salt......................................(see 7)	
Splash..................................(see 7)	

TRANSPORT	
Ferry Arrivals.........................8	A2

THE GREAT BARRIER REEF

Larger than the Great Wall of China and the only living thing visible from space, the Great Barrier Reef is one of the seven wonders of the natural world. This spectacular kaleidoscope of living colour stretches along the Queensland seaboard from just south of the tropic of Capricorn to Torres Strait, just south of New Guinea. It's the planet's biggest reef system, where in fact 2600 separate reefs form an outer ribbon parallel to the coast and lie dotted around the lagoon between this and the mainland. One BBC TV programme rated it second only to the Grand Canyon on a list of 50 Places To See Before You Die. Did we mention this reef is pretty ace?

At a Glance

Length: 2000km, from north of Bundaberg to Torres Strait
Width: 80km at its broadest
Distance from shore: 300km in the south, 30km in the north
Age: estimated between 600,000 and 18 million years old (contentious)

From Little Polyps, Mighty Reefs Grow

An industrious family of tiny animals, the coral polyp is responsible for creating the Great Barrier Reef and other reefs. All corals are primitive hollow sacs with tentacles on the top, but it is the hard, as opposed to soft, corals that are the architects and builders. These corals excrete a small amount of limestone as an outer skeleton which protects and supports their soft bodies.

As polyps die and new ones grow on top, their billions of skeletons cement together into an ever-growing natural bulwark.

Different polyps form varying structures, from staghorn and brain patterns to flat plate or table corals. However, they all need sunlight, so few grow deeper than 30m below the surface. The coral's skeletons are white, while the reef's kaleidoscopic colours come from the living polyps.

One of the most spectacular sights on the Great Barrier Reef occurs for a few nights after a full moon in late spring or early summer, when vast numbers of corals spawn. With tiny bundles of sperm and eggs visible to the naked eye, the event resembles a gigantic underwater snowstorm.

Did You Know?

Marine environments, including coral reefs, demonstrate the greatest biodiversity of any ecosystems on earth – much more so than rainforests. The Great Barrier Reef is home to marine mammals such as whales, dolphins and dugongs (sea cows). With new varieties still being found, its flora and fauna also includes:

- 1500 species of fish
- 400 types of coral
- 4000 breeds of clams and other molluscs
- 800 echinoderms, including sea cucumbers
- 500 varieties of seaweed
- 200 bird species
- 1500 different sponges
- …and six types of turtle.

Sorting the Reef from the Cays

Reefs fall into three categories: barrier or ribbon reefs, platform reefs and fringing reefs.

The barrier reef proper lies on the outer, seaward edge of the reef system, lining the edge of the continental shelf in an often-unbroken formation.

Platform reefs grow on the land side of these barrier reefs and often support coral cay islands. These occur when the reef grows to be above sea level, even at high tide; dead coral is ground down by water action to form sand, and sometimes vegetation takes root.

Many famous Great Barrier Reef islands – such as Green Island near Cairns, the Low Isles near Port Douglas, Heron Island off Gladstone and Lady Musgrave Island north of Bundaberg – are coral cays.

Closer to shore you'll find fringing reefs surrounding the hillier, continental islands. Great Keppel, most of the Whitsundays, Hinchinbrook and Dunk, for example, were once the peaks of mainland coastal ranges, but rising sea levels submerged most of these mountains, leaving only the tips exposed. Today these are good places to spot coral close to the beach. Fringing reefs also border the mainland in places, such as near Bundaberg.

Taking the Temperature of the Barrier Reef

I hear the Great Barrier Reef has been under threat lately. What's the story? Coral polyps need a water temperature of 17.5 to 28°C to grow and can't tolerate too much sediment. There are three main threats to the reef; land-based pollutants, over-fishing and the big one – global warming. Global warming is causing parts of the world's oceans to overheat occasionally, and the rise in temperature bleaches the reef. As the brightly coloured living polyps die, only the white skeletons remain. Pollution has also poisoned some coral, plus some questions persist about the long-term effects of crown-of-thorns starfish.

Some environmentalists and scientists predict that under current conditions, coral cover within the reef may be reduced to less than 5% by 2050. Because all the living organisms in the reef are symbiotic, the diverse ecosystem we see today may be gone forever.

What's being done? Fortunately it's not all doom and gloom. In July 2004, the Australian Government introduced new laws that increased 'no-take' zones, where it is forbidden to remove animal or plant life (for example no fishing), to 33.33% of the reef (it was previously only 4.5%). The Queensland Government also unveiled the Great Barrier Reef Coast Marine Park, a state park encompassing the actual coastline from just north of Bundaberg to the tip of Cape York – a total of 3600km. Although it will be several years before the success of these plans can be measured, they are certainly a huge step towards tackling the human-induced threats to the reef. On a micro level, the **Great Barrier Reef Marine Park Authority** (☎ 07-4750 0700; Reef HQ bldg, Townsville) looks after the welfare of most of the reef. It monitors bleaching and other problems and works to enforce the reef's 'no-take' zones.

Is there any way I can help? Sure. Take all litter with you, even biodegradable material like apple cores. Admire, but don't touch or harass, marine animals and be aware that if you touch or walk on coral you'll damage it (it can also create some very nasty cuts).

What's the best way to see some coral? Obviously, snorkelling and diving will get you up close

and personal. However, you can also view fish and coral from a glass-bottomed boat, a semi-submersible boat or an 'underwater observatory'. Tour operators are listed throughout this book. You can also ask the Marine Park Authority for advice, or visit its Reef HQ aquarium to see a living coral reef without leaving dry land.

What are 'bommies'? 'Bommie' is a diminutive of *bombora*, an Aboriginal word for submerged rock. It's a term used for large coral outcrops that rise up towards the surface.

And what wildlife can I realistically hope to see? Apart from all the psychedelically patterned tropical fish, there's the chance to swim with manta rays, squid, turtles and more.

Any creatures to beware of? There's nothing to be too alarmed about, but make sure to avoid scorpion fish, stonefish and jellyfish (see the boxed text, p366). No reef shark has ever attacked a diver, and while sea snakes are venomous, their fangs are at the back of their mouths, making them of little threat to humans.

Well, that's reassuring and it all sounds quite wonderful, so where do I go? It's said you could dive here every day of your life and still not see the entire Great Barrier Reef. Individual areas vary from time to time, depending on the weather or any recent damage, but places to start include:

- Cairns – the most common choice, so rather over-trafficked (p424)

- Port Douglas – gateway to the Low Isles and the Agincourt Reefs (p443)

- Lizard Island – superb diving at the Cod Hole (p453)

- Yongala shipwreck – one of Australia's best, off Townsville (p402)

- Heron Island – popular diving resort where it's wise to book ahead (p363)

- Lady Elliot Island – shipwrecks and gorgeous coral (p362)

- Fitzroy Reef Lagoon – untouched for years, tourist numbers are still limited (p363)

For more information, see Lonely Planet's *Diving & Snorkelling Australia's Great Barrier Reef*.

progressively more and more adventurous as they hike to **Monkey Beach** and **Clam Bay**. The coral here is OK (and you will see marine life), but is better around **Middle** and **Halfway Islands** (see opposite).

There are several bushwalking tracks from **Fisherman's Beach**, the main beach. The longest, and perhaps the most difficult, leads to the 2.5m 'lighthouse' near **Bald Rock Point** on the far side of the island (about three hours return).

With 18km of white-sand beaches, you don't need to go far for a swim. **Fisherman's Beach**, where the ferries come in, rarely gets crowded, and it's even quieter just round the corner at **Putney Beach**.

The **Beach Shed** (07-4925 0624; Putney Beach) and the **Mercure Watersports Hut** (Fisherman's Beach) both hire out sailboards, catamarans, motorboats and snorkelling gear, and can take you water-skiing, parasailing or camel-riding.

The **Great Keppel Island Dive Centre** (07-4939 5022; www.keppledive.com; Putney Beach) on Putney Beach offers introductory dives with all gear supplied for $100, or two qualified boat dives for $130.

Tours

Freedom Fast Cats (1800 336 244, 07-4933 6244; Rosslyn Bay marina; adult/child $55/26) Operates a coral cruise to the best location of the day (depending on tides and weather), which includes viewing through a glass-bottomed boat and fish feeding. There are also afternoon and full-day cruises.

Keppel Tourist Services (07-4933 6744; Rosslyn Bay marina; adult/child/senior/family $50/25/40/125; 9.15am & 2pm) Operates morning and afternoon coral cruises, which visit the Middle Island Underwater Observatory.

Sleeping

Keppel Lodge (07-4939 4251; info@keppellodge.com.au; s/d $90/110) This pleasant, open-plan house has four good-sized bedrooms with bathrooms branching out from a large communal lounge and kitchen. The house is available in its entirety or as individual motel-type suites.

Mercure Resort Great Keppel Island (1800 245 658; www.greatkeppelresort.com.au; r per night from $142;) In early 2005 this popular resort went through a transformation. No longer is it the 18- to 30-something party venue. With a new children's club and conference facilities the resort is aiming for a

wider market, including families, cou ples, and mature-age travellers. The reso boasts four room styles – rooms with tw queen beds, a queen and two single bed a queen and single bed, and three singl beds. It offers a gamut of facilities includ ing bars, restaurants and a nightclub. The are tennis and squash courts, a golf cours and water sports from snorkelling to skiin on offer. More than 40 of the activities ar available free to guests. The resort offer a range of package deals to make longe stays cheaper, and two meals are include in the tariff.

Great Keppel Island Holiday Village (07-4 39 8655; www.gkiholidayvillage.com.au; s/d tents $40/6 dm $27, s/d cabins $90/100) This YHA-affiliate resort is a collection of various types of ac commodation (including four- and six bed dorms and cabins that sleep four). It' friendly and relaxed and has good com munal facilities.

Keppel Haven (Keppel Tourist Services; 07-493 6744; fax 07-4933 6429; s/d tent $28/40, d $80, cabins fro $120) Although a little cramped, this plac is pleasant enough. There are simple, pe manent tents and comfortable bunkhouse nestled in established tropical greenery. has a bar and bistro and offers discoun packages including ferry transfers.

Eating

Keppel Haven Bar & Bistro (07-4933 6744; dishe $7-25; breakfast, lunch & dinner) Pleasant, breez eatery has some good-value specials tha include a glass of beer. The á la carte men offers tortillas, fish burgers, stir-fries an steaks, and you can consume your dinne with sunset views.

Island Pizza (07-4939 4699; The Esplanad dishes $6-30; dinner Tue-Sun, lunch Sat & Sun) friendly place that prides itself on a uniqu healthy pizza recipe with plenty of top pings. The pizzas are rather pricey but sti tempting. Also available are hot dogs an pastas.

Reef (Mercure Resort Great Keppel Island; mains $7-2 lunch & dinner) Within the Mercure Resor this casual bistro serves ok light lunches an hot food, including wraps, pizzas, burger and the ever-present chips.

The kiosks at Keppel Haven and Grea Keppel Island Holiday Village have a fe essentials, but if you want to cook brin your own supplies.

Entertainment

Splash is the bar in the Mercure Resort Great Keppel Island day-trippers' area. It's the place to party, with pool tables, a dance floor and live music. Resort guests can party into the night at **Salt** (admission $5; late Mon-Sat) nightclub. If patronage in the resort is down, Splash will party on and Salt won't open.

Getting There & Away

Ferries for Great Keppel leave from Rosslyn Bay Harbour, about 7km south of Yeppoon. If you have booked accommodation, check that someone will meet you on the beach to help with your luggage.

Keppel Tourist Services (☎ 07-4933 6744; adult/child/family return $32/16/80) operates ferries to the island, departing at 7.30am, 9.15am, 11.30am and 3.30pm, and returning at 8.15am, 2pm and 4.30pm. Keppel Tourist Services and **Rothery's Coaches** (☎ 07-4922 4320) run a daily bus service from Rockhampton to Rosslyn Bay, picking up from the airport ($15/30 one way/return) or accommodation in Rockhampton ($8.25/16 one way/return) by arrangement to Rosslyn Bay.

Freedom Fast Cats (☎ 07-4933 6244, 1800 336 244; family/adult/child return $78/32/16) departs the Keppel Bay Marina in Rosslyn Bay at 9am, 11.30am and 3pm, returning at 10am, 2pm and 4pm.

OTHER KEPPEL BAY ISLANDS

Although you can make day trips to the fringing coral reefs of **Middle** or **Halfway Islands** from Great Keppel Island (ask your accommodation or at Keppel Holiday Village), you can also **camp** (per person/family $4/16) on several national park islands, including **Middle**, **North Keppel** and **Miall Islands**. You'll need all your own supplies, including water. Get information and permits from the **QPWS** (www.epa.gov.au; Rockhampton ☎ 07-4936 0511; Rosslyn Bay ☎ 07-4933 6608).

Tiny, privately owned **Pumpkin Island** (☎ 07-4939 2431; sites $15, cabins $155), just south of North Keppel, has five simple, cosy cabins with water, solar power, kitchen and bathroom; bring food and linen.

Funtastic Cruises (☎ 0438 909 502) can organise camping drop-offs from Rosslyn Bay to the islands. For Pumpkin Island it costs $175 return per person, and gets cheaper per person for larger groups.

CAPRICORN HINTERLAND

According to the official road-numbering system, the Capricorn Hwy running inland from Rockhampton is Australia's very own Route 66, so get your kicks by heading for the Blackdown Tableland National Park or the even more spectacular Carnarvon National Park. Alternatively, at Emerald some 270km west of the coast, you'll find yourself on the doorstep of central Queensland's gem fields. It is best to visit in the cooler months between April and November.

Blackdown Tableland National Park

The Blackdown Tableland is a spectacular 600m sandstone plateau that rises suddenly out of the flat plains of central Queensland. This impressive national park features stunning panoramas, waterfalls, great bushwalks, Aboriginal rock art, plus some unique wildlife and plant species. The turn-off to the Blackdown Tableland is 11km west of Dingo and 35km east of the coal-mining centre of Blackwater. The 23km gravel road, which begins at the base of the tableland, isn't suitable for caravans and can be unsafe in wet weather – the first 8km stretch is steep, winding and often slippery. At the top you'll come to the breathtaking **Horseshoe Lookout**, with picnic tables, barbecues and toilets. There's a walking trail starting here to **Two Mile Falls** (2km).

The picturesque **South Mimosa Creek camping ground** (Dingo rangers ☎ 07-4986 1964; per person/family $4/16) is a self-registration camping area about 6km on from Horseshoe Lookout. It has pit toilets and fireplaces – you'll need water, firewood and/or a fuel stove. Bookings are advised.

Gem Fields

The lure of the gem fields is like the ladyluck pull of Queensland's ubiquitous pokies. In the fields west of **Emerald**, you'll hear numerous tales of fossickers unearthing sapphires, rubies or zircons worth squillions, just minutes after drifting into town. Many of these stories are even true, as the gem fields around Anakie, Sapphire, Rubyvale and Willows are the world's largest of their kind and renowned for large, rare sapphires.

To go fossicking you need a licence (adult/family $5.55/7.80) from the Emerald Courthouse or one of the gem fields' general stores

QUEENSLAND

or post offices. If you just wish to dabble, you can buy a bucket of 'wash' (mine dirt in water) from one of the fossicking parks and hand-sieve and wash it.

In **Anakie**, 42km west of Emerald, the **Gemfields Information Centre** (☎ 07-4985 4525; 1 Anakie Rd) has maps of the fields and fossicking licences. It also hires fossicking equipment.

In **Sapphire**, 10km further north, **Pat's Gems** (☎ 07-4985 4544; 1056 Rubyvale Rd; ☒ 8.30am-5pm) has buckets of dirt for $7 each or six buckets for $30. It also hires fossicking gear.

Another 8km on lies **Rubyvale**, the main town on the fields, and 2km further than that is the excellent **Miners Heritage Walk-in Mine** (☎ 07-4985 4444; Heritage Rd; adult/child $9.50/3; ☒ 9am-5pm), which has informative 20-minute underground tours throughout the day in which you descend into a maze of tunnels 18m beneath the surface.

Rubyvale Holiday Units (☎ 07-4985 4518; www .rubyvaleholiday.com.au; 35 Heritage Rd, Rubyvale; d $65-110; ☒ ☒) are spacious motel and self-contained units, about 1km north of Rubyvale.

In an attractive bush setting near Sapphire, **Sunrise Cabins** (☎ 07-4985 4281; 57 Sunrise Rd; powered/unpowered sites per 2 people $16/13, cabins $35-55) has rustic but comfortable doubles and spacious self-contained options. There are good communal amenities.

There are caravan–camping parks at Anakie, Rubyvale and Willows Gemfields.

Springsure
☎ 07 / pop 770

Springsure, 66km south of Emerald on the way to Carnarvon Gorge, has a striking backdrop of granite mountains and sunflower fields. **Virgin Rock**, an outcrop of Mt Zamia on the northern outskirts, was named after early settlers who claimed to have seen the image of the Virgin Mary in the rock face.Springsure has a motel, a couple of pubs and a caravan park.

Carnarvon National Park

Carved out over millions of years by a creek running through sandstone, this rugged national park features dramatic scenery and numerous Aboriginal rock paintings and carvings. **Carnarvon Gorge** is an amazing oasis, with river oaks, flooded gums, cabbage palms, moss gardens, deep pools and platypuses in the creek. Standing on

the valley floor, the sheer 200m rock walls towering above are simply humbling.

For most people, Carnarvon Gorge *is* the Carnarvon National Park, because the other sections – including Mt Moffatt, Ka Ka Mundi and Salvator Rosa – are pretty inaccessible.

Coming from Rolleston the road is bitumen for 70km and unsealed for 25km. From Roma via Injune and Wyseby, the road is good bitumen for about 215km then unsealed and fairly rough for the last 30km. After heavy rain, both these roads can become impassable.

The road into the park leads to an **information centre** (☎ 07-4984 4505; ☒ 8-10am, 3-5pm) and scenic picnic ground. The main walking track starts from here, following Carnarvon Creek through the gorge, with detours to various points of interest. These include the **Moss Garden** (3.6km from the picnic area), **Ward's Canyon** (4.8km), the **Art Gallery** (5.6km) and **Cathedral Cave** (9.3km). Allow *at least* a whole day for a visit. Basic groceries and ice are available at Takarakka Bush Resort (see below).

You cannot drive from Carnarvon Gorge to other sections of the park, although you can reach beautiful Mt Moffatt via an unsealed road from Injune (4WD necessary).

SLEEPING

It's best to book several months ahead, especially from April to October.

Carnarvon Gorge Wilderness Lodge (☎ 1800 64 150, 07-4984 4503; www.carnarvon-gorge.com.au; Wyseb Rd; d incl meals $390; ☒) Upmarket safari-style accommodation option located near the park entrance, offering attractive cabins nestled in the bush. There's a restaurant and a bar and the rates drop considerably for longer stays and between November and April.

Takarakka Bush Resort (☎ 07-4984 4535; www .takarakka.com.au; Wyseby Rd; powered/unpowered sites $24/18, cabins $70) About 5km from the picnic ground, this picturesque bush oasis has an open camping area and a ring of simply furnished, elevated canvas cabins (BYO linen) with private verandas. The facilities are good and the reception/store sells drinks, groceries, ice and gas.

Bookings are required for both camping options:

Carnarvon Gorge Visitor Area & Big Bend Camping Ground (☎ 07-4984 4505, 13 13 04; www.epa.qld.gov.au

sites per person/family $4/16) Isolated camping ground 10km walk up the gorge.

Mt Moffatt Camping Ground (Mt Moffatt rangers ☎ 07-4626 3581; www.epa.qld.gov.au; sites per person/family $4/16) Campers need to be self-sufficient and have a 4WD.

GETTING THERE & AWAY

CQ Travel Link (Emerald Coaches; ☎ 07-4982 1399; Old Railway Station, Clermont St, Emerald), provides transfers to/from the park and Emerald for $110 one way.

OUTBACK

Heading west from the Queensland coast across the Great Dividing Range, the legendary Outback is truly – in the well-worn words of Dorothea Mackellar– 'a sunburnt country'.

The only way to grasp any perspective of this ancient terra firma is to accept that its vast and semi-arid expanse encompasses everything 'out the back'. Miles of ochre landscape touching a smouldering sky are interrupted by grasslands and low scrub, which are drained by coolabah-lined rivers with evocative names such as the Barcoo, the Warrego and Cooper Creek. Beneath all lies the Great Artesian Basin, an enormous underground reservoir.

Although sparsely settled, the Outback is well-serviced by major roads, namely the Overlander's Way (Flinders and Barkly Hwys) and the Matilda Hwy (Landsborough Hwy and Burke Developmental Rd). Once you turn off these major arteries, however, road conditions deteriorate rapidly, services are remote and you need to be fully self-sufficient, carrying spare parts, fuel and water. Also do some pre-planning research as some sights and accommodation options (in particular the Outback stations) close from November to March, the Outback's hottest period.

Getting There & Away

AIR

Qantas and **QantasLink** (☎ 13 13 13; www.qantas .com.au) fly from Brisbane to Barcaldine ($230), Blackall ($210), Charleville ($190), Longreach ($240) and Mt Isa ($220).

Macair (☎ 13 13 23; www.macair.com.au) also flies between Brisbane and various Outback

destinations, including Birdsville ($300) via Charleville ($155), Quilpie ($220) and Windorah ($250). It also connects Mt Isa to Cairns ($255).

BUS

Greyhound Australia (☎ 13 14 99; www.greyhound .com.au) connects Mt Isa to Townsville ($125, 11 to 12 hours) and Brisbane ($155, 24 hours). From Mt Isa, buses continue to Three Ways in the NT.

TRAIN

Queensland Rail (☎ 1300 131 722; www.traveltrain .com.au) has three trains servicing the Outback, all running twice weekly. The *Spirit of the Outback* runs from Brisbane to Longreach (economy seat/sleeper $165/220, 26 hours) via Rockhampton, with connecting bus services to Winton; the *Westlander* runs from Brisbane to Charleville (economy seat/sleeper $95/145, 16½ hours), with connecting bus services to Cunnamulla and Quilpie; and the *Inlander* runs from Townsville to Mt Isa (economy seat/sleeper $110/165, 21 hours).

CHARTERS TOWERS TO CLONCURRY

The Flinders Hwy, which stretches 775km from Townsville to Cloncurry, is the major route across the top of outback Queensland. Largely, the terrain is relentlessly flat, but there are a few points of interest along the way to break the monotony. The highway was originally a Cobb & Co coach run, and along its length are small towns established as coach stopovers. **Pentland**, 105km west of Charters Towers, has pubs, fuel and camping grounds. At **Prairie**, 200km west of Charters Towers, the friendly **Prairie Hotel** (☎ /fax 07-4741 5121; Flinders Hwy; s/d from $33/44; ⊠) is filled with atmosphere and memorabilia, and even has a resident ghost.

Hughenden, a busy commercial centre on the banks of the Flinders River, bills itself as 'the home of beauty and the beast'. The beast, imprisoned in the **Flinders Discovery Centre** (☎ 07-4741 1021; 37 Gray St; adult/child $2/free), is a replica skeleton of *Muttaburrasaurus*, one of the largest and most complete dinosaur skeletons found in Australia. The museum has displays on the town's history and doubles as a visitor information centre.

The beauty is the **Porcupine Gorge National Park** (☎ 07-4741 1113; camping per person/f $4/16), an oasis in the dry country north of Hughenden. The best spot to go is **Pyramid Lookout**, about 70km north of Hughenden. You can camp here and it's an easy 30-minute walk into the gorge, with some fine rock formations and a permanently running creek.

The **Royal Hotel Resort** (☎ 07-4741 1183; 21 Moran St; s/d $60/71; 🗷) offers spotless motel units, while the venerable **Grand Hotel** (☎ /fax 07-4741 1588; 25 Gray St; s/d $25/$35; 🗷) has well-worn pub rooms and good counter meals. There's also the decent **Allan Terry Caravan Park** (☎ /fax 07-4741 1190; 2 Resolution St; powered/unpowered sites $16/14, cabins from $45), opposite the train station.

Watch for wild emus and brolgas on the Hughenden–Cloncurry stretch. **Richmond**, 112km from Hughenden, and **Julia Creek**, 144km further on, are both small towns with motels and caravan parks. Richmond has an impressive marine fossil museum and visitors centre: **Kronosaurus Korner Information Centre** (☎ 07-4741 3429; 91 Goldring St; ☉ 8.30am-4.45pm), which has more than 200 exhibits, including Australia's best vertebrate fossil, the Richmond *Pliosaur*.

From Julia Creek, the sealed Wills Developmental Rd heads north to Normanton (432km), Karumba (494km) and Burketown (467km). See the Gulf Savannah (p417) for more information on these towns.

CLONCURRY
☎ 07 / pop 2748

The centre for a copper boom in the 19th century, the Curry was the largest copper producer in the British Empire. Today it's a pastoral centre, and the town's major claim to fame is as the birthplace of the Royal Flying Doctors Service (RFDS). Australia's highest recorded temperature in the shade, 53.1°C, was measured here in 1889.

The **Mary Kathleen Park & Museum** (☎ 4742 1361; McIlwraith St; adult/child $7/3; ☉ 8am-4.30pm Mon-Fri, 9am-3pm Sat & Sun), situated on the eastern side of town, acts as a visitors centre. It is partly housed in buildings transported from the former uranium-mining town of Mary Kathleen and includes relics of the Burke and Wills expedition, and a big array of local rocks and minerals.

John Flynn Place (☎ 4742 1251; Daintree St; adult/child $8.50/4; ☉ 8am-4.30pm Mon-Fri, 9am-3pm Sat & Sun Apr-Oct) commemorates Flynn's work in setting up the invaluable Royal Flying Doc-

tors Service. The building incorporates an art gallery, cultural centre and theatre.

The attractive **Gidgee Inn** (☎ 4742 1599; gidgeeinn@bigpond.com.au; Matilda Hwy; s/d $98/104) has modern rooms, and is built from rammed red earth trimmed with corrugated iron. There's an excellent **restaurant** (mains $10-25) attached. Alternatively, you can head to the historic **Wagon Wheel Motel** (☎ 4742 1866; fax 4742 1819; 54 Ramsay St; s/d from $54/65; 🗷 🗷) with its clean and comfortable rooms, or the **Gilbert Park Tourist Park** (☎ 4742 2300; gilpark@bigpond.com.au; Matilda Hwy; powered/unpowered sites per 2 people $19/16, cabins from $70).

CLONCURRY TO MT ISA

This 121km of the Barkly Hwy has a few interesting stops and detours. Beside the **Corella River**, 44km west of Cloncurry, there's a memorial cairn to the Burke and Wills expedition, which passed here in 1861. Another 1km down the road is the **Kalkadoon & Mitakoodi Memorial**, which marks an indigenous Australian tribal boundary.

Another 9km on you will pass the (unmarked) site of **Mary Kathleen**, a uranium-mining town from the 1950s to 1982, which is now completely demolished. The turn-off to **Lake Julius**, Mt Isa's reserve water supply, is 36km past Mary Kathleen. Sitting on the Leichhardt River, the lake is a popular spot for fishing and water-skiing, and has a low-key camping resort. Nearby is **Battle Mountain**, the scene of the last stand of the Kalkadoon people in 1884. One of the last tribes to resist white settlement, the Kalkadoons were all but wiped out in a bloody massacre that marked the end of indigenous Australian resistance in the region.

MT ISA
☎ 07 / pop 20,525

Mt Isa is a town of striking beauty, with stark red ridges and olive-green clumps of spinifex. It owes its prosperity to immensely rich underground lead, zinc silver and copper ore bodies west of the city. The mine's job opportunities have attracted people from about 50 different ethnic groups, most of whom are men (there are supposedly three males to every female!). The sandy Leichhardt River divides 'townside' from 'mineside', home from work.

'The Isa', as it's known locally, is inland Queensland's major town and as authentic

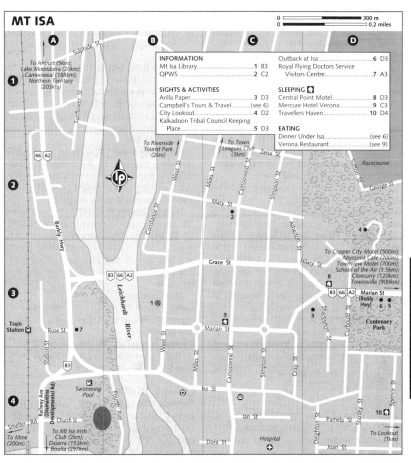

MT ISA

INFORMATION
Mt Isa Library.................................1 B3
QPWS...2 C2

SIGHTS & ACTIVITIES
Arilla Paper...................................3 D3
Campbell's Tours & Travel.........(see 6)
City Lookout.................................4 D2
Kalkadoon Tribal Council Keeping
Place...5 D3

Outback at Isa...............................6 D3
Royal Flying Doctors Service
Visitors Centre............................7 A3

SLEEPING
Central Point Motel........................8 D3
Mercure Hotel Verona.....................9 C3
Travellers Haven...........................10 D4

EATING
Dinner Under Isa.........................(see 6)
Verona Restaurant......................(see 9)

as the Outback gets. Locals stroll across the pedestrian crossings with absolute certainty that the cars will stop for them, and honking horns are usually from drivers waving hello.

Orientation & Information

Barkly Hwy, which becomes Marian St, is the main entry road. The city centre is in the area between Grace and Isa Sts, and West and Simpson Sts. **Mt Isa Airport** (☎ 4743 4598; Barkly Hwy) is roughly 5km from the town centre; a taxi to town costs around $13. **Mt Isa Library** (☎ 4744 4266; 23 West St; per hr $3) has Internet access.

Outback at Isa (see right) houses a helpful information centre, or you can find in-

formation on the area's national parks at **QPWS** (☎ 4744 7888; cnr Mary & Camooweal Sts).

Sights & Activities

The town's major attraction is **Outback at Isa** (☎ 1300 659 660, 4749 1555; www.outbackatisa.com.au; 19 Marian St; ☽ 8.30am-5pm). It features the underground **Hard Times Mine** (adult/child $45/26), where you get kitted out in fair-dinkum mining attire and head lamps and descend a purpose-built mine complete with fuming, roaring and rattling machinery. Also here is the fascinating **Riversleigh Fossil Centre** (adult/child $10/6.50), where you get to see a re-creation of Australia's prehistoric fauna, and actual fossils. The centre also houses the **Isa Experience Gallery** and **Outback Park** (adult/child $10/6.50), showcasing the natural, indigenous and mining heritage of Mt Isa. There's a good-value, two-day **Discovery Tour Pass** (adult/child $55/33), which combines all the attractions.

Arilla Paper (☎ 4743 0084; www.arillapaper.com; cnr Shackleton & Marian Sts) is an indigenous women's cooperative, where paper is handcrafted from native plants such as the hardy spinifex. There's a shop and gallery displaying the interesting products. The **Kalkadoon Tribal Council Keeping Place** (☎ 4749 1001; Marian St; admission by $2 donation; ✆ 9am-5pm Mon-Fri), adjacent to Outback at Isa, displays local indigenous art, history and artefacts.

Mt Isa puts on a mean sunset, and the **City Lookout**, off Hilary St, has spectacular views of the mine and town. At the eastern end of Pamela St is another great **lookout**.

The **Royal Flying Doctor Service Visitors Centre** (☎ 4743 2800; Barkly Hwy; admission by $2.50 donation; ✆ 9.30am-4.30pm Mon-Fri) and the **School of the Air** (☎ 4744 9100; Kalkadoon High School, Abel Smith Pde; admission by $2 donation; ✆ tours 9am & 10am Mon-Fri during school term) show how the needs of remote communities are serviced.

Lake Moondarra, 20km north of town, is a popular recreational area.

Mt Isa is also home to Australia's largest **rodeo** (www.isarodeo.com.au), held in the second weekend in August following a fortnight of festivities.

Tours

Campbell's Tours & Travel (☎ 4743 2006; www .campbellstravel.com.au; 19 Marian St; adult/child $22/11; ✆ 11am Mon-Sat) Runs fascinating two-hour surface tours of the mine.

Jabiru Adventure Tours (☎ 4749 5950; www.jabiru adventuretours.com; adult $85) Runs half-day tours, led by an indigenous guide, of the town sights and of indigenous culture, culminating in a buffet meal.

Westwing Aviation (☎ 4743 2844; www.westwing .com.au) Takes passengers on its mail-run services. Wednesday's run ($330, 9am to 5pm) has a dozen stops. Friday's run ($220, 9am to 1pm) flies southwest over the Barkly Tablelands.

Yididi Aboriginal Guided Tours (adult/child $660/330) Campbell's Tours & Travel also helps run a three-day camping safari to Boodjamulla (Lawn Hill) National Park including the Riversleigh fossil sites.

Sleeping

Townview Motel (☎ 4743 3328; fax 4749 0409; cnr Marian & Kookaburra Sts; r $65-150; ❄ ⬚) Actually, there's no view of the town, but this good

motel has a variety of rooms from budget to spacious spa suites. Its little restaurant, the Abyssinia Cafe, has a big reputation (see below).

Mercure Hotel Verona (☎ 4743 3024; www.mer cure.com.au; cnr Marian & Camooweal Sts; r from $155; ❄ ⬚) Corporate hotel with a 4½-star rating has big rooms with great views of the mine and the excellent Verona Restaurant (see below). Room prices tumble on the weekend to $99.

Copper City Motel (☎ 4743 3904; fax 4743 2290; 105 Butler St; s/d $70/80; ❄ ⬚) A friendly, clean motel in a quiet location with good undercover parking and a shaded pool. There are also elf-contained units available.

Travellers Haven (☎ 4743 0313; www.users.bigpond .net.au/travellershaven; 75 Spence St; dm/s/d $20/32/46; ❄ ⬚ ⬚) The Travellers Haven is a fairly quiet budget option with adequate rooms and facilities. A free pick-up service is offered, though it is not far from the bus terminal.

More options:

Central Point Motel (☎ 4743 0666; centralpoint@ bigpond.com; 6 Marian St; s/d $80/90) Central with top-value self-contained rooms.

Riverside Tourist Park (☎ 4743 3904; fax 4743 9417; 195 West St; powered/unpowered sites per 2 people $20/16, cabins $67; ❄ ⬚) Shady, neat park.

Eating & Drinking

Abyssinia Cafe (☎ 4743 3328; Townview Motel, cnr Marian & Kookaburra Sts; mains $16-25; ✆ dinner Mon-Sat) Located in the Townview Motel, just east of town, this cosmopolitan little café is pure delight for inquisitive palates. The very global menu boasts Ethiopian, Indian, Mexican and other far-and-away flavoured dishes. It's earned a solid reputation around town for authentic meals and modest bills.

Verona Restaurant (☎ 4743 3024; Mercure Hotel Verona, cnr Marian & Camooweal Sts; mains $23-28; ✆ breakfast & dinner) Located in Mt Isa's top corporate hotel, the Verona Restaurant is a great option for a culinary splurge. The inventive menu has an international spin, featuring good seafood and Italian cuisine. The atmosphere is a cross between elegant and functional, but the service is pure class.

Dinner Under Isa (☎ 1300 659 660; 19 Marian St; 3-course meal $69; ✆ 5-8.30pm Mon, Wed, Fri & Sat) Don a hard hat, safety specs and head lamp and enjoy a three-course dinner in the crib room

QUEENSLAND

of the Hard Times mine. Mine tour and tall stories included. The mine is licensed.

Two good clubs, where you can feast on bistro meals that are relatively kind to the wallet, are the **Town Leagues Club** (☎ 4749 5455; Ryan Rd; mains $10-20; ☺ lunch & dinner), 3km north of town, which also specialises in cheap beer, and the **Mt Isa Irish Club** (☎ 4743 2577; Nineteenth Ave), 2km south of town. The latter incorporates the **Keane's Bar & Grill** (mains $14-22; ☺ lunch & dinner) for excellent beef and seafood and frequent live music, the **Blarney Bar** (mains $10; ☺ lunch & dinner), which has a buffet, and the **Tram Stop** (mains $6-9; ☺ lunch), good for cakes and snacks. Party animals can also head downstairs to the club's popular nightclub – the **Rish** (admission $5).

Getting There & Around

AIR
Macair (☎ 13 13 23; www.macair.com.au) connects Mt Isa with Birdsville ($200), Charleville ($260) and Normanton ($180). See p375 for more flight information.

BUS
Campbell's Tours & Travel (☎ 4743 2006; www.camp bellstravel.com.au; 19 Marian St) is the long-distance bus terminal. **Greyhound Australia** (☎ 13 14 99; www.greyhound.com.au) has regular services to Townsville ($119, 11½ hours) and Longreach ($85, 8½ hours).

AICCC runs a bus service from Normanton to Mt Isa on Monday, returning on Tuesday (adult/child $110/85). You can book through Campbell's Tours & Travel. See p375 for more bus information.

CAR
For a taxi, call ☎ 4743 2333. The following car-hire firms have desks at the airport: **Avis** (☎ 4743 3733), **Hertz** (☎ 4743 4142) and **Thrifty** (☎ 4743 2911).

TRAIN
The **Queensland Rail** (☎ 1300 131 722; www.travel train.com.au) *Inlander* runs between Mt Isa and Townsville (see p375).

MT ISA TO THREE WAYS
Established in 1884 as a service centre for the vast cattle stations of the Barkly Tablelands, **Camooweal** now consists of a couple of historic buildings – **Freckleton's General Store**, in particular, is worth a visit – as well as a pub,

hostel and a few roadhouses (with extremely expensive fuel). The town is 185km from Mt Isa and 13km east of the NT border.

From Camooweal you can head north on an unsealed road to **Boodjamulla National Park**, where there are a few camp sites, and Burke-town; see p420. Eight kilometres south of town is the **Camooweal Caves National Park**, with a network of unusual caves with sinkhole openings. These have few of the usual limestone features because of the constant flooding. The caves are for experienced cavers only. Contact Mt Isa QPWS (p377) for more information on both parks.

There's nothing much for the whole 460km from Camooweal to the Three Ways junction in the NT. There's a petrol station 260km from Camooweal and you can stay nearby at **Barkly Homestead** (☎ 08-8964 4549; fax 08-8964 4543; Barkly Hwy; powered/unpowered sites per 2 people $22/14, s/d $80/90).

MT ISA TO LONGREACH
The shortest route to Longreach from Mt Isa means heading east along Barkly Hwy to the Landsborough Hwy, 14km east of Cloncurry. Here the Landsborough heads southeast, passing through McKinlay (91km), Kynuna (168km), Winton (339km) and eventually hitting Longreach (516km).

McKinlay is a tiny settlement that probably would have been doomed to eternal insignificance had it not been used as a location in the amazingly successful movie *Crocodile Dundee*.

The **Walkabout Creek Hotel** (☎ 07-4746 8424; fax 07-4746 8768; Landsborough Hwy; powered/unpowered sites $20/18, s/d $45/55; ▣) has film memorabilia and all the charm of a movie set. There are small and basic motel units a block west of the pub, or there's a camping ground out the back.

A further 74km southeast, and not much bigger than McKinlay, is **Kynuna**. It's home to **Magoffin's Matilda Expo** (☎ 07-4746 8401; Landsborough Hwy; adult/child $9/5; ☺ 8am-5pm), a gaudy and ramshackle 'museum' owned by Richard Magoffin, a real Outback character. It promises to reveal the true story behind Australia's unofficial anthem 'Waltzing Matilda'. Richard does live musical renditions of the song and two-hour shows at 7pm from April to October.

There's a lot to like about the historic little **Blue Heeler Hotel** (☎ 07-4746 8650; fax

QUEENSLAND

07-4746 8643; Landsborough Hwy, Kynuna; sites per 2 people $10, r $45-65; ⊠), from its walls covered with scrawled messages and signatures, to its unquestionably essential surf life-saving club. Accommodation ranges from pub rooms to spotless motel units, and camp sites. The nearest beach may be almost 1000km away, but each April the Blue Heeler hosts a surf life-saving carnival.

The signposted turn-off to the **Combo Waterhole**, which Banjo Paterson is said to have visited in 1895 before he wrote 'Waltzing Matilda', is off the highway about 12km east of Kynuna.

Winton
☎ 07 / pop 1321

Winton is a cattle- and sheep-raising centre, and also the railhead for transporting cattle brought from the Channel Country by road train. The town is a friendly, laidback place with two major claims to fame: the regionally inspired verse of Banjo Paterson, and the founding of Qantas airlines in 1920.

The **town library** (☎ 4657 0393; 76 Elderslie St) has Internet access.

Winton's biggest attraction is the **Waltzing Matilda Centre** (☎ 4657 1466; www.matildacentre .com.au; 50 Elderslie St; adult/child $14/12; ☯ 8.30am-5pm), which doubles as the visitors centre. Here you can also pick up the Shin Plaster pass, which covers entry to the town's attractions for $15 per person. There's a surprising number of exhibits here for a museum devoted to a song, including an indoor billabong complete with a squatter, troopers and a jolly swagman, a hologram display oozing cringe-inducing nationalism, and the **Jolly Swagman statue** – a tribute to the unknown swagmen who lie in unmarked graves in the area. There are plenty of interactive displays to keep the little ones entertained as well. The centre also houses the **Qantilda Pioneer Place**, which has a huge range of fascinating artefacts and displays on the founding of Qantas.

The **Royal Theatre** (☎ 4657 1296; 73 Elderslie St; adult/child $6/4; ☯ 8pm Wed, Apr-Sep), at the rear of the Wookatook Gift & Gem, is a wonderful open-air theatre with canvas-slung chairs, corrugated tin walls and a star-studded ceiling. It has a small museum in the projection room (admission $2) and screens old favourites such as Laurel and Hardy classics.

Arno's Wall (Vindex St), behind the North Gregory Hotel, is Winton's quirkiest attraction – a 70m-long work-in-progress, featuring a huge range of household items, from televisions to motorcycles, ensnared in the mortar.

The annual **Bush Poetry Festival**, in July, attracts entrants from all over Australia, but Winton's major festival is the five-day **Outback Festival**, held every odd year during the September school holidays.

SLEEPING & EATING
North Gregory Hotel (☎ 1800 801 611, 4657 1375; fax 4657 0106; 67 Elderslie St; dm $18, s/d $55/65, without bathroom $33/44; ⊠) This big, friendly country pub is allegedly where 'Waltzing Matilda' was first performed on 6 April 1895, although the original building burnt down in 1900. It has dozens of comfortable, old-fashioned rooms upstairs, with clean shared facilities. There's also an excellent **bistro** (mains $10-20).

Matilda Country Tourist Park (☎ 4657 1607; tma park@tpg.com.au; 43 Chirnside St; powered/unpowered sites per 2 people $20/18, cabins $70) Matilda's puts on regular campfire meals, complete with bush poetry and yarns. This camping ground, at the northern end of town, has lawn sites and good barbecue facilities.

GETTING THERE & AWAY
Greyhound Australia (☎ 13 14 99; www.greyhound .com.au) connects Winton to Brisbane ($130, 19½ hours), Mt Isa ($75, six hours) and Longreach ($28, three hours).

South of Winton
Eighty-five kilometres southwest of Winton, the friendly **Carisbrooke Station** (☎ 07-4657 3984; Cork Mail Rd; powered/unpowered sites per 2 people $16.50/11) has a wildlife sanctuary, Aboriginal paintings and bora rings (circular ceremonial grounds). Day tours of the station (available with advance notice) leave from Winton or the homestead for $110 per person (minimum of two people).

At **Lark Quarry Environmental Park** (☎ 07-4657 1812; adult/child $9/5; ☯ tours 10am, noon & 2pm) 110km southwest of Winton, there is what is thought to be the world's best-preserved evidence of a dinosaur stampede. It takes about 90 (worthwhile) minutes to drive from Winton to Lark Quarry in a conventional vehicle, but the mostly dirt road is impassable in wet weather.

Alternatively, **Diamantina Outback Tours** (☎ 07-4657 1514; www.diamantina-tour.com.au; per person $85, minimum of 4) runs day trips from Winton to Lark Quarry.

LONGREACH
☎ 07 / pop 3673
This prosperous outback town was the home of Qantas early last century, but these days it's equally famous for the Australian Stockman's Hall of Fame & Outback Heritage Centre, one of outback Queensland's biggest attractions.

Longreach's human population is vastly outnumbered by more than a million sheep, and there are a fair few cattle too.

The helpful **Visitors Information Centre** (☎ 4658 3555; 99 Eagle St; ◷ 9am-5pm Mon-Fri, 9am-1pm Sat & Sun) is opposite the **library** (☎ 4658 4104; 96a Eagle St; ◷ 9.30am-1pm Tue & Thu, 12.30-4.30pm Wed & Fri, 9am-noon Sat), which has free Internet access.

Sights
The excellent **Australian Stockman's Hall of Fame & Outback Heritage Centre** (☎ 4658 2166; www.outbackheritage.com.au; Landsborough Hwy; adult/child/family $20/10/45; ◷ 9am-5pm) is housed in a beautifully conceived building, 2km east of town towards Barcaldine. It was built as a tribute to the early explorers and stockmen, but now also encompasses several themed galleries covering Aboriginal culture, European exploration and pioneering settlers. Admission is valid for two days.

The **Qantas Founders Outback Museum** (☎ 4658 3737; www.qfom.com.au; Landsborough Hwy; adult/child/family $16/8/38; ◷ 9am-5pm) houses a life-size replica of an Avro 504K, the first aircraft owned by the fledgling airline. Interactive multimedia and working displays tell the history of Qantas. Next door, the original 1921 Qantas hangar houses a mint-condition DH-61. Towering over everything is a bright and shiny **747-200B Jumbo** (adult/child/family $12/6/25) which can be toured at additional cost.

The **Powerhouse Museum** (☎ 4658 3933; 12 Swan St; adult/child/family $5/3/13; ◷ 2-5pm Apr-Oct, variable hours Nov-Mar) displays the huge old diesel and gas-vacuum engines that were used until 1985, as well as local history relics.

Another attraction is **Banjo's Outback Theatre & Wool Shed** (☎ 1800 641 661, 4658 2360; Stork Rd; adult/child $12.50/8). It's a ramshackle place

with two-hour shows featuring bush poems, songs, yarns and shearing demonstrations most Saturday evenings, and Tuesday and Thursday mornings.

Tours
Longreach Outback Travel Centre (☎ 4658 1776; 115a Eagle St) Has a variety of tours, including a Longreach Lookabout tour (adult/child $145/128) that takes in the town's sites and ends with a dinner cruise on the Thomson River.

Outback Aussie Tours (☎ 1300 787 890; 18 Swan St) Offers tours including a combined Winton day tour that includes Carisbrooke Station and Lark Quarry (adult/child $150/80).

Festivals & Events
Longreach, along with Winton, Barcaldine and Ilfracombe, hosts **Easter in the Outback** annually. In May, on the Labour Day weekend, Longreach hosts the **Outback Muster Drovers Reunion**.

Sleeping & Eating
Old Time Cottage (☎ 4658 1550, 4658 3555; fax 4658 3733; 158 Crane St; d $75, per additional person $10; ❄) A great choice for groups and families, this quaint little corrugated-iron cottage is set in an attractive garden. Fully furnished, the self-contained cottage sleeps up to five people.

Albert Park Motor Inn (☎ 1800 812 811, 4658 2411; fax 4658 3181; Sir Hudson Fysh Memorial Dr; s/d $95/105; ❄ ♨) On the highway east of the centre, this good motel has spacious, four-star, well-appointed rooms, as well as pools and a spa. The motel's **Oasis Restaurant** (mains $15-30) has an elegant dining room and varied menu.

QUEENSLAND

Bush Verandah Restaurant (☎ 4658 2448; 120 Galah St; mains $14-20; ☒ dinner Tue-Sat) This small, licensed eatery features rustic décor and a country-style á la carte menu with beef, poultry and seafood.

Longreach Club (☎ 4658 1016; 31 Duck St; mains $10-15; ☒ lunch & dinner) The relaxed Longreach Club's restaurant is recommended for its range of inexpensive specials, including smorgasbords and roast of the day. There is also has an á la carte menu.

More accommodation options:

Longreach Motor Inn (☎ 1800 076 020, 4658 2322; fax 4658 1828; 84 Galah St; s/d $88/99; ☒ ☒) Central motel with the good Outback Restaurant (mains $14 to $28).

Central Hotel (☎ 4658 2263; 126 Eagle St; s/d without bathroom $25/40) Simple, clean rooms.

Gunnadoo Caravan Park & Cabins (☎ 4658 1781; fax 4658 0034; 12 Thrush Rd; powered/unpowered sites per 2 people $20/18, cabins $40; ☒ ☒) Neat and shady park.

Getting There & Away

Macair (☎ 13 13 23; www.macair.com.au) flies to Longreach from Townsville (one way from $210) via Winton. See p375 for more flight information.

Greyhound Australia (☎ 13 14 99; www.greyhound .com.au) connects Longreach with Winton ($28 three hours), Brisbane ($107, 17 hours) and Mt Isa ($77, eight hours). Buses stop behind the **Longreach Outback Travel Centre** (☎ 4658 1776; 115a Eagle St).

Emerald Coaches (☎ 1800 28737, 4982 4444; www .emeraldcoaches.com.au) makes the twice-weekly run travelling to and from Rockhampton ($80, 9½ hours). Buses stop at Outback Aussie Tours (p381).

See p375 for train information.

LONGREACH TO WINDORAH

The Thomson Developmental Rd is the most direct route towards Birdsville from Longreach.

The first 215km of the trip is a narrow sealed road that passes by tiny **Stonehenge**, where you'll find the **Stonehenge Hotel** (☎ 07-4658 5944; fax 07-4658 5927; Stafford St; s/d without bathroom $30/40). It also has daily meals, and sells fuel.

Jundah, 65km south of Stonehenge, is an administrative centre with a cheap caravan park, a pub and a general store. The second part of the route, from Jundah to Windorah, is mostly over unsealed roads of dirt, gravel and sand.

LONGREACH TO CHARLEVILLE

Ilfracombe

☎ 07 / pop 160

The tiny township of **Ilfracombe**, 28km east of Longreach, modestly calls itself 'the Hub of the West' and boasts the **Ilfracombe Machinery & Heritage Museum** (Landsborough Hwy; admission free), a brightly painted collection of old tractors and farm machinery and several historic buildings on the side of the highway. The charming **Wellshot Hotel** (☎ 4658 2106; Landsborough Hwy; s/d $20/40) has a wall covered with a long poem called *The Wellshot & The Bush Pub's Hall of Fame*, by Robert Raftery. The pub has clean rooms without bathrooms and good pub tucker.

Barcaldine

☎ 07 / pop 1496

Barcaldine (bar-*call*-din), at the junction of the Landsborough and Capricorn Hwys 108km east of Longreach, is known as the 'Garden City of the West', with good supplies of artesian water nourishing orchards of citrus fruits. The town also gained a place in Australian history in 1891 when it became the headquarters of a major shearers' strike. The confrontation led to the formation of the Australian Workers' Party, now the Australian Labor Party. The **Tree of Knowledge**, a ghost gum near the train station, was the organisers' meeting place and now stands as a monument to workers and their rights.

The **Visitor Information Centre** (☎ 4651 1724; Oak St) is next to the train station. **Barcaldine Video Hire** (☎ 4651 1611; 111 Oak St; per hr $6) and the **library** (☎ 4651 1170; 71 Ash St) offer Internet access.

The excellent **Australian Workers Heritage Centre** (☎ 4651 2422; www.australianworkersheritage centre.com.au; Ash St; adult/child $12/7.50; ☒ 9am-5pm Mon-Sat, 10am-5pm Sun) was built to commemorate the role of workers in forming Australian social, political and industrial movements. Set in landscaped gardens, the centre includes the Australian Bicentennial Theatre with displays tracing the history of the shearers' strike, as well as a schoolhouse, hospital and powerhouse.

The **Barcaldine Historical Museum** (☎ 4651 1310; cnr Beech & Gidyea Sts; admission $3; ☒ 7am-5pm) is in the town's former National Bank and is crammed with a fascinating collection of memorabilia, and offers mini-steam train rides once a month.

Mad Mick's (☎ 4651 1172; 84 Pine St; adult/child $10/6; ⏰ 9am-noon Apr-Sep) is a ramshackle, cluttered farmlet with a collection of old buildings and a fauna park.

SLEEPING & EATING

Ironbark Inn (☎ 4651 2311; fax 4651 2314; 115 Oak St; s/d $63/73; ☒ ☒) South of town, this motel has clean, comfortable rooms set in native gardens. Its best feature though is the **3Ls Bar & Bistro** (mains $14-20), a rustic open shed with wooden bench tables and stockmen's ropes and branding irons on the walls. It serves large steaks, pork chops and barramundi.

Blacksmith's Cottage (☎ 4651 1724; fax 4651 2243; 7 Elm St; d $60) This quaint, turn-of-the-19th-century B&B features period furniture and a modern kitchen for the self-serve breakfast.

Barcaldine's iconic iron-roofed, wooden-verandaed pubs line Oak St and make a great display.

The quintessential Artesian Hotel has the pick of patio tables in its **Drovers Inn Restaurant** (☎ 4651 1691; mains $6-15; ☰ lunch & dinner). But the Union Hotel's **Witch's Kitchen** (☎ 4651 2269; 61 Oak St; mains $14-20; ☰ lunch Mon-Fri, dinner daily) delivers the best range of bistro grills, pizzas and vegetarian dishes.

Blackall

☎ 07 / pop 1404

Blackall claims to be the site of the mythical black stump – according to outback mythology, anywhere west of Blackall was considered to be 'beyond the black stump'. The town is also famous as the site of the first artesian well to be drilled in Queensland. You'll probably agree with most travellers and say it stinks a little – the locals claim 'it's got body'.

Information on the town and the surrounding area is available from the **Blackall Visitor Information Centre** (☎ 4657 4637; www.blackall.qld.gov.au; Shamrock St; ☰ 9am-5pm). The **Blackall Woolscour** (☎ 4657 6042; Evora Rd; adult/child $9.90/5.50; ☰ 8am-4pm), 4km northeast, is the only steam-driven scour (wool cleaner) left in Queensland. Built in 1908, the scour operated until 1978, and has now been fully restored to do what it does best – get rid of sheep dags.

In the centre of town on Shamrock St, the **Jackie Howe Memorial Statue** is a tribute to the legendary shearer from Warwick (p345).

CHARLEVILLE

☎ 07 / pop 3519

In outback terms, Charleville is a veritable city and an oasis. It sits on the Warrego River, 760km west of Brisbane. The town was an important centre for early explorers – Cobb & Co had their largest coach-making factory based here

There's a **Visitor Information Centre** (☎ 4654 3057; Sturt St; ☰ 9am-5pm Apr-Sep, 9am-5pm Mon-Fri Oct-Mar) on the southern edge of town and the **library** (☎ 4654 1296; 69 Edward St; ☰ 8.30am-4pm Mon-Fri, 9am-noon Sat) has Internet access.

The **Cosmos Centre** (☎ 4654 7771; www.cosmos centre.com; adult/child/family $17/11/39; ☰ 10am-6pm, night observatory variable hours) is 2km south of the centre, off Airport Dr. Here you can tour the night sky through high-powered telescopes with an expert guide. The 90-minute sessions start soon after sunset.

Southeast of the visitors centre, the **QPWS** (☎ 4654 1255; 1 Park St; ☰ 8.30am-4.30pm Mon-Fri) runs a captive breeding programme for endangered native species. You can see yellow-footed rock wallabies here, but best is the **Bilby Show** (Racecourse Complex, Partridge St; admission $5; ☰ 6-7pm Sun, Mon, Wed & Fri Apr-Sep), which provides a fascinating insight into this rare nocturnal marsupial.

Dominating one of Charleville's main intersections, **Hotel Corones** (☎ 4654 1022; fax 4654 1756; 33 Wills St; s $25-60, tw $35-55, d $70-75, motel s/d $59/69; ☒) is a gracious old country pub. The magnificent preserved interior includes a huge public bar, leadlight windows, open fires and heritage rooms. The motel rooms are more bland. For lunch or dinner choose from the elegant dining room (mains $15 to $20) or the bar (mains $7).

THE CHANNEL COUNTRY

The remote and sparsely populated southwestern corner of Queensland, bordering the NT, South Australia (SA) and NSW, takes its name from the myriad channels that crisscross it. Rain hardly ever blesses this unforgiving corner of Australia, but water from the summer monsoons further north pours in along the Georgina, Hamilton and Diamantina Rivers and Cooper Creek. The summer heat is unbearable, so a visit is best made in winter (May to September).

For a short period after each wet season, the Channel Country becomes fertile and cattle are grazed here.

QUEENSLAND

GETTING THERE & AROUND

Some roads from the east and north to the fringes of the Channel Country are sealed, but between October and May even these can be cut off, when dirt roads become quagmires. Visiting this area requires a sturdy vehicle (4WD if you want to get off the beaten track) and some outback driving experience. Always carry plenty of drinking water and petrol, and if you're heading off the main roads notify the police.

The main road through this area is the Diamantina Developmental Rd. It runs south from Mt Isa through Boulia to Bedourie, then east through Windorah and Quilpie to Charleville. It's a long and lonely 1340km, about two-thirds of which is sealed.

Mt Isa to Birdsville

It's around 300km of sealed road from Mt Isa south to Boulia, and the only facilities along the route are at **Dajarra**, which has a pub and a roadhouse.

BOULIA
☎ 07 / pop 290

Boulia is the 'capital' of the Channel Country, and home to a mysterious supernatural phenomenon known as the **Min Min Light**, an 'earthbound UFO' resembling car headlights that hovers a metre or so above the ground before vanishing and reappearing elsewhere.

The **Min Min Encounter** (☎ 4746 3386; Herbert St; adult/child $11/7.70; ⏰ 8.30am-5pm Mon-Fri, 9am-noon Sat & Sun) features sophisticated gadgetry, imaginative sets and eerie lighting in its hourly show, which attempts to convert the nonbelievers. The centre is well worth a visit, and it doubles as the town's tourist information centre.

Boulia also lays claim to Australia's premier **camel racing** event held in mid-July.

The modern, spacious **Desert Sands Motel** (☎ 4746 3000; fax 4746 3040; Herbert St; s/d $80/90; ❄) is the town's most indulgent accommodation option. The units come with tea- and coffee-making facilities.

There's also a pub with decent rooms and food.

The sealed Kennedy Developmental Rd runs east from Boulia, 369km to Winton. The **Middleton Hotel** (☎ /fax 4657 3980; Kennedy Developmental Rd; s/d $35/45), 168km before Winton, is the only fuel stop en route. It serves meals daily and you can rent out simple dongas

(small, transportable building widely used in the Outback) without bathrooms.

BEDOURIE
☎ 07 / pop 120

From Boulia it's 200km of mainly unsealed road south to Bedourie, the administrative centre for the huge Diamantina Shire Council.

There's a caravan park and comfortable motel units at the **Simpson Desert Oasis** (☎ 47 46 1291; fax 4746 1208; Herbert St; powered/unpowered sites per 2 people $16/10, d $95; ❄), which incorporates a fuel stop, supermarket and restaurant. The **Royal Hotel** (☎ 4746 1201; fax 4746 1101; Herbert St; s/d $55/65; ❄), a charming adobe brick building built in 1880, has two motel units out the back.

Birdsville
☎ 07 / pop 120

This tiny settlement is the most remote place in Queensland, and possesses one of the country's most famous pubs, one of the most infamous horse races, and the hottest water supply.

Only 12km from the SA border, Birdsville is at the northern end of the 517km **Birdsville Track**, which leads to Marree in SA. In the late 19th century Birdsville was quite a busy place as it was the customs collection point for cattle driven south across the border via the Birdsville Track. With Federation, the charge was abolished and Birdsville became a near ghost town. In recent years a thriving cattle industry and growing tourism profile have revitalised the town. Its big event is the annual **Birdsville Races** on the first weekend in September, which attracts up to 6500 racing and boozing enthusiasts.

The **Wirrarri Centre** (☎ 4656 3300; www.diamantina.qld.gov.au; Billabong Blvd; ⏰ 8.30am-6pm Mar-Oct, 8.30am-4.30pm Mon-Fri Nov-Feb; 🖥) has tourist information and Internet access.

Don't miss the **Birdsville Working Museum** (☎ 4656 3259; Macdonald St; adult/child $7/5; ⏰ 8am-5pm Apr-Oct, tours 9am, 11am & 3pm). Inside this big tin shed is one of the most impressive private museums in Australia, with a fascinating collection of drovers' gear, shearing equipment, wool presses, road signs and much more.

Another highlight is the **Blue Poles Gallery & Caravanserai Cafe** (☎ 4656 3099; www.birdsvillestudio .com.au; Graham St; mains $17; ⏰ 9am-6pm Sun-Thu,

9am-10pm Fri, Sat & school holidays Apr-Nov), where you can inspect and buy outback art by exceptional local artist Wolfgang John and enjoy a good meal.

Dating back to 1884, the iconic **Birdsville Hotel** (☎ 4656 3244; www.theoutback.com.au; Adelaide St; s/d $80/100; ❄) faces resolutely into the Simpson Desert, having survived fire and cyclone. Tastefully renovated, it has modern motel-style units out the back, and a good restaurant (mains $15 to 18) for lunch and dinner. Friday nights are busy thanks to happy hour and the weekly 'chook raffle'.

Birdsville Track
To the south, the 517km Birdsville Track passes between the Simpson Desert to the west and Sturt's Stony Desert to the east. The first stretch from Birdsville has two routes, but only the longer, more easterly Outside Track is open these days. It crosses sandy country at the edge of the desert. Contact Birdsville's Wirrarri Centre (opposite) for road conditions, and keep friends and relatives informed of your movements.

Simpson Desert National Park
The waterless Simpson Desert occupies a massive 200,000 sq km of central Australia, and stretches across the Queensland, NT and SA borders. The Queensland section, in the state's far southwestern corner, is protected as the 10,000-sq-km Simpson Desert National Park, and is a remote, arid landscape of high red sand dunes, spinifex and canegrass.

Conventional cars can tackle the Birdsville Track quite easily, but the Simpson requires a 4WD and far more preparation. Crossings should only be tackled by parties of at least two 4WD vehicles, equipped with suitable communications to call for help if necessary. Alternatively, you can hire a satellite phone from **Birdsville police** (☎ 07-4656 3220) for $23 per day, which can be returned to **Maree police** (☎ 08-8675 8346) in SA. Permits are required to traverse the park, and are available from the Birdsville **QPWS office** (☎ 07-4652 7333; cnr Billabong Blvd & Jardine St) or from the town's petrol stations. For the park's SA sections, you need a separate permit, available through the **South Australian National Parks & Wildlife Service** (☎ 1800 816 078).

Birdsville to Charleville
The Birdsville Developmental Rd heads east from Birdsville, meeting the Diamantina Developmental Rd after 277km of rough gravel and sand. **Betoota** is the sole 'town' between Birdsville and Windorah, but there are no facilities so motorists have to carry enough fuel to cover the 395km distance.

Windorah is either very dry or very wet. The town's general store sells fuel and groceries. The **Western Star Hotel** (☎ 07-4656 3166; 15 Albert St; s/d pub rooms $30/44, motel units $75/85; ❄) has good pub rooms and motel units.

Quilpie is an opal-mining town and the railhead from which cattle are transported to the coast. It has a good range of facilities, including the **Quilpie Museum & Visitors Centre** (☎ 07-4656 2166; 51 Brolga St; ☼ 8am-5pm Mon-Fri, 9am-3.30pm Sat, 10am-4.30pm Sun mid-Apr–Oct, 8am-5pm Mon-Fri Nov–mid-Apr), two pubs, a motel, a caravan park and several petrol stations. From here it's another 210km to Charleville.

South of Quilpie and west of Cunnamulla are the remote **Yowah Opal Fields** and the town of **Eulo**, which co-hosts the **World Lizard Racing Championships** with Cunnamulla in late August. **Thargomindah**, 130km west of Eulo, has a couple of motels and a guesthouse. **Noccundra**, another 145km further west, was once a busy little community. It now has just one hotel supplying basic accommodation, meals and fuel. If you have a 4WD you can continue west to Innamincka, in SA, on the Strzelecki Track, via the site of the famous **Dig Tree**, where Burke and Wills camped in their ill-fated 1860–61 expedition.

WHITSUNDAY COAST

This is the stuff postcard dreams are made of – cloudless skies, glossy azure seas and a magnificent smear of flawless isles. This half-drowned mountain range plays host to coral gardens, sea turtles and myriad fishes. Much of the archipelago and the surrounding turquoise water belong to the Great Barrier Reef Marine Park, ensuring that this huge adventure playground stays as pristine as possible, with the notable benefit that its delights are accessible to all budgets.

Although the Whitsunday Islands steal the show, there are plenty of alternatives to sailing, swimming, snorkelling and sun-soaking. A healthy serve of national parks

QUEENSLAND

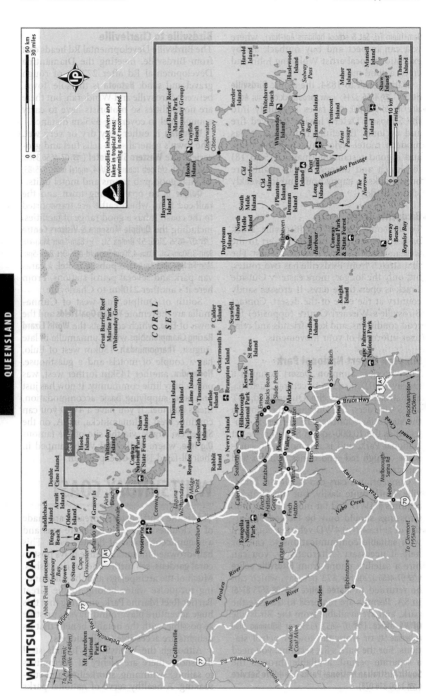

WHITSUNDAY COAST

QUEENSLAND

Crocodiles inhabit rivers and lakes in tropical areas; swimming is not recommended.

in the area provides tremendous opportunities for bushwalking, camping and platypus spotting. Then there's the partying; Airlie Beach is the gateway to the islands and chocked with restaurants, bars, clubs and heady good times.

MACKAY

☎ 07 / pop 74,000

Amidst the stretching horizons of beach along the Whitsunday Coast, Mackay catches visitors unawares with its cultural and architectural diversity and cosmopolitan ambience. It's the largest metropolitan area in the Whitsundays region and its lush, palm-lined streets hum with a relaxed café and bar scene. Across the Pioneer River the constantly transforming marina has added a new dimension to the city, with a bevy of stylish residential, tourism and dining developments.

The city's surrounding coastal plains and hinterland are carpeted in sugarcane and there are good beaches nearby. Mackay is an excellent base for visiting Eungella National Park with its famous platypuses, and for exploring the wilds of Finch Hatton Gorge and the attractive Pioneer Valley. Mackay is also the access point for ruggedly beautiful Cape Hillsborough National Park to the north, and several tropical islands.

Orientation

The blue Pioneer River wends its way through Mackay with the town settled on its southern side. Victoria St is the main strip. Long-distance buses stop at the Mackay Bus Terminal on Macallistar St.

Information

Chatline Internet (cnr Victoria & Wood Sts; per hr $6) Internet access inside an ice-cream shop.

Mackay Library (☎ 4957 1787; Gordon St; per hr $5; ☻ 9am-5pm Mon & Wed, 10am-6pm Tue, 10am-8pm Thu, 9am-3pm Fri, 10am-3pm Sat) Internet access.

Mackay Visitor Information Centre (☎ 4952 2677; www.mackayregion.com; 320 Nebo Rd; ☻ 8.30am-5pm Mon-Fri, 9am-4pm Sat & Sun) About 3km south of the centre.

QPWS (☎ 4944 7800; fax 4944 7811; cnr Wood & River Sts)

RACQ (☎ 4957 2918; 214 Victoria St; ☻ 8.30am-5pm Mon, Tue, Thu & Fri, 9am-5pm Wed, 8.30am-noon Sat)

Town Hall Visitor Information Centre (☎ 4951 4803; Sydney St; ☻ 9am-5pm Mon-Fri, to 2pm Sat & Sun)

Sights

Artspace Mackay (☎ 4957 1775; www.artspacemackay .com.au; admission free; Gordon St; ☻ 10am-5pm Tue-Sun) is an excellent contemporary gallery, showcasing local and visiting works. Enquire about current events and activities, delve deeper by consulting the extensive collection of art books or just browse the art before grazing at **foodspace** (☻ 10am-4pm Tue-Fri, 9am-4pm Sat & Sun), the in-house licensed café.

Mackay Regional Botanic Gardens (☎ 4952 7300; Lagoon St; admission free) is an impressive 'work in progress' about 3km south of the city centre. The 33-hectare site includes several themed gardens, a **Tropical Shade Garden** (☻ 8.45am-4.45pm) and **Lagoons Café** (☻ 10am-4pm).

Mackay's centre is littered with some fine Art Deco buildings. Look up when you wander the streets as most of the façades are at their finest on the second storey. Noteworthy examples include the **Mackay Town-house Motel** and the **Australian Hotel**, both on Victoria Street, and the **Ambassador Hotel** on Sydney Street. Pick up the free *Art Deco Mackay* leaflet from the Town Hall Visitor Information Centre for more information.

There are good views over the harbour from **Mt Basset**, and at **Rotary Lookout** on Mt Oscar in North Mackay. **Mackay Marina** is a pleasant place to wine and dine with a waterfront view, or to simply picnic in the park and stroll along the breakwater. **Harbour Beach**, next to it, is good for swimming, but the best beaches, about 16km north of Mackay, are **Blacks Beach**, **Eimeo** and **Bucasia**.

Illawong Fauna Sanctuary (☎ 4959 1777; fax 4959 1888; adult/child $12/6, half-day tour $60; ☻ 9am-6.30pm) is a sanctuary for sick animals and an excellent opportunity to witness native wildlife. Crocodile feeding is at 2.30pm (not to be missed), and koalas are fed at 5.15pm. It's about 43km west of Mackay, but tours include transfers. There's also the option of dinner, bed and breakfast at the sanctuary's **homestay** (per person $50; ☒).

Tours

Beyond Mackay's sugarcane sea are superb rainforest experiences and platypus spotting.

Farleigh Sugar Mill (☎ 4963 2700; admin@skillsstm .com.au; adult/child/family $17/10/40; ☻ tours 1pm Mon-Fri Jun-Nov) Two-hour tours at this mill explore the sugar-making process from harvest to cane train, but

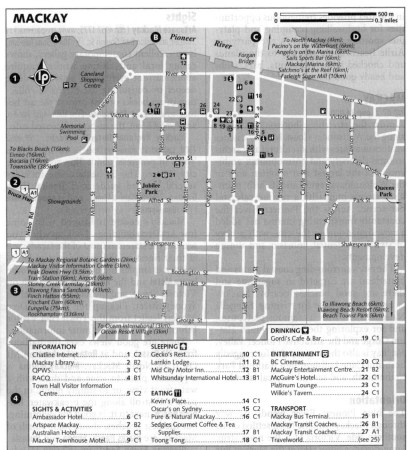

INFORMATION

Chatline Internet	1 C2
Mackay Library	2 B2
QPWS	3 C1
RACQ	4 B1
Town Hall Visitor Information Centre	5 C2

SIGHTS & ACTIVITIES

Ambassador Hotel	6 C1
Artspace Mackay	7 B2
Australian Hotel	8 C1
Mackay Townhouse Motel	9 C1

SLEEPING

Gecko's Rest	10 C1
Larrikin Lodge	11 B2
Mid City Motor Inn	12 B1
Whitsunday International Hotel	13 B1

EATING

Kevin's Place	14 C1
Oscar's on Sydney	15 C2
Pure & Natural Mackay	16 C1
Sedgies Gourmet Coffee & Tea Supplies	17 B1
Toong Tong	18 C1

DRINKING

Gordi's Cafe & Bar	19 C1

ENTERTAINMENT

BC Cinemas	20 C2
Mackay Entertainment Centre	21 B2
McGuire's Hotel	22 C1
Platinum Lounge	23 C1
Wilkie's Tavern	24 C1

TRANSPORT

Mackay Bus Terminal	25 B1
Mackay Transit Coaches	26 B1
Mackay Transit Coaches	27 A1
Travelworld	(see 25)

you need to dress for a working mill, which means long sleeves, long pants and enclosed shoes. The mill is 10km northwest of Mackay.

Jungle Johno Tours (☎ 4951 3728; larrikin@mackay .net.au; adult/child/YHA member $75/40/70) Offers highly recommended day trips to Eungella National Park, including pick-up, morning tea and lunch.

Mackay Water Taxi & Adventures (☎ 0417 073 969, 4942 7372; tjpic@mcs.net.au) Fishing charters (from $165 per person), tours to Keswick and St Bee's Islands (from $135) and snorkelling trips to the Great Barrier Reef.

Reeforest Adventure Tours (☎ 1800 500 353; www .reeforest.com; adult/child/family incl lunch $75/65/225) Explores Finch Hatton Gorge and visits the platypuses of Broken River.

Scenic Flights (Aviation Training & Transport; ☎ 4951 4300; Casey Ave) Half-hour flights from $50 per person.

Sleeping

BUDGET

Gecko's Rest (☎ 4944 1230; info@geckosrest.com.au; 34 Sydney St; dm/s/d $20/30/46; 🖳 🖳) This centrally located backpackers accommodation has comfortable, well-presented quads and triples, though some lack windows. There's a large kitchen, comfortable lounge and games area, plus a roof deck in-the-making.

Larrikin Lodge (☎ 4951 3728; fax 4957 2978; 32 Peel St; dm/tw/f $19/44/69; ⏰ 7am-2pm & 5-8.30pm) This small YHA-associated hostel in an airy, high-ceilinged timber house is clean, quiet and friendly. The owners operate Jungle Johno tours (left) and will pick you up from the bus terminal if you ring during office hours.

MIDRANGE

Ocean International (☎ 1800 635 104, 4957 2044; www.ocean-international.com.au; 1 Bridge Rd, Illawong Beach; d $130-219; ✖ ▣ ⚊) On the beach, close to the airport and only 3km south of the centre, this four-star complex overlooks Sandringham Bay and the Coral Sea. There's an excellent restaurant and cocktail bar, a spa and sauna, business centre, and harbour or airport transfer service.

Ocean Resort Village (☎ 1800 075 144, 4951 3200; www.oceanresortvillage.com.au; 5 Bridge Rd, Illawong Beach; d $79-125; ✖ ⚊) A good-value beachside resort comprising 34 self-contained apartments (studio, one- and two-bedroom) in a cool, shady setting with two pools, barbecue areas and half-court tennis.

Whitsunday International Hotel (☎ 4957 2811; fax 4951 1785; 176 Victoria St; d $66-99; ✖) This large centrally located hotel has well-maintained motel-style and self-contained rooms. There are a couple of bars, a restaurant and a nightclub on the ground floor, but the rooms are quiet.

Mid City Motor Inn (☎ 4951 1666; fax 4951 1968; 2 Macalister St; s/d $70/75; ✖ ⚊) On the banks of the river in a quiet locale, yet handy to the city centre, this spick-and-span motel has the best of both worlds.

Also recommended:

Illawong Beach Resort (☎ 4957 8427; fax 4957 8460; 73 Illawong Drive, Illawong Beach; d $120-140, extra person $16; ✖ ⚊) Manicured beachside resort with good facilities.

Beach Tourist Park (☎ 4957 4021; www.beachtourist park.com.au; 8 Petrie St, Illawong Beach; powered/unpowered sites per 2 people $24/18, cabins $48-98; ✖ ⚊) Large, modern beachfront park with excellent facilities.

Eating

Pacino's on the Waterfront (☎ 4957 8131; Mulherin Dr, Mackay Harbour; mains $15-35; ⛄ lunch & dinner Mon-Sat) This romantic Mediterranean restaurant and bar is nestled among the warehouses of the harbour and sports a breezy alfresco deck overlooking the water. Seafood is the main fare – in abundant and tasty quantities, but pastas and pizza are also served.

Kevin's Place (☎ 4953 5835; cnr Victoria & Wood Sts; mains $18-25; ⛄ lunch & dinner Mon-Sat) This heritage-listed building with ornate architecture sizzles on the inside with spicy Singaporean and Malay dishes and efficient, revved-up staff. Anything on the seafood list

is divine. Locals love this place so bookings are advised.

Oscar's on Sydney (☎ 4944 0173; cnr Sydney & Gordon Sts; mains $10-23; ⛄ breakfast, lunch & dinner) Pancakes for breakfast, pizzas and grills for lunch, more sophisticated mains in the evening – there's something for all tastes at this licensed café. Try the delicious *poffertjes*, authentic Dutch pancakes with traditional toppings ($5). Yum!

Angelo's on the Marina (☎ 4955 5600; Mulherin Dr, Mackay Marina; mains $15-33; ⛄ breakfast, lunch & dinner) A large, lively restaurant in a delightful marina setting, with an extensive range of pasta and a mouth-watering Mediterranean menu. It's fully licensed and there's a free courtesy bus for parties of six or more people, so join a group and enjoy. *Alla tua salute*! (Cheers!)

Also recommended:

Sedgies Gourmet Coffee & Tea Supplies (☎ 4957 4845; cnr Nelson & Victoria Sts; meals $5-11; ⛄ breakfast Mon-Sat, lunch Mon-Fri) Casual café with an astounding array of coffee and tea.

Pure & Natural Mackay (☎ 4957 6136; NAB Plaza, Sydney St; mains $5-10; ⛄ 7am-4.30pm Mon-Fri, 7am-3pm Sat) It's all low-fat but who cares because it tastes so good.

Toong Tong (☎ 4957 8051; 10 Sydney St; mains $12-20; ⛄ lunch & dinner) Cosy Thai restaurant with predictable, but good food.

Drinking

Gordi's Café & Bar (☎ 4951 2611; 85 Victoria St) It may be a café by day, but the open windows facing Mackay's main drag provide the perfect vantage point to enjoy a cold beer. Things get busier once evening kicks in with live music and DJs upstairs (entry $5).

Sails Sports Bar (☎ 4955 5022; Mulherin Dr, Mackay Harbour) Outdoor bar usually hums with a good crowd soaking up the alfresco drinking and convivial atmosphere on weekends.

Satchmo's at the Reef (☎ 4955 6055; Mulherin Dr, Mackay Harbour) Classy Satchmo's dishes up wine, tapas and style, but lends itself to a relaxed crowd. Boaties join other locals and tourists here and live music is a regular feature on Sunday afternoon.

Entertainment

Platinum Lounge (☎ 4957 2220; 83 Victoria St) On the 1st floor above the corner of Victoria and Wood Sts, the Platinum Lounge is a good place to unwind and to converse

QUEENSLAND

without shouting. Wednesday and Thursday nights are karaoke nights.

For live music you can head to **McGuires Hotel** (☎ 4957 7464; 17 Wood St) or **Wilkie's Tavern** (☎ 4957 2241; cnr Victoria & Gregory Sts).

Theatre and cinema in Mackay include its main venue for live performance, **Mackay Entertainment Centre** (☎ 4957 2255; Gordon St), and **BC Cinemas** (☎ 4957 3515; 30 Gordon St).

Getting There & Away

Travelworld (☎ 4944 2144; roseh@mkytworld.com.au; cnr Victoria & Macalister Sts; ⏰ 7am-6pm Mon-Fri, 7am-4pm Sat) handles all transport arrangements and is located at the bus station, where a 24-hour café also sells bus tickets.

AIR

Qantas (☎ 13 13 13; www.qantas.com.au), **Jetstar** (☎ 13 15 38; www.jetstar.com.au) and **Virgin Blue** (☎ 13 67 89; www.virginblue.com.au) all service Mackay. Flights include Brisbane ($90), Rockhampton ($140), Townsville ($180) and Sydney ($150).

BUS

Greyhound Australia (☎ 13 14 99; www.greyhound .com.au) and **Premier Motor Service** (☎ 13 34 10; www.premierms.com.au) connect Mackay with Cairns ($115, 12 hours), Townsville ($65, six hours), Airlie Beach ($26, two hours) and Brisbane ($135, 16 hours).

TRAIN

The Queensland Rail (☎ 1300 131 722; www.travel train.com.au) *Tilt Train* connects Mackay with Brisbane ($210, 12½ hours), Townsville ($95, 5½ hours) and Cairns ($165, 12 hours). The slower *Sunlander* does the same; Brisbane (economy seat/sleeper $140/195, 17 hours), Townsville (economy seat/sleeper $65/115, 6½ hours) and Cairns ($$110/165, 12½ hours). The train station is at Paget, 5km south of the city centre.

Getting Around

Avis (☎ 4951 1266), **Budget** (☎ 4951 1400) and **Hertz** (☎ 4951 3334) have counters at the airport.

Mackay Transit Coaches (☎ 4957 3330) operates local buses from two bus stops in town: at the back of Canelands Shopping Centre, and from the corner of Victoria and Gregory Sts. The visitor information centres have timetables.

For a taxi, call **Mackay Taxis** (☎ 13 10 08). Trips cost about $15 to the airport, marina or train station.

AROUND MACKAY

Pioneer Valley

You're missing a great country Queensland experience if you don't spend a couple of days enjoying the sights west of Mackay.

The Eungella Rd takes you through fertile Pioneer Valley to Marian, where you can turn off to **Kinchant Dam** and the fishing fraternity's **Kinchant Waters Leisure Resort** (☎ 07-4954 1453; powered/unpowered sites per 2 people $24/10, cabins $75). This super-casual resort is ideal for families, with canoes and aqua bikes for hire and oodles of room.

Head out of Mackay 10km on the Peak Downs Hwy to the Eungella Rd turn-off. Drive 29km along the Eungella Rd to Marian, take the Eton turn-off, driving 10km to North Eton. Turn right at Kinchant Dam Rd by the large chimney. It's 8km to the dam.

Alternatively, from Marian continue along the Eungella Rd to Mirani and visit the Illawong Fauna Sanctuary (p387).

Next stop is **Finch Hatton Gorge**. The gorge turn-off is 1.5km before the township of Finch Hatton. It's 9km into the gorge and the last 3km are on good, unsealed roads, but after heavy rain creek crossings make access difficult or impossible.

At the gorge you can try **Forest Flying** (☎ 07-4958 3359; www.forestflying.com; rides $45). Flyers whizz around the rainforest canopy sitting in a harness attached to a 340m-long cable. Keep your eyes peeled for rainforest critters as you brush through palm leaves and swing by the fruit-bat colony (August to May). Definitely book ahead.

More tranquil pursuits at the gorge include a 1.6km rainforest walk to a fantastic swimming hole beneath **Araluen Falls**, or a 2.6km walking trail to the **Wheel of Fire Falls**, and picnics at the car park. You can stay at **Finch Hatton Gorge Cabins** (☎ 07-4958 3281; sites per person $8, dm/d $15/80; 🐾), set in enchanting subtropical surrounds with a nearby creek, or there's the true bush retreat – **Platypus Bush Camp** (☎ 07-4958 3204; www.bushcamp.net; Finch Hatton Gorge; sites per person $8, dm/d $20/60) with its own swimming hole and platypus viewing.

Back on the road to Eungella, Finch Hatton is a teensy township, but the **Criterion**

Hotel (☎ 07-4958 3252; 9 Eungella Rd; mains $5-16, s/d $15/30) has spotless hotel rooms and plenty of country pub character. Alternatively, there's the **Finch Hatton Caravan Park** (☎ 07-4958 3222; Zahmel St; powered/unpowered sites per 2 people $17/14, on-site caravans from $30).

A further 20km and you reach beautiful **Eungella National Park** (*young*-gulla), meaning 'land of clouds'. Eungella has the oldest and longest stretch of subtropical rainforest in Australia and has been cut off from other rainforest areas for roughly 30,000 years. It breeds weird beasties that exist nowhere else, such as the Eungella gastric brooding frog, which incubates its eggs in its stomach and gives birth by spitting out the tadpoles!

There are excellent rainforest walks signposted on the 5km road between Eungella township and Broken River, but it's the shy platypus you'll hope to see. They live at pretty **Broken River**. You can be fairly sure of seeing platypuses most days from the viewing platform near the bridge. The best times are immediately after dawn and at dusk, but you must be patient, still and silent. Rangers lead night walks that reveal the park's party animals; ask at the QPWS office.

Broken River Mountain Retreat (☎ 07-4958 4528; fax 4958 4564; d $80-125; 🖳 🖳) has a range of lovely cedar cabins, a wood-finished lounge and the **Platypus Lodge Restaurant & Bar** (mains $18-25). There's also the lovely **QPWS Fern Flat Camping Ground** (per person/family $4/16), run on a first-come, first-served basis, near the **QPWS office** (☎ 07-4958 4552; 🕑 8am-4pm) and kiosk.

Back at Eungella township, **Eungella Chalet** (☎ 07-4958 4509; fax 07-4958 4503; s/d without bathroom $38/50, d with bathroom $72, cabins $90-110; mains $5-25; 🖳) is an old-fashioned guesthouse perched on the mountain edge with spectacular views. **Hideaway Cafe** (☎ 07-4958 4533; Broken River Rd; snacks $4-8; 🕑 9am-4pm Mon-Sun) has scrumptious homemade food. **Eungella General Store** (☎ 07-4958 4520) has snacks, groceries and fuel.

GETTING THERE & AWAY

Buses don't cover Finch Hatton or Eungella, but some organised tours do camping drop-offs (see p387 for more information). Otherwise, hire a car; you won't be sorry.

Cape Hillsborough National Park

This small coastal park, 54km north of Mackay, takes in the rocky, 300m-high Cape Hillsborough, and Andrews Point and Wedge Island, which are joined by a causeway at low tide. All cliffs, dunes, scrub, rainforest and secluded woodland, there's little to do here but relax and mingle with kangaroos, wallabies, sugar gliders and turtles. There are also remains of Aboriginal middens and stone fish-traps, which can be accessed by good walking tracks. On the approach to the foreshore area there's also an interesting boardwalk leading out through a tidal mangroves forest.

Cape Hillsborough Nature Resort (☎ 07-4959 0152; www.capehillsboroughresort.com.au; MS 895 Mackay; powered/unpowered sites per 2 people $18/13, d $39-74; 🖳 🖳) is an idyllic, low-key resort with cabin and motel accommodation and abundant wildlife. Facilities include a bar and **restaurant** (mains $12-19).

There is also the grassy **QPWS Smalleys Beach Campground** (per person/family $4/16). Register on site.

The Cumberland Islands

Of the 70-odd islands belonging to the Cumberland group, Brampton and Carlisle are the most popular. Both are mountainous national parks, joined by a sandbank, which you can wade across (about 20m) when it's low tide. The islands have forested slopes, sandy beaches, OK walks and fringing coral reefs with great snorkelling.

Brampton Island Resort (☎ 1300 134 044, 07-4951 4499; www.brampton-island.com; s $345-485, d $460-740; 🖳 🖳 🖳) is a haven for couples and

QUEENSLAND

honeymooners. The range of prices reflect varying views and facilities. Prices include meals.

Australian Helicopters (☎ 07-4951 0888; one way/return per person $100/200) fly to Brampton daily from Mackay Airport. Alternatively, the resort has its own launch (one way/return per adult $50/100, per child $25/50) that leaves Mackay Marina at 11.30am, returning at 1.15pm.

Carlisle Island is uninhabited, but there is a **QPWS camping ground** at Southern Bay, directly across from the Brampton Island Resort. You must be self-sufficient and bring your own water, but there is a free gas barbecue, toilet and picnic shelter here.

If you want real Robinson Crusoe, self-sufficient–style camping, contact the **QPWS** (☎ 07-4944 7800, 13 13 04; www.epa.qld.gov.au) about Scawfell and Goldsmith Islands. Permits can be purchased online.

AIRLIE BEACH
☎ 07 / pop 3030

The gateway to the Whitsunday Islands, Airlie defies its relatively small size by humming constantly to the tune of a party somewhere. Days simmer with buzzing beer gardens before bubbling into jumping festivities in the glut of bars, clubs, pubs and cafés. Backpackers tripping into town to embark on the mandatory Whitsunday cruise make the most of it, but yachties and local holiday-makers also congregate here. All this activity takes place on the main drag, Shute Harbour. As the picturesque streets roll up the dramatic hills in the background, the vistas and quiet swell.

Airlie boasts an excellent range of accommodation, and a glorious artificial lagoon, right on the foreshore. There's also whale-watching between July and September, and horse riding and hiking in the hinterland.

Information
Airlie Beach Visitor Information Centre (☎ 4946 6665; 277 Shute Harbour Rd; ⏱ 7.30am-8pm) Privately run centre.

Destination Whitsundays (☎ 4946 6846; 295 Shute Harbour Rd) Privately run.

Internet Centre (346 Shute Harbour Rd; per hr $2.50) Internet access.

Peterpan Adventure Travel (☎ 1800 213 225, 4948 0866; www.peterpans.com; Shop 1/398 Shute Harbour Rd; per hr $2) Internet access.

QPWS (☎ 4946 7022; fax 4946 7023; cnr Shute Harbour & Mandalay Rds; ⏱ 9am-5pm Mon-Fri) Best source of information for camping on the islands.

Whitsunday Visitor Information Centre (☎ 1800 801 252; www.whitsundaytourism.com; Bruce Hwy, Proserpine; ⏱ 10am-6pm)

Activities
Sailing opportunities are plenty (see p397 for details).

DIVING
Airlie has a reputation for being a great place to learn to dive. Costs for open-water courses with several ocean dives start at around $500; cheaper courses will probably have you spending most of your 'dives' in a pool. Generally, courses involve two or three days' tuition, meals and accommodation.

Dive companies:

Oceania Dive (☎ 1800 075 035, 4946 6032; www.oceania dive.com; 257 Shute Harbour Rd)

Pro-Dive (☎ 1800 075 035, 4948 1888; www.prodive whitsundays.com.au; 344 Shute Harbour Rd)

FISHING
Charter boat operators provide all-inclusive day trips to the outer Whitsundays. The **MV Jillian** (☎ 4948 1301) departs Abel Point Marina at Airlie Beach, and **MV Moruya** (☎ 4946 6665) departs from Shute Harbour. Both charge $120/75 per adult/child. You can hire your own boat from **Harbour Side Boat Hire** (☎ 4946 9330; Ferry Terminal, Shute Harbour; per day $80-250).

OTHER ACTIVITIES
Paddling serenely in search of an island with dolphins and turtles would have to be one of the best ways to experience the Whitsundays. **Salty Dog Sea Kayaking** (☎ 4946 1388; www .saltydog.com.au; per person half-/full-day tours $50/90) offers guided tours and kayak rental.

The Conway Range behind Airlie Beach is part national park (see p395) and part State Forest, and provides for some great walking in coastal rainforest. For info on walks, including the three-day Whitsunday Great Walk, visit QPWS (above).

Other active pursuits include tandem sky-diving with **Tandem Skydive Airlie Beach** (☎ 4946 9115; per person from $250) and parasailing with **Whitsunday Parasail** (☎ 4948 0000; per person $55). Alternatively, straddle a quad bike (a four-wheeled motorcycle) and go mental at top

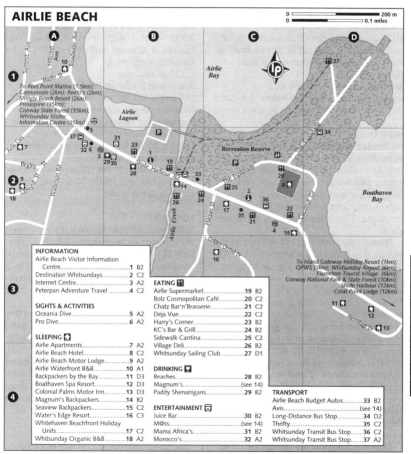

AIRLIE BEACH

0 — 200 m
0 — 0.1 miles

To Abel Point Marina (1.5km);
Cannonvale (2km); Reefo's (2km);
Shingly Beach Resort (2km);
Proserpine (35km);
Conway State Forest (35km);
Whitsunday Visitor
Information Centre (35km)

Airlie Bay

Airlie Lagoon

Recreation Reserve

Boathaven Bay

To Island Gateway Holiday Resort (1km);
QPWS (3km); Whitsunday Airport (6km);
Flametree Tourist Village (6km);
Conway National Park & State Forest (10km);
Shute Harbour (12km);
Coral Point Lodge (12km)

INFORMATION
Airlie Beach Visitor Information
   Centre...................................1 B2
Destination Whitsundays.............2 C2
Internet Centre..........................3 A2
Peterpan Adventure Travel 4 C2

SIGHTS & ACTIVITIES
Oceania Dive..............................5 A2
Pro Dive....................................6 A2

SLEEPING
Airlie Apartments.......................7 A2
Airlie Beach Hotel......................8 C2
Airlie Beach Motor Lodge............9 A2
Airlie Waterfront B&B................10 A1
Backpackers by the Bay.............11 D3
Boathaven Spa Resort...............12 D3
Colonial Palms Motor Inn..........13 D3
Magnum's Backpackers..............14 B2
Seaview Backpackers.................15 C2
Water's Edge Resort.................16 C3
Whitehaven Beachfront Holiday
   Units...................................17 C2
Whitsunday Organic B&B...........18 A2

EATING
Airlie Supermarket....................19 B2
Bolz Cosmopolitan Café.............20 C2
Chatz Bar'n'Brasserie................21 C2
Deja Vue..................................22 C2
Harry's Corner..........................23 B2
KC's Bar & Grill........................24 C2
Sidewalk Cantina......................25 C2
Village Deli...............................26 B2
Whitsunday Sailing Club.............27 D1

DRINKING
Beaches...................................28 B2
Magnum's.........................(see 14)
Paddy Shenanigans....................29 B2

ENTERTAINMENT
Juice Bar..................................30 B2
M@ss..............................(see 14)
Mama Africa's...........................31 B2
Morocco's.................................32 A2

TRANSPORT
Airlie Beach Budget Autos..........33 B2
Avis...............................(see 14)
Long-Distance Bus Stop.............34 D2
Thrifty.....................................35 C2
Whitsunday Transit Bus Stop......36 C2
Whitsunday Transit Bus Stop......37 A2

QUEENSLAND

speed (if you dare) on more than 10km of purpose-built adventure track with **Quad Bike Bush Adventures** (☎ 4946 1020;www.bushadventures .com.au; 385 Sugarloaf Rd, Sugarloaf; from $70).

Sleeping
BUDGET
Backpackers by the Bay (☎ 1800 646 994, ☎ /fax 4946 7267; www.backpackersbythebay.com; 12 Hermitage Dr; dm $22, d $55; ⊠ ▣ ☒) Away from the madding crowd, this small and quiet backpackers occupies a great vantage point on top of a hill. The atmosphere is friendly, the dorms have just four beds and the double rooms are some of the best around.

Magnum's Backpackers (☎ 4946 6266; www.mag nums.com.au; 366 Shute Harbour Rd; sites per 2 people

$15-18, dm $14-17, d $45; ⊠ ▣) This loud and large backpackers resort is smack bang in the middle of town. Cheaper dorms sit close to the bar, while the spiffier digs are surrounded by gardens. The attached bar and nightclub here (see p395) are hugely popular.

Two good camping options are **Island Gateway Holiday Resort** (☎ 4946 6228; www .islandgateway.com.au; Shute Harbour Rd, Jubilee Pocket; powered/unpowered sites $25/19, cabins $50-95; ⊠ ☒) which has shady sites and excellent facilities, and **Flametree Tourist Village** (☎ 4946 9388; www.flametreevillage.com.au; Shute Harbour Rd; powered/unpowered sites $21/17, cabins from $65; ⊠ ☒), which is situated in lovely, bird-filled gardens.

Also recommended:

Reefo's (Reef Oceania Village; ☎ 1800 800 795, 4946 6137; www.reeforesort.com; 147 Shute Harbour Rd, Cannonvale; dm $12-18, d $55; ☒ ☐ ☒) This sprawling, comfortable backpackers also features a bar, restaurant and tour desk.

Seaview Backpackers (☎ 4946 6911; seaview@mackay.net.au; 404 Shute Harbour Rd; dm $18, d $50; ☒ ☒) Central with bright and airy dorms.

MIDRANGE

Whitsunday Organic B&B (☎ 4946 7161; www .whitsundaybb.com.au; 8 Lamond St; s/d $90/120) A very stylish eco-friendly B&B, with well-appointed rooms and wholesome organic breakfasts. Dinners are also available, as is help with organising tours and wonderfully relaxing massages. There are discounts for longer stays.

Colonial Palms Motor Inn (☎ 4946 9500; fax 4946 9469; cnr Shute Harbour Rd & Hermitage Dr; d from $105; ☒ ☒) This motel is in a great location – central but quiet – and has spacious rooms, some self-contained, and a large restaurant. There's a 10% discount if you belong to a motoring club.

Airlie Beach Hotel (☎ 1800 466 233, 4964 1999; www.airliebeachhotel.com.au; cnr The Esplanade & Coconut Grove; s $90-160, d $160-170; ☒ ☒) Slick hotel is superbly located and has a range of accommodation options. There are comfortable motel-style rooms surrounding the pool and spacious hotel rooms and suites with great views in the modern high-rise. Facilities for those with disabilities are good and there are a couple of restaurants at street level.

Airlie Beach Motor Lodge (☎ 1800 810 925, 4946 6418; www.airliebeachmotorlodge.com.au; 6 Lamond St; d from $105; ☒ ☒) Tucked away in a residential pocket, this quiet motel is just a short walk from the Shute Harbour Rd action. As well as neat motel rooms there are self-contained units and a purpose-built facility for disabled guests.

Coral Point Lodge (☎ 4946 9500; fax 4946 9469; 54 Harbour Ave, Shute Harbour; d from $90; ☒ ☒) Far from the hubbub of Airlie and clinging to the ridge overlooking Shute Harbour, this pleasant spot has superb views. Some rooms are self-contained, and there's a café, which is also open to nonguests, and serves meals and snacks

Shingley Beach Resort (☎ 4948 8300; www.shin gleybeachresort.com; 1 Shingley Dr; d $115-220; ☒ ☒) These midrange and self-contained holiday apartments are close to Abel Point Marina and feature good views. There are four different room configurations, a bar and restaurant, a massage and yoga studio, and a seriously deep pool.

Other options:

Whitehaven Beachfront Holiday Units (☎ 4946 5710; fax 4946 5711; 285 Shute Harbour Rd; s/d $85/95; ☒) Cental, older-style block with well-presented apartments.

Boathaven Spa Resort (☎ 1800 985 856,4948 4948; www.boathavenresort.com; 440 Shute Harbour Rd; d $150-180; ☒ ☒) Very comfortable self-contained rooms with balconies, spas and views.

Airlie Apartments (☎ 4946 6222; www.airlieapartments .com; 22-24 Airlie Cres; d $85-120; ☒ ☒) Good-value apartments, ideal for families.

TOP END

Airlie Waterfront B&B (☎ 4946 7631; www.airliewater frontbnb.com.au; cnr Broadwater Ave & Mazlin St; d from $169; ☒) Beautifully presented and sumptuously furnished with antiques, this is a lovely relaxing option that is still convenient to the action. Two double rooms have their own private spa.

Water's Edge Resort (☎ 4948 2655; fax 4948 2755; www.watersedgewhitsundays.com.au; 4 Golden Orchid Dr; apt $190-230; ☒ ☒) A luxurious complex with Southeast Asian themes, cool stone architecture, wet-edge pools and attentive service. The one-, two- and three-bedroom apartments boast large lounges and some have spas. The views are superb, and there's also a poolside restaurant and gym.

Eating

Most of the eateries are on or just off Shute Harbour Rd.

Deja Vue (☎ 4946 5700; 301 Shute Harbour Rd; mains $21-30; ☺ dinner Tue-Sat) Tucked away in a small courtyard, this unpretentious restaurant delivers fine food with little fuss. The menu promises modern interpretations of Thai, Mediterranean, Indian and others, and the execution and presentation is faultless. The warm Indian lamb rubbed in dry spices is sensational.

Chatz Bar'n'Brasserie (☎ 4946 7223; 390 Shute Harbour Rd; mains $16-26; ☺ breakfast, lunch & dinner) There's a popular front bar, while the cosy restaurant section up the back offers seafood and Italian main courses. There are always a few inexpensive specials on the blackboard and you can get a decent breakfast or lunch here for under $10.

QUEENSLAND

Bolz Cosmopolitan Café (☎ 4946 7755; 7 Beach Plaza, The Esplanade; mains $10-25; ☺ breakfast, lunch & dinner) Sit on faux-zebra booths or the terrace at this classy little restaurant. There's pasta, pizza and more. The service can be a little erratic but the mango and prawn pizza was a delightful surprise.

Village Deli (☎ 4964 1121; 351 Shute Harbour Rd; mains $10-15; ☺ 8am-5.30pm) Tasty light meals and faaaabulous coffee are served at this casual café/deli. The mixed salad plate is great value, and big, healthy breakfasts, gelati and juices are on the go all day. Takeaway provisions and picnic boxes are a speciality.

Whitsunday Sailing Club (☎ 4946 7894; 261 Shute Harbour Rd; mains $14-32; ☺ lunch & dinner) The Sailing Club terrace is a great place for a meal and a drink. Choose from the usual steak and schnitzel culprits, off the inexpensive bistro blackboard, or select from the more upmarket Commodore's Table menu.

KC's Bar & Grill (☎ 4946 6320; 282 Shute Harbour Rd; mains $16-33; ☺ dinner & supper) KC's happy hour(s) are followed by dinner, between 6pm and 9pm, and then there is usually some live music. It's lively and licensed, and the menu has croc and roo grills as well as steak and seafood.

Also recommended:

Harry's Corner (☎ 4946 7459; 273 Shute Harbour Rd; mains $8-12; ☺ 7am-4pm) Popular little café. Huge breakfasts.

Sidewalk Cantina (☎ 4946 6425; The Esplanade; dishes $10-25; ☺ 7am-2pm, 6pm-late Thu-Mon) Café fare by day, Tex-Mex by night.

Airlie Supermarket (277 Shute Harbour Rd)

Drinking & Entertainment

Magnum's (☎ 4946 6266; Shute Harbour Rd) Attached to the hostel, this sizable pub offers punters a sea of outdoor seating at which they happily consume vast amounts of alcohol. The crowd is generally young and spirited and it's a great place to meet other travellers.

Mama Africa's (☎ 4948 0438; 263 Shute Harbour Rd) It's a shame this club, next to Panache on the Beach restaurant, doesn't open earlier; it's such a cool spot to hang out. With its zebra-striped floor, tribal motifs, kick-back lounge chairs and a vibe that taps straight into your pulse, it's no wonder Mama's rocks.

Juice Bar (☎ 4946 6465; 354 Shute Harbour Rd; ☺ 10pm-5am) Upstairs from the Irish bar Paddy Shenanigans, the bare Juice Bar pounds to dance and techno, but just about anything else is likely to pop up.

The backpacker party shuffles between **Morocco's** (☎ 4946 6001), up at the top end of Shute Harbour Rd, Magnum's and **Beaches** (☎ 4946 6244), which is in the middle of the strip.

Other recommendations:

Paddy Shenanigans (☎ 4946 5055; 352 Shute Harbour Rd)

M@ss (Magnums) Crowd-pleasing music, and foam parties.

Getting There & Away

AIR

The closest major airports are at Proserpine and on Hamilton Island. The small **Whitsunday airport** (☎ 4946 9933) is about 11km east of town. **Island Air Taxis** (☎ 4946 9933) flies to Hamilton ($60) and Lindeman ($80). **Air Whitsunday Seaplanes** (☎ 4946 9111) flies to Daydream, Long, and South Molle for $450 per flight.

BUS

Greyhound Australia (☎ 13 14 99; www.greyhound .com.au) and **Premier Motor Service** (☎ 13 34 10; www.premierms.com.au) have bus connections to Brisbane ($148, 18 hours), Mackay ($26, 2½ hours), Townsville ($46, 4 hours) and Cairns ($92, 11 hours).

Con-X-ion (☎ 1300 308 718; www.con-x-ion.com; adult/child one way $44/22) connects Mackay airport and Mackay bus terminal with Airlie Beach twice per day.

Whitsunday Transit (☎ 4946 1800) connects Proserpine (Proserpine Airport), Cannonvale, Abel Point, Airlie Beach and Shute Harbour. Buses operate from 6am to 10.30pm and stop along Shute Harbour Rd.

Getting Around

The car-rental companies are along Shute Harbour Rd.

Airlie Beach Budget Autos (☎ 4948 0300; 285 Shute Harbour Rd)

Avis (☎ 4946 6318; 366 Shute Harbour Rd)

Thrifty (☎ 4946 7727; 390 Shute Harbour Rd)

CONWAY NATIONAL PARK & STATE FOREST

Most of this mountainous park is composed of rugged ranges and valleys covered in rainforest, with a sprinkling of mangroves and open forest.

The road from Airlie Beach to Shute Harbour passes through the northern section

QUEENSLAND

of the park. Several walking trails start from near the picnic and day-use area, including a 1km circuit track to a mangrove creek. About 1km past the day-use area, on the northern side of the road, there's a 2.4km walk up to the Mt Rooper lookout, providing good views of the Whitsunday islands.

Alternatively, there's the beautiful **Cedar Creek Falls** trail in the state forest. The turn-off is on your right, 18km from Airlie Beach on the Proserpine–Airlie road. Contact QPWS (p392) in Airlie for more park and forest information.

WHITSUNDAY ISLANDS

Just about every outdoor-loving Australian dreams of soaking up the rays and reef on a yacht in the Whitsundays. The blue-green waterways surrounding these islands are marine park and fall within the Great Barrier Reef World Heritage Area that stretches from Cape York in the north to Bundaberg in the south. We're all responsible for preserving this natural wonderland for generations to enjoy, so you may kiss the fish if you can catch them, but don't feed them, and please, don't pet the coral.

The Whitsundays is a drowned landscape – these continental islands are the tips of mountains fringed with coral. The Great Barrier Reef is at least 60km from the mainland. There are more than 90 islands, most of which are uninhabited.

All but four of the islands are predominantly or completely national park, but most visitors come to stay at the resorts scattered throughout, where cheap package holidays can be booked in advance.

SLEEPING

You can pitch your tent at QPWS camping grounds on 17 of the islands, but you need to be fully self-sufficient and leave behind only footprints. Camping grounds are occasionally closed to alternate traffic between them and minimise the impact on the environment.

To organise your trip, visit the excellent QPWS office (p392), which provides permits (per person/family $4/16) and advice.

GETTING THERE & AWAY

Air

Hamilton and Lindeman islands have airports. **Island Air Taxis** (☎ 07-4946 9933; Shute Harbour Rd; ☒ 7.45am-5.30pm) offers flights to both Hamilton and Lindeman Islands ($60 one way per adult). **Air Whitsunday Seaplanes** (☎ 07-4946 9111) flies from Airlie Beach to Daydream, Long, and South Molle for $450 per flight. **Hamilton Island Aviation** (☎ 07-4946 8249) connects Hamilton with Mackay ($135), Airlie Beach ($60) and Lindeman Island ($60).

Jetstar (☎ 13 15 38; www.jetstar.com.au) connects Hamilton Island with Brisbane ($190), Sydney ($220) and Melbourne ($240). **Qantas-Link** (☎ 13 13 13; www.qantas.com.au) flies there from Cairns ($145).

Boat

Most of the cruise operators do bus pick-ups from Airlie Beach. Otherwise, the Whitsunday Transit bus goes to Shute Harbour. Leave your car at **Shute Harbour Secured Parking** (☎ 07-4946 9666; day/24hr $8/14; ☒ 6.30am-6.30pm) by the Shell petrol station.

Transfers to the islands all operate out of Shute Harbour, or Abel Point Marina near Airlie Beach. **Fantasea Ferries** (☎ 07-4946 5111; www.fantasea.au) has return fares to Hamilton Island or Daydream Island (per adult/child $60/30), and Long Island or South Molle Island ($44/22). A Three Island Discovery Pass costs $60/40/160 per adult/child/family.

Island Camping Connections (☎ 07-4946 5255) does return fares to North or South Molle, Planton or Denman Islands ($45 each); Whitsunday Island or Henning Island ($109), and Hook Island ($150).

Long Island

There's good rainforest here – the island is nearly all national park – with 13km of walking tracks and some fine lookouts. The island is about 11km long and not much more than 1.5km wide, but it's big enough to house three resorts and a **QPWS camping ground** (per person/family $4/16) in seclusion.

Peppers Palm Bay (☎ 1800 095 025, 07-4946 9233; www.peppers.com.au/palmbay; d $380-680; ☒ ☒) is a peaceful, boutique resort devoid of pesky distractions such as TV and telephones and consisting of indulgent Thai-style cabins, snuggled onto the shore of idyllic Palm Bay. Rates include a sumptuous breakfast hamper. Check for standby rates.

Otherwise, there's the secluded and beautifully informal **South Long Island Wilderness**

Lodge (☎ 07-3839 7799; www.southlongisland.com; 5-night packages per person $2990), or the well-used **Club Croc** (☎ 1800 075 125, 07-4946 9400; www.club croc.com.au; d incl all meals $240-368; 🏊 🖥), which has fairly austere rooms that cater to couples and families.

South Molle Island

The largest of the Molle group at 4 sq km, South Molle is virtually joined to Mid Molle and North Molle Islands. It has long stretches of beach, is known for its spectacular bird life and is crisscrossed by 15km

---

SAILING THE WHITSUNDAYS

Sailing the Whitsundays is simply unforgettable, and the diversity of boats and tours available in the area caters to everyone from first-timers to professionals.

When he coursed these waters in 1770, Cook wrote that 'the whole passage is one continued safe harbour'. In fact, stiff breezes and fast-flowing tides can produce some tricky conditions for small craft, yet, with a little care, the Whitsundays offer superb sailing, and bareboat (which means you rent the boat without skipper, crew or provisions) has become enormously popular.

You don't require formal qualifications to hire a yacht, but at least one person in your group must be fully competent in operating the vessel. On the first day you should receive around four hours of briefing and familiarisation with the yacht. If necessary you may require additional tutoring for around $200 per day, or you may need to hire a skipper for an hourly rate. If you lack experience, it's a good idea to hire an experienced skipper at least for the first day. The operators usually require a booking deposit of $500 to $750, and a security bond of $1000 to $2000 (depending on the boat), payable on arrival and refunded after the boat is returned undamaged. Bedding is usually supplied and provisions can also be provided. Most companies have a minimum hire period of five days.

Generally you'll pay $500 to $800 a day in the high season (September, October, December and January) for a yacht that will comfortably sleep four to six passengers. It's worth asking if the company you choose belongs to the Whitsunday Bareboat Operators Association, a self-regulatory body that guarantees certain standards.

Bareboat charter companies around Airlie Beach:

Charter Yachts Australia (☎ 1800 639 520; www.cya.com.au; Abel Point Marina)
Cumberland Charter Yachts (☎ 1800 075 101; www.ccy.com.au; Abel Point Marina)
Queensland Yacht Charters (☎ 1800 075 013; www.yachtcharters.com.au; Abel Point Marina)
Whitsunday Escape (☎ 1800 075 145, 07-4946 5222; www.whitsundayescape.com; Abel Point Marina)

There's also a bamboozling array of sailing tours, which supply professional crew and catering. It can be hard work sorting through the glossy brochures, the stand-by rates and the word of mouth, but price is usually a good indication. Cheaper companies pose a greater risk of lengthy delays, boats breaking down, unsanitary conditions, and even serious safety concerns. Look out for the tick of approval from the WCBIA (Whitsunday Charter Boat Industry Association) on the brochure. The usual package is three days/two nights, but longer and shorter cruises are possible.

Companies with good track records:

Aussie Adventure Sailing (☎ 1800 359 554; www.aussiesailing.com.au) A range of vessels including tall ships, racers, and sail and dive boats. Three-day packages from $420 per person.
Maxi Ragamuffin (☎ 1800 454 777; www.maxiaction.com.au; adult/child/concession/family/$100/50/90/250) Day cruises.
Prosail (☎ 1800 810 116; www.prosail.com.au; cnr Waterson Rd & Begley St, Airlie Beach) A range of tour vessels, as well as sailing school and diving cruises. Three-day packages from $430 per person.
Southern Cross Sailing Adventures (☎ 1800 675 790; www.soxsail.com.au; 4 The Esplanade, Airlie Beach) Adventure sailing cruises on racing yachts or sedate cruises aboard a tall ship. Three-day packages from $410 per person.

A third option is to crew a private vessel by responding to 'Crew Wanted' notices pasted up in backpackers or at the marina and yacht club. Just like hitching a ride in a car, the experience could be life affirming or life threatening. Think about yourself stuck with someone you don't know on 10m of boat, several kilometres from shore, before you actually find yourself there. Be sure to let others know where you are going, who with, and when you expect to return.

QUEENSLAND

of wonderful walking tracks. The highest point is Mt Jeffreys (198m), but the climb up Spion Kop is also worthwhile. South Molle is mainly national park, and there's a **QPWS camping ground** (per person/family $4/16) in the north, where the boats come in.

Popular with families, **South Molle Island Resort** (☎ 1800 075 080, 07-4946 9433; www.southmolleisland.com.au; d with/without meals from $350/240; 🔀 🏊) has spectacular views and children are well catered for. At high tide the jetty is one of the prettiest around.

Hook Island

The second largest of the Whitsundays at 53 sq km, Hook Island is mainly national park and blessed with great beaches and camping grounds. It also boasts some of the best diving and snorkelling locations in the Whitsundays; Crayfish Beach is an awesome spot.

Hook Island Wilderness Resort (☎ 07-4946 9380; www.hookislandresort.com; sites per person $25, dm $20-35, d with/without bathroom $130/90; 🔀 🏊) is basic, but it's also the cheapest resort in the Whitsundays. The simple units have tiny bathrooms and there's a licensed **restaurant** (mains $14-18), which serves seafood, steak and pasta.

Whitsunday Island

Whitsunday Island is food for the soul. The largest of the Whitsundays, this island covers 109 sq km and rises to 438m at Whitsunday Peak. On its southeast coast, 6km-long Whitehaven Beach is the longest and finest beach in the group (some say in the country), with good snorkelling off its southern end. *Everyone* day-trips to Whitehaven Beach, but it's magic to linger overnight.

Perhaps the most celebrated view of all the Whitsundays comes from here – looking up from Hill Inlet on Tongue Point down towards pristine Whitehaven Beach.

There are **QPWS camping grounds** (per person/family $4/16) at Dugong, Sawmill, Nari's and Joe's Beaches in the west, and at Turtle Bay and Chance Bay in the south; at the southern end of Whitehaven Beach; and Peter Bay in the north.

Daydream Island

Tiny Daydream Island, about 1km long and 500m wide, is the nearest island resort to Shute Harbour. It's a popular day-trip destination, with a wide range of water-

sports gear available for hire (free for resort guests); water-skiing is also big here.

Daydream Island Resort & Spa (☎ 1800 075 040, 07-4948 8488; www.daydream.net.au; 6-night packages $670; 🔀 🏊) is surrounded by beautifully landscaped tropical gardens with a fish-filled lagoon running through it. This large resort also has tennis courts, a gym, catamarans, windsurfers and three swimming pools. There are five grades of accommodation and most package deals include a buffet breakfast. There's also a kids club.

Hamilton Island

Hamilton Island (☎ 07-4946 9999, 1800 075 110; www.hamiltonisland.com.au; d $245-505) The busiest island in the Whitsundays, it's more like a town than a resort and the heavy development isn't everyone's cup of tea. It does, however, provide an airport, huge marina, restaurants, bars, shops and huge range of accommodation and activities. Self-catering is an option here and children will be well catered for.

Hamilton is an appealing day trip from Shute Harbour, and you can use some of the resort's facilities.

Lindeman Island

It's a bit of a hike to southerly Lindeman (mostly national park), but the rewards are lots of secluded bays and 20km of impressive walking trails. Tremendous numbers of grass trees make striking photographs and the view from Mt Oldfield (210m) is grand.

You can day-trip here with **Whitsunday Allover Cruises** (☎ 07-4946 6900; adult/child $120/60) but it's a *very* long day.

Club Med Resort (☎ 1800 258 2633, 07-4946 9333; www.clubmed.com; packages per person per night $215-310; 🔀 🏊) With its emphasis on fun, the internationally famous Club Med flourishes here. The resort has its own launch that connects with flights from the airport at Hamilton Island.

There is also a **QPWS camping ground** (per person/family $4/16).

BOWEN

☎ 07 / pop 13,200

In answer to your question, it's a mango, that huge orange blob outside the visitors centre. It's there to welcome you to Bowen, which is a thriving fruit and vegetable centre in spite of its seemingly wide, empty streets. Most travellers come here for seasonal picking work (April to August), but there are some lovely beaches and holiday accommodation just north of town at popular Horseshoe and Rose Bays.

The helpful **Bowen Visitor Information Centre** (☎ 4786 4222; www.bowentourism.com.au; ☺ 8.30am-5pm) is about 7km south of Bowen. In town, keep an eye out for some terrific **murals** that depict the town's history.

Sleeping & Eating

Murrays Bay Resort (☎ 4786 2402; fax 4786 3388; Murray Bay; d $77; ⚿) With its own palm-fringed sandy beach, this small complex of old-fashioned, but spacious and comfortable, self-contained units offers the perfect getaway-from-it-all holiday. There's an excellent palm-shaded, grassed foreshore leading down to the private beach with first-rate swimming and snorkelling.

Horseshoe Bay Resort (☎ 4786 2564; fax 4786 3460; Horseshoe Bay; powered sites $20-23, d cabins $50, self-contained units $65-100; ⚿) Right on Horseshoe Bay, this resort is nestled among the granite boulders, and with only a short walk to beaches, viewpoints and great fishing spots. The facilities are great.

Bowen's backpackers specialise in housing fruit-pickers. It's a competitive scene, so ring around to find out what deals are available. For starters, try **Bowen Backpackers** (☎ 4786 3433; fax 4786 1073; cnr Herbet & Dalrymple Sts; dm from $21, d $50; ⚿).

There are a couple of modern pubs and cafés in town, but cosy and casual **Horseshoe Bay Cafe** (☎ 4786 3280; Horseshoe Bay; mains $18-29; ☺ 10am-10pm) dishes up excellent food from a long menu.

Getting There & Away

Long-distance buses stop outside **Bowen Travel** (☎ 4786 2835; 40 Williams St). **Greyhound Australia** (☎ 13 14 99; www.greyhound.com.au) and **Premier Motor Service** (☎ 13 34 10; www.premierms .com.au) have services to/from Rockhampton ($94, eight hours), Airlie Beach ($26, 1½ hours) and Townsville ($42, three hours).

The **Queensland Rail** (☎ 1300 131 722; www .traveltrain.com.au) *Sunlander* and *Tilt Train* stop at Bootooloo Siding, 3km south of the centre. For an economy sleeper/seat on the *Sunlander*, the fare from Brisbane is $250/150.

NORTH COAST

The Outback meets the tropics on Queensland's North Coast. Townsville, the state's second-largest city, is a cheerful and fresh place, with a relaxed, waterfront café scene and an affable population. Offshore sits exquisite and accessible Magnetic Island, with unpopulated beaches and excellent bushwalking. The waters between its forested bulk and the mainland teem with hundreds of varieties of fish and coral that form part of the Great Barrier Reef. Little islands line this entire stretch of coast. Some are sacred, some uninhabited, and many are at least partly national park.

As the landscape departs the coast and heads towards the interior, the terrain becomes sunburnt and immense. The overwhelming dry is compensated for by the mountains of the Great Dividing Range, which runs parallel with the coast and forms part of the precious World Heritage–listed Wet Tropics Area.

TOWNSVILLE
☎ 07 / pop 150,000

Steeped in waves of rich foliage, Townsville is a sunny, laid-back city that mixes its casual café-latte culture with a healthy dose of the tropics. The local population is boosted by a large contingent of students, and all the residents here are staunchly proud of their home. Townsville is also one of the largest Army bases in the country and behind the city's genial character bubbles a hive of military activity. The corps and civilian worlds meld without hiccup though, and no-one looks up from their latte when faux explosions erupt from the beautiful Deco building that was Townsville's hospital, or when a truck sails gently across the sky – carried by an enormous chopper. A sweeping waterfront esplanade, excellent museums and thriving nightlife provide plenty of distraction for visitors.

Orientation

Red-rock Castle Hill (290m) presides over Townsville. Ross Creek winds about its city centre, which lies on the north side of the creek over the Dean St Bridge or Victoria Bridge (pedestrians only). The city centre is easy to get around on foot.

QUEENSLAND

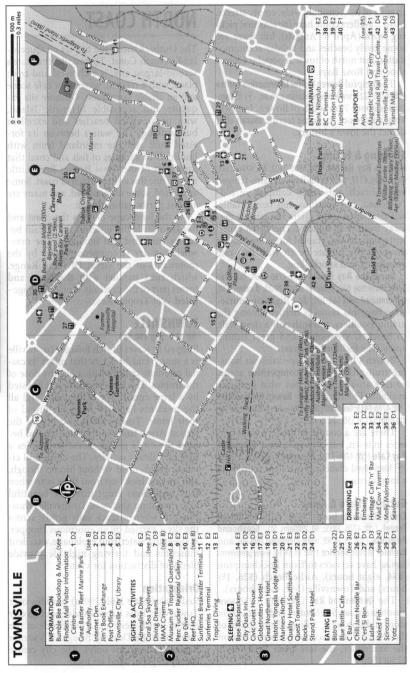

TOWNSVILLE

INFORMATION
Bumble Bee Bookshop & Music...(see 2)	
Flinders Mall Visitor Information	
Centre..**1** D2	
Great Barrier Reef Marine Park	
Authority...............................(see 8)	
Internet Den..............................**2** D2	
Jim's Book Exchange................**3** D3	
Post Office..................................**4** D3	
Townsville City Library.............**5** E2	

SIGHTS & ACTIVITIES
Adrenaline Dive..........................**6** E2	
Coral Sea Skydivers................(see 37)	
Diving Dreams...........................**7** D3	
IMAX Cinema...........................(see 8)	
Museum of Tropical Queensland.**8** E2	
Perc Tucker Regional Gallery....**9** E2	
Pro Dive....................................**10** E3	
Reef HQ..................................(see 8)	
Sunferries Breakwater Terminal..**11** F1	
Sunferries Terminal..................**12** E2	
Tropical Diving........................**13** E3	

SLEEPING
Base Backpackers.....................**14** E3	
City Oasis Inn............................**15** D2	
Civic Guest House....................**16** D3	
Globetrotters Hostel.................**17** E3	
Great Northern Hotel................**18** D3	
Historic Yongala Lodge Motel...**19** D1	
Mariners North........................**20** E1	
Quality Hotel Southbank..........**21** E3	
Quest Townsville......................**22** E3	
Rocks..**23** E2	
Strand Park Hotel.....................**24** D1	

EATING
Bistro 1..................................(see 22)	
Blue Bottle Cafe.......................**25** D1	
C Bar..**26** E2	
Chilli Jam Noodle Bar................**27** D1	
C'est Si Bon............................**28** D3	
Ladah....................................(see 24)	
Naked Fish..............................**29** F3	
Scirocco..................................**30** D1	
Yotz..**30** D1	

DRINKING
Brewery....................................**31** E2	
Embassy...................................**32** D2	
Heritage Café 'n' Bar.................**33** D3	
Mad Cow Tavern.......................**34** E2	
Molly Malones.........................**35** E2	
Seaview...................................**36** D1	

ENTERTAINMENT
Bank Niteclub...........................**37** E2	
BC Cinemas..............................**38** D3	
Criterion Hotel.........................**39** E2	
Jupiters Casino........................**40** F1	

TRANSPORT
Avis.......................................(see 35)	
Magnetic Island Car Ferry........**41** F1	
Queensland Rail Travel Centre..**42** D4	
Townsville Transit Centre........(see 14)	
Transit Mall.............................**43** D3	

Flinders St Mall, the shopping precinct, stretches to the left from the northern side of Dean Bridge, towards the train station. To the right of the bridge is Flinders St East, lined with many of the town's oldest buildings, plus eateries, nightclubs and the Sunferries terminal for Magnetic Island departures (there's another terminal on Sir Leslie Thiess Dr on the breakwater).

Information
BOOKSHOPS
Bumble Bee Bookshop & Music (☎ 4771 6091; 305 Flinders St Mall) Good travel section.

Jim's Book Exchange (☎ 4771 6020; Shaw's Arcade) Wide range of secondhand books; off Flinders St Mall.

INTERNET ACCESS
Internet Den (☎ 4721 4500; 265 Flinders Mall; per hr $5; ☼ 9am-9pm Mon-Fri, 10am-8pm Sat & Sun) Internet access.

Townsville City Library (☎ 4727 9666; 272-8 Flinders Mall; ☼ 9.30am-5pm Mon-Fri, 9am-noon Sat & Sun) Free Internet access.

POST
Australia Post (Post Office Plaza, Shop 1, Sturt St)

TOURIST INFORMATION
Flinders Mall visitor information centre (☎ 4721 3660; www.townsvilleonline.com.au; Flinders St Mall, btwn Stokes & Denham Sts; ☼ 9am-5pm Mon-Fri, 9am-12.30pm Sat & Sun) General information and diving and reef tours (www.divecruisetravel.com).

Great Barrier Reef Marine Park Authority (☎ 4750 0700; www.gbrmpa.gov.au; Reef HQ, 2-68 Flinders St East; ☼ 9am-5pm) Detailed and technical information on the Reef.

Townsville Enterprises visitor information centre (☎ 4726 2700; www.townsvilleonline.com.au; 6 the Strand; ☼ 9am-5pm Mon-Fri) Headquarters for the booth in Flinders Mall.

Sights
REEF HQ
This outstanding **aquarium** (☎ 4750 0800; www .reefhq.org.au; Flinders St East; adult/child/concession $19.50/9.50/15; ☼ 9am-5pm) is home to many of the creatures and corals that inhabit the Great Barrier Reef. In the massive central tank a dense population of vivid fish, sharks, sawfish and rays dart among one another. There are also touch tanks, and plenty of information to give you a much deeper appreciation of the reef. Plunge deeper still

into the **IMAX cinema** (☎ 4721 1481; Flinders St East; adult/child/concession $14/8/12; ☼ 10.30am-4.30pm), next door.

OTHER SIGHTS
The **Strand**, northwest of town, is a vibrant beachfront esplanade with a marina, cafés, parks and stinger enclosure. The promenade is busy with perky locals walking from end to end. At the northeast tip is the rock pool (admission free; ☼ 24hr), an enormous artificial swimming pool surrounded by lawns and sandy beaches.

The **Museum of Tropical Queensland** (☎ 4726 0600; www.mtq.qld.gov.au; Flinders St East; adult/child $9/5; ☼ 9am-5pm) reconstructs history with detailed models and interactive exhibits. A replica of the *Pandora*, which was shipwrecked off the nearby coast, is the dominant attraction, but there's also a science centre, natural history displays and indigenous Australian and Torres Strait Islander exhibits.

It's also worth popping into the contemporary **Perk Tucker Regional Gallery** (☎ 4727 9011; ptrg@townsville.qld.gov.au; cnr Denham St & Flinders Mall; admission free; ☼ 10am-5pm Mon-Fri, 10am-2pm Sat & Sun). Housed in a heritage corner building, it focuses mainly on north Queensland artists.

If you're feeling energetic, the panoramic views from the top of **Castle Hill** are worth the 2km scramble to the summit; the path to the top begins at the end of Victoria St.

The **Billabong Sanctuary** (☎ 4778 8344; www .billabongsanctuary.com.au; Bruce Hwy; adult/child $24/13; ☼ 8am-5pm), 17km south of Townsville, is a 10-hectare wildlife park containing Australian native animals and birds. There are barbecue areas, a swimming pool and a kiosk in the park, and various shows (eg hold-a-koala/wombat/python) are held throughout the day.

If you fancy a lazy picnic, head to the ornamental **Queens Gardens** (cnr Gregory & Paxton Sts) at the base Castle Hill, or **Anderson Park** (Gulliver St, Mundingburra), with plants and palms from northern Queensland and Cape York Peninsula.

About 35km southeast of Townsville on the Bruce Hwy is the turn-off to the **Australian Institute of Marine Science** (AIMS; ☎ 4753 4444; www.aims.gov.au; ☼ 8am-3pm), a fascinating marine-research facility on Cape Ferguson that conducts free, two-hour tours.

QUEENSLAND

Activities

City slickers looking for that quintessential country experience must join the cattle muster at **Woodstock Trail Rides** (☎ 4778 8888; www.woodstocktrailrides.com.au; Flinders Hwy; per person incl lunch $120). For one day you can help move 'em in and brand their hides, eat a camp-cooked lunch and down a cold beer at day's end; price includes transfer from Townsville. Trail rides and an overnight bush camp are also possible.

For adrenalin junkies, **Coral Sea Skydivers** (☎ 4772 4889; www.coralseaskydivers.com.au; 181 Flinders St East; tandem from $290) will help throw you from a plane. The tandem jump requires no prior knowledge; just a lot of guts (but not too much: there's a weight limit of 95kg).

DIVING

Apart from the Great Barrier Reef, the big attraction for divers is the stunning and spooky *Yongala* shipwreck. There are several dive companies, all offering *Yongala* options, but you need to have an openwater certificate to see it. Dive companies are only as good as their staff, who change frequently in this business. Ask other travellers for current recommendations.

Reputable PADI courses:

Adrenalin Dive (☎ 4724 0600; www.adrenalinedive .com.au; 121 Flinders St East; from $180) Yongala day trips including two dives. Also diving certification courses.

Diving Dreams (☎ 4721 2500; www.divingdreams .com; 252 Walker St; from $595)

Pro Dive (☎ 4721 1760; www.prodivetownsville.com .au; 14 Plume St, South Townsville; from $645)

Tropical Diving (☎ 1800 776 150; www.tropicaldiving .com.au; 14 Palmer St; from $130) Day trips to the reef.

Tours

Sunferries (☎ 1800 447 333; www.sunferries.com.au; Sir Leslie Thiess Dr; per person from $140) Operates day trips to the Great Barrier Reef. A certified or introductory dive costs an additional $70.

Tropical Tours (☎ 4721 6489; www.townsvilletropical tours.com.au) If superb rainforest, a beautifully restored mining town or Australia's longest waterfall tempt you, Tropical Tours has good-value day trips (from $120) that take in the Paluma Range National Park, Hidden Valley, Charters Towers or Wallaman Falls.

Sleeping

BUDGET

Great Northern Hotel (☎ 4771 6191; fax 4771 6190; 496 Flinders St; s/d $35/45; P ⊠) The rickety air-con, daggy décor and heavy bedhead-cum-storage units fixed to the wall are all part of the charm at this charismatic hotel. The best rooms open out to the broad encircling veranda. The pub downstairs dishes out healthy doses of Queensland culture.

Globetrotters Hostel (☎ 1800 008 533, 4771 3242; globetrotters@austranet.com.au; 45 Palmer St; dm $20-21; r with/without bathroom $60/50; ⊠ ▯ ⬤) Offers rooms in a comfortable old house, as well as in a newer building behind. Rooms are functional, with coin-operated air-con; a good option if you're not looking for full-moon parties and big boozy nights.

Civic Guest House (☎ 1800 646 619, 4771 5381; www.backpackersinn.com.au; 262 Walker St; dm $20; s $39-43, d & tw $42-48, r with bathroom $60; ⊠ ⬤) Behind the palms and bushes bursting out of the cyclone-wire fence is this converted home. Easy-going and sedate, the Civic hosts a free barbecue for guests on Friday night and pricier rooms have air-con.

Also recommended:

Base Backpackers (☎ 1800 628 836, 4721 2322; www.basebackpackers.com; 21 Plume St; dm/d $21/60; ⊠ ▯) Above the transit centre; basic rooms and facilities and a buzzing bar.

Rowes Bay Caravan Park (☎ 4771 3576; fax 4724 2017; Heatley Pde, Rowes Bay; powered/unpowered sites $23/12.50, cabins $55-76; ⬤) Leafy grounds; popular during holidays.

MIDRANGE

Beach House Motel (☎ 4721 1333; www.beachhouse motel.com.au; 66 the Strand; s/d $86/96; P ⊠ ⬤) Spacious bathrooms, and sleeping quarters dressed in cheerful décor are the go in these modern motel rooms. Louvred windows usher in the seabreeze from Cleveland Bay, and rooms are well equipped with mod cons.

Rocks (☎ 4771 5700; www.therocksguesthouse.com; 20 Cleveland Tce; s/d incl breakfast $90/110; ⊠) Wow! This beautifully restored historic home, replete with period furnishings and a veranda with superb bay views, is to be treasured. It comes with high ceilings, old cabinets brimming with memorabilia and sherries at six o'clock. Facilities for those with disabilities are good.

Strand Park Hotel (☎ 47507888; www.strandparkhotel .com.au; 59-60 the Strand; r $115-145; P ⊠ ⬤) Self-contained units in this waterfront complex range from standard on the ground floor, to superior and deluxe rooms with ocean views.

balconies and perhaps a spa. Downstairs you can dine at Naked Fish (below).

Quest Townsville (☎ 4772 6477; www.questapart ments.com.au; 30-4 Palmer St; apt from $130; ⚇ 🖭 P) This high-rise apartment complex houses hundreds of happy holiday-makers in its studio apartments. Rooms are serviced daily and are fully self-contained. Families are also catered to with one- and two-bedroom apartments, and a babysitting service.

Also recommended:

Bayside (☎ 4721 1688; fax 4724 1231; 102 the Strand; r from $105; P ⚇ 🖭) Comfortable one- and two-bedroom units opposite the beach.

Quality Hotel Southbank (☎ 4726 5265; www.south bankhotel.com.au; 23 Palmer St; r from $105; P ⚇ 🖳 🖭) Business travellers' haunt with practical interiors, some with ocean views.

Historic Yongala Lodge Motel (☎ 4772 4633; www .historicyongala.com.au; 11 Fryer St; r from $100-115; P ⚇ 🖭) Comfortable, clean motel rooms and self-contained units.

TOP END

Mariners North (☎ 4722 0777; www.marinersnorth .com.au; 7 Mariners Dr; apt from $165; P ⚇ 🖭) In the breakwater of the marina, this soaring apartment complex provides spectacular views of the traffic out in Cleveland Bay. The two-bedroom, two-bathroom apartments have fully equipped kitchens and laundries. Guests have free reign over the complex's tennis court and barbecue facilities.

Eating

Naked Fish (☎ 4724 4623; 60 the Strand; mains $18-24; ☯ dinner Mon-Sat) A sea of green-blue walls and a starry ceiling compliment the ocean-inspired menu at this funky eatery. Seafood sidles up to Cajun, Moroccan, tempura and other influences on the extensive menu and you can dine outside beneath a magnificent, giant fig tree.

C Bar (☎ 4724 0333; Gregory St Headland; meals $12-16; ☯ breakfast, lunch & dinner) Sublime views at this good-looking licensed restaurant enhance the simple but tasty fare. From the broad outdoor deck on the waterfront, an ordinary panini takes on extraordinary qualities, while sausages and mash become positively gourmet.

Scirocco (☎ 4724 4508; 61 Palmer St; mains $16-21; ☯ breakfast & lunch Tue-Sun, dinner Tue-Sat) The high ceilings and motif-painted walls present an understated sophistication in this refined restaurant, and the service and food rise to the occasion. Chase the pickled beetroot and goat's cheese risotto with a lime and pineapple tart for desert.

Yotz (☎ 4724 5488; Gregory St Headland, the Strand; mains $23-26; ☯ lunch & dinner) Gauguin-inspired walls and Cuban cigars create a frisky ambience at this bar and grill. Outside you can soak up panoramic harbour views, and the menu here includes tasty delicacies like lemon-and-pepper-spiced octopus or mushroom angel-hair noodles.

Ladah (☎ 4724 0402; cnr Sturt & Stanley Sts; lunch $7-10; ☯ breakfast & lunch Mon-Fri & Sun) Plant yourself on a chocolate- and cream-coloured cube at this casual city café and tuck into rice porridge and other inventive breakfasts, fresh lunches, sweet and savoury muffins, cakes and tarts. Good coffee.

C'est Si Bon (☎ 4772 5828; 48 Gregory St; meals $5-15; ☯ breakfast & lunch) Scrumptious quiches, bagels and breakfasts are consumed at the communal table that runs the length of this large café. Polished concrete floors, brushed steel and wood furnishings provide a pared-back ambience, warmed by jazzy tunes.

Also recommended:

Bistro 1 (☎ 4771 6333; 30-4 Palmer St; mains $19-24; ☯ breakfast, lunch & dinner) Licensed, casual spot serving stylish café fare and a kids menu.

Chilli Jam Noodle Bar (☎ 4721 5199; 211 Flinders St East; meals $9-11; ☯ dinner) Excellent noodle bar – eat in or takeaway.

Blue Bottle Cafe (☎ 4771 2121; cnr Gregory St & the Strand; mains $22-26; ☯ brunch & lunch Mon-Sat, dinner Tue-Sat) Large, homely café serving inventive comfort food.

Drinking

Brewery (☎ 4724 9999; 242 Flinders St) In the gorgeous old post-office building, this place pleases everybody with a sports bar, nightclub, bistro and brewery. Beer connoisseurs should definitely try one the Brewery's own: the Ned's Red Ale, Lager Lout and Belgian blonde are all good.

Embassy (☎ 4724 5000; 13 Sturt St) A sophisticated bunker in the business district of town that is velvety smooth. Dress smart and strut your stuff to the DJ, who spins funk and house vinyl. Embassy's downstairs location, split-level interior, subdued lighting and effortless chic imbue it with an in-the-know ambience.

Heritage Café 'n' Bar (☎ 4771 2799; 137 Flinders St) The Heritage is wine-bar-esque, with a sedate ambience. The large outdoor seating pen lures an after-work crowd, which lingers on well into the night.

Seaview (☎ 4771 5005; cnr the Strand & Gregory Sts) It seems the entire population jams into the huge concrete courtyard at the Seaview on a Sunday, when there's live music and entertainment.

You can get beery and raucous at **Mad Cow Tavern** (☎ 4771 5727; 129 Flinders St East) or **Molly Malones** (☎ 4771 3428; 87 Flinders St East).

Entertainment

Bank Niteclub (☎ 4771 6148; 169 Flinders St East; admission $5) Townsville's hottest nightspot is this slinky club, housed inside a superbly restored old bank building. Linger at the marble bar, or lounge in the padded chill zone. The beat is house and dance.

Brewery Club (☎ 4724 2999; 242 Flinders St East) The nightclub upstairs at this multi-functional venue features resident DJs on Friday and Saturday nights, who spin dance and progressive house as well as beats and breaks.

Other recommendations:

BC Cinemas (☎ 4771 4101; cnr Sturt & Blackwood Sts) Mainstream films.

Criterion Hotel (☎ 4721 5777; 10 the Strand) Popular nightclub with loud and leery dancing.

Jupiters Casino (☎ 4722 2333; Sir Leslie Thiess Dr) Basics: pokies, roulette, blackjack.

Getting There & Away

AIR

Virgin Blue (☎ 13 67 89; www.virginblue.com.au), **Alliance Airlines** (☎ 3212 1212; www.allianceairlines.com .au), **Macair** (☎ 13 13 13; www.macair.com.au) and **Qantas** (☎ 13 13 13; www.qantas.com.au) – and its subsidiaries – all service Townsville. Fares include Brisbane ($130), Sydney ($170), Melbourne ($240), Cairns ($150), Mackay ($180) and Mt Isa ($180).

BUS

The long-distance bus station is at the **Townsville Transit Centre** (☎ 4721 3082; transittsv@bigpond .com.au; 21 Plume St). Here you'll find agents for the major companies, including **Transit Centre Backpackers** (☎ 4721 2322), who are agents for Premier Motor Service, and **Greyhound Australia** (☎ 13 14 99, 4772 5100; www.greyhound.com.au).

Services from Townsville include Brisbane ($175, 23 hours), Rockhampton ($100, 11 hours), Airlie Beach ($55, four hours), Mission Beach ($50, four hours) and Cairns

($55, six hours). There's also a daily service to Charters Towers ($30, one hour 40 minutes) continuing to the NT.

CAR

Car-rental agencies in Townsville:

Avis (☎ 1300 137 498, 4721 2688; www.avis.com.au; 81 Flinders St)

Europcar (☎ 1300 131 390, 4762 7050; www.deltaeurop car.com.au; 305 Ingham Rd, Garbutt)

Hertz (☎ 13 30 30, 4775 5950; www.hertz.com; Stinson Ave, Garbutt)

Thrifty (☎ 4725 4600; thriftytsv@thriftytsv.com.au; 289 Ingham Rd, Garbutt)

TRAIN

The train station and **Queensland Rail Travel Centre** (☎ 4772 8358; www.traveltrain.qr.com.au; 502 Flinders St; ⊗ 9am-5pm Mon-Fri, 1-4.30pm Sat, 8.30am-4.15pm Sun, closed for lunch) are about 500m south of the centre.

The *Sunlander* connects Townsville with Brisbane (economy seat/sleeper $165/215, 24 hours), Rockhampton (economy seat $110, 11 hours) and Cairns (economy seat $60, 7½ hours). The more luxurious *Queenslander* service, which includes a sleeper and meals, is available on two services per week.

The *Inlander* heads from Townsville to Mt Isa on Wednesday and Sunday (economy seat/sleeper $115/165).

Getting Around

TO/FROM THE AIRPORT

Townsville airport is 5km northwest of the city at Garbutt. A taxi to the centre costs $20, or else **Abacus Tours** (☎ 4775 5544; one way/return $8/14) runs a shuttle to/from the CBD for all Qantas and Virgin flights.

BUS

Sunbus (☎ 4725 8482; www.sunbus.com.au) runs local bus services around Townsville. Route maps and timetables are available at the Flinders Mall visitor information centre.

TAXI

Taxis congregate outside the Transit Mall or call **Townsville Taxis** (☎ 13 10 08, 4778 9555).

MAGNETIC ISLAND

☎ 07 / pop 2500

Even at its busiest, this gorgeous island of giant granite boulders, hoop pines and swathes of eucalypts is relatively quiet. Half the island is national park and a haven for rock wallabies, bats and brushtail possums. Bird life bursts out of the bush, and it's the largest natural koala sanctuary in Queensland (some say Australia), so spotting fuzzy grey bums in the foliage is a mandatory pursuit. A good network of trails makes for some spectacular bushwalking and the

surrounding waters are also part of the precious Great Barrier Reef World Heritage Area.

Pockets of 'Maggie' have a suburban atmosphere. There's a veritable shopping complex and marina underway at Nelly Bay and a waterfront facelift at Picnic Bay, but the island remains unpretentious.

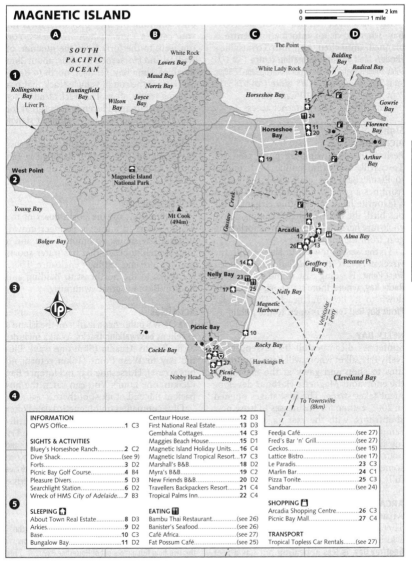

QUEENSLAND

Orientation & Information

Magnetic Island is only 8km from Townsville and roughly triangular in shape. A sealed road follows the east coast for 10km from Picnic Bay, on the island's southern point, to Horseshoe Bay in the north. A local bus ploughs the route regularly. There's a rough 8km track along the west coast leading from Picnic Bay to a wonderfully secluded beach at West Point.

All passenger ferries dock at Nelly Bay, where a visitor information centre is planned; until then, pop into Townsville's **Flinders Mall visitor information centre** (☎ 4721 3660; Flinders Mall; ☺ 9am-5pm Mon-Fri, 9am-12.30pm Sat & Sun). There's a **QPWS office** (☎ 4778 5378; Hurst St; ☺ 7.30am-4pm) at Picnic Bay.

Some hostels offer Internet access.

Sights

PICNIC BAY

Perhaps it's the twinkling night views of Townsville that draw families and couples to Picnic Bay. The mall along the waterfront has a good handful of eateries and is a favourite hang-out for that elegant, curious bird, the curlew. There's a stinger-free enclosure here and you can hire snorkelling gear from the mall.

To the west of town is **Cockle Bay**, with the wreck of HMS *City of Adelaide*, and secluded **West Point**. Heading east round the coast is **Rocky Bay**, where there's a short, steep walk down to its beautiful beach. The popular **Picnic Bay Golf Course** is open to the public.

NELLY BAY

Sunferries disgorges all its passengers at Nelly Bay, all of whom will have opportunities to shop and gawk at the marina as the enormous Magnetic Harbour development takes shape. The first stages opened in 2005, calling for businesses to lease new shopfronts, with the marina, public boat ramp and residential developments opening in stages over the coming years. Magnetic Harbour is set to transform Nelly into something of a hub for the island – hopefully a low-key one.

ARCADIA

Arcadia village has the lovely **Alma Bay** cove. There's plenty of shade, picnic tables and a kids' playground here. The main beach, **Geoffrey Bay**, is less appealing but has a reef at its southern end (QPWS discourages reef walking at low tide). It's also the access point for the car ferry, but that may change as Nelly Bay develops. Arcadia has places to stay, and a few shops and eateries.

RADICAL BAY & THE FORTS

Townsville was a supply base for the Pacific during WWII, and the **forts** were designed to protect the town from naval attack. The only ammunition they provide now is for your camera – great panoramic views. You can walk to the forts from the junction of Radical and Horseshoe Bay Rds, about 2km north of Alma Bay. Or head north to Radical Bay via the rough vehicle track that has walking tracks off it. The tracks lead to secluded Arthur and Florence Bays (great for snorkelling) and the old **searchlight station** on the headland between the two.

From Radical Bay you can walk across the headland to beautiful **Balding Bay** (an unofficial nude bathing beach) and Horseshoe Bay.

HORSESHOE BAY

Horseshoe Bay, on the north coast of the island, seems to attract a younger crowd. It has a few shops, accommodation and a long stretch of beach that has water-sports gear for hire and a stinger enclosure. There are walks to the northeast to Balding and Radical Bays for great swimming.

Activities

The QPWS publishes a leaflet on the island's excellent **bushwalking** tracks. Walks include: Nelly Bay to Arcadia (5km one way), Picnic Bay to West Point (16km return; no bus access), Horseshoe Bay to Florence Bay (2.5km, one hour). You can catch the bus back at the end of most of these.

Dive companies on Magnetic Island offer plenty of underwater action with certificate courses, and wreck and night dives. Try **Pleasure Divers** (☎ 4778 5788; www.magnetic-island .com.au/plsr-divers; 10 Marine Parade, Arcadia; per person from $220), or **Dive Shack** (☎ 4778 5690; www.dive shack.com.au; Shop 2, Marine Parade, Arcadia; per person from $250).

Tours

Barnacle Bill (☎ 4758 1237;tours $50) Bill knows the sea like the bristles on his beard; all gear is included on this two-hour fishing tour out of Horseshoe Bay.

Bluey's Horseshoe Ranch (☎ 4778 5109; 38 Gifford St, Horseshoe Bay; tours $70) Offers two-hour rides taking you through bush to the beach, where you can swim your horse.

Jazza Sailing Tours (☎ 4758 1887; www.jazza.com.au; tours $95) Snorkelling day trip on a 42ft yacht that includes boom netting and seafood lunch.

Magnetic Island Sea Kayaks (☎ 4778 5424; www .seakayak.com.au; 93 Horseshoe Bay Rd; tours from $60) Has four-hour tours departing Horseshoe Bay paddling over to Balding Bay and back. Includes breakfast.

Reef EcoTours (☎ 0419 712 579; www.reefecotours.com; adult/child $60/50) Offers a 1½ hour guided snorkel that's suitable for families.

Tropicana Tours (☎ 4758 1800; www.tropicanatours .com.au; tours $135) Operates excellent day tours with well-informed guides in a stretch 4WD. Enjoy close encounters with wildlife, and nibbles and wine at sunset on West Point.

Sleeping

Rates for a bed on Maggie increase during high season. If you're staying more than a few days, **First National Real Estate** (☎ 4778 5077; www.magneticislandfn.com.au; 21 Marine Pde, Arcadia) and **About Town Real Estate** (☎ 4778 5570; www .magneticislandrealestate.com; Shop 4/5 Bright Ave, Arcadia) manage apartments and houses ranging in price from $80 to $200 per night.

PICNIC BAY

Magnetic Island Holiday Units (☎ 4778 5246; 16 Yule St; d $94; 🅿 🖈) Set amid a leafy garden and manicured lawn, these homely self-contained units are tightly spaced. As well as the one-bedroom units, two-bedders are also available for $110.

You can also bed down at the enormous and basic **Travellers Backpackers Resort** (☎ 18 00 000 290, 4778 5166; travellers@getonit.net.au; 1 the Esplanade; dm $12-20, r with/without bathroom $55/46; 🅿 🖳 🖈), which contains a pub, bistro and resident crocodile, or take one of the bright, semi-self-contained motel rooms at **Tropical Palms Inn** (☎ 1800 777 076, 4778 5076; tropicalpalmsinn@hotmail.com; 34 Picnic St; s/d $85/92; 🅿 🖈).

NELLY BAY

Gembhala Cottages (☎ 4778 5435; 28 Mango Parkway; d from $90; 🅿 🖈) Balinese-inspired cottages sit at the end of a tropical garden that's trafficked by butterflies. It's a beautifully serene setting and inside, your accommodation boasts carved wood features, open-air bathrooms and louvre windows.

Magnetic Island Tropical Resort (☎ 1800 069 122, 4778 5955; www.magnetictropicalresort.com; 56 Yates St, Nelly Bay; d $130; 🅿 🖈) A-frame cabins with bathrooms encircle large bird-filled gardens at this attractive resort. It's so pretty weddings are a common fixture. There are also lawn tennis courts and an alluring seafood-and-steak restaurant (see Lattice Bistro, p408).

Base (☎ 1800 242 273, 4778 5777; www.baseback packers.com; 1 Nelly Bay Rd; unpowered sites per person $10, dm/d $20/70; 🖳 🖈) Although the party atmosphere prevails at this hostel, there's also enough space to escape it. Ask for a beachfront A-frame, where the Coral Sea laps just below. The beachfront decking and dining area is gorgeous and there's a dive school on site.

ARCADIA

Centaur House (☎ 1800 655 680, 4778 5668; 27 Marine Pde, Arcadia; dm/s/d $18/35/42) The beds here are romantically strung with mosquito netting and the beachfront location will make you swoon. This little hostel's rooms are all upstairs, with a shambolic shared under-croft area downstairs.

Arkies (☎ 1800 663 666, 4778 5177; www.arkieson magnetic.com; 7 Marine Pde, Arcadia; dm $15-20, d $49.50; 🅿 🖳 🖈) Short on charm but big on the hands-in-the-air party vibe, this large backpackers has a bistro and bar with loads of entertainment, including toad racing and trivia nights. The big daggy rooms were set to be refurbished during 2005.

Marshall's B&B (☎ 4778 5112; 3-5 Endeavour Rd; s/d $50/70) Marshall's friendly hosts have four basic rooms on offer in their humble home. You are welcome to use the lounge room and pleasant bird-filled garden with outdoor seating.

HORSESHOE BAY

New Friends B&B (☎ 4758 1220; 48b Horseshoe Bay Rd; s/d incl breakfast $70/90; 🖈) Lovely modern rooms with their own bathrooms are nestled in the main house, which makes for some friendly, communal living. The fabulous garden is backed by jungle palms and breakfast is a large spread.

Myra's B&B (☎ 4758 1277; 101 Swenson St; s/d incl breakfast $50/70; 🅿) Like your privacy, but don't mind a bit of wildlife? Myra's has a wee cabin at the back of the property, set in rambling bush, and a room in the main house. Myra's is a tad out of the way, but

QUEENSLAND

the owners will shuttle you to and from the ferry.

Budget options:

Bungalow Bay (☎ 1800 285 577, 4778 5577; www .bungalowbay.com.au; 40 Horseshoe Bay Rd; powered/ unpowered sites per 2 people $25/10, dm $21.50, d $57; 🖳 🞉) Rustic cedar A-frames on a natural expanse. Good facilities.

Maggies Beach House (☎ 4778 5144; www.maggies beachhouse.com.au; Pacific Dr; dm $21-26, d $52-75; 🞉 🖳 🞉) Concrete-floored functional dorms, plus a bar and Geckos restaurant (right).

Eating

Each of Magnetic's villages has its dining hub; of them, Horseshoe Bay is the most diverse.

PICNIC BAY

Fred's Bar 'n' Grill (☎ 4778 5911; Picnic Bay Mall; mains $15-20; 🞉 lunch & dinner Tue-Sat) A big corner location overlooking Picnic Bay, with seats inside and out, makes Fred's a top spot to eat and drink. This unpretentious place offers bistro favourites, such as steaks and pastas, as well as daily specials.

You can also dig into scrumptious light meals at **Café Africa** (☎ 4758 1119; Picnic Bay Mall; dishes $5-9; 🞉 breakfast & lunch), which specialises in all-day breakfasts and crepes, or the neo-hippy **Feedja Café** (☎ 4778 5833; Picnic Bay Mall; $6-10; 🞉 breakfast & lunch), which serves locally grown produce in whimsical surrounds.

NELLY BAY

Lattice Bistro (☎ 4778 5955; 56 Yates St; dishes $15-25; 🞉 dinner Thu-Tue) The Tropical Resort's open-sided restaurant sizzles up great barramundi, scallops and chicken. There's usually a veggie option and kid-friendly meal or two. Live music often serenades patrons on Thursday and Friday nights in season.

Le Paradis (☎ 4778 5044; cnr Mandalay & Sooning Sts; mains $14-20; 🞉 breakfast Sun, lunch & dinner Tue-Sun) This polished BYO restaurant offers a range of Med-inspired dishes on its extensive menu. The mostly outdoor seating is sheltered by large, angular sails and the tables are smartly dressed.

More options:

Fat Possum Café (☎ 4778 5409; 55 Spooning St; dishes $5-10; 🞉 breakfast, lunch & dinner) Cheerful café dishing up sandwiches, gourmet pies, sushi and tasty noodles.

Pizza Tonite (☎ 4758 1400; 53 Spooning St; dishes $10-12; 🞉 dinner) Yup – they do pizza, plus burgers and lasagne.

ARCADIA

Bambu Thai Restaurant (☎ 4778 5645; Bright Ave; mains $16-20; 🞉 dinner Thu-Tue) This intimate little restaurant serves boutique Thai in its back courtyard. It's BYO, and takeaway is also available. The **gallery** (🞉 10.30am-5.30pm Wed-Sun) is open for coffee and cake.

For finger-lickin' fish and chips, **Banister's Seafood** (☎ 4778 5700; 22 McCabe Cres, Arcadia; mains $5-22; 🞉 lunch & dinner) is a good takeaway, with an open-air dining area out the front.

HORSESHOE BAY

Sandbar (☎ 4778 5477; Pacific Dr; mains $15-20; 🞉 breakfast & lunch daily, dinner Wed-Sun) This licensed café-restaurant present a confident menu boasting fresh ingredients and sassy flavours. Lunch and dinner favour seafood, and breakfasts are big plates of all your favourites. There are a few outdoor tables just big enough to hold the satellite-sized plates.

Marlin Bar (☎ 4758 1588; 3 Pacific Dr; mains $10-20; 🞉 lunch daily, dinner Tue-Sat) This lively waterfront pub does decent veggie and pasta dishes and serves more meat than you could poke a cattle prod at. Order and pay at the counter, grab a number and a window seat, and your food will find you when it's ready.

Geckos (☎ 4778 5144; Pacific Dr; mains $10-18; 🞉 breakfast, lunch & dinner) The relaxed restaurant at Maggie's Beach House serves bistro-style meals all day and the bar occasionally stages live music.

Getting There & Away

Sunferries (☎ 4771 3855; www.sunferries.com.au; return per person $20; 🞉 6.45am-7pm Mon-Fri, 7am-5.30pm Sat & Sun) operates a frequent passenger ferry from the terminal on Flinders St East in Townsville, also stopping at the breakwater terminal on Sir Leslie Thiess Dr. There is car parking here (per day $4).

The **Magnetic Island Car Ferry** (Map p400; ☎ 4772 5422; Ross St, South Townsville; per person/car & 3 passengers $17/127; 🞉 7.15am-5.30pm, closes 3.45pm Sat) does the crossing six times daily from the south side of Ross Creek. It costs $127 (return) for a car and three passengers and $17 (return) for a passenger only. The ferry currently docks at Arcadia, with murmurs of it moving to Magnetic Harbour; check when you book.

Getting Around

BICYCLE

Magnetic Island is ideal for cycling. Most places to stay rent bikes for around $15 a day. Otherwise **Adventure Bike Hire** (☎ 0425 244 193) charges the same, with free delivery.

BUS

The **Magnetic Island Bus Service** (☎ 4778 5130; fares $2-4.50) ploughs between Picnic Bay and Horseshoe Bay at least 14 times per day, meeting all ferries and stopping at, or near, all accommodation.

MOKE & SCOOTER

Expect to pay around $45 per day, plus extras such as petrol and a per-kilometre fee, for a nifty little Moke (mini open-air vehicle).

Hooterz Scooterz (☎ 4778 5317; 3/11 Pacific Dr; Horseshoe Bay)

Moke Magnetic (☎ 4778 5377; www.mokemagnetic .com; Nelly Bay)

Tropical Topless Car Rentals (☎ 4758 1111; Picnic Bay)

NORTH COAST HINTERLAND

Just a couple of days' drive and you can swelter in Australia's famed Outback. The Flinders Hwy heads 800km due west from Townsville to Cloncurry.

Ravenswood

☎ 07 / pop 350

At Mingela, 88km from Townsville, think about making the 40km detour to Ravenswood. It's a tiny mining town, among scattered red-earth hills, that dates back to gold-rush days. There is little to see, but that's the point. You come here to experience the solitude of mining life. Hop on a stool at the pubs and chat over a beer; most miners are happy to welcome a fresh face.

Then visit the old **post office** and **mining & historical museum** (☎ 4770 2047; adult/child $2.20/1.10; ☼ 10am-3pm Wed-Mon), housed in the restored courthouse, police station and lock-up and hosted by the gregarious Woody.

You can sleep over at the **Imperial Hotel** (☎ 4770 2131; Macrossan St; s/d $50/60) or the **Railway Hotel** (☎ 4770 2144; Barton St; s/d $30/45), a couple of 1870s' gems, but do book ahead. The council **camping ground** (unpowered sites per 2 people $6) is a sun-battered football field.

Charters Towers

☎ 07 / pop 9400

The gold rush is over, but the locals don't seem to know it. Charters Towers thrives in isolation 130km inland from Townsville. Its main industries are cattle and mining, with a gold revival in place since the 1980s, with modern processes enabling companies to rework old deposits. This place was fabulously rich during the gold rush and still has a remarkable number of fine 19th-century homes and restored public buildings.

The gleam of gold was first spotted in 1871 in a creek bed at the foot of Towers Hill by an Aboriginal boy, Jupiter Mosman. Within a few years the surrounding area was peppered with diggings and a large town had grown. In its heyday around the end of the 19th century, Charters Towers was known as 'the World' for its wealth and diversity. It had almost 100 mines, a population of 30,000, a stock exchange and 25 pubs.

INFORMATION

Charters Towers Computers (☎ 4787 2988; 59 Gill St; ☼ 9am-5pm Mon-Fri, 9am-noon Sat) has Internet access. Otherwise, try the **library** (Gill St). **Charters Towers visitor information centre** (☎ 4752 0314; www.charterstowers.qld.gov.au; 74 Mosman St; ☼ 9am-5pm) is at the top of Gill St and runs a number of tours.

SIGHTS

A stroll down Gill and Mosman Sts will present many of Charters Towers' historically significant buildings. Almost on the corner is the picturesque **Stock Exchange Arcade** built in 1887 and now lined with shops; the 'Calling of the Card' audio presentation runs four times a day.

A wonderful place to escape in time is the **Zara Clark Museum** (☎ 4787 4661; 36 Mosman St; adult/child $4.50/2.20; ☼ 10am-3pm). The clutter of memorabilia, from old photos and farming equipment to period costumes and military items, is fascinating.

The original Australia Bank of Commerce building, built in 1891, now houses the **World Theatre** (82 Mosman St). It comprises a theatre, cinema, gift shop and restaurant.

You'll need the free cuppa to recover from the caretaker's ghost stories at **Ay Ot Lookout** (☎ 4787 2799; cnr High & Hodgkinsons Sts; admission $5; ☼ 8am-3pm). The timber building is one of

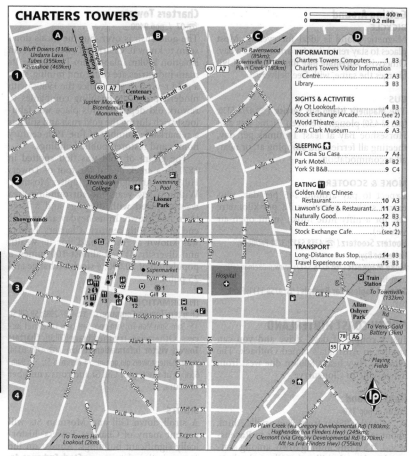

CHARTERS TOWERS

many around town built using a method known as 'balloon framing', where the walls lack external cladding, and so do not have a cavity that can lead to vermin problems. It's said to be haunted by its former owner and a mysterious young woman.

The **Venus Gold Battery** (☎ 4752 0314; Millchester Rd; admission $6; ⏱ 9.30am-4.30pm Mon-Fri), where gold-bearing ore was crushed and processed from 1872 until as recently as 1973, is the largest preserved battery in Australia. An imaginative presentation tells the story of this huge relic.

Towers Hill Lookout, the site where gold was first discovered, has inspiring views over the plain. There are interpretive panels, as well as an open-air theatre screening the

Ghosts of Gold each evening at around 7pm ($6, 20 minutes).

FESTIVALS & EVENTS
Ten Days in the Towers, held 24 April to 3 May, is the largest amateur gathering in the country, with line dancing, bush poetry and busking. More than one hundred amateur cricket teams descend on Charters Towers to play for the **Goldfield Ashes** every Australia Day weekend (late January).

SLEEPING
Park Motel (☎ 4787 1022; www.parkmotel.citysearch .com.au; 1 Mosman St; s/d $70/80; P 🞰 🞰) The guest rooms upstairs at this historic building have loads of character, high ceilings

and a resident ghost (supposedly). Downstairs is a cosy, deep-pink bar and quaint bistro, **Lissners** (mains $8-15; ☽ dinner). There are also motel rooms out the back.

York St B&B (☎ 4787 1028; 58 York St; dm/s/d $17/65/90; **P** ☒ ☎) The lofty brass beds in the Yorke's heritage-themed rooms are likely to inspire you to don a sleeping bonnet and nightshirt. These rooms, located in the main house (1880s), are busy with lace and floral patterns – the dorms are in a separate, less glorious wing. There is also a good communal country-style kitchen and wheelchair access.

Mi Casa Su Casa (☎ 4787 2146; casamiassu@hotmail .com; 21 Mill Lane; d incl breakfast $80; **P** ☒ ☎) The outdoor swimming pool and garden here are an oasis from the dusty surrounds. Four rooms are available in the house, which you'll share with three friendly dogs. You won't have to share your scrummy breakfast with anyone though.

Other recommendations:

Bluff Downs (☎ 4770 4084; www.bluffdowns.com.au; dm/d $25/150; **P** ☒) Doubles include meals.

Plain Creek (☎ 4983 5228; reid.robyn@bigpond.com; Clermont Rd; d from $100)

EATING

Stock Exchange Cafe (☎ 4787 7954; Mosman St; mains $7-10; ☽ lunch Mon-Sat May-Jan) Try not to slurp when you get to the bottom of your iced coffee – there's an echo in the charmingly restored arcade that houses this café. Stop in for a pleasant lunch of perhaps a baked potato or lasagne.

Naturally Good (☎ 4787 4211; 58 Gill St; dishes $5-8; ☽ breakfast & lunch Mon-Sat) Freshly made sandwiches and homemade cakes and pastries are the go at this super-friendly lunchtime spot. Dine in at one of the heavy wooden tables, or take away.

Lawson's Cafe & Restaurant (☎ 4787 4333; 82 Mosman St; mains $17-23; ☽ breakfast, lunch & dinner) There is something for everyone here, at any meal time. In the evening the tables are candlelit, and topped with tasty dishes such as chicken burgers, vegetable stacks or goat curry.

More options:

Redz (☎ 4787 8044; 32 Gill St; dishes $4-6; ☽ breakfast & lunch) Hip bookshop-cum-café.

Golden Mine Chinese Restaurant (☎ 4787 7609; 64 Mosman St; mains $9-12; ☽ lunch & dinner) Has an all-you-can-eat smorgasbord.

GETTING THERE & AWAY

Greyhound Australia (☎ 13 14 99; www.greyhound .com.au) has daily services from Townsville to Charters Towers ($30, one hour 40 minutes) continuing to the NT. Buses arrive and depart outside the Catholic church on Gill St.

The train station is on Enterprise Rd, 1.5km east of the centre. The twice-weekly *Inlander* runs from Townsville to Charters Towers (economy seat/sleeper $23/76, three hours).

Travel Experience.com (☎ 4787 2622; 13 Gill St) handles travel tickets.

TOWNSVILLE TO MISSION BEACH
Paluma Range National Park

Don't miss the beautiful Mt Spec–Big Crystal Creek section of this national park. It straddles the 1000m-plus Paluma Range west of the Bruce Hwy and has Australia's most southerly pocket of tropical rainforest, with wonderful coastal views. It's about 62km north of Townsville.

Take the northern access route to **Big Crystal Creek**, via the 4km road, 2km north of Mt Spec Rd. Here goannas scamper away from your approaching footsteps as you walk the few hundred metres from the picnic area to the popular Paradise Waterhole. There's a self-registration **QPWS camping ground** (per person/family $4/16) with toilets, gas barbecues and drinking water.

The southern access route, Mt Spec Rd is a dramatic narrow road with lose-your-lunch twists that weaves its way up the mountains to the village of Paluma. After 7km you will come to **Little Crystal Creek**, a great swimming spot with waterfalls, a couple of deep rock pools and a small picnic area. You'll also pass **McClelland's Lookout**, with three good walking trails.

The **Jourama Falls** area of the park is 6km along good unsealed road off the highway. The signpost is 90km north of Townsville (25km south of Ingham). Waterview Creek, walking distance from the falls (600m) has good swimming holes with loads of cute turtles, lookouts, a picnic area and a self-registration **QPWS camping ground** (per person/family $4/16) with barbecues.

Accommodation is available at **Misthaven** (☎ 07-4771 5964; d $60), a series of fabulously kitsch self-contained units in Paluma, or at **Paluma Rainforest Cottages** (☎ 07-4770 8520;

QUEENSLAND

www.palumarainforest.com.au; d $75-90). Make sure you stop at **Frosty Mango** (☎ 07-4770 8184; www .frostymango.com.au; Bruce Hwy; light meals $5-10; ⏱ 9am-5pm) at Mutarnee. It's a roadside restaurant serving everything mango-ish.

For more information, contact Ingham's QPWS or visitor information centre (below), or Townsville's visitor information centre (p401).

Ingham & Around

Littered with untenanted and untouched buildings, the clock stopped around 1950 in beautiful Ingham. You'll want to stop here for directions to spectacular **Wallaman Falls**, which lie within Lumholtz National Park, 50km west of town. The falls have the longest single drop of any in Australia at 278m. It's a dazzling sight in the wet season. There's a self-registration **QPWS camping ground** (per person/family $4/16) with a swimming hole nearby. For information, pop into the Ingham **visitor information centre** (☎ 07-4776 5211; www.hinchinbrooknq.com.au; 21 Lannercost St; ⏱ 8.45am-5pm Mon-Fri, 9am-2pm Sat & Sun) or the **QPWS office** (☎ 07-4776 1700; www.epa.qld.gov.au; 49 Cassady St; ⏱ 9am-5pm Mon-Fri).

Between Ingham and Cardwell, the Bruce Hwy briefly climbs high above the coast with tremendous views over the winding, mangrove-lined waterways known as the Everglades, which separate Hinchinbrook Island from the coast.

Lucinda, a port town 24km from Ingham, is the access point for the southern end of Hinchinbrook Island. It's worth coming down here just to see the 6km-long jetty used for shipping sugar.

Cardwell

☎ 07 / pop 1420

The idling seaside holiday town of Cardwell is one of north Queensland's oldest towns (established in 1864), yet there's surprisingly little to it. The Port Hinchinbrook marina development, 2km south of town, is the departure point for Hinchinbrook Island and may awaken this beachside stretch in years to come. For travellers with wheels, there are a bunch of great forest drives, picnic spots and walks with swimming holes in the area, including the **Cardwell Forest Drive**, a 26km round trip.

The **QPWS Reef & Rainforest Centre** (☎ 4066 88601; www.epa.qld.gov.au; ⏱ 8am-4.30pm), beside the main jetty, has a great rainforest interpretive display and information on Hinchinbrook Island and the drives.

SLEEPING

Mudbrick Manor (☎ 4066 2299; www.mudbrickmanor .com.au; Lot 13, Stony Creek Rd; d incl breakfast $100-125; Ⓟ ☒ ☒) This hand-built mudbrick home is outstanding. You'll spend lazy days on the veranda overlooking the sprawling paved courtyard or cooling off in the huge indoor lounge. Ask about the three-course dinners; you may end up staying another night.

Kookaburra Holiday Park (☎ 4066 8648; www.kook aburraholidaypark.com.au; 175 Bruce Hwy; powered/un-powered sites per 2 people $20/18, d $35-90; Ⓟ ☒ ☒) Set in attractive tropical grounds, this enormous holiday village almost outsizes Cardwell itself. There's a wide range of accommodation and out the back is the **Hinchinbrook YHA** (unpowered sites s/d $11/18, dm/s/d $18/35/40), a bright backpackers with access to the park's fabulous facilities.

Latitudz (☎ 4066 8907; Victoria St; mains $17-20, ⏱ lunch & dinner Wed-Mon) is a smart-looking café serving barramundi, oysters and other seafood. Otherwise, basic pub grub is available in the concrete courtyard of the **Marine Hotel** (☎ 4066 8662; 59 Victoria St; mains around $14, ⏱ lunch & dinner).

GETTING THERE & AWAY

All buses between Townsville and Cairns stop at Cardwell: from Townsville it costs $32 (two hours), from Cairns $31 (three hours). Cardwell is also on the Brisbane to Cairns train line; contact **Queensland Rail** (☎ 1300 131 722; www.traveltrain.qr.com.au) for details.

Hinchinbrook Island National Park

Lucky you, if you have time to explore this stunning and unspoiled wilderness. Hinchinbrook's granite mountains rise dramatically from the sea. The mainland side is thick with lush tropical forest, while long, sandy beaches and tangled mangroves curve round its eastern shores. All 399 sq km of the island is national park, and rugged Mt Bowen (1121m) is its highest peak. There's plenty of wildlife, especially pretty-faced wallabies and the iridescent-blue Ulysses butterfly.

Hinchinbrook is well known to bushwalkers and naturalists. Walking opportunities here are excellent; however, some trails may close between November and March due to adverse weather.

The highlight is the **Thorsborne Trail** (also known as the East Coast Trail), a 32km track from Ramsay Bay to Zoe Bay (with its stunning waterfall), and on to George Point at the southern tip. It's a three- to five-day walk, although you can walk shorter sections. This is the real bush experience, however. You'll need to draw water from creeks as you go (all water should be chemically purified or boiled before drinking), keep your food out of reach of the native bush rats, and keep an eye out for estuarine crocodiles in the mangroves. Take plenty of insect repellent.

Hinchinbrook Island Resort (☎ 1800 777 021, 07-4066 8270; www.hinchinbrookresort.com.au; d $165-300; 🔊) is built into the steep hillside behind Orchid Beach in the island's north. Accommodation is either in self-contained beach houses or stylish, elevated tree houses with balconies. Use of the resort's canoes, surf-skis and snorkelling gear is free, or you can just laze in a hammock on the beach.

Along the Thorsborne Trail there are six **QPWS camping grounds** (per person/family $4/16), plus the two at Macushla Bay and the Haven in the north. A limit of 40 people on the main trail at any one time necessitates booking ahead (up to one year for school holidays). Pick up the Thorsborne Trail and Hinchinbrook leaflets from the QPWS Reef & Rainforest Centre (opposite) in Cardwell. To purchase your permits and book a place, call **QPWS** (☎ 13 13 04; www.epa.qld.gov.au).

GETTING THERE & AWAY
Hinchinbrook Island Ferries (☎ 07-4066 8270; www.hinchinbrookferries.com.au) has a daily service from May to October and three services a week from November to March. Boats depart from Cardwell's Port Hinchinbrook Marina and dock at the Hinchinbrook Resort. The journey costs from $100 return. If you're walking the Thorsborne Trail a one-way transfer costs $60. Walkers usually pick up the **Hinchinbrook Wilderness Safaris'** (☎ 07-4777 8307; www.hinchinbrookwildernesssafaris.com.au; one way/return $47/57) service at the southern end.

Tully
☎ 07 / pop 2700
Tully carries the reputation as the wettest place in Australia. It holds the record for the highest annual rainfall in a populated area of

Australia – which it 'won' in 1950 when it received 7.9m. (It's no coincidence that the giant gumboot at the entrance to town is also 7.9m tall.). The big excitement here though is spending five frothy hours white-water rafting its wild river. Walkers also have good reason to stop, with 150km of new tracks, while other travellers come to pick bananas.

Day trips with **Raging Thunder Adventures** (☎ 4030 7990; www.ragingthunder.com.au/rafting.asp) or **R'n'R White Water Rafting** (☎ 4051 7777; www.raft.com.au) cost about $150 and include barbecue lunch and transfers from Mission Beach, Cairns or Port Douglas.

There are good walking opportunities in the **Tully State forests**, located 40km from Tully along Cardstone Rd. There are picnic facilities, as well as river access for swimming at Tully Gorge. It's also popular with kayakers, and the gentle burble of the Tully River can turn to rapids when the hydroelectricity company opens its floodgates. The Tully **visitor information centre** (☎ 4068 2288; www.tropicalaustralia.com.au; Bruce Hwy; 🕑 8.30am-4.45pm Mon-Fri, 9am-2.30pm Sat & Sun) has a map of all walking trails.

Sleeping options include the **Tully Motel** (☎ 4068 2233; tullymotel@bigpond.com; Bruce Hwy; s/d $65/75), with pleasant rooms, or the high-density **Banana Barracks** (☎ 4068 0455; www.bananabarracks.com; 50 Butler St; dm $18; 🔊) hostel, with a busy after-work bar and budget bistro meals.

MISSION BEACH
☎ 07 / pop 1090
Blessed with a cosy village atmosphere and the dreamiest stretch of palm-fringed sand along the northeast coast, Mission Beach is a favourite spot to chill. This collection of small settlements, including Wongaling and South Mission Beaches in the south, Mission Beach in the middle, and Bingil Bay and beautiful Garners Beach in the north, seem to exist entirely to serve you. Sophisticated restaurants and boutique B&Bs mix in with modest cafés and casual backpackers, and when you tire of languorous beach days there's a boat operator poised to ferry you out to Dunk Island or the stunning Great Barrier Reef.

Information
Mission Beach visitor information centre (☎ 4068 7099; www.missionbeachtourism.com; Porters Promenade; 🕑 9am-5pm)

QUEENSLAND

THE CASSOWARY'S PRECIOUS POO

The flightless cassowary is as tall as a grown man, has three toes, a blue-and-purple head, red wattles (fleshy lobes hanging from its neck), a helmet-like horn and unusual black feathers – that look more like ratty hair. Traditional gender roles are reversed with the male bird incubating the egg and rearing the chicks alone. The Australian cassowary is also known as the southern cassowary, though it's only found in the north of Queensland. It begins to make sense when you realise that other species are found in Papua New Guinea – to the north of Australia.

The cassowary is considered an important link in the rainforest ecosystem. It is the only animal capable of dispersing the seeds of more than 70 species of trees whose fruit is too large for other rainforest animals to digest and pass. Cassowaries swallow fruit whole and excrete the fruit's seed intact in large piles of dung, which acts as fertiliser encouraging growth of the seed. Without this process, the rainforest as we know it would look very different.

The cassowary is an endangered species; its biggest threat is loss of habitat, and eggs and chicks are vulnerable to dogs and wild pigs. A number of birds are also hit by cars: heed road signs warning drivers to be casso-wary. You're most likely to see cassowaries around Mission Beach and the Cape Tribulation section of the Daintree National Park. They can be aggressive, particularly if they have chicks. If you feel threatened do not run, give the bird right-of-way and try to keep something solid between you and it – preferably a tree.

Wet Tropics Environment Centre (☎ 4068 7179; www.wettropics.gov.au)

Sights & Activities

Mission Beach has plenty of activities on offer, from near-death experiences to more sedate options. Paddle over to Dunk Island for the day with **Coral Sea Kayaking** (☎ 4068 9154; www.coralseakayaking.com; half-/full-day tours $60/95) or bob around the coastline for half a day; trips depart South Mission Beach.

Mission Beach is one of the most popular spots in Queensland to skydive; **Jump the Beach** (☎ 4031 1822; www.jumpthebeach.com; tandem from $295) uses the sand of Mission Beach to cushion your landing.

Quick Cat (☎ 4068 7289; www.quickcatscuba.com; per person $140) operates day cruises to the outer reef, including a 45-minute stop at Dunk Island, snorkelling, lunch and a glass-bottom boat jaunt.

Experienced divers should try **Calypso Dive** (☎ 4068 8432; www.calypsodive.com; per person $160), which runs diving cruises to the Lady Bowen wreck.

Rainforest walks around Mission Beach can get exciting if you meet a southern cassowary (see above).

Sleeping

BUDGET

Treehouse (☎ 4068 7137; www.yha.com.au; Bingil Bay Rd, Bingil Bay; unpowered sites $12, dm/d $20/50; 🖳) This large timber building merges effortlessly with the lush surrounding rainforest. A generous balcony space is dotted with heavy wooden tables and it all makes for a remarkably restful and affable stay. Treehouse is a YHA-affiliated hostel.

Scotty's Mission Beach House (☎ 1800 665 567, 4068 8676; scottysbeachhouse@bigpond.com; 167 Reid Rd, Wongaling Beach; dm $19-23, d with bathroom $55 🅿 🖳 🖳) Behind a white picket fence sits this secluded pocket of accommodation with beautiful grounds and stellar facilities. The bright dorms are a beachy shade of blue.

Also recommended:

Beachcomber Coconut Caravan Village (☎ 1800 008 129, 4068 8129; big4bccv@bigpond.com.au; Kennedy Esplanade, South Mission Beach; powered/unpowered sites $28/24, d cabins $55-80; 🅿 🖳) Excellent park for families, with good facilities.

Mission Beach Backpackers Lodge (☎ 4068 8317; www.missionbeachbackpacker.com; 28 Wongaling Beach Rd; dm $18, d $40-44; 🖳 🖳) Good accommodation and hammocks around the pool.

MIDRANGE

Perrier Walk (☎ 4068 7141; www.perrierwalk.nq.nu Alexander Dr, Mission Beach; s/d $125/150; 🅿 🖳) This choice B&B is run by a landscape designer and a chef, which all makes for very scrummy scenery and breakfasts. The jungle room boasts a stone bath and a tree shower and the colourfully rendered

Mexican-style rooms are enveloped by giant exotic flowering plants.

Sanctuary (☎ 4088 6067, 1800 777 012; www.sanc tuaryatmission.com; Holt Rd, Bingil Bay; dm $33, huts s/d $60/65, cabins s/d $130/150; ☐ ☒) A rainforest boardwalk connects these minimalist huts, designed to make you feel at one with the surrounding nature. Yoga retreats and classes are regular fixtures here. 'Om' ambience aside, you can still dine on vodka and lime chicken, followed by *affogato*, in the restaurant.

Hibiscus Lodge B&B (☎ 4068 9096; hibiscuslodge@ bigpond.com; 5 Kurrajong Close, Wongaling Beach; s/d $75/120; ☒ ☒) This tidy B&B has three rooms, each with private bathroom, in a capacious modern home. Rates include a cooked breakfast, and the beautifully shaded pool makes the property unsuitable for littlies.

Mission Beach Ecovillage (☎ 4068 7534; www.eco village.com.au; Clump Point Rd, Mission Beach; d $145-155; ☒ ☒) This lovely property has 17 unassuming units, tucked away off a meandering, palm-lined path. Each has a kitchen, dining area and big beds. The deluxe room also has a spa. The freeform pool is a stunner, and you can see the beach from the bar area.

Other midrange options:

Rainforest Motel (☎ 4068 7556; www.missionbeach rainforestmotel.com; 9 Endeavour Ave, Mission Beach; d $80; ☒ ☒) Tidy rooms in a pretty courtyard.

Honeyeater Homestay (☎ 4068 8741; www.honey eater.com.au; 53 Reid Rd, Wongaling Beach; s/d $85/100; ☒) Stylish B&B with open-plan living and a tropical garden.

TOP END

Horizon (☎ 4068 8154; www.thehorizon.com.au; Explorer Dr, Mission Beach; r $220-420; ☒ ☒) Tucked away in the rainforest, this secluded resort has views out to Dunk Island and beyond. If you go for the best they've got, you could appreciate that view from your king-sized bed. There's also a tour-booking desk and restaurant.

Eating

Blarney's (☎ 4068 8472; 10 Wongaling Beach Rd, Wongaling; mains $24; ☒ dinner Tue-Sat, lunch Sun) This casual crowd-pleaser is blessed with a big backyard, bamboo-thatched ceilings and lattice screens. The á la carte menu offers tasty, hearty dishes such as beef Wellington and steak-and-kidney pie.

Friends (☎ 4068 7107; Porter Promenade, Mission Beach; mains $17-25; ☒ dinner Tue-Sun) Palms sway behind the lattice walls and candlelights flicker at this cosy restaurant. Dutiful staff cruise the low-key surrounds, serving seafood laksa and favourites including roast chicken. There's a small selection of specials, and a good wine list.

Toba (☎ 4068 7852; 37 Porter Promenade, Mission Beach; mains $21-25; ☒ dinner Wed-Sun) Toba dishes up polite portions of Asian-inspired meals, such as salmon with Chinese black vinegar, and Thai green curry. The courtyard is the main attraction though, especially the platform hut with cushioned seating. Good for small groups and couples.

Shrubbery Taverna (☎ 4068 7803; David St; mains $17-20; ☒ lunch Sat & Sun, dinner daily) Locals like the laid-back service and courtyard dining here. Balmy nights and the sound of waves washing the beach do wonders for the Mediterranean-Greek menu. And there's a happy hour-and-a-half between 4.30pm and 6pm.

Cheaper eats can be had at **Delish Niche** (☎ 40 88 6004; Porter Promenade, Mission Beach; dishes $6-10; ☒ breakfast & lunch), which serves light meals, or by heading to the supermarkets at Mission Beach and Wongaling.

Getting There & Around

Greyhound Australia (☎ 13 14 99; www.greyhound .com.au) buses stop at the Port o' Call Cafe in Mission Beach, while **Premier Motor Service** (☎ 13 34 10; www.premierms.com.au) stops at the Mission Beach Resort in Wongaling Beach. Average one-way fares are $25 to Cairns (two hours) and $45 to Townsville (3¾ hours).

The **Trans North** (☎ 4068 7400; from $3; ☒ Mon-Sat) local bus runs almost every hour between Bingil Bay and South Mission Beach; the visitors centre has timetables.

DUNK ISLAND

Dunk Island is an easy day trip from Mission Beach. It's just 4.5km off the coast and blessed with nearly 150 species of bird life and exotic butterflies in season.

Rainforest walks here will revive the spirit. From the top of Mt Kootaloo (271m; 5.6km), entrances to the Hinchinbrook Channel fan before you, or there's the rewarding but difficult island circuit (9.2km) that passes by secluded beaches. You can also check out the alternative lifestyle of **Bruce Arthur's Artists Colony** (admission $4; ✆ 10am-1pm Mon & Thu).

Day trippers can purchase a Resort Experience Pass (adult/child $40/20), available from the Watersports Centre just south of the jetty, which entitles you to lunch and an hour's use of a paddle ski.

The **Dunk Island Resort** (☎ 07-4068 8199, reservations 1800 737 678; www.dunk-island.com; s $365-520, d $500-800; ✄ ☒) sits on palm-fringed Brammo Bay and has rooms ranging from pretty nice to pretty superb. Think split-level accommodation, a huge bed and personal access to the beach. Tariffs include breakfast and dinner.

The **QPWS camping ground** (☎ 07-4068 8199; www.epa.qld.gov.au; per person/family $4/16) has nine sites with good amenities by the resort's water-sports office.

Day trippers can buy basic food and beverages from the licensed café just south of the jetty.

Getting There & Away

Macair (☎ 13 13 13; www.macair.com.au) has regular flights to/from Cairns ($190). **Mission Beach Dunk Island Connections** (☎ 07-4059 2709; www.missionbeachdunkconnections.com.au) does combination bus and boat transfers to Dunk from Cairns ($50, 2½ hours) and Port Douglas ($75, 3¾ hours).

Return ferry trips (including snorkelling) from Mission Beach cost about $22 with **Dunk Island Express Water Taxi** (☎ 07-4068 8310; Banfield Pde, Wongaling) and **Dunk Island Ferry & Cruises** (☎ 07-4068 7211; www.dunkferry.com.au; Clump Point).

You can also get here with Quick Cat or Coral Sea Kayaking; see p414.

MISSION BEACH TO CAIRNS

The scenery from Mission Beach to Cairns is wonderfully fertile. North of El Arish, you can leave the Bruce Hwy and take an alternative route to Innisfail via quaint Silkwood and Mena Creek, buried in sugar cane about 20km southwest of Innisfail.

At Mena Creek, **Paronella Park** (☎ 07-4065 3225; www.paronellapark.com.au; Japoonvale Rd, also called Old Bruce Hwy; adult/child $20/10; ✆ 9am-9.30pm) is a rambling, tropical garden with the enchanting ruins of a Spanish castle built in the 1930s. Floods, fire and the moist tropics have rendered these mossy remains almost medieval. Tours run regularly and there's a caravan park next door.

If you want to know more about sugar processing, steam trains and the slave-labour heritage of the industry, pop by the **Australian Sugar Industry Museum** (☎ 07-4063 2306; www.sugarmuseum.org.au; Bruce Hwy; adult/child/family $8/6/22; ✆ 9am-5pm Mon-Sat, 9am-3pm Sun May-Oct & 9am-5pm Mon-Fri, 9am-3pm Sat, 9am-noon Sun Nov-Apr) at Mourilyan, 7km south of Innisfail.

Innisfail

☎ 07 / pop 8530

Art Deco fans may find themselves wolf-whistling at the sight of Innisfail's beautiful buildings. This prosperous sugar city suffered a devastating cyclone in 1918, but its reconstruction came at the height of the sleek 1920s and '30s Art Deco movement.

The **visitor information centre** (☎ 4061 7422; Bruce Hwy; ☎ 9am-5pm Mon-Fri, 10am-3pm Sat & Sun), about 3.5km south of town, has a town walk brochure.

Johnstone River Crocodile Farm (☎ 4061 1121; www.crocfarm.com; Flying Fish Point Rd; adult/child $16/8; ✆ 8.30am-4.30pm, feeding times 11am & 3pm) breeds thousands of crocodiles so we can enjoy them as handbags and steak. Tours run frequently (from 9.30am) where you can watch one of the guides sit on one-tonne Gregory – the farm's fattest reptile.

About 3.5km south of town, tidy **Mango Tree Van Park** (☎ 4061 1656; mangotreepark@bigpond.com; unpowered sites/d $15/70; ☒) has two great cottage-style cabins, or there's the generic **Barrier Reef Motel** (☎ 4061 4988; www.barrierreefmotel.com.au; Bruce Hwy; s/d $75/85; ☒ ☐ ☒) with small rooms and a restaurant.

The town's hostels cater to banana plantation workers. **Codge Lodge** (☎ 4061 8055; 63 Rankin St; dm $20; ☒ ☐ ☒) is in a superb home overlooking the river. Or there's **Walkabout Motel & Backpacker** (☎ 4061 2311; motelwalkabout@bigpond.com; 20-24 Gowan Dr; dm/d $20/60; ☒), which has dowdy motel-style rooms.

From Innisfail the Palmerston Hwy winds west up to the magical Atherton Tableland, passing through the rainforest of **Palmerston (Wooroonooran National Park)**, which has creeks, waterfalls, scenic walking tracks and a self-registration **camping ground** (per person/family $4/16) at Henrietta Creek, just off the road.

Innisfail to Cairns

Australia's ancient landscape may be a pile of rubble in geological terms, but Queensland's highest peak, **Mt Bartle Frere** (1657m), is still a challenging climb. Sitting inside Wooroonooran National Park, it falls within the dramatic Bellenden Ker range, which skirts the Bruce Hwy between Innisfail and Cairns.

Experienced walkers can embark on the **Mt Bartle Frere Summit Track** (15km, two days return), which leads from the Josephine Falls car park to the summit. There's also an alternative 10km (eight-hour) return walk to Broken Nose. It's best that you don't walk alone and let someone know before you go. Pick up a trail guide from the nearest visitors centre or contact the **QPWS** (☎ 13 13 04; www.epa.qld.gov.au). Self-registration **camping** (per person/family $4/16) is permitted along the trail.

GULF SAVANNAH

The epitome of outback Australia and a true frontier, the Gulf Savannah is remote, hot and sparsely populated, with excellent fishing, extraordinary characters and a large residency of crocodiles. Here the horizons are so wide they tickle the moon and the sun. The landscape is vast and flat, embellished by sweeping grass plains, scrubby forest and an intricate network of seasonal rivers and tidal creeks that drain into the Gulf of Carpentaria. When you do stumble across a pocket of civilisation, propped up by a few locals and relics of gold-mining days, expect a warm welcome.

There are just two seasons: the Wet (December to March) and the Dry. Driving is the best way to see the region, but during the Wet, dirt roads turn to muck and sealed roads can be flooded.

Getting There & Around
AIR
Macair (☎ 13 13 13; www.macair.com.au) has services travelling between Cairns and Normanton ($190), Burketown ($250) and Mornington Island ($246); and between Mt Isa and Normanton ($200) and Burketown ($180).

BUS
Country Road Coachlines (☎ 07-4045 2794; country roadcoachlines@msn.com) has a service on Monday and Thursday from Cairns to Karumba ($125, 12 hours) via Undara ($55, 4½ hours),

Georgetown ($70), Croydon ($90) and Normanton ($118), returning on Tuesday and Friday.

AICCC runs a bus from Normanton to Mt Isa on Monday, returning on Tuesday. The adult/child one-way fare is $110/85. The Normanton terminal and booking agent is **Gulfland Souvenirs** (☎ 07-4745 1307; Normanton railway station).

CAR & MOTORCYCLE
There are two main roads into the Gulf region. The Savannah Way (or Gulf Developmental Rd) takes you from the Kennedy Hwy, south of the Atherton Tableland, across to Normanton on 450km of sealed road. The Burke Developmental Rd (Matilda Hwy) runs north from Cloncurry to Normanton (378km sealed) via the Burke & Wills Roadhouse, but it's mostly single-lane traffic and driving requires good concentration.

Other roads through the region are unsealed so before driving on any of them, make sure you seek advice on road conditions, fuel stops and what to carry with you (plenty of water!). The **RACQ** (☎ 07-4033 6711; www.racq.com.au; 520 Mulgrave St, Earlville) in Cairns is an excellent source of information.

TRAIN
The **Queensland Rail** (☎ 1300 131 722; www.travel train.com.au) *Gulflander* connects Normanton and Croydon (economy seat $48, 3½ hours) once per week.

The historic *Savannahlander* conducts four-day **tours** (☎ 07-4036 9250) along its traditional route from Cairns to Forsayth, generally between March and mid-December (weather permitting). Rates vary depending on the accommodation and tours you book so, call for details.

THE SAVANNAH WAY
Undara Volcanic National Park
The massive Undara lava tubes are one of inland Queensland's most fascinating natural attractions. They were formed around 190,000 years ago following a three-month eruption of a single shield volcano. The massive lava flows drained towards the sea, following the routes of ancient river beds, and while the surface of the lava cooled and hardened, hot lava continued to race through the centre of the flows, eventually leaving enormous basalt tubes.

QUEENSLAND

You may only visit the tubes with **Savannah Guides** (www.savannah-guides.com.au); who run full-day tours (adult/child $100/50 including lunch), half-day tours ($65/35) and two-hour introductory tours ($35/17), from the lodge.

Sitting 275km west of Cairns, the facilities for campers are excellent at **Undara Experience** (☎ 1800 990 992, 07-4097 1411; www.undara.com .au; powered & unpowered sites per 2 people $12, permanent tents $36, dm $25, s/d $100/150; ☒), but the railway carriages are a beautifully restored treat (ask about the meal packages). Bush breakfasts are outdoors with billy tea and birdsong. The bistro serves lunch and dinner, but self-caterers must bring all supplies.

Undara to Croydon

The side trips to tiny towns are what make this stretch so memorable. At Mt Surprise, you'll find the region's oldest building, the **Old Post Office Museum** (☎ 07-4062 3126; adult/child $2/50c), which has a small and quirky display of local history items. This is also a centre for gem fossicking, and local businesses can give you tips, tools and a licence to dig for the semi-precious stones. Accommodation options include two caravan parks and the **Mt Surprise Hotel** (☎ 07-4062 3118; s/d $30/50; mains $13-15; ⏰ lunch & dinner).

Tallaroo Hot Springs (☎ /fax 07-4062 1221; adult/child $9/6; ⏰ 8am-5pm Easter-Sep), 50km west of Mt Surprise, is not exactly the place to cool off, with springs that range in temperature from 52°C to 74°C. There's also a camping ground here ($11 for two adults).

Take the 150km **Explorers' Loop** southwest from Mt Surprise to the old gold-mining townships of Einasleigh and Forsayth. Spectacular **Cobbold Gorge** is 45km south of Forsayth, but can only be explored on a guided day with **Cobbold Gorge Tours** (☎ 1800 669 922, 07-4062 5470; www.cobboldgorge.com.au; adult/child $110/55), who also provide accommodation at **Cobbold Village** (powered/unpowered sites $22/11, s/d cabins $50/80; ☒ ☒). Tours include a boat cruise, agate fossicking, lunch and swimming.

The loop finishes at **Georgetown** (population 300), back on the Savannah Way. There are several places to stay, a good bakery, fuel, mechanical and tyre repairs. There's Internet access at the **Terrestrial Centre** (☎ 07-4062 1485; ⏰ 9am-5pm Apr-May, 8.30am-4.30pm Mon-Fri Oct-May; ☒), which also has information on Mt Surprise, Einasleigh and Forsayth.

Croydon

☎ 07 / pop 220

For a while there in the 1880s, everything you touched turned to gold in Croydon. Once the 'Vegas' of the Gulf Savannah, it was crammed with bars and 8000 budding millionaires, many with more muscle than cents, but the riches ran dry towards the end of WWI and the town became a skeleton of its former self.

Croydon's information centre (☎ 4745 6125; cnr Samwell & Aldridge Sts; ⏰ 8am-5pm Mon-Fri Nov-Mar; ☒), museum, craft shop and Internet café ($2.50 per 30 minutes) are housed in the historic police station alongside several other restored buildings. The centre conducts one-hour **walking tours** (☎ 4745 6125; adult/child $5.50/free; ⏰ tours 8am, 10am, 2pm & 4pm).

You can sleep on the veranda at the **Club Hotel** (☎ 4745 6184; cnr Brown & Sircom Sts; s $40, d $50-75; ☒ ☒). It's a corrugated iron pub with heaps of character, basic rooms and meals and, bless them, a pool!

Normanton

☎ 07 / pop 1450

You've hit the 'big smoke' at Normanton, a bustling centre with a handful of **historic buildings**, including the *Gulflander*'s classic Victorian-era train station. The town was established on Norman River as a port for the Cloncurry copper fields before becoming Croydon's gold-rush port. June is an excellent time to stop and enjoy the area's biggest social event, the **Normanton Rodeo & Gymkhana**. Otherwise, croc spotting, barramundi fishing and a beer at the **Purple Pub** (☎ 4745 1324; cnr Landsborough & Brown Sts) are big pastimes. The historic Burns Philp & Co Ltd store houses the **Visitor Information Centre** and **library** (☎ 4745 1065; cnr Caroline & Landsborough Sts; ⏰ 10am-6pm Mon-Fri, to 8pm Tue, 9am-2pm Sat; ☒) with Internet access ($2 per 30 minutes).

The **Normanton Caravan Park** (☎ 4745 1121; Brown St; powered/unpowered sites per 2 people $20/16, dm $25, cabins $65; ☒ ☒) is a very pleasant park with excellent cabins that have bathrooms, and a huge shaded swimming pool and artesian spa.

More accommodation:

Gulfland Motel & Caravan Park (☎ 4745 1290; 11 Landsborough St; powered/unpowered sites $20/16, s/d $80/90; ☒ ☒) Has a licensed restaurant.

Albion Hotel (☎ 4745 1218; Haig St; s/d $55/60; ☒) Motel-style rooms out the back. Counter meals.

Karumba

☎ 07 / pop 1350

Karumba may be a remote fishing village, but more and more travellers come to watch dreamy sunsets melt into the Arafura Sea over seafood platters. It's on the Gulf of Carpentaria, 79km from Normanton by a good, sealed, dual road. The Gulf offers brilliant fishing, and the surrounding wetlands and mangroves are packed with bird life and saltwater crocodiles.

There's a great bakery in town and a mobile grocery truck does the rounds for self-caterers, but you'll end up at the legendary **Sunset Tavern** (☎ 4745 9183; The Esplanade, Karumba Point; mains $11-25; ✹ 10am-midnight), which serves excellent meals outdoors.

For accommodation, you can try **Pelicans Inn** (☎ 4745 9555; www.pelicanskaramba.com.au; 2 Gilbert St, Karumba; dm $25, d $85-130; ▯ ▣), a modern, corrugated-iron building housing dorms, self-contained units, luxury bathrooms with river views and disabled-friendly rooms.

Also available:

Savannah Shores (☎ 4745 9126; www.savannahshores .com.au; The Esplanade Point; s/d $65/71; ▨ ▣) Self-contained cabins on the foreshore.

Gulf Country Van Park (☎ /fax 4745 9148; cnr Yappar St & Massey Dr; powered/unpowered sites per 2 people $22/19, s/d $40/60; ▣) Shady park with good amenities.

NORMANTON TO CLONCURRY

You'll enjoy this beautiful stretch of savannahland and red-rock country on the Matilda Hwy. Everyone stops at the **Burke & Wills Roadhouse** (☎ 07-4742 5909; powered/unpowered sites $18/10, s/d $39/50; ✹ 7am-10pm; ▨) halfway to Cloncurry, for tucker and fuel, and then pops into the **Quamby Hotel** (☎ 07-4742 5952; s/d $10/15; ▨), further on, for a cleansing beer. The hotel has one room and meals are served if weary travellers scream loudly enough.

At Cloncurry you'll find the upmarket **Gidgee Inn** (☎ 07-4742 1599; www.gidgeeinn.com.au; d/tw $100/105; ▨), built from rammed red earth, or there's the tidy **Gilbert Park Tourist Village** (☎ 07-4742 2300; powered/unpowered sites $19/16, cabins $70).

NORMANTON TO NORTHERN TERRITORY

While driving the unsealed, isolated, dusty stretch from Normanton to the NT, keep in mind that mad, ill-equipped explorers such as the doomed Burke and Wills *walked* twice these distances in summer. You can visit **Camp 119**, the northernmost camp of their wretched 1861 expedition. It's signposted 37km west of Normanton.

If you make it to **Burketown**, give yourself a clap. European settlers were no match for this feisty place and died in droves; check out the cemetery. These days, it's a favourite hangout for cattle and travellers who have read Nevil Shute's *A Town Like Alice,* part of which is set here. From September to November you can see the extraordinary natural phenomenon known as 'Morning Glory' – incredible tubular cloud formations extending the full length of the horizon that roll in from the Gulf of Carpentaria early morning.

Locals at the 130-year-old **Burketown Pub** (☎ 07-4745 5104; fax 07-4745 5146; Beames St; s/d $44, units $72/92; ▨) like a fresh face and a chat.

The **Doomadgee Aboriginal Community** (☎ 07-4745 8188), 93km west of Burketown, has a retail area and welcomes visitors, but village access is at the discretion of the community council. Further along is Hell's Gate, the last outpost of police protection for settlers heading north to Katherine in pioneer times. It was the scene of many ambushes as indigenous Australians tried to stop their lands being overrun. All weary road warriors stop at the **Hell's Gate Roadhouse** (☎ 07-4745 8258; hellsgategulfcountry@bigpond.com; on-site tents $30, s/d $70/90) for a square meal before crossing the border.

BURKETOWN TO CAMOOWEAL

You may not have planned a stop at **Gregory Downs**, but chances are you'll find the pristine Gregory River, its banks covered in luxuriant, ancient rainforest, too beautiful to pass by. It's 117km south of Burketown on the sealed Wills Developmental Rd, which becomes the Gregory Downs Camooweal Rd. Boodjamulla (Lawn Hill) National Park is a two-hour drive inland from here on a mostly well-graded, unsealed road.

The friendly **Gregory Downs Hotel** (☎ 07-4748 5566; gregorydownshotel@bigpond.com; d $75; ▨), at the main turn-off to Boodjamulla (Lawn Hill) National Park, has motel-style units and fuel. It's possible to camp free on the riverbank, but there are no amenities.

Billy Hangers General Store (☎ 07-4748 5540; ✹ 8am-6pm), opposite the pub, is crammed with goodies.

Boodjamulla (Lawn Hill) National Park

In arid country some 100km west of Gregory Downs, this prehistoric landscape is an oasis of gorges, ancient rainforest, crystal-clear green waters, creeks and tropical vegetation that indigenous Australians have enjoyed for perhaps 30,000 years. Remains of their paintings and camp sites are everywhere, and you can visit two rock-art sites.

In the southern part of the park is the World Heritage–listed **Riversleigh Fossil Field**. Some of the fossils are up to 25 million years old and include everything from giant snakes to carnivorous kangaroos.

Lawn Hill has 20km of walking tracks and an excellent national park **camping ground** (☎ 07-4748 5572; sites per person/family $4/16) that must be booked well in advance (April to September) with the park rangers. Paddling up the creek gives a wondrous perspective of the gorge and swimming near the waterfalls is heavenly. Hire canoes from Adels Grove.

Adels Grove (☎ 07-4748 5502; www.adelsgrove.com.au; sites per adult/child/family $8/4/22, s/d $85/140) camping ground is 10km east of the park entrance, set in lush surrounds by Lawn Hill Creek. In addition to camp sites, there are permanently set-up tents with beds and linen. Rates at these include dinner and breakfast Fuel and basic groceries are also available.

About 100km north of Lawn Hill, **Bowthorn Homestead** (☎ 07-4745 8132; www.bowthorn.bigpondhosting.com) offers a great opportunity to stay on a working cattle station. Rates vary according to group size and length of stay, but generally include all meals, a guided day trip and laundry service. Bookings are essential.

GETTING THERE & AWAY

The national park is 100km west of Gregory Downs, although the easiest route for 2WD vehicles is to come via the Burke & Wills Roadhouse. If you're coming from Mt Isa, the last 230km after you leave the Barkley Hwy are unsealed and often impassable after rain, and a 4WD vehicle is necessary.

Campbell's Tours & Travel (☎ 07-4743 2006; www.campbellstravel.com.au) in Mt Isa do a three-day safari (adult/child $660/330) out to Lawn Hill and Riversleigh on Tuesday and Friday, with accommodation and meals provided at Adels Grove.

FAR NORTH QUEENSLAND

Tropical, wild and rugged, Queensland's Far North proves the theory that size doesn't matter. Although small geographically, this stunning destination contains the richest pockets of biodiversity in Australia, if not the world. The dense and ancient rainforests of the Wet Tropics World Heritage Area coat the landscape, spilling out onto gorgeous beaches. Offshore lies the spectacular Great Barrier Reef Marine Park. The highland region of the Atherton Tableland forms a leafy backdrop to the coast, concealing volcanic crater lakes, waterfalls and giant strangled fig trees. Heading north is historic Cooktown, beyond which lie the dusty isolation of Cape York and the very tip of Australia, Cape York Peninsula.

Locals speak reverently about their region and will look at you with undisguised pity if you're from 'down south', which could mean only as far as Townsville. Many conform to the stereotype of the 'real' Australian: a singlet-wearing tough guy in an Akubra hat, whose idea of dressing up is to change into a newer pair of thongs. Common to most however, is a genuine respect for their fragile environment, where human impact is closely checked.

CAIRNS

☎ 07 / pop 98,981

Boasting an irrepressible energy and a lush tropical setting, Cairns is unashamedly a tourist town, and its popularity is global. The international airport here services four Japanese cities weekly; street signs are written in two to three languages, and the city's restaurants represent a huge range of world cuisines. The crowds come to visit the reef, which sits offshore and shapes the city's character. It's one of the world's most popular diving sites and the number of tour/dive/snorkel/cruise operators operating here is mind-boggling. In recent years the city has experienced a development boom, resulting in an artificial beach and cosmetically enhanced foreshore, and a theme-parkesque atmosphere.

An activity-junkie's playground, Cairns can offer you bungee jumping before breakfast, as well as tours to the Atherton Table-

---

CAIRNS REGION IN...

Two Days

The agenda for day one is to get as far away from the city as possible – on a cruise to the **Great Barrier Reef** (p425). Immerse yourself in the vivid depths and snorkel or dive. If you don't want to get wet, take a cruise with a glass-bottom boat so you can still get nose to nose with the gorgeous marine life and colourful coral.

Once the main event is taken care of, dabble around Cairns on day two. Sun up, splash about and flash some skin on the **Cairns Foreshore Promenade** and **swimming lagoon** (p424). Grab a lunchtime bite at **Fusion Organics** (p428) and then potter through the **Cairns Regional Gallery** (p424) and **Cairns Museum** (p424). For dinner treat your tastebuds at **Pier** (p428) or **Cherry Blossom** (p428).

Four Days

On day three head out early for a morning at the **Flecker Botanic Gardens** (p424), where you can take a guided tour and explore the Gondwanan Evolutionary Trail. Save the afternoon for a cultural experience at the **Tjapukai Cultural Park** (p424). Learn about the local indigenous people and witness some traditional dancing. Head back to your accommodation, freshen up and then hit the **night markets** (p429) for some shopping. Join the milieu of locals and other travellers at the capacious outdoor bar at **Gilligan's** (p429). Grab a bar snack there, or for hearty fare head to **Red Ochre Grill** (p428) for native cuisine.

On day four take in a tour of some of Cairn's surrounding sights. Catch the **Kuranda Scenic Railway** (p436) and spend the day exploring the markets and scenery of this pretty village. Get the bird's-eye view on the way back by returning on the **Skyrail** (p436). Alternatively, take a **tour** (p425) to the Atherton Tablelands, or Cape Tribulation and the magical Daintree Rainforest.

---

land, Port Douglas and beyond. In between all this fun, you'll discover it's a popular place to hook up with fellow travellers.

Orientation

Cairns' CBD is centred between the Esplanade and McLeod St and Wharf and Aplin Sts. Reef Fleet terminal is the main departure points for reef trips. Further south is Trinity Wharf, where long-distance buses arrive and depart. Cairns train station is hidden inside the Cairns Central Shopping Centre on McLeod St. Local buses (Sunbus) leave from the Lake St Transit Centre.

Information

BOOKSHOPS

Absells Chart & Map Centre (☎ 4041 2699; Andrejic Arcade, 55 Lake St) Extensive range of topographic, nautical and area maps.

Angus & Robertson (☎ 4041 0591; Shop 141, Cairns Central Shopping Centre, McLeod St) Large chain store.

Cairns Museum (☎ 4051 5582; cnr Lake & Shields Sts) Stellar collection of titles relating to the region's history, as well as local authors' works.

Exchange Bookshop (☎ 4051 1443; www.exchange bookshop.com; 78 Grafton St) New and second-hand books.

EMERGENCY

Ambulance, Fire & Police (☎ 000; ⏲ 24hr)

Cairns Police Station (☎ 4030 7000; Sheridan St)

INTERNET ACCESS

Internet access ranges from $2 to $5 per hour.

Call Station (☎ 4052 1572; 123 Abbott St)

Global Gossip (☎ 4031 6411; www.globalgossip.com; 125 Abbott St)

Inbox C@fe (☎ 4041 4677; www.inboxcafe.com.au; 119 Abbott St)

MEDICAL SERVICES

Cairns Base Hospital (☎ 4050 6333; Esplanade) Has 24-hour emergency service.

Cairns City 24 Hour Medical Centre (☎ 4052 1119; cnr Florence & Grafton Sts)

Cairns Travel Clinic (☎ 4041 1699; ctlmed@iig.com .au; 15 Lake St)

MONEY

Most of the major banks throughout the city have branches with ATMs and foreign exchange.

Amex (☎ 4051 8811; Orchid Plaza, Abbott St)

Thomas Cook (☎ 4031 3040; 13 Spence St)

QUEENSLAND

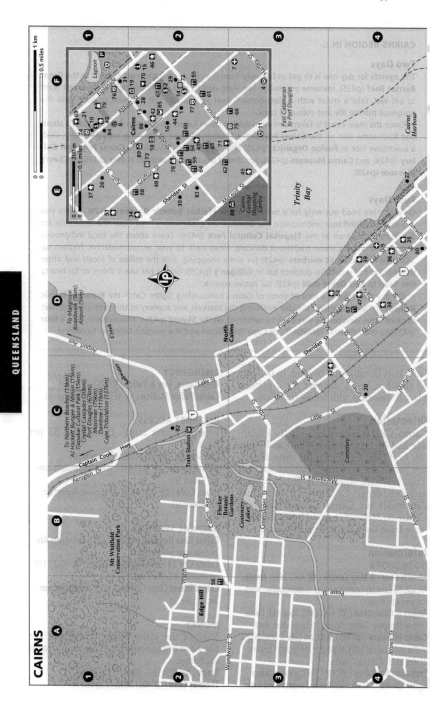

CAIRNS

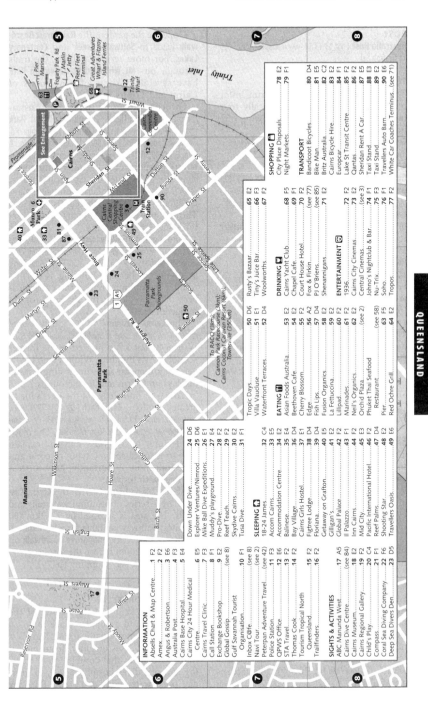

QUEENSLAND

POST

Australia Post (☎ 13 13 18; www.auspost.com; 13 Grafton St)

TOURIST INFORMATION

There are dozens of privately run 'information centres' (these are basically tour-booking agencies), but the following offer unbiased information:

Gateway Discovery Centre (☎ 4051 3588; www.tropicalaustralia.com.au; 51 Esplanade; 8.30am-6.30pm) Government run.

Gulf Savannah Tourist Organisation (☎ 4031 1631; www.gulf-savannah.com.au; 74 Abbott St; 8.45am-5pm Mon-Fri) Information on this outback region west of Cairns.

QPWS (☎ 4046 6600; www.epa.qld.gov.au; 5b Sheridan St; 8.30am-5pm Mon-Fri) National park information and permits.

Royal Automobile Club of Queensland (RACQ; ☎ 4033 6711; www.racq.com.au; 520 Mulgrave St, Earlville) Maps and information on road conditions up to Cape York. Also has a 24-hour road-report service (☎ 1300 130 595).

TRAVEL AGENCIES

Navi Tour (☎ 4031 6776, 1300 558 800; 1st fl, Orchid Plaza, 58 Lake St) Caters for Japanese tourists.

Peterpan Adventure Travel (☎ 1800 632 632; www.peterpans.com; Level 1, 90-92 Lake St) Internet access.

STA Travel (☎ 4031 4199; 9 Shields St)

Trailfinders (☎ 1300 651 900, 4041 1100; www.trailfinders.com.au; Hides Corner, Lake St)

Sights

The undisputed highlight of the **Cairns Foreshore Promenade** is the 4800-sq-m saltwater swimming **lagoon**. Like a big eye-candy convention, bodies accumulate here to cool off and bronze up. Fitness enthusiasts blade, cycle or just walk the 3km Esplanade Walking Trail, and locals and travellers meander lazily up and down the Esplanade, popping into restaurants and shops until the wee hours.

Flecker Botanic Gardens (☎ 4044 3398; Collins Ave, Edge Hill; 7.30am-5.30pm Mon-Fri, 8.30am-5.30pm Sat & Sun) are dominated by the magnificent rainforest, but there are also plots of bush-tucker plants and the Gondwanan Evolutionary Trail, which tracks the 415-million-year heritage of tropical plants. Hour-long guided walks (adult/child under 14 $10/free; 1pm Mon-Fri) through the gardens are available.

Opposite the gardens the **Rainforest Boardwalk** leads to **Saltwater Creek** and **Centenary Lakes**. For more serious walkers, the trails through out **Mt Whitfield Conservation Park** have several lookouts offering views of Cairns and Trinity Inlet.

Owned and run by indigenous Australians, the excellent **Tjapukai Cultural Park** (☎ 4042 9999; www.tjapukai.com.au; Kamerunga Rd, Carevonica; adult/child $29/14.50, incl transfers from Cairns & Palm Cove $48.50/24.25; 9am-5pm) combines interesting aspects of indigenous culture with show biz. It includes the Creation Theatre, which tells the story of creation using giant holograms and actors; there's also a Dance Theatre, as well as boomerang- and spear-throwing demonstrations.

Cairns Regional Gallery (☎ 4031 6865; www.cairnsregionalgallery.com.au; cnr Abbott & Shields Sts; adult/child under 10 $4/free; 10am-5pm Mon-Sat, 1-5pm Sun), in a gorgeous heritage building, is worth a wander. Exhibitions reflect the consciousness of the region, with an emphasis on indigenous art.

The **Cairns museum** (☎ 4051 5582; www.cairnsmuseum.org.au; cnr Lake & Shields Sts; adult/child $5/2; 10am-4pm Mon-Sat) is housed in the former School of Arts Building. While it won't blow you away, there are some interesting historic displays on Cairns and its surrounds.

Take your knowledge of the Reef's life to greater depths at **Reef Teach** (☎ 4031 7794; www.reefteach.com.au; 14 Spence St; admission $13; 10am-9pm Mon-Sat, lecture 6.15-8.30pm Mon-Sat). The madcap lecturer *talksveryfast*, and will explain how to identify specific types of coral and fish, and, more importantly, how to treat the Reef with respect.

About 20km from Cairns, the **Crystal Cascades** are a series of beautiful waterfalls and pools. The area is accessed by a 1.2km (30 minutes) pathway (suitable for wheelchairs).

There is a terrific **mangrove boardwalk** on Airport Ave, 200m before the airport.

For markets, see Shopping (p429).

Activities

DIVING & SNORKELLING

Cairns is the scuba-diving capital of the Barrier Reef and a popular place to attain PADI open-water certification. There's a plethora of courses on offer, from budget four-day courses that combine pool training and reef dives (around $320), to four-day open-water courses ($480). Five-day courses ($540 to $650) include two days' pool theory and three days' living aboard a boat, and are generally more rewarding. Find out whether prices include a medical check (around $50), daily reef tax ($5) and passport photos (around $8).

A selection of reputable schools:

Cairns Dive Centre (☎ 4051 0294; www.cairnsdive.com .au; 121 Abbott St; ☺ 8am-7pm)

Deep Sea Divers Den (☎ 4046 7333; www.diversden .com.au; 319 Draper St; ☺ 6am-6pm)

Down Under Dive (☎ 4052 8300; www.downunder dive.com.au; 287 Draper St; ☺ 7am-7pm) Multilingual instructors.

Pro-Dive (☎ 4031 5255; www.prodive-cairns.com.au; cnr Abbot & Shields Sts; ☺ 9am-9pm) Multilingual instructors.

Tusa Dive (☎ 4031 1248; www.tusadive.com; cnr Shields St & Esplanade; ☺ 8am-6pm)

More comprehensive reef trips last one to 11 days and cost roughly $200 to $3600. Liveaboard trips explore the outer and northern reefs, including Cod Hole, Homes Reef and Osprey Reef.

Operators specialising in trips for certified divers:

Coral Sea Diving Company (☎ 4041 2024; www.coral seadiving.com.au; ☺ 9am-5pm) Visibility usually 40m or more. Shark feeding offered.

Explorer Ventures/Nimrod (☎ 4031 5566; www.ex plorerventures.com; 206 Draper St; ☺ 9am-5pm Mon-Fri) Extended itineraries for far northern reefs in November.

Mike Ball Dive Expeditions (☎ 4031 5484; www.mike ball.com; 143 Lake St; ☺ 8am-6pm)

WHITE-WATER RAFTING

There's exciting white-water rafting down the Barron, Tully, Russell and North Johnstone Rivers. For tours leaving Cairns, expect to pay about $150 for a full day to Tully, $85 for a half day to the Barron River, $650/1500 for a two-/four-day trip to North Johnstone, and $130 for a full-day trip to Russell. Check whether wetsuit hire (around $10) and national park fees ($6) are included.

The major rafting companies in Cairns:

Foaming Fury (☎ 4031 3460; www.foamingfury.com.au)

Raging Thunder (☎ 4030 7990; www.ragingthunder .com.au)

R'n'R (☎ 4051 4055; www.raft.com.au)

OTHER ACTIVITIES

AJ Hackett Bungee & Minjin (☎ 4057 7188; www.aj hackett.com.au; bungee $110-140, s/tw/tr minjin swing per person $80/59/39, bungee & minjin swing $140; ☺ 10am-5pm) Swing from the trees on the minjin (a harness swing).

Fishing Cairns (☎ 4038 1144; www.fishingcairns.com.au) River fishing (half-day $75) and reef fishing (day trip $145).

Hot Air Ballooning (☎ 4039 2900; www.hotair.com .au; adult/child incl breakfast $180/124)

Skydive Cairns (☎ 4031 5466; www.skydivecairns.com .au; 59 Sheridan St; tandem jumps from 8000ft $250)

Springmount Station Horse Riding (☎ 4093 4493; www.springmountstation.com; half-/full-day rides $90/110) Includes pick-up from Cairns.

Cairns for Kids

Muddy's playground (Esplanade, btwn Minnie & Upward Sts) is suitable for all ages, with climbing nets, water-play and story-telling areas, as well as your classic slides and swings. Also on the Esplanade, the **Lagoon** (☺ 6am-10pm Oct-Mar, 7am-9pm Apr-Sep) is popular with kids and is patrolled all day. Cairns Regional Gallery (opposite) runs theme-based workshops for children aged between six and 12, during school holidays.

Central childcare facilities that offer day care are **Child's Play** (☎ 4031 1095; 38 James St; over/under 3 per day $40/45) and **ABC Manunda West** (☎ 4032 1390; 160-162 Hoare St; over/under 2 per day $40/42).

Tours

GREAT BARRIER REEF & ISLANDS

Reef tours usually include lunch, snorkelling gear (with dives an optional extra) and transfers. The cheapest tours start at around $60, but it's well worth spending more money for fewer passengers and a more secluded spot on the reef.

Compass (☎ 4051 5777, 1800 467 333; www.reeftrip.com; 100 Abbott St; per person $60) Hastings Reef and Breaking Patches. Maximum 100. Boom netting.

Great Adventures (☎ 4044 9944; www.greatadventures .com.au; adult/child/family from $165/85/415) Trips to Norman Reef, Moore Reef, Fitzroy Island or Green Island. Maximum 300 passengers.

Passions of Paradise (☎ 1800 111 346, 4041 1600; www.passions.com.au; adult/child/family $100/60/275) Upolu Cay and Paradise Reef. Maximum 65. Party reputation.

Sunlover (☎ 4050 1333, 1800 810 512; www.sunlover .com.au; adult/child/family from $145/75/355) Sails to Arlington Reef (maximum 250 passengers). Also offers semi- submersible and glass-bottom boat tour.

CAIRNS

Cairns Discovery Tours (☎ 4053 5259; www.cairnsholi day.com/scenic/cairns-discovery.htm; adult/child $50/25;

(☼ 12.45-5.45pm), which is guided by horti-culturalists, takes in Cairns, Flecker Botanic Gardens, the Royal Flying Doctors base and Palm Cove.

ATHERTON TABLELAND

Bandicoot Bicycle Tours (☎ 4055 0155; 59 Sheridan St; full day $100; ☼ Mon, Wed & Fri) Bike tours.

Food Trail Tours (☎ 4041 1522; www.foodtrailtours .com.au; adult/child incl lunch $125/90; ☼ 8am-5pm Mon-Sat) Graze on macadamias, tropical-fruit wine, ice cream and coffee.

On the Wallaby (☎ 4050 0650; www.onthewallaby .com; day/overnight tours $85/155) Activity-based tours.

Tropical Horizons Day Tours (☎ 4058 1244; www .tropicalhorizonstours.com.au; full-day tour per adult/child $125/85; ☼ 8.30am-5.15pm) Includes the Scenic Railway, Skyrail and Kuranda.

Uncle Brian's Tours (☎ 4050 0615; www.unclebrian .com.au; adult/child $85/55; ☼ 8am-8.30pm Mon-Wed, Fri & Sat) Babinda, Josephine Falls and Lake Eacham.

DAINTREE RIVER & CAPE TRIBULATION

Cape Tribulation is one of the most popular day-trip destinations from Cairns. Tour operators push the 'safari' angle, but the road is sealed (suitable for a conventional vehicle) until just before the Cape Tribulation Beach House.

Billy Tea Bush Safaris (☎ 4032 0077; www.billytea .com.au; day trips adult/child $130/90; ☼ 7.10am-6.45pm) Eco tours.

Cape Trib Connections (☎ 4041 7447; www.capetrib connections.com; day trip $110; ☼ 8am-6pm) Mossman Gorge, Cape Tribulation and Port Douglas.

Jungle Tours (☎ 4032 5600; www.adventuretours.com .au; day tours $130; ☼ 7.30am-5pm) Includes lunch and a Daintree River cruise.

COOKTOWN & CAPE YORK

Wilderness Challenge (☎ 4055 4488; www.wilderness -challenge.com.au; 2-day tours from $360; ☼ Mon, Wed & Fri) is a 4WD tour that heads to Cooktown via the inland road and returns via the Bloomfield Track (coastal route).

UNDARA LAVA TUBES

For an inland adventure, **Undara Experience** (☎ 4097 1411; www.undara.com.au; 2-day tours adult/ child $422/210; ☼ daily May-Oct, Tue & Fri Apr-Nov) has coach trips to the Undara Lava Tubes.

Sleeping

Cairns is inundated with accommodation options and range. Prices peak from 1 June

to 31 October with the tourist high season; prices quoted here are high-season rates. Lower weekly rates are always par for the course.

Accommodation agencies have up-to-date listings and can assist in locating suitable accommodation. The **Accommodation Centre** (☎ 1800 807 730, 4051 4066; www.accomcentre .com.au; cnr Sheridan & Alpin Sts) has wheelchair access and tourist information. **Accom Cairns** (☎ 1800 079 031, 4051 3200; www.accomcairns.com.au; 127 Sheridan St) gives advice on midrange, top-end and short-term rental options.

BUDGET

Gilligan's (☎ 4041 6566; www.gilligansbackpackers.com .au; 57-89 Grafton St; dm $24-28, r $80; ☒ ☒ ☒) This enormous resort-style-complex is the Ritz of all hostels. Dorms and doubles are hotel-style rooms, with a fridge and TV. Its Internet café doubles as a pizzeria, the 1000-capacity beer hall serves meals (breakfast, lunch and dinner), and the gaming room and swimming pool are licensed.

Global Palace (☎ 4031 7921; www.globalpalace.com .au; City Place, cnr Lake & Shields Sts; dm/tw/d $23/50/52; ☒ ☒ ☒) This stylish, well-groomed back-packers is housed in a lovely refurbished cinema. Dorms are devoid of bunks, there's a small rooftop pool and a classic double veranda overlooking the street. The communal areas are spacious and airy.

Cairns Girls Hostel (☎ 4051 2767; cairnsgirlshostel@ bigpond.com; 147 Lake St; dm/tw $16/36) Sorry fellas, this female-only hostel is one of the best in town. In a two-storey house, ladies enjoy two large refurbished communal kitchen and lounge areas and the service is nurturing and personalised – you'll be a name not a number here.

Tropic Days (☎ 4041 1521; www.tropicdays.com.au; 28 Bunting St; dm/d $20/45; P ✗ ☐ ☎) More like a casual B&B, this popular hostel has tasteful rooms and excellent facilities. Tariffs include a free dinner in town and Monday nights are $8 Croc BBQ affairs – an absolute bargain.

Also recommended:

Cairns Coconut Caravan Resort (☎ 4054 6644; www .coconut.com.au; cnr Bruce Hwy & Anderson Rd; powered/ unpowered sites $34/31, cabins from $65; P ☐)

Travellers Oasis (☎ 4052 1377; www.travoasis.com.au; 8 Scott St; dm/s/d $20/30/44; ✗ ☐ ☎) Boutique, low-key backpackers.

MIDRANGE

Inn Cairns (☎ 4041 2350; www.inncairns.com.au; 71 Lake St; apt $160; ✗ ☎) Urban junkies will dig these elegant inner-city style apartments, with modern furnishings and fittings. Everyone will appreciate catching the lift to the rooftop each day to watch the champagne level and sun go down simultaneously.

Shooting Star (☎ 4047 7200; www.shootingstar apartments.com.au; 117 Grafton St; r $90; P ✗ ☐ ☎) These studio-style, self-contained apartments are great value. The blue-and-white complex resembles a cluster of oversized beach boxes, and houses neat, tiled rooms. It's a good spot for couples and families, and there are also specially fitted wheelchair-accessible rooms.

Balinese (☎ 4051 9922; www.balinese.com.au; 215 Lake St; s $85, d & tw $95; P ✗ ☐ ☎) Authentic wood furnishings and ceramic pieces at this small-scale, intimate resort stay true to its moniker. It's an elegant affair and the room rate includes a basic cold breakfast, as well as access to the communal kitchen.

Mid City (☎ 4051 5050; www.midcity.com.au; 6 McLeod St; r $150; P ✗ ☐ ☎) You just might forget you're not at home after a night here. The functional apartments, with wrought-iron furnishings and terracotta-tiled floors, are serviced daily and come with superb kitchens and laundries. Each apartment also has its own balcony.

Villa Vaucluse (☎ 1800 623 263, 4051 8566; www .villavaucluse.com.au; 141-3 Grafton St; r $140; P ✗ ☎) These sturdy modern pads are private and sumptuously filled with fresh and trim fittings. There is a dash of Mediterranean in the décor, a tropical central atrium and secluded swimming pool.

Figtree Lodge (☎ 4041 0000; www.figtreelodge.com .au; 253 Sheridan St; r $105, apt $115; P ✗ ☐ ☎) Resort-style accommodation offers hotel rooms – with a beachy blue-and-white theme – and self-contained apartments. There's an Irish-themed restaurant and bar attached and you can order room service while soaking in the tub. Wheelchair-friendly rooms are available.

18-24 James (☎ 1800 621 824, 4051 4644; www.18 -24james.com.au; 18-24 James St; s $110, d & tw $140; P ✗ ☐ ☎) Catering mostly for male guests, this gay accommodation's pool area is clothing-optional and the resort's gym is apparently clothing-minimal. The handsome rooms, inclusive of airport transfer and breakfast, could represent a pot of gold at the end of that big rainbow.

Getaway on Grafton (☎ 4052 1200; 157 Grafton St; apt from $115; P ✗ ☎) These schmick one- and two-bedroom apartments all have their own kitchen and are furnished with Indonesian-style pieces. There's space enough to swing a cow…or a family, which is what the larger apartments sleep.

More midrange options:

Bay Village (☎ 4051 4622; www.bayvillage.com.au; cnr Lake & Gatton Sts; r $135-165; P ✗ ☐ ☎) Handsome two-storey resort popular with a mature crowd. On-site restaurant and tour desk.

Reef Palms (☎ 1800 815 421, 4051 2599; www.reef palms.com.au; 41-7 Digger St; r $85-125; P ✗ ☎) Crisp white apartments, some with lounge areas and spas.

TOP END

Il Palazzo (☎ 4041 2155; www.ilpalazzo.com.au; 62 Abbott St; r from $180; P ✗ ☎) This boutique high-rise hotel is quietly stylish: in a soft-focus, terracotta-urns and water-feature kind of way. Apartments feature balconies, laundries and full kitchens – although room service is always an option – right in the centre of town. The service is remarkable.

Waterfront Terraces (☎ 4031 8333; www.cairns luxury.com; 233 Esplanade; r $170-205; P ✗ ☎) This low-rise Queenslander-style building is set in neat and trim tropical grounds, just across the road from the waterfront. Handsomely furnished apartments have a separate tiled lounge and kitchen area, with one or two bedrooms.

Pacific International Hotel (☎ 4051 7888; www .pacifichotelcairns.com; 43 Esplanade; r $240; P ✗ ☎)

This is one of Cairns' original hotels. It has more of a boutique ambience, with all the good things you'd expect from an international hotel, such as three restaurants and a grand entrance foyer replete with a huge chandelier.

Eating

Cairn's multicultural visitors have brought a global influence to the city's eateries. Restaurants and cafés are spread throughout town, though many cluster together along the Esplanade to take advantage of the waterfront (you may pay extra for the privilege).

RESTAURANTS

Cherry Blossom (☎ 4052 1050; cnr Spence & Lake Sts; mains $14-24; ☺ lunch Wed-Fri, dinner Mon-Sat) This upstairs Japanese restaurant is reminiscent of an *Iron Chef* cook-off, with two chefs working at opposite ends of the restaurant floor. Among the authentic dishes such as tempura and *yakitori* you'll find item No 17: 'Aussie Animals – crocodile, kangaroo and emu in a cheese basket'.

Red Ochre Grill (☎ 4051 0100; 43 Shields St; mains $26-30; ☺ lunch Mon-Fri, dinner daily) Red Ochre's inventive menu utilises native Australian ingredients and local produce, artfully prepared to pioneer its own culinary genre. There are the animals (croc, roo and emu), but Aussie flora also appears on the menu.

Fish Lips (☎ 4041 1700; 228 Sheridan St; mains $24-27; ☺ lunch & dinner) Serving seafood done every which way but always good, Fish Lips is a convivial restaurant with professional service. You might order the barramundi served with

---

AUTHOR'S CHOICE

Pier (☎ 4031 4677; Pier Complex, Pier Point Rd; mains around $18; ☺ lunch & dinner) For instant popularity, just add water. On the marina and waterfront, it's all hands on the broad outdoor deck area of this fledgling place. Punters love to watch their boutique beer moving through the Perspex pipe overhead, almost as much as they love to watch the tide come and go. There's a handful of mains, such as salmon on papaya salad, a few pastas, starters and nibbles. Wood-fired pizzas are available until late, as is dessert: hazelnut-chocolate spread, marshmallows and coffee ice cream anyone?

---

eggplant pickle and rocket pesto, but there are meat and vegetarian options as well.

For authentic international fare head to **Marinades** (☎ 4041 1422; 43 Spence St; mains around $16; ☺ lunch Tue-Fri & dinner Tue-Sun), which dishes up delicious Indian cuisine, **La Fettuccina** (☎ 40 31 5959; 43 Shields St; mains $20-24; ☺ dinner) for saucy homemade pastas, or **Phuket Thai Seafood Restaurant** (☎ 4031 0777; 3/135 Grafton St; dishes $13-17; ☺ lunch Mon-Fri & dinner daily) for excellent Thai cuisine.

CAFÉS & QUICK EATS

Fusion Organics (☎ 4051 1388; cnr Grafton & Aplin Sts; dishes $5-10; ☺ breakfast & lunch Mon-Sat) Fusion is inspiring to the core. Its sublime Genovese coffee and juice brews will rouse even the weariest of bodies. Stellar quiches, frittata and filled breads stir the senses. Its decorous interior features local art, or there's a spacious courtyard.

Lillipad (☎ 4051 9565; 72 Grafton St; dishes $5-7; ☺ breakfast & lunch Mon-Sat) Walk down the long, narrow seating area of Lillipad, and meet the maker of your fabulously big breakfast – who toils in the kitchen, just behind the service counter. There's love in your Full Monty fry-up, your panini and your salad. Vegetarians are spoilt for choice here.

Beethoven Café (☎ 4051 0292; 105 Grafton St; dishes $5-7; ☺ breakfast Mon-Sat, lunch Mon-Fri) Make like Augustus Gloop and squeeze in a slab of poppy-seed cake or cheesecake after you've downed a huge roll or sandwich. Savoury combos include *Buendnerfleisch* (air-dried beef, Swiss cheese and gherkin), but you can get creative and invent your own.

Quick and healthy eats can be found at **Edge** (☎ 4053 2966; 1/138 Collins Ave, Edge Hill; dishes $5-8; ☺ breakfast & lunch), up the road from the Botanic Gardens, or **Tiny's Juice Bar** (☎ 4031 4331; 45 Grafton St; meals $5-8; ☺ breakfast & lunch Mon-Fri). There are lunchtime food courts at **Orchid Plaza** (Abbott St) and at the **Night Markets** (Esplanade).

SELF-CATERING

There's a **Woolworths** (Sheridan St), plus at least two supermarkets in Cairns Central Shopping Centre. **Rusty's Bazaar** (Grafton St, btwn Shields & Spence Sts; ☺ Fri & Sat) has fresh fruit and veg, herbs and honey.

Niche self-catering options:
Asian Foods Australia (☎ 4052 1510; 101-5 Grafton St) Asian goods.

Neil's Organics (☎ 4051 5688; 21 Sheridan St) Organic fruit, veg and other produce.

Drinking

The range and number of places to drink in Cairns is intoxicating. Most offer food, alcohol and some form of entertainment. Local street rag, *Barfly* (www.thefly.com.au), publishes listings and reviews.

Gilligan's (☎ 4041 6566; 57-89 Grafton St) You're guaranteed a crowd here, as the 400-odd backpackers staying in this resort complex (p426) work up a thirst; it's also popular with locals. Gilligan's is a respectable venue that features regular club nights, as well as special live music events.

Shenannigans (☎ 4051 2490; 48 Spence St) This Irish-themed pub has a public bar decked out in dark timber. There's also a huge beer garden and outdoor bistro. From Thursday to Saturday night, a band plays before a DJ moves in for the night shift.

Court House Hotel (☎ 4031 4166; 38 Abbott St) You should stay for at least one drink to do this old courthouse justice. A spacious courtyard encircles the main room, with a well-stocked bar at its centre. A mixed crew – generally suave and clean-cut – gathers at this bar.

PJ O'Briens (☎ 4031 5333; 87 Lake St) A popular pub with an Irish theme; there are 'Thank Guinness it's Friday' nights, and Wednesday's entertainment is dancing girls: not that there is anything particularly Irish about girls in bikinis dancing on the bar.

Chapel Cafe (☎ 4041 4222; Level 1, 91 Esplanade) Large groups drink and dine in the stylish surrounds of green booths lit by low-slung, low-wattage bulbs. There's a large balcony overlooking the Esplanade, which makes a stellar place for a drink. Acoustic music plays live most nights.

Other drinking options:

Cairns Yacht Club (☎ 4031 2750; 4 Wharf St) One for the leather-tanned, boat-shoes crowd.

Fox & Firkin (☎ 4031 5305; cnr Spence & Lake Sts) Relaxed pub popular with backpackers.

Entertainment

If you want to move things up a gear, head to one of Cairns' innumerable clubs. Most open around 10pm and close between 5am and 6am. That said, entry is generally refused after 3am, so get to where you're going by then. Cover charges are from $5 to $10.

1936 (28 Spence St) At its new two-level premises, 1936 is a thumping, hard venue featuring respected local and touring DJs. A second room plays funk and hip-hop. Freakquency on Friday is always popular.

Johno's Nightclub & Bar (☎ 4051 8770; cnr Abbott & Aplin Sts) Live blues and rock is the go every night at this huge venue, where a hang-glider is suspended from the roof. The World-Famous Gong Show is free every Sunday, and chipper bar staff call you 'darlin' and 'bloke'.

Soho (☎ 4051 2666; cnr Esplanade & Shields St) This funky spot features resident DJs, as well as touring local and national turntableists. Fall into the leather lounge, or prop up one of the bars.

Tropos (☎ 4031 2530; cnr Spence & Lake Sts) Wear something short, tight and white. A young, high-energy crowd drinks cocktails with names like 'attitude improvement', on an enormous balcony with pool tables.

Nu-Trix (☎ 4051 8223; 53 Spence St) Drag shows are a feature at this gay venue. The shiny metal-clad exterior acts as armour against the morning sun, keeping things dark and doofing until late.

You can catch a mainstream flick at **Cairns City Cinemas** (☎ 4031 1077; 108 Grafton St) or **Central Cinemas** (☎ 4052 1166; Cairns Central Shopping Centre).

Shopping

Every second shop in Cairns seems to sell opals, Coogi, Ken Done and made-in-Korea didgeridoos and boomerangs. For an authentic termite-made didgeridoo and other Aboriginal items your best bet is Tjapukai Cultural Park (p424).

Head to the **night markets** (Esplanade; ⏲ 4.30pm-midnight) and **Mud Markets** (Pier Marketplace; ⏲ Sat morning) for the mandatory 'Cairns Australia' T-shirt, or if you need your name on a grain of rice.

City Place Disposals (☎ 4051 6040; cnr Grafton & Shields Sts) has cheap camping and outdoor gear on offer.

Getting There & Away

AIR

Qantas (☎ 13 13 13, 4050 4000; www.qantas.com.au; cnr Lake & Shields Sts), **Virgin Blue** (☎ 13 67 89; www.virginblue.com.au) and **Jetstar** (☎ 13 15 38; www.jetstar.com.au) all service Cairns, with flights to/from Brisbane ($140), Sydney ($190),

Melbourne ($210), Darwin ($450, via Alice Springs $250) and Townsville ($150).

Macair (☎ 13 13 13; www.macair.com.au) flies to Lizard Island ($300), Dunk Island ($190) and Mt Isa ($255).

BOAT

Quicksilver (☎ 4031 4299; www.quicksilver-cruises.com; one way/return $26/39) departs from the Pier Marina at 8am for Port Douglas, and returns at 5.15pm; the journey takes 1½ hours.

BUS

Greyhound Australia (☎ 13 14 99; www.greyhound .com.au) connects Cairns with Brisbane ($200, 28½ hours), Rockhampton ($140, 17 hours) and Townsville ($53, six hours).

Premier Motor Service (☎ 13 34 10; www.premier ms.com.au) has buses to/from Innisfail ($15, 1½ hours), Mission Beach ($15, two hours), Tully ($22, 2½ hours), Ingham ($29, 3¼ hours) and Townsville ($48, 5½ hours).

Sun Palm Express (☎ 4032 4999; www.sunpalmtrans port.com) connects Cairns with Port Douglas ($25, 1½ hours), Mossman ($31, 1¾ hours) and Cape Tribulation ($45, 3¼ hours). It travels to Cooktown ($70, 5¼ hours) on the inland route Wednesday, Friday and Sunday, and via the coast road (7½ hours) Tuesday, Thursday and Saturday.

Coral Reef Coaches (☎ 4098 2600; www.coralreef coaches.com.au) also runs a daily service from Cairns to Cape Tribulation ($40, four hours) stopping in Port Douglas ($20, 1¼ hours) and Mossman ($25, two hours).

John's Kuranda Bus (☎ 0418 772 953; tickets $2) runs between Cairns and Kuranda several times daily. Buses depart from Cairns' Lake St Transit Mall. **Kuranda Shuttle** (☎ 0402 032 085; tickets $2) departs Lake St Transit Mall every two hours 9am to 3pm, and Kuranda (Therwine St) at 10am, 12.15pm and 2pm. **Whitecar Coaches** (☎ 4091 1855; tickets $4) has five departures from outside Shenannigans.

CAR & MOTORCYCLE

Hiring a car or motorcycle is the best way to travel around Far North Queensland. Most companies restrict the driving of conventional vehicles to sealed roads; if you want to travel to Cooktown via the Bloomfield Track (or the coastal route), hire a 4WD.

Rental companies in Cairns:
Britz Australia (☎ 4032 2611; www.britz.com.au; 411 Sheridan St) Hires out campervans.

Europcar (☎ 4051 4600; www.deltaeuropcar.com.au; 135 Abbott St) With an airport desk.
Sheridan Rent a Car (☎ 4051 3942; owers@top.net.au; 36 Water St)
Thrifty (☎ 1300 367 277; www.thrifty.com.au; Cairns International Airport)
Travellers Auto Barn (☎ 4041 3722; www.travellers -autobarn.com.au; 123 Bunda St) Campervans.

TRAIN

The **Queensland Rail** (☎ 1300 131 722; www.travel train.com.au; Cairns Central Shopping Centre, McLeod St) *Tilt Train* runs between Cairns and Brisbane ($285, 25 hours), as does the *Sunlander* (economy seat/sleeper $190/240, 32 hours).

See p436 for information on travelling to Kuranda.

Getting Around
TO/FROM THE AIRPORT

The airport is about 7km from central Cairns. **Australia Coach** (☎ 4048 8355; adult/child $8/4) meets all incoming flights and runs a shuttle bus to the CBD. A taxi will set you back about $15.

BICYCLE

You can hire bicycles from the following:
Bandicoot Bicycles (☎ 4041 0155; 153 Sheridan St; per day $18)
Bike Man (☎ 4041 5566; www.bikeman.com.au; 30 Florence St; per week $40)
Cairns Bicycle Hire (☎ 4031 3444; 47 Shields St; per day/week $10/40) Groovy bikes and scooters.

BUS

Sunbus (☎ 4057 7411; www.sunbus.com.au) runs regular services, in and around Cairns, that leave from the Lake St Transit Centre, where schedules for most routes are posted. Buses run from early morning to late evening. Useful destinations include: Edge Hill (Nos 6, 6a and 7), Flecker Botanic Gardens (No 7), Machans Beach (No 7), Holloways Beach (Nos 1c, 1d and 1h), Yorkeys Knob (Nos 1c, 1d and 1h), Trinity Beach (Nos 1, 1a and 2x), Clifton Beach (Nos 1 and 1B) and Palm Cove (Nos 1, 1b and 2x). All are served by the (almost) 24-hour night service (N) on Friday and Saturday.

TAXI

Black & White Taxis (☎ 4048 8333, 13 10 08) are on the corner of Lake and Shields Sts and at Cairns Central Shopping Centre.

ISLANDS OFF CAIRNS

Green Island, Fitzroy Island and Frankland Islands National Park are popular day trips. All the islands are great for snorkelling. Ferries depart from the Reef Fleet terminal in Cairns; see individual islands for departure/arrival times.

Green Island

This small coral cay has a rainforested interior with interpretive walks, hemmed by stunning beach and snorkelling just offshore. A luxury resort dominates it and the resort has a separate section for day trippers. From the shore, you can spot reef sharks, turtles and schools of tiny fish.

Activities involve swimming at the idyllic beach, or you can sip champagne and eat strawberries poolside. The gentle rainforest walk is 350m and well signposted.

Marineland Melanesia (☎ 07-4051 4032; adult/child $10/5) has an aquarium with fish, turtles, stingrays and crocodiles. There's also a collection of Melanesian artefacts.

The luxurious **Green Island Resort** (☎ 07-4031 3300; www.greenislandresort.com.au; r $480-570; ✷ ⊠) has stylish split-level rooms, each with its own private balcony. Two styles of room are available: the larger room sleeps up to four, or you can have them all to yourself and shuffle around in your complimentary slippers and bathrobe.

Great Adventures (☎ 07-4051 0455; www.great adventures.com.au; 1 Wharf St, Cairns) has regular catamaran services to Green Island ($56), departing Cairns at 8.30am, 10.30am and 1pm and returning at noon, 2.30pm and 4.30pm. **Big Cat** (☎ 07-4051 0444; www.bigcat -cruises.com.au; tours from $58) also runs half- and full-day tours, which depart Cairns at 9am and 1.15pm. Prices include the use of snorkelling gear.

Fitzroy Island National Park

A steep mountain-top peeping from the sea, Fitzroy Island has coral-littered beaches and a quaint resort. Day trippers can use the resort's facilities, and hire water-sports equipment and fishing rods. Diving courses and sea-kayak tours are run by the resort, and the most popular snorkelling spot is around the rocks at **Nudey Beach** (1.2km from the resort).

There are a number of walks, which vary in difficulty. The 20-minute **Secret Garden Walk**, with major skinks basking on rocks, is a leisurely stroll, whereas the **Lighthouse & Summit Trail** is a steep, two-hour climb.

Fitzroy Island Resort (☎ 07-4051 9588; www.fitzroy island.com.au; dm/d without bathroom $31/60, cabins with bathroom $220; ✷ ⊠) offers good accommodation. There's also a kiosk selling light snacks ($5 to $14) and a waterfront **restaurant** (meals from $12-20; ☺ breakfast, lunch & dinner).

Fitzroy Island Ferries (☎ 07-4030 7907; Reef Fleet terminal, Cairns; return adult/child $38/18) departs Cairns at 8.30am, 10.30am and 4pm, returning at 9.30am, 3pm and 5pm. Full and half-day tours, including lunch and transfers, are also available.

Sunlover Cruises (☎ 1800 810 512; www.sunlover .com.au; Reef Fleet terminal, Cairns; return adult/child $40/20) ferries cross once per day, leaving Cairns at 10am and arriving back around 5.30pm.

Frankland Islands National Park

A group of five islands surrounded by coral, the Frankland Islands have gorgeous, sandy beaches and offer a beautiful day's snorkelling. Camping is allowed in the national park, and permits are available from Cairns QPWS (p424), but you'll need to be fully self-sufficient.

Frankland Islands Cruise & Dive (☎ 07-4031 6300; www.franklandislands.com.au; adult/child $150/70) runs excellent day tours, which include a cruise down the Mulgrave River. Additionally, transfers can be arranged for campers who have the necessary QPWS permits.

CAIRNS' NORTHERN BEACHES

☎ 07 / pop 17,190

A string of communities cling to their own patch of beach on the 26km stretch of coast north of Cairns. In places where the water is too shallow to swim, residential neighbourhoods enjoy the quiet life away from the city's hum.

The following beaches, listed in order from Cairns, all have stinger nets in summer (except Machans, which has no swimming beach). If you're travelling by car, turn-offs from the highway are well signposted. Sunbus (opposite) runs regular services from Cairns.

The first suburb north of Cairns is Machans Beach; its shallow sandflats have kept it free from tourist developments. Locals enjoy fishing at the mouth of the Barron

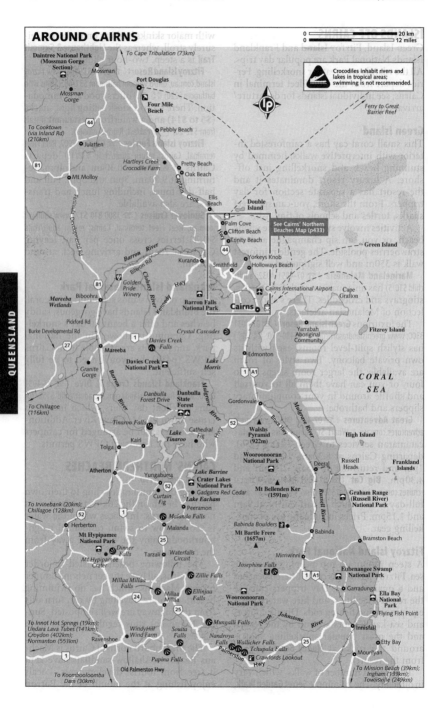

AROUND CAIRNS

0 — 20 km
0 — 12 miles

Crocodiles inhabit rivers and lakes in tropical areas; swimming is not recommended.

Daintree National Park (Mossman Gorge Section)

To Cape Tribulation (73km)

Fitzroy Island

Mossman

Mossman Gorge

Port Douglas

Ferry to Great Barrier Reef

Four Mile Beach

To Cooktown (via Inland Rd) (210km)

Pebbly Beach

Julatten

Mt Molloy

Hartleys Creek Crocodile Farm

Pretty Beach

Oak Beach

Ellis Beach

Double Island

Palm Cove

Clifton Beach

Trinity Beach

See Cairns' Northern Beaches Map (p433)

Green Island

Barron River

Biyon Rd

Kuranda

Yorkeys Knob

Holloways Beach

Clohesy River

Kennedy Hwy

Smithfield

Cairns International Airport

Cape Grafton

Golden Pride Winery

Mareeba Wetlands

Biboohra

Barron Falls National Park

Cairns

Pickford Rd

Burke Developmental Rd

Crystal Cascades

Yarrabah Aboriginal Community

Fitzroy Island

Mareeba

Davies Creek Falls

Edmonton

CORAL SEA

Granite Gorge

Davies Creek National Park

Lake Morris

Danbulla Forest Drive

Danbulla State Forest

Gordonvale

High Island

To Chillagoe (116km)

Tinaroo Falls

Cathedral Fig

Walshs Pyramid (922m)

Russell Heads

Frankland Islands

Lake Tinaroo

Wooroonooran National Park

Deeral

Kairi

Tolga

Gillies

Graham Range (Russell River) National Park

Atherton

Yungaburra

Lake Barrine

Crater Lakes National Park

Gadgarra Red Cedar

Lake Eacham

Mt Bellenden Ker (1591m)

To Irvinebank (20km); Chillagoe (128km)

Curtain Fig

Peeramon

Herberton

Malanda Falls

Babinda Boulders

Mt Bartle Frere (1657m)

Babinda

Bramston Beach

Mt Hypipamee National Park

Malanda

Dinner Falls

Tarzali

Mt Hypipamee Crater

Waterfalls Circuit

Mirriwinni

Josephine Falls

Eubenangee Swamp National Park

Garradunga

Millaa Millaa Falls

Zillie Falls

Ella Bay National Park

To Innot Hot Springs (19km); Undara Lava Tubes (141km); Croydon (402km); Normanton (553km)

Windy Hill Wind Farm

Millaa Millaa

Ellinjaa Falls

Wooroonooran National Park

North Johnstone River

Flying Fish Point

Innisfail

Ravenshoe

Souita Falls

Mungalli Falls

Nandroya Falls

Walicher Falls

Tchupala Falls

Crawfords Lookout

Etty Bay

Mourilyan

Papina Falls

Old Palmerston Hwy

Palmerston Hwy

To Mission Beach (39km); Ingham (139km); Townsville (249km)

To Koombooloomba Dam (30km)

River (a block back from the Esplanade), and keep their houses front-fence free and open to the waterfront.

Holloways Beach

The Coral Sea meets a rough ribbon of sand at a suitable depth for swimming at Holloways Beach. It's a picturesque spot with some funky cafés and bars.

Pacific Sands (☎ 4055 0277; www.pacificsandscairns .com; 1-19 Poinciana St; r $110; ✗ ⎌ P) Has pleasant two-bedroom apartments in a complex that stretches out one block back from the beach. There is also a saltwater pool and barbecue.

Cairns Beach Resort (☎ 4037 0400; www.cairns beachresort.com.au; 129 Oleander St; r $135; ✗ ⎌ P) Has very sprite two-bedroom apartments on the beachfront. Each is well-equipped with mod cons so you can focus your efforts on relaxing.

Strait on the Beach (☎ 4055 9616; 100 Oleandar St; meals $6-16; ☽ breakfast, lunch & lunch) A small shop and café with an exceptional setting, just back from the sand. It's abrilliant Sunday breakfast spot.

Coolum's on the Beach (☎ 4055 9200; cnr Hibiscus & Oleander Sts; mains $15-28; ☽ breakfast & lunch Sun, dinner daily) Next door to Strait, Coolum's is known for its Sunday Jazz sessions and inspired Mod Oz menu.

Yorkeys Knob

Yorkeys is a sprawling but low-key place with a long white-sand beach and the impressive **Yorkeys Knob Boating Club** (☎ 4055 7711; 25 Buckley St; mains $12-18; ☽ lunch & dinner daily, breakfast Sun), which dishes up grills, pastas, burgers and sea views, around the headland. If you're driving, take a spin to the top of the knob, where the views are spectacular.

Yorkeys Beach Bungalows (☎ 4055 7755; www .yorkeysbeachbungalows.com; 23 Sims Esplanade; d $80; ⎌ P) Sparsely furnished, but spacious, self-contained bungalows, set close together in leafy rainforest surrounds. A great spot for families.

York Beachfront Apartments (☎ 4055 8733; www.yorkapartments.com.au; 61-3 Sims Esplanade; r $120; ✗ ⎌ P) A midsized complex with good self-contained apartments. Sliding doors open onto private balconies and sea views.

For camping, head to the compact **Yorkeys Knob Beachfront Van Park** (☎ 4055 7201; 69-73 Sims Esplanade; powered/unpowered sites $22/18, cabins $70).

Trinity Beach

Take the Trinity Beach Rd turn-off to thriving Trinity Beach, one of Cairns' prettiest beaches. High-rise developments have long since interrupted its castaway ambience, but it's still a restful place.

Amaroo (☎ 4055 6066; www.amarooresort.com; 92 Moore St; r $170; ✗ ⎌ P) From a lofty position atop the headland, Amaroo has commanding views, tasteful self-contained apartments and a tennis court.

Roydon (☎ 4057 6512; www.roydon.com.au; 83-87 Vasey Esplanade; r $120-150; ✗ ⎌) This place is superb value. It offers huge two-bedroom, two-bathroom apartments, each with a spacious balcony and living area.

Casablanca Domes (☎ 4055 6339; www.casablanca domes.com; 47 Vasey Esplanade; s/d $80/85; ✗ ⎌) Another option is the cheap and kitschy Casablanca.

L'Unico Trattoria (☎ 4057 8855; 75 Vasey St; mains $18-23, ☽ breakfast, lunch & dinner) Stellar beachfront dining in stylish ambience. Share a gourmet pizza on the balcony.

Blue Waters at the Beach (☎ 4055 6194; 77 Vasey Esplanade; mains around $17; ☽ breakfast, lunch & dinner)

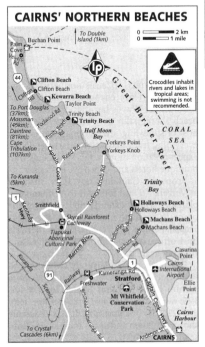

CAIRNS' NORTHERN BEACHES

Serves inventive and informal fare such as Moroccan meatballs or homemade pastas. There's also a takeaway attached.

Trinity Beach Hotel (☎ 4055 6106; Moore St; mains $6.50-15; ☷ lunch & dinner) An old pub perched high on a hill with fabulous views. Pub grub is served, but it's the cold beers that people really come for.

Clifton Beach

Local and leisurely, Clifton Beach is a good balance of residential and resort accommodation and services. It's popular with groups and families during the high season.

Clifton Palms Holiday Units (☎ 4055 3839; www .cliftonpalms.com.au; 35-41 Upolu Esplanade; cabins/units $70/110; ☷ ☷) A huge range of accommodation, including spacious, freestanding apartments backed by green hills.

Clifton Sands Holiday Units (☎ 4055 3355; 81-7 Guide St; d $75; ☷) Excellent-value one-bedroom apartments. The décor is a tad frumpy, but the apartments are spotless.

Agincourt (☎ 4055 3500; 69-73 Arlington Esplanade; r from $125; ☷ ☷ ☷) This four-storey complex on the waterfront has comfortable apartments.

Clifton Capers Bar & Grill (☎ 4055 3355; 14 Clifton Rd; mains around $18; ☷ dinner Tue-Sun) A pleasant and informal place with a large á la carte menu.

Palm Cove

The glamourpuss of Cairns' northern beaches, sultry Palm Cove encourages idleness and indulgence. Waves lap the idyllic tropical beach shore, palm trees rustle gently and a host of sprawling international resorts offer everything from massage to marriage. Don't expect isolation though, this spot teems with boutique hotels and expensive eateries.

From the Captain Cook Hwy, turn off at Veivers Rd and follow it to Williams Esplanade, which extends the length of the beach as far as the jetty. At **Paradise Village Shopping Centre** (113 Williams Esplanade) there's a post office, newsagent, moneychanger and Internet access.

Beach strolls and leisurely swims will be your chief activities, but if you need more stimuli head to **Cairns Tropical Zoo** (☎ 4055 3669; www.wildworld.com.au; Captain Cook Hwy; adult/child $25/12.50; ☷ 8.30am-5pm). It has crocodile shows (11.30am and 3pm) and a koala photo session at 2pm.

SLEEPING

Most of Palm Cove's accommodation is pricey.

Angsana Resort & Spa (☎ 4055 3000; www.angsana .com; 1 Veivers Rd; r from $455; ☷ ☷ ☷) This oh-so-chic resort has fabulous rooms, with folding louvered doors opening out to your own balcony. The décor is pure style and on site are spa treatments, two bars and a fine restaurant – **Far Horizons** (mains $17-24; ☷ breakfast, lunch & dinner).

Silvester Palms (☎ 4055 3831; www.silvesterpalms .com; 32 Veivers Rd; d from $100; ☷ ☷) These self-contained apartments, in a small block, are a refreshing alternative to the area's city-sized resorts. The communal barbecue area and fenced swimming pool make Silvester a great option for families.

Palm Cove Accommodation (☎ 4055 3797; 19 Veivers Rd; s/d $65/80) This is the only budget option in Palm Cove. Next door to the beautician, this small complex offers a limited number of rooms, which are all bright and airy.

Melaleuca Resort (☎ 4055 3222; www.melaleuca resort.com.au; 85-93 Williams Esplanade; r $180; ☷ ☷) Named after the melaleuca trees that line Palm Cove's esplanade, this is a boutique resort, with 24 self-contained apartments. Each has its own kitchen, balcony and laundry facilities. The resort is on the waterfront, behind a thatch of shady trees.

Also recommended:

Villa Paradiso (☎ 1800 683 773, 4055 3533; www.villa paradiso.com.au; 111-13 Williams Esplanade; r $280; ☷ ☷) Mediterranean-influenced apartments.

Palm Cove Camping Ground (☎ 4055 3824; 149 Williams Esplanade; powered/unpowered sites $17/13) Small beachfront park.

EATING

Blue (☎ 4055 3999; cnr Williams Esplanade & Veivers Rd; mains around $30; ☷ lunch & dinner) Wow – this hotel restaurant does delicate dishes with pizzazz (such as steamed salmon with black mussels and caviar in a champagne sauce). If that doesn't dazzle you, the wood-fired pizza might. Service is attentive and the décor is sparse and modern.

CSLC (☎ 4059 1244; Veivers Rd; meals $10-20; ☷ lunch & dinner) This locals' haunt serves decent pub grub in its fabulous garden bar. CSLC has a strict dress code: 'thongs or shoes must be worn at all times'.

For casual dining, head to **Cocky's at the Cove** (☎ 4059 1691; Veivers Rd; dishes $5-10; ☷ breakfast & lunch), which serves great breakfasts and sandwiches, or **Il Fornio Pizzeria** (☎ 4059 1666; Paradise Village; pizzas $15-17; ☺ dinner) for scrummy thin-crust pizzas.

Ellis Beach

Round the headland past Palm Cove, Ellis Beach is an absolute stunner, with a long sheltered bay.

Ellis Beach Oceanfront Bungalows (☎ 1800 637 036, 4055 3538; www.ellisbeachbungalows.com; Captain Cook Hwy; powered sites per 2 people $28-32, unpowered sites $26, cabins $75, bungalows $140-175) is a well-tended place, conveniently located right on the beach. Cabins have a private balcony.

Across the road is **Ellis Beach Bar & Grill** (☎ 4055 3534; Captain Cook Hwy; meals $8-22; ☺ lunch & dinner) which pumps out tasty burgers and has live music every Sunday. For a quiet ale, try the **SLSC** (☎ 4055 3695; Captain Cook Hwy). Soon after Ellis Beach is **Hartley's Creek Crocodile Farm** (☎ 4055 3576; www.crocodileadventures. com; adult/child $25/12.50; ☺ 8.30am-5pm). Visit at crocodile-feeding time – around 11am.

KURANDA

☎ 07 / pop 1456

Most days Kuranda is inundated with big-ticket tours full of camera-toting tourists. Purpose-built attractions and loads of B-grade merchandise make this town akin to a theme park, but this atmosphere evaporates with the crowds after 4pm. Then you can mingle with the mellow mixed community and appreciate the beautiful rainforest surrounds – the very characteristics that made it so popular in the first place.

The **Kuranda visitor information centre** (☎ 40 93 9311; www.kuranda.org; ☺ 10am-5pm) is located in Centenary Park.

Sights & Activities

Kuranda's markets remain ever popular. The original **Kuranda Markets** (☎ 4093 8772; 7 Therwine St; ☺ 9am-3pm Wed-Fri & Sun), once famous for genuine art and craft products, are supplemented by the **Heritage Markets** (☎ 4093 8060; www.kurandaline.com.au/market; Rob Veivers Dr; ☺ 9am-3pm). Between them you'll find souvenirs such as ceramics, emu oil, jewellery, food and figurines made from pistachio nuts. For genuine crafts produced by professional artists try the **Kuranda Arts Co-op** (☎ 4093 9026; www.artskuranda.asn.au; Kuranda Settlement Village, 12 Rob Veivers Dr; ☺ 10am-4pm).

Behind the train station, **Kuranda Rainforest Tours** (☎ 4093 7476; adult/child $12/6; ☺ hourly 10.30am-2.30pm) runs sedate 45-minute cruises along the Barron River. Check opening times during the Wet (October to March).

There are several signed walks in the markets, and a short walking track through **Jumrum Creek Environmental Park**, off Barron Falls Rd, which has a big population of fruit bats.

Further down, Barron Falls Rd divides: the left fork takes you to a **lookout** (wheelchair accessible) over the falls, while further along the right fork brings you to **Wrights Lookout**, which looks down at Barron Gorge National Park.

There's loads of 'wildlife' in Kuranda – albeit in zoos. **Rainforestation** (☎ 4085 5008; www.rainforest.com.au; Kennedy Hwy; adult/child $34/17; ☺ 8.30am-4pm) is an enormous tourist park with a wildlife section, river cruises and an Aboriginal show.

The **Australian Butterfly Sanctuary** (☎ 4093 7575; www.australianbutterflies.com; 8 Rob Veivers Dr; adult/child $12/5; ☺ 10am-4pm Mon-Fri) is a butterfly aviary, and is next door to **Birdworld** (☎ 4093 9188; www.birdworldkuranda.com; Heritage Markets; adult/child $12/5; ☺ 9am-4pm), which displays both native and exotic birds.

Sleeping

Kuranda B&B (☎ 4093 7151; 28 Black Mountain Rd; s/d $80/130; ☒) This excellent B&B is 20 minutes' walk from town, on Ripple Creek. There are two large rooms, each with its own bathroom and veranda overlooking the lovingly tended garden. There's a communal kitchen available, and breakfast is part of the package.

Kuranda Backpackers Hostel (☎ 4093 7355; www .kurandabackpackershostel.com; cnr Arara & Barang Sts; dm/d $18/42; ☒) Surrounded by a large garden, this agreeably rambling double-storey home has loads of communal spaces to hang about in. The environment is low-key and chummy, but you can always retreat to the reading room.

Liberty Resort (☎ 4093 7556; www.libertyresort .com.au; 3 Green Hills Rd; dm $35, r from $180; ☒ ☒) You'll feel as though you've stepped inside a magazine spread when you enter Liberty's stylish apartments. The resort is aimed at gay and lesbian travellers, though heteros are also welcome. Facilities include a gym, bar-restaurant and cinema (screening adult movies after 10.30pm).

QUEENSLAND

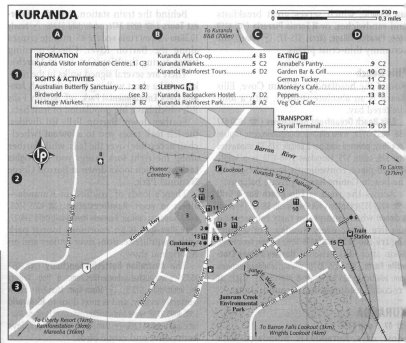

KURANDA

Kuranda Rainforest Park (☎ 4093 7316; www
.kurandarainforestpark.com.au; Kuranda Heights Rd; pow-
ered/unpowered sites per 2 people $20/17, s/d without
bathroom $30/50, units from $100;) This lovely
park, set on a rainforest block, has a great
range of accommodation. Units are self-
contained with poolside or garden views.
The park is a 10-minute walk from town.

Eating
Monkey's Cafe (☎ 4093 7451; 1 Therwine St; mains $12-
16; lunch) The fabulous garden surrounds
at Monkey's might inspire you to swing
from the trees. Specialising in big gourmet
sandwiches, this licensed café is a welcome
place to retreat and linger.

Annabel's Pantry (☎ 4093 7605; Therwine St; pies
$4-6; breakfast & lunch) Offering more var-
ieties of pie than there are letters in the al-
phabet, Annabel's has come up with some creative fillings, such as the Matilda (roo filled).
A few flimsy outdoor settings are available
to sit at.

Peppers (☎ 4093 8733; Kuranda Settlement Village,
12 Rob Veivers Dr; meals around $15; lunch & dinner
Wed-Sun) Focusing on fresh, homemade and

organic food, Peppers bakes its own bread
and serves daily specials that might include
curries, pasta or tofu with wild rice. The
gourmet pizzas are divine; try the Greek
– caramelised onion, feta, blue cheese and
oregano. You can dine in or take away.

Veg Out Cafe (☎ 4093 8483; Shop 5, 24 Coondoo St;
meals $5-10; lunch) You'll be lulled by Hare
Krishna chanting as you tuck into your
wholesome vegetarian dish here. Wheat-
and sugar-free meals are also on offer; Veg
Out is located in the Red House mall.

Also recommended:
German Tucker (☎ 4057 9688; Therwine St; dishes
$6-9; lunch) Fat kransky sausages.
Garden Bar & Grill (☎ 4093 7206; cnr Coondoo &
Arara Sts; dishes $9-13; lunch daily, dinner Mon-Sat)
Pub grub.

Getting There & Away
Kuranda Scenic Railway (☎ 4036 9288; www.trave
train.com.au; Cairns train station, Bunda St, Cairns; adult/
child/concession $35/17.50/27) winds 34km from
Cairns to Kuranda through picturesque
mountains and no less than 15 tunnels
The trip takes 1¾ hours and trains depart

Cairns at 8.30am and 9.30am Sunday to Friday (8.30am Saturday), returning from pretty Kuranda station at 2pm and 3.30pm Sunday to Friday (3.30pm Saturday).

Skyrail Rainforest Cableway (☎ 4038 1555; www.skyrail.com.au; adult/child $35/17.50; ❧ 8.15am-5.15pm) is one of the world's longest gondola cableways, at 7.5km-long. It runs from the corner of Kemerunga Rd and the Cook Hwy in Smithfield, a northern suburb of Cairns, to Kuranda (Arara St), taking 90 minutes. It includes two stops along the way and features boardwalks with interpretive panels passing the burly Barron Falls (reduced to a drip in the Dry season). The last departure from Cairns and Kuranda is at 3.30pm; transfers to/from the terminal (15 minutes' drive north of Cairns) and combination (Scenic Railway and Skyrail) deals are also available. As space is limited, only daypacks are allowed on board Skyrail.

John's Kuranda Bus (☎ 0418 772 953; tickets $2) operates a service between Cairns and Kuranda at least twice per day, and up to seven times Wednesday to Friday.

Kuranda Shuttle (☎ 0402 032 085; tickets $2) departs Cairns' every two hours between 9am and 3pm, and Kuranda (Therwine St) at 10am, 12.15pm and 2pm. **Whitecar Coaches** (☎ 4091 1855; tickets $4) has five departures from Cairns.

ATHERTON TABLELAND

Inland from the coast between Innisfail and Cairns, the lush Atherton Tableland is a region of beautiful scenery, with lakes and waterfalls, national parks and state forests, small villages and busy rural centres. The Tableland's altitude is more than 1000m in places, and one or two days here is thoroughly enjoyable.

Nonindigenous Australians and other migrants came to the Tableland in the 1870s searching for gold and (later) tin. Roads and railways were built, and logging and farming became the primary industries. The region's traditional owners, the Ngadjonji tribe of the wider Djirbal-language group, met the intrusion with violent resistance, but were themselves violently overcome.

GETTING THERE & AROUND

Hire car is the ideal way to get around as there are so many stops over short distances, but **Whitecar Coaches** (☎ 07-4091 1855) has roughly three services a day to Mareeba ($13.50, one hour), Atherton ($17.60, 1¾ hours), Herberton ($22.60, two hours) and Ravenshoe ($25.10, 2½ hours) to/from Cairns.

If you're travelling by car, be careful driving from Mareeba to Cairns as there are no fences and the Brahmin cattle certainly don't expect to move out of your way.

Mareeba
☎ 07 / pop 6900

Mareeba, the rough diamond of the Tableland, is where the rainforest meets the Outback. It's a great place to pick up seasonal work, and it has a few attractions. If you're around in July, be sure to see the **Mareeba Rodeo**.

First stop is the **Mareeba Heritage Museum & Tourist Information Centre** (☎ 4092 5674; www .mareebaheritagecentre.com.au; Centenary Park, 345 Byrnes St; museum adult/child $5/2.50; ❧ 8am-4pm), which has displays on the area's past and present commercial industries, as well as its natural surrounds.

Mareeba Wetlands (☎ 4093 2514; www.mareeba wetlands.com; adult/child $8/5; ❧ 8.30am-4pm Wed-Sun Apr-Dec) is a 20-sq-km reserve featuring wood- and grasslands, lagoons and swamps. The reserve is also a bird-lover's extravaganza and you might also see other animals such as kangaroos and freshwater crocs. Canoe tours cost $11 for an hour-long trip. To reach the wetlands, take the Pickford Rd turn-off from Biboohra, 7km north of Mareeba.

Granite Gorge (admission $2) offers waterfalls, walking trails round huge granite formations, rock-wallaby feeding and a camping ground. To reach it, follow Chewco Rd out of Mareeba for 7km; there's a turn-off to your right from there.

Coffee aficionados will love **Coffee Works** (☎ 4092 4101; www.arabicas.com.au; 136 Mason St; tour $5; ❧ 9am-4pm). For the harder stuff, **Golden Pride Winery** (☎ 4093 2750; www.goldendrop.com.au; Bilwon Rd, Bilwon; ❧ 8am-5pm) offers tastings of its sweet mango wine. Head north on the road to Mount Molloy for 11km and turn right at Bilwon Rd. It's another 2km to the winery.

Aviation and military buffs should definitely check out **Beck Museum** (☎ 4092 3979; Kennedy Hwy; adult/child $13/7; ❧ 10am-4pm).

SLEEPING & EATING

Arriga Park (☎ 4093 2114; www.bnbnq.com.au/arriga; 1720 Dimbulah Rd; r $65) Set on a sugar-cane farm and fruit orchard, this homestead has three rooms. You can soak in the outdoor spa and order home-cooked meals prepared from organic produce grown on the property. Full board is also available.

Jackaroo Motel (☎ 4092 2677; www.jackaroomotel.com; 340 Byrnes St; r $77; 🖳 ⚡) Modern motel has a great range of facilities, including a saltwater swimming pool, BBQ and laundry. Rooms are comfortable and tidy; some have wheelchair access.

Nastasi's (☎ 4092 2321; 10 Byrnes St; meals $4-7; ☺ breakfast, lunch & dinner; 🖳) If it's fried, they've got it: dim sims, fish and chips, eggs and bacon, and burgers sizzle out the door. Nastasi's also does good honest sandwiches and pizza. You can eat in (BYO) or take away.

More sleeping options:

Mareeba Motor Inn (☎ 4092 2451; Kennedy Hwy; s/d $72/77; 🖳 ⚡) Basic and functional rooms. Wheelchair access.

Riverside Caravan Park (☎ 4092 2309; 13 Egan St; per powered/unpowered sites per 2 people $14/11, on-site caravans $25-35) Shady ground on the Barron River with wheelchair facilities.

Chillagoe

☎ 07

Chillagoe's population is small, unless you count the number of termites that inhabit the rich ochre mounds dotting its arid landscape. Around town are impressive limestone caves, rock pinnacles, Aboriginal rock art and ruins of early-20th-century smelters. It's 140km west of Mareeba and close enough to make a day trip from Cairns, but an overnight stay is preferable.

The **Hub** (☎ 4094 7111; Queen St; ☺ 8am-5pm Mon-Fri, 8am-3pm Sat & Sun) is the visitors centre, and it's here that you can book QPWS **cave tours** ($11-14) of the stunning Donna (9am), Trezkinn (11am) and Royal Arch (1.30pm) limestone caves.

Chillagoe Cabins (☎ 4094 7206; www.chillagoe.com; Queen St; s/d $80/100; ⚡) are modelled on old miners' huts and fully self-contained. The friendly owners are animal carers and you may be able to pat a convalescing kangaroo. Alternatively, there's the **Chillagoe Bush Camp & Eco-Lodge** (☎ 4094 7155; Hospital Ave; s/tw $30/55, d $55-70; ⚡), with a range of cabins and a communal area with meals.

The portions are enormous at **Post Office Hotel** (☎ 4094 7119; 37 Queen St; meals $10-16; ☺ lunch & dinner), which sports graffiti from skirting board to ceiling, and a solid marble bar.

Chillagoe can be reached from Mareeba with the **Chillagoe Bus Service** (☎ 4094 7155; one way/return $33/66), which departs from Chillagoe post office at 7.30am Monday, Wednesday and Friday and returns from Mareeba train station at 1pm.

Atherton

☎ 07 / pop 5889

'Capital' of the Tableland, Atherton is a prosperous town and a handy place to regroup. **The Atherton Tableland Information Centre** (☎ 4091 4222; www.athertonsc.qld.gov.au; cnr Robert & Herberton Sts; ☺ 9am-5pm) has useful information, and **Washouse Internet café** (☎ 4091 2619; 1 Robert St; per hr $5; ☺ 9am-5pm Mon-Fri, 9am-noon Sat) has Internet access.

The best attraction in town has to be the **Crystal Caves** (☎ 4091 2365; www.crystalcaves.com.au; 69 Main St; adult/child $12.50/6; ☺ 8.30am-5pm Mon-Fri, 8.30am-4pm Sat, 10am-4pm Sun), a mineralogical museum in an artificial cave that winds for a block underground. You must wear a hard hat, and the last 'miners' need to be there one hour before closing. There is wheelchair access.

As you approach Atherton from Herberton in the southwest, the **Hou Wang Temple** (☎ 4091 6945; 86 Herberton Rd; adult/child/concession $7/2/5.50; ☺ 10am-4pm) is testament to the Chinese migrants who flooded the area to search for gold in the late 1800s. Inside are displays of objects, photographs and interpretive panels.

Lake Tinaroo

☎ 07

Picturesque Lake Tinaroo is a great spot for families and fisherfolk, who come for the excellent barramundi fishing. The enormous artificial lake and dam were originally created for the Barron River hydroelectric power scheme. **Tinaroo Falls**, at the northwestern corner of the lake, is the main settlement.

Clean and modern with lake views, **Lake Tinaroo Terraces** (☎ 4095 8555; www.laketinaroo terraces.com.au; r $80-150; ⚡) offers a range of rooms from a room with a bathroom to two-bedroom, self-contained two-storey terraces. All are superb value.

Lake Tinaroo Holiday Park (☎ 4095 8232; www
.ppawd.com/tinaroo; Dam Rd; powered/unpowered sites
$20/15, cabins $50) is a pleasant camping ground
by the lake that also has boat hire (half-
/full-day $70/80). BYO linen.

The bright and modern **Pensini's Café &
Restaurant** (☎ 4095 8242; 12 Church St; mains $17-
20; ☺ lunch daily, dinner Sat) cooks up Tableland
produce (including barramundi of course)
and serves it alongside a hefty wine list.

From the dam, the unsealed 4WD-only
Danbulla Forest Drive winds through the
Danbulla State Forest beside the lake, finally
emerging on the Gillies Hwy 4km northeast
of Lake Barrine. The road passes several spectacular self-registration lakeside **QPWS camping grounds** (☎ 13 13 04; www.epa.qld.gov.au; per person/
family $4/16).

There's a volcanic crater at **Mobo Creek**,
and 6km from the Gillies Hwy a short walk
takes you down to the **Cathedral Fig**, a gigantic strangler fig tree.

Yungaburra
☎ 07 / pop 1007
Quaint, heritage-listed and also full of 19th-
century architecture, Yungaburra's chocolate-box prettiness has made it a popular
weekend retreat for Cairns' wage slaves. It's a
romantic getaway and the perfect base from
which to explore the Atherton Tableland.

The **Yungaburra Folk Festival** (www.yungaburra
folkfestival.org) is a fabulous community event
held annually in late October. It features
music, workshops, poetry readings and kids
activities. The **Yungaburra Markets** (☎ 4095
2111; Gillies Hwy; ☺ 7am-noon) are held in town
on the fourth Saturday of every month; at
this time the town is besieged by avid craft
and food shoppers. The magnificent 500-
year-old **Curtain Fig** is a must-see. Looking
like a *Lord of the Rings* prop, it has aerial
roots that hang down to create a feathery
curtain. A wheelchair-accessible viewing
platform snakes around the tree.

SLEEPING
Kookaburra Lodge (☎ 4095 3222; www.kookaburra
-lodge.com; cnr Oak St & Eacham Rd; d $75; ✷ ☎) Be-
hind a high fence and amid a tropical garden, Kookaburra has stylish rooms fanning
out around the pale-blue pool. There are
big soft couches to sink into in the communal loungeroom. It's an intimate option,
so not suitable for small children.

Gables B&B (☎ 4095 2373; 5 Eacham Rd; r $65-75)
This historic Queenslander has a range of
rooms, including one with a spa. All rates
include a big breakfast of bread and fruit.

On the Wallaby (☎ 4095 2031; www.onthewallaby
.com; 34 Eacham Rd; unpowered sites per 2 people $10,
dm/d $20/50) The timber interiors and atten-
tive greeting are welcome and warming at
this hostel. Nature-based tours run from
here daily and packages that include transfers from Cairns and trips to the falls are
offered.

EATING
Eden House (☎ 4095 3355; 20 Gillies Hwy; mains
around $28; ☺ dinner Fri-Wed) Each dish at this
well-respected restaurant has a story: the
rib-eye is slow-cooked for four hours, and
the fish is line-caught on the Barrier Reef.
The wine list is comprehensive, and you
can dine in the garden at Eden, set beneath
a giant tree.

Flynn's (☎ 4095 2235; 17 Eacham Rd; mains $17-22;
☺ lunch Thu-Mon, dinner Thu-Sun) Plunge your fork
into some authentic French- and Italian-
style dishes at Flynn's. You can dine street-
side or on the terrace out the back. Flynn's
is BYO and cash only.

Keddie's (☎ 4095 3265; Gillies Hwy; dishes $6-12;
☺ breakfast, lunch & dinner) The broad open deck
is a great place to watch the comings and
goings of the main street. Keddie's makes
sandwiches, cooks up eggs and bacon, as
well as falafel rolls and pizza.

QUEENSLAND

Crater Lakes National Park & Around

Part of the Wet Tropics World Heritage Area, the two mirror-like volcanic lakes of Lake Eacham and Lake Barrine, off the Gillies Hwy east of Yungaburra, are beautiful swimming and picnicking spots encircled by **rainforest walking tracks**. Both lakes are national parks, but camping is not allowed.

Accessible from either lake, and 12km from Yungaburra, the native **Gadgarra Red Cedar** is more than 500 years old. On the drive there you may encounter an indignant gaggle of geese.

LAKE EACHAM

The crystal-clear waters of Lake Eacham are great for swimming and spotting turtles. The secluded area echoes with the call of whip birds cracking in lush rainforest, and there are some sensational picnic spots. Stop in to the rangers' station for information on the area or to gawk at the native python.

Bird-lovers flock to **Chambers Wildlife Rainforest Lodge** (☎ 07-4095 3754; http://rainforest-australia.com; Eacham Close; r $120; ⊠), which is embedded in the national park. There are self-contained cabins and landing platforms about the place for visiting birds – all of which enjoy celebrity status.

At **Crater Lakes Rainforest Cottages** (☎ 07-4095 2322; www.craterlakes.com.au; Eacham Close, off Lakes Dr; d incl breakfast $190-290; ⊠) Individually themed cottages come with wood-burner heating, spa baths, fully fitted kitchens and a breakfast hamper for your first morning.

Lake Eacham Caravan Park (☎ 07-4095 3730; www.lakeeachamtouristpark.com; 71 Lakes Dr; powered/unpowered sites $19/13, cabins $65), less than 2km down the Malanda road from Lake Eacham, has a pretty camping ground.

LAKE BARRINE

Spoil yourself with a Devonshire tea at **Lake Barrine Rainforest Cruise & Tea House** (☎ 07-4095 3847; Gillies Hwy; ☕ breakfast & lunch) and spot water dragons and tortoises on the 40-minute **cruise** (adult/child $12/6; 10am, 11.30am, 1.30pm, 2.30pm & 3.30pm).

Malanda

☎ 07 / pop 1022

Part of the waterfall circuit, Malanda is about 15km south of Lake Eacham. The **Malanda Falls Visitors Centre** (☎ 4096 6957; Atherton Rd; ☕ 9am-4.30pm) has thoughtful displays on the area's human and geological history, and runs guided rainforest walks ($10, by appointment) led by members of the Ngadjonji community.

On the Atherton road on the outskirts of town are **Malanda Falls**.

On the Millaa Millaa Rd, 10km from Malanda, is the tiny village of Tarzali, which offers some accommodation options.

Boutique B&B accommodation doesn't get much better than **Fur 'n' Feathers** (☎ 4096 5364; www.rainforesttreehouses.com.au; Hogan Rd, Tarzali via Malanda; d $195-480). This group of all-timber pole houses is set in a stunning and pristine patch of old-growth rainforest. The private riverfront treehouses are self-contained and perfect for spotting wildlife.

Set amid rolling pastures just 3km south of Malanda, **Fairdale Farmstay** (☎ 4096 6599; www.bnbnq.com.au/fairdale; Hillcrest Rd; s/d $65/95, cottage $110-165) offers accommodation in the family homestead or in separate self-contained cottages, which are great for families. Kids can participate in farm activities.

Malanda Lodge Motel (☎ 4096 5555; www.malandalodgemotel.com.au; Millaa Millaa Rd; s/d $80/90; ⊠ ⚑) has a good range of facilities including a restaurant and laundry. If it feels as though the solid brick walls of your room are closing in, escape to the beautiful gardens or swimming pool.

Tree Kangaroo Café (☎ 4096 6658; Atherton Rd; meals $4-10; ☕ breakfast & dinner) is next door to the Environmental Centre and serves stop-gap food.

Millaa Millaa & the Waterfall Circuit

The 16km 'waterfall circuit' near this small town, 24km south of Malanda, passes some of the most picturesque falls on the Tableland. Enter the circuit by taking Theresa Creek Rd, 1km east of Millaa Millaa on Palmerston Hwy. **Millaa Millaa Falls**, the largest of the falls, are a perfect sheet of water dropping over a fern-fringed escarpment. These are the most spectacular and have the best swimming hole. Continuing round the circuit, you reach **Zillie Falls** and then **Ellinjaa Falls**, before returning to the Palmerston Hwy just 2.5km out of Millaa Millaa. A further 5.5km down the Palmerston Hwy there's a turn-off to **Mungalli Falls**, 5km off the highway.

At **Mungalli Creek Dairy** (☎ 07-4097 2232; 254 Brooks Rd; ☕ 10am-4pm) you can sample boutique biodynamic dairy products which include yoghurt, cheese and sinfully rich cheesecake.

Mungalli Falls Rainforest Village (☎ 07-4097 2358; www.mungallifalls.com; Junction Rd; dm $25, cabins $55-85), 5km off the Palmerston Hwy, caters to groups and has beds for up to 600 people. There is a kiosk (meals $10 to $25), and horse-riding ($65 for 3½ hours) is available here.

Iskanda Park Farmstay (☎ 07-4097 2401; www .iskanda.com; Nash Rd; r $110-125), about 7km north of Millaa Millaa, has rooms in the farm's homestead. There are views over the rolling hills, and opportunities to lend a hand around the farm.

Lunch at the charming **Falls Teahouse** (☎ 07-4097 2237; www.fallsteahouse.com.au; Palmerston Hwy; meals $8-14, s $65-95, d $95-140; ☒ 10am-5pm), overlooking the rolling Tableland hills, is a treat. You might try laksa, curry, or sandwiches made from home-baked bread. Rooms are individually furnished with period fixtures and fittings. It's on the turn-off to Millaa Millaa Falls.

Mt Hypipamee National Park

Between Atherton and Ravenshoe, the Kennedy Hwy passes the eerie **Mt Hypipamee crater**, which could be a scene from a sci-fi film and is well worth stopping for. It's a scenic 800m (return) walk from the picnic area, past **Dinner Falls**, to this narrow, 138m-deep crater with its moody-looking lake far below.

Herberton

☎ 07 / pop 946

Peaceful Herberton is nestled in the crease of one of the area's rolling hills. It is a historic tin-mining town and many of its buildings are still intact.

The **visitors centre** (☎ 4096 2244; Great Northern Mining Centre, Jack's Rd), on the site of an old mine, stocks brochures outlining walks in and around town. Or you can let someone else do most of the work and let a donkey carry your gear on a trek with **Wilderness Expeditions** (☎ 4096 2266; www.wildex.com.au; day treks adult/child $125/95).

Herberton Heritage Cottage B&B (☎ 4096 2032; www.herbertoncottage.com; 2 Perkins St; s/d $120/130; ☒) has namesake-style rooms and is the best option in town. Expect lots of polished wood surfaces, potbelly heating and high comfy beds.

There are basic motel-style rooms available at the **Australian Hotel** (☎ 4096 2263; 44 Grace St; s/d $25/50, mains $12-16; ☒ lunch & dinner), which also serves counter meals.

Wild River Caravan Park (☎ 4096 2121; 23 Holdcroft Dr; powered/unpowered sites per 2 people $9/17, caravans $30, cabins $40) is on the edge of town, with an attractive aspect.

Ravenshoe

☎ 07 / pop 830

With an altitude of 904m, Ravenshoe is the highest town in Queensland. **Ravenshoe Visitor Centre** (☎ 4097 7700; www.ravenshoevisitorcentre .com.au; 24 Moore St; ☒ 9am-4pm) has maps and houses the **Nganyaji Interpretive Centre**, which explains the Jirrbal people's traditional lifestyle.

WindyHill Wind Farm is Australia's largest wind farm, with 20 wind turbines producing a clean, green energy supply. Public viewing access is available 24 hours, with views of the quiet energy source. Windy Hill can be reached either from the Kennedy Hwy from Ravenshoe, or from Millaa Millaa, along the scenic Old Palmerston Hwy.

Little Millstream Falls are 2km south of Raven-shoe on the Tully Gorge Rd, and **Tully Falls** are 24km south. About 6km past Ravenshoe and 1km off the road are the 13m-high **Millstream Falls** (no swimming), said to be the widest in Australia.

Kennedy Highway

About 32km west of Ravenshoe is the small township of **Innot Hot Springs**, where a hot spring heats up the cool waters of the town's creek. You can 'take the waters' at **Innot Hot Springs Village** (☎ 07-4097 0136; powered/ unpowered sites per 2 people $19/17, budget s/d $35/45, cabins s/d $67/77; ☒). Guests have free use of the park's seven **thermal pools** (nonguest adult/child $6/4; ☒ 8am-6pm).

PORT DOUGLAS

☎ 07 / pop 5867

Beautiful Port Douglas is a refreshingly low-rise resort town, nestled into a rich green pocket of the far north. Although it has wooed the lucrative tourist markets with its boutique accommodation, stylish eating options and swish clothing stores, the down-to-earth locals have managed to keep Port's relaxed village feel. This balance means there is excellent infrastructure,

QUEENSLAND

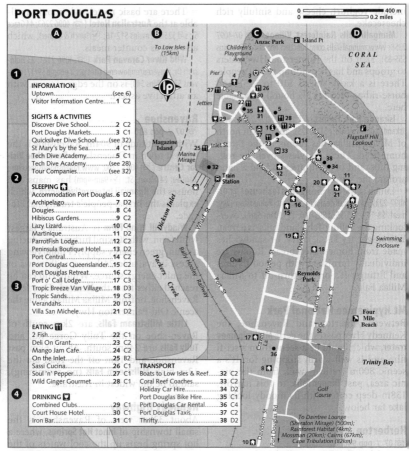

PORT DOUGLAS

all hidden behind an uninterrupted stretch of palm-fringed white-sand beach. There are some excellent sailing and fishing tours available, and you can also make trips to the Low Isles, Great Barrier Reef, Mossman Gorge, Atherton Tableland and Cape Tribulation from here.

Orientation & Information

From the Captain Cook Hwy it's 6km along a low spit of land to Port Douglas. Davidson St, the main entry road, ends at a T-intersection with Macrossan St. To the left is the town centre with most of the shops and restaurants; the beach is to the right.

Port Douglas **visitor information centre** (☎ 40 99 5599; www.reefandrainforest.com.au; 23 Macrossan St;

8am-6.30pm) has maps, and there's Internet access at **Uptown** (☎ 4099 5568; www.uptown.com .au; 48 Macrossan St; per 30min $5).

Sights & Activities

You're likely to put in at least a few hours or days on the gorgeous **Four Mile Beach**: a band of white-sand beach backed by palms that goes as far as your squinting eyes can see. You can go parasailing and jet skiing from a **waterfront hut** (☎ 4099 3175; xtraactionwater@optusnet.com.au; tandem parasail/jet-ski $60/100), or you could just lie there for hours – the Munch buggy plies the length of the beach selling ice creams and snacks.

The excellent **Rainforest Habitat** (☎ 4099 3235; www.rainforesthabitat.com.au; Port Douglas Rd;

adult/child $28/14; ☽ 8am-5.30pm) is a wildlife sanctuary that endeavours to keep and showcase native animals in enclosures that closely mimic their natural environment. Koalas, kangaroos, crocs and tree kangaroos reside here alongside parrots, wading birds and cassowaries. You can dine with the animals at **Breakfast with the Birds** (incl admission $39/19.50; ☽ 8-10.30am) or **After Dark** (adult/child $85/35; ☽ 5-9.30pm), which includes dinner and a twilight tour.

Port Douglas Markets (Anzac Park, bottom Macrossan St; ☽ 8.30am-1.30pm Sun), where you can pick up fruit and veggies and local arts and crafts, make for a leisurely Sunday morning wander along the grassy banks of Anzac Park.

St Mary's by the Sea (Anzac Park) is a tiny non-denominational white-timber chapel that was built in 1911.

Several companies offer a PADI open-water certification as well as advanced dive certificates. **Discover Dive School** (☎ 4099 6800; www.discoverdiveschool.com; Shop 6, Grant St; 4-day courses $580) and **Tech Dive Academy** (☎ 4099 6880; www.tech-dive-academy.com; 1/18 Macrossan St; 4-day courses $575) provide instruction with limited numbers per class (four to six). **Quicksilver Dive School** (☎ 4099 5050; www.quicksilverdive .au; Marina Mirage; 4-day courses $550) holds two days of its training course in Palm Cove; transfers from Port Douglas are included.

Tours
LOW ISLES TRIPS
There are several cruises to the Low Isles, a small coral cay surrounded by a lagoon and topped by a lighthouse.

Sailaway (☎ 4099 4772; www.sailawayportdouglas .com; adult/child $125/75) A maximum of 27 passengers. Great for families.

Shaolin (☎ 4099 1231; http://home.austarnet.com .au/shaolin; adult/child $135/65) A refitted Chinese junk, the Shaolin has snorkelling cruises (maximum 24).

Wavedancer (☎ 4087 2100; www.quicksilver-cruises .com; adult/child from $77/42)

FISHING & SAILING
Reef, river and land-based fishing charters operate regularly out of Port Douglas. Prices range from $80 for a half-day group tour on the Daintree River to anywhere between $2500 and $7000 per day on the mother ship. **Fishing Port Douglas** (☎ 4098 5354; www.fishingportdouglas.com.au) has details.

REEF TRIPS
The unrelenting surge of visitors to the Reef off Port Douglas has impacted on its general condition, and although you'll still see colourful corals and marine life, it has become patchy in parts. Reef trips generally include reef tax, snorkelling, transfers from your accommodation, plus lunch and refreshments. Add around $200/$180 for an introductory/certified dive.

Recommended operators:

Aristocat (☎ 4099 4727; www.aristocat.com.au; adult/child $150/105) Maximum 45 passengers.

Haba (☎ 4099 5254; www.habadive.com.au; adult/child $150/90) Maximum 40 passengers.

Quicksilver (☎ 4087 2100; www.quicksilver-cruises.com) Two boats visiting the outer reef: the Quicksmart (adult/child $145/110) with around 80 passengers and giant Wavepiercer (adult/child $185/100), which takes over 400.

Synergy 2 (☎ 4050 0675; www.synergyreef.com.au; adult/child $230/160) Maximum of 12 passengers, outer reefs tours and limo transfers.

Tallarook (☎ 4099 4990; www.tallarooksail.com; adult/child $145/105) Sails to Tongue Reef in just under two hours (maximum 25).

Wavelength (☎ 4099 5031; www.wavelength.com.au; adult/child $155/105) Snorkelling cruise only (maximum 30).

OTHER TOURS
There are numerous operators offering day trips to Cape Tribulation, some via Mossman Gorge. Many of the tours out of Cairns also go pick-ups from Port Douglas.

BTS Tours (☎ 4099 5665; return adult/child $16/8) Tours to Mossman Gorge.

Reef & Rainforest Connections (☎ 4099 5333; www.reefandrainforest.com.au; tours from adult/child $105/55) A range of day-long ecotours including Cape Trib and Bloomfield Falls, Kuranda and hot-air balloon flights.

Sleeping
Accommodation Port Douglas (☎ 4099 5355; www .accomportdouglas.com.au; 1/48 Macrossan St; ☽ 9am-5pm Mon-Sat) is an agent for many holiday rentals.

BUDGET
ParrotFish Lodge (☎ 4099 5011; www.parrotfishlodge .com; 37-9 Warner St; dm $23-26, d $75-85; ✕ ▢ ☒) This happy hostel is decorated with local mural-sized contemporary art and houses spacious dorms. The décor is extreme beach, with bright yellow walls and iridescent-blue swirling floors. There is a pool, restaurant-bar, jobs board and wheelchair access.

Dougies (☎ 4099 6200; www.dougies.com.au; 111 Davidson St; dm $25, d & tw $68; ✂ 🖥 🐾) Redefining the value of hanging out, Dougies is a laid-back resort with hammocks, yawning lawns and a cheerful bar. The rooms aren't fancy but the idea is to get out of them. Free transfers are available from Cairns on Monday, Wednesday and Saturday.

Also recommended:

Port o' Call Lodge (☎ 4099 5422; www.portocall.com .au; cnr Port St & Craven Close; dm $23-28, d $60-110; ✂ 🖥 🐾) Large YHA hostel with a range of rooms, bar and bistro. Free courtesy coach to/from Cairns Monday to Saturday.

Port Central (☎ 4051 6722; www.portcentral.com.au; 36 Macrossan St; s/d from $65/76; ✂) Central spot with no reception – just a phone link-up.

Tropic Breeze Van Village (☎ /fax 4099 5299; 24 Davidson St; powered/unpowered sites per 2 people $24/20, on-site cabins from $80) Close to the beach with shady tent sites.

MIDRANGE

Tropic Sands (☎ 4099 4533; www.tropicsands.com.au; 21 Davidson St; r $160; ✂ 🖥 🐾) Handsome open-plan rooms in a beautiful white colonial-style building. From your private balcony, you can catch a whiff of the sea or whatever's cooking in your fully equipped kitchen. There's a saltwater pool, guest laundry service, in-room TV and safe.

Hibiscus Gardens (☎ 4099 5315; www.hibiscusport douglas.com.au; cnr Mowbray & Owen Sts; r from $165; ✂ 🖥 🐾) This stylish resort features Balinese influences with its teakwood furnishing and fixtures and the occasional Buddha. The on-site spa specialises in indigenous healing techniques and products; try the Paudi head massage and quandong hair wrap.

Archipelago (☎ 40995387; www.archipelago.com.au; 72 Macrossan St; d from $130; ✂ 🐾) Very near the beach, this complex has 12 self-contained rooms spread over three levels. The upper rooms have 'filtered' views to the beach – through trees and other properties. Rooms are neat and functional, with balconies and cane furniture.

Port Douglas Retreat (☎ 4099 5053; www.port douglasretreat.com.au; 31-3 Mowbray St; apt $150; ✂ 🐾) Set the sun lounge to lying position and relax on the wide wooden decking that surrounds the swimming pool beset with palms. A total of 36 self-contained apartments sprawl over two levels in this traditional Queenslander-style complex.

Martinique (☎ 4099 6222; www.martinique.com .au; 66 Macrossan St; r $140; ✂ 🐾) This terracotta-coloured block contains lovely one-bedroom apartments; each with kitchen and private balcony. The Martinique is close to the beach and is on the main street; it has laundry facilities and landscaped gardens. Apartments are large, with some fitted for wheelchair access.

Villa San Michele (☎ 4099 4088; www.villasan michele.com.au; 39-41 Macrossan St; apt from $175; ✂ 🐾) Luxurious one- and two-bedroom self-contained apartments are barely visible above street level. Set around a courtyard swimming pool, each apartment has a large balcony and sports terracotta-tiled floors and wrought-iron furnishings.

Other midrange options:

Port Douglas Queenslander (☎ 4099 5199; www .queenslander.com.au; 8-10 Mudlo St; r $145; ✂ 🐾) Midsized complex good for families.

Lazy Lizard (☎ 4099 5900; www.lazylizardinn.com.au; 121 Davidson St; r from $135-165; ✂ 🐾) Good units serviced daily. Some have wheelchair access.

TOP END

Verandahs (☎ 4099 6650; www.verandahsportdougla .com.au; 7 Davidson St; r $275; ✂ 🐾) These oh-so stylish two-bedroom, two-bathroom apartments come replete with stainless-steel kitchens, polished floorboards, modern furnishings, and BBQs on the verandahs. Apartments are serviced daily and you can have a masseuse sent up to your room.

Peninsula Boutique Hotel (☎ 4099 9100; www .peninsulahotel.com.au; 9-13 Esplanade; s/d $300/340; ✂ 🖥 🐾) Private and luxurious, this is a hotel geared mainly towards couples and newlyweds, with special honeymoon deals available. The modern self-contained apartments are right across from Four Mile Beach. Children under 15 not catered for.

Eating

Sassi Cucina (☎ 4099 6100; cnr Wharf & Macrossan Sts; mains $28-38; ☺ breakfast, lunch & dinner) Delectable Italian eatery serves genuine pastas and risottos, pared back to just a few perfectly balanced ingredients. The coffee is deftly prepared, and the desserts are positively inspired. Italian Sassi also goes Japanese, with a fine sushi bar next door.

Mango Jam Cafe (☎ 4099 4611; 24 Macrossan St; mains $17-20; ☺ lunch & dinner) Large licensed family restaurant serves all your casual favourites, such as roast chicken, leg of lamb, crumbed calamari and lasagne. The speciality is gourmet, wood-fired pizza, which it will even deliver to your accommodation. There's also a separate kids menu.

On the Inlet (☎ 4099 5255; 3 Inlet St; mains around $25; ☺ lunch & dinner) This excellent seafood restaurant has tables spread along a sprawling deck. Your attentive waiter will recommend a wine to match your yellowfin tuna crusted in vermicelli, or salmon stacked with prawn and avocado. The pre-dinner deal (3.30pm to 5.30pm) gets you a bucket of prawns and a drink for $16.50.

Deli On Grant (☎ 4099 5852; 11 Grant St; meals $8-12; ☺ lunch) A range of boutique produce and precooked home-cooked meals to take away are on offer here. The Deli also does picnic hampers, with three hours' notice.

There are good counter meals on offer at the **Iron Bar** (below; mains $18-27; ☺ lunch & dinner) and **Court House Hotel** (right; meals $15-21; ☺ lunch & dinner)

Café options:

Wild Ginger Gourmet (☎ 4099 5972; 22 Macrossan St; dishes $4-9; ☺ lunch Wed-Sun) Gourmet sandwiches, wraps, juices and smoothies.

Soul 'n' Pepper (☎ 4099 4499; 2 Dixie St; meals $9-18; ☺ breakfast & dinner daily, lunch Mon-Sat) Outdoor café with casual service and surrounds.

Drinking

Iron Bar (☎ 4099 4776; 5 Macrossan St) The atmosphere here is so convivial that nobody seems to notice the fridge suspended from the ceiling or that the place looks like a country woolshed. Tuesday, Thursday and Sunday nights are reserved for cane-toad races.

Court House Hotel (☎ 4099 5181; cnr Macrossan & Wharf Sts) Commanding a corner location, this pub has a pleasant open-air courtyard populated by low-key drinkers. Cover bands entertain the crowd on weekends and there are pokies in the gaming room.

Daintree Lounge (☎ 4099 5888; Davidson St) In the lobby of the opulent Sheraton Mirage, you don't have to be a guest to appreciate the resort's ambience – for a few hours at least.

Combined Clubs (☎ 4099 5553; Ashford St) Mature gentlemen and their lady friends politely elbow other couples for space on the prime outdoor deck area. It's a welcoming spot for all ages though; there are even computer games to keep the kids occupied.

Getting There & Away

For more information on getting to Cairns, see p429.

Sun Palm (☎ 4084 2626; www.sunpalmtransport.com) runs daily (except Monday) services from Port Douglas to Cairns ($25, 1½ hours), Mossman ($8, 20 minutes), Cape Tribulation ($45, three hours) and Cooktown ($69, six hours).

Coral Reef Coaches (☎ 4098 2600; www.coralreefcoaches.com.au) connects Port Douglas with Mossman ($5, 20 minutes), Cow Bay ($22, two hours), Daintree Village (on request, two hours), Cape Tribulation ($30, 2½ hours) and Cairns ($20, 1¼ hours).

Quicksilver (☎ 4031 4299; www.quicksilver-cruises.com; one way/return $26/39) has a fast catamaran service that departs Port Douglas at 5.15pm, arriving in Cairns at around 6.45pm.

Getting Around

TO/FROM THE AIRPORT

Airport Connections (☎ 4099 5950; www.tnqshuttle.com; one way $23; ☺ 3.30am-4.30pm) runs an hourly shuttle-bus service to/from Cairns airport, as does **Sun Palm** (☎ 4084 2626; www.sunpalmtransport.com; adult $25), though less frequently.

BICYCLE

Pedalling around compact Port is a sensible transport method. Hire bikes from **Port Douglas Bike Hire** (☎ 4099 5799; 40 Macrossan St; per day from $15; ☺ 9am-5pm).

CAR

Port Douglas is one of the last places before Cooktown where you can hire a 4WD.

Holiday Car Hire (☎ 4099 4999; 54 Macrossan St; ☽ 8am-5.30pm Mon-Fri, 8am-noon Sat & Sun)

Port Douglas Car Rental (☎ 4099 4988; www.port carrental.com.au; 81 Davidson St; ☽ 6.30am-8.30pm Mon-Fri, 6.30am-1.30pm Sat & Sun)

Thrifty (☎ 4099 5555; www.thrifty.com; 50 Macrossan St; ☽ 9am-4pm Mon-Fri, to noon Sat & Sun)

TAXI

Port Douglas Taxis (☎ 4099 5345; 45 Warner St) offers 24-hour service.

MOSSMAN
☎ 07 / pop 1941

Shadowed by Mt Demi, this quiet town is the eye of the surrounding tourist storm. Day trippers staying in Cairns and Port Douglas come to snap a Kodak moment of the gorge, but you shouldn't miss the fine architecture of the back streets, the mellow ebb of the place and the stand of 80-year-old rain trees behind the rail tracks. The Kuku Yalanji people are the traditional owners of the stunning **Mossman Gorge**. There are some crystal-clear swimming holes, which can be treacherous after heavy rain, and a superb 2.4km **walking trail**.

Mossman QPWS (☎ 4098 2188; www.epa.qld.gov .au; Demi View Plaza, 1 Front St; ☽ 10am-4pm Mon-Fri), near the main turn-off to the gorge, has maps and information.

Excellent walks are led by Aboriginal guides and run by **Kuku-Yalanji Dreamtime Walks** (☎ 4098 2595; www.yalanji.com.au; adult/concession $17/8.50; ☽ 10am, noon & 2pm Mon-Fri).

Mossman Gorge B&B (☎ 4098 2497; www.bnbnq .com.au/mossgorge; Lot 15, Gorge View Crescent; s $65-75, d $85-95; ☒ ☒) is a gorgeous timber B&B with lavishly large verandas from which to view the dense trees of the national park. Rates include breakfast of muffins, croissants and fruits.

White Cockatoo (☎ 4098 2222; www.thewhitecock atoo.com; 9 Alchera Dr; s & d cabins $80-120; ☒ ☒) has spacious self-contained timber cabins that can sleep up to five. Part of the property operates as a nudist resort from 1 October to 1 May, and nude tours of the Reef and Daintree can also be arranged.

For fresh juices, wraps and sandwiches try **Tropical Boost** (☎ 4098 1089; 10 Front St; dishes $7-9; ☽ breakfast & lunch Mon-Sat), or visit **Goodies Cafe** (☎ 4098 1118; 33 Front St; mains around $10; ☽ lunch) for healthy meals, homemade from organic produce.

Getting There & Around

Coral Reef Coaches (☎ 4098 2800; www.coralreef coaches.com.au) stops in Mossman from Cairns ($25, two hours) and from Port Douglas ($5, 20 minutes).

Sun Palm (☎ 4084 2626; www.sunpalmtransport.com) runs regular bus services between Mossman and Cairns ($31, two hours), and Port Douglas ($8, 20 minutes).

DAINTREE VILLAGE

Surrounded by pockets of untouched rainforest, Daintree Village is the low-key tourist hub of the coastal lowland area between the Daintree and Bloomfield Rivers – also known as the Daintree Coast. It's a tidy settlement with a good range of accommodation, eating and tour options to launch visitors into the spectacular Wet Tropics World Heritage Area.

Daintree Village has a number of small tour operators:

Bruce Belcher's Daintree River Cruises (☎ 07-4098 7717; www.daintreerivercruise.com; adult/child $20/18; ☽ Mar-Jan) Eight tours daily.

Chris Dahlberg's Specialised River Tours (☎ 07-4098 7997; www.daintreerivertours.info; Daintree Village; 2hr tours $45; ☽ 6.30am Apr-Oct, 6am Nov-Jan) Specialises in bird-watching.

Crocodile Express (☎ 07-4098 6120; Daintree Village; 1½hr cruises adult/child $22/10; ☽ hourly 9.30am-3.30pm & 4pm)

Sleeping & Eating

Kenadon Homestead Cabins (☎ 07-4098 6142; www .daintreecabins.com; Dagmar St; s/d incl breakfast $80/100; ☒ ☒) Set on the fringe of a 160-hectare cattle farm, this family-owned property offers self-contained cabins, which are a good size for families and groups. Clustered together near the pool, the cabins face out to the vast pastures.

Red Mill House (☎ 07-4098 6233; www.redmillhouse .com.au; Stewart St; d $105; ☒ ☒ ☒) With a range of birds and frogs regularly stopping by, this excellent B&B plays host to more than just paying guests. The rooms are well appointed (with bathrooms), and there's a large communal lounge.

Daintree Eco Lodge & Spa (☎ 07-4098 6100; www .daintree-ecolodge.com.au; 20 Daintree Rd; s/d from $440/480; ☒ ☒ ☒) If you're looking for the sublime, well golly you'll swim in it here. Fifteen boutique villas, with private spas, are propped on stilts in the rainforest can-

---

WORLD HERITAGE LISTING – WHAT DOES IT GUARANTEE?

Far North Queensland's Wet Tropics area has amazing pockets of biodiversity. The area covers only 0.01% of Australia's surface area, but has 36% of the mammal species, 50% of the bird species, around 60% of the butterfly species and 65% of the fern species. The Wet Tropics' 3000km boundary includes diverse swamp and mangrove-forest habitats, eucalypt woodlands and tropical rainforest.

The Wet Tropics World Heritage Area stretches from Townsville to Cooktown and covers 894,420 hectares of coastal zones and hinterland. The greater Daintree rainforest reaches as far as the Bloomfield River and is protected as part of Daintree National Park.

The Daintree area has a controversial history. In 1983 the Bloomfield Track was bulldozed through sensitive coastal lowland rainforest from Cape Tribulation to the Bloomfield River, attracting international attention to the fight to save the lowland Daintree rainforests. The conservationists lost that battle, but the publicity generated by the blockade indirectly led to the federal government's moves in 1987 to nominate Queensland's wet tropical rainforests for World Heritage listing. Despite strenuous resistance by the Queensland timber industry and state government, the area was inscribed on the World Heritage List in 1988 and one of the key outcomes was a total ban on commercial logging in the area.

That may not be enough, however. The Cow Bay area that most travellers visit, an area of unique and threatened plant species, is a 1000-block real estate subdivision on freehold private land – look around and you'll see 'for sale' signs aplenty. World Heritage listing, unfortunately, doesn't affect land ownership rights or control.

Established in 1994, the Daintree Rescue Program, a buy-back scheme, has attempted to consolidate and increase public land ownership in the area, lowering the threat of land clearing and associated species extinction. State and federal governments alone have spent $23 million re-purchasing jungle properties and adding them to the Daintree National Park. It looks as though the adage of *Paradise Lost* is being stalled by local efforts, and the Daintree just could be Paradise Found…and preserved. Check out www.austrop.org.au for more information.

---

opy. Within the complex is **Blingkumu** (mains $18-23; ☺ breakfast, lunch & dinner), which serves fine, gourmet bush tucker. There are also luxurious spa treatments. Transfers from Port Douglas and Cairns available.

Papaya (☎ 07-4098 6173; Stewart St; mains $12-18; ☺ lunch & dinner Wed-Sun) Snappy bar and bistro serves a range of standard favourites, such as fish and chips, and beef pies, as well as tourist-teasers such as crocodile wontons.

Two casual eateries serving tasty fare are **Jacanas Restaurant** (☎ 07-4098 6125; Stewart St; mains $10-16; ☺ breakfast, lunch & dinner) and **Daintree Tea House Restaurant** (☎ /fax 07-4098 6161; Daintree Rd; meals from $13).

AROUND CAPE TRIBULATION

About 11km before Daintree Village and 24km from Mossman is the turn-off to the **Daintree River cable ferry** (car/motorcycle/bicycle & pedestrian $16/8/3; ☺ 6am-midnight), which runs every 15 minutes and takes two minutes to cross the river into the Cape Tribulation area. After crossing the river it's another 34km by sealed road to Cape Tribulation. The indigenous Kuku Yalanji people called

the area Kulki, but the name Cape Tribulation was given by Captain Cook after his ship ran aground on Endeavour Reef.

Part of the Wet Tropics World Heritage Area, the region from Daintree River north to Cape Tribulation is extraordinarily beautiful and famed for its ancient rainforest, sandy beaches and the rugged mountains of **Thornton Peak** (1375m) and **Mt Sorrow** (770m). It's one of the few places in the world where the tropical rainforest meets the sea.

Electricity is powered by generators in this area; few places have air-con and not everywhere has 24-hour power. Cape Trib is one of the most popular day trips from Port Douglas and Cairns, and accommodation is booked solid in peak periods.

You can get fuel and supplies at **Cow Bay Service Station & General Store** (☎ 07-4098 9127; Buchanan Creek Rd) and Mason's Store (p449), but self-caterers are better off coming prepared. Coral Reef Coaches runs daily bus services from Cairns to Cape Tribulation. For information on organised trips to the area, see Tours in Cairns (p426) and Port Douglas (p443).

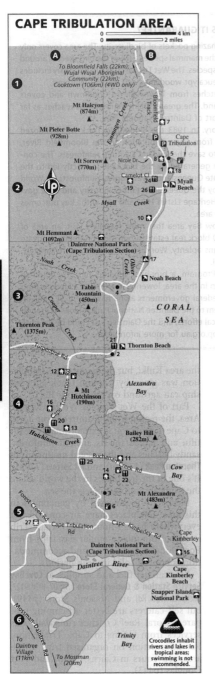

The following sections chart a route from the Daintree River to Cape Tribulation.

Cape Kimberly

Cape Kimberley Rd, 4km beyond the Daintree River crossing, leads to **Cape Kimberley Beach**, a beautiful quiet beach with **Snapper Island** just offshore, backed with tropical bush that offers shade. The small island is national park, with a fringing reef. Access to the island is by private boat; Crocodylus Village (opposite) takes a sea-kayaking tour there.

At the beach is **Koala Beach Resort** (☎ 07-4090 7500; www.koala-backpackers.com; Cape Kimberley; powered/unpowered sites $13/10, dm $18-25, d $50-85; ⊠ ⊠), a huge family-friendly camping ground with secluded sites, small cabins, a welcoming bar and a restaurant.

You'll need to obtain a permit for the **QPWS camping ground** (☎ 07-4098 2188; www.epa.qld .gov.au; per person $4) on the southwest side of Snapper Island, where there's a toilet and picnic tables. Take a fuel stove, as fires are not permitted here.

Cow Bay

Cow Bay is simply beautiful. Trees provide beach shade, and you can fish or just lie down and chill out– it doesn't get more relaxing than this.

Before the turn-off to the Jindalba Board-walk is the **Walu Wugirriga (Alexandra Range) lookout**, which has an information board and marvellous views over the **Alexandra Range**.

The **Daintree Discovery Centre** (☎ 07-4098 9171; www.daintree-rec.com.au; adult/child $20/7.50; �), 8.30am-5pm) is a rainforest interpretive centre. Its aerial walkway traverses the forest floor to a 23m tower. There are some short walks with interpretive panels and a small theatre runs films on conservation. **Jindalba Board-walk** snakes through the rainforest behind the centre.

SLEEPING & EATING

Epiphyte B&B (☎ 07-4098 9039; www.rainforestbb.com; 22 Silkwood Rd; s/d/tr $45/65/80) This spectacu-larly laid-back B&B has individually styled rooms of varying size. The encircling veran-da is festooned with hammocks and views of Thornton Peak. If you arrive unan-nounced, check the blackboard for vacan-cies and head to the beach, where you'll probably find the manager.

Crocodylus Village (☎ 07-4098 9166; www.crocodyluscapetrib.com; Buchanan Creek Rd; dm/d $20/75;) This YHA hostel has a spread of large, safari-style tents, which merge with the surrounding trees. There's a restaurant and bar, as well as a range of activities, in-cluding excellent two-day sea-kayaking tours to Snapper Island ($180).

Daintree Wilderness Lodge (☎ 07-4098 9105; www.daintreewildernesslodge.com.au; 83 Cape Tribulation Rd; r incl breakfast $250;) Seven timber cabins are separated by rainforest and connected by boardwalks. Each has a ceiling window to watch the rainforest canopy. If there's not enough action, you can always watch a DVD in your room. There's also a restaur-ant and 'jungle jacuzzi'.

Daintree Ice Cream Company (☎ 07-4098 9114; Cape Tribulation Rd; ice cream $4;) noon-5pm) Get stuck into a range of seasonal and exotic fla-vours such as wattleseed, macadamia, mango, blueberry and hazelnut. Yum!

Le Bistrot (☎ 07-4098 9016; Cape Tribulation Rd; mains 19-30;) lunch) Treats such as emu pro-sciutto and crocodile carpaccio are served in this boutique place in the thatched huts dotted around the grounds. There's also the tiny Floravilla gallery on the grounds.

More options:
Lync Haven (☎ 07-4098 9155; www.lynchaven.com.au; Cape Tribulation Rd; powered/unpowered sites $24/19,

d $140-165) Large property with basic cabins, self-con-tained bungalows, hand-reared kangaroos and a café.
Fan Palm Boardwalk Cafe (☎ 07-4098 9119; Cow Bay; mains $8-16;) breakfast, lunch & dinner) Open-air licensed café.

Cooper Creek
Cooper Creek Wilderness Cruises (☎ 07-4098 9126; www.ccwild.com; adult $30) offers day and night guided interpretive rainforest walks.

In a rainforest setting, **Daintree Deep Forest Lodge** (☎ 07-4098 9162; www.daintreedeepforestlodge.com.au; Cape Tribulation Rd; r $100-150) has two studio units and a one-bedroom unit that sleeps up to five. Each has a veranda with a barbecue for alfresco cooking.

Thornton Beach
Just a short stroll from Thornton Beach is the neo-hippy, open-air licensed **Café on Sea** (☎ 07-4098 9718; Thornton Beach; meals $10-15;) breakfast & lunch) with excellent healthy food, including delicious fish burgers.

Noah Beach
Marrdja Botanical Walk is a beautiful inter-pretive boardwalk that follows the creek through the rainforest and mangroves to a lookout over Noah Creek.

Noah Beach Camping Area (☎ 07-4098 0052; www.epa.qld.gov.au; per person/family $4/16) is a QPWS self-registration camping ground set 100m back from the beach. Big red-trunked trees provide shade for 16 sites.

CAPE TRIBULATION
Mason's Store (☎ 07-4098 0070; Cape Tribulation Rd;) 7am-7pm) is a one-stop supply shop that sells take-away food and runs tours.

Volunteers from Austrop– a local con-servation organisation– run the **Bat House** (☎ 07-4098 0063; www.austrop.org.au; Cape Tribula-tion Rd; admission $2;) 10.30am-3.30pm Tue-Sun), a nursery for fruit bats; there's always one looking to make a new friend.

Jungle Adventures (☎ 07-4098 0090; www.junglesurfingcanopytours.com; tours $25-28) runs excellent and informative night and day walks.

Sleeping & Eating
Cape Trib Beach House (☎ 07-4098 0030; www.capetribbeach.com.au; dm $25-32, r $70-135;) A pedestrian-only path buffers these A-frame rainforest huts from any hint of civilisation. The complex includes a small communal

kitchen, and **restaurant-bar** (mains $15-20; ✆ breakfast, lunch & dinner). The whole lot is right on the beach.

Rainforest Hideaway (☎ 07-4098 0108; www.rainforesthideaway.com; 19 Camelot Close; r $85-115) It's extremely private and suitable for everyone. This beautifully rambling accommodation was virtually built single-handedly by the owner. A lush backyard envelopes a rustic self-contained haven with outdoor shower.

PK's Jungle Village (☎ 07-4098 0197; www.pksjunglevillage.com; unpowered sites per person $15, dm $25, d $88-110; ✖ ▣ ■) PK's has the works: from postal facilities through to volleyball and salsa dance classes from its vibrant bar area. Dorms have eight beds, and air-conditioned rooms with bathrooms are available. There's also a **restaurant** (mains $15-20; ✆ breakfast, lunch & dinner) and communal kitchen.

Dragonfly Gallery Cafe (☎ 07-4098 0121; Lot 9, Camelot Close; mains $15-20; ✆ lunch & dinner; ■) This licensed café is in a timber pole-house with beautiful garden views. Internet access is available upstairs in the loft, and you can peruse local art displayed around the interior.

Boardwalk Cafe (dishes $6-10; ✆ breakfast, lunch & dinner) A take-away serving burgers, sandwiches and the only pizza on the Cape.

More accommodation:

Cape Trib Farmstay (☎ 07-4098 0042; www.capetribfarmstay.com; Cape Tribulation Rd; d $100) Tropical fruit with private timber cottages and joyous views. Good wheelchair access.

Cape Tribulation Camping (☎ 07-4098 0077; www.capetribcamping.com.au; powered/unpowered sites $28/22, d $50) Beach frontage and good facilities.

Coconut Beach Rainforest Resort (☎ 07-4098 0033; www.voyages.com; r $370; ✖ ■) Luxurious resort with designer rooms, a sumptuous restaurant and excellent services.

CAPE TRIBULATION TO COOKTOWN

North of Cape Tribulation, the spectacular **Bloomfield Track** is 4WD only, continuing through the forest to the Wujal Wujal Aboriginal Community on the far side of the Bloomfield River crossing. Some steep sections of the Bloomfield Track may be impassable after heavy rain; check road conditions at Mason's Store (p449) before heading off.

A must-see along the way is **Bloomfield Falls** (after crossing the Bloomfield River turn left; the car park is 1km from here). North from Wujal Wujal the track heads for

46km through the tiny settlements of **Ayton (Bloomfield)**, **Rossville** and **Helenvale** to meet the sealed Cooktown Developmental Rd, 28km south of Cooktown.

The **Lion's Den Hotel** (☎ 07-4060 3911; www.lionsdenhotel.com.au; Helensvale; unpowered sites per 2 people $7.50, dm/d $25/50; ■) is a well-known watering hole with corrugated, graffiti-covered tin walls and a slab-timber bar. You can pitch a tent or sleep in a safari-style cabin.

COOKTOWN
☎ 07 / pop 1638

Sitting at the mouth of the croc-infested Endeavour River, Cooktown has a reckless, outpost ambience. Years of isolation and hard living have imbued the locals with a laconic character and a great sense of humour. They're not afraid of hard work, and equally not shy of a smoko – say from October to June. Everything here runs on 'Cooktown time' and folk live to fish.

The Wet has traditionally cut Cooktown off from the south to all but those with 4WDs, but the completion of the sealed Cooktown Developmental Rd is expected to bring increasing recognition for the area's indigenous community and the unspoilt natural environment of wetlands, mangroves, rainforest and long, lonely beaches.

Cooktown can claim to be Australia's first nonindigenous settlement, however transient. From June to August 1770, Captain Cook beached his barque *Endeavour* here, during which time the expedition's chief naturalist, Joseph Banks, collected 186 species of Australian plants from the banks of the Endeavour River and wrote the first European description of a kangaroo.

Race relations in the area turned sour a century later when Cooktown was founded as the unruly port for the Palmer River gold rush (1873–83). Battle Camp, about 60km inland from Cooktown, was the site of a major battle between Europeans and Aborigines.

Information

Cooktown Library (☎ 4069 5009; Helen St; ▣)
Cooktown QPWS (☎ 4069 5777; Webber Esplanade; ✆ 8am-3pm Mon-Fri) Closes for lunch.
Cooktown Travel Centre (☎ 4069 5446; cooktowntravel@bigpond.com; Charlotte St; ✆ 8.30am-5pm Mon-Fri, 8.30-noon Sat) Tourist information.
Nature's Powerhouse (☎ 4069 6004; www.naturespowerhouse.info; Walker St; ✆ 9am-5pm) Info centre.

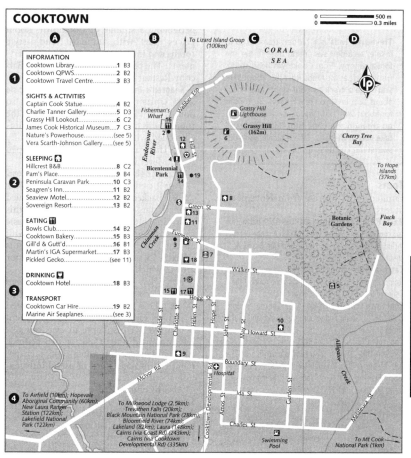

COOKTOWN

Sights

Cooktown hibernates during winter (locals call it 'the dead season'), and many attractions and tours close or have reduced hours.

Nature's Powerhouse (4069 6004; www.naturespowerhouse.info; Walker St; both galleries adult/child $2/free; 9am-5pm) is an environment interpretive centre in the **Botanic Gardens**, with two excellent galleries.

The **Charlie Tanner Gallery** (Charlie was Cooktown's 'snake man') has fantastic displays about snakes, termite mounds, crocodiles, 'only on the Cape' wildlife (the bare-backed fruit bat will give you nightmares) and inspirational stories from Taipan-bite survivors.

The **Vera Scarth-Johnson Gallery** displays a collection of intricate, beautiful botanical illustrations of the region's native plants. There are **walking trails** that lead from the gardens to the **beaches** at Cherry Tree and Finch Bays.

Housed in the imposing 1880s' St Mary's Convent, the **James Cook Historical Museum** (4069 5386; cnr Helen & Furneaux Sts; adult/child $7/2.50; 9.30am-4pm) explores Cooktown's intriguing past.

Grassy Hill lookout (162m) has spectacular 360-degree views, and its 1½km walking trail (45 minutes) leads from the summit down to the beach at Cherry Tree Bay.

Charlotte St and Bicentennial Park have a number of interesting **monuments**, including the much-photographed bronze **Captain Cook statue**.

OFF THE BEATEN TRACK

Trevathen Falls is a hidden treasure, with a safe, secluded swimming hole under the forest canopy. From Cooktown head south, turning left at Mt Amos Rd. After about 9km you'll see a track to your right; take it for about 1km until you reach a fork. Turn right for about 2km until you reach a gate. Don't go through the gate; turn left, which will take you to the falls. Take a picnic and your swimming costume. It's divine.

Tours

Limited tours operate from November to at least April.

Barts Bush Adventures (☎ 4069 6229; bartbush@ tpg.com.au; tours adult/child $165/85) A range of tours, including some to Coloured Sands and Elim Beach. Accredited Savannah guides.

Catch-a-Crab (☎ 4069 5381; cathyadams@fni.aunz .com; per person from $95) Crab-catching tours of the Endeavour and Annan Rivers; great for kids.

Cooktown Cruises (☎ 4069 5712; 2hr cruises adult/ child $25/13) Scenic Endeavour River cruises and boat hire (from $23 per hour).

Cooktown Tours (☎ 4069 5125; www.cooktowntours.com; ☻ 9am) Offers 1½-hour town tours (adult/child $20/12) and half-day trips to Black Mountain (adult/child $55/23).

Gone Fishing (☎ 4069 5980; www.fishingcooktown .com; 4hr tours from $75) River fishing tours. Private charters also available.

Guurrbi Tours (☎ 4069 5166; williegordon@fni.aunz .com; 2hr-/4hr-tours $80/105, self-drive $55/70) Unique tours run by a Nugal-warra elder, including a number of rock-art sites. Book at Pam's Place.

Marine Air Seaplanes (☎ 4069 5915; www.marineair .com.au; flights $125-175) Scenic reef flights and a Lizard Island tour ($330).

Paradise Blue (☎ 0408 183 261; www.2cooktown.com /paradise; tours $110) Snorkelling tours of the river or Great Barrier Reef.

Sleeping

Milkwood Lodge (☎ 4069 5007; www.milkwoodlodge .com.au; Annan Rd; s/d $90/110; ☻) About 2.5km south of town, these six breezy self-contained timber-pole cabins have bushland oozing up between them, and there are views from each private balcony. Cabins are spacious and split-level.

Sovereign Resort (☎ 4069 5400; www.sovereign -resort.com.au; cnr Charlotte & Green Sts; r $155-185; ☻ ☻) A well-equipped swish resort – you could sleep, eat and drink here without experiencing a smidge of Cooktown. Room prices start with standard studio-style rooms and increase to two-bedroom apartments. The complex also contains the Balcony Restaurant & Café-Bar.

Seagren's Inn (☎ 4069 5357; Charlotte St; s/d $75/85) Upstairs in a heritage building (that also houses the Pickled Gecko restaurant), the rooms here have spunk. Each is individually styled, with lots of wood and high puffy beds. There are river views from the open second-level veranda.

Hillcrest B&B (☎ 4069 5305; www.hillcrestb-b.com; 130 Hope St; guesthouse s/d/tr $40/50/70, unit s/d $60/70; ☻ ☻) Backed by a secret garden concealed beneath large greenhouse awnings, this charming old-style guesthouse has basic rooms without bathrooms, and units with air-con and private bathrooms. Breakfast is an extra $5, and there's a beautiful outdoor area in which to eat it.

Pam's Place (☎ 4069 5166; www.cooktownhostel .com; cnr Charlotte & Boundary Sts; dm/s/d $20/40/50; ☻ ☻) This comfortable YHA-associated hostel has a leafy garden and an assortment of neurotic parrots. There are also four new self-contained units ($80 for two people). All facilities are top-notch, and management can provide loads of useful information about the area.

Also recommended:

Seaview Motel (☎ 4069 5377; seaviewm@tpg.com.au; Webber Esplanade; s/d from $75/85; ☻ ☻) Low-rise motel with water frontage; tidy rooms.

Peninsula Caravan Park (☎ 4069 5107; fax 4069 5255; 64 Howard St; unpowered sites $18, s/d cabins $60/65) Lovely bush setting.

Eating & Drinking

Gill'd & Gutt'd (☎ 4069 5863; Fisherman's Wharf, Webber Esplanade; meals $8-17; ☻ lunch & dinner) This mighty takeaway dishes up fish 'n' chips in old-skool paper parcels. The fare is spectacular; barramundi or Spanish mackerel. Alternatively you can walk around to the riverside and dine in the licensed waterfront restaurant.

Pickled Gecko (☎ 4069 5357; Charlotte St; mains $16-28; ☻ lunch & dinner Apr-Sep) This licensed café offers Mod Oz cuisine in smart surrounds, downstairs from the Seagren's Inn. Thankfully the café's namesake appears only on the walls, not on the menu.

Bowls Club (☎ 4069 6173; Charlotte St; mains $12-20; ☻ dinner) Sign yourself in at the door, and join the club for the night. Apart from enormous, wholesome mains (such as fish or steak), you're able to visit the salad bar as often as you like. On weekends you might just win the meat-tray raffle.

Cooktown Hotel (☎ 4069 5308; Charlotte St; mains $10-15; ☻ lunch & dinner) Known as the Top Pub, this large hotel has character on tap and makes a pleasant place to prop for a while. There are pool tables and basic counter meals are also available.

Grab supplies from **Martin's IGA supermarket** (☎ 4069 5633; cnr Helen & Hogg Sts; ☻ 8am-6pm Mon-Sat, 10am-3pm Sun) and **Cooktown Bakery** (☎ 4069 5612; cnr Hogg & Charlotte Sts; ☻ 8am-4pm).

Getting There & Around

Sun Palm (☎ 4084 2626; sunpalmtransport.com) travels both the coastal and inland routes to Cairns ($70, Tuesday to Sunday). You can hop off in Port Douglas or Mossman on the way.

Cooktown's airfield is 10km west of town along McIvor Rd. **Skytrans** (☎ 1800 818 405, 4046 2462; www.skytrans.com.au) flies twice a day between Cooktown and Cairns (adult/child $110/55, 45 minutes).

Cooktown Car Hire (☎ 4069 5007; www.cooktown-car-hire.com; Milkwood Rainforest Lodge) rents 4WDs from $100 per day.

For a taxi call ☎ 4069 5387.

LIZARD ISLAND

☎ 07 / pop 1007

Lizard Island, the furthest north of the Great Barrier Reef resort islands, is about 100km from Cooktown. The continental island has dry, rocky and mountainous terrain, and 20-odd superb beaches, which are nothing short of sensational.

Captain Cook and his crew were the first nonindigenous people to visit the island. Having patched up the *Endeavour* in Cooktown, they sailed north and stopped here. Banks named the island after its large lizards, which are from the same family as Indonesia's Komodo dragons. Jigurru (Lizard Island) has long been a sacred place for the Dingaal Aboriginal people.

Worlds collided in 1881, when a group of Dingaal people attacked Mary Watson, wife of a man who ran a bêche-de-mer operation on the island. A Chinese worker was killed, and Mary fled the island in a bêche-de-mer boiling pot with her child and another worker. The three eventually died of thirst on a barren island to the north; Mary left a diary recording the details of their last days.

Lizard Island's beaches range from long stretches of white sand to idyllic little rocky bays. The water is crystal clear and magnificent coral surrounds the island – snorkelling here is superb. There are good dives right off the island, and the outer Barrier Reef is less than 20km away, including what is probably Australia's best-known dive, the **Cod Hole**.

Diving tours here can be arranged through **Diving Cairns** (www.divingcairns.com.au) and **Lizard Island Charters** (www.lizardislandcharters.com.au/diving-snorkelling.htm). The rates are determined by number of passengers and days.

There are also good bushwalks to **Cook's Look** (368m).

Accommodation options are extreme on Lizard Island – it's either camping or five-star luxury.

The **camping ground** (per person $4) is at the northern end of Watson's Bay; contact **QPWS** (☎ 4069 5446; www.env.qld.gov.au) in Cooktown or go online to obtain a permit. Campers must be totally self-sufficient, but there are toilets, tables and gas barbecues. Fresh water is available from a pump 250m from the site.

Expect isolation, spa treatments, private decks and an enviable location at **Lizard Island Resort** (☎ 1800 737 678, 4060 3999; www.lizardisland.com.au; Anchor Bay; s/d from $1025/1530; ☒ ☒). Rates include all meals.

Getting There & Away

Macair (☎ 13 15 28; www.macair.com.au) flies to Lizard Island from Cairns (one way from $260), and **Marine Air Seaplanes** (☎ 4069 5915; Charlotte St) has day tours ($330) from Cooktown.

CAIRNS TO COOKTOWN – THE INLAND ROAD

It's 332km (about 4½ hours' drive) from Cairns to Cooktown via this stoic and arid route. You can either access the Peninsula Developmental Rd from Mareeba, or via the turn-off just before Mossman. The road travels past rugged ironbarks and cattle-trodden land before joining the Cooktown Developmental Rd at Lakeland. From here it's another 80km to Cooktown, with just 30km left to seal – due for completion by the end of 2005.

The historical town of **Mt Molloy** marks the start of the Peninsula Developmental Rd. The **National Hotel** (☎ 07-4094 1133; Main St; s/d $25/50, mains $10-17; ✆ lunch & dinner) is a welcoming local where you can wear your work boots to lunch. Even the pickiest mother would approve of the lovely rooms upstairs.

The Palmer River gold rush (1873–83) occurred about 70km to the west, throwing up boomtowns Palmerville and Maytown; little of either remain today. You can buy horrendously expensive fuel at the **Palmer River roadhouse** (☎ 07-4060 2020; ✆ 7am-late).

South of Cooktown the road travels through the sinister-looking rock piles of **Black Mountain National Park** – a range of hills formed 260 million years ago and made up of thousands of granite boulders. Indigenous Australians call it Kalcajagga, or 'place of the spears', and it's home to unique species of frog, skink and gecko.

CAPE YORK PENINSULA

The overland pilgrimage to Cape York Peninsula – the Tip of Australia – is simply one of the greatest 4WD routes on the continent. This is one of the wildest and least populated areas of Australia, where clouds of red dust signal approaching vehicles and you'll drive many kilometres on corrugated roads to reach the next 'town', usually an isolated roadhouse. While reaching the tip is an exhilarating effort, many of the highlights of this journey are found in the detours, planned and unexpected. Along the way you'll encounter big crocs, vehicle- and character-testing roads, tropical rainforests and wetlands to rival Kakadu with their rich bird life.

If you're driving to the top, you'll need preparation and a 4WD. The ideal set-up is companion vehicles: two 4WDs travelling together so one can haul the other out of trouble if necessary. The HEMA map *Cape York & Lakefield National Park*, and the RACQ maps *Cairns/Townsville* and *Cape York Peninsula* are the best. Of the numerous books about the Peninsula, Ron and Viv Moon's *Cape York – an Adventurer's Guide* is the most comprehensive. Lonely Planet's *Queensland & the Great Barrier Reef* guide is also good.

Information & Permits

The RACQ and QPWS offices in Cairns (p424) and Cooktown (p450) have a wealth of information and are recommended starting points for planning your itinerary and to obtain permits. Once north of the Dulhunty River you will need a permit to camp on Aboriginal land, which in effect is nearly all the land north of the river. The Injinoo people are the traditional custodians of much of this land and the Injinoo Community who run the ferry across the Jardine River include a camping permit in the ferry fee.

Travelling across indigenous Australian land elsewhere on the Cape may require an additional permit from the relevant community council. **The Balkanu Cape York Development Corporation** (www.balkanu.com.au) website lists contact details for all the Cape York Aboriginal communities.

Tours

There are countless tour operators who run trips to the Cape. Tours last six to 14 days and take five to 12 passengers. Cairns is the main starting point for tours, which generally run between April and December, but dates may be affected by an early or late wet season. Most tours visit Laura, the Split Rock galleries, Lakefield National Park, Coen, Weipa, the Elliot River System (including Twin Falls), Bamaga, Somerset and Cape York itself; Thursday Island is usually an optional extra. Each tour has its own speciality (check with operators), but many offer different combinations of land, air and sea travel, and camping or motel-style accommodation. Prices include meals and fares from Cairns.

Billy Tea Bush Safaris (☎ 07-4032 0077; www.billy tea.com.au; 9-day fly/drive tours $2100, 13-day cruise/ drive $2200, 14-day overland tours $2200) A good range of tours.

Daintree Air Services (☎ 07-4034 9300, 1800 246 206; www.daintreeair.com.au; day tours $800)

Exploring Oz Safaris (☎ 1300 888 112, 07-4093 8347; www.exploring-oz.com.au; 6-day overland tours $800-1000) Takes in Musgrave Station, Coen, Wenlock River, Loyalty Beach, the Tip and Twin Falls.

Heritage 4WD Tours (☎ 07-4038 2628; www.heritage tours.com.au; 6-day fly/drive tours from $1580, 9-day cruise/drive tours from $1850) Numerous tours and accommodation options.

Oz Tours Safaris (☎ 1800 079 006, 07-4055 9535; www.oztours.com.au; 7-day fly/drive tours $1750, 12-day overland tours $2300) Numerous combinations.

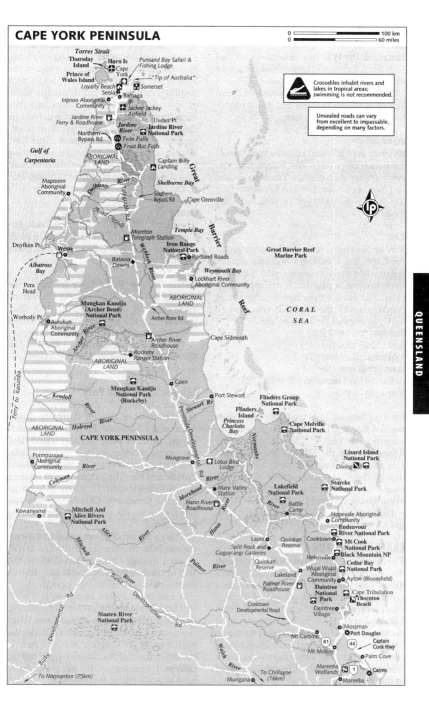

CAPE YORK PENINSULA

Crocodiles inhabit rivers and lakes in tropical areas; swimming is not recommended.

Unsealed roads can vary from excellent to impassable, depending on many factors.

Getting There & Away

AIR

QantasLink (☎ 13 13 13; www.qantas.com.au) flies daily from Cairns to Horn Island ($436 one way) and Weipa ($230 one way).

Skytrans (☎ 1800 818 405; www.skytrans.com.au) flies from Cairns to Coen and Yorke Island, and offers a charter service.

BOAT

MV Trinity Bay (☎ 07-4035 1234; www.seaswift.com.au) is a weekly cargo ferry, which departs Cairns every Friday and reaches Thursday Island and Bamaga on Sunday. The five-day return trip costs from $840 per person, including meals.

CAR

May to November is the best time to access the Cape, but conditions fluctuate according to when the Wet arrives, which is when rivers become impassable. If you're planning to head up outside these months, check road conditions with the RACQ. If you run into difficulty contact the local police:

Bamaga (☎ 07-4069 3156)
Coen (☎ 07-4060 1150)
Cooktown (☎ 07-4069 5320)
Laura (☎ 07-4060 3244)
Lockhart River Community (☎ 07-4060 7120)
Weipa (☎ 07-4069 9119)

Even as late as June and July the rivers are fast-flowing, have steep banks and frequently alter course. The Great Dividing Range runs up the spine of the peninsula, and rivers run east and west from it. Although the rivers in the south of the peninsula flow only in the Wet, those further north flow year-round.

For details on 4WD rental, see Cairns (p430) and Cooktown (p453).

LAKELAND & LAURA

The Peninsula Developmental Rd turns off the Cairns-to-Cooktown Developmental Rd at Lakeland. Facilities here include a general store with food, petrol and diesel, a small caravan park and a hotel-motel. From Lakeland it's 734km to Bamaga, almost at the top of the peninsula. The first stretch to Laura is not too bad, just some corrugation, potholes, grids and causeways – the creek crossings are bridged (although they flood in the Wet).

About 50km from Lakeland is the turnoff to **Split Rock and Guguylangi Galleries** (Split Rock/entire trail $5/10, paid into honesty box), no photography allowed. The galleries contain the best surviving examples of Quinkan rock painting, one of the most distinctive styles of Aboriginal art, and depictions here date back appoximately 14,000 years. No-one has been able to fully interpret these paintings, as the tribe who painted them were all massacred or killed by disease during the 1873 gold rush. For more information, visit **Ang-Gnarra Visitor Centre** (☎ 07-4090 3200) in Laura.

Laura

This town, 12km north of Split Rock, has a general store with food and fuel, a place for minor mechanical repairs, a post office and Commonwealth Bank agency, and an airstrip.

The **Laura Aboriginal Dance Festival** is the major event here, bringing together Aborigines from all over Cape York and other parts of Australia for three days. The festival is held in June of odd-numbered years.

The historic **Quinkan Hotel** (☎/fax 07-4060 3255; powered/unpowered sites $20/12, dm/s $15/40) offers accommodation.

Lakefield National Park

The main turn-off to Lakefield National Park is just past Laura, about a 45-minute drive.

Lakefield National Park is the second-largest national park in Queensland, and the most accessible on Cape York Peninsula. The park is best known for its **wetlands** and prolific **bird life**. The extensive river system drains into Princess Charlotte Bay on its northern perimeter. This is the only national park on the peninsula where fishing is permitted.

There's a good **QPWS camping ground** (per person/family $4/16), with showers and toilets, at Kalpowar Crossing. Contact **Laura QPWS** (☎ 4060 3260) or **Lakefield QPWS** (☎ 07-4060 3271), further north in the park, to arrange permits.

About 26km before Musgrave is the resort **Lotus Bird Lodge** (☎ 1800 674 974, 07-4060 3295; www.cairns.aust.com/lotusbird; r incl meals & tours $195).

Princess Charlotte Bay, which includes the coastal section of Lakefield National Park, is the site of some of Australia's biggest **rock-art galleries**. Unfortunately, the bay is extremely hard to reach except from the sea.

LAURA TO ARCHER RIVER ROADHOUSE

North from Laura, the roads deteriorate further. At the 75km mark, there's the Hann River crossing and **Hann River Roadhouse** (☎ 07-4060 3242; Peninsula Developmental Rd; powered sites $14, s/d $25/50, mains $10-15), a pit stop selling food, petrol and, of course, cold beers.

About 20km from here is a turn-off for the 6km drive east to **Mary Valley Station** (☎ 07-4060 3254; unpowered sites $12, s/d $30/45), a cattle property offering camping, homestead rooms and meals. It's also home to one of the largest colonies of little red flying foxes in the world, an amazing sight when they take to air in the late evening.

Another 62km on is **Musgrave**, with its historic Musgrave Telegraph Station, built in 1887, and **Musgrave Roadhouse** (☎ /fax 07-4060 3229; unpowered sites $12, s/d $40/50).

Coen, 108km north of Musgrave, has a pub, two general stores, hospital, school and police station; you can get mechanical repairs done here. Coen has an airstrip and a racecourse, where **picnic races** are held in August. **Homestead Guest House** (☎ 07-4060 1157; s/tw $40/60) has simple, clean rooms. **Exchange Hotel** (☎ 07-4060 1133; fax 07-4060 1180; s/d from $40/60; ☺ breakfast and dinner) has pub rooms.

The Archer River crossing, 65km north of Coen, used to be a real terror, but now, with its concrete causeway, is quite easy. **Archer River Roadhouse** (☎ /fax 07-4060 3266; unpowered sites per 2 people $12, s/d $45/60; ☺ 7am-10pm), on the banks of the Archer River, is a great place to stop and enjoy a cold beer and the famous Archer Burger.

Northern National Parks

Three national parks can be reached from the main track north of Coen. To stay at them you must be totally self-sufficient. Only about 3km north of Coen, before the Archer River Roadhouse, you can turn west to the remote **Mungkan Kandju National Park**. The **ranger station** (☎ 07-4060 3256) is in Rockeby, about 75km off the main track. Contact the **Coen QPWS** (☎ 07-4060 1137) for more info.

Roughly 21km north of the Archer River Roadhouse, a turn-off leads 135km through the **Iron Range National Park** to the tiny coastal settlement of Portland Roads. Although still pretty rough, this track has been improved. Register with the **ranger** (☎ 07-4060 7170) on arrival; camping is permitted at designated sites. The national park has Australia's largest area of lowland rainforest, with some animals that are found no further south in Australia.

The **Jardine River National Park** includes the headwaters of the Jardine and Escape Rivers, where explorer Edmund Kennedy was killed by Aborigines in 1848.

WEIPA

☎ 07 / pop 2502

Weipa is a bauxite-mining town of red dirt, coconut palms and intermittent danger signs. The mine here works the world's largest deposits of bauxite (the ore from which aluminium is processed).

Weipa Camping Ground (☎ 4069 7871; www.fishing cairns.com.au/page13-7c.html; powered/unpowered sites $20/18, cabins from $60; ☒) operates as the town's informal tourist office, books mine and fishing tours, and provides permits for nearby campsites. It's a relaxed camping ground by the waterfront, close to the shops and has facilities for people with disabilities.

NORTH TO THE JARDINE

After Batavia Downs there is almost 200km of rough road and numerous river crossings (the Dulhunty being the major one) before you reach the **Jardine River Ferry & Roadhouse** (☎ 07-4069 1369; ☺ 8am-5pm). From the Wenlock River there are two possible routes to the Jardine ferry: the more direct but rougher old route (Telegraph Rd, 155km), and the longer but quicker bypass roads (193km), which branch off the old route about 40km north of the Wenlock River. Don't miss **Twin Falls**, one of the most popular camping and swimming spots on the Cape; there's a signpost off the main road about 90km before the roadhouse.

The river crossing, run by the Injinoo Community Council, operates during the Dry only ($88 return, plus $11 for trailers). The fee includes a permit for bush camping in designated areas north of the river.

Stretching east to the coast from the main track is the impenetrable country of **Jardine River National Park**. The Jardine River spills more fresh water into the sea than any other river in Australia.

THE TIP

The first settlement north of the Jardine River is **Bamaga**, home to Cape York Peninsula's largest Torres Strait Islander community.

QUEENSLAND

There's a post office (and Commonwealth Bank agency), hospital, supermarket, bakery, mechanic and some places to stay.

Resort Bamaga (☎ 07-40693050; www.resortbamaga.com.au; r $180-225, mains $20-30; ❄ ☎) is the only four-star accommodation on the Cape. If you need some luxury, then this is the place. 4WD hire available.

Seisia, on the coast 5km northwest, has the central **Seisia Resort & Campground** (☎ 1800 653 243, 07-4069 3243; www.fishingcairns.com.au/page 13-7d.html; unpowered sites $22, s/d $90/115).

Northeast of Bamaga, off the Cape York track and about 11km southeast of Cape York, is **Somerset**, established in 1863 as a haven for shipwrecked sailors and a signal to the rest of the world that this was British territory. The aim was to become a major trading centre, but trading functions were moved to Thursday Island in 1879. There's nothing much left now except lovely views.

On the western side of the Tip is the scenic **Punsand Bay Safari & Fishing Lodge** (☎ 07-4069 1722; fax 07-4069 1403; unpowered sites $22, safari tents $120, cabins $170; ☎). This place is very well set up and it runs 4WD tours.

THURSDAY ISLAND & TORRES STRAIT ISLANDS

Torres Strait Islands have been a part of Queensland since 1879, the best known of them being Thursday Island (or TI as it's locally known). The 70 other islands are sprinkled from Cape York in the south to almost Papua New Guinea in the north.

Torres Strait Islanders came from Melanesia and Polynesia about 2000 years ago, bringing with them a more material culture than that of mainland Aboriginal people.

It was a claim by Torres Strait Islander Eddie Mabo to traditional ownership of Murray Island that led to the High Court handing down its groundbreaking Mabo ruling. The court's decision in turn became the basis for the Federal government's 1993 Native Title legislation; see the boxed text, p40.

Thursday Island is hilly and just over 3 sq km. It was once a major pearling centre, and the cemeteries tell the hard tale of that dangerous occupation. Some pearls are still produced here from seeded 'culture farms'. The island is a friendly, easy-going place, and its main appeal is its cultural mix – Asians, Europeans and Pacific Islanders have all contributed to its history.

Peddells Ferry Island Tourist Bureau (☎ 07-4069 1551; www.peddellsferry.com.au; Engineers Wharf; ☼ 8.30am-5pm, to noon Sat) will tell you everything you need to know.

Sights & Activities

There are fascinating reminders of Thursday Island's rich history about town. The **All Souls Quetta Memorial Church** was built in 1893 in memory of the shipwreck of the *Quetta* which struck an unchartered reef in the Adolphus Channel in 1890, with 133 lives lost.

The Japanese section of the town's cemetery is crowded with hundreds of graves of pearl divers who died from decompression sickness. The **Japanese Pearl Memorial** is dedicated to them. **Green Hill Fort**, on the western side of town, was built in 1893, when there were fears of a Russian invasion.

Sleeping & Eating

Jardine Motel (☎ 07-4069 1555; www.jardinemotel.com.au; cnr Normanby St & Victoria Pde; s/d $135/155; ❄ ☎ ☎) has four-star deluxe accommodation, and the budget **Jardine Lodge** (s/d $95/115, without bathroom $75/95), which has full use of the motel facilities. Self-contained flats are available.

Other options:

Grand Hotel (☎ 07-4069 1557; 6 Victoria Pde; s/d from $110/150) Ocean and mountain views.

Federal Hotel (☎ 07-4069 1569; Victoria Pde; s/d $95/135, d without bathroom $60; ☎) Classic Queenslander, with motel and pub rooms, harbour views and counter meals.

Rainbow Motel (☎ 07-4069 2460; fax 07-4069 2714; Douglas St; s/d $70/100) Clean, with the best burger bar.

Getting There & Around

QantasLink (☎ 13 13 13; www.qantas.com.au) flies daily from Cairns to Thursday Island ($875 return). The airport is on Horn Island.

There are regular ferry services between Seisia and Thursday Island (one way/return $40/75, one hour) run by **Peddells Ferry Service** (☎ 07-4069 1551; www.peddellsferry.com.au; Engineers Jetty, Thursday Island). In the dry season there's a service between Punsand Bay, Panjinka and Thursday Island (one way/return $40/75).

Horn Island Ferry Service (☎ 07-4069 1011) operates between Thursday Island and Horn Island. The ferries run roughly hourly between 6am and 6pm ($6 one way, 15 minutes).

There are plenty of taxis (and water taxis) on Thursday Island.

Victoria

For Victoria's compact size, it packs a mighty punch. It's Australia's smallest mainland state (roughly as big as Great Britain). The mighty Murray River squiggles its way between Victoria and New South Wales and Bass Strait forms a frothy gap between Victoria and Tasmania.

The state's geographic interior covers all spectrums, too. In the High Country brilliant autumn colours segue into snowy ski fields and back again to sleepy summer towns, haunted by pale ghost gums. Dry plains in the Western District are home to farmland and the Grampians, and the most-southern mainland tip is in the spiritually reviving Wilsons Promontory National Park. Such geographic extremes mean visitors are astonished at the bipolar climate, which wildly oscillates from windy gales to sunny skies, all between leaving the house and catching a tram! 'Four seasons in one day', Victorians will sagely remark.

Melbourne is an understated city that takes longer to know than its supposed rival, the brassy blonde with money – Sydney. But you'll learn to love Melbourne and its quirky ways. Find out how in retro bars (the upside-down lampshade is surely Melbourne's signature interior-design look?), and eat-streets lined with *baristas* foaming the creamiest lattes and most kick-ass short blacks. Around Melbourne, the hills are crisscrossed with grapevines in the wine regions of the Yarra Valley and Mornington Peninsula, and restorative mineral springs are found in the Daylesford and Hepburn Springs spa country. Wild surf pounds the coast along the death-defyingly exhilarating Great Ocean Rd, and Phillip Island plays on its incongruous reputation of hot cars and small penguins.

Come down. You'll like it. And we'll go for a pot o' Carlton.

VICTORIA

HIGHLIGHTS

- Coming a cropper at **Mt Hotham** (p585)
- Whale watching in **Warrnambool** (p545)
- Scaling rocks and hiking in the **Grampians** (p550)
- Using coffee as a recreational drug on Brunswick St, **Melbourne** (p507)
- Pretending you can sniff a 'mangosteen bouquet' during a wine tasting in the **Yarra Valley** (p528)
- Swapping your Hyundai rent-a-car for an MG after driving the **Great Ocean Road** (p535)
- Recovering from the previous highlights at **Wilsons Promontory** (p599)

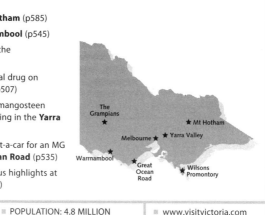

| ■ TELEPHONE CODE: 03 | ■ POPULATION: 4.8 MILLION | ■ www.visitvictoria.com |

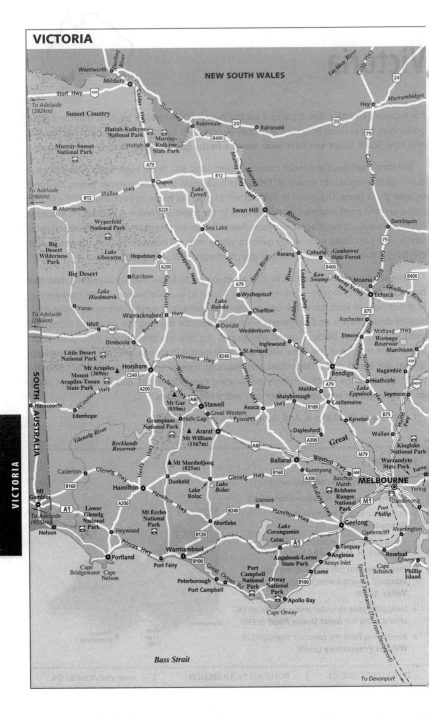

VICTORIA

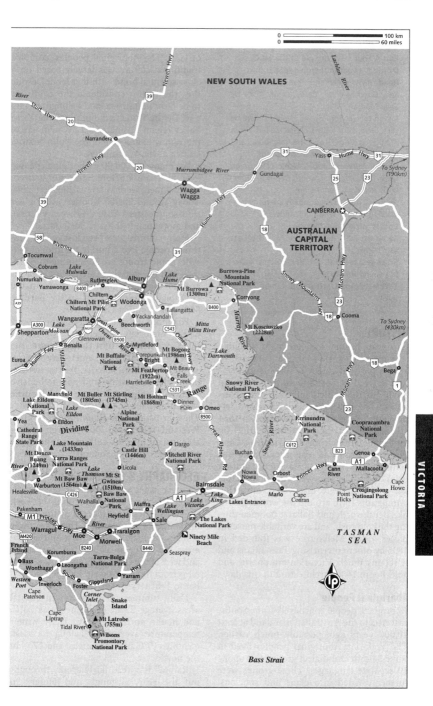

HISTORY

European history has left many tangible remains in Victoria's cities and towns. In 1803 a party of convicts, soldiers and settlers arrived at Sorrento (on Port Phillip Bay), but the settlement was soon abandoned. The first permanent European settlement in Victoria was established in 1834 at Portland (in the Western District) by the Henty family from Van Diemen's Land (Tasmania), some 46 years after Sydney was colonised. In 1851 Victoria won separation from NSW. The same year, the rich Victorian goldfields were discovered, attracting immigrants from around the world. Towns like Beechworth and Ballarat boomed during the gold rush, and are veritable museum pieces today. Melbourne was founded in 1835 by other enterprising Tasmanians and it retains much Victorian-era charm and gold-boom 1880s architecture to this day.

Aboriginal People

Aboriginal people journeyed from Southeast Asia to the Australian mainland at least 40,000 years ago, possibly much earlier. The Victorian Aboriginal peoples lived in some 38 different dialect groups that spoke 10 separate languages. These groups were further divided into clans and subclans, each with its own customs and laws, and each claiming ownership of a distinct area of land. The Aboriginal peoples' complex traditional culture was largely based on a close spiritual bond with that land. Despite this, the British considered the continent to be *terra nullius* – a land belonging to no one. Before British colonisation, the Yarra Valley region was occupied by members of the Woi wurrung clan of the Kulin Nation, known as the Wurundjeri.

As many as 100,000 Aboriginal people lived in Victoria before Europeans arrived; by 1860 there were as few as 2000 left alive. Today around 20,000 Koories (Aborigines from southeastern Australia) live in Victoria, and more than half live in Melbourne.

Many cultures have been lost and no Victorian people live a purely traditional lifestyle. Some groups are attempting to revive their cultures and there are cultural centres around the state, including those in the Grampians National Park, in the Barmah State Forest and at Cann River.

For more information about the history of the Victorian indigenous people, visit the **Koorie Heritage Trust Cultural Centre** (Map pp472-3; ☎ 03-8622 2600; www.koorieheritagetrust .com; 295 King St, central Melbourne; ☺ 10am-4pm Mon-Fri) or the interesting and comprehensive Bunjilaka indigenous centre at Melbourne Museum (p492). *Aboriginal Melbourne – The Lost Land of the Kulin People*, by Gary Presland (re-released 2001), also gives valuable insight into the culture and life of the region's original inhabitants.

GEOGRAPHY & CLIMATE

Victoria has a temperate four-seasons climate, although the distinctions between the seasons are often blurred by the unpredictability of the weather. There are three climatic regions: the southern and coastal areas, the alpine areas, and the areas north and west of the Great Dividing Range. Winter is from June to August; summer December to February.

Daily summer temperatures in coastal areas average 25°C, in alpine areas 20°C, and in the northwest 35°C. Daily winter temperatures average 14°C along the coast, a chillier 10°C in alpine areas, and 17°C in the northwest.

Rainfall is spread fairly evenly throughout the year, although mid-January to mid-March tends to be the driest period. Victoria's wettest areas are the Otway Ranges and the High Country. Because of exposure to frequent cold fronts and southerly winds, the coastal areas are subject to the most changeable weather patterns.

The weather is generally more stable north of the Great Dividing Range. The Wimmera and Mallee regions have the lowest rainfall and the highest temperatures.

It snows during the alpine high country winter; the closest snow to Melbourne is on Mt Donna Buang (p529).

INFORMATION

For more comprehensive information check out Lonely Planet's *Victoria* guide. Other useful statewide information services:

Information Victoria (Map pp472-3; ☎ 1300 366 356; 356 Collins St, central Melbourne) A government-run bookshop stocking a wide variety of publications about Melbourne and Victoria.

Melbourne Visitor Information Centre (Map pp472-3; ☎ 03-9658 9658; Federation Sq, central Melbourne; ☼ 9am-6pm)

Parks Victoria (☎ 13 19 63; www.parkweb.vic.gov.au) Manages Victoria's national parks.

Royal Automobile Club of Victoria (RACV; Map pp472-3; ☎ 13 19 55; www.racv.com.au; 422 Little Collins St, central Melbourne) Produces the excellent *Victoria Experience Guide*, full of accommodation and touring information.

Travellers' Aid Society of Victoria (Map pp472-3; ☎ 03-9654 2600; Level 2, 169 Swanston St, central Melbourne; ☼ 8am-5pm Mon-Fri) Free assistance for stranded travellers, information, advice, showers and wheelchair-access toilets.

NATIONAL PARKS

Despite its relatively small size (by Australian standards anyway), Victoria has an enormous range of national parks with vastly different weather and terrain, from the remote red sandstone ridges and dunes of the Big Desert Wilderness Park (p556) and the frostbitten peaks of the Alpine National Park (p582) to the spectacular rugged mountains of Wilsons Promontory National Park (p599).

Victoria has 39 national parks, 30 state parks and three wilderness parks, making up around 17% of the state's total area. In November 2002 the state Labor government proclaimed Victoria's new marine national parks system, which established 13 marine national parks and 11 marine sanctuaries in a bid to protect vulnerable marine plants and animals. **Parks Victoria** (☎ 13 19 63; www.parkweb.vic.gov.au), which has a useful 24-hour information line, manages Victoria's national parks.

ACTIVITIES
Boating & Sailing

Hiring a houseboat and puttering along the Murray River is a distinctly peaceful holiday. There are hire options in Mildura (p560), Swan Hill (p562) and Echuca (p564). Prices vary wildly: in the low season, a two-bedroom houseboat might cost $950 per week; in late December and January the same boat might cost $3000.

There is a whole flotilla of yacht clubs based around Melbourne's Port Phillip Bay, and plenty of schools where you can learn to sail (p496). Other popular sailing areas include the Gippsland Lakes District (p603) and Lake Eildon (p589).

Bushwalking

For national-park news and updates, and detailed descriptions of national-park trails, see the website of **Parks Victoria** (www.parkweb.vic.gov.au). For bushwalking clubs contact the **Federation of Victorian Walking Clubs** (☎ 03-9455 1876; http://home.vicnet.net.au/~vicwalk).

The High Country, with its spectacular alpine scenery and spring wildflowers, has a wide range of walks for different fitness and skill levels. Favourite stomping grounds include Mt Baw Baw National Park (p582), Mt Hotham (p585) and Mt Buffalo National Park (p586).

If coastal treks are more your pace, head south to Wilsons Promontory National Park (p601), with marked trails from Tidal River and Telegraph Bay that can take anywhere from a few hours to a couple of days. Expect squeaky white sands and aquamarine waters, pristine bushland teeming with wildlife, distinctive orange rocks and stunning coastal vistas.

Other popular areas to flex your calf muscles are the Grampians National Park (p550), with well-marked walking tracks past waterfalls and sacred Aboriginal rock-art sites; Croajingolong National Park (p610), offering rugged inland treks; and the accessible Kinglake National Park, with its thick eucalypt forest.

VICTORIA

Long-distance walks in Victoria include the **Great Southwest Walk** (www.greatsouthwestwalk .com), a 250km loop that starts near Portland; the Australian Alps Walking Track, a 760km walk from near Walhalla (p602) to Canberra; and the Victorian section of the **Bicentennial National Trail** (☎ 1300 138 724; http://home.vicnet.net.au/~bnt; PO Box 259, Oberon, NSW 2787) through the High Country.

Canoeing & Kayaking

Canoeing Victoria (☎ 03-9459 4251; www.canoevic .org.au) publicises upcoming events and offers beginners' courses.

Melbourne's Yarra River is popular with paddlers – more exciting grade-three rapids are higher up in the Warrandyte State Park.

Keen canoeists hankering for multiday trips head to the Glenelg River (p548) in the southwest. The river works its way through deep gorges with stunning riverside wildflowers and bird life.

Canoe hire costs anywhere from $35 to $75 per day, depending on the operator.

Sea kayaking around Apollo Bay (p541) offers opportunities to see wildlife such as sea lions, gannets, penguins and dolphins.

Cycling

Excellent sources of information for pedal-pushers include **Bicycle Victoria** (☎ 03-8636 8888; www.bv.com.au) and the **Melbourne Bicycle Touring Club** (☎ 03-9517 4306; www.mbtc.org.au). **Bike Paths Safe Escapes** (www.bikepaths.com.au) is a comprehensive guide to the state's best cycling tracks, featuring colour maps, useful cycling tips and a list of the best café pit stops en route. Lonely Planet's *Cycling Australia* guide covers five multiday rides in Victoria, including the Great Ocean Rd and the High Country. **Railtrails Australia** (☎ 03-9306 4846; www.railtrails.org.au) describes routes along disused railway lines.

For more information on bicycle hire in Melbourne, see p495.

Diving

Some of Victoria's diving is world class. It can get a little chilly, and 7mm wetsuits or even drysuits are needed.

Port Phillip Bay has some excellent sites. The Bellarine Peninsula is popular, with Queenscliff a good base. Other areas include Torquay, Anglesea, Lorne, Apollo Bay, Port Campbell and Portland (all on the Great Ocean Rd; p535); Flinders, Sorrento and Portsea (on the Mornington Peninsula; p530); and Wilsons Promontory (p599) and Mallacoota (p609) on the east coast.

Horse Riding

Some of the state's best riding is found in Mansfield (p590), Dinner Plain (p586) and Mt Beauty (p589) in the High Country, and a swag of companies offer visitors the chance to find their inner jackaroo. Prices average $30 for a one-hour ride, $70 for a half-day ride and $140 for a full-day ride. For trail-blazing inspiration watch the legendary 1982 romance, *The Man from Snowy River*, about Aussie 19th-century cattlemen in Victoria's High Country.

Rock Climbing

Rock climbers have plenty of tantalising cliffs and crags to conquer in Victoria. Mt Arapiles (p555), in the Western District near Horsham, is world famous for its huge variety of climbs for all skill levels, with colourful names such as Violent Crumble, Punks in the Gym and Cruel Britannia. Not far away is the Grampians National Park (p550), where rock climbing and abseiling have become increasingly popular as new areas like Mt Stapylton and Black Ian's Rock are developed. At Mt Buffalo (p586), in the Victorian Alps, there is a great variety of good granite climbs, including those on the Buffalo Gorge wall. For more information about rock-climbing sites, contact the **Victorian Climbing Club** (www.vicclimb.org.au).

Skiing & Snowboarding

Skiing in Victoria has come a long way from its modest beginnings in the 1860s when Norwegian gold miners started sliding around Harrietville in their spare time. Today it's a multimillion-dollar industry with three major and six minor ski resorts. The season officially commences in the first weekend of June; skiable snow usually arrives later in the month, and often stays until the end of September. For more information see www.visitvictoria.com /ski, and consult the **Official Victorian Snow Report** (www.vicsnowreport.com.au/report.html) or **Mountain Information Line** (☎ 1902 240 523; per min 55c) for the latest on snow, weather and road conditions.

The snowfields are northeast and east of Melbourne, scattered around the High Country. The two largest ski resorts are Mt Buller (p584) and Falls Creek (p587). Mt Hotham (p585) is smaller, but has equally good skiing, while Mt Baw Baw (p582) and Mt Buffalo (p586) are smaller resorts, popular with families and less-experienced skiers.

Resort entry fees are usually around $26 per car per day in winter; cross-country skiers pay a trail-use fee of approximately $10/5 per adult/child, plus a car entry fee of around $10. As a rough guide, you're likely to pay around $35 for equipment hire and around $85/44/225 per adult/child/family for daily lift tickets in high season (late June to mid-September). Note that hire rates are cheaper if you hire for longer periods.

Surfing

With its exposure to the Southern Ocean swell, Victoria's coastline provides quality surf.

Local and international surfers gravitate to Torquay (p535), home to legendary brands Quiksilver and Ripcurl, as well as the Surfworld Museum. Nearby, Bells Beach (p536) plays host to the Ripcurl Pro Tour every Easter.

The Shipwreck Coast (p543), west of Cape Otway as far as Peterborough, offers possibly the most powerful waves in Victoria. It faces southwest and is open to the sweeping swells of the Southern Ocean. The swell is consistently up to a metre higher than elsewhere, making it the place to go if you're after big waves.

For the less experienced, popular places with surf schools include Anglesea (p538), Lorne (p539) and Phillip Island (p533).

Telephone surf reports (☎ 1900 931 996, Mornington Peninsula ☎ 1900 983 268) are updated daily. Other useful resources for surfers include **Surfing Australia** (www.surfingaustralia.com) and **Peninsula Surf** (www.surfshop.com.au).

TOURS

If you don't feel like travelling solo, or you crave a hassle-free journey, contact **Autopia Tours** (☎ 1800 000 507, 03-9419 8878; www.autopia tours.com.au), **Go West** (☎ 03-9828 2008; www.gowest .com.au) and **Wild-Life Tours** (☎ 03-9741 6333; www .wildlifetours.com.au), which all offer day trips (starting from $65) to popular destinations,

including the Great Ocean Rd, Grampians and Phillip Island Penguin Parade. Other possibilities:

Echidna Walkabout (☎ 03-9646 8249; www.echidna walkabout.com.au) Runs nature ecotrips (from day trips to five-day expeditions) featuring bushwalking and koala spotting.

Eco Adventure Tours (☎ 03-5962 5115; www.hotkey .net.au/~ecoadven) Offers fascinating guided night walks in the Yarra Valley and the Dandenong Ranges. Ideal for animal lovers.

Ecotrek: Bogong Jack Adventures (☎ 08-8383 7198; www.ecotrek.com.au) Runs a wide range of cycling, canoeing and walking tours through the Grampians, Murray River and High Country regions.

Steamrail Victoria (☎ 03-9397 1953; www.steamrail .com.au) Gives visitors the chance to step back in time, catching a steam train and paddle steamer on a day trip to Echuca. Other destinations include Warrnambool and Hanging Rock.

Backpacker Buses

If you're travelling between Melbourne and either Sydney or Adelaide, and want to visit some of the highlights of Victoria along the way, there are some interesting hop-on, hop-off bus tour alternatives. Tours listed here travel scenic routes, some of them allowing for stopovers en route.

Groovy Grape (☎ 1800 661 177; www.groovygrape .com.au) Has three-day trips between Adelaide and Melbourne, taking in the Great Ocean Rd and the Grampians, for $260.

Oz Experience (☎ 1300 300 028; www.ozexperience .com) This backpackers' bus line is a hop-on, hop-off bus with a party atmosphere, suited to young travellers. Offers trips from Sydney to Melbourne and along the coastal road to Adelaide.

Wayward Bus (☎ 1300 653 510; www.waywardbus .com.au) Runs a variety of routes through southeastern Australia, most of them connecting Melbourne with Adelaide or Sydney. Its Classic Coast tour between Melbourne and Adelaide, along the Great Ocean Rd, costs $295 including hostel accommodation.

GETTING THERE & AROUND

Unless you're driving, Melbourne is usually the main entry and exit point for Victoria.

International and domestic flights operate from **Melbourne Airport** (www.melair.com .au) at Tullamarine. **Avalon Airport** (www.avalon airport.com.au), near Geelong, also operates domestic flights.

All bus and train services within country Victoria are operated by **V/Line** (☎ 13 61 96;

www.vline.com.au). One-way economy adult fares are quoted in this chapter but there are cheaper deals when travelling off-peak. You can buy tickets over the phone, online and at local train stations. Long-distance trains and buses all run to and from Melbourne's **Southern Cross station** (☎ 03-9670 2873; Spencer St), which was formerly known as Spencer St station. **Greyhound Australia** (☎ 13 14 99; www.greyhound.com.au), **Firefly** (☎ 1300 730 740; www.fireflyexpress.com.au) and **Premier Motor Service** (☎ 13 34 10; www.premierms.com.au) are bus companies servicing routes to/from Victoria.

If you're travelling to/from Tasmania by boat, the *Spirit of Tasmania* docks at Port Melbourne (see p518 for details).

Note that there are border restrictions preventing fruit being carried into or out of Victoria in an effort to stop the spread of fruit fly (see the boxed text, p1069, for more information).

See the Transport chapter (p1035) and Melbourne's Getting There & Away (p518) and Getting Around sections (p518) for more comprehensive details. See Tours (p465) for alternative transport routes.

MELBOURNE

☎ 03 / **pop 3.21 million**

Melbourne's residents are fuelled by the best coffee in Australia, yet the city still runs at a slow pace. Trams lumber back and forth along the city's grid, the routes radiating out as spokes from central Melbourne, and cycling is a common way to travel between suburbs. It's also becoming increasingly fashionable to buzz about town on a scooter.

The natural geographic feature of the Yarra River, bisecting the city with its wiggly border, meant that the area was prime settling land for Europeans in the 1830s, and the ornate Victorian-era architecture and leafy, established boulevards reflect this history. Cutting-edge, futuristic developments such as Federation Sq – the city's new meeting place – and the waterfront development of the Docklands provide a striking contrast, creating an artistic, architectural melange.

Character-filled neighbourhoods, such as Fitzroy, St Kilda and Carlton, hum with life

and the city just happens to produce some of the most innovative art, music, cuisine, fashion, performance, design and ideas in the country. Melburnians are also a sporty bunch (spectators, mostly) who go ballistic around AFL football finals (when the MCG is packed with a 90,000-strong crowd roaring 'BALL!') and during Spring Racing Carnival, when the country pauses to watch their horse lose the Melbourne Cup. They love to shop, eat and attend the myriad festivals that the city offers, and have a perverse sense of pride in complaining about the city's kooky, unpredictable weather.

HISTORY

In May 1835 John Batman 'bought' around 240,000 hectares of land from the Aborigines of the Kulin clan, who were the traditional owners. The concept of buying or selling land was foreign to the Aboriginal culture and in an extremely one-sided exchange they received some tools, flour and clothing.

By 1840 there were more than 10,000 Europeans living in the Melbourne area. The wealth from the goldfields built a city that was known as 'Marvellous Melbourne' and this period of prosperity lasted until the depression at the end of the 1880s.

Post-WWII Melbourne's social fabric has been greatly enriched by an influx of people and cultures from around the world. Several building booms have altered the city physically so that it's now a striking blend, with ornate 19th-century buildings sitting alongside towering skyscrapers and what seems like a million modern apartment complexes (many of them empty).

ORIENTATION

Melbourne Airport (p518), 22km from the city centre, is Melbourne's main entry point, but Jetstar airlines is also utilising Avalon Airport (p518) near Geelong. See p518 for information on travelling to/from the city's airports. If arriving by bus, you'll be dropped at the Southern Cross station coach terminal (p518). Flinders St station is the main station for suburban trains.

Melbourne hugs the shores of Port Phillip Bay, with the city centre on the north bank of the Yarra River, about 5km inland. The city centre is bordered by the Yarra to the south, Fitzroy Gardens to the east, Victoria St to the north and Spencer St to the west (although the Docklands has extended the western border and Federation Sq is changing the southeastern border).

The main streets running east–west in the city's block-shaped grid are Collins and Bourke Sts, crossed by Swanston and Elizabeth Sts. The heart of the city is Bourke St Mall and Chinatown along Little Bourke St.

Most places of interest to travellers are in the central business district (CBD) or inner suburbs and easily accessed by public transport.

Maps

The *Melbourne Visitors Map* is available at the **Melbourne Visitor Information Centre** (Map pp472-3; Federation Sq) or the **Melbourne Visitor Booth** (Map pp472-3; Bourke St Mall).

Street directories published by Melway (the most popular), Gregory's and UBD are detailed and handy if you're driving.

They can be purchased from newsagents and bookshops for around $50.

Map Land (Map pp472-3; ☎ 9670 4383; 372 Little Bourke St) has a wide selection of mapping materials.

INFORMATION
Bookshops

Borders (Map p478; ☎ 9824 2299; Jam Factory, 500 Chapel St, South Yarra)

Brunswick St Bookstore (Map pp476-7; ☎ 9416 1030; 305 Brunswick St, Fitzroy) A Fitzroy fixture with a broad selection of titles and drool-worthy art and design tomes (upstairs).

Cosmos Books & Music (Map p475; ☎ 9525 3852; 112 Acland St, St Kilda) Good selection of books and music.

Foreign Language Bookshop (Map pp472-3; ☎ 9654 2883; 259 Collins St) Foreign-language books, dictionaries, magazines and even board games.

Hares & Hyenas (Map p478; ☎ 9824 0110; 135 Commercial Rd, Prahran) This is a specialist gay and lesbian bookshop.

MELBOURNE IN...

Two Days

And your time starts...now!

Join the ranks of coffee-obsessed locals by knocking back a couple of lattes along **Brunswick St** (p507) or **Degraves St** (p505). With your heart kick-started, tackle a big-ticket culture item – perhaps the bugs at **Melbourne Museum** (p492); the Arkleys and Nolans at **National Gallery of Victoria: International** (p489); or meerkats and jungle mammals at **Melbourne Zoo** (p492).

Is it lunchtime yet? Picnic under a massive tree at the **Royal Botanic Gardens** (p490), slurp up a slithery bowl of noodles in **Chinatown** (p505), or scoff skyscraper-high cakes along Acland St in **St Kilda** (p493) – the **Monarch** (☎ 9534 2972; 103 Acland St; cakes $2-30; ☺ lunch-late) has consistently delicious *Kugelhoph* (a sponge cake marbled with spices and chocolate). Burn it off with our city **walking tour** (p496), and take in a spot of retail therapy with a monster shop along **Chapel St** (p517), or head to the wonderful **Queen Victoria Market** (p480) for consumables and cheap jeans.

Rest tired legs while sharpening your mind with a contemporary, film-buff-approved flick at the **Australian Centre for the Moving Image** (ACMI; p469). Finish off an evening with a wander around **Federation Sq** (p469), especially at dusk when the big screen is illuminated and the **Victorian Arts Centre** (p515) spire beckons theatre-goers. Hole up in a city bar – if you can find the **Croft Institute** (p513) or **Honkytonks** (p513), you're nearly a local!

Four Days

With four days to play with, you can take a jaunt outside the city perimeter. Get your bearings by ascending to the highest point in town at **Melbourne Observation Deck** (p479) in Rialto Towers. Shouting yourself hoarse at an AFL match at the **MCG** (p491) brings you back down to earth.

If it's sunny, spend time in seaside **St Kilda** (p493) and take a sojourn to **Williamstown** (p494). Other watery pursuits involve shark feeding at **Melbourne Aquarium** (p489) or a **Melbourne River Cruise** (p498) – you'll dock at **Southgate** (p506) when it's over.

In summer **Moonlight Cinema** (p514) or the **Twilight Jazz sessions** (p492) at Royal Melbourne Zoo are picnic-packing fun.

VICTORIA

Little Bookroom (Map pp472-3; ☎ 9670 1612; 185 Elizabeth St) Long-established children's book specialist.

Reader's Feast (Map pp472-3; ☎ 9662 4699; cnr Bourke & Swanston St) City bookshop with a solid range of titles, including travel guides and travel literature.

Readings (Map pp476-7; ☎ 9347 6633; 309 Lygon St, Carlton) A Carlton institution that has more than survived a Borders opening across the road.

Travellers Bookstore (Map pp476-7; ☎ 9417 4179; 294 Smith St, Collingwood) There's a travel agent on the premises.

Emergency

Dial ☎ 000 for ambulance, fire or police.

Lifeline Counselling (☎ 13 11 14; ⊙ 24hr)

Police station (Map pp472-3; ☎ 9247 5347; 228-232 Flinders Lane; ⊙ 24hr)

RACV Emergency Roadside Service (☎ 13 11 11; ⊙ 24hr)

Royal Women's Hospital Centre Against Sexual Assault (Map pp476-7; ☎ 9344 2201; Royal Women's Hospital, 132 Grattan St, Carlton; ⊙ 24hr)

Travellers' Aid Society of Victoria (Map pp472-3; ☎ 9654 2600; Level 2, 169 Swanston St; ⊙ 8am-5pm Mon-Fri) Free assistance for stranded travellers, information, advice, showers and wheelchair-access toilets.

Internet Access

Email addicts are well catered for. There are Internet cafés dotted about the CBD and inner-city suburbs, and most hostels and guesthouses have a few portals, many of which are free. Almost every hotel will have phone jacks in the room, and many now have broadband access.

E:fiftyfive (Map pp472-3; ☎ 9620 3899; 55 Elizabeth St; per hr from $2) Recently voted the most stylish Internet café by Yahoo Mail Internet Awards.

Net City (Map pp475; ☎ 9525 3411; 7/63 Fitzroy St, St Kilda; per hr from $4.50; ⊙ 9.30am-11pm)

World Wide Wash (Map pp476-7; ☎ 9419 8214; 361 Brunswick St, Fitzroy; per hr $6) Wash your clothes while you surf.

Internet Resources

http://melbourne.indymedia.org A self-published website dedicated to nonmainstream reportage.

www.melbourne.citysearch.com.au Will tell you where to eat, drink and be merry, wherever you find yourself in Melbourne.

www.melbourne.vic.gov.au The official city website.

www.thatsmelbourne.com.au Reams of information about things to see and do around town.

www.theage.com.au The home page of Melbourne's quality broadsheet newspaper.

www.visitmelbourne.com The official tourism website for the city.

Media

In Melbourne, the **Age** (www.theage.com.au) is the daily broadsheet newspaper and the **Herald Sun** (www.heraldsun.com.au) is the major tabloid. Street press thrives in Melbourne – pick up a free copy of the following from cafés, pubs, bookshops and record stores. *Beat* and *Inpress* are the main music rags with listings of gigs playing around town, music news and events. *Bnews*, *MCV* and *Melbourne Star* are the GLBTI (gay-lesbian-bisexual-transgender-intersex) papers.

Medical Services

Dental Emergency Service (Map pp476-7; ☎ 9341 1040; Royal Dental Hospital of Melbourne, 720 Swanston St, Carlton; ⊙ 8.30am-9.15pm)

Mulqueeny Midnight Pharmacy (Map p478; ☎ 9510 3977; cnr Williams Rd & High St, Prahran; ⊙ 9am-midnight)

There are three major public hospitals with 24-hour accident and emergency wards close to the city centre:

Alfred Hospital (Map pp470-1; ☎ 9276 2000; Commercial Rd, Prahran)

Royal Melbourne Hospital (Map pp470-1; ☎ 9342 7000; Grattan St, Parkville)

St Vincent's Hospital (Map pp476-7; ☎ 9288 2211; 41 Victoria Pde, Fitzroy)

Money

There are foreign-exchange booths at Melbourne Airport's international terminal, and they are open to meet all arriving flights. In the city, your best bet is probably **American Express** (Map pp472-3; ☎ 1300 139 060; 233 Collins St) which offers a commission-free service if you use its travellers cheques.

Post

Suburban branches of Australia Post are in every suburb.

Melbourne GPO (General Post Office; Map pp472-3; ☎ 13 13 18; cnr Little Bourke & Elizabeth Sts; ⊙ 8.30am-5.30pm Mon-Fri, 9am-4pm Sat, 10am-4pm Sun) Poste restante available.

Tourist Information

Information Victoria (Map pp472-3; ☎ 1300 366 356; 356 Collins St) A government-run bookshop stocking a wide variety of publications about Melbourne and Victoria.

Melbourne Visitor Booth (Map pp472-3; 9am-5pm Mon-Fri, 10am-5pm Sat & Sun) A small information booth in Bourke St Mall.

Melbourne Visitor Information Centre (Map pp472-3; ☎ 9658 9658; Federation Sq; 9am-6pm) Multilingual assistance is available for booking tours and accommodation. It runs the Melbourne Greeter Service, where volunteers offer half-day walking tours of the city – book at least three days ahead.

Met Shop (Map pp472-3; ☎ 13 16 38; Town Hall, cnr Swanston & Little Collins Sts; 8.30am-5.30pm Mon-Fri, 9am-1pm Sat) For information about Melbourne's public transport.

Travel Agencies

Flight Centre (☎ 13 13 13, 9670 0477; www.flight centre.com.au)

STA Travel (☎ 9349 2411; www.statravel.com.au)

YHA Australia (Map pp472-3; ☎ 9670 9611; www.yha.com.au; 83 Hardware Lane)

SIGHTS

Melbourne has a raft of attractions, most of which are mainly clustered in the streets and cobbled alleyways of the city centre, and extending to the inner-city suburbs. Arty Fitzroy has fashionable Brunswick St as its centrepiece, while seaside St Kilda is a flashier princess with vestiges of its seedy history slowly being eradicated. Carlton is the Italian district where Alpha Romeos growl along Lygon St; Richmond is where you head for steaming bowls of Vietnamese noodles and roast duck; maritime Williamstown is a village-style seaside port; and East Melbourne is where you'll find the 'G' – the Melbourne Cricket Ground. The burgeoning riverfront precincts of Docklands and Southgate also attract a host of happy-snapping tourists.

City Centre

FEDERATION SQUARE

A riotous explosion of steel, glass and abstract geometry, **Federation Sq** (Map pp472-3; www.fedsq.com) has become the city's new hub, creating a focal point for the city centre and connecting it with the Yarra River. Visitors and locals gather en masse and cultural events take place regularly.

The **Ian Potter Centre: National Gallery of Victoria Australia** (NGV; Map pp472-3; ☎ 8662 1553; www.ngv.vic.gov.au/ngvaustralia; Federation Sq; admission free; 10am-5pm Mon-Thu, 10am-9pm Fri, 10am-6pm Sat & Sun) houses more than 20,000 pieces of Australian art, from the colonial to modern periods. Newer works include sculptor Ricky Swallow's iMan skulls and Howard Arkley's airbrushed renditions of Melbourne suburbia. The ground floor features the popular Aboriginal and Torres Strait Islander collection. Admission is charged for temporary exhibitions.

The **Australian Centre for the Moving Image** (ACMI; Map pp472-3; ☎ 9663 2583; www.acmi.net.au; Federation Sq; 10am-6pm) is a museum dedicated to film, TV and digital media. Catch a cinematic gem, script reading or film festival at the regular **Popcorn Taxi** (www.popcorntaxi.com.au) events.

Melbourne's first new major park in over 100 years, **Birrarung Marr** (Map pp472-3; ☎ 9658 9955; Batman Ave) was built in conjunction with Federation Sq. In its centre, the **Federation Bells** play a variety of compositions. The park can be reached from the Federation Sq car park, from Batman Ave or by walking along the river. **Artplay** (Map pp472-3; ☎ 9664 7900; www.artplay.com.au) is housed in one of the old railway buildings on the site and offers creative weekend and holiday workshops for children aged between five and 12 years.

SWANSTON STREET

Swanston St boasts some fantastic architecture, including the **Manchester Unity Building** (Map pp472-3; cnr Swanston & Collins Sts), a marvellous example of 1930s modernist Gothic architecture.

Melbourne Town Hall (Map pp472-3; tour bookings ☎ 9658 9658; townhalltour@melbourne.vic.gov.au; cnr Swanston & Collins Sts) was once the main concert venue, and the 1964 balcony appearance by the Beatles was one of its most memorable 'performances'.

Built in stages from 1854, the **State Library of Victoria** (Map pp472-3; ☎ 8664 7000; www.slv.vic.gov.au; 328 Swanston St; admission free; 10am-9pm Mon-Thu, 10am-6pm Fri-Sun) boasts a Classical Revival façade and the impressive domed **La Trobe Reading Room**.

Further along, the Edwardian baroque **Melbourne City Baths** (Map pp476-7; ☎ 9663 5888; www.melbournecitybaths.com.au; cnr Swanston & Victoria Sts) originally served as the public baths in a bid to stop locals from washing themselves in the grotty Yarra.

(Continued on page 479)

VICTORIA

See Central Melbourne Map (pp472–3)

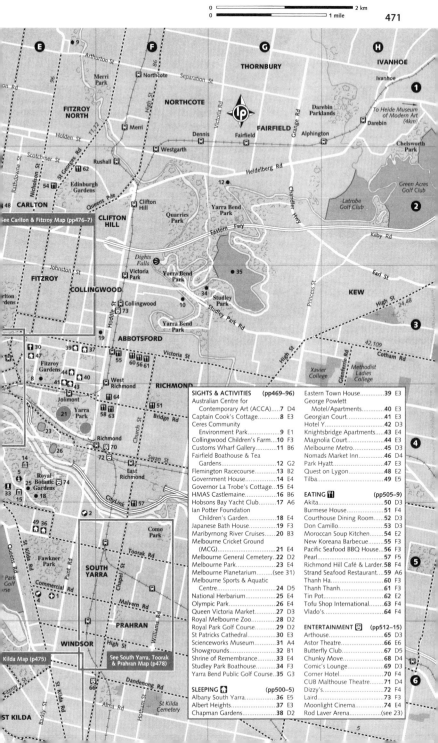

0 |===========| 2 km
0 |===========| 1 mile

THORNBURY

IVANHOE

Ivanhoe

FITZROY NORTH

NORTHCOTE

To Heide Museum of Modern Art (4km)

FAIRFIELD

Darebin Parklands

Darebin

Chelsworth Park

Dennis Fairfield

Alphington

Westgarth

Heidelberg Rd

Green Acres Golf Club

Rushall

Latrobe Golf Club

CARLTON

Edinburgh Gardens

See Carlton & Fitzroy Map (pp476–7)

CLIFTON HILL

Quarries Park

Yarra Bend Park

Kilby Rd

Clifton Hill

FITZROY

Dights Falls

Victoria Park

Yarra Bend Park

Earl St

Eastern Fwy

COLLINGWOOD

Collingwood

Studley Park

KEW

High St

Yarra Bend Park

ABBOTSFORD

Victoria St

Xavier College

Methodist Ladies College

RICHMOND

West Richmond

Fitzroy Gardens

Jolimont

Yarra Park

Richmond

East Richmond

Swan St

CityLink

Como Park

SOUTH YARRA

Toorak Rd

Royal Botanic Gardens

Fawkner Park

PRAHRAN

Malvern Rd

Chapel St

WINDSOR

High St

Dandenong Rd

Alma Rd

ST KILDA

St Kilda Cemetery

St Kilda Map (p475)

See South Yarra, Toorak & Prahran Map (p478)

SIGHTS & ACTIVITIES	(pp469–96)
Australian Centre for Contemporary Art (ACCA)	**7** D4
Captain Cook's Cottage	**8** E3
Ceres Community Environment Park	**9** E1
Collingwood Children's Farm	**10** F3
Customs Wharf Gallery	**11** B6
Fairfield Boathouse & Tea Gardens	**12** G2
Flemington Racecourse	**13** B2
Government House	**14** E4
Governor La Trobe's Cottage	**15** E4
HMAS Castlemaine	**16** B6
Hobsons Bay Yacht Club	**17** A6
Ian Potter Foundation Children's Garden	**18** E4
Japanese Bath House	**19** F3
Maribyrnong River Cruises	**20** B3
Melbourne Cricket Ground (MCG)	**21** E4
Melbourne General Cemetery	**22** D2
Melbourne Park	**23** E4
Melbourne Planetarium	(see 31)
Melbourne Sports & Aquatic Centre	**24** D5
National Herbarium	**25** E4
Olympic Park	**26** E4
Queen Victoria Market	**27** D3
Royal Melbourne Zoo	**28** D2
Royal Park Golf Course	**29** D2
St Patricks Cathedral	**30** E3
Scienceworks Museum	**31** A4
Showgrounds	**32** B1
Shrine of Remembrance	**33** E4
Studley Park Boathouse	**34** F3
Yarra Bend Public Golf Course	**35** G3

SLEEPING	(pp500–5)
Albany South Yarra	**36** E5
Albert Heights	**37** E3
Chapman Gardens	**38** D2

Eastern Town House	**39** E3
George Powlett Motel/Apartments	**40** E3
Georgian Court	**41** E3
Hotel Y	**42** D3
Knightsbridge Apartments	**43** E4
Magnolia Court	**44** E3
Melbourne Metro	**45** D3
Nomads Market Inn	**46** D4
Park Hyatt	**47** E3
Quest on Lygon	**48** E2
Tilba	**49** E3

EATING	(pp505–9)
Akita	**50** D3
Burmese House	**51** F4
Courthouse Dining Room	**52** D3
Don Camillo	**53** D3
Moroccan Soup Kitchen	**54** E2
New Koreana Barbecue	**55** F3
Pacific Seafood BBQ House	**56** F3
Pearl	**57** F5
Richmond Hill Café & Larder	**58** F4
Strand Seafood Restaurant	**59** A6
Thanh Ha	**60** F3
Thanh Thanh	**61** F3
Tin Pot	**62** E2
Tofu Shop International	**63** F4
Vlado's	**64** F4

ENTERTAINMENT	(pp512–15)
Arthouse	**65** D3
Astor Theatre	**66** E6
Butterfly Club	**67** D5
Chunky Move	**68** D4
Comic's Lounge	**69** D3
Corner Hotel	**70** F4
CUB Malthouse Theatre	**71** D4
Dizzy's	**72** F4
Laird	**73** F3
Moonlight Cinema	**74** E4
Rod Laver Arena	(see 23)

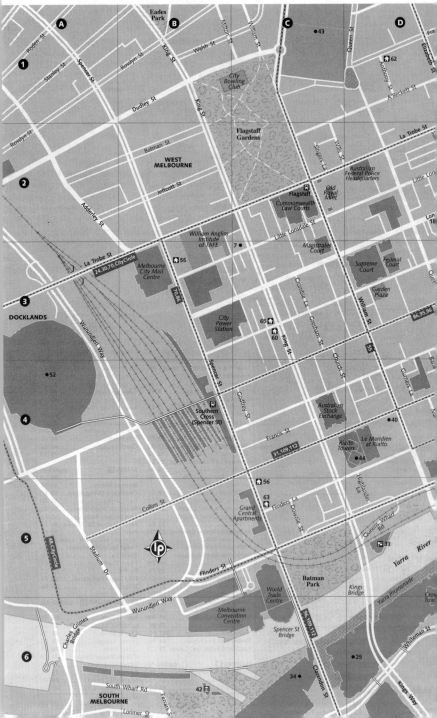

200 m
0.1 miles

E RMIT
RMIT

F

G
Royal College
of Surgeons

H
24,109
Victoria Pde

EAST
MELBOURNE

La Trobe St

Bowen St

Hayward

Bennetts La

Exploration La

99

98

Albert St

Spring St

Parliament
Gardens

St Peter's
Anglican
Church

Lonsdale St

Little Lonsdale St

Little Latrobe St

Melbourne
Central

23,24,34,CityCircle

51

Shot
Tower

121

Drewery La

96

77

123

Celestial
Ave

Tattersalls La

86

Hardware La

McKillop St

Comedy
Theatre

37

57

81

108

106

Turnbull La

93

41

St Andrews Pl

St Peters
Anglican
Church

Her
Majesty's
Theatre

88

Market
La

Exhibition St

73

85

Marthur Pl

St Francis
Church

Melbourne
Central

109

97

104

Celestial La

86

Little Bourke St

79

80

100

101

94

72

Parliament

Myer

67

10

19,57,59,60

Elizabeth St

Cohen Place

Crossley St

Liverpool St

Russell St

Meyers Pl

Windsor Pl

CityCircle

39

Treasury Pl

114

120

122

118

8

11

16

Royal La

92

Little Collins St

Nauru
House

105

31,42,109,112

113

Treasury
Gardens

45

Union La

70

110

46

49

115

17

Collins St

2

103

Collins
Place

66

Flinders St

MELBOURNE

23

Australia
on Collins

22

36

32

1

20

107

KPMG
House

83

George Pde

Grand
Hyatt

101
Collins

119

68

64

Wellington
Pde

Wellington
Pde South

5

Collins St

333 Collins

3

58

71

City
Square

78

112

116

89

90

102

Flinders St

Batman Ave

70

26

4

6

13

50

76

111

Forum
Theatre

84

Flinders St

59

117

Flinders
St

21

75

12

27

30

Federation
Square

19

Birrarrung
Marr

Flinders St

8,70,75,CityCircle

Princes
Bridge

125

35

Sandridge Bridge

124

82

87

29

Boat sheds

Alexandra
Gardens

Yarra River

Boathouse Dr

Queens
Bridge

74

48

28

Capital City Trail

Alexandra Ave

Southbank Promenade

Riverside Quay

Eureka
Tower

Cook St

Australian
Ballet
Centre

53

3,5,6,8,16,35,64,67,72

Queen
Victoria
Gardens

SOUTHBANK

City Rd

54

38

Linlithgow Ave

47

St Kilda Rd

Sturt St

Southbank Blvd

Kings
Domain

Power St

Kavanagh St

Dodds St

CityLink Burnley Tunnel

CityLink Domain Tunnel

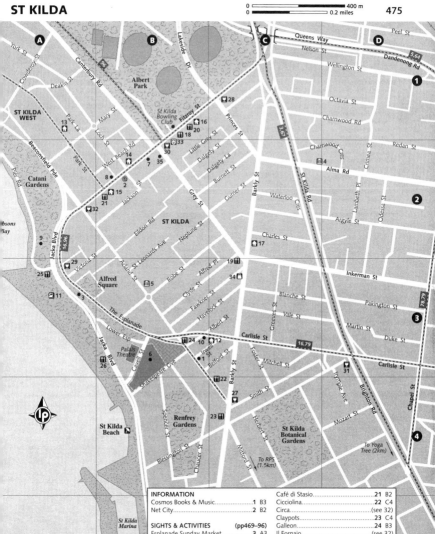

INFORMATION	
Cosmos Books & Music	**1** B3
Net City	**2** B2

SIGHTS & ACTIVITIES	(pp469–96)
Esplanade Sunday Market	**3** A3
Jewish Museum of Australia	**4** C2
Linden Art Centre & Gallery	**5** B3
Luna Park	**6** B3
Neighbours Ramsay St Tour	**7** B2
Rock 'n' Roll Skate Hire	**8** B2
Royal Melbourne Yacht Squadron	**9** A2
St Kilda Cycles	**10** B3
St Kilda Sea Baths	**11** A3

SLEEPING	(pp500–5)
Base	**12** C3
Cabana Court Motel	**13** A1
Hotel Tolarno	**14** B2
Marque	**15** B2
Medina Executive St Kilda	**16** B1
Olembia Guesthouse	**17** C2
Prince	(see 32)

EATING	(pp508–9)
Baker D Chirico	**18** B1
Bedouin Kitchen	**19** C3
Café a Taglio	**20** B1
Café di Stasio	**21** B2
Cicciolina	**22** C4
Circa	(see 32)
Claypots	**23** C4
Galleon	**24** B3
Il Fornaio	(see 32)
Soul Mama	**25** A3
Stokehouse	**26** B3

DRINKING	(pp511–12)
Doulton Bar	**27** C4
Elephant & Wheelbarrow	**28** C1
Esplanade Hotel	**29** A3
George Public Bar	**30** B2
Girl Bar	(see 32)
Greyhound Hotel	**31** D3
Mink	(see 32)
Prince of Wales	**32** A2

ENTERTAINMENT	(pp512–15)
George Cinemas	**33** B2
Prince Bandroom	(see 32)

SHOPPING	(pp516–18)
Aesop	(see 32)
Honeyweather & Speight	**34** C3

TRANSPORT	(pp518–20)
St Kilda Car Hire	**35** B2

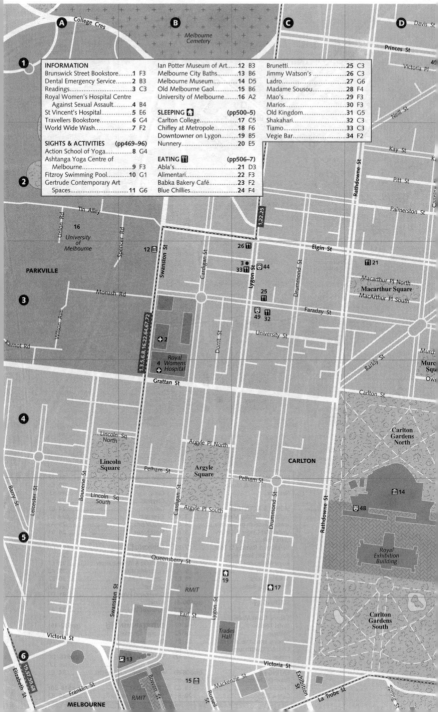

INFORMATION

Brunswick Street Bookstore	1 F3
Dental Emergency Service	2 B3
Readings	3 C3
Royal Women's Hospital Centre Against Sexual Assault	4 B4
St Vincent's Hospital	5 E6
Travellers Bookstore	6 G4
World Wide Wash	7 F2

SIGHTS & ACTIVITIES (pp469–96)

Action School of Yoga	8 G4
Ashtanga Yoga Centre of Melbourne	9 F3
Fitzroy Swimming Pool	10 G1
Gertrude Contemporary Art Spaces	11 G6
Ian Potter Museum of Art	12 B3
Melbourne City Baths	13 B6
Melbourne Museum	14 D5
Old Melbourne Gaol	15 B6
University of Melbourne	16 A2

SLEEPING (pp500–5)

Carlton College	17 C5
Chifley at Metropole	18 F6
Downtowner on Lygon	19 B5
Nunnery	20 E5

EATING (pp506–7)

Abla's	21 D3
Alimentari	22 F3
Babka Bakery Café	23 F2
Blue Chillies	24 F4
Brunetti	25 C3
Jimmy Watson's	26 C3
Ladro	27 G6
Madame Sousou	28 F4
Mao's	29 F3
Marios	30 F3
Old Kingdom	31 G5
Shakahari	32 C3
Tiamo	33 C3
Vegie Bar	34 F2

CLIFTON HILL

York St
Queens Pde
Council St

E **F** Brunswick St **G** **H**

Alexandra Pde
(Eastern Hwy)
🚻 10

Cecil St

Westgarth St

Brunswick St

Leicester St

Fitzroy St

47 🎭

🍴 34

Rose St

40 🍺
46 🎭

🍴 23

Napier St

Kerr St

George St

7 @

35 🍺
1 ●
30 🍴

9 ●

Argyle St

51 🎭

Budd St

Nicholson St

Spring St

Johnston St
50 🎭

Victoria St

Mahoney St

29 🍴

22 🍴

Chapel St

Young St

Greeves St

Bell St

56 🛍

28 🍴

Exhibition St

St David St

John St

41 🍺

🍴 112

Kent St

Moor St

37 🍺

Sackville St

38 🍺

Johnston St

Smith St

Bedford St

Perry St

54 🎭

● 6
8 ●
86

Otter St

COLLINGWOOD

Hodgson St

🍴 39

Moor St

Stanley St

Vere St

🍴 24

King William St

FITZROY

Condell St

31 🍴

Hanover St

Charles St

Atherton
Reserve

Webb St

Nicholson St

120

Brunswick St

Napier St

George St

Little Gore St

Gore St

Little Oxford St

Oxford St

Cambridge St

Dight St

John St

Palmer St

Royal La

Gertrude St

53 🎭

🏠 18

Young St

Little Napier St

86

11

36 🎭

55 🛍🍴🎭 43

42 🍺

27 🍴

Peel St

52 🎭

Wellington St

Glasshouse Rd

Langridge St

Derby St

Little Victoria St

Little Smith St

Smith St

Mason St

Victoria Pde

24,109

INFORMATION	
Borders	(see 14)
Hares & Hyenas	1 A4
Mulqueeny Midnight Pharmacy	2 D6

SIGHTS & ACTIVITIES	(p493)
Como House	3 D1

SLEEPING	(pp500–5)
Como	4 B2
Hotel Claremont	5 B2
Toorak Manor	6 D3

EATING	(pp508–9)
Borsch Vodka & Tears	7 B5
Da Noi	8 A2
Jacques Reymond	9 D6
Orange	10 B6
Prahran Market	11 A4

DRINKING	(p511)
Back Bar	12 B6
Candy Bar	13 B5

ENTERTAINMENT	(pp512–15)
Cinema Europa	14 B3
Market Hotel	15 A4
Revolver	16 B5
Xchange Hotel	17 A4

SHOPPING	(pp516–18)
Dinosaur Designs	18 B2
Greville Records	19 A5
RM Williams	20 B4

(Continued from page 469)

COLLINS STREET

Collins St is one of Melbourne's most elegant streetscapes. Its fashionable 'Paris end' is lined with plane trees (lit up beautifully with fairy lights at night), grand buildings and upmarket European boutiques (Chanel, Hermes etc). From Elizabeth to Spencer Sts, it is the home of bankers and stockbrokers.

Facing each other on the corners of Russell and Collins Sts are the 1873 decorative Gothic **Scots Church** (Map pp472–3; 140 Collins St) and the 1866 **St Michael's Uniting Church** (Map pp472–3; 120 Collins St), built in the Lombardic Romanesque style. The **Athenaeum Theatre** (Map pp472–3; 188 Collins St) dates back to 1886 and is topped by a statue of Athena, the Greek goddess of wisdom. Across the road is the magnificent **Regent Theatre** (Map pp472–3; 191 Collins St).

Block Arcade (Map pp472–3), which runs between Collins and Elizabeth Sts, was built in 1891 and is a beautifully intact 19th-century shopping arcade. Its design was inspired by the Galleria Vittorio in Milan and features intricate mosaic-tiled floors, marble columns, Victorian window surrounds and the magnificently detailed plasterwork of the upper walls. The arcade has been fully restored, and houses some specialist shops. Connecting Block Arcade with Little Collins St, **Block Place** (Map pp472–3) is a bustling lane filled with cafés, outdoor tables, an endless stream of caffeine fiends and a few clothes shops.

The block between William and King Sts provides a striking contrast between the old and the new. The Gothic façade of the three **Olderfleet Buildings** (Map pp472–3; 471-477 Collins St) has been well preserved, and **Le Meridien at Rialto** (Map pp472–3; 495 Collins St) is an imaginative five-star hotel behind the façades of two marvellous old Venetian Gothic buildings. These older buildings are dwarfed by the soaring **Rialto Towers** (Map pp472–3; 525 Collins St), Melbourne's tallest building. On the 55th floor is the justifiably popular **Melbourne Observation Deck** (Map pp472–3; ☎ 9629 8222; www .melbournedeck.com.au; adult/child/concession $12.50/7/9; ⌚ 10am-10pm), which offers spectacular 360-degree views. You can get to the top by stairs (more than 1250 of them) or by ear-popping elevator.

BOURKE STREET

The area in and around Bourke St is home to the city's main department stores and some high-street vendors. The mall section between Swanston and Elizabeth Sts is closed to traffic, and pedestrians share the **Bourke St Mall** with an assortment of buskers and trams. On the corner of Bourke and Elizabeth Sts is the **GPO building** (Map pp472–3), which suffered a fire in September 2001 and has risen from the ashes in its new incarnation of an agglomeration of specialty stores and stylish boutiques (see p517). On the other side of the mall, the **Royal Arcade** (Map pp472–3; www.royalarcade.com.au), built from 1869 to 1870, is Melbourne's oldest arcade.

SPRING STREET

The **Old Treasury Building** (Map pp472–3; ☎ 9651 2233; www.oldtreasurymuseum.org.au; Spring St; adult/concession $8.50/5; ⌚ 9am-5pm Mon-Fri, 10am-4pm Sat & Sun) was built in 1858 with basement vaults to store much of the £200 million worth of gold mined from the Victorian goldfields. It now houses three permanent exhibitions in the **Gold Treasury Museum**.

The **Windsor Hotel** (Map pp472–3; ☎ 9633 6000; www.thewindsor.com.au; 103 Spring St) is a marvellous reminder of 19th-century gold-boom Melbourne. It's still the city's grandest hotel and many of Australia's prime ministers have slept in its palatial suites.

Parliament House of Victoria (Map pp472–3; ☎ 9651 8568; www.parliament.vic.gov.au; Spring St; ⌚ Mon-Fri) runs free half-hour tours from Monday to Friday when parliament isn't in session. Ask about the second ceremonial mace that went missing from the Lower House in 1891 – rumour has it that it ended up in a brothel.

CHINATOWN

Little Bourke St has been the centre for Melbourne's Chinese community since the gold rush. In the 1850s the Chinese set up shop alongside brothels, opium dens, boarding houses and herbalists; these days the area is more salubrious and dominated by restaurants. It still retains its industrious, entrepreneurial air though, and is a sensory delight. Juicy roast ducks hang in the windows, shoe shops sport kooky shoes for tiny feet and height-giving boots, and grocers and dry-goods stores stock all manner of mushrooms and powders for Chinese cooking.

VICTORIA

The interesting **Museum of Chinese Australian History** (Map pp472-3; ☎ 9662 2888; 22 Cohen Pl; adult/concession $6.50/4.50; ☼ 10am-5pm) documents the long history of Chinese people in Australia. The entrance of the museum used to be guarded by Dai Loong, a huge Chinese dragon that has since been replaced by the 218kg Millennium Dragon, which snakes its way through the city streets during Chinese New Year (see p498). The museum also conducts two-hour walking tours around Chinatown (adult/concession $15/12) at 11am Monday to Friday.

QUEEN VICTORIA MARKET

Chaotic, friendly, multicultural – the **Queen Victoria Market** (Map pp470-1; ☎ 9320 5822; www .qvm.com.au; 513 Elizabeth St; ☼ 6am-2pm Tue & Thu, 6am-6pm Fri, 6am-3pm Sat, 9am-4pm Sun) is the grand dame of all Melbourne markets. It was officially designated as a market in 1878. The land had been put to varying uses beforehand, from cattle yards to part of Melbourne's first cemetery – an estimated 9000 bodies still remain under the car park!

Pick your way through the throng, avoiding the odd jabbing elbow and squashed fruit underfoot, to find everything from perfectly ripe Brie to next season's fashion. The bustling **night market** (☼ 5.30-10pm Wed) runs between late November and mid-February. Eating a bratwurst on a Saturday morning, while listening to musicians outside the deli, is a thigh-slappin' Melbourne must.

OLD MELBOURNE GAOL

This gruesome old gaol, now a penal **museum** (Map pp476-7; ☎ 9663 7228; Russell St; adult/child $12.50/7.50; ☼ 9.30am-5pm), is at the northern end of Russell St. In all, 135 prisoners were hanged here. It's a dark, dank, and spooky place, and its displays include death masks and histories of noted bushrangers and convicts, Ned Kelly's iconic armour and the very gallows from which Ned was hanged. There are some rather camp candlelight tours (not suitable for children under 12) of the gaol at 7.30pm on Wednesday, Friday, Saturday and Sunday (adult/child/family $60/20/13); book through **Ticketek** (☎ 13 28 49).

IMMIGRATION MUSEUM

The very inspiring **Immigration Museum** (Map pp472-3; ☎ 9927 2700; 400 Flinders St; adult/concession & child $6/free; ☼ 10am-5pm), in the Old Customs

House (1858–70), offers a sensitive historical account that mixes display and audio in a mesmerising way – it'll help you discover what makes Australians tick. The building alone is worth a visit; with its stunning Long Room, it is a magnificent piece of Renaissance Revival architecture.

DOCKLANDS

Near the rear of Southern Cross station, the **Docklands** (Map pp472-3; ☎ 1300 663 008; www.dock lands.vic.gov.au) was once a wetland and lagoon area used by Koories as a hunting ground. Until the mid-1960s it was the city's main industrial and docking area. When demand for larger berths to accommodate modern cargo vessels necessitated a move, the Docklands was left a virtual wasteland.

With its close proximity to the city centre, the area has become the focus of Melbourne's next big development boom and the city's seemingly unquenchable thirst for yet another precinct. The 52,000-seat **Telstra Dome** (Map pp472-3; ☎ 8625 7700) is the city's alternative footy arena, with a state-of-the-art sliding roof. Other sporting and entertainment events take place here on a regular basis. **Tours** (☎ 8625 7277; adult/child $13/5) of the stadium are conducted on weekdays.

The remaining precincts of the Docklands, which comprise about 200 hectares of land and water, are being developed into residential, entertainment, dining and business zones that resemble a carefully cultivated city-state of slick amenities. One interesting landmark to note on your visit here is the Webb Bridge, a sinuous structure reminiscent of a Koorie eel trap.

FITZROY & TREASURY GARDENS

The leafy **Fitzroy Gardens** (Map pp470-1; www .fitzroygardens.com; btwn Wellington Pde & Clarendon Lansdowne & Albert Sts) divide the city centre from East Melbourne and serve as a verdant retreat from city life. With their stately avenues lined with English elms, these gardens are a popular spot for weddings and photographers who immortalise brides and grooms on their big day. In the centre of the gardens are ferneries, fountains and a café By the kiosk is a miniature **Tudor village** and the **Fairies' Tree**, carved in 1932 by the write Ola Cohn. The painted carvings around the

(Continued on page 489)

Surfers Paradise (p325), Queensland

Waterfall in Lamington National Park
(p333), Queensland

Catamarans at Noosa River, Noosa (p337),
Queensland

City Botanic Gardens (p298), Brisbane

Roller coaster at Sea World (p327), Gold Coast, Queensland

The waterfront and commercial buildings of Brisbane (p290)

PAUL DYMOND

Daintree National Park (p447), Queensland

Lady Musgrave Island (p362) on the Great
Barrier Reef, Queensland

LEE FOSTER

Beaches and rainforest of Cape Tribulation (p449)

JOHN BANAGAN

Bush tucker from the Daintree (p447), Queensland

OLIVER STREWE

CHRIS MELLOR

Dingo (p358), the wild dog of Australia

Birdsville Hotel (p385), outback Queensland

Yarra River (p491), Melbourne

State Library of Victoria (p469), Melbourne

Yarra River and Southbank (p489), Melbourne

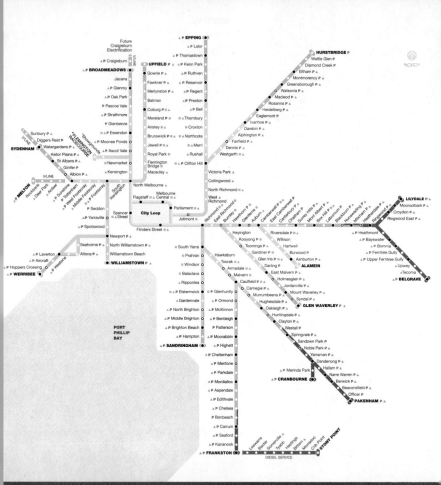

Melbourne Train Network

GLENN BEANLAND

Studley Park Boathouse (p491) on the Yarra River, Melbourne

Montsalvat chapel, Yarra Valley (p528), Victoria

CHRIS MELLOR

William Ricketts Sanctuary (p529), Dandenong Ranges, Victoria

PABLO GARCIA GASTAR

AFL football at the Melbourne Cricket Ground (p491), Melbourne

Block Place (p479), Melbourne

Royal Botanic Gardens (p490), Melbourne

(Continued from page 480)

base of the tree depict fairies, pixies, kangaroos, possums and emus.

In the northwestern corner of the gardens is the **People's Path**, which is a circular path paved with 10,000 individually engraved bricks, and is the nicest bit of whimsy in any park in Melbourne.

Captain Cook's Cottage (Map pp470-1; ☎ 9419 4677; www.cookscottage.com.au; adult/child $4/2; ☒ 9am-5pm) is actually the former Yorkshire home of the distinguished English navigator's parents. It was dismantled, shipped to Melbourne and reconstructed stone by stone in 1934. The cottage is furnished and decorated as it would have been around 1750, complete with handmade furniture and period fittings.

Nearby, the **Conservatory** (admission free; ☒ 9am-5pm), built in 1928, is looking a little dated from the outside, but the glorious floral displays and tropical-rainforest atmosphere inside are well worth a look.

The smaller **Treasury Gardens**, a popular lunchtime and BBQ spot, contain a **memorial to John F Kennedy**, who may not seem the most obvious candidate for a Melbourne memorial, but it's a soothing place to unwind regardless.

FLAGSTAFF GARDENS

The **Flagstaff Gardens** (Map pp472–3), near the Queen Victoria Market, were first known as Burial Hill – it's where most of the early settlers ended up. As the hill provided one of the best views of the bay, a signalling station was set up here. When a ship was sighted arriving from Britain, a flag was raised on the flagstaff to notify the settlers. Later, a cannon was added and fired when the more important ships arrived. The gardens are a popular alfresco lunch spot, and free lunchtime concerts are held in the warmer months.

Southbank

Across the river from the city centre you'll find the arts precinct; the Southgate complex with three levels of restaurants (p506), cafés and bars, all with city skyline and river views; and further west, Crown Casino.

ARTS PRECINCT

This small area on St Kilda Rd is the high-culture heart of Melbourne.

The **National Gallery of Victoria: International** (NGVI; Map pp472-3; ☎ 8620 2222; www.ngv.vic.gov.au; 180 St Kilda Rd; admission free; ☒ 10am-5pm) has an internationally renowned European section, with works by masters including Rembrandt, Picasso, Turner, Monet, Titian, Pissarro and van Dyck. The sculpture courtyard and gallery has some fine works such as sculptures by Auguste Rodin and Henry Moore. The gallery's full collection is too large for permanent display, so many temporary exhibits are featured. The stained-glass ceiling of the **Great Hall** took five years to create and the best way to see it is to lie on your back on the floor.

The **Victorian Arts Centre** (VAC; Map pp472-3; ☎ 9281 8000; www.vicartscentre.com.au; 100 St Kilda Rd) is made up of two separate buildings: the Melbourne Concert Hall and the Theatres Building. The interiors of both buildings are stunning. **Hamer Hall** (Map pp472–3) is a major performance venue and base for the Melbourne Symphony Orchestra (MSO). The **Theatres Building** (Map pp472–3) is topped by its distinctive Eiffel-inspired spire (illuminated at night), underneath which are housed the State Theatre, the Playhouse and the George Fairfax Studio. One-hour tours of the centre ($10) are offered at noon and 2.30pm from Monday to Saturday, and a special backstage tour for adults only ($14) is offered at 12.15pm on Sunday. Call for bookings. There's an arts and crafts **market** (☒ 10am-5pm Sun) in the Arts Centre undercroft, with a variety of goods on offer, many with an Australian bent. The **Performing Arts Museum** (admission free) in the Theatres Building has changing exhibitions on all aspects of the performing arts. The museum is open whenever the building is open.

The resolutely modern **Australian Centre for Contemporary Art** (Map pp470-1; ☎ 9654 6422; www.accaonline.org.au; 111 Sturt St; admission free; ☒ 11am-6pm Tue-Sun) often resembles a rusting hulk that has run aground. You can find cutting-edge art, or attend regular lectures, screenings and dance performances here (it's the home of the state's dance company, Chunky Move; p59).

MELBOURNE AQUARIUM

Highlights of the **Melbourne Aquarium** (Map pp472-3; ☎ 9620 0999; www.melbourneaquarium.com.au; cnr Queenswharf Rd & King St; adult/child/concession $22/12/14; ☒ 9.30am-6pm Feb-Dec, 9.30am-9pm Jan)

VICTORIA

include its floor-to-ceiling coral tank, the 360-degree fishbowl viewing area and the 2.2-million-litre oceanarium. Silky stingrays and grey nurse sharks are the big-ticket items, especially if you catch a feeding session when the divers swim with the sharks. It's hard to beat a dive with the sharks ($124 to $264, depending on your experience and equipment needs).

CROWN CASINO & ENTERTAINMENT COMPLEX

The 24-hour, nonstop cavalcade of illuminated excess that is the **Crown Casino & Entertainment Complex** (Map pp472-3; ☎ 9292 8888; www .crowncasino.com.au; Southbank; ☽ 24hr) was fleetingly the world's largest casino (it's still the biggest in the southern hemisphere) and has had an enormous effect on Melbourne. Blamed for numerous urban crises over the years (from kids left locked in cars to underworld money laundering), the casino still manages to attract plenty of customers.

MELBOURNE EXHIBITION CENTRE

The **Melbourne Exhibition Centre** (Map pp472-3; ☎ 9205 6401; www.mecc.com.au; 2 Clarendon St) is the slick-looking building situated across the street from the casino. The centre hosts trade exhibitions and fairs – everything from Sexpo to Santa's Kingdom. You may hear this building referred to as 'Jeff's Shed' by locals – a reference to former premier Jeff Kennett.

POLLY WOODSIDE MARITIME MUSEUM

The low-key **Polly Woodside Maritime Museum** (Map pp472-3; ☎ 9699 9760; Lorimer St E; adult/child/ concession $10/6/8; ☽ 10am-4pm) is on the riverfront, close to the Melbourne Exhibition Centre. An old iron-hulled sailing ship dating from 1885, the *Polly Woodside* has been lovingly restored by volunteers and is now the museum's centrepiece.

Kings Domain

Beside St Kilda Rd, which runs past the huge **Kings Domain**, stands the massive **Shrine of Remembrance** (☽ 10am-5pm), which was built as a memorial to Victorians killed in WWI. Its design was partly based on the Temple of Halicarnassus, one of the seven ancient wonders of the world.

Near the shrine is **Governor La Trobe's Cottage** (Map pp470-1; ☎ 9654 4711; cnr Birdwood Ave &

Dallas Brooks Dr; admission $2; ☽ 11am-4pm Mon, Wed, Sat & Sun), the original Victorian government house sent out from the mother country in prefabricated form in 1840. The more imposing **Government House** (Map pp470-1; ☎ 9656 9800; Government House Dr; adult/child $11/5.50; ☽ guided tours Mon, Wed & Sat, bookings essential) is where Victoria's governor resides, and is a copy of Queen Victoria's palace on England's Isle of Wight.

The **Old Melbourne Observatory** (Birdwood Ave) and National Herbarium are at the main entrance to the Royal Botanic Gardens. At the city end of the park is the **Sidney Myer Music Bowl** (Map pp470-1), a functional outdoor performance area in a natural amphitheatre.

ROYAL BOTANIC GARDENS

Certainly the finest botanic gardens in Australia, and among the finest in the world, the **Royal Botanic Gardens** (Map pp472-3; ☎ 9252 2300; www.rbg.vic.gov.au; Birdwood Ave; admission free; ☽ 7.30am-8.30pm Nov-Mar, 7.30am-5.30pm Apr-Oct) is one of Melbourne's most glorious attractions. The beautifully designed gardens sprawl beside the Yarra River, and feature plants from Australia and around the world. Mini-ecosystems, such as the cacti and succulents area, herb garden and Australian rainforest, are set amid the vast lawns. Take a book, a picnic or Frisbee; most importantly, take your time.

Along with the abundance of plant species there's a surprising amount of wildlife, including ducks, swans and eels in and around the ornamental lake, and cockatoos and possums.

The gardens are encircled by the **Tan**, a 4km running track that is Melbourne's favourite venue for joggers and walkers (and talkers). During the summer months, **Moonlight Cinema** (p514) flickers in the dark and **theatre performances** are staged.

A guided tour of the gardens departs from the **visitors centre** (☎ 9252 2429; Birdwood Ave; ☽ 9am-5pm Mon-Fri, 9.30am-5.30pm Sat & Sun) at 11am and 2pm daily except Saturday (adult/concession $4.50/3.50); bookings required. The gardens offer a variety of tours including an **Aboriginal Heritage Walk** (p498). Next door is the **National Herbarium**, which was established in 1853 and contains 1.2 million dried botanical specimens used for identification purposes.

Along the Yarra River

Melbourne's prime natural feature, the 'mighty' Yarra River, is the butt of countless jokes but it's actually a scenic river. Boat cruises depart from **Princes Walk** (just east of Princes Bridge) and **Southgate** (p498) or there's a series of cycling and walking paths.

YARRA BEND PARK

Northeast of the city centre, the Yarra River is bordered by **Yarra Bend Park** (Map pp470-1; www.parkweb.vic.gov.au), much loved by runners, rowers, cyclists, picnickers and strollers.

The **Studley Park Boathouse** (Map pp470-1; ☎ 9853 1972; Boathouse Rd, Studley Park; ☺ 9am-5pm) dates back to the 1860s, and houses a restaurant, kiosk and café. There are also boats, canoes and kayaks available for hire ($22 per hour per two-person canoe). Kane's suspension bridge takes you across to the other side of the river, and it's about a 20-minute walk from here to **Dights Falls** (Map pp470–1).

Further upriver, the **Fairfield Boathouse & Tea Gardens** (Map pp470-1; ☎ 9486 1501; www.fairfieldboathouse.com; Fairfield Park Dr, Fairfield; ☺ 9am-5pm Mon-Fri summer, 11am-4pm Mon-Fri winter, 8.30am-late Sat & Sun year-round) is a restored 19th-century boathouse with broad verandas and a garden restaurant.

Yarra Park & Melbourne Park

Yarra Park contains the Melbourne Cricket Ground (MCG) and Richmond Cricket Ground. The adjoining Melbourne Park contains the Melbourne Park National Tennis Centre, Olympic Park, Vodafone Arena and several other ovals.

MELBOURNE CRICKET GROUND

The **MCG** ('the G'; Map pp470-1; ☎ 9657 8888; www.mcg.org.au; Brunton Ave) is the temple in which sports-mad Melburnians worship their heroes. One of the world's great sporting venues, it's imbued with an indefinable combination of tradition and atmosphere. The MCG's first game of Australian Rules football was played in 1858 and in 1877 the first test cricket match between Australia and England was played here. The MCG was also the central stadium for the 1956 Melbourne Olympics, and in 2006 the opening and closing ceremonies of the Commonwealth Games will take place here. **Tours** (☎ 9657 8879; adult/concession $10/6) depart every half-hour (except on match days) from 10am to 3pm, and last for 1¼ hours.

Parkville & Carlton

Up this end of town you'll find a cosmopolitan area that blends the intellectual with the recreational, the multicultural with the mainstream.

THE YARRA RIVER

Victorians are staunchly proud of the Yarra River, which wends its way through the Yarra Valley east of Warburton, emptying into Port Phillip Bay. Its name is believed to have come from Aboriginal words meaning 'ever flowing', and it's also known as the 'upside-down river' because of its brown colour – it's muddy, but not particularly dirty.

During the gold rush, however, the river was treated appallingly: it became an open drain for raw sewage (until 1900) and a dumping ground for industrial waste. Environmental efforts in recent decades have purified the water and beautified its tree-lined banks, but recent environmental testing has discovered overly high bacteria levels in the water, prompting the minister for the environment to take action.

The river bisects Melbourne geographically and socially. 'Crossing the river' is a phrase you'll often hear bandied about by locals – the northern and western suburbs have always been working-class areas, but inner-southern and eastern suburbs are now seen as the more affluent areas, sparking a friendly rivalry. The psychological barrier of crossing the river is very real and means that inner-city 'northerners' living around Fitzroy, Collingwood, Carlton and Brunswick rarely cross to visit their 'southern' compadres in St Kilda and Prahran, and vice versa.

Cycling and walking tracks (above and p518) ramble along its scenic banks, old bridges link north to south, and there are some stunning patches of bucolic splendour. On a sunny day, when rowers stroke their oars through the water, or if you're driving towards the city on a clear night, the Yarra cuts a mighty swath.

The tree-lined Royal Pde divides these two suburbs. In Parkville there's the University of Melbourne and the Royal Melbourne Zoo; in Carlton there's the Melbourne General Cemetery and some bustling restaurants in the Italian quarter around Lygon, Drummond and Rathdowne Sts.

The once-mammoth reservation of **Royal Park** (Map pp470–1), established in the 1870s, has sports ovals, stadiums, a public golf course and the Royal Melbourne Zoo.

ROYAL MELBOURNE ZOO

The **Royal Melbourne Zoo** (Map pp470-1; ☎ 9285 9300; www.zoo.org.au; Elliot Ave, Parkville; adult/child/concession $18/9/13.50; ❧ 9am-5pm) is one of the city's most popular attractions. Established in 1861, this is the oldest zoo in Australia and the third oldest in the world. Set in spacious and attractively landscaped gardens, with broad strolling paths, the zoo's enclosures are simulations of the animals' natural habitats. The walkways pass through the enclosures – you walk through the bird aviary, cross a bridge over the lions' park, enter a tropical hothouse full of colourful butterflies and walk around the gorillas' very own rainforest. There's also a large collection of native animals in a native-bush setting, a platypus aquarium, fur seals, tigers, plenty of reptiles and lots more to see. You should allow at least half a day for your visit.

In the summer months, the zoo hosts **twilight concerts**. Roar 'n' Snore is a programme that allows you to camp at the zoo and join the keepers on their morning rounds of the animal enclosures.

UNIVERSITY OF MELBOURNE

The **University of Melbourne** (Map pp476-7; ☎ 8344 4000; www.unimelb.edu.au; Grattan St, Parkville) with its Gothic-style stone buildings is well worth a wander. The **Ian Potter Museum of Art** (Map pp476-7; ❧ 10am-5pm Tue-Fri, noon-5pm Sat & Sun) is housed in a Nonda Katsalidis–designed building on Swanston St. The museum is home to the university's large collection of 19th- and 20th-century art and features regular exhibitions of contemporary art, and lectures.

MELBOURNE MUSEUM

In the middle of Carlton Gardens, **Melbourne Museum** (Map pp476-7; ☎ 13 11 02; www.melbourne.museum.vic.gov.au; 11 Nicholson St, Carlton; adult/concession & child $6/free; ❧ 10am-5pm) is billed as 'the southern hemisphere's largest and most innovative museum'. The emphasis is on education and interaction, and the main attractions include Bunjilaka, the Aboriginal Centre; a living forest gallery; and the Australia gallery, with exhibits dedicated to that great Aussie icon Phar Lap, and another dedicated to the TV show *Neighbours* (filmed in Melbourne). The Children's Museum is a great way to keep the kids entertained awhile here.

LYGON STREET

Carlton is Melbourne's Italian quarter, and Lygon St is its backbone. Many of the thousands of Italian immigrants who came to Melbourne after WWII settled in Carlton, and Lygon St became the focal point of their community.

In among the tourist restaurants and exclusive fashion boutiques, you'll still find a few of the oldies: Tiamo and Jimmy Watson's have resisted the winds of change; and La Mama, the tiny experimental theatre started by Betty Burstall in 1967, is still going strong in Faraday St – for details, see p515.

Lygon St is one of Melbourne's liveliest streets. Day and night it is always filled with people promenading, dining, sipping cappuccinos, shopping and generally soaking up the atmosphere. Each year in late October, Lygon St hosts the lively **Lygon St Festa** (see p499), a four-day food-and-fun street party.

Fitzroy & Collingwood

Fitzroy is where Melbourne's bohemian subculture moved when the lights got too bright in Carlton.

TREAT YOURSELF

There's nothing like relaxing in a good hot bath after a day of sightseeing. **Japanese Bath House** (Map pp470-1; ☎ 9419 0268; 59 Cromwell St, Collingwood; ❧ noon-11pm Tue-Fri, noon-8pm Sat & Sun) is an authentic Japanese-style bath house with segregated areas for men and women. Each area includes a deep bath and sauna, and you can also get scrubbed to within an inch of your circulation's life. Bookings essential.

Brunswick St is probably Melbourne's liveliest street, and you shouldn't visit the city without coming here. This is where you'll find some of the best food, weirdest shops, most interesting people and coolest clothes. In particular, the blocks on either side of the Johnston St intersection have a fascinating collection of young designer and retro clothes shops, bookshops, galleries, nurseries, antique dealers, pubs (the most per capita in Victoria) and, of course, more cafés and restaurants than you can poke a fork at (see p507).

Smith St forms the border between Fitzroy and Collingwood. It has a great assortment of food stores, bookshops, pubs and restaurants, including some good veggie restaurants and some Vietnamese bakeries thrown in for good measure. The whole area has a slightly down-at-the-heels look that is sure to appeal after the polished bohemian façades of Brunswick St, though the megamart discount clothing shops, north of Johnston St, detract from this grungy appeal.

Going strong for over 20 years, **Gertrude Contemporary Art Spaces** (Map pp476-7; ☎ 9419 3406; www.gertrude.org.au; 200 Gertrude St, Fitzroy; ⏰ 11am-5.30pm Tue-Fri, 1-5.30pm Sat), a nonprofit art space, holds galleries and studios, and promotes emerging artists, with some excellent exhibitions taking place throughout the year.

In **North Fitzroy** there are a few interesting, quirky shops to explore, more historic buildings, the **Edinburgh Gardens** (Map pp470-1) and a few pubs in which to enjoy an ale.

Richmond
As Carlton is to Italy so Richmond is to Vietnam, although there are still many Greek Australians living here, hangers-on from the previous wave of immigrants to adopt the suburb.

The **Bridge Rd** and **Swan St** areas are something of a discount fashion centre, with shops where many Australian fashion designers sell their seconds and rejects, alongside the outlets of some of Melbourne's popular young designers.

South Yarra & Toorak
Welcome to the 'right' side of the river – the high-society side of town. South Yarra is

a busy, style-conscious suburb. Toorak is the ritziest suburb in Melbourne, with an exclusive cluster of shops known as **Toorak Village** along Toorak Rd. The South Yarra end of Toorak Rd is an eclectic mix of shops focused squarely on the grooming industry, from laundries and top-range designer gear (for 40-plus shoppers), to spray-on tan salons. Turn the corner to the South Yarra end of **Chapel St**, between Toorak Rd and Commercial Rd, where the action is. This is ground zero for mainstream style-conscious die-hards – it's virtually wall-to-wall clothing boutiques (with a healthy sprinkling of bars and cafés).

Overlooking the Yarra River, gracious **Como House** (Map p478; ☎ 9827 2500; www.natt rust.com.au; cnr Williams Rd & Leachdale Ave, South Yarra; adult/child $11/6.50; ⏰ 10am-5pm) is one of Australia's finest colonial mansions, built between 1840 and 1859. Aboriginal rites and feasts were still held on the banks of the Yarra when the house was first built, and an early occupant wrote of seeing a cannibal rite from her bedroom window (she was undoubtedly mistaken). Tours take place half-hourly from 10.30am to 4pm.

Prahran
Prahran is a lively blend of small Victorian workers' cottages, narrow leafy streets and high-rise, government-subsidised flats for low-income earners. It's populated by people from a broad range of ethnic backgrounds and is enlivened by a variety of cultural influences.

The Prahran sector of **Chapel St** stretches from Malvern Rd down to Dandenong Rd. The highlight of the area is the excellent **Prahran Market**. Established in 1881, it still packs in the city's gourmands today.

Commercial Rd is a focal point for Melbourne's gay and lesbian communities, and has a small collection of nightclubs, bars, pubs, bookshops and several cafés.

Running west off Chapel St beside the Prahran Town Hall, **Greville St** has a quirky collection of off-beat retro/grunge clothing shops, record shops and bookshops, and some good bars and cafés. Definitely go for a wander.

St Kilda
This lively seaside suburb has a chequered history. It became home to Russian and

Polish émigrés in the 1940s and was a prestigious address where colonial entrepreneurs built enormous mansions and Melbourne's elite took seaside holidays. Hotels were constructed, dance halls opened, sea baths and fun parks catered for the crowds, and St Kilda was *the* place to go. In the 1960s and '70s, the great unwashed moved in, attracted by the raffish atmosphere and cheap rent. It was discovered in the '90s by the macchiato crowd, and wood-fired pizza become more popular than mozza-ball soup. A dingy flat became a 'studio apartment' and real-estate prices skyrocketed.

St Kilda is still a place of extremes. If you're there on a sunny day, prepare to be swept along in a tide of humanity seeking fun, food, cakes, ale, exercise, and sex, drugs 'n' sea breezes. (For details about St Kilda Festival, see p499.)

Fitzroy St and **Acland St** are the main strips, and are packed with cafés, bars, sprawling old-school pubs and pavement tables. Acland St is particularly famed for its Continental cake shops. Following **Carlisle St**, across St Kilda Rd and into Balaclava, you'll find some great Jewish bakeries and some natty boutiques and cafés.

For some contemporary art head to the historic **Linden Art Centre & Gallery** (Map p475; ☎ 9209 6794; www.lindenarts.org; 26 Acland St; admission free; ☼ 1-6pm Tue-Sun), which also has a sculpture garden for children.

The **Jewish Museum of Australia** (Map p475; ☎ 9534 0083; 26 Alma Rd; adult/child $7/4; ☼ 10am-4pm Tue-Thu, 11am-5pm Sun) houses displays relating to Jewish history and culture, the annual cycle of festivals, and the origins of Jewish life, as well as hosting regular exhibitions.

SEASIDE ST KILDA

St Kilda pier and breakwater is a favourite spot for strollers, who used to reward themselves with a coffee or a snack at **St Kilda Pier Pavilion**, a 19th-century tearoom at the junction of the pier, which burnt down in 2003. Plans were announced in September 2004 for the tearoom's reconstruction. You can still head out along the pier.

On weekends and public holidays, a **ferry** (☎ 9682 9555; adult/child $6.50/3.25) runs from the pier across the bay to Williamstown, departing St Kilda hourly between 11.30am and 4.30pm, and leaving Williamstown hourly from 11am to 4pm.

The famous laughing face of **Luna Park** (Map p475; ☎ 9525 5033; www.lunapark.com.au; Lower Esplanade; unlimited ride ticket adult/child $33.95/23.95; ☼ 11am-6pm Sat & Sun winter; 7-11pm Fri, 11am-11pm Sat, 11am-6pm Sun summer; 11am-6pm school holidays year-round), a symbol of St Kilda since 1912, will eat you up and spit you out once you've been spun round a few times. Luna Park is an old-fashioned amusement park but that's a part of its seaside charm. The old wooden roller coaster, a beautifully crafted carousel, is a highlight.

Built in 1880, the marvellous **Esplanade Hotel** (Map p475; ☎ 9534 0211; 11 Upper Esplanade) is much loved by St Kilda's locals, with its live bands (often free), comedy nights, great pub grub and grungy atmosphere (the carpet is probably the city's stickiest and the chairs are more gaffer tape than stuffing).

The **Esplanade Sunday Market** (Map p475; Upper Esplanade; ☼ 10am-5pm Sun) features a range of open-air stalls lining the street and selling arts and crafts, often with a New Age or Australiana slant.

Williamstown

Back in 1837, Williamstown (Map pp470–1) was designated the main seaport on Port Phillip Bay. When the Yarra River was deepened and the Port of Melbourne developed in the 1880s, Williamstown became a secondary port. Tucked away in a corner of the bay, it was bypassed and forgotten for years. In the last decade or so 'Willy' has experienced a renaissance.

Nelson Pl follows the foreshore, winding around the docklands and shipyards, and is lined with historic buildings, while the yacht clubs and marinas along the waterfront add to the maritime flavour. Williamstown's other attractions include restaurants and cafés, some pubs and bars, art and craft galleries, and specialty shops.

The **Williamstown visitor information centre** (☎ 9397 3791; www.williamstowninfo.com.au; Nelson Pl; ☼ 9am-5pm) is independently operated. Between Nelson Pl and the waterfront is **Commonwealth Reserve**, a leafy park where a **craft market** (☼ 10am-4pm) is held on the first and third Sunday of each month.

Moored at Gem Pier is the **HMAS Castlemaine** (www.hmascastlemaine.com; adult/child $5/2.50; ☼ noon-5pm Sat & Sun), a WWII minesweeper built at Williamstown in 1941, which has been converted into a maritime museum.

Williamstown Railway Museum (off Map pp470-1; ☎ 9397 7412; Champion Rd; adult/child $5/2; ⊙ noon-5pm Sat, Sun & public holidays, noon-5pm Wed & school holidays) has a fine collection of old steam locomotives and mini-steam-train rides for kids.

The **Customs Wharf Gallery** (☎ 9399 9726; cnr Nelson Pl & Syme St; adult/concession $2/1; ⊙ 11am-5pm) has 13 rooms of excellent arts and crafts, including paintings, glassware, jewellery and ceramics.

The **Scienceworks Museum & Melbourne Planetarium** (☎ 9392 4800; www.scienceworks.museum.vic .gov.au; 2 Booker St, Spotswood; adult/concession $6/free, incl planetarium show $12.50/5; ⊙ 10am-4.30pm) is under the shadow of the West Gate Bridge. The Scienceworks Museum was built on the site of the Spotswood pumping station, Melbourne's first sewage works, and incorporates the historic old buildings. You can spend hours wandering around inspecting old machines, poking buttons and pulling levers, and learning all sorts of weird facts and figures. The planetarium section usually holds shows every day. The museum is a 10-minute signposted walk from Spotswood train station down Hudsons Rd.

Williamstown Beach, on the southern side of the peninsula, is a top spot for a swim. From Nelson Pl walk down Cole St or get off the train at the Williamstown Beach station and walk down Forster St.

Williamstown Ferries (☎ 9506 4144; www.williams townferries.com.au) runs ferries between Gem Pier in Williamstown and Southgate. The ferry stops at the Scienceworks Museum & Melbourne Planetarium, the *Polly Woodside* and the Melbourne Exhibition Centre/Crown Casino en route. A ferry also runs to St Kilda Pier (opposite).

ACTIVITIES

This section covers a range of activities in and around Melbourne – for more details and information on activities around the state, see p1009.

Cycling

The **Main Yarra Trail** is one of Melbourne's many inner-city bike paths constructed along the riverside green belts. At least 20 other long, urban cycle paths exist, all marked in the Melway *Greater Melbourne Street Directory*. You can get maps from the visitor centre at Federation Sq (p468) and

Bicycle Victoria (☎ 8636 8888; www.bv.com.au). In addition, **VicRoads** (www.vicroads.vic.gov.au) has printable maps.

Hire a Bike (Map pp472-3; ☎ 0412 616 633; Princes Bridge, Southbank; bikes per day $35)

St Kilda Cycles (Map p475; ☎ 9534 3074; www .stkildacycles.com.au; 11 Carlisle St, St Kilda; bikes per day $20, overnight $25)

Golf

Melbourne's sandbelt courses, such as **Royal Melbourne**, **Victoria**, **Huntingdale** and **Kingston Heath**, are world famous. It is tough to get a round at these members' courses, but there are also plenty of public courses where anyone can play. You will need to book on weekends. Green fees are around $20 for 18 holes, and most courses have clubs and buggies for hire. These are some good public courses close to town:

Royal Park Golf Course (Map pp470-1; ☎ 9387 3585; The Avenue, Parkville) Near the zoo.

Yarra Bend Public Golf Course (Map pp470-1; ☎ 9481 3729; Yarra Bend Rd, Fairfield) This is the pick of the bunch and has 27 holes. Bookings are essential.

In-line Skating

The best in-line skating tracks are found around St Kilda. **Rock 'n' Roll Skate Hire** (Map p475; ☎ 9525 3434; 22 Fitzroy St, St Kilda; per hr/day $8/25; ⊙ 10am-7pm Mon-Fri, 9am-7pm Sat & Sun) hires equipment that's in pretty good condition.

THE ART OF HEIDE

Heide Museum of Modern Art (Map p521; ☎ 9850 1500; www.heide.com.au; 7 Templestowe Rd, Bulleen; adult/child $12/8, extra for exhibitions; ⊙ 10am-5pm Tue-Fri, noon-5pm Sat & Sun) is in the outer suburb of Bulleen. It's on the site of the former home of John and Sunday Reed, under whose patronage the likes of Sir Sidney Nolan, John Perceval and Albert Tucker created a new movement in the Australian art world – the gallery has an impressive collection. Heide is set in a sprawling, informal park running down to the Yarra River. The museum is signposted off the Eastern Fwy. Otherwise, take an Eltham-line train to Heidelberg station, and catch National Bus No 291 to the corner of Manningham and Templestowe Rds and walk from there.

Sailing

There are about 20 yacht clubs around the bay and races are held most weekends (some clubs race on Wednesday as well). Some clubs welcome visitors as crew on racing boats. Following are some of the biggest clubs:

Hobsons Bay Yacht Club (Map p470-1; ☎ 9397 6393; 268 Nelson Pl, Williamstown) Volunteers get a go on weekends here.

Royal Melbourne Yacht Squadron (Map p475; ☎ 9534 0227; Pier Rd, St Kilda) Postcard-perfect location and crewing opportunities from Wednesday to Sunday.

Swimming

The bay beaches are popular during summer. St Kilda beach is busy at the first ray of sunlight, but they all get packed bum-to-bum on scorching days. Pools near the city:

Fitzroy Swimming Pool (Map pp476-7; ☎ 9417 6493; Alexandra Pde, Fitzroy; adult/concession $3.80/2.20; ☺ Nov-Mar) This is a nice outdoor local pool (50m) that was recently saved from the developers.

Melbourne City Baths (Map pp476-7; ☎ 9663 5888; cnr Swanston & Victoria Sts; adult/concession $4/3.20; ☺ year-round) This stately swimming hall has a 25m indoor pool plus a gym, spas, saunas and squash courts.

Melbourne Sports & Aquatic Centre (Map pp470-1; ☎ 9926 1555; www.msac.com.au; Albert Rd, Albert Park; adult/child $5.70/4.20; ☺ 6am-10pm year-round) With a fantastic indoor 75m 10-lane pool, several smaller pools, water slides, spa–sauna–steam room and spacious common areas. Childcare is available.

St Kilda Sea Baths (Map p475; ☎ 9525 4888; 10-18 Jacka Blvd, St Kilda; adult/child $12/6; ☺ year-round) The indoor 25m sea-water pool is a miracle worker with views out to the bay, and a soak in the hydrotherapy spa is essential.

Windsurfing & Kitesurfing

Close to the city, Elwood is a very popular kitesurfing and windsurfing area. **RPS** (Map pp470-1; ☎ 9525 6475; www.rpstheboardstore.com; 87 Ormond Rd, Elwood) can teach you the basics of either sport for $75/129 respectively per introductory outing. All gear is included in the price.

Yoga

The following places all offer drop-in classes to unkink your body. Check websites for class timetables.

Action School of Yoga (Map pp476-7; ☎ 9415 9798; www.actionyoga.com; Level 1, 275 Smith St, Collingwood) Teaches Iyengar yoga and has a solid reputation.

Ashtanga Yoga Centre of Melbourne (Map pp476-7; ☎ 9419 1598; www.ashtangamelbourne.com.au; Level 1, 110 Argyle St, Fitzroy) Rigorous Mysore-style classes, and courses for kids and teens too.

Yoga Tree (off Map p475; ☎ 9532 7418; www.yoga tree.com.au; 5 Horne St, Elsternwick) Adherents of the Bikram method will be able to sweat it out in style here.

WALKING TOUR

> **WALK FACTS**
> Distance: 2.8km
> Duration: 2½ hours

Melbourne's network of alleys, lanes and arcades, plus some of its most interesting buildings, form the basis for this classic city saunter.

Start at **Federation Sq (1**; p469) and decide whether you're in the 'love it' or 'hate it' camp. Descend the steps on the Yarra River side of Federation Sq into **Birrarung Marr (2)**, the 8.3-hectare park that has rejuvenated land formerly occupied by the Flinders St rail yards. Head back to St Kilda Rd and mosey west along Flinders St past the magnificent, domed **Flinders St station (3)** – 'under the clocks' is a popular meeting place. From here, cross over to **Young & Jackson's (4)**, one of the city's oldest hotels and home to Melbourne icon *Chloe*, the late-19th-century nude portrait.

For a coffee pit stop, travel half a block down Flinders St and turn right into Degraves St, a bustling laneway bursting with European-style cafés – **Degraves Espresso Bar (5**; p506) is the pick. Architecture buffs should continue towards Centre Pl, where you'll spy the **Majorca Building (6)**, one of the city's most sought-after slices of real estate. Fashionista detour: turn right for a window shop into the designer boutiques along Flinders Lane; **Alice Euphemia (7**; p517) will help you reinvent yourself. Follow Centre Pl through to leafy Collins St, where you'll find great architecture at No 248, **Lyric House (8)**, and No 247, **Newspaper House (9)**, with its stunning glass mosaic on the façade.

Duck through **Australia on Collins (10)** for more opportunities to use your credit card, and exit onto Little Collins St. Pop into the **Royal Arcade (11)**, built in 1869 and Mel-

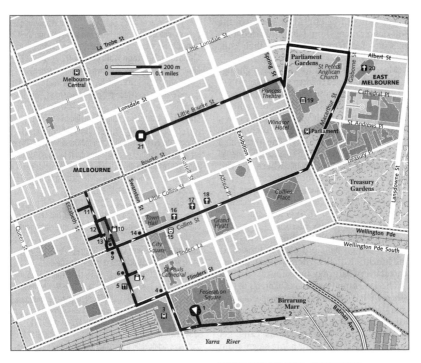

bourne's oldest arcade. Start threading your way back to Collins St by taking **Block Pl (12**; p479), which is crammed with hole-in-the-wall cafés, to **Block Arcade (13**; p479). When you emerge on Collins St, head east to the fabulous **Manchester Unity Building (14**; p469), which had the city's first escalators – its original ventilation system was cooled in summer by tonnes of ice.

Keep striding up the Collins St hill to its 'Paris end'; en route you'll pass the **Regent Theatre (15**; p515), the 1845 **Baptist Church (16)**, and **Scots (17)** and **St Michael's (18)** churches – both excellent examples of the High Victorian architecture espoused in the 1860s and 1870s.

At the top of Collins St, cross Spring St to Macarthur St, passing the back garden of **Parliament House (19**; p479), and walk towards **St Patrick's Cathedral (20)**, a Gothic Revival masterpiece. Your tummy must be grumbling by now, so from here, loop around Albert St into Spring St, and then follow your nose down Little Bourke St for steaming noodle soup in **Chinatown (21**; p479).

MELBOURNE FOR CHILDREN

Bambini, ankle-biters, wee'uns and bairns – Melbourne prefers all children to start their cultural education at an early age. The city lays on a good spread of activities geared solely towards youngsters, from low-flying raptors and kooky science exhibits to seven-gilled sharks. During school holidays many places have tailor-made early-childhood programmes. Alternatively, if Puffing Billy seems too far to go to blow off some steam, head to a park for a grassy romp.

Sights that give 'what I did on my holiday' stories backbone include the **Royal Melbourne Zoo** (p492), where meerkats cause great hilarity; the **Werribee Open Range Zoo** (p520), with its spot-the-zebra/rhino/giraffe/etc bus safari; and **Healesville Sanctuary** (p528), the best option for getting up close to Australian native animals. Overnight camps at the zoos, such as Melbourne's 'Roar 'n' Snore' and the Open Range's 'Slumber Safari', are also lots of spooky fun.

Other educational options include **Scienceworks** (p495), with lots of hands-on activities, and the **Melbourne Aquarium** (p489),

VICTORIA

where kids will be circled by sharks in the 360-degree aquarium (some harried parents may feel tempted to throw their children in!).

More casual spots for wildlife sightings include **Collingwood Children's Farm** (Map pp470-1; ☎ 9417 5806; St Heliers St, Abbotsford; adult/concession $8/4; ☽ 9am-5.30pm), a bucolic spot right by the Yarra River, with grazing goats, cows, lambs and ponies, all of which tolerate tiny hands petting their coats. The farm also runs a **Farmers' Market** (☎ 5657 2337; admission $2; ☽ 8am-1pm 2nd Sat of month), where you can stock up on local organic produce. In a similar vein, **Ceres Community Environment Park** (Map pp470-1; ☎ 9380 8861; 8 Lee St, East Brunswick; breakfast $4-15, lunch $7-11; ☽ 9.30am-4pm Sun-Fri, 9am-4pm Sat) has plenty of room for youngsters to chase chooks while parents can chow down on delicious organic breakfasts and lunchtime thalis. There's a fresh **produce market** every Saturday morning.

The **Ian Potter Foundation Children's Garden** (Map pp470-1; ☎ 9252 2300; www.rbg.vic.gov.au; Birdwood Ave; admission free; ☽ 10am-4pm Wed-Sun Apr-Oct), at the Royal Botanic Gardens, is an outdoor wonderland that kids can't get enough of. It's closed for a 'big sleep' from July to September – check the website for exact dates.

For something more riotous, **Luna Park** (p494) rides summon nerves of steel, and, in the depths of the Dandenongs, a day trip on steam train **Puffing Billy** (p529) is always a huge hit.

Lastly, almost every neighbourhood in the city will have a park with play equipment and other kids to meet and muck around with. For more information about local attractions and events, look for the free monthly publication **Melbourne's Child** (www.melbourneschild.com.au), which can be found in cafés and kid-oriented businesses all over town.

TOURS

The free monthly *Melbourne Events* guide, available at visitor information centres, has an extensive section on tours. The National Trust publishes *Walking Melbourne* ($20), particularly useful if you're interested in Melbourne's architectural heritage.

Aboriginal Heritage Walk (☎ 9252 2300; www.rbg.vic.gov.au; adult/child $16/7; ☽ tours 11am Thu & Fri, 10.30am alternate Sun) The Royal Botanic Gardens are on the ancestral lands of the Boonwurrung and Woiworung peoples, and this 90-minute tour takes you through their story. Departs from the visitor centre at the Gardens.

Chinatown Heritage Walk (Map pp472-3; ☎ 9662 2888; www.melbournechinatown.com.au/attractions_walk.html; 22 Cohen Pl; adult/concession from $15/12) A guided walking tour through historic Chinatown, with its atmospheric alleys and bustling vibe; meals also available.

City Circle trams (www.metlinkmelbourne.com.au /city_circle; admission free; ☽ 10am-6pm) This tram service runs every 10 minutes around the city centre. There are eight refurbished W-class trams, built between 1936 and 1956, painted a distinctive burgundy and gold. You can even dine on board a tram while taking a scenic night cruise around Melbourne's streets.

City Explorer (Map pp472-3; ☎ 1800 858 687; tickets from 180 Swanston St; adult/child $33/17) This service offers double-decker bus tours of Melbourne, with about 20 stops en route.

Maribyrnong River Cruises (Map pp470-1; ☎ 9689 6431; www.blackbirdcruises.com.au; Wingfield St, Footscray; adult/child from $7/4; ☽ Tue, Thu, Sat & Sun) Offers two- and one-hour cruises along the Maribyrnong River (past the Lonely Planet office!). Departures are from the end of Wingfield St in Footscray.

Melbourne River Cruises (Map pp472-3; ☎ 9681 3284; www.melbcruises.com.au; Vault 11, Banana Alley, Docklands; adult/child from $14/7.50) A one-hour cruise upstream or downstream or a 2½-hour return cruise along the Yarra River. Check with the company for departure details. Also operates a ferry between Southgate and Williamstown.

Neighbours Ramsay St Tour (Map p475; ☎ 9534 4755; www.neighbourstour.com.au; 121 Fitzroy St, St Kilda; adult/concession $30/25) A pilgrimage of sorts for many British backpackers, this tribute to the residents of the long-running soap *Neighbours* is a must-do for any devotee of Aussie kitsch. See also Elephant & Wheelbarrow, p512.

FESTIVALS & EVENTS

There's always a festival of some sort happening in Melbourne. Many are thematic, with film, comedy, theatre, sport, food and wine enticing locals and visitors to revel in Melbourne life. Check out what's on in the free *Melbourne Events* guide and at www.melbourne.vic.gov.au/events.

January

Australian Open (www.australianopen.com) One of the four Grand Slam tennis events, held at the Melbourne Park Tennis Centre.

Big Day Out (www.bigdayout.com) Nearly 40,000 revellers cut sick to over 40 alternative international and Australian rock bands at this January event.

Chinese New Year (www.melbournechinatown.com.au)
The smell of firecrackers mingles with aromas from food
stalls as the red dragon dances past. One not to be missed.
Midsumma Festival (www.midsumma.org.au) Held
Mid-January to early February. Melbourne's annual gay and
lesbian arts festival has over 100 events across the city.

February
St Kilda Festival (www.stkildafestival.com.au) This
weekend-long celebration of local arts and culture is best
when the sun's out – bring a hat and your drinking legs.

March
Antipodes Festival (www.antipodesfestival.com.au)
Celebrates Greek art, food, culture and music.
Australian Formula One Grand Prix (www.grandprix
.com.au) Albert Park gets invaded by the thoroughbreds of
the automotive world and their party-loving hangers-on.
Irish Festival Held at pubs all over the city, this pissed-up
appropriation of all things emerald reaches a Guinness-
soaked climax on St Patrick's Day (17 March) with an
open-air concert in the Royal Botanic Gardens.
Melbourne Food & Wine Festival (www.melbourne
foodandwine.com.au) The main gastronomical event of
the year takes place from mid-March to early April and is
highly regarded in Australia and overseas.
Melbourne Moomba Waterfest (www.melbourne.vic
.gov.au) Ten days of carnivals, fireworks and an outdoor art
show, as well as water skiing and a Dragon Boat Festival;
all on the Yarra River.
Melbourne Queer Film Festival (www.melbourne
queerfilm.com.au) The 10-day festival showcases gay
artists, with everything from full-length features and
animations to experimental works.

April
Anzac Day Held on the 25 April, the day begins with a
dawn service at the Shrine of Remembrance, followed by a
march for returned servicemen through the city.
International Comedy Festival (www.comedyfestival
.com.au) Locals are joined by a wealth of international acts
performing at venues all over the city.

May
Next Wave Festival (www.nextwave.org.au) Presents
over two weeks of visual and performing arts from a new
generation of artists.
St Kilda Film Festival (www.stkildafilmfestival.com.au)
Showcasing a selection of contemporary Australian short
films and videos.

July
Melbourne International Film Festival (www
.melbournefilmfestival.com.au) Two weeks of the newest
and the best in local and international film.

August
Melbourne Writers' Festival (www.mwf.com.au)
This 10-day festival covers a wide range of literary genres
and issues, with local and international authors speaking,
reading, quaffing and writing.

September
AFL Grand Final (www.afl.com.au) The AFL final is
played on the last Saturday in September. Join in with
the spirit of things and pray that it's not contested by two
out-of-town teams.
Melbourne Fringe Festival (www.melbournefringe
.com.au) Late September to mid-October. Starts with a
parade and street party on Brunswick St. Events to suit a
range of tastes and interests.
Royal Melbourne Show (www.royalshow.com.au) The
country comes to town for this large-scale agricultural fair
at the Royal Melbourne Showgrounds in Flemington.

October
Lygon St Festa (www.lygonst.com) Italian culture is
celebrated with food stalls, bands and dancers on Lygon St.
Melbourne International Arts Festival (www
.melbournefestival.com.au) The city's major arts event has
a programme that covers theatre, opera, dance and music
and revolves around an annual theme.
Oktoberfest (www.germanclubtivoli.com.au) Held at the
German Club Tivoli (291 Dandenong Rd, Windsor). I think
we know it's not for teetotallers.

GAY & LESBIAN MELBOURNE

Melbourne's GLBTI (gay-lesbian-bisexual-
transgender-intersex) scene is like Melbourne itself – understated, slightly hard
to find, but most definitely out! Free street
press is a good source of information – look
for *Melbourne Star*, **MCV** (www.mcv.net.au),
Bnews (www.bnews.net.au) and **Lesbiana**
(www.lesbiana.com.au) in various bars, clubs
and cafés. Hares & Hyenas (p467) is a gay-
and-lesbian-centric bookshop with plenty
of available information.

The **ALSO Foundation** (☎ 9827 4999;
www.also.org.au) is a very helpful community-
based organisation whose website boasts
a great services directory. If it's gay sounds
that you're after, tune in to **Joy FM** (www.joy
.org.au), Melbourne's gay radio station (and
sadly enough, Australia's only gay radio station) – you'll find it at 94.9FM.

For a list of entertainment options, see
p513. See opposite for gay and lesbian festivals and events.

VICTORIA

November
Spring Racing Carnival (www.racingvictoria.net.au) Held October to November. There are two feature races: the Caulfield Cup (Caulfield Racecourse) and the Melbourne Cup (Flemington Racecourse).

December
Carols by Candlelight (www.rvibcarolsbycandlelight .com.au) Christmas carols under the stars at the Sidney Myer Music Bowl.

International Test Match Cricket (www.mcg.org .au) Held at the MCG, the first day of the competition is Boxing Day.

SLEEPING
Melbourne's sleeping options are broad and of a high standard. During major festivals and events accommodation is scarce, so book in advance. Contrary to the rest of the book, midrange listings in Melbourne cost between $80 and $165 for a double room with bathroom. Anything higher than $165 is regarded as top end; anything less than $80 is classified as budget. Prices listed in this chapter are for high season (summer), but most places offer discounts for weekly and monthly stays.

Budget
HOSTELS
There are backpacker hostels in the city centre and most of the inner suburbs. Several of the larger hostels have courtesy buses that pick up from the bus and train terminals.

City Centre
Greenhouse Backpacker (Map pp472-3; ☎ 9639 6400; www.friendlygroup.com.au; 228 Flinders Lane; dm/s $25/55, d & tw $68; 🖳) A short walk from Flinders St station, this large, well-maintained hostel has very clean rooms, pleasant common areas and helpful staff. Security is solid.

Friendly Backpacker (Map pp472-3; ☎ 9670 1111; www.friendlygroup.com.au; 197 King St; dm $24, d & tw $68; 🖳) It manages to hum with a social vibe yet still maintains efficient, safe standards for its guests (the hostel is open and staffed 24 hours a day). Facilities are good, and there's a choice between mixed and single-sex dorms.

Melbourne Connection Travellers Hostel (Map pp472-3; ☎ 9642 4464; www.melbourneconnection.com; 205 King St; dm $22-26, d & tw $70, tr $81) Less chaotic than some of the city's larger hostels, this place has a low-key, easy-going appeal that encourages light-hearted chatter. Common areas are in good nick and 24-hour access is available.

Hotel Bakpak (Map pp472-3; ☎ 9329 7525; www .bakpakgroup.com; 167 Franklin St; dm $23-26, s/d $55/65) This behemoth offers nearly all the budget traveller could ask for – straightforward rooms sandwiched between the basement bar and rooftop entertainment area with city views. A resource centre assists in job hunting. Reception is open 24 hours.

North Melbourne
Melbourne Metro (Map pp470-1; ☎ 9329 8599; www .yha.com.au; 78 Howard St; dm from $20-28, s with/without

---

WHERE TO LAY YOUR HAT

Melbourne's city centre is an easy mosey to bars, restaurants and cinemas, and within striding distance of most of the top sights – it also has the biggest range of accommodation in all categories.

To experience a more local perspective, pepper your stay with a couple of nights in an inner suburb. Shabby-chic St Kilda is the perfect choice for sea breezes, pubs and café culture (and spotting the odd Aussie TV celebrity). Festive, arty Fitzroy lovingly nurtures its café and restaurant scene, and classic pubs grace plenty of its backstreet corners. On the fringe of the CBD, East Melbourne flaunts some of the city's best accommodation options – particularly if you're looking for an apartment or want to hear the roaring crowd at the MCG. It has a pleasant residential feel with tree-lined streets and grand old Victorian terrace houses. Carlton is Melbourne's Italian quarter; it's just out of the city centre, but an easy walk or tram ride downtown. North Melbourne, sporting a massive YHA, is best for the budget traveller, while South Yarra is at the opposite end of the sleeping spectrum with graciously restored Victorian-era mansions and a polished ambience. It's popular with hard-core shoppers, lured by the glittering window displays of nearby Chapel St and Toorak Rd. All in all, any inner-city suburb is a good choice, it just depends on which enclave best suits you.

bathroom $76/64, d $86/74; (**P**) (**⌨**) A YHA show-piece, this huge 348-bed place is well kit-ted-out and managed, and has excellent facilities, including modern bathrooms, solid kitchen, rooftop patio with BBQs and security car park. Family rooms and self-contained apartments are available.

Chapman Gardens (Map pp470-1; ☎ 9328 3595; www.yha.com.au; 76 Chapman St; dm/s from $26/52, tw & d from $56; (**⌨**) This is smaller and older than the Melbourne Metro but more inti-mate and personal in its scope. Most rooms are doubles, but there are dorms. There's a BBQ on the premises and bikes are avail-able for hire.

Fitzroy
Nunnery (Map pp476-7; ☎ 9419 8637; www.nunnery .com.au; 116 Nicholson St; dm $23-27, s $75, d & tw $100-110) This Victorian-era converted nun-nery has a friendly atmosphere and excel-lent dorms for those who are travelling in groups. The guesthouses and townhouses are great for those wanting some more space. All options here are well kitted-out and commodious.

Carlton
Carlton College (Map pp476-7; ☎ 9664 0664; www .lygonst.com; 95 Drummond St; dm $15-21, s/d without bathroom $42/50; (**P**) Fabulous old Victorian terrace houses, so typical of the area, have been transformed into small, serviceable rooms with few frills.

South Yarra
Hotel Claremont (Map p478; ☎ 9826 8000; www .hotelclaremont.com; 189 Toorak Rd; dm/s/d without bath-room $30/66/76; (**⌨**) The Claremont, a once-grand home, is now a budget hotel. Simple rooms are spotless and freshly painted, and the communal bathrooms are in excellent condition.

South Melbourne
Nomads Market Inn (Map pp470-1; ☎ 9690 2220; www.marketinn.com.au; 143 York St; dm $20-24, d $58, incl breakfast) This pleasant hostel in a con-verted pub is right beside South Melbourne Market, within walking distance of South-gate and close to tram lines. It's not really in the centre of things but is still very well located, particularly if you are into self-catering. There is a free beer on arrival and free bicycle rentals.

St Kilda
Olembia Guesthouse (Map p475; ☎ 9537 1412; www .olembia.com.au; 96 Barkly St; dm/s/d without bathroom $24/46/78; (**P**) More like a boutique hotel than a hostel, the facilities at this excellent place include a cosy guest lounge, dining room, courtyard and bike shed. Small rooms are clean and comfortable, with hand-basins and central heating. It's deservedly popular, so book ahead.

Base (Map p475; ☎ 9536 6109; www.basebackpackers .com; 17 Carlisle St; dm $23-29, d from $75; (**⌨**) Easily the flashest hostel in St Kilda, this well-run place fronts Carlisle St with a bold red feature wall and shows off inside with spar-kling facilities, natty communal areas and enough activities to keep the most revved-up backpackers happy.

CAMPING
Ashley Gardens Big 4 Holiday Village (Map pp470-1; ☎ 9318 6866; www.ashleygardens.com.au; Ashley St, Braybrook; powered & unpowered sites per 2 people $27-33, cabins from $70; (**P**) (**⌨**) Only 9km from the city centre, this is a well-run, spacious park. You can get here from the city centre via bus No 220, which departs from Flinders St station. There are also well-appointed units sleeping up to six people.

Midrange
APARTMENT HOTELS & SERVICED APARTMENTS
Melbourne has an ever-expanding range of apartment-style hotels and serviced apart-ments. More spacious than regular hotels, with their own kitchen and laundry facili-ties, this style of accommodation can be better value and more comfortable than a similarly priced hotel, especially for people travelling in a group.

Several companies manage many blocks of apartments, and you're likely to be of-fered a better deal if you speak to HQ. Try **Oakford** (☎ 1800 642 188; www.oakford.com), **Quest** (☎ 1800 334 033; www.questapartments.com.au) or **Punt Hill** (☎ 1800 331 529; www.punthill-apartments .com.au).

City Centre
Quest Fairfax House Serviced Apartments (Map pp472-3; ☎ 9642 1333; www.questapartments.com .au; 392 Little Collins St; apt from $165; (**P**) (**☷**) These apartments are centrally located but this end of Little Collins St is relatively quiet.

Apartments, with all the usual amenities, are comfortable, and the complex is well run and also offers baby-sitting services.

Pacific International Apartments (Map pp472-3; ☎ 1800 682 003; www.pacificinthotels.com.au; 318 Little Bourke St; apt from $145) These apartments occupy a lovely old heritage building right in the heart of the city, but the interior is resolutely up-to-the-minute and very comfortable. These four-star serviced apartments are well managed and well equipped.

East Melbourne

Knightsbridge Apartments (Map pp470-1; ☎ 9419 1333; www.knightsbridgeapartments.com.au; 101 George St; apt from $140; ☒) This is an excellent choice for those looking for comfortable, well-furnished accommodation, replete with thick carpets and four-poster beds. It allows you to self-cater but also puts you a fork's throw from the city's dining options. You're also within walking distance of the city's main sporting arenas. Facilities are spotless, modern and stylish.

Albert Heights (Map pp470-1; ☎ 9419 0955; www.albertheights.com.au; 83 Albert St; apt from $136; ☐ ☒) The charmingly managed Albert Heights has been getting a spruce-up and its newer 2004-style rooms are excellent. The older rooms are showing their age, but are still decent value. The small plunge pool, surrounded by greenery, is a cute way to cool off.

Eastern Town House (Map pp470-1; ☎ 9418 6666; 90 Albert St; apt from $125; ☐ ☒) This is a refurbished complex offering good-quality (albeit uninspiring) units. There's a café/bar on the ground floor, and you can walk to the city or Victoria St easily.

Carlton

Quest on Lygon (Map pp470-1; ☎ 9345 3888; www.questapartments.com.au; 700 Lygon St; apt from $154; ☐) These former one- and two-bedroom flats are opposite the Melbourne General Cemetery and have been refurbished to a good standard (with fully equipped kitchens and laundries) and are the sort of rooms that tend to fill quickly with visitors to the nearby university.

HOTELS & MOTELS

Most of the hotels and motels in this section are rated three stars, and they're comfortable but sometimes a little cramped. Doubles usually cost the same as singles.

City Centre

Duxton Hotel (Map pp472-3; ☎ 9250 1888; www.duxton.com; 328 Flinders St; r from $125; ☐ ☒ ☐) Much of this heritage-listed hotel, built in 1913, has been restored to its original splendour. Rich, dark timber panelling and ornate touches feature throughout the public areas, while modern stylings give 21st-century guests right-this-minute amenities. Staff are ever helpful, and keen to find the best deal possible.

Atlantis Hotel (Map pp472-3; ☎ 9600 2900; www.atlantishotel.com.au; 300 Spencer St; r from $135; ☐) A recent addition to the city's sleeping options at this busy end of town. There's good access to transport and city-centre sights, and rooms are pretty damn smart, with no chintz or froufrou anywhere.

Mercure Hotel Melbourne (Map pp470-1; ☎ 9205 9999; www.mercure.com.au; 13 Spring St; r from $132; ☒) The Mercure maintains a certain 'could be anywhere' sensibility in its décor and standards, but its Spring St location is a gem, with both the Paris end of town and the sporting side of things at your feet.

Hotel Y (Map pp470-1; ☎ 9329 5188; www.hotely.com.au; 489 Elizabeth St; r $80-150) This is an award-winning budget hotel run by the YWCA. The Y's facilities include a café, communal kitchen and laundry. You're also within easy reach of the Queen Victoria Market (p480). You don't need to be young, Christian or a woman to stay here either.

Victoria Hotel (Map pp472-3; ☎ 9653 0441; www.victoriahotel.com.au; 215 Little Collins St; s $56-92, d $80-155) The Vic is a Melbourne institution – it's brilliantly located, surrounded by interesting shops and great restaurants and bars. There's the option of having a room with a shared or private bathroom.

Astoria City Travel Inn (Map pp472-3; ☎ 9670 6801; www.astoriainternational.com; 288 Spencer St; r $100-130; ☐ ☒) Swathed in those matching pastel bedspread-and-curtain combos that afflict so many Australian midrange hotels, the Astoria manages to rise above the identikit doldrums by offering evidence of an admirable love of cleanliness. Parking costs $10 per night.

City Square Motel (Map pp472-3; ☎ 9654 7011; www.citysquaremotel.com.au; 67 Swanston St; s/d/tr/f $85/105/115/125) This hotel-motel has basic rooms, but is right in the centre of town. All the standard facilities, but there are no luxuries.

Hotel Enterprize (Map pp472-3; ☎ 9629 6991; www.hotelenterprize.com.au; 44 Spencer St; s $90-180; P) The Enterprize is a small and reasonably priced hotel, with good facilities for the business traveller. Amenities are strong, and the range of options should suit most travellers.

Batman's Hill (Map pp472-3; ☎ 9614 6344; www.batmanshill.com.au; 66 Spencer St; r from $155) This is a step up in quality from the budget hotels in this area, and it's in a heritage-listed building to boot. While the rooms here are diminutive in dimensions, they're solid on standards, and service is very helpful.

City Limits (Map pp472-3; ☎ 9662 2544; www.citylimits.com.au; 20-22 Little Bourke St; r incl breakfast $160; P) In the heart of the theatre district and close to Chinatown, City Limits has attractively kitted-out rooms that take full advantage of their petite dimensions. Room rates include self-catering facilities, although with Chinatown's lights winking close by you'll be hard pressed to cook for yourself.

East Melbourne

George Powlett Motel/Apartments (Map pp470-1; ☎ 9419 9488; www.georgepowlett.com.au; cnr George & Powlett Sts; s/d/tr $103/110/127; P) These are older motel-style rooms with modest kitchenettes and small balconies that allow you to hear the crowds roar at the MCG. The décor is nothing special, but rooms are clean and rates are low for this neck of the woods.

Carlton

Downtowner on Lygon (Map pp476-7; ☎ 9663 5555; www.downtowner.com.au; 66 Lygon St; r from $149; P) With its central courtyard for parking, this is a good option for those with cars, and we love the fact that its rates haven't shifted in years. Business facilities are average and some rooms have modest self-catering options.

St Kilda

Cabana Court Motel (Map p475; ☎ 9534 0771; www.cabanacourtapartments.com; 46 Park St; apt from $90; P) A little like visiting your Nanna's unit, these decent motel-style apartments are on a pretty, tree-lined street and are only a short stroll from the beach and Fitzroy St. Apartments feature kitchen facilities, TV and bathtubs and are great family value.

B&BS & BOUTIQUE HOTELS

There are some excellent B&Bs in Melbourne, many of which are at least as comfortable as a four-star hotel but charge much less. Boutique hotels are often more like large B&Bs or upmarket guesthouses.

East Melbourne

Georgian Court (Map pp470-1; ☎ 9419 6353; www.georgiancourt.com.au; 21 George St; s/d $105/119; P) The elegant façade of this friendly B&B augurs well. The interior, a little scuffed but exuding a relaxed charm, shines in the communal areas, so much so that you'll forgive your bedroom's tight corners. Cheaper rooms with spotless shared bathrooms are also available.

Magnolia Court (Map pp470-1; ☎ 9419 4222; www.magnolia-court.com.au; 101 Powlett St; r from $140) This bright and friendly place has an older wing with high ceilings and traditional-style furnishings; rooms in the new wing are of a high standard, but lack the same charm and proportions. The self-contained Victorian cottage is ideal for families (no under-threes though).

South Yarra

Tilba (Map pp470-1; ☎ 9867 8844; www.thetilba.com.au; cnr Toorak Rd W & Domain St; r from $154) This small and elegant hotel has been lovingly restored in gracious Victorian style. The 15 suites all feature old iron bedsteads, antique lamps, decorative plaster work and period-style bathrooms. It's highly recommended, with a homey, welcoming feel, although cheaper rooms are small.

Toorak Manor (Map p478; ☎ 9827 2689; www.toorakmanor.citysearch.com.au; 220 Williams Rd; d from $145) An excellent boutique hotel, this historic mansion has been impressively converted (every inch seems covered in chintz) and is set in lovely gardens. It has comfortable period-style rooms and cosy lounges.

Albany South Yarra (Map pp470-1; ☎ 9866 4485; www.thealbany.com.au; cnr Toorak Rd & Millswyn St; r from $110; P) Myriad sleeping configurations range from old-world mansion-wing glamour to more functional rooms suited to less fussy travellers. There are shared kitchen and laundry facilities.

St Kilda

Hotel Tolarno (Map p475; ☎ 9537 0200; www.hotel tolarno.com.au; 42 Fitzroy St; d from $115;) Right

VICTORIA

on Fitzroy St, rooms are small, artfully decorated and comfy, and bathrooms have been given a sparkling renovation. Choose a room at the back if you're a light sleeper.

Marque (Map p475; ☎ 8530 8888; www.rendez voushotels.com; 35 Fitzroy St; d from $160; P ⊠ ⊑) A midsized boutique property that offers a range of themed packages catering to the 'I'm worth it' demographic. Rooms are stylish and well appointed, and the location is hard to beat.

Top End

Melbourne's top-end hotels and serviced apartments combine excellent location, attractive décor and attentive service. Generally, you'll find a range of packages and deals on offer via the Internet. Parking is often of the valet variety and can incur a charge of between $12 and $25 per day.

APARTMENT HOTELS & SERVICED APARTMENTS
City Centre

Windsor Hotel (Map pp472-3; ☎ 9633 6000; www.the windsor.com.au; 103 Spring St; r from $500; P ⊠ ⊑) The queen of the scene is the stately Windsor, Melbourne's 'Grand Lady', graced by old-fashioned, haute-luxe embellishments. The rooms are just fabulous, with a great sense of history (they have accommodated luminaries such as Sir Laurence Olivier – with Vivien Leigh – Gregory Peck and even Metallica). High tea here is justifiably famous, so if you can't get a room, at least get a scone.

Punt Hill Manhattan (Map pp472-3; ☎ 1300 731 299; www.punthill.com.au; 57 Flinders Lane; apt from $221; P ⊠ ⊑) The Manhattan lives up to its name, with Soho-style loft spaces filled with super-sized sofas and beds, big windows, high ceilings and gadgetry such as DVD players. Fitness fanatics will appreciate the gym and spa. All appreciate the superfriendly service.

Fitzroy

Chifley at Metropole (Map pp476-7; ☎ 9411 8100; www.chifleyhotels.com; 44 Brunswick St; studio/apt from $195/225; P ⊠ ⊑) On the quiet end of Brunswick St, this friendly block of serviced apartments is constructed around a handy courtyard area complete with Tuscan-style pool. Rooms, with kitchens, are in excellent shape.

St Kilda

Medina Executive St Kilda (Map p475; ☎ 9536 0000; www.medinaapartments.com.au; 157 Fitzroy St; apt from $330; P ⊠) Right in the thick of St Kilda, these nattily appointed apartments can sleep up to six people. Various specials are also available at certain times of the year, making them good value for groups.

HOTELS
City Centre

Adelphi Hotel (Map pp472-3; ☎ 9650 7555; www .adelphi.com.au; 187 Flinders Lane; r from $300; ⊑) The Adelphi is showing not so much its age, but its era (the early 1990s). That said, the service is slicker than grease, with exclusivities such as the members-only rooftop bar-restaurant, the basement restaurant Ezard at Adelphi (opposite) and a cantilevered lap pool that allows you to swim right past the edge of the building and suspend yourself over Little Collins St. Magnificent.

Park Hyatt (Map pp470-1; ☎ 9224 1234; www .melbourne.park.hyatt.com; 1 Parliament Sq; r from $250; P ⊠ ⊑ ⊑) This lavish hotel has plenty of wood panelling, marble bathrooms, shiny surfaces and silky service, plus every amenity you can think of – Vichy shower anyone? Business and health facilities are excellent. Those who are mobility impaired or travelling with children are looked after royally.

Westin Melbourne (Map pp472-3; ☎ 9635 2222; www.westin.com.au; 205 Collins St; r from $299; P ⊠ ⊑ ⊑) This five-star monolith has a fabulous lobby that recalls the golden era of travel via ocean liner. Rooms are well ap-

---

AUTHOR'S CHOICE

Hotel Lindrum (Map pp472-3; ☎ 9668 1111; www.hotellindrum.com.au; 26 Flinders St; d from $360) Every inch of this sultry boutique hotel is divine, and it exudes an elegant luxury that never wanders into overdrive. Dark wood-grained furnishings are sleek and modern; the colour scheme warm, muted browns; and all areas of the hotel are lit with subtle lamplight (glaring reality is easily avoided). Wonderfully bedecked rooms overlook Federation Sq and the MCG, and offer a 'pillow menu'. Start your stay with a quality drink in the bar, and maybe a crack with a billiard cue on the full-sized table.

pointed and themed packages ('Chic Retreat' etc) will make you determined to stay for the rest of your life.

South Yarra

Como (Map p478; ☎ 9825 2222; www.mirvachotels .com.au; 630 Chapel St; r from $229; P ⊠ 🖳 🖳) The Como specialises in buffing everything to a glossy shine – from the apples in a bowl at reception to your shoes. Service is just as polished, and rooms just as plush.

St Kilda

Prince (Map p475; ☎ 9536 1111; www.theprince .com.au; 2 Acland St; r from $200; P ⊠ 🖳) This beautifully furnished boutique hotel seeps minimalist luxury – the fabulous location only adds to its appeal. Service is discreet, smart and considerate, and eating and entertainment options on the premises mean you need never leave its environs.

EATING

Melbourne is the city for food lovers. Everywhere you go, there are restaurants, cafés, delicatessens, markets, bistros, brasseries and takeaways. And a whole lot of food-literate locals who hold passionate opinions on the best places to eat a curry, roast, pizza, Peking duck or *panna cotta* (literally, 'cooked cream') and where to find the best service, décor, view and best-kept secret.

Melbourne's ethnic diversity is reflected in the inexhaustible variety of its cuisines and restaurants. Food is a local obsession, and people eat out a lot because Melburnians consider the city to be the country's eating capital (Sydneysiders will disagree just as passionately).

Reservations are recommended for the restaurants listed here.

Smoking is banned in all places where food is consumed (unless you're having a counter meal at a pub, until 2007).

City Centre & Docklands

The area in and around Chinatown – along Little Bourke St from Spring St to Swanston St – continues to be one of the city's most popular places to eat. Chinese restaurants predominate, but you can also find Greek, Indian, Japanese and Mod Oz cuisines.

Flinders Lane has plenty of cafés and wonderful little bars in the adjacent laneways. Centre Pl is the archetypal Melbourne

alleyway and it heaves with hole-in-the-wall favourites. Also check out Degraves St.

Federation Sq ('Fed Sq') has a host of eateries, most of them glam and catering to the transient tourist crowd and locals meeting up before heading out for the evening.

The Docklands is also filled with a swag of restaurants, many featuring alfresco eating areas with water views.

Flower Drum (Map pp472-3; ☎ 9662 3655; 17 Market Lane; mains $35-50, set menu per person $140; ☺ lunch Mon-Fri, dinner Mon-Sat) This is Melbourne's most famous Chinese restaurant, and a frequent winner of 'Melbourne's Best' accolades. Diners wait six weeks to score a table here and the Peking duck illustrates why. Exquisite service and an excellent wine list only add to the pleasure.

Becco (Map pp472-3; ☎ 9663 3000; 11 Crossley St; mains $23-30; ☺ lunch & dinner Mon-Sat) Serving modern Italian fare, stylish Becco is a restaurant, bar and produce store rolled into one stylish package. Service is uniformly excellent, the atmosphere comfortably sexy.

Ezard at Adelphi (Map pp472-3; ☎ 9639 6811; 187 Flinders Lane; mains $35-39; ☺ lunch Mon-Fri, dinner Mon-Sat) Ezard's flawless takes on Asian-inspired cuisine keep this basement restaurant buzzing. It's a smartly designed and staffed spot too. The tasting menu is a great way to experience the whole shebang.

Pellegrini's Espresso Bar (Map pp472-3; ☎ 9662 1885; 66 Bourke St; mains $12-14; ☺ lunch & dinner) This family-run 1950s-style espresso bar hasn't changed in years. Service is cursory, the Italian food's rudimentary and the coffee's only OK. But we love it! It oozes character, history and charm that Italo-wannabes can only dream about.

Movida (Map pp472-3; ☎ 9663 3038; 1 Hosier Lane; raciones $8.50-15; ☺ dinner daily, lunch Mon-Fri) Nab a table here and then nibble as much tapas as your heart desires – the *callos a la madrileña* (tripe) will make you swear you're in Madrid.

Yu-u (Map pp472-3; ☎ 9639 7073; 137 Flinders Lane; lunch set menu $15; ☺ lunch & dinner Mon-Fri) A certain number of four-course set lunches are made here – don't miss out. Yu-u is a rarefied world of communal seating, subdued lighting and diplomatic service. Bookings recommended.

Mo Mo (Map pp472-3; ☎ 9650 0660; basement, 115 Collins St; mains $27-39; ☺ lunch Mon-Fri, dinner Mon-Sat) You know a place is popular when it produces its own CD. Middle Eastern flavours and Australian sunniness combine to form a great experience.

Chocolate Buddha (Map pp472-3; ☎ 9654 5688; Federation Sq; meals $13-21; ✆ lunch & dinner) Organic noodles and plenty of vegetarian options keep the healthy types flocking to this fast-paced Japanese restaurant. Tables are communal, the service palm-pilot high-tech.

Supper Inn (Map pp472-3; ☎ 9663 4759; 15 Celestial Ave; mains $15-30; ✆ dinner) Open until late (2.30am) and serving some of the best late-night congee, noodles, dumplings and other Cantonese standards to a mixed crowd.

Il Solito Posto (Map pp472-3; ☎ 9654 4466; 113 Collins St; mains $24-35; ✆ breakfast, lunch & dinner) A basement place cooking sensational Italian staples with an ambience that's tough to beat. Quality wines are available by the glass and the service is top-notch.

Yamato (Map pp472-3; ☎ 9663 1706; 28 Corrs Lane; dishes $6-16) It's a tight squeeze in this popular, no-frills Japanese restaurant. Expect good-value and crunchy-fresh eats, oh, and tinny background music. Groups can book the shoes-off tatami room.

Degraves Espresso Bar (Map pp472-3; ☎ 9654 1245; 23 Degraves St; dishes $8-14; ✆ breakfast & lunch) Degraves has oodles of character – it's the one with railway-waiting-room chairs. It's great for a morning fry up, a quick sandwich or an eponymous espresso.

Mecca Bah (Map pp472-3; ☎ 9642 1300; 55a New-Quay Promenade, Docklands; mains $16-20; ✆ lunch & dinner) Architects have designed Mecca Bah to be as close to the water as is structurally sound. Diners queue for the spicy Middle Eastern fare.

Kuni's (Map pp472-3; ☎ 9663 7243; 56 Little Bourke St; mains $13-27; ✆ lunch & dinner Mon-Fri) Produces some of the best Japanese in town – grab a meat or veggie *bento* box for lunch.

Don Don (Map pp472-3; ☎ 9670 7073; 321 Swanston St; mains $5-7.50; ✆ lunch Mon-Fri) A student stronghold, Don Don dishes out discount Japanese eats to hordes of students and city workers.

Southgate & Crown Entertainment Complex

Southgate's Yarra River and city skyline views make it a prime eating destination for visitors to Melbourne. It's also only a short stroll to the galleries, theatres and gardens of Kings Domain. Next door, the Crown Casino is chock-a-block with glitzy eateries.

Walter's Wine Bar (Map pp472-3; ☎ 9690 9211; Upper Level, Southgate; mains $25-35; ✆ lunch & dinner) Walter's blends culinary flair, professional service and a justifiably famous wine list. Though wine is the main star, the Italian fare is undeniably moreish.

Mecca (Map pp472-3; ☎ 9682 2999; Mid Level, Southgate; mains $26-32; ✆ lunch & dinner) Mecca matches an elegant style with a creative North African menu. Try anything that features the words 'spiced lamb'.

Blue Train (Map pp472-3; ☎ 9696 0111; Mid Level, Southgate; mains $6-15; ✆ breakfast, lunch & dinner) This loud, gay-friendly and hugely popular place serves all the mainstream staples in a humming environment. It's a casual spot to take the kids, as there'll be something that appeals to even the fussiest eaters.

North Melbourne

Akita (Map pp470-1; ☎ 9326 5766; cnr Courtney & Blackwood Sts; mains $12-24; ✆ lunch & dinner Mon-Fri) Akita serves some of the city's best Japanese food. Small wine list, small menu, smiles all 'round – a winning formula.

Courthouse Dining Room (Map pp470-1; ☎ 9329 5394; 86 Errol St; mains $22-27; ✆ lunch Mon-Fri, dinner Mon-Sat) Fans of nouveau pub grub will be in heaven here – the international menu gets it right and service is helpful.

Don Camillo (Map pp470-1; ☎ 9329 8883; 215 Victoria St; dishes $5-14; ✆ breakfast & lunch daily, dinner Thu & Fri) This is a little Italian place that's been here for yonks (ie since the 1950s), and it serves the basics in large, tasty portions. Popular with the true superstars of Melbourne, too – footy players. See how many carbs can fit into a large man around breakfast time.

Carlton

Lygon St was once affectionately thought of as the multicultural centre of Melbourne, with its cosmopolitan immigrants and bohemian university students. Now it's fraught with restaurants sporting white linen–cloaked tables and brightly lit family-run pizzerias and pasta places.

Abla's (Map pp476-7; ☎ 9347 0006; 109 Elgin St; mains $12-17; ✆ lunch Thu & Fri, dinner Mon-Sat) An old-time favourite and arguably the best Lebanese in Melbourne. On Friday and Saturday nights there's a compulsory 13-

course banquet getting wolfed down by appreciative crowds, so put on your elasticised pants and tuck in.

Brunetti (Map pp476-7; ☎ 9347 2801; 198 Faraday St; café dishes $3-7, restaurant mains $12-23; ⟨ﾝ⟩ breakfast, lunch & dinner) A stalwart of Italian culinary obsessions, Brunetti is a large haven for those who want excellent coffee, exquisite *dolci* (sweets) and mouth-watering Roman-influenced dishes.

Jimmy Watson's (Map pp476-7; ☎ 9347 3985; 333 Lygon St; mains $19-28; ⟨ﾝ⟩ lunch Mon-Sat, dinner Tue-Sat) Wine and talk are the order of the day at this long-running wine bar–restaurant. The fare is European with a nod to special Australian ingredients such as kangaroo.

Tiamo (Map pp476-7; ☎ 9347 0911; 303 Lygon St; mains $11-16; ⟨ﾝ⟩ breakfast, lunch & dinner) This historic Lygon St institution is simply an old-fashioned Italian bistro that's popular with students and movie-goers for its fast, no-frills pastas.

Shakahari (Map pp476-7; ☎ 9347 3848; 201-203 Faraday St; mains $15-17) Vegetarians unite. Long-running Shakahari offers inspired and delicious veggie food, including some mock-meat dishes.

Fitzroy & North Fitzroy

Brunswick St is a key box to tick on your 'eating tour of Melbourne' checklist. The prevailing mood is alternative, fashionable, studenty and arty all at the same time – a far cry from its recent past, when this area was as rough as guts.

Babka Bakery Café (Map pp476-7; ☎ 9416 0091; 358 Brunswick St, Fitzroy; dishes $5-15; ⟨ﾝ⟩ breakfast & lunch Tue-Sun) Famous for its breads, pastries and eternally wholesome-looking waitresses. Also famous for its sensational breakfasts, and massive and delicious sandwiches.

AUTHOR'S CHOICE

Old Kingdom (Map pp476-7; ☎ 9417 2438; 197 Smith St, Fitzroy; mains $8-14; ⟨ﾝ⟩ dinner) It's all about the duck. The moist, succulent, fatty, crispy-skinned, exquisite Peking duck. The expert table-side slicing is a treat in itself, but it wouldn't be so theatrical without the charismatic, extroverted head waiter. Order at least a day ahead; one duck ($40) is enough for three (or two, depending on the level of your duck obsession).

Alimentari (Map pp476-7; ☎ 9416 2001; 251 Brunswick St, Fitzroy; lunch $5-12; ⟨ﾝ⟩ lunch) A café–food store serving home-cooked Lebanese and Italian fare. It's frantically busy at lunchtime – be prepared to wait as regulars file in for schnitzel wraps, spaghetti and meatballs, and lamb pies.

Moroccan Soup Bar (Map pp470-1; ☎ 9482 4240; 183 St Georges Rd, North Fitzroy; mains $10-15; ⟨ﾝ⟩ dinner Tue-Sun) This squishy, brightly coloured soup bar is a vegetarian's haven. There's no menu, just the renowned owner who rattles off a list of soups, starters and heavenly North African tagines.

Mao's (Map pp476-7; ☎ 9419 1919; 263 Brunswick St, Fitzroy; mains $10-22; ⟨ﾝ⟩ dinner Tue-Sun) Mao's is a favourite for its casual vibe, superfriendly staff, kitsch fit-out and modern twist on the classic Chinese menu. The Hunan hotpot here is smokin'.

Ladro (Map pp476-7; ☎ 9415 7575; 224 Gertrude St, Fitzroy; mains $22-27; ⟨ﾝ⟩ dinner Wed-Sun) Getting a table in Ladro requires begging, borrowing and selling your first-born. Expect to be served excellent pizza and to be rushed out the door.

Madame Sousou (Map pp476-7; ☎ 9417 0400; 231 Brunswick St, Fitzroy; mains $18-28; ⟨ﾝ⟩ breakfast, lunch & dinner) This is the sort of place that Melbourne excels at – a nod to Europe, a wink at Australia. Breakfasts here set you up magnificently.

Marios (Map pp476-7; ☎ 9417 3343; 303 Brunswick St, Fitzroy; mains $17-20; ⟨ﾝ⟩ breakfast, lunch & dinner) Snubbing the easy-come, easy-go wannabe institutions on the strip, this sceney café is one of the originals, and doesn't it know it. Come for the coffee, kick-start breakfasts and a selection of good pasta dishes.

Also recommended:

Blue Chillies (Map pp476-7; ☎ 9417 0071; 182 Brunswick St, Fitzroy; mains $19-25) Blue Chillies is an intimate spot, popular for dates. It has 'new Asian' cuisine and features nothing too unknown.

Tin Pot (Map pp470-1; ☎ 9481 5312; 284 St Georges Rd, North Fitzroy; mains $9-12; ⟨ﾝ⟩ breakfast & lunch) Great breakfasts and old-school café ambience.

Vegie Bar (Map pp476-7; ☎ 9417 6935; 380 Brunswick St, Fitzroy; mains under $10; ⟨ﾝ⟩ lunch & dinner) A wide range of vegetarian meals and snacks, and staff with attitude. Arrive early or wait in line. The pizzas rock!

Richmond

Walk down Victoria St and you'll soon realise why this area has become known as 'Little Saigon', particularly the stretch between Hoddle and Church Sts, which is lined with Asian groceries, discount shops and fishmongers.

There are myriad places to clack your chopsticks along Victoria St. There are also some other non-Asian, but highly recommended, winners in this area.

Pacific Seafood BBQ House (Map pp470-1; ☎ 9427 8225; 240 Victoria St; mains $6-25; ☯ lunch & dinner) Try the delish duck and seafood at this Chinese restaurant.

Thanh Thanh (Map pp470-1; ☎ 9428 5633; 246a Victoria St; mains $6-10.50; ☯ lunch & dinner) Best for Vietnamese favourites and delicate rice-paper rolls.

Thanh Ha (Map pp470-1; ☎ 9429 8130; 172 Victoria St; mains $7-14; ☯ lunch & dinner) It's got to be Thanh Ha for slurpy bowls of *pho* (noodle) soup.

New Koreana Barbecue (Map pp470-1; ☎ 9421 1002; 58 Victoria St; mains $10-20; ☯ lunch & dinner) Pack into the New Koreana for sizzling barbecued beef cooked at the table.

Burmese House (Map pp470-1; ☎ 9421 2861; 303 Bridge Rd; mains $15-24; ☯ dinner daily, lunch Mon-Fri) Burmese House is the master of tamarind curries and chilli crab.

Pearl (Map pp470-1; ☎ 9421 4599; 631 Church St; mains $21-27; ☯ lunch & dinner) Aptly named, this creative temple offers slick, modern dining within a stone's throw of the Yarra.

Richmond Hill Café & Larder (Map pp470-1; ☎ 9421 2808; 48 Bridge Rd; mains $11-28; ☯ breakfast & lunch daily, dinner Tue-Sat) Carefully prepared bistro fare is served at this popular bar-restaurant and *fromagerie* (cheese shop). It's owned by food icon Stephanie Alexander.

Tofu Shop International (Map pp470-1; ☎ 9429 6204; 78 Bridge Rd; dishes $3.50-11; ☯ lunch & dinner Mon-Fri, lunch Sat) Health-kickers and vegos file in for the salads, vegetables, filos and 'soyalaki'. Food is tasty, filling and cruelty-free.

Vlado's (Map pp470-1; ☎ 9428 5833; 61 Bridge Rd; set menu $68; ☯ lunch Mon-Fri, dinner Mon-Sat) This place is famous for one thing: steak. Serves are thumpin', and your iron stores will be jumpin'.

South Yarra, Toorak, Prahran & Windsor

Commercial Rd features the Prahran Market and plenty of gay-friendly eateries – its sista strip is the high-profile, style-policed Greville St. South Yarra's and Toorak's affluent eateries are dotted along Toorak Rd and Chapel St. The grungier Windsor end of Chapel St is home to cafés as comfy as your cardigan.

Prahran Market (Map p478; www.prahranmarket .com.au; 163-185 Commercial Rd, Prahran; ☯ dawn-5pm Tue & Sat, dawn-6pm Thu & Fri, 10am-3pm Sun) A top-quality produce market, with several organic-produce stores (including an organic butcher), a fresh-pasta store, bountiful delis, and a food court for grazing on the move.

Jacques Reymond (Map p478; ☎ 9525 2178; 78 Williams Rd, Prahran; 2-course menu $68, degustation menu $120; ☯ lunch Thu & Fri, dinner Tue-Sat) A real special-occasion restaurant and winner of numerous accolades. Jacques Reymond's presents mind-blowingly artful and imaginative cuisine to well-groomed diners.

Da Noi (Map p478; ☎ 9866 5975; 95 Toorak Rd, South Yarra; mains $25-35; ☯ dinner daily, lunch Fri-Sun) The seasonal menu specialises in Sardinian cuisine, which means you'll find plenty of brilliantly prepared seafood and dishes that seem to have been hunted that very day.

Borsch, Vodka & Tears (Map p478; ☎ 9530 2694; 173 Chapel St, Prahran; mains $15-19; ☯ breakfast, lunch & dinner Thu-Sun, dinner Mon-Wed) A fabulous Polish place serving around 100 strains of vodka and modern-Polish food. The ambience is shabby-chic, low-lighting and lots of sincere conversation.

Orange (Map p478; ☎ 9529 1644; 126 Chapel St, Windsor; breakfast $8.50-15, mains $23-27; ☯ breakfast, lunch & dinner) With a 1970s retro feel and tasty cross-cultural dishes, this café attracts an alternative crowd that appreciates a Bloody Mary with breakfast. Grooves are played on the turntables at night.

St Kilda

Fitzroy and Acland Sts are where you'll find the majority of cafés and restaurants. There are some mainstays by the sea, too.

Baker D Chirico (Map p475; ☎ 9534 3777; Shop 3-4, 149 Fitzroy St; loafres $4.80, mains $5-8.50; ☯ breakfast & lunch) Baker Daniel Chirico has been hailed by the media as a 'wunderkind' – his organic bread is that heavenly. Pastries are equally rapturous, and hefty lunch rolls addictive. It's only the aloof service that lets it down.

Galleon (Map p475; ☎ 9534 8934; 9 Carlisle St; meals $5-14.50; ☯ breakfast, lunch & dinner) The colour ful, homely Galleon has fuelled the creative juices of St Kilda's arts community for years with its heart-warming café fare. Just don't be in a hurry.

Café a Taglio (Map p475; ☎ 9534 1344; 157A Fitzroy St; mains $15-18, pizza slices around $6; ☽ lunch & dinner) Thin-crust pizza is served by the slice, Roman-style. A tempting array of pastas compete for attention but a couple of squares and a glass of vino will probably win out.

Café di Stasio (Map p475; ☎ 9525 3999; 31 Fitzroy St; mains $29-35; ☽ lunch & dinner) Café di Stasio thoroughly deserves its reputation as the best Italian restaurant in Melbourne. Its two-course lunch (which includes a glass of wine or coffee for $25) allows local semistarving artists to mix it with corporate types.

Il Fornaio (Map p475; ☎ 9534 2922; 2 Acland St; breakfast $2.20-13, dinner mains $17-23; ☽ breakfast, lunch & dinner) A busy, well-organised, Italian-style café that, despite all the concrete, is surprisingly cosy. Duck in for a takeaway roll, pastry or cake, or linger over fluffy scrambled eggs.

Cicciolina (Map p475; ☎ 9525 3333; 130 Acland St; mains $19-32; ☽ lunch & dinner) This dark and intimate bustling institution doesn't take reservations, and it's always packed. It's the perfect blend of style and substance, with a snug bolt hole of a bar out the back.

Claypots (Map p475; ☎ 9534 1282; 213 Barkly St; mains $10-25; ☽ lunch & dinner) It mightn't look like much from the outside, but the spicy seafood claypots here are delicious, and are influenced by international kitchens, meaning that you could share treats from Malaysia and Morocco. There are no bookings taken, so arrive early (say, 4pm!).

Bedouin Kitchen (Map p475; ☎ 9534 0888; 103 Grey St; mains $15-25; ☽ breakfast, lunch & dinner) The blood-red walls and Moroccan light fittings set the scene for sharing excellent meze dishes. Ask the staff what's special if you simply can't decide. The vegetarian options lord it over the meat dishes.

Circa (Map p475; ☎ 9536 1122; 2 Acland St; set lunch per person $30; ☽ breakfast, lunch & dinner) Part of the chichi Prince hotel (p505), which incorporates the Aurora Spa Retreat, Circa's reputation skyrocketed with the arrival of chef Andrew McConnell. Creamy-white banquettes, impeccable service and sophisticated food are its trademarks. Set-price lunches are a good way to sample the fare.

Stokehouse (Map p475; ☎ 9525 5555; 30 Jacka Blvd; mains $30-40; ☽ lunch & dinner) Right on the foreshore, the Stokehouse has the location that everyone else dreams about, with wide windows allowing every ray of light to permeate the charmingly decorated space. The upstairs restaurant's menu features classic Mod Oz interpretations of Asian and European themes.

Soul Mama (Map p475; ☎ 9525 3338; St Kilda Sea Baths, 10 Jacka Blvd; mains $13-16; ☽ lunch & dinner) Soul Mama's all-vegetarian, guilt-free, soul-warming food is presented cafeteria style – putting the glam in *bain-marie* dining. Service is fast paced, the queues long, and the sea views unrivalled.

Williamstown

Willy has a fine assortment of cafés and restaurants along Nelson Pl, catering to the hordes of day-trippers.

Strand Seafood Restaurant (Map pp470-1; ☎ 9397 7474; cnr The Strand & Ferguson St; mains $25-30; ☽ breakfast, lunch & dinner) The Strand is stylish, simple and ultramodern, with a small bar, an open-air courtyard and water views. The menu is predominantly seafood, most of it very well prepared.

Sirens (☎ 9397 7811; The Esplanade; mains $23; ☽ lunch & dinner) Located right on Williamstown beach, this converted Art Deco bathing pavilion incorporates a bistro and a more formal restaurant that leans towards Mediterranean flavours.

Self-Catering

Supermarkets, often open 24 hours or until midnight, are found in most suburbs – Coles and Safeway are the names to look out for.

Victoria St in Richmond is the place to go for cheap produce and Asian ingredients, and major markets, bursting with fresh produce and gourmet deli items, include Queen Victoria Market (p480) and Prahran Market (opposite).

For posher provisions head to the food store and food courts in David Jones and Myer (p516).

DRINKING

Melbourne has a famously lively drinking scene. You'll find bars hidden down tiny alleys, at the top of darkened staircases and perched atop most luxury hotels.

VICTORIA

Juice bars offering 'brainpower' and 'energy' supplements plus smoothies and superfood spirulina juices, are another booming industry.

City Centre

The following all offer something special, whether it be décor, drinks lists or the 'it' factor.

Gin Palace (Map pp472-3; ☎ 9654 0553; 190 Little Collins St) A sophisticated, dimly lit and beautifully furnished New York–meets–Mittel Europa cocktail bar. One killer martini and you're away.

Double Happiness (Map pp472-3; ☎ 9650 4488; 21 Liverpool St) A tiny, red-hued space, this Chinese socialist–inspired drinking den makes superb cocktails – the espresso-vodka martinis are as outrageous as communism.

Cherry (Map pp472-3; ☎ 9639 8122; AC/DC Lane) If you can find it, you're guaranteed to like this bar, hidden down a tiny cobbled alley off Flinders Lane. It's open late for dancing.

Meyers Place (Map pp472-3; ☎ 9650 8609; 20 Meyers Pl) This enchantingly small, dark bar is popular with students, office workers, artists and everyone in between. It's designed by renowned local architecture firm Six Degrees.

Troika (Map pp472-3; ☎ 9663 5461; 106 Little Lonsdale St) Troika takes its aesthetic cues from Meyers Place and inspires its devotees by never being too cool, too hot or too anything. A stylish gem that never tries too hard.

St Jerome's (Map pp472-3; 7 Caledonia Lane) Coming here on a weekend is an exercise in frustration, but stumbling upon this back-alley hidey-hole (with a great backyard) on a weeknight or afternoon is sure to thrill. The crowd's friendly, the DJs experimental.

Rue Bebelons (Map pp472-3; ☎ 9663 1700; 267 Little Lonsdale St) Earnest student types fuel up on espresso and a salad roll and custard tart at this unsigned, hanky-sized place. At night it transforms into an intimate, buzzing bar.

Robot (Map pp472-3; ☎ 9620 3646; 12 Bligh Pl) Set among humming high rises, designer Robot is a favourite for Japanese beers, sake and *nori* rolls – even Astro Boy makes an appearance. It's a cosy café by day; packed with glamorous funksters at night.

Melbourne Supper Club (Map pp472-3; ☎ 9654 6300; Level 1, 161 Spring St) The Supper Club is ideal for that fancy late-night tipple. You can recline on leather lounges while career wait-staff service all your food and drink desires. It's sophisticated, but the only stuffiness is in the armchairs.

Fitzroy

Fitzroy has a rich drinking culture and plenty of pubs and bars to support it. In and around Brunswick St is the most obvious hunting ground.

Standard (Map pp476-7; ☎ 9419 4793; 293 Fitzroy St) The décor is classic, the ornaments kitsch and the pub grub solid. Its beer garden caters to the summer crowds, while the open fire warms cold hands in winter.

Yelza (Map pp476-7; ☎ 9416 2689; 245 Gertrude St) Stepping through the door at Yelza is like entering another world, with its dim lighting, ornate furniture and tactile wallpaper. The back garden is roomier if you need breathing space from the crowded interior.

Napier Hotel (Map pp476-7; ☎ 9419 4240; 210 Napier St) A short stroll from Brunswick St, the Napier is the archetypal 'local'. It's dark and laid-back, there's a small beer garden, the pub-grub portions are massive, and sharks wage battle around the pool tables.

Polly (Map pp476-7; ☎ 9417 0880; 401 Brunswick St) Polly melds a luxe sensibility and slick service with lots of ornate carved wood and plush velvet. Ease yourself into a lounge and peruse the extensive drinks list – you're not going anywhere in a hurry.

Bar Open (Map pp476-7; ☎ 9415 9601; 317 Brunswick St) The late-night bar of choice for many locals. Downstairs is a cosy bar-café with couches plus a small courtyard. Upstairs occasionally hosts live acts, including the odd micro music gig or spoken word.

Monties (Map pp476-7; ☎ 9419 3344; 347 Smith St) A big round bar, an open space and plenty of comfy places to chill out make Monties a local's favourite. It's a casual spot for a drink, a chat and a game of stick.

Labour In Vain Hotel (Map pp476-7; ☎ 9417 5955; 197 Brunswick St) This small pub has loads of character, a tiny rooftop beer garden and some dedicated locals who appreciate the wide, old-fashioned windows that allow you to watch the world go by.

Builders Arms Hotel (Map pp476-7; ☎ 9419 0818; 211 Gertrude St) Yet another great local pub. Entertainment varies from Q&A (queer and alternative) on Thursday night, to film screenings, booty shaking, pool and live music. Grandma's Kitchen cooks up tempting food.

Prahran

Prahran is about attitude and slick style, with a lively gay scene centred on Commercial Rd. Greville St is the premier strip for a crawl.

Candy Bar (Map p478; ☎ 9529 6566; 162 Greville St) The Candy Bar is a grinding Greville St fixture. By day it's a sceney café; by night gay-flavoured patrons drink and dance to DJ-played music. If the transvestite-hosted bingo night is still happening, add that to your itinerary pronto.

Back Bar (Map p478; ☎ 9529 7899; 67 Green St) The place resembles a funeral parlour from an episode of *The Sopranos*, but the friendly welcome will make you feel as though you're part of 'the family' in the best possible way.

St Kilda

On a warm summer evening St Kilda is packed with crowded revellers – many of them English and Irish backpackers (and plenty of locals too).

Esplanade Hotel (Map p475; ☎ 9534 0211; 11 Upper Esplanade) 'The Espy' is a true Melbourne institution – don't get stuck to the festering carpets. The sprawling Espy has free live bands nightly and many competitive pool tables. Watch the sun set over the pier with a glass of something cold. Make the pilgrimage at least once!

JUST FOR NEIGHBOURS FANS   *Alan Fletcher*

For many travellers to Australia, particularly those of British origin, Melbourne is a 'must' destination because it is the home of internationally renowned TV programme *Neighbours*. A trip to Melbourne would not be complete without a trip to the legendary Ramsay St: Pin Oak Ct in Vermont South is the suburban street that has been the home of the show for 20 years.

The best way to see Ramsay St and have a proper *Neighbours* experience is by simply doing the **Official Neighbours Tour** (☎ 03-9534 4755; www.neighbourstour.com). It's the only tour approved by Grundy TV and the residents of Pin Oak Ct. If you're lucky you might see us filming and grab a photo and autograph. Two tours are available. The $25 tour runs twice daily Monday to Friday and visits Ramsay St and Erinsborough High School. The second, more-comprehensive tour costs $55 and visits the street, the school and the outside studio sets of the Lassiter's complex, Lou's Mechanics and Grease Monkeys. This tour runs on weekends and Christmas and New Year's holidays.

You'll also find some backpacker hostels that occasionally run in-house trips to Ramsay St – but always check to see if it's above board and that it's a licensed operator.

There is a variety of ways of making the pilgrimage yourself: Pin Oak Ct is in Vermont South. If you don't have wheels, take the train to Glen Waverley station and bus No 888 or 889 north (get off at Vision Dr near Burwood Hwy). Tram No 75 from Flinders St will take you all the way to the corner of Burwood Hwy and Springvale Rd; a short walk south takes you to Weeden Dr and Pin Oak Ct is third on the left. If you make the trip, please remember to respect the privacy of residents. Don't do anything in their street or front yards you wouldn't be happy with in your own street or home!

Backpacker King also runs a hugely popular **Meet Your Neighbours Trivia Night** (☎ 03-9534 4755; www.backpackerking.com.au) every Monday night at a British pub in St Kilda, where you will have the opportunity to rub shoulders and have your photo taken with your favourite *Neighbours* stars. The night is full of entertainment and prizes as well. It's held at the **Elephant & Wheelbarrow** (Map p475; 169 Fitzroy St, St Kilda). Call Backpacker King to book. After meeting the stars, fans are entertained with a one-hour concert by my band, Rythmia.

Another must-see for *Neighbours* fans is the original Robinson household studio set, which is on display at the Melbourne Museum (p492). It's a great photo op and you can read the graffiti messages from cast and crew scrawled on the back of the set.

Alan Fletcher has worked in every branch of the performing arts for 28 years. For the past 11 years he has played the role of Dr Karl Kennedy on Neighbours.

VICTORIA

Prince Bandroom (Map p475; ☎ 9536 1111; 2 Acland St) The Art Deco Prince has been a fixture of the St Kilda scene for years. The downstairs bar is where you shoot pool, and the crowd spills onto the street during warmer months. Upstairs, the bandroom hosts local and international acts and popular DJ events.

George Public Bar (Map p475; ☎ 9534 8822; 127 Fitzroy St) The narrow basement bar of the George (the 'snake pit') is an unpretentious, grungy bar swarming with backpackers and the odd local. There's a pool table and bowls of fat hot chips.

Greyhound Hotel (Map p475; ☎ 9534 4189; 1 Brighton Rd) On Saturday nights this grotty local boozer with tonnes of rough-round-the-edges charm has drag shows. Other nights you can expect live music and cheap unpretentious drinks.

Doulton Bar (Map p475; ☎ 9534 2200; Village Belle Hotel, 202 Barkly St) Slipping somewhat in its reputation as an unpretentious local boozer, the Doulton has recently become quite the pick-up joint, with local pretty boys and girls studiously avoiding looking at each other.

Mink (Map p475; ☎ 9536 1199; 2 Acland St) Tucked beneath the Prince of Wales Hotel, Mink is a plush lounge-cum-bunker with plenty of dark bordello-esque corners for an intimate rendezvous (and lots of vodka).

Elephant & Wheelbarrow (Map p475; ☎ 9534 7888; 169 Fitzroy St) This Irish chain backpacker hang-out has *Neighbours* trivia nights on Monday and thematic pub grub such as the 'Earl's Caught' fish and chips.

ENTERTAINMENT

Melbourne has a thriving nightlife and a lively cultural scene. The best source of 'what's on' is the *Entertainment Guide (EG)* in Friday's *Age*. *Beat* and *Inpress* are free music and entertainment publications that can be found in cafés, bars and other venues throughout the city. Also check online at www.melbourne.vic.gov.au/events and **Citysearch** (www.melbourne.citysearch.com.au).

Buy tickets from the following:

Ticketmaster7 (Map pp472-3; ☎ 1300 136 166; www.ticketmaster7.com; Theatres Bldg, Victorian Arts Centre, 100 St Kilda Rd; ⏰ 9am-9pm Mon-Sat) Main booking agency for theatre, concerts, sports and other events. Besides taking bookings by phone, Ticketmaster has outlets in places

like Myer, Telstra Dome, major theatres and shopping centres.

Ticketek (Map pp472-3; ☎ 13 28 49; www.ticketek .com.au; 225 Exhibition St; ⏰ 9am-5pm Mon-Fri, 9am-1pm Sat) Phone and Internet bookings for large sporting events and mainstream entertainment. Also branches in the Princess Theatre and Her Majesty's Theatre.

Half-Tix (Map pp472-3; ☎ 9650 9420; Melbourne Town Hall, cnr Little Collins & Swanston Sts; ⏰ 10am-2pm Mon & Sat, 11am-6pm Tue-Thu, 11am-6.30pm Fri) Sells half-price tickets to shows and concerts on day of performance. Cash only.

Live Music

Melbourne is widely acknowledged as the country's rock capital, and has long enjoyed a thriving pub-rock scene where bands such as AC/DC, Nick Cave & the Bad Seeds and Jet strummed their way into rock's rich tapestry. City jazz and blues venues are also listed here. Expect to pay between zilch and $30 for live performances.

Apart from the newspapers, tune into independent radio stations **3RRR** (FM102.7; www.rrr.org.au) and **3PBS** (FM106.7) for current gig guides.

ROCK
City Centre
Ding Dong Lounge (Map pp472-3; ☎ 9662 1020; 18 Market Lane) Smoky, raucous, grotty and everything a classic rock-and-roll bar should be; local and international bands play here.

Pony (Map pp472-3; ☎ 9654 5917; 68 Little Collins St) If too much rock and roll is barely enough, you can party hearty at Pony. You'll have to shout to hear yourself speak at this earringing venue.

North Melbourne
Arthouse (Map p470-1; ☎ 9347 3917; cnr Queensberry & Elizabeth Sts) At the Royal Artillery Hotel, this place hosts a wide range of acts, mostly at the heavy or punk end of the spectrum.

Fitzroy, Collingwood & Carlton
Tote (Map pp476-7; ☎ 9419 5320; 71 Johnston St, Collingwood) A mosh pit and carpet as sticky as the tar lining the lungs of the punters. Live music – metal, punk etc – plays every night except Monday at this stalwart.

Evelyn Hotel (Map pp476-7; ☎ 9419 5500; cnr Brunswick & Kerr Sts, Fitzroy) The Evelyn attracts a mixed bag of local and (occasionally) international acts, and the feel is always warm and welcoming.

Rob Roy (Map pp476-7; ☎ 9419 7180; 51 Brunswick St) On the corner of Gertrude St, this funky local has a solid roster of live pop and rock bands – some for free.

Dan O'Connell Hotel (Map pp476-7; ☎ 9347 1502; 225 Canning St, Carlton) Acoustic gigs and pints of Guinness. There are live acts most nights.

Richmond

Corner Hotel (Map pp470-1; ☎ 9427 7300; 57 Swan St, Richmond) A scungy pub and band venue that's a major player in the Melbourne music scene, hosting international and local acts. It's a good pub, too.

JAZZ

Jazz cats and blues hounds will be pleased to hear that Melbourne's jazz scene is jumpin'. *EG* has listings.

Bennetts Lane (Map pp472-3; ☎ 9663 2856; www .bennettslane.com; 25 Bennetts Lane) Hidden down a narrow lane off Little Lonsdale St, this dimly lit jazz joint is where most visiting acts perform (even Prince played a secret gig here when last in town).

Tony Starr's Kitten Club (Map pp472-3; ☎ 9650 2448; Level 1, 267 Little Collins St) This upstairs bar mixes 1950s and new-millennium style as successfully as it does its cocktails. It's got terrific atmosphere, a good menu and some great live jazz.

Dizzy's (Map pp470-1; ☎ 9428 1233; 90 Swan St, Richmond) Dizzy's offers smoke-free jazz most nights of the week and attracts some pretty big names. There are 'cry baby' sessions, for those with youngsters, on the first Saturday of the month.

Night Cat (Map pp476-7; ☎ 9417 0090; 141 Johnston St, Fitzroy) The Cat is a large, comfortable space with a great atmosphere and skew-whiff 1950s décor (a Melbourne trademark). Bands here are big and play anything from jazz to salsa.

During January, February and March, the Royal Melbourne Zoo (p492) hosts the extremely popular 'Twilights' season of open-air sessions, with jazz or big bands performing on Friday, Saturday and Sunday evenings.

Nightclubs

Melbourne's club scene is a mixed bag, and what's here today might be gone tomorrow.

Cover charges range from free to between $5 and $20.

The CBD has the largest concentration of clubs and is a good place for a club crawl, particularly if you like dancing until dawn.

Honkytonks (Map pp472-3; ☎ 9662 4555; Duckboard Pl; ☿ Wed-Sun) The bar is like a shrine to booze, the décor like an acid trip, the music sublime and the crowd secretly relieved they got past the door, no matter how nonchalant they play it.

Croft Institute (Map pp472-3; ☎ 9671 4399; 21-25 Croft Alley) Inspiring both devotion and disgust, depending on who you're talking to, the Croft is a hard-to-find laboratory of boozing and schmoozing. It's a perilous climb to the dance floor upstairs.

Lounge (Map pp472-3; ☎ 9663 2916; 243 Swanston St; ☿ Wed-Sat) Café by day, club by night. The crowd is an up-for-it mix of young students and the gainfully employed, and the music crosses the genres from electro to hip hop.

Outside the CBD you'll find many of Melbourne's alternative clubs.

Revolver (Map pp478; ☎ 9521 5985; 229 Chapel St, Prahran; ☿ nightly) Cavernous Revolver is a popular venue with Prahran's young, arty crowd. Its packed programme features DJs, bands, film nights and spoken word, and there's also an inexpensive Thai restaurant here.

Alia (Map pp476-7; ☎ 9486 0999; 83 Smith St, Fitzroy; ☿ Thu-Sun) Alia is ostensibly a club, but you'll never really feel as though you're in one. It's a mixed, easy-going spot, popular with lipstick lesbians. Decent music may well get you on the smallish dance floor.

First Floor (Map pp476-7; ☎ 9419 6380; Level 1, 393 Brunswick St, Fitzroy; ☿ Tue-Sun) A cavernous space in which to dance, drink and devote yourself to having a good time. It's a smart-looking spot, but not precious about it.

Laundry (Map pp476-7; ☎ 9419 6115; 50 Johnston St, Fitzroy) Slightly grungy and shambolic, the Laundry attracts all types and does a good job of keeping the entertainment options – DJs, pool tables, karaoke and live music – on a roll, nightly.

Gay & Lesbian Venues

Most of the newer generation of bars and clubs in Melbourne are gay- and lesbian-friendly. St Kilda, South Yarra and Prahran are the city's main 'gay precincts', with Prahran's Commercial Rd being the

VICTORIA

traditional centre of Melbourne's gay culture. Wags joke that it's not the 'gay mile', but the 'gay metre', as Melbourne certainly doesn't rival Sydney when it comes to gay nightlife – that said, it's a lot more relaxed than its northern sister. Other gay-friendly neighbourhoods include Collingwood and Abbotsford, with Northcote being a popular spot for lesbians.

Girl Bar (Map p475; ☎ 9536 1177; www.the prince.com.au; Prince of Wales, 29 Fitzroy St, St Kilda; admission $15; ☉ one Fri a month) This popular ladies' night will have you partying with the cliterati 'til the sun comes up. The Prince also has a ground-level gay bar that dates back to the 1940s – it's open daily and is free.

Peel Hotel (Map pp476-7; ☎ 9419 4762; cnr Peel & Wellington Sts, Collingwood; admission free) The Peel is one of the best-known and most popular gay venues in Melbourne, but it also attracts a lesbian crowd. It's the last stop of a big night.

Laird (Map pp470-1; ☎ 9417 2832; 149 Gipps St, Abbotsford; admission free) Men only. Lots of leather, moustaches, beer and brawn. Who's yer daddy?

Xchange Hotel (Map p478; ☎ 9867 5144; 119 Commercial Rd, Prahran; admission free-$10) A long-standing fixture on the Prahran scene, the Xchange plays host to a variety of customers and covers all the gay bases. A good, fail-safe meeting spot.

Market Hotel (Map p478; ☎ 9826 0933; 143 Commercial Rd, South Yarra; admission $10-20) A perennially popular nightclub with good house music keeping things going till the sun comes up, and then some.

Other gay- and lesbian-friendly bars include the Greyhound Hotel (p512), Alia (p513), Builders Arms Hotel (p510) and Candy Bar (p511).

Cinemas

Melbourne has plenty of mainstream cinemas playing latest releases, although if you've come from the USA or Europe they might be last season's latest. The main chains – Village, Hoyts and Greater Union – cluster around the intersection of Bourke and Russell Sts. Tickets cost around $15. Check the *EG* in Friday's *Age* or other newspapers for screenings and times.

ACMI (Map pp472-3; ☎ 9663 2583; www.acmi.net .au; Federation Sq) The fabulously high-tech cinemas here are where to see a mind-blowing

range of films, documentaries and animated features.

Astor Theatre (Map pp470-1; ☎ 9510 1414; www .astor-theatre.com; cnr Chapel St & Dandenong Rd, St Kilda) This place holds not-to-be-missed Art Deco nostalgia, with double features every night of old and recent classics.

Cinema Europa (Map p478; ☎ 9827 2440; Level 1, Jam Factory, 500 Chapel St, South Yarra) Good café and bar on the premises, comfy seats and art-house films.

Cinema Nova (Map pp476-7; ☎ 9347 5331; www .cinemanova.com.au; 380 Lygon St, Carlton) Nova has great current film releases. Cheap tickets are available on Monday.

George Cinemas (Map p475; ☎ 9534 6922; 13 Fitzroy St, St Kilda) Small cinema space but a St Kilda local.

Imax (Map pp476-7; ☎ 9663 5454; www.imax.com .au; Carlton Gardens) This theatre screens films in superwide 70mm format. Features are listed in *EG* and on the Imax website.

Kino (Map pp472-3; ☎ 9650 2100; Collins Pl, 45 Collins St) Recently refurbished and hosting good art-house releases – close to great bars too, for after-flick drinks.

Theatre

Melbourne has a number of well-regarded theatre companies, and the scene is probably the healthiest in the country, with excellent performers, a responsive public and a supportive atmosphere. The *EG* in Friday's *Age* always lists the major theatre performances, from edgy independent productions to mainstream musicals.

Melbourne prides itself on being Australia's most 'highbrow' city, so it should come as no surprise that the more tradi-

---

MOONLIGHT CINEMA

During summer the **Moonlight Cinema** (Map pp470-1; www.moonlight.com.au) has almost nightly screenings of newish and classic films in the Royal Botanic Gardens (enter via Gate F on Birdwood Ave, South Yarra). **Open Air Cinema** (Map pp472–3) screens films in the Sidney Myer Music Bowl (enter via Gate 1, Kings Domain, Linlithgow Ave). Prices are similar to standard cinemas. Bring along a rug, pillow and moonlight supper, or buy food and drinks. Tickets can also be purchased through Ticketmaster7 (p512).

tional musical and dance art forms attract enthusiastic patronage.

In 1996 Victoria's state opera company was subsumed by Opera Australia, leading to regular howls of protests about the paucity of opera performances in the state. As this book went to press there were hints the VSO would rise again – watch this space. That said, **Opera Australia** (www.opera-australia.org.au) performs regularly in Melbourne; visit its website for more details.

Classical music buffs must listen to the **Melbourne Chorale** (www.melbournechorale.com.au), a combination of two choirs that perform a variety of classical and modern works for voice. The **Melbourne Symphony Orchestra** (www.mso.com.au) performs regularly throughout the year; it has both a strong reputation and a keen fan base.

The **Australian Ballet** (www.australianballet.com.au) has a good repertoire and some sterling performers, and is based in Melbourne.

All of the above can be seen in performance at the Victorian Arts Centre, with tickets available via phone, ticket offices and the Internet.

Victorian Arts Centre (Map pp472-3; ☎ 9281 8000; www.vicartscentre.com.au; 100 St Kilda Rd, Southbank) This is Melbourne's major venue for the performing arts and where the **Melbourne Theatre Company** (MTC; Map pp472-3; ☎ 9684 4500; www.mtc.com.au) stages around 15 productions each year, from contemporary to Shakespearean.

La Mama (Map pp476-7; ☎ 9347 6948; 205 Faraday St, Carlton) This tiny, intimate forum produces new Australian works and experimental theatre, and has a reputation for developing emerging playwrights.

CUB Malthouse Theatre (Map pp470-1; ☎ 9685 5111; www.playbox.com.au; 113 Sturt St, South Melbourne) An outstanding company that stages predominantly Australian works by established and new playwrights. It was previously known as Playbox Theatre.

Princess Theatre (Map pp472-3; ☎ 9299 9800; 163 Spring St) This beautifully renovated landmark theatre is the venue for superslick musicals.

Regent Theatre (Map pp472-3; ☎ 9299 9500; 191 Collins St) A grand old venue for musicals.

Comedy

Melbourne has an extremely healthy stand-up circuit and is host to April's **International Comedy Festival** (www.comedyfestival.com.au).

Butterfly Club (Map pp470-1; ☎ 9690 2000; 204 Bank St, South Melbourne) This adorable terrace house holds a small theatre that hosts regular cabaret performances. Show over, head out the back or upstairs to a uniquely decorated bar, where surfaces are bedecked with the kitsch, the cool and the cute.

Comic's Lounge (Map pp470-1; ☎ 9348 9488; www.thecomicslounge.com.au; 26 Errol St, North Melbourne) The Comic's Lounge in North Melbourne is the only place in town with daily comedy performances, with acts ranging across the comedy spectrum for around $10.

Last Laugh Comedy Club (Map pp472-3; ☎ 9650 1977; www.comedyclub.com.au; Athenaeum Theatre, 188 Collins St) Professional stand-up on Friday and Saturday nights, with dinner-and-a-show packages available, if you want to try choking on laughter.

Sport
FOOTBALL
Australian Rules
AFL (Australian Football League; known as 'the footy') is the city's sporting obsession, with games at the **Melbourne Cricket Ground** (MCG; Map pp470-1; ☎ 9657 8888; www.mcg.org.au; Brunton Ave, Jolimont) regularly pulling crowds of between 50,000 and 80,000. If you're here between April and September try and see a match, as much for the crowd as the game. The sheer energy of the barracking at a big game is exhilarating. Despite the fervour, crowd violence is almost unknown.

Being the shrine of Aussie rules, the MCG is still widely regarded as the best place to see a match, although the newer but smaller **Telstra Dome** (Map pp472-3; ☎ 8625 7700; www.telstradome.com.au; Docklands) is an option.

Tickets can be bought at the ground for most games, and admission costs between about $15 and $20. Booking seats in advance might be necessary at big games.

Rugby
Rugby union (15 a side) has been slow to catch on in Melbourne, but the MCG and Telstra Dome attract enormous crowds to international matches.

Rugby league (13 a side) has made some impact on Melbourne's sport-mad public. **Melbourne Storm** (www.melbournestorm.com.au), the only Melbourne side in the national league, won the Grand Final in 1999, heralding wild celebrations.

April to September is the season for both codes. Melbourne Storm's home matches are played at **Olympic Park** (Map pp470-1; ☎ 9286 1600; www.mopt.com.au; Batman Ave, Jolimont).

Soccer

Soccer (football) has always had a strong fan base in Melbourne, with the Italian, Greek and Croatian communities being particularly avid followers. Contact **Football Federation Victoria** (☎ 9682 9666; www.footballfedvic.com .au) for details on home matches and venues.

CRICKET

For any cricket fan a visit to the **MCG** (Melbourne Cricket Ground; Map pp470-1; ☎ 9657 8888; www .mcg.org.au; Brunton Ave, Jolimont) is something of a pilgrimage. During summer, international test matches and one-day internationals are played here. The cricket season in Australia is from October to March. General admission to international matches is around $30 and reserved seats start at around $40, with finals costing more (and generally requiring a booking). The cricket event *par excellence* is the traditional Boxing Day test.

HORSE RACING

Horse racing takes place in Melbourne throughout the year at the racecourses at Flemington, Caulfield, Moonee Valley and Sandown.

The 3.2km **Melbourne Cup** (www.vrc.net.au), which is always run at Flemington Racecourse, brings Australia to a standstill. Cup Day is a public holiday in the Melbourne metropolitan area, but people across the nation are affected by Melbourne's spring-racing fever. Thursday after the Cup, Oaks Day, once a 'ladies' event, is now almost as popular – with both sexes – as the Cup.

MOTOR SPORTS

The **Australian Formula One Grand Prix** (☎ 9258 7100; www.grandprix.com.au/cars) is held in Albert Park in March and the World 500cc **Motorcycle Grand Prix** (www.grandprix.com.au/bikes) races at Phillip Island in October. Tickets for the Formula One Grand Prix start at $40 for a one-day general-admission ticket and $600 for a four-day reserved ticket.

TENNIS

For two weeks each January **Melbourne Park** (Map pp470-1; ☎ 9286 1244; www.mopt.com.au; Batman Ave, Jolimont) hosts the **Australian Open tennis championships** (www.ausopen.org). Top players from around the world come to compete in the year's first of the big four Grand Slam tournaments. Tickets range from about $25 for early rounds to over $100 for finals.

The **Rod Laver Arena** (Map pp470-1; www.mop .com.au; Batman Ave, Jolimont) is an enormous arena that hosts both the Australian Open tennis and populist concert tours for the likes of Sir Elton John and David Bowie. It features a retractable roof, so weather is not an issue.

SHOPPING

Melbourne offers the best shopping in Australia. The widest array of boutiques is in the city centre; the suburbs are home to a growing legion of factory outlets (try Bridge Rd and Swan St in Richmond and Smith St in Collingwood).

Bourke St Mall has the densest concentration of shops. It's home to the city's two main department stores, **David Jones** (Map pp472-3; ☎ 9643 2222; 310 Bourke St) and **Myer** (Map pp472-3; ☎ 9661 1111; 314 Bourke St). **Melbourne Central** (Map pp472-3; ☎ 9922 1100; cnr Elizabeth & Latrobe Sts) is a shopping centre with lots of mainstream shops, especially clothing. In an imposing modern skyscraper, **QV** (Map pp472-3; ☎ 9658 0100; cnr Swanston & Lonsdale Sts) is Melbourne's freshest contender and features populist commercial options and a supermarket.

Australiana

Crumpler (Map pp476-7; ☎ 9417 5338; cnr Gertrude & Smith Sts, Fitzroy) Crumpler is a local company that makes tough-as-nails bags for bicycle couriers, laptops and photography equipment. They're functional fashion accessories and 'everyone's' got a Crumpler. It's a great local souvenir you won't be ashamed to drag around the world.

Dinosaur Designs (Map p478; ☎ 9827 2600; 562 Chapel St, South Yarra) Fabulous resin *objets d'art* and jewellery moulded in organic shapes and vivid colours. It's an excellent way to brighten up your home or your body.

RM Williams (Map p478; ☎ 9510 2413; 204 Commercial Rd, Prahran) Bill Clinton doesn't consider a trip to Australia complete until he has snaffled a pair of these famously long-lasting boots. An Aussie icon, even for city slickers.

Children's Shops

Bernard's Magic Shop (Map pp472-3; ☎ 9670 9270; 211 Elizabeth St) This magical place will impress any littlies that you may have in tow. There are practical jokes galore here, as well as items that will help the more serious magician.

Gerlinki Junior (Map pp476-7; ☎ 9419 9169; 217 Brunswick St, Fitzroy) Stocking the funkiest kids' clothes in Melbourne, Gerlinki Junior is the pint-sized branch of this hip budget fashion retailer.

Honeyweather & Speight (Map p475; ☎ 9534 3380; 113 Barkly St, St Kilda) This kooky gem has wonderfully old-fashioned and unusual toys for children – pick up a pint-sized ukulele.

Clothing & Accessories

The city is your best bet for a major wardrobe upgrade. Greville St in Prahran is the strip for secondhand vintage and retro gear, as well as some designer boutiques. You can spend hours poking along Brunswick St, which sports a host of designer boutiques, retro, street wear and rave wear. Johnston and Gertrude Sts are also home to some cool designer boutiques. Chapel St in South Yarra has long had a reputation as Melbourne's premier style strip, and the street continues to be one of the most popular fashion hang-outs for the beautiful people. Expect to find top labels and top prices.

GPO Building (Map pp472-3; ☎ 9663 0066; 350 Bourke St) In September 2001 Melbourne's grand GPO went up in flames. Since then the building has been given a stunning make-over and it now houses fabulous boutiques including Leona Edmiston and Belinda La Perla, plus the ABC TV shop. This is now one of the city's classiest shopping spots.

Alice Euphemia (Map pp472-3; ☎ 9650 4300; Shop 6, 37 Swanston St, cnr Flinders Lane) The more experimental end of Melbourne fashion gets a showing here, with inventive fabrics, cuts and finishes that aim to make you look more interesting than you might actually be. Great jewellery too.

Chiodo (Map pp472-3; ☎ 9663 0044; Basement, 114 Russell St) Chiodo's menswear range features excellent basics that always have an artful (yet still wearable) twist. Fabrics are excellent, workmanship solid.

Christine (Map pp472-3; ☎ 9654 2011; 181 Flinders Lane) What did the women of Melbourne do before Christine? This treasure-trove of shoes, bags, beads and baubles will update any outfit.

City Hatters (Map pp472-3; ☎ 9614 3294; 211 Flinders St) Beside the main entrance to Flinders St station, this is the most convenient place to purchase an Aussie souvenir such as the iconic Akubra hat.

Commercial Art Galleries

Melbourne has dozens of private, commercial art galleries – the magazine **Art Almanac** (www.art-almanac.com.au), a monthly guide to all city and regional galleries, is available from newsagents. You will also find some good galleries outside the city centre, especially in the suburbs of Fitzroy (Gertrude St is an edgy delight), South Yarra and Prahran.

Anna Schwartz Gallery (Map pp472-3; ☎ 9654 6131; www.annaschwartzgallery.com.au; 185 Flinders Lane) This gallery is leader of the pack when it comes to high-profile modern-art exhibitions in a blindingly white, sometimes chilly space.

Flinders Lane Gallery (Map pp472-3; ☎ 9654 3332; www.flg.com.au; 137 Flinders Lane) Specialising in contemporary Australian (including indigenous) artists since 1990.

Gallery Gabrielle Pizzi (Map pp472-3; ☎ 9654 2944; www.gabriellepizzi.com.au; 141 Flinders Lane) Ground-breaking local exhibitions, including artists such as Christian Thompson and a host of other indigenous Australian talent.

Cosmetics & Skincare

Aesop St Kilda (Map p475; ☎ 9534 9433; 2 Acland St); City Centre (Map pp472-3; ☎ 9639 2436; 35 Albert Coates Lane, QV Bldg) The heavenly scents and luxurious unguents here will soon have you at your best. A world-famous skincare brand, and avowedly local.

Aveda Retreat on Spring (Map pp472-3; ☎ 9654 2217; 49 Spring St) This Aveda day spa stocks all the hair- and skincare preparations you could hope for, plus it offers some excellent pampering treatments.

Kleins (Map pp476-7; ☎ 9416 1221; 313 Brunswick St, Fitzroy) Stocked floor-to-ceiling with soaps, perfumes, ointments, candles and sundry pampering accessories, Kleins is an outrageously girlie shop.

VICTORIA

Music

Greville Records (Map p478; ☎ 9510 3012; 152 Greville St, Prahran) One of the last bastions of the 'old' Greville St, this fabulous music shop has such a loyal following that the great Neil Young invited the owners on stage during his last Melbourne concert.

GETTING THERE & AWAY

For comprehensive details of travel to/from Melbourne, see p1035.

Air

Most of the major airlines have direct international flights to **Melbourne Airport** (www .melair.com.au) in Tullamarine, 22km northwest of the city centre.

Qantas (☎ 13 13 13; www.qantas.com.au), **Jetstar** (☎ 13 15 38; www.jetstar.com.au) and **Virgin** (☎ 13 67 89; www.virginblue.com.au) are the main domestic carriers with flights departing from Melbourne Airport. At the time of writing, low-end, one-way fares started as follows: Sydney ($80), Brisbane ($100), Canberra ($80), Adelaide ($80), Perth ($200), Hobart ($60), Alice Springs ($240), Darwin ($225) and Cairns ($175). However, keep an eye on the Internet as one-off specials can be cheaper than the prices given here. Jetstar also offers flights from **Avalon Airport** (www .avalonairport.com.au) near Geelong; see right for more details.

Regional airlines include **QantasLink** (☎ 13 13 13; www.qantas.com.au), which has flights to Mildura (from $120) and Mt Hotham (from $110), and Burnie (from $125) and Devonport (from $125) in Tasmania. **Regional Express** (Rex; ☎ 13 17 13; www.regionalexpress .com.au) flies to Albury (from $150), Mildura (from $110) and Portland (from $185) and also runs flights to Tasmania.

Boat

The **Spirit of Tasmania** (☎ 1800 634 906; www.spirit oftasmania.com.au) sails between Melbourne and Tasmania at 9pm nightly year-round, departing from Port Melbourne's Station Pier and the Esplanade in Devonport – both arrive at around 7am.

Bus

The long-distance bus terminal in the city centre is the Southern Cross coach terminal on Spencer St. Skybus airport buses also operate from here. Greyhound Australia (p1042) and Firefly Express (p1043) are the major bus companies.

Train

Victoria's **V/Line** (☎ 13 61 96; www.vline.com.au) runs train services between Melbourne and regional Victoria, but also offers an economy service to Adelaide (adult/child $65/35) and Canberra ($60/40).

CountryLink (☎ 13 22 32; www.countrylink.nsw.gov .au) runs XPT trains between Melbourne and Sydney (economy/1st class/1st-class sleeper $115/165/245, 11 hours, two daily).

GETTING AROUND
To/From the Airport

If you're driving to/from Melbourne Airport, take the tolled Tullamarine Fwy; a 24-hour Tulla Pass costs $3.40 – contact **CityLink** (☎ 13 26 29; www.transurban.com.au) for more details. From Avalon Airport take the M1 to Melbourne.

The wheelchair-accessible **Skybus** (☎ 9335 2811; www.skybus.com.au) operates a 24-hour shuttle bus to/from the airport and central Melbourne (one way $13, every 20 minutes). Buy your ticket from the driver. You can take your bicycle, but the front wheel must be removed.

Sunbus Avalon Airport Shuttle (☎ 9689 6888; www.sunbusaustralia.com.au) meets all flights at Avalon airport and to/from the city centre (one way $14; seven daily).

A toll-inclusive taxi fare from Melbourne airport to the city centre costs around $40; from Avalon airport it's around $95.

Bicycle

Melbourne's a great city for cycling, as it's reasonably flat and there are great routes throughout the metropolitan area catering to the city's 1.2 million-odd bikes. Two of the best are the bike path that runs around the shores of Port Phillip Bay from Port Melbourne to Brighton, and the bike path that follows the Yarra River from the city for more than 20km. The visitor information centre (p468) has maps showing city paths, as does the Melway street directory.

Bicycles can be taken on suburban trains for free during off-peak times.

Slippery tram tracks are a major hazard for Melbourne cyclists. Cross them on a sufficient angle to prevent your tyre falling into the track.

For more details on cycling in Melbourne, and information on cycle rentals, see p495.

Car & Motorcycle

City parking costs from $2 per hour. Read parking signs for restrictions and times, and if your car is parked in a 'clearway' zone, which operates during peak hours, *move it*, otherwise it will be towed. The visitor information centre (p468) has information about city parking spots.

HIRE

Avis (☎ 13 63 33; www.avis.com.au), **Budget** (☎ 1300 362 848; www.budgetaustralia.com), **Delta Europcar** (☎ 1300 131 390; www.deltaeuropcar.com.au), **Hertz** (☎ 13 30 39; www.hertz.com) and **Thrifty** (☎ 1300 367 227; www.thrifty.com.au) have desks at the airport and in city-centre locations.

For cheap, secondhand rentals in varying condition try **Rent-a-Bomb** (☎ 9428 0088; www.rentabomb.com.au) and **St Kilda Car Hire** (Map p475; ☎ 9525 5900; 24 Grey St), which requires no bond and doesn't have a driver age limit. Rates start at around $35 per day at both.

TOLL ROADS

CityLink (☎ 13 26 29; www.transurban.com.au) has two main sections: the western link that runs from the Calder Hwy intersection of the Tullamarine Fwy to join the Westgate Fwy; and the southern link that runs from Kings Way, on the southern edge of the CBD, to the Monash Fwy. Both sections are toll ways.

Tolls are 'collected' electronically by overhead readers from a transponder card (an e-Tag). If you don't have an e-Tag, you can purchase a day pass ($9.65), which is valid for 24 hours from your first trip on any CityLink section, or a weekend pass ($9.65), which is valid from noon Friday to midnight Sunday. If you only intend to use the western link to travel to/from Melbourne airport, you can purchase a Tulla Pass ($3.40). Day and weekend passes can be purchased at any post office, Shell service stations, CityLink customer service centres, over the Internet or over the phone. Travelling without payment cops a $100 fine.

Motorcycles can use CityLink for free.

Public Transport

Melbourne's public transport system of buses, trains and trams is privatised. For timetables, maps and fares call the **Met Information Centre** (☎ 13 16 38; www.metlinkmelbourne .com.au). **Met Shop** (Map pp472-3; ☎ 13 16 38; Town Hall, cnr Swanston & Little Collins Sts; ◷ 8.30am-5.30pm Mon-Fri, 9am-1pm Sat) has transport information and sells tickets.

Prams and strollers are allowed on all transport free of charge.

On Friday and Saturday nights after the trams, buses and trains stop running (roughly around midnight), NightRider buses ($6) depart hourly from City Sq from 12.30am to dawn for many suburban destinations.

TICKETS

Metcards allow you to travel on any and all Melbourne bus, train and tram services, even if you transfer from one to another. Tickets are available from Metcard vending machines and counters at train stations, on board trams (tram vending machines only take coins and only dispense City Saver, two-hour and daily tickets), from retailers displaying the Met flag (usually newsagents and milk bars) and the Met Shop. You can purchase tickets directly from the driver on bus services.

The metropolitan area is divided into three zones. Zone 1 covers the city and inner-suburban area (including St Kilda) and most visitors won't venture beyond that unless they're going right out of town. Adult Zone 1 two-hour tickets cost $3.10, daily $5.90 and weekly $25.90.

City Saver tickets ($2.20) are fairly useless, only allowing you to travel two sections (check the maps on each tram giving this

---

CARS & TRAMS

Melbourne's notoriously confusing road rule is the 'hook turn'. To turn right at most city intersections, pull into the left lane, at the corner of the intersection, wait until the light of the street you're turning into changes from red to green, then complete the turn. A black-and-white sign that reads 'Right Turn from Left Only' and hangs from the overhead cables identifies these intersections.

You can only overtake a tram on the left and *always* stop behind a tram when it halts to drop off or collect passengers.

information) in the CBD without breaking your journey.

BUS

Generally, buses continue from where the trains finish, or go to places, such as hospitals, universities, suburban shopping centres and the outer suburbs, not reached by other services.

TRAIN

Suburban trains are faster than trams or buses, but they don't go to many of the inner suburbs.

Flinders St station is the main suburban terminal. During the week, trains start at 5am and finish at midnight and should run every 10 minutes during peak hour, every 15 to 20 minutes at other times, and every 30 minutes after 7pm on weekdays. On Saturday they run every half-hour from 5am to midnight; on Sunday it's every 40 minutes from 7am to 11.30pm.

The city service includes an underground City Loop, which travels to/from Parliament, Melbourne Central, Flagstaff, Southern Cross and Flinders St stations.

TRAM

Melbourne's trundling trams cover the city and inner suburbs. Tram stops are numbered from the city centre. There are also 'light rail' services to some suburbs, including St Kilda, which run along disused rail lines.

In theory, trams run along most routes about every six to eight minutes during peak hour and every 12 minutes at other times. Services are less frequent on weekends and late at night.

Be extremely careful when getting on and off a tram; by law, cars are supposed to stop when a tram stops to pick up and drop off passengers, but that doesn't always happen.

See Tours, p498, for details on the free City Circle tram.

Taxi

The main taxi ranks in the city centre are outside major hotels, outside Flinders St and Southern Cross stations, near the corner of William and Bourke Sts, on the corner of Elizabeth and Bourke Sts, and on Lonsdale St outside Myer.

Flagfall is $2.80, and the rate is $1.33 per kilometre thereafter. There is a $1 surcharge between midnight and 6am, if you place any luggage in the boot and for telephone bookings.

Yellow Cabs and Silver Top taxis have cars with wheelchair access, or phone ☎ 1300 364 050. To book a taxi, phone any of the following companies:

Black Cabs Combined (☎ 13 22 27)
Embassy Taxis (☎ 13 17 55)
Silver Top Taxis (☎ 13 10 08)
Yellow Cabs (☎ 13 19 24)

AROUND MELBOURNE

Melbourne's day-trip and overnight destinations are fully geared to accommodating metro-minibreakers. Most places in this chapter are easily accessed from Melbourne by public transport, but hiring a car (p519) is the most convenient way to explore.

Wine snobs and buffs should take to the Yarra Valley hills; surfers can catch breaks at rugged Phillip Island beaches and the Bellarine and Mornington Peninsulas; walkers and cyclists can traverse the Dandenongs. There are also wildlife sanctuaries and an open-range zoo for animal lovers.

MELBOURNE TO GEELONG

It's a one-hour drive down the Princes Fwy (M1) to Geelong. Leave Melbourne via the soaring West Gate Bridge for superlative city and bay views.

The famous **Werribee Open Range Zoo** (☎ 03-9731 9600; www.zoo.org.au; adult/child/family $19/9.50/48, combined zoo & mansion ticket $28/14/70; ☉ 9am-5pm, last entry 3.30pm) is about 30 minutes south of Melbourne. Admission includes the safari tour: plenty of emus, bison, Mongolian wild horses, rhinos, zebras and giraffes grazing on the savannah. Specialist tours include slumber or canoe safaris and the extremely popular 'Lion Behind the Scenes'.

Next door is **Werribee Park Mansion** (☎ 03-9741 2444; www.werribeepark.com.au; adult/child/family $12/6/29; ☉ 10am-4.45pm Nov-Apr, 10am-3.45pm Mon-Fri & 10am-4.45pm Sat & Sun May-Oct), surrounded by beautiful formal gardens, with picnic and BBQ areas. Audio headphones re-create the sounds of the 1870s, when the mansion was built. Dariwill Farm is a gourmet café–produce store at the mansion and the best spot to eat in the park (avoid the zoo's cafeteria).

Adjacent to the mansion is the **Victoria State Rose Garden** (admission free; ☺ 9am-5pm), with over 5500 bushes arranged in the shape of a giant Tudor rose.

Several Met trains run daily from the city to Werribee train station (daily Metcard Zones 1 and 2 $9.40). From here catch bus No 439, which runs the 5km to the zoo and mansion turn-off Monday to Saturday. Otherwise book ahead for the **Werribee Park Shuttle** (☎ 03-9748 5094; adult/child return zoo & mansion $20/10; ☺ departs 9.30am & 11am, returns 3.30pm), which departs from the Victorian Arts Centre and goes to the zoo and mansion.

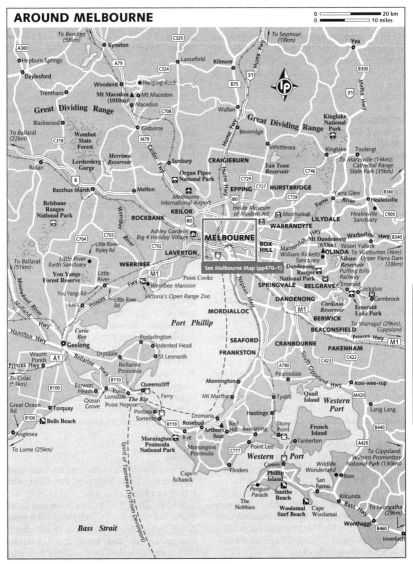

AROUND MELBOURNE

GEELONG

☎ 03 / pop 234,000

Geelong boomed during the gold rush as it was one of the main gateways to the goldfields. Today it's Victoria's largest regional city, though many see it as an extension of Melbourne, and many people commute to work from here. In recent years, the waterfront along Corio Bay has been beautified and Geelong's beaches, restaurants and bars are now extremely popular. Add to that the thriving student population from Deakin University and recent population boom (brought about by skyrocketing prices in Melbourne's housing market) and you'll find an edgy, bohemian and contemporary enclave at Geelong's heart.

Information

Geelong & Great Ocean Road Visitors Centre

(☎ 5275 5797; www.greatoceanrd.org.au/geelong; cnr Princes Hwy & St Georges Rd; ☾ 9am-5pm) About 7km north of Geelong's centre, on the left as you approach from Melbourne.

National Wool Museum visitors centre (☎ 5222 2900; 26 Moorabool St; ☾ 9.30am-5pm) A more convenient location.

Sights & Activities

Along Geelong's revamped **waterfront** you can swim, picnic, take a carousel ride, see bobbing yachts and admire the grand historic homes. A **bay walk bollards** brochure, from the information kiosk at **Cunningham's Pier**, describes Jan Mitchell's 104 famous painted bollards.

The **Geelong Art Gallery** (☎ 5229 3645; www.geelonggallery.org.au; Little Malop St; admission free; ☾ 10am-5pm Mon-Fri, 1-5pm Sat & Sun), in a gracious neoclassical building, is an inspiring regional gallery with over 4000 works of predominantly Australian art. Frederick McCubbin's *A Bush Burial* (1890) is still the gallery's most famous star.

The 1851 **Botanic Gardens** (☎ 5227 0387; www.geelongaustralia.com.au; admission free; ☾ 7.30am-5pm) are a peaceful place for a stroll or picnic. The '21st century' garden at the entrance features the region's indigenous plants.

In a historic bluestone building (1872), the **National Wool Museum** (☎ 5227 0701; www.geelongcity.vic.gov.au; 26 Moorabool St; adult/child/family $7.30/3.65/20; ☾ 9.30am-5pm) focuses on the history, politics and heritage of one of Australwlia's founding industries.

The **Ford Discovery Centre** (☎ 5227 8700; www.ford.com.au/about/discovery; cnr Gheringhap & Brougham Sts; adult/child/family $6/3/15; ☾ 10am-5pm Wed-Mon) looks at the Ford motor industry then and now, using interactive displays and exhibits. Rev-heads love the 'cars of the future' display and Bathurst-winning Falcons.

The National Trust classifies over 100 of Geelong's historic buildings. Several are open to the public, including the **Heights** (☎ 5221 3510; 140 Aphrasia St, Newtown; adult/child/family $6/3/14; ☾ 11am-4pm Wed & Sun) and **Barwon Grange** (☎ 5221 3906; Fernleigh St, Newtown; adult/child/family $5/3/12; ☾ 11am-4pm Wed & Sun).

Geelong for Children

There's a **playground** at Rippleside Park and the Art Deco **bathing pavilion** at **Eastern Beach**, but kids especially love the hand-carved **Geelong Waterfront Carousel** (☎ 5224 1547; Steampacket Pl; adult/child $3/2.50; ☾ 10.30am-5pm Mon-Fri, 10.30am-8pm Sat, 10.30am-6pm Sun), a refurbished steam-driven carousel.

Sleeping

National Hotel Backpackers (☎ 5229 1211; www.nationalhotel.com.au; 191 Moorabool St; dm/d $19/40) Upstairs at 'the Nash' (p524) is central Geelong's only backpacker accommodation. Dorms are cosy, sinks ye olde, and there's a general lack of maintenance, but there are free lockers, linen and tea/coffee.

Gatehouse on Ryrie (☎ 0417 545 196; www.bol.com.au/gatehouse/g.html; 83 Yarra St; s $80, d $95-110, incl breakfast; P ⌨) At this central, rambling guesthouse rooms are toasty warm in winter and double-glazed windows keep them quiet. Has a share kitchen, and sitting room.

Pevensey House (☎ 5224 2810; www.pevensey-house.com.au; 17 Pevensey Cres; r $110-175; P ⌨) A beautifully restored B&B with a mix of antiques and Moorish inspiration. Strengths include its position, 'tower room' panoramas and a garden Jacuzzi. Breakfast here is delectable.

Eating

You'll find a clutch of restaurants, cafés and bars around Little Malop St. For food with a view head to Corio Bay.

Go! (☎ 5229 4752; 37 Bellarine St; breakfast $3.50-7, lunch $4-8, dinner $7-12; ☾ breakfast, lunch & dinner Mon-Fri, breakfast & lunch Sat) Go! is a rollicking ride of colour and amusement. Lunchtime faves include Go!'s sausage roll and straight-up sangers, filled with meatloaf, cheddar and chutney.

Tonic (☎ 5229 8899; 5 James St; entrees from $10, mains $14-20; ☺ lunch & dinner Mon-Sat) A retro café-bar with vinyl chairs and club lounges, and a dedicated commitment to cocktails – the list numbers around 460. Meals are hearty and wholesome.

Gilligan's Fish & Chips (☎ 5222 3200; 100 Eastern Beach Rd; meals $4-17; ☺ lunch daily, dinner Thu-Sun) This colourful, licensed place, grilling flat-head for 10 years, has a jaunty sea-creature mural and a deranged shark out front.

Irrewarra Sourdough Shop & Café (☎ 5221 3909; 10 James St; breakfast $4.50-10, lunch $10-18; ☺ break-fast & lunch Mon-Fri) Authentic, handmade bread

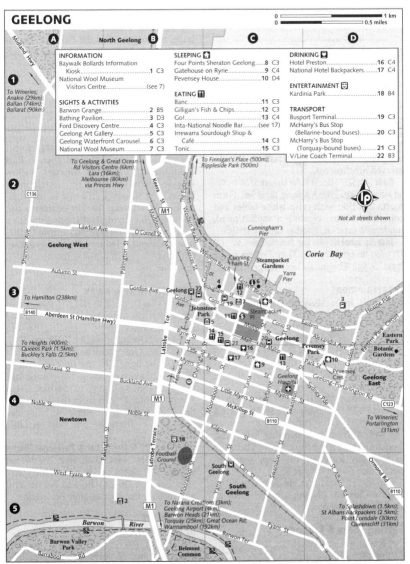

GEELONG

is what you'll find at this cosy bakery-café. Breakfast on granola and grab a fat sourdough sandwich for lunch.

Finnigans Place (☎ 5277 9266; Rippleside Park, Bell Pde; mains $20-30; ☯ lunch & dinner Wed-Sun, breakfast Sun) With views to Corio Bay, Finnigans is a busy and elegant fine-dining restaurant. Mains might include saffron linguini with banana prawns. For breakfast try thyme-infused mushrooms.

Banc (☎ 5222 3155; 53 Malop St; lunch $7.50-16, dinner mains $20-30; ☯ lunch & dinner, closed Sun) Form meets function with crisp white tables and contoured chairs, creating a sophisticated, modernist interior. Food is equally stylish.

Inta-National Noodle Bar (National Hotel; ☎ 5229 1211; 191 Moorabool St; mains $8-11; ☯ lunch Tue-Fri, dinner Tue-Sun) The meals here are generous.

Entertainment

Geelong's large student population demands a lively bar and club scene. Check Friday's *Geelong Advertiser* or the freebie *Forte* magazine for gigs.

National Hotel (☎ 5229 1211; 191 Moorabool St) Grungy op-shop décor, quirky screen projections and art installations set the youthful scene. Live bands play regularly.

Hotel Preston (☎ 5223 2366; 177 Ryrie St; lunch $8-10, dinner $10-18; ☯ to midnight Wed, 3am Thu, 5am Fri & 6am Sat) Rebar is the cruisey upstairs lounge bar with a dress code banning 'suits' and 'bogans'. There's live music from Thursday to Saturday featuring hip-hop, soul and electronica (cover charge $5).

On winter Saturdays check to see if the mighty Cats are playing a home game at **Kardinia Park** (Moorabool St).

Getting There & Around

For Jetstar air services flying from Avalon Airport, see p1039.

V/Line (☎ 13 61 96; www.vline.com.au) trains run frequently from the **Geelong train station** (☎ 5226 6525; Gordon Ave) to Melbourne ($10.20, one hour).

Four times on weekdays and twice daily on weekends V/Line buses travel to Apollo Bay ($22, 2½ hours). On Friday (and Monday in summer) a bus continues to Warrnambool ($47, seven hours).

McHarry's Bus Lines (☎ 5223 2111) operates the Bellarine Transit service with frequent buses to Torquay and the Bellarine Peninsula (below). At the time of writing McHarry's was using temporary bus stops due to roadworks. Catch Torquay-bound buses from the bus stop at the PNG building on Ryrie St; Bellarine-bound buses from the bus stop on Little Malop St.

BELLARINE PENINSULA

The laid-back Bellarine Peninsula forms the northern side of the entrance to Port Phillip. Its surf beaches, wineries, mellow seaside towns, cafés and restaurants make it a worthy stopover en route to the high-profile Great Ocean Rd. The peninsula also has accessible diving and snorkelling sites.

Accommodation prices soar from Christmas to the end of January and many caravan parks have a minimum-stay requirement at this time.

GETTING THERE & AWAY

McHarry's Bus Lines (☎ 03-5223 2111; www.mcharrys.com.au) services travel between Geelong and most peninsula towns, including Barwon Heads and Ocean Grove ($4.20), Portarlington ($5.30), Queenscliff and Point Lonsdale ($6.60, one hour). At the time of writing, the company was using temporary bus stops in Geelong due to roadworks. Catch Torquay-bound buses from the bus stop at the PNG building on Ryrie St; Bellarine-bound buses from the bus stop on Little Malop St.

Queenscliff–Sorrento Car & Passenger Ferries (☎ 03-5258 3244; www.searoad.com.au; one-way foot passenger $9, 2 adults & car $48) runs hourly services between Queenscliff and Portsea and Sorrento on the Mornington Peninsula.

Queenscliff

☎ 03 / pop 3900

Queenscliff was established for the pilot boats that steered ships through treacherous Port Phillip Heads, one of the most dangerous seaways in the world, known as 'the Rip'. The coast is littered with over 200 shipwrecks.

In the 19th century Queenscliff was a favoured holiday town for wealthy Melburnians and the Western District's squattocracy. Extravagant hotels and guesthouses of yesteryear give Queenscliff a historic charm and grandness. Today it's popular with Melburnians escaping the big smoke for a seaside minibreak.

Queenscliffe visitor information centre (☎ 5258 4843; www.queenscliffe.vic.gov.au; 55 Hesse St; ☺ 9am-5pm; ☐) is in the library in the middle of town.

SIGHTS & ACTIVITIES
Queenscliff's most impressive historic buildings line Gellibrand St. Check out the **Ozone Hotel**, **Lathamstowe** (44 Gellibrand St), **Queenscliff Hotel** and a row of old **pilots' cottages** (66-68 Gellibrand St) dating back to 1853.

Fort Queenscliff (☎ 5258 1488; cnr Gellibrand & King Sts; tours adult/child $6/4; ☺ tours 1pm & 3pm Sat & Sun) was built during the 19th century to protect Melbourne from a feared Russian invasion. Eighty-minute guided tours (the only way to see the fort) are of the military museum, magazine, cells and Black Lighthouse.

Run by rail enthusiasts, the **Bellarine Peninsula Railway** (☎ 5258 2069; www.bpr.org.au; adult/child/family return $16/8/50; ☺ trips 11.15am & 2.30pm Sun year-round, Tue & Thu school holidays, daily 26 Dec-9 Jan, Sat, Sun, Tue, Wed & Thu 10 Jan-26 Jan) has an immaculate collection of steam trains that ply the 1¾-hour return journey to Drysdale.

The **Marine Discovery Centre** (☎ 5258 3344; www.nre.vic.gov.au/mafri/discovery; 2A Bellarine Hwy; trips $20-30; ☺ 10am-4pm school holidays) runs interactive programmes, and snorkelling, canoeing and

---

BUSH DOOF David Burnett

Warbling magpies, crusty campervans pottering down dusty bush tracks, blue Australian skies arching overhead…and 120 decibels of thumping electronic bass, throbbing through the gum trees.

This superficially odd amalgamation of urban music and rural escape is at the heart of every 'bush doof' – Melbourne's particular contribution to the world of electronic dance music.

In recent years Melbourne has become the centre of Australia's thriving electronic music scene, most of the action focused on the city's many techno bars and mainstream dance clubs. However, largely unnoticed by the sweaty hordes doing the Melbourne Stomp in giant downtown venues, a parallel scene with a world audience has emerged to make southeastern Australia one of a handful of 'must visit' destinations for underground DJs from Goa to Tel Aviv.

The bush doof evolved from the outdoor 'raves' of the early 1990s – the key ingredients being dance music, a huge sound system, a few hundred 'ferals' stomping away on a dusty dirt dance floor, trippy lighting (and, as one might expect, the appropriate recreational chemicals). Small hit-and-run dance parties, intended to slip under the radar of the local constabulary, have lately become large, well-organised, multistage festivals, often featuring major international acts and two or three days of round-the-clock beats.

Hundreds of visitors from dance-crazy countries like Israel, Japan, Sweden and the UK descend on the doofs of southeastern Australia during the warmer months, and it can be hard at times to find an Aussie accent among the punters, each sporting an unnaturally wide grin. The summer of 2004–05 alone saw major international psy-trance acts such as GMS and Protoculture play to dance floors perhaps a tenth the size of their typical European audiences, in beautiful bush settings a few hours' drive from Melbourne.

Earthcore (www.earthcore.com.au), which is the largest regular outdoor event near Melbourne, and attracts as many as 10,000 people each November, held its 10th anniversary party in 2003. The **Rainbow Serpent Festival** (www.rainbowserpent.net), usually held on the Australia Day long weekend in January, is another very popular shindig.

If you're in Melbourne between November and April, keep an eye on the street press for details of upcoming doofs – event organisers often arrange buses or car pools for those without transport. Tickets range from $15 for a small party to $100 or more for the larger, multiday festivals. Byron Bay, north of Sydney, is another hub for the outdoor dance scene.

Oh, and why 'doof'? 'Cause that's what it sounds like (doof, doof, doof, doof…).

rock-pool excursions during school holidays (at other times by demand).

Sea-All Dolphin Swims (☎ 5258 3889; www.dolphinswims.com.au; Larkin Pde; adult/child sightseeing $50/40, 4hr swim $100/90; 🕑 8am & 1pm Sep-May) offers swims with seals and dolphins in Port Phillip Bay, and sightseeing tours. Otherwise take a dive with **Queenscliff Dive Centre** (☎ 5258 1188; http://divequeenscliff.com.au; 37 Learmonth St; per dive with/without gear $100/50, 2 dives $160/100).

FESTIVALS & EVENTS

The **Queenscliff Music Festival** (☎ 5258 4816; www.qmf.net.au) is held on the last weekend in November, and showcases Australian musicians of all musical genres.

SLEEPING

Queenscliff Inn (☎ 5258 4600; queenscliffinn@bigpond.com; 59 Hesse St; inn d/f incl breakfast without bathroom $110/170, YHA dm $32, tw & d $75, f $110) This spick 'n' span, two-storey Edwardian inn has period-style rooms. In the same building are four-bed YHA rooms (no bunks), some of which overlook the bay.

Seaview House (☎ 5258 1763; www.seaviewhouse.com.au; 86 Hesse St; s $85-145, d $95-180) En suite rooms are available in this cosy guesthouse. Deluxe suites come with a claw-foot bath, but all rooms have homely touches and the buffet breakfast is homemade.

Queenscliff Hotel (☎ 5258 1066; www.queenscliffhotel.com.au; 16 Gellibrand St; s $125-190, d $150-300, incl breakfast) This restored, National Trust–classified hotel is a jewel of old-world splendour. The accommodation is just as it was 100 years ago: small rooms, no telephones, no TVs. Its restaurant is a grand old dame of culinary excellence with a set menu, and its courtyard café, Café Cliffe, is the spot for a relaxed outdoor lunch.

Royal Hotel (☎ 5258 1669; 34 King St; s $35, d $70-80, tr $105) Recent renovations in some of the upstairs rooms make the Royal a top budget accommodation option. It's also a popular pub (see opposite).

EATING

Athelstane House (☎ 5258 1024; www.athelstane.com.au; 4 Hobson St; lunch $9-20, dinner mains $24-30; 🕑 lunch & dinner) Food and wine here is as stylish as

AVOIDING BED BUGS

So you're travelling alone. Along the southwest coast, operators of B&Bs and self-contained accommodation like to confirm that: 'You're on your own? Really? Just you? Right, well, um…' To many, you're an anomaly, but prices for singles are usually more negotiable. As a rule of thumb, count on the cost being about $20 less than the doubles prices quoted in this chapter. Genuinely charming singles can do even better.

The biggest bed bug is the lack of budget options. There's a good range of caravan parks along the coast, but cabins have taken over much of the camping space. Still, the newer cabins are much better than dreary motel rooms, so do consider them.

Unless you book months in advance, beds are scarce along this coast over Easter and late December/January. During this time, prices skyrocket greedily and most places have a minimum one-week stay.

In winter, you have loads more bargaining power. Rates and availability during midyear school holidays are less crazy, and the more nights you stay, the cheaper it gets.

Good-weather weekends are usually busy, and minimum two-night stays often apply at top spots like Lorne or Port Fairy on weekends throughout the year – these are noted in reviews.

Yawn, then there are the 101 pesky rate variations. The range of prices quoted in this chapter are for double rooms in low/high season. Low season is February to November, excluding school holidays, which attract a shoulder season rate (not listed), and Easter, which attracts a high-season rate, as does late December through January and public holidays (for information on holidays, see p1023). Note that price categories are a little different for the Bellarine Peninsula from the rest of the book. Budget is anything up to $90 for a double, midrange from $90 to $160 for a double, and top end anything beyond that.

For longer stays in self-contained digs, check out these websites:

Great Ocean Properties (www.greatoceanproperties.com.au)
Great Ocean Rd (www.greatoceanroad.com.au)

Athelstane looks – feast on a ploughman's in the all-day café, courtyard or deck. At dinner superb Mod Oz mains are served with inner-city professionalism.

Queenscliff Fish & Chips (☎ 5258 1312; 77 Hesse St; fish & chips $5.50-7.50; ☯ dinner daily, lunch Sat & Sun) Get your freshly grilled fish and chips wrapped in paper and eat them by the water. Naturally you'll be sharing with a boisterous flock of seagulls.

DRINKING
Royal Hotel (☎ 5258 1669; 34 King St; mains $8.50-15; ☯ lunch & dinner) For a brew and pub meal, locals head to the Royal. There's also excellent budget accommodation upstairs (see opposite).

Point Lonsdale
☎ 03 / pop 1700
Five kilometres southwest of Queenscliff, Point Lonsdale is a laid-back town with a tiny cluster of cafés, a surf beach and calmer bay beach. It's an invigorating walk from the car park at **Rip View lookout** to **Point Lonsdale pier** and the 1902 **lighthouse**. Below the lighthouse is **Buckley's Cave**, where escaped convict William Buckley lived with Aboriginal people for 32 years.

New owners at **Point Lonsdale Guest House** (☎ 5258 1142; www.pointlonsdaleguesthouse.com.au; 31 Point Lonsdale Rd; r $95-230; ☒) have revamped the decent-sized, nautical-inspired rooms. There's a communal kitchen, tennis court, games room and BBQ facilities.

Royal Park Caravan Park (☎ 5258 1765; Point Lonsdale Rd; powered sites $25-31, unpowered sites $19-23; ☯ 1 Dec-1 May) is a council-run park with lush green sites that are a dune hop to the bay.

For tucker, head to **This'n'That** (☎ 5258 2508; 59 Point Lonsdale Rd; lunch $10-15; ☯ breakfast & lunch Wed-Sun), a relaxed café, juice bar and gelati shop. It's a firm local favourite.

Barwon Heads
☎ 03 / pop 1900
Where the Barwon River meets Bass Strait, Barwon Heads is a beautiful spot with sheltered river beaches; surfers flock 2km west to **Thirteenth Beach**. It was made famous by *Seachange,* a popular TV series. There are short walks around the headland, **Bluff** (with sea-view panoramas), and scuba-diving spots under the rocky ledges below. It's a beautiful town with great cafés.

Seahaven Village (☎ 5254 1066; www.seahaven village.com.au; 3 Geelong Rd; low-season r Sun-Thu $100-160, Fri & Sat $155-190, high-season $160-225; **P** ☒) is a cluster of self-contained studios and cottages decked out in individual nautical themes. Each room is spotlessly clean and extras include electric blankets, open fires, full kitchen and entertainment systems.

For the best spots to eat, head to **Barwon Orange** (☎ 5254 1090; 60 Hitchcock Ave; breakfast & lunch $3.80-15, pizzas $7.80-16, mains $18-20; ☯ breakfast, lunch & dinner), where innovative menus and quality food earn a high distinction; the chilled **Beachnik Café & Wine Bar** (☎ 5254 3376; 48 Hitchcock Ave; breakfast $4-13, lunch $7-14, dinner $7-22; ☯ breakfast, lunch & dinner); and **Starfish Bakery** (☎ 5254 2772; 78 Hitchcock St; breakfast $6-9, lunch $5-9; ☯ breakfast & lunch), a relaxed, colourful bakery-café.

CALDER HIGHWAY
Running northwest from Melbourne to Bendigo there are a handful of sites off the Calder Hwy.

Organ Pipes National Park has some fascinating hexagonal basalt columns that form a natural outdoor amphitheatre.

Cricket enthusiasts will beg for a detour to grand old **Rupertswood** (☎ 03-9740 5020; www.rupertswood.com; Sunbury; admission by donation; ☯ 9am-5pm), birthplace of the **Ashes**, the Holy Grail of English and Australian cricket. Self-guided tours are available but it's best to call ahead. You can stay in rooms for $160 to $500.

Just north of Gisborne exit the highway for **Mt Macedon**, a 1013m-high extinct volcano, which has several **walking tracks**. The scenic route up Mt Macedon Rd takes you past mansions with beautiful gardens and there's a café and picnic grounds near the summit.

Beyond the summit turn-off, the road heads to quaint **Woodend**, or take the signed road on the right to **Hanging Rock**, the sacred site of the Wurundjeri people. The rock was a refuge for bushrangers but was made famous by Joan Lindsay's novel *Picnic at Hanging Rock* (and the subsequent film by Peter Weir), about the disappearance of a group of schoolgirls.

There are daily trains running to Woodend from Melbourne. From there, **Woodend Taxi** (☎ 03-5427 2641) can take you to the rock for about $15.

VICTORIA

THE YARRA VALLEY

One hour from Melbourne, the popular Yarra Valley is crisscrossed with walking and cycling trails, and packed with boutique wineries. **Healesville** is home to the famous Healesville Sanctuary, closest to the major wineries and 'capital' of the Lower Yarra Valley; hilly and fresh **Warburton** marks the centre of the Upper Yarra Valley.

National parks in the area include **Warrandyte State Park**, **Yarra Ranges National Park** and **Kinglake National Park**.

On the third Sunday of the month the **Yarra Valley Farmers' Market** (☎ 03-9513 0677; www.yarravalleyfood.com.au; Yering Station Winery, 38 Melba Hwy, Yering) is a sensational produce market.

Information

Warburton Water Wheel Information Centre (☎ 03-5966 9600; 3400 Warburton Hwy, Warburton; ❧ 11am-3pm Mon-Fri, 10am-5pm Sat, Sun & holidays)
Yarra Valley visitor information centre (☎ 03-5962 2600; www.yarravalleytourism.asn.au; Harker St, Healesville; ❧ 9am-5pm)

Sights & Activities

One of the best places to see Australian native fauna is the **Healesville Sanctuary** (☎ 03-5957 2800; www.zoo.org.au; Badger Creek Rd, Healesville; adult/child/family $19/9.50/50; ❧ 9am-5pm), a wildlife park set in native bushland. The Platypus House is a top spot to see these shy creatures underwater, but the real star is

---

VICTORIAN WINE REGIONS & WINERIES

Victoria is the wine hot spot of Australia, with the most number of wineries (over 500), wine regions and wine styles. The Yarra Valley, Mornington Peninsula and Geelong regions produce cool-climate, food-friendly drops such as Chardonnay, Pinot Noir and Pinot Gris. Cool-climate wines are also found in the Macedon Ranges region, which produces crisp, clear, almost sharp sparkling wines and increasingly impressive Pinot Noir. In the Rutherglen area you'll find big reds and syrupy-sweet Muscat and Tokay, while the undulating and French-influenced Pyrenees offers a considerable variety of wine styles, though flavoursome, glossy Shiraz is the area's best tipple.

Most wineries offer free tastings, although in the Yarra Valley and Mornington Peninsula some charge between $2 and $5 for the privilege – usually refundable if you purchase a bottle.

Following are some of the best places to swirl, sip and spit, but tourist offices also stock wine-touring guides for their region, with maps and more off-the-beaten-track wineries. Get busy, and have a drink for us!

TarraWarra Estate (☎ 03-5957 3510; www.tarrawarra.com.au; Healesville Rd, Yarra Glen) A striking building that melds seamlessly with the landscape. Rollicking Chardonnay is the speciality. Check out the TarraWarra art gallery and rowdy bistro for lunch, too.

Coldstream Hills (☎ 03-5964 9410; www.coldstreamhills.com.au; 31 Maddens Lane, Coldstream) Unrivalled valley views. Tangy Chardonnay, effusive Pinot Noir and silky-smooth Merlot are the star picks.

Yering Station (☎ 03-9730 0100; www.yering.com; 38 Melba Hwy, Yering) A massive, modern complex with a fine-dining restaurant, produce store and fun-loving Matt's Bar. It's where Victoria's most hedonistic Shiraz lives (the Shiraz-Viognier blend). Sparkling wine, Pinot Noir, rosé and Chardonnay are also outstanding. The Yarra Valley Farmers' Market is held here every third Sunday.

Pettaval Winery (☎ 03-5266 1120; www.pettavel.com; 65 Pettavel Rd, Waurn Ponds) The Geelong region's premier winery and fabulous restaurant – head here for a long lunch and award-winning Riesling.

Main Ridge (☎ 03-5989 2686; www.mre.com.au; 80 Williams Rd, Red Hill) Mornington Peninsula's best winery. Ripe, peachy Chardonnay and exquisite, cherried Pinot Noir are the go here.

T'Gallant (☎ 03-5989 6565; 1385 Mornington-Flinders Rd, Main Ridge) Renowned as the maker of luscious Pinot Gris ripped with tropical fruit fragrance.

All Saints Estate (☎ 02-6033 1922; All Saints Rd, Wahgunyah) In the Rutherglen region, just across the border. Buttery Chardonnays with oaky aromas are the pick.

Dalwhinnie (☎ 03-5467 2388; 448 Taltarni Rd, Moonambel) The Pyrenees region's wine star. Expensive, but beautiful Chardonnay, Pinot Noir, Cabernet and Shiraz with top views from the cellar door.

Summerfield (☎ 03-5467 2264; Moonambel) Good-value, big-flavoured, juicy red wines of great power and substance, and an intimate cellar door.

Blue Pyrenees Estate (☎ 03-5465 3202; Vinoca Rd, Avoca) Wide range of styles at a wide range of prices. Excellent sparkling wines – cleanse your mouth here after a go at some reds.

the exciting **Birds of Prey** (☼ show noon & 2pm) presentation where raptors swoop overhead and an owl catches a mouse midair.

Badger Weir, a kilometre or so past the sanctuary, is a superb picnic spot that's punctuated by lyrebird calls and has short rainforest walks.

The 38km **Lilydale to Warburton Rail Trail** (☎ 1300 368 333) follows a disused railway line from Lilydale to Warburton. It's a steady ride that takes around three hours. **Lilydale Cycles** (☎ 03-9735 5077; fax 9735 5174; 6-8 William St E; per half/full day $30/20), right next to Lilydale train station, hires bikes.

In winter, **Mt Donna Buang** (1250m), has snowy slopes for tobogganing. Below the summit, the **Rainforest Gallery** (☎ 03-5966 5996; Acheron Way; ☼ year-round) is a fantastic rainforest-canopy walk along a 40m observation platform.

Tours

Eco Adventure Tours (☎ 03-5962 5115; www.hotke .net.au/~ecoadven/aboutus.htm) Nocturnal spotlighting walks in the Healesville and Marysville area.

Yarra Valley Winery Tours (☎ 03-5962 3870; www .yarravalleywinerytours.com.au; tours $80-180) Departs from Lilydale station.

Sleeping, Eating & Drinking

Tuck Inn (☎ 03-5962 3600; www.tuckinn.com.au; 2 Church St, Healesville; r Sun-Thu $135-150, Fri & Sat $150-165) A contemporary guesthouse with five immaculate rooms sporting plush mattresses, thick linen and luxury quilts. Each has its own clean-as-a-whistle bathroom.

Healesville Hotel (☎ 03-5962 4002; www.heales villehotel.com.au; 256 Maroondah Hwy, Healesville; d Sun-Thu $80, Fri $105, Sat $120, café mains $8-16, dinner mains $24-30; ☼ breakfast, lunch & dinner) A favourite with food lovers, this iconic pub has sensational fine-dining and pub meals, a beer garden, and a food store–café, Harvest Café. Noisy and overrated accommodation is available upstairs.

Bodhi Tree Café (☎ 03-5962 4407; 317 Maroondah Hwy; mains $9-16; ☼ lunch Sat & Sun, dinner Wed-Sun) An ecofriendly café with veggie options aplenty and kid-sized pizza portions. There's mellow live music on Friday and Saturday (cover charge $3).

Getting There & Away

Suburban trains go as far as Lilydale (a Zone 1, 2 & 3 Metcard). From Lilydale train sta-tion, **McKenzie's Bus Lines** (☎ 03-5962 5088; www .mckenzies.com.au) runs to Healesville and Yarra Glen (some services continue to Healesville Sanctuary), and **Martyrs** (☎ 03-5966 2035; www .martyrs.com.au) buses run to Yarra Junction and Warburton.

THE DANDENONGS

On a clear day, the Dandenong Ranges, and their highest peak, Mt Dandenong (633m), can be seen from Melbourne. Within perfect day-trip distance, the hills are 35km east of the city. The landscape is a patchwork of exotics and natives with a lush understorey of tree ferns – it's the most accessible spot for bushwalks outside Melbourne.

Dandenong Ranges & Knox visitor information centre (☎ 03-9758 7522; www.yarrarangestourism.com; 1211 Burwood Hwy, Upper Ferntree Gully; ☼ 9am-5pm) is outside Upper Ferntree Gully train station. **Parks Victoria** (☎ 13 19 63; www.parksweb.vic .gov.au; Ferntree Gully Picnic Ground, Mt Dandenong Tourist Rd; ☼ 8am-4.30pm Mon-Fri) also has maps and advice on walking routes.

Puffing Billy (☎ 03-9754 6800; www.puffingbilly .com.au; Old Monbulk Rd, Belgrave; adult/child/family return $40/20/81) is an immensely popular attraction. A restored steam train, full of excited kids swinging their legs over the side, whistles its way through the picturesque hills and fern gullies between Belgrave and Gembrook. There are up to six departures during holidays, and three or four on other days. Puffing Billy train station is a short stroll from Belgrave train station, on Melbourne's suburban network.

Dandenong Ranges National Park, a combination of five parks, offers short walks and four-hour trails. **Sherbrooke Forest** has a towering cover of mountain ash trees. Reach the start of its eastern loop walk (10km, three hours), just 1km or so from Belgrave station, by walking to the end of Old Monbulk Rd past Puffing Billy's station. Combining this walk with a ride on Puffing Billy makes a great day out. Opposite the Alfred Nicholas Memorial Gardens is a **picnic ground** where crimson rosellas will peck birdseed from your hand (kids love it). Walks at **Ferntree Gully National Park**, home to large numbers of lyrebirds and the infamous '1000' steps, are 10 minutes' walk from Upper Ferntree Gully station.

The leafy **William Ricketts Sanctuary** (☎ 13 19 63; www.parkweb.vic.gov.au; Mt Dandenong Tourist Rd,

VICTORIA

Mt Dandenong; adult/child/family $6/2.50/14; 10am-4.30pm, closed on total fire ban days) features Ricketts' sculptures blended beautifully with damp fern gardens. His work was inspired by nature and the years he spent living with Aboriginal people. Bus No 688 runs here from Croydon train station.

Giant eucalypts tower over shady lawns and brilliant flower beds at the **National Rhododendron Gardens** (03-9751 1980; Georgian Rd, Olinda; adult/child/family Sep-Nov $7.50/2.50/17, Dec-Aug $6/2.50/15; 10am-5pm), with superb views and chirruping birds. There are groves of cherry blossoms, oaks, maples and beeches, and over 15,000 rhododendrons and 12,000 azaleas.

Ripe (03-9755 2100; 376-378 Mt Dandenong Tourist Rd, Sassafras; mains $8-16; breakfast & lunch) is a café–produce store in a cute weatherboard cottage with outdoor decking. Local produce is found in all manner of jars and bottles, and there are handmade chocolates, cheeses and deli items.

Getting There & Away

The Met's suburban trains run on the Belgrave line to the foothills of the Dandenongs (Zones 1, 2 and 3 Metcard). From Upper Ferntree Gully train station it's a 10-minute walk to the start of the Ferntree Gully section of the national park.

MORNINGTON PENINSULA

A favourite summer destination since the 1870s, the peninsula's ocean beaches, national parks and wineries make it an action-packed day trip or weekend destination. The **Peninsula visitor information centre** (03-5987 3078, 1800 804 009; www.visitmornington peninsula.org; Nepean Hwy, Dromana; 9am-5pm) is the most comprehensive source of information for this area.

GETTING THERE & AROUND

Met trains run frequently from Flinders St station to Frankston train station, where the **Portsea Passenger Service** (03-5986 5666; www.portseapas.com.au) runs bus No 788 to/from Portsea (one way $8.20, 90 minutes). **Peninsula Bus Lines** (03-9786 7088; www.buslines .com.au/peninsula) runs bus Nos 782 and 783 from Frankston train station to Flinders (one way $4.60, 90 minutes).

Car & Passenger Ferries (03-5258 3244; www .searoad.com.au; one-way foot passenger $9, 2 adults &

car $48) runs daily between Sorrento (hourly from 7am to 6pm, with reduced sailings in winter) and Queenscliff. **Inter Island Ferries** (03-9585 5730; www.interislandferries.com.au; return adult/child/bike $18/8/8) runs between Stony Point and Cowes (on Phillip Island) via French Island (every 30 minutes 8.30am to 5pm, until 7pm Friday). There are at least two trips daily year-round.

Sorrento

03 / pop 1200

Sorrento was Victoria's first official European settlement in 1803. In summer the town heaves with holiday-makers; in winter it reverts to a sleepy village. During low tide, the **rock pool** at the back beach is a safe spot for adults and children to swim and **snorkel**.

TOURS

The following tours offer dolphin swims and sightseeing, and depart from Sorrento Pier.

Moonraker Charters (5984 4211; www.moon rakercharters.com.au; adult/child sightseeing $40/35, swimming $80/65; tours 8am, noon & 4pm Oct-May, 9am & 1pm Jun-Sep)

Polperro Dolphin Swims (5988 8437; www .polperro.com.au; adult/child observing $40/30, swimming $100; tours 8.30am & 1.30pm Oct-Apr)

SLEEPING

Prices rise with the temperature, from mid-December to the end of January, and during Easter and school holidays; definitely book in advance.

Sorrento Backpackers Hostel YHA (5984 4323; www.yha.com.au; 3 Miranda St; dm $29;) The easy-to-miss Sorrento YHA receives rave reviews for its cosy ambience. It's a purpose-built hostel and facilities are of a high standard. Take bus No 788 to stop 18.

Oceanic Whitehall Guesthouse (5984 4166; www.virtualsorrento.com.au/whitehall.htm; 231 Ocean Beach Rd; r $100-200) A historic, limestone, two-storey guesthouse near the back beach, with views from its timber veranda. The majority of rooms share a bathroom.

Carmel of Sorrento (5984 3512; www.carmelof sorrento.com.au; 142 Ocean Beach Rd; s $150, d $175-200, self-contained unit $200) This historic limestone cottage, right in Sorrento, has been tastefully restored in period style. It has a cosy lounge, four Edwardian-style B&B

guestrooms with bathrooms, and two self-contained units.

Hotel Sorrento (☎ 5984 2206; www.hotelsorrento .com.au; 5-15 Hotham Rd; park r $140-275, hill apt $220-340) The legendary Hotel Sorrento has a swag of accommodation. 'Sorrento on the Park' motel rooms are overpriced and in need of a revamp, but the 'On the Hill' apartments are fab.

EATING

Stringer's (☎ 5984 2010; 2 Ocean Beach Rd; sandwiches & snacks $4-8; ☺ breakfast & lunch) Long-running Stringer's is a Sorrento staple. All the food is house-made and Mornington Peninsula wines are for sale.

Baths (☎ 5984 1500; 3278 Point Nepean Rd; mains $17-30; ☺ breakfast, lunch & dinner) A sunny café-restaurant with big breakfasts and premium waterfront views – this site used to be the sea baths.

Sunnyside Up (☎ 5984 4255; 3293 Point Nepean Rd; meals $10-17; ☺ breakfast & lunch Thu-Mon, breakfast, lunch & dinner daily in summer) A popular breakfast spot with sea views and a sun-drenched outdoor deck, where dogs look longingly at their owners for a bit of bacon.

Portsea

☎ 03 / pop 800

Portsea is where many of Melbourne's wealthiest families have built their seaside mansions. Head to the **back beach** to see **London Bridge**, an impressive natural rock formation. This ocean beach has wild surf and can be dangerous for swimming, so keep between the flags. The **front beaches** offer more-sheltered swimming spots.

Dive Victoria (☎ 5984 3155; www.divevictoria .au; 3752 Point Nepean Rd; snorkelling incl gear $65, 1/2 dives without gear $50/100) runs diving and snorkelling trips.

Portsea's beating heart is the sprawling Tudor-style **Portsea Hotel** (☎ 5984 2213; www .portseahotel.com.au; Point Nepean Rd; s $50-175, tw & d $90-200, lunch & dinner mains $17-30; ☺ breakfast, lunch & dinner). The restaurant serves massive Mod Oz meals, alongside a solid wine list, and the deck and garden overlook the bay. There's accommodation upstairs but it's noisy when bands play at weekends.

Mornington Peninsula National Park

On the tip of the peninsula is the stunning **Point Nepean** section of the **Mornington Penin-**sula National Park (☎ 13 19 63; www.parkweb.vic.gov .au; Point Nepean Rd, Portsea; ☺ 9am-5pm, to dusk Jan), originally a quarantine station and army base. **Point Nepean visitor information centre** (☎ 03-5984 4276; Point Nepean; adult/child/family walk or bicycle admission $7.20/3.20/18, one-way transport incl admission $11/6/26, return transport incl admission $13/8/34, bike hire per 3hr $15; ☺ 9am-6pm Jan, 9am-5pm Feb-Apr & Oct-Dec, 10am-5pm May-Sep) is your first port of call. You can walk or cycle to the point (12km return), or take the Point Explorer, a hop-on, hop-off bus service. There are plenty of **trails** throughout the park and at the tip is **Fort Nepean**, which was important in Australian defence from the 1880s to 1945.

On the southwestern coastline of the peninsula are beautiful rugged **ocean beaches**. It's possible to walk all the way from Portsea to Cape Schanck along them (26km, around eight hours). However, swimming at these beaches can be dangerous so its advisable to keep to the lifeguard-patrolled areas at Gunnamatta and Portsea during summer.

Cape Schanck Lightstation (☎ 03-5988 6184, 0500 527 891; adult/child/family museum only $10/6/22, museum & lighthouse $12/10/23, parking $4; ☺ 10am-4pm), built in 1859, is a spic-and-span operational lighthouse, with a kiosk, a museum, an information centre and regular guided tours.

FRENCH ISLAND

☎ 03 / pop 65

Exposed and windswept, French Island is two-thirds national park and it retains a wonderful sense of remoteness and tranquillity. Using alternative energy sources, its residents live ecologically, organically and sustainably. The main attractions are **bushwalks**, a huge variety of bird species, and one of Australia's largest **koala colonies**.

Tankerton is the main settlement and where the ferry docks. It's little more than the licensed **French Island General Store** (☎ 5980 1209; Lot 1, Tankerton Rd, Tankerton), which is the post office and has Eftpos. There's also the **French Island visitor information centre** (☎ 5980 1241; www.frenchisland.org; Lot 4, Bayview Rd, Tankerton; ☺ variable hours).

TOURS

French Island Eco Tours (☎ 1300 307 054; www .frenchislandecotours.com.au; half-/full-day tour incl ferry & lunch $65/85; ☺ Thu & Sun) Runs tours around the

VICTORIA

island and explores McLeod Eco Farm, a former prison. Tours depart from Stony Point and Cowes.

French Island Llama Expeditions (☎ 5980 1287; www .fillamas.com.au; tours $75) A quirky, relaxed tour, including walks with llamas and a gourmet picnic lunch.

SLEEPING & EATING

McLeod Eco Farm (☎ 5678 0155; www.mcleodeco farm.com; McLeod Rd; bunk room s/d $35/60, guesthouse d $65-130) A historic property (formerly the island's prison) with kitchen facilities, a lounge and an organic farm. Rooms here are basic, but the guesthouse rooms are more upmarket.

Tortoise Head Guest House (☎ 5980 1234; www .tortoisehead.net; 10 Tankerton Rd, Tankerton; s/d incl breakfast $70/140) A short walk from the ferry, it has knockout water views, but is a little worn in parts for the price. The cabins are the best value.

French Island Farm (☎ 5980 1278; www.frenchis land.org; 4 The Anchorage, Tankerton; s $80-90, d $140-160, incl breakfast) This spotless option offers 360-degree views from a sunny hill top.

Bayview Camping Ground (☎ 5980 1241; unpowered sites $10) Privately run and at the back of the general store.

Fairhaven camping ground (☎ 5980 1294; www .parkweb.vic.gov.au; unpowered sites free) On the western shore, in French Island National Park, this camping ground has a compost toilet. Fires aren't allowed and you must carry everything in and out. Bookings essential.

GETTING THERE & AROUND

Inter Island Ferries (☎ 9585 5730; www.interisland ferries.com.au; adult/child/bike $9/4/4) runs a service between Tankerton and Stony Point (10 minutes, at least two daily).

Unsealed roads make riding tough going, but you can hire **bikes** (per day $11) from the kiosk at the jetty in summer and from the general store.

PHILLIP ISLAND
☎ 03 / pop 6700

Phillip Island's main tourist drawcards are the insanely popular penguin parade and the Motorcycle Grand Prix. The island's 6700-strong winter population swells to 40,000 in summer when it's packed with holiday-makers. Phillip Island has excellent beaches, from the wild surf at Woolamai and the other south-coast beaches, to sheltered bay beaches on the north side.

Information
Phillip Island visitor information centre (☎ 5956 7447, 1300 366 422; www.phillipisland.net.au; Phillip Island Rd, Newhaven; ☯ 9am-5pm, 9am-6pm Jan) sells the Three Parks Pass (adult/child/family $28/14/72), which covers admission to the Penguin Parade, Koala Conservation Centre and Churchill Island. Tickets are also available at the individual attractions.

Sights & Activities
PHILLIP ISLAND NATURE PARK
The nature park runs the **Penguin Parade** (☎ 5951 2800; www.penguins.org.au; Summerland Beach; adult/child/family $16/8/40; ☯ 10am-last penguin show); the **Koala Conservation Centre** (☎ 5952 1307; adult/child/family $8.50/4.25/23; ☯ 10am-5pm, extended hours in summer), off Phillip Island Rd, with elevated boardwalks; and trips to **Churchill Island** (☎ 5956 7214; adult/child/family $8.50/4.25/23; ☯ 10am-4.30pm, extended hours in summer), a working farm also off Phillip Island Rd, where Victoria's first crops were planted.

The penguin complex comprises a gift shop, a café, and purpose-built concrete amphitheatres that hold up to 3800 oohing-and-aahing spectators. After sunset the little penguins emerge from the sea, and waddle resolutely up the beach to their nests. Penguin numbers swell in summer, after breeding, but they parade year-round. There are also specialised **tours** (adult $25-75) so you can get even closer to the little fellas. Book ahead in summer.

MOTOR RACING CIRCUIT
The **Motor Racing Circuit** (☎ 5952 2710; www .phillipislandcircuit.com.au; Back Beach Rd; ☯ 8.30am-5.30pm Mon-Fri) was revamped to stage the Australian Motorcycle Grand Prix in 1989. The **visitor centre** (☎ 5952 9400; ☯ 9am-5pm) runs one-hour **walking tours** (adult/child/family $12/6/28, museum & tour $16/8/38; ☯ tours 11am) and hot-car circuits of the track.

SEAL ROCKS & THE NOBBIES
Off Point Grant, the extreme southwestern tip of the island, a group of rocks called the **Nobbies** rise from the sea. Beyond these are **Seal Rocks**, inhabited by Australia's largest colony of fur seals. The rocks are most crowded during the October-to-December breeding season, when up to 6000 seals adorn the rocks. You can view the seals from boardwalks or from a boat cruise.

BEACHES

Ocean beaches on the south side of the island include **Woolamai**, a surf beach with dangerous rips and currents. More predictable surf and conditions are found at **Smiths Beach**, a popular spot with families, which caters to all levels of surfing competence. Both beaches are patrolled in summer.

Head to the quieter, sheltered northern beaches if you're not a strong swimmer or you worry about your kids in the surf.

Island Surfboards (www.islandsurfboards.com.au; surfing lesson $40, surfboard hire per hr/day $10/35; Smiths Beach ☎ 5952 3443; 65 Smiths Beach Rd; Cowes ☎ 5952 2578; 147 Thompson Ave) is one of several shops that give surfing lessons and hires out boards and wetsuits.

BIRDS & WILDLIFE

Mutton birds, also known as shearwaters, colonise in sand dunes around Cape Woolamai from around 24 September to April. Your best chance of seeing them is at the penguin parade as they fly in at dusk, or at the shearwater rookeries at Woolamai Beach.

You'll also find a wide variety of water birds, including **pelicans**, which are fed at Newhaven at 11.30am daily, in the swampland at the **Rhyll Inlet and Wetland**. There's a boardwalk and lookout here, and the **Oswin Roberts Walking Track** (two hours) takes you through the most important bird-watching areas.

At **Phillip Island Wildlife Park** (☎ 5952 2038; Thompson Ave; adult/child/family $11/5.50/30; ⏰ 10am-5pm,

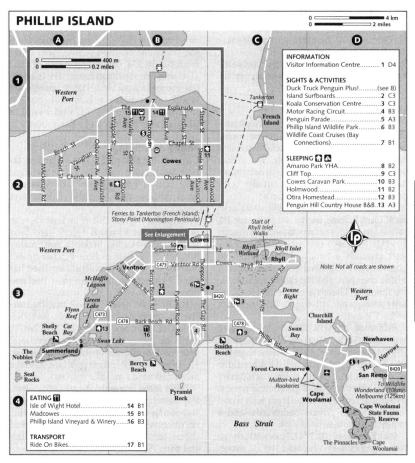

PHILLIP ISLAND

0 — 4 km
0 — 2 miles

VICTORIA

later in summer), about 1km south of Cowes, there are over 100 different species of Australian native wildlife, including koalas, cassowaries and quolls, and you can handfeed wallabies and roos. Kids love it.

Tours

Duck Truck Penguins Plus! (Amaroo Park YHA; ☎ 5952 2548; www.yha.com.au; 97 Church St; tours $145) Includes three nights' dorm accommodation, a picnic lunch, penguin parade admission, an island tour, bike hire and transport to/from Melbourne.

Wildlife Coast Cruises (☎ 5952 3501; www.bay connections.com.au; Rotunda Bldg, Jetty car park, The Esplanade, Cowes; tours $25-135; ⏱ Nov-May) Runs a cruise from Cowes jetty around Seal Rocks, and trips to French Island and Wilsons Promontory.

Festivals & Events

Australian Motorcycle Grand Prix (http://bikes .grandprix.com.au) A massive three-day event held annually in October. Phillip Island goes off!

Superbike World Championship (www.superbike.it) A classy crowd revs up in March at the three-day event to see big production bikes.

Sleeping

Phillip Island accommodation prices have distinct peaks and troughs: during motor races, Christmas, Easter and school holidays book as far ahead as possible. The visitor information centre (p532) has an accommodation booking service; you can also book online at www.phillipisland.net.au.

Amaroo Park YHA (☎ 5952 2548; www.yha.com .au; 97 Church St, Cowes; powered sites per 2 people $30, 10-/4-bed dm $23/25, 4-bed dm with bathroom $30, cabins $135-145; (P) (🖳) (🐾)) This well-run hostel has leafy grounds, a pool and a charming old homestead. The 10-bed dorms are clean, if a little cramped, and the cabins are suitable for families. There's a communal kitchen, BBQ areas, a bar, a lounge with a fireplace and a TV room.

Holmwood (☎ 5952 3082; www.holmwoodguest house.com.au; 37 Chapel St, Cowes; B&B s $140, tw & d $170, 2-bedroom townhouse $215, 3-course dinner $50; (🐾)) This delightful and well-kept boutique accommodation, with a leafy, colourful garden, offers cosy B&B guesthouse rooms; self-contained modern cottages with wood fires, spas and private courtyards; and a family townhouse.

Otira Homestead (☎ 5956 8294; www.otira.com.au; Ventnor Beach Rd, Needle's Eye; B&B d $140-150, cottages

$200) In a bucolic setting, Otira is a 1920s homestead with rooms in the main house and two- and three-bedroom cottages.

Penguin Hill Country House B&B (☎ 5956 8777; www.phillipisland.net.au/trip/penguinhill/penguinhill .html; cnr Backbeach & Ventnor Rds, Ventnor; d $130; (P)) Handy to the Nobbies and the penguin parade, this B&B has beach views from its serene, rural location. Three cosy en suite rooms are available, and guests share a sitting room.

Cliff Top (☎ 5952 1033; www.clifftop.com.au; 1 Marlin St, Smiths Beach; r $210-240) Cliff Top is on a private estate, right on Smiths Beach, with views of Bass Strait and Pyramid Rocks. There are seven stylish and luxurious rooms that each have an airy, modern ambience and a private balcony or patio.

There are a dozen or so caravan parks; most of them are in Cowes (pick up a *Caravan Parks on Phillip Island* brochure from the visitor information centre). Sites range from $25 to $38. **Cowes Caravan Park** (☎ 5952 2211; www.cowescaravanpark.com.au; 164 Church St, Cowes; powered & unpowered sites $25-37, cabins $70-105) is well run and near a sheltered beach – it has spacious grounds, shady sites, a kiosk, a BBQ, a camp kitchen and a playground.

Eating & Drinking

Cowes is the best place on the island to satiate hunger cravings. There's the standard collection of greasy-spoon takeaways and pizza palaces, plus a couple of upmarket restaurants.

Madcowes (☎ 5952 2560; 17 The Esplanade; meals $4-12; ⏱ breakfast & lunch) A breezy café–food store that cooks big brekkies and quality lunches. Breakfasts include Bircher muesli and ricotta hot-cakes with caramelised banana. At lunch, wash down a roast-beef and brie sandwich with a local wine.

Isle of Wight Hotel (☎ 5952 2301; The Esplanade; cover charge $5-8, mains $16-24, s/d/tr $65/85/105; ⏱ lunch & dinner, Splash cocktail bar 10pm-2am) A rambling pub with a front bar, a fantastic beer garden and an upstairs cocktail bar. Meals are stock-standard pub fare. Average motel rooms are on offer out back.

Phillip Island Vineyard & Winery (☎ 5956 8465; Berrys Beach Rd; platters $14-17; ⏱ 11am-6pm Nov-Mar, 11am-5pm Apr-Oct) Outside of Cowes, this winery offers velvety wines and share platters of cheese, terrine, smoked salmon, trout fillets and pâté. All come with water views.

Getting There & Around

The only direct service from Melbourne to Cowes is a **V/Line** (☎ 13 61 96; www.vline.com .au) bus departing at 3.50pm from Southern Cross station Monday to Friday (one way $17, three hours 20 minutes). Nondirect routes involve a Met train to Dandenong station and then two different coaches, or a Met train to Stony Point ($7, one hour 50 minutes, six daily), then the ferry.

Inter Island Ferries (☎ 9585 5730; www.interis landferries.com.au; adult/child/bike return $18/8/8) runs daily between Cowes and Stony Point (on the Mornington Peninsula) via French Island (every 30 minutes 9.10am to 5.25pm plus 7.45pm Friday). There are at least two trips daily year-round.

There's no public transport around Phillip Island. You can hire bicycles from **Ride On Bikes** (☎ 5952 2533; info@rideonbikes.com.au; 2-17 The Esplanade, Cowes; per half/full day $15/25) and Amaroo Park YHA (opposite).

GREAT OCEAN ROAD

The incredible Great Ocean Rd (B100) cuts its breathtaking path from Torquay to Warrnambool, every fresh twist and turn inspiring passengers to exclaim 'Oh!', and frustrated drivers to say, 'What? What's it look like?' The stunning stretch of road attracts seven million snap-happy visitors annually and is one of the world's most spectacular coastal drives, especially between Anglesea and Apollo Bay. Beyond it, the thrashing Shipwreck Coast (from Princetown to Port Fairy) inspires spooky stories of ghosts from wrecked vessels that haunt the area, and features dramatic beachscapes.

The lush green scenery of the Otway Ranges, stretching from Aireys Inlet to Cape Otway, offers revitalising landscapes for bushwalking and camping – most of the coastal section is part of the Angahook-Lorne State Park.

Taking a surfing lesson is a popular activity for would-be surfers, and there are plenty of relaxed teachers ('Paddle, paddle, keep paddling') who can give you the basics. Lessons cost about $50 for two hours.

Contact the Geelong & Great Ocean Rd Visitors Centre (p522) for maps and detailed information.

WILDLIFE ASSISTANCE

If you accidentally hit an animal or bird while driving, call **Wildlife Line** (☎ 0500 540 000). You'll be put in touch with a wildlife carer, who will either take the animal in or, if things are grim, organise to have the animal put down. Alternatively, contact the nearest police station.

Getting There & Away

Interstate visitors coming from Adelaide, Brisbane or Sydney can fly into Avalon Airport, 22km from Geelong, with **Jetstar** (☎ 13 15 38; www.jetstar.com.au) and take the door-to-door **Avalon Airport Shuttle** (☎ 03-5278 8788; www .avalonairportshuttle.com.au) along the Great Ocean Rd as far as Lorne. At the time of writing one-way flights with Jetstar to Melbourne started at: Sydney ($85), Brisbane ($100) and Adelaide ($80), but one-off specials can be cheaper than the prices given here.

V/Line (☎ 13 61 96; www.vline.com.au) trains from Melbourne's Southern Cross station travel to Geelong and then connect with V/Line buses that cruise along the Great Ocean Rd as far as Apollo Bay ($33), via Torquay ($16), Anglesea ($19) and Lorne ($27), four times daily Monday to Friday, and twice daily Saturday and Sunday. On Friday (and Monday during Christmas holidays), a V/Line bus continues around the coast from Apollo Bay to Port Campbell and Warrnambool.

Wayward Bus (☎ 1300 653 510; www.waywardbus .com.au) follows the southwest coast to South Australia (SA) as part of its Melbourne to Adelaide trip; you can do stopovers too. For more information, see p465.

McHarry's Bus Lines (☎ 03-5223 2111; www.mc harrys.com.au) has frequent bus services from Geelong to Torquay (one way $5.30).

TORQUAY

☎ 03 / pop 8000

Torquay is the capital of Australia's booming surfing industry and an OK spot to kick back if your goal is a beach 'n' book break, a surf lesson or serious shopping for surf wear or gear. Otherwise, attractions and diverse activities are light on in this beachside suburban sprawl.

The **Torquay visitor information centre** (☎ 52 61 4219; www.greatoceanroad.org/surfcoast; Surf City Plaza, Beach Rd) is at the rear of the plaza.

Sights & Activities

Next to the visitor centre is **Surfworld Australia Surfing Museum** (☎ 5261 4606; adult/child/family $8/5.50/18; ⏱ 9am-5pm), a must for those with any interest in waves.

Torquay's action revolves around gorgeous local beaches: **Fisherman's Beach**, protected from ocean swells, and **Front Beach**, ringed by shady pines and sloping lawns, are the family faves. Surf life savers patrol the frothing **Back Beach** during summer. The powerful point break at **Bells Beach**, 7km west of Torquay, is part of international surfing folklore and it's the site of a world-championship surfing contest every Easter.

Go Ride a Wave (☎ 1300 132 441; www.gorideawave .com.au; Bell St) hires surfing gear, sells second-hand equipment and offers lessons. It's next to the Plaza in Baines Cres. Other surf instructors include **Gally's Surf Coaching** (☎ 5261 3542; www.gallyssurfcoaching.com.au), **Westcoast Surf School** (☎ 5261 2241) and **Southern Exposure** (☎ 5261 2170).

Kids will appreciate **Tiger Moth World Adventure Park** (☎ 5261 5100; Blackgate Rd; adult/child under 4 $9.50/free; ⏱ 10am-5pm), 5km northeast

of Torquay. It's basically a giant play park with paddle boats, minigolf, daily air shows and joy flights in vintage aircraft.

Sleeping

Over summer and Easter, Torquay is flooded with tourists and it's hard to find anywhere to stay. Book well ahead.

Ironbark Haven B&B (☎ 5263 2224; www.iron barkhaven.com; 3 Point Addis Rd, Bells Beach/Point Addis; d low/high season $120/140) Halfway to Anglesea, it's the pretty bush setting around this rammed-earth homestead that most appeals. State-park walks begin at your back door.

Norfolk Cottage B&B (☎ 5264 8182; 22 Island Dr; d low/high season $90/130; ⌘) English country garden, homemade biscuits, plump doonas and a gourmet breakfast are yours to enjoy at this traditional B&B. The design is mock-Tudor, and the top floor is all yours, from gargantuan, beige spa room to vaulted ceiling.

Wattle Court Retreat (☎ 5261 9354; wattlecourt@ myaccess.com.au; 12 Wattle Ct, Jan Juc; d $150) In suburban Jan Juc, this bright, two-storey apartment has a wonderful bush-garden decking.

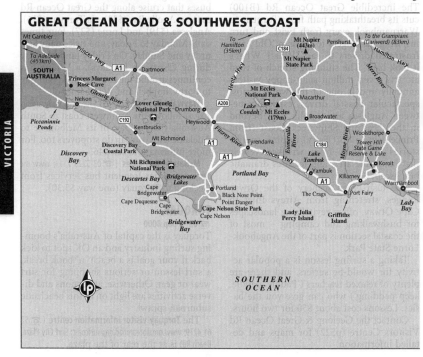

GREAT OCEAN ROAD & SOUTHWEST COAST

From your king-size bed, windows nestle you among the tree tops.

Other recommendations:

Sea-Enna Cottage (☎ 5261 4667; signific@pipeline .com.au; 21 Zeally Bay Rd; d low/high season $120/140) Vividly decorated, close to shops.

Bells Beach Lodge (☎ 5261 7070; www.bellsbeach lodge.com.au; 51-53 Surfcoast Hwy; dm from $20, d low/high season $45/60; 🖳) Neat, intimate backpackers hostel.

Torquay Public Reserve (☎ 5261 2496; powered /unpowered sites per 2 people from $25/10, cabins low/high season $65/100) Just behind Back Beach.

Torquay Holiday Resort (☎ 5261 2493; 55 Surfcoast Hwy; enquiries@torquayholidayresort.com.au; sites per 2 people from $23, cabins low/high season $49/79; 🐾) Tidy and kid-friendly.

Eating

Growlers (☎ 5264 8455; 23 The Esplanade; mains $15-26; ☽ breakfast, lunch & dinner) From the shaded veranda or dark-wood interior you have peek-a-boo views through pines to the front beach. The menu is inventive.

Imperial Rhino (☎ 5261 6780; 3 Bell St; mains $15-17; ☽ breakfast, lunch & dinner) You can match your noodle fetish (vermicelli, *hokkien*, rice stick or just plain flat) here with tossed Asian veggies, tofu or Thai red curry. It all feels very Zen: long wooden tables and bright surrounds.

Rose (☎ 5261 2038; 220 Great Ocean Rd; mains $18-26; ☽ lunch daily, dinner Thu-Mon, breakfast Sun) The Rose doubles as a function centre but its rich plumb hues set a romantic, fine-dining mood. The menu offers classic, wedding-banquet fare. On summer days, enjoy veranda views across the valley.

ANGLESEA

☎ 03 / pop 2200

Shuffling around sipping good coffee, roo watching and boogie boarding are your chores here. Anglesea is a cosy seaside village popular with families for its terrific beaches and camping. The town winds around the gum-green Anglesea River, and accommodation makes the most of tranquil bush settings. There's no visitor centre, just a lonely information booth with brochures across from the main shopping centre.

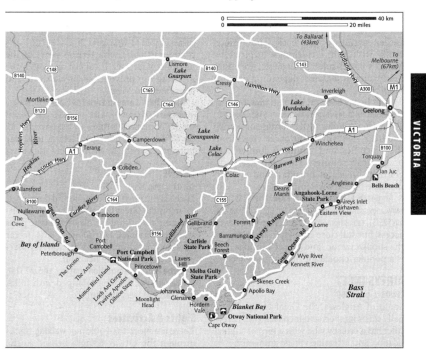

VICTORIA

Activities

Roo watch: **Anglesea Golf Club** (☎ 5263 1582; Noble St) has a resident kangaroo population that grazes blithely on the fairways as golfers fire balls off around them. There's always a posse along the Golf Links Rd, or else check the view from the club's bistro.

Hire surf or beach-play equipment from the **Anglesea Surf Centre** (☎ 5263 1530; cnr Great Ocean Rd & McMillan St) or **Go Ride A Wave** (☎ 1300 132 441; 143B Great Ocean Rd), which also gives surfing lessons, as does **Southern Exposure** (☎ 5261 2170).

Eco Logic Education & Environment Services (☎ 5263 1133; www.ecologic.net.au) guides 'marine rock-pool rambles' and night-time 'possum prowls'. Little kids love this stuff.

Sleeping

Roadknight Cottages (☎ 5263 1820; 26 Great Ocean Rd; cottages per 4 people from $155) Heading towards Lorne, these two-storey cottages have private decking with pretty native-garden settings. They're comfy and self-contained, sleeping up to six. Prices based on two-night minimum stay.

Surf Coast Spa Resort (☎ 5263 3363; www.surf coastspa.com.au; 105 Great Ocean Rd; d low/high season $95/145) Ask for the doubles with decks and garden settings up the back. These motel units, with soft furnishings inspired by Monet's pastel-splotched palette, are either pretty, or a little dated, depending on your mood.

Point Luxury B&B (☎ 5263 3738; www.thepointan glesea.com.au; d low/high season from $185/200; ✷) The style is modern Mediterranean – crisp and fresh – with dramatic ocean views from the balconies and common lounge and pretty bush settings. The king-size beds, gourmet breads at breakfast and complimentary port are welcome extras.

Anglesea Family Caravan Park (☎ 5263 1583; www.angleseafcp.com.au; Cameron Rd; sites low/high season $25/31, cabins from $65) With river and beach access, but still close enough to shuffle up to the shops in your sand-crusted thongs, this is a popular choice for budget travellers.

AIREYS INLET

☎ 03 / pop 1000

South of Anglesea, the Great Ocean Rd finally starts its spectacular coastal run. Aireys Inlet has a cruisey vibe with a hint of sophistication and a seaside village ambience.

In Aireys there are some great **beaches** backed by tall, volcanic cliffs with tidal rock pools along the foreshore. **Split Point Lighthouse** walking tracks and lookout have top views.

Great Ocean Road Adventure Tours (☎ 5289 6841; ☯ 9am-5pm) hires surfboards, mountain bikes and canoes for Painkalac Creek. Ask about bushwalks and short bus tours.

Blazing Saddles (☎ 5289 7322; per 1¼hr $35, 2¼hr $55), about 2km inland, offers horse riding in the bush and along the beach.

Sleeping

Cimarron B&B (☎ 5289 7044; www.cimarron.com.au; 105 Gilbert St; d low/high season $125/175) Cocoon and rejuvenate your spirits in this superb, rustic, yet sophisticated homestead. Loft-style doubles have vaulted ceilings and tree-top or sea views, or there's a denlike apartment. Out back, it's all state park and wildlife.

Aireys Overboard (☎ 5289 7424; www.aireysover board.com.au; Barton Ct; d low/high season $150/250; ✷) Wavelike radial-sawn weatherboards give this contemporary beach house a unique exterior. The interior is elegant – warm wood floors, log fire and double spa. Love the outdoor shower!

Seahaven B&B (☎ 5289 6408; seahavenbandb@ iprimus.com.au; 62 Wybellenna Dr; d $100; ✷) It's bright and basic with terrific views of the inlet. Fix your own breakfast and catch the morning sun on your balcony. Private and convenient to town.

Aireys Inlet Caravan Park (☎ 5289 6230; www.ai cp.com.au; 19-25 Great Ocean Rd; powered/unpowered sites from $22/20, cabins with bathroom low/high season $65/105; ▯ ✷) A neat little park lacking in shady trees but near the township's few stores.

LORNE

☎ 03 / pop 1200

Lorne is the most fashionable and developed town on the Great Ocean Rd, with some interesting restaurants and cafés, classic pubs and terrific views. During peak season, car parks and accommodation are scarce, otherwise life here is fairly peaceful.

Lorne visitor information centre (☎ 5289 1152; 144 Mountjoy Pde) is often cramped with folks, but staff are very helpful.

Sights & Activities

There are more than 50km of **walking** tracks through the Otway Ranges behind Lorne (see p542). **Eco Logic Education and Environment Services** (☎ 5263 1133; www.ecologic.net.au), based in Anglesea, organises guided walks for a minimum of two people.

At least drive to **Teddy's Lookout** and inland along the scenic Erskine Falls Rd. At **Erskine Falls**, it's an easy walk to the waterfall-viewing platform, or 250 steps down to the base. The visitor centre can also suggest scenic loop drives through the Otway Ranges.

Qdos Arts (☎ 5289 1989; www.qdosarts.com; Allenvale Rd; ☻ 10am-late, closed Wed Apr-Nov) has stunning exhibitions, striking architecture and a sculpture garden in a magical bush setting. The licensed café is excellent too.

Hire boogie boards and wetsuits from the **Lorne Surf Shop** (☎ 5289 1673; 130 Mountjoy Pde; ☻ 9am-5.30pm), or catch a surfing lesson with **Go Ride A Wave** (☎ 1300 132 441) or **Southern Exposure** (☎ 5261 2170).

Festivals & Events

Falls Festival (www.fallsfestival.com) This two-day shindig over New Year's is on a farm not too far from town. Falls assembles a top line-up of rock groups and the $100 ticket price includes camping.

Pier to Pub Swim (www.lornesurfclub.com.au) This popular event in January inspires up to 4500 swimmers to splash their way 1.2km across Loutit Bay to the Lorne Hotel.

Sleeping

Lorne has loads of accommodation for bush and beach lovers. Ask the visitor centre or

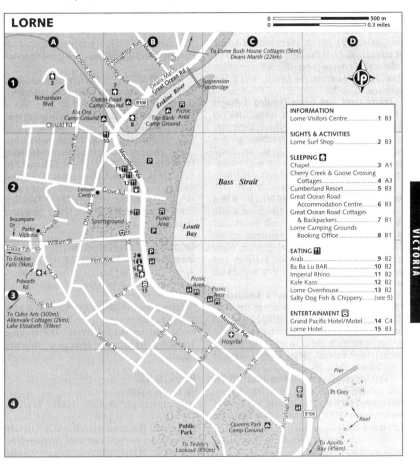

LORNE

INFORMATION
Lorne Visitors Centre................1 B3

SIGHTS & ACTIVITIES
Lorne Surf Shop........................2 B3

SLEEPING
Chapel...................................3 A1
Cherry Creek & Goose Crossing
   Cottages.............................4 A3
Cumberland Resort....................5 B3
Great Ocean Road
   Accommodation Centre.........6 B3
Great Ocean Road Cottages
   & Backpackers.....................7 B1
Lorne Camping Grounds
   Booking Office....................8 B1

EATING
Arab......................................9 B2
Ba Ba Lu BAR.........................10 B2
Imperial Rhino........................11 B2
Kafe Kaos..............................12 B2
Lorne Ovenhouse....................13 B2
Salty Dog Fish & Chippery.......(see 5)

ENTERTAINMENT
Grand Pacific Hotel/Motel.......14 C4
Lorne Hotel............................15 B3

try **Great Ocean Road Accommodation Centre** (☎ 5289 1800; www.gorac.com.au; 136 Mountjoy Pde; ⏰ 9am-5.30pm).

Great Ocean Road Cottages & Backpackers YHA (☎ 5289 1070; www.yha.com.au; 10 Erskine Ave; dm YHA members $20, nonmembers low/high season $24/30, d YHA members $50, nonmembers low/high season $60/70) This country-cosy, two-storey timber lodge nests in the gum trees with companionable cockatoos and magpies. Dorms are spacious, and doubles excellent value.

Chapel (☎ 5289 2622; thechapellorne@bigpond .com; 45 Richardson Blvd; d low/high season $150/180) Outstanding. This contemporary A-frame retreat over two levels has choice Indonesian furnishings, happy splashes of colour and bay windows that seem to tumble into forest below.

Lorneview B&B (☎ 5289 6430; www.lorneview .com.au; 677 Great Ocean Rd, Eastern View; d low/high season $120/160; ⏰) About 14km east of Lorne at Eastern View, these light, spacious, tastefully styled rooms (one with ace views) are directly across from the beach. You'll feel carefree.

Cherry Creek and Goose Crossing Cottages (☎ 5289 2107; 93-99 Polwarth Rd; cottages $100-150) These two homey cottages with eclectic furnishings are set in a lovely, rambling garden with dogs and squawking geese for company: imagine you are staying with eccentric grandparents. Kids and pets welcome.

Lorne Bush House Cottages (☎ 5289 2477; www.lornebushcottages.com.au; 1860 Deans Marsh Rd; d low/high season $140/160; ⏰) Set high on a hill, these cottages have cute loft bedrooms with superb bush, valley or ocean views. Hopefully you're a fan of golden pine, no-fuss furniture. Great for families (no pets). Minimum two-night stay applies on weekends.

Great Ocean Road Cottages & Backpackers (☎ 5289 1070; www.greatoceanroadcottages.com; 10 Erskine Ave; d low/high season $150/170; ⏰) Designed to blend into a hillside of eucalypts, these A-frame retreats are a magnet for cheeky cockatoos. Cottages sleep four or six and have basic mod cons, but bland décor.

Lorne Camping Grounds Booking Office (☎ 5289 1382; www.lorneforeshore.asn.au; 2 Great Ocean Rd; powered/unpowered sites from $22/18, cabins with bathroom low/high season $80/122) Manages bookings for five good caravan parks.

There are several motels in town, and both pubs have rooms.

Eating

ba ba lu BAR (☎ 5289 1808; 6a Mountjoy Pde; mains $18-28; ⏰ breakfast, lunch & dinner Aug-May, closed Tue-Wed in low season) Millionaires mix with backpackers at this unpretentious place, which is always set on cruise control. Flavoursome, organic (where possible) nosh is served, from authentic tapas to eclectic à la carte.

Imperial Rhino (☎ 5289 5215; 44 Mountjoy Pde; mains $15-20; ⏰ breakfast, lunch & dinner) It's the long wooden tables and ottoman squats for seats that first impress, but this licensed, contemporary concept Asian does everything well, from noodles to stir fries and sushi.

Kafe Kaos (☎ 5289 2639; 52 Mountjoy Pde; lunch $8-15; ⏰ breakfast & lunch) You come here to feel like you're hanging out in a friend's inner-urban retro pad, except it's by the beach. Standard Mod Oz lunch fare is prepared on excellent bread, and there are good vegetarian options.

Arab (☎ 5289 1435; 94 Mountjoy Pde; mains $20-24; ⏰ breakfast, lunch & dinner) They're doing something right, having opened in 1956! It's a bustling eatery that ploughs on in quiet seasons, offering simple, tasty food with no-fuss presentation and ambience to match.

For cheaper eats try the family-friendly **Lorne Ovenhouse** (☎ 5289 2544; 46A Mountjoy Pde; mains $20-25; ⏰ lunch & dinner year-round, breakfast Nov-Apr), which has gourmet wood-fired pizzas, pastas and focaccias, and the **Salty Dog Fish & Chippery** (☎ 5289 1300; Shop 1, Cumberland Resort; ⏰ lunch & dinner).

Drinking & Entertainment

Grand Pacific Hotel/Motel (☎ 5289 1609; 268 Mountjoy Pde) Striving for beachside sophistication in its sleek bar, it has cool jazz on Saturday nights all year.

Lorne Hotel (☎ 5289 1409; cnr Mountjoy Pde & Bay St) Bands play in the bottom bar most weekends, but the shaded terrace overlooking Lorne is entertainment enough on summer nights.

APOLLO BAY

☎ 03 / pop 1400

Ridiculously picturesque Apollo Bay is a fishing town and popular summer beach drop zone. It's more relaxed and less trendy than Lorne, but you can sniff development and an air of resignation among its eclectic

VICTORIA

populace. Rolling hills provide a postcard backdrop to the town, while broad white-sand beaches dominate the foreground. It's an ideal base for exploring Otway National Park.

The **Great Ocean Rd visitor information centre** (☎ 5237 6529; ☽ 9am-5pm) is on the left as you arrive from Lorne. In the same building, there's an impressive 'eco-centre' with displays on Aboriginal history, rainforests, shipwrecks and the building of the Great Ocean Rd.

Sights & Activities

It's 1.5km from town to **Marriners Lookout** (signposted) for spectacular views of the town and coast – from the car park it's about 10 minutes' climb to the lookout.

Tandem hang glide or paraglide from Marriners Lookout with **Wingsports Flight Academy** (☎ 0419 378 616), or take the high road in with a Cessna 206 flight over the Twelve Apostles with **Cape Otway Aviation** (☎ 0407 306 065; 3 Telford St; flights per person $145).

Wild Dog Trails (☎ 5237 6441; 225 Wild Dog Rd; ☽ 9am-6.30pm) has 1½- to three-hour horse rides (from $45). Meet the slippery crew banished to the **Marengo Reef Seal Colony** with **Apollo Bay Sea Kayaking** (☎ 0405 495 909; ☽ tours 10.30am & 2pm most days).

Otway Expeditions (☎ 5237 6341) runs three-hour mountain-bike rides through the Otways ($55), as well as gentle bush-bashing adventures in cross-terrain-and-water Argo Buggies (from $35).

The **Old Cable Station Museum** (☎ 5237 7441; Great Ocean Rd; admission $2.50; ☽ 2-5pm Sat, Sun & school & public holidays), has a huge collection relating to the 1859 submarine telegraph cable from Cape Otway to Tasmania.

Festivals & Events

Apollo Bay Music Festival (☎ 5237 6761; www.apollo baymusicfestival.com), in April, features blues, jazz, classical, rock and folk music, as well as street performers and markets. It's an intimate affair, attracting about 3000 locals and blow-ins. Weekend adult passes cost from $100.

Sleeping

Surfside Backpackers (☎ 5237 7263; cnr Great Ocean Rd & Gambier St; dm low/high season $18/22, d $55/60) Of the three backpackers hostels, this rambling, old, white weatherboard is the largest. It's a homely place to hang in the lounge with tumbling-surf views.

Alyeska Llama Farm Retreat (☎ 5237 6138; www.llama.asn.au/alyeska; 355 Killala Rd; lofts low/high season $125/150) Getting to know their guests is the llamas' favourite pastime, so prepare for inquisitive company. The loft is an idyllic couples' retreat with king-size bed upstairs, kitchen and lounge downstairs. Continental breakfast provided the first morning.

Spindrift B&B (☎ 5237 7410; spindrift@vicnet .net.au; 2 Marengo Cres; d $100) Who wants dibs on this incredible ocean vista? Windswept views of Mounts Bay dominate two very spacious, spotless rooms that book-end a generous guests' lounge room. Continental breakfast, plus eggs provided cheerfully.

Beacon Point Ocean View Villas (☎ 5237 6218; www.beaconpoint.com.au; 270 Skenes Creek Rd; d $150-250; ⚟) These hill-top deluxe and premium villas have great bush and ocean views, wood fires, a sensual feel and a contemporary edge. Cheaper suites have spas and daggy fabrics.

Beach Front Motel & Cottages (☎ 5237 6666; www.beachfrontmotel.com.au; d low/high season $89/215) Perfectly located at the top of the main drag, the rooms' brown brick walls, exposed beams and slanted ceilings feel rather 'ski lodge', with views onto rolling highlands.

Marengo Holiday Park (☎ 5237 6162; www.maren gopark.com.au; powered sites per 2 people low/high season $32/36, unpowered sites $17/18; d cabin $80/160) Just 2km west of town by the beach, and off the Great Ocean Rd, this is a very well-run park with spacious, motel-quality deluxe cabins. Light on shade for campers though.

Eating

Bay Leaf Café (☎ 5237 6470; 131 Great Ocean Rd; lunch mains $10-16; ☽ breakfast, lunch & dinner) Excellent spot for any meal, but the morning's pancake stacks and evening's chicken-and-leek pie are wizard. A favourite with locals for its innovative menu, real coffee, buzzy, friendly atmosphere and fair prices.

Café Nautigals (☎ 0402 825 590; 57 Great Ocean Rd; mains $14-16; ☽ breakfast, lunch & dinner; ⌨) There's a great selection of tasty, satisfying Asian noodle, rice, curry and vegetarian here, but it's the wildly warm colours and magnetic vibe that drags you in and keeps you here. A backpackers' menu includes free drink and Internet.

Café One 5 Three (☎ 5237 6518; 153 Great Ocean Rd; mains $4-10; ☽ breakfast & lunch) Light and bright with wraparound windows. Breakfast runs all day and lunches are a bread-fest: Turkish, focaccia, bagels, rolls, bruschetta and toasties.

Blue Olive (☎ 5237 7118; Great Ocean Rd; mains $15-25; ☺ lunch & dinner daily, breakfast Sat & Sun) Overlooking the rolling surf, 1km before town, the Olive has the best eating views around and a really innovative menu of international flavours. Friday nights are jam sessions and Sundays feature live music.

Chris's at Beacon Point Restaurant (☎ 5237 6411; Skenes Creek Rd; mains $30-35; ☺ lunch & dinner) A hill-top fine-dining sanctuary that overlooks Apollo Bay, 6km away. It's a beautifully designed restaurant, from its stone feature walls, sandstone floors and vaulted ceilings to its panoramic views.

CAPE OTWAY

The Cape Otway coastline is particularly beautiful, rugged and dangerous, having snapped plenty of gangly ships wide open. It's part of the Otway National Park, 21km from Apollo Bay.

About 8km along Lighthouse Rd is a signpost that points down an unsealed road. **Parker Hill**, **Point Franklin** and **Crayfish Beach** are all gorgeous, secluded spots for beach ambling (absolutely no swimming!). You can climb the **Cape Otway Lighthouse** (☎ 03-5237 9240; Lighthouse Rd; adult/child/family $10.50/5.50/26; ☺ 9am-5pm) for amazing views. It's absolutely reviving up here.

Within the Otway Ranges is Angahook-Lorne State Park – *A Guide to Walks in the Angahook-Lorne State Park* (about $5) is available from the Lorne visitor centre or Parks Victoria.

Three of the most popular walks are the Erskine Falls Walk, a 7.5km, one-way trail that descends steeply down steps to a lookout and then to the base of the falls; the Kalimna Falls Walk, an easy 9km circuit along an old timber tramway; and the Sheoak Falls Walk, a moderate to difficult 9km-return walk that takes you to the 15m drop and deep pool of the falls.

Sleeping

Lighthouse Keeper's Residence (☎ 03-5237 9240; www.lightstation.com; B&B d low/high season $145/165, studio $135/145) An airy, sandstone place with scant older-style furnishings, in keeping with the times. It sleeps up to four or can be divided for two, or there's the West Studio, which is part of the café.

Shearwater Cottages (☎ 03-5237 9290; www.shearwatercottages.com; 760 Lighthouse Rd; d low/high season $165/175) These wonderfully secluded log cabins are spacious and well-appointed – very relaxing and dog-friendly.

Bimbi Park (☎ 03-5237 9246; www.bimbipark.com.au; Manna Gum Dr; powered sites per 2 people low/high season $22/26, unpowered sites $15/18, dm $16/20, d cabin $56/75) A horse-riding ranch with great climbing trees and shade, about 3km before the lighthouse. There are good bushwalking tracks here leading to remote beaches, and 1½-hour trail rides ($40).

Bush camping (per 2 people low/high season $10/20) is allowed, but book through **Parks Victoria** (☎ 13 19 63). The visitor centre has walking maps.

PORT CAMPBELL NATIONAL PARK

This is the most photographed stretch of the Great Ocean Rd. Sheer limestone cliffs tower 70m over fierce seas. Over thousands of years, waves and tides have relentlessly thrashed the soft rock in an ongoing process of erosion and undercutting, creating a fascinating series of rock stacks, gorges, arches and blowholes.

The **Gibson Steps**, carved by hand into the cliffs in the 19th century (and more recently replaced by concrete steps), lead down to feral Gibson Beach. This beach, and others along this stretch of coast, are not recommended for swimming – you can walk along the beach, but be careful not to be stranded by high tides.

The **Twelve Apostles** are the best-known rock formations in Victoria. These lonely rocky stacks have been abandoned to the ocean by eroding headland. Today, only six apostles can be seen from the viewing platforms. There's an interpretive display at the **visitor facility**. Timber boardwalks run around the cliff tops, providing viewing platforms and seats.

West of Port Campbell, the next ocean sculpture is the **Arch**, a rocky archway offshore from Point Hesse. Nearby is **London Bridge**, albeit fallen down. It was once a double-arched rock platform linked to the mainland, but in 1990 one of the arches collapsed into the sea.

About 200m up the road, the friendly crew at **12 Apostles Helicopters** (☎ 03-5598 6161;

www.12ah.com) offers a range of tours, starting at $80 per person for an eight-minute flight. It also records a 'Skycam' video of your trip.

Nearby, at Loch Ard gorge, haunting tales of woe await. It's one of the Shipwreck Coast's most notorious sections.

Sleeping & Eating

The following options are in and around the pretty township of Port Campbell.

Ocean House Backpackers (☎ 03-5598 6492; camp inport@datafast.net.au; Cairns St; dm low/high season $20/25) Occupies the best chunk of real estate in town. Smack-bang overlooking the main beach, this hot-pink, pine-panelled house has a warm ambience and cosy guest lounge with open fireplace.

Port Campbell Cabin & Camping Park (☎ 03-5598 6492; campinport@datafast.net.au; Morris St; powered/unpowered sites per 2 people $23/20, cabins with bathroom low/high season $80/105) Neat, small and a two-minute walk to the beach and bottom end of town, these new cabins are a good option, although camp sites lack shade.

Daysy Hill Country Cottages (☎ 03-5598 6226; daysyhill@gatewaybbs.com.au; 2585 Cobden–Port Campbell Rd; d garden suite low/high season $125/135; ⊠) These lovely hill-side cedar suites, just a few minutes from town, are decked out in modern colonial-style country comfort. The rooms are part of one building or there are more private, self-contained cottages.

Eastern Reef Cottages (☎ 03-5598 6561; eastern .reef@bigpond.com; Great Ocean Rd; d low/high season $90/120; ⊠) Hooray! They accept single-night

stays in these warm, woody, open-plan A-frame cabins. No views but great for short stays. It's 600m out of town.

Waves (☎ 03-5598 6111; 29 Lord St; mains $20-26; ☺ breakfast, lunch & dinner) The only flash-looking eatery in town. At night, the seafood menu is as enticing as the contemporary ambience, buoyed by rich coral hues. Mainly fish-fillet dishes and a couple of meat options.

Nico's Pizza and Pasta (☎ 03-5598 6131; 25 Lord St; mains $15-19; ☺ dinner, lunch in summer) This pizza and pasta joint is the tasty-food 'n' chatty-ambience option. It offers schnitzels, cray and steak, and pizza with unusual toppings.

SOUTHWEST

The Great Ocean Rd ends 12km east of Warrnambool, where it meets the Princes Hwy, which continues into SA. It's a pretty stretch of road and Port Fairy is a cute place for a stopover, with plenty of windswept walks. Warrnambool is a large coastal town with a strong whaling and sealing history, and is the best place to stock up for onward travel.

WARRNAMBOOL

☎ 03 / pop 26,800

Warrnambool was originally settled as a humble whaling and sealing station. These days it feels like the major industrial and commercial centre that it is, although its historic buildings, waterways and tree-lined

---

THE SHIPWRECK COAST

The Victorian coastline between Cape Otway and Port Fairy was a notoriously dangerous stretch of water in the days of sailing ships. Navigation was exceptionally difficult due to numerous barely hidden reefs and frequent heavy fog. More than 80 vessels came to grief on this 120km stretch in just 40 years.

The most famous wreck was that of the iron-hulled clipper *Loch Ard*, which foundered off Mutton Bird Island on the final night of its voyage from England in 1878. Of the 55 people on board, only two survived. Eva Carmichael clung to wreckage and was washed into the gorge, where apprentice officer Tom Pearce rescued her. Eva and Tom were both 18 years old. The press tried to create a romantic story but nothing actually happened. Eva soon returned to Ireland and they never saw each other again.

The *Falls of Halladale*, a Glasgow barque, foundered in 1908 en route from New York to Melbourne. There were no casualties, but it lay on the reef, fully rigged and with sails set, for a couple of months. Other notable wrecks were the *Newfield* in 1892 and *La Bella* in 1905.

Divers have investigated these wrecks; relics are on display in the Flagstaff Hill Maritime Village (p545) in Warrnambool.

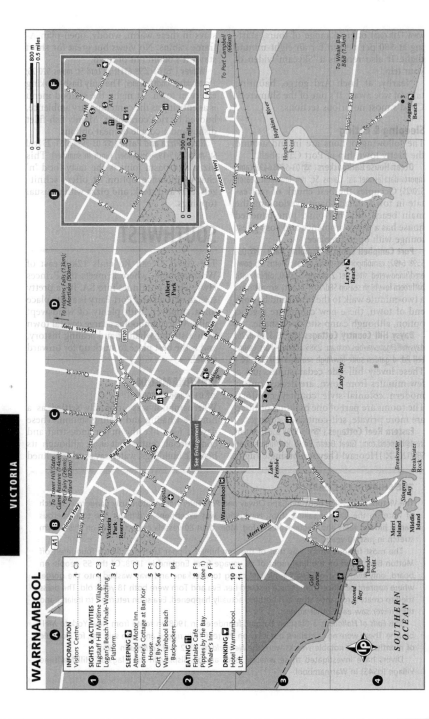

WARRNAMBOOL

INFORMATION
Visitors Centre........................1	C3

SIGHTS & ACTIVITIES
Flagstaff Hill Maritime Village...2	C3
Logan's Beach Whale-Watching	
Platform..............................3	F4

SLEEPING
Attwood Motor Inn.................4	C2
Bonnie's Cottage at Ban Kor	
House................................5	F1
Girt By Sea.........................6	C2
Warrnambool Beach	
Backpackers.......................7	B4

EATING
Fishtales Café......................8	F1
Pippies by the Bay..........(see 1)	
Whaler's Inn.......................9	F1

DRINKING
Hotel Warrnambool..............10	F1
Loft.................................11	F1

VICTORIA

SOUTHERN OCEAN

streets add appeal. There's a large student population. **Warrnambool visitor information centre** (☎ 5559 4620; Merri St; ☺ 9am-5pm), signposted off the Princes Hwy (A1), produces the handy *Warrnambool Visitors Guide*.

Sights & Activities

Warrnambool's major tourist attraction is the impressive **Flagstaff Hill Maritime Village** (☎ 5564 7841; Merri St; adult/child/family $14/5.50/35; ☺ 9am-5pm), modelled on an early Australian coastal port. See the cannon and fortifications built in 1887 to withstand the perceived threat of Russian invasion, and **Shipwrecked** (adult/child/family $23/13/63), a sound-and-laser show of the *Loch Ard*'s plunge.

Warrnambool has some excellent beaches such as the sheltered **Lady Bay**, the main swimming beach. **Logans Beach** is the best surf beach, but there are other good breaks at Levy's Beach and Second Bay (near the golf course).

The drawcard for many is the **southern right whales** that cavort making babies, breaching and fluking within sight of Warrnambool from July to September. You can try and spy the whales from Logans Beach Whale Watching Platform – you'll need 20/20 eyesight or a pair of binoculars.

Southern Right Charters and Diving (☎ 5562 5044; www.southernrightcharters.com.au) has many whale-watching and boat tours, diving and fishing charters, and shuttle services and day tours.

Walking trails in and around Warrnambool include the 3km **Heritage Trail**. The short **Thunder Point** stroll shows off the best coastal scenery in the area; it's also the starting point for the 22km coastal **Mahogany Walking Trail**.

Sleeping

Warrnambool Beach Backpackers (☎ 5562 4874; david_gilllane@hotmail.com; 17 Stanley St; dm/d $20/60) Close to the sea, this place has a huge living area, a bar, Internet access and free pick-up. It's a good place to meet people, and use of the mountain bikes and canoes is free.

Atwood Motor Inn (☎ 5562 7144; atwood@hotkey .net.au; 8 Spence St; d low/high season $88/102; ▨) In a quiet side street, yet only three minutes' walk from all the action. Small but attractively furnished doubles are excellent value in this location. Noisy neighbours are easily heard.

Girt by Sea (☎ 5562 3162; www.girtbyseabandb .com.au; 52 Banyan St; tw/d/ste $110/130/150) This restored 1856 sandstone home has been refurbished with exquisite flair. Large bathrooms boast antique vanities and red Baltic pine floors. The Southern Cross suite is special: a huge brass bed and private garden decking. There's a large, bright guest lounge and great breakfasts.

Bonnie's Cottage at Ban Kor House (☎ 5562 9461; www.bankorhouse.com.au; cottages low/high season $100/175) A quaintly renovated sandstone cottage with many original features. Love the African bedroom with its zebra cushions, pith helmet and fur throw! One block from town, two from the beach.

Eating & Drinking

Liebig St is Warrnambool's main strip and many of the eateries are along here.

Fishtales Café (☎ 5561 2957; 63 Liebig St; mains $8-15; ☺ breakfast, lunch & dinner) This upbeat, friendly eatery-takeaway has deliciously prepared fare from a dozen different burgers to fish and chips, vegetarian specials, seafood and Asian dishes and good breakfasts. Cheery courtyard.

Pippies by the Bay (☎ 5561 2188; Flagstaff Hill, Merri St; mains $26-30; ☺ lunch & dinner daily, breakfast Sat & Sun) A classy space cushioned by deep plum walls and dark wood. Offers Mod Oz cuisine, finely executed, an exceptional wine list and a view.

Whaler's Inn (☎ 5562 8391; cnr Liebig & Timor Sts; mains $12-16; ☺ lunch & dinner) It's a family friendly setup here. Meals are tasty and generous. Prices include the all-you-can-eat salad bar.

Hotel Warrnambool (☎ 5562 2377; cnr Koroit & Kepler Sts; ☺ 10.30am-midnight Mon-Tue, 10.30am-1am Wed-Sat, 10.30am-10pm Sun) The most welcoming place in town: an earthy, cavernous affair with exposed mud bricks and railway sleepers, slouchy lounge areas and a billiard table.

Loft (☎ 5561 0995; 58 Liebig St; ☺ 5.30pm-1am Wed, Fri & Sat, daily in summer) This place has a relaxed, contemporary vibe with laid-back live music on weekends. One of Warrnambool's few smoke-free zones.

Getting There & Away

The **V/Line** (☎ 13 61 96; www.vline.com.au) train station is on Merri St, at the southern end of Fairy St. There are daily services to

VICTORIA

Melbourne ($41). Connecting V/Line buses continue west to Port Fairy ($5.10), Portland ($15) and Mt Gambier ($33). Weekday buses go to Ballarat ($22) and Hamilton ($7.30).

On Friday, a bus heads along the Great Ocean Rd to Apollo Bay ($25), with connections to Geelong. There's also a service on Monday during the Christmas holidays.

The **Wayward Bus** (☎ 1300 653 510; www.waywardbus.com.au) travels from Melbourne to Adelaide following the coast all the way, and allows stopovers.

PORT FAIRY

☎ 03 / pop 2600

This seaside township was settled in 1835, and the first arrivals were whalers and seal-

ers. To this day, Port Fairy still has a large fishing fleet and a relaxed, salty feel with its old bluestone and sandstone buildings, whitewashed cottages, colourful fishing boats, and streets lined with toilet-brush pines.

The town centre is along Sackville St but the **Port Fairy visitor information centre** (☎ 5568 2682; Bank St; ⏰ 9am-5pm) is at the ocean end of Bank St.

Sights & Activities

Port Fairy has a rich and sometimes gloomy heritage that enraptures local history buffs. A brochure from the visitor centre shows a popular **Shipwreck Walk**. Then you can do the signposted **History Walk** around town, using

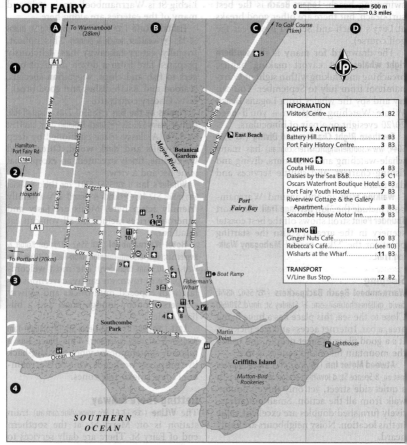

PORT FAIRY

0 — 500 m
0 — 0.3 miles

To Warrnambool (28km)

To Golf Course (1km)

Princes Hwy
Hamilton–Port Fairy Rd
Osmonds La
Griffiths St
Beach St
East Beach
Botanical Gardens
Moyne River

Hospital

Regent St
Eagle St
Grant St
Bank St
William St
Barclay St
James St
Sackville St
Princes St
Cox La
Union St
Gipps St
Wishart St
Atkinson St
Campbell St
Victoria St

To Portland (70km)

Port Fairy Bay

Fisherman's Wharf
Boat Ramp
Griffiths St

Southcombe Park

Ocean Dr

Martin Point

Lighthouse

Griffiths Island
Mutton-Bird Rookeries

SOUTHERN OCEAN

INFORMATION	
Visitors Centre	1 B2
SIGHTS & ACTIVITIES	
Battery Hill	2 B3
Port Fairy History Centre	3 B3
SLEEPING	
Couta Hill	4 B3
Daisies by the Sea B&B	5 C1
Oscars Waterfront Boutique Hotel	6 B3
Port Fairy Youth Hostel	7 B3
Riverview Cottage & the Gallery Apartment	8 B3
Seacombe House Motor Inn	9 B3
EATING	
Ginger Nuts Café	10 B3
Rebecca's Café	(see 10)
Wisharts at the Wharf	11 B3
TRANSPORT	
V/Line Bus Stop	12 B2

VICTORIA

a walk map (20c) available from the visitor centre. The **Port Fairy History Centre** (Gipps St; adult/child $3/50c; 2-5pm Wed, Sat & Sun, daily during school holidays), housed in the old bluestone court-house (complete with dusty mannequins acting out a courtroom scene), has shipping relics, old photos and costumes, and a prisoner's cell. On **Battery Hill** there's a lookout point, and cannons and fortifications that were positioned here in the 1860s.

Festivals & Events

The **Port Fairy Folk Festival** (www.portfairyfolkfestival.com), one of Australia's foremost music festivals, is held here on the Labour Day long weekend in early March.

Sleeping

Port Fairy Youth Hostel (☎ 5568 2468; 8 Cox St; www.portfairyhostel.com.au; dm YHA members/nonmembers $20/24, d $50/57;) In the rambling 1844 home of merchant William Rutledge, this friendly, relaxed and well-run hostel has a large kitchen, peaceful gardens and free cable TV.

Seacombe House Motor Inn (☎ 5568 1082; www.seacombehouse.com.au; cnr Cox & Sackville Sts; d $40) The whitewashed 'backpacker' doubles in the original upstairs section of this 1847 inn are terrific value and quite clean. With high ceilings and original paned windows, it's an authentic Port Fairy experience. Shared bathrooms are new.

Couta Hill (☎ 5568 2412; herrma2@bigpond.com; 14 Gipps St; d/f $75/85) The outside is modern but the huge double room's dark wood furniture, floral prints and lace curtains capture the historic village feel. It's very close to the wharf.

Riverview Cottage & the Gallery Apartment (☎ 5568 2964; www.riverviewonthemoyne.com.au; 17 Gipps St; d $130) Choose between a streetfront country cottage or riverfront contemporary apartment, both self-contained, and with courtyard. Both interiors are exceptionally well styled.

Daisies by the Sea B&B (☎ 5568 2355; jmrahilly@bigpond.com.au; 222 Griffiths St; d low/high season $120/150) If Port Fairy's old-world charm gives you the creeps, try these two beach bungalows about 1.5km out of town. They're as fresh as the sea breeze with absolute beach frontage, waves crashing 50m from your door. It's a snug, appealing get-away for couples.

Oscars Waterfront Boutique Hotel (☎ 5568 3022; www.oscarswaterfront.com; 41B Gipps St; d $250, premium ste $275;) Huge, wrought-iron chandeliers and parquetry floors with wide, white-tiled corridors, and a broad, shaded veranda. This overlooks the boat-speckled wharf of course.

Eating

Ginger Nuts Café (☎ 5568 2326; cnr Bank & Sackville Sts; mains $19-24; 7am-late) Ginger's is one of too few moderately priced dining options. Risotto this, shaved Parmesan that – it's the usual Mod Oz fare but delectably prepared. The wine list is good.

Rebecca's Café (☎ 5568 2533; 72 Sackville St; mains $5-12; 8am-6pm) Excellent for breakfast, light lunches are also reasonably priced, and Rebecca's has the best muffins, slices, scones, biscuits and homemade ice cream in town.

Wisharts at the Wharf (☎ 5568 1884; 29 Gipps St; mains $17-23; lunch & dinner) Wharf-side dining doesn't come prettier than this. Plump, juicy fish 'n' chips are always assured here. Adventurous presentation and flavours in very relaxed surrounds.

Getting There & Away

Daily buses between Port Fairy and Warrnambool ($5.10) connect with trains to/from Melbourne. **V/Line** (☎ 13 61 96; www.vline.com.au) has daily buses to Portland ($10.20) and Mt Gambier ($25).

PORTLAND

☎ 03 / pop 9600

Portland is the site of Victoria's first European settlement, but these days it prefers the moniker of 'Gateway to the Great South West Walk'. It's Victoria's oldest town, and was a whaling and sealing base from the early 1800s. The first permanent settlers were the Henty family, arriving from Van Diemen's Land (Tasmania) in 1834.

The **Portland visitor information centre** (☎ 5523 2671; Lee Breakwater Rd; 9am-5pm) is at the impressive-looking Maritime Discovery Centre.

Sights & Activities

The Portland **cable tram** (adult/child/family $12/6/30; 10am-4pm) plies a 3.5km route linking the vintage-car museum, botanic gardens, Maritime Discovery Centre and WWII

VICTORIA

memorial water tower by way of the waterfront. Passengers hop on and off as they please; it's a great way to get acquainted with the town.

The **Powerhouse Motor & Car Museum** (☎ 5523 5795; cnr Glenelg & Percy Sts; adult/child/family $5/1/10) has about 25 vintage Australian and American vehicles and motorbikes dating from 1920.

The fabulous **Burswood Homestead** (☎ 5523 4686; 15 Cape Nelson Rd) is a grand old place, built for Edward Henty in 1850 with 5.5 hectares of **gardens** (adult/child $3/free; ☒ 10am-5pm).

There are some good **surfing** spots around this coast, especially at sublime **Bridgewater Bay**, where a Surf Life Saving Club operates over summer on weekends and public holidays. It's a must-visit spot. The visitor centre has a guide to 15 surf breaks.

Sleeping

Bellevue Backpackers (☎ 5523 4038; Sheoke/Yellow Rock Rd; d $20) Fancy a double bed or two bunks in a dinky backyard caravan run by a lovely older couple? One for the young and young at heart, five minutes from town off the Cape Nelson Rd.

Victoria House (☎ 5521 7577; vichouse@hotkey.net .au; 5 Tyers St; d $130) This excellent two-storey bluestone dwelling, built in 1853, has been stylishly renovated and has nine heritage-style guestrooms with bathrooms, a comfy lounge, open fires and a gorgeous garden.

Whalers Cottage B&B (☎ 5521 7522; 12 Whalers Ct; d $90-130) You can't help but slide into the buff Chesterfields that adorn this old-fashioned guest lounge. Whalers is a shadowy bluestone home that has three rooms available, all with shared bathrooms.

Clifftop Accommodation (☎ 5523 1126; clifftop@ dodo.com.au; 13 Clifton Ct; d low/high season $125/130; ☒) On a sunny day, the panoramic views from your balcony are blindingly bright. These sparsely furnished rooms feel big enough to Rollerblade in, but the big brass beds look snuggly.

Burswood Homestead (☎ 5523 4686; 15 Cape Nelson Rd; s low/high season $105/125 master d $165/200, incl breakfast) Set in beautiful gardens, this resplendent place is an indulgent, antique-laden mini-mansion. Spacious master rooms have en suites. Devonshire tea is offered on arrival.

Eating

Sullys Café and Wine Bar (☎ 5523 5355; 55 Bentinck St; mains $15-18; ☒ 8am-late) 'Safe, Sustainable

Cuisine' is the catch phrase at Sullys, a narrow and pleasant nook across from the waterfront. Its produce is organic and humanely farmed, but it's also damn good.

Kopi on the Beach (☎ 5523 1822; 49 Bentinck St; mains $4-7; ☒ breakfast & lunch Mon-Sat) It's the hot-pink walls, dangling crystal mobiles, mandalas and bushcraft furniture that make you want to linger a little longer over a good latte at Kopi's. It's so reasonably priced, and the toasted tortilla sandwiches are a great light snack.

Sandilands (☎ 5523 3319; Percy St; mains $16-24 ☒ dinner, closed Tue & Sun) This elegant manor's imposing façade suggests scary sophistication but reception-centre chairs tone it down a notch. Vegetarians are well catered for here with stir-fry, pasta and risotto dishes.

Getting There & Away

There are daily **V/Line** (☎ 13 61 96; www.vline.com .au) buses between Portland and Port Fairy ($10.20), Warrnambool ($15) and Mt Gambier ($14). Buses depart from Henty St.

PORTLAND TO SOUTH AUSTRALIA

From Portland, you can either head north to Heywood and rejoin the Princes Hwy to head for SA, or you can head northwest along the slower, beautiful, coastal route known as the Portland–Nelson road. This road runs inland from the coast, but along the way there are turn-offs leading down to the beaches and into some great national parks.

Nelson

☎ 08 / pop 200

Nelson is a riverside village with a few houses, a cute general store, a friendly pub and a handful of accommodation that includes three caravan parks and a motel. It's a popular holiday and fishing spot because of its great setting on the coast and at the mouth of the **Glenelg River**, which originates in the Grampians and travels more than 400km to the coast at Nelson. A good chunk of the river flows through **Lower Glenelg National Park**, best explored by canoe.

The **visitor information centre** and **Parks Victoria** (☎ 8738 4051; ☒ 9am-5pm; ☐) share an office.

There are nine **canoeists' camping sites** between Nelson and Dartmoor, with fresh water, toilets and fireplaces. Permits for canoeing or camping cost $3 and are issued by Parks Victoria.

Nelson Boat & Canoe Hire (☎ 8738 4048; www.nelsonboatandcanoehire.com.au) can rig you up for serious camping expeditions. Canoe hire costs from $36 a day. It also does upriver canoe deliveries and pick-ups for an extra fee.

Book a leisurely 3½-hour cruise up the Glenelg River with **Nelson Endeavour River Cruises** (☎ 8738 4191; adult/child $23/10). The cruise stops at the **Princess Margaret Rose Cave** (adult/child/family $9.50/5/25), but tickets for the cave tour cost extra. Cruises depart daily in summer at 1pm, but don't operate Monday and Friday during the rest of the year. If you travel to the caves under your own steam, it's about 17km from Nelson, heading towards the border. And if you've never experienced the Tolkienesque wonderland of a cave, do take a 45-minute tour; they leave every hour between 10am and 4pm.

Simpsons Landing B&B (☎ 8738 4232; d without bathroom $80) has two cheering rooms in an A-frame, loft setup. The **Casuarina Cabins** (☎ 8738 4105; www.casuarinacabins.com.au; cabins $60; ✷) has a gorgeous bush setting, but it contrasts sharply with the stark, fluorescent-lit interior of the cabins by night. Otherwise, **Nelson Cottage** (☎ 8738 4161; cnr Kellett & Sturt Sts; d $80) has cosy enough rooms for short stays.

Nelson Hotel (☎ 8738 4011; Kellett St; mains $13-17, d $45; ☽ lunch & dinner) has a good range of vegetarian options alongside its crumbed and fried fare, and a good salad bar.

THE WESTERN DISTRICT

This region is the third-largest volcanic plain in the world and has some of the best sheep and cattle country in Australia.

Hamilton

☎ 03 / pop 9100

Hamilton, the 'Wool Capital of the World', is the major town of the Western District. The **Hamilton visitor information centre** (☎ 1800 807 056, 5572 3746; www.sthgrampians.vic.gov.au; Lonsdale St; ☽ 9am-5pm) has an interesting free guide, *Volcanoes Discovery Trail*.

The **Hamilton Art Gallery** (☎ 5573 0469; Brown St; admission by donation; ☽ 10am-5pm Mon-Sat, 2-5pm Sun) has an excellent collection of colonial art featuring Western Victoria among other exhibits. On Coleraine Rd 2km west of the cen-

tre, the **Big Woolbales** (☎ 5571 2810; Coleraine Rd; ☽ 9.30am-4pm) has wool samples and shearing demonstrations.

Sir Reginald Ansett (founder of Ansett Airlines) founded his empire in Hamilton in 1931. The **Sir Reginald Ansett Transport Museum** (☎ 5571 2767; Ballarat Rd; adult/child $4/2; ☽ 10am-4pm) has a collection of airline memorabilia, including a 1936 Fokker Universal aircraft, similar to the one Ansett used on his first flight.

SLEEPING & EATING

George Hotel (☎ 5572 1844; george-hotel@bigpond.com.au; 213 Gray St; s/d incl breakfast from $54/65, mains $8-19; ☽ lunch & dinner) Basic small units are in the centre of town, behind the hotel. Order your meal on the lacy veranda or inside the restaurant, which serves concoctions of local produce – you must order Merino chicken!

Bandicoot (☎ 5572 1688; bandicootmi@ansonic.com.au; s/d/f from $60/79/101; ✷) This cheerful place, with the ugliest-looking animal out the front (sorry conservationists), has quiet units, a bar and a restaurant.

Mourilyan (☎ 5572 4347; goldsmithmotel@hotkey.net.au; 22 Pope St; d incl breakfast from $110) This stunning period house, glittering with crystal, has a billiards room, a guest lounge, and 1870s four-poster beds, but the gourmet breakfast is totally modern.

Gilly's (☎ 5571 9111; gillys@hotkey.net.au; 106 Gray St; mains $14-19; ☽ breakfast & lunch daily, dinner Tue-Sat) This buzzing place, decorated with street signs, registration plates and big lounge chairs, serves stylish dishes and fresh yummy breakfasts.

Mt Eccles National Park

Mt Eccles erupted 19,000 years ago, and the lava flow covered the countryside in all directions, with one massive tongue flowing 30km to the coast and on another 19km out to sea. Its main features are the scenic lake, lava caves and a huge koala population. There's a **ranger's station** (☎ 5576 1338) and camp sites with toilets and showers.

THE WIMMERA

The Wimmera is an endless expanse of wheat fields and sheep properties bisected by the Western Hwy (A8), the main route between Melbourne and Adelaide.

The major attractions in the region are the Grampians National Park, Mt Arapiles State Park – Australia's most famous rock-climbing venue – and the Little Desert National Park.

Between Ararat and Stawell, you'll pass through 'blink-and-you-miss-it' Great Western, home to three wineries that offer tours and tastings.

Getting There & Away

The *Overland*, the Melbourne–Adelaide train, runs through the Wimmera, stopping at Ararat, Horsham and Dimboola (for confirmed bookings only), four times a week between 1am and 3am. **V/Line** (☎ 13 61 96; www.vline.com.au) has train/bus services between Melbourne and major towns.

From Horsham you can take a bus north to Mildura, west to Naracoorte or south to Hamilton.

STAWELL
☎ 03 / pop 6150

Stawell is famous for the **Stawell Gift**, a foot race that's been run here every Easter Monday since 1878 and attracts up to 20,000 visitors. The **Stawell Gift Hall of Fame** (☎ 5358 1326; Main St; adult/child $4/2; ☉ 9-11am Mon-Fri) is opposite the Gift Hotel and houses memorabilia from the races.

Bunjil's Shelter, along a bone-rattling bumpy road 11km south of Stawell, and signposted off the road to Pomonal, is one of the most significant Aboriginal rock-art sites in the state. Bunjil is the creator spirit of the Aboriginal people of this region.

The **Stawell visitor information centre** (☎ 1800 330 080; 50-52 Western Hwy; ☉ 9am-5pm) will book accommodation.

Sleeping & Eating

Town Hall Hotel (☎ 5358 1059; fax 5358 3355; 62 Main St; s/d without bathroom from $25/40, penthouse $150, incl breakfast) A grand old pub that has good, basic rooms with pressed-tin ceilings, a cosy guest room with TV, reasonable shared bathrooms and a back deck.

Walmsley Guest House (☎ /fax 5358 3164; 19 Seaby St; s/d from $60/85, deluxe r $130, incl breakfast) This beautiful 130-year-old building has been tastefully restored to its Victorian-era grandeur. Guests enjoy two gorgeous lounge rooms, a loungey veranda and a cooked breakfast.

Diamond House Motor Inn Restaurant (☎ 5358 3366; 24 Seaby St; s/d $70/85; mains $17-26; ☉ dinner Mon-Sat; ⊠) Hard to miss with its diamond-shaped stone-and-onyx exterior, Diamond House's rooms are wood panelled and rustic. The restaurant is meat and seafood orientated, and the cellar is full of local wine.

Stawell Park Caravan Park (☎ 5358 2709; fax 5358 2199; Western Hwy; sites per 2 people from $15, d cabin $66; ⊠ ⊠) This park, on 48 hectares of attractive bushland, has a pool and recreation room.

Café 102 (☎ 5358 4400; 102 Main St; light meals $5-9; ☉ breakfast, lunch & dinner) This buzzy little café in the centre of town churns out fresh light meals. You'll find the Grampians Produce Group goodies here too.

Getting There & Away

V/Line (☎ 13 61 96; www.vline.com.au) runs five buses daily to Ararat or Ballarat connecting with the V/Line train to Melbourne ($36). A bus service also connects Stawell with Halls Gap ($12, three daily) in the Grampians (p554).

GRAMPIANS NATIONAL PARK

The Grampians are one of Victoria's most outstanding natural features, with a rich diversity of flora and fauna, unique rock formations, Aboriginal rock art, bushwalking and climbing – something for every outdoor enthusiast. The mountains are at their best in spring, when the wildflowers (including 20 species that don't exist anywhere else in the world) are at their peak.

Orientation

The Grampians lie west of Ararat and stretch some 90km from Dunkeld in the south almost to Horsham in the north. Halls Gap, the most central town to the Grampians, has a supermarket, restaurants and cafés, and a range of accommodation.

Information

Parks Victoria (☎ 13 19 63, 03-5356 4381; www .parkweb.vic.gov.au; ☉ 9am-5pm) At the Brambuk Cultural Centre, 2.5km south of Halls Gap. Stocks plenty of maps and brochures, issues camping permits and fishing licences, and gives advice.

Visitor information centre (☎ 1800 065 599, 03-5356 4616; www.visitgrampians.com.au; Grampians Rd, Halls Gap; ☉ 9am-5pm) In Centenary Hall.

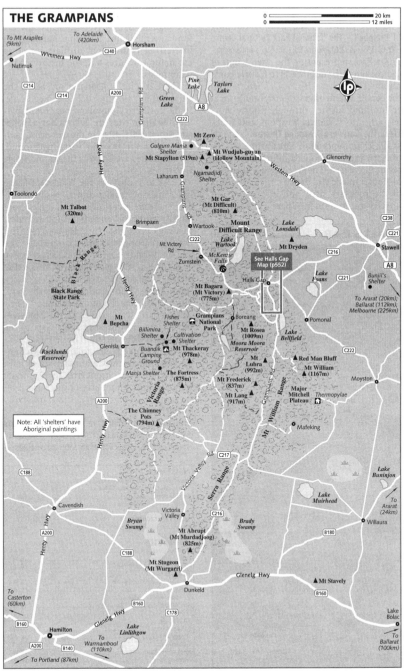

THE GRAMPIANS

Sights

You'll be drawn to the striking building of **Brambuk – The National Park Cultural Centre** (☎ 03-5356 4452; Grampians Rd, Halls Gap; admission free; ⊙ 9am-5pm), representing the open wings of the cockatoo (brambuk). Five Koorie communities, together with Parks Victoria, run the centre, which offers an insight into local culture and history through Koorie stories, art, music, dance, weapons and tools. Here the **Gariwerd Dreaming Theatre** (adult/child $4.50/2.50) presents both Dreamtime stories of Gariwerd and modern informative films about the region. There are demonstrations of Koorie music and dance, organised tours of the rock-art sites, and education and holiday programmes. There's a souvenir

shop and **café** (⊙ lunch). Outside are the native plants used by Aboriginal people for food and medicine. The front building has interesting educational displays covering the natural features and the history of the Grampians.

There is a lot of **Aboriginal rock art** in the park, but not all is publicised or accessible. In the northern Grampians, near Mt Stapylton, the main sites are **Gulgurn Manja Shelter** and **Ngamadjidj Shelter**. In the western Grampians, near the Buandik camping ground, the main sites are **Billimina Shelter** and **Manja Shelter**.

Close to Halls Gap, the **Wonderland Range** has some spectacular and accessible scenery. There are scenic drives and walks, from an easy stroll to Venus Baths (30 minutes) to a walk up to the Pinnacles Lookout (five hours). Walking tracks start from Halls Gap, and the Wonderland and Sundial car parks.

A small **wildlife park & zoo** (☎ 03-5356 4668; Pomonal Rd; adult/child/family $9/5.50/25; ⊙ 10am-5pm Wed-Mon), 3km southeast of Halls Gap, houses native and exotic animals.

There are two tracks from the Zumstein picnic area, northwest of Halls Gap, to the spectacular **McKenzie Falls**. The first track, taking two to three hours, follows the McKenzie River upstream via another set of falls. The second is a cop-out five- to 10-minute walk, for those in a hurry or just lazy.

Activities

The **Grampians Mountain Adventure Company** (GMAC; ☎ 03-5383 9218, 0427 747 047; www.grampiansadventure.com.au; instruction from $50) promises a

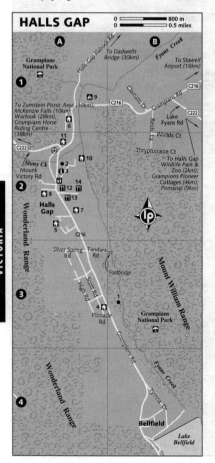

HALLS GAP

0 ——— 800 m
0 ——— 0.5 miles

VICTORIA

rock-climbing or abseiling adventure tailored to suit those who fancy a taste of the vertical world, assisted by accredited instructors.

Grampians Adventure Services (GAS; ☎ 03-5356 4556; www.g-adventures.com.au; Grampians YHA Eco-Hostel, cnr Grampians Rd & Buckler St, Halls Gap) offers rock climbing, abseiling, canoeing, bike tours, bushwalking and caving. Most activities cost $35 for beginners, and you can combine a couple in a day.

Hanging Out (☎ 03-5356 4535, 0407 684 831; www .hanginout.com.au; per person from $23) is another multiactivity adventure company offering abseiling, bushwalking and single- or multipitch climbing in groups.

There are more than 150km of **walking tracks** in the Grampians, ranging from half-hour strolls to overnight treks through difficult terrain. The rangers at Parks Victoria (p550) can provide maps and give good advice on choosing a walk. Be sure to take a map and wear appropriate footwear; take a hat and sunscreen in summer and for longer walks carry water. Before you set off, always let someone know where you're going (preferably the rangers). Water is dangerously cold in winter and it's advisable not to swim at this time.

Grampians Horseriding Centre (☎ 03-5383 9255; Brimpaen, Wartook Valley; 2hr rides $50; ☒ rides 10am & 2pm), 38km northwest of Halls Gap, gives you the opportunity to explore the forests and valleys on horseback.

Morning balloon flights are offered by **Bendigo Ballooning** (☎ 03-5358 5222; flights $175), while **Stawell Aviation Services** (☎ 03-5357 3234; flights for 3 people from $150) offers joy flights by plane.

Tours

Brambuk – The National Park Cultural Centre (☎ 03-5356 4452; Grampians Rd, Halls Gap; ☒ 9am-5pm) Offers a two-hour tour to Bunjil's Shelter (adult/child $15/8) and a half-day tour to other rock-art sites ($27/17). Bookings essential.

Grampians Central Booking Office (☎ 03-5356 46 54; 7353 Schmidt Rd, Halls Gap) A tour-booking agency in the Halls Gap general store.

Grampians Personalised Tours & Adventures (☎ 03-5356 4654, 0429 954 686; www.grampianstours.com; tours/walks from $59/15) Offers a range of 4WD tours (with off-road options), or use your feet on the discovery walks. Tours include stop-offs at picturesque locations, and lots to eat. Two- to four-day walks are available.

Sleeping

There's a helpful **booking service** (☎ 1800 246 880) at the visitor centre.

BUDGET

Grampians YHA Eco-Hostel (☎ 03-5356 4544; www.yha .com.au; cnr Grampians Rd & Buckler St, Halls Gap; dm/s/d/f $23/52/57/77) There are several ecofriendly features, such as solar electricity and water conservation, at this five-star hostel with two- or four-bed dorms. Keep an eye on the kitchen bench. Your host puts out freshly baked bread, freshly laid eggs, freshly picked herbs, and all those eco-goodies for free.

Other budget options:

Halls Gap Motel (☎ 03-5356 4209; hgmotel@netconnect.com.au; Grampians Rd, Halls Gap; s/d/f $64/76/91) One of the half-dozen or so motels in Halls Gap.

Brambuk Backpackers (☎ 03-5356 4250; www.bram buk.com.au; Grampians Rd, Halls Gap; dm/s/d $20/40/50; ☐) Light and airy with a mellow friendly feel and mountain views.

Tim's Place (☎ 03-5356 4288; www.timsplace.net; Grampians Rd, Halls Gap; dm/s/d $23/42/55; ☐) A rambling house with a cosy lounge and the local lowdown on hiking from the owner.

Camping

Parks Victoria has 13 camp sites with toilets and fireplaces, and most with at least limited drinking water. Permits ($11) cover one car and up to six people. You can self-register or pay at Brambuk – The National Park Cultural Centre (left). Bush camping is permitted anywhere except the Wonderland Range area, around Lake Wartook, and in marked parts of the Serra, Mt William and Victoria Ranges. Check with the rangers before heading off.

Parkgate Resort (☎ 03-5356 4215; www.grampians .com; Grampians Rd, Halls Gap; sites per 2 people from $24, cabin/cottage d from $75/105; ☒ ☒) This fabulous resort has everything for the kids, including a jumping pillow and playground. For adults, there are tennis courts, a camp kitchen, games and lounge rooms and free BBQs.

MIDRANGE

Pinnacle Holiday Lodge (☎ 03-5356 4249; www.pin nacleholiday.com.au; Halls Gap; r from $89; ☒ ☒) Right in the centre, this gorgeous property sits stylishly behind the Stony Creek shops. It has everything: indoor pool, tennis

VICTORIA

courts, spacious modern units and a great range of self-contained spa suites (basic up to deluxe) with gas log fires.

D'Altons Resort (☎ 03-5356 4666; www.grampians .org.au/daltonsresort; 48 Glen St, Halls Gap; standard/deluxe cottages from $100/120) These delightful timber cottages spread up the hill between the gums and kangaroos. The cottages have cosy fires, big lounge chairs and little verandas.

Grampians Pioneer Cottages (☎ 03-5356 4402; Birdswing Rd, Halls Gap; d $125-145; 🐕) Midway between Halls Gap and Pomonal are these gorgeous rustic stone or red-gum cottages. They're set in quiet bushland, some with open fires, others with spiral staircases up to bedroom attics.

TOP END

Mountain Grand Guesthouse (☎ 03-5356 4232; www .mountaingrand.com; Grampians Rd, Halls Gap; s/d incl breakfast & dinner $133/176) This gracious timber guesthouse is peaceful and friendly, with welcoming guest lounges. The bedrooms are fresh and colourful with their own spacious bathrooms. Ask about packages.

Eating

D'Arcy's (mains $23-28; 🕑 dinner) An elegant burgundy-and-white restaurant, D'Arcy's has an interesting menu – you'll love the roo coated with bush spices – and an excellent range of wines from the Grampians and Pyrenees wineries.

Morningside (mains $8.50-15; 🕑 breakfast & dinner) From the deck of this café, behind D'Arcy's, you can watch the browsing kangaroos. Inside is local artwork, and a blackboard menu with goodies like a yum cha platter.

Kookaburra Restaurant (☎ 03-5356 4222; mains $15-27; 🕑 dinner daily, lunch Sat & Sun) You'll need to book at this place, still popular after many years, if you want to try dishes like the duckling risotto. Leave room for the desserts!

Balconies (☎ 03-5356 4232; mains $16-23) This upstairs restaurant at the Mountain Grand serves fine cuisine and has live jazz on weekends. But you may need to avoid 'Polly's wicked rum & ginger pudding'. The café downstairs is more casual.

The Halls Gap **general store** (🕑 8am-8pm) has a café, takeaway and supermarket.

Getting There & Away

V/Line (☎ 13 61 96; www.vline.com.au) has a daily coach service from Melbourne to Halls Gap

($48, four hours). Three daily buses run between Halls Gap and Stawell ($12).

The road from Stawell to Halls Gap is flat, so it's an easy cycle of about 25km. It's a longer and hillier ride between Ararat and Halls Gap (via Moyston), but still fairly easy.

HORSHAM

☎ 03 / pop 13,200

First settled in 1841, Horsham is the main commercial centre of the Wimmera. There's little of interest here but it's a good base for nearby Little Desert National Park and Mt Arapiles State Park. The **Horsham visitor information centre** (☎ 5382 1832, 1800 633 218; www .horshamvic.com.au; 20 O'Callaghan's Pde; 🕑 9am-5pm) books accommodation.

The **Horsham Art Gallery** (☎ 5382 5575; www .horsham.net.au/gallery; 80 Wilson St; admission by donation; 🕑 10am-5pm Tue-Fri, 1-4.30pm Sat & Sun) houses an impressive collection of works by significant Australian artists.

The **Wool Factory** (☎ 5382 0333; 134 Golf Course Rd; adult/child $5/1.50; 🕑 8.30am-4.30pm) is a community project providing employment and skills for people with disabilities. It produces ultrafine wool and there's a walk-through sheep shed, café and shop. Tours run at 10.15am, 11am, 1.30pm and 2.30pm.

Sleeping & Eating

Royal Hotel (☎ 5382 1255; 132 Firebrace St; s/d incl breakfast $30/50, mains $14-22; 🕑 lunch & dinner) This historic hotel is the place to be on Friday and Saturday, when everybody hangs out 'til 5am. The popular bistro serves traditional steaks and pasta dishes.

Horsham House (☎ 5382 5053; 27 Roberts Ave; s/d incl breakfast $105/120, cottage d $140; 🐕) There's a happy coupling of antiques (including a billiard table) and modern amenities in this grand balconied house (1905). A detached, self-contained cottage with spa overlooks the rose garden and is popular with honeymooning couples.

Horsham Caravan Park (☎ 5382 3476; fax 5381 2170; 190 Firebrace St; sites per 2 people from $20, d cabin $60) This is a great little spot between the botanic gardens and the river, with shady sites and good facilities.

Brills (☎ 5382 1555; 77 Pynsent St; mains $25-31; 🕑 breakfast Sat & Sun, lunch Tue-Sun, dinner Wed-Sat) Fine dining from a small exclusive menu is in a glorious room with sweeping ceilings.

There's an intimate cellar, an atrium and a casual front café as well.

Getting There & Away

There are four train/bus services daily from Melbourne, changing at Ballarat ($50, 4½ hours), and two changing at Ararat.

Buses depart from the old **police station** (24 Roberts Ave) in Horsham, heading south along the Henty Hwy to Hamilton (Monday to Friday); west along the Wimmera Hwy to Naracoorte (Monday to Friday); north along the Henty Hwy to Mildura (☎ 5381 1871) on Tuesday, Thursday and Friday; and north to Rainbow via Dimboola (☎ 5352 1501) on Thursday.

To get to the Grampians, take the **V/Line** (☎ 13 61 96; www.vline.com.au) bus to Stawell and another bus from there (see p550).

MT ARAPILES STATE PARK

Mt Arapiles, 37km west of Horsham and 12km west of Natimuk, is Australia's best venue for rock climbing, with more than 2000 climbs, from basic to advanced. The park is also popular for walks. There are two short and steep walking tracks from Centenary Park to the top of Arapiles – or you can drive up.

Climbing

Several operators, including the **Climbing Company** (☎ 03-5387 1329; www.wimmera.com.au/users /climbco) and **Arapiles Climbing Guides** (☎ 03-5387 1284; users.netconnect.com.au/~climbacg), offer climbing and abseiling instruction. Group instruction and climb costs from $50 for a half day.

Arapiles Mountain Shop (☎ 03-5387 1529; 67 Main St, Natimuk) sells and hires climbing equipment, but is open sporadically.

Sleeping & Eating

Duffholme Cabins & Museum (☎ 03-5387 4246; Natimuk-Goroke Rd; dm/d $6/44) This extraordinary cottage in natural scrub is fully self-contained. The museum shows the story of three children rescued from the bush. There is plenty of wildlife around, and great scenic views of Mt Arapiles. Ring ahead to make arrangements (it's not staffed) and get directions.

National Hotel (☎ 03-5387 1300; fax 03-5387 1297; 65 Main St, Natimuk; s $22, d cabin $66, mains $10-15; ☺ lunch Mon-Sat, dinner Wed-Sat; ☷) Choose

> **TOTAL FIRE BAN**
>
> High temperatures and strong winds combine to give Victoria days of extreme fire danger in summer. To prevent bush fires there are stringent laws applying to campfires and other activities involving flames. A campfire can easily spread and wipe out huge tracts of forest and endanger lives.
>
> On days of total fire ban, no campfires of any type are allowed; you can be arrested and jailed for lighting one.
>
> It is everybody's responsibility to know when fire restrictions have been declared. To help, Parks Victoria puts up signs in camping areas, towns display warning flags and there are frequent radio messages and fire warnings in newspapers.

between comfortable little rooms and self-contained cabins. The pub serves counter meals.

Natimuk Lake Caravan Park (☎ 03-5387 1462; fax 03-5387 1567; Lake Rd; powered/unpowered sites per 2 people from $35/12) Full facilities, including BBQs and laundry, are available at this park beside Lake Natimuk, about 4km north of Natimuk.

Pines (Centenary Park; sites $2) Sitting at the foot of Mt Arapiles this camping ground, with toilets and a washbasin, makes a good base for exploring the park.

Getting There & Away

The weekday bus service between Horsham and Naracoorte will drop you at Mt Arapiles ($7.50).

DIMBOOLA
☎ 03 / pop 1550

This quaint one-horse town was made famous by Jack Hibberd's play, *Dimboola*, and the subsequent 1979 film of the same name, directed by John Duigan. It provided the ideal setting for the story line, which follows the interaction of various characters at a country wedding reception.

The town is just off the Western Hwy and has some fine old buildings.

When the **Dimboola visitor information centre** (☎ 5389 1588; dimboola@netconnect.com.au; 109 Lloyd St; ☺ 9am-5pm Tue & Fri, 6-8pm Mon, Wed & Fri, 10am-noon Sat; ☐) is closed, visit Ron and Jill at the caravan park.

VICTORIA

The Little Desert National Park starts 4km south of town. **Pink Lake** is a colourful salt lake beside the Western Hwy about 9km northwest of Dimboola. **Ebenezer Aboriginal Mission Station** was established in Antwerp, 18km north of Dimboola, in 1859. It's signposted off the Dimboola–Jeparit road.

Sleeping & Eating

Victoria Hotel (☎ 5389 1630; Lochieal St; s/d incl breakfast from $35/50, mains $12-18; �l lunch & dinner) This well-preserved 1920s pub with fantastic lace-trimmed, vine-covered veranda and renovated rooms is family owned and run. The bistro serves basic pub food.

Riverside Host Farm (☎ 5389 1550; Riverside Rd; cabins s/d from $55/77, sites per 2 people $18; ⊠) Cabins at this lovely property are on the Wimmera River – you'll be treated to a short boat trip when you arrive. There's a lavender-oil still, camp kitchen, BBQ area, canoes for hire ($10 per hour) and camping. You can take a boat tour from here into the Little Desert ($8).

Dimboola Riverside Caravan Park (☎ 5389 1416; dimboolapark@telstra.com; 2 Wimmera St; sites per 2 people from $18, d cabin from $68) The grounds of this beautiful park beside the Wimmera River are shaded by an assortment of eucalypt and pine trees.

LITTLE DESERT NATIONAL PARK

This national park may not, initially, appear very desertlike, as there's a rich diversity of plants and wildflowers. Two sealed roads between the Western and Wimmera Hwys pass through the park, or you can take the good gravel road from Dimboola.

The best-known resident here is the mallee fowl, which can be most easily seen in the aviary at the Little Desert Lodge.

There are several short walks in the eastern block. Longer walks leave from the camping ground south of Kiata, including a 12km trek south to the Salt Lake; always carry water and notify Parks Victoria (☎ 03-5389 1204) before you set out. **Oasis Desert Adventures** (☎ 0419 824 618) offers a fun way to see the desert, and learn about it. Little Desert Lodge also offers tours.

Sleeping & Eating

Little Desert Lodge (☎ 03-5391 5232; www.littledesertlodge.com.au; s/d incl breakfast from $70/95, sites $13, bunk $15, set dinner from $22; ☑ breakfast, lunch & dinner; ⊠) This very special place, 14km south of Nhill,

is run by an extraordinary man. Whimpey Reichelt is passionately involved in conservation, particularly that of the rare mallee fowl, and is regarded as one of Victoria's 'living treasures'. There are tours of the mallee fowl aviary ($8) and Little Desert National Park (half/three-quarter day $40/65), and evening spotlight walks. The complex includes camping and bunk rooms (supply own linen). There's a dining room, BBQ area and campfire.

Parks Victoria has **camping grounds** (sites per 2 people $12) at Horseshoe Bend and Ackle Bend, both on the Wimmera River south of Dimboola, and another about 10km south of Kiata. Sites have drinking water, toilets and fireplaces.

You can bush camp if you're doing overnight walks in the central and western blocks, but speak to the rangers first at the **Parks Victoria** (☎ 03-5389 1204; Wail Nursery Rd) office, south of Dimboola.

THE MALLEE

The Mallee takes its name from the mallee scrub that once covered the region. Mallee gums are canny desert survivors – root systems over 1000 years old are not uncommon – and for the Aboriginal people the region yielded plentiful food. Driving through the area you're surrounded by horizon and undulating, twisted mallee scrub. The Mallee includes the one genuinely empty part of the state (the semi-arid wilderness known as 'Sunset Country') and the sense of isolation and expanse is exhilarating. You don't have to visit central Australia to get a taste of the outback.

BIG DESERT WILDERNESS PARK

This 113,500-hectare park is a desert wilderness with no roads, tracks, facilities or water. Walking and camping are permitted but only for the experienced and totally self-sufficient. In summer temperatures are usually way too high for walking. Notify the **ranger's office** (☎ 03-5395 7221) at **Yaapeet** before heading off.

The area is mostly sand dunes, red sandstone ridges and mallee, but there's an abundance of flora and fauna and some intriguing and unusual wildlife, such as Mitchell's hopping mouse.

A dry-weather road from Murrayville on the Mallee Hwy (B12) to Nhill separates this park from the Wyperfeld National Park. Parts of the road are very rough and may be impassable after rain.

There are basic free camping sites at Big Billy Bore, the Springs, Moonlight Tank and Broken Bucket Reserve, all on the eastern side.

MURRAY-SUNSET NATIONAL PARK

This 663,000-hectare park includes the older **Pink Lakes State Park**. The lakes draw their colour from microscopic organisms that concentrate a pink pigment in their bodies.

The park is arid and mainly inaccessible. An unsealed road leads from **Linga** on the Mallee Hwy up to the Pink Lakes at the southern edge of the park, where there's a basic camping ground. Beyond this you must have a 4WD.

Rich in human history, the **Shearer's Quarters** (☎ 03-5028 1218; groups $55) has basic hostel-type accommodation on the western side of the park, accessible only by 4WD.

For more information contact the rangers in **Underbool** (☎ 03-5094 6267; Fasham St) on the Mallee Hwy, or in **Werrimull** (☎ 03-5028 1218) on the northern side of the park.

THE MURRAY RIVER

The Murray River is Australia's most important inland waterway, and forms most of the border between Victoria and NSW. The Murray flows from the Great Dividing Range in northeastern Victoria to Encounter Bay in SA, more than 2700km away, making it the third-longest navigable river in the world.

Some of Australia's earliest explorers travelled along it, and long before roads and railways crossed the land, the Murray's paddle steamers carried supplies to and from remote sheep stations. Many of the river towns carry evocative reminders of their river boat days, including historical museums, old buildings and well-preserved paddle steamers.

Getting There & Away

Regional Express (Rex; ☎ 13 17 13; www.rex.com.au; return from $250) operates daily services between Melbourne and Mildura, as does **Qantas** (☎ 13 13 13; www.qantas.com.au; return from $240).

Murraylink is a **V/Line** (☎ 13 61 96; www.vline .com.au) bus service that runs four times a week, connects all the towns along the Murray River and has connections at Bendigo, Swan Hill and Echuca. **Greyhound Australia** (☎ 13 14 99; www.greyhound.com.au) has daily services between Mildura and Adelaide ($54) or Sydney ($109).

By car or motorcycle, the main route along the Murray is the Murray Valley Hwy (B400), which starts near Mildura and follows the river all the way to Corryong. While the highway links the towns, it rarely runs right beside the river. To experience less-tamed river country, get some good maps and follow the web of back roads on the northern bank.

V/Line also has a train service to/from Melbourne to Mildura, via Swan Hill.

HATTAH-KULKYNE NATIONAL PARK

The beautiful and diverse **Hattah-Kulkyne National Park** vegetation ranges from dry, sandy mallee-scrub country to the fertile riverside areas, lined with red gum, black box, wattles and bottlebrush. The **Hattah Lakes** system fills when the Murray floods, which is great for bird-watching.

The access road is from the small town of **Hattah**, 70km south of Mildura on the Calder Hwy. The visitor information centre, 5km into the park, will tell you if the network of tracks is passable. There are two **nature drives**, the Hattah and the Kulkyne, and a network of old camel tracks, which are great for cycling. Contact **Parks Victoria** (☎ 13 19 63, www.parkweb.vic.gov.au) or the **Hattah ranger's office** (☎ 03-5029 3253).

There are **camping** (sites per 2 people $12) facilities at Lake Hattah and Lake Mournpoul, but there is limited water. Camping is also possible anywhere along the Murray River frontage, which is actually the Murray-Kulkyne State Park.

MILDURA

☎ 03 / pop 25,000

After driving for hours through desolate, unchanging stretches of golden wheat fields and silos (which you swear you've already passed), you reach this thriving regional centre. Mildura, meaning 'red soil', is a true oasis town, watered by the Murray River.

FRUIT FLY

An exclusion zone surrounding the Murray protects the fruit and vegetable crops from fruit fly and prohibits the carrying of fresh fruit (including tomatoes) into the zone. There are warning signs and disposal bins on the roads leading into the zone.

As well as being one of the richest agricultural areas in Australia, Mildura is a tourist town promoted as a place of endless blue skies and sunshine.

Information

Madec Harvest Labour Office (☎ 5021 3359; 97-99 Lime Ave) An information centre that has a full listing of fruit-picking work. Harvest season runs from about January to March, but casual work on farms and orchards is available year-round. Some farmers allow camping but often you'll need to stay in town, so transport may be necessary.

Mildura visitor information centre (☎ 5018 8380; www.visitmildura.com.au; cnr Deakin Ave & Twelfth St; ⏱ 9am-5.30pm Mon-Fri, 9am-5pm Sat & Sun) Has an accommodation booking service.

Sights & Activities

The excellent **Mildura Arts Centre & Rio Vista complex** (☎ 5018 8322; 199 Cureton Ave; adult/child $3/free; ⏱ 10am-5pm) combines an art gallery, a theatre and a historical museum at Rio Vista, a former home of William B Chaffey. This grand homestead has been beautifully preserved. The interior is set up as a series of displays depicting life in the 19th century, with period furnishings, costumes, photos, and an interesting collection of letters and memorabilia.

Available from the information centre, *The Chaffey Trail* brochure guides you around some of Mildura's more interesting sights, including the **Mildura Wharf**, the **weir** and **lock**, **Mildara Winery** and the **Old Psyche Bend Pump Station**.

PADDLE-STEAMER CRUISES

The famous **PS Melbourne** (☎ 5023 2200; Mildura wharf; 2hr cruise adult/child $22/8; ⏱ cruises 10.50am & 1.50pm Sun-Thu), an original paddle steamer, is the only one still driven by steam power – watch the operator stoke the original boiler with wood.

THE MURRAY RIVER

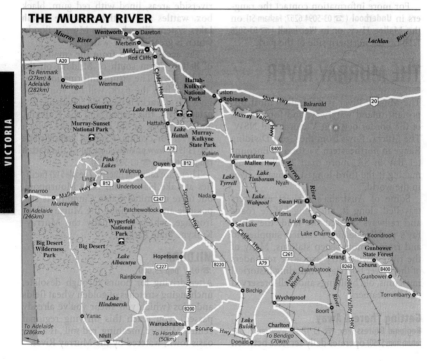

PV Rothbury (☎ 5023 2200; Mildura Wharf) offers dinner or winery cruises ($48) on Thursday, and a lunch cruise on Tuesday ($21).

Cruises depart from the Mildura Wharf, and run more often during school holiday periods.

Tours

Several Aboriginal operators run tours that concentrate on culture, history and wildlife. The best-known of these is **Harry Nanya** (☎ 5027 2076; www.harrynanyatours.com.au), whose tours include an excellent day trip to Lake Mungo National Park (adult/child $85/45) or a Wine and Dine Tour ($60). An alternative is **Jumbunna Tours** (☎ 0412 581 699), which also offers a range of tours at similar prices.

Junction Tours (☎ 0408 596 438, 5021 4424; day trips adult/child $120/92; ⏰ Mon, Wed & Fri) Day trips from Mildura to Broken Hill via Wentworth, or outback tours to Menindee from Broken Hill.

Paddleboat Coonawarra (☎ 5023 3366, 1800 645 103; www.pbcoonawarra.com.au; 5-day cruise with/without bathroom per person from $718/515) Offers three- and five-day cruises.

Sleeping

BUDGET

There are nearly 30 camping grounds and caravan parks around Mildura.

River Beach Camping Ground (☎ 5023 6879; fax 5021 5390; Cureton Ave; sites per 2 people from $8, d cabins/villas from $55/75; ⚡) It's a total outdoor experience staying in this bushland setting near Apex Beach. There are campfires, a bush kitchen, a BBQ area, a boat ramp, good swimming, walking and cycling, and a café.

Mildura International Backpackers (☎/fax 5021 0133; 5 Cedar Ave; dm $20, per week $120) All the rooms here have two beds (not bunks). Your hosts will help you find work, and they cook up a fine BBQ.

MIDRANGE

Commodore Motor Inn (☎ 5023 0241; www.commodore-mildura.com.au; cnr Deakin Ave & Seventh St; d/f from $90/130; ⚡ ⚡) Right in the centre of town, the Commodore has an indoor pool, modern décor, a cocktail garden and a quality restaurant.

Mildura Golf Club Resort (☎ 1300 366 883; www.milduragolfclub.com.au; Twelfth St; s & d from $77; ⚡ ⚡)

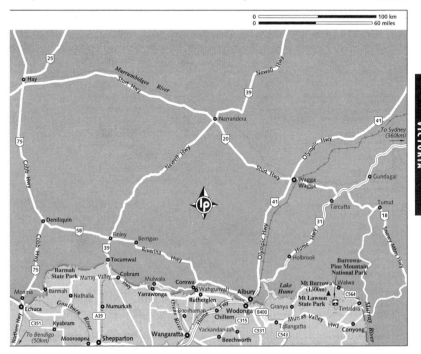

VICTORIA

This is the place for golf enthusiasts: the motel units are right on the golf course, and there's a BBQ area, great pools, abundant birdlife and a bar and bistro.

Camellia Court Holiday Apartments (☎ 5029 1555; camellia@vic.hotkey.net.au; 169 Cureton Ave; d/q/f from $96/114/135; ☒ ☒) Opposite the river, next to a playground and just along from the arts centre. The décor is totally 1970s but rooms are spacious, with kitchen, laundry, TV, dishwasher, and a pleasant pool and BBQ area.

TOP END

Olive House (☎ 0419 355 748; www.olivehouse.com.au; 170 Ninth St; d incl breakfast $145, extra person $45) This fine Federation cottage tastefully combines pressed-tin walls and ceilings, and period furnishings with a very modern bathroom that has a spa bath.

Acacia Houseboats (☎ 0428 787 250; www.acacia boats.com.au; d/q per 3 nights from $400/530) Acacia has a number of gorgeous houseboats accommodating up to eight people, with everything supplied except food and drink. Prices vary depending on the time of year.

Eating

Grand Hotel (☎ 5023 0511; cnr Deakin Ave & Seventh St) Mildura is famous for the Italian raconteur Stefano de Pieri, who has single-handedly stamped Mildura on the foodie map. All his ventures are clustered in and around (and under!) the Grand Hotel.

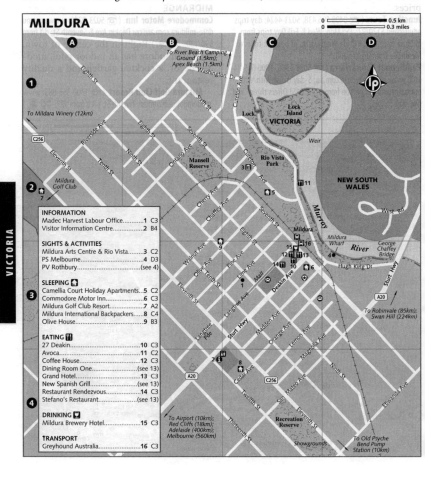

MILDURA

VICTORIA

Stefano's Restaurant (☎ 5023 0511; www.stefano.com.au; Grand Hotel, cnr Deakin Ave & Seventh St; set menu $77; ☿ dinner Mon-Sat) This is the award-winning draw card of the Grand Hotel. It's underground in a musty former wine cellar. You'll see the celebrity chef as he cooks up the set five-course northern Italian meals.

New Spanish Grill (☎ 5023 0511; Grand Hotel, cnr Deakin Ave & Seventh St; mains $15-32; ☿ dinner Tue-Sun) Simple, quality BBQ food. A carnivore's haven.

Dining Room One (☎ 5023 0511; Grand Hotel, cnr Deakin Ave & Seventh St; mains $14-35) But wait, there's more! This is the casual wine bar–café.

Avoca (☎ 5022 1444; Waterfront, Hugh King Dr; mains $19-29; ☿ breakfast Sat & Sun, lunch Tue-Sun & dinner Tue-Sat) This 1877 paddle boat is moored on the Murray. Inside it's fine dining, local wines and fish-eye river views. Its big red wheel turns every week, when it takes a cruise on the Murray. One guess who owns it.

27 Deakin (☎ 5021 3627; www.stefano.com.au; 27 Deakin Ave; mains $13-21; ☿ breakfast & lunch) A gourmet café and food store next door to a gallery. It's getting ridiculous now, so I'm just not telling you that it's owned by Stefano. This place does a fine trade in breakfasts and filled baguettes for lunch.

Restaurant Rendezvous (☎ 5023 1571; 34 Langtree Ave; mains $16.50-27; ☿ lunch & dinner Mon-Fri, dinner Sat) The warm, casual atmosphere here complements the perfectly prepared seafood, grills and unusual specials. It also features Sunraysia wines and courtyard dining.

Coffee House (☎ 5022 2900; fstrangio@optusnet.com; 26 Langtree Ave; mains $9-13; ☿ breakfast & lunch) The coffee and tea here are worth a rave, and breakfast is so good you'll come back for lunch. No wonder it's won awards.

Drinking

Mildura Brewery Hotel (16 Langtree Ave) Yes, Stefano owns this too. Set in the former Astor cinema, its beautiful renovation has made it the main nightspot in town. Shiny stainless-steel vats, pipes and brewing equipment make you thirsty for a drop. Everything kicks on from late Tuesday through to Sunday, and the substantial snacks can be bought from lunchtime.

Getting There & Away

AIR
Mildura airport is about 10km west of the town centre, off the Sturt Hwy (A20). Re-

gional Express (Rex; ☎ 13 17 13; www.rex.com.au; return from $250) operates daily services between Melbourne and Mildura, as does **Qantas** (☎ 13 13 13; www.qantas.com.au).

BUS
V/Line (☎ 13 61 96; www.vline.com.au) has a direct overnight bus ($65, 9½ hours) every night except Saturday, as well as several daily train/bus services with changes at Bendigo or Swan Hill. Its Murraylink bus service connects all the towns along the Murray River (four times weekly), including Swan Hill ($36) and Echuca ($42).

Greyhound Australia (☎ 13 14 99; www.greyhound.com.au) has daily services between Mildura and Adelaide ($54) or Sydney ($109). Long-distance buses operate from the train station on Seventh St.

SWAN HILL
☎ 03 / pop 9700
Swan Hill was named by Major Mitchell in 1836, after he was kept awake by swans in the nearby lagoon. Today Swan Hill is a major regional centre surrounded by fertile irrigated farms that produce grapes and other fruits.

The **Swan Hill visitor information centre** (☎ 5032 3033, 1800 625 373; www.swanhillonline.com; cnr McCrae & Curlewis Sts; ☿ 9am-5pm; 🖳) is just crammed with helpful maps and tourist brochures.

Sights
Swan Hill's major attraction, the **Pioneer Settlement** (☎ 5036 2410; Horseshoe Bend; adult/child $16/9; ☿ 10am-5pm Tue-Sun) is a re-creation of a riverside port town of the paddle-steamer era. Enter through the old PS *Gem*, one of the largest river boats to have served on the Murray.

The paddle steamer PS *Pyap* makes short **cruises** (adult/child $12/7; ☿ cruises 10.30am & 2.30pm) along the Murray. Every night at dusk a dramatic 45-minute **sound-and-light show** (adult/child $10/6) is held.

MV Kookaburra (☎ 5032 0003; Moulamein Rd, Murray Downs; adult/child $35/16; ☿ cruises 12.30pm Tue, Thu, Sat & Sun) has 1½-hour luncheon cruises leaving from Captain Paddy Hogg Wharf, 500m over the lift bridge on the NSW river bank.

Tyntynder Homestead (☎ 0428 500 417; Murray Valley Hwy; adult/child $8/4), 16km north of town,

VICTORIA

has a small museum of pioneering and Aboriginal relics, and reminders of the hardships of colonial life. Visits by appointment only.

Sleeping & Eating

Pioneer Settlement Lodge (☎ 5032 1093; fax 5032 1096; Horseshoe Bend; dm/d from $25/65) Watch the river flow by at this rambling lodge with glorious verandas and spacious grounds. It's basic, but there are comfortable lounge and dining areas and a BBQ pit.

Sundowner Swan Hill Resort (☎ 5032 2726; 405 Campbell St; s/d/f $114/121/217; ⊠ ⊠) The Sundowner's central courtyard is a landscaped tropical playground, featuring indoor and outdoor pools and spa. Out past the garden is minigolf, a half tennis-court and more.

Murray Downs Houseboats (☎ 5032 2160, 0428 500 066) The perfect way to experience the Murray, houseboats for eight people cost from $700 for two nights, extra nights $150. Peak rates are significantly more.

There's a great café scene down Campbell St, especially on Sunday morning.

Quo Vadis (☎ 5032 4408; 255 Campbell St; mains $15-29; ⏰ dinner) This atmospheric, fun place serves Italian favourites cooked to perfection. Next door, its takeaway or eat-outside pizza joint buzzes merrily.

Spoons (☎ 5032 2601; 387 Campbell St; meals $5-10; ⏰ breakfast & lunch) New in town, this small award-winning deli has a charming eating area and an interesting array of risottos, salads, curries and couscous.

Getting There & Away

V/Line (☎ 13 61 96; www.vline.com.au) trains run several times daily between Melbourne and Swan Hill ($52, 4½ hours) via Bendigo. There are buses 17 times weekly between Swan Hill and Mildura ($36), Echuca ($22) and Albury-Wodonga ($48).

GUNBOWER STATE FOREST

The forest, on Gunbower Island (50-odd kilometres long), stretches from Koondrook in the north to near Torrumbarry in the south. River red gum forests and swamps provide diverse habitats for the abundant bird and animal life.

Cohuna and Gunbower are the main access points, although there are tracks in from the highway; tracks on the island are impassable after rain. There are plenty of walks and many riverside camp sites.

ECHUCA

☎ 03 / pop 10,100

Echuca, which means 'the meeting of the waters', is where the Goulburn and Campaspe Rivers join the Murray River. Echuca is one of the state's most popular tourism centres: the recreational benefits of the Murray River include water skiing, paddle-steamer cruises, swimming, and houseboat holidays.

The town was founded in 1853 by ex-convict Harry Hopwood. At the peak of the river-boat era there were more than 100 paddle steamers plying the water between Echuca and outback sheep stations. The Melbourne–Echuca railway line opened in 1864 and within a decade the boom years of the river-boat trade had ended.

The **Echuca visitor information centre** (☎ 5480 7555; www.echucamoama.com; 2 Heygarth St; ⏰ 9am-5pm) has an **accommodation booking service** (☎ 1800 804 446) and sells V/Line tickets.

There are so many festivals and events in Echuca – consult calendars at www.murray-river.net/events/echuca/and www.echuca moama.com/html/whatson.htm.

Sights

HISTORIC PORT OF ECHUCA

The best feature of the **old port area** (adult/child/family $12/7.50/33, with paddle-boat cruise $24/13/60; ⏰ 9am-5pm) is that everything is original, so you're exploring living history. The attractions are spread along the waterfront. The 'passport' admits you to the three main sections: the wharf, the Star Hotel and the Bridge Hotel.

The booking office is at the entrance to the **Echuca Wharf**. In the wharf's cargo shed, dioramas depict life on the river boats and restored historic **paddle steamers** are moored alongside the wharf. Across the road at the **Star Hotel** (1867) you can escape through the underground tunnel, which helped drinkers avoid the police when the pub was a 'sly grog shop'.

At the **Bridge Hotel** (1 Hopwood Pl) your ticket admits you to a historic upstairs gallery. This pub is now a restaurant and bistro.

PORT AREA SIGHTS

At **Red Gum Works** (Murray Esplanade; admission free; ⏰ 9am-4pm) you can watch wood turners and blacksmiths at work with traditional equipment, and purchase red-gum products.

Sharp's Magic Movie House & Penny Arcade (☎ 5482 2361; Murray Esplanade; adult/child $14/8; ✇ 9am-5pm) has authentic penny-arcade machines. Don't miss the free fudge tasting! The movie house shows old movies using original equipment. Your ticket is valid all day.

There are free tastings of local wines at **Murray Esplanade Cellars** (☎ 5482 6058; Old Customs House, Murray Esplanade; ✇ 10am-5.30pm) and **Stevens Brook Estate** (☎ 5480 1916; 620 High St).

OTHER SIGHTS

Echuca Historical Museum (☎ 5480 1325; 1 Dickson St; adult/child $2/1; ✇ 11am-4pm) is in the old police station and lock-up buildings, which are classified by the National Trust. It has a collection of local history items, charts and photos from the river-boat era.

The **Great Aussie Beer Shed** (☎ 5480 6904; 377 Mary Ann Rd; ✇ 9am-5pm Sat & Sun) has wall-to-wall beer cans – mostly Australian – in a huge shed; one dates back to Federation.

Activities

As you enter the pedestrian-only Murray Esplanade, you can buy tickets for a cruise, or to explore the historic buildings along the Esplanade. A paddle-steamer cruise along the Murray is almost obligatory, and at least four steamers offer cruises; head down to the river and check out the sailing times. **PS Emmylou** (☎ 5480 2237; 1hr cruise adult/child $15/7.50) is a fully restored paddle

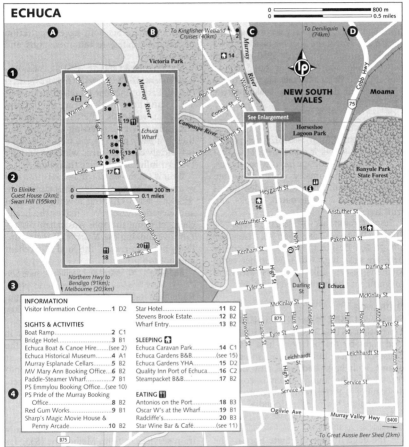

ECHUCA

steamer driven by an original engine. Overnight cruises are also available.

One-hour cruises are offered by **PS Alexander Arbuthnot** (☎ 5482 4248; adult/child $16/6), **PS Canberra** (☎ 5482 2711; adult/child $13/6), **PS Pevensey** (☎ 5482 4248; adult/child $16/6) and **PS Pride of the Murray** (☎ 5482 5244; adult/child $13/6).

PS Adelaide is the oldest wooden-hulled paddle steamer still operating anywhere in the world, and occasionally takes passengers on a cruise. **MV Mary Ann** (☎ 5480 2200) is a cruising restaurant offering lunch and dinner cruises.

Echuca Boat & Canoe Hire (☎ 5480 6208; Victoria Park boat ramp) has motor boats, kayaks and canoes for hire.

Sleeping

Hiring a houseboat is a great way to experience river life. The fully equipped boats sleep from four to 12. Rates vary according to the season and size of the boat – a boat with two double bedrooms may cost $950 per week between May and November, but $3000 in January. The **visitor information centre** (☎ 5480 7555) has full details and a **booking service** (☎ 1800 804 446).

BUDGET

Echuca Gardens YHA (☎ 5480 6522; echucagardens@ iinet.net.au; 103 Mitchell St; dm/d $20/40) This 135-year-old workers cottage has tiny bedrooms, clean old bathrooms, a country kitchen and a TV room. The exotic garden boasts ponds, statues, a veggie patch, chooks, and fruit trees.

Echuca Caravan Park (☎ 5482 2157; fax 5480 1551; 51 Crofton St; sites per 2 people from $23, d cabins from $70; ⊠ ⊒) Beside the river, the facilities here are amazing, with new timber camp kitchens, resort pool, large grassy areas and magnificent shady river red gums.

MIDRANGE

Steampacket B&B (☎ 5482 3411; fax 5482 3408; cnr Murray Esplanade & Leslie St; s/d/f from $75/85/160) Situated right by the old port, in a National Trust–classified building, the rooms are quaint, with brass bedsteads and views of the wharf. The lounge room is cosy and downstairs in the tearoom meals are served on fine china. It's even kid-friendly.

Echuca Gardens B&B (☎ 5480 6522; echucagardens@iinet.net.au; 103 Mitchell St; s/d from $90/130; ⊒) On the edge of Banyule State Forest. The

doubles with bathrooms and private balconies are artworks in progress. Breakfast is amid potted plants with fountains tinkling below. Bike hire is $15 per day.

Quality Inn Port of Echuca (☎ 5482 5666; fax 5482 5682; 465 High St; r from $130; ⊠ ⊒) The car park may look unappealing, but this huge luxury motel has swish rooms, a large heated pool and gym, and BBQ areas.

TOP END

Elinike Guest Cottages (☎ 5480 6311; www.elinike .com.au; 209 Latham Rd; d incl breakfast from $170) These are quaint little mud-brick cottages set in rambling gardens on the Murray River. Inside, the rooms are all white and lacy, and each has a small sitting room in which to enjoy your gourmet breakfast.

Eating

High and Hare Sts both have a collection of bakeries, cafés, restaurants, pubs and takeaways.

Star Wine Bar & Café (☎ 5480 1181; 45 Murray Esplanade; mains $17-22; ⏱ breakfast & lunch daily, dinner Fri & Sat) Part of the Star Hotel, this café sells snacks and light meals during the day and dinner at weekends. The bar has a moody atmosphere with interesting art work, and there's a leafy patio at the back. The food is typically cross-cultural, with just enough Eastern influence to spice things up.

Oscar W's at the Wharf (☎ 5482 5133; www.oscar ws.com.au; 101 Murray Esplanade; dinner mains $24-29; ⏱ lunch & dinner) Offering a whiff of charm and elegance, Oscar W's makes the heady claim of being the sole Australian restaurant overlooking the Murray. It seems unlikely but who cares – the food is excellent and not too pricey.

Radcliffe's (☎ 5480 6720; 2 Radcliffe St; mains $24-29; ⏱ dinner Wed-Sun) An atmospheric place, Radcliffe's has an extensive modern menu. The Tuscan courtyard is perfect for a sultry dinner in summer.

Antonios on the Port (☎ 5482 6117; 527 High St; mains $19-29; ⏱ dinner) Light bounces off the wine glasses and starched tablecloths at this sparkling Italian place. It backs onto the lovely Campaspe. Gourmet pizzas are a speciality.

Getting There & Away

V/Line (☎ 13 61 96; www.vline.com.au) has daily train services to/from Melbourne ($33, 3½ hours). V/Line's Murraylink buses run daily from the train station, connecting Echuca with Wodonga ($39), Swan Hill ($22) and Mildura ($42). A daily service is available to destinations in southern NSW.

BARMAH STATE PARK

Barmah is a significant wetland area created by the flood plains of the Murray River. It's the largest remaining red gum forest in Australia (and thus the world), and the swampy understorey is usually flooded in winter, creating a breeding area for many fish and bird species.

Dharnya Centre (☎ 03-5869 3302; admission by donation; ☼ 10.30am-4pm) is the visitor information centre and small museum with displays on Aboriginal heritage and the park, run by members of the Yorta Yorta people in partnership with Parks Victoria. Evidence of more than 40,000 years of occupation has been found nearby; however, the Yorta Yorta people's Native Title claim for the area was controversially rejected in 1998.

The park is popular for **bird-watching**, **fishing** and **walking**, although in the wet season a canoe is the best way to get around. **Gondwana Canoe Hire** (☎ 03-5869 3347), 4km past Barmah, hires canoes (per day $60).

The cruise boat **Kingfisher** (☎ 03-5869 3399; www.kingfishercruises.com.au; adult/child/family $20/14/64; ☼ cruises 11am Mon, Wed, Thu, Sat & Sun) runs two-hour cruises.

You can camp for free anywhere in the park or at the Barmah Lakes' camping area, which has tables, BBQ areas and pit toilets. There are also caravan parks and a hotel-motel in Barmah.

YARRAWONGA

☎ 03 / pop 4600

Yarrawonga has more sunshine hours than almost anywhere else in Australia. The **Yarrawonga visitor information centre** (☎ 5744 1989, 1800 062 260; Irvine Pde; ☼ 9am-5pm) is on the shores of Lake Mulwala, just beside the bridge. You can book accommodation and tours here.

The **Lady Murray** (☎ 0412 573 460) and **Paradise Queen** (☎ 0418 508 616) operate daily cruises along the lake and the Murray River.

Yarrawonga Outdoors (☎ 5744 3522; www.yarrawongaoutdoors.com.au; 7 Witt St) hires kayaks, bikes and kites. **Mulwala Waterski School** (☎ 5744 2777; www.mulwalawaterski.com.au; Melbourne St,

Mulwala) offers water-skiing instruction and parasailing, and equipment for sale and hire.

RUTHERGLEN

☎ 02 / pop 1900

Dating from gold-rush days, Rutherglen is a quaint town, and is also the centre of one of Victoria's major wine-growing districts.

The **Rutherglen visitor information centre** (☎ 6033 6300, 1800 622 871; info@rutherglenwineexperience.com.au; 57 Main St; ☼ 9am-5pm) offers an accommodation referral service and hires bikes.

Sights & Activities

Wineries are the main attraction around Rutherglen and there's a host of wineries in the area. The best are **Morris** (☎ 6026 7303; Mia Mia Rd; ☼ 9am-5pm Mon-Sat, 10am-5pm Sun), **RL Buller & Son** (☎ 6032 9660; www.buller.com.au; Three Chain Rd; ☼ 9am-5pm Mon-Sat, 10am-5pm Sun), **Stanton & Killeen Wines** (☎ 6032 9457; www.stantonandkilleenwines.com.au; Jacks Rd; ☼ 9am-5pm Mon-Sat, 10am-5pm Sun) and **Campbells** (☎ 6032 9458; www.campbellswines.com.au; Murray Valley Hwy; ☼ 9am-5pm Mon-Sat, 10am-5pm Sun). All produce superb fortified wines, while the Shiraz and Durif of Campbells, Buller, **Rutherglen Estates** (☎ 6032 8516; www.rutherglenestates.com.au; Tuileries Complex, Drummond St; ☼ 10am-6pm) and Morris can also be good. **Warrabilla Wines** (☎ 6035 7242; www.warrabillawines.com.au; Murray Valley Hwy; ☼ 10am-5pm) makes potent Shiraz and Durif wines – some of the biggest, baddest and strongest reds.

Festivals & Events

Tastes of Rutherglen (☎ 6033 6336; www.rutherglenvic.com) A major food and wine weekend held in March.

Winery Walkabout Weekend (www.rutherglenvic.com) A chance to sample all the major labels in the area; held in June.

Sleeping

Rutherglen Caravan & Tourist Park (☎ 6032 8577; www.grapevinegetaways.com.au; 72 Murray St; sites per 2 people from $13, d cabins from $40) On the banks of Lake King, there are budget or luxury cabins, spaced-out sites (true) and sparkling amenities blocks. A golf course, bowling club, playground and swimming pool are nearby.

Victoria Hotel (☎ 6032 8610; www.victoriahotelrutherglen.com.au; 90 Main St; s/d from $35/40, meals

VICTORIA

$9-16; ⊙ lunch & dinner Wed-Sun) Front rooms at this beautiful old National Trust–classified place have en suites and views over Main St. The downstairs restaurant has an interesting menu, or bar meals (from $7).

Motel Woongarra (☎ 6032 9588; www.motelwoongarra.com.au; cnr Main & Drummond Sts; s/d from $58/66) Nearest to the centre of town, Woongarra's rooms are spacious and the grounds and pool gorgeous.

Brimin Floating Lodge (☎ 6035 7245; www.briminlodge.com.au; Brimin Rd; lodges $80; ⛵) Walk along the levee, across a ramp and you're in your own little old houseboat on a billabong. Lounge on the rooftop while your lunch sizzles on the electric BBQ.

Tuileries (☎ 6032 9033; www.tuileriesrutherglen.com.au; 13 Drummond St; d incl breakfast from $165; ⛵ ⛵) Enjoy bright, uncluttered luxury in gloriously coloured modern rooms, the guest lounge and even a tennis court.

Eating

There's a great café scene all along Main St, and takeaway places or spots to fill a picnic hamper.

Café Shamrock (☎ 6032 8439; 121 Main St; dishes $18-27; ⊙ dinner daily, lunch Thu-Sat) In the historic Durham house, the Shamrock is an upbeat restaurant and piano/wine bar with live music (mostly jazz and blues) nearly every night of the week.

Rendezvous Courtyard (☎ 6032 9114; 68 Main St; mains $17-24; ⊙ dinner Thu-Tue) The menu here is Italian influenced with a vast pasta section – ideal for those with undecided taste buds. Lighter bites are available, including good-looking and imaginative salads.

Tuileries Restaurant (☎ 6032 9033; 13 Drummond St; mains $25-29; café meals $12-16; ⊙ dinner daily, café breakfast & lunch Wed-Sun) A fine-dining restaurant in an imposing building with plenty of glass and a fountain, serving Mod Oz food with lots of vegetarian options. The café on the other side of the fountain has equally exciting meals.

All the major wineries have restaurants and cafés in superb settings overlooking their vineyards, lakes and rivers. They are mostly open for lunch and snacks. The food is always outstanding, and menu choices cover all budgets:

House at Mount Prior (☎ 6026 5256; www.houseatmountprior.com; Howlong Rd; ⊙ lunch & dinner) At the Mount Prior winery.

Terrace (☎ 6033 1922; www.eldtrain.com.au/allsaints.htm; All Saints Rd, Wahgunyah; ⊙ lunch & dinner Sat) At All Saints Estate.

Lazy Grape (☎ 6033 1004; www.stleonardswine.com.au; ⊙ lunch) At St Leonards.

Pickled Sisters (☎ 6033 2377; ⊙ lunch Wed-Mon, dinner Fri & Sat) At Cofield.

Gehrig's Courtyard (☎ 6026 7296; ⊙ lunch Thu-Sun) At Gehrig Estate.

Getting There & Away

The **V/Line** (☎ 13 61 96; www.vline.com.au) bus to Wangaratta ($5.50) connects with the train to Melbourne on Wednesday, Friday and Saturday.

The Murraylink bus connecting Wodonga with Mildura stops at Rutherglen. The bus stop is at the western end of Main St.

CHILTERN
☎ 03 / pop 1100

Tiny Chiltern is one of Victoria's most historic and charming colonial townships. In fact, it's so quaint and authentic that the town is often used as a film set for period pieces.

Beryl at the **Chiltern visitor information centre** (☎ 5726 1611; 30 Main St; ⊙ 10am-4pm) is knowledgeable about the region and passionate about bird-watching in the nearby Chiltern Mt Pilot National Park.

Atheneum Library & Museum (☎ 5726 1467; Conness St; admission $2.50; ⊙ 10am-4pm Sat & Sun) is housed in the former town hall (1866).

Star Hotel/Theatre (☎ 5726 1395; cnr Main & Conness Sts; adult/child $4.50/1.50; ⊙ by appointment) was once the centrepiece of Chiltern's social and cultural life. The grapevine in the courtyard is in the *Guinness World Records* as the largest in the southern hemisphere.

WODONGA
☎ 02 / pop 31,000

Separated from its twin town, Albury, by the Murray River, Wodonga looks out on the lovely Sumsion Gardens and a lake formed off Wodonga Creek.

The **Gateway visitor information centre** (☎ 6051 3750, 1300 796 222; www.destinationalburywodonga.com.au; ⊙ 9am-5pm) has info about Victoria and NSW, and a 24-hour touch screen.

There are signed trails for the **Gateway Island Bicycle and Walking Tracks** (www.tourisminternet.com.au/wdbike1.htm) and **Wiradjuri Walkabout, Aboriginal River Walk**, which include details of Aboriginal cooking sites, camp sites, tree carvings and a birdlife sanctuary.

You'll see the main cluster of motels as you drive into town and along the main street. There are also several caravan parks. **Sanctuary Park Motel** (☎ 6024 1122; www .sanctuaryparkmotel.com.au; 11 High St; s/d/f $60/72/88; ✖ 🔲 ⚡) boasts a spa and delightful views of pelicans wandering by the lake.

Getting There & Away

There are daily **V/Line** (☎ 13 61 96; www.vline.com .au) trains to/from Melbourne ($47). V/Line buses connect Wodonga with Yarrawonga ($10) and Mildura ($64).

WODONGA TO CORRYONG

The Murray Valley Hwy continues east of Wodonga through **Tallangatta**, a small township with an interesting history. In the 1950s the rising waters of the Mitta Mitta River, a tributary of Lake Hume, flooded following construction of the Hume Weir at Tallangatta. Most of the actual township had already been relocated to what is known as New Tallangatta. There's a lookout point 7km east of the town, from which you can see the streetscape of Old Tallangatta, especially if the waters are low.

There's a turn-off 15km west of Tallangatta to the town of **Granya**. The road to the north rejoins the Murray River and follows it all the way around to Towong and **Corryong**, via **Tintaldra**, which is worth a detour if you have a day or two to spare. Rupert Bunny (1864–1947), an Australian artist with an international reputation, spent time here in the 1920s, painting *The Murray at Tintaldra* during that period. The **Tintaldra Hotel** (☎ 02-6077 9261; Main St; d $30-65) is only 100m from the bank of the Murray. It has a fine beer garden, tasty meals, basic rooms and a motel room. Camping is also an option. The main road also leads to Corryong, but by a slightly quicker and more direct route.

GOLDFIELDS

The Goldfields region is one of the state's most interesting areas, with ever-present reminders of the rich heritage of the gold-rush days. It's a blend of quaint townships, impressive regional centres and rolling countryside. Dramatic landscapes contrast from the green forests of the Wombat Ranges to red earth, bush scrub and granite country up around Inglewood.

The Goldfields Tourist Route takes in all the major gold-rush centres. This is also a great area for bike touring and horse riding, or you could even hire a gypsy caravan. **Colonial Way** (☎ 03-5438 8249; 35 Taylors Rd, Rheola; caravans per week $740-950) rents caravans pulled by Clydesdale horses.

The old diggers dug up most of the gold, but there's still gold in 'them thar hills' and metal detectors and prospecting gear can be bought or hired in many towns.

Central Victoria is also a major wine-producing area. The main regions are the Pyrenees Ranges near Avoca, the Heathcote region and around Bendigo.

BALLARAT
☎ 03 / pop 73,000

The area around Ballarat was known to the local Koories as 'Ballaarat', meaning 'resting place'. European pastoralists arrived in 1837 and the discovery of gold at nearby Buninyong in 1851 saw thousands of diggers flock to the area. After alluvial goldfields were played out, deep shaft mines were sunk, striking incredibly rich quartz reefs that were worked up until the end of WWI.

Ballarat's former prosperity is reflected in the wealth of impressive Victorian buildings throughout, which have received a little extra TLC in recent years as Melburnians have shown a willingness to move out of the city and commute.

Ballarat's 100-year-old **Begonia Festival**, in early March, attracts thousands of visitors.

Information

Ballarat visitor information centre (☎ 1800 446 633, 5320 5741; www.visitballarat.com.au; 39 Sturt St; ✖ 9am-5pm) Has an accommodation booking service.

Municipal library (cnr Sturt & Camp Sts; 🔲) Check your emails here.

Parks Victoria (☎ 5333 6782; cnr Doveton & Mair Sts)

Sights & Activities

One of Australia's finest streetscapes of Victorian architecture is Ballarat's **Lydiard St**. Impressive buildings include Her Majesty's Theatre, the art gallery and Craig's Royal Hotel.

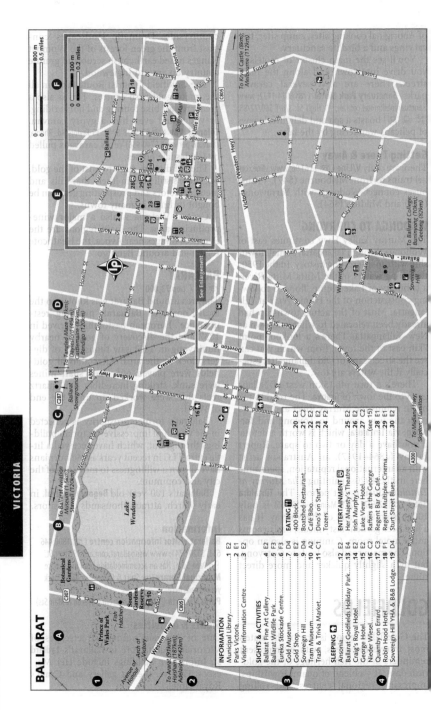

BALLARAT

Hopeful prospectors can pick up miners' rights and rent metal detectors at the **Gold Shop** (☎ 5333 4242; 8A Lydiard St N), in the old Mining Exchange building.

At the Ballarat Showgrounds there's a fine **Trash & Trivia market** (Creswick Rd; 🕑 8am-2.30pm Sun).

Timeless Tours (☎ 5342 0652) offers half-day guided tours ($30) around Ballarat's heritage sites and trips further afield.

SOVEREIGN HILL

A re-created gold-mining town of the 1860s, **Sovereign Hill** (☎ 5331 1944; www.sovereign hill.com.au; Magpie St; adult/child/family $29/14/75; 🕑 10am-5pm) is an entertaining living history museum, with actors dressed in period costumes. You can pan for gold and may find a speck or two. There are also two underground tours of re-created mines plus a gold pour, which transforms $50,000 of liquid gold into a 3kg bullion bar.

The nightly sound-and-light show **Blood on the Southern Cross** (☎ 5333 5777; adult/child/family $35/19/97) is an impressive simulation of the Eureka Stockade battle. Show times depend on when the sun sets: 9.15pm and 10.30pm in summer; 6.45pm and 8pm in winter. Bookings are essential.

GOLD MUSEUM

Sitting on a mullock heap from an old mine, the excellent **Gold Museum** (☎ 5331 1944; Magpie St; adult/child $7.50/3.50, or Sovereign Hill ticket; 🕑 9.30am-5.20pm) has imaginative displays, including gold nuggets, coins and a display on the Eureka Rebellion.

BALLARAT FINE ART GALLERY

The **Ballarat Fine Art Gallery** (☎ 5320 5858; 40 Lydiard St N; adult/child $5/free; 🕑 10.30am-5pm) is the oldest and one of the best provincial galleries in the country and houses a wonderful collection of Australian art (which includes some early colonial paintings as well as contemporary works). The gallery also has remnants of the original Eureka flag.

LAKE WENDOUREE

Formerly the Black Swamp, this large artificial lake was used for the 1956 Olympics rowing events. Wendouree Pde, which circles the lake, is where many of the city's particularly jaw-dropping and pricey houses can

be found. The old timber boat sheds along the lake's shores are equally charming.

BOTANICAL GARDENS

Ballarat's beautiful and serene botanical gardens are beside Lake Wendouree. The cottage of the poet Adam Lindsay Gordon is here. Come face to face with John Howard in the Prime Ministers' Avenue, a collection of bronze portraits.

A tourist **tramway** runs on weekend afternoons and school holidays, departing from the **tram museum** (☎ 5334 1580; South Gardens Reserve, Lake Wendouree).

EUREKA STOCKADE CENTRE

Standing on the site of the Eureka Rebellion, the **Eureka Stockade Centre** (☎ 5333 1854; Eureka St; adult/child/family $8/4/22; 🕑 9am-5pm) has multimedia galleries simulating the battle.

BALLARAT WILDLIFE PARK

This most attractive **zoo** (☎ 5333 5933; www .wildlifepark.com.au; cnr York & Fussell Sts; adult/child/family $15.50/9/42; 🕑 9am-5.30pm, tours 11am) has native animals, reptiles and a few exotics.

Sleeping

BUDGET

Sovereign Hill YHA & B&B Lodge (☎ 5333 3409; www.sovereignhill.com.au; Magpie St; dm/s/d $19/28/44; B&B lodge s/d/f from $105/126/180; 🖳) Gorgeous, heritage lodge rooms and a cosy guest lounge, with fireplace and bar, are a stroll from Sovereign Hill. The separate YHA cottage is quietly fantastic. Book well in advance.

Robin Hood Hotel (☎ 5331 3348; www.robinhood hotel.com.au; 33 Peel St N; dm/s/d $20/30/40) Right in the centre, this downmarket old local pub has spacious, high-ceilinged rooms upstairs, with good beds and crooked, clean bathrooms. Beware the karaoke on Friday and Saturday.

Ballarat Goldfields Holiday Park (☎ 1800 632 237, 5332 7888; www.ballaratgoldfields.com.au; 108 Clayton St; sites per 2 people from $22, d cabin from $60; 🖳) Close to Sovereign Hill, there's a good holiday atmosphere here and it has won several tourism awards. The cabins are like miners' cottages, and some have three bedrooms.

MIDRANGE

Craig's Royal Hotel (☎ 5331 1377; www.craigsroyal.com; 10 Lydiard St S; d $95-115, d without bathroom from $56, ste $150-300) The best of the grand old pubs was so named after it hosted visits by the Prince of Wales and the Duke of Edinburgh. This Victorian building is a wonderful place to stay. The feel is old-fashioned opulence – despite the creaky floorboards. Choose from singles with washbasin and faded floral bedspreads to fabulously grand suites with sweeping city views. It also has a restaurant.

George Hotel (☎ 5333 4866; www.ballarat.com/george; 27 Lydiard St N; s/d $70/90, without bathroom $50/65; ❲❳) In historic Lydiard St, this gorgeous pub was rebuilt in 1902 with towering ceilings and sweeping walnut staircases. The rooms are a bit more modern and include breakfast on the balcony.

Quamby on Errard (☎ 5332 2782; www.heritagehomestay.com/quamby_on_errard.htm; 114 Errard St; s/d incl breakfast from $87/135) If you're after an intimate experience, try this very sweet cottage, with its delicate antiques and gourmet breakfast.

Ansonia (☎ 5332 4678; www.ballarat.com/ansonia.htm; 32 Lydiard St S; d from $142) An upmarket retreat, this place exudes calm with its minimalist design, polished cement floors and light-filled atrium. The café serves all-day breakfasts. Rooms range from studio apartments to family suites.

Nieder Weisel (☎ 5331 8829; www.ballarat.com/niederweisel; 109 Webster St; d incl breakfast from $140, extra person $25) You'll think you're a star walking through this palatial Victorian mansion. Magnificent rooms have enormous beds and decadent bathrooms, breakfast commands silver service and warm hospitality tops it all off. Packages are available.

Eating

The main café scene is the '400 Block', on Sturt St, where tables spill out along with the coffee aroma. The cafés along here are open all day.

L'Espresso (☎ 5333 1789; 417 Sturt St) This Ballarat mainstay is a stylish, friendly and atmospheric Italian-style café in a former record store – you can choose a new CD while you wait for your espresso.

THE EUREKA REBELLION

Life on the goldfields was a great leveller, erasing social distinction as doctors, merchants, ex-convicts and labourers toiled side by side in the mud. But as the easily won gold began to run out, the diggers recognised the inequalities between themselves and the privileged few who held land and the government.

The limited size of claims and the inconvenience of licence hunts (see the boxed text, opposite), coupled with police brutality, taxation without political representation and the realisation that they could not get good farming land, fired unrest that led to the Eureka Rebellion.

In September 1854, Governor Hotham ordered that the hated licence hunts be carried out twice a week. In the following October a miner was murdered near a Ballarat hotel after an argument with the owner, James Bentley.

When Bentley was found not guilty, by a magistrate who just happened to be his business associate, a group of miners rioted over the injustice and burned his hotel. Bentley was re-tried and found guilty, but the rioting miners were also jailed, which fuelled their distrust of authority.

Creating the Ballarat Reform League, the diggers called for the abolition of licence fees, a miner's right to vote and increased opportunities to purchase land.

On 29 November about 800 miners, led by Irishman Peter Lalor, burnt their licences at a mass meeting and built a stockade at Eureka, where they prepared to fight for their rights.

On 3 December the government ordered troopers to attack the stockade. There were only 150 diggers within the makeshift barricades at the time and the fight lasted only 20 minutes, leaving 30 miners and five troopers dead.

Although the rebellion was short-lived, the miners were ultimately successful in their protest. They had won the sympathy of most Victorians and the government deemed it wise to acquit the leaders of the charge of high treason.

The licence fee was abolished. A miner's right, costing one pound a year, gave the right to search for gold and to fence in, cultivate and build a dwelling on a moderate-sized piece of land – and to vote. The rebel miner Peter Lalor actually became a member of parliament some years later.

Gee Cees Café Bar (☎ 5331 6211; 427 Sturt St) Another notable on the 400 Block is this large and popular café-bar.

Europa Café (☎ 5331 2486; 411 Sturt St) This places serves Turkish-, Mediterranean- and Spanish-inspired food on the 400 Block.

Café Bibo (☎ 5331 1255; 205 Sturt St; mains $10.50-20; ⊙ breakfast & lunch) This retro café is lined with copies of 1960s *Women's Weekly* magazines and shelves of decorated coffee cups belonging to the regulars. The breakfast is so good you'll be back for lunch.

Dino's on Sturt (☎ 5332 9711; www.ballarat.com /dinos; 212 Sturt St; mains $12-26; ⊙ breakfast, lunch & dinner) A welcoming, child-friendly and sophisticated restaurant with a menu that you'll

---

GOLD FEVER

In May 1851 EH Hargraves discovered gold near Bathurst in NSW, and sensational accounts of the find caused thousands of people to drop everything to try their luck.

News of the discovery reached Melbourne at the same time as the accounts of its influence on the people of NSW. Sydney had been virtually denuded of workers and the same misfortune soon threatened Melbourne.

A reward was offered to anyone who could find gold within 300km of Melbourne. Within a week, gold was discovered in the Yarra River but the find was soon eclipsed by a more significant discovery at Clunes. Prospectors headed to central Victoria, reversing the rush north across the Murray as fresh gold finds became an almost weekly occurrence in Victoria.

Gold was found in the Pyrenees, Warrandyte, Buninyong, and the Loddon and Avoca Rivers. Ballarat, in September 1851, produced the biggest discovery, followed by other significant finds at Bendigo, Mt Alexander, Beechworth, Walhalla, Omeo, and in the hills and creeks of the Great Dividing Range.

By the end of 1851 about 250,000 ounces of gold had been claimed. Farms and businesses lost their workforces and were often abandoned, as employers had no choice but to follow their workers to the goldfields. Hopeful miners came from England, Ireland, Europe, China and the failing goldfields of California; during 1852 about 1800 people arrived in Melbourne each week.

The government imposed a licence fee of 30 shillings a month for all prospectors. This entitled the miners to an 8-sq-foot claim in which to dig for gold and it provided the means to enforce improvised law. Any miner without a licence could be fined or imprisoned. Although this later caused serious unrest, it was successful in averting the lawlessness that had characterised the California rush.

The classic features accompanying gold fever were the backbreaking work, the unwholesome food, the hard drinking and the primitive dwellings. Amazing wealth was the luck of some but the elusive dream of others; for every story of success, there were hundreds more of hardship, despair and death.

The gold rush had its share of rogues, including the notorious bushrangers, but it also had its heroes: the martyrs of the Eureka Stockade, a miners' rebellion that eventually forced political change in the colony (see opposite).

Above all, the gold rush ushered in a fantastic era of growth and material prosperity for Victoria, opening up vast areas of country previously unexplored by colonists.

In the first 12 years of the rush, Victoria's population rose from 77,000 to 540,000. To cope with the moving population and the tonnes of gold and supplies, the development of roads and railways was accelerated.

The mining companies that followed the independent diggers invested heavily in the region over the next couple of decades. The huge shantytowns of tents, bark huts, raucous bars and police camps were eventually replaced by timber and stone buildings, which became the foundation of many of Victoria's provincial cities.

The gold towns reached the height of splendour in the 1880s. Gold gradually lost its importance but, by then, the gold towns had stable populations plus agriculture and other activities to maintain economic prosperity.

Gold also made Melbourne Australia's largest city and financial centre, a position it held for nearly half a century.

VICTORIA

love. Try traditional tomato and bread soup, or lamb shanks with kumara chips.

Boatshed Restaurant (☎ 5333 5533; www.boatshed-restaurant.com; Lake Wendouree; mains $18-27; ⓨ breakfast, lunch & dinner) Sit on the deck over the lake or stay inside with the open fire and armchairs. There's excellent coffee and an exciting menu, which, fortunately for the dozens waddling around the grounds, doesn't include duck.

Tozers (☎ 5338 8908; 101 Bridge Mall; mains $23-30; ⓨ lunch Sat, dinner Tue-Sat) Why go anywhere else? This has to be the best fine-dining venue. Try the eggs stuffed with coriander and garlic, or eye fillet with caramelised shallots.

Entertainment

With its large student population, Ballarat has a lively nightlife. You can bop 'til 5am, but you can't enter a venue after 3am.

Irish Murphy's (☎ 5331 4091; 36 Sturt St; ⓨ to 3am Wed-Sun) There's live music most nights at this atmospheric Guinness pub.

Rafters at the George (☎ 5333 4866; 27 Lydiard St N; ⓨ to late Fri & Sat) A good venue to kick back in.

Sturt Street Blues (☎ 5332 3676; cnr Sturt & Doveton Sts) A popular venue, open nightly, for blues fans of all ages.

Lake View Hotel (☎ 5331 4592; www.thelakeview .com.au; 22 Wendouree Pde; mains $13-24; ⓨ breakfast, lunch & dinner) A truly gorgeous old pub with a modernised, buzzy atmosphere, great views over the lake and good pub food.

Regent Bar & Café (☎ 5331 5507; 71 Lydiard St N; ⓨ Wed-Sun) If you're young and trendy, you'll love this upbeat place with mainstream music.

Her Majesty's Theatre (☎ 5333 5800; 17 Lydiard St S) Ballarat's main venue for the performing arts is a wonderful building.

Regent Multiplex Cinema (☎ 5331 1399; 49 Lydiard St N) This is Ballarat's main cinema complex.

Getting There & Around

Ten trains a day run from **Ballarat train station** (Lydiard St N) to Melbourne ($17, 1½ hours). Buses continue on through to Ararat ($16) and Stawell ($18).

V/Line (☎ 13 61 96; www.vline.com.au) has daily bus services from Ballarat to Geelong ($12) and Mildura ($48) via St Arnaud ($20), and weekday services to Hamilton ($30),

Maryborough ($10) and Bendigo ($22) via Daylesford ($11) and Castlemaine ($16).

Greyhound Australia (☎ 13 14 99; www.greyhound.com.au) buses stop at the train station on the Melbourne–Adelaide run.

The local bus line covers most of the town; timetables are available at the visitor information centre. The free Visitor Shuttle Bus leaves the information centre on three different routes.

The **Airport Shuttlebus** (☎ 5333 4181; www.airportshuttlebus.com.au) goes direct to Melbourne airport from Ballarat train station ($23, seven daily).

For a cab, call **Ballarat Taxis** (☎ 13 10 08).

CLUNES
☎ 03 / pop 1100

Clunes, a charming little town 32km north of Ballarat, was the site of Victoria's first significant gold discovery in June 1851. There are many fine buildings, such as the **William Barkell Arts & Historic Centre** (36 Fraser St), which is in a double-storey bluestone. The small hills around Clunes are extinct volcanoes. Nearby **Mt Beckworth** is noted for its orchids and birdlife, and you can also visit the old gold diggings of **Jerusalem** and **Ullina**.

DAYLESFORD & HEPBURN SPRINGS
☎ 03 / pop 3500

Set among the scenic hills, lakes and forests of the central highlands, delightful Daylesford and Hepburn Springs are the 'spa centre of Victoria'. The health-giving properties of the area's mineral springs were known back in the 1870s, attracting droves of fashionable Melburnians.

As well as tourists, this area attracts hedonists, spirituality seekers and escapees from the city rat race. The population is an interesting blend of alternative-lifestylers and old-timers, and there's a thriving gay and lesbian scene. Winter is peak season.

Daylesford is set around pretty Lake Daylesford. Its two main streets, Raglan and Vincent, are major café strips. Vincent St turns into Hepburn Rd at the roundabout and takes you straight through Hepburn Springs and down to the original spa resort.

The staff at the **Daylesford visitor information centre** (☎ 5321 6123; www.visitdaylesford.com; 98 Vincent St, Daylesford; ⓨ 9am-5pm) are very knowledgeable and helpful.

Sights & Activities

Swanky **Hepburn Spa Resort** (☎ 5348 2034; www
.hepburnspa.com.au; Mineral Springs Reserve, Hepburn
Springs) has all manner of pampering, primp-
ing and preening treatments to relieve sore
and aching muscles. Check out the boxed
text, p574, for more details.

The waters in the underground cavities
of the area have been absorbing minerals
and carbon dioxide for a million years.
Around the spa are several **mineral springs**,
most pretty strong in flavour, where you
can fill your own bottles. There are some
good **walking trails**; pick up maps and guides
from the visitors centre.

The **Convent Gallery** (☎ 5348 3211; Daly St,
Daylesford; admission $4.50; ☯ 10am-6pm) is a mag-
nificent 19th-century convent that's been
brilliantly converted into an art gallery-
cum-café.

Boats and kayaks can be hired at **Lake
Daylesford** and there's the even-prettier **Jubilee Lake** about 3km southeast of town.

The **Historical Society Museum** (☎ 5348 3242;
100 Vincent St, Daylesford; adult/child $3/50c; ☯ 1.30-
4.30pm Sat & Sun) is next to the visitor centre.

Don Wreford presented the Royal Vase to
Danish Crown Prince and Princess Frederik
and Mary; you can see his work at **Wreford
International Hot Art Glass Studio** (☎ 5348 1012;
39 Albert St, Daylesford; www.hotartglass.com; ☯ 11am-
5pm).

Daylesford Spa Country Tourist Railway (☎ 5348
1759; Daylesford train station; adult/child/family $7/4/19;
☯ 10am-2.45pm Sun) operates one-hour rides
on old railway trolleys and restored trains.
The **Daylesford Sunday Market** (☯ 8am-2pm Sun) is
held at the train station.

Between the antiques and collectables
shops are two good bookshops: **Avant Garden Bookshop & Gallery** (☎ 5348 1288; 46 Vincent
St, Daylesford) and **Lake Daylesford Book Barn**
(☎ 5348 3048; 1 Leggatt St, Daylesford).

Sleeping

Bookings for the region's charming guesthouses, cottages and B&Bs (many charging
30% more on weekends and stipulating a
minimum two-night stay) are made through
agencies:

Daylesford Accommodation Booking Service
(DABS; ☎ 5348 1448; www.dabs.com.au; 94 Vincent St)

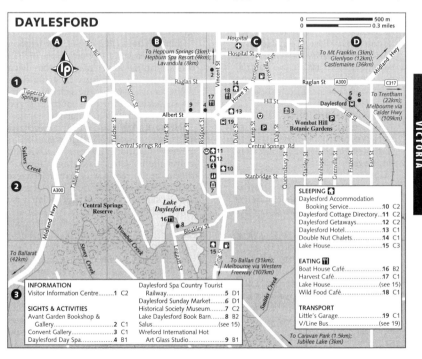

DAYLESFORD

0   500 m
0   0.3 miles

SLEEPING
Daylesford Accommodation
Booking Service...................10 C2
Daylesford Cottage Directory...11 C2
Daylesford Getaways.............12 C2
Daylesford Hotel...................13 C1
Double Nut Chalets...............14 C1
Lake House..........................15 C3

EATING
Boat Harbour Café...............16 B2
Harvest Café.......................17 C1
Lake House.....................(see 15)
Wild Food Café....................18 C1

TRANSPORT
Little's Garage.....................19 C1
V/Line Bus.....................(see 19)

INFORMATION	
Visitor Information Centre........1 C2	

SIGHTS & ACTIVITIES	
Avant Garden Bookshop &	
Gallery................................2 C1	
Convent Gallery......................3 C1	
Daylesford Day Spa.................4 B1	

Daylesford Spa Country Tourist	
Railway.................................5 D1	
Daylesford Sunday Market........6 D1	
Historical Society Museum........7 C2	
Lake Daylesford Book Barn........8 B2	
Salus..............................(see 15)	
Wreford International Hot	
Art Glass Studio...................9 B1	

VICTORIA

Daylesford Cottage Directory (☎ 5348 1255; www
.thespacountryholidayshop.com.au; 86 Vincent St)
Daylesford Getaways (☎ 5348 4422; www.dayget
.com.au; 123 Vincent St)

DAYLESFORD

Daylesford Hotel (☎ 5348 2335; fax 5348 1083; cnr Albert
& Howe Sts; r incl breakfast from $55) The old pub has
small rooms upstairs that are prettily painted.
Bathrooms are crisp and tiny, and there's a
cosy guest TV room and fantastic balcony.

Double Nut Chalets (☎ 5348 3981; www.double
nut.com; 5 Howe St; d incl breakfast from $120) The four
chalets are spacious and tasteful suites that
have gable ceilings, in a lovely garden right
in town. Each has its own kitchenette.

Lake House (☎ 5348 3329; www.lakehouse.com.au;
King St; d incl breakfast from $320; 💈) Set in ram-
bling gardens with bridges, waterfalls and
cockatoos, these welcoming units around
the lake make you feel like just staying put.
There's a guest lounge, tennis court and the
ultimate pampering of Salus healing spring
waters; see the boxed text, below.

PAMPERING SOAKS

Salus (☎ 03-5348 3329; www.lakehouse.com
.au; Lake House, King St, Daylesford) The pampering starts as you walk through a small rainforest
to your exotic jasmine flower bath in a cedar-lined
tree house overlooking the lake. Then you might
choose a lime-and-ginger salt polish before a steam
and waterfall, a rejuvenating facial and a full-body
drizzle of warm Japanese camellia oil.

Daylesford Day Spa (☎ 03-5348 2331; www
.daylesforddayspa.com.au; 25 Albert St, Daylesford)
Start with a vitamin-rich mud body mask and steam
in a body-care cocoon, before a scalp massage and
Vichy shower.

Spa House (☎ 03-5348 2202; www.thesprings
.com.au; 124 Main Rd, Hepburn Springs) Have an
algae gel wrap, based on an ancient Chinese treatment, then move into the lavender steam room, or
take a soft pack float.

Hepburn Spa Resort (☎ 03-5348 2034; www
.hepburnspa.com.au; Hepburn Mineral Springs
Reserve) Where it all began in 1896 is being
revamped during 2005. It has plunge pools, flota-
tion tanks, saunas, and a swimming pool, a salt
pool and an aero spa – every way of taking to the
waters. Finally add, say, a milk and honey wrap.
Mmm. Contact the resort about what is open during
the extensions.

Jubilee Lake Caravan Park (☎ 5348 2186; Lake
Rd; sites per 2 people from $13, d cabin from $65) Sitting
beneath tall gums beside beautiful Jubilee
Lake, this quaint park makes you feel quiet
and mellow.

HEPBURN SPRINGS

Continental House (☎ 5348 2005; www.continental
house.com.au; 9 Lone Pine Ave; dm/s/d $30/40/70, ban-
quets $15; 🍽 dinner Sat) This rambling, timber
guesthouse has a laid-back alternative vibe,
a vegan café serving excellent buffets, a
superb open-veranda sitting room and a
music room. BYO linen.

Daylesford Wildwood Youth Hostel (☎ 5348 4435;
www.mooltan.com.au/ww/wildwood.htm; 42 Main Rd; dm/s/
d from $19/32/44; 💈) In a charming cottage with
a grand lounge room, you'd never know it
was a youth hostel. The dorm rooms are average, but other rooms have grand bathtubs
and views of the lovely garden.

Mooltan Guesthouse (☎ 5348 3555; www.mooltan
.com.au; 129 Main Rd; s/d incl breakfast from $55/85) An
inviting Edwardian country home, Mooltan
has grand lounge rooms, a billiard table and
tennis court. Bedrooms open onto a broad
veranda overlooking the Mineral Springs
Reserve. There are special weekend packages and spa rooms.

Springs Retreat (☎ 5348 2202; www.thesprings
.com.au; 124 Main Rd; s/d incl breakfast from $170/185)
This charming 1930s mansion has been
brought into this century in great style.
Many rooms have private balconies, garden rooms have their own courtyards, and
pampering packages are available.

Shizuka Ryokan (☎ 5348 2030; www.shizuka
.com.au; Lakeside Dr; midweek package s/d $204/275) In-
spired by traditional places of renewal and
rejuvenation in Japan, this serene, minimalist getaway has rooms with private Japanese
gardens, tatami matting and plenty of green
tea. Packages include a superb Japanese
dinner and breakfast.

Eating

DAYLESFORD

Vincent St has a great range of food joints,
but go around the side streets for more
treats.

Wild Food Café (☎ 5348 1030; 11 Howe St; mains
$5.50-9; 🍽 breakfast & lunch Tue-Sun) This tiny
place has gone all organic and specialises
in Australian food, such as quiche with wild
lime and quandong salsa.

Harvest Café (☎ 5348 3994; 29 Albert St; dinner mains $15-22; breakfast, lunch & dinner Thu-Mon) This retro café will take you back to your student days. It has fantastic music, timber floors, blackboards, amazing prices and food to die for. Vegetarians will be in heaven.

Boat House Café (☎ 5348 1387; mains $15-19) This popular café is in an old boat shed. The setting is gorgeous, especially out on the deck where you can watch the swans while you nibble on a plate of nachos. You'll need to book on weekends.

Lake House (☎ 5348 3329; www.lakehouse.com.au; King St; mains $31-33; breakfast, lunch & dinner) Daylesford's famous Lake House restaurant is among the best in Victoria. Dine in the

beautiful dining room where picture windows overlook Lake Daylesford or lunch on the deck. Reservations are essential.

HEPBURN SPRINGS
Palais (☎ 5348 4849; www.thepalais.com.au; 111 Main Rd; mains $15-25; dinner Thu-Sun) A dazzlingly atmospheric 1920s theatre with a restaurant, café and cocktail bar. Enjoy the osso bucco or moussaka then relax in lush lounge chairs, play pool or even have a boogie. On locals' nights, meals are $10.

Springs Retreat Café (☎ 5348 2202; 124 Main Rd; mains $14-24) This spacious and bustling café fits the relaxed elegance of the Springs Retreat, with an eclectic menu that takes in lamb tagine.

Deco Restaurant (☎ 5348 2202; 124 Main Rd; mains $24-30) Across the hall from Springs Retreat Café, this elegant restaurant serves fabulous items such as spiced fillet of wild barramundi on *brandade* with sauce *vierge*.

Savoia Hotel (☎ 5348 2314; 69 Main Rd; mains $14-25; lunch & dinner) If you like your steak big and your chicken roasted, this is the place. The surrounding are as traditional as the food, with an open fire, pool table and dart board.

Getting There & Around
Daily buses connect Daylesford with the train station at Woodend ($5), from where you can continue to Melbourne by train ($15, two hours).

V/Line (☎ 13 61 96; www.vline.com.au) has weekday buses from Daylesford to Ballarat ($11), Castlemaine ($6) and Bendigo ($11). The buses run from **Little's Garage** (45 Vincent St).

A shuttle bus runs to/from Daylesford visitor information centre and Hepburn Springs spa complex four times a day (weekdays only). Local **taxis** (☎ 5348 1111) include a six-seater in the fleet.

CASTLEMAINE
☎ 03 / pop 6840
Castlemaine is a relaxed country town that's home to a diverse group of artists, and splendid architecture and gardens. The discovery of gold at Specimen Gully in 1851 radically altered the pastoral landscape of the region around Castlemaine, as 30,000 diggers worked goldfields known collectively as the Mt Alexander Diggings. The town grew up around the government

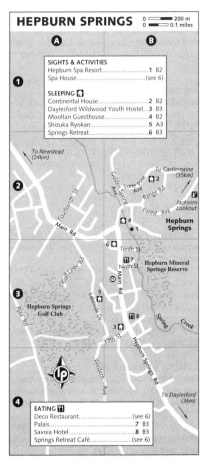

HEPBURN SPRINGS   0 — 200 m   0 — 0.1 miles

To Newstead (24km)

To Castlemaine (35km)

Jacksons Lookout

Hepburn Springs

Hepburn Mineral Springs Reserve

Hepburn Springs Golf Club

To Daylesford (3km)

VICTORIA

camp and soon became the marketplace for all the goldfields of central Victoria.

Castlemaine hosts the **State Festival** (www.castlemainefestival.com.au) in March/April in odd-numbered years, one of Victoria's leading arts events.

The **Castlemaine visitor information centre** (☎ 1800 171 888, 5470 6200; www.maldoncastlemaine.com; Mostyn St; ⏰ 9am-5pm) is in the stunning Castlemaine market building. You can buy gold-panning kits here for $6.50.

Sights

Dating from 1861, **Buda** (☎ 5472 1032; cnr Hunter & Urquhart Sts; adult/child $9/7; ⏰ noon-5pm Wed-Sun) was home to a Hungarian silversmith and his descendants for 120 years. The family's art and craft collections and personal belongings are on display.

The impressive **Castlemaine Art Gallery & Historical Museum** (☎ 5472 2292; 14 Lyttleton St; adult/student/family $4/2/8; ⏰ 10am-5pm Mon-Fri, noon-5pm Sat & Sun), in a superb Art Deco building, has a collection of colonial and contemporary Australian art; downstairs is a local history museum.

The imposing **Old Castlemaine Gaol** (☎ 5472 5311; cnr Bowden & Charles Sts; adult/child $7/3.50; ⏰ 10am-3pm) has a lingering eerie atmosphere even though the place has been renovated and looks almost attractive. Guided **tours** (adult/child $4/2) of the gaol can also be arranged.

An institution in itself, the **Restorers Barn** (Mostyn St; ⏰ 10am-5.30pm) is chock-full of interesting bric-a-brac and collectables.

Also near Chewton is the remarkable **Dingo Farm** (www.wwwins.net.au/dingofarm). Sadly, owner Bruce Jacobs died in 2004. Please visit the website for further information on the farm's operation.

Sleeping

The region has a free **accommodation booking service** (☎ 1800 171 888, 5470 5866; www.mountalexander.vic.gov.au).

Castle Motel (☎ 5472 2433; www.visitvictoria.com/castlemotel; Duke St; s/d/f 79/89/109; 🛋) Enjoy spacious rooms in soft colours and timber features, sparkling bathrooms, a delightful little pool and spa, grass and trees, and friendly people.

Midland Private Hotel (☎ 5472 1085; www.hotelmidland.net; 2 Templeton St; s/d incl breakfast from $80/120, apt d from $180) This lace-decked hotel,

which has been sheltering travellers since 1879, features a magnificent Art Deco entrance foyer and dining room, and a lounge with open fireplaces. Breakfast comes with homemade produce. The apartments are equally attractive.

Botanic Gardens Caravan Park (☎ 5472 1125; 18 Walker St; sites per 2 people from $13, d cabin from $50) Ideally situated next to the gardens and public swimming pool, this park has leafy sites, a camp kitchen, BBQs and a recreation hut.

Other wonderful sleeping experiences can be had in a cell at the **Old Castlemaine Gaol** (☎ 5470 5311; www.gaol.castlemaine.net.au; cnr Bowden & Charles Sts; per person incl breakfast $55); in bed with the stars at **Theatre Royal Back Stage** (☎ 5472 1196; www.castlemainetheatre.com; Hargraves St; d incl breakfast $195), where the rate includes as many movies as are screening; or nestled among the antiques at **Clevedon Manor** (☎ 5472 5212; clevedon@netcon.net.au; 260 Barker St; s/d from $70/100).

Eating

Saff's Café (☎ 5470 6722; 64 Mostyn St; mains $17-23; ⏰ breakfast, lunch & dinner) Fun and friendly Saff's Café serves excellent homemade bread, cakes and savouries, the best coffee in town and interesting meals such as the roti bake topped with a tomato-and-hummus crust.

Tog's Café (☎ 5470 5090; 58 Lyttleton St; mains $16-25; ⏰ breakfast & lunch daily, dinner Fri & Sat) Fashionable Tog's is a cosy spot with open fireplaces and a menu boasting Kashmiri lamb curry, great soups and salads, and unmissable hot chocolates that are works of art.

Globe Garden Restaurant (☎ 5470 5055; 81 Forest St; mains $23-32, café mains $15-18; ⏰ dinner daily, lunch Sun) Set in a historic building with a superb garden courtyard, this is a fine choice for summer dining on international cuisine. The side-room café serves great steaks. Bookings are advisable on weekends.

Getting There & Away

Daily **V/Line** (☎ 13 61 96; www.vline.com.au) trains run between Melbourne and Castlemaine ($19) and continue on to Bendigo ($7) and Swan Hill ($34).

Daily coaches run to Daylesford ($6), Maldon ($6), Ballarat ($15, except Wednesday) and Geelong ($29).

VICTORIA

MALDON

☎ 03 / pop 1230

Charming Maldon is a well-preserved relic of the gold-mining era. Its population is a tiny fraction of the 20,000 who once worked here.

The **Maldon visitor information centre** (☎ 5475 2569; www.maldoncastlemaine.com; High St; ⏰ 9am-5pm; 💻) stocks a useful *Information Guide* and *Historic Town Walk* brochure.

The **historical museum** (☎ 5474 1633; High St; ⏰ 1.30-4pm Mon-Fri, 1.30-5pm Sat & Sun), behind the visitor centre, has an interesting collection of local artefacts.

On the edge of town is the excellent **Penny School Gallery & Café** (☎ 5475 1911; www.pennyschoolgallery.com.au; 11 Church St; ⏰ 10am-5pm), exhibiting well-known artists' work.

You can take a candle-lit tour of **Carmen's Tunnel Goldmine** (☎ 5475 2667; adult/child $5/2; ⏰ 1.30-4pm Sat & Sun), which is off Parkin's Reef Rd 2.7km south of town, and was excavated in the 1880s. Railway buffs will enjoy the **Victorian Goldfields Railway** (☎ office 5470 6658, station ☎ 5475 2966; Hornsby St; adult/child/family return $16/8/40; ⏰ train rides 11.30am & 1pm Wed & Sun, also 2.30pm Sun), which has old-time **steam trains** running towards Castlemaine. Historic **Porcupine Township** (☎ 5475 1000; www.porcupinetownship.com.au; Bendigo Rd; adult/child/family $9/5.50/25; ⏰ 10am-5pm) is a quaint re-creation of a gold-mining village.

Foot-tapping folk-music fans will love the annual **Maldon Folk Festival** held in early November.

Sleeping

Heritage Cottages of Maldon (☎ 5475 1094) manages many of the area's self-contained cottages and charming B&Bs in restored old buildings.

Central Service Centre (☎ 5475 2216; Main St; s/d $40/65; 💻) This excellent option is in the unlikely setting of a former garage (the pumps are still out the front). The MG room is the funkiest choice. There's a convenient laundrette right next door.

Maldon's Eaglehawk (☎ 5475 2750; fax 5475 2914; 35 Reef St; s/d from $90/100; 💻 💻) Even motels in this town have loads of appeal. Beautiful heritage units are set in delightful grounds with little alcoves overlooking the pool, BBQ nooks and vine-trimmed verandas.

Calder House (☎ 5475 2912; www.calderhouse.com.au; 44 High St; s/d from $90/110) Step back in time at this formal and grand, yet very inviting place, right in the centre of town. It has superb features and guest rooms with four-poster beds and claw-foot baths.

Maldon Caravan Park (☎ /fax 5475 2344; Hospital St; sites per 2 people from $17, d cabin from $60; 💻) This old park straggles up through the bush. It's friendly and homely, with a bush kitchen, BBQs and a swimming pool next door.

Eating

Several cafés and tearooms along the main street serve good coffee and snacks.

Berryman's Café & Tearooms (☎ 5475 2904; 30 Main St; meals $4-9.50; ⏰ breakfast & lunch) Enjoy a light meal, snack or full-on lunch in an old tearoom environment or outside in the sun. You must try the yummy yabby pie (yabbies are farmed in the area).

Café Maldon (☎ 5475 2022; 52 Main St; mains $9; ⏰ breakfast & lunch) This trendy little place is where the locals read their papers and watch the visitors' antics. Tables are set between unusual giftware that is for sale, and couches, and with luck you'll catch some live music. The gourmet pastries are highly regarded.

Ruby's at Calder House (☎ 5475 2912; 44 High St; mains $20-27; ⏰ dinner) This is one of the state's best restaurants. Set in an elegant Victorian dining room, it serves 'creative country cuisine' using only fine local produce. Book ahead.

Getting There & Away

Castlemaine Bus Lines (☎ 5472 1455) runs two buses each weekday between Maldon and Castlemaine ($6), connecting with trains to/from Melbourne.

Castlemaine taxis (☎ 13 10 08) services the Maldon area.

MARYBOROUGH

☎ 03 / pop 7500

In 1854 gold was discovered at White Hills and Four Mile Flat. A police camp at the diggings was named Maryborough and, at the height of the gold rush, the population was over 40,000. These days it's a fairly dull place, but has some fine buildings and a few sights.

The **Maryborough visitor information centre** (☎ 1800 356 511, 5460 4511; www.centralgoldfields.com.au; cnr Alma & Nolan Sts; ⏰ 9am-5pm; 💻) has loads of helpful maps and friendly staff.

Built in 1892, magnificent **Maryborough Railway Station** (Burns St; 🕙 Wed-Mon) was described by Mark Twain as 'a train station with a town attached'. It now houses a mammoth antiques emporium, gallery and café. **Worsley Cottage** (☎ 5461 2800; 3 Palmerston St; 🕙 10am-noon Tue & Thu, 2-5pm Sun) is the historical society museum.

Have a fling at Maryborough's **Highland Gathering**, which has been held on New Year's Day since 1857.

Sleeping & Eating

There's a good foodie scene along High St.

Bull & Mouth Hotel (☎ 5461 1002; cnr High & Nolan Sts; s/d $30/40, mains $9.50-18; 🕙 lunch & dinner) Dance up the glorious staircase to these basic little rooms. The restaurant serves the best steaks in town and other quirky dishes. The weekend DJ plays dance, country and R&B.

Bella's Country House B&B (☎ 5460 5574; www .cgold.com.au/bellas/; 39 Burns St; s/d budget from $55/70, deluxe from $110) This handsome red-brick Victorian homestead has a magnificently restored interior, complete with comfy lounges and open fires. The deluxe rooms are elegant, with lashings of white linen.

Maryborough Caravan Park (☎ /fax 5460 4848; 7 Holyrood St; sites/dm/cabins from $15/20/44; 🐾) Right in town, by Lake Victoria, this family park is walking distance to the swimming pool.

Old Vault (☎ 5460 5164; 106 High St; mains $10-19; 🕙 breakfast, lunch & dinner) Enjoy the excellent coffee in this Art Deco bank building, or try an Old Vault beef burger, then kick on 'til late.

AVOCA & PYRENEES RANGES

Avoca is the centre of one of Victoria's most rapidly expanding wine-growing regions. **Mt Avoca** (760m) is the highest peak in the nearby Pyrenees Ranges. There are walking tracks on the mountain, including the 18km-long **Pyrenees Trail**, which starts from the Waterfall Picnic Area 7km west of Avoca.

The helpful **visitor information centre** (☎ 54 65 3767; www.pyreneesonline.com.au; 122 High St, Avoca; 🕙 9am-5pm) has an excellent brochure, *The Great Grape Road*. See also the boxed text, p528.

BENDIGO

☎ 03 / pop 68,700

When gold was discovered at Ravenswood in 1851, thousands of diggers converged on the fantastically rich Bendigo Diggings. The arrival of Chinese miners in 1854 had a lasting effect on Bendigo, which still has a rich Chinese heritage.

During the boom years between the 1860s and 1880s, mining companies poured money into the town, which resulted in the fine Victorian architecture that still graces Bendigo's streets today. By the 1860s, diggers were no longer tripping over surface nuggets and deep mining began. Local legend has it that you can walk underground from one side of the town to the other. These days the town is a prosperous provincial centre with one of the best regional art galleries in Australia.

Information

Bendigo visitor information centre (☎ 1800 813 153, 5444 4445; www.bendigotourism.com; 51 Pall Mall; 🕙 9am-5pm) In the historic former post office.

Parks Victoria (☎ 5444 6620; cnr Taylor St & Midland Hwy, Epsom)

Sights

The **Chinese Joss House** (☎ 5442 1685; Finn St; adult/child $3/1; 🕙 10am-5pm Thu-Mon), in North Bendigo at the end of the tramline, is one of the few practising joss houses (Chinese temples) in Victoria.

The **Goldfields Historical Chinese Cemetery** (White Hills Cemetery, Holdsworth Rd) is the oldest and most significant of its kind in Australia, with a prayer oven where paper money for the spirits of the dead was burnt.

The 500m-deep **Central Deborah Goldmine** (☎ 5443 8322; 76 Violet St; adult/child/family $17/10/46; 🕙 9.30am-5pm), worked on 17 levels, became operational in the 1940s and was connected with two Deborah shafts that date back to the 1860s. About one tonne of gold was removed before it closed in 1954.

The mine is currently being reworked and developed as one of Bendigo's major tourist attractions, with exhibits and photographs from the mid-1800s onwards. After donning hard hats and lights, you are taken 61m down the shaft to inspect the ongoing operations, complete with drilling demonstrations.

There's a combined ticket (adult/child $26/14) for the mine tour plus a ride on the Talking Tram.

Bendigo's tram system was closed down in 1972, but a number of Bendigo residents

BENDIGO

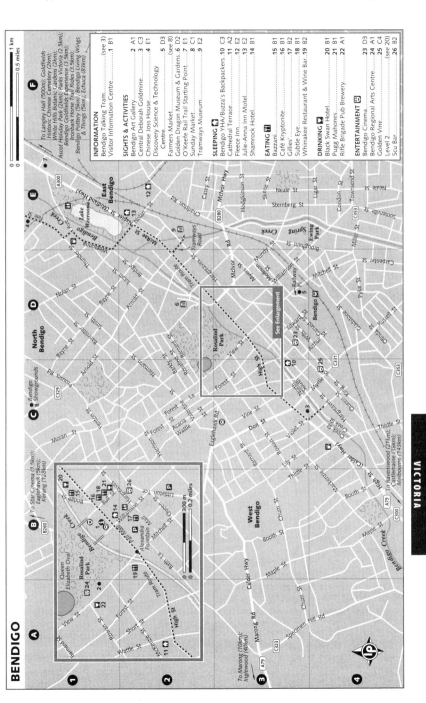

VICTORIA

took direct action and rescued the trams, which now run as a tourist feature.

The **Bendigo Talking Tram** (☎ 5443 8322; 76 Violet St; adult/child/family $13/7.50/37; ☯ 9.30am-3.30pm) runs with a commentary from the Central Deborah Goldmine, through the centre of the city, out to the **Tramways Museum** (admission free with tram ticket) and on to the Chinese Joss House. It leaves the mine every hour, or five minutes later from Alexandra Fountain in Charing Cross.

One of Victoria's largest regional galleries, the **Bendigo Art Gallery** (☎ 5443 4991; www.bendigoartgallery.com.au; 42 View St; admission by donation; ☯ 10am-5pm) has an outstanding collection of 19th-century European, colonial and contemporary Australian art and regular touring exhibitions from overseas. There are guided tours of the permanent collection at 2pm daily, and there is a swish café.

The magnificent **Shamrock Hotel** (cnr Pall Mall & Williamson St), built in 1897, is a fine example of elaborate Italianate late-Victorian architecture. The story goes that floors were regularly washed down to collect gold dust brought in on miners' boots.

There are two magnificent processional dragons, Old Loong (the oldest in the world) and Sun Loong (the longest in the world), at the excellent **Golden Dragon Museum** (☎ 5441 5044; Bridge St; adult/child/family $7/4/20; ☯ 9.30am-5pm). Old Loong arrived in 1892 for the annual Bendigo Easter Festival, and Sun Loong took over in 1970 when Old Loong retired.

The museum traces the involvement of the Chinese community in the development of Bendigo. There are also Chinese **gardens** nearby and a tearoom serving light meals.

The oldest pottery works in Australia (1858), **Bendigo Pottery** (☎ 5448 4404; Midland Hwy, Epsom; ☯ 9am-5pm) is 6km north of Bendigo. There's a café, sales gallery and historic kilns, and you can watch potters at work.

Also on site is **Bendigo Living Wings & Things** (☎ 5448 3051; adult/child/family $7/4.50/18), which has lizards, pythons, butterflies, walk-through parrot enclosures, wallabies and dingoes.

The huge **Discovery Science & Technology Centre** (☎ 5444 4400; Railway Pl; adult/child/family $9.50/7/30; ☯ 10am-5pm) has a wide range of interesting and educational exhibits.

Activities

Ironbark Horse Trail Rides (☎ 5448 3344; Watson St; per 1/2hr $30/55) organises various horse rides including the Great Australian Pub Ride to Allies Hotel in Myers Flat (with lunch $75). In the Ironbark complex, **Bendigo Goldfields Experience** (☎ 5448 4140; wwwbendigogold.com.au; Watson St) has fossicking and detecting **tours** (per half day $130) into the bush, or **gold panning** (per hr $10) at the mobile gold-panning centre.

You can hike or bike the **O'Keefe Rail Trail** (19km one way) from the corner of Midland Hwy and Baden St through bushland to Axedale.

Bendigo Showgrounds is the venue for the **Sunday Market** (☯ 8.30am-3pm) and, on the second Saturday each month, the **Farmers Market** (☯ 8am-1pm).

Festivals & Events

Bendigo Agricultural Show (www.bendigoshow.org.au) Held in October.
Bendigo Cup (www.racingvictoria.net.au/vcrc/bendigo) Part of the Spring Racing Carnival held in November.
Easter Festival Attracts thousands of visitors with its carnival atmosphere and procession of Chinese dragons.
Gold and Opal Athletics Carnival (www.vic.cycling.org.au) Attracts large crowds in March.
Swap Meet (www.bendigoswap.com.au). Perhaps Bendigo's most curious attraction: enthusiasts in search of that elusive old motorcycle or vintage-car spare part descend on the town in November.

Sleeping

There's an **accommodation booking service** (☎ 1800 813 153, 5444 4445) at the information centre.

BUDGET

Bendigo YHA/Buzza's Backpackers (☎/fax 5443 7680; 33 Creek St S; dm/s/d/f $19/32/48/60; ☐) This small, homely hostel is in a weatherboard cottage that's been opened up inside to make bright cheery rooms with all the usual amenities.

Fleece Inn (☎ 5443 3086; 139 Charleston Rd; dm/s/d incl breakfast $30/45/65; ☒) What a find. This 140-year-old ex-pub has dorm rooms with partitioned-off beds, spacious bathrooms, a carpeted balcony and back courtyard with BBQs. Smart rooms are up the grand original timber staircase.

Ascot Holiday Park (☎ 5448 4421, 1800 062 340; www.ascotholidaypark.com.au; 15 Heinz St; sites per 2 people from $20, d cabin from $65; ☒ ☒) With cabins nestled between the gardens, this excellent park has a glow about it, plus a heated spa, a camp kitchen and BBQs, mini golf, a TV lounge, everything, just north of town!

MIDRANGE

Shamrock Hotel (☎ 5443 0333; www.shamrockbendigo .com.au; cnr Pall Mall & Williamson St; r from $70, ste from $145) The Shamrock is a stunning Victorian building with stained glass, original paintings, fancy columns and a *Gone with the Wind*–style staircase. The cheaper rooms are on the small side.

Cathedral Terrace (☎ 5441 3242; 81 Wattle St; s/d incl breakfast from $105/150; ❄) For an intimate experience in olde-worlde classic Victoriana you must stay here, among the antiques and lush furnishings. A full breakfast is served in the lounge, with a view of Sacred Heart Cathedral.

Julie-Anna Inn Motel (☎ 5442 5855; fax 5441 6032; 268 Napier St; s/d/f from $117/128/177; ❄ ⬛) This upmarket motel is just across from lovely Lake Weeroona. The spacious units open onto an attractive central courtyard, with a grand dining room at the end.

TOP END

Langley Hall (☎ 5443 3693; www.langleyhall.com .au; 484 Napier St; s/d incl breakfast from $120/155; ❄) Built in 1904, Langley Hall offers unfussy opulence. Sweep up the grand staircase to magnificent suites, opening onto expansive verandas. Downstairs, enjoy the elegant and comfortable parlour, drawing room and billiard room.

Eating

Bendigo has an excellent range of cafés, pubs and restaurants. Bull St (off Pall Mall) has a great café scene.

Gillies' (Hargreaves St Mall) The pies here are among the best in Australia. At this Bendigo institution, you queue at the little window, order one of their five or so varieties, and then sit in the mall to eat it.

Subtle Eye (☎ 0402 328 339; 68 Bull St; mains $6.80-9; ❄ breakfast & lunch) A funky modern place with a tiny menu and top coffee. At night the tables go outside and it turns into a cocktail bar that's open until 1am Tuesday to Saturday.

Café Kryptonite (☎ 5443 9777; Pall Mall; mains $15-28; ❄ lunch & dinner) No wonder it's popular, with a good buzz – the food's great.

Tuscan pork sausages with apple will warm the tum.

Bazzani (☎ 5441 3777; www.bazzani-bendigo.com; 2 Howard Pl; mains $25-29; ❄ lunch & dinner) This stylish, friendly venue has a diverse and innovative menu, a separate bar, a smoking room and local wines sold from the cellar.

Whirrakee Restaurant & Wine Bar (☎ 5441 5557; 17 View Point; mains $13-28; ❄ dinner Tue-Sat) The owner/head chef serves excellent Mod Oz cuisine (such as kangaroo sirloin with creamed parsnip!). Downstairs there's a small wine bar with cosy sofas.

Drinking

Pugg Mahones (☎ 5443 4916; 224 Hargreaves St) Pugg's has Guinness (and many other beers) on tap, a great atmosphere, a beer garden and live music Thursday to Saturday.

Rifle Brigade Pub Brewery (☎ 5443 4092; 137 View St; mains $16-20) A popular old pub brewing Ironbark Dark, Old-fashioned Bitter and Rifle Lager. Enjoy top pub food in the shady courtyard.

Black Swan Hotel (☎ 5444 0944; 6 Howard Pl) A trendy place for a drink in a very old pub.

Entertainment

Level 2 (☎ 5444 0944; Upstairs, Black Swan Hotel, 6 Howard Pl; ❄ Fri & Sat) Plays house dance for 18 to 35 year olds.

Scu Bar (☎ 5441 6888; 238 Hargreaves St) This is the place to be for mainstream dance music on Friday and Saturday nights.

Golden Vine (☎ 5443 6063; 135 King St) Popular jam sessions are the go on Tuesday nights; top bands play on Wednesday, Friday and Saturday.

Bendigo Regional Arts Centre (☎ 5441 5344; www.bendigo.vic.gov.au; 50 View St) Bendigo's main venue for the performing arts.

Bendigo Cinema (☎ 5442 1666; www.cinema.ben digo.net.au; 107 Queen St) Shows the usual diet of mainstream films.

Star Cinema (☎ 0408 337 277; Old Town Hall, Peg Leg Rd, Eaglehawk; adult/child $11/6.60) Screens classic and art-house flicks.

Getting There & Around

V/Line (☎ 13 61 96; www.vline.com.au) runs 11 trains daily from Melbourne ($25, two hours). One train continues on to Swan Hill ($28). Other stops include Castlemaine ($7) and Kyneton ($12).

VICTORIA

Buses from Bendigo, departing outside the train station, include daily services to Castlemaine ($6) and to Mildura ($55) via Swan Hill ($28); weekday services to Ballarat ($22) and Geelong ($35); and Monday to Saturday services to Echuca ($8).

Walkers Buslines (☎ 5443 9333) and **Christian's Buslines** (☎ 5447 2222) service the area (two-hour tickets $1.30). Timetables are available at the visitor centre.

For a taxi call **Bendigo Associated Taxis** (☎ 13 10 08).

THE HIGH COUNTRY

Grab your bike, throw the skis on the roof, and get set for an action-packed trip to Victoria's High Country, where the air is clear and the mountain scenery invigorating and spectacular. The High Country isn't particularly high – the highest point, Mt Bogong, only reaches 1986m.

Although there are plenty of activities to do in the High Country, it's the ski resorts that have really put this area on the map. Skiers and snowboarders flock here from Melbourne and the outlying areas during the winter months, eager to indulge in a little adrenaline-fuelled snow sport.

The ski season officially launches, with or without snow, on the Queen's Birthday long weekend in June and runs until mid-September. The best deals are to be found in June and September (low season), with late July to August (high season) the busiest and most expensive time.

Others may prefer the year-round slothful delights of wine tasting, and during the summer (October onwards) there are outdoor activities such as horse riding, canoeing and abseiling.

Eildon and the gateway towns (Mansfield, Myrtleford, Harrietville and Bright) are in the northwestern foothills. Omeo is the High Country's southeastern gateway town.

Getting There & Away

V/Line (☎ 13 61 96; www.vline.com.au) operates services to major alpine towns, and there are also connecting services from Benalla and Wangaratta. Services vary seasonally.

During winter roads can become impassable. Check road conditions with the **Official**

Victorian Snow Report (www.vicsnowreport.com.au /report.html) before heading out. Snow chains, widely available for hire, must be carried during winter even if there's no snow – heavy penalties apply if you don't.

ALPINE NATIONAL PARK

Declared a national park in December 1989, the 646,000-hectare Alpine National Park joins the high country areas of Victoria, NSW and the Australian Capital Territory (ACT).

Recreation and ecotourism opportunities in the area are outstanding, particularly snow sports in the winter. Dispersed **bush camping** is available in areas running off 4WD and walking tracks, while on principal roads the use of designated camping areas is encouraged. The area's many walking tracks include the **Australian Alps Walking Track**, which extends 655km through the park from Walhalla to the outskirts of Canberra.

The park is a spectacular and fragile environment, and the vegetation throughout is quite diverse. In spring and summer the slopes are carpeted with beautiful wildflowers. More than 1100 plant species have been recorded in the park, including 12 that are unique to Australia.

SKI RESORTS

The closest snowfield to Melbourne is **Mt Donna Buang**, 95km east via Warburton, though it's mainly for sightseeing or tobogganing families.

The following snowfields offer cross-country skiing but lack accommodation:

Lake Mountain (☎ 03-5963 3288) Ski region, 120km northeast of Melbourne via Marysville, with 37km of beginners to advanced cross-country trails.

Mt Stirling (☎ 03-5777 0815) An excellent cross-country area a few kilometres northeast of Mt Buller, with over 60km of mostly advanced trails and a ski school.

Mt St Gwinear (☎ 03-5165 3204) Cross-country trails on this mountain, 171km from Melbourne via Moe, connect with Mt Baw Baw.

Mt Bogong Tough back-country skiing on Mt Bogong, Victoria's highest mountain. Accessed via Mt Beauty, 350km northeast of Melbourne; requires a long hike.

MT BAW BAW

☎ 03 / elevation 1564m

This small ski resort, in the centre of the Baw Baw National Park, is a relaxed option for beginners and families, and is seldom

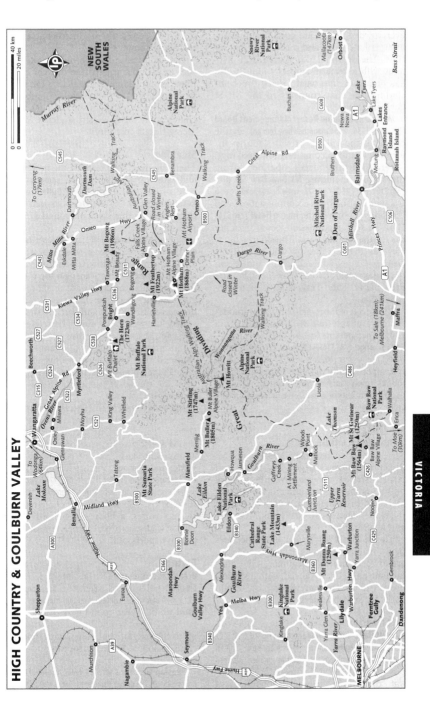

overcrowded. There are good beginner-to-intermediate runs, and a couple of harder runs. The downhill skiing area is 25 hectares with a vertical drop of 140m. It also has plenty of **cross-country skiing** trails, including one that connects to the Mt St Gwinear trails.

The **Mt Baw Baw Alpine Resort Management Board** (☎ 5165 1136; www.mountbawbaw.com.au), in the centre of the village, provides tourist information and accommodation bookings. Several ski-hire places operate during the season, including **Mt Baw Baw Ski Hire** (☎ 5165 1120, 1800 629 578; www.bawbawskihire.com.au), which also books accommodation, and IDS Snow Sports in the **Alpine Hotel** (☎ 5165 1155). Ski season admission fees are $26 per car for the day car park. The ski lifts operate only if there is snow and day tickets cost $63/33 per adult/child; lift-and-lesson packages cost $85/60. The new Frantic Frog Super Tube Park is $20 for a five-ride ticket.

In the ski season, ski-club accommodation is available midweek/weekends from $30/50 per person (minimum two nights). **Kelly's Lodge** (☎ 5165 1129; www.kellyslodge.com.au; Frostii Lane; summer $60, ski season $77-180, meals $8-16) is a superfriendly place and one of the few lodges open year-round. You can cook in the shared kitchen or have a meal in the café.

MT BULLER
☎ 03 / elevation 1805m

Three hours' drive from Melbourne, Mt Buller is Victoria's largest and busiest ski resort. There's an extensive lift network on the mountain, including a chairlift that takes you from the day car park directly to the slopes. **Cross-country trails** link Mt Buller and Mt Stirling.

The downhill skiing area is 180 hectares (snow making covers 44 hectares), and runs are divided into 25% beginner, 45% intermediate and 30% advanced, with a vertical drop of 400m. There are several cool terrain parks for snowboarders.

Information

The **Mt Buller Resort Management Board** (☎ 5777 6077; www.mtbuller.com.au; 8.30am-5pm Mon-Fri in ski season, 10am-4pm Sat & Sun in summer) shares premises with the village post office on Summit Rd. In winter the information office is at the Clock Tower. There's Internet access in the Abom complex.

Gate admission fees during the ski season are $27 per car for the day car park, more for longer stays. Lift tickets for a full day cost $85/44 per adult/child. Combined lift-and-lesson packages start at $122. Discounts apply for university students. Sightseeing tickets cost $16/9.

Sleeping

There are over 7000 beds on the mountain and rates vary depending on seasons and type of accommodation. **Mt Buller Central Reservations** (☎ 1800 039 049) books lodge accommodation that starts at around $75 per person.

Mt Buller YHA Lodge (☎ /fax 5777 6181; The Avenue; dm members/nonmembers midweek $52/62, weekend $57/67) Open only during winter, this is one of the least expensive places on the mountain. Although the dorms are small, there's good quality bedding, facilities (kitchen, drying room, TV etc) and friendly staff.

Duck Inn (☎ 5777 6236; www.duckinnmtbuller.com; 18 Goal Post Rd; dm/tw/d incl breakfast from $70/95/100) An intimate guesthouse with a range of accommodation from dorm rooms to doubles. There's a good restaurant here (guess what the special is!) as well as a ski- and clothing-hire store.

Andre's at Buller (☎ 5777 6966; www.andresatbuller.com; Cobbler Lane; d incl breakfast summer/ski season from $140/240) The luxurious architecturally designed Andre's is open year-round and boasts an excellent ski-in, ski-out position during winter and glorious summer sunsets.

Mercure Grand Chalet Hotel (☎ 5777 6566; www.mtbullerchalet.com.au; Summit Rd; d summer $180-210, ski season $240-380; ⌘) Features a range of swanky suites, a library, a billiard table, several well-regarded eateries and an impressive sports centre.

Eating

Breathtaker Signature Restaurant (☎ 5777 6377; Breathtaker All Suite Hotel, 8 Breathtaker Rd; mains $17-33; ⌛ dinner daily winter, Wed-Sun summer) The food at this year-round fine-dining restaurant (the only one in the region) lives up to the magnificent views, with its delicious fusion of Asian, European and Mod Oz cuisine.

Pension Grimus (☎ 5777 6396; Breathtaker Rd; mains $25-30; ⌛ dinner daily, lunch Sat & Sun in the ski season only) Traditional Austrian fare includes Wiener schnitzel and Salzburger *nockerl* (hazelnut and choc-chip soufflé). Pension Grimus also has very comfortable boutique apartments.

There's a licensed supermarket in the Moloney's building in the village centre (closed in summer) or otherwise there are various fast-food eateries on the slopes and in the village, including **Cattleman's Café** (☎ 5777 7800; Bourke St).

Getting There & Around

V/Line (☎ 13 61 96; www.vline.com.au) has buses twice daily from Melbourne to Mansfield ($33); **Mansfield-Mt Buller Buslines** (☎ 5775 2606, winter ☎ 5775 6070) runs year-round daily buses up to Mt Buller (adult/child return $38/25).

Ski-season car parking is below the village; a 4WD taxi service transports people from the overnight car park to their accommodation in the village (adult/child one way $12/8).

Day-trippers park in the Horse Hill day car park and can take the quad chairlift into the skiing area, or the free day-tripper shuttle-bus service between the day car park and the village. Ski hire and lift tickets are available at the base of the chairlift.

For the ultimate rock-star arrival to the snow, chopper into Mt Buller with **Helicopters Victoria** (☎ 9416 9999), which charges $2950 (return, including lift passes) for up to seven people.

MT HOTHAM

☎ 03 / elevation 1868m

Serious hikers and skiers head to Mt Hotham, which is the starting point for some stunning alpine walks between November and May, and home to 320 hectares of downhill runs, with a vertical drop of 428m. About 80% of the ski trails are intermediate or advanced. The Big D is open for **night skiing** every Wednesday and Saturday, and the village chairlift also runs between late December and early January and over Easter.

Off-piste skiing in steep and narrow valleys is good. **Cross-country skiing** is also good with 35km of trails winding through tree-lined glades.

You can obtain good walking notes from Parks Victoria in Omeo and Bright. The most popular walk is to Mt Feathertop, but there are many others to choose from.

Information

Mt Hotham Alpine Resort Management Board (☎ 5759 3550; www.mthotham.com.au; ⏰ 8am-5pm daily ski season, Mon-Fri other times) is at the village administration centre.

The ski-season admission fee is $26 per car. Lift tickets cost $85/43/69 per adult/child/student. Lift-and-lesson packages are $120 for adults.

Sleeping

There are three booking agencies: **Mt Hotham Reservation Centre** (☎ 1800 354 555; www.hotham.net.au; Hotham Central) operates year-round; **Mt Hotham Accommodation Service** (☎ 1800 032 061, 5759 3636; www.mthothamaccommodation.com.au; Lawlers Apartments) operates during ski season only; and **Mt Hotham Central Reservations** (☎ 1800 657 547, 5759 3522; www.mthotham-centralres.com.au) can book local and off-mountain accommodation throughout the year.

Hotham Heights Chalets (☎ 1800 354 555, 5759 3522; Great Alpine Rd; chalets summer $280, low/high ski season $750/1600) Sleeping up to 13 of your pals, these ultramodern apartments have it all: an entertainment system, a spa, views, a fully equipped kitchen, an open fire and wonderfully soft lounges.

Gravbrot Ski Club (☎ 5759 3533; www.gravbrot.com; Great Alpine Rd; d low/high ski season $90/190) The price at this homely place includes all meals and predinner nibbles, making it startlingly good value for the ski fields. You need to bring your own linen or sleeping bag.

Karnulurra Ski Club (☎ 5759 2517; karnbook@dragnet.com; d low/high ski season $110/150) Another laid-back lodge with a great location next to the Big D lift and a well-equipped kitchen for self-caterers.

Arlberg (☎ 5986 8200; www.ski.com.au/arlberg.hotham; Great Alpine Rd; s & d ste per 2 nights $600-760; 🐕) Smack bang in the centre of all the action, the multilevel Arlberg has a family bistro, a heated indoor pool, a sauna and a spa. There are also organised activities for the kids.

Eating & Drinking

General Store (☎ 5759 3523; Great Alpine Rd; mains $11-16; ⏰ lunch & dinner) Usually the only place to stay open over part (not all) of the summer. It does tasty pizzas and counter meals and it's one of the more popular watering holes during the ski season.

Summit Bar (☎ 5759 3503; Snowbird Inn, Great Alpine Rd) Can get rather raucous, being the bar of choice for the young snowboarding pack, during its daily 'Jug Frenzy' sessions.

Some of the better eateries in the winter months (all closed in summer) are **Swindlers** (☎ 5759 4421; Hotham Central), which is also the place for an après-ski Gluhwein, the Austrian-inspired **Zirky's** (☎ 5759 3542; Great Alpine Rd), and **Chiones** (☎ 5759 3626; Hotham Central), which features an impressive Mod Oz menu and a lovely deck.

For self-caterers, there is a small supermarket next to Big D, plus a few kiosks and takeaways.

Getting There & Around

Mt Hotham is 373km northeast of Melbourne and can be reached either via the Hume Fwy (M31) and Harrietville (4½ hours), or via the Princes Hwy (A1) and Omeo (5½ hours). Contact **Mount Hotham Resort Management Board** (MHRMB; ☎ 5759 3550) to check winter road conditions before deciding which route to take (note that wheel chains must be carried).

In winter, **Trekset** (☎ 1800 659 009, 9370 9055; www.mthothambus.com.au) has daily buses from Melbourne to Mt Hotham, via Wangaratta, Myrtleford, Bright and Harrietville.

A free shuttle runs frequently around the resort from 7am to 3am; a separate shuttle service also operates to Dinner Plain. The free 'zoo cart' takes skiers from their lodges to the lifts between 8am and 6pm.

Mt Hotham airport (☎ 5159 6777) services Mt Hotham and Dinner Plain. **QantasLink** (☎ 13 13 13) flies here throughout the week in the ski season from Melbourne (one way from $250) and Sydney (from $155).

The Helicopter Lift Link (return $94, with a lift ticket) takes six minutes to fly to Falls Creek, but operates only on clear days.

DINNER PLAIN

☎ 03 / elevation 1520m

Eleven kilometres east of Mt Hotham village, the stylish alpine resort of Dinner Plain is lovely winter and summer with its attractive 'high country' architecture and endless outdoor activities. The entire village, inspired by early cattle farmers' huts,

was built in the mid-1980s from corrugated iron and local timber and stone.

There are excellent cross-country trails around the village, including the **Hotham–Dinner Plain Ski Trail** (10km one way). There is a beginners' lift; one-day tickets cost $35/30 per adult/child.

Molony Ski Hire (☎ 5159 6450; 7.30am-6pm) has full hire options, and **Dinner Plain Ski School** has ski and snowboard packages available. It's a short 20-minute drive to Mount Hotham or visitors can use the convenient shuttle-bus service.

In summer the village is an ideal base for hiking (notes are available from Parks Victoria in Hotham), or horse riding with **Dinner Plain Trail Rides** (☎ 5159 7241; www.dinnerplaintrailrides.com; 1hr/half day/full day $50/110/160, Nov-Jun).

Sleeping & Eating

There are 200 chalets and lodges to choose from – for bookings contact either **Dinner Plain Central Reservations** (☎ 1800 670 019, 5159 6451; www.dinnerplain.com; Big Muster Dr) or **Dinner Plain Accommodation** (☎ 5159 6696; info@accom.dinnerplain.com.au; Big Muster Dr).

Crystal Creek Resort (☎ 5159 6422; www.crystalcreekresort.com; Big Muster Dr; s/d summer $80/110, winter $145/210;) Originally an Australian army retreat, this sprawling complex is now a well-run hotel with all the comforts (spa, sauna, restaurant/bar and Samoyed snow dog) but a definite lack of pretension compared with flashier accommodation at the big ski resorts.

High Plain Lodge (☎ 5159 6455; www.highplains.com.au; d $90-130 summer, d incl breakfast ski season from $110-170, lunch mains $6.50-15, dinner mains $18-25; Big Muster Dr) Superior motel-style accommodation with comfy rooms and cable TV. There's a decent bar and restaurant here.

Dinner Plain Hotel (☎ 5159 6462; mains $9-18) Looks somewhat like an overgrown mountain hut, with its split-level interior of huge timber poles and slabs, plus roaring open fires. The bistro has had good reports, particularly the pizzas.

MT BUFFALO

☎ 03 / elevation 1500m

Mt Buffalo is Victoria's smallest ski resort and is managed by Parks Victoria. However, a private operator manages Mt Buffalo Chalet and Lodge, the ski lifts, the handful of downhill runs, along with some more-challenging cross-country skiing areas that are popular with beginners and families.

There are two skiing areas, Cresta Valley and Dingo Dell. Cresta is the main area, and has five lifts. The downhill skiing area is 27 hectares, and the eight runs are predominantly beginner and intermediate, with a vertical drop of 157m. Within Mt Buffalo Lodge there's a café, kiosk and ski hire. Cresta Valley is the starting point for many of the **cross-country trails**. Dingo Dell is ideal for beginners and has a day-visitor shelter with a kiosk and ski school. It's usually open only on weekends.

In summer visitors here can enjoy over 90km of walking tracks, **hang gliding** and **rock climbing**.

Information

Mt Buffalo is about four hours' drive from Melbourne. The main access road leads off the Great Alpine Rd at Porepunkah.

The admission fee to Mt Buffalo National Park is $9.30 per car ($12.90 in winter, but only if ski lifts are operating) and payable at the Mt Buffalo Entrance Station. Lift tickets are priced according to the number of lifts open (adult $25 to $50, child $12.50 to $25), and there are lift-and-lesson packages (adult/child $55/39).

Track information and camping permits and payments can be organised at the **Entrance Station** (☎ 5756 2328). For further information contact **Parks Victoria** (☎ 5755 1466) in Porepunkah.

Activities

Adventure Guides Australia (☎ 5728 1804; www .adventureguidesaustralia.com.au) offers abseiling, caving and rock climbing alpine-style, basically meaning the worse the conditions (rain, snow etc) the better – though you're only 200m from a hot coffee at Mt Buffalo Chalet! It also has ski touring/snow camping and other activities from $77 to $100 per half day.

Horse riding, climbing, abseiling, guided walks and hang gliding can be arranged through **Mt Buffalo Chalet** (☎ 1800 037 038). It also rents mountain bikes.

Eagle School of Microlighting (☎ 5750 1174; www.eagleschool.com.au) has powered hang gliding (from $95 to $155), and tandem flights ($250).

Sleeping & Eating

Mt Buffalo Chalet (☎ 1800 037 038, 5755 1500; www .mtbuffalochalet.com.au; s/d from $105/160, without bathroom from $85/120, incl breakfast; 🖃) Built in 1909, this rambling mountain guesthouse has four different types of simple bedrooms, large lounges and games rooms with open fires. During ski season and January, all accommodation includes dinner and breakfast. Mt Buffalo Chalet Café is open daily to the public, while the chalet's dining room, in the former ballroom, is reserved for houseguests. The chalet's café offers a High Tea ($12 per person) with scones and jam between 11.30am and 4pm.

Remote camping is possible at Rocky Creek, which has pit toilets only. Strict conditions apply; organise a permit through **Parks Victoria** (☎ 5756 2328) at the Mt Buffalo Entrance Station. **Lake Catani** (sites $17) also has a summer camping ground, with toilets and showers. During peak periods you must book.

Getting There & Around

There is no public transport to the plateau, though a **V/Line** (☎ 13 61 96; www.vline.com.au) bus from Melbourne to Bright ($43, one per day Monday, Tuesday, Thursday and Friday), can drop you at Porepunkah, near the base of the mountain. Transport from Wangaratta train station can be arranged for chalet and lodge guests.

FALLS CREEK

☎ 03 / elevation 1780m

Falls Creek is arguably the most fashion-conscious and upmarket ski resort in Australia, and combines a picturesque alpine setting among the snow gums with impressive skiing and infamous après-ski entertainment. Hordes of city folk make the 4½-hour journey from Melbourne at weekends during the ski season.

The skiing is spread over two main areas, the Village Bowl and Sun Valley. There are 19 lifts: 17% beginner, 60% intermediate and 23% advanced runs. The downhill area covers 451 hectares with a vertical drop of 267m. Night skiing in the Village Bowl operates several times a week.

You'll also find some of Australia's best **cross-country skiing** here. A **trail** leads around Rocky Valley Pondage to old cattlemen's huts, and the more adventurous can tour to the white summits of Nelse, Cope and Spion Kopje. These also provide walking routes in summer.

Information

The **Falls Creek visitor information centre** (☎ 1800 033 079, 5758 3490; www.fallscreek.com.au; ☺ 9am-5pm) is on the right-hand side as you enter the resort, at the bottom of the Gully chairlift, and has plenty of information on the whole region including Mt Buffalo.

The daily admission fee is $24 per car during the ski season only. There are lift tickets for a full day (adult/child/student $85/43/69), and combined lift-and-lesson packages ($121/83/90).

Sleeping

Accommodation can be booked via several agencies including **Falls Creek Central Reservations** (☎ 1800 033 079, 5758 3733; www.fallscreek .com.au; Bogong High Plains Rd), **Mountain Multiservice** (☎ 1800 465 566, 5758 3499; www.mountainmulti service.com.au; Schuss St) and **Go Snow Go Falls Creek** (☎ 1800 253 545, 9873 5474; www.albury.net .au/~gosnow).

Alpha Lodge (☎ 5758 3488; www.alphaskilodge .com.au; 5 Parallel St; dm $26-90, d & tw from $105) This spacious lodge is set up with a sauna and a large lounge with panoramic views. Self-caterers will have a field day in the communal kitchen, which has eight cooking stations.

Julians Lodge (☎ 5758 3211; www.julianslodge .com; 18 Slalom St; dm/d low ski season $85/95, high ski season $140/160; ☒) This warm, laid-back lodge has been in the same family for 45 years. The price includes dinner and breakfast plus unmissable predinner nibbles.

Frueauf Village (☎ 1300 300 709; www.fvfalls.com .au; d per 2 nights summer from $300, low/high ski season from $400/950; ☐) The 25 luxurious, architect-designed apartments have everything an alpine chalet needs and more (free Internet access, private outdoor hot tubs) plus the funky Milch café (right) and Glo cinema downstairs.

Eating

Mo's Restaurant at Feathertop (☎ 5758 3232; mains $14-30; 14 Parallel St; ☺ dinner) This inviting restaurant features red-gum furniture, private alcoves and mood lighting. Bookings are recommended.

Summit Ridge (☎ 5758 3800; 8 Schuss St; mains $14-30; ☺ dinner) Another great dinner option, this rustic restaurant in the Summit Ridge apartments boasts an extensive wine list. High-country fine dining meets crisp Asian flavours. Bookings are essential.

Milch Café Wine Bar (☎ 5758 3770; 4 Schuss St; mains $12-18; ☺ 8am-1am) The hip place to see and be seen, with flavoursome Middle Eastern meze and an expansive wine list. In winter, this place is packed with skiers conducting postmortems of their runs.

Café Max (☎ 5758 3347; 27 Falls Creek Rd; ☺ breakfast, lunch & dinner) This very social café in the Village Bowl serves up tasty Mod Oz dishes all day. Après-ski drinks are served between 4pm and 6pm.

In the **Snowland Shopping Centre** (☎ 5758 3318; 9 Slalom St), at the bottom of Halleys Comet chairlift, a licensed supermarket and the **Wombat Café** (☎ 5758 3666) are open year-round. In the ski season the usual kiosks are open.

Getting There & Around

Falls Creek is 375km and a 4½-hour drive from Melbourne. During the winter, **Pyle's Coaches** (☎ 5754 4024; www.pyles.com.au) operates buses daily between Falls Creek and Melbourne (one way/return $78/125) and also runs services to and from Albury ($44/70) and Mt Beauty ($25/40).

The Over-Snow Taxi service (return $25) operates between the car parks and the lodges from 8am to midnight (until 2am on Friday night). Car parking for day visitors is at the base of the village, next to the ski lifts.

If you want to ski Mt Hotham for the day, jump on the Helicopter Lift Link for $94 return if you have a valid lift ticket.

EILDON

☎ 03 / pop 700

The small, one-pub town of Eildon is a popular recreation and holiday base for Lake Eildon and the surrounding **Lake Eildon National Park**. It was built in the 1950s to house Eildon Dam project workers.

On Main St there's the small **Eildon visitor information centre** (☎ 5774 2909; www.lakeeildon .com; ☺ 10am-2pm Sat-Mon, to 5pm Fri).

Activities

Lake Eildon has a shoreline of over 500km and is one of Victoria's favourite watersports playgrounds.

Kids love the touch-and-feel tanks at the **Freshwater Discovery Centre** (☎ 5774 2208; Goulburn Valley Hwy; adult/child/concession $5.50/3/3; ⏰ 11am-4pm Fri-Mon, 11am-4pm daily during school holidays).

Horse trails are run by **Rubicon Valley Horse-riding** (☎ 5773 2292; www.rubiconhorseriding .com.au; Rubicon Rd, Thornton; 2/3hr $55/75).

If you want to practise your angling, try the **Goulburn Valley Fly Fishing Centre** (☎ 5773 2513; www.goulburnvlyflyfishing.com.au) or **Blackridge Flyfishing School** (☎ 5774 2825; www.flyflickers.com; 785 Back Eildon Rd).

Eildon Lake Charters (☎ 5774 2871; 55 Joe Taylor Rise) rents boats and runs water-skiing and sightseeing trips.

Sleeping & Eating

Robyn's Nest (☎ 5774 2525; 13 High St; d incl breakfast $100-140) This plush 'adults only' B&B swears it has the most comfortable beds in Eildon. If you decide to get up, the private balconies have superb views of the Eildon Valley and Mt Trobrek.

Golden Trout Hotel/Motel (☎ 5774 2508; 1 Riverside Dr; s/d from $60/70, meals $8-30) Try to secure a room with a Goulburn River view here. The pub has a decent bistro with a nice sun deck.

Lake Eildon Marina & Houseboat Hire (☎ 5774 2107; 190 Sugarloaf Rd; www.houseboatholidays.com.au) and **High Country Houseboats** (☎ 5777 3899; www .ahch.com.au) both rent out 10- to 12-berth houseboats from around $2100 to $4500 per week during high season.

Coco's Restaurant & Bar (☎ 5774 2866; lunch mains $9-13, dinner mains $17-23; ⏰ lunch & dinner Wed-Sun) overlooks the boat harbour, while **Taste of Eildon** (☎ 5774 2642; 7 High St; mains $8-16; ⏰ 9am-5pm Thu-Mon, dinner summer) is a café, gallery, and gourmet food and wine shop in the old general store.

Getting There & Away

V/Line (☎ 13 61 96; www.vline.com.au) runs daily services from Melbourne to Eildon (one way $22, 3¼ hours), Marysville and Alexandra (three hours, Monday, Wednesday and Thursday).

MT BEAUTY

☎ 03 / pop 1650

Mt Beauty and its twin town of Tawonga South are the gateway to the Falls Creek ski resort and the Bogong High Plains.

The **Alpine Discovery Centre** (☎ 1800 808 277; www.visitmtbeauty.com.au; 31 Bogong High Plains Rd; ⏰ 9am-5pm) has an **accommodation booking service** (☎ 1800 033 079; accommodation@mtbeauty .com.au). The brand-new information centre also houses displays that highlight the region's history.

Activities

The pretty 2km **Tree Fern Walk** and the slightly longer **Peppermint Walk** both start from **Mountain Creek Picnic and Camping Ground**, on Mountain Creek Rd, off the Kiewa Valley Hwy. For information on longer walks in the area, visit the Alpine Discovery Centre.

Rocky Valley Bikes (☎ 5754 1118; www.rockyvalley .com.au; Kiewa Valley Hwy) offers mountain-bike trips for all levels. Bike hire is also available from $22 per day.

Bogong Horseback Adventures (☎ 5754 4849; www.bogonghorse.com.au; Mountain Creek Rd; half-/full-/3-day trips $70/$140/825, 5-day packhorse $1375) runs excellent trips over the Bogong High Plains.

The Kiewa Valley is world-renowned for **trout fishing** from spring to autumn. For fly-fishing trips, try **Peter Panozzo Guided Fishing Tours & Lessons** (☎ 5754 4522; 18 Nelse St; per hr per 2 people $40).

Sleeping

Braeview (☎ 5754 4756; www.braeview.com.au; 4 Stewarts Rd; s/d incl breakfast $99/110, spa cottage s/d from $160/190) Choose between traditional B&B rooms (with a scrumptious country breakfast on the balcony overlooking the gardens) and self-contained cottages or apartments with spa.

Springfield Cottage (☎ 5754 1112; springfield@ netc.net.au; 186 Simmonds Creek Rd, Tawonga South; s/d incl breakfast $90/125) This Japanese-themed B&B is curiously furnished, but has a sun-drenched garden and views to Mt Bogong.

Dreamers (☎ 5754 1222; www.dreamers1.com; Kiewa Valley Hwy, Tawonga South; d $160-290; 🐾) For high-country luxury accommodation at its best, try this enchanting collection of superbly designed timber-and-stone cottages surrounding a peaceful lagoon.

Tawonga Caravan Park (☎ 5754 4428; Mountain Creek Rd, Tawonga South; powered/unpowered sites $20/18, cabins from $55) Turn off the Kiewa Valley Hwy at the Bogong Hotel in Tawonga to find this caravan park by the Kiewa River.

VICTORIA

Eating & Drinking

Roi's Diner Restaurant (☎ 5754 4495; 177 Kiewa Valley Hwy, Tawonga South; mains $18-25; ⊙ dinner Thu-Sun) An unassuming timber shack on the highway, Roi's is an award-winning restaurant offering exceptional modern Italian cuisine.

Mt Beauty Bakery & Café (☎ 5754 4870; cnr Hollands & Kiewa Sts; meals $4-8; ⊙ 6.30am-6.30pm) This swish bakery-bar-café with a sunny outdoor area offers a big range of cakes, focaccias and antipasto.

Bogong Hotel (☎ 5754 4482; 169 Kiewa Valley Hwy; ⊙ lunch Sun, dinner Thu-Mon) The obvious spot for a beer, it also has a relaxed bistro with lovely views of the snow-capped mountains. Bookings recommended.

Getting There & Away

V/Line (☎ 13 61 96; www.vline.com.au) operates a train/bus service from Melbourne via Wangaratta ($50, twice weekly). **Pyle's Coaches** (☎ 5754 4024; www.pyles.com.au) operates buses to Albury (one way $15, once daily Monday to Friday) and to Falls Creek daily in winter (one way $20).

MANSFIELD

☎ 03 / pop 2550

Mansfield is an all-seasons destination, with a plethora of activities from skiing at Mt Buller to late-spring horse trail rides through the mountains. Mansfield makes a great base for a weekend or a longer stay.

The graves of the three Mansfield police officers killed by Ned Kelly and his gang in 1878 at Stringybark Creek rest in **Mansfield cemetery**, at the end of Highett St.

The visitor information centre, **Mansfield-Mt Buller High Country Reservations** (☎ 5775 2518, 1800 039 049; www.mansfield-mtbuller.com.au; Old Railway Station, Maroondah Hwy; ⊙ 9am-5pm, 8am-9pm ski season), books accommodation.

Activities

Global Ballooning (☎ 9428 5703; www.globalballooning.com.au; flights incl champagne breakfast $285) Enjoy spectacular sunrise views of Mt Buller from a hot-air balloon.

High Country Camel Treks (☎ 5775 1591; Rifle Butts Rd; per hr $20) Offers hourly and overnight treks, 7km south of town.

High Country Horses (☎ 5777 5590; www.highcountryhorses.com.au; 10 McCormacks Rd, Merrijig; 2hr rides $50, half-day $75, full-day $140-180, overnight $400)

Rides around Merrijig or overnight trips across Mt Stirling, camping in a cattleman's hut at Razorback.

High Country Scenic Tour (☎ 5777 5101; www.highcountryscenictours.com.au; ⊙ Nov-May) If you want to get off-road this group has exciting day tours from $110 per person.

Kestral Aviation (☎ 0428 376 619) Runs helicopter joy flights.

Mansfield Mountain Bike Tours (☎ 5775 2380, 1800 815 810; 2hr rides $35, half-day $80; ⊙ Oct-Apr) Adventure bike tours.

Watson's Mountain Country Trail Rides (☎ 5777 3552; www.watsonstrailrides.com.au; 3 Chains Rd, Boorolite; 1/2hr $30/50) Make like *The Man from Snowy River* and take a trail ride on the Great Dividing Range, 22km from Mansfield. One of the highlights is the downhill area that is featured in the 1982 film.

Sleeping

Mansfield Backpackers' Inn & Travellers Lodge (☎ 5775 1800; www.mansfieldtravellodge.com; 112 High St; dm $23, d $85-95, ste $125-135; ☒) There's superior dorm accommodation in this restored heritage building, or modern motel rooms (prices drop midweek). Includes a well-stocked kitchen.

Wappan Station (☎ 5778 7786; www.wappanstation.com.au; Royal Town Rd, Maindample; cottage d from $90, shearer's quarters adult/child $30/15; ☒) Experience life on a 40.5-sq-km sheep and cattle farm at Wappan Station, on the banks of Lake Eildon. It has newly renovated self-contained cottages and more basic twin-share rooms.

Tavistock House (☎ 5775 1024; cnr High & Highett Sts; www.tavistockhouse.com.au; d midweek/weekend incl bottle of wine $120/135) In the centre of town, this lovely conversion of the historic former Westpac building has three spacious rooms decked out in Victorian-era style (no TV, phone or radio here).

Highton Manor (☎ 5775 2700; www.hightonmanor.com.au; 140 Highton Lane; stable/manor d incl breakfast $120/235; ☒) Built in 1896, this stately two-storey manor has motel-style rooms in the former stables, and lavish period rooms in the main house. The impressive gardens are great for a stroll.

Eating

Magnolia Gourmet Country House (☎ 5779 1444; 190 Mt Buller Rd; mains $24-26; ⊙ dinner Thu-Sat) The locals' pick for fine dining in Mansfield – try the robust high-country beef with mash and mushrooms. Magnolia House is also a

B&B, which is a good thing to remember after demolishing one of the signature desserts – you won't be able to move!

Mansfield Regional Produce Store (☎ 5889 1404; 68 High St; mains $7-15; ☼ breakfast & lunch daily, dinner Fri) This rustic store, with its array of delicious homemade produce and artisan breads, is a great place to shop if you're self-catering. Take a seat by the fire or get to know the locals over a coffee and baguette at the communal tables.

Sweet Potato (☎ 5775 1955; 50 High St; mains $10-18; ☼ 10.30am-2pm & dinner Thu-Mon) There's a relaxed vibe at this cosy licensed café, which serves Mod Oz cuisine with some spicier Asian fusion dishes.

Bon Appetit (☎ 5775 2951; 39-41 High St; mains $5-12; ☼ 9.30am-6pm Mon-Fri, 9am-5pm Sat) This inexpensive deli café serves up gourmet surprises in a sunny courtyard. The vanilla slices are justifiably famous.

Getting There & Away

V/Line (☎ 13 61 96; www.vline.com.au) buses run twice daily (once Sunday) from Melbourne (one way $33). **Mansfield-Mt Buller Bus Lines** (☎ 5775 2606) runs twice-daily buses for skiers from Mansfield to Mt Buller ($35 return).

HARRIETVILLE

☎ 03

Harrietville is a picturesque little town nestled at the foot of Mt Feathertop. During ski season a bus shuttles between the town and Mt Hotham, so it's a good spot for slightly cheaper off-mountain accommodation.

Ski and wheel-chain hire is available from Harrietville Hotel/Motel and **Hoy's** (☎ 5779 2658).

Harrietville is the starting and finishing point for various **alpine walking tracks**, including the popular Mt Feathertop walk, Razorback Ridge and Dargo High Plains walks. Several small companies, including **Higher Ground Adventures** (☎ 5759 2754), lead day walks to Mt Feathertop ($150 per four-person group) but they specialise in longer overnight trips, which are self-catering ($250, two nights including equipment).

In late November the annual **Blue Grass Festival** (http://bluegrass.org.au/Festivals/harrietville /index.cfm) takes over the town. Early December heralds the **Lawnmowing Grand Prix**, a classy affair of lawnmower and snowmobile races.

Sleeping & Eating

Pick & Shovel Cottage (☎ 5759 2627; 1 Pick & Shovel Rise; d midweek/weekend incl breakfast $125/140; ⛄) This lovely cottage combines style with olde-worlde charm and is professionally run by a helpful couple. Generous breakfast and complimentary champagne are an added bonus.

Shady Brook Cottages (☎ 5759 2741; www.shady brook.com.au; Mountain View Walk; d midweek/weekend incl breakfast from $110/130) Shady Brook is in 4.85 hectares of secluded bush at the foot of Mt Hotham. There are two alpine-style cottages, both with spas and spacious verandas for contemplating the stunning surroundings.

Big Shed Café (☎ 5759 2672; Great Alpine Rd, Smoko; meals $7-15; ☼ 10am-5pm Wed-Mon) A popular spot down the road towards Bright. This tobacco shed started out as a fruit-and-veggie store before reinventing itself as a gourmet café with great views of Mt Feathertop.

Getting There & Away

No public transport operates to Harrietville. During the ski season a bus connects Harrietville with Mt Hotham (return $20, twice daily). **Mountain View Holiday Retreat** (☎ 5759 2530) sells tickets and is the pick-up point. The road to Mt Hotham is sometimes closed because of snow in winter.

BRIGHT

☎ 03 / pop 1900

Spectacular in autumn, this picturesque leafy town in the foothills of the alps is popular year-round. Bright is perfectly positioned to enjoy the Alpine National Park, skiing at Falls Creek and Mt Hotham, and a wide range of outdoor adventure activities. Great local produce and a sophisticated restaurant scene make it well worth staying the night.

The **Bright visitor information centre** (☎ 1300 551 117; www.brightescapes.com.au; 119 Gavan St; ☼ 9am-5pm) has a very busy accommodation booking service as well as Parks Victoria information.

Bright Autumn Festival (☎ 5755 2275; www.bright autumnfestival.org.au) is at the end of April/early May.

Activities

There are plenty of **walking trails** around Bright, including the 3km loop **Canyon Walk**,

VICTORIA

which starts from Star Rd Bridge and follows the Ovens River. The 4km **Cherry Walk** heads from Centenary Park in the other direction along the Ovens, and a 6km track to **Wandiligong** follows Morses Creek.

The **Murray to Mountains Rail Trail** travels 30km from the old train station to Myrtleford via Porepunkah. Bike rental and tours are available from **Cyclepath Adventures** (☎ 5750 1442; 74 Gavan St; hire per hr $12, half/full day $18/24; ⏱ 9am-5pm Mon-Fri, 10am-4pm Sat & Sun).

Alpine Paragliding (☎ 5755 1753; www.alpine paragliding.com; 100 Gavan St; ⏱ Oct-Jun) has 20-minute tandem flights for $150. **Bright Microlights** (☎ 5750 1555; 10/30min flights $70/155) offers powered hang-glider flights.

Sleeping

Bright has an abundance of accommodation but it's advisable to book ahead.

Bright Hikers Backpackers' Hostel (☎ 5750 1244; backpackers@brighthikers.com.au; 4 Ireland St; dm/s/tw $21/30/44; 🖥) This efficient, clean, well-set-up hostel in the middle of town has a cosy lounge for winter nights, and its huge veranda is perfect for summer days in the hammock. Knowledgeable staff are an added bonus.

Elm Lodge Motel (☎ 5755 1144; elmlodge@bigpond .net.au; 2 Wood St; s $55-75, d $70-130; 🐾) This restored 1950s pine mill has rooms for all budgets, located only a few minutes' walk from the town centre. The gardens are beautifully landscaped and the owners superfriendly.

Eucalypt Mist B&B (☎ 5755 1336; 152A Delaney Ave; d $115-135) This attractive B&B has only two elegantly decorated suites. It's a short walk into town – that's if you can leave the veranda overlooking the gorgeous bird-filled garden.

Ashwood House Cottages (☎ 5755 1081; ashwood@ netc.net.au; 22A Ashwood Ave; d $145; 🐾) Three unique, corrugated-iron cottages set in bushland down by the Ovens River. All have creature comforts such as entertainment system, double spa and log fires.

Odd Frog (☎ 5755 2123; www.theoddfrog.com; 3 McFadyens Lane; d $130-180) Designed and built by the young architect–interior designer owners, these contemporary, ecofriendly studios feature light, breezy spaces and fabulous outdoor decks.

Villa Gusto (☎ 5756 2000; www.villagusto.com.au; 630 Buckland Valley Rd, Buckland; d incl breakfast $220-325) An exquisite Tuscan-inspired villa, this class joint is run by Italy enthusiasts who stop at nothing to ensure you are well cared for. It includes a superb restaurant (dinner Thursday to Sunday).

Eating & Drinking

Simone's Restaurant (☎ 5755 2266; 98 Gavan St; mains $26-30; ⏱ dinner Tue-Sun) Owner and chef Patrizia Simone serves outstanding Italian food, with a focus on local ingredients and seasonal produce, in the rustic dining room of a heritage-listed house. Bookings essential.

Sasha's of Bright (☎ 5750 1711; 2D Anderson St; mains $18-30; ⏱ dinner) Seriously good and incredibly hearty European cooking. There's also a reasonably priced, regional wine list.

Jackie's (☎ 5750 1303; 6 Ireland St; dishes $5-12; ⏱ 8am-3pm) Jackie's fresh juices are delicious; the breakfasts are excellent and generous. Lunches aren't as exciting, but it's a cosy place to sit.

Food Wine Friends (☎ 5750 1312; 2/6 Ireland St; dishes $8-15; ⏱ 10am-5pm) A foodie haven where you can shop for regional goodies while tucking into espresso and light dishes such as smoked-trout bruschetta.

Getting There & Away

V/Line (☎ 13 61 96; www.vline.com.au) runs trains from Melbourne to Wangaratta; the connecting bus service continues to Beechworth and Bright (both $47 one way, daily). During the ski season a regular bus operates from Bright to Mt Hotham (one way/return $25/35, 1½ hours).

MYRTLEFORD

☎ 03 / pop 2700

Near the foot of Mt Buffalo, Myrtleford is yet another 'gateway to the alps'. The helpful **Alpine Visitor Centre** (☎ 1800 991 044; www .alpinevic.com.au; Great Alpine Rd) has information and a booking service for the area. Other attractions include the cycling track and two local wineries.

Sleeping & Eating

Myrtle Creek Farmstay Cottages (☎ 5753 4447; www.myrtlecreekcottages.com; d incl breakfast $150, extra child $25) Feed the horses and fluffy alpacas at this hands-on farmstay. Bed down in self-contained log cabins, each with a spa and well-equipped kitchen.

Alpine Enoteca Restaurant (☎ 1800 991 044; Great Alpine Rd; mains $9-16; ☟ lunch daily, dinner Wed-Sun) Locals love this casual bistro in the Alpine Information Centre. Enjoy its airy ambience and chilled music as you hoe into a big bowl of risotto or pasta.

MILAWA GOURMET REGION

Milawa, a one-pub town, has had a renaissance as a regional gourmet centre, boasting notable wineries, fine restaurants and several local food producers.

Brown Brothers Vineyard (☎ 03-5720 5547; www.brownbrothers.com.au; Bobinawarrah Rd, Milawa; ☟ 9am-5pm) produced its first vintage in 1889 and is still run by the same family. The swanky complex features a tasting room, an excellent restaurant and picnic and BBQ facilities.

Milawa Mustard (☎ 03-5727 3202; Old Emu Inn, The Cross Roads, Milawa; ☟ 10am-5pm) offers tastings of 18 seeded mustards. The **Olive Shop** (☎ 03-5727 3887; oliveshop@ozemail.com.au; Snow Rd, Milawa; ☟ 10am-5pm Thu-Mon) has locally produced olive oil for sale as well as delicious tapenades.

At Oxley, there are several wineries including **John Gehrig Wines** (☎ 03-5727 3395; ☟ cellar door 9am-5pm). At **King Valley Cellar** (☎ 03-5727 3777; Snow Rd, Oxley), part of the King River Café (right), tastings of Pizzini, Chrismont and Moyhu wines are encouraged, and other King Valley wines are also on sale.

The **Milawa Cheese Company** (☎ 03-5727 3588; milawacheese@netc.net.au; Factory Rd, Milawa; ☟ 9am-5pm), 2km north of Milawa, offers tastings and a café. It excels at soft and washed-rind cheeses.

Sleeping
Will Oak B&B (☎ 03-5727 3292; Tetleys Lane; www.willoaks.com.au; d $120-140) A working cattle property 3km from Oxley. Art books, magazines, herbal teas and real coffee can all be found in the modern timber cottage, with views to Mt Buffalo. The two-course breakfast gets fantastic reports.

Lindenwarrah Country House (☎ 03-5720 5777; www.lindenwarrah.com.au; Bobinawarrah Rd, Milawa; d incl breakfast $280-360; ☒) Surrounded by vineyards, this Moroccan-inspired boutique hotel has simple but impeccably stylish rooms. The restaurant here (right) is also recommended.

Eating
Milawa Factory Bakery & Restaurant (☎ 03-5727 3589; Factory Rd, Milawa; mains $20-25; ☟ lunch daily, dinner Fri & Sat) An absolute must-stop on the 'Gourmet Road'. Fringed by grape vines, the old loading-dock area makes a pleasant place to stop for lunch from the stone-oven bakery.

Epicurean Centre (☎ 03-5720 5540; www.brownbrothers.com.au; Brown Brothers Vineyard, Bobinawarrah Rd, Milawa; 2-4 courses plus wine per person $34-55; ☟ 11am-3pm) This rustic place is a total wine and food experience. Brown Brothers wines are carefully matched with each dish, with an emphasis on regional produce.

King River Café (☎ 03-5727 3461; www.kingrivercafe.com.au; Snow Rd, Oxley; mains $15-22; ☟ 10am-3pm Mon, 10am-late Wed-Sun) Blink and you'll miss this old general store that is now *the* place to stop for coffee, or a reasonably priced meal, en route to the snow.

Restaurant Merlot (Lindenwarrah Country House, Bobinawarrah Rd, Milawa; mains $26-32; ☟ breakfast daily, lunch Fri-Sun, dinner Thu-Sun) At boutique-hotel Lindenwarrah (left), this restaurant garners good reports.

BEECHWORTH
☎ 03 / pop 2950

Rated by the National Trust as one of Victoria's two 'notable' towns, Beechworth is a living legacy of the 1860s gold-rush era. Many of the distinctive honey-coloured public buildings remain, including the courthouse and jail where Ned Kelly was charged and remanded for the murder of two Mansfield policemen.

The helpful **Beechworth visitor information centre** (☎ 1300 366 321, 5728 8065; www.beechworth.com; 103 Ford St; ☟ 9am-5pm), in the Old Shire Hall, books accommodation and activities, and has information on scenic walks and wineries in the area.

Sights & Activities
Beechworth's **historic and cultural precinct** (☎ 1300 366 321; www.beechworthprecinct.com.au) consists of many interesting old buildings including the excellent **Burke Museum** (☎ 5728 8067; Loch St; adult/child/family $5.50/3/15; ☟ 9am-5pm), showing gold-rush relics and an arcade with 16 shop fronts preserved as they were over 140 years ago.

The **Beechworth Courthouse** (Ford St; adult/child/family $4/2/10; ☟ 9am-5pm) is notable for Ned

VICTORIA

Kelly's first court appearance. See the cell where Ned was held in the basement behind the **Shire Hall**.

The new **Chinese Cultural Centre** (☎ 5728 2866; adult/child/family $3/1/8; ☺ 10am-4pm Wed-Mon) displays the history of the 6000 Chinese who came to the area in the 1850s to seek their fortune.

The **Powder Magazine** (Gorge St; adult/child/family $2.50/1.50/6) was an 1859 storage area for gunpowder. View the *Echoes of History* video at the **1858 Town Hall** (Ford St) roughly half-hourly. The precinct ticket covers the whole experience (adult/child/family $13/5.50/30). Ask at the visitor centre about free tours, as well as Ned Kelly trial re-enactments.

Sleeping

There's a host of B&Bs and self-contained cottages in the area. The visitor centre will book for you.

Old Priory (☎ 5728 1024; 8 Priory Lane; dm/s/d $40/50/80, cottages $105, incl breakfast) This historic convent has lovely gardens and a range of accommodation. It can often be overrun by school groups, so check first when booking.

Bank Mews (☎ 5728 2223; www.thebankrestaurant .com; 86 Ford St; d incl breakfast $160) The original stables and coach house of this historic building have been renovated to house four swish suites overlooking an attractive courtyard and garden.

Kinross (☎ 5728 2351; kinross@dragnet.com.au; 34 Loch St; s $125-135, d $150-165, incl breakfast; ⌨) A former presbyterian minister's house, this elegant B&B retains many of its original 1850s features, while allowing for modern trappings such as TV and Internet.

Beechworth House (☎ 5728 2322; www.beech worth.com; 5 Dingle Rd; s $110-150, d $150-185 both incl breakfast) A very comfortable and peaceful guesthouse with delicious breakfasts. The glorious gardens feature a lake, birds, roses and views. One of the owners is a chef and will make dinner on request.

Country Charm Swiss Cottages (☎ 5728 2435; www.swisscottages.com.au; 22 Malakoff Rd; d incl breakfast $170-215) These private self-contained timber cottages are ideal for families and have excellent views of the Beechworth Gorge and Woolshed Valley.

Eating

Gigi's (☎ 5728 2575; 69 Ford St; mains $17-26; ☺ breakfast & lunch Thu-Tue, dinner Mon, Tue & Thu-Sat) This shopfront café and produce store can be on the snooty side, but hearty Italian dishes such as spinach and scallop risotto are deservedly popular.

Bank (☎ 5728 2223; 86 Ford St; mains $20-28; ☺ dinner daily, lunch Sun) Sophisticated dining amid the antique interior of this former bank building makes for a memorable culinary experience. Duck, ostrich and buffalo all make an appearance on the creative Mod Oz menu. Try regional wines by the glass; check out the cellar in the old vault.

Green Shed Bistro (☎ 5728 2360; 37 Camp St; mains $18-25; ☺ lunch Fri-Sun, dinner Wed-Thu) This former printery is now a cosy place to warm your hands by the fire and check out the busy open kitchen.

Beechworth Bakery (☎ 5728 1132; 27 Camp St; ☺ 6am-7pm) It's certainly worth elbowing the locals and tourists out of the way at this place, which is famous interstate, for a delicious pie, though the coffee is ordinary.

Beechworth Provender (☎ 5728 2650; 18 Camp St) Absolutely crammed with delectable local produce such as Milawa cheeses, wines, chutneys and antipasto.

Getting There & Away

V/Line (☎ 13 61 96; www.vline.com.au) has daily services between Melbourne and Beechworth ($41). **Wangaratta Coachlines** (☎ 5722 1843) run to major centres nearby. Tickets for V/Line, CountryLink and Greyhound Australia buses can be booked at **Beechworth Animal World** (☎ 5728 1374; 36 Camp St).

YACKANDANDAH

☎ 02 / pop 600

An old gold-mining town set amid beautiful hills and valleys, Yackandandah has been classified by the National Trust. There's information in the church hall on High St. Pick up the free *A Walk in High Street* brochure, detailing the history of the shops. The glossy *Yackandandah Touring Guide* has information on the wider area.

Other options apart from curio shopping – try **Vintage Sounds Restoration** on Wyndham St – include trout fishing on Yackandandah Creek; a visit to the **Lavender Patch** (☎ 6027 1603; Beechworth Rd; ☺ 9am-5.30pm) for some lavender ice cream; and the studio-gallery **Kirby's Flat Pottery** (☎ 6027 1416; ☺ 10.15am-5.30pm Sat & Sun), 4km south of Yackandandah.

The unsealed 14km **Yackandandah Scenic Forest Drive** begins at Bells Flat Rd and travels over former gold-mining territory, much of which is now Stanley State Forest.

Built in 1863, the **Star Hotel** (☎ 6027 1493; 30 High St; d incl breakfast $45, mains $8.50-19) is an old country pub with renovated rooms and pub grub. **Karililla** (☎ 6027 1788; Ben Valley Lane; d $130) is a homestead about 5km from town, and offers genuine country hospitality, a generous breakfast and lovely gardens.

OMEO
☎ 03 / pop 300

Nestled among hills thick with bushland, pretty Omeo is the southern access route to Mt Hotham. The road is sometimes snowbound in winter; always check conditions before heading this way. In the gold-rush days of the 1850s, Omeo was one of the toughest and most remote goldfields in the state.

There's an unofficial visitors centre in the **German Cuckoo Clock Shop** (☎ 5159 1552; www.omeoregion.com.au; Great Alpine Rd; ☒ 9.30am-5.30pm). The Historical Park has a mud map to the **Oriental Claims Walk**.

The scenic Victoria Falls Camping Area, off the Great Alpine Rd, 18km west of Omeo, has pit toilets and a picnic area, while **Omeo Caravan Park** (☎ 5159 1351; Old Omeo Hwy; powered/unpowered sites per 2 people $18/15, d cabin from $55) is alongside the Livingstone River.

Omeo Bankhouse (☎ 5159 1405; omeoregion.com.au/bankhouse; 154 Day Ave; up to 10 people $200) is a restored two-storey bank that easily accommodates up to 10 people with its airy rooms, well-equipped kitchen and large backyard.

Golden Age Motel & Bar (☎ 5159 1344; Day Ave; s/d from $70/90) is an Art Deco pub that has been converted into B&B-style accommodation. Its **restaurant** (mains $13-18; ☒ Mon-Sat) serves reliable fare of steaks, salads and soups.

You won't need dinner after hoeing into a veggie bake at **Gracie's Tea Rooms** (☎ 5159 1428; 174 Day Ave; dishes $8-13), a great little lunch stop.

Getting There & Away
Omeo Bus Lines (☎ 5159 4231) runs Monday to Friday between Omeo and Bairnsdale ($28 one way, two hours). During the ski season **O'Connell's Bus Lines** (☎ 5159 1377) operates a winter service to Dinner Plain and Mt Hotham from Friday to Sunday; it also has inexpensive bunkhouse accommodation in Omeo.

ANGLERS REST

About 30km north of Omeo is Anglers Rest.

Beside the Cobungra River you'll find the **Blue Duck Inn Hotel** (☎ 03-5159 7220; Omeo Hwy; d from $65), which is popular with anglers, canoeists and bushwalkers. Self-contained units sleep up to six people, there's a bar that also serves meals, and a good BBQ area right by the river.

GOULBURN VALLEY & HUME FREEWAY REGION

You can put your foot down on the Hume Fwy (M31) as it isn't particularly scenic and the speed limit is usually 110km, although there are a few attractions off the freeway.

West of the Hume is the Goulburn Valley, Victoria's fruit bowl. The valley's other main crop is wine, and several wineries are worth a visit, notably the impressive Tahbilk and Mitchelton wineries near Nagambie.

East of the freeway are the foothills of the High Country.

GLENROWAN
☎ 03 / pop 350

Ned Kelly's legendary bushranging exploits came to their bloody end here in 1880. The story of Ned and his gang has become an industry in this small town and you can't drive through Glenrowan without being confronted by the legend.

Sights
The highlight of Glenrowan is **Kellyland** and its over-the-top **theatre** (☎ 5766 2367; Gladstone St; adult/child/family $16/10/45; ☒ 9.30am-4.30pm). The story is told in different rooms by a cast of surprisingly lifelike computerised characters (it may be too scary for young children).

The 400-million-year-old **Warby Range State Park** extends about 25km north of Glenrowan and provided Ned Kelly and his gang with many vantage points.

VICTORIA

Sleeping & Eating

Glenrowan Kelly Country Motel (☎ 5766 2202; Main St; s/d/f from $55/70/90; 🅿 💻) Spacious yellow rooms look out on a small garden and BBQ area.

Glenrowan Bushland Caravan Park (☎ 5766 2288; Warby Range Rd; sites per 2 people from $15, d cabin from $38) In a relaxed bushland setting 2km north of town, this place is interesting with its many long-term residents. The turn-off is just north of Kellyland.

Glenrowan Hotel (☎ 5766 2255; Main St; mains $7.50-15; 🕑 lunch & dinner) It's free of Kelly paraphernalia, but you'd swear the air was the same that Kelly breathed. Fortunately there's a courtyard.

WANGARATTA

☎ 03 / pop 15,500

Wangaratta (also known as Wang) is at the junction of the Ovens and King Rivers. Its name comes from two local Aboriginal words meaning 'resting place of the cormorants'. Wangaratta is the turn-off for the Great Alpine Rd, which leads to the High Country, and is the home of the world-famous **Wangaratta Jazz Festival** (☎ 1800 803 944; www.wangaratta-jazz.org.au).

The **Wangaratta visitor information centre** (☎ 5721 5711, 1800 801 065; Murphy St; 🕑 9am-5pm; 💻) is in the old library.

Sights & Activities

At the **Wangaratta Cemetery** you'll find the grave of notorious bushranger Dan 'Mad Dog' Morgan. It contains most of Morgan's remains: his head was taken to Melbourne for a study of the criminal mind, and the scrotum was supposedly fashioned into a tobacco pouch.

A bicycle and walking trail, the **Murray to the Mountains Rail Trail**, connects Wangaratta with Beechworth and Bright using disused railway lines. Maps are available at the information centre.

Sleeping

Pinsent Hotel (☎ 5721 2183; 20 Reid St; s/d $35/70) This pub has had major renovations so the old rooms upstairs are as swish as at any motel. The bistro serves well-presented pub meals.

Millers Cottage (☎ 5721 5755; 26 Parfitt Rd; s/d from $62/68; 🅿 💻) This motel, on the northern side of town, has small comfortable rooms in a large garden, with a pool, playground and BBQ.

Gateway Wangaratta (☎ 5721 8399, 1800 033 439; www.wangarattagateway.com.au; 29-37 Ryley St; s/d/f from $109/119/144; 🅿 💻) At this modern motel there are good standard rooms and more-expensive suites with spas. Rooms are spacious, or head for the cocktail lounge, restaurant, dance floor, gym, spa or sauna. Disabled facilities are available.

Painters Island Caravan Park (☎ 5721 3380; Pinkerton Cres; sites per 2 people from $19, d cabin from $50; 🅿) Set in 10 hectares of lovely grounds on the banks of the Ovens River, you can lose yourself in this friendly place, just two

---

THE KELLY GANG

Ned Kelly is probably Australia's greatest folk hero. His life and death have been embraced as part of the national culture, and have inspired a range of artists, including author Peter Carey, who wrote *True History of the Kelly Gang,* and painter Sidney Nolan, who produced a series of iconic works.

Before he became a cult hero, Edward 'Ned' Kelly was a common horse thief. Born in 1855, Ned was first arrested when he was 14 and spent the next 10 years in and out of jails. In a shoot out at Stringybark Creek, Ned and his gang killed three police officers, and a reward was posted for their capture. The gang robbed banks at Euroa and Jerilderie, making a mockery of the police by locking them in their own cells and wearing their uniforms during the hold-up.

On 27 June 1880 the gang held 60 people captive in a hotel at Glenrowan. Surrounded by police, the gang were under siege for hours while wearing heavy armour made from plough-shares. Ned was shot in the legs and captured, and his gang, along with several of their hostages, were killed.

Ned Kelly was brought to Melbourne, tried and hanged on 11 November 1880. His last words were said to be 'Such is life.' His death mask, armour and the gallows on which he died are on display in the Old Melbourne Gaol (p480).

minutes from town. There's a playground, BBQ and camp kitchen.

Eating

Scribblers Coffee Lounge (☎ 5721 3945; 66 Reid St; meals $8-16; ✶ breakfast & lunch) This friendly spot with outdoor seating has a varied menu including pastas and interesting quiches, pies and cakes.

Rusty Dog Café (☎ 5722 4392; cnr Reid & Ovens Sts; mains $12-25; ✶ breakfast & lunch, dinner Tue-Sat) You'll feel right at home in this modern café, and you'll love the fresh salads, steaks, seafood baskets and variety of local wines.

Café Martini (☎ 5721 9020; 87 Murphy St; mains $10-22; ✶ dinner daily, lunch Mon-Sat) This big and bustling restaurant is known for its wood-fired pizzas. Eat upstairs or down, the food will still be good.

Vine Hotel (☎ 5721 2605; www.tourismInternet.com .au/wgvine.htm; Detour Rd; mains $12-24; ✶ lunch & dinner Wed-Sun) This charming old pub hasn't changed much since Ned Kelly and his gang used to drink here. After a meal, check out the small history museum in the basement.

Getting There & Away

Wangaratta train station is just west of the town centre in Norton St. Daily **V/Line** (☎ 13 61 96; www.vline.com.au) trains from Melbourne ($36) continue on to Wodonga ($14).

V/Line buses run daily from Wangaratta to Rutherglen ($6).

SHEPPARTON

☎ 03 / pop 56,500

Shepparton is the regional centre of the Goulburn Valley, and fruit-picking work is the main attraction. The **Shepparton visitor information centre** (☎ 5831 4400, 1800 808 839; Wyndham St; ✶ 9am-5pm) is at the southern end of the Victoria Park Lake. **McPherson Media** (☎ 5832 8000; 194 High St; per hr $6.60) offers Internet access.

Sights

Shepparton City Historical Museum (cnr High & Welsford Sts; adult/child $2/1; ✶ 1-4pm Sun or by appointment) is divided into sections devoted to transport, local agriculture, colonial clothing, shopping and communications. The huge 100-year-old four-faced post-office clock chimes on the hour.

Shepparton Art Gallery (☎ 5832 9861; Eastbank Centre, 70 Welsford St; ✶ 10am-4pm) has an impressive permanent collection of Australian art as well as regular temporary exhibitions.

The **Bangerang Keeping Place** (Parkside Dr; ✶ 9am-4pm Mon-Fri) has displays on the area's original Aboriginal owners.

Sleeping

Hotel Australia (☎ 5821 4011; cnr Maude & Fryers Sts; s/d $33/55) This grand yellow pub, with its wide protected verandas, has basic old rooms upstairs with their own exit down to a little courtyard. Live bands play here Thursday to Saturday nights.

Overlander Hotel-Motel (☎ 5821 5622; overland@ cv.quik.com.au; 97 Benalla Rd; s/d from $63/73; ✶ ✶) This looks like any big pub, but the motel units are spacious and quiet, with views of rolling paddocks. The central courtyard has a small pool and picnic area, and the dining room has a kids' play area.

Tirana Motel (☎ 5831 1766; 33 Wyndham St; s/d $78/88; ✶) This clean, well-run motel is probably the best value in town. The hosts are very friendly, and the high wall along the street blocks traffic noise.

Sherbourne Terrace Motel (☎ 5821 4977; 109 Wyndham St; s/d from $99/110; ✶ ✶) This large and modern motel has standard and VIP spa rooms, a bistro and a cocktail bar. The upstairs rooms here have attractive balconies and there's an outdoor pool in a pleasant garden.

Victoria Lake Holiday Park (☎ 5821 5431; info@ viclakeholidaypark.com.au; Wyndham St; sites per 2 people from $18, d cabin from $62) Right beside Victoria Lake, this friendly place has plenty of grass and trees, bicycle paths and walkways. New luxury cabins have balconies out to the lake.

Eating

Lemon Tree Café (☎ 5822 2300; 98 Fryers St; mains $13-19; ✶ breakfast & lunch Mon-Sat) It's a friendly

---

FRUIT PICKING

From January to April it's fruit-picking season, but start looking for work in December. Winter work in the vineyards is available from June to August. The **Worktrainers Harvest Office** (☎ 1800 802 277; 361 Wyndham St) arranges employment. Some orchards offer basic accommodation or tent sites.

VICTORIA

place with wonderful breakfast items such as French toast with bacon and maple syrup, and an interesting lunch menu with spicy lamb kofta.

Letizia's Café, Bar & Restaurant (☎ 5831 8822; 67 Fryers St; mains $18-24; ☺ breakfast, lunch & dinner) This open, friendly place has a pleasant casual air, but there's nothing casual about its Asian-influenced food. If you want Mod Oz, try the grilled pesto chicken.

Cellar 47 (☎ 5831 1882; 170 High St; mains $20-25; ☺ lunch & dinner Mon-Sat) With its sleek black-and-glass bar, this smart restaurant is a long-standing favourite. The menu includes Italian and Australian dishes.

Getting There & Away

Shepparton train station is east of the town centre. There are daily **V/Line** (☎ 13 61 96; www.vline.com.au) trains and buses to/from Melbourne ($28), and buses to/from Cobram ($10).

V/Line buses also connect with Wodonga ($29) and Benalla ($9) daily, and with Mildura ($48) and Bendigo ($12) three times a week.

NAGAMBIE

☎ 03 / pop 1300
Nagambie is on the shores of **Lake Nagambie**, created by the construction of the Goulburn Weir back in 1887. This area's main attractions are its wineries and water sports.

The **Nagambie visitor information centre** (☎ 5794 2647, 1800 444 647; www.nagambielakestourism.com.au; 145 High St; ☺ 9am-5pm) provides a great range of information, along with free tastings and a small shop selling souvenirs and maps.

Two of the best-known wineries in Victoria, **Tahbilk Winery** (☎ 5794 2555; ☺ 9am-5pm Mon-Sat, 11am-5pm Sun), off Goulburn Valley Hwy, and **Mitchelton Wines** (☎ 5794 2710, 5736 2222; Mitchellstown Rd; ☺ 10am-5pm), are just south of town. A great way to visit both these wineries is to take a cruise with **Goulburn River Cruises** (☎ 5794 2877; per person $19; ☺ Sep-May).

GIPPSLAND

Gippsland sprawls across the southeastern corner of Australia and is packed full of national parks, lakes, deserted coastline and some of the most diverse wilderness, scenery and wildlife on the continent. The western part is divided into the Latrobe Valley, a coal-mining and electricity-generating centre, and South Gippsland, which includes the beautiful Wilsons Promontory National Park. East Gippsland, backed by the wild forests of the Great Dividing Range, includes the Lakes District and the Wilderness Coast.

Getting There & Away

The two major routes through Gippsland are the Princes Hwy (which joins the M1 in Melbourne) and the South Gippsland Hwy. Many places of interest, such as Mallacoota, Marlo, Cape Conran and Bemm River, are off the Princes Hwy.

Most minor roads are unsealed and some in state parks are closed during the wetter winter months. Check road conditions with **Parks Victoria** (☎ 13 19 63; www.parks.vic.gov.au) and keep an eye out for logging trucks.

BUSES

V/Line (☎ 13 61 96; www.vline.com.au) has daily bus services along the Princes Hwy (A1) from Bairnsdale to Narooma in NSW and also Lakes Entrance via Lake Tyers (east of Lakes Entrance). Another service, which runs twice a week, follows the Princes Hwy as far as Cann River, then proceeds north to Canberra in the ACT. **Premier** (☎ 13 34 10) has daily services from Melbourne travelling along the Princes Hwy to Sydney.

There are also regular V/Line buses from Traralgon to Sale via Maffra; Melbourne to Yarram, which stop along the South Gippsland Hwy; and Melbourne to Inverloch, which stop along the Bass Hwy.

Omeo Buslines (☎ 03-5159 4231) runs between Bairnsdale and Omeo ($28) on weekdays.

TRAINS

Bairnsdale is the end of the V/Line train link from Melbourne. Daily services from Melbourne to Bairnsdale stop at all major towns along the Princes Hwy.

SOUTH GIPPSLAND

From Melbourne, the South Gippsland Hwy passes through the beautiful 'blue' rounded hills of the Strzelecki Ranges and is the quickest route to Wilsons Promontory. An alternative coastal route is even more scenic, with some stunning ocean views.

Korumburra

☎ 03 / pop 3040

The first sizable town along the South Gippsland Hwy is Korumburra, situated on the edge of the Strzelecki Ranges. **Prom Country Information Centre** (☎ 1800 630 704, 5655 2233; www.promcountrytourism.com.au; South Gippsland Hwy) is on the way out of town next to Coal Creek.

Coal Creek Heritage Village (☎ 5655 1811; www .coalcreekvillage.com.au; adult/child/family $11/6/30; ☻ 10am-4.30pm) is a reasonable re-creation of a 19th-century mining town. The V/Line coach stops outside.

South Gippsland Railway (☎ 1800 442 211, 5658 1111; adult/child/family return $12/7/35) runs heritage diesel trains along scenic tracks from Kor-

umburra to neighbouring towns on Sunday and public holidays (four services).

There are several wineries in the area including award-winning **Paradise Enough** (☎ 5657 4241;175 Stewart's Rd, Kongwak; ☻ 10am-5pm Thu-Mon), 16km from Korumburra, off Korumburra-Inverloch Rd.

WILSONS PROMONTORY NATIONAL PARK

The superb habitats and activities of the 'Prom', including more than 80km of walking tracks, some wonderful beaches and abundant wildlife, make it one of the most popular national parks in all of Australia. The wildlife found around Tidal River is very tame.

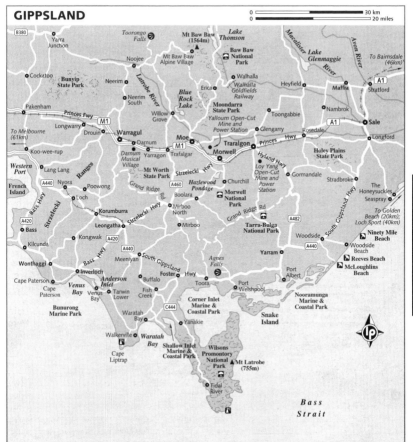

GIPPSLAND

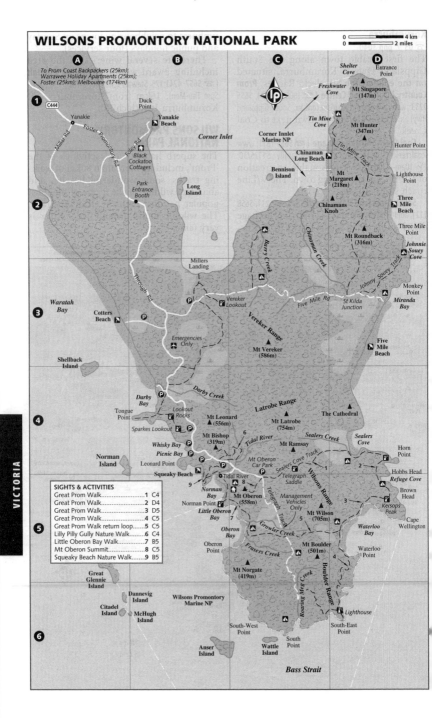

WILSONS PROMONTORY NATIONAL PARK

VICTORIA

Information

The only access road leads to **Tidal River** on the western coast, which has the Parks Victoria office and education centre, a petrol station, a general store (with Internet access), an open-air cinema (summer only), camp sites, cabins, lodges and facilities.

Parks Victoria (☎ 1800 350 552, 03-5680 9555; www.parkweb.vic.gov.au; Tidal River; ☒ 8am-4.30pm) in Tidal River takes accommodation reservations and issues camping permits for outside the Tidal River area. Day entry to the park is $9.30, which is included in camping fees.

Activities

BUSHWALKING

The Prom's diverse walking tracks will take you through swamps, forests, marshes, valleys of tree ferns and long beaches lined with sand dunes. The park office has details of walks, from 15-minute strolls to overnight and longer hikes. For some serious exploration, buy a copy of *Discovering the Prom* ($15).

The northern area of the park is much less visited. Most walks in this 'wilderness zone' are overnight or longer, and mainly for experienced bushwalkers. Wood fires are not permitted anywhere in the park.

Tours

Taking a tour is one of the best ways of seeing the wildlife, such as wombats, close up. **Bunyip Tours** (☎ 03-9531 0840; www.bunyiptours .com; 2-/3-/4-day tour $225/345/425) Runs all-inclusive ecofriendly hiking tours of the Prom from Melbourne. ISIC and IYHA members receive discounts.

High Spirit Outdoor Adventures (☎ 03-9391 8188; www.highspirit.com.au) Operates day tours ($80) to the Prom from Melbourne.

Sleeping

HOSTELS

Prom Coast Backpackers (☎ 03-5682 2171; http://gip psland.com/web/WarraweeHolidayApartments; 40 Station Rd, Foster; dm/d/f $25/60/75) While there are no hostels in the park, in nearby Foster this cosy renovated cottage has a small kitchen and lounge and sleeps 10. Ask the friendly owners about a lift to the Prom (around $10).

Warrawee Holiday Apartments (☎ 03-5682 2171; http://gippsland.com/web/WarraweeHolidayApartments; d/f from $80/100) These homely and spacious apartments are next door to Prom Coast Backpackers and under the same management.

HUTS, CABINS & UNITS

Black Cockatoo Cottages (☎ 03-5687 1306; www.black cockatoo.com; 60 Foley Rd, Yanakie; d $120) In nearby Yanakie, you can take in glorious views of the Prom without leaving your very comfortable bed in these private, stylish, self-contained cottages.

There are **self-contained huts** (4-6 beds from $55), two-bedroom **cabins** ($144) and **units** ($104) located in the park and booked through **Parks Victoria** (☎ 1800 350 552, 03-5680 9516).

CAMPING

Bookings are essential for Tidal River's 480 camp sites during holiday periods.

TOP FIVE PROM WALKS

From November to Easter a free shuttle bus operates between the Tidal River visitors' car park and the Mt Oberon car park (a nice way to start the Prom Circuit Walk). Return times and distances are given:

Great Prom Walk This is the most popular long-distance hike, a moderate 45km circuit across to Sealers Cove from Tidal River, down to Refuge Cove, Waterloo Bay, the lighthouse and back to Tidal River via Oberon Bay. Allow two to three days, and coordinate your walks with tide times, as creek crossings can be hazardous. It's possible to visit or stay at the lighthouse by prior arrangement with the park office.

Lilly Pilly Gully Nature Walk An easy 5km (two-hour) walk through heathland and eucalypt forests, with lots of wildlife. Or take the longer route through stringy-bark forest (6km, two to three hours).

Mt Oberon Summit Starts from the Telegraph Saddle car park. A moderate-to-hard 7km (2½-hour) walk, it's an ideal introduction to the Prom, and the panoramic views from the summit are excellent.

Little Oberon Bay An easy-to-moderate 8km (three-hour) walk over sand dunes covered in coastal tea trees; you'll be rewarded with beautiful views over Little Oberon Bay.

Squeaky Beach Nature Walk Another easy stroll of 5km returning through coastal tea trees and banksias to a sensational white-sand beach. Go barefoot on the beach to find out where the name comes from.

VICTORIA

During high season sites for up to three adults (or two adults and two children) and one car cost $20, plus $4.20 per extra adult and $6 per extra car. At other times, rates are slightly cheaper.

There are another 11 bush-camping areas around the Prom, all with pit or compost toilets and most with water. Overnight hikers need camping permits (adult/child $6.50/3.25), which should be booked ahead through the park office.

Getting There & Away

There's no direct public transport between Melbourne and the Prom, though Prom Coast Backpackers (see p601) in Foster, about 60km north of Tidal River, can usually organise a lift to the Prom for its guests (about $10).

WEST GIPPSLAND & THE LATROBE VALLEY

From Melbourne, the Princes Hwy follows the power lines past dairy country to their source in the Latrobe Valley. The region between Moe and Traralgon contains one of the world's largest deposits of brown coal, which is consumed by power stations at Yallourn, Morwell and Loy Yang.

Yarragon

If you stop to shop anywhere along the highway, make it Yarragon. The town has successfully reinvented itself over the years into a Gippsland mecca for quality art and gifts, and gourmet produce, and the area wears the moniker of **Gippsland Gourmet Deli Country** (www.gourmetgippsland.com).

Walhalla

☎ 03 / pop 23

Tiny Walhalla, 46km north of Moe, was one of Victoria's great gold-mining towns in the 19th century. Today just 23 people live here and, despite the inevitable heritage décor (the sepia-photo salesman has evidently been in town), it remains one of the most scenic of Victoria's historic towns.

WARNING

There are many mine shafts in the area so keep to the marked tracks.

SIGHTS & ACTIVITIES

Take the circuit walk anticlockwise from the information shelter as you enter town. This passes the main sights before climbing the hill to follow the old timber tramway and heading back down to the car park. The tramway also leads to the **Australian Alps Walking Track**, which goes to Canberra. There are other walks to Thomson Bridge, Poverty Point or on to the Baw Baw Plateau.

Long Tunnel Extended Gold Mine (☎ 5165 6259; adult/child $9/6.50), off Walhalla-Beardmore Rd, runs guided tours at 1.30pm weekdays and noon, 2pm and 3pm Saturday, Sunday and school holidays.

You can also take a 25-minute ride into Walhalla on the **Walhalla Goldfields Railway** (☎ 5126 4201, info line ☎ 9513 3969; adult/child/family return $15/10/35). Trains depart at 11.30am, 1.20pm and 3.10pm from Thomson Bridge on Wednesday, Saturday, Sunday and school holidays.

Copper Mine Adventure (☎ 5134 6875; www.mountaintopexperience.com; tour $15) operates rugged 1½-hour 4WD trips along old coach roads to a disused mine, on Wednesday and most weekends.

SLEEPING & EATING

There are good bush-camping areas along Stringer's Creek.

Rawson Village (☎ 5165 3200; 1 Pinnacle Dr, Rawson; lodge s/d from $34/48, motel d from $82) South of Walhalla, Rawson Village has high-standard accommodation for a healthy range of prices. Lodge rooms sleep up to six.

Walhalla Star Hotel (☎ 5165 6262; www.starhotel.com.au; Main Rd; d from $169, mains $19-23; ☯ dinner) The rebuilt historic Star offers stylish boutique-hotel accommodation with sophisticated designer décor and king-size beds. Nonguests should reserve a table at Parker's restaurant, within the hotel.

Windsor House (☎ 9882 5985, 5165 6237; www.windsorhouse.com.au; d incl breakfast from $150) The clock turns back more than a century when you step into this B&B with four-poster beds, open fires and a library of old books. This building was originally a guesthouse during Walhalla's heyday and has been restored to its former glory.

Walhalla Lodge Family Hotel (☎ 5165 6226; mains $12-15; ☯ lunch daily, dinner Wed-Mon) Prints of old Walhalla decorate this cosy one-room pub serving good-enough pub fare.

Miner's Café (☎ 5165 6227; dishes $4.50-10.50; ☺ lunch) This small café, next to the general store, also has takeaway food.

Grand Ridge Road

The winding Grand Ridge Rd traverses the top of the Strzelecki Ranges, running from midway between Warragul and Korumburra to midway between Traralgon and Yarram, providing a fabulous excursion through fertile farmland that was once covered with forests of giant mountain ash trees. Pick it up north of Korumburra or south of either Trafalgon or Moe. The only place of any size along the route is the pretty township of **Mirboo North**, home to Gippsland's only brewery, the unassuming **Grand Ridge Brewery** (☎ 03-5668 1647) in the historic Butter Factory building.

One of the last remnants of original southern Gippsland forest is tucked in a rainforest gully 30km south of Traralgon in the **Tarra-Bulga National Park**. Camping isn't allowed in the park, but you can stroll to the **Cyathea Falls** or picnic in the northern section, on Grand Ridge Rd, where there's a **visitor information centre** (☎ 03-5196 6166; ☺ 10am-4pm Sat, Sun & holidays) and the 2km **Fern Gully Nature Walk**.

THE LAKES DISTRICT

Gippsland's Lakes District is the largest inland waterway system in Australia. There are three main lakes that interconnect: Lake King, Lake Victoria and Lake Wellington. The 'lakes' are actually shallow lagoons, separated from the ocean by a narrow strip of sand dunes known as Ninety Mile Beach.

Sale

☎ 03 / pop 12,850

Apart from some nicely restored old buildings and a few new bars and restaurants, this once-busy port town, active during the paddle-steamer era, has little to excite the traveller. Sale is the centre of the **Gippsland Wetlands**, where lakes, waterways and billabongs harbour more than 130 species of water bird. Two kilometres south of Sale, on the South Gippsland Hwy, is the Sale Common Wildlife Refuge with a wetlands boardwalk.

The **Sale visitor information centre** (☎ /fax 5144 1108; www.gippslandinfo.com.au; 8 Foster St; ☺ 9am-5pm; ☐) is on the Princes Hwy, on the Melbourne side of town. For **Parks Victoria** (☎ 5144 3048; 1 Lacey St; ☺ Mon & Fri) turn right at Foster St into Guthridge St.

Ninety Mile Beach

Ninety miles (144km) of pristine and seamless sandy beach is backed by dunes, swamplands and lagoons, stretching from Seaspray to Lakes Entrance. The beach is great for surf fishing and walking but can be dangerous for swimming, except at Seaspray, where it's patrolled. There are kangaroos and emus here so drive slowly, especially at night.

Camping is permitted at designated sites between Seaspray and Golden Beach. Seaspray has general stores, the **Seaspray Caravan Park** (☎ 03-5146 4364; powered sites per 2 people $16, d cabins $48), the only park near the beach, and **Ronnie's Tea Rooms** (☎ 03-5146 4420; 13 Trood St; coffee & cake $5.50; ☺ Sat, Sun & holidays).

Kangaroos graze on front lawns at **Loch Sport**, surrounded by lake, ocean and bush, with some good swimming areas. The bright and friendly **Marina Hotel** (☎ 03-5146 0666; mains $15-24; ☺ lunch & dinner) has great sunset views and decent Tuscan-style seafood.

A spit of land surrounded by lakes and ocean, **Lakes National Park** covers coastal bushland and is reachable by road from adjoining Loch Sport, or by boat from Paynesville (5km).

There's a **Parks Victoria office** (☎ 03-5146 0278; ☺ variable hours) at the park entrance near Loch Sport. The only camping is at **Emu Bight** (sites for up to six people $14); book through the park office.

Mitchell River National Park

About 42km northwest of Bairnsdale, this park has some beautiful green valleys, camping areas and lovely hiking, including the two-day, 18km **Mitchell River Walking Track**. Its best-known feature is the **Den of Nargun**, a small cave that, according to Aboriginal stories, is haunted by a strange, half-stone creature, the Nargun.

Bairnsdale

☎ 03 / pop 10,670

Bustling Bairnsdale is the major town of this district. The **Bairnsdale visitor information centre** (☎ 1800 637 060, 5152 3444; www.egipps .vic.gov.au; 240 Main St; ☺ 9am-5pm) can book accommodation and there's also a **Parks Victoria** (☎ 5152 0600; 73 Calvert St) office here.

SIGHTS

The **Krowathunkoolong Keeping Place** (☎ 5152 1891; 37-53 Dalmahoy St; adult/child $3.50/2.50; ☯ 9am-5pm Mon-Fri), behind the train station, is a Koorie cultural centre that explores Gunai (Kurnai) daily life before and after white settlement.

On the edge of town, the **MacLeod Morass Boardwalk** is a stunning wetland reserve with walking tracks and bird hides.

Howitt Park is the starting point for the **East Gippsland Rail Trail**, a popular bike and walking track that leads northeast to **Bruthen**, 30km away, and now extends through state forest to Lakes Entrance.

SLEEPING & EATING

There are numerous motel options on the highway (Main St).

Riversleigh Country Hotel (☎ 5152 6966; fax 5152 4413; 1 Nicholson St; s/d incl breakfast from $114/159, lunch $12-19, dinner $21-25; ☯ lunch Thu-Fri, dinner Mon-Sat; ⊠) Elegant rooms at this Victorian-era boutique hotel have brass beds, crisp linen and antique furnishings to transport you back to a bygone era. Breakfast is served in the sunny conservatory.

Mitchell Gardens Holiday Park (☎ 5152 4654; http://gippsland.com/web/MGHP; powered/unpowered sites per 2 people $20/17, d cabin from $44) East of the town centre on the banks of the Mitchell River, this friendly park has shade for cabins and full sun for tents. Holiday units ($74), actually deluxe cabins, have river views.

Larrikin's Café Deli (☎ 5153 1421; 2 Wood St; breakfast $6-14, meals $9-16; ☯ breakfast & lunch Mon-Sat) This local bastion of fine food and coffee, in converted 1880s stables, has stunning views of farmland. Typical city-café fare with flair includes colourful vegetable stacks and silky-smooth lemon tart.

Metung

☎ 03 / pop 520

The unhurried charm of this picturesque village on Bancroft Bay is contagious. Its shoreline is dotted with jetties and small wooden craft.

The historic ketch **Spray** (☎ 0428 516 055; Metung Hotel Jetty; adult/child/family $32/10/74) runs 4½-hour picnic cruises (BYO lunch) to various

lake destinations; cruises depart at 11am daily and you can book tickets at Metung Village Store.

Boats ($110 per day) and yachts (from $1945 per week) are available from **Riviera Nautic** (☎ 5156 2243; www.rivieranautic.com.au; 185 Metung Rd).

For a dip, head to the safe swimming beach next to Lake King Jetty.

SLEEPING & EATING

Holiday homes and other accommodation are available through **Metung Accommodation** (Slipway Villas; ☎ 5156 2861; www.metungaccommodation.com).

Arendell Holiday Units (☎ 5156 2507; 30 Mairburn Rd; d/f $66/77; ⊠) These comfortable timber cottages are very 1970s and don't have water views but they sit a pleasant walk from the beach and town centre. Prices double during Christmas school holidays.

Metung Hotel (☎ 5156 2206; Kurnai Ave; meals $16-26; ☯ lunch & dinner) The pub takes prime position, with its large wooden terrace and garden overlooking Bancroft Bay – the perfect spot for an afternoon Guinness. It serves good pub food and the children's meals ($4.50) are the cheapest in Gippsland.

Little Mariners (☎ 5156 2077; 57 Metung Rd; meals $10-30; ☯ breakfast Fri-Sun, lunch Wed-Sun, dinner Tue-Sun) Book ahead for dinner at the town's most popular restaurant, serving quality Mod Oz cuisine, or drop in for a coffee and cake.

Lakes Entrance

☎ 03 / pop 5500

In season, Lakes Entrance is a packed-out tourist town, as witnessed by the ugly strip of motels, caravan parks and shops lining the Esplanade. Its saving grace is its picturesque location on the gentle waters of Cunninghame Arm, backed by sand dunes and small fishing boats.

INFORMATION

Hai Q (☎ 5155 4247; cnr Myer St & The Esplanade; ⊠)
Lakes Entrance visitor information centre (☎ 1800 637 060, 5155 1966; www.lakesandwilderness.com.au; cnr Princes Hwy & Marine Pde; ☯ 9am-5pm) Has plenty of information on the area.

ACTIVITIES

A footbridge crosses the Cunninghame Arm inlet from the east of town to the ocean and

Ninety Mile Beach. From December to Easter paddle boats, canoes and sailboats can be hired by the footbridge. Guided walks to spot nocturnal wildlife, in the company of an experienced naturalist, are run by **Wildlife at Night** (☎ 5156 5863; Wyungara Nature Sanctuary; adult/child/family $22/13/55).

Surfing lessons with equipment are available from the **Surf Shack** (☎ 5155 4933; 507 The Esplanade; 2hr lesson $40).

Several outfits organise cruises:

Corque (☎ 5155 1508) Popular 4½-hour lunch cruise to Wyanga Park Winery (adult $40, child $5 to $18), dinner cruises and Sunday brunch.

Mulloway Fishing Charters (☎ 5155 3304, 0427 943 154) Regular three-hour fishing cruises ($40) in the lake from the jetty opposite 66 Marine Pde.

Peels Tourist & Ferry Services (☎ 5155 1246; Post Office Jetty) Daily two-hour cruises (adult/child $26/13) exploring Reeves Channel, Bancroft Bay and Lake King. A daily four-hour cruise also runs to Metung ($39 with lunch) at 11am.

SLEEPING

Riviera Backpackers (☎ 5155 2444; www.yha.com.au; The Esplanade; dm from $19, s/d from $30/38; 🖳 🐀) The YHA, east of town, is a good, clean hostel with a large kitchen and pool table. V/Line and other buses stop nearby on the Esplanade.

Kalimna Woods (☎ 5155 1957; www.kalimnawoods .com.au; Kalimna Jetty Rd; d $95-140; 🐾) Retreat from the town centre, 2km away, to rainforest, gardens, possums, birds, wood fires and spas. Log cottages with timber furnishings and fluffy towels are spacious and very comfortable.

Goat & Goose (☎ 5155 3079; www.goatandgoose .com; 16 Gay St; d incl breakfast $130-160) Bass Strait views are maximised at this wonderfully unusual, multistorey, timber pole-frame house. The owners are friendly and the rooms (all with spas) are gorgeously quaint. No children.

Eastern Beach Caravan Park (☎ 5155 1581; powered/unpowered sites per 2 people $18/15) This park is refreshingly old style, with a bush setting by the Eastern Beach walking track into town (30 minutes). Prices almost double in peak season.

EATING & DRINKING

Fisherman's Co-op (☎ 5155 1688; Bullock Island; 🕙 9am-5pm) You'll find the coop on the right-hand side of Princes Hwy, when entering Lakes Entrance from the west. This is where the fishing boats unload their catch – fish, prawns and shellfish can be bought cheaply in the shop.

L'Ocean (☎ 5155 2253; 19 Myer St) There are a few excellent fish-and-chip shops in Lakes including this award-winning one, which caters for the gluten-free diet and vegetarian crowds.

Charnwood Antiques Café (☎ 5155 2348; cnr The Esplanade & Bulmer St; 🕙 breakfast & lunch) Cosily nestled between antiques and crafts, this café serves a mouthwatering selection of cakes and biscuits.

Nautilus (☎ 5155 1400; mains $23-47; 🕙 dinner Tue-Sat) Fine food (mainly caught by the local fishing fleet) and an exclusively Gippsland wine list dominate the menu in this glass-sided barge moored on the water.

Kalimna Hotel (☎ 5155 1202) For a drink with views, you can't beat this hotel, off the highway on the Melbourne side of Lakes Entrance.

EAST GIPPSLAND & THE WILDERNESS COAST

Much of this region wasn't cleared for agriculture and contains some of the most remote and spectacular national parks in the state, making logging in these ancient forests a hot issue.

Unexciting Orbost is the major town and gateway to the Snowy River and Errinundra National Parks, and the Wilderness Coast. The magnificent coastal areas of Cape Conran, Mallacoota and Croajingolong are all uncrowded, unspoiled and undeveloped.

Buchan

☎ 03 / pop 400

Buchan, a beautiful town in the foothills of the Snowy Mountains, is chiefly known for its spectacular limestone cave system.

SIGHTS & ACTIVITIES

Guided tours, alternating between **Royal Cave** and **Fairy Cave**, are run by **Parks Victoria** (☎ 5162 1900; adult/child/family $12/6/31). The rangers also offer hard-hat guided tours to **Federal Cave** during the high season.

Snowy River Expeditions (☎ 5155 9353; Karoonda Park, Gelantipy) runs one-, two- or four-day rafting trips on the Snowy ($130 per day all inclusive), abseiling or caving trips.

VICTORIA

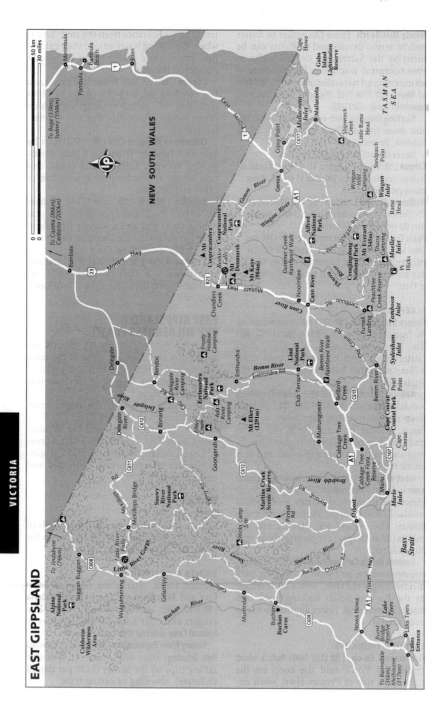

EAST GIPPSLAND

VICTORIA

Buchan Bus 'n' Freight (☎ 5155 0356; buchanbusn freight@hotmail.com; ☺ tours Nov-Apr) operates four-day East Gippsland Wilderness tours ($540) from Bairnsdale or Lakes Entrance visiting Buchan Caves and Snowy River and Errinundra National Parks.

SLEEPING & EATING
Buchan Lodge Backpackers (☎ 5155 9421; www.buchan lodge.com; Saleyard Rd; dm incl breakfast $20) There are good facilities here, including a fully equipped kitchen, large dining room and BBQ. It's a great spot for lounging about and taking in the country views.

Ontos (☎ 5155 0275; ontos@net-tech.com.au; Gelantipy Rd, West Tree; units s/d incl breakfast $40/50, cabins incl breakfast $80; ☺ lunch & dinner) Ontos' rustic wooden cabins have pot-belly stoves and sleep up to six. Healthy breakfasts include homemade bread, and dinner is also served.

Natural Healing & Spiritual Centre (☎ 5155 0245; 2337 Gelantipy Rd, West Tree; s/d incl meals $125/250) Overlooking bush and mountains from a lovely timber home, this is the place for a complete de-stress. Vegetarian meals, taken on bush walks, and kinesiology natural-healing treatments are the go.

Buchan Caves Caravan Park (☎ 5162 1900; Buchan Caves Reserve; powered/unpowered sites per 2 people $16/$12, d cabin $55; ☒) This picturesque camping ground has a camp kitchen and open fireplaces.

Caves Hotel (☎ 5155 9203; mains $14-19; ☺ dinner daily, lunch Tue-Sun) A pretty timber pub serving well-recommended steaks.

Snowy River National Park
Dominated by gorges that are carved by the Snowy River, this is one of Victoria's most isolated and spectacular parks.

The main access roads are Buchan Jindabyne Rd from Buchan, and Bonang Rd (C612) from Orbost, and they are joined by McKillops Rd in the north, crossing the Snowy River at **McKillops Bridge**.

About 25km before the bridge, on the Gelantipy Rd, are **Little River Falls** and **Little River Gorge** lookouts. The latter, a 500m-deep gorge, is the deepest in Victoria.

Bushwalking and canoeing are popular but be prepared as conditions can change suddenly. The classic canoe or raft trip down the Snowy River, from McKillops Bridge to a finish point near Buchan, takes at least four days.

Either side of McKillops Bridge are camp sites, toilets and fireplaces, and access to sandy river beaches.

For information contact the park offices at **Deddick** (☎ 02-6458 0290), **Buchan** (☎ 03-5162 1900; adult/child/family $12/6/31), **Orbost** (☎ 03-5161 1222; cnr Nicholson & Salisbury Sts) or **Bairnsdale** (☎ 03-5152 0600; 73 Calvert St).

SLEEPING & EATING
Karoonda Park (☎ 03-5155 0220; Gelantipy Rd, Karoonda Park, Gelantipy; dm/d incl breakfast $24/58, cabins incl breakfast $95, 3-course meals $14; ☒ ☐ ☒) This cattle and sheep property and horse-riding ranch at Gelantipy, 40km north of Buchan, also has YHA accommodation. Fully catered packages are available and the owners may have work going. Activities available include abseiling ($20 per hour), horse riding ($30 per hour), wild caving ($30 per 1½ hours) and white-water rafting.

Tranquil Valley Lodge & Delegate River Tavern (☎ 02-6458 8009; tranquility_lodge@bigpond.com; Bonang Hwy, Delegate River; sites/cabins from $15/50, d cabin with/without bathroom $72/50, meals $13-15) Tranquil Valley Lodge, behind the Delegate River Tavern, has a terrific bush setting with lots of activities in the vicinity, including fishing and canoeing. Some log cabins have river frontage. Basic pub grub is aimed at meat eaters.

Errinundra National Park
The Errinundra Plateau contains Victoria's largest cool-temperate rainforest. The national park covers just 25,100 hectares of the rainforest, but really should be much larger – unfortunately many areas around the park are still being logged.

The Bonang Rd passes the western side of the park, while the Errinundra Rd, from Club Tce, runs through the centre. Both roads are unsealed, steep, winding and often closed in winter – check with **Parks Victoria** (☎ 02-6458 1456; ☺ 8am-4.30pm Mon-Fri) at Bendoc, or at **Cann River** (☎ 03-5158 6351) or **Orbost** (☎ 03-5161 1222; cnr Nicholson & Salisbury Sts).

Camping areas are at Delegate River on the Gap Rd connecting Bonang Rd with Bendoc, Frosty Hollow on the Hensleigh Creek Rd, Ada River on the Errinundra Rd, and Goongerah. There's a petrol station and general store at Bonang, a pub at Bendoc and another pub and cabins at Delegate River (see above).

VICTORIA

Orbost

☎ 03 / pop 2100

Orbost, by the Snowy River, is mainly a service centre for the surrounding farming and forest areas. There's an edgy feel in this town, where tensions between environmentalists and loggers can run high. The Princes Hwy passes just south of the town, the Bonang Rd, heads north towards the Snowy River and Errinundra National Parks, and Marlo Rd follows the Snowy River south to Marlo, and continues along the coast to Cape Conran.

The Orbost Newsagent doubles as the **Orbost visitor information centre** (☎ 5154 2424; 152-156 Nicholson St). Close by, **Parks Victoria** (☎ 5161 1222; cnr Nicholson & Salisbury Sts) has information on road conditions if you're heading up into the forests.

SLEEPING

Commonwealth Hotel (☎ 5154 1077; 159 Nicholson St; s/d without bathroom incl breakfast $30/40, mains $15-21; ☻ lunch & dinner Mon-Sat) Predictable pub rooms with shared lounge are on offer at this sprawling old hotel. The bar downstairs is a popular local hang-out.

Snowy River Cottage (☎ 0438 083 014; snowyriver cottage@dodo.com.au; 6 Nicholson St; s/d $80/100) This refurbished old-style cottage, set in a pretty garden opposite Forest Park, has the nicest accommodation close to the town centre. There's a two-night minimum stay.

Marlo

☎ 03 / pop 350

Marlo is a sleepy settlement at the mouth of the Snowy River, 15km south of Orbost.

Tabbara Lodge (☎ 5154 8231; 1 Marlo Rd; d from $50; ☻) has self-contained wood-lined rooms, decorated with country crafts in shady gardens containing BBQs and a playground. It's on the right as you enter town.

Marlo Hotel & Country Retreat (☎ 5154 8201; 17 Argyle Pde; d from $120, mains $16; ☻ lunch & dinner) offers indulgent suites with king-size beds, comfy sofas and antique furniture, and with either a spa or fireplace. A massive veranda overlooks the jaw-dropping spot where the Snowy River flows into the sea. The restaurant has a varied bistro-style menu.

Cape Conran Coastal Park

Cape Conran is one of the most beautiful spots in the state. The 19km coastal route

from Marlo to Cape Conran is especially pretty and there are some great beaches, including the safest surfing beach in the region. A rough track 4km east leads from the cape to the mouth of the Yeerung River, which is another good spot for swimming, canoeing and fishing. There are no shops at Cape Conran.

SLEEPING

Parks Victoria (☎ 03-5154 8438; www.conran.net.au; Yeerung Rd) manages the accommodation at Cape Conran.

Banksia Bluff Camping Area (sites up to 4 people $15) Right on the foreshore, the camping ground has toilets, cold showers and fireplaces; bring drinking water if you don't like the taste of bore water.

Cape Conran Cabins & Lodge (4-8–person cabins from $100) These well-equipped, large cabins resemble oversized cubby houses with cosy nooks for sleeping. They have an airy, beachcomber feel and are just a short walk to the beach. BYO linen.

Cann River

☎ 03 / pop 250

Cann River is at the junction of the Princes and Monaro Hwys heading north into NSW. There are petrol stations, motels, a supermarket, a hotel and a caravan park here, as well as several places to grab a quick bite. Consult the **Parks Victoria office** (☎ 5158 6351) about roads in the Croajingolong National Park and walking within the park.

Coopracambra National Park

Remote and undeveloped Coopracambra (38,300 hectares) retains its original ecosystem virtually intact and supports many rare and endangered species. The landscape is rugged and spectacular, with deep gorges where the earliest fossil evidence of four-footed creatures was discovered. The only access is a 4WD track, which runs from the Monaro Hwy to Genoa. Beehive Falls are 2km from the Monaro Hwy, 28km north of Cann River.

The beautifully furnished, ecofriendly **Coopracambra Cottage** (☎ 03-5158 8277; www.mal lacoota.com; d $60) is 16km northwest of Genoa. The pastureland setting has emus, kangaroos, wombats, many birds and mountain views. The owners can take visitors on tours through the National Park.

Gipsy Point

☎ 03

Idyllic Gipsy Point is a tiny settlement at the head of the Mallacoota Inlet.

The friendly **Gipsy Point Lodge** (☎ 1800 063 556, 5158 8205; www.gipsypoint.com; self-contained cottages/guesthouses per person incl meals $105/145, 3-course meals $55; ☷ dinner; ☷), in a peaceful setting overlooking the river and gardens, has canoes and rowboats for guests, and motorboat hire ($75 per day). Nonguests should book ahead for the well-recommended dinner.

Mallacoota

☎ 03 / pop 1040

Low-key Mallacoota, which is surrounded by the Croajingolong National Park, becomes a crowded family holiday spot at Christmas and Easter.

Parks Victoria (☎ 5161 9500; cnr Buckland & Allan Drs; ☷ 9.30am-noon & 1-3.30pm Mon-Fri) is opposite the main wharf. **Mallacoota Information Shed** (☎ 5158 0800; www.mallacoota.com; Main Wharf; ☷ 10am-4pm), the green shed on the wharf, is operated by friendly volunteers and has a handy map of the 7km Mallacoota walking track.

ACTIVITIES

The 300km shoreline of Mallacoota Inlet is backed by national park. There are plenty of great short **walks** (from 30 minutes to four hours) around town, the inlet, and in the bush.

A number of operators offer **cruises** and boat hire:

Mallacoota Hire Boats (☎ 0438 447 558) Just left of the main wharf; hires out canoes ($15 per hour) and motor boats (half/full day $70/110). No licence is required.

Porkie Bess (☎ 5158 0109, 0408 408 094; 2hr cruise $25) A 1940s wooden boat offering fishing trips and cruises around the lakes, and ferry services for hikers ($10 per person, minimum four).

Wilderness Coast Ocean Charters (☎ 0418 553 809) Runs trips to Gabo Island ($60) and the Skerries ($100) to view the seal colony off Wingan Inlet. Whales are sometimes spotted between September and November.

SLEEPING

Prices vary significantly with the seasons; book ahead for Christmas or Easter.

Mallacoota Hotel Motel & Backpackers (☎ 5158 0455; inncoota@speedlink.com.au; 51-55 Maurice Ave; dm $22, motel s/d/f from $55/66/75; ☷ ☷) It's nothing

fancy but offers good value for this pack-'em-in tourist town. Motel rooms are large while backpackers' rooms are a bit shabby but share a good kitchen.

Karbeethong Lodge (☎ 5158 0411; www.karbeethonglodge.com.au; 16 Schnapper Point Dr; d with/without bathroom from $85/65, f $95/75) A sense of serenity prevails as you rest on the broad verandas of this early-1900s timber guesthouse overlooking Mallacoota Inlet. The large guest lounge and dining room have open fires and period furnishings; pastel-toned bedrooms are small.

Adobe Mudbrick Flats (☎ 5158 0329; www.adobeholidayflats.com.au; 17 Karbeethong Ave; d/f $65/80) At this creative and comfortable mud-brick village, the eco-rule of not feeding the wildlife isn't followed, so expect a squawk-fest of birds outside your door waiting to be fed. You may even see the elusive lyrebird. The flats sleep four people; linen costs extra.

Mallacoota Houseboats (☎ 5158 0775; houseboats low/high season 3-night minimum $750/1250, extra night $100/200) These clean and cosy houseboats are a divine way to explore Mallacoota's waterways. They sleep up to six and have a kitchen, toilet and shower. There's a BBQ on the deck for a bit of alfresco dining.

Mallacoota Foreshore Caravan Park (☎ 5158 0300; camppark@vicnet.net.au; powered/unpowered sites per 2 people $18/14, caravan d $50) Grassy sites extend along the foreshore, with sublime views of the lake and its resident population of black swans and pelicans. Prices increase by 50% at Christmas and Easter.

EATING

Croajingolong Café (☎ 5158 0098; Allan Dr; mains $6.50-11; ☷ breakfast & lunch Tue-Sun) Overlooking the inlet, this friendly café is a perfect place to linger over a latte, and watch the world move slowly by. The menu offers some innovations and they do great fruit smoothies. Try the veggie brekky ($10) or the chicken with sage and mushroom on a bed of noodles ($8). No credit cards.

Pub Bistro (☎ 5158 0455; 51-55 Maurice Ave; mains $14-26; ☷ lunch & dinner) For hearty meals. Sample porterhouse in seafood sauce ($26) and the rich profiterole mousse cake ($7.50). Bands play at the pub regularly in summer.

Tide Restaurant (☎ 5158 0100; cnr Maurice Ave & Allan Dr; mains $17-25) Has a long history of serving quality food from its prime lakeside spot but was closed at the time of writing.

VICTORIA

GETTING THERE & AWAY

Mallacoota is 23km off the Princes Hwy. Buses stop at Genoa, where some accommodation places and tour operators may pick you up by arrangement. At the time of writing, the **Mallacoota Information Shed** (☎ 5158 0800) was planning a shuttle-bus service.

Croajingolong National Park

The coastal wilderness park of Croajingolong (87,500 hectares) is one of Australia's finest national parks. It stretches for about 100km from Bemm River to the NSW border and includes unspoiled beaches, inlets and forests. The 200m sand dunes at Thurra are the highest on the mainland. Mallacoota Inlet is the largest and most accessible area. There's plentiful wildlife in the park, including huge goannas.

Walkers must be suitably equipped for long-distance walking, with sufficient maps and information on conditions. Contact

Parks Victoria (Cann River ☎ 03-5158 6351, Mallacoota ☎ 03-5158 0219) for information, road conditions, overnight hiking and camping permits, and track notes. All access roads from the Princes Hwy, except Mallacoota Rd, are unsealed and can be very rough; check conditions with Parks Victoria.

The main camping areas are at Wingan Inlet, Shipwreck Creek, Thurra River and Mueller Inlet. You may need to bring water so check with Parks Victoria. You'll also need to book during the main holiday seasons; camping fees cost up to $17 a site.

Point Hicks was the first part of Australia to be spotted by Captain Cook in 1770. Experience the windy and isolated ruggedness that the lighthouse keepers used to know, plus get a seagull's view when you climb to the top of the remote but basic **Point Hicks Lighthouse** (☎ 03-5158 4268; pointhicks@bigpond .com; up to 8 people from $210), with ocean views and wood fires. There's a two-night minimum stay; bring all your own food.

Tasmania

Tasmania has slowly come to realise that it has a certain rarity in abundance: huge, undeveloped areas that are empty, wild and beautiful. Lately the state's tourism officials have been making a lot of noise in their efforts to put Tassie (as it's affectionately known) on the tourist map, and it seems to be working. And well it should – it may be an island off an island at the bottom of the world, but Tasmania's diversity and relatively small size make it an outstanding holiday destination, particularly for those with a penchant for the great outdoors, gourmet produce, friendly locals or an intriguing history.

History buffs will enjoy the rich legacy of Tasmania's abject convict era that is evident throughout the state, and can bed down at night in historic cottages reborn as gracious guesthouses. City-slickers visiting Hobart, and to a lesser extent Launceston, will be thrilled to find all the urban delights they seek (plush hotels, gastronomic temples, a thriving arts scene), but with a lot less attitude and loads more charm than many mainland destinations. Foodies will rejoice over the wines, the cheeses, the fruits – and especially the seafood. And few visitors will fail to be entranced by natural vistas such as Wineglass Bay on the Freycinet Peninsula, majestic Cradle Mountain, or the Nut looming over Stanley.

Although Tasmania provides plenty of excuses to sit back and do little more than roll your eyes across such fine landscape, that same landscape lends itself to any number of outdoor pursuits, from bushwalking to white-water rafting. You haven't fully experienced Tasmania until you've ventured into the mountains and onto the rivers, oceans and cliffs that are this beautiful island's greatest attractions.

HIGHLIGHTS

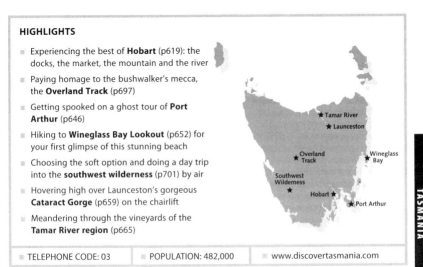

- Experiencing the best of **Hobart** (p619): the docks, the market, the mountain and the river
- Paying homage to the bushwalker's mecca, the **Overland Track** (p697)
- Getting spooked on a ghost tour of **Port Arthur** (p646)
- Hiking to **Wineglass Bay Lookout** (p652) for your first glimpse of this stunning beach
- Choosing the soft option and doing a day trip into the **southwest wilderness** (p701) by air
- Hovering high over Launceston's gorgeous **Cataract Gorge** (p659) on the chairlift
- Meandering through the vineyards of the **Tamar River region** (p665)

★ Tamar River
★ Launceston
★ Overland Track
Wineglass Bay
Southwest Wilderness ★
Hobart ★
★ Port Arthur

TASMANIA

▪ TELEPHONE CODE: 03   ▪ POPULATION: 482,000   ▪ www.discovertasmania.com

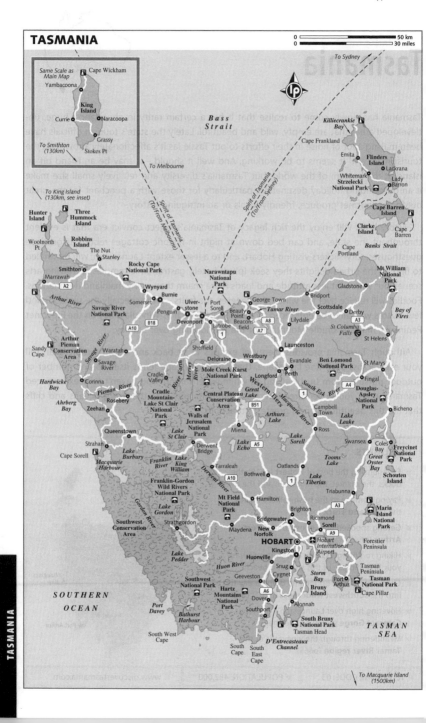

HISTORY

The first European to see Tasmania was the Dutch navigator Abel Tasman, who arrived in 1642 and named it Van Diemen's Land after the governor of the Dutch East Indies.

European contact with the Tasmanian coast became more frequent after the First Fleet arrived at Sydney Cove in 1788, mainly because ships heading to the colony of New South Wales from the west had to sail around Tasmania. In 1798 Matthew Flinders circumnavigated Van Diemen's Land, proving it was an island.

In 1803 Risdon Cove, on the Derwent River, became the site of Australia's second colony. One year later the settlement was moved to the present site of Hobart. Although convicts were sent with the first settlers, penal settlements weren't built until later: at Macquarie Harbour (Strahan) in 1822, at Maria Island in 1825 and at Port Arthur in 1830. For more than three decades, Van Diemen's Land was the most feared destination for British convicts.

In 1856 transportation to Van Diemen's Land was abolished. In an effort to escape the stigma of its dreadful penal reputation, Van Diemen's Land officially became known as Tasmania, after the Dutch navigator.

Gold was discovered in the 1870s and prospectors randomly explored most of the state in search of mineral wealth. The subsequent exploitation of natural resources inevitably clashed with environmental preservation. This clash became a source of public debate in the 1960s and '70s, when bushwalkers and conservationists unsuccessfully fought to stop the flooding of Lake Pedder for hydroelectric schemes. Again in the 1980s this issue became hugely controversial – this time the burgeoning Green movement successfully campaigned against flooding the wild Franklin River for similar purposes. The uneasy balance between conservation interests and industry (especially logging and mining) continues today.

Aboriginal People

Since European settlement the story of Tasmania's indigenous people has been an unhappy one. The state's Aborigines became separated from the mainland more than 10,000 years ago when sea levels rose due to the thawing of the last Ice Age. Geographically isolated, their culture diverged from that of their mainland counterparts.

Tasmania's European settlers fenced off sections of fertile land for farming. As the Aborigines lost more and more of their traditional hunting grounds, battles erupted between Aborigines and settlers. In 1828 martial law was declared by Lieutenant-Governor Arthur, and Aboriginal tribes were forced at gunpoint from districts settled by whites.

Between 1829 and 1834 all remaining indigenous Tasmanians were resettled in a reserve on Flinders Island, to be 'civilised' and Christianised. Most of them died of despair, poor food or respiratory disease. Of the 135 taken to the island, only 47 survived to be transferred to Oyster Cove in Tasmania's south in 1847. Within 32 years, the entire Aboriginal population at Oyster Cove had perished.

European sealers had been working in Bass Strait since 1798 and, although they occasionally raided tribes along the coast, their contact with Aboriginal people was mainly based on trade. Aboriginal women were also traded and many sealers settled on Bass Strait islands with these women and had families.

By 1847 an Aboriginal community, with a lifestyle based on both Aboriginal and European ways, had emerged on Flinders and other islands in the Furneaux group. Although the last full-blooded Tasmanian Aborigine died in the 19th century, the strength of this community helped save the race from total extinction. Today thousands of descendants of members of this community still live in Tasmania.

GEOGRAPHY & CLIMATE

Tasmania's population is concentrated on the north and southeast coasts, where the undulating countryside is rich and fertile and the coast is accessible and inviting. By contrast, the southwest and west coasts are wild and remote. For much of the year, large seas batter the west coast and rainfall is high. Inland, the rich forests and mountains of Tasmania's west and southwest form one of the world's last great wilderness areas, almost all of it a World Heritage–listed region.

Tasmania has four distinct seasons, although storms can bring wintry conditions at any time of year. In summer the days are generally warm rather than hot, while the nights are mild. Conditions are usually good up until March, when temperatures drop. The rest of autumn is generally characterised by cool, sunny days and occasional frosty nights. Winter is wet, cold and stormy, particularly in the west. Overcast days are common in the east, despite its lower rainfall. Snow lies on the higher peaks but is usually only deep enough for the state's two ski resorts to operate spasmodically. Spring is windy and storms still sweep the island, but in between the sun shines and gradually warmth returns.

INFORMATION

The main tourism authority is **Tourism Tasmania** (☎ 03-6230 8235, 1800 806 846; www.discover tasmania.com), which disseminates loads of information and has a useful website.

On the mainland, government-operated **Tasmanian travel centres** (☎ 1300 655 145; www .tastravel.com.au; Sydney Map pp94-5; 60 Carrington St; Melbourne Map pp472-3; 259 Collins St) provide information on all things Tasmanian and are able to book accommodation, tours and transport.

In Tasmania itself, there are visitor information centres in major towns. At these centres, visitors should pick up the free bimonthly newspaper *Tasmanian Travelways* (www.travelways.com.au). It contains comprehensive state-wide listings of accommodation, activities, public transport and vehicle hire, and an indication of current costs.

Other useful information sources include the following:

Parks & Wildlife Service (PWS; ☎ 1300 315 513; www.parks.tas.gov.au) Great website detailing walks, camp sites, activities and other facilities in the state's magical national parks and reserves.

Royal Automobile Club of Tasmania (RACT; ☎ 13 27 22; www.ract.com.au) Provides roadside assistance in the event of car breakdown, plus directories of accommodation and a range of maps.

NATIONAL PARKS

If you want high-quality national parks, you've come to the right place! A greater percentage of land is national park or reserve in Tasmania than in any other Australian state. Tasmania currently has 19 national parks, comprising more than 1.4 million hectares, or nearly 21% of the state's total land area.

In 1982 Tasmania's four largest national parks (Southwest, Franklin-Gordon Wild Rivers, Cradle Mountain-Lake St Clair and Walls of Jerusalem) and much of the Central Plateau were placed on the Unesco World Heritage list. This listing acknowledges that these parks comprise one of the last great temperate wilderness areas left in the world.

An entry fee is charged for all of Tasmania's national parks; a pass is needed whether there is a collection booth or not. Passes are available at most park entrances, at many visitor information centres, on board the *Spirit of Tasmania* ferries, and at the state-wide offices of **Service Tasmania** (☎ 1300 135 513; www.service.tas.gov.au).

A 24-hour pass to any number of parks costs $20 per car (including up to eight passengers) or $10 per individual (arriving by bus, or for bushwalkers, cyclists and motorcyclists). The best value for most travellers is the eight-week pass, which costs $50 per vehicle or $30 per individual.

The **Parks & Wildlife Service** (PWS; www.parks.tas .gov.au) website is excellent. In the peak season (mid-December to mid-February) PWS rangers run free family-friendly activities at the major national parks, including walks, talks and slide shows.

ACTIVITIES

For information on activities, adventure tourism and various tour operators, the following are good online resources:

Networking Tasmanian Adventures (www.tasman ianadventures.com.au) Lists a number of operators and activities, categorised as either 'wild' (eg scuba diving, white-water rafting, abseiling) or 'mild' (eg fishing, scenic flights, river cruises).

Parks & Wildlife Service (www.parks.tas.gov.au) Click on 'outdoor recreation'.

Tourism Tasmania (www.discovertasmania.com) Click on 'Things to Do & See'.

Bushwalking

The best-known of Tasmania's many superb bushwalks is the Overland Track through Cradle Mountain-Lake St Clair National Park (p697). Lonely Planet's *Walking in Australia* has a large section on some of Tasmania's best (longer) walks. Even if you're not going bush for days on end, you can still experience Tassie's famed wilderness on foot – the excellent *Tasmania's Great Short Walks* brochure (free from visitor information centres) lists 60 of the state's best short walks, with durations from 10 minutes to all day. Travellers interested in long or short walks should check out the website of the **Parks & Wildlife Service** (www.parks .tas.gov.au/recreation/bushwalking.html).

On long walks, it's extremely important to remember that, in any season, a fine day can quickly deteriorate, so warm clothing, waterproof gear, a tent and a compass are vital. Tasmap produces an excellent series of maps available from Hobart, or at **Service Tasmania** (Map p624; www.service.tas.gov.au; ☎ 1300 135 513; 134 Macquarie St) and the **Tasmanian Map Centre** (Map p624; ☎ 03-6231 9043; www.map-centre.com.au; 100 Elizabeth St), as well as state-wide outdoor-equipment stores.

Loads of books have been written specifically for walkers in Tasmania. There are many excellent shops selling bush gear, and a few youth hostels hire out equipment and/ or guided bushwalking tours.

Caving

Tasmania's caves are widely considered to be among the most impressive in Australia. The caves at Hastings (p643), Gunns Plains (p675) and Mole Creek (p673) are open to the public daily; both Mole Creek and Hastings offer the chance to get down and dirty on adventure caving tours.

Fishing

All you need to know to go fishing in Tasmania is to be found at www.fishonline.tas .gov.au.

The sparsely populated Lake Country, on Tasmania's Central Plateau, is a region of glacial lakes, crystal-clear streams and world-class fishing. It's home to the state's best-known spots for both brown and rainbow trout. There are dozens of operators that can help you organise guides, lessons or fishing trips – the website of **Trout Guides & Lodges Tasmania** (www.troutguidestasmania.com.au) is a great starting point.

Rafting, Canoeing & Kayaking

Tasmania is well known for its challenging white-water rafting on the wild Franklin River (p696).

Sea-kayaking is popular from Kettering (p638), on the Freycinet Peninsula (p652) and around the docks of Hobart (p626).

Rock Climbing & Abseiling

Some excellent cliffs have been developed for rock climbing, particularly along the east coast, where the weather is usually best. The Organ Pipes on Mt Wellington (near Hobart; p625), the Hazards at Coles Bay (p652) and Launceston's Cataract Gorge (p659) offer excellent climbing. The magnificent rock formations and coastal cliffs on the Tasman Peninsula are spectacular, but may be impossible to climb if the ocean swell is too big.

If you want to rock climb or abseil with an experienced instructor, try one of the following companies:

Aardvark Adventures (☎ 0408 127 714; www.aardvark adventures.com.au)

Freycinet Adventures (☎ 03-6257 0500; www .adventurestasmania.com)
Tasmanian Expeditions (☎ 1300 666 856, 03-6334 3477; www.tas-ex.com)

Sailing

There are many good anchorages in the D'Entrecasteaux Channel south of Hobart, a wide, deep and beautiful place to sail. For casual berths in Hobart (overnight or weekly), contact the **Royal Yacht Club of Tasmania** (☎ 03-6223 4599; www.ryct.org.au), in Sandy Bay, or the **Hobart Ports Corporation** (☎ 03-6235 1000; www.hpc.com.au), which manages berths in the heart of town.

If you're an experienced sailor, hire a yacht from **Yachting Holidays** (☎ 03-6224 3195; www.yachtingholidays.com.au), based in Hobart. Charter of a six-berth vessel is $650 per day, with reduced rates for long rentals or in the off-peak (May to November) period. Skippered charter is also available.

Scuba Diving

There are some excellent scuba-diving sites on the east coast, and around Rocky Cape on the north coast; there are also shipwrecks around King and Flinders Islands.

TOURING YOUR TASTEBUDS

One of the highlights of travelling in Tasmania is sampling fine local fare, especially fresh seafood, luscious fruits, great dairy products and excellent cool-climate wines. If you intend expanding your waistline while you're here, two recommended publications are *Graeme Philip's Guide to the Wine & Food of Tasmania*, updated annually (around $15 from many visitor information centres, newsagents and bookshops), and *Tasmania Wine & Food – Cellar Door & Farm Gate Guide*, a free brochure published by Tourism Tasmania and available at most visitor information centres and online (www .discovertasmania.com – click on 'things to do & see', then 'wine & food'). Both publications have details of the best restaurants, cafés, wineries and farm stores around the state, classified by region, plus details of wine and food annual events. The Tourism Tasmania brochure also has a helpful chart detailing when particular foods are in season.

Diving courses are considerably cheaper than on the mainland. **Dive Tasmania** (☎ 03 6265 2251; divetas@eaglehawkdive.com.au) is an industry organisation with information or a number of affiliated diving businesses Otherwise, contact dive operators in Eaglehawk Neck (p644), Bicheno (p654), King Island (p702) and Flinders Island (p704) Equipment can also be rented by licensed divers from dive shops located in Hobart and Launceston.

Skiing

Despite Tassie's southerly latitude, snowfalls tend to be light and unreliable. There are two minor ski resorts: Ben Lomond (p669) 60km southeast of Launceston, and Mt Mawson in Mt Field National Park (p637) 80km northwest of Hobart. Both offer cheaper, though much less-developed, ski facilities than the main resorts in Victoria and New South Wales.

Surfing

Tasmania has plenty of good surf beaches Close to Hobart, the best spots are Clifton Beach and the surf beach en route to South Arm. The southern beaches of Bruny Island (p639), particularly Cloudy Bay, are also good. The east coast from Bicheno north to St Helens has good surf when conditions are favourable. The greatest spot of all is Marrawah (p680) on the west coast; the waves here are often huge as the ocean is uninterrupted all the way to South America.

Websites to check on surf reports and conditions are www.surftasmania.com and www.tassiesurf.com.

Swimming

The north and east coasts have plenty of sheltered white-sand beaches offering excellent swimming, although the water can be rather cold (read: freezing!).

Our favourite spots for beach-bumming include Wineglass Bay (p652) and the stunning beaches of the Freycinet Peninsula, the long and inviting Binalong Bay outside St Helens (p656), and the small but perfectly formed Boat Harbour Beach (p679).

There are also pleasant beaches near Hobart, such as Bellerive and Sandy Bay, but these tend to receive some urban pollution, so it's better to head further south towards Kingston and Blackmans Bay, or east to

Seven Mile Beach, for safe swimming. On the west coast, the surf can be ferocious and the beaches are not patrolled.

TOURS

Many travel agents can help you arrange a package deal from the mainland that usually includes transport to Tasmania (either by air or sea), car rental and accommodation. Contact Tourism Tasmania or the travel centres in Sydney and Melbourne (see p614).

Once you're in Tasmania, there are operators who can guide you to the highlights, and many more who can offer a wilderness experience or activity-based tour. Most trips depart from Hobart, but some operators have tours out of Devonport and Launceston. Many businesses are listed in the relevant sections of this chapter. Some other suggestions:

Bottom Bits Bus (☎ 1800 777 103, 03-6229 3540; www.bottombitsbus.com.au) Day trips out of Hobart from $89, or a three-day tour ($345) taking in the far south.

Island Cycle Tours (☎ 1300 880 334, 03-6234 4951; www.islandcycletours.com) Guided cycling trips – day trips from Hobart, budget-minded walking and cycling tours (from one to 10 days), and 'indulgence' trips (three to seven days).

Island Escape Tours (☎ 1800 133 555, 03-6344 9799; www.islandescapetours.com) Launceston-based company offering day trips ($75 to $110) and longer tours. Offers participants the chance to break a tour and rejoin the next bus.

Tasmanian Expeditions (☎ 1300 666 856, 03-6334 3477; www.tas-ex.com) Excellent range of activity-based tours, from half a day to 16 days, with a choice of bushwalking, river-rafting, rock climbing, cycling and kayaking, or a combo of these.

Tiger Trails (☎ 03-6234 3931; www.tigertrails.green .net.au) Green-focused group offering guided walks in areas such as the Tarkine wilderness, Maria Island and along the South Coast Track.

Under Down Under (☎ 1800 064 726, 03-6362 2237; www.underdownunder.com.au) Nature-based, backpacker-friendly trips, including a two-day tour into the Tarkine wilderness ($259).

GETTING THERE & AWAY

Stringent rules are in place to protect the disease-free status of Tasmania's agriculture. Visitors must discard all plants, fruit and vegetables prior to their arrival (even if they're only travelling from mainland Australia).

Air

There are no direct international flights to/from Tasmania. Airlines with services between Tasmania and the Australian mainland include the following:

Jetstar (☎ 13 15 38; www.jetstar.com.au) Direct flights from Melbourne, Sydney, Brisbane and Adelaide to Hobart; also from Melbourne, Sydney and Brisbane to Launceston.

Qantas (☎ 13 13 13; www.qantas.com.au) Direct flights from Sydney and Melbourne to Hobart, and from Melbourne to Launceston. QantasLink (the regional subsidiary) offers flights from Melbourne to Burnie/Wynyard and Devonport.

Regional Express (REX; ☎ 13 17 13; www.regional express.com.au) Flies from Melbourne to Devonport, Burnie/Wynyard and King Island.

Virgin Blue (☎ 13 67 89; www.virginblue.com.au) Direct flights from Melbourne, Sydney, Brisbane and Adelaide to Hobart, and from Melbourne and Sydney to Launceston.

Regular domestic fares are available on Qantas, while Virgin Blue and Jetstar offer some good bargains, usually (but not always) cheaper than Qantas. Lowest one-way prices from Melbourne to Tassie are in the $69 to $150 range; from Sydney costs $89 to $160, from Brisbane $149 to $200, and from Adelaide $129 to $155.

There are also air links from Tasmania to King Island (p703) and Flinders Island (p704).

Boat

There are three *Spirit of Tasmania* ferries operated by **TT-Line** (☎ 13 20 10; www.spiritof tasmania.com.au); two cruise nightly in either direction between Melbourne and Devonport (10 hours), the third sails generally twice per week between Sydney and Devonport (21 to 22 hours).

All fares depend on whether you're travelling in the peak (mid-December to late January), shoulder (late January to April, and September to mid-December) or off-peak season (May to August), and there's a range of cabin options. Child, student, pensioner and senior discounts apply. Some cabins are wheelchair-accessible.

If you're prone to seasickness, be warned that Bass Strait can be very rough!

Tasmania ferry terminals details: **Devonport** (The Esplanade, East Devonport), **Melbourne** (Station Pier, Port Melbourne), **Sydney** (47-51 Hickson Rd, Darling Harbour; entry via Gate D8N).

TASMANIA

MELBOURNE–DEVONPORT

At 9pm year-round, overnight ferries leave from Melbourne and Devonport, arriving at their destinations at 7am. Additional daytime sailings are scheduled during the peak and shoulder seasons (from mid-December to April). Prices (per adult) are as follows:

Fare type	Peak season	Shoulder season	Off-peak season
cruise seat	$145	$115	$108
4-berth cabin	$215	$196	$187
tw cabin	$260	$220	$210
daytime sailings (seats only)	$145	$99	n/a
standard vehicles & campervans up to 5m length	$55	$10	$10
bicycles	$6	free	free

SYDNEY–DEVONPORT

In 2004 TT-Line began sailing between Sydney and Devonport. At the time of research, the future of this service was in doubt due to low passenger numbers. Services range from one sailing a week in either direction from June to August, to three per week over the Christmas and New Year period. Further changes may be on the cards; it's best to check the current schedule on the website.

Unlike the Melbourne ferries, Sydney fares include a buffet dinner and brunch.

Fare type	Peak season	Shoulder season	Off-peak season
dm-style bed	$270	$255	$230
4-berth cabin	$420	$400	$360
tw cabin	$490	$465	$420
standard vehicles & campervans up to 5m length	$55	$10	$10
bicycles	$6	free	free

GETTING AROUND
Air

Air travel within the state is not common. Of use to bushwalkers may be the air services to/from the southwest. **Par Avion** (☎ 03-6248 5390; www.paravion.com.au) and **Tasair** (☎ 03-6248 5088, 1800 062 900; www.tasair.com.au) fly between Hobart and remote Melaleuca for around $150 one way.

There are also air links from Tasmania to King Island (p703) and Flinders Island (p704).

Bicycle

Tasmania is a good size for exploring by bicycle and you can hire touring bikes in both Hobart (p635) and Launceston (p665). If you plan to cycle between Hobart and Launceston via either coast (the east coast is a favourite cycling destination), count on it taking 10 to 14 days. For a full circuit of the island, you should allow 18 to 28 days.

If you're planning a trip, the website of **Bicycle Tasmania** (www.biketas.org.au) is a good source of information. Click on 'rides by region' for details of two- and three-week circuits.

Bus

Tasmania has a reasonable bus network connecting major towns and centres, but weekend services are infrequent.

The main bus lines are **Redline Coaches** (☎ 03-6336 1446, 1300 360 000; www.tasredline.com.au) and **TassieLink** (☎ 03-6271 7320, 1300 300 520; www.tassielink.com.au), and between them they cover most of the state. TassieLink's *Main Road Express* is designed to work with the Bass Strait ferry schedules; it provides an early-morning express service from Devonport to Launceston and Hobart, and an afternoon service in the opposite direction to meet evening boat departures.

To give some idea of the fares and travel times around the state, a one-way trip from Devonport to Launceston costs around $18 (1½ hours); Hobart to Launceston around $27 (2½ hours); Hobart to Queenstown is $52 (five hours); Hobart to Dover $17 (1¾ hours); and Launceston to Bicheno $26 (2½ hours).

There are smaller operators offering useful bus services on important tourist routes (eg between Bicheno and Coles Bay, or within the Cradle Mountain-Lake St Clair region); details of these are given in the relevant sections of the chapter.

TRAVEL PASSES

TassieLink has an Explorer Pass for seven/10/14/21 days that must be used within 10/15/20/30 days and costs $172/205/237/280. The pass is valid on all scheduled services for unlimited kilometres and can be bought from most travel agents, or directly from TassieLink. If you intend to buy an Explorer Pass, ask for timetables in advance or check TassieLink's website and plan your itinerary carefully.

Redline offers its own form of pass, the Tassie Pass, with unlimited travel on its services for seven/10/14/21 days at a cost of $135/160/185/219. The Redline network is not as comprehensive as that of TassieLink, so it's definitely worth checking Redline's websites and timetables to ascertain the worth of the pass before you purchase.

Car & Campervan
There's no doubt that travelling by car is the best option in Tasmania. Although you can bring cars from the mainland, renting may be cheaper (particularly for shorter trips); rates are considerably lower here than on the mainland. Before you decide, find out if you'll be covered for driving on unsealed roads (a number of Tasmania's natural attractions lie off such roads).

Large international firms such as Avis, Budget and Thrifty have booking desks at airports and offices in major towns. They have standard rates from about $70 to $80 for high-season, multi-day hire of a small car. By booking in advance and choosing smaller cars, rates can be as low as $60 per day for one week's hire (outside the high season).

Small local firms rent older cars for as little as $35 a day, depending on the season and length of rental. It's normal for these smaller companies to ask for a bond of upwards of $300. With some companies you can collect your car from the airport or ferry terminal. Some operators:

Lo-Cost Auto Rent (www.locostautorent.com) Hobart (☎ 03-6231 0550); Launceston (☎ 03-6334 6202); Devonport (☎ 03-6427 0796)

Rent-a-Bug (www.rentabug.com.au) Hobart (☎ 03-6231 0300); Launceston (☎ 03-6334 3427); Devonport (☎ 03-6427 9444)

Selective Car Rentals (☎ 03-6234 3311; www .selectivecarrentals.com.au) Office in Hobart.

Campervans and motorcycles can also be rented:

Tasmanian Campervan Hire (☎ 1800 807 119, 03-6248 9623; www.tascamper.com)

Tasmanian Motorcycle Hire (☎ 03-6391 9139; www .tasmotorcyclehire.com.au)

> ### WARNINGS FOR DRIVERS
> There are a few road hazards to be aware of as you cruise around the state. Watch out for the wildlife and, if possible, avoid driving between dusk and dawn as this is when marsupials are most active (you'll undoubtedly notice lots of roadkill on your travels). One-lane bridges on country roads, and log trucks piled high and speeding around sharp corners, also demand caution. Finally, in cold weather be wary of 'black ice', an invisible layer of ice over the bitumen, especially on the shaded side of mountain passes.

HOBART

☎ 03 / pop 128,600

Hobart is Australia's second-oldest city and its southernmost capital. Straddling the mouth of the Derwent River and backed by the towering bulk of Mt Wellington, Hobart has embellished its rich colonial heritage and splendid natural beauty with the youthful, lively atmosphere of numerous festivals and inner-city bars and restaurants. Its attractive Georgian buildings, busy harbour, relaxed populace and serene surrounding districts make it one of Australia's most stress-free and enjoyable capitals.

HISTORY
The first inhabitants of the area were the semi-nomadic Aboriginal Mouheneer tribe. The first European colony in Tasmania was founded in 1803 at Risdon Cove, but a year later it was decided that a site 10km below Risdon and on the opposite shore was a better place to settle. Hobart began as a village of tents and huts with a population of 262 Europeans (178 of whom were convicts).

ORIENTATION
Hobart is sandwiched between the steep hills of Mt Wellington and the wide Derwent River. The city centre is fairly small and easy to navigate, with its streets (many with one-way traffic only) arranged in a grid pattern around the Elizabeth St Mall; the visitor information centre, banks and the main post office are on Elizabeth St, and the main shopping area extends west from the mall.

Salamanca Pl, a row of Georgian warehouses, is along the southern waterfront, and just south of this is Battery Point, Hobart's well-preserved early colonial district. If you follow the river south from Battery Point you'll come to Sandy Bay, the site of Hobart's university and the landmark Wrest Point Hotel & Casino.

The northern side of the city centre is bounded by the recreation area known as the Domain (short for Queen's Domain), which includes the Botanical Gardens. From here the Tasman Bridge crosses the river to the eastern suburbs and the airport (16km from the city centre).

Maps

The visitor information centre can supply basic maps. The best maps of Hobart are the *Hobart & Surrounds Street Directory* ($18) and the capital maps in the UBD *Tasmania Country Road Atlas* ($30). You can usually purchase these and other good maps at larger newsagents and bookshops.

Travellers with disabilities can get a copy of the useful *Hobart CBD Mobility Map* at the visitor information centre; it's a guide to the relevant facilities and access.

Sources for maps in Hobart:

Service Tasmania (Map p624; ☎ 1300 135 513; www.service.tas.gov.au; 134 Macquarie St)

Tasmanian Map Centre (Map p624; ☎ 6231 9043; www.map-centre.com.au; 100 Elizabeth St) Stocks a range of maps to guide bushwalking exploits.

Visitor information centre (Map p624; ☎ 6230 8233; tasbookings@tasvisinfo.com.au; cnr Davey & Elizabeth Sts; 🕑 8.30am-5.30pm Mon-Fri, 9am-5pm Sat, Sun & public holidays)

INFORMATION

Bookshops

Fullers (Map p624; ☎ 6224 2488; www.fullersbookshop.com.au; 140 Collins St) Great range of literature and travel guides, plus a café upstairs.

Hobart Book Shop (Map p624; ☎ 6223 1803; 22 Salamanca Sq) Excellent range of Tasmania-specific titles and works by Tassie writers.

Tasmanian Map Centre (Map p624; ☎ 6231 9043; www.map-centre.com.au; 100 Elizabeth St) Specialises in maps and guidebooks.

Wilderness Society Shop (Map p624; ☎ 6234 9370; Shop 8, The Galleria, 33 Salamanca Pl) Environmental publications, wildlife posters, videos, maps and calendars.

Emergency

Police, fire & ambulance (☎ 000)

Police (Map p624; ☎ 6230 2111; 37-43 Liverpool St)

Internet Access

Drifters Internet Café (Map p624; ☎ 6224 6286; Shop 9/33 Salamanca Pl)

Mouse on Mars (Map p624; ☎ 6224 0513; 27 Salamanca Pl)

Pelican Loft (Map p624; ☎ 6234 2225; 1st fl, 35a Elizabeth St)

Service Tasmania (Map p624; ☎ 1300 135 513; www.service.tas.gov.au; 134 Macquarie St) Free 30-minute access.

HOBART IN...

Two Days

Start with a stroll around the city's oldest and prettiest neighbourhood, **Battery Point** (p622) – morning tea at **Jackman & McRoss** (see the boxed text, p632) will sustain you for exploration of the stores and galleries of nearby **Salamanca Place** (p622). Spend the afternoon brushing up on history at the **Tasmanian Museum & Art Gallery** (p623) before a promenade along the **waterfront** (p631), followed by a fresh seafood dinner.

On day two stretch your legs and take in the fantastic views from **Mt Wellington** (p625), then come down to earth with dinner and drinks along the **North Hobart restaurant strip** (p633).

Four Days

Follow the two-day itinerary, then venture north to the **Cadbury factory** (p623), followed by lunch at **Moorilla Estate** (p625) – these can be done as part of a **river cruise** (p628). Walk off any over-indulgence at the lovely, leafy **Botanical Gardens** (p625).

If you're feeling energetic, day four could see you taking on the **'pedal 'n' paddle'** challenge (p626) – descending Mt Wellington by bike, followed by kayaking around the docks – or taking an easy day trip to nearby **Richmond** (p636) or **Mt Field National Park** (p637).

TASMANIA

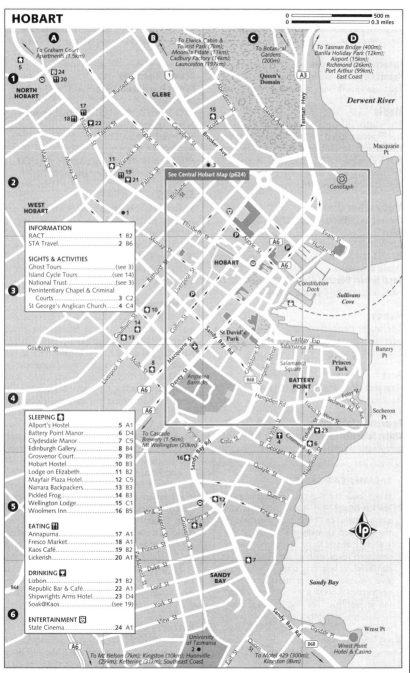

HOBART

| 0 | | 500 m |
| 0 | | 0.3 miles |

INFORMATION
RACT..................................1 B2
STA Travel..........................2 B6

SIGHTS & ACTIVITIES
Ghost Tours..........................(see 3)
Island Cycle Tours..................(see 14)
National Trust.......................(see 3)
Penintentiary Chapel & Criminal
  Courts..............................3 C2
St George's Anglican Church......4 C4

SLEEPING
Allport's Hostel...................5 A1
Battery Point Manor................6 D4
Clydesdale Manor...................7 C5
Edinburgh Gallery..................8 B4
Grosvenor Court....................9 B5
Hobart Hostel.....................10 B3
Lodge on Elizabeth................11 B2
Mayfair Plaza Hotel...............12 C5
Narrara Backpackers...............13 B3
Pickled Frog......................14 B3
Wellington Lodge..................15 C1
Woolmers Inn......................16 B5

EATING
Annapurna.........................17 A1
Fresco Market.....................18 A1
Kaos Café.........................19 B2
Lickerish.........................20 A1

DRINKING
Lizbon............................21 B2
Republic Bar & Café...............22 A1
Shipwrights Arms Hotel............23 D4
Soak@Kaos.........................(see 19)

ENTERTAINMENT
State Cinema......................24 A1

See Central Hobart Map (p624)

NORTH HOBART

GLEBE

WEST HOBART

HOBART

BATTERY POINT

SANDY BAY

Derwent River

Queen's Domain

Botanical Gardens

St David's Park

Princes Park

Battery Pt

Macquarie Pt

Sullivans Cove

Constitution Dock

Salamanca Square

Anglesea Barracks

University of Tasmania

Wrest Point Hotel & Casino

Wrest Pt

Sandy Bay

To Graham Court Apartments (1.5km)

To Elwick Cabin & Tourist Park (7km); Moonlila Estate (11km); Cadbury Factory (14km); Launceston (197km)

To Tasman Bridge (400m); Barilla Holiday Park (12km); Airport (15km); Richmond (26km); Port Arthur (99km); East Coast

To Cascade Brewery (1.5km); Mt Wellington (20km)

To Mt Nelson (7km); Kingston (10km); Huonville (29km); Kettering (31km); Southeast Coast

To Motel 429 (300m); Kingston (8km)

Cenotaph

TASMANIA

State Library (Map p624; ☎ 6233 7529; 91 Murray St) Offers 30-minute sessions free for Australians, $5.50 for international visitors.

Internet Resources
Hobart City (www.hobartcity.com.au)
Tasmania's South (www.tasmaniasouth.com)

Media
The visitor information centre stocks lots of free Tassie tourist publications that invariably highlight Hobart attractions. Hobart's main newspaper, the *Mercury*, is good for discovering what's on where – the Thursday edition lists entertainment options.

Medical Services
Chemist on Collins (Map p624; ☎ 6235 0257; 93 Collins St; ◷ daily)
City Doctors Surgery & Travel Clinic (Map p624; ☎ 6231 3003; 93 Collins St; ◷ Mon-Sat) Access through Chemist on Collins.
Royal Hobart Hospital (Map p624; ☎ 6222 8423; 48 Liverpool St; ◷ 24hr) Use Argyle St entry for emergencies.

Money
The major banks have large branches on or near the Elizabeth St Mall, plus branches in many suburbs.

Post
Main post office (Map p624; cnr Elizabeth & Macquarie Sts)

Tourist Information
Visitor information centre (Map p624; ☎ 6230 8233; tasbookings@tasvisinfo.com.au; cnr Davey & Elizabeth Sts;

◷ 8.30am-5.30pm Mon-Fri, 9am-5pm Sat, Sun & public holidays) Houses loads of brochures, maps and information, plus a booking service for the entire state (booking fee charged).

Travel Agencies
Qantas Travel Centre (Map p624; ☎ 6237 4900; 130 Collins St)
RACT (Map p621; ☎ 6232 6300, 13 27 22; www.ract.com.au; cnr Murray & Patrick Sts)
STA Travel (Map p621; ☎ 1300 360 960; Student Union Bldg, University of Tasmania, Sandy Bay)
YHA (Map p624; ☎ 6234 9617; yhatas@yhatas.org.au; 1st fl, 28 Criterion St) YHA's Tasmanian head office.

SIGHTS
Most of Hobart's main sights are in or near the city centre and waterfront area, largely within walking distance of each other. There are also a few must-see historic houses, wineries and a brewery on the outskirts of town, plus the mountain that looms over it all, Mt Wellington.

Salamanca Place
The row of beautiful sandstone warehouses on the harbour-front at Salamanca Place (Map p624) is a prime example of Australian colonial architecture. Dating back to the whaling days of the 1830s, these warehouses were the centre of Hobart Town's trade and commerce. Today, they have been tastefully developed to house restaurants, cafés and shops selling everything from vegetables to antiques. Visitors can enjoy the obvious tourist appeal of eating, drinking and browsing, or go behind the scenes to find the vibrant and creative arts community based here.

The nonprofit **Salamanca Arts Centre** (SAC; Map p624; ☎ 6234 8414; www.salarts.org.au; Salamanca Pl) is housed in seven sandstone warehouses east of Salamanca Sq and is home to more than 75 arts-related organisations and individuals, including retail outlets, galleries, artists' studios, performing arts venues and public spaces.

To reach Battery Point from Salamanca Pl, climb up **Kelly's Steps**, wedged between two warehouses about halfway along the main block of buildings.

Battery Point
Behind Princes Wharf and Salamanca Pl is the historic core of Hobart, the old port area known as Battery Point (Map p624).

> **SALAMANCA MARKET**
>
> Every Saturday the open-air **Salamanca Market** (Map p624; ◷ 8.30am-3pm Sat) is held along Salamanca Pl, and browsing through the hundreds of stalls is a feature of any visit to Hobart. Many stalls offer locally produced items such as jams and sauces, handmade accessories, creative woodwork and ceramics, and occasional attention-getting curios or collectibles. There's a buzzing atmosphere, entertainment provided by buskers and other street performers while you devour local produce from market stalls or nearby cafés, and excellent people-watching. Don't miss it!

TASMANIA

Its name comes from the gun battery that stood on the promontory by the guardhouse (1818). During colonial times this area was a colourful maritime village.

Today Battery Point's pubs, churches, conjoined houses and narrow winding streets have been lovingly preserved and are a delight to wander around. Highlights of the area include **Arthur Circus**, a circle of quaint little cottages built around a village green, and **St George's Anglican Church** (Map p621; Cromwell St). To help with your exploration, purchase the *Battery Point and Sullivan's Cove Trail of Discovery* ($2) pamphlet from the visitor information centre.

Narryna Heritage Museum (Map p624; ☎ 6234 2791; 103 Hampden Rd; adult/child $6/3; ☙ 10.30am-5pm Tue-Fri, 2-5pm Sat & Sun, closed Jul) is a fine Georgian sandstone mansion built in 1836, set in beautiful grounds and containing a treasure-trove of domestic colonial artefacts.

Historic Buildings

One of the things that makes Hobart exceptional among Australian cities is its wealth of remarkably well-preserved old buildings. There are more than 90 buildings classified by the National Trust and 60 of these, featuring some of Hobart's best Georgian architecture, are on Macquarie and Davey Sts. More information can be obtained from the local office of the **National Trust** (Map p621; ☎ 6223 5200; www.tased.edu.au/tasonline/nattrust/; cnr Brisbane & Campbell Sts; ☙ 9am-1pm Mon-Fri).

The court rooms, cells, tunnels and gallows of the **Penitentiary Chapel & Criminal Courts** (Map p621; ☎ 6231 0911; cnr Brisbane & Campbell Sts; tours adult/child/family $8/6/16; ☙ 10am, 11.30am, 1pm, 2.30pm) can be explored via the excellent National Trust–run tours. One-hour **ghost tours** (☎ 0417 361 392; adult/child $8.80/5.50; ☙ after sunset) are also held here most nights; they're popular, so bookings are essential.

Close to the city centre is **Parliament House** (Map p624; Murray St), built in 1835 and originally used as a customs house. Hobart's prestigious **Theatre Royal** (Map p624; 29 Campbell St) was built in 1837 and is the oldest theatre in Australia; see p634 for details.

There are free 20-minute tours behind the scenes of Hobart's **Town Hall** (Map p624; ☎ 6238 2711; Macquarie St; ☙ tours 2.45pm Tue, 10.45am Thu), built in the 1860s. The tours depart from the town hall's foyer – turn up five minutes before the start time.

Museums

The rewarding **Tasmanian Museum & Art Gallery** (Map p624; ☎ 6211 4177; www.tmag.tas.gov.au; 40 Macquarie St; admission free; ☙ 10am-5pm) incorporates Hobart's oldest building, the Commissariat Store (1808). The museum section features an Aboriginal display and relics from the state's colonial heritage, while the gallery has a collection of Tasmanian colonial art. Free guided tours take place at 2.30pm Wednesday to Sunday.

The **Maritime Museum of Tasmania** (Map p624; ☎ 6234 1427; www.maritimetas.org; 16 Argyle St; adult/child/family $6/4/16; ☙ 10am-5pm), in the historic Carnegie building, has an interesting, salt-encrusted collection of photos, paintings, models and relics highlighting Tasmania's shipping past. Upstairs from the museum is the **Carnegie Gallery** (admission free; ☙ 10am-5pm), exhibiting contemporary Tasmanian art, craft, design and photography.

The most unexpected attraction at Moorilla Estate, a vineyard and restaurant 12km north of town, is the world-class **Moorilla Museum of Antiquities** (off Map p621; ☎ 6277 9999; www.moorilla.com.au; 655 Main Rd, Berriedale; admission free; ☙ 10am-4pm), displaying a wealth of antiquities brought together from private collections. Displays include mosaics dating from the Roman Empire, sculptures and tribal art from Africa, gold jewellery and pre-Columbian figures from Central America, and an excellent Egyptian section featuring a mummy case dating from around 600 BC.

Tastes of Hobart

Visitors can admire Tassie's gastronomic prowess by sampling locally produced edibles at the following popular attractions.

CADBURY CHOCOLATE FACTORY

This attraction is a must for sweet-tooths. The **Cadbury factory** (off Map p621; ☎ 6249 0333, 1800 627 367; www.cadbury.com.au; Cadbury Rd, Claremont; adult/child/family $12.50/6.50/31.50) offers guided tours weekdays except public holidays, every half-hour from about 8am to 2.30pm (subject to demand; bookings essential). Fully enclosed footwear is required. Participants get to enjoy samples along the way, and can buy low-priced products at the completion of the tour. The factory is some 15km north of the city centre; many companies offer day trips and river cruises that incorporate this tour (see p628), but you can also book directly with Cadbury and make your own way there.

CASCADE BREWERY

Australia's oldest brewery, **Cascade** (off Map p621; ☎ 6224 1117; 140 Cascade Rd; tours adult/child/family $16/7/38; ⏰ tours 9.30am, 10am, 1pm & 1.30pm Mon-Fri except public holidays), was established in its photogenic location on the southwestern edge of the city centre in 1832. It's still in use today, producing tasty beverages (beer and soft drinks) for nationwide consumption. Brewery tours last 1½ hours, involve plenty of stair climbing, and include free samples at the end. Visitors should wear

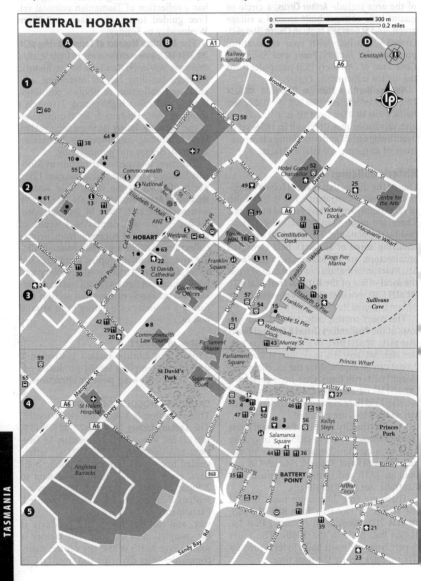

CENTRAL HOBART

flat, enclosed shoes and long trousers (no shorts or skirts); bookings are essential.

MOORILLA ESTATE
Moorilla Estate (off Map p621; ☎ 6277 9900; www .moorilla.com.au; 655 Main Rd, Berriedale; ☼ 10am-5pm) can be found in the suburbs around 12km north of Hobart's centre, on the banks of the Derwent River. It's a fascinating place with a number of reasons for visiting – its vineyard, restaurant (open for lunch only), super-swish accommodation and stunning museum (p623). At the estate's new tasting rooms you can sample and purchase some top-quality wines (including excellent pinot noir).

Natural Attractions
Just by the Tasman Bridge, the small but beguiling **Royal Tasmanian Botanical Gardens** (off Map p621; admission free; ☼ 8am-6.30pm Oct-Mar, 8am-5.30pm Apr & Sep, 8am-5pm May-Aug), established in 1818, features more than 6000 exotic and native plant species. After wandering through the flora, you can explore their world in more detail in the **Botanical Discovery Centre** (☎ 6234 6299; admission free, donations welcome; ☼ 9am-5pm), which also houses a gift shop, kiosk and restaurant.

Hobart is dominated by 1270m-high **Mt Wellington**, which has fine views and many good walking tracks – the *Mt Wellington Walks* map ($4.40; available at the visitor information centre) has all the details. The mountain's summit is about 22km out of town: to get here, you can either drive up winding roads, take a guided tour, or travel on local bus 48 or 49 to Fern Tree at the base of the mountain and from here it's an often-stunning walk to the top (five to six hours return, via the Springs and the Organ Pipes).

Many tour companies include Mt Wellington in their bus-tour itineraries (see p627); another option is the **Mt Wellington Shuttle Bus Service** (☎ 0417 341 804; per person $25), which departs from central Hobart three times daily. City pick-ups can be arranged, but bookings are essential.

See Kayaking on p626 for information on bike trips down the mountain.

There are also wonderful views from **Mt Nelson**, a good alternative when Mt Wellington is in cloud. A restaurant is beside the old signal station here, and there are also barbecues and picnic tables.

ACTIVITIES
Cycling
A useful navigational tool is the *Hobart Bike Map* (around $4), available from the visitor information centre and most bike shops. It contains details of the city's cycle paths and road cycling routes.

If you fancy a ride, hire a bicycle from central **Bike Hire Tasmania (Appleby Cycles)** (Map

TASMANIA

p624; ☎ 6234 4166, 0400 256 588; www.bikehiretasmania
.com.au; 109 Elizabeth St; ⊗ Mon-Sat). It offers city or
touring bikes by the hour, day or week, with
city bikes from $7/20 per hour/day (touring
bikes available from $252 per week).

Island Cycle Tours (Map p621; ☎ 1300 880 334, 6234
4951; www.islandcycletours.com; 281 Liverpool St), operating out of the Pickled Frog backpack-
ers, organises a great range of guided trips.
Try the popular three-hour descent of Mt
Wellington ($65, including transport to the
summit, bikes and safety equipment), a one-
day cycle to Mt Field ($120), or five days
exploring the east coast (from $690). It also
hires out bikes and gear (touring bikes from
$30/140 per day/week),

Kayaking

Kayaking around the docks in Hobart,
particularly at twilight, is a lovely way to
sightsee. Your best bet is **Island Cycle Tours**
(Map p621; ☎ 1300 880 334, 6234 4951; www.islandcycle
tours.com; 281 Liverpool St; adult/child incl meal $100/95;
⊗ daily Dec-Mar), which offers half-day 'pedal 'n'
paddle' combo trips. Tours run other times
according to demand (minimum numbers
apply), and involve a descent of Mt Wellington on two wheels, and a two-hour paddle
around the waterfront. You can do just the
paddling for $50.

WALKING TOUR

No surprises here – this amble through
Hobart's prime sightseeing locations starts
at **Salamanca Place** (p622), the town's tourist hub.

While port activity has largely moved
away from the Salamanca area, restoration
work has preserved one of Hobart's best
vistas. The sandstone Georgian warehouses
were built from about 1835, replacing earlier
wooden structures. The majority of these
warehouses are now home to trinket-filled
speciality and craft shops, and restaurants,
cafés and bars perfect for people-watching
and grazing on fine Tassie food and wine.

Moving east, a gap in the warehouses
leads to **Kellys Steps** (**1**; 1839), which link the
waterfront area with the residential neigh-

bourhood known as **Battery Point** (**2**; p622).
You can take the steps to Kelly St, lined with
small cottages (1850s), but for now, continue your walk along Salamanca Pl past the
incongruous old silo buildings (now luxury
apartments).

At Runnymede St, either continue straight
ahead to Princes Park or turn right and wander past **Lenna of Hobart** (**3**; 1880), a splendid Italianate building that's now a hotel.
Continuing up Runnymede, you encounter
the chocolate-box scene of **Arthur Circus (4)**, a
circle of pretty Georgian houses set around
a small village green.

Runnymede St ends at Hampden Rd, the
main thoroughfare through Battery Point.
Turn right for some window-shopping and
to peruse the restaurant menus to plan your
evening meal. Pop into **Jackman & McRoss** (**5**;
p632), a Hobart institution, for a cuppa and
delectable baked goods. Hampden Rd and
surrounds have numerous buildings for
the period-architecture buff, but the highlight would have to be **Narryna** (**6**; p623),
built in 1836 and now home to a heritage
museum.

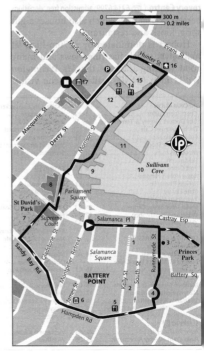

WALK FACTS

Distance: approximately 3km
Duration: 2½ to three hours

Just beyond Narryna, Hampden Rd meets busy Sandy Bay Rd; veer right and continue along Sandy Bay Rd to **St David's Park (7)**. This was Hobart Town's original cemetery, which became an overgrown eyesore and was turned into a park in 1926. Here you'll find gravestones dating from the earliest days of the colony.

Across Salamanca Pl from St David's Park is **Parliament House (8**; 1835). Originally, this building was the Customs House for Hobart Town; it became Parliament House in 1856. Stroll through the manicured gardens of Parliament Sq, in front of Parliament House, to **Watermans Dock (9)**. From here you can walk along the waterfront of **Sullivans Cove (10)**. Just beyond Watermans Dock are the terminals for harbour cruises, while the large **Elizabeth St Pier (11)** is prime real estate housing upmarket accommodation and restaurants. Cross the drawbridge over the entrance to **Constitution Dock (12)** – this place really comes alive when yachties celebrate the finish of the famous Sydney to Hobart Yacht Race around New Year.

Moored along the northeastern side of the dock are a number of inexpensive **floating takeaway seafood stalls (13**; p631) – it's an obligatory holiday activity to sit in the sun munching fresh fish and chips while watching the busy harbour. Nearby is **Mures Fish Centre (14**; p631), a mecca for seafood-lovers, and **Victoria Dock (15)**, home to much of Hobart's fishing fleet.

Walk up to Hunter St and pop into the stylish new **Henry Jones Art Hotel (16**; p630) for a sticky-beak. It's housed in creatively converted Georgian warehouses that once held the IXL jam factory, headed by one Henry Jones. Entrepreneurial Mr Jones was once the largest private employer in Tasmania, with interests in jam, fruit, timber, mining and shipping. There's a bar, restaurant and café here, if you're feeling peckish, plus a couple of galleries.

From Hunter St it's a short walk back along the waterfront to Salamanca Pl or west to Elizabeth St and the mall, with the option of calling in at the nearby **Tasmanian Museum & Art Gallery (17**; p623) to soak up some culture.

HOBART FOR CHILDREN

Parents don't need to empty their wallets to keep the troops entertained in Hobart.

The Friday-night free music in the **Salamanca precinct** (p634) is a fabulous family-friendly affair, and Saturday's **Salamanca Market** (see the boxed text, p622) has street performers to amuse all ages. The docks area is also ideal for wandering and/or for impromptu picnicking – the **floating fish 'n' chip stalls** (p631) provide a budget way to keep a family well fed.

Rainy-day attractions worth seeking out to satisfy your child (and inner child) are the **Cadbury Chocolate Factory** (p623) and the Discovery Centre at the **Botanical Gardens** (p625).

Activities in and around the capital also hold family appeal – take a boat cruise; do a nature walk and enjoy great views from Mt Wellington or Mt Nelson; rent a bike and explore the cycling paths. The minute you head out of town the child-friendly options increase, with an abundance of animal parks, beaches, caves, nature walks and mazes to explore.

TOURS
Bus Tours

Bottom Bits Bus (☎ 1800 777 103, 6229 3540; www .bottombitsbus.com.au) This backpacker-oriented company caters to smaller groups and has a program of day trips out of Hobart, including to Port Arthur, Freycinet Peninsula, Mt Field National Park, or the Tahune Forest AirWalk and Hastings Caves. All trips are good value at $89.

Gregory Omnibuses (☎ 6236 9116) Offers sightseeing on an old London double-decker bus, including a busy day trip visiting the Cascade brewery and Cadbury factory, as well as a river cruise (adult/child $76/38). Alternatively, the City Hopper Explorer day pass (adult/child $25/13) allows you an independent, hop-on-hop-off experience visiting the major sights (as far as the Cascade Brewery, Wrest Point Hotel & Casino or Botanical Gardens). This service runs daily from December to May.

Tigerline Coaches (☎ 6272 6611, 1300 653 633; www .tigerline.com.au) Day and half-day bus tours in and around Hobart are operated by Tigerline, and it has free pick-up from many city hotels and hostels. Its half-day trips include jaunts to Mt Wellington and various city sights (adult/child $46/28), the Cadbury factory ($46/28) and Richmond ($52/32). Full-day destinations include Port Arthur ($77/46), Mt Field National Park ($99/60) and the Tahune Forest AirWalk ($89/54).

Cruises

Several boat cruise companies operate from the Franklin Pier, Brooke St Pier and Watermans Dock area (Map p624), offering a variety of cruises in and around the harbour. Note that timetables can be unreliable and schedules change regularly.

Cruise Company (☎ 6234 9294; ⊙ 10am Mon-Fri) One of the most popular cruises is the Cruise Company's four-hour Cadbury Cruise (adult/child $45/20) which leaves from Brooke St Pier; the boat chugs to the Cadbury factory, where you disembark and tour the premises before returning to the city centre.

Derwent River Cruises (☎ 6223 1914; ⊙ 11am Mon-Fri) Sailings offered include a four-hour trip north, visiting the Cadbury Chocolate Factory and Moorilla Estate (adult/child $50/27), and lunch ($30/15) and dinner ($40/20) cruises on the harbour.

Captain Fell's Historic Ferries (☎ 6223 6893) Offers good-value lunch (from $20 adult) and dinner ($32) cruises, plus an array of sightseeing packages offering ferry, coach or double-decker bus trips (or a combination of these transport modes).

Guided Walks

Hobart Historic Tours (☎ 6278 3338; www.hobarthistorictours.com.au; tours adult/child $24.50/12) conducts a highly informative two-hour **Historic Walk** (⊙ 10am daily Sep-May, winter on request), and also a fun two-hour **Historic Pub Tour** (⊙ 5pm Sun-Thu, winter on request), taking in three watering holes with historic ambience. Bookings and inquiries can be made at the visitor information centre (p622), which is also the departure point for the tours.

FESTIVALS & EVENTS

December–January

Hobart Summer Festival (www.hobartsummerfestival .com.au) Hobart's premier festival, centred around the Hobart waterfront. It lasts two weeks and incorporates numerous festivities, including major New Years' Eve celebrations for revelling sailors, locals and visitors alike.

Sydney to Hobart Yacht Race (http://rolexsydney hobart.com) The arrival (29 December to 2 January) in Hobart of the yachts competing in this annual race is celebrated with lots of noise and colour. Winning yachts arrive in time for New Year's Eve celebrations.

Taste of Tasmania A week-long celebration of Tassie's gastronomic prowess.

February

Royal Hobart Regatta Major aquatic carnival held over three days.

Australian Wooden Boat Festival (www.australian woodenboatfestival.com.au) Biennial event (odd-numbered years) to coincide with the Regatta. The festival showcases Tasmania's boat-building heritage and maritime traditions.

March–April

Ten Days on the Island (www.tendaysontheisland .com) Biennial event (odd-numbered years) which usually runs from late March until early April and is Tasmania's premier cultural festival, a state-wide celebration of local and international 'island culture'.

June

Antarctic Midwinter Festival (www.antarctic -tasmania.info) Celebrate the winter solstice at this new, 10-day Hobart festival, designed to highlight, inform, educate and celebrate Tasmania's connection with the Antarctic.

October

Royal Hobart Show Large festival showcasing the state's primary industries.

SLEEPING

The best areas to stay in Hobart are the docks, Salamanca Pl and neighbouring Battery Point, though the prices are high and the vacancy rates low.

The central business district and immediate surrounds is where you'll find most hostels and pubs offering budget rooms, plus a decent array of midrange and top-end hotels. There's not a great deal of atmosphere to the area at night, but from most places it's only a 10-minute walk to the waterfront and Salamanca Pl.

Away from the water on the other side of the city centre, but still reasonably close to town, are the adjoining suburbs of North Hobart and New Town. Here you'll find a couple of hostels, good B&Bs and moderately priced motels within walking distance of a cluster of lively restaurants and cafés.

Accommodation in the affluent waterside suburb of Sandy Bay is also generally well-priced. Sandy Bay Rd is long and winding, so if you don't want to be too far from town, check distances from the city centre before making a booking.

If you're planning to visit in January, you should book well ahead.

Budget

HOSTELS

Allport's Hostel (Map p624; ☎ 6231 5464; 432 Elizabeth St; www.tassie.net.au/~allports; dm/d/tr/f $20/60/70/70; ⌨ P) Within walking distance of the restaurant strip of North Hobart is this bright, cheery hostel, housed in a two-storey Italianate mansion. The atmosphere is relaxed and the facilities first-rate, including two kitchens, laundry and spacious common rooms. The friendly owner offers bushwalking equipment for hire.

Narrara Backpackers (Map p621; ☎ 6231 3191; nigel ruddock@hotmail.com; 88 Goulburn St; dm/s/d $19/24/40; 🖳 P) Central, well-maintained backpackers with the appealing atmosphere of a large group house and good facilities. It's run by an affable bloke with lots of regional knowledge and bushwalking advice. By the time you read this there should also be another hostel under the same management, **Hobart Hostel** (Map p621; ☎ 6234 6122; cnr Goulburn & Barrack Sts), in a former pub and with similar prices.

Hollydene Lodge (Map p624; ☎ 6234 6434; www .hollydene.com.au; 55 Campbell St; dm/d/f $22/48/87; 🖳 P) Huge, conveniently central hostel with lots of basic rooms and a roll-call of communal facilities, including barbecue area, games room, laundry, comfy lounge and large kitchen. Weekly rates available – this place hosts lots of overseas students.

Pickled Frog (Map p621; ☎ 6234 7977; www.the pickledfrog.com; 281 Liverpool St; dm $19-22, s/d $30/50, incl breakfast; 🖳 P) Big red ramshackle hostel that's well placed for the city centre and has a young, social vibe. There's an in-house bar and lounge for meeting fellow travellers. Extras include bike hire and good tour info.

Central City Backpackers (Map p624; ☎ 6224 2404; www.centralbackpackers.com.au; 138 Collins St; dm $18-22, s/d $36/48; 🖳) In the heart of the central business district, this rambling hostel has loads of communal space, OK rooms, friendly staff and extras such as baggage storage and bike hire.

CAMPING & CABINS
There are no camping grounds within walking distance of the city centre.

Barilla Holiday Park (off Map p621; ☎ 1800 465 453, 6248 5453; www.barilla.com.au; 75 Richmond Rd, Cambridge; powered/unpowered sites per 2 people $21.50/16.50, cabins $63-73; 🖳 P) An excellent option for those with their own transport. It's a midway point between Hobart (13km) and Richmond (14km) and close to the airport and great wineries. It has nice grounds and well-kept cabins, plus an on-site restaurant.

Elwick Cabin & Tourist Park (off Map p621; ☎ 6272 7115; www.islandcabins.com.au; 19 Goodwood Rd, Glenorchy; powered/unpowered sites per 2 people

$20/17, cabins $50-89; P) The nearest camping area to town (about 8km north of the centre). Well equipped, with a range of cabins but limited powered sites (book ahead).

Midrange
GUESTHOUSES & B&BS
Edinburgh Gallery (Map p621; ☎ 6224 9229; www .artaccom.com.au; 211 Macquarie St; s $90, d $100-150; 🖳 P) This funky, art-filled and affordable boutique hotel is owned by a writer and an artist who have put their stamp on an old Federation home in the western part of the city centre. Some rooms are without a bathroom, all have eclectic décor (try for a veranda suite). Excellent winter reductions (May to September) see savings of up to 30%.

Battery Point Manor (Map p621; ☎ 6224 0888; www.batterypointmanor.com.au; 13-15 Cromwell St; d incl breakfast $100-195; P) Take in the magic views from the outdoor terrace at this homely manor, built c 1834. There's a range of large rooms in the manor, some with king-size beds and views over the Derwent River, as well as a separate two-bedroom cottage.

Lodge on Elizabeth (Map p621; ☎ 6231 3830; www.thelodge.com.au; 249 Elizabeth St; s/d incl breakfast from $120/140; 🖳 P) Value-for-money guesthouse in an elevated position in North Hobart, not far from the restaurant strip. Rooms in this grand Georgian manor are decorated with antiques and there are some spa rooms. In the courtyard there's also a self-contained spa cottage ($190, two-night minimum).

Wellington Lodge (Map p621; ☎ 6231 0614; www .wwt.com.au/wellingtonlodge; 7 Scott St; s $90, d $110-130; P) Next to Queen's Domain in the small northern suburb of Glebe (the easiest access is via Aberdeen St). The welcoming owners have four comfortable, well-priced rooms in a restored Victorian townhouse set in magnificent gardens.

HOTELS
Astor Private Hotel (Map p621; ☎ 6234 6611; www .astorprivatehotel.com.au; 157 Macquarie St; d $120-160, s/d without bathroom $55/80) This large central 1920s guesthouse has retained much of its character, full of stained-glass windows, old furniture and family-run charm. There are old-style rooms (some suitable for families), plus brand new and very appealing rooms.

Harrington's 102 (Map p624; ☎ 6234 9277; www
.harringtons102.com.au; 102 Harrington St; r incl breakfast
$95-140) After the shock of the ultra-bright
colours in the reception area, you'll find
the rooms here are well equipped but small.
Still, the price is good and you're within
walking distance of everywhere. Winter
rates can drop to a bargain $70.

MOTELS
No surprises that the best motel options are
out of the city centre. Central motels have
décor well past their use-by dates, but the
places listed – all in Sandy Bay – are a cut
above the rest.

Woolmers Inn (Map p621; ☎ 6223 7355, 1800 030
780; www.woolmersinn.com.au; 123-127 Sandy Bay Rd; d from
$130; ℗) A superior choice, with modern
décor and a location not too far from the
action. It has spacious studio and two-
bedroom units, all with kitchenette, cable
TV and video. Some units have facilities for
people with disabilities.

Mayfair Plaza Motel (Map p621; ☎ 6220 9900; www
.mayfairplaza.com.au; 236-244 Sandy Bay Rd; r $109-149;
🖳 ℗) Another good choice, with cavern-
ous modern rooms opening onto an attractive atrium. There are bonuses such as free
cable TV and complimentary guest laundry, plus an in-house business centre.

Motel 429 (off Map p621; ☎ 6225 2511; www.motel
429.com.au; 429 Sandy Bay Rd; d $105-155; ℗) Not
far from the casino, this motel is the recent recipient of a smart makeover. Selling
features include friendly staff, water views
from the deluxe rooms and a small gym
with spa and sauna.

**APARTMENT HOTELS &
SERVICED APARTMENTS**
For your money, Hobart's best midrange
options are its self-contained flats and units
with fully equipped kitchens – perfect for
longer stays and for families and small
groups, even if the last two options listed
here are a little out of the centre.

Avon Court Holiday Apartments (Map p624; ☎ 6223
4837, 1800 807 257; www.view.com.au/avon; 4 Colville St; d
$130-170, extra adult/child $30/16; ℗) If you overlook
the dated furnishings, these spacious apartments in the heart of Battery Point represent
excellent value. Larger apartments can sleep
up to six.

Graham Court Apartments (off Map p621; ☎ 6278
1333, 1800 811 915; www.grahamcourt.com.au; 15 Pirie

St, New Town; d $95-133, extra adult/child $23/17; ℗)
In a quiet residential area in the northern
suburbs, this large block of well-maintained
apartments is set in leafy gardens. Units
range from one to three bedrooms and are
perfect for families, with a large playground
on the premises, cots and high chairs available and a babysitting service for when you
need a break! Units accessible by people
with disabilities are available.

Grosvenor Court (Map p621; ☎ 6223 3422; www
.grosvenorcourt.com.au; 42 Grosvenor St, Sandy Bay; d $99-
139, q $149-220; ℗) Grosvenor Court features
a large block of studio and two-bedroom
units, all furnished with heritage-style décor
and blackwood furniture. Helpful owners,
DVD/CD players in each apartment, a barbecue area and guest laundry make this a
good home away from home.

Top End
Compared with other Australian capital
cities, top-end accommodation in Hobart
is quite reasonable, generally starting at
around $150 per double (and if your budget
stretches to $200 you can afford something
quite special). As well as the typical big-city
hotels, in this price range you'll find historic guesthouses and cottages – especially
in Battery Point – and modern apartments
in great waterside spots or in the heart of
Salamanca Pl.

Henry Jones Art Hotel (Map p624; ☎ 6210 7700,
1300 665 581; www.thehenryjones.com; 25 Hunter St;
r $240-270, ste $310-850; ℗) Super-stylish HJs
has been wowing guests since it opened in
mid-2004. This harbourside hotel is housed
in restored warehouses and oozes sophistication – but it's not intimidating (this
is Hobart after all, not Sydney). Service,
décor (including modern art on many spare
walls), facilities and downstairs distractions
(bar, restaurant, café) are all first-rate.

Somerset on Salamanca (Map p624; ☎ 6220
6600, 1800 766 377; www.the-ascott.com; 8 Salamanca Pl;
apt from $220; ℗) This option has a similar
upmarket pedigree to its pier-bound sister
establishment, Somerset on the Pier (see
the boxed text, opposite), offering modern,
well-equipped apartments close to the fun
of Salamanca. It's managed by Somerset
on the Pier: everything from inquiries to
check-in should be directed there.

Colville Cottage (Map p624; ☎ 6223 6968; www
.colvillecottage.com.au; 32 Mona St; s/d from $135/160)

Our favourite B&B in Battery Point, with its welcoming, elegant interior, full of colonial heritage but without the clutter. Sit back and enjoy the lovely cottage gardens from the shady verandas.

Clydesdale Manor (Map p621; ☎ 6223 7289; www .clydesdale-accommodation.com.au; 292 Sandy Bay Rd, Sandy Bay; d $150-200; P) This quality guesthouse bills itself as the 'quintessential Hobart destination for discerning adults', so leave the offspring behind and enjoy the warm hospitality, elegant furnishings and gourmet breakfasts.

EATING

Hobart's central business district has some excellent spots for brunch and lunch, but evening options are generally better closer to the water or historic precincts. The waterfront streets, docks and piers are the collective epicentre of the city's restaurant scene, and quality seafood is on offer everywhere you look. Salamanca Pl is an excellent choice for cafés and restaurants, especially brunch-time during the Saturday market. For the most diverse selection of eateries, head to Elizabeth St in North Hobart, a cosmopolitan strip of pubs, cafés and restaurants. City-wide, pubs serve up dependable, if somewhat predictable, meals that usually represent good value.

City Centre

Criterion St Café (Map p624; ☎ 6234 5858; 10 Criterion St; meals $6-12; ☺ breakfast & lunch Mon-Sat) Coffeelovers, vegetarians and fans of creative café fare will be impressed by this light, bright eatery. It serves breakfast from 7.30am, followed by an array of salads, pasta, sandwiches and cakes.

Nourish (Map p624; ☎ 6234 5674; 129 Elizabeth St; meals $7.50-11; ☺ Mon-Sat) A godsend for people with food allergies and intolerances. The menu at this café features tasty dishes (curries, salads, stir-fries, risotto, burgers) that are all gluten-free and largely dairy-free too. Vegetarians and vegans also catered for.

Choux Shop (Map p624; ☎ 6231 0601; 4 Victoria St; meals $5-10; ☺ breakfast & lunch Mon-Fri) A fantastic, newly-opened bakery-café that's become the new lunch hotspot thanks to its superb array of pastries, sandwiches, savoury tarts and quality coffee and tea.

Sirens (Map p624; ☎ 6234 2634; 6 Victoria St; lunch $8-13, dinner $16-23; ☺ lunch Mon-Fri, dinner Tue-Sat)

Sirens is a gem, serving up creative vegetarian and vegan food in a warm, welcoming space, accompanied by excellent service and impeccable ethics. But don't be misled – it's not all long-haired earnest types producing lentil stews; there's some sophisticated cooking going on in the kitchen. Who knew vegetarian food could taste this good?!

The most central option for self-caterers is **City Supermarket** (Map p624; 148 Liverpool St; ☺ 8am-7pm Mon-Fri, 9am-6pm Sat, 9am-5pm Sun).

Waterfront Area

Constitution Dock has a number of permanently moored barges that serve as floating takeaway seafood stalls (you can't miss them), which are a good option for a dockside picnic.

Mures (Map p624; ☎ 6231 2121; www.mures.com .au; Victoria Dock) Mures is a Hobart institution. On the ground level you'll find a fishmonger and an inexpensive, family-friendly bistro, the **Lower Deck** (meals $7-13; ☺ lunch & dinner), which serves meals for the masses: fish and chips, salmon burgers, crumbed scallops and so on. The **Upper Deck** (mains $20-28; ☺ lunch & dinner) is a fancier restaurant with great harbour views and well-prepared seafood dishes.

Orizuru Sushi Bar (Map p624; ☎ 6231 1790; Victoria Dock; sushi $7-10, mains $18-28; ☺ lunch & dinner Mon-Sat) Also part of the Mures complex, this much-praised sushi bar uses fresh seafood to great effect in delicate sushi creations and other popular Japanese dishes.

Fish Frenzy (Map p624; ☎ 6231 2134; Elizabeth St Pier; meals $8.50-18.50; ☺ lunch & dinner) Munch waterside on fish and chips (of course), spicy calamari salad or a fish burger, making your choice from a simple menu of fresh seafood and ordering at the counter. This is a casual, affordable and always-busy eatery; note that no bookings are taken.

T-42° (Map p624; ☎ 6224 7742; Elizabeth St Pier; mains $15-25; ⊙ breakfast, lunch & dinner) A favourite among Hobart's fashionable crowd, especially late in the week, is this cool waterfront bistro/wine bar. There is an innovative menu selection, good service, an extensive wine list, and lounges for a bit of reclining after dining. Dinner bookings recommended.

Steam Packet Restaurant (Map p624; ☎ 6210 7706; Hunter St; breakfast & lunch $8-16, dinner $23-34; ⊙ breakfast, lunch & dinner) A new addition to the waterfront scene, inside the glam Henry Jones Art Hotel. Breakfast dishes can get pricey – lunch is better value and options include salads, local oysters and fish and chips. Dinner sees prices climb again, but the produce is high quality.

Sticky Fingers (Map p624; ☎ 6223 1077; Murray St Pier; snacks $4-8; ⊙ Tue-Sun) Fun, kid-friendly place for a pitstop, full of sweet treats like sundaes, smoothies, cakes, crepes and loads of flavoured ice cream and gelati.

Salamanca

This historic area has something to please everyone: bright cafés for people-watching over coffee, good restaurants, cosy pubs and quick snacks.

Retro Café (Map p624; ☎ 6223 3073; 31 Salamanca Pl; mains $8-12; ⊙ breakfast & lunch) Top spot for Saturday brunch among the market stalls. There are huge breakfasts on offer, plus excellent coffee and blackboard specials of bagels, salads, burgers and assorted lunchtime faves, served to a diverse and interesting clientele.

AUTHOR'S CHOICE

Jackman & McRoss (Map p624; ☎ 6223 3186; 57-59 Hampden Rd; ⊙ breakfast & lunch) Be sure to pop in to this perfect neighbourhood bakery-café, even if it's just to admire the display cabinet full of delectable pies, tarts, baguettes and pastries. Stop by for an early-morning croissant and coffee, and you may well find you return for quiche or soup for lunch, and then a pastry for afternoon tea.

Sugo (Map p624; ☎ 6224 5690; 9 Salamanca Sq; mains $8.50-15; ⊙ breakfast & lunch) Tomato-red walls, good coffee and a menu heavy with Italian influences (pasta, pizza, risotto, *panini*) make this a *perfetto* café choice.

Machine Laundry Café (Map p624; ☎ 6224 9922; 12 Salamanca Sq; mains $8-15; ⊙ breakfast & lunch) Bright, retro-style café where you can wash your dirty clothes while discreetly adding fresh juice, soup or coffee stains to your clean ones (there's an on-site laundry).

Vietnamese Kitchen (Map p624; ☎ 6223 2188; 61 Salamanca Pl; mains $7.50-12; ⊙ lunch & dinner) Cheap and cheerful eatery where you can happily overlook the daggy décor because the food and prices are just right. Two mains from the *bain-marie* plus rice or noodles costs all of $7.50. There are also cooked-to-order prawn and tofu dishes, and noodle soups.

Say Cheese (Map p624; ☎ 6224 2888; 7 Salamanca Sq; mains $10.50-16.50; ⊙ breakfast & lunch) A friendly deli-café serving hearty breakfasts and great platters of cheese (of course), dips or antipasto – and even a kids' platter. Lots of wine options too. Leave room for the lemon cheesecake.

Self-caterers after picnic supplies should head to **Wursthaus** (Map p624; ☎ 6224 0644; 1 Montpellier Retreat; ⊙ daily) for superb deli produce, or to the **fresh fruit market** (Map p624; 41 Salamanca Pl; ⊙ 7am-7pm), which also stocks groceries.

Battery Point

With a few exceptions, options in Battery Point are situated along the main drag, Hampden St.

Shipwrights Arms Hotel (Map p621; ☎ 6223 5551; 29 Trumpeter St; mains $15-24; ⊙ lunch & dinner Mon-Sat) Known locally as Shippies, this is a landmark 1834 yachties pub, popular with locals for its generously portioned seafood meals and beer garden perfect for lazy summer afternoons.

Kelleys Seafood Restaurant (Map p624; ☎ 6224 7225; cnr James & Knopwood Sts; lunch $12.50-28, dinner $23-38; ⊙ lunch Mon-Fri, dinner daily) An institution in Hobart, and well hidden in an 1849 sailmaker's cottage in the back streets of Battery Point. Offers lots of creatures fresh from the sea – the accidental occy (tenderised and grilled octopus) is a trademark dish. Bookings advised.

Restaurant Gondwana (Map p624; ☎ 6224 9900; cnr Hampden Rd & Francis St; dinner mains $25-33; ⊙ lunch

Tue-Fri, dinner Mon-Sat) This place gets lots of recommendations from discerning Hobartians and has a menu of contemporary Mod Oz fare, utilising locally sourced produce for dishes including macadamia-crusted blue eye, twice-roasted duck and poached wild scallops. Lunch is a little easier on the wallet. Bookings recommended.

North Hobart

Elizabeth St in North Hobart (between Burnett St and Federal Rd in particular, but with a few worthy options three blocks south) is a great hunting ground for restaurants, with a reputation for good-value cuisine reflecting a range of nationalities. There's no shortage of Asian and pizza joints.

Lickerish (Map p621; ☎ 6231 9186; 373 Elizabeth St; mains $24-28; ☺ dinner Tue-Sat) One of our favourite Tassie meals was enjoyed at this gorgeous restaurant. The chef takes great local produce and gives it a winning twist with primarily Asian and Middle Eastern touches, and the results – together with the excellent service – are impressive. Bookings advised.

Annapurna (Map p621; ☎ 6236 9500; 305 Elizabeth St; mains $10-15; ☺ lunch Mon-Fri, dinner daily) It seems like half of Hobart lists Annapurna as their favourite eatery – hence it's well worth booking. It offers a variety of northern and southern Indian cuisine, and the *masala dosa* (south Indian style of crepe filled with curried potato) is a crowd favourite. Takeaway available.

Republic Bar & Café (Map p621; ☎ 6234 6954; 299 Elizabeth St; mains $13-20; ☺ lunch Wed-Sun, dinner daily) A great pub with friendly atmosphere, an interesting mixed crowd, regular live music (see p634) and a kitchen producing what was recently voted the best pub food in Tasmania.

Kaos Café (Map p621; ☎ 6231 5699; 237 Elizabeth St; meals $12-19; ☺ lunch & dinner) A few blocks south of our other recommendations, this laid-back, gay-friendly café busies itself with a fine assortment of dishes, including burgers, salads and risotto, serving until late (mostly around 11.30pm).

Self-caterers should also find most of what they need at **Fresco Market** (Map p621; 346 Elizabeth St; ☺ 8.30am-8pm).

DRINKING

Salamanca Pl is home to some fine pubs and bars – lots of outdoor imbibing when the weather is warm, or cosy open fires and lounges in winter. See p628 for information on a guided pub tour, with lots of historical tales and drinking involved.

Knopwood's Retreat (Map p624; ☎ 6223 5808; 39 Salamanca Pl) Follow the 'when in Rome…' advice and head for Knopwood's, a perennial Hobart favourite. It's usually hidden behind a solid mass of Friday-night drinkers loitering on the pavement section (well, it's been 'a Friday night institution since 1829', if you believe its publicity).

Hope & Anchor Tavern (Map p624; ☎ 6236 9982; 65 Macquarie St) Make time to call into this atmospheric old pub, dating from 1807. The downstairs bar (open from 3pm) has lounges and a range of bar snacks; upstairs is a gorgeous, museum-like bar and dining room.

Republic Bar & Café (Map p621; ☎ 6234 6954; 299 Elizabeth St, North Hobart) Don't miss everybody's favourite local in North Hobart, doing as good pubs should – serving great food and alcohol-flavoured beverages, as well as putting on regular live music.

Shipwrights Arms Hotel (Map p621; ☎ 6223 5551; 29 Trumpeter St, Battery Point) Sink a few beers with the yachties and Battery Point locals at this beloved 1834 pub, known affectionately as Shippies.

Bar Celona (Map p624; ☎ 6224 7557; 24 Salamanca Sq) By day a café with decent lunch menu, of an evening a popular wine bar (no meals). On Friday and Saturday nights, the upstairs loft-style lounge – called Elevation – is a cruisy little space with DJ.

T-42° (Map p624; ☎ 6224 7742; Elizabeth St Pier) This waterfront place is popular for its food (see opposite) but draws a mass of barflies to its minimalist interior with plenty of booze and funky background music.

IXL Long Bar at Henry Jones (Map p624; ☎ 6210 7700; 25 Hunter St) Prop yourself at the bar of this fab new hotel and check out Hobart's fashionable folk over cocktails.

Lizbon (Map p621; ☎ 6234 9133; 217 Elizabeth St, North Hobart) A cool new wine bar, boasting excellent wines by the glass, antipasto platters, smooth tunes and cosy nooks and crannies.

Soak@Kaos (Map p621; ☎ 6231 5699; 237 Elizabeth St, North Hobart) A great choice for an intoxicating late afternoon or evening. Gay-friendly Soak is an intimate little lounge bar attached to Kaos Café (left), where you can consume burgers or cake from the café alongside pretty cocktails, while listening to the resident DJ on Friday and Saturday until 3am.

ENTERTAINMENT

The *Mercury* newspaper lists most of Hobart's entertainment options in the 'Pulse' section of its Thursday edition. Also check out the online gig guide at www.nakeddwarf .com.au.

LIVE Tasmania (www.livetasmania.com), a joint project of a number of performing arts groups, can help you find live theatre, dance or music performances during your time in Hobart.

Live Music

Republic Bar & Café (Map p621; ☎ 6234 6954; www .republicbar.com; 299 Elizabeth St, North Hobart) The Republic is a fine, raucous Art Deco pub hosting live music every night (usually, but not always, free entry). It's the No 1 live-music pub in town, with an always-interesting line-up and an understandably loyal following.

New Sydney Hotel (Map p624; ☎ 6234 4516; 87 Bathurst St) Mostly free, low-key Irish folk, jazz and blues usually plays from Tuesday to Saturday, but the occasional pub-rock outfit and end-of-week crowds add a few decibels. It has 10 beers on tap and is a sociable place for a drink or three.

Irish Murphy's (Map p624; ☎ 6223 1119; 21 Salamanca Pl) As you'd expect of an Irish-themed

---

AUTHOR'S CHOICE

The best live music in Hobart is held every Friday year-round from 5.30pm to 7.30pm at **Salamanca Arts Centre courtyard** (see p622), just off Wooby's Lane – and it's free (donations welcome). This community event started about five years ago and has come to be known as Rektango – but that's a bit of a misnomer, as Rektango is the name of a band that occasionally plays here. The bands vary from month to month, and could play anything from African beats to rockabilly to folk or gypsy-latino. This is a fantastic family-friendly affair with loads of atmosphere. Drinks are available (including sangria in summer, mulled wine in winter), dancing is optional…

---

pub anywhere in the world – often crowded, lively, friendly and well stocked with Guinness. There's free live music on offer from Wednesday to Sunday.

Other bar/pub gig options (all free) include those at the **Telegraph Hotel** (Map p624; ☎ 6234 6254; 19 Morrison St) and the nearby **Customs House Hotel** (Map p624; ☎ 6234 6645; 1 Murray St), where live music usually plays Wednesday to Sunday nights.

Theatres & Concert Halls

Theatre Royal (Map p624; box office ☎ 6233 2299, 1800 650 277; www.theatreroyal.webcentral.com.au; 29 Campbell St) Live theatre can be enjoyed at a number of venues around town, including this venerable theatre, which staged its first performance in 1837 and today stages a range of music, ballet, theatre and opera.

Federation Concert Hall (Map p624; ☎ 6235 3633, 1800 001 190; 1 Davey St) Welded to the Hotel Grand Chancellor, this concert hall has the external aesthetics of a huge aluminium can and is home to the Tasmanian Symphony Orchestra (www.tso.com.au).

Cinemas

State Cinema (Map p621; ☎ 6234 6318; www.state cinema.com.au; 375 Elizabeth St, North Hobart) Screens mainly independent local and international flicks.

Village Cinemas (Map p624; ☎ 6234 7288; 181 Collins St) Large inner-city complex showing mainstream releases.

Nightclubs

It has to be said – few people come to Hobart for its nightlife! Still, there is action if you know where to find it. Anyone looking to tap into the (admittedly small and low-key) gay scene should head along to Kaos Café (p633) and make inquiries.

Round Midnight & Syrup (Map p624; ☎ 6223 8249; 39 Salamanca Pl; ☯ Thu-Sat) A great place for late-night drinks and a mixture of live music and DJs playing to the techno/house crowd, above Knopwood's Retreat. Sharing the premises is Syrup, the best bar-club in town.

Isobar (Map p624; ☎ 6231 6600; 11 Franklin Wharf; ☯ 10pm-5am Wed, Fri & Sat) Downstairs at Isobar is a popular bar, while Isobar – The Club is a 1st-floor venue that generally plays commercial music, and blows hot and cold with the locals.

SHOPPING

Most of Hobart's speciality shops and services are in the city centre. The main shopping area extends west from the mall on Elizabeth St and arcades dot the inner-city blocks.

The best shopping for fine Tasmanian arts and crafts is in the numerous shops and galleries on Salamanca Pl, and at the renowned market held here every Saturday – see the boxed text, p622. The market is also the place to sample and buy fine Tasmanian produce – or just head to the nearest supermarket for superb local cheeses, sauces, jams, fudge and assorted digestibles.

There's a plethora of stores on Elizabeth St, between Melville and Bathurst Sts, catering to outdoorsy types wanting to explore a state overflowing with wilderness.

GETTING THERE & AWAY
Air

There are no direct international flights to/ from Tasmania. Airlines with services between Hobart and the mainland are **Qantas** (Map p624; ☎ 13 13 13; www.qantas.com.au; 130 Collins St), **Jetstar** (☎ 13 15 38; www.jetstar.com.au) and **Virgin Blue** (☎ 13 67 89; www.virginblue.com.au). At time of writing, low-return, one-way fares from Hobart started at: Melbourne ($70), Sydney ($110), Brisbane ($150) and Adelaide ($90).

Only Qantas has an office in town, the other airlines are based at the airport.

Bus

See p618 for general information on intrastate bus services.

The main bus companies (and their terminals) operating to/from Hobart are **Redline Coaches** (Map p621; ☎ 1300 360 000; www .tasredline.com.au; Transit Centre, 199 Collins St) and **TassieLink** (Map p624; ☎ 1300 300 520; www.tassielink .com.au; Hobart Bus Terminal, 64 Brisbane St).

Additionally, **Hobart Coaches** (☎ 13 22 01; www.hobartcoaches.com.au) has regular services to/from Richmond, New Norfolk and Kingston, and south along the D'Entrecasteaux Channel and to Cygnet. Timetable and fare information is available from the Metro office inside Hobart's main post office on the corner of Elizabeth and Macquarie Sts.

GETTING AROUND
To/From the Airport

The airport is 16km east of the centre. The **Airporter shuttle bus** (☎ 0419 382 240; adult/child $9.70/4.80) runs between the city (via various places to stay) and the airport. Bookings for city pick-ups are essential.

A taxi between the airport and city centre should cost $32 (6am to 8pm weekdays) or $37 (all other times).

Bicycle

See p625 for details of bicycle rental in Hobart.

Bus

Metro (☎ 13 22 01; www.metrotas.com.au) operates the local bus network, there's an information desk dispensing timetables inside the main post office on the corner of Elizabeth and Macquarie Sts. Most buses leave from this area of Elizabeth St, or from around the edges of nearby Franklin Sq.

One-way fares vary according to the distance travelled (from $1.50 to $3.40). For $3.90 (or $11 per family), you can buy an unlimited-travel Day Rover ticket that can be used after 9am Monday to Friday, and all day Saturday, Sunday and public holidays.

Car

There is timed, metered parking in the CBD and around popular tourist areas (such as Salamanca and the waterfront). For longer-term parking, large garages (signposted) in the CBD offer inexpensive rates.

There are many car-rental firms in Hobart; most have representation at the airport. The large multinationals (including Avis, Budget, Thrifty) have desks inside the terminal; smaller local companies have representation in the car park area. Some of the cheaper local firms, with daily rental rates starting around $30:

Lo-Cost Auto Rent (Map p624; ☎ 6231 0550, 1800 647 060; www.rentforless.com.au; 105 Murray St)

Rent-a-Bug (Map p624; ☎ 6231 0300, 1800 647 060; www.rentforless.com.au; 105 Murray St)

Selective Car Rentals (Map p624; ☎ 6234 3311, 1800 300 102; www.selectivecarrentals.com.au; 47 Bathurst St)

Taxi

You shouldn't have too much trouble hailing a cab or finding a taxi rank in the busy, touristed areas. Fares are metered. Call **City Cabs** (☎ 13 10 08), or **Maxi-Taxi Services** (☎ 6234 3573) can provide vehicles that accommodate people with disabilities.

TASMANIA

AROUND HOBART

You won't have to travel too far from Hobart to swap the cityscape for great natural scenery, sandy beaches and historic sites. Reminders of Tasmania's convict history await at Richmond, and the waterfalls, wildlife and fantastic short walks of Mt Field National Park are an easy day trip.

Without your own set of wheels, day trips to places around Hobart are offered by a number of companies (see p627).

RICHMOND

☎ 03 / pop 750

Richmond is just 27km northeast of Hobart and, with more than 50 buildings from the 19th century, is arguably Tasmania's premier historic town. Straddling the Coal River on the old route between Hobart and Port Arthur, Richmond was once a strategic military post and convict station. It has transformed into a tourist destination and is a lovely spot for a day trip. It's also quite close to the airport, so is a good overnight option if you have an early flight to meet.

Information is available online at www.richmondvillage.com.

Sights & Activities

The much-photographed **Richmond Bridge** (Wellington St), built by convicts in 1823, is the town's historical centrepiece. The northern wing of the remarkably well-preserved **Richmond Gaol** (☎ 6260 2127; Bathurst St; adult/child/family $5.50/2.50/14; ☺ 9am-5pm) was built in 1825, five years before the penitentiary at Port Arthur.

There's an interesting **model village** (☎ 6260 2502; off Bridge St; adult/child/family $7.50/3.50/18.50; ☺ 9am-5pm) of Hobart Town in the 1820s, re-created from the city's original plans. The detail of the 60-plus miniature buildings and Hobart's shrunken population is excellent.

Other places of historical interest include: the 1836 **St John's Church** (off Wellington St), the first Roman Catholic church in Australia; the 1834 **St Luke's Church of England** (Edwards St); the 1825 **courthouse** (Forth St); the 1826 **old post office** (Bridge St); and the 1888 **Richmond Arms Hotel** (Bridge St).

Richmond is at the centre of Tasmania's fastest-growing wine region, known as the Coal River Valley, and there are wineries to be found in all directions. **Meadowbank Estate** (☎ 6248 4484; www.meadowbankwines.com.au; 699 Richmond Rd, Cambridge; lunch mains $21-27; ☺ 10am-5pm), 9km from Richmond, is home to an acclaimed restaurant, plus an art gallery, a children's play area, and an area for tastings and sales. Lunch is served daily, with coffee and snacks available throughout the day.

Sleeping & Eating

There's precious little budget lodging in Richmond. The majority of accommodation is in self-contained historic cottages.

Richmond Cabin & Tourist Park (☎ 6260 2192; www.richmondcabins.com; Middle Tea Tree Rd; powered/unpowered sites per 2 people $24/16, on-site caravans $42, cabins $55-85; ☒) This friendly park is a little out of town. It offers the town's cheapest accommodation in neat, no-frills cabins, while kids will be happy with the indoor pool and games room.

Richmond Colonial Accommodation (☎ 6260 2570; www.richmondcolonial.com; 4 Percy St; d $130-150, extra adult/child $25/15) Manages a number of well-equipped, family-friendly historic cottages in town. All are self-contained and have a roll-call of colonial touches.

Millhouse on the Bridge (☎ 6260 2428; www.millhouse.com.au; 2 Wellington St; d $160-220) The 1850s mill by the historic bridge has been masterfully restored and transformed into a luxury guesthouse. Helpful owners, a large breakfast spread and extensive gardens have made this one of the state's most appealing B&Bs.

Richmond Wine Centre (☎ 6260 2619; 27 Bridge St; mains $10.50-22.50; ☺ breakfast & lunch daily, dinner Wed-Sat) Don't be misled by the name – this place dedicates itself to fine food as well as wine. Select an outdoor table then peruse the extensive menu, where Tassie produce reigns supreme.

Ma Foosies (☎ 6260 2412; 46 Bridge St; dishes $4.50-15; ☺ breakfast & lunch Thu-Tue) Cosy tearoom offering late breakfasts and an array of light meals, including ploughman's lunch, grilled *panini*, quiche and lasagne.

Richmond Arms Hotel (☎ 6260 2109; 42 Bridge St; mains $12-29; ☺ lunch & dinner) This laid-back pub has a good menu selection (including a kids' menu) and better-than-average pub grub. There's also a decent selection of local wines.

Getting There & Away

The **Richmond Tourist Bus** (☎ 0408 341 804) runs a twice-daily service from Hobart ($25 return) that gives you three hours to explore Richmond before returning.

A far cheaper option is to catch a scheduled bus: **Hobart Coaches** (☎ 13 22 01; www.hobartcoaches.com.au) runs three buses per day (Monday to Friday only) to/from Richmond ($5.40/8.70 one way/return, 20 to 30 minutes).

MT FIELD NATIONAL PARK

☎ 03 / pop 170 (National Park township)

Mt Field, 80km northwest of Hobart, was declared a national park in 1916 and is well known for its spectacular mountain scenery, alpine moorlands and lakes, rainforest, waterfalls and abundant wildlife.

The park's **visitor information centre** (☎ 6288 1149; Lake Dobson Rd; ⏲ 8.30am-5pm Nov-Apr, 9am-4pm May-Oct) houses a café and displays on the origins of the park, plus information on walks. There are excellent day-use facilities in the park, including barbecues, shelters and a children's playground.

Skiing in the park is also an option, when nature sees fit to deposit snow (an infrequent event in recent years). Snow reports are available online at www.ski.com.au /reports/mawson, or via a recorded message service (☎ 6288 1166).

To reach the magnificent 40m-high **Russell Falls**, take the easy 20-minute walk from behind the visitor information centre. The path is suitable for prams and most wheelchair-users. There are also easy walks to Lady Barron and Horseshoe Falls, as well as much longer bushwalks.

A couple of kilometres east of Mt Field is **Something Wild** (☎ 6288 1013; www.somethingwild .com.au; adult/child $10/5; ⏲ 10am-5pm), a wildlife sanctuary with the aim of rehabilitating orphaned and injured wildlife, and providing a home for animals unable to be released. You can visit the animal nursery, see native wildlife, and probably spot one of the platypuses residing in the sanctuary's grounds.

Sleeping & Eating

Land of the Giants Campground (powered/unpowered sites per 2 people $20/25) A privately run, self-registration camping ground with good facilities (toilets, showers, laundry and free barbecues) just inside the park. Bookings not required. Site prices are additional to national park entry fees.

Russell Falls Holiday Cottages (☎ 6288 1198; Lake Dobson Hwy; d $85, extra adult/child $15/10) In a great location next to the park's entrance and off the main road, these spotless cottages have very dated furnishings but are roomy and well equipped.

Giants' Table & Cottages (☎ 6288 2293; www .giantstable.com; Junee Rd; s/d $50/70, cottage d $120-135, extra person $30) There is also good accommodation 12km east, at Maydena, in this complex of revamped workers' cottages in a rural setting. You have the option of renting a room in a cottage with communal bathroom, kitchen and lounge, or hiring an entire four-bedroom house (sleeping up to 10 people, breakfast provisions supplied). Also on this 10-hectare riverside site is a **restaurant** (mains $17-22; ⏲ lunch & dinner Nov-Apr) serving huge portions from a creative menu. From May to October the restaurant's opening hours are varied; it's best to call in advance.

Possum Shed (☎ 6288 1477; Gordon River Rd; meals $7-13.50) Well worth stopping at en route to Mt Field is this lovely little riverside café at Westerway, about 8km east. Here you'll find a craft shop, outdoor seating, a resident platypus (sightings not guaranteed) and excellent lunches and snacks.

Getting There & Away

Public transport connections to the park are unfortunately irregular. From December through March **TassieLink** (☎ 1300 300 520; www.tassielink.com.au) runs one bus on Tuesday, Thursday and Saturday from Hobart to Mt Field (1¾ hours, $26); bookings are essential.

KINGSTON

☎ 03 / pop 12,910

Kingston, 12km south of Hobart, is basically a sprawling outer suburb of the city. It's home to the headquarters of the **Australian Antarctic Division** (☎ 6232 3209; www.aad .gov.au; 203 Channel Hwy; admission free; ⏲ 9am-5pm Mon-Fri), the department administering Australia's 42% portion of the frozen continent. There's a fine display here on the exploration and ecology of Antarctica.

Kingston Beach is a popular swimming and sailing spot, with attractive wooded cliffs at each end of a long arc of white sand.

Further south by road are **Blackmans Bay**, another good beach, and **Tinderbox Marine Reserve**, where you can snorkel along an underwater trail marked with submerged information plates.

The Kingston Beach area is a relaxed base for travellers exploring Hobart and the southeast – it takes only 10 minutes to drive to the capital.

Kingston Beach Motel (☎ 6229 8969; 31 Osborne Esplanade; d $110, extra person $20) has an old-style motel exterior but revamped rooms (with kitchenettes) directly opposite the beach. Cheaper rates apply in the off-season or for longer stays.

Next door, **Tranquilla** (☎ 6229 6282; 30 Osborne Esplanade; d $110, extra person $20) offers a self-contained unit that can sleep up to four.

Citrus Moon Café (☎ 6229 2388; 23 Beach Rd; mains $8-14) is a bright, retro-style café with a predominantly vegetarian menu.

Hobart Coaches (☎ 13 22 01; www.hobartcoaches .com.au) runs regular services (bus No70 and 80) from Hobart to Kingston Beach and Blackmans Bay ($2.50 one way).

THE SOUTHEAST

This slice of the state has much to offer, particularly if you have your own transport and enjoy driving through idyllic countryside and browsing roadside produce stores. South of Hobart are the scenic timber- and fruit-growing areas of the Huon Valley and the enticing D'Entrecasteaux Channel, as well as beautiful Bruny Island and the Hartz Mountains National Park. Once mainly an apple-growing region, the area has now diversified and produces a range of other fruits, Atlantic salmon and wines, as well as catering to the growing tourism industry.

Information about the region can be found online at www.huontrail.org.au and www.farsouth.com.au.

Getting There & Around

The region south of Hobart has two distinct areas: the peninsula, which includes Kettering and Cygnet, and the coastal strip where the Huon Hwy links Huonville to Cockle Creek.

Hobart Coaches (☎ 13 22 01; www.hobartcoaches .com.au) runs several buses on weekdays from Hobart south to Kettering ($7.10, 45 min-

utes) and Woodbridge ($7.30, one hour). A bus also runs once each weekday from Hobart to Snug and inland across to Cygnet ($8.80, one hour).

TassieLink (☎ 1300 300 520; www.tassielink.com .au) buses tootle along the Huon Hwy from Hobart through Huonville ($9, one hour) Franklin ($10, one hour) and Geevestor ($13, 1½ hours) to Dover ($17, 1¾ hours).

From December to March on Monday Wednesday and Friday, TassieLink run buses along the Huon Hwy from Hobart all the way to the end of the road at Cockle Creek ($57, 3½ hours). The service returns to Hobart from Cockle Creek on the same days.

For details of the ferry service to Bruny Island, see p641.

KETTERING
☎ 03 / pop 295

The small, picturesque port of Kettering shelters a popular marina for fishing boats and yachts, as well as the Bruny Island ferry terminal. It's a reasonable place to base yourself for regional explorations, and an essential stop for any kayakers.

The **visitor information centre** (☎ 6267 4494 www.tasmaniaholiday.com; 81 Ferry Rd; ☉ 9am-5pm) by the ferry terminal has information on accommodation and services on Bruny Island (including notes on walks and a self-guided driving tour). There's also a café here.

At the marina is **Roaring 40's Ocean Kayaking** (☎ 6267 5000, 1800 653 712; www.roaring40skayaking .com.au; Ferry Rd), Tassie's leading kayaking tour operator. The company offers gear rental to experienced kayakers, and organises a smorgasbord of kayaking trips to suit all levels of experience. A half-day tour exploring Oyster Cove costs $80; a full day on D'Entrecasteaux Channel costs $150 including lunch. Overnight trips at venues such as Lake St Clair, Lake Pedder, the Freycinet Peninsula or the southwest wilderness are also available.

In a great setting with views across the boat-cluttered harbour, the **Oyster Cove Inn** (☎ 6267 4446; oyster.cove@tassie.net.au; Ferry Rd; s/c without bathrooms $45/80) is a large pub offering a mixture of budget singles and bigger rooms. It also has a good **restaurant** (mains $16-26) with an extensive menu and local wine selections, and a more casual bar and outdoor deck.

Just north of town, **Herons Rise Vineyard**
(☎ 6267 4339; www.heronsrise.com.au; Saddle Rd; d $130-
150, extra person $30) has two upmarket, self-
contained cottages, each with log fire, set in
delightful gardens. Breakfast provisions are
supplied (dinner by prior arrangement).

BRUNY ISLAND
☎ 03 / pop 520
Bruny Island is almost two islands, joined by
an isthmus where mutton birds and other
waterfowl breed. It's a beautiful and sparsely
populated retreat, renowned for varied wildlife (including fairy penguins). For info, visit
www.brunyisland.net.

Too many visitors try unsuccessfully to
cram their experience of Bruny into a day

or less. If you can, stay for a few days to
explore the island's superb coastal scenery, fine swimming and surf beaches, good
fishing, and the walking tracks within the
spectacular **South Bruny National Park**.

Tourism is important to the island's economy, though as yet there are no large resorts,
just self-contained cottages and guesthouses.
A car or bicycle is essential for getting around.
Supplies are available at the well-stocked Adventure Bay general store and there are small
shops at Alonnah and Lunawanna (but not
in the northern part of the island at the time
of research).

The **Bligh Museum of Pacific Exploration**
(☎ 6293 1117; 876 Main Rd, Adventure Bay; adult/child
$4/2; ☺ 10am-3pm) details the local exploits of

THE SOUTHEAST

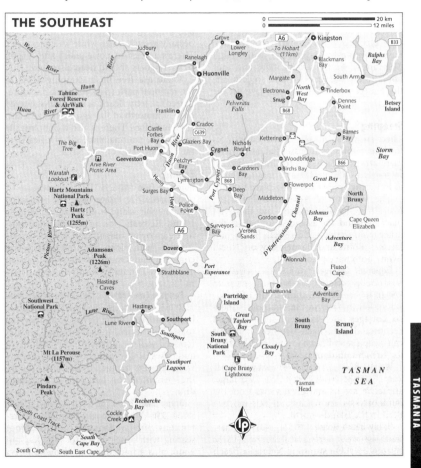

explorers such as Bligh, Cook and Furneaux. Also of interest is South Bruny's **lighthouse**, built in 1836. Visits are restricted to the surrounding **reserve** (🕑 10am-4pm), which has impressive panoramas of the rugged coast.

From October to April, **Bruny Island Charters** (☎ 6293 1465; www.brunycharters.com.au) operates highly recommended three-hour tours of the island's stunning southeast coastline, taking in rookeries, seal colonies, bays, caves and towering sea cliffs. Trips leave the Adventure Bay jetty at 11am daily and cost $85/45 per adult/child; for $145/100 the company offers a full-day tour from Hobart including transfers, the cruise, morning tea and lunch. Bookings are essential.

Travellers without their own transport might wish to take advantage of the **Bruny Island Bus Service** provided by Bruny Island Charters. For $48, passengers can get a return bus trip from Hobart to Adventure Bay, morning tea, admission to the Bligh Museum of Pacific Exploration, and four hours to explore (enough time to complete the Fluted Cape Walk, or just laze on the beach).

Sleeping

There are numerous self-contained cottages for hire; bookings are essential, as owners/managers and their keys are not always easily located – the visitor information centre at Kettering (p638) is a good place to start.

The township of Adventure Bay is the main accommodation area, but there are places around the island. Alonnah is the other main settlement on South Bruny, and Dennes Point and Barnes Bay on North Bruny both have places to stay.

Explorers' Cottages (☎ 6293 1271; www.brunyisland.com; Lighthouse Rd, Lunawanna; d $120, extra person $25) In a secluded location south of Lunawanna on the way to the lighthouse, these six cottages offer excellent self-contained accommodation. Each two-bedroom unit can sleep six and has a lounge and kitchen, log fire and outdoor deck.

Wainui B&B (☎ 6260 6260; www.wainuibandb.com; 87 Main Rd, Dennes Point; d $130) Two large, attractive rooms and great views from the outdoor deck are features of this modern B&B in the island's north.

Bruny Beach House (☎ 5243 8486; www.brunybeachhouse.com; 91 Nebraska Rd, Dennes Point; d $120, extra person $10) On stunning Nebraska Beach in the north is this large, good-value beach house sleeping four. It's got all the facilities you could need, plus a great deck from which to enjoy the views. There's a two-night minimum stay.

Captain James Cook Memorial Caravan Park (☎ 6293 1128; www.capcookolkid.com.au; Main Rd, Adventure Bay; powered/unpowered sites per 2 people $15/12, on-site caravans $32-40, cabins $80-90) Great beachside location, plus welcoming owners and good facilities (including new cabins with access for travellers with disabilities). Fishing charters also available.

Adventure Bay Holiday Village (☎ 6293 1270; www.adventurebayholidayvillage.com.au; Main Rd, Adventure Bay; powered/unpowered sites per 2 people $16/14, on-site caravans $32, cabins $50-95) Beside the beach at the end of Adventure Bay Rd (3km past the general store), with cabins to suit all budgets and pretty grounds filled with wildlife (especially at dusk, when white wallabies visit). There's a strict no-noise policy after 11pm, so party-goers should head elsewhere.

There are free bush camping areas in the national park (national park passes required) at Jetty Beach, a beautiful sheltered cove 3km north of the lighthouse, and also at Cloudy Bay. There is also a camping site outside the national park at Neck Beach, at the southern end of The Neck.

Eating

Hothouse Café (☎ 6293 1131; 46 Adventure Bay Rd; snacks & meals $7-20; 🕑 from 10am) The best lunch spot on the island is this café at Morella Island Retreats. It's in a converted hothouse enjoying magnificent views over the isthmus, with plenty of birds to keep you company and a menu of interesting snacks and meals. Dinner is usually an option here in January.

Penguin Café (☎ 6293 1352; Adventure Bay; meals $6.50-16.50; 🕑 10am-5pm, also dinner Sat; 🖳) Found beside the Adventure Bay store and offering toasted focaccias, interesting hot lunches (curried wallaby, anyone?), Devonshire tea and cakes. It also caters to holiday-makers with hampers for picnics or dinner (bookings essential for hampers or Saturday dinners).

Bruny Island Hotel (☎ 6293 1148; Alonnah; main $12.50-18.50; 🕑 lunch & dinner) Friendly, unpretentious pub in Alonnah, with outdoor seating with water views to help you unwind, plus a fine, well-priced menu heavy on local seafood. There's also a kids' menu, and a decent bar area.

Getting There & Around

Access to the island is via **car ferry** (☎ 6272 3277) from Kettering – there are at least 10 services daily. Fares are for return trips: a car costs $25 ($30 on public holidays and public holiday weekends) and bicycles $3; there's no charge for foot passengers.

At least two weekday-only buses from Hobart to Kettering, run by **Hobart Coaches** (☎ 13 22 01; www.hobartcoaches.com.au), will stop on request at the Kettering ferry terminal, but the ferry terminal on Bruny Island is a long way from anywhere and travellers will need their own transport once there.

WOODBRIDGE
☎ 03 / pop 250

Established in 1874 and originally called Peppermint Bay due to the area's peppermint gums, Woodbridge was eventually renamed by a landowner nostalgic for his old home in England. It's a quiet village now on the tourist map thanks to the sleek development known as **Peppermint Bay** (☎ 6267 4088; www.peppermintbay.com.au; 3435 Channel Hwy). Right on the water end and enjoying wonderful views, Peppermint Bay houses a gourmet food store; the upmarket, à la carte **Dining Room** (mains $25-30; ☽ lunch daily, dinner Sat), bookings advised; and the more casual **Local Bar & Terrace** (meals $10-17; ☽ lunch daily, dinner Tue-Sat, closed Mon in winter). The emphasis is on local produce, so you'll find seafood, fruits, meats, cheeses and other foodstuffs from just down the road, used to fantastic effect.

To stay down this way, visit the **Old Woodbridge Rectory** (☎ 6267 4742; www.rectory .alltasmanian.com; 15 Woodbridge Hill Rd; d $120-130), a friendly place with flower-filled gardens and two large rooms with bathroom.

CYGNET
☎ 03 / pop 800

This small township was originally named Port de Cygne Noir (Port of the Black Swan) by Rear-Admiral D'Entrecasteaux because of the many swans seen on the bay. Youthfully reincarnated as Cygnet (a young swan), the town and surrounding area has numerous orchards, and there is fruit-picking work for backpackers in the warmer months.

If you're in the area, don't miss driving the scenic coastal road (the C639) between Cradoc and Cygnet. The direct route along the Channel Hwy between these two towns is about 7km; the Cygnet Coast Rd makes the journey considerably longer (27km) but is well worthwhile.

Huon Valley (Balfes Hill) Backpackers (☎ 6295 1551; www.balfeshill.alltasmanian.com; 4 Sandhill Rd, Cradoc; dm/d/f $20/50/75; 🖳), off the Channel Hwy 4.5km north of town, has decent rooms, good facilities, extensive grounds and a great view from the large communal area. It's especially busy from November to May, when the host helps backpackers find fruit-picking work. Offers courtesy bus to/from Cygnet bus stop.

There are three pubs in Cygnet offering food and rooms. The top pick for a feed is **Red Velvet Lounge** (☎ 6295 0466; 87 Mary St; meals $8-12; ☽ 10am-6pm; 🖳), a funky wholefood store and café serving deliciously healthy meals to a diverse clientele.

HUONVILLE
☎ 03 / pop 1708

Huonville straddles the banks of the Huon River and is only a short drive from lovely vineyards and small towns. This small, busy town on the picturesque Huon River is another apple-growing centre; the valuable softwood, Huon pine, was discovered here.

The **visitor information centre** (☎ 6264 1838; Esplanade; ☽ 9am-5pm) is by the river on the road south to Cygnet. Also here is the booking desk for **Huon River Jet Boats** (☎ 6264 1838; www.huonjet.com), which offers frenetic jet-boat rides (adult/child $55/35) or more sedate river cruises (adult/child $35/20).

The nearby township of Ranelagh (3km west of Huonville) is home to the beautiful vine-surrounded environs of **Home Hill**

(☎ 6264 1200; www.homehillwines.com.au; 38 Nairn St; ⊙ 10am-5pm), producers of award-winning wines. Tastings are free; there is also an excellent restaurant here.

At Grove, 6km north of Huonville, the **Huon Apple & Heritage Museum** (☎ 6266 4345; 2064 Main Rd; adult/child $5/2.50; ⊙ 9am-5pm Sep-May, 10am-4pm Jun-Aug) has displays on 500 varieties of apples and 19th-century apple-picking life. Not far away is **Doran's Jam Factory** (☎ 6266 4377; Pages Rd; ⊙ 10am-4pm), where you can see jam being made, taste and purchase some, and also eat at JJ Café (the spiced apple butter is a taste sensation).

Two kilometres northwest of Huonville is **Matilda's of Ranelagh** (☎ 6264 3493; www.matilda sofranelagh.com.au; 44 Louisa St, Ranelagh; d $150-200), one of Tasmania's finest heritage B&Bs. There are more good accommodation options further south, in Franklin and Castle Forbes Bay.

GEEVESTON

☎ 03 / pop 830

Geeveston is an important base for the timber industry, and the gateway to Hartz Mountains and the popular Tahune Forest AirWalk.

The **Forest & Heritage Centre** (☎ 6297 1836; www.forestandheritagecentre.com.au; Church St; ⊙ 9am-5pm; 🖳) incorporates the visitor information centre, displays on all aspects of forestry, and a gallery where local craftspeople have taken to wood with artistic fervour. Buy your ticket here for the Tahune Forest AirWalk (you can also buy tickets at the airwalk itself, but it's well worth stopping in here to pick up a map detailing the short walks you can do en route).

Head 29km out of town to the **Tahune Forest Reserve**, where there are camping and picnic areas. The reason most people come here is to stroll along the very popular **Tahune Forest AirWalk** (☎ 6297 0068; adult/child/family $11/7/30; ⊙ 9am-5pm), nearly 600m of horizontal steelwork suspended at an average height of 20m above the forest floor. There is access to the walk for people with disabilities, and there's a café and gift shop here. You'll need your own transport to visit the airwalk; alternatively, take a day trip from Hobart (p617).

You won't miss **Bob's Bunkhouse** (☎ 6297 1069; cnr Huon Hwy & School Rd; dm/tw $20/50; 🖳) on the highway. This backpackers is painted

bright blue and houses clean, comfy rooms and good facilities.

Bears B&B (☎ 6297 0110; www.bearsoverthemoun tain.com; 2 Church St; d $89-125) is the most central accommodation, attached to an antique and collectibles store and decorated with a whimsical bear theme. If features friendly hosts and well-equipped rooms.

Kyari (☎ 6297 1601; Church St; meals $8-20; ⊙ breakfast & lunch Wed-Mon, dinner Fri & Sat) is a streamlined modern café with all-day breakfasts, enticing café fare, a kids' menu and an outdoor deck. If you're heading out to the airwalk or national park, consider picking up one of Kyari's picnic hampers.

HARTZ MOUNTAINS NATIONAL PARK

If you prefer your wilderness a little less pre-packaged than that of the Tahune Forest Reserve, head to Hartz Mountains. This national park, classified as part of the World Heritage Area, is only 84km from Hobart and is popular with weekend walkers and day-trippers. The park is renowned for its rugged mountains, glacial lakes, gorges, alpine moorlands and dense rainforest. The area is subject to rapid changes in weather, so even on a day walk take waterproof gear and warm clothing.

There are some excellent isolated viewpoints and walks in the park. **Waratah Lookout** is only 24km from Geeveston and is an easy five-minute walk from the road. Other shortish walks on well-surfaced tracks include **Arve Falls** (20 minutes return) and **Lake Osborne** (40 minutes return). The walk to **Lake Esperance** (two hours return, moderate grade) takes you through some truly magnificent high country.

There are no camping facilities in the park, but basic day-visitor facilities exist (ie toilets, shelter, picnic tables, barbecue).

DOVER

☎ 03 / pop 570

This picturesque fishing port is a good spot to stay while you're exploring the far south. In the late 19th century, the processing and exporting of timber was Dover's major industry, nowadays fish factories employ locals to harvest Atlantic salmon, which is exported throughout Asia.

There's not much by way of attractions in Dover itself, but there are lots of activities in the beautiful surrounding wilderness (ask around about fishing charters – at the time of research these were in a state of flux). If you're heading further south, buy petrol and food supplies here.

Far South Wilderness Lodge & Backpackers (☎ 6298 1922; Narrows Rd, Strathblane; dm/d $22/60; 💻) offers some of the finest budget accommodation in Tasmania, with a superb waterfront bush setting, quality accommodation, a strong environmental focus, and mountain bikes and sea kayaks for rent.

Dover Beachside Tourist Park (☎ 6298 1301; www.dovercaravanpark.com.au; unpowered sites per 2 people $20/16, on-site caravans/cabins from $38/75) is a well-maintained park opposite a sandy beach, with plenty of greenery and spotless facilities.

Driftwood Holiday Cottages (☎ 6298 1441, 1800 353 983; www.farsouth.com.au/driftwood; Bayview Rd; d $150-200, f $210-300) offers modern and self-contained studio units or three large, family-friendly houses that accommodate four to eight guests. Each of the options boasts all mod cons and has a veranda or outdoor area from which to enjoy the great bay views.

The cosy **Dover Woodfired Pizza & Eatery** (☎ 6298 1905; Main Rd; mains $10-19; 🕑 dinner Tue-Sun) offers traditional and gourmet wood-fired pizzas as well as baked spuds and filling pasta dishes. Eat in or takeaway.

HASTINGS

☎ 03 / pop 300

The **Hastings Caves & Thermal Springs** (☎ 6298 3209; 🕑 9am-5pm Mar, Apr & Sep-Dec, 9am-6pm Jan & Feb, 10am-4pm May-Aug) facility attracts visitors to this once-thriving logging and wharf town, 21km south of Dover.

The spectacular main cave is in the lush vegetation of the Hastings Caves State Reserve, 10km inland from Hastings and well signposted from the Huon Hwy. Guided **cave tours** (adult/child/family $20/10/49) leave on the hour, the first an hour after the visitor centre opens and the last an hour before it closes. Admission includes a 45-minute tour of the main cave, plus entry to the **thermal swimming pool**, filled daily with warm water (28°C) from a thermal spring (you can elect to visit the pool only for adult/child/family $5/3/12). Other facilities include a visitor centre and café, plus BBQs and picnic areas. No public transport runs out this way.

Additional guided 'adventure caving' tours are available in the area (no experience required). **Southern Wilderness Eco Adventure Tours** (☎ 6297 6368, 0427 976 368; www.tasglow-wormadventure.com.au) visits a cave with a thriving glow-worm population. These highly rated tours last 3½ hours, include all equipment, and run daily at 1pm and 6pm (weather and minimum numbers permitting).

COCKLE CREEK

The most southerly drive you can make in Australia is along the 19km gravel road from Lune River to **Cockle Creek** and beautiful **Recherche Bay**. This is an area of spectacular mountain peaks and endless beaches, ideal for camping and bushwalking. It's also the start (or end) of the challenging **South Coast Track**, which, with the right preparation and a week or so to spare, will take you to Melaleuca (or, combined with the Port Davey Track, all the way to Port Davey in the southwest; see p701).

TASMAN PENINSULA

The Arthur Hwy runs 100km from Hobart through Sorell to Port Arthur, one of the state's most popular tourist sites. The Tasman Peninsula is famous for the convict ruins at Port Arthur as well as for its magnificent 300m-high cliffs, beautiful beaches and bays, and stunning bushwalks, much of which now constitutes the Tasman National Park.

Inside the entrance building of the Port Arthur historic site, there's a **regional information counter** (☎ 03-6251 2371; www.portarthur-region .com.au). There is also a helpful information office located in central Hobart at the **Port Arthur Region Travel Shop** (☎ 03-6224 5333; 49a Salamanca Pl).

Getting There & Around

Regional public-transport connections are surprisingly poor. **TassieLink** (☎ 1300 300 520; www.tassielink.com.au) links Hobart and the Tasman Peninsula; there is a weekday bus service connecting Hobart with Port Arthur ($21.20, 2¼ hours) during school terms, and one afternoon service from Hobart three times a week in the school holidays. Buses make stops at all the main towns on the peninsula.

Those without their own transport might prefer to join a coach tour out of Hobart: **Bottom Bits Bus** (☎ 1800 777 103, 6229 3540; www .bottombitsbus.com.au) Operates a small-group day trip to the area twice a week. The price ($89) includes entry to the Port Arthur historic site plus the evening ghost tour, and the tour visits some of the natural attractions of the peninsula, such as the Tessellated Pavement and Tasmans Arch. **Tigerline Coaches** (☎ 1300 653 633; www.tigerline .com.au) Organises a day tour (per adult/child $77/46) which includes entry to the historic site.

SORELL

☎ 03 / pop 1730

Settled in 1808, this is one of Tasmania's oldest towns, but its aura of history has diminished over time. There's a great pitstop here, however: the **Sorell Fruit Farm** (☎ 6265 2744; www.sorellfruitfarm.com; 174 Pawleena Rd; ☒ 8.30am-5pm late Oct–May), where you can pick your own fruit from a huge variety grown on the property; you can also enjoy a snack in the tearooms. To find the farm, head east through Sorell following the signs for Port Arthur; just after exiting the town you'll find Pawleena signposted on your left.

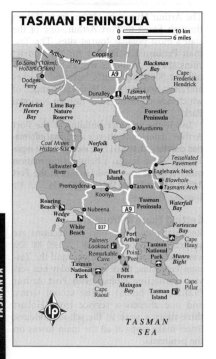

EAGLEHAWK NECK TO PORT ARTHUR

Most tourists associate the Tasman Peninsula only with the Port Arthur historic site, but there are loads more attractions (natural and otherwise) down here. Bushwalkers should get hold of a copy of *Peninsula Tracks* by Peter & Shirley Storey, which contains track notes to 35 walks in the area. The *Convict Trail* booklet ($2.50), available from visitor information centres in the area, covers the peninsula's key historic sites.

As you approach Eaglehawk Neck from the north, turn east onto Pirates Bay Dr to the **lookout** – there's a wonderful view of Pirates Bay and the rugged coastline beyond. Near Eaglehawk Neck are the incredible coastal formations of the **Tessellated Pavement**, the **Blowhole**, **Tasmans Arch** and **Waterfall Bay**. South of Port Arthur is **Remarkable Cave**.

There are some spectacular walks in the **Tasman National Park**. From Fortescue Bay, the best walk is east to **Cape Hauy** (four to five hours return) – a well-used path leads out to sea cliffs with sensational views of sea stacks.

You can visit the remains of the **penal outstations** at Eaglehawk Neck, Koonya, Premaydena and Saltwater River, and the restored ruins of the **Coal Mines Historic Site**.

The **Tasmanian Devil Park** (☎ 03-6250 3230; adult/child/family $20/10/49.50; ☒ 9am-5pm) in Taranna is a wildlife rescue centre with plenty of native birds and animals. There are feedings of the little devils (at 10am, 11am and 1.30pm) and a show featuring birds of prey (at 11.15am and 3.30pm). Admission is pricey, so be sure to visit at feeding time and for the bird show to get your money's worth.

Other options for exploring the area's attractions:

Eaglehawk Dive Centre (☎ 03-6250 3566; www .eaglehawkdive.com.au; 178 Pirates Bay Dr, Eaglehawk Neck) Underwater explorations, diving courses and equipment rental.

Hire It With Denis (☎ 03-6250 3103; hirewithdenis@hotmail.com; 6 Andersons Rd, Port Arthur) About 5km north of the historic site. Offers rental of canoes, kayaks, bikes, tents and more.

Seaview Riding Ranch (☎ 03-6250 3110; 60 Firetower Rd, Koonya) Horse-riding for all ages and skill levels, from beginners to advanced. Signposted off the main road from Taranna.

Tasmanian Sea Charters (☎ 1300 554 049; www .tasmanseacharters.com) Three-hour cruises (with commentary) along the peninsula's east coast, wildlife spotting from Eaglehawk Neck to Cape Hauy. Cruises depart from Eaglehawk Jetty.

Sleeping

Eaglehawk Neck Backpackers (☎ 03-6250 3248; 94 Old Jetty Rd, Eaglehawk Neck; sites per person $7, dm $18) Simple, endearing hostel in a peaceful location to the west of the isthmus. Apart from bunks, it also has a tiny camping area and bike hire is available for guests ($5).

Teraki Cottages (☎ 03-6250 3436; 996 Arthur Hwy; s $60-70, d $70-80, extra adult $20) Some of the best-value accommodation on the peninsula, sign-posted at the southern end of Taranna. These three spotless, self-contained cottages have loads of rustic charm, including a quiet bush setting and open fires. No credit cards.

Lufra Hotel (☎ 03-6250 3262; www.lufrahotel.com; Pirates Bay Dr, Eaglehawk Neck; s $65-75, d $80-120) There are great views from the water-facing rooms at this modernised hotel, perched above the Tessellated Pavement. The rooms are modest but comfortable; some have undergone refurbishment. There are good eating options downstairs.

Osprey Lodge (☎ 03-6250 3629; www.view.com.au /osprey; 14 Osprey Rd, Eaglehawk Neck; ste & unit $160-200) Spoil yourself in luxurious surrounds, not far from the beach. You can choose from a suite or self-contained unit, but you may find yourself spending a lot of time in the guest lounge, with its idyllic views.

Fortescue Bay Campground (☎ 03-6250 2433; Tasman National Park; sites per person $11) This remote and captivating area is 12km off the highway on an unsealed road. It lacks powered sites, but firewood is available and there are fireplaces, gas BBQs, toilets and cold showers. National park entry fees apply in addition to camping fees; book ahead for the summer period.

Eating

Eaglehawk Café (☎ 03-6250 3331; Arthur Hwy, Eaglehawk Neck; mains $7-15; ☺ breakfast & lunch) One of the peninsula's nicest dining options is this stylish café just south of Eaglehawk Neck. It's open until 6pm. There's attractive décor, art on the walls (by local artists), and a fine menu of breakfast, lunch, wines by the glass, or just coffee and cake. B&B rooms are also available.

Mussel Boys (☎ 03-6250 3088; 5927 Arthur Hwy; mains $16-23; ☺ brunch, lunch & dinner) Open from 10am, this bright, fresh café-restaurant has a menu worth stopping for. Try beetroot and goat-cheese ravioli, then macadamia-crusted trevalla or beer-battered fresh fish fillets.

PORT ARTHUR
☎ 03 / pop 170

In 1830 Governor Arthur chose the Tasman Peninsula as the place to confine prisoners who had committed further crimes in the colony. He called the peninsula a 'natural penitentiary' because it was connected to the mainland by a strip of land less than 100m wide – Eaglehawk Neck. To deter escape, ferocious guard dogs were chained in a line across the isthmus and a rumour circulated that the waters on either side were shark-infested.

Between 1830 and 1877, approximately 12,500 convicts served their sentences at Port Arthur. For some it was a living hell, but those who behaved often lived in better conditions than they had endured in England and Ireland.

The penal establishment of Port Arthur became the centre of a network of penal stations on the peninsula, but it was much more than just a prison town, with its fine buildings and thriving industries built on convict labour, including timber milling, shipbuilding, coal mining, shoemaking and brick and nail production.

Australia's first railway literally 'ran' the 7km between Norfolk Bay and Long Bay: convicts pushed the carriages along the tracks. A semaphore telegraph system allowed instant communication between Port Arthur, the penal outstations and Hobart. Convict farms provided fresh vegetables, a boys' prison was built at Point Puer to reform and educate juvenile convicts, and a church was erected.

Port Arthur was reintroduced to tragedy in April 1996 when a gunman opened fire on visitors and staff, killing 35 people and injuring several others. The gunman was finally captured after burning down a local guesthouse and subsequently imprisoned. There is now a poignant memorial garden at the site.

The **Port Arthur Historic Site** (☎ 6251 2310, 1800 659 101; www.portarthur.org.au; adult/child/family $24/11/52; ☺ tours & buildings 9am-5pm, grounds 8.30am-dusk) is one of Tasmania's premier tourist attractions. The visitor centre includes an information counter, café, restaurant and gift shop. Downstairs is an excellent interpretation gallery, where you can follow the convicts' journey from England to Tasmania. Buggy transport around the site can be arranged for people with restricted mobility; ask at the information counter.

Guided tours of the site (included in the entry fee) are worthwhile and leave regularly from outside the visitor centre. You can visit all the restored buildings, including the Old Asylum (now a museum and café) and the Model Prison. The admission ticket, valid for two consecutive days, also entitles you to a short harbour cruise circumnavigating (but not stopping at) the **Isle of the Dead**. Should you wish to visit this island on a 40-minute guided tour to see the remaining headstones and hear some of the stories, it costs an additional $10/6.50/29 per adult/child/family. Note that the cruises and Isle of the Dead tours don't operate in August.

Another extremely popular tour is the 90-minute, lantern-lit **ghost tour** (adult/child/family $15.50/9.50/40), which leaves from the visitor centre nightly at dusk and takes in a number of historic buildings, with guides telling of some rather spine-chilling occurrences.

Tasmanian Seaplanes (☎ 6250 1077; www.tas-seaplane.com) is based at the site and offers scenic seaplane flights along the spectacular local coastline, starting at $65/30 per adult/child for 20 minutes.

Sleeping

Roseview Youth Hostel (☎ 6250 2311; Champ St; dm/d $19/44; 🖳) With a great location at the edge of the historic site, this YHA hostel has OK facilities and crowded dorms but a rough-around-the-edges charm. To get here, continue 500m past the Port Arthur turn-off and turn left at the sign for the hostel into Safety Cove Rd.

Comfort Inn Port Arthur (☎ 6250 2101, 1800 030 747; www.portarthur-inn.com.au; 29 Safety Cove Rd; d $120-168) Motel with flash views over the historic site and unremarkable motel accommodation (some rooms have been recently refurbished and have a spa). There are also good dining options (see right). Ask about packages including accommodation, dinner, breakfast and a ghost tour of Port Arthur (from $218 for two).

Port Arthur Villas (☎ 6250 2239, 1800 815 775; www.portarthurvillas.com.au; 52 Safety Cove Rd; d $112-140) Not far from the Comfort Inn, this place has affordable, older-style self-contained units sleeping up to four. There's a lovely garden and outdoor barbecue area.

Sea Change Safety Cove (☎ 6250 2719; www.safetycove.com; 425 Safety Cove Rd; d $140-166) Whichever way you look from this guesthouse there are fantastic views – of peninsula cliffs, the neighbouring beach or of bushland. It's 5km south of Port Arthur, just off the sandy sweep of Safety Cove Beach. There are a couple of B&B rooms, plus a large, homey self-contained unit that can sleep five.

Port Arthur Caravan & Cabin Park (☎ 6250 2340, 1800 620 708; www.portarthurcaravan-cabinpark.com.au; Garden Point Rd; powered/unpowered sites per 2 people $19/17, dm $15, cabins $85-95) Spacious, attractive and well-equipped park about 2km before Port Arthur, not far from a sheltered beach.

Eating

At the historic site there are a couple of daytime food options, including the Museum Coffee Shop in the Old Asylum and the bustling Port Café, inside the visitor centre, which serves café food and the usual takeaway suspects.

Felons (☎ 6251 2310; visitor centre; mains $15-26; 🕑 dinner) Felons, with the catchy slogan 'dine with conviction', is a good choice before you head off on a ghost tour. It is an upmarket dinner spot serving creative options with a seafood emphasis. Reservations are advised here.

Comfort Inn Port Arthur (☎ 6250 2101, 1800 030 747; www.portarthur-inn.com.au; 29 Safety Cove Rd) There are two dining options inside the pub at this motel complex and they enjoy great views over the historic site. The **Convict Kitchen** (mains $12-18; 🕑 lunch & dinner) serves up standard pub fare such as schnitzel, roast of the day, fish and chips, and steak, and has a kids' menu, while the **Commandant's Table** (mains $17-28, 🕑 dinner) offers more formal dining and menu options to match.

MIDLANDS

The English trees and hedgerows give Tasmania's Midlands an English-countryside feel. The area's agricultural potential contributed to Tasmania's rapid settlement, and coach stations, garrison towns, stone villages and pastoral properties soon sprang up as convict gangs constructed the main road between Hobart and Launceston.

The course of the Midland Hwy (called the Heritage Highway in many tourist publications) has changed slightly from its original route and many of the historic towns are now bypassed, but it's worth making a few detours to enjoy the Georgian architecture, pretty gardens and antique shops found in each of them.

Getting There & Around

Redline Coaches (☎ 1300 360 000; www.tasredline.com.au) runs along the Midland Hwy several times a day; you can disembark at any of the main towns provided you're not on an express service. The fare from Hobart to Launceston is $27.50 (about 2½ hours).

The one-way fare between Oatlands and Launceston/Hobart is $19.90/15.40; Ross is $13.90/20.60; Campbell Town is $12/23.30.

OATLANDS

☎ 03 / pop 550

Oatlands is home to Australia's largest collection of Georgian architecture – on the main street alone, there are 87 historic buildings. Many historic properties are now being spruced up and contain galleries and craft stores. The helpful **visitor information centre** (☎ 6254 1212; 85 High St; 🕑 9am-5pm) is home to an interesting history room.

Much of the sandstone for Oatlands' early buildings, including that used for the 1829 **courthouse** (Campbell St), came from the shores of the town's **Lake Dulverton**, now a wildlife reserve. Nearby **Callington Mill** (☎ 6254 0039; Mill Lane; admission free; 🕑 9am-4pm), off High St, was built in 1837 and used until 1891. Restoration work was begun after a century of neglect, but for the past few years the project has moved in fits and starts. There's not a lot to do except for a vigorous climb of the 15m-high mill tower.

Oatlands Lodge (☎ 6254 1444; 92 High St; s/d $90/110) is the pick of the town's accommodation. It's warm and inviting, with a huge breakfast spread (and dinners served by arrangement). At the northern end of the main street, **Blossom's Georgian Tea Rooms** (☎ 6254 1516; 116 High St; light meals $3-10.50; 🕑 Thu-Mon) exudes old-fashioned warmth and is a good place for a cuppa.

ROSS

☎ 03 / pop 266

This ex-garrison town, about 120km from Hobart, is wrapped firmly in colonial charm and history. It was established in 1812 to protect travellers journeying on the main north–south road and was an important coach staging post.

The visitor information centre is housed in the **Tasmanian Wool Centre** (☎ 6381 5466; Church St; 🕑 9am-5pm). There's good online information at www.rosstasmania.com.

Sights & Activities

The town is famous for the convict-built **Ross Bridge** (1836), one of the oldest, most beautiful bridges in Australia. Daniel Herbert, a convict stonemason, was granted a pardon for his detailed work on the 186 panels decorating the arches.

In the heart of town is a crossroads that can lead you in one of four directions: temptation (represented by the Man O'Ross Hotel), salvation (the Catholic church), recreation (the town hall) and damnation (the old jail).

Historic buildings include the 1832 **Scotch Thistle Inn** (Church St), now a private residence; the **Barracks** (Bridge St), restored by the National Trust and also a private residence; the 1885 **Uniting Church** (Church St); **St John's Anglican Church** (cnr Church & Badajos Sts), built in 1868; and the still-operating **post office** (26 Church St), dating from 1896.

The **Tasmanian Wool Centre** (☎ 6381 5466; www.taswoolcentre.com.au; Church St; 🕑 9am-5pm) is home to a craft shop, wool exhibition and **museum** (admission by donation).

The **Ross Female Factory** (admission free; 🕑 9am-5pm) was one of only two female prisons in Tasmania during the convict period, and today only one building is still standing. There's little to see inside, but the descriptive signs and stories give a good idea of what life was like for these women. Walk to the site along the track near the Uniting Church, next to the Wool Centre.

Sleeping & Eating

Ross Caravan Park & Cabins (☎ 6381 5224; http://caravanpark.rosstasmania.com; Bridge St; powered/unpowered sites per 2 people $16/13, cabins without bathroom

$40-65) An appealing patch of green, adjacent to Ross Bridge. The row of simple conjoined cabins here each sleep two to four people and have cooking facilities. Reception is at the neighbouring Best Western Ross Motel.

Man O'Ross Hotel (☎ 6381 5445; www.manoross .com.au; cnr Church & Bridge Sts; s/d without bathroom & incl breakfast $70/85) Accommodation prices at this lovely old pub are a bit steep given that there are no private bathroom facilities but the rooms are bright and modernised. Evening dining options in Ross are slim, so you may well find yourself eating here too (dinner mains $10.50 to $21.50). There's a leafy courtyard to enjoy in fine weather.

Ross Bakery Inn (☎ 6381 5246; www.rossbakery .com.au; 15 Church St; s/d $90/120) You can wake up to brekky fresh from a 100-year-old wood-fired oven if you stay in this friendly 1830s coaching house, attached to the Ross Village Bakery. The small, cosy rooms are well equipped, and there's a guest lounge with open fire. By day, visitors can overdose on carbs at the Ross Village Bakery – choose from soup, salads and all manner of pies, but leave room for something sweet.

CAMPBELL TOWN

☎ 03 / pop 880

Campbell Town, 12km north of Ross, is another former garrison settlement on the Midland Hwy. Unlike Oatlands and Ross, however, the highway passes right through town, making it a popular loo-and-snack stop between Launceston and Hobart (or between Cradle Mountain and the east coast).

The town has many buildings well over 100 years old; most can be seen by travelling along High St and returning along Bridge St. They include **St Luke's Church of England** (High St), constructed in 1835; the 1840 **Campbell Town Inn** (100 High St); the 1834 **Fox Hunters Return** (132 High St); and the 1878 **old school** (Hamilton St) in the current school's grounds. There are also a couple of good antique shops in town.

Stay among all the history at the **Grange** (☎ 6381 1686; www.thegrangecampbelltown.com.au; Midland Hwy; s/d $99/132), a rather grand-looking guesthouse built in 1847. The best choice in town to refuel is bustling **Zeps** (☎ 6381 1344; 92 High St; meals $7-22; ☼ breakfast, lunch & dinner; ☐), serving brekky, *panini*, pasta and other café fare throughout the day, with pizzas and additional blackboard specials of an evening.

EAST COAST

Tasmania's scenic east coast, known as the 'sun coast' because of its mild, sunny climate, devotes itself to long, sandy beaches, fine fishing and that special sort of tranquillity that occurs only by the ocean. The light-hued granite peaks and glorious bays of Freycinet Peninsula are among the state's most attractive features, but even from the highway the water views are often magnificent.

Getting There & Around

BICYCLE

Arguably the most popular cycle route in Tasmania, a trip along the east coast makes for a wonderfully varied ride. Traffic in the area is usually light and the hills are not too steep, particularly if you follow the coastal highway from Chain of Lagoons to Falmouth (to the east of St Marys).

BUS

The main bus companies serving the east coast are **Redline Coaches** (☎ 1300 360 000; www .tasredline.com.au) and **TassieLink** (☎ 1300 300 520; www.tassielink.com.au).

Redline runs one service each weekday from Launceston to Swansea ($28, two hours), the Coles Bay turn-off ($31.10, 2½ hours) and Bicheno ($31.70, 2¾ hours) – and return – via the Midland Hwy and the inland B34 linking road. Services from Hobart connect with these buses (change buses at Campbell Town, where you'll have to wait anything from five minutes to three hours depending on your particular service). Redline also runs daily services (except Saturday) from Launceston to St Helens (and vice versa) along the A4 via St Marys (from Launceston/St Helens to St Marys the fare is $20.20/5.10). Again, Hobart buses connect with this service, at Conara on the Midland Hwy.

TassieLink runs three times per week between Hobart and Bicheno ($27.70, three hours) via Orford ($15, 1½ hours), Triabunna ($16, 1½ hours), Swansea ($22.60, 2¼ hours) and the Coles Bay turn-off

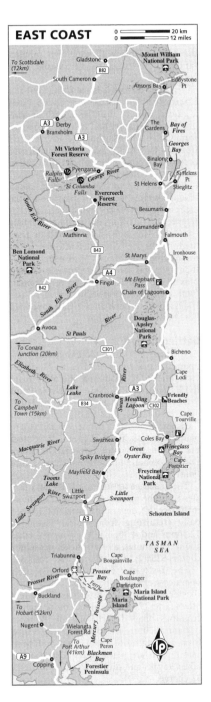

EAST COAST

($26.90, three hours); on Friday and Sunday this service presses on further north to St Helens ($40.30, four hours).

TassieLink also runs one bus each weekday (three times per week during school holidays) from Hobart to Swansea via Richmond, Orford and Triabunna. TassieLink also has a twice-weekly service between Launceston and Bicheno ($26, 2½ hours) via the A4, calling at St Marys (from Launceston/Bicheno it costs $18.70/8.30).

Neither Redline nor TassieLink services the Freycinet Peninsula. For this route you must rely on **Bicheno Coach Service** (☎ 03-257 0293), which runs from Bicheno to Coles Bay (see p653), connecting with Redline and TassieLink services at the Coles Bay turn-off.

Note that all the services are limited at weekends.

ORFORD
☎ 03 / pop 500

Orford is a small seaside town on the Prosser River; the area has good fishing and swimming and some excellent walks. South of town (signposted from the southern end of the bridge over the river) are **Shelly Beach** and **Spring Beach**, popular swimming and surfing spots. There's a 2km cliff-top walk between the two beaches.

Prosser Holiday Units (☎ 6257 1427; cnr Tasman Hwy & Charles St; d $85, extra adult/child $20/10) offers family-friendly, self-contained highway-side units. They're good value, each featuring a spacious interior and room for up to five people.

Readers speak highly of **Sanda House** (☎ 6257 1527; www.orfordsandahouse.com.au; 33 Walpole St; d $90-130), a B&B in Orford's oldest house (a stone cottage dating from 1840).

EAST COAST SHORTCUT

For east coast explorers, it's worth knowing that there's an interesting shortcut between the Tasman Peninsula and Orford, a road leaving the Tasman Hwy at Copping and following 35km of gravel north through Wielangta Forest. Portions of the forest have been reserved for recreational use and contain a couple of good walking tracks. You're also likely to encounter a few logging trucks on your way.

Scorchers on the River (☎ 6257 1033; 1 The Esplanade; meals $7-18; ⏲ 10am-9pm) is a cheerful café-restaurant on the south side of the river, specialising in wood-fired pizza. In summer, ask here about canoes for rent for river exploration.

TRIABUNNA

☎ 03 / pop 925

Just 8km north of Orford is the larger community of Triabunna. Except for the great backpacker joint here, it doesn't make a particularly appealing overnight stop – Orford is a better, more picturesque option.

There's a helpful **visitor information centre** (☎ 6257 4772; cnr Charles St & The Esplanade; ⏲ 10am-4pm) on the waterfront. It can provide information on chartering boats for fishing, plus walks and activities in the area, and is the best source of information if you plan to visit Maria Island.

Udda Backpackers (☎ 6257 3439; udda@southcom .com.au; 12 Spencer St; sites/s/d $18/25/40) is an excellent, laid-back YHA hostel that gives you a warm rural welcome and offers spotless rooms. The Udda is in 'east' Triabunna; head over the bridge and keep left, following the signs. Alternatively, call ahead to arrange pick-up from the Triabunna bus stop.

MARIA ISLAND NATIONAL PARK

This peaceful, car-free island (Ma-*rye*-ah Island) was declared a national park in 1972. It features some magnificent natural scenery: forests, fern gullies, fossil-studded sandstone and limestone cliffs, and beautiful beaches. It has some invigorating walks, while mountain bikers have plenty of great trails to ride, bird-watchers have plenty to look at, and snorkellers and divers are in for a treat in the waters of the island's marine reserve. Visitors require a national park pass.

The visitor information centre in Triabunna (above) can help you with pre-trip information. On the island, various brochures are available from the **visitors reception area** in the old commissariat store (close to where the ferry docks).

From 1825 to 1832, **Darlington** was Tasmania's second penal colony (the first was Sarah Island near Strahan). The remains of the penal village, including the **commissariat store** (1825), the **mill house** (1846) and

the **coffee palace** (1888), are well preserved and easy to explore. There are no shops on the island so bring all your own supplies (and no, the 'coffee palace' doesn't serve coffee!).

The four-day **Maria Island Walk** (☎ 03-6227 8800; www.mariaislandwalk.com.au; per person $1550) is a guided walk of the island, with an emphasis on its nature and history. Trips run from October to May and include transfers from Hobart to the island, all meals, and accommodation (in beachfront tents and in an historic house in Darlington).

For independent visitors, **camping** (sites per adult/child/family $4.40/2.20/11) is possible by the creek to the east of Darlington (bookings not required). The rooms in the old **penitentiary** (☎ 03-6257 1420; dm/6-bed unit $8.80/22) in Darlington have been converted into very basic, unpowered bunkhouses. Visitors must take their own gas lamp and portable cooker, plus all utensils. The units are very popular (with school groups as well as travellers) and it's essential to book ahead. Coin-operated hot showers are available.

Getting There & Away

At the time of research there were two boats operating passenger services to Maria Island: one from Triabunna, the other from the Eastcoaster Resort on Louisville Point Rd, a few kilometres north of Orford. However, it's unlikely that visitor numbers to the island can sustain two services. If you're planning a visit, the best idea is to contact the Triabunna visitor information centre (left) beforehand to confirm boat departure points and times.

The **Triabunna service** (☎ 0427 100 104) operates from the marina near the visitor information centre, departing 9.30am and 1.30pm daily (returning from Maria Island at 12.30pm and 4.30pm). The journey takes about 50 minutes, a return ticket per adult/child is $25/12; to transport a bike costs $2.

The **Eastcoaster Express** (☎ 03-6257 1589) operates from the wharf next to the Eastcoaster Resort. The Eastercoaster Express offers faster (25 minutes) and more regular crossings: boats depart Louisville Point at 9.30am, 1.30pm and 3.15pm, and return from Darlington at 10am, 2pm and 4pm. The return fare per adult/child is $25/12; bikes, kayaks and dive tanks incur an extra $2 charge.

SWANSEA

☎ 03 / pop 550

An appealing holiday town located on the western shore of Great Oyster Bay, Swansea is popular with visitors for the local camping, boating, fishing and surfing, not to mention the superb views across to Freycinet Peninsula.

Settled during the 1820s, Swansea has a number of interesting historic buildings, including the original 1860 **council chambers** (Noyes St), still in use, and the red-brick 1838 **Morris' General Store** (13 Franklin St), still trading. The community centre dates from the 1860s and houses a **museum of local history** (☎ 6257 8215; Franklin St; adult/child $3/1; ☉ 9am-5pm Mon-Sat).

At the **Swansea Bark Mill & East Coast Museum** (☎ 6257 8382; 96 Tasman Hwy; adult/child/family $6/3.80/14.50; ☉ 9am-5pm), a restored mill displays working models of equipment used in the processing of black-wattle bark, a basic ingredient that is used in the tanning of heavy leathers. The adjoining museum features displays of Swansea's early history. There's also a café, souvenir shop and some visitor information.

Sleeping & Eating

Swansea has an abundance of high-quality accommodation; because it's a holiday-maker magnet, prices are generally higher here than in most other coastal towns.

Swansea Holiday Park at Jubilee Beach (☎ 6257 8177; www.swansea-holiday.com.au; Shaw St; powered/unpowered sites per 2 people $18/16, cabin $80-140; ☐ ☒) This neat, spruced-up park has family-friendly facilities and a beachfront location on the way out of town, heading north. Prime camping sites are right on the beach; some self-contained cabins have a spa.

Freycinet Waters (☎ 6257 8080; www.freycinet waters.com.au; 16 Franklin St; s $100-130, d $120-150) Friendly B&B with definite seaside ambience. The three in-house rooms (one with spa) are well equipped and come with private deck for enjoying the water views (plus cooked breakfast), or there's a modern self-contained unit on offer (breakfast provisions included).

Redcliffe House (☎ 6257 8557; www.redcliffehouse .com.au; 13569 Tasman Hwy; s $110, d $126-160, incl breakfast) A warm and welcoming option, Redcliffe is a charmingly restored farmhouse 1.5km north of town beside the Meredith River. You'll have no choice but to relax, with large gardens, barbecues, DVDs and cooked breakfasts to enjoy.

Tubby & Padman (☎ 6257 8901; www.tubbyand padman.com.au; 20 Franklin St; d cottage ste $150-160, d unit $130-140, extra person $30) This place gets our vote thanks to its fabulous décor and fine attention to detail. Inside the richly renovated 1840s cottage are heritage suites built for romance – but if you're travelling with family or in a group with no time for such shenanigans, opt for one of the two modern, two-bedroom, self-contained units behind the cottage.

Left Bank (☎ 6257 8896; cnr Main & Maria Sts; light meals $5-16; ☉ Wed-Mon Sep-Apr, Thu-Mon May-Jul, closed Aug) Behind the bright red door, the Left Bank is one of the east coast's best pitstops. Choose from breakfast dishes, toasted *panini*, pasta and salads, plus a lemon tart worth travelling miles for.

Kate's Berry Farm (☎ 6257 8428; Addison St; cakes $6-8; ☉ daily) About 3km south of Swansea, this fruit farm is home to a store selling jams, wines, sauces and divine ice cream, and a café serving perfect afternoon tea fodder.

Blue House (☎ 6257 8446; 10 Franklin St; lunch $8-20, dinner $20-27; ☉ lunch Fri-Mon, dinner daily) This sleek new restaurant has a menu of creative, well-prepared meals, heavy on local seafood (but not exclusively so). The fancy fish 'n' chips (grilled blue-eye trevalla with salad and hand-cut potato chips) was one of the best meals we've eaten in Tassie. Bookings advised.

COLES BAY & FREYCINET NATIONAL PARK

☎ 03 / pop 120

The small township of Coles Bay is dominated by the spectacular 300m-high pink granite outcrops known as The Hazards. The town is the gateway to many white-sand beaches, secluded coves, rocky cliffs and excellent bushwalks in the Freycinet National Park.

Information

Park information is available from the helpful **national park visitor centre** (☎ 6256 7000; freycinet@parks.tas.gov.au; ☉ 8am-5pm May-Oct, 8am-6pm Nov-Apr) at the park entrance. From late December to February, inquire here about the free ranger-led activities (eg walks, talks

TASMANIA

and slide shows). There is park information also available online at www.parks.tas.gov.au/natparks/freycinet.

Town maps and general tourist information is available in most stores in Coles Bay. Jack-of-all-trades **Coles Bay Trading** (☎ 6257 0109; 1 Garnet Ave; ⏲ 8am-6pm Mar-Nov, 7am-7pm Dec-Feb) is the general store and post office. It houses a café and ATM.

The **Iluka Holiday Centre** (☎ 6257 0115; Coles Bay Esplanade) has a store with ATM and fuel, plus a bistro and takeaway food outlet.

You can hire camping equipment from **Freycinet Adventures** (☎ 6257 0500; www.adventures tasmania.com; 2 Freycinet Dr). An excellent online guide to the area is at www.freycinetcoles bay.com.

Sights & Activities

The Freycinet National Park, incorporating Freycinet Peninsula, beautiful Schouten Island and the Friendly Beaches (on the east coast, north of Coles Bay), is noted for its coastal heaths, orchids and other wildflowers, and for its wildlife, including black cockatoos, yellow wattlebirds, honeyeaters and Bennett's wallabies.

For a walker it's paradise, with attractions such as a two-day, 31km circuit of the peninsula, and many shorter tracks. The best known of these walks is to the famously beautiful **Wineglass Bay**. The walk to the white sand and crystal-clear water of the beach itself takes 2½ to three hours return; alternatively, walk along the same track only as far as **Wineglass Bay Lookout** (one to 1½ hours return, and some 600 steps each way), with its mesmerising, postcard-perfect vista.

Shorter walks include the 500m-long easy lighthouse boardwalk at **Cape Tourville**, which affords great coastal panoramas (including a less-strenuous glimpse of Wineglass Bay) and is suitable for some wheelchair-users and folks with prams.

On any long walk remember to sign in (and out) at the registration booth at the car park. A national parks pass is required.

Tours

Aside from all the walks, the following companies offer you the chance to see Freycinet from a different angle:

All4Adventure (☎ 6257 0018; www.all4adventure .com.au; Coles Bay Esplanade) Offers 4WD tours and fun

quad-bike tours that vary in length (a one-hour sunset trip costs $60).

Freycinet Adventures (☎ 6257 0500; www.adventures tasmania.com; 2 Freycinet Dr) You can participate in a range of great activities through this local company – rock climbing and abseiling (from $95), sea-kayaking (from $55), mountain-biking (from $55) and multiday walks and paddle trips.

Freycinet Air (☎ 6375 1694; www.freycinetair.com .au) Offers scenic flights over the park, departing from the airstrip near Friendly Beaches. Flights start at $82 for 30 minutes.

Freycinet Experience (☎ 6223 7565, 1800 506 003; www.freycinet.com.au) From October to April, this Hobart-based company offers four-day guided walks on the peninsula ($1975) with a degree of comfort and style. The price includes food, wine, accommodation, boat trips and return transport from Hobart.

Freycinet Sea Charters (☎ 6257 0355; www .freycinetseacharters.com) Cruises (from two- to six-hours' duration) leave daily from Coles Bay jetty to experience the scenery and wildlife of the peninsula; prices start at around $60. Fishing charters are also available, as is a handy pick-up and drop-off service for campers and walkers.

Sleeping

Accommodation is at a premium at Christmas, January and Easter; book well ahead for these periods. Owing to the popularity of the area, you'll also find prices higher here than in other parts of the state.

BUDGET

Iluka Holiday Centre (☎ 6257 0115, 1800 786 512; www.ilukaholidaycentre.com.au; Coles Bay Esplanade; powered/unpowered sites $25/20, on-site caravans $55-65, cabins & units $80-130, extra adult/child $15/10) This large, busy park is well maintained and has good amenities, plus a shop, pub and bakery next door. There are decent self-contained cabin options, but it's wise to book well ahead for these.

Iluka Backpackers (☎ 6257 0115, 1800 786 512; www.ilukaholidaycentre.com.au; Coles Bay Esplanade; dm/d $20/52) Also at the Holiday Centre is this popular YHA hostel that's light on for character but very clean and with a large kitchen.

Small camping grounds worth walking to for their scenery include **Wineglass Bay** (around 1½ hours from the car park), **Hazards Beach** (two to three hours), **Cooks Beach** (4½ hours) and **Bryans Beach** (5½ hours). Further north, at **Friendly Beaches**, are two basic camp sites with pit toilets. There's little reliable drinking water at any of these sites or elsewhere on the peninsula, so carry your own. While there are no camping fees at these sites, national park entry fees apply. Note that the park is a fuel-stove only area, and campfires are not permitted.

Richardsons Beach at the national park entrance is the main **camping ground** (☎ 6256 7000; freycinet@parks.tas.gov.au; powered/unpowered sites per adult $6.60/5.50). Facilities here include powered sites, toilets and water, however, there are no showers. Camping here is extremely popular, and sites for the period from mid-December to Easter are determined by a ballot drawn on 1 October (applications must be made by post, fax or email before 30 September). Some dates may remain unfilled after the ballot, so it's still worth inquiring about vacancies. During the peak period there is limited, first-come-first-served tent space available in the designated backpacker camping area (no vehicle access, no bookings taken), but this fills quickly. Outside of the ballot period, advance bookings are taken and recommended.

MIDRANGE

Freycinet Rentals (☎ 6257 0320; www.freycinetren tals.com; 5 Garnet Ave, Coles Bay) If you're looking for holiday accommodation in Coles Bay, this is the best place to start. The managers have 14 houses/units of varying sizes (sleeping up to six) on their books. All feature kitchen, laundry, lounge, TV and video, and barbecue. Summer prices range from $130 to $180 for two people (extra adult costs $15 to $25, extra child $5 to $15). Prices are lower in the off season (from May to August) and for longer stays. Check the website for more detailed information and pictures of each property.

TOP END

Sheoaks on Freycinet (☎ 6257 0049; www.sheoaks .com; 47 Oyster Bay Crt; s/d incl breakfast $135/165) Readers have reported great things about this new B&B. It's a stylish, modern house enjoying fantastic views of Great Oyster Bay. Friendly, knowledgeable hosts, well-equipped rooms and first-class breakfasts complete the package. Packed lunches (for walkers) and evening meals can be arranged. This B&B is not suitable for kids. To get here, take Hazards View Rd (about

6km before Coles Bay), then turn left at Oyster Bay Crt.

Freycinet Lodge (☎ 6257 0101; www.freycinetlodge .com.au; cabin s & d $260-395, extra person $54) Situated within the national park at the southern end of Richardsons Beach, this lodge has 60 plush, private cabins with balconies set in bushland, some with self-catering facilities and/or spas, several with access for people with disabilities. Activities and guided walks are organised for guests, and there are good on-site eating choices.

Eating

Freycinet Bakery & Café (☎ 6257 0272; Shop 2, Coles Bay Esplanade; meals $3-10, pizzas $9-24; ☺ 8am-7.30pm; ▣) Fuel your walking with this bakery's all-day brekky options, or choose from pies and pastries, focaccias, and cakes galore. Pizzas are served after 5pm.

Iluka Tavern (☎ 6257 0429; Coles Bay Esplanade; mains $10-24; ☺ lunch & dinner) A sociable and family-friendly place, serving good-value pub lunches and dinners daily. It's also home to a popular bar, bottle shop and occasional live music in summer.

Richardsons Bistro (☎ 6257 0101; Freycinet Lodge; mains $7-20; ☺ from 10am daily, dinner Nov-Apr) This casual option is at Freycinet Lodge; here the punters can select from a menu of café-style fare and uncomplicated dinner dishes. Nab a table on the deck for alfresco dining and glorious views.

The Bay (☎ 6257 0101; Freycinet Lodge; mains $19-28.50; ☺ dinner) The Bay is Freycinet Lodge's more formal offering, and bookings are essential. As you'd expect, service and views are top-notch, as are the menu selections. Leave room for dessert.

Getting There & Away

Bicheno Coach Service (☎ 6257 0293, 0419 570 293) runs buses between Bicheno, Coles Bay and the national park, connecting with east-coast Redline Coaches and TassieLink services at the Coles Bay turn-off. If coming from Hobart, take TassieLink; it costs $26.90 to the turn-off. From Launceston, opt for Redline Coaches; its fare to the turn-off is $31.10.

From May to November there are usually three Bicheno–Coles Bay buses on weekdays and at least one on Saturday and Sunday. The one-way fare from Bicheno to Coles Bay is $9.30 ($7.70 from the highway turn-off to Coles Bay).

Getting Around

It's more than 5km from Coles Bay to the national park walking tracks car park. **Bicheno Coach Service** (☎ 6257 0293, 0419 570 293) does the trip three times each weekday and once on Saturday and Sunday; bookings are essential. The one-way/return cost from Coles Bay township to the car park is $4.50/8. Park entry fees apply.

Cycling is also a good way to get around the area. You can hire a bike from **Freycinet Adventures** (☎ 6257 0500; 2 Freycinet Dr; per half/full day $20/30).

BICHENO

☎ 03 / pop 700

Bicheno has all the attributes of a successful holiday resort, including soporific water views, a mild climate and abundant sunshine. Fishing is the community's mainstay and the local fleet shelters in a tiny, picturesque harbour called The Gulch. With reasonable prices for food and accommodation, it's a good place to unwind for a few days.

The **visitor information centre** (☎ 6375 1500; 69 Burgess St; ☉ 10am-4pm Mon-Fri, 1-4pm Sat & Sun) can help with information on what to do in the area. Opening hours are longer in the high season.

Sights & Activities

The 3km **Foreshore Footway** extends from Redbill Point to the Blowhole; the best stretch is from the Sea Life Centre east to **Peggys Point**, taking you through The Gulch and along to the **Blowhole**, where there's a large, sea-rocked granite boulder. You return along footpaths with panoramic views over town. In whaling days, passing whales were spotted from **Whalers Hill**. Commercial whaling depleted the animal's population, and these days it's only the occasional lucky visitor who enjoys a whale sighting.

There's a **fairy penguin rookery** (☎ 6375 1333; tours adult/child $18/9) at the northern end of Redbill Beach. The best way to learn about the birds and avoid overly disturbing them is to take the one-hour tour that leaves nightly at dusk from the surf shop on the main road in the centre of town; bookings are essential.

For something different, **Le Frog Trike Rides** (☎ 6375 1777) offers passenger rides on a three-wheeled trike (a cross between a motorbike and convertible car) in and around town (with a French driver – hence the name). Prices start at $12 for a 10-minute 'sampler' cruise around Bicheno, then move upwards in duration and cost.

The helpful owners of **Bicheno Dive Centre** (☎ 6375 1138; www.bichenodive.com.au; 2 Scuba Crt; ☉ 9am-5pm) hire diving equipment and organise underwater trips, including to dive sites in the nearby Governor Island Marine Reserve.

Seven kilometres north of town is the 52-hectare, family-friendly **East Coast Natureworld** (☎ 6375 1311; www.natureworld.com.au; adult/child/family $12.90/6.60/34.80; ☉ 9am-5pm), which boasts a walk-through aviary and lots of free-roaming native animals.

A few kilometres south of the animal park is the turn-off to **Douglas-Apsley National Park**. This park protects a large, undisturbed dry eucalypt forest and has a number of waterfalls and gorges; birds and animals are prolific here. There's rough road access to Apsley Gorge in the park's south, where there's a waterhole with excellent swimming.

Sleeping & Eating

Bicheno Hostel (☎ 6375 1651; 11 Morrison St; dm $19-21, d $53-60; ☐) With its young, enthusiastic owners, good facilities and friendly, laid-back atmosphere, this hostel is the best choice for budget accommodation. One lodge houses dorms, the other has double rooms – try for the front room with large balcony and sea views.

Bicheno East Coast Holiday Park (☎ 6375 1999; bichenoecholidaypark@bigpond.com; 4 Champ St; powered/unpowered sites from $18/16, on-site caravans $35-45, cabins & units $55-105) This neat, well-maintained park has a central location, friendly managers, all the requisite amenities and a range of old and new cabins.

Old Tram Road B&B (☎ 6375 1298; ronmer@intas .net; 3 Old Tram Rd; d $135-145) The best B&B in town, with two large, comfortable rooms only 100m from the beach, accessed via a private track from the lovely back garden. The gourmet cooked breakfasts will get you started.

Sandpiper Ocean Cottages (☎ 6375 1122; www .sandpiper.au.com; Tasman Hwy; d $133-143, extra person $33) A top choice for comfort and seclusion. These three cottages are 8km north of Bicheno on Denison Beach. Each modern two-bedroom cottage sleeps five and features large balconies from which to enjoy the peaceful surrounds.

White Dog Café (☎ 6375 1266; Burgess St; light meals $5-9.50; ☽ breakfast & lunch) At the rear of the Silver Sands Resort is this bright and breezy place, serving classic café fare at very reasonable prices. The deck here boasts water views and is the perfect spot for breakfast (served all day) in the sun.

For something quick, simple and tasty, **Freycinet Café & Bakery** (☎ 6375 1972; cnr Burgess & Morrison Sts) has pies, focaccia and other freshly baked treats, and **Cod Rock Café** (☎ 6375 1340; 45 Foster St) does fish and chips cooked to order.

Getting There & Away

See p648 for details of bus services between Hobart/Launceston and Bicheno.

Bicheno Coach Service (☎ 6257 0293, 0419 570 293) runs between Bicheno and Coles Bay, departing from the Freycinet Bakery & Café. The fare is $9/17.50 one way/return to Coles Bay, $11/20 to the national park walking tracks' car park.

ST MARYS

☎ 03 / pop 590

St Marys is a sleepy little town near the Mt Nicholas range, 10km inland of the Tasman Sea. A visit here entails peaceful countryside wanderings that take in waterfalls, state forest and hilly heights.

St Marys Seaview Farm (☎ 6372 2341; www .seaviewfarm.com.au; German Town Rd; dm $20-25, units $60) is the kind of place you visit for a night but end up staying a week. It's in a peaceful, remote setting, surrounded by forest and with blissful views of coastline and mountains. The cosy backpackers cottage has a kitchen and lounge for all guests, and there are great-value units with bathroom. You'll find Seaview Farm at the end of a dirt track, 8km from St Marys – take Franks St opposite St Marys Hotel, which becomes German Town Rd. Bring along your own supplies; note that the farm doesn't allow kids under 12.

Crepe-fanciers have been known to go troppo over **Mount Elephant Pancake Barn** (☎ 6372 2263; Mt Elephant Pass; savoury pancakes $12-17, sweet pancakes $8-10; ☽ 8am-6pm), 9km south of town off the highway to Bicheno. In the scenic mountain location, take your pick from a range of tasty but overpriced pancakes. No credit cards.

THE NORTHEAST

It's remarkable that the northeast receives so little attention from visitors: it's seductively close to the Pipers River vineyards, yet it boasts some of Tasmania's most secluded white-sand beaches. It encompasses the pretty seaside town of St Helens, the evocatively named Bay of Fires, waterfalls, a wildlife-rich national park, and miles and miles of scenic coastline (with great fishing opportunities and, needless to say, outstanding seafood). A good source of information is www.netasmania.com.au.

Getting There & Around

The main bus company that services Tasmania's northeast is **Redline Coaches** (☎ 1300 360 000; www.tasredline.com.au), which runs daily except Saturday between Launceston and St Helens ($25.10, 2½ hours), via St Marys. It also runs buses daily except Saturday from Launceston to Scottsdale ($13.50, 1¼ hours).

TassieLink (☎ 1300 300 520; www.tassielink.com .au) has two services weekly between Hobart and St Helens ($40.30, four hours), via the east coast.

ST HELENS

☎ 03 / pop 2000

St Helens, sprawled around Georges Bay, is an old whaling town first settled in 1830. Its interesting and varied past is recorded in the memorabilia and photographs contained in the **History Room** (☎ 6376 1744; 61 Cecilia St; ☽ 9am-5pm Mon-Fri, to noon Sat year-round, also 10am-2pm Sun Sep-Apr), which shares its space (and phone lines) with the town's visitor information centre. Here you can pick up a number of useful handouts on fishing, scenic drives and walks in the area.

St Helens is Tasmania's largest fishing port, with a big fleet afloat in the bay and a great reputation for its seafood. Visitors can charter boats for game fishing or take a lazy cruise. **Ahoy! Boat Hire** (☎ 0418 140 436; www.our .net.au/~chrinsy/ahoy.html; ☽ Oct-May) is on the waterfront, behind the Bayside Inn, and hires out kayaks, canoes, motor boats, sail boats and fishing tackle.

TASMANIA

Although the town's beaches aren't particularly good for swimming, there are excellent scenic beaches at **Binalong Bay** (11km north, accessed along Binalong Bay Rd), **Jeanneret Beach** and **Sloop Rock** (about 15km north; take Binalong Bay Rd then the turn-off to The Gardens for both), **Stieglitz** (7km east on St Helens Point), and at St Helens and Humbug Points. Also out on St Helens Point are the spectacular **Peron Dunes** (8km east).

About 26km west of St Helens you'll encounter the turn-off to tiny **Pyengana**, well worth a detour for a trio of attractions: a pub in a paddock; an excellent cheese factory and café; and the scenic **St Columba Falls**. At around 90m, the falls are among the state's highest; there's a 20-minute return walk from the car park to their base.

Sleeping & Eating

You can sleep very well in St Helens for a lot less than other parts of the east coast.

St Helens Youth Hostel (☎ 6376 1661; 5 Cameron St; dm/d/f $18/40/55) Although the rooms at this friendly, central YHA are nothing flash, the facilities (laundry, bike hire etc) are very good.

St Helens Caravan Park (☎ 6376 1290; sthelenscp@ hotmail.com; Penelope St; powered/unpowered sites per 2 people $22/17, on-site caravans $35-45, cabins $55-85) This park has a pleasant bushland setting to the south of town, and good, family-friendly amenities (including games room and playground).

Kellraine Units (☎ 6376 1169; 72 Tully St; d/tr/q $55/75/95) This unassuming collection of large, self-contained units is the best value for money in St Helens (possibly in northern Tassie). The units are next to the highway, about 800m northwest of the centre. Each roomy unit has a kitchen, laundry, video, and living and dining areas (one has wheelchair access).

Bay of Fires Character Cottages (☎ 6376 8262; www.bayoffirescottages.com.au; Binalong Bay Rd; d $130, extra adult/child $25/15) In a million-dollar location opposite a stunning beach some 11km from St Helens is this welcoming enclave of eight colourful, modern, one- to three-bedroom cottages. All have full kitchen and laundry, plus barbecue and private balcony. There is also a neighbouring café and store. Boat tours along the coast can also be arranged here.

Captain's Catch (☎ 6376 1170; Marine Pde; takeaway meals $9-14; ☼ lunch) Order superbly cooked fish and chips from this small kiosk and picnic by the water (doing battle with the seagulls, of course). It also sells fresh, uncooked fish and seafood (including crays).

Fidler's on the Bay (☎ 6376 2444; cnr Tasman Hwy & Jason St; mains $19-26; ☼ dinner Mon-Sat May-Nov, lunch & dinner Mon-Sat Dec-Apr) This highly regarded restaurant showcases the region's fine seafood, particularly in its famed starter: 'a trip around the bay' (featuring scallops, calamari, oysters and salmon). Bookings advised.

BAY OF FIRES

A minor road (Binalong Bay Rd) heads northeast from St Helens to meet the coast at the start of the Bay of Fires, and then continues north up to **The Gardens**. The bay's northern end is reached via the C843, the road to the settlement of Ansons Bay and Mt William National Park.

Early explorers named the bay after seeing Aboriginal fires along the shore. Now a coastal reserve, it's a series of glorious white-sand beaches, rocky headlands, heathlands and lagoons. The ocean beaches provide some good surfing and the lagoons safe swimming; be careful when swimming in the ocean as there are many rips.

For those who like their wilderness experiences to involve some element of sophistication, **Bay of Fires Walk** (☎ 03-6391 9339; www.bayoffires.com.au) conducts a fully catered four-day walk ($1495) from Boulder Point south to Ansons Bay. Trips run from November to May, and accommodation includes two nights at the company's magnificent eco-friendly lodge.

There are some beautiful free camping spots along the bay, though usually without toilets or fresh water. There are good options immediately north of Binalong Bay, accessed by road from St Helens (take the turn-off to The Gardens). In the northern reaches, particularly recommended are the sheltered beachfront sites at Policemans Point, reached by a turn-off before Ansons Bay.

MT WILLIAM NATIONAL PARK

This little-known park consists of long sandy beaches, low ridges and coastal heathlands – it's best to visit during spring and early summer, when the heathland wild-flowers are at their colourful best. The highest point, Mt William (one to 1½ hours return on foot from the car park), is only 216m yet provides some fine views. The area was declared a national park in 1973, primarily to protect the endangered Forester kangaroo, which have since flourished here. Activities on offer in the area include bird-watching and wildlife-spotting, fishing, swimming, surfing and diving.

The impressive **Eddystone lighthouse**, at Eddystone Point, was built of granite blocks in the 1890s. A small picnic spot here overlooks a beach of red-granite outcrops, while a short drive away, beside a lovely tannin-stained creek and yet another magnificent arc of white sand and aqua water, is the idyllic, free camping ground of **Deep Creek**.

Camping in the park is very basic, with only pit toilets, bore water and fireplaces – there's no power and you must bring your own drinking water and wood. Camping is also allowed at four areas at **Stumpys Bay** and **Musselroe Top Camp**. National park entry fees apply.

The park is well off the main roads and can be accessed from the north or south. The northern end is 17km from Gladstone; the southern end is around 60km from St Helens. Try to avoid driving here at night as that's when animals are most active.

SCOTTSDALE & AROUND
☎ 03 / pop 2000

Scottsdale, the largest town in the northeast, services some of Tasmania's richest agricultural and forestry country. The **visitor information centre** (☎ 6352 6520; 88 King St, Scottsdale; ☺ 9am-5pm Mon-Fri, 9am-3pm Sat & Sun) is inside the Forest EcoCentre, a striking place built by Forestry Tasmania. The centre stocks loads of good handouts on drives, walks and accommodation in the area.

Anabel's of Scottsdale (☎ 6352 3277; 46 King St, Scottsdale; s/d $99/140, extra adult $20) has a high-standard restaurant inside a lovely old Federation home, plus modern motel units looking out on a lovely overgrown garden.

Bridestowe Estate Lavender Farm (☎ 6352 8182; www.bridestoweestates.com.au; 296 Gillespies Rd; ☺ 9am-5pm daily Nov-Apr, 10am-4pm Mon-Fri May-Jul & Sep-Oct, by appointment Aug) is near Nabowla, 22km west of Scottsdale. During the lavender's spectacular flowering season, from mid-December to late January, admission is $4 per adult (children free), which covers a guided tour; at other times admission is free. You can purchase numerous lavender products here, and sample lavender-flavoured muffins or ice cream at the café.

Bridport, 21km northwest of Scottsdale, is a popular, laid-back beach resort where there's plenty of accommodation. The Southern Shipping Company runs a weekly ferry from here to Flinders Island (p704).

Platypus Park Country Retreat (☎ 6356 1873; www.platypuspark.com.au; Ada St, Bridport; d $70-140) has self-contained family-friendly units enhanced by sunny verandas and rustic views.

Flying Teapot (☎ 6356 1918; 1800 Bridport Rd; light meals $7-15; ☺ Wed-Sun, closed winter) is a novel café about 3km south of Bridport, overlooking a private airstrip.

PIPERS RIVER REGION

Travelling west from Bridport on the B82 brings you to this well-known and highly regarded wine-producing region, where several wineries provide tastings and cellar-door sales.

Established in 1974, **Pipers Brook** (☎ 03-6382 7527; www.pbv.com.au; 1216 Pipers Brook Rd; tastings $3; ☺ 10am-5pm) is the best-known grape-squeezer in Tasmania; here you can try Pipers Brook Vineyard and Ninth Island wines. The architecturally arresting winery houses a **café** (mains around $20; ☺ lunch). Also at the estate, visit the **Jansz Wine Room** (☎ 03-6382 7066; ☺ 10am-4.30pm), where you can taste Jansz's great range of 'methode Tasmanoise' sparkly.

Some 15km away, south of Pipers River, **Bay of Fires Wines** (☎ 03-6382 7622; 40 Baxters Rd, Pipers River; tastings free; ☺ 10am-5pm) offers tastings plus a stylish **restaurant** (mains $12-35) serving quality Tasmanian produce indoors or alfresco.

LAUNCESTON

☎ 03 / pop 66,750

Launceston may be Tasmania's second-largest city, but life here is at a relaxed big-country-town pace. The town still lags behind Hobart in the cosmopolitan stakes, but in recent years has shaken off its weary, tired image with plenty of social invigoration, tourist development and the opening of sophisticated new eateries. It's a pleasant place to spend a low-key few days, and there are a number of worthwhile attractions in the surrounding areas, from wine regions to historic villages.

ORIENTATION

The compact city centre is arranged in a grid pattern centred on The Mall, on Brisbane St between Charles and St John Sts. Two blocks north, on Cameron St, there's another pedestrian mall in the centre of Civic Sq, around which many public buildings are found. Flanking the old seaport, north of Royal Park, are new developments, including a string of riverfront eateries and a hotel. There's plenty of greenery scattered throughout the town; west of central

Launceston is Cataract Gorge, a magnificent, naturally rugged ravine that is one of the city's major tourist drawcards.

INFORMATION

Bank branches (with ATMs) are mainly located on St John St or Brisbane St near the mall.

Birchalls (Map p662; ☎ 6331 3011; 118-120 Brisbane St, Launceston) Considered Australia's oldest bookshop (c 1844).

Cyber King (Map p662; ☎ 0417 393 540; 113 George St)

iCaf Internet Café (Map p662; ☎ 6334 6815; 22 Quadrant Mall; per 15min $2; ⏰ 9am-5.30pm Mon-Fri, 10am-2pm Sat)

Launceston City Council (www.discoverlaunceston .com)

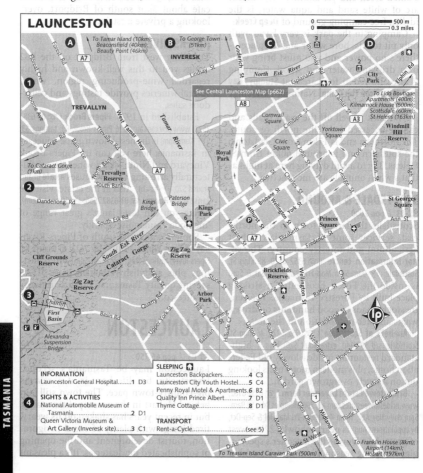

LAUNCESTON

0 ————— 500 m
0 ————— 0.3 miles

INFORMATION	
Launceston General Hospital	1 D3

SIGHTS & ACTIVITIES	
National Automobile Museum of Tasmania	2 D1
Queen Victoria Museum & Art Gallery (Inveresk site)	3 C1

SLEEPING 🏠	
Launceston Backpackers	4 C3
Launceston City Youth Hostel	5 C4
Penny Royal Motel & Apartments	6 B2
Quality Inn Prince Albert	7 D1
Thyme Cottage	8 D1

TRANSPORT	
Rent-a-Cycle	(see 5)

Main post office (Map p662; 107 Brisbane St)
Visitor information centre (Map p662; ☎ 6336 3133,
1800 651 827; www.gatewaytas.com.au; cnr St John &
Cimitiere Sts; ⏱ 9am-5pm Mon-Fri, to 3pm Sat, to noon
Sun & public holidays) Recently taken up residence on
Cornwall Sq, the centre houses racks of pamphlets, and
handles state-wide accommodation, tour and transport
bookings.

SIGHTS & ACTIVITIES
Cataract Gorge
A 10-minute walk west of the city centre
is the magnificent **Cataract Gorge** (Map p658;
☎ 6331 5915; www.launcestoncataractgorge.com.au;
⏱ 9am-dusk). Near-vertical cliffs crowd the
banks of the South Esk River as it enters
the Tamar and the area around the gorge is
a wildlife reserve.

Two walking tracks, one on either side of
the gorge, lead from Kings Bridge up to First
Basin, where you'll find a **swimming pool** (admission free; ⏱ Nov-Mar), picnic grounds, a good
restaurant with sociable peacocks loitering
outside, and trails leading up to the vista-
packed Cataract and Eagle Eyrie lookouts.
The gorge walk takes about 30 minutes; the
northern trail is the easier, while the southern track has some steep climbs as it passes
along the clifftops. The gorge is well worth
visiting at night when it's floodlit.

Both a suspension bridge and a **chairlift**
(one way adult/child $7/5, return $8.50/6; ⏱ 9am-dusk)
cross the waters of the First Basin. A good
walking track (45 minutes each way) leads
further up the gorge to Second Basin and
Duck Reach.

Queen Victoria Museum & Art Gallery
The **Queen Victoria Museum & Art Gallery**
(☎ 6323 3777; www.qvmag.tas.gov.au; adult/child $10/
free; ⏱ 10am-5pm) has two branches, one at a
site purpose-built for the museum in 1891
at **Royal Park** (Map p662; 2 Wellington St), and the
other at the revamped **Inveresk railyards** (Map
p658; 2 Invermay Rd). Both have cafés and access
for wheelchairs. The one-off admission fee
allows access to both sites.

The child-friendly Royal Park branch includes exhibitions on the island's Aboriginal
inhabitants and Tasmanian fauna, a splendid joss house donated by the descendants
of Chinese settlers, and a **planetarium** (adult/
child/family $5/3/12; ⏱ shows 3pm Tue-Sat).

The Inveresk site houses an impressive art
gallery, Aboriginal shell necklaces, stories of

Tasmania's migration history and authentic
railway workshops.

Boag's Brewery
Boag's beer (the beer of choice for most
northern Tasmanians – southerners are
loyal to Cascade, brewed in Hobart) has
been brewed at this site on William St since
1881. Guided tours (90 minutes) operate
from the irresistibly named **Boag's Centre
for Beer Lovers** (Map p662; ☎ 6332 6300; www.boags
.com.au; 39 William St; adult/child $16/12; ⏱ tours 9am &
11am Mon-Fri, also 2pm Fri), opposite the brewery.
Bookings are essential.

Other Attractions
The **Design Centre of Tasmania** (Map p662; ☎ 6331
5506; www.twdc.org.au; cnr Brisbane & Tamar Sts;
⏱ 9.30am-5.30pm), on the edge of City Park,
is a retail outlet displaying high-quality
work by Tasmanian craftspeople. The **Wood
Design Collection** (☎ 6334 6558; adult/child/family
$2.20/1.10/5.50), also incorporated into the
centre, showcases designs by locals.

The oxymoronic **National Automobile Museum
of Tasmania** (Map p658; ☎ 6334 8888; 86 Cimitiere St;
adult/child/family $8.50/4.50/21.50; ⏱ 9am-5pm Sep-May,
10am-4pm Jun-Aug) will please motor enthusiasts –
it's one of Australia's best presentations of
classical and historic relics, with a ground
floor devoted to four-wheelers and a loft full
of classic motorbikes.

The National Trust–classified **Old Umbrella Shop** (Map p662; ☎ 6331 9248; 60 George St;
admission free; ⏱ 9am-5pm Mon-Fri, to noon Sat) was
built from Tasmanian blackwood in the
1860s and still displays old brollies. Along
with an assortment of gifts, local crafts and
souvenirs this rare period treat is worth
walking into if only to sample the friendly
service of a bygone era.

Well signposted some 8km south of the
city, **Franklin House** (off Map p658; ☎ 6344 7824; 413
Hobart Rd, Breadalbane; adult/child $7.70/free; ⏱ 9am-
5pm Oct-Mar, to 4pm Apr-Sep) is one of Launceston's most attractive Georgian homes. Built
in 1838, it is now beautifully restored and
furnished by the National Trust.

Parks & Reserves
The 13-hectare **City Park** (Map p662) is a
fine example of a Victorian garden and features an elegant fountain, a bandstand, a
fabulous Japanese macaque enclosure and a
glass conservatory dating from 1832. **Princes**

TASMANIA

Square (Map p662; btwn Charles & St John Sts) features a bronze fountain bought at the 1855 Paris Exhibition.

Other public parks and gardens include **Royal Park** (Map p662), near the junction of North Esk and Tamar Rivers – it includes a river-edge boardwalk taking in the Cataract Gorge Reserve, Ritchies Mill, Home Point and the new seaport development.

A 10-minute drive north of the city is **Tamar Island** (☎ 6327 3964; West Tamar Hwy; adult/child/family $2/1/5; ☼ 9am-dusk), where you'll find a 2km wheelchair-friendly boardwalk through a significant wetlands reserve, teeming with birdlife.

TOURS

Call at the visitor information centre to get the lowdown on tours available within and beyond Launceston.

Cataract Cruises (Map p662; ☎ 6334 9900; Cataract Gorge cruise adult/child $15/6) Operates good-value 50-minute cruises which operate hourly from 9.30am to 3.30pm; from the same departure point as Tamar River Cruises.

Coach Tram Tours (☎ 6336 3133, 0419 004 802) Operates tours that depart from the visitor information centre, which also handles bookings. Among its offerings is a three-hour tour of the city's key attractions ($32/24/90 per adult/child/family), which leaves daily at 10am May to December (also at 2pm January to April). It also runs excursions around the Tamar Valley and Beauty Point.

Ghost tour (☎ 0421 819 373; adult/family $20/45) In the evening, get spooked on a 90-minute ghost tour around the city's back alleys and lanes, conducted by professional theatrical guides. Tours depart from the front of the **Royal Oak Hotel** (Map p662; ☎ 6331 5346; 14 Brisbane St) at dusk and bookings are essential.

Historic walk (☎ 6336 3133; adult/child $15/11) This old favourite includes a one-hour guided taking in the city centre's architecture, departing from the visitor information centre at 9.45am Monday to Friday.

Tamar River Cruises (Map p662; ☎ 6334 9900; www .tamarrivercruises.com.au; Home Point Pde; Cataract Gorge cruise adult/child/family $15/8/38) Based at Home Point in Royal Park, this company conducts excellent 50-minute cruises through the Cataract Gorge. Other package cruises are also available; bookings are recommended.

FESTIVALS & EVENTS

Australian Three Peaks Race (www.threepeaks.org .au) A four-day nonstop nautical rush in March to sail from Beauty Point (north of Launceston) to Hobart, pausing for teams of runners to jump ashore to scale three mountains along the way.

Festivale (www.festivale.com.au) Three days in mid-February devoted to eating, drinking, arts and entertainment, staged in City Park.

Royal Launceston Show Old hands show off their herds in October.

SLEEPING
Budget

Launceston Backpackers (Map p658; ☎ 6334 2327; www.launcestonbackpackers.com.au; 103 Canning St; dm $18-19, d with/without bathroom $65/55; ☐) Buzzing with a friendly vibe is this well-managed hostel, housed in an impressive Federation building. The staff are amicable, offering great advice on local attractions, and the rooms are clean and spacious.

Launceston City Youth Hostel (Map p658; ☎ 6344 9779; tasequiphire@email.com; 36 Thistle St; dm/s/f $15/22/40) This is a rambling, private hostel 2km south of the city centre. It's a sound choice – unless you're adverse to the strict single-sex dorm policy. The hostel rents out bicycles (see p665) and bushwalking gear.

Irish Murphy's (Map p662; ☎ 6331 4440; cnr Brisbane & Bathurst Sts; dm/d without bathroom $17/35) This pub has good cheap bunks, an appealing common room and a balcony to pose on. It also has a downstairs bar that becomes particularly lively when bands are performing.

Treasure Island Caravan Park (off Map p658; ☎ 6344 2600; 94 Glen Dhu St; powered/unpowered sites per 2 people $20/19, on-site caravans $46, cabins $70-80) About 2.5km south of Launceston, this park has good facilities but is in a somewhat noisy location beside the highway.

Midrange
GUESTHOUSES & B&BS

Kilmarnock House (off Map p658; ☎ 6334 1514; www .kilmarnockhouse.com; 66 Elphin Rd; s $85, d $135-150, f $170) This National Trust–listed 1905 Edwardian mansion houses gracious accommodation. Turned blackwood-timber staircase rails lead to elegant, antique-furnished rooms. The rate includes a generous breakfast and kids are welcome.

Hillview House (Map p662; ☎ 6331 7388; cnr George & Canning Sts; s $85, d $115-125) This impressive National Trust–listed house (c 1840) offers exceptional views over the city, river and valley. It exudes charm and comfort with well-furnished rooms; guests can enjoy a fully cooked or continental breakfast.

Fiona's B&B (Map p662; ☎ 6334 5965; www.fionas -bnb.com.au; 141a George St; s/d $90/124, ste $135-255)

Fiona's is a hospitable B&B set in a lush garden setting, with immaculate modern rooms. The rates include a full breakfast and many of the rooms have either a balcony or private courtyard.

Ashton Gate (Map p662; ☎ 6331 6180; www.ashton gate.com.au; 32 High St; s $90, d $120-150) This thoroughly welcoming and refreshing Victorian B&B provides a sense of home; each room is beautifully furnished, and there's also a self-contained apartment in the Old Servant's Quarters.

HOTELS & MOTELS
Quality Inn Prince Albert (Map p658; ☎ 6331 7633; www.qualityinnprincealbert.com.au; cnr Tamar & William Sts; d $135-280) The Italianate façade hides an widely extravagant affair. The rooms are spacious and elegant and every room boasts high-quality French-polished woodwork. Cooked or continental brekky is available.

Sandor's on the Park (Map p662; ☎ 6331 2055, 1800 030 140; 3 Brisbane St; d $85-105) Well positioned opposite City Park, Sandor's provides neat and tidy rooms, including family rooms. Facilities here include TV, fridge, tea- and coffee-making facilities, and free in-house movies.

Old Bakery Inn (Map p662; ☎ 6331 7900, 1800 641 264; oldbakeryinn@bestwestern.com.au; cnr York & Margaret Sts; r from $125) Established for over 130 years and now run by the Best Western crew, this old bakery offers heritage accommodation in comfortable, stylish and charming rooms that include all the mod cons. There's also a self-contained suite in the Loft.

Penny Royal Motel & Apartments (Map p658; ☎ 6331 6699, 1800 060 954; www.leisureinns.com.au; 147 Paterson St; motel r from $134, 1-/2-bedroom apt from $133/163) A short walk from Cataract Gorge, the Penny Royal has motel rooms trying to take in the heritage, old-world look of dark-wood furniture and exposed ceiling timbers, plus a picturesque row of comfortable modern apartments.

SELF-CONTAINED UNITS & COTTAGES
Adina Place (Map p662; ☎ 6331 6866, 1800 030 181; adinacityview@bigpond.com; 50 York St; s/d from $105/135) Near Windmill Hill Reserve, Adina Place offers smart and tidy studio apartments, two-bedroom units and spa suites; continental brekky is provided.

Thyme Cottage (Map p658; ☎ 6331 1906; www.thymecottage.com.au; 31 Cimitiere St; d $110-155) This

delightful 1880s heritage cottage is decorated with antiques and exudes warmth and charm. It includes modern facilities, provides full breakfast provisions and welcomes anklebiters.

Canning Cottage (Map p662; ☎ 6331 4876; 26-28 Canning St; d $95) These two fully-furnished, two-bedroom cottages are conjoined buildings situated on the one lot. Both are very snug, with plenty of steep steps and narrow doorways.

Top End
Waratah on York (Map p662; ☎ 6331 2081; www.waratahonyork.com.au; 12 York St; d $172-260) Set in an 1862 Victorian Italianate mansion, the Waratah is an opulent and unashamedly old-fashioned B&B (and gay-friendly, to boot). Its luxurious heritage rooms are fully equipped and the executive spa suites all have panoramic views.

Peppers Seaport Hotel (Map p662; ☎ 6345 3333; www.seaport.com.au; 28 Seaport Blvd; d $250-504) Built in the shape of a ship on the site of an old dry dock, this new glam hotel epitomises the recent dockside developments. The hotel's contemporary design extends to the deluxe rooms (accentuated by natural timbers and muted tones). The rooms and suites are spacious, include all the mod cons, and most of them have balconies with spectacular views.

Lido Boutique Apartments (Map p662; ☎ 6334 5988; www.thelido.com.au; 47-49 Elphin Rd; d apt incl breakfast $190-294, extra person $40) Offering designer boutique apartments with 1930s flair and elegance, the Lido houses deluxe quarters of varying sizes (one to three bedrooms), and 'Japanese Imperial' suites with full-sized

AUTHOR'S CHOICE

Hatherley House (Map p662; ☎ 6334 7727; www.hatherleyhouse.com.au; 43 High St; ste incl breakfast $250-300) Oozing style and sophistication, Hatherley House is one of Tasmania's finest boutique hotels. The décor is a striking combination of antique and ultra-modern inside a beautifully restored 1830s mansion, set in lovely gardens. Great attention to detail has been paid in furnishing the suites, with king-sized beds, artworks, fireplaces and sleek bathrooms (some with spa). Leave the kiddies at home

TASMANIA

TASMANIA

CENTRAL LAUNCESTON

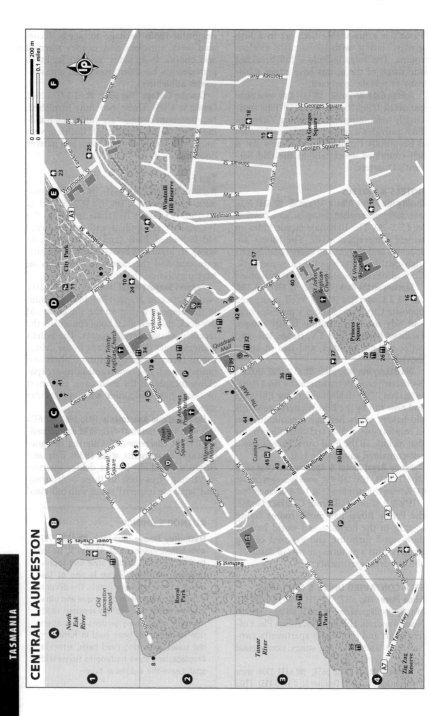

spa and king-sized bed. All apartments have modern amenities.

EATING
Restaurants
Stillwater (Map p662; ☎ 6331 4153; 2 Bridge Rd, in Ritchies Mill; lunch $8-20, dinner $20-30; ☺ breakfast, lunch & dinner) Having scratched a few notches in its awards belt, this is where you come to impress and be impressed. Set in the stylishly renovated 1840s Ritchies flour mill beside the Tamar River, culinary delights include all manner of seafood and meat dishes, vegetarian options and a comprehensive wine list. By day it's a relaxed café churning out breakfast (smoked salmon bagels, homemade muesli) and lunch (roast pumpkin pizza, Thai lamb salad). Of an evening the restaurant struts its stuff. Book ahead.

Fee & Me (Map p662; ☎ 6331 3195; www.feeandme.com.au; cnr Charles & Frederick Sts; 3-/4-/5-courses per course $19/17/15; ☺ dinner Mon-Sat) This restaurant does outstanding, innovative and up-market cuisine, which has been handsomely awarded year after year. Located in the National Trust–registered Morton House, Fee & Me specialises in fine dining and an interesting degustation menu structure – all dishes are entrée size and brackets of dishes move from light to rich; most diners choose between three and five courses, depending on appetite. Book ahead.

Sushi Shack (Map p662; ☎ 6331 4455; 134 York St; sushi dishes $3.50-15; ☺ lunch & dinner Mon-Sat) This is *the* spot for fresh sushi. Tempting you with classic Japanese mains, such as yakisoba, crispy tempura and teriyaki delights, your best bet is to be here every Wednesday and Thursday night for the all-you-can-eat sushi fest ($18).

Hallam's Waterfront (Map p662; ☎ 6334 0554; 13 Park St; mains $23.50-28.50; ☺ lunch & dinner) Adjacent to the Tamar Yacht Club and decked out with the requisite nautical theme, this riverfront place has friendly service and specialises in super-fresh seafood. There's also a takeaway attached, catering to gourmet fish 'n' chip lovers.

Jailhouse Grill (Map p662; ☎ 6331 0466; cnr Wellington & York Sts; mains $15-20; ☺ dinner daily, also lunch Fri) A favourite of the meat-and-three-veg aficionados, this wood-fired grilling mecca takes your choice of steak (eye fillet, scotch, rump or porterhouse) and cooks it just the way you like it. It doesn't do a bad job with the chicken and seafood dishes either.

Cafés & Quick Eats
Pierre's (Map p662; ☎ 6331 6835; 88 George St; mains $15-26; ☺ breakfast, lunch & dinner Mon-Sat) Choices at wonderful Pierre's involve either light meals (bagels, focaccias, burgers or pasta) or more substantial and innovative mains. Early risers can expect sumptuous croissants, home-made fruit loaf or any choice of brekky-style eggs. Finally, in the finest café tradition, the desserts are an experience and the coffee – pure class.

Ric's Café Bar (Map p662; 35/39 Cameron St; mains $13-25; ☺ breakfast, lunch & dinner) By day this sophisticated new venue dishes out an array of café fare; options include an extensive seafood menu, pizza, or something special

TASMANIA

such as a moussaka that's bound to line your tummy. It also provides late-night entertainment (see below).

Fish 'n' Chips (Map p662; ☎ 6331 1999; 30 Seaport Blvd; meals $10-15; ☑ lunch & dinner) Perched on the riverfront, this modern affair has fresh fish 'n' chips (from around $6), seafood salads and antipasto platters. Kids are bound to get into a feathered fist-fight with a seagull or two in the alfresco dining area.

Konditorei Café Manfred (Map p662; ☎ 6334 2490; 106 George St; mains $10-16; ☑ breakfast & lunch) This eatery allows you to gorge yourself on really good baked goods (gourmet breads, tarts, tortes) and plenty of creative vegetarian dishes at either a downstairs table or upstairs on the weather-proofed terrace.

Fresh (Map p662; 6331 4299; 178 Charles St; mains $8-16; ☑ breakfast & lunch) This all-welcoming retro-arty place, opposite Princes Sq, offers tasty vegetarian snacks, including terrific pizza, bruschetta and a plug-your-stomach brekky 'with the works'.

Pasta Resistance Too (Map p662; ☎ 6334 3081; 23 Quadrant Mall; lunch $4.50-6; ☑ breakfast & lunch) An excellent lunch spot, this tiny, no-frills place has a great range of freshly made pasta and sauces at near-to-nothing prices, which is why it's often packed.

DRINKING & ENTERTAINMENT

Most of Launceston's entertainment options are advertised in the local-based daily newspaper the *Examiner*.

Ursula's on Brisbane (Map p662; ☎ 6334 7033; 63 Brisbane St) This cosmopolitan and stylish wine and tapas bar is great for grazing while sipping through choice Tassie wines. Soak up the Euro ambience on comfy leather sofas; the savvy are onto this one.

Ric's Café Bar (Map p662; 35/39 Cameron St) By night this eatery (see p663) dons a different cap and entertains the cool set with funky jazz bands.

Saloon Bar (Map p662; ☎ 6331 7355; 191 Charles St) Part of the Hotel Tasmania complex, this bar has décor that's a mixture of *The Good, the Bad and the Ugly*, but it does have a mixture of DJs and mainly cover bands strutting their stuff Wednesday to Saturday nights.

Irish Murphy's (Map p662; ☎ 6331 4440; cnr Brisbane & Bathurst Sts) This excellent watering hole is stuffed full of Emerald Isle paraphernalia and has live music Thursday through Sat-

urday nights (and you can eavesdrop on the Sunday arvo jam sessions).

Princess Theatre (Map p662; ☎ 6323 3666; 57 Brisbane St) Built in 1911 and including the smaller Earl Arts Centre, this theatre stages an eclectic mix of drama, dance and comedy, drawing acts from across Tasmania and the mainland.

GETTING THERE & AWAY
Air

There are regular direct flights between Launceston and Melbourne, Sydney and Brisbane (see p617). **Qantas** (Map p662; ☎ 13 13 13; www.qantas.com.au; cnr Brisbane & Charles Sts) has an office in the centre of town.

Bus

The main bus companies operating out of Launceston are **Redline Coaches** (☎ 1300 360 000; www.tasredline.com.au) and **TassieLink** (☎ 1300 300 520; www.tassielink.com.au); the terminal for both is at **Cornwall Square Transit Centre** (Map p662; cnr St John & Cimitiere Sts), at the rear of the visitor information centre.

Redline runs buses to Bicheno ($28, 2¾ hours), Burnie ($24, 2¾ hours), Deloraine ($10, 45 minutes), Devonport ($18, 1½ hours), George Town ($9, 45 minutes), Hobart ($25, 2½ hours), Stanley ($37, four hours), St Helens ($25, 2¾ hours) and Swansea ($22, two hours).

TassieLink operates a regular city express service linking Launceston with Devonport ($18, 1¼ hours), tying in with the ferry schedules, and Hobart ($24, 2½ hours). It services the north and west from Launceston, including Sheffield ($20, two hours), Cradle Mountain ($46.50, three hours), Queenstown ($56.50, six hours) and, after a break in Queenstown, Strahan ($64.50, 8¾ hours). TassieLink also runs a twice-weekly service between Launceston and Bicheno ($26, 2½ hours) – this is increased to four times weekly in summer.

Tamar Valley Coaches (Map p662; ☎ 6334 0828; 4 Cuisine Lane), off Brisbane St, operates bus services along the West Tamar Valley, stopping at Rosevears ($3.20), Beaconsfield ($6.40) and Beauty Point ($7.20, one hour).

GETTING AROUND
To/From the Airport

Launceston airport is 15km south of the city. A **shuttle bus** (☎ 0500 512 009; adult/child

$10/5) runs a door-to-door airport service. A taxi to the city costs about $30.

Bicycle

Rent-a-Cycle (Map p658; ☎ 6344 9779; tasequiphire@ email.com; 36 Thistle St), at the Launceston City Youth Hostel (p660), has a good range of touring/mountain bikes from $12/18 per day (ask for weekly or monthly rates), plus camping equipment for hire and lots of bushwalking advice.

Seaport Boat & Bike Hire (Map p662; ☎ 6331 89 99; hire@jmc.com.au; 26 Seaport Blvd) has bikes for rent (from $10/40 per hour/day), plus canoes ($10/50 per hour/day) and motorboats ($35/155 per hour/day) for river exploration. Touring bikes are also available for longer-term hire.

Bus

The local bus service is run by **Metro** (☎ 13 22 01; www.metrotas.com.au); the main departure points are on the two blocks of St John St between Paterson and York Sts. For $3.60 you can buy a daily pass that can be used after 9am Monday to Friday and all day Saturday, Sunday and public holidays. Most routes, however, don't operate in the evening and Sunday services are limited.

Car

There are plenty of car-rental firms in Launceston. All the major firms have desks at the airport, and most also have an office in town. The bigger ones include **Europcar** (Map p662; ☎ 6331 8200, 1800 030 118; 112 George St) and **Thrifty** (Map p662; ☎ 6333 0911, 1800 030 730; 151 St John St). Cheaper operators include **Economy Car Rentals** (Map p662; ☎ 6334 3299; 27 William St), with prices starting at $31 per day (older cars, rentals of at least seven days) and **Lo-Cost Auto Rent** (Map p662; ☎ 1800 647 060; www.rentforless.com.au; 174 Brisbane St), with a good selection of vehicles and starting rates from $30 to $45 daily.

AROUND LAUNCESTON

TAMAR VALLEY

The Tamar River links Launceston with its ocean port, wending its way north through lovely orchards, pastures, forests and vineyards. The best way to explore this area is to skip the highways and hug the quieter

minor roads that weave through rural hamlets. Crossing the river near Deviot is Batman Bridge, the only bridge on the lower reaches of the Tamar.

The Tamar Valley and nearby Pipers River (p657) are among Tasmania's main wineproducing areas, heartily embracing the notion of eat, drink and be merry.

GETTING THERE & AROUND

For cyclists, the ride north along the Tamar River is a gem.

On weekdays, **Tamar Valley Coaches** (☎ 03-6334 0828; 4 Cuisine Lane) runs three to five buses per day from Launceston up and down the West Tamar Valley, with stops including Rosevears ($3), Beaconsfield ($6.50) and Beauty Point ($7, one hour).

Redline Coaches (☎ 1300 360 000; www.tasredline .com.au) has three buses on weekdays along the eastern side of the Tamar between Launceston and George Town ($8.60, 45 minutes).

The **Shuttlefish ferry** (☎ 03-6383 4479, 0412 485 611; www.shuttlefishferry.com.au; one way adult/child $9/5, return $16/9; ☸ Wed-Mon Oct-May) is an ondemand passenger service making regular trips across the Tamar River between Beauty Point and George Town (25 minutes). Bookings are essential.

Rosevears

☎ 03 / pop 160

Rosevears is a tiny, picturesque riverside settlement nestled on a side road off the West Tamar Hwy. This area is definitely one for wine buffs, as it's home to three very good wineries.

Strathlynn (☎ 6330 2388; www.pbv.com.au; 95 Rosevears Dr; tastings $3; ☸ 10am-5pm) is an outlet for Pipers Brook Vineyard (p657) and is home to a highly polished **restaurant** (mains $18-28; ☸ lunch) with lovely views.

Nearby is the low-key **St Matthias Vineyard** (☎ 6330 1700; www.moorilla.com.au; 113 Rosevears Dr; free tastings; ☸ 10am-5pm), where you can sample Moorilla favourites with cheese and antipasto.

Back on the main road, you'll encounter the sizable hilltop headquarters of **Rosevears Estate** (☎ 6330 1800; www.rosevearsestate .com.au; Waldhorn Dr; tastings $2; ☸ 10am-5pm), a prestigious wine-maker that conducts winery tours for $3.30 per person. Its stylish **restaurant** (mains $16.50-28; ☸ lunch daily, dinner Wed-Sat) offers a contemporary menu, and

TASMANIA

rather than drink and drive, you can stay here in luxurious self-contained **cottages** (1-/2-bedroom cottages $225/380).

The other attraction in town is of the feathered variety: the **Waterbird Haven Trust** (☎ 6394 3744; Rosevears Dr; adult/child $5/3; ☷ 9am-dusk) is a nonprofit sanctuary for marine birds.

And if you haven't overdone it on all the vino and fine food, **Rosevears Waterfront Tavern** (☎ 6394 4074; 215 Rosevears Dr; mains $15-20; ☷ lunch & dinner) has good meals and a scenic terrace.

Beauty Point & Around
☎ 03 / pop 1500
Beauty Point is where you'll find the fascinating **Seahorse World** (☎ 6383 4111; www.sea

horseworld.com.au; Beauty Point Wharf; adult/child/family $15/8/40; ☷ 9.30am-4.30pm), based around a seahorse farm where the tiny critters are grown to supply aquariums worldwide and eventually, it's hoped, the Chinese-medicine market. There's an interesting one-hour tour where you get up close to the fascinating *hippocampus abdominalis* (pot-bellied seahorse). The **café** (mains $10-18; ☷ breakfast & lunch) here enjoys outstanding views over the Tamar.

Next to Seahorse World, the new venture **Platypus House** (☎ 6383 4884; www.platypushouse .com.au; Inspection Head Wharf; adult/child/family $15/8/40; ☷ 9am-4pm) seemed a little underdeveloped when we visited. The one-hour guided tour consisted of only two platy-

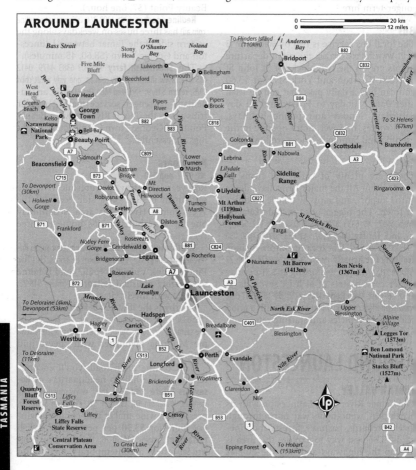

AROUND LAUNCESTON

puses on show and no butterflies in the much-touted Butterfly House.

North of Beauty Point, at the mouth of the Tamar River, are the quiet holiday and fishing resorts of **Greens Beach** and **Kelso**, each with waterside caravan parks, and south is the once-thriving but now somewhat subdued gold-mining town of Beaconsfield. Here you can visit the **Grubb Shaft Gold & Heritage Museum** (☎ 6383 1473; West St; adult/family $8/20; 9.30am-4.30pm Oct-Apr, 10am-4pm May-Sep), once Tasmania's largest gold mine. The museum's hands-on interactive exhibits are kid-friendly.

There's a decent selection of accommodation in Beauty Point. **Tamar Cove** (☎ 6383 4375; 4421 Main Rd; r $55-65), on the way into town, is an old-style motel that's benefited from a facelift and the addition of a good **restaurant** (mains $12-21; lunch & dinner) that attracts hungry crowds to its bright interior and alfresco terrace.

George Town
☎ 03 / pop 5600

George Town, on the eastern shore of the Tamar River, close to the heads, is historically significant as the site where Lieutenant Colonel Paterson landed in 1804 to establish a beachhead against a feared French occupation, leading to the European settlement of northern Tasmania. The **visitor information centre** (☎ 6382 1700; Main Rd; 9am-5pm) is on the main road as you enter from the south.

The **Grove** (☎ 6382 1336; cnr Cimitiere & Elizabeth Sts; adult/child $7.50/3.50; 10am-5pm mid-Sep–mid-May, 10.30am-3pm Mon-Fri mid-May–mid-Sep) is an extensively restored Georgian bluestone residence built in 1835 and now classified by the National Trust. Lunch and light refreshments are available in the tearooms here, served in the spirit of the past by staff in period costume.

Seal & Sea Adventure Tours (☎ 6382 3452, 0419 357 028; www.sealandsea.com) offers three- to four-hour trips out to the seal colony at Tenth Island in a glass-bottom boat, with an enthusiastic and knowledgeable guide at the helm; trips cost $121 per person for two people, $94 per person for groups of three to six. River cruises and fishing and dive charters can also be arranged.

Your best option for both food and a bed is the **Pier Hotel** (☎ 6382 1300; www.pierhotel

.com.au; 5 Elizabeth St; r with/without bathroom $110/55, villas from $150). At the top of the price scale you'll get modern riverside lodgings in motel units or self-contained villas, or for considerably less you can choose pleasant pub-style accommodation. The popular **bistro** (mains $12-20; lunch & dinner) has outdoor seating and a modernised pub menu.

Low Head
☎ 03 / pop 465

North of George Town is Low Head, which provides the navigation aids for ships to enter the Tamar. The **pilot station** (Low Head Rd) is Australia's oldest (established in 1805) and houses an interesting **maritime museum** (☎ 6382 2826; adult/child/family $5/3/20; 9am-6pm), cluttered with historical items and displays. At the head itself, the grounds of the 1888 **lighthouse** (grounds to 6pm) provide great views over the river mouth and surrounding area.

Penguins return to their burrows near the lighthouse at dusk and can be viewed via **Nocturnal Tours** (☎ 0418 361 860; www.penguin tours.com.au; adult/child $14/8). Tours take place nightly. There's good surf at **East Beach** on Bass Strait and safe swimming in the river.

Low Head Beachfront Holiday Village (☎ 6382 1000; 40 Gunns Pde; powered/unpowered sites per 2 people $18/15, cabins $60-75) has claimed a good location on East Beach for its multitude of bush sites and pine-drenched cabins.

At the **pilot station** (☎ 6382 1143, 1800 008 343; Low Head Rd; d from $90) you can stay in roomy, well-equipped colonial cottages.

HADSPEN & CARRICK
☎ 03 / pop 1730

Hadspen, 15km southwest of Launceston, is home to some attractive 19th-century buildings, and just west of here, off Old Bass Hwy, is the National Trust–owned **Entally House** (☎ 6393 6201; adult/child/family $7.70/5.50/15.40; 10am-4pm), one of Tasmania's best-known historic homes. Built in 1819 and named after a Calcutta suburb, it's set in beautiful grounds and creates a vivid period picture of rural affluence.

The **Red Feather Inn** (☎ 6393 6331; 42 Main St; mains from $19; dinner) is an atmospheric old inn from 1844 with low ceilings and a rabbit warren of rooms. There's a fine menu featuring staples such as steak and seafood, plus vegetarian options.

Just 4km west of Hadspen is tiny Carrick, on the old highway to Deloraine. Carrick's most prominent feature is the 1846 four-storey, ivy-smothered **Carrick Mill** (☎ 6393 6922; 67 Bass Hwy; mains around $12; ⊗ 11am-late), now a magnificent pub with a lovely beer garden.

WESTBURY
☎ 03 / pop 1300
The historic town of Westbury, 32km west of Launceston, has a few quirky attractions. It's best known for its **White House** (☎ 6393 1171; King St; adult/child/family $7.70/3/15; ⊗ 10am-4pm Tue-Sun), situated on the Village Green and built in 1841. It features collections of colonial furnishings, vintage cars, an intricate doll's house and a collection of 19th-century toys. The on-site **bakery** (⊗ 9am-4pm Tue-Sun) is well worth a visit for the freshest and tastiest hot bread this side of Bass Strait.

Westbury Maze (☎ 6393 1840; Bass Hwy; adult/child/family $5.50/4.50/20; ⊗ 10am-5pm Sep-Jul) is a large hedge maze which will appeal to children (or your inner child), plus a tearoom.

Nearby, **Pearn's Steam World** (☎ 6397 3313; 65 Bass Hwy; adult/child $5/2; ⊗ 9am-4pm) is filled with antique steam engines and relics.

Call into the **John Temple Gallery** (☎ 6393 1666; Bass Hwy; admission free; ⊗ 10am-5pm) to purchase or just admire John's panoramic photographs of Tasmania's wilderness.

Fitzpatricks Inn (☎ 6393 1153; fitzpatricksinn@ bigpond.com; 56 Bass Hwy; s/d $55/85) has good-value rooms set in a pretty garden behind a large, white, porticoed building dating from 1833.

Hobnobs (☎ 6393 2007; 47 William St; ⊗ lunch Wed-Sun, dinner Thu-Sat) is a classy café-restaurant with a fabulous courtyard, set in a 1860s National Trust–listed building.

LONGFORD
☎ 03 / pop 2830
Longford, a National Trust–classified town 27km south of Launceston, is best known for its proximity to two historic estates. **Woolmers** (☎ 6391 2230; www.woolmers.com.au; Woolmers Lane; adult/child $18/5; ⊗ 10am-4.30pm) was built in 1819 and now nurtures a two-hectare rose garden. The admission price includes a one-hour guided tour of the homestead, plus a self-guided tour of the grounds.

Nearby is **Brickendon** (☎ 6391 1383; www .brickendon.com.au; Woolmers Lane; adult/child/family

$9/3.50/27; ⊗ 9.30am-5pm Tue-Sun), dating from 1824, with heritage gardens and an authentic farming village.

Both these estates offer self-contained accommodation in restored colonial-era **cottages** (d $110-180).

Country Club Hotel (☎ 6391 1155; 19 Wellington St; s/d $30/40, unit $60) is a welcoming place offering good-value budget rooms (some with bathroom) and a self-contained unit. Downstairs, the bistro dishes up hearty pub tucker.

JJ's Bakery & Old Mill Café (☎ 6391 2364; 52 Wellington St; mains $10-20; ⊗ 7am-5pm), in the restored Old Emerald flour mill, produces a wide variety of light snacks and delicious baked goods.

EVANDALE
☎ 03 / pop 1035
One of Tasmania's most impressive National Trust–classified towns, Evandale is 22km south of Launceston in the South Esk Valley, near Launceston's airport. Many of its 19th-century buildings are in excellent condition and it's a pretty place for a stroll. A large country **market** (Falls Park; ⊗ 9am-1pm Sun) is held weekly. The volunteer-staffed **visitor information centre** (☎ 6391 8128; 18 High St; ⊗ 10am-3pm) has lots of information about the region.

In keeping with its olde-world atmosphere, the town hosts the **Evandale Village Fair & National Penny Farthing Championships** (www .evandalevillagefair.com) in February each year.

Ten kilometres south of Evandale, off Nile Rd, is the National Trust–listed property of **Clarendon** (☎ 6398 6220; adult/family $7.70/15.40; ⊗ 10am-5pm Sep-May, 10am-4pm Jun-Aug), a grand French neoclassical mansion built in 1838 and surrounded by impressive parklands. There are also three self-contained cottages ($100) available for accommodation.

Clarendon Arms Hotel (☎ 6391 8181; 11 Russell St; s/d without bathroom $40/65) is a classic country hotel. It has murals downstairs depicting the area's history, good-value meals, budget accommodation and a leafy beer garden.

Grandma's House (☎ 6381 8088; www.grand mashouse.com.au; 10 Rodgers Lane; d $140, extra person $35) accommodates up to seven people in a two-storey, self-contained cottage set in pretty gardens.

Atmospheric **Ingleside Bakery Café** (☎ 6391 8682; 4 Russell St; mains $7-20; ⊗ breakfast & lunch churns out light lunches of soups, gourmet sandwiches and pies, and also displays a selection of arts and antique items.

BEN LOMOND NATIONAL PARK

This 165-sq-km park, which is 55km south-east of Launceston, includes the entire Ben Lomond Range and is best known for its skiing. It's a popular spot for sightseers and walkers as well as skiers, however, as the scenery is magnificent year-round. The park is particularly noted for its alpine wildflowers, which run riot during spring and summer.

There's accommodation here year-round at Tasmania's highest-altitude pub, the **Creek Inn** (☎ 03-6390 6199; s/d/f $40/75/115). There's also a fully licensed restaurant. During the ski season (usually early July to late September) there's also a kiosk and ski shop; lift tickets and equipment hire cost considerably less than they do on the mainland.

During the ski season, there's a morning bus service running from Launceston to the top of the mountain, returning in the late afternoon; inquire at Launceston's visitor information centre for further details. Outside the ski season, driving is your only transport option. The route up to the alpine village from the mountain's base includes Jacob's Ladder, a very steep climb on an unsealed road with six hairpin bends – care should be taken, and snow chains are required in winter.

THE NORTH

Gently rolling hills and farmlands extend from the Tamar Valley north of Launceston and west to the Great Western Tiers. In this region travelling is touring; there's no such thing as getting from A to B. The best way to explore is to leave the highways and follow the quiet minor roads through small towns that are set in mountainous areas or by the lovely coastline.

Getting There & Around

Redline Coaches (☎ 1300 360 000; www.tasredline.com .au) has several services daily from Launceston to Devonport ($19, 1¼ hours), Ulverstone ($23.10), Penguin ($23.80) and Burnie ($26.80, two to 2½ hours); bookings are required for all stops. Redline also runs four weekday services from Launceston to Deloraine ($10, 45 minutes) – one service continues to Mole Creek ($14.30, 1¼ hours).

TassieLink (☎ 1300 300 520; www.tassielink.com .au) runs a daily express service that picks up passengers from the Bass Strait ferry terminal in Devonport in the morning and then heads to Launceston ($18, 1¼ hours) and Hobart ($45, four hours); this service also runs daily in reverse from Hobart, reaching Devonport in time for the nightly ferry sailing. TassieLink also runs from Launceston and Devonport to Cradle Mountain via Sheffield, and has a service from Devonport that heads west to Burnie, with onward connections to Zeehan, Queenstown and Strahan.

DEVONPORT

☎ 03 / pop 25,000

The dominant feature of Devonport, Tassie's third-largest city, is the lighthouse-topped Mersey Bluff, from where there are fine views of the coastline. The compact lighthouse was built in 1889 to aid navigation for the expanding port, which is still important today, handling much of the produce from northern Tasmania's agricultural areas.

Devonport is a common entry point for visitors to Tasmania, with its terminal for the ferry services plying Bass Strait from both Melbourne and Sydney. Devonport's visitors are usually arriving or departing rather than staying.

Information

Backpacker's Barn (☎ 6424 3628; www.backpackers barn.com.au; 10-12 Edward St; ☺ 9am-6pm Mon-Fri, to noon Sat) Head here for information about bushwalking and tours; also has an excellent bushwalking shop with plenty of gear for sale or hire, and handles accommodation, tour, car rental and bus bookings.

Café Natur (☎ 6424 1917; 10-12 Edward St; ☐)There's Internet access at this café at the front of the Backpacker's Barn.

Online access centre (☎ 6424 9413; 21 Oldaker St; per 30min/hr $3/5; ☐) This Internet source is in the library.

Visitor information centre (☎ 6424 8176; tourism@dctc.tas.gov.au; 92 Formby Rd; ☺ 7.30am-5pm or 9pm) In the centre of town, across the river from the ferry terminal, this centre is open to meet all ferry arrivals; the 9pm closure applies when there are day crossings of the Melbourne ferry, which arrive at 7pm.

Sights & Activities

The impressive Aboriginal culture centre and museum, **Tiagarra** (☎ 6424 8250; Bluff Rd; adult/child/family $3.60/2.50/10; ☼ 9am-5pm), which means 'keep', is on the road to the lighthouse. This museum has a rare collection of more than 250 indigenous rock engravings, thought to date around 10,000 years, some of which can be seen by following the marked geological trail on the bluff.

The **Devonport Maritime Museum** (☎ 6424 7100; 6 Gloucester Ave; adult/child/family $3/1/6; ☼ 10am-4.30pm Tue-Sun Oct-Mar, 10am-4pm Tue-Sun Apr-Sep) is in the old harbourmaster's residence near the foreshore and has an excellent display of maritime paraphernalia, including old and new model ships.

The National Trust–administered **Home Hill** (☎ 6424 3028; 77 Middle Rd; adult/child/family $7.50/5.50/15.40; ☼ 2-4pm Tue-Thu, Sat & Sun), located about 3km south of town, was the former residence of Joseph and Dame Enid Lyons. Joseph Lyons is the only Australian to have been both a state premier (1923–28) and prime minister of Australia (1932–39), and in 1943 Dame Enid Lyons made history when she became the first woman to be sworn in as a member of the House of Representatives.

The **Don River Railway** (☎ 6424 6335; www .donriverrailway.com.au; Forth Main Rd; adult/child/family $10/6/25; ☼ 9am-5pm), 4km west of town on the Bass Hwy, features a collection of steam locomotives and passenger carriages, and

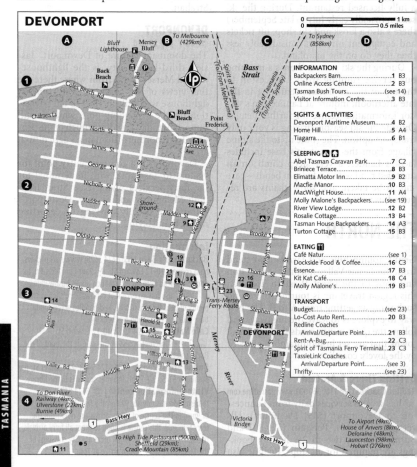

DEVONPORT

INFORMATION
Backpackers Barn.....................................1 B3
Online Access Centre...............................2 B3
Tasman Bush Tours...........................(see 14)
Visitor Information Centre.......................3 B3

SIGHTS & ACTIVITIES
Devonport Maritime Museum.........4 B2
Home Hill..5 A4
Tiagarra..6 B1

SLEEPING
Abel Tasman Caravan Park.............7 C2
Briniece Terrace......................................8 B3
Elimatta Motor Inn.................................9 B2
Macfie Manor...10 B3
MacWright House..................................11 A4
Molly Malone's Backpackers.......(see 19)
River View Lodge..................................12 B2
Rosalie Cottage.....................................13 B4
Tasman House Backpackers.............14 A3
Turton Cottage......................................15 B3

EATING
Café Natur.......................................(see 1)
Dockside Food & Coffee.....................16 C3
Essence...17 B3
Kit Kat Café..18 C4
Molly Malone's.....................................19 B3

TRANSPORT
Budget..(see 23)
Lo-Cost Auto Rent...............................20 C3
Redline Coaches
    Arrival/Departure Point..............21 B3
Rent-A-Bug...22 C3
Spirit of Tasmania Ferry Terminal...23 C3
TassieLink Coaches
    Arrival/Departure Point..............(see 3)
Thrifty..(see 23)

you can ride a vintage train (30 minutes return) along the banks of the Don River.

Southeast along the Bass Hwy (follow the signs for Launceston), about 8km out of Devonport, you'll come upon the **House of Anvers** (☎ 6426 2958; anvers@bigpond.com.au; 9025 Bass Hwy, Latrobe; ⏱ 7am-5pm), which produces velvety smooth Belgian-style chocolates and truffles. You can watch production (Monday to Saturday), sample and buy the results and check out the chocolate museum. Its café supplies crispy croissants and *pain au chocolat* (of course), among other delights.

Tours

Tasman Bush Tours (☎ 6423 2335; www.tasmanbush tours.com; 114 Tasman St), operating out of Tasman House Backpackers (below), offers guided walks in remote parts of the state (eg the Walls of Jerusalem and Southwest National Parks), including a six-day trek along the Overland Track (see p697).

Sleeping

With ferries operating daily (and twice daily in high season), Devonport is a busy place and accommodation can often be hard to come by if you haven't booked ahead.

BUDGET

Molly Malone's (☎ 6424 1898; mollymalones@vantage group.com.au; 34 Best St; dm $15, d with/without bath-room $50/30) There's nothing fancy about this central option, located above an Irish pub, but it has clean, basic dorms and a comfy lounge. The downstairs crowds can get a little rowdy Friday and Saturday night.

MacWright House (☎ 6424 5696; 115 Middle Rd; dm/s from $20/25) This YHA offers simple, clean accommodation and a friendly vibe. It's 3km from the city centre, about a 40-minute walk or a five-minute bus ride (Bus 40).

Tasman House Backpackers (☎ 6423 2335; www .tasmanhouse.com; 114 Tasman St; dm/tw $13/30, d with/ without bathroom $40/35) This sprawling hostel is actually the converted nurses' quarters of the old regional hospital. It's a 15-minute walk from town (or transport can be arranged when booking). Camping and hiking equipment is available for hire.

Abel Tasman Caravan Park (☎ 6427 8794; www .tigerresortstas.com.au; 6 Wright St; powered/unpowered sites per 2 people $20/15, on-site caravans $45, cabins $65) Offering very clean facilities, this busy

park has a good beachfront location in East Devonport, just five minutes from the ferry terminal.

MIDRANGE

Briniece Terrace (☎ 6423 4441; lovey@hotkey.net.au; 3-5 Archer St; d from $140) These boutique one-bedroom self-contained apartments (c 1891) in a grand, restored Victorian terrace have fireplaces, a spa and lots of room in which to stretch out, including balconies over the Strait. Kitchens are well equipped and beds very comfy; overall a good choice.

River View Lodge (☎ 6424 7357; www.river viewlodge.com.au; 18 Victoria Pde; s/d $65/80, without bathroom $50/70, incl breakfast) This foreshore-situated lodge is a friendly, old-fashioned place opposite a strip of picnic table–dotted greenery. The rooms with bathroom are good value.

Elimatta Motor Inn (☎ 6424 6555; 15 Victoria Pde; s $65-75, d & tw $80-85) Elimatta isn't anything to write home about, with ordinary and basic motel-style rooms, but the staff are friendly, it's well managed and it's an easy walk from the city centre.

Macfie Manor (☎ 6424 1719; 44 Macfie St; s $85, d $95-110) Offering B&B close to the city centre is this beautiful two-storey Federation building, superbly furnished. Guests have the option of staying in a room with its own bathroom or in a cosy terrace apartment.

Devonport Historic Cottages (☎ 1800 240 031; www.devonportcottages.com; d incl breakfast from $140) This company manages the self-contained **Rosalie Cottage** (66 Wenvoe St) and **Turton Cottage** (28 Turton St). Both are comfortable and are fitted out with all mod cons, but are restored with period furniture and lots of memorabilia to keep the heritage atmosphere. There are ample breakfast provisions and log fires to doze in front of.

Eating

Dockside Food & Coffee (☎ 6427 9127; 25 Murray St; meals $6-12; ⏱ breakfast & lunch) Just the thing as you stumble bleary-eyed off the ferry, this place offers an all-day no-limits hot brekky ($9.50) – just what the doctor ordered – plus tasty focaccias and filling pancakes.

Kit Kat Café (☎ 6427 8437; Tarleton St; meals $4-15; ⏱ breakfast, lunch & dinner) This lovely place offers hearty cooked breakfasts or great burgers. It also does hot fresh rolls or you can tuck into a fresh scallop pie for around $4.

Café Natur (☎ 6424 1917; 10-12 Edward St; lunch $6-10; ✆ breakfast & lunch Mon-Sat) This café, at the front of the Backpacker's Barn (p669), does fresh, healthy burgers, salads, focaccias and soups, including vegan and gluten-free meals.

Molly Malone's (☎ 6424 1898; 34 Best St; mains $10-18; ✆ lunch & dinner) This authentically fake Irish den has a bistro with plenty of fish, roasts, stews and grills; wash it all down with a Guinness or two, or three.

Essence (☎ 6424 6431; 28 Forbes St; mains $25-45; ✆ lunch Tue-Fri, dinner Tue-Sat) This strangely suburban-industrial neighbourhood isn't where you'd expect to find one of Devonport's best restaurants, but you'll be impressed by the menu of carefully prepared local produce. For a meal that's easier on the pocket but just as tasty, come for lunch.

High Tide (☎ 6424 6200; 17 Devonport Rd; lunch $10-15, dinner $16-28; ✆ lunch & dinner) Just south of town off the road to Latrobe, this modern waterfront restaurant has a range of dishes, including lots of seafood - savour the views and food from the outdoor deck.

Rooke St's northern end has a few interesting eateries, including **Rialto Gallery Restaurant** (☎ 6424 6793; 159 Rooke St; mains from $15; ✆ lunch & dinner Tue-Sat), serving prompt platefuls of pasta, lasagne and other Italian standards, and **Mallee Grill** (☎ 6424 4477; 161 Rooke St; mains $15-25; ✆ lunch Mon-Fri, dinner daily) – definitely one for the carnivores, with a menu heavy on steaks.

Getting There & Away

AIR
There are regular flights to/from Melbourne with **Qantas** (☎ 13 13 13; www.qantas.com.au; one way from $120) and **Regional Express** (Rex; ☎ 13 17 13; www.regionalexpress.com.au; one way from $100).

Tasair (☎ 6248 5088; www.tasair.com.au) flies between Devonport and King Island (one way from $160) via Burnie/Wynyard.

BOAT
See p617 for details of the ferry services (☎ 13 20 10; www.spiritoftasmania.com.au) between Melbourne, Sydney and Devonport. The ferry terminal is on the Esplanade in East Devonport.

BUS
See p618 for details of services operated by **Redline Coaches** (☎ 1300 360 000; www.tasredline

.com.au) from Launceston to Devonport and on to Burnie, and also for details of the **TassieLink** (☎ 1300 300 520; www.tassielink.com.au) services that shuttle disembarking and embarking ferry passengers to/from Launceston, Hobart and Burnie.

TassieLink also runs from Launceston to Devonport and then via Sheffield to Cradle Mountain, and has a service from Devonport that heads west to Burnie, with onward connections to western destinations such as Zeehan, Queenstown and Strahan.

Redline Coaches has its terminal opposite the Backpacker's Barn on Edward St, and will also stop at the ferry terminal when the ferry is in, while TassieLink coaches pull up outside the Devonport visitor information centre and the *Spirit of Tasmania* terminal.

If none of the scheduled services suit your particular bushwalking needs, charter a minibus from **Maxwells** (☎ 6492 1431, 0418 584 004) or through the Backpacker's Barn (p669).

Getting Around
The airport is 5km east of town. A **shuttle bus** (☎ 0400 035 995; per person $10) runs between the airport/ferry terminals, the visitor information centre and your accommodation. Bookings are essential. Alternatively, a **taxi** (☎ 6424 1431) to/from the airport will cost $12 to $15.

A small ferry (one way $2; ✆ 9am-5pm Mon-Sat in winter, 8am-6pm Mon-Sat in summer) departs on demand from opposite the post office, docking on the eastern side of the river beside the ferry terminal.

Devonport has plenty of cheap car-rental firms, such as **Rent-a-Bug** (☎ 6427 9034; 5 Murray St) and **Lo-Cost Auto Rent** (☎ 6424 9922, 1800 802 724; 22 King St), where high-season rates for older cars start at $35. **Budget** (☎ 6427 0650, 13 27 27) and **Thrifty** (☎ 6427 9119, 1800 030 730) have representatives at the airport and ferry terminal.

DELORAINE
☎ 03 / pop 2032
Deloraine is Tasmania's largest inland town and is a great base from which to explore the surrounding area, with features such as a charming rural town centre, riverside picnic areas, a superb setting at the foot of the Great Western Tiers and proximity to Cradle Mountain.

If you're travelling during spring, it's worth noting that Deloraine's annual four-day **craft fair** is a hugely popular event, drawing tens of thousands of visitors in late October and/or early November (when accommodation can book out from Launceston to Devonport).

The **visitor information centre** (☎ 6362 3471; 98 Emu Bay Rd; 9am-5pm), near the roundabout at the top of the main street, shares its premises with the **Deloraine Folk Museum & Yarns: Artwork in Silk** (adult/child/family $7/2/15). 'Yarns' is a magnificent four-panel, hand-dyed silk depiction of life in the area, and a worthwhile audio-visual display explains its design and construction (involving some 300 locals and taking three years to complete).

Many of the town's Georgian and Victorian buildings have been restored. Those of interest include **St Mark's Anglican Church** (East Westbury Pl), built in 1859, and, 2km east of town, the 1853 **Bowerbank Mill** (4455 Meander Valley Hwy), now a gallery.

Sleeping & Eating

The visitor information centre has details of country guesthouses and self-contained cottages in the area.

Highview Lodge YHA (☎ 6362 2996; 8 Blake St; dm/d/f from $19/45/56) This welcoming hillside YHA hostel has warm, timber-floored confines and friendly staff. It's a relatively steep walk from town, but the compensation includes some incredible views of the Great Western Tiers. There are also bikes for hire.

Bush Inn (☎ 6362 2365; 7 Lake Hwy; r per person without bathroom $20) The Bush Inn has good-value, simple pub accommodation in very spacious rooms at hostel prices.

Highland Rose (☎ 6362 2634; highlandrose.bb@ bigpond.com; 47 West Church St; d $95-105) The name stems from the Scottish owner and the pretty garden, and this hospitable, home-style B&B has two simple, comfortable rooms; the full cooked breakfast is served in the attractive sunroom.

Arcoona (☎ 6362 3443; www.arcoona.com; East Barrack St; s $165, d $185-220) Arcoona is a grand old hilltop home, set amid enchanting gardens on the eastern side of the river. Originally the town doctor's residence and then the district hospital, its credentials as a luxury B&B now include king-size beds, a spa suite and a billiards room.

Scooters (☎ 6362 3882; 53-55 Emu Bay Rd; mains $15-18; breakfast, lunch & dinner) Scooters is a well-managed licensed restaurant with contemporary tastes, issuing excellent seasonal dishes that include venison sausages, char grills and mushroom risotto; it also has a kids' menu.

Deloraine Delicatessen & Gourmet Foods (☎ 6362 2127; 36 Emu Bay Rd; mains $5-10; breakfast & lunch Mon-Sat) A fine place for late-morning baguettes, bagels and focaccias, with a variety of tasty fillings. Its coffee is superb, and it does dairy- and gluten-free meals, too.

MOLE CREEK

☎ 03 / pop 213

About 25km west of Deloraine is tiny Mole Creek, and in its vicinity you'll find spectacular limestone caves, apiaries producing leatherwood honey, and an excellent wildlife park. Many of the area's features are now protected within the **Mole Creek Karst National Park**.

Sights & Activities

Marakoopa Cave, a wet cave 15km from Mole Creek, features two underground streams and a glow-worm display. **King Solomon Cave** is a dry cave with amazing calcite crystals that reflect light; it has few steps in it, making it the better cave for the less energetic. In the high season, there are at least five tours in each cave daily between 10am and 4pm. A visit to each cave costs $11/5.50/27.50 per adult/child/family; current tour times are prominently displayed on access roads, or call **Mole Creek Caves** (☎ 6363 5182). Wear warm clothes on the tours (temperatures inside average 9ºC).

There are also some magnificent wild caves in the area. **Wild Cave Tours** (☎ 6367 8142; www.wildcavetours.com) offers half-/full-day adventures for $85/170 including caving gear (book ahead; only 14 years and over). Take spare clothing and a towel, as you'll get wet.

The leatherwood tree only grows in the damp western part of Tasmania, so honey made from its flower is unique to the state. At **R Stephens Leatherwood Honey Factory** (☎ 6363 1170; 25 Pioneer Dr; admission free; 9am-4pm Mon-Fri Jan-Apr), visitors can taste and purchase the sticky stuff.

Off the main road, a few kilometres east of the township, is the first-rate, family-friendly

Trowunna Wildlife Park (☎ 6363 6162; adult/child $14/7.50; ☼ 9am-8pm Jan, to 5pm Feb-Dec, tours 11am, 1pm & 3pm), which specialises in Tasmanian devils, wombats and koalas. The park runs an informative 75-minute tour where you get to pat, feed or even hold the critters.

Sleeping & Eating

Mole Creek Hotel (☎ 6363 1102; Pioneer Dr; s $45, d with/without bathroom $65/75, incl breakfast) A classic small-town pub with bright upstairs rooms. Downstairs is the **Tiger Lair Café-Bar** (mains $10-15; ☼ lunch & dinner), dedicated to the Tasmanian tiger and serving up hearty portions of pub standards.

Mole Creek Guest House & Restaurant (☎ 6363 1399; 100 Pioneer Dr; s from $100, d $120-140, incl breakfast) This is a friendly, comfy place to stay, with nicely presented rooms. The more-expensive rooms are larger and have a bathroom. It also rents out **Engadine** (d $100), a self-contained cottage, while its **Laurelberry Restaurant** (☎ 6363 1399; mains $16-22; ☼ breakfast, lunch & dinner Wed-Sun, breakfast & lunch Mon & Tue) offers good eating options.

WALLS OF JERUSALEM NATIONAL PARK

This remote national park comprises a series of glacial valleys and lakes on top of the Central Plateau and is part of the Tasmanian Wilderness World Heritage Area. It has wild alpine flora and rugged dolerite peaks, and is a favourite of experienced bushwalkers who prefer an isolated and spectacular hiking challenge. The most popular walk in the park is the full-day trek to the 'Walls'; you can also camp in the park.

If you prefer a guided walk, **Tasmanian Expeditions** (☎ 1300 666 856, 03-6334 3477; www.tas-ex.com) operates an eight-day trip for $1240 (runs November to April) that combines Cradle Mountain and the Walls of Jerusalem.

The quickest access to the Walls is from Sheffield or Mole Creek. From Mole Creek take the B12 west, then the C138 south and finally the C171 (Mersey Forest Rd) to Lake Rowallan; remain on this road, following the 'C171' and/or 'Walls of Jerusalem' signs to the start of the track.

SHEFFIELD & AROUND

☎ 03 / pop 982

In the 1980s, a group of locals got together to figure out a way of improving Sheffield's dour economic prospects, and some clever folk came up with the idea of decorating the town with murals, mainly depicting the history of the local pioneers. The first of the township's large, colourful mural was so well received by visitors that over the years around 50 of these impressive artworks have been daubed in town and a dozen in the surrounding district. The **visitor information centre** (☎ 6491 1036; Pioneer Cres; ☼ 8.30am-5pm), just off the main street, has maps with mural locations plus information on the region.

A must-see attraction in town, and one that will delight kids (and adults), is the **Tiger's Tale** (☎ 6491 1075; 38a Main St; theatre adult/child/family $5/3/13; ☼ 9am-5pm). It's a unique animatronic theatre and robot display of high-tech comedic drama; its main feature is a 10-minute performance in which the Tasmanian tiger comes to life through computer-controlled robotics.

Kentish Hills Retreat (☎ 6491 2484; www.kentishhills.com.au; 2 West Nook Rd, Sheffield; d $85-142), on the western edge of town offers modern motel units which are attractive and well equipped; most feature a video and kitchenette, some units have spas, and all have access to an outdoor barbecue area.

Central eating options include bakeries, tearooms and the refreshingly cosmopolitan **Coffee on Main** (☎ 6491 1893; 43 Main St; mains $10-15; ☼ breakfast, lunch & dinner), an art-filled gallery-café. You could always try **Hotel Sheffield** (☎ 6491 1130; 38 Main St; mains $10-16; ☼ lunch & dinner) for good-value counter-meal options and a lively local atmosphere to boot.

The scenery surrounding Sheffield is another of the town's great attractions, with **Mt Roland** (1234m) dominating the peaceful farmlands, and thick forests and fish-filled rivers. Nearby is beautiful **Lake Barrington**, a major rowing venue. **Tasmazia** (☎ 6491 1934; 500 Staverton Rd; adult/child $15/8; ☼ 10am-4pm Mar-Nov, 9am-5pm Dec-Feb), at the wonderfully named Promised Land, near Lake Barrington, combines mazes, a model village, lavender farm and pancake parlour.

Gowrie Park, 14km southwest of Sheffield, is at the foot of Mt Roland, making it an excellent base for walks up the mountain or for a rural retreat. The settlement here is home to **Mt Roland Budget Backpackers** (☎ 6491 1385; www.users.bigpond.com/weindorfers.com; Claude Rd; powered sites $5, dm $10), which offers basic camping and good-value hostel-style accommodation. Adjacent to the backpackers and run by the same people are the four self-contained **Gowrie Park Wilderness Cabins** (d from $66). The settlement is also home to the outstanding **Weindorfers** (mains $10-26.50; ☺ brunch, lunch & dinner Oct-May), a nostalgic, rustic cabin-style restaurant with top-notch hearty fare.

ULVERSTONE & AROUND
☎ 03 / pop 9795

The coastal town of Ulverstone has a relaxed, uncommercial atmosphere and has good surrounding attractions. The **visitor information centre** (☎ 6425 2839; 13 Alexandra Rd; ☺ 9am-5pm) is a treasure trove of knowledge.

At Gunns Plains, 25km south of Ulverstone, there are entertaining guided tours (on the hour) of the spectacular **Gunns Plains Caves** (☎ 6429 1388; adult/child $10/5; ☺ 10am-4pm). Also in Gunns Plains is **Wings Farm Park** (☎ 6429 1151; www.wingsfarmpark.com.au; 137 Winduss St; adult/child $12.50/6; ☺ 10am-4pm), a low-key, family-oriented place where you can interact with farm and native animals, check out reptiles or the animal nursery. There's also accommodation here (camping and cabins).

On the southern side of Gunns Plains, the River Leven emerges from a 250m-deep gorge. To view the gorge, follow the roads through Nietta to the **Leven Canyon Lookout**, 41km from Ulverstone. A 15-minute track leads to the sensational gorge-top lookout.

Sleeping & Eating

Ulverstone Caravan Park (☎ 6425 2624; 57 Water St; powered/unpowered sites $20/17, on-site caravans $45, units from $70) Near both the water and the town centre, this large park has plenty of greenery and sheltered camp sites, plus good amenities.

Waterfront Inn (☎ 6425 1599; Tasman Pde; s/d $70/95) Across the river from the town centre, this motel has a crowd of economical waterfront rooms, including spa and family units. It also has a wonderful on-site restaurant.

Ocean View Guesthouse (☎ 6425 5401; 1-3 Victoria St; s $75-130, d $100-150) If you're looking for well-appointed, heritage-style rooms, try this guesthouse, 100m from the beach and an easy walk from the town centre.

Pedro's the Restaurant (☎ 6425 6663; Wharf Rd; mains $20-40; ☺ lunch & dinner) Sitting on the port where its own boats bring in the daily catch, Pedro's is an appealing place specialising in upmarket seafood dishes (the paradise platter is top-notch and worth every penny; $75). Next door is **Pedro's Takeaway** (☎ 6425 5181; ☺ 11am-8pm), serving fab fresh fish 'n' chips.

PENGUIN
☎ 03 / pop 3050

This pretty little seaside town (complete with a large concrete penguin posing for countless photo ops on the foreshore, with smaller artificial penguins adorning rubbish bins along the main street) attracts as

---

A TIGER'S TALE

The story of the Tasmanian tiger (*Thylacinus cynocephalus* or thylacine), a striped carnivore once widespread in Tasmania, currently has two different endings.

Version one has it that thylacines were hunted to extinction by European settlers in the 19th and early 20th centuries, and that the last tiger died in miserable captivity in Hobart's Beaumaris Zoo in 1936. Those who put their faith in the thylacine's extinction point out that no living specimen has been conclusively discovered since then, regardless of hundreds of alleged 'sightings'.

Version two maintains that thylacines continue a furtive existence deep in the Tasmanian wilderness (alongside Elvis, we wonder?). Advocates of this theory refute that they live in a state of fanciful denial over the tiger's demise.

The physical mystique of a large nocturnal hunter that carried its young in a pouch and had a large, powerful jaw, combined with the conveniently perpetuated enigma of its existence, has made the tiger prime corporate fodder – Tasmanian companies have plastered the animal's picture on everything from beer bottles to TV network promos.

You can see black-and-white footage of a tiger in captivity at the Tasmanian Museum & Art Gallery in Hobart (p623). In *Thylacine: The Tragic Tale of the Tasmanian Tiger*, David Owen traces the history of the animal and examines the reasons for its decline, accompanied by excellent illustrations and anecdotes.

many visitors for its glorious roadside garden displays as for its fantastic beaches.

If driving from Ulverstone, take the old Bass Hwy (signposted 'Scenic Route'). As you approach Penguin, the countryside takes on a gentrified feel as cottage gardens, a narrow-gauge railway track and the seaside squeeze themselves into the scene. The **historic train service** (☎ 6432 3400) runs between Burnie, Penguin and Ulverstone on the second and fourth Sunday of each month, coinciding with Penguin's large **market** (☼ 9am-3.30pm Sun), which has some 150 stalls.

If you like the relaxed feel of the town, treat yourself to a night at the stylish **Madsen Guesthouse** (☎ 6437 2588; 64 Main St; $ d 110-150; ☒). The top rate will get you the large, elegantly furnished front room, complete with sea views; there's also a friendly café here.

Groovy Penguin Café (☎ 6437 2101; 74 Main Rd; mains $8-13; ☼ breakfast & lunch Wed-Sun) is a living artwork filled with kitsch paraphernalia and magnificent views of the ocean, where super-nice staff serve great food.

THE NORTHWEST

Swept clean by the winds of the Roaring Forties and washed annually by more than 2000mm of rain, the magnificent northwest coast boasts heaths, wetlands and dense rainforests of Gondwana times. Its story stretches back 35,000 years to when giant kangaroos and wombats were not yet extinct, and Aboriginal tribes took shelter in the caves on the coast, where they left a remarkable legacy of rock engravings and middens.

Getting There & Around

AIR

The airport for the region is in Wynyard, and is known as both Wynyard and Burnie airport. There are regular flights to/from Melbourne with **Qantas** (☎ 13 13 13; www.qantas .com.au) and **Regional Express** (Rex; ☎ 13 17 13; www.regionalexpress.com.au); see p617 for details.

Tasair (☎ 03-6248 5088; www.tasair.com.au) flies between Devonport and King Island via Burnie/Wynyard (one way from $160).

BUS

Redline Coaches (☎ 1300 360 000; www.tasredline .com.au) runs several buses daily from Hobart

to Launceston ($26.50, one way, 2½ hours) – these usually connect with a service running from Launceston along the north coast to Devonport ($18, one to 1½ hours) and Burnie ($28, two to 2½ hours).

From Burnie, Redline also runs two times each weekday to Wynyard ($3.40, 20 minutes), the Boat Harbour turn-off ($6, 30 minutes), Stanley ($15.60, one hour) and Smithton ($15.60, 1½ hours).

TassieLink (☎ 1300 300 520; www.tassielink.com .au) runs a Wednesday and Friday service from Devonport's ferry terminal to Burnie ($10, one hour), with onward connections to the west coast.

There are no public transport services to Marrawah or Arthur River.

CAR & MOTORCYCLE

The main route from the north to the west coast is the Murchison Hwy (A10) from Somerset (just west of Burnie) to Queenstown. The Western Explorer is the name given to an alternative inland route from Smithton to the west coast that incorporates a difficult 50km section between Arthur River and Corinna. Although this road can be negotiated by vehicles without 4WD and is promoted as a tourist route, bear in mind that it's remote, mostly unsealed and can be potholed, so the journey shouldn't be attempted in bad weather or at night. Make sure you get petrol at Marrawah (in the north) or Zeehan (in the south), because petrol is unavailable between these points.

At Corinna, there is a vehicle ferry (p690) across the Pieman River, from where you can continue on to Zeehan and the rest of the west coast.

BURNIE

☎ 03 / pop 20,000

Burnie, Tasmania's fourth-largest city, sits on the shores of Emu Bay – its deepwater port has led to cargo shipping becoming an important part its economy. Assisted by various attractions and the odd nearby glade, Burnie has developed an appealing coastal atmosphere, despite the fact that visible evidence of the town's heavy industry doesn't make a great first impression on visitors.

The **visitor information centre** (☎ 6434 6111; Little Alexander St; ☼ 9am-5pm Mon-Fri, 1.30-4.30pm Sat

& Sun) is attached to the Pioneer Village Museum and is a good source of information on Tassie's northwest region.

Sights & Activities

The absorbing **Pioneer Village Museum** (☎ 6430 5746; Little Alexander St; adult/child $6/2.50; ☼ 9am-5pm Mon-Fri, 9am-4pm Sat, Sun & public holidays) is an authentic indoor re-creation of a village streetscape from the 1900s. It includes a blacksmith, printer, stage coach depot and bootmaker.

In the visitor centre at the cheese-maker **Lactos Tasmania** (☎ 6433 9255; 145 Old Surrey Rd; ☼ 9am-5pm Mon-Fri, 10am-4pm Sat & Sun), you can taste, and of course purchase, sundry speciality cheeses.

On the same road as Lactos is the **Creative Paper Mill** (☎ 6430 7717; www.creativepapermill.org; Old Surrey Rd; admission free; ☼ 10am-4pm daily Oct-Apr, to 4pm Mon-Sat May-Sep), where paper is made by hand. There are paper products for sale (including novel new stuff made from 'roo poo!) and artworks on show; paper-making tours are conducted regularly (adult/child/family $10/6/28).

There are a number of gardens, waterfalls and viewpoints in the Burnie area. **Fern Glade**, just 3km from the city centre, is a peaceful riverside spot offering picnic areas, walks and the chance to spot a platypus. During summer, get down here by 6.30pm on Monday, Wednesday or Friday, when free, guided platypus-spotting excursions take place.

For more wildlife-spotting, there's also a boardwalk from Burnie's foreshore that leads from Hilder Pde to the western end of West Beach, where there's a **penguin observation centre**. Over summer you can observe free the shy birds at dusk if they choose to make an appearance.

Sleeping

Beachfront Voyager Motor Inn (☎ 6431 4866, 1800 355 090; 9 North Terrace; r $120-155) Opposite the surf lifesaving club on the main section of West Beach is this motel. It has large, very well-equipped rooms; those with a balcony overlooking the beach are recommended.

Apartments Down Town (☎ 6432 3219; www.apart mentsdowntown.com.au; 52 Alexander St; s/d apt $109/145)

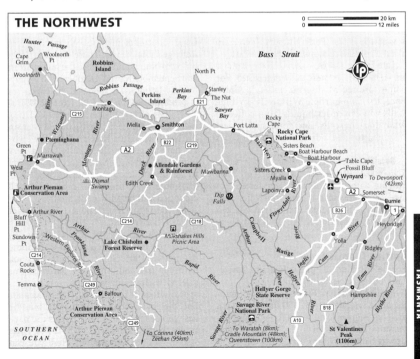

THE NORTHWEST

TASMANIA

This option lives in a bygone era, a classic Art Deco era to be precise. Its stylish, spacious and well-equipped apartments, with two or three bedrooms, are full of the trimmings of the 1930s and make a pleasant change from the colonial timewarp offered by other guesthouses.

Glen Osborne House (☎ 6431 9866; 9 Aileen Cres; s/d from $80/110) It may be set in the suburban hills in Burnie's south, but there's nothing suburban about this B&B. It provides high-standard hospitality in a lavish, National Trust–listed 1885 Victorian house with established gardens. Note that Aileen Cres runs off Mount St.

Burnie Holiday Caravan Park (☎ 6431 1925; 253 Bass Hwy, Cooee; powered/unpowered sites per 2 people $20/15, dm $36, on-site caravans $42, cabins $75-85) Four kilometres west of the city centre, this well-managed park has two budget lodge rooms (four to six bunks) equipped with fridge and stove, decent camping sites and a range of cabins.

Eating

Grove Country Kitchen (☎ 6431 9779; 63 West Park Grove; mains $5-14; ☽ breakfast & lunch) This is a great place for light meals, served in the pleasant interior or on the outdoor deck. It's at the West Park Nursery (drive up West Park Grove alongside Burnie Park).

Café Europa (☎ 6431 1897; cnr Cattley & Wilson Sts; mains $6-15; ☽ breakfast, lunch & dinner) For some carefree Mediterranean-style ambience, try Café Europa. Within its sky-blue walls you can order liquids from coffee to wine and cocktails, and food such as croissants, toasted Turkish bread and tapas platters.

Bocelli's (☎ 6431 8441; 63 Mount St; mains around $20; ☽ lunch Mon-Fri, dinner Mon-Sat) You'll be singing with joy after you have tasted Bocelli's full à la carte menu, which includes delicious lamb shanks, marinated chicken and smoked salmon salads, and tasty veggie risottos.

Getting There & Away

See p676 for details of Redline and Tassie-Link bus services to/from Burnie.

From Monday to Friday, except on public holidays, **Metro** (☎ 13 22 01; www.metrotas .com) has regular local buses to Penguin, Ulverstone and Wynyard ($3.40 each), which depart from bus stops on Cattley St.

WYNYARD
☎ 03 / pop 4510

Sheltered by the impressive Table Cape and Fossil Bluff, the agreeable small town of Wynyard sits both on the seafront and the banks of the Inglis River. Although there's not much to see in the town itself, it's a good base from which to explore the attractions in the area.

There's a **visitor information centre** (☎ 6442 4143; Goldie St; ☽ 9.30am-4.30pm Mon-Sat, 12.30-4.30pm Sun) dispensing lots of brochures on the surrounding region, including information on good scenic walks and drives. At the time of research there were plans to relocate the visitor information centre to a new building, which would also house a veteran car collection.

Fossil Bluff is 3km from Wynyard, signposted from the roundabout on which the Wynyard Hotel sits – the route winds through several side-streets, so keep your eyes peeled for the signs. It's where the oldest marsupial fossil ever found in Australia was unearthed (estimated at 20 million years old). The soft sandstone here features numerous shell fossils deposited when the level of Bass Strait was much higher.

Other attractions in the area include **Table Cape**, about 4km north of Wynyard; it has unforgettable views. There's also a tulip farm (in bloom and open to the public from late September to mid-October) and a lighthouse (dating from 1888) on the cape.

Beach Retreat Tourist Park (☎ 6442 1998; 30 Old Bass Hwy; sites per 2 people $16, budget s/d $20/35, motel unit/cabin $65/70) is a well-situated park on the beach and close to town. Friendly owners have upgraded the facilities to a very high standard and there's accommodation to suit most tastes and budgets. The spotless motel-style units and cabins are well equipped and brightly decorated.

By the Inglis River about 1.5km out of town, **Alexandria B&B** (☎ 6442 4411; alexandria@ ozemail.com.au; 1 Table Cape Rd; s/d from $130/150; ☒) is in a well-groomed Federation-style home dating from 1905. Guests can enjoy the pool, barbecue area and impressive gardens, plus river views from the veranda.

A number of restaurants, cafés and pubs line the main street of Wynyard, but the best choice for a good fishy feed is the nautically themed **Buckaneers** (☎ 6442 4104; 4 Inglis St; mains $11-23; ☽ lunch & dinner). Here you can buy fresh fish and seafood, order succulent fish and chips to take away or enjoy a more formal meal of fresh catches in the attached restaurant.

BOAT HARBOUR BEACH
☎ 03 / pop 400

The tiny holiday resort of Boat Harbour Beach, which is 14km northwest of Wynyard and 3km off the Bass Hwy, is perched on a beautiful bay with gleaming white sand and crystal-clear water – as you descend towards the town the views across the water are breathtaking.

Boat Harbour Beach Resort (☎ 6445 1107; The Esplanade; motel r $79-109, executive spa unit $175; ⊠) is a revived and refurbished 1960s motel with accommodation ranging from tiny 'economy' motel rooms, to larger rooms nearer the beach, to self-contained executive spa units.

Jolly Rogers (☎ 6445 1710; The Esplanade; mains $10-25; ⊠ breakfast, lunch & dinner Sep-May) is an inviting beachside eatery.

Nearby, bordering the coastal heathlands of the small **Rocky Cape National Park**, is **Sisters Beach**, an 8km expanse of bleached sand with safe swimming and good fishing.

STANLEY
☎ 03 / pop 600

Nestled at the foot of the extraordinary Circular Head (better known as the Nut), Stanley is a charming fishing village with a range of accommodation and attractions; it's a lovely spot to unwind for a few days.

The **visitor information centre** (☎ 6458 1330; 45 Main Rd; ⊠ 9am-5pm Mon-Fri, 10am-4pm Sat & Sun) is on the left-hand side of the road as you head into town. Its knowledgeable staff can offer extensive advice on the region.

Sights & Activities
THE NUT

This striking 152m-high volcanic rock formation, thought to be 13 million years old, can be seen for miles around. It's a steep 20-minute climb to the top, but the view is definitely worth it. For the less energetic, a **chairlift** (☎ 6458 1286; adult/child/family $9/7/25; ⊠ 9.30am-5.30pm Oct-May, 10am-4pm Jun-Sep) also operates, weather permitting. At the top you can take a leisurely stroll from one lookout to the next; at the base there's a cheery café.

OTHER ATTRACTIONS

The old bluestone building on the seafront was originally the 1844 **Van Diemen's Land Company Store** (Wharf Rd), and is now an interesting gallery. The company's headquarters were at gracious **Highfield** (☎ 6458 1100; Green Hills Rd; adult/child/family $6/4/14, grounds only $2; ⊠ 10am-4pm), 2km north of Stanley, which includes the elegant homestead, barns, stables, workers' cottages and a chapel. There are guided and self-guided tours, plus an after-dark tour by lamplight from October to April ($10/5/25 per adult/child/family; bookings essential).

Back in town, near the wharf is the mid-19th-century **Ford's Store**, a particularly fine old bluestone building that used to be a grain store and is now a restaurant. Other buildings of historical interest include **Lyons Cottage** (☎ 6458 1145; 14 Alexander Tce; admission by donation; ⊠ 10am-4pm Nov-Apr, 11am-3pm May-Oct), the birthplace of former prime minister Joseph Lyons, and **St James' Presbyterian Church** (Fletcher St), which was bought in England and transported to Stanley in 1885. By the church, the **Discovery Centre** (Church St; adult/child $3/50c; ⊠ 10am-4pm) is a one-room folk museum filled with Circular Head photos and artefacts.

Tours

Stanley Seal Cruises (☎ 0419 550 134; www.users .bigpond.com/staffordseals; adult/child $40/17; ⊠ daily) You can see around 200 Australian fur seals sunning themselves on Bull Rock, near Stanley, by taking a 75-minute cruise provided by this company. The cruises depart from the wharf, weather permitting. There are also combined platypus and penguin tours for $45/15.

Wilderness to West Coast Tours (☎ 6458 2038; www.wildernesstasmania.com) This Stanley-based company has platypus-spotting excursions (per adult/child $30/15) and penguin-viewing tours (per adult/child $15/5) when the birds appear at either end of Godfreys Beach from late September until February. Its full-day 4WD wilderness tours (per person for two people $225, for three or more people $195) take in rainforest and the Edge of the World areas (includes gourmet lunch), or you can join a tag-along tour in your own 4WD for $99 per person.

Sleeping

Dovecote Motel & Restaurant (☎ 6458 1300; www .dovecote.com.au; 58 Dovecote Rd; d $90-145) A little way out of town, this friendly place has an assortment of standard motel rooms and self-contained units, most endowed with

TASMANIA

million-dollar views of The Nut and the town from their balconies (the cheapest rooms lack the view). The restaurant features local produce and has well-priced options.

There are oodles of B&Bs and self-contained cottages dotted in and around Stanley. They range in price from $80 to $170 per double in summer, though you should bargain at other times. Some close in winter. Some recommendations:

Stanley Hotel (☎ 6458 1161; 19 Church St; s/d $55/80, without bathroom $35/55) Refurbished to within an inch of its life, this pub offers comfortable, spacious and modern accommodation. The bathroom facilities have been updated and are so clean they shine. The rooms with views to the Nut or beach are good value.

Stanley Cabin & Tourist Park (☎ 6458 1266; www .stanleycabinpark.com.au; Wharf Rd; powered sites per 2 people $20, unpowered sites $18-22, on-site caravans from $40, cabins $55-100) On a great bayfront site, this park is loaded with amenities and has well-serviced caravans and cabins (you pay extra for waterfront camp sites). This place is also home to the no-frills **Stanley YHA** (dm $20); guests can use the campers' kitchen.

Abbey's Cottages (☎ 1800 222 397; www.stanley tasmania.com; d $80-160, extra person $10-25) Offers a range of self-contained units and cottages in town, of varying sizes, standards and prices – check the website.

Captain's Cottage (☎ 6458 3075; www.captainscottage stanley.com.au; 30 Alexander Tce; d $160, extra adult/child $35/25) Heritage-listed, self-contained cottage (sleeps six) with water views.

Eating

Hurseys Seafood (☎ 6458 1103; 2 Alexander Tce; ⏲ 9am-6pm) This place is awash with tanks filled with live sea creatures (including crayfish) for the freshest of takeaways. The complex includes **Kermies Café** (meals $5-12), serving quick meals and fish-and-chip takeaways, and upstairs is **Julie & Patrick's** (mains $18-28; ⏲ dinner), a more formal restaurant where the menu is, naturally, heavy on seafood.

Sealer's Cove (☎ 6458 1414; 2 Main Rd; mains $10-18.50; ⏲ dinner Tue-Sun) If you're not too keen on seafood, head along to this inviting BYO place, where you'll get an extensive selection of pizza, pasta and salad dishes, plus excellent desserts.

Moby Dicks (☎ 6458 1329; 5 Church St; mains $8-16; ⏲ breakfast) This new breakfast bar is a unique and charming take on the humble breaking

of the fast. Until 11am you can have your eggs done pretty much any way you like.

SMITHTON & AROUND
☎ 03 / pop 3320

Smithton, 22km from Stanley, serves one of Tasmania's largest forestry areas. Thirty kilometres southwest of Smithton (just off the A2), Forestry Tasmania has set up the alluringly named **Dismal Swamp** (☎ 6456 7199; www.tasforestrytourism.com.au/pages/site_nw_dismal .html; adult $10; ⏲ 9am-5pm), essentially a 110m-long slide providing a thrilling descent into a blackwood sinkhole (not for those aged under 13 years). It incorporates a treetop interpretation centre constructed mostly of blackwood, and gives visitors the opportunity to wander through the swamp floor along a boardwalk maze, with contemporary sculptures planted among the ferns. There's a café and a small gift shop.

The serenely beautiful **Allendale Gardens & Rainforest** (☎ 6456 4216; B22 Rd, Edith Creek; adult/child $7.50/3.50; ⏲ 9am-6pm Oct-Apr) is on the B22 road, 12km south of Smithton towards Edith Creek. It has five acres of bird-filled gardens and 26 hectares of old temperate rainforest to lose yourself in, plus a café serving Devonshire teas.

MARRAWAH
☎ 03 / pop 370

Marrawah, an untrammelled delight, is where the wild Southern Ocean occasionally throws up the remains of ships wrecked on the dangerous and rugged west coast. Marrawah's nearby beaches and rocky outcrops can be hauntingly beautiful, particularly at dusk, and the seas are often huge. The **West Coast Classic**, an excellent round of the state's surfing championships, is regularly decided here, as is a round of the state's windsurfing championships.

Marrawah has a tavern supplying daily counter meals (but not accommodation) and a general store selling petrol and supplies. There's a free, basic camping area at beautiful Green Point, 2km from Marrawah.

Glendonald Cottage (☎ 6457 1191; 79 Arthur River Rd; s/d from $70/85, extra person $25) is a comfortable self-contained cottage sleeping up to five; the owner also conducts excellent wildlife tours in the area.

(Continued on page 689)

RICHARD NEBESKY

Sovereign Hill (p569), Ballarat, Victoria

Port Fairy (p546), Victoria

CHRISTOPHER GROENHOUT

PAUL SINCLAIR

The Grampians National Park (p550), Victoria

Walhalla (p602), Victoria

CHRISTOPHER GROENHOUT

JOHN HAY

Yarra Valley wine region (p528), Victoria

Lakes Entrance (p604), Victoria

CHRI

CHRIS MELLOR

View from Mt Wellington (p625) over Hobart

RICHARD I'ANSON

Arthur Circus at Battery Point (p622), Hobart

Tamar River, Launceston (p657), Tasmania

RICHARD I'ANSON

Strahan harbour (p693), Tasmania

LINDSAY BROWN

Salamanca Market (p622), Hobart

RICHARD I'ANSON

Royal Tasmanian Botanical Gardens (p625), Hobart

King Solomon Cave (p673), Mole Creek, Tasmania

Cascade Brewery (p624), Hobart

Ross Bridge (p647), Tasmania

Convict church, Port Arthur (p645), Tasmania

Richmond (p636), Tasmania

Penny Royal World near Cataract Gorge (p659), Launceston, Tasmania

Barossa Valley vineyards (p750),
South Australia

Granite Island (p739), Victor Harbor,
South Australia

Sea lion on beach, Kangaroo Island (p743), South Australia

Torrens River, Adelaide (p713)

SkyCity Casino (p730), Adelaide

Mt Lofty Botanic Gardens (p733), Adelaide Hills

(Continued from page 680)

ARTHUR RIVER

☎ 03 / pop 110

The sleepy settlement of Arthur River, 14km south of Marrawah, is mainly a collection of holiday houses belonging to people who come here to fish. **Gardiner Point**, signposted off the main road on the southern side of the old timber bridge, has been locally christened the **Edge of the World** because the sea stretches uninterrupted all the way to Argentina.

Apart from the excellent fishing, travellers also come to take a scenic cruise on the Arthur River. There are two operators: **Arthur River Cruises** (☎ 6457 1158; www.arthurrivercruises .com; adult/child $65/25) departs daily (minimum numbers permitting) at 10am and returns at 3pm, cruising upriver to the confluence of the Arthur and Frankland Rivers, where passengers enjoy a BBQ and a rainforest walk; **AR Reflections River Cruises** (☎ 6457 1288; 4 Gardiner St; adult/child $60/35) departs 10.15am daily for a 5½-hour return trip, where participants also get a guided rainforest walk; a morning luncheon is provided, as well as a BBQ back in the township.

For those keen on self-exploration, **Arthur River Canoe & Boat Hire** (☎ 6457 1312), at the jetty, hires boats for $18/110 per hour/day; canoes or dinghies from $60 per day; and kayaks for $8/40 per hour/day.

From Arthur River you can drive 110km south to Corinna on the narrow, unsealed Western Explorer. This rough road passes through the wild and often spectacular **Arthur Pieman Conservation Area**, part of the incredible, 3500-sq-km **Tarkine wilderness** – conservation groups are still seeking World Heritage Area protection for this diverse region. Before heading off, get fuel in Marrawah as there's no petrol available until either Zeehan or Waratah; also get the latest on the road's condition from the **Arthur River Parks & Wildlife Service** (PWS; ☎ 6457 1225).

There are several basic **camping grounds** (sites $5) located in the area; self-register at the PWS office. There are also a few decent self-catering accommodation options in Arthur River, but no eateries (there is only a kiosk with limited supplies on Gardiner St).

Arthur River Holiday Units (☎ 6457 1288; 2 Gardiner St; s/d from $70/90) has comfortable, well-equipped riverside units ranging in size from one to three bedrooms.

Further up the same road, **Sunset Holiday Villas** (☎ 6457 1197; 23 Gardiner St; s/d $75/90) offers two units that share a balcony and views of the beach (stunning at sunset).

THE WEST

Nature at its most awe-inspiring is the attraction of Tasmania's magnificent west coast. Formidable mountains, button-grass plains, ancient rivers, tranquil lakes, dense rainforests and a treacherous coast are all compelling features of this beautiful region, much of which is now a World Heritage Area.

Prior to 1932, when the road from Hobart to Queenstown was built, the only way into the area was by sea, through the dangerously narrow Hells Gates into Macquarie Harbour, near Strahan. Despite such near-inaccessibility, early European settlement brought explorers, convicts, soldiers, loggers, prospectors, railway gangs and fishermen, while the 20th century brought outdoor adventurers, naturalists and environmental crusaders.

It was over the west's wild rivers, beautiful lakes and tranquil valleys that battles between environmentalists and governments raged. In the 1980s, the proposed damming of the Franklin and Lower Gordon Rivers caused one of the greatest, longest-running environmental debates in Australia's history, and subsequently led to the boom of ecotourism around Strahan.

See www.westcoast.tas.gov.au for information on the region.

Getting There & Around

TassieLink (☎ 1300 300 520; www.tassielink.com.au) runs five buses per week from Hobart to Bronte Junction ($29.20, 2½ hours), Lake St Clair ($40.60, three to 3½ hours), Derwent Bridge ($34.90, 3¾ hours), Queenstown ($51, five to 5½ hours) and Strahan ($59, 6½ to 8½ hours, times varying due to Queenstown stopover); there are return services along this route on the same days.

From Launceston, TassieLink buses run three to four times per week to Devonport ($18, 1½ hours), Sheffield ($20, two hours), Gowrie Park ($23.50, 2¼ hours), Cradle Mountain ($46.50, three hours), Zeehan ($49, 5½ hours), Queenstown ($56.50, seven

TASMANIA

hours) and Strahan ($64.50, 8¾ hours); again, there are return services on the same days.

Drivers heading north along the rugged Western Explorer road should fill up at Zeehan or Waratah, as there's no fuel at either Savage River or Corinna, only at distant Marrawah.

CORINNA

☎ 03

Tiny Corinna, on the northern bank of the Pieman River, was once a thriving gold-mining settlement, but nowadays people come for the serenity, scenery and the **Pieman River Cruises** (☎ 6446 1170; adult/child $50/25), a laid-back, more rustic alternative to the

crowded, mass-produced Gordon River cruises out of Strahan. The four-hour cruises pass an impressive gorge and forests of eucalypts, ferns and Huon pines on the way to Pieman Heads. The cruises depart at 10.30am daily; bookings are essential.

The *Fatman* **ferry** (☎ 6446 1170; standard vehicle/caravan $20/25, motorcycles & bicycles $11; 9am-5pm Apr-Sep, to 7pm Oct-Mar) slides across the Pieman on demand.

ZEEHAN

☎ 03 / pop 1120

Zeehan has experienced its fair share of highs and lows, with its fortunes intrinsically linked to those of local mining. By the late 19th century Zeehan had become

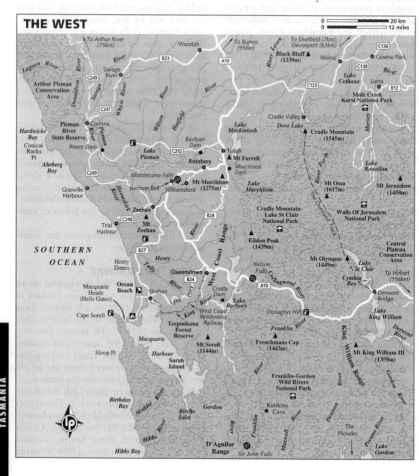

THE WEST

0 — 20 km
0 — 12 miles

a booming silver-mining centre known as Silver City, with a population that peaked at nearly 10,000. In its heyday Zeehan had 26 hotels and its Gaiety Theatre seated 1000.

In 1908, however, the mines began to fail and the town declined. With the reopening and expansion of the Renison Tin Mine at nearby Renison Bell, Zeehan experienced a revival in the late 1960s, but it remains a small and sleepy place (if you arrive here on a Sunday afternoon you could be forgiven for believing you saw some tumbleweed roll down the main street). It's a convenient overnight stop if you're planning on driving the 50km to Corinna to take a cruise.

It's worth noting that the historic part of Main St is at the northern end of town, not the bit you see when entering from Strahan or Queenstown. Buildings that remain from the boom days include the once-famous **Grand Hotel** (encompassing the Gaiety Theatre), the **post office**, the **bank** (all on Main St) and **St Luke's Church** (Belstead St). The **Gaiety Theatre** is slowly being restored, and enthusiasts can tour it and hear some of its fascinating history; contact **Silver City Info/Tours** (☎ 6471 5095, 0438 716 389; 129 Main St; theatre tours adult/child $6.50/4.50). The office is opposite the theatre and also acts as an information centre on the region.

For an excellent insight into the workings of a mine, visit the **West Coast Pioneers Memorial Museum** (☎ 6471 6225; Main St; adult/family $9/20; ◷ 9am-5pm), which also features an interesting mineral collection and a pictorial history of the west coast.

Trial Harbour, the original port for Zeehan, is a beautiful place for bush camping, while the sandy desert-like expanses of the **Henty Dunes** should not be missed on the drive from Zeehan to Strahan.

Hotel Cecil (☎ 6471 6221; Main St; s $40, d with/without bathroom $55/65, cottages $85) has small, spotless hotel rooms and, on an adjacent block, three comfortable, cosy self-contained miners' cottages. It also serves **pub meals** (mains $12-20; ◷ dinner).

Heemskirk Motor Hotel (☎ 1800 639 876; Main St; r from $90), at the eastern entrance to town, won't win any architectural design awards, but it has decent-sized motel rooms and includes a **bistro** (mains $12-19; ◷ lunch & dinner).

Otherwise there are slim pickings for diners. The coffee lounge inside the Pioneers Museum is good for a light lunch.

QUEENSTOWN

☎ 03 / pop 3400

The final, winding descent into Queenstown from the Lyell Hwy is unforgettable for its denuded 'moonscape' hills and deep, eroded gullies testifying to the destruction of the local environment by mining. These days mining activities are monitored and sulphur emissions are controlled, and in recent years patches of green have begun appearing on the slopes.

Queenstown is now busy occupying itself with tourism. Unlike its overcommercialised sister town, Strahan, Queenstown has more of an authentic pioneer village atmosphere popular with visitors for its rich social and industrial history, augmented by the completion of the West Coast Wilderness Railway, breathing new life into the township.

The Galley Museum now houses the **visitor information centre** (☎ 6471 1483; 1-7 Driffield St), a treasure trove of local knowledge.

Sights & Activities

The town's biggest attraction is the **West Coast Wilderness Railway**, a recently restored line that traverses some of the west's most pristine wilderness along a 35km stretch between Queenstown and Strahan. The station is on Driffield St, opposite the Empire Hotel. For more information on the railway, see the boxed text, p692.

The **Eric Thomas Galley Museum** (☎ 6471 1483; 1-7 Driffield St; adult/child/family $4/2.50/10; ◷ 9.30am-6pm Mon-Fri, 12.30-6pm Sat & Sun Oct-Mar, 10am-5pm Mon-Fri, 1-5pm Sat & Sun Apr-Sep) started life as the Imperial Hotel in 1898. It now counts among its features an intriguing collection of old photographs with wonderfully idiosyncratic captions written by the photographer, Eric Thomas.

For panoramic views of town, follow Hunter St uphill, turn left onto Bowes St, then do a sharp left onto Latrobe St to a small car park, from where a short, steep track leads to the summit of **Spion Kopf Lookout**. The geological wound of **Iron Blow**, the original but now abandoned open-cut mine, can be seen from a lookout off the Lyell Hwy.

The open-cut section of the Mt Lyell Mine is no longer worked, but mining continues deep beneath the massive West Lyell crater. The mine can be seen as part of 2½-hour

TASMANIA

underground excursions with **Douggies Mine Tours** (☎ 6471 1472; tours $58; ⏱ tours 8.15am, 10.15am, 1.15pm). The minimum age for tour participants is 12 years. Bookings are essential.

Sleeping & Eating

Queenstown Cabin & Tourist Park (☎ 6471 1332; 17 Grafton St; powered/unpowered sites per 2 people $22/18, dm $15, on-site caravans $45, cabins $75) About 500m south of the town centre, this park covers most price brackets. It has a lodge with decent budget rooms, spotless caravans and cabins, and good amenities.

Empire Hotel (☎ 6471 1699; empirehotel@tassie .net.au; 2 Orr St; s $30, d with/without bathroom $50/40) The majestic, century-old Empire has basic but clean, good-value rooms in a prime location. It's also a good choice for a meal, with its heritage **dining room** (mains $12-17; ⏱ lunch & dinner) serving a changing menu of hearty pub standards.

Chancellor Inn Queenstown (☎ 6471 1033; www .ghihotels.com; Batchelor St; d $115) There are a number of generic motels in town – this is the top pick. It has comfortable, refurbished rooms, all mod cons and a buffet breakfast; adjacent is the Old Prospector restaurant, which offers hearty meals with a cosy ambient wood fire.

Penghana (☎ 6471 2560; 32 The Esplanade; d with/without bathroom from $150/110) Built in 1898 for the first general manager of the Mt Lyell Mining Company, this upmarket guesthouse, accessed via Preston St, stands grandly above the town amid a surprising number of trees (surprising, given that this is Queenstown). Guest facilities include a lounge with open fire, bar and billiard table, and a grand dining room in which to enjoy chef-prepared à la carte meals (Wednesday to Sunday).

There's not a great deal of choice for eating out. Takeaway stores line the main

---

WEST COAST WILDERNESS RAILWAY

The restoration of the century-old railway line between Queenstown and Strahan is enabling passengers to jump aboard a refurbished locomotive to explore the pristine wilderness of the area, passing through dense forest and crossing wild rivers and 40 restored bridges, with stops at a few historic stations en route.

The rack-and-pinion line was the reason why the company that mined Mt Lyell for so long was called the Mt Lyell Mining *and* Railway Company. For the mining to be profitable, a railway connecting Mt Lyell with the port of Teepookana on King River, and later with Strahan, was vital. Construction began in 1894 and by its completion had cost the mining company over half its capital investment and covered 35km of rugged terrain.

Opened in 1896 and extended to Strahan in 1899, the line ran along the Queen River and up to Rinadeena Saddle, before heading down through magnificent rainforest to the King River. Here it crossed a stunning, curved 400m-long bridge high above the water, before continuing on to Teepookana and Regatta Point.

The Abt system (named after its inventor) was used to cover terrain too steep for the standard haulage of large quantities of ore. In this arrangement, a third toothed rack rail is positioned between the two conventional rails, and locomotives are equipped with geared pinion wheels that lock into the rack rail, allowing trains to climb and descend gradients they'd otherwise be unable to negotiate fully loaded.

The railway eventually closed in 1963 and fell into disrepair. Today the entire track is magnificently restored and steam and diesel locomotives take passengers along its full length. The trains depart from Queenstown and Strahan at the same times (10am and 3pm daily) and meet in the heart of the rainforest at Dubbil Barrel station. The entire journey takes a little over four hours and passengers can then take a later train or a bus back to their point of origin. Alternatively, travellers can ride to the track's half-way point at Dubbil Barril, change trains and return to the point of departure. Costs for riding the full length one way, or for a return journey to Dubbil Barril, are $97/54.50 per adult/child. The bus option costs an additional $14/7, or to ride both ways on the railway costs $194/109.

Make inquiries or purchase tickets at either the **Queenstown Station** (☎ 6471 1700; Driffield St), in the centre of town, or the **Regatta Point Station** (☎ 6471 4300), on the waterfront 1.5km south of Strahan's centre.

street, and **Dotties Coffeeshop** (☎ 6471 1700; Driffield St; ☺ breakfast, lunch & dinner), inside the train station, is the best choice for café fare.

STRAHAN
☎ 03 / pop 600

Strahan, 40km southwest of Queenstown on Macquarie Harbour, is the only sizable town on the rugged west coast.

Treacherous seas, the lack of natural harbours and high rainfall discouraged early settlement of the region until Macquarie Harbour was discovered by sailors searching for the source of the Huon pine that frequently washed up on southern beaches. In those days, the area was inaccessible by land and difficult to reach by sea, and in 1821 these dubious assets prompted the establishment of a brutal penal settlement on Sarah Island, in the middle of the harbour. Its main function was to isolate the worst of the colony's convicts and to use their muscle to harvest the huge stands of Huon pine nearby. The convicts worked upriver 12 hours per day, often in leg irons, felling the pines and rafting them back to the island's sawpits, where they were used to build ships and furniture. In 1834, however, after the establishment of the 'escape-proof' penal settlement at Port Arthur, Sarah Island was abandoned.

Today, Strahan's harbourside main street is undeniably attractive, but in a somewhat artificial and overcommercialised manner. The town's true appeal lies in the natural and historical attractions around it rather than in the town itself, and as such it draws droves of visitors seeking a wilderness-in-comfort experience aboard a seaplane, Gordon River cruise or the wilderness railway.

Information
The architecturally innovative **visitor information centre** (☎ 6471 7622; strahan@tasvisinfo .com.au; The Esplanade; ☺ 10am-8pm Dec-Mar, to 6pm Apr-Nov) offers information on accommodation options, attractions and activities in the town.

There's a **Parks & Wildlife Service office** (PWS; ☎ 6471 7122; ☺ 9am-5pm Mon-Fri; ☐) in the old Customs House on the foreshore. The same building also houses the post office and on-line access centre. There's an ATM outside the Fish Café on the main street.

Sights & Activities
Beyond the Huon-pine reception desk at the visitor information centre is **West Coast Reflections** (☎ 6471 7622; The Esplanade; adult/child $4.50/free; ☺ 10am-8pm Dec-Mar, to 6pm Apr-Nov), a creative and thought-provoking display on the history of the west, including a refreshingly blunt appraisal of environmental disappointments and achievements.

The visitor info centre stages **The Ship That Never Was** (☎ 6471 7622; The Esplanade; adult/child $12.50/2.50; ☺ 5.30pm year-round, also 8.30pm in Jan) daily in its amphitheatre. It's an entertaining pantomime-style show telling the story of the last ship built at Sarah Island, and the convicts who stole it and escaped. The show has something to please all ages, including audience participation for the kids.

Hogarth Falls is a pleasant one-hour return walk through the rainforest alongside the platypus-inhabited Botanical Creek. Start at People's Park.

Other natural attractions include the impressive 33km-long **Ocean Beach**, 6km from town, where the sunsets have to be seen to be believed. Due to rips and undertows, swimming isn't recommended. From October to April the dunes behind the beach become a **mutton bird rookery**, when the birds return from their winter migration. About 14km along the road from Strahan to Zeehan are the spectacular **Henty Dunes**, a series of 30m-high sand dunes. Ask at the Gordon River Cruises office about hiring sandboards and toboggans to ride these natural beauties.

Next to the caravan park is **West Strahan Beach**, with a gently shelving sandy bottom that provides safe swimming.

Tours
See the boxed text, opposite for information about the West Coast Wilderness Railway between Strahan and Queenstown.

FOUR-WHEEL MOTORCYCLING
Dune Buggy Tours (☎ 6471 7622, 0419 508 175) offers 35- to 40-minute controlled guided hooning over Henty Dunes on four-wheeled motorbikes ($40). There's a 12km/h speed limit and participants must have a full driving licence.

GORDON RIVER CRUISES
Both the following companies offer popular river cruises that include a rainforest walk

at Heritage Landing, views of – or passage through – Hells Gates (the narrow entrance to Macquarie Harbour), and a land tour of Sarah Island, the former penal settlement. The major difference between the companies is that Gordon River Cruises has reserved seating, and World Heritage Cruises doesn't (the latter is more first-in-best-dressed).

Gordon River Cruises (☎ 6471 4300, 1800 628 286; www.strahanvillage.com.au; The Esplanade) Offers 5½-hour cruises departing at 8.30am daily, and also at 2.30pm over summer. The cost depends on where you sit (you'll find most people get up and wander about anyway) and whether meals are involved: standard seats without food cost from $80/45/205 per adult/child/family. It offers a buffet lunch on board for $15/12 per adult/child. Don't be sucked in to paying extra for 'better' seats – they're not worth it.

World Heritage Cruises (☎ 6471 7174, 1800 611 796; www.worldheritagecruises.com.au; The Esplanade) Runs a six-hour cruise departing 9am from October through April ($65/25/165 per adult/child/family), and also at 2pm in summer. There are shorter cruises offered from October to April (departing 9am, returning 1.30pm) which cost $60/22/145 per adult/child/family, but note that they doesn't stop at Sarah Island. A good-value buffet lunch is available onboard (adult/child $12/6).

JET-BOAT RIDES

Wild Rivers Jet (☎ 6471 7174; www.wildriversjet.com .au; The Esplanade) runs 50-minute jet-boat rides on the hour from 9am to 4pm up the rain-forest-lined gorges of the King River. The experience costs $55/33/155 per adult/child/family (minimum two people; bookings are recommended).

SAILING

West Coast Yacht Charters (☎ 6471 7422; www.tasad ventures.com/wcyc; The Esplanade) offers overnight sightseeing cruises on the Gordon River on board the 60-foot steel ketch *Stormbreaker*. It's a more personal way to experience the river as the boat carries only 10 passengers. One night, including a visit to Sarah Island and all meals, costs $290/145 per adult/child. Two-day/two-night cruises are $390/195 per adult/child. Also available are three-hour fishing trips ($45/20) and a 2½-hour evening cruise ($70/50, including crayfish dinner) on Macquarie Harbour.

SCENIC FLIGHTS

The following companies offer daily flights over the area (weather and numbers permitting); trips should be booked ahead.

Seair Adventure Charters (☎ 6471 7718; www .adventureflights.com.au; Strahan Wharf) Conducts light-plane and helicopter flights over the region. Light-plane options include 45-minute flights over Frenchmans Cap, the Franklin and Gordon Rivers, and Sarah Island ($160/90 per adult/child), or 65-minute flights over the Cradle Mountain region ($175/90); there's a 60-minute helicopter flight over the Teepookana Forest ($165/90).

Wilderness Air (☎ 6471 7280; wildair@tassie.net.au; The Esplanade) Offers excellent 80-minute seaplane flights ($150/90 per adult/child), departing regularly from the wharf area, that fly up the Gordon River to Sir John Falls, where the plane lands so you can enjoy a rainforest walk.

SEA-KAYAKING

At the time of research, **Strahan Adventures** (☎ 6471 7275; www.adventurestasmania.com; The Esplanade) was not operating its kayak tours, but interested parties might like to ask around to see if tours have restarted.

Sleeping

Although Strahan has a range of accommodation, places are often full in summer and it's wise to book ahead. There is a dearth of budget lodgings – most options in town are priced at the higher end of the scale, but outside the high season you should be able to negotiate reasonable stand-by discounts.

BUDGET

West Coast Yacht Charters (☎ 6471 7422; www.tas adventures.com/wcyc; The Esplanade; dm adult/child $40/20, d $80) If you're hankering to sleep in a floating bunk on a wharf-moored yacht, then this is a great option. Because the yacht is used for charters, it has late check-in and early check-out (be prepared to check in after 7.30pm and disembark before 9am). The yacht isn't moored every night (overnight cruises on Gordon River are available), so you'll need to book ahead. Prices include continental breakfast and linen is supplied.

Strahan Youth Hostel (☎ 6471 7255; 43 Harvey St; dm $20, tw & d $50, cottages $75) Don't be fooled by the old YHA signage; it's not affiliated with YHA any longer. It may be in a nice bush setting around 15 minutes' walk from the town centre, but the hostel has very plain bunks and doubles, and tiny, ordinary A-frame cabins; the cottages are self-contained. The bathroom facilities could do with a decent scrub, too.

Strahan Caravan & Tourist Park (☎ 6471 7239; cnr Innes & Andrew Sts; powered/unpowered sites per 2 people $25/20, on-site caravans $50, cabins $75) A well-maintained beachfront park that's only a short distance from the heart of the village and offers good-value accommodation and facilities.

MIDRANGE & TOP END
Strahan Village (☎ 6471 4200, 1800 628 286; www .strahanvillage.com.au; d $140-290, extra person $30) Much of the accommodation in the centre of town is run by this conglomerate, which has its booking office (open daily) under the clock tower on the Esplanade. It has dozens of rooms on offer, including a group of terraces and cottages on the waterfront (some with self-catering facilities, some with spas), and the Hilltop Motor Inn, a refurbished motel high above the town with good views. The lowest rates will get you a standard room at the motel, the highest a deluxe spa terrace in the town, but there are a number of options in-between.

Cedar Heights (☎ 6471 7717; cedarheights@vision.net .au; 7 Meredith St; s/d from $85/100) These timber cabins with private courtyards are set back in a quiet street away from the bustle.

Regatta Point Villas (☎ 6471 7103; The Esplanade; d from $120) Near the West Coast Wilderness Railway station at Regatta Point and managed by the local tavern, this place offers eight roomy, self-contained units with fair views.

Gordon Gateway (☎ 6471 7165, 1300 134 425; www .gordongateway.com.au; The Esplanade, Regatta Point; studios $135, chalets $210, ste $220) In a scenic hillside location on the way to Regatta Point, this place has modern, well-outfitted, fully self-contained studio units (including a barrier-free room) and several larger A-frame chalets (with spa); all units have excellent views out to Macquarie Harbour and the township.

Risby Cove (☎ 6471 7572; www.risby.com.au; The Esplanade; d with/without spa $195/200) This eye-catchingly modern complex on the foreshore, 500m east of the town centre, has lodgings in fine suites overlooking the marina, including two right on the water's edge. There are bikes and dinghies for hire, plus a gallery and high-quality restaurant on site.

Franklin Manor (☎ 6471 7311; www.franklinmanor .com.au; The Esplanade; d $185-260) Not far from Risby Cove, this 1896 manor is a charming hideaway situated in lovely grounds. Visitors will appreciate the elegant rooms (the top rooms have king-sized beds, open fireplaces and spa), underground wine cellar, cooked breakfasts and the superb on-site restaurant (see below). There are also rustic cottages to accommodate larger parties (sleeping up to five), two with self-catering facilities.

Eating
Banjo's Bakehouse (☎ 6471 7794; The Esplanade; pizzas from $10; ☻ 6am-8.30pm) Popular central bakery serving a wonderful breakfast menu along with snacks such as sandwiches, hot chunky pies and other savouries and pastries. You'll have to wait until after 6pm for its oven-baked pizzas.

Hamer's Hotel (☎ 6471 7191; The Esplanade; meals $13-25; ☻ lunch & dinner) This family-friendly joint serves commendable counter meals and grill options, including vegetarian dishes. Carnivores can enjoy unique meals such as wallaby sirloin, or tuck into some seafood feasts. Its public bar is a good spot to down a couple of beers.

Fish Café (☎ 6471 4386; The Esplanade; meals $5-10; ☻ breakfast, lunch & dinner) This bustling café does a good trade in fresh, succulent seafood, chips, burgers, pies and rolls. Good options include the generous fisherman's box – a medley of seafood and chips ($10), a Strahan souvlaki with chicken ($6), the crumbed flounder ($4) and battered Tasmanian scallops ($1.80 each); eat in or be prepared for battle with the seagulls.

Regatta Point Tavern (☎ 6471 7103; The Esplanade; mains $16-18; ☻ lunch & dinner) If you want to eat with the locals away from the glitz, make your way to this pub near the railway terminus, 2km around the bay from Strahan's centre. It serves hearty seafood and steak meals in its bistro; there's also a kiddies' menu.

Franklin Manor (☎ 6471 7311; The Esplanade; mains $30-35; ☻ dinner) For sheer holiday indulgence, head to this fine restaurant for fabulous local produce carefully prepared by the Michelin-starred French chef. The degustation menus offer great value, with four/seven courses costing $85/125, and you can indulge yourself further with selections from the acclaimed wine list. Bookings are essential.

TASMANIA

Getting There & Around

Buses arrive at and depart from the visitor information centre; see p689 for details.

Strahan Taxis (☎ 0417 516 071) has services to surrounding attractions such as Henty Dunes ($25 per taxi, maximum four people). **Risby Cove** (☎ 6471 7572) rents out bicycles ($10/20 per half/full day).

FRANKLIN-GORDON WILD RIVERS NATIONAL PARK

This environmentally awesome, World Heritage–listed park includes the catchment areas of the Franklin and Olga Rivers and part of the Gordon River, as well as exceptional bushwalking and climbing. The park's most significant peak is **Frenchmans Cap** (1443m; a three- to five-day walk). The park also boasts a number of unique plant species and the major indigenous Australian archaeological site at **Kutikina Cave**.

Much of the park is deep river gorges and impenetrable rainforest, but the Lyell Hwy traverses its northern end and there are a few short walks starting from the road. These include hikes to **Donaghys Hill** (40 minutes return), from where you can see the Franklin River and the magnificent white-quartzite dome of Frenchmans Cap, and a stroll to **Nelson Falls** (20 minutes return).

Rafting

Rafting the wild Franklin River makes for a sensational but hazardous journey; for the inexperienced, there are tour companies offering complete rafting packages. Whether you go with an independent group or a tour operator, you should contact the park rangers at the **Lake St Clair visitor information centre** (☎ 6289 1172; Cynthia Bay; ⊙ 8am-7pm Dec & Jan, to 8pm Feb, to 5pm Mar-Nov) or the **Queenstown Parks & Wildife Service office** (PWS; ☎ 6471 2511; Penghana Rd) for current information on permits, regulations and environmental considerations. You should also check out the detailed Franklin rafting notes online at www.parks.tas.gov.au – go to 'Outdoor Recreation', then 'Boating, Kayaking & Rafting Notes'.

All expeditions should register at the booth at the junction of the Lyell Hwy and the Collingwood River, 49km west of Derwent Bridge. Rafting the length of the river, starting at Collingwood River and ending at Sir John Falls, takes between eight and 14 days (it's also possible to do shorter trips on different sections of the river). From the exit point, you can be picked up by a **Wilderness Air** (☎ 6471 7280; wildair@tassie.net.au) seaplane or paddle a further 22km downriver to meet a Gordon River cruise boat at Heritage Landing.

Tours run mainly from December to March. Tour companies with complete rafting packages:

Rafting Tasmania (☎ 6239 1080; raftingtas@ozemail .com.au) Has five-/seven-/10-day trips costing $1400/1650/2150.

Tasmanian Expeditions (☎ 1300 666 856, 6334 3477; www.tas-ex.com) Another operator with nine-/11-day trips for $2190/2450.

Water By Nature (☎ 1800 111 142, 0408 242 941; www.franklinrivertasmania.com) This new operator (formerly Peregrine) provides five-/seven-/10-day trips for $1390/1690/2250.

CRADLE MOUNTAIN-LAKE ST CLAIR NATIONAL PARK

Tasmania's best-known national park is the superb 1262-sq-km World Heritage area of Cradle Mountain-Lake St Clair. Its spectacular mountain peaks, deep gorges, lakes, tarns and wild moorlands extend from the Great Western Tiers in the north to Derwent Bridge on the Lyell Hwy in the south. It's one of the most glaciated areas in Australia and includes Mt Ossa (1617m) – Tasmania's highest peak – and Lake St Clair, Australia's deepest (over 200m) natural freshwater lake.

The preservation of this region as a national park is due in part to Gustav Weindorfer, an Austrian who fell in love with the area. In 1912 he built a chalet out of King Billy pine, called it Waldheim (German for 'Forest Home') and, from 1916, lived there permanently. Today, bushwalkers huts stand near his original chalet at the northern end of the park and the area is named Waldheim, after his chalet.

There are plenty of day walks in both the Cradle Valley and Cynthia Bay (Lake St Clair) regions, but it's the spectacular 80.5km Overland Track between the two that has turned this park into a bushwalkers' mecca.

Information

All walking tracks in the park are signposted, well defined and easy to follow, but it's still advisable to carry a map, which can be purchased at the park's visitor information centres.

CRADLE VALLEY

There are now two visitor information centres. Immediately opposite the Cradle Mountain Tourist Park & Campground and 3km north of the park's northern boundary is the new **Cradle information centre** (☎ 6492 1110; Cradle Mountain Rd; ☽ 8.30am-4.30pm) with its vast car park. This is the starting point for the bus shuttle service (p700) into the national park, here you can purchase park passes, bushwalking information, food and fuel.

Within the park boundaries itself lies the **Cradle Mountain visitor centre** (☎ 6492 1133; ☽ 8am-5pm Jun-Aug, 8am-6pm Sep-May), which is run by the Parks and Wildlife Service and provides extensive bushwalking information and informative displays about the flora, fauna and history of the park.

Whatever time of the year you visit, be prepared for cold, wet weather in the Cradle Valley area. On average it rains here on seven days out of 10, is cloudy eight days in 10, the sun shines all day only one day in 10 and it snows on 54 days each year!

LAKE ST CLAIR

Occupying one wing of a large building at Cynthia Bay, on the southern boundary of the park, is the **Lake St Clair visitor information centre** (☎ 6289 1172; ☽ 8am-7pm Dec & Jan, to 8pm Feb, to 5pm Mar-Nov), with good advice and displays on the park.

At the adjacent, separately run **Lakeside St Clair Wilderness Park** (☎ 6289 1137; www.lake stclairwildernessholidays.com.au; ☽ 8am-5pm Mar-Nov, to 7pm or 8pm Dec-Feb), you can book a range of accommodation (p699), a seat on a ferry or cruise (p700), or hire dinghies.

Sights & Activities
THE OVERLAND TRACK
A handy pocket-sized reference for the walk is *The Overland Track – A Walkers Notebook* ($10), published by the Parks & Wildlife Service and detailing all sections of the track and the flora and fauna that live there. It can be ordered online – visit

---

DEFORESTATION IN TASMANIA *Senator Bob Brown*

Tasmania's wild and scenic beauty, along with a human heritage dating back 30,000 years, is a priceless heritage available to all of us. The waterfalls, wild rivers, lovely beaches, snow-capped mountains, turquoise seas and wildlife are abundant and accessible for locals and visitors alike.

Because we are all creations of nature – that curl on our ears is fashioned to pick up the faintest sounds from the forest floor – we are all bonded to the wilds. No wonder that in this anxiety-ridden world there is such a thirst for remote, pristine, natural places. Yet around the world, wilderness is the fastest disappearing resource and Tasmania is no exception.

This year 150,000 truck-loads of the island's native forests, including giant eucalypt species which produce the tallest flowering plants on earth, will arrive at the woodchip mills en route to Japan. After logging, the forests are firebombed and every fur, feather and flower is destroyed. These great forests, built of carbon, are one of the world's best hedges against global warming. They are carbon banks. Yet they are being looted, taken from our fellow creatures and all who come after us. The log trucks on Tasmania's highways are enriching banks of a different kind.

Over two decades ago, people power saved Tasmania's wild Franklin and Lower Gordon Rivers (opposite) which nowadays attract hundreds of thousands of visitors to the west coast. Those visitors, in turn, bring jobs, investment and local prosperity. Saving the environment has been a boom for the economy and employment.

The rescue of Tasmania's forests relies on each of us, and there are plenty of ways we can help. We can help with letters or phone calls to newspapers, radio stations, or politicians; with every cent donated to the forest campaigners; and in every well-directed vote. The tourist dollar speaks loudly in Tasmania, so even overseas travellers, who cannot vote, should take the opportunity to write letters to our newspapers and politicians. With each step we take, we move toward ending this destruction of Tasmania's wild and scenic heritage.

Senator Bob Brown was elected to the Tasmanian parliament in 1983 and first elected to the Senate in 1996. His books include The Valley of the Giants. *Read more about Bob Brown at www.bobbrown.org.au*

www.parks.tas.gov.au/publications/general
.html.

A good source of planning information is the website of the Parks & Wildlife Service – go to www.parks.tas.gov.au/rec reation/tracknotes/overland.html for helpful tips. Another useful website is www.over landtrack.com.au.

The best time to walk the Overland Track is during summer, when flowering plants are most prolific (also December to April sees longer daylight hours and warmer aver age temperatures), although spring and autumn also have their attractions. You can walk the track in winter, but only if you're very experienced.

Walkers sometimes start at Dove Lake, but the recommended route actually begins at Ronny Creek, a walk of around 5km from the visitor centre. The trail is well marked its entire length and, at an easy pace, takes around five or six days to complete. There are many secondary paths leading up to mountains such as Mt Ossa or other natural features, so the length of time you actually take is only limited by the amount of supplies you can carry.

There are unattended huts along the track that you can use for overnight accommodation, but in summer they fill quickly so be sure you carry a tent. Campfires are banned so you must also carry a fuel stove.

The walk itself is extremely varied, negotiating high alpine moors, rocky scree, gorges and tall forest. Once you reach Cynthia Bay, you have the option of radioing Lakeside St Clair Wilderness Park from Narcissus Hut on the northern end of Lake St Clair for a ferry to come and pick you up, saving a five- to six-hour walk, at a cost of $20 per person.

More detailed descriptions of the walk are given in Lonely Planet's *Tasmania* and *Walking in Australia* guides.

OTHER BUSHWALKS

There are dozens of short walks in the park. For visitors to Cradle Valley, behind the visitor centre is an easy but quite spectacular 10-minute circular boardwalk through the adjacent rainforest, called the **Rainforest Walk**; it's more than suitable for wheelchairs and prams. There's another boarded path nearby leading to **Pencil Pine Falls** and on to **Knyvet Falls** (25 minutes return), as well as the **Enchanted Nature Walk** alongside Pencil Pine Creek (25 minutes return). The boardwalk running the 8.5km-long **Cradle Valley walk** between the visitor centre and Dove Lake is also suitable for those in wheelchairs. Walks also start from **Dove Lake**; the best walk in the area is the circuit of the lake itself, which takes two to three hours.

At Cynthia Bay, the **Larmairremener tabelti** is an Aboriginal culture walk that winds through the traditional lands of the Larmairremener, the indigenous people of the region. The walk (one hour return) starts

---

CHANGES ARE ON TRACK

In 1953 it's estimated that less than 1000 people walked the Overland Track; by 2004 the Overland Track was pounded by around 9000 people, so it should come as no great surprise that in order to preserve the delicate ecology of the area and to avoid environmental degradation and overcrowding some changes to the conditions for walking the track are required. The idea of people turning up without notice and hiking the track will cease, particularly during the peak walking season.

Three major changes have been introduced:

- A booking system for the peak walking period (November to April), with departure dates for walkers now subject to a quota.

- Visitors from November to April are required to walk the track from north to south (Cradle Mountain to Lake St Clair).

- Fees of $100 ($80 for children and seniors) have been introduced to cover costs of the sustainable management of the track. This is in addition to national park entry fees. Fees apply only from November to April, and only to those walking the entire Overland Track.

For further information about the Overland Track, visit the website www.overlandtrack.com.au.

at the visitor information centre. One way to do some good walking here is to catch the ferry service to either Echo Point Hut or Narcissus Hut and walk back to Cynthia Bay along the lake shore. From Echo Point it's about three to five hours' walk back, and from Narcissus Hut it's about five to six hours.

Tours

Most travellers to Tasmania consider Cradle Mountain a must-see, so almost every tour operator in the state offers day trips or longer tours to the area (including guided walks along the Overland Track). Some recommendations:

Craclair (☎ 6339 4488; www.craclair.com.au) The company most experienced at running guided bushwalking tours in this national park; among its many offerings is an eight-day tour along the Overland Track for $1485 per person (all packs, sleeping bags, tents, jackets and overtrousers are supplied). Also runs shorter trips.

Cradle Mountain Huts (☎ 6391 9339; www.cradle huts.com.au) If camping isn't for you, from November to May you can take a six-day, small-group guided walk along the Overland Track which includes accommodation in private huts. The $1995 fee per person also includes meals, national park entry fees and transfer to/from Launceston.

Tasman Bush Tours (☎ 6423 2335; www.tasmanbush tours.com) Offers a six-day package for $980. This includes camping gear, park pass, food, ferry tickets to Lake St Clair and transport to/from Devonport.

Tasmanian Expeditions (☎ 6334 3477, 1800 030 230; www.tas-ex.com) Does an eight-day trip for $1240 (runs November to April) combining Cradle Mountain and the Walls of Jerusalem National Park (p674).

TigerLine (☎ 6271 7333, 1300 653 633; www.tigerline .com.au) For the less energetic, this company has a day trip (adult/child $113/68) to Cradle Mountain from Launceston via Sheffield.

SCENIC FLIGHTS

An entirely sedentary way to see the region's sights is to take a helicopter flight with **Seair Adventure Charters** (☎ 6492 1132; www.adventureflights.com.au; Cradle Mountain Rd; flights Sep-Jun). Flights leave from the airstrip next to Cradle Wilderness Café; flights lasting 50 minutes cost $185/110 per adult/child.

Sleeping & Eating
CRADLE VALLEY

Cradle Mountain Tourist Park & Campground (☎ 6492 1395, 1800 068 574; www.cosycabins.com /cradle; Cradle Mountain Rd; powered/unpowered sites per 2 people $25/20, dm $25, cabins $95-125) Situated 2.5km from the national park entrance, this busy bushland complex has camping sites, a decent YHA hostel, self-contained cabins and more upmarket cottages (with spa). It pays to book in advance.

Waldheim Cabins (☎ 6492 1110; cradle@parks.tas .gov.au; d $70, extra adult $25) These basic four- to eight-bunk huts are found near Gustav Weindorfer's original hut some 5km into the national park. Each contains gas stove, cooking utensils and wood or gas heater, but no bedding. Bathroom facilities are shared. Check-in and bookings are handled by the Cradle information centre.

Cradle Mountain Highlanders Cottages (☎ 6492 1116; www.cradlehighlander.com.au; Cradle Mountain Rd; d $105-180, extra person $25-35) The hospitable Highlanders has rustic timber cottages in a beautiful setting. It's a friendly, family-run operation and each cottage is different, although all come equipped with kitchen (and breakfast provisions) and lounge area. The more luxurious have a wood-fired heater and a spa.

Cradle Mountain Lodge (☎ 6492 1303; www.cradle mountainlodge.com.au; Cradle Mountain Rd; d $230-580, extra person $60; 🖳) This gloriously swish resort, right by the entrance to the park, is huge – nearly 100 cabins surround the main lodge. There are three standards of cabin, in sizes to suit couples or families. Each has tea- and coffee-making facilities and fridge (no kitchens); prices include an extensive buffet breakfast. There are log fires in all cabins, and pricier suites have CD players and spa baths. There's a spa retreat here too, and you can undertake a plethora of activities (guided and self-guided).

As well as a cosy bar and library area, Cradle Mountain Lodge is home to the **Highlander** (mains $19-26; 🌙 dinner), a fine-dining restaurant offering well-prepared dishes (bookings advised). Also here is the **Tavern Bar & Bistro** (mains $12-19; 🌙 lunch & dinner), serving pub-style meals in a casual setting.

Cradle Wilderness Café (☎ 6492 1400; Cradle Mountain Rd; mains $7-20; 🌙 9am-5pm Mar-Nov, to 8pm Dec-Feb) has a good range of satisfying meals, plus takeaways. The café also sells petrol and alcohol.

Self-caterers should stock up before heading to Cradle Valley; minimal supplies are sold at the café, the tourist park and Cradle Mountain Lodge.

TASMANIA

CYNTHIA BAY & DERWENT BRIDGE

Lakeside St Clair Wilderness Holidays (☎ 6289 1137; www.lakestclairwildernessholidays.com.au; Cynthia Bay; powered/unpowered sites per 2 people $15/12, dm $25, cabins $196) This place has its office at Cynthia Bay by the visitor information centre, adjacent to the shop and café it also manages. It has a lakeside camping ground not far away, plus Spartan dorm rooms and high-quality self-contained cabins. The **café** (mains $4-10; ☯ 8am-5pm, to 6pm in summer) serves light meals such as toasted sandwiches, or more substantial fare, including burgers, plus a range of takeaways.

Derwent Bridge Wilderness Hotel (☎ 6289 1144; Lyell Hwy, Derwent Bridge; dm $25, d $85-105) If you've got any sense, the moment you step off the Overland Track you'll head here for a beer, a steak and some big talk about your big walk. The accommodation is nothing special (only the more expensive rooms have bathrooms) but the welcoming lounge bar has a high, timber-beamed ceiling, pool table and massive open fire. Meals (breakfast, lunch and dinner) are impressive – better than the usual pub offerings – with dinner mains costing $17 to $25.

Derwent Bridge Chalets (☎ 6289 1000; www.troutwalks.com.au; Lyell Hwy, Derwent Bridge; d $155-200, extra adult $35) There are a half-dozen roomy self-contained cottages to choose from here, each with bush views from the back porch. The immaculate cottages can sleep up to eight and are well equipped, with full kitchen, laundry and wood or gas heaters; some also have a spa. The cheaper option here, and good for one-night stays, is one of the newer studio units with kitchenette, which are known as **Travellers Rest Cabins** (d from $115).

Getting There & Away

See p689 for details of **TassieLink** (☎ 1300 300 520; www.tassielink.com.au) services to Cradle Mountain and Lake St Clair. TassieLink also offers packages whereby it drops you off at one end of the Overland Track and picks you up at the other. There are myriad options depending on where you're coming from/going to, so call TassieLink for prices; the packages must be booked.

Maxwells (☎ 6492 1431, 0418 584 004) runs services on demand from Devonport to Cradle Mountain (one to four passengers $160/five

or more $40 per passenger), Launceston to Cradle Mountain ($240/60) via the Walls of Jerusalem (p674), and Devonport and Launceston to Lake St Clair ($280/70).

You might be able to find a more convenient or cheaper transport option by talking to staff at bushwalking shops or hostels.

Getting Around

CRADLE VALLEY

Immediately opposite the Cradle Mountain Tourist Park & Campground is the new Cradle information centre with its vast car park. From here free shuttle buses leave at 15-minute intervals (mid-September to late May) stopping at the visitor centre inside the park, Ronny Creek (near Waldheim Chalet) and then on to Dove Lake. Visitors can alight at any bus stop along the way. Contact the information centre for the shuttle's reduced winter timetable.

Maxwells (☎ 6492 1431, 0418 584 004) provides an on-demand year-round shuttle service for $9 per person (one way), picking up passengers from the campground and other accommodation venues. Bookings are essential.

CYNTHIA BAY

Also run by **Maxwells** (☎ 6289 1125, 0418 328 427) is an on-demand service between Cynthia Bay/Lake St Clair and Derwent Bridge ($7 per person one way).

Lakeside St Clair Wilderness Park (☎ 6289 1137; www.lakestclairwildernessholidays.com.au; one way/return $20/25) runs a ferry service between Cynthia Bay and Narcissus Hut, at the northern end of Lake St Clair. The boat departs at least three times daily (usually 9am, 1pm and 3pm); bookings are essential and you can expect to pay more if there are fewer than four people on board. If you're using the ferry service at the end of your Overland Track hike, you *must* radio the ferry operator when you arrive at Narcissus Hut.

At the time of research some proposed changes to the ferry system included a new cruise boat, due to start operating two-hour cruises of the lake, while the taxi ferry service as it currently exists would provide a service for bushwalkers only. Contact the Lakeside St Clair Wilderness Park for details.

THE SOUTHWEST

SOUTHWEST NATIONAL PARK

There are few places left in the world as isolated and untouched as Tasmania's southwest wilderness, the state's largest national park. It's home to some of the world's last tracts of virgin temperate rainforest and these contribute much to the grandeur and extraordinary diversity of this ancient area.

The southwest is the habitat of the endemic Huon pine, which lives for more than 3000 years, and of the swamp gum, the world's tallest hardwood and tallest flowering plant. About 300 species of lichen, moss and fern – some of which are rare and endangered – dapple the rainforest in many shades of green; glacial tarns are seamless silver mirrors on the jagged mountains; and in summer, the alpine meadows are picture-perfect with wildflowers and flowering shrubs. Through it all run the wild rivers, with rapids tearing through deep gorges and waterfalls plunging over cliffs.

Bushwalking

The best-known walks in the park are the 70km **Port Davey Track** used by walkers between Scotts Peak Rd and Melaleuca (four or five days' duration), and the considerably more popular 85km **South Coast Track** between Cockle Creek and Melaleuca.

The South Coast Track takes six to eight days to complete and hikers should be well prepared for the often vicious weather. Light planes are used to airlift bushwalkers into the southwest, and there is vehicle access and public transport to/from Cockle Creek, at the park's southeastern edge. Detailed notes to the South Coast Track are available in Lonely Planet's *Walking in Australia*, and information is available on the website of the **Parks & Wildlife Service** (PWS; www.parks.tas.gov.au/recreation/tracknotes/scoast.html).

Getting There & Around

A popular way to tackle the South Coast Track is to fly into remote Melaleuca and walk out. **Par Avion** (☎ 03-6248 5390; www.paravion .com.au) and **Tasair** (☎ 03-6248 5088; www.tasair .au) offer air services to bushwalkers, flying between Hobart and Melaleuca for around $150 one way.

For those who like your creature comforts, there is a soft option – scenic flights out of Hobart over the southwest, with time spent on the ground. Par Avion's offerings start with a basic scenic flight (no landing) for $150. You're better off spending a little extra and taking the four-hour option ($170), which includes a landing at Melaleuca and a short boat trip here. Tasair's speciality is a 2½-hour flight ($176) that includes 30 minutes on the ground, with a beach landing at Cox Bight (if weather conditions are right) or at Melaleuca.

From December through March, **TassieLink** (☎ 1300 300 520; www.tassielink.com.au) runs three buses a week from Hobart to Scotts Peak ($64, four hours), and between Hobart and Cockle Creek ($57, 3½ hours). Bookings are essential.

LAKE PEDDER & STRATHGORDON
☎ 03 / pop 75

At the northern edge of the southwest wilderness lies Lake Pedder, once a spectacularly beautiful natural lake considered the ecological jewel of the region. In 1972, however, it was flooded to become part of the Gordon River power development. Together with nearby Lake Gordon, Pedder now holds 27 times the volume of water that's in Sydney Harbour and is the largest inland freshwater catchment in Australia.

Built to service employees during construction of the Gordon River Power Scheme, tiny Strathgordon is the base from which to visit Lakes Pedder and Gordon. About 12km west of the township is the **Gordon Dam lookout and visitor information centre** (☎ 6280 1134; ⏰ 10am-5pm Nov-Apr, 11am-3pm May-Oct), located at the 140m-high Gordon Dam and providing info on the scheme. The views from the dam walls are spectacular.

Accommodation-wise, your only options are the free **Teds Beach Campground** beside Lake Pedder (toilets and electric barbecues; no fires permitted), or the newly renovated **Lake Pedder Chalet** (☎ 6280 1166; www.lakepedderchalet .com.au; d $50-100). Also at the Chalet is a **restaurant** (lunch $7-11, dinner $14-21; ⏰ breakfast, lunch & dinner) serving well-priced meals in a dining room with excellent lake views. To help you explore the area, the Chalet offers bike and boat hire, rod and tackle rental, and fishing, lake and wildlife-spotting tours.

No bus services run to Strathgordon.

TASMANIA

BASS STRAIT ISLANDS

You might well feel that Tasmania moves at a slower pace compared to the mainland states, but there are two land masses in Bass Strait that offer the chance to drop back a further few notches.

Tasmania has two groups of islands, the Hunter and Furneaux Groups, at the western and eastern entrances of Bass Strait, respectively. Once the transient homes of sealers, sailors and prospectors, today these islands are rich in wildlife and natural beauty and offer a peaceful retreat for those keen to get well off the beaten track.

A good idea for visiting King or Flinders Islands is to purchase a package that includes flights, car rental and accommodation. Make inquiries with the airlines listed here, or contact Tourism Tasmania or travel centres in Melbourne and Sydney (for contact details see p614).

KING ISLAND
☎ 03 / pop 1765

King Island guards the western end of Bass Strait. Only 64km long and 27km wide, this island's beaches, rocky coastline, seafood and dairy fare, and bucolic atmosphere more than compensate for its size.

Discovered in 1798, King Island was soon known as a breeding ground for seals and sea elephants, later hunted close to extinction by brutal sealers and sailors known as the Straitsmen.

Over the years, the stormy seas of Bass Strait have claimed many ships and there are several wrecks around the island. The worst accident occurred in 1845 when the *Cataraqui*, an immigrant ship, went down with 399 people aboard.

The main township is Currie on the west coast, and other notable settlements are Naracoopa on the east coast and Grassy in the southeast. Currie has an ATM.

Pre-trip information can be obtained from **King Island Tourism** (☎ 6462 1313, 1800 645 014; www.kingisland.org.au). For tourist information once you reach the island, visit the **Trend** (☎ 6462 1360; Edward St, Currie; ☼ 9am-6.30pm).

Sights & Activities

King Island's four **lighthouses** guard against its treacherous coasts. The 48m Cape Wick-ham lighthouse is the tallest in the southern hemisphere and is worth visiting for the view of the surrounding coast. The others are at Currie, Stokes Point and south of Naracoopa.

The **King Island Historical Museum** (☎ 6462 1698; Lighthouse St, Currie; adult/child $4/1; ☼ 2-4pm Sep-Jun), housed in what was once the lighthouse-keeper's cottage, features many maritime and local-history displays but is particularly fond of the remnants of maritime disasters.

King Island is probably best known for its dairy produce (especially heavenly, award-winning cheeses). **King Island Dairy** (☎ 6462 1348; www.kidairy.com.au; North Rd, Loorana; ☼ 12.30-4.30pm, closed Sat Oct-Apr, closed Wed & Sat May-Sep), 8km north of Currie (just beyond the airport), has tastings and sales for *from-age* connoisseurs.

Crayfish and kelp are other valuable exports for the island. On Netherby Rd is the only **kelp-processing plant** in Australia; from the roadside you can see kelp drying on racks.

Diving among the local marine life and shipwrecks is recommended. **Swimming** at deserted beaches or in freshwater lagoons, **surfing** and **fishing** are all popular. If you're interested in a drier pastime, try **bushwalking**. There is abundant **wildlife** here, including a small colony of fairy penguins at Grassy.

Tours

King Island Coaches (☎ 6462 1138, 1800 647 702; www.kingislandgem.com.au; 95 Main St, Currie) Offers various half-/full-day island explorations ($40/80), as well as an evening tour to view fairy penguins ($40).

King Island Dive Charters (☎ 6461 1133; www.kingislanddivecharter.com.au) Offers single boat dives for $75, and can arrange good-value three- to seven-day packages.

Sleeping

Boomerang by the Sea (☎ 6462 1288; www.bythesea.com.au; Golf Club Rd, Currie; s/d $99/120) Boomerang has decent, well-equipped motel rooms that enjoy superb ocean views across the golf course. It's only a short stroll into town, and there's a high-quality restaurant on site.

Baudins Cottages (☎ 6461 1110; baudins@kingisland.net.au; The Esplanade, Naracoopa; d $121-154, extra person $40) On the beachfront at Naracoopa with fine views across Sea Elephant Bay, Baudins has four one- and two-bedroom self-contained units. The guest facilities include the use of fishing rods and mountain bikes.

Contact King Island Tourism or see its website for more on sleeping options, including self-contained houses for rent.

Bass Caravan Park & Cabins (☎ 6462 1260; www .kingislandgem.com.au; 100 Main St, Currie; on-site caravan per 2 people $45, cabin $98) A few kilometres from the beach, this small park offers a handful of on-site caravans with bathroom, plus two-bedroom cabins with kitchen and bathroom.

Eating

There are good eating options in Currie within walking distance of most accommodation. There are also two supermarkets on Main St.

King Island Bakery (☎ 6462 1337; 5 Main St, Currie; snacks $3-6; ☺ from 6am) An excellent spot for picnic fodder. Sells lots of freshly baked goods, including raved-about gourmet pies with fillings such as crayfish, camembert and asparagus, and King Island beef.

Boomerang by the Sea (☎ 6462 1288; Golf Club Rd, Currie; mains from $22; ☺ dinner daily Sep-Apr, Mon-Sat May-Oct) Recognised as one of the island's best eating options, this restaurant has ocean views and serves up delicious, locally sourced produce (anything featuring local cheese, seafood or beef is a sure bet).

Baudins (☎ 6461 1110; The Esplanade; mains $20-25; ☺ dinner) On the eastern side of the island, the colonial-style Baudins serves beef, seafood and other well-prepared local edibles in its restaurant on the bay.

Getting There & Away

Flying is the only way to get to King Island. **Regional Express** (Rex; ☎ 13 17 13; www.regionalex press.com.au) flies from Melbourne, as does **King Island Airlines** (☎ 9580 3777; www.kingislandair .com.au) – the latter flies to/from a small suburban airport (Moorabbin) in Melbourne's southeast. Return flights cost $300 to $400.

Tasair (☎ 6248 5088; www.tasair.com.au) flies from Devonport and Burnie/Wynyard to King Island (around $365 return from both destinations). Connecting flights from Hobart to Burnie are usually available.

Getting Around

There is no public transport on the island. Hire-car companies will meet you at the airport, but vehicles should be booked in advance. **King Island Car Rental** (☎ 6462 1282, 1800 777 282; kicars@kingisland.net.au; 2 Meech St, Currie) has cars from $62 per day; you can hire bikes from the **Trend** (☎ 6462 1360; Edward St, Currie).

FLINDERS ISLAND

☎ 03 / pop 925

Flinders Island is the largest of the 52 islands that comprise the Furneaux Group, and is rich in natural attractions. First charted in 1798 by the British explorer Matthew Flinders, the Furneaux Group became a base for the Straitsmen, who slaughtered seals in their tens of thousands.

The most tragic part of Flinders Island's history, however, was its role in the virtual annihilation of Tasmania's Aboriginal people between 1829 and 1834. Of the 135 survivors who were forcibly removed from the Tasmanian mainland to Wybalenna (meaning 'Black Man's House') to be 'civilised and educated', only 47 survived to make the journey to Oyster Cove near Hobart in 1847.

The island's main industries are farming, fishing and seasonal mutton-birding. The island supports a wide variety of **wildlife**, including many bird species, the best known being the protected Cape Barren goose.

The principal town on Flinders Island is Whitemark, and Lady Barron in the south is the main fishing area and deep-water port. Planning a visit can be done with the help of the **Flinders Island Area Marketing & Development Office** (☎ 6359 2380, 1800 994 477; www.flindersislandonline.com.au); on the island, locals are the best sources of information. There are no ATMs, but most businesses have Eftpos facilities.

Sights & Activities

Today, all that remains of the unfortunate settlement at **Wybalenna** is the cemetery and the chapel, restored by the National Trust. In 1999 the site was returned to the descendants of the indigenous people who lived there.

Not far from Wybalenna, at Emita, is the **Furneaux Museum** (☎ 6359 2010; adult/child $4/free; ☺ 1-5pm daily late Dec-Jan, 1-5pm Sat & Sun rest of year), which houses a variety of Aboriginal artefacts (including beautiful shell necklaces), sealing and shipwreck relics, and a display on the mutton-bird industry.

TASMANIA

Bushwalking is popular here and many visitors climb **Mt Strzelecki** – the walk starts about 12km south of Whitemark on Trousers Point Rd, and the well-signposted track (four to five hours return) culminates in spectacular views enjoyed at a height of 756m.

There are beautiful **beaches** around the island (particularly the west coast – be sure to visit Trousers Point), and several **scuba diving** locations off the northern and western coasts. In many places you can enter these from the beach or shelving rocks. Rock and beach **fishing** are popular all year. A more unusual pastime is **fossicking** for Killiecrankie diamonds – actually fragments of topaz – on the beach and creek at Killiecrankie Bay.

Tours

Flinders Island Adventures (☎ 6359 4507; jamesluddington@bigpond.com) Can arrange fishing charters, evening cruises to view mutton birds ($30), half- or full-day 4WD tours ($90/156 per person), cruises around the outer islands, and other customised touring options.

Flinders Island Dive (☎ 6359 8429; flindersdive@yahoo.com) Offers half-/full-day diving charters from $100/160 per person, as well as fishing trips, diving courses and equipment hire.

Sleeping

Interstate Hotel (☎ 6359 2114; interstatehotel@trump.net.au; Patrick St, Whitemark; s $22-60, d $38-90) In the centre of Whitemark is this pub, built in 1911 and renovated in heritage style. It's a comfortable place offering an array of rooms and facilities, from no-frills budget options to better-standard rooms with private shower and TV.

Furneaux Tavern (☎ 6359 3521; potboil@bigpond .com; Franklin Pde, Lady Barron; s/d $80/110, extra person $30) The tavern in Lady Barron has 10 spacious motel units set in native gardens behind the bar-restaurant. Note that some road signage still refers to this place as the Flinders Island Lodge.

Silas Beach (☎ 6359 3521; Franklin Pde, Lady Barron; d $130, extra person $35) In an absolute waterfront location and enjoying great views is this modern three-bedroom holiday house, sleeping six and providing all the comforts of home. Book through the tavern.

Flinders Island Cabin Park (☎ 6359 2188; fi_cabin park@yahoo.com.au; Bluff Rd; sites per person $7, d cabin $50-95, extra person $15) About 4km north of

Whitemark, situated close to the airport. On offer are a handful of affordable, family-sized brick cabins, some with private bathroom. The park isn't signposted from the main road – go down the road for Bluff Point, and it's the first property on the left.

There is free **camping** in a lovely campground on Trousers Point, where facilities include toilets and gas barbecues (no powered sites, no showers).

Eating

Flinders Island Bakery (☎ 6359 2105; Lagoon Rd, Whitemark; sandwiches & pies $4; ☺ Mon-Fri) For lunch, how about a salad roll or chunky lamb curry pie, followed by decent coffee and a slice of lemon tart? Open on weekends in summer.

Interstate Hotel (☎ 6359 2114; Patrick St, Whitemark; lunch $10, dinner $16-25; ☺ lunch Mon-Fri, dinner Mon-Sat) Drop into this gracious old pub in the centre of Whitemark, the hub of island life. Its dining room serves a range of well-priced lunches and dinners, with the usual array of pub dishes and a welcome emphasis on local seafood.

Furneaux Tavern (☎ 6359 3521; Franklin Pde, Lady Barron; bar mains $8-12, restaurant mains $22-32; ☺ bar lunch & dinner daily, restaurant lunch & dinner Wed-Sun) This is your only option for meals in Lady Barron, but the tavern looks after everyone with its great views, social bar, cheap, filling bar meals such as burgers or fish and chips, and a restaurant menu featuring the stars of the local produce scene.

There's a **supermarket** (☎ 6359 2010; Patrick St; ☺ 9am-5.30pm Mon-Fri, 9am-12.30pm Sat) in Whitemark, and general stores (open seven days) in Lady Barron and Killiecrankie.

Getting There & Away

AIR

Airlines of Tasmania (☎ 6359 2312, 1800 144 460; www.airtasmania.com.au) offers daily scheduled services between Launceston and Flinders Island ($281 return), as well as services to Moorabbin in Victoria three times a week ($395 return).

FERRY

Southern Shipping Company (☎ 6356 1753; s.ship .co@microtech.com.au) operates a weekly ferry service (departing Monday) from Bridport in Tasmania's northeast to Flinders

Island; the ferry then continues on to Port Welshpool in Victoria on demand (usually operating once a month). A return trip to Flinders Island costs $85 per person (a vehicle costs from $475 to $845, depending on the size of the vehicle), and the journey will take around eight hours. Advance bookings are essential.

Getting Around

There is no public transport on the island. Hire-car companies will meet you at the airport but bookings are essential. **Bowman-Lees Car Hire** (☎ 6359 2388), in Whitemark, rents vehicles for $60 to $80 per day. Flinders Island Cabin Park (see opposite) has cars for similar rates, as well as bikes.

South Australia

South Australia (SA) is ripe for exploration, so select a gear and choose your own pace for adventure. Each portion of SA reveals a new land for discovery, its liberating expanses of sky and coastline making it perfect for the ultimate road trip or to explore under your own steam – hiking along the Heysen Trail or pedalling the Mawson Trail. Carved like the skin of a weathered sage, SA's timeless, rugged features are distinct– the ancient, majestic Flinders Ranges, the opal fields and troglodytic moonscape around Coober Pedy, the vast Outback and an uncluttered coastline harbouring sheltered bays and sandy beaches.

Spot southern right whales on their annual pilgrimage to SA's waters or mingle with the migratory birds at the Coorong, Bool Lagoon, and the expansive sweep of Lake Eyre in flood. And these are just some of many opportunities to meet and mingle with the wildlife – magical Kangaroo Island offers it up at every turn, with resident seals and sea lions, leafy sea dragons, little penguins, raucous cockatoos, wallabies and roos.

Charming Adelaide, perched between white sandy beaches and picturesque hills comes as a surprise to many, its hefty appetite for hedonism evident in supreme arts festivals, at cricket matches played on atmospheric Adelaide Oval and in the fabulous bustle, colours and aromas of the Central Market. Gourmet food and wine is serious business in SA and exploration of its renowned wine regions, such as the Barossa Valley, Coonawarra, the Clare Valley and McLaren Vale, is a must.

HIGHLIGHTS

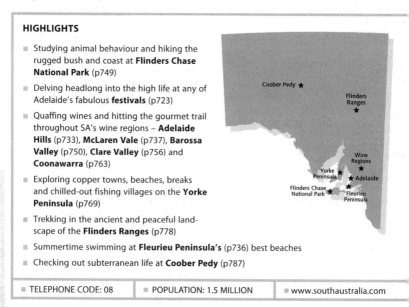

- Studying animal behaviour and hiking the rugged bush and coast at **Flinders Chase National Park** (p749)

- Delving headlong into the high life at any of Adelaide's fabulous **festivals** (p723)

- Quaffing wines and hitting the gourmet trail throughout SA's wine regions – **Adelaide Hills** (p733), **McLaren Vale** (p737), **Barossa Valley** (p750), **Clare Valley** (p756) and **Coonawarra** (p763)

- Exploring copper towns, beaches, breaks and chilled-out fishing villages on the **Yorke Peninsula** (p769)

- Trekking in the ancient and peaceful landscape of the **Flinders Ranges** (p778)

- Summertime swimming at **Fleurieu Peninsula's** (p736) best beaches

- Checking out subterranean life at **Coober Pedy** (p787)

- TELEPHONE CODE: 08   - POPULATION: 1.5 MILLION   - www.southaustralia.com

SOUTH AUSTRALIA FACTS

Eat: Any and all fresh produce and local gourmet delights

Drink: Coopers beer, and anything from the vine

Read: *The Dog Fence* by James Woodford, *Storm Boy* by Colin Thiele, *All Things Bright and Beautiful* by Susan Mitchell

Listen to: Paul Kelly, Jimmy Barnes, Archie Roach and Ruby Hunter, and The Pogues' song titled 'South Australia'

Watch: *The Tracker, Shine, Gallipoli, Pitch Black, Breaker Morant, Storm Boy*

Avoid: Drinking the 'not so tasty' water

Locals' nickname: Croweaters

Swim at: Port Elliot (p741)

Strangest festival: Womadelaide and the Adelaide Fringe

Tackiest tourist attraction: 'Larry the Giant Lobster', a wonderful, large and looming roadside crustacean (p760)

HISTORY

South Australia was declared a province and open for business on 28 December 1836, the day the first British 'settlers' landed at Holdfast Bay. A site about 10km inland was chosen for the state capital. The first governor, Captain John Hindmarsh, named Adelaide after the wife of the then British monarch, William IV.

While the eastern states struggled with the problems of a convict society, SA's settlers were free citizens. The founders based the colony on an idealistic 19th-century theory of systematic colonisation and social engineering; land was sold at set prices by the British government to help establish mainly skilled and young married couples. The ideal was that equal numbers of these men and women would be free from religious and political persecution to create a truly egalitarian new world.

At first, progress was slow and only British government funds saved the colony from bankruptcy, yet it became self-supporting by the mid-1840s and self-governing by 1856.

Following the successful crossing of the continent by local explorers, SA won the contract to lay the Overland Telegraph from Port Augusta to Darwin, connecting Australia to the world by telegram (1872), and later, telephone.

South Australia's socially progressive history is long, including 'firsts' such as: pioneering the legalisation of trade unions (1876) and opening the first community-run hotel in British Empire; allowing women to stand for parliament (1894); being one of the first places in the world to give women the vote; and being the first state in Australia to grant driving licences, outlaw racial and gender discrimination, legalise abortion and decriminalise gay sex.

Aboriginal People

It is estimated that there were 12,000 Aboriginal people in SA at the beginning of the 19th century. In the decades following white settlement, many were either killed by the settlers or died from starvation and introduced diseases. Except in the northwest, which was mainly unsuitable for pastoral development, Aborigines were usually forcibly dispossessed of their traditional lands. As a result, there was a general movement of Aborigines to missions and other centres where they could find safety and obtain food rations.

Many of the state's 21,000 Aboriginal people live in urban centres. In 1966, SA became the first state to grant Aboriginal people title to their land. In the early '80s most of the land situated west of the Stuart Hwy and north of the railway to Perth was transferred to Aboriginal ownership. Cultural clashes still occur, exemplified in SA by the politically and culturally divisive Hindmarsh Bridge controversy, pitting Aboriginal beliefs against development.

Some great opportunities to learn about Aboriginal culture and beliefs include the Ngarrindjeri-run Camp Coorong (p760) in the southeast and the Adnyamathanha-run Iga Warta (p784) in the northern Flinders Ranges. In Adelaide, there is Tandanya – National Aboriginal Cultural Institute (p717); the Australian Aboriginal Cultures Gallery in Adelaide's South Australian Museum (p717); indigenous-guided Tauondi Aboriginal Cultural Tours (p722); and Cleland Wildlife Park (p733) in Adelaide Hills.

The seminal *Survival in Our Own Land*, edited by Christobel Mattingley and Ken Hampton, contains historical accounts by Nungas (South Australian Aboriginal people). It is available from good bookshops in Adelaide.

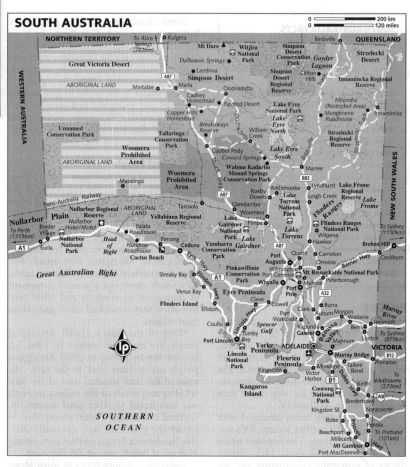

GEOGRAPHY & CLIMATE

South Australia is sparsely settled, with over 80% of its population living in Adelaide and a handful of major rural centres. The state's productive agricultural regions are clustered in the south and in the Murray River irrigation belt. As you travel further north or west the terrain becomes increasingly drier and more inhospitable; the outback, which takes up more than 75% of the state's area, is largely semidesert.

More than 80% of the land area is less than 300m above sea level, and few points rise above 700m. The only hills of real note are Mt Lofty and Flinders Ranges, which form a continuous spine running 800km from southeast of Adelaide into the interior.

The state's most important watercourse is the Murray River, which rises in the Australian Alps and meets the sea by Lake Alexandrina. South Australia is by far the driest Australian state – over 80% of SA normally receives less than 250mm annual rainfall. The state's low and unreliable rainfall has resulted in water from the Murray being piped over long distances to ensure the survival of many communities, including Adelaide. In fact, around 90% of South Australians depend either wholly or partly on the river for their water supply. The continuing deterioration of the Murray's water quality and flow rates is thus of major concern to the state.

South Australia has a Mediterranean climate of hot, dry summers and cool winters, with most rain falling between May and August. Heat is the major climatic extreme, with daily maximums around 38°C common in the outback from October to April.

INFORMATION

Environment Shop (Map p714; ☎ 08-8204 1910; www.parks.sa.gov.au; 77 Grenfell St, Central Adelaide; ⏰ 9am-5pm Mon-Fri) Run by the Department for Environment & Heritage (DEH), this shop is a great resource for comprehensive parks information, passes, maps and nature books. The free *South Australia's National Parks* guide lists details on each park and its facilities.

Houseboat Hirers Association (☎ 08-8395 0999; www.houseboat-centre.com.au) Its booklet *SA Houseboat Holidays* is available from the SATC.

Royal Automobile Association (RAA; Map p714; ☎ 08-8202 4600; www.raa.net; 55 Hindmarsh Sq, Central Adelaide) South Australia's automobile association sells SA-specific travel publications.

South Australian Tourism Commission visitor information centre (SATC; Map p714; ☎ 1300 655 276, 08-8303 2033; www.southaustralia.com; 18 King William St, Central Adelaide; ⏰ 8.30am-5pm Mon-Fri, 9am-2pm Sat & Sun) This centre has an extensive range of regional information. Advance bookings for tours and shows can also be made here. There are SATC outlets in most Australian capital cities; check its website for details.

For more in-depth coverage of SA, pick up a copy of Lonely Planet's *Adelaide & South Australia* guidebook.

The SATC publishes booklets for all aspects of travel within the state, including B&B listings. Useful websites include: www.bnbbookings.com, www.ozbedandbreakfast.com and www.sabnb.org.au.

NATIONAL PARKS

Around 22% of SA's land area is under some form of official conservation management and include national parks, recreation parks, wildlife reserves, waterways and regional reserves. The largest areas are in the outback. South Australia's Flinders Chase National Park (Kangaroo Island; see p749), Flinders Ranges National Park (p782) and the Great Australian Bight Marine Park (p777) are some of Australia's better-known national parks.

The DEH manages the state's conservation areas and sells day passes and camping permits ($7 per vehicle). The latter offers a good deal as it includes a day pass. A 'Four Week Holiday Parks Pass' ($20 per vehicle) covers entry to some of the most popular parks, excluding the desert parks.

ACTIVITIES

Seekers of wilderness experiences or an adrenalin rush will find a smorgasbord of choices in the rugged hills, wide open spaces and expansive coastline of SA. Adelaide's outdoor gear suppliers (p731) can provide gear, as well as details on outdoor pursuits and operators around the state.

South Australian Trails (www.southaustraliantrails.com) has a wealth of information on activities in the great outdoors, including horse riding, canoeing, hiking, cycling and diving, with safety tips, maps and useful links.

Bushwalking

The state's national parks and conservation areas have thousands of kilometres of

---

THE HEYSEN TRAIL

The 1200km Heysen Trail (named after Hans Heysen, a famous South Australian landscape artist) starts at Cape Jervis, south of Adelaide. It then winds along the ridgetops of the Mt Lofty and Flinders Ranges and finishes in Parachilna Gorge north of Wilpena Pound. It passes through some of the state's major scenic and historical highlights, and traverses two of its finest conservation areas: the Mt Remarkable and Flinders Ranges National Parks.

Although designed as a long-distance route, the many access points along the way make it ideal for half- and full-day walks. For the most part, it's clearly marked, and apart from a handful of very steep or rough areas the going is seldom difficult for fit and experienced walkers. Due to fire restrictions, the trail is closed between December and April.

Australia's longest dedicated walking trail has a dedicated team at **Friends of the Heysen Trail** (Map p714; ☎ 08-8212 6299; www.heysentrail.asn.au; 10 Pitt St, Central Adelaide; ⏰ 10.30am-2.30pm Mon, Tue & Thu, to 1.30pm Wed, 9.30am-1.30pm Fri), who welcome walkers to join their periodic excursions. Maps are available from the **Environment Shop** (Map p714; ☎ 08-8204 1910; www.parks.sa.gov.au; 77 Grenfell St, Central Adelaide; ⏰ 10am-5pm Mon-Fri), and outdoor-gear shops (see p731).

marked trails traversing spectacular scenery and native flora. Close to Adelaide there are many walks to suit all abilities in the Mt Lofty Ranges, including those at Belair National Park and Morialta Conservation Park.

In the Flinders Ranges there are excellent walks in the Mt Remarkable (p759) and Flinders Ranges National Parks (p782), and further north in the Arkaroola-Mt Painter Wildlife Sanctuary (p784).

Canoeing & Sailing

Abundant wildlife, good fishing, magnificent river scenery and quiet places to camp make the Murray River (p764) and Coorong (p760) popular canoeing spots. **Canoe South Australia** (☎ 08-8240 3294; www.canoesa.asn .au; Aquatics Reserve, Old Port Rd, West Lakes) lists state clubs, equipment and events.

There is good sailing all along Adelaide's shoreline in Gulf St Vincent; **Yachting South Australia** (Map p714; ☎ 08-8410 2117; www.sa.yachting .org.au; 300 Morphett St, Central Adelaide; ⊙ 9am-5pm Mon-Fri) has great information including contacts for all SA's sailing clubs, courses and boating events.

Diving

South Australia's underwater world hides a great diversity of life. There are reefs supporting sponge beds and jetties, wrecks, and drop-offs; and caves sporting fish, colourful sponges, nudibranchs and soft corals. To set your gills twitching visit www.dive -southaustralia.com.

Off the Gulf St Vincent coast, the Rapid Bay jetty is renowned for its abundant marine life (including leafy sea dragons) and has been the location for underwater film shoots. Scuttled in 2002, the intact HMAS *Hobart* is the new 'burb for marine critters and is now regarded as one of the country's best wreck dives. Obtain permits (single/ double dives $50/95) from **Dolphin Dive** (☎ 08-8558 2733; www.diveexhmashobart.com; 52 Main St, Normanville; ⊙ 9am-5pm), which also rents gear and runs dive certification courses.

At Dangerous Reef, off Port Lincoln, those pushing the fear factor can look a white pointer shark in the eye – and teeth – from the safety (?) of a suspended diving cage (see p775).

Other good diving areas include most jetties around the Yorke Peninsula and the reefs off Port Lincoln.

One of the best freshwater dives in the world is at Piccaninnie Ponds (p762) near Mt Gambier in the southeast, where trained and certificated divers can explore the legendary formations, huge caverns and deep sink holes in incredibly clear water. Ewens Ponds Conservation Park near Mr Gambier is also excellent.

Rock Climbing

Rock spiders happy with cliffs between 10m to 15m in height will enjoy the gorges in Morialta Conservation Park and Onkaparinga River Recreation Park.

Advanced lead climbers head for the Flinders Ranges (p778) – Moonarie, on the southeastern side of Wilpena Pound, has cliffs reaching 120m. Buckaringa Gorge, close to Quorn and Hawker, is another favourite for the skilled.

Swimming & Surfing

Uncrowded, white and sandy swimming beaches stretch right along the coast, with the safest generally being on Gulf St Vincent (p739) and Spencer Gulf. Anywhere exposed to the Southern Ocean and Investigator Strait, which separates Kangaroo Island from the mainland, may have strong rips and undertows. If seeking tanline-free bathing, head to the nudist beach at Maslins Beach South, 40km south of Adelaide.

Surfers descend on any area exposed to the Southern Ocean's rolling swells. The closest surf to Adelaide of any real consequence is near Victor Harbor at Waitpinga Beach, Middleton and Port Elliot. Pennington Bay has the most consistent surf on Kangaroo Island. Pondalowie, on the 'foot' of Yorke Peninsula, has the state's most reliable strong breaks. Other notable sites are scattered between Port Lincoln, at the southern tip of Eyre Peninsula, and include famous Cactus Beach in the far west.

Waxheads can get the scoop around the state with plenty of details on surf breaks at www.surfsouthoz.com. The **surf report** (Gulf St Vincent Coast ☎ 1902 241 018, Surf Coast ☎ 1900 931 543) is updated regularly.

You can learn to surf (around $40 including gear) with the following companies: **South Coast Surf Academy** (☎ 0414 341 545; www .danosurf.com.au) **Surf & Sun Safaris** (☎ 1800 786 386; www.surfnsun .com.au)

Whale Watching

Between July and September, migrating **southern right whales** often come within a few hundred metres of shore as they pass along the ocean coast to breeding grounds in the Great Australian Bight. Once roaming the seas in prolific numbers, the unrestrained slaughter of southern right whales in the 19th century reduced this whale population from 100,000 to just a few hundred by 1935. Although considered an endangered species, they are fighting back and the population worldwide may be as high as 4000. From late June to September, many southern rights migrate to the warmer waters along Australia's southern coast to breed, with around 100 whales born each year. Hot spots for whale watching include Victor Harbor (p739), Port Lincoln, Elliston and Yalata at Head of Bight (p777), on the far west coast. Find out about current whale action on ☎ 1900 931 223.

TOURS

Whatever your interest or destination, there's probably a tour to suit it. Many run from Adelaide while others start in regional areas (see regional sections for details). **Tourabout Adelaide** (☎ 08-8333 1111; www.tourabout adelaide.com.au) offers private tours, bilingual guides and innovative themed tours around the state.

Around Adelaide

There is a huge variety of tours covering the Adelaide Hills, Fleurieu Peninsula (p738) and Barossa Valley (p752), all departing from Adelaide. When choosing one of the many wine tours check the number of wineries to be visited and ensure that you won't spend half of the day at tourist shops.

There is a gamut of coach tours (adult/child from $40/30) to choose from. Destinations include Hahndorf and the Cleland Wildlife Park, the Barossa Valley and McLaren Vale, Victor Harbor, the Murray River and the Coorong. Day trips to the southern Flinders Ranges and Kangaroo Island are very rushed and not recommended. Coach-tour operators include the following:

Adelaide Sightseeing (☎ 08-8231 4144; www .adelaidesightseeing.com.au)

Great Sights (☎ 1300 850 850; www.greatsights .com.au)

Premier Stateliner (☎ 08-8415 5500; www.premier stateliner.com.au)

A great way to get from 'A to B' and see the sights on the way is to join an 'off-the-beaten-track' 4WD tour or to take a backpacker-style bus. Most backpacker hostels have travel agencies or booking offices that specialise in the cheaper end of the market (see p723).

Some operators:

Adelaide Eco Tours (☎ 1800 639 933) One-day nature and wildlife tours ($150) to the Fleurieu Peninsula, including wine tasting.

Prime Mini Tours (☎ 08-8276 1600; www.primemini tours.com; ☷ Tue-Thu) Runs excellent tours to places such as the Barossa Valley (from $65, including lunch); Hahndorf, Victor Harbor and McLaren Vale (from $54); winery-focused McLaren Vale and Adelaide Hills ($95); Wildlife ($92), including dinner at Warrawong; and Murray River ($82), including cruise and lunch.

Outback

Outback tours usually include the Flinders Ranges; Coober Pedy; and Uluru (Ayers Rock), in the Northern Territory (NT). Operators:

Groovy Grape Getaways Australia (☎ 1800 661 177, 08-8371 4000; www.groovygrape.com.au) Three-day tours Melbourne–Adelaide ($285) along the Great Ocean Rd, seven-day tours Adelaide–Alice Springs ($750), stopping in the Flinders Ranges, Coober Pedy and Uluru. Includes all meals, camping ground charges and national park entry fees. Small groups.

Heading Bush (☎ 1800 639 933; www.headingbush .com) These rugged, small-group, 10-day Adelaide to Alice Springs expeditions (with/without VIP or YHA membership $1195/1400) are all-inclusive. Tours travel through the Flinders Ranges, William Creek, Coober Pedy, the Simpson Desert and Aboriginal communities, into the NT, Uluru and West MacDonnell Ranges.

Nullarbor Traveller (☎ 08-8390 3297; www.the-travel ler.com.au) Relaxed camping and hostelling trips between Adelaide and Perth (seven/nine days $770/990), which include bushwalking, surfing, whale watching, accommodation, national park entry fees, and almost all meals. Swimming with sea lions and dolphins is also possible.

Swagabout Tours (☎ 0408 854 3737; www.swagabout tours.com.au) Runs a range of great tours to take you off the beaten track, from one-day Clare Valley tours ($90 including lunch) to three-day Flinders Ranges tours (from $550), five-day whale watching at Head of Bight (from $900) and Adelaide to Alice Springs trips (five/10 days from $810/1800). The tours are all inclusive, in tent or motel accommodation.

Wayward Bus Touring Company (☎ 1800 882 823; www.waywardbus.com.au) Melbourne–Adelaide via the Coorong and Great Ocean Rd ($295, 3½ days); weekly Adelaide–Alice Springs ($790, eight days; $180, three days) via the Clare Valley, Flinders Ranges, Oodnadatta Track, Coober Pedy and Uluru; and to Kings Canyon. Includes sightseeing; food kitties are extra.

GETTING THERE & AROUND
Air
International flights and flights from other Australian cities fly in and out of **Adelaide Airport** (www.aal.com.au; noise tax $4), 7km west of the city centre. Budget, Hertz, Avis and Thrifty have car-rental desks at the airport.

See the individual Getting There & Away sections for details on small airlines servicing country destinations.

Regional operators:

Airlines of SA (☎ 13 13 13; www.airlinesofsa.com.au) Flies twice each weekday from Adelaide to Port Augusta ($140).

Emu Airways (☎ 08-8234 3711) Flies between Kingscote, Kangaroo Island and Adelaide (around $125).

O'Connor Airlines (☎ 13 13 13, 08-8723 0666; www.oconnor-airlines.com.au) Flies between Adelaide, Melbourne, Mildura, Mt Gambier and Whyalla.

Regional Express (Rex; ☎ 13 17 13; www.regionalexpress.com.au) Flies between Adelaide and Kingscote on Kangaroo Island ($120), Coober Pedy ($167), Ceduna (from $305), Mt Gambier ($205), Port Lincoln ($185), Olympic Dam and Whyalla ($165), and also to Broken Hill (New South Wales; $260). Special fares are often 30% off the full price.

Bus
Bus travel is generally the cheapest way of getting from one point to another (other than hitching, which we don't recommend), and there are some good deals available. Many travellers prefer to see SA by bus because it's one of the best ways to come to grips with the state's size – also, the bus companies have far more comprehensive route networks than the railway system. Plenty of companies team interstate transport with good value touring; see Tours (p711) and Backpacker Buses (p1043).

Adelaide's **central bus station** (Map p714; 101-111 Franklin St, Central Adelaide) has terminals and ticket offices for all major interstate and statewide services, and has left-luggage lockers. For bus timetables, see the **Bus SA** (www.bussa.com.au) website. Discounts are available for holders of backpacker association or international student ID cards.

Firefly Express (☎ 1300 730 740; www.fireflyexpress.com.au; ⊗ 7am-8.30pm) departs at 7.30am and 8.30pm for Melbourne ($50, 11 hours) and Sydney ($100, 24 hours).

Greyhound Australia (☎ 13 14 99; www.greyhound.com.au; ⊗ 6am-8.30pm) has services between Adelaide and Melbourne ($65, 11 hours), Sydney ($145, 25 hours) via Broken Hill or Renmark, Alice Springs ($220, 21 hours) and Perth ($290, 35¼ hours). All buses have air-conditioning, toilets and videos, and smoking is forbidden. Australian and international students, VIP and Nomads card holders, and children under 14 receive a 10% discount.

Premier Stateliner (☎ 08-8415 5555; www.premierstateliner.com.au; ⊗ 7am-9pm) operates a statewide bus service.

V/Line (☎ 13 61 96, 08-8231 7620; www.vlinepassenger.com.au; ⊗ 7.30am-5pm Mon-Fri) runs daily bus/train services to Melbourne ($62, 11½ hours), and Sydney ($155, 21 hours). Melbourne passengers take the train to/from Bendigo in Victoria.

See individual destination sections for bus companies operating in the region.

Car & Motorcycle
If you're travelling by car, Australian quarantine points are at Border Village, and also at Ceduna for those heading east, to/from Western Australia (WA); on the Mallee Hwy at Pinnaroo and on the Sturt Hwy between Mildura and Renmark on the Victorian border; and at Oodla-Wirra, on the Barrier Hwy from Broken Hill into New South Wales (NSW). Transporting honey to Kangaroo Island is a no-no, to protect the island's pure-strain honey-production industry.

To hitch a ride (sharing petrol costs) or buy a second-hand car, check out notice boards at the hostels (see Hitching, p1069).

Train
The interstate train terminal is at Railway Tce, Keswick, just southwest of the city centre. **Skylink** (☎ 08-8332 0528; www.skylinkadelaide.com; ⊗ bookings 7am-10pm) will pick up pre-booked passengers on its airport–city runs (adult/child $4/2).

Great Southern Railway (☎ 13 21 47, 08-8213 4444; www.trainways.com.au; ⊗ 7.30am-8pm Mon-Fri,

8am-6pm Sat, 9am-5pm Sun) operates all train services in and out of SA. Backpackers are eligible for huge discounts (around 50%) and cheap six-month passes ($450) with appropriate ID.

The following trains depart from Adelaide regularly:

Ghan To Alice Springs (economy seat/twin-berth sleeper $215/680, 19 hours).

Ghan To Darwin (economy seat/twin-berth sleeper $440/1390, 47 hours).

Indian Pacific To Perth (economy seat/twin-berth sleeper $310/960, 39 hours).

Indian Pacific To Sydney (economy seat/twin-berth sleeper $223/450, 25 hours).

Overland To Melbourne (economy seat/twin-berth sleeper $60/150, 11 hours).

The fastest service between Sydney and Adelaide is Speedlink (around 20 hours) – you travel from Sydney to Albury on the XPT train, and from Albury to Adelaide on a V/Line bus.

ADELAIDE

☎ 08 / pop 1,467,300

You only need scratch the surface of the quiet achiever of Australian cities to tap into its hedonistic vein. This epicurean playground boasts world-renown major events, spanning the cultured and cerebral, artistic and gastronomic, petrol-burning and sports crazed. A vibrant student population ensures easy-on-the-pocket appeal which coaxes the community out to dine. The pleasure-seeking spirit flows from varied cuisines and magnificent wines through to the healthy live music and bar scene and numerous galas that celebrate a thriving arts community. During the innovative Adelaide Fringe Festival, the artistic flair of this historically progressive, yet still conservative, city truly emerges.

The traditional owners of the Adelaide area are the Kaurna people, whose territory extends south towards Cape Jervis and north towards Port Wakefield. Early European colonists ('free settlers') began to arrive in 1836, creating a lush, European-style capital, while successive waves of settlers have added to the cosmopolitan mix.

Adelaide is just a cycle away from native bushland hiking in the Mt Lofty Ranges and a rattling tram ride from long stretches of sand on which to sunbathe around Glenelg. The city makes an excellent base for trips into the nearby wine regions, surf lessons on the Fleurieu Peninsula and hikes through the wildlife lair of Kangaroo Island.

ORIENTATION

Adelaide's compact city centre is laid out on an orderly grid bordered by North, East, South and West Tces. King William St is the main thoroughfare dissecting the city and most cross streets change their name here. Victoria Sq, the city's geographical centre, has bus stops and the Glenelg tram terminus. Franklin St, which runs off the square, has Adelaide's central bus station.

ADELAIDE IN…

Two Days

Head to the **Central Market** (p726) for breakfast on the go, then if the city is in the grips of a festival, join the fun. Otherwise, head off on a **walking tour** (p721) of the city's sights, perusing artworks and exhibitions along the way. Wind up at the **National Wine Centre** (p720) – for education of course – before dining at a (prebooked) restaurant on **Gouger St** (p726) and checking out a couple of the city's atmospheric bars. On day two, visit the **Jam Factory Craft & Design Centre** (p717) or the **Bradman Collection** (p719) and take a tour of the **Haigh's Chocolate Visitors Centre** (p718) before hopping on a tram for sundowners in **Glenelg** (p718).

Four Days

Follow the two-day itinerary, then pick up some gourmet fare from the **Central Market** (p726) and journey to the nearby **Adelaide Hills** (p733), **McLaren Vale** (p737) or **Barossa Valley** (p750) wine regions. Next day, explore the **South Australian Museum** (p717) and **Tandanya – National Aboriginal Cultural Institute** (p717), then take in a cabaret – perhaps at the **Weimar Room** (p729).

CENTRAL ADELAIDE

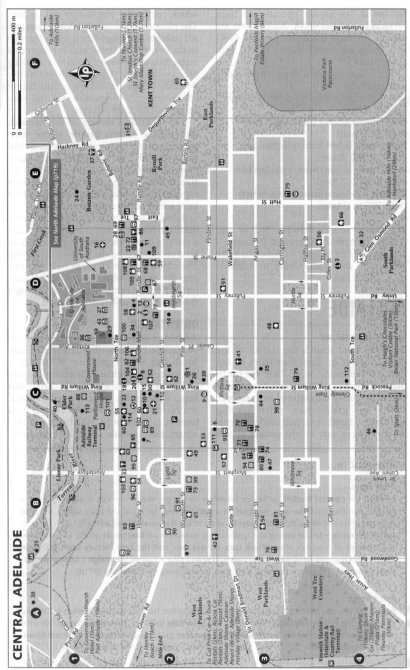

Rundle St, lined with cafés, restaurants, bookshops, retro clothing shops and independent cinemas, is the social centre for all ages. Heading west the street becomes Rundle Mall, the main shopping strip. Across King William St, Rundle Mall turns into Hindley St, with its mix of bars, dance clubs and strip joints.

Elegant North Tce hosts a string of magnificent public buildings, including the art gallery, museum, state library and the University of Adelaide. Continue north and you're in the lush north parklands, with the Festival Centre; King William Rd then crosses into North Adelaide at the Torrens River, which has walking and cycling paths.

See Getting There & Around (p732) for details on getting to the city centre from the airport and train station.

Maps

Central Adelaide maps available from the visitor information centre (see Tourist Information, p716) should be ample for navigating your way around central Adelaide. If you need something more in-depth, pick up a RAA, Hema or Westprint map, available from the RAA and all bookshops. The **Map Shop** (Map p714; ☎ 8231 2033; mercator@mapshop .net.au; 6 Peel St) stocks a range of SA maps, as well as charts and guides, for walking, hiking and touring.

INFORMATION
Bookshops

ABC Shop (Map p714; ☎ 8410 0567; Level 2, Myer Centre, Rundle Mall)
Dymocks Booksellers (Map p714; ☎ 8223 5380; 136 Rundle Mall)

Imprints Bookseller (Map p714; ☎ 8231 4454; 107 Hindley St) The book-lover's bookshop – quality literature with a great selection of biographies.

Map Shop (Map p714; ☎ 8231 2033; 6-20 Peel St) Has a comprehensive selection of maps.

Mary Martin's Bookshop (Map p714; ☎ 8359 3525; 249 Rundle St; ◷ 10am-late) An Adelaide institution.

Emergency

Ambulance (☎ 000, 13 29 62)

Fire (☎ 000, 8204 3600)

Lifeline (24hr counselling ☎ 13 11 14, 8202 5820)

Police station (Map p714; ☎ 000, 8303 0525; 26 Hindley St)

RAA Emergency Roadside Assistance (☎ 13 11 11, 8202 4600)

Rape & Sexual Assault Service (Map p714; ☎ 8226 8777/87; 55 King William St)

Internet Access

Adelaide City Council (Map p714; ☎ 8203 7203; 25 Pirie St; access free; ◷ 8.30am-5.30pm)

State Library of South Australia (Map p714; bookings ☎ 8207 7250; www.slsa.sa.gov.au; cnr North Tce & Kintore Ave; access free; ◷ 9.30am-8pm Mon-Wed & Fri, 9.30am-6pm Thu, noon-5pm Sat & Sun) Book ahead!

Zone Internet Café (Map p714; ☎ 8223 1947; 238 Rundle St; per min 10c; ◷ 9.30am-11pm)

Internet Resources

The following websites are worth a look for information on Adelaide:

Adelaide Review (www.adelaidereview.com.au)

City of Holdfast Bay (www.coastaladelaide.com.au)

Media

Adelaide's daily tabloid is the parochial *Advertiser* ('Tiser'), though the *Age*, the *Australian* and the *Financial Review* are widely available. The free fortnightly *Adelaide Review* (www.adelaidereview.com.au) has highbrow articles (often covering the city's history and current social issues), and culture and arts sections. The *Independent* comes out on Sunday, with some articles from the UK paper of the same name.

Medical Services

Emergency Dental Service (☎ 8272 8111; ◷ Sat, Sun & after hours) Provides dentist contact details.

Royal Adelaide Hospital (Map p714; ☎ 8222 4000; North Tce)

Simpsons Pharmacy (Map p714; ☎ 8231 6333; cnr West Tce & Waymouth St; ◷ 7am-midnight Mon-Sat, 9am-midnight Sun)

Traveller's Medical & Vaccination Centre (Map p714; ☎ 8212 7522; 29 Gilbert Pl; ◷ 9am-5pm Mon, Tue, Thu & Fri, 9am-7pm Wed, 9am-12.30pm Sat)

Women & Children's Hospital (Map p719; ☎ 8161 7000; 72 King William Rd, North Adelaide)

Womens Information Service (Map p714; ☎ 8303 0590; www.wis.sa.gov.au; Station Arcade, 136 North Tce; ◷ 8am-6pm Mon-Fri, 9am-5pm Sat; 🖳) Practical information and counselling services.

Money

Banks and ATMs are prevalent throughou the city centre, particularly on and aroun Rundle Mall.

To change foreign currencies (out of hours head to the airport or casino):

American Express (Amex; Map p714; ☎ 1300 139 060 Shop 32, Rundle Mall; ◷ 9am-5pm Mon-Fri, to noon Sat

Thomas Cook (Map p714; ☎ 8231 6977; Shop 4, Rundle Mall; ◷ 9am-5pm Mon-Fri, 10am-4pm Sat)

Post

Main post office (Map p714; ☎ 13 13 18; 141 King William St) Handles poste restante; have mail addressed to you c/o Poste Restante, Adelaide 5001.

Tourist Information

Disability Information & Resource Centre (DIRC; Map p714; ☎ 8223 7522/79; www.dircsa.org.au; 195 Gilles St; ◷ 9am-5pm Mon-Fri) Provides information on accommodation, venues, tourist destinations and travel agencies for people with disabilities.

Information kiosk (Map p714; Rundle Mall; ◷ 10am-5pm Mon-Thu, 10am-8pm Fri, 10am-3pm Sat, 11am-4pm Sun) Provides Adelaide-specific information and free walking tours at 9.30am from Monday to Friday. Found at the King William St end of the mall.

South Australian Tourism Commission visitor information centre (SATC; Map p714; ☎ 1300 655 276, 8303 2033; www.southaustralia.com; 18 King William St; ◷ 8.30am-5pm Mon-Fri, 9am-2pm Sat & Sun) Abundantly stocked with leaflets and publications on Adelaide and SA. There's also a booking service and BASS ticket-selling outlet.

SIGHTS

Most of Adelaide's sights are strung alon North Tce or within walking distance o the city centre. Many visitors also eithe stay in or take a day to explore beachsid Glenelg (p718), and the nearby Baross Valley (p750), Adelaide Hills (p733) an McLaren Vale (p737) regions.

The **Discover Adelaide Card** (☎ 8400 2222; www .adelaidecard.com.au; card $48) can be an economi cal way of seeing the city's sights; check the appeal and book through BASS (at the SATC visitor information centre).

Art Galleries

The superb **Art Gallery of South Australia** (Map p714; ☎ 8207 7000; www.artgallery.sa.gov.au; North Tce; admission free, restaurant sandwiches $7, mains $21.90; 🕙 10am-5pm) represents all the big names in Australian art, has an impressive international art collection (including Rodin) and hosts temporary exhibitions. You could easily return here over a couple of days but if you have limited time, perhaps start with the Southern Australian landscapes in the Australian galleries. Guided tours (free) run at 11am and 2pm weekdays, 11am and 3pm weekends. Peruse the great bookshop and indulge your other senses at the top-notch restaurant, with a menu inspired by the current exhibition.

Discover **public artworks** on a walk around the city and along Hindley St (maps available at the visitor information centre). Adelaide's arts precinct oscillates around the West End.

Some galleries with quality contemporary exhibits:

Jam Factory Craft & Design Centre (Map p714; ☎ 8410 0727; www.jamfactory.com.au; Lion Arts Centre, cnr Morphett St & North Tce) Quality local arts and crafts and a glass-blowing studio.

Experimental Art Foundation (Map p714; ☎ 8211 7505; www.eaf.asn.au; Lion Arts Centre, North Tce) Has a focus on innovation.

Greenaway Art Gallery (Map p714; ☎ 8362 6354; 39 Rundle St, Kent Town; 🕙 11am-6pm Tue-Sun)

Museums

The enthralling exhibits of the **South Australian Museum** (Map p714; ☎ 8207 7368; www.samuseum.sa.gov.au; North Tce; admission free, kids meals $5-6, breakfast & lunch $5.50-12.50; 🕙 10am-5pm) include Australia's natural history, whales and Antarctic explorer Sir Douglas Mawson (with expedition footage). The absorbing Aboriginal Cultures Gallery displays artefacts of the Ngarrindjeri people of the Coorong and lower Murray and explores the story of Dreamtime spirit ancestor Ngurunderi, and how the Murray was created. The Balaena Café runs the length of an enormous sperm-whale skeleton and serves value-packed meals.

The fascinating **Migration Museum** (Map p714; ☎ 8207 7580; www.history.sa.gov.au; 82 Kintore Ave; admission by donation; 🕙 10am-5pm Mon-Fri, 1-5pm Sat & Sun), next door to the State Library, tells the stories of migrants who came from all over the world to make SA their home. There's information on more than 100 nationalities in its database, along with poignant personal stories.

Tandanya – National Aboriginal Cultural Institute

Visit this **indigenous cultural centre** (Map p714; ☎ 8224 3200; www.tandanya.com.au; 253 Grenfell St; adult $4; 🕙 10am-5pm) to learn about the local Kaurna people. It has fun, interactive displays on living with the land; offers free didgeridoo shows (noon Monday to Friday) and Torres Strait Islander dances (noon Saturday and Sunday); and has galleries, a café, and art and crafts.

CHAMPION OF THE POOR: A SAINT IN THE MAKING

Mary MacKillop (1842–1909) was beatified in 1995 and is to be canonised as Australia's first saint.

A fierce defender of equality, Mary was co-founder (with Father Julian Woods) of the Order of the Sisters of St Joseph of the Sacred Heart, which started Australia's first free schools, orphanages and a home for fallen women. She lived in Adelaide for 16 years, during which time conflict with SA's Catholic hierarchy led to her excommunication, though she was reinstated just five months later.

At the time of her death, Mary's order had founded 117 schools and 11 charitable homes in Australia and New Zealand. Sites associated with her include **St Mary's Convent** (Map p714; 253 Franklin St), where she was excommunicated, and **St Ignatius Church** (off Map p714; Queen St, Norwood) where she assisted at Mass during this exile. **St Joseph's Convent** (off Map p714; 286 Portrush Rd, Kensington) houses the **Mary MacKillop Centre** (☎ 8364 5311; cnr High & Phillips Sts, Kensington; admission $3; 🕙 10am-4pm Mon, Tue, Thu, Fri, 1.30-4pm Sun), which displays historic photos, artefacts, and a leaflet describing eight significant pilgrimage sites.

SOUTH AUSTRALIA

Haigh's Chocolates Visitors Centre

If you're craving chocolate, you need settle only for the best at the iconic **Haigh's Chocolates Visitors Centre** (off Map p714; ☎ 8372 7077; www.haighschocolates.com; 154 Greenhill Rd, Parkside; admission free; ☉ 8.30am-5.30pm Mon-Fri, 9.30am-4.45pm Sat). Dedicated to fine chocolate production, Haigh's takes you through the life-cycle of chocolate on tours of the factory (1pm and 2pm Monday to Saturday, 20 minutes); samples are included, and bookings for the tour are essential. Take bus No 190, 191, 191B or 192 from King William St. Get off at stop 1 on Unley Rd just over Greenhill Rd.

Parks & Gardens

The city and North Adelaide are surrounded in a green swath of attractive parkland, garden and large trees.

Stroll, jog or find yourself a grassy patch to read a book in the splendid, city-fringe **Adelaide Botanic Garden** (Map p714; www.botanicgardens.sa.gov.au; North Tce; ☉ 8am-sunset Mon-Fri, 9am-sunset Sat, Sun & public holidays). Highlights here include a unique prefabricated palm house (1877), the **Museum of Economic Botany** (check out its stencilled ceiling), and the 1988 **Bicentennial Conservatory** (adult/child/family $3.30/1.70/8; ☉ 10am-5pm), which recreates a tropical rainforest environment. Free 1½-hour guided walks depart from the kiosk at 10.30am on Monday, Tuesday, Friday and Sunday.

Old-money **North Adelaide** (a pretty suburb with bluestone cottages, pubs and alfresco restaurants) is separated from the city by the Torrens River and the **North Parklands** (Map p719). On Montefiore Hill stands the **statue of Colonel William Light**, Adelaide's disputed founder. In the afternoon, there's a nice view from here of the city's gleaming office towers rising above the trees, with the Adelaide Hills making a scenic backdrop.

Rymill Park (Map p714) in the East Parklands, has a boating lake, a 600m running track and possums in the trees (the possums emerge at night). The South Parklands contain the **Veale Gardens**, with streams and flowerbeds. The restful Japanese **Himeji Gardens** (Map p714; ☎ 8203 7483; South Tce) blends two styles of Japanese garden: *senzui* (lake and mountain) and *kare senzui* (dry garden). Sporting grounds west of the city complete Adelaide's ring of green.

Adelaide Zoo

Around 1400 exotic and native mammals, birds and reptiles reside at the **zoo** (Map p719; ☎ 8267 3255; www.adelaidezoo.com.au; Frome Rd, North Adelaide; adult/child/family $15/9/48; ☉ 9.30am-5pm). There are free tours and a children's petting zoo, but the major attraction is the Southeast Asian rainforest exhibit. You can take a water cruise to the zoo from Elder Park, in front of the Festival Centre, on **Popeye** (Map p714; ☎ 8295 4747; cruises adult/child return $8/4.50; ☉ departs hourly 11am-3pm Mon-Fri, every 20min 10.30am-4.30pm Sat & Sun).

Glenelg

In relaxed, seaside **Glenelg** (off Map p714; www.glenelgholiday.com.au), also called 'The Bay', locals mingle happily with tourists strolling the promenade; weekend crowds devour mountains of ice cream; and a bustling alfresco café strip leads to a great swimming beach. Take a vintage tram from Victoria Sq in the city centre for the sunset views. **Beach Hire** (☎ 8294 1477; ☉ sunny days Sep-Apr), nearby the visitor information centre, hires out deck chairs, umbrellas, wave skis and bodyboards.

You can pick up second-hand books between beach stops at **Glenelg Book Exchange** (☎ 8294 6407; 2c Moseley St). For fast Internet connections, head to **Kappy's Bettanet Internet Café** (☎ 8294 8977; 55 Jetty Rd; per 15min/1hr $2/5; ☉ 7.30am-10.30pm), attached to a great café. **Glenelg visitor information centre** (☎ 8294 5833; Glenelg foreshore; ☉ 9am-5pm Mon-Fri, 10am-3pm Sat & Sun), behind the town hall, also provides Internet access.

Shark victim turned shark advocate Rodney Fox promotes understanding of the much-maligned creature and its position in the delicate ocean ecosystem at **Rodney Fox Shark Experience** (☎ 8376 3373; www.rodneyfox.com.au; Glenelg Town Hall, Moseley Sq; adult $6.50; ☉ 10am-5pm). It offers a fascinating insight into the 'smoke and mirrors' of the filming of *Jaws*.

The proclamation of SA was read in 1836 at **Old Gum Tree** on MacFarlane St, and Governor Hindmarsh and the first colonists landed on the beach nearby. Also in 1836, the original free European settlers travelled from England on **HMS Buffalo**; a full-sized replica sits on the Patawalonga, north of Moseley Sq. The **Bay Discovery Centre** (☎ 8179 9504; Moseley Sq; admission free; ☉ 10am-5pm) depicts life and hardships experienced by the first European settlement and addresses the plight of the local Kaurna Aboriginal people, who lost both their land and voice.

Glenelg to Port Adelaide

Henley Beach, also on the sea, is much smaller and quieter than Glenelg, but has the best pub on the coast: the **Ramsgate Hotel** (☎ 8356 5411; 328 Seaview Rd, Henley Beach). Take bus Nos 130 to 137 from Grenfell and Curry Sts.

You could easily spend a day wandering around the gentrified warehouses and sprawling museums of **Port Adelaide** (off Map p714). The **Maritime Museum** (☎ 8207 6255; 126 Lipson St; adult/child/family $8.50/3.50/22; ☺ 10am-5pm) features several vintage ships including the *Nelcebee*, the third-oldest ship on Lloyd's shipping register. There's also a computer register of early migrants. Combined tickets ($15/6/35) also cover the next-door **National Railway Museum** (☎ 8341 1690; www.natrailmuseum.org.au; Lipson St; ☺ 10am-5pm), which has a huge collection of railway memorabilia. The **South Australian Aviation Museum** (☎ 8240 1230; www.saam.org.au; cnr Ocean Steamers Rd & Honey St; adult/child/family $6/3/15; ☺ 10.30am-4.30pm) has an impressive collection of old birds.

Australian Museum of Childhood (☎ 8240 5200; 95 Dale St, Port Adelaide; admission $3.50; ☺ 11am-4pm Sat & Sun) is an overflowing toy box with toys from the 1890s through to *Mouse Trap* and today's faves. And the best part? You can actually play with them.

West-bound bus Nos 151, 152 or 153 will get you to Port Adelaide from North Tce, or you can take the train.

Other Sights

Cricket fans can pour over the personal items of cricketing legend Sir Donald Bradman at the **Bradman Collection** (Map p714; ☎ 82 07 7271; Institute Bldg, cnr North Tce & Kintore Ave; admission free; ☺ 9.30am-6pm Mon-Thu, 9.30am-8pm Fri, noon-5pm Sat & Sun). Tours ($6.50) run at 11.30am and 12.30pm weekdays. Continue the theme north of the Torrens River at the **Adelaide Oval** (Map p719; ☎ 8300 3800; www.cricketsa.com.au; King William Rd, North Adelaide), where a statue of 'the Don' graces this most picturesque of Test cricket grounds. Adelaide Oval/Museum tours (adult/student $10/5,

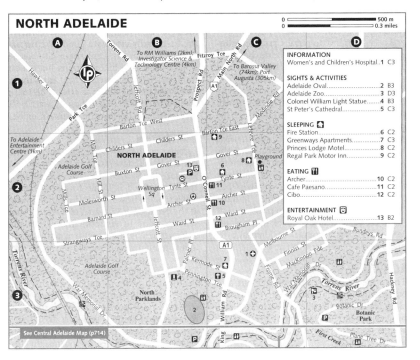

two hours) depart at 10am Monday to Friday and 2pm Sunday from the south gate on War Memorial Dr.

Built in 1878 and decommissioned in 1988, the **Old Adelaide Gaol** (Map p714; ☎ 8231 4062; www.adelaidegaol.org.au; Gaol Rd, Thebarton; adult/student $7/5.50; ◔ 11am-4pm Mon-Fri, 11am-3.30pm Sun) displays a range of homemade escape devices. Commentary tapes are provided for self-guided tours, or take a guided tour on Sunday at 11am and 1pm. Spooky ghost tours are run by appointment.

Architect **Edmund Wright's house** (Map p714; 59 King William St; admission free; ◔ 9am-4.30pm), built in 1876, was originally constructed for the Bank of SA (you can view the historic foyer and reception area) in an elaborate Renaissance style with intricate decoration. His other buildings include the imposing 1863–66 **Adelaide Town Hall** (Map p714; King William St), located between Flinders and Pirie Sts and built in 16th century Renaissance style with the faces of Queen Victoria and Prince Albert carved into the façade, and the **main post office**, diagonally opposite, commenced in 1867 and altered in 1891.

Fully justify shopping with a cultural stroll through the restored **shopping arcades** running off of Rundle Mall.

Adelaidians love to put the rather patronising moniker of 'the city of churches' into perspective by pointing out that pubs and clubs far outnumber churches. However, among the most impressive churches are the 1838 **Holy Trinity Church** (Map p714; ☎ 8212 3611; 87 North Tce), the first Anglican church in the state; the 1869–76 **St Peter's Cathedral** (Map p719; ☎ 8267 4551; cnr King William Rd & Pennington Tce, North Adelaide); and 1856 **St Francis Xavier Cathedral** (Map p714; ☎ 8231 3551; Victoria Sq.). Nearby on Victoria Sq, other important early buildings include the 1847–50 **Magistrate's Court** (Map p714); the 1869 **Supreme Court** (Map p714); and the 1839 **Old Treasury Building** (Map p714).

On the eastern side of town, **Norwood** (off Map p714), has a popular residential café, pub and shopping street (The Parade).

ACTIVITIES

There are plenty of ways to get out and enjoy Adelaide's mild climate – from cycling trails and sunning at beaches, to sipping wines and munching at the market. When there's a festival on in town, get into it.

If you squint…no, it still doesn't look like Venice, but paddling along in an original **gondola** (Map p714; ☎ 8358 1800; www.adelaidegondola.com.au; 2 people per 30min $60) on the Torrens River may still float your boat. Boats depart from Red Ochre Restaurant near the weir and golf course. You can order a bottle of wine and take up to four people for the ride.

For a bit of pampering, head to the **Jurlique International Day Spa** (Map p714; ☎ 8410 7180; www.jurlique.com.au; 22-38 Rundle Mall Plaza, Rundle Mall), where aromatherapy baths use certified organic and biodynamic herbs that are grown in the hills.

Cycling & Walking

Free 1½-hour **guided walks** of the peaceful Botanic Gardens depart from the information kiosk Monday, Tuesday, Friday and Sunday. The kiosk also stocks free trail guides. Self-guided walks such as 'Historical Walking Trails' tell the story of Adelaide's many fine buildings, while others cover **public art**, and the wonderful riverside **Linear Park** – a 40km walking/cycling path that wends its way mainly along the Torrens River from the beach to the foot of the Adelaide Hills. Adelaide is a relatively cyclist-friendly city, with good bike tracks, and cycle lanes on some main city roads. You can take your bike on trains, but not on trams or buses. Hire equipment from **Linear Park Mountain Bike Hire** (Map p714; ☎ 8223 6271; Elder Park; bikes & in-line skate hire per day/week $20/80; ◔ 9am-5pm), just below the Festival Centre.

Wine Tasting

Perched on the city's doorstep, the historic **Penfolds Magill Estate Winery** (off Map p714; ☎ 8301 5569; 78 Penfolds Rd, Magill; ◔ 10.30am-4.30pm Mon-Fri, 11am-5pm Sat & Sun) is home to perhaps Australia's best-known wine. Enjoy a tasting at the cellar door (the area of a winery that sells its wine to visitors), indulge at the gourmet restaurant – with a tailor-made menu matching the wines, and great city views – or partake in the 'Great Grange Tour', visiting Grange cottage (the original Penfold family home) and get a taste of the iconic Penfolds Grange, among others. You can take a self-guided tour at the **National Wine Centre of Australia** (Map p714; ☎ 8222 9222; www.wineaustralia.com.au; cnr Botanic & Hackney Rds; ◔ 10am-6pm). You'll get a good insight into all the issues winemakers contend with, and can even have your own virtual vintage rated.

WALKING TOUR

Take a stroll along leafy North Tce, Adelaide's cultural boulevard lined with fine buildings and many of the city's finest sights.

Starting at the grand old **Botanic Hotel (1)**, head west along North Tce to 1845 **Ayers Historic House (2**; ☎ 8223 1234; 288 North Tce; adult/child $8/5; ☺ 10am-4pm Tue-Fri, 1-4pm Sat & Sun). This elegant residence of early South Australian premier Sir Henry Ayers, after whom Ayers Rock (Uluru) in the NT was named, now features period furnishings and costume displays.

WALK FACTS

Distance: 4.5km
Duration: Allow a full day browsing and grazing

Down the road is a small campus of the **University of South Australia (3)**. Next door is the more imposing façade of the **University of Adelaide (4)**, founded in 1874, which was the first university in Australia to admit women to degree courses.

Further west along North Tce is the impressive **Art Gallery of South Australia (5**; p717), an easy spot in which to lose a few hours. Next door is the **South Australian Museum (6**; p717), with good Aboriginal and natural-history displays, and a café alongside a giant whale skeleton.

Near the corner of Kintore Ave is the **State Library of South Australia (7)** and its 1836 **Institute Building (8**; p719) – the oldest building on North Tce, housing Don Bradman's cricketing memorabilia. From here head down Kintore Ave to the fascinating **Migration Museum (9**; p717).

Back on North Tce, pass the **National War Memorial (10)** and continue west, following the stone wall surrounding the grounds of the 1838 **Government House (11)** to the **South African War Memorial (12)** at King William Rd. Opposite, you'll see the elegant façade of

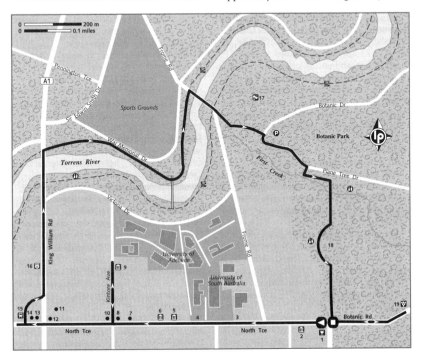

Parliament House (13), featuring 10 marble Corinthian columns. It was built in two stages: the west wing was completed in 1889 and the east wing in 1939. Continue along North Tce to **Old Parliament House (14**; ☎ 8212 6881; ☯ 10am-5pm Mon-Fri, noon-5pm Sat & Sun), set up in its original state and boasting a restaurant, then onto the grand **Railway Station (15)**, now home to the casino. Loop past intriguing street art to cut through to the **Adelaide Festival Centre (16**; p729), then down to the Torrens River. Meander east along the walking path to Frome Rd, and the entrance to the **Adelaide Zoo (17**; p718).

Head south along Frome Rd, turning left onto a footpath to follow the fence of the zoo. Take the right fork, Plane Tree Dr, and follow it to the gate of the stunning **Adelaide Botanic Garden (18**; p718). Continue generally south following the signs to the main gate on North Tce, and head east to the **National Wine Centre (19**; p720). If you have time, toast a hard day's sightseeing back at the **Botanic Bar (1**; p729), or indulge at **Botanic Café (1**; p727).

ADELAIDE FOR CHILDREN

During school holidays, the **South Australian Museum** (p717), **State Library of South Australia**, **Art Gallery of South Australia** (p717), **Adelaide Zoo** (p718) and **Botanic Garden** (p718) run inspired kid- and family-oriented programmes with accessible and interactive general displays. The **Investigator Science & Technology Centre** (off Map p719; ☎ 8410 1115; www.investigator .org.au; Regency Institute of Tafe, Days Rd, Regency Park; adult/child $8.50/5.50; ☯ 9am-5pm Mon-Fri) has live demonstrations and makes science fun, or perhaps take drooling munchkins on a tour of **Haigh's Chocolate** (p718) factory.

Port Adelaide (see p719) has some great museums to spark youthful intrigue.

At **Glenelg** (p718), you can hire all manner of water toys for an active day at the beach.

The free monthly paper *Adelaide's Child* (www.adelaideschild.com.au) is available at cafés and libraries, contains a comprehensive events calendar. *Adelaide for Kids: A Guide for Parents*, by James Muecke, has comprehensive details and is available at bookshops.

Books on tape are perfect for keeping travelling kids happy. You can find them at the **ABC Shop** (Map p714; ☎ 8410 0567; Level 3, Myer Centre, Rundle Mall). Nearby, the **Australian Geographic Shop** (Map p714; ☎ 8211 7700; Myer Centre, Rundle Mall) stocks nature-based books, toys and activities (including bug-eye lenses, strap-on kangaroo tails and southern hemisphere night-sky charts) for fun interaction.

Dial-An-Angel (☎ 8267 3700) is a company providing nannies and babysitters to all areas of Adelaide.

TOURS

Adelaide Explorer (☎ 8364 1933; www.adelaide explorer.com.au) You can travel between most city sights on the free city buses (see p732), or on this jump-on/jump-off tram-bus. Tickets cover the city and coast (adult/child $30/10) or city only ($25/10) and are valid for two days; there are three departures daily. Pick up a brochure at the visitor information centre.

Adelaide's Top Food & Wine Tours (☎ 8263 0265; www.topfoodandwinetours.com.au) Uncovers SA's gastronomic soul with dawn tours of the buzzing Central Market, on which stallholders introduce their varied produce. See the website for changing tour details.

Falie Charters (☎ 8341 2004; www.falie.com.au) Runs dolphin trips from Port Adelaide in the tall ship *Falie*.

Port Dock Brewery Hotel (☎ 8240 0187; www .portdockbreweryhotel.com.au; 10 Todd St, Port Adelaide) Tours of the brewery and cellar can be arranged at this pub, which brews its own distinctive beers.

Port River Dolphin Cruises (☎ 8447 2366) Runs dolphin cruises from Port Adelaide.

Prime Mini Tours (☎ 8276 1600; www.primemini tours.com; ☯ Tue-Thu) Runs City & Brewery Tours ($50, 5½ hours) that combine the Rodney Fox Shark Experience, Haigh's Chocolates and the South Australian Brewing Company.

Susie's Boutique Tours (☎ 0417 841 008; www .susiestours.com.au; ☯ 9.30am Tue, Thu-Sat) Runs two-hour market tours ($30), including tastings and 10% discount at stalls.

Tauondi Aboriginal Cultural Tours (☎ 8341 2777; tours $10-15) These 45-minute Aboriginal guided tours examine plants and their uses in the Botanic Gardens (Wednesday to Friday and Sunday), Dreaming stories in Cleland Wildlife Park (p733), and the Aboriginal Cultures Gallery in the South Australian Museum. Bookings are essential.

Temptation Sailing (☎ 0412 811 838; www.dolphin boat.com.au; Holdfast Shores Marina, Glenelg) Head out on a catamaran to swim with dolphins ($98, 3½ hours) or spot dolphins ($48, 3½ hours).

Tourabout Adelaide (☎ 8333 1111; www.tourabout adelaide.com.au; 2hr tours $25) Brings to life Adelaide's founders, shakers, shapers and landmarks in the following guided walks: Adelaide's Cultural Heritage (Friday), West Tce Cemetery (first Sunday in the month) and West End Arts walks (Thursday). Bookings essential.

FESTIVALS & EVENTS

Adelaide is Australia's festival epicentre with a continuous high-calibre stream of fantastic international and local events. These attract performers and audiences from around the world, particularly for the Glenelg Jazz Festival and the Adelaide Festival of the Arts. At the Adelaide Fringe Festival, Aussie stand-up comedians are joined by their European and American counterparts and other headline acts from the Edinburgh Fringe Festival.

January
Jacob's Creek Tour Down Under One hundred of the world's best cyclists sweat their Lycra to the limit over this week's six races and street parties. Stages 1 to 5 race through 55 of the state's towns with a grand finale in Adelaide.

March
Adelaide Festival of Arts (www.adelaidefestival.com.au) Culture vultures absorb international and Australian dance, drama, opera and theatre performances on even-numbered years.

Adelaide Fringe (www.adelaidefringe.com.au) A biennial independent arts festival (even-numbered years), second only to Edinburgh Fringe.

Clipsal 500 (www.clipsal500.com.au) Rev heads (lovers of cars) rejoice as Adelaide's streets become a four-day Holden versus Ford racing track.

Womadelaide (www.womadelaide.com.au) One of the world's best live music events with more than 400 musicians and performers from around the globe. Held on odd-numbered years.

April–July
Adelaide Cabaret Festival (www.cabaretfringe.com) The only one of its kind in the country; held in mid-June.

Adelaide's Festival of Ideas (www.adelaidefestival.com.au) The glorious, the good and the innovative from around the world descend on Adelaide for a biennial talkfest (odd-numbered years) in July.

Medieval Festival Held in April at Carrick Hill, this celebration of Middle Ages culture includes jousting and other knightly activities, such as feasting.

August
South Australian Living Artists Festival (www.salafestival.com) Innovative exhibitions and displays across the city.

September
Royal Adelaide Show (www.adelaideshowground.com.au) Agricultural and horticultural displays and entertainment.

October
Bartercard Glenelg Jazz Festival First-class New Orleans and Australian jazz bands.

Classic Adelaide Rally (www.classicadelaide.com.au) Full of lovingly maintained machines.

Feast Festival (www.feast.org.au) A three-week lesbian and gay cultural festival with a carnival, theatre performances, talks and dances.

November
Credit Union Christmas Pageant (www.cupageant.com.au) An Adelaide institution for more than 70 years – floats, bands and marching troupes take over the city streets for a day.

Mitsubishi Horse Trials (www.adelaidehorsetrials.com.au) An Olympic-level event held in the city-centre parklands.

December
Bay Sports Festivals A large sports fest held in Glenelg, including beach volleyball, an aquathon, a surf carnival, hockey and gridiron.

SLEEPING

Adelaide is very easy to get around, and staying outside the compact central business district (CBD) is a practical option. For example, attractive and peaceful North Adelaide is a five-minute bus ride or a 2km walk into town, while the city beach suburbs (Glenelg in particular) are a 30-minute bus or tram ride from town.

Last-minute specials on hotel rooms, booked within two weeks of occupancy dates, are available through a plethora of discount websites and provide heavy reductions – often over 50%. Many also offer weekend B&B packages.

Book ahead for any beachside accommodation during December and January and expect prices to rise during all school holidays.

Budget

A couple of city pubs have rooms, but the centrally located hostels offer the best value. Caravan parks offer excellent-value cabins, often including kitchens and linen – for more information contact the SATC visitor information centre.

HOSTELS & GUESTHOUSES
Many hostels tempt with free apple pie or cheesecake for supper and most have dedicated TV rooms (with a selection of movies) and a well-stocked guest kitchen. They generally provide linen and offer a free service to/from the airport, bus and train stations, and have their own travel agencies or will book tours and car hire. Most places have shared bathrooms, though some rooms at budget places do have private facilities.

Glenelg Beach Resort (☎ 8376 0007; www.glenelg beachhostel.com.au; 7 Moseley St, Glenelg; dm $25, d/f incl breakfast from $60/70; 🖳) With a fabulous beachside location, this charming terrace dates from 1879 and is Adelaide's budget golden child. Fan-cooled rooms sport period details and are bunk-free. There's nightly entertainment in the bar, an open fireplace and large plasma TV screen in the lounge, a pool room with jukebox, and a courtyard garden. Rates include airport pick-ups.

Adelaide Central YHA (Map p714; ☎ 8414 3010; www .yha.com.au; 135 Waymouth St; dm/d from $20/60, non-YHA members extra $5; P ⊠ 🖳) While the YHA is not known for its overly gregarious guests, you will get plenty of sleep in the spacious and comfortable rooms. It's surrounded by great bars and nightspots, and has gleaming facilities, excellent communal areas with a pool table, TV rooms, free nightly movies and bike hire ($10).

My Place (Map p714; ☎ 8221 5299; 257 Waymouth St; www.adelaidehostel.com.au; dm incl breakfast $20, d incl breakfast & TV $54; P 🖳) This place has a wonderfully welcoming atmosphere just a stumble away from pubs and Light Sq nightspots, a cosy TV room, a sauna and a plant-rimmed terrace on which to laze. Affable staff will get you out on the town with evening adventures to local pubs – particularly good for solo travellers. Rates include a daily bus to Glenelg. Bike hire here is $10 per day.

Backpack Oz (Map p714; ☎ 8223 3551; www.back packoz.com.au; cnr Wakefield & Pulteney Sts; dm/s/d incl breakfast $22/55/60; ⊠ 🖳) This gleaming family-run hostel in a former hotel has spacious dorms and a guesthouse over the road (great for couples). Guests can get a coldie (cold beer) and shoot some pool at the converted bar.

Other backpacker hostels:
Adelaide Backpackers Inn (Map p714; ☎ 8223 6635; 118 Carrington St; dm/s/tw/d incl breakfast & supper $20/44/50/55; ⊠ 🖳) A relaxed and ultraclean place with roomier dorms than most and an annexed guesthouse across the road (try to get a window room when staying at the guesthouse).

Blue Galah Backpackers Hostel (Map p714; ☎ 8231 9295; www.bluegalah.com.au; Level 1, 62 King William St; dm/tw from $22/64; 🖳) A friendly spot with a grand old balcony slap bang in the city centre. Rooms are clean if a little cramped, and some lack windows.

Cannon St Backpackers (Map p714; ☎ 1800 069 731, 8410 1218; www.cannonst.com.au; 110 Franklin St; dm/tw $20/55; P 🖳) A frat house–style party place, most popular for its backpackers bar. Some bemoan the tattiness and lack of sleep.

HOTELS
Princes Lodge Motel (Map p719; ☎ 8267 5566; princeslodge@senet.com.au; 73 Lefevre Tce, North Adelaide; s with bathroom $48, d with/without bathroom incl breakfast $85/66, f $92; P ⊠) In a grand old house overlooking parkland and the hills, this friendly but tired lodging is close to chichi North Adelaide's restaurants and within walking distance of the city.

Hampshire Hotel (Map p714; ☎ 8231 5169; 110 Grote St; dm/d without bathroom $23/60) Diagonally opposite the Central Market, the Hampy provides gay-friendly accommodation in basic rooms with kitchen, and various entertainment from Tuesday to Saturday.

CAMPING & HOLIDAY PARKS
Adelaide Shores Caravan Resort (off Map p714; ☎ 8356 7654; www.adelaideshores.com.au; 1 Military Rd, West Beach; sites $25, caravans/cabins from $50/65; P ⊠ 🖳 ⚑) Nestled behind dunes on a lovely beach with a walking/cycling track extending to Glenelg (3.4km) in one direction and Henley Beach (3.5km) in the other, this is a great spot to be in the summer. There are lush sites, glistening amenities and passing dolphins. The attached **Adelaide Shores Holiday Village** (off Map p714; ☎ 8355 7360; cabins from $85, 2-bedroom units/villas from $120/150; P ⊠ ⚑) has comfortable self-contained family accommodation, playgrounds, pools and a communal leisure centre.

Midrange
Motels in this range are generally of the 3½-star variety with TV, fridge, and sometimes a microwave. They're dotted all over Adelaide; 'motel alley' along Glen Osmond Rd in the southeast is a main arterial, so some places can be noisy. For extra calm,

consider places in leafy North Adelaide, 2km north of the city centre.

APARTMENTS

Holiday apartments in and around Adelaide are listed under 'Apartments & Flats' and 'Apartments – Serviced' in the *Yellow Pages*.

Director's Studios (Map p714; ☎ 8213 2500; www.savillesuites.com.au; 259 Gouger St; d/studio $115/130; P ✗) These warm and unfussy classically styled rooms are on the west business side of town. Studio rooms contain kitchenettes. Children under 14 can stay for free.

Greenways Apartments (Map p719; ☎ 8267 5903; www.greenwaysapartments.com; 45 King William Rd, North Adelaide; 1-/2-/3-bedroom apt $90/125/170; P ✗) Within good strolling distance of the city centre, these standard apartments have rates reduced by $10 for stays of more than three days.

Quest on King William (Map p714; ☎ 8217 5000; www.questapartments.com.au; 82 King William St; 1-/2-bedroom apt from $145/190; P ✗) These immaculate apartments have kitchenettes, and some have DVD players. There are also laundries on site.

Glenelg Letting Agency (☎ 8294 9666; www.baybeachfront.com.au; 742 Anzac Hwy, Glenelg; d apt $100-130) This company lets out Baybeachfront, Bayswaterfront and Bayview apartments – these bright, comfortable and modern apartment buildings are situated on the seafront, on Adelphi Tce and in central Glenelg. There's a minimum three-night stay.

B&BS

Pick up a **South Australian B&B** (www.sabnb.org.au) brochure for details of private B&Bs in and around the city.

Adelaide Old Terraces (☎ 8364 5437; www.adelaideoldterraces.com.au; d incl continental breakfast $140-200; P) Asian antiques and provincial furniture give these heritage-listed cottages plenty of character. **Florence's Cottage** (Map p714; 14 Ely St) and **Wisteria Terrace** (Map p714; 25 Blackburn St) can sleep up to seven people and there's a minimum two-night stay.

North Adelaide Heritage Group (☎ 8272 1355; www.adelaideheritage.com; cottages $140-360; ✗) manages a range of beautifully refurbished cottages around Adelaide. The 1866 bluestone **Fire Station** (Map p719; 80 Tynte St, North Adelaide) was operational during Victorian times – line up to book the Fire Engine Suite, outfitted with a genuine red and shiny fire engine.

MOTELS & HOTELS

Majestic Roof Garden Hotel (Map p714; ☎ 8100 4400; www.majestichotels.com.au; 55 Frome St; d/tw from $130/145, extra person $30; P ✗) This new city-centre motel has attractive, boutique-style minimalist rooms and a gym.

Festival Lodge (Map p714; ☎ 8212 7877; 140 North Tce; s/d incl breakfast $90/110; P ✗) While its old-style (yet immaculate) rooms may not be of the boutique variety found elsewhere along this strip, Festival Lodge has affordable rooms in a prime position opposite the casino and a hop from the Festival Centre.

Royal Coach Motor Inn (Map p714; ☎ 8362 5676; www.royalcoach.com.au; 24 Dacquetteville Tce, Kent Town; d from $145, extra adult/child $15/10; P ✗ ☙) Just a stroll through Rymill Park from the East End and CBD, these bright rooms have a queen-sized bed and a sofa. There's a Grecianlike indoor pool, and one child can stay for free.

Strathmore Hotel (Map p714; ☎ 8238 2900; www.strath.com.au; 129 North Tce; d incl breakfast from $115; P ✗) Huddled between larger entities, this traditional hotel with a wrought-iron balcony is directly opposite the train station and casino. Its attractive and good-value renovated rooms have all the mod cons.

Motels with standard, comfortable facilities in and around the city centre:

Adelaide Paringa Motel (Map p714; ☎ 8231 1000; www.macbitz.net.au/paringa; 15 Hindley St; s incl breakfast $99, d incl breakfast $125-150, extra adult/child $20/5; P ✗ ☙) In a heritage building at the heart of hyper Hindley St.

Mercure Grosvenor Hotel (Map p714; ☎ 8407 8888; www.mercuregrosvenorhotel.com.au; 125 North Tce; economy/standard d $110/195; P ✗) Opposite the casino, compact room configurations at this hotel feature a double or two single beds. Children under 16 stay free.

Regal Park Motor Inn (Map p719; ☎ 8267 3222; www.regalpark.com.au; 44 Barton Tce East, North Adelaide; d from $100; P ✗ ☙ ☙) Overlooking parkland in quiet, elegant North Adelaide. There's a children's playground on site.

Recommended motels in Glenelg:

Taft Motor Inn (☎ 8376 1233; 18 Moseley St, Glenelg; motel d from $95, 1-/2-bedroom apt from $127/137; P ✗ ☙) Some of these comfortable motel rooms and apartments come with kitchenettes and there's a BBQ and playground on site. Transport from the airport, railway and bus stations is provided.

AUTHOR'S CHOICE

Hotel Richmond (Map p714; ☎ 8223 4044; www.hotelrichmond.com.au; 128 Rundle Mall; d from $250; P ✦ 🖳) This chic hotel in a grand 1920s building has minimalist boutique-style rooms with king-sized beds, marble bathrooms and American oak and Italian furnishings. Oh, and that hotel rarity – opening windows. Rates include breakfast, movies and newspapers. Business services and babysitting are also available.

Best Western Ensenada Motor Inn (☎ 8294 5822; www.ensenada.com.au; 13 Colley Tce, Glenelg; d with/without kitchenette from $150/120, extra person $15; ✦ 🖳) Located opposite the beach near the Jetty Rd shops and eateries. Check the Ensenada's website for special deals.

Top End

The following hotels are right in the city centre. Most offer package deals on weekends, when room prices are generally a fair bit cheaper than during the week. It's worth checking bargain hotel-booking websites (such as www.needitnow.com) for discounts of over 50% off rack rates. Generally, children under 12 stay free.

Rockford Adelaide (Map p714; ☎ 8211 8255; www .rockfordhotels.com.au; 164 Hindley St; standard/refurbished d $155/165, spa ste $195-245, extra person $20; P ✦ 🖳 ≋) Rooms in this contemporary, boutique-style hotel are decorated in warm, natural tones that are as smooth as chocolate. In all but the cheaper doubles, expect bathrobes, complimentary champagne and chocolates. Riverside rooms have balconies. Guests have use of the nearby gym.

Radisson Playford Hotel & Suites (Map p714; ☎ 8213 8888; www.Radisson.com/adelaideau; 120 North Tce; midweek d from $205, weekend B&B d from $185; P ✦ 🖳 ≋) Be sure to check for special deals at this award-winning five-star boutique hotel, which has opulent, luxurious rooms and a gym.

Stamford Grand Hotel (☎ 8376 1222; www.stam ford.com.au; Moseley Sq, Glenelg; d city/ocean views from $180/220; P ✦) At the top of the comfort scale, this towering beachside luxury hotel overlooks Gulf St Vincent. Packages are available.

EATING

Dining out in Adelaide sits high on the social register – aided by low prices and high standards. Foodies flock to Gouger St, where you can sample food from every continent, try the Central Market's delights, and get some of the gutsiest Chinese food around in Chinatown.

Pull up a people-watching pew at the lively Italian and Thai alfresco cafés and restaurants in Rundle St, or relax at the quiet cluster of good restaurants on nearby Hindmarsh Sq. Diverse cafés sit alongside sleaze on Hindley St, while chic restaurants with gourmet accolades huddle on Hutt St.

Across the river in North Adelaide, Melbourne and O'Connell Sts have a healthy offering, including Italian bistros, gourmet providores and cool pubs with great food and live music.

City Centre

GOUGER ST & CENTRAL MARKET

You can pretty much take your pick from any of the restaurants along this strip and be guaranteed a great meal – from Argentine to Vietnamese and everywhere in between.

Central Market (Map p714; cnr Gouger & Grote Sts; ⏰ 7am-5.30pm Mon-Thu, 7am-9pm Fri, 7am-3pm Sat) Adelaide's main market, near Victoria Sq, is good value for all types of food. Don't miss the Providore and a sample from the Yoghurt Company. Tacked on the market's western end is Chinatown, with a collection of cafés doing fast and furious trade (especially Friday night) and bursting with contented diners slurping soup and noodles.

Chinatown Café (Map p714; ☎ 8231 2230; Shop 38-41 Moonta St, Chinatown; meals $5.50-6.80; ⏰ 10.30am-4.30pm Sun-Thu & Sat, to 8.30pm Fri) Straight up mixed-Asian favourites and no-fuss décor. The massive laksa ($5.50) is a winner. Most dishes come with a vegetarian option.

Lucia's Pizza & Spaghetti Bar (Map p714; ☎ 8231 2303; 2 Western Mall, Central Market; meals $6-7.50; ⏰ 7am-5pm Mon-Thu, 7am-9pm Fri, 7am-3pm Sat) This little piece of Italy is an Adelaide institution (operating since 1957) renowned for some of the finest coffee in town. Breakfast and value-packed tucker are served during market hours. All sauces are homemade – try Friday's lasagne special, or the homemade pizzas.

Nu's Thai (Map p714; ☎ 8470 2288; 117 Gouger St; mains $10-30; ☘ lunch Thu & Fri, dinner Tue-Sun) A contemporary Thai restaurant regarded as the best in town – despite a change in ownership – serving dishes such as crispy chilli barramundi.

Guacho's Argentinian Restaurant (Map p714; ☎ 8231 2299; 91 Gouger St; mains $22.50-29.50; ☘ lunch Mon-Fri, dinner daily) Only carnivores need apply – you'll get the finest dose in this Argentinian meat house.

Ying Chow Chinese Restaurant (Map p714; ☎ 8211 7998; 114 Gouger St; mains $7.50-14; ☘ 5pm-late daily, lunch Friday) Behind the utilitarian décor hides a culinary gem. It's not your typical Chinese restaurant – rather than ubiquitous Cantonese, the cuisine is styled from the Guangzhou region and the flavours are delightful. Try Eshan chicken or aniseed tea duck ($12). It gets packed nightly, but it's worth the wait – or you can grab a takeaway. For lunch, head to action-packed sister restaurant **Ky Chow** (Map p714; ☎ 8221 5411; 82 Gouger St; mains $7-13; ☘ lunch Mon-Fri, dinner daily), which serves dishes such as duck with sundried Chinese bayberries ($9).

EAST END

The eastern end of Rundle St (off Rundle Mall) and its side streets burst with lively alfresco cafés and restaurants, craft and furniture shops, and designer clothing stores.

Exeter (Map p714; ☎ 8223 2623; 246 Rundle St; snacks $1.20-5.50, meals $10-17; ☘ lunch & dinner) This atmospheric pub has inspired meals ranging from venison vindaloo and roo fillets to chicken laksa and tofu burgers.

Austral (Map p714; ☎ 8223 4660; 205 Rundle St; bar menu $7.50-15) This pub serves excellent food, including nachos, schnitzels, grills and Thai curry.

Amalfi Pizzeria Ristorante (Map p714; ☎ 8223 1948; 29 Frome St; mains $12-22; ☘ lunch Mon-Fri, dinner Mon-Sat) Regulars swear by the pizza and pasta at this buzzing Adelaide institution that's just off Rundle St. It's often difficult to get in, but hang around because it's worth the wait.

Botanic Café (Map p714; ☎ 8224 0925; 4 East Tce; mains $17-25; ☘ lunch & dinner) Order from a seasonal menu styled from the best regional produce in this swish, contemporary hot spot opposite the Botanic Gardens. On Friday and Saturday nights, it turns into a buzzing tapas bar.

Jasmin Indian Restaurant (Map p714; ☎ 8223 7837; 31 Hindmarsh Sq; mains $19.50; ☘ lunch Tue-Fri, dinner Tue-Sat) Mrs Singh's mouthwatering North Indian cuisine garners a full house and keeps Jasmin among Australia's top 100 restaurants. If you like it hot, try the vindaloo.

Sprouts (Map p714; ☎ 8232 6977; 39 Hindmarsh Sq; meals $11-17) Vegetarians and vegans – you're in good company here. Famous herbivores are prominently named at the entry to this small, stylish dining room, which serves dishes such as Cajun spiced tofu and mushroom crepe wraps.

WEST END

Adelaide's original 'sin strip' is on the artsy-alternative side of town, with plenty of good eateries and cool clubs among glittery bars.

Garage Bar & Dining (Map p714; ☎ 8212 9577; 163 Waymouth St, Light Sq; lunch mains $12-20; ☘ 8am-3pm Mon-Fri, 11am-4pm Sun) Generous portions of Modern Australian (Modern Oz) and Asian food are served at this favoured lunch and brunch venue.

Great-value bar meals are served with a good casual vibe to a mixed crowd at **Worldsend Hotel** (Map p714; ☎ 8231 9137; 208 Hindley St; bar meals $7-11, dining room mains $16-19; ☘ lunch & dinner) and the **Prince Albert** (Map p714; ☎ 8212 7912; 154 Wright St; mains $10-18), where schnitzels loom large.

AROUND THE CENTRE

La Trattoria (Map p714; ☎ 8212 3327; 346 King William St; mains from $12; ☘ lunch Mon-Fri, dinner daily) A tried and tested favourite for pizza and pasta.

AUTHOR'S CHOICE

Good Life (pizzas $12.50-18.90; ☘ lunch Tue-Fri, dinner Tue-Sun; City Map p714; ☎ 8223 2618; 170 Hutt St; Glenelg ☎ 8376 5900; Level 1, cnr Jetty Rd & Moseley St) Sensational organic pizzas disappear in record time at these casually stylish sister pizzerias. Thin crusts are piled high with tasty toppings such as spicy garlic-and-venison *mettwurst* (German sausage) with kalamata and green split olives. Fancy roast duck with shiitake mushrooms and spring-onion ginger jam? You can even get dessert pizzas. Book ahead.

Spats (off Map p714; ☎ 8272 6170; 108 King William Rd, Hyde Park; desserts $7.50; ☺ 6.30pm-late) Cosy up on a couch for wicked desserts, hot chocolates and liqueur coffees.

Hawker's Corner (Map p714; cnr West Tce & Wright St; meals $6-12; ☺ lunch & dinner Tue-Sun) Pick up cheap Asian dishes here.

There's great eating in buzzing cafés and restaurants on Hutt St.

North Adelaide

Quality cafés and restaurants line Melbourne and O'Connell Sts, the main thoroughfares into the city.

Cafe Paesano (Map p719; ☎ 8239 0655; cnr O'Connell & Tynte Sts; breakfast $4-11.50, mains $12-21; ☺ breakfast, lunch & dinner) This jovial Italian bistro has alfresco dining on the pavement, and huge portions. Entrées are ample.

Archer (Map p719; ☎ 8361 9300; 47 O'Connell St; bar menu $7.50-14.50, mains $20-26; ☺ lunch & dinner) Meat-rich Mod Oz cuisine is served in the refined library of this deconstructionist-style pub, with a long accompanying list of fine SA wines. Burgers, curries and grills are served in the bar, which has Victorian and WA microbrews on tap.

Royal Oak Hotel (Map p719; ☎ 8267 2488; 123 O'Connell St; mains $16-23) Kick back on the back seat of an old car or under wall-mounted flying brass instruments at this eclectic, retro pub. Order from the hearty menu, or share a meze platter ($17). There's live music (p731), particularly jazz.

Cibo (Map p719; ☎ 8267 2444; 10 O'Connell St; mains $27-31; ☺ lunch & dinner) Smart dining Italian style, with attentive yet unfussed service, a refined atmosphere and a dedicated pizza oven. The two-course lunch deals ($25) include a glass of wine from the great wine list.

Glenelg & Seaside Suburbs

Glenelg's Jetty Rd and marina have plenty of restaurants of varied cuisines to cruise and choose. The lively square at Henley Beach is also surrounded by hip restaurants and cafés.

Cafe Zest (☎ 8295 3599; 2A Sussex St, Glenelg; breakfast $4-8.90, lunch mains $6.90-11.90; ☺ breakfast & lunch) This itty-bitty gallery-cum-café has a laid-back atmosphere and meals with a twist. Baguettes and bagels are crammed with taste-bud tingling combos, and good coffee is served with a home-baked treat.

Café Blu (☎ 8350 6688; Ramada Pier Hotel, 16 Holdfast Promenade, Glenelg; meals $12.50-21.50; ☺ lunch & dinner) Enthusiastically reputed to have 'the best (bleep) margarita pizza on the planet'.

Scampi's (☎ 8376 6200; Foreshore, Glenelg; mains $20-30; ☺ lunch & dinner) Book a table by the window and watch the sun go down over the bay while feasting on seafood.

Ramsgate Hotel (☎ 8356 5411; 328 Seaview Rd, Henley Beach; mains $8-22) Located on Henley's bustling square, the Ramsgate is the best pub on the coast. To get here, take bus Nos 130 to 137 from Grenfell and Curry Sts.

Grange Jetty Kiosk (☎ 8235 0822; cnr Jetty Rd & The Esplanade, Grange; mains $12-22; ☺ breakfast Sun, lunch Wed-Mon, dinner Wed-Sat) The popular Grange has a seafood-heavy menu. Floodlit dunes and the lights of the jetty make it a romantic spot at night. Take bus No 130 or 137 from Grenfell St and get off at stop 29A.

Lipson Café (☎ 8341 0880; 117 Lipson St, Port Adelaide; breakfast $2-8.50, lunch $4-14; ☺ breakfast & lunch) In a converted warehouse opposite the Maritime Museum, in Port Adelaide, the Lipson Café keeps the arty community ticking over with great food in generous proportions.

Self-Catering

Central Market (Map p714; cnr Gouger & Grote Sts; ☺ 7am-5.30pm Mon-Thu, 7am-9pm Fri, 7am-3pm Sat) You can find just about everything at the Central Market's 250-odd shops – abundant and fresh organic fruit and vegetables, bread, cheese, seafood and gourmet produce – you name it. Good luck making it out without succumbing to the temptation here. Bargain hunters should head down on Tuesday afternoon or after lunch on Saturday.

Supermarkets:

Coles (Map p714; Central Market Arcade, cnr King William & Gouger Sts)

Woolworths (Map p714; 86 Rundle Mall) Has an attached liquor store.

DRINKING

To get a true Adelaide experience, head for the bar and order a schooner (half-pint) or pint of the local brew – Coopers – or a glass of one of SA's impressive wines. Most pubs feature a 'happy hour' with reduced-price drinks at some stage in the evening.

In Hindley St, grunge and sleaze collide with student energy, and groovy bars sit amid adult bookshops and strip joints. Here you'll find a few uni student hangouts like the **Worldsend Hotel** (Map p714; ☎ 8231 9137; 208 Hindley St), which also serves bar meals (see West End, p727) and the cool, ambient **Supermild Lounge Bar** (Map p714; ☎ 8212 9699; 182 Hindley St).

On Rundle, to the east, cafés spill onto footpaths and groovy bars behind simple paint-peeling doors open up in the evening. Atmospheric pubs attract punters with cold beers at sunset, dotted on corners throughout North Adelaide and the city centre, at Glenelg and along Adelaide's beaches.

Well-trained baristas crank out great espresso coffee all over town; head for the ubiquitous Cibo Express cafés if you need a good fast fix. For a quickie, pause at the street-side counter at **Short Black** (Map p714; ☎ 8410 9390; 87 Hindley St).

T Bar (Map p714; ☎ 8410 5522; 44 Gouger St; breakfast $2.50-7.50, lunch $6-7.50, tea $2.50-3; ☒ breakfast & lunch) Take a side-step out of the market and indulge at this 140-variety tea emporium, which also serves coffee, cakes and meals.

Botanic Bar (Map p714; ☎ 8227 0799; 309 North Tce) Cocktails sink to soulful beats and a ruby-red glow suffuses this retro bar–cum–stately manor in Adelaide's East End.

Archer (Map p719; ☎ 8361 9300; 47 O'Connell St, North Adelaide) A great place for a drink, with a room for every mood – from the jovial front bar (with sports screen) to the fireside lounge with Chesterfields, snooker room and upbeat music room – with DJs on weekends.

Governor Hindmarsh Hotel (off Map p714; ☎ 8340 0744; www.thegov.com.au; 59 Port Rd, Hindmarsh) A renowned live-music venue with atmospheric bars attracting a mixed crowd of all ages (and flavours).

Other eclectic spots:

Apothecary 1878 (Map p714; ☎ 8212 9099; 118 Hindley St) Get a dose from this old dispensary turned wine bar.

Garage Bar (Map p714; ☎ 8212 9577; 163 Waymouth St, Light Sq) Kick back at this groovy converted garage bar with darts, pool and fusbol. Oh, and you can eat here, too (see West End, p727).

Fumo Blu (Map p714; ☎ 8232 2533; www.fumoblu .com.au; Rundle St) A hip underground cigar bar/club with a tropical fish tank, super-dry martinis and Moët by the glass.

In Glenelg's **Holdfast Shores Marina** (www.hold fastshores.com.au), the sassy **Salt Wine Bar** (☎ 8376 6887; Holdfast Shores, Glenelg; mains $18-24) pulls in punters to dine or just for drinks, while **Pier One Bar** (☎ 8350 6688; Ramada Pier Hotel, 16 Holdfast Promenade, Glenelg) is a good spot for sundowners – especially for sports fans.

ENTERTAINMENT

Arts-connoisseur Adelaide has a phenomenal cultural life that compares favourably with much larger cities. The free monthly *Adelaide Review* (www.adelaidereview.com) features theatre and gallery listings, and on Thursday and Saturday the *Advertiser* (www.theadvertiser.com.au) newspaper lists events, cinema programmes and gallery details. The Theatre Association of South Australia compiles the **Adelaide Theatre Guide** (☎ 8272 6726; http://theatreguide.tripod.com), a comprehensive site with dates, venues, booking details and reviews of comedy, drama and musical events and other performance arts.

Bookings for big events can be made through **BASS** (Map p714; ☎ 13 12 46; www.bass.sa.com .au; SATC visitor information centre, 18 King William St) and the riverside **Adelaide Festival Centre** (Map p714; ☎ 8216 8600; www.afct.org.au; King William Rd). The latter is the hub of performing arts in SA, hosting touring and local plays, festival events, concerts and musicals. The **State Theatre Company** (www.statetheatre.sa.com.au) is based here.

Other theatre venues include **Her Majesty's Theatre** (Map p714; ☎ 8212 8600; 58 Grote St) and the **Lion Theatre & Bar** (Map p714; ☎ 8212 9200; Lion Arts Centre, 13 Morphett St).

The multipurpose **Adelaide Entertainment Centre** (off Map p719; Port Rd, Hindmarsh) hosts everything from ballet to opera to big-name concerts.

Nightclubs

The scene is ever changing, though the West End and Light Sq are a pretty safe

---

AUTHOR'S CHOICE

Weimar Room (Map p714; ☎ 8410 4700; 27 Hindley St; admission $10-16; ☒ 8pm-2am Fri-Sun) This *über*-cool European-style cabaret venue has a 'rough-around-the-edges, turn-of-the-20th-century' chic and a range of shows including flamenco, tango, theatre sports, jazz, big bands and cabaret acts. You can also eat here, and the bar serves absinthe.

bet for club activity. Pick up a copy of *Onion* from pubs, cafés and music shops for 'dance news and fat reviews'.

Garage Bar (Map p714; ☎ 8212 9577; 163 Waymouth St, Light Sq) Has a good vibe, and a resident DJ on weekends (for details on dining here, see West End, p727).

Savvy (Map p714; ☎ 8221 6030; 149 Waymouth St, Light Sq) Gets pumping with commercial house music, featuring DJs and guests. It's very popular with the 18 to 25 set.

Heaven Nightclub complex (Map p714; ☎ 8216 5216; www.heaven.com.au; 7 West Tce; ❧ 8pm-6am) Nectar for clubbers – different bars play different music including retro, R&B, house and dance.

Also in the city:

Minke Bar (Map p714; ☎ 8211 8088; 142 Hindley St; ❧ from 9pm Wed-Sun) A grungy-but-cool New York–style bar.

Moskva Vodka Bar West (Map p714; ☎ 8211 9007; 192 Hindley St; ❧ from 9pm Wed-Sun) A West End club with a packed, chandelier-decorated dance floor and watermelon martinis.

Mars Bar (Map p714; ☎ 8231 9639; 120 Gouger St; ❧ 10.30pm-late Wed-Sat) A popular dance club.

Casinos

SkyCity Casino (Map p714; ☎ 8218 4100; North Tce; ❧ 10am-4pm Mon-Thu, 10am-6am Fri-Sun) Housed in the grand old train station, this casino has all the flashing lights, trilling machines, two-up games and psychedelic carpet you could ask for. There are two bars, two restaurants and a café. Smart casual dress is required (but clean jeans are OK).

Cinemas

Check the entertainment pages in the *Advertiser* for what's on around town. Cinemas slash ticket prices on Tuesday.

Nova Cinema (Map p714; ☎ 8232 3434; 251 Rundle St; adult/concession $13.50/9.50) and **Palace East End Cinemas** (Map p714; ☎ 8232 3434; 274 Rundle St; adult/concession $13.50/9.50) both feature new-release independent, art-house and foreign-language films, as well as some mainstream flicks.

Academy Cinema City (Map p714; ☎ 8223 5000; Hindmarsh Sq; tickets $14) Screens the usual new-release mainstream films.

Glenelg Cinema Centre (☎ 8294 3366; 119 Jetty Rd, Glenelg; adult/child/concession/$14/9.50/10.50) Screens mainly mainstream films, and offers movie-and-meal deals with local restaurants.

Moonlight Cinema (Map p714; ☎ 1900 933 899; www.moonlight.com.au; Adelaide Botanic Garden, North Tce; adult/concession $14/10; ❧ mid-Dec–mid-Feb) In summer, pack a picnic and mosquito repellent, and spread out on the lawn to watch old and new classics under the stars.

Mercury Cinema (Map p714; ☎ 8410 1934; Lion Arts Centre, 13 Morphett St) This cinema publishes a quarterly calendar detailing its upcoming art-house films and festival screenings. Pick up a calendar at cafés or the visitor information centre.

Gay & Lesbian Venues

For details on the local scene, pick up a copy of *Blaze* (www.blazemedia.com.au), available around the city; reviews, community news and popular gay and lesbian venues are listed on its website.

Some venues worth checking out:

Hampshire Hotel (Map p714; ☎ 8231 5169; 110 Grote St) Hosts various themed party nights and entertainment from Tuesday to Saturday (for more on the hotel, see p724).

Queen's Arms Hotel (Map p714; ☎ 8211 8000; 88 Wright St) Nightly entertainment.

Edinburgh Castle Hotel (Map p714; ☎ 8410 1211; 233 Currie St) Has a dance floor, bistro and beer garden.

Mars Bar (Map p714; ☎ 8231 9639; 120 Gouger St; ❧ 10.30pm-late Wed-Sat) A popular and lively gay-and-lesbian dance club with drag shows on weekends.

Skin@Club199 (Map p714; ☎ 8232 2733; 199 North Tce; ❧ 3am-9am Sun) If your engines are still firing after a big night out, head to Skin for recovery.

Church (Map p714; ☎ 8223 4233; Synagogue Pl, Rundle St) A big club in the centre of the action, enjoyed by all persuasions.

Live Music

To get your finger on the pulse, grab a copy of free street press papers *Rip it Up* or *db* – available at record shops, hotels, cafés and nightspots – they have listings and reviews of bands and DJs playing around town. Dedicated websites provide up-to-date listings for Adelaide's jazz (www.jazz.adelaide .onau.net) scene, **Adelaide Symphony Orchestra** (Map p714; ☎ 8233 6233; www.aso.com.au; 91 Hindley St), and general events at **South Australian Music Online** (www.musicsa.com.au).

Governor Hindmarsh Hotel (off Map p714; ☎ 8340 0744; www.thegov.com.au; 59 Port Rd, Hindmarsh; cover charge varies) Live-music fans should check out the line-up at 'The Gov' when heading into town. It received the Australian 'Live music venue of the year award' and features some legendary local and international acts. The odd Irish fiddle band sits around in the bar, and a back venue hosts folk, jazz, blues, salsa, reggae and dance music.

Royal Oak Hotel (Map p719; ☎ 8267 2488; 123 O'Connell St, North Adelaide) A great pub with a lively crowd and a variety of music including lounge and jazz (for details on dining here, see p728).

Other pubs offering good live music include the laid-back cool **Grace Emily Hotel** (Map p714; ☎ 8231 5500; 232 Waymouth St), **Austral Hotel** (Map p714; ☎ 8223 4660; 205 Rundle St), on Friday and Saturday nights, and **Exeter Hotel** (Map p714; ☎ 8223 2623; 246 Rundle St).

Sport

Sport is a huge part of the city's daily life, encompassing everything from lawn bowls to spectacular international one-day cricket matches.

Adelaide hosts a number of world class international events that take over the city streets and turn into big parties, including tennis matches, car racing and one-day and Test cricket matches. For cricket match details, check the *Advertiser* (www.thead vertiser.news.com.au) and local TV sports news.

Australian Football League (AFL) rules the city, with two local competitive teams: the Adelaide Crows and Port Power, the latter were premiership winners in 2004. The Redbacks are the state's cricket team and basketball has the Adelaide 36ers.

SHOPPING

High street shops and department stores (including Myer, David Jones and Harris Scarfe) line Rundle Mall. The beautiful old arcades running between the mall and Grenfell St retain their original splendour and house plenty of eclectic little shops. Rundle St and the lanes running off it are home to boutique and retro clothing shops; you'll also find some on Norwood Pde in Norwood.

Once you try Haigh's Chocolates, considered Australia's finest chocolates, you'll be ducking into every branch you pass.

Tourist tat souvenir shops lurk around Rundle Mall and nearby King William St. For something more stylish, consider heading to **Tandanya – National Aboriginal Cultural**

Institute (Map p714; ☎ 8224 3200; 253 Grenfell St), the Aboriginal cultural institute (see p717), or seek out beautiful local art and crafts at the **Jam Factory Craft & Design Centre** (Lion Arts Centre Map p714; ☎ 8410 0727; cnr Morphett St & North Tce; Rundle Mall Map p714; ☎ 8211 9777; 44-60 Rundle Mall). Other good spots selling textiles, artworks, and accessories by established and emerging artists and designers include **T'Arts** (Map p714; ☎ 8232 0265; 10G Gays Arcade, Adelaide Arcade, Rundle Mall) and **Urban Cow Studio** (Map p714; ☎ 8232 6126; 11 Frome St).

A collection of opal shops around King William St and the end of Rundle Mall sell opals mined out of Coober Pedy. **Opal Field Gems** (Map p714; ☎ 8212 5300; 33 King William St) has a mock-up opal mine and a free museum attached to its shop.

RM Williams (off Map p719; ☎ 8269 3752; 5 Percy St, Prospect) About 2km north of North Adelaide, sells handmade boots (women/men $250/220), first crafted for stockmen in the early 1800s. June sales can halve the price.

Outdoor gear shops are conveniently grouped on Rundle St, including **Mountain Designs** (Map p714; ☎ 8232 0690; 203 Rundle St), **Annapurna** (Map p714; ☎ 8223 4633; 210 Rundle St) and **Paddy Palin** (Map p714; ☎ 8232 3155; 228 Rundle St).

GETTING THERE & AWAY
Air
Adelaide is connected by regular air services to all Australian capitals. **Qantas** (Map p714; ☎ 13 1313; www.qantas.com.au; 144 North Tce) and **Virgin Blue** (☎ 13 67 89; www.virginblue.com.au) operate flights between Adelaide and other capital cities and major centres; approximate one-way fares start at: Melbourne ($80), Sydney ($150), Perth ($250), Alice Springs ($180) and Darwin ($295).

For more details on travelling to and from Adelaide see the Transport chapter (p1035).

Bus
Adelaide's **central bus station** (Map p714; 101-111 Franklin St) has terminals and ticket offices for all major interstate and state-wide services, and it has left-luggage lockers. See p712 for details of services to and from Adelaide.

Car & Motorcycle
If you want to hitch a ride (sharing petrol costs) or buy a second-hand car, check out the hostel notice boards.

HIRE

The *Yellow Pages* lists over 20 vehicle rental companies in Adelaide, including all the major nationals. Some don't allow cars to be taken to Kangaroo Island. Expect to pay about $45 a day (less for longer rentals) for car hire with the cheaper companies:

Acacia Car Rentals (off Map p714; ☎ 8234 0911; 91 Sir Donald Bradman Dr, Hilton) Cheap rentals for travel within a 100km radius.

Access Rent-a-Car (Map p714; ☎ 1800 812 580, 8359 3200; 60 Frome St)

Cut Price Car-&-Truck Rentals (off Map p714; ☎ 8443 7788; cnr Sir Donald Bradman Dr & South Rd, Mile End South)

Explore (Map p714; ☎ 8231 2223; explorecoachlines@bigpond.com.au; 101 Franklin St)

Hawk-Rent-A-Car (Map p714; ☎ 1800 004 295, 8371 2824; 101 Franklin St)

Wicked Campers (☎ 1800 246 869; 07-3257 2170; www.wickedcampers.com.au) Fitted-out caravans from $48/60 per day for one/eight weeks' rental.

Show & Go (off Map p714; ☎ 8376 0333; 236 Brighton Rd, Somerton Park), 21km southwest of town, has motor scooters (from $55 a day) and motorcycles from 250cc (from $69) to 1000cc (from $169). You need a car driving licence to rent a scooter, while a full motorcycle licence is required for the bikes – a motorcycle learner's licence is acceptable for 250cc bikes.

Train

The interstate **train terminal** (Map p714; Railway Tce, Keswick) is just southwest of the city centre. See p712 for details of train services to and from Adelaide.

GETTING AROUND
To/From the Airport & Train Station

Skylink (☎ 8332 0528; www.skylinkadelaide.com; adult/child one way $7.50/2.50) runs hourly shuttles between the airport and the city centre. Shuttles go via Keswick interstate train station (adult/child one way $4/1.50), if prebooked. Shuttles leaving the airport run from 6.15am to 9.40pm and those from the city run from 5.30am to 9pm. Most hostels will pick you up and drop you off if you're staying with them. Taxis charge around $17 to travel between the airport and city centre.

Bicycle

Hire bikes from hostels or **Linear Park Mountain Bike Hire** (Map p714; ☎ 8223 6271; Elder Park; ⏰ 9am-5pm), just below the Festival Centre. Bikes (including helmets, locks and bike maps) and in-line skates cost $20/80 per day/week.

Glenelg Cycles (☎ 8294 4741; 754 Anzac Hwy, Glenelg; ⏰ 9am-5pm Mon-Fri, 9am-4pm Sat & Sun) hires out bikes for $18 per day. In Port Adelaide, try **Lipson Bike Hire** (☎ 8240 0463; 118 Lipson St, Port Adelaide).

Public Transport

The **Adelaide Metro Information Centre** (Map p714; ☎ 8210 1000; www.adelaidemetro.com.au; cnr King William & Currie Sts; ⏰ 8am-6pm Mon-Sat, 10.30am-5.30pm Sun) has timetables and sells tickets for the integrated metropolitan buses, trains and the Glenelg tram. Tickets can also be purchased on board, at staffed train stations, and in delis and newsagents. There are day-trip tickets ($6.20) and two-hour peak ($3.30) and off-peak ($2) tickets. Train tickets can be bought from vending machines on board trains, or at staffed train stations. The peak travel time is before 9am and after 3pm. Bee Line and City Loop buses are free.

Bee Line (No 99B) runs in a loop from the Glenelg tram terminus at Victoria Sq, up King William St and around the corner past the train station to the City West campus of the University of South Australia. It leaves the square every five minutes on weekdays from 7.40am to 6pm (9.20pm Friday), every 15 to 17 minutes on Saturday from 8.27am to 5.30pm, and every 15 minutes on Sunday from 10am to 5.30pm.

City Loop (No 99C) runs clockwise and anticlockwise around the margins of the CBD from the train station, passing the Central Market en route. It generally runs every 15 minutes on weekdays between 8am and 6pm (9pm Friday), and every 30 minutes on Saturday between 8.15am and 5.15pm, and Sunday between 10am and 5.15pm.

Wandering Star Service (☎ 8210 1000; tickets $6; ⏰ 12.30am-5am Fri & Sat) will pick you up from designated spots/nightclubs and deliver you to your front door within most city suburbs, including Adelaide Hills, Glenelg and Marion Plaza nightclubs.

Vintage trams rattle between Moseley Sq (Glenelg) and Victoria Sq (Central Adelaide) approximately every 15 minutes from 6am to 11.50pm.

Suburban trains depart from **Adelaide Railway Terminal** (Map p714; ☎ 8210 1000; North

Tce), by the Casino. The five metro routes are: Belair via Goodwood and Blackwood; Gawler via North Adelaide and Ovingham; Grange; Noarlunga via Goodwood, Marion, Brighton and Seacliff; and Outer Harbor via Port Adelaide, Glanville and Largs.

Taxi
There are licensed taxi ranks all over town, or you can call **Adelaide Independent Taxis** (☎ 13 22 11, for wheelchair users ☎ 1300 360 940) or **Suburban Taxis** (☎ 13 10 08).

ADELAIDE HILLS

Centred in the Mt Lofty Ranges, the Adelaide Hills are a 30-minute drive from the city. Even in the driest summer months they offer cooler temperatures than the city and lush woodland shade. Winding and narrow roads lead you through gentrified villages, leafy hills and farmed valleys past carts of fresh produce for sale, stone cottages, olive groves and vineyards. Wineries dotted throughout the hills are gaining accolades for their cool-climate wines.

The Hills' numerous conservation and wildlife parks have walking trails, stunning views and the chance to view and interact with native fauna.

It's worth hiring a car for a full day to take in early morning views and breakfast at Mt Lofty Summit and a guided wildlife walk at sunset. Take a good map, as signage is lacking and it's easy to get lost.

Information
Adelaide Hills visitor information centre Mt Lofty Summit (☎ 08-8370 1054; www.visitadelaidehills.com .au; 🕑 9am-5pm); Hahndorf (☎ 1800 353 323; 41 Main St; 🕑 9am-5pm Mon-Fri, 10am-4pm Sat & Sun) Has oodles of info and can assist with B&B accommodation; the Hahndorf centre has Internet access ($2 per 15 minutes).

Sights & Activities
PARKS & GARDENS
Just a 12km ride or drive from the city (or taking bus No 105 from Currie St to stop 26, then walking the extra 1km), you can follow walking trails that wend through the woodlands, rugged gorges and waterfalls of **Morialta Conservation Park**.

Make like Dr Doolittle and walk with Australian fauna at **Cleland Wildlife Park** (☎ 08-8339 2444; www.environment.sa.gov.au/parks/cleland; Summit Rd, Cleland; adult/student $12/9; 🕑 9.30am-5pm). You can feed the kangaroos (roos) and emus, and have your photograph taken with a koala ($12, 2pm to 4pm). The hissing Tasmanian devils are particularly fascinating to watch when they are active at feeding time. You could easily spend a good few hours at Cleland Wildlife Park. Dusk **wildlife** and **Aboriginal tours** (adult $20) run with minimum numbers only, so you'll need to call ahead. A café here sells light lunches and snacks. Public transport to the park is limited; take bus No 163F from Grenfell St at 9.52am, 10.52am or 12.52pm and get off at Crafers for a connecting No 823 service to the wildlife park.

From the Cleland Wildlife Park, you can walk through the bush (2km) or drive up to **Mt Lofty Summit** (727m), which has beautiful views over Adelaide and the Gulf of St Vincent. From here continue south for 1.5km to the stunning **Mt Lofty Botanic Garden** (☎ 08-8370 8370; www.dehaa.sa.gov.au/botanicgardens /mtlofty.html; 🕑 8.30am-4pm Mon-Fri, 10am-6pm Sat & Sun). The garden's gates are Mawson Dr and Lampert Rd.

The main attraction of leafy Mylor is **Warrawong Earth Sanctuary** (☎ 08-8370 9422; www .warrawong.com; Stock Rd, Mylor; restaurant mains around $19; 🕑 breakfast, lunch & dinner), about 3km from town and the first of the feral-free Earth Sanctuaries set up to protect endangered native wildlife. Book ahead for the excellent 1½-hour guided walks (adult/child/family $22/17.50/59) at dawn (Friday to Sunday) and sunset (nightly). Accommodation/walk/dinner packages in luxury tents are available (adults $150); accommodation per child costs $12, not including tours and meals. The huge windows in the restaurant give close-up views of many native birds, including rainbow lorikeets. From Adelaide, turn off the freeway at Stirling and follow the signs from the Stirling roundabout. A taxi from Stirling is about $12.

WINERIES
The first exported Australian wine was a case of Adelaide Hills' hock, sent to Queen Victoria in 1845. There are now around a dozen cellar doors in the area, including Petaluma's **Bridgewater Mill Winery & Restaurant** (☎ 08-8339 3422; www.bridgewatermill.com.au;

Mt Barker Rd, Bridgewater; mains around $30; cellar door ⏱ 10am-5pm), situated in a beautifully restored 200-year-old flour mill, complete with an award-winning restaurant overlooking Cox's Creek and 'The Old Rumbler' waterwheel. See Hahndorf (p736) and Adelaide to Birdwood (opposite) for other Hills' wineries.

Tours

SCENIC SELF-DRIVES

If you have a car, a good tour of the Hills' loops from Adelaide to the northern Hills area, leaving the city via North Tce, Botanic Rd and then Payneham Rd and continuing on to Lower North East Rd. This scenic route takes you via **Chain of Ponds Wines**

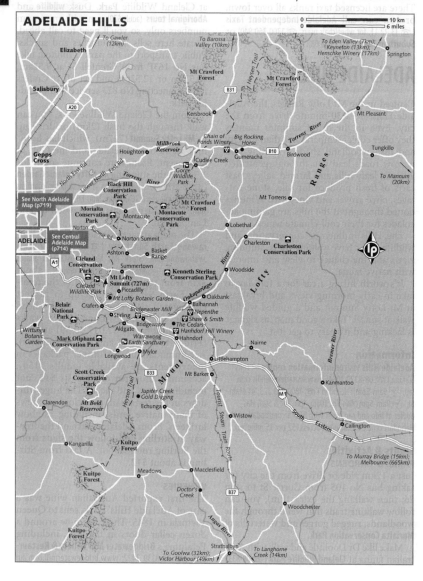

ADELAIDE HILLS

0 — 10 km
0 — 6 miles

and the **Big Rocking Horse** to Birdwood, from where you could continue north to the **Barossa Valley**, or head south through sheep and alpaca country to **Hahndorf**, returning to Adelaide via the South Eastern Fwy.

For a smaller loop focusing on the region's beautiful national parks, you can turn into Magill Rd instead of Payneham Rd and onto Norton Summit Rd to check out **Morialta Conservation Park**, which has walking trails, waterfalls and a rugged gorge. Then continue south to **Cleland Wildlife Park**, **Mt Lofty Summit**, the stunning **Mt Lofty Botanic Gardens** and **Belair National Park**, before heading back to Adelaide via Crafers and the freeway.

Sleeping & Eating

The rustic and basic cottages in national parks along the Heysen Trail at Mt Lofty, Norton Summit, Mylor and Kuitpo offer a fantastic opportunity to get out into nature. Make bookings at the **Adelaide Central YHA** (Map p714; ☎ 08-8414 3000; www.yha.com.au; 135 Waymouth St, Central Adelaide; cottages Mon-Thu $60, Fri-Sun $80) and bring your own linen.

Budget accommodation is slim on the ground in the Hills' B&B territory. Most B&Bs range from $120 to $210 and are invariably pricier on weekends. Pick up a **South Australian B&B** (www.sabnb.org.au) brochure or contact the **Hahndorf visitor information centre** (☎ 08-8388 1185) for bookings.

Burnslea Log Cabin (☎ 08-8388 5803; burnslealc@yahoo.com; Leslie Creek Rd, Mylor; d $85) Secluded in leafy Mylor, this cosy, self-contained log cabin is separated from the friendly, travel-wise owner's home. It comes with breakfast provisions and alpaca petting.

Mount Lofty Railway Station (☎ 08-8339 7400; www.mlrs.com.au; 2 Sturt Valley Rd, Stirling; d B&B $95, without bathroom $65, f from $110) The *Overland* whooshes through this converted heritage-listed train station (providing simple self-contained accommodation) in otherwise quiet Stirling village. Breakfast provisions are included.

Fuzzies Farm (☎ 08-8390 1111; fuzzyt@ozemail.com.au; Norton Summit; cabins per week $90) In a great setting at the edge of Morialta Conservation Park, 15km east of Adelaide, this friendly organic farm has self-contained bushland cabins and a café. You can pick up tips on animal care, organic gardening and building construction. Bookings are essential.

Organic Market & Café (☎ 08-8339 7131; 5 Druids Ave, Stirling; meals $3.50-12; ⏰ breakfast & lunch) Hill types flock to this vibrant and lively café off Mt Barker Rd. Gorge on plump savoury or sweet muffins and great coffee, and leave feeling virtuous and healthy. The Portuguese custard tarts are wicked.

Jimmies (☎ 08-8339 1534; 6 Main St, Crafers; mains $10.50-18; ⏰ breakfast & lunch Sat & Sun, dinner daily) A lively evening spot loved for its wood-fired oven pizzas. There's also live jazz on Thursday night.

Aldgate Pump Hotel (☎ 08-8339 2015; 1 Strathalbyn Rd, Aldgate; mains $13-24; ⏰ lunch & dinner) A charming pub with a fascinating history and an unconventional menu packed with surprises.

Bistro 49 (☎ 08-8339 4416; 49 Mt Barker Rd, Stirling; mains $17.50-24.50; ⏰ lunch & dinner Wed-Sun) Enjoy relaxed elegance and great food, including diahes such as herb-roasted venison with sweet-potato mash and juniper glaze, or mushroom ragout.

Getting There & Around

Public transport to the Hills is very limited. The best options are to hire a car or take an organised coach tour from Adelaide (p711).

Bus Nos 840 and 164F depart hourly for Hahndorf from Adelaide ($3.40, 70 minutes). There are few No 823 buses from Crafers to Mt Lofty Summit and Cleland Wildlife Park.

For taxi service, contact **Hilltop Taxis & Hire Cars** (☎ 08-8388 2211).

ADELAIDE TO BIRDWOOD

Heading out of Adelaide along Lower North East Rd, the celebrated **Chain of Ponds Wines** (☎ 08-8389 1415; www.chainofponds.com.au; Main Adelaide Rd, Gumeracha; lunch mains $17-24; cellar door ⏰ 11am-4pm Mon-Fri, 10.30am-4.30pm Sat & Sun) is about 35km from the city centre. A few kilometres further on, the very stationary **Big Rocking Horse** is another fascinating example of giant Aussie kitsch, though this time constructed of corrugated iron rather than deteriorating fibreglass. In the historic Birdwood Mill about 6km further on, the **National Motor Museum** (☎ 08-8568 5006; www.history.sa.gov.au; Shannon St, Birdwood; adult $9; ⏰ 9am-5pm) has an impressive collection of immaculate vintage and classic cars and motorcycles.

At the **Birdwood Wine & Cheese Centre** (☎ 08-8568 5067; 22 Shannon St, Birdwood) you can taste the wines of boutique producers or pick up a picnic hamper (two/four people $25/45).

HAHNDORF
☎ 08 / pop 1842

You could be forgiven for thinking you've arrived slap-bang in the centre of a German theme park when you reach Hahndorf. Located 28km southeast of Adelaide, it's the oldest surviving German settlement in Australia. Along the main street European trees flirt with gums and cascades of colourful flowers flow from half-wine barrels in front of antique, vintage and knick-knack shops. Settled in 1839 by Lutherans who left Prussia to escape religious persecution, the town took its name from the ship's captain, Hahn; *dorf* is German for village.

The 1857 **Hahndorf Academy** (☎ 8388 7250; 68 Main St; ☽ 10am-5pm Mon-Sat, noon-5pm Sun) houses an art gallery with rotating exhibitions and several original sketches by Sir Hans Heysen, once a famed landscape artist and resident of Hahndorf. The attached **German Immigration Museum** is worth the gold coin donation. It illustrates the early life of German settlers in the Adelaide Hills and has an extensive collection of bizarrely carved pipes.

You'll see more than 300 of Sir Hans' original works on a tour through his studio and house, the **Cedars** (☎ 8388 7277; Heysen Rd; tours $8; ☽ 11am, 1pm & 3pm Sun-Fri), about 2km northwest of Hahndorf.

Pick your own strawberries between November and May from the famous **Beerenberg Strawberry Farm** (☎ 8388 7272; Mount Barker Rd; ☽ 9am-5pm), also renowned for its plethora of jams, chutneys and sauces.

You can reach some quality wineries in the Hahndorf area from Balhannah Rd, off Main St in the centre of town, including **Shaw & Smith** (☎ 8398 0500; Lot 4 Jones Rd, Balhannah; ☽ 10am-4pm Sat & Sun), **Nepenthe Wines** (☎ 8388 4439; Jones Rd, Balhannah; ☽ 10am-4pm) and **Hahndorf Hill Winery** (☎ 8388 7512; Lot 10 Pains Rd, Hahndorf; ☽ 10am-5pm).

Sleeping & Eating

The B&B accommodation in Hahndorf and its surrounds can be booked through the Adelaide Hills visitor information centre.

Hahndorf Resort (☎ 1800 350 143; www.hahndorfresort.com.au; 145 Main St, Hahndorf; powered/unpowered sites per 2 people $16.50/15, cabins from $50, d motel $95, chalets $100-145; ✶ ☐ ☎) In keeping with the local theme, Bavarian-style chalets encircle this sprawling resort, complete with tennis courts, a swimming pool and a fauna park. Located 1.5km from town, bus Nos 840 and 164F stop at the gate. Half-/full-day bike hire costs $7.50/15.

Hahndorf Inn Motor Lodge (☎ 8388 1000; 35 Main St; tw/d/f $95/100/130, Sat night extra $10; ✶ ☎) Behind the Hahndorf Inn in the centre of town, you'll find comfortable motel rooms of the exposed brick era. Facilities include an indoor pool, BBQ and laundry.

Wurst, sauerkraut, pretzels, strudel and German beer abound in Hahndorf.

Café Dalila (☎ 8388 1072; 23 Main St; dishes $8-14; ☽ breakfast & lunch) Delightful results come out of a French, Israeli and Middle Eastern mix in a scrumptious range of baguettes, platters and supreme soups.

Casalinga (☎ 8388 7877; 49 Main St; pizza & pasta $10-16.90, mains $18-20; ☽ dinner) This friendly local haunt pumps out pizza, pasta and the like, made from the best ingredients. Live acoustic music on Friday.

Hahndorf Inn (☎ 8388 1000; 35A Main St; breakfast $4.50-15, mains $10-22; ☽ breakfast, lunch & dinner) Fancy a meal of cheese Krasky, Vienna sausage, sauerkraut and apple strudel? Gather around a wine barrel with a stein of German beer (on tap) and soak up the friendly buzz.

FLEURIEU PENINSULA

South of Adelaide, the Fleurieu (*floo*-ree-oh) Peninsula is a mecca for vacationing and day-tripping Adelaidians, and for good reason: the coastline has fantastic vast beaches that never feel crowded, while the adjacent rolling hills of the lower Mt Lofty Ranges create vivid, contrasting landscapes. The area's residential and inland farming communities have maintained their idiosyncratic character, with the inevitable tourist hustle kept to a few towns. Deep Creek Conservation Park and Onkaparinga River Recreational Park are equipped with beautiful bouncing fauna, and boutique wineries are dotted like little liquid gems throughout the whole peninsula.

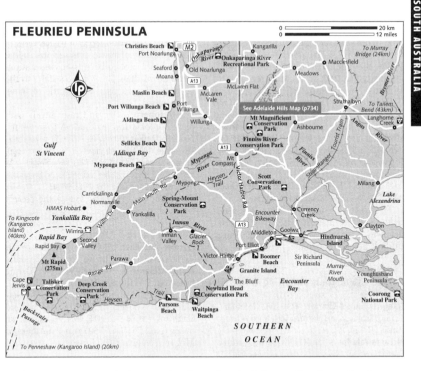

FLEURIEU PENINSULA

The region was named after Napoleon's naval minister and the man responsible for financing explorer Nicholas Baudin's Australian expedition. In the early days, settlers on the peninsula ran a smuggling business, but this was replaced by whaling in 1837 from Encounter Bay. Protected baby whales and their doting mothers can now be watched capering off the southern beaches.

MCLAREN VALE WINE REGION

Infiltrated by worshippers of the gourmet gods, McLaren Vale (37km from Adelaide) has plenty of ways to delight the senses. Most of the 48 wineries with cellar-door sales are within a few minutes' drive or satisfying bike ride from the town centre. The area is particularly well suited to red wines.

McLaren Vale & Fleurieu visitor information centre (☎ 08-8323 9944; www.mclarenvale.info/; Main Rd; ☺ 9am-5pm Mon-Fri, 10am-5pm Sat & Sun), at the northern end of McLaren Vale, shares space with **Stump Hill Café & Wine Bar** (☎ 08-8323 8999), which offers tastings from local wineries

that don't have cellar doors. For Internet access, try **McLaren Vale Video** (☎ 08-8323 8503; 165 Main Rd).

McLaren Vale's main events are its **Wine Bushing Festival** (late October or early November) and **Sea and the Vines Festival** (June long weekend).

Sights & Activities

Wineries with great wines available for cellar door tastings include, among others: **Wirra Wirra**, home of the sensational 'wood henge'; **Fox Creek Wines**, which produces a top Shiraz – the Last Chance Reserve Shiraz; **Coriole Vineyards**, with delightful gardens, cheeses and olives; and **Chapel Hill**, which has beautiful views. You can cover all bases by teaming your tastings with perfectly matched dishes and good atmosphere at some great cellar door–restaurant combos, including **d'Arry's Verandah** (☎ 08-8323 8710; www.darenberg.com.au; Osborne Rd) restaurant at d'Arenberg and **Woodstock Winery & Coterie** (☎ 08-8323 0156; Douglas Gully Rd).

A great way to see the area and sample its delights is to both hire a bike (per three hours/one day $21/30) and buy a cheese box (from $10 per person) from **Blessed Cheese** (☎ 08-8323 7958; www.blessedcheese.com.au; 150 Main St), then hit the old railway line **walking and cycling track** from McLaren Vale to Willunga, 6km south.

Pick up a *McLaren Vale Heritage Trail* brochure from the visitor information centre for a guided stroll through town, stopping along the way at **Dridan Fine Arts** (☎ 08-8323 9866; www.dridanfinearts.com.au; Hardy's Tintara, Main Rd; ☾ 10am-5pm), which displays fine local artisans' work.

Smooth is the word at **David Medlow Chocolates** (☎ 08-8323 8818; McLaren on the Lake, Kangarilla Rd; ☾ 10am-5pm), from the Belgian chocolates to the soft pectin fruit gels, but you won't get away from wines here – a vintage Shiraz in dark Belgian chocolate, perhaps?

Tours

For details of tours departing from Adelaide, see p711.

Integrity Tours & Charter (☎ 08-8382 9755, 0402 120 361) Runs tours that also cover Goolwa and Victor Harbor.

McLaren Vale Tours (☎ 0414 784 666; www.mclarenvaletours.com.au) Allows you to create your own tour ($50 per person, 3½ hours aided with suggestions for boutique wineries and gourmet producers in the Vale).

Southern Spirit (☎ 0407 223 361) Organises tours and has a limousine and minibus for hire.

Sleeping & Eating

The visitor information centre can advise on and book B&B accommodation throughout the southern vales.

McLaren Vale Motel (☎ 1800 631 817, 08-8323 8265; www.mclarenvalemotel.com.au; Caffrey St; s/d from $90/105, per child $10; ☒ ☐ ☒) This single-level motel has spacious units, a palm-fringed central pool in which to lounge around between winery visits, and complimentary laundry facilities. The motel is close to the visitor information centre, and is a digestive walk from main street restaurants.

McLaren Vale Lakeside Caravan Park (☎ 08-8323 9255; www.mclarenvale.net; Field St; powered/unpowered sites per 2 people $22/18, caravans/cabins with bathroom from $50/75; ☒) In a pretty rural setting by a creek close to town, this pristine place with excellent facilities provides the only budget accommodation in McLaren Vale and has information on possible work at wineries.

Salopian Inn (☎ 08-8323 8769; cnr Willunga & McMurtrie Rds; mains $16-30; ☾ lunch Thu-Tue, dinner Fri & Sat) Just out of town, this serious foodie haunt has a 'not-to-be-missed' reputation. Head down the stone cottage's stairs to the cellar to choose your own bottle of wine. Book ahead.

For superb coffee and tasty meals with plenty of local and regional SA ingredients, head to **Market 190** (☎ 08-8323 8558; www.market 190.com.au; 190 Main Rd; meals $6-14; ☾ 8am-6pm), **Blessed Cheese** (☎ 08-8323 7958; www.blessedcheese .com.au; 150 Main St; dishes around $8; ☾ breakfast & lunch) or **Tin Shed Café** (☎ 08-8323 7343; 225 Main Rd; meals $3.90-10.90; ☾ breakfast & lunch), the cosiest tin shed in town.

Getting There & Around

Premier Stateliner (☎ 08-8415 5555; www.premier stateliner.com.au) runs up to four buses daily from Adelaide to McLaren Vale ($6.70, one hour) and Willunga ($7.10, 70 minutes). Regular suburban trains run between Adelaide and Noarlunga Centre and several **SouthLink** (☎ 08-8186 2888; www.southlink.com.au) buses (Nos 751 and 752) run from here to McLaren Vale and Willunga.

WILLUNGA

☎ 08 / pop 1200

Intriguing, arty Willunga took off in 1840 when high-quality slate was mined nearby and exported all around Australia. Today, the restored old buildings in this quiet, pretty little town house gourmet eateries and galleries showcasing the work of established and emerging fine artists. The town comes into full bloom during its **Almond Blossom Festival** in July.

Willunga is nearby to the **Kuitpo Forest** to the northeast and small conservation parks to the southeast, including **Mt Magnificent Conservation Park**, 13km from Willunga.

Sleeping & Eating

Willunga Hotel (☎ 8556 2135; High St; s/d without bathroom $30/60, dishes $16-20; ☾ lunch & dinner) Straight-up pub rooms are the go here, along with a TV lounge. Simple pub meals are served in the old-style bistro.

Citrus & Sea & Vines Cottages (☎ 8295 8659; www.seavinescottage.com; d from $160; ☒) These beautifully restored stone cottages have the perfect proportions of cosiness and style. Breakfast provisions, complimentary wine, log fires and blooming cottage gardens are included. There's a minimum two-night stay ($340) on weekends.

Willunga House B&B (☎ 8556 2467; www.willungahouse.com.au; 1 St Peters Tce; d $160-220; 🖳) If you're looking for a real splurge, this graceful old mansion off the main street might just be the place. Indulge in breakfast feasts overlooking the gardens.

Willie Hill Café (☎ 8556 2379; 27 High St; breakfast $3.90-10.50, mains $8.50-14.50; ⏲ breakfast, lunch & dinner) All your prayers will be answered at this eclectic café–cum–art space in a decommissioned stone church. Cleanse your palate with tangy, freshly pressed juices and there'll be no room for guilt.

Russell's (☎ 8556 2571; pizzas $12-16; ⏲ dinner Fri) It may resemble a ramshackle chicken coup, but it's the place to be on Friday evening for wood-fired pizza. No one minds the wait for a meal – it's all about the atmosphere.

GULF ST VINCENT BEACHES

There are superb swimming beaches along the Gulf St Vincent coastline, extending from **Christies Beach**, popular with experienced surfers, onto the partially nudist and gay hang-out (at the southern end) of **Maslin Beach**. Nearby **Port Willunga** is home to acclaimed cliff-top restaurant the **Star of Greece** (☎ 08-8557 7420; The Esplanade; mains $20-35; ⏲ lunch), serving fabulous seafood and sensational views. **Sellicks Beach** is home of jovial pub the **Victory** (☎ 08-8556 3083; Main South Rd; mains $12-22), also with fine views, good food and an impressive cellar. Beyond here the coastline becomes rockier. There are good beaches at **Carrickalinga** and **Normanville**.

See p710 for information on diving along this coast.

Deep Creek Conservation Park runs along the south coast near Cape Jervis and the Kangaroo Island ferry terminal, with walking tracks (including the Heysen Trail) and bush camping areas.

Ferries for Kangaroo Island (see p745) depart from Wirrina and Cape Jervis.

VICTOR HARBOR

☎ 08 / pop 8968

A row of towering pines lines the foreshore of this magnet for holiday-makers and retirees seeking sun, water sports and golf courses. Victor Harbor (www.victor.sa.gov.au), 84km south of Adelaide, overlooks

Granite Island and Encounter Bay, where Matthew Flinders and Baudin had an historic meeting in 1802. Victor was founded as a sealing and whaling centre in 1837 but the unrestrained slaughter of southern right whales, on which the industry was based, eventually made operations unfeasible, and they ceased in 1864.

A 10-minute drive gets you to the fabulous beaches of Middleton and Goolwa, beloved of surfers and beach layabouts of all ages. Or hire a bicycle – the 23km sealed Encounter Bikeway follows the coastline between Victor Harbor's Bluff and Goolwa.

Victor Harbor is protected from the angry Southern Ocean by lichen-covered, boulder-strewn Granite Island, connected to the mainland by a causeway.

Information

Victor Harbor visitor information centre (☎ 8552 5738; www.tourismvictorharbor.com.au; ⏲ 9am-5pm; 🖳) Found at the mainland end of the Granite Island causeway, this centre can book accommodation and tours and has Internet access.

Sights & Activities

Between June and September, you may be lucky enough to see a **southern right whale** swimming near the causeway. Victor Harbor is on the migratory path of these splendid animals. Head to the Bluff for a good lookout point. The **South Australian Whale Centre** (☎ 8552 5644; www.sawhalecentre.com; 2 Railway Tce; adult/student $6/4.50; ⏲ 11am-4.30pm), opposite the causeway, has awe-inspiring displays of Victor's largest visitors. Engaging kids' programmes ($6) are run during holidays.

You can ride over the causeway to Granite Island on the 1894 double-decker **horse-drawn tram** (one way adult/child/family $4/3/12; ⏲ trips every 40min 10am-4pm).

The island has the 'Kaiki Walk' (1.5km circuit, 40 minutes) and is a rookery for penguins. **Granite Island Nature Park** (☎ 8852 7555; www.graniteisland.com.au) runs the **Penguin Centre** (adult/child/family $4/2/10; ⏲ 12.30-3.30pm Sat, Sun & holidays), which details the little penguins' breeding, habits and behaviour. **Granite Island Eco Tours** (☎ 8552 7555) operate various **dolphin and seal cruises** (adult/child $40/28), and one-hour **guided walks** (adult/child/family $12.50/9/36; ⏲ walks winter/summer 6pm/9pm) to witness the penguins haul out of the water then along the north shore between the causeway and jetty after sunset. These walks leave from the centre at dusk (leave your camera flash behind). You can also watch sharks being fed through underwater windows, depending upon visibility of the water, at the **Below Decks Shark Aquarium** (adult $15; 11am-5pm). Contact **Regardless** (0413 854 511) about whale and dolphin cruises.

Back on the mainland, the **Encounter Coast Discovery Centre** (8552 5388; 2 Flinders Pde; adult/concession/child/family $4/3/2/10; 1-4pm), opposite the Causeway, explores local history from pre-European times to around 1900 and includes the **Old Customs House & Station Master's Residence** (1866), set up in its original state.

Sleeping

Holiday apartments are a particularly good option for longer stays; contact **LJ Hooker** (8552 1944; www.ljhooker.com.au; 73 Ocean St) or **Fleurieu Booking Office** (1800 241 033, 8552 1033; fpbo.com.au; 66 Ocean St). Book B&Bs through the visitor information centre.

Anchorage (8552 5970; anchoragevh@ozemail .com.au; cnr Coral St & Flinders Pde; s/d incl breakfast from $85/120;) This heritage-listed grand villa on the seafront is the pick of the bunch. Most of its comfortable rooms are on the beachside, some with balconies overlooking the bay. The spa rooms are pretty swish. Budget rooms also available.

Hotel Victor (8552 1288; www.victorhotels.com .au; cnr The Esplanade & Albert Pl; s/d from $95/105, extra $12 Sat, bar meals $12-20; breakfast, lunch & dinner) There are often attractive packages (including dinner, pokie vouchers and golf transport) for these standard, compact motel rooms. Book ahead to nab a room overlooking Granite Island.

Whalers Inn Resort (8552 4400; www.whalers innresort.com.au; 121 Franklin Pde; d with/without balcony $170/100;) Out under the Bluff, this upmarket spot has sublime views overlooking the bay and islands, particularly from its restaurant/cocktail bar and upmarket rooms. Work out on the croquet lawn and tennis courts.

Victor Harbor Beachfront Caravan & Tourist Park (8552 1111; 114 Victoria St; sites per 2 people from $26, cabins with/without bathroom $68/56, villas $80) This grassy, treed spot has a playground and BBQs but is a bit of a hike from town on the grottier end of Victor's beach.

Eating

Original Victor Harbor Fish Shop (8552 1273; 20 Ocean St; lunch & dinner) This eat-in or take-away option was runner-up for the 2003 best fish and chips in SA award, but covers all bases with schnitzels, hamburgers, *yiros* (souvlaki) and roast chicken.

Anchorage Café (8552 5970; cnr Coral St & Flinders Pde; mains $14.50-22.50; breakfast, lunch & dinner) This is the salties' lair, with fishing nets trawling from the ceiling and a bar hewn from the hull of an old wooden whaling boat. It has a great atmosphere and a seafood-dominated Mediterranean-Greek meets Mod-Oz menu. Tuck into Devonshire tea or coffee and cake ($6.50) between meals. The beachside terrace benches are perfect for sundowners, year-round.

Beach House Café (8552 4417; 62 Franklin Rd, Encounter Bay; 9in pizzas $9-14, curries around $12; dinner) Is it Italian-style Indian or the other way around? You decide over your own butter chicken 'pizza with personality'. The beachside position overlooking Wright Island and the Bluff is spot on.

Getting There & Around

Premier Stateliner (08-8415 5555; www.premier stateliner.com.au) runs buses to Victor Harbor from Adelaide and continuing to Goolwa.

For details of bus connections to Kangaroo Island ferries departing from Cape Jervis and Wirrina, near Yankalilla, see p745.

Victor Harbor Cycles & Skates (8552 1417; 73 Victoria St; 9am-5.30pm Mon-Fri, 9am-noon Sat) rents out bikes for $10/25 per hour/day ($15 per day for rentals of more than three days). Helmets and locks are included, and baby seats ($5) are available. Book within office hours for weekend delivery.

You can rent cars through **Victor Rent-a-car** (8552 1033; 66 Ocean St). For taxi service, call the **Peninsular Taxi Group** (131 008, 8552 2622).

Steamranger Tourist Railway (8552 2782; www.steamranger.org.au; Victor Harbor Station), more scenic train rides than an actual mode of transport, runs the **Cockle Train** (one way/return $16/23), along the scenic Encounter Coast between Goolwa and Victor Harbor via Port Elliot every Sunday. **Southern Encounter** (return adult/child/family $52/31/135) does a return trip from Mt Barker to Victor Harbor via Strathalbyn, Goolwa and Port Elliot on alternate Sundays.

PORT ELLIOT

☎ 08 / pop 1527

On Encounter Bay just 8km east of Victor Harbor, Port Elliot is the most charming of the towns along this stretch. Its historic heart synchronises with a bohemian verve, and the picturesque **Horseshoe Bay** offers a sheltered swimming beach and a cliff-top walk – great for spying whales in season. There's a surf life-saving club, and well-maintained showers beside the bowls club. **Commodore Point** at the eastern end is a good surf spot for experienced surfers, but there are better ones at nearby **Boomer Beach**, **Knights Beach** and **Middleton Beach**.

For surf-gear hire, head to **Southern Surf Shop** (☎ 8554 2376; 36 North Tce) or **Big Surf Australia** (☎ 8554 2399; Main Rd, Middleton); see p710 for details of surfing lessons. Those feeling less energetic can pick up a second-hand book at the **Bargain Barn** (☎ 8554 2103; 43 The Strand).

Sleeping & Eating

Holiday rentals can be organised through **Dodd & Paige** (☎ 8554 2029; 51 The Strand).

Royal Family Hotel (☎ 8554 2219; rfhotel@chariot .net.au; 32 North Tce; s/d without bathroom $30/40, mains $9-16; ⏲ lunch & dinner; ⚄) There are clean and simple time-warped rooms and a lounge at this family pub. The trad-pub food is popular with locals – Friday is schnitzel night while Sunday boasts roasts.

Arnella by the Sea (☎ 8554 3611; narnu@bigpond .com; 28 North Tce; dm/s/d $25/30/60) Fans of shabby-chic will love the cosy rooms, housed in Port Elliott's oldest building. There's a communal lounge and the kitchen has the works – or you can cook on the garden BBQ.

Thomas Henry B&B (☎ 8554 3388, 8 Charteris St; s/d $120/150) This lovely, doily-free old guesthouse has spacious fan-cooled rooms near a good whale-spotting cliff. In warm weather, you can eat the large cooked breakfast outside under the grape vines.

Trafalgar House B&B (☎ 8554 3888; www.trafal garhouse.com.au; cnr The Strand & Freeling St; d B&B from $125, cottage from $120) At the top of the hill equidistant from cafés, the beach and a whale-spotting cliff, this serene cottage has a log fire and lovely garden.

Port Elliot Tourist Park (☎ 8554 2134; www.port elliotcaravanpark.com.au; Middleton Rd; powered/unpowered sites per 2 people $28/24, cabins/units/cottages from $75/98/120, per extra person $7) In an unbeatable position nestled behind sand dunes on Horseshoe Bay, this grassy park has a laundry and all the Big-4 facilities. As with anywhere along the coast, it can be a touch on the windy side.

Flying Fish (1 The Foreshore; takeaway $9-14.50, mains $26-30; ⏲ lunch Sun-Thu, dinner Fri & Sat) Sit down for lunch and you'll be here all day – the views are sublime. Otherwise, grab a quality takeaway of Coopers-battered flathead (a type of fish) and chips and head back to the sand.

There's also a supermarket, takeaway joints and the *über*-popular Port Elliot Bakery on North Tce, which is the main street through town.

Getting There & Away

Premier Stateliner (☎ 8415 5555; www.premier stateliner.com.au) has daily services between Adelaide and Port Elliot ($16, two hours), linking the town to Victor Harbor and Goolwa.

GOOLWA

☎ 08 / pop 4345

A restful and unassuming place, Goolwa has the best beach on the southern coast. Water sports, fishing, skydiving and simple beach-pleasures are the preferred pastimes of locals and visitors alike. Whales (and dolphins) can be seen in season and artists revel in the glorious sunsets.

At the point where Australia's largest river, the Murray, enters the ocean, Goolwa initially grew with the developing river trade. In the 1880s, a new railway line to Adelaide from Murray Bridge spelt the end for Goolwa as a port town. However, boat building is a continuing art, celebrated in the biennial (March in odd-numbered years) **Wooden Boat Festival**.

Signal Point visitor information centre (☎ 8555 3488; The Wharf; ⏲ 9am-5pm) has plenty of literature and an interpretive centre (adult/child/family $5.50/2.75/13.20) with interactive displays on the life and ecology of the Murray River.

Sights & Activities

Goolwa Museum (☎ 8555 2221; 11 Porter St; adult/child $2.50/50c; ⏲ 2-4.30pm Tue-Thu, Sat & Sun, daily school holidays) sheds light on the town's past, the Murray River and ships that have come to grief nearby.

On the waterfront, a short walk upstream from the main wharf, is the **Goolwa Maritime Gallery**.

Head to **Barrell Surf & Skate** (☎ 8555 5422; 10C Cadell St) for gear hire (long-board/bodyboard/wetsuit $20/10/15). Jet skis, catamarans and sailboards can be hired on the waterfront between the wharf and the barrage. A bird-watching hide towards the **Goolwa Barrage** (⏰ 8am-5pm) spies on activity where fresh water meets the sea.

You can cycle along the stunning coastline from Goolwa to Victor Harbor on the **Encounter Bikeway Trail** (23km); maps are available at the visitor information centre.

Hindmarsh Island Bridge links the mainland with **Hindmarsh Island**. Development and sacred sites collided and disputes over the building of this aesthetically bland bridge continued for years, dividing local opinion, Aboriginal communities and the state's academic and political powerhouses. You can drive down to the Murray River mouth to see dredges working 24/7 to prevent the mouth from silting up. Tip: slather on mosquito repellent – those mozzies are voracious!

Tours

Spirit Australia Cruises (☎ 1800 442 203, 8555 2203; www.coorongcruises.com.au; Main Wharf) runs ecocruises on the Murray and Coorong Rivers, including lunch and guided walks. The MV *Aroona* takes cruises on the lower Murray (adult/child $35/20), while you can explore the Murray Mouth and Coorong on MV *Wetlands Explorer* (one day adult/child $75/45), a 4½-hour Coorong Discovery Cruise (adult/child $70/52), and a six-hour Coorong Adventure Cruise (adult/child $84/57). A five-day Great Murray River Run cruise to/from Border Cliffs costs $940 per person with a coach return. Bookings are essential.

Sleeping & Eating

Holiday rentals in and around Goolwa and Hindmarsh Island are managed by **LJ Hooker** (☎ 8555 1785; www.ljhooker.com.au/goolwa; 25 Cadell St) and the **Professionals** (☎ 8555 2122; www.professionalsgoolwa.com.au; 1 Cadell St), which has a good range of choices available at the lower end. Houses accommodating six people range from $250 to $700 per week in the off-season, and $450 to $1500 a week during December, January and Easter. Linen is required. Contact the visitor information centre (p741) for details on Goolwa's B&Bs, many of which are situated in beautifully refurbished cottages.

Narnu Farm (☎ 8555 2002; Monument Rd, Hindmarsh Island; cottages from $95; ⛹) This family-oriented, pioneer-style farm offers rustic cottages and plenty of animal activity.

Goolwa Central Motel (☎ 8555 1155; www.goolwacentral.bestwestern.com.au; 30 Cadell St; s/d from $110/120; ⛹ 🏊) These standard motel rooms in the centre of town are sparsely furnished, though the Kilkenny and Guinness served in the attached Irish pub should colour things up nicely.

Goolwa Caravan Park (☎ 1800 130 353, 8555 2737; www.goolwacaravanpark.com.au; Noble Ave; powered/unpowered sites per 2 people $20/16, cabins from $70; ⛹ 🏊) A swish park close to the river, 3.5km from town, with boat access to the river. Canoes, aquabikes and bicycle hire are available for guests.

Goolwa boasts three bakeries and plenty of fast-food joints.

Café Lime (☎ 8555 5522; 1/11 Goolwa Tce; dishes $8-14; ⏰ breakfast & lunch Fri-Wed) Take away a cone of salt and pepper squid with lime salted fries ($9.50), or nab a table to indulge in corn bread, baguettes and lip-smacking hot dishes. Espresso perfecto.

Hector's (☎ 8555 5885; Main Wharf; breakfast $4.50-10.50, mains $13.50-16; ⏰ breakfast, lunch & dinner Tue-Sun) Head to this breezy wharf-side haven for relaxed snacks and mixed café fare.

Beach House Café (☎ 8555 5055; Cadell St; 9in pizzas $9.60-14.50, curries $11.50-13; ⏰ dinner Thu-Sun) Wood-fired 'pizzas with a difference'. This sister of the Victor Harbor operation (p740) serves up treats such as tandoori lamb pizza with mozzarella and mango chutney.

Pub meals are served at Goolwa's two 1850s hotels: **Goolwa Hotel** (☎ 8555 2012; 7 Cadell St; mains $10-18; ⏰ lunch & dinner), adorned with the figurehead from the *Mozambique*, wrecked at the Murray Mouth in 1864, and nearby **Corio Hotel** (☎ 8555 2011; Railway Tce; mains $11-26; ⏰ lunch & dinner), with slightly more-upmarket meals.

Getting There & Around

Premier Stateliner (☎ 8415 5555; www.premierstateliner.com.au) runs several daily buses between Adelaide and Goolwa ($16, two hours).

For steam-train timetables, see p740.

KANGAROO ISLAND

Kangaroo Island, 13km off SA's coast, is part wildlife wonderland of birds, native animals and ocean-based creatures, and part significant agricultural region. Its wild, rugged coastline shelters beaches edged with turquoise seas, while the interior contains native forest and bush, 30% of which is maintained as conservation or national parks. Kangaroo Island's isolation from European diseases and feral species has greatly protected the island's native wildlife.

Many island place names are in French, attributed to the first thorough survey of its coast carried out in 1802 and 1803 by French explorer Nicholas Baudin. He found the island uninhabited, though archaeologists have since found evidence of Aboriginal habitation of about 2250 years ago. Baudin's English counterpart, Matthew Flinders, named the island after his crew enjoyed a feast of kangaroo meat here.

A motley collection of whalers, sealers, escaped convicts and ship deserters began to make their homes on the island. They brought Aboriginal women from Tasmania, and abducted others from the mainland. Before long, Kangaroo Island had a reputation as one of the most lawless and vicious places in the British Empire. The worst scoundrels were rounded up in 1827, and thereafter a rough sort of respectability was achieved.

South Australia's first official settlement was established on Kangaroo Island at Reeves Point (near Kingscote, in the island's northeast) in 1836. It struggled on for two years, but the lack of fresh water led most of the colonists to moved to Adelaide. Those who were left embarked on a semi-subsistence lifestyle.

While here, be sure to try the island's local produce, including fresh seafood and marron (a freshwater crayfish), honey produced by a pure strain of Ligurian bees, jams from indigenous fruits, sheep-milk cheeses, local wines and eucalyptus oil.

Information

The Royal Society of SA's *Natural History of Kangaroo Island* gives comprehensive

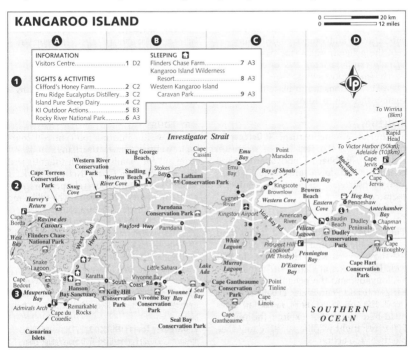

(though densely scientific) coverage of the island's natural history. *The Southern Land – Kangaroo Island*, by Jean M Nunn, gives an historical account of the island. You can get these from the visitor information centre near Penneshaw and the visitor information centre in Flinders Chase National Park.

There are banking facilities in Kingscote and Penneshaw (in the island's northeast). For medical assistance, contact the **Kangaroo Island Medical Clinic** (☎ 08-8553 2037; 64 Murray St, Kingscote) or **Kangaroo Island Hospital** (☎ 08-8553 4200; The Esplanade, Kingscote).

Bear in mind that mobile phone reception is only available in Kingscote, Penneshaw, American River, the airport and some areas of Emu Bay.

The **visitor information centre** (☎ 08-8553 1185; www.tourkangarooisland.com.au; ☺ 9am-5pm Mon-Fri, 10am-4pm Sat & Sun) is well stocked, and operated by knowledgeable staff. This rich asset provides good maps; books accommodation; and sells park entry tickets and Island Parks Passes. It's just outside Penneshaw on the road to Kingscote.

DEH (☎ 08-8553 2381; www.parks.sa.gov.au; 37 Dauncey St, Kingscote) also sells Island Parks Passes (adult/child/student/family $42/25/31/110), which cover DEH entry fees for all conservation areas and ranger-guided tours except the penguin walks (the passes do not include camping fees). Passes can also be purchased at most sights.

Fire restrictions are in place from 1 December through to 30 April.

Activities

Seeking an adrenalin rush? **KI Outdoor Actions** (☎ 08-8559 4295; South Coast Rd, Vivonne Bay) rents out surfboards, bodyboards, sand boards (to surf down some dunes), kayaks and windsurfers – along with a guide, if required.

Tours

The DEH operates guided tours and walks at the sea lion colony at Seal Bay, the show cave at Kelly Hill Caves, the historic lighthouses at Cape Borda and Cape Willoughby, and the penguin rookeries at Kingscote and Penneshaw. **KI Outdoor Actions** (☎ 08-8559 4295; South Coast Rd, Vivonne Bay) takes quad-bike tours that explore the outfit's 500 acres; night wildlife-spotting tours see plenty of roo action.

PACKAGE TOURS

The ferry operators (see Getting There & Away, opposite) and various Adelaide-based tour operators offer packages ex-Adelaide with coach and ferry passage; competition is fierce, so shop around to pick up a good deal. A plethora of one- to three-day coach tours (generally including accommodation and meals) are run by the following:

Adelaide Sightseeing (☎ 08-8231 4144; www .adelaidesightseeing.com.au) Takes some small group tours that visit the main sights.

Adventure Tours (☎ 1300 654 604; www.adventure tours.com.au) Has popular two-/three-day ex-Adelaide tours (from $320/445).

Camp Wild Adventures (☎ 08-8132 1333; www .campwild.com.au) Two-/three-day small-group wildlife safaris ($320/370) ex-Penneshaw including sand boarding, swimming, surfing and all the main sights. There are discounts for hostel memberships.

Kangaroo Island Ferry Connections (Map p714; ☎ 13 13 01, 08-8202 8688; www.sealink.com.au; 440 King William St, Central Adelaide) This range of day tours (from Kangaroo Island/Adelaide $99/181) can also be picked up on the island. The one-day tour from Adelaide is only for those extremely short on time. Overnight trips with two day tours cost $302.

Surf 'n' Sun (☎ 1800 786 386; www.surfnsun.com.au) Three-day 4WD tours ($340) with a strong focus on wildlife include snorkelling and a surfing lesson and depart from Adelaide.

Wayward Bus Touring Company (☎ 1300 653 510; www.waywardbus.com.au) Has backpacker-oriented two-day tours ($310) covering all the major sights; stays can be extended.

DAY TOURS

See the visitor information centre or tourism website (www.tourkangarooisland .com.au) for details of coach tours to Seal Bay and Flinders Chase National Park. If money is no object, several operators specialise in luxury 4WD tours. The following operators run small-group tours:

Adventure Charters of Kangaroo Island (☎ 08-8553 9119; www.adventurecharters.com.au) Small group, off-the-beaten-track 4WD tours (adult/child per day $295/200), exploring the various habitats and landscapes of Kangaroo Island. Great lunch spread…

Alkirna Nocturnal Tours (☎ 08-8553 7464; www .alkirna.com.au) Naturalist-led night tours view nocturnal creatures around American River (adult/child $52/34, two hours).

KI Discovery Tours (☎ 1800 228 2112; www.aust dreaming.com.au) Personalised 4WD tours (adult/child including lunch $198/148) to private areas just outside the national park.

KI Ferries (☎ 13 22 33) Day tours ($93) to Seal Bay and Flinders Chase National Park, or central sights (eucalyptus distillery, sheep dairy, beehives and wildlife park).

DIVING TOURS

The island's two operators cater for novice and experienced divers:

KI Diving Safaris (☎ 08-8559 3225; www.kidiving safaris.com; ☒) Charter operators offering double dives from Western River Cove ($250, including equipment) and various multiday packages with land- or boat-based accommodation. Hire gear is also available ($65).

KI Diving Services (☎ 08-8553 1072; www.kidiving .com) Offers 'discover scuba' half-day dives for novices ($89, including all gear), double boat dives ($138 including tank and weights, $30 extra for gear hire), and three-day Professional Association of Diving Instructors (PADI) Open-Water certification courses ($415 including full gear).

Sleeping

There are basic camping grounds within the Flinders Chase National Park and at American River, Antechamber Bay, Browns Beach, Stokes Bay, Vivonne Bay and Western River.

The main settlements of Kingscote and Penneshaw offer a range of accommodation including caravan parks, hostels, hotels and guesthouses, while American River has several motels and rental apartments. Just outside Flinders Chase National Park (p750), you'll also find the full range of accommodation. Packages can offer good value, particularly through the less frequented winter months.

Some of the most atmospheric accommodation can be found in the remote historic cottages for rent through **DEH** (☎ 08-8559 7235; www.environment.sa.gov.au/parks/; basic huts per person $15-20, cottages per 2 people $75-120). These range from basic huts to the lightkeepers' cottages (with bathrooms and lounges) at Cape Willoughby, Cape Borda and Cape du Couedic. Six-bed Mays Homestead and the basic Postmans Cottage are at Rocky River. Each has heating and some sort of cooking facilities.

There are plenty of B&Bs on Kangaroo Island, with plenty in the four-star range. These can be booked through the visitor information centre and **Ferry Island Connections** (☎ 1800 018 484, 08-8553 1233; www.ki-ferrycon nections.com). For stays of more than a few

nights, the best value can be found in **holiday house rentals** (d from $70) around the island, including the beach settlements of Emu Bay and Vivonne Bay. For listings, contact the visitor information centre or **Century 21** (☎ 08-8553 2688; www.century21.com.au/kangaroois land; 66 Dauncey St, Kingscote).

Getting There & Away

For flights between Adelaide and Kingscote (around $125), contact **Emu Airways** (☎ 08-8234 3711; www.emuairways.au), **Regional Express** (Rex; ☎ 13 17 13; www.regionalexpress.com.au) or **Great Western Airlines** (☎ 08-8355 9299).

If you don't have your own vehicle, catch the bus from Adelaide to Cape Jervis or Wirrina (near Yankalilla), and ferry across to the island. You can then hire a car (previously booked for collection) from the ferry terminus at Penneshaw or Kingscote. Bookings are essential.

Kangaroo Island Ferries (☎ 13 22 33; www.ki ferries.com.au) operates at least two daily ferries each way between Wirrina and Kingscote (one way adult/child/bicycle/car $30/14/5/64). Bus services to/from Adelaide (adult/child $14.50/8) and Goolwa/Victor Harbor ($9.50/5) are timed for each ferry.

Kangaroo Island Sealink (☎ 13 13 01) operates three vehicular ferries between Cape Jervis and Penneshaw daily (one way passenger/bicycle/car $32/5.50/70). It also operates a bus service connecting with ferry departures at Cape Jervis, with buses from Adelaide's central bus station (adult/student $18/15, two hours), and Goolwa and Victor Harbor ($12, 40 minutes).

Getting Around

Kangaroo Island is a big place and there is no public transport. Unless you're taking a tour, the only feasible way to get around is to bring or hire your own transport.

The island's main roads are sealed; some gravel roads can give you a wild ride if it's been a while since grading, including those to Cape Willoughby, Cape Borda and smaller coastal areas. To avoid coming to grief, overturning or 'going bush' on corners, take it slow. Roos and wallabies often leap onto roads, particularly from dusk to dawn; keep your speed under 70km/h at these times.

Petrol is available in Kingscote, Penneshaw, American River, Parndana, and in the west of the island at Vivonne Bay and Kangaroo Island Wilderness Resort (see Sleeping, p749), though this can be intermittent.

TO/FROM THE AIRPORT
The airport is 14km from Kingscote; a **shuttle bus** (☎ 08-8553 2390) connects the airport and Kingscote ($12).

TO/FROM THE FERRY LANDINGS
The **Sealink Shuttle** (☎ 13 13 01) connects with most ferries, linking Kingscote and American River with Penneshaw ($11). Bookings are essential.

CAR & MOTORCYCLE HIRE
Not all Adelaide car-rental companies will rent cars for Kangaroo Island trips. Due to the cost of transporting a car on the ferry, it is more economical (if you are going to hire a car) to make your way to Kangaroo Island and hire a car on the island – but book ahead. Car-hire companies:
Budget (☎ 08-8553 3133; www.budget.com.au; Kingscote airport)
Hertz (☎ 1800 088 296, 8553 2390; Kingscote airport)
Kirks Car Rentals (☎ 08-8598; 0011; thebookingoffice @Yankalilla.net.au) Has late-model vehicles, from Penneshaw and American River.

KINGSCOTE
☎ 08 / pop 1693
The quiet seaside town of Kingscote is the island's main settlement and sits 60km from Penneshaw and 117km from Flinders

Chase National Park. Most services are based here.

Stock up on reading material at **Lori's Web Book Exchange** (☎ 8553 9093; Dauncy St; ☼ 10am-5.30pm Wed-Fri, 9.30am-5.30pm Sat) and check your emails at the **library** (☎ 8553 2015; Dauncey St) for free.

Sights & Activities
The **tidal pool** about 500m south of the jetty is the best place in town to swim. However, most locals head out to the lovely **Emu Bay**, 18km away.

Hope Cottage Museum (☎ 8553 2656; Centenary Ave; admission $5; ☼ 1-4pm Feb-Dec, 10am-4pm Jan), built in 1857, overlooks Reeves Point and has some interesting memorabilia including a eucalyptus-oil distillery and an old lighthouse.

Each evening at 7.30pm and 8.30pm (9pm and 9.40pm during daylight saving) rangers take visitors on a fabulous **Discovering Penguins Walk** (adult/child $8/6.50). Tours depart outside the Ozone Hotel.

For a taste of what's lurking in the waters around Kangaroo Island (sea horses, seastars, giant cuttlefish etc), take a one-hour tour of the penguin colony and saltwater aquariums at the **KI Marine Centre** (☎ 8553 3112; Kingscote Wharf; adult/child $10/5; ☼ tours 7.30pm & 8.30pm, & 9.30pm daylight savings). Near the wharf, **bird feeding** (adult/child $2/free; ☼ 5pm) attracts around 40 of those majestic (if somewhat comical) beaked battleships – pelicans – as well as a Pacific gull or two.

WATCHING WILDLIFE ON KANGAROO ISLAND

Kangaroo Island's geographical isolation has mercifully kept it free from dingoes, rabbits and foxes. Thanks to this, native wildlife thrives in the island's pristine environment, and some threatened mainland species, such as the koala, platypus and ringtail possum, have been introduced to ensure their survival.

Kangaroos and Cape Barren geese are easily spotted at **Flinders Chase National Park**. If you're lucky you may see a platypus here as well.

Koalas can usually be seen at **Hanson Bay Sanctuary**. You can spot sea lions at **Seal Bay** and you're almost guaranteed a sighting of New Zealand fur seals at **Admirals Arch**. Sea lions are pale and large, while seals are smaller, darker and more lively. Echidnas, Tamar wallabies, goannas and possums are found around the island.

Divers will see leafy sea dragons – a beautiful species of sea horse – particularly off the northern coastline. Dolphins sometimes come in to Pelican Lagoon at **American River**. Southern right and minke whales are often spotted during the whale-watching season (June to September) – ask at the visitor information centre for whale-watching locations.

Bird life includes little penguins and pelicans, black cockatoos and black swans, as well as many other species.

KI Gallery (☎ 8553 2868; 1 Murray St; ☺ 10am-5pm) has an excellent selection of local arts and crafts.

In Cygnet River, 12km from Kingscote, **Island Pure Sheep Dairy** (☎ 8553 9110; Gum Creek Rd, Cygnet River; adult/child $5/4; ☺ 1-5pm) will take you on a journey through cheese production. You can also taste its highly regarded yoghurts and cheeses and watch sheep being milked (from 3pm).

Sleeping & Eating

KI Central Accommodation (☎ 8553 2787; 19 Murray St; dm/d without bathroom $20/50) Near Kingscote's main strip, this small and well-maintained hostel has a homey communal lounge and kitchen.

Queenscliffe Family Hotel (☎ 8553 2254; 57 Dauncey St; s/d incl breakfast $70/80, lunch mains $6.50-12.50, dinner mains $10-19.50; ☺ lunch & dinner) The comfortable, old rooms at this pub can get noisy if over the bar. Bistro dishes range from grills and island seafood to stir-fries and a curry of the day.

Ozone Hotel (☎ 1800 083 133, 8553 2249; www .ozonehotel.com; Kingscote Tce; d/tr/f from $114/127/165, lunch mains $7.50-8.50, dinner mains $11-27; ☺ breakfast, lunch & dinner; ✖ 🖳 🖭) Opposite the foreshore with million-dollar waterfront views, the Ozone has modern rooms, a pool and spa. The bistro menu features some of the best food in town (mostly grills and seafood) and there are plenty of Kangaroo Island wines to try at the bar.

Kangaroo Island Seaview Motel (☎ 8553 2368; www.seaview.net.au; 51 Chapman Tce; s/d/f $120/135/180) Soak up the views at this charming and central old-style guesthouse overlooking the bay. Choose from comfortable rooms with shared facilities or motel units (some with kitchens).

Kingscote Nepean Bay Tourist Park (☎ 8553 2394; www.kingscotetourist.citysearch.com.au; Third Ave; powered/unpowered sites per 2 people $20/17; cabins with/without bathrooms from $75/45) In Brownlow, about 3km southwest of Kingscote, you'll find the full camping-resort range of accommodation and good facilities. There's a breezy coastal walking trail from here to Kingscote.

Roger's Deli (☎ 8553 2053; Dauncey St; meals $4-16; ☺ breakfast & lunch) You can get all manner of tasty burgers, daily specials, sweet things and coffee at this bakery-deli-newsagency. There are deli foods to take away, too.

Bella (☎ 8553 0400; 54 Dauncey St; lunch $7-15, small pizzas $11-13.50, mains $15-25; ☺ noon-late) Dine indoors or alfresco at Bella's popular Italian café–restaurant–pizza bar, which also sells takeaway pizza and hot BBQ chickens.

AMERICAN RIVER
☎ 08 / pop 250

Between Kingscote (37km away) and Penneshaw (32km away), this small settlement takes its name from the American sealers who built a boat here in 1804. The town is on a small peninsula and shelters an inner bay (named **Pelican Lagoon** by Flinders), which is now an aquatic reserve. **Fishing** is the main recreation, with boat charters readily available.

You can watch **pelican feeding** at 5pm down on the wharf.

Nestled among trees, opposite the foreshore, **Island Coastal Units** (☎ 8553 7010; www .kangaroo-island-au.com/coastalunits; d cabins from $66, self-contained units from $95) are equipped with TVs, fans and heating; the units also contain kitchens. BBQs and meatpacks are available.

Sit on the balcony of your self-contained cabin and watch the birds on Eastern Cove at **Ulonga Lodge** (☎ 8553 7171; www.ulonga.com .au; The Esplanade; cabins $105, 2-bedroom cottage $135; breakfast for 2 $25). There's a café and rowboats for guests to paddle around in, while the knowledgeable owners can book tours and fishing trips.

Kangaroo Island Lodge (☎ 8553 7053; www.ki lodge.com.au; The Esplanade; d $140-180, extra person $23; breakfast buffet from $14, dinner mains $21-25; ☺ breakfast & dinner; ✖ 🖭) has comfortable motel suites with fridge and TV overlooking the pool or American River. The bar and restaurant, the latter serving island specialities and seafood, are open to all.

PENNESHAW & DUDLEY PENINSULA
Looking across Backstairs Passage to the Fleurieu Peninsula, Penneshaw (population 400) is the arrival point for ferries from Cape Jervis, and dolphins can often be seen from the jetty.

There are not many places where locals can boast fairies in the bottom of their gardens. But you'll hear 'fairy' penguins clacking their safety call, a cross between a duck and dog yap, all over this quiet town at night.

Grimshaw's Corner Store & Cafe (cnr Third St & North Tce, Penneshaw) has an ATM and the **post office** (Nat Thomas St, Penneshaw; 9am-5pm Mon-Fri & 9-11am Sat) acts as a bank agency, with Eftpos cash-withdrawal facilities.

Sights & Activities

On the foreshore near the ferry terminal, **Penneshaw Penguin Centre** (08-8553 1103; tours adult/child/family $8/6.50/20; tours 7.30pm & 8.30pm winter, 8.30pm & 9.30pm summer), allows for close-up, unobtrusive views of the **little penguins** that nest along the shore as they ply the penguin highway. This is possibly the best place to see them in Australia. Book ahead and leave camera flashes behind.

Artefacts from local shipwrecks and early settlement memorabilia is on display at **Penneshaw Maritime & Folk Museum** (Howard Dr, Penneshaw; adult/child/family $3/2/7; 10am-noon & 3-5pm Mon, Wed & Sat).

The **Cape Willoughby Lightstation** (08-8553 1191; Willoughby Rd, Cape Willoughby), 28km southeast of town, first operated in 1852 and is now used as a weather station. Tours (adult/child/family $10.50/6.50/28) run at 11.30am, 12.30pm and 2pm, and also 3.15pm and 4pm in holiday periods.

About 24km out of Penneshaw towards Kingscote, you come to a steep staircase leading up to **Prospect Hill**, from where Flinders mapped the coast. There are panoramic views north towards American River and south over **Pennington Bay**, one of the island's best surfing and surf-fishing spots.

Sleeping & Eating

The visitor information centre (see p744) issues camping permits for bush sites at Chapman River, Brown Beach and American River.

Kangaroo Island Seafront (08-8553 1028; www.seafront.com.au; 49 North Tce, Penneshaw; d/tr from $120/145, chalets $195, cottages $175, restaurant mains $16.50-24.50; breakfast & dinner;) This hilltop hotel has pretty standard motel-style rooms in the original guesthouse. Nestled behind native trees, secluded self-contained chalets and cottages sleep up to three and six people respectively. The attached beachy Sorrento's Restaurant serves Kangaroo Island produce and local seafood.

Seaview Lodge (08-8553 1132; www.seaviewlodge.com.au; Willoughby Rd; tw & d $155, 3-course din-

ner $55) This gracious B&B is in a beautifully restored 1860 farm homestead with cottage gardens and lovely ocean views. Some rooms boast four-poster beds and fireplaces.

Penguin Walk YHA Hostel (08-8553 1344; www.yha.com.au; 33 Middle Tce, Penneshaw; dm/d without bathroom $23/60, d/tr with bathroom $75/90;) The YHA's spacious, tiled rooms have linen, and there are large luggage lockers. There's also a small communal kitchen and lounge, a laundry, and resident penguins in the garden overlooking Hog Bay.

Penguin Stop Café (08-8553 1211; Middle Tce, Penneshaw; dishes $7-12; 10am-5pm Mon-Fri, 9am-4pm Sat) Kangaroo Island's gourmet specialists serve up local produce in snapping-fresh lunches and mouthwatering cakes. Pre-order picnic hampers to sample the island's fare on the go.

NORTH COAST ROAD

The 5km-long, white sandy beach at **Emu Bay**, situated 18km from Kingscote, is one of the island's best spots for swimming. About 36km further west, **Stokes Bay** features a beautiful beach, a penguin rookery and a large rock pool that is reachable through a natural tunnel among huge boulders. Note that there's a dangerous rip located outside the pool.

Other good beaches include **Snelling Beach** and **Western River Cove**.

Sleeping & Eating

Plenty of fully equipped holiday rentals are available in Emu Bay – many of which are built on the hill and maximise stunning views of the bay. You'll need to bring your own supplies. For details, see Sleeping, p745, or contact the following:

Wintersun (08-8553 5163; www.emubayholidays.com.au; Emu Bay; d from $100, per extra person $15;) Neat and modern two-bedroom beachside units and three-bedroom houses.

Emu Bay Holiday Homes (08-8553 5241; www.emubaysuperviews.com.au; r per person from $35) Cosy (and a bit frilly) cabins and holiday homes on a property set back a bit from the beach, but with expansive views. A cot and highchair are available.

Kangaroo Island Experience & Rock Pool Cafe (08-8559 2277; www.kiexperience.com; Stokes Bay; unpowered sites per 2 people $10, luxury tents d $130) At Stokes Bay, you can dine alfresco on seafood with a glass of local wine.

SOUTH COAST ROAD

The south coast is rough and wave swept compared with the north.

A detour off Hog Bay or Birchmore Rds takes you past the **Emu Ridge Eucalyptus Distillery** (☎ 08-8553 8228; Willsons Rd, MacGillivary; 🕙 9am-2pm), a self-sufficient operation extracting eucalyptus oil from the Kangaroo Island narrow-leaf mallee. The attached craft gallery sells lots of eucalyptus oil products.

It's almost worth swimming the Backstairs Passage for the honey ice-cream at nearby **Clifford's Honey Farm** (☎ 08-8553 8295; Elsegood Rd, MacGillivary; 🕙 9am-5pm), and to taste a few of the honeys made by the last remaining colony of pure Ligurian bees – the mallee variety is like liquid gold.

At **Seal Bay Conservation Park** (☎ 08-8559 4207; tours adult/child/family $12.50/7.50/24), 60km southwest of Kingscote, ranger-guided tours stroll the beach alongside a large colony of (mostly sleeping) Australian sea lions. Tours (beach and boardwalk) depart from here between 9am and 4.15pm (7pm during summer holidays).

Back on South Coast Rd, the next turn-off on your left (just before the Eleanor River, about 7km from the Seal Bay road) will take you to **Little Sahara**, a vast expanse of white sandhills.

Further west, **Vivonne Bay** is a quiet settlement with a general store and beautiful sweeping beach. It's a good surfing spot but seek local advice before plunging in as there are some fierce undertows. KI Outdoor Action, just east of town, offers plenty of activities (see Activities, p744).

Getting close to Flinders Chase National Park is **Kelly Hill Conservation Park** (☎ 08-8559 7231; show caves adult/child/family $10.50/6.50/28), a series of dry limestone caves that were 'discovered' in the 1880s by a horse named Kelly, which fell into them through a hole. Tours leave every 45 minutes between 10am and 4.15pm, more regularly during school holidays. Adventure caving tours (adult/child/family $26.50/16/71) depart at 2pm; book ahead. The **Hanson Bay Walk** (9km) weaves past mallee scrub and freshwater wetlands to fine coastal views at the mouth of South West River at Hanson Bay.

Sleeping & Eating

Flinders Chase Farm (☎ 08-8559 7223; chillers@internode.on.net; West End Hwy; dm/cabins $20/50, d & tw 70)

There's a casual charm to this farm, about 10 minutes' drive from Rocky River, with rustic 'love shacks', dorms in wooden buildings, and tropical bathrooms. There's a good outdoor kitchen and campfire area, and roaming kangaroos.

Kangaroo Island Wilderness Resort (☎ 08-8559 7275; www.austdreaming.com.au; South Coast Rd; dm $40, d $120-180, ste $270-330, bar meals $10-20, restaurant mains $29-28; 🍴 💻) This well-planned eco-resort on the national park's boundary provides its guests with an overwhelming wildlife experience. Typical counter meals (such as schnitzel and grills) are available at the wall-less Bushman's Bar, while the restaurant serves Mod-Oz cuisine with plenty of local ingredients. Limited groceries, takeaway foods and petrol are available at the shop.

Western Kangaroo Island Caravan Park (☎ 08-8559 7201; www.westernki.com.au; South Coast Rd; powered/unpowered sites per 2 people $21/17, self-contained cabins $90-120; 🍴) Just a few minutes' drive east of Rocky River, this ultrafriendly, farm-based caravan park has a camp kitchen and laundry. Check out the koala walk and the very cool telephone cabin in an old bakery truck. The shop sells limited groceries, tasty homemade heat-and-eat meals and (for guests only) beer and wine.

FLINDERS CHASE NATIONAL PARK

Occupying the western end of the island, Flinders Chase is one of SA's most significant national parks. Much of the park is mallee scrub, but there are some beautiful, tall sugar-gum forests, particularly around Rocky River and the Ravine des Casoars, 5km south of Cape Borda. There's wild, often spectacular, scenery right around the coast, reached via roads and walking tracks.

The **Flinders Chase visitor information centre** (☎ 08-8559 7235; Rocky River; 🕙 9am-5pm summer, 10am-5pm rest of year) supplies useful information and park maps, has excellent displays on the changing landscape of the island, stocks souvenirs and books on the island and has a good café and toilets.

Sights & Activities

Once a farm, **Rocky River National Park** is a great spot to see wildlife, with plenty of roos, wallabies and Cape Barren geese lining the inbound road. Good walks start

SOUTH AUSTRALIA

from behind the visitor information centre, including one to potentially view the elusive platypus (4.5km return).

From Rocky River the road leads south to a 1906 lighthouse perched on top of wild and remote **Cape du Couedic**. A boardwalk leads down to **Admirals Arch** (a spectacular archway formed by pounding seas) and passes through a colony of New Zealand fur seals, which are fascinating to watch once you get used to the ripe smell.

At Kirkpatrick Point, 2km east of Cape du Couedic, **Remarkable Rocks** is a cluster of huge, weather-sculpted granite boulders perched on a dome that swoops down to the sea.

On the northwestern corner of the island, **Cape Borda** (☎ 08-8559 3257) features an 1858 lighthouse atop soaring cliffs. Guided tours (adult/child/student $10.50/6.50/28) depart at 11am, 12.30pm and 2pm, with extra tours at 3.15pm and 4pm during summer holidays. At nearby **Harvey's Return** there are great views and a poignant cemetery on the cliff top. From here you can drive to **Ravine des Casoars**, where a beautiful walking trail (6.5km return) leads down to the coast. This lovely spot was named by Baudin after the dwarf emus he saw there (*casoars* means 'cassowaries'). The species became extinct soon after European settlement.

Sleeping & Eating

Within Flinders Chase, the main **camp site** (unpowered sites with car & up to 5 people $19.50, per extra person $5.50) is at Rocky River, with shower facilities, roaming wildlife, walking tracks and the luxury of the visitor information centre's **Chase café** (dishes $5.50-12.50; 9am-5pm), which serves hot and cold dishes. There are also basic sites at **Snake Lagoon**, **West Bay** and **Harveys Return** (sites with car & up to 5 people $6.50, per person $4). Keep all food secured in your car if you have one. The DEH has some beautiful refurbished heritage accommodation at Rocky River, Cape du Couedic and Cape Borda; see Sleeping (p745) for details.

See p749 for options just outside the national park.

BAROSSA VALLEY

The Barossa Valley, 55km northeast of Adelaide, is Australia's best-known wine district. Its gnarled old vineyards have been producing wines for around 160 years – about 65,000 tonnes of grapes are now crushed here annually (a quarter of the Australian vintage) producing some immensely quaffable red wines. International judges agree, rating wines such as Penfolds Grange, the Barossa Valley Estate's Black Pepper Shiraz, Two Hand's Area and Henschke's Hill of Grace (from nearby Eden Valley) highly on a world scale. The region's 60 wineries all lie within easy reach of each other.

The rolling landscape is dotted with modest Lutheran churches and old cottages that date back to the original settlement of 1842. Fleeing religious persecution in Prussia and Silesia, these first settlers weren't actually wine makers, but came clutching vines that are the origin of today's full and silky red wines. Prior to WWI, place names in the Barossa sounded even more Germanic, but during the war many names were patriotically anglicised.

If you have the time, make your own way up to the Barossa, as many of the wineries are within walking/cycling distance and you'll get a greater variety and choice than if you take a tour.

Try a scenic drive: about 7km southwest of Lyndoch, en route from Adelaide (via Gawler), you'll find the famous Whispering Wall, a concrete dam wall with amazing acoustics. Normal conversations held at one end can be heard clearly at the other, 150m away – so sing your lungs out! Turn off the main road southeast of Tanunda and take the drive through the sleepy hamlet of Bethany, the first German settlement in the valley, and via Menglers Hill Lookout for a superb view over the valley before reaching Angaston (possibly detouring to Eden Valley) and Nuriootpa. This route runs through beautiful, rural country featuring large gums. From Nuriootpa, take the palm-fringed road to Seppeltsfield and Marananga, before heading back to Tanunda.

Information

The **Barossa council library** (9am-5pm Mon-Fri, to noon Sat; Tanunda 83 Murray St; Nuriootpa 10 Murray St) has free Internet access.

The **visitor information centre** (☎ 1300 852 982, 08-8563 0600; www.barossa-region.org; 66 Murray St, Tanunda; 9am-5pm Mon-Fri, 10am-4pm Sat & Sun) stocks a plethora of info on local sights, B&B

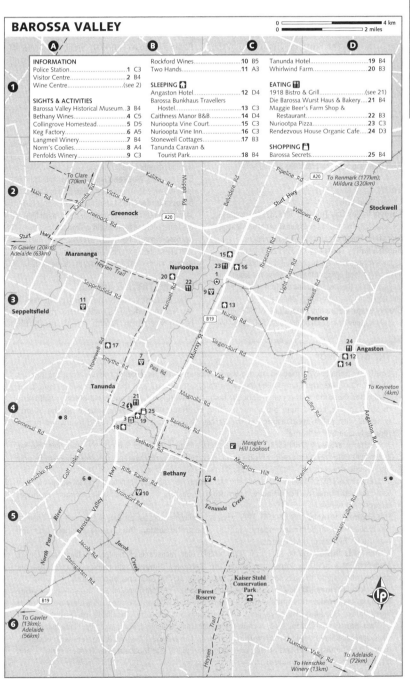

BAROSSA VALLEY

0 ——— 4 km
0 ——— 2 miles

INFORMATION
Police Station...........................1 C3
Visitor Centre...........................2 B4
Wine Centre.........................(see 2)

SIGHTS & ACTIVITIES
Barossa Valley Historical Museum..3 B4
Bethany Wines..........................4 C5
Collingrove Homestead............5 D5
Keg Factory..............................6 A5
Langmeil Winery.......................7 B4
Norm's Coolies.........................8 A4
Penfolds Winery........................9 C3

Rockford Wines.......................10 B5
Two Hands.............................11 A3

SLEEPING
Angaston Hotel.......................12 D4
Barossa Bunkhaus Travellers
  Hostel.................................13 C3
Caithness Manor B&B..............14 D4
Nuriootpa Vine Court...............15 C3
Nuriootpa Vine Inn..................16 C3
Stonewell Cottages..................17 B3
Tanunda Caravan &
  Tourist Park..........................18 B4

Tanunda Hotel........................19 B4
Whirlwind Farm......................20 B3

EATING
1918 Bistro & Grill...............(see 21)
Die Barossa Wurst Haus & Bakery....21 B4
Maggie Beer's Farm Shop &
  Restaurant...........................22 B3
Nuriootpa Pizza......................23 C3
Rendezvous House Organic Cafe..24 D3

SHOPPING
Barossa Secrets......................25 B4

accommodation, wineries and contacts for vineyard work. All you want to know about the history of the Barossa, viticulture in the region, and wines in general is covered at the attached **Wine Centre** (admission $2.50).

There are ATMs in the main street in Tanunda and Nuriootpa.

If you fancy some self-indulgence, there are loads of excellent luxury cottages and self-contained B&Bs offering bubbling spas and great two-night deals. The visitor information centre has details, or try the **Barossa B&B Booking Service** (☎ 1800 227 677).

Tours

Organised tours:

Barossa Valley Day Tour (☎ 08-8262 6900; tours $60; ☺ tours Sat) This tour takes in five wineries and Maggie Beer's Farm Shop & Restaurant – a good mixture.

Barossa Valley Tours (☎ 08-8563 2233, 0417 852 453; www.barossavalleytour.com; full-day tours $39, incl lunch $47) A local operator that will whisk you around the major sights in the area, including a selection of wineries, and stop for a two-course lunch (optional).

Groovy Grape Getaways Australia (☎ 1800 661 177; www.groovygrape.com.au; tours incl BBQ lunch $65)

Fun backpacker tours from Adelaide that include the Whispering Wall, Big Rocking Horse and a few wineries.

Prime Mini Tours (☎ 1300 667 650; www.primemini tours.com; tours incl lunch $65) One of the best one-day tours from Adelaide.

Festivals & Events

For full details on events, contact the **visitor information centre** (☎ 1300 852 982, 08-8563 0600; www.barossa-region.org).

Barossa Music Festival (www.barossa.org) Two weeks of wine and picnics in October to accompany theatre, and classical, chamber and jazz music.

Barossa Jazz Weekend Indulge in jazz, and gourmet food and wine at various cellar doors; held in August.

Barossa Under the Stars Entertainers such as Rod Stewart and Cliff Richard have yodelled by moonlight at this winery-hosted festival held in February.

Barossa Vintage Festival A week-long colourful festival with brass bands, maypole dancing, wineries' tug-of-war contests, etc; begins Easter Monday in odd-numbered years.

Getting There & Around

There are several routes to the Barossa Valley from Adelaide, with the most direct being via Main North Rd through Eliza-

---

THE GOOD DROP

South Australia is well marked on the world wine map for its excellent wines from the regions of, among others, the Clare Valley, McLaren Vale, Coonawarra and the Barossa Valley. Here's the deal when heading to the cellar door for tastings – swirl, sniff, sup and swill before swallowing or spitting out. Listed here are some exciting boutique wineries, which make up the 50-odd wineries with cellar-door tastings in the Barossa Valley, together with world-renowned names regularly quaffed at home.

Bethany Wines (☎ 08-8563 2086; www.bethany.com.au; Bethany Rd, Tanunda; ☺ 10am-5pm Mon-Sat, 1-5pm Sun) Offering a stunning hillside vista, this friendly family winery makes a killer white port and classic dry reds.

Henschke (☎ 08-8564 8223; www.henschke.com.au; Henschke Rd, Keyneton; ☺ 9am-4.30pm Mon-Fri 9am-noon Sat) In nearby Eden Valley, 14km from Angaston, the home of 'Hill of Grace' produces exceptional wines.

Langmeil Winery (☎ 08-8563 2595; www.langmeilwinery.com.au; cnr Para & Langmeil Rds, Tanunda; ☺ 10.30am-4.30pm) Some legendary wines in a beautiful setting. Pre-arrange a winery tour and explore its history and vineyards.

Penfolds Wines (☎ 08-8568 9290; www.penfolds.com; Tununda Rd, Nuriootpa; ☺ 10am-5pm Mon-Fri, 11am-5pm Sat & Sun) You know the name. The 'Barossa Ultimate Tasting Experience' ($100 per person) allows you to pass some Grange Hermitage across your lips; book ahead.

Rockford Wines (☎ 08-8563 2720; Krondorf Rd, Tanunda; ☺ 11am-5pm Mon-Sat) The converted stone building itself makes this small winery's cellar door a picturesque winner. It's widely noted for its Black Shiraz. Fabulous chutneys, jams and mustards are also often available for tasting.

Two Hands (☎ 08-8562 4566; www.twohandswines.com; Neldner Rd, Marananga; ☺ 11am-5pm Wed-Fri, 10am-5pm Sat & Sun) People swoon with delight over the wonderful wines (complete with eccentric names and labels) produced at this boutique winery. Try the Moscata, the 'Garden series'…and all the others – they're fabulous.

beth and Gawler. More picturesque routes go through the Torrens Gorge, then via either Williamstown or Birdwood. If you're coming from the east and want to tour the wineries before hitting Adelaide, take the scenic route via Springton and Eden Valley to Angaston.

Barossa Valley Coaches (☎ 08-8564 3022) has twice daily (once on Sunday) return services from Adelaide to Tanunda ($13, 1½ hours), Nuriootpa ($14, two hours) and Angaston ($15, two hours).

Premier Stateliner (☎ 08-8415 5555; www.premier stateliner.com.au) runs services to Nuriootpa from Adelaide ($7.40, two hours) three times daily.

Cycling is a good way to get around the Barossa, particularly along the Para Rd Trail, a dirt trail which wends its way past wineries. Hire bikes from the Bunkhaus Travellers Hostel ($10) in Nuriootpa, or Tanunda Caravan & Tourist Park (half-/full day $15/20) and Barossa Secrets (daily/overnight $16.50/25) in Tanunda.

Barossa Valley Taxis (☎ 08-8563 3600) has a 24-hour service.

TANUNDA
☎ 08 / pop 3865

It's worth taking a wander around Tanunda, the most Germanic of the towns in the centre of the valley. It has some fine old Lutheran churches, and early cottages around **Goat Square** on John St. This was the site of the original *ziegenmarkt*, a meeting and market place laid out as the original centre of Tanunda in 1842.

The **Barossa Valley Historical Museum** (☎ 8563 0507; 47 Murray St; admission $4; 🕑 11am-5pm Mon-Sat, 1-5pm Sun) has exhibits on the valley's early settlement. A few galleries and antique shops line the main street, while **Barossa Secrets** (☎ 8563 0665; 91 Murray St; 🕑 10am-4.30pm) sells local produce, and fascinating things made out of lavender and old oak wine barrels.

You can watch artisans making kegs and other wooden items at the **Keg Factory** (☎ 8563 3012; St Halletts Rd; 🕑 8am-4.30pm Mon-Sat, 10am-4.30pm Sun), 4km south of town.

At **Norm's Coolies** (☎ 8563 2198; Barossa Valley Way; adult $8; 🕑 shows 2pm Mon, Wed & Sat), at Breezy Gully Farm, off Gomersal Rd, about 3km from Tanunda, you can watch trained sheepdogs going through their paces.

See the Barossa Valley introduction, p750 for a scenic drive loop via Bethany, Angaston and Marananga.

Sleeping & Eating
Most accommodation in the Barossa centres on Tanunda.

Tanunda Hotel (☎ 8563 2030; 51 Murray St; s/d $50/60, mains $13-18, 🕑 lunch & dinner) This family-run hotel in the centre of town has comfortable rooms and a broad menu.

Stonewell Cottages (☎ 8563 2019; www.stonewell cottages.com.au; Stonewell Rd; cottages $135-160; 🔀) These award-winning, waterfront, vineyard spa retreats offer comfort and tranquillity along with generous offerings of wine, port and edible goodies.

Tanunda Caravan & Tourist Park (☎ 8563 2784; www.tanundacaravantouristpark.com.au; Barossa Valley Way; powered/unpowered sites per 2 people $22/17, caravans from $38, cabins from $58; 🖳) Just a short walk from the town and pub, this place has good facilities, and a camp kitchen and laundry. It also hires out bikes (half-/full day $15/20) so that you can explore nearby wineries.

There's a supermarket, bakery and takeaway food shops in the centre of town.

Die Barossa Wurst Haus & Bakery (☎ 8563 3598; 86A Murray St; breakfast $3.50-9, meals $8-12.50; 🕑 7.30am-5pm Mon-Fri, 7.30am-4pm Sat & Sun) At this deli-cum-bakery home of *mettwurst* (Bavarian sausage) and cheeses, the pies, value-packed all-day breakfasts, German cakes and apple strudel are gobbled up in record time. Delve into the region's heritage with a Bavarian Feast roll ($12.50) with wurst, sauerkraut, potato salad and mustard.

1918 Bistro & Grill (☎ 8563 0405; 94 Murray St; mains $19-26; 🕑 lunch & dinner) This local institution has an atmospheric setting, but is not one for vegetarians or those with picky appetites. Steamed-pudding lovers will rejoice.

NURIOOTPA
☎ 08 / pop 3865

At the northern end of the valley, the small town of Nuriootpa is surrounded by vineyards. You can follow the Para Rd Trail cycling and walking path along the river to a number of cellar doors.

Sleeping & Eating
Barossa Bunkhaus Travellers Hostel (☎ 8562 2260; Barossa Valley Way; dm/d $17/50; 🔀 summer only) Rest

SOUTH AUSTRALIA

glazed eyes at this relaxed, friendly vine-fringed hostel, 1km south of town. It has a well-appointed kitchen, BBQs and wood fires and is a great base for winery exploration by foot or bike (cycle hire from $8).

Nuriootpa Vine Inn & Vine Court (☎ 8562 2133; www.vineinn.com.au; 14 & 49 Murray St; d $95-115; 🏊 🛎) As both have pools and are within walking distance of a couple of good wineries, these otherwise standard motels become *very* attractive!

Whirlwind Farm (☎ 8562 2637; www.whirlwindbb .com; Samuel Rd; d $140; 🏊) This farmhouse B&B just near Maggie Beer's restaurant has a guest wing with wooden beams, attractive airy rooms and a large veranda for contemplating life or snoozing with the papers after breakfast.

Nuriootpa Pizza (☎ 8562 1896; 51 Murray St; small pizzas $8.50-11.50; ⏰ 4-10.30pm Mon-Wed, noon-late Thu-Sun) Thick- or thin-style pizzas, pasta, fish and chips, *yiros* (souvlaki), burgers and more are served up at this 'jack-of-all-cuisines' fast-food joint. Can't decide? Cover a few options with the 'chicken and chips' pizza.

Maggie Beer's Farm Shop & Restaurant (☎ 8562 4477; www.maggiebeer.com.au; Pheasant Farm Rd; lunch mains $25; ⏰ 10.30am-5pm) Seasonal specialities are dished up in celebrity-gourmet Maggie's kitchen – she's famous for her pheasant dishes. Book ahead for a table overlooking the water, or cruise in for great coffee and taste Maggie's gourmet produce and Beer Brothers wines.

ANGASTON

☎ 08 / pop 1933

On the eastern side of the valley, the quiet town of Angaston, named after George Fife Angas, one of the area's pioneers, has a couple of galleries and studios along its main street.

About 7km from town, magnificent **Collingrove Homestead** (☎ 8564 2061; Angaston Rd, Eden Valley; admission $8; ⏰ 1-4.30pm Mon-Fri, 11am-4.30pm Sat & Sun) was built by Angas' son in 1856 and is now owned by the National Trust of Australia. Devonshire teas are served daily and formal banquets can be organised upon request.

Sleeping & Eating

Angaston Hotel (☎ 8564 2428; 59 Murray St; B&B per person $35, mains $9-16; ⏰ breakfast, lunch & dinner)

Traditional hotel rooms at 'the corner pub', are clean and as comfortable as at grandma's house. Pub grub features steak and grills, and schnitzel any way you like it.

Caithness Manor B&B (☎ 8564 2761; www.caith ness.com.au; 12 Hill St West; d $170; 🏊 🖥 🛎) Propped on a hillside overlooking the town, the friendly hosts of this refurbished girls' school offer cosy B&B rooms, a pool, hot spa and BBQ deck.

Rendezvous House Organic Café (☎ 8564 3533; 22 Murray St; mains $8-18; ⏰ breakfast, lunch & dinner) Oh, yum! Enrapture your taste buds with flavoursome organic food amid casual arty chic. Carnivores, vegans and vegetarians are all catered for.

Vintners Bar Grill (☎ 8564 2488; Nuriootpa Rd; mains $18-25; ⏰ lunch & dinner) Regional produce and simple elegance go hand-in-hand at this Barossa landmark, with beautiful views across surrounding vineyards.

MID-NORTH

The area between Adelaide and Port Augusta is generally known as the Mid-North. It's a mixed bunch of landscapes and lifestyles, dominated by vast farms producing wheat and fine wool. The Clare Valley is lined with boutique wineries producing classic Riesling and Shiraz, and there are a number of townships from the copper-mining era, such as Auburn, Burra, Kapunda and Mintaro, whose streetscapes have changed little over the past 100 years.

Getting There & Away

Two main routes from Adelaide run through the Mid-North. One runs to Gawler then on through Burra to Peterborough. From there you can head west to Port Augusta, northwest to the Flinders Ranges or continue along the Barrier Hwy to Broken Hill in NSW.

The second route heads through Port Wakefield and on to Port Augusta on the Spencer Gulf. You can then travel northeast to the Flinders Ranges, southwest to the Eyre Peninsula, north to Alice Springs or west towards the Nullarbor and WA.

Barossa Valley Coaches (☎ 08-8564 3022) depart for Kapunda ($16, 4½ hours) on weekdays, which involves a 3¾-hour stopover in Gawler.

Mid-North Passenger Service (☎ 08-8823 2375) departs Adelaide daily for Auburn ($15, 2¼ hours), Clare ($22, 2½ hours) and Peterborough ($28, five hours). Other services include Burra ($22, 3½ hours) from Monday to Friday, Jamestown ($26, 4½ hours) from Tuesday to Sunday and Orroroo ($32, five hours) on Wednesday, Friday and Sunday.

Premier Stateliner (☎ 08-8415 5555; www.premierstateliner.com.au) runs daily buses from Adelaide to Port Wakefield ($17, 1½ hours), Port Pirie ($31, three hours) and Port Germein ($40, 3½ hours).

Yorke Peninsula Coaches (☎ 08-8823 2375) departs from Adelaide once a day (Sunday to Friday) to Auburn ($16, 2½ hours), Clare ($22, three hours) and Peterborough ($30, five hours). Buses for Orroroo ($34, 5½ hours) leave Monday, Wednesday and Friday and for Burra ($23, 3½ hours) on Monday and Friday.

KAPUNDA

☎ 08 / pop 2303

This is a welcoming and friendly little town, just outside the Barossa Valley and 80km north of Adelaide. A rich deposit of highest-grade copper was found here in 1842, making Kapunda the first copper-mining town in Australia. Famous cattle king Sir Sidney Kidman ran properties covering 340,000 sq km and had horse sales reputed to be the largest in the world.

Kapunda visitor information centre (☎ 8566 2902; kapundatouristinfo@bigpond.com; 7 Hill St; ☼ 9am-4pm) dispenses information and has a witty display depicting Kapunda life past and present. Upstairs is the appealing **Kapunda Gallery** (☎ 8566 3368; ☼ 9am-4pm).

Superb **murals** of past heroes and (grinning) local personalities can be found outside the post office (Main St) and inside the Sir John Franklin Hotel.

In the big old Baptist church, the **Kapunda Museum** (☎ 8566 2286; 11 Hill St; adult/child $5/2; ☼ 1-4pm) is one of the state's best folk museums. Entry to **Bagot's Fortune** (☎ 8566 2286; 5 Hill St), in the *Kapunda Herald* printing office down the street, is included in the price – this mining interpretation centre has displays on the Cornish, Welsh, Irish and German pioneers and the different roles they played in the town's development.

Map Kernow (or 'Son of Cornwall' in old Cornish), an 8m-high bronze statue, stands at the Adelaide end of town as a tribute to pioneer miners.

Sleeping & Eating

Contact the visitor information centre for details on B&Bs in and around town.

Sir John Franklin Hotel (☎ 8566 3233; 63 Main St; s/d $25/55, meals $8-15; ☼ lunch & dinner) This amiable hotel has budget rooms, cheap bar meals and a great front bar. Check out the brilliant caricatures on the bar walls.

Peppertrees B&B (☎ 8566 2776; 47 Clare Rd; s/d $95/120; ☼) You can't get much better than this: your own suite of beautiful rooms in a classic Australian bluestone, set in pretty gardens. It's child-free and rates include champagne and full breakfast. Book ahead.

Kapunda Tourist & Leisure Park (☎ 8566 2094; www.kapundatouristpark.com; 3 Montefiore St; unpowered sites $18, cabins from $65; ☼) There are plenty of trees, birds and shade, if few facilities, at this park. It's within walking distance of the town centre and golf course.

Wheatsheaf Hotel (☎ 8566 2198; www.wheatsheaf1855.com; Burra Rd, Allendale North; mains $12-22; ☼ brunch, lunch & dinner) This unpretentious bistro with art-bedecked walls serves dishes of local produce that draw in the locals and is a much-coveted brunch spot (from 11am). It's 5km from Kapunda.

Caffeine hounds should head to **Fresh Fields** (☎ 8566 3222; 39 Main St; mains $10-14; ☼ breakfast, lunch & dinner) for huge all-day breakfasts, and **Kapunda Bakery Café** (☎ 8566 2739; cnr Smedley & Main Sts; snacks $3; ☼ breakfast & lunch) for freshly baked goods.

AUBURN

☎ 08 / pop 334

This sleepy township, 24km south of Clare, is reminiscent of an old European village. The few streets are lined with beautifully preserved stone buildings, a timeless pub and a French restaurant. Auburn was the birthplace of CJ Dennis, one of Australia's best-known colonial poets.

The brilliant 25km **Riesling Trail** starts at the restored Auburn Train Station, now a café and cellar door. Clare Valley's largest winery is Auburn's **Taylor's Wines** (☎ 8849 2008; Taylors Rd; ☼ 9am-5pm Mon-Fri, 10am-4pm Sat & Sun).

Sleeping & Eating

Auburn BnB Hotline (☎ 0400 257 597, 0419 824 488) is a free accommodation booking service.

Auburn Shiraz Motel (☎ 8849 2125; auburn.shiraz@ bigpond.com; Main North Rd; s/d $55/65; ☒) This proudly renovated motel has nine bright, spotless units, and friendly hosts.

Rising Sun Hotel (☎ 8849 2015; rising@capri.net .au; Main North Rd; s B&B $50-75, d $82-130, pub mains $6.50-15.50, steakhouse mains $11-23; ☺ lunch & dinner; ☒) The Rising Sun is an understated but classic pub, and is one of Auburn's major attractions. Its friendly atmosphere is matched with great new-style pub food and elegant rooms. Inquire about packages, and book ahead.

Tatehams (☎ 8849 2030; tatehams@capri.net.au; Main North Rd; d $165, mains $29, 2-4 courses $48-90; ☺ lunch & dinner Wed-Sun) This award-winning gourmet restaurant/winery is one of the best in the state and produces French-Swiss cuisine (including snails in champagne), expertly matched to its wines. Only the two- to five-course dining option is available on weekends. Be sure to make a reservation. Stay in the charming self-contained B&B cottages.

CLARE VALLEY WINE REGION

An intimate and sociable atmosphere pervades the small family and boutique wineries distributed throughout the valley's heartland. The Clare Valley stretches from Auburn in the south to Jamestown in the north, but is concentrated around Clare (population 2815). Between Clare and Auburn, the pretty village of Mintaro has an atmospheric pub and a couple of great restaurants.

The **visitor information centre** (☎ 08-8842 2131; www.clarevalley.com.au; 229 Main St; ☺ 9am-5pm Mon-Sat, 10am-4pm Sun) is in Clare. For casual work during March and April, contact the wineries directly.

Clare itself has a number of interesting buildings, including an impressive **Catholic church** (Victoria Rd). The first police station and courthouse date from 1850 and are preserved as the National Trust of Australia **Old Police Station Museum** (☎ 08-8842 2376; cnr Victoria & Neagles Rock Rds; adult/child $6/2; ☺ 10am-noon & 2-4pm Sat, Sun & school holidays).

You can walk or ride past some of the district's finest wineries on the **Riesling Trail**, which meanders through the valley from Auburn to Clare. The wonderful **artists' galleries** in the area are worth a peek as you pedal by.

Wineries

Wineries here produce some of the best Riesling, as well as some grand Semillon and Shiraz. There are around 35 winery cellar doors in the valley, including the following:

Annie's Lane at Quelltaler (☎ 08-8843 0003; www .annieslane.com.au; Quelltaler Rd, Watervale; ☺ 8.30am-5pm Mon-Fri, 11am-4pm Sat) Its glorious flagship wines are Copper Trail Shiraz and Riesling. It has a welcoming cellar door and a winery museum and gallery.

Grosset (☎ 08-8849 2175; www.grosset.com; King St, Auburn; ☺ 10am-5pm Wed-Sun Sep) If you're here in September, get in quick – wines sell out within six weeks.

Kirrihill Estate (☎ 08-8842 4087; www.kirrihillwines .com.au; Wendouree Rd, Clare; ☺ 10am-4pm) Established in 1998, this young winery has outstanding Shiraz, Sauvignon Blanc and Semillon to suit the seafood specialities of upstairs' enticing Salt n Vines Bar & Bistro.

Jim Barry (☎ 08-8842 2261, 8842 3752; Main North Rd, Clare; ☺ 9am-5pm Mon-Fri, 9am-4pm Sat & Sun) A local icon. The flagship Armagh Shiraz will be too pricey for many; however, the superb Riesling and golden Chardonnays are very good value.

Sevenhill Cellars (☎ 08-8843 4222; www.sevenhill cellars.com.au; College Rd, Sevenhill; ☺ 9am-4.30pm Mon-Fri, 10am-4pm Sat) About 7km south of Clare, this was the valley's first winery, established in 1851 by Jesuit priests. It still produces communion wine, as well as a very good Verdelho. The 1875 St Aloysius Church adjoins the winery.

Skillogalee (☎ 08-8843 4270; www.skillogalee.com; Trevarrick Rd, Sevenhill; ☺ 10am-5pm) A delightful family winery with top-range elegant Rieslings, spicy Shiraz and fabulous food. Indulge yourself with a long lunch on the shady veranda.

Taylors (☎ 08-8849 2008; www.taylorswines.com.au; Taylors Rd, Auburn; ☺ 9am-5pm Mon-Fri, 10am-4pm Sat & Sun) One of the region's largest wineries. Ignore the unfortunate mock-castle roof, because this winery does produce wines fit for royalty. The Shiraz wines are winners.

Festivals & Events

Clare Show (☎ 08-8842 2374; Sep) The largest one-day show in SA celebrates with concert bands, Irish dancers, Bavarian dancers, performing dogs and bell ringers.

Clare Valley Gourmet Weekend (☎ 08-8842 2131) One of the valley's major events, held on a May long weekend; a festival of wine, food and music hosted by local wineries.

Romería del Rocío Spanish Festival (☎ 08-8842 2131) A colourful four-day event in April, with much clicking of heels and fingers.

Sleeping & Eating

There are numerous B&Bs throughout the valley; ask at the visitor information centre in Clare and book well ahead. The caravan park is opposite the local motorcycle club grounds.

Taminga Hotel (☎ 08-8842 2808/2461; 302 Main St, Clare; s/d $23/45) This friendly town pub has basic rooms, and a garden grill and bar during the summer.

Riesling Trail Country Cottages (☎ 0412 265 031; www.rieslingcottages.com.au; d $130; 🏊) Luxuriously appointed self-contained cottages in a choice of locations offer lovely views near the Riesling Trail. Spa baths, breakfast provisions and wood fires are the norm.

Clare Valley Cabins (☎ 08-8842 1155; www.clarevalleycabins.com.au; Hubbe Rd, Clare; d $100; 🏊) In a bush setting 6km from Clare, these secluded and comfortable cabins come with breakfast and BBQ provisions. Mountain bikes and massages (normal/full-body $45/65) are also available.

Mintaro Mews (☎ 08-8843 9001, 0400 484 242; http://users.chariot.net.au/~minmews; Burra St, Mintaro; B&B per person $60, mains $20-24; 🍴 lunch & dinner) Often the first place in Mintaro to get booked out, this quaint spot has an award-winning restaurant with a self-select wine cellar. Accommodation and meal packages are great deals.

Coffee & Cork (☎ 08-8842 3477; 12 Main North Rd, Clare; mains $19-24; 🍴 breakfast Sat & Sun, lunch Wed-Sun, dinner Wed, Fri & Sat) Duck into this local haunt for coffee and book ahead for the popular Mod Oz dinners.

Salt n Vines Bar & Bistro (☎ 08-8842 1796; Kirrihill Estate, Clare; mains $18-25; 🍴 lunch & dinner Thu-Sun) This light and airy hillside bar/restaurant has good food (seafood is a speciality) and a balcony on which to enjoy it with a bottle of excellent Kirrihill Estate Shiraz or Riesling.

Magpie & Stump Hotel (☎ 08-8843 9014/9191; Burra St, Mintaro; mains $15-19; 🍴 lunch daily, dinner Mon-Sat) This atmospheric 1851 hotel has soul-humming food, log fires and a beer garden.

Getting Around

Clare Valley Cycle Hire (☎ 08-8842 2782, 0418 802 077; 32 Victoria Rd, Clare; 🕒 8am-6pm) has rates for a half-/full day ($17/25). The operators will also collect any wine you buy along the way.

Clare Valley Taxis (☎ 13 10 08; 261 Main North Rd, Clare; 🕒 8am-6pm Sun-Thu, 24hr Fri & Sat with bookings) can drop off or pick up along the Riesling Trail.

BURRA

☎ 08 / pop 1106

This attractive little town is bursting at the seams with historic sites. Burra was a centre for copper mining from 1847 to 1877, with various British ethnic groups forming their own distinctive communities – the Cornish being the most numerous. The hardship of that era can especially be felt in the dugouts (underground rooms that miners excavated for themselves and their families).

By one account, the district of Burra Burra takes its name from the Hindi word for 'great', and from another account, it comes from the Aboriginal name of the creek.

Information

Visitor information centre (☎ 8892 2154; www.visitburra.com; 2 Market Sq; 🕒 9am-5pm) This helpful centre sells the Burra Heritage Passport ($25), which includes the *Discovering Historic Burra* booklet (describing 49 sites on an 11km heritage trail) and admission to eight (locked) sights and four museums. Children are admitted free.

Sights & Activities

Burra has many substantial stone buildings, tiny Cornish cottages and numerous other reminders of the mining days. All the following attractions are included in the Burra Passport or have free admission.

Market Square Museum (Market Sq; adult/child $4.50/2.50; 🕒 11.30am-1.30pm Thu, 2.15-3.30pm Sat & Sun) has a shop, a post office and a house set up as they may have looked between 1880 and 1930.

The 33 attached cottages on **Paxton Square** were built for Cornish miners in the 1850s; some of these are available for accommodation (see Paxton Square Cottages, p759). One of the cottages, **Malowen Lowarth** (☎ 8892 2577; Kingston St; adult/child $4.50/2.50; 🕒 2-4pm Sat, 9.30am-12.30pm Sun), has furnishings and a garden that are in the 1850s style.

Morphett's Enginehouse Museum (☎ 8892 2244; adult/child $4.50/2.50; 🕒 11am-1pm Mon, Wed & Fri, 11am-2pm Sat & Sun), off Market St, is a reconstructed three-storey Cornish enginehouse that once pumped water from the mine. The enginehouse is on the grounds of the original mine site, now converted into the open-air **Burra Mine Museum**. Information boards detail the history of the mine.

At **Bon Accord Complex** (☎ 8892 2056; Railway Tce; adult/child $4.50/2.50; 🕒 1-3pm Mon-Fri, 1-4pm Sat

& Sun), a Scottish mining enterprise found underground water instead of the copper they were mining for. Not to be deterred, the canny Scots sold the site to the town, and the property supplied Burra's water until 1966. The site is now an interpretive centre.

In Burra's early days, nearly 1500 people lived in **dugouts** along the creek. A couple of these have been preserved. Other interesting old buildings accessed with the Burra Heritage Passport key include **Redruth Gaol** (Tregony St), the **Old Police Lock-Up** (Tregony St) and the old **Smelter Works** (Smelts Rd).

Thorogoods Apple Wines (☎ 8892 2669; www .thorogoods.com.au; ❂ noon-4.30pm) turns out a range of great light and delicate apple-derived drinks, from cider to liquor. It's signposted from John Barker St.

Gaslight Collectable & Old Books (☎ 8892 3003; 20 Market Sq; ❂ 10am-5pm) is grail for book-lovers; browsers can leaf through this shop's treasures while savouring the coffee aromas and soothing classical music. Or munch on one of the yummy cakes.

Sleeping & Eating

Burra's historic houses and cottages provide atmospheric B&B accommodation (doubles with/without breakfast for around $120/100). The town's five hotels all serve bar meals, and some offer budget accommodation. The visitor information centre acts as a booking agent for all accommodation.

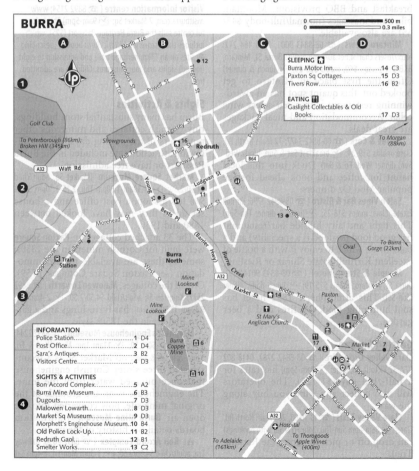

BURRA

| | 0 | 500 m |
| 0 | | 0.3 miles |

SLEEPING 🏠
Burra Motor Inn...................14 C3
Paxton Sq Cottages................15 D3
Tivers Row...........................16 B2

EATING 🍴
Gaslight Collectables & Old
Books...............................17 D3

To Peterborough (86km);
Broken Hill (345km)

To Morgan
(88km)

To Burra
Gorge (22km)

**Burra
North**

Mine
Lookout

Mine
Lookout

**Burra
Copper
Mine**

St Mary's
Anglican Church

To Thorogoods
Apple Wines
(400km)

To Adelaide
(161km)

Hospital

INFORMATION
Police Station..............................1 D4
Post Office.................................2 D4
Sara's Antiques...........................3 B2
Visitors Centre............................4 D3

SIGHTS & ACTIVITIES
Bon Accord Complex....................5 A2
Burra Mine Museum.....................6 B3
Dugouts....................................7 D3
Malowen Lowarth.......................8 D3
Market Sq Museum......................9 D3
Morphett's Enginehouse Museum..10 B4
Old Police Lock-Up.....................11 B2
Redruth Gaol.............................12 B1
Smelter Works...........................13 C2

Paxton Square Cottages (☎ 8892 2622; paxton cottages@bigpond.com.au; Kingston St; d $65) These pristine, historic cottages are sparsely furnished but have reasonable cooking facilities. Each house sleeps up to six people and one has fittings for disabled people.

Tivers Row (☎ 8892 2461; www.burraheritagecot tages.com.au; 8-18 Truro St; B&B d $120) This row of Cornish cottages has been beautifully restored and have pretty courtyard gardens. History buffs will relish the lovingly chosen period furnishings. Book through **Sara's Antiques** (1 Young St; ☎ 8892 2461).

Burra Motor Inn (☎ 8892 2777; Market St; s/d $80/90; ❂ ❑) The most modern motel in town offers large rooms overlooking the creek. Book well ahead for weekends.

PETERBOROUGH & ORROROO

Those heading onto the Flinders Ranges or Sydney may pass through **Peterborough** (population 1683), a dusty agricultural service town that's very proud of its rail heritage. One of nature's odd little quirks, **Magnetic Hill**, is around 10km from the town centre. Follow signs from the Orroroo and Jamestown junction. A giant magnet marks the spot where your car (with its engine shut off) will roll up a hill completely unaided! The town has a **caravan park** (☎ 08-8651 2545) and **motor inn** (☎ 08-8651 2078).

The small agricultural town of **Orroroo** (population 504) has a restored **Early Settlers Cottage** (☎ 08-8658 1219; cnr Fouth & South Sts), and **Aboriginal rock carvings** accessed by a walking track from the Lion's Picnic Grounds at Pekina Creek. More recently, two sentimental poems (dated 1896 and 1901) were engraved in the rock further down the track by a man called David McDonald.

MT REMARKABLE NATIONAL PARK

This steep, rugged park, near Melrose (265km north of Adelaide) straddles the southern Flinders Ranges between Wilmington and the coast. There's a large, attractive bush camping area at Mambray Creek on the eastern side of the range.

From **Wilmington** (population 250), on the other (western) side of the park, you can access some nice bushwalks in the park, including the **Heysen Trail** (see the boxed text, p709). One short walk is through colourful **Alligator Gorge** (admission per car $6.50), with walls that are only 2m apart in places.

Hancocks Lookout, just north of the park and on the way to Horrocks Pass from Wilmington, offers excellent views of Spencer Gulf. The 7km detour (one way) is well worth it.

PORT GERMEIN

☎ 08 / pop 279

On the Spencer Gulf coast south of Port Augusta, Port Germein has the longest wooden jetty in Australia, from which dolphins are often seen frolicking. You'll understand why the jetty was built when the tide goes out: there is a 1283m-long walk across the beach to reach the sea!

You can head east from Port Germein to cut through the mountains via the beautiful **Germein Gorge** to Murray Town and north to Melrose.

SOUTHEAST

Along the rugged wind- and salt-parched southeast coast (Limestone Coast), you'll find tranquil harbours with fishing and holiday towns, and some great swimming and surfing beaches. From Robe to Mt Gambier, the road passes through a sea of plantation forests, interspersed with the odd patch of cleared farmland or stand of gum trees.

You can gorge on salt-water fare along the Limestone Coast; October to April is crayfish (rock lobster) season. Don't miss the opportunity to slurp the superb *terra rossa* (red soil) reds of the Coonawarra wine belt or to walk around the enigmatic volcanic crater lakes at Mt Gambier. For regional information, see www.thelime stonecoast.com.

Getting There & Away

Regional Express (☎ 13 17 13; www.regionalexpress .com.au) and **O'Connor Airlines** (☎ 13 13 13, 08-8723 0666; www.oconnor-airlines.com.au) fly daily between Adelaide and Mt Gambier ($225).

Dukes Hwy provides the most direct route between Adelaide and Melbourne (729km), via Bordertown, but the coastal Princes Hwy route, which runs adjacent to the Coorong National Park, is definitely more scenic.

Premier Stateliner (☎ 08-8415 5555; www.premier stateliner.com.au; central bus station, Franklin St, Central Adelaide) runs a Sunday to Friday coastal bus service between Adelaide and Mt Gambier ($55, 6½ hours) via the Coorong (Meningie: $26, two hours), Kingston Southeast($41, four hours), Robe ($46, 4½ hours) and Beachport ($50, five hours). A daily inland route travels to Bordertown ($40, four hours), Naracoorte ($50, five hours), and Penola ($50, six hours). Premier also runs services between Mt Gambier and Penola ($11, 30 minutes).

V/Line (☎ 13 61 96, 1800 817 037) runs a combined bus and train service between Mt Gambier and Melbourne ($60; 6½ hours) on weekdays.

Wayward Bus Touring Company (☎ 1300 653 510; www.waywardbus.com.au) also travels this stretch (see p712).

COORONG NATIONAL PARK

The dunes, lagoons, freshwater soaks and ephemeral lakes of the Coorong form a wetland of international importance and support vast numbers of water birds. From the mouth of the Murray River, the Coorong stretches 145km southeast and is rarely more than 4km in width. *Storm Boy*, a film about a young boy's friendship with a pelican, based on the novel of the same name by Colin Thiele, was shot in the Coorong. Pelicans are evident at Jack Point and elsewhere in the park, as are ducks, waders and swans. The Ngarrindjeri people are still closely connected to this area; the name Coorong is derived from the Ngarrindjeri word 'Karangk', meaning 'long neck'. Travelling through at sunset is serenely beautiful.

The easiest access point to the ocean is a 3km drive from the Princes Hwy at 42 Mile Crossing, 19km south of Salt Creek. From here, it's a 1.3km 4WD or walk to a great view of the Southern Ocean. When roads are dry, you can take the dirt Old Coorong Rd as an alternative to the Princes Hwy.

Permits for bush camp sites ($6.50 per car) are available from the roadhouse at Salt Creek and the **DEH** (☎ 08-8575 1200; 34 Main St, Meningie; ☼ 9am-5pm Mon-Fri), which also has general park and trail information.

MENINGIE

☎ 08 / pop 897

On Lake Albert – a large arm of Lake Alexandrina – Meningie is a popular sailboarding spot and the main town in the centre of the Coorong.

Coorong Nature Tours (☎ /fax 8574 0037; www .coorongnaturetours.com; Dadd Rd, Narrung; adult/child $150/110) offers excellent 4WD and bushwalking eco-tours.

At stunning Point Hack, off the Princes Hwy about 25km south of Meningie, is the Ngarrindjeri-owned **Coorong Wilderness Lodge** (☎ 8575 6001; powered/unpowered sites per 2 people $10/20, cabins $65, meals $13; ☼ lunch Mon-Fri). Here you can enjoy bush-tucker and bush-medicine walks ($7 per hour) and kayak tours ($20 per hour, kayaks per half-/full day $30/50), as well as bush-food meals of Coorong mullet, fresh damper and kangaroo meatballs. Book ahead.

Run by the Ngarrindjeri Lands & Progress Association, **Camp Coorong** (☎ 8575 1557; www .ngarrindjeri.net; Princes Hwy; sites/dm/cabins $10/22/55; ☒), 10km south of Meningie, is a great place for those keen to learn about Aboriginal history. Simple, modern cabins and dorms are great value, and there are also laundry and kitchen facilities. Book in advance, ask about linen hire and bring your own food. The Cultural Museum here and cultural walks (from $33 per hour) are run by an informed and passionate Ngarrindjeri guide.

Lake Albert Caravan Park (☎ /fax 8575 1411; lacp@lm.net.au; 25 Narrung Rd; unpowered sites per 2 people $18, cabin with/without bathroom $50/65) is an older park right on the lake with some shady sites.

MENINGIE TO ROBE

Kingston Southeast (SE) is the proud hometown of 'Larry the Giant Lobster'. Satisfy your 'cray'-vings (sorry!) at **Lacepede Lobster** (☼ 9am-6pm), a swimmingly fresh takeaway by the jetty. Between here and Robe, gently undulating farmland is interspersed with plantation pine forests and the occasional vineyard around Mt Benson, near Cape Jaffa.

ROBE

☎ 08 / pop 965

This relaxed and charming fishing port gets inundated with sun-, sand- and surf-seekers in summer.

The **Robe visitor information centre** (☎ 8768 2465; www.robe.sa.gov.au; Mundy Tce; ☼ 9am-5pm Mon-Fri, 10am-4pm Sat & Sun) has free Internet access and an interesting photo display on Robe's heritage.

The town is blessed with quaint limestone cottages, a protected sandy swimming beach near the town centre, and **Long Beach** (2km from town off the Kingston SE road) – a good sailboarding and surfing spot. The beachfront walking trail has interpretational signs, while other marked trails meander through the coastal dunes at **Little Dip Conservation Park**, extending 13km south of town.

Dating from 1846, and one of the state's first settlements, Robe's citizens made a fortune in the late 1850s when the Victorian government instituted a $10-per-head tax on Chinese gold miners. Many Chinese miners circumvented this by landing at Robe and walking hundreds of kilometres to the Victorian goldfields; 10,000 arrived in 1857 alone. The **Chinamen's Wells** along the route they took are a reminder of that time.

Wilsons at Robe (☎ 8768 2459; 5 Victoria St) sells local and Australian coastal-inspired art and craft.

Sleeping & Eating

In summer, there's stiff competition for Robe's seemingly abundant accommodation. Most motel rooms are around $95 per night. Inquire about self-contained units and upmarket B&Bs (some in historic homes) at the visitor information centre.

Caledonian Inn (☎ 8768 2029; caled@seol.net.au; Victoria St; s/d without bathroom $45/60, units $120, meals $13-20; ☽ lunch & dinner) An ivy-covered façade hides this beachside inn and its atmospheric Scottish bar. The rooms are light and cosy, and bar meals service mainly carnivores and seafood fans.

Lake View Motel & Flats (☎ 8768 2100; apt s/d $83/93, motel s/d $93/103; ☒) While the motel itself looks a little dated from the outside, there are surprisingly spacious and cheerful rooms here – some come with basic cooking facilities. A guest laundry and BBQ are also available.

Robe Cricklewood (☎ 8768 2137; www.robe.sa.gov .au/cricklewood; 24 Wollundry Rd; d $150; ☒) Soak up the atmosphere at this beautifully refurbished cottage with cathedral ceilings and exposed beams, and, from the balcony, take in views over Robe's lake.

Robe Long Beach Caravan Park (☎ 8768 2237; www.robelongbeach.com.au; 70 The Esplanade; unpowered sites per 2 people $21, cabin with/without bathroom

from $70/44, chalets $88; ☒ ☐ ☒) This fabulous park right near the beach has some of the best accommodation in town. Its hefty facilities include basketball and tennis courts, arcade machines, a covered BBQ area and a crayfish boiler!

Wild Mulberry Café (☎ 8768 5276; 46 Victoria St; meals $7-16.50; ☽ breakfast & lunch) Tasty gourmet lunches and decadent cakes are baked on site at this soulful café. Situated in a limestone cottage, it also serves all-day cooked breakfasts and Robe-roasted Mahalia coffee.

Robe Seafood & Takeaway (Victoria St) Dine alfresco on the foreshore with freshly hooked and cooked takeaway.

Gallerie (☎ 8768 2256; cnr Victoria & Davenport Sts; mains $22-30; ☽ breakfast, lunch & dinner, closed Tue & Wed winter) Home of Dawson Estate wines, this popular place has an open fire and lots of polished wood and glass, and serves plenty of pasta and seafood. The deck is perfect for outdoor munching.

BEACHPORT

☎ 08 / pop 407

Tranquil Beachport's milky turquoise waters and beautiful location make it a great chill-out spot. There's a decent surf beach, or you can float like never before on the hyper-saline Pool of Siloam. There's a **visitor information centre** (☎ 8735 8029; Millicent Rd; ☽ 9am-5pm Mon-Fri, 11am-2pm Sat & Sun), a couple of caravan parks and Bompa's, which has accommodation, a cosy bar and a café.

The giant sand dunes of **Canunda National Park** lie 22km south of town and feature 4WD tracks, Boandik Aboriginal middens (traces of old camp sites), and cliff-top walks. You can camp near Southend ($7 per vehicle).

Beachport Motor Inn (☎ 8735 8070; beachportmotel@bigpond.com; cnr Railway Tce & Lanky St; d/unit $70/85; ☒), within 300m of the town beach, has neat and compact rooms.

A hop from the beach, **Bompa's** (☎ 8735 8333; bombas@bipond.com; 3 Railway Tce; dm/d $25/95, cottages from $120, mains $11-24; ☽ breakfast, lunch & dinner; ☒) is an all-in-one small hotel and cosy licensed restaurant/café. Dorms have TVs, but book ahead to beat the tour groups.

Beachfront B&B (☎ 8735 8340, 0419 842 401; triz@ seol.net.au; d $130; ☒) provides a choice of continental or cooked breakfast for one or two lucky couples.

Southern Ocean Tourist Park (☎ 8735 8153; sotp@
seol.net.au; Somerville St; sites per 2 people $15, cabins $55)
is grassy and well-maintained and sits shel-
tered behind a hill near the town centre. The
children's playground is a winner.

MT GAMBIER
☎ 08 / pop 22,751

Mount Gambier (486km from Adelaide,
471km from Melbourne) appears like a
lush oasis built on the slopes of an extinct
volcano. Its crater – Blue Lake – is a stunning sight in an almost implausible shade
of sapphire during summer. There are some
excellent walking and biking trails around
the Crater Lakes. Underground caves attract trolls and cave divers who can venture
under Mt Gambier itself, while fishing fans
head for Valley Lake, Glenelg River or the
seas off Port MacDonnell.

Mt Gambier's bus station is at the **Shell
Blue Lake service station** (☎ 8725 5037; 100 Commercial St West).

Information
Mt Gambier visitor information centre (☎ 8724
9750, 1800 087 187; Jubilee Hwy East; ☺ 9am-5pm)
Provides details on the region.

Sights & Activities
Mt Gambier has three volcanic craters, two
with lakes. Perhaps the most surprising
thing about the **Blue Lake**'s blueness is that
there doesn't seem to be a definitive reason
for it. At its deepest point it's about 204m
and has an encircling 3.6km scenic drive.
Boardwalks (over Valley Lake) and cycling
and walking trails crisscross the lakes.

The Mt Gambier district is well known
for its numerous caves. There are pretty,
floodlit sunken gardens in the **Umpherston
Sinkhole** and volunteers take tours, on the
hour, down to the water table in the **Engel-
brecht Cave** (☎ 8725 5493; adult/child $6/3; ☺ sum-
mer), a popular cave-diving spot. Scuba
divers can attain cave-diving qualifications
(three-day courses); book at the visitor information centre. Contact the **Gambier Dive
Centre** (☎ 8723 4255; gambierdive@corprite.net; 60
Commercial St West) for course information and
requisite dive experience.

The surrounding region has some fine
walks, including the path to the top of **Mt
Schank**, an extinct volcano off the Mt Gambier road. The rugged coastline to the west

of **Port MacDonnell** is worth a visit, while **Piccaninnie Ponds** is another popular cave diving and snorkelling spot – for information
contact the **DEH** (☎ 8735 1177; www.environment
.sa.gov.au).

Hire bicycles from **Bats Bike Hire** (☎ 0418
133 407; ☺ 7am-6pm Nov-Mar, 8am-5pm Apr-Oct),
whose staff will drop off and pick up at
tourism spots (half-/full day $10/20).

Attached to the visitor information cen-
tre is a **discovery centre** (Jubilee Hwy East; adult/child
$10/5; ☺ 9am-5pm) featuring a replica of the
historic brig *Lady Nelson*, complete with
sound effects and taped commentary. It
documents the devastating impact of European settlement on the local Aboriginal
people.

Tours
Acquifer Tours (☎ 8723 1199; cnr Bay Rd & John
Watson Dr; adult/child $6/3; ☺ 9am-2pm Sep-Oct) runs
hourly tours through the Blue Lake's aqui-
fer system, in a glass-panelled lift.

Sleeping, Eating & Drinking
Mt Gambier has numerous midrange motor
inns, but many have tired and gloomy
rooms, so check them out first. There are
six caravan parks and some old hotels in
the town's busy centre.

Jail (☎ 8723 0032; www.jailbackpackers.com; Lang-
lois Dr; dm/tw $22/56) Become a jailbird for the
night in these converted cells (which were
operational as jail cells until 1995).

Arkana Motor Inn (☎ 8725 5433; www.users
.bigpond.com/arkanamotorinn; 201 Commercial St East;
s/d/units $80/85/120; ☒ ☐ ☒) One of the best
places around – this inn has bright and
modern rooms, cable TV and a heated pool
and spa. Book ahead for great family deals
on units.

Clarendon Chalets (☎ 8726 8306, 0418 838 926;
www.clarendonchalets.com; Clarke Rd; d $120; ☒)
These four stunning chalets with combus-
tion fires and spas are set in a lovely garden
and walnut orchard 7km south of town.
There are BBQs and bikes for hire.

Blue Lake Holiday Park (☎ 1800 676 028, 8725
9856; www.bluelakeholidaypark.com.au; Bay Rd; unpowered
sites per 2 people $19, cabins/units/bungalows $65/75/96;
☒ ☒) This gardenlike park, adjacent to
walking and cycling trails and close to the
Blue Lake, has great facilities for kids.

Sage & Muntries Café (☎ 8724 8400; sagemunt@
bigpond.net.au; 78 Commercial St West; mains $19-26;

breakfast, lunch & dinner) Quality mixed cuisine is served at this popular licensed café. Dishes include souped-up 'bangers and mash' and melt-in-the-mouth homemade pasta.

Redfins Seafood & Grill (☎ 8725 0611; 2 Commercial St West; lunch specials from $5, mains $18-25; lunch daily, dinner Mon-Sat) Mt Gambians relish these seafood dinners – Coffin Bay oysters are a speciality. Lunchtime specials (from $5) run Monday to Friday.

Sorrentos Café (☎ 8723 0900; 6 Bay Rd; mains $14-24; breakfast, lunch & dinner) All-day brekkies ($8.50) are served along with pasta and risotto in this attractive old stone building.

For good-value pub grub, try **Flanagan's Hotel** (☎ 8725 1671; 6 Ferris St; mains $9-14; lunch & dinner) and the **Commercial Hotel** (☎ 8725 3006; 76 Commercial St West; mains $9-14; lunch & dinner).

COONAWARRA WINE REGION

The red-gum country between Mt Gambier and Border Town has some of the richest fodder-growing and grazing land in SA, as well as the peaceful and compact wine region (25 sq km) around Coonawarra and Padthaway that produces supreme Shiraz and Cabernet Sauvignon. Along with plenty of cellar doors, there's the protected bird sanctuary of the Bool Lagoon, and the unique Naracoorte Caves.

The **visitor information centre** (☎ 08-8737 2855; www.wattlerange.sa.gov.au; 27 Arthur St; 8.30am-5pm Mon-Fri, 10am-5pm Sat, 9.30am-4pm Sun) is in Penola.

Penola

☎ 08 / pop 1222

Penola is famous as a winery region and for its link with the Sisters of St Joseph of the Sacred Heart, the order co-founded in 1867 by Mother Mary MacKillop (see p717). The **Mary MacKillop Interpretive Centre** (☎ 8737 2092; cnr Portland St & Petticoat Lane; admission $3.50; 10am-4pm) features the 1867 **Woods-MacKillop Schoolhouse** and information on the first Australian school to welcome children from lower socioeconomic backgrounds (co-founded by MacKillop and Father Julian Tenison Woods). Quaint old slab **cottages** on Petticoat Lane are open to the public.

Most of the region's 22 or so wineries with cellar doors are off Riddoch Hwy:

Balnaves of Coonawarra (☎ 8738 2946; www .balnaves.com.au; Riddoch Hwy, Coonawarra; 9am-5pm Mon-Fri, 10am-5pm Sat & Sun) Producer of some of the district's best wines.

Majella (☎ 8736 3055; www.majellawines.com.au; Lynn Rd, Coonawarra; 10am-4.30pm) If it were possible to liquefy Christmas pudding, it would taste like this winery's warm and spicy Cabernet Sauvignons.

Padthaway Estate (☎ 8765 5039; Riddoch Hwy, Coonawarra; 10am-4pm) Stop to taste the rich and sultry Padthaway reds, then stay on for lunch or overnight at this historic homestead that's surrounded by vineyards.

Wynns Coonawarra Estate (☎ 8736 2225; www .wynns.com.au; Memorial Dr, Coonawarra; 10am-5pm) The founding winery in the Coonawarra, Wynns is renowned for its truly peppery Shiraz, and also produces fragrant Rieslings and fantastic golden Chardonnays.

Zema Estate (☎ 8736 3219; www.zema.com.au; Riddoch Hwy, Coonawarra; 9am-5pm) This hutlike cellar door pours peppery Shiraz and rich Cabernet Sauvignons.

SLEEPING & EATING

Penola has dolled-up plenty of its historic cottages to offer atmospheric B&B and self-contained accommodation. For listings, contact **Coonawarra Discovery** (☎ 1800 600 262; www.coonawarradiscovery.com). Penola also has a nice but oldish caravan park.

Heyward's Royal Oak Hotel (☎ 8737 2322; 31 Church St; s/tw/d $44/77/88, mains $13-18; lunch & dinner;) Locals pack in the bar to chomp great schnitzels and seafood at this atmospheric heritage hotel with open wood fires. Nice bedrooms have wooden four-poster beds and share bathroom facilities.

Cobb & Co Cottages (☎ 8737 2526; www.cobbnco .com; 2 Portland St; d $125;) Tucked away from the main street, these three bright, attractive two-bedroom spa cottages are a five-minute walk from Penola's restaurants and pub.

Chardonnay Lodge & Poplars Restaurant (☎ 87 36 3309; www.chardonnaylodge.com.au; Riddoch Hwy; s/d $120/140, breakfast & lunch $9, mains $24-28; breakfast, lunch & dinner;) This top-notch motel has lovely gardens and sits within walking distance of five wineries. There's an attached café/restaurant.

Irises Café (☎ 8737 2967; 48 Church St; mains $9.50-16.50; breakfast, lunch & dinner) This BYO (bring your own alcohol) and licensed café serves homemade soups, crusty-topped pies, pastas, stuffed croissants and a filling, juicy apple crumble.

NARACOORTE

☎ 08 / pop 4785

Settled in the 1840s, Naracoorte is one of the oldest towns in the state and one of the largest in the southeast region.

The **Naracoorte visitor information centre** (☎ 8762 1518, 1800 244 421; www.naracoortetourism .com.au; MacDonnell St; ◷ 9am-4pm) is housed in an old flour mill.

The **Bool Lagoon Game Reserve** is a Wetland of International Importance and is usually home to 155 bird species, including 79 water birds. To get here, take the Naracoorte Rd heading north, and after about 35km turn west onto Bool Lagoon Rd and follow for 7km.

Sleeping & Eating

Naracoorte Backpackers (☎ 8762 3835; www.nara coortebackpackers.com.au; 4 Jones St; dm per week $130; ▣) The manager of this hostel acts as a casual labour contractor for local vineyards, and provides transport for working travellers. The facilities are enough to get by with for a few weeks or so.

William MacIntosh Motor Lodge (☎ 8762 1644; willnara@bigpond.com; Adelaide Rd; d/tw $105/120, mains $17-22; ◷ lunch & dinner; ▣ ▣) This lodge has neat and pleasant rooms and a licensed restaurant.

Naracoorte Holiday Park (☎ 8762 2128; www .naracoorteholidaypark.com.au; 81 Park Tce; powered sites per 2 people $21, caravans/cabins $62/73) This immaculate park has spotless accommodation and distractions such as a miniature train, minigolf course and swimming lake.

NARACOORTE CAVES NATIONAL PARK

About 12km southeast of Naracoorte, off the Penola road, is the only SA World Heritage–listed site. The fossil deposits and limestone cave formations here featured in the David Attenborough series *Life on Earth* (BBC). The signage is sporadic, so take a good map.

The excellent **Wonambi Fossil Centre** (☎ 08-8762 2340; naracoortecaves@saugov.sa.gov.au; Hynam-Caves Rd ◷ 9am-5pm winter, 9am-sunset summer) houses a re-creation of the rainforest environment that covered this area 200,000 years ago. The centre has life-sized reconstructions of extinct animals, painstakingly put together. Some models grunt and move.

Book here also for the ranger-guided cave tours (9.30am to 3.30pm) through the nearby **Victoria Fossil Cave**, **Alexandra Cave** and **Blanche Cave**. **Wet Cave** can be seen on a self-guided tour.

Adventure tours to undeveloped caves in the area (wear sneakers or trainers and old

clothes) start at $28 for novices and $60 for a minimum of four advanced explorers.

It is worth visiting the **Bat Cave** on summer evenings to see the southern Bentwing bats make a spectacular departure en masse. The cave is not open to the public, but infrared TV cameras allow you to see inside.

All the preceding options, including the Bat Cave and Wonambi Fossil Centre, are priced as follows: single-cave tours adult/child $11/$6.50; two-cave tours $17.50/10.50. For further details check out www .environment.sa.gov.au/parks/naracoorte.

DUKES HIGHWAY

The last town on the SA side of the border with Victoria is **Bordertown** (population 2340). This town is the birthplace of former Labor prime minister Bob Hawke, and there's a bust of Bob outside the town hall. On the left as you enter from Victoria there is a wildlife park, with various species of Australian fauna, including rare white kangaroos dozing behind a wire fence.

MURRAY RIVER

Australia's greatest river starts in the Snowy Mountains, the Australian Alps, and for most of its length forms the boundary between NSW and Victoria. It meanders for 650km through SA, first heading west to Morgan and then turning south towards Lake Alexandrina.

En route, the river is tapped to provide domestic water for Adelaide and country towns as far away as Whyalla and Woomera, and for agricultural use across SA, NSW and Victoria (it's over-draining threatening a dire situation of salination and the silting of the Murray Mouth). Between the Victorian border and Blanchetown (SA), the usual vista of immense dry bush and farmlands is interrupted by a lush-green oasis of grapevines and citrus trees of the Riverina – irrigation having turned this previously unproductive land into an important agricultural region.

North of the river, the Murray River National Park and Chowilla Regional Reserve form part of the renowned Unesco Bookmark Biosphere Reserve. These are major breeding grounds for the state's waterfowl and other birds.

The Murray has a fascinating history. Before the advent of railways, it was Australia's Mississippi, with paddle-steamers carrying trade from the interior down to the coast. Several of these shallow-draught vessels have been restored and you can re-live the past on cruises of a few hours or several days.

There are many places along the Murray where the road crosses over the river by vehicle ferry. These are free and usually run 24 hours a day – phones are supplied to call the operator if the ferry is unattended.

Sights & Activities
HOUSEBOAT HIRE
The best way to explore the aura and mystique of the Murray River is by the water, and in full comfort. Houseboats can be booked in Adelaide and most riverside towns, but book well ahead, especially between October and April. The **Houseboat Hirers Association** (☎ 08-8395 0999; www.houseboat-centre.com.au; 7 Gollop Cres, Redwood Park, Adelaide) have a houseboat holiday brochure detailing each boat and can make free bookings on your behalf. Prices vary hugely, but in the 'normal season' you can expect to pay from around $210 per person per week depending on such factors as size of the boat, number of people and duration of hire. Prices are usually considerably cheaper in winter.

WATER PURSUITS
If you fancy the idea of splashing around on the water, this is the region in which to do it. A few caravan parks hire out canoes, and operators based in Mannum (see p766) and Barmera (see p767) will hire and deliver all manner of equipment to suit most water activities.

For general fishing info, mud maps and equipment try **Hook, Line & Sinker** (☎ 08-8582 2488; hlsinker@riverland.net.ay; 8 Denny St, Berri; ☉ 9am-5pm Mon-Fri, 9am-1.30pm Sat, 10am-2pm Sun).

Getting There & Away
Greyhound Australia (☎ 13 20 30; www.greyhound.com.au) passes through Barmera ($36, four hours), Berri ($41, 4¼ hours) and Renmark ($46, 4¾ hours) on the way to Sydney.

Murray Bridge Passenger Service (☎ 08-8415 5579) runs from Adelaide to Murray Bridge ($15, 1¼ hours) and Mannum ($20, 2½ hours) from Monday to Friday.

THE FRUITS OF YOUR LABOUR

The fruit- and grape-growing centres of Waikerie, Barmera, Loxton, Berri and Renmark are always seeking seasonal workers during harvest times. If you have a valid working visa and don't mind hard physical labour, ask at the backpacker hostels at Berri, Kingston-on-Murray, Loxton, Barmera and Murray Bridge, which all act as labour contractors. Also try Berri's private job agencies: **Rivskills** (☎ 08-8582 2188), **Riverland Personnel** (☎ 08-88586 5888; rivper@riverland.net.au) and Waikerie's **Select Labour Hire & Staff Recruitment** (☎ 08-8541 2407).

Premier Stateliner (☎ 08-8415 5555; www.premierstateliner.com) has daily services from Adelaide to Murray Bridge ($13, one hour), on its Mt Gambier service; its Riverland service stops in Waikerie ($30, 2½ hours), Kingston Hotel-on-Murray (Kingston OM; $35, three hours), Berri ($38, 3½ hours), Loxton, Barmera and Renmark ($38, four hours).

MURRAY BRIDGE
☎ 08 / pop 13,500
South Australia's largest river town is in dairy country. There's plenty of milk but little of interest for many visitors, though it makes a good base for fishing trips or to pick up hired boats. The **Murray Bridge visitor information centre** (☎ 8539 1142; mbvc@rcmb.sa.gov.au; 3 South Tce; ☉ 8.30am-5.30pm Mon-Fri, 10am-4pm Sat & Sun) has great regional information and details on river cruise operators:
MV Barrangul (☎ 0407 395 385; adult/family $12/30; ☉ daily) Departs from Sturt Reserve and offers lunch and dinner cruises upon bookings.
Proud Australia Nature Cruises (☎ 8231 9472; www.proudmary.com.au; Woodland Reserve, Mypolonga; adult/child $24/14; ☉ 11am Fri) Has a range of cruises aboard the *Proud Mary*.
River Boat Cruises South Australia (☎ 8532 2292; www.captainproud.com; cruises $12; ☉ Fri-Mon & Wed) Short cruises or lunch and dinner cruises (book ahead) on the *Captain Proud* and *Dragonfly* depart from Murray Bridge Wharf.

Open-range **Monarto Zoological Park** (☎ 8534 4100; www.monartozp.com.au; Princes Hwy, Monarto; adult/child/family $16/10/52; ☉ 10am-5pm), 20km west of town, has Australian and African creatures including herds of zebras and giraffes. A one-hour safari bus tour and guided walking trail are included in the price. **Murray Bridge Passenger Service** (☎ 8415 5533; 101 Franklin St, Central Adelaide; adult/child $30/15; ☺ departs 9am & returns 12.45pm Mon-Fri, departs noon & returns 3.45pm Sat) offers the only public transport to the park.

MANNUM TO WAIKERIE

The picturesque town of **Mannum** (population 2195), 84km east of Adelaide is the unofficial houseboat-hiring capital for the region. The *Mary Ann*, Australia's very first riverboat, was built here in 1853 and made the first paddle-steamer trip up the Murray. River cruise and houseboat bookings can be made at the **Mannum visitor information centre** (☎ 08-8569 1303; www.psmarion.com; 6 Randell St; ☺ 9am-5pm Mon-Fri, 10am-4pm Sat, Sun & public holidays). The centre incorporates the **Mannum Dock Museum of River History** (adult/child $5/2), featuring the Ngarrindjeri Aboriginal communities and the restored 1897 paddle-steamer PS *Marion*.

Breeze Holidays (☎ 08-8569 2223; www.breeze .com.au; Main St, Mannum) hires out canoes ($10 per hour); fishing gear including rod, tackle and yabby nets ($5 per hour); and a ski boat, driver and lessons ($120 per hour).

From Mannum to Swan Reach, you can take the eastern riverside detour via Bowhill, Purnong and Nildottie. Around 9km from Swan Reach, the Murray makes a tight meander known as **Big Bend**, a beloved spot for artists and photographers, with the sweeping curves of the river and glowing ochre-coloured cliffs.

Sleepy old **Swan Reach** (population 255), in picturesque river country 70km southwest of Waikerie, is a bit of a conundrum. There are not many swans, but there are plenty of pelicans.

A citrus-growing centre, **Waikerie** takes its name from the Aboriginal for 'anything that flies', after the teeming bird life on nearby lagoons and the river. Get binoculars out and start counting – 180 bird species (including six endangered breeds) have been recorded at the **Gluepot Reserve** (☎ 08-8892 9600; gluepot@riverland.net.au; Gluepot Rd; cars per day/ overnight $6/11; ☺ 8am-6pm). This mallee scrub area 64km north of Waikerie (off Lunn Rd) was set up by Birds Australia, and is part of Unesco's Bookmark Biosphere Reserves.

Sleeping & Eating

Waikerie Hotel/Motel (☎ 08-8541 2999; www.waiker iehotel.com; 2 McCoy St, Waikerie; d hotel/motel from $65/75, lunch $5-21, dinner $7-21; ☺ lunch & dinner; ✿) This central accommodation has clean, good-value rooms and serves decent pub tucker in the front bar or bistro.

Mannum House B&B (☎ 08-8569 2631; www.man numhouse.com.au; 33 River Lane, Mannum; d $135; ✿) Bliss out in the lounge overlooking the river and feast on the voluminous cooked breakfast at this cosy spot.

Heritage Centre B&B (☎ 08-8569 1987; 49 Randell St, Mannum; s/d $95/120; ✿) This cute cottage behind the old Mannum bank has the remarkable feature of a 20 million-year-old fossil wall. To the trained eye, markings depict global catastrophes such as the Ice Age!

Mannum Caravan Park (☎ 08-8569 1402, mann park@lm.net.au; Purnong Rd, Mannum; unpowered sites per 2 people $15, cabins from $58, linen $10; ✿) This riverside, older-style park is a five-minute walk from the main street. The adjacent Purnong Road Bird Sanctuary is a great spot to see water birds.

Mallyons on the Murray (☎ 08-8543 2263; Renmark–Morgan Rd; lunch $11; ☺ 10am-4pm Thu-Mon Aug-Jun) About 20km from Morgan on the Renmark Rd, this licensed and BYO bush café and organic veggie outlet was originally an 1841 resthouse for cattle drovers on the overland run from NSW.

BARMERA

☎ 08 / pop 1946

Barmera was once on the overland stock route from NSW and sits on the shores of the serene Lake Bonney. This wide and attractive freshwater lake has small sandy beaches, and is popular for swimming and water sports. World land-speed record holder Donald Campbell attempted to break his water-speed record on this lake in 1964.

Barmera visitor information centre (☎ 8588 2289; barmeravic@hotkey.net.au; Barwell Ave; ☺ 9am-5.15pm Mon-Fri, 9am-noon Sat, 10am-1pm Sun) is really a travel agent and booking service for coach companies.

Sights & Activities

Lake Bonney is very popular for swimming and water sports, and even has a nudist beach at **Pelican Point Nudist Resort** (☎ 8588

7366; bookings essential) on the lake's western shore. The lake is ringed by large dead red gums, whose stark branches are often festooned with cormorants.

Country music is a big deal here, with the **South Australian Country Music Festival & Awards** (☎ 8588 1030; www.riverlandcountrymusic.com) in June, and the **Country Music Hall of Fame** (☎ 8588 1463; Barwell Ave; adult/child $2/1) across from the visitor information centre.

On the Morgan Rd 19km northwest of town, the evocative 1859 **Overland Corner Hotel** (☎ 8588 7021; Old Coach Rd; meals $11-17; ☿ 11am-10pm Mon-Sat, 11am-8pm Sun) is named after a bend in the Murray River where drovers and travellers once camped. It is a great pub and has a resident museum, ghost and beer garden. An 8km self-guided **nature trail** leads down to the river from the pub past an ochre quarry and fossils. Pick up a map (50c) at the bar.

Wildlife reserves with walking trails can be found at **Moorook** (on the road to Loxton) and **Loch Luna** across the river from Kingston OM; the latter backs onto the Overland Corner Hotel. Both reserves have nature trails and are good spots for bird-watching and canoeing. For camping permits, contact the **DEH** (☎ 8595 2111) in Berri. Ecofriendly **Banrock Station winery** (☎ 8583 0299; www.banrockstation.com.au; Holmes Rd, Kingston OM; ☿ 10am-5pm) is signposted off Sturt Hwy at Kingston OM, and its stylish wine-tasting centre and restaurant overlook a beautiful wetland. A 2.5km wetland walk to a bird-hide leaves from the centre, and is very popular with twitchers. Bookings essential.

Sleeping & Eating

Barmera Backpackers (☎ 8588 3007; www.yha.com.au; 6 Bice Street; dm per night/week $17/115, tr per person $22; ☒ ☐) This small, bright and cheerful YHA is centrally based and takes international (or card-holding) backpackers. The manager also acts as a labour contractor. A grassed backyard with seating is a nice place in which to relax.

Barmera Lake Resort-Motel (☎ 8588 2555; lake resort@riverland.net.au; Lakeside Dr; s/d $60/70, mains $10-20; ☿ lunch & dinner; ☒ ☐) Right on the lake, this motel offers good value and facilities including a BBQ, laundry, tennis court and on-site Café Mudz.

Barmera Country Club (☎ 8588 2888; counbarm@ozemail.com.au; Hawdon St; s $94, d with/without spa

$142/112, dinner mains $15-25; ☿ dinner; ☒ ☐) Slightly faded but with grand facilities, this country club backs onto the golf course and is within putting distance of floodlit tennis courts and heated spas.

Lake Bonney Holiday Park (☎ 8588 2234; fax 8588 1974; Lakeside Dr; unpowered sites per 2 people $15, camp/park cabins $38/60; ☒) This spacious lakeside park has small swimming beaches, an electric BBQ and laundry, and large areas in which children can run around. It's within walking distance of town.

LOXTON
☎ 08 / pop 3358

Charming Loxton, on the Murray River loop, is a great place to while away a day or two or to stop at and boost travel funds. You can canoe from here across to the Katarapko Creek section of the Murray River National Park (a major breeding ground for waterfowl).

The friendly **Loxton visitor information centre** (☎ 8584 7919; www.loxtontourism.com.au; Bookpurnong Tce; ☿ 9am-5pm Mon-Fri, 9am-12.30pm Sat, 1-4pm Sun; ☐) has national park information, and a small art and craft gallery. Ask for film listings for its drive-in cinema.

Sights & Activities

The town's major attraction is **Loxton Historical Village** (☎ 8584 7194; www.loxtonhistoricalvillage.com.au; Scenic Dr; adult/child/family $8/4/21; ☿ 10am-4pm Mon-Fri, 10am-5pm Sat & Sun), with over 30 fully furnished buildings from days gone by.

Katarapko Game Reserve is prized by bird and nature-lovers and is accessible by water only. **Canoes** can be hired from Loxton Riverfront Caravan Park (see Sleeping & Eating, p768).

Curious types can check out the **Tree of Knowledge** by the caravan park, which is marked with flood levels from previous years.

Sleeping & Eating

Harvest Trail Lodge (☎ 8584 5646; www.harvesttrail.com; 1 Kokoda Tce; dm per night/week for workers $27/140, d $45; ☒ ☐) The four-bed dorms at this hostel have TVs and fridges and there is a great balcony-BBQ area. The staff will find you work, and shunt you to and from jobs for free.

Loxton Community Hotel/Motel (☎ 1800 656 686, 8584 7266; www.loxtonhotel.com.au; East Tce; hotel s/d $57/77, motel s/d $80/90, meals $8-20; lunch & dinner;) These immaculate rooms offer the best value in the region with some great weekend and golf deals. Pub-style meals are served in the bar and bistro.

Loxton Riverfront Caravan Park (☎ 8584 7862; loxtoncp@hotkey.net.au; Riverfront Rd; unpowered sites $13, cabins with/without bathroom $55/40;) At Habels Bend, 2km from town, this peaceful riverside park is surrounded by beautiful red gums. Canoes can be hired ($7/30 per hour/day) and there's a free nine-hole par-three golf course.

BERRI

☎ 08 / pop 4241

This attractive but surprisingly low-key town – once a refuelling stop for wood-burning paddle-steamers – takes its name from the Aboriginal term *berri berri*, meaning 'big bend in the river'. It virtually closes down at night, perhaps due to the mainly transient working population. Berri is the regional centre for both state government and agricultural casual labour agencies.

The **Berri visitor information centre** (☎ 8582 2188; Riverview Dr; 9am-5pm Mon-Fri, 10am-4pm Sat & Sun) is by the river.

Sights & Activities

Water-based activities and bushwalking are popular in the area.

On and around the base of Berri Bridge, check out the excellent **murals and totem poles** created by local artists. **Country Arts SA** (☎ 8584 5807; 23 Wilson St; admission free; 9.30am-4.30pm Mon-Fri) displays local and travelling exhibitions.

Berri Estates (☎ 8582 0340; Old Sturt Hwy; cellar door 9am-5pm Mon-Fri, 10am-4pm Sat & Sun) at Glossop, 7km west of Berri, claims to be one of Australia's biggest wineries, although perhaps it's not one of the most attractive.

Road access to the beautiful Katarapko Creek section of the **Murray River National Park** is through Berri or Winkie (near Glossop). This beautiful stretch of river is a great area for **bush camping** ($6.50), and for canoeing and bird-watching.

Sleeping & Eating

Berri Backpackers (☎ 8582 3144; Sturt Hwy; dm/dm per week for workers $20/120;) On the Barmera side of town, this hostel is beloved of pleasure-seeking international travellers,

who revel in the Balinese surroundings and hippy environment. Among other facilities on the huge grounds are a sauna, soccer field, tennis court, bicycles and canoes. There's seasonal work available in local the orchards and vineyards.

Berri Resort Hotel (☎ 8582 1411; www.berrire sorthotel.com; Riverview Dr; hotel s/d $55/70, motel s/d $110/120, meals $11-18; breakfast, lunch & dinner;) While motel rooms are on the pricey side here, children under 13 stay for free and there's a gym. The lively pub/restaurant serves tasty bistro food.

Berri Riverside Caravan Park (☎ 8582 3723; www .berricaravanpark.com.au; Riverview Dr; unpowered sites per 2 people $17, dm/cabins $28/50;) This well-maintained and popular park opposite the river is big on greenery and the facilities are spotless.

RENMARK

☎ 08 / pop 4470

Renmark is the first major river town across from the NSW border and is 254km from Adelaide. It doesn't have the friendliness of nearby Loxton and Barmera, and social drinking can start early on the riverfront.

The **Renmark visitor information centre** (☎ 8586 6704; www.renmarkparinga.sa.gov.au; 84 Murray Ave; 9am-5pm Mon-Fri, 9am-4pm Sat, 10am-4pm Sun) has a free interpretive centre and the recommissioned 1911 paddle-steamer PS *Industry*.

Renmark River Cruises (☎ 8595 1862; www.ren markrivercruises.com.au; Main Wharf; adult/child/family $28/12/60; Tue-Sun) offers two-hour cruises past the Murray River cliffs on the MV *Big River Rambler*. The company also conducts guided tours by motorised dinghy ($59 per person, minimum two people).

Upstream from town, the huge **Chowilla Regional Reserve** (part of the sprawling Unesco Bookmark Biosphere Reserve) is great for bush camping, canoeing and bushwalking. Access is along the north bank from Renmark or along the south bank from Paringa. For details, contact the **DEH** (☎ 8595 2111; Vaughan Tce, Berri).

Canoes ($5 per hour) can be hired from Renmark Riverfront Caravan Park (see following).

Sleeping & Eating

Renmark Hotel/Motel (☎ 8586 6755; www.renmark hotel.com.au; Murray Ave; hotel s/d $60/70, motel s/d

$80/90, mains $14.50-22; ☺ breakfast, lunch & dinner; ✗ ☐) The clean rooms are good value in this huge hotel, which also serves meals.

Renmark Riverfront Caravan Park (☎ 8584 7862; renrivcarapk@riverland.net.au; Sturt Hwy; unpowered sites per 2 people $19, unpowered cabins $35-60, powered cabins $55-60; ☒) This neatly manicured park sits idyllically on the river 1km east of town and seems to be geared for long-term workers.

YORKE PENINSULA

With agriculture as its primary industry, the Yorke Peninsula (www.yorkepeninsula .com.au) is also a weekend destination of choice for more-adventurous Adelaidians. Beaches are tucked behind farmlands and families gather at holiday shacks to enjoy the solitude and fishing. Every October experienced surfers compete in the **Cutloose Ripcurl Yorke's Classic**, from celebrated points on the striking **Innes National Park** coastline. Emus, kangaroos, ospreys and sea eagles inhabit this unspoilt park, and southern right whales and dolphins pass by its coastline.

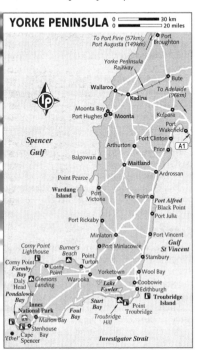

The area's economy was originally based on the so-called Copper Triangle – Moonta (the mine), Wallaroo (the smelter) and Kadina (the service town), following a copper boom in the early 1860s. Many miners were from Cornwall in England, and the area still retains a Cornish flavour – notably in the Cornish pasty. A Cornish festival, **Kernewek Lowender**, is held here in alternate years during May (complete with wheelbarrow races). If you drink enough traditional beer you may see a *piskey* – a mischievous sprite believed to bring good fortune.

The boom peaked around the turn of the century, but in the early 1920s rising labour costs and a slump in copper prices closed all of the peninsula's mines.

The regional **visitor information centre** (☎ 1800 654 991, 08-8821 2333; www.coppercoast.sa.gov .au; 50 Moonta Rd, Kadina; ☒ 9am-5pm Mon-Fri, 10am-3.30pm Sat & Sun) is in Kadina.

Getting There & Around

Amazingly, there is no public transport to take you to the end of the peninsula.

Excel Rent-a-Car (☎ 08-8821 2777; Adelaide Rd, Kadina) is at Kadina Gateway Motor Inn.

Premier Stateliner (☎ 08-8645 9911; www.premierstateliner.com.au) operates a bus from Adelaide to Kadina, Wallaroo, Moonta, Port Hughes and Moonta Bay (all $21, two to three hours) twice daily on weekdays and daily on weekends.

Yorke Peninsula Coaches (☎ 08-8823 2375) will take you as far as Warooka or Yorketown. It runs daily from Adelaide's central bus station to Yorketown either along the east coast or down the centre of the peninsula.

WEST COAST

The west coast, facing onto Spencer Gulf, has several quiet swimming beaches and the small Copper Triangle historic towns of Kadina, Wallaroo and Moonta, which are all within a short drive of each other.

Weary travellers can kick off their hiking boots and kick back in **Port Broughton**, a mellow holiday town around 50km northeast of Kadina and Wallaroo. Swim, fish and chill.

Kadina

☎ 08 / pop 3745

The town of Kadina has a number of historic sites. **Kadina Heritage Museum** (☎ 8821

2333; Moonta Rd; adult/child/concession $8/2/6; ⏰ 9am-5pm Mon-Fri, 10am-2pm Sat & Sun), in the visitor information centre complex, illustrates the lifestyle of the mining folk and includes the restored Matta House (1863), old farming machinery, a blacksmith's shop and details on the Matta Matta mine.

There's also the **Banking & Currency Museum** (☎ 8821 2906; 3 Graves St; adult/child $5/2; ⏰ 10am-4.30pm Sun-Thu Jul-May), housed in an old bank; you can still buy and sell coins here.

Wallaroo

☎ 08 / pop 2720

Wallaroo was a major port during the copper boom, and has the Copper Triangle's best beach. The big stack, one of the great chimneys from the copper smelters (built in 1861) still stands, but today the port's main function is the exporting of agricultural products.

The solid ex–post office holds the **Heritage & Nautical Museum** (☎ 8823 2015; Jetty Rd; adult/child $5/2; ⏰ 2-4pm Tue, Thu, Sat & Sun, 10.30am-4pm Wed), with tales of the English square-rigged sailing ships that serviced this region.

There's plenty of fishing or just boat-based sightseeing to be had around the area.

Sonbern Lodge Motel (☎ 8823 2291; 18 John Tce; s $28-67, d $44-84), once a grand former-temperance hotel (relax – it's licensed now), is an old-fashioned charmer right down to the pool table and antique wind-up phone. Upstairs are basic pub-style rooms while private motel units are at the back.

The basic **Office Beach Holiday Cabins & Caravan Park** (☎ 8823 2722; 11 Jetty Rd; powered/unpowered sites per 2 people $20/17, cabins $55, units $80-105; 🐾) is on the beach near the main jetty, and has an outdoor kitchen.

The town's five hotels have counter meals and there are also several takeaways, bakeries and tearooms.

Moonta

☎ 08 / pop 3084

In the late 19th century the copper mine at Moonta, 18km south of Wallaroo, was the richest mine in Australia.

Moonta Tourist Office (☎ 8825 1891; Kadina-Moonta Rd; ⏰ 9am-5pm) has a good selection of history pamphlets, and details on walks around **Moonta Heritage Site** (Arthurton Rd), 1km east of town.

At its peak, the town's grand old school had 1100 pupils on its rolls, but these days it's the excellent **Moonta Mines Museum** (☎ 8825 1891; Verran Tce; adult/child $5/2; ⏰ 1.30-4pm Wed, Fri, Sat & Sun). **Moonta Mines Sweet Shop** is across the road. On weekends, a **tourist railway** (adult/child $5/2) runs from the museum to Kadina and Bute (50 minutes).

Nearby is an evocative and fully restored **Miner's Cottage** (☎ 8825 1891; Verco St; adult/child $2.50/1; ⏰ 1.30-4pm Wed, Sat & Sun).

Just 3km from town on the Wallaroo Rd, a section of the 1980s **Wheal Hughes Copper Mine** (☎ 8825 1892; Moonta–Wallaroo Rd; adult/child/concession $22/11/8; ⏰ tours by appointment) has been reopened, offering a look into a modern mine.

SLEEPING & EATING

Moonta Bay Patio Motel (☎ 8825 2473; 196 Bay Rd, Moonta Bay; s/d/tr $78/90/100, mains $16-26; ⏰ lunch & dinner; 🐾) Soak up the tremendous views over Moonta Bay from this pleasant beachside hotel. It's 3km from town but you needn't move – the fully-licensed restaurant serves tasty meals.

Peppertree Cottage (☎ 8825 2680; 85 Wallaroo Rd; s/d $90/120; 🐾) This quiet weekend-away star has plenty of creature comforts, no TV for distraction and a private pool. There are huge cooked breakfasts and evening meals available.

Moonta Bay Top Tourist Park (☎ 8825 2406; Foreshore, Moonta Bay; powered/unpowered sites per 2 people $23/21, cabins $66-73, cabins with spa $109) Handy to the jetty, this family-friendly park has some good luxury cabins that include spas for a splurge.

In a region worshipping the Cornish pasty, three bakeries vie for top pastry honours, including **Cornish Kitchen** (☎ 8825 3030; 16 Ellen St). Other cafés are near the jetties in the adjoining seaside towns of Port Hughes and Moonta Bay.

EAST COAST

The east coast road from the top of Gulf St Vincent down to Stenhouse Bay near Cape Spencer is generally within 1km to 2km of the sea. En route, tracks and roads lead to sandy beaches and secluded coves.

There are many small coastal townships usually with a caravan park, cabins or camping ground, including tranquil **Port Vincent**. Good off-season deals for couples, families and friends can be made at the central and friendly **Port Vincent Holiday Cabins** (☎ 08-8853 7411; abins@netyp.com.au; 12 Main St; d $85; 😢).

Further south, **Edithburgh** has a tidal swimming pool in a small cove; from the cliff tops you can look across to **Troubridge Island lighthouse** and **conservation park**. Overnight stays ($80 per person, minimum two nights) with sole occupancy of the island are also available in the old **lighthouse keeper's cottage** (☎ 08-8852 6290; q $320). Migratory birds stop to visit the island's permanent inhabitants, an enchanting fairy penguin colony.

The district's inland business and administrative centre, **Yorketown** (population 750), is a friendly place and you may find accommodation here when the seaside resorts are full during summer.

INNES NATIONAL PARK

The southern tip of the peninsula, marked by Cape Spencer, is part of the **Innes National Park** (admission per car $6.50). The park has spectacular coastal scenery as well as good fishing, reef diving and surfing. You'll go a long way to find quieter emus! **Stenhouse Bay**, just outside the park, and **Pondalowie Bay**, within the park, are the principal settlements. Pondalowie Bay is the base for a large lobster-fishing fleet and also has a fine surf beach hosting regular surfing events. Beaches are swimmable, but keep an eye on the swell and wind direction.

The remaining hull ribs of the steel barque *Ethel,* a 711-tonne ship that ran aground in 1904, rise forlornly from the sands – her anchor is mounted in a memorial on the cliff top above the beach. Just past the Cape Spencer turn-off, a sign on the right directs you to the ruins of the **Inneston Historic Site**. Inneston was a gypsum-mining community that was abandoned in 1930.

There are a number of sheltered **bush camp sites** (per car $6.50-16, depending on facilities) that are close to nice beaches. Alternatively, comfortable heritage **lodges** (per night $80-110) at Inneston and Stenhouse Bay sleep four or 10 people and have showers and cooking facilities. Drinking water is limited, so bring your own in summer. Book ahead at the **DEH** (☎ 08-8854 3200; Stenhouse Bay; 🕒 9am-4.30pm Mon-Fri, 10.30am-2pm Sat & Sun).

Rhino's Tavern (☎ 08-8854 4066; Stenhouse Bay; 🕒 lunch & dinner) serves steaks and whiting and a taste-bud zapping curry.

EYRE PENINSULA & WEST COAST

The Eyre Peninsula's wide, triangular shape points south between Spencer Gulf and the Great Australian Bight, engulfing golden beaches backed by rugged cliffs. It takes its name from Edward John Eyre, the hardy explorer who, in 1841, made the first overland crossing between Adelaide and Albany (WA).

This major agricultural region is considered by gourmands to be the Barossa Valley of seafood, while rich iron-ore deposits from the Middleback Ranges are processed and shipped from the busy port of Whyalla. The coastline along the peninsula is pocked with sheltered bays and pleasant little port towns, popular as summer holiday and recreational fishing spots. Along the spectacular wild western side are important breeding grounds for the southern right whale, the Australian sea lion and the great white shark – the scariest scenes in the film *Jaws* were shot here.

Surfers from around the world are drawn to many excellent breaks along the coast, including the famous Cactus Beach. However it's not for the faint-hearted. The ocean rips can be vicious and sharks are a constant threat; in 2000, two surfers were taken within two days off of Cactus Beach and Elliston, and others have since perished. Ask the locals about safe swimming beaches.

The devastating bushfires on the Eyre Peninsula in January 2005 were Australia's deadliest since the 1983 Ash Wednesday blaze, claiming homes, stock and lives.

You can take the Eyre Hwy from Port Augusta to Ceduna (468km), though the coast road via Port Lincoln (763km) is much more interesting.

For further information, visit www.tep .com.au.

Tours

Nullarbor Traveller (☎ 08-8390 3297; www.the-traveller .com.au) runs relaxed camping and hostelling trips between Adelaide and Perth (seven/nine days $770/990) which include bushwalking, surfing and whale watching. Prices include accommodation, national park entry fees and almost all meals.

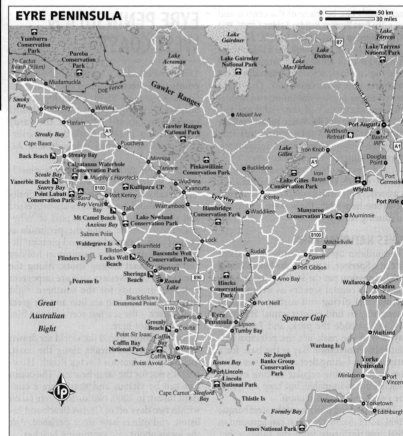

EYRE PENINSULA

Getting There & Away

AIR

Airlines of SA (☎ 13 13 13; www.airlinesofsa.com.au) flies daily from Adelaide to Port Lincoln ($225) and Port Augusta ($140).

O'Connor Airlines (☎ 13 13 13; www.oconnor-airlines.com.au) flies daily from Adelaide to Whyalla ($102).

Rex (☎ 13 17 13; www.regionalexpress.com.au) has flights daily from Adelaide to the destinations of Ceduna (one way $129), Port Lincoln and Whyalla ($165).

BUS

Greyhound Australia (☎ 13 14 99; www.greyhound .com.au) passes through Ceduna daily on its way to Perth ($287, 26 hours).

Premier Stateliner (☎ 08-8645 9911; www.prem ierstateliner.com.au) has daily buses from Adelaide to Port Augusta ($48, four hours), Whyalla ($78, five hours), Port Lincoln ($80, 8½ hours), Ceduna ($90, 12 hours) and Streaky Bay ($84, 10 hours).

TRAIN

For details of train and bus services in the region, see opposite.

PORT AUGUSTA

☎ 08 / pop 13,194

The Aboriginal name *kurdnatta* (heaps of sand) aptly describes this unremarkable transport hub. Shipping booms in the 1880s made this a centre for trade, which was re-enforced when it was made the headquarters for the Transcontinental Railway to Perth. Today, the town remains a major crossroads for travellers. A bit sad and tatty, Port Augusta was thrown into politically charged controversy with the establishment of Baxter Detention Centre.

From town, roads head west across the Nullarbor to WA, north to Alice Springs in the NT, south to Adelaide and east to Broken Hill in NSW. With railway lines converging here, trains can be caught to Alice Springs and Darwin, the east and west coasts, Adelaide and Melbourne.

The **Port Augusta visitor information centre** (☎ 1800 633 060, 8641 0793; www.portaugusta.sa.gov .au; 41 Flinders Tce; ☺ 9am-5.30pm Mon-Fri, 10am-4pm Sat & Sun; ☐) is the major information outlet for the Flinders Ranges, the outback and the Eyre Peninsula.

Sights & Activities

Get a taste of how a phenomenal medical service operates: visit the **Royal Flying Doctor Service** (☎ 8642 2044; 4 St Vincent St; admission by donation; ☺ 10am-3pm Mon-Fri). It's due to relocate to the hangar at the airport in the future.

Off the Stuart Hwy, **Australian Arid Lands Botanic Garden** (☎ 8641 104; ☺ gardens 7am-sunset, visitor information centre 9am-5pm Mon-Fri, 10am-4pm Sat & Sun) covers more than 250 hectares of sandhills and clay flats. You can walk the trails and learn about local plant life and you'll definitely see Sturt's desert pea, the state's floral emblem. A bush café serves snacks.

Homestead Park Pioneer Museum (☎ 8642 2035; Elsie St; adult/child $2.50/1.50; ☺ 9am-noon Mon-Fri, 1-4pm Sat & Sun) features an original 1870s log-cabin homestead.

Adjoining the visitor information centre, the interpretative **Wadlata Outback Centre** (41 Flinders Tce; adult/child $8.50/5.50; ☺ 9am-5.30pm Mon-Fri, 10am-4pm Sat & Sun) has many excellent exhibits, particularly the Flinders Ranges and Outback Tunnel of Time, which traces the histories of the Aboriginal and European people. Right next door, the **Fountain Gallery** (☎ 8642 4557; 43 Flinders Tce; admission free; ☺ 10am-4pm Mon-Fri) is an intimate space with works by local and indigenous artists.

Sleeping & Eating

There are plenty of motels in Port Augusta, but little quality budget accommodation. Hotels are the best bet for meals.

Hotel Flinders (☎ 8642 2544; 39 Commercial Rd; dm/s/d/tr $16.50/50/66/77, mains $14-22; ☺ lunch Mon-Fri, dinner Mon-Sun) It's hard to beat the Flinders for its variety of pub rooms; better ones have private bathrooms and TVs. It also has one of the more innovative pub menus.

Blue Fox Lodge (☎ 8641 2960; 8-10 Victoria Pde; dm $18-20) The town's only real hostel has cramped rooms but also cosy living areas with videos and a BBQ area. Staff can pick up guests from the bus station.

Comfort Inn Augusta Westside (☎ 8642 2488; 3 Loudon St; s $98-160, d $106-160; ☒ ☒) Handy to the gulf and the town centre, this excellently appointed hotel has all the mod cons, including spas in the better rooms.

Standpipe Golf Motor Inn (☎ 8642 4033; cnr Stuart Hwy & Hwy 1; s $67-100, d $74-110, mains $9-19; ☒) Comfy '70s-era units drop in price on weekends at this friendly place. Order from European or Indian menus in its restaurant.

Shoreline Caravan Park (☎ 8642 2965; Gardiner Ave; powered/unpowered sites per 2 people $16/11, on-site caravans $33, cabins/units $55/65) Well positioned near the water, this park has loads of good facilities, including TV and games rooms, plus a great BBQ area.

Getting There & Away

AIR

Airlines of SA (☎ 13 13 13; www.airlinesofsa.com.au) has flights twice each weekday to/from Adelaide ($140).

BUS

You can book tickets for Premier Stateliner at the **bus station** (☎ 8642 5055; 23 Mackay St) but not for Greyhound Australia.

Greyhound Australia (☎ 13 14 99; www.greyhound .com.au) travels daily to Perth ($290, 30 hours), Alice Springs ($210, 14 hours) via Coober Pedy ($80, six hours), and Darwin ($440, 35 hours).

Premier Stateliner (☎ 8642 5055; www.premier stateliner.com.au) runs daily to Adelaide ($39, four hours), Port Lincoln ($55, 4½ hours) and Ceduna ($75, 6½ hours).

Yorke Peninsula Coaches (☎ 1800 625 099, 8666 2255; adult/child $5/2.50) head north to Quorn, Wilmington and a few smaller towns in the southern Flinders on Friday.

TRAIN

The *Ghan* and *Indian Pacific* trains pass through Port Augusta en route to mainland capitals, stopping at **Stirling Rd Station** (☎ 8642 6699). **Great Southern Railways** (☎ 13 21 47; www .trainways.com.au) offers excellent backpacker deals and discounts.

Full-fare options departing from Port Augusta include: Adelaide (seat $38, four hours); Alice Springs (seat/twin-share/1st-class sleeper $175/550/680, 16 hours, Friday and Sunday); Darwin (seat/twin-share/1st-class sleeper $410/1280/1600, 43 hours, Friday and Sunday); Perth (seat/twin-share/1st-class sleeper $280/850/1060, 33 hours, Thursday and Sunday); and Sydney (seat/twin-share/1st-class sleeper $270/590/740, 32 hours, Friday and Tuesday).

For a more-scenic trip, **Pichi Richi Railway** (☎ 8633 0380; www.prr.org.au) goes to Quorn ($34, 1¾ hours) and back on Saturday.

WHYALLA

☎ 08 / pop 21,271

An hour's drive from Port Augusta, Whyalla is the second-largest city in the state and is a major steel-producing centre (with a deep-water port) that also supports oil and gas refineries. As the vast spread of towering chimneys, hideous portworks and furnaces lurch into view, you'll be relieved to know that Whyalla is also a nuclear-free zone.

Whyalla visitor information centre (☎ 8645 7900; www.whyalla.sa.gov.au; Lincoln Hwy; ☉ 10am-4pm) is adjacent to the **Maritime Museum** (☉ 10am-4pm), which features the 650-tonne, WWII corvette HMAS *Whyalla*. Museum tours are conducted on the hour between 11am and 3pm.

Tours of the **OneSteel works** (2½hr tours adult/child/concession $17/8/16; ☉ tours 1pm) depart from the visitor information centre. Long trousers, long-sleeved shirts and closed footwear are essential.

Divers are attracted here between May and August to witness the spawning of thousands of **giant cuttlefish** (see www.cuttlefishcapital.com.au for more information). These dancing chameleons of the sea gather around Point Lowly and Black Point, where you can snorkel or dive to watch their graceful courtship.

WYHALLA TO PORT LINCOLN

The pleasant little town of Cowell is near Australia's only large jade deposit. You can purchase a wide range of jade products

from the **Cowell Jade Motel** (☎ 08-8629 2002; Lincoln Hwy; s/d/tr from $75/80/90), a classic old pub with a fine view of the town and harbour at the northern end of town. Oysters are farmed locally – they're sold at several places for as little as $5.50 a dozen.

The Lincoln Hwy keeps you close to the coast all the way to Port Lincoln and passes by **Arno Bay**, a small beach resort with a pub and caravan park. A further 33km on is picturesque **Port Neill**, a pleasant little seaside town with a vintage-vehicle museum.

South again is **Tumby Bay**, with its long curving white-sand beach, a National Trust of Australia **museum** (☎ 08-8688 2198; Lipsom Rd; adult $2; ☉ 2.30-4.30pm Fri & Sat), and a number of old buildings around town. **Hales Mini Mart** (☎ 08-8688 2584; 1 Bratten Way; ☉ 7am-9pm) hires out boats ($35 per day).

PORT LINCOLN

☎ 08 / pop 12,664

Prosperous, bustling Port Lincoln, at the southern end of the Eyre Peninsula, is 662km from Adelaide. The first settlers arrived in 1839 and the town has grown to become the tuna-fishing capital of Australia and a popular holiday spot, complete with marina and numerous sea-based activities.

The annual **Tunarama Festival** (☎ 8682 1300) runs over the Australia Day weekend in January and celebrates every aspect of the tuna-fishing industry. It's an entertaining weekend with tuna tossing, keg rolling, slippery-pole climbing, boat-building races, stalls and bands.

Information

Port Lincoln visitor information centre (☎ 8683 3544; www.visitportlincoln.net; 3 Adelaide Pl; ☉ 9am-5pm; ☐) This excellent centre has national parks information and sells park passes.

Sights & Activities

Port Lincoln is well situated on Boston Bay. There are a number of historic buildings, including **Mill Cottage** (☎ 8682 4650; 20 Flinders Hwy; adult/child $4/50c; ☉ 2-4.30pm Mon, Wed & Sat), built in 1866.

The **Seahorse Farm** (☎ 8683 4866; 5 Mallee Cr; adult/child/concession $10/7/8.50; ☉ tours 3pm) breeds cute critters for the pet market. The 40-minute tour shows off leafy sea dragons, SA's state marine emblem. Book tours at the visitor information centre.

There are some good surfing and diving spots near the town. For information about the best areas, contact the **Port Lincoln Skin-Diving & Surfing Centre** (☎ 8682 4428; 1 King St; ☺ 9am-5.30pm Mon-Fri, to 12.30pm Sat), where licensed divers can hire scuba equipment (around $80 for one-day hire).

The visitor information centre handles bookings for various tours and activities including **boat charters** and **yacht cruises** around Boston Bay to off-shore islands, and **whale-watching** tours. Land-based tours include a day tour of the town and spectacular Whalers Way and a 4WD tour exploration of Coffin Bay Peninsula.

For the ultimate waterborne adventure, **Calypso Star Charter** (☎ 8364 4428; www.calypso starcharter.com.au; 1-day dive $517) offers the chance to cage dive with notorious great white sharks or less-threatening sea lions.

Sleeping & Eating

There are plenty of hotels, motels and holiday flats in and around town, and restaurants in the city centre.

Grand Tasman Hotel (☎ 8682 2133; 94 Tasman Tce; s/d $50/60, bistro mains $16-14, restaurant mains $17-30; ☺ lunch & dinner) The swanky re-fit downstairs at this foreshore hotel didn't make it upstairs but the rooms are clean with worn beds and big TVs. Local seafood is served in the bistro.

Limani Motel (☎ 8682 2200; www.limanimotel.com .au; 50 Lincoln Hwy; d $95) Don't be confused by the two-level parking complex at the entrance, as oceanfront rooms in this great little spot are excellently appointed. Staff are cheery, and helpful with local touring plans.

Kirton Point Caravan Park (☎ 8682 2537; Hindmarsh St; powered/unpowered sites $21/8, 4-bed camp cabins $35, caravans/cabins $51/64) On the water close to the town centre, this roomy place has great facilities, boat-launching jetties and a green park with pelicans.

AROUND PORT LINCOLN

Better known as Whalers Way, **Cape Carnot** is 32km south of Port Lincoln and features beautiful and rugged coastal scenery. It's privately owned but you can visit with a 24-hour permit ($25 per car) from most petrol stations or the Port Lincoln visitor information centre. The permit includes camping at Redbanks or Groper Bay.

These places also sell permits to **Mikkira Station & Koala Sanctuary** (☎ 08-8685 6020; Fishery Bay Rd; day permit/camping $12/17), the Eyre Peninsula's first sheep station and home to abundant bird life including the attractive Port Lincoln parrot. Pop-culture trivia: it was recently used on the US *Survivor* TV series.

The beautiful beaches at **Sleaford Bay** are a 3km detour off the road to Whalers Way, but a strong rip means it's best not to swim.

Also south of Port Lincoln is **Lincoln National Park**, with a magnificent coastline that includes quiet coves with safe swimming and pounding surf beaches. There's self-registration for entry on the way in ($6.50 per car including one night's camping). Most of the park's vehicle tracks are suitable for conventional vehicles but you will need a 4WD to visit tranquil **Memory Cove** – the visitor information centre in Port Lincoln keeps the keys to the gate on this track for would-be happy campers ($16 per car).

PORT LINCOLN TO STREAKY BAY
Coffin Bay
☎ 08 / pop 453

Ominous-sounding Coffin Bay (named by Matthew Flinders to honour Sir Isaac Coffin) basks languidly in the warm sun and calm bay waters, but becomes inundated with holiday-makers in January. Oysters from the nearby beds are exported worldwide, but you won't pay more than $6 a dozen around town.

From here you can visit wild coastal scenery along the ocean side of Coffin Bay Peninsula, which is entirely taken up by **Coffin Bay National Park** (per car $6.50). Access for conventional vehicles is limited within the park – you can get to scenic **Point Avoid** (a good surf break) and **Yangie Bay** quite easily, but otherwise you'll need a 4WD.

Bird life, including some unusual migratory species, is a feature of the **Kellidie Bay Conservation Park**, just outside Coffin Bay township.

Several places along the peninsula allow bush camping – generally with difficult access ($7 per car.) For holiday shacks, contact **Century 21 Real Estate** (☎ 8685 4063; www.century21 .com.au/coffinbay; 61 Esplanade; cottages $45-180).

Coffin Bay Hotel (☎ 8685 4111; Shepperd Ave; d $85, mains around $18; ☺ lunch & dinner; ☒) has roomy units and serves standard counter meals.

There are plenty of good sites nestled among sheoaks and tea trees at **Coffin Bay Caravan Park** (☎ 8685 4170; Shepperd Ave; powered/unpowered sites per 2 people $20/15, on-site caravans $37, cabins $50, cottage $60). The amenities are well kept and there are golf clubs for hire ($5).

Oysterbeds Restaurant (☎ 8685 4000; Shepperd Ave; mains $19-25; ☒ lunch & dinner Wed-Sat) is the best dining option in town, serving the finest local seafood.

Coffin Bay to Point Labatt

Just past **Coulta**, 40km north of Coffin Bay, there's good surfing at **Greenly Beach**. About 15km south of **Elliston** (a small resort and fishing town on peaceful Waterloo Bay), **Locks Well** is one of several good salmon-fishing spots along this wild coast. A long steep stairway – called **Staircase to Heaven** – leads from the car park here down to the gorgeous beach. **Elliston** has a beautiful swimming beach and a well-regarded fishing jetty (best for tommy ruff or whiting) as well as accommodation, a pub and a bakery.

Just north of Elliston, take the 7km detour to **Anxious Bay** and **Salmon Point** for some dramatic ocean scenery – en route you'll pass **Blackfellows**, with some of the west coast's best surfing breaks. From here you can see distant **Flinders Island**, where there's a sheep station and tourist accommodation.

At **Venus Bay** there are quiet beaches, plenty of pelicans and a small caravan park.

About 38km before Streaky Bay, the turnoff to **Point Labatt** takes you to one of the few permanent colonies of sea lions on the Australian mainland. You can view them from the cliff-top above the colony – take binoculars.

A few kilometres down the Point Labatt road are **Murphy's Haystacks**. This is the most impressive collection of inselbergs (colourful, weather-sculpted granite outcrops which are millions of years old) on the peninsula.

STREAKY BAY

☎ 08 / pop 1081

This endearing little town takes its name from the streaks of seaweed Flinders saw in the bay. Still visible at low tide, the seagrass attracts ocean critters, making for some first-class fishing. Tourist informa-

tion is available from **Stewarts Roadhouse** (☎ 8626 1126; www.streakybay.sa.gov.au; 15 Alfred Tce; ☒ 6.30am-9pm).

The **Streaky Bay Museum** (☎ 8626 1142; Montgomery Tce; adult/child $3.50/50c, ☒ 2-4pm Tue & Fri) features a fully furnished pug-and-pine hut and an iron lung. The museum is also open by appointment.

There's some grand cliff scenery around the coast here. **Back Beach**, 4km west of Streaky Bay, is good for surfing, and **Yanerbie**, at the northern end of Sceale Bay, has a swimming beach and white Sahara-like dunes.

There are lots of oyster farms out this way, as well as further along the coast at sleepy **Smoky Bay**. You can get fresh oysters from several outlets from as little as $8 a dozen.

Sleeping & Eating
Streaky Bay Community Hotel/Motel (☎ 8626 1008; 35 Alfred Tce; dm $20-24, hotel s/d $60/75, motel s/d $80/95, meals $8-16; ☒ lunch & dinner) This comfortable classic in the centre of town serves impressive *bain-marie*-based cuisine in its bistro.

Headland House (☎ 8626 1315; 5 Flinders Dr; s/d $85/95; ☒) Scenic Headland is a plush place with a full-sized pool table, large continental breakfasts and a fan collection from across the globe.

Foreshore Tourist Park (☎ 8626 1666; Wells St; powered/unpowered sites per 2 people $20/18, units $45-75, cabins $65-70) About 1km west of town, this friendly caravan park is by a safe swimming beach. The adjoining kiosk serves good takeaways.

CEDUNA

☎ 08 / pop 2588

Just past the junction of the Eyre and Flinders Hwys, Ceduna marks the end of the Eyre Peninsula and the start of the long lonely drive across the Nullarbor Plain into WA. The town was established in 1896, although there had been a whaling station on St Peter Island, off nearby Cape Thevenard, back in 1850.

The **Ceduna visitor information centre** (☎ 1800 639 413, 8625 2780; 58 Poynton St; ☒ 9am-5.30pm Mon-Fri, 9am-noon Sat; ☐) is located in Traveland Ceduna, and onward coach tickets can be obtained here.

Ceduna Museum (☎ 8625 2210; 2 Park Tce; adult/child $3.50/2; ☒ 10am-noon Mon, Tue & Thu-Sat, & 2-

4pm Wed & Thu) has pioneer exhibits as well as artefacts and newspaper clippings from the British atomic weapons programme at Maralinga.

The sea-inspired works of local indigenous artists from along the coast are featured at **Ceduna Aboriginal Arts & Culture Centre** (☎ 8625 2487; cnr Eyre Hwy & Kuhlmann St; admission free; ⏰ 9am-5pm Mon-Fri).

Sleeping & Eating

There are four caravan parks in Ceduna; ask about them at the visitor information centre.

East West Motel (☎ 8625 2101; www.eastwest ceduna.com.au; 66-76 McKenzie St; s $55-100, d $65-105, mains $13-26; ⏰ lunch & dinner; ⚅) Definitely one of the slicker places in town, with fancy Anna's Restaurant and simple motel rooms through to deluxe apartments that include DVD players.

Ceduna Foreshore Hotel/Motel (☎ 8625 2008; O'Loughlin Tce; powered/unpowered sites per 2 people $20/17; cabins $50-70; hotel s/d $30/40, motel s/d $75/85, mains $9-14; ⏰ lunch & dinner; ⚅) The caravan park offers picturesque ocean views while weary motel rooms include cable TV. Bistro meals represent the best value in town, from simple, fresh seafood to laksa, crepes and deep-fried Camembert.

Greenacres Backpackers (☎ 8625 3811; 12 Kuhlmann St; dm incl breakfast $17) This small hostel is marked by hubcaps nailed to trees.

Oyster Bar (☎ 8626 9086; Eyre Hwy; meals $8; ⏰ 9.30am-6pm Mon-Sat, 1-6pm Sun) Slurp down a few molluscs and enjoy a glass of wine near the (not very) Big Oyster.

CEDUNA TO THE WESTERN AUSTRALIA BORDER

It's 480km from Ceduna to the WA border and the only places with tourist facilities are at Penong (73km from Ceduna), Nundroo Roadhouse (151km), Yalata Roadhouse (202km), Nullarbor Hotel (294km) and Border Village.

Wheat and sheep paddocks line the road to Nundroo Roadhouse, after which you're in attractive mallee until 50km beyond Yalata Roadhouse. Here the trees start to become sparser; they peter out into a sea of shrubby bluebush 20km later. This is the true Nullarbor (derived from the Latin for 'no trees') and you travel through this surreal landscape for the next 40km or so.

Turn off the highway at **Penong** (population 200), and follow the 20km dirt road to Point Sinclair and **Cactus Beach**, with one of Australia's most famous surfing breaks. Although Caves is the best break for experienced surfers, be warned that the locals don't take kindly to tourists dropping in. There's **bush camping** (per person $8) on private property close to the breaks; bring your own drinking water in summer.

The whale-watching platforms at Head of Bight, afford spectacular views of a major breeding ground for **southern right whales**, which migrate here from Antarctica in June. You can see them from July to September. The breeding area is protected by the **Great Australian Bight Marine Park**, the world's second largest marine park after the Great Barrier Reef.

Head of Bight is on Aboriginal land – you can get entry permits ($8) and whale information from the **Yalata Roadhouse** and at the **White Well Ranger Station** on the way in to the viewing area. The signposted turn-off is 78km west of Yalata, and 14km east of the **Nullarbor Hotel/Motel**.

You can also inspect **Murrawijinie Cave**, a large overhang behind the Nullarbor Hotel/ Motel. There are several signposted coastal lookouts along the top of the 80m-high **Bunda Cliffs**.

Watch out for animals on the road if you're driving through here at night.

If you're heading west into WA, dump all fruit, vegetables, cheese and plants as per quarantine regulations, and put your watch back 1½ hours (2½ hours during daylight saving – from the last Sunday in October to the last Sunday in March).

Sleeping & Eating

There are basic caravan parks, budget and air-conditioned motel-style accommodation, restaurants and fuel sales at a number of places; you can also camp for free in roadside rest areas.

Nundroo Hotel/Motel (☎ 08-8625 6120; Eyre Hwy, Nundroo; dm/d/tr $10/77/90; ⚅) If you're heading west, Nundroo has this hotel/motel and the last mechanical repair service until Norseman, 1038km away.

Yalata Roadhouse (☎ 08-8625 6807; www.wangka wilurrara.com/yalata; Eyre Hwy, Yalata; unpowered sites $6, d $65; ⏰ roadhouse 8am-8pm) The roadhouse offers basic motel-style rooms, basic meals

www.lonelyplanet.com

and has a huge range of Aboriginal art for sale.

Nullarbor Hotel/Motel (☎ 08-8625 6271; Eyre Hwy, Nullarbor; unpowered sites per 2 people $11, dm/s/d/tr $19/80/100/115; ⏲ 7am-11pm) This licensed hotel, 146km from the Yalata Roadhouse, is a service centre and offers meals. It's close to the Head of Bight for whale watching.

Border Village Motel (☎ 08-9039 3474; fax 08-9039 3473; Eyre Hwy, Border Village; unpowered sites per 2 people $12, dm/s/d/f $25/80/90/85; ✹ ▢ ✹) This rebuilt motel has a variety of modern rooms and cabins and a licensed restaurant. The motel is on the WA–SA border, 186km west of the Nullarbor Hotel/Motel.

Fowlers Bay Caravan Park (☎ 08-8625 6143; powered/unpowered per 2 people sites $17/14, on-site caravans $35-40) There's basic accommodation, a shop and takeaway food in this veritable ghost town with heritage buildings, good fishing and impressive coastal dunes. Take the turn-off to Fowlers Bay, 106km from Ceduna.

FLINDERS RANGES

The glowing red and purple folds of the majestic Flinders Ranges are the most spectacular sight in SA. Beloved of artists and bushwalkers alike, this ancient colossus rises from the northern end of the Spencer Gulf and runs 400km north into the arid outback. It's a superb area for wildlife and unique geological formations or for simply appreciating the outstanding beauty of the Australian bush. In the far north, the ranges are hemmed in by sand ridges and barren salt lakes.

As in many other dry regions of Australia, the vegetation here is surprisingly diverse and colourful. In the early spring, after good rains, the country is carpeted with wildflowerss. During summer, the days can be searingly hot, but the nights usually cool down to a pleasant temperature. Winter and early spring are probably the best times to visit, although there are attractions at any time of the year.

In 1802, when Matthew Flinders landed near Port Augusta, several Aboriginal tribes lived in the region. You can visit some of their sites: the cave paintings at Yourambulla (near Hawker) and Arkaroo (near Wilpena); and the rock carvings at Sacred Canyon (near Wilpena) and remote Chambers Gorge.

Bushwalking is a major attraction of the area, but this is wild, rugged country and care should be taken before setting out. Wilpena Pound, the Arkaroola-Mt Painter Wildlife Sanctuary and Mt Remarkable National Park (see p759) all have excellent walks, many of them along marked trails. The Heysen Trail (see the boxed text, p709) ends in Parachilna Gorge, near Blinman, having come up through the Flinders.

For further information visit www.southernflinders.com.au or www.flindersranges.com.

Information

DEH (☎ 08-8648 5300, desert parks inquiries ☎ 1800 816 078; www.parks.sa.gov.au; 9 McKay St, Port Augusta; ⏲ 8.45am-5pm Mon-Fri) Provides information on the southern Flinders (ie south of Quorn).

Port Augusta visitor information centre (☎ 1800 633 060, 08-8641 0793; www.portaugusta.sa.gov.au; 41 Flinders Tce, Port Augusta; ⏲ 9am-5.30pm Mon-Fri, 10am-4pm Sat & Sun; ▢) Good general and park-trail information.

Wilpena Pound visitor information centre (☎ 08-8648 0048; admin@wilpenapound.com.au; ⏲ 8am-6pm) At the Flinders Ranges National Park headquarters, this centre dispenses information on the park and surrounding region and sells park passes (per day/month/year $6.50/21/77), which are also available at self-service stations.

You'll need a good map of the area because there are many back roads and a variety of road surfaces. According to local experts, Westprint puts out the most accurate touring map, Hema is recommended and the RAA's map is also very good. Westprint and Hema's maps can be found at most map shops and bookshops, while RAA maps can be purchased from its own outlets.

Tours

A number of operators offer different types of tours from Adelaide; check with visitor information centres. See also Tours, p711 for details of longer tours that include the Flinders Ranges on their itineraries.

You may prefer to take a bus from Adelaide (see Bus, p781) and then pick up tours departing from Port Augusta (p772), Hawker (p781), Quorn (p781), Wilpena Pound (p783), Iga Warta (p784) and Arkaroola (p784). Local visitor information centres

FLINDERS RANGES

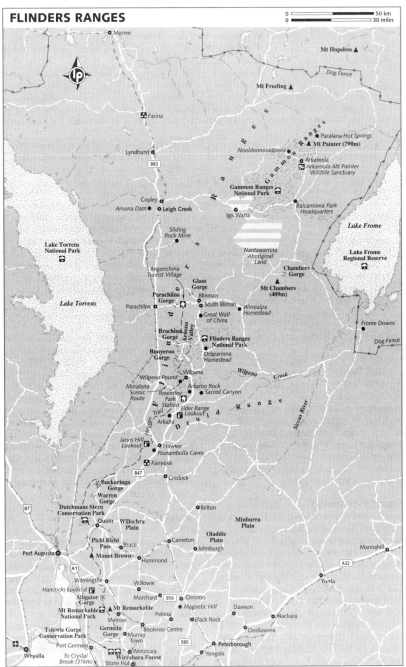

0   50 km
0   30 miles

Marree

Mt Hopeless ▲

Dog Fence

Mt Freeling ▲

Farina

Paralana Hot Springs

Lyndhurst

Nooldoonooldoona   ▲ Mt Painter (790m)

Arkaroola

B83

Arkaroola-Mt Painter
Wildlife Sanctuary

Gammon Ranges
National Park

Copley

Aroona Dam ● ● Leigh Creek

Iga Warta

Balcanoona Park
Headquarters

Lake Frome

Sliding
Rock Mine

Lake Torrens
National Park

Nantawarrina
Aboriginal
Land

Lake Frome
Regional Reserve

Angorichina
Tourist Village

Glass
Gorge

Chambers
Gorge

Parachilna
Gorge

Blinman

Mt Chambers
(409m)

Lake Torrens

Parachilna

South Blinman

Wirrealpa
Homestead

Great Wall
of China

Frome Downs

Brachina
Gorge

Flinders Ranges
National Park

Dog Fence

Bunyeroo
Gorge

Oraparinna
Homestead

Wilpena   Creek

Wilpena Pound

Wilpena

Moralana
Scenic
Route

Arkaroo Rock
● Sacred Canyon

Rawnsley
Park
Station

D r u i d   R a n g e

Siccus River

Elder Range
Lookout

Trail

Arkaba

Jarvis Hill
Lookout

Hawker
Yourambulla Caves

Kanyaka

B47

Cradock

Buckaringa
Gorge

Warren
Gorge

Belton

Dutchmans Stern
Conservation Park

87

Quorn   Willochra
Plain

Minburra
Plain

Pichi Richi
Pass

Bruce

Carrieton

Oladdie
Plain

Mannahill

Port Augusta

Mount Brown ▲

Hammond

Johnburgh

A1

A32

Yunta

Wilmington

Willowie

Handocks Lookout

Morchard

B56

Orroroo

Alligator
Gorge

Magnetic Hill

Dawson

Mt Remarkable ▲ Mt Remarkable

Pekina

Nackara

Mt Remarkable
National Park

Melrose

Black Rock

Oodlawirra

Germein
Gorge

Booleroo Centre

Telowie Gorge
Conservation Park

Murray
Town

Port Germein

Peterborough

Whyalla

*To Crystal
Brook (31km)*

Wirrabara
Wirrabara Forest
Stone Hut

B80

Yongala

ADNYAMATHANHA DREAMING George Dunford

The concepts of land and nature are integral in the culture of the traditional owners of the Flinders Ranges, collectively called Adnyamathanha (or 'Hill People'). The Adnyamathanha exchanged and elaborated on stories to explain their spectacular local geography.

The creation of the walls of Ikara (Wilpena Pound), for example, are the bodies of two Akurra (giant snakes), who coiled around Ikara during an initiation ceremony, gobbling up most of the participants. The snakes were so full after their feast that they could not move and willed themselves to die, creating the landmark. Because of its traditional significance, the Adnyamathanha prefer that visitors don't climb St Mary Peak, which is reputedly to be the head of the female snake.

In a different story, another Akurra drank Lake Frome dry, then weaved his way across the land, creating creeks and gorges. Wherever he stopped, he created a large waterhole, including Arkaroola Springs. The sun warmed the salty water in his stomach, causing it to rumble, a noise which can still be heard today in the form of flowing underground spring water.

Colour is essential to the Adnyamathanha, as they use the area's red ochre in traditional ceremonies and medicine. Traditional stories say that the colour is from Marrukurli, dangerous dogs who were killed by Adnu, the bearded dragon. When Adnu killed the black Marrukurli the sun went out and he was forced to throw his boomerang in every direction to re-awaken the sun. It was only when he threw it to the east that the sun returned. Meanwhile, the blood of the Marrukurli had seeped into the earth to create sacred ochre deposits.

You can find out more about Adnyamathanha legends by following one of the Dreaming Trails, which are explained in the helpful *South Australian Aboriginal Dreaming of the Flinders Ranges* brochure, available at visitor information centres. The trails themselves take in Iga Warta, Arkaroola and other sacred sites in the Flinders.

---

and backpacker hostels will have details of these.

Ecotrek (☎ 08-8383 7198; www.ecotrek.com.au) Leads seven-day professionally guided, specialised walking tours (from $1300) inclusive of meals, beds and wine. Cycling trips are available, too.

Mulpa Tours (☎ 08-8520 2808; www.mulpatours.com.au) Provides an indigenous insight into the Flinders Ranges on its tours (two to five days, from $710).

Swagabout Tours (☎ 0408 845 378; www.swagabout tours.com.au) Runs tours of the Flinders Ranges (three/four days $550/710) and longer overland outback tours between Adelaide and Alice Springs.

SCENIC SELF-DRIVES

If you have a vehicle, you can make a loop taking you around an interesting section of the central part of the ranges. From Wilpena Pound continue north through the Flinders Ranges National Park past Oraparinna Homestead, then veer west through Brachina Gorge to the main Leigh Creek road.

Brachina Gorge has a self-guided geology trail with information signs en route – pick up a leaflet from the Wilpena Pound visitor information centre (p778). You can then either turn back to Hawker (directly or via the Moralana Scenic Route), or head north to Parachilna and take the scenic road east through Parachilna Gorge and Blinman, before heading south back to Wilpena through the national park.

If you want to see the spectacular northern ranges, head east from South Blinman to Wirrealpa Homestead, from where you swing north via Chambers Gorge to meet the Frome Downs road south of Balcanoona. Continue up to Arkaroola, then head back to the sealed road through Gammon Ranges National Park via Weetootla Gorge. You'll need a car with decent clearance to take this route.

Sleeping

Motels, hotels, hostels and self-contained cottages (around $75 per night) can normally be found in the townships. Old working (farming) stations have budget rooms, which are favoured by backpacker tours, and most hotels cater for both budget and midrange travellers. Book ahead to beat the tour groups.

Visitor information centres have comprehensive listings, or contact the **Flinders Ranges Accommodation Booking Service** (☎ 1800 777 880, 08-8648 4022; www.frabs.com.au).

Getting There & Around

Port Augusta (see p773) is the main transport hub for travel to and from the Flinders Ranges, with regular air, bus and train services.

BUS

Yorke Peninsula Coaches (☎ 08-8823 2375) head north from Adelaide to Peterborough ($28, five hours) from Sunday to Friday and to Orroroo ($31, 5½ hours) on Monday, Wednesday and Friday.

CAR & MOTORCYCLE

There are good sealed roads all the way north to Wilpena Pound and Leigh Creek. The Marree road skirting the western edge of the Flinders Ranges is sealed to Lyndhurst.

Check with DEH offices for current information, as gravel roads can be closed by heavy rain. For recorded information on road conditions in the Flinders Ranges and the outback, call ☎ 1300 361 033.

QUORN

☎ 08 / pop 1005

At about 330km north of Adelaide and 40km northeast of Port Augusta, friendly Quorn is the picturesque gateway to the Flinders and is the area's main service town. It retains the atmosphere of its pioneering days, when it became an important railway town after the completion of the Great Northern Railway in 1878.

The **Quorn visitor information centre** (☎ 8648 6419; www.flindersrangescouncil.sa.gov.au; 3 Seventh St; 9am-5pm Mon-Fri, 9am-4pm Sat & Sun) is next to the council chambers.

The railway closed in 1957, but now a vintage tourist train – often pulled by a steam engine – follows the old *Ghan* railway route through the scenic Pichi Richi Pass to Port Augusta and Woolshed. **Pichi Richi Railway** (☎ 8633 0380; www.prr.org.au; Train Station, Railway Tce) operates most Saturdays from April to November (one way to Port Augusta adult/child $34/12). Train buffs should ask about tours ($8) of the **workshop/museum** when the trains are running.

There are several good walks in Pichi Richi Pass out on the Port Augusta road, including the **Waukerie Creek Trail** and the **Heysen Trail** (p709). Closer to town are walks at **Dutchman's Stern** and **Devil's Peak**.

Tours

Some small operators offer 4WD trips, which go off road and really allow you to see the Flinders in its full glory.

Ozzie's Bush Track Tours (☎ 8648 6567; www.aboutozzietours.com; 22 Pool St; half-/full-day tours $78/140, 3-/5-day tours $480/890) Offers a range of tours, from a popular half-day tour to nearby Dutchmans Stern Conservation Park to five-day tours of Arkaroola and Wilpena Pound, with a local who imparts plenty of bush knowledge.

Tracks Adventure Tours (☎ 1800 639 933, 8648 6655; www.users.bigpond.com/headbush; 1-/4-day tours $119/800) Runs good-value tours with interesting itineraries, including the popular Wilpena Pound trek – a one-day wonder that gives you a good look at this magnificent area.

Sleeping & Eating

Quorn's four hotels have counter or dining-room meals, and a few other eateries around town provide good snack options.

Transcontinental Hotel (☎ 8648 6076; 15 Railway Tce; s/d $32/55;) This friendly place with standard rooms is the pick of the town's four hotels for accommodation.

Andu Lodge (☎ 1800 639 933, 8648 6655; www.users.bigpond.com/headbush; 12 First St; dm/s/d/f $20/30/50/75) A former hospital serves as the town's YHA hostel with clean rooms and a help-yourself attitude to videos and breakfasts. Mountain bikes are available and Wallaby Track Adventure Tours also runs from here, offering good tips for exploring the area.

Flinders Ranges Motel (☎ 8648 6016; cnr West & Railway Tce; s/d $80/85) Comfortable motel units come with small fridges and TVs at this restored old mill.

Willows State Bank (☎ 8648 6391; 37 First St; d $120) Set in a magnificent restored bank, this building retains its period charm without sacrificing luxury. Downstairs rooms share a huge living area, kitchen and full laundry, while intimate upstairs rooms share a charming sitting room and veranda.

Quorn Caravan Park (☎ 8648 6206; Silo Rd; powered/unpowered sites per 2 people $20/17, on-site caravans $38, cabins $45-62;) This large shaded park is just behind the train station and is a wildlife haven for kookaburras, galahs and the odd kangaroo.

HAWKER

☎ 08 / pop 298

Only 55km south of Wilpena Pound, Hawker is the last outpost of civilisation for many on their way out to the Strzelecki Track and makes for a popular pit stop.

The main visitor information outlet is in **Hawker Motors** (☎ 8648 4014; www.hawkermotors .com.au; cnr Wilpena & Craddock Rds; ⌨).

Sights

About 10km south of Hawker are the impressive **Kanyaka ruins**, all that's left of a sheep station founded in 1851. Close by, picturesque **Kanyaka Waterhole** is overlooked by the so-called **Death Rock**.

There are Aboriginal rock paintings 12km south of Hawker at **Yourambulla Caves**, comprising three rock shelters high up on the side of Yourambulla Peak; the first one is a 1km walk from the car park. **Jarvis Hill Lookout** is about 6km west of Hawker and affords good views over the town and north to Wilpena Pound.

Tours

SCENIC SELF-DRIVES

The **Moralana Scenic Route** is a return-trip drive from Hawker, taking in the magnificent scenery along the Elder and Wilpena Pound ranges. The turn-off is 24km from Hawker on the Wilpena road, then 28km along an unsealed road (best taken in the morning to avoid sun glare) that joins up with the sealed Hawker to Leigh Creek road. From here it's 46km back to Hawker.

Sleeping & Eating

Hawker Hotel/Motel (☎ 8648 4102; Elder Tce; hotel s/ d $30/55, motel s/d $70/80) This budget-conscious establishment has no-frills hotel rooms and self-contained motel rooms.

Flinders Ranges Caravan Park (☎ 8648 4266; Leigh Creek Rd; powered/unpowered sites per 2 people $21/18, cabins $45-75) About 1km from town on the Leigh Creek road, this spacious and friendly place has a good campers' kitchen, and lots of trees. It also offers half-/full-day tours $80/115.

Outback Chapmanton Motel (☎ 8648 4100; 1 Wilpena Rd; s/d $80/86, units 90; ▨) This established motel offers the best rooms in town, with the two-bedroom units making for a good family stay.

For city-style café fare duck into **Hawker General Store** (☎ 8648 4005; cnr Cradock & Wilpena Rds; lunches $4-10); for something more atmospheric, try the **Old Ghan Restaurant** (☎ 8648 4176; Leigh Creek Rd; mains $19-22; ◷ 10.30am-late

Wed-Sun) in the old train station. Expect first-rate tucker such as roo medallions with wattleseed and mustard.

WILPENA POUND

The large natural basin of Wilpena Pound is the best-known feature of the ranges and the main attraction in SA's treasured **Flinders Ranges National Park**. Covering about 80 sq km, it is generally accessible via the narrow gap through which Wilpena Creek exits the pound. On the outside, the external wall soars almost sheer for 500m; inside, the basin slopes away from the encircling ridge top.

There is plenty of wildlife in the park, particularly euros (hill kangaroos), red and grey kangaroos, and birds – everything from rosellas, galahs and budgerigars to emus and wedge-tailed eagles. You may even see endangered yellow-footed rock wallabies, whose numbers are increasing now that fox and rabbit populations are being controlled. **Brachina Gorge** is a good spot to see these beautiful animals.

Sacred Canyon, with its many petroglyphs (rock carvings), is 20km east from the visitor information centre on a rough road. To the north and still within the national park are striking scenic attractions, such as **Bunyeroo Gorge**, **Brachina Gorge** and the **Aroona Valley** (head anticlockwise from the junction of Brachina Gorge and Blinman Rds for a 110km round-trip of these sights). There are several bush-camping areas, most accessible by 2WD. The 20km **Brachina Gorge Geological Trail** (you follow it in your car) features an outstanding geological sequence of exposed sedimentary rock.

See p778 for park information and entry details. A shuttle bus ($3.50 return) will take you from the Wilpena Pound Resort (opposite) to within 1km of the soaring Wilpena Pound wall.

Bushwalking

Solo walks are not recommended. Also be sure that you are adequately equipped – particularly with drinking water, maps and sun protection. It's worth noting that searches are no longer initiated by rangers – so let someone know where you're headed and when you expect to return from your walk.

The park has a number of marked walking trails (marked with blue triangles;

Heysen Trail sections are indicated by red markers) and these are listed in a free DEH leaflet. Topographical maps (scale 1:50,000) are available from the visitor information centre.

Most walks start from the visitor information centre near the main camp site and vary from short walks suitable for families to longer multiday treks for experienced and super-fit trekkers. One of the latter is **St Marys Peak** and **Tanderra Saddle** from which you can enjoy the white glimmer of **Lake Torrens** off to the west, the beautiful Aroona Valley to the north, and the pound spread out below your feet.

For the rest of us mere mortals, a popular four-hour walk (6½km) to **Ohlssen Bagge** takes you to the top of the mountain that sits on the rim above the resort. The views here are tremendous, as are the views in spring from the **Arkaroo Rock**, which is about 10km south of Wilpena off the Hawker road. It takes around one hour (3km) to walk from the car park to the rock shelter, where there are well-preserved Aboriginal paintings.

Wangara Hill lookout is a 7km return walk and **Cooinda** is the bush-camping area within the pound.

Tours

Wilpena Pound visitor information centre (p778) has details of 4WD tours (half-/full day from $55/75) operating in the area, and books tours. It can also recommend tag-along tour operators (4WD self-drive).

Derek's 4WD Tours (☎ 0417 175 770; www.dereks 4wdtours.com) does several good off-road trips (half-/full day from $70/135), including the Skytrek drive out of Hawker.

Wilpena Pound Resort (below) offers popular scenic flights, with cheaper 20- and 30-minute flights covering Wilpena and immediate surrounds (from $80), and longer flights such as the five-hour trip to Lake Eyre and William Creek ($750).

Sleeping & Eating

Groceries, last-minute camping requirements and takeaway food are available at the well-stocked store in the visitor information centre.

Wilpena Pound Resort (☎ 1800 805 802, 08-8648 0004; www.wilpenapound.com.au; powered/unpowered sites per 2 people $22/16, permanent tents $75, dm/s/d

$25/120/130; ⚅ 🖳 🖭) Rooms come with TVs and 1980s décor. The camping ground is set in pleasant bush with good facilities; those lacking camping gear can overnight in the permanent tents, which sleep up to four people.

Rawnsley Park Station (☎ 08-8648 0030; www .rawnsleypark.com.au; Wilpena Rd; powered/unpowered sites per 2 people $17/24, caravans $48, units $83-103, lunch & dinner $6-21; ⚅ lunch & dinner; ⚅ 🖳) Off the Hawker road, about 20km south of Wilpena and close to the pound's outer edge, this friendly park has great accommodation and is popular with backpacking tours. There are several good bushwalks from here, and you can also take horse trail rides (one/two hours $45/60), 4WD tours (half-/full day $85/130), or hire mountain bikes. The licensed restaurant does good bush tucker with quirky names.

BLINMAN
☎ 08 / pop 16

This quaint hamlet on the circular route around the Flinders Ranges National Park was a copper-mining centre from the 1860s to the 1890s.

About 1km north of town is the historic **Blinman copper mine**, which has walking trails and interpretive signs.

Chunky cobblestones, historic photos and capacious luxury rooms are combined in the excellently renovated classic **Blinman Hotel** (☎ 8648 4867; www.blinmanhotel.com.au; Main St; dm/s/d $20/90/100, mains $12-20; ⚅). The kitchen serves up bush-flavoured dishes such as saltbush-wrapped chicken breast ($18) or char-grilled eucalyptus lamb ($19).

AROUND BLINMAN

Dramatic **Chambers Gorge**, 64km to the northeast of Blinman towards Arkaroola, features a striking gallery of Aboriginal rock carvings (from the car park it's an 8.3km walk). From **Mt Chambers** you can see over Lake Frome to the east and all along the Flinders Ranges from Mt Painter in the north to Wilpena Pound in the south.

An inspiring scenic drive links Blinman with Parachilna to the west, where there's the wonderful and renowned **Prairie Hotel**. This route takes you through **Parachilna Gorge** and past some lovely picnic and camping spots – the gorge marks the northern end of the **Heysen Trail** (p709).

Sleeping & Eating

Prairie Hotel (☎ 08-8648 4844; www.prairiehotel
.com.au; Parachilna; cabins $60-80, ste d $195, meals $9-
15; ☯ lunch & dinner; ☒ ▨) This busy hotel
at tiny Parachilna (population 5) is a real
oasis of luxury in the harsh outback. Tastefully appointed rooms with private facilities
and dorm rooms share a swimming pool.
Don't miss a meal in the hotel – an imaginative menu features gourmet bush tucker
(emu pâté on damper, or croc steaks, for
starters).

Angorichina Tourist Village & Store (☎ 08-
8648 4842; Parachilna Gorge; unpowered sites per 2 people
$18, dm $13, s/d on-site caravans $25/36, units $65) This
dusty park in Parachilna Gorge boasts a
magnificent setting, with steep hills all
around. Be aware: dorms are often booked
out by backpacker tours. You can also hire
mountain bikes.

LEIGH CREEK & COPLEY

Leigh Creek (population 690) was developed in 1980 when the original settlement
was demolished to make way for mining.
The huge open-cut coal mine supplies Port
Augusta's power station. Landscaping has
created a green suburban environment,
reminiscent of Canberra, but in the desert.
The sweet old railway town of Copley (population 100), 5km north of Leigh Creek, is on
the turn-off to Arkaroola.

Approximately 60km beyond Copley the
Aborigine-run **Iga Warta** (☎ 08-8648 3737; www
.igawarta.com; Arkaroola Rd; walks/tours $29/63, un-
powered sites $15) offers 4WD cultural tours
focusing on the surrounding country and
Aboriginal history. There are also bush-
tucker walks ($29) and campfire stories
($20). Anyone can use the camp sites, with
tents and swags for hire.

From Leigh Creek, you can also visit the
scenic **Aroona Dam**, 10km to the west, and
Gammon Ranges National Park, 100km to the
east.

For information on Gammon Ranges
National Park, contact the local **DEH** (☎ 08-
8648 4829; Balcanoona) or the **DEH office** (☎ 08-
8648 5300, desert parks inquiries ☎ 1800 816 078; www
.parks.sa.gov.au; 9 McKay St, Port Augusta; ☯ 8.45am-
5pm Mon-Fri).

Sleeping & Eating

Leigh Creek Tavern (☎ 08-8675 2025; Leigh Creek
Town Shopping Centre, Leigh Creek; s/d $110/135, cabins

$80, meals $8-20; ☒ ☒) This central inn offers
luxury cabins and motel rooms, and has a
good restaurant.

Copley Caravan Park (☎ 08-8675 2288; www.copley
caravan.com.au; Railway Tce West, Copley; unpowered sites
per 2 people $18, cabins with/without bathroom $80/60;
☒) This small, friendly park offers guests
a good bonfire cook-up for dinner.

Quandong Café & Bush Bakery (☎ 08-8675 2683;
Railway Tce, Copely; ☯ 8.30am-5pm Easter-Nov) This is
the big attraction in Copley – it's the home
of great quandong (a native fruit) pies and
other bakery goodies.

ARKAROOLA
☎ 08

Once a sheep station, **Arkaroola-Mt Painter
Wildlife Sanctuary** sprawls across rugged and
spectacular country near the northern end
of the Flinders Ranges.

You can stay in the **resort** (☎ 1800 676 042,
8648 4848; www.arkaroola.com.au; Arkaroola Rd Camp;
powered/unpowered sites per 2 people $20/15, cabins $45,
lodges $65-145; ☒), which offers good facili-
ties, a cosy bar/restaurant, small supermarket and service station.

You can take a guided or tag-along tour,
or do your own thing. Most of the places
of interest are accessible to conventional
vehicles, with some hiking involved. Dirt
roads and tracks lead to **Paralana Hot Springs**,
rock pools at **Bararranna Gorge** and **Echo Camp**,
and to water holes at **Arkaroola** and **Nooldoonooldoona**.

One of Arkaroola's highlights is the resort's four-hour **Ridgetop Tour** ($85), along a
4WD track through wild mountain coun-
try. Another excellent tour allows you to
view the heavens through a high-powered
telescope at Arkaroola's **Dodwell & Oliphant
Astronomical Observatories** ($30).

OUTBACK

The area north of Eyre Peninsula and the
Flinders Ranges stretches into the vast,
empty red spaces of SA's outback. Although
sparsely populated and often difficult to
travel through, it is possible to head here if
you're properly prepared.

Note that fuel outlets, repair facilities and
spare parts are often extremely limited, so
be prepared in case of breakdown. Always
travel with two spare tyres and enough

water for several days; 5L per person per day in winter, 10L in summer.

The many brave (some foolhardy) explorers who mapped the state, and equipped it with communication systems, managed to cross the 'big red' without air-conditioned vehicles! However, for us softies, it's not wise to stray far from the few main roads without a 4WD or camels.

Entry permits are required for a large part of the northwest (which is either Aboriginal land, desert park or the Woomera Prohibited Area).

Information
Desert Parks Hotline (☎ 1800 816 078) Call for information on the outback roads, or check with the state automobile associations.
Port Augusta visitor information centre (☎ 08-8641 0793, 1800 633 060; www.portaugusta.sa.gov.au; 41 Flinders Tce; ☒ 9am-5.30pm Mon-Fri, 10am-4pm Sat & Sun)

NATIONAL PARK PERMITS
For information on national parks and an update on the park permit system, contact **DEH** (☎ 08-8648 5020, desert parks inquiries ☎ 1800 816 078; www.parks.sa.gov.au; 9 McKay St, Port Augusta).

To visit most of the outback's conservation areas you need a Desert Parks Pass ($90 per vehicle). It's valid for a year and includes an excellent information book, detailed routes and area maps. If you're just visiting Cooper Creek in the Innamincka Regional Reserve, Lake Eyre in the Lake Eyre National Park or Dalhousie Springs in the Witjira National Park, you need only buy a day/night permit ($18 per vehicle).

Desert Parks Passes are available from the following locations:
Adelaide RAA (Map p714; ☎ 08-8202 4600; www.raa .net; 55 Hindmarsh Sq, Central Adelaide); Environment Shop (Map p714; ☎ 08-8204 1910; www.parks.sa.gov.au; 77 Grenfell St, Central Adelaide; ☒ 9am-5pm Mon-Fri)
Alice Springs Shell Mt Gillen service station (☎ 08-8952 23476; Larapinta Dr, Alice Springs)
Birdsville Mobil service station and police station.
Coober Pedy Underground Books (Map p787; ☎ 08-8672 5558; Post Office Hill Rd, Coober Pedy; ☒ 8.30am-5pm Mon-Fri, 10am-4pm Sat)
Hawker Hawker Motors (☎ 08-8648 4014; Wilpena Rd, Hawker)
Innamincka Trading Post (☎ 08-8675 9900; fax 8675 9920)
Marree Outback Roadhouse (☎ 08-8675 9900; Railway Tce, North Marree)

Mt Dare Homestead (☎ 08-8670 7835; Witjira National Park)
Oodnadatta Pink Roadhouse (☎ 08-8670 7822; Main St, Oodnadatta; ☒ 8am-5.30pm); Oodnadatta Hotel (☎ /fax 08-8670 7804; oodnadattahotel@bigpond.com; Main St, Oodnadatta)
Port Augusta Wadlata Outback Centre (☎ 08-8641 0793, 1800 633 060; www.portaugusta.sa.gov.au; 41 Flinders Tce, Port Augusta; ☒ 9am-5.30pm Mon-Fri, 10am-4pm Sat & Sun)
William Creek William Creek Store & Campground (☎ 08-8670 7746; www.williamcreekcampground.com; Oodnadatta Track)

Tours
There are a number of six- to 10-day tours ex-Adelaide and ex–Alice Springs that explore the outback. These take in the Flinders Ranges, Oodnadatta Track, Coober Pedy, Uluru and Kings Canyon. See Tours, p711.

Getting There & Around
AIR
Regional Express (Rex; ☎ 13 17 13; www.regionalex press.com.au) flies daily between Adelaide and Coober Pedy ($170), and Olympic Dam ($149).

BUS
Greyhound Australia (☎ 13 14 99; www.greyhound .com.au) runs a daily passenger coach between Adelaide and Alice Springs, stopping at Pimba ($93, 6½ hours), Glendambo ($103, 7½ hours) and Coober Pedy ($130, 10½ hours). Fares to Coober Pedy from Alice Springs/Port Augusta cost $130/80.

Premier Stateliner (☎ 08-8415 5555; www.prem ierstateliner.com.au) runs from Port Augusta to Roxby Downs ($47, three hours) via Woomera ($35, 1¾ hours) daily except Saturday.

CAR & MOTORCYCLE
The Stuart Hwy is sealed all the way from Port Augusta to Darwin. The highway is a long, often boring drive and the temptation to get it over with quickly has resulted in many high-speed collisions between cars and cattle, sheep, kangaroos and wedge-tailed eagles. Take care, particularly at night.

If you want to travel to NT by a more adventurous route, there's the **Oodnadatta Track**. This option takes you from Port Augusta through the Flinders Ranges to Leigh

Creek, Lyndhurst, Marree and Oodnadatta before joining the Stuart Hwy at Marla, about 180km south of the NT border. For most of the way it runs close to the defunct *Ghan* train line.

The Oodnadatta Track is sealed as far as Lyndhurst, then you are on dirt (and often rough and dusty dirt, at that) all the way to Marla. There are several routes across to the Stuart Hwy: from Lake Eyre south via Roxby Downs to Pimba; from William Creek west to Coober Pedy; and from Oodnadatta either south to Coober Pedy or west to Cadney Homestead (a roadhouse on the Stuart Hwy). With a 4WD you can keep going up the old railway line from Oodnadatta to Alice Springs, visiting Witjira National Park and Old Andado Homestead (NT) on the way.

If you don't have your own vehicle, it's also possible to catch a bus to Roxby Downs (right) or Coober Pedy (opposite) from Adelaide and hire a 4WD from there to explore Lake Eyre and the Oodnadatta Track.

Two other routes of interest to outback travellers are the legendary **Birdsville Track** (p792) and **Strzelecki Track** (p792). These days the tracks have been so much improved that it's usually quite feasible to travel them in any car that's in good condition and has reasonable ground clearance.

The SA outback includes much of the **Simpson Desert** and the harsh, rocky landscape of the **Sturt Stony Desert**. There are also huge salt lakes that fill with water every once in a long while. **Lake Eyre**, used by Donald Campbell for his attempt on the world's land-speed record in the 1960s, filled to capacity in 1974. Since then it has had water in it a number of times, including 2000 and 2004.

When soaking rain does fall on this usually dry land the effect can be amazing – flowers bloom and plants grow at a breakneck pace in order to complete their life cycles before the drought returns. There is even a species of water-holding frog that goes into suspended animation, remaining in the ground for years on end, only to pop up when the rains come again.

On a much more mundane level, roads can either be washed out or turned into gluelike mud. Venture into the wrong place after heavy rain and you may be stuck for days – or even weeks.

TRAIN

For information on the *Ghan*, see p1069.

WOOMERA

☎ 08 / pop 1000

Just off the Stuart Hwy, Woomera is a rather drab-looking government town with its roots in early British weapons testing and space rocket programmes. More recently, it's been in the news as a proposed low-level nuclear waste dump and for its controversial detention centre (a centre for refugees awaiting judgement by the federal government).

In the small **Woomera Heritage Centre** (☎ 8673 7042; Dewrang Ave; ☯ 9am-5pm) there's a (sanitised) display of Woomera's past, present and projected future roles. Outside is a collection of old military aircraft, rockets and missiles. Coffee and sandwiches are available in the Outback Diner.

Olympic Dam Tours (☎ 8671 0788; www.flinders outback.com/odtours; 4hr tours $45) takes in the town, Koolymilka camp and the rocket launch site at Lake Hart.

The friendly **Woomera Travellers' Village** (☎ 8673 7800; www.woomera.com; Wirruna Ave; powered/unpowered sites per 2 people $22/16, dm from $25, cabins/units from $58/68; ☒) has a well-maintained range of accommodation.

Originally built to house the space programme personnel, **Eldo Hotel** (☎ 8673 7867; Kotara Ave; s/d $83/100, mains $12-24; ☯ breakfast Mon-Fri, lunch & dinner daily; ☒) has comfortable rooms with shared facilities and serves counter or restaurant meals.

ROXBY DOWNS & ANDAMOOKA

Following along the Torrens Track (92km from the Stuart Hwy via Woomera) you'll find the thriving mining town of Roxby Downs (population 3620; www.roxbydowns.com), a service centre for the **Olympic Dam** uranium, copper, silver and gold mine. About 30km by sealed road from Roxby Downs, Andamooka (population 498) is a rough-and-ready opalmining town, known for dark matrix opal. The contrast between this frontier town and leafy Roxby is breathtaking and even makes Coober Pedy look like a metropolis.

GLENDAMBO

☎ 08 / pop 20

Glendambo, 113km northwest of Pimba and 252km southeast of Coober Pedy, is a service centre on the Stuart Hwy. It has a good pub, motel, two roadhouses and a caravan park. Fuel is available from 6am to midnight.

If you're heading north, remember that there are no refuelling stops between here and Coober Pedy.

COOBER PEDY
☎ 08 / pop 2624

The lure of opal has brought people from all over the world to charismatic Coober Pedy – the opal capital of Australia, if not the world. It's 535km north of Port Augusta, along the Stuart Hwy.

The name Coober Pedy is from an Aboriginal language and is said to mean 'white man's hole in the ground'. About half the population, comprising more than 40 nationalities, lives in dugouts (underground rooms) to shelter from the extreme climate: daytime summer temperatures can soar to over 50°C and the winter nights are freezing cold. Apart from the dugouts, there are more than 250,000 mine shafts in the area. Although these days the shafts are fenced off, it pays to keep your eyes open!

Opal was discovered here by a teenage boy in 1915, and the chance of a strike has since lured people from all over the world to live here. If you stay for any length of time, you'll hear outrageous stories of fortunes made and lost, shady deals, intrigues, vendettas and crazy old-timers. Every few years someone makes a million-dollar find, but

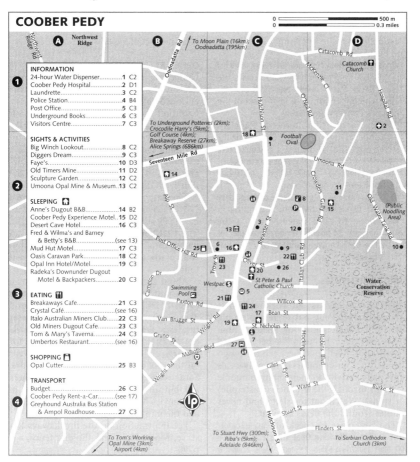

COOBER PEDY

INFORMATION
24-hour Water Dispenser............1 C2
Coober Pedy Hospital................2 D1
Laundrette...............................3 C2
Police Station...........................4 B4
Post Office...............................5 C3
Underground Books...................6 C3
Visitors Centre..........................7 C3

SIGHTS & ACTIVITIES
Big Winch Lookout....................8 C2
Diggers Dream..........................9 C3
Faye's...................................10 D3
Old Timers Mine......................11 D2
Sculpture Garden....................12 C3
Umoona Opal Mine & Museum..13 C2

SLEEPING
Anne's Dugout B&B.................14 B2
Coober Pedy Experience Motel..15 D2
Desert Cave Hotel....................16 C3
Fred & Wilma's and Barney
  & Betty's B&B....................(see 13)
Mud Hut Motel........................17 C3
Oasis Caravan Park..................18 C2
Opal Inn Hotel/Motel...............19 C3
Radeka's Downunder Dugout
  Motel & Backpackers.............20 C3

EATING
Breakaways Cafe......................21 C3
Crystal Café.........................(see 16)
Italo Australian Miners Club......22 C3
Old Miners Dugout Cafe...........23 C3
Tom & Mary's Taverna.............24 C3
Umbertos Restaurant............(see 16)

SHOPPING
Opal Cutter.............................25 B3

TRANSPORT
Budget...................................26 C3
Coober Pedy Rent-a-Car.........(see 17)
Greyhound Australia Bus Station
  & Ampol Roadhouse..............27 C3

some miners spend decades hard at work and make very little for their efforts.

Coober Pedy is in an extremely inhospitable environment and the town's appearance reflects this: water is expensive and the rainfall scant, so even in the middle of winter the town looks dried out and dusty. It's not as ramshackle as it used to be, but even so you could never describe it as attractive. In fact, the town looks a bit like the end of the world, making it the perfect locale for 'end of the world' films such as *Mad Max III* and *Stark*, and otherworldly movies including *Red Planet* and the sci-fi cult film, *Pitch Black*.

Information

Coober Pedy visitor information centre (☎ 1800 637 076; www.opalcapitaloftheworld.com.au; District Council offices, Hutchison St; ⏰ 8.30am-5pm Mon-Fri) is diagonally opposite the Ampol Roadhouse and bus station.

Underground Books (☎ 8672 5558; Post Office Hill Rd; ⏰ 8.30am-5pm Mon-Fri, 10am-4pm Sat) sells the Desert Parks Pass (yearly pass $90 per vehicle), which is required to visit most of the outback's conservation areas.

You can access the Internet at Radeka's Downunder Dugout Motel & Backpackers (see opposite) and there's a **Launderette** (Hutchison St) attached to the real estate agent. **Coober Pedy Hospital** (☎ 8672 5009; Hospital Rd) has a 24-hour emergency room.

Bottled water is an expensive commodity here. For those headed into the outback, it's cheapest to refill water bottles at the coin-operated **24-hour water dispenser** (per 30L 20c) by the **Oasis Caravan Park** (☎ 8672 5169; Seventeen Mile Rd).

Sights & Activities
OPAL MINING
There are hundreds of working mines around Coober Pedy but there are no big operators. When somebody makes a find, dozens of miners home in like bees around a honey pot. Keen fossickers can have a go themselves; tour operators or friendly locals may invite you out to their claim to noodle (fossick) through the mullock (waste pile) for stones. Watch out for shafts and never wander around the fields at night.

The best place to check out an excavation is **Tom's Working Opal Mine** (☎ 1800 196 500; tours adult/child $15/5; ⏰ tours 10am, 2.30pm &

4pm), 1km north of town, where visitors are encouraged to fossick through the mullock for their fortunes.

The **Umoona Opal Mine & Museum** (☎ 8672 5288; Hutchison St; tours $10; ⏰ 8am-7pm) is a large complex right in the centre of town, with informative tours of the mine and displays of Aboriginal mythology and traditions, as well as exhibitions on the early mining days.

DUGOUT HOMES
Many of the early dugout homes were simply worked-out mines; now, however, they're usually cut specifically as residences and some residents open them for viewing.

Faye's (☎ 8672 5029; Old Water Tank Rd; admission $4.50; ⏰ 9am-5pm Mon-Sat) was hand-dug by three women in the 1960s, while **Diggers Dream** (☎ 8672 5442; Nayler Pl; admission $4; ⏰ sunrise-sunset) has a more contemporary décor.

OTHER ATTRACTIONS
Underground worshippers can choose from five underground churches, including the curious **Serbian Orthodox Church** (⏰ 11am-6pm), found off the Stuart Hwy. You can tee off at the unique bare-earth **golf course**, or take in views over the town from the prominent **Big Winch Lookout**. Further south there's a **sculpture garden** (admission by donation) with bizarre art and some leftover props from the film *Pitch Black*.

The fascinating **Old Timers Mine** (☎ 8672 5555; Crowders Gully Rd; adult/child $10/5; ⏰ 9am-5pm) has opals still embedded in the rock walls. The 1916 mine was rediscovered when an underground home extended into a labyrinth of low tunnels, which make for a great tour.

About 2km northwest of town, you can watch potters at work at **Underground Potteries** (☎ 8672 5226; Rowe St; ⏰ 8.30am-6pm). Around 3km further on, an old-school character resides at **Crocodile Harry's** (☎ 8672 5872; Seventeen Mile Rd; admission $2; ⏰ 9am-6pm), known for its large collection of women's underwear on the roof and Harry's strange sculpture. Some readers have found it sleazy, others sad, but this quirky dugout has featured in the movies *Mad Max III* and *Ground Zero*, and the miniseries *Stark*.

For information on the Breakaways Reserve, Moon Plain and the dog fence, see p790.

Tours

Several operators run half-day tours that will take you into an opal mine, underground home and the Serbian church, while others head out to the Breakaways and distant stations.

Desert Cave Hotel (☎ 8672 5688; Hutchison St; adult/child $52/26) Half-day tours leave from this hotel (right), taking in the town's attractions, the dog fence and Moon Plain.

Desert Diversity Tours (☎ 1800 069 911, 8672 5226; www.desertdiversity.com) One-day ecotours to the Painted Desert ($145) and Lake Eyre ($155); book through Underground Books (opposite). If you really want to get the expanse into perspective and visit small, remote outback communities, travel with the **mail run** (tours $125; ✆ Mon & Thu) along 600km of dirt roads on its round trip (12 hours) from Coober Pedy to Oodnadatta and William Creek. Book ahead.

Martin's Star Gazing (☎ 8672 5223; adult/child $22/11) Readers rave about Martin's tour, which explores the night heavens from Moon Plain.

Oasis Tours (☎ 8672 5169; adult/child $30/15) Three-hour town tours that include fossicking.

Opal Cave Tag-Along Tours (☎ 8672 5028; adult $15-20) Provides one-hour in-car guides.

Radeka's Downunder Dugout Motel & Backpackers (☎ 8672 5223; Oliver St; tours $40/20) A popular town tour from this motel (below), this tour includes fossicking for opals, and visiting the Breakaways and Harry's.

Stuart Range Tours (☎ 8672 5179; adult/child $40/20) Morning town tours cover Coober Pedy's history and lifestyle; afternoon tours include the Breakaways.

Sleeping

BUDGET

Radeka's Downunder Dugout Motel & Backpackers (☎ 8672 5223; www.radekadownunder.com.au; Oliver St; underground dm/tw $22/55, motel s/d $80/90; ✂ 🖳) This backpacker mecca has bunks in open alcoves, and pleasant private rooms. It has a good kitchen, bar, restaurant and laundry. Free airport and bus-station transfers are provided if you book in advance.

Riba's (☎ 8672 5614; William Creek Rd; underground/above-ground sites per person $7.50/11, powered sites $18) Just 5km from town, Riba's offers the unique option of underground camping or above ground for traditionalists. Cool underground extras include a TV lounge, free showers and an interesting one-hour evening tour ($16, included in the cost of camping).

Oasis Caravan Park (☎ 8672 5169; Seventeen Mile Rd; powered/unpowered sites per 2 people $23/19, r $34, cabins $70-89) Reasonably central to the action with shade, shelter and an undercover swimming pool.

MIDRANGE

Mud Hut Motel (☎ 1800 646 962, 8672 3003; www.mudhutmotel.com.au; St Nicholas St; s/d/units $90/105/145; ✂) The walls look rustic, and with good reason – they're actually packed earth. And despite the grubby name, this is one of the cleanest places in town. Units are well tricked-out with cooktops and large fridges, and there's an attached restaurant and bar.

Coober Pedy Experience Motel (☎ 8672 5777; www.cooberpedyexperience.com.au; Crowders Gully Rd; dm/d $24/126) This subterranean treasure is the largest place in town yet maintains its homey feel and has good facilities. The wholesomeness of the next-door Revival Church pervades this place.

Opal Inn Hotel/Motel (☎ 8672 5054; Hutchison St; powered/unpowered sites per 2 people $25/20, hotel s/d $65/70, motel s $73-103, motel d $80-110; ✂ 🖳) Central to the action, this jack-of-all-trades offers basic but clean pub rooms and motel-style accommodation. It also provides excellent information packs. The saloon bar serves counter meals and has pool tables and cable TV.

Fred & Wilma's and Barney & Betty's B&B (☎ 8672 5028; Hutchison St; d $110) You can make bookings for these cute Flintstones-inspired places through the Umoona Opal Mine & Museum. Fred & Wilma's is underground, while Barney & Betty's is above ground, but both places come with full kitchens and fold-out beds.

Anne's Dugout B&B (☎ 8672 5541; Koska St; www.annesdugoutbandb.com; d/f incl breakfast without bathroom $80/110) A real dugout experience amid relics from the 1960s mine. The delightful owner provides lots of interesting historical titbits to digest with a hefty cooked breakfast and homemade quandong jam.

TOP END

Desert Cave Hotel (☎ 8672 5688; www.desertcave.com.au; Hutchison St; d $187; ✂ 🖳) Fancy oasis-style luxury? With a pool, gym, in-house movies, formidable minibar and great restaurant (see Umberto's Restaurant, p790), this underground palace won't disappoint. Staff are well informed and there are plenty of tours to choose (see Tours, left), departing from reception.

Eating & Drinking

Breakaways Cafe (☎ 8672 3177; Hutchison St; meals $5-9; ✆ 7am-8pm) A friendly and popular café serving value-packed cooked breakfasts, burgers, and specials such as schnitzel with salad ($7.50).

Tom & Mary's Taverna (☎ 8672 5622; Hutchison St; meals $6-15; ✆ lunch & dinner) This popular Greek spot with faux wood panelling and vinyl chairs does everything from *yiros* (souvlaki) and hearty Greek salads to pastas.

Italo Australian Miners Club (Italian Club; ☎ 8672 5101; Italian Club Rd; mains with salad bar $10; ✆ dinner Wed-Sat) The local institution for steak and schnitzels from Wednesday to Saturday nights, and a good place for a beer at other times.

Old Miners Dugout Cafe (☎ 8672 3552; 335 Trow St; lunch $6-17, dinner $10-24; ✆ lunch & dinner Mon-Sat) You pay a little extra for the underground ambience, but the menu is internationally imaginative and the food tasty.

Upmarket **Umberto's Restaurant** (☎ 8672 5688; www.desertcave.com.au; Hutchison St; mains $18-26; ✆ dinner), which offers dishes such as kangaroo served in a juniper *jus*, and **Crystal Café** (☎ 8672 5688; www.desertcave.com.au; Hutchison St; breakfast $3.50-11, lunch $6-12; ✆ breakfast & lunch) are at the Desert Cave Hotel (p789). Start your day at the café with a maple syrup pancake stack ($8.50) and good coffee. The Sunday lunch buffet ($14.50) is a local favourite.

Shopping

There are numerous reputable – and some not so reputable – opal outlets in town. It's best to shop around and be wary of anyone offering too-good-to-be-true discounts. Some of the best buys are found at the **Opal Cutter** (☎ 8672 3086; Post Office Hill Rd), but you should definitely compare a few prices around town before purchasing.

Getting There & Around

Coober Pedy sits just off the Stuart Hwy 846km northwest of Adelaide and 686km south of Alice Springs (NT). See p785 for transport details. Most motels and hostels meet you at the airport if you ring ahead.

You can rent cars – including 4WDs and camping vehicles – from **Budget** (☎ 8672 5333; cpdbudget@ozemail.com.au; Oliver St) and **Coober Pedy Rent-a-Car** (☎ 8672 3003; Mud Hut Motel, St Nicholson St). Budget offers handy one-way rentals, though you'll pay an extra rate over 100km.

COOBER PEDY TO MARLA

Breakaways Reserve is a stark but colourful area of mesa hills and scarps off the Stuart Hwy about 31km north of Coober Pedy – you turn off the highway 22km from town. Here you'll find the white-and-yellow formation known as the **Castle**, which featured in the films *Mad Max III* and *The Adventures of Priscilla, Queen of the Desert*. Entry permits ($4 per person) are available at the tourist office or Underground Books in Coober Pedy at the self-registration station. Late afternoon is the best time for photographs.

An interesting loop of 70km on mainly unsealed road from Coober Pedy takes in the Breakaways, the **dog fence** and the tablelike **Moon Plain** on the Coober Pedy–Oodnadatta road. The Coober Pedy visitor information centre has leaflets.

If you're heading for Oodnadatta, turning off the Stuart Hwy at Cadney Homestead, 151km northwest of Coober Pedy, gives you a shorter run on dirt roads than the routes via Marla or Coober Pedy. En route you pass through the aptly named and stunning **Painted Desert**.

Cadney Homestead (☎ 08-8670 7994; www.cadneyhomestead.com.au; Stuart Hwy; powered sites per 2 people $20, cabins/motel d $33/$100; ❄) has grassy camp sites, cabins with air-con ($5 for linen hire) or motel rooms and organises tours of the Painted Desert.

About 32km east of Cadney Homestead, **Copper Hills Tourist Park** (☎ 08-8670 7995; Painted Desert Hwy; unpowered sites $6, dm $12, cabins $30) is a great place to appreciate the desert's unique atmosphere while you camp by a peaceful billabong.

MARLA

☎ 08 / pop 150

In the mulga scrub, about 160km south of the NT border, Marla replaced Oodnadatta as the official regional centre when the *Ghan* railway line was re-routed in 1980. The rough-and-ready **Mintabie** opal field is on Aboriginal land, 35km west, and the recently opened **Lambina** opal field is 75km northeast. Fuel and provisions are available in Marla 24 hours a day.

Marla Travellers Rest (☎ 8670 7001; powered/unpowered sites per 2 people $17/10, cabins s/d $30/40, d $75-85, mains $6-10; ✆ café 7am-9pm; ❄) has spacious motel rooms and a pool. The café does basic meals.

MARREE

☎ 08 / pop 80

Sleepy Marree is at the southern end of the Birdsville and Oodnadatta Tracks, and was a major centre for the Afghan camel trains that serviced the outback from the 1870s to the 1930s. There are still a couple of date palms, an incongruously large pub, and relics of the old *Ghan* train.

The township has modern travellers' facilities, and really fires up during the **Marree Australian Camel Cup** (first Saturday in July).

Reminders of the area's non-European history are at the **Arabunna People's Community Centre & Museum** (☎ 8675 8351; admission by donation; ☼ Mon-Fri 8am-5pm), which includes an informative video and several cultural displays.

One of the best land-based tours of the area is **Reg Dodd's Arabunna Tours** (☎ 8675 8351; 1-day tour $90), which take in Lake Eyre and provide insight into the Aboriginal history of the area, with a BBQ lunch thrown in.

Sleeping & Eating

Marree Hotel (☎ 8675 8344; www.marreehotel.com; Railway Tce; s/d $50/70, meals around $17; ☼ breakfast, lunch & dinner; ✖) This rather grand hotel in the town centre has old-style pub rooms and can also organise flights ($170, one hour) over **Lake Eyre** and **Marree Man**, the huge outline of an Aboriginal warrior that people unknown etched into the desert sands in 1998.

Oasis Caravan Park (☎ 8675 8352; Railway Tce; powered/unpowered sites per 2 people $15/12, s/d $37/55; ✖) The Oasis, in the town centre, has several good camp sites as well as motel-style rooms with TVs and fridges. The park also has a café and shop.

MARREE TO OODNADATTA

Around 60km west of Marree at **Alberrie Creek** is the **Mutonia Sculpture Park** (admission by donation) which is definitely worthy of some contemplation.

Coward Springs (☎ 08-8675 8336; www.cowardsprings.com.au; unpowered sites per 2 people $14), roughly 130km west of Marree, is the first stop at the old Coward Springs railway siding. There's a beautiful natural warm-water spa and incongruous wetland in the desert, created by a bore sunk here in 1886. You can take a dip in the spa ($2) or camp in the basic camping ground – there are toilets

and showers. You can ride a **camel**, or do a five-day camel trek to Lake Eyre in the cooler months ($185 per day). A few kilometres back down the road towards Marree, the **Wabma Kadarbu Mound Springs Conservation Park** includes artesian mound springs such as the Bubbler and Blanche Cup.

In another 70km you'll hit William Creek (population 12) about halfway between Oodnadatta and Marree. Claims are made that this town, consisting of a classic pub and store, is Australia's smallest. It's best enjoyed at weather-beaten **William Creek Hotel** (☎ 08-8670 7880; www.williamcreekhotel.net.au; Oodnadatta Track; unpowered sites $7, dm $14, unit d $60, mains $8-14; ☼ breakfast, lunch & dinner; ✖), a fair-dinkum outback pub with a dusty camping ground, modest motel rooms and a bunkhouse. It also sells fuel, cold beer, basic provisions and meals, and stocks spare tyres.

Across the road from the pub, there's good camping facilities and takeaway food at **William Creek Store & Camp Ground** (☎ 08-8670 7746; www.williamcreekcampground.com; Oodnadatta Track; powered/unpowered sites per 2 people $20/15; s $40, tw & d $49; ☼ Mar-Nov; ✖).

OODNADATTA

☎ 08 / pop 200

Reverend John Flynn, founder of the Royal Flying Doctor Service (RFDS), established the Australian outback's first hospital (1912) in Oodnadatta, where the main road and the old railway line diverged.

The old train station (by far the most impressive building in town) has been converted into an interesting little **museum**. Pick up the key from the pub or roadhouse.

The heart of the town today is the **Pink Roadhouse** (☎ 1800 802 074, 8670 7822; www.pinkroadhouse.com.au; Main St; ☼ 8am-5.30pm), which is an excellent source for advice about track conditions, and about attractions in any direction. Its mud maps are authoritative and can be found on its colourful website. The owners, Adam and Lynnie Plate, have spent a lot of time and effort putting road signs and kilometre pegs over a huge area in this district – even in the inhospitable Simpson Desert. They also run the attached **Adam & Lynnie's Oodnadatta Caravan Park** (unpowered sites per 2 people $15, on-site caravans $28, s/d/cabins $38/48/80; ✖), which has basic camping through to self-contained cabins and serves meals.

Transcontinental Hotel (☎ 8670 7804; http:webeze .com.au/oodnadatta; Main St; s/d/tw $40/65/70; ⚡) has reasonably good pub rooms.

From Oodnadatta you can head north-west to Marla (209km).

BIRDSVILLE TRACK

Running 520km from Marree in SA to Birdsville (p384), just across the border in Queensland, this old droving trail is one of the best outback routes in Australia. Cattle were walked down the Birdsville Track from southwest Queensland to Marree to be loaded onto trains until motor transport took over from the drovers in the 1960s. Now the cattle are trucked out in road trains. These days, it is generally feasible to travel it in any well-prepared, conventional vehicle, though it's worth bearing in mind that traffic is anything but heavy – particularly in summer.

The only refuelling stop is 205km north of Marree (315km to Birdsville) at **Mungeranie Hotel** (☎ 08-8675 8317; s/d $45/70; ⏱ 8am-8pm), which offers camping, decent rooms, mechanical repairs, meals and a large hot-spring pool in which to soak away the road weariness.

The track is more or less at the meeting point between the sand dunes of the Simpson Desert to the west and the desolate wastes of Sturt Stony Desert to the east. There are ruins of a couple of homesteads along the track, and artesian bores gush out boiling-hot salty water at many places. At Clifton Hills, about 200km south of Birdsville, the track splits, with the main route going around the eastern side of Goyder Lagoon.

Remember to take plenty of water with you – even locals have become lost here and then perished from thirst.

STRZELECKI TRACK

The Strzelecki Track spans 460km from Lyndhurst, about 80km south of Marree, to the tiny outpost of Innamincka, meandering through the sandhills of the Strzelecki Regional Reserve. Discovery of oil and gas at **Moomba** (a closed town to travellers) saw the upgrading of the road from a camel track to a decent dirt road, though heavy transport travelling along it makes for bone-rattling corrugation. The new Moomba–Strzelecki Track is better kept, but longer and less interesting than the old track, which follows Strzelecki Creek. Accommodation, provisions and fuel are available at Lyndhurst and Innamincka, but there's nothing in between.

The track skirts the northern Flinders Ranges, crossing the **dog fence**, a fence that stretches for thousands of kilometres across southeastern Australia, originally erected as a barrier against sheep-killing dingoes.

INNAMINCKA

☎ 08 / pop 10

At the northern extreme of the Strzelecki Track, Innamincka is on Cooper Creek close to where the ill-fated 1860 expedition of Robert O'Hara Burke and William John Wills came to its tragic end. The famous **Dig Tree** marks the expedition's base camp and although the word 'dig' is no longer visible, the expedition's camp number is still visible. The Dig Tree is over the Queensland border, though memorials and markers – commemorating where Burke and Wills died, and where sole-survivor King was found – are downstream in SA. There's also a memorial where AW Howitt's rescue party made its base on the creek.

Cooper Creek flows only after heavy soaking rains fall over central Queensland, but it has deep, permanent waterholes and the semipermanent **Coongie Lakes**, which is part of the **Innamincka Regional Reserve** and a significant habitat for aquatic fauna and water birds.

The old **Australian Inland Mission Hospital** now houses the **DEH** (☎ 8675 9909; ⏱ 8am-6pm) ranger's office and displays on the reserve.

Prior to European settlement, the area had a large Aboriginal population, so relics such as middens and grinding stones can be seen around the area.

Westprint's *Innamincka-Coongie Lakes* map is a good source of information on the Innamincka area.

You can take 2WD vehicles over the unsealed road to Birdsville via 1883 **Cordillo Downs Homestead**, which has a huge stone shearing shed.

Sleeping & Eating

Innamincka Hotel (☎ 8675 9901; fax 8675 9961; dm/s/ d/tr $30/50/70/90, mains $15-24; ⏱ breakfast, lunch & dinner; ⚡) This old-style hotel has good motel-style rooms as well as a basic bunkhouse for the budget conscious. Choose between takeaways and hefty counter meals – the Wednesday night bush BBQs and Sunday night roasts ($18) are a real treat for bigger bellies. Canoe and dinghy hire is available.

Innamincka Trading Post (☎ 8675 9900; fax 8675 9920; s/d/tr $45/70/100; ☒) This place has three two-bedroom cabins sleeping up to four people. There's also a BBQ, and fuel and provisions are also sold here.

Cooper Creek Homestay (☎ 8675 9591; fourmatth ews@bigpond.com.au; s/d $60/80; ☒ breakfast, lunch & dinner; ☒) About 400m from Cooper Creek, the friendly family here offers rooms in their home. The three-course evening feast ($30) is cooked over an open fire and eaten under the stars.

There are plenty of shady **bush camping** (per vehicle, per night $20) spots along Cooper Creek – see the ranger or Innamincka Trading Post for a permit. You can also camp on the **town common** (per vehicle, per night $5); there are pit toilets and an honesty box for fees. For a donation to the Progress Association you can use the shower, toilet and laundry facilities (no washing machines here) outside the Trading Post.

Northern Territory

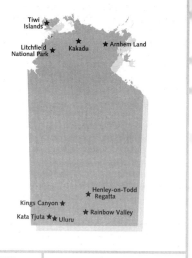

The Northern Territory (NT) is a revelation, a place of such natural and cultural distinction that, despite the best intentions of the local tourism industry, no amount of open-jawed crocodile photos, didgeridoo CDs or videos of 4WDs emerging from clouds of red dust can prepare you for it. Sometimes you'll be ambushed by visual splendour, such as when you stare into the grand maw of Kings Canyon, glance across a plain of spinifex to see Chambers Pillar stretching up from the horizon, or watch dozens of startled flying foxes take flight from the canopy of a monsoon forest. But much of the NT's beauty steals up on you only after days of exposure to its mesmerising, deceptive emptiness: the silhouette of desert oaks against a dusky sky, water lilies painting the surface of a billabong, a goanna ambling down a dry creek bed or ancient scratchings of Aboriginal art under a sandstone overhang.

Visitors quickly learn to savour the landscape, from the desert-pegged contours of Uluru and the sheer escarpment of Arnhem Land to the tropical Top End's mangrove swamps. They cruise Yellow Water looking for the eyeballs of a saltie (saltwater crocodile) off the muddy riverbank, walk the rugged gorges that indent the MacDonnell Ranges, and paddle across rock pools and under waterfalls in Litchfield National Park. They appreciate the fascinating complexities of Aboriginal culture by standing among burial poles on the Tiwi Islands, buying the artistic output of remote communities and viewing fine exhibitions in museums and cultural centres. And they kick back in pubs in the Outback, beer gardens in Alice and foreshore cafés in Darwin, digesting past experiences and eager for more Territorial travel.

HIGHLIGHTS

- Climbing the walls of awesome **Kings Canyon** (p867)

- Being transfixed by colossal **Uluru** (Ayers Rock; p871) and **Kata Tjuta** (The Olgas; p872)

- Floating dreamily across a beautiful water hole in **Litchfield National Park** (p822)

- Studying Ubirr's rock art before gazing out across timeless **Kakadu** (p828)

- Snorting outback dust on a 4WD trip to **Rainbow Valley** (p866)

- Visiting Aboriginal communities with a local guide in **Arnhem Land** (p832) and on the **Tiwi Islands** (p819)

- Helping Aussies laugh at themselves during the **Henley-on-Todd Regatta** (p853)

Tiwi Islands ★
Litchfield National Park ★　★ Kakadu　★ Arnhem Land
Henley-on-Todd Regatta ★
Kings Canyon ★
Kata Tjuta ★★ Uluru　★ Rainbow Valley

| ▪ TELEPHONE CODE: 08 | ▪ POPULATION: 200,000 | ▪ www.ntexplore.com.au |

NORTHERN TERRITORY FACTS

Eat: Freshly caught/cooked barramundi

Drink: A 'handle' (285mL) or 'schooner' (425mL) of ice-cold beer

Read: Robyn Davidson's *Tracks*, Bill Neidjie's *Gagudju Man*

Listen to: Blekbala Mujik (pop, reggae), NoKTuRNL (rock, rap), Plonker (punk)

Watch: *Crocodile Dundee, Yolngu Boy*

Avoid: Stingers, salties, dehydration

Locals' nickname: Top Enders, Centralians

Swim at: Crocodile-free Litchfield water holes (p822)

Strangest festival: Darwin's Beer Can Regatta (p809), Alice Spring's Henley-on-Todd Regatta (p853)

Tackiest tourist attraction: Charlie the water buffalo, well and truly stuffed at the Adelaide River Inn (p823)

HISTORY

It's believed that Australian Aborigines have occupied the Australian land mass for at least 50,000 years and possibly for up to 70,000 years, though the continent's interior was not inhabited until about 24,000 years ago. The first significant contact with outsiders occurred in the 18th century with fishermen from Sulawesi in modern-day Indonesia.

Early attempts to settle the Top End were mainly due to British fears that the French or Dutch might get a foothold in Australia. Forts were established at places like Melville Island and Fort Wellington (on the Cobourg Peninsula) between 1824 and 1838, but all were subsequently abandoned. Then in 1845, German explorer Ludwig Leichhardt reached Port Essington overland from Brisbane and aroused prolonged interest in the Top End.

The process of white settlement in the NT was slower but just as troubled and violent as elsewhere in Australia. By the early 20th century, most Aboriginal people were confined to government reserves or Christian missions. Some took employment as stockmen or domestic servants on cattle stations (often to retain the connection to their land), while others lived on the edges of towns, taking on low-paid work, with alcohol abuse a common problem. Only a few were able to maintain much of their traditional way of life.

During the 1960s, Aboriginal people began to demand more rights. In 1963 the people of Yirrkala on the Gove Peninsula protested against plans for bauxite mining in the area. They failed to stop the mining, but the way they presented their case – producing sacred objects and bark paintings that showed their right to the land under Aboriginal custom – was a milestone.

In 1966, a group of Aboriginal stockmen, led by Vincent Lingiari, went on strike on Wave Hill Station, in protest over the low wages and poor conditions that they received compared with white stockmen. They were soon joined by others and before long only stations that gave Aboriginal workers good conditions were provided with workers by Lingiari and other Gurindji elders. A federal court decision granting equal wages to Aboriginal workers took effect in December 1968.

In 1976, the Aboriginal Land Rights (NT) Act was passed in Canberra. It handed over all reserves and mission lands in the NT to the Aboriginal people and allowed Aboriginal groups to claim government land with which they had traditional ties – provided the land wasn't already leased, in a town or set aside for some other special purpose.

Today, Aboriginal people own about half of the land in the NT, including Kakadu and Uluru–Kata Tjuta National Parks, which are leased back to the federal government. Minerals on Aboriginal land are still government property, though the landowners' permission for exploration and mining is usually required and has to be paid for. Around 30% of the Territory's 200,000 people are Aborigines.

While non-Aboriginal Australia's awareness of the need for reconciliation with the Aboriginal community has increased in recent years, there are still huge gulfs between the cultures. It's often difficult for short-term visitors to make meaningful contact with Aborigines because they generally prefer to be left to themselves. The impressions given by Aboriginal people on the streets of Alice Springs, Katherine and Darwin, where social problems and alcohol abuse among a few people can present an unpleasant picture, are not indicative of Aboriginal communities as a whole.

Tours to Aboriginal lands, some operated by the communities themselves, are

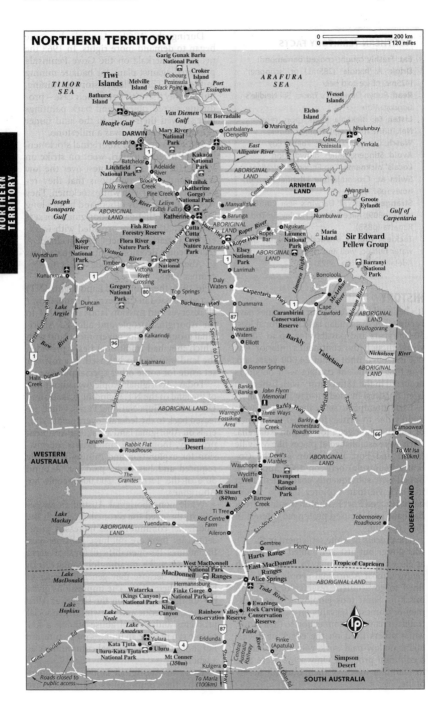

NORTHERN TERRITORY

gradually becoming more acceptable, as communities feel more inclined to share their culture. Benefits are twofold: financial gain, not only from the tours but from selling arts and crafts direct to the public; and educating non-Aboriginal people about traditional culture and customs, helping to alleviate the problems caused by the ignorance and misunderstandings of the past.

GEOGRAPHY & CLIMATE

Although roughly 80% of the NT is in the tropics – the Tropic of Capricorn lies just north of Alice Springs – only the northern 25%, known as the Top End, has anything that resembles the popular idea of a tropical climate. It's a distinct region of savanna woodlands and rainforest pockets – in the northeast, the Arnhem Land plateau rises

ABORIGINAL FESTIVALS & EVENTS

There are many annual Aboriginal festivals worth attending. Although the festivals are usually held on restricted Aboriginal land, permit requirements are generally waived for them; this applies to most of the festivals listed below. Bear in mind that alcohol is banned in many communities.

Tiwi Grand Final

Held at the end of March on Bathurst Island, this sporting event is the culmination of a season of Australian Rules football between Aboriginal communities from around the Top End. The Islanders are passionate followers of the game and the final is a major spectacle, with planeloads of people flying in from Darwin for the day.

Merrepen Arts Festival

Nauiyu Nambiyu, on the banks of the Daly River, is the venue for the Merrepen Arts Festival, held on the first weekend in June. Several local Aboriginal communities, such as Wadeye, Nauiyu and Peppimenarti, display their arts and crafts.

Barunga Festival

For four days including the Queen's Birthday long weekend in June, Barunga, 80km east of Katherine, hosts Aboriginal people from around 40 communities. There are displays of traditional arts and crafts, as well as dancing and athletics competitions. Bring your own camping equipment; alternatively, visit for the day from Katherine.

Alice Springs Beanie Festival

This arts and crafts festival, held over several days in mid-June, brings together communities from around central Australia and celebrates the work of indigenous artists. The 'beanie' is a knitted woollen hat.

Oenpelli Open Day

Gunbalanya (Oenpelli), in Arnhem Land, across the East Alligator River from Jabiru, has an open day in August. This event gives visitors a chance to buy local artefacts and watch sports, concerts and dancing events.

Garma Festival

This four-day festival (www.garma.telstra.com) is held in August in northeastern Arnhem Land. It's an important, large-scale celebration of Yolngu culture and includes ceremonial performances, bushcraft lessons, a *yidaki* (didgeridoo) master class and an academic forum.

National Aboriginal & Torres Strait Islander Art Award

Each year (usually August to October), an exhibition of works entered for this award is held at the Museum & Art Gallery of the Northern Territory (p803) in Darwin. It attracts entries from around the country.

abruptly from the plain and continues to the Gulf of Carpentaria. Much of the southern 75% of the Territory consists of desert or semiarid plain.

The Top End's climate is described in terms of the Dry and the Wet, with year-round maximum temperatures of 30°C to 34°C and minimums between 19°C and 26°C. Roughly, the Dry lasts from April to September, and the Wet from October to March, with the heaviest rain falling from January onwards.

In the centre, temperatures are much more variable, plummeting below freezing on winter nights (June to August) and soaring above 40°C on summer days (December to March).

The most comfortable time to visit both the centre and the Top End is June and July, though the centre is pleasant as early as April. The Top End has its good points during the Wet – everything is green, and there are spectacular electrical storms and relatively few tourists. However, the combination of heat and high humidity can be unbearable, dirt roads are often impassable and some national parks are either totally or partially closed.

INFORMATION

The **NT Tourist Commission** (NTTC; www.nttc.com.au) doesn't operate any tourist offices, but works through travel agencies and its comprehensive website. There are regional visitor information centres in Darwin, Katherine, Tennant Creek and Alice Springs; see the relevant sections for details.

Comprehensive information on the Territory is also provided in Lonely Planet's *Northern Territory* guidebook.

Helpful websites:

Automobile Association of the Northern Territory (AANT; www.aant.com.au)

Bed & Breakfast and Farmstay NT Inc (www.bed-and-breakfast.au.com)

Parks & Wildlife Commission (www.nt.gov.au/ipe/pwcnt/)

Permits

You need to purchase permits in order to enter Aboriginal land. Sometimes permits won't be necessary if you stay on recognised public roads that cross Aboriginal territory. However, if you leave the main road by more than 50m, even if you're only going

into an Aboriginal settlement for fuel and provisions, you may need a permit.

Three land councils process permit requests: the Central Land Council deals with all land south of a line drawn between Kununurra (Western Australia) and Mt Isa (Queensland); the Northern Land Council is responsible for land north of that line; and the Tiwi Land Council deals with Bathurst and Melville Islands (at the time of writing, travellers could only visit the Tiwi Islands on a tour, with the permit included in the tour price). Permits can take four to six weeks to be processed, although for Gunbalanya (Oenpelli) they are issued on the spot in Jabiru ($13.20).

Central Land Council (Map p846; ☎ 08-8951 6211; 33 Stuart Hwy, Alice Springs, postal address: PO Box 3321, Alice Springs, NT 0871; permits issued ☺ 8am-noon & 2-4pm Mon-Fri)

Northern Land Council (www.nlc.org.au); Darwin (Map p801; ☎ 08-8920 5100; 9 Rowling St, Casuarina, NT 0810); Jabiru (☎ 08-8979 2410; Flinders St, Jabiru, NT 0886); Katherine (Map p834; ☎ 08-8972 2799; 5 Katherine Tce, Katherine NT 0850); Nhulunbuy (☎ 08-8987 2602; Endeavour Sq)

Tiwi Land Council (Map p801; ☎ 08-8981 4898; Unit 5, 3 Bishop St, Stuart Park, Darwin NT 0820)

NATIONAL PARKS

The NT has some of Australia's wildest, best-known national parks, with familiar names like Kakadu (p824) and Uluru–Kata Tjuta (p869) – both of these parks have World Heritage listing. Other places that bequeath visitors superb travel memories in the Top End include: Litchfield National Park (p822), punctuated by magnificent rocky swimming holes; the proposed Mary River National Park (p820), with outstanding wetlands and birdlife; the rugged gorges that comprise Nitmiluk (Katherine Gorge) National Park (p838); and the sandstone splendour of Keep River National Park (p840), on the Western Australia (WA) border.

In central Australia, Watarrka (Kings Canyon) National Park (p867) is centred on the outrageously picturesque Kings Canyon, while the West MacDonnell National Park (p861) encompasses spectacular gorge country and offers excellent bushwalking, including the renowned Larapinta Trail (p862).

The Parks & Wildlife Commission (left) produces national park factsheets, available on its website or from its various offices.

ACTIVITIES

Bushwalking

The territory's national parks offer well-maintained tracks of varying lengths and degrees of difficulty, which expose walkers to some marvellous sights, smells and sounds. Extended overnight hikes include the Giles Track (p867) in Watarrka, the Jatbula Trail (p838) from Nitmiluk National Park to Edith Falls, the Larapinta Trail (p862) in the West MacDonnell Ranges, or you can mark up your own topographical maps for Litchfield (p822) and Kakadu National Parks (p830) – permits are required.

Fishing

The most popular Top End fish is the barramundi, a perch that often grows over 1m long. Landing the pugnacious 'barra' is a challenge, but it's only half the fun; the other half is eating it. Key locales for barramundi and other sporting fish include Borroloola, Daly River and Mary River. The minimum size limit on barramundi is 55cm.

The bag size for mud crabs is 13/14cm for males/females. To tell if your crab is full of meat as opposed to having just started moulting (growing into a new shell), press the top of the shell and see how much it flexes. Also look for worn claws and a dirty shell: sharp teeth and a clean shell mean the crab has recently moulted.

For information contact the **Recreational Fishing Office** (Map p804; ☎ 08-8999 2372; The Esplanade) in Darwin.

Fossicking

Fossicking for agate, amethyst, garnet, jasper, zircon and gold is a popular activity in the NT, although it's really only an option if you have a 4WD. Some good places to try include Gemtree and the Harts Range in central Australia, Pine Creek for gold, and Brock's Creek (37km southwest of Adelaide River) for topaz, tourmaline, garnet and zircon.

You must first obtain a fossicking permit (free) and permission from the land owner or leaseholder on freehold land and mineral leases. The **Department of Business, Industry & Resource Development** (www.minerals.nt.gov.au; Darwin Map p804; ☎ 08-8999 6443; The Esplanade; Alice Springs ☎ 08-8951 8177) has information on permits, geological maps and fossicking guides.

> **THE CANE TOAD COMETH**
>
> It must've seemed like a good idea at the time. The time was 1935 and the idea involved the release of 100 Central American cane toads in Gordonvale, Queensland, in order to eat a beetle with an unpopular appetite for sugar cane. Unfortunately, no-one anticipated the cane toad's voracious appetite (both for food and breeding) or the poisonous glands that make it a fatal meal for unsuspecting predators. Equipped with these assets and a bad case of wanderlust, the toads have been making their way west ever since. As of early 2005, they had come to within 70km of Darwin, insinuating themselves into the ecosystems of Kakadu and Nitmiluk National Parks along the way. The toads pose a serious threat to native frogs, quolls and goannas, and pretty much anything they decide to eat or that decides to eat them. There's some good news, however, in the form of the native Dahl's aquatic frog *(Litoria dahlii)*, which ate young cane toads in recent scientific tests without any ill effects. At the time of writing, the two species were due to confront each other in the wild, in nature's remake of *Alien vs Predator*.

Swimming

The cool waterfalls, water holes and rejuvenating thermal pools throughout the NT are perfect spots to revitalise travel-weary flesh. Litchfield National Park, in the Top End, and the West MacDonnell Ranges, in the centre, are particularly rewarding.

Saltwater crocodiles inhabit both salt and fresh waters in the Top End (though there are quite a few safe, natural swimming holes). Before taking a plunge, read the signs and seek local advice. If in doubt, don't risk it. Box jellyfish populate the sea from October to May.

TOURS

A plethora of tours operate around the Red Centre and Top End. See the various sections in this chapter for details, and listen to word of mouth from other travellers. Tours into Arnhem Land, originating in Kakadu, Darwin or Katherine, offer spectacular experiences but are costly due to the area's remoteness.

NORTHERN TERRITORY

Adventure Tours Australia (☎ 1300 654 604, 08-8309 2277; www.adventuretours.com.au) Runs tours throughout the Territory, ranging from one to 10 days.

Anangu (☎ 08-8956 2123; www.anangutours.com.au) Tours around Uluru guided by the traditional owners.

Australian Pacific Touring (APT; ☎ 1800 891 121; www.aptouring.com.au) Has a trip from Darwin to Kakadu (adult/child $175/90) that includes a Yellow Water trip.

Darwin Day Tours (☎ 1300 721 365) Offers day trips to Kakadu (adult/child $165/130) and Katherine ($150/75).

Emu Run (☎ 08-8953 7057; www.emurun.com.au) Operates tours to the East and West MacDonnell Ranges from Alice Springs.

Goanna Eco Tours (☎ 1800 003 880, 08-8927 2781; www.goannaecotours.com.au) Runs tours from Darwin into Litchfield National Park.

Kakadu Animal Tracks (☎ 08-8979 0145; www .animaltracks.com.au) If you are inside Kakadu, supplement your own transport with a wildlife and Aboriginal cultural tour, or a cruise on the sublime Yellow Water.

Magela Cultural & Heritage Tours (☎ 08-8979 2114) Discover Arnhem Land rock-art sites and Aboriginal culture.

Manyallaluk Cultural Tours (☎ 08-8975 4727) Experience Aboriginal culture near Katherine.

Nitmiluk Tours (☎ 1800 089 103; nitmiluk@bigpond .com) Runs cruises through Katherine's serpentine gorge.

Sahara Outback Tours (☎ 08-8953 0881; www .saharatours.com.au) Run 4WD camping tours from the Alice to the centre's top sights.

Tiwi Tours (☎ 1300 721 365, 08-8922 2777; www .aussieadventure.com.au) Indulge in a one- or two-day tour to the Tiwi Islands.

Wilderness 4WD Adventures (☎ 1800 808 288, 08-8941 2161; www.wildernessadventures.com.au) Takes small-group tours into Kakadu.

GETTING THERE & AROUND

Darwin International Airport (☎ 08-8920 1805) is the NT's sole international air gateway. Direct overseas flights descend here from Brunei, East Timor, Indonesia and Malaysia.

The Darwin (p815), Alice Springs (p857) and Uluru (p876) sections of this chapter detail interstate transport. For an overview of countrywide transport, see the Transport chapter (p1039).

Travellers must surrender all fruit, vegetables, nuts, and honey at the Northern Territory/Western Australia border.

Air

Airnorth (☎ 1800 627 474; www.airnorth.com.au) connects Darwin with Gove Peninsula (in the far northeast), and with Broome and Kununurra

in WA. **Qantas** (☎ 13 13 13; www.qantas.com.au) flies between Darwin and most other Australian capital cities, as well as to Gove, Alice Springs and Yulara. **Virgin Blue** (☎ 13 67 89; www.virginblue .com.au) has direct flights from Darwin to Melbourne, Sydney and Brisbane.

Bus

Greyhound Australia (☎ 13 14 99; www.greyhound .com.au) regularly services the main road routes, including Kakadu and Uluru; see Getting There & Away in the relevant sections for details.

Backpacker buses cover vast distances while savouring the sights along the way. See the Darwin (p815) and Alice Springs (p858) bus sections for details.

Car & Motorcycle

Proceed with great care when travelling off the beaten track. Before leaving sealed roads, check road conditions via the 24-hour **road information service** (☎ 1800 246 199), the **Automobile Association of the Northern Territory** (AANT; www.aant.com.au; Darwin Map p804; ☎ 08-8981 3837; 79-81 Smith St; Alice Springs ☎ 08-8981 3837) and visitor information centres. Note that areas self-designated as 'alcohol-free' do not allow *any* alcohol to be brought in, even if the alcohol is unopened. You can actually be fined if it's found in your vehicle.

Traffic may be fairly light and many roads dead straight, but watch out for the four great NT road hazards – speed (there are no speed limits on the open road), driver fatigue, road trains and animals (domestic livestock and native animals).

Roadhouses offering fuel, food (sometimes dubious) and accommodation appear at regular intervals along the main highways. The price of fuel climbs the further you get from Darwin or Alice Springs.

Train

The famous *Ghan* train now shunts into Darwin, with stops at Alice Springs and Katherine. See p858 for timetable and fare details.

DARWIN

☎ 08 / pop 71,350

Darwin is a thoroughly likable modern place with a laid-back, tropical spirit, attributes

DARWIN

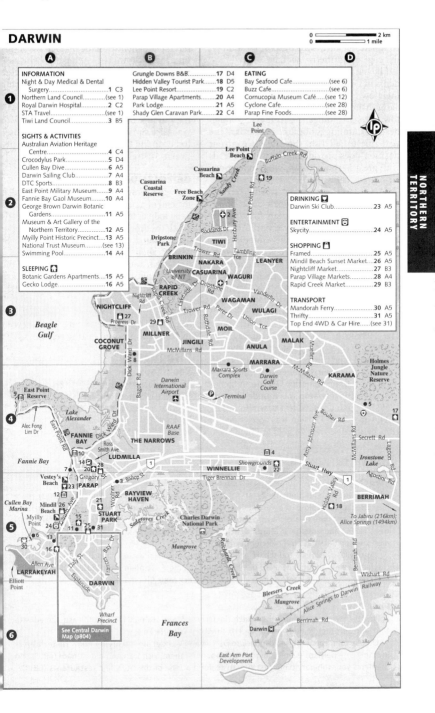

0 — 2 km
0 — 1 mile

NORTHERN
TERRITORY

Lee
Point

Lee Point
Beach

Buffalo Creek Rd

Casuarina
Beach

19

Casuarina
Coastal
Reserve

Free Beach
Zone

Sandy Creek

Lee Point Rd

Henbury Ave

Rocklands Dr

Dripstone
Park

Trower Rd

TIWI

Tambling
Tce

BRINKIN

2

NAKARA

LEANYER

University
of NT

CASUARINA

WAGURI

**RAPID
CREEK**

Dripstone Rd

Lakeside Dr

1

WAGAMAN

Nightcliff
Rd

NIGHTCLIFF

27

Progress Dr

29

Trower Rd

Rapid Creek

Parer Dr

WULAGI

Rothdale Rd

Union Tce

Vanderlin Dr

MOIL

**Beagle
Gulf**

MILLNER

JINGILI

Rd

ANULA

**COCONUT
GROVE**

8

Dick Ward Dr

McMillans Rd

MARRARA

McMillans Rd

MALAK

KARAMA

Holmes
Jungle
Nature
Reserve

Bagot Rd

Marrara Sports
Complex

Darwin
Golf
Course

Mueller Rd

**East Point
Reserve**

Lake
Alexander

Alec Fong
Lim Dr

East Point Rd

**FANNIE
BAY**

Dick Ward Dr

Darwin
International
Airport

P — Terminal

RAAF
Base

Amy Johnson Ave

Boulter Rd

5

17

Secrett Rd

Fannie Bay

10

Ross
Smith Ave

THE NARROWS

4

**Ironstone
Lake**

Agostini Rd

14
20
28

LUDMILLA

1

WINNELLIE

Showgrounds

22

Stuart Hwy

**Vestey's
Beach**

7
23

Gregory St

PARAP

3 Bishop St

Tiger Brennan Dr

**Cullen Bay
Marina**

12

Mindil 26
Beach

21

Woolner Rd

**BAYVIEW
HAVEN**

18

BERRIMAH

**Myilly
Point**

24

15
11

**STUART
PARK**

25 31

Sadgroves Creek

**Charles Darwin
National Park**

Reichardt Creek

Hidden Valley Rd

To Jabiru (216km);
Alice Springs (1494km)

30

6
13

16

Daly St

Frances Bay Dr

Mangrove

LARRAKEYAH

Allen Ave

Elliott
Point

Esplanade

DARWIN

Wharf
Precinct

**Frances
Bay**

Berrimah Rd

Bleesers Creek

Mangrove

Alice Springs to Darwin Railway

Wishart Rd

Darwin

Berrimah Rd

See Central Darwin
Map (p804)

East Arm Port
Development

it seems to have consciously developed in complete defiance of its outpost location on the edge of northern Australia.

Like most far-flung Territorians, residents of Darwin are accustomed to making their own fun, which is why the nightlife along Mitchell St is so successfully geared towards self-indulgence. And even though beach swimming is out for two-thirds of the year due to jellyfish, the city's oceanfront position does provide breezy walking trails with great harbour views, plus some popular bayside cafés.

The volatile wet season weather creates some fantastic storms, when dark clouds scud overhead and lightning fires up the atmosphere – locals know a storm is about to begin in earnest when the wind picks up. At other times, the climate is conducive to sitting out in a sunny beer garden and planning trips to nearby Top End highlights such as Kakadu and Litchfield National Parks, the Tiwi Islands and Arnhem Land.

HISTORY

The harbour occupied by present-day Darwin was discovered by Europeans when in 1839 John Lort Stokes aboard the *Beagle*, named it Port Darwin after a former shipmate, evolutionist Charles Darwin. A settlement called Palmerston was founded here in 1869; its name chanced to Darwin in 1911.

The growth of Darwin was accelerated in 1871 by the discovery of gold at Pine Creek,

about 200km south, but it was WWII tha put it permanently on the map. It was at thi time that the town became an important bas for Allied action against the Japanese in th Pacific. Darwin was attacked 64 times durin the war and at least 243 people died.

Since the completion in February 2004 c the rail link between Adelaide and Darwi via Alice Springs, the city is a step close to becoming the main port connection be tween Australia and Asia.

ORIENTATION

Darwin's centre is a compact, orderly grid a the end of a peninsula. The Stuart Hwy doe a big loop entering the city and finally head south to become Daly St. The main shoppin area, around the pedestrian-only Smith S Mall, is about 500m southeast of Daly St.

Darwin's airport is 12km northeast of th centre, while the train station is about 18km to the east; see p816 for transport details.

Maps

Maps NT (see opposite) can equip you witl maps of Darwin and nearby regions.

INFORMATION
Bookshops

Angus & Robertson (Map p804; ☎ 8941 3489; Shop T18, Galleria Shopping Centre, Smith St Mall) Fiction, nonfiction and regional travel publications.
Bookworld (Map p804; ☎ 8981 5277; Centrepoint Arcade, 48-50 Smith St) New releases.

DARWIN IN...

Two Days

Observe the fish-feeding frenzy at **Aquascene** (p805), then visit **Cullen Bay** (p813) for a lazy breakfast. Explore the fascinating **Museum & Art Gallery of the Northern Territory** (opposite) en route to a picnic at **East Point Reserve** (p806). Wander through the **botanic gardens** (p805) and emerge at **Mindil Beach Sunset Market** (p815) for an evening snack, before a nightcap (or three) at an inner-city **bar** (p813).

On day two, explore the **wharf precinct** (p806) and have a late alfresco lunch overlooking the jetty. Learn about Australia's pearling culture at the **Australian Pearling Exhibition** (p806) and then ease yourself into some canvas at the **Deckchair Cinema** (p814).

Four Days

Follow the two-day itinerary, then catch the ferry to **Mandorah** (p817). Become acquainted with Northern Territory ecology at the superb **Territory Wildlife Park** (p821).

On day four, catch the sea cat back to Darwin and wander around **Myilly Point Historic Precinct** (p805) – perhaps even indulge in afternoon tea there. Visit Darwin's oldest **gaol** (p805) and then end your itinerary dining on superb seafood at one of the city's fine **restaurants** (p811).

Maps NT (Map p804; ☎ 8999 7032; 1st fl, Nichols Pl, cnr Cavenagh & Bennett Sts) Government-run map agency.

NT General Store (Map p804; ☎ 8981 8242; 42 Cavenagh St) This store (see Shopping p815) also sells maps and travel guides.

Read Back Book Exchange (Map p804; ☎ 8981 0099; Star Village, Smith St Mall) Second-hand books and CDs.

Emergency
AANT Road Service (☎ 13 111)
Ambulance (☎ 000)
Fire (☎ 000)
Lifeline Crisis Line (☎ 13 11 14)
Poisons Information Centre (☎ 13 11 26) Provides 24-hour advice, including info on stingers.
Police (Map p804; ☎ 000; Knuckey St)

Internet Access
Internet cafés charge around $4 to $6 per hour. Most hostels have their own Internet access.

Some options:

Global Gossip (Map p804; ☎ 8942 3044; 44 Mitchell St)
Internet Outpost (Map p804; ☎ 8981 0720; 69 Mitchell St)
NT Tours & Travel Internet Cafe (Map p804; Harry Chan Arcade, 60 Smith St)

Internet Resources
Darwin City Council (www.darcity.nt.gov.au)
Tourism Top End (www.tourismtopend.com.au /attractions/darwincity.htm)

Media
The local broadsheet is the *Northern Territory News* ($1), which often takes tabloid news to new depths.

Medical Services
Guardian Pharmacy (Map p804; ☎ 8981 9202; Smith St Mall; ☒ 9am-6pm Mon-Fri, to 5pm Sat, to 2pm Sun)
Night & Day Medical & Dental Surgery (Map p804; medical ☎ 8927 1899, dental ☎ 8927 9418; Shop 31, Casuarina Shopping Centre, Trower Rd, Casuarina; ☒ 8am-late Mon-Sat, 9am-late Sun)
Royal Darwin Hospital (Map p801; ☎ 8922 8888; Rocklands Dr, Tiwi)
Travel Doctor (Map p804; ☎ 8981 7492; 1st fl, 43 Cavenagh St; appointments ☒ 8.30am-noon & 1.30-3.30pm Mon-Fri)

Money
There are several banks with 24-hour ATMs on or near the Smith St Mall. The following places change cash and travellers cheques:

American Express (Amex; Map p804; ☎ 13 13 98; Westpac Bank, 24 Smith St Mall)
Bureau de Change (Map p804; 69 Mitchell St)
Travelex (Map p804; ☎ 8981 6182; Star Village, 32 Smith St Mall)

Post
Post office (Map p804; cnr Cavenagh & Edmunds Sts; ☒ 9am-5pm Mon-Fri, 9am-12.30pm Sat) Check the poste restante folder on the bench.

Tourist Information
The **visitor information centre** (Map p804; ☎ 8936 2499; www.tourismtopend.com.au; cnr Knuckey & Mitchell Sts; ☒ 8.30am-5pm Mon-Fri, 9am-3pm Sat, 10am-3pm Sun), run by Tourism Top End, books tours and accommodation throughout the NT service providers within its organisation. Top End national park factsheets are available, as are Kakadu park passes.

Free tourist publications available include *Destination Darwin & the Top End*, which is published twice-yearly, and the *Top End Holiday Guide*, an annual guide to regional attractions.

Travel Agencies
Darwin has plenty of agencies, and most hostels and many hotels have their own tour desks. The following are reliable:
Flight Centre (Map p804; ☎ 8941 8002; 24 Cavenagh St)
STA Travel (Map p801; ☎ 8928 0944; 247 Trower Rd, Casuarina Shopping Centre, Trower Rd, Casuarina)

SIGHTS
Museum & Art Gallery of the Northern Territory
Head north of town to Fannie Bay for the superb **museum and art gallery** (Map p801; ☎ 8999 8201; Conacher St, Fannie Bay; admission to permanent exhibition free, fees vary for visiting exhibits; ☒ 9am-5pm Mon-Fri, 10am-5pm Sat & Sun), which is bright, well presented and full of interesting displays. A highlight is the NT Aboriginal art collection, with carvings and bark paintings from the Tiwi Islands and Arnhem Land. The gallery also features visiting exhibitions.

Considerable space is devoted to Cyclone Tracy, with photographs, newsreel and radio coverage from Christmas Day, 1974. You can even step into a darkened room and hear a frightening recording from the night of the cyclone.

Pride of place among the stuffed birds and animals undoubtedly goes to 'Sweetheart',

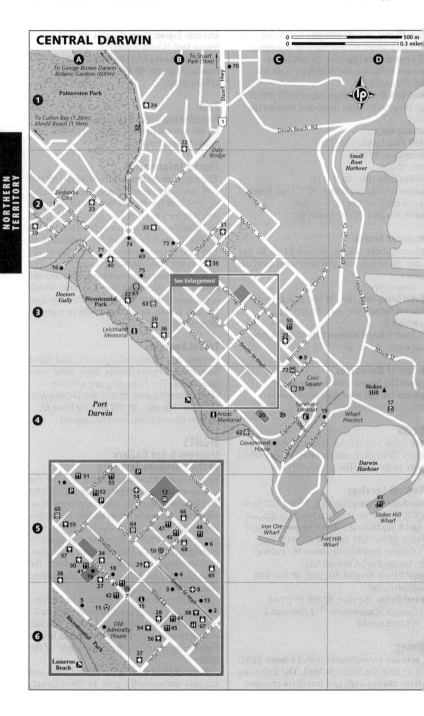

CENTRAL DARWIN

NORTHERN TERRITORY

a 5m-long, 780kg saltwater crocodile who
became a Top End personality after numerous encounters with fishing dinghies on the
Finniss River south of Darwin. He died during his capture in 1979. It's rumoured that
Sweetheart looked much bigger in real life
and that he lost weight during the taxidermy
process.

The museum has a good bookshop and
café. Bus Nos 4 and 6 travel close by, or get
there on the Tour Tub (p809).

Aquascene

For more than 40 years, fish have headed to
Aquascene (Map p804; ☎ 8981 7837; www.aquascene
.com.au; 28 Doctors Gully Rd; adult/child/family $7/4/20;
☑ variable) for a feed at high tide. Visitors get
to dole out trays of bread to hordes of mullet, catfish, batfish and big milkfish, plus the
odd tuskfish and manta ray. It's a fascinating sight and children love it. Aquascene is
open only for the high tide feedings; check
website for details.

George Brown Darwin Botanic Gardens

Sloping down to the waterfront northwest
of the centre, the **botanic gardens** (Map p801;
☎ 8999 5535; Geranium St; admission free; ☑ 24hr) are
superb and contain more than 1600 plant
species. There's a self-guided Aboriginal
plant-use walk through a monsoon vine
forest, a reconstructed old Wesleyan church
(it once sat on Knuckey St) and a coastal
section over the road, between Gilruth Ave
and Fannie Bay.

It's an easy 15-minute cycle to the gardens from the city centre.

Myilly Point Historic Precinct

At the northwestern end of Smith St, in
Burnett Pl, is this small but important precinct of four houses (Map p801) built in
the 1930s. The buildings, known as Burnett
houses, are elevated and feature asbestos-
cement louvres and casement windows, so
the ventilation can be regulated according
to weather conditions. Burnett House contains a **National Trust museum** (Map p801; ☎ 8981
0165; admission by donation; ☑ 10am-1pm Mon-Sat,
10am-6pm Sun). Indulge in a dainty high tea
($7.50) on a Sunday afternoon.

Fannie Bay Gaol Museum

This interesting **museum** (Map p801; ☎ 8999
8201; East Point Rd; admission free; ☑ 10am-4.30pm)
was Darwin's main jail from 1883 to 1979.
Wander around the old cells and see a gallows constructed for two hangings in 1952.

The minimum security section was used at various times for juveniles, lepers and Vietnamese refugees. A brochure available at the entrance details a self-guided walk.

East Point Reserve

This spit of land north of Fannie Bay (Map p801) is particularly nice in the late afternoon when wallabies come out to feed and the sun sets across the bay. There are walking and cycling paths, plus a road to the tip of the point.

On the point's northern side is a series of **wartime gun emplacements** and the small **East Point Military Museum** (Map p801; ☎ 8981 9702; www.epmm.com.au; adult/child/family $10/5/28; ☺ 10am-5pm), entered through a gun battery command post and devoted to Darwin's WWII activities.

Parliament House

Dominating the streetscape at the end of Mitchell St is the boxlike **Parliament House** (Map p804; ☎ tours 8946 1425; ☺ 9am-6pm Mon-Fri, tours 9am & 11am Sat), with an overhanging roof that evokes the grandeur of Southeast Asian architecture. Wander around the cavernous

---

CYCLONE TRACY

The statistics of this disaster are frightening. Cyclone Tracy built up over Christmas Eve 1974 and by midnight the winds began to reach their full fury. At 3.05am the airport's anemometer failed, just after it recorded a wind speed of 217km/h. It's thought the peak wind speeds were as high as 280km/h. In all, 66 people died. Of Darwin's 11,200 houses, 50% to 60% were destroyed either totally or beyond repair, and only 400 survived relatively intact.

Much criticism was levelled at the design and construction of Darwin's houses, but plenty of places at least a century old, and built as solidly as you could ask for, also toppled before the awesome winds. The new and rebuilt houses have been cyclone-proofed with steel reinforcements and roofs that are firmly pinned down.

Most people say that next time a cyclone is forecast, they'll jump into their cars and head down the Track (the Stuart Hwy) – and come back afterwards to find out if their houses really were cyclone-proof!

---

interior; the free tours (45 minutes) mu. be booked. The building also houses th **Northern Territory Library**.

The nearby **Supreme Court building** contains some fine Aboriginal artworks.

Wharf Precinct

The old **Stokes Hill Wharf** (Map p804; belo' the cliffs at the southern end of the centr is worth exploring. At the end of the jett is the **Arcade** (Map p804), an old warehous housing a food centre that's great for a alfresco lunch or a cool drink on a balm evening.

Back on the mainland, the precinct als features old **oil-storage tunnels** (Map p804; ☎ 898 6333; adult/child $4.50/2.50; ☺ 9am-5pm May-Sep, 10an 2pm Tue-Sun Oct–mid-Dec & late-Dec–Apr), dug int the cliff face during WWII.

Much of the waterfront land may b destined for a massive (some locals say ill conceived) redevelopment that will yiel a convention centre, wave pool and mor than 1000 apartments.

INDO-PACIFIC MARINE

Individual ecosystems are left alone t flourish at this **aquarium** (Map p804; ☎ 898 1294; Wharf Precinct; adult/concession/family $16/14/3' ☺ 10am-5pm) – the water in the main tan hasn't been changed for 15 years. This fas cinating marine-life facility has stonefist starfish, coral, sea horses, clown fish, bo' jellyfish and other remarkable creatures. Tr to visit when feedings take place (call fo exact times). Unfortunately, the tanks lac explanatory labels, though the proprieto' will happily explain each exhibit.

The **Coral Reef by Night show** (show $75) is hel' here at 7pm on Wednesday, Friday and Sun day, and includes a seafood dinner. Boo' ahead and re-confirm your booking on th relevant day.

AUSTRALIAN PEARLING EXHIBITION

Housed in the same building as the aquar ium is the **Australian Pearling Exhibition** (Ma p804; ☎ 8999 6573; adult/child/family $6.60/3.30/17 ☺ 10am-5pm), with explanations of how pre cious pearls are harvested and fashioned b' the Territory's pearling industry.

Crocodylus Park

There are hundreds of giant reptiles a this **breeding complex** (Map p801; ☎ 8922 4500

McMillans Rd, Berrimah; adult/child/family $25/13/65;
9am-5pm). Tours include a feeding demonstration and a chance to cuddle a baby croc. A minizoo houses lions and other big cats, spider monkeys, turtles and large birds including ostriches and cassowaries, while a museum covers all things croc-related. Admission is steep, but worthwhile if your visit coincides with a tour, held at 10am, noon and 2pm.

Take bus No 5 from Darwin.

Australian Aviation Heritage Centre
About 10km from Darwin's centre, the city's **aviation museum** (Map p801; ☎ 8947 2145; 557 Stuart Hwy, Winnellie; adult/child/family $11/6/28; 9am-5pm) is a large hangar crammed with aircraft and memorabilia. The mammoth American B52 bomber dwarfs the other aircraft, which include the wreck of a Japanese Zero fighter shot down in 1942. Guided free one-hour tours (after you've paid the admission fee) occur at 10am and 2pm.

Bus Nos 5 and 8 run along the Stuart Hwy.

ACTIVITIES
Cycling
Darwin is a compact city with an excellent network of bicycle tracks. The main track runs from the northern end of Cavenagh St to Fannie Bay, Coconut Grove, Nightcliff and Casuarina.

Most hostels hire out bicycles; the usual charge is $5/15 per hour/day. **Kakadu Dreams** (Map p801; ☎ 8981 3266; 50 Mitchell St) also rents out bicycles.

Diving
Darwin Harbour offers excellent diving due to the wrecks from WWII and Cyclone Tracy, which are now encrusted with coral and support plentiful marine life.

Cullen Bay Dive (Map p801; ☎ 8981 3049; www .divedarwin.com; 66 Marina Blvd, Cullen Bay) organises double boat dives year-round with all gear provided for $160. Basic Open-Water Professional Association of Diving Instructors (PADI) courses cost $650.

Sailing
Only members can visit the **Darwin Sailing Club** (Map p801; ☎ 8981 1700; Atkins Dr, Fannie Bay), but anyone permanently residing more than 100km from Darwin can get temporary

membership (free) on the spot. Although you can't charter boats here, you can meet local sailing enthusiasts; there's a race programme from April to November.

Swimming
Darwin has many beaches but safe swimming is not possible between October and May because of box jellyfish. Popular beaches outside the stinger season include **Mindil** and **Vestey's** on Fannie Bay (Map p801), and **Mandorah**, across the bay from town (see p817).

A stretch of the 7km **Casuarina Beach**, (Map p801) beyond the northern suburbs, is a nude beach. You can swim year-round without fear of stingers in the western part of **Lake Alexander** (Map p801), an easy cycle from the centre at East Point.

The main public **swimming pool** (Map p801; ☎ 8981 2662; Ross Smith Ave, Parap; adult/child $3/1.40; 6am-7.30pm Mon-Fri, 8am-6pm Sat, 10am-6pm Sun) has a partly shaded 50m pool and a children's play pool.

Tennis & Volleyball
At **DTC Sports** (Darwin Tennis Centre; Map p801; ☎ 8985 2844; cnr Bagot & Old McMillans Rds, Coconut Grove) you can hire beach volleyball courts ($22 to $48 per hour, including ball hire) and tennis courts ($16 to $24 per hour, ball and racquet hire $2). Call ahead for opening times.

WALKING TOUR
Despite the destruction caused by WWII and Cyclone Tracy, Darwin still retains several historic buildings. The National Trust produces the booklet *A Walk through Historical Darwin,* available from the visitor information centre.

Start in the heart of the city at Smith St Mall. Near its southern end is the historic **Victoria Hotel** (1; the Vic; p813), a popular nightspot. Walking southeast along Smith St to the historic part of town you'll find the ruins of the **Old Palmerston Town Hall** (2; 1883), which was virtually destroyed by Tracy, despite its solid Victorian construction. Opposite is the former mining exchange, **Brown's Mart** (3; p814), built in 1885, which was also cyclone-damaged but now houses a theatre.

On the other side of Civic Sq is **Christ Church Cathedral (4)**, originally built in 1902. Only the porch, added in 1944, remained

NORTHERN TERRITORY

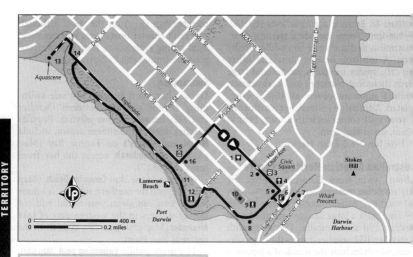

WALK FACTS

Distance: 3.5km
Duration: one hour

after the cyclone, and a contemporary cathedral has since been built around it. On the corner of Smith St and the Esplanade, the original **police station** and **courthouse** (**5**; 1884) were badly damaged in the cyclone, but have been restored and are now used as government offices.

Cross the Esplanade for **Survivors' Lookout** (**6**), perched atop the cliff. It has interesting interpretive displays, complete with WWII photos of Japanese bombing missions over Darwin. Steps from here lead down the cliff to Kitchener Dr and the WWII **oil-storage tunnels** (**7**; p806).

Back on the Esplanade, **Government House** (**8**), built in stages from 1870, was known as the Residency until 1911 and has been (temporarily) damaged by numerous cyclones. Across the road is a **monument** (**9**) to the completion of the Overland Telegraph Line – the line linked a submarine cable from Java (Indonesia) with the telegraph line from Adelaide, putting Australia in instant communication with Britain for the first time.

Set back from the Esplanade is the modern **Parliament House** (**10**; p806). From here, the Esplanade runs along the length of the city centre. Turn off into the green expanse of **Bicentennial Park** (**11**) at Herbert St, where

you'll pass the **Anzac Memorial** (**12**). From her you can walk all the way along the south western edge of the gardens.

At the park's northern end, a footpat leads down to **Doctors Gully** (**13**), though thi is really only worthwhile during fish-feedin time at Aquascene (p805). From the gully, **boardwalk** (**14**) leads up through a small patc of remnant vegetation to Daly St, where yo can get back on the Esplanade and continu southeast to the city centre. At Knuckey S you reach two historic buildings: **Lyons Cot tage** (**15**), the British-Australian Telegrap Residence and now a museum; and **Old Ad miralty House** (**16**), an early Darwin residenc raised on stilts.

Turn left onto Knuckey St, then righ on Smith St and you're back in the mall and ready to pop into the Vic for a col drink.

DARWIN FOR CHILDREN

Darwin is a relatively youthful city and a such is very child-friendly. Families ca enjoy food and refreshments at the city' **markets** (p815), load up on a meal of fish and chips at **Cullen Bay** (p813), and picni at **East Point Reserve** (p806) and the **botani gardens** (p805).

Many of Darwin's attractions inspir kids' enthusiasm: they can feed fish at **Aqua scene** (p805); interact with displays at th **Museum & Art Gallery of the Northern Territor** (p803); get up close to all manner of wil animals at the **Territory Wildlife Park** (p821) squeeze the life out of your hand at **Crocody-lus Park** (p806); and stick their faces into the viewing bubbles adorning the main tank at **Indo-Pacific Marine** (p806).

For professional short-term child care, try looking up 'Baby Sitters' and 'Child Care Centres' in the *Yellow Pages* telephone directory.

TOURS

The visitor information centre and most places to stay have plenty of tour information for Darwin and the Top End; where possible, contact the operator directly.

Aboriginal Cultural Tours

See p819 for information on tours highlighting the culture of the Aboriginal community on Bathurst Island.

City Sights

Darwin Day Tours (☎ 1300 721 365) operates an afternoon city tour (adult/child $55/40) that takes in all the major attractions and can be linked with a harbour cruise ($90/65).

Tour Tub (☎ 8985 6322; www.tourtub.com) This open-sided minibus does a circuit of the city, calling at the major places of interest. You can hop on or off anywhere along its route. Stops include Aquascene (at fish-feeding times), the Wharf Precinct, the Museum & Art Gallery, Fannie Bay Gaol, Parap markets and the botanic gardens. There's a set fare (adult/child $25/15) per day. Buses leave from the Knuckey St end of Smith St Mall and normally operate hourly from 9am to 4pm, but bookings may be required when business slows during the Wet.

Harbour Cruises

You'll find plenty of harbour cruise operators at Cullen Bay marina. Most cruises last two to three hours, depart daily (however, most stop during the wet season) and include nibbles and a glass of sparkling wine for around $50.

Anniki (☎ 8941 4000; www.australianharbourcruises .com.au) Three-hour sunset cruises on this pearling lugger depart at 5pm (adult/child $50/30).

City of Darwin Cruises (☎ 0417 855 829; www.darwin cruises.com) This outfit's two catamarans do one-hour cruises ($35) at 10am and 2.30pm, and a two-hour cruise (from $45) at noon, plus a two-hour sunset cruise ($45); cruises depart from either Cullen Bay or the Wharf Precinct.

Darwin Cruises & Charters (☎ 8942 3131) The *Tum-laren* sunset dinner cruise (adult/child $70/50) departs at 5pm; the BBQ (barbecue) lunch cruise (adult/child $55/35) leaves at noon.

Spirit of Darwin (☎ 8981 3711; www.spiritofdarwin .net) This modern passenger boat that takes two-hour sightseeing cruises ($32) at 1.40pm and 5.40pm daily.

FESTIVALS & EVENTS

Beer Can Regatta A cheerfully strange festival in mid-July featuring races for boats made entirely of beer cans, off Mindil Beach.

Darwin Cup Carnival The running of the Darwin Cup in July/August is the highlight of this racing carnival.

Darwin Fringe Festival Local performing and visual arts festival in July/August.

Darwin Rodeo Whips crack in August as international teams compete in numerous events.

Darwin to Bali Yacht Race The city is abuzz in July in the days leading up to this hotly contested race.

Festival of Darwin A two-week, mainly outdoor festival in August highlighting Darwin's unique cultural mix.

Royal Darwin Show This agricultural show, on the fourth Friday to Saturday of July, features all manner of rides and competitions.

SLEEPING

If you want to make the most of the tropical atmosphere, try one of Darwin's peaceful camping and caravan parks that are scattered around the suburbs. There's a gaggle of nightlife-infatuated hostels along Mitchell St, and quieter options northwest of the centre towards Cullen Bay. Many places pick up from the bus or train stations or the airport if pre-arranged, and most turn the air-conditioning on only at night.

Most midrange accommodation can be found around the centre and to the north in Stuart Park and Parap, both of which have excellent apartment choices. Pleasant B&Bs with rural touches are located in the suburban fringe.

Most of Darwin's facility-laden top-end hotels are on the Esplanade, making best use of the prime views across the bay. The rare places that lack a swimming pool will have a spa in which to cool off. During the wet season, prices can plummet by as much as 50%.

Budget
HOSTELS & LODGES
Darwin International YHA (Map p804; ☎ 8981 3995; darwinyha@yhant.org.au; 69 Mitchell St; dm $16-20, s & d $50-70; ❄ 🖳 🖭) Despite its rooms looking a little worn, and a TV room that can get uncomfortably hot, the YHA receives high praise from backpackers. They like its

central location, large pool, friendly staff and 1st-floor kitchen with an open-air dining area.

Cavenagh (Map p804; ☎ 1300 851 198, 8941 6383; www.thecavenagh.com; 12 Cavenagh St; dm $16-20, s from $55, d $55-90; 🛇 🖵 🗩) Cavenagh has arranged its clean, comfortable and relatively spacious rooms around an enticing central pool. Dorms are either four-bed (each dorm comes with its own fridge) or 16-bed. The on-site café-bar does $10 lunch specials.

Gecko Lodge (Map p801; ☎ 1800 811 250; www.geckolodge.com.au; 146 Mitchell St; dm $17-20, d from $55; 🛇 🗩) This lodge promises and delivers a laid-back time, aided by its small size (only 30 beds), friendly management, and an overgrown garden and sheltered deck that give it a cosy, tropical feel. A pancake breakfast and filtered coffee are included in the room price.

Melaleuca on Mitchell (Map p804; ☎ 8941 7800; info@melaleucaonmitchell.com.au; 52 Mitchell St; dm from $25, r from $90; 🛇 🖵 🗩) This newish hostel is zealously expanding down Mitchell St, with a café and beer garden (sorry, 'alfresco tavern') slated for construction when we visited. The rooms here are well maintained but bland. The rooftop pool is crowded with sun-tanning backpackers.

Park Lodge (Map p801; ☎ 8981 5692; 42 Coronation Dr, Stuart Park; s/d from $50/60; 🛇 🗩) This peaceful lodge's breeze-block buildings contain an airy sitting room (above reception) and simple but well-priced rooms, each with a fridge, balcony and coffee-/tea-making facilities.

Other recommendations:

Frogshollow Backpackers (Map p804; ☎ 1800 068 686, 8941 2600; www.frogs-hollow.com.au; 27 Lindsay St; dm from $22, d from $60; 🛇 🖵 🗩) Only a short walk from central business district (CBD) hubbub.

Chilli's Backpackers (Map p804; ☎ 1800 351 313, 8980 5800; www.chillis.com.au; 69A Mitchell St; dm from $18, d with/without bathroom $55/50; 🛇 🖵) There's usually a party in progress here, or one's about to start.

CAMPING & CARAVANNING

Hidden Valley Tourist Park (Map p801; ☎ 8947 1422; www.hvtp.com.au; 15 Hidden Valley Rd, Berrimah; powered/unpowered sites per 2 people $25/23, cabins $75-125; 🛇 🗩) The location of this particular hidden valley is clearly signposted off the highway, somewhat reducing its mystique. Nonetheless, the grounds are lovely and the immaculate cabins have their own decks.

Lee Point Resort (Map p801; ☎ 8945 0535; fax 894 0642; Lee Point Rd; powered/unpowered sites per 2 peopl $25/22, cabins $80; 🛇) This spacious, seclude and friendly park is 800m from the Le Point beach and 15km north of the city The facilities here are excellent and eac powered site has a private bathroom.

Shady Glen Caravan Park (Map p801; ☎ 898 3330; www.shadyglen.com.au; cnr Farrel Cres & Stuart Hwy powered/unpowered sites per 2 people $24/21, cabins with without bathroom $100/75; 🛇 🗩) You get a littl bit of highway noise here, but not enough to distract you from the leafy grounds an good facilities. The on-site shop sells basi supplies, as well as alcohol (until to 6pm).

Midrange

The resorts and tourist parks listed unde Camping & Caravanning (left) also offe comfortable motel-style units and self contained cabins.

APARTMENTS

Botanic Gardens Apartments (Map p801; ☎ 894 0300; botanic@octa4.net.au; 17 Geranium St, Stuart Park motel d from $110, apt $140-280; 🛇 🗩) Highl recommended apartment complex flanke by Carpentaria palms and overlooking th serene botanic gardens; top-most room command views of Fannie Bay. All apart ments are spacious and have a full kitchen laundry and balconies.

Parap Village Apartments (Map p801; ☎ 180 620 913, 8943 0500; pva@paspaley.com.au; 39-45 Para Rd, Parap; d $160-240; 🛇 🗩) Strung out along gorgeous, tropical garden–covered plot op posite Parap Village are these outstandin two- and three-bedroom apartments. Th complex has a pair of shaded saltwater pool and BBQs; baby-sitting can be arranged.

Alatai Holiday Apartments (Map p804; ☎ 180 628 833, 8981 5188; www.alataiapartments.com.au; cn McMinn & Finniss Sts; studios from $90, 1-/2-/3-bedroo apt from $120/180/260; 🛇 🗩) A modern com plex on the edge of the CBD, with its self contained apartments arranged around wide central courtyard filled with tropica flora. A baby-sitting service is available.

B&Bs

Steeles at Larrakeyah (Map p804; ☎ 8941 3636; www .steeles-at-larrakeyah.com.au; 4 Zealandia Cres, Larrakeyah d $150; 🛇 🗩) Steeles' Spanish Mission–styl B&B is positioned midway between the city centre, Cullen Bay and Mindil Beach. Ther re only two bedrooms for rent, each with a private entrance.

Grungle Downs B&B (Map p804; ☎ 8947 4440; www .grungledowns.com.au; 945 McMillan's Rd, Knuckey Lagoon; d from $110; 🖭 🕭) This is an attractive, modern B&B on a one-hectare property out past Crocodylus Park (p806). It has a large inground pool and a self-contained cottage where you can lodge your family and even your pets.

MOTELS & MOTELS

Value Inn (Map p804; ☎ 8981 4733; www.valueinn.com .au; 50 Mitchell St; d from $95; 🅿 🖭 🕭) This motel offers decent rates for such a central place, especially considering there's off-street parking and each room has a TV and fridge. When reception is unattended you can check in next door at Melaleuca on Mitchell (same owner), but be warned that this can entail a $5 surcharge.

Top End Hotel (Map p804; ☎ 1800 626 151, 8981 6511; cnr Mitchell & Daly Sts; d from $100; 🖭 🕭) Handy for those who want to roll into bed after delving into the hotel's nocturnal entertainments. Each comfortable motel room opens onto the pool and garden, and is surprisingly quiet.

Asti Motel (Map p804; ☎ 8981 8200; 7 Packard Pl; d from $100; 🖭 🕭) What Asti's chunky multistorey blocks lack in glamour, it makes up for in cleanliness and proximity to the city centre and Cullen Bay. You can buy snacks and beer from reception.

Mirambeena Resort (Map p804; ☎ 1800 891 100, 8946 0111; 64 Cavenagh St; d from $160; 🖭 🖵 🕭) Mirambeena looks as though it's been around for a while, and it has plenty of private land and OK facilities. You can find betterstandard (and cheaper) rooms in Darwin, but the larger deluxe rooms and townhouses are worth consideration by families and large groups.

Palms City Resort (Map p804; ☎ 1800 829 211, 8982 9200; www.citypalms.com; 64 The Esplanade; d from $140-250; 🖭 🕭) An attractive, greenery-filled resort across the road from harbourfront parkland. The 'superior' motel rooms are worth the extra cash if you appreciate space. All villas come with electric BBQs.

More choices:

Mediterranean Hotel (Map p804; ☎ 1800 357 760, 8981 7771; www.mediterraneanhtl.com.au; 81 Cavenagh St; d from $145; 🖭 🕭) Comfortable modern suites with spa baths cost $20 extra.

Cherry Blossom Hotel (Map p804; ☎ 8981 6734; 108 The Esplanade; d $95; 🖭 🕭) A modest, friendly place, and the cheapest option on the Esplanade.

Top End

Darwin Central Hotel (Map p804; www.darwincentral.com.au; ☎ 8944 9000; 21 Knuckey St; d from $220; 🖭 🕭) This is a thoroughly modern hotel that's addicted to style and is riddled with mod cons. It has excellent accessibility for disabled travellers, a plunge pool and a prime CBD location.

Holiday Inn (Map p804; ☎ 8980 0800; www.holiday-inn.com.au; The Esplanade; r from $200; 🖭 🖵 🕭) Appended to the Darwin Entertainment Centre, the Holiday Inn consumes a large plot of land off the Esplanade, giving some rooms great water views. It's crammed with five-star facilities, including the city's largest pool, and is one of Darwin's busiest hotels.

Other options:

Saville (Map p804; ☎ 1300 881 686, 8943 4333; www .savillesuites.com.au; 88 The Esplanade; d from $220, 1-/2-bedroom apt from $260/370; 🖭 🖵 🕭) Pay less for city views, more for stunning harbour views.

Novotel Atrium (Map p804; ☎ 8941 0755; www.novotel.com.au; 100 The Esplanade; d $200-250; 2-bedroom apt $320; 🖭 🖵 🕭)

Crowne Plaza Darwin (Map p804; ☎ 1800 891 107, 8982 0000; 32 Mitchell St; d from $180; 🖭 🖵 🕭)

EATING

Chomp your way around Darwin, starting with the cheap nosh in the transit centre arcade and in the bustling markets, and continuing with the fresh variety of café fare and the exotic concoctions whipped up at top restaurants. The standard and variety of eateries in Darwin tops that of anywhere else in the NT. There are plenty of options around Mitchell St and the city centre, or head down to the Wharf Precinct or Cullen Bay for water views.

City Centre & Wharf Precinct

RESTAURANTS

Hanuman (Map p804; ☎ 8941 3500; 28 Mitchell St; mains $10-27; ☒ lunch & dinner Mon-Fri, dinner Sat & Sun) Hanuman has an accomplished, much-awarded menu of Thai, Nonya and Indian cookery. There's not much difference between lunch and dinner offerings except for the addition of tandoori meals at night. The signature dish of oysters (around $25) is superb.

Ten Litchfield (Map p804; ☎ 8981 1024; 10 Litchfield St; mains $8-18; ☒ lunch & dinner Mon-Fri, dinner Sat & Sun) This bustling side-street restaurant has a split personality, alternating between a daytime espresso bar-café (Ten Litchfield) and a night-time steak and seafood emporium (Tim's Surf 'n' Turf). It's a favourite of local office workers, who talk water-cooler politics in the shady garden over creative curries and baguettes.

Go Sushi (Map p804; ☎ 8941 1008; 5/28 Mitchell St; mains $12-25; ☒ lunch & dinner Mon-Sat) Perch yourself at the central counter, order a cold Sapporo or Asahi, and pluck plates ($3.50 to $5.50) from the 'sushi train'. You can also get a variety of sushi combinations and large tempura, sashimi and teriyaki dishes.

Crustaceans (Map p804; ☎ 8981 8658; Stokes Hill Wharf; mains $25-55; ☒ dinner Mon-Sat) Freshly expired barramundi, lobster, croc and oysters are plated up at this reputable seafood restaurant at the end of Stokes Hill Wharf, where diners look out over the choppy waters of Frances Bay from their 1st-floor perch.

Salvatore's (Map p804; ☎ 8941 9823; 21 Knuckey St; mains $9-20; ☒ breakfast, lunch & dinner) For such a small place, Salvatore's has an exceptionally large menu. Hearty breakfasts include pancakes and there are numerous tasty gourmet pizzas and pastas, a high proportion of which have the word 'creamy' in their descriptions.

Vietnam Saigon Star (Map p804; ☎ 8981 1420; 60 Smith St; mains $9-17; ☒ lunch & dinner Mon-Sat, dinner Sun) A simple, somewhat pricey Vietnamese eatery, but with a huge menu of traditional fare – 120-plus choices with pork, fish and squid as core ingredients. Vegetarians have about a dozen selections.

CAFÉS

Relish (Map p804; ☎ 8941 1900; 35 Cavenagh St; meals $ 10; ☒ breakfast & lunch Mon-Fri) This is a cosy retrea for lovers of caffeine, healthy breakfasts, an focaccias and 'melts' (toppings melted on ciabatta bread). Walls are cheerily plastere with event fliers and bright artwork.

Roma Bar (Map p804; ☎ 8981 6729; 30 Cavenag St; meals $5-11; ☒ breakfast & lunch Mon-Fri, lunch S & Sun) A small, appealingly casual café se ving good coffee and fresh sandwiches, an providing magazines and newspapers (suc as the *Guardian Weekly*) for customers t peruse while they eat. A good place to re search local arts happenings.

Moorish Cafe (Map p804; ☎ 8981 0010; 37 Knuck St; mains $13-27; ☒ breakfast, lunch & dinner Mon-Sat) looks mostly like a stock-standard moder café, but there's something relaxing abou its deep, airy interior and comfy padde wall-benches. Besides a nice mixture of wel prepared mains, it also doles out reasonabl priced tapas ($6 to $8).

Cafe Uno (Map p804; ☎ 8942 2500; 69 Mitchell S mains $10-27; ☒ breakfast, lunch & dinner) Its exte ior might be jammed between backpacke oriented shopfronts, but Uno's interior i suave, dressed in rich colours and Impres sionist art. The efficient staff take orders fo satisfying salads, pastas, pizzas and dessert and numerous wines and cocktails.

Simply's (Map p804; ☎ 8981 4765; Star City Arcad 32 Smith St Mall; meals $4-9; ☒ lunch Mon-Fri) This a no-frills vegetarian/vegan sandwich ba serving a variety of salads, smoothies, juice and hot food such as lentil rissoles an moussaka.

PUBS

Rorke's Drift (Map p804; ☎ 8941 7171; 46 Mitchell S mains $10-20; ☒ lunch & dinner) The menu at thi popular pub begins with roast-beef roll steak sandwiches and bangers and mash and then gets meatier. Tables crowd onto th pavement and into a patchy beer garden.

Lizards Bar & Grill (Map p804; ☎ 8981 6511; To End Hotel, cnr Mitchell & Daly Sts; mains $9-25; ☒ lunch dinner) The foliage-cloaked outdoor deckin here is a good place to wolf down a parmi giana or a barra fillet. Dinner mains start a $17; 500g of T-bone steak will cost you $25

Pubs like the Vic (opposite), Blue Heele Bar (p814) and Kitty O'Shea's (p814) pre pare a limited choice of filling meals fo between $5 and $10.

SELF-CATERING

Coles (Map p804; ☎ 8941 8055; Mitchell Centre, 55-59 Mitchell St) supermarket is open 24 hours, while **Woolworths** (Map p804; ☎ 8941 6111; cnr Cavenagh & Whitfield Sts) is open until midnight most nights.

Cullen Bay & Fannie Bay

The Cullen Bay marina is full of yachts and is surrounded by some generically trendy cafés, where self-conscious regulars pose on outdoor decks. Fannie Bay has a museum-piece café.

Buzz Cafe (Map p801; ☎ 8941 1141; The Slipway, Cullen Bay; mains $15-25; ☺ breakfast, lunch & dinner) This is a multilevel waterfront café with great food, a long wine list and distinctive design features: handmade teak and mahogany furniture, a lava bar and revealing men's toilets. Perfect for a leisurely brunch.

Cornucopia Museum Café (Map p801; ☎ 8981 1002; Museum & Art Gallery of the Northern Territory, Conacher St, Fannie Bay; mains $8-20; ☺ lunch) After browsing the museum's fine collection, head to Cornucopia's outdoor deck to enjoy the lovely view over Vestey's Beach while sipping wine and eating something from the varied menu – perhaps one of the delicious crepes.

Bay Seafood Cafe (Map p801; ☎ 8981 8789; 2/57 Marina Blvd, Cullen Bay; meals $8-20; ☺ lunch & dinner) Unlike just about every other eatery in the area, this place doesn't worry about its looks. It just concentrates on making good fish and chips.

Parap

Cyclone Cafe (Map p801; ☎ 8941 1992; Urquhart St, Parap; meals $5-10; ☺ breakfast & lunch Mon-Sat) A tiny, locally popular café beside the post office in Parap Village, with corrugated-

---

AUTHOR'S CHOICE

Twilight on Lindsay (Map p804; ☎ 8981 8631; 2 Lindsay St; mains $10-27; ☺ lunch & dinner Tue-Fri, dinner Sat) This is a memorably atmospheric restaurant tucked away under the raised floor of a pre–Cyclone Tracy house, where ceiling fans swirl air among painted support timbers. The excellent menu has distinct Asian touches and is brimming with fresh NT ingredients. There are not many tables, so book ahead for dinner.

---

iron walls and a rust-coloured floor that lend it the appealingly eccentric look of a ramshackle bush shed. It has a long list of coffee styles, including an excellent 'hypercino' (super-strong), and a menu of melts, burritos, eggs and cakes.

Parap Fine Foods (Map p804; ☎ 8981 8597; 40 Parap Rd, Parap) Stock up here on fine coffee, deli meats and gourmet preserves like Kakadu plum jam. To show it has the common touch, Parap Fine Foods also stock plenty of everyday brands.

DRINKING

Most of the bars popular with travellers are on Mitchell St, all within a short walk (or long stumble) of each other.

Rorke's Drift (Map p804; ☎ 8941 7171; 46 Mitchell St) Set in a former cinema, Rorke's has a certain unkempt grandeur lent it by a golden ceiling and royal green lamp shades that overlook a scattering of wooden tables and floorboards worthy of an old saloon. See Pubs opposite for details of its pub grub menu.

Victoria Hotel (The Vic; Map p804; ☎ 8981 4011; 27 Smith St Mall) This old, stone-walled hotel has seen many a drinker staggering out. The atmosphere of the downstairs bar is tainted by the inane warbling of poker machines. More agreeable is the high-ceilinged upstairs space, which has pool tables, frequent live bands and a balcony overlooking the mall.

Darwin Ski Club (Map p804; ☎ 8981 6630; Conacher St, Fannie Bay) This clubhouse for water-skiers on palm tree–fringed Vestey's Beach is a sublime little spot for sundowners in the Dry. The café serves good cheap tucker. Interstate or international visitors get issued with a free, one-month membership.

Top End Hotel (Map p804; ☎ 8981 6511; cnr Mitchell & Daly Sts) The busy little entertainment enclave at this hotel (p811) has several clubs and bars, including **Lizards Bar & Grill** (☎ 8981 6511), an eatery (see Pubs, opposite) with a great beer garden that's dominated by a huge stone horseshoe bar. It pulls in revellers of all ages.

Shenanigans (Map p804; ☎ 8981 2100; 69 Mitchell St) To be sure, you know what's coming before setting foot inside this Irish theme pub: dark wood, dim lighting, barrels and benches to sit at, and the sight of Guinness dribbling down many chins.

Other popular city watering holes:

Duck's Nuts (Map p804; ☎ 8942 2122; 76 Mitchell St) Ordinary-looking bar but can be insanely popular with a young crowd on the weekend.

Kitty O'Shea's (Map p804; ☎ 8941 7947; cnr Herbert & Mitchell Sts) Relatively quiet, heavy on the wood varnish and drenched in Kilkenny and Caffrey's.

Blue Heeler Bar (Map p804; ☎ 8941 7494; 10 Mitchell St) A rustic saloon bar with a thing for loud rawwwk songs.

Pub Bar (Map p804; ☎ 8941 1113; 32 Mitchell St) A small tavern-style space with pool tables, a loud jukebox and free DJ-led theme nights.

ENTERTAINMENT

Darwin has some lively haunts, with bands performing at several venues and a selection of nightclubs in which to lose your hearing. Other tastes are also catered for, with theatre, films, concerts and a casino.

For info on upcoming events, pick up the free, widely distributed monthly publication *Fresh*. You'll also find up-to-date entertainment listings in the Friday edition of the *Northern Territory News*, or check the noticeboard at **Roma Bar** (Map p804; ☎ 8981 6729; 30 Cavenagh St).

Nightclubs

Discovery (Map p804; ☎ 8942 3300; 89 Mitchell St; admission $5-10; ☺ 9pm-late Fri & Sat) A multilevel venue with a changing roster of DJs and usually a queue of clubbers waiting outside. It's fronted by a blokey, run-of-the-mill bar called Lost Arc.

Throb (Map p804; ☎ 8942 3435; 64 Smith St; admission usually $10; ☺ from 10pm Thu-Sat) A gay- and lesbian-friendly upstairs nightclub and cocktail bar,

---

where party-goers can enjoy regular drag shows and theme nights – bare flesh is a recurring theme.

Retro (Map p804; ☎ 8981 6511; Top End Hotel, cnr Mitchell & Daly Sts; weekend admission usually $5) Located in the Top End Hotel enclave, Retro is a large dance club that occasionally hosts live bands. It gets busy on Tuesday when cheap drinks are on offer. Accessed through Retro is another DJ-hosted space called Beachcombers, where major dance parties are staged.

Live Music

Just about every pub and bar in town has some form of live music, mostly on Friday and Saturday nights. Places that keep their microphones busy include the Lizards Bar & Grill (see p812), Shenanigans (p813), Blue Heeler Bar (left), the Vic (p813) and Duck's Nuts (left).

Theatre

Brown's Mart (Map p804; ☎ 8981 5522; Harry Chan Ave; Bamboo Lounge admission $5-10) Built in the 1880s as a warehouse, this is now an eclectic performance venue hosting plays, stand-up comedy and even dance parties. An arty crowd frequently congregates here on a Friday night for Bamboo Lounge, which may include anything from a short film festival to touring bands. It's all-inclusive, hassle-free and has a bar.

Darwin Entertainment Centre (Map p804; ☎ box office 8980 3333; www.darwinentertainment.com.au; 93 Mitchell St; ☺ box office 10am-5.30pm Mon-Fri & from 1hr before performances) Comedy, theatre, musicals, gala fashion events and major concerts all take to the stages inside this low-rise performing arts complex.

Cinemas

Darwin City Cinemas (Map p804; ☎ 8981 3111; www .birch.com.au; 76 Mitchell St; adult/child/concession $14/11/ 9.80) This is a five-theatre complex screening latest release films, usually of the mass-appeal, big-budget variety.

Casinos

Skycity (Map p801; ☎ 8943 8888; Gilruth Ave) Its name implies height but Skycity is resolutely hunkered low to the ground. The poker machine areas chatter away 24 hours a day. Anticipating *Goldfinger*-style villains, the casino bans hats of any description.

SHOPPING

The city centre is filled with outlets selling Top End arts and crafts, including bark paintings from western Arnhem Land, and carvings and screen printing by Tiwi Islanders. Trawl Darwin's fabulous markets (see the boxed text, right) for anything from jewellery and pottery to stock-whips.

Raintree Aboriginal Fine Arts Gallery (Map p804; ☎ 8941 9933; 20 Knuckey St) In business for more than 20 years, this is a knowledgeable purveyor of widely sourced Aboriginal art. Modern art connoisseurs should check out the gallery section, where some canvases cost upwards of $9000.

Mason Gallery (Map p804; ☎ 8981 9622; 21 Cavenagh St) Not far from the Raintree, Mason Gallery also stocks fine, large-scale Aboriginal canvases.

Aboriginal Fine Arts Gallery (Map p804; ☎ 8981 1315; 1st fl, cnr Mitchell & Knuckey Sts) Located above Global Gossip, this gallery sells art from Arnhem Land and the central desert region, including the work of high-profile artists. There's also a large selection of didgeridoos downstairs.

Framed (Map p801; ☎ 8981 2994; 55 Stuart Hwy, Stuart Park) This is a wonderful bazaar of contemporary arts that stocks glasswork, ceramics, sculptures, silkwork, paintings and jewellery brought in from all over Australia. It's a labyrinthine place, with small corridors revealing some mesmerising display rooms. It also hosts significant exhibitions.

Craft Territory (Map p804; ☎ 8942 1622; foyer, Parliament House, Mitchell St) Sells all kinds of locally crafted goods, from woven baskets to pearl jewellery and silk scarves. Worth trawling through for gifts.

Paspaley Pearls (Map p804; ☎ 8982 5555; 19 Smith St Mall) Sells top-quality handcrafted strands of beautiful South Sea pearls, farmed from the otherwise humble *pinctada maxima* (oyster). Enter via Bennett St.

Australian Crocodile Products (Map p804; ☎ 8941 4470; Paspaley Pearls Bldg, 19 Smith St Mall) This company takes the hides of some unfortunate salties, dyes them several colours (including a shade of brown curiously called 'camel') and stitches them into handbags, belts, wallets and much more.

NT General Store (Map p804; ☎ 8981 8242; 42 Cavenagh St) This store has shelves piled high with camping and bushwalking gear.

> ### TO MARKET, TO MARKET
>
> As the sun descends to the horizon, residents and tourists descend on **Mindil Beach Sunset Market** (Map p801; www.mindilbeachsunset markets.com; Mindil Beach; ☼ 5-10pm Thu May-Oct & 4-9pm Sun mid-May–Oct) and its 200-plus tantalising food stalls, all found off Gilruth Ave. There's usually Thai, Sri Lankan, Indian, Chinese, Malaysian, Greek, Portuguese and more, all at about $4 to $6 a serve. Visitors top off meals with fruit salad, decadent cakes, luscious crepes or any type of jerky imaginable, before cruising past crafts stalls bulging with handmade jewellery, tie-dyed clothes, pummelling masseurs and wares from Southeast Asia. An outdoor cinema is set up here on the first Thursday of each month that the market is open.
>
> Similar stalls can be found at the **Parap Village Markets** (Map p801; ☎ 8942 0805; Parap Rd, Parap; ☼ 8am-2pm Sat) and **Nightcliff Market** (Map p801; Progress Dr, Nightcliff; ☼ 8am-2pm Sun). **Rapid Creek Market** (Map p801; Rapid Creek Rd, Rapid Creek; ☼ 5pm-10pm Fri, 8am-2pm Sun) is reminiscent of an Asian marketplace, with a heady mixture of spices and the scent of jackfruit and durian.

GETTING THERE & AWAY

Air

International and interstate flights operate out of Darwin. Prices quoted here for all carriers are for low-end, one-way fares. One-off prices can sometimes be cheaper.

Qantas (☎ 13 13 13; www.qantas.com.au) has direct daily services to Adelaide (one way from $295), Alice Springs (from $210), Brisbane (from $205), Cairns (from $310), Melbourne (from $275), Perth (from $270) and Sydney (from $235).

Virgin Blue (☎ 13 67 89; www.virginblue.com.au) flies daily direct to Melbourne (one way from $225), Sydney (from $235) and Brisbane (from $180).

Airnorth (☎ 1800 627 474; www.airnorth.com.au) links Darwin with Broome (one way from $290), Kununurra (from $180) and Gove Peninsula (from $200). Smaller routes are flown by local operators; ask your travel agent.

Bus

You can travel to Darwin via bus on the Queensland route through Mt Isa to Three

Ways; the Western Australian route from Broome and Kununurra; or straight up the Track (the Stuart Hwy) from Alice Springs. **Greyhound Australia** (☎ 13 14 99; www.greyhound .com.au; transit centre, 69 Mitchell St; ☺ info counter 6am-3.45pm Mon-Fri, 6am-1.30pm Sat & Sun) runs daily services via Katherine on all of these routes. Examples of one-way fares from Darwin include: Alice Springs (adult/child $240/195, 21 hours), Brisbane ($440/350, 47 hours), Broome ($310/250, 27 hours), Katherine ($70/55, 4½ hours), Kununurra ($165/130, 9½ hours), Mt Isa ($290/230, 21 hours), Perth ($630/500, 60 hours) and Tennant Creek ($175/140, 13½ hours). Beware of services that schedule long waits for connections in Tennant Creek or Mt Isa.

Backpacker-type buses offer good alternative transport, as they stop at many sights along the way. **Desert Venturer** (☎ 1800 079 119; www.desertventurer.com.au) makes four-day trips between Darwin and Cairns ($390, food kitty $75) via the Atherton Tablelands, Cape Crawford and Katherine between March and November.

Car & Campervan

If you're planning to buy or sell a car for the next leg of your journey, check the noticeboards at hostels and Internet cafés, and talk to other travellers about their experiences.

Hiring a campervan for a week or two of touring can be worthwhile when you consider that cooking facilities and accommodation are included. Britz: Australia has a large range of 4WD campervans from around $140/170 per day (two-/four-berth). It costs an extra $35 to $50 per day to reduce the insurance excess to a few hundred dollars, otherwise you must pay a $5000 deposit. **Backpacker Campervans** (☎ 1800 670 232; www.backpackercampervans.com) has budget-priced three-berth campervans from $75 per day.

Train

Adult fares for the weekly *Ghan* train service travelling from Darwin to Alice Springs, via Katherine, are $240/880/1150 one way for 'Daynighter' seats/sleeper cabins/1st-class ('Gold Kangaroo') sleepers; Darwin–Adelaide fares are $440/1390/1830. Bookings are recommended and can be made through **Trainways** (☎ 13 21 47; www.gsr.com.au). Discounted fares are sometimes offered.

Darwin's train station is 15km east of the centre, down Berrimah Rd. A shuttle bus meets all services; it departs from the transit centre and costs $9.

GETTING AROUND
To/From the Airport
Darwin International Airport (☎ 8920 1805) is 12km northeast of the city centre. The **airport shuttle bus** (☎ 8981 5066) will pick you up or drop you off almost anywhere in the city centre for $8/15 one way/return. A taxi from the airport to city centre is around $20.

Car
Darwin has numerous budget car-rental operators, as well as all major national and international companies:
Avis (Map p804; ☎ 8981 9922; www.avis.com.au; 89 Smith St)
Britz: Australia (Map p804; ☎ 8981 2081; www.britz .com; 44 Stuart Hwy, Stuart Park) Also acts as an agent for Maui and Backpacker Campervan Rentals.
Budget (Map p804; ☎ 8981 9800; www.budget.com.au; cnr Daly St & Doctors Gully Rd)
Europcar NT (Map p804; ☎ 1800 811 541, 8941 0300; www.europcarnt.com.au; 77 Cavenagh St)
Hertz (Map p804; ☎ 13 30 39, 8941 0944; www.hertz .com.au; cnr Smith & Daly Sts)
Nifty Rent-A-Car (Map p804; ☎ 8981 2999; 86 Mitchell St)
Thrifty (Map p801; ☎ 8924 0000; www.rentacar.com .au; 64 Stuart Hwy, Stuart Park) Partnered with Territory Rent-A-Car.
Top End 4WD & Car Hire (Map p801; ☎ 8941 2922; www.topend4wd.com.au; 1 Westralia St, Stuart Park)

For driving around Darwin, small cars are cheap enough: Nifty and Delta have them from $40 per day. But most companies offer only 100km free and charge about 27.5c per additional kilometre; outside of Darwin, 100km won't get you very far. Some companies do deals that give you enough mileage to get to Kakadu and back with three or four days' rental (from around $90 per day). Bear in mind that if you book a rental car through a travel agency you could possibly get those unlimited kilometres for no additional charge.

You may be able to get some good deals for extended vehicle hire through Thrifty, especially on one-way hire.

There are also plenty of 4WD vehicles for rent, but you usually have to book ahead

Expect to pay from $200 per day for a sturdy, go-anywhere vehicle such as a Toyota Land-cruiser.

There's plenty of parking on Darwin's inner-city streets. Smith St Mall is for pedestrians only.

Public Transport

Darwinbus (☎ 8924 7666; City Bus Interchange, Harry Chan Ave; info counter 8am-12.45pm & 1.45-5pm Mon-Fri) runs a comprehensive service from its small depot.

Fares work on a zone system; one-/six-zone single trips cost $1.40/2.80 per adult (70c/$1.40 per child). Or alternatively, you can buy unlimited all-zone daily/weekly passes (Tourcards) for $5/25 ($2.50/13 per child). Tourcards can be bought from the interchange and some newsagencies; ditto single-trip fares, which can also be bought on the bus.

Most buses claim 'easy access' in that they can lower their steps to the curb. Bus No 4 (to Fannie Bay, Nightcliff, Rapid Creek and Casuarina) and No 6 (Fannie Bay, Parap and Stuart Park) are useful for getting to Mindil Beach, the Museum & Art Gallery, Fannie Bay Gaol Museum and East Point. Bus Nos 5 and 8 travel along the Stuart Hwy to Berrimah.

The **Tour Tub** (☎ 8985 6322; www.tourtub.com) minibus tours Darwin's sights throughout the day and you can hop on and off along the route (see p809).

Taxi

As well as a regular **taxi service** (☎ 13 10 08), Darwin has two taxi bus services – **Arafura Shuttle** (☎ 8981 3300) and **Unique Minibus** (☎ 8928 1100) – that will take you anywhere in the central area for a flat $3 ($5 for two people), and elsewhere, such as Fannie Bay and East Point, for a fixed fee. Double-check rates when you book, as anything outside a 4km radius of the centre incurs extra charges, in which case a standard taxi may be cheaper.

AROUND DARWIN

Tours

Several operators visit the jumping croco-diles at Adelaide River and the Territory Wildlife Park on the Cox Peninsula Rd. See

Litchfield (p822) for details of tours from Darwin.

Australian Pacific Touring (APT; ☎ 1800 891 121; www.aptouring.com.au) This operator has numerous excursions from Darwin, including a day tour to Nitmiluk (Katherine Gorge) and Leliyn (Edith Falls; adult/child $150/75) that includes a gorge cruise, and one to Kakadu (adult/child $175/90) that includes a Yellow Water trip.

Darwin Day Tours (☎ 1300 721 365) Offers various full- and half-day trips. The full-day 'Wildlife Spectacular' (adult/child $135/105) takes in the Territory Wildlife Park, Darwin Crocodile Farm, a Jumping Croc cruise and Fogg Dam. A half-day trip to the Territory Wildlife Park costs $60/45; there are also day trips to Litchfield National Park ($100/85), Kakadu ($165/130) and Katherine ($150/75).

MANDORAH
☎ 08

Mandorah is a popular beach resort on the tip of the Cox Peninsula, most easily reached by a 20-minute **Sea Cat** (☎ 8978 5015) boat ride across Darwin Harbour from Cullen Bay Ferry Terminal. Ferries cross about 10 times daily; return fares are $18/9.50/50 per adult/child/family.

You can stay at the **Mandorah Beach Hotel** (☎ 8978 5044; mandorahbeachhotel@bigpond; Cox Peninsula; powered/unpowered sites per 2 people $15/12, d $90;), which has a large pool and also serves meals.

HOWARD SPRINGS NATURE PARK

This forest-fringed **nature park** (admission free; 8am-8pm) is Darwin's nearest crocodile-free swimming hole. Swimming around you are long-necked turtles, catfish and barramundi. There's also a separate toddlers' pool. It can get uncomfortably crowded, but on a quiet day (especially early in the morning) it's very pleasant. From Darwin, turn left 24km down the Stuart Hwy, beyond Palmerston, and continue for 11km.

If you want to stay the night, **Howard Springs Holiday Park** (☎ 1800 831 169, 08-8983 1169; www.howardspringscaravanpark.com.au; 170 Whitewood Rd; powered/unpowered sites per 2 people $24/19, budget r $40, cabins $80-90;) has good facilities.

DARWIN CROCODILE FARM

Head 35km south of Darwin and you'll come across this **crocodile farm** (☎ 08-8988 1450; www.crocfarm.com.au; Stuart Hwy; adult/child $10/5.50; 9am-4pm). Many of the 8000 or so salt-water and freshwater crocodiles removed from NT waters (because they've become

NORTHERN TERRITORY

NORTHERN TERRITORY

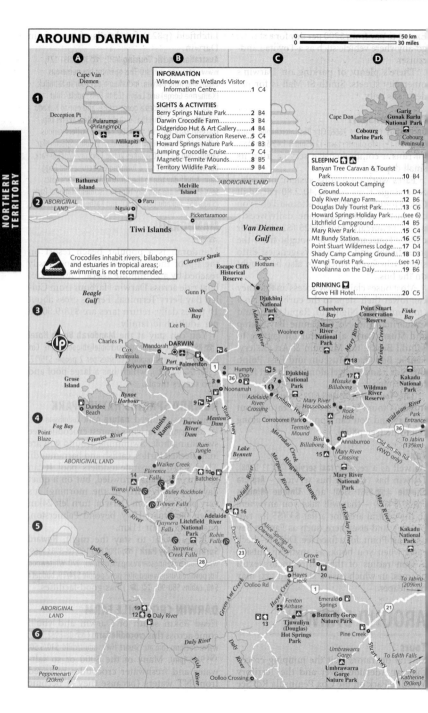

AROUND DARWIN

0   50 km
0   30 miles

INFORMATION
Window on the Wetlands Visitor
  Information Centre...................1 C4

SIGHTS & ACTIVITIES
Berry Springs Nature Park.............2 B4
Darwin Crocodile Farm..................3 B4
Didgeridoo Hut & Art Gallery........4 B4
Fogg Dam Conservation Reserve...5 C4
Howard Springs Nature Park..........6 B3
Jumping Crocodile Cruise..............7 C4
Magnetic Termite Mounds.............8 B5
Territory Wildlife Park....................9 B4

SLEEPING
Banyan Tree Caravan & Tourist
  Park...10 B4
Couzens Lookout Camping
  Ground......................................11 D4
Daly River Mango Farm................12 B6
Douglas Daly Tourist Park.............13 C6
Howard Springs Holiday Park......(see 6)
Litchfield Campground..................14 B5
Mary River Park............................15 C4
Mt Bundy Station.........................16 C5
Point Stuart Wilderness Lodge.....17 D4
Shady Camp Camping Ground.....18 D3
Wangi Tourist Park.................(see 14)
Woolianna on the Daly.................19 B6

DRINKING
Grove Hill Hotel............................20 C5

Crocodiles inhabit rivers, billabongs
and estuaries in tropical areas;
swimming is not recommended.

a hazard to people) end up here. This is no rest home, though – many of the beasts are killed each year for their skin and meat. The best time to visit is for feeding at 2pm.

TIWI ISLANDS

The Tiwi Islands – Bathurst and Melville – are two large, flat islands about 80km north of Darwin and are the home of the Tiwi Aboriginal people. A British settlement in the 1820s at Fort Dundas (near Pularumpi) on Melville Island failed partly because of poor relations with the locals. The main settlement on the islands is Nguiu, in the southeast of Bathurst Island, founded in 1911 as a Catholic mission – most Tiwi are Christian due to the influence of European missionaries. On Melville Island the main settlements are Pularumpi and Milikapiti.

Most Tiwi Islanders live on Bathurst Island and follow a nontraditional lifestyle. Some Tiwi return to their traditional lands on Melville Island for several weeks each year. Melville Island is also home to descendants of the Japanese pearl divers who regularly visited here early last century, and people of mixed Aboriginal and European parentage who were gathered here under government policy over a half-century ago.

Isolated from mainland developments until relatively recently, Tiwi culture has retained several unique features. Perhaps the best known are the *pukumani* (taboo) burial poles, which are carved and painted with symbolic and mythological figures, and erected around graves. The Tiwi now produce highly acclaimed art for sale, mainly bark painting, textile screen printing, batik and pottery, using traditional designs and motifs. Visitors can buy pieces directly from the artists for reasonable prices.

Travellers are only permitted to visit the islands on a tour. **Tiwi Tours** (☎ 1300 721 365, 08-8922 2777; www.aussieadventure.com.au) employs many Tiwi Islanders and is the main operator. Although interaction with the local community tends to be limited to your guides and the craft workshops and showrooms in Nguiu, the tours are fascinating and come highly recommended.

A one-day tour to Bathurst Island from Darwin (adult/child $310/170) includes visits to the early Catholic mission buildings and the exhibit-filled Patakijiyali Museum, morning tea with loquacious Tiwi women, swimming in a beautiful water hole and a trip to a *pukumani* burial site. An overnight tour staying at a private bush camp ($570/500) allows you to get a better feel for the people and culture. Prices include charter flights, permits, meals and, on the two-day tour, accommodation.

Another option is the **Arafura Pearl** (☎ 08-8941 1991; seacat@bigpond.com), a catamaran running day trips to Bathurst Island (adult/child from $240/170) from Darwin's Cullen Bay ferry terminal between March and November. It's cheaper than Tiwi Tours' day trip,

---

TOP-END CROCS

Australia has two types of crocodile: the freshwater, also called a 'freshie' (*Crocodylus johnstoni*) and the estuarine crocodile (*Crocodylus porosus*), better known as the saltwater or 'saltie'. Both are found in the northern part of the country, including the Northern Territory (NT). Mary River is said to have the world's greatest concentration of saltwater crocs. After a century of being hunted, crocodiles are now protected in the wild in the NT, though they are farmed for their valuable skin and meat. However, such is the current concentration of crocs in places like the East Alligator River, in Kakadu, that the NT government has suggested culling both salties and freshies at the rate of 1000 (each) per year. The proposal is highly controversial, partly because it's reportedly meant to encourage the creation of crocodile hunting safaris for tourists.

The smaller freshwater croc is endemic to Australia and is found in freshwater rivers and billabongs, while the larger saltwater croc, found throughout Southeast Asia and parts of the Indian subcontinent, can be found in or near almost any body of water, fresh or salt. Freshwater crocs, which have narrower snouts and rarely exceed 3m in length, are harmless to people unless provoked, but saltwater crocs, which grow to 5m and longer, are extremely dangerous.

Ask locally before swimming or even paddling in any Top End waterways. Attacks on humans by salties in recent years have been well documented. Warning signs are posted alongside many dangerous stretches of water.

but you spend much less time on the island, most of it in Nguiu.

Australian Rules football is a passion among the Tiwi people and the Tiwi Grand Final in March is a huge event (for more information, see the boxed text, p797). In November 2004, major celebrations were sparked by the unveiling of new lighting towers at Stanley Tipiloura Oval on Bathurst Island, which have allowed night-time games for the first time.

ARNHEM HIGHWAY

The Arnhem Hwy branches off towards Kakadu 33km southeast of Darwin. At this intersection is the **Didgeridoo Hut & Art Gallery** (☎ 08-8988 4457; 1 Arnhem Hwy), where you can watch indigenous artists from Kakadu and Arnhem Land at work, and purchase didgeridoos.

About 10km further along the highway is the small town of Humpty Doo, the naming of which is subject to dozens of local theories. Fronting the highway is **Humpty Doo Hotel** (☎ 08-8988 1372; cnr Zamia Rd & Arnhem Hwy; mains $10-30; lunch & dinner). Stop for a counter meal and a beer in its concrete-floored front bar.

About 15km beyond Humpty Doo is the turn-off to **Fogg Dam Conservation Reserve**, home to several thousand water pythons who feed on the local population of dusky rats. There are three short nature walks, including one along the dam wall past pontoons of lotus lilies to the Pandanus Lookout (one hour return, 2.5km).

Window on the Wetlands visitor information centre (☎ 08-8988 8188; 7.30am-7pm) sits atop Beatrice Hill, by the Arnhem Hwy 3km past the Fogg Dam turn-off. It's the headquarters for the proposed Mary River National Park (see right) and has interactive displays detailing northern coastal wetlands and local Aboriginal history. There are great views from the upper level, including occasional glimpses of water buffalo in an adjacent field.

Jumping-croc cruises depart from the Adelaide River Crossing. These cruises involve the dangling of bits of meat on the ends of poles, to entice huge saltwater crocodiles to rise out of the water. The whole thing is a bit of a circus, but it's a startling sight. The **Adelaide River Queen** (☎ 08-8988 8144; www.jumpingcrocodilecruises.com.au; adult/child

$36/20) runs 1½-hour cruises at 9am, 11am, 1pm and 3pm from May to August, and 9am, 11am and 2.30pm from September to April. About 2km past the Window on the Wetlands, along an unsealed road, is the **Jumping Crocodile Cruise** (☎ 08-8988 4547; www.jumpingcrocodile.com.au; adult/child/family $25/12/65), which stages one-hour tours at 9am, 11am, 1pm and 3pm year-round (the 9am cruise includes a light breakfast).

An alternative route to Cooinda (in Kakadu) is via the unsealed Old Jim Jim Rd, 19km beyond the Bark Hut Inn (below). Make sure your entry permit is current and note that this route is often impassable in the Wet. The entrance to Kakadu National Park is 19km further along the highway.

Sleeping & Eating

There are several places to stay between Window on the Wetlands and the entrance to Kakadu.

Mary River Park (☎ 1800 788 844, 08-8978 8877; www.maryriverpark.com.au; Arnhem Hwy; powered/unpowered sites per 2 people $22/18, dm $30, cabins without bathroom $95, mains $10-22; lunch & dinner;   ) Claiming over 200 bushy hectares, this impressive park has a warehouse-sized restaurant-bar with a great outside deck, and organises croc spotting and sunset dinner cruises. However, the cabins are minuscule and not a great deal.

Bark Hut Inn (☎ 08-8978 8988; Arnhem Hwy, Annaburroo; powered/unpowered sites per 2 people $22/16, s/d/f from $45/60/120, mains $10-20; breakfast, lunch & dinner;   ) This is an atmospheric roadhouse adorned with boar and buffalo heads, a restaurant and a lovely deep pool. Campers note: at the time of writing, the camp kitchen was not functional. The budget cabins are 'dongas', small rooms containing only a bed.

MARY RIVER NATIONAL PARK

At the time of writing, the Mary River National Park was still waiting on a bureaucratic rubber stamp for the park to come into official existence. Its holdings will extend north and south of the Arnhem Hwy and consist of a number of wetland areas, including Mary River Crossing, Wildman River Reserve, Shady Camp, Mary River Conservation Reserve and Stuart's Tree Historical Reserve. There are also significant monsoon and paperbark forests. This area offers excellent fishing and wildlife-spotting opportunities and is far less visited than nearby Kakadu.

Access to the park's northern region is via Point Stuart Rd, an often rough dirt track (the first 16km is sealed) heading north off the Arnhem Hwy 22km east of Annaburroo. Rock Hole is 19km west of this road, and Shady Camp is 55km north of the highway.

Sleeping & Eating

Point Stuart Wilderness Lodge (☎ 08-8978 8914; powered/unpowered sites per 2 people $15/12, r $140, dm/ tw without bathroom $25/70; 🔁 🖭) Part of an old cattle station, this camp, 1km off Point Stuart Rd, caters mainly to fishing parties and tour groups. All rooms have air-con, and rooms with bathrooms can sleep four people. There's a restaurant-bar, and wallabies congregate on the lawns in the afternoon.

Mary River Houseboats (☎ 08-8978 8925; Corroboree Billabong; 6-/8-berth houseboats for 2 days $500/570, per extra day $180/260) Groups should consider hiring a houseboat for a leisurely exploration of the Mary River. A $300 bond is required. The turn-off to the houseboat berth is 1km east of Corroboree Park, then 20km along an unsealed road. Houseboats are hired out only during the Dry.

There are basic **camping grounds** (adult/child/ family $3.30/1.65/7.70) at Couzens Lookout and Shady Camp.

STUART HIGHWAY TO LITCHFIELD NATIONAL PARK
Territory Wildlife Park & Berry Springs Nature Park

The turn-off to Berry Springs is 48km down the Track from Darwin; it's then 10km to the **Territory Wildlife Park** (☎ 08-8988 7200; www .territorywildlifepark.com.au; Cox Peninsula Rd; adult/ concession/family $18/9/40; 🕒 8.30am-6pm, last admission 4pm). Set on 400 hectares of bushland, this wonderful open-air park features a wide variety of northern Australian birds, mammals, reptiles and fish. The habitats are beautifully re-created, including wetlands and tropical rainforest environments.

One highlight is the walk-through aquarium, replicating a Top End river system and featuring a saltwater croc and enormous barramundi. Another is the nocturnal house, containing the energetic spinifex-hopping mouse and other night dwellers. There's also

a reptile house, aviaries and nature trails. Put aside a half-day to explore it, especially if you want to attend some of the regular ranger presentations, including the excellent birds of prey show (10am) and training session (3pm).

You can either walk around the 4km perimeter road, or hop on and off the shuttle train that runs every 15 to 20 minutes and stops at all exhibits. Wheelchairs are available and strollers can be hired.

Close by is **Berry Springs Nature Park** (admission free; 🕒 8am-6.30pm), a beautiful series of swimming holes that includes a stunning main pool and thermal falls. Wood-fired BBQs are provided for picnickers and there's also a visitor information centre and a café (closed during the Wet).

Batchelor
☎ 08 / pop 730

Litchfield's southern access road passes through this small town, 84km down the Track from Darwin, then another 14km west. This winding road, which once serviced the now-closed Rum Jungle uranium and copper mine, is a favourite of motorcyclists and gets the odd road train servicing cattle stations beyond Litchfield's western boundary. Batchelor is only 18km from the Litchfield National Park's eastern boundary. Signs throughout town mark the way to the **Coomalie Cultural Centre** (☎ 8939 7404; cnr Awillia & Nurndina Sts; 🕒 10am-4pm Tue-Sat Apr-Sep, 10am-4pm Tue-Fri Oct-Mar), a gallery of colourful indigenous art.

SLEEPING & EATING
Batchelor Butterfly & Bird Farm (☎ 8976 0199; www.butterflyfarm.net; 8 Meneling Rd; d from $70, mains $10-20; 🕒 breakfast, lunch & dinner; 🔁 🖭) This commercial butterfly farm is devoted to relaxation and serenity, as evidenced by a scattering of Buddhas, the wide verandas and numerous private corners in which to lounge. Guesthouse rooms share facilities and are ultracosy. Meals in the restaurant include lentil burgers, nasi goreng, pancakes and fresh fruit salad.

Jungle Drum Bungalows (☎ 8976 0555; 10 Meneling Rd; d from $110; 🔁 🖭) This has a small grouping of modern cabins, each fitted out with a double bed and two bunks. There's also a restaurant and an adjacent pool shadowed by palm trees.

Banyan Tree Caravan & Tourist Park (☎ 8976 0330; www.banyan-tree.com.au; Litchfield Park Rd; powered/unpowered sites per 2 people $20/18, budget s/d from $40/45, cabin s/d from $70/75, meals $4-15; ☺ lunch & dinner; ❌ ▣) Located 12km from Batchelor towards Litchfield, this fine park has a centuries-old banyan tree watching over it. There are good-value budget rooms, a barrier-free cabin and a licensed café. Bring binoculars to spy on the abundant birdlife.

Batchelor Resort Caravillage (☎ 1800 260 166, 8976 0166; www.batchelor-resort.com; Rum Jungle Rd; powered/unpowered sites per 2 people $26/24, cabins from $100; ❌ ▣ ▣) The Caravillage has plenty of flat, tree-studded land on which to pitch a tent and stare vacantly up at the stars. Amenities include a bar, restaurant and shop. The resort's Rum Jungle Motor Inn offers clean but uninspiring rooms ($140 per room).

Batchelor General Store (☎ 8976 0045; Nurndina St; ☺ 8am-6.30pm) This well stocked store also sells takeaway.

LITCHFIELD NATIONAL PARK

Much of the Tabletop Range – a wide sandstone plateau surrounded by cliffs – lies within this magnificent park, 115km south of Darwin. Four waterfalls drop off the plateau's edge, spilling into idyllic water holes surrounded by patches of rainforest. The prime activity here is simply wandering from one pristine swimming hole to another – when you're not bushwalking or setting up camp, that is. You can swim in all of Litchfield's water holes year-round except for Wangi (*wong*-guy) Falls, which admits the odd saltie when the water level is high enough; pay attention to any signposted warnings. Avoid visiting the park on weekends in the Dry, as it's a very popular day-trip destination for locals.

SCRUB TYPHUS

Scrub typhus is spread by a tiny mite that lives in long grass, and several cases have been associated with Litchfield National Park. The danger is small, but cover up your legs and feet if you're going to walk in this habitat. If you fall ill after visiting the park, advise your doctor that you've been to Litchfield – scrub typhus symptoms include headaches, backaches, fever and a black scab at the bite site.

The two routes to Litchfield from the Stuart Hwy join up and loop through the park. The southern access road via Batchelor is all sealed, while the northern access route, off the Cox Peninsula Rd, is partly unsealed and may be impassable in the Wet.

About 17km after entering the park from Batchelor, there's a field of **magnetic termite mounds**, resembling a bush graveyard. The termites build their mounds in a narrow north–south orientation to catch the heat of the morning and afternoon sun. There's an information display and boardwalk here.

Another 6km further along is the turn-off to **Buley Rockhole** (2km), where water cascades through a series of rocky water holes. This turn-off also takes you to **Florence Falls** (5km), which is accessed by a 15-minute walk via a trail leading to a deep, beautiful pool surrounded by monsoon forest. Both are superb for lazing: just lie on the rocks like a lizard, then roll into the cool water. There's a walking track (45 minutes, 1.6km) between the two places that follows Florence Creek.

About 18km beyond the turn-off to Florence Falls is the turn-off to **Tolmer Falls**, which are a 450m walk off the road. A 1.5km loop track (45 minutes) offers beautiful views of the valley.

It's a further 7km along the main road to the turn-off for Litchfield's most popular attraction, **Wangi Falls**, 1.5km up a side road. The falls flow year-round and fill a beautiful swimming hole bordered by extensive picnic areas and roosting fruit bats. Bring swimming goggles so that you can spot the local fish.

The park offers plenty of bushwalking, including the **Tabletop Track**, a circuit of the park that takes three to five days to complete depending on how many side-tracks you follow.

Tours

Many companies offer trips to Litchfield from Darwin. Most day tours cost from $90 to $110 and include pick-up from your accommodation, as well as swimming, morning tea and lunch.

Goanna Eco Tours (☎ 1800 003 880, 08-8927 2781; www.goannaecotours.com.au) runs a one-day tour (adult/child $110/95) that includes a jumping-croc cruise on the *Adelaide River Queen*, lunch and rental of a swimming mask.

Inquire at Monsoon Cafe (see Sleeping & Eating, below) about cruises on McKeddies Billabong, an extension of Reynolds River.

Sleeping & Eating

There are good **camp sites** (adult/child/family $6.60/3.30/15.40) with toilets and fireplaces at Florence Falls, Florence Creek (4WD required), Buley Rockhole, Wangi Falls and Tjaynera Falls (Sandy Creek; 4WD required). There are more-basic **camp sites** (adult/child/family $3.30/1.65/7.70) at Surprise Creek Falls, and also at Walker Creek, where camping involves bushwalking to a series of magnificent, isolated riverside sites.

Litchfield Campground (☎ 08-8978 2077; monsoon .café@bigpond.com; Litchfield Park Rd; unpowered sites per vehicle $5-10, safari tents per person $10-25, meals $5-15; ☺ breakfast & lunch Apr-Sep, lunch Oct-Mar) Various bush camping options are available here, just north of the Wangi Falls turn-off. Choose your own private clearing or stay in a two- or six-bunk canvas safari tent. The Monsoon Cafe here serves nine types of burger, as well as salads and milkshakes.

Nearby is the sparsely grassed **Wangi Tourist Park** (☎ 08-8978 2185; wangitouristpark@bigpond .com; Litchfield Park Rd; powered/unpowered sites per 2 people $22/17).

Get refreshments at Wangi Falls courtesy of **Wangi Kiosk** (meals $3.50-9; ☺ 8.30am-4.30pm).

ADELAIDE RIVER TO KATHERINE
Adelaide River
☎ 08 / pop 230

This sleepy settlement is 111km south of Darwin. It has an immaculately landscaped **cemetery** (Memorial Tce) that's filled with modest plaques dug into the ground, dedicated to the servicepeople who died during the 1942–43 Japanese air raids on northern Australia. This stretch of the highway is dotted with WWII airstrips.

Mt Bundy Station (☎ 8976 7009; mt.bundy@octa4 .net.au; Haynes Rd; powered/unpowered sites per 2 people $18/16, s $25, d & tw $50-150; ⛽ 🍽) is a beautiful property, 3km from town, which is threaded with walking trails and saturated with peace and quiet. The spotless bunkhouse has a fully equipped kitchen, and the cosy rooms (mostly twin share) are fantastic value. There's also a cottage that sleeps seven people and a house sleeping up to 20. Horse rides cost $30 per hour.

The local pub, **Adelaide River Inn** (☎ 8976 7047; Memorial Tce; powered/unpowered sites per 2 people $15/10, cabins $65, meals $7-22; ☺ breakfast, lunch & dinner; 🍽), is hiding behind the roadhouse. It has comfortable rooms and serves mountainous mains and good-value breakfasts in its bistro. Charlie the water buffalo, who shot to stardom in *Crocodile Dundee*, stands (stuffed) atop the bar.

Old Stuart Highway

Just south of Adelaide River, a sealed section of the old Stuart Hwy (now called Dorat Rd) does a scenic, little-trafficked loop south before rejoining the main road after 52km. Beautiful **Robin Falls** are a short, rocky scramble 15km along this road. The falls, set in a monsoon-forested gorge, dwindle to a trickle in the Dry, but are spectacular in the Wet.

The turn-off to **Daly River** (below) is 14km further. But to reach **Tjuwaliyn (Douglas) Hot Springs Park**, turn south from Dorat Rd onto Oolloo Rd and continue for 35km. The springs are a further 7km down a dirt track (usually OK for 2WD vehicles). The nature park includes a section of the Douglas River and several hot springs – a bit hot for a dip at 40°C to 60°C, but there's a good spot for bathing where the hot spring water mixes with the cool water from the Douglas River near the camp-site river entrance. The **camping ground** (adult/child/family $6.60/3.30/15.40) has pit toilets, BBQs and drinking water.

Butterfly Gorge Nature Park is about 17km beyond Tjuwaliyn (Douglas) Hot Springs – you'll need a 4WD and even then the road is closed for much of the wet season. True to its name, butterflies sometimes swarm in the paperbark-lined gorge.

A further 7.5km south along Oolloo Rd from the Tjuwaliyn turn-off is **Douglas Daly Tourist Park** (☎ 08-8978 2479; douglasdalypark@bigpond .com; Oolloo Rd; powered/unpowered sites per 2 people $25/20, tw/f $40/75, cabins $110; 🍽), a picturesque place with grassy camp sites, varied birdlife, and fine river swimming at the lovely **Arches**, accessed by an often-rutted dirt track. There's a small store-bar selling fuel and cooked meals.

Daly River
☎ 08 / pop 620

The big attraction at historic Daly River, 109km west of the Stuart Hwy, is the prospect of hooking a 'barra'. But even if you're not into fishing, it's a pleasant spot in which to while away several days. There are numerous fishing tour operators, and boat hire (half-/full day from $100/160) is available at accommodation places. The river is infested with saltwater crocodiles.

Locally made arts and crafts are exhibited at **Merrepen Arts** (☎ 8978 2533; ☽ 8am-5pm Mon-Fri), the Naniyu Nambiyu Aboriginal community's exemplary gallery and resource centre. Visitors are welcome to the community, without needing a permit. It's reached via a well-signed turn-off 6km before the Daly River crossing. The Merrepen Arts Festival, held on the first weekend of June, celebrates local Aboriginal arts and music.

The camping ground at **Daly River Mango Farm** (☎ 8978 2464; www.mangofarm.com.au; sites per 2 people $26, d $65-120; ☒), on the Daly River 7km from the crossing, is shaded by a magnificent grove of 90-year-old mango trees. Other accommodation includes budget rooms and a two-bedroom unit ($220). Set dinners, from sausage sizzles to fish and chips, are offered several nights a week.

Also on the banks of the river, **Woolianna on the Daly** (☎ 8978 2478; Woolianna Rd; powered/unpowered sites per 2 people $26/22, flats per person $65-85; ☒) has a beautiful, shady green lawn for camping, beds in multibedroom self-contained flats, and lots of mango trees. It's 15km down a dirt road that's signposted just before town.

Eat something from the small, meat-packed menu in the open-air courtyard at **Daly River Roadside Inn** (☎ 8978 2418; Daly River Rd; mains $14-25; ☽ lunch & dinner), or quench your thirst on a hot day at the tiny, pool table–equipped front bar.

Pine Creek
☎ 08 / pop 470

Laid-back Pine Creek has some interesting old timber and corrugated-iron buildings that survive from an 1870s gold rush. The area is said to have the NT's widest variety of bird species. The Kakadu Hwy branches off the Stuart Hwy at Pine Creek, connecting it to Cooinda and Jabiru.

The **train station** (1888), off Main Tce at the northwest end of town, has a display on the old Darwin to Pine Creek railway (1889–1976), and a lovingly restored steam engine. **Pine Creek Museum** (Railway Pde; adult/

child $2.20/free; ☽ 10am-5pm Mon-Fri), housed in the 1889 repeater station, contains mining memorabilia and old telegraph equipment.

Pine Creek Diggers Rest Motel (☎ 8976 1442; 3. Main Tce; s/d $80/90; ☒) has tidy self-contained cabins (sleeping one to five people) that peer out of tranquil, tropical garden surrounds. There's a laundrette out the front and the motel acts as the town's unofficial info centre.

The relaxed **Pine Creek Hotel** (☎ 8976 1288; 40 Moule St; d from $85, meals $8-24; ☽ lunch & dinner ☒) has standard motel rooms at its rear. A lengthy list of dinners and some great-value lunches are served in its recently renovated dining room.

Tentatively modelled on an American diner, with red vinyl booths and Hollywood memorabilia adorning the walls, **Mayse's** (☎ 8976 1241; 40 Moule St; meals $6-16; ☽ breakfast & lunch) is named after local publican Mayse Young, who spent 50 years behind the bar. Tasty meals range from all-day breakfasts to pizzas.

Around Pine Creek

A dirt road follows the old railway line east of the highway between the towns of Hayes Creek and Pine Creek. This is the original 'north road', which was in use before the 'new road' (now the old Stuart Hwy) was built. It's pretty rough in parts, especially after rain, but the detour is worthwhile to see the 1930s **Grove Hill Hotel** (☎ 08-8978 2489). The pub, built entirely of corrugated iron to prevent it from being eaten by termites, is part museum, part watering hole.

About 3km along the Stuart Hwy south of Pine Creek is the turn-off to pretty **Umbrawarra Gorge Nature Park**, 30km southwest along a dirt road (often impassable in the Wet). There's a basic **camping ground** (adult/child/family $3.30/1.65/7.70), and croc-free pools in which to swim, 1km from the car park.

KAKADU & ARNHEM LAND

KAKADU NATIONAL PARK

The extraordinary Kakadu National Park shelters a bewildering variety of habitats and wildlife, and some of Australia's most significant rock-art sites. It stretches more

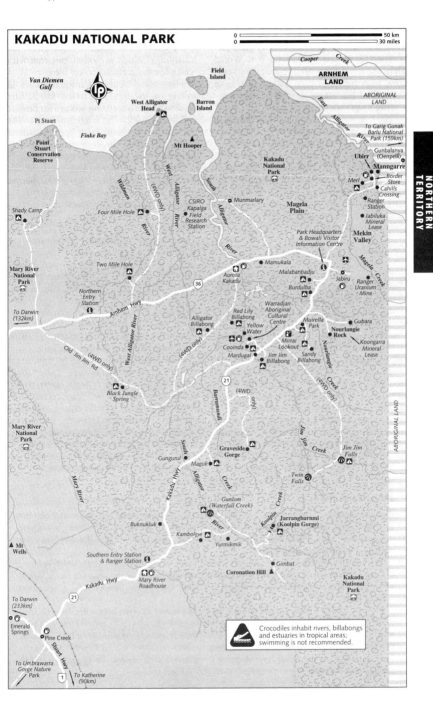

KAKADU NATIONAL PARK

0 ————————— 50 km
0 ————————— 30 miles

NORTHERN TERRITORY

Crocodiles inhabit rivers, billabongs and estuaries in tropical areas; swimming is not recommended.

than 200km south from the coast and 100km from east to west, with its main entrance 153km east of Darwin. It is World Heritage listed for both its natural and cultural importance (a rare distinction). Give yourself at least three days to begin appreciating its grandeur.

The name Kakadu comes from Gagudju, which is a local Aboriginal language. Much of Kakadu is Aboriginal land, leased to the government for use as a national park. There are several Aboriginal settlements here, and about one-third of the park rangers are Aboriginal people. Enclosed by the park, but not part of it, are several tracts of land designated for other purposes, principally uranium mining.

Geography

The circuitous Arnhem Land escarpment, a dramatic 30m- to 200m-high sandstone cliff line, forms the natural boundary between Kakadu and Arnhem Land and winds 500km through eastern and southeastern Kakadu.

Creeks cut across the rocky plateau and, in the wet season, tumble off it as thundering waterfalls. They then flow across the lowlands to swamp Kakadu's vast northern flood plains. From west to east, the rivers are: the Wildman, West Alligator, South Alligator and East Alligator (the latter forming the eastern boundary of the park). Such is the difference between dry and wet seasons that areas that are perfectly dry in September will be submerged in 3m of water several months later. As the waters recede, some loops of wet-season watercourses become cut off, but don't dry up. These are billabongs, which are often carpeted with water lilies and attract water birds.

The coastal zone has long stretches of mangrove swamp, important for halting erosion and as a breeding ground for birdlife and marine life. The southern part of the park is dry lowlands with open grassland and eucalypts. Pockets of monsoon rainforest crop up throughout the park.

Over 80% of Kakadu is savanna woodland. It has more than 1000 plant species, many still used by Aboriginal people for food and medicinal purposes.

Climate

The average maximum temperature in Kakadu is 34°C, year-round. The Dry season is roughly April/May to September/October, and the Wet, when most of Kakadu's average rainfall of 130mm falls, is from October/November to March/April. The transition from Dry to Wet transforms the landscape. As wetlands and waterfalls grow, unsealed roads become impassable, cutting off some highlights like Jim Jim Falls.

Local Aboriginal people recognise six seasons in the annual cycle:

Gunumeleng The 'build-up' to the Wet, starting in October. Humidity increases, the temperature rises to 35°C or more and mosquitoes reach near-plague proportions. By November, the thunderstorms have started, billabongs are replenished and water birds and fish disperse.

Gudjeuk The Wet proper continues through January, February and March, with violent thunderstorms and flora and fauna thriving in the hot, moist conditions.

JABILUKA MINE

Uranium was discovered at Jabiluka in 1971, and an agreement to mine was negotiated with the local Aboriginal people. Mine development was delayed due to oscillating federal government mining policy until 1996, by which time concern had grown that Aboriginal elders had been coerced into signing the agreement.

The Jabiluka mine became the scene of sit-in demonstrations during 1998, which resulted in large-scale arrests. A Unesco delegation inspected the mine site and reported that it would endanger Kakadu's World Heritage listing, a finding later contradicted by an Independent Science Panel.

In April 2004, the fate of the controversial mine seemed to have been effectively decided when multinational mining company, Energy Resources of Australia (ERA), entered into an agreement that there would be no development of the project without the consent of the traditional landowners, the Mirrar people, and, since then, the decline tunnel leading into the deposit has been backfilled. As the Mirrar have staged a David and Goliath–style battle against the mine's construction for many years, it's unlikely their position will change.

Banggereng In April, storms (known as 'knock 'em down' storms) flatten the spear grass, which during the course of the Wet has shot up to 2m high.
Yekke The season of mists, when the air starts to dry out, extends from May to mid-June. The wetlands and waterfalls still have a lot of water and most of the tracks are open.
Wurrgeng & Gurrung The most comfortable time, weather-wise, is the late Dry, in July and August. This is when wildlife, especially birds, gather in large numbers around shrinking billabongs, and when most tourists visit.

Wildlife

Kakadu has about 25 frog species, 51 freshwater fish species, 60 types of mammals, 120 types of reptile, 280 bird species (one-third of native Australian species) and at least 10,000 insect types. This list is frequently added to and some rarer species are unique to the park.

Only a fraction of these creatures reveal themselves to visitors, since many are nocturnal or are few in number. So take advantage of walks led by park rangers (mainly in the Dry). Cruises of the East Alligator River and Yellow Water Billabong enable you to see the water life.

BIRDS

Kakadu's abundant water birds and their beautiful wetland homes are a highlight of Kakadu. This is one of the chief refuges in Australia for several species, including the magpie goose, green pygmy goose and Burdekin duck. Other fine water birds include pelicans, darters and the jabiru, with its distinctive red legs and long beak. Herons, egrets, cormorants, wedge-tailed eagles, whistling kites and black kites are common. The open woodlands harbour rainbow bee-eaters, kingfishers and the endangered bustard. Majestic white-breasted sea eagles are seen near inland waterways. At night, you might hear barking owls calling – they sound just like dogs. The raucous call of the spectacular red-tailed black cockatoo is often considered to be the sound of Kakadu.

At Mamukala, 8km east of the South Alligator River on the Arnhem Hwy, is a wonderful observation building, plus bird-watching hides and a 3km walking track.

FISH

You can't miss the silver barramundi, which creates a distinctive swirl near the water's surface. It can grow to over 1m in length and changes its sex from male to female at the age of five or six years.

MAMMALS

Several types of kangaroo and wallaby inhabit the park; the shy black wallaroo is unique to Kakadu and Arnhem Land. You may see a sugar glider in wooded areas in the daytime. Kakadu has 26 bat species, four of them endangered. If you're driving at night, watch out for wildlife crossing the road, especially the destructive wild pig.

REPTILES

Twin Falls and Jim Jim Falls have resident freshwater crocodiles, while the dangerous saltwater variety is found throughout the park.

Kakadu's other reptiles include the frilled lizard and five freshwater turtle species, of which the most common is the northern snake-necked turtle. Kakadu has many snakes, though most are nocturnal and rarely encountered. The striking Oenpelli python was first seen by non-Aboriginal people in 1976.

Rock Art

Kakadu is one of Australia's richest, most accessible repositories of rock art. There are more than 5000 sites, which date from 20,000 years to 10 years ago. The vast majority of these sites are off-limits or inaccessible, but two of the finest collections are the galleries at Ubirr and Nourlangie.

The rock paintings have been classified into three roughly defined periods: Pre-estuarine, which is from the earliest paintings up to around 6000 years ago; Estuarine, which covers the period from 6000 to around 2000 years ago, when rising sea levels brought the coast to its present level; and Freshwater, from 2000 years ago until the present day.

For local Aboriginal people, these rock-art sites are a major source of traditional knowledge and represent their historical archives. Recent paintings, some which were executed in the 1980s, connect the local community with the artists. Older paintings are believed by many Aboriginal people to have been painted by spirit people, and depict stories that connect the people with creation legends and the development of Aboriginal law.

As the paintings are all done with natural, water-soluble ochres, they are very susceptible to water damage. Therefore, drip-lines of clear silicon rubber have been laid on the rocks above the paintings, to divert rain. As the most accessible sites receive up to 4000 visitors a week, boardwalks have been erected to keep the dust down and to keep people at a suitable distance from the paintings.

Orientation

The sealed Arnhem Hwy stretches 120km east from the Stuart Hwy to Kakadu's entrance, and another 107km to Jabiru. The sealed Kakadu Hwy, which leads to Nourlangie, Cooinda and Pine Creek, turns south off the Arnhem Hwy shortly before Jabiru.

Information

Fuel is available at Kakadu Resort, Border Store (Ubirr), Jabiru and Cooinda. Jabiru also has a supermarket, a post office and a Westpac bank.

Bowali visitor information centre (☎ 08-8938 1121; www.ea.gov.au/parks/kakadu; Kakadu Hwy; 🕒 8am-5pm) has beautifully presented walk-through displays that sweep you across the land, explaining Kakadu's ecology from Aboriginal and non-Aboriginal perspectives – look out for Monty the python. There's a 25-minute audio-visual presentation on Kakadu's seasons (screened hourly from 9am to 4pm), a theatre showing documentaries (from 8.30am to 3.30pm), a café, a gift shop and a resource centre with various reference books. The centre is 2.5km south of the Arnhem Hwy. A pleasant 2km walk leads here from Jabiru, starting opposite Gagudju Crocodile Holiday Inn.

Northern Land Council office (☎ 08-8979 2410; Flinders St) in Jabiru issues permits ($13.20) to visit the Injalak Arts & Crafts Centre (p832) in Gunbalanya (Oenpelli), a 30-minute trip into Arnhem Land that crosses the East Alligator River.

Warradjan Aboriginal Cultural Centre (☎ 08-8979 0051; 🕒 9am-5.30pm Sep-Jun, 7.30am-6pm Jul & Aug), near Cooinda, reveals the culture of the park's traditional owners through creation stories; displays of items such as clapsticks and sugarbag holders; rock-art samples; and an introduction to the moiety system (internal tribal division) and skin names. The building's circular structure symbolises how Aboriginal people sit in a circle when meeting and is also reminiscent of the *warradjan* (pig-nosed turtle), hence the centre's name. A theatre screens videos and there's also a gallery. Warradjan is an easy walk (15 minutes, 1km) from the Cooinda resort.

ENTRY FEES

The park entry fee of $16 (children under 16 free) entitles you to stay in the park for seven days and is paid at the park entry stations (open 7am to 7pm); if you arrive outside of these times, just buy your ticket at a visitor information centre when it opens.

Ubirr

Ubirr is an outcrop of the Arnhem escarpment, famous for its spectacular Aboriginal **rock-art site** (🕒 8.30am-sunset Apr-Nov, 2pm-sunset Dec-Mar). It lies 39km north of the Arnhem Hwy. About 2km before Ubirr is a ranger station with an unstaffed visitor information centre.

Shortly before Ubirr you pass the Border Store (p831). Nearby, a couple of **walking tracks** skirt the East Alligator River.

Guluyambi Cruises (☎ 1800 089 113) runs 1¾-hour Aboriginal-guided cruises on the East Alligator River (adult/child $35/15), where you'll learn about Aboriginal culture and the relationship Aborigines have with the land. Tours depart the upstream boat ramp at 9am, 11am, 1pm and 3pm from May to October. During the Wet, Guluyambi op-

THE RAINBOW SERPENT

The story of the Rainbow Serpent is common in Aboriginal tradition across Australia, although the story varies from place to place.

In Kakadu the serpent is a woman, Kurangali, who painted her image on the rock wall at Ubirr while on a journey through this area. The journey forms a creation path that links the places she visited: Ubirr, East Alligator River and various places in Arnhem Land.

To the traditional owners of the park, Kurangali is the most powerful spirit. Although she spends most of her time resting in billabongs, if disturbed she can be destructive, causing floods and earthquakes. One local story has it that she even eats people.

erates half-day tours (adult/child $100/80) that include a boat transfer across picturesque Magela Creek and a bus drive to Ubirr; BYO (bring your own) lunch. It departs at 10am and provides the only means by which visitors can reach Ubirr when the river is at its highest.

From Ubirr car park, an easy 1km path loops through the main natural galleries formed out of the natural rock. The highlight is the main gallery with its large array of well-preserved X-ray-style wallabies, possums, goannas, tortoises and fish, plus some *balanda* (white men) with hands on hips, an intriguing Tasmanian tiger and *mimi* (spirit people). Also of major interest is the Rainbow Serpent painting and the picture of the Namarkan sisters, shown with string pulled taut between their hands. The Ubirr paintings are in many different styles and were painted over a period spanning from 20,000 years ago to the 20th century.

A 250m-long side track leads to **Nardab Lookout**, which has magnificent 360-degree views. Sitting atop the rocks here and gazing out over the wetlands, particularly as the sun lowers itself behind the Arnhem Land escarpment, is a wonderfully scenic and calming experience.

All road access is sealed, although low-lying areas may still be inundated during the Wet.

Jabiru

☎ 08 / pop 1780

Jabiru, built to accommodate Ranger uranium mine workers, is Kakadu's major service centre, with a bank, newsagent, medical centre, supermarket, bakery and service station. About 6km east is Jabiru airport and the Ranger uranium mine. Minibus tours of the mine (adult/child $20/10) are run by **Kakadu Parklink** (☎ 1800 089 113) at 10.30am and 1.30pm weekdays from May to October.

Nourlangie

The sight of this looming outlier of the Arnhem Land escarpment makes it easy to understand its ancient importance to Aboriginal people. Its long, red sandstone bulk, striped in places with orange, white and black, slopes up from surrounding woodland to fall away at one end in stepped cliffs. Below is Kakadu's best-known collection of rock art.

The name Nourlangie is a corruption of Nawulandja, an Aboriginal word that refers to an area bigger than the rock itself. The Aboriginal name for the higher parts of the rock outcrop is Burrunggui, while the lower area is called Anbangbang. Nourlangie is at the end of a 12km sealed road (open 8am to sunset) that turns east off Kakadu Hwy, 21km south of Arnhem Hwy.

This corner of Kakadu has other attractions. From the main car park, a circuit of 2km takes you first to the **Anbangbang rock shelter**, used for 20,000 years as a refuge from heat and wet-season thunderstorms. From the natural gallery, a short walk leads to **Gunwarddehwarde lookout**, with views of the Arnhem Land escarpment and Lightning Dreaming (Namarrgon Djadjam), the home of Namarrgon. The 12km **Barrk Sandstone bushwalk** follows the rock's base; track notes are available at Bowali visitor information centre.

Heading back towards the highway are turn-offs to three other places of interest. The first, on the left about 1km from the main car park, leads to the lily-carpeted **Anbangbang billabong**. The second, also on the left, leads to a short walk up to **Nawulandja lookout**, with views back over Nourlangie Rock. The third turn-off, a dirt track on the right, takes you to the outstanding **Nanguluwur**, a little-visited rock-art gallery.

A further 6km along this road, you'll reach the beginning of a 3km walk to **Gubara (Baroalba Springs)**, an area of shaded pools in monsoon forest.

Jim Jim Falls & Twin Falls

These two spectacular waterfalls are along a 4WD dry-season track that turns south off the Kakadu Hwy between the Nourlangie and Cooinda turn-offs. It's about 57km from the turn-off to Jim Jim Falls (the last 1km on foot) and a further 10km to Twin Falls, where the last few hundred metres are through the water up a snaking, forested gorge.

Jim Jim Falls, a sheer 215m drop, is awesome after rain, but its waters can shrink to nothing by about June. Twin Falls flows year-round.

Note that the track to Jim Jim Falls and Twin Falls is often still closed in late May and even into June. The only way to see them in the Wet is via a scenic flight.

Yellow Water & Cooinda

The turn-off to the Cooinda accommodation complex and the superb Yellow Water wetlands is 47km down the Kakadu Hwy from the Arnhem Hwy intersection. It's then 4.5km to the Warradjan Aboriginal Cultural Centre (p828), a further 1km to the Yellow Water turn-off, and another 1km to Cooinda.

The **boat trip** (☎ 08-8979 0145; www.gagudju -dreaming.com) on Yellow Water Billabong is one of the highlights of a Kakadu visit, involving a slow, ethereal cruise down Jim Jim Creek and then along the South Alligator River, along the way spotting territorial salties, freshwater mangroves and melaleucas (paperbarks), and wild birds like eagles, brolgas and kites. The dawn trip is the best as the birds are most active and the light is perfect. Two-hour cruises cost $45/17 per adult/child and depart at 6.45am, 9am and 4.30pm from April to November. Shorter (1½-hour) cruises leave at 11.30am, 1.15pm and 2.45pm from April to November, and 8.30am, 11.45am, 1.30pm and 3.30pm from December to March, and cost $40/15. The tickets are purchased at Gagudju Lodge Cooinda (see opposite), where a shuttle bus can deliver you to the departure point. Book a day ahead during busy times.

Cooinda to Pine Creek

Just south of the Yellow Water and Cooinda turn-off, the Kakadu Hwy heads southwest out of the park to Pine Creek, 160km away. On the way there's a turn-off to the superb escarpment waterfall and plunge pool at **Gunlom (Waterfall Creek)**. It's 37km along a good dirt road.

Activities

BUSHWALKING

Kakadu is rewarding but tough bushwalking country, with marked tracks ranging from 1km to 12km in length. For the more adventurous there are numerous possibilities, especially in the park's drier southern and eastern sections – prepare well, tell people where you're going and don't walk alone. A good short track is the **Manngarre Walk** (one hour, 1.6km) at Cahills Crossing, which winds through monsoon vine forest inhabited by hundreds of flying foxes; keep your mouth shut when looking up (trust us on this!).

Darwin Bushwalking Club (☎ 08-8985 1484) welcomes visitors and may be able to help with information. It has walks most weekends, often in Kakadu.

Tours

Meals and entry fees are generally (but not always) included in tour prices.

Arnhemlander (☎ 1800 089 113, 08-8979 2411) This company is managed by descendants of Big Bill Neidjie, who was a well-known Aboriginal elder in the park, and employs knowledgeable and companionable guides to lead fascinating trips to Gunbalanya (Oenpelli). On weekends, and when the level of the East Alligator River is too high for a safe crossing, it instead takes you to see wonderful rock art and wildlife on private, otherwise inaccessible land adjacent to Ubirr. Both tours cost $185/145 per adult/child and operate from May to October. Its booking agents have sometimes neglected to mention that only weekday tours go into Arnhem Land, so double-check the tour's destination when you book.

Kakadu Animal Tracks (☎ 08-8979 0145; www .animaltracks.com.au) Runs unique seven-hour tours (adult/child $135/85) combining a wildlife safari and an Aboriginal cultural tour; tours depart Cooinda at 1pm from May to mid-October.

Magela Cultural & Heritage Tours (☎ 08-8979 2114; magela@austarnet.com.au) This Aboriginal-owned outfit does various small-group 4WD tours from Jabiru, visiting Arnhem Land escarpment country and rock-art sites with an emphasis on Aboriginal culture.

Wilderness 4WD Adventures (☎ 1800 808 288, 08-8941 2161; www.wildernessadventures.com.au) Offers small-group 4WD camping tours into Kakadu (three/five days $430/690).

Willis's Walkabouts (☎ 08-8985 2134; www .bushwalkingholidays.com.au) Organises bushwalks of two days or more, guided by knowledgable Top End walkers.

Several companies run 4WD trips to Jim Jim Falls and Twin Falls from Cooinda and Jabiru, including lunch and paddling gear, for around $120 to $135:

Kakadu Park Connections (☎ 08-8979 0388; kakaduconnection@hotmail.com)

Lord's Kakadu & Arnhemland Safaris (☎ 08-8948 2200; www.lords-safaris.com) Also runs trips to Gunbalanya (Oenpelli) (adult/child $180/130).

SCENIC FLIGHTS

The view of Kakadu from the air is spectacular. Here are two reputable outfits:

Kakadu Air (☎ 1800 089 113, 08-8979 2411) Jabiru-based Kakadu Air takes half-/one-hour fixed-wing flights for $90/150. It also offers half-hour helicopter tours of the

escarphment and Mekin Valley for around $180, or you can zoom over Jim Jim Falls and Twin Falls for $420.
North Australian Helicopters (☎ 1800 898 977; www.northaustralianhelicopters.com.au) Offers similar half-hour helicopter tours to Kakadu Air.

Sleeping & Eating

The accommodation prices in Kakadu vary tremendously depending on the season – resort rates can drop by as much as 50% during the Wet.

SOUTH ALLIGATOR

This is the first resort you'll pass if entering the park along the Arnhem Hwy.
Aurora Kakadu (☎ 08-8979 0166; www.aurora -resorts.com.au; Arnhem Hwy; powered & unpowered sites per 2 people $15, r $100-175; mains $17-26; 🔀) Several kilometres west of the South Alligator River, this resort has sprawling manicured gardens with shady trees and plenty of birdlife. The rooms are comfortable, and there's a pool, tennis court, laundry, restaurant and bar.

UBIRR

About 3km from Ubirr is the **Border Store** (☎ 08-8979 2474; 🕑 8am-4pm Mon-Sat & 8am-2pm Sun Apr–mid-Dec), for supplies and snacks.

JABIRU

Kakadu Lodge (☎ 1800 811 154, 08-8979 2422; klodge@auroraresorts.com.au; Jabiru Dr; powered/unpowered sites per 2 people $25/20, lodge r from $135, cabins from $190, dinner mains $20; 🕑 breakfast & dinner; 🔀 💻 🏊) This is a well-tended resort that has a popular pool area flanked by the Croc & Quoll Bar & Bistro. Numerous birds pay flying visits and a family of dingoes are frequent visitors. Lodge rooms are expensive (in typical Kakadu fashion) but in good

shape, and facilities like the camp kitchen are excellent. There are only a dozen cabins; book these well ahead.
Lakeview Park (☎ 08-8979 3144; www.lakeview kakadu.com.au; Lakeside Cres; r $85-180; 🔀) Accommodation at this attractive, palm-festooned place includes 'bush bungalows' (fan-cooled safari tents sleeping four) and self-contained, two-bedroom cabins. To reach it, turn left into Lakeside Cres at the Mobil service station on Leichhardt St.
Gagudju Crocodile Holiday Inn (☎ 1300 666 747, 08-8979 2800; www.gagudju-crocodile.holiday-inn.com; Flinders St; d from $150, mains $20-33; 🕑 breakfast, lunch & dinner; 🔀 💻 🏊) Viewed from the air, this hotel forms the shape of a 250m crocodile, arguably a pointless design feature considering most visitors arrive by car. The rooms were recently refurbished and are very comfortable; get one on the ground floor beside the pool. The high-ceilinged Escarpment Restaurant serves creative upmarket mains with bush-tucker embellishments.

Jabiru has a shopping centre with several budget eating options.

COOINDA

Gagudju Lodge Cooinda (☎ 08-8979 0145; reservations@gagudjulodge.cooinda.com.au; powered/unpowered sites per 2 people $30/15, budget/hotel r from $70/210; 🔀 💻 🏊) Being the main accommodation near Yellow Water Billabong, the capacities of the lodge's shady camping ground, tiny budget rooms and comfortable hotel rooms are regularly tested. The eateries here include the open-air **Barra Bar & Bistro** (meals $8-17; 🕑 lunch & dinner), which is vulnerable to mosquito attacks, and the pricier **Mimi's** (mains $22-35; 🕑 dinner Apr-Sep). The pool area is great, though the water is kept warm, and there's a shop selling fuel and basic supplies.

CAMPING UNDER THE STARS IN KAKADU

Although you can pitch a tent on the manicured lawns of Aurora Kakadu (above), Kakadu Lodge (above) or Gagudju Lodge Cooinda (above), nothing beats rolling out a swag or setting up a tent at one of Kakadu's 14 designated camping areas. Most of the sites offer basic bush camping (free), but four of the **camping grounds** (adult/child $5.40/free) have amenities like flush toilets and hot showers. These are at Merl, near the Border Store at Ubirr; Muirella Park, several kilometres south of the Nourlangie turn-off and then 6km off the Kakadu Hwy; Mardugal, just off the Kakadu highway 1.5km south of the Cooinda turn-off; and Gunlom (Waterfall Creek), 37km down a dirt road that branches off Kakadu Hwy near the southern entry gate. Only the Mardugal site is open during the Wet.

If you're camping in a swag you'll need a well-maintained mosquito net.

KAKADU HIGHWAY

Mary River Roadhouse (☎ 08-8975 4564; fax 8975 4730; Kakadu Hwy; powered/unpowered sites per 2 people $15/13, budget/motel room $30/90, mains $10-20; ☺ lunch & dinner; ☒) Located just outside the park's southern entrance, this friendly roadhouse has a variety of decent accommodation and a bistro, plus cheaper takeaway that includes lentil burgers. This place can get busy in the Wet, when backpacker buses bypass Kakadu's drenched camping grounds to overnight here.

Getting There & Around

In the Dry you can easily get to most of the sites in a conventional vehicle, excluding Jim Jim Falls and Twin Falls, which are also off-limits to many 4WD hire vehicles (check your policy). Sealed roads lead from Kakadu Hwy to Nourlangie, the Muirella Park camping area and to Ubirr. Other roads are mostly dirt and are blocked for varying periods during the Wet and early Dry.

Even without your own wheels, it's still possible to explore Kakadu independently at your leisure and at a discount. Getting around on a bus pass alone is frustrating, but you can see a lot by combining transport to Jabiru, Ubirr and Cooinda with a couple of tours, such as a trip to the Jim Jim Falls, the Yellow Water cruise and an Aboriginal cultural tour. Camping gear can be hired inexpensively in Darwin, which is also the place to stock up on nonperishable food.

Jabiru has an airport, but at the time of writing it serviced only tour-group charter flights and sightseeing tours.

Greyhound Australia (☎ 13 14 99; www.greyhound.com.au) has a daily service between Darwin and Cooinda via Jabiru. The bus leaves Darwin at 6.30am, Jabiru at 10.15am, and arrives at Cooinda at 12.30pm. It departs from Cooinda at 2.30pm, Jabiru at 4pm, and arrives in Darwin at 7pm. Tickets cost $55/110 one way/return.

Many tours (p830) depart from Darwin for Kakadu – some combine Kakadu with Mary River, Litchfield, Katherine and Arnhem Land.

ARNHEM LAND ABORIGINAL LAND TRUST

The entire eastern half of the Top End is the Arnhem Land Aboriginal Reserve, a vast, virtually undisturbed area with spectacular scenery and superb rock art. Apart from Gunbalanya (Oenpelli), the remote Garig Gunak Barlu National Park (on the Cobourg Peninsula) and Gove Peninsula, Arnhem Land is virtually closed to independent travellers. Much of this is Yolngu country, featured in the film *Yolngu Boy* (2001).

TOURS

Don't pass up the opportunity to head into the unique terrain of Arnhem Land.

Brookes Australia Tours (☎ 08-8948 1306; www.brookesaustralia.com.au) This company transports you in comfort to remote northwestern Arnhem Land. There's a range of options, from one-day fly-in/fly-out tours from Darwin ($900) to extended tours.

Davidson's Arnhemland Safaris (☎ 08-8927 5240; www.arnhemland-safaris.com) Takes people to its safari camp at Mt Borradaile, north of Gunbalanya (Oenpelli), with meals, guided tours, fishing and comfortable accommodation all provided. The daily price is around $450 if two of you make a booking; a one-person booking can cost upwards of $1000 per day. Transfers from Darwin can be arranged.

Nomad Charters (☎ 08-8987 8085; www.nomadcharters.com.au) This outfit, based in Nhulunbuy, runs sightseeing and fishing tours and overnight camping trips around Gove Peninsula.

See also Magela Cultural & Heritage Tours, Lord's Kakadu & Arnhemland Safaris and the Arnhemlander (p830).

Gunbalanya (Oenpelli)

☎ 08 / pop 1300

The drive into this Aboriginal community, along a 17km dirt road from Kakadu, traverses the wildly interesting East Alligator River flood plain, which rivals anything within Kakadu itself. The **Injalak Arts & Crafts Centre** (☎ 8979 0190; Oenpelli St; ☺ Mon-Sat) sells high-quality Aboriginal artefacts at very reasonable prices. It's both a workplace and a shopfront for artists and craftspeople producing traditional paintings on bark and paper, didgeridoos, pandanus weavings and baskets, and screen-printed fabrics. All sales of these authentic pieces directly benefit the community. The **Northern Land Council** (☎ 8979 2410; Flinders St, Jabiru) issues permits ($13.20) to visit Injalak.

See the boxed text, p797, for details of the Gunbalanya (Oenpelli) open day in August.

Cobourg Peninsula

This remote wilderness includes **Cobourg Marine Park** and **Garig Gunak Barlu National Park**. Entry is by permit only.

The ruins of the early settlement known as Victoria can be visited on **Port Essington**, a superb 30km-long natural harbour on the peninsula's northern side.

At Black Point (Algarlarlgarl) there's a **ranger station** (☎ 08-8979 0244) with a visitor information centre and the **Garig Store** (☎ 08-8979 0455; ☥ 4-6pm Mon-Sat), which sells basic provisions, ice and camping gas; credit cards and Eftpos are accepted.

PERMITS

The track to Cobourg passes through part of Arnhem Land and, because the Aboriginal owners restrict the number of vehicles going through to 20 at any one time, you're advised to apply up to a year ahead for the necessary transit permit ($232 per vehicle, valid for seven days), which includes camping fees for the national park. Permits are only issued for travel between May and October and can be obtained from the **Parks & Wildlife Commission** (☎ 08-8999 4814; PO Box 496, Palmerston, NT 0831). If you book accommodation through a lodge (such as Cobourg Beach Huts), it will arrange a permit for you.

SLEEPING

There's a good, shady camping ground about 100m from the shore at **Smith Point** (unpowered sites free). Facilities include a shower, toilet, BBQs and limited bore water; generators are allowed in one area.

Cobourg Beach Huts (☎ 08-8979 0455; www.cobourgbeachhuts.com.au; d $220; ☒) This is a grouping of four secluded, self-contained huts, each of which can sleep up to six people. There are louvred window-walls, solar-powered lights, bush showers and compost toilets.

GETTING THERE & AWAY

The quickest route here is by private charter flight, which can be arranged by accommodation providers. However, this will leave you without transport when you arrive.

The track to Cobourg starts at Gunbalanya (Oenpelli) and is accessible by 4WD vehicles only – it's closed in the Wet, usually opening early May. The 270km drive to Black Point from the East Alligator River takes four to six hours and must be completed in one day.

Straight after the Wet, the water level at Cahills Crossing can be high, and you can only drive across the ford about an hour either side of the low tide. Check the tide chart included with your permit, or at the Bowali visitor information centre in Kakadu.

Eastern Arnhem Land

The Gove Peninsula offers fine beaches and fishing. Nhulunbuy (population 4000) is a remote community on the peninsula, built to service the **bauxite-mining centre** (☎ 08-8987 5345), which runs free tours (bookings essential) on Friday morning.

There are Aboriginal art and craft centres at Nhulunbuy and Yirrkala. **Nambara Arts & Crafts Aboriginal Gallery** (☎ 08-8987 2811; Melville Bay Rd) sells art and crafts from northeast Arnhem Land and often has artists in residence. **Buku Larrnggay Mulka Art Centre & Museum** (☎ 08-8987 1701; Yirrkala; museum admission $2), 20km southeast of Nhulunbuy, is a major repository of bark paintings, carved totems and other artefacts.

Groote Eylandt, a large island off the east Arnhem Land coast, is also Aboriginal land and has a large manganese mining operation. Alyangula (population 670) is the main settlement here.

PERMITS

Overland travel through Arnhem Land from Katherine requires a permit (free); contact the Northern Land Council (see p798).

Dhimurru Land Management Aboriginal Corporation (☎ 08-8987 3992; www.dhimurru.com.au; Arnhem Rd, Nhulunbuy) issues recreation permits ($22, valid for two months) for visits to Nhulunbuy and associated recreation areas. It also publishes a useful visitors' guide ($10), available at its office.

GETTING THERE & AWAY

Airnorth (☎ 1800 627 474; www.airnorth.com.au) flies from Darwin to Nhulunbuy ($260), Groote Eylandt ($260) and Gove Peninsula (from $200). **Qantas** (☎ 13 13 13; www.qantas.com.au) also flies between Darwin and Gove (one way from $185).

In Nhulunbuy, you can hire bikes and vehicles to explore the coast. There are some fine beaches, but beware of crocodiles.

NORTHERN TERRITORY

KATHERINE TO ALICE

The Stuart Hwy from Darwin to Alice Springs is known as 'the Track' and until WWII it was just that – a dirt track connecting the Territory's two main towns, roughly following the Overland Telegraph Line. It's now sealed and adorned with historical plaques at roadside stops.

The stretch of highway between Katherine and Alice Springs can be a dull drive, but there are notable diversions along the way, such as Mataranka's thermal pool, Daly Waters' pub, Tennant Creek's mining history and the frequently photographed Devil's Marbles.

KATHERINE

☎ 08 / pop 6720

Apart from Tennant Creek, Katherine is the only town of any real size between Darwin and Alice Springs. It's a bustling place with a productive Aboriginal arts community – many of the didgeridoos and other artworks sold in Alice and Darwin come from around here. The town's population has grown rapidly in recent years, mainly because of the establishment of the large Tindal air-force base south of town.

Katherine has long been an important stopping point, as the river it's built on and named after is the first permanent source of running water north of Alice Springs. It's been a mixed blessing, because floods have

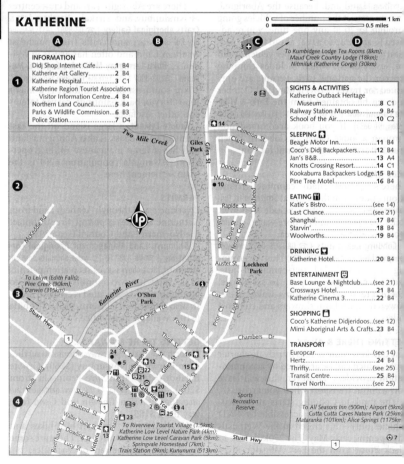

KATHERINE

0 ━━━━━━ 1 km
0 ━━━━━━ 0.5 miles

INFORMATION
Didj Shop Internet Cafe............**1** B4
Katherine Art Gallery.............**2** B4
Katherine Hospital.................**3** C1
Katherine Region Tourist Association
Visitor Information Centre....**4** B4
Northern Land Council............**5** B4
Parks & Wildlife Commission...**6** B3
Police Station.......................**7** D4

To Kumbidgee Lodge Tea Rooms (8km);
Maud Creek Country Lodge (18km);
Nitmiluk (Katherine Gorge) (30km)

SIGHTS & ACTIVITIES
Katherine Outback Heritage
Museum.........................**8** C1
Railway Station Museum..........**9** B4
School of the Air..................**10** C2

SLEEPING
Beagle Motor Inn....................**11** B4
Coco's Didj Backpackers........**12** B4
Jan's B&B.............................**13** A4
Knotts Crossing Resort...........**14** C1
Kookaburra Backpackers Lodge..**15** B4
Pine Tree Motel....................**16** B4

EATING
Katie's Bistro.......................(see 14)
Last Chance........................(see 21)
Shanghai..............................**17** B4
Starvin'...............................**18** B4
Woolworths..........................**19** B4

DRINKING
Katherine Hotel.....................**20** B4

ENTERTAINMENT
Base Lounge & Nightclub.........(see 21)
Crossways Hotel.....................**21** B4
Katherine Cinema 3................**22** B4

SHOPPING
Coco's Katherine Didjeridoos..(see 12)
Mimi Aboriginal Arts & Crafts..**23** B4

TRANSPORT
Europcar..............................(see 14)
Hertz...................................**24** B4
Thrifty.................................(see 25)
Transit Centre.......................**25** B4
Travel North.........................(see 25)

Two Mile Creek
Giles Park
Cameron St
Clarke Cres
Giles St
Donegan
McDonald St
Rapide St
Dakota Cres
Heron Cres
Dove Cres
Lockheed Rd
Auster St
Lockheed Park
Cox Cres
Lockheed Rd
Prior Ct

To Leliyn (Edith Falls);
Pine Creek (90km);
Darwin (315km)

Katherine River
O'Shea Park
O'Shea Tce
Fourth St
Chambers Dr
Third St
Second St
Stuart Hwy
McKeddie Rd
Ackaba Rd

First St
Warburton St
Giles St
Lindsay St
Railway Tce
Katherine Tce
Shepherd St
Stutterd St
Walter Young St
Dowling St
Lucy St
Riverbank Rd
Victoria Hwy
Pearce St

Sports
Recreation
Reserve

To All Seasons Inn (500m); Airport (5km);
Cutta Cutta Caves Nature Park (25km);
Mataranka (101km); Alice Springs (1175km)

To Riverview Tourist Village (1.5km);
Katherine Low Level Nature Park (4km);
Katherine Low Level Caravan Park (5km);
Springvale Homestead (7km);
Train Station (9km); Kununurra (513km)

Stuart Hwy

caused plenty of damage over the years. The devastating surge on Australia Day 1998 inundated the surrounding countryside, leaving a water line up to 2m high on the town's buildings.

Katherine is a good place to recharge on the long drive north or south (or west down the Victoria Hwy to WA). It's also the gateway to the spectacular Nitmiluk (Katherine Gorge) National Park.

Orientation & Information

Katherine's main street, Katherine Tce, is the Stuart Hwy on its way through town. Giles St, the road to Nitmiluk National Park, branches off to the northeast in the middle of town.

Didj Shop Internet Cafe (☎ 0415 461 759; cnr Giles St & Railway Tce; per hr $6) Has Internet access.

Katherine Art Gallery (☎ 8971 1051; 12 Katherine Tce; per hr $6) Has Internet access.

Katherine Hospital (☎ 8973 9211; Giles St) Located 2.5km north of town.

Katherine Region Tourist Association visitor information centre (☎ 8972 2650; www.krta.com .au; cnr Stuart Hwy & Lindsay St; ☉ 8.30am-5pm Mon-Fri, 9am-2pm Sat & Sun) This helpful office stocks information on all areas of the NT and the Kimberley and Gulf regions, as well as park notes.

Parks & Wildlife Commission (☎ 8973 8866; 32 Giles St) Has park notes available.

Police station (☎ 8973 8000; Stuart Hwy) Southeast of town.

Transit Centre (Katherine Tce; per 15min $2) Has Internet access.

For information on getting to/from the airport (7km from town) and train station (9km from town), see p837.

Sights & Activities

Katherine Low Level Nature Park is a great spot on the banks of the Katherine River, just off the Victoria Hwy 4km from town. It has a popular dry-season swimming hole and thermal pools that are best enjoyed in the early morning, before the crowds arrive. A cycle-walking path links the nature park with town.

The 'classroom' of the **School of the Air** (☎ 8972 1833; www.schools.nt.edu.au/ksa; Giles St; adult/child $5/2; ☉ mid-Mar–mid-Dec) covers around 800,000 sq km, with kids living on remote stations and in Aboriginal communities being taught via radio and web hook-ups.

Guided tours usually include listening in on a live lesson and start at 9am, 10am, 11am, 1pm and 2pm from Monday to Friday.

Katherine Outback Heritage Museum (☎ 8972 3945; Giles St; adult/child $3.50/1; ☉ 10am-4pm Mon-Fri, 10am-1pm Sat & 2-5pm Sun Mar-Oct, 10am-1pm Mon-Fri, 10am-1pm Sat & 2-5pm Sun Nov-Feb), in the old airport terminal building 3km northeast of the town centre, has a good selection of old photos, including some of the 1998 flood. You can also inspect the Gypsy Moth biplane flown by Dr Clyde Fenton, the pioneering flying doctor. There are picnic tables and a BBQ in the adjacent park.

In 1879, Ernest Giles established **Springvale Homestead** (☎ 8972 1355; Shadforth Rd), 7km southwest of town. It's claimed to be the NT's oldest cattle station. You're welcome to wander around the homestead, take the free tour at 3pm from May to September, or stay overnight (see p836).

The National Trust–run **Railway Station Museum** (Railway Tce; admission $2; ☉ 1-3pm Mon-Fri May-Sep) lies within the original station building (built 1926) and has historical displays revealing the station's WWII functions.

Tours

See the tourist office or **Travel North** (☎ 8971 9999; www.travelnorth.com.au; Transit Centre, Katherine Tce) for local tour options.

Gecko Canoeing (☎ 8972 2224; www.geckocanoeing .com.au) runs exhilarating canoe trips during the Dry along remote stretches of the Katherine, Daly and Flora Rivers. One-/three-day trips cost $180/600, including meals and transport. The 10-day expedition combining a five-day hike along the awesome Jatbula Trail in Nitmiluk (Katherine Gorge) National Park, with canoeing, is $1980.

Sleeping

BUDGET

Kookaburra Backpackers Lodge (☎ 1800 808 211, 8971 0257; kookaburra@nt-tech.com.au; cnr Lindsay & Third Sts; dm from $19, d & tw without bathroom from $50; ☒ ☐) This popular hostel in a converted motel has gregarious owners who organise sociable BBQ-centred gatherings where the odd guitar and didgeridoo make an appearance. There are single- and mixed-sex dorms. The units each have three TV- and fridge-equipped rooms arranged around a shared kitchen and bathroom. You can also hire bikes and canoes here.

Katherine Low Level Caravan Park (☎ 8972 3962; lowlevel@austarnet.com.au; Shadforth Rd; powered/unpowered sites per 2 people $25/20, cabins from $90; ❄ ▨) Just across the river off the Victoria Hwy, 5km from town, this park has a vast expanse of attractive lawn on which to park your tent or campervan. It also has a large pool, spacious cabins (including one with wheelchair access), a bistro and a kiosk.

Riverview Tourist Village (☎ 8972 1011; www.riverviewtouristvillage.com.au; 440 Victoria Hwy; powered/unpowered sites per 2 people $21/17, backpacker s/d $20/30, s cabins $50-65, d cabins $65-80; ❄ ▨) Lots of mature trees shade this pretty park, and guests can access Katherine's thermal pools via a 500m path at the back of the property. Facilities include free BBQs, and rooms are well-maintained. Backpacker rooms fill up quickly during the mango-picking season (October to November).

Beagle Motor Inn (☎ 8972 3998; fax 8972 3725; 2 Fourth St; s/d $70/80; ❄) Has OK rooms (several with wheelchair access), a bar-café and a nice pool area with a sun shade. Beagles, however, have not been spotted.

Other options:

Coco's Didj Backpackers (☎ 8971 2889; coco@21firstst.com.au; 21 First St; unpowered sites per 2 people $18, dm $16; ❄) A down-to-earth, artist-friendly and unapologetically idiosyncratic hostel; not the place for party animals.

Springvale Homestead (☎ 8972 1355; Shadforth Rd; powered/unpowered sites $17/16, s/d from $30/55; ❄ ▨) In a relaxing bush setting on the Katherine River. Lots of natural distractions for kiddies.

MIDRANGE

Jan's B&B (☎ 8971 1005; jcomelybbaccom@yahoo.com.au; 13 Pearce St; d without bathroom $85-120; ❄ ▯ ▨) This is an excellent accommodation option, with comfy B&B rooms. There's also a large guesthouse sleeping up to 12 people (one double bed, and bunk beds making up the balance) and guests have access to a pool table, piano, spa and pool.

Knotts Crossing Resort (☎ 1800 222 511, 8972 2511; www.knottscrossing.com.au; cnr Giles & Cameron Sts; powered/unpowered sites $25/20, d $75-150; ❄ ▯ ▨) Over 100 rooms are spread across this well-landscaped resort. Plenty of thought went into the design of the cabins, which are compact but open-plan rather than compartmentalised, and there are spacious family rooms. It has a pair of pools and an excellent bistro, Katie's Bistro (right).

Pine Tree Motel (☎ 8972 2533; pinetree2@bigpond.com; 3 Third St; s/d from $75/95; ❄ ▨) Good standard motel accommodation is offered here, accompanied by an on-site restaurant and a small pool in which to splash. Bus tours sometimes pull in here, so book ahead in peak season.

Maud Creek Country Lodge (☎ 8971 1814; maudcreekcountrylodge@bigpond.com; Gorge Rd; d from $110; ❄ ▨) Swimming, bushwalking, fishing, bird-watching and just lazing around are the activities of choice at picturesque Maud Creek Station, where the accommodation is planted in a tropical garden. There's a communal kitchen for guests to share.

All Seasons Inn (☎ 8972 1744; www.accorhotels.com.au; Stuart Hwy; d $140-155; ❄ ▯ ▨) This plush set-up is beside the highway about 2km out of town. Grab one of the deluxe rooms as they cost only a little more than the standard rooms but are much bigger. Good walk-in rates are often available.

Eating

Kumbidgee Lodge Tea Rooms (☎ 8971 0699; Gorge Rd; mains $6-17; ☺ breakfast, lunch & dinner) Eleven or so kilometres from town along the gorge road is this popular eatery, where people masticate happily in the open air or under a covered patio. On Sunday there's a queue for the all-you-can-eat breakfast ($10).

Starvin' (☎ 8972 3633; 32 Katherine Tce; meals $7-16; ☺ dinner Mon-Sat) Customers take the name of this licensed café to heart and proceed to stuff their stomachs with filling pastas, salads and a range of gourmet pizzas.

Last Chance (☎ 8972 1022; Crossways Hotel, 2 Katherine Tce; mains $9-20; ☺ lunch & dinner) The bistro of Crossways Hotel (opposite) serves good-value meals such as meatballs with onions and gravy, as well as a long list of other well-cooked pub fare. Grab yourself a table in the beer garden.

Shanghai (☎ 8972 3170; cnr Katherine Tce & Murphy St; mains $6-17; ☺ lunch & dinner Mon-Fri, dinner Sat & Sun) Serves a satisfying variety of Chinese meals, from sweet-and-sour concoctions to soups and noodles, including some vegetarian dishes. You can eat in or take away.

Katie's Bistro (☎ 8972 2511; Knotts Crossing Resort, cnr Giles & Cameron Sts; mains $18-26; ☺ dinner) Katherine's best restaurant, part of the Knotts Crossing Resort (left) has a menu dominated by Territory fauna such as crocodile, barramundi and buffalo, with some vegetarian choices as well. Eat in the breezy dining room or out in the garden.

Woolworths (☎ 8972 3055; Katherine Tce) The cheapest place for you to stock up within hundreds of kilometres. It has a liquor shop and a bakery.

Drinking

Katherine Hotel (☎ 8972 1622; 5 Katherine Tce) is a popular drinking hole with a roomy front bar, a beer garden and occasional live music.

Entertainment

Crossways Hotel (☎ 8972 1022; 23 Katherine Tce) The front bar here usually closes midafternoon, after which patrons pile around the corner to play pool or drink in the beer garden of the bistro area. Adjacent to the front bar is **Base Lounge & Nightclub** (admission lounge free, nightclub $5; lounge ⏰ 5pm-late Thu-Sat, nightclub ⏰ 11pm-late Fri & Sat).

Katherine Cinema 3 (☎ 8971 2555; www.katherine cinemas.com.au; 20 First St; adult/child/concession $13/8/9.70) Usually a half-dozen motion pictures are on offer at any one time. Tickets are discounted every Wednesday.

Shopping

Mimi Aboriginal Arts & Crafts (☎ 8971 0036; 6 Pearce St) This Aborigine-owned cooperative sells quality goods mainly from the Katherine region, but also from Arnhem Land and the desert and Kimberley regions.

Coco's Katherine Didjeridoos (☎ 8971 2889; 21 First St) Situated at Coco's Didj Backpackers (opposite) this outlet has a shed full of authentic Aboriginal art and didgeridoos (plain and decorated) uniquely carved out in different musical keys. Also worth a browse is Katherine Art Gallery (see Information, p835) and Didj Shop Internet Cafe (see Information, p835) which has a small collection of didgeridoos and some high-quality art, plus good coffee.

Getting There & Around

Katherine airport is 7km south of town. However, at the time of writing, Airnorth had suspended its Katherine services and no other airline had taken over the route.

Buses travelling between Darwin and Alice Springs, Queensland or WA stop at Katherine's **Transit Centre** (☎ 8971 9999; Katherine Tce). Typical fares from Katherine: Alice Springs ($200, 15 hours), Darwin ($70, 4½ hours) and Kununurra ($100, 7¾ hours).

Car-rental outfits include **Thrifty** (☎ 8972 3183; Transit Centre, 6 Katherine Tce), **Hertz** (☎ 8971 1111; cnr Katherine & O'Shea Tces) and **Europcar** (☎ 8971 2777; Knotts Crossing Resort, Cameron St).

For taxis, call **Katherine Taxis** (☎ 8972 1777).

The *Ghan* train travels between Adelaide and Darwin, stopping at Katherine;

NORTHERN TERRITORY

BUYING A DIDGERIDOO

Didgeridoos are one of the most popular forms of souvenir Aboriginal art purchased by tourists. Not only are they artworks in themselves, but they are also an instrument with important cultural significance.

Traditionally, didgeridoos were only used by Aborigines from the Top End. They were made from a single piece of eucalypt (often woollybutt) that was naturally hollowed out by termites only found in this part of Australia. Authentic didgeridoos are still made this way: reasonably straight, termite-hollowed pieces of wood are gathered, cleaned out, cut to the required length (which affects the key of the drone) and painted. Often the mouthpiece is moulded with beeswax. When shopping for a didg, take a look inside and run your finger around the inner edge – it should be rough and uneven, otherwise it has probably been bored out by a drill. Ask what type of wood was used and where it came from.

Many retail didgeridoos are 'fakes', mass-produced in factories and outrageously overpriced. The best place to buy a genuine didgeridoo is in the NT. Expect to pay $200 to $350 (or more) for a reasonably sized didg. Ask for a certificate of authenticity if it is claimed that it was made and decorated by an Aboriginal artist.

It's worth looking for didgeridoos in the Alice. However, if you're heading further north, it's cheaper to buy them closer to the source. Katherine is the main regional centre for many Aboriginal artists making their traditional instrument. If you buy a didgeridoo, ask for a quick lesson – most vendors are more than happy to oblige.

see p858 for timetable and fare details. The train station is off the Victoria Hwy, 9km southwest of town. **Travel North** (☎ 8971 9999), based at the Transit Centre, runs shuttles between the station and town ($5/8 one way/return).

AROUND KATHERINE
Cutta Cutta Caves Nature Park

There are impressive karst (limestone) rock formations outside these tropical caves, 27km southeast of Katherine along the Stuart Hwy. Several types of bat roost in the main cave, including the endangered orange horseshoe and ghost bats. Take the 45-minute **guided tour** (☎ 08-8972 1940; adult/child $13/6.30) held at 9am, 10am, 11am, 1pm, 2pm and 3pm; they're generally held year-round, though the caves can flood in the Wet.

Manyallaluk

Formerly the 3000-sq-km Eva Valley cattle station, **Manyallaluk** (☎ 08-8975 4727) abuts the eastern edge of Nitmiluk (Katherine Gorge) National Park. The land is owned by the Jawoyn Aboriginal people, some of whom lead highly regarded cultural tours. You'll learn about traditional bush tucker, spear throwing and playing a didgeridoo on the one-day trip ($145), which includes transport to/from Katherine, lunch and tea. The cost is less ($110) if you have your own vehicle. The on-site **Art & Craft Centre** (☉ 9am-5pm Mon-Fri) sells items made by artists in the community. No permits are needed to visit Manyallaluk, but alcohol is prohibited.

Nitmiluk (Katherine Gorge) National Park

Remote and beautiful Nitmiluk (Katherine Gorge) comprises 13 gorges, separated from each other by rapids and carved out by the Katherine River, which begins in Arnhem Land. The gorge walls aren't high, but they are rugged and sheer. Further downstream the river becomes the Daly River, flowing into the Timor Sea 80km southwest of Darwin. The difference in water levels between the Wet and Dry is staggering. During the dry season the gorge waters are calm, but from November to March they can become a raging torrent, so swimming and canoeing are restricted.

Swimming in the gorge is safe except when it's in flood. Usually the only croco-diles around are the freshwater variety, more often seen in the cooler months. The surrounding countryside is excellent for walking.

INFORMATION

Nitmiluk Centre (☎ 08-8972 1253; ☉ 7am-7pm Apr-Sep, 7am-5pm Oct-Mar) Found at the gorge, this centre has informative displays on the park's geology, wildlife, traditional Jawoyn owners and European history.

Parks & Wildlife Commission (☎ 08-8972 1886) Has a desk at the Nitmiluk Centre, dispensing info sheets on the walking tracks that meander through the picturesque country south of the gorge, descending to the river at various points. Some tracks pass Aboriginal rock paintings that are up to 7000 years old. Register here between 7am and 1pm for overnight walks and camping permits ($3.30 per person per night, plus a $50 refundable deposit).

LELIYN (EDITH FALLS)

Reached via a turn-off from the Stuart Hwy 45km north of Katherine, then 20km down a sealed road, these pretty waterfalls cascade through three pools. It's a beautiful spot for walking, swimming and camping.

Leliyn Camp Ground (☎ 08-8975 4869; adult/child/family $8/4/20), a ranger-staffed site at the main pool, has shady camping areas, toilets, showers and a laundry. The kiosk sells basic supplies and cooks light meals like burgers during the Dry; only snack food is on offer during the Wet.

ACTIVITIES & TOURS
Bushwalking

The park has fabulous marked bushwalking tracks, ranging from 2km stretches to 20km overnight hikes. The **Jatbula Trail** is a 66km, five-day hike over the Arnhem Land escarpment from Nitmiluk (Katherine Gorge) National Park to Leliyn (Edith Falls). Along the way, this marvellous trail treats you to rainforests, an impressive waterfall at Northern Rockhole, fine swimming at Biddlecombe Cascades, Jawoyn rock paintings at the Amphitheatre, and scenic Sandy Camp Pool.

Canoeing

A leisurely paddle is by far the best way to appreciate the peacefulness and beauty of the gorge. You can stop anytime you like for a swim, and you may even spot a freshie (freshwater crocodile) sheltering near the bank. In the Dry you'll have to carry your canoe over rocks to get from one gorge to the next. **Nitmiluk Tours** (☎ 1800 089 103, 08-8972 1253; nitmiluk@bigpond.com) hires out single/double canoes for a half day ($33/50), while full-day hire is $70/45 per adult/child; hire includes life jackets and a waterproof drum to keep possessions dry. Three-day canoeing trips ($500) depart 9am Tuesday. Tours leave from the boat ramp, which is by the main car park, 500m beyond Nitmiluk Centre.

You can also hire canoes overnight for $135/90 per adult/child, plus $3.30 for an overnight camping permit and a $50 refundable deposit.

Gorge Cruises

A less energetic way to get out on the water is with a cruise, also run by **Nitmiluk Tours** (☎ 1800 089 103, 08-8972 1253; nitmiluk@bigpond.com). The two-hour cruise (adult/child $40/16) goes to the second gorge and visits a rock-art gallery. It leaves at 9am, 11am, 1pm and 3pm. The four-hour trip (adult/child $60/26) goes to the third gorge and includes a swim and refreshments. It leaves at 9am from April to late October, plus at 11am and 1pm from May to August. Finally, there's an eight-hour trip ($100 per person) that takes you up to the fifth gorge, and involves a 5km walk and a BBQ lunch. It departs 9am from May to October. All trips leave from the boat ramp.

During the Wet, when the water level is above 2m, power boats (adult/child $50/35) speed to the end of the third gorge.

Helicopter Flights

Buzz the gorge with **Sky Safari** (☎ 1800 089 103, 08-8971 9999). A 10-minute sweep of three gorges costs $60, while a 25-minute flight through all 13 gorges costs $145. Book at Nitmiluk Centre.

FESTIVALS & EVENTS

The Red Cross–organised **Katherine River Canoe Marathon** takes place in June.

SLEEPING & EATING

Nitmiluk Caravan Park (☎ 08-8972 1253; fax 8971 0715; unpowered sites per adult/child $9/5.50, powered sites per 2 people $22) Situated beside the gorge entrance, this busy park has plenty of grass and shade, plus BBQs and a laundry. Wallabies and goannas come calling. You need to book and pay at the visitor information centre.

Nitmiluk Restaurant (Nitmiluk Centre; meals $5-12; breakfast & lunch) There are burgers, salads and big breakfasts available here, as well as assorted takeaway items. During the Dry, evening meals are often served on the big outside deck, sometimes accompanied by live music.

GETTING THERE & AWAY

It's 30km by sealed road from Katherine to the gorge.

Travel North (☎ 8971 9999) shuttle services run from Katherine's transit centre to the gorge at 8am, 12.15pm and 4.15pm, and then back to town at 9am, 1pm and 5pm. The one-way cost is $14/7 per adult/child (return $21/11).

KATHERINE TO WESTERN AUSTRALIA

The Victoria Hwy stretches 513km, linking Katherine to Kununurra in WA. It winds past beautiful sandstone outcrops and as you approach the WA border you start to see the distinctive, bulbous baobab trees found in much of Australia's northwest.

All fruits, vegetables, nuts and honey must be left at the quarantine inspection post on the border. Western Australian time is 1½ hours behind NT time.

Flora River Nature Park

Limestone tufa outcrops form bars across the Flora River acting as dams to create small waterfalls in this interesting, scenic little park, most of which is a mixture of savanna and woodland. There's a **camping ground** (adult/child/family $5/2/12) at Djarrung with an amenities block, and there are boat and canoe ramps across the tufa. The Flora River has crocs, so there's no swimming.

The park turn-off is 90km southwest of Katherine; the park entrance is a further 36km along a good dirt road.

Victoria River Crossing

The low sandstone cliffs surrounding the spot where the highway crosses the Victoria River create a dramatic setting. The **Victoria River Wayside Inn** (☎ 08-8975 0744; Victoria Hwy; powered/unpowered sites per 2 people $20/15, s from $35, d $65-85, meals $6-19; breakfast, lunch & dinner) has decent motel rooms behind the roadhouse, which cooks up mixed grills and veggie burgers. Boat cruises and fishing tours depart from here during the Dry.

Much of this area forms the eastern section of Gregory National Park. Just west of the crossing is **Joe Creek**, where you can picnic surrounded by reddish-brown cliffs and take a 1.7km loop track along the base of the escarpment.

Timber Creek
☎ 08 / pop 300

Situated 286km southwest of Katherine, Timber Creek is the only town between Katherine and Kununurra. Here you can take a cruise of the majestic Victoria River, or jump in a tinny (a small, aluminium fishing dinghy) to catch some barramundi.

A baobab tree marked by early explorer AC Gregory is at **Gregory's Tree Historical Reserve**, west of town.

Max's Tours operates a 3½-hour cruise (adult/child $60/30) that heads down the Angalarri River and into the broad Victoria River to enthuse over salties, water birds and the escarpment of the Yambarran Ranges. Trips run at 4pm Monday to Saturday from April to September; book at the **Croc Stock Shop** (☎ 8975 0850; www.maxsvictoriarivercruise.com; Victoria Hwy).

Northern Air Charter (☎ 8975 0628; www.flynac.com.au) flies over the Bungle Bungles in WA and various NT sites on its way to/from WA, including Keep River National Park and the mouth of the Victoria River. It also flies over Sara Henderson's 'Bullo Station', made famous in her books (she died in early 2005, after a battle with cancer). At $270, it's better value than flights starting in WA.

Timber Creek Gunanu Tourist Park (☎ 8975 0722; fax 8975 0772; Victoria Hwy; powered/unpowered sites per 2 people $19/13, d from $70;) Also known as Fogarty's and by the mysterious moniker Circle F, this complex includes the Timber Creek Hotel and the Wayside Inn (both have bars and bistros). It has well-treed grounds, budget rooms, and cabins with/without bathroom. The Wayside's motel rooms are better (though more expensive) than those at the hotel.

Gregory National Park

This little-visited national park sits at the transitional zone between the tropical and semiarid regions. It covers 12,860 sq km, consisting of the eastern (Victoria River) section and the much larger Bullita section in the west, and offers good fishing, bird-watching and bushwalking. The 90km 4W **Bullita Stock Route** (closed December to Apr) takes around eight hours, although it's be ter to break the journey at one of the tw marked (free) camping grounds. Conta the **Parks & Wildlife Commission** (☎ 08-8975 08 in Timber Creek before heading into th Bullita section.

Just off the highway at Sullivan Cree 17km east of Victoria River Crossing, a basic **camping ground** (adult/child/family $3.3 1.65/7.70).

Keep River National Park

This remote park is noted for its stun ning sandstone formations and beautif desolation, and has some excellent wal including the **Jinumun Track** through Kee River Gorge. You can reach the park's ma points by conventional vehicle during th Dry. **Aboriginal art** can be seen near the c park at the end of the road.

The park entrance is 3km shy of the W border. A **rangers station** (☎ 08-9167 8827) li 3km into the park from the main highwa and there are basic, sandstone-surrounde **camping grounds** (adult/child/family $3.30/1.65/7.7 at Gurrandalng (15km into the park) an Jarrnarm (28km). Water is available ne the park entrance and at Jarrnarm.

MATARANKA
☎ 08 / pop 500

The main attractions of Mataranka, 105k southeast of Katherine, are its thermal po and nearby Elsey National Park.

Sights & Activities

Mataranka's crystal-clear **thermal pool** is in pocket of rainforest 10km from town. It a great place to revitalise but don't expe a secluded oasis – the pool is reached via boardwalk from Mataranka Homestead R sort and it can get mighty crowded. Abou 200m away (follow the boardwalk from th resort) is the **Waterhouse River**, where yo can rent canoes for $10 per hour.

Outside the homestead entrance is replica of the **Elsey Station Homestead**, con structed for the filming of Jeannie Gunn famous story of her early 20th-century stir in the Top End, *We of the Never Never*.

The relatively untouristed **Elsey Nation Park** adjoins the thermal pool reserve an offers great camping, fishing and walkin long the Waterhouse and Roper Rivers. **Bitter Springs** is a lovely thermal pool within the national park, accessed via Martin Rd from Mataranka town. The blue-green colour of the 34°C water is due to dissolved limestone particles. There's a 120m-long section that you can snorkel or swim up.

In Mataranka town, the **Museum of the Never Never** (adult/child $2.50/2; 8.30am-4.30pm Mon-Fri) has displays on the northern railway, WWII and local history.

About 7km south of the Roper junction is the turn-off to **Elsey Cemetery**, with the graves of characters like 'the Fizzer' who came to life in the novel We of the Never Never. The **Back to the Never Never Festival** is held in Mataranka in May and features art shows and a rodeo.

Roper River Cruises (0427 754 804) departs from 12 Mile Yards in Elsey National Park at 4pm for explorations of this remote waterway, returning at sunset. Tickets per adult/child/family cost $25/10/65; bookings are essential. Bring your own (BYO) drinks and towel.

Sleeping & Eating

Mataranka Cabins (8975 4838; fax 8975 4814; Martins Rd; powered/unpowered sites per 2 people from $17/12, cabins from $80;) Located only a few hundred metres from the Bitter Springs car park, with a front yard decorated by an amazing colony of termite mounds. Each modern, well-equipped cabin has an open-plan layout and a small deck, and sleeps up to six people.

Mataranka Homestead Resort (8975 4544; Homestead Rd; powered/unpowered sites per 2 people $22/18, dm $17, d $60-100, meals $5-22; lunch & dinner;) Just 100m from the thermal pool, this 'resort' is more like an outback pub, but with more rooms. Dorms are clean but dishevelled and only have a fan – air-con is reserved for motel rooms and cabins. The shared kitchen is also on the rustic side. The resort bistro is in the bar area, where staff work hard to keep up with patrons.

Jalmurak Campground (John Hauser Dr; adult/child/family $6.60/3.30/16) This tranquil camping ground is at 12 Mile Yards on the Roper River. It's 12km down John Hauser Dr, accessed from the road to Mataranka Homestead Resort. There's a walking track leading 4km to Mataranka Falls. You can hire canoes here from $6 per hour.

Stockyard Gallery (8975 4530; Roper Tce; meals $5-10; breakfast & lunch) Framed by bougainvillea and other blooming plants, this fine gallery-café serves light meals like toasted sandwiches, muffins and cheesecake. While digesting, browse the contemporary paintings or, if you feel inclined, buy yourself a stockwhip. This is also the town's de facto visitor information centre.

Getting There & Away

Greyhound Australia (13 14 99; www.greyhound.com.au) buses stop in Mataranka en route to Katherine and Alice Springs. **Travel North** (1800 089 103; www.travelnorth.com.au) runs half-day tours ($80/65 per adult/child), including lunch, from Katherine.

BARKLY TABLELAND & GULF COUNTRY

Roper Highway

Not far south of Mataranka on the Stuart Hwy, the mostly sealed Roper Hwy strikes 175km eastwards to **Roper Bar**, on the Roper River. It's mainly visited by fishing enthusiasts and there's accommodation at **Roper Bar Store** (08-8975 4636; unpowered sites per 2 people $15, d from $80). Roper Bar is an access point into southeastern Arnhem Land, or you can continue south to Borroloola through Limmen National Park (carry two spare tyres).

Carpentaria & Tablelands Highways

Just south of Daly Waters, the sealed Carpentaria Hwy (Hwy 1) heads 378km east to Borroloola, near the Gulf of Carpentaria and one of the NT's top barramundi fishing spots. After 267km the Carpentaria Hwy meets the sealed Tablelands Hwy at Cape Crawford, where you'll find an outback oasis, the **Heartbreak Hotel** (08-8975 9928; fax 08-8975 9993; Carpentaria Hwy; powered/unpowered sites per 2 people $20/12, dm $20, s $55-60, d $65-70, meals $5-22; breakfast, lunch & dinner;). Treat yourself to a camp site under a palm tree and a meal from the kitchen, and slurp a beer while reading the poems on the front porch. From here it's a desolate 374km south across the Barkly Tablelands to the Barkly Hwy and **Barkly Homestead Roadhouse** (08-8964 4549; www.barklyhomestead.com.au; powered/unpowered sites per 2 people $23/14, s/d $80/95). Both places pump petrol. Although both highways are sealed, they're narrow and may be cut off during the Wet.

The picturesque **Caranbirini Waterhole** in the Carabirini Conservation Reserve is 44km before Borroloola on the Carpentaria Hwy – follow the **Barrawulla loop walk** (1½ hours, 2km) to see an eerie collection of sandstone pillars.

Borroloola

☎ 08 / pop 770

Borroloola, or 'Land of the Paperbarks', is akin to heaven for fishing fans, but unless you're keen on baiting a hook (the barramundi season peaks from February to April) or doing remote road trips, then you'll be driving a long way for little reason. The town's varied history is displayed at **Borroloola Museum** (☎ 8975 4149; Robinson Rd; admission $2; ☽ 8am-5pm Mon-Fri), within the 1886 police station.

Offshore from Borroloola is **Barranyi National Park**, which is worth a visit.

Cape Crawford Tourism (☎ 8975 9611; www.capecrawfordtourism.com.au) operates three-hour tours ($200) to the nearby Lost City sandstone formations; it includes a scenic flight. **Sea-Eagle Fishing Tours** (☎ 8975 8980) runs full-day fishing tours, including lunch.

SLEEPING & EATING

Borroloola Guesthouse (☎ 8975 8883; www.handr.com.au; cnr Robinson Rd & Broad St; s $50-90, d $65-105; ☒) This breezy guesthouse and cabin complex is located down the street opposite the pub's lounge bar. It has good common areas and a BBQ in the very relaxed garden.

McArthur River Caravan Park (☎ 8975 8734; Robinson Rd; powered/unpowered sites per 2 people $22/20, cabins $100; ☒) A basic park beside the McArthur River, with shady sites and presentable self-contained cabins. It's only a short walk from the pub, if you're feeling dry.

Borroloola Hotel (☎ 8975 8766; Robinson Rd; meals $8-26; ☽ lunch & dinner) This is town's only eating option (besides the takeaway available at the general stores). It serves the usual pub fare of burgers, chops and mixed grills within a lounge bar that's heavily reinforced with steel mesh.

MATARANKA TO TENNANT CREEK

Larrimah

☎ 08 / pop 20

At one time the railway line from Darwin came as far as Birdum, 8km south of the sleepy highway settlement of Larrimah. The

Larrimah Museum (Mahoney St; admission by donatio. ☽ 7am-9pm) is in the former telegraph re peater station opposite the Larrimah Hote and is worth a look, though some of the dis play text needs updating, particularly the b that says 'The dream of a transcontinenta rail link remains unfulfilled' (see The Gha boxed text, p859).

Larrimah Hotel & Caravan Park (☎ 8975 993 Mahoney St; powered/unpowered sites per 2 people $10/ s/d $28/40; ☒) is a cheerfully rustic and quirk pub offering very basic rooms, rather bar camping sites and meals. It's identifiable b the large pink panther out the front.

Fran's Devonshire Teahouse (☎ 8975 9945; Stua Hwy; meals $4-12; ☽ breakfast & lunch) is run b loquacious Fran, who's a dab hand at pi and pastry making. Devotees travel lon distances down the Stuart Hwy for decer coffee and delicious light fare – try the bu falo, spinach and cheese pie. It's hard t miss due to its tangle of roadside signage.

Daly Waters

☎ 08

About 3km off the highway and 160kr south of Mataranka is Daly Waters, an im portant staging post in the early days c aviation – Amy Johnson landed here an it was used as a refuelling stop betwee Sydney and Singapore. The **Daly Wate Aerodrome**, at its busiest during WWII, ha an historical display in the old hangar, an explorer John McDouall Stuart carved a initial 'S' on a nearby signposted tree.

Daly Waters Pub (☎ 8975 9927; powered/unpov ered sites per 2 people $14/10, s from $35, d $50-95, mea $5-18; ☽ breakfast, lunch & dinner; ☒) has an un orthodox approach to interior decoration with its walls plastered in foreign currency T-shirts, stubby (375mL bottle of beer holders, farming equipment, underwear pretty much everything except wallpape It also lays claim to being 'oldest pub i the Territory', as its liquor licence has bee valid since 1893. It's a highly social plac with reasonable accommodation and a bus kitchen. The toilet block is a bit of a wild life refuge – there's often a frog in the bo Fuel is usually cheaper here than on th highway.

Daly Waters to Three Ways

Heading south, you encounter the fascin ating one-time droving town of **Newcastl**

Waters, 3km west of the highway. Its atmospheric, historic buildings include the Junction Hotel, cobbled together from abandoned windmills in 1932. South of the cattle town of **Elliott**, the land just gets drier and drier and the vegetation sparser. Further south is **Renner Springs**, generally accepted as the dividing line between the seasonally wet Top End and the dry centre.

Break up your road trip at **Banka Banka Station** (☎ 08-8964 4511; bankabankastn@bigpond.com; Stuart Hwy; unpowered sites per adult/child $6/3), a historic cattle station 100km north of Tennant Creek. It supplies a grassy camping area, marked walking tracks (one leading to a tranquil water hole) and a small kiosk selling refreshments, including beer. Over winter, the owner gives a slide show and talk on station life most nights.

Three Ways

Three Ways, 537km north of Alice, is the junction of the Stuart and Barkly Hwys, from where you can head south to Alice, north to Darwin (988km) or east to Mt Isa in Queensland (643km).

Threeways Roadhouse (☎ 08-8962 2744; Stuart Hwy; powered/unpowered sites per 2 people $20/15, d from $70, meals $6-18; ☼ breakfast, lunch & dinner; ✹ ☎) has a bar, restaurant and accommodation, but if you've made it this far then Tennant Creek, only 26km away, has better accommodation options and cheaper fuel.

TENNANT CREEK

☎ 08 / pop 3290

Tennant Creek is the only sizable town on the Stuart Hwy between Katherine and Alice Springs. Many travellers spend a night here to break up their journey and to see the town's few attractions, as well as the nearby Devil's Marbles.

The Warumungu people know Tennant Creek as Jurnkurakurr, the intersection of a number of Dreaming tracks; the Dreaming is a complex concept that forms the basis of Aboriginal spirituality, incorporating the creation of the world and the spiritual energies operating around us.

It's rumoured that Tennant Creek was first settled when a wagon carrying beer broke down here in the early 1930s and the drivers decided to make themselves comfortable while they consumed the freight fittingly, on the spot now occupied by the

Tennant Creek Hotel). The truth is somewhat more prosaic: Tennant Creek was Australia's last gold-rush town. Unusually, most of the gold deposits weren't found in quartz but in jet-black ironstone.

Nobles Nob on Peko Rd, 16km east of town, was the country's biggest open-cut gold mine until mining ceased in 1985. A substantial new gold-mining venture started up in 2003 at the Chariot mine, 9km west of town. But judging by the air of disrepair clouding parts of Tennant Creek's main street, it doesn't look like much of this nouveau wealth is heading into town.

Information
Police station (☎ 8962 4444; Paterson St)
Switch.com (☎ 8962 3124; 163 Paterson St; access per 20min $2; ☼ 8.30am-5pm Mon-Fri, 9am-2pm Sat) Has Internet access.
Tennant Creek hospital (☎ 8962 4399; Schmidt St)
Tennant Creek visitor information centre (☎ 8962 3388; www.tennantcreektourism.com.au; Peko Rd; ☼ 9am-5pm May-Sep, 9am-5pm Mon-Fri & 9am-noon Sat Oct-Apr) Inconveniently located at the Battery Hill Mining Centre 1.5km east of town, but the staff is very helpful.
Travel World (☎ 8962 2211; 62 Paterson St) Sells airline tickets and long-distance bus tickets.

Sights & Activities
For 50 years from the 1930s, gold-bearing ore was crushed and treated at **Battery Hill Mining Centre** (☎ 8962 1281; Peko Rd; adult/child/family $24/16/50; ☼ 9am-5pm), 1.5km east of town. Tours of the gold battery are held at 11am and 5pm, and an underground mine tour departs at 9.30am (with an extra tour at 2pm from April to August). There's also a **Minerals Museum**. The admission price gives access to all of the above, or you can just choose one of the tours (adult/child/family $15/8/30) or a visit to the Minerals Museum only (adult/family $2/5).

Nyinkka Nyunyu (☎ 8962 2211; www.nyinkkanyunyu.com.au; Paterson St; adult/child $7.50/3.75; ☼ 8am-5pm Mon-Fri & 9am-4pm Sat May-Sep, 9am-5pm & 10am-2pm Sat Oct-Apr) is an excellent Aboriginal art and culture centre, with absorbing displays on contemporary art, traditional objects (some recently returned by state museums), bush medicine and regional history. A cosy café in the centre sells burgers and focaccias ($4 to $8).

Have a picnic and plunge into the cooling water at **Mary Ann Dam**, 5km north of town.

NORTHERN TERRITORY

NORTHERN
TERRITORY

About 7km north of here are the green-roofed stone buildings of the old **telegraph station**, looking as isolated and forlorn as it must have 100 years ago. This is one of only four of the original 12 stations remaining in the Territory (the others are at Barrow Creek, Alice Springs and Powell Creek). The station's telegraph functions ceased in 1935 when a new office opened. Pick up a key for the telegraph station from the visitor information centre.

The small, National Trust–run **Tuxworth-Fullwood Museum** (Schmidt St; admission free, donations appreciated; ⊕ 2-4pm Tue-Fri May-Sep) has displays of local memorabilia and reconstructed mining scenes.

The **Warrego Fossicking Area** is 60km west of town along Warrego Rd. A permit (free) must be obtained from the Tennant Creek visitor information centre.

Tours

Devil's Marbles Tour (☎ 0418 891 711) There are several trips (from $60) out to these unusual rock formations. The standard day tour includes a BBQ lunch (vegetarians are catered for), and there's also a sunrise visit.

Kraut Downs Station (☎ 8962 2820) Learn about bush tucker and medicine on a half-day tour ($28) – you can also try whip-cracking and wash down a witchetty grub (in season) with billy tea and damper. The station owners will pick you up from your accommodation.

Sleeping

BUDGET

Tourist's Rest Tennant Creek Hostel (☎ 8962 2719; www.touristrest.com.au; cnr Leichhardt & Windley Sts; unpowered sites per 2 people $16, dm $18, d & tw $40; ☒ 🖳 🗊) A small hostel with basic but clean rooms and a rough-around-the-edges appeal. The camping area is tiny, so get in early. Late check-out is good news for those dehydrated from the night before.

Juno Horse Centre (☎ 8962 2783; unpowered sites per 2 people $12; 🗊) This atmospheric camping ground is planted in scrub land some 8km past the visitor information centre, off Peko Rd, and has a swimming pool made out of a squatter's tank. Inquire about the horseback cattle muster and track rides.

Outback Caravan Park (☎ 8962 2459; outback@ swtch.com.au; Peko Rd; powered/unpowered sites per 2 people $20/18, cabins $50-75; ☒ 🗊) Lots of trees and birdsong inhabit this friendly caravan park, which has a well-stocked kiosk and also pumps petrol. Pay $5 extra for the

standard cabin – budget cabins are locate in a more-exposed (less-shaded) corner the park.

MIDRANGE

Desert Sands (☎ 8962 1346; fax 8962 1014; 780 Pate son St; s/d from $70/75; ☒ 🗊) This multistore complex at the southern end of town offe terrific value for money. The budget pric snag you a scrupulously clean room with i own fully equipped kitchen, TV (with i house movies) and a bathroom with a wash ing machine.

Bluestone Motor Inn (☎ 8962 2617; capefire bigpond.com; Stuart Hwy; s $90-95, d $95-105, ☒ 🗊 The hexagonal 'lodge' rooms at this high standard motel, opposite Desert Sands, li at the back of the property and are mor spacious and have bigger beds than th standard rooms. The inn also has a goo restaurant.

Eldorado Motor Inn (☎ 8962 2402; Paterson S d from $95; ☒ 🗊) There's no sign of legend ary treasure at Eldorado, just comfortabl brick motel rooms encircling a pool. Th on-site restaurant-bar will suit those wh don't feel like venturing out at night.

Eating

Ta Rah Cafe (☎ 8962 3790; Transit Centre, 151 Pate son St; meals $7-14; ⊕ breakfast, lunch & dinner) Th smart, recently established café serves a excellent variety of light and heavy meal plus juices, pastries and good coffee. It open long hours to greet all bus arrivals.

Margo Miles Steakhouse (☎ 8962 2227; Tenna Creek Hotel, 146 Paterson St; mains $15-23; ⊕ lunch dinner) Serving Territory standards such a T-bone, chicken parmigiana and barra mundi, this pleasant, uncluttered pub din ing room also has a shortlist of gourme pizzas and a growing wine list. Wet you whistle next door in the beer garden at th lively Jackson's Bar.

Getting There & Away

The **airport** (☎ 8962 2894; www.ntapl.com.au; Irvin St) is in the northwest part of town. **Abo ginal Air Services** (☎ 8953 5000; www.aboriginala .com.au) flies to/from Alice Springs ($250).

All long-distance buses stop at the Tran sit Centre on Paterson St. Greyhound Aus tralia tickets are sold at the **Thrifty** (☎ 89 2358) counter. Fares from Tennant Creek t Alice Springs/Darwin are $125/175.

To rent a car, contact **Thrifty** (☎ 8962 2358; Transit Centre, 151 Paterson St) or **Hertz** (☎ 8962 2459; Outback Caravan Park, Peko Rd). Bike rental is available at **Bridgestone** (☎ 8962 2361; 52 Paterson St) for $5/10 per half-/full day.

TENNANT CREEK TO ALICE SPRINGS

The huge granite boulders that are strewn in precarious piles beside the Stuart Hwy, 105km south of Tennant Creek, are called the **Devil's Marbles**. They are called Karlukarlu by the local Warumungu Aboriginal people, who believe the rocks to be the eggs of the Rainbow Serpent (see the boxed text, p828). According to scientists, they are the remains of molten lava eroded over millions of years. This area is beautiful at sunset, when the boulders exude a rich glow. The **camping ground** (adult/child/family $3.30/1.65/7.70) has remarkably hard ground, pit toilets and fireplaces.

At Wauchope (*war*-kup), 10km south of the Devil's Marbles, are the well-kept rooms of the **Wauchope Hotel** (☎ 08-8964 1963; Stuart Hwy; powered/unpowered sites per 2 people $16/12, s/d from $30/70, dinner $15-20; ☼ breakfast, lunch & dinner; ☒). It serves decent meals and rents bicycles ($10 per day) so that you can pedal out to the Devil's Marbles.

If you're wondering where aliens prefer to stage abductions in Australia, it's at the UFO-friendly town of Wycliffe Well, 17km south of Wauchope. **Wycliffe Well Roadhouse & Holiday Park** (☎ 1800 222 195, 08-8964 1966; Stuart Hwy; powered/unpowered sites per 2 people $24/20, cabins $35-105, dinner $15-20; ☼ breakfast, lunch & dinner; ☒ ☐ ☒) is thus decorated with alien figures and newspaper clippings ('That UFO Was Chasing Us!'), though the backroom King Kong shrine defies explanation. On a more down-to-earth note, the park has pleasant lawn camp sites, a kids' playground, a café and an outstanding range of international beer.

Heading south, you reach **Barrow Creek**. The old telegraph repeater station here was attacked by Kaytetye Aboriginal people in 1874 and the station master and linesman were killed – their graves are by the road. A great many Aboriginal people died in the inevitable reprisals. The trademark of many old pubs along the Stuart Highway is a cluttered quirkiness, and the **Barrow Creek Hotel** (☎ 08-8956 9753; Stuart Hwy; powered/unpowered sites per 2 people $10/6, s from $25, d from $50) is no exception. Its interior is so festooned

with photos, bumper stickers and knick-knacks that there's barely any wall space left. There is also an area available for tents and campervans.

The highway continues through **Ti Tree**, where you'll find an art gallery and café called **Red Sands** (☎ 08-8956 9738; Stuart Hwy) that primarily displays work from the Utopia homelands. Utopia is a community to the northeast of Alice Springs set up on traditional land reclaimed in 1977 from the former Utopia station. The community has nurtured some fine indigenous artists, particularly female painters. Artists work here daily and prices for paintings and didgeridoos are some of the most competitive you'll find in the Territory. There's a pricier branch of this gallery in Alice Springs.

About 12km south of Ti Tree is the **Red Centre Farm** (Shatto Mango; ☎ 08-8956 9828; www .redcentrefarm.com; Stuart Hwy; ☼ 8am-7pm), which harvests mangoes from its 1700-tree orchard to produce ice cream, jam, wine and other treats.

About 70km north of Alice, the Plenty Hwy heads off to the east towards the **Harts Range**. The main reason to detour is to fossick in the **gemfields** about 78km east of the Stuart Hwy, which are well known for garnets and zircons. Join a tag-along tour ($60) from **Gemtree Caravan Park** (☎ 08-8956 9855; www.gemtree.com.au).

ALICE SPRINGS

☎ 08 / pop 24,640

In its 125-year history, 'the Alice' has gone from a simple telegraph station on the Overland Telegraph Line to central Australia's key town. Along the way it built a reputation as a tough place for any stranger to find themselves in, particularly in the rough old pubs that used to line Todd St. But nowadays it has a much less volatile personality. It's settled into a new role as service provider for the hordes of tourists keen to taste the outback charms of the MacDonnell Ranges and a certain big rock to the south. The town itself has fascinating remnants of the pioneering days, plus some excellent ecological attractions, museums and important modern institutions such as the Royal Flying Doctor Service Base and the School of the Air.

NORTHERN
TERRITORY

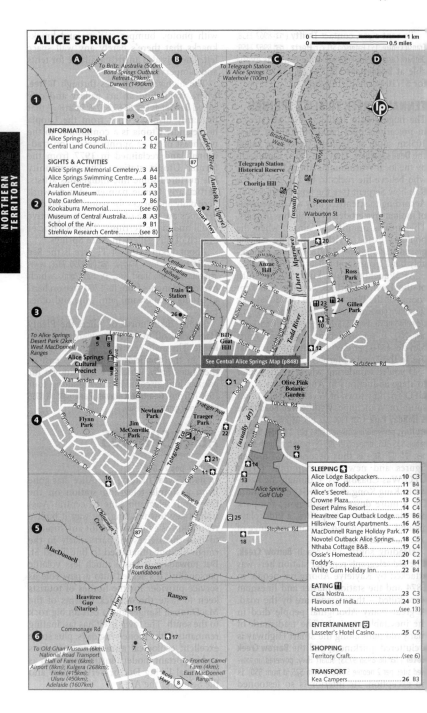

ALICE SPRINGS

0 — 1 km
0 — 0.5 miles

INFORMATION
Alice Springs Hospital..................1 C4
Central Land Council.....................2 B2

SIGHTS & ACTIVITIES
Alice Springs Memorial Cemetery..3 A4
Alice Springs Swimming Centre.....4 B4
Araluen Centre................................5 A3
Aviation Museum............................6 A3
Date Garden...................................7 B6
Kookaburra Memorial.................(see 6)
Museum of Central Australia..........8 A3
School of the Air............................9 B1
Strehlow Research Centre..........(see 8)

SLEEPING
Alice Lodge Backpackers...............10 C3
Alice on Todd...............................11 B4
Alice's Secret...............................12 C3
Crowne Plaza...............................13 C5
Desert Palms Resort......................14 C4
Heavitree Gap Outback Lodge......15 B6
Hillsview Tourist Apartments.......16 A5
MacDonnell Range Holiday Park..17 B6
Novotel Outback Alice Springs.....18 C5
Nthaba Cottage B&B.....................19 C4
Ossie's Homestead.......................20 C2
Toddy's.......................................21 B4
White Gum Holiday Inn................22 B4

EATING
Casa Nostra.................................23 C3
Flavours of India.........................24 D3
Hanuman...............................(see 13)

ENTERTAINMENT
Lasseter's Hotel Casino................25 C5

SHOPPING
Territory Craft..........................(see 6)

TRANSPORT
Kea Campers...............................26 B3

See Central Alice Springs Map (p848)

The telegraph station was built near a permanent water hole in the bed of the normally dry Todd River. The river was named after Charles Todd, superintendent of telegraphs back in Adelaide, and the water hole was named after Alice, his wife. A town called Stuart was first established here in 1888 as a railhead for a proposed railway line. When the name was officially changed to Alice Springs in 1933 (everyone had been calling it Alice anyway), the population had just reached 200. Even in the 1950s Alice Springs was still a tiny town with a population in the hundreds, but there has been rapid growth in the past two decades.

The Alice Springs area is known as Mparntwe to its traditional residents, the Arrernte Aboriginal people. All the topographical features of the town were formed by the creative ancestral beings – the Yeperenye, Ntyarlke and Utnerrengatye caterpillars – as they crawled across the landscape from Emily Gap (Anthwerrke), in the East MacDonnell Ranges.

ORIENTATION

The centre of Alice Springs is a compact and uniform grid just five streets wide, bounded by the (usually dry) Todd River on one side and the Stuart Hwy on the other.

Todd St is a pedestrian mall from Wills Tce to Gregory Tce. Greyhound Australia buses pull in on the corner of Gregory and Railway Tces.

INFORMATION
Bookshops
Big Kangaroo Books (Map p848; ☎ 8953 2137; 79 Todd Mall) Specialises in Australian titles.
Boomerang Book Exchange (Map p848; ☎ 8952 8922; Shop 10, Reg Harris Lane) Good assortment of preloved books.
Department of Infrastructure, Planning & Environment (Map p848; ☎ 8951 9200; 1st fl, Alice Plaza, Todd Mall) Sells maps of the NT.
Dymocks (Map p848; ☎ 8952 9111; Alice Plaza, Todd Mall) General reading material.
Helene's Books & Things (Map p848; ☎ 8953 2465; 113 Todd St) Bursting with well-thumbed second-hand paperbacks.

Emergency & Medical Services
Alice Springs Hospital (Map p848; ☎ 8951 7777; Gap Rd)

Ambulance (☎ 000)
Fire (☎ 000)
Lifeline Crisis Line (☎ 13 11 14)
Police station (☎ 000, 8951 8888; Parsons St)

Internet Access
Alice's Internet cafés charge between $2 and $4 per hour.
Internet Outpost (Map p848; ☎ 8952 8730; Melanka Backpackers, 94 Todd St)
Outback Email (Map p848; ☎ 8955 5288; Outback Travel Shop, 2A Gregory Tce)
Todd Internet Cafe (Map p848; ☎ 8953 8355; 82 Todd St)

Money
Major banks and ATMs can be found in and around Todd Mall in the town centre.

Post
Post office (Map p848; ☎ 13 13 18; 31-33 Hartley St; ☼ 8.15am-5pm Mon-Fri) All the usual services are available here.

Tourist Information
Central Australian Tourism visitor information centre (Map p848; ☎ 8952 5800; www.centralaustralian tourism.com; Gregory Tce; ☼ 8.30am-5.30pm Mon-Fri, 9am-4pm Sat & Sun) This very helpful centre can load you up with stacks of brochures and the free *Central Australia Visitor Guide* booklet. Updated weather forecasts and road conditions are posted on the wall, and national parks information is also available. Central Australian Tourism also has a counter at the airport.

DANGERS & ANNOYANCES
Avoid walking alone late at night on poorly lit backstreets. Get a taxi back to your accommodation if you're out late.

SIGHTS
Alice Springs Desert Park
Situated at the foot of the MacDonnell Ranges on the outskirts of town is the superb **Alice Springs Desert Park** (☎ 8951 8788; www .alicespringsdesertpark.com.au; Larapinta Dr; adult/concession/family $18/9/40; ☼ 7.30am-6pm), a wonderful walk-through lesson in the key habitats of the central Australian environment. Explore sand country, woodlands and desert river ecologies, and meet some of the residents. This predominantly open-air park also touches on the relationship that Aboriginal people have traditionally had with the land.

NORTHERN TERRITORY

NORTHERN TERRITORY

CENTRAL ALICE SPRINGS

0 ____ 300 m
0 ____ 0.2 miles

INFORMATION	
Big Kangaroo Books..........................1 B3	
Boomerang Book Exchange...............2 A3	
Central Australian Tourism Visitor	
Information Centre.......................3 B4	
Dept of Infrastructure, Planning &	
Environment..............................4 C4	
Dymocks....................................(see 4)	
Helene's Books & Things...................5 C6	
Internet Outpost............................6 B6	
Outback Email..............................7 A3	
Police Station...............................8 C4	
Post Office..................................9 C5	
Todd Internet Cafe........................10 C6	
SIGHTS & ACTIVITIES	
Alice Springs Reptile Centre.............11 B6	
Royal Flying Doctor Service Base.....12 B6	
SLEEPING 🏠	
Alice Springs Plaza Hotel..............(see 6)	
Aurora Alice Springs......................13 C5	
Desert Rose Inn............................14 B4	

Elkira Motel................................15 B5	
Pioneer YHA Hostel.......................16 D5	
Todd Tavern...............................17 D4	
EATING 🍴	
Afghan Traders............................18 D5	
Al Fresco...................................19 D4	
Bi-Lo......................................(see 4)	
Bluegrass Restaurant......................20 C6	
Bojangles..................................21 C6	
Cafe Mediterranean Bar Doppio......22 B3	
Coles......................................23 B4	
Country Health Store......................24 C5	
Firkin & Hound............................25 C4	
Gourmet Bakehouse.......................26 B4	
Oscar's....................................27 C4	
Overlanders Steakhouse..................28 B3	
Pub Cafe..................................(see 17)	
Red Dog...................................29 B3	
Red Ochre Grill............................30 B3	
Sultan's Kebabs............................31 A3	
Tea Shrine.................................32 A3	
Woolworths...............................33 A3	

DRINKING	
Melanka Party Bar......................(see 6)	
ENTERTAINMENT 🎫	
Alice Springs Cinemas....................34 D4	
Sean's Irish Bar............................35 B5	
Sounds of Starlight Theatre.............36 B3	
SHOPPING 🛍	
Aboriginal Australia Art & Cultural	
Centre..................................37 B6	
Alice Disposals............................38 B3	
CAAMA Shop..............................39 C6	
Gallery Gondwana.........................40 B3	
K-Mart....................................41 B5	
Leaping Lizards Gallery...................42 B3	
Lone Dingo...............................43 C5	
Mbantua Gallery...........................44 A3	
Red Sand Art Gallery..................(see 40)	
Todd Mall Market.........................45 B3	
TRANSPORT	
Airport Shuttle Bus Office...............46 B3	
Avis.......................................47 A3	
Budget....................................48 B3	
Greyhound Australia......................49 B5	
Hertz......................................50 B6	
Outback Auto Rentals....................51 C6	
Qantas....................................52 C5	
Taxi Rank.................................53 B3	
Thrifty....................................54 B6	

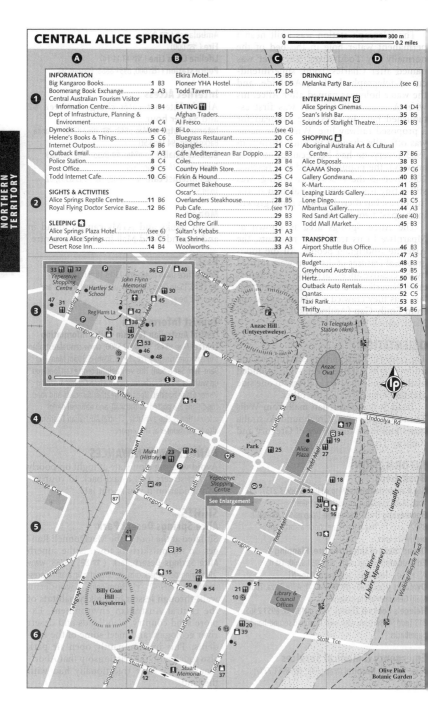

Self-contained exhibits include the **aquarium**, where you examine life around a water hole in the form of catfish, yabbies and burrowing frogs. The **nocturnal house** displays fascinating arid-zone mammal species – some of them endangered or extinct in the Australian wild – such as bilbies, thorny devils, kowari (marsupial mice) and carnivorous ghost bats. There are birds of prey exhibitions at 10am and 3.30pm. Ranger talks are held at various exhibits throughout the day.

A café serves refreshments and the gift shop hires out strollers.

It's an easy 2.5km cycle out to the park. Alternatively, **Desert Park Transfers** (☎ 8952 4667) does return trips for $30/20/77 per adult/concession/family; the price includes the park entrance fee.

Alice Springs Cultural Precinct

Several of the town's historical and cultural attractions feature at the **Alice Springs Cultural Precinct** (Map p846; ☎ 8951 1120; www.ascp.com.au; cnr Larapinta Dr & Memorial Ave; precinct pass adult/child/family $8/5/24; ☉ most attractions 10am-5pm), all connected by a walking path. Entry is at the **Araluen Centre**, where you can buy a 'precinct pass' covering all the attractions.

ARALUEN CENTRE
Beautiful stained-glass windows grace the foyer of this **centre** (☎ 8951 1120), which contains a quartet of fine galleries and a café. The **Albert Namatjira Gallery** features paintings by Namatjira as well as his mentor Rex Battarbee and other artists from the Hermannsburg school. The other galleries showcase paintings from the central desert region and other contemporary art, including travelling exhibitions. A doorway leads through to the **sculpture garden**.

MUSEUM OF CENTRAL AUSTRALIA & STREHLOW RESEARCH CENTRE
Housed in a building partly constructed of a massive rammed-earth wall, the **Museum of Central Australia** (☎ 8951 1121) has fascinating exhibits on natural history, including local megafauna fossils, stuffed reptiles and marsupials, regional meteorite impacts and Aboriginal culture.

Located upstairs in the same building is the **Strehlow Research Centre** (☎ 8951 1111), commemorating the work of Professor Theodor George Henry Strehlow among the Arrernte

people, particularly at the Hermannsburg Mission where he was born. It houses the most comprehensive collection of Aboriginal spirit items (known as *tjurunga*) in the country. These were entrusted to Strehlow for safekeeping by the Arrernte people years ago when they feared their traditional life was under threat. These items cannot be viewed by an uninitiated male or *any* female, and are kept in a vault in the centre. There is, however, a display detailing the works of Strehlow and the culture of the Arrernte.

KOOKABURRA MEMORIAL & AVIATION MUSEUM
A small circular building houses the wreck and story of the **Kookaburra**, a tiny plane that crashed in the Tanami Desert in 1929 while searching for Charles Kingsford-Smith and his co-pilot Charles Ulm, who had gone down in their plane, the *Southern Cross*. Keith Anderson and Bob Hitchcock perished in the desert, while Kingsford-Smith and Ulm were rescued.

Nearby, the **Aviation Museum** is in the Connellan Hangar, Alice's original aerodrome. There are exhibits on pioneer aviation in the Territory and, of course, the famous Royal Flying Doctor Service (the old plane out the front belonged to John Flynn – founder of the service).

ALICE SPRINGS MEMORIAL CEMETERY
This **cemetery** is adjacent to the aviation museum and contains the graves of some prominent locals.

The most famous grave is that of **Albert Namatjira**; it's the sandstone one in the middle section to the left as you enter the cemetery. The headstone features a terracotta tile mural of three of Namatjira's Dreaming sites in the MacDonnell Ranges. The glazes forming the mural design were painted on by Namatjira's granddaughter, Elaine, while the rest were painted by other members of the Hermannsburg Potters.

Other graves located in the cemetery include that of **Harold Lasseter**, who perished in 1931 while trying to relocate the rich gold reef he supposedly found west of Uluru 20 years earlier. The grave of anthropologist **Olive Pink**, who spent many years working with the Aboriginal people of the central deserts, is also here. A number of the original Afghan cameleers are also buried here.

Olive Pink Botanic Garden

There's a fine collection of native shrubs and trees – all of them varieties found within a 500km radius of Alice Springs – at the **Olive Pink Botanic Garden** (Map p846; ☎ 8952 2154; www.opbg.com.au; Tuncks Rd; admission free, donations appreciated; ☻ 10am-6pm). Short walks in the reserve include the climb to the top of Meyer's Hill (35 minutes return) in the Sadadeen Range, from where there's a fine view over town. The hill is known to the Arrernte people as Tharrarltneme and is a registered sacred site. Looking to the south, in the middle distance is a small ridge running east to west: this is Ntyarlkarle Tyaneme, one of the first sites created by the caterpillar ancestors (the name indicates that this was the place where the caterpillars crossed the river). There is a visitor information centre and the Garden Cafe, both open until 4pm.

Royal Flying Doctor Service Base

All communities and stations within a 600km radius of town are serviced by Alice's **Royal Flying Doctor Service base** (RFDS; Map p848; ☎ 8952 1129; www.flyingdoctor.net; Stuart Tce; adult/child $6/2.50, meals $5-15; base ☻ 9am-4pm Mon-Sat, 1-4pm Sun, café ☻ 9am-4pm Mon-Sat).

Entry is by the half-hour tours that run continuously all day. Tours include a 10-minute video, a squiz at an operational control room, and a wander through a museum with historical displays that include ancient medical gear.

The café, housed in the RFDS's original communications base, serves great pies, salads and desserts. The souvenir shop is a good place to pick up gifts; proceeds go towards the base's operational costs.

Alice Springs Reptile Centre

If you want to see everything from bulbous, green tree frogs to numerous lizards and venomous snakes, head for this **reptile centre** (Map p848; ☎ 8952 8900; www.reptilecentre.com.au; 9 Stuart Tce; adult/child $8/4; ☻ 9.30am-5pm). It provides a rare opportunity to see the enormous, magnificently patterned perentie lizard, and a 3.3m saltie is viewable via an underwater passage. Reptile handling takes place at 11am, 1pm and 3.30pm.

School of the Air

Using a combination of satellite-linked web cams and HF radio, the **School of the Air** (Map p846; ☎ 8951 6834; www.assoa.nt.edu.au; 80 Head St; adult/concession/family $4/3/14; ☻ 8.30am-4.30pm Mon-Sat, 1.30-4.30pm Sun) broadcasts lessons to children living on remote outback stations – over an area of 1.3 million sq km. Informal tours of the facility (included in admission price) begin with an interesting video screening and you can watch a live broadcast during school terms (8.30am to 2pm Monday to Friday).

Telegraph Station Historical Reserve

Laying the Overland Telegraph Line across Australia's harsh centre was no easy task, as you'll discover at the small museum at the old, evocative **Telegraph Station** (☎ 8952 3993; Heritage Dr; adult/child/concession/family $7/3.75/5.50/20; ☻ 8am-5pm). The station was constructed from local stone in the early 1870s and operated until 1932. It later served as a welfare home for Aboriginal children of mixed descent, until 1963.

Guided tours operate between 9am and 4.30pm (in winter only). There is also an informative station map that guides you through restored homestead buildings, a blacksmith shop and the telegraph station itself. The original **Alice Springs** (Thereyurre to the Arrernte Aboriginal people), a semi-permanent water hole in the Todd River, is just behind the station.

The station is part of a 450-hectare **historical reserve** (☻ 8am-9pm), with a grassy picnic area, free BBQs, tables and some shady gum trees. A fact sheet for the reserve details its walking tracks.

From the centre of town, it's an easy 3km walk or cycle to the station, which lies north of town; follow the path on the western side of the riverbed.

Frontier Camel Farm

Situated about 4km along Ross Hwy, southeast of Heavitree Gap, is the **Frontier Camel Farm** (☎ 8953 0444; www.cameltours.com.au; Ross Hwy; adult/child/family $6/3/12; ☻ 9am-5pm), where you can ride one of these enigmatic animals. Guided by their Afghani masters, camels were the main form of transport through the desert before the railways were built. The museum includes a video on wild camels and many fascinating exhibits, including one on the Imperial Camel Corps, which served in the Middle East in WWI. See Camel Riding, right for details of camel rides, and also Tours, p853) if you'd like to take a camel to dinner or breakfast.

Date Garden

The unyielding rows of palms at the **Date Garden** (Map p846; ☎ 8953 7558; Palm Circuit; admission free; ◷ 9am-6pm) constitute Australia's first date plantation. The 'fauna park' is thinly populated, but it's still a peaceful place to bring kids. Buy date-infused ice cream and scones in the café.

Old Ghan Museum & National Road Transport Hall of Fame

At the MacDonnell siding, 10km south of Alice Springs on the Stuart Hwy, a group of local railway enthusiasts have restored a collection of *Ghan* locomotives and carriages on a stretch of disused siding from the old narrow-gauge railway track. The **Old Ghan Museum** (☎ 8955 5047; Norris Bell Ave; adult/child/family $5.50/3.50/14; ◷ 9am-5pm) has an interesting collection of railway memorabilia.

Next door is the **National Road Transport Hall of Fame** (☎ 8952 7161; Norris Bell Ave; adult/child/family $8/5/22; ◷ 9am-5pm), great for budding truckers and anyone interested in highway and off-road history. It has a huge shed jammed with restored Macks and a vintage car collection, as well as a couple of road trains and the bush-basher used by Lasseter's descendants in an unsuccessful attempt to find his elusive gold reef.

ACTIVITIES
Ballooning

Fancy quietly sailing through the desert skies at sunrise? Balloon flights cost from $200 for a 30-minute flight, which includes breakfast.

Local operators:

Ballooning Downunder (☎ 1800 801 601; www .ballooningdownunder.com.au)

Outback Ballooning (☎ 1800 809 790, 8952 8723; www.outbackballooning.com.au)

Spinifex Ballooning (☎ 1800 677 893, 8953 4800; www.balloonflights.com.au)

Bushwalking

If you really want to get to know this country, head for the bush. Several easy walks radiate from the Olive Pink Botanic Gar-

den and the Telegraph Station, which marks the start of the first stage of the Larapinta Trail.

Alice Springs Bushwalkers Association (☎ 8953 1956; http://home.austarnet.com.au/longwalk) is an informal group of local bushwalkers that schedules a wide variety of walks in the area; check out the website.

For info on guided Larapinta Trail walks, see p862. For details about hiring or buying camping gear see Shopping, p857.

Camel Riding

Frontier Camel Farm (☎ 8953 0444; www.cameltours .com.au; Ross Hwy; adult/child/family $6/3/12; ◷ 9am-5pm) stages short rides (adult/child $10/6) from 10am to noon, plus between 1pm and 2.30pm from April to October. A one-hour ride down the Todd River ($50/25, including museum entry and transfers) takes place at 9.30am and 2pm, with a sunset ride at 4.30pm from May to September and at 5.30pm from October to April.

Also offering desert plods on camelback is **Pyndan Camel Tracks** (☎ 0416 170 164; www.cameltracks.com), which does a one-hour ride for $30/15 per adult/child.

Cycling

Alice is a flat town, so grab a bike and plenty of water and be off with you – down the excellent track along the Todd River to the Telegraph Station, to the Alice Springs Desert Park, or along the designated track to Simpsons Gap. **Alice Bike Hire** (☎ 0407 324 697) offers half-/full-day rental for $12/24, including delivery and collection. Several accommodation places also hire out bikes.

Swimming

If your hotel/hostel pool has become too familiar, go to the **Alice Springs Swimming Centre** (☎ 8953 4633; Speed St; adult/child $3.30/1.70; ◷ 6am-7pm Mon-Fri, 10am-7pm Sat & Sun).

WALKING TOUR

You can do an easy town walk taking in most of the heritage buildings. Starting in Todd Mall, you'll find the **John Flynn Memorial Church (1)**, which commemorates the man who founded the flying doctor service. Next door, this theme continues at **Adelaide House** (**2**; ☎ 8952 1856; Todd Mall; adult/child $4/3; ◷ 10am-4pm Mon-Fri, 10am-noon Sat), built in the 1920s as the town's first hospital and now a

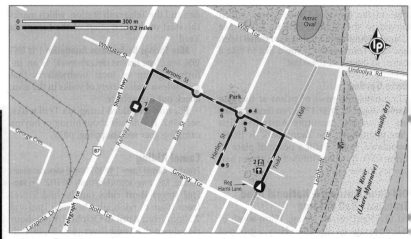

WALK FACTS

Distance: 1km

Duration: 30 minutes

memorial museum to Flynn. Walk north and take a left on Parsons St. On the left is the squat **Residency** (**3**; cnr Hartley & Parsons Sts; admission by donation; 10am-2pm Mon-Fri), dating from 1926–27. It was originally the home of central Australia's first governor and has been refurbished to reflect the period.

Across the road is the Old Courthouse, which was in use until 1980 and now houses the **National Pioneer Women's Hall of Fame** (**4**; ☎ 8952 9006; www.pioneerwomen.com.au; 27 Hartley St; adult/child $2.20/free; 10am-5pm Feb–mid-Dec), a thought-provoking tribute to pioneering women from all over Australia, with a special section on outback heroines.

Turn left onto Hartley St and walk 150m; just south of the car park is the **Hartley St School** (**5**; ☎ 8952 5950; admission free; 10.30am-2.30pm Mon-Fri, 9.30am-12.30pm Sat) and National Trust office. Historical displays here include a re-created early classroom.

Back on Parsons St, to the northwest, is the original **Stuart Town Gaol** (**6**; Parsons St; adult/child $2.20/free; 10am-12.30pm Mon-Fri, 9.30am-noon Sat Mar-Nov), squeezed between the modern law courts and the police station. It was the town's main jail from 1909 to 1938; if you walk down the path behind the jail, a **mural** tells the history of local policing. Continue

along Parsons St, turn left at Railway Tce and you'll come to another giant **mural** (**7**) on the back wall of the supermarket, which depicts the history of Alice Springs.

ALICE SPRINGS FOR CHILDREN

Children love the animal magnetism of **Alice Springs Desert Park** (p847), with its secretive Nocturnal House; the **Alice Springs Reptile Centre** (p850), where fascinating creatures live behind glass; and the **Frontier Camel Farm** (p850), where they can ride through the desert high up on camelback. Calm them down with a date-flavoured ice cream at the **Date Garden** (p851) and a lesson in outback schooling at the **School of the Air** (p850).

For professional short-term child care, look up 'Baby Sitters' and 'Child Care Centres' in the *Yellow Pages* directory. **Baby Equipment Hire** (☎ 0413 239 997; www.babyehire .com.au) delivers porta-cots, backpacks and prams to your accommodation.

TOURS

Aboriginal Australia Art & Cultural Centre (Map p848; ☎ 8952 3408; 125 Todd St) This centre runs a half-day Aboriginal desert-discovery tour (adult/child $85/50) that includes morning tea and a dance performance.
Dreamtime Tours (☎ 8955 5095; www.rstours.com .au) Operates the popular 'Dreamtime & Bushtucker Tour' (adult/child $80/40), which gives you a chance to meet some Warlpiri Aboriginal people and learn a little about their traditional life. You can tag along on the same tour with your own vehicle for $60/30.

Take a Camel out to Breakfast or Dinner (☎ 8953 0444; Ross Hwy; adult/child breakfast $80/45, dinner $105/75) These popular tours combine a one-hour camel ride with a meal at the Frontier Camel Farm (p850).

There's at least one trip daily to the major attractions around Alice Springs: Uluru–Kata Tjuta National Park (Ayers Rock and the Olgas), Kings Canyon, Palm Valley, the West and East MacDonnell Ranges, Simpsons Gap and Standley Chasm. See the respective sections for details of operators. Tours further afield, such as those to Rainbow Valley and Chambers Pillar, operate less frequently. Most follow similar routes and you see much the same on them all, although the price will determine the level of service and degree of comfort you experience.

FESTIVALS & EVENTS
Most of the local community gets involved in the Alice's many colourful activities.

Alice Springs Cup The Pioneer Park Racecourse is a surprisingly good track and through the cooler months it hosts a series of horse races. The Alice Springs Cup in May is the main event. Contact the **Alice Springs Turf Club** (☎ 8952 4977; www.alicespringsturfclub.org.au) for a programme.

Alice Springs Rodeo Held at Blatherskite Park in August. During the rodeo, the town fills up with bow-legged stockmen swaggering around in 10-gallon hats, cowboy shirts, moleskin jeans and RM Williams' Cuban-heeled boots.

Beanie Festival See the boxed text (p797) for information on this annual festival held in mid-June.

Camel Cup (www.camelcup.com.au) A series of camel races in mid-July.

Finke Desert Race (www.finkedesertrace.com.au) A three-day event held on the Queen's Birthday weekend in June along the Old South Rd from Alice to Finke – 218km of rough road. It attracts all sorts of rev heads (lovers of cars) and gives the town a carnival atmosphere.

Henley-on-Todd Regatta (www.henleyontodd.com.au) This September event draws the biggest crowds of all. Holding a series of boat races on the normally dry bed of the Todd River – they say that if you see the Todd River flow three times, you're a local – is a typically Australian light-hearted denial of reality. The boats are all bottomless: the crews' legs stick through and they simply run down the course.

SLEEPING
Alice has a surfeit of accommodation scattered throughout the town centre and strung out to the south along Gap Rd. Many places have at least one wheelchair-accessible room, and nearly all have a pool or cool spa in which to chill out.

Budget
HOSTELS
Pioneer YHA Hostel (Map p848; ☎ 8952 8855; alice pioneer@yhant.org.au; cnr Parsons St & Leichhardt Tce; dm/d from $23/65; 🅿 🖥 🕸) A pleasant hostel set up in a former cinema and now devoted to backpacker cameos. Days are often spent lazing on canvas chairs around the pool. It has a small kitchen, comfy lounge and heaps of info on local sights and activities.

Toddy's (Map p846; ☎ 1800 027 027, 8952 1322; www .toddys.com.au; 41 Gap Rd; dm $18, d $45-65; 🅿 🖥 🕸) This is a popular, lively backpackers where the backyard pool area is the centre of social attention – the poolside bar probably has something to do with it. Breakfast is included in the price.

Also recommended:

Ossie's Homestead (Map p846; ☎ 1800 628 211, 8952 2308; www.ossieshomestead.com.au; cnr Lindsay Ave & Warburton St; dm $17-19, r $45; 🅿 🖥 🕸) Cosy, relaxed, quiet (no TV) and with a cold pool.

Alice's Secret (Map p846; ☎ 1800 783 633, 8952 8686; www.asecret.com.au; 6 Khalick St; dm/s/tw/d $18/35/45/50; 🅿 🖥) Another relaxed hostel, with a spa in which to soak, and fire-twirling lessons; bicycle hire costs $7/12 per half-/full day.

Alice Lodge Backpackers (Map p846; ☎ 1800 351 925, 8953 1975; www.alicelodge.com.au; 4 Mueller St; dm $18-22, s/d from $40/50; 🅿 🕸) The main house is a little tatty, but the renovated caravans out the back provide privacy and are popular.

HOTELS
Todd Tavern (Map p848; ☎ 8952 1255; www.toddtavern .com.au; 1 Todd Mall; d $50-60; 🅿) So long as you can handle the noise of drinkers enjoying their obsession, and can live without a television for one night, the weathered rooms in this tavern are OK for a budget-minded stay.

CAMPING & CARAVANNING
Most camping grounds are on the outskirts of Alice.

MacDonnell Range Holiday Park (Map p846; ☎ 1800 808 373, 8952 6111; www.macrange.com.au; Palm Pl; powered/unpowered sites per 2 people $27/23, cabins $55-140; 🅿 🖥 🕸) This is a well-maintained park in a quiet locale outside town. It has excellent facilities, including a trio of pools and a distraction-filled recreation room.

The budget cabin comes without bathroom or linen.

Heavitree Gap Outback Lodge (Map p846; ☎ 1800 896 119, 8950 4444; www.auroraresorts.com.au; Palm Circuit; powered/unpowered sites per 2 people $20/18, bunkhouse from $65, motel d from $90; ✗ 🖳 🖳) Black-footed rock wallabies descend to feed at this gap in the range south of town. Reception is encircled by two tiers of motel rooms and four-bed bunkhouse rooms, all of which have basic cooking facilities. Meals are available at the nearby tavern and supplies at the on-site supermarket. A free shuttle runs regularly into town and back.

Midrange

See Camping & Caravanning (p853) for information on comfortable motel units and cabins at resorts.

APARTMENTS
Alice on Todd (Map p846; ☎ 8953 8033; www.aliceontodd.com; cnr Strehlow St & South Tce; studio/1-/2-bedroom apt from $100/120/150; ✗ 🖳 🖳) Spacious modern apartments, each with their own balcony, arranged around a pool on a plot of land adjacent to the dusty trough of Todd River. Stand-by and long-term rates are available.

Hillsview Tourist Apartments (Map p846; ☎ 0407 602 379; www.hillsviewapartments.com; 16 Bradshaw Dr; d from $110; ✗ 🖳) The Hillsview has well-equipped two-bedroom apartments looking out towards the West MacDonnells. It's particularly good value for four-person groups as you can share an apartment for as little as $150.

B&Bs
Nthaba Cottage B&B (Map p846; ☎ 8952 9003; www.nthabacottage.com.au; 83 Cromwell Dr; s $125, d $125-155; ✗) Settle into this nice cottage with its own sitting room, or take a less-expensive room (with private entrance) in the owners' house. With a bit of notice, a fruit platter and almost anything else you fancy for breakfast can be whipped up.

HOTELS & MOTELS
Anything with a landscaped garden and a nice pool seems to be called a resort, but most have a range of accommodation and standard motel-style rooms.

Desert Rose Inn (Map p848; ☎ 8952 1411; www.desertroseinn.com.au; 15 Railway Tce; d from $60; ✗ 🖳)

An old-style motel with good-value rooms, particularly for travellers seeking low rates. Budget doubles come with their own shower, wash basin, TV and small fridge; toilet facilities are shared.

Elkira Motel (Map p848; ☎ 8952 1222; 65 Bath St; d from $85; ✗ 🖳 🖳) Elkira's décor is getting older by the minute, but it has good facilities (including a buffet restaurant), helpful staff and a central location opposite a well-stocked supermarket. Deluxe rooms have balconies and queen-sized beds and are more appealing than the standard rooms on the ground floor.

Aurora Alice Springs (Map p848; ☎ 1800 089 644, 8950 6666; asp@auroraresorts.com.au; 11 Leichhardt Tce; d from $130; ✗ 🖳) Has all the requisite facilities of a modern hotel and is a mere lurch from Todd Mall, though it feels strangely down at heel. It's located opposite Todd River, but don't get your hopes up for water views unless there's a flash flood.

Alice Springs Plaza Hotel (Map p848; ☎ 8952 2233; www.melanka.com.au; 94 Todd St; s/d from $90/95; ✗ 🖳 🖳) Put visions of a swank hotel out of your mind – this place is part of the Melanka Backpackers complex and has the same rather drab university-residence aesthetic as the hostel section. However, the price isn't too bad for centrally located midrange accommodation, and each room has a TV and fridge.

White Gum Holiday Inn (Map p846; ☎ 8952 5144; fax 8953 2092; 17 Gap Rd; s/d from $75/85; ✗) The motel units here are noticeably weathered and have aged fittings. But it's clean and you get a kitchen (two hotplates, a sink and fridge) in which to cook.

Top End
Most of the top-end accommodation is east of the river and provides shuttle buses to town.

Novotel Outback Alice Springs (Map p846; ☎ 1300 656 565, 8952 6100; www.novotel.com.au; 46 Stephens Rd; d from $140; ✗ 🖳) This flash resort has been refurbished in recent years and is chockers with mod cons and leisure facilities. Active types can jump into the pool or gym, or onto the tennis court. It's across from Alice's golf course and so accommodates many fashion-challenged visitors.

Bond Springs Outback Retreat (☎ 8952 9888; www.outbackretreat.com.au; d incl gourmet breakfast $230-280; ✗ 🖳) Experience the combination of outback station life and imported luxury at this retreat – head about 15km north on the Stuart Hwy, then turn right down a dirt road (not signposted; look for a 'T' sign) and travel another 6.5km. Choose between well-appointed, self-contained cottages or a suite in the homestead.

Crowne Plaza (Map p846; ☎ 1300 666 545, 8950 8000; www.crowneplaza.com.au; 82 Barrett Dr; d from $150; [icons]) Suffers a little from an excessive application of exterior concrete, but has several hundred well-turned-out rooms, a nice greenery-fringed pool area, and a restaurant proficient in spicy Asian meals. Can get booked up by conventioneers.

EATING

Alice has a reasonable range of eateries and most places make an effort (though not necessarily a successful one) to appease vegetarians. If you've travelled from Melbourne or Sydney, you'll be astounded to find the prices here can top them. For information on dining tours, see p853.

Restaurants

Casa Nostra (Map p846; ☎ 8952 6749; cnr Undoolya Rd & Stuart Tce; mains $13-22; [icon] dinner Tue-Sun) Only an authentic Italian restaurant would dare fuse red-and-white-checked tablecloths, a plastic grape vine and a soundtrack of European country and western. This old-fashioned but relaxed family eatery makes Mama proud with tasty, good-value pizzas, pastas and meat dishes.

Hanuman (Map p846; ☎ 8953 7188; Crowne Plaza hotel, 82 Barrett Dr; mains $16-30; [icon] lunch & dinner Mon-Fri, dinner Sat & Sun) Expertly prepared Thai and Indian dishes such as green chicken, red duck and beef masaman curries predominate in this outstanding restaurant. Some say the décor is exotic, while others think the faux-gold statuary is a little overdone.

Red Ochre Grill (Map p848; ☎ 8952 9614; Todd Mall; mains $11-30; [icon] lunch & dinner) There's nothing hugely original in this restaurant's menu of modernised Australian bush tucker. However, the casual open-plan interior is a good place for a long munch, as is the shady courtyard, and there are usually a few Asian meals thrown into the mix.

Sultan's Kebabs (Map p848; ☎ 8953 3322; cnr Hartley St & Gregory Tce; takeaway $7-9, mains $14-17; [icon] lunch & dinner) Unassuming Sultan's cooks a good variety of Turkish pizzas, kebabs,

dips and other treats such as *sutlac* (creamy sweet rice cooked over several hours). Belly dancers show you an effective way of encouraging digestion from 8pm on Friday and Saturday.

Al Fresco (Map p848; ☎ 8953 4944; Todd Mall; meals $8-25; [icon] lunch & dinner) Located in the cinema complex on Todd Mall, this breezy café has numerous pastas and sauces to mix and match, and also serves meaty meals like chicken parmigiana. Lunches can be significantly cheaper than dinners.

Flavours of India (Map p846; ☎ 8952 3721; 20 Undoolya Rd; mains $10-16; [icon] dinner) This is an ultraplain establishment serving up a decent range of reasonably priced tandoori, seafood and vegetarian dishes. Worth trying, even if the outside looks like a minimum security prison.

Oscar's (Map p848; ☎ 8953 0930; Todd Mall; mains $12-28; [icon] breakfast Sat & Sun, lunch & dinner daily) Serves a big, hearty menu of pastas, salads and Oz delicacies such as surf 'n' turf (meat served with seafood). It is a favourite of families and older travellers, who seem to prefer its semiformal atmosphere and wide-ranging but familiar menu. It offers a good selection of wines.

Overlanders Steakhouse (Map p848; ☎ 8952 2159; 72 Hartley St; mains $19-30; [icon] dinner) This vine-wreathed restaurant lets you accompany your mignon (bacon wrapping and mushroom sauce) with chunks of either beef, chicken, kangaroo, camel or buffalo. Gluttons should order the six-meat 'Drover's Blowout' ($50).

Cafés

Cafe Mediterranean Bar Doppio (Map p848; ☎ 8952 6525; Fan Arcade; mains $8-13; [icon] breakfast & lunch) A lively, unpretentious café (except for the name), where conversation is vigorous, the Alice arts scene is well represented, and the kitchen cranks out a wholesome assortment of pita pizzas, focaccias, salads and breakfasts, plus an impressive list of juices.

Tea Shrine (Map p848; ☎ 8952 4339; Yeperenye shopping centre, Hartley St; meals $4-9; ☺ lunch Mon-Sat) Tea fanciers can refresh themselves in this temple of the brewed leaf while eating some modest (but tasty) snacks, breakfasts and curries. A pot of any tea – from English breakfast to herb- and fruit-infused blends – is $4.50.

Red Dog (Map p848; ☎ 8953 1353; 64 Todd Mall; meals $7-10; ☺ breakfast & lunch) This is a popular, Australiana-decorated place dishing out budget breakfasts, burgers and steaks. The ice cream and lolly counters usually have a child or three jammed up against them.

Pubs

Pub Cafe (Map p848; ☎ 8952 1255; Todd Tavern, 1 Todd Mall; mains $10-22; ☺ breakfast, lunch & dinner) The place for pub grub, with everything from cheap roasts and even cheaper bar snacks like the gourmet pie floater, to rump steak topped with Moreton Bay bugs. You can take your meals at barrel tables in the pub, in the slightly more formal bistro, or alfresco in the mall.

Bojangles (Map p848; ☎ 8952 2873; 80 Todd St; mains $15-35; ☺ lunch & dinner) A variety of Aussie tucker – which has included diced camel marinated in Guinness – is served in a back room of this busy pub. A couple of veggie dishes attempt to balance out all the cooked flesh.

Firkin & Hound (Map p848; ☎ 8953 3033; 21 Hartley St; mains $11-25; ☺ lunch & dinner) The cosy dining room at the rear of this English-theme pub

emphasises UK fare like beef-and-Guinness pie and beef Wellington, plus some trans-Atlantic competition like American ribs.

Self-Catering

Large supermarkets include **Coles** (Map p848; ☎ 8952 5166; Bath St; ☺ 24hr), **Woolworths** (Map p848; ☎ 8953 0988; 40 Hartley St) and **Bi-Lo** (Map p848; ☎ 8952 6110; Alice Plaza, Todd Mall).

Gourmet Bakehouse (Map p848; ☎ 8953 0041; Coles Complex, Bath St) has made-to-order sandwiches, pies, cakes and sourdough bread.

Afghan Traders (Map p848; ☎ 8955 5560; Leichtodt Plaza) is replete with organic and other health foods – follow the laneway behind the ANZ bank, or duck through Springs Plaza from Todd Mall. Also bursting with vitality is the **Country Health Store** (Map p848; ☎ 8952 5157; 20 Parsons St).

DRINKING

Bojangles (Map p848; ☎ 8952 2873; 80 Todd St) Hard-drinking pub aiming for an antipodean Wild West look, but the liberal touches of corrugated iron, the Meatloaf shrine and old the Holden bonnet on the ceiling make it look more like the Confused West. There's a DJ most nights playing last century's hits, and an acoustic show on Sunday. Head here for hearty meals (left).

Firkin & Hound (Map p848; ☎ 8953 3033; 21 Hartley St) This is a low-lit, subdued Brit tavern; a pleasant place to sink a chilly brew or down some pub grub (left). There was no live music at the time of writing, but this may change in the future.

Todd Tavern (Map p848; ☎ 8952 1255; 1 Todd Mall) Busy local watering hole (with accommodation – see p853) at the top end of Todd Mall. There's often a jam session here on Monday night and live music several times a week.

Melanka Party Bar (Map p848; ☎ 8952 4744; 94 Todd St) Where backpackers like to get conspicuously trashed, all in the name of cultural bonding, of course. Free live music plays Thursday to Sunday.

ENTERTAINMENT

The gig guide in the entertainment section of the *Centralian Advocate* (published every Tuesday and Friday) lists what's on in and around town.

Alice Springs Cinemas (Map p848; ☎ 8952 4999; Todd Mall; adult/child $14/9.50) Latest release movies make themselves at home here. All tickets are discounted on Tuesday (adult/child $9.50/7.50). Some hostels offer two-for-one movie ticket deals.

Araluen Centre (Map p848; ☎ 8951 1120; Larapinta Dr) This fine arts centre, part of the Alice Springs Cultural Precinct (p849), stages performances of theatre, music and dance. The main theatre also screens art-house flicks and film festivals from around 7pm most Sundays (adult/concession $11/9).

Lasseter's Hotel Casino (Map p846; ☎ 8950 7777; 93 Barrett Dr) Lasseter's is filled with low-tech entertainment and bored attendees of the convention centre next door. The casino is named after a man who died a terrible death in his quest for riches – go figure.

Live Music
Sean's Irish Bar (Map p848; ☎ 8952 1858; 51 Bath St) This diminutive, slightly dishevelled place hosts live music and the odd jam session from Friday to Sunday, as well as the ear-straining strains of traditional Irish karaoke on Thursday.

Sounds of Starlight Theatre (Map p848; www .soundsofstarlight.com; ☎ 8953 0826; 40 Todd Mall; adult/concession/family $25/20/80) This is a unique musical performance evoking the spirit of the outback with a didgeridoo and various Latin American instruments. Performances are held at 8pm on Tuesday, Friday and Saturday between April and November.

SHOPPING
Alice is the centre for Aboriginal arts and crafts from all over central Australia. It has plenty of art galleries and other shops specialising in such wares, particularly along Todd Mall. There's a forest of didgeridoos here (though it's an instrument not traditionally played in this part of the Territory), but if you're heading north, save your didgeridoo purchase for later in the journey – Katherine has plenty of outlets (see Shopping, p837 and the boxed text, p837).

Mbantua Gallery (Map p848; ☎ 8952 5571; 71 Gregory Tce) Sells ceramics, baskets woven from date-palm fronds, and an enormous range of traditional art, mostly by artists from the Utopia region northeast of Alice.

Leaping Lizards Gallery (Map p848; ☎ 8952 5552; Reg Harris Lane) Has an innovative stockpile of contemporary arts and crafts, including paintings, woodwork, DIY arts packs for kids, outback photography and some super-funky handbags.

Territory Craft (Map p846; ☎ 8952 4417; Alice Springs Cultural Precinct, Larapinta Dr) This is a retail gallery for Territorian artists working with glass, enamel, fibre and many other materials. Visit the studio out the back to see how the wares are made, and to talk to the artisans.

Aboriginal Australia Art & Cultural Centre (Map p848; ☎ 8952 3408; 125 Todd St) Sells a range of desert art, contains cultural displays and offers didgeridoo lessons ($15). The centre also runs a desert-discovery tour (see Tours, p852), and there are plans to eventually relocate to 86 Todd St.

Central Australian Aboriginal Media Association (CAAMA; Map p848; ☎ 8951 9710; 101 Todd St) Stocks Aboriginal books, CDs and cassettes, painted ceramics and various products with local Aboriginal designs.

Todd Mall Market (Map p848; ☎ 8952 9299; Todd Mall; ⏰ 9am-1pm every 2nd Sun Feb-Dec) Lines the pedestrian zone with stalls selling crafts, food and knick-knacks.

Two good commercial outlets for contemporary Aboriginal art are **Gallery Gondwana** (Map p848; ☎ 8953 1577; 43 Todd Mall) and **Red Sand Art Gallery** (Map p848; ☎ 8953 7222; 45 Todd Mall), a pair of stylish art spaces a short distance apart in Todd Mall. For general items, try **K-Mart** (Map p848; ☎ 8952 8188; Bath St). For camping and hiking gear, head to **Alice Disposals** (Map p848; ☎ 8952 5701; Reg Harris Lane) or **Lone Dingo** (Map p848; ☎ 8953 3866; 24 Parsons St), which hires out all manner of camping gear, including sleeping bags and camping stoves from $5/25 per day/week and tents from $10/50. For a small surcharge staff will deliver hired equipment to your accommodation.

GETTING THERE & AWAY
Air
Qantas (Map p848; ☎ 13 13 13; www.qantas.com.au; cnr Todd Mall & Parsons St) flies daily between Alice and Adelaide (one way from $180), Darwin (from $210), Melbourne (from $260), Perth (from $290), Sydney (from $210) and Yulara (from $120).

Virgin Blue (☎ 13 67 89; www.virginblue.com.au) flies from Alice Springs to Adelaide ($200), Brisbane ($300), Melbourne (from $240) and Sydney (from $190) daily.

Aboriginal Air Services (☎ 8953 5000; www.aboriginalair.com.au) flies between Alice Springs and Tennant Creek ($250).

Bus

Greyhound Australia (Map p848; ☎ 13 14 99, 8952 7888; www.greyhound.com.au; cnr Gregory & Railway Tces) has daily services from Alice Springs to Adelaide ($220, 21 hours), Cairns ($410, 36 hours), Coober Pedy ($130, nine hours), Darwin ($240, 21 hours), Katherine ($200, 15 hours), Mt Isa ($240, 14 hours), Tennant Creek ($125, eight hours) and Uluru ($75, 5½ hours).

Backpacker buses cover the distance while savouring sights along the way. **Desert Venturer** (☎ 1800 079 119; www.desertventurer.com.au) makes three-day runs ($330, food kitty $55) between Cairns and the Alice thrice weekly. **Groovy Grape Getaways Australia** (☎ 1800 661 177; www.groovygrape.com.au) has a two-day Alice to Adelaide run via Coober Pedy ($160), plus longer camping trips from Adelaide to Alice Springs. The **Wayward Bus Touring Company** (☎ 1300 653 510, 8410 8833; www.waywardbus .com.au) has a 'Just the Centre' trip ($330, plus Uluru park entry) taking in Kings Canyon, Uluru and Rainbow Valley, while its 'Territory Explorer' ($280) is a road trip between Alice and Darwin.

Car & Motorcycle

Alice Springs is a long way from everywhere. From Mt Isa, in Queensland, it's 1180km; from Darwin to Alice Springs is 1476km (15 hours); and from Alice Springs to Yulara via the sealed Lasseter Hwy is 441km (4½ hours).

These are outback roads, but you're not yet in the real, outer outback, where a breakdown can mean big trouble. Nevertheless, it's wise to have your vehicle prepared, particularly as you won't get a mobile phone signal outside Alice or Yulara. Carry drinking water and emergency food at all times.

Most of the car-rental companies in Alice Springs have 4WDs for hire. Rentals don't come cheap, as most firms offer only 100km free a day, which won't get you far. Local operator **Outback Auto Rentals** (Map p848; www .outbackautorentals.com.au; ☎ 8953 5333; 78 Todd St) has small cars from $55 per day.

Many rental companies have counters at the airport:

Avis (Map p848; ☎ 8953 5533; 52 Hartley St)
Britz: Australia (☎ 8952 8814; cnr Stuart Hwy & Power St)
Budget (Map p848; ☎ 13 27 27, 8952 8899; Shop 6, Capricornia Centre, Gregory Tce)

Hertz (Map p848; ☎ 8952 2644; 76 Hartley St)
Kea Campers (Map p848; ☎ 8955 5525; 7 Kidman St)
Thrifty (Map p848; ☎ 8952 9999; cnr Stott Tce & Hartley St)

Train

In Alice, tickets for the classic, Australia-crossing *Ghan* can be booked through **Trainways** (☎ 13 21 47; www.trainways.com.au) or **Travelworld** (Map p848; ☎ 8953 0488; 40 Todd Mall). Discounted fares are sometimes offered, especially in the low season (February through June). Bookings are recommended on this popular route.

You can travel by reclining 'Daynighter' seat (no sleeper, no meals), 'Red Kangaroo' sleeper cabin (with shared facilities, no meals) and 'Gold Kangaroo' sleeper cabin (self-contained, all meals provided).

The train leaves Adelaide bound for Alice Springs at 5.15pm on Friday and Sunday, arriving in the Alice at noon the next day. From Alice Springs, the departure for Adelaide is at 12.45pm Thursday and 2pm Saturday, arriving about 9am the next day on both routes. Adult fares for the Alice–Adelaide ride in Daynighter/Red Kangaroo cabin/ Gold Kangaroo cabin are $215/680/890.

The *Ghan* train departs Alice Springs for Darwin at 4.10pm on Monday, arriving in Katherine at 8am Tuesday and in Darwin at 4.30pm Tuesday. The service from Darwin departs at 10am on Wednesday, leaves Katherine at 6.20pm, and arrives in Alice Springs at 9.20am Thursday. The stopovers in Katherine last four to five hours. Fares for the Alice–Darwin trip are $240/880/1150. The Adelaide–Darwin fares are $440/1390/1830. The cost of embarking/disembarking at Katherine is the equivalent of doing so at Darwin.

It's also possible to put your car on the *Ghan*. The cost from Adelaide to Alice Springs is $390; from Adelaide to Darwin is $800; and from Alice to Darwin is $450.

The *Ghan* is met in Adelaide by the *Indian Pacific*, which travels to/from Sydney, and the *Overland*, which travels to/from Melbourne.

GETTING AROUND

Alice Springs is compact enough to get to most parts of town on foot, and you can reach quite a few of the closer attractions by bicycle.

THE GHAN

The *Ghan* is one of Australia's great railway adventures, and is the centrepiece of a saga that started in 1877 when it was decided to build a railway line from Adelaide to Darwin. It took more than 50 years to reach Alice Springs, and the final 1500km of track to Darwin was only ready to receive an inaugural trip in February 2004. The reason the project took so long was that a big mistake was made right at the start: the line was built in the wrong place.

This grand error resulted from the theory that because all the creek beds north of Marree were bone dry, and because nobody had seen rain, there wasn't going to be rain in the future. In fact, the initial stretch of line was laid across a flood plain and when the rain came, even though it soon dried up, the line was simply washed away. In the century or so that the original *Ghan* line existed, this was a regular occurrence.

Compounding this problem was the fact that the line's foundations were flimsy, the grading was too steep and it meandered hopelessly – which explains why the old *Ghan*'s top speed was a flat-out 30km/h. Early rail travellers went from Adelaide to Marree on the broad-gauge line, changed there to narrow gauge as far as Oodnadatta, then made the final journey to Alice Springs by camel train. Afghani cameleers pioneered outback transport and it was from them that the *Ghan* took its name.

In 1929, the line was extended to Alice Springs, but the *Ghan* was still chronically slow and unreliable. Worst of all, heavy rainfall could strand it at either end or even in the middle. Parachute drops of supplies to stranded train travellers became part of outback lore and on one occasion the *Ghan* rolled in 10 days late.

By 1980, a new standard gauge line had been laid from Tarcoola (northwest of Port Augusta) to Alice Springs, in a spot where rain wouldn't wash it out. In 1982 the old *Ghan* made its last run and the old line was subsequently torn up. One of its last appearances was in the film *Mad Max III*.

To/From the Airport

Alice Springs airport is 12km south of the town. It's about $28 by taxi.

An **airport shuttle** (Map p848; ☎ 8953 0310; Gregory Tce) meets flights and picks up and drops off at city accommodation for $12/20 one way/return.

Public Transport

BUS

The public bus service, **Asbus** (☎ 8952 5611), departs from outside the Yeperenye shopping centre on Hartley St. Buses run about every 1½ hours from 7.45am to 6pm Monday to Friday, and from 9am to 12.45pm on Saturday. A short trip is $2.20. There are three routes of interest to travellers: No 1 has a detour to the cultural precinct; No 3 passes the School of the Air; and No 4 passes many southern hotels and caravan parks along Gap Rd and Palm Circuit. The visitor information centre has free timetables.

The **Alice Wanderer Centre Sightseeing** (☎ 1800 722 111, 8952 2111; www.alicewanderer.com.au) bus does a loop around 16 major sights, including the old Telegraph Station, School of the Air, the Old Ghan Museum and the cultural precinct. You can get on and off wherever you like; daily tickets cost $35. It runs every 70 minutes from 9am to 4pm from opposite the visitor information centre on Gregory Tce, and you can arrange to be picked up from your accommodation.

Taxi

Taxis congregate near the corner of Todd St and Gregory Tce (Map p848). To book one, call ☎ 13 10 08 or ☎ 8952 1877.

Train

The Alice's train station is 800m northwest of Todd St, on a side road off Larapinta Dr. The **airport shuttle** (☎ 8953 0310) runs between the station and town centre ($5/8 one way/return). Taxis charge about $6 for this trip.

THE MACDONNELL RANGES

The MacDonnell Ranges, full of superb scenery, gorges, water holes and walking tracks, stretch themselves out to the east and west of Alice Springs. The sheer walls of the many gorges harbour rocky water holes that nourish wildlife and spring wildflowers. The most practical option for many is to visit the ranges as part of a big group, but the only way to truly succumb to the region's peaceful nature is via some solo exploration.

There are many places you can visit within a day, but if you have time, immerse yourself in the local beauty by camping or staying at a homestead. Walks range from sightseeing strolls to the challenge of the Larapinta Trail. There's no public transport to either the East or West MacDonnell Ranges, though some of the closer gorges are accessible by bicycle or on foot.

EAST MACDONNELL RANGES

The East MacDonnell Ranges stretch for 100km east of Alice Springs, intersected by a series of scenic gaps and gorges that see far fewer visitors than the West MacDonnell Ranges. The sealed Ross Hwy, accessible through Heavitree Gap south of town, leads to most of the highlights. About 100km from Alice Springs, the dirt Arltunga Rd becomes the Arltunga Tourist Dr (also known as the Gardens Rd) northwest of Arltunga and rejoins the Stuart Hwy 50km north of Alice Springs; this rougher section sometimes requires a 4WD. There are currently no shops in the East MacDonnell Ranges, so take all provisions with you.

Emily & Jessie Gaps Nature Park

Both of these gaps are associated with the Eastern Arrernte Caterpillar Dreaming trail. **Emily Gap**, 16km out of town, is a pleasant spot with rock art and a fairly deep water hole in the narrow gorge. Known to the Arrernte as Anthwerrke, this is one of the most important Aboriginal sites in the Alice Springs area because it was from here that the caterpillar ancestral beings of Mparntwe originated (see the Alice Springs' introduction, p845). The gap is a sacred site with some well-preserved paintings on the eastern wall – in the wet season you may have to wade or swim to reach them. **Jessie Gap**, 8km further, is an equally scenic and usually much quieter place. Both sites have toilets.

Corroboree Rock Conservation Reserve

Past Jessie Gap you drive over eroded flats before entering a valley between red ridges. **Corroboree Rock**, 51km from Alice Springs, is one of many strangely shaped outcrops scattered over the valley floor. Despite the name, it's doubtful the rock was ever used as a corroboree area, but it is associated with the Perentie Dreaming trail. The perentie is one of the world's largest lizards, growing in excess of 2.5m, and takes refuge within the area's rockfalls. However, you're unlikely to see one outside the Alice Springs Reptile Centre (see p850). The rock is looped by a walking track (15 minutes) and there's a toilet.

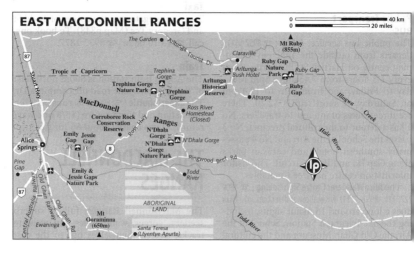

EAST MACDONNELL RANGES

| 0 | 40 km |
| 0 | 20 miles |

Trephina Gorge Nature Park

About 70km from Alice Springs you cross the sandy bed of Benstead Creek and shadow a lovely stand of red gums for the 6km from the creek crossing to the Trephina Gorge turn-off – it's then another 8km to the gorge. If you only have time for a couple of stops in the East MacDonnell Ranges, make Trephina Gorge Nature Park one of them. The contrast between pale sand in dry river beds, red and purple tones of the valley walls, white tree trunks, eucalyptus-green foliage and blue sky is spectacular. You'll also find deep swimming holes and abundant wildlife. Just before the gorge itself is **Trephina Bluff**. Another main attraction is the delightful **John Hayes Rockhole**, 9km from the Trephina Gorge turn-off (the last 4km is suitable for 4WDs only).

The **Trephina Gorge Walk** (one hour, 2km, moderate) loops around the gorge's rim. The **Ridgetop Walk** (six hours, 10km one way, difficult) traverses the view-hidden ridges from the gorge to the rockhole; the 8km return along the road takes 1½ hours.

There's a **rangers station** (☎ 08-8956 9765) and **camping grounds** (adult/child/family $3.30/1.65/7.70) at Trephina Gorge, the Bluff and John Hayes Rockhole.

N'Dhala Gorge Nature Park

Shortly before the Ross River Homestead (a former resort now under redevelopment), a strictly 4WD-only track leads 11km south to N'Dhala Gorge. Around 5900 ancient Aboriginal petroglyphs (rock carvings) and some rare endemic plants decorate a deep, narrow gorge, although the art isn't easy to spot. There's a small, exposed **camping ground** (adult/child/family $3.30/1.65/7.70).

It's possible to turn off before the gorge and head to the Ringwood Homestead Rd, then west to rejoin the Ross Hwy 30km east of Alice Springs.

Arltunga Historical Reserve

Situated at the eastern end of the MacDonnell Ranges, 110km east of Alice Springs, is the old gold-mining ghost town of **Arltunga**. Its history, from the discovery of alluvial (surface) gold in 1887 until mining activity petered out in 1912, is fascinating. **Old buildings**, a couple of **cemeteries** and the many deserted **mine sites** in this parched landscape give visitors an idea of what life was like for

miners here. There are walking tracks (the Government Works area has the best collection of remnant drystone buildings) and old mines to explore (now hosting bat colonies), so bring a torch (flashlight).

The unstaffed **visitor information centre** (☎ 08-8956 9770; 🕑 8am-5pm) has many displays and old photographs of the gold-extracting process, plus a slideshow on the area's history, and drinking water and toilets. There's no camping in the reserve itself, but the nearby **Arltunga Bush Hotel** (☎ 08-8956 9797; sites per adult/child $8/4) has a camping ground with showers, toilets, BBQ pits and picnic tables. The hotel itself is closed and sells no provisions.

The 40km section of unsealed road between the Ross Hwy and Arltunga can be impassable after heavy rain. Including side trips, a complete loop from Alice Springs to Arltunga and back would be over 300km. From Arltunga it's possible to loop back to the Alice along the Arltunga Tourist Dr.

Ruby Gap Nature Park

This remote, little-visited park rewards visitors with wild and beautiful scenery. The sandy bed of the Hale River is purple in places due to thousands of tiny garnets. The garnets caused a 'ruby rush' here in the 19th century and some miners did well out of it until it was discovered that the 'rubies' were, in fact, virtually worthless garnets. It's an evocative place and is well worth the effort required to reach it – speaking of which, you'll need a high-clearance 4WD. The water holes at Glen Annie Gorge are usually deep enough for a cooling dip.

Camping (adult/child/family $3.30/1.65/7.70) is permitted anywhere along the river; BYO drinking water and firewood. Allow two hours each way for the 44km trip from Arltunga. It's essential to get a map from the Parks & Wildlife Commission and register with the **Overnight Walker Registration Scheme** (☎ 1300 650 730). A refundable deposit of $50/200 per individual/group is payable by credit card over the phone or cash at the visitor information centre in Alice to offset the cost of a search should anything go wrong.

WEST MACDONNELL RANGES

Spectacular gorges and fine walks define the West MacDonnell Ranges, which hold many of the features the centre is renowned for. Their easy access by conventional vehicles makes them especially popular with day-trippers. Heading west from the Alice, Namatjira Dr turns northwest off Larapinta Dr 6km beyond Standley Chasm and is sealed all the way to Glen Helen Gorge, 132km from town. From the dirt road beyond, there is a turn-off south through Tylers Pass to Tnorala (Gosse Bluff), which meets up with the Mereenie Loop Rd. Larapinta Dr continues southwest from Standley Chasm to Hermannsburg (sealed), then the Mereenie Loop Rd (a dirt road) loops all the way to Kings Canyon.

All the sites mentioned in this section lie within the **West MacDonnell National Park**, except for Standley Chasm, which is privately owned. There are ranger stations at Simpsons Gap and Ormiston Gorge.

ACTIVITIES
Bushwalking
There are many excellent bushwalking tracks in the ranges. Anyone attempting an overnight walk should register with the **Overnight Walker Registration Scheme** (☎ 1300 650 730).

TOURS
Emu Run (☎ 08-8953 7057; www.emurun.com.au) does full-day trips from Alice Springs to the West MacDonnell Ranges (adult/child $100/50) among its comprehensive tours of the region.

Larapinta Trail
Larapinta Trail is a 12-stage, 242km track of varying degrees of difficulty along the backbone of the West MacDonnells, stretching from the Telegraph Station in Alice Springs to Mt Sonder, beyond Glen Helen Gorge. The following sections each take one to two days to navigate and pass many of the attractions in the West MacDonnells:

Section 1 Alice Springs Telegraph Station to Simpsons Gap (24km)
Section 2 Simpsons Gap to Jay Creek (25km)
Section 3 Jay Creek to Standley Chasm (14km)
Section 4 Standley Chasm to Birthday Waterhole (18km)
Section 5 Birthday Waterhole to Hugh Gorge (16km)
Section 6 Hugh Gorge to Ellery Creek (31km)
Section 7 Ellery Creek to Serpentine Gorge (14km)
Section 8 Serpentine Gorge to Ochre Pits (20km)
Section 9 Ochre Pits to Ormiston Gorge (30km)

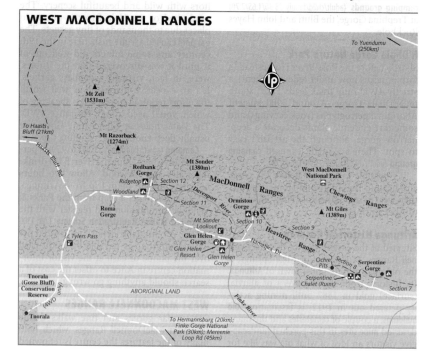

WEST MACDONNELL RANGES

Section 10 Ormiston Gorge to Glen Helen (13km)
Section 11 Glen Helen to Redbank Gorge (29km)
Section 12 Redbank Gorge to Mt Sonder (16km return)

Detailed track notes and maps are available on the website of the **Parks & Wildlife Commission** (www.nt.gov.au/ipe/pwcnt) and at the visitor information centre in Alice Springs (which charges $6.60 for complete set of notes and maps). There's no public transport out to this area, but transfers can be arranged through the **Alice Wanderer Centre Sightseeing** (☎ 1800 722 111, 08-8952 2111; www.alicewanderer .com.au) bus; see the website for the various costings.

Trek Larapinta (☎ 08-8953 2933; www.treklarapinta .com.au) has transport and catering for one-day walks ($135) and overnight walks ($200 for one night, $300 for two days/one night).

Simpsons Gap
Westbound from Alice Springs on Larapinta Dr you soon come to **John Flynn's Grave**. The flying doctor's final resting place is topped by a boulder donated by the Arrernte people. Opposite the car park is the start of the **cyc-**

ling track to Simpsons Gap, a pleasant three-to four-hour return ride.

By road, **Simpsons Gap** (☼ 5am-8pm) is 22km from Alice Springs and 8km off Larapinta Dr. It's a popular picnic spot and has some good walks. This towering gap in the range is the result of 60 million years of effort by a river – a river that rarely runs. There are often rock wallabies in the jumble of rocks either side of the gap. While here, test out the gap's excellent echo capabilities.

The visitor information centre is 1km from the park entrance.

Standley Chasm (Angkerle)
Fifty kilometres west of Alice Springs is **Standley Chasm** (☎ 08-8956 7440; adult/child $6.50/5.50; ☼ 8am-6pm), probably the most spectacular gap in the area. This narrow chasm slices neatly through the rock and is bordered by tall cliffs that burn red in the noon-day sun, which is when most camera-toting tourists arrive; early or late in the day it is much more peaceful. The rocky path into the gorge (15 minutes) follows a creek bed lined with ghost gums and cycads. You can continue to

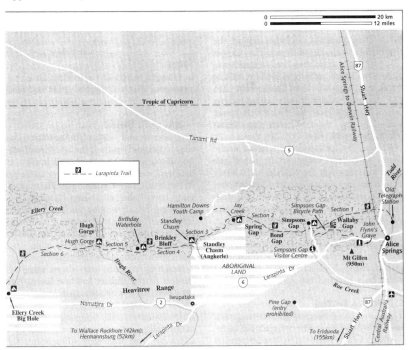

a second chasm (one hour return). There's a kiosk, picnic facilities and toilets.

Namatjira Drive

Not far beyond Standley Chasm you can choose the northwesterly Namatjira Dr or the more southerly Larapinta Dr. West along Namatjira Dr is another series of gorges and gaps in the range. **Ellery Creek Big Hole** is 91km from Alice Springs and has a large permanent water hole – a great (and popular) place for a swim on a hot day, but the usually shaded water is freezing. Thirteen kilometres further on is narrow **Serpentine Gorge**, which has a water hole at the entrance (no swimming) and a great lookout at the end of a short steep track.

The **Ochre Pits** line a dry creek bed 11km west of Serpentine and were a source of paints for Aboriginal people. The various coloured ochres – mainly yellow, white and red-brown – are weathered limestone, with iron oxide stains creating the colouring.

The car park for the large, rugged **Ormiston Gorge** is 24km beyond the ochre pits. It's the most impressive chasm in the West MacDonnells and well worth a couple of hours. There's a water hole and the gorge curls around to the enclosed **Ormiston Pound**. When the pound's water holes dry up, the fish burrow into the sand, going into a sort of suspended animation and reappearing after rain. There are some excellent **walking tracks**, including the **Ghost Gum Lookout** path (20 minutes), which affords brilliant views down the gorge, and the **Pound Walk** (three to four hours, 7.5km). There's also a **visitor information centre** (☎ 08-8956 7799).

About 2km further is the turn-off to the scenic **Glen Helen Gorge**, where the Finke River cuts through the MacDonnells. Only 1km past Glen Helen is a good **lookout** over Mt Sonder, which was a popular painting subject for Albert Namatjira – sunrise and sunset are particularly impressive.

The road is gravel and often rough beyond this point, but if you continue northwest for 25km you'll reach the multihued, cathedral-like **Redbank Gorge**, a permanent water hole 161km from Alice Springs.

SLEEPING & EATING

There are basic **camping grounds** (adult/child/family $3.30/1.65/7.70) at Ellery Creek Big Hole, Redbank Gorge and 6km west of Serpentine

Gorge at Serpentine Chalet (a 4WD or high-clearance 2WD vehicle is recommended to reach the chalet). The **camping area** (adult, child/family $6.60/3.30/15.40) at Ormiston Gorge has good facilities, including a small **kiosk** (☯ 10am-4pm Mon-Sat). All fees are payable to an honesty box.

At **Glen Helen Resort** (☎ 08-8956 7489; res@glen helen.com.au; Namatjira Dr; powered/unpowered shady sites per 2 people $23/20, dm/d from $20/150, meals $7-32 ☯ lunch & dinner; ☒), there's been a homestead on this superb site, with the sheer walls of the gorge as a spectacular backdrop, since 1905 – the current building dates mainly from the 1980s. This comfortable, remote retreat has a restaurant-bar serving à la carte meals or BBQ packs that you can cook yourself. Also on offer are helicopter flights (from $40).

SOUTH OF ALICE SPRINGS

You can make some interesting diversions off the road south from Alice Springs. There are also attractions to the east of the Stuart Hwy, but to visit most of these you will require a 4WD.

Tours

Emu Run (☎ 08-8953 7057; www.emurun.com.au) has a day tour that visits Palm Valley and Hermannsburg (adult/child $100/50).

LARAPINTA DRIVE

The spectacular James Ranges form an east–west band south of the West MacDonnell Ranges. While not as well known as the MacDonnells, the ranges contain some of the centre's best attractions: Hermannsburg, Palm Valley and Kings Canyon.

Taking the alternative road to the south from Standley Chasm, Larapinta Dr crosses the Hugh River before reaching the **Wallace Rockhole** turn-off, 18km off the main road and 109km from Alice Springs.

You'll be virtually guaranteed some seclusion at the **Wallace Rockhole Tourist Park** (☎ 08-8956 7993; www.wallacerockholetours.com.au; powered & unpowered sites per 2 people $20, cabins $100; ☒), owned by the Arrernte Aboriginal community and situated at the end of a 18km dirt road branching off Larapinta Dr.

It conducts an excellent rock-art tour ($9/5 per adult/child) and sells locally made artwork and ceramics.

Back on Larapinta Dr, shortly before Hermannsburg, is the **Namatjira Monument**. Albert Namatjira, the Aboriginal artist who made the stunning purple, blue and orange hues of this region famous in his watercolours, lived at the Hermannsburg Mission. Namatjira supported many in his community with the income from his work. In 1957, he was the first Aboriginal person to be granted Australian citizenship. Due to this, he was permitted to buy alcohol at a time when it was illegal for Aboriginal people to do so. Remaining true to his kinship responsibilities, he broke nonindigenous laws and was jailed for six months in 1958 for supplying alcohol to his community. He died the following year, aged only 57.

Hermannsburg
☎ 08 / pop 460

Only 8km beyond the Namatjira Monument you reach the Hermannsburg Aboriginal settlement, 125km from Alice Springs. Although the town is restricted Aboriginal land, permits are not required to visit the historic precinct and town shop.

The **Hermannsburg Mission** was established by German Lutheran missionaries in 1872 and operated for more than 100 years. The complex, on land that was returned to the Aranda people, includes a museum and a

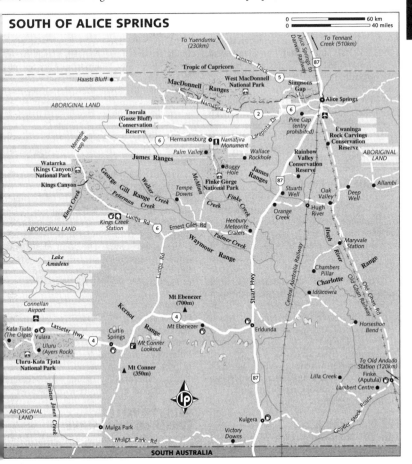

SOUTH OF ALICE SPRINGS

gallery with some Albert Namatjira originals. Entry tickets (adult/child/family $5/4/14) are sold at the **Kata-Anga Tea Rooms** (☎ 8956 7402; meals $5-9; ☒ 9am-4pm Mar-Nov, 9am-4pm Wed-Sun Dec–mid-Dec & mid-Jan-Feb), which serves Devonshire teas and a delightful apple strudel. On sale at the tea rooms are a range of paintings and prints, plus distinctive ceramic works by the **Hermannsburg Potters**, a collective of Aranda artists.

Finke Gorge National Park

From Hermannsburg, a 4WD track follows the Finke River 12km south to the Finke Gorge National Park. **Palm Valley**, famous for the rare, stately central Australian red cabbage palm *(Livistona mariae)*, is the most popular attraction. The main gorge has high red cliffs, majestic river red gums and plenty of sand, tailor-made for beautiful short bushwalks. There's a **rangers station** (☎ 08-8956 7401), and a shady **camping ground** (adult/child/family $6.60/3.30/16) has a serene setting opposite red sandstone ridges and has hot showers and flush toilets.

A 4WD vehicle is essential to bump along the sandy Finke River bed and rocky access road. If you're up for some serious 4WDing, a rough track meanders through the picturesque Finke Gorge to **Boggy Hole**, about 2½ hours from Hermannsburg.

Mereenie Loop Road

From Hermannsburg, you can continue west to the Areyonga turn-off (no visitors) and then take the Mereenie Loop Rd to **Kings Canyon**. This dirt road is suitable for robust conventional vehicles and is a scenic way of reaching Kings Canyon. Motorcycles and bicycles are not allowed.

To travel the loop road you need a Central Land Council permit, as it passes through Aboriginal land. The permit includes the informative *Mereenie Tour Pass* booklet, which details the local Aboriginal culture and has a route map. The permits ($2.20) are issued on the spot (usually only on the day of travel) at the visitor information centre in Alice Springs, and from Glen Helen Homestead, Kings Canyon Resort reception and Hermannsburg service station.

THE OLD GHAN ROAD

The 'Old South Rd', which runs close to the old *Ghan* railway line, is pretty rough and may require a 4WD after rain. It's only 39km from Alice Springs to **Ewaninga**, where prehistoric Aboriginal petroglyphs are carved into sandstone. The rock carvings found here and at N'Dhala Gorge (p861) are thought to have been made by Aboriginal tribes who lived here before those currently in the centre.

The eerie, sandstone **Chambers Pillar**, southwest of Maryvale Station, rises 50m above its surrounding plain and is carved with the names and visit dates of early explorers – and, unfortunately, some much less worthy modern-day graffitists. To the Aboriginal people of the area, Chambers Pillar is the remains of Itirkawara, a powerful gecko ancestor. It's 160km from Alice Springs and a 4WD is required for the last 44km from the turn-off at Maryvale Station. There's a basic **camping ground** (adult/child/family $3.30/1.65/7.70).

Back on the main track south, you eventually arrive at **Finke (Aputula)**, a small Aboriginal community 230km from Alice Springs. When the old *Ghan* was running, Finke was a thriving little town; these days it seems to have drifted into a permanent torpor, except when the **Finke Desert Race** is staged (p853). Fuel is sold at the basic **Aputula Store** (☎ 08-8956 0968; ☒ 9am-noon & 2-4pm Mon-Fri, 9am-noon Sat), which is also the outlet for the **Aputula Art Centre**.

From Finke, you can turn west along the Goyder Stock Route to join the Stuart Hwy at Kulgera (150km), or east to Old Andado station on the edge of the Simpson Desert (120km). Just 21km west of Finke, and 12km north of the road along a signposted track, is the **Lambert Centre**. The point marks Australia's geographical centre and features a 5m-high replica of the flagpole found on top of Parliament House in Canberra.

Tours

Outback Experience (☎ 08-8953 2666; www.outback experience.com.au) is currently the only operator with a day tour ($150) taking in Chambers Pillar, Ewaninga and Rainbow Valley (see below). This highly recommended excursion is chaperoned by a guide with a detailed knowledge of, and affinity with, the area.

RAINBOW VALLEY CONSERVATION RESERVE

This series of free-standing sandstone bluffs and cliffs, in shades ranging from cream to ed, is one of central Australia's more extraordinary sights. A marked walking trail takes you past claypans and in between the multihued outcrops to the aptly named Mushroom Rock. Rainbow Valley is most striking in the early morning or at sunset, but the area's stupefying silence will overwhelm you whatever time of day you are here.

The park lies 22km off the Stuart Hwy along a 4WD track that's 75km south of Alice Springs. It has a basic **camping ground** (adult/child/family $3.30/1.65/7.70).

STUARTS WELL

Climb onto a camel at Stuarts Well, 90km south of Alice Springs. At **Camel Australia** (☎ 08-8956 0925; www.camels-australia.com.au) you can take a short ride around the yard for $5/4 per adult/child, a 30-minute jaunt for $25/20 or a full day for $150/110. Multiday safaris through the gaps and gorges of the James Ranges can also be arranged.

Jim's Place (☎ 08-8956 0808; fax 8956 0809; powered/unpowered sites per 2 people $17/14, bunkhouse $20-30, s $70, d $55-85) is run by well-known outback identity Jim Cotterill, who along with his father opened up Kings Canyon to tourism. Ask about Dinky the singing dingo.

ERNEST GILES ROAD

The Ernest Giles Rd heads off to the west of the Stuart Hwy about 140km south of Alice. This shorter but rougher route to Kings Canyon is often impassable after heavy rain and is not recommended for conventional vehicles. The section along the Luritja Rd to Kings Canyon is sealed.

Henbury Meteorite Craters

Eleven kilometres west of the Stuart Hwy, a dusty corrugated track leads 5km off Ernest Giles Rd to this cluster of 12 small craters, formed after a meteor fell to earth 4700 years ago. The largest of the craters is 180m wide and 15m deep.

There are no longer any fragments of the meteorites at the site, but the Museum of Central Australia in Alice Springs (p849) has a small chunk that weighs 46.5kg.

There are some very basic, exposed **camp sites** (adult/child/family $3.30/1.65/7.70), which verge on unbearable when the flies are out in force.

WATARRKA (KINGS CANYON) NATIONAL PARK

Continuing west along Ernest Giles Rd, or detouring from the Lasseter Hwy, brings you to the Watarrka (Kings Canyon) National Park, which includes one of the most spectacular sights in central Australia – the sheer, 100m-high walls of **Kings Canyon**.

There's a **rangers station** (☎ 08-8956 7488) 22km east of the canyon.

The **Kings Creek Walk** (2km return) follows the rocky creek bed to a raised platform with amphitheatre-like views of the towering canyon rim. Walkers are rewarded with awesome views on the **Kings Canyon Rim Walk** (four hours, 6km loop, strenuous). After a steep climb up a 100m-high cliff face, the walk skirts the canyon's rim and then enters the **Garden of Eden** – do the short walk to the rockpool at the end of this stunning gorge, which is decorated with prehistoric cycads. The next section of the walk winds through a maze of giant eroded domes. Watch your step here as the cliffs are unfenced and the wind can be strong. A kiosk in the car park sells drinks and ice cream. A guided walk ($2) around the canyon rim departs from the car park at 6.30am weekdays; make a booking for the walk at Kings Canyon Resort reception.

Off Luritja Rd, between Kings Creek Station and the turn-off to the canyon, is the **Kathleen Springs Walk** (1½ hours, 2.6km return), a pleasant wheelchair-accessible track leading to a water hole at the head of a gorge.

The **Giles Track** (overnight, 22km one way, easy) is a marked track that meanders along the George Gill Range between the canyon and Kathleen Springs. You can register for the walk with the **Overnight Walker Registration Scheme** (☎ 1300 650 730).

You can reach Kings Canyon from Alice Springs via the unsealed Mereenie Loop Rd (see opposite), a drive of 325km. This road is rough but usually passable with conventional vehicles when it's dry.

Tours

For information about tours that combine Kings Canyon and Uluru, see p869.

AAT Kings (☎ 08-8956 2171; www.aatkings.com) Runs guided walks of the canyon rim that depart from the Mobil Service Station at Kings Canyon Resort and cost $45/22 per adult/child.

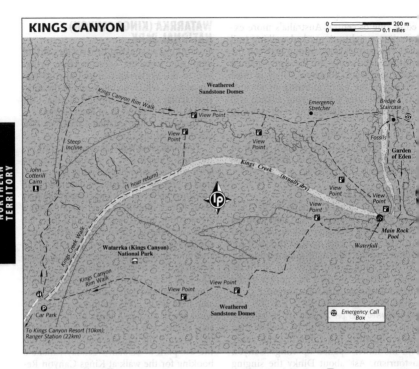

KINGS CANYON

Weathered Sandstone Domes
Kings Canyon Rim Walk
View Point
Emergency Stretcher
Bridge & Staircase
Steep Incline
View Point
View Point
Fossils
Garden of Eden
John Cotterill Cairn
(1 hour return)
Kings Creek (usually dry)
View Point
View Point
View Point
View Point
Waterfall
Main Rock Pool
Watarrka (Kings Canyon) National Park
Kings Canyon Rim Walk
View Point
View Point
Weathered Sandstone Domes
Emergency Call Box
Car Park
To Kings Canyon Resort (10km); Ranger Station (22km)

Kings Creek Station (☎ 08-8956 7474) Runs scenic flights over Kings Canyon starting from $60.

Professional Helicopter Services (☎ 08-8956 7873) Offers scenic helicopter flights.

Sleeping & Eating

Kings Canyon Resort (☎ 1300 139 889, 08-8956 7442; www.voyages.com.au; Luritja Rd; powered/unpowered sites per 2 people $32/28, dm from $45, d $120-300;) This resort is spread out on bushy terrain 10km west of the canyon. Dorms have four beds and budget rooms have shared facilities. Comfy but unexceptional hotel units fan out behind the reception building. The grassy camping ground has lots of shade. Fuel is available and there's an ATM at reception.

The resort has several eating options. The **Desert Oaks Cafe** (meals $8-13; lunch;) serves decent light meals such as focaccias, salads and quiche, while **Carmichael's** (breakfast $18-23, dinner $45; breakfast & dinner) does an evening seafood buffet. The **Outback BBQ** (mains $15-30; dinner) is filled with the aroma of pizza and meaty grills, and you can listen to fair dinkum Aussie singers here – alternatively, head to the resort's George Gill Bar.

Kings Creek Station (☎ 08-8956 7474; www.king creekstation.com.au; Luritja Rd; unpowered sites per adul child $12/6.50, with power extra $3.10, cabins per adult/chil $55/34;) Located outside the nationa park's eastern boundary, 35km from th canyon, this station has pristine camp site among desert oaks. Tiny 'cabins' have can vas walls and two single bunks, and can ge uncomfortably hot; the price includes baco and eggs in the morning. There's also came rides (one-hour ride $50), quad bikes (one hour ride $70) and, from March to Octobe a stock camp show with animal handlin and whip cracking ($20). There's fuel, ic and limited stores at the **shop** (7am-7pm).

LASSETER HIGHWAY

The Lasseter Hwy connects the Stuart Hw with Uluru–Kata Tjuta National Park, 244kr to the west from the turn-off at Erldund. There are a couple of roadhouses along th way, plus a lookout for **Mt Conner** (350m), large mesa (table-top mountain) that som eager souls mistake for Uluru. Local Abor ginal people know it as Artula, home of th ice men.

Curtin Springs Station (☎ 08-8956 2906; curtinas@ ozemail.com.au; Lasseter Hwy; powered/unpowered sites $11/free, s/d $70, without bathroom $35/45, f $110, meals $6-20; ☺ breakfast, lunch & dinner; ☒) is the last stop before Yulara, and if you're on a budget it's not a bad alternative to staying at the expensive Ayers Rock resort. The un-powered site price is fixed regardless of how many people huddle onto it, and the family room can squeeze in six people. There's a bar and restaurant, camel rides, and cattle station tours that head out to Mt Conner. Showers cost $1.

ULURU–KATA TJUTA NATIONAL PARK

This entire area is of deep cultural signifi-cance to the traditional owners, the Pitjantja-tjara and Yankunytjatjara Aboriginal peoples (who refer to themselves as Anangu). To them, the Ayers Rock area is known as Uluru and the Olgas as Kata Tjuta. The national park is leased to Environment Australia (the federal government's national parks body), who administers it in conjunction with the traditional owners.

Unfortunately, most of the group tours squeeze in a quick afternoon climb of Uluru, photos at sunset, a morning at the Olgas the next day and then off – 24 hours in total, if you're lucky. But considering the effort it takes to get out here and the walks and other activities you can do, you should ideally plan on spending several days in the Uluru–Kata Tjuta area. The ever-changing appearance of the Rock itself, be it glow-ing enigmatically in the twilight or streaked with waterfalls after a stormy downpour, is another reason to linger.

Information

Uluru–Kata Tjuta National Park Cultural Centre (☎ 08-8956 3138; ☺ 7am-5.30pm Apr-Oct, 7am-6pm Nov-Mar) is 1km before Uluru on the road from Yulara. Some tour buses don't stop here but hightail it straight to Uluru, which is a shame because the centre is an excel-lent resource for anyone who wants to un-derstand the area better. The two inspiring buildings represent the ancestral figures of Kuniya and Liru and contained within them are two main display areas, both with

multilingual information. The Tjukurpa display features Anangu art and *tjukurpa* (Aboriginal law, religion and custom), while the Nintiringkupai display focuses on the history and management of the na-tional park.

The cultural centre also encompasses the Aborigine-owned **Maruku Art & Crafts** (☎ 08-8956 2558; ☺ 8.30am-5.30pm) and **Walkatjara Art Centre** (☎ 08-8956 2537; ☺ 8.30am-5.30pm), where you can see artists from the Maruku and Mutitjulu communities at work. Everything is created in the surrounding desert region and certificates of authenticity are issued with most artworks. Since you're buying dir-ectly from the artists, these are good places to buy souvenirs such as 'tjanpi' baskets – the tjanpi is a type of lizard that lives in spinifex, the hardy plant from which the baskets are woven.

Ininti Cafe & Souvenirs (☎ 08-8956 2214; meals $3.50-10; ☺ 7am-5.15pm) sells tourist trinkets (think emu-emblazoned ties) and a small range of books on Aboriginal culture and the park's flora and fauna. The attached café serves ice cream, pies and light meals like lasagne.

The **Liru Walk** (45 minutes, 2km) leads from the Cultural Centre to the start of the Base and Mala Walks.

There's also a visitor information centre in Yulara (see p873).

ENTRY FEES

The park is open from 30 minutes before sunrise to sunset. Three-day entry permits to the national park ($25/free per adult/child under 16) are available from the park entry station on the road from Yulara to Uluru.

Tours

Several of the outfits mentioned here – AAT Kings, Anangu Tours, Discovery Eco-tours, Ayers Rock Scenic Flights, Ayers Rock Helicopters and Professional Helicop-ter Services – have counters at the Tour & Information Centre in Yulara (see p873).

AAT KINGS

Major operator **AAT Kings** (☎ 8956 2171; www .aatkings.com) runs a range of daily coach tours. Generally, it can work out cheaper to use the Uluru Express (see p876) or to hire a car between a group.

NORTHERN TERRITORY

The Rock Pass ($220/110 per adult/child) is valid for three days and includes a guided base tour, sunset, climb, sunrise and Cultural Centre visit, plus park entry fee. The Rock Super Pass ($270/135) also includes a Valley of the Winds walk (at Kata Tjuta) and a BBQ.

All of these activities are also available in differing forms: base tour ($45/23), sunrise tour ($45/22), sunset ($36/18), sunrise and base ($75/38), sunrise and climb and base ($100/50). These prices don't include the park entry fee.

For Kata Tjuta viewing, the Explorer Pass ($165/85) includes a base tour, Uluru sunrise and sunset, and the Valley of the Winds walk.

ANANGU TOURS
Owned and operated by Anangu from the Mutitjulu community, **Anangu Tours** (☎ 08-8956 2123; www.ananangutours.com.au) offers a range of tours led by an Anangu guide and gives an insight into the land through Anangu eyes.

The daily, five-hour Aboriginal Uluru Tour ($110/75 per adult/child) starts with sunrise over Uluru and breakfast at the Cultural Centre, followed by a guided stroll down the Liru Walk (including demonstrations of bush skills such as spear-throwing).

The Kuniya Sunset Tour ($85/60, 4½ hours) departs at 2.30pm (3.30pm between November and February) and includes a visit to Mutitjulu Waterhole and the Cultural Centre, finishing with sunset viewing of Uluru.

Both trips can be combined over 24 hours with an Anangu Culture Pass ($175/120). Self-drive options are also available for $55/27. You can join an Aboriginal guide at 8.30am (7.30am from November to January and 8am from February and October) for the morning walk or at 3.30pm (4.30pm from November to February) for the Kuniya tour.

DISCOVERY ECOTOURS
There are several possibilities offered by **Discovery Ecotours** (☎ 8956 2563; www.ecotours.com.au), including a five-hour Uluru circumambulation and breakfast for $110/85 per adult/child; Spirit of Uluru is a four-hour, vehicle-based version for the same price. The Kata Tjuta & Dunes Tour includes a walk into Olga Gorge and sunset at Kata

Tjuta for $85/65. The company also runs tour to Mt Conner (see Lasseter Highway p868) with dinner at the Curtin Spring Homestead ($210/160).

FROM ALICE SPRINGS
All-inclusive camping tours taking in Ulur and Kings Canyon start at $350/460 fo two/three days; the price climbs when othe types of accommodation are involved.

Compare each company's vehicles, grou size and types of meals before deciding:
Adventure Tours Australia (☎ 8309 2277; www.adventuretours.com.au)
Mulga's Adventures (☎ 1800 359 089, 08-8952 1545 www.mulgas.com.au)
Sahara Outback Tours (☎ 08-8953 0881; www.saharatours.com.au)

MOTORCYCLE TOURS
If you like the wind in your hair (or face) then **Uluru Motorcycle Tours** (☎ 08-8956 2019) ca accommodate you with trips to Uluru an Kata Tjuta on the back of a motorcycle. A trip to Uluru/Kata Tjuta at sunrise or other wise is $145. Half-day rental of a late-mode bike costs $435.

SCENIC FLIGHTS
While the enjoyment of those on the groun may be diminished by the constant buzz c light aircraft and helicopters overhead, fo those actually up there it's an unforgettabl experience. There are no child concession on any helicopter flights, which make then an expensive proposition for families.
Ayers Rock Helicopters (☎ 08-8956 2077) A 15-minute buzz of Uluru costs $100; to include Kata Tjuta costs $180.
Ayers Rock Scenic Flights (☎ 08-8956 2345) Prices start from $135 for a 40-minute flight over Uluru and Kata Tjuta; it costs $310 for a two-hour flight that also takes in Lake Amadeus and Kings Canyon.
Professional Helicopter Services (PHS; ☎ 08-8956 2003) Charges $105 for its Uluru flight and $205 for its 30-minute Uluru and Kata Tjuta flight.

DINING TOURS
Sounds of Silence (☎ 8957 7448; adult/child $130/65 runs a four-hour dinner tour that transport you 7km from town for a unique desert ex perience. You'll watch the sun set on Ulur and Kata Tjuta while sipping champagne listening to the didgeridoo and munching canapés, then chew dinner under the stars

bookings are essential. If you're more of a morning person, try the similarly styled, 2½-hour **Sunrise Breakfast** (☎ 1300 134 044; adult/child $95/50).

ULURU (AYERS ROCK)

Nothing in Australia is as readily identifiable as Uluru (Ayers Rock). Australia's favourite postcard image is 3.6km long and rises a towering 348m from the surrounding sandy scrubland (867m above sea level). If that's not impressive enough, it's believed that two-thirds of the rock lies beneath the sand. If your first sight of Uluru is during the afternoon, it appears as an ochre-brown colour, scored and pitted by dark shadows. As the sun sets, it illuminates the rock in burnished orange, then a series of deeper and darker reds before it fades into charcoal. A performance in reverse, with marginally fewer spectators, is given at dawn. Don't assume, however, that a distant glimpse of this geological marvel will suffice – a close-up, extended viewing of the rock's contours is a must.

Uluru is often called the world's biggest monolith, but it's only the runner up – first prize goes to Mt Augustus (Burringurrah) in WA, which is 2½ times the size of Uluru.

Activities

ULURU WALKS

There are walking tracks around Uluru, and guided walks explain into the area's plants,

---

CLIMBING ULURU

Many visitors consider climbing Uluru to be a highlight – almost a rite of passage – of a trip to the centre. For the Anangu, the path up the side of the rock is part of the route taken by ancestral Mala men on their arrival at Uluru, and as such has great spiritual significance. The Anangu are the custodians of these lands and take responsibility for the safety of visitors. Any injuries or deaths that occur on the rock (and they do occur) are a source of distress to them. For these reasons, the Anangu don't climb and they ask that you don't either. If you compare climbing Uluru to, say, clambering over the altar in Notre Dame Cathedral or striding through a mosque during prayer, it's not hard to understand the Anangu perspective – it's a question of respect.

This respect should also be extended to the stones littering the ground around the rock. Those who pocket a stony souvenir at Uluru, which is essentially stealing from a protected site, can be charged with a criminal offence and fined up to $5500.

---

wildlife, geology and mythology. All the walks are flat and are suitable for wheelchairs. Several areas of the utmost spiritual significance to Anangu are off-limits to visitors – these are marked with fences and signs. Photography of sacred sites is also forbidden.

ULURU (AYERS ROCK)

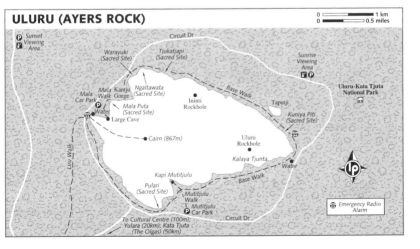

The *Insight into Uluru* brochure ($1), available at the Cultural Centre, details self-guided walks.

Base Walk (10km)

You can spend three to four hours walking around the base of Uluru at a leisurely pace (if you're pushed for time, you can do it in two hours), dwelling on the monolith's caves, paintings, sandstone folds and geological abrasions along the way. As most people are too rushed (and too busy tackling the climb) to do this walk, you'll often find a bit of solitude.

Mala Walk (2km return)

This walk starts from the base of the climbing point and takes about one hour to complete at an easy pace. There are interpretive signs explaining the *tjukurpa* of the Mala (hare-wallaby people), which is of great importance to the Anangu. A ranger-guided walk (free) along this route departs at 10am (8am from October to April) from the car park. It's not necessary to book ahead; just turn up.

Mutitjulu Walk (1km return)

Mutitjulu is a permanent water hole a short walk from the car park on the southern side of Uluru. The *tjukurpa* tells of the clash between two ancestral snakes: Kuniya and Liru. You'll learn more about the Kuniya *tjukurpa* and the food and medicinal plants found here with Anangu Tours (p870).

THE CLIMB

If you insist on climbing (see the Climbing Uluru boxed text, p871), take note of the warnings. It's a demanding 1.6km round trip that takes about two hours return to the memorial cairn, allowing for a good rest at the top, and there have been numerous deaths from falls and heart attacks. Be sun smart, take plenty of water and be prepared to turn around if it all gets too much. The first part of the walk is the steepest and most arduous, and there's a chain to cling to. The climb is often closed (sometimes at short notice) due to strong winds, rain, mist and Anangu business, and on days forecast to reach 36°C or more.

KATA TJUTA (THE OLGAS)

About 30km west of Uluru, you'll find Kata Tjuta (the Olgas), a striking collection of rounded monoliths. Many visitors find them just as captivating as their prominent neighbour. The tallest rock, **Mt Olga** (546m; 1066m above sea level) is approximately 200m higher than Uluru. Kata Tjuta means 'many heads' and is of great *tjukurpa* significance, so climbing on the domed rocks is definitely not on.

The main walking track here is the **Valley of the Winds**, a 7.4km loop trail (two to four hours) that winds through beautiful gorges and yields wonderful views of surreal boulders. It's not particularly arduous, but take plenty of water and sun protection. Starting this walk at first light may

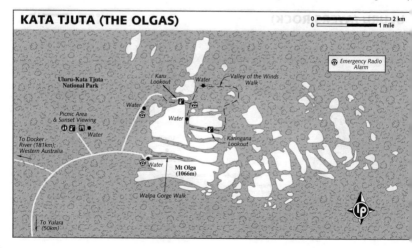

KATA TJUTA (THE OLGAS)

reward you with solitude, enabling you to appreciate the sounds of the wind and bird calls carried up the valley. The short (2.6km return) signposted track beneath towering rock walls into the pretty **Walpa Gorge** is especially beautiful in the afternoon when sunlight floods the gorge.

There's a picnic and sunset-viewing area with toilet facilities just off the access road a few kilometres west of the base of Kata Tjuta. Like Uluru, the Olgas are at their glorious, blood-red best at sunset.

HEADING WEST

A lonely sign at the western end of the Kata Tjuta access road points out that there's a hell of a lot of nothing if you travel west – although, if suitably equipped, you can travel all the way to Kalgoorlie and on to Perth in WA. It's 180km to Docker River, an Aboriginal settlement on the road west, and about 1500km to Kalgoorlie. You need a permit from the Central Land Council for this trip – for more information, see the Great Central Road section (p1066).

YULARA (AYERS ROCK RESORT)

☎ 08 / pop 2530 (including Mutitjulu)

Yulara is the service village for the Uluru–Kata Tjuta National Park and has effectively turned one of the world's least hospitable regions into an easy and comfortable place to visit. Lying just outside the national park, 20km from Uluru and 53km from Kata Tjuta, the complex is the main – though expensive and bland – base for exploring the area's renowned attractions. Opened in 1984, the village was designed to blend in with the local environment and is a low-rise affair nestled between the dunes. Yulara supplies the only accommodation, food outlets and other services available in the region; demand certainly keeps pace with supply and you'll have little choice but to part with lots of money to stay in anything other than a tent here.

Orientation & Information

Yulara is built around the vaguely circular Yulara Dr. Heading clockwise along it, everything is on your left, starting with the Desert Gardens Hotel, visitor information centre and Emu Walk Apartments, followed by the resort shopping centre, which is built around an outdoor eating area and contains most of the town's facilities (including a photo shop). Further around the ring road is Sails in the Desert hotel, a medical centre and the Royal Flying Doctor Service, a police station, camping ground, petrol station and the Outback Pioneer Hotel & Lodge. The useful *Welcome to Ayers Rock Resort* flier is available at the visitor information centre and at hotel desks.

ANZ (☎ 13 13 14) Has two ATMs in town.

Post office (☎ 8956 2288; Resort Shopping Centre; ✆ 9am-6pm Mon-Fri, 10am-2pm Sat & Sun) An agent for the Commonwealth and National Australia banks.

Tour & Information Centre (☎ 8957 7324; Resort Shopping Centre; ✆ 8am-8.30pm) Most tour operators and car-hire firms have desks at this centre. The central desk provides general information about the park and takes bookings for other tours.

Visitor information centre (☎ 8957 7377; ✆ 9am-5.30pm) Contains displays on the geography, wildlife and history of the region, and sells books and regional maps. Information is also available at the national park's Cultural Centre.

There are coin-operated Internet kiosks in the Tour & Information Centre and at all accommodation.

Sights & Activities

Frontier Camel Tours (☎ 8956 2444; www.cameltours .com.au) has a depot just south of Yulara with a small museum and camel rides. A popular ride is the 'Camel to Sunrise', a 2½-hour tour that includes a saunter through the dunes before sunrise, billy tea and a chat about camels for $95; equally popular is the sunset equivalent, which costs the same. There's also the 'Camel Express', a 1½-hour excursion (including a 45-minute ride) departing at noon and costing $60.

Stroll through **Mulgara Gallery** (found off reception, in the Sails in the Desert hotel), where quality handmade Australian arts and crafts are displayed. Each month brings a new artist in residence.

The **Night Sky Show** (☎ 8956 2563; adult/child/ family $32/24/95) takes an informative look at Anangu and Greek astrological legends, with views of the startlingly clear outback night sky through telescopes and binoculars. Trips in English are at 8.30pm, with a further session at 7.30pm from May to August and 10.15pm from September to April. Prices also include pick-up from your accommodation. Bookings (essential) can be made through Discovery Ecotours (p870), which has a counter in the Tour & Information Centre.

Bike hire is available at **Ayers Rock Resort Campground** (☎ 8957 7001) for $7/20 per hour/day; a $200 deposit is required.

Tours

Most local operators have desks at the **Tour & Information Centre** (☎ 8957 7324; Resort Shopping Centre; ⏱ 8am-8.30pm) in Yulara.

See p869 for details of individual tour operators.

Sleeping

If there's anything to put a dampener on your visit to Uluru, it's the high cost of accommodation and eating at Yulara. But you'll just have to lie back and think of England – unless, that is, you have your own transport and are tempted by the free camping and relatively inexpensive rooms at Curtin Springs Station (p868).

Bookings for accommodation (other than for the camping ground) are made through **central reservations** (☎ 1300 139 889; www.voyages

.com.au). Substantial discounts are usually offered if you stay for three nights or more and you can also save a reasonable amount through Internet sites offering discount accommodation. Book ahead during the high season.

Outback Pioneer Hotel & Lodge (dm $33-40, d $170-400; 🍽 🖵 🏊) Supplies the full gamut of accommodation, from four-bed mixed sex dorms and 20-bed unisex dorms to budget rooms (budget for Yulara, that is) with/without bathroom, and standard hotel rooms. Rooms are a decent size and pricier ones are equipped with a TV and fridge.

Lost Camel Hotel (d from $390; 🍽 🖵 🏊) The funky (though small) rooms available here come with very comfy beds and stereos – TV addicts, however, will have to head for the plasma screen at reception. A fine courtyard pool and a bar inspire you to do very little.

Emu Walk Apartments (1-/2-bedroom apt from $420/520; 🍽) Comfort and uniformity are the chief characteristics of these modern apartments, each with a lounge room (with TV) and a well-equipped kitchen. The one-

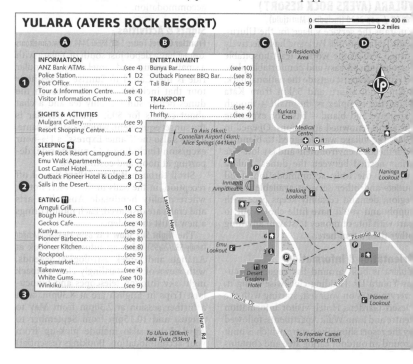

YULARA (AYERS ROCK RESORT)

0 ——— 400 m
0 ——— 0.2 miles

INFORMATION
ANZ Bank ATMs...................(see 4)
Police Station...........................1 D2
Post Office...............................2 C2
Tour & Information Centre......(see 4)
Visitor Information Centre........3 C3

SIGHTS & ACTIVITIES
Mulgara Gallery.....................(see 9)
Resort Shopping Centre...........4 C2

SLEEPING 🛏
Ayers Rock Resort Campground..5 D1
Emu Walk Apartments...............6 C2
Lost Camel Hotel......................7 C2
Outback Pioneer Hotel & Lodge..8 D3
Sails in the Desert....................9 C2

EATING 🍴
Arnguli Grill..........................10 C3
Bough House.........................(see 8)
Geckos Cafe..........................(see 4)
Kuniya...................................(see 9)
Pioneer Barbecue...................(see 8)
Pioneer Kitchen.....................(see 8)
Rockpool................................(see 9)
Supermarket..........................(see 4)
Takeaway...............................(see 4)
White Gums...........................(see 10)
Winikku.................................(see 9)

ENTERTAINMENT
Bunya Bar.............................(see 10)
Outback Pioneer BBQ Bar........(see 8)
Tali Bar................................(see 9)

TRANSPORT
Hertz....................................(see 4)
Thrifty..................................(see 4)

To Residential Area

Kurkara Cres
Medical Centre
Yulara Dr
Kiosk
Naninga Lookout

To Avis (4km); Connellan Airport (4km); Alice Springs (441km)

Inmapiti Amphitheatre
Imalung Lookout

Lasseter Hwy

Emu Lookout

Perentie Rd

Desert Gardens Hotel

Yulara Dr

Pioneer Lookout

To Uluru (20km); Kata Tjuta (53km)

Uluru Rd

To Frontier Camel Tours Depot (1km)

NORTHERN TERRITORY

bedroom apartment accommodates four people, while the two-bedroom version sleeps six. Check in at the Desert Gardens Hotel reception.

Sails in the Desert (d $520, spa $610, ste $920; 🗙 📇 🗩) This luxurious five-star hotel has several restaurants, a piano bar and plenty of sunbathing sites around the pool. Standard rooms are spread over three levels, so request an upper berth if you want a balcony to lean over. The spa rooms have spas on private patios.

Ayers Rock Resort Camp Ground (☎ 8957 7001; camp.ground@ayersrockresort.com.au; powered/unpowered sites per 2 people $27/26, cabins $150; 🗙 📇 🗩) A sprawling camping ground with good facilities, including a kiosk, free BBQs and amenities for disabled travellers. During the peak season, it fills up with dusty campervans, tents and tourists, and the inevitable pre-dawn convoy heading for Uluru can provide an unwanted wake-up call. The cabins (shared facilities) sleep six people and are cramped but OK for groups trying to budget. Unpowered sites cannot be prebooked.

Eating

For information on dining tours, see p870.

Pioneer Barbecue (Outback Pioneer Hotel & Lodge; BBQ $17-25, salads $16; 🕑 dinner) Kangaroo skewers, veggie burgers, steaks and emu sausages are among the meats you can grill yourself at this lively tavern, and the deal includes all the salad you can eat. In the same complex is the **Pioneer Kitchen** (meals $7-9; 🕑 lunch & dinner), doing brisk business in burgers and kiddy meals, and the **Bough House** (breakfast $20-24, dinner $40; 🕑 breakfast & dinner), a family-style place that piles buffet tables high with 'Australiana' foodstuffs.

Geckos Cafe (Resort Shopping Centre; mains $16-28; 🕑 lunch & dinner) No culinary surprises here, just a tried-and-true menu of pizzas, pastas and salads served either in the roomy interior or on the deck outside. It doesn't take bookings so just wander in any time, though beware of large and raucous early-afternoon tour groups. Attached to Geckos is an ice-cream parlour also serving juices and thickshakes.

White Gums (☎ 8957 7888; Desert Gardens Hotel; dinner $45; 🕑 breakfast & dinner) is a pleasant and low-lit restaurant that puts on a substantial evening buffet, including a large selection of salads. Also in the Desert Gardens is **Arnguli Grill** (☎ 8957 7888; mains $27-40; 🕑 lunch & dinner), which has some good à la carte choices but will not satisfy those of the vegetarian persuasion. Reservations are required for both eateries.

The port of call for upmarket dining is Sails in the Desert hotel. **Rockpool** (3 dishes $40, plus dessert $45; 🕑 lunch & dinner) serves tapas-style dishes on the poolside patio. **Winkiku** (☎ 8956 2200; breakfast $18-33, dinner $55; 🕑 breakfast & dinner) is a buffet specialist, with the evening spread dedicated to seafood and a meat-filled carvery; kids under 15 eat for free if accompanied by an adult. Yulara's most sophisticated restaurant, **Kuniya** (☎ 8956 2200; mains $40-50; 🕑 dinner), offers a tour of Australia on a plate, from Bathurst Island barramundi to Tasmanian crayfish; you're required to dress up, so leave the thongs and singlet by the pool. Reservations are required for Winkiku and Kuniya.

Takeaway (☎ 8957 7768; Resort Shopping Centre; meals $4-15; 🕑 breakfast, lunch & dinner) Serves gourmet pies, pre-packaged sandwiches and salads, a range of burgers (including kangaroo and vegetarian versions) and barbecued chook. Apart from self-catering, this is your best bet for an inexpensive meal.

The well-stocked **supermarket** (☎ 8957 7395; Resort Shopping Centre; 🕑 8.30am-9pm) has a salad bar and delicatessen and sells picnic portions, fresh fruit and vegetables, meat and camping supplies.

Entertainment

Outback Pioneer BBQ Bar (Outback Pioneer Hotel & Lodge) Modelled on a big iron shed, this convivial bar is filled with beer-splattered benches and the sounds of Barnesy straining

---

GROG

Please be aware that alcohol (grog) is a problem among some of the local Mutitjulu Aboriginal people living near Uluru. It is a 'dry' community and, at the request of the Aboriginal leaders, the liquor outlet in Yulara has agreed not to sell alcohol to Aboriginal people. For this reason, you may be approached at Yulara by Aboriginal people who want you to buy grog on their behalf. The community leaders appeal to you not to do so.

his voice in his Cold Chisel glory days. It has pool tables, live music nightly (usually solo acoustic gigs) and minimal dress standards – and few other standards for that matter. You can buy takeaway alcohol here from noon to 9pm.

Tali Bar (Sails in the Desert Hotel) The cocktails ($15) at this bar include locally inspired mixtures like 'Desert Oasis', or you can eschew these pretenders for a classic, well-shaken Manhattan. The piano gets a workout most nights from 8pm. Dress up after sunset.

Bunya Bar (Desert Gardens Hotel) This is a rather characterless hotel bar, but it knows the importance of well-chilled beer and the cocktails are several dollars cheaper than at Tali Bar.

Evening entertainment is also provided by the **Night Sky Show** (see p873) and the **Sounds of Silence** (see p870).

Getting There & Away

AIR

Connellan airport is about 6km north from Yulara. **Qantas** (☎ 13 13 13; www.qantas.com.au) has direct flights from Alice Springs (one way from $120), Cairns (from $335), Perth (from $260) and Sydney (from $220). Non-direct flights from the aforementioned cities (detouring through other capitals) are much more expensive.

BUS

Greyhound Australia (☎ 13 14 99; www.greyhound.com .au) has daily services between Alice Springs and Uluru ($75, 5½ hours). Services between Adelaide and Uluru ($250) connect with the bus from Alice Springs at Erldunda.

Australian Pacific Touring (APT; ☎ 1800 891 121; www.aptouring.com.au) does one-way transfers from Alice Springs to Yulara ($110), departing from Alice at 6.30am and arriving at Yulara at noon.

CAR & MOTORCYCLE

The road from the Alice to Yulara is sealed, with regular food and petrol stops along the way. Yulara is 441km from Alice Springs (241km west of Erldunda on the Stuart Hwy), and the whole journey takes about four to five hours.

If you don't have your own vehicle, renting a car in Alice Springs to go to Uluru and back can be expensive – between four people, however, it's cheaper than taking a bus. For details, see Getting There & Away, (p858).

Getting Around

A free shuttle bus meets all flights and drops-off at all accommodation points around the resort.

The resort itself sprawls a bit, but it's not too large to get around on foot. A free shuttle bus runs between all accommodation points, the shopping centre and Frontier Camel Tours depot (when prebooked) every 20 minutes from 10.30am to 6pm and 6.30pm to 12.30am.

Uluru Express (☎ 8956 2152; www.uluruexpress .com.au) falls somewhere between a shuttle bus service and an organised tour. It provides return transport from the resort to Uluru for $35/20 per adult/child (sunrise only $40/20). Morning shuttles to Kata Tjuta cost $50/25; afternoon shuttles include a stop at Uluru for sunset and cost $55/30.

Hiring a car will give you the flexibility to visit the Rock and the Olgas as often and whenever you want. Car-hire companies **Hertz** (☎ 8956 2244) and **Thrifty** (☎ 8956 2030) have counters at the Tour & Information Centre in the resort shopping centre – both also have desks located at the airport, as does **Avis** (☎ 8956 2487). Hertz is usually the cheapest option, with standby rates for small cars starting at around $65 per day, with 100km free.

Western Australia

Ever heard the expression 'bigger than Texas'? It applies here. You could fit Texas into Western Australia (WA) and still have room for New Zealand. There are other large numbers too: 12,000km of magnificent coastline and more species of wildflowers than the rest of the world. Perth has the most poker machine-free pubs in an Australian capital city and more restaurants per head than anywhere else. Western skies blaze with more days of sunshine and certainly more visible stars than most places.

East-coast Australians who have visited speak of the west with a kind of reverence. They tell of wondrous weather and white wine. And surfing (the waves and the menu). They describe incredible natural beauty: a tropical north, ancient rock-art galleries, vast central plains where five broad rivers meet, and a south with giant trees and billion-year-old outcrops of granite. The names are equally pleasing: the Pilbara, Wanna Munna, the Kimberley, Esperance.

Travellers can find themselves traversing infinite roads through forest, mulga scrub or desert. They can lose themselves in leisure or azure water. They can explore the kind of red, sweeping outback that Australia is so famous for – where all that glitters was once gold. They can learn of the oldest culture in the world and how it has been challenged, but never erased, by the newest (in some places in WA, contact with Aboriginal people was as recent as 70 years ago). From the bottom of Southeast Asia to the Southern Ocean 2600km away, there's a lot of space and not many people, but WA is far from empty.

WESTERN AUSTRALIA

HIGHLIGHTS

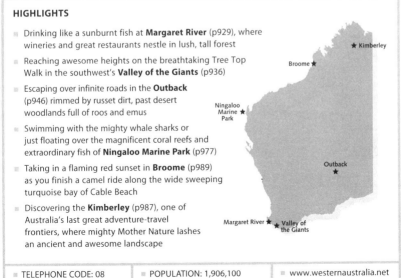

- Drinking like a sunburnt fish at **Margaret River** (p929), where wineries and great restaurants nestle in lush, tall forest

- Reaching awesome heights on the breathtaking Tree Top Walk in the southwest's **Valley of the Giants** (p936)

- Escaping over infinite roads in the **Outback** (p946) rimmed by russet dirt, past desert woodlands full of roos and emus

- Swimming with the mighty whale sharks or just floating over the magnificent coral reefs and extraordinary fish of **Ningaloo Marine Park** (p977)

- Taking in a flaming red sunset in **Broome** (p989) as you finish a camel ride along the wide sweeping turquoise bay of Cable Beach

- Discovering the **Kimberley** (p987), one of Australia's last great adventure-travel frontiers, where mighty Mother Nature lashes an ancient and awesome landscape

★ Kimberley

Broome ★

Ningaloo Marine ★ Park

Outback ★

Margaret River ★ ★ Valley of the Giants

- TELEPHONE CODE: 08   - POPULATION: 1,906,100   - www.westernaustralia.net

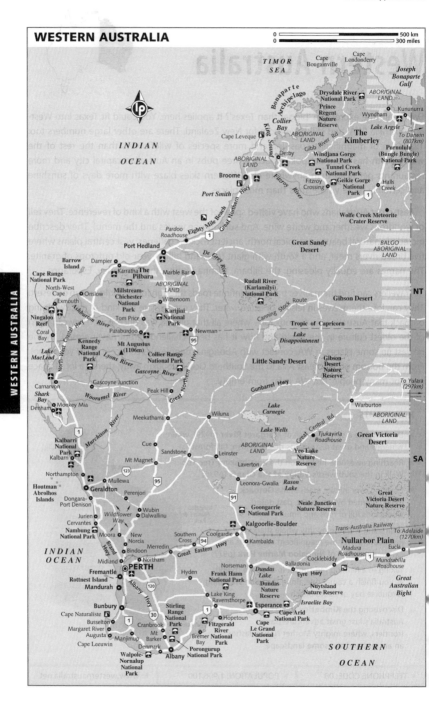

WESTERN AUSTRALIA

WESTERN AUSTRALIA

0 ——————— 500 km
0 ——————— 300 miles

TIMOR SEA

Cape Bougainville
Cape Londonderry

Joseph Bonaparte Gulf

Bonaparte Archipelago

Drysdale River National Park
ABORIGINAL LAND

Prince Regent Nature Reserve

Kununurra
To Darwin (807km)
Lake Argyle
Wyndham

Collier Bay

King Sound

Cape Leveque

Derby

ABORIGINAL LAND

Gibb River Rd

The Kimberley

Windjana Gorge National Park
Tunnel Creek National Park

Purnululu (Bungle Bungle) National Park

ABORIGINAL LAND

Broome

Port Smith

Fitzroy River

Fitzroy Crossing

Geikie Gorge National Park
Halls Creek

Wolfe Creek Meteorite Crater Reserve

BALGO ABORIGINAL LAND

Pardoo Roadhouse

Eighty Mile Beach

Great Northern Hwy

Great Sandy Desert

INDIAN OCEAN

Port Hedland

De Grey River

Barrow Island
Dampier
Marble Bar

Cape Range National Park
North-West Cape
Onslow

Karratha
The Pilbara

ABORIGINAL LAND

Rudall River (Karlamilyi) National Park

Gibson Desert

NT

Exmouth

Millstream-Chichester National Park
Wittenoom

Canning Stock Route

Ningaloo Reef

Tom Price
Karijini National Park

Coral Bay

Paraburdoo
Newman

Tropic of Capricorn

Lake MacLeod

Kennedy Range National Park
Mt Augustus (1106m)
Collier Range National Park

Lyons River
Gascoyne River

Lake Disappointment

Little Sandy Desert

Gibson Desert Nature Reserve

To Yulara (297km)

Carnarvon

Wooramel River

Gascoyne Junction
Peak Hill

Great Northern Hwy

Gunbarrel Hwy

Shark Bay
Denham
Monkey Mia

Murchison River

Meekatharra

Wiluna

Lake Carnegie

Warburton

ABORIGINAL LAND

Great Victoria Desert

Kalbarri National Park
Kalbarri

Cue
Sandstone
Leinster

Lake Wells

Great Central Rd

Tjukayirla Roadhouse

Mt Magnet

ABORIGINAL LAND

Yeo Lake Nature Reserve

SA

Northampton

Mullewa

Laverton

Rason Lake

Houtman Abrolhos Islands

Geraldton
Perenjori

Leonora-Gwalia

Neale Junction Nature Reserve

Great Victoria Desert Nature Reserve

Dongara-Port Denison

Wubin
Dalwallinu

Goongarrie National Park

Jurien
Cervantes

Wildflower Way

Kalgoorlie-Boulder

Trans-Australia Railway

To Adelaide (1270km)

Nambung National Park

Moora
New Norcia

Southern Cross
Coolgardie

Kambalda

Nullarbor Plain

Madura Roadhouse
Eucla

Mundrabilla Roadhouse

INDIAN OCEAN

Merredin

Great Eastern Hwy

Midland
Bindoon
Northam

PERTH

Hyden

Frank Hann National Park

Norseman

Dundas Lake

Dundas Nature Reserve

Balladonia

Eyre Hwy

Cocklebiddy

Nuytsland Nature Reserve

Great Australian Bight

Fremantle
Rottnest Island
Mandurah

Albany Hwy

Lake King
Ravensthorpe

Israelite Bay

Bunbury

Cape Naturaliste
Busselton
Margaret River
Augusta

Blackwood River

Stirling Range National Park

Cranbrook

Mt Barker

Hopetoun

Fitzgerald River National Park

Cape Le Grand National Park

Cape Arid National Park

Esperance

Manjimup
Denham

Bremer Bay

Cape Leeuwin
Walpole-Nornalup National Park
Albany
Porongurup National Park

SOUTHERN OCEAN

WESTERN AUSTRALIA FACTS

Eat: Crayfish (western rock lobster), marron, chilli mussels

Drink: A 'middy' (285mL) of Emu Bitter or Redback beer, or Houghton's White Burgundy wine

Read: Ron and Viv Moon's *The Kimberley: An Adventurer's Guide*, Tim Winton's *Dirt Music*, Robert Drewe's *The Shark Net*

Listen to: John Butler Trio, Eskimo Joe, Downsyde

Watch: *Rabbit-Proof Fence, Japanese Story*

Avoid: Telling the locals that the eastern states are bigger and better (well they're not bigger are they?)

Locals' nickname: Sandgropers

Swim at: Como, Scarborough, Cottesloe, City Beach (p891)

Strangest festival: Charitable teams push wheelbarrows full of iron ore over 120km (Whim Creek is the starting point) in the Blackrock Stakes (www.blackrockstakes.pilbara.net.au)

Tackiest tourist attraction: Burswood Casino (Perth), Big Croc at Wyndham (p1002)

HISTORY

Archaeological records indicate that Aboriginal people entered Australia in the northwest. Later findings show they were in a peaceful trading relationship with Macassan trepang fishers, from Sulawesi in Southeast Asia, from at least the 17th century. WA was close to the Indian Ocean trading routes – guns, slaves, home wares, hay and rats (some with two legs) all sailed past and regularly sank off this coast. Dutchman Dirk Hartog was one of the first-known Europeans to land here in 1616. Countryman Abel Tasman charted parts of the coastline in 1644, but who could blame him if some of his charts read 'these partes unknowne'? There were undoubtedly spouting whales on his parchment too.

Aboard the prophetically named *Cygnet*, William Dampier filled in the cartographic gaps in 1688 and again in 1699, from the Swan River to as far north as Broome. The race between the French and the English to explore and invade tempted British authorities to ignore reports of a barren, treacherous place. They sent Sydney-based Major Edmund Lockyer and a team of troops and convicts to set up base at King George Sound (present-day Albany) in 1826. Lockyer and co were well received by the local Minang Noongar people.

Just when transportation was finishing up in other parts of Australia, over 10,000 convicts were sent to slow-growing WA. Postsentence, they established local businesses and were in effect a sizable, stable wave of settlers.

Late in the 19th century, someone stubbed their toe and the state's fortunes changed forever. Gold put WA on the map and finally gave it the population to make it a viable offshoot of the distant eastern colonies. Prosperity and proud isolation led to a 1933 referendum for secession: Western Australians voted two to one in favour of leaving the Commonwealth. Although it didn't eventuate, the people retained a strong independent streak.

The victorious shout 'G'day from WA!' was especially audible after *Australia II* sailed to victory in the 1983 America's Cup. In the early 1990s, political and corporate scandals rocked the boat and sent some modern-day criminals sailing into prison. Fortunately some of the best writers in Australia were starting to reach other shores in this period, putting WA on the literary map.

Aboriginal People

Stone tools from a campfire confirm that indigenous Australians lived as far south as present-day Perth at least 40,000 years ago. Despite their resistance, dispossession, poor treatment and continuous presence, the white obsession with dates often puts Aboriginal people in the past. Yet theirs is ultimately a story of survival.

With 58,496 people (16% of the nation's total Aboriginal population), WA is still home to one of the strongest indigenous communities in Australia today. The Pilbara and Kimberley regions in the north are home to a large number of Aboriginal people, and in many towns there, indigenous folk make up most of the population.

As elsewhere in Australia, colonisation irrevocably changed indigenous ways of life in WA. Across the state, the experience was uniform: confrontations led to massacres or jail (see p909). Conflict and assimilation policies plagued Aboriginal people, with tales of 'blackbirding', incarceration, illness, death and loss of basic rights. Forced off their traditional lands, some communities were practically wiped out by European disease. The Western Australian Aborigines Act (1905) allowed authorities to remove children, control employment and restrict movement.

After WWII many Aboriginal people banded together in protest against their appalling treatment on cattle stations, in their first public displays of political consciousness. One such resistance legend was Jandamarra (see the boxed text, p1001). In 1972 there was a full repeal of repressive legislation. Since then more than 120 native-title claims have been made by Aboriginal people across the state (mainly on Crown land) with many of these still going through mediation.

Today's people use several names to refer to themselves. The Noongar live in the southwest. In the southwestern desert regions the people are collectively known as Wongi, and Yamatji is a popular term for folk in other parts. Some of the greatest Aboriginal footballers and many visual artists of national acclaim come from WA.

GEOGRAPHY & CLIMATE

WA is Australia's largest state, comprising one-third of its land mass. In the north much of the landscape is barren. The Great Sandy Desert fringes the central-west coast. The Nullarbor, a vast dry plain, sweeps across the south and over the border into South Australia (SA). The southwestern corner of the state is a fertile area of forest and vineyards, and is only small in comparison to the size of the rest of WA.

Interesting variations in landscape include the Kimberley, in the extreme north of the state, which is a wild and rugged area with a convoluted coastline and stunning inland gorges.

The Pilbara, in the northwest of the region, is magnificent ancient-rock and gorge country from which the state derives vast mineral wealth. Away from the coast most of WA is simply a huge empty stretch of outback: along with the Nullarbor Plain and the Great Sandy Desert, the Gibson and Great Victoria Deserts cover much of the state.

It's tropical in the north, where the dry and wet seasons replace winter and summer. The Dry lasts from June to August and the Wet from December to February, with monsoonal rain falling from January onwards. The rain can render roads impassable and Port Hedland weathers a cyclone at least every two years. In the interior the climate is semi-arid and arid. The southwest of WA is temperate. It's often above 25°C here while the average temperature along the Kimberley Coast is a heavenly 28°C. Up in the Pilbara temperatures can soar to a nose-bleeding 48°C.

INFORMATION

See the excellent website of the **Western Australian Tourism Commission** (www.westernaustralia .net) for general statewide information. Most country towns have their own helpful visitor centres.

The **Royal Automobile Club of Western Australia** (RACWA; Map p888; ☎ 08-9421 4444; www .rac.com.au; 228 Adelaide Tce, Central Perth) produces the terrific *Western Australia Experience Guide*, full of accommodation and touring information. Download free basic maps (with distances, en route facilities and road conditions) from its website.

Lonely Planet's *Western Australia* guidebook gives more comprehensive information about the state.

Permits

To travel through Aboriginal land in WA, you need a permit issued by the **Department of Indigenous Affairs** (Map p888; ☎ 08-9235 8000; www.dia.wa.gov.au; 197 St Georges Tce, Central Perth). Applications can be lodged on the Internet. For information on Aboriginal Culture Tours see p882.

NATIONAL PARKS

Most of the state's important natural attractions are protected as national parks. The majority are managed by the **Department**

of Conservation & Land Management (CALM; Map pp886-7; ☎ 08-9334 0333; www.naturebase.net; Hackett Dr, Crawley), with offices throughout the state. In recent times up to 30 new national parks have been created to protect old-growth forests in the southwest, but many of these are still being gazetted and having their boundaries pegged out. Contact CALM for an update.

You can camp in designated areas of some parks (usually $15 per night for two people). Helpful maps, pamphlets and local signage are all produced by CALM.

ACTIVITIES

Bird-Watching
Ornithologists delight in the variety of species found in WA. There are Birds Australia observatories in Eyre (p955) and Broome (p995). Yalgorup National Park (p926) and the Kepwari trail, part of the Kepwari Wetland Wonderland (p944), are important habitats for a wide variety of water birds. Twitchers also descend on the Kimberley in the Wet.

Bushwalking
You can contact the many bushwalking clubs in Perth through the umbrella organisation **Federation of Western Australia Bushwalking Clubs** (☎ 08-9362 1614).

The best bushwalking areas in WA include the Stirling Range and Porongurup National Parks (p938), both northeast of Albany. Good walking tracks abound in the coastal parks in the south and southwest, such as Walpole-Nornalup (p935), Fitzgerald River (p943), Cape Le Grand (p946) and Cape Arid (p946). To the north are the Kalbarri (p968), Karijini (p959) and Purnululu National Parks (p1002), which provide a rugged walking environment.

There are also good walks through the hills around Perth. Real enthusiasts undertake the 1000km **Bibbulmun Track** (www.bibbulmun track.org.au) from Perth's outskirts to Albany. Catering for walkers of all abilities, it goes through seven rural communities and the loveliest natural areas of the southwest: take a gentle wander or have an eight-week adventure.

Beware you don't spread 'dieback', a fungal disease that rots the roots of plants. Observe 'no go' road signs and clean the soil from your boots before and after each walk.

Cycling
Rivalling the famous Bibb Track is the new **Munda Biddi Mountain Bike Trail** (www.mundabiddi .org.au), which will eventually take off-road cyclists some 900km from Mundaring on Perth's outskirts through the beautiful scenic southwest to Albany on the south coast. The third stage was complete as far as Denmark at the time of writing. **CALM** (☎ 08-9334 0333) has more info, including map packs ($15).

Two-wheel enthusiasts always love the easy climes of Rottnest Island (p909) and Perth (p891). For more tips, check out the **Bicycle Transportation Alliance** (Map pp884-5; ☎ 08-9420 7210; www.multiline.com.au/~bta; City West Lotteries House, 2 Delhi St, West Perth).

Since 1896, when the first bicycle crossing was made, the Nullarbor has continued to entice tenacious cyclists who relish a tremendous physical and mental challenge (1219km in the heat). Preparation and planning are essential (see p954).

Diving
The stunning reefs of the Ningaloo Marine Park (p977), artificial reefs created by sunken ships at Albany (p941) and Dunsborough (p929) and older shipwrecks along the coast between Geraldton and Exmouth are all popular.

Introductory scuba-diving courses for noncertified divers often occur in the waters off Perth, before moving to more challenging or remote spots like Rottnest Island. **Malibu Dive** (☎ 08-9292 5111; www.rottnestdiving.com.au) takes you out for a day that includes equipment hire, an instructor and lunch.

Fishing
WA is a fishing paradise. Heading down the lengthiest coastline in Australia, popular places to drop a line are at Kununurra, the Northwest Cape, Broome, the Dampier Archipelago, Shark Bay, Denham, Geraldton, Houtman Abrolhos Islands and Albany.

Recreational fishing licences ($21 to $36) are required to catch marron (freshwater crayfish) or rock lobsters, to use a fishing net; or to freshwater angle in the southwest. There's an annual licence covering all fishing activities ($72). Buy one from the **Department of Fisheries** (Map p888; ☎ 08-9482 7333; www.fish.wa.gov.au; SGIO Bldg, 168-170 St Georges Tce, Central Perth), or one of its regional offices. Saltwater angling and crabbing come free.

WESTERN AUSTRALIA

Rock Climbing & Caving

The southern sea cliffs of Wilyabrup, West Cape Howe and the Gap, and the huge cliffs of the Stirling and Porongurup Ranges attract plenty of climbers. Those with a head for heights will also enjoy scaling the lookout trees in the Valley of the Giants (p936).

The caves of the Margaret River region, for example near Yallingup (p929), and the lesser-known 'holes' of Cape Range National Park (p981) offer plenty of opportunities for cavers.

Sailing, Canoeing & Kayaking

WA was briefly the home of sailing's greatest prize, the America's Cup, and sailing is popular, especially on the sheltered Swan River. All hands are on deck with **Leeuwin Ocean Adventure Foundation** (Map pp904-5; ☎ 08-9430 4105; www.leeuwin.com; B Berth, Victoria Quay, Fremantle; tours adult/child $99/55). Set sail in its tall ship for full summer days or at twilight ($55).

Canoeing Western Australia (☎ 08-9285 8501; www.canoe.org.au) will provide information on the many good canoeing and kayaking rivers in the state.

Surfing

The southwestern beaches, from Cape Naturaliste (p928) to Margaret River (p930; where the Masters is held), are the sites of some epic wave action. Another surfari is the stretch from Geraldton to Kalbarri, particularly Jakes Corner (p968; experienced surfers only). If you're stuck in the city, don't despair. Trigg, Scarborough (p891) and Rottnest Island (p911) are nearby. *Down South Surfing Guide* is free at the Dunsborough and Busselton visitor centres, or check conditions at www.dpi.wa.gov.au/coastaldata.

Lancelin and Ledge Point are long-term hang-outs for sailboarders and kitesurfers. Windsurfers adore the windy conditions along Perth's city beaches and up in blustery Geraldton.

TOURS

There are dozens of tours through WA to suit all tastes and budgets.
Dr Marion Hercock's Explorer Tours (☎ 08-9361 0940; www.explorertours.com.au) Ranging from nine to 26 days (from $1675), 4WD tours take (up to 10) travellers along the routes of 19th-century explorers.
Easyrider Backpacker Tours (Map p888; ☎ 08-9226 0307; www.easyridertours.com.au; 144 William St, Central Perth) Has a hop-on, hop-off bus – a fun, relaxed way to travel and meet people.
H2 Overland Surf Adventures (☎ 0438 658 059; www.h2osurfadventure.com; 4-/2-day tours incl meals & equipment $479/250) A constant favourite with readers, who appreciate the guides' skill in surf coaching and camping under the stars.
Nullarbor Traveller (☎ 1800 816 858; www.the-traveller.com.au) Offers leisurely seven-day ($735) and nine-day ($945) minibus camping trips between Perth and Adelaide, taking in national parks and fun activities.
Travelabout Outback Adventures (☎ 08-9244 1200; www.travelabout.au.com) Travellers get the chance to go bush to see the state's natural wonders, from one-day Pinnacles trips ($125) to a 24-day odyssey from Perth to Darwin ($3299).
Western Travel Bug (☎ 08-9204 4600, 1800 627 488; www.travelbug.com.au) A southwest specialist with an eco flavour. Separate day trips to the Pinnacles, Wave Rock and Margaret River each cost $98/70 per adult/child, while a four-day southwest tour is $495/400. Ask about YHA/VIP discounts.

Aboriginal Culture Tours

Across the state are a number of fascinating tours that incorporate aspects of Aboriginal life and culture (for details of tours, see the relevant sections later in this chapter).

In the Kimberley, there are operations run by the Lombadina Aboriginal community and Middle Lagoon, both in the Dampier Peninsula, and Bungoolee Tours in Fitzroy Crossing.

The Purnululu Aboriginal Corporation and CALM jointly manage the Purnululu (Bungle Bungle) National Park, one of the first attempts in Australia to balance the needs of local people with the demands of tourism. At Geikie Gorge, near Fitzroy Crossing, **Darngku Heritage Cruises** (☎ 08-9191 5552) offers a river cruise and cultural tour.

In the Pilbara there's a visitor centre in the Karijini (Hamersley Range) National Park (p959) and an information centre on Yinjibarndi people's culture in the Millstream Homestead.

GETTING THERE & AWAY

Qantas operates direct flights between Perth airport and Singapore, Tokyo, Denpasar (Bali), Jakarta, Hong Kong and Johannesburg. South African Airways flies direct between Perth and Johannesburg. Singapore Airlines, Malaysia Airlines, Thai Airways and Garuda Indonesia all have direct flights from Perth to their home countries.

See the Getting There & Away sections for Perth (p901), Broome (p995) and Kalgoorlie-Boulder (p952) for information on domestic transport into WA by air, bus and train.

GETTING AROUND

For information on getting around Perth, see p902. Extra Western Australian tourist information on all forms of transport is available if you email travel@tourism.wa.gov.au.

Air

Qantas (☎ 13 13 13; www.qantas.com.au) has regular flights to Broome and Kalgoorlie; it's also worth checking Internet specials to Broome with **Virgin Blue** (☎ 13 67 89; www.virginblue.com .au). **Skywest** (☎ 1300 660 088; www.skywest.com.au) operates flights to many regional centres, including Albany, Esperance, Exmouth, Carnarvon and Kalgoorlie. Two- to 21-day advance-purchase tickets are cheaper, and students are eligible for discounts. **Golden Eagle Airlines** (☎ 08-9172 1777; www.goldeneagleair lines.com/regional) has daily flights between Broome, Fitzroy Crossing and Halls Creek, plus services to Port Hedland (three weekly). **Skippers** (☎ 1300 729 924; www.skippers.com.au) flies Perth–Kalbarri and then on to Shark Bay.

Bus

Greyhound Australia (☎ 13 14 99; www.greyhound .com; ☉ 7am-9pm) buses run from Perth along the coast to Broome ($319, 10 hours) and Darwin ($630, 60 hours), and from Perth to Adelaide on Fridays ($293, 36 hours) via Kalgoorlie ($131, eight hours). Most people buy a Kilometre Pass (2000/5000/10,000km for $328/681/1259) or one of the set-route passes. Students and YHA/VIP card holders are eligible for discounts. With Kilometre Passes, bear in mind that Greyhound Australia deducts double the kilometres for side trips off the main highway, such as those to the Pinnacles, Kalbarri and Monkey Mia.

Perth Goldfields Express (☎ 1800 620 440; www .goldrushtours.com.au/express.html) goes from Perth to Laverton via Kalgoorlie. **Integrity Coach Lines** (☎ 08-9226 1339; www.integritycoachlines.com.au) runs between Perth and Port Hedland, with a 10% discount for YHA/VIP card holders.

South West Coachlines (☎ 08-9324 2333), in the Transperth City Busport, runs services from Perth to southwestern towns such as Augusta, Bunbury, Busselton, Dunsborough, Nannup and Margaret River.

Transwa (☎ 1300 662 205; www.transwa.wa.gov.au) goes to Albany, Augusta, Esperance, Hyden, Kalgoorlie, Pemberton and York, and north to Geraldton, Kalbarri and Meekatharra. There's a 10% discount for concession card holders, including YHA/VIP members.

Car

To really see and explore this enormous state, and for flexibility, many people end up hiring or buying a car (see p1044). Bear in mind that WA is not only enormous it's also sparsely populated, so make safety preparations if you plan to travel any significant distance (for more information on outback travel see p1065).

There are many spectacular, enticing areas of the state that don't have sealed roads, and a 4WD will come in handy. For instance, you'll need a 4WD to see any of the spectacular Kimberley, even in the Dry (you can hire one in Broome or Kununurra).

For up-to-date road information across the state, call ☎ 1800 013 314.

Train

Transwa (☎ 1300 662 205; www.transwa.wa.gov.au) operates WA's domestic rail network. It provides services between Perth and Kalgoorlie *(Prospector)*, Northam *(AvonLink)* and Bunbury *(Australind)*; for details, see the individual destinations.

PERTH

☎ 08 / pop 1,380,000

On experiencing Perth's temperate vibrancy and bountiful beaches, with the rich southern wilderness and wineries at its feet, some travellers wonder why Australians settled for the east coast at all. The southwestern coastline and its capital – the world's most remote city of its size – have all you could want. Most Western Australians concur by choosing to call Perth home.

Politically and socially, you could say this is a place with a lot of ocean but not many waves. Yet can we blame Perth for being fascinated with its own tanned navel, beer and boats? Founded on the great riches in its soil, its fortune these days amounts to constant sunshine, great food, a relaxed pace, natural beauty and space. Even the dogs have their own beach here.

WESTERN AUSTRALIA

WESTERN AUSTRALIA

GREATER PERTH

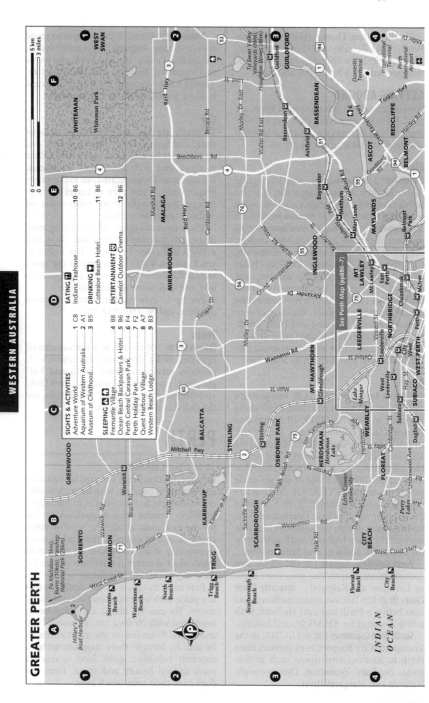

SIGHTS & ACTIVITIES

Adventure World...............................	1 C8
Aquarium of Western Australia...........	2 A1
Museum of Childhood.........................	3 B5

SLEEPING

Fremantle Village..............................	4 B8
Ocean Beach Backpackers & Hotel.....	5 B6
Perth Central Caravan Park................	6 F4
Perth Holiday Park............................	7 F2
Quest Harbour Village........................	8 A7
Western Beach Lodge........................	9 B3

EATING

Indiana Teahouse..............................	10 B6

DRINKING

Cottesloe Beach Hotel.......................	11 B6

ENTERTAINMENT

Camelot Outdoor Cinema..................	12 B6

0   5 km
0   3 miles

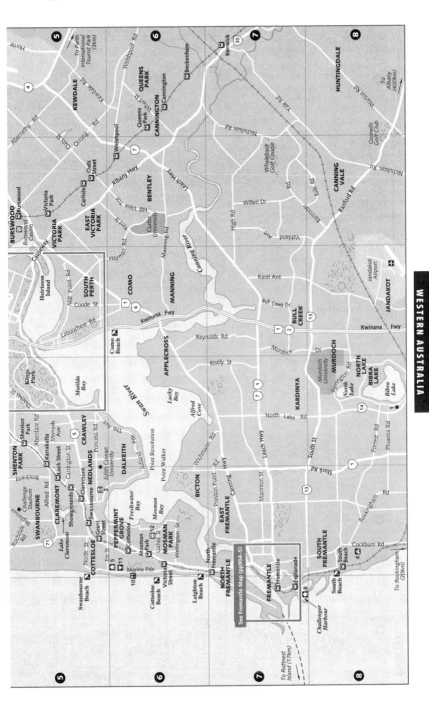

See Fremantle Map (pp904–5)

WESTERN AUSTRALIA

WESTERN AUSTRALIA

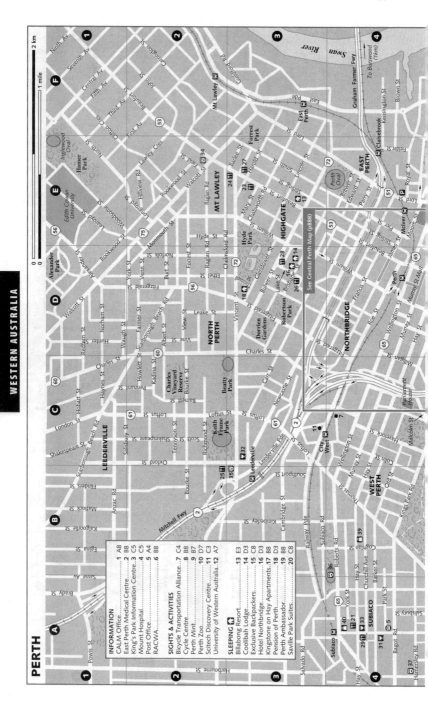

PERTH

INFORMATION	
CALM Office	1 A8
East Perth Medical Centre	2 B8
King's Park Information Centre	3 C5
Mount Hospital	4 C5
Post Office	5 A4
RACWA	6 B8

SIGHTS & ACTIVITIES	
Bicycle Transportation Alliance	7 C4
Cycle Centre	8 B8
Perth Mint	9 B7
Perth Zoo	10 D7
Scitech Discovery Centre	11 C3
University of Western Australia	12 A7

SLEEPING	
Billabong Resort	13 E3
Coolbah Lodge	14 D3
Exclusive Backpackers	15 C8
Hotel Northbridge	16 D3
Kingstone on Hay Apartments	17 B8
Pension of Perth	18 D3
Perth Ambassador	19 B8
Saville Park Suites	20 C8

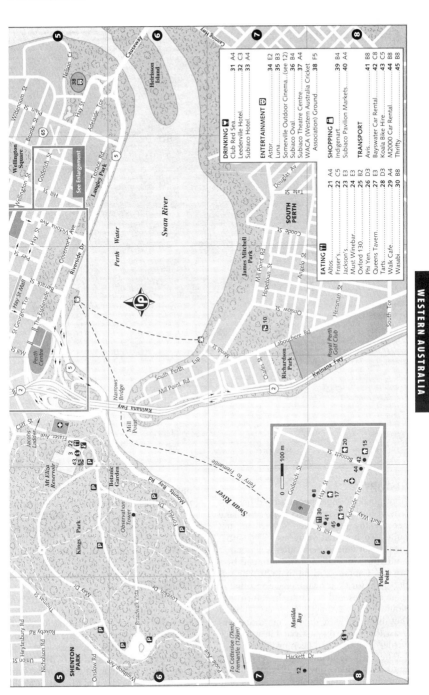

WESTERN AUSTRALIA

DRINKING 🍺
Club Red Sea.................................31 A4
Leederville Hotel...........................32 C3
Subiaco Hotel................................33 A4

ENTERTAINMENT 🎭
Astor...34 E2
Luna...35 B3
Somerville Outdoor Cinema....(see 12)
Subiaco Oval.................................36 B4
Subiaco Theatre Centre.................37 A4
WACA (Western Australia Cricket
    Association) Ground..................38 F5

SHOPPING 🛍️
Indigenart.....................................39 B4
Subiaco Pavilion Markets..............40 A4

TRANSPORT
Avis...41 B8
Bayswater Car Rental....................42 C8
Koala Bike Hire..............................43 C5
M2000 Car Rental.........................44 B8
Thrifty...45 B8

EATING 🍴
Altos...21 A4
Fraser's...22 C5
Jackson's.......................................23 E3
Must Winebar................................24 E3
Oxford 130....................................25 B2
Phi Yen...26 D3
Queens Tavern..............................27 E3
Tarts...28 D3
Walk Cafe.....................................29 A4
Wasabi..30 B8

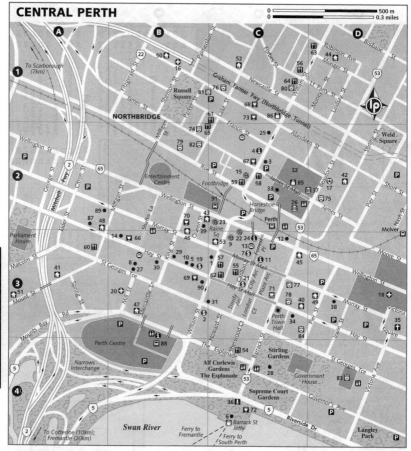

CENTRAL PERTH

WESTERN AUSTRALIA

HISTORY

Aboriginal Noongar peoples lived here for tens of thousands of years before this land became the Swan River Settlement, not quite two hundred years ago. The settlement (later named Perth after a dignitary's hometown in Scotland) was founded by a hopeful Captain Stirling in 1829. The settlers paid for their own passage and that of their families and servants. In return they would receive 200 acres for every labourer they brought with them. This didn't appease them once they arrived. Life was much harder than they had been promised.

The early settlement grew very slowly until 1850, when convicts alleviated the labour shortage and boosted the population.

Convict labour was also responsible for constructing the city's substantial buildings (Government House and the Perth Town Hall are two of them). The discovery of gold in the 1890s increased Perth's population fourfold in a decade and initiated a building bonanza.

ORIENTATION

Perth lazes by the wide blue swath of the Swan River to its south. To the east it stretches towards a gentle backdrop of hills and the vineyards of the Swan Valley. In the city centre, the glass towers of the central business district (CBD) sparkle on the suited drag of St Georges Tce. North of here, the Hay and Murray St Malls and arcades are abuzz with shoppers who spill over into the streets and eateries of Northbridge, Leederville and Highgate. The high green expanse of King's Park oversees Perth's western end. Beyond, to the northwest of the city, are the Indian Ocean, stylish Subiaco and the packed beachside suburbs of Cottesloe and Scarborough. Fremantle ('Freo') is only twenty minutes south by car, along Mounts Bay Rd.

INFORMATION
Bookshops
There are large chain stores on the Hay and Murray St Malls.

All Foreign Languages Bookshop (Map p888; ☎ 9321 9275; 101 William St) Travel books, language guides, books in languages other than English.

Arcane Bookshop (Map p888; ☎ 9328 5073; 212 William St, Northbridge) An eclectic collection for an arty audience.

Boffins Bookshop (Map p888; ☎ 9321 5755; 806 Hay St) Australiana, technical books and travel.

Elizabeth's Secondhand Bookshop (Map p888; ☎ 9481 8848; 820 Hay St) Secondhand books and mags. Orders in from other stores.

Map World (Map p888; ☎ 9322 5733; sales@perthmap .com.au; 900 Hay St) State, regional and bushwalking maps, and language guides.

Emergency
Dial ☎ 000 for ambulance, fire or police.
Lifeline (☎ 13 11 14) Crisis counselling.
Police station (Map p888; ☎ 9222 1111; Curtin House, 60 Beaufort St)
RACWA Roadside Assistance (☎ 13 11 11)
Sexual Assault Resource Centre (☎ 9340 1828) Crisis line open 24 hours.

Internet Access
There's plenty of Internet access along William St between Murray and Wellington Sts. Tour companies and backpacker centres are a good cheap option, with fast connection speeds and travel tips or advice if you need it. Try the following:

Backpackers Travel Centre (Map p888; ☎ 9228 1877; 223 William St, Northbridge)
Outback Travel Centre (Map p888; ☎ 9228 3812; 197 William St, Northbridge)
Traveller's Club (Map p888; ☎ 9226 0660; 555-559 Wellington St)

Medical Services
East Perth Medical Centre (Map pp886-7; ☎ 9221 4242; 168 Adelaide Tce; ⏱ 8.30am-3pm) GPs, physiotherapist and traveller vaccinations.
Lifecare – Dentist (Map p888; ☎ 9221 2777; Forrest Chase; ⏱ 8am-8pm) In the main train station.

Perth Women's Centre (Map p888; ☎ 9227 9032; 122 Aberdeen St; ❂ Mon-Thu 9am-4.30pm) Travellers can drop in for crisis or drug and alcohol counselling, multicultural women's advocacy and doctor referrals.

Royal Perth Hospital (Map p888; ☎ 9224 2244; Victoria Sq) Close to the city centre.

Travel Medicine Centre (Map p888; ☎ 9321 7888; 5 Mill St; ❂ 8am-5.30pm Mon-Fri)

Money

All the major banks have branches in Perth with foreign-currency facilities generally open from 9.30am to 4pm Monday to Thursday (until 5pm Friday).

American Express (Amex; Map p888; ☎ 1300 132 639; 109 St Georges Tce)

Thomas Cook (Map p888; ☎ 9321 7811; 760 Hay St)

Travelex (Map p888; ☎ 9481 7900; 704 Hay St Mall) Provides foreign exchange.

Post

Main post office (GPO; Map p888; ☎ 9237 5460; Forrest Pl; ❂ 8am-5.30pm Mon-Fri, 9am-12.30pm Sat)

Tourist Information

i-City Information Kiosk (Map p888; ☎ 1300 361 351; cnr Forrest Pl & Murray St Mall; ❂ 10am-4pm Mon-Thu & Sat, to 8pm Fri, noon-4pm Sun, closed public holidays) Hosts are dressed in blue and green; easy to find in the mall.

Western Australian Visitors Centre (Map p888; ☎ 1300 361 351; www.westernaustralia.net; Albert Facey House, Forrest Pl; ❂ 8.30am-6pm Mon-Thu, 8.30am-7pm Fri, 8.30am-12.30pm Sat; 🖳) Offers a booking service for accommodation and tours, and multiple brochures on Perth and WA. Closes an hour earlier on weekdays in winter.

Free guides to the city include *What's On in Perth & Fremantle*, available from visitor centres, hostels and hotels.

Travel Agencies

Backpackers Travel Centre (Map p888; ☎ 9228 1877; www.backpackerstravel.net.au; 223 William St, Northbridge; 🖳) Budget travel and tours, Internet access and a hotel and hostel booking service.

Outback Travel Centre (Map p888; ☎ 9228 3812; www.goworknetwork.com.au; 197 William St; ❂ 10.30am-5pm Mon-Fri, 12-4pm Sat & Sun) As well as tours and info, arranges work on farms, in pubs, roadhouses, resorts, nannying and labouring for travellers.

Traveller's Club (Map p888; ☎ 9226 0660; www.travellersclub.com.au; 555-559 Wellington St) Look for the corrugated-iron frontage, a well-established bulletin board and plenty of friendly staff advice on discount travel, tours and work. Sells VIP cards.

PERTH IN...

Two Days

Get out and explore Perth with a **walking tour** (p892), winding your way up to vast **King's Park** (opposite) for a picnic. Dine out on international cuisines in racy **Northbridge** (p897), close to the city. In the morning jump on the train to **Freo** (p903). After some **museum** (p903) meandering, make a beeline for an ale at **Little Creatures** (p907). Be sure to find the **Fremantle Markets** (p903) if it's the weekend.

Four Days

Do the two-day thing and stay in Freo. Cruise across to **Rottnest Island** (p909) on the morning ferry for a sunny day of cycling, snorkelling and quokka spotting. Spend your last day at **Cottesloe** (p892), where you can warm the soles of your feet on the windowsill of the **Ocean Beach Hotel** (p899), as the sun sets over the Indian Ocean.

YHA Travel Shop (Map p888; ☎ 9227 5122; 259 William St, Northbridge) Adjoins Northbridge's YHA Britannia.

SIGHTS

To quote one local, 'Perth's getting bigger than the eight streets it used to be'; however there's still plenty to do in those streets. Attractions are all within easy reach of the city centre, and many have their own stops on the free Central Area Transit (CAT) bus service route (p902). See the Walking Tour (p892) for a pedestrian's perspective of Perth.

Perth Cultural Centre

Just north of the Perth train station, between James St Mall and Roe St, you'll find the state museum, gallery, library and the Perth Institute of Contemporary Arts.

Take your sweet time in the **Western Australian Museum** (Map p888; ☎ 9427 2700; www.museum.wa.gov.au; James St Mall; admission by donation; ❂ 9.30am-5pm), which offers insights into the state's geology and early history (both Aboriginal and European). Kids will love the prehistoric megafauna display. Highlights include the gallery of Aboriginal culture and a collection of the world's butterflies. There are free guided tours at 11am and 2pm.

The **Art Gallery of Western Australia** (Map p888; ☎ 9492 6600; www.artgallery.wa.gov.au; 47 James St; admission free; ۩ 10am-5pm) has a brilliant collection of Aboriginal artworks. There's also a fine permanent exhibition of European, Australian and Asia-Pacific art, regular temporary exhibitions and a fabulous gift shop.

The **Perth Institute of Contemporary Arts** (PICA; Map p888; ☎ 9227 6144; www.pica.org.au; 51 James St; ۩ 11am-8pm Tue-Sun) is all about new media and the promotion of local artists, photographic exhibitions and awards. Ask about performances in the Blue Room (sorry, no nudity).

Aquarium of Western Australia

Not far north of the city, the **Aquarium of Western Australia** (AQWA; Map pp884-5; ☎ 9447 7500; Hillary's Boat Harbour, West Coast Dr, Hillarys; adult/child/ family $24/13/65; ۩ 10am-5pm year-round, to 9pm Wed Dec-Apr) has an afternoon's worth of entertainment in the seal gallery alone! Watch them training above the water (1.30pm) and then make eye contact through the windows below. You can explore 12,000km of WA's coastline condensed into the mini-aquariums, where, unlike other aquariums, all the coral is living. You'll never get as close to a shark and still feel so calm as in the 98m-long moving-tunnel aquarium, where fish, turtles and huge stingrays glide around and over you. Snorkellers and divers can pay for a shark experience *inside* the tank ($90 plus equipment hire). From September to December, whale-watching trips are also available.

To get here from the Perth train station, take the Joondalup train to Warwick Station, then bus No 423 to Hillarys.

King's Park

The green hill-top crown of **King's Park and Botanic Garden** (Map pp886-7; ☎ 9480 3659; King's Park Rd, West Perth) is set in the midst of 4 sq km of natural bushland. The garden boasts over 2500 Western Australian plant species, many of them in full flower during the October **wildflower festival**. The relatively new Federation Walkway meanders 620m along the eastern boundary of the park, taking in views of the river.

Next to the car park is a kiosk and the **information centre** (☎ 9480 3659; ۩ 9.30am-4pm). There are free guided walks at 10am and 2pm daily. It's a 1.5km walk (p892) or a quick drive up the hill of St Georges Tce from the city centre. If you are laden with picnic gear, take the Red CAT bus service to the entrance or hop on the Perth Tram (p894).

Perth Mint

The **Mint** (Map p888; ☎ 9421 7223; 310 Hay St; adult/ child $7/3.50; ۩ 9am-4pm Mon-Fri, closes 1pm Sat & Sun) retains its solid Victorian place right in the city. It gains in stature when you realise how many Western Australian fortunes were made from gold and mining. Maybe the Perth expression 'mint' (meaning excellent) comes from this history. See the 11.5kg Golden Beauty (worth $200,000), a nugget which might buy you a bathroom in a beachside suburb.

Greater Perth

Good grief, is that Heath? Mr Ledger was born here in **Guildford**, a handsome stopoff before the **Swan Valley vineyards**. Dotted along the river to the Upper Swan, many are open for tastings and cellar sales. Start at the original, **Houghton Wines** (off Map pp884-5; ☎ 9274 5100; Dale Rd, Middle Swan; ۩ 10am-5pm).

Lake Monger (Map pp884–5) in Wembley, northwest of the city centre, is a hang-out for black swans, the emblem of Perth.

Cottesloe, west of Perth, has a small, popular width of beach and beachfront cafés. Further north is **Scarborough** ('Scabs' to the locals – nice!), with a long, white beach, better surf and more development.

ACTIVITIES
Cycling

Need to rent some wheels? Try the **Cycle Centre** (Map p888; ☎ 9325 1176; 282 Hay St; per day $18). Bicycle routes follow the Swan River all the way to Fremantle and along the Indian Ocean coast. Download city cycling maps from the website of the **Department for Planning and Infrastructure** (☎ 9216 8558; www .dpi.wa.gov.au).

Swimming & Surfing

Some of the best city beaches in Australia include those on the Indian Ocean coast. It seems most Perthites are devoted to some kind of water activity: swimming, surfing, fishing, cray potting or yachting. You'll see windsurfers practically flying on the afternoon wind and kitesurfers colouring the beach sky. Weekend snorkellers head to Marmion Marine Park near Scarborough.

WESTERN AUSTRALIA

Cottesloe Beach (Map pp884–5) is a swimming spot popular with families, as is **Swanbourne**. **Scarborough**, further north, is a wide beach with nightlife on its increasingly commercial shores. It sports a permanent population of surfers, bodyboarders and gnarly waves. The comparatively quiet **City** and **Floreat Beaches** are in between. On your way to Yanchep National Park, **Sorrento** is relaxed and beautiful. Surf's often up at **Trigg Island**, though it can get rough. Close to town, surf-free beaches on the Swan River include **Crawley**, **Peppermint Grove** and **Como** (Map pp884–5).

Catch any nonexpress Fremantle-bound train for Cottesloe and Swanbourne – in each case there's a bit of a walk to get to the beach itself. Alternatively, bus No 71 or 72 (destination Cottesloe) from the City Busport will get you to Cottesloe and Swanbourne. For Scarborough, take bus No 400 from the Wellington St bus station.

Whale Watching

Humpback whales pass by Perth on their annual journey to Antarctic waters from September to December, offering visitors to the city a once-in-a-lifetime encounter. **Mills Charters** (☎ 9246 5334; www.millscharters.com.au; adult/child $45/25) runs an informative three-hour whale-watching trip from Hillary's Boat Harbour. To get to Hillary's, take the train to Warwick and bus No 423 from there. Other whale-watching operators are **Rottnest Express** (☎ 9335 6406) and **Oceanic Cruises** (☎ 9325 1191), which both leave from Fremantle.

Yoga

If you're in need of a stretch and some time out from WA's obsession with all things outdoors, head for the **Yoga School of WA** (Map p888; ☎ 9381 9916; www.yoga.com.au; 10 Queen St).

WALKING TOUR

'Our cities…are mere plagiarisms from the Old World' observed Sir Walter Murdoch in 1930. This can no longer be said of Perth. The city's clean, has wide streets on a predictable grid and is unmistakably 20th century – you have to look hard to find the architectural bastions of older times. But Perth's water and its greenery are the real features of today's capital. King's Park makes a fitting end to this walk: from up there you'll really get the lay of the land and a brilliant view.

Start by looping through the busy shopping precinct. Walk across the raised walkway from airy, elegant Perth train station. Head across Murray St Mall, through City Arcade and briefly across Hay St Mall to wander down **Trinity Arcade (1)**, one of the older arcades. Then do a U-turn up London Court, for a touch of kitsch, and back onto Hay St Mall. Turn left onto Barrack St and right when you reach Murray St, heading east. The **Fire Safety and Education Museum (2)**, on the corner of Irwin and Murray Sts, was Perth's all-important fire-bobby headquarters from 1900 to 1979. Further down the street you'll see the beautiful arching fig tree over the redbrick **Perth Hospital (3)** buildings, and **St Mary's Cathedral (4)** ahead of you. Step inside for a moment's glass-lit serenity, although today's interior is humble in comparison to its grand Gothic beginnings (in 1863). Wander down the slope of Victoria Ave and cross Adelaide Tce, past **Perth Concert Hall (5)**. Take the path down into the Stirling Gardens: **Government House (6)** is on your left. Further down the hill you'll come across the Georgian structure of one of Perth's oldest buildings: the 1836 **courthouse (7)**, next to the Supreme Court.

LOCAL COLOUR

Look just beyond Cottesloe shoreline and you'll see a marker bobbing about: the Cottesloe Bell. This little piece of history was the mainstay of a shark net in the 1950s. It's also the trophy for the annual tussle between the Surf Life Saving Clubs of Cottesloe and North Cottesloe. The clubs have long been swept up in a fierce current of competition. Every year, the winners proudly daub the Bell in team colours. However, more than once, pranksters armed with paint have swum out in the middle of the night and changed the colours back. This has been known to happen up to three times during the week after the comp.

You can see life savers training on the beach in summer. You'll appreciate their presence on those rare days here when rips can take hundreds of people further out than they'd planned. The life savers will get to you first if you're between the red and yellow flags.

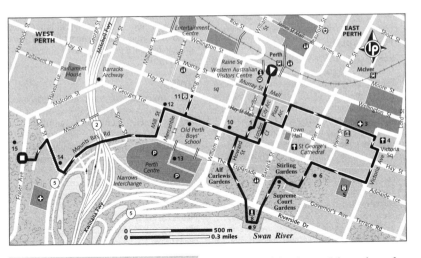

WESTERN AUSTRALIA

Make for the river and the Christmas-green spire of the **Swan Bell Tower** (**8**; ☎ 9218 8183; adult/concession $6/4; ◷ 10am-4.15pm), which is home to bells from the Academy of St Martin-in-the-Fields. Stop in for a bite to eat with a view at the **Barrack St Jetty** (**9**) restaurants. Here you can jump aboard a boat tour to Rottnest Island, the Swan Valley or Fremantle.

Now walk back up steep little Howard St and turn left onto St Georges Tce, where you'll see the magnificent contrast of old Perth and new in the **Palace Hotel** (**10**), now Bank West, and its new tower on your right. Continue west along St Georges Tce, the epicentre of the CBD. At King St detour right towards **His Majesty's Theatre** (**11**; p900), where there are foyer tours during the day. Back on St Georges Tce, you'll see the old-school bricks of the **Cloisters** (**12**), now an office, to your right.

The last part of the walk requires a bit of energy, a love of steps and a head for heights. Head left down Mill St and where it meets Mounts Bay Rd note the gigantic new **Perth Centre** (**13**), which is planned to expand right down to the water's edge. Walk along the curve of Mounts Bay Rd, under the overpass, and cross over to the

hotel side of the thoroughfare; after a few hundred metres you'll see **Jacob's Ladder** (**14**), a steep climb to Cliff St and the massive **King's Park** (**15**; p891). From up here the view of Perth and its surrounds is unrivalled. Relax on the grass under graceful gums and watch the river from above. Walk back across the footbridge on Mount St, or take the Red CAT bus from Mounts Bay Rd (outside the hospital) to return to the city centre.

PERTH FOR CHILDREN
The sunshine here will suit kids to a tee. There's plenty to do outdoors: cycle along the riverfront, spend days at the beach, or jump on a ferry to Rottnest Island (p894).

The **King's Park Federation Walkway** (King's Park; admission free; ◷ 9am-5pm) winds along and above the river and is safe for kids (and not too long). It showcases many of the colourful plants, trees and flowers that are only found in WA. Bring a ball and have a kick on an expanse of free and easy lawn here. Explore the huge park with **Koala Bike Hire** (Map pp886-7; ☎ 9321 3061; Fraser Ave, King's Park; per hr/day $6/18; ◷ 9.30am-4pm, to 6pm Sat & Sun), on the western side of the main car park. If you're here in the late afternoon, have a special sundown picnic at the **Moonlight Cinema** (☎ 1300 551 908; www.moonlight.com.au; King's Park; adult/child/concession $15/10/12) and watch a flick in the open air (Tuesday to Sunday nights from December to March, gates open 6pm). Check the website for the programme.

WESTERN AUSTRALIA

TOO DEADLY!

Yirra Yaakin (☎ 08-9202 1966; www.yirrayaa kin.asn.au; 65 Murray St) is one of Australia's leading indigenous theatre companies. In a great tradition of 30 years of Western Australian indigenous theatre, which began with playwright Jack Davis, it has attracted black actors, writers and directors from all over the country. Among its performances are kids' shows, which travel to schools and communities around WA. It also does *Welcome to Country,* the diplomatic ceremony, which is performed by Aboriginal elders and acknowledges the homelands and ongoing presence of Australia's Aboriginal people. In 2005 the company is also involved in the International Arts Festival opening ceremony. Check out upcoming shows for children on its website.

On the rare rainy day, self-confessed nerds will dig the excellent **Scitech Discovery Centre** (Map pp886-7; ☎ 9481 5789; www.scitech.org.au; cnr Railway Pde & Sutherland St, West Perth; adult/child $12/8; ⊗ 10am-5pm). Displays include a planetarium, puppet shows and interactive exhibits. From Perth train station, catch the free train to City West on the Fremantle line.

The **Museum of Childhood** (Map pp884-5; ☎ 9442 1373; Edith Cowan University, Bay Rd, Claremont; adult/child $4/3; ⊗ 10am-4pm Mon-Fri, 2-5pm Sun) has a bonza collection of old-fashioned toys and games of the kind grandma played with, a bush school from the 1920s and visiting exhibitions, such as the clock from ABC TV's *Playschool.*

Perth Zoo (Map pp886-7; ☎ 9474 0444; www.perth zoo.wa.gov.au; 20 Labouchere Rd, South Perth; adult/child/family $15/7.50/40; ⊗ 9am-5pm) is an exciting ferry ride across the Swan River from the city. Never smile at an estuarine crocodile, even if it has a grin the size of Steve Irwin's. You can smile at numbats though. Bus No 35 (No 108 on the weekend) will get you there from the City Busport, or catch the more pleasant South Perth ferry across the Swan from the Barrack St Jetty (return $2.20).

Little kids can pat baby koalas while the older ones 'go fully sick' on the rides at **Adventure World** (Map pp884-5; ☎ 9417 9666; www .adventureworld.net.au; Progress Dr, Bibra Lake; adult/child/family $36/30/112; ⊗ 10am-5pm Oct-Apr), an amusement park 15km south of the city.

If you're here in November, kids aged five to 16 will enjoy the **Awesome Festival** (www .awesomearts.com), a programme of the contemporary arts.

TOURS

There are countless tours on offer, so head to the visitors centre (p890) or one of the budget traveller centres for a full list of options.

Perth Tram (Map p888; ☎ 9322 2006; adult/child $20/10) This hop-on, hop-off tram is a speedy way to tour some of the city's main attractions (with commentary) between the Burswood Casino and King's Park. It leaves 565 Hay St at least six times daily (or pick it up en route).

Planet Perth (☎ 9225 6622; www.planettours.com.au) Offers some great day trips, including a popular wine-tasting tour on Tuesday and Friday ($45), an after-dark trip into Caversham Wildlife Park on Monday ($45) or horse-riding trips ($70) on Monday and Thursday afternoon. Offers YHA/VIP discounts.

Tourist Trifecta (☎ 9322 2006; www.perthtram.com .au; adult/child $60/30) Combines a Perth Tram tour, return cruise up the Swan River with Captain Cook Cruises, and a ride on the Fremantle Tram in between.

Many companies offer day trips to the Pinnacles and Wave Rock, and extended trips (from two days) to the southwest. See p882 for more information.

Cruises

Several cruise companies run tours from Barrack St Jetty, including **Captain Cook Cruises** (Map p888; ☎ 9325 3341; www.captaincook cruises.com.au), **Boat Torque** (☎ 9221 5844; www .boattorque.com.au) and **Oceanic Cruises** (☎ 9325 1191; www.oceaniccruises.com.au). All offer lunch and dinner cruises on the Swan River, winery visits and trips to Fremantle and Rottnest Island (p909).

Captain Cook Cruises (Pier 5) does a three-hour river cruise around Perth and Fremantle (adult/child $29/14), which will satisfy real-estate obsessed Australians from the East. There's also a day cruise to the Swan Valley vineyards (adult/child $99/58) and a zoo tour combined with a sightseeing cruise (you can use the tickets on separate days). Oceanic Cruises' Carnac Island Luncheon Eco Cruise (adult/child $79/39), from October to April, includes a guided beach walk with a marine biologist, snorkelling and a buffet lunch.

FESTIVALS & EVENTS

Artrage (www.artrage.com.au) Contemporary arts and local culture showcased in October.

Fremantle Arts Festival (www.fremantlefestivals.com.au) November. Culture galore.

Gay Pride March (www.pridewa.asn.au) October.

Perth International Arts Festival (www.perthfestival.com.au) Music, drama, dance and films in November.

Perth Royal Show (www.perthroyalshow.com.au) Late September. If you'd rather be with the animals.

SLEEPING
Budget
HOSTELS

Perth's backpacker scene is jumping. There's a bed to suit every taste and budget (many more places than we can list). In the massive, well-established bunk halls you'll have to trade new paint for plenty of company, endless activities and a fun time. The newer, swisher breed of hostel is quieter, with good facilities and quality sheets. Most hostels give a $1 discount for VIP, YHA or Nomads cards and are much cheaper the longer you stay. Internet access is usually available for $3 to $5 per hour. Sometimes Australians will be asked to prove they are travelling, as some places have a pro-international-guest policy that bans dodgy locals from rocking up and expecting a cheap bed. All sleeping options have shared facilities unless otherwise stated.

City

Billabong Backpackers Resort (Map pp886-7; ☎ 9328 7720; www.billabongresort.com.au; 381 Beaufort St; dm/d $22/62; 🖳 🏊) Your 'tanned and hot at three o'clock' radar will be busy at this boisterous youth hall – all primary colours, surfing lessons, three floors' worth of dorm-style bunks and a former car park posing as a beach-volleyball court. Beware the beer-holding bunyips by the pool.

Globe Backpackers (Map p888; ☎ 9321 4080; 553-561 Wellington St; dm/d $24/65, s & tw $55; 🗽 🖳 🏊) Comparing Globe to the others is like user-pays education versus the old pipe-smoking universities of the 1970s. The new kid on the block features refurbished Tokyo-style hidey holes. All bathrooms are private and many rooms have their own TV. A pool counteracts the feeling of industrious impersonality.

Grand Central Backpackers (Map p888; ☎ 9421 1123; grandcentralbp@hotmail.com; 379 Wellington St; dm/s/d $18/36/50; 🖳) Ignore the peeling ex-

terior. This former hotel is enormous and bright inside with a low-key vibe. Cheaper weekly rates are available.

Exclusive Backpackers (Map pp886-7; ☎ 9221 9991; exclusiv@pielink.com; 158 Adelaide Tce; dm/s/d $15/35/50, d with bathroom $50-55; 🗽 🖳) The owners are eccentric but caring. New rooms out the back are spartan and clean with the luxury of air-con and TV.

Northbridge

Governor Robinson's (Map p888; ☎ 9328 3200; www.govrobinsons.com.au; 7 Robinson Ave; dm/d $20/55; 🗽 🖳) A serene scene awaits you at this renovated cottage with dark jarrah floors, small dorms and the best hostel bathrooms this side of Fremantle. Warning: no TV! What'll you do? Talk, read, sleep or explore Perth.

Underground Backpackers (Map p888; ☎ 9228 3755; underground@electrolley.com.au; 268 Newcastle St; dm $19-22, tw & d $60; 🅿 🗽 🖳 🏊) You can't help but meet people – lots of 'em – at this 170-bed hostel. Guests kick back in the bar or in the TV room.

Coolibah Lodge (Map pp886-7; ☎ 9328 9958; www.coolibahlodge.com.au; 194 Brisbane St; dm/s/d $20/39/52; 🖳) A warren-like, laid-back pad to meet people, among the plants or in the courtyard. The hostel has a bar and offers nightly activities, such as quizzes, drink cards and pool comps, and a job-search and tours desk.

Britannia YHA (Map p888; ☎ 9328 6121; britannia@yhawa.com.au; 253 William St; dm/s/d from $19/35/60, nonmembers extra $3.50; 🖳) This is the original sprawling YHA, complete with mess hall and drinks machine. Don't expect anything flash except the service. Single rooms are as cheap as you get; top-floor rooms look back across Northbridge.

AUTHOR'S CHOICE

oneworld backpackers (Map p888; ☎ 9228 8206; 162 Aberdeen St, Northbridge; www.oneworldbackpackers.com.au; dm/d $21/41; 🅿 🖳) A sister-brother team has set up this down-to-earth lodge on the edge of the North-bridge mandala: a clean stay in a warm, bohemian atmosphere. Eco-aware practices include solar hot water, biodegradable cleaning, native gardens, recycling, support for local artists…these guys eat karma on their (free) morning toast. Watch 'em lead the way.

Cottesloe & Scarborough

Ocean Beach Backpackers (Map pp884-5; ☎ 9384 5111; www.obh.com.au/backpackers; cnr Marine Pde & Eric St, Cottesloe; dm/s/d $21/60/65; P ⬛) The pool tables, outside benches and bar are never empty at this bright beachside hostel behind the famous hotel (p899). Travellers flock like seagulls to the dorms with private bathrooms and fridge.

Western Beach Lodge (Map pp884-5; ☎ 9245 1624; 6 Westborough St, Scarborough; dm $17, d with/without bathroom $50/40; P ⬛) Beach bums will be happy to find this cosy, clean, converted house so close to the sand. There are some great little takeaway joints nearby.

CAMPING

Most Perth caravan parks are in the suburbs, so having your own transport is always handy. Ask at the visitors centre for a full list of options.

Perth Holiday Park (Map pp884-5; ☎ 9279 6700; www.aspenparks.com.au; 91 Benara Rd, Caversham; powered/unpowered sites per 2 people $25/20, cabins $56-97; ⬛) In the Swan Valley, this park has a full complement of amenities, including a pool and a kids' playground.

Perth Central Caravan Park (Map pp884-5; ☎ 9277 1704; fax 9479 4434; 34 Central Ave, Ascot; sites per 2 people $18, cabins $80-90) Just 8km east of the city and swimmingly located close to the river.

Midrange

There's a selection of midrange hotels within spitting distance of each other on the intimate, clean inner blocks of the city. All options given include private bathrooms, unless stated otherwise.

GUESTHOUSES

Pension of Perth (Map pp886-7; ☎ 9228 9049; www.pensionperth.com.au; 3 Throssell St, Highgate; s/d incl breakfast $115/135; P ⬛) Across the road from lovely Hyde Park, with all its plane trees, ponds and paths. Guests love the gourmet breakfasts, chocolates, and the little fragrant details in the rooms here. Winter discounts apply.

Emperor's Crown (Map p888; ☎ 9227 1400; 295 Stirling St, Northbridge; dm/s/d $22/75/90; ⬛) This fortress is part of a new generation of accommodation that caters for travellers, families, groups *and* corporate types. Two minutes from the train station, it has outstanding facilities: a large communal kitchen, rooms with spacious en suites, DVDs, easy net access and an adjoining café that serves great scrambled eggs.

HOTELS

Melbourne (Map p888; ☎ 9320 3333; www.melbournehotel.com.au; cnr Hay & Milligan Sts; d $130-240; P ✖ ⬛) An elegant old remnant of goldrush Perth, this city-centre beauty (1897) has been renovated in rich heritage style. There's a thriving downstairs café, bar and restaurant. Ask about weekend rates and packages.

Hotel Northbridge (Map pp886-7; ☎ 9328 5254; 210 Lake St, Northbridge; www.hotelnorthbridge.com.au; s/d $40/50, boutique d $160-180; P ✖) This grand old hotel (1912), with its sweeping balcony and Gold Plate–lauded restaurant, sits atop the Northbridge action. There are renovated spa rooms in the boutique section. Long-term visitors should ask for the well-priced travellers' rooms tucked away up by the balcony, overlooking Perth.

Ocean Beach Hotel (Map pp884-5; ☎ 9384 2555; www.obh.com.au; cnr Marine Pde & Eric St, Cottesloe; d/tw/ste $120/135/165; P ✖ ⬛) Treat yourself to a view of the Indian Ocean sunset. Contemporary rooms have all the mod cons, and a deluxe suite is an arm twister with its spa and sea vistas.

Perth Ambassador (Map pp886-7; ☎ 9325 1455; 196 Adelaide Tce; s/d $120/140, 4-bed ste $250; ✖) Mirror ceilings in the lobby, 5th-floor spa, views of the Swan and an apricot-coloured penthouse suite (couples to share?). This is where Imran Khan would have stayed in 1983.

Hotel Ibis (Map p888; ☎ 9322 2844; gm@htlibis.com.au; 334 Murray St; d $90-140, ste $180; ✖ ⬛) Tastefully furnished, reasonably priced and well run, the Ibis won't start a revolution but it's good value.

Miss Maud (Map p888; ☎ 9325 3900; www.missmaud.com.au; 300 Murray St; s/d $99/139) Anyone with a love of Scandinavia, kitsch, or, bless it, *The Sound of Music* will find a few of their favourite things in the alpine murals, dainty rooms and rooftop sunbathing. Room 160 is still Miss Maud's favourite after 33 years. The smorgasbord breakfast is enough to feed a goat herd.

Emerald Hotel (Map p888; ☎ 9481 0866; www.emeraldhotel.com.au; 24 Mount St; r $95; P ✖ ⬛) Newly painted and close to the new Perth Centre, this is a good option if you're here for the boat show. There's a spa, sauna and gym in the basement. The lower floors are quiet.

Kingstone on Hay Apartments (Map pp886-7; ☎ 9325 7933; www.kingstoneonhay.com.au; 273 Hay St; 2-bed ste $148-169; P ☒ ☐ ☒) Here to see a man about a dog? These comfy apartments, at the eastern end of the city, offer corporate rates. After work there's a gym and your own balcony with a view of the river at sunset.

Also recommended:

Criterion Hotel (Map p888; ☎ 9325 5155, 1800 245 155; www.criterion-hotel-perth.com.au; 560 Hay St; s/d incl breakfast $110/140; P ☒) Restored Art Deco building in the centre.

Wentworth Plaza (Map p888; ☎ 9481 1000; wentport@fchotels.com.au; 300 Murray St; s/d $95/120; P ☒) Next to the Moon & Sixpence, and within staggering distance of other English pubs.

MOTELS & HOLIDAY APARTMENTS

In a state where cars are crucial, motels abound. For listings see the useful *Western Australia Accommodation & Tours Listing*, available from the visitors centre. Most places have cheaper weekly rates available.

Riverview on Mount Street (Map p888; ☎ 9321 8963; www.riverview.au.com; 42 Mount St; studio/riverside apt $85/95; P ☒ ☐) Located about halfway up the jacaranda-lined hill to King's Park, this is a cut above the rest. Apartments are simply styled and there's reliable morning coffee downstairs at the café (right).

Top End

Saville Park Suites (Map pp886-7; ☎ 9267 4888; www.savillesuites.com; 201 Hay St; 1-/2-bedroom ste from $170/200; P ☒ ☒) Tuscan-orange, palatial and staffed accordingly, this is a classy option for the new breed of 'soft adventure' travellers (you get a driver with your 4WD). The rooftop saltwater pool has views of Perth and the restaurant a Gold Plate award. Rates are on the up.

Medina Grand (Map p888; ☎ 9217 8000; www.medinaapartments.com.au; 33 Mounts Bay Rd; studio/d/ste $161/182/213; P ☒ ☒) One of the newer hotels, the Medina is dwarfed by the Perth Centre. If you can forgive the radiant lime hue, you'll enjoy the spacious rooms with high ceilings, a stylin' lap pool, classy accommodation for families, and the service at the Metro Bar.

EATING

City

Balthazar (Map p888; ☎ 9421 1206; 6 The Esplanade; mains $20-34; ☺ lunch & dinner) A deliciously closeted interior by day and a little bit Euro by night, this foodie haven has a wondrous wine list and passionate staff. If you meet someone in Perth, take them here for the third date.

Mount St Café (Map p888; ☎ 9485 6566; 42 Mount St; mains $9.50-18; ☺ breakfast & lunch) Languish here in the sunshine over eggs Benedict, on your way up to a day in King's Park – take some local picnic produce with you.

Fraser's (Map pp886-7; ☎ 9481 7100; Fraser Ave, King's Park; mains $15-32; ☺ lunch & dinner) People propose to each other up here…blame the view. The Mod Oz food marries Asian and French influences. Book an outside table so the breeze may caress you.

For Japanese try the genuinely tasty takeaway from **Wasabi** (Map pp886-7; ☎ 9225 6868; 323 Hay St; ☺ lunch) or the reputable **Matsuri** (Map p888; ☎ 9322 7737; QV1 Bldg, 250 St Georges Tce; mains $13-18; ☺ lunch & dinner), a minimalist eatery with food fit for a samurai.

If you need a quick bite, fill up on international cuisine for under $10. Down an escalator from the Hay St Mall is the **Metro Food Hall** (Map p888; cnr Hay & William Sts). Off the Hay St Mall is the slightly more upmarket **Carillon Arcade Food Hall** (Map p888; Carillon Arcade). Get your fill of burgers, hot chips and sundaes on the east side of William St, between Murray and Hay Sts.

Northbridge

In our experience Northbridge is the pulse of Perth (and its taste buds). With either fantastic plastic or just loose change, you'll satisfy most cravings here.

Toledo (Map p888; ☎ 9227 9222; 35 Lake St; mains $4-25; ☺ lunch & dinner) Get out your castanets! All-you-can-eat pizza ($10) and share-the-love tapas are popular with big groups on hot summer nights here.

Maya Masala (Map p888; ☎ 9328 5655; cnr Lake & Francis Sts; mains $13-19; ☺ dinner Tue-Sun) This warm hub is a favourite for superquick service and authentic Southern Indian *dosa* (massive crepes with delicious fillings). If you still have room, there are trillions of traditional sweets to choose from.

Red Teapot (Map p888; ☎ 9228 1981; 413 William St; mains $8-18; ☺ dinner Mon-Sat) This groovy little architect-designed spot has an extensive menu of Hong Kong–style dishes, such as Fragrant Prosperous Chicken. BYO, cash only, and book like crazy.

Thai Elephant (Map p888; ☎ 9227 5738; 323 William St; mains $11-20; ✷ dinner) Like its name, this hard-working restaurant hasn't forgotten its reliable, fragrant recipes and is still a favourite with locals.

Phi Yen (Map pp886-7; ☎ 9227 1032; 205 Lake St; ✷ lunch & dinner) A little walk before dinner will take you to venerable Vietnamese at the top of Northbridge, for seafood dishes.

Tarts (Map pp886-7; ☎ 9328 6607; 212 Lake St; mains $7-14; ✷ breakfast & lunch) Swedish language students, ornamental orange blossom, ladies who lunch and buy each other whisks…look deeper for the heart of Tarts, which is the provedore (local Western Australian produce, yum). The 'bellyfull' breakfast ($15) ensures the café is packed like a hamper on weekends.

Govinda's Restaurant (Map p888; ☎ 9227 1684; 200 William St; dishes $2-6; ✷ noon-2.30pm & 5-6pm Mon-Fri) An institution for budget-conscious vegetarians, who practically roll out of the simple cafeteria after the wholesome, Hare Krishna, all-you-can-eat lunch (still $6).

Self-caterers can stock up at **City Fresh Fruit Company** (Map p888; 393 William St), with healthy fruit and veg, or the pungent Continental deli at **Kakulas Bros** (Map p888; 14 William St; ✷ Mon-Sat), which stocks a huge selection of European imported goods.

Leederville

Oxford St offers up more than a few cafés and a laid-back groove. Good food followed by a film at the local Luna cinema (opposite) is a tempting combo.

Oxford 130 (Map pp886-7; 130 Oxford St; breakfast & snacks $5.50-12) One of the best breakfasts we've found in Perth: simple, casual and fresh. Hip locals pull up a stool by the open windows while the staff do what they're great at.

See opposite for a selection of Leederville's finest establishments.

Subiaco

Wander down the gentrified slope of Rokeby Rd in 'Subi' and enjoy the shop windows and window shoppers.

Subiaco Hotel (Map pp886-7; ☎ 9381 3069; 465 Hay St; mains $19-25; ✷ breakfast, lunch & dinner) Another gem in the crown of pubs circling Perth,

and the food is also royally good: try the tasting platter. Breakfasting magnates are commonly sighted, but don't let that put you off your croissant.

Walk Café (Map pp886-7; ☎ 9381 2466; Shop 5, 9 Rokeby Rd; meals $8-23; ✷ breakfast, lunch & dinner) If you have a car, it's worth the trip here for breakfast. Sit out under the trees and watch Subi strut by as you devour delectable corn fritters.

Altos (Map pp886-7; ☎ 9382 3292; 424 Hay St; meals $16-33; ✷ dinner) There's a mix of traditional and modern Italian on the menu, but Ada's handmade gnocchi melts in the mouth.

Greater Perth

A food strip worth the trip is Beaufort St, Mt Lawley. Catch bus No 67 or wander up from Northbridge through Highgate.

Indiana Teahouse (Map pp884-5; ☎ 9385 5005; Marine Pde, Cottesloe; mains $17-32; ✷ lunch & dinner) It's a bit overpriced but we'd pay just to sit by the window in this atmospheric villa (which dropped out of the sky during time travel from colonial India) on the beach. A G&T in the late rays of the sun is a must.

Must Winebar (Map pp886-7; ☎ 9328 8255; 519 Beaufort St, Highgate; mains $15-30; ✷ lunch & dinner) This bar-restaurant is fond of itself, but has reasons to be: the fresh fare and wine list sampled by a throng of Perth's beautiful business people. One word – scallops.

Queens Tavern (Map pp886-7; ☎ 9328 7374; 520 Beaufort St, Highgate; mains $12-25; ✷ lunch & dinner) Once a coach house (1899), Queens is now an alehouse for all seasons. Experience the cooling 'Arizona mist' in the beer garden where sprays of fine droplets evaporate just before they reach the punters below. When it's chilly, find one of the fireplaces upstairs.

AUTHOR'S CHOICE

Jackson's (Map pp886-7; ☎ 9328 1177; www .jacksonsrestaurant.com.au; 483 Beaufort St, Highgate; mains $20-38, degustation $110; ✷ lunch & dinner) You'll want to kiss the excellent wait staff, or chef Hugh Jackson himself, after you have tried all 10 dishes on the 'Dego', the famous degustation menu. Over three hours, morsel after scrumptious morsel arrives on the table like artworks on small white canvases. In between, your glass is refreshed with wines that complement the food.

DRINKING

You won't be in Perth long before you hear about the legendary Sunday Sesh (Sunday Session). Everyone within cooee of a pub heads there for a long afternoon of beer and conversation (not necessarily in that order). While it seems all the pubs in the Western suburbs have been turned into old folks' homes, there's an ever-growing scene in Northbridge.

Brass Monkey Bar & Brasserie (Map p888; ☎ 9227 9596; 209 William St, Northbridge) Outdoors mingles with in at this fantastic pub, which boasts cavernous class and a shade-dappled beer garden. Caps and comb-overs, ties and tats, T-shirts and G-strings: all agree the beer is as good as the food. Tiny tots are welcome too.

Universal Bar (Map p888; ☎ 9227 6771; 221 William St, Northbridge; ☼ 4pm-late) Open-fronted, bold and hip to the funk with live music Monday to Saturday. Go the bar snacks.

Deen (Aberdeen Hotel; Map p888; ☎ 9227 9361; 84 Aberdeen St, Northbridge; ☼ 5pm-1am Mon, 3pm-2am Fri, 5pm-2am Sat) You're sure to hear the Aussie anthem *Land Down Under* (number-one DJ request). Even if you actually know what a Vegemite sandwich is, don't leave town without attending Monday's backpacker night. Beyond the crazy front bar there are pool tables and six separate bar zones.

Shed (Map p888; ☎ 9228 2200; 81 Aberdeen St, Northbridge; ☼ noon-midnight Wed-Fri, noon-2am Sat & Sun) A new pub aiming for Oz appeal: it's all outdoor bars, sandstone and water-tank features.

Though quiet compared to Northbridge, the city also has some places worth seeking out.

Hudson's Bar & Gallery (Map p888; ☎ 9322 1088; 76 King St) Bastion of the local art community, this successful urban space lends itself to different media, subsidising exhibitions with Cosmopolitan cocktails. Friday night's the night; openings are on Saturday.

Box Deli (Map p888; ☎ 9322 6744; 918 Hay St) A contemporary bar attracting a self-satisfied crowd that clusters in its intimate transit lounge, drinking lychee cocktails.

écucina (Map p888; ☎ 94811020; www.ecucina .com.au; 777 Hay St) Overlooking Perth's version of Central Park, this café-bar-restaurant is a good place in which to rest and look at some evergreens while you down a strong, long black.

Also worth a gander are the **Moon & Sixpence** (Map p888; ☎ 9481 1000; 300 Murray St), an English-style pub with many a backpacker; and **Lucky Shag** (Map p888; ☎ 9221 0203; Barrack St Jetty), where office workers are liable to get a cold beer and some waterfront breeze down their suits.

The beachside pubs are famous for their Sunday Sesh. Get a tan in the middle of the pub at Cottesloe's open-windowed institution the **Ocean Beach Hotel** (OBH; Map p884-5; ☎ 9384 5111; 1 Eric St, Cottesloe) or the equally popular **Cottesloe Beach Hotel** (The Cott; Map pp884-5; ☎ 9383 1100; 104 Marine Pde, Cottesloe).

In the 'burbs, the **Leederville Hotel** (Map pp886-7; ☎ 9286 0150; 742 Newcastle St, Leederville) is funky on Friday and on Wednesday nights it's packed. Other popular venues for a Sunday Session are the **Subiaco Hotel** (The Subi; Map pp886-7; ☎ 9381 3069; cnr Rokeby Rd & Hay St, Subiaco) and Mt Lawley's **Queens Tavern** (Map p888; ☎ 9328 7267; 520 Beaufort St, Highgate).

The city centre's **Java Juice** (Map p888; Hay St) keeps hangovers and diets happy.

ENTERTAINMENT

Northbridge, Leederville, Subiaco and Fremantle are the main places to go after dark. **Xpress** (www.xpressmag.com.au), the free weekly entertainment mag, produces a gig and clubbing guide, and it's available at music shops and on the net. Check the *West Australian* for theatre, cinema and nightclub events.

Cinemas

Luna (Map pp886-7; ☎ 9444 4056; www.lunapalace.com .au; 155 Oxford St, Leederville) Retro Luna shows the latest indie flicks in its outdoor courtyard cinema (double features on Monday, $9.50).

Camelot Outdoor Cinema (Map pp884-5; ☎ 9370 1777; Memorial Hall, Lochee St, Mosman Park; ☼ Dec-Apr) Not far from Cottesloe, Camelot offers wood-fired pizzas, a fully licensed bar and nightly movies under the stars.

Somerville Outdoor Cinema (UWA; Map pp886-7; ☎ 6488 6000; adult/concession $15/10) Get your fix of cult films and world movies under the pines at the University of WA.

Cinema Paradiso (Map p888; ☎ 9227 1771; 164 James St, Northbridge) Screens film festivals and quality art-house films.

Astor (Map pp886-7; ☎ 9370 1777; 659 Beaufort St, Mt Lawley) This sister cinema to Cinema Paradiso holds cry-baby sessions and a seniors' movie and lunch, monthly.

WESTERN AUSTRALIA

Mainstream films screen at **Greater Union** (Map p888; www.greaterunion.com.au), **Hoyts** (Map p888; www.hoyts.ninemsn.com.au) and suburban cinemas; budget night is called 'tightarse Tuesday'.

Classical Music & Theatre

Catch the latest hit plays at the historic **His Majesty's Theatre** ('the Maj'; Map p888; ☎ 9265 0900; ☟ 8.30am-5pm, open later during shows), the modern **Playhouse Theatre** (Map p888; ☎ 9325 3344; 3 Pier St) or the **Subiaco Theatre Centre** (Map pp886-7; ☎ 9382 3385; 180 Hamersley Rd, Subiaco). Regular classical concerts and recitals by local and international acts are usually performed at the **Perth Concert Hall** (Map p888; ☎ 9231 9900; www.perthconcerthall.com.au; 5 St Georges Tce). Session times and programmes appear daily in the *West Australian*, or book tickets for all four through **BOCS ticketing** (☎ 1800 193 300).

Gay & Lesbian Venues

Highlights of a gay year include the Big Gay Out in February and Pride Week in October. The **Arcane Bookshop** (p889) has free copies of the fortnightly gay and lesbian newspaper **OutinPerth** (www.outinperth.com) the magazine **Women out West** (www.womenoutwest.com.au). Both feature the latest venues, news and events.

Grapeskin (Map p888; ☎ 9227 9596; 209 William St, Northbridge) Next to the Brass Monkey, this bacchanalian place has captured a magnificent cocktail genie behind the bar who can fulfil your every wish. Rub up against a rainbow crowd of gays and straights.

eurobar (Map p888; ☎ 9227 5244; cnr Lake & Aberdeen Sts, Northbridge) A friendly spot with a penchant for pop. Shows on Sunday night feature the 'lady' who inspired the big Australian movie *Priscilla Queen of the Desert*.

Court Hotel (Map p888; ☎ 9328 5292; 50 Beaufort St) This drag-show venue has had an extension in the direction of the beer garden. New Year's Eve features big identities.

Nightclubs & Live Music

You can't miss the clubs of Northbridge: look for the usual queues, door bitches and hair products. There's free admission and cheap drinks during the week, but the weekend means cover charges and a ban on shorts.

Paramount (Map p888; ☎ 9228 1344; 163 Lake St) Live bands, techno, doof – your night will have many phases. Surfie types and clubbers join forces and share poisons at this multilevel pub-club, which has cheap entry and grog specials.

Office Nightclub (Map p888; ☎ 9228 0077; cnr Aberdeen & Parker Sts; ☟ 8pm-late Wed-Sat) Get there early to avoid the cover charge 'cos you'll pay for the overpriced drinks. Then play like you don't have to work at this popular revamped club. There are alternating live bands and DJs here.

Metro City (Map p888; ☎ 9228 0500; 146 Roe St Northbridge) Perth's biggest city nightclub (why are they always called Metro?) has great architecture inside (the glass top floor is for members, of course). Ring for upcoming events at this intimate band and dance-party venue that's on the edge between the city and Northbridge.

Moon (Map p888; ☎ 9328 7474; 323 William St Northbridge) For a little taste of Australia's east coast on its west, slink in here for jazz and retro tunes which filter through until sunrise. It's better for drinking than eating.

Float to Subiaco for cosmopolitan **Club Red Sea** (Map pp886-7; ☎ 9382 2022; Rokeby Rd, Subiaco) and its co-club Under the Sea. We also loved the hip bar scene of Beaufort St.

Sport

In summer hoards head for the **WACA** (Western Australian Cricket Association ground; Map pp886-7, ☎ 9265 7222; Nelson Cres, East Perth) to catch the drama of one-day and test-match cricket.

Come winter (or WA's attempt at the season), lovely **Subiaco Oval** (Map pp886-7) is the place to be. Join Australian Rules football fans in watching the Dockers (Fremantle's beloved team) and the Eagles (Perth's West Coast Eagles) tough it out in the annual derby (but home rivalry vanishes when either team takes on the other Australian states). Sports fans can also watch the Perth Wildcats tear up the court in the National Basketball League (NBL), or Perth Glory's skills in the National Soccer League. There's also one of Australia's newest Rugby Super 12 franchises here. Check the *West Australian* for game details and venues.

SHOPPING

The Hay and Murray St Malls border the city's shopping heartland, while James St Mall has a stylish selection of boutique shops. Opals and souvenirs for home can be found along the London Court arcade. The new Harbour Town complex just west of the CBD, at City West station, has a kazillion clothing outlets. Upmarket Subiaco's Rokeby Rd and Hay St boast high fashion and classy souvenirs.

Leederville's Oxford St is the place for groovy boutiques and eclectic music and bookshops.

Vinnie's Retro (Map p888; ☎ 9228 4877; 267 William St, Northbridge; ☼ 9am-4.30pm) Here's a lion of a wardrobe for when you feel like hitting the town in plaid or sparkles. There's even a wedding dress section if you want special treatment.

Indigenart (Map pp886-7; ☎ 9388 2899; 115 Hay St) For those with an interest in art or indigenous culture.

Subiaco Pavilion Markets (Map pp886-7; cnr Roberts & Rokeby Rds, Subiaco; ☼ Thu-Sun) It's worth a wander around the small stalls of jewellery, and there's a food hall on the city side.

Galleria Arts & Craft Market (Map p888; Perth Cultural Centre, James St; ☼ 9am-5pm Sat & Sun) When in the city check out this weekend market.

GETTING THERE & AWAY
Air
Qantas (Map p888; ☎ 13 13 13; www.qantas.com.au; 55 William St) has direct economy flights to/from Adelaide (one way from $230), Alice Springs (from $270), Darwin (from $265), Melbourne (from $220), Sydney (from $265) and Brisbane (from $305). Within WA, Qantas also flies to Broome (one way from $265) and Kalgoorlie ($155). **Virgin Blue** (☎ 13 67 89; www.virginblue.com.au) also offers flights to/from Adelaide (one way from $170), Sydney (from $220), Melbourne (from $200), Brisbane (from $250) and Broome (from $200). Of course fares are changeable, so check both the Qantas and Virgin Blue websites for up-to-the-minute discounts and special deals.

Skywest (☎ 1300 660 088; www.skywest.com.au) flies to many regional centres, including Albany, Esperance, Exmouth, Carnarvon and Kalgoorlie.

Bus
Greyhound Australia (☎ 13 14 99; www.greyhound.com; ☼ 7am-9pm) has daily buses from Perth's Wellington St bus station, heading north to Darwin and east to Adelaide via Kalgoorlie. The **Nullarbor Traveller** (☎ 1800 816 858; www.the-traveller.com.au) runs leisurely minibus trips between Adelaide and Perth.

Transwa (☎ 1300 662 205; www.transwa.wa.gov.au) has bus services from the East Perth train station to many regional destinations and as far as Esperance, Kalbarri and Kalgoorlie. **Integrity** (☎ 9226 1339) runs regular northbound buses from the Wellington St bus station as far as Broome. **South West Coachlines** (☎ 9324 2333) runs daily buses between the City Busport and Bunbury and Margaret River. **Perth Goldfields Express** (☎ 1800 620 440) has buses to/from Laverton via Kalgoorlie, while **Easyrider Backpacker Tours** (Map p888; ☎ 9226 0307; www.easyridertours.com.au; 144 William St) has hop-on, hop-off services in the southwest, and along the coastal route to Broome and on to Darwin.

Car
No matter which way you look at it, or where you're coming from, driving to Perth from any other state involves desert and is a bloody long way (around 4400km from Sydney). However if you've got your own wheels and companions to share the driving and the fuel costs, it's still probably the cheapest way of getting to Perth. It's certainly the best way to see the country.

Train
The *Indian Pacific* travels twice weekly each way between Sydney and Perth via Kalgoorlie. One-way fares from Adelaide to Perth for an economy 'daynighter' seat/economy sleeper/1st-class sleeper (including meals)/concession sleeper are $310/960/1250/850, while fares from Sydney are $515/1250/1640/1178. The *Indian Pacific* departs from East Perth train station at 11.55am on Monday and Friday. You can make rail connections in Adelaide for the *Overland* to Melbourne and for the *Ghan* to Alice Springs. Book your tickets through **Great Southern Railways** (☎ 13 21 47; www.gsr.com.au).

The *AvonLink* commuter service from Perth to Northam (via Midland and Toodyay), and the *Prospector* to Kalgoorlie, arrive and depart from the East Perth terminal. The *Prospector* has at least one service in each direction daily, and the full trip takes eight hours. It leaves Perth around 7.15am Monday to Saturday and at 2.10pm on Sunday. The 2½-hour *Australind* service to Bunbury departs from Perth train station at 9.30am and 5.55pm daily. Reservations can be made with **Transwa** (☎ 1300 662 205).

WESTERN AUSTRALIA

WESTERN AUSTRALIA

GETTING AROUND

Perth is easy to get around, with an efficient, fully integrated public transport system that is free in the city centre. The zone involves Transperth buses and trains within the area bounded by Northbridge (Newcastle St) in the north, the river in the south, King's Park in the west and the Causeway in the east. For more info on services, see below.

To/From the Airport

Perth's domestic and international terminals are about 11km and 15km from the city centre. **Swan Taxis** (☎ 13 13 88) can get you to the city from the terminals for around $22 and $28, respectively.

The privately run **Airport-City Shuttle Bus** (☎ 9277 7015) meets all incoming domestic and international flights, and provides transport to/from the city centre, hotels and hostels ($11/13 one way to domestic/international terminal). Call for more information on hotel and hostel pick-ups and timetables.

Alternatively, catch Transperth bus No 37 every half-hour from the domestic airport to the City Busport for $3.

Car & Motorcycle

HIRE

Better deals are available from the smaller operators, but make sure you read the small print and know what your insurance covers you for. **Bayswater Car Rental** (Map pp886-7; ☎ 9325 1000; www.bayswatercarrental.com.au; 160 Adelaide Tce) offers cheaper rates and no-fuss white cars. For sporty banana-yellow and good deals on unlimited kilometres, try **M2000 Car Rental** (Map pp886-7; ☎ 9325 4110; 166 Adelaide Tce), across the road.

Avis (Map pp886-7; ☎ 13 63 33), **Budget** (Map p888; ☎ 13 27 27), **Hertz** (Map p888; ☎ 13 30 39) and **Thrifty** (Map pp886-7; ☎ 9464 7444; reservations@thrifty.com.au) are all represented in Perth (including at the airport).

Public Transport

Transperth (☎ 13 62 13; www.transperth.wa.gov.au; ☯ 7.30am-5.30pm Mon-Fri) operates the city's public buses, trains and ferries, and has information offices in the Plaza Arcade (off the Hay St Mall), Perth train station, the City Busport on Mounts Bay Rd and Wellington St bus station. The Plaza Arcade office also opens from 8am to 5pm on Saturday, and the City Busport office from noon to 4pm

on Sunday. A single ticket allows you to travel on all forms of transport. Family day tickets are awesome value at $7.50.

BOAT

Transperth ferries (☎ 13 62 13) depart every half-hour, on the hour, from 7am to 7pm daily from the Barrack St Jetty to the zoo (one way adult/child $1.30/50c).

BUS

You can get to most sights in the inner city with the free CAT bus services in the city centre, running from 6.50am to 6.20pm on weekdays. The lumbering (red, blue or yellow) buses are state-of-the-art and have displays and audio services at the stops, which tell you when the next bus is due. There's a bit of a longer wait on weekends (every 15 to 35 minutes from 10am).

Maps of the routes are readily available all over the city. The Red CAT operates east–west from the WACA in East Perth to Outram St (next to King's Park) and back, every five minutes. The Blue CAT operates north–south from Barrack St Jetty to Northbridge, every seven minutes. Special Friday, Saturday and Sunday night services carry the party crowd from the city to Northbridge, and run every 15 minutes to 1am. The Yellow CAT goes east–west on Wellington St, to/from East Perth.

On regular buses, a short ride within one zone is $3, two zones $3.20 and three zones $5. Zone 1 covers the inner suburbs (including Subiaco and Claremont) and Zone 2 extends all the way west to Fremantle. Zone 3 extends to the outer suburbs, including Armadale. A MultiRider ticket gives 10 journeys for the price of nine, and a DayRider (available after 9am on weekdays) costs $7.50.

TRAIN

Transperth (☎ 13 62 13) also operates the Fastrak suburban train lines to Armadale, Fremantle, Midland and the northern suburb of Joondalup, from around 5.20am to midnight Monday to Friday, with reduced services on the weekend. There's free train travel (in the free transit zone) between the Claisebrook and City West train stations.

All local trains leave from the Perth train station on Wellington St. Your rail ticket can also be used on Transperth buses and ferries within its zone.

FREMANTLE

☎ 08 / pop 25,000

When you first walk through the close streets of this historic port town, on the mouth of the Swan River, you almost expect a piped theme tune to emerge from hidden speakers ('It's a small world after all'?). Consistent colonial architecture and a relaxed, alternative *joie de vivre* make Fremantle a highlight of WA. While you're there you'll be swept up in the quality museums, music and arts scene and the happening hippies, ferals and freaks, all beetling around the café strip and monumental pubs. This charisma is as refreshing as the Fremantle Doctor, the afternoon breeze that whistles through on a slow, hot afternoon. You'll grow sentimental for 'Freo' as soon as you've left.

HISTORY

Noongar people used this area for ceremony and trade. Charles Fremantle and the HMS *Challenger* arrived in 1829, but the new European settlement made little progress until it began taking in convicts in the 1850s. Just 50 years ago, not many people here would willingly admit their convict ancestry. Now it's a different story: the locals of Fremantle take pride in their heritage and the historic buildings that convict and Aboriginal labour helped to construct.

As a port, Fremantle was ineffective until the Irish engineer CY O'Connor (p955) built an artificial harbour in the 1890s (see his statue on South Fremantle Beach). However, this land was sacred to the local Noongar people and they put a curse on him. In the 1950s, Freo became the first port of call for postwar migrant ships.

Development after victory in the America's Cup forever transformed Freo from a sleepy port into a vibrant city, where Perth now spends its weekends.

INFORMATION

Chart & Map Shop (☎ 9335 8665; 14 Collie St) Maps and travel books, with excellent staff.

etech (☎ 9239 8112; 53 South Tce; per hr $3; ☺ 8.30am-7.30pm Mon-Fri, 10am-6pm Sat & Sun; ▢) Part of local TAFE. Quiet access and tech help.

Fremantle Public Hospital (☎ 9431 3333; Alma St)

Fremantle visitor information centre (☎ 9431 7878; fax 9431 7755; Town Hall, King's Sq; ☺ 9am-5pm Mon-Fri, 10am-3pm Sat, noon-3pm Sun)

WA Naturally (☎ 9430 8600; 47 Henry St) CALM's outdoor and nature information centre.

SIGHTS
Maritime Museums

The new **Western Australian Maritime Museum** (☎ 9431 8444; www.mm.wa.gov.au; Victoria Quay; adult/child $12/5, with submarine tour $15/5; ☺ 9.30am-5pm) looks like a ship in full sail, but once inside, you're in the belly of a whale. Apart from *Australia II*, complete with kooky models of its crew, you can learn about fishing, pearling, whaling and trade. High and dry next door is the 90m-long submarine HMAS *Ovens*, which gives an insight into life on a sub during WWII. One-hour tours are popular, so book early.

Near the waterfront is the fascinating **Shipwreck Museum** (☎ 9431 8444; 1 Cliff St; admission by donation; ☺ 9.30am-5pm). The gruesome story of the mutiny on the *Batavia*, and its majestic recovered hull, are well worth investigating. Free tours are held at 10am and 3pm daily. Aboriginal-heritage walking tours (adult/child $10/5) leave from the front entrance at 11.30am Wednesday, Friday and Sunday.

Markets

On the weekend, make sure you check out the lively **Fremantle Markets** (cnr South Tce & Henderson St; ☺ 9am-9pm Fri, 9am-5pm Sat, 10am-5pm Sun). The National Trust–listed building (1897) houses trinkets, art, things to make you smell good, seafood and fresh fruit. Indulge in a massage or find unusual souvenirs, including toys.

Tucked away in a relaxed, distinctly Australian corner of the shed, the **Fremantle Markets Bar** (☺ 10am-9pm Fri-Sun) is where musicians play acoustic sets every hour and drinks are poured every minute. See the owner if you want to perform and earn a bit of spindoola (money).

Grab a snack in the food court or browse the stalls in the popular dockside **E Shed Markets** (E Shed, Victoria Quay; ☺ 9am-6pm Fri-Sun).

Fremantle History Museum & Arts Centre

The **history museum** (☎ 9430 7966; www.museum.wa.gov.au; 1 Finnerty St; admission by donation; ☺ 10.30am-4.30pm Sun-Fri, 1-5pm Sat) and **arts centre** (☎ 9432

WESTERN AUSTRALIA

FREMANTLE

WESTERN AUSTRALIA

INFORMATION
Chart & Map Shop..................1 C6
etech 2 D6
Fremantle Public Hospital........3 D6
Visitors Centre.......................4 D5
WA Naturally (CALM)..............5 C6

SIGHTS & ACTIVITIES
E Shed Markets.......................6 C5
Fremantle History Museum &
    Arts Centre..........................7 E3
Fremantle Markets...................8 D5
Fremantle Motor Museum.........9 B5
Fremantle Tram......................10 D5
HMAS Ovens Submarine..........11 B5
Leeuwin Ocean Adventure
    Foundation..........................12 B5
Old Fremantle Prison...............13 E5
Round House...........................14 B6
St John's Anglican Church........15 D5
Samson House.........................16 E4
Shipwreck Museum..................17 C6
Western Australian Maritime
    Museum...............................18 B5

SLEEPING
Fremantle Colonial
    Accommodation....................19 E5
Fremantle Hotel.......................20 D6
Norfolk Hotel..........................21 D6
Old Firestation Backpackers......22 C5
Pirates....................................23 D6
Port Mill Bed & Breakfast.........24 D6
Sundancer Backpackers............25 C5
Terrace Central B&B.................26 D6

EATING
Bengal.................................(see 22)
Gino's...................................27 D5
Han's Café.............................28 C6
Harvest..................................29 E1
Old Shanghai Food Market......30 D5
Pizza Bella Roma....................31 D5
Roma....................................32 C5

DRINKING
Fremantle Markets Bar.............33 D6
Left Bank Bar & Café...............34 F2
Little Creatures.......................35 C6
Sail & Anchor Hotel.................36 D5

ENTERTAINMENT
Clink...................................(see 31)
Fly by Night Musician's Club....37 D5
Hoyts Millennium....................38 C6
Hoyts Queensgate...................39 D5
Kulcha...............................(see 27)
Luna SX.................................40 D6
Metropolis..........................(see 31)
Mojo's...................................41 E1
Swan Basement......................42 E1

SHOPPING
Indigenart...........................(see 25)
Kakulas Sister.........................43 C5
New Edition Bookshop.............44 D5

TRANSPORT
East St Jetty............................45 E2
Northport Terminal..................46 A5
Overseas Passenger Terminal....47 D3
Rottnest Ferry........................48 B5

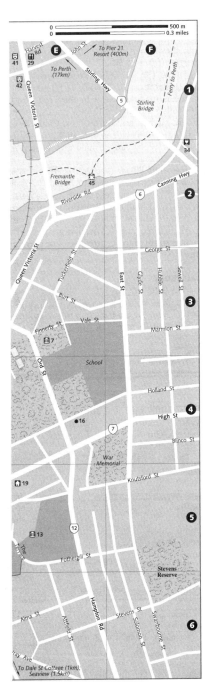

9555; www.fac.org.au; admission free; 10am-5pm) were the site of a lunatic asylum in the 1860s. These days madness and its brilliant sister, creativity, are celebrated with exhibitions, 'create courses', a courtyard full of summer music and a fabulous café. The museum has exhibits on Fremantle's black and white history, and the ships that first 'discovered' the western coast of Australia.

Round House

The oldest public building in WA (1831) is the **Round House** (Arthur Head, High St; admission by gold coin donation; 10.30am-3.30pm). In 1829 the 700-strong population of Freo needed a prison, and this carefully designed, 12-sided stone structure became the first permanent building. It was the site of the colony's first hanging, that of a 15-year-old boy who had shot his boss's son. Later the building was used to hold Aboriginal prisoners before they were incarcerated on Rottnest Island. In a nasty irony, before settlement the site was a ceremonial meeting place for the Noongar people.

Old Fremantle Prison

In 1842 boys and men were shipped from the Isle of Wight to construct this hilltop **prison** (9336 9200; www.fremantleprison.com; 1 The Terrace; day tours adult/child $15/7.20, night tours $18/8.80; 11am-5pm, night tours Wed & Fri 7pm), which practically sits on top of Fremantle's Cappuccino Strip. It then went on to become a maximum-security institution until 1991. Visitors can trace their convict heritage in the museum here, or attend a facts-packed tour of the main cell blocks (every half-hour). If you are totally unflappable, you may be able to endure the 1½-hour candlelight tour without an accident in your pantaloons.

Gold-Rush Landmarks

A visit to some of the buildings of this period hints at what it was like a century ago. **Samson House** (61 Ellen St; donation requested $3; 1-5pm Sun, closed public holidays), was the residence of a wine merchant, and then two mayors, none of whom ever threw anything out; it's like stepping into your great uncle's lounge room. Other buildings of note are the 1887 **Fremantle Town Hall** (Kings Sq) and the nearby 1882 **St John's Anglican Church** (cnr Adelaide & Queen Sts), near the visitor centre.

WESTERN AUSTRALIA

Fremantle Motor Museum

On Victoria Quay, the **museum** (☎ 9336 5222; www.fremantlemotormuseum.net; B Shed, Victoria Quay; adult/child/family $9.50/5/23; ⌚ 9.30am-5pm) houses a private collection of wheels owned by one mining magnate. British racers, historic motorcycles, a Ferrari and the first Holden prototype are all licensed and still grace the track. Even Wally's chariot from the much-loved Australian movie *Crocodile Dundee* has made its way here. That's not a ute, *this* is a ute.

TOURS

Capricorn Kayak Tours (☎ 9433 3802; www .capricornkayak.com.au; trips $130) From September to June, this Fremantle-based company offers full-day kayaking trips around Penguin and Seal Islands, leaving from Fremantle at 8am. See p882 for details of other kayaking trips.

Fremantle Tram (☎ 9339 8719; www.tramswest.com .au; ⌚ 10am to 4pm) A good way to see all the historical spots in one ride. Daily 45-minute tours with commentary (adult/child/family $10/3/20) depart from the town hall on the hour. There's also the 1½-hour Top of the Port tour ($15/5/30). The Friday-night Ghostly Tour includes fish and chips, and slips through little-known graveyards, the prison and the Round House (adult/child $44/30; book ahead).

FESTIVALS & EVENTS

Blessing of the Fleet October.

Busker's Festival April.

Festival of Fremantle This 10-day festival in November is the city's largest annual event, featuring street parades, concerts, exhibitions and free performances.

Sardine Festival Fun for foodies in January, with gourmet yabbies, crocodile, seafood and sardines on offer.

SLEEPING

Budget

If you're staying for a while, weekly rates are a whole lot cheaper here.

Sundancer Backpackers (☎ 1800 061 144; www .sundancerbackpackers.com; 80 High St; dm $17-20, d with/ without bathroom $70/50; ⌘) Close to the station, the first thing you see at this welcoming heritage pad is the residents' bar. Shortly afterwards you might discover the funky murals, pool table, outdoor spa and free DVDs.

Old Firestation Backpackers (☎ 9430 5454; www .old-firestation.net; 18 Phillimore St; dm/d $17/45; ⌘) Behold, is this a dorm with natural light and fresh currents of air? It feels secure here

and the girls have their own space. Along with the toga parties, surf trips and free net, they'll keep you fed with BBQs ($5) and curries (from $3.50).

Pirates (☎ 9335 6635; www.planetbackpack.com .au; 11 Essex St; dm $19-21, d $65; ⌘) This small fish has made a splash in the Freo pond. It's fully renovated with new management, linen, kitchen and bathrooms. Cabin boys will enjoy 200 videos and an Xbox, while outdoor types can be hale and hearty in the BBQ area.

Fremantle Village (Map pp884-5; ☎ 9430 4866; www.fremantlevillage.com.au; Lot 1, Cockburn Rd, South Fremantle; powered/unpowered sites per 2 people $24/22, cabins $74) Although its little domes look like a termite village, this is the only caravan park in Freo and it's well organised. It's 3.5km south of the centre by car, or you can the CAT to Stop 18.

Midrange

Norfolk Hotel (☎ 9335 5405; fax 9430 5908; 47 South Tce; s/d $85/95, without bathroom $45/65) The location is tops, and the no-frills pub rooms (plump pillows, no TV) are on top of the action. The sandstone courtyard below is full of feasting and merriment all weekend.

Fremantle Hotel (☎ 9430 4300; fax 9335 2636; cnr Cliff & High Sts; s/tw $60/90, d with/without bathroom $95/80) This smokily atmospheric hotel, with its haunting dark wood staircase, has been family operated almost all of its 106 years. The rooms are understated but well priced. You will still find old locals in the bar downstairs.

Terrace Central B&B (☎ 9335 6600; portfremantle@ bigpond.com; 83-85 South Tce; s/d ind breakfast $118/128; ⌘) Aladdin, the resident border collie, and his dad, Barry, preside (with devoted attention) over this terrace, close to the Cappuccino Strip. Individually decorated, the eight rooms now have en suites. Out the back, there are spanking new two-/three-bed units ($180).

Dale Street Cottage (☎ 9331 6875, 0413 685 902; 2A Dale St, South Fremantle; d $77-130) The wood-beamed lounge feels like a friend's home. There's even a garage for your beloved vehicle. Sleeps up to seven ($15 per extra person).

Fremantle Colonial Accommodation (☎ 9430 6568; fremantle.col@westnet.net.au; 215 High St; B&B s/d $127, 2-bed apt $132, cottages from $160; ⌘) Choose between the frilly terrace rooms with big beds or self-contained accommodation in three heritage, former wardens' cottages adjoining the hill-top prison.

Port Mill Bed & Breakfast (☎ 9433 3832; www .babs.com.au/portmill; 3/17 Essex St; s/d incl breakfast from $140/150) Old sandstone, curlicued balconies, red geraniums, white bedspreads…this convict-built court is the love child of Tuscany and Freo.

Top End

Pier 21 Resort (☎ 9336 2555; www.pier21resort.com .au; 9 John St, North Fremantle; d $157-177, 2-bed apt $210; P ✗ ⊠) Hiding in residential North Freo, right on the Swan River, this compact resort (of sorts) is accessible from the path along the river. The rooms have a holiday feel and there's free tennis for the kiddiewinks.

Quest Harbour Village (☎ 9430 3888; Mews Rd, Challenger Harbour; d from $185; P ✗) Right on the water, at the end of the marina, is Freo's breeziest accommodation. You're paying for the berth in these no-fuss rooms: sit on your own deck and hear the clink of the masts in an apartment with a spa ($250).

EATING
Cappuccino Strip

People-watching from pavement tables on the South Tce Cappuccino Strip is a legitimate lifestyle here.

Gino's (☎ 9336 1464; 1 South Tce; mains $9-24; ✑ breakfast, lunch & dinner) Queue up for great coffee, a seat-on-the-street and a patriarch's handle on the Freo scene. Morning pastries over the paper are *de rigueur* for locals.

Pizza Bella Roma (☎ 9335 1554; 14 South Tce; mains $12-26; ✑ dinner) It's an almighty claim to make, but some say this Italian joint does the best pizza in Freo. Settle back by the window to watch the South Tce crowds mill by and you'll be served with alacrity.

Han's Café (☎ 9433 5668; Shop 1, 27 Collie St; mains $4-15; ✑ lunch & dinner) You'll see Han's Cafés everywhere in Perth: it's like a chain, but it's justifiably popular. This one is newer than the rest and does healthy, generous serves of authentic Asian cuisines.

Old Shanghai Food Market (4 Henderson St; mains $5-14; ✑ lunch & dinner) You'll be lucky to get a seat because the locals adore this food hall off South Tce, next to the markets. Good food in large portions, 'til 9pm most nights.

West End, Harbour & North of the River

Little Creatures (☎ 9430 5555; www.littlecreatures .au; 40 Mews Rd; mains $13-20; ✑ breakfast, lunch & dinner) No matter how they vote, what they wear or whether they have hair, people swear by the fresh, excellent Mod Oz food here (wood-fired pizzas, chilli mussels $17).

Harvest (☎ 9336 1831; 1 Harvest Rd, North Fremantle; mains $11-30; ✑ dinner) A richly decorated bungalow is the setting for the sumptuous food at this restaurant, which feels like one big dinner party. The desserts will curl your toes.

Roma (☎ 9335 3664; 9 High St; mains $10-23; ✑ dinner) On your way to the Round House you might come across this unassuming Italian place, straight outta 1954. The food is *buonissimo*. Chicken Parmigiana shares the menu with *zuppa di mare* made with fresh local seafood.

Bengal (☎ 9335 2400; 18 Phillimore St; mains $17-21; ✑ dinner Tue-Sun) Underneath the Old Firestation Backpackers, this licensed Indian has tasty curries and a fun atmosphere. In backpacker spirit there's free Internet here, or free delivery there.

DRINKING

Little Creatures (☎ 9430 5555; www.littlecreatures .com.au; 40 Mews Rd) Outstanding. In every way. The staff are Freo's best and fairest. The pale ale is award winning, and the hangar-sized active brewery-bar-restaurant is pumping and pouring day and night. You'll want to come back, and back again.

Sail & Anchor Hotel (The Sail; ☎ 9335 8433; www .sailandanchor.com.au; 64 South Tce) The gigantic front bar of Australia's first brewery-pub is proud to pour boutique beers on tap, such as its Indian Pale Ale. Sample six award-winning beers on a brewery tour ($10), then head up the glorious stairs to Top Deck.

Left Bank Bar & Café (☎ 9319 1315; 15 Riverside Rd) Don't expect anything too bohemian – you're more likely to see football players than Parisian artists here on the river. The Lefty is famous for its Sunday Sesh and in the morning you can recover here over a decent brekky.

Seaview (☎ 9335 2259; 282 South Tce, South Fremantle) Owned by three Dockers football players, this is the ultimate sporto pub, throwing a little tapas and a huge Sunday-friendly beer garden into the fray.

ENTERTAINMENT

Freo's live music scene is legendary. This is where local Aussie musician John Butler and his trio planted the seeds of their wild musical tree, and the home of the 'Freo Sound', where bands like Eskimo Joe and Little Birdy emerged. There are as many local bands as there are types of beer here – like Juncadelic, who play on top of garbage bins! – and enough cool venues to make Freo worth a band safari on weekends.

Mojo's (☎ 9430 4010; 237 Queen Victoria St; ❂ 7pm-late Tue-Sun) Across the river in North Fremantle, this indie-music venue is all about rock and the local scene.

Swan Basement (☎ 9335 2725; cnr Tydeman Rd & Queen Victoria St) In the old Swan Hotel across the bridge, groovers go underground to this soundproof venue for late gigs.

Fly by Night Musician's Club (☎ 9430 5976; www .flybynight.org; Parry St) Variety is the key here, from international acts to local sets (with hip-hop, trance and jazz in between). It's smoke-free. Book ahead for big names.

Kulcha (☎ 9336 4544; www.kulcha.com.au; 13 South Tce; tickets $12, at the door $14) Live music, workshops, visiting artists, drumming classes – if it has a pulse it's alive upstairs at Kulcha. Check the website or the posters on the door.

Clink (54 South Tce; admission $3; ❂ 8pm-late) How appropriate: an underground dance club in an old jail cell. Rapscallions, gals and sailors spend their doubloons on rum and dance to jailhouse pop – nothing's changed!

Metropolis (☎ 9336 1880; 58 South Tce; ❂ 8pm-5am Fri, 9pm-6am Sat, 9pm-1am Sun) There are lines up the street for this dance club, especially on Saturday. If you wear a skirt that's more like a belt, you should get in.

Luna SX (☎ 9430 5999; Essex St) screens the latest art-house and independent films. For blockbusters, try **Hoyts Millennium** (Collie St) or **Hoyts Queensgate** (6 William St).

SHOPPING

Indigenart (☎ 9335 2911; 82 High St) This is the best place to purchase indigenous Australian art. Proceeds and royalties go to the artists themselves through community art centres, a major source for community development. The superb gallery space holds central and western desert dot paintings, X-ray art, totemic pieces from the Tiwi Islands, and contemporary works. Staff are knowledgeable.

MINTOX

Maybe it's because they're a long way from anywhere, but Western Australians have concocted some remarkable expressions all of their own.

- Black budgie: a (large) blowfly
- Deadly treadly: a wonderful bicycle
- Down south: the area from Dunsborough to Augusta
- Fanta pants: a red-headed person
- Mintox: if 'mint' means good, for some reason 'mintox' means strongly good
- Sesh: the Sunday session of drinking at a pub
- Wingwong on a goose's bridle: an object whose purpose is unclear

---

New Edition Bookshop (☎ 9335 2383; 50 South Tce; ❂ 10am-10pm) Open late, this is your destination for quality fiction.

Kakulas Sister (☎ 9430 4445; 29-31 Market St) Related to the Northbridge store, here's where you'll find great cheese and other foodstuffs of a Mediterranean persuasion.

GETTING THERE & AROUND

The **Fremantle Airport Shuttle** (☎ 9335 1614) leaves for the airport eight times daily from 8.15am to 9.15pm, picking up passengers at their accommodation ($25 per person, bookings essential). It also runs shuttle services from the airport to Fremantle 24 hours. It costs $20 per person, $30 for two and $35 for a family of four.

The train between Perth and Fremantle runs every 10 minutes or so throughout the day ($3). Bus Nos 105, 106 and 111 from the City Busport in Perth go along St Georges Tce to Fremantle via Canning Hwy. Bus Nos 103 and 104 depart from St Georges Tce and head to Fremantle station via the north side of the river.

Oceanic Cruises (☎ 9325 1191) has daily ferries at 8.45am, 10am, noon and 2pm from Perth's Barrack St Jetty to Freo; they depart at 11am, 1pm, 3.15pm and 5.30pm for the return journey (one way adult/child $14/9, return $22/12).

There is a plethora of one-way streets and parking meters in Freo. It's easy enough to travel by foot or on the free CAT bus service, which takes in all the major sites on a continuous route every 10 minutes from 7.30am to 6pm on weekdays and 10am to 6pm on the weekend.

AROUND PERTH

ROTTNEST ISLAND

☎ 08 / pop 200

From Boxing Day until the first week of February, the only way you can stay on 'Rotto' is if you're lucky in the yearly ballot. Published in the *West Australian* every June, it's a litmus test for the island's popularity with both travellers and locals. However Rotto is still worth a day trip: there's native wildlife to spot, aqua shoals and white sand to explore, and bikes for hire on this 'car-free paradise'. In fact, there's more than a bit of traffic: people on bikes of all sizes and descriptions; the new train; food vans; luggage forklifts from the ferries; boats; and the building equipment you'd expect from a $4 million upgrade of accommodation and disabled access at Longreach and Fays Bays in 2005.

Away from Thomson Bay, the island's largest settlement, it's cruisy and quiet, and this is emphasised by the cry of roaming peacocks. Look back across the ocean in all its hues to the tiny city skyline of Perth, where only seven towers are visible. Vlamingh Lookout offers up a panorama of the island itself.

History

Dutch explorer Willem de Vlamingh declared this 11km sand hill 'a paradise' when he came upon it in 1696. Prior to that it was known as Wadjemup to the Noongar people, whose connection with it stretched back 7000 years, when the island was connected to the mainland.

Europeans settled here in 1831. Not long after it became a prison for Aboriginal men, transported from as far away as Port Hedland for minor crimes such as stealing sheep. These men constructed the older buildings, including the museum (1857). Many died in appalling, windowless conditions: the Wadjemup Aboriginal Cemetery contains 360 Aboriginal men. Some sites on today's island are still significant to Aboriginal people and others are heritage-listed.

Rottnest was later the site of a boys' reformatory for delinquents as young as 15. Around this time the governor's residence, now the Quokka Arms, was built (1848) and tourism took off at the turn of the century.

Information

Ranger (☎ 0419 951 635) Out of hours in an emergency you can call the ranger.
Rottnest Island Authority (☎ 9432 9111) At the end of the jetty. Has post and banking facilities, and a small shop.
Rottnest Island visitor information centre
(☎ 9372 9752; www.rottnest.wa.gov.au; ♥ 7.30am-5.15pm, to 8pm Fri; 💻) Almost all accommodation on Rotto needs to be booked through here. Also provides tour and transport bookings, rental moorings, detailed maps and useful info on summer events.

Sights & Activities

All year round, the small but informative **museum** (☎ 9372 9753; Kitson St; admission by gold coin donation; ♥ 11am-4pm) has exhibits about the natural and human history of the island. Arm yourself with some holiday reading at the library.
    Lomas Cottage (admission free; ♥ 10.30am-12.30pm) was the residence of a convict from a rich English family. Disowned by them after deserting as a soldier, he was transported and ensconced here in relative comfort in the

---

IT'S JUST NOT CRICKET

Quokkas, a small nocturnal marsupial of the wallaby family, are native to southwest WA and Rottnest Island. As the explorer Vlamingh observed, they do indeed look a little plagueish, with their pointy faces and hairless tails. He called the island Rottnest (meaning 'rat nest') after them. However these small, sweet, social animals are largely restricted in their population (10,000) to this A-class reserve in the Indian Ocean. They live in extended families of 20 to 150 and hang around the salt lakes and water sources on the island. Rumour has it that 'quokka Soccer', where small furry objects fly, is common during Schoolies' Week (postschool celebrations), but we hope this is just an urban myth related by witty Perthonalities. In any case, kick some goals by alerting the **Rottnest Island Authority** (☎ 08-9432 9111) if you see any fun and games of this nature.

WESTERN AUSTRALIA

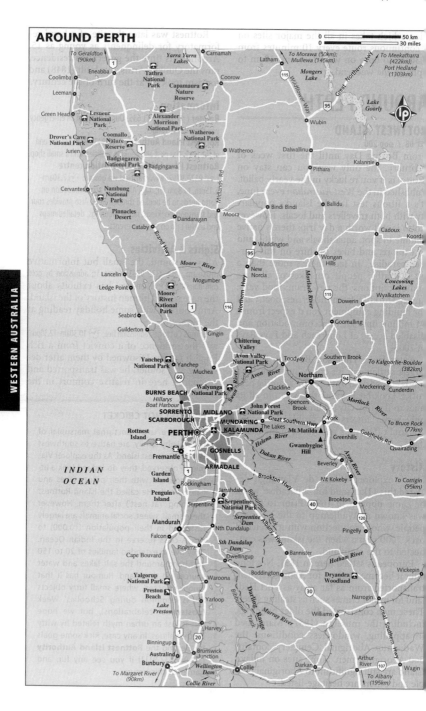

AROUND PERTH

WESTERN AUSTRALIA

0 — 50 km
0 — 30 miles

hope he'd never come back. It backfired: a resentful Lomas popped home to set fire to the family mansion.

Nearby, the **Quod** (1838 to 1931), a design of prison resembling the Round House in Fremantle, housed Aboriginal prisoners for nearly a hundred years. Reports suggest it's haunted, though it's now part of the Rottnest Lodge accommodation.

Trains head west from Thomson Bay for a two-hour tour of the well-preserved guns and tunnels of the **Oliver Hill Gun Emplacement** (adult/concession/child/family $16/11/7.70/39; 4 tours daily), west of Thomson Bay. Planned in 1934 before WWII began, by 1937 it was ready to defend Perth and its port-city Fremantle. It was thought the enemy would come by sea via the only safe passage, which was past Rottnest.

Most visitors come for Rottnest's **beaches** and water activities. Surfing is big at Strickland, Salmon and Stark Bays at the west end, while swimmers prefer the Basin (protected by a ring of reefs), Longreach and Geordie Bays. Excellent visibility in the temperate waters, coral and shipwrecks all appeal to snorkellers and scuba divers.

Malibu Dive (9292 5111; www.rottnestdiving.com.au; Thomson Bay) offers a range of snorkelling ($80) and diving day trips ($150 to $185 for noncertified divers, including two dives and lunch). Scuba-diving courses take you from Perth sites to the waters of Rotto (four-day open-water course $385). Hire kayaks (single/double $15/20 per hour) or self-drive glass-bottom boats ($18 per half-hour) from **Time-Out Watercraft Hire** (0413 181 322); it's an environmentally friendly way to check out the sea life, including stingrays.

The **Family Fun Park** (9292 5156; adult/child/concession $8/6.50/5; trampolines per 10min $2.50; 9am-5.15pm) is the spot for putt-putt and trampolines; bigger golfers can hire clubs and buggies from **Rottnest Bike Hire** (9292 5105). Nearby is the **Picture Hall** (adult/concession $8/7), which shows recent releases nightly in an old corrugated-iron hall, or for a night in you can hire machines and videos from the visitor centre and the Family Fun Park.

Tours
Astro Tours (0417 949 958) At night, explore the clearest of starry skies with Astro Tours; can cater tours for kids.
Capricorn Kayak Tours (1800 625 688; www .capricornkayak.com.au; full day $129; 1-3pm Tue-

Sun) There's much more to Rotto than its landmass – sea kayaking and snorkelling are a great way to experience this pristine place. Capricorn has a variety of ecofriendly tours, including the two-hour Short and Sweet tour ($44), or the three-hour Bays and Beaches ($117 with ferry ticket).
Coach tours (adult/child $22/11) The visitor centre runs daily two-hour tours, narrated by the driver, to Wadjemup lighthouse and the island's west end.
Rottnest Voluntary Guides (9372 9757; tours free) These guides are willing to talk your ear off about local history, including indigenous heritage, the buildings around you, quokkas, daring sailors and wrecks. Walking tours start from the ranger's office (near the visitor centre) at 11am and 2pm daily.

Festivals & Events
On Saturdays in January and February there's music on the Rotto wind, with twilight concerts on Heritage Common by Western Australian performers. Then in mid-February, March and early April you can be a dedicated fin-spotter during the **Channel Swim** from Cottesloe, the **Open Water Classic** and the **Rottnest Triathlon**.

Sleeping
Something about Rottnest makes it feel like a school camp. Maybe it's the uniformly terracotta, rendered buildings – including the accommodation blocks, with names like 'Tern' and 'Shark' – or the kids weaving through on bikes as people relax on their verandas. There's no air-con as it's always a few degrees cooler than Perth, and no baths or spas while the island is on its own water supply. Prices given here are for high season (it's much cheaper at other times, and for longer stays).

Rottnest Island Accommodation (9432 9111; reservations@rottnest.wa.gov.au; 1st/2nd night 4-bed cottages $335/150, 4-bed oceanfront villas from $220/125, 4-bed bungalows $80/40, 6-bed cabins $105/55) The self-contained accommodation here includes 250 cottages, villas, bungalows and cabins in Thomson Bay and around Geordie, Fays and Longreach Bays, about half of which have been refurbished. Rooms with a view are the most expensive. Ask about off-peak and weekly rates, and rooms sans view or refurbishment. Book (up to a year) in advance, especially after Christmas.

Kingstown Barracks YHA (9372 9780; fax 9372 9715; dm/d $22/50;) Almost 2km from the jetty, this military-style accommodation feels bleak and sun drenched but the rooms

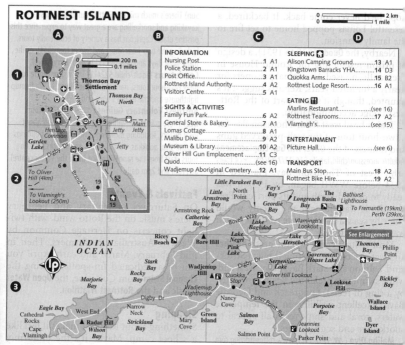

ROTTNEST ISLAND

INFORMATION

Nursing Post	**1** A1
Police Station	**2** A1
Post Office	**3** A1
Rottnest Island Authority	**4** A2
Visitors Centre	**5** A1

SIGHTS & ACTIVITIES

Family Fun Park	**6** A2
General Store & Bakery	**7** A1
Lomas Cottage	**8** A1
Malibu Dive	**9** A2
Museum & Library	**10** A1
Oliver Hill Gun Emplacement	**11** C3
Quod	(see 16)
Wadjemup Aboriginal Cemetery	**12** A1

SLEEPING

Alison Camping Ground	**13** A1
Kingstown Barracks YHA	**14** D3
Quokka Arms	**15** B2
Rottnest Lodge Resort	**16** A1

EATING

Marlins Restaurant	(see 16)
Rottnest Tearooms	**17** A2
Vlamingh's	(see 15)

ENTERTAINMENT

Picture Hall	(see 6)

TRANSPORT

Main Bus Stop	**18** A2
Rottnest Bike Hire	**19** A2

are cool enough and readers like the food. Book at the visitor centre.

Rottnest Lodge Resort (☎ 9292 5161; www .rottnestlodge.com.au; Kitson St; tw/d/f incl breakfast from $180/250/465; 🖳 🖳) A swish resort feel is emphasised by the oasis-like pool, Courthouse cocktail bar and colonial-style wicker. However some of the rooms here are pretty standard, such as those in the Quod (a former prison). The lakeside options are new.

Quokka Arms (☎ 9292 5011; www.rottnest.wa.gov .au; Bedford Ave; s/d from $140/180) Looking like a giant sand castle, the turreted former governor's summer residence is now a sprawling hotel. The bayside rooms have their own beachfront courtyards (ask about midweek specials). Prices are set to rise in 2005.

Allison camping ground (☎ 9432 9111; Thomson Bay; sites per person $8) Tall tuarts shade this sandy camping ground, 'Tentland', which has an ablution block and gas BBQs.

Eating

Rottnest Tearooms (☎ 9292 5171; Thomson Bay; mains $18-30; 🕒 breakfast, lunch & dinner) This elegant building with a sea vista is a great spot to

watch island life at any stage of the day, although the adjoining kiosk charges 'captive audience' prices for a piece of fish ($7.50) Kids play on equipment nearby while adults relax in the airy deck-style surrounds.

Vlamingh's (☎ 9292 5011; Quokka Arms, Bedford Ave; mains $20-28; 🕒 breakfast, lunch & dinner) Fresh-off-the-boat seafood is a speciality in this enormous à la carte mid-Victorian restaurant, which looks out to sea. There's music here on weekends, December to April.

Marlins Restaurant (☎ 9292 5161; Rottnest Lodge Resort; mains $21-30; 🕒 breakfast, lunch & dinner) Recommended for poolside ambience.

The hub at Thomson Bay has a busy **general store** (🕒 8am-7pm), surf shops and benches under the shade of large fig trees. Peacocks wander past all the pie-munchers. The bakery is well stocked and there's even a beauty salon if you forgot to wax.

Getting There & Away

There are daily ferries to Rottnest from Fremantle (30 minutes) and a handful of daily

(Continued on page 921)

Aboriginal rock art (p60)

Carved and painted pole of the Tiwi people,
Melville Island (p819), Northern Territory

Jim Jim Falls (p829), Kakadu National Park, Northern Territory

Mindil Beach Sunset Market (p815), Darwin

RICHARD

Aboriginal art collection at the Museum and Art Gallery of the Northern Territory, Darwin (p803)

WI

The *Ghan* train (p859)

Aboriginal didgeridoo player at Nightcliff
Market (p815), Darwin

Uluru (Ayers Rock; p871), Northern Territory

RICHARD

Alice Springs (p845) from Anzac Hill, Northern Territory

Devil's Marbles (p845), near Tennant Creek,
Northern Territory

KRZYSZTOF DYDYNSKI

Leliyn (Edith Falls), Nitmiluk (Katherine
Gorge) National Park (p838), Northern
Territory

ANDREW MARSHALL & LEANNE WALKER

Beach near Margaret River (p929), Western
Australia

Rottnest Island (p909), Western Australia

Lucky Bay in the Cape Le Grand National Park (p946), Western Australia

Perth cityscape (p883)

The Bank West building dwarfs the former
Palace Hotel (p893) in Perth

Fremantle harbour (p903), Western Australia

Karri trees, Warren National Park (p934),
Western Australia

Lake Cave at Yallingup (p929), Western Australia

The Pinnacles, Pinnacles Desert (p922), Western Australia

Whale shark, Exmouth (p979), Western Australia

Bottlenose dolphins, Monkey Mia (p972), Western Australia

(Continued from page 912)

services from Perth (1½ hours). The companies listed have similar prices: adult/child/backpacker about $50/20/45 for same-day return from Fremantle; $65/23/60 from Perth. It's $5 extra for an extended stay. Concession cards get the backpacker rate. There are also transport and accommodation packages.

Boat Torque (☎ 9430 5844; www.boattorque.com.au) Runs at least nine daily ferries from Fremantle, departing from either Victoria Quay's C Shed or the Northport terminal. From Perth's Barrack St Jetty there are services at 8.45am, 9.45am and 2pm.

Oceanic Cruises (☎ 9430 5127) Offers six daily ferries each way from Victoria Quay's B Shed, and an 8am service from the East St Jetty in Fremantle. From the Barrack St Jetty in Perth, ferries leave at 8.45am, 10am, noon and 2pm.

Rottnest Air Taxi (☎ 1800 500 006) enables incredible views on a same-day return flight to Rotto (four-/six-seater planes) from Perth's Jandakot Airport (from $60 per person).

Getting Around

Bayseeker (adult/child all-day ticket $7/3.50) bus service leaves Thomson Bay every half-hour from 8.40am to 4.40pm to circle the island, stopping at the most beautiful bays and beaches.

A free shuttle to Geordie Bay, Kingstown and the airport leaves from the main jetty in Thomson Bay between 8.15am and 9pm.

If there are more than two of you, hire a yellow five-seater pedal car from **Rottnest Bike Hire** (☎ 9292 5105; Thomson Bay; bikes per hr adult/child $9/8 with $25 deposit, per day $20/17; ☺ 8.30am-5.15pm). Bikes are cheaper if you want them over several days; prices include locks and helmets. Hire your own two-person tricycle taxi in the form of a **Boogie Bug** (☎ 0421 796 878; one way $10-20) to zip between settlements. Watch out for quokkas!

NORTH OF PERTH

The coast north of Perth is windswept and barren, and although the sprawling sands look inviting, these beaches are much better for water sports. Popular with day-trippers is **Yanchep National Park**, which is situated 51km north of Perth. It's a pretty bushland park with plentiful wildlife, including a protected colony of koalas. Visitors can explore the limestone **Crystal Cave**, paddle boats on **Loch McNess** and wander down the **Yaberoo Budjara Aboriginal Heritage Trail**.

Lancelin

☎ 08 / pop 600

Wind worshippers get some serious whoopee in Lancelin's blowy bay. Sailboards screaming across the choppy waters and kitesurfers kicking up the wind and waves are a wonderful spectacle. This once-sleepy cray-fishing town has become a mecca for windsurfers and kitesurfers in summer, particularly during January's three-day Ocean Classic (the popular Ledge Point to Lancelin race). It's not uncommon for European windsurfers to hang out here for months, giving Lancelin a bleached, cosmopolitan air.

SIGHTS & ACTIVITIES

Head to the beach and watch the gun windsurfers do their stuff. If you're inspired, **Werner's Hot Spot** (☎ 9655 1553) offers lessons for newbies ($15 to $20) and hires out the latest boards (from $25 per hour) and gear from a Kombi parked at the beach between October and March (phone at other times). Thrill seekers can learn kitesurfing for $70 per hour.

Desert Storm Adventures (☎ 9655 2550; www.desertstorm.com.au; adult/child $40/25) takes delighted (sometimes shrieking) travellers on a wild ride through the dunes daily.

SLEEPING & EATING

Windsurfer Beach Chalets (☎ 9655 1454; fax 9655 2454; 1 Hopkins St; d $110) These airy, self-contained chalets by the beach are open plan, sleep six (extra child/adult $10/20) and are extremely good value. A modern, functional design, with everything supplied, means you only need to bring a towel. Call ahead and ask about any deals that may be on offer.

Lancelin Lodge YHA (☎ 9655 2020; www.lancelinlodge.com.au; Hopkins St; dm $20, d/f $55/70; ☐ ☐) With clean, well-kept common areas, hammocks for lazing and a volleyball court for sporty types, this purpose-built lodge also has great kitchen facilities and an open fire in winter. Rooms are small but comfy and dorms sleep a maximum of eight.

Lancelin Caravan Park (☎ /fax 9655 1056; Hopkins St; powered/unpowered sites per 2 people $22/18, on-site caravans $75) As close to the beach as you can get, this tidy, quiet park also has ageing on-site caravans set up for families. For the best grass and shaded sites veer to the left as you enter and head to the East Camp.

WESTERN AUSTRALIA

Endeavour Tavern (☎ 9655 1052; Gingin Rd; mains $15-20; ☺ lunch & dinner) The views are priceless at this classic beachfront pub, with a beer garden, a grassy area and an excellent climbing tree for the kiddies. Don't let the occasional pong that wafts over from the seafood company next door put you off the local seafood on the menu.

Mira Mare (☎ 9655 1699; Miragliotta St; ☺ lunch & dinner daily, breakfast Sat & Sun) For Italian fare check out the new kid on the block.

GETTING THERE & AWAY

Lancelin is 130km north of Perth. **Catch-a-bus** (☎ 9655 2020) is a shuttle service (one way $25) run by the YHA, with frequent drop-offs and pick-ups in Perth (around Northbridge).

A 4WD-only coast road continues up to Cervantes.

Cervantes & Pinnacles Desert
☎ 08

The popularity of Cervantes (population 480), a busy cray-fishing port, has soared in recent years – quite justifiably. From sleepy backwater to prime tourist puller, this tiny town offers clear turquoise waters, brilliant fishing and great beaches for kids and grown-ups, and is the entry point for the eerie **Pinnacles Desert**.

The **Pinnacles visitor information centre** (☎ 9652 7700; www.turquoisecoast.org; Cadiz St, Cervantes; ☺ 9am-5pm Mon-Sat, 10am-4pm Sun) provides a wealth of information on the area as well as a free tour and accommodation booking service. There's Internet access at **Thirsty Point Liquor** (Cadiz St, Cervantes; per hr $6; ☐).

SIGHTS & ACTIVITIES

Part of the large coastal **Nambung National Park** (bus passenger $3.40, car $9), the **Pinnacles** are made up of thousands of peculiar limestone pillars resembling termite nests that jut out of the desert floor like so many soldiers, some towering up to 5m. Dawn and dusk, when crowds are low, the heat is bearable, and purple and orange hues provide a haunting note to the scene (as well as good photographic conditions), are the best times to visit. The park is also the scene of an impressive wildflower display between August and October.

The park is 17km along a sealed road from Cervantes, and has a good gravel road that loops through the main concentrations of the Pinnacles.

Nearby are two clean white-sand beaches, **Kangaroo Point** and **Hangover Bay**, which offer a cooling dip after your visit and also great beach fishing.

TOURS

Fun and informative trips into the Pinnacles, offered by **Turquoise Coast Enviro Tours** (☎ 9652 7047; www.pinnacletours.info; 59 Seville St, Cervantes; half-day Pinnacles tour $35, full-day regional tour $110), leave daily at 8am and 2½ hours before sunset.

SLEEPING & EATING

All accommodation is in Cervantes, where there's an ATM and a supermarket.

Cervantes Lodge/Pinnacles Beach Backpackers (☎ 1800 245 232, 9652 7377; www.cervanteslodge.com .au; 91 Seville St; dm $22, d $60-90; ☒ ☐ ☒) This versatile lodging, close to the beach, has good options. The backpackers hostel has clean and tidy four- to eight-bed dorms, a well-equipped kitchen and plenty of space to lounge around. The classy lodge next door houses double rooms (think polished floors, high ceilings, private bathrooms).

Cervantes Holiday Homes (☎ /fax 9652 7115; cnr Malaga Ct & Valencia Rd; 1-/2-/3-bedroom apt per 2 people from $65, extra person $10) These good-value, stand-alone holiday units are classic holiday accommodation – simple, well worn and spacious with a full kitchen, comfy lounges and TV. Linen is $6 per person.

Cervantes Pinnacles Motel (☎ 9652 7145; pinn acles@bigpond.com; 7 Aragon St; d with/without kitchenette $129/118; ☒ ☒) An orderly place with low-slung units, manicured lawns and a great swimming pool, it's the best-appointed option in town. Rooms are in good nick and are very comfy, if slightly claustrophobic.

Don Quixote's (☎ 9652 7377; mains $25-35; ☺ lunch daily, dinner Thu-Mon) This restaurant at Cervantes Lodge/Pinnacle Backpackers serves fine seafood, which is nicely complemented by its Spanish wines.

Seabreeze Cafe (Cadiz St; meals $6-30; ☺ lunch & dinner) If it's cray season (November to June), Seabreeze has succulent crayfish from $24.

Ronsard Bay Tavern (☎ 9652 7009; Cadiz St; mains $15-24) Another option that has a decent selection of burgers, seafood and pasta dishes, all served with a cheery smile.

GETTING THERE & AWAY

Cervantes is 257km north of Perth. **Grey-hound Australia** (☎ 13 14 99; www.greyhound.com.au)

CHRISTMAS & COCOS (KEELING) ISLANDS   *Virginia Jealous*

Christmas Island
☎ 08 / pop 1300

Christmas Island (CI), sighted and named by a passing ship on 25 December 1643, is one of Australia's remote Indian Ocean Territories. It's a distant 2300km northwest of Perth and 360km south of Jakarta, Indonesia, and is 135 sq km in size. A rugged limestone mountain, CI was eventually settled in 1888 to mine phosphate and this is still the main economic activity. Its people are a mix of Chinese, Malays and European-Australians, a blend reflected in the island's food, languages, customs and religions. Several Singapore-style colonial buildings remain, as do traces from the three-year Japanese occupation in WWII. Self-guided heritage walking trails track the island's human history.

Natural history is likewise varied here, with 63% of Christmas Island protected as national park. There is tall rainforest on the plateau, and a series of limestone cliffs and terraces that attract endemic nesting seabirds, including the gorgeous golden-bosun and rare Abbott's booby. Christmas Island is famous for the spectacular annual migration in November/December of millions of red land crabs, travelling from the forest down to the coast to breed. They cover everything in sight on their migration routes – roads are closed, and playing a round of golf is particularly tricky during this period. Marine life is dramatic, with bright corals and fish on the fringing reefs, attracting snorkellers in the dry season (roughly April to November), when international yachties also drop anchor. Divers come throughout the year for the drop-off, wall and cave dives, and are especially drawn to the possibility of diving with seasonal whale sharks (roughly October to April). A sea swell can bring decent surf during the wet season (roughly December to March).

The island had its 15 minutes of fame in August 2001 when a Norwegian container ship, the MV *Tampa*, with its cargo of 438 rescued asylum seekers, was refused permission to land. A temporary detention centre is operational for the few remaining would-be refugees, and an 800-bed 'immigration reception and processing centre' has been under construction on and off since early 2003. Rumour has it that, if completed, it's as likely to be used as a strategic military base instead.

National Jet Systems flies a circle from Perth, via the Cocos (Keeling) Islands, two or three times a week ($1700 return, five to seven hours depending on route). Book through **Qantas** (☎ 13 13 13). There is usually a weekly charter flight to/from Indonesia or Singapore; for current arrangements check with **CI Travel** (☎ 08-9164 7168; xch@citravel.com.au). Visa requirements are as for Australia, and Australians should bring their passports. There is no public transport.

Visitor accommodation is in self-contained units, motel-style rooms or resort-style suites from $80 to $100 per room, or check out the cheaper combined flight and accommodation packages. Expect to pay around $5 to $10 for lunch, and $20 for dinner, at any of the several Chinese and European-Australian restaurants.

Christmas Island visitor information centre (☎ 08-9164 8382; www.christmas.net.au) can coordinate accommodation, diving, fishing and car hire. Visit its website for links to travel agents offering packages, and detailed island information.

Cocos (Keeling) Islands
☎ 08 / pop 600

Some 900km further west are the tiny (14 sq km) Cocos (Keeling) Islands (CKI), a necklace of low-lying islands around a blue lagoon that inspired Charles Darwin's theory of coral atoll formation. The islands were settled by John Clunies-Ross in 1826 (and briefly by a huge contingent of British forces during WWII); the Clunies-Ross family remained in control of the islands' coconut plantations and their Malay workers until 1978, when CKI became part of Australia's Indian Ocean Territories. Now a population of about 500 Malays and 100 European-Australians live on the two settled islands. It's a *very* low-key place in which to walk, snorkel, dive, fish, surf and relax. Check out the two island-information websites www.cocos-tourism.cc and www.cocos-solutions.com.

has daily services to Perth ($33, 3¾ hours) and Geraldton ($33, 2¾ hours), leaving from the BP Roadhouse.

SOUTH OF PERTH

Holiday homes, tranquil fishing spots and sleepy towns contour the soft lines of the coast south of Perth, where many Western Australians spend a lazy week each year at the beach.

GETTING THERE & AWAY

Transperth city buses buzz back and forth between Perth and Rockingham many times a day. Catch bus No 920 or 126 from Fremantle ($5.50, 45 minutes), or bus No 866 from Perth's City Busport ($5.50, one hour). For Mandurah, catch bus No 107 from Perth ($7.80, 70 minutes). **South West Coachlines** (☎ 08-9324 2333) also does drop-offs at Mandurah ($14).

The *Australind* train service stops at Pinjarra ($10.90, 1¼ hours) twice daily. Unfortunately, there's no public transport to Dwellingup.

Rockingham

☎ 08 / pop 66,000

Rockingham is worth visiting for the dolphins, ice cream and a great sheltered beach for kids who love aqua. It's easy to drive right past this naval base that's 47km south of Perth, and surrounded by suburban houses that hunker down in the sun. Its main attraction is the offshore Shoalwater Islands Marine Park, where you can watch wildlife such as sea lions, penguins, silver gulls and fairy terns. For information about the islands contact the **Rockingham visitor information centre** (☎ 9592 3464; 43 Kent St; ☽ 9am-5pm, to 4pm Sat & Sun).

Rockingham Dolphins (☎ 9591 1333; www.dolphins .com.au; tours $155; ☽ daily Sep-Mar), moored at the Palm Beach jetty, takes small groups of people to swim for hours with a group of wild bottlenose dolphins. If you'd rather stay high and dry, there's a Dolphin Watch Tour on the comfort of the boat (adult/child $67/34, daily September to May). There's a free shuttle bus from Perth.

From October to May, Fremantle-based **Capricorn Kayak Tours** (☎ 1800 625 688; www.capricorn kayak.com.au; ☽ Tue, Thu, Sat & Sun) takes visitors out on full-day tours (deluxe/budget $119/88) to see Australian sea lions on Seal Island.

Penguin & Seal Island Cruises (☎ 9528 2004; www.pengos.com.au; 153 Arcadia Dr, Shoalwater) runs a variety of wildlife-watching trips daily. The Penguin Experience (adult/child $16/13) includes a short ferry trip to Penguin Island, where you are free to explore, swim or snorkel, and visit the Discovery Centre. There's also a 45-minute cruise of both islands ($32/23) and a snorkel cruise ($38/28).

Central budget accommodation with basic facilities is available at the **Palm Beach Caravan Park** (☎ 9527 1515; cnr Fisher & Lake Sts; caravan sites per 2 people $20, cabins $55).

Amid greenery, right on the esplanade, **Comfort Suites Beachside** (☎ 9529 3777; 58 Kent St; ste from $155, 2-bed ste $180; ☒) consists of secure self-contained apartments.

Sunsets (☎ 9528 1910; The Boardwalk, Palm Beach; mains $13-30; ☽ lunch & dinner) is open late for dinner on warm summer nights; there's a dish for everybody and it's right on the beach.

La Gelataria (☎ 9528 1533; 2/1 Rockingham Beach Rd; treats $3-9.50; ☽ to 11pm) is the one-stop dessert shop that has melted Palm Beach hearts, with locally made ice cream, sundaes, Italian sweets and crepes.

Mandurah

☎ 08 / pop 48,000

This sleepy waterside town 74km south of Perth on the Mandurah Estuary has expanded at the waistline to let in big boats, palm trees, waterfront mansions and retirees living large on luxury estates. It still has a dreamy appeal.

The terrific waterfront **Mandurah visitor information centre** (☎ 9550 3999; www.peeltour.net .au; 75 Mandurah Tce) has transport schedules, maps, booking assistance and offers Transwa services.

Getting out on the water is a must here. There are regular dolphin sightings and birdlife enlivens the Peel Inlet and the narrow coastal salt lakes to the south. **Kwillana Dreaming** (☎ 0408 845 881, 9535 4444; day tours $60) can share something of the local Noongar culture. Readers recommend its ecotours, which canoe on the Murray River estuary in an area that has been ceded back to its traditional owners. One-hour **estuary cruises** (adult/child $11/5.50) leave from the jetty near the visitor centre on the half-hour, or hire a motorised dinghy yourself from **Mandurah Boat Hire** (☎ 9535 5877).

The premier regional **Mandurah Performing Arts Centre** (☎ 9550 3900; www.manpac.com.au; Ormsby Tce) is next to the **Reading Cinema** (☎ 9535 2800; 7 James Service Pl) on the boardwalk.

SLEEPING & EATING

From resorts to hidden B&Bs, rates can vary according to season. If you have wheels, go a little further out to these places.

Yalgorup Eco Park (☎ 9582 1320; www.ecopark .com.au; 8 Henry Rd, Melros Beach; powered/unpowered sites per 2 people $20/17, budget cabins $55, luxury cabins from $120; ▣) Guests camp behind sand dunes overlooking a spectacular beach at this quality park, which has a range of accommodation, a tennis court and a playground. It's a 15-minute drive south of town, across the Dawesville Channel on Melros Beach.

Blue Bay Holiday Lodge (☎ 9535 3781; www.blue baymotel.com.au; Robert Point; powered/unpowered sites per 2 people $20/17, d $55) Cross the old bridge at the end of the Terrace to get to pretty, restful Robert Point and wake up by the beach.

Reading Room Book Café (☎ 9535 1633; 15 Mandurah Tce; mains $12-18; ◷ lunch) Bookish, eccentric and couch-oriented; if you're game, tuck into a bowl of Tim Winton's wedgies ($7).

Café Pronto (☎ 9535 1004; cnr Pinjarra Rd & Mandurah Tce; mains $11-33; ◷ lunch & dinner) At the end of Mandurah Tce, there's cold beer at the wooden bar, wood-fired pizzas and warm seafood salad. Chill out on the veranda.

Brighton Hotel (☎ 9534 8864; 10-12 Mandurah Tce; mains $20-30; ◷ breakfast, lunch & dinner) Decks for views onto the estuary, four bars and a garden with beer are all on tap at this spanking-new, curvaceous number.

Pinjarra

☎ 08 / pop 2000

A drive-through town 86km south of Perth, petite Pinjarra is on a Murray River flood plain that fills to the brim every 84 years or so. Most of its available historical information neglects to mention the bloody massacre of 1834, when colonists turned on a large group of the Bindjareb Noongar tribe in reprisal for a series of raids and the killing of a servant.

The beautiful old 'Edenvale' **visitor information centre** (☎ 9531 1438; cnr George & Henry Sts; ◷ 8.30am-4.30pm Mon-Fri, 9am-4pm Sat, 9.30am-4pm Sun) fronts the **Heritage Tearooms** (☎ 9531 2273; 1 George St; mains $5-12).

Wander through a large aviary and hand-feed the lorikeets at **Bellawood Parrots** (☎ 9531 1457; Ravenswood Sanctuary, off Sutton St; adult/child $7.50/5; ◷ 10am-4pm Wed-Mon). Here there are 50 of Australia's 55 parrot species.

Nearby **Coopers Cottage** offers insights into the life of local farmer Joseph Cooper and has crafts; nose out a feed at **Redcliffe Barn**.

The **Pinjarra Motel** (☎ 9531 1811; fax 9531 1355; 131 South Western Hwy; s/d from $60/75; ▣) is plain but convenient, with mandatory palms by the minuscule pool.

Setting off down the South Western Hwy, cheese lovers should stop to try the flavoursome cow's milk varieties at **HaVe** (☎ 9729 3949; www.harveycheese.com; Wokalup).

Dwellingup

☎ 08

Heading inland to peaceful Dwellingup, you leave the coast road for the cool relief of hilly farming country, wide and rich with trees. As is the danger here, the tiny timber town 24km from Pinjarra was destroyed by bushfire in 1961. Rebuilt, it's now a focal point for bushwalkers and canoeists, who are drawn to its jarrah forests and meandering Murray River. Pick up *Bushwalking Trails* ($2.50) from the jovial **Dwellingup visitor information centre** (☎ 9538 1108; Marrinup St; ◷ 10am-3pm, to 4pm Sat & Sun).

In a building that's shaped like three gum leaves, the magnificent **Forest Heritage Centre** (☎ 9538 1395; Acacia St; adult/child/family $5.50/2.20/11; ◷ 10am-5pm) has an interpretive forest exhibition, a skilled woodwork gallery-shop and a tree-top walk. The recipient of an ongoing grant for its excellent work in providing local training, the **School of Fine Wood** (☎ 9538 1395) has creative workshops here (guitar making, kids' programmes) that are gaining a reputation. If you're seeking an alternative holiday with new skills thrown in, basic accommodation is also available (adult/child $20/5.50).

Dwellingup Adventures (☎ 9538 1127) offers a series of canoeing adventures, including self-guided Murray River trips (two-person canoe half/full day $60/70) with pick-up. Overnight camping trips and combined bushwalking and canoeing options are also popular.

Berryvale Lodge (☎ 9538 1239; www.berryvale lodge.com.au; off South Western Hwy; s/d $70/100) is a country family home, 1km west of town, where you can sleep a deep sleep in an attic-style room. Awake to kookaburras, a breakfast cooked any way you like and fresh berries from the farm. Give Marcia notice if you'd like dinner ($20).

Muffins, chocolates, cakes…have what you like for breakfast or lunch at the **Mill House Café & Chocolate Co** (☎ 9538 1122; McLarty St; mains $12-23; ⏰ breakfast & lunch daily, dinner Fri & Sat).

Yalgorup National Park

Around 50km south of Mandurah is the beautiful Yalgorup National Park, a region of woodlands, tranquil lakes and coastal sand dunes. Ornithologists will be in their element and amateur scientists can visit the distinctive thrombalites on the shores of Lake Clifton.

SOUTHWEST

Two prominent capes and countless national parks, including the magnetic 'tall trees' region, are the lush green and aqua setting for a ravishing region that satisfies everyone. Wild bottlenose dolphins and whales frolic and relax offshore. Eager surfers ride the waves. Inland there are sublime wineries and spring wildflowers. This picturesque stretch of coast is so popular with Perth weekenders that you can find yourself milling among crowds at the height of summer.

Getting There & Away

Tramway (☎ 1300 662 205) buses go daily from Perth to Bunbury ($22, three hours), Busselton ($26, 4¼ hours), Dunsborough ($28, 4½ hours), Yallingup ($29, 4¾ hours), Margaret River ($30, 5½ hours) and Augusta ($36, six hours).

There are also six buses a week from Perth to Pemberton ($37, 5½ or eight hours); some go via Bunbury and Bridgetown ($32, 4½ hours) and some take the longer cape route via Margaret River and Augusta. There's also a daily service from Albany to Pemberton ($25, three hours).

South West Coach lines (☎ 08-9324 2333) also services the region daily from Perth to Bunbury ($21), Busselton ($25), Dunsborough ($27), Margaret River ($28) and Augusta ($34). From Monday to Friday it has services to Bridgetown ($28), Nannup ($29) and Manjimup ($32).

The *Australind* train travels twice daily in both directions between Perth and Bunbury ($22, 2½ hours). It leaves Perth at 9.30am and 6.15pm, and departs from Bunbury at 6am and 2.45pm.

BUNBURY

☎ 08 / pop 28,000

Industrial Bunbury is more Cape Barren goose than Southwest swan, but wild dolphins are the famous draw card here and many readers have been thrilled by swimming with them. You can probably catch some live music too, or chill out on the gentle surf beach close to town.

Start with a morning visit to the **Dolphin Discovery Centre** (☎ 9791 3088) at Koombana Bay. Nearby is the **Mangrove Boardwalk**, located by the shores of bird-haven Leschenault Inlet.

The **Bunbury visitor information centre** (☎ 9721 7922; Carmody Pl; ⏰ 9am-5pm Mon-Sat, 9.30am-4.30pm Sun) is situated in the old 1904 train station. Check your email in the Old Station Coffee Lounge next door. Nearby, **Bunbury City Transit** (☎ 9791 1955) will help you get around.

Sleeping

Wander Inn YHA (☎ 9721 3242; wanderinnbp@yahoo .com; 16 Clifton St; dm/s/d from $22/35/50; 🖳) Nestled between town and beach, this is the perfect place to hang out for a while. Ask about evening sunset cruises ($30 to $35), which include dolphin spotting and fishing.

Fawlty Towers (☎ 9721 2427; fawltyby@iinet.net .au; 205 Ocean Dr; s/d $65/75; 🍴 🖳) This beachfront motel is thankfully more like Sybil than Basil: attentive service, spotless rooms and well-managed facilities.

Rose Hotel (☎ 9721 4533; fax 9721 8285; cnr Victoria & Wellington Sts; s/d $48/70, motel s/d $75/90) Hark back to an older world upstairs and eat in the palm-potted ambience of the ground-floor restaurant, or there's a twee motel wing.

Prince of Wales (☎ 9721 2016; fax 9791 1984; 41 Stephen St; s/d $50/70, without bathroom $40/60) Basic hotel rooms are available in this central hotel that's well known for its live music (expect plenty of noise on the weekend).

Eating & Drinking

The long strip of Victoria St will satisfy both hunger and thirst, with many more options than we can list.

SOUTHWEST

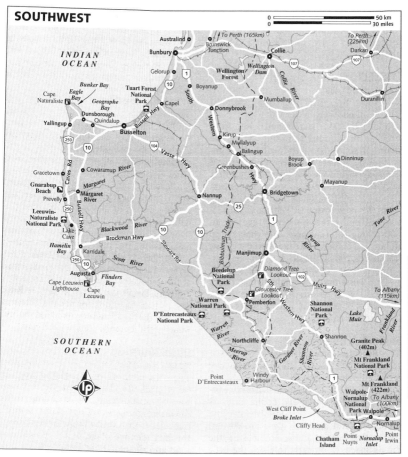

Benessé (83 Victoria St; mains $5-12; ☻ breakfast & lunch) If coffee is your drug of choice, you'll be well chuffed at this zappy little spot, replete with a cake cabinet and light meals.

Jane's Jungle Juice (☎ 9791 8808; 52 Victoria St; wraps $5.90; ☻ lunch) Cheap healthy lunches and jazzy juices.

White Elephant II (☎ 9721 6522; 65 Victoria St; mains $16-20; ☻ dinner) Craving a curry? Salivating for a satay? Banquets here do both $26 per person).

Reef Hotel (☎ 9791 6677; 12 Victoria St) A younger crowd bangs on in the beer garden over the free BBQ on Friday nights.

There's a heritage front bar with plenty on tap at the **Rose** (☎ 9721 4533). Bunbury's main Sunday Sesh is at **Fitzgerald's** (☎ 9791 2295; 22 Victoria St) with DJs and bands. For weekend indie bands and local talent try the **Prince of Wales** (☎ 9721 2016; 41 Stephen St).

DONNYBROOK

☎ 08 / pop 1650

Check out the green-apple street lights along the main road of this low-key country town on the fringe of the forest region. If you're seeking casual work, hit town for some apple-picking work from late October to June. The **Donnybrook visitor information centre** (☎ 9731 1720; South Western Hwy; ☻ 9am-5pm) is centrally located in the Old Railway Station on the South Western Hwy.

Brook Lodge Backpackers (☎ 9731 1520; www .brooklodge.com.au; 3 Bridge St; dm/d $20/45; ☐), on

WESTERN AUSTRALIA

two acres, is popular with travellers drawn to this region's Big Apple. It often accommodates long-termers so it's smart to book ahead.

BUSSELTON

☎ 08 / pop 11,000

According to locals, 'everything starts at Busselton and gets better from here'. Surrounded by calm waters and white-sand beaches, the famous 2km-long jetty is the main attraction. It's entrenched in the resort town's culture too: every week the local newspaper showcases a resident and their jetty story (wedding proposals, childhood fishing memories, shark sightings). Along with the jetty swim in February, Busselton has embraced some new events: an 800-strong international iron man comp in late November, and the **South Bound** (www .sunsetevents.com.au) music festival held in January.

The **Busselton visitor information centre** (☎ 9752 1288; 38 Peel Tce; ☒ 8.30am-5pm Mon-Fri, 9am-4pm Sat, 10am-3pm Sun) has plenty of local tips and information.

Sights & Activities

The **Busselton Jetty Experience** (☎ 9754 0900; adult/child $20/12) means you can keep dry while enjoying a view previously only enjoyed by divers, at the new **Underwater Observatory**. Right at the end of the jetty, its descending staircase windows display the colourful coral and rich algae growth 8m below the surface, made possible by the jetty's shade. Book early to catch the little train that takes you out there, and walk back in your own time if you wish.

Keen divers can always explore the underwater world here and at Dunsborough's HMAS *Swan* wreck with **Busselton Naturaliste Diving Academy** (☎ 9752 2096; www.natdive.com; 103 Queen St). There's good snorkelling at the Gazebo and the Sandbar, 1km out, where you can see wobbegongs, rays, and schools of whiting and herring.

Sleeping, Eating & Drinking

A number of guesthouses are within walking distance of the jetty.

Observatory Guesthouse (☎ 9751 3336; www .observatory-guesthouse.com; 7 Brown St; s/d $85/95; ☒) This cheery guesthouse has all the comforts of home: grab a beach towel for an early morning swim and return for a cooked brekky on the deck.

Kinvarra Park Lodge (☎ 9755 4203; kinvarra@swisp .net.au; Pries Rd, Vasse; s/d incl breakfast $85/110) Just off the Busselton Hwy, this private gem has large modern rooms and parklike gardens in which kangaroos laze.

Jacaranda Guesthouse (☎ 9752 1246; jacaranda @westnet.com.au; 30 West St; s/d/tr incl breakfast $70/95/135) Summer's busy at this elegant white house with en suite rooms, a pretty garden, a spa and satellite TV.

Goose (☎ 9754 7700; www.thegoose.com.au; mains $14-28; ☒ breakfast, lunch & dinner) An old Busselton favourite has laid the proverbial golden one, right by the jetty. Beachy and open, this is first-class seaside dining. Try the pancakes with berry coulis for brekky, or seafood chowder (owner Rhys' favourite). Sunday Sessions with live music are on the cards.

Vasse Pub (☎ 9752 8560; 44 Victoria St; mains $13-28; ☒ lunch & dinner) Mingle with the lovely locals at this renovated pub on the main street.

Gelato Buonissimo (☎ 9751 1477; 13 Bussell Hwy; ☒ 10am-9pm) Look for banana-coloured paint on the highway and you'll find mouthwatering homemade Italian ice cream.

DUNSBOROUGH

☎ 08 / pop 2500

There's a plethora of accommodation options available along Caves Rd, on your way to Dunsborough. An expanding coastal town that lounges on Cape Naturaliste, it's managed to grow fast without going through the bad teenage stage of too much junk food and mismatching colours. It's a great base for beaches and the nearby wineries. For accommodation and tour tips, see the **Dunsborough visitor information centre** (☎ 9755 3299; Seymour Blvd; ☒ 9am-5pm Mon-Fri, 9am-4pm Sat, 10am-4pm Sun) in the shopping centre.

Sights & Activities

Northwest of Dunsborough, Cape Naturaliste Rd leads to excellent beaches such as **Meelup**, **Eagle Bay** (also known locally as 'Ego Bay') and exclusive **Bunker Bay**, some fine coastal lookouts and the tip of **Cape Naturaliste**, which has a **lighthouse** (☎ 9755 3955; adult/child $7/3; ☒ 9.30am-4.30pm) and a network of walking tracks.

From September to December, marvel at humpback and southern right whales from the lookouts over Geographe Bay, or on two-hour cruises with **Dunsborough Charters** (☎ 0419 244 804; www.dunsboroughcharters.com.au; adult/child $45/25). Scenic **Sugarloaf Rock** is the southernmost nesting colony of the rare red-tailed tropic bird.

The wreck of the Australian frigate HMAS *Swan* was sunk in Geographe Bay in 1997 specifically for diving. **Cape Dive** (☎ 9756 8778; 222 Naturaliste Tce) runs snorkelling trips (with/without equipment $50/40) and diving ($160 for two dives with equipment provided).

Sleeping & Eating

Dunsborough Beach House YHA (☎ 9755 3107; dunsboroughyha@hotmail.com; 201 Geographe Bay Rd, Quindalup; dm/s $20/30, d & tw $50; ▣) The super-clean, brightly painted, party-time YHA has a stunning beachfront location about 2km southeast of Dunsborough. Look for the three tall Norfolk pines in front.

Dunsborough Inn (☎ 9756 7277; dunnsinn@wn .com.au; 50 Dunn Bay Rd; dm/s/tr $22/32/70, d with/without bathroom $85/55; ▣) Spotless and modern, this purpose-built budget inn has a large communal kitchen, recreation room, disabled facilities plus several self-contained units. The friendly owners run a shuttle bus to nearby beaches for long-termers.

Dunsborough Rail Carriages & Farm Cottages (☎ 9755 3865; www.dunsborough.com; Commonage Rd; 2-person carriages from $100, cottages from $130) For novelty value, these charming rail carriages, set on 40 hectares of bushland, win hands down. If you need more space, ask for the roomier farm cottages.

inji bar (☎ 9755 3657; Naturaliste Tce; mains $8-16; Ⓨ lunch & dinner) This hip bar has a café-style menu and entertainment on weekends.

Three Bears Bar (☎ 9755 3657; cnr Caves Rd & Naturaliste Tce) This is a happy tale: Goldilockses of both sexes, a range of beers on tap and live music on weekends.

Olive Pit (☎ 9755 2438; cnr Commonage Rd & Brushwood Brook Dr; Ⓨ 10.30am-5pm) Stock up on predinner snacks here: marinated olives, tapenades, *dukkah* (a spicy paste of nuts and seeds) and wonderful olive oils.

YALLINGUP

☎ 08 / pop 500

A tiny settlement surrounded by surf mist, coves and deep olive green coastal vegetation, this is legendary surfer Taj Burrow's territory and the place Australian cricketers have their holiday homes. However that's a secret. In the local Noongar language, '-up' means 'place of', and Yallingup means 'place of love'. Nearby is the **Ngilgi Cave** (Ⓨ 9.30am-4pm) of Aboriginal legend. Other dark attractions are **Giant's Cave** (not for the faint-hearted or unfit) and **Lake Cave** (Ⓨ 9.30am-3.30pm).

The **Wardan Aboriginal Centre** (☎ 9756 6566; www.wardan.com.au; Injidup Springs Rd; Ⓨ 10am-4pm, Wed-Mon), 6km south, is a place of stories, bush tucker, dancers, didgeridoo and other aspects of the local Wardandi culture.

Sleeping, Eating & Drinking

Caves House Hotel (☎ 9755 2131; www.caveshouse .com.au; Caves Rd; d $80-180) You can choose to stay in standard rooms in the classic Art Deco lodge or luxurious Jacuzzi units in a separate house. Both are loved by Lonely Planet travellers from around the world.

Yallingup Beach Holiday Park (☎ 9755 2164; Valley Rd; powered/unpowered sites per 2 people $40/20, on-site caravans $50, cabins $100-200) Hire a beach cabin across the road from the water, or bung on a BBQ (with free wood) overlooking the bay. Take a woolly hat in October and you'll fit right in. Mainly families are welcome here in summer.

Surfside Café & Restaurant (☎ 9755 2133; Valley Rd; mains $22-30; Ⓨ dinner Thu-Sun) Wolf down after-surf brekky or, at the other end, watch the sunset sky over a steak. The adjoining kiosk does a mean burger during the day.

Wicked Ale Brewery (☎ 9755 2848; Hemsley Rd; Ⓨ 11am-4pm Sun-Thu, 10am-6pm Sat & Sun) 'An oasis of beer in a desert of wine' (we just had to quote them). These guys dare you to sample chilli, chocolate or mama's ginger beers, or the very exotic 'bad frog' (presumably it jumped in the mix) citrus beer.

MARGARET RIVER

☎ 08 / pop 6000

One can not live on cheese and chocolate alone. Actually, we take that back. There are so many tasting opportunities around here you'll need a glass of wine at the end of it all. Hugely popular Margaret River also serves up some of the best surfing in Australia, wild coastal caves, sophisticated restaurants and internationally acclaimed vineyards scattered throughout richly forested land. The town itself, known as 'Margs', is an affable enclave of cafés and accommodation that satisfies both surfies and the slickest suits.

WESTERN AUSTRALIA

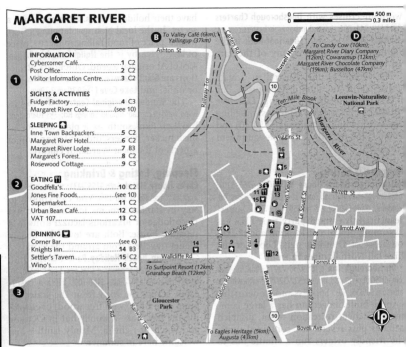

MARGARET RIVER

INFORMATION	
Cybercorner Café	**1** C2
Post Office	**2** C2
Visitor Information Centre	**3** C2

SIGHTS & ACTIVITIES	
Fudge Factory	**4** C3
Margaret River Cook	(see 10)

SLEEPING	
Inne Town Backpackers	**5** C2
Margaret River Hotel	**6** C2
Margaret River Lodge	**7** B3
Margaret's Forest	**8** C2
Rosewood Cottage	**9** C3

EATING	
Goodfella's	**10** C2
Jones Fine Foods	(see 10)
Supermarket	**11** C2
Urban Bean Café	**12** C3
VAT 107	**13** C2

DRINKING	
Corner Bar	(see 6)
Knights Inn	**14** B3
Settler's Tavern	**15** C2
Wino's	**16** C2

The **Margaret River visitor information centre** (☎9757 2911; Bussell Hwy; ⏱9am-5pm) has lots of useful information and an impressive wine centre. For a pin-drop-quiet place to check your email, try the **Cybercorner Café** (Willmott Ave; ⏱8am-8pm Mon-Sat, 1-5pm Sun), now with wireless access.

Sights & Activities

You'll find yourself zipping up and down Caves Rd (stretching from Yallingup to Augusta) and the Bussell Hwy, taking in countless attractions on the way. There are galleries, caves and, of course, a cloistered vineyard at the end of many a dirt turn-off. The best **surfing** beaches here are Margaret River Mouth, Gnarabup, Suicides (south side) and Redgate. Josh at **Surf Academy** (☎9975 73850; 2hr lessons $40) knows his breaks and will introduce you to the waves.

Eagles Heritage (☎9757 2960; Boodjidup Rd; adult/child $9/5; ⏱10am-5pm), 5km south of town, is a natural wildlife centre for birds of prey. Flight displays are at 11am and 1.30pm.

Put on your tasting hat at **Margaret River Dairy Company** (☎9755 5400; cnr Bussell Hwy & Harman's Rd, Cowaramup; ⏱9.30am-5pm), famous for its smooth club cheddar and yoghurt. At the **Margaret River Chocolate Company** (☎9755 6555; Harman's South Rd, Willyabrup; ⏱9am-5pm), sample a bag of red-gum honey crunch or a rum rebellion truffle, but try not to loiter by the choc buds. If too much is barely enough, the **Fudge Factory** (☎9758 8881; 152 Bussell Hwy) and **Candy Cow** (cnr Bussell Hwy & Bottrill St, Cowaramup) are 10 minutes north of Margaret River.

Margaret River Cook (☎9758 8990; www.the margaretrivercook.com.au; Shop 2, 99 Bussell Hwy; classes $65-80), right in town, has cooking classes where you can eat your own Australian creations.

Tours

Book at the visitor centre for your designated driver and guide to the sensational wineries.

Bushtucker Tours (☎9757 1084; www.bushtucker tours.com) A five-hour 4WD Great Wine Food Forest Adventure ($55) to five wineries with a gourmet lunch of wild foods.

Margaret River Tours (☎0419 917 166; www .margaretrivertours.com) Offers half-day and full-day options ($50/85).

Outdoor Discoveries (☎ 0407 084 945) Takes experienced and wannabe bushwalkers, canoeists, abseilers, cavers and rock climbers on activities in the local area.

Wine for Dudes (☎ 9758 8699; www.winefordudes .com; tour $55) Includes pick-up and drop-off, a tour of a working winery, lunch and *boules* – awesome.

Sleeping

Surfpoint Resort (☎ 9757 1777; www.surfpoint.com .au; Riedle Dr, Gnarabup; dm $23, tw & d with/without bathroom $85/75; 🖳) On Gnarabup Beach, 12km west of town, is a backpackers hostel loved by both readers and the industry. It has a large communal kitchen, recreation areas and a courtesy bus to/from town. Did we mention *el primo* beachfront location?

Inne Town Backpackers (☎ 9757 3698; innetown@ westnet.com.au; 93 Bussell Hwy; dm/d $22/60; 🖳) Diagonally across from the visitor centre, this hill haven is a bit chaotic but secure, and ace for activities (including lounging on the deck watching the house pool comp). They'll give you a map and bike, and send you off to explore the forest and river trails.

Margaret River Lodge (☎ 9757 9532; www.mr lodge.com.au; 220 Railway Tce; dm/s/d from $20/40/55, non-members extra $3.50; 🖳 🖳) The rammed-earth YHA with peachy facilities, including an organic veggie garden, is about 1.5km southwest of town. It's a favourite with readers.

Margaret River Hotel (☎ 9757 2655; www.marg aretriverhotel.com.au; 139 Bussell Hwy; s/d/f $90/150/180) The elegantly aged dark-wood rooms with mammoth spas oversee the action in the downstairs restaurant under the vines. The family balcony room is great value, but it could be a bit noisy on Friday nights, when the Corner Bar corners the market.

Rosewood Cottage (☎ 9757 2845; 54 Wallcliffe Rd; s/d from $90/100; 🖳) The flowery theme of the gardens extends into the cottage, and amiable owners preserve the peace with a child-free rule. Be sure to ask them about the area.

Margaret's Forest (☎ 9758 7188; www.assured hospitality.com.au; 96 Bussell Hwy; s & d ste $148-185, 2-bedroom apt $195-310; 🖳) These lovely, new and central corrugated-iron and wood townhouses have their backs to the road and their faces to the forest. Spa suites attract couples but there are business and group rates on offer too.

Eating

Sniff out a feast along the Bussell Hwy, which is the town centre. The wineries also go hand in hand with their beloved fine foods (see below).

Urban Bean Café (☎ 9757 3480; 157 Bussell Hwy; mains $4.50-12; ☽ breakfast & lunch) The croissants are really just an excuse to have more than one coffee (and what a coffee!) here at the top of the strip, surrounded by locals.

Goodfella's Café (☎ 9757 3184; 97 Bussell Hwy; mains $13-20; ☽ dinner) If De Niro were in town he'd be eating these pizzas at his own table, no questions asked. Don't miss Tuesday's pizza-and-a-glass-of-wine night ($14).

Vat 107 (☎ 9758 8877; 107 Bussell Hwy; mains $16-32; ☽ dinner) Fancy a well-heeled wine to combine with your shiny-toed food? Step into 107 for some well-rehearsed hospitality and become the waiter's friend.

Jones Fine Foods (☎ 9758 8990; Shop 2, 99 Bussell Hwy; mains $10.50-14) This well-stocked and proportioned establishment has a fridge full of takeaway gourmet meals made daily by the Margaret River Cook herself (opposite). Heat up or stock up.

Valley Café (☎ 9757 3225; cnr Carters & Caves Rds; mains $14-29; ☽ breakfast, lunch & dinner, Wed-Sun) Set on a 2-hectare bush block 6km out of town, the Valley Café is renowned for its creative food and flamboyant drag revues ($55).

Drinking

Sauvignon Blanc is the favoured variety in this region. You can still get a beer in town though.

TOP FIVE WINERIES WITH RESTAURANTS

A number of great vineyards in Margaret River have an equally good name for their dining, so you can say 'I'll have food with that wine'. Some places to sip and sup:

Clairault (☎ 08-9755 6655; Caves Rd, Willyabrup) Closer to Yallingup and family owned.

Redbrook Winery (cnr Caves & Metricup Rds, Wilyabrup) Great whites from the region's biggest producer.

Brookland Valley (☎ 08-9755 6250; Caves Rd, Willyabrup) Drop crumbs to the ducks on the lake below the excellent Flutes restaurant.

Lamonts (☎ 08-9755 2434; Gunyulgyup Valley Dr) The eating here is matched by the great food at the owner's other restaurant in the Swan Valley.

Vasse Felix (☎ 08-9756 5000; Harman's Rd S, Cowramup) The first major winery in the area.

Settler's Tavern (☎ 9757 2398; 114 Bussell Hwy) Are you up for the Metallica tribute? Or just some local big hair? Bands, big brews and a burger royale in the middle of town.

Corner Bar (☎ 9757 2655; Margaret River Hotel, 139 Bussell Hwy) Revive yourself on Friday night at the corner, watching Margs walk past. A beer in fine weather is a fine thing here.

Knight's Inn (☎ 9757 2655; Margaret River Resort, 40 Walcliffe Rd) Just off the main drag, lap up a lazy afternoon drink with the locals at Knight's. On Monday kids eat free and Tuesday is backpacker night.

Wino's (☎ 9758 7155; 85 Bussell Hwy) The bona fide–best wine list resides in this little tapas bar (great food for all wallets). There's French wine worth a baron's small fortune, but we recommend the local drop.

KARRIDALE
☎ 08
Beyond the crowds of Margaret River is a little wooded town with increasing appeal. If you've got time and your own transport, pop over to fishing hot spot Hamelin Bay to watch the large stingrays patrol the shallows.

Rex the kelpie dog will sound your arrival to **Brilea Cottages** (☎ 9758 5001; B&B d $85, 2-bed cottages $130, incl breakfast), set on a red-dirt-and-vines family farm. These self-contained cottages have enormous spa bathrooms and DVDs. Walk around the property or head over to the tavern across the highway.

Stop for lunch at the stunning stone winery with an inland view, **Hamelin Bay Wines** (☎ 9758 6779; www.hbwines.com.au; 116 McDonald Rd). Kids can play badminton while you have a coffee or a ploughman's lunch ($25).

AUGUSTA
☎ 08 / pop 2000
Australia's most southwesterly point is Cape Leeuwin, where the Southern and Indian Oceans meet. Augusta, 5km north, is still a sleepy, weathered hollow due to national park restrictions. It's nature that takes precedence here, not people. Whale watching occurs between late May and September.

Take the winding road to the historic **lighthouse** (☎ 9758 1920; admission $7; ☯ 9am-4pm), perching on Cape Leeuwin. Not far away is a photogenic salt-encrusted **water wheel**.

The **Matthew Flinders memorial** on Leeuwin Rd commemorates Flinders' mapping of the Australian coastline, and offers wonderful lighthouse photo ops. The **Augusta Historical Museum** (Blackwood Ave; adult/child $2/50c; ☯ 10am-noon & 2-4pm Oct-Apr, 10am-noon May-Sep) has interesting exhibits on whales and shipwrecks.

Helicopter scenic flights (☎ 0427 825 682; Leeuwin/Hamelin Bay $65/130) offers a bird's eye view of the coast; head up and away.

Miss Flinders (☎ 0439 424 455; cruises $20) and **Sea Dragon** (☎ 9758 4003; adult/child $30/10) cruises both have women who know a heck of a lot about the Blackwood River area at the helm.

In town, the **Augusta visitor information centre** (☎ 9758 0166; 75 Blackwood Ave; ☯ 9am-5pm, to 1pm Sat & Sun) is in the main street.

It sounds like **Baywatch Manor Resort** (☎ 9758 1290; www.baywatchmanor.com.au; 88 Blackwood Ave; dm/s $20/50, d with/without bathroom from $70/55) gives out red swimming costumes, but this is not a party place. Like Augusta itself it's very chilled out, and has very good facilities. The daggiest upstairs room in the southwest has possibly the best view of the inlet's coastal colours. The hosts are travellers at heart.

Augusta Bakery (☎ 9758 1664; 121 Blackwood Ave; light meals $5.50-11; ☯ breakfast & lunch daily, dinner Fri) also has great views of the inlet. Vanilla slices, cakes with fresh cream and a buzzing breakfast make it better than your average bakehouse. On pizza night (5.30pm to 8.30pm), try the seafood-stacked 'Flinders' ($24).

SOUTHERN FORESTS
For sentimentalists, the hot smell of the Australian forest, with its monolithic trunks and the saffron and black of bushfires past, has emotional impact. This is powerful land, tall and crowded with jarrah, marri and karri trees. It's almost a relief to occasionally emerge into the open spaces of wheat-coloured farm country. Recognising the importance of these forests and the viability of a fast-growing ecotourism industry, the government has scaled down native forest logging. Former timber towns Nannup, Bridgetown, Pemberton and Northcliffe are slowly moving to new industries and ways of thinking.

CALM offices (Nannup Map p927; ☎ 08-9756 1101; Warren Rd; Pemberton Map p927; ☎ 08-9776 1207; Kennedy St) can help with maps and information on new national parks (p881).

Nannup
☎ 08 / pop 520
Nannup's idyllic bush setting, 290km from Perth on the Blackwood River, appeals to

bushwalkers and people wanting to chill out. The **Folk in the Forest** festival is held on the Labour Day long weekend, in early March.

Walkers should check out the 17km **Timberline Trail**, which follows the old railway line out to Barrabup Pool, the local swimming hole. You can camp here and there are BBQ facilities.

One of Australia's great canoe trips is the descent of the Blackwood River from the forest to the sea. In the old police station (1922), the **Nannup visitor information centre** (☎ 9756 1211; Brockman St; 9am-5pm) can recommend tours. Check your email at the **Telecentre** (Warren Rd).

Stroll up Warren Rd and browse through its many craft shops, furniture galleries and secondhand stores. Garden lovers meander through the residential **Blythe Gardens** (Brockman St; admission by gold coin donation; dawn-dusk).

SLEEPING & EATING

Black Cockatoo (☎ 9756 1035; 27 Grange Rd; dm $19, s/d from $30/45) Near the river, this peaceful hostel gets rave reviews from travellers, who come for a night and stay for a week. Sustainable living practices include picking your own herbs and reading back issues of *Rolling Stone* magazine under a tree.

Nannup Hotel (☎ 9756 1080; 12 Warren Rd; s/tw/d $35/50/60) You could do much worse than stay at this well-swept, 105-year-old jarrah hotel. The upstairs rooms hark back to the simple ways of olden days.

Mulberry Tree (☎ 9756 3038; 62 Warren Rd; mains $23-30; lunch daily, dinner Tue-Sun) Choose between an afternoon-tea stopover amid petunias, or decent hearty food from 6pm at this cottage restaurant and café. It's BYO.

Good Food Shop (☎ 9756 1351; 15 Warren Rd; mains $4-12; lunch) Tempeh, local marron and trout burgers are to be found until 4pm at this health-conscious place.

Bridgetown

☎ 08 / pop 2100

In late November each year, 20,000 folk from around the country rock in for the **Blues at Bridgetown** (☎ 9761 1280) festival, held in the midst of karri forest and apple orchards. On the Blackwood River, gorgeous Bridgetown itself has an array of charming eateries and old buildings, including the mud-and-clay **Bridgedale House** (Hampton St; admission $3; 10am-2pm Sat & Sun), built by the

area's first settler in 1862. There's a history display at the **Bridgetown visitor information centre** (☎ 9761 1740; Hampton St; 9am-5pm).

Sunnyhurst Winery (☎ 9761 4525; Doust St; 10am-6pm) features a country garden and handmade wines, while the **Cidery** (☎ 9761 2204; 43 Gifford St; 11am-4pm Wed-Sun, 7.30pm-late Fri & Sat) wets everyone's whistle with both alcoholic and nonalcoholic cider tastings on offer.

The Blackwood River valley features burrawangs (grass trees) and large granite boulders. In **Boyup Brook**, 31km northeast of Bridgetown, there's a flora reserve and **Harvey Dickson's Country Music Centre** (☎ 9765 1125), with some 2000 titles. Nearby is **Norlup Pool**, with glacial rock formations.

SLEEPING & EATING

Ford House (☎ 9761 1816; www.members.westnet .com.au/ford.house; Eedle Tce; s/d from $50/110) We were enamoured of this garden maze of superb accommodation. The cosy nook of the single-bed Bookcase, the tasteful Cook's Retreat, and the gracious new quarters of Aislinn House impress with their themed attention to detail. Tongue and Groove Café holds over 60 lavish functions a year, including midwinter Christmas dinner, in 'The Barn' (decorated as if a team of elves project-managed it).

Nelson's of Bridgetown (☎ 9761 1641; www.nel sonsofbridgetown.com.au; 38 Hampton St; d $70-115) This Federation-style hotel has a range of accommodation from naff 1980s budget rooms to flowery deluxe options and executive spa units. There's a tennis court.

Barking Cow (☎ 0415 689 886; Hampton St; mains $6-11; breakfast & lunch Mon-Thu, dinner Sat & Sun) Graze over gourmet lunches, gluten-free breads and preservative-free vegetarian food in this urban little café, or savour Yallingup coffee.

Bygone Days (☎ 9761 2221; Hampton St; mains $6-11; dinner Thu-Mon) Surf 'n' Turf ($20) is among the homemade-style meals at the warm, sparsely decorated café, which also does takeaway ($12 to $15).

Pemberton

☎ 08 / pop 800

Pemberton the wondertown. In the midst of the stunning Karri Forest Explorer drive, surrounded by vineyards, this pretty place is making a name for itself in wine making and nature-based tourism. If you arrive in town too late, however, it will be nuts and berries for you.

INFORMATION

The **Pemberton information centre** (☎ 9776 1133; www.pembertontourist.com.au; Brockman St; ☒ 9am-5pm) sells a Pemberton map ($3.95) and several touring maps and bushwalking books. It also incorporates a small pioneer museum from the old logging days. Learn about the wildlife here at the **Karri Forest Discovery Centre** (admission by donation). Internet access is available at the Telecentre next door and you can buy national park passes and great maps from the visitor centre or the **CALM office** (☎ 9776 1207; Kennedy St).

SIGHTS & ACTIVITIES

Readers rave about the 60m shimmy up the former lookout **Gloucester Tree** in the Gloucester National Park, 3km from town. The **Dave Evans Bicentennial Tree** in the splendorous **Warren National Park**, 12km to the south, is also climb worthy. If you are a groundhog at heart, it's still worth the trip to watch others exercise their courage and to feed bronze-wing pigeons by hand. See the boxed text, p938, for more about lookout trees.

The **Big Brook Dam**, 6km northeast, is a favourite local hang-out, with a small swimming beach, an excellent 3.5km track circling the dam, and regal stands of karri.

Wend through marri and karri forests on the scenic **Pemberton Tramway** (☎ 9776 1322; www.pemtram.com.au; Pemberton Railway Station). Trams leave for Warren River (adult/child $18/9) at 10.45am and 2pm daily, and for Northcliffe (adult/child $48/24) at 10.15am on the third Saturday of each month. Steam trains run from Easter to November.

The **Lavender-Berry Farm** (☎ 9776 1661; Browns Rd) is purple to all people, with berry, lavender or honey ice cream ($2.50), lavender soap, oils, ornaments and hundreds of miniature lavender mice.

In lush gardens, the **Fine Woodcraft Gallery** (☎ 9776 1399; Dickinson St; ☒ 9am-5pm) has furniture made by clever people with lathes.

TOURS

Pemberton Discovery Tours (☎ 9776 0484; adult/child $60/40) Whisks visitors off on half-day 4WD adventures, which stop at the spectacular Yeagarup Dunes, drive down remote beaches and include some munchies.

Pemberton Hiking & Canoeing Company (☎ 9776 1559; half-/full-day trips $45/90) Has ecotours that include a walk through old-growth forest and canoeing through Warren National Park.

SLEEPING

Pemberton Backpackers YHA (☎ /fax 9776 1105; pembertonbackpackers@wn.com.au; 7 Brockman St; dm/s/d/f $20/35/60/70) Readers always have good things to say about this busy YHA in the town centre. Ask for a free day-walk map.

Pemberton Hotel (☎ 9776 1017; fax 9776 1600; 66 Brockman St; s/d/f $90/120/145) The architect-designed motel units, which look like stacked railway sleepers, contain king-size bed comfort. Next door is the original capacious pub, with locals at its front bar.

Glenhaven B&B (☎ 9776 0028; glenhaven@wn.com.au; 25 Browns Rd; s/d $70/95) The Scottish invented shortbread, did ye noo? Afternoon tea and breakfasts are both generous in cottagey style here, 3km from town.

Marima Cottages (☎ /fax 9776 1211; Warren National Park, Old Vasse Rd; cottages from $145, with spa $175) Secluded and favoured by kangaroos in the morning, there are only four cottages on 40 hectares of karri forestland here.

You can also get away from it all at **camp sites** (per 2 people $10) in Warren National Park; contact **CALM** (☎ 9776 1207) for details.

EATING

Keep your eye out for local trout and marron on the menu at wineries.

Gloucester Ridge Vineyard & Restaurant (☎ 9776 1035; Burma Rd; mains $20-30; ☒ lunch & dinner) Around the corner from the Gloucester Tree, this picturesque place will bring you back down to the earthy delights of a seasonal menu.

Café Mazz (☎ 9776 1017; 66 Brockman St; mains $16-28; ☒ dinner Wed-Sat) Attached to the hotel, bustling Mazz is no-nonsense, but ambient, with dishes and a wine list to match.

Coffee Connection (☎ 9776 1159; Dickinson St; mains $8-10; ☒ lunch) An afternoon's coffee and a selection of chocolates and cakes can be found at this tranquil café in bird-filled gardens on the town's fringes.

Shannon National Park

Some of the region's most magnificent karri country can be found in this 535-sq-km national park, 53km south of Manjimup. As you travel over such long shadow-striped roads it begins to feel like you're in a frame of time-lapse photography. The 48km **Great Forest Trees Drive** leads you through the old-growth forest with the bonus of on-board commentary, if you tune your radio in to

100FM when you see the signs. The full-colour *Great Forest Trees Drive* ($15) is a detailed map and drive guidebook that's available from CALM; see also the CALM website (www.calm.wa.gov.au). As you'd expect from a region renowned for its pristine forests, Shannon National Park offers some excellent bushwalking opportunities, including a section of the Bibbulmun Track.

There's a fine **camping ground** (sites per 2 people $13) on the spot where the original timber-milling village used to be. The ground also has **huts** ($15) equipped with potbelly stoves; all fees are on a self-registration basis.

Northcliffe
☎ 08 / pop 240
Mountain bikers skid to a halt at quiet Northcliffe to find a bed after a tough day's ride in the annual Karri Cup. A minuscule town 31km south of Pemberton, it's ringed by bushwalking and bike trails through lush forest and farming country.

Find out about walks at the **Northcliffe visitor information centre** (☎ 9776 7203; Wheatley Coast Rd; ⏰ 9.30am-4pm Mon-Fri, 10am-2pm Sat & Sun), next door to the **pioneer museum** (⏰ 10am-2pm, limited hours Jun-Aug). The cliffs of the fine **D'Entrecasteaux National Park** are accessible 30km south from here.

At the **Bibbulmun Break Motel** (☎ 9776 6060; bibbulmunbreak@bigpond.com; 14 Wheatley Coast Rd; s/d incl breakfast $55/77), stay in one of only four whisper-quiet rooms with en suites and sleep-inducing beds.

Round Tu-It Holiday Park (☎ 9776 7276; roundtu-it@westnet.com.au; Muirillup Rd; dm $15, B&B s/d $45/65, powered sites per 2 people $20) is a hobby farm run by a kind-hearted couple with a one-eyed devotion for orphaned baby roos, who they raise in their lounge room. An experience like no other is to be had here in their homely abode, basic dorm rooms or caravans.

GREAT SOUTHERN

Great Southern is a unique wilderness area. Stunning coastline, 386,000 hectares of forest and the famous Valley of the Giants are the highlights. Stretching from Walpole-Nornalup in the west to Cape Arid, east of Esperance, the area is a nature lover's paradise, with spectacular (and often empty) beaches, and some of the best mountainous

national parks in Australia, exemplified by the ecological 'islands' of the dramatic Stirling Range and the ancient granite spires of the Porongurups.

Getting There & Away
Skywest (☎ 1300 660 088; www.skywest.com.au) has daily flights from Perth to Albany ($230) and Esperance ($280).

Transwa (☎ 1300 662 205) offers a daily service from Perth to Albany (via Bunbury) that uses a combination of the *Australind* and road coach ($55). It passes through Walpole ($48) and Denmark ($50), and the journey takes about 8½ hours. Another daily bus service from Perth to Albany ($45, six hours) travels inland via Williams and stops in Mt Barker ($37, 5½ hours).

Transwa also has daily buses from Perth to Esperance ($64, 10 hours), two buses a week from Albany to Esperance ($47) and three buses a week between Esperance and Kalgoorlie ($41, five hours).

WALPOLE-NORNALUP AREA
If driving from the west into the thickly forested **Walpole-Nornalup National Park**, keep an eye out for the sign to the Diamond Tree Lookout. A seedling in 1795, and now 52m high, this beauty is your introduction to the great beasts of trees further east. If you have the guts to climb it, you must have koala somewhere in your family.

Just west of Walpole is the turn-off to wild Mandalay Beach, 8km down a bush track. It's named after a Norwegian barque that was beached here in a storm on its way from South Africa to Albany in 1911. The crew survived for five days before local farmers found them. Every 10 years the wreck appears on the white beach, unveiled by the wind.

Other scenic drives include Knoll Dr and Hilltop Rd (and a lovely walk leading to the **Giant Tingle Tree**). Walpole is a tranquil pit stop around 14km from the Tree Top Walk and not far from the Bibbulmun Track, while Nornalup is even smaller and just minutes from the giants.

Stop at the info-rich **visitor information centre** (☎ 08-9840 1111; ⏰ 9am-5pm, to 4pm Sat & Sun) and **CALM** (☎ 08-9840 1027), both on the South Coast Hwy. There's a shady picnic ground here too, and you can grab a sandwich across the road.

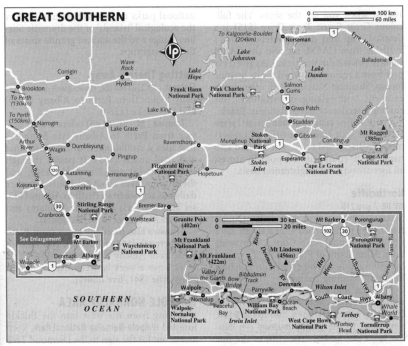

One of the top ecotour guides in Australia takes knowledgeable, funny, stimulating tours on the **WOW Wilderness Cruise** (☎ 08-9840 1036; adult/child $30/14; ⏰ 10am), a 2½-hour trip through the inlets and river systems in the area.

Valley of the Giants

Unique to this small region of southwestern WA, tingle tingle trees live for up to 400 years, and can grow to 60m tall and as wide as 16m around the base. It's no wonder some families in earlier times found them a likely home. For decades people have made the short trek down the 6km Valley of the Giants Rd, eager to see the 'Ancient Empire' that was here long before Europeans turned up. Now you can get up amongst it on the **Tree Top Walk** (☎ 08-9840 8263; adult/child/family $6/2.50/14; ⏰ 8am-5.15pm Dec-Jan, 9am-4.15pm Feb-Nov), a 600m-long structure that leads you into the canopy. The views and the sensation are great, but so is the height (40m): even the mighty steel supports sway with the wind up here. If you are shy of high diving boards, this is not the

walk for you. Try the 600m ground-level **Ancient Empire** boardwalk through a grove of equally colossal tingles.

CALM (☎ 08-9840 1027; adult/child $12/5) runs guided Forest by Night tours in summer, when visitors can watch starlit creatures rustle the canopy.

Sleeping & Eating

See the Walpole office of **CALM** (☎ 08-9840 1027) for camping options in the Walpole-Nornalup National Park.

Walpole Lodge (☎ 08-9840 1244; www.walpolelodge.com.au; cnr Pier St & Park Ave; dm/d $21/56; 🖳) 'Mike' the baby magpie was being nursed back to health at this friendly, roomy post at the edge of the bush with mountain-bike hire and a social pool table. Kids welcome ($10).

Rest Point Holiday Village (☎ 08-9840 1032; www.restpoint.com.au; Rest Point Rd; cabins from $60) About 2km from town, right on the shore of the Walpole Inlet, the green chalets in a forest setting have access to the river where pelicans drift. Explore with boats and canoes.

Redman's Riverside Retreat (☎ 08-9840 1255; fax 08-9840 1388; South Coast Hwy; 2-/3-bed chalets

$99/110) There's peace, privacy (except for the kangaroos) and plenty to do when staying at these self-contained chalets. Fish the Frankland River from the jetty, or sink a quiet sunset beer there. The enthusiastic hosts really know and love the area.

Wellington House (☎ 08-9840 1103; www.wellingtonhouse.com.au; Station Rd; s/d $90/100) Wander around this lovely property with sizable country-style rooms, 4km from the Conspicuous Cliffs and the beach. Decking overlooks a sloping garden and natural forest.

Nornalup Tea House (☎ /fax 08-9840 1422; South Coast Hwy; mains $16-24; ☼ lunch & dinner Wed-Mon) Teahouses in Nepal are traditionally places of travellers' rest, and you can't miss the welcoming lights of this elegant restaurant – nor should you forgo its food and wine. The worldly owners are taking the responsible tourism reins, using local organic produce, and grey water on the surrounding gardens.

DENMARK
☎ 08 / pop 2000

Where the forest meets the sea and hippies meet each other…idyllic Denmark. Fish, surf, or drop out for a while. Head for the hills for alternative lifestyle: there's everything from alpacas to art galleries. Or meander through the village itself, a former timber town gone green and growing at 5% a year.

The **Denmark visitor information centre** (☎ 98 48 2055; Strickland St; ☼ 9am-5pm) is in the RSL Memorial Hall, while the nearby **Telecentre** (Strickland St; ☼ 10am-4pm Mon-Fri; ☐) offers Internet access. It has public toilets and a baby-change room behind.

Sights & Activities
If you have wheels, explore **Scotsdale Rd**, lined with orchards, vineyards, berry farms and craft studios, and **Mt Shadforth Rd**, with galleries, potters' shops and luxury retreats.

William Bay National Park, 15km west of Denmark, has spectacular coastal scenery and safe swimming beaches at **Madfish Bay** and **Green's Pool**. Nearby hikes include the **Mokare Trail** (a 3km circuit along the Denmark River) and the **Wilson Inlet Trail** (6km, starting from the river mouth). **Elephants Rocks** are worth a nosey too. Closer to town, walk to sheltered **Ocean Beach**, which is popular with surfers.

Mike's Surfing Lessons (☎ 9848 2057; group/private lessons $35/50, hire $10) are recommended.

Doing it for love not money, Mike can't wait to teach you how to stand up for two hours. He's good at it, too.

Little River Discovery Tours (☎ 9848 2604) has 4WD day trips to the Valley of the Giants (adult/child $80/37) and the isolated beaches of West Cape Howe National Park ($75/35).

Sleeping
Blue Wren Travellers' Rest YHA (☎ 9848 3300; bluewrenrest@yahoo.com.au; 17 Price St; dm/tw $19/50, nonmembers extra $2; ☐) Fresh, clean and friendly, the Blue Wren is where you'll find local knowledge, communal lounging areas, free bikes and a loyal old Labrador. There's disabled access.

Riverbend Chalets (☎ 9848 1044; East River Rd; sites per 2 people $19-22, d $75-86) Pick your own veggies, plums and nectarines or pop some strawberries in your champagne. The chalets are a bit 'Norwegian Wood'. Families will love the acres of lawn, and the caravan park is peaceful (there are on-site cabins for a cheap overnight price of $45). No pets.

Mt Lindsay View (☎ 9848 1933; mtlindesayview@westnet.com.au; cnr Mt Shadforth & McNabb Rds; s/d $105/120) Locals and readers are quick to recommend a hill-top stay, especially the marvellous breakfasts.

Koorabup Motel (☎ 9848 1044; www.koorabup.com.au; South Coast Hwy; s/d $88/98) Next to the tavern, with rammed-earth, high-ceilinged accommodation, this is a great spot to pull in for the night.

Rivermouth Caravan Park (☎ /fax 9848 1262; 1 Inlet Dr; powered/unpowered sites per 2 people $17/14, on-site caravans $36, cabins $45-65) Budget travellers should check out this option under fig trees on the river bend, 1km south of town.

Eating
Café Lime (☎ 9848 2899; Strickland St; mains $5-13; ☼ breakfast & lunch) The groove is great over eggs on summery Saturday mornings at this fresh little café. Juices, healthy lunches… everything's yum, especially the staff.

Figtree Café (☎ 9848 2051; 27 Strickland St; mains $5-8; ☼ breakfast & lunch year-round, dinner Dec-Feb) Fine food and the arts are at the heart of things in this courtyard eatery. The blueberry whips have healing qualities.

Denmark Pizza (☎ 9848 2479; cnr Walker & Strickland Sts; pizzas $10-20) These guys deliver and their tasty pizzas experiment with wheat-free bases.

Observatory (☎ 9848 2600; www.karrimia.com
.au; Mt Shadforth Rd; mains $11-33; ☻ lunch & dinner)
A few kilometres up the hill, Observatory
serves so-so food, but you cannot beat the
view (even if you had a very big stick and
were trained in vista-combat). Coffee and
cake, mountains and sea ($7).

If you are cooking for yourself, stock up
at the **Denmark Bakery** (Strickland St) and the
impressive **Denmark Liquor Store** (☎ 9848 1145),
which focuses expertly on over 70 regional
wines.

MT BARKER
☎ 08 / pop 1650

Bare as a babe's bum, Mt Barker (50km
north of Albany) is nevertheless the gateway
town to the increasingly visited Porongurup and Stirling Range National Parks. It's
also the hub for the rapidly growing local
wine industry. You'll see the name Plantagenet everywhere in the region – nutty
King George III was convinced at one point
that he had French lineage and colonial WA
humoured him. **Plantagenet Wines** (☎ 9851
2150; Albany Hwy) is in the middle of town,
Goundrey Wines (☎ 9851 1777; Muirs Hwy) 10km
west. For a list of vineyards and cellar-door
opening times, see the **Mt Barker visitor information centre** (☎ 9851 1163; Albany Hwy; ☻ 9am-
5pm Mon-Fri, 9am-3pm Sat, 10am-3pm Sun) in the old
train station.

Historical sites worth a visit include the
picturesque 1873 **St Werburgh's Chapel** (☎ 9857
6041; St Werburgh's Rd) and the **Old Police Station
Museum** (Albany Hwy; adult/child $5/free; ☻ 10am-4pm
Sat, Sun & school holidays), which houses a collection of historical memorabilia. Enjoy panoramic views of the area from the **Mt Barker
Lookout**, 5km south of town.

THE GIANT GUARDS

Like professional basketballers in a nightclub, Lookout Trees in the southwestern
forests stand above the average canopy.
Since early colonial times they have been
used as strategic points to spot approaching bushfires. Vicious steel spikes were
scaled by nimble fellas. Light planes took
over in 1972, yet there are still days when
high winds make flying dangerous and the
trees once again become the protectors of
their own wilderness.

Aptly named **Chill Out Backpackers** (☎ 985
2798; 79 Hassell St; dm/s/d $20/25/45) is a terrifi
abode that sleeps seven and feels more lik
a B&B (minus breakfast) than a hostel.

Rayanne Homestead (☎ 9851 1562; fax 9851 244(
Porongurup Rd; s/d incl breakfast $60/80), on the town'
fringes offers small, modern rooms opening
onto a sprawling wraparound veranda.

Mount Barker Caravan Park (☎ 9851 1691; fa
9851 2691; Albany Hwy; powered/unpowered sites per
people $17/15, dm $20, cabins with/without bathroom
$60/50) is a quiet, spick-and-span park wit
friendly owners and comfortable cabins.

Taste Mt Barker (☎ 9851 2500; fax 9851 282; 2
Langton Rd; platters $9.50-24; ☻ lunch) is a barn-lik
café with hampers ($40) and snacks, sucl
as *dukkah* and olive oil ($7.50). It has a
fridge full of local wines that you can sam
ple, served by resident Scot Patricia – she'
tell you it's her birthday and join you.

PORONGURUP & STIRLING RANGE
The region north of Albany is one of spec
tacular natural beauty with two rugged
mountainous national parks to explore
National park fees apply to vehicles enter
ing both parks. For further informatior
contact Albany's **CALM office** (☎ 08-9842 450(
120 Albany Hwy) or the rangers at **Porongurup Na
tional Park** (☎ 08-9853 1095) and **Stirling Rang
National Park** (☎ 08-9827 9230).

Porongurup National Park
Striking granite outcrops hint at this area'
formation 200 million years ago, wher
tectonic plates collided. Above the ground
towering karri trees and excellent bus
tracks are worth exploring. Trails includ
Castle Rock (two hours) and the challengin
Devil's Slide and Marmabup Rock walk (thre
hours). There's a scenic 6km drive alon
the park's northern edge, starting at th
ranger's residence.

Porongurup Shop & Tearooms (☎ 08-9853 111(
homebake@omninet.net.au; Porongurup Rd; dm/s/d per per
son $20) runs a great backpackers hostel that i
also family friendly. Pick-ups from Alban
or Mt Barker are available (book ahead).

Children are more than welcome at **Bo
ganup Homestead** (☎ 08-9853 1049; RMB 1340 Po
ungurup; d $95), a must-stay in the area wit
self-contained units in a 1920s guesthouse
on a 202-hectare working sheep farm.

The **Sleeping Lady B&B** (☎ /fax 08-9853 111
Porongurup Rd; powered/unpowered sites per 2 peop

FAMILIAR LANDSCAPES

Beloved Australian author Tim Winton makes no secret of his love for WA. Its coast and people wind and spark through the majority of his 25 books. The following in particular will give you a strong sense of place:

- *Shallows* (1984) – the fictional town of Angelus is based on the real-life southwestern community of Albany, where Tim spent his late childhood and teenage years. The novel explores the conflict here between whaling and conservation, and the town's convict history.

- *Cloud Street* (1991) – a magnificent, funny, ambitious, beautiful, brawling family saga set in the suburbs of Perth, including Mt Lawley where Winton was born. Somehow this book is familiar territory for all Australians. It bottles and shelves the essence of this country.

- *Dirt Music* (2001) – fictional White Point is probably based on a coastal cray-potting town ('fish deco') north of Perth, where Winton lived with his family. This is a novel of loneliness, regret, redemption…and music! The CD soundtrack to the book charts the Western Australian landscape and a northbound passage all the way up to Cape Leveque.

$18/16, cabins $60) is on the temperate northern slopes of the ranges; there's a beaut, private spot among orchards. For adults and older kids only.

Pitch a tent at the popular **Porongurup Range Tourist Park** (☎ /fax 08-9853 1057; Porongurup Rd; powered/unpowered sites per 2 people $18/16, cabins $60), close to the entrance of the national park.

Stirling Range National Park

Ever seen a Queen of Sheba orchid or a Stirling Bell? The spectacular wildflower season blooms from late August to early December. Rising abruptly from the surrounding flat and sandy plains, photographers will be captivated by the Stirling Range's propensity to change colour through blues, reds and purples. Try to squeeze in at least one half-day walk to Toll Peak (plentiful wildflowers), Toolbrunup Peak (for views and a good climb) or Bluff Knoll (1073m, the highest peak in the range).

An array of accommodation lies in a tranquil setting at **Stirling Range Retreat** (☎ 08-9827 9229; www.stirlingrange.com.au; Chester Pass Rd; powered/unpowered sites per 2 people $22/18, dm $19, cabins $79-85, chalets $105-125) on the northern boundary of the park. Ecotourism is the go and TV is a no-no. The licensed Bluff Knoll café is opposite.

Lily (☎ 08-9827 9205; www.thelily.com.au; Chester Pass Rd; d from $97), 11km further down the road, is a replica Dutch flour-producing windmill with a restaurant nearby. If not bowled over by that, check out the gingerbread cottage–looking accommodation. Sweet.

Those looking to get right off the beaten track will relish **Trio Park Campground** (☎ 08-9827 9270, 0427 279 270; triopark@westnet.com.au; Salt River Rd; powered/unpowered sites per 2 people $24/20), with powered sites, on a corner of the Byrnes' wheat farm. A bush setting, wildflowers and a mountainous backdrop make a good starting point from which to explore the Stirlings. Local farmers sometimes drop in for a chat.

ALBANY

☎ 08 / pop 29,900

Albany is a city of two tales: the stately, peeling old quarter and its rampant offspring to the north, a new, hectic sprawl of malls and fast food. Established shortly before Perth in 1826, the oldest European settlement in the state is now the bustling commercial centre of the southern region. The area was occupied by Aboriginal people long before Europeans arrived and there is much evidence of their earlier presence, especially around Oyster Harbour.

There's a vague sense of menace or, at the very least, a power in the solid grey granite landscape. This is a place that's seen weather and the violence of whaling on its white beaches and rugged coastline. Serene King George Sound is popular with divers and whales, who find a safer passage through here these days.

Information

Albany Rest Centre (cnr Stirling Tce & York St) If you are in need of a quick shower, this place can accommodate; it also has toilets, disabled facilities and baby-change rooms.

Albany visitor information centre (☎ 9841 1088, 1800 644 088; Proudlove Pde; ⊙ 9am-5pm) In the old train station; offers accommodation and tour tips.
CALM (☎ 9842 4500; Albany Hwy)
RACWA (Albany Hwy)
Stirling Terrace Book Café (☎ 9841 4611; 168 Stirling Tce; ⊙ 9am-5pm Mon-Sat, to 8pm Thu, 10am-4pm Sun) Has a special section on local and WA writers.

Sights
HISTORIC BUILDINGS
Near the foreshore you'll see the buildings of the old historic precinct. This area is relatively quiet, as if the town's boom years belong to another time. A free walking-tour brochure of Albany's colonial buildings is available from the visitor centre.

The phantasmal 'History and Mystery night-time tour of the **Old Gaol** (☎ 9841 140 Lower Stirling Tce; adult/child $4/2.50, tour $10; ⊙ 10am 4.15pm) is a good way to spook yourself wit less. Daytime entry includes a visit to tin **Patrick Taylor Cottage** (☎ 9841 6174; Duke St; ⊙ 1 4.15pm), believed to be the oldest colonia dwelling in WA (1832).

Albany Residency Museum (☎ 9841 4844; Residency Rd; adult/child $3/1; ⊙ 10am-5pm), built in the 1850s, explores the social history of th region through seafaring subjects and Abori ginal artefacts.

Near the museum is a full-blown replic of the **Brig Amity** (adult/child $3/1; ⊙ 9am-5pm which brought Albany's founders to the are in 1826. See how people made a farm living

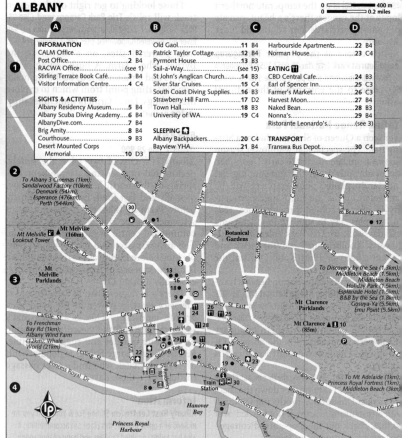

INFORMATION	
CALM Office..............................**1** B2	
Post Office..............................**2** B4	
RACWA Office......................(see 1)	
Stirling Terrace Book Café......**3** B4	
Visitor Information Centre......**4** C4	
SIGHTS & ACTIVITIES	
Albany Residency Museum......**5** B4	
Albany Scuba Diving Academy....**6** B4	
AlbanyDive.com......................**7** B4	
Brig Amity..............................**8** B4	
Courthouse..............................**9** B3	
Desert Mounted Corps	
Memorial..............................**10** D3	

Old Gaol..............................**11** B4	
Patrick Taylor Cottage............**12** B4	
Pyrmont House......................**13** B3	
Sail-a-Way..........................(see 15)	
St John's Anglican Church......**14** B3	
Silver Star Cruises................**15** C4	
South Coast Diving Supplies....**16** B3	
Strawberry Hill Farm............**17** D2	
Town Hall..............................**18** B3	
University of WA....................**19** C4	
SLEEPING	
Albany Backpackers................**20** C4	
Bayview YHA..........................**21** B4	

Harbourside Apartments..........**22** B4	
Norman House......................**23** C4	
EATING	
CBD Central Cafe..................**24** B3	
Earl of Spencer Inn................**25** C3	
Farmer's Market....................**26** C3	
Harvest Moon......................**27** B4	
Naked Bean........................**28** B3	
Nonna's..............................**29** B4	
Ristorante Leonardo's............(see 3)	
TRANSPORT	
Transwa Bus Depot..............**30** C4	

at **Strawberry Hill Farm** (☎ 9841 3735; 170 Middleton Rd; adult/child/family $3.30/2.20/8.30; ☻ 10am-4pm), a National Trust–listed property. The tea-rooms do a debonair Devonshire tea.

Other historic sites include **St John's Angli-can Church** (cnr York St & Peels Pl), the elegant **Pyr-mont House** (110 Serpentine Rd), the **courthouse** (cnr Grey St W & York St) and the **Town Hall** (217 York St).

OTHER ATTRACTIONS

Slow down to a turtle's pace (20km/h) at much-loved **Middleton Beach**, popular for swimming, sunbathing and some great ac-commodation options. It's not often that you see a sign saying 'please dry off excess water before entering' but that's how it is at the little eateries right on the beach at family-friendly **Emu Point** – a beautiful, clean, enclosed swimming area with rewarding fishing and boating, 4km east.

The **Desert Mounted Corps Memorial** sits atop **Mt Clarence**, which you can climb along a track accessible from the end of Grey St E. Enjoy panoramic views from the lookout tower on **Mt Melville**; there's a signposted turn-off from Serpentine Rd. There's also a **whale-watching walk** from Marine Dr on Mt Adelaide to the harbour entrance (45 minutes return).

The **Princess Royal Fortress** (Marine Dr; adult/child $4/2; ☻ 7.30am-5.30pm) on Mt Adelaide was built in 1893 as a strategic defence post, and today boasts restored buildings, gun emplacements and fine views.

Activities

Albany's appeal as a top-class diving desti-nation grew after the 2001 scuttling of the warship HMAS *Perth* to create an artificial reef for divers. There's plenty of competi-tion for business among the companies in town. The following offer a range of dive courses and guided dives to the wreck and reefs:

Albany Scuba Diving Academy (☎ 9842 3101; cnr Proudlove Pde & York St)

AlbanyDive.com (☎ 9842 6886; www.albanydive.com; cnr York St & Stirling Tce; ☐) For info on diving, whale watching, rock climbing and kayaking in the area.

South Coast Diving Supplies (☎ 9841 7176; www .divealbany.com.au; 84 Serpentine Rd)

If blowing bubbles below is not really your thing, the semisubmersible underwater viewing vessel, the **Albany Reef Explorer** (☎ 0418

950 361), does several one-hour cruises daily (adult/child $24/15).

Tours

From July to October, southern right whales are often spotted near the bays and coves of King George Sound.

Albany Motorcycle Touring Co (☎ 9841 8034; tours $5-30) You can tour around town or along scenic coastline on the back of a Harley Davidson.

Escape Tours (☎ 9844 1945; adult/child half-day tours $40/30, full-day $80/60) Operates half-day bus tours of historic Albany or the peninsula. Full-day tours head to the Tree Top Walk, West Cape Howe and the Porongurups, among other destinations.

Kalgan Queen Scenic Cruises (☎ 9844 1949; kalqueen@albanyis.com.au; adult/child $36/20; ☻ cruise 9am) Leaves at 9am on the dot from the Emu Point boat pens, to cruise the Kalgan River and Oyster Harbour in search of wildlife. Be sure to book.

Sail-a-Way (☎ 0409 107 180; ☻ cruises 9.30am & 1.30pm) Gives informative themed cruises – take the Ex-plorer's Trip (2½ hours, $45), which retraces the route and stories of the explorers; the Rockstar (three hours, $45), which examines the billion-year-old coastline; the Twilight Cruise (two hours, $25); or sail out to see the whales (if no sightings, you can come back free until you do see one).

Silver Star Cruises (☎ 0428 936 711; adult/child $45/30; ☻ cruises 9.30am & 1pm) Runs 2½-hour whale-watching trips around King George Sound from the town jetty.

Sleeping
BUDGET

Albany Backpackers (☎ 9841 8848; www.albanyback packers.com.au; cnr Stirling Tce & Spencer St; dm $22, d & tw $50, nonmembers extra $3-5; ☐) Fabbo free arvo coffee and cake are served at this rambling joint, which is the pick of the backpackers hostels for activities, free net cards and a terrific laundry. Crazy murals painted by travellers make every wall an experience.

Bayview YHA (☎ 9842 3388; albany@yhawa.com.au; 49 Duke St; dm/d $20/50, nonmembers extra $3.50; ☐) BBQs, beer tickets and beach trips: 500m from town, this huge old sloping place on stilts has sea views from the four-bed dorms.

Happy Days Caravan Park (☎ 9844 3267; happydays@omninet.net.au; Millbrook Rd; powered/un-powered sites per 2 people $22/20, cabins $50-70) Read-ers have enjoyed a wood-fired BBQ by the friendliest of owners here, a few kilometres out of Albany, and beside the King River.

Middleton Beach Holiday Park (☎ 9841 3593, 1800 644 674; www.holidayalbany.com.au; Flinders Pde; powered/unpowered sites per 2 people $27/26, cabins from

$80) Another top option is this beachfront park, which is located 3km from the town centre. Prices are reduced in low season.

MIDRANGE

Harbourside Apartments (☎ 9842 1769; www.albany harbourside.com.au; 8 Festing St; d & tw $110, per extra adult/child $15/10, up to 8) These old stone cottages (1890) with fantastic new additions could well be haunted, but they're so nicely appointed you'll be prepared to share (ghost, you shall sleep in the bath tonight). In fact this is top accommodation for bigger families or groups.

Norman House (☎ 9841 5995; www.westnet.com .au/normanhouse; 28 Stirling Tce; s/d incl breakfast $65/90) With the scent of magnolia out the front, richly coloured carpets and a homely air, this eight-bedroom guesthouse offers a very relaxed stay. Wake to a full cooked breakfast overlooking a shambolic but lovely backyard.

Middleton Beach

Drive around the head, overlooking granite outcrops and beautiful sheltered beaches, to Middleton Beach.

Discovery by the Sea (☎ 9842 5535; www.discovery inn.com.au; 9 Middleton Rd; s/d/f $40/65/75) Elegant in a wickery way, this place caters to 'baby-boomer backpackers' – meaning people who have never given up travelling. Families will also like it here, 50m from the sand.

B&B by the Sea (☎ 9844 1135; www.bbythesea .com.au; 7 Griffiths St; d $110-130) This small place has the admiration of B&B owners as far away as Nornalup. It's adjacent to coastal walking tracks. Gourmet breakfast is served on the balcony. Couples only.

Esplanade Hotel (☎ 9842 1711; www.albanyespla nade.com.au; cnr Adelaide Cres & Flinders Pde; d from $175, self-contained apt from $160) 'Oh I do like to be beside the seaside…' Hum the old ditty to yourself as you book into an extremely comfortable room at this grand overseer of the strand. The pub is famous for its Sunday Session.

Eating & Drinking

Stirling Tce, York St and Frederick St are the eat streets here. If you're cooking for yourself, the fresh **farmer's market** (☎ 0417 983 428; Aberdeen St; ☽ 8am-noon) is worth a wander to find some local produce on a Saturday morning.

Naked Bean (☎ 9841 1815; 14 Peels Pl; mains $8-15 ☽ breakfast & lunch Mon-Sat) Tall windows flood light across this buzzing breakfast spot. Locals chat over crumbly cake and coffee. Kids are welcome.

Harvest Moon (☎ 9841 8833; 82 Stirling Tce; meals $5-15; ☽ lunch) Winter brings open fires and homemade soups to this vegetarian café and secondhand bookshop. Maxine's brown-rice bake and carrot cake rock.

Nonna's (☎ 9841 4626; 135 Lower York St; mains $8.50-23; ☽ dinner) While away an evening in the warmth of conversation over sumptuous homemade pastas, cold carafes and *molto bene* gelati.

CBD Central Café (☎ 9842 9551; cnr York & Grey Sts E; mains $13-30; ☽ breakfast, lunch & dinner Mon-Sat) A small, welcoming restaurant with a touch of urban about it (we mean a cake cabinet and a more-than-decent wine list). There's free ice cream for kids who eat their dinner – you won't have any trouble finishing yours.

Ristorante Leonardo's (☎ 9841 1732; 164 Stirling Tce; mains $17-32; ☽ dinner) Local fresh produce is served with an Italian influence – can you honestly walk past pear, currant and grappa pudding with King Island double cream?

Earl of Spencer Inn (☎ 9841 1322; cnr Earl & Spencer Sts; mains $11-28; ☽ dinner) Lit up on the hill overlooking Princes Royal Harbour, this cosy, colonial-style pub is full locals here for an Old Speckled Hen ale. Seek out the well-populated patch of beer garden during the day.

Legends Bar & Bistro (☎ 9842 1711; Esplanade Hotel, cnr Adelaide Cres & Flinders Pde, Middleton Beach; ☽ lunch & dinner) Stagger up from the beach to grab an ale or a tasty counter meal at this bistro in the Esplanade Hotel.

Gosuya-Ya (☎ 9844 1111; 1 Mermaid Ave; mains $14-23; ☽ lunch & dinner Tue-Sat) Don't miss lunch ('til 2pm)! Down some raw fish after a swim in Oyster Harbour (a sashimi set includes rice, miso soup and green tea) or come back and take your time over a sundown meal on the decking.

Getting Around

Love's (☎ 9841 1211; adult/child $2/90c) runs bus services around town along the Albany Hwy from Peel Pl to the main roundabout, and to Middleton Beach, Emu Point and Bayonet Head on weekdays and Saturday morning.

AROUND ALBANY

Whale World

On an isolated, bleak promontory of extreme natural beauty, **Whale World** (☎ 08-9844 4021; www.whaleworld.org; Frenchman Bay Rd; adult/child/family $18/9/45; ☺ 9am-5pm, tours hourly 10am-4pm) should really be called 'Whaling World'. Its focus is still more on the industry than the mammals themselves, nearly 15,000 of which were caught and their every part (from oil to ivory) processed here at Cheynes Beach Whaling Station between 1963 and 1978. Documentaries screen in the old oil tanks. Scramble over a rusting former whale chaser outside.

En route to Whale World, about 12km from Albany, stop off to take a look at the **Albany Wind Farm** (Frenchman Bay Rd), the biggest in the southwest and an eerily striking sight as you get closer.

National Parks & Reserves

South of Albany, off Frenchman Bay Rd, is the **Torndirrup National Park**. Its beauty is matched only by its treachery: people have drowned here (one in 2004). Don't take lightly the warning signs at the **Gap**, the **Natural Bridge** and the **Blowholes**; tragic accidents still occur thanks to carelessness and strong wind gusts. Other popular spots in the park are **Jimmy Newhill's Harbour** and **Salmon Holes**, which is popular with surfers, although these coves are quite dangerous. Southern right whales can be seen from the cliffs during the season.

You can explore many habitats in the excellent natural areas along the coast west and east of Albany. **West Cape Howe National Park**, 30km west, is a favourite with naturalists, bushwalkers, rock climbers and anglers.

East of Albany is **Two People's Bay**, a nature reserve with a good swimming beach, scenic coastline and a small colony of noisy scrub birds, a species once thought extinct.

One of the best of the national parks, but the least visited, is **Waychinicup**, which is 65km east of Albany, and features its own population of noisy scrub birds and several other endangered animals.

ALBANY TO ESPERANCE

From Albany, the South Coast Hwy (Hwy 1) runs northeast along the coast before turning inland to skirt the Fitzgerald River National Park and ending in Esperance.

Fitzgerald River National Park

This 3300-sq-km park contains half of the orchid species in WA (more than 80 species, 70 of which occur nowhere else), 22 mammal species, 200 species of birds and 1700 species of plants. It's also the blossoming ground of the royal hakea *(Hakea victoria)* and qualup bell *(Pimelia physodes)* flowers. Walkers will discover beautiful coastline, sand plains, the rugged coastal hills (known as 'The Barrens') and deep, wide river valleys. You might be lucky enough to see whales and their calves from the shore at Point Ann.

The overnight wilderness bushwalking route from Fitzgerald Beach to Whalebone Beach is recommended, though there's no track and no water. Call the **ranger** (☎ 08-9835 5043) before you set out, and clean your shoes at the start and finish of each walk to avoid the spread of dieback fungus.

Access to the park is from Bremer Bay (west) and Hopetoun (east), or from Hwy 1 along Devils Creek, Quiss and Hamersley Rds. Readers have commented on the park's good natural camping sites. For more information, contact the Albany **CALM office** (☎ 08-9842 4500).

Ravensthorpe

☎ 08 / pop 350

Hwy 1 runs smack bang through the middle of Ravensthorpe, which started out as the centre of the Phillips River goldfield. Copper mining followed and modern nickel mines are a prospect, but this is farming country, in an area which is two-thirds natural bushland.

Tourist information and locally knitted beanies are available from the **Going Bush Information Stop** (☎ 9838 1277; Morgan St; ☺ 9am-4.30pm).

After a long drive, you can relax in quiet units and enjoy room-service continental breakfast at **Ravensthorpe Motel** (☎ 9838 1366; South Coast Hwy; s/d $50/64). It's not far from the road but the sound of trucks is sort of comforting when you feel like you've been hit by one.

Ravensthorpe Caravan Park (☎ 9838 1050; fax 9838 1465; South Coast Hwy; powered/unpowered sites per 2 people $17/12, on-site caravans from $22, cabins from $35) is a tidy place and offers camping and cabins in a bush setting. Several of the cabins have limited disabled access.

WESTERN AUSTRALIA

The **Palace Motor Hotel** (☎ 9838 1005; fax 9838 1200; 28 Morgan St; hotel s/d $22/38, motel s/d $50/66; ⏰ lunch & dinner) is full of farmers feasting. This gold-rush relic has very basic rooms upstairs, and dishes up traditional counter meals in its downstairs bar and bistro.

The **Ravy Country Kitchen** (☎ 9838 1163; Morgan St; mains $6-12; ⏰ lunch) cooks up reliable pies, cakes and other country fare.

Hopetoun
☎ 08 / pop 350

Windswept, remote Hopetoun, 50km south of Ravensthorpe, was once the port for the Phillips River goldfield and served sealers, whalers and early settlers. These days it's a favourite with retirees who love the heat. The eastern gateway to the Fitzgerald River National Park, Hopetoun has fine beaches and bays. In September there's a wildflower show here with over 800 species. You can get here via the rebuilt Culham Inlet causeway, a well-graded gravel road through breathtaking scenery.

The town has a wide central strip, Veal St, with only a few businesses on it. The **Hopetoun visitor information centre** (☎ 9838 3228) is one of those, or check your email at the **Telecentre** (☎ 9838 3062). Warning: if you roll into town late, you'll be having toothpaste for dinner.

The spacious rammed-earth rooms at **Hopetoun Motel & Chalet Village** (☎ 9838 3219; cnr Veal & Canning Sts; motel d/tw from $80/85, chalets $150) have thick walls and wide bull-nose verandas. Unless you're missing the traffic, ask for a room away from the main road.

Grab some country tucker at **Taste of the Toun** (☎ 9838 3222; Veal St; meals $5-14; ⏰ lunch), where you can get a no-fuss, home-style quiche or a burger. Dinner finishes early.

At **Deck** (☎ 9448 0200; cnr Veal & Clarke Sts; snacks $3-9; ⏰ breakfast & lunch Dec-Apr; 🖳) there's a deep shady veranda to sit and slurp your smoothie on. Coffee is of the watery volcanic variety, but the ice cream's luscious. There are pretty souvenirs available at the gift-bookshop.

ESPERANCE
☎ 08 / pop 8650

Esperance sits quietly on the Bay of Isles, a clear landscape of aquamarine waters and squeaky white beaches, but the town's charm is not immediately visible. At first glance, the Norfolk Pines are the only stately reminder that Esperance has been around just as long as Perth (1863). Many of the buildings were shifted to Esperance from other locales. A port during the gold rush of the 1890s, it was quiet in the years afterwards, becoming a farming centre only when trace elements were added to the soil in the 1950s.

A favourite holiday destination for people who enjoy the sense of community here, the pristine coastal environment of the Recherche Archipelago is also home to colonies of fur seals, penguins and a variety of sea birds.

Information
CALM (☎ 9071 3733; 92 Dempster St)
Visitor information centre (☎ 9071 2330; Dempster St; ⏰ 8.45am-5pm; 🖳) Can book tours to the islands and surrounding national parks, as well as onward transport.

Sights & Activities

The **Esperance Aquarium** (☎ 9071 7222; 53 The Esplanade; admission $9; ⏰ 10am-5pm) is a fantastic little boutique aquarium run by two divers who are dedicated environmentalists. Among the healthy sea life in their 14 natural ecosystem tanks are a pregnant male seahorse, tall-fin batfish, 'Dory and Nemo', and lumbering southern rock lobsters.

A visit to the **Cannery Art Centre** (☎ 9071 3599; Norseman Rd; ⏰ 10am-4pm Mon-Fri) yields exhibitions and local artists' work. The **Kickarts Fest** (January) features sand sculpture, kite making or drama workshops for kids.

In town, the **museum** (cnr Dempster & James Sts; adult/child $3/1; ⏰ 1.30-4.30pm) has a collection of old local things from the 1800s. Slightly younger are a few pieces of *Skylab*, the US space station that crashed on the Nullarbor in 1979. Behind the visitor centre is the knick-knacky **Museum Park Period Village** (⏰ 10am-4pm Mon-Fri, to 1pm Sat).

A street back from the Esplanade, groovy **Fenwick 3 Cinema** (☎ 9072 1355; 105-107 Dempster St) shows mainstream flicks.

Try to find time for the 36km **Great Ocean Drive**, west of town. Stunning lookouts and beaches entice you to stop at **Blue Haven** and **Twilight Bay**. **Pink Lake** is a favourite with photographers. Via Lakes Rd, the **Kepwari Wetland Wonderland** has 59 species of water birds and a trail (3.6km).

Esperance is renowned for its **fishing** – try catching your dinner from the jetty. There's good **diving** around the islands, and the wrecks of the *Sanko Harvest* and the *Lapwing* are worth exploring. **Esperance Diving & Fishing** (☎ 9071 5111; 72 The Esplanade) runs trips and hires out equipment. **Esperance Boat Hire** (☎ 0419 834 232) has dinghies for day hire ($120 including fuel).

Tours

Cruises on the Bay of Isles are a must. **MacKenzie's Island Cruises** (☎ 9071 5757; www .emerge.net.au/~macruise; 71 The Esplanade; adult/child $55/20) Runs morning wildlife tours that get close to wild fur seals, sea lions, Cape Barren geese, and (if luck's on their side) dolphins. After morning tea, watch sea eagles swoop down to seize hand-fed fish. Full-day trips ($80/35) are available on Wednesday and Sunday.

Vacation Country Tours (☎ 9071 2227) Daily trips around Esperance, including a town-and-coast tour ($31) and a Cape Le Grand tour ($50).

Sleeping

BUDGET

Esperance Backpackers (☎ 9071 4724; esperanceback packers@bigpond.com; 14 Emily St; dm/d from $19/48; 🖳) This clean, timber, two-storey pad is family run. Beach fishing ($45) is a speciality here and they hire out golf clubs. Free pick-up and drop-off.

Esperance Guesthouse (☎ 9071 3396; fax 9072 0298; 23 Daphne St; dm/d $20/45; 🖳) Lovely people run this suburban backpackers hostel with beds instead of bunks. It feels like a home, right down to the table-tennis set up in the garage and free bikes. It's boiling inside during summer, but in winter there's a potbelly stove and homemade hot bread. Rates drop after the first night.

Blue Waters Lodge YHA (☎ 9071 1040; yhaesper ance@hotmail.com; 299 Goldfields Rd; dm/s/d/f from $18/30/45/70; 🖳) About 1.5km out of town, this rambling, plain lodge has large communal areas and beaut bay views from the balcony.

There are six caravan parks around Esperance, including **Esperance Seafront Caravan Park** (☎ 9071 1251; Goldfields Rd; powered/unpowered sites per 2 people $21/18, on-site caravans $55), which has an enviable beachfront position.

Getting across to **Woody Island** (sites per person $9, 2-person tent $31) is not so budget, but if you want a real beachy-wildlife-castaway kind of experience, there's nowhere better. BYO tent or rent a permanently erected tent with mattresses (see also below for details on safari huts). Contact **MacKenzie's Island Cruises** (☎ 9071 5757) for details.

MIDRANGE

Old Hospital Motel (☎ 9071 3587, 0419 449 871; oldesp@emerge.net.au; William St; s/d/f $80/90/120) Centrally located and run by a garrulous, fun couple, these corrugated buildings from 1896 are superclean and comfortable inside. The deluxe upstairs is all blue and white and cool tiled floors.

All Seasons Esplanade (☎ 9071 2257; fax 9071 2331; 73 The Esplanade; d $88) The owners are modest, but this really is a comfortable little 1960s motel that's had a serious upgrade. Everything's in great nick and there's a TV/DVD in the bedroom too! Hello takeaway dinner.

Beach House Apartments (☎ 9071 5313; www .wn.com.au/espbeachhouse; 20 The Esplanade; 1-/2-bedroom apt from $125/150; ✷) Little A-frame beachside numbers with a great view are stylishly furnished and close to town.

Esperance Seaside Apartments (☎ 9072 0044; www.esperanceseaside.com; 14-16 The Esplanade; 1-/2-bedroom apt from $140/190; ✷) It's a challenge to stay here in high season, but you might get a taste of luxury two-storey living with home touches. Hire bikes or catch the afternoon air currents over a balcony BBQ. The three-bedroom places ($250) sleep up to eight.

Woody Island Eco Stay (☎ 9071 5757; d $62-92) A tranquil 16km out into the ocean, there's a row of hillside safari huts on elevated wooden platforms with queen-size beds (cheaper with own linen). Look out over Shearwater Bay at dawn (with the birds).

Eating

Taylor Street Tearooms (☎ 9071 4317; Taylor St Jetty; mains $13-30; ✷ breakfast, lunch & dinner) The name doesn't convey the loveliness of the location or the meals. The veranda is one of the best in town for a zephyr-cooled glass of wine.

Loose Goose (☎ 9071 2320; 9A Andrew St; mains $11-30; ✷ dinner) Honk if you could handle a T-bone steak. This BYO joint will be your idea of a great evening out.

Onshore (☎ 9071 2575; 105 Dempster St; snacks $3-11; ✷ lunch & dinner Thu-Sun) Affluence in Esperance will sniff out this new café–gift shop. Next to the Fenwick 3 Cinema, it does lunch and the coffee is very good.

Ocean Blues (☎ 9071 7101; 19 The Esplanade; mains $10-21; ✷ breakfast & lunch) Wander up from the

drink to this beach deli. As well as a sizable breakfast ($15), there are burgers and focaccias.

West Beach Deli & Café (☎ 9071 4622; 71 Phillips St; mains $4-22; ✷ lunch & dinner) Try the surf 'n' turf or a lentil burger here, off Twilight Beach Rd.

AROUND ESPERANCE

If you've got any more than a day in this beautiful part of the world, don't miss a drive down to the magnificent **Cape Le Grand National Park**, extending from about 20km to 60km east of Esperance. The park boasts dramatic coastal scenery, excellent walking tracks and some of the best beaches in the state. Holiday-makers head here in summer for good fishing, camping and swimming at **Lucky Bay** and **Le Grand Beach**. Day-trippers should try to squeeze in the steep (but worthwhile) climb to the top of **Frenchman's Peak** for breathtaking views.

Further east is the coastal **Cape Arid National Park**, a rugged, isolated park with abundant flora and fauna, good bushwalking and beaches at the start of the Great Australian Bight. Much of the park is accessible only by 4WD.

Other national parks in the area include **Stokes**, located 92km west of Esperance, with an inlet, long beaches and rocky headlands, and **Peak Charles**, situated 130km north. For more information on all of these parks, contact **CALM** (☎ 08-9071 3733; 92 Dempster St, Esperance).

If you are heading into national parks take plenty of water, as there's little or no fresh water in these isolated areas. Also, be wary of spreading dieback (clean your shoes before and after each hike). Entry fees apply to vehicles ($9).

There are limited-facility camp sites at **Cape Le Grand** (per 2 people $12.50) and **Cape Arid** (per 2 people $10); apply for permits at the park entrances. There are basic camp sites at **Stokes** (☎ 08-9076 8541; per 2 people $10) and **Peak Charles** (☎ 08-9071 3733; free).

SOUTHERN OUTBACK

Ghost towns located to the north, the famous Nullarbor Plain to the east and Kalgoorlie-Boulder a nugget in between. Stretching across to SA and up to the Northern Territory (NT), this is the outback Australia that many travellers come to see – a remote, dry land of dramatic landscapes and sprinkles of gold-rush history. The red desert landscape seems barren but is far from it. Aboriginal people have lived here for an age, while ample fortunes were sought and made in a tiny glint of decades.

History

The government in long-suffering Perth was in raptures when gold was discovered at Southern Cross in 1887. In one of the world's last great gold rushes, the next few years drew prospectors from other states – and other nations. Some 50 towns immediately rose up in the Eastern Goldfields, but the area's population dwindled along with the gold itself, and these days Kalgoorlie-Boulder is the only real survivor. In diminished towns, prodigious structures from early last century still stand unwavering in the heat. The region is fascinating to explore.

It was a harsh life on the goldfields. Enthusiasm, or greed, sometimes outweighed common sense. Diseases like typhoid ran through mining camps. Inadequate water, housing, food and medical supplies lead to a dusty death for many.

The 1903 Golden Pipeline (p955) was a lifeline for the towns it passed through and it filled Kalgoorlie with the sense of a future, with or without gold.

COOLGARDIE

☎ 08 / pop 1260

Just hours after Arthur Bayley rode into Southern Cross in 1892 and dumped 554 ounces of gold on the mining warden's counter, the greatest movement of people in Australian history began. Bayley had found the gold at Fly Flat, the site that became Coolgardie, and is now the turn-off for Kalgoorlie. By 1898 more than 16,000 people would make it the third-largest town in WA.

The most excellent **Coolgardie visitor information centre** (☎ 9026 6090; Warden's Ct, Bayley St; ☺ 9am-4pm) shares a beautiful pink stone building with the **Goldfields Museum** (adult/child $4/1.10; ☺ 9am-5pm), which houses a model of

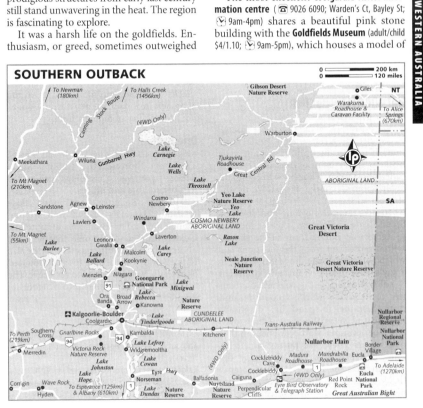

SOUTHERN OUTBACK

the city at its peak. Check your email at the nearby **Telecentre** (☻ 9am-1pm; 🖳).

One kilometre west of Coolgardie is the **town cemetery** (Great Eastern Hwy) with many old graves, such as that of assassinated explorer Tagh Mohomed. Legend has it half the population of Coolgardie knocked off the other half, or succumbed to the dust during the gold rush.

On New Year's Eve, you might be lucky enough to be poolside at the 'black tie and black thongs' evening at the **Coolgardie Motel** (☎ 9026 6080; hodgesbeverley@hotmail.com; 53 Bayley St; s/d $60/75; 🕿), where the Lazy Sundays Kitchen has a great local rep.

Readers have recommended the clean sites, cabins and facilities at **Coolgardie Tourist Village** (☎ 9026 6009; fax 9026 6714; 99 Bayley St; powered/unpowered sites per 2 people $18/14, on-site caravans $40, d $71, 2-person chalets $66).

Greyhound Australia (☎ 13 14 99) passes through Coolgardie on the Perth to Adelaide run ($265), with the Perth to Coolgardie segment costing $116. **Perth Goldfields Express** (☎ 1800 620 440) has a similar service from Perth to Coolgardie, but is cheaper at $120. **Golden Lines** (☎ 9021 2655) runs from Kalgoorlie to Coolgardie (adult/child $6/3) Monday to Friday.

KALGOORLIE-BOULDER
☎ 08 / pop 30,500

After cruising along endless roads rimmed by red dirt and green straggly scrub (sometimes blackened by bushfires), punctuated by the pitiful remains of roos and the occasional ghost town, it's a shock to come suddenly upon Kalgoorlie. It's a town of wide streets and scant trees, with giant pubs on its corners. People move up and down the broad shade of Hannan St under the huge verandas that extend from all the shops – a little protection from the ferocious sun, which hammers home the fact that you are a day's drive inland on this arid continent.

Kal still feels like the wild west: a frontier town where workers come straight from the mines to spend their disposable income and sit at the bars in their overalls. The 'skimpie' staff serve beer in their underwear. There are tattoos and gambling and brothels. The electronic display high on the Palace Hotel constantly flicks shares and the price of gold and nickel in a red horizontal stream. But ul-

timately this is still a country town, with churches, schools and a community that these days relies as much on tourist gold as the mine's.

Due to eastern Australians migrating here for some warmth, Kal's peak season is actually in winter.

History
Long-time prospector Paddy Hannan set out from Coolgardie in search of another gold strike, and proved that sometimes beggars can be choosers. He stumbled across the surface gold that sparked the 1893 gold rush, and inadvertently chose the site of Kalgoorlie for a township.

When surface sparkles subsided, the miners dug deeper, extracting the precious metal from the rocks by costly and complex processes. Kalgoorlie quickly prospered, and the town's magnificent public buildings, constructed at the end of the 19th century, are evidence of its fabulous wealth. The streets were wide enough to turn a camel train.

Despite its slow decline after WWI, Kal is still the largest producer of gold in Australia, with giant mining conglomerates operating open-cut mines in the Golden Mile. Gone are the old headframes and corrugated iron shacks – these enormous homes on the approach to Kalgoorlie attest to the ongoing profitability of modern mining.

Orientation
Kalgoorlie itself is a grid of broad streets. The main thoroughfare, Hannan St, is flanked by imposing buildings such as hotels, restaurants and offices.

Although Kalgoorlie sprang up close to Paddy Hannan's original find, mining soon shifted a few kilometres away to the Golden Mile, a square mile that was one of the richest gold-mining areas for its size in the world. The satellite town of Boulder, 5km south, was developed to service it. The two towns amalgamated into Kalgoorlie-Boulder city in 1989 .

Information
CALM office (☎ 9021 2677; Post Office Bldg, Hannan St)
Kalgoorlie Regional Hospital (☎ 9080 5888; Piccadilly St)
Kalgoorlie visitor information centre (☎ 9021 1966; 250 Hannan St; ☻ 8.30am-5pm, to 9am Sat & Sun) Has a free map of Kal and will do your booking for you.

WESTERN AUSTRALIA

KALGOORLIE-BOULDER

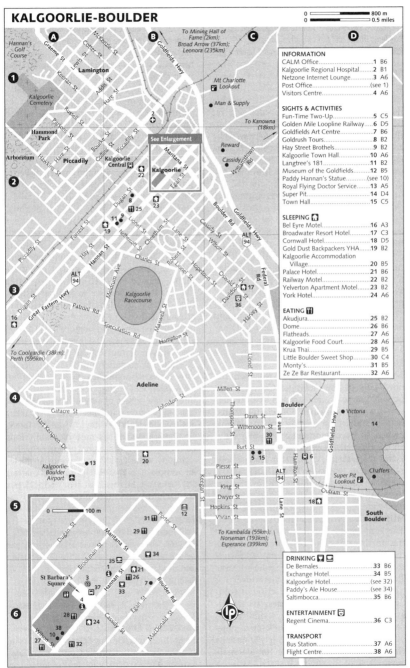

WESTERN AUSTRALIA

Netzone Internet Lounge (☎ 9091 4178; Shop 6, St Barbara's Sq; ☽ 10am-7pm, to 5pm Sat & Sun; ▣) Excellent facilities and fast connection speeds.

RACWA office (☎ 9021 1511; cnr Porter & Hannan Sts)

Sights

MINING HALL OF FAME

Was your grandad born in a tent while his mother lay back and prayed luck was on her side? If so it's essential to check out the **Mining Hall of Fame** (☎ 9091 4074; www.mining hall.com; Eastern Bypass Rd; adult/concession/child/family $20/16/12/50; ☽ 9am-4.30pm), 2km north of town. Explore the harsh conditions of the goldfields in the lean-to camps on the hot dirt. Inside, the impressive, interactive exhibits focus on the Western Australian mining industry, in the context of mining across the whole of Australia. Native title for indigenous Australians is explained and discussed. Visitors can ride a lift cage 36m underground and are taken on a guided tour around the crosscuts of the mine. Watch gold-pouring demonstrations and try your hand at panning for gold. Underground tours run at 10am, noon, 2pm and 3.20pm daily (remember to wear fully enclosed shoes). There's a café here too.

SUPER PIT

The working mine is a coin's toss from the north edge of town: a Grand-Canyonesque, fiercely scarred valley striated by different-coloured levels of earth. Once a punctured field of individual mining leases, it's now owned by a conglomerate that blasts out all the bits left between the original shafts. From the **lookout** (☎ 9022 1100; Outram St; www .superpit.com.au; ☽ 7am-7pm), watch trucks descend in a zigzag until they're toy sized at its floor.

MUSEUM OF THE GOLDFIELDS

The 31m-high Ivanhoe mine headframe at the northeastern end of Hannan St marks the entrance to the **museum** (☎ 9021 8533; 17 Hannan St; admission by donation; ☽ 10am-4.30pm). Take the lift to the top for views over the town. Inside you'll find a selection of goldfields implements and stories, an underground vault full of gold watches, and a restored miner's cottage. Pick up a copy of the *One Hundred Women of the Eastern Goldfields* brochure ($2.50) for a female perspective of the town's history.

OTHER ATTRACTIONS

Travel the famous Golden Mile on the **Golden Mile Loopline Railway** (☎ 9093 3055; adult/child $9.90/5.50; ☽ departs 10am, 11.45am Sun). The ramshackle 'Rattler' sets off from Boulder train station on its one-hour journey to the power station, complete with commentary.

The game of two-up was a highlight for gamblers on the goldfields. Take a wad of Monopoly money to **Fun-Time Two-Up** (☎ 9093 3467; Sheffield's Bar & Grill, 140 Burt St, Boulder; admission $5; ☽ 3pm Wed & Sun) and see how it was played.

The amazing work of the **Royal Flying Doctor Service** (☎ 9093 7595; Kalgoorlie-Boulder Airport; admission by donation; ☽ 10am-3pm Mon-Fri) is explained during tours on the hour (last one at 2pm).

One of Kal's more (in)famous 'attractions' is **Hay St**, a wide road with scrappy trees and a few weirdly painted brothels. Working women once beckoned passing men into their galvanised-iron doorways, but there didn't seem to be much making hay while the sun shone when we were here. Instead, the workers sit solemnly behind windows as tourists do a slow drive past. One of the brothels, the renovated **Langtree's 181** (☎ 9026 2181; 181 Hay St; admission $45; ☽ tours 11am, 3pm & 7pm), runs frank tours of the premises.

There's an art gallery upstairs in the decorative Edwardian **town hall** (☎ 9021 9809; cnr Hannan & Wilson Sts; ☽ 8.30am-4.55pm Mon-Fri), while outside is a replica of a **statue of Paddy Hannan** grasping a water bag. Meanwhile, the gallery at the **Goldfields Arts Centre** (☎ 9088 6905, Egan St; ☽ 10am-4pm Mon-Fri) has monthly exhibitions by local, state and national artists.

Fly over the Golden Mile with **Goldfields Air Services** (GAS; ☎ 9093 2116) and **AAA Charters** (☎ 9093 4115). Flights cost from $50/25 per adult/child (minimum of two people).

Tours

4WD Tours (☎ 0419 915 670; half-/full-day tours $120/165) Takes visitors into the outback to fossick for gold and visit the ghost towns north of Kal. Full-day wildflower tours are also available from August to November for $130.

Goldrush Tours (☎ 1800 620 440; 16 Lane St) The main local operator with tours of Kal (adult/child $25/5) and Coolgardie ($55/10). Book through the visitor centre.

Festivals & Events

Busy times include the **Kalgoorlie Race Round** and the 2300m Kalgoorlie Cup in early September, a real spectacle for fans of horse racing and wildflowers. The Mining Expo and **Royal Show** makes October busy. It may sound like a gnome convention, but the Diggers & Dealers mining conference (August) brings magnates from across Australia. Don't expect to find a bed easily at any of these times.

Boulder Market Day (Burt St; 9am-1.30pm) is on the third Sunday of the month, but the people-watching along Burt St and the big brass band are better than the stalls themselves. There are free Super Pit tours by bus (10am to 11.30am).

Sleeping
BUDGET
Golddust Backpackers YHA (9091 3737; www.kalgoorliebackpackers.com; 192 Hay St; dm/s $18/30, d & tw $45, nonmembers extra $2-5;) It's easy come, easy go here at this down-to-earth den of activity with dark caves of rooms (ask for the honeymoon double). Staff will help you find work in the mining and associated industries all year round.

Kalgoorlie Accommodation Village (9039 4800, 1800 004 800; www.resortparks.com.au; 286 Burt St, Boulder; powered/unpowered sites per 2 people $28/14, chalets $91, spa units from $104;) In leafy surrounds Boulder's park has a wide choice of accommodation, from basic camp sites to A-frame chalets and spa units.

Bel Eyre Motel (9021 4455; fax 9021 3744; 4 Great Eastern Hwy; d/tw $78/118, garden/spa rooms $98/108) Standard rooms here are markedly better out the back, away from the road, where you can actually hear the in-house movies.

MIDRANGE
In the heady gold-rush days, Kal had a pub on every corner, and several still offer comfy lodgings today. Be warned that weekend crowds in some pubs can be noisy.

York Hotel (/fax 9021 2337; 259 Hannan St; s/d/tr $40/65/84) Memorable architecture inside and out, and music in the crowded front bar. The accommodation revolves around an incredible central staircase, which is worth a look even if you don't stay here.

Palace Hotel (9021 2788; www.palacehotel.com.au; cnr Hannan & Maritana Sts; dm/s/d $18/65/85, executive s/d $85/100, all incl breakfast;) Go for the balcony berths at this rambling historic hotel with beds for all budgets, including refurbished executive options. A young Herbert Hoover (31st US president) donated the enormous antique mirror that stands in the foyer.

Cornwall Hotel (9093 2510; cornwallhotel@bigpond.com; 25 Hopkins St, Boulder; s/d $40/65) Quaint, with dark old-fashioned rooms, this tiny hotel is all shut up from the heat. Inside lives an incredibly hard-working chef, who has an ear for history and an eye for detail, and caters for mine managers on leave…and you.

Railway Motel (9088 0000; www.railwaymotel.com.au; 51 Forrest St; d Fri-Sun $100, Mon-Thu $120;) A dip in the pool and a full cooked breakfast in the morning make the Railway a good stop.

TOP END
Broadwater Resort Hotel (1800 198 001; www.broadwaters.com.au; 21 Davidson St; studio $136-145, d $168, 2-bed apt $243;) Convincingly five-star, this modern Australian is palatial and a step up for accommodation in Kal. All rooms have spas and exec suites have two king beds. After a long journey it might be worth the extra gold to really put your feet up alfresco by the pool. Prices slide on weekends.

Yelverton Apartment Motel (9022 8181; www.theyelverton.com.au; 210 Egan St; apt $165-185;) These lacy apartments, each with a giant spa bathroom, bedroom, kitchen and living room with complimentary Foxtel, are secreted away in the back streets. Make like a lizard in the lounge bar or by the lap pool.

Eating
Kalgoorlie's main drag has several reliable pubs that offer generous counter meals, but the following places stand out from the crowd.

Ze Ze Bar Restaurant (9021 3046; Kalgoorlie Hotel, cnr Hannan & Wilson Sts; mains $12-22; lunch & dinner) Inventive, wood-fired pizzas can't be made quickly enough for thriving Ze Ze's full booths and upstairs balcony. Try the Moroccan lamb with minted yoghurt.

Akudjura (9091 3311; 418 Hannan St; mains $9.90-32; dinner) We recommend you skip the main just so you can try the tantalising tasting plates (entrée/dessert $15/19). The restaurant service is pleasantly 'outback'; the food aims for city style and gets a bull's-eye.

Dome (9386 3099; Hannan St; mains $5-14; breakfast & lunch) The reliable statewide chain injects reasonable prices and decent coffee into the Kal foodie scene. The cakes are its recipe for success; also try the tandoori chicken sandwich.

Krua Thai (☎ 9091 5227; 84 Hannan St; mains $13-18; ⓨ dinner) Wonders never cease: yummy Thai in the outback, with happy serviettes and service.

Monty's (☎ 9022 8288; cnr Hannan & Porter Sts; mains $15-30; ⓨ 24hr) Italian-style Monty's is the last drink after the pubs shut and the last stop before the town's edges fray into the Super Pit.

If you're looking for something faster, try the **Kalgoorlie Food Court** (Hannan St) or popular fish 'n' chippery **Flatheads** (28 Wilson St).

The **Little Boulder Sweet Shop** (☎ 9093 0011; 41 Burt St, Boulder; ⓨ 9am-5.30pm Mon-Fri, 9am-2pm Sat) has old-fashioned Aussie lollies and your favourites from the UK, New Zealand, USA and Holland.

Drinking

On weekends, locals seem to migrate on a slow pub crawl up Hannan St…why not put on your mining hat and join them?

Federal Hotel (1 Hannan St) For a taste of the original Kalgoorlie pub, try here.

Kalgoorlie Hotel (☎ 9021 3046; 319 Hannan St) Also known as Judd's, this is the place to be for a big night out in Kal with rockin' bands and a totally up-for-it crowd. There are several bars and a jukebox.

Exchange Hotel (☎ 9021 3046; 135 Hannan St) At the other end of the street is this wild west saloon bar. Sport reigns on TV and workers are found on both sides of the bar.

Paddy's Ale House (☎ 9021 2833; Exchange Hotel, 135 Hannan St) Next door to the Exchange, and where couples populate the dance floor.

De Bernales (☎ 9021 4534; 193 Hannan St) Nicely shady and full of ladies (of the nonskimpie variety). Check out the Bill-and-Monica mural while you sip your wine.

Palace Hotel (☎ 9021 2788; cnr Hannan & Maritana Sts) Houses the recently renovated Corner Bar at the front, all designer corrugated iron and splashes of purple.

Saltimbocca (☎ 9022 8028; Hannan St; ⓨ 8am-3pm) Coffee and smoothies are dealt from this tiny doorway halfway along the northern side of Hannan St.

Entertainment

Catch a movie at **Regent Cinemas** (☎ 9021 2199; cnr Davidson & Oswald Sts). In summer, there are outdoor screenings at the **Twilight Outdoor**

Cinema (Hammond Park). Call the Regent for details.

Getting There & Away
AIR

Skywest (☎ 1300 660 088; www.skywest.com.au) and **Qantas** (☎ 13 13 13; www.qantas.com.au) fly between Perth and Kalgoorlie at least twice each day (full fare $274, but there are regular specials available). Qantas also offers flights to most of the major Australian capital cities. **Flight Centre** (☎ 9091 1999; www.flightcentre.com.au; 169 Hannan St) can assist with bookings.

BUS

Greyhound Australia (☎ 13 14 99; www.greyhound.com.au) buses stop in Kalgoorlie daily between Perth and Adelaide. **Perth Goldfields Express** (☎ 1800 620 440) has a service from Perth to Kal, continuing north to Menzies ($32 from Kal), Leonora ($43) and Laverton ($64) on Sunday, Wednesday and Friday. Services on Tuesday, Thursday and Saturday run between Perth and Kal only ($77).

Transwa (☎ 1300 662 205) runs a bus three times a week to/from Esperance (five hours), twice via Kambalda and once via Coolgardie; it costs $22 to Norseman and $41 to Esperance. Buses stop outside the visitor centre on Hannan St.

TRAIN

The daily *Prospector* service from Perth takes around eight hours ($60). The *Indian Pacific* train also goes through Kal on Wednesday and Saturday (for Perth) and Monday and Friday (for Adelaide).

Getting Around

There's a regular bus service between Kal and Boulder, operated by **Golden Lines** (☎ 9021 2655) between 8am and 6pm Monday to Friday, and Saturday mornings (adult/child $1.90/80c).

NORTH OF KALGOORLIE-BOULDER

Fascinating ghost towns and near-ghost towns dot the landscape in this remote region. The road north is surfaced from Kal all the way to Leonora-Gwalia (235km), Laverton (359km) and Leinster (361km). Off the main road, traffic is virtually nonexistent and rain can quickly close dirt roads.

Head 18km east along an unsealed road to the cemetery and the processing plant at **Kanowna**. One hundred years ago it swarmed with miners, and had 16 hotels and an hourly train service to Kal.

Cold beer and pub grub is served up by one of just five locals at the **Broad Arrow Tavern** (☎ 08-9024 2058; 🕑 11am-late). This place (37km north of Kalgoorlie-Boulder) was once a thriving community of 15,000 people.

Menzies, 132km north of Kal, has a train station with a 120m-long platform. If you're sick of driving, you could sprint it.

The largest service centre for mining exploration and the pastoral industry in the area is **Leonora** (population 3500). Don't miss the recently restored abandoned miners' camps and State Hotel at **Gwalia**, where the Sons of Gwalia gold mine was managed by US-president-to-be Herbert Hoover at the end of the 19th century. The old mine office now houses the **Gwalia Historical Museum** (☎ 08-9037 7210; admission $3; 🕑 10am-4pm).

South of here, 25km off the main road to Laverton, is **Kookynie**, where a true outback pub experience can be had at the 1901 **Grand Hotel** (☎ 08-9031 3010; Menzies-Kookynie Rd; s/d $55/88). Have a serious breakfast before setting out in the morning.

The surfaced road ends at the town of **Laverton** (population 500). 'The gateway to the desert' crouches on the edge of the Great Victoria Desert. It's only 1710km to Alice Springs via the Great Central Rd (part of the Outback Hwy).

Ask the Kalgoorlie visitor centre about the **Golden Quest Discovery Trail** (www.golden questtrail.com). By car, you can explore 25 major sites of the region over 965km. Along the way there's many a tale of the tough pioneers who made their mark. Some 525km of the track is unsealed, so don't forget to ask about road conditions and safe-travel tips.

Laverton to Giles

From here on in, make sure you take precautions relevant to travel in such an isolated area. Tell someone reliable of your travel plans and take adequate supplies of water, food, petrol and spare parts. Don't even consider travelling between November and March, when the heat is extreme, nor after heavy rain. See p954 for more information about travelling in this area.

Along the way there's dirt every shade of red, from fire engine to russet. The unsealed road from Laverton to Yulara (near Uluru) via Warburton is dressed with a rich landscape of spinifex, mulga and desert oaks. The surface is well maintained and suitable for conventional vehicles, although a 4WD would give a much smoother ride.

Petrol and supplies are available at Laverton, Warburton, Docker River and Yulara. Towards Warburton (about 315km from Laverton), **Tjukayirla Roadhouse** (☎ 08-9037 1108; Great Central Rd; sites per 2 people $12, s/d $38/76) has fuel and supplies and offers basic accommodation. Meals are also possible if you book ahead.

As this road passes through Aboriginal land, transit permits are required from the **Central Land Council** (☎ 08-8951 6211) in Alice Springs for the NT section, and from the **Department of Indigenous Affairs** (☎ 08-9235 8000; www.dia.wa.gov.au) in Perth for the WA end. Transit permits are free and can be arranged online. Allow two to three weeks for your application to be processed. It's prohibited to leave the main road when travelling through Aboriginal lands.

SOUTH OF KALGOORLIE-BOULDER

Kambalda

☎ 08 / pop 1200

This major nickel-mining town 55km south of Kalgoorlie-Boulder has two town centres, Kambalda East and Kambalda West, about 4km apart.

Landsailers on **Lake Lefroy** have apparently been clocked skimming over the dry salt-pans at 100km/h. Confirm this rumour at the **Kambalda visitor information centre** (☎ 9027 0192; Emu Rocks Rd, Kambalda West). The **Red Hill Lookout** offers sweeping views.

Kambalda Caravan Park (☎ 9027 1582; powered/unpowered sites per 2 people $18/15; 🕑 7-9am & 4.30-7pm Mon-Sat) is in shade-dappled scrub.

Norseman

☎ 08 / pop 600

From Norseman you can head south to Esperance or north to Kalgoorlie, or begin the intrepid trek across the Eyre Hwy (Nullarbor). Along these lengthy roads you're likely to see taxis with bull bars, or a family of emus crossing.

Facilities in town are set up for quick stopovers. Not far from the corrugated iron camels is the **Norseman visitor information centre** (☎ 9039 1071; 68 Robert St; ⏰ 9am-5pm). At the back is a rest park with showers and BBQ facilities (7am to 6pm). A permit ($5.50) from the visitor centre allows you to try your hand at **gemstone fossicking** on a property about 12km north of town. Check your email at the nearby **Telecentre** (Robert St; per hr $6).

We liked one display at the **Historical Collection** (☎ 9039 1593; Battery Rd; adult/child $2/1; ⏰ 10am-1pm Mon, Wed, Thu & Sat) – nothing in it but a piece of rock and a note: 'Dear Bruce, don't know what this is, but I've got more at home.'

There are excellent views of the town and the surrounding salt lakes from the **Beacon Hill Lookout**, on the Old Mines Rd past the mountainous tailings dumps. For stunning sunrise and sunset photo opportunities, amateur photographers should head for the dry, expansive **Lake Cowan**, situated north of town.

SLEEPING & EATING

Lodge 101 (☎ /fax 9039 1541; 101 Prinsep St; dm/s/d $20/35/55) Familiar ambience, comfy rooms and a free feed on the BBQ make an impression on weary desert travellers.

Great Western Motel (☎ 9039 1633; fax 9039 1692; Prinsep St; s/d/tr $80/92/105; ✲ ✲) An oasis of a pool and deep verandas define this outback stay.

Norseman-Eyre Hotel (☎ 9039 1023; fax 9039 1130; 90 Roberts St; s $74, d $78-86, incl breakfast, mains $12-18; ✲) Workers pull in here on those 45°C days. It offers filling counter meals for lunch or dinner.

Gateway Caravan Park (☎ /fax 9039 1500; 23 Prinsep St; powered/unpowered sites per 2 people $20/16, dm $15, cabins $75, without bathroom $55-60) Excellent cabin accommodation in a quiet bushland spot makes this a great midrange option. Campers are also well catered for, with clean facilities and a camp kitchen.

EYRE HIGHWAY

London to Moscow, or Perth to Adelaide? There's not much difference, distance wise. The 2700km Eyre Hwy crosses the southern edge of the vast **Nullarbor Plain** – a place travellers seem to want to cross just to prove they can. Be prepared for an almost meditative drive that takes days and needs a damn good supply of water and 1980s cassettes. The Trans Australia Railway runs across the true Nullarbor Plain, while the highway is mainly to the south of the treeless area.

John Eyre deserves having a highway named after him because he was the first of his kind to cross the stretch in 1841. After a telegraph line was laid (1877), miners en route to the goldfields trekked across the vacuous plain under its negligible shade. In 1912 the first car made it across. By 1941 the rough-and-ready transcontinental highway carried a handful of vehicles a day. In 1969 the Western Australian government surfaced the road as far as the South Australian border. Finally, in 1976, the last stretch was surfaced and now it runs close to the coast on the SA side, with the Nullarbor region ending dramatically at the cliffs of the Great Australian Bight.

From Norseman it's 725km to the South Australian border, near Eucla, and a further 480km to Ceduna (meaning 'a place to sit down and rest' in the local Aboriginal language) in SA. They aren't kidding! From Ceduna, it's still another 793km to Adelaide (a *long* day's drive) via Port Augusta.

Crossing the Nullarbor

Do outback rescue services a big favour and take some simple precautions. This is not the place to run out of petrol: high fuel prices range from 15 to 30 cents a litre above city prices and the longest distance between fuel stops is about 200km. Carry some drinking water (an active adult needs 5L per day in hot weather) in the unfortunate case you do have to sit it out by the roadside. Getting help for a mechanical breakdown can be expensive and time consuming, so make sure your vehicle is in good shape, you've got good tyres and at least a basic kit of simple spare parts. Be sure to book ahead if you're going to break up the drive with an overnight stay at one of the roadhouses.

Norseman to Eucla

The first settlement you reach from Norseman is **Balladonia**, 193km to the east. The **Balladonia Hotel Motel** (☎ 08-9039 3453; Eyre Hwy; powered/unpowered sites per 2 people $19/12, dm $17, s/d from $76/91) offers camping, backpacker beds and four-star rooms. It has a bar, café, shady playground, roadhouse facilities and scraps of the Skylab space station in its small interactive historical museum.

Between Balladonia and **Caiguna** is one of the longest stretches of straight road in the world (145km), known as the **90 Mile Straight**. If you need a break, get some shut-eye at the **John Eyre Motel** (☎ 08-9039 3459; Eyre Hwy; powered/unpowered sites per 2 people $18/12, s with/without bathroom $79/55, d $95/69; ⚡).

At **Cocklebiddy** you will find the stone ruins of an Aboriginal mission and the largest of the Nullarbor caves, **Cocklebiddy Cave**, which is situated some 10km northwest. With a 4WD, you can travel the 32km south to **Twilight Cove**, with its dramatic 75m-high limestone cliffs. There's accommodation, fuel and supplies all available at the **Wedgetail Inn Cocklebiddy** (☎ 08-9039 3462; Eyre Hwy; powered/unpowered sites per 2 people $18/11, budget s/d/tr $51/68/81, motel s/d/tr $79/95/106).

Birds Australia's **Eyre Bird Observatory** (☎ 08-9039 3450; eyrebirdobs@bigpond.com) is housed in the former Eyre Telegraph Station, which is located 50km south of Cocklebiddy on the Bight. Full board is $80/40 per adult/child (with reductions after the first night). Return transport from Cocklebiddy is available for overnight guests ($28 for day-trippers); otherwise, you will need a 4WD with good clearance.

Madura, 83km east of Cocklebiddy, has a population of seven and is close to the Hampton Tablelands (just out of town is a scenic lookout). The one-stop shop for fuel, a shower ($3), beer, a meal or a bed is the **Madura Roadhouse** (☎ 08-9039 3464; Eyre Hwy; powered/unpowered sites per 2 people $18/12, budget s/d $60/70, motel s/d $80/100; ⚡).

In **Mundrabilla**, 116km to the east, is the friendly **Mundrabilla Motel Hotel** (☎ 08-9039 3465; Eyre Hwy; powered/unpowered sites per 2 people $15/10, motel s/d/f $70/85/105; ⚡).

Just before the SA border is **Eucla**, surrounded by stunning sand dunes and pristine beaches. Around 5km south of town are the photogenic ruins of an old **telegraph station** (1877), gradually being engulfed by the dunes. Camp sites and spacious rooms are available at the **Eucla Motor Hotel** (☎ 08-9039 3468; Eyre Hwy; powered/unpowered sites per 2 people $15/6, budget s/d $25/45, motel s/d $75/90; ⚡).

There are strict quarantine restrictions when crossing the border, so scoff your fruit and vegetables before you get there; checkpoints are at Eucla and Ceduna.

Eucla to Ceduna
See p777 for details of the section of highway between the border and Ceduna.

MIDLANDS

Increasingly known as the 'heartlands', this gigantic rural region expands from the base of the Pilbara down to the Wheatbelt towns some 300km or so south of the Great Eastern Hwy. Visitors come to see its vast empty landscapes, glorious displays of spring wildflowers and dramatic geological formations – particularly the iconic Wave Rock (Map p947).

GREAT EASTERN HIGHWAY
CY O'Connor's **Golden Pipeline** (www.goldenpipeline.com.au) carried precious water 560km from Mundaring Weir in the Perth foothills to the goldfields. It finally flowed in 1903 – another miraculous feat of the troubled Irishman's engineering (he took his own life before it was completed). Its construction was impressive even by today's standards. Today the Great Eastern Hwy follows the path of the pipeline, stretching east from Perth through barren but beautiful countryside, all the way to Kalgoorlie-Boulder. Country towns en route are convenient places to stop, stretch your legs and enjoy some historical sites.

Stop off at the impressive farming **museum** (Forrest St; adult/child $4/1.50; ⏰ 10am-4pm) at **Cunderdin**, 64km east of Northam.

Merredin
☎ 08 / pop 2900
Merredin's main claim to fame is temporarily playing host to the world's longest road train – 45 trailers stretching over half a kilometre. The turn-off to Wave Rock is just east of town. Visitors use the town as a base during wildflower season, from August to October.

The **Merredin visitor information centre** (☎ 9041 1666; Barrack St; ⏰ 9am-5pm Mon-Fri, 11am-1pm Sat, 11am-2pm Sun) is an abundant source of information on the area.

A range of accommodation is available at the agreeable **Merredin Caravan Park** (☎ /fax 9041 1535; 2 Oats St; powered sites per 2 people $20, on-site caravans $45, cabins/villas $60/70).

Gabbi's Coffee Lounge (☎ 9041 1713; Barrack St; ⏰ 9am-8pm Mon-Sat; 💻) serves up a wicked superdog ($5). It has Internet and toilets around the side.

Southern Cross

☎ 08 / pop 2900

When it came to gold, Southern Cross flared and died like a miner's match on a cold desert night. Further east, it's still the site of mining memorabilia and artefacts in the **Yilgarn History Museum** (Antares St; adult/child $2.50/50c; ☺ 9.30am-noon & 1.30-4pm Mon-Sat, 1.30-4pm Sun), in the old courthouse. Survive the sizzle at the **swimming pool** (Antares St; adult/child $2.50/1.50; ☺ 11am-6.30pm).

An obvious remnant of the golden days, the **Palace Hotel** (☎ 9049 1555; fax 9049 1509; Antares St; basic s $25-60, d with/without bathroom $80/70) has rooms and meals (three courses $16).

Southern Cross Caravan Park (☎ 9049 1212; powered sites per 2 people $19, cabins/caravans $50/35), on the western side of town, consists of miraculously tenacious trees and red dirt to park on.

WAVE ROCK & HYDEN

☎ 08 / pop 190

Hyden, 340km east of Perth, is the base from which to see the astounding natural sculpture of Wave Rock (15m high and 110m long). The eroded crest is streaked with mineral colours from a natural spring. Hand prints of Aboriginal people, whose association with this place goes back as far as legend, can be seen nearby. Many people do the 700km-return day trip from Perth simply to stand under the rock in a 'hang ten' pose. If you want to linger longer, wander around other interesting rock formations such as the **Breakers**, **Hippo's Yawn** and the **Humps**. Legendary **Mulka's Cave**, 21km away, was the long-ago place of an outcast who could not hunt and turned to eating children.

The **Wave Rock visitor information centre** (☎ 9880 5182; ☺ 9am-5.30pm) is in the Wave Rock Wildflower Shoppe opposite the site.

There's a restaurant, gym and solar-heated pool at **Hyden Hotel Motel** (☎ 9880 5052; fax 9880 5041; 2 Lynch St; s/d/ste $90/110/160).

Wave Rock Caravan Park (☎ 9880 5022; wave rock@wn.com.au; Wave Rock Rd; powered/unpowered sites per 2 people $20/17, cabins $75, 2-bedroom cottages $116), an inviting stay not far from the rock, has camp sites and cabins in a bushland setting.

A bus runs from Perth to Hyden every Tuesday ($37, five hours), with the return service to Perth each Thursday. Book with **Transwa** (☎ 1300 662 205).

OTHER WHEATBELT TOWNS

If you stop at any town of size around here (Map p910), you'll find a pub with counter meals, a caravan park, some silos silhouetted against the sky and a sense that time…might…stop.

Kokerbin (Aboriginal for 'high place') is a granite rock formation 45km west of Bruce Rock. **Corrigin** has a **folk museum** (☎ 08-9063 2066; Brookton Hwy; ☺ 10am-4pm Sun, also by request) and a **miniature railway** (☎ 08-9063 2176; Campbell St; ☺ 10am-4pm Sun), but it's the **Dog Cemetery** (Brookton Hwy), 5km west, that will have you howling. Lassie, Shep, Dusty, Trigger and many more working dogs dug their last holes here.

Narrogin (population 4500), 189km southeast of Perth, is an agricultural centre with a **courthouse museum** (☎ 08-9881 2064; Egerton St; ☺ 9.30am-4.30pm Mon-Fri, 9.30am-noon Sat). The **Narrogin visitor information centre** (☎ 08-9881 2064) is next door to the museum.

Eucalypt woodlands once covered most of the Wheatbelt. Some 26km north of Narrogin is the magnificent **Dryandra Woodland**, the remnants of an environment in which numbats, many species of birds and wildflowers survive today.

Wickepin, about 45km northeast of Narrogin, is the setting of *A Fortunate Life*, the much-loved, school-of-hard-knocks autobiography of Albert Facey. The **Albert Facey Homestead** (☎ 08-9888 1010; Wagin Rd; adult/child $2.50/1; ☺ 10am-4pm) is worth a visit for anyone who's read it.

Rammin' home Australia's record in the area of ugly big things is the 15m-high fibreglass **merino**, 228km southeast of Perth in **Wagin** (population 1350). It does have a rival in the one in Goulburn, New South Wales (see p237). The visitor centre is at **Wagin Historical Village** (☎ 08-9861 1232; Showground Rd).

The world water-speed record was shattered (444.66km/h) in 1964 by Donald Campbell near **Dumbleyung**, 40km east of Wagin. Today, only birds race across the lake.

A large Muslim community, originally from Christmas Island (see the boxed text, p923), live in **Katanning**, south of Wagin. It has a mosque, which was built in 1980. The **Katanning visitor information centre** (☎ 08-9821 2634; Clive St; ☺ 10am-4pm Mon-Fri, to noon Sat) is in the old flour mill here.

BLOOMING WILDFLOWERS

WA is famed for its 8000 species of wildflower, which bloom in greatest number between August and October. Even some of the driest regions put on a colourful display after a little rainfall, and at any time of the year.

The southwest has over 3000 species, many of which are unique to this region. They're commonly known as everlastings because the petals stay attached after the flowers have died. You can find flowers almost everywhere in the state, but the jarrah forests in the southwest are particularly rich. The coastal national parks north of Perth, such as Fitzgerald River and Kalbarri, also have brilliant displays, as do the Stirling Ranges. Near Perth, the Badgingarra, Alexander Morrison, Yanchep and John Forrest National Parks are excellent choices. There's also a wildflower display in King's Park, Perth. As you go further north, they tend to flower earlier in the season. Common flowering plants include various species of banksia, wattle, mountain bell, Sturt's desert pea, kangaroo paw and many orchids.

WILDFLOWER WAY

Between August and October, one of the best places to see WA's famous carpet of wildflowers is in the area north of Perth, where three roads run roughly parallel towards Geraldton. This area is notable for its varieties of everlasting daisy, kangaroo paw, foxgloves, wattles, featherflowers, banksias and the gorgeous low-lying wreath *Leschenaultia* (see also the boxed text, above). Multiday tours are available, but only botany freaks would enjoy them – most folk are better off with their own wheels and planning their own blooming adventure.

Three main routes head north to Geraldton. Notable stops along the Brand Hwy between Midland and Dongara include **Moore River National Park**, **Badgingarra National Park**, **Coomallo Nature Reserve** and **Lesueur National Park**, which requires a 4WD. Towns along the way include Cataby, Badgingarra and Eneabba. This road also connects you to the Pinnacles and several coastal towns, which have the area's best accommodation – see p961.

From Bindoon on the Great Northern Hwy, the Midland Rd heads to Dongara, passing **Alexander Morrison National Park**, **Capamauro Nature Reserve** and **Depot Hill Reserve**, and the towns of Moora, Watheroo, Coorow and Mingenew. The **Yarra Yarra Lakes**, near Carnamah, are noted for their birdlife.

The stretch between Wubin, on the Great Northern Hwy, and Mullewa, east of Geraldton, has fewer formal wildflower areas, but there's plenty to see in the fields and along the verges as you drive. The surrounds of the tiny towns of **Tardun**, **Canna** and **Morawa** are the best places to look, and there are desolate gold-mining ghost towns near **Perenjori**.

Pick up a free copy of the *Wildflower Holiday Guide* from the **Western Australian Visitors Centre** (☎ 1300 361 351, 08-9483 1111; www .westernaustralia.com; Albert Facey House, Forrest Pl, Perth) for more detailed information.

Getting There & Away

Transwa (☎ 1300 662 205; www.transwa.wa.gov.au) has three Perth–Geraldton bus services through this area. The daily N1 service follows the Brand Hwy via Cataby ($21, 2¼ hours) and Dongara–Port Denison ($41, 5¼ hours). The N2 service runs four times weekly via Moora ($23, three hours) and Mingenew ($43, 5½ hours). The N3 goes via Wubin ($34, four hours) and Mullewa ($53, 7½ hours). **Greyhound Australia** (☎ 13 14 99; www.greyhound.com.au) also runs regular services up the Brand Hwy.

GREAT NORTHERN HIGHWAY

Stretching from Perth to Port Hedland via a succession of small mining and agricultural towns, this highway is the quickest way to get up north. It's also the designated route for long-haul road trains, so be prepared for gruesome roadkill. On the city's outskirts, Perth's suburban spaces are quickly replaced by gently undulating brown pastureland dotted with eucalypts; but you've really left the urban grime behind when you hit the red, red dirt scrubland that characterises the Pilbara. The highlight is the awesome gorge country of Karijini National Park, which is worth a couple of days' exploration. New Norcia, with it's monastic heritage and fabulous pub, is a top place to stay overnight. Unless you're in a hurry or have a love of mining towns, the coastal road certainly has more highlights.

Getting There & Away

Qantas (☎ 13 13 13; www.qantas.com.au) links Perth with Newman (from $210) daily.

    Integrity (☎ 1800 226 339, 08-9226 1339; www.integritycoachlines.com.au) shuttles between Perth and Port Hedland via the Great Northern Hwy, Tuesday and Friday (northbound) and Wednesday and Saturday (southbound). From Perth the bus stops at New Norcia ($25, two hours), Mt Magnet ($90, seven hours), Cue ($100, 8¾ hours), Meekatharra ($115, 10 hours) and Newman ($180, 16 hours).

    Transwa (☎ 1300 662 205; www.transwa.wa.gov.au) has a northbound (Monday) and southbound (Tuesday) service between Perth and Meekatharra.

NEW NORCIA

☎ 08 / pop 80

The only monastic town in Australia, the small, meditative community of New Norcia is a historical oddity. Established by the Spanish Benedictine order in 1846 to proselytise among Aboriginal groups in the region, its work soon turned to raising orphans after European diseases ravaged the local communities. Today it remains a working monastery, and many of the town's stunning buildings are registered by the National Estate. The monastery's renowned breads and olive oil pull the crowds from far and wide and are available in the museum shop.

    It's worth coming to New Norcia just to poke your head inside the **New Norcia Museum & Art Gallery** (☎ 9654 8056; Great Northern Hwy; adult/child $6.50/free; ☻ 9.30am-5pm Aug-Oct, 10am-4.30pm Nov-Jul), even if you're not into God. It details the town's intriguing history, including the missionaries' early work and their first meetings with indigenous Australians, often depicted through some fascinating B&W photos and rather biased commentary. Its art collection includes minor works by Charles Blackman and Pro Hart, plus a cartoon fragment attributed to the circle of Raphael. Don't miss *The Rule of Saint Benedict: chapter XL The Measure of Drink,* which was created to stop monks grumbling over how much wine they can swig a day.

    The museum also runs excellent two-hour **town tours** (adult/child $14/5.50; ☻ 11am & 1.30pm) that take in the frescoed interior of chapels and other cloistered places. These tours give an insight into how the order has evolved and is adapting to the 21st century.

NEW NORCIA TO NEWMAN

More than 400km to the north is **Mt Magnet**, where mining is the town's lifeblood. Situated some 11km north of town are the ruins of **Lennonville**. Approximately 80km to the north of Lennonville, the old gold-mining town of **Cue** is the route's architectural highlight – a pretty little town of stone buildings, corrugated roofs and a sense of time gone by. **Walga Rock**, situated 48km to the west, has a gallery of Aboriginal art, and **Wilgie Mia**, located 64km northwest of Cue via Glen Station, is the site of a 30,000-year-old Aboriginal red-ochre quarry.

    Another 116km north of Cue, **Meekatharra** has little for the traveller. Further north, the mining town of **Newman** is an incongruous piece of modern suburbia. It's bland, but has all the facilities and is the place to stock up for further travels.

Sleeping & Eating

Meekatharra's accommodation offers little value for money, and you're better off pushing on to Cue or Newman.

AUTHOR'S CHOICE

New Norcia Hotel (☎ 08-9654 8034; hotel@newnorcia.wa.edu.au; Great Northern Hwy; s/d $70/80) Set back from the highway and built along epic lines, with towering ceilings, stately banisters and sweeping verandas, this is a unique Western Australian pub. The massive divided stairwell and pressed-metal ceilings are architectural highlights, and there's no better place for a cold drink in the evening than the vast front veranda, where you can observe the swaying eucalypts as the sun sets. The rooms are plain and clean, the staff very friendly and it's well worth spending at least a night.

Auski Inland Motel (☎ 08-9981 1433; fax 08-9981 1478; Main St, Meekatharra; r $120; ▨) The best rooms in Meekatharra are found at this serene hotel.

Miners Rest (☎ 08-9963 4380; fax 08-9963 4390; Thurckle Cove, Mt Magnet; s/d incl breakfast $55/60; ▨) These ageing but well-kept units on the eastern edge of town have a kitchen and are great value. There's also a coin-operated laundry and BBQ here. Head east down the Sandstone road and follow the signs.

Queen of the Murchison Hotel (☎ 08-9963 1625; fax 08-9963 1206; Great Northern Hwy, Cue; s/d incl breakfast $75/95; ▨) The standout accommodation choice along the whole highway, this classic old pub has been converted to a spacious, unlicensed B&B with well-appointed rooms, pristine amenities and home-cooked evening meals.

Seasons Hotel Newman (☎ 08-9177 8666; www .seasonshotel.com.au; Newman Dr, Newman; budget s/d $42/57, motel r $140; ▨ ▣) Attractively furnished motel rooms in a peaceful garden setting are of a high standard here, with Foxtel, a good-sized living area and plenty of beauty condiments to wash away a hard day's travel.

Red Sands Tavern (☎ 08-9177 8866; Newman Dr, Newman; mains $15-26; ☀ lunch & dinner) On the way into Newman, this tavern has a spacious, modern bistro area that's especially good for families and has a children's playground outside.

The roadhouse in Cue serves plenty of hot meals. There are also caravan parks at most towns along the Great Northern Hwy. The following are recommended:

Cue Caravan Park (☎ 08-9963 1107; Great Northern Hwy, Cue; powered/unpowered sites per 2 people $18/10) Shady eucalypts and a healthy strip of grass. Also a campfire and large stone BBQ.

Dearlove's Caravan Park (☎ 08-9175 2802; dearlovescp@benet.net.au; Cowra Dr, Newman; powered/ unpowered sites per 2 people $22/15, r per person from $35; ▨ ▣) Lots of clean donga accommodation here. It's often used by local workers, so book ahead.

KARIJINI NATIONAL PARK

Almost 200km northwest of Newman, **Karijini National Park** (bus passenger $4, car $9) is famous for its magnificent sheer gorges and beautiful swimming holes, as well as a carpet of wildflowers in early spring. It's best visited in the Wet, when the water's flowing, the waterfalls are more spectacular, the swimming

holes are deeper (a perfect foil for the unrelenting sun) and there are generally fewer people around to detract from the beauty. The downside is that flash floods occur after heavy rain, and you'll need to take care when walking along cliff faces and into gorges. There are unfenced sections along the cliff tops and the rocks can be very slippery near the water. Most of the attractions are in the park's north, off the 67km-long Banjima Dr, a rough and rocky dirt road that's hard on conventional vehicles.

The excellent **Karijini visitor information centre** (☎ 08-9189 8121; Banyjima Dr; ☀ 9am-4pm Apr-Oct, 10am-2pm Nov-Mar), in the northeastern corner of the park, is run by the traditional owners of Karijini, the Banyjima people. It interprets the story of the land, and includes exhibits on flora and fauna.

Entering Banjima Dr from the east, you soon reach the turn-off to **Dales Gorge** (sealed road for 6km). A short, sharp descent takes you to **Fortescue Falls** and the beautiful swimming hole of **Circular Pool**. There's a pleasant walk along the cliff top here.

Next is Kalamina Rd and a 30-minute walk into the depths of **Kalamina Gorge**, where there's a small shady pool. Another 11km along is Joffre Falls Rd, which leads to **Knox Gorge**, and passes a lookout over the spectacular Joffre Falls.

The final turn-off is Weano Rd, which takes you to the park's signature attraction, **Oxers Lookout**, from where there are extraordinary views of the junction of the Red, Weano, Joffre and Hancock Gorges. It's one of Australia's great sights. To get down into the gorges proper, take the steps down to Handrail Pool in **Weano Gorge** (stopping for a swim), or the more difficult but dramatic walk down into stunning **Hancock Gorge**.

Other attractions here include **Rio Tinto Gorge** and **Hamersley Gorge** off Nanutarra-Wittenoom Rd in the park's northwest, and **Wittenoom Gorge** in the far north (see the boxed text, p961). It's reached by an 11km sealed road that takes you past old asbestos mines, small gorges and pretty pools. Avoid the road if there's been rain, as there are several creek crossings to negotiate and flash flooding is a real possibility.

Tours

Given the park's remote location and unforgiving roads, it's well worth considering

WESTERN AUSTRALIA

joining a tour. **Lestok Tours** (☎ 08-9189 2032; www.lestoktours.com.au) has good one-day tours of the gorges from Tom Price (adult/child $110/55), as well as a tour of the enormous Hamersley Iron mine ($17/8.50). There are also longer trips from Karratha (p982) and Port Hedland (p986).

Sleeping & Eating

Auski Tourist Village (☎ 08-9176 6988; 08-fax 9176 6973; Great Northern Hwy; powered/unpowered sites per 2 people $22/12, budget s/d $45/55, motel s/d $115/125; ✷) On the highway, 35km north of the Karijini Dr turn-off, this is really a roadhouse with some convenient accommodation. Camp sites are grassy and there are plenty of trees to huddle under in summer. Motel

rooms have the usual comforts, and you'll need to book budget rooms in advance.

Wittenoom Guest House (☎ 08-9189 7060; Gregory St, Wittenoom; dm/tw without bathroom $10/20; ✷) This slightly ramshackle place has 1950s furniture, a few homely rooms and a long dorm. It's clean, friendly and probably the cheapest place in the state, although it's a fair way from the park's major attractions.

Within the park there is a basic **camping ground** (☎ 08-9189 8157; sites per 2 people $10) at Dales Gorge and the privately run **Savannah Camp Ground** (☎ 08-9189 8013; sites per person/family $10/25) about 4km up Weano Rd.

The mining town of Tom Price, 120km west of the Great Northern Hwy, also has some accommodation, including **Tom Price**

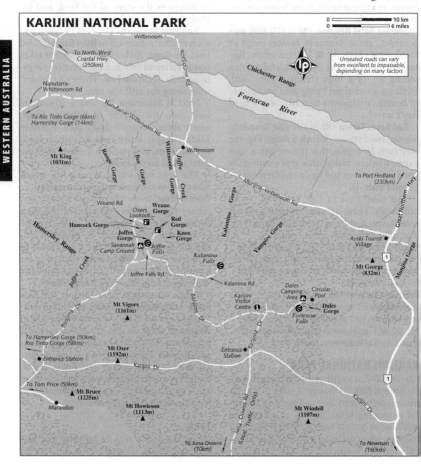

KARIJINI NATIONAL PARK

WITTENOOM WARNING

At the northern end of Karijini National Park, the ghost town of Wittenoom (population 25) is officially classified as 'abandoned' – and doesn't even appear on some maps – as a result of a series of deaths linked to the local blue asbestos mine. However, some hardy residents have refused to depart, and they offer accommodation, tours and counterpropaganda on the alleged dangers of the town. Although the mine closed in 1966, there is a potential health risk from airborne asbestos fibres in the township, and in the Wittenoom and Yampire Gorges. Avoid disturbing asbestos tailings in the area and keep your car windows closed on windy days. If you are concerned, seek medical advice before going to Wittenoom.

Tourist Park (☎ 08-9189 1515; Mt Nameless; powered/unpowered sites per 2 people $22/17, dm $20, cabins $95-115; 🅿 🖭), which has top facilities and a good range of cabin accommodation.

Getting There & Away

Access to the park is via Karijini Dr, which leaves the Great Northern Hwy 226km south of Port Hedland and 162km northwest of Newman. **Integrity** (☎ 1800 226 339; www.integrity coachlines.com.au) buses from Perth stop at Auski Tourist Village ($180, 19 hours, Tuesday and Friday), 35km north of the turn-off.

The direct, unsealed Tom Price Railway Rd takes you between Tom Price and Karratha, but it's a private road and you must get a (free) permit from the visitor centre at **Tom Price** (☎ 08-9188 1112; 497 Sirus St) or **Karratha** (☎ 08-9144 4600; Karratha Rd).

CENTRAL WEST COAST

The further north you head, the longer the distances stretch between settlements and roadhouses and, seemingly, no matter how far you travel in a day, it's a mere thumbnail on a map of the immense west coast. The North-West Coastal Hwy (Hwy 1) winds its way through some of WA's most striking and diverse areas. The Batavia coastal region is marked by precolonial shipwrecks, stout heritage buildings, cray fishing and Perth holiday-makers lapping

up the sun on pristine beaches. This area is also ablaze with wildflowers between July and November. The priceless treasure of World Heritage–listed Shark Bay is a unique area of wildlife, unspoilt beaches, blue skies and azure waters. Where else in the world can you feed wild dolphins in the morning, go dugong and tiger shark spotting in the afternoon and have the chance to spot a bilby on your way home?

Getting There & Away

Skywest (☎ 1300 660 088; www.skywest.com.au) links Perth with Carnarvon and has daily flights from Perth to Geraldton, with links to Exmouth and Karratha. **Skippers** (☎ 1300 729 924; www.skippers.com.au) offers a Perth–Kalbarri service that goes on to Shark Bay three times a week.

Greyhound Australia (☎ 13 14 99; www.greyhound .com.au) has daily north- and southbound buses between Perth and Dongara ($40, 5¾ hours), Geraldton ($50, 6¾ hours), Overlander Roadhouse (for Denham and Monkey Mia; $100, 10¾ hours) and Carnarvon ($125, 13 hours). Its Perth–Exmouth service takes you into Kalbarri ($95, eight hours, three weekly). **Transwa** (☎ 1300 662 205; www .transwa.wa.gov.au) follows three routes to Geraldton: via the Brand Hwy, Mullewa and Mingenew.

JURIEN BAY TO DONGARA-PORT DENISON

A newish road runs straight up the coast from Cervantes, passing through the small coastal towns of **Jurien Bay**, **Green Head** and **Leeman** on the way to Dongara-Port Denison. Stop off at the Molah Hill Lookout 11km north of Cervantes to drink in some truly awesome 360-degree views of the countryside. (It's wheelchair accessible too.)

Apart from an unbroken run of magnificent white-sand beaches and great fishing, the main attractions are the **Lesueur National Park**, which is home to one of the most diverse and rich wildflower areas of WA (access is via a 4WD track off Cockleshell Gully Rd), and excellent tours to Australian sea-lion populations on offshore islands.

Jurien Sealion Charters (☎ 08-9652 1109; www .juriencharters.com; Jurien Marina; half-day tours adult/child $75/30) takes you snorkelling near the island colonies and also offers whale-watching tours in season (September to December).

At Green Head, **Sea Lion Charters** (☎ 08-9953 1012; tours $75/35) offers similar tours.

Jurien Bay Tourist Park (☎ 08-9652 1595; Roberts St, Jurien Bay; powered/unpowered sites per 2 people $20/19, on-site caravans $55, chalets $120) is a well-developed park right on the beach with some *very* classy chalets.

DONGARA-PORT DENISON

☎ 08 / pop 3000

Dongara-Port Denison is distinguished by the huge fig trees that line Moreton Tce, and Point Leander at the marina, as well as an alluring historical heritage, fine beaches and top fishing. The foreshore has plenty of grass and a terrific walk-cycle way that follows the coast north, giving you a bird's-eye view.

In the old post office, the **Dongara visitor information centre** (☎ 9927 1404; www.lobstercapital .com.au; 9 Waldeck St; ⏰ 9am-5pm Mon-Fri, 9am-2pm Sat & Sun) has information on the town's historical buildings, including the striking but derelict flour mill, built in 1894. Fast Internet access is available at **Arrowsmith** (☎ 9927 2155; 33 Moreton Tce; per 30min $4; 💻).

Next door to the visitor centre, in the old police station, is the **Irwin District Museum** (Waldeck St; admission $2.50; ⏰ 10am-4pm Mon-Fri), which has small historical displays in its cells. Just over the Irwin River is **Russ Cottage** (Point Leander Dr; adult/child $2.50/50c; ⏰ 10am-noon Sun), built in 1870 and the birthplace of WA's first white baby. Further still is **Port Denison**, with its marina full of crayfish boats.

Sleeping & Eating

Priory Lodge Historic Inn (☎ /fax 9927 1090; priory@ dodo.com.au; 11 St Dominics Rd; s/d incl breakfast $45/70; 🍽 🍷) Built on the Irwin River in 1881, the atmospheric priory started life as a hotel, before serving as a nunnery and girls' school. It's now fully restored and boasts a cosy bar and bistro, period furniture, deep verandas and bucket loads of character. Rooms are large and airy with simple furniture and polished floorboards.

Dongara Marine Holiday Units (☎ 9927 1486; dongaramarinaunits@bigpond.com.au; 4 George St, Port Denison; units $80; 🍽) The best option for families or groups, these spacious, modern units are just up from the marina and sleep seven. They have all the mod-con trappings, a private courtyard and a BBQ. Add an extra $20 on at peak times and $17 for each extra person.

Dongara Backpackers (☎ 9927 1581; dongara backpack@westnet.com.au; cnr Waldeck & Walton Sts; dm/d $19/50; 💻) Next to a bakery, Dongara Backpackers has a great suburban location. A small, friendly hostel, it's in a colonial house with rooms around a kitchen and TV lounge, and has rather quaint additional (tiny) rooms in a 1906 train carriage parked out the back.

Southerleys (☎ 9927 2207; 60 Point Leander Dr, Port Denison; bar/restaurant mains $15/25; ⏰ lunch & dinner) A favourite with locals, the restaurant at this pub has fine seafood dining. The well-prepared dishes include local crayfish and Thai peppered prawns. Decent bang-up counter meals are also served in the excellent courtyard or at the bar. It's all very family friendly.

Toko's Restaurant (☎ 9927 1497; cnr Moreton Tce & Point Leander Dr; mains $9-25; ⏰ breakfast, lunch & dinner) A good spot for those with a romantic twinkle in their eye, Toko's is a cosy little eatery with overwrought décor. It dishes out Asian food, delectable scotch fillets, plenty of seafood and a couple of veggie options; bookings are requested.

Getting There & Away

Greyhound Australia (☎ 13 14 99; www.greyhound .com.au) buses to Broome and Perth stop at the Shell roadhouse on Brand Hwy. **Transwa** (☎ 1300 662 205; www.transwa.wa.gov.au) buses stop outside the visitor centre.

GREENOUGH

☎ 08 / pop 100

Just south of Geraldton, Greenough was once a busy little mining town, but today is notable for its host of National Trust buildings (mostly between 1860 and 1890).

Greenough visitor information centre (☎ 9926 1084; Brand Hwy; ⏰ 9am-5pm) has tourist information and there are 11 well-restored 19th-century **buildings** (adult/child $5/3.50; ⏰ tours by arrangement) clustered around it. Across the road, the **Pioneer Museum** (☎ 9926 1058; Brand Hwy; adult/child $4.50/free; ⏰ 10am-4pm) is a convincing recreation of an 1860s farmhouse, complete with cellar, butchery, two-hole dunny and creepy models of children in the bedroom.

Hampton Arms Inn (☎ 9926 1057; hamptonarms@ westnet.com.au; Company Rd; d incl breakfast $75, mains $12-16) is a classic pub (1863) with tons of charm set among sprawling eucalypts; it's great for a beer, a counter meal or an overnight stay in an old-fashioned room with many original fittings. Attached is a bookshop that specialises in rare and out-of-print books. Drop in at lunchtime for a ploughman's or veggie nutloaf.

Transwa (☎ 1300 662 205; www.transwa.wa.gov .au) services heading north and south stop at the Greenough turn-off on the Brand Hwy.

GERALDTON
☎ 08 / pop 23,400

Geraldton, the midwest's major town and cray-fishing centre, is a fine place with a pleasant town centre right on the waterfront, great eating and entertainment options, and a cracking museum. This aside, it is a good base to see the Batavia Coast's many sights and for trips to the beautiful Abrolhos Islands.

Information

There are several banks and ATMs along the main drag, Marine Tce.

Geraldton Regional Hospital (☎ 9956 2222; Shenton St)

Geraldton visitor information centre (☎ 9921 3999; www.geraldtontourist.com.au; Bill Sewell Complex, Chapman Rd; ⏰ 8.30am-4.30pm Mon-Fri, 9am-4.30pm Sat & Sun; 🖳) The staff here are very amiable. Pick up a *Heritage Trail* leaflet if you want to explore the town's historic architecture.

Harvey World Travel (☎ 9921 7377; Chapman Way Arcade; per hr $8; 🖳)

Sights

The **Western Australian Museum Geraldton** (☎ 9921 5080; www.museum.wa.gov.au; 1 Museum Pl; admission by donation; ⏰ 10am-4pm), WA's largest regional museum, has an excellent waterside home and a good series of exhibits on the region's Aboriginal, pioneer, natural and economic history. Don't miss the Shipwreck Gallery, which details the gruesome story of the *Batavia*.

Magnificent, towering **St Francis Xavier Cathedral** (Cathedral Ave; admission free, tours $2; ⏰ tours 10am Mon & 2pm Fri) will catch your eye on the way into town. It's one of a number of buildings in the midwest designed by Monsignor John Hawes (see the boxed text, p965). Completed in 1938, its external features include twin towers with arched openings, an enormous central dome and a cone-roofed tower.

Geraldton Regional Art Gallery (☎ 9964 7170; 24 Chapman Rd; admission free; ⏰ 10am-4pm Tue-Sat, 1-4pm Sun), situated in the old town hall, has a reasonable permanent collection on display, including several works by Norman Lindsay, as well as a rolling series of temporary exhibitions in a well-designed space.

The **Old Geraldton Gaol Craft Centre** (☎ 9921 1614; Bill Sewell Complex, Chapman Rd; admission free; ⏰ 10am-4pm) has a few frilly crafts for sale, but more compelling are the tiny, grim cells that housed prisoners from 1858 all the way to 1986.

At **Geraldton Fisherman's Co-op** (☎ 9921 7084; Geraldton Harbour; admission by donation; ⏰ tours 9.30am Mon-Fri mid-Nov–Jun) you get to see exactly how a live rock lobster gets from the ocean floor to a Hong Kong restaurant table. Located nearby are a couple of places on Connell Rd where you can get a lobster fresh off the boat.

On a small hill overlooking the town is the **HMAS Sydney Memorial** (follow the signs from George St), commemorating the loss of 645 men and the ship after a skirmish with the German ship *Kormoran* in November 1941. There are brilliant views over the town and water.

Festivals & Events

Batavia Celebrations June.

Geraldton Windsurfing Classic January.

Seajazz Festival March.

Sunshine Festival October.

Sleeping

BUDGET

Foreshore Backpackers YHA (☎ 9921 3275; foreshore bp@hotmail.com; 172 Marine Tce; dm/s/d $20/27/45; 🖳 🛒) Location, location, location – that's what it's all about at this large, friendly and character-filled place, smack bang in the middle of town. It's an ageing hostel with high-ceilinged, small rooms (maximum of four beds) but it's good honest accommodation. There's a large kitchen, snorkelling equipment, cool verandas with sea views and tours.

Batavia Backpackers (☎ 9964 3001; fax 9964 3611; cnr Chapman Rd & Bayly St; dm/s/d $18/25/42; 🖳) Just behind the visitor centre in a superb National Trust building, this place has worn but very clean and tidy dorms with high ceilings and plenty of cupboard space. The upstairs balcony is a top spot in the evening. Solo female travellers are well catered for and the friendly owners are very helpful.

MIDRANGE & TOP END

Champion Bay B&B (☎ 9921 7624; www.westnet.com.au/championbay; 31 Snowdon St; d with/without bath-

room $110/90) In a 110-year-old roomy family home atop a sharp hill, with sweeping views of the bay, this is a welcoming place that has a friendly owner and tastefully decorated rooms. Think polished floors, period furniture and a nautical feel. Try to get the upstairs room for the views and take your breakfast on the balcony.

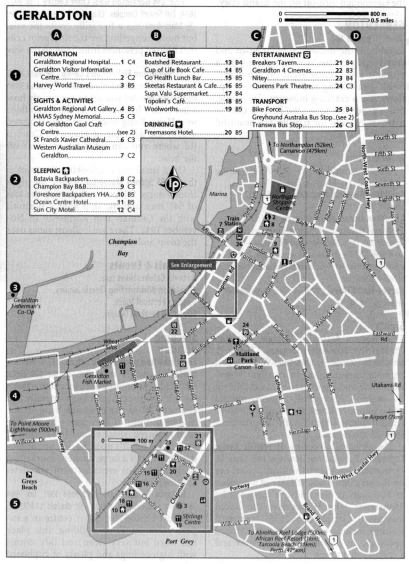

GERALDTON

0 — 800 m
0 — 0.5 miles

INFORMATION
Geraldton Regional Hospital......1 C4
Geraldton Visitor Information
Centre....................................2 C2
Harvey World Travel..................3 B5

SIGHTS & ACTIVITIES
Geraldton Regional Art Gallery..4 B5
HMAS Sydney Memorial.............5 C3
Old Geraldton Gaol Craft
Centre................................(see 2)
St Francis Xavier Cathedral........6 C3
Western Australian Museum
Geraldton..............................7 C2

SLEEPING
Batavia Backpackers..................8 C2
Champion Bay B&B....................9 C3
Foreshore Backpackers YHA.....10 B5
Ocean Centre Hotel.................11 B5
Sun City Motel........................12 C4

EATING
Boatshed Restaurant...............13 B4
Cup of Life Book Cafe.............14 B5
Go Health Lunch Bar...............15 B5
Skeetas Restaurant & Cafe.....16 B5
Supa Valu Supermarket..........17 B4
Topolini's Café.......................18 B5
Woolworths...........................19 B5

DRINKING
Freemasons Hotel...................20 B5

ENTERTAINMENT
Breakers Tavern......................21 B4
Geraldton 4 Cinemas...............22 B3
Nitey...................................23 B4
Queens Park Theatre..............24 C3

TRANSPORT
Bike Force.............................25 B4
Greyhound Australia Bus Stop..(see 2)
Transwa Bus Stop..................26 C3

Sun City Motel (☎ 9921 6111; www.clubsun.iinet .net.au; 137 Cathedral Ave; r with/without kitchenette $85/60; ⚡) This place offers the best-value motel accommodation close to town. It's a little frayed around the edges and the non-smoking policy borders on paranoia, but rooms (with in-house movies and fridges) are clean, a good size and excellent value. Ask about the more luxurious rooms currently being built.

Albrolhos Reef Lodge (☎ 9921 3811; www.modnet .com.au/~abrolhosreef; 126 Brand Hwy; budget/A-frame/ deluxe d $75/115/90; ⚡ ⚡) On the fringe of town, Abrolhos has a range of units; most will find something that suits the budget here. The rule of thumb is the more you fork out the more modern and extensive the facilities (especially the kitchenettes) and the springier the beds. The enticing Tarcoola Beach is a short walk away.

Ocean Centre Hotel (☎ 9921 7777; www.ocean centrehotel.com.au; cnr Foreshore Dr & Cathedral Ave; d from $90, ste with spa from $150; ⚡) You pay more for the sea views and luxury at this modern, spotless hotel in the centre of town right on the seafront. All rooms are well appointed, have sparkling bathrooms and, for the extremely lazy, come with bar fridge.

Eating

Skeetas Restaurant & Cafe (☎ 9964 1619; 101 Foreshore Dr; snacks $12-16, mains $17-24; ⏰ breakfast, lunch & dinner) You'll always get a table at this sprawling place across from the beach. Pull out a stylish number from the luggage and slip into some sophistication (sandgroper-style) at trendy Skeetas, where locals meet for a natter. Try the kangaroo fillet and sweet potato mash dressed in wattle-seed mousse *lavosh* (bread) with wild berry *jus* from the Mod Oz menu.

Topolini's Cafe (☎ 9964 5866; 158 Marine Tce; pizzas $12-17, mains $20-26; ⏰ lunch & dinner) This breezy, chirpy little place has friendly staff, a Mediterranean feel, delightful Italian nosh and to-die-for desserts. This licensed eatery also offers dinner-movie deals for $26, and half-price pasta on Monday. A good wine list tops it off.

Boatshed Restaurant (☎ 9921 5500; 357 Marine Tce; mains $26-32; ⏰ dinner) Arguably Geraldton's top seafood restaurant, the Boatshed has nautical décor and plenty of fishy goodness (it should be fresh – the fish market is next door). Try the oysters any way you like 'em.

For light meals, decent coffee and fresh, healthy fare, duck into **Go Health Lunch Bar** (☎ 9965 5200; 122 Marine Tce; light meals $8-14; 💻) with its fresh juices, espresso and delectable sangers, or **Cup of Life Book Cafe** (☎ 9965 5088; 84 Marine Tce; ⏰ breakfast & lunch; 💻), which is a favourite with readers and has a play area for kids.

Geraldton also has plenty of supermarkets, including **Supa Valu Supermarket** (Marine Tce) and **Woolworths** (Stirlings Centre, Chapman Rd).

Drinking

Freemason's Hotel (☎ 9964 3457; 79 Marine Tce) The big, breezy Freo is the best pub in town

---

MONSIGNOR JOHN HAWES

The architect-cum-priest Monsignor John Hawes, who was born in Richmond, England, in 1876, has left a magnificent legacy of buildings in the midwest. He trained as an architect in London, then, following his ordination as an Anglican priest in 1903, worked in the London slums as a missionary. He then went to the Bahamas where he helped rebuild a number of churches.

Two years later he converted to Catholicism and went to study in Rome. He came to Australia in 1915 at the invitation of the Bishop of Geraldton and worked as a country pastor in the Murchison goldfields. For the next 24 years he worked tirelessly as a parish priest at Mullewa and Greenough while designing 24 buildings, 16 of which were built.

His best works are the Church of Our Lady of Mt Carmel and the Priest House in Mullewa, the Church of the Holy Cross in Morawa, the Church of St Joseph in Perenjori and the beautiful, inspiring St Francis Xavier Cathedral in Geraldton.

Hawes left Australia in 1939 and went to Cat Island in the Bahamas and lived as a hermit. He died in a Miami hospital in 1956 and his body was brought back to a tomb he had built for himself on Cat Island.

The *Monsignor Hawes Heritage Trail* pamphlet ($4.50) is available from the visitor centre in Geraldton.

for a drink, with great Western Australian beers like the honeyed Beez Neez on tap and a decent wine list. Its terrace seating and relaxed atmosphere makes it popular with all ages and persuasions.

Entertainment

The *Geraldton Guardian* has weekend entertainment listings on Friday.

Freemason's Hotel (☎ 9964 3457; 79 Marine Tce) Pulls some great guitar bands.

Breakers Tavern (☎ 9921 8925; 41 Chapman Rd) Attracts a wild and woolly crowd and is a little less polished than Freemason's. Bands bash out a tune Friday and Saturday night.

Nitey (☎ 9921 1400; 60 Fitzgerald St) The place to show the locals your latest moves and dance, dance, dance 'til you can't dance no more.

Geraldton 4 Cinemas (☎ 9965 0568; cnr Marine Tce & Fitzgerald St; adult/child $13/8) Has four screens showing the latest movie releases.

Queens Park Theatre (☎ 9956 6662; www.mid westevents.com.au; cnr Cathedral Ave & Maitland St) For concerts, plays and comedy.

Getting There & Around

Skywest (☎ 1300 660 088; www.skywest.com.au) has direct flights to/from Perth daily ($105), as well as daily flights to Carnarvon ($150).

Skippers (☎ 1300 729 924; www.skippers.com.au) also flies to Perth and has links to Kalbarri.

Greyhound Australia (☎ 13 14 99; www.greyhound .com.au) buses run daily from the Bill Sewell Complex to Perth ($50, 6¾ hours), as well as Broome ($255, 26 hours) and all points in between. **Transwa** (☎ 1300 662 205; www.transwa .wa.gov.au) also goes daily to Perth and three times weekly to Kalbarri ($21). Transwa buses stop at the old train station.

Geraldton Bus Service (☎ 9923 1100) operates eight routes to local suburbs (1½-hour ticket $2). **Bike Force** (☎ 9921 3279; 54 Marine Tce) hires out good bikes (per day/week $15/70).

HOUTMAN ABROLHOS ISLANDS

Known locally as 'the Abrolhos', this archipelago is about 60km off the coast of Geraldton and takes in more than 100 coral islands. They are home to sea-lion colonies and a host of sea birds, plus hefty golden orb spi-

---

A BLOODY BUSINESS

During the 17th century, the easiest way for ships of the Dutch East India Company to get to Batavia (Jakarta) in Java was to head due east from the Cape of Good Hope and then hoon up the Western Australian coast to Indonesia. However, the many offshore reefs and island groups made this a risky business, and the whole area is littered with wrecks, including the ill-fated *Batavia*.

On 4 June 1629 the *Batavia* ran aground on the inhospitable Abrolhos Islands (*abre los vos* means 'open your eyes'!). The ship's commander, Francisco Pelsaert, took most of the officers and passengers to the mainland to search for water, leaving 268 people behind, including a sizable body of soldiers. An undermerchant named Jeronimus Cornelisz, who had agitated against the commander during the voyage, saw his chance to act. Tricking the soldiers into relinquishing their arms, he banished them to a nearby island and instituted a reign of terror that resulted in the death of 125 men, women and children before Pelsaert returned.

The first murders were carried out under the pretext of saving water supplies, but Cornelisz and his small band of followers became increasingly arbitrary and brutal, taking concubines and raping and murdering indiscriminately. Pelsaert eventually returned after three months (having been forced to travel all the way to Batavia for help) with more soldiers. He summarily executed Cornelisz, and dumped some of his men at Wittecarra Gully, just south of modern-day Kalbarri, making them the first white men on mainland Australia.

Another notable wreck was the *Zuytdorp*, which ran aground beneath the towering cliffs about 65km north of Kalbarri in 1712. Wine bottles, other relics and the remains of fires have been found on the cliff top, and the discovery of the extremely rare Ellis van Creveld syndrome (short-limbed dwarfism characterised by physical deformities; rife in Holland at the time the ship ran aground) in Aboriginal children suggests that *Zuytdorp* survivors lasted long enough to introduce the gene to Australia.

Relics from these shipwrecks, and others, can be seen in the Western Australian Museum Geraldton (p963) and Shipwreck Museum (p903) in Fremantle. The latter has a gallery devoted entirely to the *Batavia* that's well worth a look.

PRINCE LEONARD'S LAND

Down a dusty, dirt road, 75km northwest of Northampton, lies the independent land of the **Hutt River Province Principality** (☎ /fax 08-9936 6035; www.huttriver.net). Australia's 'second-largest country' was created on 21 April 1970 when farmer Len Casley, disgusted with government quotas on wheat production, seceded from the Commonwealth of Australia under a (hastily closed) legal loophole.

Despite concerted attempts by the Western Australian government to legally overturn the secession, more than 30 years later HRH Prince Leonard and Princess Shirley remain the monarchs of the only principality in the world declared without bloodshed. Their 75-sq-km property features a post office, gift shop and deadpan collection of flags, stamps, letters, medallions and other paraphernalia to lend legitimacy to the province. Similarly, the province also has its own flag, postal system, constitution and armed forces, although the latter plays a strictly ceremonial role. You can become naturalised if you like – the province has 13,000 citizens worldwide and a five-year passport costs $250. The downside for the 20 or so permanent residents is that they have no entitlement to Australian government health or social security benefits, although neither do they pay tax.

Visitors are encouraged, but call ahead to ensure that one of the royals is in residence. After all, how often do you get the chance of taking a guided tour led by a genuine royal?

---

ders, carpet pythons and the small tammar wallaby. However, much of the beauty of the Abrolhos lies beneath the water, where *Acropora* coral abounds and (thanks to the warm Leeuwin Current) a rare and spectacular mix of tropical and temperate fish species thrives. The beautiful but treacherous reefs surrounding the islands have also claimed many ships over the years, including the ill-fated *Batavia* – see the boxed text, opposite.

As the islands are protected and have no tourist facilities, it's not possible to stay on them overnight. You can visit from Geraldton by boat or air. **Geraldton Air Charters** (☎ 08-9923 3434) has scenic flights ($165) or day trips that include lunch and snorkelling gear ($200); **Shine Aviation** (☎ 08-9923 3600) has similar tours. **Odyssey Expeditions** (☎ 0428 382 505) is among the boat operators that charge from $100 for a fishing and snorkelling day trip.

NORTHAMPTON TO KALBARRI
Lovely **Northampton** is a National Trust–classified town with many historic buildings. The **Old Convent** (☎ 08-9934 1692; 61 Hampton Rd; dm/s/d $12/15/30), a magnificent old stone building with sweeping wooden verandas that were designed by Monsignor Hawes and then converted to a backpackers hostel, is a great place to stay. Next door is the striking **St Mary's Church** (another Hawes building), a dignified and slender structure made from weathered red stone.

The coastal road is the more scenic option to get to Kalbarri, and passes through the tiny coastal towns of **Horrocks** and **Port Gregory**, and the superb coastal gorges located in the southern reaches of **Kalbarri National Park** (p968).

The **Port Gregory Caravan Park** (☎ 08-9935 1052; powered/unpowered sites per 2 people $20/17, on-site caravans $48, cabins from $60;) has to be a contender for the friendliest caravan park in WA and is only too happy to dispense tourist info on the town. You'll also get you a rundown of the excellent fishing in the area (tailor, snapper, groper, mulloway and coral trout can all be caught here). Keep the camera at hand for some snaps of the pink lake just before you pull into town. Horrocks also has a **caravan park** (☎ 08-9934 3039; powered/unpowered sites per 2 people $19/16, on-site caravans $42) that fronts onto a quiet and attractive beach.

KALBARRI
☎ 08 / pop 2000
Picture-perfect with its alluring coastal playground, Kalbarri doesn't really have a low season – it's always popular. Activities, adventure, sightseeing and outdoor fun abound in this striking little town with its turquoise waters and abundance of tourist facilities. It lies at the mouth of the Murchison River and the stunning gorges of Kalbarri National Park are rightly billed as its prime puller.

Information

There are ATMs in the supermarket and Gilgai Tavern, and at the shopping centre.

CALM office (☎ 9937 1140; Ajana-Kalbarri Rd; ☺ 8am-4pm Mon-Fri)

Kalbarri Cafe & Takeaways (Kalbarri Shopping Centre; per hr $6; ▣)

Kalbarri visitor information centre (☎ 1800 639 468, 9937 1104; ktb@wn.com.au; Grey St; ☺ 9am-5pm) Always bustling; books tours and accommodation.

Traveller's Book Exchange & Internet Cafe (☎ 9937 2676; 42 Grey St; per hr $5; ▣) Next to the post office.

Sights & Activities

KALBARRI NATIONAL PARK

This arid **national park** (per car $9) boasts over 1000 sq km of bushland, scenic gorges on the Murchison River and rugged coastal cliffs. To get to the gorges from Kalbarri, head 11km east along Ajana-Kalbarri Rd to the turn-off, then follow the long stretches of dirt to the impressive gorges of the **Loop** (29km) and **Z-Bend** (25km). More accessible and just as attractive are two lookouts, **Hawk's Head** and **Ross Graham**. The turn-off to both is another 24km along Ajana-Kalbarri Rd. The park has a particularly fine display of **wildflowers** between July and November, including banksia, grevillea and kangaroo paw.

South of town there's a string of rugged cliff faces, including **Red Bluff**, **Rainbow Valley**, **Pot Alley**, **Eagle Gorge** and **Natural Bridge**. A **walking-cycling path** from town goes as far

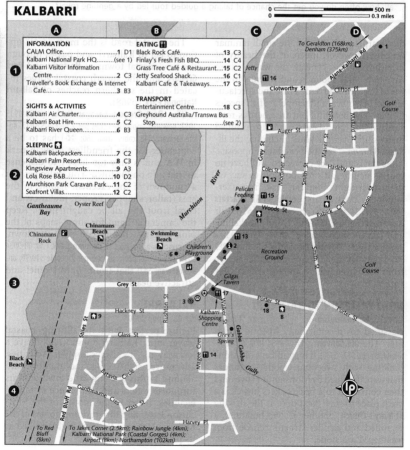

KALBARRI

0 _____ 500 m
0 _____ 0.3 miles

INFORMATION	
CALM Office	1 D1
Kalbarri National Park HQ	(see 1)
Kalbarri Visitor Information Centre	2 C3
Traveller's Book Exchange & Internet Cafe	3 B3

SIGHTS & ACTIVITIES	
Kalbarri Air Charter	4 C3
Kalbarri Boat Hire	5 C2
Kalbarri River Queen	6 B3

SLEEPING	
Kalbarri Backpackers	7 C2
Kalbarri Palm Resort	8 C3
Kingsview Apartments	9 A3
Lola Rose B&B	10 D2
Murchison Park Caravan Park	11 C2
Seafront Villas	12 C2

EATING	
Black Rock Café	13 C3
Finlay's Fresh Fish BBQ	14 C4
Grass Tree Café & Restaurant	15 C2
Jetty Seafood Shack	16 C1
Kalbarri Cafe & Takeaways	17 C3

TRANSPORT	
Entertainment Centre	18 C3
Greyhound Australia/Transwa Bus Stop	(see 2)

To Geraldton (168km);
Denham (375km)

To Red Bluff (8km)

To Jakes Corner (2.5km); Rainbow Jungle (4km); Kalbarri National Park (Coastal Gorges) (4km); Airport (8km); Northampton (102km)

as **Jakes Corner**, one of the state's best surfing breaks, or you can take a morning shuttle bus to **Natural Bridge** and walk or cycle back to town. From August to November it may be possible to spot **humpback whales** passing by, while **dolphins** can be seen year-round.

OTHER SIGHTS & ACTIVITIES

Rainbow Jungle (☎ 9937 1248; Red Bluff Rd; adult/child $10/3.50; ⏰ 9am-5pm Mon-Sat, 10am-5pm Sun), 4km south of town, is a fine bird park and parrot-breeding centre. The walk-in aviary is a highlight but be careful you don't get pooped on from above! The miniwaterfalls and extensive greenery almost give it a Zen-like quality. You'll be astounded by the variety and beauty of Australian parrots and their cousins.

For water activities on the Murchison River, **Kalbarri Boat Hire** (☎ 9937 1245) is on the foreshore and hires kayaks, rowboats, windsurfers and sailboats ($10 to $20 per hour).

Other activities include **abseiling** at Z-Bend, **sandboarding** and **camel safaris**; see the visitor centre for details.

Tours

There's a host of daily tours covering scenic, adventure and wildlife activities (including whale-watching tours).

For a leisurely look around, cruises are run by **Murchison River Cruises** (☎ 9937 1393) and **Kalbarri River Queen** (☎ 9937 1104); both boats have on-board bars, and tours are roughly $30 for two to three hours.

Also recommended:

Kalbarri Adventure Tours (☎ 9937 1677; www .kalbarritours.com.au) Popular all-day bushwalking and canoeing trips through the national park (adult/child $65/50).

Kalbarri Air Charter (☎ 9937 1130; Grey St) Does 20-minute flights over the Murchison River gorges (adult/child $45/30) and longer tours.

Sleeping

Kalbarri Backpackers (☎ 9937 1430; kalbarriback packers@wn.com.au; cnr Woods & Mortimer Sts; dm/d $20/55, motel d $105, 2-bedroom units $90; ✂ 🖳 🕭) One of the best backpackers hostels around with a plethora of accommodation options that include fully self-contained units (great value for groups). On the downside dorms are jam-packed with beds, but this is compensated for by great facilities, including free use of BBQs and snorkel gear, bike hire ($10 per day) and a huge number of tours.

Lola Rose B&B (☎ 9937 2224; fax 9937 2324; 21 Patrick Cres; r with/without bathroom $85/75; ✂) The best midrange deal in town, Lola Rose is friendly and spacious with a generous shared lounge and kitchen. There's even a measure of privacy as the managers live off-site.

Kingsview Apartments (☎ 9937 1274; cnr Stiles & Hackney Sts; d $185 ✂) Managing seclusion, yet close to town and blessed with gorgeous views, these beautiful, modern and roomy apartments are decked out with luxurious touches, tasteful décor and kitchens worthy of a gourmet chef.

Kalbarri Palm Resort (☎ 1800 819 029, 9937 2333; www.bestwestern.com.au/kalbarri; 8 Porter St; 2-bedroom apt $110, d with spa $150; ✂ 🕭) A large, family-oriented place, the apartments here are very schmick and great value for groups. Spread over three levels, you get a master bedroom with walk-in robes, balcony and a washing machine. Deluxe and spa rooms come with bigger beds. There are also tennis courts and even an indoor cricket court.

Also recommended:

Murchison Park Caravan Park (☎ 9937 1005; fax 9937 1415; cnr Woods & Grey Sts; powered/unpowered sites per 2 people $22/18, cabins $60; ✂) Almost spilling out onto the surrounding roads, the most central of Kalbarri's parks.

Seafront Villas (☎ 9937 1025; www.kalbarriseafront villas.com.au; 108 Grey St; 1-/2-bedroom villas from $90/110; ✂) Spacious, modern, self-contained villas on the waterfront; there are few better places for sitting out in the evening with a cold drink.

Eating

Black Rock Café (☎ 9937 1062; 80 Grey St; breakfast $4-12, mains $12-35; ⏰ breakfast, lunch & dinner) A casual place that takes its food seriously (check out the quotes on the specials board), and with plenty of outdoor seating overlooking the water, Black Rock is Kalbarri's best eatery. Choose from generous brekkies, gourmet sandwiches (the open prawn sandwich is scrumptious) and salads at lunchtime, and a varied Mod Oz menu in the evening. The wine list is well priced, and all wine is available by the glass.

Grass Tree Café & Restaurant (☎ 9937 2288; 94 Grey St; mains $11-33; ⏰ lunch & dinner) Readers rave about this place. A delightful eatery with excellent outside dining and a varied and innovative menu. There's an Asian-fusion theme to the menu with seafood featuring as well as pasta dishes. Try the bruschetta of shrimps for lunch or the oriental spiced lamb rack for dinner.

Finlay's Fresh Fish BBQ (Magee Cres; mains $13-20; ☺ dinner Tue-Sun) This ultra-laid-back and often raucous place is in a tree-shaded sand garden, and gives you Australiana in spades. Mismatched cutlery and crockery, BYO booze (and glass if you don't fancy a plastic tumbler) and large serves of seafood or steak makes for a great night, but get in early – you can't reserve a table.

Jetty Seafood Shack (☎ 9937 1067; 1/108 Grey St; meals from $9; ☺ lunch & dinner) This basic take-away, opposite the little marina, has an excellent rep for the quality of its seafood, and has good-value combo packs ($14 to $26), which are ideal for a picnic on the river. You can also buy fresh snapper here, if you want to fire up the BBQ.

Getting There & Around

The airport is 10km south of town. **Skippers** (☎ 1300 729 924; www.skippers.com.au) flies to/from Perth ($240) three times weekly and on to Shark Bay ($100).

Greyhound Australia (☎ 13 14 99; www.greyhound .com.au) buses head for Perth ($95, eight hours) and Exmouth ($130, 10½ hours). **Transwa** (☎ 1300 662 205; www.transwa.wa.gov.au) has services to Perth three times weekly. Both leave from the visitor centre.

Bicycles can be rented from the **Entertainment Centre** (☎ 9937 1105; Porter St) for $20 per day.

SHARK BAY AREA

Is Shark Bay paradise? If you're reading this on the 130km detour off the highway to get here, you'll be thinking, 'yeah right', but if you're reading this as you leave, you may be scratching your head and thinking, 'they may have a point here'.

The turquoise waters, brilliant blue skies and tiny population of this remote peninsula make it an idyllic destination, giving visitors a sense of being rewarded when they finally arrive. And rewarded they will be…by the captivating Shark Bay World Heritage and Marine Park with its spectacular beaches, important sea-grass beds, great fishing, ancient stromatolites and famously predictable dolphins of Monkey Mia.

Among 16 endangered species in the area are dugongs (more than 10% of the world's population), loggerhead turtles, western barred bandicoots and bilbies (see also the boxed text, opposite).

Overlander Roadhouse to Denham

Leaving the highway just past the Overlander Roadhouse, the first turn-off (about 27km along) takes you to **Hamelin Pool**, a marine reserve containing the world's best-known colony of **stromatolites**. These microbes are almost identical to organisms that existed 1900 million years ago and evolved into more complex life. They are extremely fragile, so there's a boardwalk that allows you to view them without causing further harm; it's best to visit at low tide when they're not completely submerged.

Information on the stromatolites (including a live specimen) forms part of the display in the nearby 1884 **Telegraph Station** (☎ 08-9942 5905; adult/child $5/free; ☺ 9am-5.30pm), which served as a telephone exchange until 1977. You'll see fossils from the area and viewing is by informal tour, which takes about half an hour. **Hamelin Pool Caravan Park** (☎ 08-9942 5905; powered/unpowered sites per 2 people $18/16) offers food (sandwiches $4.50), basic facilities and a decent grassed area to pitch your tent.

Another 35km along is the turn-off to **Nanga Bay Holiday Resort** (☎ 08-9948 3992; nangabay@wn.com.au; powered/unpowered sites $24/18, dm $20, 2-bed cabins $65, motel d $125; ⌘). It's a peaceful place with a broad range of accommodation and good facilities, including a pool, tennis courts, spa, shop, bar and restaurant. It caters mainly to families, fishing fans and grey nomads.

Just 5km away, the cockleshells at stunning **Shell Beach** are 10m deep in some places and in the past were used as building materials. The water is only knee-deep for at least 100m out, and the 'hypersalinity' of the whole bay is evident here – as you'll find out if you accidentally swallow some. There are superb cliff-top views at **Eagle Bluff**, halfway between Nanga and Denham.

Denham

☎ 08 / pop 1140

The most westerly town in Australia, Denham was established as a pearling port, but tourism is the main breadwinner today. An unspoilt little place, it is a convenient base for lazing around the shallow turquoise waters, and has a great beach for kids.

INFORMATION

Almost all visitor facilities are on Knight Tce, across from the pale-green waters of the bay. There is an ATM at Heritage Resort.

CALM (☎ 9948 1208; 89 Knight Tce; ☼ 8am-5pm Mon-Fri) Has plenty of information on the World Heritage area.

Denham visitor information centre (☎ 9948 1253; 71 Knight Tce; ☼ 9am-5pm) Staff at this privately run centre can book tours.

Shark Bay Telecentre (☎ 9948 1787; 67 Knight Tce; per hr $10; ☼ Tue-Sun; ⌨)

SIGHTS

On the way into town, **Ocean Park** (☎ 9948 1765; www.oceanpark.com.au; Denham Hamelin Rd; adult/child $7/3; ☼ 10am-4pm) is a locally run aquaculture farm featuring an artificial lagoon stocked with sharks, pink snapper, turtles and stingrays, which are fed every afternoon. An oceanarium and touch pool are under construction.

The huge **wind turbines** west of Denham provide over half of the town's electricity.

TOURS

Majestic Tours (☎ /fax 9948 1627; www.ozpal.com /majestic) Full-day 4WD tours into François Péron National Park ($125), Hamelin Pool and Shell Beach ($125), and just Shell Beach ($65).

Shark Bay Air Charter (☎ 9948 1773; tours $50-115) Offers three tours of the region, which range from 15 to 45 minutes and can take in Dirk Hartog Island, Zuytdorp Cliffs, Useless Loop and the Salt Lakes.

Shark Bay Coaches & Tours (☎ 9948 1081) Day tours from $55 and has been recommended by readers.

SLEEPING & EATING

Bay Lodge (☎ 1800 812 780, 9948 1278; www.baylodge .info; 113 Knight Tce; dm $20, d & tw from $50, 2-bed-room apt from $100; ✂ ⌨ ☎) Across from the beach, this shell-brick YHA hostel is very well set up and has a large range of accommodation. Nothing seems like too much trouble for the friendly owners and dorms are actually an apartment with three, four or five beds and shared facilities, while three-room bungalows have their own kitchen and bathroom. There's a free daily bus to Monkey Mia.

Shark Bay Holiday Cottages (☎ /fax 9948 1206; www.sharkbaycottages.com.au; 3-13 Knight Tce; 1-/2-/3-bedroom cottages from $80/90/100; ✂ ☎) These cottages are nothing flash, but they're fully self-contained and across from the beach, which makes them good value. Boats can also be hired here.

Heritage Resort (☎ 9948 1133; heritageresort@ bigpond.com.au; cnr Knight Tce & Durlacher St; d & tw with/without sea view $140/120; ✂ ☎) Denham's upmarket option offers identical, spacious rooms with queen-size beds and balconies overlooking the beach. It discounts heavily when things are slow. There's also a bistro here featuring seafood.

Old Pearler Restaurant (☎ 9948 1373; Knight Tce; mains $10-30; ☼ lunch & dinner) A cosy place built

---

PROJECT EDEN

Degraded by decades of poor farming practices and infested with feral foxes, cats, goats and rabbits, only 10 years ago Peron Peninsula was an ecological basket case. Today, however, the area is the subject of Australia's largest and most ambitious ecosystem regeneration programme, Project Eden.

Established in 1995, the CALM project is attempting to eradicate the feral animals, re-establish populations of endemic species and develop techniques that can be applied to other degraded arid zones in Australia. The key has been the isolation of the peninsula from mainland Australia, with an electric fence at the isthmus preventing feral species from repopulating, and most of the foxes and cats have been destroyed through baits and traps.

A breeding centre in François Péron National Park has collected breeding pairs of rare marsupials from the offshore Dorre and Bernier Islands, as well as zoos and rehabilitation centres across Australia, and is breeding bilbies, rufous hare wallabies, banded hare wallabies, western barred bandicoots and woylies for release into the wild.

To date the results have been mixed. Although woylie, mallee fowl and bilby populations appear to be surviving (thriving in the case of the mallee fowl), the reintroduction of the wallabies was not successful due to continued cat predation. Future planned releases include the western barred bandicoot, Shark Bay mouse and phascogales. If you're interested in the project, **CALM** (☎ 08-9948 1208; 89 Knight Tce, Denham) has plenty of information.

from Hamelin Pool shell blocks, Old Pearler has good-value lunches, and a rather more expensive seafood, steak and pasta evening menu with a couple of veggie dishes thrown in for good measure. In crayfish season you'll get half a cray and salad for $16; readers have recommended the cheesecakes.

There are also supermarkets, a bakery and takeaways along Knight Tce.

GETTING THERE & AROUND
Skippers (☎ 1300 729 924; www.skippers.com.au) flies to Kalbarri ($100) and to Perth ($190) five times a week.

There are shuttle buses ($30, 1½ hours, Monday, Thursday and Saturday) from Denham and Monkey Mia that connect with the north- and southbound **Greyhound Australia** (☎ 13 14 99; www.greyhound.com.au) services at the Overlander Roadhouse on the main highway.

Shark Bay Coaches & Tours (☎ 9948 1081) runs a daily bus to Monkey Mia ($20 return) that leaves from the Caltex service station on Knight Tce; bookings are essential.

François Péron National Park
About 4km from Denham, on Monkey Mia Rd, is the turn-off to the wild **François Péron National Park** (bus passenger $4, car $9), renowned for its untouched beaches, dramatic cliffs, salt lakes and rare marsupial species (see the boxed text, p971). There's a visitor centre at the old Peron Homestead, 6km from the main road, where a former artesian bore has been converted to a soothing 35°C hot tub. **Camp sites** (per 2 people $10) with limited facilities are at Big Lagoon, Gregories, Bottle Bay and Herald Bight.

The sandy road to the homestead is generally suitable only for 4WD vehicles; check conditions with **CALM** (☎ 08-9948 1208; 89 Knight Tce; ☉ 8am-5pm Mon-Fri) in Denham. See p971 for 4WD tour operators that go into the park.

Monkey Mia
☎ 08
A sprawling beach resort 26km northeast of Denham, **Monkey Mia** (adult/child/family $6/2/12) has become world-famous for the bottlenose dolphins that turn up like clockwork every day. It's so popular these days that the morning feeding session can be a bit of a circus, but you will get a good look at these attractive creatures. Always

observe the rules of behaviour outlined in your entry brochure; in particular don't touch the dolphins, as they can contract viruses from humans, and always follow the ranger's instructions. There is a swimming area next to the interaction zone. If a dolphin joins you, let it swim around you while you stay still. Never chase or approach a dolphin, as it may cause it distress, particularly if it's accompanied by a calf.

The **Dolphin Information Centre** (☎ 9948 1366; ☉ 7.30am-4pm), near the beach viewing area, has lots of information on dolphins, including regular videos, and occasional evening talks by wildlife researchers.

There's a general store selling groceries, a shop hiring **snorkelling gear** (per half/full day $12/20), an ATM inside the Boughshed Restaurant and a couple of Internet terminals. A beach wheelchair is available.

TOURS
Aristocat II (☎ 9948 1446; www.monkey-mia.net) Offers similar cruises to *Shotover* (following). The sunset cruise ($50) is a great way to unwind with a drink.
Shotover (☎ 1800 241 481, 9948 1481; www.monkey miawildsights.com.au) This former ocean-racing catamaran offers a range of short wildlife cruises ($35 to $60), where you'll see dugongs, dolphins, turtles and, in summer, tiger sharks and sea snakes.
Wula Guda Nyinda (☎ 0429 708 847) Offers tours that give the Aboriginal perspective, and include bush tucker and animal tracking. The 1½-hour tours depart at 9am on Saturday and Sunday (adult/child $20/15).

SLEEPING & EATING
Monkey Mia is not a town, but simply the resort and beachfront. It offers a good range of accommodation, which is reasonably priced considering it's the only show in town. The same cannot be said for the eateries, so if you're on a tight budget consider bringing your own food.
Monkey Mia Dolphin Resort (☎ 1800 653 611, 9948 1320; www.monkeymia.com.au; powered/unpowered sites per 2 people $29/18, on-site caravans from $50, cabins $100, motel r from $175; ☒ ☐ ☒) The bustling, compact resort is set around a great paddling beach and the famous home of the dolphins. The top-end accommodation is not great value, but the beachfront villas have a divine location. On-site caravans are a bargain but pretty beat-up. Park homes are better value and have cooking facilities.

Dolphin Lodge & Backpackers (4-/7-bed dm $19/22, r $65, units $175) This new lodge offers up some very schmick accommodation that caters for both ends of the market. Functional dorms come with lockable drawers (bring a padlock), while the small and fairly plain rooms sleep up to four and share a bathroom with one other room. These rooms also come with a fan, but they're upstairs so usually catch a good breeze anyway. There are large, shared cooking facilities at the backpackers hostel.

Bough Shed Restaurant & Cocktail Bar (☎ 9948 1171; breakfasts $4-13, lunches $14-19, dinner mains $29-35; ☽ breakfast, lunch & dinner) A great setting, with tables that spill out onto the grassed area overlooking the beach, is spoilt by poor-value meals, although the Mod Oz menu is interesting enough. There's a bar (no takeaways).

Peron Cafe (meals $7-14) Nearby, Peron has burgers, sandwiches and salads.

Monkey Bar/Cafe (Dolphin Lodge & Backpackers) This is a cheaper, more atmospheric spot to munch on a burger or pasta dish ($8 to $15). It's also a decent, if more raucous, waterfront spot for a beer.

GETTING THERE & AWAY
The only public transport to Monkey Mia from Denham is by shuttle bus (see opposite for more information).

CARNARVON
☎ 08 / pop 6900
At the mouth of the Gascoyne River, Carnarvon is a sleepy town – its main attraction is a lack of attractions, which makes it a perfect spot to laze away a day or two, and enjoy some excellent seafood dining and great-value accommodation. There's also fruit-picking work in season, and you'll probably learn more about a banana than you ever thought possible. If you're passing through on the weekend, drop into the Saturday fresh-produce **market** (Civic Centre; ☽ 8am-noon May-Oct) for some bargain fruit and veg.

Information
Carnarvon visitor information centre (☎ 9941 1146; Civic Centre, Robinson St; ☽ 8.30am-5pm Mon-Fri year-round, 9am-noon Sat Nov-Mar, 9am-2pm Sat, 10am-2pm Sun Apr-Oct) Excellent, in-depth information on the town and region.

Gascoyne Photographics (☎ 9941 3366; 24 Robinson St; per hr $4; ☐)
Post office (Camel Lane)
Wise Owl Book Exchange (Babbage Island Rd) Large selection of secondhand books.

Sights & Activities
You can catch a little diesel train called the **Coffee Pot** (adult/child $5.50/3.50) along **One Mile Jetty**, where locals fish for mulloway; you can also walk the jetty's length (adult/child $3/2). A restored **steam train** occasionally runs from the end of the town footbridge to the **historic precinct**; check with the visitor centre to see if it's running. Also in the precinct is the **Lighthouse Keeper's Cottage Museum** (☎ 9941 3423; admission $1) with a small collection of pioneer and railway artefacts, as well as the old lighthouse itself; call for opening hours.

Tours
Trust us, you will learn more about a banana at **Westoby Banana Plantation** (☎ 9941 8003; 500 Robinson St) than you ever thought possible (or healthy!), and you'll have a laugh doing it on the 45-minute tour ($5.50). For those who are without wheels, **Carnarvon Bus Charter** (☎ 9941 3336) will take you there for $2 return.

Sleeping
Carnarvon Family B&B (☎ 9941 4794; jjdwyer@bigpond.net.au; 23 Wheelock Way; s/d $80/90, dinner $20; ☒) Just out of the centre this homely place, with its bright rooms and cheery welcome, takes good care of visitors. Guests can use a private sitting room; the bathroom, which has a spa, is a big draw!

Sea Change House (☎ 9941 4794; 75 Olivia Tce; house from $100) The Carnarvon Family also lets out this three-bedroom house, situated right across from the water, as fully self-contained accommodation or as a B&B offering a bit more privacy. The owners are very willing to accommodate families at either of the two places (there is a small surcharge for kids).

Gascoyne Hotel (☎ 9941 1412; gascoynehotelwn.com.au; 88 Olivia Tce; s/d/tw $70/80/90; ☒) Honest, brick motel rooms come with fridge and TV at this attractive old pub. Rooms are a little bit tired, but good value and only a short stumble from the bar, which has the delectable James Squire beer on tap; the

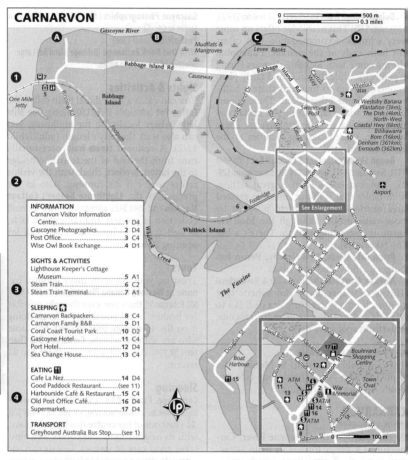

CARNARVON

attached Good Paddock restaurant serves seafood and steak.

Coral Coast Tourist Park (☎ 9941 1438; coral coastpk@westnet.com.au; 108 Robinson St; powered/un-powered sites per 2 people $21/18, units $55-95; ☒ ☒) This well-organised and friendly place is located within walking distance of town. The units here are simple, but they're well decked out and in good nick. You'll also find that there's plenty of grass and shade available for camping.

Port Hotel (☎ 9941 1704; Robinson St; 2- & 3-bed r per night/week $25/110) Watch this space – the old beat-up Port Hotel has recently changed hands and at the time of writing was undergoing a serious make-over to include backpacker accommodation.

Carnarvon Backpackers (☎ /fax 9941 1095; 97 Olivia Tce; dm $18-20, tw $50; ☒ ☐) Given the negative feedback about this place, Port Hotel could be a welcome alternative.

Eating

Old Post Office Cafe (☎ 9941 1800; 10 Robinson St; pizza $15-23; ☺ dinner Tue-Sat) 'Voted in the Top Five Pizzas in the World' – their words not ours, but certainly tasty pizza and fine gelati make this a great spot for a casual meal. It's licensed and there are cheap takeaway deals, but the wooden veranda tables are just the job for a touch of people-watching on a steamy evening.

Cafe La Nez (☎ 9941 1252; 16 Robinson St; light meals $6-10; ☺ breakfast daily, lunch Mon-Sat) On the main drag, this is a good little café with outdoor seating, juices, focaccia, wraps and salads, plus coffee and cake.

There's a supermarket and a couple of takeaways in the Boulevard shopping centre.

Getting There & Away

Skywest (☎ 1300 660 088; www.skywest.com.au) flies to Perth ($200) daily, and has less-frequent flights to Geraldton and Exmouth. Daily **Greyhound Australia** (☎ 13 14 99; www.greyhound .com.au) buses to Perth ($125, 13 hours) and Broome ($190, 20 hours), via Port Hedland, stop at the visitor centre.

GASCOYNE AREA

Good beaches south of Carnarvon include **Eundoo Creek** (the turn-off is 20km down the North-West Coastal Hwy), and **Bush Bay** and **New Beach** (the turn-off is 37km south of Carnarvon); all are accessed via reasonable dirt roads.

Heading north, it's a fair detour to the frenzied **blowholes**, 49km off the main highway along a sealed road, but they are worth a look, as is the rocky, windswept coastline. Keep a sharp eye on the ocean, as people have been killed by king waves here. Just 1km south is a gorgeous, turquoise **lagoon** with coral and tropical fish, best admired via a snorkel and flippers. If you can't drag yourself away there's basic **camping** (sites $5.50). Around 7km to the north of the blowholes, the **HMAS Sydney Memorial** commemorates the ship sunk here by the German raider *Kormoran* in 1941.

Another couple of kilometres brings you to **Quobba Station** (☎ /fax 08-9948 5098; www.quob ba.com.au; powered/unpowered sites per 2 people $18/16, fishing shacks from $38, chalets from $80), an attractive oceanfront property with plenty of basic accommodation, a shop and legendary fishing.

Remote Gascoyne Junction, 177km east of Carnarvon on a good unsealed road (in the process of being upgraded), is in the gemstone-rich **Kennedy Range**. The classic old **Junction Hotel** (☎ 08-9943 0504; fax 08-9943 0564; s/d $55/65, units tw $40) has motel-style rooms and a friendly front bar. From here, the adventurous can continue northeast another 300km to Mt Augustus (Burringurrah) National Park to see **Mt Augustus**, the biggest, but certainly not the most memor-

able, rock in the world. Highlights include the outstanding Aboriginal rock paintings and the rock can be climbed in a day.

Mt Augustus Outback Tourist Resort (☎ 08-9943 0527; powered/unpowered sites per 2 people $22/18, donga d $70, units $175; ☒) is right at the base of Mt Augustus and has good facilities and a licensed restaurant.

CORAL COAST & PILBARA

This mesmerising area of north WA showcases the best of the state's natural wonder alongside the most awesome of its economic endeavours, which here involve digging some seriously big holes. There's even some historical charm thrown in for good measure – and graceful historic stone buildings, battered by over 100 years of extreme weather, have a certain allure when they are planted in red-dirt country alongside turquoise water under big blue skies.

The Coral Coast extends from Coral Bay to Onslow, and includes Ningaloo Marine Park, which protects the world's largest west-coast reef, a rival to the Great Barrier Reef in beauty and biodiversity and far more accessible. The Pilbara region is an arid, expansive landscape that clangs with mining machinery and shudders with ancient memories (the world's oldest rocks are here) and natural wonder. It stretches along the coast from Onslow to Port Hedland and inland

WESTERN AUSTRALIA

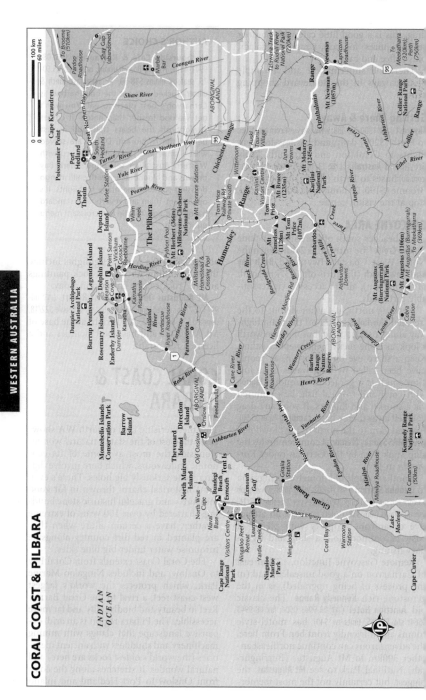

beyond the superb Millstream-Chichester National Park.

Getting There & Away

Skywest (☎ 1300 660 088; www.skywest.com.au) has daily flights from Perth to Port Hedland, sometimes via Karratha. There are also daily Perth–Exmouth flights via Carnarvon twice a week. **Qantas** (☎ 13 13 13; www.qantas .com.au) flies from Perth to Karratha and QantasLink has a service to Port Hedland.

Greyhound Australia (☎ 13 14 99; www.grey hound.com.au) has three services a week from Perth to Exmouth ($190, 19¾ hours), via Coral Bay ($190, 18¼ hours). There are also daily services from Perth (with connecting shuttles into Exmouth) stopping at Karratha ($195, 22½ hours) and Port Hedland ($225, 25½ hours). From Port Hedland buses continue to the Kimberley.

NINGALOO MARINE PARK

The stunning Ningaloo Marine Park is a natural wonder that is perhaps the state's most precious natural resource. In recognition of this, the state government has extended the boundaries of the park.

The reef is amazingly accessible, lying only 100m offshore from some parts of the peninsula, and is home to a staggering variety of marine life. Over 220 species of coral have been recorded in the waters, ranging from the slow-growing bommies to delicate branching varieties, and for eight or nine nights after the full moon in March there is a synchronised mass spawning of coral, with a soup of eggs and sperm being released into the water.

It's this coral that attracts the park's most popular visitor, the underwater giant *Rhiniodon typus,* otherwise known as the whale shark. Ningaloo is the only place in the world where these creatures reliably appear each year, making it a mecca for marine biologists and visitors alike. The largest fish in the world, it can weigh up to 21 tonnes, although most weigh between 13 and 15 tonnes, and reach up to 18m long, but this gentle giant is content to feed on plankton and small fish. There are also more than 500 species of fish, plus sharks, enormous manta rays, humpback whales, turtles and dugongs. Even if the whale sharks aren't about when you visit, there's always something fabulous to see here:

March–May Coral spawning.
March–June Whale sharks.
June–November Manta rays.
June/July & October/November Humpback whales.
November–March Turtle nesting and hatching.

The area's two centres are tiny Coral Bay (the only settlement on the park's coastline) and functional Exmouth, a further 140km to the northeast on the continental side of the peninsula. The western side of the peninsula beyond Exmouth has a string of superb beaches, many with small camping grounds right on the water.

For more information on the park, contact **CALM** (☎ 08-9949 1676; 20 Nimitz St, Exmouth).

Whale Shark Tours

Swimming with a whale shark is what many people are here for. Full-day whale shark tours cost around $320 and operate out of both Exmouth (up to eight boats) and Coral Bay (two boats). There's not much between them – Exmouth operators have shorter travel times and also adhere to a 'no sighting policy' (ie you can go on the next available trip if a whale shark isn't spotted), but Coral Bay operators have a higher encounter rate and you don't have to battle seven other boats and scores of people to reach a shark. Outside the whale shark season, half-day manta ray tours are a pretty good substitute and cost around $125, including snorkelling gear, wetsuit and snacks. You need to be a capable swimmer to get the most out of either experience.

Most operators also offer dive trips ($70 to $150) and courses (around $450 for PADI Open Water Certificates, plus medical), although conservation laws prevent you from diving with the whale sharks. Snorkelling equipment is available for around $10/15 per half/full day and it's possible to 'snuba' dive using an air hose for $50 per person.

Good dive spots include the **Labyrinth** and **Blizzard Ridge** in Lighthouse Bay, the **Navy Pier** near Bundegi Beach (one of Australia's top dive sites) and the **Muiron Islands**, 10km northeast of the cape. The last is a breeding sanctuary for green, loggerhead and hawksbill turtles.

Recommended operators:
Coral Bay Adventures (☎ 08-9942 5955; www.coral bayadventures.com.au; Coral Bay)

WESTERN AUSTRALIA

CHANGES TO NINGALOO MARINE PARK

In late 2004 the state government announced extensions to the area covered by the Ningaloo Marine Park: it now encapsulates the whole of the Ningaloo Reef with the southern boundary extending to Red Bluff (it used to end at Amherst Point) in the southwest. From here the park stretches all the way to Bundegi Reef in the northeast, at the tip of the North-West Cape.

The move hasn't been without controversy as recreational fishing has been banned in some areas (sanctuary zones, where fishing is not permitted, have been increased to 34% of the park), particularly around Exmouth, causing an outcry among the fishing-mad locals. If you want to throw a line in the water you should pick up the useful *Ningaloo Marine Park & Murion Islands* map from CALM, which details all the various zones.

The Ningaloo Marine Park now covers an area of 264,000 hectares, and the government will pursue World Heritage listing in the hope that careful management of this precious resource will ensure the economic security of many of the communities of the northwest (tourist numbers have doubled in the past 10 years to around 200,000). For more information, check out www .ningaloocoast.wa.gov.au.

Exmouth Diving Centre (☎ 08-9949 1201; www .exmouthdiving.com.au; Exmouth)

Ningaloo Blue (☎ 1800 811 338, 08-9949 1119; www .ningalooblue.com.au; Exmouth)

Ningaloo Reef Dive (☎ 08-9942 5824; www.ningaloo reefdive.com; Coral Bay)

Three Islands Marine (☎ 08-9949 1994; www.whale sharkdive.com; Exmouth)

There are plenty of other water- and land-based tours from Coral Bay (right), Exmouth (opposite) and Cape Range National Park (p981).

CORAL BAY

☎ 08 / pop 120

At the southern end of Ningaloo Marine Park, this is a tiny, chilled-out community on the edge of a picturesque bay with stunning beaches. Coral reefs lie just off the town beach, making it brilliant for snorkelling, swimming and sunbathing, and it's a good base for outer-reef and wildlife-spotting trips.

After a proposal to build a colossal marine resort was rejected here in 2003, the state government has earmarked new coastal development around Coral Bay to be small scale and low impact only. The Save Ningaloo Campaign (www.save-ningaloo.org), instrumental in rallying opposition to the original development, will no doubt be watching events carefully over the coming years.

There's no visitor centre in Coral Bay, but there are plenty of booking offices that can give you information. Coral Bay's two small shopping centres have supermarkets

with Eftpos facilities and ATMs, while Internet access is available at **Fins Cafe** (☎ 9942 5900; per 30min $3; 🖳).

The beach is the focus of activity and there are many water-based activities on offer here. You can hire snorkels ($15 per day), boogie boards ($6 per hour) and glass-bottomed canoes ($18 per hour).

Tours

Glass Bottom Boats (☎ 9942 5885) and **Sub-Sea Explorer** (☎ 9942 5955) allow you to see beneath the waves without getting wet (one-hour tours adult/child $30/15); both also offer two-hour snorkelling cruises ($40/19).

Coral Bay Adventures (☎ 9942 5955) offers 30-minute scenic flights over Ningaloo Reef (from $55).

ATV Eco Tours (☎ 9942 5873) and **Quad Treks** (☎ 9948 5190) both have a range of self-drive quad-bike tours around the bay, including snorkelling ($70) and sunset ($65) tours.

Also on offer by many of the tour companies are **turtle ecocruises** (adult/child $60/35), which are becoming increasingly popular.

Sleeping & Eating

You'll need to book accommodation ahead during school holidays.

Ningaloo Reef Resort (☎ 9942 5934; www.coral bay.org/resort.htm; motel s/d $135/155, units s/d $150/165; 🅿 🖳 🛋) Right on the beach, this place is that most rare of beasts – a decent resort. Laid-back, comfortable and well-appointed, it has several levels of accommodation (plenty of options for families), including self-contained units, plus the town pub, bottle shop and a beautiful grassed area that fronts the bay and has great views.

Ningaloo Club (☎ 9948 5100; www.ningalooclub .com; dm $20-25, d & tw $85-90, without bathroom $65-70; ✻ ⌨ ☎) This excellent, purpose-built hostel has a modern demeanour and boasts a great pool, first-rate common area with pool tables, lockable cabinets in the dorms (four or 10 beds), a poolside bar area, free movie nights and a well-equipped kitchen.

Peoples Park Caravan Village (☎ 9942 5933; peoplesparkcoralbay@bigpond.com; powered sites per 2 people $29, 1-/2-bedroom cabins $175/195) This is a small, attractive park with lush lawns close to the beach (prime spots are oceanfront – but no tents). Cabins are fully decked out but there are only seven, so get in early.

Bayview Holiday Village (☎ 9385 6655, 9948 5100) It's dearer than its giant, older rival, but is far nicer.

Shades Restaurant (☎ 9942 5934; takeaways $4-9, mains $17-28; ✻ dinner) At Ningaloo Reef Resort, Shades is licensed with takeaway food during the day and upmarket bistro meals for dinner (bookings essential), including whole crayfish in season. There's also a good kiddies' menu.

Reef Cafe (☎ 9942 5882; Bayview Holiday Village; mains $17-26; ✻ dinner) Opens nightly to dole out a variety of dishes including tasty pizzas.

Fins Cafe (☎ 9942 5900; Coral Bay Shopping Village; dinner mains $19-28; ✻ breakfast, lunch & dinner; ⌨) Has good-value brekkies and lunches (burgers, kebabs) to offset the upmarket seafood menu at night (BYO alcohol). There's also plenty of shade and a decent cup of coffee.

There's a bakery and supermarket in the shopping centre.

EXMOUTH

☎ 08 / pop 2500

Wandering emus, palm trees laden with screeching cockatoos, and a burning sun all give Exmouth a somewhat surreal but very Australian edge. On closer inspection, with its haphazard layout, it feels like a town that's never convinced itself it is a town, and is more a collection of buildings. Established in 1967 to support the nearby naval communications base, Exmouth today, due primarily to its location, is a creature of tourism.

Information

Blue's Internet Café (☎ 9949 1119; cnr Kennedy & Thew Sts; per hr $6; ⌨) Fast access.

CALM (☎ 9949 1676; 20 Nimitz St; ✻ 8.15am-5pm Mon-Fri) Can supply maps and guides to the national park.

Challenge Bank (Maidstone Cres) This is an ATM.

D&A Hire Bookshop (☎ 9949 1425; cnr Murat Rd & Pellew St; ✻ Tue-Sun) Good selection of secondhand books.

Exmouth visitor information centre (☎ 1800 287 328, 9949 1176; www.exmouth-australia.com; Murat Rd; ✻ 8.30am-5pm) Has plenty of information and books tours.

What Scooters (☎ 9949 4748; 102 Murat Rd; per hr $4; ⌨)

Sights & Activities

The town is not the attraction here but rather its proximity to Cape Range National Park and Ningaloo Reef. There are also good beaches within cycling or driving distance. **Town Beach** is OK, but **Bundegi Beach**, 12km north, is more attractive and has a licensed kiosk for sunset drinks, while clothing-optional **Mauritius Beach**, 21km from Exmouth near Vlamingh Head Lighthouse, is also popular.

Catch a movie under the stars at **Ningaloo Starlight Cinema** (☎ 9949 1553; Harold Holt Naval Base, Murat Rd; adult/child $11/7), which screens movies during high season – book your beanbag.

Tours

Apart from Ningaloo Marine Park cruises and dives (p977), tours from Exmouth include gulf and gorge safaris and some other water-based options:

Capricorn Kayak Tours (☎ 1800 625 688, 9949 4431; www.capricornkayak.com.au) A range of coastal and camping tours between April and mid-October, including a sunset BBQ (adult/child $50/40) or full-day tour ($130/105).

Neil McLeod's Ningaloo Safari Tours (☎ 9949 1550; www.ningaloosafari.com; adult/child full day $155/115, half day $65/50) Well-regarded trips through Ningaloo Reef, Cape Range National Park and Vlamingh Head. Sunset turtle tour ($45/35) between November and March.

Ningaloo Coral Explorer (☎ 9949 4499) Two-hour coral-viewing and snorkelling tour at 2pm daily from Bundegi Beach (adult/child $40/19).

There are plenty of **fishing charters** and **whale-watching tours** available, plus **camel treks, quad-bike tours** and **surfing lessons**; see the visitor centre for details.

Sleeping

Ningaloo Lodge (☎ 1800 880 949, 9949 4949; www .ningaloolodge.com.au; Lefroy St; d & tw $70-90; ✻ ☎) With straight-up-and-down ageing motel-style rooms (check the mattress is OK), a huge communal kitchen, BBQ and TV room, Ningaloo Lodge offers the best-value midrange accommodation in town.

Sea Breeze Resort (☎ 9949 1800; www.seabreeze resort.com.au; s/d $125/130; ✳ ☎) Out at the naval base, 6km north of town, Sea Breeze is in a converted barracks block, but you'd hardly know it. The large motel rooms, with in-house movies and data ports, are stylishly furnished and there's a bar with regular happy hour, and a restaurant. Rates tend to fluctuate so call in advance.

Ningaloo Club (☎ 9949 1805; www.ningaloochase .com.au; Market St; dm/d $24/50, deluxe r $165; ☐ ☎) Affiliated with the place of the same name in Coral Bay, and about 4km south of town, the safari tents here are very comfy and house two to eight beds. The facilities are superb, including a terrific whale-/dolphin-spotting deck and a pool area surrounded by hammocks. Kick off your shoes and chill.

Potshot Hotel Resort (☎ 9949 1200; www.potshot resort.com; Murat Rd; dm $20, d & tw $60, motel s/d from $80/90, apt d from $145; ✳ ☐ ☎) This sprawling resort offers several levels of accommodation (including Excape Backpackers), plus

two restaurants, four bars and a bottle shop. The cheaper motel rooms are pretty basic but good value for Exmouth.

Osprey Apartments (☎ 9949 1200; www.potshot resort.com; Murat Rd; 2-/3-bedroom units $185/205, d with spa $160; ✳) Just across the road from Potshot and operated by the resort, these luxury, fully self-contained, corrugated apartments are Exmouth's best.

Ningaloo Caravan & Holiday Resort (☎ 1800 652 665, 9949 2377; reception@exmouthresort.com; Murat Rd; powered/unpowered sites per 2 people $26/21, 1-/2-/3-bedroom chalets from $100/140/155; ✳ ☐ ☎) The best of the caravan parks, this shady resort has modern facilities, a café, a dive shop and bike hire. The chalets are extremely well equipped and very stylish.

Winston's Backpackers (Murat Rd; dm $20, d & tw $60) Attached to the Ningaloo Caravan & Holiday Resort, this hostel has OK four-bed dorms and the run of the park's facilities.

Eating

Whaler's Restaurant (☎ 9949 2416; 5 Kennedy St; mains $18-24; ☀ lunch & dinner) There's a great menu here that includes Asian-inspired seafood

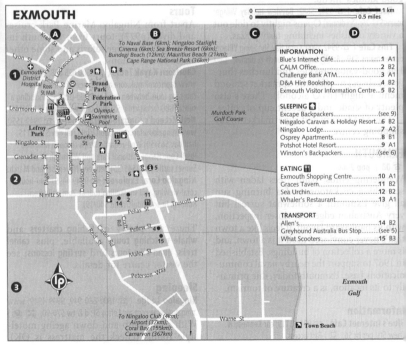

EXMOUTH

dishes, best enjoyed on the breezy veranda. Conveniently, it's licensed and BYO and is also open for brekky in summer.

Graces Tavern (☎ 9949 1000; Murat Rd; mains $10-26; ☺ lunch & dinner; ☐) A modern, family-friendly place with a large dining room and great outdoor tables. The bistro menu has great chef's specials that normally involve a fish, a steak or a pasta dish. Graces is popular and its upmarket pub-grub dining, together with its Redback beer on tap, make it a favourite spot for a meal.

Sea Urchin (☎ 9949 1249; Maidstone Cres; mains $13-18; ☺ lunch & dinner) In a relaxing shaded garden, the cutesy Urchin predictably dishes out seafood mains but also does other dishes, such as laksa, curries and even lasagne. It's all done pretty well, it's BYO and you can takeaway.

There's also a café, bakery and Chinese restaurant at Exmouth shopping centre, along with two supermarkets.

Getting There & Away

There are daily **Skywest** (☎ 1300 660 088; www.skywest.com.au) flights to Carnarvon and on to Perth ($200).

All buses stop at the visitor centre. **Greyhound Australia** (☎ 13 14 99; www.greyhound.com.au) has three buses a week from Perth ($190, 19¾ hours). Or you can hop off the daily Greyhound Perth–Darwin bus at the Giralia turn-off and pick up the Exmouth shuttle there ($35, one hour). From Exmouth, regular services include Kalbarri ($130, 10½ hours), Overlander (for Denham; $105, eight hours) and Coral Bay ($55, 1¾ hours).

Getting Around

The **Airport Shuttle Bus** (☎ 9949 4623; adult/child $18/9) meets all flights.

There are several car-hire outfits, including **Allen's** (☎ 9949 2403; Nimitz St), which charges from $50 per day for secondhand cars.

Ningaloo Caravan & Holiday Resort (per half/full day $5.50/9) hires out bikes.

What Scooters (☎ 9949 4748; 102 Murat Rd; per day $33) provides zippy little mopeds to get around.

CAPE RANGE NATIONAL PARK

This 510-sq-km park runs down the west coast of the peninsula and includes a variety of flora and fauna, rugged scenery, several gorges (the Shothole, Charles Knife and Yardie Creek) plus Owl's Roost Cave. The high-light, however, is the sensational swimming and snorkelling available off every beach.

The modern and informative **Milyering visitor information centre** (☎ 08-9949 2808; milyering@calm.wa.gov.au; ☺ 9am-3.45pm), in the north near the park entrance, houses a comprehensive display of the area's natural and cultural history, and has useful maps and publications.

From Tantabiddi, at the northern end of the park, **Ningaloo Ecology Cruises** (☎ 08-9949 2255; www.ecology.com.au; adult/child $40/10) has two-hour coral-viewing and snorkelling cruises, including free transfers from Exmouth.

One of the park's highlights is the **snorkel drift** at Turquoise Bay, 60km from Exmouth. From the Drift Loop car park, walk about 200m south of the beach side, then go about 30m to 50m into the water and allow the current to carry you across to the sand bar side of the bay while you admire the coral formations and fish below. Make sure you get out at the sand bar – and watch out for strong currents near the gap in the reef.

Those in 4WDs can continue south to Coral Bay via the coast (check at the visitor centre that Yardie Creek is passable).

There are compact **camping grounds** (sites per 2 people $10) dotted along the coast within the park (mainly concentrated in the north) and accessible from the main sealed road running north–south. Facilities and shade are usually minimal, but most have pit toilets; good options include Ned's Camp, Mesa Camp, Lakeside and Turquoise Bay.

Ningaloo Reef Retreat (☎ 1800 999 941, 08-9949 4073; www.ningalooreefretreat.com; swag s $155, wilderness tents $215) is a real getaway; this wilderness experience in the dunes near the entrance to Mandu Mandu Gorge Rd allows you to camp out in swags under the stars or in a more civilised safari tent. Rates are per person, including all food (DIY cooking), Exmouth transfers, park fees, guided nature walks and snorkelling – take a sleeping bag. You can also take a turtle snorkel ($60) or

> **WARNING**
>
> While swimming and snorkelling are the highlights of Cape Range, please be aware that strong currents do occur at beaches everywhere in the park, but particularly in Turquoise Bay. Be vigilant.

WESTERN AUSTRALIA

kayak and snorkel ($90) at the resort. The Ningaloo Reef bus stops here.

Getting There & Away

For those without transport, the **Ningaloo Reef bus** (☎ 1800 999 941) is the best way to get to/from the park. It leaves Exmouth shopping centre at 8.20am (daily April to October, and Monday, Tuesday, Friday and Saturday only November to March) returning from Ningaloo Reef Retreat at 1.30pm. En route it stops at Vlamingh Head Lighthouse ($6), Tantabiddi ($10), Milyering ($20), Turquoise Bay ($20) and Mandu Mandu Gorge.

KARRATHA

☎ 08 / pop 9500

Karratha and neighbouring Dampier make an excellent reprieve from the road and a good place to recharge the batteries. While nothing to write to the folks about, Karratha is a neat, orderly town with great facilities and makes an excellent place for visits to Millstream-Chichester National Park. The lush greenery in town contrasts strongly with the red dirt and blue skies of the Pilbara. Karratha developed alongside the Hamersley Iron and Woodside LNG projects in the 1960s and '70s.

Information

CALM (☎ 9143 1488; Anderson Rd; ☺ 8am-5pm Mon-Fri) Information on Millstream-Chichester National Park.

Karratha Outdoors & Dive Centre (☎ 9185 2299; 1435 Warambie Rd; per hr $7.50; ☐)

Karratha visitor information centre (☎ 9144 4600; www.pilbara.com; Karratha Rd; ☺ 8.30am-5pm Mon-Fri, 9am-4pm Sat & Sun Apr-Nov, 9am-5pm Mon-Fri, 9am-noon Sat Dec-Mar; ☐)

AUSTRALIA'S NUCLEAR ISLANDS

The Montebello Islands, a group of about 100 flat, limestone islands 200km southwest of Dampier, have the dubious distinction of being the site of Britain's first nuclear tests in Australia, in 1952. These days the islands are a conservation park with thriving land and marine fauna. The radiation warning signs remain, along with commemorative plaques, but the islands are considered safe to visit. The best way is to charter a boat from Dampier.

Sights

The 3.5km **Jaburara Heritage Trail** acknowledges the traditional owners, starts by the visitor centre (pick up a copy of the *Jaburara Heritage Trail* leaflet for $2), and gives pointers to carvings and other significant sites. Plenty of indigenous artefacts remain in the area, such as middens, carvings, grindstones and etchings. Ensure you have plenty of water.

Practically a suburb of Karratha, **Dampier** (population 2000), 20km west on King Bay, overlooks the 41 islands of the Dampier Archipelago – a fishing mecca. It's also a Hamersley Iron town and the region's main port facility. Just to the north, **Burrup Peninsula** has some 10,000 Aboriginal rock engravings depicting fish, turtles, kangaroos and a Tasmanian tiger. The best place to see them is near **Hearson's Cove**, a fine swimming beach.

Tours

Snappy Gum Safaris (☎ 9185 2141; www.snappygum.karratha.com) operates well-regarded four-day camping trips to Karijini National Park ($490) that also include the Millstream-Chichester National Park. Also available are day tours of Millstream-Chichester ($130), which depart at least three times weekly in season.

There are plenty of **industrial tours** available as well as **fishing charters** through the beautiful Dampier Archipelago or Montebello Islands; enquire at the visitor centre.

Sleeping & Eating

As in most mining towns, there are no accommodation bargains in Karratha.

Mercure Inn (☎ 9185 1155; www.accorhotels.au; Searipple Rd; d from $130; ☒ ☐) Probably the best value of Karratha's motels, this place has luxury rooms with bar fridge, superduper air-con and a concoction of comforts. Rates change depending on the day, how busy they are, the rotation of the earth…call ahead.

Karratha Backpackers (☎ 9144 4904; www.kisser.net.au/backpackers; 110 Wellard Way; dm/d $20/50; ☒ ☐) This is a very basic hostel, with tired rooms and just passable bathrooms surrounding a small courtyard. The kitchen is good, however, and there's coin-operated air-con, a TV room and tours to the Burrup Peninsula and Roebourne area.

Pilbara Holiday Park (☎ 1800 451 855, 9185 1855; Rosemary Rd; powered/unpowered sites per 2 people $27/22, units from $103; ⊞ ⊡) A forest of young euca-lypts greets campers at the most central of the area's parks, which offers renovated shower blocks, grassed camp sites, a camp-ers' kitchen, TV room and café. The cheaper units are pretty small, but who cares when the air-con works a treat?

Gecko's (☎ 9185 3111; International Hotel, Dampier Rd; mains $17-29; ◷ lunch & dinner) A modern, convivial bar with outdoor seating, decent grub and the local game of whatever on the box. This place is a good blend of con-temporary and traditional Aussie design. Pastas, steaks, fish and chips and salads fea-ture, but the locals come for the infamous ribs.

Barnacle Bob's (☎ 9183 1053; The Esplanade, Damp-ier; mains $10-20; ◷ dinner) Overlooking Dampier Harbour, Bob's has great sunset views to go along with a good list of seafood dishes.

Hearson's Bistro (☎ 9185 1155; Mercure Inn, Searipple Rd; mains $18-26; ◷ breakfast, lunch & dinner) A good steak and seafood place (veggie option too) that's popular with the locals.

Getting There & Away

Skywest (☎ 1300 660 088; www.skywest.com.au) has four weekly flights from Perth to Karratha (from $235), some going on to Port Hed-land. **Qantas** (☎ 13 13 13; www.qantas.com.au) also flies direct from Perth to Karratha.

Greyhound Australia (☎ 13 14 99; www.greyhound .com.au) has daily services to Perth ($195, 22½ hours) and Broome ($115, 11 hours) from the Shell petrol station on Searipple Rd.

ROEBOURNE AREA

Around 40km east of Karratha, **Roebourne** (population 970) is the oldest town in the Pilbara (1866) and home to a large Abori-ginal community. Once a grazing and cop-per-mining centre, it has some fine old buildings, including the **Old Gaol** (☎ 08-9182 1060; Queen St; ◷ 9am-4pm Mon-Fri, 9am-3pm Sat & Sun May-Oct, 9am-3pm Mon-Fri Nov-Apr) – which is now the visitor centre and museum – **Holy Trinity Church** (1894), and **Victoria Hotel**, the last of five original pubs.

Just west of the town of Roebourne, the Point Sampson–Roebourne Rd heads north to Cossack and Point Samson. **Cossack**, at the mouth of the Harding River, was the district's main port from the mid- to late 19th century, but was supplanted by Point Samson and then abandoned. Today, how-

ever, its few stout, stone buildings (1870–98) in the red landscape, opposite turquoise waters, have given it a new lease on life. Attractions include the **Courthouse Museum** (adult/child $2/1; ◷ 9am-4pm), which celebrates the town's halcyon days with historical memorabilia and some B&W photos, and **Cheeditha Aboriginal Gallery** (☎ 08-9182 1060; ◷ 9am-4pm) in the old Galbraiths Store. Be-yond town the pioneer cemetery has a tiny Japanese section dating from the days when Cossack was WA's first major pearl-fishing town. **Cossack Adventure Cruises** (☎ 08-9187 0296) offers trips up the mangrove-lined Harding River and out to Jarman Island ($75, four hours).

Point Samson (population 250) also had its day in the sun as the area's main port, before Dampier shouldered it aside. Today it's an attractive seaside town that buzzes with 4WDs, boats and fishing fans. There's good **snorkelling** off the Point Samson and Honeymoon Cove beaches.

Sleeping & Eating

Cossack Backpackers (☎ 08-9182 1190; dm $22, f $44) In the atmospheric old police barracks, this is the place to chill out for a few days' swim-ming and reading. The austere rooms are kept neat as a pin, and you'll need to bring your own food as the nearby Strand Café isn't open for dinner.

Point Samson Lodge Resort (☎ 08-9187 1052; www.pointsamson.com; 56 Samson Rd; motel/apt d $170/180; ⊞) A pristine and welcoming place with top-notch rooms in cooling tropical grounds. The rooms are all different so ask to see a few. New superdeluxe rooms with spa will be available by the time you read this ($380).

Ta Ta's (Point Samson Lodge Resort, 56 Samson Rd; mains $15-30) Has a seafood (try the chowder) and Thai menu and generous brekkies.

Strand Café (☎ 08-9182 1550; light meals $5-11; ◷ breakfast & lunch) Near Cossack Backpack-ers. There's also a small Aboriginal art gal-lery in the café with some works for sale.

Moby's Kitchen (☎ 08-9187 1435; mains $11-20) At Samson Point, Moby's has excellent takeaway fish and chips.

Samson Beach Trawler's Tavern (☎ 08-9187 1414; mains $17-28) Above Moby's Kitchen, this more upmarket tavern has sweeping views of the bay from its veranda and a great vibe – perfect for a sunset session.

WHIM CREEK CLASSIC

Situated just off the main highway, 82km from Roebourne and 118km from Port Hedland, is Whim Creek Hotel, a classic, historic Aussie outback pub complete with corrugated iron, cold beer, chatty locals and bucket loads of character. Have a recce of the old B&W photos on the walls; the destructive force of cyclones is documented in the images of the damage caused by cyclone John, which ripped through here in 1999. The beer garden has a great wooden-bench seating area, plenty of grass and an aviary of some of WA's more exotic and colourful-looking parrots. There are counter meals available all day ($10) and a joey was hopping around the bar when we called in.

MILLSTREAM-CHICHESTER NATIONAL PARK

Around 150km south of Roebourne, this 2000-sq-km park is well worth the detour. The permanent waterholes of the Fortescue River are the attractions here, creating cool, lush oases in the midst of stony plateaus and basalt ranges.

Millstream visitor information centre (☎ 08-9184 5144; ☾ 8am-4pm) was once the homestead of a pastoral station and now has good information on the park's history and ecosystems, and on its traditional owners, the Yinjibarndi people.

In the park's north, the captivating **Python Pool** is linked to Mt Herbert by the **Chichester Range Camel Trail** (8km one way, three hours). Further south, **Chinderwarriner Pool** and **Crossing Pool** are the highlights, featuring shady palms and lilies. Other walks in the park include the **Murlunmunyjurna Trail** (5km, 1½ hours return) and the **Mt Herbert Track** (600m, 45 minutes return). Pick up a map from the visitor centre.

There are basic **camp sites** (☎ 08-9184 5144; sites per 2 people $10) at Snake Creek, Crossing Pool and Deep Reach Pool, which have fireplaces and pit toilets. Regular tours of the park leave from Karratha (p982).

MARBLE BAR

☎ 08 / pop 360

Reputed to be the hottest place in Australia, Marble Bar is 222km southeast of Port Hedland and the centre of a 377,000-sq-km

shire that's larger than New Zealand. **Ironclad Hotel** (☎ 9176 1066; www.geocities.com/ironcladhotel; 15 Francis St; dm $20, donga s/d $70/80, motel s/d $90/100, mains $16-22) is a classic old pub that's the heart and soul of the town, and has pool tables, a beer garden and counter meals.

PORT HEDLAND

☎ 08 / pop 15,000

Port Hedland is not going to win a beauty pageant – the 'brown town' is an antidote to the lovely, charming rural town with graceful historic stone buildings. Instead, Port Hedland is a web of steel, a working, industrial town; the population is here to make money and you are here because you're interested in mining (great big machinery and ore being loaded onto impossibly large tankers gliding in and out of the port right off the edge of town) or you're just passing through.

The helpful **Port Hedland visitor information centre** (☎ 9173 1711; www.discoverwest.com; 13 Wedge St; ☾ 8.30am-4.30pm Mon-Fri, 9am-4pm Sat, 10am-2pm Sun May-Oct, 9am-4pm Mon-Fri, 10am-2pm Sat Nov-Apr; ▣) has loads of info on the town. There are ATMs on Wedge St.

Sights & Activities

You can survey the town and port from the 26m-high **observation tower** (adult/child $2.50/1.50) behind the visitor centre, where you have to pay and sign a waiver (you'll need enclosed shoes). Just to the north, Goode St is the best place to view Port Hedland's own **Staircase to the Moon** (see the boxed text, p986).

Dalgety House Museum (☎ 9173 4311; cnr Wedge & Anderson Sts; admission $3) has splendid displays and recorded dialogues that bring the town's Aboriginal and settler history to life. Check with the visitor centre for opening hours.

The **Courthouse Art Centre & Gallery** (☎ 9173 1064; 16 Edgar Street; admission free; ☾ 9am-4.30pm Mon-Fri) has some interesting temporary art exhibitions (changing monthly) as well as local and Aboriginal art and craft for sale.

Between October and March **flatback turtles** nest on some of the nearby beaches, including Cooke Point, Cemetery and Pretty Pool. Ask at the visitor centre for the turtles' location, but be extremely careful not to spook them and keep your torch switched off.

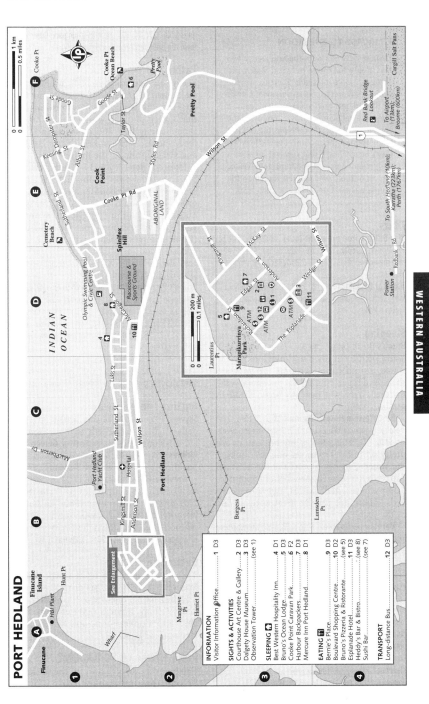

PORT HEDLAND

WESTERN AUSTRALIA

INFORMATION
Visitor Information Office................1 D3

SIGHTS & ACTIVITIES
Courthouse Art Centre & Gallery......2 D3
Dalgety House Museum...................3 D3
Observation Tower........................(see 1)

SLEEPING
Best Western Hospitality Inn............4 D1
Bruno's Ocean Lodge......................5 D3
Cooke Point Caravan Park...............6 F2
Harbour Backpackers......................7 D3
Mercure Inn Port Hedland...............8 D1

EATING
Bernie's Place...............................9 D3
Boulevard Shopping Centre............10 D2
Bruno's Pizzeria & Ristorante.........(see 5)
Esplanade Hotel...........................11 D3
Heddy's Bar & Bistro.....................(see 8)
Sushi Bar...................................(see 7)

TRANSPORT
Long-distance Bus.......................12 D3

STAIRCASE TO THE MOON

If you're between Karratha and Derby two days after a full moon between March and October, don't miss the Staircase to the Moon. It's a pretty cool experience, named for the red-and-gold stairway effect caused when the reflections of the moon hit the rippling mud flats. Broome has the biggest celebration of the monthly spectacle when Town Beach has a real carnival air with a lively evening market and food stalls. Visitor centres in the towns can tell you when the Staircase is next on show.

Tours

BHP Billiton iron ore plant tours (adult/child $18/10; ☻ Mon-Sat) Departs from the visitor centre. You can also take the extended version, which includes a town tour ($30/14).

Harbour Backpackers (☎ 9173 4455; www.harbour lodge.com.au) Recommended for its tours of Karijini National Park.

Sleeping

Bruno's Ocean Lodge (☎ 9173 2635; 7 Richardson St; motel d $75; ☻) In town and overlooking the water, Bruno's motel rooms are in good shape and represent the best midrange value in town. You will need to book ahead in season.

Best Western Hospitality Inn (☎ 9173 1044; www .hospitalityinnporthedland.com.au; Webster St; r ind break-fast $130; ☻) These low-slung brick units are pretty schmick. Try to get one overlooking the water (No 41 is best) for the view, of course, but also as they are better appointed. Rooms have small patios and queen-size beds. There are usually great specials late in the year.

Harbour Backpackers (☎ 9173 4455; www.harbour lodge.com.au; 11 Edgar St; dm $18, d & tw $42; ☻ 🖵) Very close to town, this small, chummy place has a few rooms around a TV lounge, plus a shady front terrace and sushi bar (right). Air-con is free in all the rooms at night.

Also recommended:

Mercure Inn Port Hedland (☎ 9173 1511; www .mercure.com.au; cnr Lukis & McGregor Sts; d $165; ☻) Refurbished rooms (upstairs are the best) and a good position on the water.

Cooke Point Caravan Park (☎ 9173 1271; www .fleetwood.com.au; cnr Athol & Taylor Sts; powered/ unpowered sites per 2 people $28/22, motel d $79, units $100-127; ☻ 🖳) Neat-as-a-pin park. Buses into town run every few hours (weekdays only).

Eating

Heddy's Bar & Bistro (☎ 9173 1511; cnr Lukis & McGregor Sts; mains $19-27; ☻ lunch & dinner) At the Mercure Inn, this is a huge, glitzy, bustling place that's very popular with locals, who don their Sunday best and come for a decent feed. Pastas, wok-cooked dishes, seafood and steak dominate the menu.

Esplanade Hotel (☎ 9173 1798; Anderson St; meals $15-26; ☻ lunch & dinner) At this hotel is a good selection of sizable counter meals (including grilled barramundi), a cavernous courtyard, outside bar and thumping sound system. If you want to see how Port Hedland plays (think skimpies), spend an evening here.

Also recommended:

Sushi Bar (Harbour Backpackers, 11 Edgar St; lunches $7.50) Good sushi lunches.

Bruno's Pizzeria & Ristorante (☎ 9173 2047; 7 Richardson St; mains $11-25; ☻ dinner) Pleasant, licensed spot that serves generous portions of basic Italian fare.

Bernie's Place (☎ 9173 4342; Port Plaza, Edgar St; curries $4-8; ☻ lunch) Tasty, homemade curries, available sit-in or takeaway.

There is a supermarket and café at the **Boulevard shopping centre** (cnr Wilson & McGregor Sts).

Getting There & Away

Skywest (☎ 1300 660 088; www.skywest.com.au) has daily flights from Perth to Port Hedland ($240), sometimes via Karratha. **Golden Eagle Airlines** (☎ 9140 1181; www.goldeneagleairlines.com) has three weekly flights to Broome ($415).

Greyhound Australia (☎ 13 14 99; www.grey hound.com.au) has daily buses to Perth ($225, 25½ hours) and Broome ($80, 7½ hours). **Integrity** (☎ 9226 1339; www.integritycoachlines.com .au) motors up and down the Great Northern Hwy to/from Perth ($195) twice a week.

Getting Around

The airport is 13km from town; **Hedland Taxis** (☎ 9172 1010) charges around $25 each way. **Hedland Bus Lines** (☎ 9172 1394) runs limited weekday services between Port Hedland and Cooke Point, and on to South Hedland ($3).

PORT HEDLAND TO BROOME

The highway stays inland for the 601km to Broome, passing through fairly monotonous bushland. However, the coastline just to the west is remote and unspoilt, and there are a few good places to break the journey.

Pardoo Roadhouse (☎ 08-9176 4916; powered/unpowered sites per 2 people $21/18, donga s/d $48/58; ❄ ❅) has some grassy camp sites, fairly plain budget rooms with fridge, laundry facilities, and a restaurant, and is 150km from Port Hedland.

Situated not far from Pardoo Roadhouse (154km) is the turn-off to **Cape Keraudren Reserve**, a great fishing spot with **camp sites** (per vehicle $5).

Eighty Mile Beach Caravan Park (☎ 08-9176 5941; powered/unpowered sites per 2 people $25/19, cabins $70, beachside units $135) is right on a beautiful shell-covered beach, 245km from Port Hedland. This popular park has shady sites, fresh water, a bakery and terrific fishing.

Port Smith Caravan Park (☎ 08-9192 4983; powered/unpowered sites per 2 people $24/14, donga d $60, 6-bed units $130) is on a tidal lagoon, 477km from Port Hedland. It has good swimming and fishing, a shop and a nine-hole bush golf course.

RUDALL RIVER NATIONAL PARK

WA's most isolated national park, Rudall River (Karlamilyi) is a breathtakingly beautiful desert region of 15,000 sq km, 300km east of Newman, and is still occupied by the Martu people. This unforgiving country features low-lying ranges and salt lakes, split by the seasonal, gum-lined Rudall River. There are no facilities, but you can rough camp. Only those in totally self-sufficient 4WD vehicles should attempt this trip.

THE KIMBERLEY

WA's rough, uncut gemstone, the rugged Kimberley is the state's adventure-travel highlight and, in Broome, contains its most exotic and intriguing northern rural town. The dramatic splendour of the countryside (great rivers, thunderous waterfalls, deep chasms and bulging boab trees, plus deadly saltwater crocodiles in most of the river systems) will sear itself in your mind. One of Australia's last great frontiers, the Kimberley of the 21st century is still a lightly travelled and remote area. Even many sandgropers have failed to penetrate its inner labyrinth. A place of climatic extremes typical of the tropics, this magnificent region is worth seeing any time of year, but in the Wet, when tours slow to a trickle and many sealed roads (and therefore attractions) are closed, you'll need to do much more planning to see the regional sights.

Tours

There are many multiday tours between Broome and Kununurra or Darwin that explore the Kimberley (although they often don't run in the Wet). The price usually includes all park fees, food and equipment. Representative operators:

Flak Track Tours (☎ 08-8894 2228; www.flaktrak .com) A range of tours between Broome and Kununurra, including Mitchell Plateau and Gibb River Rd gorges (nine days $2520), and Purnululu National Park and Gibb River Rd gorges (eight days $1920).

WET OR DRY?

The climatic extremes of the Kimberley make for very different travel experiences, depending on the time of year you visit. The best, but busiest, time to visit is April to September (the Dry). There's little rain, the temperatures are low and all the roads are likely to be open. By October it's already getting hot as the build-up starts, and throughout the Wet (roughly November to March) temperatures of more than 40°C are common.

Probably the Wet's major drawback is the closure of the Gibb River Rd, which blocks exploration of the magnificent northern Kimberley. In addition, opening hours for visitor centres and attractions are reduced and tours run less frequently or not at all. Otherwise, the Wet is definitely not to be sneezed at. It's as hot as blazes, and humid to boot, but the locals are more relaxed, there's plenty of elbowroom and the lack of crowds makes accommodation prices plummet. And when the rains do arrive, you'll be glad you were here to see the spectacle – low, black clouds come at a pace, dumping massive volumes of water during huge thunderstorms with awesome lightning displays. Rivers and creeks can rise rapidly and become impassable torrents within 15 minutes.

Kimberley Adventure Tours (☎ 1800 083 368, 08-9191 2655; www.kimberleyadventures.com.au) Darwin to Broome, taking in Edith Falls, Lake Argyle, Purnululu (Bungle Bungle) National Park and Gibb River Rd (nine days $1400).

Other operators:
Aussie Off Road Tours (☎ 08-9192 3617; www.aussie offroadtours.com.au)

Kimberley Wild (☎ 08-9193 7778; www.kimberley wild.com.au)
Kimberley Wilderness Adventures (☎ 1800 675 222, 08-9277 8444; www.kimberleywilderness.com.au)

Getting There & Away

Qantas (☎ 13 13 13; www.qantas.com.au) has daily flights from Perth to Broome (from $200).

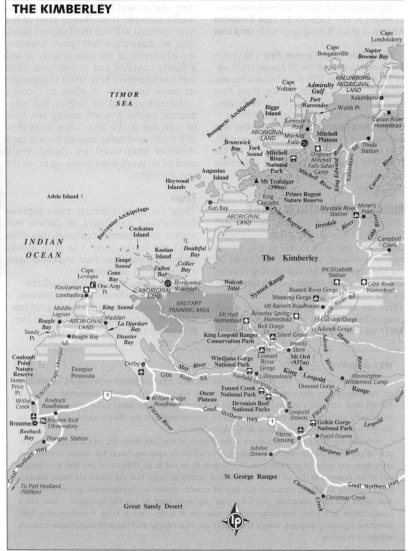

THE KIMBERLEY

There are a couple of direct flights per week to Kununurra from $295 one way. Partner airline **Airnorth** (☎ 8920 4001; www.airnorth .com.au) flies from Broome to Darwin (from $420) and Kununurra (from $320), as well as Kununurra to Darwin (from $245). **Golden Eagle Airlines** (☎ 9172 1777; www.goldeneagle airlines.com) has daily flights from Broome to

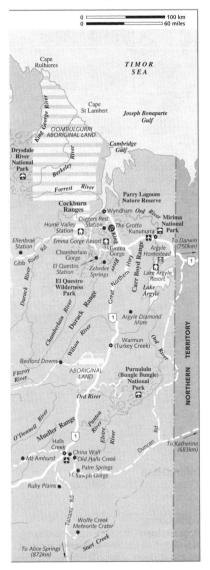

Fitzroy Crossing ($300) and Halls Creek ($375), plus services to Port Hedland ($415, three weekly). It also flies between Broome and Derby ($190, Monday to Saturday).

Greyhound Australia (☎ 13 14 99; www.greyhound .com.au) stops at the Broome visitor centre on its daily Perth–Darwin service. From Darwin, destinations include Kununurra ($185, 9½ hours), Derby ($270, 23½ hours) and Broome ($310, 27 hours). From Broome, fares include Perth ($320, 32¾ hours), Port Hedland ($80, 7½ hours), Derby ($55, 2¾ hours) and Kununurra ($185, 14¾ hours).

BROOME
☎ 08 / pop 14,000

Although a mere pinprick on the colossal north Western Australian coast, Broome looms large in the Australian psyche. Broome is synonymous with exotic, tropical beaches and the outdoors, and Aussies get a dreamy, faraway look in their eyes at the mention of it. WA's isolation has served it well in the case of the north's largest town, helping to preserve Broome's frontier feel despite a well-developed local tourist industry. Gourmet restaurants, all-star resorts and the nouveau riche have detracted from its outback appeal, but instead you'll find a unique culture unlike anywhere else in the state. Broad, white sandy beaches, emerald waters lapping at the feet of mangrove bushes, a historic and well-preserved town centre with a cosmopolitan air and an optimistic beat, blend with the north's languid, laid-back nature. If you can't relax here, we'd suggest therapy. It's a great spot to visit any time of the year with facilities for backpackers right through to those who prefer their cocktails by the saltwater pool. It's also the gateway to the superb wilderness, wildlife and indigenous culture of the vast Kimberley region.

History
Established as a pearling centre by Japanese entrepreneurs in the 1880s, Broome soon attracted communities of Chinese traders and Malay divers, with the latter joining many local Aboriginal people in the dangerous side of the business. Pearling peaked in the early 20th century, when the town's 400 luggers supplied 80% of the world's mother-of-pearl. Today only a handful of boats still operate, with pearl farms having largely replaced open-sea diving.

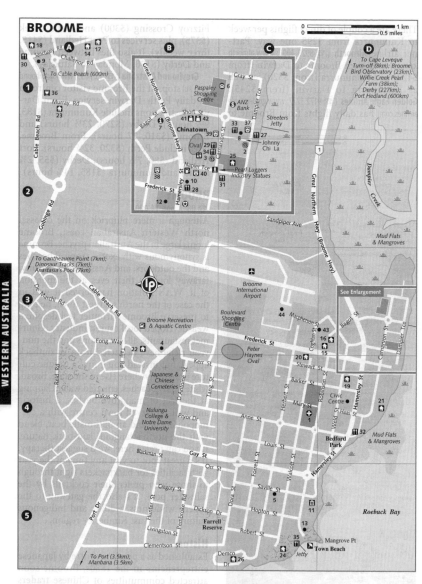

BROOME

WESTERN AUSTRALIA

Orientation

Broome's historical and commercial centre, known as Chinatown, is on the eastern coast of the Dampier Peninsula. Frederick St heads west from here towards Cable Beach. Most of Broome's accommodation, restaurants and sights are found around Chinatown and in the area south down to Town Beach.

Information

There are ATMs in both Carnarvon and Short Sts.

BOOKSHOPS

Magabala Books (☎ 9192 1991; www.magabala.com; 15 Saville St) A rich selection of novels, poetry, biographies and Kimberley history, all written by indigenous Australians.

INFORMATION		Cable Beach Backpackers	17	A1	DRINKING		
Broome Hospital	1 C4	Cable Beach Club	18	A1	Diver's Tavern	36	A1
Chinatown Music Internet Café	2 C2	Courthouse B&B	19	D4	Palms Café Bar	(see 21)	
Internet Outpost	3 B2	Kimberley Klub	20	C4	Roebuck Bay Hotel	(see 25)	
Kimberley Camping Hire	4 B3	Mangrove Resort Hotel	21	D4	Sunset Bar	(see 18)	
Magabala Books	5 C5	Ocean Lodge	22	B3			
Post Office	6 C1	Palm Grove Holiday Resort	23	A1	ENTERTAINMENT		
Visitor Information Centre	7 B1	Roebuck Bay Caravan Park	24	C5	Nippon Inn	37	C1
Woody's Book Exchange	8 C1	Roebuck Bay Hotel Motel &			Sun Cinemas	38	B2
		Backpackers	25	C2	Sun Pictures	39	B1
SIGHTS & ACTIVITIES		Waterfront B&B	26	C5	Tokyo Joe's	40	B2
Broome Crocodile Park	9 A1						
Broome Cycles	10 B2	EATING			SHOPPING		
Broome Historical Society Museum	11 C5	2 Rice	27	C1	Gecko Gallery	41	B1
Courthouse	12 B2	Aarli Bar	28	B2	Monsoon Gallery	(see 32)	
Markets	(see 12)	Bloom's	29	B2	Short Street Gallery	42	B1
Pioneer Cemetery	13 C5	Cable Beach Sandbar & Grill	30	A1			
		Fragipanis Cafe Restaurant	31	C2	TRANSPORT		
SLEEPING		Matso's Café & Brewery	32	D4	Avis	43	D3
Blue Seas Resort	14 A1	Shady Lane Cafe	33	C1	Europcar	44	C3
Broome Motel	15 D3	Son Ming	34	B2	Greyhound Australia Bus Stop	(see 7)	
Broome's Last Resort	16 D3	Town Beach Cafe	35	C5			

Woody's Book Exchange (☎ 9192 8999; Johnny Chi Lane) Decent selection of used titles.

INTERNET ACCESS
Chinatown Music Internet Café (☎ 9192 1443; 20 Dampier Tce; per hr $6; 🖳)
Internet Outpost (☎ 9193 6534; 16 Carnarvon St; per hr $6; 🖳)

MEDICAL SERVICES
Broome Hospital (☎ 9192 9222; Robinson Street)

POST
Post office (Paspaley shopping centre)

TOURIST INFORMATION
Broome visitor information centre (☎ 9192 2222; www.broomevisitorcentre.com.au; cnr Great Northern Hwy & Bagot St; 🕑 8am-5pm Mon-Fri year-round, 9am-1pm Sat & Sun Jan-Mar, 9am-4pm Sat & Sun Apr-Dec) The unflappable and wonderfully helpful staff can book accommodation and tours.
Kimberley Camping Hire (☎ 9193 5354; cnr Frederick St & Cable Beach Rd) A wide range of equipment, including portable fridges, for those going bush.

Sights & Activities
CABLE BEACH
About 4km west of town, **Cable Beach** is one of Australia's finest beaches and has azure waters and a classic, wide, white sandy beach as far as the eye can see. At the northern end (in the suburb of the same name), you can hire surfboards, surf skis and other beach equipment from caravans in the dunes. The long sweep of Cable Beach ends at **Gantheaume Point**, 7km south of Broome. The striking cliffs have eroded into curious shapes, revealing beautiful layers of reds, oranges and yellows that give off a lovely hue at sunset, and at very low tides, 120-million-year-old **dinosaur tracks** are exposed (if the tide's in, there are casts on the cliff top). **Anastasia's Pool** is a rock pool that was built by the lighthouse keeper to soothe his wife's arthritis.

Just back from Cable Beach is **Broome Crocodile Park** (☎ 9192 1489; Cable Beach Rd; adult/child $19/10; 🕑 10am-5pm Mon-Fri, 2-5pm Sat & Sun Apr-Nov, 3.30-5.15pm daily Dec-Mar, tours at 11am & 3pm), which has crocs up to 5m in length, an 80-year-old senior-citizen croc and cute hatchlings to fondle. Try to time your visit with a tour to get the most out of your experience, particularly during the afternoon, when feeding takes place. A new Wildlife Farm was due to open in late 2005 incorporating the current park, but at a new facility; ask at the visitor centre for details.

CHINATOWN & TOWN BEACH
For an indication of Broome's diverse ethnic mix, particularly obvious in its excellent eateries, take a stroll around Chinatown – the old part of Broome. Most of the aesthetically pleasing wood and corrugated-iron buildings that line Carnarvon St and Dampier Tce now house restaurants, shops and galleries.

At **Pearl Luggers** (☎ 9192 2059; 31 Dampier Tce; admission free, tours adult/child $19/9; 🕑 tours 11am & 2pm) you can mosey around two restored pearl boats, but you'll need to join the tour to see the museum: a storehouse of equipment and photographs that provide an interesting insight into Broome's pearling past. Ask about a new tour that should be running in 2006 and involves going out onto the water in a restored pearl lugger.

WESTERN AUSTRALIA

Broome's relatively long and fascinating story is detailed in the intriguing **Broome Historical Society Museum** (☎ 9192 2075; Saville St; adult/child $5/1; 10am-1pm Nov-May, 10am-4pm Mon-Fri & 10am-1pm Sat & Sun Jun-Oct). The museum is refreshingly honest in dealing with indigenous issues. Samples of Aboriginal Dreamtime stories contrast strongly with the cruelty of Broome's early settler days, illustrated by photos of Aboriginal people in chain gangs. The sometimes-forgotten history of the Japanese air raids on north WA is explored, revealing accounts such as the Carnot Bay Incident in 1942, which may compel you to go searching for diamonds on nearby beaches…

There's a **pioneer cemetery** at the end of Robinson St, while another **cemetery**, near Cable Beach Rd, has a large Japanese section, and testifies to the dangers of pearl diving. In 1914 alone, 33 divers tragically died of the bends.

Back towards Chinatown, the 1888 **courthouse** (cnr Hammersley & Frederick Sts) once housed the transmitting equipment for the old cable station (the cable ran to Banyuwangi on Java) and is the venue for a popular Saturday morning **market** (see the boxed text, below).

PORT OF BROOME

A visit to the **Manbana** (☎ 9192 3844; Murakami Rd, Port of Broome; tours adult/child $15/8; tours at 10.30am & 1.30pm) aquaculture centre is highly recommended. The strong links between indigenous people and the sea and waterways of the Kimberley are explored through laid-back and informative tours. Ingenious traditional fishing methods are explained and there are touch tanks where you get to hold a number of slimy sea creatures (the kids will love it!). You'll see enormous barramundi (which the guide lovingly compares to puppies) hand fed and get a rundown of the trochus project

---

DON'T MISS THE MARKET!

A bubbly market with local crafts and food is held outside the courthouse on Saturday morning. This is a great place to buy a print of that perfect Broome sunset. Keep an eye out for discounted tours, cheap mangoes (in season) and to-die-for fruit smoothies.

(shell-like creatures that are bred here in huge hatcheries and then distributed back into the wild). You'll also get to see scorpion, stone and other hazardous fish close up.

Tours

There are tours galore in and around Broome. The visitor centre has full details and makes bookings.

Astro Tours (☎ 9193 5362; tours $60) A close-up of the night sky.

Broome Day Tours (☎ 1800 801 068; adult/child $55/35) Half-day tours of Broome Peninsula.

Mamabulanjin Tours (☎ 9192 2660; adult/child $55/30) Half-day indigenous perspective on Broome and its history.

Outback Ballooning (☎ 1800 809 790; www.outback ballooning.com.au; adult $280) Get a bird's-eye view over the bay and desert with the Broome Balloon Flight.

Ships of the Desert (☎ 9192 6383) One of several operators providing sunset camel tours ($30) of the area.

Trike Flights (☎ 0407 010 772; per 30min incl instruction $165, per hr $230) For those with an adventurous spirit, get the adrenalin flowing by learning the basics of microflight.

You can also take a hovercraft ride, fishing charter or art-and-craft tour; see the visitor centre for details. Tours of Dampier Peninsula (p996), the Kimberley (p987) and the Devonian Reef National Parks (p1000) also operate out of Broome. During the Wet, enquire at the visitor centre as many of these tour companies close for the season.

Festivals & Events

The people of Broome love nothing more than a good party and there are plenty of festivals. Exact dates vary from year to year – contact the visitor centre for more information. Some highlights:

Dragon Boat Classic March/April.

Mango Festival November.

Shinju Matsuri Festival of the Pearl; held July/August.

Stompen Ground Aboriginal music festival held in September/October.

Sleeping

The cost of Broome's accommodation skyrockets during the Dry. If you're here in the Wet, compare deals as competition is fierce. High-season prices are listed in this section.

TOP FIVE SUNSET SPOTS

There are lots of top places to take in a memorable Broome sunset but the following are our favourites:

■ Sunset Bar at the Cable Beach Club (p994) – Anywhere is good along Cable Beach, but you can't beat the hint of decadence at this well-heeled bar. It's also a good spot to see the camel trains as they come off the beach just as the sun is dipping.

■ Matso's Café & Brewery (p995) – Although great for a drink anytime, it's somehow close to perfect in the evening.

■ Gantheaume Point (p991) – Grab your fave bottle of wine, a couple of glasses, a rug and set up shop on the colourful cliffs here. Ideal for couples.

■ Palms Café Bar at the Mangrove Resort Hotel (p994) – This place just makes you feel special: where else can you sip a cocktail as you watch the sun set over the mangroves, while playing a game of giant chess?

■ Roebuck Bay Caravan Park (below) – Park yourself on the grass overlooking the wide sweep of the bay and watch the sun set over green waters.

BUDGET

Cable Beach Backpackers (☎ 1800 655 011, 9193 5511; www.cablebeachbackpackers.com; 12 Sanctuary Rd; dm $19, d & tw $65; ✗ ▢ ⬚) This easy-going place is the spot to head for if you want to spend your time relaxing by the beach. The tiny pool invites frolicking about with other travellers, while hammocks complement its laid-back vibe. Choose from clean dorms or roomy doubles in the original house.

Kimberley Klub (☎ 9192 3233; www.kimberleyklub .com; 62 Frederick St; dm $23-25, d & tw $75; ✗ ▢ ⬚) A large setup and a well-run operation within walking distance to town, it's more budget resort than backpackers hostel. There's plenty of greenery, large common areas, a tour desk and a poolside bar. The Klub is not as personal as other places, but the excellent facilities will ensure boredom isn't a problem. Dorms have no air-con but they're in good shape.

Broome's Last Resort (☎ 1800 801 918, 9193 5000; www.broomeslastresort.com.au; 2 Bagot St; dm $21-24, d & tw $65; ✗) Close to the town centre, this fine old veranda-ed place is *the* spot to party. A great pool and smallish outdoor area (complete with bar, of course) make it very sociable. In its own words, 'there are piss-ups every night'.

Roebuck Bay Caravan Park (☎ 9192 1366; Walcott St; powered/unpowered sites per 2 people $24/20, on-site caravans d $60; ✗) A ramshackle caravan park bursting with greenery right on Town Beach. There are excellent on-site caravans (with air-con, gas stove and TV), which are a little rough and ready, but roomy. Try asking for No 41A – the view is unbeatable. There are also some excellent grassy camp sites overlooking the green waters of Roebuck Bay.

MIDRANGE

Courthouse B&B (☎ 9192 2733; www.thecourthouse .com.au; 10 Stewart St; r incl breakfast $150-170; ✗ Mar-Dec; ✗ ⬚) If you like personal touches – Aussie style – this is the place for you. Your space is very much integrated with your hosts', who will probably pull up a pew while you eat breakfast. An open, airy, laid-back ambience, tropical gardens, a pool and a BBQ area nudge guests into total relaxation.

Palm Grove Holiday Resort (☎ 1800 803 336, 9192 3336; www.palmgrove.com.au; Murray Rd; powered/un-powered sites per 2 people $30/26, studio d $130, cabins $150; ✗ ▢ ⬚) Across from Cable Beach the upmarket, caravan park–style studios and two-bedroom cabins here are modern and spacious. They all have fully equipped kitchens, TV and front balcony, and some have spas. Most cabins are surrounded by a collage of greenery enhancing a sense of privacy.

Roebuck Bay Hotel Motel & Backpackers (☎ 18 00 098 824, 9192 1221; www.roey.com.au; Carnarvon St; 4-/8-/12-bed dm $18/17/15, budget/standard/superior motel d $110/120/130; ✗ ⬚) Smack bang in the middle of Chinatown, the Roey's rooms are in good shape, although the budget rooms back onto the rowdy live-music area. You

WESTERN AUSTRALIA

get a lot more space, and sink-in-and-smile beds, in the superior rooms. Proximity to the pub is the main attraction of its dorm rooms.

Also recommended:

Broome Motel (☎ 1800 683 867, 9192 7775; www .broomemotel.com.au; 51-57 Frederick St; motel d $99, f apt $130; 🞩) Central and popular, with small rooms in good nick.

Ocean Lodge (☎ 1800 600 603, 9193 7700; www .oceanlodge.com.au; 1 Cable Beach Rd; d & tw $110, f $130; 🞩 🖳 🖭) Rooms are a little tired, the service is indifferent, but it has some of the cheapest rates in the off season.

Blue Seas Resort (☎ 1800 637 415, 9192 0999; www .blueseasresort.com.au; 10 Sanctuary Rd; 4-person apt $205; 🞩 🖭) Excellent value for families; near Cable Beach.

TOP END

Cable Beach Club (☎ 1800 199 099, 9192 0400; www .cablebeachclub.com; Cable Beach Rd; d $220-460; 🞩 🖳 🖭) A $7 million refurbishment has turned this resort into something special. Beautifully designed and offering first-class service, it still manages a laid-back edge. Understated, rustic rooms with corrugated-iron walls blend perfectly into the dark red polished-wood furniture – it's all very tasteful, and there are excellent-value package deals in the Wet.

Mangrove Resort Hotel (☎ 1800 094 818, 9192 1303; www.mangrovehotel.com.au; Carnarvon St; d from $185; 🞩 🖭) A good spot for those with a romantic twinkle in their eye. There's a range of luxury accommodation here, from flashy motel-style rooms to suites with spas and jaw-dropping views of the coast.

AUTHOR'S CHOICE

Waterfront B&B (☎ 9192 6661; www.broome bb.com; 10 Demco Dr; r incl breakfast $130-150; 🕑 Apr-Jan; 🞩 🖭) Overlooking Roebuck Bay, this place is a real treat. The two Mediterranean-inspired, understated, luxury rooms (one with waterbed) peer out through lush vegetation onto a lap pool and – here's the best bit – in between is a shared outdoor bathroom…you can shower under the stars (don't worry, it's discreet!). Little extras such as a huge breakfast and robes in your room make this place a favourite. No kids, no smokers.

Eating

Broome has the only decent restaurant scene between Perth and Darwin, so frustrated foodies should take full advantage. Note that many places keep shorter opening hours in the Wet.

Aarli Bar (☎ 9192 5529; cnr Frederick & Hamersley Sts; breakfasts $14, mains $10-15; 🕑 breakfast, lunch & dinner) A small place with a big menu; the tapas selection gives diners variety, while the wood-fired pizzas will satisfy the most persistent hunger pangs. Delicious whole-fish meals to share (from $50) are also on offer. And besides, where else in town can you get char-grilled figs with spicy ricotta and honey for breakfast?

Bloom's (☎ 9193 6366; 31 Carnarvon St; entrées $5-10, mains $14-20; 🕑 breakfast, lunch & dinner) Bloom's is busy and popular casual dining, set in an old atmospheric timber building. There's an innovative tapas menu ($5 to $7) and they do delicious things with salads, salmon and mussels, and much, much more. Try the tasty salt-and-pepper crispy calamari – perfect with a vodka granita.

Cable Beach Sandbar & Grill (☎ 9193 5090; Cable Beach Rd; mains $15-22; 🕑 breakfast, lunch & dinner) In a prime spot overlooking an immaculately clipped lawn and the azure waters of Cable Beach, this breezy, licensed place prepares decent seafood and steak meals. Good nippers' nosh is available and remember, no singlets, thongs or nudity after 7pm, but before 7pm…

Town Beach Cafe (☎ 9193 5585; Robinson St; mains $18-25; 🕑 breakfast, lunch & dinner) Right on Town Beach, this BYO café has plenty of outdoor tables to enjoy both the seafood menu and the cool breeze off the water. Arrive early during the Dry to get a table, and cross your fingers that the succulent tiger prawns are on the menu.

2 Rice (☎ 9192 1395; 26 Dampier Tce; sushi $7.80, curries $14; 🕑 breakfast, lunch & dinner) Chilled-out, comfy and licensed, 2 Rice serves quality Asian food, and Broome is one place in country WA where Asian food *doesn't* mean a chop suey knocked up by a bloke called Trevor. The menu includes Thai, Malay and Japanese dishes deftly assembled from authentic ingredients. There's eat-in or takeaway.

Also recommended:

Son Ming (☎ 9192 2192; Carnarvon St; mains $13-18; 🕑 lunch & dinner) Good spot for a quick feed before a movie at Sun Pictures. BYO.

Matso's Café & Brewery (☎ 9193 5811; 60 Hamersley St; mains $16-25; 🕒 lunch & dinner) Life doesn't get any better in Broome than the relaxed dining in this heritage-listed building overlooking Roebuck Bay. Broome's only brewery has a great selection of boutique beers (if you're here in November, try a Mango Ale with its superb, limey, lingering finish) and a Mod Oz menu in the evening. There's terrific outdoor seating and a roomy bar inside which is surrounded by vivid paintings of scenes of the Top End hanging from corrugated walls. A recommended Indian curry selection ($19), traditionally prepared by a former chef from Kerala (watch the fiery mango chutney!), is on offer during the Wet.

Fragipanis Cafe Restaurant (☎ 9193 6766; 5 Napier Tce; mains $13-17; 🕒 breakfast, lunch & dinner) Offers Mediterranean-inspired food. Tuesday and Wednesday nights mean $14 pasta specials.

Shady Lane Cafe (☎ 9192 2060; Johnny Chi Lane; breakfasts $6-11, lunches $7-12; 🕒 breakfast & lunch) Generous serves are well complemented by fresh juices.

Drinking

See the boxed text, p993, for the best places in town for a drink while watching a flaming sun dip over the water.

Roebuck Bay Hotel (☎ 9192 1221; 45 Dampier Tce) The Roey is a barn of an Aussie pub, smack in the centre of town – it's great for meeting locals and shooting some stick.

Diver's Tavern (☎ 9193 6066; 12 Cable Beach Rd) Slightly more civilised than the Roey, Diver's has a popular Wednesday open-mic night – $5 pints and a free sausage sizzle draw the punters, who are a good mix of locals and travellers.

Entertainment

Sun Pictures (☎ 9192 1077; 27 Carnarvon St; adult/child $14/8) The world's oldest open-air cinema (1916) and a real gem. Settling back on a deck chair to watch the latest flick here is an absolute must.

Sun Cinemas (☎ 9192 3199; 3 Weld St; adult/child $14/8.50) There are two screens here.

The Roebuck Bay Hotel (above) and Diver's Tavern (above) are good spots for live music – drop by to find out who's playing.

To shake your tush to great Aussie tunes, **Tokyo Joe's** (☎ 9193 7222; 52 Napier Tce) and the more upmarket **Nippon Inn** (☎ 9192 1941; Dampier Tce) are the clubs in town. Cover charges are around $6 (sometimes free before 11pm) and they pump till the early hours.

Shopping

Monsoon Gallery (☎ 9193 5379; www.monsoongallery .com.au; Hammersley St) Serious art lovers should make a beeline for this place to admire leading Western Australian contemporary works of art, including some cracking local landscape paintings and exquisite pottery.

Gecko Gallery (☎ 9192 8909; www.geckogallery .com; 9 Short St) Has a broad range of local and regional Aboriginal art (some cheaper souvenir pieces are available).

Short St Gallery (☎ 9192 2658; www.shortstgallery .com; 7 Short St) Next door, and similar to Gecko Gallery.

If you're after pearls, boutiques line Dampier Tce and Short St.

Getting There & Away

Broome is a regional hub with flights or links to all Australian capitals including Perth ($250) and major towns, as well as towns throughout the Kimberley. **Greyhound Australia** (☎ 13 14 99; www.greyhound.com.au) stops at the visitor centre. See p988 for details.

Getting Around

The **Town Bus** (☎ 9193 6585; adult/child $2.70/1) links Chinatown with Cable Beach every hour, via most of Broome's places to stay. From April to December there is also a daily Nightrider service (adult $3.50).

Just Broome (☎ 9192 6636) has hire cars from $33 a day (delivered to your door), but they're for local use only; check that the aircon works. Try also **Avis** (☎ 9193 5980; Coghlan St) or **Europcar** (☎ 9193 7788; Broome Airport). If you're after a 4WD, check the daily kilometre allowance, as the charges can be ruinous.

Good mountain bikes are available for hire from **Broome Cycles** (☎ 9192 1871; 2 Hamersley St) for $18/70 per day/week. If you need a cab, contact **Chinatown Taxis** (☎ 1800 811 772).

AROUND BROOME
Broome Bird Observatory

In an isolated spot on the mud flats of Roebuck Bay, this beautiful **observatory** (☎ 08-9193 5600; www.birdsaustralia.com.au; Crab Creek Rd; adult/child

$5/free) is a vital staging post for hundreds of types of migratory species, including 49 wader species (nearly a quarter of the world's total species). An incredible 800,000 birds arrive in Broome each year. If you've any interest in wildlife, this place is well worth a visit. Excellent tours from the observatory/Broome cost $50/75, or you can do a one-hour introductory tour (from the observatory only; $12). There's a range of **accommodation** (powered/unpowered sites per person $14/11, donga s/d $30/35, d $50-60, self-contained chalets from $100).

The observatory is located 25km from Broome – access is via a good dirt road (fine for 2WD cars), although it may be closed in the Wet.

Dampier Peninsula

A wonderful area of striking coastal vistas and tiny Aboriginal communities, the Dampier Peninsula offers activities and unique cultural experiences, all readily accessible from Broome with a 4WD or by tour. The turn-off to the 200km-long dirt Cape Leveque Rd is 7km east of Broome off the highway. This narrow 4WD track is pretty rough, and can be impassable in the Wet, but this just adds to the attraction, as does the simple accommodation – unless you're on a tour, you'll need to be completely self-sufficient.

Many people head straight for the 'resorts' of Middle Lagoon and Kooljaman, but most of the Aboriginal communities offer accommodation, plus cultural, fishing and mud-crabbing tours. The *Dampier Peninsula Travellers Guide* details options; pick up a copy from the Broome visitor centre, where you can check on the condition of the road and book accommodation and tours.

The first turn-off (Manari Rd) takes you past **Willie Creek Pearl Farm** (☎ 08-9193 6000), which can be visited on a half-day bus tour from Broome (adult/child $60/30) or you can join the tour at the farm ($30/12). Another 40km north is **Coulomb Point Nature Reserve**, which protects unique pindan vegetation and the rare bilby.

Back on the main road, it's around 100km to Beagle Bay, most notable for the extraordinary mother-of-pearl altar in the local **church** (☎ 08-9192 4913; admission $5). There's a shop and fuel is available weekdays, but there's no accommodation.

Next is **Middle Lagoon** (☎ 08-9192 4002; day entry per car $8; powered/unpowered sites per 2 people $32/26, beach shelters $45, cabins $125), a simple spot right on the beach run by a friendly local couple and boasting fantastic swimming, snorkelling and fishing.

Between Middle Lagoon and Cape Leveque are the turn-offs to **La Djarardr Bay** (☎ 08-9192 4896; sites per 2 people $25; guided walks from $33), **Maddarr** (☎ 08-9192 6070; sites per 2 people incl guided walks $100, day pass $50), **Lombadina** (☎ 08-9192 4936; dm $44, units $154, guided walks $33-99, boat tours $154; ☯ fuel Mon-Fri) and **Mudnunn** (☎ 08-9192 4121; sites per 2 people $28, mud-crabbing $55). For these communities, everything needs to be booked in advance and permits may be required (available from the Broome visitor centre). Some communities may encourage you to visit only on weekdays.

Cape Leveque, at the tip of the peninsula, is a magnificent spot, with wonderful beaches and stunning red cliffs. **Kooljaman** (☎ 08-9192 4970; www.kooljaman.com.au; powered/unpowered sites per 2 people $32/28, beach shelters $50, units $90, safari tents $190) is an unhurried, spacious place that gets very busy in season, but can be almost deserted off season. Try to get a beach shelter (you'll need to book); they're open air, right on the beach and each has its own BBQ – a steak, a coldie and a sunset, and all is well with the world. Other facilities include mud-crabbing tours, dinghy hire, snorkelling (no crocs so far!) and a basic shop.

TOURS

In the Wet contact the Broome visitor centre as they keep track of which companies are heading out. Some tour operators:

Aussie Off Road Tours (☎ 08-9192 3617; www.aussieoffroadtours.com.au; two-day tours $365)

Golden Eagle Airlines (☎ 08-9191 1132; www.goldeneagleairlines.com) Scenic flights from Derby ($285).

Kimberley Wild (☎ 08-9193 7778; www.kimberleywild.com.au; one-day tours $209)

DERBY

☎ 08 / pop 5000

The administrative centre for West Kimberley, this laid-back town shuffles along at a languid pace, making it ideal if you want to escape Broome's hustle and bustle. Strategically, it's well placed as the western entrance to the Gibb River Rd, the spectacular gorges of the Devonian Reef National Parks and the remote islands of the Buccaneer Archipelago. On a peninsula jutting into King Sound, 219km from Broome, Derby is surrounded by huge tidal mud flats, baked hard in the Dry and occasionally flooded by king tides.

Information

Most shops and services are located in the town centre on Loch and Clarendon Sts. It's here you'll find the post office and ATM.

Derby Telecentre (☎ 9193 1272; Clarendon St; per 15min/hr $2.25/9; 🖳))

Derby visitor information centre (☎ 1800 621 426, 9191 1426; www.derbytourism.com.au; 2 Clarendon St; 🕑 8.30am-4.30pm Mon-Fri year-round, 9am-4pm Sat & Sun Jun-Aug, 9am-1pm Sat & Sun Apr, May & Sep, 9am-noon Sat Oct-Mar; 🖳)

Sights & Activities

The **Boab Prison Tree** (admission free; 🕑 24hr), 7km south of town, is probably Derby's most famous attraction. With a girth of 14m and a hollow trunk, it's said to be over 1000 years old. It was used as a prison or holding bay by blackbirders, settlers who captured and used Aboriginal people in the pearling industry. It serves as a stark reminder of crimes against indigenous people in WA and holds an air of ancient majesty and sadness. Prisoners were held here en route to the grim **Old Derby Gaol** (Loch St; admission free; 🕑 24hr), next to the police station. You can examine the rusty iron rings that are bolted into the floors here, and were used to chain prisoners to the ground. **Wharfinger's House Museum** (cnr Loch & Elder Sts; admission by gold coin do-

nation; 🕑 8.30am-4.30pm Mon-Fri year-round, 9am-4pm Sat & Sun Jun-Aug, 9am-1pm Sat & Sun Apr, May & Sep, 9am-noon Sat Oct-Mar) has historic displays (get the key from the visitor centre). It won't set your world on fire, but it's pioneer, battler stuff and is good for killing an hour. Derby's lofty **wharf** is a good fishing spot and the best place to see the town's colossal tidal flow – generally there's about 11m difference between high and low.

The **Boab Festival**, held in July, features concerts, sports (including mud footy) and street parades.

Derby's greatest drawcard is its access to the natural splendour of **King Sound** and the **Buccaneer Archipelago**, a combination of remote coastline and uninhabited islands that offer amazing walking, swimming, fishing, bird-watching and camping opportunities.

Tours

Operators of sea safaris into the Buccaneer Archipelago, ranging from four to 15 days, include **Buccaneer Sea Safaris** (☎ 9191 1991; www.buccaneerseasafaris.com) and **One Tide Charters** (☎ 9193 1358; www.onetide.com). Prices start at around $1400 for four days, all inclusive, and you will need to book and pay well in advance.

Ask at the visitor centre about the popular four-hour **Horizontal Falls Fly-Cruise** ($270), which takes in a flight to Talbot Bay and then a cruise to the startling horizontal falls.

Tours are also available to the fabulous Windjana Gorge and Tunnel Creek.

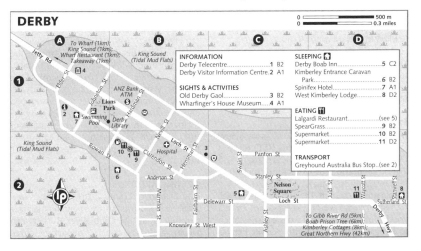

Sleeping

Derby Boab Inn (☎ 9191 1044; Loch St; budget s/d $50/80, deluxe $80/120; ❄ ⛱) The rooms at this professionally run place are possibly the best deal in town. The budget rooms are fairly basic with creaky floors but are comfy enough. The motel-style rooms are 1970s-era, have been well looked after with bright décor, and are pretty good value for the Kimberley.

West Kimberley Lodge (☎ 9191 1031; Sutherland St; s/d $70/80, without bathroom $60/65, powered sites per 2 people $24; ❄) Rooms are well kept at this neat place, although the ones without a bathroom can be a little claustrophobic. This is compensated for by lush gardens and a great BBQ area. There's also an orderly camping ground with the ablutions block holding pride of place (apparently people from all over Australia comment on this facility).

Spinifex Hotel (☎ 9191 1233; Clarendon St; spinifex hotel@westnet.com.au; dm $20, budget s/d $50/55, motel $60/75; ❄) The good news for budget travellers is that Derby's first backpackers hostel is currently being built – the bad news is that if it's not yet open, your only budget option in town is this place. The four-bed dorms here are dark, very basic and not altogether clean. They're OK if you don't mind roughing it for a night or two. The budget rooms are also pretty tired and flyblown. The Spinny seems to do a fair bit of business from folk too pissed to drive home from the pub.

Also recommended:

Kimberley Cottages (☎ 9191 1114; www.kimberley cottages.com.au; Windjana Rd; 2-/3-bedroom chalets $125/165, s $35; ❄) On a farm 8km from town off the Gibb River Rd. Fully self-contained cottages perfect for small groups.

Kimberley Entrance Caravan Park (☎ 9193 1055; kecp@westnet.com.au; Rowan St; powered/unpowered sites per 2 people $24/18) Friendly owners and plenty of shade. Sites 153 to 179 are best for sunsets over the tidal flats.

Eating

Wharf Restaurant (☎ 9191 1195; mains $15-25; ☽ Dry) Right on the jetty, this BYO place is Derby's best, with lush tropical gardens and a good reputation for its seafood (including takeaways after 11am).

Lalgardi Restaurant (☎ 9191 1044; Derby Boab Inn, Loch St; mains $18-25; ☽ lunch & dinner) Puts a good spin on traditional Aussie dishes, such as kangaroo flavoured with pepper berries

and served with smoked-corn relish. It also does sushi, salads and a vegetable calzone.

SpearGrass (☎ 9191 2725; Clarendon St; meals $5-10; ☽ breakfast & lunch; ❄) This small lunch bar serves up decent sandwiches, wraps, souvlakis, burgers and, of course, pies. There's simple dining inside or some shady outdoor seating.

There are supermarkets on Loch and Clarendon Sts.

Getting There & Away

Golden Eagle (☎ 9191 1132; www.goldeneagle.com; Derby airport) flies between Derby and Broome ($190). Daily **Greyhound Australia** (☎ 13 14 99; www.greyhound.com.au) buses to Darwin and Perth stop at the visitor information centre. The Gibb River Express runs between Derby and Kununurra (below) along the Gibb River Rd.

GIBB RIVER ROAD

The 664km dirt 'back road' from Derby to Wyndham/Kununurra is more direct than the Great Northern Hwy by several hundred kilometres. However, it can be extremely rough after rain and is generally closed altogether during the Wet – it's definitely not recommended for conventional vehicles. Even if you plan to stay at stations along the way, you should carry several days' food and water in case you get stranded.

If you want just a taste of back-country adventure, try the 'tourist loop' that takes you 125km along the Gibb River Rd from Derby to the Fairfield Leopold Downs Rd turn-off, and then another 124km past Windjana Gorge and Tunnel Creek to the Great Northern Hwy, 43km west of Fitzroy Crossing.

Before you head off, grab a copy of the indispensable *Gibb River & Kalumburu Roads Travellers Guide* ($4) from any of the regional visitor centres. It has useful advice, plus accommodation (generally dinner, bed and breakfast – DBB), sights and tour information. Some tours also take in parts of this area (p987). Please note that camp-site prices are for two people unless otherwise indicated.

GETTING AROUND

The **Gibb River Express** (☎ 08-9169 1880; www .gibbriverbus.com.au) is an excellent bus service running along the Gibb River Rd between Derby and Kununurra, departing three times a week. You can purchase a hop-on, hop-off ticket for $280, good for three months. The service usually runs from May through to mid-September, depending on weather conditions.

Derby to Mt Barnett Roadhouse

The Lennard River bridge is crossed at 120km and the Yamarra Gap in the King Leopold Range is at 145km. The 5km-long **Lennard River Gorge**, 8km off Gibb River Rd, has a waterfall and refreshing pool.

At 184km is the turn-off to the beautiful **Mt Hart Wilderness Lodge** (☎ 08-9191 4645; www.mthart.com.au; DBB $180), 50km up a rough, 4WD road.

About 26km past the Mt Hart turn-off is **Bell Gorge**, 29km down a 4WD track. It's one of the region's finest, with a picturesque waterfall, and you can camp nearby at **Silent Grove** (adult/child $9/2).

Mornington Wilderness Camp (☎ 08-9191 7406; mornington@australianwildlife.org; sites/DBB $20/185), on the Fitzroy River, is 100km south of the 247km mark and has tours, a bar and canoe hire, while **Beverley Springs Homestead** (☎ 08-9191 4646; beverleysprings@bigpond.com; sites/DBB $33/155) is a working station in gorge country, 43km north of the 251km mark.

Horseshoe-shaped **Galvans Gorge** has a swimming hole less than 1km off the road at the 286km mark.

Mt Barnett Roadhouse (☎ /fax 08-9191 7007; sites $20), at the 306km point, is owned by Kupingarri Aboriginal community and has fuel and a general store. **Manning Gorge** lies 7km along an easy dirt track and camping is by a lovely water hole.

Mt Barnett to Wyndham – Kununurra Road

Barnett River Gorge is another good swimming spot, 5km off the 328km mark. Another 10km along is the turn-off to **Mt Elizabeth Station** (☎ /fax 08-9191 4644; mt.elizabeth@bigpond .com; sites/DBB $22/160), a working station 30km off the road.

At 406km you reach the Kalumburu turn-off. The road then continues through magnificent scenery; at 579km there are excellent views of the Cockburn Ranges to the north, the Cambridge Gulf and the Pentecost and Durack Rivers. About 2km further is **Home Valley Station** (☎ /fax 08-9161 4322; sites/DBB $20/110), which offers 4WD and

fishing tours of the local area, and at 590km is the **Pentecost River** crossing, which can be dodgy when the water is up.

At 614km the million-acre **El Questro Wilderness Park** (☎ 08-9169 1777; www.elquestro.com.au; sites $30; ☑ Apr-Nov) is the best-known station in the Kimberley – so well known there's an entry fee (Wilderness Park/Emma Gorge $15/7.50).

Attractions include **El Questro Gorge**, **Zebedee Springs**, boat rides up **Chamberlain Gorge** and spectacular **Emma Gorge** (at 623km) where a 40-minute walk takes you to a pool with a high waterfall. Luxurious accommodation is split between the **El Questro Homestead** (s/d incl all meals from $850/1700) and **Emma Gorge Resort** (cabins $135, 4-bedroom bungalows $220), both of which have a restaurant and bar. At 630km you cross King River and at 647km you finally hit the bitumen road; Wyndham lies 48km to the northwest, Kununurra 52km east.

KALUMBURU ROAD

This dirt road traverses extremely rocky terrain in an isolated area. Distances are given from the junction of the Gibb River and Kalumburu Rds, 419km from the Derby Hwy and 248km from the Wyndham–Kununurra road.

You need two permits to visit the Kalumburu community. The first is free, and available in advance online at www.dia.wa.gov .au, or from **Department of Indigenous Affairs offices** (Perth ☎ 08-9235 8000; Broome ☎ 08-9192 2865; Derby ☎ 08-9191 2066; Kununurra ☎ 08-9168 2550). The second is issued by the **Kalumburu community** (☎ 08-9161 4300; kac10@bigpond.com; ☑ 8am-noon, 1.30-4pm Mon-Fri) in advance or on arrival. It costs $35 per car and is good for seven days.

Please note that camping prices are for two people unless indicated otherwise.

Gibb River Road to Mitchell Plateau

After crossing the Gibb River at 3km and Plain Creek at 16km, **Drysdale River Station** (☎ 08-9161 4326; www.drysdaleriver.com.au; powered/ unpowered sites $28/22, d & tw $100) is the first fuel stop, at 59km, and has supplies, meals and **scenic flights** (from $200). The homestead is 1km down a side road.

At 62km you can turn off to **Miners Pool** (sites $15), also operated by Drysdale River Station. It's 3.5km to the river, and the last 200m is slow going.

The Mitchell Plateau turn-off is at 162km, from where it's 70km to the turn-off to the spectacular, multitiered **Mitchell Falls**. The falls are 16km downhill and you have to walk the final 3km; allow a full day for the walk. In the Dry the water falls from the centre of the terraces. In the Wet, however, they are vastly different. The muddied water stretches from escarpment to escarpment and thunders down submerged terraces. A scenic flight is a great way to see this spectacle. The road continues another 39km north to the coast.

There are several accommodation options in the area, including basic **camp sites** ($18) at King Edward River and Mitchell Plateau, and **Ungolan-Mitchell Falls Safari Camp** (☎ 1800 675 222; DBB $130), at the turn-off to the falls. See the *Gibb River & Kalumburu Roads Travellers Guide* for alternatives.

Mitchell Plateau Turn-Off to Kalumburu

From the Mitchell Plateau turn-off, the road heads northeast and crosses **Carson River** at 247km. Another 20km brings you to the **Kalumburu Aboriginal community** (☎ 08-9161 4333; sites $20, motel s/tw $50/75), about 5km from the mouth of the King Edward River and King Edward Gorge. The picturesque mission sits among giant mango trees and coconut palms, and has a shop, food and **fuel** (◷ 7.15-11.15am & 1.30-4pm Mon-Fri).

Drysdale River National Park

Very few people get into WA's northern-most national park, 100km south of Kalumburu. It's one of the most remote in Australia (there's no road access, but you can bushwalk) and is home to ancient Bradshaw art figures and more recent Wandjina figures, plus waterfalls, gorges and many rare plants and animals. Visitors must register with **CALM** (☎ 08-9168 4200; Ivanhoe Rd) at Kununurra and get a permit from the **Kalumburu Aboriginal Corporation** (☎ 08-9161 4300).

DEVONIAN REEF NATIONAL PARKS

West Kimberley has three national parks featuring beautiful gorges that were once part of a western coral 'great barrier reef' in the Devonian era, 350 million years ago. Windjana Gorge and Tunnel Creek National Parks are accessed via Fairfield Leopold Downs Rd (which links the Great Northern Hwy and Gibb River Rd), while Geikie Gorge National Park is just northeast of the town of Fitzroy Crossing.

The walls of **Windjana Gorge** soar 100m above the Lennard River, which rushes through in the Wet but becomes a series of pools in the Dry. You'll almost certainly see freshwater crocodiles sunning themselves on sand banks or gliding through pools. Bring plenty of water, especially if you intend to make the 7km return walk from the **camping ground** (sites $18) to the end of the gorge.

Three kilometres from the river are the ruins of **Lillimooloora**, an early homestead and a police outpost that dates from 1893. It was here that Aboriginal tracker Jandamarra shot Constable Richardson (see the boxed text, opposite).

Tunnel Creek is a 750m-long passage, 3m to 15m wide, created by the creek cutting through a spur of the Napier Range. You can walk all the way along it in the Dry, but you'll need a torch and a change of shoes (preferably sandals); be prepared to wade through cold, knee-deep water in places. There are several Aboriginal paintings at either end. There's no camping here.

The magnificent **Geikie Gorge**, cut through the Devonian Reef by the Fitzroy River, is 18km north of Fitzroy Crossing on a sealed road. There are creeks to be crossed and the park can be inaccessible in the Wet. The best way to see it is by boat (see below).

Tours

Tours of the gorges run from Broome, Derby and Fitzroy Crossing. Tour operators to Windjana and Tunnel Creek include the following:
Bungoolee Tours (☎ 08-9191 5355; full-day tour $160) A company run by Aboriginal people and operating from Fitzroy Crossing. Rock art is the highlight.

JANDAMARRA

Derby, Windjana Gorge, Tunnel Creek and Lillimooloora were the setting for the legendary exploits of the outlaw Aboriginal tracker Jandamarra, who was nicknamed Pigeon. As a teenager, Jandamarra, a member of the Bunuba tribe, was a highly skilled stockman working on the Lennard River Station. His skills eventually led to him becoming an armed tracker working with the local police to capture Aboriginal people who were spearing sheep.

In October 1894 Pigeon's tribal loyalty got the better of him – he shot a police colleague at Lillimooloora, freed the captured tribesmen and escaped to lead a band of dissident Bunuba people, who evaded search parties for almost three years. Despite being seriously wounded in a shoot-out at Windjana Gorge only a month after his escape, Pigeon survived and continued to taunt the settlers with raids and vanishing acts.

Pigeon killed another four men and in 1897 was finally trapped and killed near his Tunnel Creek hide-out. For the full story, get a copy of the *Pigeon Heritage Trail* ($2.50) from the Derby or Broome visitor centres, or the fascinating *Jandamarra and the Bunuba Resistance* by Howard Pedersen and Banjo Woorunmurra.

Derby Bus Service (☎ 1800 621 426; full-day tour $100) From Derby and Broome.

Kimberley Wild (☎ 08-9193 7778; full-day tour $195) From Broome.

Tours to Geikie Gorge are also on offer:

Broome Day Tours (☎ 1800 801 068; full-day tour $210)

CALM (☎ 9191 5121; 1hr tour adult/child $20/2.50; ☺ tours 8am, 9.30am, 11am & 3pm Apr-Nov) From Fitzroy Crossing; a number of cruises per day; changes monthly.

Darngku Heritage Cruises (☎ 08-9191 5552; half-/full-day tours $60/120) Well-regarded walk-view-cruise from Fitzroy Crossing between April/May and September.

FITZROY CROSSING
☎ 08 / pop 1500

This tiny settlement, where the Great Northern Hwy crosses the Fitzroy River, is a handy place for a breather from the road, as well as a good spot to join a tour of the nearby attractions, such as Geikie and Windjana Gorges. It's also home to the Gooniyandi, Bunuba, Walmajarri and Wangkajungka communities.

The old town site and pub are northeast of the present town and the excellent **Fitzroy Crossing visitor information centre** (☎ 9191 5355; ☺ 8am-5pm Apr-Oct, 9am-4.30pm Mon-Fri Nov-Mar) is on the highway.

Crossing Inn (☎ 9191 5080; crossinginn@bigpond .com.au; Skuthorpe Rd; powered/unpowered sites $15/11, motel s/d $93/110; ☒), more or less a tin shed, is the oldest pub in the Kimberley, and features paintings by local students (art gallery opening soon). Now, who the hell lives out here anyway? To find out, meet the locals in the outside garden bar.

Fitzroy River Lodge (☎ 9191 5141; fitzroyriverlodge@ bigpond.com; Great Northern Hwy; powered/unpowered sites $24/21, safari tent d & tw $130, motel d $175, 6-person apt $293; ☒ ☐ ☒) is a decent if pricey accommodation oasis, 2km east of town. The contemporary self-contained apartments, which could have been flown straight from Perth, are ideal for families or groups. This is all complemented by bars and a **bistro** (mains $14-26) – if you're not comfy here, you really are fussy.

Fitzroy Crossing is 392km east of Broome. **Golden Eagle Airlines** (☎ 9191 1132; www.goldeneagle airlines.com; Derby) has flights to Broome ($300) and Halls Creek ($150) Monday to Saturday.

Greyhound Australia (☎ 13 14 99; www.greyhound .com.au) has daily buses to Perth and Darwin, and stops at the visitor centre between 1am and 2.30am. Stops include Broome ($115, six hours) and Kununurra ($140, eight hours).

HALLS CREEK
☎ 08 / pop 1590

On the edge of the Great Sandy Desert, Halls Creek is a small town with communities of Kidja, Jaru and Gooniyandi people. The town has quite a user-friendly layout, with most services on the highway or Roberta Ave. Pick up local information at **Halls Creek visitor information centre** (☎ 9168 6262; Great Northern Hwy ☺ 8am-4pm, reduced hours Wet). Check your email at the **Telecentre** (Library, Great Northern Hwy; per 20min $2; ☐).

From here there are tours and flights to the Wolfe Creek Meteorite Crater and Purnululu (Bungle Bungle) National Park, while **China Wall**, 5km east and about 1.5km off the road, is a small but picturesque subvertical quartz vein. You can walk the length of it if the weather is OK.

Halls Creek Motel (☎ 9168 6001; hallscreekmotel@ westnet.com.au; 194 Great Northern Hwy; dongas $30-50, r $88-110; ⊠) is a low, huddled group of buildings with refurbished motel rooms and two types of donga (sharing facilities with two or 12 other rooms); it's the best value in town. Licensed **Russian Jacks** (mains $18-28) has a simple, filling menu and a decent outdoor area.

JKs Cafe (Great Northern Hwy; meals $4-9; ⏰ breakfast & lunch), next to the visitor centre, is the best spot in town for breakfast or lunch. Sandwiches and burgers are served under a shady veranda or in air-con comfort.

Golden Eagle (☎ 9172 1777; www.goldeneagleair lines.com) has flights to Fitzroy Crossing and Broome ($340), Monday to Saturday. **Greyhound Australia** (☎ 13 14 99; www.greyhound.com .au) buses run to Perth and Darwin via Kununurra ($91, 4½ hours) and stop at the Poinciana Roadhouse.

WOLFE CREEK METEORITE CRATER

The 835m-wide and 50m-deep Wolfe Creek meteorite crater is the second largest in the world. To the local Jaru people, the crater, called Kandimalal, marks the spot where a huge snake emerged from the ground.

The Wolfe Creek Crater turn-off is 16km west of Halls Creek; from there it's 137km south along the rough, rocky Tanami Track. A 4WD with food, water and fuel supplies is definitely recommended. Otherwise, **Oasis Air** (☎ 08-9168 6462) has a one-hour flight over the crater from Halls Creek ($145).

PURNULULU (BUNGLE BUNGLE) NATIONAL PARK

The 3000-sq-km **Purnululu (Bungle Bungle) National Park** (per car $9) contains the extraordinary Bungle Bungle Range, with its famous striped rock towers, and attracts huge numbers of visitors during the Dry. Amazingly, these formations were only 'discovered' during the 1980s (although the Kidja people were pretty familiar with them). The Bungle Bungles were added to the World Heritage list in 2003. The word *purnululu* means 'sandstone' in the local Kidja dialect, and *bungle bungle* is thought to be a misspelling of *bundle bundle*, a common grass.

The distinctive rounded rock towers ar made of sandstone and rough conglomer ates, and their stripes reflect the amount o water the layers accept: the rock within th dark stripes is more permeable, allowin algae to flourish, while the less permeabl lighter layers are created by iron and man ganese stains. The park is also noted for it Aboriginal art galleries, plus the beautifu pools hidden within the gorges and the ric wildlife they attract, including nailtail wal labies and over 130 bird species.

The park's main attractions all requir some legwork to reach. **Echidna Chasm** in th north and **Cathedral Gorge** in the south ar about an hour's walk from the car parks The soaring **Piccaninny Gorge** is an 18km round trip that takes eight to 10 hours t walk; this makes for a good overnight trip The restricted gorges in the northern part o the park can be seen only from the air.

The park is open only between April and December. If you're driving, the turn-of from the highway is 53km south off War mun. It's then 52km along a rough 4WD track to the Three Ways junction. From here it's 20 minutes north to **Kurrajong Cam** and 45 minutes south to **Walardi Camp**; both have water and toilets, and camping cost $18 for two people.

Tours

Both Kununurra Backpackers and Kim berley Croc Backpackers (p1004) offer **4W camping tours** (two/three days $320/475), or, fo something more swish, **East Kimberley Tour** (☎ 08-9168 2213; www.eastkimberleytours.com.au) ha overnight fly-in tours with cabin accommodation for $995. Several operators also include Purnululu in multiday Kimberley tours; see p987 for details.

Helicopters and light planes offer scenic flights. **Slingair Heliwork WA** (☎ 08-9169 1300; www .slingair.com.au) charges $225/200 from Warmun/Purnululu for a 30-minute chopper flight. **Oasis Air** (☎ 08-9168 6462) has 80-minute plane flights from Halls Creek ($170).

WYNDHAM

☎ 08 / pop 1000

A historic little town wedged in some beautiful countryside, sleepy Wyndham is at the junction of five rivers. It has one of only two crocodile farms in WA, and the 20m concrete croc that greets visitors at the entrance of the town reassures that Wyndham doesn't take itself too seriously.

The friendly folk at **Kimberley Motors** (☎ 9161 1281; Great Northern Hwy; ☎ 6am-6pm) dish out tourist info, including a useful town map.

Wyndham Crocodile Farm (☎ 9161 1124; Barytes Rd; adult/child $15/10; ☼ 8.30am-4pm Dry) has some monstrous specimens, as well as a breeding programme and Komodo dragons. It's best to visit at feeding time (11am).

Five Rivers Lookout on Mt Bastion (with a view of the King, Pentecost, Durack, Forrest and Ord Rivers entering the Cambridge Gulf) is awesome! Almost-360-degree jaw-dropping views include water slicing through the brown, red and mottled-green land – it's unforgettable.

Warriu Dreamtime Park (Koolama St) features enormous statues of a local family with their domestic animals – quite a striking sight. About 15km from Wyndham is **Parry Lagoons Nature Reserve**, a beautiful wetland that teems with birds during the Wet, and the **Grotto**, a peaceful pool surrounded by lush vegetation in a small gorge.

Wyndham Town Hotel (☎ 9161 1003, 9161 1202; O'Donnell St; s/d $90/100, mains $20-24; ☒) has a pool table, a piano and plenty of character. Battered rooms come in different sizes (No 27 is good) and a mishmash of furniture that will have interior designers in a tizz. This place has a homely feel – aged but friendly.

Gulf Breeze Guest House (☎ /fax 9161 1401; Foreshore Rd; s/tw $35/50; ☒) is a compact, basic place at Wyndham Port, very close to the pub.

Wyndham Caravan Park (☎ 9161 1064; Baker St; powered/unpowered sites per 2 people $19/16; donga s/d $35/45) is a great little place with lots of beautiful eucalypts to pitch your tent under, a peaceful location and a campers' kitchen. And, best of all, the largest boab tree in captivity – over 2000 years old!

Wyndham is 60km north of the Great Northern Hwy and your own wheels are the best way to get there. **Triangle Tours** (☎ 9168 1272; adult/child $165/90) runs one-day tours from Kununurra.

KUNUNURRA
☎ 08 / pop 6000

Purposely planned, intelligently set out and flanked by the Lily Creek Lagoon and the diminutive Mirima National Park, Kununurra comes as a tiny urban relief,

if you've been travelling through the Kimberley. Apart from the services and facilities it offers, there's a much better vibe here – far more upbeat. Founded in 1960 as the centre for the Ord River irrigation scheme, tourism has developed quickly, thanks to its nearby attractions.

Information
There are ATMs around the town centre. There's 90 minutes' time difference between Kununurra and the NT.

CALM (☎ 9168 4200; Ivanhoe Rd) Situated opposite the Showgrounds.

Kununurra Hospital (☎ 9168 1522)

Kununurra Telecentre (☎ 9169 1868; Coolibah Dr; per hr $8; ▢)

Kununurra visitor information centre (☎ 9168 1177; www.eastkimberley.com.au; Coolibah Dr; ☼ 8am-5pm Mon-Sat, 9am-4pm Sun Dry, 9am-4pm Mon-Fri, 9am-1pm Sat Wet) One of the Kimberley's best – has lots of information and can book tours.

Western Australia Quarantine & Inspection Service (☎ 9168 7354) Strict quarantine restrictions apply in WA and especially the East Kimberley (don't bring fruit etc).

Sights & Activities
Lily Creek Lagoon is a miniwetlands next to town with lots of birdlife, and has a 'celebrity' tree park (there's even a tree planted by Rolf Harris). Lake Kununurra, also called the **Diversion Dam**, has picnic spots and is popular with water skiers and boating enthusiasts. There are good views from **Kelly's Knob**, a favourite sunset viewpoint on the town's northern fringe. Be careful of lightning strikes during storms. **Waringarri Aboriginal Arts Centre** (Speargrass Rd; ☼ 8am-5pm Dry, 8.30am-4pm Mon-Fri Wet, closed Dec) is an Aboriginal community shop with arts and crafts for sale – you'll often find artists working here.

Only 2km from the town centre, **Mirima National Park** (car $9) is a wonderful area of rugged sedimentary formations, steep gorges and some great views, and is a good spot to while away half a day. Drop into CALM for a map, advice on walking trails and information on the latest conditions in the park.

The visitor centre has details, including a map, of a beautiful self-guided drive around the Ivanhoe irrigation area, northwest of town. Highlights include the **Hoochery**

(☎ 9168 2467; www.hoochery.com.au; 243 Weaber Plains Rd; admission free; ⏰9am-4pm Mon-Fri, to noon Sat, reduced hours Wet) where you can taste Ord River Rum.

Tours

Alligator Airways (☎ 1800 632 533; www.alligatorairways.com.au) Fly over Purnululu (Bungle Bungle) National Park (two hours for $200).

Go Wild Adventure Tours (☎ 1300 663 369) Also offers excellent canoe trips along with abseiling tours to Kelly's Knob ($60) and the Grotto ($110).

Kununurra Backpackers (☎ 1800 641 998, 9169 1998; www.adventure.kimberley.net.au; 24 Nutwood Cres) Offers popular, self-guided canoe trips ($145) on the Ord River, between Lake Argyle and Diversion Dam (55km).

Kununurra Cruises (☎ 9168 1718) To get the most out of sunset consider a BBQ dinner cruise on Lily Creek Lagoon ($55).

Slingair (☎ 1800 095 500; www.slingair.com.au) Another flights operator.

Sleeping

Lakeview Apartments (☎ 9168 0000; lakeviewapartments@wn.com.au; 224 Victoria Hwy; 1-/2-/3-bedroom apt $165/187/253; 🅿️) The royalty of self-

contained apartments, these generously proportioned 'little houses' come with two lounge sofas, a dining suite and more mod cons than you'd find in Retravision. Its location across from the lake makes it great for walks.

Ivanhoe Village Caravan Resort (☎ 9169 1995; cnr Ivanhoe Rd & Coolibah Dr; powered/unpowered site $30/24, standard/deluxe cabins $90/125; 🅿️🖥️🅿️) This rather pretentiously named caravan park is a beauty. Meticulously manicured lawns, lush gardens and an intelligent lay out gets this place full marks. The well priced cabins are in very good shape with modern furnishings and outdoor patios. Campers can even get sites with their own bathroom.

Kununurra Backpackers (☎ 1800 641 998, 9169 1998; www.adventure.kimberley.net.au; 24 Nutwood Cres; dm/d $18/50; 🅿️🖥️🅿️) Run by backpackers for backpackers, this excellent hostel has a large adventure centre, and is a great place to relax with its lovely outdoor area that includes a hammock and even a small waterfall. The hostel is close to Mirima National Park.

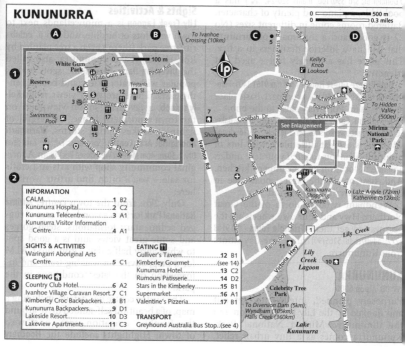

KUNUNURRA

Also recommended:

Country Club Hotel (☎ 9168 1024; www.countryclub hotel.com.au; 47 Coolibah Dr; motel d/units $170/230; ❊ 🖵 🏊) In a veritable tropical jungle (the crickets are deafening). Reminiscent of a colonial-era setup with a great bar overlooking the pool and tennis courts.

Lakeside Resort (☎ 1800 786 692, 9169 1092; www.lakeside.com.au; Casuarina Way; powered/un powered sites, $24/20, cabins $125, motel d & tw $155; ❊ 🖵 🏊) On the shore of the lagoon. Self-contained, smallish cabins and low-slung motel units in good nick.

Kimberley Croc Backpackers (☎ 1300 136 702, 9168 2702; www.yha.com.au; cnr Konkerberry Dr & Tristania St; dm $20-22, d & tw $55; ❊ 🖵 🏊) Four-, six- and eight-bed dorms are small but very clean and air conditioned.

Eating

Stars in the Kimberley (☎ 9168 1122; 4 Papuana St; mains $20-32; ❤ lunch & dinner) Tuscan-inspired décor, well-spaced tables, prompt service, decent coffee and a good Mod Oz menu fusing international flavours make this the stand-out choice in Kununurra. Call ahead during the Wet as hours can be erratic.

Gulliver's Tavern (☎ 9168 1666; Cottontree Ave; mains $20-25; ❤ lunch & dinner) Try the excellent seafood at the bistro here. Crayfish, Moreton Bay bugs, oysters and prawns are all presented in a variety of tasty, well-prepared dishes. The convivial bar also dishes out reasonable bar food.

Also recommended:

Valentine's Pizzeria (☎ 9169 1167; 4 Cottontree Ave; pizzas $13-19; ❤ dinner) Fresh pizza delivered to your room. Also dabbles in Mexican cuisine.

Kununurra Hotel (☎ 9168 0400; 37 Messmate Way; mains $10-28; ❤ lunch & dinner) Decent counter meals of the burger-and-wedges variety, or sink your teeth into more sophisticated restaurant fare.

At Kununurra shopping centre, **Rumours Patisserie** (☎ 9168 2071; breakfasts $9.50-11, lunches $4-8; ❤ breakfast & lunch) is a great spot to grab a big brekky or a selection of rolls, wraps and sandwiches (the sticky treats will tempt most mortals), while **Kimberley Gourmet** (lunches $5-10; ❤ lunch) does a decent coffee and similar café fare.

There are two supermarkets in town (the one in the shopping centre is open until 10pm).

Getting There & Around

Airnorth (☎ 8920 4001; www.airnorth.com.au) flies daily to Broome (from $300) and Darwin (from $245). **Qantas** (☎ 13 13 13; www.qantas .com.au) has a direct flight from Perth twice weekly (one way from $295).

Greyhound Australia (☎ 13 14 99; www.greyhound .com.au) has daily buses to Darwin and Perth that stop at the visitor centre. Destinations include Katherine ($100, 7¾ hours), Halls Creek ($90, 4½ hours), Derby ($180, 11¾ hours) and Broome ($185, 14¾ hours).

LAKE ARGYLE

Created by the Ord River Dam, Lake Argyle is the second-biggest storage reservoir in Australia, holding somewhere between nine and 18 times as much water as Sydney Harbour, depending on who you ask. The scenery is spectacular, with high, steep, red ridges plunging into the lake's blue waters.

Argyle Downs Homestead Museum (☎ 08-9167 8088; Parker Rd; admission $3; ❤ 7am-4pm Mar-Oct) has memorabilia from the good old days, as well as Aboriginal artefacts and a small cemetery.

Lake Argyle Cruises (☎ 08-9168 7687; www.lake argyle.com) offers morning/sunset/six-hour cruises for $40/50/125. Bring your swimming gear with you. **Triple J Tours** (☎ 08-9168 2682; www.triplejtours.net.au) has tours that include a visit to Argyle Homestead, a cruise on Lake Argyle, and a boat trip back to Kununurra on the Ord River.

Lake Argyle Resort (☎ 08-9168 7360; paradise@ lakeargyle.com; Parker Rd; powered/unpowered sites $25/18, motel d $55-75), right by the lake, was undergoing a major refurbishment at the time of writing, with new villa accommodation expected to be available late 2005.

WESTERN AUSTRALIA

Directory

CONTENTS

ACCOMMODATION

It's easy to get a good night's sleep in Australia, which offers everything from the tent-pegged confines of camping grounds and the communal space of hostels to gourmet breakfasts in guesthouses, chaperoned farmstays and everything-at-your-fingertips resorts, plus the gamut of hotel and motel lodgings.

The accommodation listings in this book are organised into budget, midrange and top-end sections. These listings are in order of author preference, based on a mixture of atmosphere, cleanliness, facilities, location and authorial mood of the day. Places that primarily offer tent and campervan sites (eg camping grounds and holiday parks) appear either at the end of the budget listings or at the tail of the accommodation section.

We generally treat any place that charges up to $50 per single or $100 per double as budget accommodation. Midrange facilities are usually in the range of $100 to $150 per double, while the top-end tag is mostly applied to places charging more than $150 per double. In more expensive areas such as metropolitan Sydney and Melbourne, however, budget can mean paying up to $120 per double, and midrange places can charge up to $170 for a double.

In most areas you'll find seasonal price variations. During the high season over summer (December to February) and at other peak times, particularly school and public holidays, prices are usually at their highest, whereas outside these times you will find useful discounts and lower walk-in rates. One exception is the Top End, where the Wet season (roughly October to March) is the low season, and prices can drop substantially. Another exception is the ski resorts whose peak season is winter.

High-season prices are quoted in this guidebook unless otherwise indicated. For more information on climatic seasons, see p1014; for specific details on each state or territory see Geography & Climate at the start of each destination chapter.

The weekend escape is a notion that figures prominently in the Australian psyche, meaning accommodation from Friday night through to Sunday can be in greater demand (and pricier) in major holiday areas.

B&Bs

The local bed-and-breakfast (guesthouse) birth rate is climbing rapidly. New places are opening all the time and the options include everything from restored miners' cottages, converted barns, rambling old houses, upmarket country manors and beachside bungalows to a simple bedroom in a family home. In areas that tend to attract weekenders – quaint historic towns, wine regions, accessible forest regions such as the Blue Mountains in New South Wales (NSW)

PRACTICALITIES

▪ Videos you buy or watch will be based on the PAL system, also used in New Zealand and most of Europe.

▪ Leaf through the daily *Sydney Morning Herald,* Melbourne's *Age* or the national *Australian* broadsheet.

▪ Find tabloid titillation in the *Daily Telegraph* (Sydney), *Herald Sun* (Melbourne) and *Courier Mail* (Brisbane) papers.

▪ Switch on the box to watch the ad-free ABC, the government-sponsored and multicultural SBS, or one of three commercial TV stations, namely Seven, Nine and Ten.

▪ Use a three-pin adaptor (different to British three-pin adaptors) to plug into the electricity supply (230V AC, 50Hz).

---

and the Dandenongs in Victoria – B&Bs are often upmarket and will charge a small fortune for stays between Friday and Sunday in high season. Tariffs are typically in the $80 to $150 (per double) bracket, but can be much higher.

Local tourist offices can usually provide a list of places. For some online information, try www.babs.com.au.

Camping & Caravanning

The cheapest accommodation lies outdoors, where the nightly cost of camping for two people is usually between $15 and $25, slightly more for a powered site. Whether you're packing a tent, driving a campervan or towing a caravan ('house trailer' in North American–speak), camping in the bush is a highlight of travelling in Australia. In the outback and northern Australia you often won't even need a tent, and nights spent around a camp fire under the stars are unforgettable. Staying at designated sites in national parks normally costs between $4 and $9 per person. Note that most city camping grounds lie at least several kilometres from the town centre.

Almost all caravan or holiday parks are equipped with hot showers, flushing toilets and laundry facilities, and frequently a pool. Many have old on-site caravans for rent, but these are being replaced by on-site cabins. Cabin sizes and facilities vary, but expect to pay $60 to $100 for two people in a cabin with a kitchenette. If you intend doing a lot of caravanning/camping, consider joining one of the major chains like **Big 4** (www.big4.com.au), which offers discounts at member parks.

Hostels

Hostels are a highly social but low-cost fixture of the Australian accommodation scene. In some areas, travellers may find hostels have reinvented themselves as 'inns', 'lodges' or 'guesthouses', partly to broaden their appeal beyond backpackers. Not all dorms are same-sex rooms – double-check this if you're after a single-sex dorm.

The website www.allbackpackers.com.au lists hostels around the country.

HOSTEL ORGANISATIONS

There are around 140 hostel franchisees of **VIP Backpacker Resorts** (☎ 1800 724 833, 07-3395 6111; www.backpackers.com) in Australia and many more overseas. Membership entitles you to a $1 discount on accommodation and a 5% to 15% discount on other products such as air and bus transport, tours and activities. A one-/two-year membership that's purchased direct from a participating hostel or an agent dealing in backpacker travel costs $35/49. An extra $6 is charged for postage if you order membership through the VIP website.

Nomads Backpackers (☎ 02-9232 7788; www .nomadsworld.com; Level 7, Dymocks Bldg, 428 George St, Sydney) has several dozen franchisees in Australia alone. Like VIP, membership ($39 for 12 months) entitles you to numerous discounts. You can join at participating hostels, backpacker travel agencies, online, or via the Nomads head office.

Australia has over 140 hostels that are part of the Youth Hostels Association (YHA). The **YHA** (Map pp94-5; ☎ 02-9261 1111; www.yha .com.au; 422 Kent St, Sydney, NSW 2000) is part of the **International Youth Hostel Federation** (IYHF;

www.hihostels.com), also known as Hostelling International (HI), so if you're already a member of that organisation in your own country, your membership entitles you to YHA rates in the relevant Australian hostels. Nightly charges are between $10 and $30 for members; most hostels also take non-YHA members for an extra $3.50. Preferably, visitors to Australia should purchase a HI card in their country of residence, but you can also buy one at major local YHA hostels at a cost of $37 for 12 months; see the HI website for further details. Australian residents can become full YHA members for $55/85/115 for one/two/three years; join online, at a state office or at any youth hostel.

YHA hostels provide varying levels of accommodation, from the austere simplicity of wilderness hostels to city-centre buildings with a café-bar and some en suite rooms. Most of the accommodation is in small dormitories (bunk rooms), although many hostels also provide twin rooms and even doubles. They have 24-hour access, cooking facilities, a communal area with a TV, laundry facilities and, in larger hostels, travel offices. There's often a maximum-stay period (usually five to seven days). Bed linen is provided (sleeping bags are not welcomed due to hygiene concerns) in all hostels except those in wilderness areas, where you'll need your own sleeping sheet.

INDEPENDENT HOSTELS

Australia has numerous independent hostels, with fierce competition for the backpacker dollar prompting high standards and plenty of enticements like free breakfasts, courtesy buses and discount meal vouchers. In cities, some places are run-down hotels trying to fill empty rooms; the unrenovated ones are often gloomy and depressing. Other might be converted motels, where each four-to-six-bed unit has a fridge, TV and bathroom, but communal areas and cooking facilities may be lacking. There are also purpose-built hostels, often with the best facilities but sometimes too big and impersonal –avoid 'we love to party' places if you're in an introspective mood. The best places tend to be the smaller, more intimate hostels where the owner is also the manager.

A new trend in hostels is represented by **base Backpackers** (www.basebackpackers.com), an up-market hostel chain that emphasises comfort

and extensive facilities – one of its innovations is a women-only floor.

Independent backpacker establishments typically charge $19 to $27 for a dorm bed and $40 to $65 for a twin or double room (usually without bathroom), often with a small discount if you're a member of YHA, VIP or Nomads.

Some places will only admit overseas backpackers; this mainly applies to city hostels that have had problems with locals sleeping over and bothering the backpackers. Hostels that discourage or ban Aussies say it's only a rowdy minority that makes trouble, and will often just ask for identification in order to deter potential troublemakers, but it can be annoying and discriminatory for genuine people trying to travel in their own country. Also watch out for hostels catering expressly to working backpackers, where wages and facilities can be minimal but rent can be high.

Hotels & Motels

Except for pubs, the hotels that exist in cities or well-touristed places are generally of the business or luxury variety (insert the name of your favourite chain here), where you get a comfortable, anonymous and mod con-filled room in a multistorey block. These places tend to have a pool, restaurant/café, room service and various other facilities. For these hotels we quote 'rack rates' (official advertised rates), though significant discounts can be offered when business is quiet.

Motels (or motor inns) offer comfortable midrange accommodation and are found all over Australia. Prices vary and there's rarely a cheaper rate for singles, so motels are better for couples or groups of three. Most motels are modern, low rise and have similar facilities (tea- and coffee-making, fridge, TV, air-con, bathroom) but the price will indicate the standard. You'll mostly pay between $60 and $120 for a room.

Pubs

For the budget traveller, hotels in Australia are the ones that serve beer, and are commonly known as pubs (from the term 'public house'). In country towns, pubs are invariably found in the town centre. Many pubs were built during boom times, so they're often among the largest, most extravagant buildings in town. In tourist areas some of these pubs have been restored as heritage buildings, but generally the rooms remain small, old fashioned and weathered, with a long amble down the hall to the bathroom. You can sometimes rent a single room at a country pub for not too much more than a hostel dorm, and you'll also be in the social heart of the town. But if you're a light sleeper, avoid booking a room right above the bar and check whether a band is playing downstairs that night (especially on Friday and Saturday nights).

Standard pubs have singles/doubles with shared facilities starting at around $35/55, more if you want a private bathroom. Few have a separate reception area – make inquiries in the bar.

Rental Accommodation

The ubiquitous holiday flat resembles a motel unit but either has a kitchen or cooking facilities. It can come with two or more bedrooms and is often rented on a weekly basis – higher prices are often reserved for shorter stays. For a two-bedroom flat, you're looking at anywhere from $60 to $100 per night. The other alternative in major cities is to take out a serviced apartment.

If you're interested in a shared flat or house for a long-term stay, delve into the classified advertisements sections of the daily newspapers; Wednesday and Saturday are usually the best days. Notice boards in universities, hostels, bookshops and cafés are also worth browsing.

Other Accommodation

Scattered across the country are lots of less-conventional and, in some cases, uniquely Australian accommodation possibilities.

Many of the country's farms offer a bed for a night. At some you sit back and watch other people raise a sweat, while others like to get you involved in day-to-day activities. At a couple of remote outback stations you can stay in homestead rooms or shearer's quarters and try activities such as horse riding. Check out some options on the website of **Australian Farm Tourism** (www.australiafarmhost .com); state tourist offices can also tell you what's available.

Back within city limits, it's sometimes possible to stay in the hostels and halls of residence normally occupied by university students, though you'll need to time your stay to coincide with the longer uni holiday periods.

Coober Pedy in South Australia (SA), meanwhile, is famed for its underground dwellings, a couple of which have been turned into hostels, guesthouses and even camping sites. And wannabe sailors can investigate houseboat hire on easily navigable watercourses such as the Murray River in SA and Victoria (for details on accommodation options visit www.murray-river.net /homepage.htm), or the Hawkesbury River in NSW; the cost can be reasonable if you have a big enough group.

ACTIVITIES

Although Australia provides plenty of excuses to sit back and do little more than roll your eyes across some fine landscape, that same landscape lends itself very well to any number of energetic pursuits, whether it's on the rocks, wilderness trails and mountains of dry land, or on the offshore swells and reefs. The following is a general rundown of what's possible; for specifics, read the individual activities entries in each state and territory chapter.

Adrenalin-Charged Activities

Bungee jumping is popular on the northeast coast, with elastic entertainment on the Gold Coast (p327) and in Cairns (p425).

Fantastic sites for rock climbing and abseiling include the Blue Mountains (p152) in NSW, Victoria's Mt Arapiles (p555) and Mt Buffalo in the High Country (p586), the spectacular Hazards at Coles Bay (p652) on Tasmania's east coast, the Warrumbungle National Park (p214) in northwest NSW and West Cape Howe National Park (p943) in Western Australia (WA). Local professionals can set you up with equipment and training. For online info on rock climbing in Australia, visit www.climbing.com.au or www.rock.com.au.

Tandem paragliding flights are available anywhere there are good take-off and landing points and thermal winds. A good place to learn is Bright (p592) in the Victorian High Country, and the national paragliding championships are held annually in Manilla (p202) in NSW.

Skydiving and parachuting are also widely practised, and most clubs are listed in the *Yellow Pages* telephone directory.

Hot-air ballooning is less adventurous but worth doing for sleepy dawn views. Catch a flight in most capital cities and fine locales like Alice Springs (p851) and the Hunter Valley (p166).

Bird-Watching

Australia is a twitchers' haven, with a wide variety of habitats and bird life, particularly water birds. **Birds Australia** (☎ 03-9882 2622; www.birdsaustralia.com.au) runs feathered-friend observatories and nonprofit reserves in the Northern Territory (NT), SA and WA, and publishes the informative quarterly magazine *Wingspan*.

Bushwalking

You can follow fantastic trails through many national parks. Notable walks include the Overland Track (p697) and the South Coast Track (p701) in Tasmania, the Australian Alps Walking Track (p582) in Victoria's High Country, the Thorsborne Trail (p412) across Hinchinbrook Island in Queensland, the Heysen Trail (p709) in SA, the Larapinta Trail (p862) in the Centre, Mt Kosciuszko (p232) in NSW and the Bibbulmun Track (p881) in WA.

Walking in Australia by Lonely Planet provides good detailed information about bushwalking around the country.

Cycling

Avid cyclists have access to lots of great cycling routes and touring country for day, weekend or even multiweek trips, while very experienced pedallers can consider trips through the dry Centre or (if they've got a bit of spare time) a circumnavigation of the country. Most large cities have a recreational bike-path system and an abundance of bike-hire places. The rates charged by most outfits for renting road or mountain bikes (not including the discounted fees offered by budget accommodation to their guests) are anywhere from $8 to $14 per hour, and $18 to $40 per day. Security deposits can range from $50 to $200, depending on the rental period.

Most states have helpful bicycle organisations that provide maps and advice; see p1040 in the Transport chapter and each destination chapter for more on cycling in Australia. See Lonely Planet's *Cycling Australia* for other useful contacts and details of popular routes. More information and news on local pedal power is available online at www.bicycles.net.au.

Diving & Snorkelling

There's excellent scuba diving along the Great Barrier Reef (p425). Courses by the **Open-water Professional Association of Diving Instructors** (PADI; www.padi.com) typically cost $320 to $650 for three to five days, depending on how much time you actually spend on the reef. You'll need to procure a medical certificate (about $50) for all certified PADI courses.

In WA the Ningaloo Reef (p977) is every bit as interesting as the east-coast reefs, without the tourist numbers, and diving courses are available at Coral Bay (p977) and Exmouth (p977). In the southern waters around Melbourne, Adelaide, Perth, Tasmania and NSW you can dive around shipwrecks and with seals and dolphins; courses and tours are generally cheaper in the south, too. And don't forget you can cheaply hire a mask, snorkel and fins.

CONSIDERATIONS FOR RESPONSIBLE BUSHWALKING

Please consider the following when hiking, to help preserve the ecology and beauty of Australia:

■ Do not urinate or defecate within 100m of any water sources. Doing so can lead to the transmission of serious diseases and pollutes precious water supplies.

■ Use biodegradable detergents and wash at least 50m from any water sources.

■ Avoid cutting wood for fires in popular bushwalking areas as this can cause rapid deforestation. Use a stove that runs on kerosene, methylated spirits or some other liquid fuel, rather than stoves powered by disposable butane gas canisters.

■ Hill sides and mountain slopes are prone to erosion; it's important to stick to existing tracks.

Fishing

Barramundi fishing is hugely popular across the Top End and ocean fishing is possible right around the country, from a pier or a beach, or on an organised deep-sea charter. There are many fine rivers and lakes where you can fish for trout, redfin and perch. There are particularly good fishing rivers and lakes in Tasmania (p615), and Cooktown (p452) in far north Queensland also attracts a bit of attention.

The uninitiated may think the website **Fishnet** (www.fishnet.com.au) is devoted to stockings, but those keen on all aspects of Australian fishing know better.

Horse & Camel Riding

Exploring the bush on horseback has a peaceful edge over the ruckus of engine-powered transport. In Victoria you can go horse riding in the High Country (p464) and follow the spectacular routes of the Snowy Mountains cattle people. In northern Queensland you can ride horses through rainforests and along sand dunes, and swim with them in the sea. There are also sundry riding opportunities in Australia's north and west.

Camel riding is an offbeat alternative, especially in central Australia and outback SA where there are camel farms. Originally brought in from the Middle East to be used as transport in Australia's harsh desert environment, camels now run wild all over the interior. A sunset camel ride on Cable Beach is *de rigueur* in Broome (p992), while at Stuart's Well (p867), south of Alice Springs, you can take rides lasting from a five-minute plod to a five-day desert expedition.

Skiing & Snowboarding

Australia has a small but enthusiastic skiing industry, with snowfields straddling the NSW–Victoria border. The season is relatively short, however, running from about mid-June to early September, and snowfalls can be unpredictable. The top places to ski are Thredbo (p235) and Perisher (p235) in NSW's Snowy Mountains, and Falls Creek (p587) and Mt Hotham (p585) in Victoria's High Country. Equipment can be hired at the snowfields.

The website www.ski.com.au has links to major resorts and snow reports.

Surfing

World-class waves can be ridden all around Australia, from Queensland's Gold Coast (p327), the beaches in Sydney (p112) and Victoria's Bells Beach (p536) to Marrawah (p680) in Tasmania, SA's Cactus Beach (p777) and Margaret River (p930) in WA – you could spend your whole trip shuttling a board from one break to another.

(More) Water Sports

Most major beach resorts will rent out windsurfing gear and there are outfits on the east coast offering parasailing (behind a speedboat) and jet boating. The places with the most activities on offer are those with the most visitors, such as Airlie Beach (p392), Cairns (p424) and the Gold Coast (p323) in Queensland.

Sailing is a popular activity around the islands of the Great Barrier Reef (see the boxed text, p397) and all along the east coast, where you can take lessons or sometimes just pitch in and help crew a yacht. The best places for info are the local sailing clubs.

There are several good trips in Australia, with the best of these being enjoyed on the upper Murray River (p231) in southern NSW, the Nymboida River (p183) in northern NSW, the Tully River (p289) in north Queensland and the Franklin River (p696) in Tasmania. Canoeing and kayaking can be enjoyed on rivers at Katherine Gorge (p838) in the NT, Barrington Tops National Park (p172) in NSW, the Coorong (p760) in SA and Blackwood River (p932) in the southern region of WA. Sea kayaking is big around Tasmania's D'Entrecasteaux Channel (p638) and Freycinet Peninsula (p652).

Whale & Dolphin Watching

Southern right and humpback whales pass close to Australia's southern coast on their migratory route between the Antarctic and warmer waters. Whale-watching cruises get you relatively close to these magnificent creatures. The best spots are Eden (p229) in southern NSW, the mid-north coast of NSW, Warrnambool (p543) in Victoria, Albany (p941) on WA's southwest cape and numerous places in SA (p711). Whale-watching season is roughly May to October on the west coast and in southwestern Victoria, September to November on the east coast, and June to September off the SA coast.

WHERE TO SURF IN AUSTRALIA Andrew Tudor

Bells Beach, Cactus, Margaret River, the Superbank – mention any of them in the right company and stories of surfing legend will undoubtedly emerge. That these breaks are renowned the world over is hardly surprising; the Superbank hosts the first event on the WCT (World Championship Tour) calendar, and Bells Beach the second, with Bells having recently become the longest-serving host of a WCT event. Cactus dangles a lure of remote mystique, while Margaret River is a haunt for surfers chasing the bigger wave.

While the aforementioned might be jewels, they are dot points in the sea of stars that Australia has to offer. Little wonder – the coastline is vast, touching either the Indian, Southern or South Pacific Oceans. With that much potential swell, an intricate coastal architecture, and the right conditions, you'll find anything from innocent beach breaks to gnarly reefs not far from all six Australian state capitals.

For daily surf reports, cams and forecasts, look up www.coastalwatch.com, or call the **Surf & Snow Line** (☎ 1900 911 525). For more information, news, events and surf schools, look up www.surfingaustralia.com.

New South Wales

It's hard to know where to begin: name practically any coastal town in NSW and there will be good surf nearby.

Popular spots:

- Manly through Avalon, otherwise known as Sydney's northern beaches (p112; surf report www.realsurf.com).
- Byron Bay (p192), Lennox Head (p189) and Angourie Point (p187) on the far north coast.
- Nambucca Heads (p180) and Crescent Head (p179) on the mid-north coast.
- The areas around Jervis Bay and Ulladulla (p226) on the south coast.

Queensland

By now every surfer in the world has heard of the Superbank. Just in case you haven't, it was formed in recent years, when the Tweed River entrance was dredged and a fixed sand bypass was put in place. A happy accident. The resulting sandbar is 2km long, give or take, and it's said that on the right swell you can ride a wave the entire length. The Superbank stretches from Snapper Rocks to Kirra Point (p331) and effectively replaces the breaks of Rainbow Bay, Greenmount Point, Coolangatta Beach and the Kirra groins.

Other areas:

- Along with Superbank, Burleigh Heads (p330; surf cam and report www.burleighcam.com.au) through to Surfers Paradise (p327) on the Gold Coast.
- North Stradbroke Island (p320), just north of Surfers Paradise.
- Caloundra (p335), Alexandra Heads near Maroochy (p336) and Noosa (p339), on the Sunshine Coast.

South Australia

Recent shark attacks have made Cactus Beach (p777), west of Ceduna on remote Point Sinclair, something of a bogeyman for surfers, if there is such a thing. Still, it's without doubt SA's best-known surf spot and remains internationally recognised for its quality and consistency. If you're game, it'll be worth it.

Other areas to check:

- Streaky Bay (p776), Venus Bay (p776) and Elliston (p776) on the western side of the Eyre Peninsula.
- Pennington Bay, which has the most consistent surf on Kangaroo Island (p748).

▧ Pondalowie Bay and Stenhouse Bay on the Yorke Peninsula tip in Innes National Park (p771).

▧ Victor Harbor (p739), Port Elliot (p741) and Middleton Beach at Port Elliot on the southern side of the Fleurieu Peninsula (surf cam and reports www.surfsouthoz.com).

Tasmania

Tasmania has some fine surfing and for years it enjoyed relative anonymity among the global surf community. Recently, the publicity surrounding the arrival of Shipstern Bluff on the world surfing stage has blown Tassie's cover. However, this wave is remote and dangerous and not recommended for the faint-hearted; indeed, it's not recommended at all unless you can magic some expert guidance.

That said, there are plenty of breaks to choose from, but be sure to pack a full-length wetsuit.

Other areas:

▧ Marrawah (p680) on the exposed northwest coast can offer huge waves.

▧ St Helens (p655) and Bicheno (p654) on the east coast (surf report www.eastsurf.com.au/).

▧ Eaglehawk Neck (p644) on the Tasman Peninsula.

▧ Closer to Hobart, Cremorne Point and Clifton Beach (surf cam and news www.coastview .com.au/site/surfing).

Victoria

Bells Beach is arguably the spiritual home of Australian surfing; hell, there's even a museum dedicated to Australian surfing history in nearby Torquay. When the wave is on, well, few would argue, but the break is notoriously inconsistent.

Just as well there are many other excellent breaks throughout the state. Phillip Island, the Mornington Peninsula and the Great Ocean Rd are all within a two-hour drive from Melbourne (surf report www.surfshop.com.au).

Popular spots:

▧ Woolamai, Surfies Point, Smiths Beach and Cat Bay on Phillip Island (p533).

▧ Point Leo, Flinders, Gunnamatta (p531), Rye and Portsea (p531) on the Mornington Peninsula.

▧ On the southwest coast, Barwon Heads (p527), Torquay (p535), Bells Beach (p536) and numerous spots along the Great Ocean Rd.

▧ Further south, on the Shipwreck Coast, the areas around Port Campbell (p542) and Peterborough.

Western Australia

The surf on offer in WA is simply awesome. North of Perth there are reefs that produce world-class lefts, while south of Perth, Margaret River can be huge.

Margaret River (p930), Gracetown and Yallingup (p929) are southwest of Perth on the stretch of coast between Cape Leeuwin and Cape Naturaliste. The entire stretch is simply littered with quality breaks. For details on the great surf WA has to offer, surf cams and reports, check out www.srosurf.com.

Other areas:

▧ Trigg Point and Scarborough Beach (p891) just north of Perth.

▧ Further north at Geraldton (p963), Kalbarri (p967) and Carnarvon (p374).

▧ Down south at Denmark (p937), Albany (p939) and Hopetoun (p944) on the southern ocean.

Andrew Tudor is a Lonely Planet employee and an avid surfer.

Dolphins can be seen year-round along the east coast at Jervis Bay (p225), Port Stephens (p169) and Byron Bay (p189), all in NSW; off the coast of WA at places like Bunbury (p926), Rockingham (p924), Esperance (p945) and Monkey Mia (p972); and off the Victorian coast at Sorrento (p530) and at Mallacoota in Gippsland (p609).

BUSINESS HOURS

Hours vary a little from state to state but most shops and businesses open about 9am and close at 5pm Monday to Friday, with Saturday hours usually from 9am to either noon or 5pm. Sunday trading is becoming increasingly common but is currently limited to major cities and, to a lesser extent, regional Victoria. In most towns there are usually one or two late shopping nights a week, normally Thursday and/or Friday, when doors stay open until about 9pm. Most supermarkets are open till at least 8pm and are sometimes open 24 hours. Milk bars (bars) and convenience stores often open until late.

Banks are normally open from 9.30am to 4pm Monday to Thursday and until 5pm on Friday. Some large city branches are open from 8am to 6pm weekdays, and a few are also open until 9pm on Friday. Post offices are open from 9am to 5pm Monday to Friday, but you can also buy stamps on Saturday morning at post office agencies (operated from newsagencies) and from Australia Post shops in all the major cities.

Restaurants typically open at noon for lunch and between 6pm and 7pm for dinner; most dinner bookings are made for 7.30pm or 8pm. They normally dish out food until at least 9pm – later on Friday and Saturday. That said, the main restaurant strips in large cities keep longer hours throughout the week. Cafés tend to be all-day affairs that either close around 5pm or continue into the night. Pubs usually serve food from noon to 2pm and 6pm to 8pm. Pubs and bars often open for drinking at lunchtime and continue well into the evening, particularly from Thursday to Saturday.

Nearly all attractions across Australia are closed on Christmas Day.

CHILDREN

All cities and most major towns have centrally located public rooms where mothers (and sometimes fathers) can go to nurse their baby or change its nappy; check with the local tourist office or city council for details. While many Australians have a relaxed attitude about breast feeding or nappy changing in public, some do frown on it.

Most motels and the better-equipped caravan parks have playgrounds and swimming pools, and can supply cots and baby baths – motels may also have in-house children's videos and child-minding services. Top-end hotels and many (but not all) mid-range hotels are well versed in the needs of guests with children. B&Bs, on the other hand, often market themselves as sanctuaries from all things child related. Many cafés and restaurants lack a specialised children's menu, but many others do have kids' meals, or will provide small serves from the main menu. Some also supply high chairs.

If you want to leave Junior behind for a few hours, some of Australia's numerous licensed childcare agencies offer casual care. Check under 'Baby Sitters' and 'Child Care Centres' in the *Yellow Pages* telephone book, or phone the local council for a list. Licensed centres are subject to government regulation and usually adhere to high standards; to be on the safe side, avoid unlicensed ones.

Child concessions (and family rates) often apply to accommodation, tours, admission fees, and transport, with some discounts as high as 50% of the adult rate. However, the definition of 'child' varies from under 12 to under 18 years. Accommodation concessions generally apply to children under 12 years sharing the same room as adults. On the major airlines, infants travel free provided they don't occupy a seat – child fares usually apply between the ages of two and 11 years.

Australia has high-standard medical services and facilities, and items such as baby food formula and disposable nappies are widely available in urban and regional centres. Major hire-car companies will supply and fit booster seats, charging around $18 for up to three days' use, with an additional daily fee for longer periods.

Lonely Planet's *Travel with Children* contains plenty of useful information.

CLIMATE CHARTS

Australia's size means there's a lot of climatic variation, but without severe extremes. The southern third of the country has cold (though generally not freezing)

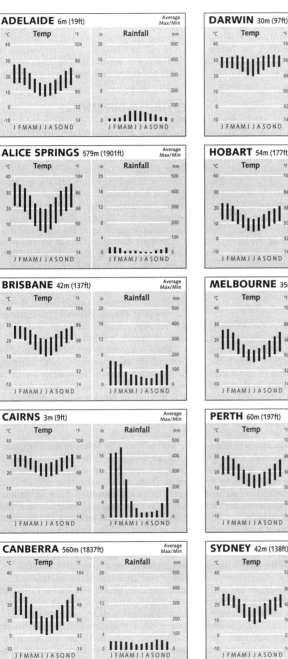

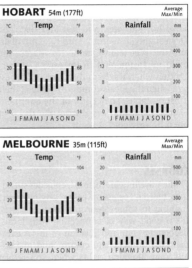

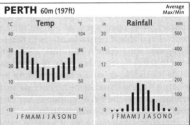

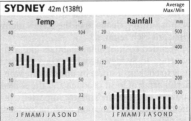

ADELAIDE 6m (19ft) — Average Max/Min

DARWIN 30m (97ft) — Average Max/Min

ALICE SPRINGS 579m (1901ft) — Average Max/Min

HOBART 54m (177ft) — Average Max/Min

BRISBANE 42m (137ft) — Average Max/Min

MELBOURNE 35m (115ft) — Average Max/Min

CAIRNS 3m (9ft) — Average Max/Min

PERTH 60m (197ft) — Average Max/Min

CANBERRA 560m (1837ft) — Average Max/Min

SYDNEY 42m (138ft) — Average Max/Min

DIRECTORY

winters (June to August). Tasmania and the alpine country in Victoria and NSW get particularly chilly. Summers (December to February) are pleasant and warm, sometimes quite hot. Spring (September to November) and autumn (March to May) are transition months, much the same as in Europe and North America.

As you head north the climate changes dramatically, but seasonal variations become fewer until, in the far north around Darwin and Cairns, you're in the monsoon belt where there are basically just two seasons: hot and wet, and hot and dry. The Dry roughly lasts from April to September, and the Wet from October to March; the build-up to the Wet (from early October) is often when the humidity is at its highest and when the locals confess to being at their most irritable. The centre of the continent is arid – hot and dry during the day, but often bitterly cold at night.

See When to Go (p25) for further information on Australia's seasons.

COURSES

While travelling in Australia, consider spending a few days or even weeks receiving expert training in some rewarding local activities. It's a good way of connecting with locals, deepening your appreciation of the Australian environment and culture, and increasing your bragging rights when you return home.

You can learn how to dive around the country, with open-water and shore diving courses available at coastal locations in nearly every state and territory. You could also learn how to stand up on a thin piece of fibreglass while it's sliding down the face of a wave by taking a surfing lesson or two. There are surf schools around the country, though the east coast has the greatest concentration.

If you enjoy having a bit of a tipple, take a wine appreciation course at SA's National Wine Centre of Australia (p720), located within sniffing distance of the state's many vineyard-rich regions.

Well-fed cosmopolitan habitats like Melbourne and Sydney are where you can learn how to cook up a storm by utilising the wonderful array of local produce and the skilled cookery of Australia's many imported ethnic cuisines. For more on cooking courses, see p80.

Appreciate indigenous culture by learning how to play a didgeridoo, throw a spear or recognise edible flora and natural medicines out in the bush. This is possible in several places across the Top End, such as at the Northern Territory Aboriginal community of Manyallaluk (p838).

CUSTOMS & QUARANTINE

For information on customs regulations contact the **Australian Customs Service** (☎ 1300 363 263, 02-6275 6666; www.customs.gov.au).

When entering Australia you can bring most articles in free of duty provided that customs is satisfied they are for personal use and that you'll be taking them with you when you leave. There's a duty-free quota per person of 2.25L of alcohol, 250 cigarettes and dutiable goods up to the value of $900.

There are duty-free stores at international airports and in their associated cities. Treat them with healthy suspicion: 'duty-free' is one of the world's most overworked catch phrases and it's often just an excuse to sell things at prices you can easily beat with a little shopping around. Alcohol and cigarettes are certainly cheaper duty-free, though, as they are heavily taxed in Australia.

When it comes to prohibited goods, be particularly conscientious about carrying drugs, which customs authorities are adept at sniffing out – unless you want to make a first-hand investigation of conditions in Australian jails, don't bring illegal drugs in with you. And note that all medicines must be declared.

You will also be asked to declare on arrival all goods of animal or plant origin (wooden spoons, straw hats, the lot) and show them to a quarantine officer. The authorities are naturally keen to protect Australia's unique environment and important agricultural industries by preventing weeds, pests or diseases getting into the country.

Most food is also prohibited, particularly meat, cheese, fruit, vegetables and flowers, plus there are restrictions on taking fruit and vegetables between states; see the boxed text, p1069. And if you lug in a souvenir, such as a drum with animal hide for a skin, or a wooden article (though these items are not strictly prohibited, they are subject to inspection) that shows signs of insect damage, it won't get through. Some items may require treatment to make them safe before they are allowed in.

Weapons and firearms are either prohibited or they will require a permit and safety testing. Other restricted goods include products made from protected wildlife species (such as animal skins, coral or ivory), unapproved telecommunications devices and live animals.

Australia takes quarantine very seriously. All luggage is screened or X-rayed – if you fail to declare quarantine items on arrival and are caught, you risk an on-the-spot fine of up to $220, or prosecution, which may result in much more significant fines and possible imprisonment. For more information on quarantine regulations contact the **Australian Quarantine and Inspection Service** (AQIS; ☎ 1800 020 504, 02-6272 3933; www .aqis.gov.au). See also the boxed text, above.

DANGERS & ANNOYANCES
Animal Hazards
Judging by Australia's remarkable profusion of dangerous creatures, Mother Nature must have been really pissed off when she concocted the wildlife. Apart from the presence of poisonous snakes and spiders, the country has also had its share of shark and crocodile attacks and, to top it off, is home to the world's deadliest creature, the box jellyfish (right). Travellers don't need to be constantly alarmed, however – you're unlikely to see many of these creatures in the wild, much less be attacked by one. For some reassuring statistics, see the boxed text, p1018.

Hospitals have antivenin on hand for all common snake and spider bites, but it helps to know what it was that bit you.

BOX JELLYFISH
There have been numerous fatal encounters between swimmers and these large jellyfish on the northern coast. Also known as the sea wasp or 'stinger', their venomous tentacles can grow up to 3m long. You can be stung during any month, but the worst time is from November to the end of April, when you should stay out of the water unless you're wearing protective clothing such as a 'stinger suit', available from swimwear and sporting shops in the stinger zone. The box jellyfish also has a tiny, lethal relative called an irukandji, though to date only one north-coast death has been directly attributed to it.

For information on treating box jellyfish stings, see p1074.

CROCODILES
In northern Australia, saltwater crocodiles ('salties') are a real danger. As well as living around the coast they can be found in estuaries, creeks and rivers, sometimes a long way inland. Observe safety signs or ask locals whether an inviting water hole or river is croc-free before plunging in – these precautions have been fatally ignored in the past.

INSECTS
For four to six months of the year you'll have to cope with those two banes of the Australian outdoors: the fly and the mosquito ('mozzie'). Flies aren't too bad in the cities but they start getting out of hand in the outback. In central Australia the flies emerge with the warmer spring weather (late August), particularly if there has been good winter rain, and last until the next frosts kill them off. Flies also tend to be bad in various coastal areas. The humble fly net fits on a hat and is very effective (albeit utterly unfashionable). Widely available repellents such as Aerogard and Rid may also help to deter the little bastards, but don't count on it.

Mozzies are a problem in summer, especially near wetlands in tropical areas, and some species are carriers of viral infections; see p1073. Try to keep your arms and legs covered as soon as the sun goes down and make liberal use of insect repellent. For details of what ticks can get up to, see p1074.

SNAKES

There are many venomous snakes in the Australian bush, the most common being the brown and tiger snakes, but few are aggressive – unless you're interfering with one, or have the misfortune to stand on one, it's extremely unlikely that you'll be bitten. The golden rule if you see a snake is to do a Beatles and *let it be*.

For information on treating snake bites, see p1075.

SPIDERS

The deadly funnel-web spider is found in NSW (including Sydney) and its bite is treated in the same way as a snake bite. Another eight-legged critter to stay away from is the black one with a distinctive red stripe on its body, called the redback spider for obvious reasons; for bites, apply ice and seek medical attention. The white tail is a long, thin black spider with, you guessed it, a white tail, and has a fierce bite that can lead to local inflammation and ulceration. The disturbingly large huntsman spider, which often enters homes, is harmless, though seeing one for the first time can affect your blood pressure.

Bushfires & Blizzards

Bushfires are a regular occurrence in Australia. In hot, dry and windy weather, be extremely careful with any naked flame – cigarette butts thrown out of car windows

---

A BIT OF PERSPECTIVE

There's approximately one shark-attack fatality per year in Australia, and a similar number of croc-attack deaths. Blue-ringed octopus deaths are even rarer – only two in the last century – and there's only ever been one confirmed death from a cone shell. Jellyfish do better, disposing of about two people each year. However, you're still over 100 times more likely to drown than be killed by one of these creatures.

On land, snakes kill one or two people per year (about the same as bee stings, or less than one-thousandth of those killed on the roads). There hasn't been a recorded death from tick bite for over 50 years, nor from spider bites in the last 20.

---

have started many a fire. On a total fire ban day it's forbidden even to use a camping stove in the open; the penalties are severe.

When a total fire ban is in place, bushwalkers should delay their trip until the weather improves. If you're out in the bush and you see smoke, even a long way away, take it seriously – bushfires move quickly and change direction with the wind. Go to the nearest open space, downhill if possible. A forested ridge, on the other hand, is the most dangerous place to be.

More bushwalkers actually die of cold than in bushfires. Even in summer, temperatures can drop below freezing at night in the mountains and the weather can change very quickly. Blizzards in the mountains of Tasmania, Victoria and NSW can occur at almost any time of the year, even January. Exposure in even moderately cool temperatures can sometimes result in hypothermia – for more information on hypothermia and how to minimise its risk, see p1076.

Crime

Australia is a relatively safe place to visit but you should still take reasonable precautions. Don't leave hotel rooms or cars unlocked, and don't leave your valuables unattended or visible through a car window. Sydney, the Gold Coast, Cairns and Byron Bay all get a dishonourable mention when it comes to theft, so keep a careful eye on your belongings in these areas.

Some pubs in Sydney and other major cities carry posted warnings about drugged drinks, after several reported cases in the past few years of women accepting a drink from a stranger only to later fall unconscious and be sexually assaulted. Women are advised to refuse drinks offered by strangers in bars and to drink bottled alcohol rather than from a glass.

On the Road

Australian drivers are generally a courteous bunch, but risks can be posed by rural petrol heads, inner-city speedsters and, particularly, drunk drivers. Potential dangers on the open road include animals, such as kangaroos, which can leap out in front of your vehicle (mainly at dusk); fatigue, caused by travelling long distances without the necessary breaks; and excessive speed. Driving on dirt roads can also be tricky if you're not used to them. For more information on road conditions see p1068, and for more on road hazards, p1068.

Swimming

Popular beaches are patrolled by surf life savers and patrolled areas are marked off by flags (for details see the boxed text, above). Even so, surf beaches can be dangerous places to swim if you aren't used to the conditions. Undertows (or 'rips') are the main problem. If you find yourself being carried out by a rip, the important thing to do is just keep afloat; don't panic or try to swim against the rip, which will exhaust you. In most cases the current stops within a couple of hundred metres of the shore and you can then swim parallel to the shore for a short way to get out of the rip and make your way back to land.

A number of people are also paralysed every year by diving into waves in shallow water and hitting a sand bar; check the depth of the water before you leap.

DISABLED TRAVELLERS

Disability awareness in Australia is pretty high and getting higher. Legislation requires that new accommodation meets accessibility standards, and discrimination by tourism operators is illegal. Many of Australia's key attractions, including many national parks, provide access for those with limited mobility and a number of sites have also begun addressing the needs of visitors with visual or aural impairments; contact attractions in advance to confirm the facilities. Tour operators with accessible vehicles operate from most capital cities. Facilities are improving in accommodation places, but there are still far too many older (particularly 'historic') establishments where the necessary upgrades haven't been done.

DISCOUNT CARDS

The **International Student Travel Confederation** (ISTC; www.istc.org) is an international collective of specialist student travel organisations. It's also the body behind the internationally recognised International Student Identity Card (ISIC), which is issued only to full-time students aged 12 years and over, and gives the bearer discounts on accommodation, transport and admission to various attractions. The ISTC also produces the International Youth Travel Card (IYTC or Go25), which is issued to people who are between 12 and 26 years of age and not full-time students, and gives equivalent benefits to the ISIC. A similar ISTC brainchild is the International Teacher Identity Card (ITIC), available to teaching professionals. All three cards are chiefly available from student travel companies.

Senior travellers and travellers with disabilities who reside in Australia are eligible for concession cards; most states and territories issue their own version and these can be used Australia-wide. Senior and disabled travellers who live overseas will generally find that the cards issued by their respective countries are not 'officially' recognised in Australia, but that most places (though not all) will still acknowledge such a card and grant a concession where one applies.

Travellers over 60 years of age (both Australian residents and visitors) will simply need to present current age-proving identification to be eligible for discounts of up to 70% off regular air fares.

AUSTRALIA FOR THE TRAVELLER WITH A DISABILITY

Information

Reliable information is the key ingredient for travellers with a disability and the best source is the **National Information Communication and Awareness Network** (Nican; ☎ /TTY 02-6285 3713, TTY 1800 806 769; www.nican.com.au; 4/2 Phipps Cl, Deakin, ACT 2600). It's an Australia-wide directory providing information on access issues, accessible accommodation, sporting and recreational activities, transport and specialist tour operators.

The website of **Tourism Australia** (www.australia.com) publishes detailed, downloadable information for people with disabilities – look under 'Plan Your Trip', then 'Special Interest Travel', then 'Disabled Travellers' – including travel and transport tips and contact addresses of organisations in each state. For more on the organisation, see p1030.

Another source of quality information is the **Disability Information & Resource Centre** (DIRC; Map p714; ☎ 08-8236 0555, TTY 08-8223 7579; www.dircsa.org.au; 195 Gilles St, Adelaide, SA 5000). The website of **e-bility** (www.e-bility.com/travel/) provides lots of info on accessible holidays in Australia, including listings of tour operators and accommodation.

The publication **Easy Access Australia** (www.easyaccessaustralia.com.au) by Bruce Cameron is available from various bookshops and provides details on easily accessible transport, accommodation and attraction options.

The comprehensive website www.toiletmap.gov.au lists over 14,000 public and private toilets, including those with disabled access.

Air

Accepted only by Qantas, the **Carers Concession Card** (☎ 13 13 13, TTY 1800 652 660; www.qantas .com.au) entitles a disabled person and the carer travelling with them to a 50% discount on full economy fares; call Nican for eligibility and an application form. All of Australia's major airports

---

EMBASSIES & CONSULATES

Australian Embassies & Consulates

The website of the **Department of Foreign Affairs & Trade** (www.dfat.gov.au) provides a full listing of all Australian diplomatic missions overseas.

Canada Ottawa (☎ 613-236 0841; www.ahc-ottawa.org; Suite 710, 50 O'Connor St, Ottawa, Ontario K1P 6L2) Also in Vancouver and Toronto.

France Paris (☎ 01 40 59 33 00; www.france.embassy .gov.au; 4 Rue Jean Rey, 75724 Cedex 15, Paris)

Germany Berlin (☎ 030-880 08 80; www.australian -embassy.de; Wallstrasse 76-79, Berlin 10179) Also in Frankfurt.

Indonesia Jakarta (☎ 0212 550 5555; www.austembjak .or.id; Jalan HR Rasuna Said Kav C15-16, Kuningan, Jakarta Selatan 12940) Also in Medan (Sumatra) and Denpasar (Bali).

Ireland Dublin (☎ 01-664 5300; www.australianem bassy.ie; 7th fl, Fitzwilton House, Wilton Terrace, Dublin 2)

Japan Tokyo (☎ 0352 324 111; www.australia.or.jp; 2-1-14 Mita, Minato-Ku, Tokyo 108-8361) Also in Osaka, Nagoya, Sendai, Sapporo and Fukuoka City.

Malaysia Kuala Lumpur (☎ 032 146 5555; www.aus tralia.org.my; 6 Jalan Yap Kwan Seng, Kuala Lumpur 50450) Also in Penang, Kuching (Sarawak) and Kota Kinabalu (Sabah).

Netherlands The Hague (☎ 0703 10 82 00; www.aus tralian-embassy.nl; Carnegielaan 4, The Hague 2517 KH)

New Zealand Wellington (☎ 04-473 6411; www.aus tralia.org.nz; 72-76 Hobson St, Thorndon, Wellington); Auckland (☎ 09-921 8800; Level 7, Price Waterhouse Coopers Bldg, 186-194 Quay St, Auckland)

Singapore Singapore (☎ 6836 4100; www.singapore .embassy.gov.au; 25 Napier Rd, Singapore 258507)

Thailand Bangkok (☎ 0 2287 2680; www.austembassy .or.th; 37 South Sathorn Rd, Bangkok 10120)

UK London (☎ 020-7379 4334; www.australia.org.uk; Australia House, The Strand, London WC2B 4LA) Also in Edinburgh.

USA Washington DC (☎ 202-797 3000; www.austemb .org; 1601 Massachusetts Ave NW, Washington DC 20036-2273) Also in Los Angeles, New York and other major cities.

Embassies & Consulates in Australia

The main diplomatic representations are in Canberra. There are also representatives in other major cities, particularly from countries with a strong link to Australia such as the USA, the UK or New Zealand, or in cities with important connections, such as Darwin, which has an Indonesian consulate.

Addresses of major offices include the following. Look in the *Yellow Pages* phone

have dedicated parking spaces, wheelchair access to terminals, accessible toilets and 'skychairs' to convey passengers onto planes via 'airbridges'.

Car Hire

Avis and Hertz offer hire cars with hand controls at no extra charge for pick-up at capital cities and the major airports, but advance notice is required.

The international wheelchair symbol (blue on a white background) for parking in allocated bays is recognised. Maps of central business districts showing accessible routes, toilets etc are available from major city councils, some regional councils and at visitor centres.

Taxi

Most taxi companies in major cities and towns have modified vehicles that will take wheelchairs.

Train

In NSW, CountryLink's XPT trains have at least one carriage (usually the buffet car) with a seat removed for a wheelchair and an accessible toilet. Queensland Rail's *Tilt Train* from Brisbane to Cairns has a wheelchair-accessible carriage.

Melbourne's suburban rail network is accessible and V/Line's country trains and stations are equipped with ramps. Some rural services employ hoist-equipped accessible coaches; 24 hours' advance booking is required. **V/Line Disability Services** (☎ 03-9619 2300) is at Southern Cross station. The **Travellers' Aid Society** (☎ 03-9670 2873), also at Southern Cross station, provides a meet-and-greet service (arrange this in advance).

directories of the capital cities for a more complete listing.

Canada Canberra (Map p266; ☎ 02-6270 4000; www .dfait-maeci.gc.ca/australia; Commonwealth Ave, Canberra, ACT 2600); Sydney (Map pp94-5; ☎ 02-9364 3000; Level 5, 111 Harrington St, Sydney, NSW 2000)

France Canberra (Map p266; ☎ 02-6216 0100; www .ambafrance-au.org; 6 Perth Ave, Yarralumla, ACT 2600); Sydney (Map pp94-5; ☎ 02-9261 5779; www.consul france-sydney.org; Level 26, St Martins Tower, 31 Market St, Sydney, NSW 2000)

Germany Canberra (Map p266; ☎ 02-6270 1911; www .germanembassy.org.au; 119 Empire Circuit, Yarralumla, ACT 2600); Sydney (Map pp92-3; ☎ 02-9328 7733; 13 Trelawney St, Woollahra, NSW 2025); Melbourne (Map pp470-1; ☎ 03-9864 6888; 480 Punt Rd, South Yarra, Vic 3141)

Ireland Canberra (Map p266; ☎ 02-6273 3022; irishemb@cyberone.com.au; 20 Arkana St, Yarralumla, ACT 2600); Sydney (Map pp94-5; ☎ 02-9231 6999; Level 30, 400 George St, Sydney, NSW 2000)

Japan Canberra (Map p266; ☎ 02-6273 3244; www .japan.org.au; 112 Empire Circuit, Yarralumla, ACT 2600); Sydney (Map pp94-5; ☎ 02-9231 3455; Level 34, Colonial Centre, 52 Martin Pl, Sydney, NSW 2000)

Malaysia Sydney (Map pp92–3; ☎ 02-9327 7596; 67 Victoria Rd, Bellevue Hill, NSW 2023)

Netherlands Canberra (Map p266; ☎ 02-6220 9400; www.netherlands.org.au; 120 Empire Circuit, Yarralumla, ACT 2600); Sydney (Map pp92-3; ☎ 02-9387 6644; Level 23, 500 Oxford St, Bondi Junction, NSW 2022)

New Zealand Canberra (Map p266; ☎ 02-6270 4211; www.nzembassy.com/australia; Commonwealth Ave, Canberra, ACT 2600); Sydney (Map pp94-5; ☎ 02-8256 2000; Level 10, 55 Hunter St, Sydney, NSW 2001)

Singapore Canberra (Map p266; ☎ 02-6273 3944; 17 Forster Cres, Yarralumla, ACT 2600)

Thailand Canberra (Map p266; ☎ 02-6273 1149; rtecanberra@mfa.go.th; 111 Empire Circuit, Yarralumla, ACT 2600); Sydney (Map pp94-5; ☎ 02-9241 2542; http://thaisydney.idx.com.au; Level 8, 131 Macquarie St, Sydney, NSW 2000)

UK Canberra (Map p266; ☎ 02-6270 6666; http://bhc .britaus.net/default.asp; Commonwealth Ave, Yarralumla, ACT 2600); Sydney (Map pp94-5; ☎ 02-9247 7521; 16th fl, 1 Macquarie Pl, Sydney, NSW 2000); Melbourne (Map pp472-3; ☎ 03-9652 1600; 17th fl, 90 Collins St, Melbourne, Vic 3000)

USA Canberra (Map p266; ☎ 02-6214 5600; http://us embassy-australia.state.gov/index.html; 21 Moonah Pl, Yarralumla, ACT 2600); Sydney (Map pp94-5; ☎ 02-9373 9200; Level 59, 19-29 Martin Pl, Sydney, NSW 2000); Melbourne (Map pp470-1; ☎ 03-9526 5900; Level 6, 553 St Kilda Rd, Melbourne, Vic 3004)

It's important to realise what your own embassy – the embassy of the country of which you are a citizen – can and can't do to help you if you get into trouble. Generally speaking, it won't be much help in emergencies if the trouble you're in is even remotely your own fault. Remember that while in Australia you are bound by Australian laws. Your embassy will not be sympathetic if you end up in jail after committing a crime locally, even if such actions are legal in your own country.

In genuine emergencies you might get some assistance, but only if other channels have been exhausted. For example, if you need to get home urgently, a free ticket is exceedingly unlikely – the embassy would expect you to have insurance. If you have all your money and documents stolen, it might assist with getting a new passport, but a loan for onward travel is out of the question.

FESTIVALS & EVENTS

Some of the most enjoyable Australian festivals are also the most typically Australian – like the surf life-saving competitions on beaches all around the country during summer, or outback race meetings, which draw together isolated communities. There are also some big city-based street festivals, sporting events and arts festivals that showcase comedy, music and dance, and some important commemorative get-togethers.

Details of festivals and events that are grounded in a single place – be it a city, town, valley or reserve – are provided throughout the destination chapters of this book. The following events are pursued throughout a particular region or state, or even around the country.

January & February
Big Day Out (www.bigdayout.com) This huge open-air music concert tours Sydney, Melbourne, Adelaide, Perth and the Gold Coast, stopping over for one day in each city. It attracts big-name international acts and dozens of local bands and DJs.

April
Ten Days on the Island (www.tendaysontheisland .org) Major biennial Tasmanian cultural festival. Held in odd-numbered years in venues around the state.
Targa Tasmania (www.targa.org.au) Six-day rally for exotic cars that runs around the entire state, appropriating 2000km of roads as it goes.

May
Sorry Day (www.journeyofhealing.com) On 26 May each year, the anniversary of the tabling in 1997 of the *Bringing Them Home* report, concerned Australians acknowledge the continuing pain and suffering of indigenous Australians affected by Australia's one-time child-removal practices and policies. Events are held in most cities countrywide.

July
Naidoc Week Communities across Australia celebrate the National Aboriginal and Islander Day of Celebration (inaugurated in 1957), from the annual Naidoc Ball (held in a different location each year) to local street festivals.

December
Sydney to Hobart Yacht Race (http://rolexsydney hobart.com) Sydney Harbour is a fantastic sight as hundreds of boats farewell competitors in the gruelling Sydney to Hobart Yacht Race.

FOOD

Australia is not renowned for having a unique cuisine, but many people are surprised by the range and wealth of food available in restaurants, markets, delicatessens (delis) and cafés, especially in the major cities but often in far less populated surrounds as well. This fine dining is in large part due to the abundance of reasonably priced fresh produce, including seafood. Many people from different cultures have also made their home here, bringing with them a huge range of ethnic cuisines that are now part of the country's culinary repertoire.

Vegetarian eateries and vegetarian selections in nonvegie places (including menu choices for vegans and coeliac sufferers) are becoming more common in large cities and are forging a stronger presence in the smaller towns visited by tourists, though rural Australia – as exemplified by pub grub – mostly continues its stolid dedication to meat. Those who enjoy a pre- or postdigestive puff will need to go outside, as smoking has been made illegal in most enclosed public places in all Australian states and territories, including indoor cafés, restaurants, clubs and (sometimes only at meal time) pub dining areas.

When it comes to cities, the eating recommendations provided in this book are often broken down into the main food-infatuated areas or suburbs. The innovative food offered in top-quality Australian eateries doesn't necessarily cost a fortune. Best value are the modern cafés where you can get a good meal in casual surroundings for under $20. A full cooked breakfast at a café costs around $10. Some inner-city pubs do offer upmarket restaurant-style fare, but most pubs serve standard (often large-portion) bistro meals, usually in the $10 to $19 range, and these are served in the dining room or lounge bar. Bar (or counter) meals, which are eaten in the public bar, usually cost between $6 and $10. Generally, breakfast is served between 6am and 11am, lunch lasts from around noon 'til 3pm, and dinner usually starts after 6pm.

It's common but by no means obligatory to tip in restaurants and upmarket cafés if the service warrants it – a gratuity of between 5% and 10% of the bill is the norm.

See also the Food & Drink chapter (p73) for more on Australian cuisine.

GAY & LESBIAN TRAVELLERS

Australia is a popular destination for gay and lesbian travellers, with the so-called 'pink tourism' appeal of Sydney especially big, thanks largely to the city's annual, high-profile and spectacular Sydney Gay & Lesbian Mardi Gras. Throughout the country, but particularly on the east coast, there are tour operators, travel agents and accommodation places that make a point of welcoming gays and lesbians.

Certain areas are the focus of the gay and lesbian communities, among them Cairns (p420) and Noosa (p337) in Queensland; Oxford St and King's Cross in Sydney (see the boxed text, p136); the Blue Mountains (p149), Hunter Valley (p164) and south coast in NSW; the Melbourne suburbs of Prahran, St Kilda and Collingwood (see the boxed text, p499); Daylesford and Hepburn Springs (p572) in Victoria; and Perth (p883).

Major gay and lesbian events include the aforementioned **Sydney Gay & Lesbian Mardi Gras** (www.mardigras.org.au) held annually in February and March, Melbourne's **Midsumma Festival** (www.midsumma.org.au) from mid-January to mid-February, and Adelaide's **Feast** (www.feast .org.au) held in November.

In general Australians are open minded about homosexuality, but the further into the country you get, the more likely you are to run into overt homophobia. Having said that, you will find active gay communities in places like Alice Springs and Darwin. Even Tasmania, once a bastion of sexual conservatism, now actively encourages gay and lesbian tourism. Homosexual acts are legal in all states but the age of consent between males varies: in the Australian Capital Territory (ACT), Victoria, NSW and WA it's 16 years; in SA and Tasmania it's 17; and in NT and Queensland it's 18.

Publications & Contacts

All major cities have gay newspapers, available from gay and lesbian venues and from newsagents in popular gay and lesbian residential areas. Gay lifestyle magazines include *DNA, Lesbians on the Loose, Women Out West,* the monthly *Queensland Pride* and the bimonthly *Blue*. Perth has the free *OutinPerth* and Adelaide has *Blaze*.

The website of **Gay and Lesbian Tourism Australia** (Galta; www.galta.com.au) has general information. Other helpful websites include **Queer Australia** (www.queeraustralia.com.au) and the Sydney-based **Pinkboard** (www.pinkboard.com.au). Gay telephone counselling services (you'll find them in most capital cities) are often a useful source of general information.

Tour Operators

Tour operators that cater to gay and lesbian travellers:

Parkside Travel Adelaide (☎ 08-8274 1222; 70 Glen Osmond Rd, Parkside, SA 5063)

Present Australia Sydney (☎ 08-8568 4000; www .presentaustralia.com; 1 Missenden Rd, Camperdown, NSW 2050)

Tas Vacations Hobart (☎ 1800 030 160, 08-6234 4666; www.tasvacations.com; 1st fl, 11-17 Argyle St, Hobart, Tas 7000)

Tearaway Travel Melbourne (☎ 03-9510 6644; 52 Porter St, Prahran, Vic 3181)

HOLIDAYS
Public Holidays

The following is a list of the main national and state public holidays (* indicates holidays that are only observed locally). As the timing can vary from state to state, check locally for precise dates.

National

New Year's Day 1 January
Australia Day 26 January
Easter (Good Friday to Easter Monday inclusive) March/April
Anzac Day 25 April
Queen's Birthday (except WA) Second Monday in June
Queen's Birthday (WA) Last Monday in September

Christmas Day 25 December
Boxing Day 26 December

Australian Capital Territory
Canberra Day March*
Bank Holiday First Monday in August
Labour Day First Monday in October

New South Wales
Bank Holiday First Monday in August
Labour Day First Monday in October

Northern Territory
May Day First Monday in May
Show Day (Alice Springs) First Friday in July*; (Tennant Creek) Second Friday in July*; (Katherine) Third Friday in July*; (Darwin) Fourth Friday in July*
Picnic Day First Monday in August

Queensland
Labour Day First Monday in May
RNA Show Day (Brisbane) August*

South Australia
Adelaide Cup Day Third Monday in May*
Labour Day First Monday in October
Proclamation Day Last Tuesday in December

Tasmania
Regatta Day 14 February
Launceston Cup Day February*
Eight Hours Day First Monday in March
Bank Holiday Tuesday following Easter Monday
King Island Show March*
Launceston Show Day October*
Hobart Show Day October*
Recreation Day (northern Tasmania only) First Monday in November*

Victoria
Labour Day Second Monday in March
Melbourne Cup Day First Tuesday in November*

Western Australia
Labour Day First Monday in March
Foundation Day First Monday in June

School Holidays
The Christmas holiday season, from mid-December to late January, is part of the summer school holidays – it's the time you are most likely to find transport and accommodation booked out, and long, restless queues at tourist attractions. There are three shorter school holiday periods during

the year, but they vary by a week or two from state to state. They fall roughly from early to mid-April, late June to mid-July, and late September to early October.

INSURANCE
Don't underestimate the importance of a good travel insurance policy that covers theft, loss and medical problems – nothing is guaranteed to ruin your holiday plans quicker than an accident or having that brand new digital camera stolen. Most policies offer lower and higher medical-expense options; the higher ones are chiefly for countries that have extremely high medical costs, such as the USA. There is a wide variety of policies available, so compare the small print.

Some policies specifically exclude designated 'dangerous activities' such as scuba diving, bungee jumping, motorcycling, skiing and even bushwalking. If you plan on doing any of these things, make sure the policy you choose fully covers you for your activity of choice.

You may prefer a policy that pays doctors or hospitals directly rather than requiring you to pay on the spot and claim later. If you have to claim later make sure you keep all documentation. Check that the policy covers ambulances and emergency medical evacuations by air.

See also Before You Go (p1071) in the Health chapter. For information on insurance matters relating to cars that are bought or rented, see p1065.

INTERNET ACCESS
Internet addicts will find it fairly easy to get connected throughout Australia.

Internet Cafés
Local cybercafés aren't as futuristic as their name implies, and connection speeds and prices vary significantly, but they all offer straightforward Internet access. Most public libraries also have Internet access, but this is provided primarily for research needs, not for travellers to check their email – so head for a cybercafé first. You'll find Internet cafés in cities, sizable towns and pretty much anywhere else that travellers congregate. The cost ranges from $3 per hour in cut-throat places in Sydney's King's Cross to $10 per hour in more remote locations. The average is about $6 per hour, usually with a

minimum of 10 minutes' access. Most youth hostels and backpacker places can hook you up, as can many hotels and caravan parks. Telecentres (community centres providing web access and other hi-tech facilities to locals and visitors) provide Internet access in remote areas of WA, SA and NSW, while Tasmania has set up access centres in numerous local libraries and schools.

Free web-based email services include **Yahoo** (www.yahoo.com), **MSN Hotmail** (www.hotmail .com) and **Excite** (www.excite.com).

Hooking Up

If you've brought your palmtop or notebook computer and want to get connected to a local ISP (Internet Service Provider), there are plenty of options, though some ISPs limit their dial-up areas to major cities or particular regions. Whatever enticements a particular ISP offers, make sure it has local dial-up numbers for the places where you intend to use it – the last thing you want is to be making timed STD calls every time you connect to the Internet. If you're based in a large city, there's no problem. Telstra (BigPond) uses a nationwide dial-up number at local call rates. Some major ISPs:

Australia On Line (☎ 1300 650 661; www.ozonline .com.au)

CompuServe (www.compuserve.com.au) Users who want to access the service locally can check the website or phone CompuServe Pacific (☎ 1300 555 520) to get the local dial-up numbers.

iPrimus (☎ 1300 850 000; www.iprimus.com.au)

OzEmail (☎ 13 28 82; www.ozemail.com.au)

Primus-AOL (☎ 1800 265 265; www.primusonline .com.au) Has dial-up numbers in all capitals and many provincial cities.

Telstra BigPond (☎ 13 12 82; www.bigpond.com)

Australia uses RJ-45 telephone plugs and Telstra EXI-160 four-pin plugs, but neither is universal – electronics shops such as Tandy and Dick Smith should be able to help. You'll also need a plug adaptor, and a universal AC adaptor will enable you to plug in without frying the innards of your machine. Most midrange accommodation and all top-end hotels will have sockets but you will be hit with expensive call charges. In most cheaper places you'll probably find that phones are hard-wired into the wall.

Keep in mind that your PC-card modem may not work in Australia. The safest option is to buy a reputable 'global' modem before you leave home or buy a local PC-card modem once you get to Australia.

For a list of useful Australia-savvy websites, see p28.

LEGAL MATTERS

Most travellers will have no contact with the Australian police or any other part of the legal system. Those that do are likely to experience it while driving. There is a significant police presence on the country's roads, with the power to stop your car and ask to see your licence (you're required to carry it), check your vehicle for roadworthiness, and insist that you take a breath test for alcohol – needless to say, drink-driving offences are taken very seriously here.

First offenders caught with small amounts of illegal drugs are likely to receive a fine rather than go to jail; nonetheless the recording of a conviction against you may affect your visa status. If you remain in Australia beyond the life of your visa, you will officially be an 'overstayer' and could face detention and expulsion, and then be prevented from returning to Australia for up to three years.

If you are arrested, it's your right to telephone a friend, relative or lawyer before any formal questioning begins. Legal Aid is available only in serious cases and only to the truly needy (for links to Legal Aid offices see www.nla.aust.net.au). However, many solicitors do not charge for an initial consultation.

MAPS

Good-quality road and topographical maps are plentiful. The various state motoring organisations are a dependable source of road maps, while local tourist offices usually supply free maps, though the quality varies.

Lonely Planet publishes handy fold-out city maps of Sydney and Melbourne. City street guides, such as those produced by Ausway (publishers of *Melway* and *Sydway*), Gregorys and UBD are useful for in-depth urban navigation, but they're expensive, bulky and only worth getting if you intend to do a lot of city driving.

Bushwalkers and others undertaking outdoor activities for which large-scale maps are essential should browse the topographic sheets published by **Geoscience Australia** (☎ 1800 800 173, 02-6249 9111; www.ga.gov.au). The more popular sheets are usually available over the counter at shops selling specialist bushwalking gear and outdoor equipment.

MONEY
ATMs, Eftpos & Bank Accounts

Branches of the ANZ, Commonwealth, National, Westpac and affiliated banks are found all over Australia, and many provide 24-hour automated teller machines (ATMs). But do not expect to find ATMs *everywhere*, certainly not off the beaten track or in very small towns. Most ATMs accept cards issued by other banks and are linked to international networks.

Eftpos (Electronic Funds Transfer at Point Of Sale) is a convenient service that many Australian businesses have embraced. It means you can use your bank card (credit or debit) to pay directly for services or purchases, and often withdraw cash as well. Eftpos is available practically everywhere these days, even in outback roadhouses where it's a long way between banks. Just like an ATM, you need to know your Personal Identification Number (PIN) to use it.

OPENING A BANK ACCOUNT

If you're planning to stay in Australia a while (on a Working Holiday Maker visa for instance) it makes sense to open up a local bank account. This is easy enough for overseas visitors provided it's done within six weeks of arrival. Simply present your passport and provide the bank with a postal address and they'll open the account and send you an ATM card.

After six weeks it's much more complicated. A points system operates and you need to score a minimum of 100 points before you can have the privilege of letting the bank take your money. Passports or birth certificates are worth 70 points; an international driving licence with photo earns you 40 points; and minor IDs, such as credit cards, get you 25 points. You must have at least one ID with a photograph. Once the account is open, you should be able to have money transferred across from your home account (for a fee, of course).

Some financial institutions offer travellers the option of setting up an Australian

bank account with them before embarking on a international trip. For one example of this, see the details of Citibank's 'Traveller Account' on its website (www.citibank .com.au/tnt).

If you don't have an Australian Tax File Number (TFN), interest earned from your funds will be taxed at a rate of up to 47%. See p1033 for tax-related information.

Credit & Debit Cards

Arguably the best way to carry most of your money around is in the form of a plastic card. Australia is well and truly a card-carrying society; its is becoming unusual to line up at a supermarket checkout, petrol station or department store and see someone actually paying with cash these days. Credit cards such as Visa and MasterCard are widely accepted for everything from a hostel bed or a restaurant meal to an adventure tour, and are pretty much essential (in lieu of a large deposit) for hiring a car. They can also be used to get cash advances over the counter at banks and from many ATMs, depending on the card, though these transactions incur immediate interest. Charge cards such as Diners Club and American Express (Amex) are not as widely accepted.

The obvious danger with credit cards is maxing out your limit and going home to a steaming pile of debt and interest charges. A safer option is a debit card with which you can draw money directly from your home bank account using ATMs, banks or Eftpos devices. Any card connected to the international banking network (Cirrus, Maestro, Plus and Eurocard) should work, provided you know your PIN. Fees for using your card at a foreign bank or ATM vary depending on your home bank; ask before your leave.

The most flexible option is to carry both a credit and a debit card.

Currency

Australia's currency is the Australian dollar, made up of 100 cents. There are 5c, 10c, 20c, 50c, $1 and $2 coins, and $5, $10, $20, $50 and $100 notes. Although the smallest coin in circulation is 5c, prices are often still marked in single cents and then rounded to the nearest 5c when you come to pay.

Cash amounts equal to or in excess of the equivalent of A$10,000 (in any currency) must be declared on arrival or departure.

In this book, unless otherwise stated, all prices given in dollars refer to Australian dollars. For an idea of local costs, see p26.

Exchange Rates

In recent times the Australian dollar has increased in value against the US dollar, buying upwards of US$0.75. See the Quick Reference on the inside front cover for a list of exchange rates.

Exchanging Money

Changing foreign currency or travellers cheques is usually no problem at banks throughout Australia or at licensed money-changers such as Travelex or Amex in cities and major towns.

Taxes & Refunds

The Goods and Services Tax (GST) is a flat 10% tax on all goods and services – accommodation, eating out, transport, electrical and other goods, books, furniture, clothing etc. There are exceptions, however, such as basic foods (milk, bread, fruits and vegetables etc). By law the tax is included in the quoted or shelf prices, so all prices in this book are GST-inclusive. International air and sea travel to/from Australia is GST-free, as is domestic air travel, when purchased outside Australia by nonresidents.

If you purchase new or secondhand goods with a total minimum value of $300 from any one supplier no more than 30 days before you leave Australia, you are entitled under the Tourist Refund Scheme (TRS) to a refund of any GST paid. The scheme doesn't apply to all goods but mainly to those taken with you as hand luggage or worn onto the plane or ship. Also note that the refund is valid for goods bought from more than one supplier, but only if at least $300 is spent in each. For more details, contact the **Australian Customs Service** (☎ 1300 363 263, 02-6275 6666; www.customs.gov.au).

Travellers Cheques

The ubiquity and convenience of internationally linked credit and debit card facilities in Australia means that travellers cheques are not heavily relied upon. Nevertheless, Amex, Thomas Cook and other well-known international brands of travellers cheques are easily exchanged. Transactions at their bureaux are commission-free if you use their cheques, while local banks charge hefty fees (often in excess of $7 per transaction) for the same service. You need to present your passport for identification when cashing travellers cheques.

There are no notable restrictions on importing or exporting travellers cheques.

POST
Letters

Australia's postal services are efficient and reasonably cheap. It costs 50c to send a standard letter or postcard within the country. **Australia Post** (www.auspost.com.au) has divided international destinations into two regions: Asia/Pacific and 'Rest of World'; airmail letters up to 50g cost $1.20 and $1.80, respectively. The cost of a postcard (up to 20g) is $1.10 and an aerogram to any country is 95c.

Parcels

There are four international parcel zones. You can send parcels by seamail to anywhere in the world except countries in the Asia/Pacific region (including New Zealand); it's cheap but they can take forever. A 1/1.5/2kg parcel costs $16/22/29. Each 500g over 2kg costs $3.50 extra, with a maximum of 20kg.

Economy airmail rates for 1/1.5/2kg parcels to Zone A (New Zealand) are $14/19/25; to Zone B (Asia/Pacific) costs $16/23/29; to Zone C (USA/Canada/Middle East) costs $20/28/37; and to Zone D (Rest of World) costs $22/32/40.

Sending & Receiving Mail

All post offices hold mail for visitors. You need to provide some form of identification (such as a passport) to collect mail. You can also have mail sent to you at city Amex offices if you have an Amex card or travellers cheques.

See p1014 for post office opening times.

SHOPPING

Australians are fond of spending money, a fact evidenced by the huge variety of local- and international-brand shops, and the feverish crowds that gather at every clearance sale. Big cities can satisfy most consumer appetites with everything from high-fashion boutiques to secondhand emporiums, while many smaller places tend towards speciality retail, be it home-grown produce, antiques or arts and crafts.

Markets are a great place to shop and most cities have at least one permanent bazaar, such as Hobart's Salamanca Market (p622). Melbourne and Sydney have a couple – try the Queen Victoria Market (p480) in Melbourne or the Paddington Market (p139) in Sydney. Alternative markets on the NSW north coast, such as the one at Nimbin (p199), are also worth poking around.

You may be able to get a refund on the tax you pay on goods; see p1027.

Aboriginal Art & Artefacts

An Aboriginal artwork or artefact makes an evocative reminder of your trip. By buying authentic items you are supporting Aboriginal culture and helping to ensure that traditional and contemporary expertise and designs continue to be of economic and cultural benefit for Aboriginal individuals and their communities. Unfortunately, much of the so-called Aboriginal art sold as souvenirs is ripped off, consisting of appropriated designs illegally taken from Aboriginal people; or it's just plain fake, and usually made overseas by underpaid workers.

The best place to buy artefacts is either directly from the communities that have art-and-craft centres or from galleries and outlets that are owned, operated or supported by Aboriginal communities. There are also many reputable galleries that have long supported the Aboriginal arts industry, usually members of the **Australian Commercial Galleries Association** (ACGA; www.acga.com.au), and that will offer certificates of authenticity with their goods.

Regardless of its aesthetic worth, a painting purchased for its investment potential without a certificate of authenticity from either a reputable gallery or community art centre will probably be hard to resell at a later time, even if it's attributed to a well-known artist.

Didgeridoos are in high demand, but you should decide whether you want a decorative piece or a functional musical instrument. The didgeridoos on the market are not always made by Aboriginal people, which means that at a nonsupportive souvenir shop in Darwin or Cairns you could pay anything from $250 to $400 or more for something that looks pretty but is little more than a painted bit of wood. From a community outlet such as Manyallaluk (p838) in the NT, however, you could expect to pay $200 to $350 for a functional, authentic didgeridoo painted with natural pigments such as ochre.

Australiana

The cheapest souvenirs, usually mass produced and with little to distinguish them, are known collectively by the euphemism 'Australiana'. They are supposedly representative of Australia and its culture, but in reality are just lowest-common-denominator trinkets, often made in Asia rather than Australia (check the label).

Genuine Australian offerings include the seeds of native plants – try growing kangaroo paws (see the boxed text, p957, for more information on Australia's unique wildflowers) back home (if your own country will allow them in). You could also consider a bottle of fine Australian wine, honey (leatherwood honey is one of many powerful local varieties), macadamia nuts (native to Queensland) or Bundaberg Rum, with its unusual sweet flavour.

Clothing

Modern Australian fashion collections that are in demand include Collette Dinnigan, Ty & Melita, Morrissey, Sass & Bide, Tsubi and Akira Isogawa. For a rustic look, try wrapping yourself in a waterproof Driza-Bone coat, an Akubra hat, moleskin pants and Blundstone boots; RM Williams is a well-known bush-clothing brand.

Surf-wear labels such as Rip Curl, Quiksilver, Mambo and Billabong make good buys. You can pick up printed T-shirts, colourful board shorts and the latest beach and street fashion from surf and sports shops all over the country, especially on the east coast. Rip Curl and Quiksilver were both born in Torquay, Victoria, in the 1960s and are now internationally renowned surf brands, marketing wetsuits, boards and surf wear.

Opals & Gemstones

The opal, Australia's national gemstone, is a popular souvenir, as is the jewellery made with it. It's a beautiful stone but buy wisely and shop around, as quality and prices vary widely from place to place. Coober Pedy (p788) in SA and Lightning Ridge (p214) and White Cliffs (p247) in NSW are opal-mining towns where you can buy the stones or fossick for your own.

On the Torres Strait Islands (p458) look out for South Sea pearls, while in Broome (p989) in WA, cultured pearls are sold in many local shops.

Australia is a mineral-rich country and semiprecious gemstones such as topaz, garnets, sapphires, rubies, zircon and others can sometimes be found lying around in piles of dirt at various locations. The gem fields around Anakie, Sapphire and Rubyvale in Queensland's Capricorn Hinterland (p373) are a good place to shop for jewellery and gemstones, and there are sites around rural and outback Australia where you can pay a few dollars and fossick for your own stones. On Flinders Island (p704), Killiecrankie 'diamonds' (actually topaz) are the stone of choice.

TELEPHONE

The two main telecommunication companies are **Telstra** (www.telstra.com.au) and **Optus** (www.optus.com.au). Both are also major players in the mobile (cell) market, along with **Vodafone** (www.vodafone.com.au) – other mobile operators include **AAPT** (www.aapt.net.au) and **Orange** (www.orange.net.au).

Domestic & International Calls
INFORMATION & TOLL-FREE CALLS
Numbers starting with ☎ 190 are usually recorded information services, charged at anything from 35c to $5 or more per minute (more from mobiles and payphones). To make a reverse-charge (collect) call from any public or private phone, dial ☎ 1800-REVERSE (738 3773), or ☎ 12 550.

Toll-free numbers (prefix ☎ 1800) can be called free of charge from almost anywhere in Australia – they may not be accessible from certain areas or from mobile phones. Calls to numbers beginning with ☎ 13 or ☎ 1300 are charged at the rate of a local call – the numbers can usually be dialled Australia-wide, but may be applicable only to a specific state or STD district. Telephone numbers beginning with either ☎ 1800, ☎ 13 or ☎ 1300 cannot be dialled from outside Australia.

INTERNATIONAL CALLS
Most payphones allow ISD (International Subscriber Dialling) calls, the cost and international dialling code of which will vary depending on which provider you are using. International calls from Australia are cheap and subject to specials that reduce the rates even more, so it's worth shopping around – look in the *Yellow Pages* for a list of providers.

When calling overseas you will need to dial the international access code from Australia (☎ 0011 or ☎ 0018), the country code and then the area code (without the initial 0). So for a London telephone number you'll need to dial ☎ 0011-44-20, then the number. In addition, certain operators will have you dial a special code to access their service.

Some country codes:

Country	International Country Code
France	☎ 33
Germany	☎ 49
Ireland	☎ 353
Japan	☎ 81
Netherlands	☎ 31
New Zealand	☎ 64
UK	☎ 44
USA & Canada	☎ 1

If dialling Australia from overseas, the country code is ☎ 61 and you need to drop the 0 in state/territory area codes.

LOCAL CALLS
Calls from private phones cost 18c to 30c, while local calls from public phones cost 40c; both involve unlimited talk time. Calls to mobile phones attract higher rates and are timed. Blue phones or gold phones that are found in pubs, hotel lobbies and other businesses usually cost a minimum of 50c for a local call.

LONG-DISTANCE CALLS & AREA CODES
For long-distance calls, Australia uses four STD (Subscriber Trunk Dialling) area codes. These STD calls can be made from any public phone and are cheaper during off-peak hours, generally between 7pm and 7am. Long-distance calls (ie to more than about 50km away) within these areas are charged at the long-distance rate, even though they

have the same area code. The main area codes are as follows:

State/Territory	Area code
ACT	☎ 02
NSW	☎ 02
NT	☎ 08
QLD	☎ 07
SA	☎ 08
TAS	☎ 03
VIC	☎ 03
WA	☎ 08

Area code boundaries don't necessarily co-incide with state borders; NSW, for example, uses each of the four neighbouring codes.

Mobile (Cell) Phones
Local numbers with the prefixes ☎ 04xx or ☎ 04xxx belong to mobile phones. Australia's two mobile networks, digital GSM and digital CDMA, service more than 90% of the population but leave vast tracts of the country uncovered. The east coast, south-east and southwest get good reception, but elsewhere (apart from major towns) it's haphazard or nonexistent.

Australia's digital network is compatible with GSM 900 and 1800 (used in Europe), but generally not with the systems used in the USA or Japan. It's easy and cheap enough to get connected short-term as the main service providers have prepaid mobile systems. Buy a starter kit, which may include a phone or, if you have your own phone, a SIM card (around $15) and a prepaid charge card. The calls tend to be dearer than with standard contracts, but there are no connection fees or line-rental charges and you can buy the recharge cards at convenience stores and newsagents. Shop around.

Phonecards
A variety of phonecards can be bought at newsagents, hostels and post offices for a fixed dollar value (usually $10, $20 etc) and can be used with any public or private phone by dialling a toll-free access number and then the PIN number on the card. Some public phones also accept credit cards.

TIME
Australia is divided into three time zones: the Western Standard Time zone (GMT/

UTC plus eight hours) covers WA; Central Standard Time (plus 9½ hours) covers the NT and SA; and Eastern Standard Time (plus 10 hours) covers Tasmania, Victoria, NSW, the ACT and Queensland. There are minor exceptions – for instance, Broken Hill (NSW) is on Central Standard Time.

So when it's noon in WA, it's 1.30pm in the NT and SA, and 2pm in the rest of the country. When it's noon in Sydney, the time in London is 3am (April to October) or 1am (November to March), and in New York it's 10pm (April to October) or 8pm (November to March) the previous day. For more on international timing, see the map of world time zones on the last page of the book.

'Daylight saving', for which clocks are put forward an hour, operates in most states during the warmer months (October to March). However, things can get pretty confusing, with WA, the NT and Queensland staying on standard time, while in Tasmania daylight saving starts a month earlier than in SA, Victoria, the ACT and NSW.

TOURIST INFORMATION
Australia's highly self-conscious tourism in-frastructure means that when you go looking for information, you can easily end up being buried neck deep in brochures, booklets, maps and leaflets, or get utterly swamped with detail during an online surf.

Local Tourist Offices
Within Australia, tourist information is disseminated by various regional and local offices. In this book, the main state and ter-ritory tourism authorities are listed in the introductory Information section of each destination chapter. Almost every major town in Australia seems to maintain a tour-ist office of some type and in many cases they are very good, with friendly staff (often volunteers) providing local info not readily available from the state offices. If booking accommodation or tours from local offices, bear in mind that they often only promote businesses that are paying members of the local tourist association. Details of local tourism offices are given in the relevant city and town sections throughout this book.

Tourist Offices Abroad
The government body charged with im-proving foreign tourist relations is called

Tourism Australia (Map pp94-5; ☎ 02-9360 1111; www.australia.com). A good place to start some pretrip research is on its website, which has information in 10 languages (including French, German, Japanese and Spanish).

Tourism Australia agents can supply various publications on Australia, including a number of handy fact sheets on topics such as camping, fishing, skiing, disabled travel and national parks, plus a handy map for a small fee. This literature is only distributed overseas, but local travellers can download and print the information from the Tourism Australia website.

Some countries with Tourism Australia offices:

Germany (☎ 069-274 00622; Neue Mainzer Strasse 22, Frankfurt D 60311)

Japan (☎ 0352 140 720; Australian Business Centre, New Otani Garden Court Bldg 28F, 4-1 Kioi-cho Chiyoda-ku, Tokyo 102-0094)

New Zealand (☎ 09-915 2826; Level 3, 125 The Strand, Parnell, Auckland)

Singapore (☎ 6255 4555; 101 Thomson Rd, United Sq 08-03, Singapore 307591)

Thailand (☎ 0 2670 0640; 16th fl, Unit 1614, Empire Tower, 195 S Sathorn Rd, Yannawa, Sathorn, Bangkok 10120)

UK (☎ 020-7438 4601; 6th fl, Australia House, Melbourne Place/Strand, London WC2B 4LG)

USA (☎ 310-695 3200; Suite 1150, 6100 Center Dr, Los Angeles CA 90045)

VISAS

All visitors to Australia need a visa – only New Zealand nationals are exempt, and even they receive a 'special category' visa on arrival. Application forms for the several types of visa are available from Australian diplomatic missions overseas (p1020), travel agents or the website of the **Department of Immigration & Multicultural & Indigenous Affairs** (Dimia; ☎ 13 18 81; www.immi.gov.au).

Electronic Travel Authority (ETA)

Many visitors can get an ETA through any travel agent or overseas airline registered with the International Air Transport Association (IATA). They make the application directly when you buy a ticket and issue the ETA, which replaces the usual visa stamped in your passport – it's common practice for travel agents to charge a fee, in the vicinity of US$15, for issuing an ETA. This system is available to passport holders of some 32 countries, including the UK, the USA and Canada, most European and Scandinavian countries, Malaysia, Singapore, Japan and South Korea.

You can also apply for the ETA online (www.eta.immi.gov.au), which attracts a nonrefundable service charge of $20.

Tourist Visas

Short-term tourist visas have largely been replaced by the ETA. However, if you are from a country not covered by the ETA, or you want to stay longer than three months, you'll need to apply for a visa. Standard visas (which cost $65) allow one (in some cases multiple) entry, for a stay of up to three months, and are valid for use within 12 months of issue. A long-stay tourist visa (also $65) can allow a visit of up to a year.

Visa Extensions

Visitors are allowed a maximum stay of 12 months, including extensions. Visa extensions are made through Dimia and it's best to apply at least two or three weeks before your visa expires. The application fee is $170 and is nonrefundable, even if your application is rejected.

Working Holiday Maker (WHM) Visas

Young (aged 18 to 30), single visitors from Belgium, Canada, China, Cyprus, Denmark, Estonia, Finland, France, Germany, Hong Kong, Ireland, Italy, Japan, Korea, Malta, the Netherlands, Norway, Sweden, Taiwan and the UK are eligible for a WHM visa, which allows you to visit for up to two years and gain casual employment.

The emphasis of this visa is on casual and not full-time employment, so you're only supposed to work for any one employer for a maximum of three months. This visa can only be applied for at Australian diplomatic missions abroad and you can't change from a tourist visa to a WHM visa once you're in Australia. You can also apply for this visa online at www.immi.gov.au/e_visa/visit.htm.

You can apply for this visa up to a year in advance, which is worthwhile as there's a limit on the number issued each year. Conditions include having a return air ticket or sufficient funds for a return or onward fare, and an application fee of $170 is charged. For details of what sort of employment is available and where, see p1033.

WOMEN TRAVELLERS

Australia is generally a safe place for women travellers, although the usual sensible precautions apply. It's best to avoid walking alone late at night in any of the major cities and towns. And if you're out on the town, always keep enough money aside for a taxi back to your accommodation. The same applies to outback and rural towns where there are often a lot of unlit, semi-deserted streets between you and your temporary home. When the pubs and bars close and there are inebriated people roaming around, it's not a great time to be out and about. Lone women should also be wary of staying in basic pub accommodation unless it looks safe and well managed.

Sexual harassment is an ongoing problem, be it via an aggressive cosmopolitan male or a rural bloke living a less-than-enlightened pro forma bush existence. Stereotypically, the further you get from 'civilisation' (ie the big cities), the less enlightened your average Aussie male is probably going to be about women's issues. Having said that, many women travellers say that they have met the friendliest, most down-to-earth blokes in outback pubs and remote roadhouse stops. And cities still have to put up with their unfortunate share of 'ocker' males who regard a bit of sexual harassment as a right, and chauvinism as a desirable trait.

Lone female hitchers are tempting fate – hitching with a male companion is safer. See Crime (p1018) for a warning on drugged drinks, and the boxed text on p397 for some cautionary words on crewing private boats.

WORK

If you come to Australia on a tourist visa then you're not allowed to work for pay – working for approved volunteer organisations (for details see p1034) in exchange for board is OK. If you're caught breaching your visa conditions, you can be expelled from the country and placed on a banned list for up to three years.

Equipped with a WHM visa (see p1031), you can begin to sniff out the possibilities for temporary employment. Casual work can often be found during peak season at the major tourist centres. Places like Alice Springs in the Centre, Cairns and various resort towns along the Queensland coast, and the ski fields of Victoria and NSW are

all good prospects when the country is in holiday mode.

Many travellers have found work cleaning or attending the reception desk at backpacker hostels, which usually means free accommodation. Most hostels, however, are now employing their own locally based staff.

Seasonal fruit picking (harvesting) relies on casual labour and there is something to be picked, pruned or farmed somewhere in Australia all year round. It's hard work that involves early-morning starts, and you're usually paid by how much you pick (per bin, bucket or whatever). Expect to earn $50 to $60 a day to start with, more when you get quicker at it. Some work, such as pruning or sorting, is paid by the hour at around $12 or $13. If you're looking for fruit-picking work, the **Harvest Hotline** (☎ 1300 720 126) can connect you with the relevant regions.

Other prospects for casual employment include factory work, labouring, bar work, waiting tables, domestic chores at outback roadhouses, nanny work, working as a station hand (jackaroo/jillaroo) and collecting for charities. People with computer, secretarial, nursing and teaching skills can find work temping in the major cities by registering with a relevant agency.

Though there are certainly many possibilities for picking up short-term work in Australia, finding something suitable will not always be easy, regardless of how straightforward it may look from afar on work-touting websites. Be prepared to hunt around for worthwhile opportunities, and make your own wellbeing the priority if you find yourself subjected to unsatisfactory conditions.

Information

The Internet is a good place to research work opportunities. **Australian Job Search** (www.jobsearch.gov.au) is a Commonwealth government agency with plenty of jobs on offer, including a 'Harvest Trail' for backpackers to follow around the country. At the time of research, there were over 8500 jobs listed on the website for Sydney alone.

One of the country's busiest employment websites is www.mycareer.com.au, while a good website for travellers with general information on working in Australia is www.workoz.com.

Backpacker accommodation, magazines and newspapers are good resources for local work opportunities. **Workabout Australia** (www.workaboutaustralia.com.au) by Barry Brebner gives a state-by-state breakdown of seasonal work opportunities.

Casual Employment Seasons

The following tables list the main times and regions where casual employment, mainly fruit picking, is a possibility:

New South Wales

Industry	Time	Region(s)
tomatoes	Jan-Mar	Forbes
grapes	Feb-Mar	Griffith, Hunter Valley
apples	Feb-Apr	Orange, Batlow, Gundagai
asparagus	Oct-Dec	Jugiong (northeast of Gundagai)
cotton	Oct-Jan	Narrabri
bananas	Nov-Jan	North Coast
cherries	Nov-Jan	Orange, Batlow, Young
apples	Dec-Jan	Forbes
citrus	Dec–Mar	Griffith

Northern Territory

Industry	Time	Region(s)
tourism	May-Sep	Darwin, Alice Springs, Katherine
mangoes	Oct-Nov	Darwin, Katherine

Queensland

Industry	Time	Region(s)
grapes	Jan-Apr	Stanthorpe
apples	Feb-Mar	Warwick
tourism	Apr-Oct	Cairns
fishing trawlers	May-Aug	Cairns
vegies	May-Nov	Bowen
asparagus	Aug-Dec	Warwick
tomatoes	Oct-Dec	Bundaberg
mangoes	Dec-Jan	Atherton, Mareeba
bananas	year-round	Tully, Innisfail

South Australia

Industry	Time	Region(s)
tomatoes	Jan-Feb	Riverland
grapes	Feb-Apr	Riverland, Barossa, Clare
peaches	Feb-Jun	Riverland
apples/pears	Feb-Jul	Adelaide Hills
citrus	May-Dec	Berri, Riverland
pruning	Aug-Dec	Adelaide Hills
apricots	Dec	Riverland

Tasmania

Industry	Time	Region(s)
strawberries/ raspberries	Jan-Apr	Huonville
apples/pears	Mar-Apr	Huon/Tamar Valleys
grapes	Mar-Apr	Tamar Valley
cherries	Dec-Jan	Huonville

Victoria

Industry	Time	Region(s)
tomatoes	Jan-Mar	Shepparton, Echuca
grapes/oranges	Jan-Mar	Mildura
peaches/pears	Feb-Apr	Shepparton
apples	Mar-May	Bendigo
ski fields	June-Oct	Wangaratta/Alps
strawberries	Oct-Dec	Echuca, Dandenongs
cherries	Nov-Dec	Dandenongs

Western Australia

Industry	Time	Region(s)
grapes	Feb-Mar	Albany, Margaret River, Mt Barker, Manjimup
apples/pears	Feb-Apr	Donnybrook, Manjimup
prawn trawlers	Mar-June	Carnarvon
bananas	Apr-Dec	Kununurra
vegies	May-Nov	Kununurra, Carnarvon
tourism	May-Dec	Kununurra
flowers	Sep-Nov	Midlands
lobsters	Nov-May	Esperance
bananas	year-round	Carnarvon

Paying Tax

Even with a TFN (Tax File Number), non-residents (including WHM visa holders) pay a considerably higher rate of tax than Australian residents, especially those on a low income. For a start, there's no tax-free threshold – you pay tax on every dollar you earn, starting at 29% on an annual income of up to $21,600 ($415 per week), then roughly 30% up to $58,000, 42% from $58,000 to $70,000, and 47% above $70,000.

Because you have been paid wages in Australia, you must lodge a tax return with the

Australian Taxation Office (ATO; ☎ 13 28 61; www.ato .gov.au). Check its website for details of what you need to do, including what happens if you plan on leaving Australia before the end of the financial year (30 June). To lodge a tax return, you will need your TFN and also a Group Certificate (an official summary of your earnings and tax payments) provided by your employer – give them written advice at least 14 days in advance that you want the certificate on your last day at work, otherwise you may have to wait until the end of the financial year.

If you have had tax deducted as you earn, it's unlikely you'll be entitled to a tax refund when you leave Australia. However, if you have had tax deducted at 47% because you did not submit a TFN, you will be entitled to a partial refund of the tax paid.

Superannuation

As part of the government's compulsory superannuation scheme, if you're earning more than $450 per calendar month your employer must make contributions on your behalf to a retirement or superannuation (super) fund. These contributions are at the rate of 9% of your wage, and the money must remain in the fund until you reach 'preservation age' (no embalming fluid is involved), which is currently 60 years.

Current legislation does not allow for the early release of superannuation funds. Find out the latest from the ATO and the relevant super fund with which your contributions have been lodged.

Tax File Number

If you have a WHM visa, you should apply for a TFN. Without it, tax will be deducted from any wages you receive at the maximum rate (around 47%). Apply for a TFN online via the **ATO** (www.ato.gov.au); it takes about four weeks to be issued.

Volunteer Work

Mainly involved in recruiting Australians to work overseas, **Australian Volunteers International** (AVI; Darwin ☎ 08-8941 9743; www.ozvol .org.au) does also place skilled volunteers into Aboriginal communities in northern and central Australia. Most of the placements are paid contracts for a minimum of a year and you will need a work visa. There are, however, occasional short-term placements, especially in the medical or accounting fields, and short-term unskilled jobs, usually helping out at community-run roadhouses.

The nonprofit **Conservation Volunteers Australia** (☎ 1800 032 501, 03-5330 2600; www.conservationvolunteers.com.au; Greenhill Enterprise Centre cnr University Dr & Enterprise Grove, Mt Helen, Ballarat Vic 3350) organises practical conservation projects such as tree planting, walking-track construction and flora and fauna surveys. It's an excellent way to get involved with conservation-minded people and visit some interesting areas of the country.

Most projects are either for a weekend or a week and all food, transport and accommodation is supplied in return for a small contribution to help cover costs ($30 per day). Many travellers join a Conservation Experience package of either four or six weeks ($815 and $1200), both of which comprise several different projects; additional weeks can be added for $200 per seven-day block.

Willing Workers on Organic Farms (WWOOF; ☎ 03-5155 0218; www.wwoof.com.au) is well established in Australia. The idea is that you do a few hours work each day on a farm in return for bed and board, often in a family home. Almost all places have a minimum stay of two nights.

There are about 1200 WWOOF associates in Australia, mostly in Victoria, NSW and Queensland. As the name states, the farms are supposed to be organic (including permaculture and biodynamic growing), but that isn't always so. Some places aren't even farms – you might help out at a pottery or do the books at a seed wholesaler. Whether participants in the scheme have a farm or just a vegie patch, most are concerned to some extent with alternative lifestyles.

You can join online or through various WWOOF agents (see the website for details) for a fee of $50/60 per single/couple. You'll get a membership number and a booklet that lists participating enterprises.

Transport

CONTENTS

THINGS CHANGE ...

The information in this chapter is particularly vulnerable to change. Check directly with the airline or a travel agent to make sure you understand how a fare (and ticket you may buy) works and to be aware of the security requirements for international travel. Shop carefully. The details given in this chapter should be regarded as pointers and are not a substitute for your own careful, up-to-date research.

GETTING THERE & AWAY

They don't call Australia the land 'down under' for nothing. It's a long way from just about everywhere, and getting here is usually going to mean a long-haul flight. That 'over the horizon' feeling doesn't stop once you're here either – the distances between key cities (much less opposing coastlines) can be vast, requiring a minimum of an hour or two of air time but up to several days of highway cruising or dirt-road jostling to traverse.

ENTERING THE COUNTRY

Disembarkation in Australia is a straightforward affair, with only the usual customs declarations (p1016) and the fight to be first to the luggage carousel to endure. However, recent global instability has resulted in conspicuously increased security in Australian airports, in both domestic and international terminals, and you may find that customs procedures are now more time-consuming.

Passport

There are no restrictions when it comes to citizens of foreign countries entering Australia. If you have a visa (p1031), you should be fine.

AIR

There are lots of competing airlines and a wide variety of air fares to choose from if you're flying in from Asia, Europe or North America, but you'll still pay a lot for a flight. Because of Australia's size and diverse climate, any time of year can prove busy for inbound tourists – if you plan to fly at a particularly popular time of year (Christmas is notoriously difficult for Sydney and Melbourne) or on a particularly popular route (such as Hong Kong, Bangkok or Singapore to Sydney or Melbourne), make your arrangements well in advance of your trip.

The high season for flights into Australia is roughly over the country's summer (December to February), with slightly less of a premium on fares over the shoulder months (October/November and March/April). The low season generally tallies with the winter months (June to August), though this is actually the peak tourist season in central Australia and the Top End.

Airports & Airlines

Australia has several international gateways, with Sydney and Melbourne being the busiest. The full list of international airports follows:

Adelaide (code ADL; ☎ 08-8308 9211; www.aal.com.au)

Brisbane (code BNE; ☎ 07-3406 3190; www.brisbane airport.com.au)

Cairns (code CNS; ☎ 07-4052 9703; www.cairnsport .com.au/airport)

Darwin (code DRW; ☎ 08-8920 1811; www.ntapl.com.au)

Melbourne (Tullamarine; code MEL; ☎ 03-9297 1600; www.melbourne-airport.com.au)

Perth (code PER; ☎ 08-9478 8888; www.perthairport .net.au)

Sydney (Kingsford Smith; code SYD; ☎ 02-9667 9111; www.sydneyairport.com.au)

Australia's overseas carrier is Qantas, which is regarded as one of the world's safest airlines and flies chiefly to runways across Europe, North America, Asia and the Pacific. It's one of a dozen international airlines that have already placed orders for the new double-decker Airbus A380, the biggest aircraft ever built and which is set to lumber into the skies sometime in 2006.

A subsidiary of Qantas, Australian Airlines flies between the prime east-coast destination of Cairns (with connections to the Gold Coast) and Japan, Hong Kong and Singapore. It also flies nonstop between Bali and Perth, Sydney and Melbourne.

Airlines that visit Australia include the following (all phone numbers listed here are for dialling from within Australia):

Air Canada (airline code AC; ☎ 1300 655 767; www.aircanada.ca; hub Pearson International Airport, Toronto)

Air New Zealand (airline code NZ; ☎ 13 24 76; www.airnz.com.au; hub Auckland International Airport)

Air Paradise International (airline code AD; ☎ 13 66 66; www.airparadise.co.id; hub Ngurah Rai, Denpasar)

Australian Airlines (airline code AO; ☎ 1300 799 798; www.australianairlines.com.au; hub Kingsford Smith Airport, Sydney)

British Airways (airline code BA; ☎ 1300 767 177; www.britishairways.com; hub Heathrow Airport, London)

Cathay Pacific (airline code CX; ☎ 13 17 47; www.cathaypacific.com; hub Hong Kong International Airport)

Emirates (airline code EK; ☎ 1300 303 777; www.emirates.com; hub Dubai International Airport)

Freedom Air (airline code SJ; ☎ 1800 122 000; www.freedomair.com; hub Auckland International Airport)

Garuda Indonesia (airline code GA; ☎ 1300 365 330; www.garuda-indonesia.com; hub Soekarno-Hatta International Airport, Jakarta)

Gulf Air (airline code GF; ☎ 1300 366 337; www.gulfairco.com; hub Abu Dhabi International Airport)

Hawaiian Airlines (airline code HA; ☎ 02-9244 2377; www.hawaiianairlines.com.au; hub Honolulu International Airport, Hawaii)

Japan Airlines (airline code JL; ☎ 02-9272 1111; www.jal.com; hub Narita Airport, Tokyo)

KLM (airline code KL; ☎ 1300 303 747; www.klm.com; hub Schiphol Airport, Amsterdam)

Lufthansa (airline code LH; ☎ 1300 365 727; www.lufthansa.com; hub Frankfurt Airport)

Malaysia Airlines (airline code MH; ☎ 13 26 27; www.malaysiaairlines.com; hub Kuala Lumpur International Airport)

Pacific Blue (airline code DJ; ☎ 13 16 45; www.flypacificblue.com; hub Brisbane Airport)

Qantas (airline code QF; ☎ 13 13 13; www.qantas.com.au; hub Kingsford Smith Airport, Sydney)

Royal Brunei Airlines (airline code BI; ☎ 1300 721 271; www.bruneiair.com; hub Bandar Seri Begawan Airport)

Singapore Airlines (airline code SQ; ☎ 13 10 11; www.singaporeair.com.au; hub Changi International Airport, Singapore)

South African Airways (airline code SA; ☎ 1800 221 699; www.flysaa.com; hub Johannesburg International Airport)

Thai Airways International (airline code TG; ☎ 1300 651 960; www.thaiairways.com.au; hub Bangkok International Airport)

United Airlines (airline code UA; ☎ 13 17 77; www.unitedairlines.com.au; hub Los Angeles International Airport)

Tickets

Automated online ticket sales work well if you're doing a simple one-way or return trip on specified dates, but are no substitute for a travel agent with the lowdown on special deals, strategies for avoiding stopovers and other useful advice.

Paying by credit card offers some protection if you unwittingly end up dealing with a rogue fly-by-night agency, as most card issuers provide refunds if you can prove you didn't get what you paid for. Alternatively, buy a ticket from a bonded agent, such as one covered by the **Air Travel Organiser's Licence** (ATOL; www.atol.org.uk) scheme in the UK. If you have doubts about the service provider, at the very least call the airline and confirm that your booking has been made.

INTERCONTINENTAL (RTW) TICKETS

If you are flying to Australia from the other side of the world, round-the-world (RTW) tickets can be real bargains. They're generally put together by the three biggest airline alliances – **Star Alliance** (www.staralliance.com), **Oneworld** (www.oneworldalliance.com) and **Skyteam** (www.skyteam.com) – and give you a limited period (usually a year) in which to circumnavigate the globe. You can go anywhere the participating airlines go, as long as you stay within the prescribed kilometre extents or number of stops and don't backtrack when flying between continents. Backtracking is generally permitted within a single continent, though with certain restrictions; see the relevant websites for details.

An alternative type of RTW ticket is one put together by a travel agent. These are usually more expensive than airline RTW fares but allow you to devise your own itinerary.

RTW tickets start around UK£850 from the UK and US$1850 from the USA.

CIRCLE PACIFIC TICKETS

A Circle Pacific ticket is similar to a RTW ticket but covers a more limited region, using a combination of airlines to connect Australia, New Zealand, North America and Asia, with stopover options in the Pacific islands. As with RTW tickets, there are restrictions on how many stopovers you can take.

ONLINE TICKET SITES

For online ticket bookings, including RTW fares, start with the following websites:

Air Brokers (www.airbrokers.com) This US company specialises in cheap tickets. To fly Los Angeles–Tokyo–Beijing–Shanghai–Hong Kong–Auckland–Christchurch–Sydney–Los Angeles costs around US$2200.

Cheap Flights (www.cheapflights.com) Informative site with specials, airline information and flight searches from the USA and other regions.

Cheapest Flights (www.cheapestflights.co.uk) Cheap worldwide flights from the UK; get in early for the bargains.

Expedia (www.expedia.msn.com) Microsoft's travel site; mainly USA related.

Flight Centre International (www.flightcentre.com) Respected operator handling direct flights, with sites for Australia, New Zealand, the UK, the USA, Canada and South Africa.

Flights.com (www.flights.com) International site for flights; offers cheap fares and an easy-to-search database.

Roundtheworldflights.com (www.roundtheworld flights.com) This excellent site allows you to build your own trips from the UK with up to six stops. A four-stop trip including Asia, Australia, New Zealand and the USA costs from £900.

STA Travel (www.statravel.com) Prominent in international student travel but you don't have to be a student; site linked to worldwide STA sites.

Travel.com.au (www.travel.com.au) Good Australian site; look up fares and flights to/from the country.

Travel Online (www.travelonline.co.nz) Good place to check worldwide flights from New Zealand.

Travelocity (www.travelocity.com) US site that allows you to search fares (in US dollars) to/from practically anywhere.

Asia

Most Asian countries offer competitive airfare deals, but Bangkok, Singapore and Hong Kong are the best places to shop around for discount tickets.

Flights between Hong Kong and Australia are notoriously heavily booked. Flights to/from Bangkok and Singapore are often part of the longer Europe-to-Australia route so they are also in demand. Plan your preferred itinerary well in advance.

Some typical one-way fares to Sydney are US$350 from Singapore, US$340 from Penang or Kuala Lumpur, and US$340 from Bangkok. From Tokyo fares start at US$750 but are often much higher. From east-coast Australia, return fares to Singapore and Kuala Lumpur range from $850 to $1600, to Bangkok from $900 to $1600, and to Hong Kong from $950 to $1800.

You can get cheap short-hop flights between Darwin and Indonesia, a route serviced by Garuda Indonesia, Qantas and Airnorth (see p1039). Air Paradise International operates regular flights between Denpasar in Bali and most Australian state capitals, with fares out of Australia from around $900 ($750 from Perth).

Royal Brunei Airlines flies between Darwin and Bandar Seri Begawan, while Malaysia Airlines flies from Kuala Lumpur.

Excellent bargains are sometimes available in Hong Kong. Some Asian agents:

Phoenix Services (☎ 2722 7378) Based in Hong Kong.

STA Travel Bangkok (☎ 02-236 0262; www.statravel .co.th); Singapore (☎ 6737 7188; www.statravel.com.sg); Tokyo (☎ 03-5391-2922; www.statravel.co.jp)

Canada

The air routes from Canada are similar to those from mainland USA, with most Toronto and Vancouver flights stopping in one US city such as Los Angeles or Honolulu before heading on to Australia.

The air fares sold by Canadian discount air-ticket sellers (consolidators) tend to be about 10% higher than those sold in the USA. **Travel Cuts** (☎ 866-246-9762; www.travel cuts.com) is Canada's national student travel agency and has offices in all major cities.

One-way fares out of Vancouver to Sydney or Melbourne cost from C$1300/1500 in the low/high season. From Toronto, one-way fares cost from around C$1300/1600.

In the low season, fares from Australia start at around $1900 return from Sydney to Vancouver. In the high season, fares start around $2100.

TRANSPORT

Continental Europe

From major European destinations, most flights travel to Australia via one of the Asian capitals. Some flights are also routed through London before arriving in Australia via Singapore, Bangkok, Hong Kong or Kuala Lumpur.

In Germany good travel agencies include the Berlin branch of **STA Travel** (☎ 030-2859 8264; www.statravel.de). One-way fares from Frankfurt start around €900/1200 in the low/high season.

A good option in the Dutch travel industry is **Holland International** (☎ 0900-8858; www .hollandinternational.nl). From Amsterdam return fares start around €1400.

In France try **Usit Connect Voyages** (☎ 01 43 29 69 50; www.usitconnections.fr) or **OTU Voyages** (☎ 01 40 29 12 22; www.otu.fr) – both of these companies are student/youth specialists and have offices in many French cities. Other recommendations include **Voyageurs du Monde** (☎ 01 40 15 11 15; www.vdm.com/vdm) and **Nouvelles Frontiéres** (☎ 08 25 00 08 25; www.nouvelles -frontieres.fr/nf); the details given are for offices in Paris, but again both companies have branches elsewhere. Fares from Paris in the low/high season cost from €900/1200.

Return air fares from Australia to key European hubs like Paris and Frankfurt usually cost between $1700 and $2500.

New Zealand

Air New Zealand and Qantas operate a network of flights linking key New Zealand cities with most major Australian gateway cities, while quite a few other international airlines include New Zealand and Australia on their Asia-Pacific routes.

Another trans-Tasman option is the no-frills budget airline Freedom Air, an Air New Zealand subsidiary that offers direct flights between destinations on Australia's east coast and main New Zealand cities.

Pacific Blue, a subsidiary of budget airline Virgin Blue, flies between both Christchurch and Wellington and several Australian cities, including Perth, Hobart and Adelaide.

If you book early enough and do your homework, you can pay around $180 for a one-way fare from Sydney or Melbourne to either Auckland, Christchurch or Wellington, though you could be charged anything up to $370; return fares cost between $350 and $700.

From key New Zealand cities, you'll ordinarily pay between NZ$220 and NZ$270 for a one-way ticket to an Australian east-coast city, with a return flight costing NZ$430 to NZ$570.

There's usually not a significant difference in price between seasons, as this is a popular route year-round.

For reasonably priced fares, try one of the numerous branches of **STA Travel** (☎ 0508 78. 872; www.statravel.co.nz). Another good option is **House of Travel** (www.houseoftravel.co.nz); see the website for contact telephone numbers for its dozens of New Zealand offices.

UK & Ireland

There are two routes from the UK: the western route via the USA and the Pacific; and the eastern route via the Middle East and Asia. Flights are usually cheaper and more frequent on the latter. Some of the best deals around are with Emirates, Gulf Air, Malaysia Airlines, Japan Airlines and Thai Airways International. British Airways, Singapore Airlines and Qantas generally have higher fares but may offer a more direct route.

Discount air travel is big business in London. Advertisements for travel agencies appear in the travel pages of the weekend broadsheet newspapers, in *Time Out*, in the *Evening Standard* and in the free magazine *TNT*.

Popular agencies in the UK include the ubiquitous **STA Travel** (☎ 0870 160 0599; www .statravel.co.uk), **Trailfinders** (☎ 020-7628 7628; www .trailfinders.co.uk) and **Flight Centre** (☎ 0870 499 0040; www.flightcentre.co.uk).

Typical direct fares from London to Sydney are UK£400/600 one way/return during the low season. At peak times such as mid-December, fares go up by as much as 30%.

From Australia you can expect to pay from $1000/1650 one way/return in the low season to London and other European capitals (with stops in Asia on the way) and upwards of $1100/1800 in the high season.

USA

Most of the flights between the North American mainland and Australia travel to/from the USA's west coast, with the bulk routed through Los Angeles but some coming through San Francisco. Numerous airlines offer flights via Asia or various Pacific islands.

San Francisco is the ticket consolidator capital of America, although good deals can be found in Los Angeles, New York and other big cities.

STA Travel (☎ 800-781 4040; www.statravel.com) has offices all over the USA.

Typically a return ticket to Australia from the west coast will start from US$1100/1400 in the low/high season; fares from the east coast start at US$1400/1700.

Return fares from Australia to the US west coast cost around $1850, and to New York from $2000.

SEA

It's possible (though by no means easy or safe) to make your way between Australia and countries such as Papua New Guinea and Indonesia, and between New Zealand and Australia and some smaller Pacific islands, by hitching rides or crewing on yachts – usually you have to at least contribute towards food. Try asking around at harbours, marinas and sailing clubs.

Good places on the Australian east coast include Coffs Harbour, Great Keppel Is-

land, Airlie Beach and the Whitsundays, and Cairns – basically anywhere boats call. Darwin could yield Indonesia-bound possibilities. A lot of boats move north to escape the winter, so April is a good time to look for a berth in the Sydney area.

There are no passenger liners operating to/from Australia and finding a berth on a cargo ship is difficult – that's if you actually wanted to spend months at sea aboard an enormous metal can.

GETTING AROUND

AIR

Time pressures combined with the vastness of the Australian continent may lead you to consider taking to the skies at some point in your trip. Nicotine fiends should note that all domestic flights are nonsmoking.

Airlines in Australia

Qantas is the country's chief domestic airline, represented at the so-called 'budget' end of the national air-travel market by its

AUSTRALIAN AIR FARES

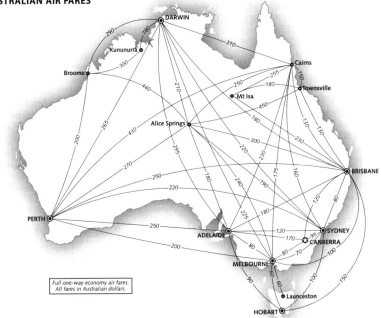

Full one-way economy air fares.
All fares in Australian dollars.

subsidiary Jetstar. Another highly competitive carrier that flies all over Australia is Virgin Blue. Keep in mind if flying with Jetstar or Virgin Blue that these no-frills airlines close check-in 30 minutes prior to a flight.

Australia also has many smaller operators flying regional routes. In many places, such as remote outback destinations or islands, these are the only viable transport option. Many of these airlines operate as subsidiaries or commercial partners of Qantas.

Some regional airlines:

Aboriginal Air Services (☎ 08-8953 5000; www .aboriginalair.com.au) Flies between Alice Springs and Tennant Creek.

Airlines of South Australia (☎ 1800 018 234; www .airlinesofsa.com.au) Connects Adelaide with Port Lincoln and Port Augusta; part of the RegionalLink consortium (see entry following).

Airnorth (☎ 1800 627 464; www.airnorth.com.au) Flies across northern Australia between Darwin, Kununurra, Broome and Gove; also flies across the Timor Sea to Dili (East Timor) and Kupang (West Timor, Indonesia); a member of the RegionalLink consortium.

Alliance Airlines (☎ 1300 130 092; www.allianceair lines.com.au) Connects Brisbane, Townsville, Mt Isa and Adelaide.

Australian Airlines (☎ 1300 799 798; www.australian airlines.com.au) This Qantas subsidiary flies between Cairns and both the Gold Coast and Sydney.

Emu Airways (☎ 1800 182 353; www.emuairways.com .au) This RegionalLink member flies between Adelaide and Kangaroo Island.

Golden Eagle Airlines (☎ 08-9172 1777; www.golden eagleairlines.com) Flies from Broome to Port Hedland, Fitzroy Crossing, Halls Creek and Derby.

Jetstar (☎ 13 15 38; www.jetstar.com.au) Budget-oriented Qantas subsidiary flying around 15 east-coast destinations from Cairns to Hobart, and also to Adelaide.

Macair (☎ 13 13 13; www.macair.com.au) Commercially partnered with Qantas, this Townsville-based airline flies throughout western and northern Queensland.

O'Connor (☎ 13 13 13, 08-8723 0666; www.oconnor -airlines.com.au) Another Qantas partner, flying between Melbourne, Adelaide, Mildura, Mount Gambier and Whyalla.

OzJet (☎ 03-9373 8523; www.ozjet.com.au) New business-class carrier targeting corporate fliers and initially flying between Melbourne, Sydney, Adelaide and Canberra.

Qantas (☎ 13 13 13; www.qantas.com.au) Australia's chief domestic airline.

QantasLink (☎ 13 13 13; www.qantas.com.au) Flying across Australia under this Qantas subsidiary brand is a collective of regional airlines that includes Eastern Australia Airlines, Airlink and Sunstate Airlines.

Regional Express (Rex; ☎ 13 17 13; www.regional express.com.au) Flies to Sydney, Melbourne, Adelaide, Devonport and around 25 other destinations in New South Wales (NSW), Victoria, South Australia (SA) and Tasmania.

RegionalLink (www.regionallink.com.au) Consortium of regional carriers that includes Airnorth, Emu Airways and Airlines of South Australia (see entries preceding). Eventually member airlines will all be serviced through one booking number, but they currently retain separate numbers and their planes feature a mixture of individual and RegionalLink livery.

Skippers (☎ 1300 729 924; www.skippers.com.au) Flies between a half-dozen Western Australia (WA) destinations, including Perth, Kalbarri, Geraldton and Shark Bay.

Skywest (☎ 1300 660 088; www.skywest.com.au) Flies from Perth to many western towns, including Albany, Esperance, Exmouth, Carnarvon, Kalgoorlie and Broome, plus Darwin up north.

Virgin Blue (☎ 13 67 89; www.virginblue.com.au) Highly competitive, Virgin Blue flies all over Australia – Virgin fares are cheaper if booked online (discount per ticket $10).

Air Passes

With discounting being the norm these days, air passes are not great value. Qantas' **Boomerang Pass** (☎ 13 13 13) can only be purchased overseas and involves buying coupons for either short-haul flights (up to 1200km, eg Hobart to Melbourne) from $160 one way, or multizone sectors (including New Zealand and the Pacific) from $300. You must purchase a minimum of two coupons before you arrive in Australia, and once here you can buy more.

Regional Express has the **Rex Backpacker** (☎ 13 17 13) scheme, where international travellers clutching a VIP, YHA, ISIC or IYTC card (Australian residents are not eligible) pay $500/950 for one/two months' worth of unlimited travel on the airline; it applies to standby fares only.

BICYCLE

Australia has much to offer cyclists, from leisurely bike paths winding through most major cities to thousands of kilometres of good country roads where you can wear out your chain wheels. 'Mountainous' is not an adjective that applies to this country. Instead, there's lots of flat countryside and gently rolling hills – that said, mountain bikers can find plenty of forestry trails and high country.

Bike helmets are compulsory in all states and territories, as are white front lights and red rear lights for riding at night.

If you are bringing in your own bike, check with your airline for costs and the degree of dismantling and packing required. Within Australia, bus companies require you to dismantle your bike and some don't guarantee that it will travel on the same bus as you. On trains supervise the loading, if possible tie your bike upright, and check for possible restrictions: most inter-city trains carry only two to three boxed bikes per service.

Eastern Australia was settled on the principle of not having more than a day's horse ride between pubs, so it's possible to plan even ultralong routes and still get a shower at the end of each day. Most riders carry camping equipment but, on the east coast at least, it's feasible to travel from town to town staying in hostels, hotels or caravan parks.

You can get by with standard road maps but, as you'll probably want to avoid both highways and low-grade unsealed roads, the government series is best. The 1:250,000 scale is the most suitable, though you'll need a lot of maps if you're going far. The next scale up, 1:1,000,000, is adequate and is widely available in speciality map shops.

Carry plenty of water to avoid dehydration. Cycling in the summer heat can be made more endurable by wearing a helmet with a peak (or a cap under your helmet), using plenty of sunscreen, not cycling in the middle of the day, and drinking lots of water (not soft drinks). It can get very cold in the mountains, so pack appropriate clothing. In the south, beware the blistering hot northerlies that can make a north-bound cyclist's life hell in summer. The southeast trade winds begin to blow in April, when you can have (theoretically at least) tailwinds all the way to Darwin.

Outback travel needs to be properly planned, with the availability of drinking water the main concern – those isolated water sources (bores, tanks, creeks and the like) shown on your map may be dry or undrinkable, so you can't depend entirely on them. Also make sure you've got the necessary spare parts and bike-repair knowledge. Check with locals if you're heading into remote areas, and let someone know where you're headed before setting off.

Information

The national cycling body is the **Bicycle Federation of Australia** (☎ 02-6249 6761; www.bfa.asn .au). Each state and territory has a touring organisation that can also help with cycling information and put you in touch with touring clubs.

Bicycle New South Wales (☎ 02-9281 4099; www .bicyclensw.org.au)

Bicycle Queensland (☎ 07-3844 1144; www.bq.org .au)

Bicycle SA (☎ 08-8232 2644; www.bikesa.asn.au)

Bicycle Tasmania (www.biketas.org.au)

Bicycle Transportation Alliance (☎ 08-9420 7210; www.multiline.com.au/~bta) In WA.

Bicycle Victoria (☎ 03-8636 8888; www.bv.com.au)

Northern Territory Cycling Association (☎ 08-8932 2869; www.nt.cycling.org.au)

Pedal Power ACT (☎ 02-6248 7995; www.pedalpower .org.au)

For more information, see Lonely Planet's *Cycling Australia*.

Purchase

If you arrive in the country without a set of wheels and want to buy a reliable new road cycle or mountain bike, your absolute bottom-level starting point is $400 to $500. To set yourself up with a new bike, plus all the requisite on-the-road equipment such as panniers, helmet etc, your starting point becomes $1500 to $2000. Second-hand bikes are worth checking out in the cities, as are the post-Christmas sales and mid-year stocktakes, when newish cycles can be heavily discounted.

Your best bet for reselling your bike is via the **Trading Post** (www.tradingpost.com.au), which is distributed in newspaper form in many urban centres and also has a busy online trading site.

BOAT

There's a hell of a lot of water around Australia but unless you're fortunate enough to hook up with a yacht, it's not a feasible way of getting around. The only regular passenger services of note are run by **TT-Line** (☎ 1800 634 906; www.spiritoftasmania.com.au), which dispatches three high-speed, vehicle-carrying ferries – *Spirit of Tasmania I, II & III* – between Devonport and both Sydney and Melbourne. See p617 for more details.

TRANSPORT

BUS

Australia's extensive bus network makes a relatively cheap and reliable way to get around, though it can be a tedious means of travel and requires planning if you intend to do more than straightforward city-to-city trips. Most buses are equipped with air-con, toilets and videos, and all are smoke-free zones. The smallest towns eschew formal bus terminals for a single drop-off/pick-up point, usually outside a post office, newsagent or shop.

A national bus network is provided by **Greyhound Australia** (☎ 13 14 99; www.greyhound .com.au), which recently ended its association with the bus company McCafferty's. Fares purchased online are roughly 5% cheaper than over-the-counter tickets; fares purchased by phone incur a $4 booking fee.

Due to convoluted licensing arrangements involving some regional bus operators, there are some states and smaller areas in Australia – namely SA, Victoria and parts of NSW and northern Queensland – where you cannot buy a Greyhound ticket to travel between two destinations within that state/area. Rather, your ticket needs to take you out of the region or across a state/territory border. For example, you cannot get on a Greyhound bus in Melbourne (Victoria) and get off in Ballarat (Victoria), but you can travel from Melbourne to Bordertown (SA). This situation does not apply to bus passes (p1044), which can be used freely.

PRINCIPAL BUS ROUTES & RAILWAYS

Small regional operators running key routes or covering a lot of ground include the following:

Firefly Express (☎ 1300 730 740; www.fireflyexpress .com.au) Runs between Sydney, Melbourne and Adelaide.

Integrity Coach Lines (☎ 1800 226 339; www .integritycoachlines.com.au) Heads north from Perth up to Port Hedland.

Premier Motor Service (☎ 13 34 10; www.prem ierms.com.au) Runs along the east coast between Cairns and Melbourne.

Premier Stateliner (☎ 08-8415 5555; www.premier stateliner.com.au) Services towns around SA.

Redline Coaches (☎ 1300 360 000; www.tasredline .com.au) Services Hobart and Tasmania's northern and eastern coasts.

TassieLink (☎ 1300 300 520; www.tassielink.com .au) Crisscrosses Tasmania, with extra summer links to bushwalking locales.

Transwa (☎ 1300 662 205; www.transwa.wa.gov.au) Hauls itself around the southern half of WA.

V/Line (☎ 13 61 96; www.vline.com.au) Runs to most major towns and cities in Victoria.

Backpacker Buses

While the companies offering transport options for budget travellers in various parts of Australia are pretty much organised-tour operators, they do also get you from A to B (sometimes with hop-on, hop-off services) and so can be a cost-effective alternative to the big bus companies. The buses are usually smaller, you'll meet lots of other travellers, and the drivers sometimes double as tour guides; conversely, some travellers find the tour-group mentality and inherent limitations don't suit them. Discounts for card-carrying students and members of hostel organisations are usually available.

Adventure Tours Australia (☎ 1300 654 604; www .adventuretours.com.au) This company does budget tours in all states except NSW. A two-day Red Centre tour starting/finishing in Alice Springs and taking in Uluru, Kata Tjuta and Kings Canyon costs $350 (plus national park entry fees), while an eight-day trip from Perth to Broome costs $1200.

Autopia Tours (☎ 1800 000 507; www.autopiatours .com.au) Autopia runs three-day trips along the Great Ocean Rd from Melbourne to Adelaide via the Grampians for $170, not including accommodation or meals (both can be arranged). The 3½-day Melbourne–Sydney tour goes via the Snowy Mountains, Canberra and the Blue Mountains ($195).

Desert Venturer (☎ 1800 079 119; www.downunder tours.com) Treks across the top of Australia. Does a three-

day Cairns–Alice Springs trip ($330, plus $55 to cover meals) and a four-day Cairns–Darwin excursion ($390, plus $75 for food). Both itineraries can be started from either end.

Easyrider Backpacker Tours (☎ 1300 308 477; www .easyridertours.com.au) A true hop-on, hop-off bus, but you can also do trips as tours. It covers the west coast from Albany to Broome, with trips out of Perth, and also offers trips from Broome to Darwin. The Southern Curl goes Perth–Margaret River–Albany–Perth ($210) in three days. A trip from Perth to Exmouth costs $310, Exmouth to Broome costs $290, and Broome to Darwin costs $510.

Groovy Grape (☎ 1800 661 177; www.groovygrape .com.au) This SA-based operator, formerly dedicated to Barossa Valley tours, also offers a seven-day Adelaide–Alice Springs camping trip for an all-inclusive $750, a two-day Boomerang return (with a night in Coober Pedy) for $160, and a three-day Great Ocean Rd trip between Adelaide and Melbourne for $290.

Island Escape Tours (☎ 1800 133 555; www.island escapetours.com) Tasmania-based company offering everything from one-day tours of Bruny Island ($95) to seven-day circumnavigations of Tasmania ($800). Ask about hop-on, hop-off options.

Nullarbor Traveller (☎ 08-8390 3297; www .the-traveller.com.au) This small company runs relaxed minibus trips across the Nullarbor. There's a nine-day Adelaide–Perth trip ($1000) via the southern forests, while the seven-day return journey ($780) goes straight through Kalgoorlie. Prices include accommodation (camping and hostels), entry fees and most meals.

Oz Experience (☎ 1300 300 028; www.ozexperience .com) This is one of those hop-on, hop-off services you will either love or hate. In the past many travellers have complained about seat availability and a boozy culture, while others rave about it as a highly social experience. The Oz Experience network covers central, northern and eastern Australia. Travel is one-directional and passes are valid for up to 12 months with unlimited stops. A Sydney–Cairns pass is $420, and from Cairns right around the east coast and up the Centre to Darwin (or vice versa) is $1530.

Wayward Bus (☎ 1300 653 510; www.waywardbus .com.au) Most trips with this reputable company allow you to get on or off where you like. The eight-day Face the Outback run travels from Adelaide to Alice Springs via Wilpena Pound, the Oodnadatta Track, Coober Pedy and Uluru ($790 including meals, camping and hostel charges; national park entry fees cost an extra $25). Classic Coast is a 3½-day trip along the Great Ocean Rd between Adelaide and Melbourne (from $300).

Wild-Life Tours (☎ 03-9741 6333; www.wildlifetours .com.au) This company offers various trips ex-Melbourne, including Adelaide and Sydney runs. Melbourne to Adelaide can be done in two to five days ($145 to $240).

TRANSPORT

Bus Passes

The following Greyhound passes are subject to a 10% discount for members of YHA, VIP, Nomads and other approved organisations, as well as card-carrying seniors/pensioners.

AUSSIE EXPLORER PASS

This popular pass gives you from one to 12 months to cover a set route – there are 23 in all and the validity period depends on the distance of the route. You don't have the go-anywhere flexibility of the Kilometre Pass (you can't backtrack), but if you can find a route that suits you it generally works out cheaper.

The Aussie Highlights pass allows you to loop around the eastern half of Australia from Sydney, taking in Melbourne, Adelaide, Coober Pedy, Alice Springs, Darwin, Cairns, Townsville, the Whitsundays, Brisbane and Surfers Paradise for $1470, including tours of Uluru–Kata Tjuta and Kakadu National Parks. Or there are one-way passes, such as the Aussie Reef & Rock, which goes from Sydney to Alice Springs (and Uluru) via Cairns and Darwin (and Kakadu) for $1130; the Top End Explorer, which takes in Cairns to Darwin (and Kakadu) for $470; and the Western Explorer from Perth to Darwin ($630).

AUSSIE KILOMETRE PASS

This is the simplest pass and gives you a specified amount of travel, starting at 2000km ($330) and going up in increments of 1000km to a maximum of 20,000km ($2310). The pass is valid for 12 months and you can travel where and in what direction you like, and stop as many times as you like. For example, a 2000km pass will get you from Cairns to Brisbane, 4000km ($560) from Cairns to Melbourne, and 12,000km ($1480) will cover a loop from Sydney through Melbourne, Adelaide, central Australia, Darwin, Cairns and back to Sydney. On the west coast you'll need 3000km to get from Perth to Broome and 5000km from Perth to Darwin.

Phone at least a day ahead to reserve a seat if you're using this pass, and bear in mind that side-trips or tours off the main route (eg to Kakadu, Uluru or Shark Bay) may be calculated at double the actual kilometre distance.

Classes

There are no separate classes on buses, and the vehicles of the different companies all look pretty similar and are equipped with air-con, toilets and videos. Smoking isn't permitted on Australian buses.

Costs

Following are the average, nondiscounted, one-way bus fares on some well-travelled Australian routes.

Route	Adult/Child/Concession
Adelaide–Darwin	$445/360/400
Adelaide–Melbourne	$60/45/55
Adelaide–Perth	$290/230/260
Brisbane–Cairns	$200/160/180
Canberra–Melbourne	$70/55/65
Canberra–Sydney	$35/30/30
Sydney–Brisbane	$100/80/90
Sydney–Melbourne	$65/50/60

Reservations

Over summer, school holidays and public holidays, book well ahead on the more popular routes, including intercity and east-coast services. Make a reservation at least a day in advance if you're using a Greyhound pass.

CAR & MOTORCYCLE

Australia is a vast, mostly sparsely populated country where public transport is often neither comprehensive nor convenient, and can sometimes be nonexistent. Anyone whose experience of Australia is limited to travelling the east coast might hotly dispute this, but on the whole it's true. Many travellers find that the best way to see the place is to purchase a car, and it's certainly the only way to get to those interesting out-of-the-way places without taking a tour.

Motorcycles are another popular way of getting around. The climate is good for bikes for much of the year, and the many small trails from the road into the bush lead to perfect spots to spend the night. Bringing your own motorcycle into Australia will entail an expensive shipping exercise, valid registration in the country of origin and a Carnet De Passages en Douanes – this is an internationally recognised customs document that allows the holder to import

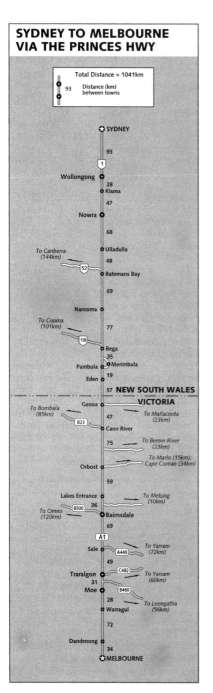

SYDNEY TO MELBOURNE VIA THE PRINCES HWY

Total Distance = 1041km

93 Distance (km) between towns

- SYDNEY
- 93
- 1
- Wollongong
- 28
- Kiama
- 47
- Nowra
- 68
- Ulladulla
- To Canberra (144km)
- 48
- 52
- Batemans Bay
- 69
- Narooma
- To Cooma (101km)
- 77
- 18
- Bega
- 35
- Pambula — Merimbula
- Eden — 19
- 57 **NEW SOUTH WALES**
- Genoa — **VICTORIA**
- To Bombala (85km)
- 47 To Mallacoota (23km)
- B23
- Cann River
- 75 To Bemm River (23km)
- To Marlo (15km)/Cape Conran (34km)
- Orbost
- 59
- Lakes Entrance — To Metung (10km)
- To Omeo (120km) — B500 — 36
- Bairnsdale
- 69
- A1
- Sale — To Yarram (72km)
- A440
- 49
- Traralgon — C482 — To Yarram (60km)
- 31
- Moe — B460
- 28 To Leongatha (56km)
- Warragul
- 72
- Dandenong
- 34
- MELBOURNE

their vehicle without paying customs duty or taxes. To get one, apply to a motoring organisation/association in your home country. You'll also need a rider's licence and a helmet. A fuel range of 350km will cover fuel stops up the Centre and on Hwy 1 around the continent. The long, open roads are tailor-made for large-capacity machines above 750cc.

Automobile Associations

The national **Australian Automobile Association** (www.aaa.asn.au) is the umbrella organisation for the various state and territory associations, which handle day-to-day operations such as providing emergency breakdown services, excellent touring maps and detailed guides to accommodation and camping grounds.

State/territory organisations have reciprocal arrangements with other Australian states and with similar organisations overseas. So if you're a member of the NRMA in NSW, for example, you can use RACV facilities in Victoria. Similarly, if you're a member of the AAA in the USA, you can use any of the Australian organisations' facilities. Bring proof of your membership with you.

Association details for each state:

Automobile Association of the Northern Territory (AANT; ☎ 08-8981 3837; www.aant.com.au)

National Roads & Motorists Association (NRMA; ☎ 13 11 22; www.nrma.com.au) In NSW and Australian Capital Territory (ACT).

Royal Automobile Association of South Australia (RAA; ☎ 08-8202 4600; www.raa.net)

Royal Automobile Club of Queensland (RACQ; ☎ 13 19 05; www.racq.com.au)

Royal Automobile Club of Tasmania (RACT; ☎ 13 27 22; www.ract.com.au)

Royal Automobile Club of Victoria (RACV; ☎ 13 19 55; www.racv.com.au)

Royal Automobile Club of Western Australia (RACWA; ☎ 13 17 03; www.rac.com.au)

Driving Licence

You can generally use your home country's driving licence in Australia, as long as it's in English (otherwise you'll need a certified translation) and carries your photograph for identification. You can also use an International Driving Permit (IDP), which must be supported by your home licence. It's easy enough to get an IDP – just go to your

TRANSPORT

home country's automobile association and they issue it on the spot. The permits are valid for 12 months.

Fuel & Spare Parts

Fuel (predominantly unleaded and diesel) is available from service stations sporting well-known international brand names. LPG (liquefied petroleum gas) is not always stocked at more remote roadhouses; if you're on gas it's safer to have dual-fuel capacity.

Prices vary from place to place but basically fuel is heavily taxed and continues to hike up, much to the disgust of local motorists. Unleaded petrol is now hovering around $1 a litre even in the cities. Once out into the country, prices soar – in outback Northern Territory (NT) and Queensland they can go as high as $1.45 a litre. Distances between fill-ups can be long in the outback but there are only a handful of tracks where you'll require a long-range fuel tank. On main roads there'll be a small town or roadhouse roughly every 150km to 200km. Note, though, that while many roadhouses on main highways are open 24 hours, this does not apply to every fuel stop and you can't always rely on a service station being open in the dead of night.

The further you get from the cities, the better it is to be in a Holden or a Ford. If you're in an older vehicle that's likely to require a replacement part, life is much simpler if it's a make for which spare parts are more readily available. VW Kombi vans were once the quintessential backpackers'

wheels, but they're notoriously bad for breaking down and difficult to find parts for, and so are a poor choice for remote Australia.

Hire

For cheaper alternatives to the car-hire prices charged by big-name international firms, try one of the many local outfits. Remember, though, that if you want to travel a significant distance you will want unlimited kilometres, and that cheap car hire often comes with serious restrictions.

You must be at least 21 years old to hire from most firms – if you're under 25 you may have to pay a surcharge. It's cheaper if you rent for a week or more and there are often low-season and weekend discounts. Credit cards are the usual payment method.

Big firms sometimes offer one-way rentals (eg pick up a car in Adelaide and leave it in Sydney) but there are many limitations, including a substantial drop-off fee, particularly for one-way rentals into or out of the NT or WA.

Major companies offer a choice: either unlimited kilometres, or 100km or so a day free plus so many cents per kilometre over this. Daily rates in cities or on the east coast are typically about $55 to $60 daily for a small car (Holden Barina, Ford Festiva, Hyundai Excel), about $65 to $80 daily for a medium car (Mitsubishi Magna, Toyota Camry, Nissan Pulsar), or $85 to $100 daily for a big car (Holden Commodore, Ford Falcon), all including insurance.

LRP RIP

In 2002 Australia discontinued the use of leaded fuel and introduced lead replacement petrol (LRP) to cater to older-model cars unable to run on unleaded petrol (ULP) – the cars in question are those pre-1986 vehicles that need lead or lead substitute in their fuel to prevent erosion of the engine valve seats. However, LRP is now being phased out due to declining demand and stocks are expected to dry up permanently by the end of 2005. In lieu of an expensive engine overhaul, drivers of older cars that relied on LRP will have to fill up with unleaded or premium unleaded petrol (generally, the higher the octane rating the better) and then manually top up their tanks with a valve-protecting additive. This additive comes in a small plastic dispenser and is sold at most service stations.

If you're planning to buy a car in Australia that was manufactured before 1986, look up the model on the website of the **Australian Institute of Petroleum** (www.aip.com.au/health/lead_guide) to see whether it accepts ULP or not. If it doesn't, and you're planning a long road trip through remote areas, stock up on the additive before heading off, as we encountered several roadhouses in central Australia that had sold out of the product.

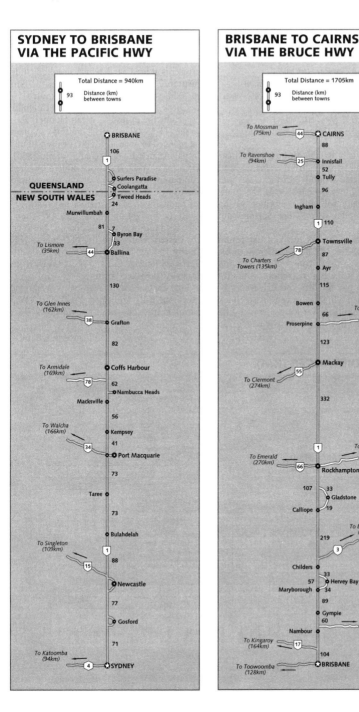

SYDNEY TO BRISBANE VIA THE PACIFIC HWY

Total Distance = 940km

93   Distance (km) between towns

BRISBANE

106

Surfers Paradise
Coolangatta
Tweed Heads

QUEENSLAND
NEW SOUTH WALES

24

Murwillumbah

81
7   Byron Bay
33
To Lismore (35km)   44   Ballina

130

To Glen Innes (162km)   38   Grafton

82

To Armidale (169km)   78   Coffs Harbour
62
Nambucca Heads
Macksville

56

To Walcha (166km)   34   Kempsey
41
Port Macquarie

73

Taree

73

Bulahdelah

To Singleton (109km)   15
88

Newcastle

77

Gosford

71

To Katoomba (94km)   4   SYDNEY

BRISBANE TO CAIRNS VIA THE BRUCE HWY

Total Distance = 1705km

93   Distance (km) between towns

To Mossman (75km)   44   CAIRNS
88
To Ravenshoe (94km)   25   Innisfail
52
Tully
96
Ingham
110
Townsville
87
To Charters Towers (135km)   78
Ayr
115
Bowen   To Airlie Beach (36km)
66
Proserpine
123
Mackay
To Clermont (274km)   55
332
To Yeppoon (40km)
To Emerald (270km)   66   Rockhampton
107   33
Gladstone
Calliope   19
To Bundaberg (53km)
219   3
Childers
33
57   Hervey Bay
Maryborough   34
89
Gympie
60   To Noosa (21km)
Nambour
To Kingaroy (164km)   17
104
To Toowoomba (128km)   BRISBANE

TRANSPORT

Major companies such as those listed here have offices or agents in most urban centres:

Avis (☎ 13 63 33; www.avis.com.au)

Budget (☎ 1300 794 344; www.budget.com.au)

Delta Europcar (☎ 1300 131 390; www.deltaeuropcar .com.au)

Hertz (☎ 13 30 39; www.hertz.com.au)

Thrifty (☎ 1300 367 227; www.thrifty.com.au)

You will usually be able to hire a small car with limited kilometres from a smaller local company from around $45 per day. **Apex** (☎ 1800 804 392; www.apexrentacar.com.au) is a good-value company with offices located in the mainland capital cities, Alice Springs and Cairns.

For a less orthodox form of car rental check out **Ezi-Ride** (☎ 07-5559 5938; www.ezi-ride .com), an organised car-pooling scheme that brings together travellers who are prepared to pay for lifts and drivers looking for cash-paying passengers. Also check out the possibilities for long-distance lifts on the virtual notice board www.needaride .com.au.

4WD & CAMPERVAN HIRE

A small 4WD like a Suzuki Vitara or Toyota Rav4 is $85 to $100 a day. A Toyota Landcruiser is at least $150, which should include insurance and some free kilometres (100km to 200km a day, or sometimes unlimited).

Check the insurance conditions carefully, especially the excess, as it can be onerous – in the NT $5000 is typical, but this can often be reduced to around $1000 (or even to nil) by paying an extra daily charge (around $50). Even for a 4WD, insurance offered by most companies may not cover damage caused travelling 'off-road', meaning anywhere that isn't a maintained bitumen or dirt road.

Hertz, Budget and Avis have 4WD rentals, with one-way rentals possible between the eastern states and the NT. In the NT, **Thrifty** (☎ 1800 891 125) has partnered with Territory Rent-A-Car and rents 4WDs from Darwin and Alice Springs.

Britz Rentals (☎ 1800 331 454; www.britz.com) hires out fully equipped 2WD and 4WD campervans. The high-season costs start

(Continued on page 1065)

ROAD DISTANCES (KM)

MAINLAND AUSTRALIA

	Adelaide	Albany	Alice Springs	Birdsville	Brisbane	Broome	Cairns	Canberra	Cape York	Darwin	Kalgoorlie	Melbourne	Perth	Sydney	Townsville
Albany	2649														
Alice Springs	1512	3573													
Birdsville	1183	3244	1176												
Brisbane	1942	4178	1849	1573											
Broome	4043	2865	2571	3564	5065										
Cairns	3079	5601	2396	1919	1705	4111									
Canberra	1372	4021	2725	2038	1287	5296	2923								
Cape York	4444	6566	3361	2884	2601	5076	965	3888							
Darwin	3006	5067	1494	2273	3774	1844	2820	3948	3785						
Kalgoorlie	2168	885	3092	2763	3697	3052	5234	3540	6199	4896					
Melbourne	728	3377	2240	1911	1860	4811	3496	637	4461	3734	2896				
Perth	2624	411	3548	3219	4153	2454	6565	3996	7530	4298	598	3352			
Sydney	1597	4246	3109	2007	940	5208	2634	289	3599	3917	3765	862	3869		
Townsville	3237	5374	2055	1578	1295	3770	341	2582	1306	2479	4893	3155	5349	2293	
Uluru	1559	3620	441	1617	2290	3012	2837	2931	3802	1935	3139	2287	3595	2804	2496

TASMANIA

	Bicheno	Cradle Mountain	Devonport	Hobart	Launceston
Cradle Mountain	383				
Devonport	283	100			
Hobart	186	296	334		
Launceston	178	205	105	209	
Queenstown	443	69	168	257	273

These are the shortest distances by road; other routes may be considerably longer.
For distances by coach, check the companies' leaflets.

Road Maps

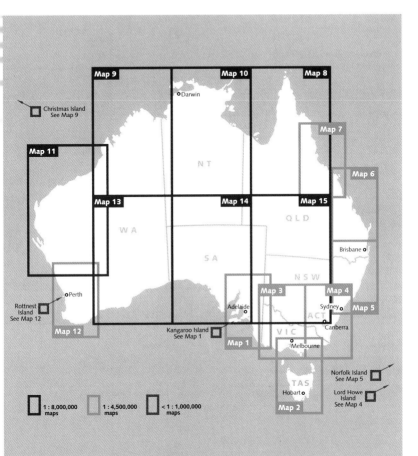

POPULATION

☼	**CANBERRA**	National Capital
◉	**SYDNEY**	State Capital
●	**Geelong**	>100 000
●	**Bathurst**	25 000 - 100 000
●	**Geraldton**	7 500 - 25 000
●	Roxby Downs	2 000 - 7 500
●	Yarrawonga	750 - 2 000
●	Rankins Springs	< 750
●	*Kalumburu*	Aboriginal Community

TRANSPORTATION

	Freeway
sealed unsealed	Primary Road
	Secondary Road
	Other Road
	Track
64	Distance in Kilometres
	Railway
39 A8	Route numbers

BOUNDARIES

	State Border
	Aboriginal Land
	National Park
	State/Other Park

NATURAL FEATURES

	Coastline
	River, Creek
	Intermittent River
	Lake
	Intermittent Lake
	Swamp
	Spring
	Reef
▲ *Mt Connor*	Hill/Mountain
	Military/Prohibited Area
	Fence

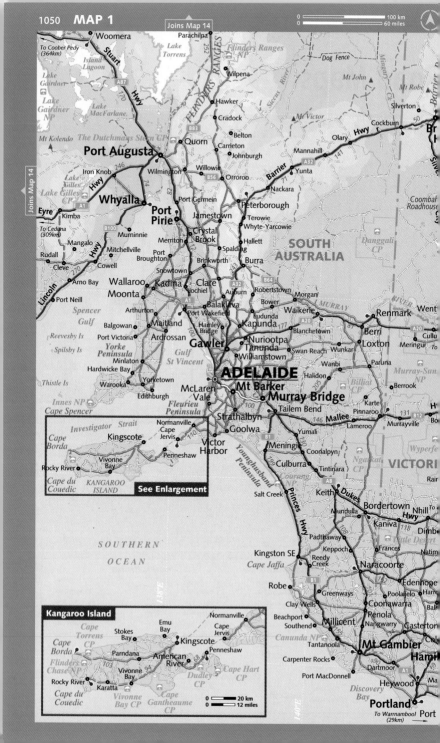

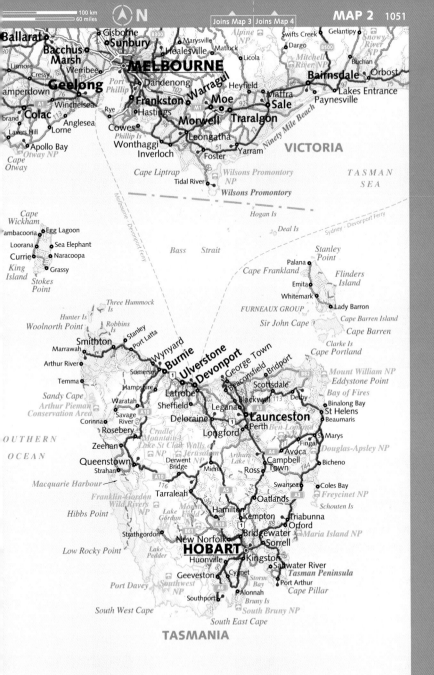

MAP 2 1051

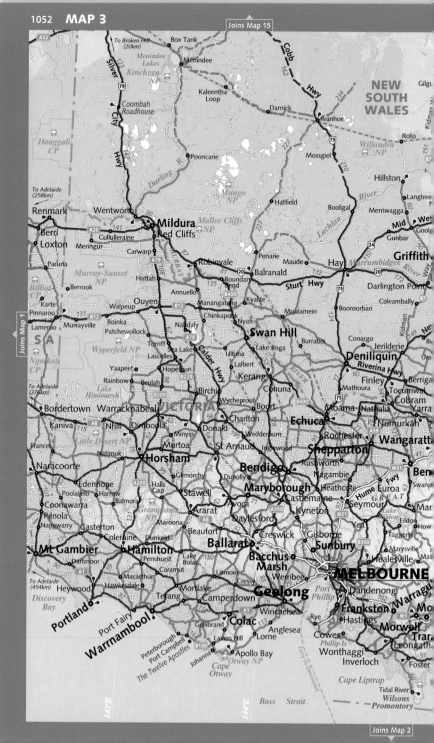

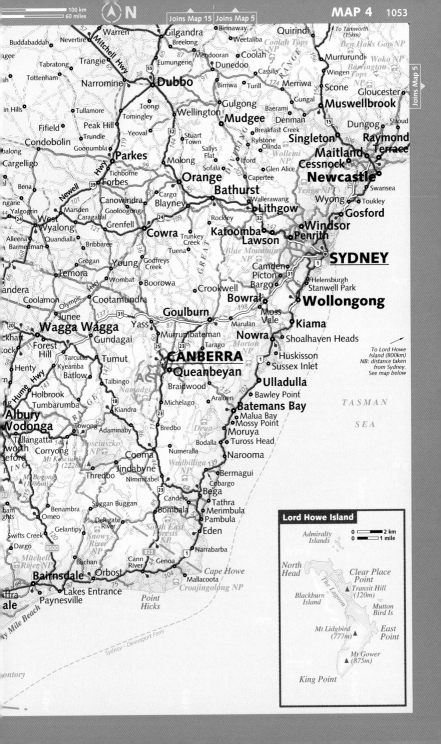

100 km
60 miles

N

Buddabaddah
Nevertire   Warren   Gilgandra   Birriway   Quirindi   To Tamworth (15km)
agee   Tabratong   Trangie   Breelong   Weetaliba   Coolah Tops   Ben Halls Gap NP
ah   Mitchell Hwy   Eumungerie   Mendooran   Coolah   NP   Murrurundi   Woko NP
Tottenham   Narromine   Dubbo   Dunedoo   Cassilis   Merriwa   Wingen   Barrington Tops
in Hills   Tullamore   Toongi   Birriwa   Turill   Gungal   Scone   NP   Gloucester
Fifield   Peak Hill   Tomingley   Wellington   Gulgong   Baerami   Muswellbrook
Trundle   Yeoval   Mudgee   Denman   Dungog   Stroud
Condobolin   Goonumbla   Stuart Town   Breakfast Creek   Singleton   Raymond
balong   Parkes   Sallys Flat   Rylstone   Maitland   Terrace
Cargelligo   Tichborne   Molong   Olinda   Cessnock
al   Bena   Forbes   Sofala   Ilford   Wollemi   Newcastle
ngarie   Yalgogrin   Newell Hwy   Orange   Glen Alice   NP   Swansea
West   Marsden   Canowindra   Cargo   Bathurst   Capertee   Yengo NP
Wyalong   Caragabal   Blayney   Wallerawang   Wyong   Toukley
Alleena   Quandialla   Grenfell   Rockley   Lithgow   Gosford
Barmedman   Bribbaree   Cowra   Trunkey Creek   Katoomba   Windsor
Grogan   Young   Godfreys Creek   Tuena   Lawson   Penrith
Temora   Wombat   Boorowa   Blue Mountains NP   Camden   SYDNEY
andera   Coolamon   Olympic Hwy   Cootamundra   Crookwell   Picton   Bargo   Helensburgh
Junee   Yass   Bowral   Stanwell Park
ckhart   Wagga Wagga   Murrumbateman   Goulburn   Moss Vale   Wollongong
ock   Forest Hill   Gundagai   Marulan   Kiama
Henty   Tarcutta   Tumut   Tarago   Nowra   Shoalhaven Heads
Kyeamba   Batlow   CANBERRA   Morton NP   To Lord Howe Island (800km)
Albury   Holbrook   Talbingo   Queanbeyan   Huskisson   NB: distance taken from Sydney. See map below
Wodonga   Tumbarumba   Braidwood   Sussex Inlet
Tallangatta   Towong   ACT   Ulladulla   TASMAN
worth   Corryong   Kiandra   Namadgi   Michelago   Araluen   Bawley Point
eford   Adaminaby   Bredbo   Deua NP   Batemans Bay   SEA
Mt Kosciuszko (2228m)   Cooma   Malua Bay
Thredbo   Jindabyne   Numeralla   Mossy Point
ING   Mt Bogong (1986m)   Nimmitabel   Moruya
Mt Kosciuszko   Bodalla   Tuross Head
Benambra   Suggan Buggan   Wadbilliga NP   Narooma
ham   Omeo   Candelo   Cobargo   Bermagui
ghts   Gelantipy   Delegate River   Bega
Swifts Creek   Dargo   Snowy River NP   Bombala   Tathra
Mitchell River   Buchan   South East Forests NP   Merimbula
Bairnsdale   Orbost   Cann River   Genoa   Pambula
iffra   Lakes Entrance   Narrabarba   Eden
ale   Paynesville   Cape Howe   Mallacoota
y Mile Beach   Point Hicks   Croajingolong NP
ontory   Sydney - Devonport Ferry

Lord Howe Island

Admiralty Islands   0 ——— 2 km   0 ——— 1 mile
North Head   The Lagoon   Clear Place Point
Blackburn Island   Transit Hill (120m)   Mutton Bird Is
Mt Lidgbird (777m)   East Point
Mt Gower (875m)
King Point

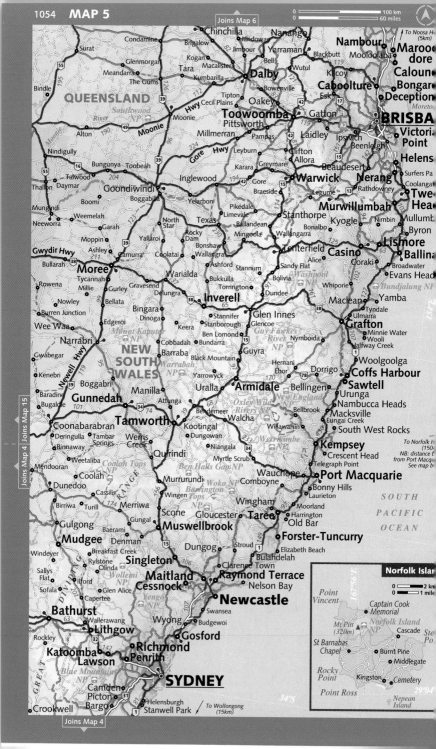

Joins Map 6

0   100 km
0   60 miles

To Noosa He
(5km)

QUEENSLAND

Southwood
NP

Chinchilla
Nanango
Nambour
Maroo
dore
Condamine
Brigalow
Jandowae
Jimbour
Yarraman
Blackbutt
Mooloolab
Caloun
Surat
Kogan
Bell
Wutul
Kilcoy
Caboolture
Bongar
Glenmorgan
Macalister
Bowenville
Esk
Deception
Meandarra
Tara
Kumbarilla
Dalby
119
The Gums
Tipton
Cecil Plains
Oakey
Gatton
17
BRISBA
Alton
Moonie
Toowoomba
42
Nindigully
Pittsworth
Laidley
Ipswich
Victori
Point
Millmerran
Pampas
42
Beenleigh
M1
Bungunya
Toobeah
Leyburn
Clifton
Allora
Helens
Talwood
204
Karara
Greymare
Beaudesert
Thallon
Daymar
Inglewood
194
42
Gore
Warwick
Nerang
Surfers Pa
Boomi
Braeside
15
Rathdowney
13
Coolanga
Mungindi
Goondiwindi
Legume
Twe
Neeworra
Boggabilla
Yelarbon
Stanthorpe
Murwillumbah
Hea
Weemelah
Garah
Texas
Pikedale
Limevale
Kyogle
Nimbin
Mullumb
Moppin
North
Star
Ballandean
Bonalbo
Byron
Yallaroi
Rocky
Dam
Mingoola
Wallangarra
Tenterfield
Casino
Lismore
Ashley
211
Bonshaw
Wallangra
Sandy Flat
Alice
Coraki
Ballina
Bullarah
Camurra
Coolatai
Ashford
Bolivia
Whiporie
Broadwater
Moree
Warialda
Bukkulla
Dundee
Evans Head
Tycannah
Gurley
Gravesend
Torrington
Stannum
Macleay
Yamba
Millie
Delungra
Inverell
Washpool
Tyndale
Bellata
65
Bundjalung NP
Bingara
Dinoga
Stannifer
Glen Innes
Ulmarra
Wee Waa
Keera
Stanborough
Glencoe
Grafton
Gwabegar
Edgeroi
Ben Lomond
15
Nymboida
Minnie Water
Wooli
Narrabri
Cobbadah
Bundarra
Guyra
Hernani
Halfway Creek
Kenebri
Barraba
Black Mountain
Ebor
78
Dorrigo
Woolgoolga
Boggabri
Yarrowyck
170
Coffs Harbour
Manilla
Uralla
Armidale
Bellingen
Sawtell
Baradine
Attunga
Bendemeer
Urunga
Bugaldie
Gunnedah
34
Walcha
Nambucca Heads
Coonabarabran
Kootingal
Bellbrook
Macksville
Deriabri
Tambar
Springs
74
Tamworth
Dungowan
Willawarrin
Eungai Creek
South West Rocks
Binnaway
Werris
Creek
Niangala
To Norfolk I
(150
Weetaliba
Qurrindi
Myrtle Scrub
Kempsey
Mendooran
Coolah
Murrurundi
34
Wauchope
Crescent Head
Telegraph Point
Dunedoo
Cassilis
Wingen
Comboyne
Port Macquarie
Birriwa
Turill
Merriwa
Gungal
Wingham
Moorland
Bonny Hills
Laurieton
Gulgong
Baerami
Scone
Gloucester
Taree
Harrington
Old Bar
Mudgee
Denman
Muswellbrook
Stroud
Forster-Tuncurry
Windeyer
Breakfast Creek
Dungog
Elizabeth Beach
Singleton
Bulahdelah
Ilford
Glen Alice
Maitland
Clarence Town
Bathurst
Capertee
Cessnock
Raymond Terrace
Nelson Bay
Wallerawang
Newcastle
Rockley
Lithgow
Swansea
Gosford
Richmond
Katoomba
Wyong
Budgewoi
Lawson
Penrith
Crookwell
Camden
Picton
SYDNEY
Bargo
Helensburgh
Stanwell Park
To Wollongong
(15km)

**NEW
SOUTH
WALES**

Newell Hwy

Gwydir Hwy

Gore Hwy

Norfolk Islar

0   2 km
0   1 mile

Point
Vincent
Captain Cook
Memorial
Mt Pitt
(320m)
Norfolk Island
NP
Cascade
St Barnabas
Chapel
Burnt Pine
Middlegate
Rocky
Point
Kingston
Cemetery
Point Ross
Nepean
Island

Joins Map 4

Joins Map 15

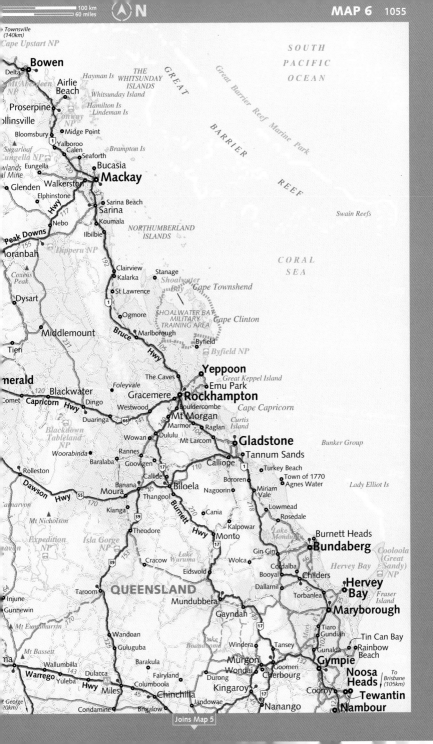

MAP 6 1055

100 km
60 miles

N

*Townsville
(140km)*
Cape Upstart NP

Bowen
Delta

*Mt Aberdeen
NP*

Airlie
Beach

Proserpine
ollinsville

Hayman Is
*THE
WHITSUNDAY
ISLANDS*
Whitsunday Island

*Hamilton Is
Lindeman Is*

Bloomsbury
Midge Point
Conway
NP
Yalboroo
Calen
Seaforth

Brampton Is

*Sugarloaf
ungella NP*
Eungella
al Mine

Bucasia
Mackay
Walkerston

Glenden
Elphinstone

Sarina Beach
Sarina
Koumala

Nebo

Ilbilbie

*NORTHUMBERLAND
ISLANDS*

Peak Downs
loranbah

Clairview
Kalarka
St Lawrence

Stanage

*Shoalwater
Bay* *Cape Townshend*

*CORAL
SEA*

*Coxens
Peak*

Dysart

Ogmore

*SHOALWATER BAY
MILITARY
TRAINING AREA*

Cape Clinton

Middlemount

Bruce
Marlborough

Tieri

Byfield
Byfield NP

emerald

Hwy

The Caves
Yeppoon
Great Keppel Island

Blackwater
Comet **Capricorn**
Foleyvale
Gracemere
Emu Park

Dingo
Hwy
Rockhampton

Duaringa
Westwood
Bouldercombe

Mt Morgan

Cape Capricorn

Wowan
Marmor
Raglan

*Blackdown
Tableland
NP*

Dululu

Mt Larcom
Gladstone

Bunker Group

Wooroobinda
Rannes
Goovigen

*Curtis
Island*

Tannum Sands

Baralaba

Calliope
Turkey Beach

Callide
Bororen
Town of 1770
Agnes Water

Lady Elliot Is

Rolleston
Dawson
Banana
Biloela
Moura
Thangool

Miriam
Vale

Kianga
Nagoorin

Lowmead
Rosedale

amarvon

Mt Nicholson

Theodore

Cania

Kalpowar
Monto

*Lake
Monduran*

Burnett Heads
Bundaberg

*Expedition
NP*

*Isla Gorge
NP*

Cracow
*Lake
Wuruma*

Gin Gin
Wolca

*Cooloola
(Great
Sandy)
NP*

Hervey Bay

Injune

Eidsvold
Cordalba
Booyal
Childers

Gunnewin

Taroom

Dallarnil
Torbanlea
**Hervey
Bay**

Mt Eumamurrin

QUEENSLAND
Mundubbera
*Fraser
Island*
Maryborough

Gayndah

Tiaro
Gundiah

Wandoan
Guluguba

Windera
Tansey

Tin Can Bay
Gunalda
**Rainbow
Beach**

Mt Bassett

Barakula

Murgon
Wondai
Goomeri
Gympie

na
Wallumbilla
743
Dulacca
Fairyland
Durong
Cherbourg

**Noosa
Heads**

Warrego
Yuleba
Columboola
Hwy
Miles

Kingaroy
Cooroy
*To
Brisbane
(105km)*
Tewantin

*George
?0km)*

Chinchilla
Jandowae
Condamine
Bigalow
Nanango
Nambour

Joins Map 5

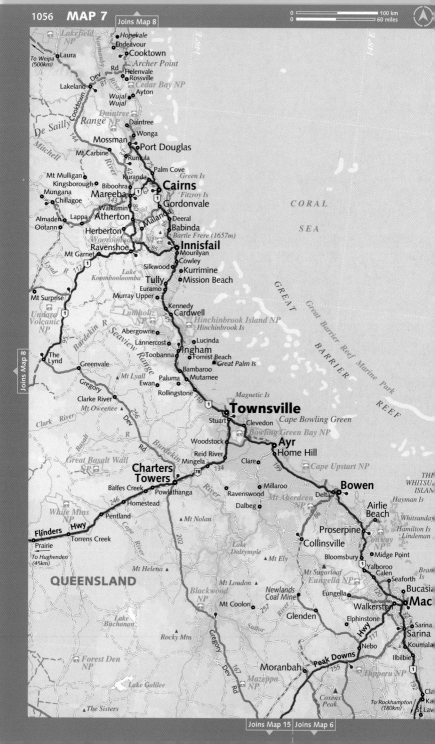

Joins Map 8

0 ———— 100 km
0 ———— 60 miles

Lakefield NP

To Weipa (500km)
Laura
Hopevale
Endeavour
Cooktown
Archer Point
Lakeland
Helenvale
Rossville
Ayton
Wujal Wujal
Cedar Bay NP

De Sailly *Range*

Daintree NP

Daintree
Wonga

Mossman
Mt Carbine
Rumula
Port Douglas
Palm Cove
Kuranda
Green Is

Mt Mulligan
Kingsborough
Mungana
Chillagoe
Biboohra
Mareeba
Walkamin
Atherton
Cairns
Gordonvale
Fitzroy Is

Almaden
Ootann
Lappa
Herberton
Deeral
Babinda
▲ Bartle Frere (1657m)

Mt Garnet
Ravenshoe
Innisfail
Mourilyan
Cowley
Kurrimine
Silkwood
Tully
Mission Beach

Mt Surprise
Lake Koomboloomba
Euramo
Murray Upper
Kennedy
Cardwell
Hinchinbrook Island NP
Hinchinbrook Is

Undara Volcanic NP

Lumholtz NP

Abergowrie
Lannercost
Lucinda
Toobanna
Ingham
Forrest Beach
Great Palm Is

The Lynd
Greenvale
Bambaroo
▲ Mt Lyall
Paluma
Ewan
Mutarnee
Rollingstone

Seaview Range

CORAL

SEA

GREAT

Great Barrier Reef Marine Park

BARRIER

REEF

Gregory
▲ Mt Oweenee
Magnetic Is

Clark River
Stuart
Townsville
Cape Bowling Green
Clevedon
Bowling Green Bay NP

Great Basalt Wall NP

Woodstock
Reid River
Mingela
Ayr
Home Hill
Clare
Cape Upstart NP

Charters Towers
Balfes Creek
Powlathanga
Ravenswood
Millaroo
Clare
199
Delta
Bowen

Homestead
134
Dalbeg
▲ Mt Aberdeen NP
Airlie Beach
Hayman Is
THI WHITSU ISLAN

Flinders **Hwy**
Pentland
▲ Mt Nolan
Mt Ely
Proserpine
Collinsville
Hamilton Is
Lindeman
Whitsunday

Prairie
Torrens Creek
Lake Dalrymple
Bloomsbury
Midge Point
Conway NP

To Hughenden (45km)

QUEENSLAND

Mt Helena ▲
Mt Loudon ▲
Newlands Coal Mine
Glenden
▲ Mt Sugarloaf
Eungella NP
Yalboroo
Calen
Seaforth
Bucasia
Mac

Mt Coolon
Eungella
Walkerston
Sarina
Bran

Blackwood NP

Lake Buchanan
257
Glenden
Elphinstone
Sarina
Koumala

Rocky Mtn
Nebo
Ilbilbie
Dipperu NP

Forest Den NP

Lake Galilee
Moranbah
Peak Downs
155
To Rockhampton (180km)
Cla
Ka
St Lav

▲ The Sisters
Mazeppa NP
Coxens Peak

Joins Map 15 | Joins Map 6

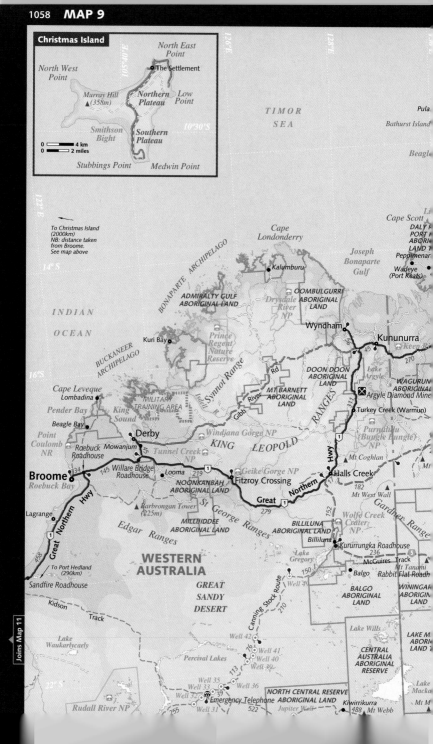

Christmas Island

North East
Point

North West
Point

The Settlement

Murray Hill
▲ (358m)

*Northern
Plateau*

Low
Point

*Smithson
Bight*

*Southern
Plateau*

0 ———— 4 km
0 ———— 2 miles

Stubbings Point   Medwin Point

*TIMOR
SEA*

Pula

Bathurst Island

Beagle

To Christmas Island
(2000km)
NB: distance taken
from Broome.
See map above

Cape
Londonderry

Cape Scott

*Joseph
Bonaparte
Gulf*

DALY
PORT
ABORI
LAND

Peppimenar

Kalumburu

Wadeye
(Port Keats)

BONAPARTE ARCHIPELAGO

ADMIRALTY GULF
ABORIGINAL LAND

Drysdale
River
NP

OOMBULGURRI
ABORIGINAL
LAND

Wyndham

Kununurra

Keen

*INDIAN
OCEAN*

Kuri Bay

*Prince
Regent
Nature
Reserve*

Sir
Synnot Range

Rd

DOON DOON
ABORIGINAL
LAND

45

56

Lake
Argyle

270

WAGURIN
ABORIGINAL

*BUCKANEER
ARCHIPELAGO*

MILITARY
TRAINING AREA

MT BARNETT
ABORIGINAL
LAND

MT
BARNETT
ABORIGINAL
LAND

RANGES

311

Argyle Diamond Mine

Cape Leveque
Lombadina

Pender Bay

Beagle Bay

*King
Sound*

River

Gibb

R

Turkey Creek (Warmun)

*Purnululu
(Bungle Bungle)
NP*

Point
Coulomb
NR

Derby

Windjana Gorge NP

KING

LEOPOLD

Mt Coghlan

Mt

Roebuck
Roadhouse

Mowanjum

Tunnel Creek
NP

Broome

Roebuck Bay

145

Willare Bridge
Roadhouse

34

Looma

219

1

Geike Gorge NP

NOONKANBAH
ABORIGINAL LAND

Fitzroy Crossing

Great

Northern

Halls Creek

47

Hwy

182

Mt West Wall

Gardner Range

Lagrange

Great Northern Hwy

1

458

St George Ranges

279

1

MILLIJIDDEE
ABORIGINAL LAND

Barbrongan Tower
(225m)

Edgar Ranges

BILLILUNA
ABORIGINAL LAND

Billiluna

152

Wolfe Creek
Crater
NP

Kururrungka Roadhouse

236

To Port Hedland
(290km)

Sandfire Roadhouse

**WESTERN
AUSTRALIA**

*GREAT
SANDY
DESERT*

*Lake
Gregory*

150

McGuires Track

Balgo

Mt Tanami

Rabbit Flat Roadh

WININGAN
ABORIGIN
LAND

Kidson

Track

BALGO
ABORIGINAL
LAND

Well 4

210

Canning Stock Route

*Lake
Waukarlycarly*

Percival Lakes

Well 42

Well 41
Well 40
Well 39

76

113

Lake Wills

CENTRAL
AUSTRALIA
ABORIGINAL
RESERVE

LAKE M
ABORI
LAND

Well 35

Well 33

Well 36

Rudall River NP

Well 31

Emergency Telephone

265

NORTH CENTRAL RESERVE
ABORIGINAL LAND

Jupiter Well

522

Kiwirrkurra

488 Mt Webb

Lake
Macka

Mt

Joins Map 11

ARAFURA SEA

Cobourg
Peninsula
Croker
Island

Island
rti
taramoor

Garig Gunak
Barlu NP

Van Diemen Gulf

Braithwaite
Point

WESSEL
ISLANDS

Marchinbar Is

Guluwuru Is

Maningrida

Galiwinku

Nhulunbuy

DARWIN
Palmerston
Noonamah

Oenpelli

Ramingining

Dhupuma

Jabiru
Nourlangie

Gapuwiyak

Gove
Peninsula

Garrthalala

Bark Hut Inn
Adelaide River

Mt Gilruth

Kakadu
NP

Arnhem
Land

ARNHEM LAND
ABORIGINAL
LAND TRUST

Cape Grey

Mary River Roadhouse

Bulman

Mt Marumha

Alyangula

Butterfly
Gorge
NP

Pine Creek

Mt Furner

Numbulwar

Angurugu

GULF

Nitmiluk
(Katherine Gorge)

Beswick

Katherine

Roper
Bar

Ngukurr

Port Roper

GROOTE
EYLANDT

OF

CARPENTARIA

Stuart
Hwy

Mataranka

Maria Is

MARRA ABORIGINAL LAND TRUST

regory
NP

Victoria
Hwy

Elsey
NP

HODGSON DOWNS
ABORIGINAL LAND

SIR EDWARD
PELLEW GROUP

Larrimah

ALAWA
ABORIGINAL
LAND TRUST

Vanderlin Is

Victoria
R

Daly Waters

Borroloola

Top Springs

Dunmarra

Mt Brown

Darwin

Alice Springs to

BARKLY TABLELAND

Cape Crawford

GARAWA
ABORIGINAL
LAND TRUST

Mornington Is

Gununa

Kalkarindji

Mt Seale

Newcastle Waters

Elliott

NORTHERN
TERRITORY

Tablelands
Hwy

Hell's Gate
Roadhouse

Mt Reid

Lake
Woods

Railway

WAANYI /
GARAWA
ABORIGINAL
LAND

Doomadgee

jamanu

Mirrinyungu

Renner Springs

Mt Hawker

Tarrabool
Lake

Mt Morgan

Mt Steiglitz

Gregory
Downs
Hotel

Dawn Hill
NP

mecke

KARLANTUPA NORTH
ABORIGINAL LAND TRUST

Lake
Sylvester

Mt Lamb

Mt Oxide

NTRAL DESERT
ABORIGINAL
AND TRUST

Threeways

Barkly

Barkly Homestead Roadhouse

Gunpowder

TANAMI

DESERT

Tennant Creek

MUNGKARTA
ABORIGINAL
LAND TRUST

Hwy

Wunura Store

Camooweal

Camooweal
Caves
NP

KARLANTUPA SOUTH
ABORIGINAL
LAND TRUST

Devils Marbles
Conservation Reserve

WAKAYA ABORIGINAL
LAND TRUST

Mt Isa

Mt Solitaire

Mt Rawlins

Wycliffe Well

Wauchope

Davenport Range
NP

Alpurrurulam

QLD

WIRLYAJARRAYI
ABORIGINAL
LAND

Ali-Curung

Mt Theo

Barrow Creek

Stuart

Mt Alone

Urandangi

Dajarra

Mt Leichhardt

Honeymoon
Bore

Sandover

Mt Hogarth

ewell

Yuendumu

Hwy

Ti Tree

Mt Dixon

Arlparra Store

Hwy

Mt Guide

To Boulia
(147 km)

Tanami
Rd

Aileron

Urapuntja

Mt Sainthill

Leslie Peak

Tilmouth Well Roadhouse

To Alice
Springs
(68 km)

Plenty

Hwy

Joins Map 14

MAP 12 1061

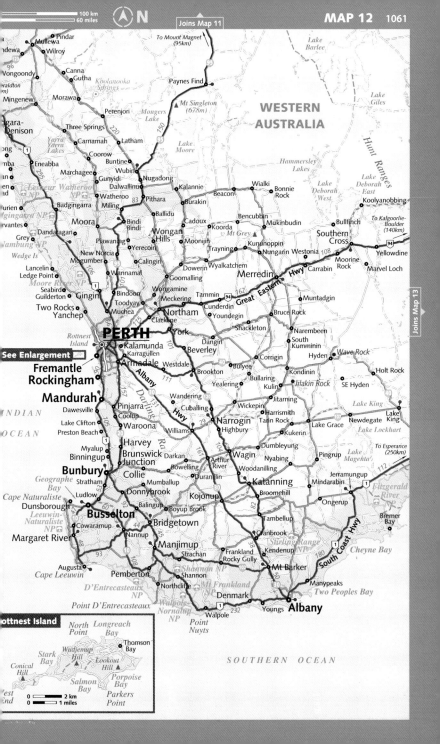

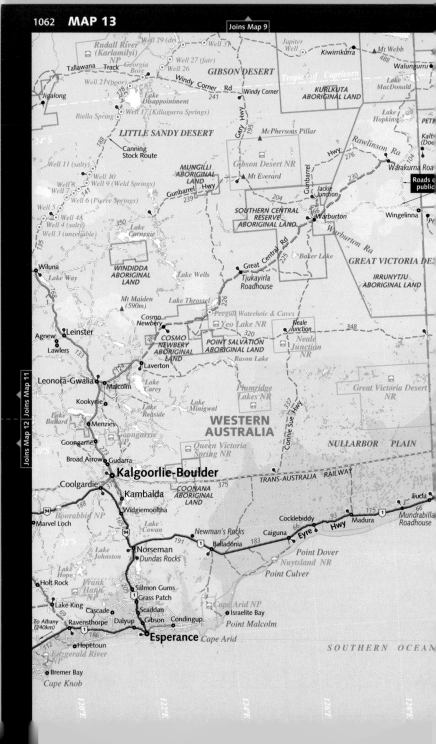

Joins Map 9

Rudall River (Karlamilyi) NP

Well 29 (dry) Well 31 Jupiter Well Kiwirrikurra Mt Webb 488 Walungurru

Tallawana Track Georgia Bore Well 27 (fair) GIBSON DESERT Tropic of Capricorn KURLKUTA ABORIGINAL LAND Lake MacDonald

Jigalong Well 21 (poor) Well 26 Windy Corner Rd 241 Windy Corner

178 Lake Disappointment PET

24°S 188 Biella Spring Well 17 (Killagurra Springs) Lake Hopkins Kalt (Doc

LITTLE SANDY DESERT McPhersons Pillar Rawlinson Ra 104

Canning Stock Route Gibson Desert NR Hwy 276 Warakurna Roa

Well 11 (salty) MUNGILLI ABORIGINAL LAND Mt Everard Gunbarrel 230 Roads public

Well 8 Well 10 Well 9 (Weld Springs) 195 Jackie Junction

Well 7 141 Gunbarrel Hwy 239 204 66 Warburton Wingelinna

Well 6 (Pierre Springs) SOUTHERN CENTRAL RESERVE ABORIGINAL LAND Warburton Ra

Well 5 Well 4A 350 Lake Carnegie 225 Baker Lake GREAT VICTORIA DE:

Well 4 (salty) Well 3 (unreliable) 135 IRRUNYTJU ABORIGINAL LAND

Wiluna Lake Way WINDIDDA ABORIGINAL LAND Lake Wells Great Central Rd Tjukayirla Roadhouse

198 Mt Maiden (590m) Lake Throssel 226 Peegull Waterhole & Caves

Agnew Leinster Cosmo Newberry Yeo Lake NR Neale Junction 348

Lawlers 133 COSMO NEWBERY ABORIGINAL LAND 320 Neale Junction NR

Leonora-Gwalia 124 Laverton POINT SALVATION ABORIGINAL LAND Rason Lake

Malcolm Lake Carey Plumridge Lakes NR Great Victoria Desert NR

Kookynie Lake Reaside Lake Minigwal WESTERN AUSTRALIA 337

Lake Ballard Menzies Goongarrie Queen Victoria Spring NR Connie Sue Hwy NULLARBOR PLAIN

Goongarrie 30°S

Broad Arrow Gudarra **Kalgoorlie-Boulder**

Coolgardie COONANA ABORIGINAL LAND 375 TRANS-AUSTRALIA RAILWAY

94 Kambalda Eucla

Boorabbin NP Widgiemooltha Cocklebiddy 93 Madura 115 1 Mundrabilla

Marvel Loch 188 Lake Cowan Newman's Rocks Caiguna 66 Eyre Hwy Roadhouse

94 Norseman 791 Balladonia 183 Point Dover

Lake Johnston Dundas Rocks 1 Nuytsland NR Point Culver

Lake Hope Holt Rock Point Malcolm SOUTHERN OCEAN

Frank Hann NP Salmon Gums Cape Arid NP

Lake King Cascade Grass Patch Scaddan Israelite Bay

Ravensthorpe Dalyup Gibson Condingup Point Malcolm

To Albany (240km) 1 186 **Esperance** Cape Arid

Hopetoun Fitzgerald River 712

Bremer Bay Cape Knob

Joins Map 12 Joins Map 11

120°E 122°E 124°E 126°E 128°E

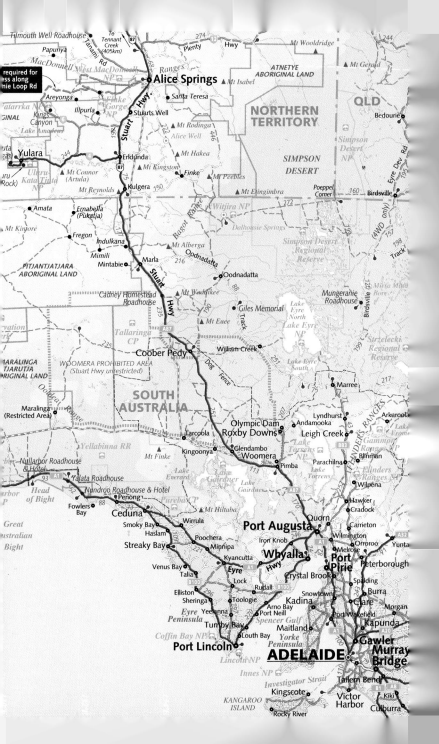

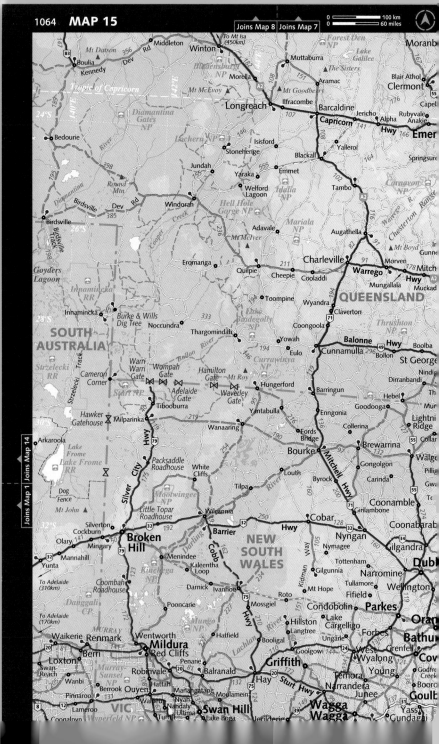

Joins Map 8 | Joins Map 7

0 — 100 km
0 — 60 miles

Joins Map 1 | Joins Map 14

(*Continued from page 1048*)

from around $100 (two-berth) or $170 (four-berth) per day for a minimum hire of five days (with unlimited kilometres), but the price climbs steadily from there. To reduce the insurance excess from $5000 to a few hundred dollars costs an extra $35 per day for a 2WD and $50 per day for a 4WD. One-way rentals are also possible.

Many other places rent campervans, especially in Tasmania and the Top End. Check out **Backpacker Campervans** (☎ 1800 670 232; www.backpackercampervans.com) and the loud colour schemes of **Wicked Campers** (☎ 1800 246 869; www.wickedcampers.com.au).

Insurance

In Australia, third-party personal injury insurance is included in the vehicle registration cost, ensuring that every registered vehicle carries at least minimum insurance. We recommend extending that minimum to at least third-party property insurance – minor collisions can be amazingly expensive.

When it comes to hire cars, understand your liability in the event of an accident. Rather than risk paying out thousands of dollars, you can take out your own comprehensive car insurance or (the usual option) pay an additional daily amount to the rental company for an 'insurance excess reduction' policy. This reduces the excess you must pay in the event of an accident from between $2000 and $5000 to a few hundred dollars.

Be aware that if travelling on dirt roads you will not be covered by insurance unless you have a 4WD. Also, most companies' insurance won't cover the cost of damage to glass (including the windscreen) or tyres.

Outback Travel

You can drive all the way around Australia on Hwy 1 and through the Centre from Adelaide to Darwin without leaving sealed roads. However, if you really want to see outback Australia, there are plenty of routes that breathe new life into the phrase 'off the beaten track'.

While you may not need 4WD or fancy equipment to tackle most of these roads, you do need to be carefully prepared for the isolation and lack of facilities. Vehicles should be in good condition and have reasonable ground clearance. Always carry a tow rope so that some passing good Samaritan can pull your broken-down car to the next garage.

When travelling to very remote areas, such as the central deserts, it's advisable to carry a high-frequency (HF) radio transceiver equipped to pick up the Royal Flying Doctor Service bases. A satellite phone and Global Positioning System (GPS) finder can also be handy. Of course, all this equipment comes at a cost, but travellers have perished in the Australian desert after breaking down. Always carry plenty of water. In warm weather allow 5L per person per day and an extra amount for the radiator, carried in several containers.

Do not attempt the tougher routes during the hottest part of the year (October to April inclusive) – apart from the risk of heat exhaustion, simple mishaps can lead to tragedy at this time. Conversely, there's no point going anywhere on outback dirt roads if there has been recent flooding. Get local advice before heading off into the middle of nowhere. For more information regarding Australia's climate see p1014.

OUTBACK ROAD SHOW

On many outback highways you'll see thundering road trains – huge trucks (a prime mover plus two or three trailers) up to 50m long. These things don't move over for anyone and it's like something out of a *Mad Max* movie to have one bearing down on you at 120km/h. When you see a road train approaching on a narrow bitumen road, slow down and pull over – if it has to put its wheels off the road to pass you, the resulting shower of stones will almost certainly smash your windscreen. When trying to overtake one, allow plenty of room (about a kilometre) to complete the manoeuvre. Road trains throw up a lot of dust on dirt roads, so if you see one coming it's best to pull over and stop until it's gone past.

And while you're on outback roads, don't forget to give the standard bush wave to oncoming drivers – it's simply a matter of lifting the index finger off the steering wheel to acknowledge your fellow motorist.

TRANSPORT

If you do run into trouble in the back of beyond, don't wander off – stay with your car. It's easier to spot a car than a human from the air, and you wouldn't be able to carry a heavy load of water very far anyway. SA police suggest you carry two spare tyres (for added safety) and, if stranded, try to set fire to one of them (let the air out first) – the pall of smoke will be seen for miles.

Before you set out, let family, friends or your car-hire company know where you're going and when you intend to be back.

OUTBACK TRACKS

Birdsville Track

Running 517km from Marree in SA to Birdsville just across the border of Queensland, this old droving trail (p792) is one of Australia's best-known outback routes. It's generally feasible to travel it in any well-prepared, conventional vehicle.

Canning Stock Route

This old 1700km-long cattle-droving trail runs southwest from Halls Creek to Wiluna in WA. The route crosses the Great Sandy Desert and Gibson Desert and, since the track is entirely unmaintained, it's a route to be taken very seriously. Like the Simpson Desert crossing, you should travel only in a well-equipped 4WD party. Nobody does this trip in summer.

Gibb River Road

This 'short cut' between Derby and Kununurra runs through the heart of the spectacular Kimberley in northern WA – it's 710km, compared with about 920km via Hwy 1. The going is much slower but the surroundings are so beautiful you'll probably find yourself lingering anyway. Although badly corrugated in places, it can usually be negotiated without too much difficulty by conventional vehicles in the dry season (May to November); it's impassable in the Wet.

Great Central Road

This route runs west from Uluru to Laverton in WA, from where you can drive down to Kalgoorlie and on to Perth. The road is well maintained and is normally OK for conventional vehicles, but it's pretty remote. It passes through Aboriginal land for which travel permits must be obtained in advance – see Permits, p798 (NT) and

p880 (WA) for details. It's almost 1500km from Yulara (the town nearest Uluru) to Kalgoorlie. For 300km, from near the Giles Meteorological Station, this road and the Gunbarrel Hwy run on the same route. Taking the old Gunbarrel (to the north of Warburton) to Wiluna in WA is a much rougher trip requiring a 4WD.

Oodnadatta Track

Running mainly parallel to the old Ghan railway line through Alice Springs, this track (p785) is comprehensively bypassed by the sealed Stuart Hwy to the west. It's 429km from Marree to Oodnadatta, then another 216km to the Stuart Hwy at Marla. So long as there is no rain, any well-prepared conventional vehicle should be able to manage this fascinating route.

Peninsula Developmental Road

This road up to the tip of Cape York (p453) has a number of river crossings, such as the Jardine, that can only be made in the dry season. Only those in 4WD vehicles should consider the journey to Cape York, via any route. The shortest route from Cairns is 1000km, but a worthwhile alternative is Cooktown to Musgrave via Lakefield National Park, which then meets up with the main route.

Plenty & Sandover Highways

These remote routes run east from the Stuart Hwy north of Alice Springs to Boulia or Mt Isa in Queensland. They're normally suitable for conventional vehicles, though are often rough.

Simpson Desert

The route crossing the Simpson Desert from the Stuart Hwy to Birdsville (p385) is a real test of driver and vehicle. A 4WD is definitely required and you should be in a party of at least three vehicles equipped with HF radios.

Strzelecki Track

This track (p792) covers much the same territory as the Birdsville Track, starting south of Marree at Lyndhurst and going to Innamincka, 460km northeast and close to the Queensland border. It was at Innamincka that the hapless explorers Burke and Wills died. This route has been much improved due to work on the Moomba gas fields.

Tanami Track

Turning off the Stuart Hwy just north of Alice Springs, this route goes northwest across the Tanami Desert to Halls Creek in WA. The road has been extensively improved in recent years and conventional vehicles are normally OK, although there are sandy stretches on the WA side and it's very corrugated if it hasn't been graded for a while. Be warned that the Rabbit Flat roadhouse in the middle of the desert is open only from Friday to Monday, so if you don't have long-range fuel tanks, plan your trip accordingly. Get advice on road conditions in Alice Springs.

Purchase

You should be able to buy a 1982 to 1984 XE Ford Falcon station wagon in good condition for between $1500 and $2500, while an XF Falcon (1985 to 1986) costs around $3000 to $3500; both models are popular with backpackers. Japanese cars of a similar size and age are more expensive, but old Mitsubishi Sigmas and Nissan Bluebirds are usually cheap and reliable. If there are only two of you, a panel van with a mattress in the back is a good option – it's cheaper than a campervan and more comfortable to sleep in than a station wagon.

See the boxed text (p1046) for information on a fuel issue with older-model cars.

You can buy a vehicle through a car dealer, but it's much cheaper if you buy one through car markets, automobile auctions or privately through newspapers or traveller notice boards. Buying through a car dealer does have the advantage of some sort of guarantee, but this is not much use if you're buying a car in Sydney for a trip to Perth.

Sydney, Perth, Fremantle and Darwin are particularly good places to buy cars from backpackers who have finished their trip. These vehicles will have done plenty of kilometres but often come complete with camping gear, Eskies, water containers, tools and road maps. The large car markets in the aforementioned cities (plus Melbourne) are worth investigating too. See the Sydney section (p142) for the situation at this popular starting/finishing point.

When it comes to buying or selling a car, every state has its own regulations, particularly in regard to registration (rego). In Victoria, for example, a car needs a compulsory safety check (Certificate of Roadworthiness) before it can be registered in the new owner's name. In NSW and the NT, safety checks are compulsory every year when it's time to renew the registration. Stamp duty has to be paid when you buy a car and, as this is based on the purchase price, it's not unknown for buyer and seller to agree privately to understate the price.

Note that it's much easier to sell a car in the same state that it's registered in, otherwise you (or the buyer) must re-register it in the new state, and that's a hassle. Vehicles with interstate plates are particularly hard to get rid of in WA.

The start of winter (June) is a good time to begin looking for a second-hand motorcycle. Australian newspapers and the local bike-related press have classified advertisement sections; $3500 should get you something that will take you around the country, provided you know a bit about bikes. The main drawback is that you'll have to try to sell it again afterwards.

BUY-BACK DEALS

One way of getting around the hassles of buying and selling a vehicle privately is to enter into a buy-back arrangement with a car or motorcycle dealer. However, dealers may find ways of knocking down the price when you return the vehicle (even if it was agreed to in writing), often by pointing out expensive repairs that allegedly will be required to gain the dreaded roadworthiness certificate needed in order to transfer the registration.

A company specialising in buy-back arrangements on a range of cars and campervans is **Travellers Auto Barn** (☎ 1800 674 374; www.travellers-autobarn.com.au), which has offices in Sydney, Melbourne, Brisbane and Cairns. The buy-back arrangement is guaranteed in writing: the basic deal is 50% of the purchase price if you have the vehicle for eight weeks, 40% for up to six months, or 30% for up to 12 months. You can probably get better value if you purchase and/or sell on your own, but the convenience of a guaranteed buy-back is handy.

That said, Lonely Planet has received a number of complaints from travellers about this service. We strongly urge you to get an independent mechanical check before you buy and to be satisfied with all aspects of the deal before you commit to it – and talk to other travellers about their experiences with this firm.

Another option for motorcycles and cars is **Car Connection** (☎ 03-5473 4469; www .carconnection.com.au), which is based in Castlemaine but will provide transport to/from Melbourne. Rather than outlaying the full amount and then selling the vehicle back, you post a bond that is actually less than the value of the vehicle (a credit-card imprint is fine) and only pay a fixed 'user fee' for any period up to six months. A Ford Falcon station wagon or Yamaha XT600 trail bike will cost $2200 for any period up to six months; a diesel Toyota Landcruiser, suitable for serious outback exploration, costs around $5000; and a campervan costs $6000. Information and bookings are also handled by the company's Germany-based agent, **Travel Action GmbH** (☎ 0276-47824).

Buy-back arrangements are also possible with large motorcycle dealers in major cities. They're usually keen to do business, and basic negotiating skills allied with a wad of cash (say, $8000) should secure an excellent second-hand road bike with a written guarantee that they'll buy it back in good condition minus around $2000. **Better Bikes** (☎ 02-9718 6668; www.betterbikes.com.au; 605 Canterbury Rd, Belmore) is a Sydney dealer offering buy-back deals.

Road Conditions

Australia has few multilane highways, although there are stretches of divided road (four or six lanes) in some particularly busy areas, including the Princes Hwy from Murray Bridge to Adelaide, most of the Pacific Hwy from Sydney to Brisbane, and the Hume and Calder Hwys in Victoria. Elsewhere the major roads are all sealed two-laners.

You don't have to get far off the beaten track to find dirt roads. In fact, anybody who sets out to see the country in reasonable detail should expect some dirt-road travelling. And if you seriously want to explore the more remote Australia, you'd better plan on having a 4WD and a winch. A few basic spare parts, such as fan belts and radiator hoses, are worth carrying if you're travelling in places where traffic is light and garages are few and far between.

Motorcyclists should beware of dehydration in the dry, hot air – carry at least 5L o water on remote roads in central Australia and drink plenty of it, even if you don' feel thirsty. If riding in Tasmania (a to motorcycling destination) or southern an eastern Victoria, you should be prepared for rotten weather in winter and rain a any time of year. It's worth carrying som spares and tools even if you don't know how to use them, because someone else often does. Carry a workshop manual fo your bike and spare elastic (octopus) strap for securing your gear.

Road Hazards

The 'roadkill' that you unfortunately see lot of in the outback and alongside roads in many other parts of the country is mostly the result of cars and trucks hitting animal at night. Many Australians avoid travelling altogether once the sun drops because o the risks posed by animals on the roads.

Kangaroos are common hazards on country roads, as are cows and sheep in the unfenced outback – hitting an animal of this size can make a real mess of your car Kangaroos are most active around dawn and dusk. They often travel in groups, so if you see one hopping across the road in front of you, slow right down, as its friends may be just behind it.

If you're travelling at night and a large animal appears in front of you, hit the brakes, dip your lights (so you don't continue to dazzle and confuse it) and only swerve if it's safe to do so – numerous travellers have been killed in accidents caused by swerving to miss animals.

Another hazard is driver fatigue. Driving long distances (particularly in hot weather) can be so tiring that you might fall asleep at the wheel. It's not uncommon and the consequences can be unthinkable. So on a long haul, stop and rest every two hours or so – do some exercise, change drivers or have a coffee.

Road Rules

Australians drive on the left-hand side of the road and all cars are right-hand drive. An important road rule is 'give way to the right' – if an intersection is unmarked (unusual), you must give way to vehicles entering the intersection from your right.

The general speed limit in built-up areas is 60km/h, but this has been reduced to 50km/h (and in some cases 40km/h) on residential streets in most states – keep an eye out for signs. Near schools, the limit is 40km/h in the morning and afternoon. On the open highway it's usually 100km/h or 110km/h. In the NT there's no speed limit outside built-up areas, except along the Lasseter Hwy to Uluru, where the limit is 110km/h. The police have speed radar guns and cameras and are fond of using them in strategically concealed locations.

Oncoming drivers who flash their lights at you may be giving you a friendly warning of a speed camera ahead, or they may be telling you that your headlights are not on. It's polite to wave back if someone does this. Try not to get caught doing it yourself, since it's illegal.

All new cars in Australia have seat belts back and front and it's the law to wear them; you're likely to get a fine if you don't. Small children must be belted into an approved safety seat.

Drink-driving is a real problem, especially in country areas. Serious attempts to reduce the resulting road toll are ongoing and random breath-tests are not uncommon in built-up areas. If you're caught with a blood-alcohol level of more than 0.05% expect a hefty fine and the loss of your licence.

PARKING

One of the major problems with driving around cities like Sydney and Melbourne (or popular tourist towns like Byron Bay) is finding somewhere to park. Even if you do find a spot there's likely to be a time restriction, meter (or ticket machine) or both. It's one of the great rorts in Australia that for overstaying your welcome (even by five minutes) in a space that may cost only a few dollars to park in, local councils are prepared to fine you anywhere from $50 to $120. Also note that if you park in a 'clearway' your car will be towed away or clamped – look for signs. In the cities there are large multistorey car parks where you can park all day for between $10 and $25.

Many towns in NSW have a peculiar form of reverse-angle parking, a recipe for disaster if ever there was one. If in doubt, park your car in the same direction and at the same angle as other cars.

HITCHING

Hitching is never entirely safe in any country in the world, and we don't recommend it. Travellers who decide to hitch should understand that they are taking a small but potentially serious risk. People who do choose to hitch will be safer if they travel in pairs and let someone know where they are planning to go.

In Australia, the hitching signal can be a thumbs up or a downward-pointed finger.

TRAIN

Long-distance rail travel in Australia is something you do because you really want to – not because it's cheaper or more convenient, and certainly not because it's fast. That said, trains are more comfortable than buses, and on some of Australia's long-distance train journeys the romance of the rails is alive and kicking. The *Indian Pacific* across the Nullarbor Plain and the *Ghan* from Adelaide to Darwin are two of Australia's great rail journeys.

Rail services within each state are run by that state's rail body, either government or private – see the introductory transport section of the relevant state or territory chapter for details.

INTERSTATE QUARANTINE

When travelling in Australia, whether by land or air, you'll come across signs (mainly in airports, in interstate train stations and at state borders) warning of the possible dangers of carrying fruit, vegetables and plants (which may be infected with a disease or pest) from one area to another. Certain pests and diseases – such as fruit fly, cucurbit thrips, grape phylloxera and potato cyst nematodes, to name a few – are prevalent in some areas but not in others, and so for obvious reasons authorities would like to limit them spreading.

There are quarantine inspection posts on some state borders and occasionally elsewhere. While quarantine control often relies on honesty, many posts are staffed and officers are entitled to search your car for undeclared items. Generally they will confiscate all fresh fruit and vegetables, so it's best to leave shopping for these items until the first town past the inspection point.

TRANSPORT

The three major interstate services in Australia are operated by **Great Southern Railways** (☎ 13 21 47; www.gsr.com.au), namely the *Indian Pacific* between Sydney and Perth, the *Overland* between Melbourne and Adelaide, and the *Ghan* between Adelaide and Darwin via Alice Springs.

Costs

Following are some standard one-way train fares. Note that prices from Melbourne to Perth or Adelaide are up to 15% higher than the fares for travelling in the opposite direction.

Adelaide–Darwin Adult/child/concession in a travel seat $440/200/220, from $1390/840/840 in a cabin.

Adelaide–Melbourne Adult/child/concession in a travel seat $60/35/45, from $150/95/95 in a cabin.

Adelaide–Perth Adult/child/concession in a travel seat $310/140/160, from $960/580/580 in a cabin.

Brisbane–Cairns $190 per adult (economy seat).

Canberra–Melbourne $95 per adult (economy seat); involves a bus ride from Canberra to Cootamundra, then a train to Melbourne.

Canberra–Sydney $50 per adult (economy seat).

Sydney–Brisbane $115 per adult (economy seat).

Sydney–Melbourne $115 per adult (economy seat).

Sydney–Perth Adult/child/concession in a travel seat $520/240/260, from $1250/810/810 in a cabin.

Reservations

As the railway-booking system is computerised, any station (other than those on metropolitan lines) can make a booking for any journey throughout the country. For reservations call ☎ 13 22 32; this will connect you to the nearest main-line station.

Discounted tickets work on a first-come, first-served quota basis, so it helps to book in advance.

Train Passes

The **Great Southern Railways Pass** (☎ 13 21 47; www.gsr.com.au), which is available only to non-Australian residents equipped with a passport, allows unlimited travel on the rail network for a period of six months. The pass costs $590/450 per adult/concession (relatively inexpensive considering the amount of ground you could cover over the life of the pass), but note that you'll be travelling in a 'Daynighter' reclining seat and not a cabin. You need to prebook all seats at least 24 hours in advance.

CountryLink (☎ 13 22 32; www.countrylink.info) is a rail and coach operation that visits destinations in NSW, the ACT, Queensland and Victoria, and offers two passes to foreign nationals with valid passports. The **East Coast Discovery Pass** (☎ 13 22 32) allows one-way economy travel between Melbourne and Cairns (in either direction) with unlimited stopovers, and is valid for six months – the full trip costs $400, while Sydney to Cairns is $310 and Brisbane to Cairns is $230. The **Backtracker Rail Pass** (☎ 13 22 32; www.backpacker railpass.info) allows for travel on the entire CountryLink network and has four versions: a 14-day/one-/three-/six-month pass costing $220/250/270/380 respectively.

Health Dr David Millar

Healthwise, Australia is a remarkably safe country in which to travel, considering that such a large portion of it lies in the tropics. Tropical diseases such as malaria and yellow fever are unknown; diseases of insanitation such as cholera and typhoid are unheard of. Thanks to Australia's isolation and quarantine standards, even some animal diseases such as rabies and foot-and-mouth disease have yet to be recorded.

Few travellers to Australia will experience anything worse than an upset stomach or a bad hangover, and, if you do fall ill, the standard of hospitals and health care is high.

BEFORE YOU GO

Since most vaccines don't produce immunity until at least two weeks after they're given, visit a physician four to eight weeks before departure. Ask your doctor for an International Certificate of Vaccination (otherwise known as 'the yellow booklet'), which will list all the vaccinations you've received. This is mandatory for countries that require proof of yellow fever vaccination upon entry (sometimes required in Australia, see Required & Recommended Vaccinations, right), but it's a good idea to carry a record of all your vaccinations wherever you travel.

Bring medications in their original, clearly labelled, containers. A signed and dated letter from your physician describing your medical conditions and medications, including generic names, is also a good idea. If carrying syringes or needles, be sure to have a physician's letter documenting their medical necessity.

INSURANCE

If your health insurance doesn't cover you for medical expenses abroad, consider getting extra insurance – check www.lonely planet.com for more information. Find out in advance if your insurance plan will make payments directly to providers or if it will reimburse you later for overseas health expenditures. (In Australia, as in many countries, doctors expect payment at the time of consultation. Make sure you get an itemised receipt detailing the service and keep the contact details of the health provider. See p1072 for details of health care in Australia.)

REQUIRED & RECOMMENDED VACCINATIONS

If you're entering Australia within six days of having stayed overnight or longer in a yellow fever–infected country, you'll need proof of yellow fever vaccination. For a full list of these countries visit the **World Health Organization** (WHO; www.who.int/wer/) website or the **Centers for Disease Control & Prevention** (www.cdc.gov/travel/yb/outline.htm#2) website.

If you're really worried about health when travelling, there are a few vaccinations you could consider for Australia. The WHO recommends that all travellers should be covered for diphtheria, tetanus, measles, mumps, rubella, chickenpox and polio, as well as hepatitis B, regardless of their destination. Planning to travel is a great time to ensure that all routine vaccination cover is complete. The consequences of these diseases can be severe, and while Australia has high levels of childhood vaccination coverage, outbreaks of these diseases do occur.

MEDICAL CHECKLIST

- Antibiotics
- Antidiarrhoeal drugs (eg loperamide)
- Acetaminophen (paracetamol) or aspirin
- Anti-inflammatory drugs (eg ibuprofen)
- Antihistamines (for hayfever and allergic reactions)
- Antibacterial ointment in case of cuts or abrasions
- Steroid cream or cortisone (for poison ivy and other allergic rashes)
- Bandages, gauze, gauze rolls
- Adhesive or paper tape
- Scissors, safety pins, tweezers
- Thermometer
- Pocket knife
- DEET-containing insect repellent for the skin
- Permethrin-containing insect spray for clothing, tents and bed nets
- Sun block
- Oral rehydration salts
- Iodine tablets or water filter (for water purification)

INTERNET RESOURCES

There is a wealth of travel health advice to be found on the Internet. For further information, **Lonely Planet** (www.lonelyplanet .com) is a good place to start. The **WHO** (www .who.int/ith) publishes a superb book called *International Travel and Health,* which is revised annually and is available online at no cost. Another website of general interest is **MD Travel Health** (www.mdtravelhealth.com), which provides complete travel health recommendations for every country and is updated daily.

It's usually a good idea to consult your government's travel health website before departure, if one is available:

Australia (www.dfat.gov.au/travel)
Canada (www.travelhealth.gc.ca)
UK (www.doh.gov.uk/traveladvice)
USA (www.cdc.gov/travel)

FURTHER READING

Lonely Planet's *Healthy Travel Australia, New Zealand & the Pacific* is a handy, pocket-sized guide packed with useful information including pre-trip planning, emergency first aid, immunisation and disease information and what to do if you get sick on the road. *Travel with Children,* from Lonely Planet, includes advice on travel health for younger children. Other recommended reference include *Traveller's Health* by Dr Richar■ Dawood (Oxford University Press) and *Inter■ national Travel Health Guide* by Stuart ▶ Rose, MD (Travel Medicine Inc).

IN TRANSIT

DEEP VEIN THROMBOSIS (DVT)

Blood clots may form in the legs (deep vei■ thrombosis) during plane flights, chiefly be■ cause of prolonged immobility. The longe■ the flight, the greater the risk. Though mos■ blood clots are reabsorbed uneventfully some may break off and travel through th■ blood vessels to the lungs, where they coul■ cause life-threatening complications.

The chief symptom of DVT is swelling o■ pain of the foot, ankle or calf, usually – bu■ not always – on just one side. When a bloo■ clot travels to the lungs, it may cause ches■ pain and breathing difficulties. Traveller■ with any of these symptoms should imme■ diately seek medical attention.

To prevent the development of DVT o■ long flights, you should walk about th■ cabin, perform isometric compressions o■ the leg muscles (ie flex the leg muscles whil■ sitting), drink plenty of fluids and avoi■ alcohol and tobacco.

JET LAG & MOTION SICKNESS

Jet lag is common when crossing more tha■ five time zones, and it results in insomnia, fa■ tigue, malaise or nausea. To avoid jet lag, try drinking plenty of (nonalcoholic) fluids an■ eating light meals. On arrival, expose yoursel■ to sunlight and readjust your schedule (fo■ meals, sleep etc) as soon as possible.

Antihistamines such as dimenhydrinat■ and meclizine are usually the first choic■ for treating motion sickness. Their mai■ side effect is drowsiness. A herbal alterna■ tive is ginger, which works like a charm fo■ some people.

IN AUSTRALIA

AVAILABILITY & COST OF HEALTH CARE

Health insurance is essential for all travel■ lers. While health care in Australia is of a■ high standard and is not overly expensive■

by international standards, considerable costs can build up and repatriation is extremely expensive. Make sure your existing health insurance will cover you – if not, organise extra insurance.

Australia has an excellent health-care system. It's a mixture of privately run medical clinics and hospitals alongside a system of public hospitals funded by the Australian government. The Medicare system covers Australian residents for some of their health-care costs. Visitors from countries with which Australia has a reciprocal health-care agreement are eligible for benefits specified under the Medicare programme. There are agreements currently in place with New Zealand, the UK, the Netherlands, Sweden, Finland, Italy, Malta and Ireland – check the details before departing from these countries. In general the agreements provide for any episode of ill-health that requires prompt medical attention. For further information, visit www.health.gov.au/pubs/mbs/mbs3 /medicare.htm.

There are excellent, specialised, public health facilities for women and children in Australia's major centres.

Over-the-counter medications are widely available at privately owned chemists throughout Australia. These include pain-killers, antihistamines for allergies, and skin-care products.

You may find that medications readily available over the counter in some countries are only available in Australia by prescription. These include the oral contraceptive pill, most medications for asthma and all antibiotics. If you take medication on a regular basis, bring an adequate supply and ensure you have details of the generic name as brand names may differ between countries.

Health Care in Remote Areas

In Australia's remote locations, it is possible there'll be a significant delay in emergency services reaching you in the event of serious accident or illness. Do not underestimate the vastness between most major outback towns; an increased level of self-reliance and preparation is essential.

Consider taking a wilderness first-aid course, such as those offered at the **Wilderness Medicine Institute** (www.wmi.net.au). Take a comprehensive first-aid kit that is appropriate for the activities planned, and ensure that you have adequate means of communication. Australia has extensive mobile phone coverage but additional radio communication is important for remote areas. The **Royal Flying Doctor Service** (www.rfds.org.au) provides an important back-up for remote communities.

INFECTIOUS DISEASES
Bat Lyssavirus
This disease is related to rabies and some deaths have occurred after bites. The risk is greatest for animal handlers and vets. The rabies vaccine is effective, but the risk of travellers contracting bat lyssavirus is very low.

Dengue Fever
Dengue Fever occurs in northern Queensland, particularly from October to March, during the wet season. Also known as 'breakbone fever', because of the severe muscular pains that accompany it, this viral disease is spread by a species of mosquito that feeds primarily during the day. Most people recover in a few days but more severe forms of the disease can occur, particularly in residents who are exposed to another strain of the virus (there are four types) in a subsequent season.

Giardiasis
Giardiasis is widespread in waterways around Australia. Drinking untreated water rom streams and lakes is not recommended. Use water filters and boil or treat water with iodine to help prevent the disease. Symptoms consist of intermittent bad-smelling diarrhoea, abdominal bloating and wind. Effective treatment is available (tinidazole or metronidazole).

Hepatitis C
This is still a growing problem among intravenous drug users. Blood transfusion services fully screen all blood before use.

HIV
In Australia, human immuno-deficiency virus (HIV) rates have stabilised and levels are similar to other Western countries. Clean needles and syringes are widely available at all chemists.

HEALTH

Malaria

Although isolated cases have occurred in northern Queensland, malaria is not an ongoing problem in Australia. The risk to travellers is low.

Meningococcal Disease

This disease occurs worldwide and is a risk if you have prolonged stays in dormitory-style accommodation. A vaccine exists for some types of this disease, namely meningococcal A, C, Y and W. There is no vaccine presently available for the viral type of meningitis.

Ross River Fever

The Ross River virus is widespread throughout Australia and is spread by mosquitoes living in marshy areas. In addition to fever, it causes headache, joint and muscular pains and a rash, and resolves after five to seven days.

Sexually Transmitted Diseases (STDs)

Rates of STD infection are similar to most other Western countries. The most common symptoms are pain while passing urine, and a discharge. Infection can be present without symptoms, so seek medical screening after any unprotected sex with a new partner. Throughout the country you'll find sexual health clinics in all of the major hospitals. Always use a condom with any new sexual partner. Condoms are readily available in chemists and through vending machines in many public places, including toilets.

Tick Typhus

Cases of tick typhus have been reported throughout Australia, but are predominantly found in Queensland and New South Wales. A week or so after being bitten, a dark area forms around the bite, followed by a rash and possible fever, headache and inflamed lymph nodes. The disease is treatable with antibiotics (doxycycline), so see a doctor if you suspect you have been bitten.

Viral Encephalitis

Also known as Murray Valley encephalitis virus, this is spread by mosquitoes and is most common in northern Australia, especially during the wet season (October to March). This potentially serious disease is normally accompanied by headache, muscle pains and sensitivity to light. Residual neurological damage can occur and no specific treatment is available. However, the risk to most travellers is low.

TRAVELLERS' DIARRHOEA

Tap water is universally safe in Australia. All water other than tap water should be boiled, filtered or chemically disinfected (with iodine tablets) to prevent travellers' diarrhoea and giardia.

If you develop diarrhoea, be sure to drink plenty of fluids – preferably an oral rehydration solution containing lots of salt and sugar. A few loose stools don't require treatment but if you start having more than four or five stools a day, you should begin taking an antibiotic (usually a quinolone drug) and an antidiarrhoeal agent (such as loperamide). If diarrhoea is bloody, persists for more than 72 hours or is accompanied by fever, shaking chills or severe abdominal pain, you should seek medical attention.

ENVIRONMENTAL HAZARDS
Bites & Stings
MARINE ANIMALS

Marine spikes, such as those found on sea urchins, stonefish, scorpion fish, catfish and stingrays, can cause severe local pain. If this occurs, immediately immerse the affected area in hot water (as high a temperature as can be tolerated). Keep topping up with hot water until the pain subsides and medical care can be reached. The stonefish is found only in tropical Australia, from northwestern Australia around the coast to northern Queensland. An antivenin is available.

Marine stings from jellyfish such as box jellyfish and Irukandji also occur in Australia's tropical waters, particularly during the wet season (October to March). The box jellyfish and the Irukandji have an incredibly potent sting and have been known to cause fatalities. Warning signs exist at affected beaches, and stinger nets are in place at the more popular beaches. Never dive into water unless you have checked – with local beach life-savers – that it's safe. 'Stinger suits' (full-body Lycra swimsuits) prevent stinging, as do wetsuits. If you are stung, first aid consists of washing the skin with vinegar to prevent further discharge of remaining stinging cells, followed by rapid transfer to a hospital; antivenin is widely available.

SHARKS & CROCODILES

Despite extensive media coverage, the risk of shark attack in Australian waters is no greater than in other countries with extensive coastlines. There's also low risk of an attack by tropical sharks on scuba divers in northern Australian waters. Great white sharks are now few in number in the temperate southern waters. Check with surf life-saving groups about local risks.

The risk of crocodile attack in tropical northern Australia is real but predictable and largely preventable. Discuss the local risk with police or tourist agencies in the area before swimming in rivers, water holes and in the sea.

SNAKES

Australian snakes have a fearful reputation that is justified in terms of the potency of their venom, but unjustified in terms of the actual risk to travellers and locals. Snakes are usually quite timid in nature and, in most instances, will move away if disturbed. They have only small fangs, making it easy to prevent bites to the lower limbs (where 80% of bites occur) by wearing protective clothing (such as gaiters) around the ankles when bushwalking. The bite marks are very small and may even go unnoticed.

In all cases of confirmed or suspected bites, preventing the spread of toxic venom can be achieved by applying pressure to the wound and immobilising the area with a splint or sling before seeking medical attention. Firmly wrap an elastic bandage (you can improvise with a T-shirt) around the entire limb, but not so tight as to cut off the circulation. Along with immobilisation, this is a life-saving first-aid measure.

SPIDERS

Australia has a number of poisonous spiders. The Sydney funnel-web spider causes severe local pain, as well as generalised symptoms (vomiting, abdominal pain, sweating). An antivenin exists, so apply pressure to the wound and immobilise the area before transferring to a hospital.

Redback spiders are found throughout the country. Bites cause increasing pain at the site, followed by profuse sweating and generalised symptoms (including muscular weakness, sweating at the site of the bite, nausea). First aid includes application of ice or cold packs to the bite, then transfer to hospital.

White-tailed spider bites may cause an ulcer that is very slow and difficult to heal. Clean the wound thoroughly and seek medical assistance.

Heat Exhaustion & Heatstroke

Very hot weather is experienced all year round in northern Australia and during the summer months for most of the country. Conditions vary from tropical in the Northern Territory and Queensland to hot desert in northwestern Australia and central Australia. When arriving from a temperate or cold climate, remember that it takes two weeks for acclimatisation to occur. Before the body is acclimatised, an excessive amount of salt is lost in perspiration, so increasing the salt in your diet is essential.

Heat exhaustion occurs when fluid intake does not keep up with fluid loss. Symptoms include dizziness, fainting, fatigue, nausea or vomiting. The skin is usually pale, cool and clammy. Treatment consists of rest in a cool, shady place and fluid replacement with water or diluted sports drinks.

Heatstroke is a severe form of heat illness that occurs after fluid depletion or extreme heat challenge from heavy exercise. This is a true medical emergency, with heating of the brain leading to disorientation, hallucinations and seizures. Prevent heatstroke by maintaining an adequate fluid intake to ensure the continued passage of clear and copious urine, especially during physical exertion.

A number of unprepared travellers die from dehydration each year in outback Australia. This can be prevented by following some simple rules:

- Carry sufficient water for any trip, including extra in case your vehicle breaks down.
- Always let someone, such as the local police, know where you are going and when you expect to arrive.
- Carry communications equipment of some form.
- Stay with the vehicle rather than walking for help.

HEALTH

Hypothermia

Hypothermia is a significant risk, especially during the winter months in southern parts of Australia. Despite the absence of high mountain ranges, strong winds produce a high chill factor that can result in hypothermia even in moderately cool temperatures. Early signs include the inability to perform fine movements (such as doing up buttons), shivering and a bad case of the 'umbles' (fumbles, mumbles, grumbles, stumbles). The key elements of treatment include moving out of the cold, changing out of any wet clothing into dry clothes with windproof and waterproof layers, adding insulation and providing fuel (water and carbohydrate) to allow shivering, which builds the internal temperature. In severe hypothermia, shivering actually stops – this is a medical emergency requiring rapid medical attention in addition to the above measures.

Insect-Borne Illnesses

Various insects can be a source of irritation and, in Australia, may be the source of specific diseases (dengue fever, Ross River fever). Protection from mosquitoes, sandflies, ticks and leeches can be achieved by a combination of the following strategies:

- Wearing loose-fitting, long-sleeved clothing.
- Application of 30% DEET to all exposed skin and repeating every three to four hours.
- Impregnation of clothing with permethrin (an insecticide that kills insects but is believed to be safe for humans).

Surf Beaches & Drowning

Australia has exceptional surf, particularly on the eastern, southern and western coasts. Beaches vary enormously in their underwater conditions: the slope offshore can result in changeable and often powerful surf. Check with local surf life-saving organisations and be aware of your own expertise and limitations before entering the water.

Ultraviolet (UV) Light Exposure

Australia has one of the highest rates of skin cancer in the world. Monitor your exposure to direct sunlight closely. Ultraviolet exposure is greatest between 10am and 4pm, so avoid skin exposure during these times. Always use 30+ sunscreen, apply it 30 minutes before going into the sun and repeat application regularly to minimise damage.

Glossary

AUSTRALIAN ENGLISH

Any visitor from abroad who thinks that
Australian (that's 'Strine') is simply a weird-
sounding variant of English is in for a surprise. For starters, many Australians don't
speak Australian at home – they speak
Italian, Lebanese, Vietnamese, Turkish or
Greek. These languages then influence the
way they speak English.

The colloquial language may lose you
in a strange maze of Australian words.
The meaning of some words in Australia
is completely different from that in other
English-speaking countries – some commonly used words have been shortened almost beyond recognition, while others are
derived from Aboriginal languages, or from
the slang used by early convict settlers.

There is a slight regional variation in the
Australian accent, while the difference between city and country speech is mainly a
matter of speed. Some of the most famed
Aussie words are hardly heard at all –
'mates' are more common than 'cobbers'.
If you want to pass for an Aussie, just try
speaking slightly nasally, shortening any
word of more than two syllables and then
adding a vowel to the end of it, making
anything you can into a diminutive and
peppering your speech with expletives.

Lonely Planet's *Australian Phrasebook* is
an introduction to both Australian English
and some Aboriginal languages. The list
that follows may also help.

ACT – Australian Capital Territory
Akubra – a type of hat found occasionally on farmers but mostly in souvenir shops
arvo – afternoon
ATM – Automated Teller Machine, public cash dispenser operated by banks
Aussie rules – Australian Rules football, a game resembling rugby, played by teams of 18

B&B – 'bed and breakfast' accommodation
back o' Bourke – back of beyond, middle of nowhere
bail out – to leave
Banana Bender – resident of Queensland
barbie – barbecue (also 'BBQ')
barrack – cheer on team at sporting event, support

bastard – general form of address which can mean many things, from high praise or respect ('He's the bravest bastard I know!') to dire insult ('You bastard!'); avoid use if unsure
bathers – swimming costume (in Victoria)
battler – struggler, someone who tries hard
BBQ – barbecue (also 'barbie')
beaut, beauty, bewdie – great, fantastic
bevan – *bogan* (in Queensland)
bikies – motorcyclists
billabong – waterhole in a riverbed formed by waters receding in the *Dry*
billy – tin container used to boil water in the *bush*
bitumen – surfaced road
block, do your – lose your temper
bloke – man
blokey – exhibiting characteristics considered typically masculine
blowies, blow flies – large flies
blow-in – stranger
bludger – lazy person, one who refuses to work
blue – argument or fight
body board – half-sized surfboard
bogan – unsophisticated person
bonzer – great, *ripper*
boogie board – see *body board*
boomer – very big; a particularly large male kangaroo
boomerang – a curved, flat, wooden instrument used by Aborigines for hunting
booner – see *bogan* (in ACT)
booze bus – police van used for random breath testing for alcohol
bot – to scrounge or obtain by begging or borrowing ('bot a cigarette')
bottle shop – liquor shop, off-licence
brekky – breakfast
Buckley's – no chance at all
bull dust – fine, sometimes deep dust on *outback* roads; also bullshit
bullroarer – secret instrument often used in Aboriginal men's initiation ceremonies; a long piece of wood on a string swung around the head to create an eerie roar
bunyip – mythical bush spirit
'burbs – outer suburbs of a city
burl – have a try ('give it a burl')
bush tucker – native foods
bush, the – country, anywhere away from the city
bushbash – to force your way through pathless bush
bushranger – Australia's equivalent of the outlaws of the American Wild West

bushwalking – hiking

BYO – 'bring your own'; a restaurant licence permitting customers to drink *grog* they've purchased elsewhere

camp oven – large, cast-iron pot with lid, used for cooking on an open fire

cark it – to die

cask wine – wine packaged in a plastic bladder surrounded by a cardboard box (a great Australian invention)

catch ya later – goodbye, see you later

chiga – *bogan* (in Tasmania)

chocka – completely full, from 'chock-a-block'

chook – chicken

chuck a U-ey – make a U-turn, turn a car around within a road

clap stick – percussion instrument used in Aboriginal societies, either sticks (one or two) or a pair of boomerangs

clobber – to hit; clothes

clout – to hit

cobber – (archaic) see *mate*

cocky – small-scale farmer

come good – turn out all right

cool drink – soft drink (in Western Australia)

coolamon – Aboriginal wooden carrying dish

corroboree – Aboriginal festival or gathering for ceremonial or spiritual reasons

counter meal – pub meal

cow cocky – small-scale cattle farmer

cozzie – swimming costume (in New South Wales)

crack a mental, crack the shits – lose one's temper

crook – ill or substandard

Crow Eater – resident of South Australia

crikey – an exclamation of surprise, as in 'crikey these shorts are tight!'

cut lunch – sandwiches

dag – dirty lump of wool at a sheep's rear; also an affectionate or mildly abusive term for a socially inept person

daks – trousers

damper – bush loaf made from flour and water, often cooked in a *camp oven*

dead horse – tomato sauce

dead set – true, dinkum

deli – *milk bar* (in South Australia and Western Australia); also delicatessen

didgeridoo – wind instrument made from a hollow piece of wood, traditionally played by Aboriginal men

digger – (archaic, from Australian and New Zealand soldiers in WWI) see *mate*

dill – idiot

dilly bag – Aboriginal carry bag

dinkum – honest, genuine

dinky-di – the real thing

dip out – to miss out or fail

dob in – to inform on someone

donga – small, transportable building widely used in the *outback*

Dreamtime – complex concept that forms the basis of Aboriginal spirituality, incorporating the creation of the world and the spiritual energies operating around us; 'Dreaming' is often the preferred term as it avoids the association with time

drongo – worthless or stupid person

dropbear – imaginary Australian bush creature

Dry, the – dry season in northern Australia (April to October)

duco – car paint

dunny – outdoor lavatory

earbash – to talk nonstop

eftpos – Electronic Funds Transfer at Point of Sale; widespread service that lets you use your bank card (credit or debit) to pay for services or purchases, and often withdraw cash

Esky – large insulated box for keeping food and drinks cold

fair dinkum – see *dinkum*

fair go! – give us a break!

flag fall – minimum charge for hiring a taxi

flake – shark meat

flat out – very busy or fast

flog – sell; steal

football, footy – for Mexicans, Crow Eaters, Taswegians and Sand Gropers: Aussie Rules. For Banana Benders and Cockroaches: rugby league. Almost never soccer.

fossick – hunt for gems or semiprecious stones

freshie – freshwater crocodile (usually harmless, unless provoked); new *tinny* of beer

furphy – rumour or false story

galah – noisy parrot, thus noisy idiot

game – brave

gander – to look ('have a gander')

g'day – good day, traditional Australian greeting

gibber – Aboriginal word for a stone or rock, hence gibber plain or desert

give it away – give up

good on ya! – well done!

grazier – large-scale sheep or cattle farmer

grog – general term for alcoholic drinks

grouse – very good

hicksville – derogatory term usually employed by urbanites to describe a country town

homestead – residence of a *station* owner or manager

hoon – idiot, hooligan

how are ya? – standard greeting (expected answer: 'Good, thanks, how are you?')

humbug – the begging of cigarettes and drinks

icy pole – frozen lollipop, ice lolly
iffy – dodgy, questionable
indie – independent music

jackaroo – male trainee on an *outback station*
jillaroo – female trainee on an *outback station*
jocks – men's underpants
journo – journalist
jumped-up – self-important, arrogant

kali – jumbo-sized boomerang
karri – Australian eucalyptus tree
kick the bucket – to die
kiwi – New Zealander
knacker – testicle
knackered – broken, tired
knock – to criticise, deride
knocker – one who knocks; woman's breast
Kombi – a classic (hippies') type of van made by Volkswagon
Koories – Aboriginal people of southeastern Australia
Kooris – Aboriginal people of NSW

lair – layabout, ruffian
lamington – square of sponge cake covered in chocolate icing and desiccated coconut
larrikin – hooligan, mischievous youth
lay-by – to put a deposit on an article so the shop will hold it for you
lemon – faulty product, a dud
little ripper – extremely good thing; see also *ripper*
lob in – drop in (to see someone)
lollies – sweets, candy
loo – toilet
lurk – scheme

marron – large freshwater crayfish
mate – general term of familiarity, correctly pronounced 'maaaaate'
Mexicans – Victorians
milk bar – small shop selling milk and other basic provisions; see also *deli*
mobile phone – cell phone
Moreton Bay bug – small, edible crustacean
mozzies – mosquitoes
Murri – collective term used to identify Aborigines from Queensland

nature strip – strip of land where trees and bushes are grown alongside a road
never-never – remote country in the *outback*
no-hoper – hopeless case
no worries! – no problems! That's OK!
noodle – to fossick through discarded dirt for opal missed by the miner

Noongar – collective term used to identify Aborigines from Western Australia
NSW – New South Wales
NT – Northern Territory
Nunga – collective term used to identify Aborigines from South Australia

ocker – uncultivated or boorish Australian; a *knocker* or derider
oi oi oi – the second stanza of the traditional Australian ballad that starts 'Aussie Aussie Aussie'
off-sider – assistant, partner
outback – remote part of the *bush, back o' Bourke*

paddock – fenced area of land, usually intended for livestock
PADI – Professional Association of Diving Instructors
pastoralist – large-scale *grazier*
pavlova – traditional Australian meringue, fruit and cream dessert, named after Russian ballerina Anna Pavlova
pay out – to make fun of, deride
perve – to gaze with lust
pie floater – meat pie served in green pea soup; a South Australian favourite
piker – someone who doesn't pull their weight, or chickens out
piss – beer
piss turn, piss up – boozy party
piss weak – no good, gutless
pissed – drunk
pissed off – annoyed
plonk – cheap wine
pokies – poker machines
Pom – English person
postie – mailperson
pot – large beer glass (in Victoria); beer gut; to sink a billiard ball

Queenslander – high-set weatherboard house, noted for its wide veranda
quokka – small wallaby

rapt – delighted, enraptured
rarrk – cross-hatching designs used in Arnhem Land paintings and body art
ratbag – friendly term of abuse
ratshit – lousy
reckon! – you bet! absolutely!
rego – (car) registration
rellie – (family) relative
ridgy-didge – original, genuine
ring-in – substitute or outsider
rip – a strong ocean current or undertow
ripper – good; see also *little ripper*
road train – semitrailer truck towing several trailers

roos – kangaroos
root – to have sexual intercourse
rooted – tired, broken
ropable – very bad-tempered or angry
RS – see *ratshit*
RSL – Returned Servicemen's League or community venue operated by same

SA – South Australia
saltie – saltwater crocodile (the dangerous one)
Salvo – member of the Salvation Army
Sand Groper – resident of Western Australia
sanger – sandwich
scallops – fried potato cakes (in Queensland and New South Wales); shellfish
schooner – large beer glass (in New South Wales and South Australia)
scrub – see *bush*
sea wasp – (deadly) box jellyfish
sealed road – bitumen road
session – lengthy period of heavy drinking
shanks's pony – to travel on foot
shark biscuit – inexperienced surfer
sheila – woman
she'll be right – no problems, no worries
shellacking – comprehensive defeat
shonky – unreliable
shoot through – to leave in a hurry
shout – to buy a round of drinks ('Your shout!')
sickie – day off work ill (or malingering)
skimpy – scantily clad female bar person
slab – two dozen *stubbies* or *tinnies*
smoko – tea break
snag – sausage
sparrow's fart – dawn
spindoola – money
station – large farm
stickybeak – nosy person
stinger – (deadly) box jellyfish
stolen generations – Aboriginal and Torres Strait Islander children forcibly removed from their families during the government's policy of assimilation
story – tale from the Dreamtime that taps into the concepts of legend, myth, tradition and the law; carries much more weight than an ordinary historical account
strides – trousers, *daks*
stroppy – bad-tempered

Stubbies – popular brand of men's work shorts
stubby – 375mL bottle of beer
sundowner – alcoholic drink consumed at sunset
surf'n'turf – a slab of steak topped with seafood, usually served in pubs
swag – canvas-covered bed roll used in the *outback*; a large amount

take the piss – friendly derision
tall poppies – achievers (*knockers* like to cut them down)
tea – evening meal
thingo – thing, whatchamacallit, doovelacki, thingamajig
thongs – flip-flops, an *ocker*'s idea of formal footwear
tinny – 375mL can of beer; small, aluminium fishing dinghy (in the Northern Territory)
tjukurpa – Aboriginal law, religion and custom
togs – swimming costume (in Queensland and Victoria)
too right! – absolutely!
Top End – northern part of the Northern Territory
true blue – *dinkum*
tucker – food
two-pot screamer – person unable to hold their drink
two-up – traditional heads-or-tails coin gambling game

unsealed road – dirt road
ute – utility; pick-up truck

WA – Western Australia
wag – to skip school or work
walkabout – lengthy solitary walk
weatherboard – timber cladding on a house
Wet, the – rainy season in the north (November to March)
whinge – to complain, moan
whoop-whoop – *outback*, miles from anywhere
wobbly – disturbing, unpredictable behaviour
woomera – stick used by Aborigines to propel spears
wowser – someone who doesn't believe in having fun, spoilsport, teetotaller

yabbie – small freshwater crayfish
yakka – work
yobbo – uncouth, aggressive person
yonks – a long time
youse – plural form of 'you' (pronounced 'yooze'), used by the grammatically challenged

Behind the Scenes

THIS BOOK

Lonely Planet's *Australia* was first published in 1977, with LP co-founder Tony Wheeler covering the entire country on his own. In the 28 years since then, we've sent hundreds of different authors out to far-flung corners of Australia to bring us editions two through 13. (It's surprising Australia's travel industry isn't heartily sick of mysterious travellers turning up unannounced and asking to see 'one of your single rooms, and one of the doubles too just in case my partner joins me later'.)

This lucky 13th edition represents the research efforts of a grand total of 30 different authors, although the writing talents of 'only' 10 of them were used to present the literary masterpiece you hold in your hands. As well as the authors you'll see on pp21–4, we acknowledge here the tireless research efforts of Lindsay Brown, Simone Egger and Miriam Raphael (Queensland); Susie Ashworth, Sally O'Brien, Jocelyn Harewood, Cathy Lanigan, Lisa Mitchell and Miriam Raphael (Victoria); Gina Tsarouhas (Tasmania); and George Dunford and Jill Kirby (South Australia).

THANKS from the Authors

Paul Smitz A big thanks to all the people I met on and off the road who helped me pretend to know what I was doing, from patient visitor centre staff and national park rangers to tour guides, fellow travellers, loquacious locals and passing strangers. In Canberra, ta to the usual suspects for accommodation, conversation, friendship and hangovers, including Judy, Tom, Julie, Jane, Cathie, Ian, Mandy, Michael, Steve, Carlos and Jose. In the Top End, thanks to Trish and family for the backyard valet service and the generous hospitality. Thanks also to LP inhouse folk – particularly Errol and Corie – for doing all that important behind-the-scenes stuff (inventing whimsical new guidelines, approving payments, playing solitaire etc), and to my fellow authors for all the hard work and for putting up with a barrage of bad jokes every time my fingers hit the keyboard. Special thanks to the enigmatic woman who refuses to see the irony in the fact that Don McLean survived the Day the Music Died.

Carolyn Bain Many thanks to Errol Hunt and Stefanie Di Trocchio at Lonely Planet for giving me the chance to revisit such a great destination. Professional hat-doffing goes to coordinating author supremo Paul Smitz, and to Gina Tsarouhas, my fab co-author on LP's recent *Tasmania* guide. In Tassie, boundless gratitude to all the friendly locals, mainland refugees and fellow travellers who took time out for a chat and a cuppa, and who shared lots of insights and info. Finally, much love and thanks to Helen Aucote, Sally O'Keefe, Rosalind Gilsenan and Sally O'Brien, who all flew south for fun and games (and restaurant visits).

Sandra Bao Sydney is full of gracious and very helpful folks whose contributions greatly aided my work during the research of this book. I met them everywhere I went, and their friendliness made this LP gig one of my best ever. But I'd like to thank one person especially for his help and companionship –

THE LONELY PLANET STORY

The story begins with a classic travel adventure: Tony and Maureen Wheeler's 1972 journey across Europe and Asia to Australia. There was no useful information about the overland trail then, so Tony and Maureen published the first Lonely Planet guidebook to meet a growing need.

From a kitchen table, Lonely Planet has grown to become the largest independent travel publisher in the world, with offices in Melbourne (Australia), Oakland (USA) and London (UK). Today Lonely Planet guidebooks cover the globe. There is an ever-growing list of books and information in a variety of media. Some things haven't changed. The main aim is still to make it possible for adventurous travellers to get out there – to explore and better understand the world.

At Lonely Planet we believe travellers can make a positive contribution to the countries they visit – if they respect their host communities and spend their money wisely. Every year 5% of company profit is donated to charities around the world.

my friend Dilip Varma. A quick nod also to Sydney's very helpful tourist staff and to fellow NSW authors Ryan Ver Berkmoes and Paul Smitz. And, as always, thanks to Mom, Dad and Daniel for behind-the-scenes support. Last, but not least, my husband Ben's help made this project possible. I couldn't have done it nearly as well without you by my side, sweetie – even when you were back home!

Simone Egger Kudos to Verity Campbell who wrote last edition's Culture chapter. Thanks to Errol, Kate and Katrina at Lonely Planet.

Susannah Farfor Utmost thanks to navigator Ian Malcolm – surf buddy, hiker, feaster and Shiraz quaffer extraordinaire. Warm thanks for the great local knowledge from Elizabeth and Melanie Dankel, Mark Potter, Annie McColl and family, Jason and Louise James, cellar door staff and the many friendly South Australians who went out of their way to answer oodles of questions. Thanks also to George Dunford and Jill Kirby for their South Australia research.

Alan Murphy A very big thanks to my family and in particular my parents, Alan and Nan, who joined me for research trips to The Kimberley, New Norcia and Lancelin, and gave me an insight into the 'senior but active' travel perspective. Visitor centres were a welcoming fountain of information (particularly those in Geraldton, Carnarvon, Broome, Fitzroy Crossing and Kununurra) and I am indebted to their patience at my dogged and persistent questioning. Lastly to all the people I met on the road, from those happy to divulge their travel tales to those just abiding by the rule of the northwest and nodding, catching my eye and murmuring 'how's it goin' mate', my heartfelt thanks.

Nina Rousseau First of all I would like to thank the authors of the *Victoria* guide, whose witty, concise and brilliant research I made great use of here. Enormous, multitudinous thanks to Susie Ashworth, Sally O'Brien, Lisa Mitchell, Cathy Lanigan, Jocelyn Harewood, Miriam Raphael and Campbell Mattinson. Next, thanks to coordinating author Smitzy del Mar and the exceedingly patient Errol Hunt. Special thanks to Jo Tayler, Susannah Farfor, George Dunford (walky-talky support) and travelling companion Jo Argent. As always, thanks to Luc McKenna, for being Luc.

Simon Sellars Thanks to Daniel New for braving the coast with me. And to Rachel Thorpe, George

Dunford and Andrés Vaccari for everything else. At Lonely Planet, thanks to Stefanie Di Trocchio, Errol Hunt, Csanad Csutoros, Hunor Csutoros and Michael Day for invaluable insider trading.

Justine Vaisutis First and foremost I'd like to thank my colleagues Simone Egger, Miriam Raphael and Lindsay Brown for their outstanding research and text, which made the compilation of the Queensland chapter infinitely easier. I'd also like to thank all the tourist offices in Queensland and their dedicated staff for assistance and information along the way. On the home front I'd like to say cheers to Aidy for her support during the write-up of my chapter, and to my mum for always being there. Thanks too to all the readers who sent in invaluable letters and advice, and last but not least, to Paul Smitz, Errol Hunt and Corie Waddell who made this such a fun project to be a part of.

Ryan Ver Berkmoes Huge thanks go to Errol Hunt, Corie Waddell and many others in the Lonely Planet Melbourne office. These amazing people worked miracles (at no small cost to their own sanity) so I could divert my energies to the beachside tragedies after the Indian Ocean tsunami. I am also indebted to the many fine folks in NSW (especially Larry Buttrose) who helped me understand the multitude of pleasures possible. And special mention must go to Janet Brunckhorst, who put Wagga Wagga on the map for me. Thanks too to Miriam Raphael and Jane Rawson for giving me some damn fine text to mess with. And of course it's not complete without Erin Corrigan, who exposed me to everything I could love in the NSW sands.

Meg Worby Thanks to Jimi Ellis and Kate McLeod for their expatriate enthusiasm. Thanks to my dear friend Lauren Walter, whose Sandgroper pals shared their local knowledge: Karen and Mike in Freo, Gina in Cottesloe, Jodie in Subiaco, Bee and Si in Busselton. Thanks to Angelo for cool insights on this hot state. At LP, thank you again Errolio for the gig – and to stars Paul, Corie, Hunor and Katrina for bringing it all together. Thanks to Dad and Lynny for support and Australian Studies nous during write-up. And to Charles, a brilliant travel partner with a mintox sense of humour.

CREDITS

Commissioning Editor Errol Hunt
Coordinating Editor Katrina Webb
Coordinating Cartographer Julie Sheridan
Coordinating Layout Designer John Shippick
Managing Cartographer Corinne Waddell

Assisting Editors Sasha Baskett, Victoria Harrison, Joanne Newell, Kate Evans, Sarah Bailey, Kate Whitfield, Yvonne Byron, Helen Koehne, Margedd Heliosz
Assisting Cartographers Jacqueline Nguyen, Laurie Mikkelsen, Valentina Kremenchutskaya, Csanad Csutoros, Barbara Benson
Assisting Layout Designers Pablo Gastar, Mick Ruff, Laura Jane, Kaitlin Beckett, Jim Hsu, Jacqueline McLeod
Cover Designer Daniel New
Colour Designer Steven Cann
Indexer Yvonne Byron
Project Managers Glenn van der Knijff, Ray Thomson

Thanks to the authors for coping with what was (as usual) a monumental and sometimes bamboozling task. Special thanks to Simon Sellars, who agreed over a jug of cold beer to hit the road at short notice for a lengthy, tricky research gig. Also thanks to Stefanie Di Trocchio, Marg Toohey, Helen Christinis, Bruce Evans, Stephanie Pearson, Brigitte Ellemor, Jennifer Garrett, Jane Thompson, Paul Piaia, Celia Wood, Sally Darmody, Glenn Beanland and the LPI team.

THANKS from Lonely Planet

Many thanks to the hundreds of travellers who used the last edition and wrote to us with helpful hints, useful advice and interesting anecdotes:

A Marleen Aabel-Kaag, Ashman Abdulov, Julie Ackerman, John Adams, Liam Addison, Daniel Aeberli, Olof Aerts, Kim Ahrend, Cindy Albracht, G W Albury, Declan Alcock, Jenna Alembick, Caroline Alison, Joanne Allday, Chritian Amon, Susie Anderson, Helene Andersson, Frida Andrae, Greg Andrews, Julia Anten, Kalle Anttila, Helene Apper, Matthew Aquilina, Katie Armitage, Neil Armour, Olivia Astorino, Carl Atkin, Kieron Attenborough, George Avery **B** Heike Baars, Ditte Baek, Gavin Baggott, Nikki Baker, Peter Baldacchino, Rinse Balk, Frederic Balussaud, Robert & Emma Barker, Annette Barlow, Silke Baron, Ann Barrett, Della Barton, Kate Barton, Nadine Baxter-Smallwood, John Bayley, Lisa Beavis, Silke Beissel, Caroline Bell, Jackie Bell, Daniel Benavithis, Jim Benedek, Geoff Benson, Erik Berge, Thomas Berger, Megan Berkle, Mara Berkun, Carole Bernard, Richard Bernard, Tom Berry, Bob & Jessica Berryman, Ivan Bevan, Gabriela Bezada, Marc Biedermann, Susan Birtles, Lisa Bisgaard, Diana Bishop, Natasha Blackmore, Adam Blackwell, Brendon Blake, Bastian Blankenburg, Michael Bonnet, Jorma Bosch, Therese Bourke, Duncan Box, Brendan Boyd, Marcus Boynton, Audrey & Roy Bradford, Robert Bradford, Peter Brady, Tom Brailsford, Paula Brand, Kirsten Brandin, Felicity Branton, Nicole Brenner, Jayne Bretherton, Catherine Brewer, Emma Bridge, Nicky Brine, Maree Brooks, Mark Brooks, Adam Brown, James Brown, Oliver Bruttel, Matt Buchan, Chris Buchanan, Howard Buck, Claudia Buehrer, Vanessa Burgess, Stefan Burkhardt, Kelly Burns, Dawn Byrne, Sinead Byrne **C** Andrew Caballero-Reynolds, Anthony Cairns, Kirsty Cambridge, Amanda Campbell, Cindy Campbell, Matthew Campbell-Ellis, Sarah Cantwell, John Capes, Mary Carney, Gregory Carroll, Jane Carroll, Mary Carroll, Wayne Carroll, Dave Cartwright, Debbie Cashmore, Robert Cats, Robert Chamberlain, Justin Charlebois, Auore Chatelain, Donna Chojnacki, Bart Claeys, Caroline Clancy, Simon Clark, Gary Clarke, David Clegg, Louise Clemenson, Richard Clements, Henry Clifford, Cheryl Clothier, Elroy Cocheret, Maurice Coffey, Valerie Coignard, Tom Cok, Margreet Colenbrander, Sandra Colenbrander, Marie Colfer, Michael Collins, Elaina Conneely, Gael Connell, Ray Cook, Ben Cooksey, A Corben, Bruce Cormack, Tom Coulis, Lynne Coupethwaite, Lee Cousins, Kate Cowmeadow, Laura D Crank, Michelle Cranston, Victoria Craven, Dianne Cresswell, Gabor Csonka, Joy Cullen, K Cullen, Scott Cunningham, Jennifer Cupitt, Rachel Curley, Marie Curnow, Lynne Curry, Hannah Czeschinski **D** Paul Dale, Jan-Hendrik Damerau, Johnson Daniel, Joan Darcy, Svenja Dassbach, Elke Dausch, Sarah Jane Davis, Andrew Dawes, Tasha D'Cruz, Cora de Koning, Helen de Wolfe, Mara Deacon, Sarah Deas, Claire Dedman, Brendon Deeley, Jacinta Deevey, Thomas Denck, Danielle Derks, Isabelle Deven, Massimo Dibartolo, Ester Dick, Matthias Dietrich, Francis Dillon, Jenna Dillon, Karyn Dirse, Angela DiVirgilio, Paul Dixon, Ed Dobosz, Eddie Dolan, Michelle Donaldson, Greg Dorahy, John Downe, Anna Drylie, Till Dudda, Matthias Duemmler, Karl Dungan, Andrew Dye **E** Annette Eakes, Sandra Eastern, Cindy Eaton, Scott Eaton, Peter & Emma Ebeling, Roger Paul Edmonds, Nicola Edmondson, Glenda Edwards, Ken & Ilyse Edwards, Karina Ekdal, P A Elliot, Charlotte Elliott, Alistair English, Blake Erickson, Matt Evans, Richard Eyre **F** Anne Lise Faero, Ian Fair, Sally Fankhauser, Sascha Farnell, Toby Ferguson, Aletta Filippidou, R S Finn, Daniel Flemmer, Alexia Floyd, Louise Forbes, Andrew Forsyth, Claire Fossey, Jamie Foxley, Luc Frans, Alena Friedrich, Flair Friesen, Jack Fuller, Debra Fulton **G** Sonia Gagnon, Anna Garling, Allison Garrett, Florian Gebkenjans, Roy Geddes, Trish George, Cathy Georgeson, Anja Gertz, Igo Geurtjens, Diego Ghirardi, Dave Gibbon, Marnie Gibson, Linda Giddy, Helen Gillman, Melanie Ginger, Davis Givan, Anne Glazier, Rob Gleeson, Michelle Godwin, Nadine Golding, Dorte Gollek, Annette Gordon, Jules & Laura Gorgone, Deirdre Grace, Gemma Grace, Scott Graham, Alistair Gray, Debbie Green, Dave Greene, Natalie Greenway, Asser Gregersen, Simi Grewal, Patrick Griessen, Astrid Gueldner, Bernard Guillelmon, Jane Guillelmon, Trey Guinn, Charlie Gwilliam **H** Tina Haas, Lisa Anna Haeger, Robin Haig, Tim Haldenby, Sarah Hales, Robyn Hall, Liz Hallett, Emanuel Hallgren, Alex Hamilton, Christine & John Hamilton, Jim Hamilton, Nick Hammink, Carly Hammond, Meg Hammond, Sonya Hammond, Siobhan Hanbury-Aggs, Elizabeth Hardy, Ilse Harms, Ian Harrison, Stacey Harrison, Elin Hartelius, Marie Hatjoullis, Rosie Hatton, Ian Hawkins, Mary Jo Hazard, Jamey Heit, Inger Helene, Kaisa Helenius, David Helesic, Karri Helin, Peter Hendrikson, Kerry Hennigan, Gundi Herget, Tara Hernandez, Jim Hewins, Pam Hewins, Christoph Hezel, John Hickey, Diane Hill, Lucy Hill, Suzanne Hill, Tessa Hill, Jo Hillis, Matthias Hils, Robin Hingley, C J Hinke, Kate Hinze, Sandra Hirsch, Danijela Hlis, Rob Hodge, Geoff & Carol Hodgson, Arjen Hoekzema, Johnny Hoffman, Bernd Hoffmann, Matt Hogg, Natalie Hohmann, Calvin Holbrook, Kaylen Holmes, Lesley & David Holmes, Simon Holmes, Leonie Hooghart, Guy Hook, Jennifer Hooper, Nessa Horewitch, Aziza Horsham, Antti

Hovila, Jenny Howard, Sue Hoylen, Sophie Hughes, Alda Hummelinck, Jim Humphreys, Julia Humphries, Quentin & Ann Hunter, Gaston & Nynke Hupkens, Mike Hurrell, John Hutton **I** Jan IJmker, Kay Imf, Markus Imhof, Stuart Ingram, Stephen Ireland, Julie Ison, Ilan Ivory **J** Becks Jackson, Ian Jackson, Karen Jackson, Alice James, Steve James, Marc Jarnet, Martin Jehle, Neil Jenkinson, Rob Jenneskens, P S Johnson, Andrea Jones, Rick Jones, Tim Jones, William Jones, Kristi Jordan, Ilma Joukes, Tamara Jungwirth **K** Eveline van Kampen, Nasrin Kashfi, Melanie Kasischke, Kaori Kawamura, Maayke & Erik Kazemier, Carmen Keating, Daniel Keenan, Sarah Keenan, Amy Kelly, Katherine Kelly, Michael Kelly, Peter Kelly, Sinead Kennedy, Jenny Kerr, Katleen Kerremans, David Kerry, Carla Kersten, Samir Khimji, Nabeel KHuweis, Robert Kiely, Esther Killat, Carol King, Richard King, Lee Kitson, Anne-Marie Kleijberg, Maureen Klijn, Anke Klostermeyer, Oli Kneer, Katie & Simon Knight, Michael Knoll, Christoph Knop, Julia Koch, Lindsay Koehler, Bram Koopman, Barry Kowal, Marthe Kramer, Mark Kranz Moshinsky, Sidra Kranz Moshinsky, Tatiana Krause, Matthias Kretschmer, Udo Kreuz, Daniel Kusterer, Alie Kwint **L** Jessica Lake, Gayle Lamb, Roger Lamb, Robert Lambeaux, Terry Lambeth, Ashley Lanahan, Adrian Land, Jan Lane, Garry & Carol Larkin, Karl Larson, Andrew Lashier, Carl Lauren, Simon Lavender, Alicia Lazzarini, Zoe Le Grand, Kitty Lee, Susie Leeves, Hanna Lempola, Julie Lennox, Dirk Lenzkes, Ivor Leonard, Mun Yi Leong, Robert Leslie, Naiara Lewe, Joe Lewelling, Natalie Lewis, Peter Lewis, Steven Lim, Markus Linckelmann, K A Lindemann, Gary Liniker, Bron Littlewood, Penny Liu, Joep Lobee, Geoff & Judith Lomas, Cathie Longbottom, Rosemary Longmore, Martin Lorger, Nina Lovell, Jeffrey Lowe, Sheana Loxton, Sally Loyall, Robyn Ludwig, Martin Lundgren, Teagan Lundy-Stern, Christine Luthy, Jean-Denis Lutz, E Lynch **M** Lorna Macgougan, Neil Maciver, Jim & Monica McMaster, Justine Macnamara, Abby Macnaughton, Patrick Maddigan, Rebecca Maier, Jon Malcolm, Andrew Mannell, Neil Manning, Orlaith Mannion, Malin Markestedt, Rinske Marse, Beth Marsh, Jonathan Marsh, Mark Martelletti, Pam Martin, Emilie Martinet, Andrea Masnata, Dan Massey, Kevin Masters, Lisa Masters, Linda Math, Rebecca Mathershaw, Kate Matthews, Najida Matthews, Lily Mayhew, Bill Maynard, Breid Mc Loone, Kerry McArthur, Craig McBain, Maureen McCarthy, Gavin Mcdonagh, Jane McDonnell, Niall McDonough, Catherine McGowan, Hazel Mcgrouther, Mary Rose Mcintyre, Phil Mckenzie, Ralph McLean, Paul McLennan, Adam McMillan, Shane McNamara, Roseanne Medda, Marco Melges, Steve Melhuish, Tony Menendez, Robbie A Meriales, Kimberly Merris, Debra Metcalf-Harrison, Aaron Michie, Martin Mickan, Juan Mier, Arlene Miller, Marilyn Miller, Gillian Millett, Selena Mirams, Kelly Mitchell, Melody Miyashiro, Natalie Mock, Yasantha Monerawela, Linda Moolenaar, Michael P Moore, Michele Moore, Damian Moran, Caroline Morgan, Nia Morgan, Corinne Mori, John Morley, Andrew Morris, Keith Morris, Jamie Moss, Fiona Moug, Sarah Mountcastle, Hubert Mueller, Stefan Mueller, Kellie Mundie, Jennifer Mundy-Nordin, Maarten Munnik, Avril Murphy, Patrick Murphy, Sam Musumeci, Darren Myles **N** Jay Nagler, Natalia Naomi, Julia Neumann, Terry Newman, Amy Newton, Helen Newton, Deirdre Ni Dhea, Anne Nicolas, Tony Nicolle, Ulf Niederwemmer, Kelly Noyce, Andrea Nunan, Andreas Nyenhuis **O** Justin Obyrne, Margaret O'Connell, Daniel Ohlsson, Shigeru Okada, Leigh Oliver, Lars Olsen, John O'Neill, Marcel Oosting, Kim Oostveen, Alexandra Overbeck, Alexandra & Klaus-Oliver Welsow Overbeck, Rhys Owen, Sara Owen, Simon Owen **P** Rebecca Palmer, Jan-Michael Panhoff, Marianne Pank Fischer, W R Pankhurst, Adam Papish, Eleanor Parry, Ron Parry, Ron & Jen Parry, Jo Patel, S Pathirana, Drew Paton, Pattaraplurk Pattarachote, Neil Pattemore, Stephanie Payne, Stephanie Payten, E A Payton, Naomi Peachey, Jill Pearce, Tamsyn Pearson, Lena Pedersen, Will Pegg, Birte Peters, Kevin Philipson, Scott Phillips, Tatjana & Daniel Piffaretti, Sara Pike, Mark Pinan, Krissy Piper, Mike Pomfrey, Elizabeth Pope, Bianca Popelier, Wiebke Poppinga, Marcel Post, Valerie Poulard, Sarah Price, Beth Primeau, Zoe Prince, Erin Prior, Florian Proepper, Suzanne Prymek, Hayley Pyle **R** Carole Rainsford, John & Eileen Randall, Tom Rayner, Helen & Nigel Read, Peter Regenberg, Marianne Reimann, Rebecca Reis, Jim Revell, Gail Revesz, Diane Revill, Dan Richards, Kim Richardson, Esther Ricken, Julia Ridealgh, Stefan Rieger, Jeremy Rigby, Sally Rigden, Corinna Ritter, Emilie Robert, Jenny Roberts, Jane Rodgers, Wladyslaw Romanowicz, Fiona Roscoe, Emelie Rosen, Erik Rosness, Gail Ross, Domi Rossi, Michelle Rostant, Edith Rothermel, Val Rowe, Andrew Rumsey, Joni Ruokolainen, Vicky Rushton, Cian Rutzinsky, Fintan Ryan, Kate Ryan **S** Louise S, Charlotte Sadd, Chistian Sadler, Andreas Sahlstrom, Matthew Salisbury, Darren Salter, George Salter, Kay & Paul Sammon, Samineh Sanatkar, Anja Sandreid, Melissa Santos, Patricia Sanz-Munoz, Felix Sattler, Kevin Sayer, Gerry & Christine Scanlon, Maarten Schellingerhout, Mark Schlagboehmer, Robert Schmeer, Adrian Schmid, Thomas Schnaffer, Jochen Schneider, Sandra Schneider, Philippa Schnitzler, Pamela & Gerhard Schoene, Lisa Schreiber, Roland Schreiber, Maren Schrock, Randolph Schuette, Frank Schulte, Elke Schunck, Edwin Schuurman, Jessica Scully, Matthew Scully, Mary Sealey, William Seccombe, Marion Senior, Bo Soo Seo, Kathrin Seyer, Leila Shabankareh, Hilary Shaw, Ed Sheldon, Chip Sherman, Susanne Sherman, Susan & James Shields, Bettina Short, Daniel Sieber, Kristin Jo Siess, Lorna Simpson, David Sinclair, Teran Sittner, Ina Skafte, Susanne Skujat, Anze Slosar, Robyn Small, Irene Smereka, James Smith, Nicola Smith, Wendy Smith, Mathew Sorenson, Stefano Sori, Andy Sparrow, Michaela Spettmann, Martin Staal, Matt Stead, Rebecca Steadman, Simon Stebbing, Lis Stedman, Anastasia Stephens, John Stevenson, Diana Stewart, Katie Stewart, Johannes Stoffels, Rita Stooss, Neil Stopforth, Sue Story, Sam Stott, Bill & Ann Stoughton, Robert Strauch, Grant Straw, Helene Stromme, Craig Sugden, Martin Sullivan, Alastair Suren, Soren Svendsen, Marian Svinth, Peter Swan, Marian Swart, Eileen Synnott, Kuba Szczepanik **T** Alaa Taher, Rachel Tailford, George Tam, Muei Hoon Tan, Matty Taylor, A Teale, Jean-Pierre Tennant, John Terry, Tim Tettenborn, Jamie Textor, Vee Thakur, Louie Tham, Elke Thoma, Rich Thomas, Kate Thompson, Kerri Thompson, Les G Thompson, Louise Thornber, Rhonda Tomlin, Cara Torrington, Amanda Townsend, Alberto Trentini, Steve Trigg, Markus Troendle, Claire Tucak, Amanda Tucker, Ivo Turris **U** Christian Ufo, Keith Upton **V** Isabel Heim Vadis, Maria Vagunda, Lore van Dale, Miranda van Damme, Kim van den Anker, Deborah van der Beek,

Vincent van der Meer, Stefan van der Meeren, Jeroen van der Weijden, Irene van Eyk, Alex Van Gool, Kim van Rijbroek, Kim & Jan van Rijbroek, Ron Van Son, Heidi Van Spaandonk, Sonja van Veen, Peter van Velzen, Suzan van Wezel, Alessandro Vecchini, R Veldmaat, Andrea Venturelli, Inge Verheijden, Clem Vetters, Lea Vivarelli, Sascha Von Kanel **W** Stefan Waibel, Bernhard Waldvogel, Tanja Walinschur, Sarah Walker, Tom Walker, Hanna Wallenwein, Rachael Wallis, David Walsh, Georgia Walters-Helps, Andy Ward, James Ward, Anthony Warren, Melisssa Watson, Jenny Watts, Christine Webb, Mary Weeder, Jeroen van der Weijden, Sinead Weldon, Alexi Welsh, Ken Wendle, Annelies Wessels, Maartje Wessels, Wayne West, Jantien Wester, Debbie Westwell, Marion White, James Whitford, James & Katie Whitford, Joyce & Kenneth Why, Sheryle Whybrow, Nick Whyles, Daniel Wickie, Stuart Wilcox, Paula Wilkinson, Susanne Willems, Catrin Williams, Craig Williams, Sue Williams, Vicky Williams, Alan Williamson, Greta Wills, Katrina Willsher, Andy Wilson, Carol Wilson, Leah Wilson, Ronald Wilson, Ruth & Jane Wilson, Stuart Wilson, Aileen & Frank Wolterink, James Wood, Kerry Woodcock, Donald Woods, Jessica Worlock, Martin Wranik, Deanne Wright, Sally Wright, Christian Wuensch, Thom Wuyts **Y** Ivan Young, Jenny Young **Z** Ivana Zajickova, Michael Zavelberg, Mark Zee, Bernhard Zeimetz, Elad Zicherman, Yvonne Zuidam, Froukje Zumbrink

ACKNOWLEDGEMENTS

Many thanks to the following for the use of their content: CityRail's Sydney Suburban Network Map © 2005 CityRail; Sydney Ferries Corporation Network Map © 2004 Sydney Ferries Corporation; Melbourne Train Network Map © 2005 Metlink.

SEND US YOUR FEEDBACK

We love to hear from travellers – your comments keep us on our toes and help make our books better. Our well-travelled team reads every word on what you loved or loathed about this book. Although we cannot reply individually to postal submissions, we always guarantee that your feedback goes straight to the appropriate authors, in time for the next edition. Each person who sends us information is thanked in the next edition – and the most useful submissions are rewarded with a free book.

To send us your updates – and find out about Lonely Planet events, newsletters and travel news – visit our award-winning website: **www.lonelyplanet.com/feedback**.

Note: We may edit, reproduce and incorporate your comments in Lonely Planet products such as guidebooks, websites and digital products, so let us know if you don't want your comments reproduced or your name acknowledged. For a copy of our privacy policy visit www.lonelyplanet.com/privacy.

BEHIND THE SCENES

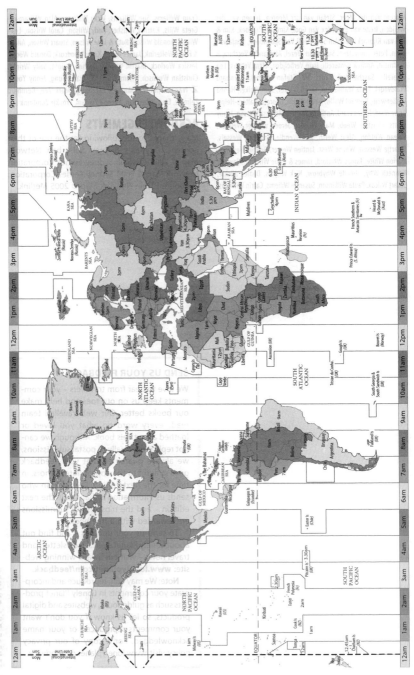

Index

000 Map pages
000 Location of colour photographs

INDEX

000 Map pages
000 Location of colour photographs

MAP LEGEND
ROUTES

Tollway	One-Way Street
Freeway	Street Mall/Steps
Primary Road	Tunnel
Secondary Road	Walking Tour
Tertiary Road	Walking Tour Detour
Lane	Walking Trail
Under Construction	Walking Path
Track	Pedestrian Overpass
Unsealed Road	

TRANSPORT

Ferry	Rail
Metro	Rail (Underground)
Bus Route	Tram

HYDROGRAPHY

River, Creek	Canal
Intermittent River	Water
Swamp	Lake (Dry)
Mangrove	Lake (Salt)
Reef	Mudflats

BOUNDARIES

State, Provincial	Regional, Suburb
Marine Park	Cliff

AREA FEATURES

Airport	Mall
Area of Interest	Market
Beach, Desert	Park
Building	Reservation
Campus	Rocks
Cemetery, Christian	Sports
Forest	Urban
Land	

POPULATION

CAPITAL (NATIONAL)	CAPITAL (STATE)
Large City	Medium City
Small City	Town, Village

SYMBOLS

Sights/Activities
- Beach
- Castle, Fortress
- Christian
- Diving, Snorkelling
- Islamic
- Jewish
- Monument
- Museum, Gallery
- Point of Interest
- Pool
- Ruin
- Skiing
- Surfing, Surf Beach
- Trail Head
- Winery, Vineyard
- Zoo, Bird Sanctuary

Eating
- Eating

Drinking
- Drinking
- Café

Entertainment
- Entertainment

Shopping
- Shopping

Sleeping
- Sleeping
- Camping

Transport
- Airport, Airfield
- Bus Station
- Cycling, Bicycle Path
- General Transport
- Parking Area
- Petrol Station
- Taxi Rank

Information
- Bank, ATM
- Embassy/Consulate
- Hospital, Medical
- Information
- Internet Facilities
- Police Station
- Post Office, GPO
- Telephone
- Toilets

Geographic
- Lighthouse
- Lookout
- Mountain, Volcano
- National Park
- Pass, Canyon
- Picnic Area
- River Flow
- Waterfall

LONELY PLANET OFFICES

Australia
Head Office
Locked Bag 1, Footscray, Victoria 3011
☎ 03 8379 8000, fax 03 8379 8111
talk2us@lonelyplanet.com.au

USA
150 Linden St, Oakland, CA 94607
☎ 510 893 8555, toll free 800 275 8555
fax 510 893 8572, info@lonelyplanet.com

UK
72–82 Rosebery Ave,
Clerkenwell, London EC1R 4RW
☎ 020 7841 9000, fax 020 7841 9001
go@lonelyplanet.co.uk

Published by Lonely Planet Publications Pty Ltd
ABN 36 005 607 983

© Lonely Planet 2005

© photographers as indicated 2005

Cover photographs by Lonely Planet Images: Young Aboriginal dancer from the Pormpuraaw community of Cape York Peninsula, Queensland, Oliver Strewe (front); The Sydney Opera House, Sydney, New South Wales, Jenny Snapper (back). Many of the images in this guide are available for licensing from Lonely Planet Images: www.lonelyplanetimages.com